F·I·NA·NC·E, I·N·S·U·R·A·N·C·E, & R·E·A·L EST·A·TE USA

USA

Third Edition

**Industry Analyses,
Statistics, and Leading Organizations**

A *W*ard's Business Directory™

F·I·N·A·N·C·E,
I·N·S·U·R·A·N·C·E,
& R·E·A·L E·S·T·A·T·E
USA

Third Edition

Industry Analyses,
Statistics, and Leading Organizations

- A comprehensive guide to statistics on the finance, insurance, and real estate industries—covering 36 major sectors and their activities

- Combines diverse federal and private sources of data in a unique, synthesized, analyzed format

- Includes more than 2,600 corporate participants with addresses, names, and sales or asset performance

- State data, rankings, and maps

- Covers local data on 2,500 counties

Gary Alampi, Editor
Arsen J. Darnay, Editor

GALE

DETROIT · NEW YORK · TORONTO · LONDON

Arsen J. Darnay, *Editor*
Gary Alampi, *Coeditor*

Editorial Code and Data, Inc. Staff

Nancy Ratliff, *Technical Support*
Helen S. Fisher, *Advisor*

Gale Research Staff

Kristin Hart, *Coordinator*
Mary Beth Trimper, *Production Director*
Shanna Heilveil, *Production Assistant*

Cynthia Baldwin, *Product Design Manager*
Bernadette M. Gornie, *Cover Designer*
C. J. Jonik, *Desktop Publisher*

Finance, Insurance, and Real Estate, U.S.A. is published by Gale Research Inc. under license from Information Access Company. Ward's Business Directory is a trademark of Information Access Company.

Ward's Business Directory™ utilizes an intensive research approach. Information on companies listed in the directory was gathered from annual reports, questionnaires, banks, trade commissions, newsletters, government documents, and telephone interviews. When sales data are unavailable from private companies, Ward's offers an estimate based on several considerations. Estimates are so noted with an asterisk (*).

While an extensive verification and proofing process preceded the printing of this directory, Information Access Company makes no warranties or representation regarding its accuracy or completeness, and each subscriber or user of the directory understands that Information Access Company disclaims any liability for any damages (even if Information Access Company has been advised of such damages) in connection with its use.

ISBN 0-8103-6452-2
ISSN 1066-7350

Printed in the United States of America
Published in the United States by Gale Research

TABLE OF CONTENTS

Finance, Insurance, and Real Estate by State continued:

Finance, Insurance, and Real Estate by County 472

Finance, Insurance, and Real Estate by County continued:

Highlights

Finance, Insurance, and Real Estate, USA (*FIRE USA*), now in its third edition, has been completely updated, with time series extended by two years. *FIRE USA* presents comprehensive information on 36 standard industrial classifications (SICs) of these financially oriented industries.

- Detailed information on 24 four-digit and 12 three-digit SIC classifications.

- Most current data available on industrial activity at this level of detail covering the span of the F.I.R.E. industries.

- Statistical data series on establishments, employment, and payroll now from 1988 through 1993 for most industries.

- Financial performance data on all but two of the industries. Detailed presentations on selected industries to 1994.

- Revenue data consistently for the U.S. industry and for states, for the first time in this edition. Data are from the new 1992 Census of the F.I.R.E. sector.

- Graphic illustration of trends in establishments, employment, and payroll.

- More than 2,900 company listings, arranged by sales, revenues, or assets. Up to 100 companies are listed per 4-digit SIC industry, showing company name, address, telephone, name of the chief executive officer, sales, revenues, or assets, and employment.

- Occupational data for industry groups in 1994 (a two-year update), showing major occupations employed by the group and trends in employment to the year 2005 (projection year remains unchanged).

- Input-Output tables for the 1982 benchmark year.

- State rankings and detailed state industry data for 1992 and 1993. State tables are provided with each industry and illustrated with maps. In addition, a section in Part II is devoted to state tables by SIC.

- Detailed data for 3,100 counties for 1992 and 1993, arranged by state, county, and SIC.

Introduction

Finance, Insurance, and Real Estate, USA (*FIRE USA*), in its third edition, presents statistics on 36 industries drawn from a variety of federal, industry, and association sources. These data are combined with information on leading public and private corporations obtained from *Ward's Business Directory of U.S. Private and Public Companies.*

FIRE USA is a unique synthesis of relevant data from County Business Patterns, the Federal Deposit Insurance Corporation, the Federal Reserve System, industry association sources, *Input-Output Study of the U.S. Economy*, and the Industry-Occupation Matrix, produced by the U.S. Department of Labor. Data on leading private and public corporations are drawn from *Ward's*, as mentioned above. Together, these materials, in preanalyzed presentation, provide a one-stop, well-indexed access to the most recently available data on finance, insurance, and real estate (F.I.R.E.) in the United States.

Features

The third edition is a comprehensive update of the book. Two additional years of data have been added. National, state, and county tables have all been updated. The new 1992 Economic Census data are incorporated for the first time. New company information is presented. The base year of the occupational data has been moved to 1994. Only the Input-Output tables remain unchanged —because this series renews (at best) every five years. Data are presented in analyzed format and illustrated by graphics and maps. Specific features include:

- Coverage of 36 industries, including 12 industries at the 3-digit SIC level and 24 at the 4-digit SIC level (1987 SIC classification).

- National, state, and county data. State data include ratios and data for every industry as well as state rankings for all F.I.R.E. categories. County data include data on 3,100 counties.

- Up to 100 leading companies in each 4-digit industry in the F.I.R.E. classifications, complete with addresses, telephone numbers, names of chief executive officers, and sales or asset information to permit ranking of participants.

- Consistent, analytically presented data permitting comparisons across the F.I.R.E. industries.

- Data series from 1988 through 1993 plus selected data series up to and including 1994.

- Input-Output (I-O) data for the U.S. economy showing relationships between industries.

- Occupational data for 1994 with projections to the year 2005.

- Maps and graphics to aid the user in viewing industry locations and trends.

'The Most Current Data Available'

FIRE USA reports the most current data available at the time of the book's preparation. The objective is to present hard information—data based on actual surveys by authoritative bodies—about all F.I.R.E. industries on a comparable basis.

Scope and Coverage

FIRE USA presents statistical data on 36 F.I.R.E. industries nationally, in all 50 states (when the industry is present), and in 3,100 counties. Data are also presented on 68 occupational groupings employed in the F.I.R.E. industries and more than 2,900 public and private companies.

Data are shown for the years 1988 to 1993. Revenue data, for the U.S. and states, is shown for 1992 from the Economic Census. These data were not collected before by the Bureau of the Census in this consistent format. Occupational data are presented for 1992 and projected (by the Department of Labor) to the year 2005. Input-Output data for 1982 are taken from the latest I-O study (released in 1991). Corporate data are drawn from the 1996 edition of *Ward's Business Directory*.

FIRE USA follows the 1987 classification conventions published by the Office of Management and Budget (*Standard Industrial Classification Manual: 1987*).

The SIC convention divides economic activity hierarchically into major industry groups (2-digit code), industry groups (3-digit), and industries (4-digit). Most data presented in *FIRE USA* are shown at the 4-digit industry level (24 industries). The 3-digit groups are used in those instances where federal sources do not provide detail below the 3-digit level (12 industries). Occupational data are reported at the 3-digit level or in groups of 3-digit industries.

Organization and Content

FIRE USA is in two parts. Part I shows national and state industry profiles; Part II presents state summaries and county data by state.

In Part I, each industry is presented as follows:

1. Introductory text
2. Table of establishments, employment, and payroll
3. Graphic of establishments, employment, and payroll
4. Table of inputs and outputs for the industry
5. Table of occupations employed by the industry
6. Table of state-by-state data on establishments, employment, and payroll
7. Maps of establishments, employment, and payroll
8. Table of leading companies

In the case of seven industries, additional tables are presented; they are drawn from federal and association sources. The content of these tables varies from industry to industry; they are all listed in the Table of Contents.

Each industry begins on a new page. The order of graphics and tables is invariable. In a few instances, tables are split between pages.

Part II presents state and county data on the F.I.R.E. industries as follows:

1. State Rankings for 1992, drawn from the Economic Census
2. Finance, Insurance, and Real Estate by State, 1992 and 1993
3. Finance, Insurance, and Real Estate by County, 1992 and 1993

The State Rankings section shows all F.I.R.E. industries by state. Rankings are provided based on establishments, employment, revenues, and payroll per employee. State data are organized alphabetically by state. Within each state, data are shown by SIC. County data are shown alphabetically within each state. Within each county, data are arranged by SIC.

The four indexes are:

*   Standard Industrial Classification (SIC) Code Index
*   Keyword Index

- Company Index
- Occupation Index

The SIC Index is in two parts. The first part is arranged in SIC code sequence followed by the name of the industry and the page number on which it begins; the second part is arranged alphabetically by industry name.

For detailed information on *FIRE USA*'s industry profiles and indexes, please consult the "Overview of Sources and Contents."

Acknowledgments

FIRE USA includes copyrighted statistical tabulations obtained from the National Association of Realtors. The Association was most forthcoming in its support of this project by generously giving permission to reprint portions of its proprietary data base.

Comments and Suggestions Are Welcome

Comments on or suggestions for improvement of the usefulness, format, and coverage of *FIRE USA* are always welcome. Although every effort is made to maintain accuracy, errors may occasionally occur; the editor will be grateful if these are called to his attention. Please contact:

Editor
FIRE, USA
Gale Research Inc.
835 Penobscot Building
Detroit, MI 48226-4094
Phone: (313) 961-2242
          (800) 347-GALE
Fax: (313) 961-6815

Overview of Sources and Contents

Discussion of Sources

Unlike other sectors of the economy, the sector made up of Finance, Insurance, and Real Estate (F.I.R.E.) had not been documented by the quadrennial censuses of business—until 1992. The Department of Commerce (DOC) had announced its intention of conducting a full survey of F.I.R.E. in 1991. The 1992 data collection effort, one presumes, was stimulated by the savings and loan crisis. These new data are presented in this edition of *FIRE USA* for the first time.

One federal data collection effort, County Business Patterns (CBP) survey, includes the F.I.R.E. industries. The CBP is also a program of DOC's Bureau of the Census; it collects data every year on establishment counts, employment, and payroll. It falls short of a complete economic census—such as the Census of Manufactures—by excluding performance figures (shipments, assets, investment, cost data). It also covers certain Standard Industrial Classifications (SICs) at aggregated levels only (3-digit rather than 4-digit). Nevertheless, County Business Patterns is a consistent, yearly survey that reports data by SIC. For these reasons, the CBP continues to be used as the "spine" of *FIRE USA*—but is now augmented by Economic Census data for 1992.

One of the reasons why the Bureau of the Census has not focused on the F.I.R.E. industries is because other federal agencies have been collecting data on some of the more important F.I.R.E. industries. Therefore, duplication of effort—including the burden of reporting—has been avoided. For instance, the Federal Deposit Insurance Corporation (FDIC) publishes *Statistics on Banking* and also reports on those savings banks that it insures. The National Credit Union Administration (NCUA) performs a similar task in relation to federally insured credit unions. These and other agencies, however, have their functional orientations; the data they receive are not published in a consistent format across the entire F.I.R.E. spectrum; institutional classifications are not by SIC. And many industries are not covered by a regulatory agency or else data are not normally published in any detail.

FIRE USA includes data from some of these agencies as well as data from industry associations. As a consequence, County Business Patterns data are supplemented by financial information in seven important areas: Banking, Savings and Loans, Credit Unions, Life Insurance, Health Insurance, and Real Estate. These data, which follow the SIC presentations of some industries in special sections, have their own and variable formats. The names and addresses of sources for these special tables are provided at the beginning of each special section. Each table is listed in the Table of Contents.

Three other sources of data are included. These will be familiar to users of other titles in this series (*Manufacturing USA, Service Industries USA*). They are tables of leading companies drawn from *Ward's Business Directory of U.S. Private and Public Companies* (*Ward's*), 1996; the *Input-Output Study of the U.S. Economy* from the Department of Commerce, and the *Industry-Occupation Matrix*, published by the Department of Labor's Bureau of Labor Statistics (BLS).

The total presentation, drawn from these sources, provides the most comprehensive and consistent view of this sector ever presented.

SIC Classification

Data in *FIRE USA* are classified using the SIC structure published in the *Standard Industrial Classification Manual: 1987*, Office of Management and Budget. Data series from 1988 to 1993 are shown in this SIC format throughout the book—whether the source is County Business Patterns or the 1992 Economic Census.

Use of Abbreviations and Symbols

Throughout *FIRE USA*, the same symbols or abbreviations are used to denote certain circumstances. The abbreviation "nec" stands for "not elsewhere classified"—terminology used by the Bureau of the Census to indicate "catch-all" categories. Groupings of activities that cannot be classified under one of the approved industrial categories are combined with others under one of the "nec" industries.

The symbol (000) is used to indicate the omission of zeroes; "$ mil." is used to denote that the values are in millions of dollars. "1st Q" means the first quarter of the year. The symbol (D) is used to indicate that data, although available, have been withheld by the government to avoid disclosure of competitive information. Data suppression in these cases is legislatively mandated.

The abbreviation "na" is used to indicate "not available." The dash (-) is used to mark instances where data cannot be calculated; the symbol usually occurs in cases where a percentage would be present if data were present.

A number of abbreviations are used in the Leading Companies tables to show company type and to annotate the sales or assets column. These are explained in the source note for each table and also in this section.

In the special tables, acronyms are explained in the source note.

Arrangement and Contents of Tables and Graphics

FIRE USA is in two parts. Part I presents industry summaries, arranged by SIC number; Part II presents additional data on states and counties within each state.

Contents of Part I

Each chapter in Part I is made up of the following eight elements:

1. Introductory text
2. Table of establishments, employment, and payroll
3. Graphic on facing page
4. Table of inputs and outputs for the industry or for a larger grouping of industries
5. Table of occupations employed by the industry or for a larger grouping of industries
6. Table of U.S. and state-by-state data on revenues and other accounts
7. Maps on facing page
8. One or more tables of leading companies (one table for each 4-digit SIC)

For some industries, additional tables, headed by a brief explanatory text, follow the standard elements of the chapter.

An explanation of each element follows:

1. Introductory Text

The text describes the industry, providing a definition of its activities and a listing of the industry's component SICs (if more than one 4-digit SIC is included) and activity components. The text is adapted, with occasional minor changes, from the *Standard Industrial Classification Manual: 1987*, Office of Management and Budget, Washington, D.C. Where appropriate, information is added reflecting changes in the industry's structure that occurred after the publication of the manual.

2. Table of Establishments, Employment, and Payroll

The table provides information for 1988 through 1993. The source of the data is County Business Patterns for the years 1988-1993. Four elements of information are provided. These are—

- Establishment counts
- Mid-March employment figures
- 1st quarter wages, annualized, in millions of dollars
- 1st quarter payroll per employee, annualized
- Annual payroll, in millions of dollars

The same presentation is provided for all establishments of the industry and then for establishments with 1 to 4, 5 to 9, 10 to 19, 20 to 49, 50 to 99, 100 to 249, 250 to 499, 500 to 999, and 1000 or more employees.

First quarter wages are annualized, i.e., they are multiplied by 4 so that they are comparable to annual payroll. Payroll per employee is also a calculated value; it is based on mid-March employment figures, annualized, divided by employment. This provides an estimate of annual pay per employee; the value is an estimate because payroll and employment may have increased or decreased in subsequent quarters.

3. Graphic of Establishments, Employment, and Payroll

On the page facing the table just described are three graphics illustrating change in establishments, mid-March employment figures, and annual payroll—from 1988 through 1993. The graphs are curves drawn to logarithmic scale so that regardless of the magnitude of the values used, the slope of the curves may be compared. Source of the data is the Table of Establishments, Employment, and Annual Payroll; only data for All Establishments are graphed.

4. Table of Inputs and Outputs

One of the more useful tools for tracing economic activity from industry to industry and from one economic sector to another is an economic data structure known as the input-output table. For this reason, *FIRE USA* provides an extract from the *Benchmark Study of the U.S. Economy*, 1982, published in the fall of 1991 by the Department of Commerce. Input-output studies are expensive, complex enterprises; consequently, such data are published infrequently and at a substantial lag in time; nevertheless, these data show the fundamental structural relationships between economic activities and are a useful if imprecise adjunct to market, developmental, locational, and other analyses.

The Table of Inputs and Outputs is an extraction. It records only those transactions between F.I.R.E. industries and other sectors of the economy that represent at least one tenth of one percent of total inputs to an industry or outputs from an industry. All lesser transactions are suppressed in order to conserve space.

The table has two parts. The first part (column 1) shows economic sectors or industries that supply an industry with goods and services (inputs); the second part (column 2) shows economic sectors or industries that purchase the outputs of the industry (outputs). (Since some of the economic units shown are not "industries"—for instance State and Local Government—the term "sector" is used to denote such economic entities.) Within each part, the sector/industry is shown first followed by a percentile of input or output; the final entry categorizes the sector/industry by type (Manufacturing, Wholesale or Retail Trade, Services, Utilities, etc.).

The Input-Output accounts are based on the 1977 SIC structure which was in force in 1982. For presentation in *FIRE USA*, data have been associated with the 1987 SIC structure as closely as possible; the user, however, must keep in mind that two different schemes of classification have been coordinated; therefore, some distortions are likely.

The sectors/industries in each part of the table are sorted in descending order of importance: the largest supplying and purchasing sectors/industries are placed at the top of the table. If the percentile is the same, the data are sorted in alphabetical order by the name of the activity.

The user should note the following when using this table:

- Most industries buy from and sell to themselves. These transactions may at times be the largest inputs and one of the larger outputs of an industry. The reason for this phenomenon is simply that a 4-digit industry is very often composed of many specialized industries that supply each other in a cascade of components.

- Not all inputs to an industry are shown—only those that account for 0.1% or more of inputs.

- Some of the output categories used in the Input-Output Study hide the ultimate user. Examples are Exports and Gross Private Fixed Investment. This limitation derives from the manner in which the Input-Output accounts are organized.

- The input and output ratios are not likely to be accurate for industries where there has been dramatic change (technological or other) since the early 1980s.

5. Table of Occupations Employed by Industry Group

FIRE USA presents data on 68 occupations employed by F.I.R.E. industries. The information presented is an extract from the Industry-Occupation Matrix produced by the Bureau of Labor Statistics (BLS), Department of Labor. BLS has reorganized this matrix for the most recent issue. The number of occupational groups that now fall into the scope of *FIRE USA* has been reduced somewhat as a consequence.

The Occupations Employed table presents an extract; showing the entire matrix would have required too much space. Thus only those occupations are included that represent 1% or more of total employment in an industry. The advantage of this method is that the data are kept manageable while most of an industry's employment is defined by occupation. The disadvantage is that certain occupations, although employed by an industry, do not make the "cutoff" of 1% of total employment. For example, many industries employ janitors, but the occupation is large enough to be reported only in a few.

The data are shown for 1994 in percent of total employment for an industry group (3-digit industry level or groupings of 3-digit industries). Also shown is the Bureau of Labor Statistics' projection of the anticipated growth or decline of the occupation to the year 2005. This value is reported as a percent change to 2005; a value of 5.5, for instance, means that overall employment in the industry group will increase 5.5% between 1994 and 2005. A negative value indicates a corresponding decline. Note that these are not rates of annual change.

BLS does not provide occupational data at the 4-digit SIC level. Consequently, the same Occupations Employed table is reproduced for each industry that is in the same 3-digit grouping. This approach has been adopted so that the user will find the occupations associated with a 4-digit industry together with other data on that industry.

The user should note the following:

- As already stated, the occupations shown are a subset of total occupations employed: those that account for 1% or more of employment in the industry group.

- Since the data are for groups, some occupations listed will appear out of place in a particular 4-digit industry; that is because those occupations are employed by a related 4-digit industry in the same group.

- Growth or decline indicated for an occupation within an industry group does not mean that the occupation is growing or declining overall. The overall pattern is that service occupations, especially those associated with medicine and health, are growing. Manufacturing occupations, especially those associated with old industries or those threatened by the overseas migration of their jobs, are declining.

6. U.S. and State Data on Industry Revenues and Other Accounts

This table presents all the data available from the first-ever Economic Census of F.I.R.E. held in 1992. For this reason, the U.S. total is shown at the top of each table. State data follow. Categories covered are Establishments, Employment, Payroll, and Revenues. These columns are followed by ratios as follows: Employees per Establishment, Revenue per Establishment, Payroll per Establishment, Revenue per Employee, and Payroll per Employee.

Note, please, that data for 1992 displayed in the Table of Establishments, Employment, and Payroll will be comparable with but not exactly the same as data in this table. The reason is simply that the County Business Patterns and the Economic Census are two different surveys. The 1992 Economic Census results are, it is believed, much more accurate.

Variant of the State Table

Two industries, *SIC 6732 - Educational, Religious, etc. Trusts* and *SIC 6733 - Trusts, nec*, were not covered by the 1992 Economic census. For these two industries, state data are repeated from the last edition under the heading of *State-by-State Data on Establishments, Employement, and Payroll*.

This variant format provides five data elements for 1989 and 1991 from County Business Patterns. The elements are (1) number of establishments, (2) employment, (3) payroll per employee, (4) annual payroll, shown in millions of dollars, and (5) payroll per establishment. The last column shows percent change in employment between 1989 and 1991.

Payroll per employee is calculated by dividing the value of 1st Quarter payroll, annualized, by the value of mid-March employment to provide an estimate of earnings per employee in each state for each year. Multiplying employment by payroll per employee will not necessarily produce the value shown under payroll; payroll is total annual payroll. Both employment and payroll used to obtain the pay/employee ratio may have changed. For some states, data are withheld; in such cases, usually only establishment counts are available.

7. Map Graphics

Three maps plot the results of the state table or its variant on the page facing the table. Two maps are provided for each of three categories—establishments, employment, and revenues or payroll (variant); in all cases, the data are for 1992 or 1991 (variant) only.

State maps (left column) are shaded to differentiate between (1) states where the industry's presence is roughly proportional to its population (grey), (2) states where the industry's presence is more than its share of the nation's population (dark), or (3) states where the industry's presence is less than its population proportion (open dots). States left blank do not have any establishments in the industry. Average values (grey shading) are shown when a state's establishment count, employment, or revenue is 15% more or less than the state's population proportion. States for which data are withheld are assumed to be average (grey).

Regional maps (right column) are shaded to indicate absolute rank in the category; only the first, second, and third regions are shaded; if no data for the category are available, establishment counts are used to shade the regions; establishment counts are always available.

The regional boundaries are those of the Census Regions and are named, from left to right and top to bottom as follows:

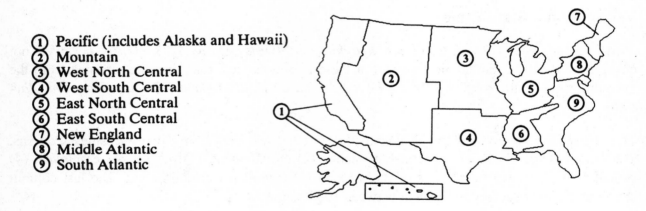

① Pacific (includes Alaska and Hawaii)
② Mountain
③ West North Central
④ West South Central
⑤ East North Central
⑥ East South Central
⑦ New England
⑧ Middle Atlantic
⑨ South Atlantic

In the case of the Pacific region, all parts of the region are shaded (including Alaska and Hawaii), even if the basis for the ranking is the industry's predominance in California (the usual case).

Although regional data are only mapped and not reported in a separate table, the data provided in the table give all the necessary information for constructing a regional table.

8. Table(s) of Leading Companies

One or more tables of Leading Companies are provided for each industry but one (*SIC 6732, Educational, Religious, etc. Trusts*). Since the *Ward's* data are classified by 4-digit SIC, *FIRE USA* preserves this detail by providing separate tables for each 4-digit SIC in those cases where basic data are more aggregated. Up to 100 company names are provided per table. More than 2,900 company entries are listed in *FIRE USA*.

The listings are sorted in descending order of sales or total assets and show the company name, address, name of the chief executive officer, telephone number, company type, sales (in millions of dollars) and employment (in thousands of employees). The number of companies shown, their total sales/assets, and total employment are given at the top of the table for the user's convenience.

The data are from *Ward's Business Directory of U.S. Private and Public Companies* for 1996. Public and private corporations, divisions, subsidiaries, joint ventures, and corporate groups are shown. Thus, a listing for an industry may show the parent company as well as important divisions and subsidiaries of the same company (usually in different locations).

While this method of presentation has the disadvantage of duplication (the sales of a parent corporation include the sales of any divisions listed separately), it has the advantage of providing the user with information on major components of an enterprise at different locations. In any event, the user should not assume that the sum of the sales, assets, or employment shown in the Leading Companies table represents the total sales (or employment) of an industry. Using sales/assets to employment ratios from the table however, is one possible method of estimating the economic size of an industry which has no special tables to provide better measurements.

The company type (private, public, division, etc.) is shown in the table under the column headed "Co Type," thus providing the user with a means of roughly determining the total "net" sales, assets, or employment represented; this can be accomplished by adding all values and then deducting values corresponding to divisions and subsidiaries of parent organizations also shown in the table. The code used is as follows:

P - Public Corporation
R - Private Corporation
S - Subsidiary
D - Division
J - Joint Venture
G - Corporate Group

An asterisk (*) placed behind the sales volume or an asset value indicates an estimate; the absence of an asterisk indicates that the sales value has been obtained from annual reports, other formal submissions to regulatory bodies, or from the corporation. The symbol "<" appears in front of some employment values to indicate that the actual value is "less than" the value shown. Thus the value of "<0.1" means that the company employs fewer than 100 people.

Special Tables

Additional statistical tables are provided following *SIC 6020, Commercial Banks*; *SIC 6030, Savings Institutions*; *SIC 6060, Credit Unions*; *SIC 6310, Life Insurance*; *SIC 6321, Accident and Health Insurance*; *SIC 6370, Pension, Health, and Welfare Funds*; and *SIC 6530, Real Estate Agents and Managers*.

Sources for these tables are the Federal Deposit Insurance Corporation, the Federal Reserve System, the National Credit Union Administration, the Council of Life Insurance, and the National Association of Realtors. Some of these sources drew their data from other public and private sources; these are indicated in the source notes of each table where appropriate. Data from the Council of Life Insurance and the National Association of Realtors have been reproduced by permission; the editors are grateful for permission to use these data to add value to *FIRE USA*.

Each special section begins with a brief textual annotation. The names and addresses of sources are also provided so that the interested user can obtain more detailed information.

Contents of Part II

Part II of *FIRE USA* is divided into a short section of State Rankings tables, a somewhat longer tabulation of Finance, Insurance, and Real Estate by State, and a long section of Finance, Insurance, and Real Estate by County.

State Rankings

This section holds five tables showing data for all F.I.R.E. industries on Establishments, Employment, Revenues, and Pay per Employee for all states and the District of Columbia. Data are shown for 1992 and are drawn from the new 1992 Economic Census. Each table shows the states in a different sort order based on (1) population rank, (2) establishment count rank, (3) employment rank, (4) revenue rank, and (5) pay per employee rank. In each table, the column used for ranking is shown in bold type. Columns show actual data for each category, absolute rank, and per capita rank. Sort is by absolute rank.

The employment column represents mid-March employment in 1991. Pay per employee is calculated by dividing 1st Quarter payroll, annualized, by mid-March employment figures. Per capita ratios were calculated by dividing data fields by the population of that state in 1991.

Finance, Insurance, and Real Estate by State

This section lists data for each state, in SIC order, for the years 1992 and 1993. The tabulation permits an overall assessment of F.I.R.E. industries in each state. Categories covered are establishments, employment, pay per employee, and annual payroll. In the blocks showing establishments and annual payroll, a column is provided showing the industry's size relative to the United States as a whole ("% U.S.") in 1993. The value of 0.9%, for instance, for *SIC 6020, Commercial Banks* means that the state had 0.9 percent of the nation's total establishments (or payroll) for that industry in 1993.

States are shown in alphabetical order. SICs within each state presentation are shown in SIC order. The source of the data is County Business Patterns for 1992 and 1993.

Finance, Insurance, and Real Estate by County

This section is organized in the same manner as the state tabulations just described with the exception that entities reported on are counties and the percentile columns show "% of State" rather than "% of U.S." Data are drawn from the County Business Patterns because, unfortunately, the 1992 Economic Census did not report details at levels below the Metropolitan Area.

Counties are shown in alphabetical order; for this reason, no separate index of counties is provided. Within each county, data are presented in SIC order. SIC categories for which data were suppressed or not available for both 1992 and 1993 are not displayed. In the case of some counties, the only data available were for the F.I.R.E. industries as a whole.

In Alaska, subdivisions are boroughs or areas; in Louisiana, subdivisions are parishes rather than counties. In Virginia, the DOC provides, in addition to counties, data for independent cities; other independent cities are Baltimore, MD; Carson City, NV; and St. Louis, MO. The District of Columbia is reported as a separate entity.

Indexes

Unlike most government documents, *FIRE USA* is thoroughly indexed. In addition to fulfilling their primary purpose of directing users to the analyzed industries by supplying page numbers, *FIRE USA*'s indexes also provide SIC codes. All page numbers (or ranges) are indicated by the letter "p." All SIC codes (or ranges) are preceded by the letters "SIC."

SIC Index

Part one of the index is ordered numerically using the 1987 SIC sequence beginning with the first F.I.R.E. industry, *SIC 6010, Central Reserve Depository Institutions* and ending with *SIC 6799, Investors, not elsewhere classified*. This part is immediately followed by an alphabetical listing by industry name—from *Accident and Health Insurance (6321)* to *Trusts, nec (6733)*; each industry name is followed by its SIC and then the page number on which it begins.

Keyword Index

The Keyword Index has nearly 800 alphabetically arranged entries identifying services, activities, and agencies related to F.I.R.E. The names were largely but not exclusively obtained from the SIC Manual. Additional keywords have been added as required. Each term is followed by one or more SIC codes indicating the industry or industries in which the term is used. The references following each entry are arranged in SIC order.

Company Index

This index shows more than 2,900 company names arranged in alphabetical order; company names that begin with a numeral ("1st," etc.) precede company names that begin with the letter A. Company names are followed by page references and a listing of SICs (within brackets). Some company names are abbreviated.

Occupation Index

The Occupation Index shows 68 occupational groups. Where multiple occupations are part of a group, they are shown separately in the index. Alphabetical rotation is also shown (Registered nurses, Nurses, registered). All told, the index has 143 entries. The index does not attempt to refer the user to every industry in which an occupation occurs; that approach would render the index unwieldy. The total number of 3-digit industries employing the occupation is shown, in parentheses, following the name of the occupation; thereafter, the top ten (or fewer) industry groups are shown in their order of importance; the most important group (that which employs the largest number) is shown first.

The user should note that—

- Occupations are reported by 3-digit industry group; a reference to industry 632, for instance, means that the user can find the occupation under *SIC 6321, Accident and Health Insurance* as well as *6324, Hospital and Medical Service Plans.*

- Only those occupations are included which represent at least 1% of employment in a 3-digit industry group. As an example, many "Librarians, professional" are employed by F.I.R.E. industries; but as highly specialized professionals among others, their numbers do not reach the "reporting threshold" used in *FIRE USA.*

User's Guide

Finance, Insurance, and Real Estate, USA (FIRE USA) provides the user with a wealth of data and a framework for doing many kinds of assessments and analyses. The nature of the work, of course, will depend on the user's need and specific context. For this reason, all the possible uses of such a book cannot be fully described. The purpose of this section is to provide examples of use.

By their nature and function, the F.I.R.E. industries play an enabling and supporting role in the economy. They provide funding; underwrite risk; manage properties for use by others; buy, sell, and hold assets; guarantee loans or bond performance; etc. For this reason sophisticated uses of the book in economic, policy, or planning studies would typically involve using other resources as well, including the three other books in this series, *Manufacturing USA*, *Service Industries USA*, and *Wholesale and Retail Trade USA*. The examples that follow do not attempt to depict using *FIRE USA* in analytical studies.

Finding an SIC

The caller may begin by saying something like this: "We're a bonding organization. We provide job completion bonds. We have to fill out this form, and they want to know our SIC. Can you help?" A typical way to fulfill such a request is to identify the SIC associated with an activity or company. Under Bonding in the Keyword Index, job completion guarantee is shown to be *SIC 6350, Surety Insurance*. A quick reading of the introductory text for the SIC confirms that the SIC does, indeed, include "bonding for guaranteeing job completion."

Providing Magnitude Information

FIRE USA is a convenient resource for answering questions on how big an industry is or what the wages in an industry might be. The question "How big is the Savings & Loan industry?" can be answered rapidly by finding Savings and Loan Associations in the Keyword Index; references are to *SIC 6010* and *6030*; looking further in the index, it becomes clear that Savings banks and Savings institutions are both in *SIC 6030*. Examination of tables in that chapter reveals the number of employees in 1992 (341,920), payroll ($8.4 billion), revenues ($92.3 billion) and earnings per employee ($24,700 per year). These data are from the U.S. and State Data table, U.S. total line.

employees in 1992 (341,920), payroll ($8.4 billion), revenues ($92.3 billion) and earnings per employee ($24,700 per year). These data are from the U.S. and State Data table, U.S. total line. State data can also be found in the table. And in the special tables provided, data are given for such categories as total assets, equity, income, expenses, and profits.

Looking for Trends

With more years available in this edition, the user can spot trends more easily by using national or state tabulations or graphs as well as special tables in areas where they are available.

Answering Geographical Questions

The combined use of indexes, maps, the State table, and the Leading Companies table can help the reference librarian respond quickly and effectively to questions about the concentration of the industry at the state and local levels. A look at the maps provided for *Savings Institutions (SIC 6030)* shows that West Coast states have a proportionally high concentration of this industry (among others). The industry is present in all states.

The State Rankings tables can be used to determine the rank of each state among all F.I.R.E. industries using number of establishments, employment, payroll, or pay per employee. Arkansas, for instance, ranks 33rd in establishments, 37th in employment, 36th in revenues, and 39th in payroll per employee. The state ranks 33rd in population.

The F.I.R.E. by State or County tables are useful in pinpointing salient facts about each F.I.R.E. SIC.

Finding Companies

The Keyword Index, used in conjunction with the Leading Companies tables, gives the reference-provider a way to identify one or more companies within an industry or state. A caller, for instance, may be trying to find a mobile home site operator in Michigan. The Keyword Index points to *SIC 6510, Real Estate Operators and Lessors*. A look through the Leading Companies tables shows eight entries for *SIC 6515, Mobile Home Site Operators*. None is listed for Michigan; but one entry in a neighboring state, Ohio, may be a good point of contact for the caller.

Helping Job Seekers

FIRE USA provides a painless means of matching occupations to industries and companies—provided, of course, that the occupations fall into the F.I.R.E. category and are employed in reasonable numbers. A newlywed couple, moving from Missouri to Florida to be nearer the wife's family, attempt to identify potential employers of property managers (she is working in that occupation now). Their desire is to relocate in the Miami area. The Occupation Index identifies 3-digit SICs 651 and 653 as the two largest employers of this specialty. A look at companies in *SIC 6510, Real Estate Operators and Lessors* produces five companies (3 in North Miami Beach, 2 in Miami)—which should serve as a starting point.

Estimating Financial Data

With the availability of revenue data for all but two of the 36 industries covered in *FIRE USA* (*SICs 6732, 6733*), estimating the financial performance of industries in this sector has become a little easier: at least one year's worth of "hard" census data is available and can be used to estimate other years. For example:

Suppose you want to estimate the size of *SIC 6510 - Real Estate Operators and Lessors* in 1993 as measured in revenues. A single value, revenues for 1992, is available, $74.0695 billion, from the U.S. and State Data table. You would use this value to obtain an industry revenue figure for 1996 as follows:

1. Calculate change in employment between 1992 and 1993 using the Establishments, Employment and Payroll table. The change is 3.4%.

2. Apply this figure to the employment item in the U.S. and State Data table: 462,546 x 1.034 = 478,273.

3. In 1992, revenues per employee were $160,128. Apply this value to the result in 2. above: 478,273 x 160,128 = $76.5849 billion. This is a reasonable estimate for 1993 revenues.

You can apply a similar approach to developing longer-range projections as well. Using the Establishments, Employment, and Payroll table (County Business Patterns), you can develop various growth factors for this industry. Employment has grown 1.4% in the last five years; payroll is up 13.9 percent, etc. Using such data, you can estimate 1997 revenues, say, by applying growth factors to the 1992 census datum.

Such analyses are, of course, bound to be imprecise. But in the absence of better numbers, such exercises can sometimes provide enough of an answer to guide research in the right direction.

Analyzing Occupational Trends

The Occupation table provides occupations within an industry group for 1994 as well as projections of growth or decline to the year 2005. These data can be used effectively in identifying areas of potential problems for the employee or for the employer.

Generally, higher skill levels are growing, lower skills declining. For example, *Typists and word processors* and *Bookkeeping, auditing, and accounting clerks* are declining occupations in most industries; but more so in some than others. *Computer programmers* are still growing in number to the year 2005—more rapidly in some industries than in others. *Book-keeping clerks*, examining *FIRE USA*, can clearly see (in *SIC 6310, Life Insurance*, for example) that employment of *Accountants and auditors* is projected to grow significantly. The path to job security, evidently, lies in upgrading skills from the clerical to the professional level. Employers, plotting human resource strategies, can predict in this same industry that competition for people with higher skills in the data processing area will become sharp. The number of *Computer programmers* will decrease, but demand for *Systems Analysts* will increase dramatically—and much more in other industries than in Life Insurance.

In addition to the examples listed above, the state and county data provide statistics for a variety of geographical analyses. These might involve comparing counties (or groups of counties aggregated into urban areas) with each other, identifying gaps to be filled in services by expansion, etc. Users who wish to see additional examples illustrated in subsequent editions need but to write to the editor.

F·I·N·A·N·C·E,
I·N·S·U·R·A·N·C·E,
& R·E·A·L E·S·T·A·T·E
USA

Third Edition

Industry Analyses,
Statistics, and Leading Organizations

SIC 6010

CENTRAL RESERVE DEPOSITORY INSTITUTIONS

Central reserve depository institutions are organizations engaged primarily in receiving deposits from banks and providing advances to such institutions. Reserve depositories generally do not take deposits or make advances to other enterprises and individuals. Included in this category are the Federal Reserve Banks and their branches (SIC 6011), which serve as regional reserve and rediscounting institutions for their members, and Central Reserve Depository Institutions, not elsewhere classified (SIC 6019), which include institutions that are not part of the Federal Reserve System but provide analogous services to savings banks, savings and loan associations, or credit unions. SIC 6019 includes the Central Liquidity Facility, the Federal Home Loans Banks, and the National Credit Union Administration (NCUA).

ESTABLISHMENTS, EMPLOYMENT, AND PAYROLL

	1988	1989		1990		1991		1992		1993		% change 88-93
		Value	%	Value	%	Value	%	Value	%	Value	%	
All Establishments	101	97	-4.0	118	21.6	142	20.3	150	5.6	75	-50.0	-25.7
Mid-March Employment	25,631	25,952	1.3	30,513	17.6	29,074	-4.7	28,706	-1.3	26,448	-7.9	3.2
1st Quarter Wages (annualized - $ mil.)	680.1	734.4	8.0	894.5	21.8	909.1	1.6	951.8	4.7	912.9	-4.1	34.2
Payroll per Emp. 1st Q. (annualized)	26,535	28,300	6.6	29,315	3.6	31,267	6.7	33,158	6.0	34,516	4.1	30.1
Annual Payroll ($ mil.)	691.4	737.7	6.7	901.9	22.3	917.2	1.7	964.0	5.1	902.9	-6.3	30.6
Establishments - 1-4 Emp. Number	10	8	-20.0	11	37.5	18	63.6	15	-16.7	8	-46.7	-20.0
Mid-March Employment	(D)	16	-	13	-18.8	35	169.2	33	-5.7	12	-63.6	-
1st Quarter Wages (annualized - $ mil.)	(D)	0.3	-	0.2	-6.1	0.6	129.0	0.5	-8.5	0.3	-48.5	-
Payroll per Emp. 1st Q. (annualized)	(D)	16,500	-	19,077	15.6	16,229	-14.9	15,758	-2.9	22,333	41.7	-
Annual Payroll ($ mil.)	(D)	0.5	-	0.8	76.5	0.9	13.4	0.9	-4.6	1.4	58.4	-
Establishments - 5-9 Emp. Number	11	7	-36.4	8	14.3	8	-	22	175.0	(D)	-	-
Mid-March Employment	(D)	(D)	-	56	-	59	5.4	155	162.7	(D)	-	-
1st Quarter Wages (annualized - $ mil.)	(D)	(D)	-	2.3	-	1.3	-41.7	3.3	149.6	(D)	-	-
Payroll per Emp. 1st Q. (annualized)	(D)	(D)	-	41,071	-	22,712	-44.7	21,574	-5.0	(D)	-	-
Annual Payroll ($ mil.)	(D)	(D)	-	2.7	-	1.1	-58.9	3.4	204.9	(D)	-	-
Establishments - 10-19 Emp. Number	14	18	28.6	13	-27.8	17	30.8	17	-	(D)	-	-
Mid-March Employment	200	246	23.0	189	-23.2	(D)	-	275	-	(D)	-	-
1st Quarter Wages (annualized - $ mil.)	5.2	6.3	21.3	4.3	-32.4	(D)	-	6.7	-	(D)	-	-
Payroll per Emp. 1st Q. (annualized)	25,960	25,610	-1.3	22,519	-12.1	(D)	-	24,305	-	(D)	-	-
Annual Payroll ($ mil.)	5.4	7.2	33.7	4.6	-35.6	(D)	-	7.5	-	(D)	-	-
Establishments - 20-49 Emp. Number	11	11	-	20	81.8	20	-	24	20.0	8	-66.7	-27.3
Mid-March Employment	(D)	(D)	-	599	-	607	1.3	691	13.8	251	-63.7	-
1st Quarter Wages (annualized - $ mil.)	(D)	(D)	-	18.1	-	21.4	18.0	29.4	37.5	5.8	-80.2	-
Payroll per Emp. 1st Q. (annualized)	(D)	(D)	-	30,264	-	35,249	16.5	42,576	20.8	23,219	-45.5	-
Annual Payroll ($ mil.)	(D)	(D)	-	19.6	-	23.4	19.3	28.6	22.4	5.8	-79.8	-
Establishments - 50-99 Emp. Number	9	10	11.1	10	-	30	200.0	19	-36.7	7	-63.2	-22.2
Mid-March Employment	640	752	17.5	702	-6.6	2,013	186.8	1,321	-34.4	494	-62.6	-22.8
1st Quarter Wages (annualized - $ mil.)	15.1	16.6	9.9	18.6	11.9	60.6	226.8	38.3	-36.9	15.3	-59.9	1.6
Payroll per Emp. 1st Q. (annualized)	23,594	22,059	-6.5	26,433	19.8	30,126	14.0	28,990	-3.8	31,069	7.2	31.7
Annual Payroll ($ mil.)	15.0	15.6	3.9	18.9	21.2	55.9	195.1	35.7	-36.1	15.2	-57.3	1.2
Establishments - 100-249 Emp. Number	23	20	-13.0	25	25.0	20	-20.0	25	25.0	24	-4.0	4.3
Mid-March Employment	3,851	3,516	-8.7	4,453	26.6	(D)	-	3,838	-	3,550	-7.5	-7.8
1st Quarter Wages (annualized - $ mil.)	94.4	94.4	-0.0	127.6	35.1	(D)	-	121.5	-	117.4	-3.4	24.3
Payroll per Emp. 1st Q. (annualized)	24,526	26,850	9.5	28,646	6.7	(D)	-	31,663	-	33,068	4.4	34.8
Annual Payroll ($ mil.)	95.1	86.4	-9.1	121.9	41.0	(D)	-	118.5	-	114.9	-3.1	20.8
Establishments - 250-499 Emp. Number	10	10	-	17	70.0	16	-5.9	15	-6.3	12	-20.0	20.0
Mid-March Employment	3,631	3,666	1.0	6,289	71.5	(D)	-	4,851	-	3,961	-18.3	9.1
1st Quarter Wages (annualized - $ mil.)	82.6	88.3	7.0	165.8	87.8	(D)	-	141.4	-	117.6	-16.8	42.4
Payroll per Emp. 1st Q. (annualized)	22,736	24,091	6.0	26,370	9.5	(D)	-	29,147	-	29,689	1.9	30.6
Annual Payroll ($ mil.)	82.5	88.3	7.0	164.4	86.2	(D)	-	149.3	-	115.6	-22.6	40.0
Establishments - 500-999 Emp. Number	5	6	20.0	6	-	4	-33.3	4	-	(D)	-	-
Mid-March Employment	(D)	(D)	-	(D)	-	3,372	-	3,225	-4.4	(D)	-	-
1st Quarter Wages (annualized - $ mil.)	(D)	(D)	-	(D)	-	100.7	-	108.9	8.1	(D)	-	-
Payroll per Emp. 1st Q. (annualized)	(D)	(D)	-	(D)	-	29,878	-	33,759	13.0	(D)	-	-
Annual Payroll ($ mil.)	(D)	(D)	-	(D)	-	106.4	-	109.1	2.5	(D)	-	-
Estab. - 1000 or More Emp. Number	8	7	-12.5	8	14.3	9	12.5	9	-	9	-	12.5
Mid-March Employment	12,639	12,109	-4.2	(D)	-	13,997	-	14,317	2.3	14,255	-0.4	12.8
1st Quarter Wages (annualized - $ mil.)	360.3	368.0	2.1	(D)	-	478.4	-	501.8	4.9	524.1	4.4	45.4
Payroll per Emp. 1st Q. (annualized)	28,509	30,392	6.6	(D)	-	34,179	-	35,048	2.5	36,765	4.9	29.0
Annual Payroll ($ mil.)	366.0	375.3	2.5	(D)	-	481.2	-	510.9	6.2	528.5	3.4	44.4

Source: County Business Patterns, U.S. Department of Commerce, Washington, D.C., for 1988 through 1993. Payroll per employee is calculated using mid-March employment and 1st Quarter wages, annualized. Annual payroll, also shown, may not equal the annualized 1st Quarter wages. Columns headed by a percent sign (%) indicate change from the previous year. *na* stands for not available. The symbol (D) indicates that data are withheld by the source to avoid disclosure of competitive information. A dash (-) indicates that data are not available or cannot be calculated.

ESTABLISHMENTS
Number

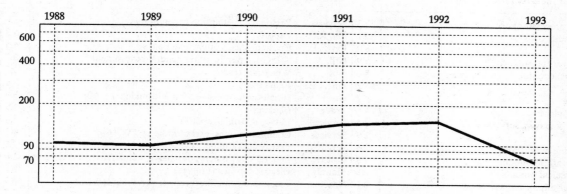

MID-MARCH EMPLOYMENT
Number

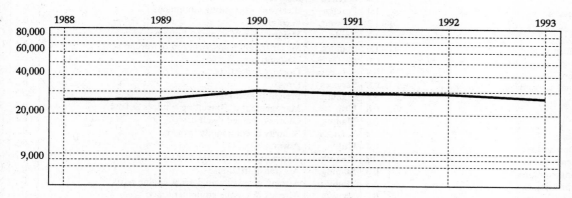

ANNUAL PAYROLL
$ million

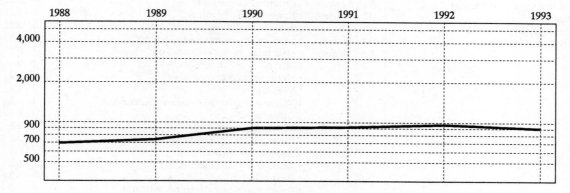

INPUTS AND OUTPUTS FOR ALL BANKING SECTORS - SICs 601, 602, 603, 608, and 609

Economic Sector or Industry Providing Inputs	%	Sector	Economic Sector or Industry Buying Outputs	%	Sector
Computer & data processing services	13.3	Services	Personal consumption expenditures	43.5	
Security & commodity brokers	10.1	Fin/R.E.	Exports	5.3	Foreign
Real estate	8.0	Fin/R.E.	Credit agencies other than banks	4.5	Fin/R.E.
Communications, except radio & TV	5.9	Util.	S/L Govt. purch., other general government	3.7	S/L Govt
Motor freight transportation & warehousing	5.8	Util.	Wholesale trade	3.7	Trade
Banking	5.7	Fin/R.E.	Real estate	3.6	Fin/R.E.
U.S. Postal Service	4.7	Gov't	Retail trade, except eating & drinking	3.3	Trade
Eating & drinking places	4.5	Trade	Banking	1.9	Fin/R.E.
Equipment rental & leasing services	3.4	Services	Eating & drinking places	1.4	Trade
Advertising	2.9	Services	Communications, except radio & TV	1.1	Util.
Accounting, auditing & bookkeeping	2.8	Services	Petroleum refining	1.1	Manufg.
Maintenance of nonfarm buildings nec	2.8	Constr.	Federal Government purchases, nondefense	1.0	Fed Govt
Blankbooks & looseleaf binders	2.5	Manufg.	Electric services (utilities)	0.9	Util.
Management & consulting services & labs	2.4	Services	Engineering, architectural, & surveying services	0.7	Services
Federal Government enterprises nec	2.1	Gov't	Meat animals	0.7	Agric.
Insurance carriers	2.1	Fin/R.E.	Aircraft	0.6	Manufg.
Photographic equipment & supplies	1.7	Manufg.	Apparel made from purchased materials	0.5	Manufg.
Electric services (utilities)	1.6	Util.	Crude petroleum & natural gas	0.5	Mining
Detective & protective services	1.5	Services	Gas production & distribution (utilities)	0.5	Util.
Legal services	1.4	Services	Insurance carriers	0.5	Fin/R.E.
Noncomparable imports	1.4	Foreign	Electronic computing equipment	0.4	Manufg.
Petroleum refining	1.2	Manufg.	Feed grains	0.4	Agric.
Wholesale trade	1.2	Trade	Maintenance of nonfarm buildings nec	0.4	Constr.
Manifold business forms	1.0	Manufg.	Motor freight transportation & warehousing	0.4	Util.
Credit agencies other than banks	0.9	Fin/R.E.	Dairy farm products	0.3	Agric.
Personnel supply services	0.9	Services	Doctors & dentists	0.3	Services
Business/professional associations	0.8	Services	Drugs	0.3	Manufg.
Commercial printing	0.8	Manufg.	Freight forwarders	0.3	Util.
Air transportation	0.6	Util.	Management & consulting services & labs	0.3	Services
Envelopes	0.6	Manufg.	Owner-occupied dwellings	0.3	Fin/R.E.
Electrical repair shops	0.4	Services	Security & commodity brokers	0.3	Fin/R.E.
Transit & bus transportation	0.4	Util.	Advertising	0.2	Services
Electronic components nec	0.3	Manufg.	Agricultural chemicals, nec	0.2	Manufg.
Electronic computing equipment	0.3	Manufg.	Air transportation	0.2	Util.
Engraving & plate printing	0.3	Manufg.	Aircraft & missile engines & engine parts	0.2	Manufg.
Manufacturing industries, nec	0.3	Manufg.	Aircraft & missile equipment, nec	0.2	Manufg.
Paper mills, except building paper	0.3	Manufg.	Broadwoven fabric mills	0.2	Manufg.
Periodicals	0.3	Manufg.	Chemical & fertilizer mineral	0.2	Mining
Services to dwellings & other buildings	0.3	Services	Coal	0.2	Mining
Textile bags	0.3	Manufg.	Computer & data processing services	0.2	Services
Automotive rental & leasing, without drivers	0.2	Services	Electronic components nec	0.2	Manufg.
Hotels & lodging places	0.2	Services	Hotels & lodging places	0.2	Services
Sanitary services, steam supply, irrigation	0.2	Util.	Industrial buildings	0.2	Constr.
Carbon paper & inked ribbons	0.1	Manufg.	Laundry, dry cleaning, shoe repair	0.2	Services
Newspapers	0.1	Manufg.	Machinery, except electrical, nec	0.2	Manufg.
			Medical & health services, nec	0.2	Services
			Motor vehicles & car bodies	0.2	Manufg.
			Newspapers	0.2	Manufg.
			Nonfarm residential structure maintenance	0.2	Constr.
			Office buildings	0.2	Constr.
			Oil bearing crops	0.2	Agric.
			Photographic equipment & supplies	0.2	Manufg.
			Radio & TV broadcasting	0.2	Util.
			Radio & TV communication equipment	0.2	Manufg.
			Railroads & related services	0.2	Util.
			Residential 1-unit structures, nonfarm	0.2	Constr.
			Semiconductors & related devices	0.2	Manufg.
			Water transportation	0.2	Util.

Continued on next page.

INPUTS AND OUTPUTS FOR ALL BANKING SECTORS - SICs 601, 602, 603, 608, and 609 - Continued

Economic Sector or Industry Providing Inputs	%	Sector	Economic Sector or Industry Buying Outputs	%	Sector
			Arrangement of passenger transportation	0.1	Util.
			Automotive repair shops & services	0.1	Services
			Blast furnaces & steel mills	0.1	Manufg.
			Bottled & canned soft drinks	0.1	Manufg.
			Business services nec	0.1	Services
			Commercial printing	0.1	Manufg.
			Cyclic crudes and organics	0.1	Manufg.
			Equipment rental & leasing services	0.1	Services
			Food grains	0.1	Agric.
			Malt beverages	0.1	Manufg.
			Metal office furniture	0.1	Manufg.
			Miscellaneous plastics products	0.1	Manufg.
			Motion pictures	0.1	Services
			Pipe, valves, & pipe fittings	0.1	Manufg.
			Pipelines, except natural gas	0.1	Util.
			Portrait, photographic studios	0.1	Services
			Prepared feeds, nec	0.1	Manufg.
			Primary aluminum	0.1	Manufg.
			Residential additions/alterations, nonfarm	0.1	Constr.

Source: Benchmark Input-Output Accounts for the U.S. Economy, 1982, U.S. Department of Commerce, Washington, D.C., July 1991. Data, as reported in the source, are organized by the 1977 SIC structure in use in 1982 but have been matched, as closely as is possible, to the 1987 SIC structure used in this book. Activities with the same percentage are sorted alphabetically by name of activity.

OCCUPATIONS EMPLOYED BY BANKING AND CLOSELY RELATED FUNCTIONS, NEC

Occupation	% of Total 1994	Change to 2005	Occupation	% of Total 1994	Change to 2005
Bank tellers	8.1	32.9	Clerical support workers nec	2.4	6.3
General office clerks	7.2	13.3	Loan officers & counselors	2.3	45.0
Management support workers nec	6.8	32.9	Computer programmers	2.2	7.6
Clerical supervisors & managers	5.8	35.9	Systems analysts	2.1	112.6
Adjustment clerks	5.0	79.4	Sales & related workers nec	2.0	32.9
Secretaries, ex legal & medical	4.2	21.0	Credit analysts	1.9	6.3
Cashiers	4.2	29.6	Securities & financial services sales workers	1.7	32.8
Bookkeeping, accounting, & auditing clerks	3.8	-0.3	Managers & administrators nec	1.5	32.8
General managers & top executives	3.7	26.1	Data entry keyers, ex composing	1.5	-2.0
Financial managers	3.2	32.9	Computer operators, ex peripheral equipment	1.4	-24.5
Accountants & auditors	3.1	32.9	Guards	1.1	19.6
Duplicating, mail, & office machine operators	2.7	-22.5	Brokerage clerks	1.0	46.2
Loan & credit clerks	2.7	19.6			

Sources: Industry-Occupation Matrix, Bureau of Labor Statistics. These data relate to one or more 3-digit SIC industry groups rather than to a single 4-digit SIC. The change reported for each occupation to the year 2005 is a percent of growth or decline as estimated by the Bureau of Labor Statistics. The abbreviation *nec* stands for not elsewhere classified.

U.S. AND STATE DATA ON INDUSTRY REVENUES AND OTHER ACCOUNTS FOR 1992

State	No. of Estab.	Employment	Payroll ($ mil.)	Revenues ($ mil.)	Empl./ Estab.	Revenue/ Estab. ($)	Payroll/ Estab. ($)	Revenue/ Empl. ($)	Payroll/ Empl. ($)
UNITED STATES	67	26,334	870.4	29,571.7	393	441,369,149	12,991,388	1,122,949	33,053
California	3	2,260	83.2	4,549.0	753	516,321,333	27,740,000	2,012,816	36,823
Colorado	2	392	11.2	18.9	196	9,442,000	5,624,500	48,173	28,696
Florida	2	676	19.3	30.1	338	15,030,000	9,633,000	44,467	28,500
Georgia	2	1,350	49.2	1,780.6	675	890,317,000	24,585,000	1,318,988	36,422
Illinois	2	1,994	73.8	2,449.2	997	224,619,500	36,919,500	1,228,304	37,031
Indiana	1	155	4.8	554.8	155	554,750,000	4,840,000	3,579,032	31,226
Maryland	1	433	11.5	321.3	433	321,307,000	11,537,000	742,048	26,644
Massachusetts	2	1,686	55.1	1,887.6	843	943,789,500	27,527,000	1,119,560	32,654
Michigan	1	426	11.6	440.6	426	440,563,000	11,581,000	1,034,185	27,185
Minnesota	2	1,086	35.9	431.2	543	215,580,000	17,939,000	397,017	33,037
Missouri	4	1,828	60.8	1,100.9	457	275,217,750	15,198,000	602,227	33,256
New Jersey	1	185	5.1	558.0	185	557,951,000	5,087,000	3,015,951	27,497
New York	3	4,167	153.3	8,259.7	1,389	753,224,000	51,108,000	1,982,163	36,795
North Carolina	1	419	10.2	310.9	419	310,917,000	10,230,000	742,045	24,415
Ohio	5	1,342	42.7	1,462.7	268	292,531,200	8,535,200	1,089,908	31,800
Pennsylvania	4	2,244	65.6	1,354.9	561	338,730,750	16,411,000	603,798	29,253
Tennessee	3	419	9.8	76.2	140	25,406,000	3,258,000	181,905	23,327
Texas	5	1,818	59.9	1,516.4	364	303,275,000	11,976,400	834,090	32,938
Virginia	2	1,138	44.5	825.2	569	412,597,000	22,270,000	725,127	39,139
Washington	2	277	9.4	689.6	139	344,815,000	4,701,000	2,489,639	33,942

Source: 1992 Economic Census, U.S. Department of Commerce, Washington, D.C. This is the only table that shows revenue data as collected by the Bureau of the Census in an Economic Census. The symbol (D) indicates that data are withheld by the source to avoid disclosure of competitive information. A dash (-) indicates that data are not available or cannot be calculated.

ESTABLISHMENTS 1992 - STATE AND REGIONAL CONCENTRATION

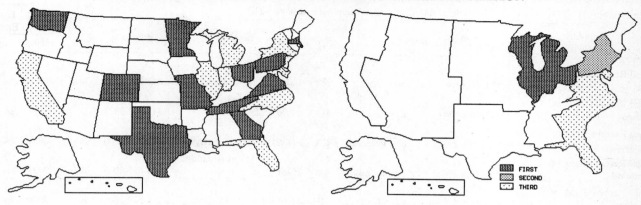

EMPLOYMENT 1992 - STATE AND REGIONAL CONCENTRATION

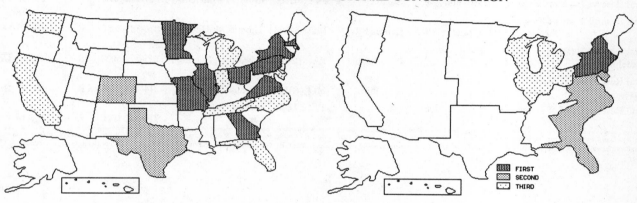

REVENUES 1992 - STATE AND REGIONAL CONCENTRATION

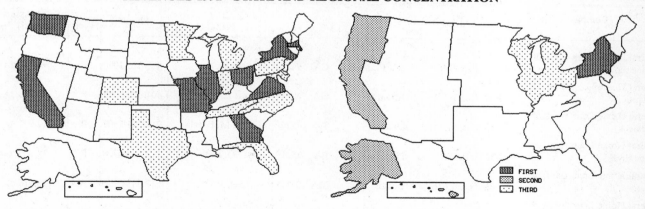

States with the darkest shading indicate those states which have proportionately more establishments, employment, or revenues than would be indicated by the state's population. States with light shading are states with proportionately fewer establishments, less employment, and lower revenues than population distribution. States shaded grey are within 15 percent of the state's population proportion in these categories. States for which no data are available are shown as average (grey). *Regions* are shaded to indicate absolute rank in the category. If no data for the category are available, establishment counts are used to shade the regions. Source of the data is the table on the facing page.

LEADING COMPANIES - SIC 6011 - Federal Reserve Banks

Number shown: **11**   Total sales/assets ($ mil): **407,621**   Total employment (000): **22.3**

Company Name	Address				CEO Name	Phone	Co. Type	Sales/Assets ($ mil)	Empl. (000)
Federal Reserve Bank of New York	33 Liberty St.	New York	NY	10045	William J. McDonough	212-720-5000	R	160,707 TA	4.0
Federal Reserve Bank of Chicago	P.O. Box 834	Chicago	IL	60690	Silas Keehn	312-322-5322	R	47,400 TA	2.0
Federal Reserve Bank of San Francisco	P.O. Box 7702	San Francisco	CA	94120	Robert T. Parry	415-974-2000	R	38,122 TA	2.5
Federal Reserve Bank of Richmond	P.O. Box 27622	Richmond	VA	23261	J. Alfred Broaddus Jr.	804-697-8000	R	33,080 TA	2.6
Federal Reserve Bank of Cleveland	P.O. Box 6387	Cleveland	OH	44101	Jerry L. Jordan	216-579-2000	R	22,684 TA	1.4
Federal Reserve Bank of Atlanta	104 Marietta St. N.W.	Atlanta	GA	30303	Robert P. Forrestal	404-521-8500	R	22,573 TA	2.4
Federal Reserve Bank of Boston	600 Atlantic Ave.	Boston	MA	02106	Cathy E. Minehan	617-973-3000	R	20,000 TA	1.5
Federal Reserve Bank of Kansas City	925 Grand Ave.	Kansas City	MO	64198	Thomas M. Hoenig	816-881-2000	R	16,493 TA	1.7
Federal Reserve Bank of Philadelphia	10 Independence Mall	Philadelphia	PA	19106	Edward G. Boehne	215-574-6000	R	16,059 TA	1.4
Federal Reserve Bank of St. Louis	P.O. Box 442	St. Louis	MO	63166	Thomas C. Melzer	314-444-8444	R	15,387 TA	1.2
Federal Reserve Bank of Dallas	P.O. Box 655906	Dallas	TX	75265	Robert D. McTeer Jr.	214-922-6000	R	15,116 TA	1.6

Source: Ward's Business Directory of U.S. Private and Public Companies, 1996. Company type codes: P - Public, R - Private, S - Subsidiary, D - Division, J - Joint Venture, A - Affiliate, G - Group. If the dollar values shown are not sales, the following codes apply: TA - Total Assets; OR - Operating Revenues; GB - Gross Billings. * - estimated dollar value. < - less than; *na* - not available.

LEADING COMPANIES - SIC 6019 - Central Reserve Depositories, nec

Number shown: **12**   Total sales/assets ($ mil): **188,737**   Total employment (000): **2.1**

Company Name	Address				CEO Name	Phone	Co. Type	Sales/Assets ($ mil)	Empl. (000)
Federal Home Loan Bank of San Francisco	P.O. Box 7948	San Francisco	CA	94120	M. Schultz	415-616-1000	R	49,900 TA	0.2
Federal Home Loan Bank of Atlanta	P.O. Box 105565	Atlanta	GA	30348	Robert E. Showfety	404-888-8000	R	24,616 TA	0.2
Federal Home Loan Bank of Dallas	P.O. Box 619026	Dallas	TX	75261	George M. Barclay	214-714-8500	R	17,991 TA	0.1
Federal Home Loan Bank of Pittsburgh	601 Grant St.	Pittsburgh	PA	15219	James D. Roy	412-288-3400	R	14,120 TA*	0.2
Federal Home Loan Bank of Boston	1 Financial Ctr.	Boston	MA	02111	Michael A. Jessee	617-542-0150	R	13,916 TA	0.1
Federal Home Loan Bank of Indianapolis	P.O. Box 60	Indianapolis	IN	46206	Martin L. Heger	317-465-0200	R	13,646 TA	0.1
Federal Home Loan Bank of Seattle	1501 4th Ave.	Seattle	WA	98101	James R. Faulstich	206-340-2300	R	12,701 TA	<0.1

Company type codes: P - Public, R - Private, S - Subsidiary, D - Division, J - Joint Venture, A - Affiliate, G - Group. If the dollar values shown are not sales, the following codes apply: TA - Total Assets; OR - Operating Revenues; GB - Gross Billings. * - estimated dollar value. < - less than. *na* - not available.

Continued on next page.

LEADING COMPANIES - SIC 6019 - Central Reserve Depositories, nec
Continued

Company Name	Address				CEO Name	Phone	Co. Type	Sales/Assets ($ mil)	Empl. (000)
Federal Home Loan Bank of Des Moines	907 Walnut St.	Des Moines	IA	50309	Thurmond C. Connell	515-243-4211	R	11,650 TA	0.3
Federal Home Loan Bank of Chicago	111 E. Wacker Dr.	Chicago	IL	60601	Alex J. Pollock	312-565-5700	R	10,943 TA	0.1
Federal Home Loan Bank of Cincinnati	P.O. Box 598	Cincinnati	OH	45201	Charles L. Thiemann	513-852-7500	R	9,965 TA	0.3
Federal Home Loan Bank of Topeka	P.O. Box 176	Topeka	KS	66601	Frank A. Lowman	913-233-0507	R	9,265 TA	0.2
Federal Home Loan Bank of New York	1 World Trade Ctr.	New York	NY	10048	Alfred A. Dellibovi	212-441-6600	R	23 TA	0.2

Source: *Ward's Business Directory of U.S. Private and Public Companies*, 1996. Company type codes: P - Public, R - Private, S - Subsidiary, D - Division, J - Joint Venture, A - Affiliate, G - Group. If the dollar values shown are not sales, the following codes apply: TA - Total Assets; OR - Operating Revenues; GB - Gross Billings. * - estimated dollar value. < - less than; *na* - not available.

SIC 6020

COMMERCIAL BANKS

The category of Commercial Banks includes banks and trust companies that accept deposits from the public. SIC 6020 is further subdivided into (1) National Commercial Banks (SIC 6021), which are commercial banks and trust companies that accept deposits and are chartered under the National Bank Act; (2) State Commercial Banks (SIC 6022), which are commercial banks and trust companies that accept deposits and are chartered by states or territories; and (3) Commercial Banks, not elsewhere classified (SIC 6029), which are commercial banks that accept deposits and do not operate under federal or state charter. Trust companies engaged in fiduciary business but not regularly engaged in deposit banking are classified as SIC 6091 and included, in this book, under Functions Closely Related to Banking (SIC 6090).

ESTABLISHMENTS, EMPLOYMENT, AND PAYROLL

	1988	1989		1990		1991		1992		1993		% change 88-93
		Value	%	Value	%	Value	%	Value	%	Value	%	
All Establishments	49,567	51,284	3.5	52,303	2.0	61,395	17.4	65,049	6.0	62,629	-3.7	26.4
Mid-March Employment	1,454,561	1,463,412	0.6	1,472,304	0.6	1,606,240	9.1	1,576,334	-1.9	1,528,258	-3.0	5.1
1st Quarter Wages (annualized - $ mil.)	33,983.8	35,982.0	5.9	37,903.8	5.3	42,661.1	12.6	44,325.8	3.9	42,770.8	-3.5	25.9
Payroll per Emp. 1st Q. (annualized)	23,364	24,588	5.2	25,745	4.7	26,560	3.2	28,120	5.9	27,987	-0.5	19.8
Annual Payroll ($ mil.)	32,120.0	33,620.7	4.7	35,567.3	5.8	39,720.3	11.7	42,518.2	7.0	42,099.7	-1.0	31.1
Establishments - 1-4 Emp. Number	5,468	5,776	5.6	5,971	3.4	6,686	12.0	9,464	41.5	9,220	-2.6	68.6
Mid-March Employment	14,493	14,980	3.4	(D)	-	17,647	-	26,404	49.6	24,677	-6.5	70.3
1st Quarter Wages (annualized - $ mil.)	305.6	366.5	19.9	(D)	-	485.5	-	643.7	32.6	584.5	-9.2	91.3
Payroll per Emp. 1st Q. (annualized)	21,083	24,463	16.0	(D)	-	27,513	-	24,380	-11.4	23,687	-2.8	12.3
Annual Payroll ($ mil.)	440.8	489.9	11.1	(D)	-	554.6	-	705.4	27.2	664.6	-5.8	50.8
Establishments - 5-9 Emp. Number	14,508	15,325	5.6	15,871	3.6	18,545	16.8	22,048	18.9	20,664	-6.3	42.4
Mid-March Employment	102,108	107,765	5.5	111,483	3.5	131,253	17.7	153,187	16.7	143,829	-6.1	40.9
1st Quarter Wages (annualized - $ mil.)	1,721.4	1,981.2	15.1	2,170.6	9.6	2,686.4	23.8	3,165.0	17.8	2,834.9	-10.4	64.7
Payroll per Emp. 1st Q. (annualized)	16,859	18,384	9.0	19,470	5.9	20,468	5.1	20,661	0.9	19,710	-4.6	16.9
Annual Payroll ($ mil.)	1,765.2	1,978.7	12.1	2,177.0	10.0	2,624.9	20.6	3,199.7	21.9	2,913.3	-8.9	65.0
Establishments - 10-19 Emp. Number	15,281	15,672	2.6	15,653	-0.1	21,323	36.2	19,210	-9.9	18,497	-3.7	21.0
Mid-March Employment	205,230	210,625	2.6	209,283	-0.6	286,850	37.1	255,785	-10.8	247,056	-3.4	20.4
1st Quarter Wages (annualized - $ mil.)	3,656.4	3,983.6	8.9	4,214.6	5.8	5,987.8	42.1	5,530.5	-7.6	5,152.4	-6.8	40.9
Payroll per Emp. 1st Q. (annualized)	17,816	18,913	6.2	20,138	6.5	20,874	3.7	21,622	3.6	20,855	-3.5	17.1
Annual Payroll ($ mil.)	3,679.9	3,950.5	7.4	4,157.0	5.2	5,766.2	38.7	5,504.1	-4.5	5,255.1	-4.5	42.8
Establishments - 20-49 Emp. Number	9,534	9,785	2.6	10,034	2.5	10,666	6.3	10,112	-5.2	10,096	-0.2	5.9
Mid-March Employment	286,477	292,384	2.1	301,951	3.3	311,243	3.1	297,617	-4.4	298,874	0.4	4.3
1st Quarter Wages (annualized - $ mil.)	5,406.8	5,706.5	5.5	6,144.3	7.7	6,720.5	9.4	6,888.8	2.5	6,777.6	-1.6	25.4
Payroll per Emp. 1st Q. (annualized)	18,873	19,517	3.4	20,349	4.3	21,593	6.1	23,147	7.2	22,677	-2.0	20.2
Annual Payroll ($ mil.)	5,348.6	5,610.2	4.9	6,055.4	7.9	6,414.4	5.9	6,841.3	6.7	6,772.7	-1.0	26.6
Establishments - 50-99 Emp. Number	2,905	2,851	-1.9	2,895	1.5	2,376	-17.9	2,408	1.3	2,384	-1.0	-17.9
Mid-March Employment	197,165	193,665	-1.8	194,832	0.6	158,975	-18.4	161,400	1.5	160,499	-0.6	-18.6
1st Quarter Wages (annualized - $ mil.)	3,958.6	4,078.2	3.0	4,216.1	3.4	3,820.7	-9.4	4,206.5	10.1	4,148.4	-1.4	4.8
Payroll per Emp. 1st Q. (annualized)	20,077	21,058	4.9	21,640	2.8	24,033	11.1	26,063	8.4	25,847	-0.8	28.7
Annual Payroll ($ mil.)	3,853.2	3,954.6	2.6	4,081.0	3.2	3,597.8	-11.8	4,086.8	13.6	4,110.4	0.6	6.7
Establishments - 100-249 Emp. Number	1,271	1,272	0.1	1,288	1.3	1,110	-13.8	1,141	2.8	1,131	-0.9	-11.0
Mid-March Employment	187,493	186,359	-0.6	190,303	2.1	167,159	-12.2	170,084	1.7	169,461	-0.4	-9.6
1st Quarter Wages (annualized - $ mil.)	4,265.6	4,397.5	3.1	4,771.9	8.5	4,602.1	-3.6	4,860.4	5.6	4,830.3	-0.6	13.2
Payroll per Emp. 1st Q. (annualized)	22,751	23,597	3.7	25,075	6.3	27,531	9.8	28,576	3.8	28,504	-0.3	25.3
Annual Payroll ($ mil.)	4,054.4	4,168.3	2.8	4,508.7	8.2	4,232.4	-6.1	4,670.9	10.4	4,755.4	1.8	17.3
Establishments - 250-499 Emp. Number	334	343	2.7	337	-1.7	388	15.1	367	-5.4	347	-5.4	3.9
Mid-March Employment	114,191	117,633	3.0	117,946	0.3	133,507	13.2	125,541	-6.0	122,838	-2.2	7.6
1st Quarter Wages (annualized - $ mil.)	2,916.1	3,214.3	10.2	3,482.6	8.3	4,009.3	15.1	4,121.1	2.8	4,369.2	6.0	49.8
Payroll per Emp. 1st Q. (annualized)	25,537	27,325	7.0	29,527	8.1	30,030	1.7	32,827	9.3	35,569	8.4	39.3
Annual Payroll ($ mil.)	2,779.3	3,001.2	8.0	3,267.5	8.9	3,672.8	12.4	3,900.3	6.2	4,266.2	9.4	53.5
Establishments - 500-999 Emp. Number	158	153	-3.2	158	3.3	174	10.1	174	-	175	0.6	10.8
Mid-March Employment	109,345	105,802	-3.2	110,948	4.9	123,327	11.2	121,128	-1.8	120,841	-0.2	10.5
1st Quarter Wages (annualized - $ mil.)	3,159.5	3,183.6	0.8	3,600.5	13.1	4,012.2	11.4	3,975.8	-0.9	4,266.6	7.3	35.0
Payroll per Emp. 1st Q. (annualized)	28,895	30,090	4.1	32,452	7.8	32,533	0.3	32,823	0.9	35,307	7.6	22.2
Annual Payroll ($ mil.)	2,830.5	2,858.7	1.0	3,236.9	13.2	3,727.6	15.2	3,771.2	1.2	4,089.3	8.4	44.5
Estab. - 1000 or More Emp. Number	108	107	-0.9	96	-10.3	127	32.3	125	-1.6	115	-8.0	6.5
Mid-March Employment	238,059	234,199	-1.6	(D)	-	276,279	-	265,188	-4.0	240,183	-9.4	0.9
1st Quarter Wages (annualized - $ mil.)	8,593.9	9,070.7	5.5	(D)	-	10,336.6	-	10,933.9	5.8	9,806.8	-10.3	14.1
Payroll per Emp. 1st Q. (annualized)	36,100	38,731	7.3	(D)	-	37,414	-	41,231	10.2	40,831	-1.0	13.1
Annual Payroll ($ mil.)	7,368.1	7,608.6	3.3	(D)	-	9,129.6	-	9,838.6	7.8	9,272.7	-5.8	25.8

Source: County Business Patterns, U.S. Department of Commerce, Washington, D.C., for 1988 through 1993. Payroll per employee is calculated using mid-March employment and 1st Quarter wages, annualized. Annual payroll, also shown, may not equal the annualized 1st Quarter wages. Columns headed by a percent sign (%) indicate change from the previous year. *na* stands for not available. The symbol (D) indicates that data are withheld by the source to avoid disclosure of competitive information. A dash (-) indicates that data are not available or cannot be calculated.

ESTABLISHMENTS
Number

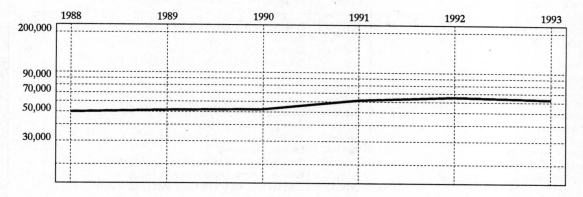

MID-MARCH EMPLOYMENT
Number

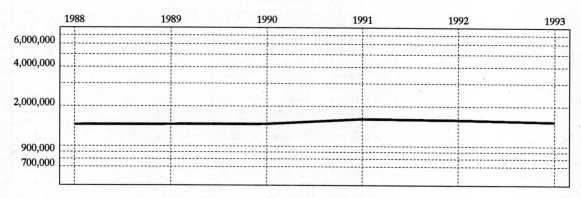

ANNUAL PAYROLL
$ million

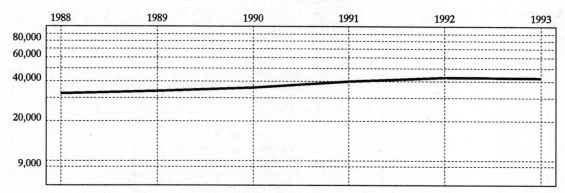

INPUTS AND OUTPUTS FOR ALL BANKING SECTORS - SICs 601, 602, 603, 608, and 609

Economic Sector or Industry Providing Inputs	%	Sector	Economic Sector or Industry Buying Outputs	%	Sector
Computer & data processing services	13.3	Services	Personal consumption expenditures	43.5	
Security & commodity brokers	10.1	Fin/R.E.	Exports	5.3	Foreign
Real estate	8.0	Fin/R.E.	Credit agencies other than banks	4.5	Fin/R.E.
Communications, except radio & TV	5.9	Util.	S/L Govt. purch., other general government	3.7	S/L Govt
Motor freight transportation & warehousing	5.8	Util.	Wholesale trade	3.7	Trade
Banking	5.7	Fin/R.E.	Real estate	3.6	Fin/R.E.
U.S. Postal Service	4.7	Gov't	Retail trade, except eating & drinking	3.3	Trade
Eating & drinking places	4.5	Trade	Banking	1.9	Fin/R.E.
Equipment rental & leasing services	3.4	Services	Eating & drinking places	1.4	Trade
Advertising	2.9	Services	Communications, except radio & TV	1.1	Util.
Accounting, auditing & bookkeeping	2.8	Services	Petroleum refining	1.1	Manufg.
Maintenance of nonfarm buildings nec	2.8	Constr.	Federal Government purchases, nondefense	1.0	Fed Govt
Blankbooks & looseleaf binders	2.5	Manufg.	Electric services (utilities)	0.9	Util.
Management & consulting services & labs	2.4	Services	Engineering, architectural, & surveying services	0.7	Services
Federal Government enterprises nec	2.1	Gov't	Meat animals	0.7	Agric.
Insurance carriers	2.1	Fin/R.E.	Aircraft	0.6	Manufg.
Photographic equipment & supplies	1.7	Manufg.	Apparel made from purchased materials	0.5	Manufg.
Electric services (utilities)	1.6	Util.	Crude petroleum & natural gas	0.5	Mining
Detective & protective services	1.5	Services	Gas production & distribution (utilities)	0.5	Util.
Legal services	1.4	Services	Insurance carriers	0.5	Fin/R.E.
Noncomparable imports	1.4	Foreign	Electronic computing equipment	0.4	Manufg.
Petroleum refining	1.2	Manufg.	Feed grains	0.4	Agric.
Wholesale trade	1.2	Trade	Maintenance of nonfarm buildings nec	0.4	Constr.
Manifold business forms	1.0	Manufg.	Motor freight transportation & warehousing	0.4	Util.
Credit agencies other than banks	0.9	Fin/R.E.	Dairy farm products	0.3	Agric.
Personnel supply services	0.9	Services	Doctors & dentists	0.3	Services
Business/professional associations	0.8	Services	Drugs	0.3	Manufg.
Commercial printing	0.8	Manufg.	Freight forwarders	0.3	Util.
Air transportation	0.6	Util.	Management & consulting services & labs	0.3	Services
Envelopes	0.6	Manufg.	Owner-occupied dwellings	0.3	Fin/R.E.
Electrical repair shops	0.4	Services	Security & commodity brokers	0.3	Fin/R.E.
Transit & bus transportation	0.4	Util.	Advertising	0.2	Services
Electronic components nec	0.3	Manufg.	Agricultural chemicals, nec	0.2	Manufg.
Electronic computing equipment	0.3	Manufg.	Air transportation	0.2	Util.
Engraving & plate printing	0.3	Manufg.	Aircraft & missile engines & engine parts	0.2	Manufg.
Manufacturing industries, nec	0.3	Manufg.	Aircraft & missile equipment, nec	0.2	Manufg.
Paper mills, except building paper	0.3	Manufg.	Broadwoven fabric mills	0.2	Manufg.
Periodicals	0.3	Manufg.	Chemical & fertilizer mineral	0.2	Mining
Services to dwellings & other buildings	0.3	Services	Coal	0.2	Mining
Textile bags	0.3	Manufg.	Computer & data processing services	0.2	Services
Automotive rental & leasing, without drivers	0.2	Services	Electronic components nec	0.2	Manufg.
Hotels & lodging places	0.2	Services	Hotels & lodging places	0.2	Services
Sanitary services, steam supply, irrigation	0.2	Util.	Industrial buildings	0.2	Constr.
Carbon paper & inked ribbons	0.1	Manufg.	Laundry, dry cleaning, shoe repair	0.2	Services
Newspapers	0.1	Manufg.	Machinery, except electrical, nec	0.2	Manufg.
			Medical & health services, nec	0.2	Services
			Motor vehicles & car bodies	0.2	Manufg.
			Newspapers	0.2	Manufg.
			Nonfarm residential structure maintenance	0.2	Constr.
			Office buildings	0.2	Constr.
			Oil bearing crops	0.2	Agric.
			Photographic equipment & supplies	0.2	Manufg.
			Radio & TV broadcasting	0.2	Util.
			Radio & TV communication equipment	0.2	Manufg.
			Railroads & related services	0.2	Util.
			Residential 1-unit structures, nonfarm	0.2	Constr.
			Semiconductors & related devices	0.2	Manufg.
			Water transportation	0.2	Util.

Continued on next page.

INPUTS AND OUTPUTS FOR ALL BANKING SECTORS - SICs 601, 602, 603, 608, and 609 - Continued

Economic Sector or Industry Providing Inputs	%	Sector	Economic Sector or Industry Buying Outputs	%	Sector
			Arrangement of passenger transportation	0.1	Util.
			Automotive repair shops & services	0.1	Services
			Blast furnaces & steel mills	0.1	Manufg.
			Bottled & canned soft drinks	0.1	Manufg.
			Business services nec	0.1	Services
			Commercial printing	0.1	Manufg.
			Cyclic crudes and organics	0.1	Manufg.
			Equipment rental & leasing services	0.1	Services
			Food grains	0.1	Agric.
			Malt beverages	0.1	Manufg.
			Metal office furniture	0.1	Manufg.
			Miscellaneous plastics products	0.1	Manufg.
			Motion pictures	0.1	Services
			Pipe, valves, & pipe fittings	0.1	Manufg.
			Pipelines, except natural gas	0.1	Util.
			Portrait, photographic studios	0.1	Services
			Prepared feeds, nec	0.1	Manufg.
			Primary aluminum	0.1	Manufg.
			Residential additions/alterations, nonfarm	0.1	Constr.

Source: Benchmark Input-Output Accounts for the U.S. Economy, 1982, U.S. Department of Commerce, Washington, D.C., July 1991. Data, as reported in the source, are organized by the 1977 SIC structure in use in 1982 but have been matched, as closely as is possible, to the 1987 SIC structure used in this book. Activities with the same percentage are sorted alphabetically by name of activity.

OCCUPATIONS EMPLOYED BY COMMERCIAL BANKS, SAVINGS INSTITUTIONS, CREDIT UNIONS

Occupation	% of Total 1994	Change to 2005	Occupation	% of Total 1994	Change to 2005
Bank tellers	27.8	-29.8	General managers & top executives	3.0	-4.0
Clerical supervisors & managers	6.5	12.9	Management support workers nec	2.6	1.2
Loan officers & counselors	6.4	8.8	Clerical support workers nec	1.4	-19.1
Financial managers	6.2	16.3	Accountants & auditors	1.4	-14.0
New accounts clerks, banking	5.8	1.2	Securities & financial services sales workers	1.3	11.3
Loan & credit clerks	5.2	-9.0	Adjustment clerks	1.3	5.3
General office clerks	3.9	-32.6	Statement clerks	1.1	-39.6
Bookkeeping, accounting, & auditing clerks	3.7	-24.1	Duplicating, mail, & office machine operators	1.0	-41.0
Secretaries, ex legal & medical	3.6	-18.1			

Sources: Industry-Occupation Matrix, Bureau of Labor Statistics. These data relate to one or more 3-digit SIC industry groups rather than to a single 4-digit SIC. The change reported for each occupation to the year 2005 is a percent of growth or decline as estimated by the Bureau of Labor Statistics. The abbreviation nec stands for not elsewhere classified.

U.S. AND STATE DATA ON INDUSTRY REVENUES AND OTHER ACCOUNTS FOR 1992

State	No. of Estab.	Employ-ment	Payroll ($ mil.)	Revenues ($ mil.)	Empl./ Estab.	Revenue/ Estab. ($)	Payroll/ Estab. ($)	Revenue/ Empl. ($)	Payroll/ Empl. ($)
UNITED STATES	62,761	1,506,055	41,206.5	318,076.7	24	5,068,064	656,562	211,199	27,361
Alabama	1,051	23,634	532.8	3,779.9	22	3,596,465	506,909	159,934	22,542
Alaska	127	2,623	72.7	414.8	21	3,265,961	572,252	158,131	27,707
Arizona	828	20,336	576.8	2,517.2	25	3,040,051	696,582	123,779	28,362
Arkansas	831	13,532	285.2	1,978.1	16	2,380,384	343,224	146,179	21,077
California	5,746	145,006	4,224.7	29,229.7	25	5,086,962	735,237	201,576	29,134
Colorado	584	15,977	409.7	2,751.3	27	4,711,146	701,553	172,204	25,644
Connecticut	656	16,568	485.3	2,746.3	25	4,186,502	739,723	165,762	29,289
Delaware	212	22,219	620.2	9,405.4	105	44,365,179	2,925,476	423,305	27,913
District of Columbia	207	4,286	140.3	1,022.1	21	4,937,502	677,657	238,465	32,729
Florida	3,211	74,700	1,763.2	12,904.5	23	4,018,837	549,101	172,751	23,603
Georgia	1,789	41,591	1,066.0	7,205.4	23	4,027,587	595,841	173,243	25,630
Hawaii	251	8,163	237.5	1,619.1	33	6,450,550	946,068	198,345	29,090
Idaho	332	6,523	150.4	864.9	20	2,605,130	453,048	132,593	23,059
Illinois	2,064	82,220	2,471.0	14,489.4	40	7,020,068	1,197,211	176,227	30,054
Indiana	1,765	35,194	759.0	5,490.1	20	3,110,556	430,003	155,996	21,565
Iowa	1,013	18,368	427.2	3,323.4	18	3,280,725	421,751	180,933	23,260
Kansas	901	15,573	363.1	2,567.1	17	2,849,179	402,973	164,844	23,315
Kentucky	1,098	23,445	519.4	4,029.7	21	3,670,024	473,065	171,878	22,155
Louisiana	1,196	23,430	526.0	3,426.1	20	2,864,606	439,807	146,226	22,450
Maine	335	5,030	118.4	810.5	15	2,419,296	353,570	161,126	23,548
Maryland	1,452	30,524	798.2	5,188.4	21	3,573,312	549,751	169,979	26,151
Massachusetts	1,065	40,388	1,263.7	10,537.1	38	9,894,017	1,186,551	260,897	31,288
Michigan	2,559	52,750	1,243.6	8,987.0	21	3,511,922	485,969	170,370	23,575
Minnesota	1,137	25,980	724.5	4,639.4	23	4,080,429	637,224	178,578	27,888
Mississippi	863	13,396	291.7	1,900.2	16	2,201,896	338,044	141,851	21,778
Missouri	1,430	34,060	758.8	5,487.0	24	3,837,034	530,611	161,097	22,278
Montana	199	4,171	94.6	668.1	21	3,357,307	475,422	160,178	22,683
Nebraska	648	11,702	269.8	2,154.9	18	3,325,427	416,381	184,146	23,057
Nevada	337	6,516	149.6	2,049.4	19	6,081,255	443,819	314,516	22,954
New Hampshire	191	3,579	79.9	1,064.1	19	5,570,984	418,356	297,306	22,326
New Jersey	2,147	42,069	1,101.1	7,315.2	20	3,407,166	512,837	173,885	26,173
New Mexico	408	8,157	171.0	1,104.3	20	2,706,728	419,042	135,386	20,960
New York	3,714	155,855	6,889.6	70,480.3	42	18,976,928	1,855,034	452,217	44,205
North Carolina	2,096	40,769	995.4	7,462.1	19	3,560,150	474,903	183,033	24,416
North Dakota	267	4,171	98.9	742.4	16	2,780,438	370,419	177,985	23,712
Ohio	3,079	61,814	1,504.8	13,621.7	20	4,424,073	488,738	220,366	24,344
Oklahoma	737	17,354	417.0	2,544.9	24	3,453,014	565,805	146,645	24,029
Oregon	755	14,781	339.4	2,217.4	20	2,936,903	449,589	150,014	22,965
Pennsylvania	3,774	81,401	1,927.0	14,990.9	22	3,972,162	510,599	184,162	23,673
Rhode Island	172	7,453	184.1	1,769.7	43	10,288,849	1,070,355	237,446	24,702
South Carolina	847	13,929	317.0	2,207.1	16	2,605,765	374,236	158,452	22,757
South Dakota	315	8,104	170.0	3,279.9	26	10,412,508	539,797	404,731	20,982
Tennessee	1,597	28,929	713.2	4,938.4	18	3,092,284	446,587	170,707	24,653
Texas	2,904	87,156	2,308.7	14,406.4	30	4,960,897	795,017	165,295	26,490
Utah	447	8,891	214.6	1,152.7	20	2,578,747	480,107	129,648	24,138
Vermont	220	3,770	79.9	537.0	17	2,440,714	363,000	142,429	21,183
Virginia	2,144	36,348	853.7	6,255.1	17	2,917,480	398,168	172,089	23,486
Washington	1,173	22,941	584.3	3,647.1	20	3,109,171	498,098	158,976	25,468
West Virginia	495	10,842	217.4	1,624.4	22	3,281,600	439,248	149,824	20,054
Wisconsin	1,282	27,393	635.7	4,113.9	21	3,208,966	495,888	150,180	23,208
Wyoming	110	2,444	60.5	415.5	22	3,777,127	550,309	170,002	24,768

Source: 1992 Economic Census, U.S. Department of Commerce, Washington, D.C. This is the only table that shows revenue data as collected by the Bureau of the Census in an Economic Census. The symbol (D) indicates that data are withheld by the source to avoid disclosure of competitive information. A dash (-) indicates that data are not available or cannot be calculated.

ESTABLISHMENTS 1992 - STATE AND REGIONAL CONCENTRATION

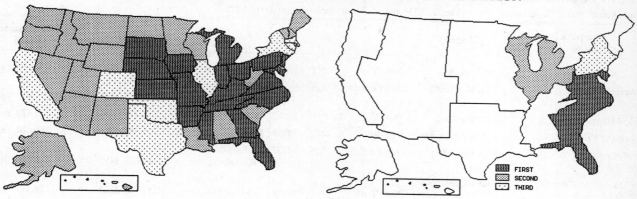

EMPLOYMENT 1992 - STATE AND REGIONAL CONCENTRATION

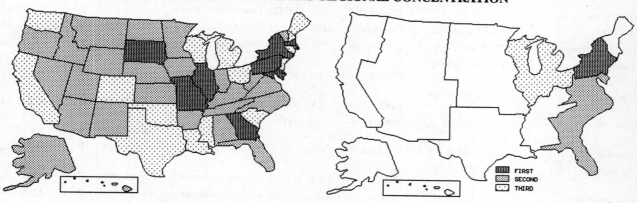

REVENUES 1992 - STATE AND REGIONAL CONCENTRATION

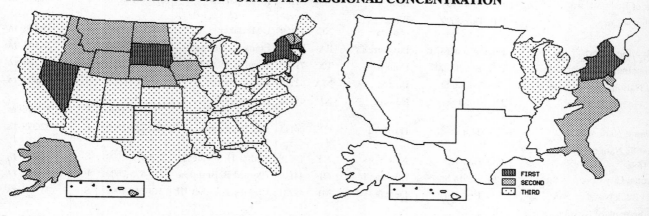

States with the darkest shading indicate those states which have proportionately more establishments, employment, or revenues than would be indicated by the state's population. States with light shading are states with proportionately fewer establishments, less employment, and lower revenues than population distribution. States shaded grey are within 15 percent of the state's population proportion in these categories. States for which no data are available are shown as average (grey). *Regions* are shaded to indicate absolute rank in the category. If no data for the category are available, establishment counts are used to shade the regions. Source of the data is the table on the facing page.

LEADING COMPANIES - SIC 6021 - National Commercial Banks

Number shown: **100**   Total sales/assets ($ mil): **3,235,864**   Total employment (000): **1,272.6**

Company Name	Address				CEO Name	Phone	Co. Type	Sales/Assets ($ mil)	Empl. (000)
Citibank N.A.	399 Park Ave.	New York	NY	10043	John S. Reed	212-559-1000	S	250,489 TA	82.6
BankAmerica Corp.	P.O. Box 37002	San Francisco	CA	94137	Richard M. Rosenberg	415-622-3456	P	215,475 TA	98.6
Chemical Banking Corp.	270 Park Ave.	New York	NY	10017	Walter V. Shipley	212-270-6000	P	171,423 TA	42.1
NationsBank Corp.	100 N. Tryon St.	Charlotte	NC	28255	Hugh L. McColl Jr.	704-386-5000	P	169,604 TA	61.5
Bank of America	P.O. Box 37000	San Francisco	CA	94137	Richard M. Rosenberg	415-622-3456	S	136,693 TA	70.0
Chase Manhattan Corp.	1 Chase Manhattan Plz.	New York	NY	10081	Thomas G. Labrecque	212-552-2222	P	98,197 TA	34.4
Banc One Corp.	100 E. Broad St.	Columbus	OH	43271	John B. McCoy	614-248-5944	P	88,923 TA	48.8
First Union Corp.	2 First Union Ctr.	Charlotte	NC	28288	E. E. Crutchfield Jr.	704-374-6565	P	77,314 TA	33.0
PNC Bank Corp.	1 PNC Plz.	Pittsburgh	PA	15222	Thomas H. O'Brien	412-762-2666	P	62,080 TA	21.1
KeyCorp Inc.	127 Public Sq.	Cleveland	OH	44114	Victor J. Riley Jr.	216-689-3000	P	59,631 TA	17.0
First Interstate Bancorp.	P.O. Box 54068	Los Angeles	CA	90054	William E.B. Siart	213-614-3001	P	55,813 TA	27.4
First Chicago Corp.	1 First National Plz.	Chicago	IL	60670	Richard L. Thomas	312-732-4000	P	52,560 TA	17.4
Wells Fargo and Co.	420 Montgomery St.	San Francisco	CA	94163	Carl E. Reichardt	415-477-1000	P	52,513 TA	19.7
Norwest Corp.	Norwest Ctr.	Minneapolis	MN	55479	Richard M. Kovacevich	612-667-1234	P	50,782 TA	35.0
Fleet Financial Group Inc.	50 Kennedy Plz.	Providence	RI	02903	Terrence Murray	401-278-5800	P	48,757 TA	21.5
NBD Bancorp Inc.	611 Woodward Ave.	Detroit	MI	48226	Thomas H. Jeffs II	313-225-1000	P	47,111 TA	1.8
SunTrust Banks Inc.	P.O. Box 4418	Atlanta	GA	30302	James B. Williams	404-588-7711	P	42,709 TA	19.9
Barnett Banks Inc.	P.O. Box 40789	Jacksonville	FL	32203	Charles E. Rice	904-791-7720	P	41,278 TA	18.9
Republic New York Corp.	452 5th Ave.	New York	NY	10018	Walter H. Weiner	212-525-6100	P	41,068 TA	5.5
Bank of Boston Corp.	P.O. Box 1987	Boston	MA	02105	Ira Stepanian	617-434-2200	P	40,588 TA	18.6
Wachovia Corp.	P.O. Box 3099	Winston-Salem	NC	27150	L.M. Baker	910-770-5000	P	39,188 TA	15.5
Mellon Bank Corp.	Mellon Bank Ctr.	Pittsburgh	PA	15258	Frank V. Cahouet	412-234-5000	P	38,644 TA	24.3
NationsBank of Texas N.A.	P.O. Box 831000	Dallas	TX	75283	Hugh L. McColl Jr.	214-508-6262	S	37,109 TA	20.7
First National Bank of Boston	100 Federal St.	Boston	MA	02110	Ira Stepanian	617-929-6000	S	36,887 TA	14.3
First Fidelity Bancorp.	550 Broad St.	Newark	NJ	07102	Anthony P. Terracciano	201-565-3200	P	36,216 TA	12.0
Shawmut National Corp.	777 Main St.	Hartford	CT	06115	Joel B. Alvord	203-728-2000	P	32,399 TA	9.6
Republic National Bank of New York	P.O. Box 423	New York	NY	10018	Walter H. Weiner	212-525-5000	S	32,395 TA	3.2
National City Corp.	1900 E. 9th St.	Cleveland	OH	44114	Edward B. Brandon	216-575-2000	P	32,114 TA	20.3
NBD Bank N.A.	P.O. Box 116	Detroit	MI	48231	Charles T. Fisher III	313-225-1000	S	31,494 TA	8.1
NationsBank of North Carolina N.A.	P.O. Box 120	Charlotte	NC	28255	Hugh L. McColl Jr.	704-386-5000	S	31,280 TA	7.7
Comerica Inc.	100 Renaissance Ctr.	Detroit	MI	48243	Eugene A. Miller	313-222-3300	P	30,295 TA	12.7
CoreStates Financial Corp.	P.O. Box 7618	Philadelphia	PA	19101	Terrence A. Larsen	215-973-3100	P	29,325 TA	13.7

Company type codes: P - Public, R - Private, S - Subsidiary, D - Division, J - Joint Venture, A - Affiliate, G - Group. If the dollar values shown are not sales, the following codes apply: TA - Total Assets; OR - Operating Revenues; GB - Gross Billings. * - estimated dollar value. < - less than. *na* - not available.

Continued on next page.

LEADING COMPANIES - SIC 6021 - National Commercial Banks
Continued

Company Name	Address				CEO Name	Phone	Co. Type	Sales/Assets ($ mil)	Empl. (000)
National Westminster Bancorp Inc.	10 Exchange Pl.	Jersey City	NJ	07302	John Tugwell	201-547-7000	S	29,000 TA	8.1
National City Bank of Cleveland	P.O. Box 5756	Cleveland	OH	44101	David A. Daberko	216-575-2000	S	28,834 TA	3.2
First Union Corporation of Florida	P.O. Box 2080	Jacksonville	FL	32231	Byron Hodnett	904-361-2265	S	27,933 TA	9.9
Boatmen's Bancshares Inc.	800 Market St.	St. Louis	MO	63101	Andrew B. Craig III	314-466-6000	P	26,654 TA	14.4
First Bank System Inc.	P.O. Box 522	Minneapolis	MN	55480	John F. Grundhofer	612-973-1111	P	26,219 TA	12.0
Society National Bank	P.O. Box 6179	Cleveland	OH	44101	Henry L. Meyer III	216-689-3000	S	24,571 TA	4.9
Continental Bank Corp.	231 S. LaSalle St.	Chicago	IL	60697	Thomas C. Theobald	312-828-2345	P	22,240 TA	4.2
First Union National Bank of North Carolina	301 S. Tryon St.	Charlotte	NC	28288	Frank H. Dunn Jr.	704-374-6161	S	21,956 TA	7.6
CoreStates Bank N.A.	P.O. Box 7618	Philadelphia	PA	19101	Terrence Larson	215-973-3100	S	21,889 TA	10.7
U.S. Bancorp	8534 E. Kemper Rd.	Cincinnati	OH	45249	Gerry B. Cameron	513-247-0300	P	21,416 TA	12.9
NationsBank of Florida N.A.	P.O. Box 31590	Tampa	FL	33631	R. Eugene Taylor	813-882-1100	S	21,391 TA	5.1
First of America Bank Corp.	211 S. Rose St.	Kalamazoo	MI	49007	Daniel R. Smith	616-376-9000	P	21,230 TA	13.3
Sun Banks Inc.	200 S. Orange Ave.	Orlando	FL	32801	Wendell H. Colson	407-237-4141	S	21,006 TA	7.9
Texas Commerce Bancshares Inc.	P.O. Box 2558	Houston	TX	77002	Marc J. Shapiro	713-236-4865	S	20,890 TA	9.5
Wachovia Bank of North Carolina N.A.	P.O. Box 3099	Winston-Salem	NC	27150	J. Walter McDowell	919-770-5000	S	20,287 TA	5.2
Southern National Corp.	200 W. 2nd St.	Winston-Salem	NC	27101	John A. Allison	919-773-7200	P	19,855 TA	7.7
Texas Commerce Bank N.A.	P.O. Box 2558	Houston	TX	77252	Marc J. Shapiro	713-236-4865	S	19,805 TA	9.2
ABN AMRO North America Inc.	135 S. La Salle St.	Chicago	IL	60603	Harrison F. Tempest	312-443-2000	S	18,935 TA	5.3
Northern Trust Corp.	50 S. La Salle St.	Chicago	IL	60675	David W. Fox	312-630-6000	P	18,562 TA	6.6
Huntington Bancshares Inc.	Huntington Ctr.	Columbus	OH	43287	Frank Wobst	614-480-8300	P	17,771 TA	8.2
Harris Bankcorp Inc.	111 W. Monroe St.	Chicago	IL	60603	Alan G. McNally	312-461-2121	S	16,809 TA	6.3
National Westminster Bank USA	175 Water St.	New York	NY	10038	John Tugwell	212-602-1000	S	16,662 TA	3.7
First Bank N.A.	601 2nd Ave. S.	Minneapolis	MN	55402	John Grundhofer	612-973-1111	S	15,803 TA	4.2
Seattle-First National Bank	P.O. Box 3586	Seattle	WA	98124	John Rindlaub	206-358-3000	S	15,458 TA	7.2
UJB Financial Corp.	P.O. Box 2066	Princeton	NJ	08543	T. Joseph Semrod	609-987-3200	P	15,429 TA	6.1
NationsBank of Georgia N.A.	P.O. Box 4899	Atlanta	GA	30303	Jim Lientz	404-581-2121	S	15,308 TA	4.4
AmSouth Bancorp.	P.O. Box 11007	Birmingham	AL	35288	John W. Woods	205-320-7151	P	15,293 TA	7.0
Fifth Third Bancorp.	38 Fountain Square Plz	Cincinnati	OH	45263	George A. Schaefer Jr.	513-579-5300	P	14,957 TA	6.0
Key Bank of New York N.A.	P.O. Box 748	Albany	NY	12201	James Menzies	518-486-8500	S	14,945 TA	6.3
Trust Company of Georgia	P.O. Box 4418	Atlanta	GA	30302	Edward P. Gould	404-588-7711	S	14,880 TA	4.5
SouthTrust Corp.	P.O. Box 2554	Birmingham	AL	35290	Wallace D. Malone Jr.	205-254-5000	P	14,708 TA	7.0
Shawmut Bank Connecticut N.A.	777 Main St.	Hartford	CT	06115	Gunnar S. Overstrom Jr.	203-728-2000	S	14,500 TA	5.4

Company type codes: P - Public, R - Private, S - Subsidiary, D - Division, J - Joint Venture, A - Affiliate, G - Group. If the dollar values shown are not sales, the following codes apply: TA - Total Assets; OR - Operating Revenues; GB - Gross Billings. * - estimated dollar value. < - less than. *na* - not available.

Continued on next page.

LEADING COMPANIES - SIC 6021 - National Commercial Banks

Continued

Company Name	Address				CEO Name	Phone	Co. Type	Sales/Assets ($ mil)	Empl. (000)
Beneficial Corp.	301 N. Walnut St.	Wilmington	DE	19801	Finn M. W. Caspersen	302-425-2500	P	14,377 TA	8.5
Crestar Financial Corp.	P.O. Box 26665	Richmond	VA	23261	Richard G. Tilghman	804-782-5000	P	14,010 TA	7.0
First Union Corporation of Virginia	201 S. Jefferson St.	Roanoke	VA	24011	Warner N. Dalhouse	703-563-7580	S	13,945 TA	7.0
Integra Financial Corp.	4 PPG Pl.	Pittsburgh	PA	15222	William F. Roemer	412-644-7669	P	13,800 TA	5.6
Firstar Corp.	777 E. Wisconsin Ave.	Milwaukee	WI	53202	Roger L. Fitzsimonds	414-765-4321	P	13,794 TA	9.7
Midlantic Bank N.A.	80 Park Plz.	Newark	NJ	07102	Gary J. Scheuring	201-266-6000	S	13,293 TA	6.0
Shawmut Bank N.A.	1 Federal St.	Boston	MA	02211	Allen Sanborn	617-292-2000	S	12,900 TA	5.0
Marshall and Ilsley Corp.	770 N. Water St.	Milwaukee	WI	53202	James B. Wigdale	414-765-7801	P	12,432 TA	8.6
LaSalle National Corp.	135 S. La Salle St.	Chicago	IL	60603	Ted Roberts	312-443-2000	S	12,385 TA	3.5
Mercantile Bancorporation Inc.	P.O. Box 524	St. Louis	MO	63166	Thomas H. Jacobsen	314-425-2525	P	12,242 TA	5.7
First Security Corp.	79 S. Main St.	Salt Lake City	UT	84130	Spencer F. Eccles	801-246-5706	P	12,149 TA	7.6
Wachovia Bank of Georgia N.A.	P.O. Box 4148	Atlanta	GA	30302	G. Joseph Prendergast	404-332-5000	S	11,976 TA	3.0
Huntington National Bank	P.O. Box 1558	Columbus	OH	43216	W. Lee Hoskins	614-476-8300	S	11,969 TA	3.9
Bank One, Arizona N.A.	P.O. Box 71A620	Phoenix	AZ	85001	Richard J. Lehmann	602-221-2900	S	11,936 TA	5.4
NationsBank of Virginia N.A.	P.O. Box 27025	Richmond	VA	23261	Randolph W. McElroy	804-788-2000	S	11,678 TA	5.9
Maryland National Bank	P.O. Box 987	Baltimore	MD	21203	Frank P. Bramble Sr.	410-244-5000	S	11,376 TA	4.7
United States National Bank of Oregon	P.O. Box 4412	Portland	OR	97208	John D. Eskildsen	503-275-6111	S	11,327 TA	6.7
First Empire State Corp.	P.O. Box 223	Buffalo	NY	14240	Robert G. Wilmers	716-842-5138	P	10,529 TA	4.5
First Tennessee National Corp.	P.O. Box 84	Memphis	TN	38101	Ralph Horn	901-523-4444	P	10,522 TA	6.5
Central Fidelity Banks Inc.	P.O. Box 27602	Richmond	VA	23261	Lewis N. Miller Jr.	804-782-4000	P	10,054 TA	3.5
Boatmen's National Bank of St. Louis	P.O. Box 236	St. Louis	MO	63166	Samuel B. Hayes III	314-554-6000	S	9,998 TA	2.9
MBNA America Bank N.A.	400 Christiana Rd.	Newark	DE	19713	Charles M. Cawley	302-456-8588	S	9,672 TA	10.8
Central Fidelity Bank N.A.	8000 Franklin Farms Dr	Richmond	VA	23229	Lewis N. Miller Jr.	804-697-7145	S	9,595 TA	0.2
First Tennessee Bank N.A.	165 Madison Ave.	Memphis	TN	38103	Ronald Terry	901-523-4444	S	9,432 TA	5.3
Star Banc Corp.	425 Walnut St.	Cincinnati	OH	45202	Jerry A. Grundhofer	513-632-4000	P	9,391 TA	3.5
Compass Bancshares	15 S. 20th St.	Birmingham	AL	35233	D. Paul Jones Jr.	205-933-3000	P	9,123 TA	4.0
First Maryland Bancorp.	25 S. Charles St.	Baltimore	MD	21201	Frank P. Bramble	410-244-4000	S	9,106 TA	4.6
First Union National Bank of Georgia	55 Park Pl.	Atlanta	GA	30303	David M. Carroll	404-827-7100	S	9,083 TA	2.5
West One Bancorp.	P.O. Box 8247	Boise	ID	83733	Daniel R. Nelson	208-383-7000	P	8,977 TA	4.8
LaSalle National Bank	135 S. LaSalle St.	Chicago	IL	60603	Norman R. Bobins	312-443-2000	S	8,802 TA	1.0
AmSouth Bank N.A.	P.O. Box 11007	Birmingham	AL	35288	John W. Woods	205-326-5120	S	8,714 TA	3.9
Michigan National Corp.	P.O. Box 9065	Farmington Hills	MI	48333	Robert J. Mylod	313-473-3000	P	8,692 TA	4.9
NationsBank of South Carolina N.A.	P.O. Box 727	Columbia	SC	29222	Joel A. Smith III	803-765-8011	S	8,427 TA	2.4

Company type codes: P - Public, R - Private, S - Subsidiary, D - Division, J - Joint Venture, A - Affiliate, G - Group. If the dollar values shown are not sales, the following codes apply: TA - Total Assets; OR - Operating Revenues; GB - Gross Billings. * - estimated dollar value. < - less than. *na* - not available.

Continued on next page.

LEADING COMPANIES - SIC 6021 - National Commercial Banks
Continued

Company Name	Address				CEO Name	Phone	Co. Type	Sales/Assets ($ mil)	Empl. (000)
First Union National Bank of Virginia	P.O. Box 13327	Roanoke	VA	24040	Warner N. Dalhouse	703-563-7000	S	8,319 TA	4.2
Michigan National Bank	P.O. Box 9065	Farmington Hills	MI	48334	Douglas Ebert	313-473-3000	S	8,253 TA	4.2
Commerce Bancshares Inc.	P.O. Box 13686	Kansas City	MO	64199	David W. Kemper	816-234-2000	P	8,036 TA	4.2

Source: *Ward's Business Directory of U.S. Private and Public Companies*, 1996. Company type codes: P - Public, R - Private, S - Subsidiary, D - Division, J - Joint Venture, A - Affiliate, G - Group. If the dollar values shown are not sales, the following codes apply: TA - Total Assets; OR - Operating Revenues; GB - Gross Billings. * - estimated dollar value. < - less than; *na* - not available.

LEADING COMPANIES - SIC 6022 - State Commercial Banks
Number shown: **100**   Total sales/assets ($ mil): **2,671,249**   Total employment (000): **945.6**

Company Name	Address				CEO Name	Phone	Co. Type	Sales/Assets ($ mil)	Empl. (000)
BankAmerica Corp.	P.O. Box 37002	San Francisco	CA	94137	Richard M. Rosenberg	415-622-3456	P	215,475 TA	98.6
Chemical Banking Corp.	270 Park Ave.	New York	NY	10017	Walter V. Shipley	212-270-6000	P	171,423 TA	42.1
J.P. Morgan and Company Inc.	60 Wall St.	New York	NY	10260	Dennis Weatherstone	212-483-2323	P	154,917 TA	15.2
Chemical Bank	270 Park Ave.	New York	NY	10017	Walter V. Shipley	212-270-6000	S	135,742 TA	25.5
Morgan Guaranty Trust Company of New York	60 Wall St.	New York	NY	10260	Dennis Weatherstone	212-483-2323	S	124,384 TA	12.1
Chase Manhattan Corp.	1 Chase Manhattan Plz.	New York	NY	10081	Thomas G. Labrecque	212-552-2222	P	98,197 TA	34.4
Bankers Trust New York Corp.	280 Park Ave.	New York	NY	10017	Eugene B. Shanks Jr.	212-250-2500	P	97,016 TA	14.5
Banc One Corp.	100 E. Broad St.	Columbus	OH	43271	John B. McCoy	614-248-5944	P	88,923 TA	48.8
Bankers Trust Co.	130 Liberty St.	New York	NY	10006	Charles S. Sanford Jr.	212-250-2500	S	74,820 TA	11.7
PNC Bank Corp.	1 PNC Plz.	Pittsburgh	PA	15222	Thomas H. O'Brien	412-762-2666	P	62,080 TA	21.1
KeyCorp Inc.	127 Public Sq.	Cleveland	OH	44114	Victor J. Riley Jr.	216-689-3000	P	59,631 TA	17.0
First Interstate Bancorp.	P.O. Box 54068	Los Angeles	CA	90054	William E.B. Siart	213-614-3001	P	55,813 TA	27.4
Norwest Corp.	Norwest Ctr.	Minneapolis	MN	55479	Richard M. Kovacevich	612-667-1234	P	50,782 TA	35.0
Bank of New York Company Inc.	48 Wall St.	New York	NY	10286	J. Carter Bacot	212-495-1784	P	48,879 TA	15.4
Fleet Financial Group Inc.	50 Kennedy Plz.	Providence	RI	02903	Terrence Murray	401-278-5800	P	48,757 TA	21.5
NBD Bancorp Inc.	611 Woodward Ave.	Detroit	MI	48226	Thomas H. Jeffs II	313-225-1000	P	47,111 TA	1.8
SunTrust Banks Inc.	P.O. Box 4418	Atlanta	GA	30302	James B. Williams	404-588-7711	P	42,709 TA	19.9
Barnett Banks Inc.	P.O. Box 40789	Jacksonville	FL	32203	Charles E. Rice	904-791-7720	P	41,278 TA	18.9
Bank of Boston Corp.	P.O. Box 1987	Boston	MA	02105	Ira Stepanian	617-434-2200	P	40,588 TA	18.6
First Fidelity Bancorp.	550 Broad St.	Newark	NJ	07102	Anthony P. Terracciano	201-565-3200	P	36,216 TA	12.0
Shawmut National Corp.	777 Main St.	Hartford	CT	06115	Joel B. Alvord	203-728-2000	P	32,399 TA	9.6

Company type codes: P - Public, R - Private, S - Subsidiary, D - Division, J - Joint Venture, A - Affiliate, G - Group. If the dollar values shown are not sales, the following codes apply: TA - Total Assets; OR - Operating Revenues; GB - Gross Billings. * - estimated dollar value. < - less than. *na* - not available.

Continued on next page.

LEADING COMPANIES - SIC 6022 - State Commercial Banks

Continued

Company Name	Address				CEO Name	Phone	Co. Type	Sales/Assets ($ mil)	Empl. (000)
National City Corp.	1900 E. 9th St.	Cleveland	OH	44114	Edward B. Brandon	216-575-2000	P	32,114 TA	20.3
Comerica Inc.	100 Renaissance Ctr.	Detroit	MI	48243	Eugene A. Miller	313-222-3300	P	30,295 TA	12.7
CoreStates Financial Corp.	P.O. Box 7618	Philadelphia	PA	19101	Terrence A. Larsen	215-973-3100	P	29,325 TA	13.7
Boatmen's Bancshares Inc.	800 Market St.	St. Louis	MO	63101	Andrew B. Craig III	314-466-6000	P	26,654 TA	14.4
First Bank System Inc.	P.O. Box 522	Minneapolis	MN	55480	John F. Grundhofer	612-973-1111	P	26,219 TA	12.0
Comerica Bank Inc.	100 Renaissance Ctr.	Detroit	MI	48243	Eugene A. Miller	313-222-3300	S	24,913 TA	10.2
State Street Bank and Trust Co.	P.O. Box 351	Boston	MA	02101	Marshall N. Carter	617-786-3000	S	22,778 TA	10.2
State Street Boston Corp.	P.O. Box 351	Boston	MA	02101	Marshall N. Carter	617-786-3000	P	21,730 TA	11.1
U.S. Bancorp	8534 E. Kemper Rd.	Cincinnati	OH	45249	Gerry B. Cameron	513-247-0300	P	21,416 TA	12.9
First of America Bank Corp.	211 S. Rose St.	Kalamazoo	MI	49007	Daniel R. Smith	616-376-9000	P	21,230 TA	13.3
Sun Banks Inc.	200 S. Orange Ave.	Orlando	FL	32801	Wendell H. Colson	407-237-4141	S	21,006 TA	7.9
ABN AMRO North America Inc.	135 S. La Salle St.	Chicago	IL	60603	Harrison F. Tempest	312-443-2000	S	18,935 TA	5.3
Northern Trust Corp.	50 S. La Salle St.	Chicago	IL	60675	David W. Fox	312-630-6000	P	18,562 TA	6.6
Huntington Bancshares Inc.	Huntington Ctr.	Columbus	OH	43287	Frank Wobst	614-480-8300	P	17,771 TA	8.2
Harris Bankcorp Inc.	111 W. Monroe St.	Chicago	IL	60603	Alan G. McNally	312-461-2121	S	16,809 TA	6.3
Union Bank	350 California St.	San Francisco	CA	94104	Kanetaka Yoshida	415-705-7000	P	16,761 TA	6.9
UJB Financial Corp.	P.O. Box 2066	Princeton	NJ	08543	T. Joseph Semrod	609-987-3200	P	15,429 TA	6.1
Meridian Bancorp Inc.	35 N. 6th St.	Reading	PA	19601	Samuel A. McCullough	610-655-2000	P	15,053 TA	6.9
Fifth Third Bancorp.	38 Fountain Square Plz	Cincinnati	OH	45263	George A. Schaefer Jr.	513-579-5300	P	14,957 TA	6.0
Trust Company of Georgia	P.O. Box 4418	Atlanta	GA	30302	Edward P. Gould	404-588-7711	S	14,880 TA	4.5
SouthTrust Corp.	P.O. Box 2554	Birmingham	AL	35290	Wallace D. Malone Jr.	205-254-5000	P	14,708 TA	7.0
Northern Trust Co.	50 S. La Salle St.	Chicago	IL	60675	David W. Fox	312-630-6000	S	14,700 TA	4.8
Crestar Financial Corp.	P.O. Box 26665	Richmond	VA	23261	Richard G. Tilghman	804-782-5000	P	14,010 TA	7.0
Midlantic Corp.	P.O. Box 600	Edison	NJ	08818	Garry J. Scheuring	908-321-8000	P	13,293 TA	6.0
Signet Banking Corp.	P.O. Box 25970	Richmond	VA	23260	Robert M. Freeman	804-747-2000	P	12,931 TA	7.3
Meridian Bank	P.O. Box 1102	Reading	PA	19603	Ezeciel S. Ketchum	215-655-2000	S	12,845 TA	5.2
Regions Financial Corp.	P.O. Box 10247	Birmingham	AL	35202	J. Stanley Mackin	205-326-7060	P	12,839 TA	6.0
BanPonce Corp.	P.O. Box 362708	San Juan	PR	00936	Richard L. Carrion	809-765-9800	P	12,778 TA	7.5
Bancorp Hawaii Inc.	P.O. Box 2900	Honolulu	HI	96846	H. Howard Stephenson	808-537-8111	P	12,586 TA	4.4
Bank of Hawaii	P.O. Box 2900	Honolulu	HI	96846	H. Howard Stephenson	808-537-8111	S	12,462 TA	3.1
Marshall and Ilsley Corp.	770 N. Water St.	Milwaukee	WI	53202	James B. Wigdale	414-765-7801	P	12,432 TA	8.6
LaSalle National Corp.	135 S. La Salle St.	Chicago	IL	60603	Ted Roberts	312-443-2000	S	12,385 TA	3.5
Mercantile Bancorporation Inc.	P.O. Box 524	St. Louis	MO	63166	Thomas H. Jacobsen	314-425-2525	P	12,242 TA	5.7
Crestar Bank	P.O. Box 26665	Richmond	VA	23261	Richard G. Tilghman	804-782-5000	S	12,233 TA	6.1

Company type codes: P - Public, R - Private, S - Subsidiary, D - Division, J - Joint Venture, A - Affiliate, G - Group. If the dollar values shown are not sales, the following codes apply: TA - Total Assets; OR - Operating Revenues; GB - Gross Billings. * - estimated dollar value. < - less than. *na* - not available.

Continued on next page.

LEADING COMPANIES - SIC 6022 - State Commercial Banks
Continued

Company Name	Address				CEO Name	Phone	Co. Type	Sales/Assets ($ mil)	Empl. (000)
Harris Trust and Savings Bank	P.O. Box 755	Chicago	IL	60690	Philip A. DeLaney	312-461-2121	S	11,944 TA	4.2
Banco Popular de Puerto Rico	P.O. Box 362708	San Juan	PR	00936	Richard L. Carrion	809-765-9800	S	11,384 TA	4.5
BayBanks Inc.	175 Federal St.	Boston	MA	02110	William M. Crozier Jr.	617-482-1040	P	10,771 TA	5.9
First Tennessee National Corp.	P.O. Box 84	Memphis	TN	38101	Ralph Horn	901-523-4444	P	10,522 TA	6.5
Trust Company Bank	P.O. Box 4418	Atlanta	GA	30302	Edward P. Gould	404-588-7711	S	10,373 TA	2.7
Central Fidelity Bank	P.O. Box 27602	Richmond	VA	23261	Lewis L. Miller Jr.	804-782-4000	S	9,981 TA	3.5
Bank of America Arizona	P.O. Box 16290	Phoenix	AZ	85011	David S. Hanna	602-597-5000	S	9,260 TA	3.8
Branch Banking and Trust Co.	P.O. Box 1847	Wilson	NC	27893	John A. Allison	919-399-4291	S	9,179 TA	3.7
BB and T Financial Corp.	P.O. Box 1847	Wilson	NC	27894	John A. Allison	919-399-4291	P	9,173 TA	4.4
Compass Bancshares	15 S. 20th St.	Birmingham	AL	35233	D. Paul Jones Jr.	205-933-3000	P	9,123 TA	4.0
First Maryland Bancorp.	25 S. Charles St.	Baltimore	MD	21201	Frank P. Bramble	410-244-4000	S	9,106 TA	4.6
Signet Bank-Virginia	P.O. Box 25970	Richmond	VA	23260	Robert M. Freeman	804-747-2000	S	9,008 TA	3.5
West One Bancorp.	P.O. Box 8247	Boise	ID	83733	Daniel R. Nelson	208-383-7000	P	8,977 TA	4.8
Manufacturers and Traders Trust Co.	1 M & T Plz.	Buffalo	NY	14240	Robert G. Wilmers	716-842-4200	S	8,813 TA	3.5
Old Kent Financial Corp.	1 Vandenberg Ctr.	Grand Rapids	MI	49503	David J. Wagner	616-771-5000	P	8,700 TA	5.0
Michigan National Corp.	P.O. Box 9065	Farmington Hills	MI	48333	Robert J. Mylod	313-473-3000	P	8,692 TA	4.9
Greenwood Trust Co.	12 Read's Way	New Castle	DE	19720	J. Nathan Hill	302-323-7184	R	8,649 TA	1.3
Commerce Bancshares Inc.	P.O. Box 13686	Kansas City	MO	64199	David W. Kemper	816-234-2000	P	8,036 TA	4.2
Sanwa Bank California	P.O. Box 54445	Los Angeles	CA	90054	Hiroya Nobuhara	213-896-7000	S	7,975 TA	2.7
First Virginia Banks Inc.	6400 Arlington Blvd.	Falls Church	VA	22042	Barry J. Fitzpatrick	703-241-4000	P	7,865 TA	5.0
Integra Bank/Pittsburgh	4th Ave. & Wood St.	Pittsburgh	PA	15278	Gayland B. Cook	412-644-8111	S	7,500 TA	1.8
First Hawaiian Inc.	P.O. Box 3200	Honolulu	HI	96847	Walter A. Dods Jr.	808-525-7000	P	7,269 TA	3.0
Fifth Third Bank	38 Fountain Square Plz	Cincinnati	OH	45263	George A. Schaefer Jr.	513-579-5300	S	6,875 TA	3.1
ONBANCorp Inc.	P.O. Box 4983	Syracuse	NY	13221	Robert J. Bennett	315-424-4400	P	6,723 TA	1.1
Third National Corp.	P.O. Box 305110	Nashville	TN	37230	John W. Clay Jr.	615-748-4000	S	6,605 TA	2.6
First Commerce Corp.	P.O. Box 60279	New Orleans	LA	70160	Ian Arnof	504-561-1371	P	6,559 TA	3.2
United Jersey Bank	210 Main St.	Hackensack	NJ	07602	T. Joseph Semreo	201-646-5000	S	6,357 TA	1.8
Union Planters Corp.	P.O. Box 387	Memphis	TN	38147	Benjamin W. Rawlins Jr.	901-383-6000	P	6,318 TA	3.5
First Hawaiian Bank	P.O. Box 3200	Honolulu	HI	96847	Walter A. Dods Jr.	808-525-7000	S	6,276 TA	2.7
Synovus Financial Corp.	P.O. Box 120	Columbus	GA	31902	James H. Blanchard	706-649-2387	P	6,115 TA	4.8
First Citizens Bancshares Inc.	P.O. Box 151	Raleigh	NC	27602	Frank B. Holding Jr.	919-755-7000	P	6,099 TA	3.3
Mercantile Bankshares Corp.	P.O. Box 1477	Baltimore	MD	21203	H. Furlong Baldwin	410-237-5900	P	5,938 TA	2.8
United Missouri Bancshares Inc.	P.O. Box 419226	Kansas City	MO	64141	R. Crosby Kemper	816-860-7000	P	5,767 TA	3.7
Compass Bank	P.O. Box 10566	Birmingham	AL	35296	D. Paul Jones Jr.	205-933-3000	S	5,734 TA	2.8
First USA Inc.	2001 Bryan Twr.	Dallas	TX	75201	John C. Tolleson	214-746-8700	P	5,491 TA	1.8
Summit Bancorp.	1 Main St.	Chatham	NJ	07928	Robert G. Cox	201-701-2666	P	5,467 TA	1.6

Company type codes: P - Public, R - Private, S - Subsidiary, D - Division, J - Joint Venture, A - Affiliate, G - Group. If the dollar values shown are not sales, the following codes apply: TA - Total Assets; OR - Operating Revenues; GB - Gross Billings. * - estimated dollar value. < - less than. *na* - not available.

Continued on next page.

LEADING COMPANIES - SIC 6022 - State Commercial Banks

Continued

Company Name	Address				CEO Name	Phone	Co. Type	Sales/Assets ($ mil)	Empl. (000)
Summit Bank	1 Main St.	Chatham	NJ	07928	Robert G. Cox	201-701-2666	S	5,467 TA	1.6
Provident Bancorp Inc.	1 E. 4th St.	Cincinnati	OH	45202	Allen L. Davis	513-579-2000	P	5,411 TA	1.8
First Citizens Bank and Trust Co.	P.O. Box 151	Raleigh	NC	27602	James B. Hyler Jr.	919-755-7000	S	5,395 TA	3.6
Citizens Financial Group Inc.	1 Citizens Plz.	Providence	RI	02903	Mark J. Formica	401-456-7000	S	5,084 TA	2.2
Sumitomo Bank of California	320 California St.	San Francisco	CA	94104	Tadaichi Ikagawa	415-445-8000	P	5,000 TA	1.4
Dauphin Deposit Bank and Trust Co.	P.O. Box 2961	Harrisburg	PA	17105	Christopher R. Jennings	717-255-2121	S	4,996 TA	2.2
Dauphin Deposit Corp.	213 Market St.	Harrisburg	PA	17101	William J. King	717-255-2121	P	4,996 TA	2.2
Zions Bancorp.	1380 Kennecott Bldg.	Salt Lake City	UT	84133	Harris H. Simmons	801-524-4787	P	4,934 TA	2.8
Liberty National Bancorp Inc.	P.O. Box 32500	Louisville	KY	40232	Malcolm B. Chancey Jr.	502-566-2000	P	4,917 TA	2.3

Source: Ward's Business Directory of U.S. Private and Public Companies, 1996. Company type codes: P - Public, R - Private, S - Subsidiary, D - Division, J - Joint Venture, A - Affiliate, G - Group. If the dollar values shown are not sales, the following codes apply: TA - Total Assets; OR - Operating Revenues; GB - Gross Billings. * - estimated dollar value. < - less than; *na* - not available.

LEADING COMPANIES - SIC 6029 - Commercial Banks, nec

Number shown: **3**   Total sales/assets ($ mil): **478**   Total employment (000): **0.1**

Company Name	Address				CEO Name	Phone	Co. Type	Sales/Assets ($ mil)	Empl. (000)
Hurley State Bank	811 E. 10th St.	Sioux Falls	SD	57103	Robert L. Wieseneck	605-336-5661	S	470 TA	<0.1
Treasury Bank Ltd.	1155 15th St.	Washington	DC	20005	Kevin B. Coyne	202-872-8899	R	8 TA*	<0.1
Commercial Bank of San Francisco	333 Pine St.	San Francisco	CA	94104	Robert A. Fuller	415-627-0333	R	0 TA	<0.1

Source: Ward's Business Directory of U.S. Private and Public Companies, 1996. Company type codes: P - Public, R - Private, S - Subsidiary, D - Division, J - Joint Venture, A - Affiliate, G - Group. If the dollar values shown are not sales, the following codes apply: TA - Total Assets; OR - Operating Revenues; GB - Gross Billings. * - estimated dollar value. < - less than; *na* - not available.

FINANCIAL DATA ON BANKS AND TRUSTS

The following seven tables show additional data on banks and trusts obtained from the Federal Deposit Insurance Corporation (FDIC) and the Federal Reserve System as published in the *Statistical Abstract of the United States 1995*. Much more detailed information on banks and trusts is available from the Office of Corporate Communications, FDIC, 550 17th Street, N.W., Washington, D.C. 20429 or from the Federal Reserve System, Publications Services, Mail Stop 128, Board of Governors of the Federal Reserve System, Washington, DC 20551.

BANKING OFFICES, BY TYPE OF BANK: 1980 TO 1994

As of December 31. Includes Puerto Rico and outlying areas. Covers all FDIC-insured commercial banks and all Bank Insurance Fund-insured savings banks as well as those State-chartered Savings Association Insurance Fund-insured savings banks that are regulated by the FDIC. Data for 1980 include automatic teller machines which were reported by many banks as branches.

Item	1980	1985	1988	1989	1990	1991	1992	1993	1994
All banking offices	57,232	60,890	63,960	64,570	66,945	67,783	67,777	68,664	70,284
Number of banks	15,330	14,809	13,629	13,201	12,819	12,390	11,997	11,552	11,060
Number of branches	41,902	46,081	50,331	51,369	54,126	55,393	55,780	57,112	59,224
Commercial banks, total	53,649	57,764	60,200	60,796	63,160	64,006	63,903	64,078	65,594
Member, Federal Reserve System	29,985	33,854	35,763	36,755	38,201	39,449	39,271	39,639	40,998
National banks	24,217	27,844	29,270	30,019	31,279	31,771	31,064	30,879	31,633
State banks	5,768	6,010	6,493	6,736	6,922	7,678	8,207	8,760	9,365
Insured nonmember banks	23,664[1]	23,910	24,437	24,041	24,959	24,557	24,632	24,439	24,596
Savings banks, insured	3,583[1]	3,126	3,760	3,774	3,785	3,777	3,874	4,586	4,690

Source: U.S. Federal Deposit Insurance Corporation, 1980, *Annual Report* and, beginning 1985, *Statistics on Banking*, annual. *Note:* 1. Includes noninsured banks.

SELECTED FINANCIAL INSTITUTIONS - NUMBER AND ASSETS: 1993

As of December. FDIC = Federal Deposit Insurance Corporation.

ASSET SIZE	Number of Institutions			Assets (bil. dol.)		
	F.D.I.C.-insured		Credit unions[2]	F.D.I.C.-insured		Credit unions[2]
	Commercial banks	Savings institutions[1]		Commercial banks[3]	Savings institutions[1]	
Total	10,958	2,262	12,317	3,706.2	1,000.9	277.2
Less than $5.0 million	[4]	[4]	6,553	[4]	[4]	11.4
$5.0 million to $9.9 million	[4]	[4]	1,851	[4]	[4]	13.2
$10.0 million to $24.9 million	2,217[4]	191[4]	1,845	35.9[4]	3.1[4]	29.6
$25.0 million to $49.9 million	2,789	343	952	101.5	12.9	33.2
$50.0 million to $99.9 million	2,782	514	560	197.7	37.4	38.6
$100.0 million to $499.9 million	2,543	900	507	502.6	202.2	99.5
$500.0 million to $999.9 million	245	140	36	174.4	96.6	24.5
$1.0 billion to $2.9 billion	187	116	11	305.6	190.9	15.6
$3.0 billion or more	195	58	2	2,388.5	457.8	11.6
PERCENT DISTRIBUTION						
Total	100.0	100.0	100.0	1000	100.0	100.0
Less than $5.0 million	[4]	[4]	53.3	[4]	[4]	4.1
$5.0 million to $9.9 million	[4]	[4]	15.0	[4]	[4]	4.8
$10.0 million to $24.9 million	20.2[4]	8.4[4]	15.0	0.9[4]	0.3[4]	10.7
$25.0 million to $49.9 million	25.5	15.2	7.7	2.7	1.3	12.0
$50.0 million to $99.9 million	25.4	22.7	4.5	5.3	3.7	13.9
$100.0 million to $499.9 million	23.2	39.8	4.1	13.6	20.2	35.9
$500.0 million to $999.9 million	2.2	6.2	0.3	4.7	9.7	8.8
$1.0 billion to $2.9 billion	1.7	5.1	0.1	8.3	19.1	5.6
$3.0 billion or more	1.8	2.6	(Z)	64.5	45.7	4.2

Source: Except as noted, U.S. Federal Deposit Insurance Corporation, *Statistics on Banking, 1993. Notes:* Z Less than 0.05 percent. 1. Excludes institutions in Resolution Trust Corporation conservatorship. 2. Source: National Credit Union Administration, *National Credit Union Administration Year-end Statistics 1993.* Excludes nonfederally insured State charted credit unions and federally insured corporate credit unions. 3. Includes foreign branches of U.S. banks. 4. Data for institutions with assets less than $10 million included with those with assets of $10.0 million to $24.9 million.

BIF-INSURED COMMERCIAL AND SAVINGS BANKS CLOSED OR ASSISTED DUE TO FINANCIAL DIFFICULTIES AND PROBLEM BANKS: 1988 TO 1994

Banks are closed either permanently or temporarily by order of supervisory authorities or by directors of banks. B.I.F. = Bank Insurance Fund.

ITEM	Unit	1988	1989	1990	1991	1992	1993	1994
Total banks closed or assisted	Number	221	207	169	127	122	41	13
Assets, closed and assisted banks	Bil. dol.	52.6	29.4	15.7	63.2	44.2	3.5	1.4
Deposits, closed and assisted banks	Bil. dol.	37.2	24.1	14.5	53.8	41.2	3.1	1.2
Problem banks[1]	Number	1,406	1,109	1,046	1,090	863	474	265
Assets, problem banks	Bil. dol.	352	236	409	610	465	269	42

Source: U.S. Federal Deposit Insurance Corporation, *Annual Report, The FDIC Quarterly Banking Profile,* and *Failed Bank Cost Analysis Report,* 1994. *Notes:* NA Not available. 1. BIF-insured commercial and savings banks considered to be problem banks by the supervisory authorities, end-of-period.

INSURED COMMERCIAL BANKS - ASSETS AND LIABILITIES

In billions of dollars, except as indicated. As of Dec. 31. Includes outlying areas. Except as noted, includes foreign branches of U.S. banks.

Item	1988	1989	1990	1991	1992	1993	1994[1]
Number of banks	13,137	12,713	12,345	11,926	11,462	10,958	10,450
Assets, total	3,131	3,299	3,389	3,431	3,506	3,706	4,011
Net loans and leases	1,886	2,004	2,055	1,998	1,977	2,097	2,306
Real estate loans	675	762	830	851	868	923	998
Home equity lines of credit[2]	40	51	61	70	73	73	(NA)
Commercial and industrial loans	600	618	615	559	536	539	589
Loans to individuals	378	401	404	392	385	419	487
Farm loans	30	31	33	35	35	37	39
Other loans and leases	265	261	242	227	216	239	251
Less: Reserve for losses	47	54	56	55	54	53	52
Less: Unearned income	16	15	14	11	9	7	6
Investment securities	536	559	605	691	773	837	823
Other	709	736	730	742	755	773	882
Domestic office assets	2,726	2,897	2,999	3,033	3,110	3,258	(NA)
Foreign office assets	405	402	390	398	396	448	(NA)
Liabilities and capital, total	3,131	3,299	3,389	3,431	3,506	3,706	4,011
Noninterest-bearing deposits[3]	479	483	489	480	541	572	572
Interest-bearing deposits[4]	1,952	2,065	2,162	2,207	2,158	2,182	2,302
Subordinated debt	17	19	24	25	34	37	41
Other liabilities	486	526	496	486	510	618	783
Equity capital	197	205	219	232	263	297	312
Domestic office deposits	2,117	2,237	2,357	2,383	2,412	2,424	2,442
Foreign office deposits	315	312	293	305	287	330	432

Source: U.S. Federal Deposit Insurance Corporation. *The FDIC Quarterly Banking Profile, Annual Report,* and *Statistics on Banking,* annual. *Notes:* NA Not available. 1. Preliminary. 2. For one- to four-family residential properties. 3. Prior to 1985, demand deposits. 4. Prior to 1985, time and savings deposits.

INSURED COMMERCIAL BANKS - INCOME AND SELECTED MEASURES OF FINANCIAL CONDITION

In billions of dollars, except as indicated. Includes outlying areas. Includes foreign branches of U.S. banks.

Item	1988	1989	1990	1991	1992	1993	1994[1]
Interest income	272.3	317.3	320.4	289.2	255.2	245.1	257.8
Interest expense	165.0	205.1	204.9	167.3	121.8	105.7	111.3
Net interest income	107.2	112.2	115.5	121.9	133.4	139.3	146.6
Provisions for loan losses	17.2	31.0	32.1	34.3	26.0	16.8	10.9
Noninterest income	45.0	50.9	54.9	59.7	65.6	75.0	76.2
Noninterest expense	101.3	108.1	115.7	124.8	130.9	139.7	144.2
Income taxes	10.0	9.5	7.7	8.3	14.5	19.8	22.4
Securities gain/loss, net	0.3	0.8	0.5	3.0	4.0	3.1	-0.6
Extraordinary gains, net	0.8	0.3	0.6	0.7	0.4	2.1	-
Net income	24.8	15.6	16.0	17.9	32.0	43.1	44.7
RATIOS OF CONDITION							
Return on assets[2] (percent)	0.82	0.49	0.48	0.53	0.93	1.20	1.15
Return on equity[3] (percent)	13.19	7.71	7.45	7.94	12.98	15.35	14.63
Equity capital to assets (percent)	6.28	6.21	6.45	6.75	7.51	8.00	7.78
Nonperforming assets	67.1	75.4	98.1	102.2	91.5	69.2	(NA)
Nonperforming assets to assets (percent)	2.14	2.30	2.94	3.02	2.54	1.61	1.01
Net charge-offs[4]	18.6	22.9	29.7	32.9	25.6	17.5	11.2
Net charge-offs to loans and leases (percent)	1.00	1.16	1.43	1.59	1.27	0.85	0.50
Net interest margin[5] (percent)	4.02	4.02	3.94	4.11	4.41	4.40	4.36
Percent of banks losing money	14.7	12.5	13.4	11.6	6.9	4.9	3.8

Source: U.S. Federal Deposit Insurance Corporation, *Annual Report; Statistics on Banking*, annual; and *FDIC Quarterly Banking Profile. Notes:* - Represents or rounds to zero. NA Not available. 1. Preliminary. 2. Net income (including securities transactions and nonrecurring items) as a percentage of average total assets. 3. Net income as a percentage of average total equity capital. 4. Total loans and leases charged off (removed from balance sheet because of uncollectibility), less amounts recovered on loans and leases previously charged off. 5. Interest income less interest expense as a percentage of average earning assets (i.e. the profit margin a bank earns on its loans and investments).

INSURED COMMERCIAL BANKS, 1993, AND BANKS CLOSED OR ASSISTED, 1994

In billions of dollars, except as indicated. Includes foreign branches of U.S. banks.

State	Commercial Banks, 1993[1]			Banks closed or assisted, 1994[2]	
	Number	Assets	Deposits	Number	Deposits
Total	10,957	3,705.9	2,753.9	13	1.2
U.S.	10,941	3,683.7	2,737.5	13	1.2
Northeast	718	1,227.2	839.6	4	0.5
New England	183	166.1	121.2	4	0.5
ME	20	8.7	6.8	-	-
NH	26	7.4	5.8	-	-
VT	20	5.8	4.8	-	-
MA	61	97.7	70.0	2	0.2
RI	10	13.5	10.0	-	-
CT	46	32.9	23.6	2	0.3
M.A.	535	1,061.1	718.4	-	-
NY	175	770.5	493.9	-	-
NJ	99	100.3	84.4	-	-
PA	261	190.4	140.1	-	-
Midwest	4,808	817.9	633.3	1	(Z)
East North Central	2,102	566.6	433.2	-	-
OH	263	132.9	96.5	-	-
IN	237	61.5	49.5	-	-
IL	958	212.0	161.2	-	-
MI	208	106.0	81.6	-	-
WI	436	54.2	44.4	-	-
West North Central	2,706	251.3	200.0	1	(Z)
MN	573	62.3	47.9	-	-
IA	530	38.7	32.0	-	-
MO	490	68.5	55.7	-	-
ND	141	8.1	7.1	-	-
SD	121	19.2	11.0	-	-
NE	361	24.1	20.9	-	-
KS	490	30.3	25.5	1	(Z)
South	4,131	1,072.3	811.6	-	-
South Atlantic	1,384	617.3	437.1	-	-
DE	36	85.8	34.9	-	-
MD	94	52.0	40.7	-	-
DC	18	13.3	9.8	-	-
VA	165	74.4	57.5	-	-
WV	148	19.9	16.6	-	-
NC	71	104.0	70.3	-	-
SC	78	27.7	20.6	-	-
GA	399	90.1	63.3	-	-
FL	375	150.2	123.4	-	-
East South Central	891	173.9	139.6	-	-
KY	309	45.5	35.1	-	-
TN	250	57.0	46.6	-	-
AL	214	46.9	37.4	-	-
MS	118	24.4	20.5	-	-
West South Central	1,856	281.1	235.0	-	-
AR	257	26.0	22.8	-	-
LA	217	40.1	34.0	-	-
OK	371	31.0	27.0	-	-
TX	1,011	184.0	151.2	-	-

[Continued]

INSURED COMMERCIAL BANKS, 1993, AND BANKS CLOSED OR ASSISTED, 1994
[Continued]

State	Commercial Banks, 1993[1]			Banks closed or assisted, 1994[2]	
	Number	Assets	Deposits	Number	Deposits
West	1,284	566.3	453.0	8	0.7
Mountain	702	141.7	112.0	-	-
MT	117	7.9	6.8	-	-
ID	21	10.9	8.3	-	-
WY	55	5.2	4.5	-	-
CO	322	34.4	30.0	-	-
NM	81	12.8	11.2	-	-
AZ	37	37.1	29.7	-	-
UT	48	15.4	11.2	-	-
NV	21	18.0	10.2	-	-
Pacific	582	424.6	341.0	8	0.7
WA	87	41.4	34.5	-	-
OR	45	27.4	21.4	-	-
CA	425	328.5	267.0	8	0.7
AK	8	5.0	3.8	-	-
HI	17	22.3	14.3	-	-
AM	1	0.1	(Z)	-	-
PR	12	21.5	15.8	-	-
GU	2	0.6	0.6	-	-
Pacific Islands	1	0.1	(Z)	-	-

Source: U.S. Federal Deposit Insurance Corporation, *Annual Report*; *Statistics on Banking*, annual; and *FDIC Quarterly Banking Profile*. *Notes:* - Represents zero. Z Less than $50 million. 1. As of December 31. 2. Includes Bank Insurance Fund-insured savings banks.

INSURED COMMERCIAL BANKS - SELECTED MEASURES OF FINANCIAL CONDITION: 1994

In percent, except as indicated. Preliminary.

Asset Size and Region	Number of banks	Return on assets	Return on equity	Equity capital to assets	Nonper-forming assets to total assets	Net charge-offs to loans and leases	Percentage of banks losing money
Total	10,450	1.15	14.63	7.78	1.01	0.50	3.8
Less than $100 million	7,258	1.13	11.36	9.84	0.86	0.24	4.3
$100 million to $1 billion	2,800	1.20	13.48	8.80	0.92	0.37	2.6
$1 billion to $10 billion	328	1.31	16.04	7.94	0.90	0.54	3.7
$10 billion or more	64	1.06	15.01	7.01	1.13	0.57	1.6
Northeast[1]	834	1.07	14.71	7.33	1.28	0.75	6.2
Southeast[2]	1,740	1.18	14.78	7.84	0.72	0.27	3.6
Central[3]	2,272	1.13	14.08	7.88	0.66	0.29	3.3
Midwest[4]	2,622	1.46	16.76	8.43	0.68	0.46	1.7
Southwest[5]	1,857	1.12	13.49	8.16	0.67	0.16	2.9
West[6]	1,125	1.24	14.48	8.33	1.33	0.58	9.7

Source: U.S. Federal Deposit Insurance Corporation. *The FDIC Quarterly Banking Profile*, Fourth Quarter 1994. *Notes:* 1. CT, DE, DC, ME, MD, MA, NH, NJ, NY, PA, PR, RI, and VT. 2. AL, FL, GA, MS, NC, SC, TN, VA, and WV. 3. IL, IN, KY, MI, OH, and WI. 4. IA, KS, MN, MO, NE, ND, and SD. 5. AR, LA, NM, OK, and TX. 6. AK, AZ, CA, CO, HI, ID, MT, NV, OR, Pacific Islands, UT, WA, and WY.

SIC 6030

SAVINGS INSTITUTIONS

Savings institutions are divided into federally chartered (SIC 6035) and state-chartered (SIC 6036) organizations. Popularly called the Savings & Loans, the S&Ls, or "thrifts", they are institutions that accept deposits and make loans. These institutions may be insured by the Federal Deposit Insurance Corporation's (FDIC) Bank Insurance Fund ("BIF-insured") or by FDIC's Savings Association Insurance Fund ("SAIF-insured"). The FDIC's Deposit Insurance Fund was renamed the Bank Insurance Fund; SAIF has taken over the functions of the Federal Savings and Loan Insurance Corporation (FSLIC). These changes were made upon enactment of the Financial Institutions Reform, Recovery, and Enforcement Act of 1989 (FIRREA), Public Law 101-73, 103 Stat. 183.

ESTABLISHMENTS, EMPLOYMENT, AND PAYROLL

	1988	1989		1990		1991		1992		1993		% change 88-93
		Value	%	Value	%	Value	%	Value	%	Value	%	
All Establishments	20,158	21,953	8.9	21,689	-1.2	22,211	2.4	21,089	-5.1	19,330	-8.3	-4.1
Mid-March Employment	383,698	434,730	13.3	416,571	-4.2	393,715	-5.5	355,035	-9.8	318,553	-10.3	-17.0
1st Quarter Wages (annualized - $ mil.)	7,786.1	9,186.5	18.0	9,049.6	-1.5	9,066.6	0.2	8,850.2	-2.4	7,983.4	-9.8	2.5
Payroll per Emp. 1st Q. (annualized)	20,292	21,132	4.1	21,724	2.8	23,028	6.0	24,928	8.2	25,062	0.5	23.5
Annual Payroll ($ mil.)	7,727.3	8,997.3	16.4	8,791.9	-2.3	8,809.5	0.2	8,758.8	-0.6	8,254.4	-5.8	6.8
Establishments - 1-4 Emp. Number	4,044	4,182	3.4	4,146	-0.9	3,904	-5.8	4,414	13.1	3,863	-12.5	-4.5
Mid-March Employment	(D)	12,246	-	(D)	-	11,271	-	12,843	13.9	10,755	-16.3	-
1st Quarter Wages (annualized - $ mil.)	(D)	223.5	-	(D)	-	231.5	-	270.4	16.8	229.4	-15.2	-
Payroll per Emp. 1st Q. (annualized)	(D)	18,254	-	(D)	-	20,540	-	21,055	2.5	21,328	1.3	-
Annual Payroll ($ mil.)	(D)	285.5	-	(D)	-	256.8	-	270.8	5.4	272.3	0.6	-
Establishments - 5-9 Emp. Number	8,211	8,617	4.9	8,562	-0.6	8,738	2.1	8,610	-1.5	7,935	-7.8	-3.4
Mid-March Employment	55,058	58,174	5.7	57,612	-1.0	59,939	4.0	57,836	-3.5	53,507	-7.5	-2.8
1st Quarter Wages (annualized - $ mil.)	868.8	968.9	11.5	1,023.6	5.6	1,104.1	7.9	1,099.0	-0.5	1,005.6	-8.5	15.8
Payroll per Emp. 1st Q. (annualized)	15,779	16,656	5.6	17,768	6.7	18,421	3.7	19,002	3.2	18,794	-1.1	19.1
Annual Payroll ($ mil.)	886.0	979.5	10.6	1,010.4	3.2	1,103.2	9.2	1,122.0	1.7	1,058.9	-5.6	19.5
Establishments - 10-19 Emp. Number	4,591	5,034	9.6	5,019	-0.3	6,238	24.3	4,888	-21.6	4,553	-6.9	-0.8
Mid-March Employment	60,566	66,183	9.3	66,205	0.0	82,152	24.1	64,151	-21.9	60,090	-6.3	-0.8
1st Quarter Wages (annualized - $ mil.)	969.4	1,134.9	17.1	1,208.9	6.5	1,569.1	29.8	1,339.2	-14.7	1,205.9	-10.0	24.4
Payroll per Emp. 1st Q. (annualized)	16,006	17,147	7.1	18,259	6.5	19,100	4.6	20,876	9.3	20,068	-3.9	25.4
Annual Payroll ($ mil.)	982.6	1,136.3	15.6	1,184.6	4.2	1,564.8	32.1	1,334.5	-14.7	1,266.0	-5.1	28.8
Establishments - 20-49 Emp. Number	1,929	2,445	26.7	2,430	-0.6	2,181	-10.2	2,086	-4.4	1,961	-6.0	1.7
Mid-March Employment	(D)	72,932	-	73,061	0.2	63,087	-13.7	61,267	-2.9	58,051	-5.2	-
1st Quarter Wages (annualized - $ mil.)	(D)	1,460.1	-	1,502.6	2.9	1,355.1	-9.8	1,497.5	10.5	1,406.3	-6.1	-
Payroll per Emp. 1st Q. (annualized)	(D)	20,020	-	20,566	2.7	21,481	4.4	24,441	13.8	24,226	-0.9	-
Annual Payroll ($ mil.)	(D)	1,425.8	-	1,439.5	1.0	1,325.3	-7.9	1,508.4	13.8	1,464.3	-2.9	-
Establishments - 50-99 Emp. Number	739	960	29.9	876	-8.8	596	-32.0	623	4.5	615	-1.3	-16.8
Mid-March Employment	51,137	66,286	29.6	60,112	-9.3	40,970	-31.8	42,697	4.2	42,112	-1.4	-17.6
1st Quarter Wages (annualized - $ mil.)	1,078.8	1,441.0	33.6	1,360.8	-5.6	1,012.1	-25.6	1,203.8	18.9	1,151.0	-4.4	6.7
Payroll per Emp. 1st Q. (annualized)	21,097	21,740	3.0	22,637	4.1	24,704	9.1	28,193	14.1	27,331	-3.1	29.5
Annual Payroll ($ mil.)	1,070.5	1,396.6	30.5	1,322.5	-5.3	989.6	-25.2	1,179.8	19.2	1,190.9	0.9	11.2
Establishments - 100-249 Emp. Number	481	549	14.1	502	-8.6	393	-21.7	330	-16.0	299	-9.4	-37.8
Mid-March Employment	72,203	81,383	12.7	75,050	-7.8	59,990	-20.1	50,183	-16.3	45,871	-8.6	-36.5
1st Quarter Wages (annualized - $ mil.)	1,688.2	1,905.1	12.8	1,774.8	-6.8	1,578.8	-11.0	1,448.8	-8.2	1,371.3	-5.3	-18.8
Payroll per Emp. 1st Q. (annualized)	23,381	23,409	0.1	23,648	1.0	26,317	11.3	28,870	9.7	29,896	3.6	27.9
Annual Payroll ($ mil.)	1,603.6	1,824.3	13.8	1,692.4	-7.2	1,514.9	-10.5	1,436.5	-5.2	1,377.3	-4.1	-14.1
Establishments - 250-499 Emp. Number	122	126	3.3	107	-15.1	117	9.3	101	-13.7	76	-24.8	-37.7
Mid-March Employment	41,785	43,089	3.1	34,496	-19.9	39,057	13.2	34,704	-11.1	25,963	-25.2	-37.9
1st Quarter Wages (annualized - $ mil.)	1,009.3	1,070.7	6.1	844.2	-21.2	1,060.3	25.6	981.9	-7.4	836.7	-14.8	-17.1
Payroll per Emp. 1st Q. (annualized)	24,155	24,850	2.9	24,472	-1.5	27,147	10.9	28,294	4.2	32,227	13.9	33.4
Annual Payroll ($ mil.)	987.0	1,006.9	2.0	775.0	-23.0	976.6	26.0	940.5	-3.7	879.3	-6.5	-10.9
Establishments - 500-999 Emp. Number	32	32	-	37	15.6	34	-8.1	27	-20.6	22	-18.5	-31.3
Mid-March Employment	20,999	21,960	4.6	(D)	-	21,844	-	17,714	-18.9	14,043	-20.7	-33.1
1st Quarter Wages (annualized - $ mil.)	552.9	590.9	6.9	(D)	-	640.0	-	561.2	-12.3	489.9	-12.7	-11.4
Payroll per Emp. 1st Q. (annualized)	26,332	26,907	2.2	(D)	-	29,298	-	31,682	8.1	34,885	10.1	32.5
Annual Payroll ($ mil.)	537.5	576.4	7.2	(D)	-	619.1	-	518.6	-16.2	510.8	-1.5	-5.0
Estab. - 1000 or More Emp. Number	9	8	-11.1	10	25.0	10	-	10	-	6	-40.0	-33.3
Mid-March Employment	13,335	12,477	-6.4	13,453	7.8	15,405	14.5	13,640	-11.5	8,161	-40.2	-38.8
1st Quarter Wages (annualized - $ mil.)	331.9	391.4	17.9	402.9	2.9	515.5	28.0	448.4	-13.0	287.3	-35.9	-13.4
Payroll per Emp. 1st Q. (annualized)	24,887	31,368	26.0	29,949	-4.5	33,464	11.7	32,877	-1.8	35,199	7.1	41.4
Annual Payroll ($ mil.)	318.0	366.1	15.1	399.2	9.1	459.2	15.0	447.7	-2.5	234.6	-47.6	-26.3

Source: County Business Patterns, U.S. Department of Commerce, Washington, D.C., for 1988 through 1993. Payroll per employee is calculated using mid-March employment and 1st Quarter wages, annualized. Annual payroll, also shown, may not equal the annualized 1st Quarter wages. Columns headed by a percent sign (%) indicate change from the previous year. na stands for not available. The symbol (D) indicates that data are withheld by the source to avoid disclosure of competitive information. A dash (-) indicates that data are not available or cannot be calculated.

ESTABLISHMENTS
Number

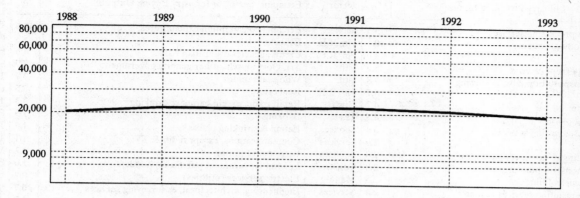

MID-MARCH EMPLOYMENT
Number

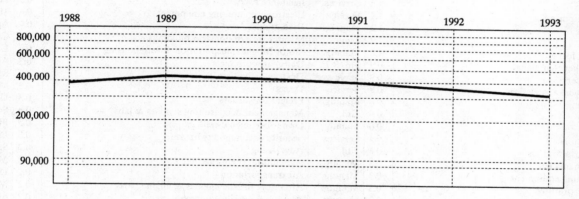

ANNUAL PAYROLL
$ million

INPUTS AND OUTPUTS FOR ALL BANKING SECTORS - SICs 601, 602, 603, 608, and 609

Economic Sector or Industry Providing Inputs	%	Sector	Economic Sector or Industry Buying Outputs	%	Sector
Computer & data processing services	13.3	Services	Personal consumption expenditures	43.5	
Security & commodity brokers	10.1	Fin/R.E.	Exports	5.3	Foreign
Real estate	8.0	Fin/R.E.	Credit agencies other than banks	4.5	Fin/R.E.
Communications, except radio & TV	5.9	Util.	S/L Govt. purch., other general government	3.7	S/L Govt
Motor freight transportation & warehousing	5.8	Util.	Wholesale trade	3.7	Trade
Banking	5.7	Fin/R.E.	Real estate	3.6	Fin/R.E.
U.S. Postal Service	4.7	Gov't	Retail trade, except eating & drinking	3.3	Trade
Eating & drinking places	4.5	Trade	Banking	1.9	Fin/R.E.
Equipment rental & leasing services	3.4	Services	Eating & drinking places	1.4	Trade
Advertising	2.9	Services	Communications, except radio & TV	1.1	Util.
Accounting, auditing & bookkeeping	2.8	Services	Petroleum refining	1.1	Manufg.
Maintenance of nonfarm buildings nec	2.8	Constr.	Federal Government purchases, nondefense	1.0	Fed Govt
Blankbooks & looseleaf binders	2.5	Manufg.	Electric services (utilities)	0.9	Util.
Management & consulting services & labs	2.4	Services	Engineering, architectural, & surveying services	0.7	Services
Federal Government enterprises nec	2.1	Gov't	Meat animals	0.7	Agric.
Insurance carriers	2.1	Fin/R.E.	Aircraft	0.6	Manufg.
Photographic equipment & supplies	1.7	Manufg.	Apparel made from purchased materials	0.5	Manufg.
Electric services (utilities)	1.6	Util.	Crude petroleum & natural gas	0.5	Mining
Detective & protective services	1.5	Services	Gas production & distribution (utilities)	0.5	Util.
Legal services	1.4	Services	Insurance carriers	0.5	Fin/R.E.
Noncomparable imports	1.4	Foreign	Electronic computing equipment	0.4	Manufg.
Petroleum refining	1.2	Manufg.	Feed grains	0.4	Agric.
Wholesale trade	1.2	Trade	Maintenance of nonfarm buildings nec	0.4	Constr.
Manifold business forms	1.0	Manufg.	Motor freight transportation & warehousing	0.4	Util.
Credit agencies other than banks	0.9	Fin/R.E.	Dairy farm products	0.3	Agric.
Personnel supply services	0.9	Services	Doctors & dentists	0.3	Services
Business/professional associations	0.8	Services	Drugs	0.3	Manufg.
Commercial printing	0.8	Manufg.	Freight forwarders	0.3	Util.
Air transportation	0.6	Util.	Management & consulting services & labs	0.3	Services
Envelopes	0.6	Manufg.	Owner-occupied dwellings	0.3	Fin/R.E.
Electrical repair shops	0.4	Services	Security & commodity brokers	0.3	Fin/R.E.
Transit & bus transportation	0.4	Util.	Advertising	0.2	Services
Electronic components nec	0.3	Manufg.	Agricultural chemicals, nec	0.2	Manufg.
Electronic computing equipment	0.3	Manufg.	Air transportation	0.2	Util.
Engraving & plate printing	0.3	Manufg.	Aircraft & missile engines & engine parts	0.2	Manufg.
Manufacturing industries, nec	0.3	Manufg.	Aircraft & missile equipment, nec	0.2	Manufg.
Paper mills, except building paper	0.3	Manufg.	Broadwoven fabric mills	0.2	Manufg.
Periodicals	0.3	Manufg.	Chemical & fertilizer mineral	0.2	Mining
Services to dwellings & other buildings	0.3	Services	Coal	0.2	Mining
Textile bags	0.3	Manufg.	Computer & data processing services	0.2	Services
Automotive rental & leasing, without drivers	0.2	Services	Electronic components nec	0.2	Manufg.
Hotels & lodging places	0.2	Services	Hotels & lodging places	0.2	Services
Sanitary services, steam supply, irrigation	0.2	Util.	Industrial buildings	0.2	Constr.
Carbon paper & inked ribbons	0.1	Manufg.	Laundry, dry cleaning, shoe repair	0.2	Services
Newspapers	0.1	Manufg.	Machinery, except electrical, nec	0.2	Manufg.
			Medical & health services, nec	0.2	Services
			Motor vehicles & car bodies	0.2	Manufg.
			Newspapers	0.2	Manufg.
			Nonfarm residential structure maintenance	0.2	Constr.
			Office buildings	0.2	Constr.
			Oil bearing crops	0.2	Agric.
			Photographic equipment & supplies	0.2	Manufg.
			Radio & TV broadcasting	0.2	Util.
			Radio & TV communication equipment	0.2	Manufg.
			Railroads & related services	0.2	Util.
			Residential 1-unit structures, nonfarm	0.2	Constr.
			Semiconductors & related devices	0.2	Manufg.
			Water transportation	0.2	Util.

Continued on next page.

INPUTS AND OUTPUTS FOR ALL BANKING SECTORS - SICs 601, 602, 603, 608, and 609 - Continued

Economic Sector or Industry Providing Inputs	%	Sector	Economic Sector or Industry Buying Outputs	%	Sector
			Arrangement of passenger transportation	0.1	Util.
			Automotive repair shops & services	0.1	Services
			Blast furnaces & steel mills	0.1	Manufg.
			Bottled & canned soft drinks	0.1	Manufg.
			Business services nec	0.1	Services
			Commercial printing	0.1	Manufg.
			Cyclic crudes and organics	0.1	Manufg.
			Equipment rental & leasing services	0.1	Services
			Food grains	0.1	Agric.
			Malt beverages	0.1	Manufg.
			Metal office furniture	0.1	Manufg.
			Miscellaneous plastics products	0.1	Manufg.
			Motion pictures	0.1	Services
			Pipe, valves, & pipe fittings	0.1	Manufg.
			Pipelines, except natural gas	0.1	Util.
			Portrait, photographic studios	0.1	Services
			Prepared feeds, nec	0.1	Manufg.
			Primary aluminum	0.1	Manufg.
			Residential additions/alterations, nonfarm	0.1	Constr.

Source: Benchmark Input-Output Accounts for the U.S. Economy, 1982, U.S. Department of Commerce, Washington, D.C., July 1991. Data, as reported in the source, are organized by the 1977 SIC structure in use in 1982 but have been matched, as closely as is possible, to the 1987 SIC structure used in this book. Activities with the same percentage are sorted alphabetically by name of activity.

OCCUPATIONS EMPLOYED BY COMMERCIAL BANKS, SAVINGS INSTITUTIONS, CREDIT UNIONS

Occupation	% of Total 1994	Change to 2005	Occupation	% of Total 1994	Change to 2005
Bank tellers	27.8	-29.8	General managers & top executives	3.0	-4.0
Clerical supervisors & managers	6.5	12.9	Management support workers nec	2.6	1.2
Loan officers & counselors	6.4	8.8	Clerical support workers nec	1.4	-19.1
Financial managers	6.2	16.3	Accountants & auditors	1.4	-14.0
New accounts clerks, banking	5.8	1.2	Securities & financial services sales workers	1.3	11.3
Loan & credit clerks	5.2	-9.0	Adjustment clerks	1.3	5.3
General office clerks	3.9	-32.6	Statement clerks	1.1	-39.6
Bookkeeping, accounting, & auditing clerks	3.7	-24.1	Duplicating, mail, & office machine operators	1.0	-41.0
Secretaries, ex legal & medical	3.6	-18.1			

Sources: Industry-Occupation Matrix, Bureau of Labor Statistics. These data relate to one or more 3-digit SIC industry groups rather than to a single 4-digit SIC. The change reported for each occupation to the year 2005 is a percent of growth or decline as estimated by the Bureau of Labor Statistics. The abbreviation nec stands for not elsewhere classified.

U.S. AND STATE DATA ON INDUSTRY REVENUES AND OTHER ACCOUNTS FOR 1992

State	No. of Estab.	Employ- ment	Payroll ($ mil.)	Revenues ($ mil.)	Empl./ Estab.	Revenue/ Estab. ($)	Payroll/ Estab. ($)	Revenue/ Empl. ($)	Payroll/ Empl. ($)
UNITED STATES	20,544	341,920	8,445.6	92,322.2	17	4,493,877	411,097	270,011	24,700
Alabama	192	2,041	41.6	480.3	11	2,501,422	216,667	235,313	20,382
Alaska	3	-	(D)	(D)	(D)	(D)	(D)	(D)	(D)
Arizona	96	909	17.9	166.8	9	1,737,083	185,990	183,454	19,642
Arkansas	129	1,409	30.3	282.1	11	2,186,798	235,225	200,211	21,536
California	2,982	59,775	1,716.2	17,724.2	20	5,943,718	575,515	296,515	28,711
Colorado	189	1,943	40.3	389.7	10	2,062,153	213,492	200,590	20,767
Connecticut	734	15,222	369.7	3,785.6	21	5,157,545	503,668	248,695	24,287
Delaware	39	538	15.3	180.0	14	4,615,564	392,538	334,586	28,455
District of Columbia	79	914	25.7	309.8	12	3,921,278	324,785	338,929	28,072
Florida	1,362	20,084	472.3	5,901.4	15	4,332,899	346,776	293,836	23,517
Georgia	323	5,379	130.2	1,171.4	17	3,626,498	403,111	217,765	24,206
Hawaii	150	2,293	61.4	545.5	15	3,636,460	409,140	237,884	26,765
Idaho	44	343	8.4	116.6	8	2,650,136	191,886	339,959	24,615
Illinois	965	20,126	468.9	5,475.5	21	5,674,110	485,864	272,062	23,296
Indiana	355	5,433	117.8	1,279.5	15	3,604,124	331,856	235,499	21,684
Iowa	206	2,137	46.0	502.6	10	2,440,029	223,291	235,211	21,525
Kansas	189	2,381	52.8	1,100.6	13	5,823,238	279,603	462,239	22,194
Kentucky	239	2,468	57.6	638.7	10	2,672,502	241,134	258,804	23,351
Louisiana	162	2,306	50.3	531.5	14	3,280,765	310,247	230,479	21,795
Maine	165	2,659	59.1	523.5	16	3,172,806	358,473	196,883	22,244
Maryland	435	8,265	210.1	1,990.2	19	4,575,067	483,071	240,793	25,425
Massachusetts	1,075	20,449	534.9	5,013.6	19	4,663,844	497,590	245,177	26,158
Michigan	547	8,305	201.1	2,611.6	15	4,774,373	367,636	314,459	24,214
Minnesota	207	4,444	105.8	1,040.5	21	5,026,763	511,314	234,145	23,817
Mississippi	139	1,704	35.8	306.4	12	2,203,978	257,489	179,785	21,004
Missouri	389	4,929	103.5	1,390.4	13	3,574,270	266,064	282,084	20,998
Montana	62	639	13.9	117.5	10	1,894,387	224,629	183,806	21,795
Nebraska	171	1,970	48.1	659.4	12	3,856,117	281,053	334,719	24,396
Nevada	97	1,366	34.4	318.0	14	3,277,990	354,608	232,771	25,181
New Hampshire	245	4,062	91.7	865.9	17	3,534,469	374,098	213,182	22,564
New Jersey	1,026	15,366	382.2	4,235.4	15	4,128,066	372,490	275,634	24,871
New Mexico	41	-	(D)	(D)	(D)	(D)	(D)	(D)	(D)
New York	1,454	37,325	892.6	10,343.0	26	7,113,488	613,866	277,107	23,913
North Carolina	507	5,750	139.2	1,443.2	11	2,846,586	274,639	250,995	24,216
North Dakota	56	-	(D)	(D)	(D)	(D)	(D)	(D)	(D)
Ohio	1,124	15,082	335.5	3,834.2	13	3,411,228	298,505	254,225	22,246
Oklahoma	177	2,380	46.1	697.8	13	3,942,277	260,226	293,186	19,353
Oregon	229	2,556	64.3	634.0	11	2,768,603	280,860	248,048	25,163
Pennsylvania	957	12,465	279.0	2,979.2	13	3,113,060	291,534	239,005	22,383
Rhode Island	65	1,829	42.0	330.4	28	5,082,523	646,369	180,625	22,971
South Carolina	328	5,001	111.8	954.1	15	2,908,857	340,970	190,783	22,363
South Dakota	64	560	10.2	122.8	9	1,919,156	159,687	219,332	18,250
Tennessee	241	3,157	69.4	706.3	13	2,930,585	287,801	223,716	21,970
Texas	660	10,472	269.7	4,227.6	16	6,405,520	408,615	403,709	25,753
Utah	33	-	(D)	(D)	(D)	(D)	(D)	(D)	(D)
Vermont	49	1,081	26.1	192.2	22	3,921,592	531,939	177,759	24,112
Virginia	525	6,772	159.5	1,754.0	13	3,340,956	303,859	259,008	23,557
Washington	482	7,198	228.7	2,246.8	15	4,661,332	474,546	312,137	31,777
West Virginia	46	609	11.6	138.3	13	3,007,283	252,217	227,151	19,051
Wisconsin	482	7,273	160.0	1,524.7	15	3,163,210	332,017	209,634	22,004
Wyoming	28	-	(D)	(D)	(D)	(D)	(D)	(D)	(D)

Source: 1992 Economic Census, U.S. Department of Commerce, Washington, D.C. This is the only table that shows revenue data as collected by the Bureau of the Census in an Economic Census. The symbol (D) indicates that data are withheld by the source to avoid disclosure of competitive information. A dash (-) indicates that data are not available or cannot be calculated.

ESTABLISHMENTS 1992 - STATE AND REGIONAL CONCENTRATION

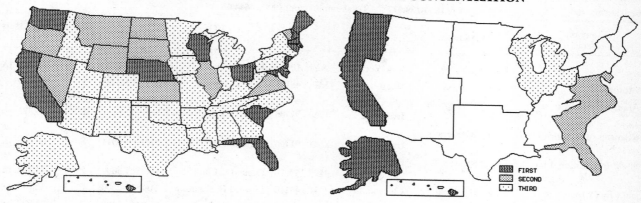

EMPLOYMENT 1992 - STATE AND REGIONAL CONCENTRATION

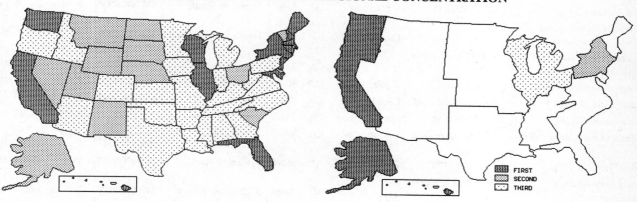

REVENUES 1992 - STATE AND REGIONAL CONCENTRATION

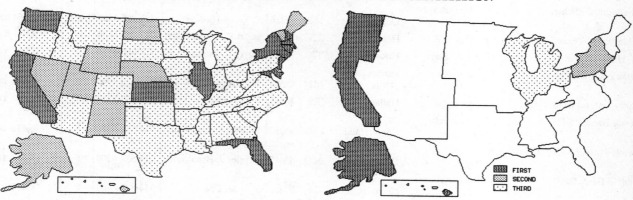

States with the darkest shading indicate those states which have proportionately more establishments, employment, or revenues than would be indicated by the state's population. States with light shading are states with proportionately fewer establishments, less employment, and lower revenues than population distribution. States shaded grey are within 15 percent of the state's population proportion in these categories. States for which no data are available are shown as average (grey). *Regions* are shaded to indicate absolute rank in the category. If no data for the category are available, establishment counts are used to shade the regions. Source of the data is the table on the facing page.

LEADING COMPANIES - SIC 6035 - Federal Savings Institutions

Number shown: **100**   Total sales/assets ($ mil): **1,120,077**   Total employment (000): **644.0**

Company Name	Address				CEO Name	Phone	Co. Type	Sales/Assets ($ mil)	Empl. (000)
Citicorp	399 Park Ave.	New York	NY	10043	John S. Reed	212-559-1000	P	250,489 TA	82.6
Ford Motor Co.	P.O. Box 1899	Dearborn	MI	48121	Alex Trotman	313-322-3000	P	128,439	337.8
H.F. Ahmanson and Co.	4900 Rivergrade Rd.	Irwindale	CA	91706	Charles R. Rinehart	818-960-6311	P	53,726 TA	9.9
Home Savings of America F.S.B.	4900 Rivergrade Rd.	Irwindale	CA	91706	Richard H. Deihl	818-960-6311	S	48,000 TA	8.5
Household International Inc.	2700 Sanders Rd.	Prospect Heights	IL	60070	Donald C Clark	708-564-5000	P	34,338 TA	15.5
National City Corp.	1900 E. 9th St.	Cleveland	OH	44114	Edward B. Brandon	216-575-2000	P	32,114 TA	20.3
Golden West Financial Corp.	1901 Harrison St.	Oakland	CA	94612	Marion O. Sandler	510-446-3420	P	28,829 TA	4.4
World Savings and Loan Association	1901 Harrison St.	Oakland	CA	94612	Herbert M. Sandler	510-446-6000	S	28,029 TA	4.3
First of America Bank Corp.	211 S. Rose St.	Kalamazoo	MI	49007	Daniel R. Smith	616-376-9000	P	21,230 TA	13.3
ABN AMRO North America Inc.	135 S. La Salle St.	Chicago	IL	60603	Harrison F. Tempest	312-443-2000	S	18,935 TA	5.3
American Savings and Loan Association	17877 Von Karman Ave.	Irvine	CA	92714	Mario J. Antoci	714-252-7083	S	18,552 TA	3.0
Huntington Bancshares Inc.	Huntington Ctr.	Columbus	OH	43287	Frank Wobst	614-480-8300	P	17,771 TA	8.2
Glendale Federal Bank F.S.B.	700 N. Brand Blvd.	Glendale	CA	91203	Stephen J. Trafton	818-500-2000	P	16,803 TA	3.4
First Nationwide Bank	135 Market St.	San Francisco	CA	94105	John M. Devine	415-904-0110	S	15,483 TA	3.5
California Federal Bank F.S.B.	5700 Wilshire Blvd.	Los Angeles	CA	90036	Edward G. Harshfield	213-932-4321	P	14,182 TA	2.3
Regions Financial Corp.	P.O. Box 10247	Birmingham	AL	35202	J. Stanley Mackin	205-326-7060	P	12,839 TA	6.0
Standard Federal Bank	2600 W. Big Beaver Rd.	Troy	MI	48084	Thomas R. Ricketts	810-643-9600	P	12,077 TA	3.1
Dime Bancorp Inc.	589 5th Ave.	New York	NY	10017	Lawrence J. Toal	212-326-6170	P	9,996 TA	1.7
Dime Savings Bank of New York F.S.B.	589 5th Ave.	New York	NY	10017	Richard Parsons	212-326-6170	S	9,276 TA	2.0
First Federal of Michigan	1001 Woodward Ave.	Detroit	MI	48226	C. Gene Harling	313-965-1400	S	9,264 TA	1.3
Bank United of Texas F.S.B.	P.O. Box 1370	Houston	TX	77251	Barry C. Burkholder	713-963-6500	S	8,901 TA	2.9
USAT Holdings Inc.	3200 S.W. Fwy.	Houston	TX	77027	Barry C. Burkholder	713-965-6920	R	8,901 TA	2.9
Michigan National Corp.	P.O. Box 9065	Farmington Hills	MI	48333	Robert J. Mylod	313-473-3000	P	8,692 TA	4.9
Guaranty Federal Bank F.S.B.	8333 Douglas Ave.	Dallas	TX	78225	Kenny Jastrow	214-360-3360	S	8,500 TA	1.6
Roosevelt Bank F.S.B.	900 Roosevelt Pkwy.	Chesterfield	MO	63017	Stanley J. Bradshaw	314-532-6200	S	8,432 TA	1.0
Roosevelt Financial Group Inc.	900 Roosevelt Pkwy.	Chesterfield	MO	63017	Stanley J. Bradshaw	314-532-6200	P	8,432 TA	1.0
Household Bank F.S.B.	4301 MacArthur Blvd.	Newport Beach	CA	92660	Ron McGee	714-833-0367	S	8,400 TA	2.1
FirstFed Michigan Corp.	1001 Woodward Ave.	Detroit	MI	48226	C. Gene Harling	313-965-1400	P	8,399 TA	1.3
Coast Federal Bank F.S.B.	1000 Wilshire Blvd.	Los Angeles	CA	90017	Robert L. Hunt II	213-362-2000	S	8,197 TA	1.7
Coast Savings Financial Inc.	1000 Wilshire Blvd.	Los Angeles	CA	90017	Ray Martin	213-362-2000	P	8,197 TA	1.7

Company type codes: P - Public, R - Private, S - Subsidiary, D - Division, J - Joint Venture, A - Affiliate, G - Group. If the dollar values shown are not sales, the following codes apply: TA - Total Assets; OR - Operating Revenues; GB - Gross Billings. * - estimated dollar value. < - less than. *na* - not available.

Continued on next page.

LEADING COMPANIES - SIC 6035 - Federal Savings Institutions
Continued

Company Name	Address				CEO Name	Phone	Co. Type	Sales/Assets ($ mil)	Empl. (000)
Fleet Bank of Connecticut	1 Constitution Plz.	Hartford	CT	06115	Frederick C. Copeland	203-244-5000	S	6,770 TA	2.1
Charter One Financial Inc.	1215 Superior Ave.	Cleveland	OH	44114	Charles J. Koch	216-589-8320	P	6,130 TA	1.4
LaSalle Talman Bank F.S.B.	30 W. Monroe St.	Chicago	IL	60603	Theodore H. Roberts	312-726-8915	S	5,851 TA	1.4
Commercial Federal Corp.	2120 S. 72nd St.	Omaha	NE	68124	William A. Fitzgerald	402-554-9200	P	5,521 TA	1.1
Commercial Federal Bank	P.O. Box 1103 DTS	Omaha	NE	68101	William A. Fitzgerald	402-554-9200	S	5,521 TA	1.1
First Financial Bank F.S.B.	1305 Main St.	Stevens Point	WI	54481	John C. Seramur	715-341-0400	S	5,104 TA	1.8
First Financial Corp.	1305 Main St.	Stevens Point	WI	54481	John C. Seramur	715-341-0400	P	5,104 TA	1.8
TCF Financial Corp.	801 Marquette Ave.	Minneapolis	MN	55402	William A. Cooper	612-370-7000	P	5,026 TA	3.5
FirstMerit Corp.	III Cascade Plz.	Akron	OH	44308	Howard L. Flood	216-384-8000	P	4,924 TA	3.4
Chevy Chase Bank F.S.B.	8401 Connecticut Ave.	Chevy Chase	MD	20815	Alexander R.M. Boyle	301-986-7000	R	4,900 TA	2.5
Astoria Federal Savings and Loan Association	1 Astoria Federal Plz.	Lake Success	NY	11042	George L. Engelke Jr.	516-327-3000	S	4,643 TA	0.8
Astoria Financial Corp.	1 Astoria Federal Plz.	Lake Success	NY	11042	George L. Engelke Jr.	516-327-3000	P	4,643 TA	0.8
Collective Bank	P.O. Box 316	Egg Harbor City	NJ	08215	Thomas H. Hamilton	609-965-1234	S	4,593 TA	0.9
Collective Bancorp Inc.	P.O. Box 316	Egg Harbor City	NJ	08215	Thomas H. Hamilton	609-965-1234	P	4,589 TA	0.9
CSF Holdings Inc.	1221 Brickell Ave.	Miami	FL	33131	Charles B. Stuzin	305-577-0400	P	4,576 TA	0.9
Long Island Bancorp Inc.	201 Old Country Rd.	Melville	NY	11747	John J. Conefry Jr.	516-547-2000	P	4,516 TA	1.2
Long Island Savings Bank F.S.B.	201 Old Country Rd.	Melville	NY	11747	John J. Conefry Jr.	516-547-2000	S	4,516 TA	1.2
Third Federal Savings and Loan Association of Cleveland	7007 Broadway Ave.	Cleveland	OH	44105	Marc A. Stefanski	216-441-6000	R	4,500 TA	0.6
Sovereign Bancorp Inc.	1130 Berkshire Blvd.	Wyomissing	PA	19610	Jay S. Sidhu	215-320-8400	P	4,495 TA	1.0
Sovereign Bank F.S.B.	P.O. Box 37	Wyomissing	PA	19603	Jay S. Sidhu	215-723-6711	S	4,495 TA	1.0
Citizens Federal Bank F.S.B.	1221 Brickell Ave.	Miami	FL	33131	Charles B. Stuzin	305-577-0400	S	4,437 TA	0.9
Brooklyn Bancorp Inc.	211 Montague St.	Brooklyn	NY	11201	Richard A. Kraemer	718-780-0400	P	4,161 TA	0.8
CrossLand Federal Savings Bank	211 Montague St.	Brooklyn	NY	11201	Richard A. Kraemer	718-780-0400	S	4,161 TA	0.8
FirstFed Financial Corp.	401 Wilshire Blvd.	Santa Monica	CA	90401	William S. Mortensen	310-319-6000	P	4,157 TA	0.5
St. Paul Bancorp Inc.	6700 W. North Ave.	Chicago	IL	60635	Joseph C. Scully	312-622-5000	P	4,100 TA	1.1
St. Paul Federal Bank for Savings	6700 W. North Ave.	Chicago	IL	60635	Patrick J. Agnew	312-622-5000	S	4,100 TA	1.1
Capitol Federal Savings and Loan Association	700 Kansas Ave.	Topeka	KS	66603	John C. Dicus	913-235-1341	R	4,000 TA	0.6
Northeast Federal Corp.	50 State House Sq.	Hartford	CT	06103	Kirk W. Walters	203-280-1000	P	3,920 TA	0.9
Northeast Savings F.A.	50 State House Sq.	Hartford	CT	06103	Kirk W. Walters	203-280-1000	S	3,900 TA	0.9
Washington Federal Inc.	425 Pike St.	Seattle	WA	98101	Guy C. Pinkerton	206-624-7930	P	3,830 TA	0.5
Washington Federal Savings	425 Pike St.	Seattle	WA	98101	Guy C. Pinkerton	206-624-7930	S	3,830 TA	0.5

Company type codes: P - Public, R - Private, S - Subsidiary, D - Division, J - Joint Venture, A - Affiliate, G - Group. If the dollar values shown are not sales, the following codes apply: TA - Total Assets; OR - Operating Revenues; GB - Gross Billings. * - estimated dollar value. < - less than. na - not available.

Continued on next page.

LEADING COMPANIES - SIC 6035 - Federal Savings Institutions
Continued

Company Name	Address				CEO Name	Phone	Co. Type	Sales/Assets ($ mil)	Empl. (000)
Citadel Holding Corp.	600 N. Brand Blvd.	Glendale	CA	91203	Richard M. Greenwood	818-956-7100	P	3,719 TA	0.9
Fidelity Federal Bank F.S.B.	600 N. Brand Blvd.	Glendale	CA	91203	Richard M. Greenwood	818-956-7100	S	3,719 TA	0.9
San Francisco Federal Savings and Loan Association	88 Kearny St.	San Francisco	CA	94108	Roger L. Gordon	415-955-5800	S	3,719 TA	0.7
SFFed Corp.	88 Kearny St.	San Francisco	CA	94108	Roger L. Gordon	415-955-5800	P	3,719 TA	0.7
First Federal Bank of California	401 Wilshire Blvd.	Santa Monica	CA	90401	William S. Mortenson	310-319-6000	S	3,674 TA	0.6
American Savings of Florida F.S.B.	17801 N.W. 2nd Ave.	Miami	FL	33169	Stephen D. Taylor	305-653-5353	P	3,561 TA	0.7
TCF Bank Minnesota F.S.B.	801 Marquette Ave.	Minneapolis	MN	55402	Thomas A. Cusick	612-370-7000	S	3,447 TA	2.0
ITT Federal Bank F.S.B.	5 Park Plz.	Irvine	CA	92714	Graham Williams	714-757-1999	S	3,266 TA	0.2
Bay View Capital Corp.	2121 S. El Camino Real	San Mateo	CA	94403	James E. Tecca	415-573-7300	P	3,166 TA	0.5
Bay View Federal Bank F.S.B.	2121 S. El Camino Real	San Mateo	CA	94403	James E. Tecca	415-573-7300	S	3,166 TA	0.5
American Savings Bank F.S.B.	915 Fort St. Mall	Honolulu	HI	96813	Wayne K. Minami	808-531-6262	S	3,116 TA	0.7
FirsTier Financial Inc.	1700 Farnam St.	Omaha	NE	68102	David A. Rismiller	402-348-6000	P	3,100 TA	1.6
Southwest Gas Corp.	P.O. Box 98510	Las Vegas	NV	89193	Michael O. Maffie	702-876-7011	P	3,090 TA	2.4
ALBANK Financial Corp.	10 N. Pearl St.	Albany	NY	12207	Herbert G. Chorbajian	518-445-2100	P	2,940 TA	0.9
Albany Savings Bank F.S.B.	P.O. Box 70	Albany	NY	12201	Herbert G. Chorbajian	518-432-2200	S	2,940 TA	0.9
Temple-Inland Inc.	P.O. Drawer N	Diboll	TX	75941	Clifford J. Grum	409-829-1313	P	2,938	15.0
Columbia First Bank F.S.B.	1560 Wilson Blvd.	Arlington	VA	22209	Thomas J. Schaefer	703-247-5000	P	2,849 TA	0.5
Adam Corp.	1111 Briarcrest Dr.	Bryan	TX	77802	Don Adam	409-776-1111	R	2,800 TA	1.0
AmWest Savings Association	P.O. Box 8100	Bryan	TX	77805	Bob Shofstahl	409-361-6200	S	2,800 TA	1.0
Webster Financial Corp.	1st Federal Plz.	Waterbury	CT	06702	James C. Smith	203-755-1422	P	2,762 TA	0.9
First Federal Bank F.S.B.	P.O. Box 191	Waterbury	CT	06726	James C. Smith	203-755-1422	S	2,750 TA	0.9
Western Financial Savings Bank	23 Pasteur Rd.	Irvine	CA	92713	Stephen Prough	714-727-1000	S	2,750 TA*	1.0
Westcorp	P.O. Box 19733	Irvine	CA	92718	Ernest S. Rady	714-727-1000	P	2,742 TA	1.1
CNB Bancshares Inc.	P.O. Box 778	Evansville	IN	47705	H. Lee Cooper	812-464-3400	P	2,648 TA	1.6
Great Lakes Bancorp F.S.B.	401 E. Liberty St.	Ann Arbor	MI	48104	Robert J. Delonis	313-769-8300	P	2,607 TA	1.1
Loyola Capital Corp.	1300 N. Charles St.	Baltimore	MD	21201	Joseph W. Mosmiller	410-787-3100	P	2,468 TA	0.8
Coral Gables Fedcorp Inc.	P.O. Box 141488	Coral Gables	FL	33114	Walter F. Hinson III	305-447-4711	P	2,464 TA	0.8
Coral Gables Federal Savings and Loan Association	P.O. Box 141488	Coral Gables	FL	33114	Walter F. Hinson III	305-447-4711	S	2,464 TA	0.8
Leader Federal Bank for Savings	P.O. Box 275	Memphis	TN	38101	Ronald W. Stimpson	901-578-2454	S	2,448 TA	0.8
Leader Financial Corp.	158 Madison Ave.	Memphis	TN	38103	Ronald W. Stimpson	901-578-4300	P	2,448 TA	0.8
Dollar Bank	3 Gateway Ctr.	Pittsburgh	PA	15222	Stephen C. Hansen	412-261-4900	R	2,315 TA	1.0
Local Federal Bank F.S.B.	P.O. Box 26020	Oklahoma City	OK	73126	Robert Irbin	405-841-2100	S	2,300 TA	0.4
Local Financial Corp.	P.O. Box 26020	Oklahoma City	OK	73126	Bruce S. Sherman	405-841-2100	R	2,300 TA	0.4

Company type codes: P - Public, R - Private, S - Subsidiary, D - Division, J - Joint Venture, A - Affiliate, G - Group. If the dollar values shown are not sales, the following codes apply: TA - Total Assets; OR - Operating Revenues; GB - Gross Billings. * - estimated dollar value. < - less than. *na* - not available.

Continued on next page.

LEADING COMPANIES - SIC 6035 - Federal Savings Institutions

Continued

Company Name	Address				CEO Name	Phone	Co. Type	Sales/Assets ($ mil)	Empl. (000)
Loyola Federal Savings Bank	1300 N. Charles St.	Baltimore	MD	21201	Joseph W. Mosmiller	410-332-7000	S	2,222 TA	0.7
First Heights Bank F.S.B.	2727 N. Loop W.	Houston	TX	77248	Robert E. Zambie	713-869-3411	S	2,185 TA	0.5
First Savings Bank F.S.B.	301 College St.	Greenville	SC	29601	Luther C. Boliek	803-458-2000	P	2,086 TA	0.9
Fidelity New York F.S.B.	1000 Franklin Ave.	Garden City	NY	11530	Thomas V. Powderly	516-746-8500	S	2,018 TA	0.3
Citizens Federal Bank F.S.B.	1 Citizens Federal Ctr	Dayton	OH	45402	Jerry L. Kirby	513-223-4234	S	2,013 TA	0.6
First Financial Bancorp.	300 High St.	Hamilton	OH	45011	Stanley N. Pontius	513-867-4700	P	1,923 TA	1.1

Source: Ward's Business Directory of U.S. Private and Public Companies, 1996. Company type codes: P - Public, R - Private, S - Subsidiary, D - Division, J - Joint Venture, A - Affiliate, G - Group. If the dollar values shown are not sales, the following codes apply: TA - Total Assets; OR - Operating Revenues; GB - Gross Billings. * - estimated dollar value. < - less than; na - not available.

LEADING COMPANIES - SIC 6036 - Savings Institutions, ex Federal

Number shown: **100**   Total sales/assets ($ mil): **369,397**   Total employment (000): **126.9**

Company Name	Address				CEO Name	Phone	Co. Type	Sales/Assets ($ mil)	Empl. (000)
Republic New York Corp.	452 5th Ave.	New York	NY	10018	Walter H. Weiner	212-525-6100	P	41,068 TA	5.5
Bank of Boston Corp.	P.O. Box 1987	Boston	MA	02105	Ira Stepanian	617-434-2200	P	40,588 TA	18.6
Great Western Financial Corp.	9200 Oakdale Ave.	Chatsworth	CA	91311	James F. Montgomery	818-775-3411	P	38,348 TA	17.0
Southern National Corp.	200 W. 2nd St.	Winston-Salem	NC	27101	John A. Allison	919-773-7200	P	19,855 TA	7.7
Washington Mutual Inc.	1201 3rd Ave.	Seattle	WA	98101	Kerry K. Killinger	206-461-2000	P	18,457 TA	4.4
Washington Mutual Bank	1201 3rd Ave.	Seattle	WA	98101	Kerry K. Killinger	206-461-2000	S	15,827 TA	4.7
Metropolitan Financial Corp.	333 S. 7th St.	Minneapolis	MN	55435	Norman M. Jones	612-928-5000	P	7,007 TA	2.6
GP Financial Corp.	41-60 Main St.	Flushing	NY	11355	Thomas S. Johnson	718-670-7600	P	6,677 TA	1.4
Green Point Savings Bank	807 Manhattan Ave.	New York	NY	11222	Thomas S. Johnson	718-670-7600	S	6,677 TA	1.4
People's Bank of Bridgeport	850 Main St.	Bridgeport	CT	06604	David E.A. Carson	203-338-7001	S	6,484 TA	2.5
People's Mutual Holdings Inc.	850 Main St.	Bridgeport	CT	06604	David E.A. Carson	203-579-7171	P	6,484 TA	2.5
People's Bank	850 Main St.	Bridgeport	CT	06604	David E.A. Carson	203-338-7171	P	6,400 TA	2.2
Republic Bank for Savings	415 Madison Ave.	New York	NY	10017	John A. Pancetti	212-688-3000	S	6,100 TA	1.0
Emigrant Savings Bank	5 E. 42nd St.	New York	NY	10017	Philip Milstein	212-850-4000	R	6,060 TA	1.3
Citizens Financial Group Inc.	1 Citizens Plz.	Providence	RI	02903	Mark J. Formica	401-456-7000	S	5,084 TA	2.2
Citizens Savings Bank	1 Citizens Plz.	Providence	RI	02903	Mark J. Formica	401-456-7000	S	5,084 TA	2.2
Hudson City Savings Bank	W. 80 Century Rd.	Paramus	NJ	07652	Leonard Gudelski	201-967-1900	R	4,895 TA	0.8
Downey Savings and Loan Association	3501 Jamboree Rd.	Newport Beach	CA	92660	Stephen W. Prough	714-854-0300	P	4,651 TA	1.1
OnBank and Trust Co.	P.O. Box 4950	Syracuse	NY	13221	Robert J. Bennett	315-424-4400	S	4,414 TA	1.0
Rochester Community Savings Bank	40 Franklin St.	Rochester	NY	14604	Leonard S. Simon	716-258-3000	P	4,189 TA	1.7

Company type codes: P - Public, R - Private, S - Subsidiary, D - Division, J - Joint Venture, A - Affiliate, G - Group. If the dollar values shown are not sales, the following codes apply: TA - Total Assets; OR - Operating Revenues; GB - Gross Billings. * - estimated dollar value. < - less than. na - not available.

Continued on next page.

LEADING COMPANIES - SIC 6036 - Savings Institutions, ex Federal

Continued

Company Name	Address				CEO Name	Phone	Co. Type	Sales/Assets ($ mil)	Empl. (000)
Farm and Home Financial Corp.	10100 N. Exec. Hills	Kansas City	MO	64153	John Morton III	816-891-7778	P	3,742 TA	0.6
Alleghany Corp.	Park Avenue Plz.	New York	NY	10055	John J. Burns Jr.	212-752-1356	P	3,588 TA	9.1
Centerbank	60 N. Main St.	Waterbury	CT	06702	Robert J. Narkis	203-578-7000	P	3,064 TA	1.3
Peoples Heritage Financial Group Inc.	P.O. Box 9540	Portland	ME	04112	William J. Ryan	207-761-8500	P	2,800 TA	1.0
Security Bank S.S.B.	P.O. Box 3082	Milwaukee	WI	53203	William G. Schuett Sr.	414-273-1900	S	2,574 TA	1.1
Security Capital Corp.	P.O. Box 3097	Milwaukee	WI	53203	William G. Schuett Sr.	414-273-8090	P	2,574 TA	1.1
Fortune Bancorp Inc.	P.O. Box 6100	Clearwater	FL	34618	John R. Torell III	813-538-1000	P	2,551 TA	0.8
Fortune Bank	P.O. Box 6100	Clearwater	FL	34618	Roy J. McCraw Jr.	813-538-1000	S	2,551 TA	0.8
Greater New York Savings Bank	1 Penn Plz.	New York	NY	10119	Gerard C. Keegan	212-613-4000	P	2,500 TA	0.7
NBB Bancorp Inc.	P.O. Box 5000	New Bedford	MA	02742	Robert McCarter	508-996-5000	P	2,451 TA	0.5
New Bedford Institution for Savings	P.O. Box 5000	New Bedford	MA	02742	Robert M. McCarter	508-996-5000	S	2,451 TA	0.5
Coastal Banc Savings Association	8 Greenway Plz.	Houston	TX	77046	Manuel J. Mehos	713-623-2600	P	2,300 TA	0.3
South Boston Savings Bank	460 W. Broadway	South Boston	MA	02127	Peter H. Hersey	617-268-2500	S	2,204 TA	0.2
Ohio Savings Bank	1801 E. 9th St.	Cleveland	OH	44114	Robert Goldberg	216-696-2222	S	2,161 TA	0.9
Ohio Savings Financial Corp.	1801 E. 9th St.	Cleveland	OH	44114	Robert Goldberg	216-696-2222	R	2,161 TA	0.9
Boston Bancorp.	460 W. Broadway	South Boston	MA	02127	Peter H. Hersey	617-268-2500	P	2,033 TA	0.2
Eastern Bank Corporation Inc.	270 Union St.	Lynn	MA	01901	Stanley J. Lukowski	617-599-2100	R	2,021 TA	0.7
New Haven Savings Bank	P.O. Box 302	New Haven	CT	06502	Charles Terrell	203-787-1111	R	1,879 TA	0.4
Franklin First Savings Bank	P.O. Box 449	Wilkes-Barre	PA	18773	Thomas H. van Arsdale	717-821-7100	S	1,874 TA	0.4
East New York Savings Bank	350 Park Ave.	New York	NY	10022	Atwood Collins III	212-350-2500	S	1,777 TA	0.3
Shawmut Bank NH	P.O. Box 9524	Manchester	NH	03108	Robert Keller	603-485-6500	S	1,750 TA	0.6
First Republic Bancorp Inc.	388 Market St.	San Francisco	CA	94111	James H. Herbert II	415-392-1400	P	1,707 TA	0.1
Provident Savings Bank	830 Bergen Ave.	Jersey City	NJ	07306	Paul Pantozzi	201-333-1000	R	1,700 TA	0.5
F.N.B. Corp.	Hermitage Sq.	Hermitage	PA	16148	Thomas M. Tuggle	412-981-6000	P	1,686 TA	0.8
First Republic Thrift and Loan	101 Pine St.	San Francisco	CA	94111	James H. Herbert II	415-392-1400	S	1,643 TA	0.1
Bankers Savings	P.O. Box 509	Perth Amboy	NJ	08862	Joseph P. Gemmell	908-442-4100	S	1,622 TA	0.2
North Side Savings Bank	170 Tulip Ave.	Floral Park	NY	11001	Thomas M. O'Brien	516-488-6900	P	1,541 TA	0.3
Worcester County Institution for Savings	365 Main St.	Worcester	MA	01608	Harold Cabot	508-831-4000	S	1,457 TA	0.5
CB Bancshares Inc.	P.O. Box 3709	Honolulu	HI	96811	James M. Morita	808-546-2411	P	1,440 TA	0.4
Northwest Bancorp M.H.C.	P.O. Drawer 128	Warren	PA	16365	John O. Hanna	814-726-2140	R	1,427 TA	0.6
Northwest Savings Bank	P.O. Drawer 128	Warren	PA	16365	John O. Hanna	814-726-2140	P	1,427 TA	0.6
Republic Bancorp Inc.	P.O. Box 70	Owosso	MI	48867	Jerry D. Campbell	517-725-7337	P	1,400 TA	1.0
Staten Island Savings Bank	P.O. Box 137	Staten Island	NY	10304	Harry P. Doherty	718-447-7900	R	1,376 TA	0.3
Sterling Financial Corp.	N. 120 Wall St.	Spokane	WA	99201	Harold B. Gilkey	509-458-3711	P	1,374 TA	0.5

Company type codes: P - Public, R - Private, S - Subsidiary, D - Division, J - Joint Venture, A - Affiliate, G - Group. If the dollar values shown are not sales, the following codes apply: TA - Total Assets; OR - Operating Revenues; GB - Gross Billings. * - estimated dollar value. < - less than. *na* - not available.

Continued on next page.

LEADING COMPANIES - SIC 6036 - Savings Institutions, ex Federal
Continued

Company Name	Address				CEO Name	Phone	Co. Type	Sales/Assets ($ mil)	Empl. (000)
Citizens Commercial and Savings Bank	1 Citizens Banking Ctr	Flint	MI	48502	David A. Thomas Jr.	810-766-7500	S	1,303 TA	0.9
Gateway Bank	P.O. Box 120	Norwalk	CT	06854	Reginald DeKoven III	203-845-7700	S	1,276 TA	0.5
Gateway Financial Corp.	P.O. Box 120	Norwalk	CT	06854	Reginald DeKoven III	203-845-7700	P	1,276 TA	0.5
Northwestern Savings and Loan Association	2300 N. Western Ave.	Chicago	IL	60647	Henry R. Smogolski	312-489-2300	S	1,254 TA	0.4
DS Bancor Inc.	33 Elizabeth St.	Derby	CT	06418	Harry P. DiAdamo Jr.	203-736-9921	P	1,227 TA	0.3
California Financial Holding Co.	501 W. Weber Ave.	Stockton	CA	95203	David K. Rea	209-948-6870	P	1,202 TA	0.4
Derby Savings Bank	33 Elizabeth St.	Derby	CT	06418	Harry P. DiAdamo Jr.	203-736-9921	S	1,194 TA	0.3
Queens County Bancorp Inc.	38-25 Main St.	Flushing	NY	11354	Joseph R. Ficalora	718-359-6400	P	1,171 TA	0.3
Queens County Savings Bank	38-25 Main St.	Flushing	NY	11354	Joseph R. Ficalora	718-359-6400	S	1,171 TA	0.3
American Savings Bank	P.O. Box	New Britain	CT	06050	Robert T. Kenney	203-225-6431	R	1,165 TA	0.3
Binghamton Savings Bank	P.O. Box 1056	Binghamton	NY	13902	William H. Rincker	607-779-2552	S	1,159 TA	0.4
BSB Bancorp Inc.	P.O. Box 1056	Binghamton	NY	13902	William H. Rincker	607-779-2552	P	1,159 TA	0.4
Midfirst Bank S.S.B.	P.O. Box 26750	Oklahoma City	OK	73126	John Laisle	405-840-7600	R	1,100 TA	0.7
Stockton Savings Bank	212 N. San Joaquin St.	Stockton	CA	95202	David K. Rea	209-948-6870	S	1,058 TA	0.3
Andover Bank	P.O. Box 2005	Andover	MA	01810	Gerald T. Mulligan	508-749-2000	S	1,058 TA	0.3
Harris Savings Bank	P.O. Box 1711	Harrisburg	PA	17105	William J. McLaughlin	717-236-4041	P	1,058 TA	0.4
Sterling Savings Association	N. 120 Wall St.	Spokane	WA	99201	Harold B. Gilkey	509-458-3711	S	1,039 TA	0.4
AnchorBank S.S.B.	25 W. Main St.	Madison	WI	53703	Douglas J. Timmerman	608-252-8700	S	1,004 TA	0.6
Cambridge Savings Bank	P.O. Box 380206	Cambridge	MA	02238	James P. Ingram	617-864-8700	R	944 TA	0.2
Medford Savings Bank	29 High St.	Medford	MA	02155	Arthur H. Meehan	617-395-7700	P	915 TA	0.3
Wesco Financial Corp.	315 E. Colorado Blvd.	Pasadena	CA	91101	Charles T. Munger	818-449-2345	P	915 TA	0.3
Peoples Bancorp of Worcester Inc.	120 Front St.	Worcester	MA	01608	Woodbury C. Titcomb	508-791-3861	P	891 TA	0.3
Peoples Savings Bank	120 Front St.	Worcester	MA	01608	Woodbury C. Titcomb	508-791-3861	S	891 TA	0.3
Advest Group Inc.	280 Trumbull St.	Hartford	CT	06103	Allen Weintraub	203-525-1421	P	885 TA	1.5
Parkvale Financial Corp.	4220 William Penn Hwy.	Monroeville	PA	15146	Robert J. McCarthy Jr.	412-373-7200	P	874 TA	0.2
Parkvale Savings Bank	4220 William Penn Hwy.	Monroeville	PA	15146	Robert J. McCarthy Jr.	412-373-7200	S	874 TA	0.2
Jefferson Savings and Loan Association	P.O. Box 17	Ballwin	MO	63022	David V. McCay	314-227-3000	S	861 TA	0.1
Jefferson Savings Bancorp Inc.	P.O. Box 17	Ballwin	MO	63022	David V. McCay	314-227-3000	P	861 TA	0.1
Hawthorne Savings and Loan Association	13658 Hawthorne Blvd., 400	Hawthorne	CA	90250	Scott Braly	310-973-8964	S	849 TA	0.2

Company type codes: P - Public, R - Private, S - Subsidiary, D - Division, J - Joint Venture, A - Affiliate, G - Group. If the dollar values shown are not sales, the following codes apply: TA - Total Assets; OR - Operating Revenues; GB - Gross Billings. * - estimated dollar value. < - less than. *na* - not available.

Continued on next page.

LEADING COMPANIES - SIC 6036 - Savings Institutions, ex Federal

Continued

Company Name	Address				CEO Name	Phone	Co. Type	Sales/Assets ($ mil)	Empl. (000)
MASSBANK Corp.	123 Haven St.	Reading	MA	01867	Gerard H. Brandi	617-662-0100	P	844 TA	0.3
MASSBANK for Savings	123 Haven St.	Reading	MA	01867	Gerard H. Brandi	617-662-0100	S	844 TA	0.3
InterWest Savings Bank	P.O. Box 1649	Oak Harbor	WA	98277	Steven M. Walden	206-679-4181	P	839 TA	0.4
Andover Bancorp Inc.	61 Main St.	Andover	MA	01810	Gerald T. Mulligan	508-749-2000	P	832 TA	0.2
Richmond County Savings Bank	1214 Castelton Ave.	Staten Island	NY	10310	Michael Manzulli	718-448-2800	R	828 TA	0.3
Family Bancorp.	P.O. Box 431	Haverhill	MA	01830	David D. Hindle	508-374-1911	P	818 TA	0.3
Quincy Savings Bank	1200 Hancock St.	Quincy	MA	02169	Charles R. Simpson Jr.	617-471-3500	P	812 TA	0.3
Civista Corp.	P.O. Box 24110	Canton	OH	44701	Richard G. Gilbert	216-456-7757	P	798 TA	0.4
First Savings Bank	339 State St.	Perth Amboy	NJ	08861	Joseph F. Yewaisis	908-442-2770	P	798 TA	0.3
Savings Bank of Utica	233 Genesee St.	Utica	NY	13501	William L. Schrauth	315-768-3000	R	796 TA	0.3
Shadow Lawn Savings Bank S.L.A.	241 Monmouth Rd.	West Long Branch	NJ	07764	Stephen M. Graham	908-222-1100	S	788 TA	0.3
Co-operative Bank of Concord	125 Nagog Park	Acton	MA	01720	David E. Bradbury	508-635-5000	P	783 TA	0.3
Compass Bank for Savings	P.O. Box 2101	New Bedford	MA	02740	Kevin G. Champagne	508-994-5000	R	773 TA	0.3
Salem Five Cents Savings Bank	210 Essex St.	Salem	MA	01970	William Mitchelson	508-745-5555	R	770 TA	0.3
CFX Bank	P.O. Box 746	Keene	NH	03431	Peter J. Baxter	603-352-2502	S	770 TA	0.4
First Western Financial Corp.	2700 W. Sahara Ave.	Las Vegas	NV	89102	Anne Bacon	702-871-2000	P	759 TA	0.3
CFX Corp.	P.O. Box 429	Keene	NH	03431	Peter J. Baxter	603-352-2502	P	756 TA	0.4

Source: Ward's Business Directory of U.S. Private and Public Companies, 1996. Company type codes: P - Public, R - Private, S - Subsidiary, D - Division, J - Joint Venture, A - Affiliate, G - Group. If the dollar values shown are not sales, the following codes apply: TA - Total Assets; OR - Operating Revenues; GB - Gross Billings. * - estimated dollar value. < - less than; *na* - not available.

FINANCIAL DATA ON SAVINGS & LOANS

The next two tables, drawn from the *Statistical Abstract of the United States 1995*, present additional data on Savings & Loans.

Until 1990, the FDIC insured a subset of all savings and loan institutions; the majority were insured by the Federal Savings and Loan Insurance Corporation (FSLIC). As a consequence of the Financial Institutions Reform, Recovery, and Enforcement Act of 1989 (FIRREA), signed into law on August 9, 1989, the FDIC has taken over insuring all savings and loans under the FDIC Savings Association Insurance Fund (SAIF).

Much more detailed information is available from the Office of Corporate Communications, FDIC, 550 17th Street, N.W., Washington, D.C. 20429.

INSURED SAVINGS INSTITUTIONS - FINANCIAL SUMMARY

In billions of dollars, except number of institutions. As of December 31. Includes Puerto Rico, Guam, and Virgin Islands. Covers SAIF (Savings Association Insurance Fund)- and BIF (Bank Insurance Fund)- insured savings institutions. Minus sign (-) indicates debt or loss.

Item	Insured Savings Institutions[1]					RTC Conservatorships[4]			
	1990	1991	1992[2]	1993[2]	1994[2,3]	1991	1992	1993	1994
Number of institutions	2,816	2,560	2,390	2,262	2,152	91	81	63	2
Assets, total	1,267	1,119	1,030	1,001	1,009	44	37	22	2
Loans and leases, net	816	727	648	626	635	24	17	10	1
Liabilities, total	1,200	1,051	956	923	929	48	42	27	2
Deposits	987	907	828	774	737	37	31	18	1
Equity capital	68	69	74	78	80	-4	-4	-5	(Z)
Interest and fee income	117	98	78	66	63	3	1	1	(Z)
Interest expense	91	70	46	35	33	3	1	1	(Z)
Net interest income	26	28	32	32	30	(Z)	(Z)	(Z)	(Z)
Net income	-5	1	7	7	6	-2	-3	-2	-2

Source: U.S. Federal Deposit Insurance Corporation, *Statistics on Banking*, annual and *FDIC Quarterly Banking Profile. Notes:* Z Less than $500 million. 1. Excludes institutions in RTC conservatorship. 2. Excludes one self-liquidating institution. 3. Preliminary. 4. RTC=Resolution Trust Corporation. These savings institutions are members of the Savings Association Insurance Fund.

INSURED SAVINGS INSTITUTIONS - FINANCES, BY ASSET SIZE: 1993

In billions of dollars, except as indicated. See headnote, previous table. Excludes institutions in Resolution Trust Corporation conservatorships.

Item	Total	Less than $100 million	$100 million to $1 billion	$1 billion or more	Item	Total	Less than $100 million	$100 million to $1 billion	$1 billion or more
Number of institutions	2,262	1,048	1,040	174	Equity capital	78	5	26	48
Assets, total	1,001	53	299	649					
Investment securities	276	12	83	181	Interest and fee income	66	3	21	42
Loans and leases, net[1]	626	34	186	406	Interest expense	35	2	10	22
Real estate loans	595	33	178	384	Net interest income	32	1	11	20
Commercial and					Provisions for loan losses	4	(Z)	2	3
industrial loans	10	(Z)	3	7	Noninterest income	7	(Z)	2	5
Loans to individuals	38	2	10	26	Noninterest expense	25	1	8	16
Less: Reserve for					Net operating income,				
losses	8	(Z)	2	6	pretax	10	(Z)	4	6
Liabilities, total	923	48	273	601	Securities gain/loss, net	(Z)	(Z)	(Z)	(Z)
Deposits	774	46	249	478	Income taxes	4	(Z)	2	2
Noninterest-bearing	29	1	8	20	Net income	7	(Z)	3	4
Interest-bearing	745	45	241	459	Net charge-offs[2]	4	(Z)	(Z)	4

Source: U.S. Federal Deposit Insurance Corporation, *Statistics on Banking, 1993. Notes:* Z Less than $500 million. 1. Includes other items, not shown separately. 2. Total loans and leases charged off (removed from balance sheet because of uncollectibility), less amounts recovered on loans and leases previously charged off.

SIC 6060

CREDIT UNIONS

Credit unions are classified as (1) federally chartered (SIC 6061), also called Federal Credit Unions and (2) not federally chartered (SIC 6062), also called State Credit Unions, not federally charted. These are cooperative thrift and loan associations, accept deposits, and are organized to finance the credit needs of their members. Credit unions are usually associations of employees working for an institution (agency, company) or members of some organization (e.g. a labor union). National Credit Union Administration (NCUA), an independent federal agency, supervises and insures more than 8,500 federal credit unions and insures nearly 4,350 state-chartered credit unions.

ESTABLISHMENTS, EMPLOYMENT, AND PAYROLL

	1988	1989		1990		1991		1992		1993		% change 88-93
		Value	%	Value	%	Value	%	Value	%	Value	%	
All Establishments	3,582	3,721	3.9	3,650	-1.9	12,356	238.5	13,177	6.6	15,306	16.2	327.3
Mid-March Employment	44,861	47,747	6.4	50,642	6.1	114,313	125.7	122,924	7.5	147,359	19.9	228.5
1st Quarter Wages (annualized - $ mil.)	753.0	847.6	12.6	944.8	11.5	2,127.7	125.2	2,448.1	15.1	2,867.4	17.1	280.8
Payroll per Emp. 1st Q. (annualized)	16,785	17,752	5.8	18,656	5.1	18,613	-0.2	19,915	7.0	19,458	-2.3	15.9
Annual Payroll ($ mil.)	778.2	873.9	12.3	959.1	9.7	2,160.0	125.2	2,516.4	16.5	3,015.0	19.8	287.4
Establishments - 1-4 Emp. Number	2,269	2,329	2.6	2,186	-6.1	5,655	158.7	7,025	24.2	7,998	13.9	252.5
Mid-March Employment	(D)	4,578	-	(D)	-	12,839	-	16,253	26.6	18,466	13.6	-
1st Quarter Wages (annualized - $ mil.)	(D)	54.1	-	(D)	-	180.0	-	247.9	37.7	281.1	13.4	-
Payroll per Emp. 1st Q. (annualized)	(D)	11,826	-	(D)	-	14,020	-	15,254	8.8	15,221	-0.2	-
Annual Payroll ($ mil.)	(D)	67.9	-	(D)	-	191.4	-	257.8	34.7	309.2	19.9	-
Establishments - 5-9 Emp. Number	554	596	7.6	638	7.0	3,151	393.9	3,011	-4.4	(D)	-	-
Mid-March Employment	(D)	(D)	-	4,158	-	21,225	410.5	19,889	-6.3	(D)	-	-
1st Quarter Wages (annualized - $ mil.)	(D)	(D)	-	67.4	-	386.9	473.7	365.4	-5.6	(D)	-	-
Payroll per Emp. 1st Q. (annualized)	(D)	(D)	-	16,221	-	18,231	12.4	18,373	0.8	(D)	-	-
Annual Payroll ($ mil.)	(D)	(D)	-	69.0	-	393.9	471.1	375.7	-4.6	(D)	-	-
Establishments - 10-19 Emp. Number	318	325	2.2	332	2.2	2,296	591.6	1,830	-20.3	2,199	20.2	591.5
Mid-March Employment	4,302	4,409	2.5	4,487	1.8	30,824	587.0	24,831	-19.4	29,814	20.1	593.0
1st Quarter Wages (annualized - $ mil.)	69.8	73.3	5.1	76.8	4.8	579.7	654.4	486.0	-16.2	558.7	14.9	700.7
Payroll per Emp. 1st Q. (annualized)	16,219	16,631	2.5	17,124	3.0	18,806	9.8	19,573	4.1	18,738	-4.3	15.5
Annual Payroll ($ mil.)	71.0	74.9	5.6	79.1	5.5	584.9	639.7	495.6	-15.3	588.5	18.7	728.9
Establishments - 20-49 Emp. Number	225	239	6.2	247	3.3	1,081	337.7	964	-10.8	1,200	24.5	433.3
Mid-March Employment	(D)	(D)	-	7,334	-	30,252	312.5	28,731	-5.0	35,485	23.5	-
1st Quarter Wages (annualized - $ mil.)	(D)	(D)	-	134.0	-	572.7	327.5	591.2	3.2	701.6	18.7	-
Payroll per Emp. 1st Q. (annualized)	(D)	(D)	-	18,267	-	18,930	3.6	20,577	8.7	19,772	-3.9	-
Annual Payroll ($ mil.)	(D)	(D)	-	135.3	-	577.4	326.9	603.1	4.5	738.6	22.5	-
Establishments - 50-99 Emp. Number	123	130	5.7	134	3.1	120	-10.4	255	112.5	324	27.1	163.4
Mid-March Employment	8,819	9,030	2.4	9,240	2.3	8,252	-10.7	16,709	102.5	21,619	29.4	145.1
1st Quarter Wages (annualized - $ mil.)	155.7	171.4	10.1	188.1	9.7	173.0	-8.0	371.7	114.9	463.7	24.8	197.8
Payroll per Emp. 1st Q. (annualized)	17,655	18,986	7.5	20,356	7.2	20,959	3.0	22,246	6.1	21,450	-3.6	21.5
Annual Payroll ($ mil.)	160.0	170.3	6.5	187.6	10.2	172.6	-8.0	384.1	122.5	475.2	23.7	197.0
Establishments - 100-249 Emp. Number	80	85	6.3	96	12.9	43	-55.2	82	90.7	89	8.5	11.2
Mid-March Employment	11,776	12,468	5.9	14,332	15.0	(D)	-	11,774	-	12,188	3.5	3.5
1st Quarter Wages (annualized - $ mil.)	215.1	238.0	10.7	288.7	21.3	(D)	-	278.1	-	282.8	1.7	31.5
Payroll per Emp. 1st Q. (annualized)	18,266	19,093	4.5	20,145	5.5	(D)	-	23,619	-	23,199	-1.8	27.0
Annual Payroll ($ mil.)	217.3	241.4	11.1	282.8	17.2	(D)	-	278.9	-	289.6	3.8	33.3
Establishments - 250-499 Emp. Number	12	16	33.3	16	-	9	-43.8	(D)	-	17	-	41.7
Mid-March Employment	(D)	4,734	-	4,968	4.9	(D)	-	(D)	-	5,100	-	-
1st Quarter Wages (annualized - $ mil.)	(D)	88.6	-	98.5	11.2	(D)	-	(D)	-	118.3	-	-
Payroll per Emp. 1st Q. (annualized)	(D)	18,717	-	19,826	5.9	(D)	-	(D)	-	23,202	-	-
Annual Payroll ($ mil.)	(D)	89.5	-	99.5	11.2	(D)	-	(D)	-	128.2	-	-
Establishments - 500-999 Emp. Number	-	-	-	-	-	-	-	-	-	-	-	-
Mid-March Employment	-	-	-	-	-	-	-	-	-	-	-	-
1st Quarter Wages (annualized - $ mil.)	-	-	-	-	-	-	-	-	-	-	-	-
Payroll per Emp. 1st Q. (annualized)	(D)	(D)	-	(D)	-	(D)	-	-	-	-	-	-
Annual Payroll ($ mil.)	-	-	-	-	-	-	-	-	-	-	-	-
Estab. - 1000 or More Emp. Number	1	1	-	1	-	1	-	(D)	-	(D)	-	-
Mid-March Employment	(D)	(D)	-	(D)	-	(D)	-	(D)	-	(D)	-	-
1st Quarter Wages (annualized - $ mil.)	(D)	(D)	-	(D)	-	(D)	-	(D)	-	(D)	-	-
Payroll per Emp. 1st Q. (annualized)	(D)	(D)	-	(D)	-	(D)	-	(D)	-	(D)	-	-
Annual Payroll ($ mil.)	(D)	(D)	-	(D)	-	(D)	-	(D)	-	(D)	-	-

Source: County Business Patterns, U.S. Department of Commerce, Washington, D.C., for 1988 through 1993. Payroll per employee is calculated using mid-March employment and 1st Quarter wages, annualized. Annual payroll, also shown, may not equal the annualized 1st Quarter wages. Columns headed by a percent sign (%) indicate change from the previous year. na stands for not available. The symbol (D) indicates that data are withheld by the source to avoid disclosure of competitive information. A dash (-) indicates that data are not available or cannot be calculated.

ESTABLISHMENTS
Number

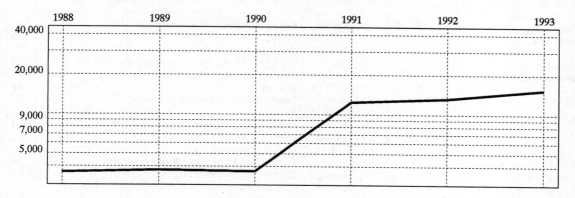

MID-MARCH EMPLOYMENT
Number

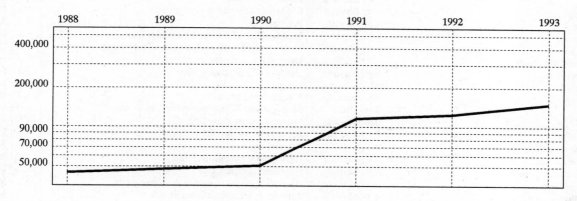

ANNUAL PAYROLL
$ million

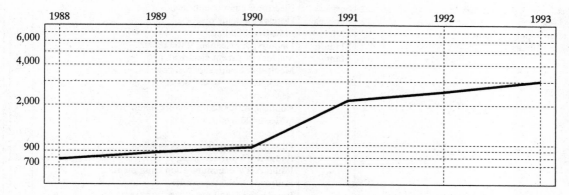

INPUTS AND OUTPUTS FOR ALL BANKING SECTORS - SICs 601, 602, 603, 608, and 609

Economic Sector or Industry Providing Inputs	%	Sector	Economic Sector or Industry Buying Outputs	%	Sector
Computer & data processing services	13.3	Services	Personal consumption expenditures	43.5	
Security & commodity brokers	10.1	Fin/R.E.	Exports	5.3	Foreign
Real estate	8.0	Fin/R.E.	Credit agencies other than banks	4.5	Fin/R.E.
Communications, except radio & TV	5.9	Util.	S/L Govt. purch., other general government	3.7	S/L Govt
Motor freight transportation & warehousing	5.8	Util.	Wholesale trade	3.7	Trade
Banking	5.7	Fin/R.E.	Real estate	3.6	Fin/R.E.
U.S. Postal Service	4.7	Gov't	Retail trade, except eating & drinking	3.3	Trade
Eating & drinking places	4.5	Trade	Banking	1.9	Fin/R.E.
Equipment rental & leasing services	3.4	Services	Eating & drinking places	1.4	Trade
Advertising	2.9	Services	Communications, except radio & TV	1.1	Util.
Accounting, auditing & bookkeeping	2.8	Services	Petroleum refining	1.1	Manufg.
Maintenance of nonfarm buildings nec	2.8	Constr.	Federal Government purchases, nondefense	1.0	Fed Govt
Blankbooks & looseleaf binders	2.5	Manufg.	Electric services (utilities)	0.9	Util.
Management & consulting services & labs	2.4	Services	Engineering, architectural, & surveying services	0.7	Services
Federal Government enterprises nec	2.1	Gov't	Meat animals	0.7	Agric.
Insurance carriers	2.1	Fin/R.E.	Aircraft	0.6	Manufg.
Photographic equipment & supplies	1.7	Manufg.	Apparel made from purchased materials	0.5	Manufg.
Electric services (utilities)	1.6	Util.	Crude petroleum & natural gas	0.5	Mining
Detective & protective services	1.5	Services	Gas production & distribution (utilities)	0.5	Util.
Legal services	1.4	Services	Insurance carriers	0.5	Fin/R.E.
Noncomparable imports	1.4	Foreign	Electronic computing equipment	0.4	Manufg.
Petroleum refining	1.2	Manufg.	Feed grains	0.4	Agric.
Wholesale trade	1.2	Trade	Maintenance of nonfarm buildings nec	0.4	Constr.
Manifold business forms	1.0	Manufg.	Motor freight transportation & warehousing	0.4	Util.
Credit agencies other than banks	0.9	Fin/R.E.	Dairy farm products	0.3	Agric.
Personnel supply services	0.9	Services	Doctors & dentists	0.3	Services
Business/professional associations	0.8	Services	Drugs	0.3	Manufg.
Commercial printing	0.8	Manufg.	Freight forwarders	0.3	Util.
Air transportation	0.6	Util.	Management & consulting services & labs	0.3	Services
Envelopes	0.6	Manufg.	Owner-occupied dwellings	0.3	Fin/R.E.
Electrical repair shops	0.4	Services	Security & commodity brokers	0.3	Fin/R.E.
Transit & bus transportation	0.4	Util.	Advertising	0.2	Services
Electronic components nec	0.3	Manufg.	Agricultural chemicals, nec	0.2	Manufg.
Electronic computing equipment	0.3	Manufg.	Air transportation	0.2	Util.
Engraving & plate printing	0.3	Manufg.	Aircraft & missile engines & engine parts	0.2	Manufg.
Manufacturing industries, nec	0.3	Manufg.	Aircraft & missile equipment, nec	0.2	Manufg.
Paper mills, except building paper	0.3	Manufg.	Broadwoven fabric mills	0.2	Manufg.
Periodicals	0.3	Manufg.	Chemical & fertilizer mineral	0.2	Mining
Services to dwellings & other buildings	0.3	Services	Coal	0.2	Mining
Textile bags	0.3	Manufg.	Computer & data processing services	0.2	Services
Automotive rental & leasing, without drivers	0.2	Services	Electronic components nec	0.2	Manufg.
Hotels & lodging places	0.2	Services	Hotels & lodging places	0.2	Services
Sanitary services, steam supply, irrigation	0.2	Util.	Industrial buildings	0.2	Constr.
Carbon paper & inked ribbons	0.1	Manufg.	Laundry, dry cleaning, shoe repair	0.2	Services
Newspapers	0.1	Manufg.	Machinery, except electrical, nec	0.2	Manufg.
			Medical & health services, nec	0.2	Services
			Motor vehicles & car bodies	0.2	Manufg.
			Newspapers	0.2	Manufg.
			Nonfarm residential structure maintenance	0.2	Constr.
			Office buildings	0.2	Constr.
			Oil bearing crops	0.2	Agric.
			Photographic equipment & supplies	0.2	Manufg.
			Radio & TV broadcasting	0.2	Util.
			Radio & TV communication equipment	0.2	Manufg.
			Railroads & related services	0.2	Util.
			Residential 1-unit structures, nonfarm	0.2	Constr.
			Semiconductors & related devices	0.2	Manufg.
			Water transportation	0.2	Util.

Continued on next page.

INPUTS AND OUTPUTS FOR ALL BANKING SECTORS - SICs 601, 602, 603, 608, and 609 - Continued

Economic Sector or Industry Providing Inputs	%	Sector	Economic Sector or Industry Buying Outputs	%	Sector
			Arrangement of passenger transportation	0.1	Util.
			Automotive repair shops & services	0.1	Services
			Blast furnaces & steel mills	0.1	Manufg.
			Bottled & canned soft drinks	0.1	Manufg.
			Business services nec	0.1	Services
			Commercial printing	0.1	Manufg.
			Cyclic crudes and organics	0.1	Manufg.
			Equipment rental & leasing services	0.1	Services
			Food grains	0.1	Agric.
			Malt beverages	0.1	Manufg.
			Metal office furniture	0.1	Manufg.
			Miscellaneous plastics products	0.1	Manufg.
			Motion pictures	0.1	Services
			Pipe, valves, & pipe fittings	0.1	Manufg.
			Pipelines, except natural gas	0.1	Util.
			Portrait, photographic studios	0.1	Services
			Prepared feeds, nec	0.1	Manufg.
			Primary aluminum	0.1	Manufg.
			Residential additions/alterations, nonfarm	0.1	Constr.

Source: Benchmark Input-Output Accounts for the U.S. Economy, 1982, U.S. Department of Commerce, Washington, D.C., July 1991. Data, as reported in the source, are organized by the 1977 SIC structure in use in 1982 but have been matched, as closely as is possible, to the 1987 SIC structure used in this book. Activities with the same percentage are sorted alphabetically by name of activity.

OCCUPATIONS EMPLOYED BY COMMERCIAL BANKS, SAVINGS INSTITUTIONS, CREDIT UNIONS

Occupation	% of Total 1994	Change to 2005	Occupation	% of Total 1994	Change to 2005
Bank tellers	27.8	-29.8	General managers & top executives	3.0	-4.0
Clerical supervisors & managers	6.5	12.9	Management support workers nec	2.6	1.2
Loan officers & counselors	6.4	8.8	Clerical support workers nec	1.4	-19.1
Financial managers	6.2	16.3	Accountants & auditors	1.4	-14.0
New accounts clerks, banking	5.8	1.2	Securities & financial services sales workers	1.3	11.3
Loan & credit clerks	5.2	-9.0	Adjustment clerks	1.3	5.3
General office clerks	3.9	-32.6	Statement clerks	1.1	-39.6
Bookkeeping, accounting, & auditing clerks	3.7	-24.1	Duplicating, mail, & office machine operators	1.0	-41.0
Secretaries, ex legal & medical	3.6	-18.1			

Sources: Industry-Occupation Matrix, Bureau of Labor Statistics. These data relate to one or more 3-digit SIC industry groups rather than to a single 4-digit SIC. The change reported for each occupation to the year 2005 is a percent of growth or decline as estimated by the Bureau of Labor Statistics. The abbreviation nec stands for not elsewhere classified.

U.S. AND STATE DATA ON INDUSTRY REVENUES AND OTHER ACCOUNTS FOR 1992

State	No. of Estab.	Employment	Payroll ($ mil.)	Revenues ($ mil.)	Empl./ Estab.	Revenue/ Estab. ($)	Payroll/ Estab. ($)	Revenue/ Empl. ($)	Payroll/ Empl. ($)
UNITED STATES	15,665	139,762	2,872.0	21,390.4	9	1,365,491	183,342	153,049	20,550
Alabama	305	2,589	49.6	379.5	8	1,244,305	162,770	146,587	19,175
Alaska	63	919	21.5	128.4	15	2,038,159	341,968	139,721	23,443
Arizona	155	1,728	35.4	231.2	11	1,491,600	228,400	133,795	20,487
Arkansas	86	-	(D)	(D)	(D)	(D)	(D)	(D)	(D)
California	1,293	16,641	408.9	2,859.3	13	2,211,402	316,249	171,825	24,572
Colorado	266	2,757	50.8	373.7	10	1,404,906	190,805	135,548	18,409
Connecticut	307	1,817	41.7	341.6	6	1,112,577	135,951	187,981	22,970
Delaware	55	-	(D)	(D)	(D)	(D)	(D)	(D)	(D)
District of Columbia	100	963	25.4	185.4	10	1,853,890	254,470	192,512	26,425
Florida	540	6,754	136.1	1,055.8	13	1,955,269	252,015	156,329	20,149
Georgia	308	2,281	46.8	349.8	7	1,135,769	151,964	153,361	20,520
Hawaii	136	1,262	28.7	268.4	9	1,973,772	210,963	212,704	22,735
Idaho	120	848	12.6	83.5	7	695,592	105,400	98,433	14,915
Illinois	767	4,691	90.2	635.4	6	828,395	117,661	135,446	19,238
Indiana	455	4,207	79.3	575.5	9	1,264,804	174,358	136,792	18,857
Iowa	274	1,829	31.3	225.3	7	822,128	114,252	123,162	17,116
Kansas	190	-	(D)	(D)	(D)	(D)	(D)	(D)	(D)
Kentucky	173	1,167	21.9	153.3	7	886,410	126,364	131,404	18,733
Louisiana	351	1,963	33.8	289.9	6	826,026	96,242	147,700	17,209
Maine	138	-	(D)	(D)	(D)	(D)	(D)	(D)	(D)
Maryland	229	-	(D)	(D)	(D)	(D)	(D)	(D)	(D)
Massachusetts	450	4,200	90.2	793.1	9	1,762,396	200,393	188,828	21,471
Michigan	778	8,369	168.8	1,118.1	11	1,437,098	217,015	133,596	20,174
Minnesota	289	2,269	44.1	310.7	8	1,075,166	152,588	136,943	19,435
Mississippi	150	727	13.0	98.9	5	659,240	86,767	136,019	17,902
Missouri	231	1,902	35.7	265.9	8	1,151,247	154,597	139,820	18,776
Montana	104	-	(D)	(D)	(D)	(D)	(D)	(D)	(D)
Nebraska	118	-	(D)	(D)	(D)	(D)	(D)	(D)	(D)
Nevada	60	-	(D)	(D)	(D)	(D)	(D)	(D)	(D)
New Hampshire	55	-	(D)	(D)	(D)	(D)	(D)	(D)	(D)
New Jersey	372	1,921	41.5	347.2	5	933,336	111,505	180,740	21,593
New Mexico	88	1,117	20.9	143.3	13	1,628,034	237,409	128,261	18,704
New York	735	6,156	129.4	1,134.4	8	1,543,346	176,113	184,269	21,027
North Carolina	326	3,015	56.9	474.9	9	1,456,850	174,607	157,523	18,880
North Dakota	93	-	(D)	(D)	(D)	(D)	(D)	(D)	(D)
Ohio	805	5,251	93.4	639.3	7	794,221	116,027	121,757	17,787
Oklahoma	138	1,790	37.7	255.5	13	1,851,449	273,261	142,737	21,067
Oregon	206	2,185	47.8	309.1	11	1,500,272	231,883	141,444	21,862
Pennsylvania	878	5,054	96.7	874.1	6	995,604	110,156	172,960	19,137
Rhode Island	83	-	(D)	(D)	(D)	(D)	(D)	(D)	(D)
South Carolina	182	1,704	35.2	250.2	9	1,374,615	193,264	146,819	20,642
South Dakota	76	469	7.7	44.2	6	582,224	101,026	94,348	16,371
Tennessee	389	-	(D)	(D)	(D)	(D)	(D)	(D)	(D)
Texas	1,049	10,091	206.4	1,473.9	10	1,405,100	196,763	146,066	20,454
Utah	230	2,242	40.6	264.7	10	1,150,709	176,478	118,048	18,104
Vermont	60	-	(D)	(D)	(D)	(D)	(D)	(D)	(D)
Virginia	381	5,891	138.0	1,071.6	15	2,812,622	362,220	181,906	23,427
Washington	328	4,290	95.6	694.8	13	2,118,442	291,549	161,969	22,291
West Virginia	136	-	(D)	(D)	(D)	(D)	(D)	(D)	(D)
Wisconsin	521	4,250	71.2	458.0	8	879,155	136,576	107,774	16,743
Wyoming	43	-	(D)	(D)	(D)	(D)	(D)	(D)	(D)

Source: 1992 Economic Census, U.S. Department of Commerce, Washington, D.C. This is the only table that shows revenue data as collected by the Bureau of the Census in an Economic Census. The symbol (D) indicates that data are withheld by the source to avoid disclosure of competitive information. A dash (-) indicates that data are not available or cannot be calculated.

ESTABLISHMENTS 1992 - STATE AND REGIONAL CONCENTRATION

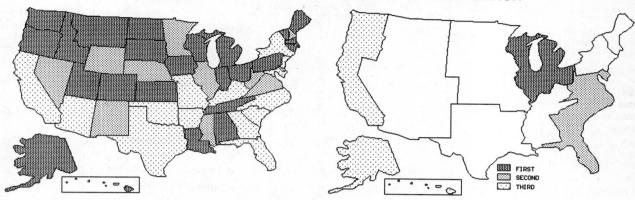

EMPLOYMENT 1992 - STATE AND REGIONAL CONCENTRATION

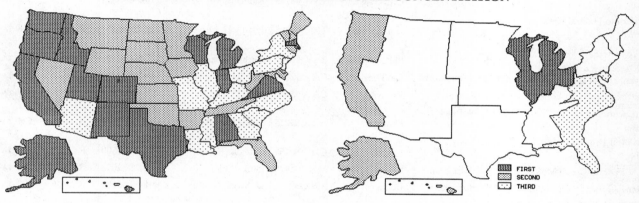

REVENUES 1992 - STATE AND REGIONAL CONCENTRATION

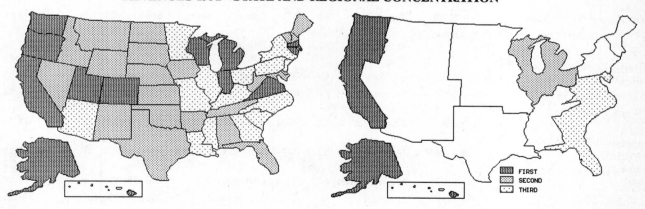

States with the darkest shading indicate those states which have proportionately more establishments, employment, or revenues than would be indicated by the state's population. States with light shading are states with proportionately fewer establishments, less employment, and lower revenues than population distribution. States shaded grey are within 15 percent of the state's population proportion in these categories. States for which no data are available are shown as average (grey). *Regions* are shaded to indicate absolute rank in the category. If no data for the category are available, establishment counts are used to shade the regions. Source of the data is the table on the facing page.

LEADING COMPANIES - SIC 6061 - Federal Credit Unions

Number shown: **100**   Total sales/assets ($ mil): **31,114**   Total employment (000): **13.6**

Company Name	Address				CEO Name	Phone	Co. Type	Sales/Assets ($ mil)	Empl. (000)
Navy Federal Credit Union	P.O. Box 3000	Merrifield	VA	22119	Thomas J. Hughes	703-255-8000	R	8,000 TA	3.2
Pentagon Federal Credit Union	P.O. Box 1432	Alexandria	VA	22313	Ronald L. Snellings	703-838-1000	R	1,785 TA	0.6
American Airlines Employees Federal Credit Union	P.O. Box 619001	Dallas	TX	75261	John M. Tippets	817-963-6000	R	1,657 TA	0.2
Orange County Teachers Federal Credit Union	P.O. Box 11547	Santa Ana	CA	92711	Rudy Hanley	714-258-4000	R	1,224 TA	0.5
Suncoast Schools Federal Credit Union	P.O. Box 11904	Tampa	FL	33680	Perry M. Dawson	813-621-7511	R	1,200 TA	0.4
LMSC Federal Credit Union	P.O. Box 3643	Sunnyvale	CA	94088	Don McClure	408-742-2801	R	1,123 TA	<0.1
Eastern Financial Federal Credit Union	700 S. Royal Poinciana	Miami Springs	FL	33166	Donald L. Hersman	305-882-5000	R	865 TA	0.3
Randolph-Brooks Federal Credit Union	P.O. Box 2097	Universal City	TX	78148	Randy Smith	210-945-3333	R	830 TA*	0.4
San Antonio Federal Credit Union	P.O. Box 1356	San Antonio	TX	78295	Jeffrey H. Farver	210-734-1414	R	788 TA	0.5
Police and Fire Federal Credit Union	901 Arch St.	Philadelphia	PA	19107	Anthony LaRosa	215-931-0300	R	597 TA	0.2
Mission Federal Credit Union	P.O. Box 919023	San Diego	CA	92191	Hal Stephens	619-546-2000	R	588 TA	0.4
Travis Federal Credit Union	P.O. Box 2069	Vacaville	CA	95696	John F. Gonge	707-449-4000	R	569 TA	0.3
Desert Schools Federal Credit Union	6633 N. Black Canyon	Phoenix	AZ	85015	James Hysell	602-433-7000	R	524 TA	0.2
Bellco First Federal Credit Union	P.O. Box 6611	Englewood	CO	80155	Douglas Ferraro	303-689-7800	R	500 TA	0.2
N.W.A. Federal Credit Union	4 Appletree Sq.	Bloomington	MN	55425	Paul V. Parish	612-726-2073	R	404 TA	0.2
Keesler Federal Credit Union	P.O. Box 7001	Biloxi	MS	39534	D. Scott Broome	601-385-5500	R	393 TA	0.2
State Employees Federal Credit Union in Albany	P.O. Box 12189	Albany	NY	12212	Patrick G. Calhoun	518-452-8183	R	380 TA	0.2
Premier America Federal Credit Union	19867 Prairie St.	Chatsworth	CA	91311	Robert Dottai	818-772-4000	R	356 TA	0.2
MacDill Federal Credit Union	P.O. Box 19100	Tampa	FL	33686	Robert L. Fisher	813-837-2451	R	350 TA	0.2
Navy Orlando Federal Credit Union	3075 N. Alafaya Trail	Orlando	FL	32826	Edward Baranowski	407-277-5045	R	350 TA	0.2
Pacific IBM Employees Federal Credit Union	P.O. Box 530953	San Jose	CA	95153	Daryl Tanner	408-256-4566	R	350 TA	0.1
GTE Federal Credit Union	P.O. Box 10550	Tampa	FL	33679	Bucky Sebastian	813-871-2690	R	342 TA	0.2
Fort Worth Federal Credit Union	819 Taylor St.	Fort Worth	TX	76102	Richard Howdeshell	817-335-2525	R	318 TA	<0.1
OmniAmerican Federal Credit Union	P.O. Box 150099	Fort Worth	TX	76108	Larry E. Duckworth	817-246-0111	R	304 TA	0.2
AT and T Family Federal Credit Union	P.O. Box 26000	Winston-Salem	NC	27114	Clyde Padgett	910-659-1955	R	300 TA	0.2
Fibre Federal Credit Union	P.O. Box 1234	Longview	WA	98632	Dennis Curtin	206-423-8750	R	279 TA	0.1
Arizona Federal Credit Union	P.O. Box 11990	Phoenix	AZ	85061	Michael Hale	602-242-0002	R	270 TA	0.2
Indiana Federal Credit Union	P.O. Box 47769	Indianapolis	IN	46247	Edward Lechner	317-788-0366	R	270 TA	0.2

Company type codes: P - Public, R - Private, S - Subsidiary, D - Division, J - Joint Venture, A - Affiliate, G - Group. If the dollar values shown are not sales, the following codes apply: TA - Total Assets; OR - Operating Revenues; GB - Gross Billings. * - estimated dollar value. < - less than. *na* - not available.

Continued on next page.

LEADING COMPANIES - SIC 6061 - Federal Credit Unions
Continued

Company Name	Address				CEO Name	Phone	Co. Type	Sales/Assets ($ mil)	Empl. (000)
Aberdeen Proving Ground Federal Credit Union	P.O. Box 1176	Aberdeen	MD	21001	Nancy Stubbs	410-272-4000	R	262 TA	0.2
Central Florida Educators' Federal Credit Union	P.O. Box 2189	Orlando	FL	32802	Thomas J. Powers Jr.	407-896-9411	R	245 TA	0.2
Cummins Federal Credit Union	P.O. Box 789	Columbus	IN	47202	Loretta Burd	812-376-9771	R	225 TA	0.1
First Financial Federal Credit Union	P.O. Box 90	West Covina	CA	91790	Richard Ghysels	818-814-4611	R	222 TA	0.1
Austin Area Teachers Federal Credit Union	P.O. Box 14867	Austin	TX	78761	Hal Coffman	512-302-6800	R	220 TA	0.1
Los Angeles Federal Credit Union	300 S. Glendale Ave.	Glendale	CA	91205	Steven McDiffett	818-242-8640	R	220 TA*	0.1
Direct Federal Credit Union	P.O. Box 9123	Needham Heights	MA	02194	David C. Breslin	617-455-6500	R	204 TA	<0.1
Finance Center Federal	P.O. Box 26501	Indianapolis	IN	46226	Ken Hawkins	317-543-5800	R	203 TA	0.2
Merrimack Valley Federal Credit Union	1475 Osgood St.	North Andover	MA	01845	Duncan M. MacLeod	508-975-4095	R	200 TA	<0.1
Indiana Telco Federal Credit Union	P.O. Box 50738	Indianapolis	IN	46250	John Jeter	317-845-8383	R	197 TA	0.1
First City Savings Federal Credit Union	P.O. Box 2007	Glendale	CA	91209	Robert Ciuzik	818-546-2489	R	191 TA	0.1
University of Colorado Federal Credit Union	2935 Baseline Rd.	Boulder	CO	80303	Jan Hesalroad	303-443-4672	R	187 TA	0.1
Lackland Federal Credit Union	2250 Bong	San Antonio	TX	78236	Tony Lema	210-673-5610	R	170 TA*	<0.1
Evansville Teachers Federal Credit Union	P.O. Box 5129	Evansville	IN	47716	Michael Phipps	812-477-9271	R	167 TA	<0.1
Heritage Trust Federal Credit Union	P.O. Box 118000	Charleston	SC	29423	Quince E. Cody	803-552-4040	R	160 TA	0.1
Fort Knox Federal Credit Union	P.O. Box 1000	Fort Knox	KY	40121	William J. Rissel	502-942-0254	R	156 TA	0.1
Continental Federal Credit Union	5933 W. Century Blvd.	Los Angeles	CA	90045	Gary R. Swensson	310-337-0212	R	149 TA	<0.1
Ethicon Employees Federal Credit Union	P.O. Box 151	Somerville	NJ	08876	Eugene T. Reilly Jr.	908-218-3200	R	138 TA	<0.1
Georgia Federal Credit Union	652 N. Indian Creek Dr	Clarkston	GA	30021	Mack D. Ivey	404-292-6868	R	130 TA	<0.1
Campus Federal Credit Union	P.O. Box 16049	Baton Rouge	LA	70893	John W. Milazzo	504-388-8841	R	127 TA	<0.1
Unit Number 1 Federal Credit Union	P.O. Box 830	Lockport	NY	14095	Patricia LaRocca	716-434-2290	R	127 TA	<0.1
Whittier Area Federal Credit Union	P.O. Box 200	Whittier	CA	90608	David Gunderson	310-698-8326	R	121 TA	<0.1
CinFed Employees Federal Credit Union	550 Main St.	Cincinnati	OH	45202	John D. Leahy	513-333-3800	R	115 TA	0.1
Miramar Federal Credit Union	P.O. Box 45309	San Diego	CA	92145	William R. Moyer	619-695-9494	R	106 TA	<0.1
Community Federal Credit Union	P.O. Box 8050	Plymouth	MI	48170	James Cantrell	313-453-1200	R	100 TA	<0.1
LOC Federal Credit Union	22981 Farmington Rd.	Farmington	MI	48336	Dennis DeWitt	810-474-2200	R	100 TA*	<0.1

Company type codes: P - Public, R - Private, S - Subsidiary, D - Division, J - Joint Venture, A - Affiliate, G - Group. If the dollar values shown are not sales, the following codes apply: TA - Total Assets; OR - Operating Revenues; GB - Gross Billings. * - estimated dollar value. < - less than. *na* - not available.

Continued on next page.

LEADING COMPANIES - SIC 6061 - Federal Credit Unions

Continued

Company Name	Address				CEO Name	Phone	Co. Type	Sales/Assets ($ mil)	Empl. (000)
Deer Valley Federal Credit Union	13430 N. Black Canyon	Phoenix	AZ	85029	Rod Eickelberg	602-862-6151	R	99 TA	<0.1
IBM Rocky Mountain Employees Federal Credit Union	2142 N. Main St.	Longmont	CO	80501	Thomas Evers	303-440-4706	R	92 TA	<0.1
Sacramento Credit Union	P.O. Box 2351	Sacramento	CA	95812	Jerrold A. Kinlock	916-444-6070	R	90 TA	<0.1
Coosa Pines Federal Credit Union	Hwy. 235 N.	Childersburg	AL	35044	Charles W. Evans	205-378-5559	R	77 TA	<0.1
Greater Texas Federal Credit Union	6411 N. Lamar Pl.	Austin	TX	78752	Tommy D. Seargeant	512-458-2558	R	74 TA	<0.1
Massachusetts Federal Credit Union	P.O. Box 850623	Braintree	MA	02185	Leonard Broderick	617-843-5626	R	73 TA	<0.1
Schenectady Teachers Federal Credit Union	1776 Union St.	Schenectady	NY	12309	Rachele Granka	518-393-1326	R	68 TA	<0.1
Florida Commerce Federal Credit Union	P.O. Box 6416	Tallahassee	FL	32314	Ronald Fye	904-488-0035	R	65 TA	<0.1
Edwards Federal Credit Union	10 S. Muroc Dr.	Edwards	CA	93524	Thomas G. Craft	805-258-4407	R	60 TA	<0.1
Mutual Security Federal Credit Union	P.O. Box 347	Wilton	CT	06897	Larry Holderman	203-761-2410	R	60 TA	<0.1
HAR-CO Maryland Federal Credit Union	30 Hickory Ave.	Bel Air	MD	21014	Ann Marie Navin	410-838-9090	R	58 TA	<0.1
Bay Gulf Federal Credit Union	P.O. Box 271990	Tampa	FL	33688	John E. Simmonds	813-932-1301	R	57 TA	<0.1
GenFed Federal Credit Union	85 Massillon Rd.	Akron	OH	44312	Stephen F. Halas	216-784-5451	R	57 TA	<0.1
Denver Municipal Federal Credit Union	6700 E. Colfax Ave.	Denver	CO	80220	Carla Hedrick	303-399-1173	R	55 TA	<0.1
Midwest United Credit Union	8100 N.E. U.S. Hwy. 69	Pleasant Valley	MO	64068	D. Pat Yokley	816-454-1250	R	55 TA	<0.1
American River Federal Credit Union	P.O. Box 500	Orangevale	CA	95662	Bob Steponovich	916-985-6700	R	54 TA	<0.1
Pocatello Railroad Federal Credit Union	P.O. Box 1450	Pocatello	ID	83204	Carl A. Lytle	208-232-5746	R	54 TA*	<0.1
Motor Parts Federal Credit Union	2955 University Dr.	Auburn Hills	MI	48326	Donald Major	810-340-9310	R	51 TA	<0.1
United BN Federal Credit Union	777 Main St.	Fort Worth	TX	76102	Peter D. Gates	817-333-2344	R	50 TA	<0.1
Denver Fire Department Federal Credit Union	2201 Federal Blvd.	Denver	CO	80211	Alan R. Hoch	303-458-6129	R	47 TA	<0.1
Burbank Federal Credit Union	1715 W. Magnolia Blvd.	Burbank	CA	91510	Margaret Holliday	818-846-5143	R	41 TA	<0.1
Hambuco Federal Credit Union	314 N. Erie Hwy.	Hamilton	OH	45011	Gareda J. Guecking	513-867-1550	R	36 TA	<0.1
Security One Federal Credit Union	P.O. Box 5583	Arlington	TX	76010	Pamela Stephens	817-273-5900	R	35 TA	<0.1
Raychem Employees Federal Credit Union	P.O. Box 3449	Redwood City	CA	94064	Christine L. Brown	415-361-3090	R	33 TA	<0.1
Consumer Electronics Employees Federal Credit Union	P.O. Box 629	Marion	IN	46953	George C. Dixon	317-662-5300	R	28 TA	<0.1
Owensboro Federal Credit Union	P.O. Box 1189	Owensboro	KY	42302	Stephen B. Sharp	502-683-1054	R	26 TA	<0.1

Company type codes: P - Public, R - Private, S - Subsidiary, D - Division, J - Joint Venture, A - Affiliate, G - Group. If the dollar values shown are not sales, the following codes apply: TA - Total Assets; OR - Operating Revenues; GB - Gross Billings. * - estimated dollar value. < - less than. *na* - not available.

Continued on next page.

LEADING COMPANIES - SIC 6061 - Federal Credit Unions

Continued

Company Name	Address				CEO Name	Phone	Co. Type	Sales/Assets ($ mil)	Empl. (000)
Obelisk Federal Credit Union	710 Pillsbury Ln.	New Albany	IN	47150	Ralph M. Lilly	812-944-1325	R	25 TA	<0.1
Anne Arundel County Employee Federal Credit Union	2666 Riva Rd.	Annapolis	MD	21401	Richard Stoll	410-222-7283	R	24 TA	<0.1
Orlando Postal Service Credit Union	301 E. Michigan St.	Orlando	FL	32806	John Blount	407-425-2561	R	22 TA	<0.1
Daniels-Sheridan Federal Credit Union	P.O. Box 1160	Scobey	MT	59263	Patricia P. Audet	406-487-5391	R	22 TA	<0.1
Gulf States Federal Credit Union	P.O. Box 945110	Maitland	FL	32794	Bernard Arvin	407-831-8844	R	18 TA	<0.1
Maricopa County Employees Federal Credit Union	721 N. 3rd St.	Phoenix	AZ	85004	Paul H. Mercer	602-252-6831	R	18 TA	<0.1
Northwest United Federal Credit Union	P.O. Box 547	Arvada	CO	80001	Patricia G. Tinucci	303-424-5037	R	18 TA	<0.1
Columbine Federal Credit Union	P.O. Box 5888	Denver	CO	80217	Charles G. Eskew	303-843-2089	R	16 TA	<0.1
A N G Federal Credit Union	P.O. Box 170204	Birmingham	AL	35217	Joyce A. Baldwin	205-841-4525	R	14 TA	<0.1
MMD Federal Credit Union	2110 E. Galbraith Rd.	Cincinnati	OH	45215	William Hudak	513-948-7777	R	10 TA	<0.1
Baptist Federal Credit Union	1600 N.E. Loop 410	San Antonio	TX	78209	Judith A. Murphy	210-822-8691	R	10 TA	<0.1
Albany Federal Employees C.U. nion	P.O. Box 3012	Albany	GA	31706	Connie Mancuso	912-439-1448	R	8 TA	<0.1
Louisiana National Guard Federal Credit Union	57 Jackson Barracks	New Orleans	LA	70146	Annabeth Hellmers	504-277-0288	R	8 TA	<0.1
Rarin Federal Credit Union	Rough and Ready Island	Stockton	CA	95203	Don Messerschmidt	209-944-0423	R	8 TA*	<0.1
Sentinel Communications Employees Federal C.U.	633 N. Orange Ave.	Orlando	FL	32801	Timothy J. Brennan	407-420-5691	R	8 TA*	<0.1
Texas Associations of Professionals Federal C.U.	9110 I-10 W.	San Antonio	TX	78230	Paula Walpole	210-593-1200	R	8 TA	<0.1
Local 142 Federal Credit Union	P.O. Box 12067	San Antonio	TX	78212	Angela Johnson	210-226-4536	R	7 TA	<0.1
Auto Parts Employees Credit Union	1216 Everman Pkwy.	Fort Worth	TX	76140	Charlotte Douglas	817-293-8412	R	7 TA	<0.1
Georgia Methodist Federal Credit Union	P.O. Box 8008	Atlanta	GA	31106	James R. Mitchell	404-378-6538	R	7 TA	<0.1
SEI-US Employees Federal Credit Union	P.O. Box 1466	Pocatello	ID	83204	Dale Higgins	208-233-4395	R	5 TA	<0.1

Source: *Ward's Business Directory of U.S. Private and Public Companies*, 1996. Company type codes: P - Public, R - Private, S - Subsidiary, D - Division, J - Joint Venture, A - Affiliate, G - Group. If the dollar values shown are not sales, the following codes apply: TA - Total Assets; OR - Operating Revenues; GB - Gross Billings. * - estimated dollar value. < - less than; *na* - not available.

LEADING COMPANIES - SIC 6062 - State Credit Unions

Number shown: **86**   Total sales/assets ($ mil): **19,957**   Total employment (000): **9.1**

Company Name	Address				CEO Name	Phone	Co. Type	Sales/Assets ($ mil)	Empl. (000)
State Employee's Credit Union	900 Wade Ave.	Raleigh	NC	27605	Jim Blaine	919-839-5003	R	3,689 TA	1.9
U.S. Central Credit Union	7300 College Blvd.	Overland Park	KS	66210	James R. Bell	913-661-3800	R	2,700 TA	0.2
Golden 1 Credit Union	P.O. Box 15966	Sacramento	CA	95852	Stan Hollen	916-732-2900	R	1,558 TA	0.7
Patelco Credit Union	156 2nd St.	San Francisco	CA	94105	Ed Callahan	415-442-6200	R	800 TA	0.2
State Employees Credit Union of Maryland Inc.	8503 LaSalle Rd.	Towson	MD	21286	Robert A. Smith	410-494-8030	R	740 TA	0.4
Wisconsin Corporate Central Credit Union Inc.	P.O. Box 469	Hales Corners	WI	53130	Mark Schroeder	414-425-5555	R	579 TA	<0.1
Space Coast Credit Union	P.O. Box 2470	Melbourne	FL	32902	Gregory Thomas	407-724-5730	R	524 TA	0.3
Portland Teachers Credit Union	P.O. Box 3750	Portland	OR	97208	John Beckwith	503-228-8255	R	515 TA	0.3
Brockton Credit Union	P.O. Box 720	Brockton	MA	02403	James W. Blake	508-586-2080	R	430 TA	0.2
Credit Union ONE	450 E. 9 Mile Rd.	Ferndale	MI	48220	Armando R. Cavazos	810-398-1210	R	347 TA	0.3
Baxter Credit Union	1425 Lake Cook Rd.	Deerfield	IL	60015	Mike Valentine	708-940-6300	R	320 TA	0.1
First Community Credit Union	15715 Manchester Rd.	Ellisville	MO	63011	Donald C. Berra	314-256-9292	R	313 TA	0.2
Anheuser-Busch Employees Credit Union	1001 Lynch St.	St. Louis	MO	63118	J. David Osborn	314-771-7700	R	306 TA	0.2
Motorola Employees Credit Union West	P.O. Box 3489	Scottsdale	AZ	85271	Peter DiSylvester	602-441-5900	R	296 TA	0.1
United Cooperative Bank	P.O. Box 9020	West Springfield	MA	01090	Raymond J. Labbe	413-787-1700	R	286 TA	0.1
Los Angeles Police Credit Union	P.O. Box 10188	Van Nuys	CA	91410	Stephen M. Endaya	818-787-6520	R	280 TA	<0.1
Oregon Telco Credit Union	2121 S.W. 4th Ave.	Portland	OR	97201	Wayne Gaylin	503-227-5571	R	276 TA	<0.1
Gasco Credit Union	810 S. Flower St.	Los Angeles	CA	90017	Lynn Bowers	213-244-2274	R	270 TA	<0.1
Workers' Credit Union	P.O. Box 900	Fitchburg	MA	01420		508-345-1021	R	250 TA	0.1
Detroit Teachers Credit Union	7700 Puritan	Detroit	MI	48238	Robert T. Lynch	313-345-7200	R	235 TA	0.1
University and State Employees Credit Union	10045 Mesa Rim Rd.	San Diego	CA	92121		619-535-1676	R	205 TA	<0.1
San Bernardino County Central Credit Union	P.O. Box 735	San Bernardino	CA	92402	Larry R. Sharp	909-881-3355	R	203 TA	0.2
Coast Central Credit Union	2650 Harrison Ave.	Eureka	CA	95501	Dean Christensen	707-445-8801	R	197 TA	0.1
San Antonio Teachers Credit Union	10730 Gulfdale	San Antonio	TX	78279	Leon Ewing	210-342-8484	R	189 TA	0.1
Telhio Credit Union	96 N. 4th St.	Columbus	OH	43215	Jerry Jackson	614-221-3233	R	187 TA	<0.1
Webster Credit Union	P.O. Box 778	Webster	MA	01570	Michael Lussier	508-943-1433	R	185 TA	<0.1
Educational Employees Credit Union	P.O. Box 11628	Tacoma	WA	98411	Jeff L. Kline	206-926-4000	R	185 TA	0.1
Boston Edison Employees Credit Union	P.O. Box 62	Boston	MA	02199	Thomas J. Kenny	617-424-3770	R	172 TA	<0.1
Educators Credit Union	1400 N. Newman Rd.	Racine	WI	53406	Eugene Szymczak	414-886-5900	R	160 TA	0.1
Educational Community Credit Union	P.O. Box 2600	Jacksonville	FL	32232	John W. Wallace	904-354-8537	R	151 TA	0.1

Company type codes: P - Public, R - Private, S - Subsidiary, D - Division, J - Joint Venture, A - Affiliate, G - Group. If the dollar values shown are not sales, the following codes apply: TA - Total Assets; OR - Operating Revenues; GB - Gross Billings. * - estimated dollar value. < - less than. *na* - not available.

Continued on next page.

LEADING COMPANIES - SIC 6062 - State Credit Unions
Continued

Company Name	Address				CEO Name	Phone	Co. Type	Sales/Assets ($ mil)	Empl. (000)
Credit Union of Denver	P.O. Box 261420	Lakewood	CO	80226	Wayne Harubin	303-234-1700	R	147 TA	0.1
Huron River Area Credit Union	2350 W. Stadium Blvd.	Ann Arbor	MI	48103	Gerald Gilikin Jr.	313-769-9830	R	140 TA*	<0.1
Sierra Central Credit Union	820 Plaza Way	Yuba City	CA	95991	Ed Waite	916-671-3000	R	137 TA	0.1
Listerhill Employees Credit Union	P.O. Box 566	Sheffield	AL	35660	Cyril B. Mann	205-383-9204	R	136 TA	0.1
Arizona Central Credit Union	P.O. Box 11650	Phoenix	AZ	85061	Gerald Merrill	602-264-6421	R	134 TA	<0.1
Group Health Credit Union	P.O. Box 19340	Seattle	WA	98109	Joseph W. Veneziani	206-298-9394	R	134 TA	0.1
Whatcom Educational Credit Union	P.O. Box 9750	Bellingham	WA	98227	Wayne Langei	206-676-1168	R	130 TA	<0.1
Valley Credit Union	2635 Zanker Rd.	San Jose	CA	95134	Anthony Jones	408-955-1300	R	129 TA	<0.1
Rhode Island State Employees Credit Union	160 Francis St.	Providence	RI	02903	Paul Filippone	401-751-7440	R	120 TA	0.1
Financial Center Credit Union	P.O. Box 8369	Stockton	CA	95208	L. Dennis Duffy	209-948-6024	R	116 TA	<0.1
First South Credit Union	P.O. Box 54217	Millington	TN	38054	W. Craig Esrael	901-873-2300	R	116 TA	<0.1
Co-op Services Credit Union	29550 Five Mile Rd.	Livonia	MI	48154	Robert L. Huston	313-522-3700	R	114 TA	<0.1
Kemba Cincinnati Credit Union	1011 W. 8th St.	Cincinnati	OH	45203	William Lowes	513-762-4830	R	101 TA	<0.1
Granite State Credit Union	P.O. Box 6420	Manchester	NH	03108	Denise Blanchette	603-668-2221	R	100 TA	<0.1
Landmark Credit Union	2775 S. Moorland Rd.	New Berlin	WI	53151	Ron Kase	414-797-0890	R	100 TA*	0.1
SOC Credit Union	4555 Corporate Dr.	Troy	MI	48098	Eldon Thompson	313-641-0088	R	100 TA	<0.1
Denver Postal Credit Union	P.O. Box 1346	Arvada	CO	80001	Patricia Cosby	303-422-6221	R	91 TA	<0.1
Gates Credit Union	305 E. Mississippi Ave	Denver	CO	80210	John Mann	303-744-3535	R	83 TA	<0.1
Portland Postal Employees Credit Union	12630 S.E. Division St	Portland	OR	97216	H. Lee Hardiman	503-760-5304	R	72 TA	<0.1
Hospital and Health Services Credit Union	2100 Commonwealth Blvd	Ann Arbor	MI	48105	Larry Colbert	313-769-4621	R	64 TA*	<0.1
Northeast Catholic Credit Union	16012 E. Seven Mile	Detroit	MI	48205	Lloyd Schlaf	313-521-4725	R	64 TA*	<0.1
Jefferson County Teachers Credit Union	P.O. Box 2385	Birmingham	AL	35201	Joseph Shaw	205-226-3900	R	62 TA	<0.1
Fort Worth City Credit Union	2309 Montgomery St.	Fort Worth	TX	76107	William B. Gordon	817-732-2803	R	61 TA	<0.1
Kemba Columbus Credit Union	4220 E. Broad St.	Columbus	OH	43213	Gerald Guy	614-235-2395	R	60 TA	<0.1
Hawthorne Credit Union	1519 N. Naper Blvd.	Naperville	IL	60563	Carl Sorgatz	708-369-4070	R	57 TA	<0.1
Aerospace Community Credit Union	1550 Country Club Plz.	St. Charles	MO	63303	Nina G. Pilger	314-947-0044	R	54 TA	<0.1
Municipal Employees Credit Union of San Jose	140 Asbury St.	San Jose	CA	95110	Judith A. Larson	408-294-8800	R	52 TA	<0.1
Arsenal Credit Union	8651 Watson Rd.	St. Louis	MO	63119	Linda G. Allen	314-962-6363	R	50 TA	<0.1
Oakland Catholic Credit Union	255 E. Maple Rd.	Troy	MI	48083	Doreen A. Martin	810-689-7400	R	50 TA	<0.1
Deere Community Credit Union	P.O. Box 319	Ankeny	IA	50021	Dennis Skelton	515-289-1822	R	45 TA	<0.1

Company type codes: P - Public, R - Private, S - Subsidiary, D - Division, J - Joint Venture, A - Affiliate, G - Group. If the dollar values shown are not sales, the following codes apply: TA - Total Assets; OR - Operating Revenues; GB - Gross Billings. * - estimated dollar value. < - less than. *na* - not available.

Continued on next page.

LEADING COMPANIES - SIC 6062 - State Credit Unions
Continued

Company Name	Address				CEO Name	Phone	Co. Type	Sales/Assets ($ mil)	Empl. (000)
Greater Cleveland Fire Fighters Credit Union Inc.	2300 St. Clair Ave.	Cleveland	OH	44114	Karen A. McNamara	216-621-4644	R	45 TA	<0.1
Cincinnati Central Credit Union	1717 Western Ave.	Cincinnati	OH	45214	William Herring	513-241-2050	R	44 TA	<0.1
Boulder Valley Credit Union	5505 Arapahoe Rd.	Boulder	CO	80303	Anne Marie Bradford	303-442-8850	R	42 TA	<0.1
First Class American Credit Union	P.O. Box 2135	Fort Worth	TX	76113	Russell Back	817-332-7947	R	40 TA	<0.1
Coors Credit Union	816 Washington Ave.	Golden	CO	80401	Barbara Cecil	303-279-6414	R	39 TA	<0.1
Craftsman Credit Union	2444 Clark St.	Detroit	MI	48209	Mario Maraldo	313-554-9300	R	34 TA	<0.1
Health Services Credit Union	6900 Southpoint Dr. N.	Jacksonville	FL	32216	Maurice Pilver	904-296-1292	R	34 TA	<0.1
American Electronic Association Credit Union	505 N. Mathilda Ave.	Sunnyvale	CA	94086	Tim Kramer	408-720-8953	R	32 TA	0.2
Trans Air Credit Union	10895 Natural Bridge	Bridgeton	MO	63044	Robert Matteson	314-429-0018	R	30 TA	<0.1
School Employees Credit Union	P.O. Box 12217	Kansas City	KS	66112	LLoyd Nugent	913-334-4200	R	28 TA	<0.1
Peoples Credit Union	680 N.E. 124th St.	North Miami	FL	33161	Gail E. Siebe	305-893-4880	R	24 TA	<0.1
Missouri Central Credit Union	340 S.W. Blue Pkwy.	Lee Summit	MO	64063	Ray Becker	816-246-0002	R	22 TA	<0.1
Sacramento District Postal Employees Credit Union Co.	1620 35th Ave.	Sacramento	CA	95822	David Van Leer	916-395-1505	R	22 TA	<0.1
Brewery Credit Union	1351 N. Martin Luther	Milwaukee	WI	53212	John E. Milner	414-273-3170	R	17 TA	<0.1
Midland Area Credit Union	784 Poseyville Rd.	Midland	MI	48640	Janis L. Barrett	517-839-0770	R	16 TA	<0.1
First Service Credit Union	7630 W. Bluemound	Milwaukee	WI	53208	Scott Bliss	414-342-7660	R	15 TA	<0.1
OCHA Credit Union	200 S. Manchester Ave.	Orange	CA	92668	Ruth Whitmarsh	714-456-0525	R	15 TA	<0.1
Hospitality USA Credit Union	6390 E. Thomas Rd.	Scottsdale	AZ	85251	Karen Van Brocsccia	602-423-8500	R	14 TA	<0.1
Wisconsin Education Association Credit Union	P.O. Box 8003	Madison	WI	53708	Sue Cowan	608-274-9828	R	13 TA	<0.1
Campus Credit Union	1845 Fairmount	Wichita	KS	67206	Cynthia S. Rohner	316-689-3666	R	11 TA	<0.1
Michigan Services Credit Union	30200 Telegraph Rd.	Bingham Farms	MI	48025	Elizabeth J. Morehouse	810-540-8200	R	11 TA*	<0.1
Simplot Employees Credit Union	P.O. Box 1059	Caldwell	ID	83606	Vernon Smith	208-454-4286	R	11 TA	<0.1
Fellowship Credit Union	P.O. Box 39055	San Antonio	TX	78218	Pam Jones	210-599-4488	R	10 TA*	<0.1
Fernald Environment Mgmnt Projects Credit Union Inc.	P.O. Box 247	Ross	OH	45061	Collen L. Uhl	513-738-6306	R	9 TA	<0.1
Health Credit Union	P.O. Box 2648	Birmingham	AL	35202	Felix Hartley	205-930-1213	R	8 TA	<0.1
Public Employees Credit Union	1839 N. Government Way	Coeur D'Alene	ID	83814	Diane C. Larson	208-667-7722	R	6 TA	<0.1

Source: *Ward's Business Directory of U.S. Private and Public Companies*, 1996. Company type codes: P - Public, R - Private, S - Subsidiary, D - Division, J - Joint Venture, A - Affiliate, G - Group. If the dollar values shown are not sales, the following codes apply: TA - Total Assets; OR - Operating Revenues; GB - Gross Billings. * - estimated dollar value. < - less than; na - not available.

FINANCIAL DATA ON CREDIT UNIONS

The following eight tables present financial data on federal, state, and corporate credit unions, from 1986 or 1990 through 1994. The data were obtained from the National Credit Union Administration (NCUA), Washington, D.C. 20456.

SELECTED DATA FOR FEDERAL CREDIT UNIONS

December 31, 1935 to 1994.

Year	Charters issued	Charters canceled	Net change	Total outstanding	Inactive credit unions	Active credit unions	Members	($000)		
								Assets[1]	Shares[1]	Loans outstanding
1935[1]	828		828	906	134	772	119,420			
1936	956	4	952	1,858	107	1,751	309,700	2,372	2,228	1,834
1937	638	69	569	2,427	114	22,313	483,920	9,158	8,511	7,344
1938	515	83	432	2,859	99	2,760	632,050	19,265	17,650	15,695
1939	529	93	436	3,295	113	3,182	850,770	29,629	26,876	23,830
1940	666	76	590	3,855	129	3,756	1,127,940	47,811	43,327	37,673
1941	583	89	494	4,379	151	4,228	1,408,880	72,530	65,806	55,818
1942	187	89	98	4,477	332	4,145	1,356,940	106,052	97,209	69,485
1943	108	321	-213	4,264	326	3,938	1,311,620	119,591	109,822	43,053
1944	69	285	-216	4,048	233	3,815	1,306,000	127,329	117,339	35,376
1945	96	185	-89	3,959	202	3,757	1,216,625	144,365	133,677	34,438
1946	157	151	6	3,965	204	3,761	1,302,132	153,103	140,614	35,155
1947	207	159	48	4,013	168	3,845	1,445,915	173,166	159,718	56,801
1948	341	130	211	4,224	166	4,058	1,628,339	210,376	192,410	91,372
1949	523	101	422	4,646	151	4,495	1,819,606	258,412	235,008	137,642
1950	565	83	482	5,128	144	4,984	2,126,823	316,363	285,001	186,218
1951	533	75	458	5,586	188	5,398	2,463,898	405,835	361,925	263,736
1952	692	115	577	6,163	238	5,925	2,853,241	504,715	457,402	299,756
1953	825	132	693	6,856	278	6,578	3,255,422	662,409	597,374	415,062
1954	852	122	730	7,586	359	7,227	3,598,790	854,232	767,571	573,974
1955	777	188	589	8,175	369	7,806	4,032,220	1,033,179	931,407	681,970
1956	741	182	559	8,734	384	8,350	4,502,210	1,267,427	1,135,165	863,042
1957	662	194	468	9,202	467	8,735	4,897,689	1,529,202	1,366,258	1,049,189
1958	586	255	331	9,533	503	9,030	5,209,912	1,788,768	1,589,191	1,257,319
1959	700	270	430	9,963	516	9,447	5,643,248	2,034,866	1,812,017	1,379,724
1960	685	274	411	10,374	469	9,905	6,087,378	2,352,813	2,075,055	1,666,526
1961	671	265	406	10,780	509	10,271	6,542,603	2,669,734	2,344,337	2,021,463
1962	601	284	317	11,097	465	10,632	7,007,630	3,028,294	2,673,488	2,245,223
1963	622	312	310	11,407	452	10,955	7,499,747	3,429,805	3,020,274	2,560,722
1964	580	323	257	11,664	386	11,278	8,092,030	3,916,541	3,452,615	2,911,159
1965	584	270	324	11,978	435	11,543	8,640,560	4,559,438	4,017,393	3,349,068
1966	701	318	383	12,361	420	11,941	9,271,967	5,165,807	4,538,461	3,864,809
1967	636	292	344	12,705	495	12,210	9,873,777	5,668,941	4,944,033	4,323,943
1968	662	345	317	13,022	438	12,584	10,508,504	6,208,158	5,420,633	4,677,480
1969	705	323	382	13,404	483	12,921	11,301,805	6,902,175	5,986,181	5,398,052
1970	563	412	151	13,555	578	12,977	11,966,181	7,793,573	6,713,385	6,328,720
1971	400	461	-61	13,494	777	12,717	12,702,135	8,860,612	7,628,805	6,969,006
1972	311	672	-361	13,133	425	12,708	13,572,312	10,533,740	9,191,182	8,071,201
1973	364	523	-159	12,974	286	12,688	14,665,890	12,513,621	10,956,007	9,424,180
1974	367	369	-2	12,972	224	12,748	15,870,434	14,568,736	12,597,607	11,109,015
1975	373	334	39	13,011	274	12,737	17,066,428	16,714,673	14,370,744	12,729,653
1976	354	387	-33	12,978	221	12,757	18,623,862	20,208,536	17,529,823	14,868,840
1977	337	315	22	13,000	250	12,750	20,426,661	24,395,896	21,130,293	18,311,204
1978	348	298	50	13,050	291	12,759	23,259,284	29,563,681	25,576,017	22,633,860
1979	286	336	-50	13,000	262	12,738	24,789,647	34,760,098	29,802,504	27,686,584
								36,467,850	31,831,400	28,547,097

[Continued]

SELECTED DATA FOR FEDERAL CREDIT UNIONS
[Continued]

Year	Charters issued	Charters canceled	Net change	Total outstanding	Inactive credit unions	Active credit unions	Members	($000)		
								Assets[1]	Shares[1]	Loans outstanding
1980	170	368	-198	12,802	362	12,440	24,519,087	40,091,855	36,263,343	26,350,277
1981	119	554	-435	12,367	398	11,969	25,459,059	41,905,413	37,788,699	27,203,672
1982	114	556	-442	11,925	294	11,631	26,114,649	45,482,943	41,340,911	28,184,280
1983	107	736	-629	11,296	320	10,976	26,798,799	54,481,827	49,889,313	33,200,715
1984	135	664	-529	10,767	219	10,548	28,191,922	63,656,321	57,929,124	42,133,018
1985	55	575	-520	10,247	122	10,125	29,578,808	78,187,651	71,616,202	48,240,770
1986	59	441	-382	9,865	107	9,758	31,041,142	95,483,828	87,953,642	55,304,682
1987	41	460	-419	9,446	45	9,401	32,066,542	105,189,725	96,346,488	64,104,411
1988	45	201	-156	9,290	172	9,118	34,438,304	114,564,579	104,431,487	73,766,200
1989	23	307	-284	9,006	185	8,821	35,612,317	120,666,414	109,652,600	80,272,306
1990	33	410	-377	8,629	118	8,511	36,241,607	130,072,955	117,891,940	83,029,348
1991	14	291	-277	8,352	123	8,229	37,080,854	143,163,749	130,163,749	84,150,334
1992	33	341	-308	8,044	128	7,916	38,205,128	162,543,659	146,078,403	87,632,808
1993	42	258	-216	7,828	132	7,696	39,755,596	172,854,187	153,505,799	94,640,348
1994	39	224	-185	7,643	146	7,497	40,841,438	182,541,535	160,236,822	110,093,504

Source: National Credit Union Administration, *1994 Annual Report*, Alexandria, Va., p. 42. *Note:* 1. Data for 1935-44 are partly estimated.

FEDERAL CREDIT UNION DATA 10 YEAR SUMMARY, 1986 TO 1994

December 31. Dollar amounts in millions.

	1986	1987	1988	1989	1990	1991	1992	1993	1994
Number of credit unions	9,758	9,401	9,118	8,821	8,511	8,229	7,916	7,696	7,497
Number of members	31,041,142	32,066,542	34,438,304	35,612,317	36,241,607	37,080,854	38,205,128	39,755,596	40,841,438
Assets	95,484	105,190	114,565	120,666	130,073	143,940	162,544	172,854	182,542
Loans outstanding	55,305	64,104	73,766	80,272	83,029	84,150	87,633	94,640	110,094
Shares	87,954	96,346	104,431	109,653	117,892	130,164	146,078	153,506	160,237
Reserves[1]	3,312	3,725	4,216	4,690	5,158	5,539	6,176	6,976	7,621
Undivided earnings	2,506	3,023	3,567	4,072	4,594	5,338	6,793	8,338	9,582
Gross income	9,416	10,158	11,173	12,420	13,233	13,559	13,301	12,946	13,489
Operating expenses	3,115	3,585	3,931	4,364	4,730	5,068	5,329	5,578	5,961
Dividends	5,506	5,624	6,148	6,910	7,372	7,184	5,876	5,038	5,200
Reserve transfers	250	237	232	265	222	170	191	186	246
Net income	626	688	799	781	841	1,087	1,897	2,096	1,908

Source: National Credit Union Administration, *1994 Annual Report*, Alexandria, Va., p. 40. *Note:* 1. Does not include the allowance for loan losses.

FEDERAL CREDIT UNION DATA - PERCENT CHANGE - 1986 TO 1994

December 31. Dollar amounts in millions.

	1986	1987	1988	1989	1990	1991	1992	1993	1994
Total assets	22.1	10.2	8.9	5.3	7.8	10.7	12.9	6.3	5.6
Loans outstanding	14.6	15.9	15.1	8.8	3.4	1.3	4.1	8.0	16.3
Savings	22.8	9.5	8.4	5.0	7.5	10.4	12.2	5.1	4.4
Reserves	14.8	12.5	13.2	11.2	10.0	7.4	11.5	13.0	9.2
Undivided earnings	21.5	20.6	18.0	14.2	12.8	16.2	27.3	22.7	14.9
Gross income	10.4	7.9	10.0	11.2	6.5	2.5	-1.9	-2.7	4.2
Operating expenses	16.5	15.1	9.7	11.0	8.4	7.1	5.1	4.7	6.9
Dividends	8.2	2.1	9.3	12.4	6.7	-2.6	-18.2	-14.3	3.2
Net reserve transfers	-11.3	-5.2	-2.1	14.2	-16.1	-23.8	12.7	-2.6	32.3
Net income	20.2	9.9	16.1	-2.3	7.6	29.3	74.5	10.5	-9.0

Source: National Credit Union Administration, *1994 Annual Report*, Alexandria, Va., p. 40.

FEDERAL CREDIT UNION DATA - SIGNIFICANT RATIOS - 1986 TO 1994

December 31. Dollar amounts in millions.

	1986	1987	1988	1989	1990	1991	1992	1993	1994
Reserves to assets	3.5	3.5	3.7	3.9	4.0	3.8	3.8	4.0	4.2
Reserves and undivided earnings to assets	6.1	6.4	6.8	7.3	7.5	7.6	8.0	8.9	9.4
Reserves to loans	6.1	5.8	5.7	5.8	6.2	6.6	7.0	7.4	6.9
Loans to shares	62.9	66.5	70.6	73.2	70.4	64.6	60.0	61.7	68.7
Operating expense to gross income	33.1	35.3	35.2	35.1	35.7	37.4	40.1	43.1	44.2
Salaries and benefits to gross income	14.1	14.6	14.8	14.7	15.0	15.7	17.4	19.4	20.2
Dividends to gross income	58.5	55.4	55.0	55.6	55.7	53.0	44.2	38.9	38.5
Yield on average assets	10.8	10.1	10.2	10.6	10.6	9.9	8.7	7.7	7.6
Cost of funds to average assets	6.4	5.6	5.7	6.0	5.9	5.3	3.9	3.1	3.0
Gross spread	4.5	4.5	4.5	4.6	4.6	4.6	4.8	4.6	4.6
Net income divided by gross income	6.6	6.8	7.2	6.3	6.4	8.0	14.3	16.2	14.1
Yield on average loans	12.7	11.6	11.3	11.5	11.4	11.2	10.4	9.4	8.7
Yield on average investments	7.9	7.7	7.9	8.4	8.3	7.0	5.5	4.6	5.1

Source: National Credit Union Administration, *1994 Annual Report*, Alexandria, Va., p. 40.

STATE CREDIT UNION FINANCIAL DATA - 1986 TO 1994

December 31. Dollar amounts in millions.

	1986	1987	1988	1989	1990	1991	1992	1993	1994
Number of credit unions	4,935	4,934	4,760	4,552	4,349	4,731	4,737	4,621	4,494
Number of members	17,362,780	17,998,921	18,518,969	18,939,127	19,453,940	21,619,223	23,859,447	23,996,751	24,292,589
Assets	52,244	56,972	60,740	63,175	68,133	83,133	98,767	104,316	106,928
Loans outstanding	30,834	35,436	39,977	42,373	44,102	49,268	53,727	57,695	65,763
Shares	48,097	52,083	55,217	57,658	62,082	75,626	89,648	93,482	94,792
Reserves[1]	2,147	2,423	2,612	2,872	3,047	3,620	4,238	4,754	4,905
Undivided earnings	1,253	1,458	1,651	1,945	2,241	2,952	3,910	4,862	5,569
Gross income	5,117	5,483	5,973	6,529	6,967	7,878	8,182	7,878	7,954
Operating expenses	1,655	1,884	2,078	2,216	2,412	2,860	3,203	3,302	3,473
Dividends	3,004	3,049	3,290	2,930	3,908	4,203	3,664	3,109	3,145
Reserve transfers	201	184	158	150	118	98	121	114	143
Net income	288	355	470	457	509	711	1,207	1,347	1,146

Source: National Credit Union Administration, *1994 Annual Report*, Alexandria, Va., p. 41. *Note:* 1. Does not include the allowance for loan losses.

STATE CREDIT UNION DATA - PERCENT CHANGE - 1986 TO 1994

December 31. Dollar amounts in millions.

	1986	1987	1988	1989	1990	1991	1992	1993	1994
Total assets	25.8	9.0	6.6	4.0	7.8	22.0	18.8	5.6	2.5
Loans outstanding	17.8	14.9	12.8	6.0	4.1	11.7	9.1	7.4	14.0
Savings	26.8	8.3	6.0	4.4	7.7	21.8	18.5	4.3	1.4
Reserves	20.6	12.9	7.8	10.0	6.1	18.8	17.1	12.2	3.2
Undivided earnings	17.7	16.4	13.2	17.8	15.2	31.7	32.5	24.3	14.5
Gross income	13.5	7.2	8.9	9.3	6.7	13.1	3.9	-3.7	1.0
Operating expenses	21.3	13.8	10.3	6.6	8.8	18.6	12.0	3.1	5.2
Dividends	11.9	1.5	7.9	-10.9	33.4	7.5	-12.8	-15.1	1.2
Net reserve transfers	-11.5	-8.5	-14.1	-5.1	-21.3	-16.9	23.5	-5.8	25.4
Net income	12.5	23.3	32.4	-2.8	11.4	39.7	69.8	11.6	-14.9

Source: National Credit Union Administration, *1994 Annual Report*, Alexandria, Va., p. 41.

STATE CREDIT UNION DATA - SIGNIFICANT RATIOS - 1986 TO 1994

December 31. Dollar amounts in millions.

	1986	1987	1988	1989	1990	1991	1992	1993	1994
Reserves to assets	4.1	4.3	4.3	4.5	4.5	4.4	4.3	4.6	4.6
Reserves and undivided earnings to assets	6.5	6.8	7.0	7.6	7.8	7.9	8.2	9.2	9.8
Reserves to loans	7.0	6.8	6.5	6.8	6.9	7.3	7.9	8.2	7.5
Loans to shares	64.1	68.0	72.4	73.5	71.0	65.1	59.9	61.7	69.4
Operating expense to gross income	32.3	34.4	34.8	33.9	34.6	36.3	39.1	41.9	43.7
Salaries and benefits to gross income	13.9	14.5	14.5	14.4	14.7	15.4	16.9	19.0	20.0
Dividends to gross income	58.7	55.6	55.1	44.9	56.1	53.4	44.8	39.5	39.5
Yield on average assets	11.2	10.4	10.1	10.5	10.6	10.4	9.0	7.8	7.5
Cost of funds to average assets	6.4	5.5	5.5	5.9	6.0	5.6	4.1	3.1	3.0
Gross spread	4.5	4.3	4.6	4.6	4.6	4.6	4.6	4.7	4.5
Net income divided by gross income	5.6	6.5	7.9	7.0	7.3	9.0	14.8	17.1	14.4
Yield on average loans	12.7	11.1	11.2	11.4	11.4	11.8	10.8	9.5	8.6
Yield on average investments	8.0	7.5	7.9	8.4	8.5	7.4	5.7	4.7	4.9

Source: National Credit Union Administration, *1994 Annual Report*, Alexandria, Va., p. 41.

CORPORATE CREDIT UNIONS - KEY STATISTICS

December 31. Dollar amounts in millions.

	1990	1991	1992	1993	1994
Number	31	33	35	37	39
Assets	25,493.8	31,014.8	37,823.7	39,058.8	34,307.8
Loans	1,172.4	1,172.8	1,159.2	1,199.2	1,686.6
Shares	20,012.3	25,856.9	31,891.2	31,392.4	27,566.6
Reserves	218.0	315.1	412.2	466.8	598.1
Undivided earnings	96.9	120.1	159.7	191.2	289.3
Gross income	1,904.1	1,928.3	1,746.7	2,268.2	1,813.1
Operating expenses	54.9	70.6	79.81	97.8	114.0
Interest on borrowing	323.9	285.5	238.6	334.8	280.6
Dividends and interest on deposits	1,465.5	1,457.6	1,291.61	1,674.2	1,338.5
Reserve transfers	27.8	40.4	45.01	61.5	31.5
Net income	32.5	74.2	91.71	99.9	48.5

Source: National Credit Union Administration, *1994 Annual Report*, Alexandria, Va., p. 13. *Notes:* To prevent double counting, U.S. Central Credit Union is excluded from totals.

SIC 6080

FOREIGN BANKS & BRANCHES & AGENCIES

Foreign Banks and Branches and Agencies of Foreign Banks are divided into SIC 6081, Branches and Agencies of Foreign Banks and SIC 6082, Foreign Trade and International Banking Institutions.

SIC 6081 represents establishments that specialize in commercial loans, especially to finance trade. They are funded typically by large interbank deposits rather than retail deposits. Federally licensed agencies of foreign banks may not accept deposits; federal branches may accept deposits, but if they accept deposits in denominations of $100,000 or less, federal deposit insurance is required. Foreign-owned banks engaged primarily in accepting retail deposits from the public are classified as SIC 6020.

SIC 6082 includes federally or state-chartered foreign trade companies organized to aid or finance foreign trade. The category also includes banking institutions (federal or state charter) which engage in banking only outside the United States.

ESTABLISHMENTS, EMPLOYMENT, AND PAYROLL

	1988	1989		1990		1991		1992		1993		% change 88-93
		Value	%	Value	%	Value	%	Value	%	Value	%	
All Establishments	265	250	-5.7	235	-6.0	473	101.3	480	1.5	561	16.9	111.7
Mid-March Employment	12,763	13,920	9.1	13,317	-4.3	21,627	62.4	23,248	7.5	27,710	19.2	117.1
1st Quarter Wages (annualized - $ mil.)	549.5	639.6	16.4	661.3	3.4	1,114.1	68.5	1,369.6	22.9	1,827.1	33.4	232.5
Payroll per Emp. 1st Q. (annualized)	43,050	45,950	6.7	49,659	8.1	51,515	3.7	58,912	14.4	65,937	11.9	53.2
Annual Payroll ($ mil.)	568.5	660.7	16.2	662.7	0.3	1,150.7	73.6	1,393.0	21.1	1,810.8	30.0	218.5
Establishments - 1-4 Emp. Number	49	38	-22.4	41	7.9	73	78.0	42	-42.5	41	-2.4	-16.3
Mid-March Employment	(D)	80	-	72	-10.0	(D)	-	98	-	95	-3.1	-
1st Quarter Wages (annualized - $ mil.)	(D)	4.2	-	3.8	-9.9	(D)	-	7.0	-	7.4	5.1	-
Payroll per Emp. 1st Q. (annualized)	(D)	52,400	-	52,444	0.1	(D)	-	71,837	-	77,853	8.4	-
Annual Payroll ($ mil.)	(D)	5.6	-	5.9	5.3	(D)	-	7.0	-	8.2	17.4	-
Establishments - 5-9 Emp. Number	23	23	-	20	-13.0	53	165.0	59	11.3	(D)	-	-
Mid-March Employment	(D)	(D)	-	(D)	-	387	-	400	3.4	(D)	-	-
1st Quarter Wages (annualized - $ mil.)	(D)	(D)	-	(D)	-	22.0	-	51.4	133.9	(D)	-	-
Payroll per Emp. 1st Q. (annualized)	(D)	(D)	-	(D)	-	56,734	-	128,400	126.3	(D)	-	-
Annual Payroll ($ mil.)	(D)	(D)	-	(D)	-	26.8	-	32.4	21.1	(D)	-	-
Establishments - 10-19 Emp. Number	46	43	-6.5	34	-20.9	80	135.3	101	26.3	(D)	-	-
Mid-March Employment	695	661	-4.9	(D)	-	(D)	-	1,435	-	(D)	-	-
1st Quarter Wages (annualized - $ mil.)	50.5	31.7	-37.3	(D)	-	(D)	-	74.7	-	(D)	-	-
Payroll per Emp. 1st Q. (annualized)	72,639	47,885	-34.1	(D)	-	(D)	-	52,081	-	(D)	-	-
Annual Payroll ($ mil.)	36.4	36.0	-1.1	(D)	-	(D)	-	80.8	-	(D)	-	-
Establishments - 20-49 Emp. Number	73	67	-8.2	69	3.0	159	130.4	151	-5.0	172	13.9	135.6
Mid-March Employment	(D)	2,138	-	2,166	1.3	5,141	137.3	4,630	-9.9	5,260	13.6	-
1st Quarter Wages (annualized - $ mil.)	(D)	89.3	-	99.9	11.9	241.8	142.1	226.1	-6.5	280.1	23.9	-
Payroll per Emp. 1st Q. (annualized)	(D)	41,770	-	46,122	10.4	47,043	2.0	48,838	3.8	53,257	9.0	-
Annual Payroll ($ mil.)	(D)	88.2	-	93.0	5.5	251.7	170.6	238.4	-5.3	287.3	20.5	-
Establishments - 50-99 Emp. Number	42	44	4.8	37	-15.9	60	62.2	74	23.3	87	17.6	107.1
Mid-March Employment	2,922	3,276	12.1	2,724	-16.8	4,278	57.0	5,240	22.5	6,113	16.7	109.2
1st Quarter Wages (annualized - $ mil.)	120.7	148.9	23.4	130.0	-12.7	198.4	52.7	274.3	38.2	353.2	28.8	192.7
Payroll per Emp. 1st Q. (annualized)	41,294	45,437	10.0	47,724	5.0	46,388	-2.8	52,343	12.8	57,784	10.4	39.9
Annual Payroll ($ mil.)	132.8	162.8	22.6	129.4	-20.5	209.6	62.0	288.1	37.4	361.3	25.4	172.0
Establishments - 100-249 Emp. Number	24	23	-4.2	23	-	33	43.5	37	12.1	44	18.9	83.3
Mid-March Employment	3,745	3,649	-2.6	3,827	4.9	4,875	27.4	5,073	4.1	6,749	33.0	80.2
1st Quarter Wages (annualized - $ mil.)	142.5	177.4	24.5	205.4	15.8	260.9	27.0	281.9	8.0	430.2	52.6	201.9
Payroll per Emp. 1st Q. (annualized)	38,049	48,614	27.8	53,683	10.4	53,518	-0.3	55,569	3.8	63,736	14.7	67.5
Annual Payroll ($ mil.)	157.8	179.9	14.0	205.2	14.0	254.4	24.0	300.9	18.3	441.8	46.8	180.0
Establishments - 250-499 Emp. Number	7	11	57.1	10	-9.1	12	20.0	13	8.3	17	30.8	142.9
Mid-March Employment	(D)	3,425	-	3,354	-2.1	(D)	-	4,582	-	5,971	30.3	-
1st Quarter Wages (annualized - $ mil.)	(D)	160.8	-	166.3	3.4	(D)	-	329.3	-	541.0	64.3	-
Payroll per Emp. 1st Q. (annualized)	(D)	46,952	-	49,590	5.6	(D)	-	71,860	-	90,598	26.1	-
Annual Payroll ($ mil.)	(D)	157.1	-	168.7	7.4	(D)	-	313.4	-	482.2	53.9	-
Establishments - 500-999 Emp. Number	1	1	-	1	-	3	200.0	3	-	(D)	-	-
Mid-March Employment	(D)	(D)	-	(D)	-	1,692	-	1,790	5.8	(D)	-	-
1st Quarter Wages (annualized - $ mil.)	(D)	(D)	-	(D)	-	77.8	-	124.9	60.6	(D)	-	-
Payroll per Emp. 1st Q. (annualized)	(D)	(D)	-	(D)	-	45,953	-	69,777	51.8	(D)	-	-
Annual Payroll ($ mil.)	(D)	(D)	-	(D)	-	86.3	-	132.0	52.9	(D)	-	-
Estab. - 1000 or More Emp. Number	-	-	-	-	-	-	-	-	-	-	-	-
Mid-March Employment	-	-	-	-	-	-	-	-	-	-	-	-
1st Quarter Wages (annualized - $ mil.)	-	-	-	-	-	-	-	-	-	-	-	-
Payroll per Emp. 1st Q. (annualized)	(D)	(D)	-	(D)	-	(D)	-	-	-	-	-	-
Annual Payroll ($ mil.)	-	-	-	-	-	-	-	-	-	-	-	-

Source: County Business Patterns, U.S. Department of Commerce, Washington, D.C., for 1988 through 1993. Payroll per employee is calculated using mid-March employment and 1st Quarter wages, annualized. Annual payroll, also shown, may not equal the annualized 1st Quarter wages. Columns headed by a percent sign (%) indicate change from the previous year. *na* stands for not available. The symbol (D) indicates that data are withheld by the source to avoid disclosure of competitive information. A dash (-) indicates that data are not available or cannot be calculated.

ESTABLISHMENTS
Number

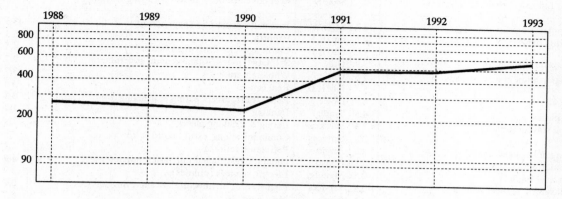

MID-MARCH EMPLOYMENT
Number

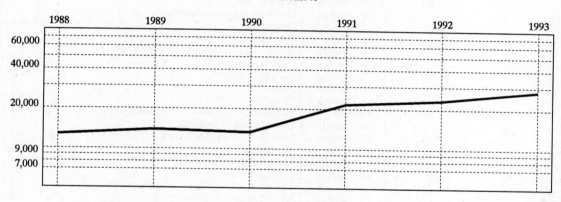

ANNUAL PAYROLL
$ million

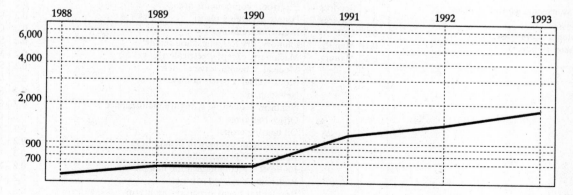

INPUTS AND OUTPUTS FOR ALL BANKING SECTORS - SICs 601, 602, 603, 608, and 609

Economic Sector or Industry Providing Inputs	%	Sector	Economic Sector or Industry Buying Outputs	%	Sector
Computer & data processing services	13.3	Services	Personal consumption expenditures	43.5	
Security & commodity brokers	10.1	Fin/R.E.	Exports	5.3	Foreign
Real estate	8.0	Fin/R.E.	Credit agencies other than banks	4.5	Fin/R.E.
Communications, except radio & TV	5.9	Util.	S/L Govt. purch., other general government	3.7	S/L Govt
Motor freight transportation & warehousing	5.8	Util.	Wholesale trade	3.7	Trade
Banking	5.7	Fin/R.E.	Real estate	3.6	Fin/R.E.
U.S. Postal Service	4.7	Gov't	Retail trade, except eating & drinking	3.3	Trade
Eating & drinking places	4.5	Trade	Banking	1.9	Fin/R.E.
Equipment rental & leasing services	3.4	Services	Eating & drinking places	1.4	Trade
Advertising	2.9	Services	Communications, except radio & TV	1.1	Util.
Accounting, auditing & bookkeeping	2.8	Services	Petroleum refining	1.1	Manufg.
Maintenance of nonfarm buildings nec	2.8	Constr.	Federal Government purchases, nondefense	1.0	Fed Govt
Blankbooks & looseleaf binders	2.5	Manufg.	Electric services (utilities)	0.9	Util.
Management & consulting services & labs	2.4	Services	Engineering, architectural, & surveying services	0.7	Services
Federal Government enterprises nec	2.1	Gov't	Meat animals	0.7	Agric.
Insurance carriers	2.1	Fin/R.E.	Aircraft	0.6	Manufg.
Photographic equipment & supplies	1.7	Manufg.	Apparel made from purchased materials	0.5	Manufg.
Electric services (utilities)	1.6	Util.	Crude petroleum & natural gas	0.5	Mining
Detective & protective services	1.5	Services	Gas production & distribution (utilities)	0.5	Util.
Legal services	1.4	Services	Insurance carriers	0.5	Fin/R.E.
Noncomparable imports	1.4	Foreign	Electronic computing equipment	0.4	Manufg.
Petroleum refining	1.2	Manufg.	Feed grains	0.4	Agric.
Wholesale trade	1.2	Trade	Maintenance of nonfarm buildings nec	0.4	Constr.
Manifold business forms	1.0	Manufg.	Motor freight transportation & warehousing	0.4	Util.
Credit agencies other than banks	0.9	Fin/R.E.	Dairy farm products	0.3	Agric.
Personnel supply services	0.9	Services	Doctors & dentists	0.3	Services
Business/professional associations	0.8	Services	Drugs	0.3	Manufg.
Commercial printing	0.8	Manufg.	Freight forwarders	0.3	Util.
Air transportation	0.6	Util.	Management & consulting services & labs	0.3	Services
Envelopes	0.6	Manufg.	Owner-occupied dwellings	0.3	Fin/R.E.
Electrical repair shops	0.4	Services	Security & commodity brokers	0.3	Fin/R.E.
Transit & bus transportation	0.4	Util.	Advertising	0.2	Services
Electronic components nec	0.3	Manufg.	Agricultural chemicals, nec	0.2	Manufg.
Electronic computing equipment	0.3	Manufg.	Air transportation	0.2	Util.
Engraving & plate printing	0.3	Manufg.	Aircraft & missile engines & engine parts	0.2	Manufg.
Manufacturing industries, nec	0.3	Manufg.	Aircraft & missile equipment, nec	0.2	Manufg.
Paper mills, except building paper	0.3	Manufg.	Broadwoven fabric mills	0.2	Manufg.
Periodicals	0.3	Manufg.	Chemical & fertilizer mineral	0.2	Mining
Services to dwellings & other buildings	0.3	Services	Coal	0.2	Mining
Textile bags	0.3	Manufg.	Computer & data processing services	0.2	Services
Automotive rental & leasing, without drivers	0.2	Services	Electronic components nec	0.2	Manufg.
Hotels & lodging places	0.2	Services	Hotels & lodging places	0.2	Services
Sanitary services, steam supply, irrigation	0.2	Util.	Industrial buildings	0.2	Constr.
Carbon paper & inked ribbons	0.1	Manufg.	Laundry, dry cleaning, shoe repair	0.2	Services
Newspapers	0.1	Manufg.	Machinery, except electrical, nec	0.2	Manufg.
			Medical & health services, nec	0.2	Services
			Motor vehicles & car bodies	0.2	Manufg.
			Newspapers	0.2	Manufg.
			Nonfarm residential structure maintenance	0.2	Constr.
			Office buildings	0.2	Constr.
			Oil bearing crops	0.2	Agric.
			Photographic equipment & supplies	0.2	Manufg.
			Radio & TV broadcasting	0.2	Util.
			Radio & TV communication equipment	0.2	Manufg.
			Railroads & related services	0.2	Util.
			Residential 1-unit structures, nonfarm	0.2	Constr.
			Semiconductors & related devices	0.2	Manufg.
			Water transportation	0.2	Util.

Continued on next page.

INPUTS AND OUTPUTS FOR ALL BANKING SECTORS - SICs 601, 602, 603, 608, and 609 - Continued

Economic Sector or Industry Providing Inputs	%	Sector	Economic Sector or Industry Buying Outputs	%	Sector
			Arrangement of passenger transportation	0.1	Util.
			Automotive repair shops & services	0.1	Services
			Blast furnaces & steel mills	0.1	Manufg.
			Bottled & canned soft drinks	0.1	Manufg.
			Business services nec	0.1	Services
			Commercial printing	0.1	Manufg.
			Cyclic crudes and organics	0.1	Manufg.
			Equipment rental & leasing services	0.1	Services
			Food grains	0.1	Agric.
			Malt beverages	0.1	Manufg.
			Metal office furniture	0.1	Manufg.
			Miscellaneous plastics products	0.1	Manufg.
			Motion pictures	0.1	Services
			Pipe, valves, & pipe fittings	0.1	Manufg.
			Pipelines, except natural gas	0.1	Util.
			Portrait, photographic studios	0.1	Services
			Prepared feeds, nec	0.1	Manufg.
			Primary aluminum	0.1	Manufg.
			Residential additions/alterations, nonfarm	0.1	Constr.

Source: Benchmark Input-Output Accounts for the U.S. Economy, 1982, U.S. Department of Commerce, Washington, D.C., July 1991. Data, as reported in the source, are organized by the 1977 SIC structure in use in 1982 but have been matched, as closely as is possible, to the 1987 SIC structure used in this book. Activities with the same percentage are sorted alphabetically by name of activity.

OCCUPATIONS EMPLOYED BY BANKING AND CLOSELY RELATED FUNCTIONS, NEC

Occupation	% of Total 1994	Change to 2005	Occupation	% of Total 1994	Change to 2005
Bank tellers	8.1	32.9	Clerical support workers nec	2.4	6.3
General office clerks	7.2	13.3	Loan officers & counselors	2.3	45.0
Management support workers nec	6.8	32.9	Computer programmers	2.2	7.6
Clerical supervisors & managers	5.8	35.9	Systems analysts	2.1	112.6
Adjustment clerks	5.0	79.4	Sales & related workers nec	2.0	32.9
Secretaries, ex legal & medical	4.2	21.0	Credit analysts	1.9	6.3
Cashiers	4.2	29.6	Securities & financial services sales workers	1.7	32.8
Bookkeeping, accounting, & auditing clerks	3.8	-0.3	Managers & administrators nec	1.5	32.8
General managers & top executives	3.7	26.1	Data entry keyers, ex composing	1.5	-2.0
Financial managers	3.2	32.9	Computer operators, ex peripheral equipment	1.4	-24.5
Accountants & auditors	3.1	32.9	Guards	1.1	19.6
Duplicating, mail, & office machine operators	2.7	-22.5	Brokerage clerks	1.0	46.2
Loan & credit clerks	2.7	19.6			

Sources: Industry-Occupation Matrix, Bureau of Labor Statistics. These data relate to one or more 3-digit SIC industry groups rather than to a single 4-digit SIC. The change reported for each occupation to the year 2005 is a percent of growth or decline as estimated by the Bureau of Labor Statistics. The abbreviation nec stands for not elsewhere classified.

U.S. AND STATE DATA ON INDUSTRY REVENUES AND OTHER ACCOUNTS FOR 1992

State	No. of Estab.	Employ-ment	Payroll ($ mil.)	Revenues ($ mil.)	Empl./ Estab.	Revenue/ Estab. ($)	Payroll/ Estab. ($)	Revenue/ Empl. ($)	Payroll/ Empl. ($)
UNITED STATES	632	34,310	2,263.5	62,689.7	54	99,192,587	3,581,492	1,827,156	65,972
California	126	3,385	211.4	9,869.5	27	78,329,452	1,678,040	2,915,661	62,462
Colorado	1	-	(D)	(D)	(D)	(D)	(D)	(D)	(D)
Florida	58	2,236	89.1	1,206.1	39	20,794,897	1,536,655	539,403	39,860
Georgia	18	337	21.5	922.4	19	51,243,667	1,191,944	2,737,050	63,665
Illinois	55	2,011	122.4	4,296.6	37	78,120,109	2,225,673	2,136,552	60,871
Massachusetts	7	-	(D)	(D)	(D)	(D)	(D)	(D)	(D)
New Jersey	2	-	(D)	(D)	(D)	(D)	(D)	(D)	(D)
New York	307	25,009	1,749.3	45,073.6	81	146,819,577	5,698,036	1,802,296	69,947
North Carolina	1	-	(D)	(D)	(D)	(D)	(D)	(D)	(D)
Pennsylvania	7	303	10.0	153.8	43	21,976,429	1,433,429	507,706	33,116
Texas	25	439	26.1	524.4	18	20,974,880	1,045,120	1,194,469	59,517
Washington	8	154	8.0	181.8	19	22,721,125	999,250	1,180,318	51,909
Wisconsin	1	-	(D)	(D)	(D)	(D)	(D)	(D)	(D)

Source: 1992 Economic Census, U.S. Department of Commerce, Washington, D.C. This is the only table that shows revenue data as collected by the Bureau of the Census in an Economic Census. The symbol (D) indicates that data are withheld by the source to avoid disclosure of competitive information. A dash (-) indicates that data are not available or cannot be calculated.

ESTABLISHMENTS 1992 - STATE AND REGIONAL CONCENTRATION

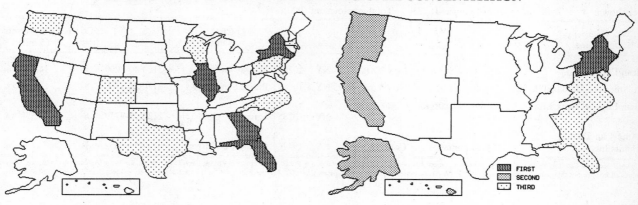

EMPLOYMENT 1992 - STATE AND REGIONAL CONCENTRATION

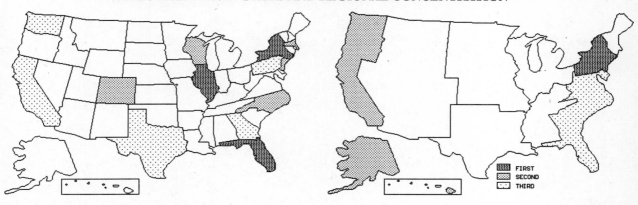

REVENUES 1992 - STATE AND REGIONAL CONCENTRATION

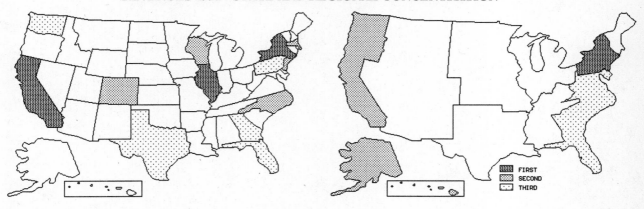

States with the darkest shading indicate those states which have proportionately more establishments, employment, or revenues than would be indicated by the state's population. States with light shading are states with proportionately fewer establishments, less employment, and lower revenues than population distribution. States shaded grey are within 15 percent of the state's population proportion in these categories. States for which no data are available are shown as average (grey). *Regions* are shaded to indicate absolute rank in the category. If no data for the category are available, establishment counts are used to shade the regions. Source of the data is the table on the facing page.

LEADING COMPANIES - SIC 6082 - Foreign Trade & International Banks

Number shown: **4**   Total sales/assets ($ mil): **41,733**   Total employment (000): **76.7**

Company Name	Address				CEO Name	Phone	Co. Type	Sales/Assets ($ mil)	Empl. (000)
American Express Co.	200 Vesey St.	New York	NY	10285	Harvey Golub	212-640-2000	P	14,282 OR	72.4
French American Banking Corp.	P.O. Box 127	New York	NY	10008	Pierre Schneider	212-978-5700	S	13,890 TA	0.3
American Express Bank Ltd.	American Express Twr.	New York	NY	10285	Steven D. Goldstein	212-298-3759	S	13,559 TA	4.0
Euro American Trading Merchants Inc.	37 Centennial St.	Collegeville	PA	19426	Herbert D. Moyer	610-454-0854	R	2 OR	<0.1

Source: *Ward's Business Directory of U.S. Private and Public Companies*, 1996. Company type codes: P - Public, R - Private, S - Subsidiary, D - Division, J - Joint Venture, A - Affiliate, G - Group. If the dollar values shown are not sales, the following codes apply: TA - Total Assets; OR - Operating Revenues; GB - Gross Billings. * - estimated dollar value. < - less than; *na* - not available.

SIC 6090

FUNCTIONS CLOSELY RELATED TO BANKING

This grouping includes Nondeposit Trust Facilities (SIC 6091) and Functions Related to Depository Banking, not elsewhere classified (SIC 6099).

The trust companies included in SIC 6091 are engaged in fiduciary business (managing funds entrusted to them by others) but not regularly engaged in deposit banking. Some of these establishments hold limited amounts of special types of deposits; their uninvested trust funds are also classified as deposits; but they are not engaged in conventional banking. Trusts may have either national or state charters. Title insurance companies—which operate under charters that limit them to real estate title or mortgage loan activities—are classified as SIC 6361 and are not included here.

SIC 6099 includes a wide range of functions related to deposit banking, including automated clearinghouses, check cashing agencies, check clearinghouse associations, deposit brokers, electronic funds transfer, escrow institutions other than real estate, fiduciary agencies which are not trusts or real estate, foreign currency exchanges, money order issuers, regional clearinghouse associations, representatives of foreign banks that are not agencies or branches, safe deposit companies, tax certificate sale and redemption agencies, and travelers' check issuers.

ESTABLISHMENTS, EMPLOYMENT, AND PAYROLL

	1988	1989 Value	%	1990 Value	%	1991 Value	%	1992 Value	%	1993 Value	%	% change 88-93
All Establishments	2,598	2,275	-12.4	2,778	22.1	3,790	36.4	4,515	19.1	4,692	3.9	80.6
Mid-March Employment	37,877	40,013	5.6	43,937	9.8	48,428	10.2	50,898	5.1	45,967	-9.7	21.4
1st Quarter Wages (annualized - $ mil.)	1,043.3	1,248.3	19.7	1,404.0	12.5	1,649.7	17.5	1,801.4	9.2	1,554.6	-13.7	49.0
Payroll per Emp. 1st Q. (annualized)	27,544	31,198	13.3	31,956	2.4	34,064	6.6	35,393	3.9	33,820	-4.4	22.8
Annual Payroll ($ mil.)	1,038.8	1,243.1	19.7	1,362.8	9.6	1,567.2	15.0	1,735.7	10.7	1,637.2	-5.7	57.6
Establishments - 1-4 Emp. Number	1,431	1,239	-13.4	1,626	31.2	2,392	47.1	2,959	23.7	2,971	0.4	107.6
Mid-March Employment	(D)	2,665	-	3,316	24.4	5,035	51.8	6,190	22.9	6,681	7.9	-
1st Quarter Wages (annualized - $ mil.)	(D)	53.7	-	72.9	35.6	105.0	44.2	135.9	29.4	142.4	4.8	-
Payroll per Emp. 1st Q. (annualized)	(D)	20,167	-	21,976	9.0	20,864	-5.1	21,956	5.2	21,311	-2.9	-
Annual Payroll ($ mil.)	(D)	64.6	-	88.9	37.6	127.6	43.4	146.0	14.4	164.9	13.0	-
Establishments - 5-9 Emp. Number	635	535	-15.7	597	11.6	896	50.1	1,026	14.5	1,149	12.0	80.9
Mid-March Employment	4,191	(D)	-	3,881	-	5,549	43.0	6,395	15.2	7,333	14.7	75.0
1st Quarter Wages (annualized - $ mil.)	83.9	(D)	-	86.9	-	113.8	31.0	134.4	18.1	147.4	9.6	75.6
Payroll per Emp. 1st Q. (annualized)	20,024	(D)	-	22,395	-	20,513	-8.4	21,023	2.5	20,101	-4.4	0.4
Annual Payroll ($ mil.)	93.0	(D)	-	91.9	-	116.8	27.1	136.3	16.7	160.3	17.7	72.3
Establishments - 10-19 Emp. Number	263	252	-4.2	277	9.9	250	-9.7	272	8.8	(D)	-	-
Mid-March Employment	3,470	3,306	-4.7	3,676	11.2	(D)	-	3,458	-	(D)	-	-
1st Quarter Wages (annualized - $ mil.)	79.4	87.6	10.3	100.3	14.4	(D)	-	105.8	-	(D)	-	-
Payroll per Emp. 1st Q. (annualized)	22,891	26,502	15.8	27,275	2.9	(D)	-	30,595	-	(D)	-	-
Annual Payroll ($ mil.)	85.4	90.5	6.0	98.4	8.7	(D)	-	106.9	-	(D)	-	-
Establishments - 20-49 Emp. Number	145	124	-14.5	151	21.8	131	-13.2	138	5.3	169	22.5	16.6
Mid-March Employment	(D)	3,702	-	4,489	21.3	4,110	-8.4	4,337	5.5	5,044	16.3	-
1st Quarter Wages (annualized - $ mil.)	(D)	106.2	-	138.3	30.3	152.8	10.5	173.3	13.4	210.8	21.6	-
Payroll per Emp. 1st Q. (annualized)	(D)	28,679	-	30,812	7.4	37,186	20.7	39,970	7.5	41,786	4.5	-
Annual Payroll ($ mil.)	(D)	108.2	-	131.2	21.2	144.5	10.2	161.0	11.4	227.6	41.4	-
Establishments - 50-99 Emp. Number	68	67	-1.5	58	-13.4	45	-22.4	53	17.8	59	11.3	-13.2
Mid-March Employment	4,630	4,604	-0.6	3,963	-13.9	2,943	-25.7	3,724	26.5	3,789	1.7	-18.2
1st Quarter Wages (annualized - $ mil.)	126.0	130.8	3.8	144.3	10.3	139.8	-3.2	184.8	32.2	168.1	-9.0	33.4
Payroll per Emp. 1st Q. (annualized)	27,218	28,407	4.4	36,418	28.2	47,486	30.4	49,613	4.5	44,374	-10.6	63.0
Annual Payroll ($ mil.)	118.1	127.4	7.9	125.9	-1.2	126.9	0.8	167.1	31.7	148.7	-11.0	25.9
Establishments - 100-249 Emp. Number	31	32	3.2	42	31.3	38	-9.5	30	-21.1	35	16.7	12.9
Mid-March Employment	4,294	4,957	15.4	6,382	28.7	6,003	-5.9	4,770	-20.5	5,391	13.0	25.5
1st Quarter Wages (annualized - $ mil.)	133.5	159.8	19.7	214.1	34.0	217.9	1.8	170.1	-21.9	236.0	38.7	76.8
Payroll per Emp. 1st Q. (annualized)	31,090	32,228	3.7	33,555	4.1	36,301	8.2	35,670	-1.7	43,784	22.7	40.8
Annual Payroll ($ mil.)	122.6	146.5	19.6	207.1	41.3	188.5	-9.0	170.3	-9.6	276.6	62.4	125.6
Establishments - 250-499 Emp. Number	12	14	16.7	13	-7.1	17	30.8	(D)	-	11	-	-8.3
Mid-March Employment	4,234	5,120	20.9	4,985	-2.6	6,019	20.7	(D)	-	3,913	-	-7.6
1st Quarter Wages (annualized - $ mil.)	139.1	157.9	13.5	133.0	-15.8	214.9	61.6	(D)	-	105.0	-	-24.5
Payroll per Emp. 1st Q. (annualized)	32,863	30,845	-6.1	26,682	-13.5	35,706	33.8	(D)	-	26,840	-	-18.3
Annual Payroll ($ mil.)	119.6	153.7	28.5	134.1	-12.7	203.5	51.7	(D)	-	100.1	-	-16.3
Establishments - 500-999 Emp. Number	10	9	-10.0	10	11.1	19	90.0	13	-31.6	10	-23.1	-
Mid-March Employment	6,092	6,339	4.1	6,923	9.2	13,237	91.2	9,874	-25.4	6,939	-29.7	13.9
1st Quarter Wages (annualized - $ mil.)	165.9	246.9	48.8	290.8	17.8	523.8	80.1	362.6	-30.8	293.2	-19.1	76.8
Payroll per Emp. 1st Q. (annualized)	27,232	38,949	43.0	42,006	7.8	39,574	-5.8	36,720	-7.2	42,258	15.1	55.2
Annual Payroll ($ mil.)	165.6	236.2	42.6	257.3	9.0	483.9	88.0	349.4	-27.8	273.9	-21.6	65.4
Estab. - 1000 or More Emp. Number	3	3	-	4	33.3	2	-50.0	(D)	-	(D)	-	-
Mid-March Employment	(D)	(D)	-	6,322	-	(D)	-	(D)	-	(D)	-	-
1st Quarter Wages (annualized - $ mil.)	(D)	(D)	-	223.4	-	(D)	-	(D)	-	(D)	-	-
Payroll per Emp. 1st Q. (annualized)	(D)	(D)	-	35,335	-	(D)	-	(D)	-	(D)	-	-
Annual Payroll ($ mil.)	(D)	(D)	-	228.1	-	(D)	-	(D)	-	(D)	-	-

Source: County Business Patterns, U.S. Department of Commerce, Washington, D.C., for 1988 through 1993. Payroll per employee is calculated using mid-March employment and 1st Quarter wages, annualized. Annual payroll, also shown, may not equal the annualized 1st Quarter wages. Columns headed by a percent sign (%) indicate change from the previous year. na stands for not available. The symbol (D) indicates that data are withheld by the source to avoid disclosure of competitive information. A dash (-) indicates that data are not available or cannot be calculated.

ESTABLISHMENTS
Number

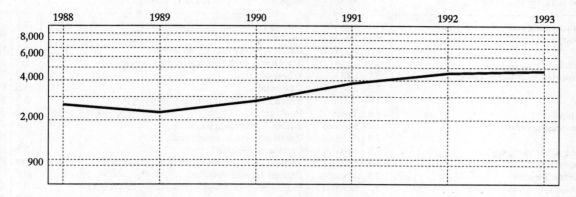

MID-MARCH EMPLOYMENT
Number

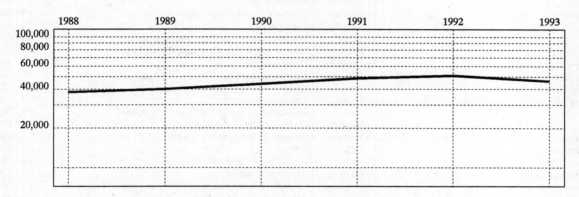

ANNUAL PAYROLL
$ million

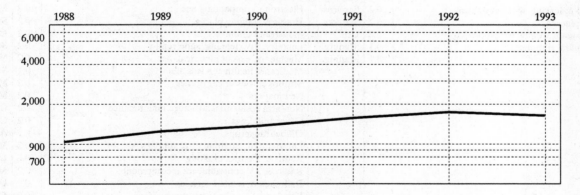

INPUTS AND OUTPUTS FOR ALL BANKING SECTORS - SICs 601, 602, 603, 608, and 609

Economic Sector or Industry Providing Inputs	%	Sector	Economic Sector or Industry Buying Outputs	%	Sector
Computer & data processing services	13.3	Services	Personal consumption expenditures	43.5	
Security & commodity brokers	10.1	Fin/R.E.	Exports	5.3	Foreign
Real estate	8.0	Fin/R.E.	Credit agencies other than banks	4.5	Fin/R.E.
Communications, except radio & TV	5.9	Util.	S/L Govt. purch., other general government	3.7	S/L Govt
Motor freight transportation & warehousing	5.8	Util.	Wholesale trade	3.7	Trade
Banking	5.7	Fin/R.E.	Real estate	3.6	Fin/R.E.
U.S. Postal Service	4.7	Gov't	Retail trade, except eating & drinking	3.3	Trade
Eating & drinking places	4.5	Trade	Banking	1.9	Fin/R.E.
Equipment rental & leasing services	3.4	Services	Eating & drinking places	1.4	Trade
Advertising	2.9	Services	Communications, except radio & TV	1.1	Util.
Accounting, auditing & bookkeeping	2.8	Services	Petroleum refining	1.1	Manufg.
Maintenance of nonfarm buildings nec	2.8	Constr.	Federal Government purchases, nondefense	1.0	Fed Govt
Blankbooks & looseleaf binders	2.5	Manufg.	Electric services (utilities)	0.9	Util.
Management & consulting services & labs	2.4	Services	Engineering, architectural, & surveying services	0.7	Services
Federal Government enterprises nec	2.1	Gov't	Meat animals	0.7	Agric.
Insurance carriers	2.1	Fin/R.E.	Aircraft	0.6	Manufg.
Photographic equipment & supplies	1.7	Manufg.	Apparel made from purchased materials	0.5	Manufg.
Electric services (utilities)	1.6	Util.	Crude petroleum & natural gas	0.5	Mining
Detective & protective services	1.5	Services	Gas production & distribution (utilities)	0.5	Util.
Legal services	1.4	Services	Insurance carriers	0.5	Fin/R.E.
Noncomparable imports	1.4	Foreign	Electronic computing equipment	0.4	Manufg.
Petroleum refining	1.2	Manufg.	Feed grains	0.4	Agric.
Wholesale trade	1.2	Trade	Maintenance of nonfarm buildings nec	0.4	Constr.
Manifold business forms	1.0	Manufg.	Motor freight transportation & warehousing	0.4	Util.
Credit agencies other than banks	0.9	Fin/R.E.	Dairy farm products	0.3	Agric.
Personnel supply services	0.9	Services	Doctors & dentists	0.3	Services
Business/professional associations	0.8	Services	Drugs	0.3	Manufg.
Commercial printing	0.8	Manufg.	Freight forwarders	0.3	Util.
Air transportation	0.6	Util.	Management & consulting services & labs	0.3	Services
Envelopes	0.6	Manufg.	Owner-occupied dwellings	0.3	Fin/R.E.
Electrical repair shops	0.4	Services	Security & commodity brokers	0.3	Fin/R.E.
Transit & bus transportation	0.4	Util.	Advertising	0.2	Services
Electronic components nec	0.3	Manufg.	Agricultural chemicals, nec	0.2	Manufg.
Electronic computing equipment	0.3	Manufg.	Air transportation	0.2	Util.
Engraving & plate printing	0.3	Manufg.	Aircraft & missile engines & engine parts	0.2	Manufg.
Manufacturing industries, nec	0.3	Manufg.	Aircraft & missile equipment, nec	0.2	Manufg.
Paper mills, except building paper	0.3	Manufg.	Broadwoven fabric mills	0.2	Manufg.
Periodicals	0.3	Manufg.	Chemical & fertilizer mineral	0.2	Mining
Services to dwellings & other buildings	0.3	Services	Coal	0.2	Mining
Textile bags	0.3	Manufg.	Computer & data processing services	0.2	Services
Automotive rental & leasing, without drivers	0.2	Services	Electronic components nec	0.2	Manufg.
Hotels & lodging places	0.2	Services	Hotels & lodging places	0.2	Services
Sanitary services, steam supply, irrigation	0.2	Util.	Industrial buildings	0.2	Constr.
Carbon paper & inked ribbons	0.1	Manufg.	Laundry, dry cleaning, shoe repair	0.2	Services
Newspapers	0.1	Manufg.	Machinery, except electrical, nec	0.2	Manufg.
			Medical & health services, nec	0.2	Services
			Motor vehicles & car bodies	0.2	Manufg.
			Newspapers	0.2	Manufg.
			Nonfarm residential structure maintenance	0.2	Constr.
			Office buildings	0.2	Constr.
			Oil bearing crops	0.2	Agric.
			Photographic equipment & supplies	0.2	Manufg.
			Radio & TV broadcasting	0.2	Util.
			Radio & TV communication equipment	0.2	Manufg.
			Railroads & related services	0.2	Util.
			Residential 1-unit structures, nonfarm	0.2	Constr.
			Semiconductors & related devices	0.2	Manufg.
			Water transportation	0.2	Util.

Continued on next page.

INPUTS AND OUTPUTS FOR ALL BANKING SECTORS - SICs 601, 602, 603, 608, and 609 - Continued

Economic Sector or Industry Providing Inputs	%	Sector	Economic Sector or Industry Buying Outputs	%	Sector
			Arrangement of passenger transportation	0.1	Util.
			Automotive repair shops & services	0.1	Services
			Blast furnaces & steel mills	0.1	Manufg.
			Bottled & canned soft drinks	0.1	Manufg.
			Business services nec	0.1	Services
			Commercial printing	0.1	Manufg.
			Cyclic crudes and organics	0.1	Manufg.
			Equipment rental & leasing services	0.1	Services
			Food grains	0.1	Agric.
			Malt beverages	0.1	Manufg.
			Metal office furniture	0.1	Manufg.
			Miscellaneous plastics products	0.1	Manufg.
			Motion pictures	0.1	Services
			Pipe, valves, & pipe fittings	0.1	Manufg.
			Pipelines, except natural gas	0.1	Util.
			Portrait, photographic studios	0.1	Services
			Prepared feeds, nec	0.1	Manufg.
			Primary aluminum	0.1	Manufg.
			Residential additions/alterations, nonfarm	0.1	Constr.

Source: Benchmark Input-Output Accounts for the U.S. Economy, 1982, U.S. Department of Commerce, Washington, D.C., July 1991. Data, as reported in the source, are organized by the 1977 SIC structure in use in 1982 but have been matched, as closely as is possible, to the 1987 SIC structure used in this book. Activities with the same percentage are sorted alphabetically by name of activity.

OCCUPATIONS EMPLOYED BY BANKING AND CLOSELY RELATED FUNCTIONS, NEC

Occupation	% of Total 1994	Change to 2005	Occupation	% of Total 1994	Change to 2005
Bank tellers	8.1	32.9	Clerical support workers nec	2.4	6.3
General office clerks	7.2	13.3	Loan officers & counselors	2.3	45.0
Management support workers nec	6.8	32.9	Computer programmers	2.2	7.6
Clerical supervisors & managers	5.8	35.9	Systems analysts	2.1	112.6
Adjustment clerks	5.0	79.4	Sales & related workers nec	2.0	32.9
Secretaries, ex legal & medical	4.2	21.0	Credit analysts	1.9	6.3
Cashiers	4.2	29.6	Securities & financial services sales workers	1.7	32.8
Bookkeeping, accounting, & auditing clerks	3.8	-0.3	Managers & administrators nec	1.5	32.8
General managers & top executives	3.7	26.1	Data entry keyers, ex composing	1.5	-2.0
Financial managers	3.2	32.9	Computer operators, ex peripheral equipment	1.4	-24.5
Accountants & auditors	3.1	32.9	Guards	1.1	19.6
Duplicating, mail, & office machine operators	2.7	-22.5	Brokerage clerks	1.0	46.2
Loan & credit clerks	2.7	19.6			

Sources: Industry-Occupation Matrix, Bureau of Labor Statistics. These data relate to one or more 3-digit SIC industry groups rather than to a single 4-digit SIC. The change reported for each occupation to the year 2005 is a percent of growth or decline as estimated by the Bureau of Labor Statistics. The abbreviation nec stands for not elsewhere classified.

U.S. AND STATE DATA ON INDUSTRY REVENUES AND OTHER ACCOUNTS FOR 1992

State	No. of Estab.	Employ- ment	Payroll ($ mil.)	Revenues ($ mil.)	Empl./ Estab.	Revenue/ Estab. ($)	Payroll/ Estab. ($)	Revenue/ Empl. ($)	Payroll/ Empl. ($)
UNITED STATES	4,836	51,708	1,681.3	8,006.1	11	1,655,527	347,673	154,833	32,516
California	929	7,104	302.7	1,042.8	8	1,122,544	325,864	146,797	42,614
Colorado	83	-	(D)	(D)	(D)	(D)	(D)	(D)	(D)
Florida	310	2,508	76.0	366.1	8	1,180,816	245,187	145,954	30,306
Georgia	136	975	29.1	119.9	7	881,574	214,206	122,968	29,879
Illinois	662	5,152	139.5	442.1	8	667,810	210,745	85,809	27,079
Indiana	25	121	2.7	10.6	5	422,120	107,240	87,215	22,157
Maryland	75	-	(D)	(D)	(D)	(D)	(D)	(D)	(D)
Massachusetts	58	-	(D)	(D)	(D)	(D)	(D)	(D)	(D)
Michigan	59	342	6.3	26.3	6	445,102	107,102	76,787	18,477
Minnesota	49	1,717	51.5	263.7	35	5,382,510	1,050,531	153,607	29,980
Missouri	59	3,082	82.9	282.7	52	4,791,254	1,405,407	91,721	26,904
New Jersey	110	-	(D)	(D)	(D)	(D)	(D)	(D)	(D)
New York	555	9,871	407.5	1,242.8	18	2,239,294	734,229	125,905	41,282
North Carolina	62	-	(D)	(D)	(D)	(D)	(D)	(D)	(D)
Ohio	112	1,051	26.7	145.4	9	1,298,446	238,714	138,369	25,439
Pennsylvania	176	1,476	42.9	157.6	8	895,574	243,835	106,789	29,075
Tennessee	46	-	(D)	(D)	(D)	(D)	(D)	(D)	(D)
Texas	518	2,264	51.3	481.6	4	929,707	98,975	212,716	22,645
Virginia	74	887	27.6	178.7	12	2,415,324	372,527	201,504	31,079
Washington	106	792	25.5	135.5	7	1,278,057	240,528	171,053	32,192
Wisconsin	47	-	(D)	(D)	(D)	(D)	(D)	(D)	(D)

Source: 1992 Economic Census, U.S. Department of Commerce, Washington, D.C. This is the only table that shows revenue data as collected by the Bureau of the Census in an Economic Census. The symbol (D) indicates that data are withheld by the source to avoid disclosure of competitive information. A dash (-) indicates that data are not available or cannot be calculated.

ESTABLISHMENTS 1992 - STATE AND REGIONAL CONCENTRATION

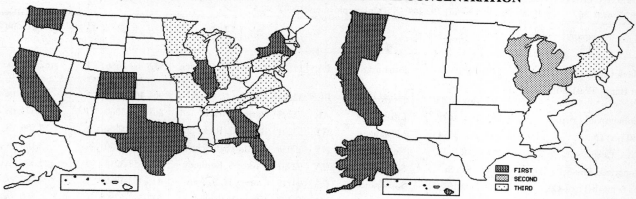

EMPLOYMENT 1992 - STATE AND REGIONAL CONCENTRATION

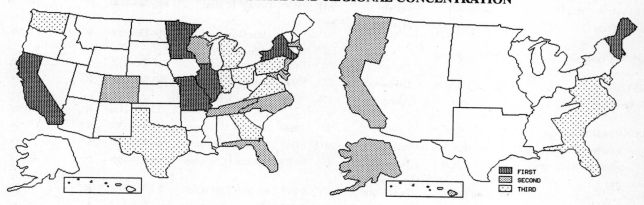

REVENUES 1992 - STATE AND REGIONAL CONCENTRATION

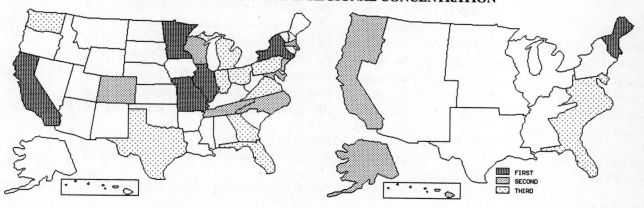

States with the darkest shading indicate those states which have proportionately more establishments, employment, or revenues than would be indicated by the state's population. States with light shading are states with proportionately fewer establishments, less employment, and lower revenues than population distribution. States shaded grey are within 15 percent of the state's population proportion in these categories. States for which no data are available are shown as average (grey). *Regions* are shaded to indicate absolute rank in the category. If no data for the category are available, establishment counts are used to shade the regions. Source of the data is the table on the facing page.

LEADING COMPANIES - SIC 6091 - Nondeposit Trust Facilities

Number shown: **36**   Total sales/assets ($ mil): **92,069**   Total employment (000): **42.6**

Company Name	Address				CEO Name	Phone	Co. Type	Sales/Assets ($ mil)	Empl. (000)
PNC Bank Corp.	1 PNC Plz.	Pittsburgh	PA	15222	Thomas H. O'Brien	412-762-2666	P	62,080 TA	21.1
Barnett Banks Trust Company N.A.	P.O. Box 40200	Jacksonville	FL	32203	Michael C. Baker	904-464-2877	S	13,000 TA	0.6
First Commercial Corp.	P.O. Box 1471	Little Rock	AR	72203	Barnett Grace	501-371-7000	P	4,374 TA	3.5
Firstar Trust Co.	P.O. Box 2054	Milwaukee	WI	53201	Blaine E. Rieke	414-765-5000	S	3,500 TA	0.5
U.S. Trust Corp.	114 W. 47th St.	New York	NY	10036	H. Marshall Schwarz	212-852-1000	P	3,186 TA	1.9
First American Financial Corp.	114 E. 5th St.	Santa Ana	CA	92701	Parker S. Kennedy	714-558-3211	P	1,398 TA	10.7
Charles Schwab Trust Co.	P.O. Box 193931	San Francisco	CA	94119	Harvey A. Rowen	415-403-5999	S	1,200 TA	<0.1
Piper Trust Co.	222 S. 9th St.	Minneapolis	MN	55402	Karen M. Bohn	612-342-6290	S	800 TA	<0.1
Participants Trust Co.	40 Rector St.	New York	NY	10006	John Sceppa	212-312-6500	R	326 TA	0.1
Capital Guardian Trust Co.	333 S. Hope St.	Los Angeles	CA	90071	James F. Rothenberg	213-486-9200	S	320 TA*	0.2
Great Bay Bankshares Inc.	P.O. Box 919	Dover	NH	03820	Donald R. Hatt	603-749-4149	P	319 TA	0.2
Boatmen's Trust Co.	1 Boatmen's Plz.	St. Louis	MO	63102	John Peters MacCarthy	314-231-9300	S	314 TA	1.1
Pennsylvania Trust Co.	100 Matsonford Rd.	Radnor	PA	19087	Richardson T. Merriman	215-975-4300	S	270 TA	<0.1
GEMISYS Corp.	3605 S. Teller St.	Lakewood	CO	80235	Darrall E. Robbins	303-969-6000	R	220 TA*	0.1
Austin Trust Co.	100 Congress Ave.	Austin	TX	78701	William J. Hudspeth Jr.	512-478-2121	R	175 TA	<0.1
LaSalle National Trust N.A.	P.O. Box 729	Chicago	IL	60690	James B. Wynsma	312-443-2300	S	157 TA	0.2
Investors Fiduciary Trust Co.	127 W. 10th St.	Kansas City	MO	64105	Thomas McCrossan	816-474-8786	S	87 TA	0.3
Trust Company of Washington	P.O. Box 3096	Bellevue	WA	98009	William H. Sperber	206-637-1856	R	85 TA	<0.1
American Stock Transfer and Trust Co.	40 Wall St.	New York	NY	10005	Michael Karfunkel	212-936-5100	R	66 OR*	0.2
Marshall and Ilsley Trust Co.	1000 N. Water St.	Milwaukee	WI	53202	Morry O. Birnbaum	414-765-8200	S	47 TA	0.3
First Trust Corp.	717 17th St.	Denver	CO	80202	Gordon Rockafellow	303-293-2223	S	35 TA	0.6
Huntington Trust Company N.A.	41 S. High St.	Columbus	OH	43218	Norman A. Jacobs	614-480-5345	S	24 TA	0.3
Fleet Trust Co.	45 East Ave.	Rochester	NY	14604	Sandra M. Democh	716-546-9085	S	24 TA	0.2
Columbian Financial Corp.	4701 W. 110th St.	Overland Park	KS	66211	Sam McCaffree	913-491-1061	R	20 TA	<0.1
IAA Trust Co.	808 IAA Dr.	Bloomington	IL	61701	John White Jr.	309-557-2111	S	11 TA	<0.1
Imperial Trust Co.	201 N. Figueroa	Los Angeles	CA	90012	Michael J. Vaughan	213-627-5600	S	6 TA	<0.1
North American Trust Co.	P.O. Box 84419	San Diego	CA	92138	L. Mark Fingerl	619-891-5378	S	5 TA	<0.1
Amcore Trust Co.	501 7th St.	Rockford	IL	61110	Glen Wilson	815-961-7119	S	4 TA	<0.1
NBD Trust Company of Florida N.A.	11300 U.S. Hwy. 1	North Palm Beach	FL	33408	Frederick H. Gravelle	407-627-9400	S	3 TA	<0.1
AmalgaTrust Company Inc.	1 W. Monroe St.	Chicago	IL	60603	Eugene P. Heytow	312-822-3162	S	3 TA	<0.1
Camelback Trust Co.	7373 N. Scottsdale Rd.	Scottsdale	AZ	85253	Chris Olson	602-955-2829	S	3 TA*	<0.1
First Midwest Trust Company N.A.	121 N. Chicago St.	Joliet	IL	60431	Paul Gantzert	815-740-7700	S	2 TA	<0.1
Constitution Trust Co.	P.O. Box 1049	Dover	NH	03820	John D. Griffiths	603-749-0303	S	1 TA	<0.1
Columbian Trust Co.	4701 W. 110th St.	Overland Park	KS	66211	Carl McCaffree	913-491-1061	S	1 TA	<0.1

Company type codes: P - Public, R - Private, S - Subsidiary, D - Division, J - Joint Venture, A - Affiliate, G - Group. If the dollar values shown are not sales, the following codes apply: TA - Total Assets; OR - Operating Revenues; GB - Gross Billings. * - estimated dollar value. < - less than. *na* - not available.

Continued on next page.

LEADING COMPANIES - SIC 6091 - Nondeposit Trust Facilities
Continued

Company Name	Address				CEO Name	Phone	Co. Type	Sales/Assets ($ mil)	Empl. (000)
Security Trust Co.	925 B. St.	San Diego	CA	92101	J. Paul Spring	619-239-3091	S	1 TA	<0.1
First Trust of MidAmerica	410 W. 8th St.	Kansas City	MO	64105	Kevin R. Ingrem	816-221-6988	R	1 TA	<0.1

Source: Ward's Business Directory of U.S. Private and Public Companies, 1996. Company type codes: P - Public, R - Private, S - Subsidiary, D - Division, J - Joint Venture, A - Affiliate, G - Group. If the dollar values shown are not sales, the following codes apply: TA - Total Assets; OR - Operating Revenues; GB - Gross Billings. * - estimated dollar value. < - less than; *na* - not available.

LEADING COMPANIES - SIC 6099 - Functions Related to Deposit Banking
Number shown: **29**   Total sales/assets ($ mil): **100,917**   Total employment (000): **327.3**

Company Name	Address				CEO Name	Phone	Co. Type	Sales/Assets ($ mil)	Empl. (000)
AT and T Corp.	32 Avenue of the Americas	New York	NY	10013	Robert E. Allen	212-605-5500	P	67,156 OR	308.7
First Bank System Inc.	P.O. Box 522	Minneapolis	MN	55480	John F. Grundhofer	612-973-1111	P	26,219 TA	12.0
Student Loan Corp.	P.O. Box 22944	Pittsford	NY	14692	Stephen C. Biklen	716-248-7187	P	4,347 TA	0.7
HUBCO Inc.	1000 MacArthur Blvd.	Mahwah	NJ	07430	Kenneth T. Neilson	201-236-2600	P	1,377 TA	0.6
BTI Services Inc.	6420 S. Point Pkwy.	Jacksonville	FL	32216	David Graham	904-281-7100	S	840 TA*	0.5
Comdata Holdings Corp.	5301 Maryland Way	Brentwood	TN	37027	George L. McTavish	615-370-7000	P	283 TA	1.9
Electronic Transaction Corp.	19803 N. Creek Pkwy.	Bothell	WA	98011	Timothy C. Birk	206-365-6711	S	160 TA*	0.1
Plus System Inc.	P.O. Box 5060	Denver	CO	80217	Denny D. Dumler	303-486-7587	R	86 TA*	<0.1
Maestro Latin America Inc.	801 Brickell Ave.	Miami	FL	33131	Richard Child	305-539-2330	S	84 TA*	<0.1
ACE Cash Express Inc.	1231 Greenway Dr.	Irving	TX	75038	Raymond C. Hemming	214-550-5000	P	59 TA	0.9
Internet Inc.	11800 Sunrise Valley	Reston	VA	22091	David A. O'Conner	703-620-1000	R	50 TA*	<0.1
Checkfree Corp.	P.O. Box 897	Columbus	OH	43216	Peter J. Kight	614-898-6000	R	47*	0.3
National Payment Corp.	100 W. Kennedy Blvd.	Tampa	FL	33602	Timothy N. Tracey	813-222-0333	R	40 TA*	<0.1
Pay-O-Matic Corp.	160 Oak Dr.	Syosset	NY	11791	Rayman Mustafa	516-496-4900	P	38 TA	0.6
Noonan, Astley and Pearce Inc.	10 Exchange Pl.	Jersey City	NJ	07302	Joseph Sciametta	201-200-4500	S	37 TA*	0.3
Arizona Clearing House Association	P.O. Box 37967	Phoenix	AZ	85069	Paul Finch	602-995-6900	R	22 TA	<0.1
Financial Information Technologies Inc.	P.O. Box 3903	Tampa	FL	33601	Robert Christensen	813-273-9065	R	16 TA	<0.1
Michigan Safe Deposit Co.	30555 Northwestern Hwy	Farmington Hills	MI	48334	Doug Hexer	810-626-8998	R	16 TA	<0.1
Foreign Exchange Ltd.	415 Stockton St.	San Francisco	CA	94108	Randy Roberts	415-677-5107	S	11 TA	<0.1
Check Express Inc.	5201 W. Kennedy Blvd.	Tampa	FL	33609	Larry F. Lang	813-289-2888	P	7 TA	<0.1

Company type codes: P - Public, R - Private, S - Subsidiary, D - Division, J - Joint Venture, A - Affiliate, G - Group. If the dollar values shown are not sales, the following codes apply: TA - Total Assets; OR - Operating Revenues; GB - Gross Billings. * - estimated dollar value. < - less than. *na* - not available.

Continued on next page.

LEADING COMPANIES - SIC 6099 - Functions Related to Deposit Banking

Continued

Company Name	Address				CEO Name	Phone	Co. Type	Sales/Assets ($ mil)	Empl. (000)
Cash Station Inc.	188 W Randolph St 1405	Chicago	IL	60601	Stephen S. Cole	312-977-1150	R	6 TA	<0.1
Tele-Trip Company Inc.	Mutual of Omaha Plz.	Omaha	NE	68175	Tom Sawicz	402-351-5742	S	5 TA•	0.3
GulfNet Inc.	2250 Gause Blvd. E.	Slidell	LA	70461	Del R. Tonguette	504-643-0300	R	4 TA	<0.1
Balfour Investors Inc.	45 Rockefeller Plz.	New York	NY	10111	Harry Freund	212-489-7077	R	2 TA	<0.1
Cirrus System Inc.	1 Westbrook Corp. Ctr.	Westchester	IL	60154	G. Henry Mundt III	708-449-4000	S	2 TA•	<0.1
Money Access Service Corp.	25209 Country Club	North Olmsted	OH	44070	Steven E. Dawe	216-779-2100	S	1 TA	0.1
TeleCheck Inc.	3500 188th St. S.W.	Lynnwood	WA	98037	Judy Martin	206-775-3220	S	1 TA•	<0.1
Star System Inc.	401 W. A St.	San Diego	CA	92101	Ronald V. Congemi	619-234-4774	R	1 TA•	<0.1
Kansas Electronic Transfer System Inc.	1900 N. Amidon St.	Wichita	KS	67203	Richard Schopf	316-838-4411	R	0 TA	<0.1

Source: Ward's Business Directory of U.S. Private and Public Companies, 1996. Company type codes: P - Public, R - Private, S - Subsidiary, D - Division, J - Joint Venture, A - Affiliate, G - Group. If the dollar values shown are not sales, the following codes apply: TA - Total Assets; OR - Operating Revenues; GB - Gross Billings. • - estimated dollar value. < - less than; *na* - not available.

SIC 6110

FEDERAL & FEDERALLY SPONSORED CREDIT

This SIC groups federal agencies and those sponsored by the federal government engaged in guaranteeing, insuring, or making loans. Federally sponsored credit agencies are established under federal legislation but are not regarded as part of the federal government; they are often owned by their members or borrowers. The category includes banks for cooperatives, the Commodity Credit Corporation, Export-Import Bank, Farmers Home Administration, Federal Home Mortgage Corporation, Federal Intermediate Credit Bank, federal land banks, Federal National Mortgage Association, Government National Mortgage Association, National Consumer Cooperative Bank, Rural Electrification Administration, Student Loan Marketing Association, and the Synthetic Fuels Corporation.

ESTABLISHMENTS, EMPLOYMENT, AND PAYROLL

	1988	1989		1990		1991		1992		1993		% change 88-93
		Value	%	Value	%	Value	%	Value	%	Value	%	
All Establishments	2,754	581	-78.9	577	-0.7	787	36.4	828	5.2	1,375	66.1	-50.1
Mid-March Employment	88,652	17,802	-79.9	13,529	-24.0	16,147	19.4	15,351	-4.9	22,271	45.1	-74.9
1st Quarter Wages (annualized - $ mil.)	1,973.3	556.1	-71.8	422.3	-24.1	521.6	23.5	507.0	-2.8	1,014.7	100.2	-48.6
Payroll per Emp. 1st Q. (annualized)	22,259	31,238	40.3	31,218	-0.1	32,304	3.5	33,025	2.2	45,561	38.0	104.7
Annual Payroll ($ mil.)	2,051.5	513.0	-75.0	396.7	-22.7	498.2	25.6	485.0	-2.6	909.9	87.6	-55.6
Establishments - 1-4 Emp. Number	487	199	-59.1	220	10.6	337	53.2	396	17.5	664	67.7	36.3
Mid-March Employment	1,176	505	-57.1	588	16.4	(D)	-	1,077		1,857	72.4	57.9
1st Quarter Wages (annualized - $ mil.)	27.9	14.6	-47.8	16.8	15.3	(D)	-	31.0		58.2	87.8	108.6
Payroll per Emp. 1st Q. (annualized)	23,728	28,863	21.6	28,592	-0.9	(D)	-	28,769	-	31,341	8.9	32.1
Annual Payroll ($ mil.)	192.9	17.4	-91.0	19.3	11.0	(D)	-	31.0	-	62.1	100.5	-67.8
Establishments - 5-9 Emp. Number	437	153	-65.0	160	4.6	238	48.8	248	4.2	424	71.0	-3.0
Mid-March Employment	(D)	998	-	1,050	5.2	1,561	48.7	1,600	2.5	2,739	71.2	-
1st Quarter Wages (annualized - $ mil.)	(D)	28.4	-	28.0	-1.6	43.1	54.2	47.7	10.7	90.9	90.5	-
Payroll per Emp. 1st Q. (annualized)	(D)	28,493	-	26,636	-6.5	27,621	3.7	29,840	8.0	33,203	11.3	-
Annual Payroll ($ mil.)	(D)	26.9	-	27.7	2.8	44.1	59.6	48.4	9.6	84.9	75.5	-
Establishments - 10-19 Emp. Number	562	91	-83.8	83	-8.8	129	55.4	98	-24.0	167	70.4	-70.3
Mid-March Employment	7,796	1,227	-84.3	1,121	-8.6	1,654	47.5	1,250	-24.4	2,092	67.4	-73.2
1st Quarter Wages (annualized - $ mil.)	163.5	34.8	-78.7	32.7	-6.1	50.2	53.6	37.8	-24.6	80.6	113.1	-50.7
Payroll per Emp. 1st Q. (annualized)	20,970	28,346	35.2	29,128	2.8	30,326	4.1	30,250	-0.3	38,512	27.3	83.7
Annual Payroll ($ mil.)	170.2	34.0	-80.0	33.2	-2.2	48.2	44.9	40.4	-16.1	69.2	71.2	-59.3
Establishments - 20-49 Emp. Number	803	74	-90.8	64	-13.5	44	-31.3	51	15.9	75	47.1	-90.7
Mid-March Employment	25,121	2,282	-90.9	1,956	-14.3	1,224	-37.4	1,394	13.9	2,011	44.3	-92.0
1st Quarter Wages (annualized - $ mil.)	523.2	86.3	-83.5	72.8	-15.6	49.1	-32.5	61.1	24.3	82.1	34.4	-84.3
Payroll per Emp. 1st Q. (annualized)	20,828	37,825	81.6	37,243	-1.5	40,150	7.8	43,825	9.2	40,829	-6.8	96.0
Annual Payroll ($ mil.)	512.7	69.2	-86.5	61.4	-11.3	48.6	-20.8	53.7	10.6	70.4	31.0	-86.3
Establishments - 50-99 Emp. Number	310	32	-89.7	24	-25.0	14	-41.7	10	-28.6	17	70.0	-94.5
Mid-March Employment	21,405	2,114	-90.1	1,584	-25.1	(D)	-	675	-	1,190	76.3	-94.4
1st Quarter Wages (annualized - $ mil.)	449.2	67.4	-85.0	54.1	-19.7	(D)	-	22.6	-	54.4	141.3	-87.9
Payroll per Emp. 1st Q. (annualized)	20,985	31,864	51.8	34,167	7.2	(D)	-	33,416	-	45,738	36.9	118.0
Annual Payroll ($ mil.)	426.6	60.3	-85.9	46.5	-22.9	(D)	-	20.7	-	51.9	151.0	-87.8
Establishments - 100-249 Emp. Number	128	14	-89.1	16	14.3	9	-43.8	9	-	13	44.4	-89.8
Mid-March Employment	18,749	2,254	-88.0	2,722	20.8	1,715	-37.0	1,679	-2.1	2,397	42.8	-87.2
1st Quarter Wages (annualized - $ mil.)	399.8	67.8	-83.0	84.1	23.9	66.2	-21.2	56.7	-14.4	119.1	110.1	-70.2
Payroll per Emp. 1st Q. (annualized)	21,325	30,101	41.2	30,892	2.6	38,615	25.0	33,768	-12.6	49,695	47.2	133.0
Annual Payroll ($ mil.)	372.3	63.2	-83.0	80.1	26.6	64.8	-19.0	51.6	-20.5	113.0	119.2	-69.6
Establishments - 250-499 Emp. Number	20	11	-45.0	7	-36.4	9	28.6	10	11.1	5	-50.0	-75.0
Mid-March Employment	6,308	3,296	-47.7	2,452	-25.6	3,174	29.4	3,818	20.3	1,737	-54.5	-72.5
1st Quarter Wages (annualized - $ mil.)	207.5	111.8	-46.1	88.2	-21.1	92.4	4.7	100.8	9.1	96.7	-4.1	-53.4
Payroll per Emp. 1st Q. (annualized)	32,891	33,925	3.1	35,985	6.1	29,105	-19.1	26,410	-9.3	55,650	110.7	69.2
Annual Payroll ($ mil.)	174.2	105.8	-39.2	80.7	-23.7	94.0	16.4	107.7	14.6	79.9	-25.8	-54.1
Establishments - 500-999 Emp. Number	6	6	-	3	-50.0	6	100.0	6	-	7	16.7	16.7
Mid-March Employment	4,008	(D)	-	2,056	-	3,841	86.8	3,858	0.4	4,091	6.0	2.1
1st Quarter Wages (annualized - $ mil.)	101.0	(D)	-	45.6	-	130.8	186.8	149.2	14.1	142.3	-4.7	40.9
Payroll per Emp. 1st Q. (annualized)	25,192	(D)	-	22,189	-	34,063	53.5	38,685	13.6	34,772	-10.1	38.0
Annual Payroll ($ mil.)	100.2	(D)	-	47.8	-	115.1	140.6	131.6	14.4	127.0	-3.5	26.7
Estab. - 1000 or More Emp. Number	1	1	-	-	-	1	-	-	-	3	-	200.0
Mid-March Employment	(D)	(D)	-	-	-	(D)	-	-	-	4,157	-	-
1st Quarter Wages (annualized - $ mil.)	(D)	(D)	-	-	-	(D)	-	-	-	290.4	-	-
Payroll per Emp. 1st Q. (annualized)	(D)	(D)	-	(D)	-	(D)	-	-	-	69,862	-	-
Annual Payroll ($ mil.)	(D)	(D)	-	-	-	(D)	-	-	-	251.4	-	-

Source: County Business Patterns, U.S. Department of Commerce, Washington, D.C., for 1988 through 1993. Payroll per employee is calculated using mid-March employment and 1st Quarter wages, annualized. Annual payroll, also shown, may not equal the annualized 1st Quarter wages. Columns headed by a percent sign (%) indicate change from the previous year. *na* stands for not available. The symbol (D) indicates that data are withheld by the source to avoid disclosure of competitive information. A dash (-) indicates that data are not available or cannot be calculated.

ESTABLISHMENTS
Number

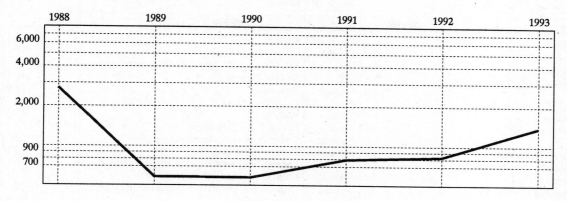

MID-MARCH EMPLOYMENT
Number

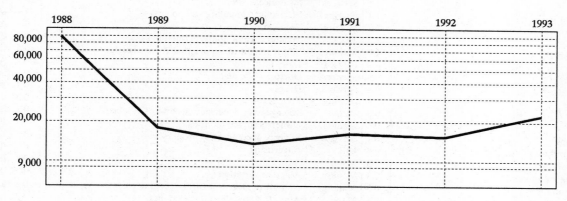

ANNUAL PAYROLL
$ million

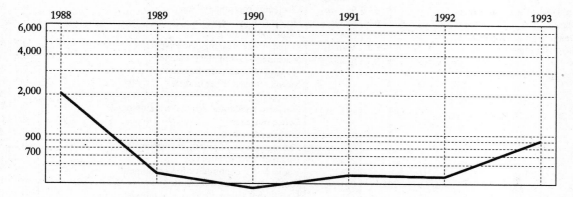

INPUTS AND OUTPUTS FOR ALL BANKING SECTORS - SICs 601, 602, 603, 608, and 609

Economic Sector or Industry Providing Inputs	%	Sector	Economic Sector or Industry Buying Outputs	%	Sector
Computer & data processing services	13.3	Services	Personal consumption expenditures	43.5	
Security & commodity brokers	10.1	Fin/R.E.	Exports	5.3	Foreign
Real estate	8.0	Fin/R.E.	Credit agencies other than banks	4.5	Fin/R.E.
Communications, except radio & TV	5.9	Util.	S/L Govt. purch., other general government	3.7	S/L Govt
Motor freight transportation & warehousing	5.8	Util.	Wholesale trade	3.7	Trade
Banking	5.7	Fin/R.E.	Real estate	3.6	Fin/R.E.
U.S. Postal Service	4.7	Gov't	Retail trade, except eating & drinking	3.3	Trade
Eating & drinking places	4.5	Trade	Banking	1.9	Fin/R.E.
Equipment rental & leasing services	3.4	Services	Eating & drinking places	1.4	Trade
Advertising	2.9	Services	Communications, except radio & TV	1.1	Util.
Accounting, auditing & bookkeeping	2.8	Services	Petroleum refining	1.1	Manufg.
Maintenance of nonfarm buildings nec	2.8	Constr.	Federal Government purchases, nondefense	1.0	Fed Govt
Blankbooks & looseleaf binders	2.5	Manufg.	Electric services (utilities)	0.9	Util.
Management & consulting services & labs	2.4	Services	Engineering, architectural, & surveying services	0.7	Services
Federal Government enterprises nec	2.1	Gov't	Meat animals	0.7	Agric.
Insurance carriers	2.1	Fin/R.E.	Aircraft	0.6	Manufg.
Photographic equipment & supplies	1.7	Manufg.	Apparel made from purchased materials	0.5	Manufg.
Electric services (utilities)	1.6	Util.	Crude petroleum & natural gas	0.5	Mining
Detective & protective services	1.5	Services	Gas production & distribution (utilities)	0.5	Util.
Legal services	1.4	Services	Insurance carriers	0.5	Fin/R.E.
Noncomparable imports	1.4	Foreign	Electronic computing equipment	0.4	Manufg.
Petroleum refining	1.2	Manufg.	Feed grains	0.4	Agric.
Wholesale trade	1.2	Trade	Maintenance of nonfarm buildings nec	0.4	Constr.
Manifold business forms	1.0	Manufg.	Motor freight transportation & warehousing	0.4	Util.
Credit agencies other than banks	0.9	Fin/R.E.	Dairy farm products	0.3	Agric.
Personnel supply services	0.9	Services	Doctors & dentists	0.3	Services
Business/professional associations	0.8	Services	Drugs	0.3	Manufg.
Commercial printing	0.8	Manufg.	Freight forwarders	0.3	Util.
Air transportation	0.6	Util.	Management & consulting services & labs	0.3	Services
Envelopes	0.6	Manufg.	Owner-occupied dwellings	0.3	Fin/R.E.
Electrical repair shops	0.4	Services	Security & commodity brokers	0.3	Fin/R.E.
Transit & bus transportation	0.4	Util.	Advertising	0.2	Services
Electronic components nec	0.3	Manufg.	Agricultural chemicals, nec	0.2	Manufg.
Electronic computing equipment	0.3	Manufg.	Air transportation	0.2	Util.
Engraving & plate printing	0.3	Manufg.	Aircraft & missile engines & engine parts	0.2	Manufg.
Manufacturing industries, nec	0.3	Manufg.	Aircraft & missile equipment, nec	0.2	Manufg.
Paper mills, except building paper	0.3	Manufg.	Broadwoven fabric mills	0.2	Manufg.
Periodicals	0.3	Manufg.	Chemical & fertilizer mineral	0.2	Mining
Services to dwellings & other buildings	0.3	Services	Coal	0.2	Mining
Textile bags	0.3	Manufg.	Computer & data processing services	0.2	Services
Automotive rental & leasing, without drivers	0.2	Services	Electronic components nec	0.2	Manufg.
Hotels & lodging places	0.2	Services	Hotels & lodging places	0.2	Services
Sanitary services, steam supply, irrigation	0.2	Util.	Industrial buildings	0.2	Constr.
Carbon paper & inked ribbons	0.1	Manufg.	Laundry, dry cleaning, shoe repair	0.2	Services
Newspapers	0.1	Manufg.	Machinery, except electrical, nec	0.2	Manufg.
			Medical & health services, nec	0.2	Services
			Motor vehicles & car bodies	0.2	Manufg.
			Newspapers	0.2	Manufg.
			Nonfarm residential structure maintenance	0.2	Constr.
			Office buildings	0.2	Constr.
			Oil bearing crops	0.2	Agric.
			Photographic equipment & supplies	0.2	Manufg.
			Radio & TV broadcasting	0.2	Util.
			Radio & TV communication equipment	0.2	Manufg.
			Railroads & related services	0.2	Util.
			Residential 1-unit structures, nonfarm	0.2	Constr.
			Semiconductors & related devices	0.2	Manufg.
			Water transportation	0.2	Util.

Continued on next page.

INPUTS AND OUTPUTS FOR ALL BANKING SECTORS - SICs 601, 602, 603, 608, and 609 - Continued

Economic Sector or Industry Providing Inputs	%	Sector	Economic Sector or Industry Buying Outputs	%	Sector
			Arrangement of passenger transportation	0.1	Util.
			Automotive repair shops & services	0.1	Services
			Blast furnaces & steel mills	0.1	Manufg.
			Bottled & canned soft drinks	0.1	Manufg.
			Business services nec	0.1	Services
			Commercial printing	0.1	Manufg.
			Cyclic crudes and organics	0.1	Manufg.
			Equipment rental & leasing services	0.1	Services
			Food grains	0.1	Agric.
			Malt beverages	0.1	Manufg.
			Metal office furniture	0.1	Manufg.
			Miscellaneous plastics products	0.1	Manufg.
			Motion pictures	0.1	Services
			Pipe, valves, & pipe fittings	0.1	Manufg.
			Pipelines, except natural gas	0.1	Util.
			Portrait, photographic studios	0.1	Services
			Prepared feeds, nec	0.1	Manufg.
			Primary aluminum	0.1	Manufg.
			Residential additions/alterations, nonfarm	0.1	Constr.

Source: *Benchmark Input-Output Accounts for the U.S. Economy, 1982*, U.S. Department of Commerce, Washington, D.C., July 1991. Data, as reported in the source, are organized by the 1977 SIC structure in use in 1982 but have been matched, as closely as is possible, to the 1987 SIC structure used in this book. Activities with the same percentage are sorted alphabetically by name of activity.

OCCUPATIONS EMPLOYED BY FEDERAL AND BUSINESS CREDIT INSTITUTIONS

Occupation	% of Total 1994	Change to 2005	Occupation	% of Total 1994	Change to 2005
Bill & account collectors	10.6	79.9	Accountants & auditors	2.9	33.3
Loan officers & counselors	6.8	11.9	Securities & financial services sales workers	2.7	33.3
Adjustment clerks	6.5	79.9	Correspondence clerks	2.3	-6.7
Secretaries, ex legal & medical	6.1	21.3	Clerical support workers nec	2.2	6.6
Loan & credit clerks	5.3	20.0	Managers & administrators nec	1.6	33.2
Clerical supervisors & managers	4.9	36.3	Computer programmers	1.6	7.9
General managers & top executives	4.8	26.4	Systems analysts	1.4	113.3
General office clerks	4.8	13.6	Receptionists & information clerks	1.3	33.3
Financial managers	4.3	33.3	Data entry keyers, ex composing	1.3	-1.6
Bookkeeping, accounting, & auditing clerks	4.3	-0.0	Credit checkers	1.3	-10.1
Management support workers nec	3.8	33.3	Sales & related workers nec	1.2	33.3
Credit analysts	3.5	6.6			

Sources: *Industry-Occupation Matrix*, Bureau of Labor Statistics. These data relate to one or more 3-digit SIC industry groups rather than to a single 4-digit SIC. The change reported for each occupation to the year 2005 is a percent of growth or decline as estimated by the Bureau of Labor Statistics. The abbreviation *nec* stands for not elsewhere classified.

U.S. AND STATE DATA ON INDUSTRY REVENUES AND OTHER ACCOUNTS FOR 1992

State	No. of Estab.	Employ-ment	Payroll ($ mil.)	Revenues ($ mil.)	Empl./ Estab.	Revenue/ Estab. ($)	Payroll/ Estab. ($)	Revenue/ Empl. ($)	Payroll/ Empl. ($)
UNITED STATES	1,349	21,298	833.1	28,092.0	16	20,824,313	617,532	1,318,997	39,114
Alabama	33	-	(D)	(D)	(D)	(D)	(D)	(D)	(D)
Arizona	5	-	(D)	(D)	(D)	(D)	(D)	(D)	(D)
Arkansas	23	216	4.7	33.3	9	1,446,087	205,609	153,981	21,894
California	64	1,201	48.2	1,791.4	19	27,990,953	753,484	1,491,608	40,152
Colorado	25	-	(D)	(D)	(D)	(D)	(D)	(D)	(D)
Connecticut	3	-	(D)	(D)	(D)	(D)	(D)	(D)	(D)
Delaware	2	-	(D)	(D)	(D)	(D)	(D)	(D)	(D)
District of Columbia	4	-	(D)	(D)	(D)	(D)	(D)	(D)	(D)
Florida	32	-	(D)	(D)	(D)	(D)	(D)	(D)	(D)
Georgia	42	643	26.6	1,452.6	15	34,586,857	634,429	2,259,173	41,440
Hawaii	1	-	(D)	(D)	(D)	(D)	(D)	(D)	(D)
Idaho	19	-	(D)	(D)	(D)	(D)	(D)	(D)	(D)
Illinois	46	-	(D)	(D)	(D)	(D)	(D)	(D)	(D)
Indiana	52	-	(D)	(D)	(D)	(D)	(D)	(D)	(D)
Iowa	34	-	(D)	(D)	(D)	(D)	(D)	(D)	(D)
Kansas	34	-	(D)	(D)	(D)	(D)	(D)	(D)	(D)
Kentucky	54	402	14.4	346.0	7	6,408,111	266,981	860,791	35,863
Louisiana	27	108	3.5	17.4	4	642,593	129,407	160,648	32,352
Maine	5	-	(D)	(D)	(D)	(D)	(D)	(D)	(D)
Maryland	16	-	(D)	(D)	(D)	(D)	(D)	(D)	(D)
Massachusetts	5	-	(D)	(D)	(D)	(D)	(D)	(D)	(D)
Michigan	36	278	8.3	58.2	8	1,616,333	231,028	209,309	29,917
Minnesota	44	940	52.0	837.2	21	19,027,136	1,180,795	890,632	55,271
Mississippi	38	110	3.3	21.9	3	576,079	86,184	199,009	29,773
Missouri	42	510	9.6	178.0	12	4,238,738	227,524	349,073	18,737
Montana	11	-	(D)	(D)	(D)	(D)	(D)	(D)	(D)
Nebraska	34	-	(D)	(D)	(D)	(D)	(D)	(D)	(D)
Nevada	3	-	(D)	(D)	(D)	(D)	(D)	(D)	(D)
New Hampshire	2	-	(D)	(D)	(D)	(D)	(D)	(D)	(D)
New Jersey	6	109	4.0	43.0	18	7,168,333	662,333	394,587	36,459
New Mexico	9	60	1.9	12.5	7	1,388,000	216,333	208,200	32,450
New York	32	364	10.7	128.6	11	4,018,594	333,750	353,283	29,341
North Carolina	84	-	(D)	(D)	(D)	(D)	(D)	(D)	(D)
North Dakota	28	341	9.3	47.7	12	1,704,071	331,107	139,924	27,188
Ohio	53	-	(D)	(D)	(D)	(D)	(D)	(D)	(D)
Oklahoma	24	168	4.8	13.4	7	556,583	201,792	79,512	28,827
Oregon	12	-	(D)	(D)	(D)	(D)	(D)	(D)	(D)
Pennsylvania	39	-	(D)	(D)	(D)	(D)	(D)	(D)	(D)
Rhode Island	1	-	(D)	(D)	(D)	(D)	(D)	(D)	(D)
South Carolina	19	-	(D)	(D)	(D)	(D)	(D)	(D)	(D)
South Dakota	16	-	(D)	(D)	(D)	(D)	(D)	(D)	(D)
Tennessee	54	-	(D)	(D)	(D)	(D)	(D)	(D)	(D)
Texas	119	1,599	48.0	2,084.6	13	17,518,050	403,160	1,303,720	30,004
Utah	1	-	(D)	(D)	(D)	(D)	(D)	(D)	(D)
Vermont	6	-	(D)	(D)	(D)	(D)	(D)	(D)	(D)
Virginia	40	-	(D)	(D)	(D)	(D)	(D)	(D)	(D)
Washington	14	-	(D)	(D)	(D)	(D)	(D)	(D)	(D)
West Virginia	11	45	1.3	14.7	4	1,337,818	119,000	327,022	29,089
Wisconsin	39	414	11.2	65.4	11	1,677,821	286,103	158,056	26,952
Wyoming	6	-	(D)	(D)	(D)	(D)	(D)	(D)	(D)

Source: 1992 Economic Census, U.S. Department of Commerce, Washington, D.C. This is the only table that shows revenue data as collected by the Bureau of the Census in an Economic Census. The symbol (D) indicates that data are withheld by the source to avoid disclosure of competitive information. A dash (-) indicates that data are not available or cannot be calculated.

ESTABLISHMENTS 1992 - STATE AND REGIONAL CONCENTRATION

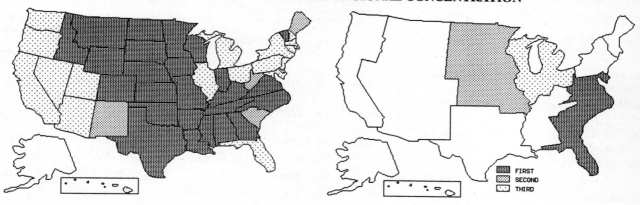

EMPLOYMENT 1992 - STATE AND REGIONAL CONCENTRATION

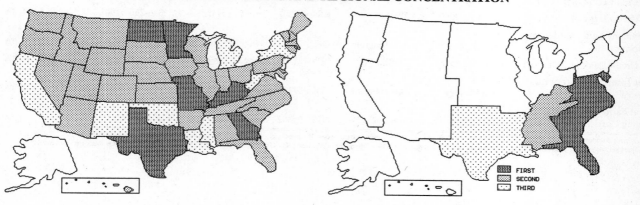

REVENUES 1992 - STATE AND REGIONAL CONCENTRATION

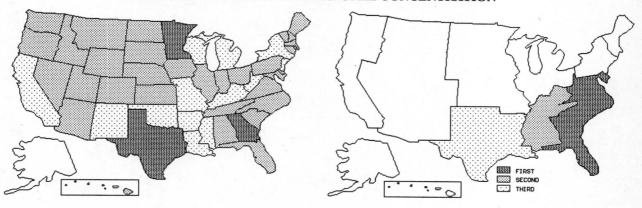

States with the darkest shading indicate those states which have proportionately more establishments, employment, or revenues than would be indicated by the state's population. States with light shading are states with proportionately fewer establishments, less employment, and lower revenues than population distribution. States shaded grey are within 15 percent of the state's population proportion in these categories. States for which no data are available are shown as average (grey). *Regions* are shaded to indicate absolute rank in the category. If no data for the category are available, establishment counts are used to shade the regions. Source of the data is the table on the facing page.

LEADING COMPANIES - SIC 6111 - Federal & Federally Sponsored Credit

Number shown: **14**   Total sales/assets ($ mil): **420,380**   Total employment (000): **16.6**

Company Name	Address				CEO Name	Phone	Co. Type	Sales/Assets ($ mil)	Empl. (000)
Federal National Mortgage Association	3900 Wisconsin Ave. N	Washington	DC	20016	Lawrence M. Small	202-752-7000	P	216,979 TA	3.2
Federal Home Loan Mortgage Corp.	8200 Jones Branch Dr.	McLean	VA	22102	Leland C. Brendsel	703-903-2000	P	106,199 TA	3.0
Student Loan Marketing Association	1050 Thomas Jefferson	Washington	DC	20007	Lawrence A. Hough	202-333-8000	P	46,509 TA	4.5
CoBank	P.O. Box 5110	Denver	CO	80217	Douglas D. Sims	303-740-4000	R	13,000 TA	0.5
AgAmerica	P.O. Box TAF-C5	Spokane	WA	99220	James Kirk	509-838-9289	R	7,217 TA	<0.1
Farm Credit Bank of Columbia	P.O. Box 1499	Columbia	SC	29202	Maxey D. Love Jr.	803-799-5000	R	5,608 TA	1.4
Western Farm Credit Bank	P.O. Box 13106	Sacramento	CA	95813	James M. Cirona	916-485-6000	R	5,239 TA	0.9
Farm Credit Bank of Omaha	206 S. 19th St.	Omaha	NE	68102	James D. Kirk	402-348-3333	R	4,290 TA	0.8
Farm Credit Bank of Texas	P.O. Box 15919	Austin	TX	78761	Arnold R. Henson	512-465-0400	R	4,063 TA	0.3
Farm Credit Bank of Wichita	P.O. Box 2940	Wichita	KS	67201	Jerold L. Harris	316-266-5100	R	3,896 TA	0.9
Government National Mortgage Association	451 7th St. S.W.	Washington	DC	20410	Dwight P. Robinson	202-708-0926	S	3,683 TA	<0.1
Farm Credit Bank of Baltimore	P.O. Box 1555	Baltimore	MD	21203	Gene L. Swackhamer	410-329-5500	R	3,642 TA	0.9
Hemar Insurance Corporation of America	3900 W. Technology	Sioux Falls	SD	57106	Kevin Moehn	605-361-5051	R	49 TA	<0.1
Federal Farm Credit Banks Funding Corp.	10 Exchange Pl.	Jersey City	NJ	07302	James A. Brickley	201-200-8000	R	6 TA	<0.1

Source: Ward's Business Directory of U.S. Private and Public Companies, 1996. Company type codes: P - Public, R - Private, S - Subsidiary, D - Division, J - Joint Venture, A - Affiliate, G - Group. If the dollar values shown are not sales, the following codes apply: TA - Total Assets; OR - Operating Revenues; GB - Gross Billings. * - estimated dollar value. < - less than; *na* - not available.

SIC 6140

PERSONAL CREDIT INSTITUTIONS

Personal credit institutions are engaged in providing loans to individuals. The SIC also includes organizations engaged primarily in financing retail sales made on the installment plan and those financing automobile loans for individuals. The category includes consumer finance companies, industrial loan "banks" and loan companies not engaged in deposit banking, installment sales finance organizations other than banks, loan companies and societies, Morris plans not engaged in deposit banking, mutual benefit associations, and personal finance companies.

ESTABLISHMENTS, EMPLOYMENT, AND PAYROLL

	1988	1989		1990		1991		1992		1993		% change 88-93
		Value	%	Value	%	Value	%	Value	%	Value	%	
All Establishments	25,629	25,258	-1.4	24,960	-1.2	20,049	-19.7	19,887	-0.8	17,003	-14.5	-33.7
Mid-March Employment	212,806	217,801	2.3	236,318	8.5	175,823	-25.6	158,519	-9.8	151,920	-4.2	-28.6
1st Quarter Wages (annualized - $ mil.)	4,776.5	5,138.1	7.6	5,735.0	11.6	4,627.4	-19.3	4,458.7	-3.6	3,722.8	-16.5	-22.1
Payroll per Emp. 1st Q. (annualized)	22,445	23,591	5.1	24,268	2.9	26,318	8.4	28,127	6.9	24,505	-12.9	9.2
Annual Payroll ($ mil.)	4,636.5	4,962.8	7.0	5,547.4	11.8	4,560.0	-17.8	4,487.1	-1.6	3,846.8	-14.3	-17.0
Establishments - 1-4 Emp. Number	15,031	14,693	-2.2	13,804	-6.1	11,240	-18.6	12,069	7.4	9,766	-19.1	-35.0
Mid-March Employment	(D)	36,791	-	35,187	-4.4	29,789	-15.3	32,084	7.7	25,079	-21.8	-
1st Quarter Wages (annualized - $ mil.)	(D)	671.0	-	655.6	-2.3	647.6	-1.2	732.0	13.0	556.8	-23.9	-
Payroll per Emp. 1st Q. (annualized)	(D)	18,239	-	18,633	2.2	21,741	16.7	22,816	4.9	22,203	-2.7	-
Annual Payroll ($ mil.)	(D)	732.1	-	697.5	-4.7	670.4	-3.9	768.5	14.6	624.9	-18.7	-
Establishments - 5-9 Emp. Number	6,886	6,692	-2.8	6,760	1.0	5,975	-11.6	5,560	-6.9	4,678	-15.9	-32.1
Mid-March Employment	42,631	41,643	-2.3	42,883	3.0	37,321	-13.0	34,182	-8.4	28,871	-15.5	-32.3
1st Quarter Wages (annualized - $ mil.)	791.1	817.2	3.3	853.6	4.4	815.0	-4.5	814.9	-0.0	622.5	-23.6	-21.3
Payroll per Emp. 1st Q. (annualized)	18,558	19,624	5.7	19,904	1.4	21,838	9.7	23,841	9.2	21,561	-9.6	16.2
Annual Payroll ($ mil.)	784.1	790.9	0.9	849.1	7.4	804.5	-5.3	818.1	1.7	648.4	-20.7	-17.3
Establishments - 10-19 Emp. Number	1,829	1,871	2.3	2,240	19.7	1,552	-30.7	1,113	-28.3	1,448	30.1	-20.8
Mid-March Employment	24,397	24,989	2.4	29,619	18.5	20,386	-31.2	14,660	-28.1	19,639	34.0	-19.5
1st Quarter Wages (annualized - $ mil.)	497.1	541.7	9.0	635.9	17.4	484.5	-23.8	406.6	-16.1	343.2	-15.6	-31.0
Payroll per Emp. 1st Q. (annualized)	20,376	21,678	6.4	21,470	-1.0	23,764	10.7	27,736	16.7	17,475	-37.0	-14.2
Annual Payroll ($ mil.)	500.6	532.2	6.3	626.1	17.6	487.7	-22.1	402.5	-17.5	334.6	-16.9	-33.2
Establishments - 20-49 Emp. Number	1,235	1,313	6.3	1,383	5.3	823	-40.5	760	-7.7	778	2.4	-37.0
Mid-March Employment	37,251	39,910	7.1	41,615	4.3	24,986	-40.0	22,899	-8.4	22,060	-3.7	-40.8
1st Quarter Wages (annualized - $ mil.)	834.8	928.9	11.3	1,007.9	8.5	688.2	-31.7	680.9	-1.1	526.0	-22.7	-37.0
Payroll per Emp. 1st Q. (annualized)	22,409	23,274	3.9	24,220	4.1	27,542	13.7	29,734	8.0	23,844	-19.8	6.4
Annual Payroll ($ mil.)	829.2	923.2	11.3	980.6	6.2	688.8	-29.8	674.0	-2.1	529.5	-21.4	-36.1
Establishments - 50-99 Emp. Number	471	504	7.0	558	10.7	319	-42.8	260	-18.5	209	-19.6	-55.6
Mid-March Employment	31,743	34,729	9.4	38,275	10.2	22,075	-42.3	17,969	-18.6	14,462	-19.5	-54.4
1st Quarter Wages (annualized - $ mil.)	784.4	892.3	13.8	1,024.6	14.8	727.6	-29.0	609.1	-16.3	439.2	-27.9	-44.0
Payroll per Emp. 1st Q. (annualized)	24,710	25,693	4.0	26,770	4.2	32,962	23.1	33,897	2.8	30,366	-10.4	22.9
Annual Payroll ($ mil.)	773.7	874.2	13.0	1,001.1	14.5	729.8	-27.1	627.7	-14.0	450.7	-28.2	-41.7
Establishments - 100-249 Emp. Number	128	142	10.9	170	19.7	87	-48.8	80	-8.0	75	-6.3	-41.4
Mid-March Employment	16,820	19,347	15.0	24,023	24.2	(D)	-	11,808	-	10,858	-8.0	-35.4
1st Quarter Wages (annualized - $ mil.)	430.9	530.2	23.1	762.1	43.7	(D)	-	415.3	-	317.8	-23.5	-26.3
Payroll per Emp. 1st Q. (annualized)	25,617	27,407	7.0	31,726	15.8	(D)	-	35,168	-	29,265	-16.8	14.2
Annual Payroll ($ mil.)	409.5	497.9	21.6	679.4	36.5	(D)	-	376.8	-	316.6	-16.0	-22.7
Establishments - 250-499 Emp. Number	38	31	-18.4	28	-9.7	34	21.4	27	-20.6	26	-3.7	-31.6
Mid-March Employment	13,008	10,358	-20.4	9,758	-5.8	11,226	15.0	8,888	-20.8	9,330	5.0	-28.3
1st Quarter Wages (annualized - $ mil.)	392.2	331.3	-15.5	326.8	-1.3	363.0	11.1	288.8	-20.4	269.5	-6.7	-31.3
Payroll per Emp. 1st Q. (annualized)	30,151	31,984	6.1	33,494	4.7	32,332	-3.5	32,491	0.5	28,887	-11.1	-4.2
Annual Payroll ($ mil.)	359.6	297.4	-17.3	299.8	0.8	351.1	17.1	286.3	-18.5	264.8	-7.5	-26.4
Establishments - 500-999 Emp. Number	9	10	11.1	15	50.0	14	-6.7	13	-7.1	16	23.1	77.8
Mid-March Employment	6,135	(D)	-	(D)	-	9,330	-	9,005	-3.5	11,533	28.1	88.0
1st Quarter Wages (annualized - $ mil.)	276.6	(D)	-	(D)	-	274.4	-	254.5	-7.3	342.4	34.6	23.8
Payroll per Emp. 1st Q. (annualized)	45,089	(D)	-	(D)	-	29,407	-	28,257	-3.9	29,686	5.1	-34.2
Annual Payroll ($ mil.)	176.0	(D)	-	(D)	-	262.7	-	276.5	5.3	349.9	26.6	98.8
Estab. - 1000 or More Emp. Number	2	2	-	2	-	5	150.0	5	-	7	40.0	250.0
Mid-March Employment	(D)	(D)	-	(D)	-	(D)	-	7,024	-	10,088	43.6	-
1st Quarter Wages (annualized - $ mil.)	(D)	(D)	-	(D)	-	(D)	-	256.6	-	305.5	19.0	-
Payroll per Emp. 1st Q. (annualized)	(D)	(D)	-	(D)	-	(D)	-	36,537	-	30,286	-17.1	-
Annual Payroll ($ mil.)	(D)	(D)	-	(D)	-	(D)	-	256.7	-	327.4	27.6	-

Source: County Business Patterns, U.S. Department of Commerce, Washington, D.C., for 1988 through 1993. Payroll per employee is calculated using mid-March employment and 1st Quarter wages, annualized. Annual payroll, also shown, may not equal the annualized 1st Quarter wages. Columns headed by a percent sign (%) indicate change from the previous year. *na* stands for not available. The symbol (D) indicates that data are withheld by the source to avoid disclosure of competitive information. A dash (-) indicates that data are not available or cannot be calculated.

ESTABLISHMENTS
Number

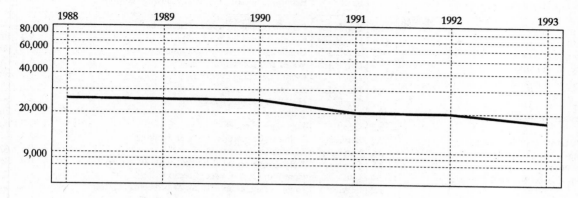

MID-MARCH EMPLOYMENT
Number

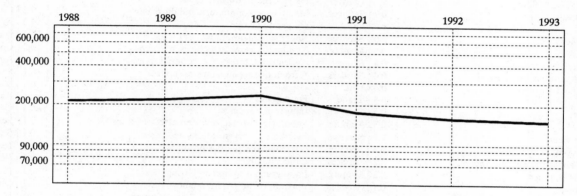

ANNUAL PAYROLL
$ million

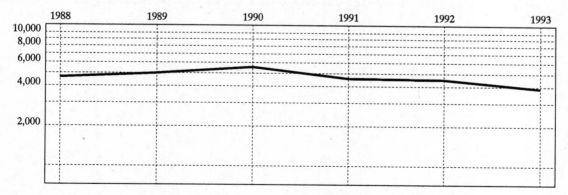

INPUTS AND OUTPUTS FOR CREDIT AGENCIES OTHER THAN BANKS - SICs 606, 611, 614-16

Economic Sector or Industry Providing Inputs	%	Sector	Economic Sector or Industry Buying Outputs	%	Sector
Banking	21.4	Fin/R.E.	Personal consumption expenditures	56.2	
Security & commodity brokers	17.4	Fin/R.E.	Eating & drinking places	9.2	Trade
Computer & data processing services	6.5	Services	Credit agencies other than banks	6.8	Fin/R.E.
Credit agencies other than banks	5.9	Fin/R.E.	Water transportation	4.4	Util.
Federal Government enterprises nec	5.6	Gov't	Owner-occupied dwellings	3.6	Fin/R.E.
Real estate	5.5	Fin/R.E.	Air transportation	2.2	Util.
Eating & drinking places	4.1	Trade	Hotels & lodging places	1.9	Services
Communications, except radio & TV	3.6	Util.	Banking	1.7	Fin/R.E.
U.S. Postal Service	3.3	Gov't	Insurance carriers	1.7	Fin/R.E.
Management & consulting services & labs	2.9	Services	Retail trade, except eating & drinking	1.5	Trade
Accounting, auditing & bookkeeping	2.6	Services	Meat animals	0.5	Agric.
Equipment rental & leasing services	2.5	Services	Automotive rental & leasing, without drivers	0.4	Services
Motor freight transportation & warehousing	2.4	Util.	Communications, except radio & TV	0.4	Util.
Advertising	1.9	Services	Engineering, architectural, & surveying services	0.4	Services
Insurance carriers	1.5	Fin/R.E.	Management & consulting services & labs	0.4	Services
Legal services	1.3	Services	Feed grains	0.3	Agric.
Electric services (utilities)	1.2	Util.	Job training & related services	0.3	Services
Petroleum refining	1.0	Manufg.	Real estate	0.3	Fin/R.E.
Commercial printing	0.9	Manufg.	S/L Govt. purch., other general government	0.3	S/L Govt
Maintenance of nonfarm buildings nec	0.9	Constr.	Dairy farm products	0.2	Agric.
Detective & protective services	0.7	Services	Maintenance of nonfarm buildings nec	0.2	Constr.
Air transportation	0.6	Util.	Oil bearing crops	0.2	Agric.
Hotels & lodging places	0.6	Services	Religious organizations	0.2	Services
Manifold business forms	0.6	Manufg.	Residential 1-unit structures, nonfarm	0.2	Constr.
Business/professional associations	0.4	Services	Agricultural, forestry, & fishery services	0.1	Agric.
Services to dwellings & other buildings	0.4	Services	Automotive repair shops & services	0.1	Services
Transit & bus transportation	0.4	Util.	Drugs	0.1	Manufg.
Wholesale trade	0.4	Trade	Food grains	0.1	Agric.
Business services nec	0.3	Services	Industrial buildings	0.1	Constr.
Envelopes	0.3	Manufg.	Labor, civic, social, & fraternal associations	0.1	Services
Personnel supply services	0.3	Services	Membership organizations nec	0.1	Services
Photographic equipment & supplies	0.3	Manufg.	Miscellaneous plastics products	0.1	Manufg.
Automotive rental & leasing, without drivers	0.2	Services	Office buildings	0.1	Constr.
Manufacturing industries, nec	0.2	Manufg.	Photographic equipment & supplies	0.1	Manufg.
Electrical repair shops	0.1	Services	Portrait, photographic studios	0.1	Services
Periodicals	0.1	Manufg.	Radio & TV communication equipment	0.1	Manufg.
Sanitary services, steam supply, irrigation	0.1	Util.	Transit & bus transportation	0.1	Util.
			Wholesale trade	0.1	Trade

Source: Benchmark Input-Output Accounts for the U.S. Economy, 1982, U.S. Department of Commerce, Washington, D.C., July 1991. Data, as reported in the source, are organized by the 1977 SIC structure in use in 1982 but have been matched, as closely as is possible, to the 1987 SIC structure used in this book. Activities with the same percentage are sorted alphabetically by name of activity.

OCCUPATIONS EMPLOYED BY PERSONAL CREDIT INSTITUTIONS

Occupation	% of Total 1994	Change to 2005	Occupation	% of Total 1994	Change to 2005
Loan officers & counselors	12.5	43.9	Bank tellers	3.4	31.9
Bill & account collectors	10.7	31.9	Bookkeeping, accounting, & auditing clerks	3.1	-1.1
Loan & credit clerks	10.4	18.7	Management support workers nec	2.4	31.9
Financial managers	9.4	31.9	Credit analysts	2.4	5.5
General office clerks	7.8	12.5	Secretaries, ex legal & medical	2.3	20.1
Adjustment clerks	6.7	78.0	Securities & financial services sales workers	1.7	31.9
Clerical supervisors & managers	4.7	34.9	Sales & related workers nec	1.5	31.9
General managers & top executives	4.2	25.1	Accountants & auditors	1.1	31.9
Cashiers	4.0	58.3			

Sources: Industry-Occupation Matrix, Bureau of Labor Statistics. These data relate to one or more 3-digit SIC industry groups rather than to a single 4-digit SIC. The change reported for each occupation to the year 2005 is a percent of growth or decline as estimated by the Bureau of Labor Statistics. The abbreviation nec stands for not elsewhere classified.

U.S. AND STATE DATA ON INDUSTRY REVENUES AND OTHER ACCOUNTS FOR 1992

State	No. of Estab.	Employ-ment	Payroll ($ mil.)	Revenues ($ mil.)	Empl./ Estab.	Revenue/ Estab. ($)	Payroll/ Estab. ($)	Revenue/ Empl. ($)	Payroll/ Empl. ($)
UNITED STATES	16,900	158,790	4,281.4	47,668.4	9	2,820,618	253,337	300,198	26,963
Alabama	460	2,457	55.7	513.9	5	1,117,241	121,041	209,170	22,661
Alaska	8	-	(D)	(D)	(D)	(D)	(D)	(D)	(D)
Arizona	180	8,700	233.7	1,525.5	48	8,475,228	1,298,261	175,350	26,861
Arkansas	23	394	10.3	140.9	17	6,125,870	446,913	357,602	26,089
California	1,754	18,265	528.6	6,071.3	10	3,461,403	301,388	332,401	28,942
Colorado	232	3,292	84.4	701.9	14	3,025,228	363,802	213,200	25,639
Connecticut	108	3,187	146.0	1,929.6	30	17,866,620	1,351,889	605,458	45,812
Delaware	67	2,127	49.8	554.4	32	8,274,597	742,940	260,648	23,402
District of Columbia	6	-	(D)	(D)	(D)	(D)	(D)	(D)	(D)
Florida	774	11,122	277.1	2,638.6	14	3,409,105	358,023	237,246	24,915
Georgia	1,101	6,000	149.0	1,388.1	5	1,260,797	135,334	231,356	24,834
Hawaii	100	419	11.7	140.3	4	1,402,510	116,800	334,728	27,876
Idaho	67	319	7.6	80.9	5	1,207,373	113,552	253,586	23,850
Illinois	564	8,015	291.1	3,228.0	14	5,723,473	516,138	402,750	36,320
Indiana	400	4,511	107.8	1,576.2	11	3,940,380	269,425	349,402	23,890
Iowa	133	1,024	32.9	169.8	8	1,276,677	247,692	165,818	32,171
Kansas	151	997	25.7	361.8	7	2,395,881	170,331	362,867	25,797
Kentucky	343	1,745	35.5	260.2	5	758,659	103,598	149,123	20,363
Louisiana	849	3,543	75.5	592.3	4	697,698	88,951	167,188	21,315
Maine	10	117	3.6	68.6	12	6,861,000	356,900	586,410	30,504
Maryland	278	2,975	85.4	865.1	11	3,112,000	307,317	290,802	28,717
Massachusetts	173	2,313	64.3	581.3	13	3,360,156	371,931	251,322	27,818
Michigan	167	5,147	156.3	5,379.8	31	32,214,653	935,850	1,045,239	30,365
Minnesota	205	2,586	63.8	697.1	13	3,400,620	311,327	269,577	24,680
Mississippi	488	2,097	44.8	396.3	4	812,006	91,900	188,965	21,386
Missouri	293	2,178	53.3	741.8	7	2,531,795	182,041	340,595	24,489
Montana	25	191	4.5	68.6	8	2,742,480	181,840	358,963	23,801
Nebraska	63	385	9.5	112.1	6	1,780,063	150,413	291,283	24,613
Nevada	73	356	8.9	135.6	5	1,857,397	121,877	380,871	24,992
New Hampshire	46	328	8.8	100.8	7	2,191,435	191,043	307,335	26,793
New Jersey	269	2,701	82.9	983.1	10	3,654,818	308,145	363,993	30,689
New Mexico	135	776	18.6	172.6	6	1,278,148	137,970	222,358	24,003
New York	443	8,195	319.5	2,395.0	18	5,406,400	721,255	292,256	38,989
North Carolina	732	7,617	169.1	1,559.2	10	2,130,122	231,033	204,706	22,202
North Dakota	16	130	3.4	53.3	8	3,328,813	210,188	409,700	25,869
Ohio	715	8,819	191.0	2,606.6	12	3,645,656	267,092	295,571	21,654
Oklahoma	588	2,418	44.3	376.9	4	641,024	75,405	155,882	18,337
Oregon	161	934	24.8	269.7	6	1,675,379	153,894	288,797	26,528
Pennsylvania	685	3,984	124.4	1,480.9	6	2,161,826	181,552	371,700	31,216
Rhode Island	47	248	6.6	68.2	5	1,450,340	140,213	274,863	26,573
South Carolina	892	3,856	80.0	607.9	4	681,516	89,732	157,654	20,758
South Dakota	22	461	9.6	152.9	21	6,948,909	437,091	331,618	20,859
Tennessee	538	3,870	95.4	786.1	7	1,461,240	177,307	203,139	24,649
Texas	1,400	11,011	276.4	2,935.5	8	2,096,801	197,450	266,599	25,105
Utah	113	2,297	40.8	477.5	20	4,225,920	361,035	207,892	17,761
Vermont	3	-	(D)	(D)	(D)	(D)	(D)	(D)	(D)
Virginia	427	2,582	64.8	590.7	6	1,383,461	151,801	228,791	25,104
Washington	244	1,445	41.5	475.4	6	1,948,352	169,967	328,995	28,700
West Virginia	82	406	9.7	72.5	5	884,598	117,756	178,663	23,783
Wisconsin	230	1,905	42.9	457.9	8	1,990,870	186,561	240,367	22,524
Wyoming	17	-	(D)	(D)	(D)	(D)	(D)	(D)	(D)

Source: 1992 Economic Census, U.S. Department of Commerce, Washington, D.C. This is the only table that shows revenue data as collected by the Bureau of the Census in an Economic Census. The symbol (D) indicates that data are withheld by the source to avoid disclosure of competitive information. A dash (-) indicates that data are not available or cannot be calculated.

ESTABLISHMENTS 1992 - STATE AND REGIONAL CONCENTRATION

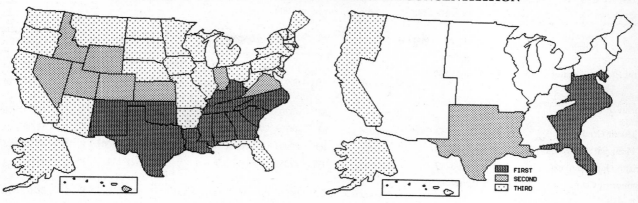

EMPLOYMENT 1992 - STATE AND REGIONAL CONCENTRATION

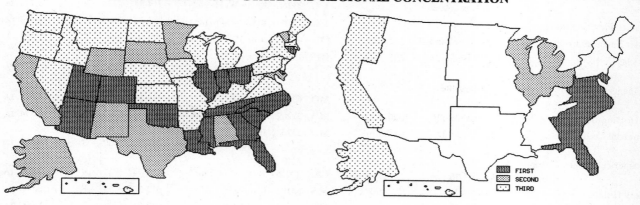

REVENUES 1992 - STATE AND REGIONAL CONCENTRATION

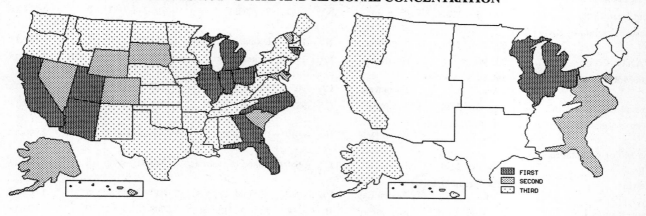

States with the darkest shading indicate those states which have proportionately more establishments, employment, or revenues than would be indicated by the state's population. States with light shading are states with proportionately fewer establishments, less employment, and lower revenues than population distribution. States shaded grey are within 15 percent of the state's population proportion in these categories. States for which no data are available are shown as average (grey). *Regions* are shaded to indicate absolute rank in the category. If no data for the category are available, establishment counts are used to shade the regions. Source of the data is the table on the facing page.

LEADING COMPANIES - SIC 6141 - Personal Credit Institutions

Number shown: 82   Total sales/assets ($ mil): **614,988**   Total employment (000): **232.4**

Company Name	Address				CEO Name	Phone	Co. Type	Sales/Assets ($ mil)	Empl. (000)
General Electric Capital Corp.	260 Long Ridge Rd.	Stamford	CT	06927	Gary C. Wendt	203-357-4000	S	117,939 TA	18.6
General Motors Acceptance Corp.	3044 W. Grand Blvd.	Detroit	MI	48202	Robert T. O'Connell	313-556-1508	S	80,751 TA	19.3
Ford Motor Credit Co.	P.O. Box 1732	Dearborn	MI	48121	William E. Odom	313-323-1200	S	58,967 TA	8.6
Fleet Financial Group Inc.	50 Kennedy Plz.	Providence	RI	02903	Terrence Murray	401-278-5800	P	48,757 TA	21.5
American General Corp.	P.O. Box 3247	Houston	TX	77253	Harold S. Hook	713-522-1111	P	43,982 TA	12.7
Transamerica Corp.	600 Montgomery St.	San Francisco	CA	94111	Frank C. Herringer	415-983-4000	P	36,050 TA	10.7
Household International Inc.	2700 Sanders Rd.	Prospect Heights	IL	60070	Donald C Clark	708-564-5000	P	34,338 TA	15.5
Associates Corporation of North America	P.O. Box 660028	Dallas	TX	75266	Kevin W. Hughes	214-541-4000	S	32,200 TA	17.0
Associates First Capital Corp.	P.O. Box 660237	Dallas	TX	75266	Keith W. Hughes	214-541-4000	S	32,200 TA	17.0
Chrysler Financial Corp.	27777 Franklin Rd.	Southfield	MI	48034	John P. Tierney	810-948-3888	S	14,402 TA	3.1
Beneficial Corp.	301 N. Walnut St.	Wilmington	DE	19801	Finn M. W. Caspersen	302-425-2500	P	14,377 TA	8.5
ITT Financial Corp.	645 Maryville Centre	St. Louis	MO	63131	Frank J. Schultz	314-542-3636	S	11,619 TA	5.0
CCC Holdings Inc.	300 St. Paul Pl.	Baltimore	MD	21202	R. S. Willumstad	410-332-3000	S	8,894 TA	5.0
Commercial Credit Co.	300 St. Paul Pl.	Baltimore	MD	21202	Robert B. Willumstad	410-332-3000	S	8,894 TA	5.0
Transamerica Finance Group Inc.	1150 S. Olive St.	Los Angeles	CA	90015	Richard H. Finn	213-742-4321	S	8,832 TA	5.3
EduServ Holding Corp.	85 E. 7th Pl.	St. Paul	MN	55101	Carl Keil	612-227-6735	R	8,000 TA	1.2
EduServ Technologies Inc.	85 E. 7th Pl.	St. Paul	MN	55101	Carl Keil	612-227-6735	S	8,000 TA	1.2
American General Finance Inc.	P.O. Box 59	Evansville	IN	47701	Daniel Leitch III	812-424-8031	S	7,641 TA	6.5
Norwest Financial Inc.	206 8th St.	Des Moines	IA	50309	David C. Wood	515-248-7462	S	6,125 TA	6.1
Student Loan Corp.	P.O. Box 22944	Pittsford	NY	14692	Stephen C. Biklen	716-248-7187	P	4,347 TA	0.7
Rochester Community Savings Bank	40 Franklin St.	Rochester	NY	14604	Leonard S. Simon	716-258-3000	P	4,189 TA	1.7
ADVANTA Corp.	300 Welsh Rd.	Horsham	PA	19044	Dennis Alter	215-657-4000	P	3,113 TA	1.8
Toyota Motor Credit Corp.	190001 S. Western Ave.	Torrance	CA	90509	Shingi Sakai	310-787-1310	S	2,950 TA•	1.2
Fleetwood Enterprises Inc.	P.O. Box 7638	Riverside	CA	92513	John C. Crean	909-351-3500	P	2,370	14.0
Household Retail Services	700 N. Wood Dale Rd.	Wood Dale	IL	60191	Paul Miller	708-350-4000	S	2,000 TA	0.8
Nissan Motor Acceptance Corp.	P.O. Box 2870	Torrance	CA	90509	Takao Miyashita	310-719-8000	S	1,720 TA	0.7
Aristar Inc.	8900 Grand Oaks Cir.	Tampa Bay	FL	33637	Mike M. Pappas	813-632-4500	S	1,605 TA	2.5
Mercury Finance Co.	40 Skokie Blvd.	Northbrook	IL	60062	John N. Brincat	708-564-3720	P	1,036 TA	1.5
Finance Enterprises	P.O. Box 3979	Honolulu	HI	96812	Clifford Yee	808-548-3311	R	860 TA	0.4
Alfa Corp.	P.O. Box 11000	Montgomery	AL	36191	Goodwin L. Myrick	334-288-3900	P	846 TA	2.1
NOVUS Credit Services Inc.	2500 Lake Cook Rd.	Riverwoods	IL	60015	Nancy S. Donovan	708-405-0900	S	740 TA•	0.3

Company type codes: P - Public, R - Private, S - Subsidiary, D - Division, J - Joint Venture, A - Affiliate, G - Group. If the dollar values shown are not sales, the following codes apply: TA - Total Assets; OR - Operating Revenues; GB - Gross Billings. • - estimated dollar value. < - less than. *na* - not available.

Continued on next page.

LEADING COMPANIES - SIC 6141 - Personal Credit Institutions
Continued

Company Name	Address				CEO Name	Phone	Co. Type	Sales/Assets ($ mil)	Empl. (000)
Oakwood Homes Corp.	P.O. Box 7386	Greensboro	NC	27417	Nicholas J. St. George	919-855-2400	P	506	3.6
American Credit Services Inc.	228 E. Main St.	Rochester	NY	14604	Mike Halloway	716-238-8867	S	490 TA*	0.2
Midland Co.	537 E. Pete Rose Way	Cincinnati	OH	45202	J.P. Hayden Jr.	513-721-3777	P	483 TA	1.0
American Home Funding Inc.	2812 Emerywood Pkwy.	Richmond	VA	23233	Paul S. Reid	804-756-6800	S	450 TA	0.3
Credit Acceptance Corp.	25505 W. Twelve Mile	Southfield	MI	48084	Donald A. Foss	313-353-2700	P	426 TA	0.3
Kentucky Finance Company Inc.	Kincaid Towers	Lexington	KY	40507	H.C. Baker	606-253-5800	S	350 TA	0.8
Transamerica Financial Services	1150 S. Olive St.	Los Angeles	CA	90015	Al Miech	213-742-4321	S	330 TA*	0.2
EquiCredit Corporation of America	P.O. Box 53077	Jacksonville	FL	32201	John T. Hayt	904-398-7581	S	326 TA	0.6
Fleetwood Credit Corp.	P.O. Box 87024	Yorba Linda	CA	92686	Lawrence F. Pitroff	714-921-3400	S	326 TA	0.1
Fidelity Acceptance Corp.	330 2nd Ave. S.	Minneapolis	MN	55401	Florian A. Stang	612-338-5479	S	300 TA	0.7
Pacific Crest Capital Inc.	30343 Canwood St.	Agoura Hills	CA	91301	Gary L. Wehrle	818-865-3300	P	249 TA	<0.1
Pacific Crest Investment and Loan	30343 Canwood St.	Agoura Hills	CA	91301	Gary L. Wehrle	818-865-3300	S	249 TA	<0.1
1st Franklin Corp.	P.O. Box 880	Toccoa	GA	30577	Ben F. Cheek III	706-886-7571	P	136 TA	0.5
Miles Homes Inc.	4700 Nathan Ln.	Minneapolis	MN	55446	Peter R. DeGeorge	612-553-8300	P	127	0.3
Finance Co.	240 Corporate Blvd.	Norfolk	VA	23502	George R. Kouri	804-466-1222	S	126 TA	0.3
TFC Enterprises Inc.	240 Corporate Blvd.	Norfolk	VA	23502	George R. Kouri	804-466-1222	P	126 TA	0.3
Olympic Financial Ltd.	7825 Washington Ave. S	Minneapolis	MN	55439	Jeffrey C. Mack	612-942-9880	P	124 TA	0.2
AmeriCredit Corp.	200 Bailey Ave.	Fort Worth	TX	76107	Clifton H. Morris Jr.	817-332-7000	P	122 TA	0.2
AmeriCredit Financial Services Inc.	200 Bailey Ave.	Fort Worth	TX	76107	Michael R. Barrington	817-332-7000	S	122 TA	0.2
Guardian National Acceptance Corp.	19080 W. 10 Mile Rd.	Southfield	MI	48075	William Dingwall	313-352-4300	R	120 TA*	<0.1
Regional Acceptance Corp.	3004 S. Memorial Dr.	Greenville	NC	27834	William R. Stallings Sr.	919-756-2148	P	117 TA	0.1
CenCor Inc.	P.O. Box 26098	Kansas City	MO	64196	Dennis C. Berglund	816-221-9744	P	112 TA	0.3
Century Acceptance Corp.	P.O. Box 26098	Kansas City	MO	64196	Dennis C. Berylund	816-221-9744	S	110 TA	0.3
AutoFinance Group Inc.	601 Oakmont Ln.	Westmont	IL	60559	A.E. Steinhaus	708-655-7100	P	108 TA	0.1
Eaglemark Financial Services Inc.	150 S. Wacker Dr.	Chicago	IL	60606	Steven F. Deli	312-368-9501	R	100 TA	0.1
Maytag Financial Services Corp.	403 W. 4th St. N.	Newton	IA	50208	E. Matt Elliot	515-791-8800	S	100 TA	<0.1
Mego Financial Corp.	4310 Paradise Rd.	Las Vegas	NV	89109	Robert Nederlander	702-737-3700	P	100 TA	0.8
First Consumers National Bank	9300 S.W. Gemini Dr.	Beaverton	OR	97008	Greg Aube	503-520-8200	S	99 TA	0.5
Computer Power Inc.	P.O. Box 2388	Jacksonville	FL	32204	David M. Hicks	904-350-1400	R	86 OR	0.8
World Acceptance Corp.	P.O. Box 6429	Greenville	SC	29606	Charles D. Walters	803-277-4570	P	84 TA	0.7

Company type codes: P - Public, R - Private, S - Subsidiary, D - Division, J - Joint Venture, A - Affiliate, G - Group. If the dollar values shown are not sales, the following codes apply: TA - Total Assets; OR - Operating Revenues; GB - Gross Billings. * - estimated dollar value. < - less than. *na* - not available.

Continued on next page.

LEADING COMPANIES - SIC 6141 - Personal Credit Institutions

Continued

Company Name	Address				CEO Name	Phone	Co. Type	Sales/Assets ($ mil)	Empl. (000)
Eagle Finance Corp.	1509 N. Milwaukee Ave.	Libertyville	IL	60048	Charles F. Wonderlic	708-680-4900	P	71 TA	0.1
Litchfield Financial Corp.	789 Main Rd.	Stamford	VT	05352	Donald R. Dion Jr.	802-694-1200	P	64 TA	<0.1
KBK Capital Corp.	301 Commerce	Fort Worth	TX	76102	Robert J. McGee	817-335-7557	P	62 TA	<0.1
KBK Financial Inc.	301 Commerce	Fort Worth	TX	76102	Robert J. McGee	817-335-7557	S	62 TA	<0.1
Great Western Consumer Finance Group	8900 Grand Oak Cir.	Tampa	FL	33637	Michael M. Pappas	813-632-4500	S	54 TA*	2.0
Saturn Financial Services Inc.	2 Concourse Pkwy.	Atlanta	GA	30328	Donald Kombs	404-394-1900	R	54 TA*	<0.1
H.W. Kaufman Financial Group Inc.	30833 Northwestern Hwy	Southfield	MI	48034	Herbert W. Kaufman	810-932-9000	P	52	0.5
AMGRO Inc.	472 Lincoln St.	Worcester	MA	01605	Eleanor T. Raye	508-757-1628	S	45 TA	<0.1
Walshire Assurance Co.	3350 Whiteford Rd.	York	PA	17402	Kenneth R. Taylor	717-757-0000	P	43 TA	<0.1
Taylor Chevrolet Inc.	P.O. Box 10	Lancaster	OH	43130	Milton J. Taylor	614-653-2091	R	36	0.1
Northstar Guarantee Inc.	444 Cedar St.	St. Paul	MN	55101	Taige P. Thornton	612-290-8780	R	33 TA	<0.1
United Group Inc.	5960 Fairview Rd.	Charlotte	NC	28210	Bill G. Beaver	704-554-9280	P	31 TA	0.1
American Life Resources Group Inc.	420 Jefferson Ave.	Miami	FL	33139	Steven Simon	305-534-0101	S	30 TA	<0.1
First Virginia Credit Services Inc.	6402 Arlington Blvd.	Falls Church	VA	22042	John F. Chimento	703-241-3101	S	24 TA*	<0.1
ProCard Inc.	14062 Denver W. Pkwy.	Golden	CO	80401	Stanley Anderson	303-279-2255	R	24 TA	<0.1
Standard Funding Corp.	335 Crossways Park Dr.	Woodbury	NY	11797	Alan J. Karp	516-364-0200	P	19 TA	<0.1
Construction Materials Inc.	12400 Olive	Kansas City	MO	64146	Ray Goffinet	816-942-9783	R	16	<0.1
National Affiliated Finance Company Inc.	P.O. Box 12190	Alexandria	LA	71315	Richard E. Peck	318-473-4355	S	9 TA	<0.1
Student Education Loan Marketing Corp.	10390 Santa Monica	Los Angeles	CA	90025	Ron Warren	310-551-1892	R	6 TA*	<0.1
Royal Premium Budget Inc.	P.O. Box 257	Southfield	MI	48037	Herbert W. Kaufman	810-932-9020	S	2 TA	<0.1
Broadmont Association	P.O. Box 12828	Tucson	AZ	85732	Richard B. O'Reilly	602-747-8000	R	1 TA*	<0.1

Source: Ward's Business Directory of U.S. Private and Public Companies, 1996. Company type codes: P - Public, R - Private, S - Subsidiary, D - Division, J - Joint Venture, A - Affiliate, G - Group. If the dollar values shown are not sales, the following codes apply: TA - Total Assets; OR - Operating Revenues; GB - Gross Billings. * - estimated dollar value. < - less than; *na* - not available.

SIC 6150

BUSINESS CREDIT INSTITUTIONS

Business credit institutions are engaged in making loans to agricultural and other business enterprises; establishments engaged primarily in home or personal financing are excluded. The group is divided into SIC 6153, Short Term Business Credit Institutions, Except Agricultural and SIC 6159, Miscellaneous Business Credit Institutions.

SIC 6153 includes establishments that lend money to business enterprises for relatively short periods of time. The category covers short-term lenders to business, credit card collection service agencies, factors of commercial paper, financing of dealers by motor vehicle manufacturers' organizations, the buying of installment notes, dealers in installment paper, mercantile financing, purchasers of accounts receivable and commercial paper, purchasers and sellers of trust deeds, and working capital financers.

SIC 6159 includes establishments engaged primarily in furnishing intermediate or long-term general and industrial credit. The category includes agricultural loan companies, automobile finance leasing, farm mortgage companies, finance leasing of equipment and vehicles, general and industrial loan institutions, intermediate investment "banks", investment companies, livestock loan companies, general or industrial loan institutions, machinery and equipment finance leasing, pari-mutuel totalizator equipment finance leasing and maintenance, production credit associations in agriculture, and truck finance leasing.

ESTABLISHMENTS, EMPLOYMENT, AND PAYROLL

	1988	1989		1990		1991		1992		1993		% change 88-93
		Value	%	Value	%	Value	%	Value	%	Value	%	
All Establishments	3,633	3,681	1.3	3,719	1.0	4,085	9.8	4,369	7.0	4,828	10.5	32.9
Mid-March Employment	86,222	85,082	-1.3	87,608	3.0	100,612	14.8	99,276	-1.3	100,482	1.2	16.5
1st Quarter Wages (annualized - $ mil.)	2,916.3	2,896.8	-0.7	3,179.5	9.8	3,729.3	17.3	4,198.5	12.6	4,295.5	2.3	47.3
Payroll per Emp. 1st Q. (annualized)	33,823	34,047	0.7	36,292	6.6	37,066	2.1	42,292	14.1	42,749	1.1	26.4
Annual Payroll ($ mil.)	2,676.0	2,762.6	3.2	3,098.2	12.1	3,427.8	10.6	3,889.4	13.5	4,126.6	6.1	54.2
Establishments - 1-4 Emp. Number	1,921	2,008	4.5	2,013	0.2	2,151	6.9	2,450	13.9	2,737	11.7	42.5
Mid-March Employment	(D)	4,093	-	4,005	-2.2	(D)	-	4,726	-	4,844	2.5	-
1st Quarter Wages (annualized - $ mil.)	(D)	143.9	-	156.1	8.4	(D)	-	189.2	-	195.1	3.1	-
Payroll per Emp. 1st Q. (annualized)	(D)	35,164	-	38,972	10.8	(D)	-	40,042	-	40,280	0.6	-
Annual Payroll ($ mil.)	(D)	169.9	-	165.6	-2.5	(D)	-	228.0	-	235.5	3.3	-
Establishments - 5-9 Emp. Number	746	705	-5.5	741	5.1	859	15.9	787	-8.4	838	6.5	12.3
Mid-March Employment	(D)	4,564	-	4,815	5.5	(D)	-	5,128	-	5,432	5.9	-
1st Quarter Wages (annualized - $ mil.)	(D)	162.9	-	176.4	8.3	(D)	-	207.2	-	216.2	4.4	-
Payroll per Emp. 1st Q. (annualized)	(D)	35,700	-	36,645	2.6	(D)	-	40,402	-	39,809	-1.5	-
Annual Payroll ($ mil.)	(D)	156.2	-	164.1	5.1	(D)	-	197.5	-	223.9	13.3	-
Establishments - 10-19 Emp. Number	419	454	8.4	438	-3.5	491	12.1	497	1.2	544	9.5	29.8
Mid-March Employment	5,640	6,124	8.6	5,946	-2.9	6,803	14.4	6,703	-1.5	7,534	12.4	33.6
1st Quarter Wages (annualized - $ mil.)	236.5	252.4	6.7	248.7	-1.5	275.3	10.7	297.5	8.1	351.1	18.0	48.5
Payroll per Emp. 1st Q. (annualized)	41,928	41,214	-1.7	41,826	1.5	40,468	-3.2	44,386	9.7	46,608	5.0	11.2
Annual Payroll ($ mil.)	192.6	220.9	14.7	219.9	-0.5	268.6	22.2	291.5	8.5	343.4	17.8	78.3
Establishments - 20-49 Emp. Number	336	311	-7.4	293	-5.8	344	17.4	385	11.9	409	6.2	21.7
Mid-March Employment	10,445	9,677	-7.4	8,932	-7.7	10,498	17.5	11,848	12.9	12,492	5.4	19.6
1st Quarter Wages (annualized - $ mil.)	363.8	350.0	-3.8	356.8	1.9	440.2	23.4	610.5	38.7	526.4	-13.8	44.7
Payroll per Emp. 1st Q. (annualized)	34,829	36,167	3.8	39,944	10.4	41,929	5.0	51,530	22.9	42,138	-18.2	21.0
Annual Payroll ($ mil.)	346.2	340.5	-1.6	345.5	1.5	410.6	18.8	544.0	32.5	529.6	-2.7	53.0
Establishments - 50-99 Emp. Number	86	73	-15.1	86	17.8	98	14.0	116	18.4	141	21.6	64.0
Mid-March Employment	6,175	5,137	-16.8	5,726	11.5	6,682	16.7	7,979	19.4	9,637	20.8	56.1
1st Quarter Wages (annualized - $ mil.)	211.8	173.4	-18.1	203.1	17.1	293.1	44.3	374.8	27.9	458.7	22.4	116.6
Payroll per Emp. 1st Q. (annualized)	34,296	33,754	-1.6	35,462	5.1	43,858	23.7	46,972	7.1	47,600	1.3	38.8
Annual Payroll ($ mil.)	195.7	164.1	-16.2	187.4	14.2	247.7	32.2	301.7	21.8	426.7	41.4	118.0
Establishments - 100-249 Emp. Number	71	77	8.5	85	10.4	69	-18.8	60	-13.0	84	40.0	18.3
Mid-March Employment	10,999	11,699	6.4	13,196	12.8	10,781	-18.3	9,474	-12.1	12,740	34.5	15.8
1st Quarter Wages (annualized - $ mil.)	423.6	463.0	9.3	540.2	16.7	384.1	-28.9	372.0	-3.2	611.8	64.5	44.4
Payroll per Emp. 1st Q. (annualized)	38,514	39,579	2.8	40,938	3.4	35,627	-13.0	39,264	10.2	48,020	22.3	24.7
Annual Payroll ($ mil.)	383.0	428.5	11.9	447.4	4.4	335.5	-25.0	359.8	7.2	542.9	50.9	41.7
Establishments - 250-499 Emp. Number	33	33	-	41	24.2	41	-	43	4.9	50	16.3	51.5
Mid-March Employment	11,511	11,704	1.7	14,417	23.2	14,029	-2.7	14,606	4.1	17,040	16.7	48.0
1st Quarter Wages (annualized - $ mil.)	426.0	393.2	-7.7	488.3	24.2	699.7	43.3	750.5	7.3	765.9	2.0	79.8
Payroll per Emp. 1st Q. (annualized)	37,012	33,595	-9.2	33,872	0.8	49,877	47.3	51,381	3.0	44,945	-12.5	21.4
Annual Payroll ($ mil.)	353.0	362.2	2.6	457.5	26.3	562.6	23.0	628.4	11.7	665.0	5.8	88.4
Establishments - 500-999 Emp. Number	13	12	-7.7	12	-	19	58.3	19	-	14	-26.3	7.7
Mid-March Employment	9,411	8,708	-7.5	7,986	-8.3	12,323	54.3	13,945	13.2	10,873	-22.0	15.5
1st Quarter Wages (annualized - $ mil.)	329.0	281.2	-14.5	354.3	26.0	421.7	19.0	577.0	36.8	372.0	-35.5	13.1
Payroll per Emp. 1st Q. (annualized)	34,962	32,291	-7.6	44,359	37.4	34,218	-22.9	41,376	20.9	34,216	-17.3	-2.1
Annual Payroll ($ mil.)	305.1	264.4	-13.4	386.0	46.0	408.8	5.9	553.1	35.3	378.5	-31.6	24.1
Estab. - 1000 or More Emp. Number	8	8	-	10	25.0	13	30.0	12	-7.7	11	-8.3	37.5
Mid-March Employment	23,223	23,376	0.7	22,585	-3.4	29,688	31.5	24,867	-16.2	19,890	-20.0	-14.4
1st Quarter Wages (annualized - $ mil.)	634.7	676.7	6.6	655.6	-3.1	827.5	26.2	819.8	-0.9	798.2	-2.6	25.8
Payroll per Emp. 1st Q. (annualized)	27,332	28,950	5.9	29,028	0.3	27,872	-4.0	32,969	18.3	40,130	21.7	46.8
Annual Payroll ($ mil.)	615.4	656.1	6.6	724.7	10.5	811.2	11.9	785.2	-3.2	781.2	-0.5	26.9

Source: County Business Patterns, U.S. Department of Commerce, Washington, D.C., for 1988 through 1993. Payroll per employee is calculated using mid-March employment and 1st Quarter wages, annualized. Annual payroll, also shown, may not equal the annualized 1st Quarter wages. Columns headed by a percent sign (%) indicate change from the previous year. na stands for not available. The symbol (D) indicates that data are withheld by the source to avoid disclosure of competitive information. A dash (-) indicates that data are not available or cannot be calculated.

ESTABLISHMENTS
Number

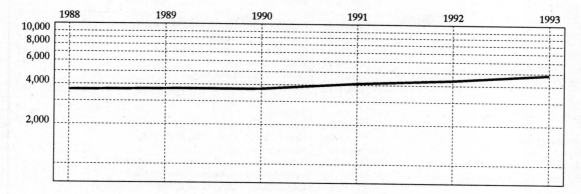

MID-MARCH EMPLOYMENT
Number

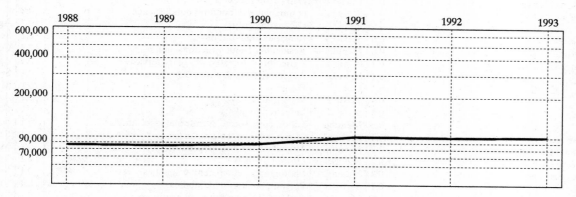

ANNUAL PAYROLL
$ million

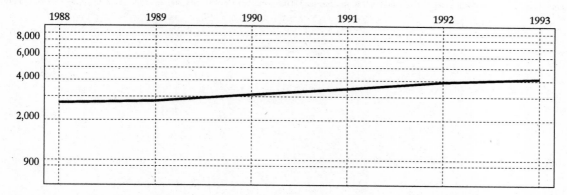

INPUTS AND OUTPUTS FOR CREDIT AGENCIES OTHER THAN BANKS - SICs 606, 611, 614-16

Economic Sector or Industry Providing Inputs	%	Sector	Economic Sector or Industry Buying Outputs	%	Sector
Banking	21.4	Fin/R.E.	Personal consumption expenditures	56.2	
Security & commodity brokers	17.4	Fin/R.E.	Eating & drinking places	9.2	Trade
Computer & data processing services	6.5	Services	Credit agencies other than banks	6.8	Fin/R.E.
Credit agencies other than banks	5.9	Fin/R.E.	Water transportation	4.4	Util.
Federal Government enterprises nec	5.6	Gov't	Owner-occupied dwellings	3.6	Fin/R.E.
Real estate	5.5	Fin/R.E.	Air transportation	2.2	Util.
Eating & drinking places	4.1	Trade	Hotels & lodging places	1.9	Services
Communications, except radio & TV	3.6	Util.	Banking	1.7	Fin/R.E.
U.S. Postal Service	3.3	Gov't	Insurance carriers	1.7	Fin/R.E.
Management & consulting services & labs	2.9	Services	Retail trade, except eating & drinking	1.5	Trade
Accounting, auditing & bookkeeping	2.6	Services	Meat animals	0.5	Agric.
Equipment rental & leasing services	2.5	Services	Automotive rental & leasing, without drivers	0.4	Services
Motor freight transportation & warehousing	2.4	Util.	Communications, except radio & TV	0.4	Util.
Advertising	1.9	Services	Engineering, architectural, & surveying services	0.4	Services
Insurance carriers	1.5	Fin/R.E.	Management & consulting services & labs	0.4	Services
Legal services	1.3	Services	Feed grains	0.3	Agric.
Electric services (utilities)	1.2	Util.	Job training & related services	0.3	Services
Petroleum refining	1.0	Manufg.	Real estate	0.3	Fin/R.E.
Commercial printing	0.9	Manufg.	S/L Govt. purch., other general government	0.3	S/L Govt
Maintenance of nonfarm buildings nec	0.9	Constr.	Dairy farm products	0.2	Agric.
Detective & protective services	0.7	Services	Maintenance of nonfarm buildings nec	0.2	Constr.
Air transportation	0.6	Util.	Oil bearing crops	0.2	Agric.
Hotels & lodging places	0.6	Services	Religious organizations	0.2	Services
Manifold business forms	0.6	Manufg.	Residential 1-unit structures, nonfarm	0.2	Constr.
Business/professional associations	0.4	Services	Agricultural, forestry, & fishery services	0.1	Agric.
Services to dwellings & other buildings	0.4	Services	Automotive repair shops & services	0.1	Services
Transit & bus transportation	0.4	Util.	Drugs	0.1	Manufg.
Wholesale trade	0.4	Trade	Food grains	0.1	Agric.
Business services nec	0.3	Services	Industrial buildings	0.1	Constr.
Envelopes	0.3	Manufg.	Labor, civic, social, & fraternal associations	0.1	Services
Personnel supply services	0.3	Services	Membership organizations nec	0.1	Services
Photographic equipment & supplies	0.3	Manufg.	Miscellaneous plastics products	0.1	Manufg.
Automotive rental & leasing, without drivers	0.2	Services	Office buildings	0.1	Constr.
Manufacturing industries, nec	0.2	Manufg.	Photographic equipment & supplies	0.1	Manufg.
Electrical repair shops	0.1	Services	Portrait, photographic studios	0.1	Services
Periodicals	0.1	Manufg.	Radio & TV communication equipment	0.1	Manufg.
Sanitary services, steam supply, irrigation	0.1	Util.	Transit & bus transportation	0.1	Util.
			Wholesale trade	0.1	Trade

Source: Benchmark Input-Output Accounts for the U.S. Economy, 1982, U.S. Department of Commerce, Washington, D.C., July 1991. Data, as reported in the source, are organized by the 1977 SIC structure in use in 1982 but have been matched, as closely as is possible, to the 1987 SIC structure used in this book. Activities with the same percentage are sorted alphabetically by name of activity.

OCCUPATIONS EMPLOYED BY FEDERAL AND BUSINESS CREDIT INSTITUTIONS

Occupation	% of Total 1994	Change to 2005	Occupation	% of Total 1994	Change to 2005
Bill & account collectors	10.6	79.9	Accountants & auditors	2.9	33.3
Loan officers & counselors	6.8	11.9	Securities & financial services sales workers	2.7	33.3
Adjustment clerks	6.5	79.9	Correspondence clerks	2.3	-6.7
Secretaries, ex legal & medical	6.1	21.3	Clerical support workers nec	2.2	6.6
Loan & credit clerks	5.3	20.0	Managers & administrators nec	1.6	33.2
Clerical supervisors & managers	4.9	36.3	Computer programmers	1.6	7.9
General managers & top executives	4.8	26.4	Systems analysts	1.4	113.3
General office clerks	4.8	13.6	Receptionists & information clerks	1.3	33.3
Financial managers	4.3	33.3	Data entry keyers, ex composing	1.3	-1.6
Bookkeeping, accounting, & auditing clerks	4.3	-0.0	Credit checkers	1.3	-10.1
Management support workers nec	3.8	33.3	Sales & related workers nec	1.2	33.3
Credit analysts	3.5	6.6			

Sources: Industry-Occupation Matrix, Bureau of Labor Statistics. These data relate to one or more 3-digit SIC industry groups rather than to a single 4-digit SIC. The change reported for each occupation to the year 2005 is a percent of growth or decline as estimated by the Bureau of Labor Statistics. The abbreviation *nec* stands for not elsewhere classified.

U.S. AND STATE DATA ON INDUSTRY REVENUES AND OTHER ACCOUNTS FOR 1992

State	No. of Estab.	Employ- ment	Payroll ($ mil.)	Revenues ($ mil.)	Empl./ Estab.	Revenue/ Estab. ($)	Payroll/ Estab. ($)	Revenue/ Empl. ($)	Payroll/ Empl. ($)
UNITED STATES	5,038	86,526	3,459.2	36,552.8	17	7,255,413	686,623	422,448	39,979
Alabama	36	-	(D)	(D)	(D)	(D)	(D)	(D)	(D)
Alaska	5	-	(D)	(D)	(D)	(D)	(D)	(D)	(D)
Arizona	86	-	(D)	(D)	(D)	(D)	(D)	(D)	(D)
Arkansas	18	33	0.6	3.4	2	187,056	32,778	102,030	17,879
California	755	10,505	452.1	4,562.7	14	6,043,323	598,860	434,337	43,040
Colorado	122	2,202	67.7	453.5	18	3,717,189	555,311	205,948	30,767
Connecticut	86	3,005	199.3	4,106.7	35	47,751,942	2,317,558	1,366,611	66,326
Delaware	53	504	10.9	332.3	10	6,270,094	204,962	659,355	21,554
District of Columbia	24	-	(D)	(D)	(D)	(D)	(D)	(D)	(D)
Florida	270	4,651	158.1	1,526.7	17	5,654,270	585,526	328,242	33,991
Georgia	210	3,863	136.2	1,442.4	18	6,868,629	648,781	373,392	35,269
Hawaii	22	-	(D)	(D)	(D)	(D)	(D)	(D)	(D)
Idaho	12	-	(D)	(D)	(D)	(D)	(D)	(D)	(D)
Illinois	307	8,114	354.0	3,728.0	26	12,143,404	1,152,984	459,456	43,624
Indiana	51	-	(D)	(D)	(D)	(D)	(D)	(D)	(D)
Iowa	41	1,670	48.9	368.4	41	8,986,317	1,193,171	220,622	29,293
Kansas	51	-	(D)	(D)	(D)	(D)	(D)	(D)	(D)
Kentucky	41	762	18.5	134.4	19	3,277,341	451,220	176,340	24,278
Louisiana	57	225	6.5	80.3	4	1,408,158	113,351	356,733	28,716
Maine	10	-	(D)	(D)	(D)	(D)	(D)	(D)	(D)
Maryland	95	-	(D)	(D)	(D)	(D)	(D)	(D)	(D)
Massachusetts	129	1,942	94.3	736.9	15	5,712,465	731,093	379,458	48,564
Michigan	127	2,351	112.1	2,067.7	19	16,281,173	882,709	879,502	47,684
Minnesota	100	1,382	58.8	571.8	14	5,718,270	588,440	413,768	42,579
Mississippi	26	232	4.4	35.5	9	1,367,154	168,538	153,216	18,888
Missouri	85	1,947	64.8	410.3	23	4,826,824	761,847	210,724	33,260
Montana	13	-	(D)	(D)	(D)	(D)	(D)	(D)	(D)
Nebraska	33	-	(D)	(D)	(D)	(D)	(D)	(D)	(D)
Nevada	41	-	(D)	(D)	(D)	(D)	(D)	(D)	(D)
New Hampshire	18	-	(D)	(D)	(D)	(D)	(D)	(D)	(D)
New Jersey	185	4,186	207.7	1,863.9	23	10,075,384	1,122,724	445,281	49,619
New Mexico	26	606	11.5	81.1	23	3,118,269	440,577	133,787	18,903
New York	485	11,727	588.9	4,930.5	24	10,165,889	1,214,282	420,436	50,220
North Carolina	117	1,338	45.9	437.9	11	3,742,915	392,410	327,295	34,314
North Dakota	8	16	0.6	7.4	2	925,125	80,125	462,563	40,063
Ohio	152	2,251	75.6	689.3	15	4,534,829	497,664	306,217	33,605
Oklahoma	43	567	14.6	309.1	13	7,188,279	338,558	545,143	25,675
Oregon	64	1,224	42.1	435.2	19	6,800,266	657,719	355,569	34,391
Pennsylvania	145	2,590	101.4	1,268.2	18	8,745,931	699,241	489,637	39,147
Rhode Island	5	-	(D)	(D)	(D)	(D)	(D)	(D)	(D)
South Carolina	44	-	(D)	(D)	(D)	(D)	(D)	(D)	(D)
South Dakota	16	-	(D)	(D)	(D)	(D)	(D)	(D)	(D)
Tennessee	73	1,695	38.7	293.0	23	4,014,274	530,329	172,886	22,840
Texas	418	5,988	192.7	1,967.8	14	4,707,696	461,100	328,627	32,188
Utah	37	-	(D)	(D)	(D)	(D)	(D)	(D)	(D)
Vermont	6	-	(D)	(D)	(D)	(D)	(D)	(D)	(D)
Virginia	89	1,629	59.3	710.9	18	7,987,157	666,236	436,376	36,400
Washington	112	1,147	44.8	502.9	10	4,490,205	399,670	438,451	39,026
West Virginia	9	15	0.2	1.2	2	131,444	25,556	78,867	15,333
Wisconsin	77	644	22.6	225.7	8	2,930,649	293,065	350,404	35,040
Wyoming	3	-	(D)	(D)	(D)	(D)	(D)	(D)	(D)

Source: 1992 Economic Census, U.S. Department of Commerce, Washington, D.C. This is the only table that shows revenue data as collected by the Bureau of the Census in an Economic Census. The symbol (D) indicates that data are withheld by the source to avoid disclosure of competitive information. A dash (-) indicates that data are not available or cannot be calculated.

ESTABLISHMENTS 1992 - STATE AND REGIONAL CONCENTRATION

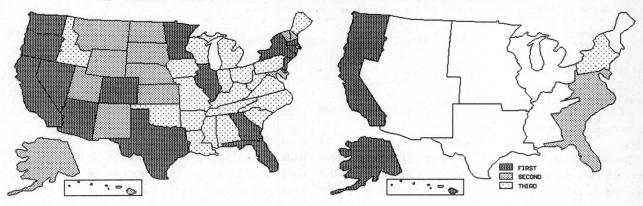

EMPLOYMENT 1992 - STATE AND REGIONAL CONCENTRATION

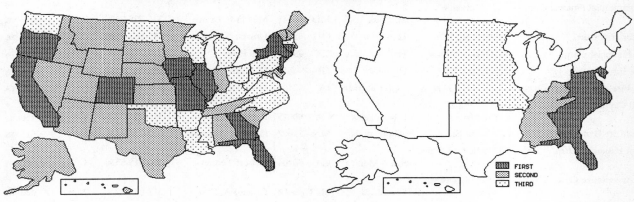

REVENUES 1992 - STATE AND REGIONAL CONCENTRATION

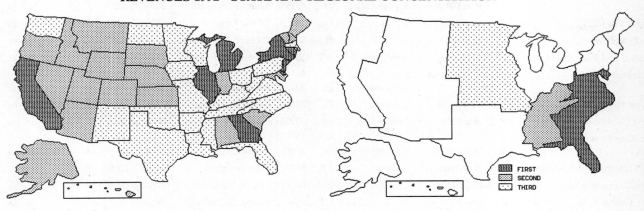

States with the darkest shading indicate those states which have proportionately more establishments, employment, or revenues than would be indicated by the state's population. States with light shading are states with proportionately fewer establishments, less employment, and lower revenues than population distribution. States shaded grey are within 15 percent of the state's population proportion in these categories. States for which no data are available are shown as average (grey). *Regions* are shaded to indicate absolute rank in the category. If no data for the category are available, establishment counts are used to shade the regions. Source of the data is the table on the facing page.

LEADING COMPANIES - SIC 6153 - Short-Term Business Credit

Number shown: 51   Total sales/assets ($ mil): 277,931   Total employment (000): 204.4

Company Name	Address				CEO Name	Phone	Co. Type	Sales/Assets ($ mil)	Empl. (000)
General Electric Capital Corp.	260 Long Ridge Rd.	Stamford	CT	06927	Gary C. Wendt	203-357-4000	S	117,939 TA	18.6
American Express Travel Related Services Company Inc.	American Express Twr.	New York	NY	10285	Harvey Golub	212-640-5130	S	40,464 TA	51.0
Associates Corporation of North America	P.O. Box 660028	Dallas	TX	75266	Kevin W. Hughes	214-541-4000	S	32,200 TA	17.0
Dean Witter, Discover and Co.	2 World Trade Ctr.	New York	NY	10048	Philip J. Purcell	212-392-2222	P	27,662 TA	26.6
American Express Credit Corp.	1 Rodney Sq.	Wilmington	DE	19801	Vincent P. Lisanke	302-594-3350	S	16,868 TA	<0.1
American Express Co.	200 Vesey St.	New York	NY	10285	Harvey Golub	212-640-2000	P	14,282 OR	72.4
Sears Roebuck Acceptance Corp.	3711 Kennett Pike	Greenville	DE	19807	Keith E. Trost	302-888-3100	S	7,031 TA	<0.1
Norwest Financial Inc.	206 8th St.	Des Moines	IA	50309	David C. Wood	515-248-7462	S	6,125 TA	6.1
ITT Commercial Finance Corp.	655 Maryville Centre	St. Louis	MO	63141	Melvin F. Brown	314-725-2525	S	4,000 TA	1.5
Ohio Casualty Corp.	136 N. 3rd St.	Hamilton	OH	45025	Lauren N. Patch	513-867-3000	P	3,739 TA	4.0
Lomas Financial Corp.	P.O. Box 655644	Dallas	TX	75265	Jess Hay	214-879-4000	P	1,078 TA	2.1
Finance Enterprises	P.O. Box 3979	Honolulu	HI	96812	Clifford Yee	808-548-3311	R	860 TA	0.4
United Fire and Casualty Co.	P.O. Box 73909	Cedar Rapids	IA	52401	Scott McIntyre Jr.	319-399-5700	P	828 TA	0.6
Foothill Capital Corp.	11111 Santa Monica	Los Angeles	CA	90025	Peter E. Schwab	310-996-7000	S	750 TA	0.1
National City Bancorp.	75 S. 5th St.	Minneapolis	MN	55402	David L. Andreas	612-340-3183	P	614 TA	0.3
Fremont Financial Corp.	2020 Santa Monica Blvd	Santa Monica	CA	90404	Robert Tenney	310-315-5550	S	600 TA	0.2
Credit Acceptance Corp.	25505 W. Twelve Mile	Southfield	MI	48084	Donald A. Foss	313-353-2700	P	426 TA	0.3
Computer Calling Technologies Inc.	135 E. Ortega St.	Santa Barbara	CA	93101	Donald Sledge	805-963-2423	S	310 TA*	0.3
Premium Financing Specialists Inc.	P.O. Box 13367	Kansas City	MO	64199	Tom Charbonneau	816-391-2350	R	280 TA	0.1
NationsBank Card Services	P.O. Box 7029	Dover	DE	19903	Eileen Friars	302-672-4200	D	260 TA*	0.3
Idaho First Bank	P.O. Box 8167	Boise	ID	83707	Richard D. Williams	208-386-3640	D	226 TA	0.1
Rosenthal and Rosenthal Inc.	1370 Broadway	New York	NY	10018	Imre J. Rosenthal	212-356-1400	R	190 TA	0.2
Capital Factors Inc.	1799 W. Oakland Park	Fort Lauderdale	FL	33311	John Kiefer	305-730-2900	S	161 TA	<0.1
Mesirow Financial Holdings Inc.	350 N. Clark St.	Chicago	IL	60610	Lester A. Morris	312-670-6000	R	150 TA*	0.5
Barnett Card Services Corp.	P.O. Box 2166	Jacksonville	FL	32232	Cynthia A. Graham	904-464-3000	S	109 TA	0.6
Prime Rate Premium Finance Corp.	P.O. Box 100507	Florence	SC	29501	James Lingle	803-669-0937	S	100 TA	<0.1
Tokai Financial Services Inc.	1055 Westlakes Dr.	Berwyn	PA	19312	Don Campbell	215-651-5000	R	100 TA	0.5
PROMPT Finance Inc.	P.O. Box 9119	Concord	MA	01742	Eric N. Wickfield	508-369-8078	S	87 TA	<0.1
Center Capital Corp.	P.O. Box 1177	Avon	CT	06001	Joseph M. Murphy	203-674-0600	S	66 TA*	<0.1
Leasing Solutions Receivables Inc.	10 Almaden Blvd.	San Jose	CA	95113	Steven L. Yeffa	408-995-6565	S	63 TA*	<0.1
Systran Financial Service Corp.	P.O. Box 3289	Portland	OR	97208	Ed Foehl	503-293-6400	R	55 TA	<0.1

Company type codes: P - Public, R - Private, S - Subsidiary, D - Division, J - Joint Venture, A - Affiliate, G - Group. If the dollar values shown are not sales, the following codes apply: TA - Total Assets; OR - Operating Revenues; GB - Gross Billings. * - estimated dollar value. < - less than. *na* - not available.

Continued on next page.

LEADING COMPANIES - SIC 6153 - Short-Term Business Credit
Continued

Company Name	Address				CEO Name	Phone	Co. Type	Sales/Assets ($ mil)	Empl. (000)
AMGRO Inc.	472 Lincoln St.	Worcester	MA	01605	Eleanor T. Raye	508-757-1628	S	45 TA	<0.1
Metro Financial Services	P.O. Box 38604	Dallas	TX	75238	Richard Worthy	214-363-4557	R	45 TA	<0.1
Creekwood Capital Corp.	1010 Lamar St.	Houston	TX	77002	Steve Rosencranz	713-759-9070	R	37 TA	<0.1
Working Assets Funding Service	701 Montgomery St.	San Francisco	CA	94111	Laura Scher	415-788-0777	R	35 OR	<0.1
Chicorp Financial Services Inc.	208 S. La Salle St.	Chicago	IL	60604	Timothy O'Gorman	312-855-5880	S	25 TA*	<0.1
Sitco Corp.	P.O. Box 5164	San Ramon	CA	94583	Howard T. Goodman	510-830-4777	R	20 TA	<0.1
Xerox Financial Services Inc.	100 1st Stamford Pl.	Stamford	CT	06904	Stuart B. Ross	203-325-6600	S	20 TA*	<0.1
Merchant Factors Corp.	1450 Broadway	New York	NY	10018	Walter Kaye	212-840-7575	R	19 TA	<0.1
Global Acceptance Corp.	2004 Hogback Rd.	Ann Arbor	MI	48105	Robert A. Shaw	313-971-1570	R	15 TA	<0.1
Mazon Associates Inc.	1425 Greenway Dr.	Irving	TX	75038	John Mazon	214-550-0111	R	12 TA	<0.1
MTB Bank. Trading Alliance Div.	90 Broad St.	New York	NY	10004	Anthony K. Brown	212-858-3450	D	7 TA*	<0.1
Nissan Capital of America Inc.	399 Park Ave.	New York	NY	10022	Yasuro Osawa	212-572-9100	S	7 TA*	<0.1
Victor Capital Group L.P.	885 Third Ave.	New York	NY	10022	Craig Hatkoff	212-593-5400	R	6 TA	<0.1
Command Credit Corp.	189 Sunrise Hwy.	Rockville Centre	NY	11570	William G. Lucas	516-764-1117	P	4 TA	<0.1
Foxmoor Industries Ltd.	3801 E. Florida Ave.	Denver	CO	80210	W. Ross C. Corace	303-759-4626	P	3 TA	<0.1
Caribou Capital Corp.	6300 S. Syracuse Way	Inglewood	CO	80111	Douglas H. Kelsall	303-694-6956	R	2 TA	<0.1
Chase-Cavett Services Inc.	4646 Poplar	Memphis	TN	38117	Will Chase	901-684-1129	R	2 TA	<0.1
Euro American Trading Merchants Inc.	37 Centennial St.	Collegeville	PA	19426	Herbert D. Moyer	610-454-0854	R	2 OR	<0.1
DFH Business Consulting Inc.	4400 S.W. 72nd Ter.	Davie	FL	33314	Daniel F. Herz	305-370-6200	R	2 OR	<0.1
Bristol Trade Finance Inc.	4809 Cole Ave., #350	Dallas	TX	75205	Joel T. Williams III	214-528-2888	R	1 TA	<0.1

Source: Ward's Business Directory of U.S. Private and Public Companies, 1996. Company type codes: P - Public, R - Private, S - Subsidiary, D - Division, J - Joint Venture, A - Affiliate, G - Group. If the dollar values shown are not sales, the following codes apply: TA - Total Assets; OR - Operating Revenues; GB - Gross Billings. * - estimated dollar value. < - less than; *na* - not available.

LEADING COMPANIES - SIC 6159 - Miscellaneous Business Credit Institutions

Number shown: **100**   Total sales/assets ($ mil): **836,140**   Total employment (000): **1,388.2**

Company Name	Address				CEO Name	Phone	Co. Type	Sales/Assets ($ mil)	Empl. (000)
General Electric Capital Services Inc.	260 Long Ridge Rd.	Stamford	CT	06927	Gary C. Wendt	203-357-6978	S	211,730 TA	25.0
General Motors Corp.	3044 W. Grand Blvd.	Detroit	MI	48202	John F. Smith Jr.	313-556-5000	P	154,951	692.8
General Electric Capital Corp.	260 Long Ridge Rd.	Stamford	CT	06927	Gary C. Wendt	203-357-4000	S	117,939 TA	18.6
AT&T Corp.	32 Avenue of the Americas	New York	NY	10013	Robert E. Allen	212-605-5500	P	67,156 OR	308.7
Chrysler Corp.	12000 Chrysler Dr.	Highland Park	MI	48288	Robert J. Eaton	313-956-5741	P	52,224	121.0
Ford Holdings Inc.	The American Rd.	Dearborn	MI	48121	Stanley Seneker	313-322-1639	S	34,755 TA	17.0
Associates Corporation of North America	P.O. Box 660028	Dallas	TX	75266	Kevin W. Hughes	214-541-4000	S	32,200 TA	17.0
Associates First Capital Corp.	P.O. Box 660237	Dallas	TX	75266	Keith W. Hughes	214-541-4000	S	32,200 TA	17.0
Chrysler Financial Corp.	27777 Franklin Rd.	Southfield	MI	48034	John P. Tierney	810-948-3888	S	14,402 TA	3.1
IBM Credit Corp.	P.O. Box 10399	Stamford	CT	06904	James J. Forese	203-973-5100	S	10,042 TA	0.9
Textron Inc.	40 Westminster St.	Providence	RI	02903	James F. Hardymon	401-421-2800	P	9,683	53.0
Westinghouse Electric Corp.	11 Stanwix St.	Pittsburgh	PA	15222	Michael H. Jordan	412-244-2000	P	8,848	84.4
AT and T Credit Holdings Inc.	2 Gatehall Dr.	Parsippany	NJ	07054	Thomas C. Wajnert	201-606-3500	S	8,022 TA	2.7
AT&T Capital Corp.	44 Whippany Rd.	Morristown	NJ	07962	Thomas C. Wajnert	201-397-3000	P	8,022 TA	2.7
Norwest Financial Inc.	206 8th St.	Des Moines	IA	50309	David C. Wood	515-248-7462	S	6,125 TA	6.1
GFC Financial Corp.	1850 N. Central Ave.	Phoenix	AZ	85077	Samuel L. Eichenfield	602-207-4900	P	5,834 TA	0.9
Philip Morris Capital Corp.	800 Westchester Ave.	Rye Brook	NY	10573	Hans G. Storr	914-335-1155	S	5,236 TA	0.1
Finova Capital Corp.	95 Rte. 17 S.	Paramus	NJ	07652	Sam Eichenfield	201-368-1045	S	5,200 TA	0.3
Caterpillar Financial Services Corp.	3322 W. End Ave.	Nashville	TN	37203	James S. Beard	615-386-5800	S	4,400 TA	0.4
John Deere Capital Corp.	1 E. 1st St.	Reno	NV	89501	Michael P. Orr	702-786-5527	S	4,290 TA	0.8
John Deere Credit Co.	1 E. 1st St.	Reno	NV	89501	Michael P. Orr	702-786-5527	S	4,290 TA	0.8
Farm Credit Services of Mid-America	P.O. Box 34390	Louisville	KY	40232	Don Winters	502-566-3718	R	4,210 TA*	0.7
Pitney Bowes Credit Corp.	201 Merritt 7	Norwalk	CT	06856	Michael Cretelli	203-846-5600	S	3,618 TA	0.8
ADVANTA Corp.	300 Welsh Rd.	Horsham	PA	19044	Dennis Alter	215-657-4000	P	3,113 TA	1.8
AT&T Capital Leasing Services Inc.	P.O. Box 9104	Framingham	MA	01701	James Tenner	508-620-0099	S	2,380 TA	0.7
Whirlpool Financial Corp.	553 Benson Rd.	Benton Harbor	MI	49022	James LeBlanc	616-926-5500	S	2,146 TA	0.8
McDonnell Douglas Finance Corp.	4060 Lakewood Blvd.	Long Beach	CA	90808	George M. Rosen	310-627-3100	S	1,930 TA	0.1
McDonnell Douglas Financial Services Corp.	4060 N. Lakewood Blvd.	Long Beach	CA	90808	George M. Rosen	310-627-3000	S	1,794 TA	0.1
PACCAR Financial Corp.	P.O. Box 1518	Bellevue	WA	98009	T. Ronald Morton	206-462-4100	S	1,771 TA	0.2
United Carriers Corp.	P.O. Box 4070	Newark	OH	43055	R.A. Barnes	614-349-8144	R	1,750 TA*	0.3
Navistar Financial Corp.	2850 W. Golf Rd.	Rolling Meadows	IL	60008	John J. Bongiorno	708-734-4000	S	1,672 TA	0.4

Company type codes: P - Public, R - Private, S - Subsidiary, D - Division, J - Joint Venture, A - Affiliate, G - Group. If the dollar values shown are not sales, the following codes apply: TA - Total Assets; OR - Operating Revenues; GB - Gross Billings. * - estimated dollar value. < - less than. *na* - not available.

Continued on next page.

LEADING COMPANIES - SIC 6159 - Miscellaneous Business Credit Institutions
Continued

Company Name	Address				CEO Name	Phone	Co. Type	Sales/Assets ($ mil)	Empl. (000)
GATX Capital Corp.	4 Embarcadero Ctr.	San Francisco	CA	94111	Joseph C. Lane	415-955-3200	S	1,240 TA	0.2
Leasing Dynamics Inc.	30033 Clemens Rd.	Westlake	OH	44145	Bob Kendall	216-899-2900	S	1,220 TA	0.2
ADVANTA Leasing Corp.	1020 Laurel Oak Rd.	Voorhees	NJ	08043	Albert Lindenberg	609-782-7300	S	1,020 TA	0.2
Mission First Financial	18101 Von Karmen Ave.	Irvine	CA	92715	Thomas R. McDaniel	714-757-2400	S	1,008 TA	<0.1
Oxford Resources Corp.	270 S. Service Rd.	Melville	NY	11747	Michael Pascucci	516-777-8000	P	906 TA	0.3
United Fire and Casualty Co.	P.O. Box 73909	Cedar Rapids	IA	52401	Scott McIntyre Jr.	319-399-5700	P	828 TA	0.6
Clark Credit Corp.	500 Circle Dr.	Buchanan	MI	49107	Dick Goble	616-697-4000	S	800 TA	0.2
Farm Credit Leasing Services Corp.	5500 Wayzata Blvd.	Minneapolis	MN	55416	Rolf E. Haugen	612-378-1733	R	700 TA	0.2
Norwest Equipment Finance Inc.	733 Marquette Ave.	Minneapolis	MN	55479	James R. Renner	612-667-9702	S	580 TA*	0.1
PEC Israel Economic Corp.	511 5th Ave.	New York	NY	10017	Frank Klein	212-687-2400	P	384 TA	<0.1
Southeastern Michigan Gas Enterprises Inc.	P.O. Box 5026	Port Huron	MI	48061	Ward N. Kirby	810-987-2200	P	372 TA	0.5
Circle Business Credit Inc.	P.O. Box 44901	Indianapolis	IN	46244	David McCellan	317-767-0077	S	351 TA*	<0.1
Security Pacific Executive-Professional Services Inc.	14707 E. 2nd Ave.	Aurora	CO	80011	Richard Rushton	303-363-7600	S	350 TA*	<0.1
Ampal-American Israel Corp.	1177 Ave. of the Amer.	New York	NY	10036	Lawrence Lefkowitz	212-782-2100	P	343 TA	<0.1
Mid-North Financial Services Inc.	205 W. Wacker Dr.	Chicago	IL	60606	Al Hanna	312-641-0660	R	318 TA	<0.1
Gillco Inc.	7611 Bellaire Blvd.	Houston	TX	77036	Ramsay H. Gillman	713-776-7000	R	270	0.8
D'Accord Holdings Inc.	1 Embarcadero Ctr.	San Francisco	CA	94111	Christopher W. Gould	415-981-3812	R	230 TA*	<0.1
USL Capital Corp.	733 Front St.	San Francisco	CA	94111	James G. Duff	415-627-9000	S	214 OR	0.7
Ruan Leasing Co.	3200 Ruan Ctr.	Des Moines	IA	50309	Gary Alvord	515-245-2500	R	180 TA	1.8
Ameritech Credit Corp.	2550 W. Golf Rd.	Rolling Meadows	IL	60008	R. Scott Horsley	708-290-5000	S	170 TA	<0.1
D'Accord Inc.	1 Embarcadero Ctr.	San Francisco	CA	94111	Christopher Gold	415-981-3812	S	170 TA*	<0.1
Money Store Investment Corp.	3301 C St.	Sacramento	CA	95816	Lawrence J. Wodarski	916-446-1829	S	170 TA*	0.3
Copelco Financial Services Group Inc.	1700 Suckle Plz.	Pennsauken	NJ	08110	Ian J. Berg	609-665-6400	S	165 TA	0.5
Chancellor Fleet Corp.	745 Atlantic Ave.	Boston	MA	02111	Stephen G. Morison	617-728-8500	S	130 TA	<0.1
Hyster Credit Co.	222 S.W. Columbia St.	Portland	OR	97201	William F. Burke	503-321-5400	D	130 TA*	<0.1
First Community Financial Corp.	3550 N. Central Ave.	Phoenix	AZ	85012	James Adamany	602-265-7714	R	110 TA*	<0.1
First New England Financial Corp.	1000 Bridgeport Ave.	Shelton	CT	06484	Jim Foley	203-944-2810	S	110 TA*	<0.1
Rush Enterprises Inc.	P.O. Box 200105	San Antonio	TX	78220	Marvin Rush	210-661-4511	R	110*	0.3

Company type codes: P - Public, R - Private, S - Subsidiary, D - Division, J - Joint Venture, A - Affiliate, G - Group. If the dollar values shown are not sales, the following codes apply: TA - Total Assets; OR - Operating Revenues; GB - Gross Billings. * - estimated dollar value. < - less than. *na* - not available.

Continued on next page.

LEADING COMPANIES - SIC 6159 - Miscellaneous Business Credit Institutions

Continued

Company Name	Address				CEO Name	Phone	Co. Type	Sales/Assets ($ mil)	Empl. (000)
HPSC Inc.	470 Atlantic Ave.	Boston	MA	02210	Raymond R. Doherty	617-574-4240	P	103 TA	<0.1
Chase Community Development Corp.	2 Chase Manhattan Plz.	New York	NY	10081	Mark A. Willis	212-552-8519	S	102 TA	<0.1
Horrigan American Inc.	P.O. Box 13428	Reading	PA	19612	Arthur A. Haberberger	215-775-3134	R	100 TA•	0.1
Maytag Financial Services Corp.	403 W. 4th St. N.	Newton	IA	50208	E. Matt Elliot	515-791-8800	S	100 TA	<0.1
New York Business Development Corp.	P.O. Box 738	Albany	NY	12201	Robert W. Lazar	518-463-2268	R	100 TA	<0.1
Sirrom Capital Corp.	511 Union St.	Nashville	TN	37219	George M. Miller II	615-256-0701	P	91 TA	<0.1
PROMPT Finance Inc.	P.O. Box 9119	Concord	MA	01742	Eric N. Wickfield	508-369-8078	S	87 TA	<0.1
Eagle Finance Corp.	1509 N. Milwaukee Ave.	Libertyville	IL	60048	Charles F. Wonderlic	708-680-4900	P	71 TA	0.1
EnCap Investment L.L.C.	6688 N. Central Expwy.	Dallas	TX	75206	David B. Miller	214-696-6700	R	71 TA•	<0.1
Amstat Corp.	12760 High Bluff Dr.	San Diego	CA	92130	Bob Cohrs	619-794-6333	R	70 TA•	<0.1
Evergreen Community Development Association	1310 Smith Tower	Seattle	WA	98104	Jim MacDonald	206-622-3731	R	64 TA•	<0.1
Integra Business Credit Co.	801 Penn Ave.	Pittsburgh	PA	15222	Denis Burke	412-456-2452	S	60 TA	<0.1
Freeman Spogli and Co.	11100 Santa Monica	Los Angeles	CA	90025	Bradford Freeman	310-444-1822	R	58 TA•	<0.1
Associated Leasing Inc.	P.O. Box 10	Menomonee Falls	WI	53052	Peter c. Bapes	414-253-2300	S	52 TA•	<0.1
Allied Financial Corp.	1583 Beacon St.	Brookline	MA	02146	Andre Danesh	617-734-7771	R	51 TA	<0.1
Sterling Industrial Loan Association	5516 Falmouth St.	Richmond	VA	23230	William Bower	804-644-2361	S	35 TA	<0.1
Emergent Group Inc.	P.O. Box 17526	Greenville	SC	29606	John M. Sterling Jr.	803-235-8056	P	35 OR	0.3
John Hancock Leasing Corp.	P.O. Box 111	Boston	MA	02117	John M. Butler	617-572-6000	S	34 TA	<0.1
PDS Financial Corp.	6442 City West Pkwy.	Minneapolis	MN	55344	Johan P. Finley	612-941-9500	P	31 TA	<0.1
Massachusetts Minority Enterprise Investment Corp.	100 Franklin St.	Boston	MA	02110	Tom Schumpert	617-338-0425	R	29 TA	<0.1
Harvey Cadillac Co.	2600 28th St. S.E.	Grand Rapids	MI	49512	H.A. Duthler	616-949-1140	R	28	<0.1
AAA Interair Inc.	P.O. Box 522230	Miami	FL	33152	Doug Potter	305-889-6111	S	26	<0.1
Chicorp Financial Services Inc.	208 S. La Salle St.	Chicago	IL	60604	Timothy O'Gorman	312-855-5880	S	25 TA•	<0.1
Griffin and Associates Leasing Inc.	2730 San Pedro N.E.	Albuquerque	NM	87110	Joan Rosley-Griffin	505-889-6318	R	23 TA	<0.1
MCC Financial Corp.	8180 Greensboro Dr.	McLean	VA	22102	Jim Walker	703-847-6595	R	23 TA•	<0.1
American Industrial Loan Association	3420 Holland Rd.	Virginia Beach	VA	23452	Allen Wyckle	804-430-1400	R	20 TA	<0.1
Citizens Commercial Leasing Corp.	1 Citizens Banking Ctr	Flint	MI	48502	Susan McClary	810-768-4815	S	17 TA•	<0.1
Shealy's Truck Center Inc.	P.O. Box 13484	Columbia	SC	29201	C.B. Shealy	803-771-0176	R	15	<0.1

Company type codes: P - Public, R - Private, S - Subsidiary, D - Division, J - Joint Venture, A - Affiliate, G - Group. If the dollar values shown are not sales, the following codes apply: TA - Total Assets; OR - Operating Revenues; GB - Gross Billings. • - estimated dollar value. < - less than. *na* - not available.

Continued on next page.

LEADING COMPANIES - SIC 6162 - Mortgage Bankers and Correspondents
Continued

Company Name	Address				CEO Name	Phone	Co. Type	Sales/Assets ($ mil)	Empl. (000)
General Electric Capital Mortgage Services Inc.	3 Executive Campus	Cherry Hill	NJ	08034	Alan Hainey	609-661-6100	S	1,310 TA*	1.2
Margaretten and Company Inc.	205 Smith St.	Perth Amboy	NJ	08861	Felix M. Beck	908-324-4000	S	1,203 TA	2.0
Margaretten Financial Corp.	205 Smith St.	Perth Amboy	NJ	08861	Felix M. Beck	908-324-4000	P	1,203 TA	2.0
Lomas Financial Corp.	P.O. Box 655644	Dallas	TX	75265	Jess Hay	214-879-4000	P	1,078 TA	2.1
U.S. Home Corp.	P.O. Box 2863	Houston	TX	77252	Robert J. Strudler	713-877-2311	P	995 OR	1.4
Metropolitan Mortgage and Securities Company Inc.	W. 929 Sprague Ave.	Spokane	WA	99204	C. Paul Sandifur Jr.	509-838-3111	R	982 OR	0.3
Plaza Home Mortgage Corp.	1820 E. 1st St.	Santa Ana	CA	92705	Jack French	714-564-3010	P	953 TA	0.9
Money Store Inc.	2840 Morris Ave.	Union	NJ	07083	Marc Turtletaub	908-686-2000	P	910 TA	1.4
York Financial Corp.	101 S. George St.	York	PA	17405	Robert W. Pullo	717-846-8777	P	888 TA	0.5
ARCS Mortgage Inc.	26541 Agoura Rd.	Calabasas	CA	91302	Howard J. Levine	818-880-2600	S	880 TA*	0.8
Meridian Mortgage Corp.	744 W. Lancaster Ave.	Wayne	PA	19087	Russel J. Kunkel	215-971-6000	S	870 TA	0.5
PHH US Mortgage Corp.	6000 Atrium Way	Mount Laurel	NJ	08054	H. Robert Nagel	609-439-6000	S	840 TA	1.1
NVR Inc.	7601 Lewinsville Rd.	McLean	VA	22102	Dwight C. Schar	703-761-2000	P	821 OR	1.5
North American Mortgage Co.	3883 Airway Dr.	Santa Rosa	CA	95403	John F. Farrell Jr.	707-546-3310	P	765 TA	2.4
Medallion Mortgage Co.	P.O. Box 9369	San Jose	CA	95157	Walter Muir	408-985-1000	R	760 TA	0.7
Poughkeepsie Savings Bank F.S.B.	249 Main Mall	Poughkeepsie	NY	12601	Joseph B. Tockarshewsky	914-431-6200	P	728 TA	0.2
Merrill Lynch Credit Corp.	4802 Deer Lake Dr. E.	Jacksonville	FL	32246	Kevin O'Hanlon	904-928-6000	S	680 TA*	0.6
Sterling Financial Corp.	P.O. Box 10608	Lancaster	PA	17605	John E. Stefan	717-295-7551	P	633 TA	0.4
Commerce Group Inc.	211 Main St.	Webster	MA	01570	Arthur J. Remillard Jr.	508-943-9000	P	600 TA	1.2
ADVANTA Mortgage Corporation USA	16875 W. Bernardo Dr.	San Diego	CA	92127	Milt Riseman	619-674-1800	S	560 TA	0.2
Home Lending Associates Inc.	950 Andover Park E.	Tukwila	WA	98188	Dave Zehm	206-575-8875	R	540 TA*	0.5
Shawmut Mortgage Co.	433 S. Main St.	West Hartford	CT	06110	John J. Spear	203-240-6829	S	500 TA*	0.4
SNMC Management Corp.	2974 Lyndon B. Johnson	Dallas	TX	75234	Jim Witherow	214-484-5600	R	500 TA	0.9
First Franklin Financial Corp.	2150 N. 1st St.	San Jose	CA	95131	William D. Dallas	408-955-9600	R	490 TA*	0.5
AmSouth Mortgage Co.	P.O. Box 847	Birmingham	AL	35201	Michael Padalino	205-326-4600	S	484 TA	0.8
Primark Corp.	8251 Greensboro Dr.	McLean	VA	22102	Joseph E. Kasputys	703-790-7600	P	477 OR	3.4
Railroad Financial Corp.	P.O. Box 2933	Wichita	KS	67201	Robert D. Taylor	316-269-0300	P	461 TA	0.3
Wendover Funding Corp.	725 N. Regional Rd.	Greensboro	NC	27409	Jeffrey S. Taylor	910-668-7000	S	460 TA*	0.4
George Mason Bankshares Inc.	11185 Main St.	Fairfax	VA	22030	Bernard H. Clineburg	703-352-1100	P	457 TA	0.2
Fleet Real Estate Funding Corp.	P.O. Box 11988	Columbia	SC	29211	Robert Golitz	803-253-7900	S	400 TA	0.9
Oxford First Corp.	7300 Old York Rd.	Philadelphia	PA	19126	Lewis Collin	215-782-7000	S	390 TA	0.3

Company type codes: P - Public, R - Private, S - Subsidiary, D - Division, J - Joint Venture, A - Affiliate, G - Group. If the dollar values shown are not sales, the following codes apply: TA - Total Assets; OR - Operating Revenues; GB - Gross Billings. * - estimated dollar value. < - less than. *na* - not available.

Continued on next page.

LEADING COMPANIES - SIC 6162 - Mortgage Bankers and Correspondents

Continued

Company Name	Address				CEO Name	Phone	Co. Type	Sales/Assets ($ mil)	Empl. (000)
Guild Mortgage Co.	P.O. Box 85304	San Diego	CA	92186	Martin Gliesch	619-560-7711	R	380 TA*	0.4
BancBoston Mortgage Corp.	7301 Baymeadows Way	Jacksonville	FL	32256	Joe K. Pickett	904-281-3000	S	370 TA	0.9
Loan America Financial Corp.	8100 Oak Ln.	Hialeah	FL	33016	Charles B. Stuzin	305-557-9282	P	368 TA	0.4
Kaufman and Broad Mortgage Co.	21900 Burbank Blvd.	Woodland Hills	CA	91367	Daniel Schreiner	818-887-2275	S	356 TA	0.2
EQ Services Inc.	235 Peachtree St, N.E.	Atlanta	GA	30303	Paul S. Klick III	404-654-2000	S	350 TA	0.3
Continental Homes Holding Corp.	7001 N. Scottsdale Rd.	Scottsdale	AZ	85253	Donald R. Loback	602-483-0006	P	349 OR	0.2
Ampal-American Israel Corp.	1177 Ave. of the Amer.	New York	NY	10036	Lawrence Lefkowitz	212-782-2100	P	343 TA	<0.1
NBD Mortgage Co.	P.O. Box 331755	Detroit	MI	48232	Thomas McDowell	313-828-2307	S	340 TA	0.6
Mission Hills Mortgage Corp.	1403 N. Tustin Ave.	Santa Ana	CA	92701	Jay Ledbetter	714-972-3832	R	320 TA*	0.3
SouthTrust Mortgage Corp.	P.O. Box 532060	Birmingham	AL	35253	Larry Hamilton	205-254-8308	S	310 TA*	0.3
ICM Mortgage Corp.	6061 S. Willow Dr.	Greenwood Village	CO	80111	Jeffery D. LeClaire	303-740-3323	S	305 TA	0.2
Arbor National Holdings Inc.	333 Earle Ovington	Uniondale	NY	11553	Ivan Kaufman	516-357-7400	P	294 TA	0.9
Arbor National Mortgage Inc.	615 Merrick Ave.	Westbury	NY	11590	Ivan Kaufman	516-832-7200	S	294 TA	0.9
SunTrust Mortgage Inc.	P.O. Box 100100	Atlanta	GA	30348	Robert W. Hearn Jr.	404-955-6000	S	280 TA*	0.3
Temple-Inland Mortgage Corp.	P.O. Box 40	Austin	TX	78767	Herb Lloyd	512-477-6561	S	270 TA*	0.3
Centennial Bancorp.	P.O. Box 1560	Eugene	OR	97440	Richard C. Williams	503-342-3970	P	258 TA	0.2
AccuBanc Mortgage Corp.	12377 Merit Dr.	Dallas	TX	75251	William R. Starkey Sr.	214-458-9200	R	257 TA	0.6
Resource Bancshares Mortgage Group Inc.	P.O. Box 7486	Columbia	SC	29202	Edward J. Sebastian	803-790-4500	P	238 TA	0.4
First Advantage Mortgage Corp.	8910 Rte. 108	Columbia	MD	21045	Al Kocourek	410-964-4800	R	230 TA	0.3
Consolidated Mortgage Corp.	1 W. 1st. Ave.	Conshohocken	PA	19004	Bill Siderio	610-397-0333	S	210 TA*	0.2
Fleet Management and Recovery Corp.	245 Summer St.	Boston	MA	02209	Georgina Macdonald	617-573-5008	S	210 TA*	0.2
Midwest Mortgage Services Inc.	1901 S. Meyers Rd.	Oakbrook Terrace	IL	60181	Leonard Giblin	708-495-0090	S	200 TA*	0.2
AGM Financial Services Inc.	111 3rd Ave. S.	Minneapolis	MN	55401	Gerald Glaser	612-339-8700	R	185 TA	<0.1
Hamilton Financial Corp.	525 Market St.	San Francisco	CA	94105	William Kirschenbaum	415-597-5600	S	174 TA	0.4
Hamilton Financial Services Corp.	525 Market St.	San Francisco	CA	94105	William Kirschenbaum	415-597-5600	P	174 TA	0.4
First Eastern Mortgage Corp.	100 Brickstone Sq.	Andover	MA	01810	Richard F. Kalagher	508-749-3100	S	170 TA*	0.2
Shelter Mortgage Corp.	4000 W. Brown Deer Rd.	Milwaukee	WI	53209	Jill Belcomis	414-355-3000	S	170 TA*	0.2
Central Fidelity Mortgage Corp.	828 Main St.	Lynchburg	VA	24504	Bryant W. Baird Jr.	804-847-9252	S	160 TA*	0.2
Universal Lending Corp.	6775 E. Evans Ave.	Denver	CO	80224	Peter Lansing	303-758-4969	R	160 TA*	0.2
Central Resource Group Inc.	611 5th Ave.	Des Moines	IA	50309	Alfred P. Moore	515-242-2384	S	154 OR	0.8
Financial Resources Group Inc.	2 University Plz.	Hackensack	NJ	07602	Murray L. Beer	201-489-6120	R	150 TA	0.2

Company type codes: P - Public, R - Private, S - Subsidiary, D - Division, J - Joint Venture, A - Affiliate, G - Group. If the dollar values shown are not sales, the following codes apply: TA - Total Assets; OR - Operating Revenues; GB - Gross Billings. * - estimated dollar value. < - less than. *na* - not available.

Continued on next page.

LEADING COMPANIES - SIC 6162 - Mortgage Bankers and Correspondents
Continued

Company Name	Address				CEO Name	Phone	Co. Type	Sales/Assets ($ mil)	Empl. (000)
Sterling National Mortgage Company Inc.	77 Brant Ave.	Clark	NJ	07066	Linda Valentine	908-499-8200	R	150 TA	<0.1
First Virginia Mortgage Co.	6402 Arlington Blvd.	Falls Church	VA	22042	P. Thomas May Jr.	703-241-3201	S	140 TA*	0.1
Alliance Mortgage Co.	4500 Salsbury Rd.	Jacksonville	FL	32216	Gary Meeks	904-281-6000	R	120 TA*	0.2
Express America Holdings Corp.	9060 E. Via Linda St.	Scottsdale	AZ	85258	Robert W. Stallings	602-661-3577	P	120 TA	0.2
Boatmen's Mortgage Corp.	222 S. Central Ave.	Clayton	MO	63105	William Carson	314-889-7333	S	109 TA	<0.1
EnTrust Funding Co.	2000 Riveredge Pkwy.	Atlanta	GA	30328	Al Kocourek	404-980-4700	D	104 TA	<0.1
First of America Mortgage Co.	1 First of America	Kalamazoo	MI	49009	David L. Stimpson	616-376-8535	S	103 TA	0.6
Independence Mortgage Corp.	2699 Lee Rd.	Winter Park	FL	32789	Douglas Turner	407-645-0065	S	100 TA	0.1
Gulf Pacific Mortgage Corp.	5100 Poplar Ave.	Memphis	TN	38137	Ronald Carol	901-767-3400	D	100 TA*	0.1
HomeBanc Mortgage Corp.	5775 Glenridge Bldg. E	Atlanta	GA	30328	Robert S. Cannon	404-303-4280	S	100 TA	0.3
MortgageAmerica Inc.	3535 Grandvia Pkwy.	Birmingham	AL	35243	John Johnson	205-970-3000	R	100 TA*	0.1

Source: *Ward's Business Directory of U.S. Private and Public Companies*, 1996. Company type codes: P - Public, R - Private, S - Subsidiary, D - Division, J - Joint Venture, A - Affiliate, G - Group. If the dollar values shown are not sales, the following codes apply: TA - Total Assets; OR - Operating Revenues; GB - Gross Billings. * - estimated dollar value. < - less than; na - not available.

LEADING COMPANIES - SIC 6163 - Loan Brokers
Number shown: **23**   Total sales/assets ($ mil): **452**   Total employment (000): **2.6**

Company Name	Address				CEO Name	Phone	Co. Type	Sales/Assets ($ mil)	Empl. (000)
National Auto Credit Inc.	30000 Aurora Rd.	Solon	OH	44139	Sam J. Frankino	216-349-1000	P	219 OR	1.6
Nationwide Secondary Marketing Inc.	7770 W. Oakland Park	Fort Lauderdale	FL	33351	Howard Kaye	305-748-7700	R	31 OR	<0.1
Koenig and Strey Inc.	3201 Old Glenview Rd.	Wilmette	IL	60091	Thomas E. Koenig	708-729-5050	R	30 OR	0.5
Manhattan Mortgage Co.	425 Park Ave.	New York	NY	10022	Ellen Bitton	212-593-4343	R	27 OR*	<0.1
Fairway Capital Corp.	285 Governors St.	Providence	RI	02906	Arnold Kilberg	401-454-7500	R	21 OR*	<0.1
Homes for South Florida Inc.	1390 Brickell Ave.	Miami	FL	33131	Marie Lee	305-579-3076	R	21 OR*	<0.1
NBR Mortgage Company Inc.	P.O. Box 1987	Santa Rosa	CA	95402	John H. Downey	707-573-4880	S	19 TA*	<0.1
Meredith and Grew Inc.	160 Federal St.	Boston	MA	02110	Thomas J. Hynes Jr.	617-330-8000	R	16 OR	0.2
USGI Holdings Inc.	P.O. Box 6003	Norwalk	CT	06852	William C. Gow	203-849-4500	R	14 OR	<0.1
BISYS Loan Service Inc.	5373 W. Alabama St.	Houston	TX	77056	Larry Litton Sr.	713-960-9676	S	11 OR*	0.1
Randall Mortgage Inc.	670 N. Orlando Ave.	Maitland	FL	32757	Al Feldman	407-539-1551	R	9 OR*	<0.1
Michael V. Coratolo and Associates Inc.	502 La Guardia Pl.	New York	NY	10012	Michael V. Coratolo	212-254-9800	R	5 OR	<0.1

Company type codes: P - Public, R - Private, S - Subsidiary, D - Division, J - Joint Venture, A - Affiliate, G - Group. If the dollar values shown are not sales, the following codes apply: TA - Total Assets; OR - Operating Revenues; GB - Gross Billings. * - estimated dollar value. < - less than. *na* - not available.

Continued on next page.

LEADING COMPANIES - SIC 6163 - Loan Brokers

Continued

Company Name	Address				CEO Name	Phone	Co. Type	Sales/Assets ($ mil)	Empl. (000)
Southern Dallas Development Corp.	1201 Griffin St. W.	Dallas	TX	75215	Jim Reid	214-428-7332	R	5 OR	<0.1
Equivest Finance Inc.	7777 Davie Rd.	Hollywood	FL	33024	Murray Bacal	305-433-5434	P	4 OR	<0.1
Banker's Portfolio Exchange Inc.	2200 E. River Rd.	Tucson	AZ	85718	Sherry Neasham	602-299-5399	R	3 OR•	<0.1
DRG Financial Corp.	5125 MacArthur Blvd. N	Washington	DC	20016	Donald M. DeFranceaux	202-965-7000	R	3 OR•	<0.1
LJM Realty Advisors Inc.	18500 Von Karman Ave.	Irvine	CA	92715	Guy K. Johnson	714-660-1999	R	3 OR	<0.1
Baltimore Financial Corp.	P.O. Box 192011	San Francisco	CA	94119	Joseph Moore	415-435-9621	R	2 OR	<0.1
Elite Financial Group Inc.	2400 W. Cypress Creek	Fort Lauderdale	FL	33309	Bill C. Stamper	305-938-4366	R	2 OR	<0.1
Federal Services Corp.	3330 Oakwell Ct.	San Antonio	TX	78218	Charles Leone III	210-829-0279	R	2 OR•	<0.1
Gallatin Realty Co.	409 S. Division	Ann Arbor	MI	48104	Jeffrey R. Gallatin	313-994-1202	R	2 OR	<0.1
Mortgage Resource Inc.	14430 S. Outer 40	Chesterfield	MO	63017	Steven Carrico	314-576-5577	R	2 OR	<0.1
Specialty Group	3205 E. McKnight Dr.	Pittsburgh	PA	15237	Ned Sokoloff	412-369-1555	R	1 OR	<0.1

Source: Ward's Business Directory of U.S. Private and Public Companies, 1996. Company type codes: P - Public, R - Private, S - Subsidiary, D - Division, J - Joint Venture, A - Affiliate, G - Group. If the dollar values shown are not sales, the following codes apply: TA - Total Assets; OR - Operating Revenues; GB - Gross Billings. • - estimated dollar value. < - less than; *na* - not available.

SIC 6210

SECURITY BROKERS AND DEALERS

SIC 6210 includes establishments primarily engaged in the purchase, sale, and brokerage of securities; the SIC also includes investment bankers primarily engaged in originating, underwriting, and distributing issues of securities. Excluded from the SIC are establishments engaged in issuing shares of mutual and money market funds, unit investment trusts, and face-amount certificates; these operations are in SIC 6720, Investment Offices.

The SIC group includes agents for mutual funds; brokers for and dealers in bonds, notes, oil and gas leases, oil royalties, mineral leases and royalties, mortgages (rediscounting), securities, tax certificates, and stock options; distributors of securities; floor traders; investment bankers; investment firms engaged in general brokerage; and sellers of partnership shares in real estate syndicates.

ESTABLISHMENTS, EMPLOYMENT, AND PAYROLL

	1988	1989 Value	%	1990 Value	%	1991 Value	%	1992 Value	%	1993 Value	%	% change 88-93
All Establishments	13,343	13,313	-0.2	15,894	19.4	17,032	7.2	18,690	9.7	19,616	5.0	47.0
Mid-March Employment	332,743	312,550	-6.1	308,078	-1.4	295,412	-4.1	310,823	5.2	309,943	-0.3	-6.9
1st Quarter Wages (annualized - $ mil.)	35,225.7	27,171.6	-22.9	26,669.6	-1.8	23,152.6	-13.2	30,333.8	31.0	28,631.3	-5.6	-18.7
Payroll per Emp. 1st Q. (annualized)	105,865	86,935	-17.9	86,568	-0.4	78,374	-9.5	97,592	24.5	92,376	-5.3	-12.7
Annual Payroll ($ mil.)	22,630.4	20,306.5	-10.3	20,777.4	2.3	21,082.3	1.5	26,383.4	25.1	28,896.8	9.5	27.7
Establishments - 1-4 Emp. Number	6,498	6,592	1.4	8,144	23.5	8,921	9.5	10,322	15.7	11,219	8.7	72.7
Mid-March Employment	10,970	10,885	-0.8	14,882	36.7	16,533	11.1	19,055	15.3	18,538	-2.7	69.0
1st Quarter Wages (annualized - $ mil.)	587.6	561.4	-4.5	864.8	54.0	917.8	6.1	1,078.0	17.5	1,202.9	11.6	104.7
Payroll per Emp. 1st Q. (annualized)	53,568	51,576	-3.7	58,108	12.7	55,513	-4.5	56,574	1.9	64,890	14.7	21.1
Annual Payroll ($ mil.)	567.5	752.3	32.6	867.7	15.3	936.4	7.9	1,162.8	24.2	1,342.8	15.5	136.6
Establishments - 5-9 Emp. Number	2,017	1,883	-6.6	2,466	31.0	2,648	7.4	2,844	7.4	2,669	-6.2	32.3
Mid-March Employment	13,281	12,489	-6.0	16,485	32.0	17,706	7.4	18,810	6.2	17,831	-5.2	34.3
1st Quarter Wages (annualized - $ mil.)	807.6	812.5	0.6	1,297.0	59.6	1,358.7	4.8	1,636.9	20.5	1,560.9	-4.6	93.3
Payroll per Emp. 1st Q. (annualized)	60,808	65,056	7.0	78,680	20.9	76,735	-2.5	87,025	13.4	87,537	0.6	44.0
Annual Payroll ($ mil.)	666.8	715.5	7.3	1,041.4	45.5	1,138.7	9.3	1,303.6	14.5	1,406.2	7.9	110.9
Establishments - 10-19 Emp. Number	1,861	1,858	-0.2	2,150	15.7	2,279	6.0	2,276	-0.1	2,359	3.6	26.8
Mid-March Employment	25,491	25,660	0.7	29,621	15.4	31,275	5.6	31,343	0.2	32,656	4.2	28.1
1st Quarter Wages (annualized - $ mil.)	1,700.2	1,676.7	-1.4	2,100.9	25.3	2,286.1	8.8	2,734.5	19.6	2,746.7	0.4	61.6
Payroll per Emp. 1st Q. (annualized)	66,698	65,343	-2.0	70,927	8.5	73,098	3.1	87,246	19.4	84,111	-3.6	26.1
Annual Payroll ($ mil.)	1,352.1	1,405.6	4.0	1,735.5	23.5	2,077.5	19.7	2,319.9	11.7	2,581.6	11.3	90.9
Establishments - 20-49 Emp. Number	1,822	1,851	1.6	2,042	10.3	2,135	4.6	2,142	0.3	2,235	4.3	22.7
Mid-March Employment	55,661	57,001	2.4	63,165	10.8	65,471	3.7	65,892	0.6	68,734	4.3	23.5
1st Quarter Wages (annualized - $ mil.)	4,206.5	4,159.0	-1.1	4,905.7	18.0	4,925.8	0.4	5,728.0	16.3	6,204.5	8.3	47.5
Payroll per Emp. 1st Q. (annualized)	75,574	72,964	-3.5	77,665	6.4	75,237	-3.1	86,930	15.5	90,268	3.8	19.4
Annual Payroll ($ mil.)	3,154.5	3,298.5	4.6	3,949.1	19.7	4,459.0	12.9	5,035.5	12.9	5,658.3	12.4	79.4
Establishments - 50-99 Emp. Number	687	688	0.1	694	0.9	669	-3.6	705	5.4	757	7.4	10.2
Mid-March Employment	46,696	46,348	-0.7	46,340	-0.0	44,942	-3.0	47,492	5.7	50,889	7.2	9.0
1st Quarter Wages (annualized - $ mil.)	4,453.3	3,813.3	-14.4	3,733.8	-2.1	3,473.5	-7.0	4,447.8	28.1	4,710.6	5.9	5.8
Payroll per Emp. 1st Q. (annualized)	95,369	82,275	-13.7	80,575	-2.1	77,288	-4.1	93,655	21.2	92,567	-1.2	-2.9
Annual Payroll ($ mil.)	3,018.6	2,821.7	-6.5	2,935.1	4.0	3,168.1	7.9	3,998.6	26.2	4,516.2	12.9	49.6
Establishments - 100-249 Emp. Number	306	292	-4.6	261	-10.6	269	3.1	285	5.9	276	-3.2	-9.8
Mid-March Employment	46,586	43,877	-5.8	38,612	-12.0	40,222	4.2	42,556	5.8	41,204	-3.2	-11.6
1st Quarter Wages (annualized - $ mil.)	4,422.5	3,506.7	-20.7	3,297.0	-6.0	2,892.0	-12.3	3,873.9	34.0	3,904.9	0.8	-11.7
Payroll per Emp. 1st Q. (annualized)	94,932	79,920	-15.8	85,388	6.8	71,900	-15.8	91,031	26.6	94,769	4.1	-0.2
Annual Payroll ($ mil.)	2,914.3	2,855.5	-2.0	2,617.1	-8.4	2,917.1	11.5	3,585.3	22.9	4,018.5	12.1	37.9
Establishments - 250-499 Emp. Number	91	93	2.2	82	-11.8	66	-19.5	65	-1.5	50	-23.1	-45.1
Mid-March Employment	31,649	32,437	2.5	29,235	-9.9	22,067	-24.5	22,184	0.5	17,460	-21.3	-44.8
1st Quarter Wages (annualized - $ mil.)	2,427.5	2,278.8	-6.1	2,031.5	-10.9	1,568.2	-22.8	1,868.4	19.1	1,377.3	-26.3	-43.3
Payroll per Emp. 1st Q. (annualized)	76,700	70,253	-8.4	69,490	-1.1	71,065	2.3	84,223	18.5	78,882	-6.3	2.8
Annual Payroll ($ mil.)	1,730.7	1,906.4	10.2	1,850.7	-2.9	1,595.6	-13.8	1,979.5	24.1	1,755.9	-11.3	1.5
Establishments - 500-999 Emp. Number	33	34	3.0	36	5.9	28	-22.2	35	25.0	35	-	6.1
Mid-March Employment	20,757	20,939	0.9	23,575	12.6	17,817	-24.4	23,192	30.2	22,879	-1.3	10.2
1st Quarter Wages (annualized - $ mil.)	1,849.9	2,105.1	13.8	2,708.1	28.6	1,697.8	-37.3	2,678.8	57.8	2,045.1	-23.7	10.6
Payroll per Emp. 1st Q. (annualized)	89,121	100,533	12.8	114,870	14.3	95,292	-17.0	115,507	21.2	89,390	-22.6	0.3
Annual Payroll ($ mil.)	1,277.4	1,399.2	9.5	1,713.9	22.5	1,315.0	-23.3	2,262.3	72.0	2,374.0	4.9	85.8
Estab. - 1000 or More Emp. Number	28	22	-21.4	19	-13.6	17	-10.5	16	-5.9	16	-	-42.9
Mid-March Employment	81,652	62,914	-22.9	46,163	-26.6	39,379	-14.7	40,299	2.3	39,752	-1.4	-51.3
1st Quarter Wages (annualized - $ mil.)	14,770.6	8,258.2	-44.1	5,730.8	-30.6	4,032.7	-29.6	6,287.3	55.9	4,878.4	-22.4	-67.0
Payroll per Emp. 1st Q. (annualized)	180,897	131,261	-27.4	124,142	-5.4	102,408	-17.5	156,017	52.3	122,720	-21.3	-32.2
Annual Payroll ($ mil.)	7,948.4	5,151.7	-35.2	4,066.9	-21.1	3,475.0	-14.6	4,735.9	36.3	5,243.2	10.7	-34.0

Source: County Business Patterns, U.S. Department of Commerce, Washington, D.C., for 1988 through 1993. Payroll per employee is calculated using mid-March employment and 1st Quarter wages, annualized. Annual payroll, also shown, may not equal the annualized 1st Quarter wages. Columns headed by a percent sign (%) indicate change from the previous year. *na* stands for not available. The symbol (D) indicates that data are withheld by the source to avoid disclosure of competitive information. A dash (-) indicates that data are not available or cannot be calculated.

ESTABLISHMENTS
Number

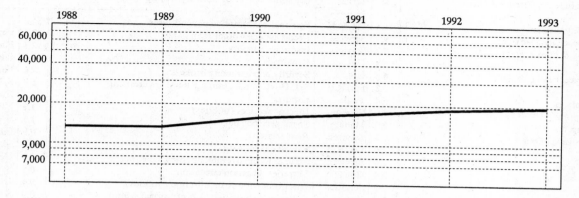

MID-MARCH EMPLOYMENT
Number

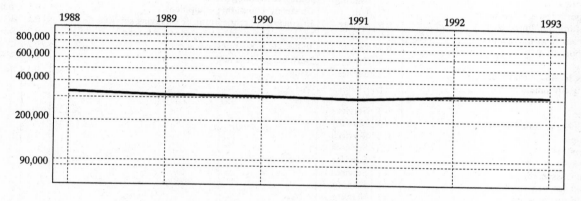

ANNUAL PAYROLL
$ million

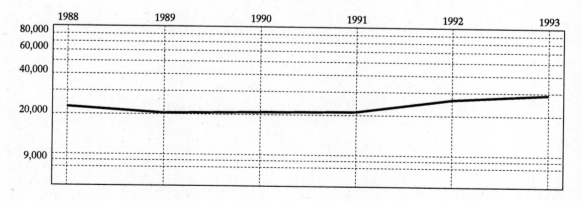

INPUTS AND OUTPUTS FOR SECURITY AND COMMODITY BROKERS - SIC GROUP 62

Economic Sector or Industry Providing Inputs	%	Sector	Economic Sector or Industry Buying Outputs	%	Sector
Security & commodity brokers	21.8	Fin/R.E.	Personal consumption expenditures	35.2	
Computer & data processing services	9.7	Services	Credit agencies other than banks	12.5	Fin/R.E.
Accounting, auditing & bookkeeping	8.2	Services	Insurance carriers	12.3	Fin/R.E.
Air transportation	6.8	Util.	Banking	11.7	Fin/R.E.
Communications, except radio & TV	6.8	Util.	Security & commodity brokers	7.6	Fin/R.E.
Real estate	6.2	Fin/R.E.	S/L Govt. purch., other general government	5.8	S/L Govt
Eating & drinking places	5.4	Trade	Exports	2.8	Foreign
Noncomparable imports	4.0	Foreign	Electric services (utilities)	1.3	Util.
Commercial printing	3.0	Manufg.	Social services, nec	1.1	Services
Detective & protective services	2.7	Services	Real estate	0.9	Fin/R.E.
Banking	2.6	Fin/R.E.	Petroleum refining	0.8	Manufg.
Hotels & lodging places	2.4	Services	State & local government enterprises, nec	0.8	Gov't
U.S. Postal Service	2.4	Gov't	Libraries, vocation education	0.5	Services
Advertising	2.2	Services	Gas production & distribution (utilities)	0.4	Util.
Imports	2.0	Foreign	Colleges, universities, & professional schools	0.3	Services
Petroleum refining	1.7	Manufg.	Communications, except radio & TV	0.3	Util.
Legal services	1.6	Services	Retail trade, except eating & drinking	0.3	Trade
Photofinishing labs, commercial photography	1.5	Services	Child day care services	0.2	Services
Management & consulting services & labs	0.9	Services	Crude petroleum & natural gas	0.2	Mining
Manifold business forms	0.7	Manufg.	Eating & drinking places	0.2	Trade
Motor freight transportation & warehousing	0.7	Util.	Electronic computing equipment	0.2	Manufg.
Maintenance of nonfarm buildings nec	0.6	Constr.	Engineering, architectural, & surveying services	0.2	Services
Sanitary services, steam supply, irrigation	0.6	Util.	Management & consulting services & labs	0.2	Services
Transit & bus transportation	0.5	Util.	Railroads & related services	0.2	Util.
Wholesale trade	0.5	Trade	Business services nec	0.1	Services
Automotive rental & leasing, without drivers	0.4	Services	Drugs	0.1	Manufg.
Electronic computing equipment	0.4	Manufg.			
Insurance carriers	0.4	Fin/R.E.			
Business services nec	0.3	Services			
Photographic equipment & supplies	0.3	Manufg.			
Electrical repair shops	0.2	Services			
Personnel supply services	0.2	Services			
Automotive repair shops & services	0.1	Services			
Business/professional associations	0.1	Services			
Manufacturing industries, nec	0.1	Manufg.			
Paper mills, except building paper	0.1	Manufg.			

Source: Benchmark Input-Output Accounts for the U.S. Economy, 1982, U.S. Department of Commerce, Washington, D.C., July 1991. Data, as reported in the source, are organized by the 1977 SIC structure in use in 1982 but have been matched, as closely as is possible, to the 1987 SIC structure used in this book. Activities with the same percentage are sorted alphabetically by name of activity.

OCCUPATIONS EMPLOYED BY SECURITY AND COMMODITY BROKERS AND DEALERS

Occupation	% of Total 1994	Change to 2005	Occupation	% of Total 1994	Change to 2005
Securities & financial services sales workers	34.9	46.3	Sales & related workers nec	2.2	33.0
Brokerage clerks	13.6	6.4	Computer programmers	1.6	7.8
Management support workers nec	7.7	47.3	Accountants & auditors	1.4	33.0
Secretaries, ex legal & medical	7.3	21.1	Receptionists & information clerks	1.3	33.0
General office clerks	3.6	13.5	Marketing & sales worker supervisors	1.3	33.0
General managers & top executives	3.2	26.2	Bookkeeping, accounting, & auditing clerks	1.1	-0.2
Clerical supervisors & managers	3.1	36.1	Clerical support workers nec	1.1	6.4
Financial managers	2.7	53.0			

Sources: Industry-Occupation Matrix, Bureau of Labor Statistics. These data relate to one or more 3-digit SIC industry groups rather than to a single 4-digit SIC. The change reported for each occupation to the year 2005 is a percent of growth or decline as estimated by the Bureau of Labor Statistics. The abbreviation *nec* stands for not elsewhere classified.

U.S. AND STATE DATA ON INDUSTRY REVENUES AND OTHER ACCOUNTS FOR 1992

State	No. of Estab.	Employ- ment	Payroll ($ mil.)	Revenues ($ mil.)	Empl./ Estab.	Revenue/ Estab. ($)	Payroll/ Estab. ($)	Revenue/ Empl. ($)	Payroll/ Empl. ($)
UNITED STATES	17,787	299,953	26,252.8	88,171.4	17	4,957,071	1,475,953	293,951	87,523
Alabama	144	1,420	95.5	211.5	10	1,468,472	662,868	148,915	67,220
Alaska	18	-	(D)	(D)	(D)	(D)	(D)	(D)	(D)
Arizona	234	2,570	156.9	393.7	11	1,682,359	670,444	153,180	61,044
Arkansas	123	1,758	114.2	315.3	14	2,563,203	928,114	179,337	64,936
California	1,826	29,342	2,332.2	6,121.2	16	3,352,268	1,277,238	208,617	79,485
Colorado	358	-	(D)	(D)	(D)	(D)	(D)	(D)	(D)
Connecticut	275	-	(D)	(D)	(D)	(D)	(D)	(D)	(D)
Delaware	53	-	(D)	(D)	(D)	(D)	(D)	(D)	(D)
District of Columbia	93	-	(D)	(D)	(D)	(D)	(D)	(D)	(D)
Florida	1,019	12,948	902.7	2,428.1	13	2,382,798	885,865	187,525	69,717
Georgia	399	4,404	323.6	892.2	11	2,236,163	810,927	202,595	73,470
Hawaii	44	-	(D)	(D)	(D)	(D)	(D)	(D)	(D)
Idaho	80	-	(D)	(D)	(D)	(D)	(D)	(D)	(D)
Illinois	1,147	18,390	1,561.7	4,721.3	16	4,116,253	1,361,520	256,734	84,919
Indiana	274	-	(D)	(D)	(D)	(D)	(D)	(D)	(D)
Iowa	226	1,338	73.8	174.9	6	774,075	326,735	130,748	55,188
Kansas	199	-	(D)	(D)	(D)	(D)	(D)	(D)	(D)
Kentucky	156	1,344	77.4	238.5	9	1,529,096	495,981	177,484	57,569
Louisiana	196	1,689	121.2	245.7	9	1,253,332	618,316	145,443	71,753
Maine	49	409	22.9	58.7	8	1,198,041	466,714	143,531	55,914
Maryland	194	-	(D)	(D)	(D)	(D)	(D)	(D)	(D)
Massachusetts	321	-	(D)	(D)	(D)	(D)	(D)	(D)	(D)
Michigan	421	4,763	301.7	736.1	11	1,748,534	716,734	154,552	63,352
Minnesota	332	6,285	436.5	1,291.5	19	3,890,151	1,314,732	205,494	69,450
Mississippi	86	-	(D)	(D)	(D)	(D)	(D)	(D)	(D)
Missouri	354	-	(D)	(D)	(D)	(D)	(D)	(D)	(D)
Montana	81	-	(D)	(D)	(D)	(D)	(D)	(D)	(D)
Nebraska	161	1,158	68.3	169.1	7	1,050,180	424,050	146,009	58,957
Nevada	59	-	(D)	(D)	(D)	(D)	(D)	(D)	(D)
New Hampshire	61	-	(D)	(D)	(D)	(D)	(D)	(D)	(D)
New Jersey	683	13,466	1,009.6	3,387.0	20	4,959,064	1,478,227	251,525	74,976
New Mexico	76	-	(D)	(D)	(D)	(D)	(D)	(D)	(D)
New York	3,132	108,402	12,296.7	50,387.3	35	16,087,911	3,926,155	464,819	113,436
North Carolina	361	3,115	201.4	471.5	9	1,305,967	557,828	151,350	64,647
North Dakota	57	-	(D)	(D)	(D)	(D)	(D)	(D)	(D)
Ohio	498	6,101	420.3	989.2	12	1,986,369	843,896	162,139	68,884
Oklahoma	226	1,346	78.3	190.6	6	843,496	346,385	141,627	58,160
Oregon	208	1,987	118.3	309.5	10	1,487,995	568,572	155,764	59,518
Pennsylvania	603	-	(D)	(D)	(D)	(D)	(D)	(D)	(D)
Rhode Island	40	-	(D)	(D)	(D)	(D)	(D)	(D)	(D)
South Carolina	158	-	(D)	(D)	(D)	(D)	(D)	(D)	(D)
South Dakota	57	-	(D)	(D)	(D)	(D)	(D)	(D)	(D)
Tennessee	273	3,445	239.3	539.7	13	1,977,095	876,498	156,675	69,458
Texas	1,190	12,510	1,046.1	2,495.5	11	2,097,044	879,058	199,479	83,619
Utah	85	-	(D)	(D)	(D)	(D)	(D)	(D)	(D)
Vermont	27	-	(D)	(D)	(D)	(D)	(D)	(D)	(D)
Virginia	297	3,448	237.7	629.5	12	2,119,650	800,202	182,580	68,927
Washington	388	4,103	260.4	749.3	11	1,931,170	671,188	182,621	63,471
West Virginia	58	407	27.4	65.0	7	1,120,069	472,034	159,617	67,268
Wisconsin	333	3,201	213.7	530.9	10	1,594,219	641,643	165,847	66,750
Wyoming	54	-	(D)	(D)	(D)	(D)	(D)	(D)	(D)

Source: 1992 Economic Census, U.S. Department of Commerce, Washington, D.C. This is the only table that shows revenue data as collected by the Bureau of the Census in an Economic Census. The symbol (D) indicates that data are withheld by the source to avoid disclosure of competitive information. A dash (-) indicates that data are not available or cannot be calculated.

ESTABLISHMENTS 1992 - STATE AND REGIONAL CONCENTRATION

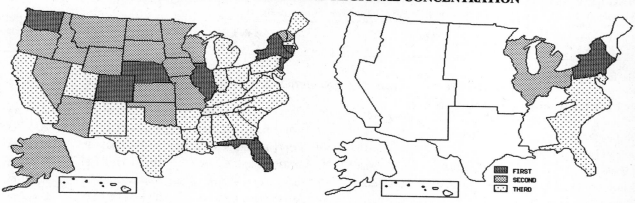

EMPLOYMENT 1992 - STATE AND REGIONAL CONCENTRATION

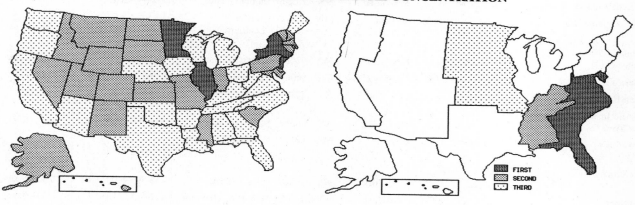

REVENUES 1992 - STATE AND REGIONAL CONCENTRATION

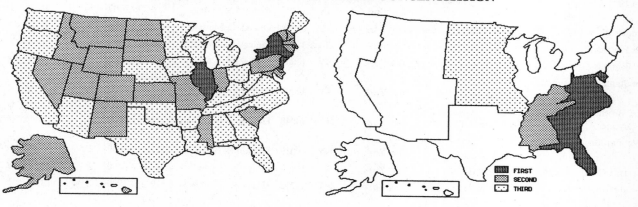

States with the darkest shading indicate those states which have proportionately more establishments, employment, or revenues than would be indicated by the state's population. States with light shading are states with proportionately fewer establishments, less employment, and lower revenues than population distribution. States shaded grey are within 15 percent of the state's population proportion in these catego-ries. States for which no data are available are shown as average (grey). *Regions* are shaded to indicate absolute rank in the category. If no data for the category are available, establishment counts are used to shade the regions. Source of the data is the table on the facing page.

LEADING COMPANIES - SIC 6163 - Loan Brokers

Number shown: **100**　　　Total sales/assets ($ mil): **1,108,868**　　　Total employment (000): **792.2**

Company Name	Address				CEO Name	Phone	Co. Type	Sales/Assets ($ mil)	Empl. (000)
Prudential Insurance Company of America	751 Broad St.	Newark	NJ	07102	Arthur F. Ryan	201-802-6000	R	313,660 TA	100.0
General Electric Capital Services Inc.	260 Long Ridge Rd.	Stamford	CT	06927	Gary C. Wendt	203-357-6978	S	211,730 TA	25.0
Equitable Companies Inc.	787 7th Ave.	New York	NY	10019	Richard H. Jenrette	212-554-1234	P	98,991 TA	13.1
Bankers Trust New York Corp.	280 Park Ave.	New York	NY	10017	Eugene B. Shanks Jr.	212-250-2500	P	97,016 TA	14.5
Barnett Banks Inc.	P.O. Box 40789	Jacksonville	FL	32203	Charles E. Rice	904-791-7720	P	41,278 TA	18.9
Metropolitan Life Insurance Co.	1 Madison Ave.	New York	NY	10010	Harry Kamen	212-578-2211	R	40,100 TA	55.0
Dean Witter, Discover and Co.	2 World Trade Ctr.	New York	NY	10048	Philip J. Purcell	212-392-2222	P	27,662 TA	26.6
CS First Boston Inc.	55 E. 52nd St.	New York	NY	10055	John M. Hennessy	212-909-2000	R	26,663 OR	1.5
ConAgra Inc.	1 ConAgra Dr.	Omaha	NE	68102	Philip B. Fletcher	402-595-4000	P	23,512	87.3
Merrill Lynch and Company Inc.	250 Vesey St.	New York	NY	10281	Daniel P. Tully	212-449-1000	P	18,233 OR	43.8
St. Paul Companies Inc.	385 Washington St.	St. Paul	MN	55102	Douglas W. Leatherdale	612-221-7911	P	17,496 TA	12.6
New England Mutual Life Insurance Co.	501 Boylston St.	Boston	MA	02117	Robert A. Shafto	617-578-2000	R	16,582 TA	3.0
SunAmerica Inc.	1 SunAmerica Ctr.	Century City	CA	90067	Eli Broad	310-772-6000	P	14,656 TA	4.3
American Express Co.	200 Vesey St.	New York	NY	10285	Harvey Golub	212-640-2000	P	14,282 OR	72.4
Mutual Life Insurance Company of New York	1740 Broadway	New York	NY	10019	Michael I. Roth	212-708-2000	R	14,166 TA	5.1
BayBanks Inc.	175 Federal St.	Boston	MA	02110	William M. Crozier Jr.	617-482-1040	P	10,771 TA	5.9
Morgan Stanley Group Inc.	1251 Ave. of the Amer.	New York	NY	10020	John J. Mack	212-703-4000	P	9,376 OR	9.7
Salomon Inc.	7 World Trade Ctr.	New York	NY	10048	Robert E. Denham	212-747-7000	P	8,799 OR	8.6
Lehman Brothers Holdings Inc.	3 World Financial Ctr.	New York	NY	10285	Richard S. Fuld Jr.	212-298-2000	P	8,692 OR	9.3
Lehman Brothers Inc.	3 World Financial Ctr.	New York	NY	10285	Richard S. Fuld Jr.	212-298-2000	S	8,692 OR	9.3
Salomon Brothers Inc.	7 World Trade Ctr.	New York	NY	10048	Deryck C. Maughan	212-747-7000	S	8,224 OR	8.7
Synovus Financial Corp.	P.O. Box 120	Columbus	GA	31902	James H. Blanchard	706-649-2387	P	6,115 TA	4.8
Kidder, Peabody Group Inc.	10 Hanover Sq.	New York	NY	10005	Michael A. Carpenter	212-510-3000	S	4,861 OR	5.0
Morgan Stanley and Company Inc.	1251 Ave. of the	New York	NY	10020	Richard B. Fisher	212-703-4000	S	4,156 OR	8.7
Salomon Brothers Holding Company Inc.	7 World Trade Ctr.	New York	NY	10048	Deryck C. Maughan	212-783-7000	S	4,135 OR	4.1
PaineWebber Group Inc.	1285 Avenue of the Americas	New York	NY	10019	Donald B. Marron	212-713-2000	P	3,964 OR	16.6
Bear Stearns Companies Inc.	245 Park Ave.	New York	NY	10167	James E. Cayne	212-272-2000	P	3,441 OR	7.3
Prudential Securities Inc.	199 Water St.	New York	NY	10292	Hardwick Simmons	212-214-1000	S	3,400 OR	17.0
Smith Barney Shearson Holdings Inc.	1345 Ave. of the Amer.	New York	NY	10105	Robert F. Greenhill	212-399-6000	S	3,366 OR	29.9
Smith Barney Shearson Inc.	1345 Ave. of the Amer.	New York	NY	10105	Robert F. Greenhill	212-399-6000	S	3,366 OR	29.9

Company type codes: P - Public, R - Private, S - Subsidiary, D - Division, J - Joint Venture, A - Affiliate, G - Group. If the dollar values shown are not sales, the following codes apply: TA - Total Assets; OR - Operating Revenues; GB - Gross Billings. * - estimated dollar value. < - less than. *na* - not available.

Continued on next page.

LEADING COMPANIES - SIC 6163 - Loan Brokers
Continued

Company Name	Address				CEO Name	Phone	Co. Type	Sales/Assets ($ mil)	Empl. (000)
PaineWebber Inc.	1285 Ave. of the Amer.	New York	NY	10019	Donald B. Marron	212-713-2000	S	3,364 OR	13.6
American Express Financial Advisors Inc.	IDS Tower 10	Minneapolis	MN	55440	David R. Hubers	612-671-3131	S	3,156 OR	7.7
National Western Life Insurance Co.	850 E. Anderson Ln.	Austin	TX	78752	Robert L. Moody	512-836-1010	P	2,915 TA	0.2
Bear, Stearns and Company Inc.	245 Park Ave.	New York	NY	10167	James Cayne	212-272-2000	S	2,670 OR*	5.9
Goldman Sachs and Co.	85 Broad St.	New York	NY	10004	Stephen Friedman	212-902-1000	R	2,530 OR*	9.0
PacifiCorp Holdings Inc.	700 N.E. Multnomah St.	Portland	OR	97232	F.W. Buckman	503-464-6000	S	2,000 OR	5.0
Pulte Corp.	33 Bloomfield Hills	Bloomfield Hills	MI	48304	Robert K. Burgess	313-647-2750	P	1,941 TA	3.4
Victoria Bankshares Inc.	1 O'Connor Plz.	Victoria	TX	77902	Charles R. Hardlicka	512-573-5151	P	1,746 TA	1.0
Kemper Financial Companies Inc.	120 S. LaSalle St.	Chicago	IL	60603	Charles M. Kierscht	312-781-1121	S	1,242 OR	2.8
A.G. Edwards Inc.	1 N. Jefferson Ave.	St. Louis	MO	63103	Benjamin F. Edwards III	314-289-3000	P	1,178 OR	10.7
Charles Schwab Corp.	101 Montgomery St.	San Francisco	CA	94104	Charles R. Schwab	415-627-7000	P	965 OR	6.1
ALLIED Group Inc.	701 5th Ave.	Des Moines	IA	50391	Douglas L. Andeson	515-280-4211	P	893 TA	2.1
Advest Group Inc.	280 Trumbull St.	Hartford	CT	06103	Allen Weintraub	203-525-1421	P	885 TA	1.5
Donaldson, Lufkin and Jenrette Inc.	140 Broadway	New York	NY	10005	John S. Chalsty	212-504-3000	S	840 OR*	3.0
Franklin Resources Inc.	777 Mariners Island	San Mateo	CA	94404	Charles B. Johnson	415-312-3000	P	827 OR	4.1
Kemper Securities Inc.	77 W. Wacker Dr.	Chicago	IL	60606	James R. Boris	312-574-6000	S	674 OR	3.6
Alex. Brown Inc.	135 E. Baltimore St.	Baltimore	MD	21202	A.B. Krongard	410-727-1700	P	628 OR	2.2
Twentieth Century Companies Inc.	P.O. Box 419200	Kansas City	MO	64141	James E. Stowers Sr.	816-531-5575	R	540 OR*	1.8
Raymond James Financial Inc.	880 Carillon Pkwy.	St. Petersburg	FL	33716	Thomas A. James	813-573-3800	P	507 OR	2.3
Cantor, Fitzgerald Securities Corp.	1 World Trade Ctr.	New York	NY	10048	Howard Lutnick	212-938-5000	R	470 OR*	1.7
Inter-Regional Financial Group Inc.	60 S. 6th St.	Minneapolis	MN	55402	Irving Weiser	612-371-7750	P	457 OR	3.0
First Chicago Capital Markets Inc.	1 First National Plz.	Chicago	IL	60670	John Gilchrist	312-732-5600	S	443 OR	0.3
Alex. Brown and Sons Inc.	135 E. Baltimore St.	Baltimore	MD	21202	Alvin B. Krongard	410-727-1700	S	440 OR*	2.0
Enterprise Diversified Holdings Inc.	1 Riverfront Plz.	Newark	NJ	07102	Paul H. Way	201-596-6761	S	440 OR	0.4
Piper Jaffray Companies Inc.	222 S. 9th St.	Minneapolis	MN	55402	Addison L. Piper	612-342-6000	P	397 OR	2.7
Gruntal and Company Inc.	14 Wall St.	New York	NY	10005	Howard Silverman	212-267-8800	S	388 OR	1.9
Legg Mason Inc.	P.O. Box 1476	Baltimore	MD	21202	Raymond A. Mason	410-539-0000	P	372 OR	2.9
Piper Jaffray Inc.	P.O. Box 28	Minneapolis	MN	55440	Addison L. Piper	612-342-6000	S	360 OR*	2.5

Company type codes: P - Public, R - Private, S - Subsidiary, D - Division, J - Joint Venture, A - Affiliate, G - Group. If the dollar values shown are not sales, the following codes apply: TA - Total Assets; OR - Operating Revenues; GB - Gross Billings. * - estimated dollar value. < - less than. *na* - not available.

Continued on next page.

LEADING COMPANIES - SIC 6163 - Loan Brokers

Continued

Company Name	Address				CEO Name	Phone	Co. Type	Sales/Assets ($ mil)	Empl. (000)
Gruntal Financial Corp.	14 Wall St.	New York	NY	10005	Howard Silverman	212-267-8800	S	350 OR	2.0
Meridian Investments	10220 River Rd.	Potomac	MD	20854	John P. Casey	301-983-5000	R	350 OR	<0.1
Cowen and Co.	Financial Sq.	New York	NY	10005	Joseph Cohen	212-495-6000	R	330 OR*	1.2
Jefferies Group Inc.	11100 Santa Monica	Los Angeles	CA	90025	Frank E. Baxter	310-445-1199	P	316 OR	0.7
Quick and Reilly Group Inc.	26 Broadway	New York	NY	10004	Leslie C. Quick Jr.	212-747-1200	P	315 OR	0.7
J.J.B. Hilliard, W.L. Lyons Inc.	P.O. Box 32760	Louisville	KY	40232	Gilbert L. Pamplin	502-588-8400	R	280 OR*	1.0
Nomura Securities International Inc.	2 World Financial Ctr.	New York	NY	10281	Max C. Chapman	212-208-9300	S	280 OR*	1.0
Tucker Anthony Inc.	200 Liberty St.	New York	NY	10281	Thomas Tasquale	212-225-8000	S	280 OR*	1.0
Dain Bosworth Inc.	60 S. 6th St.	Minneapolis	MN	55402	Irving Wiser	612-371-2711	S	255 OR	1.7
Affiliated Financial Services Inc.	7840 E. Berry Pl.	Englewood	CO	80111	Richard J. Graham	303-770-4429	R	250 OR	<0.1
Morgan Keegan Inc.	50 Front St.	Memphis	TN	38103	William W. Deupree Jr.	901-524-4100	P	232 OR	1.2
Congress Financial Corp.	1133 Avenue of the Americas	New York	NY	10036	Robert A. Miller	212-840-2000	S	230 OR*	0.9
John Nuveen Co.	333 W. Wacker Dr.	Chicago	IL	60606	Richard J. Franke	312-917-7700	P	220 OR	0.6
Wertheim Schroder and Company Inc.	787 7th Ave.	New York	NY	10019	James A. Harmon	212-492-6000	R	220 OR*	0.8
Morgan Keegan and Company Inc.	50 Front St.	Memphis	TN	38103	William W. Deupree	901-524-4100	S	209 OR	1.2
McDonald and Company Securities Inc.	800 Superior Ave.	Cleveland	OH	44114	William B. Summers Jr.	216-443-2300	S	205 OR	1.0
Lazard Freres and Co.	1 Rockefeller Plz.	New York	NY	10020	Michel A. David-Weill	212-632-6000	R	190 OR*	0.7
Advest Inc.	280 Trumbull St.	Hartford	CT	06103	Allen Weintraub	203-525-1421	S	187 OR	1.5
McDonald and Company Investments Inc.	800 Superior Ave.	Cleveland	OH	44114	William B. Summers Jr.	216-443-2300	P	178 OR	1.1
Raymond, James and Associates Inc.	880 Carillon Pkwy.	St. Petersburg	FL	33716	Thomas S. Franke	813-573-3800	S	170 OR*	1.3
Vero Group	1000 Louisiana	Houston	TX	77002	Mark Haukohl	713-655-0071	R	170 OR	0.1
American Southwest Financial Corp.	2390 E. Camelback Rd.	Phoenix	AZ	85016	Michael H. Feinstein	602-381-8960	R	162 OR	<0.1
Cargill Investor Services Inc.	233 S. Wacker Dr.	Chicago	IL	60606	Hal Hansen	312-460-4000	S	160 OR*	0.6
Dillon, Read and Company Inc.	535 Madison Ave.	New York	NY	10022	John Birkelund	212-906-7000	R	160 OR*	0.6
Mabon Securities Corp.	1 Liberty Plz.	New York	NY	10006	Salvatore Trani	212-732-2820	R	160 OR*	0.8
Ohio Co.	155 E. Broad St.	Columbus	OH	43215	Walter R. Chambers	614-464-6811	R	160 OR*	0.6
Mayer and Schweitzer Inc.	111 Pavonia Ave. E.	Jersey City	NJ	07310	Herb Schweitzer	201-963-9100	S	157 OR	0.2
Fidelity Federal Bancorp Inc.	18 N.W. 4th St.	Evansville	IN	47708	Jack Cunningham	812-424-0921	P	152 TA	<0.1
Interstate/Johnson Lane Inc.	P.O. Box 1012	Charlotte	NC	28201	James H. Morgan	704-379-9000	P	151 OR	1.1
Rauscher Pierce Refsnes Inc.	700 N. Pearl St.	Dallas	TX	75201	David A. Smith	214-978-0111	S	150 OR	0.9
AIM Distributors Inc.	11 Greenway Plz.	Houston	TX	77046	Charles T. Bauer	713-626-1919	S	150 OR*	0.6
AIM Management Group Inc.	11 Greenway Plz.	Houston	TX	77046	Charles T. Bauer	713-626-1919	R	150 OR*	0.6

Company type codes: P - Public, R - Private, S - Subsidiary, D - Division, J - Joint Venture, A - Affiliate, G - Group. If the dollar values shown are not sales, the following codes apply: TA - Total Assets; OR - Operating Revenues; GB - Gross Billings. * - estimated dollar value. < - less than. *na* - not available.

Continued on next page.

LEADING COMPANIES - SIC 6163 - Loan Brokers
Continued

Company Name	Address				CEO Name	Phone	Co. Type	Sales/Assets ($ mil)	Empl. (000)
First Institutional Securities Corp.	470 Colfax Ave.	Clifton	NJ	07013	George Liss	201-778-9700	R	150 OR	0.1
American Capital Marketing Inc.	P.O. Box 1411	Houston	TX	77251	Don Powell	713-993-0500	D	140 OR	0.5
Royal Alliance Associates Inc.	733 3rd Ave.	New York	NY	10017	Gary W. Krat	212-551-5100	S	140 OR	0.1
Benham Management International Inc.	1665 Charleston Rd.	Mountain View	CA	94043	James M. Benham	415-965-8300	R	130 OR*	0.5
Sutro and Company Inc.	201 California St.	San Francisco	CA	94111	George McGough	415-445-8500	S	130 OR	0.6
Pioneer Group Inc.	60 State St.	Boston	MA	02109	John F. Cogan Jr.	617-742-7825	P	129 OR	1.1
Chicago Corp.	208 S. La Salle St.	Chicago	IL	60604	J.A. Wing	312-855-7600	R	120 OR*	1.0
Daiwa Securities America Inc.	200 Liberty St.	New York	NY	10281	K. Yoneyama	212-341-5400	S	120 OR*	0.5
Southwest Securities Group Inc.	1201 Elm St.	Dallas	TX	75270	Robert A. Buchholz	214-651-1800	P	114 OR	0.5
INVEST Financial Corp.	5404 Cypress Ctr.	Tampa	FL	33609	D. Mark Olson	813-289-5721	S	110 OR	0.3

*Source: Ward's Business Directory of U.S. Private and Public Companies, 1996. Company type codes: P - Public, R - Private, S - Subsidiary, D - Division, J - Joint Venture, A - Affiliate, G - Group. If the dollar values shown are not sales, the following codes apply: TA - Total Assets; OR - Operating Revenues; GB - Gross Billings. * - estimated dollar value. < - less than; na - not available.*

SIC 6220

COMMODITY CONTRACTS BROKERS, DEALERS

SIC 6220 includes all establishments involved in commodity contract trading. These establishments are primarily engaged in buying and selling commodity contracts on either a spot or future basis for their own account or for the accounts of others. The establishments are members—or are associated with members—of recognized commodity exchanges. Companies engaged in the actual buying and selling of the commodities themselves (versus contracts in these commodities) are classified as Wholesale Trade and are not included in this book.

The categories that make up SIC 6220 include commodity brokers and dealers, futures brokers and dealers, and traders in commodity contracts.

ESTABLISHMENTS, EMPLOYMENT, AND PAYROLL

	1988	1989 Value	%	1990 Value	%	1991 Value	%	1992 Value	%	1993 Value	%	% change 88-93
All Establishments	1,236	1,127	-8.8	1,158	2.8	1,412	21.9	1,391	-1.5	1,468	5.5	18.8
Mid-March Employment	15,288	15,641	2.3	14,736	-5.8	12,837	-12.9	12,942	0.8	12,504	-3.4	-18.2
1st Quarter Wages (annualized - $ mil.)	757.4	750.4	-0.9	720.6	-4.0	597.7	-17.0	645.2	7.9	560.1	-13.2	-26.0
Payroll per Emp. 1st Q. (annualized)	49,540	47,977	-3.2	48,898	1.9	46,564	-4.8	49,851	7.1	44,794	-10.1	-9.6
Annual Payroll ($ mil.)	665.4	693.8	4.3	710.7	2.4	611.8	-13.9	726.2	18.7	724.2	-0.3	8.8
Establishments - 1-4 Emp. Number	843	731	-13.3	760	4.0	976	28.4	972	-0.4	1,041	7.1	23.5
Mid-March Employment	1,336	1,144	-14.4	1,150	0.5	1,467	27.6	1,587	8.2	1,555	-2.0	16.4
1st Quarter Wages (annualized - $ mil.)	73.2	59.4	-18.8	58.3	-2.0	64.0	9.9	72.4	13.1	67.8	-6.4	-7.4
Payroll per Emp. 1st Q. (annualized)	54,799	51,965	-5.2	50,661	-2.5	43,632	-13.9	45,636	4.6	43,583	-4.5	-20.5
Annual Payroll ($ mil.)	95.8	78.6	-17.9	80.2	2.0	91.5	14.2	102.7	12.2	105.3	2.5	9.9
Establishments - 5-9 Emp. Number	154	173	12.3	159	-8.1	179	12.6	183	2.2	(D)	-	-
Mid-March Employment	1,002	1,118	11.6	1,011	-9.6	1,188	17.5	1,229	3.5	(D)	-	-
1st Quarter Wages (annualized - $ mil.)	55.7	48.7	-12.5	40.3	-17.2	47.1	16.7	54.2	15.2	(D)	-	-
Payroll per Emp. 1st Q. (annualized)	55,605	43,585	-21.6	39,889	-8.5	39,616	-0.7	44,127	11.4	(D)	-	-
Annual Payroll ($ mil.)	48.9	54.0	10.3	45.1	-16.4	54.3	20.3	57.1	5.3	(D)	-	-
Establishments - 10-19 Emp. Number	119	104	-12.6	125	20.2	135	8.0	115	-14.8	110	-4.3	-7.6
Mid-March Employment	(D)	1,431	-	1,714	19.8	1,854	8.2	1,514	-18.3	1,508	-0.4	-
1st Quarter Wages (annualized - $ mil.)	(D)	62.6	-	77.5	23.8	95.7	23.5	80.9	-15.4	69.9	-13.6	-
Payroll per Emp. 1st Q. (annualized)	(D)	43,732	-	45,209	3.4	51,631	14.2	53,458	3.5	46,377	-13.2	-
Annual Payroll ($ mil.)	(D)	58.8	-	82.7	40.6	99.2	20.1	85.5	-13.8	92.1	7.7	-
Establishments - 20-49 Emp. Number	66	66	-	64	-3.0	73	14.1	76	4.1	74	-2.6	12.1
Mid-March Employment	2,086	2,043	-2.1	2,037	-0.3	2,260	10.9	2,246	-0.6	2,288	1.9	9.7
1st Quarter Wages (annualized - $ mil.)	106.6	94.4	-11.5	107.6	14.0	98.9	-8.1	127.3	28.7	114.4	-10.1	7.3
Payroll per Emp. 1st Q. (annualized)	51,120	46,203	-9.6	52,815	14.3	43,740	-17.2	56,657	29.5	49,986	-11.8	-2.2
Annual Payroll ($ mil.)	94.4	92.7	-1.8	91.0	-1.7	94.8	4.2	114.6	20.9	131.0	14.3	38.8
Establishments - 50-99 Emp. Number	25	26	4.0	26	-	27	3.8	24	-11.1	22	-8.3	-12.0
Mid-March Employment	1,749	1,843	5.4	1,695	-8.0	1,717	1.3	1,680	-2.2	1,618	-3.7	-7.5
1st Quarter Wages (annualized - $ mil.)	129.1	102.0	-21.0	67.3	-34.0	75.7	12.5	60.3	-20.4	89.1	47.6	-31.0
Payroll per Emp. 1st Q. (annualized)	73,816	55,329	-25.0	39,710	-28.2	44,116	11.1	35,910	-18.6	55,046	53.3	-25.4
Annual Payroll ($ mil.)	86.0	83.6	-2.7	82.7	-1.0	80.0	-3.3	65.7	-17.9	96.0	46.1	11.7
Establishments - 100-249 Emp. Number	19	16	-15.8	15	-6.3	16	6.7	15	-6.3	12	-20.0	-36.8
Mid-March Employment	3,300	2,832	-14.2	2,536	-10.5	(D)	-	2,300	-	1,871	-18.7	-43.3
1st Quarter Wages (annualized - $ mil.)	171.2	136.1	-20.5	152.7	12.2	(D)	-	182.3	-	85.6	-53.1	-50.0
Payroll per Emp. 1st Q. (annualized)	51,870	48,064	-7.3	60,213	25.3	(D)	-	79,252	-	45,738	-42.3	-11.8
Annual Payroll ($ mil.)	144.4	134.1	-7.1	151.8	13.2	(D)	-	210.7	-	146.3	-30.6	1.3
Establishments - 250-499 Emp. Number	8	6	-25.0	5	-16.7	5	-	(D)	-	5	-	-37.5
Mid-March Employment	2,608	(D)	-	1,599	-	(D)	-	(D)	-	1,756	-	-32.7
1st Quarter Wages (annualized - $ mil.)	91.5	(D)	-	109.7	-	(D)	-	(D)	-	64.4	-	-29.6
Payroll per Emp. 1st Q. (annualized)	35,095	(D)	-	68,580	-	(D)	-	(D)	-	36,692	-	4.6
Annual Payroll ($ mil.)	81.5	(D)	-	91.4	-	(D)	-	(D)	-	72.5	-	-11.1
Establishments - 500-999 Emp. Number	2	5	150.0	4	-20.0	1	-75.0	(D)	-	(D)	-	-
Mid-March Employment	(D)	(D)	-	2,994	-	(D)	-	(D)	-	(D)	-	-
1st Quarter Wages (annualized - $ mil.)	(D)	(D)	-	107.2	-	(D)	-	(D)	-	(D)	-	-
Payroll per Emp. 1st Q. (annualized)	(D)	(D)	-	35,814	-	(D)	-	(D)	-	(D)	-	-
Annual Payroll ($ mil.)	(D)	(D)	-	85.7	-	(D)	-	(D)	-	(D)	-	-
Estab. - 1000 or More Emp. Number	-	-	-	-	-	-	-	-	-	-	-	-
Mid-March Employment	-	-	-	-	-	-	-	-	-	-	-	-
1st Quarter Wages (annualized - $ mil.)	-	-	-	-	-	-	-	-	-	-	-	-
Payroll per Emp. 1st Q. (annualized)	(D)	(D)	-	(D)	-	(D)	-	-	-	-	-	-
Annual Payroll ($ mil.)	-	-	-	-	-	-	-	-	-	-	-	-

Source: County Business Patterns, U.S. Department of Commerce, Washington, D.C., for 1988 through 1993. Payroll per employee is calculated using mid-March employment and 1st Quarter wages, annualized. Annual payroll, also shown, may not equal the annualized 1st Quarter wages. Columns headed by a percent sign (%) indicate change from the previous year. na stands for not available. The symbol (D) indicates that data are withheld by the source to avoid disclosure of competitive information. A dash (-) indicates that data are not available or cannot be calculated.

ESTABLISHMENTS
Number

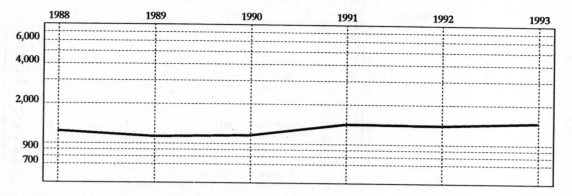

MID-MARCH EMPLOYMENT
Number

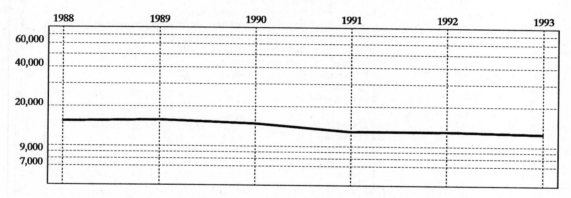

ANNUAL PAYROLL
$ million

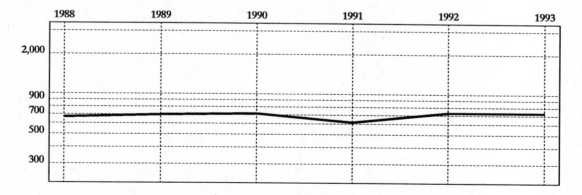

INPUTS AND OUTPUTS FOR SECURITY AND COMMODITY BROKERS - SIC GROUP 62

Economic Sector or Industry Providing Inputs	%	Sector	Economic Sector or Industry Buying Outputs	%	Sector
Security & commodity brokers	21.8	Fin/R.E.	Personal consumption expenditures	35.2	
Computer & data processing services	9.7	Services	Credit agencies other than banks	12.5	Fin/R.E.
Accounting, auditing & bookkeeping	8.2	Services	Insurance carriers	12.3	Fin/R.E.
Air transportation	6.8	Util.	Banking	11.7	Fin/R.E.
Communications, except radio & TV	6.8	Util.	Security & commodity brokers	7.6	Fin/R.E.
Real estate	6.2	Fin/R.E.	S/L Govt. purch., other general government	5.8	S/L Govt
Eating & drinking places	5.4	Trade	Exports	2.8	Foreign
Noncomparable imports	4.0	Foreign	Electric services (utilities)	1.3	Util.
Commercial printing	3.0	Manufg.	Social services, nec	1.1	Services
Detective & protective services	2.7	Services	Real estate	0.9	Fin/R.E.
Banking	2.6	Fin/R.E.	Petroleum refining	0.8	Manufg.
Hotels & lodging places	2.4	Services	State & local government enterprises, nec	0.8	Gov't
U.S. Postal Service	2.4	Gov't	Libraries, vocation education	0.5	Services
Advertising	2.2	Services	Gas production & distribution (utilities)	0.4	Util.
Imports	2.0	Foreign	Colleges, universities, & professional schools	0.3	Services
Petroleum refining	1.7	Manufg.	Communications, except radio & TV	0.3	Util.
Legal services	1.6	Services	Retail trade, except eating & drinking	0.3	Trade
Photofinishing labs, commercial photography	1.5	Services	Child day care services	0.2	Services
Management & consulting services & labs	0.9	Services	Crude petroleum & natural gas	0.2	Mining
Manifold business forms	0.7	Manufg.	Eating & drinking places	0.2	Trade
Motor freight transportation & warehousing	0.7	Util.	Electronic computing equipment	0.2	Manufg.
Maintenance of nonfarm buildings nec	0.6	Constr.	Engineering, architectural, & surveying services	0.2	Services
Sanitary services, steam supply, irrigation	0.6	Util.	Management & consulting services & labs	0.2	Services
Transit & bus transportation	0.5	Util.	Railroads & related services	0.2	Util.
Wholesale trade	0.5	Trade	Business services nec	0.1	Services
Automotive rental & leasing, without drivers	0.4	Services	Drugs	0.1	Manufg.
Electronic computing equipment	0.4	Manufg.			
Insurance carriers	0.4	Fin/R.E.			
Business services nec	0.3	Services			
Photographic equipment & supplies	0.3	Manufg.			
Electrical repair shops	0.2	Services			
Personnel supply services	0.2	Services			
Automotive repair shops & services	0.1	Services			
Business/professional associations	0.1	Services			
Manufacturing industries, nec	0.1	Manufg.			
Paper mills, except building paper	0.1	Manufg.			

Source: Benchmark Input-Output Accounts for the U.S. Economy, 1982, U.S. Department of Commerce, Washington, D.C., July 1991. Data, as reported in the source, are organized by the 1977 SIC structure in use in 1982 but have been matched, as closely as is possible, to the 1987 SIC structure used in this book. Activities with the same percentage are sorted alphabetically by name of activity.

OCCUPATIONS EMPLOYED BY SECURITY AND COMMODITY BROKERS AND DEALERS

Occupation	% of Total 1994	Change to 2005	Occupation	% of Total 1994	Change to 2005
Securities & financial services sales workers	34.9	46.3	Sales & related workers nec	2.2	33.0
Brokerage clerks	13.6	6.4	Computer programmers	1.6	7.8
Management support workers nec	7.7	47.3	Accountants & auditors	1.4	33.0
Secretaries, ex legal & medical	7.3	21.1	Receptionists & information clerks	1.3	33.0
General office clerks	3.6	13.5	Marketing & sales worker supervisors	1.3	33.0
General managers & top executives	3.2	26.2	Bookkeeping, accounting, & auditing clerks	1.1	-0.2
Clerical supervisors & managers	3.1	36.1	Clerical support workers nec	1.1	6.4
Financial managers	2.7	53.0			

Sources: Industry-Occupation Matrix, Bureau of Labor Statistics. These data relate to one or more 3-digit SIC industry groups rather than to a single 4-digit SIC. The change reported for each occupation to the year 2005 is a percent of growth or decline as estimated by the Bureau of Labor Statistics. The abbreviation *nec* stands for not elsewhere classified.

U.S. AND STATE DATA ON INDUSTRY REVENUES AND OTHER ACCOUNTS FOR 1992

State	No. of Estab.	Employ-ment	Payroll ($ mil.)	Revenues ($ mil.)	Empl./ Estab.	Revenue/ Estab. ($)	Payroll/ Estab. ($)	Revenue/ Empl. ($)	Payroll/ Empl. ($)
UNITED STATES	1,450	12,893	706.5	2,558.2	9	1,764,308	487,219	198,421	54,795
Alabama	4	31	0.5	4.1	8	1,029,500	130,000	132,839	16,774
Alaska	1	-	(D)	(D)	(D)	(D)	(D)	(D)	(D)
Arizona	4	7	0.3	0.9	2	232,500	71,500	132,857	40,857
Arkansas	5	19	0.3	0.7	4	132,200	57,600	34,789	15,158
California	62	264	13.3	87.7	4	1,415,129	213,742	332,341	50,197
Colorado	17	-	(D)	(D)	(D)	(D)	(D)	(D)	(D)
Connecticut	18	-	(D)	(D)	(D)	(D)	(D)	(D)	(D)
Delaware	2	-	(D)	(D)	(D)	(D)	(D)	(D)	(D)
District of Columbia	2	-	(D)	(D)	(D)	(D)	(D)	(D)	(D)
Florida	41	388	18.4	39.1	9	954,561	449,780	100,869	47,528
Georgia	14	113	4.9	12.4	8	885,857	352,929	109,752	43,726
Hawaii	2	-	(D)	(D)	(D)	(D)	(D)	(D)	(D)
Idaho	4	-	(D)	(D)	(D)	(D)	(D)	(D)	(D)
Illinois	530	7,284	334.8	1,242.5	14	2,344,332	631,668	170,579	45,962
Indiana	13	-	(D)	(D)	(D)	(D)	(D)	(D)	(D)
Iowa	48	196	8.3	24.1	4	502,021	171,979	122,944	42,117
Kansas	32	-	(D)	(D)	(D)	(D)	(D)	(D)	(D)
Kentucky	5	12	0.3	1.5	2	306,000	66,400	127,500	27,667
Louisiana	4	10	0.3	0.7	3	185,750	77,500	74,300	31,000
Maryland	1	-	(D)	(D)	(D)	(D)	(D)	(D)	(D)
Massachusetts	5	-	(D)	(D)	(D)	(D)	(D)	(D)	(D)
Michigan	5	11	0.6	1.9	2	389,200	127,800	176,909	58,091
Minnesota	32	88	3.5	14.7	3	459,219	110,031	166,989	40,011
Mississippi	5	-	(D)	(D)	(D)	(D)	(D)	(D)	(D)
Missouri	25	-	(D)	(D)	(D)	(D)	(D)	(D)	(D)
Montana	8	-	(D)	(D)	(D)	(D)	(D)	(D)	(D)
Nebraska	17	40	1.4	5.0	2	293,647	81,059	124,800	34,450
Nevada	2	-	(D)	(D)	(D)	(D)	(D)	(D)	(D)
New Hampshire	1	-	(D)	(D)	(D)	(D)	(D)	(D)	(D)
New Jersey	43	228	16.2	50.5	5	1,174,372	376,512	221,482	71,009
New Mexico	3	-	(D)	(D)	(D)	(D)	(D)	(D)	(D)
New York	309	2,776	185.5	533.2	9	1,725,560	600,443	192,074	66,836
North Carolina	5	16	0.2	1.1	3	221,600	46,600	69,250	14,563
North Dakota	5	-	(D)	(D)	(D)	(D)	(D)	(D)	(D)
Ohio	14	39	0.9	1.8	3	130,571	62,714	46,872	22,513
Oklahoma	20	76	2.4	5.2	4	259,850	118,000	68,382	31,053
Oregon	7	12	0.4	1.5	2	208,143	59,714	121,417	34,833
Pennsylvania	11	-	(D)	(D)	(D)	(D)	(D)	(D)	(D)
Rhode Island	2	-	(D)	(D)	(D)	(D)	(D)	(D)	(D)
South Carolina	4	-	(D)	(D)	(D)	(D)	(D)	(D)	(D)
South Dakota	12	-	(D)	(D)	(D)	(D)	(D)	(D)	(D)
Tennessee	20	83	5.8	26.4	4	1,320,600	290,300	318,217	69,952
Texas	48	147	10.2	22.6	3	471,063	212,458	153,816	69,374
Utah	2	-	(D)	(D)	(D)	(D)	(D)	(D)	(D)
Vermont	1	-	(D)	(D)	(D)	(D)	(D)	(D)	(D)
Virginia	7	19	1.0	1.8	3	254,429	145,429	93,737	53,579
Washington	17	28	1.1	3.2	2	187,824	64,765	114,036	39,321
Wisconsin	10	41	1.4	3.1	4	309,500	144,900	75,488	35,341
Wyoming	1	-	(D)	(D)	(D)	(D)	(D)	(D)	(D)

Source: 1992 Economic Census, U.S. Department of Commerce, Washington, D.C. This is the only table that shows revenue data as collected by the Bureau of the Census in an Economic Census. The symbol (D) indicates that data are withheld by the source to avoid disclosure of competitive information. A dash (-) indicates that data are not available or cannot be calculated.

ESTABLISHMENTS 1992 - STATE AND REGIONAL CONCENTRATION

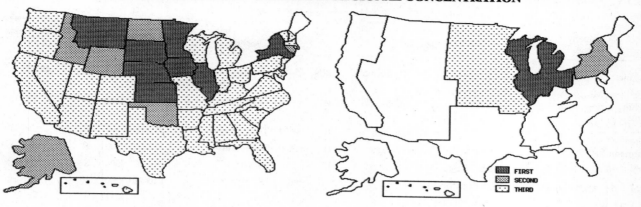

EMPLOYMENT 1992 - STATE AND REGIONAL CONCENTRATION

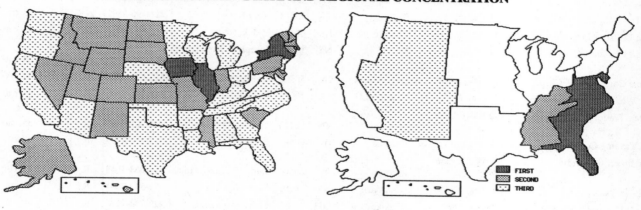

REVENUES 1992 - STATE AND REGIONAL CONCENTRATION

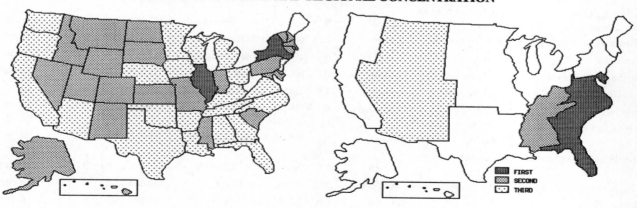

States with the darkest shading indicate those states which have proportionately more establishments, employment, or revenues than would be indicated by the state's population. States with light shading are states with proportionately fewer establishments, less employment, and lower revenues than population distribution. States shaded grey are within 15 percent of the state's population proportion in these categories. States for which no data are available are shown as average (grey). *Regions* are shaded to indicate absolute rank in the category. If no data for the category are available, establishment counts are used to shade the regions. Source of the data is the table on the facing page.

LEADING COMPANIES - SIC 6211 - Security Brokers and Dealers

Number shown: **44**   Total sales/assets ($ mil): **51,153**   Total employment (000): **74.9**

Company Name	Address				CEO Name	Phone	Co. Type	Sales/Assets ($ mil)	Empl. (000)
Cargill Inc.	P.O. Box 9300	Minneapolis	MN	55440	Whitney Macmillan	612-475-7575	R	48,000	70.5
Metropolitan Mortgage and Securities Company Inc.	W. 929 Sprague Ave.	Spokane	WA	99204	C. Paul Sandifur Jr.	509-838-3111	R	982 OR	0.3
Refco Group Ltd.	111 W. Jackson Blvd.	Chicago	IL	60604	Tone Grant	312-930-6500	R	390 OR*	0.5
Geldermann Inc.	440 S. La Salle St.	Chicago	IL	60605	James Curley	312-663-7500	R	310 OR*	0.4
First Options of Chicago Inc.	440 S. La Salle St.	Chicago	IL	60605	Al Salem	312-362-3000	S	273 OR*	0.9
Carter Marketing Group Inc.	1845 Brinston Ave.	Troy	MI	48083	Mark Carter	810-740-3900	R	110 OR*	0.2
Trout Trading Co.	3 First National Plz.	Chicago	IL	60602	Monroe Trout	312-372-9262	R	110 OR	0.2
Gerald Metals Inc.	P.O. Box 10134	Stamford	CT	06904	Gerald L. Lennard	203-329-4700	R	100 OR	0.7
MilBrands Inc.	16415 Addison Rd.	Dallas	TX	75248	Richard K. Ryalls	214-931-2500	S	80 OR	<0.1
Darci International Group Inc.	15400 Knoll Tr.	Dallas	TX	75248	Veni Rastogi	214-490-3893	S	78 OR	<0.1
Sakura Dellsher Inc.	30 S. Wacker Dr.	Chicago	IL	60606	Hideki Neda	312-930-0001	R	66 OR*	<0.1
Ore and Chemical Corp.	520 Madison Ave.	New York	NY	10022	Joseph E. Robertson Jr.	212-715-5200	S	64 OR*	<0.1
Farmers Commodities Corp.	P.O. Box 4887	Des Moines	IA	50306	Hal Richard	515-223-3788	R	59 OR*	0.2
Brody White and Company Inc.	4 World Trade Ctr.	New York	NY	10048	Steve Bergan	212-504-7500	R	55 OR*	<0.1
McVean Trading and Investm. Inc.	850 Ridge Lake Blvd.	Memphis	TN	38120	Charles McVean	901-761-8400	R	55 OR*	<0.1
Siegel Trading Company Inc.	118 N. Clinton Ave.	Chicago	IL	60661	Frank Mazza	312-236-6789	R	47 OR*	<0.1
TransMarket Group Inc.	141 W. Jackson Blvd.	Chicago	IL	60604	James G. McCormick	312-663-4848	R	47 OR*	<0.1
Allied Deals Inc.	230 5th Ave.	New York	NY	10001	Viren Rastogi	212-532-7644	R	40 OR	<0.1
Auglaize Farmers Cooperative	P.O. Box 360	Wapakoneta	OH	45895	Larry Hammond	419-738-2137	R	40	<0.1
AIOC Corp.	230 Park Ave.	New York	NY	10169	Alan Clingman	212-949-0600	R	39 OR*	<0.1
Vincent Commodities Corp.	P.O. Box 620481	Middleton	WI	53562	Ronald M. Vincent	608-831-4447	R	32 OR	<0.1
Alaron Trading Corp.	822 W. Washington Blvd	Chicago	IL	60607	Steven Greenberg	312-563-8000	R	31 OR*	<0.1
Rand Financial Services Inc.	30 S. Wacker Dr.	Chicago	IL	60606	Jeff Ouinto	312-559-8800	S	30 OR	0.1
FSI Futures Inc.	55 John St.	New York	NY	10038	Robin Rodriguez	212-619-5959	S	15 OR	<0.1
Baldwin Financial Corp.	209 S. La Salle St.	Chicago	IL	60604	William Taki Jr.	312-553-6100	R	14 OR*	<0.1
Johnston Grain and Seed Co.	1133 N. Bowie	Seguin	TX	78155	Art Johnston	210-379-5547	R	13	<0.1
Allendale Inc.	P.O. Box 1586	Crystal Lake	IL	60039	Paul J. Georgy	815-455-5010	R	11 OR	<0.1
DKB Financial Futures Corp.	10 S. Wacker Dr. #1835	Chicago	IL	60606	Kunio Yamanishi	312-466-1700	S	9 OR	<0.1
McKeany-Flavell Company Inc.	11 Embarcadero W.	Oakland	CA	94607	Michael Ruffolo	510-832-2866	R	9 OR*	<0.1
Allied Brokerage Group Inc.	1359 Broadway	New York	NY	10018	Alan Miller	212-564-9170	R	8 OR*	<0.1
Klein-Berger Co.	P.O. Box 609	Stockton	CA	95201	Bob Corlern	209-948-6802	S	6 OR*	<0.1
Commodity Improvisors Inc.	350 Old Country Rd.	Garden City	NY	11530	Daniel Reddington	516-248-9714	R	5 OR	<0.1
Simmons Brothers International Inc.	3019 Roseborough	Marshall	TX	75670	Mitch Simmons	903-935-6071	R	4 OR*	<0.1

Company type codes: P - Public, R - Private, S - Subsidiary, D - Division, J - Joint Venture, A - Affiliate, G - Group. If the dollar values shown are not sales, the following codes apply: TA - Total Assets; OR - Operating Revenues; GB - Gross Billings. * - estimated dollar value. < - less than. *na* - not available.

Continued on next page.

LEADING COMPANIES - SIC 6211 - Security Brokers and Dealers
Continued

Company Name	Address				CEO Name	Phone	Co. Type	Sales/Assets ($ mil)	Empl. (000)
Barex World Trade Corp.	777 W. Putnam Ave.	Greenwich	CT	06830	Stanley Rosenstock	203-531-1059	R	3 OR*	<0.1
Commodities Resource Corp.	P.O. Box 15087	Minneapolis	MN	55415	George Kleinman	612-333-7575	R	3 OR*	<0.1
FINEX	4 World Trade Ctr.	New York	NY	10048	Jacqueline Ewing	212-938-2629	D	3 OR	<0.1
RWA Financial Services Inc.	3307 Northland Dr.	Austin	TX	78731	Randall W. Allen	512-459-3911	R	3 OR	<0.1
EBCO U.S.A. Inc.	6613 N. Meridian St.	Oklahoma City	OK	73116	Paul Smart	405-720-0313	R	3 OR	<0.1
Keystone Trading Corp.	5420 Milwaukee Ave.	Chicago	IL	60630	Brian McGuire	312-763-8401	R	2 OR	<0.1
Ingredient Quality Consultants Inc.	4370 S. Tamiami Trail	Sarasota	FL	34231	Wayne Whittaker	813-921-6595	R	1 OR	<0.1
I.J. Cohen Company Inc.	P.O. Box 8378	Shawnee Mission	KS	66208	Phillip L. Gershon	913-648-6668	R	1 OR*	<0.1
Simonds-Shields-Theis Grain Co.	4800 Main St.	Kansas City	MO	64112	Steven O. Theis	816-561-4155	R	1 OR	<0.1
TW Energy Consulting Inc.	4800 Main St.	Kansas City	MO	64112	Peter Van Cleve	816-531-5455	R	0 OR	<0.1
Phoenixx International Resources Inc.	4955 Steubenville Pike	Pittsburgh	PA	15205	Paul Helsel	412-787-6363	R	0 OR*	<0.1

*Source: Ward's Business Directory of U.S. Private and Public Companies, 1996. Company type codes: P - Public, R - Private, S - Subsidiary, D - Division, J - Joint Venture, A - Affiliate, G - Group. If the dollar values shown are not sales, the following codes apply: TA - Total Assets; OR - Operating Revenues; GB - Gross Billings. * - estimated dollar value. < - less than; na - not available.*

SIC 6230

SECURITY AND COMMODITY EXCHANGES

SIC 6230 includes establishments whose principal activity is to furnish space and other facilities to members for the purpose of buying, selling, or trading in stocks, stock options, bonds, or commodity contracts. Commodity contract exchanges, futures exchanges, security exchanges, stock exchanges, and stock option exchanges are all classified as SIC 6230.

ESTABLISHMENTS, EMPLOYMENT, AND PAYROLL

	1988	1989		1990		1991		1992		1993		% change 88-93
		Value	%	Value	%	Value	%	Value	%	Value	%	
All Establishments	129	142	10.1	150	5.6	133	-11.3	142	6.8	105	-26.1	-18.6
Mid-March Employment	7,544	7,507	-0.5	9,149	21.9	8,268	-9.6	8,624	4.3	7,373	-14.5	-2.3
1st Quarter Wages (annualized - $ mil.)	375.7	352.2	-6.2	485.3	37.8	404.1	-16.7	437.1	8.1	407.4	-6.8	8.5
Payroll per Emp. 1st Q. (annualized)	49,795	46,919	-5.8	53,048	13.1	48,881	-7.9	50,682	3.7	55,261	9.0	11.0
Annual Payroll ($ mil.)	324.5	322.4	-0.6	450.3	39.7	398.6	-11.5	437.9	9.8	414.2	-5.4	27.7
Establishments - 1-4 Emp. Number	67	65	-3.0	69	6.2	60	-13.0	68	13.3	68	-	1.5
Mid-March Employment	114	114	-	108	-5.3	(D)	-	121	-	81	-33.1	-28.9
1st Quarter Wages (annualized - $ mil.)	13.0	5.1	-60.7	5.4	6.3	(D)	-	6.3	-	6.0	-5.7	-53.8
Payroll per Emp. 1st Q. (annualized)	113,614	44,702	-60.7	50,148	12.2	(D)	-	52,430	-	73,877	40.9	-35.0
Annual Payroll ($ mil.)	15.0	10.3	-31.6	8.7	-15.8	(D)	-	8.4	-	6.5	-21.8	-56.6
Establishments - 5-9 Emp. Number	18	21	16.7	18	-14.3	20	11.1	26	30.0	(D)	-	-
Mid-March Employment	(D)	145	-	110	-24.1	(D)	-	176	-	(D)	-	-
1st Quarter Wages (annualized - $ mil.)	(D)	9.0	-	6.9	-23.4	(D)	-	12.0	-	(D)	-	-
Payroll per Emp. 1st Q. (annualized)	(D)	61,793	-	62,400	1.0	(D)	-	68,114	-	(D)	-	-
Annual Payroll ($ mil.)	(D)	9.6	-	5.8	-39.6	(D)	-	11.1	-	(D)	-	-
Establishments - 10-19 Emp. Number	8	11	37.5	15	36.4	13	-13.3	9	-30.8	5	-44.4	-37.5
Mid-March Employment	(D)	157	-	212	35.0	175	-17.5	123	-29.7	65	-47.2	-
1st Quarter Wages (annualized - $ mil.)	(D)	6.3	-	11.9	88.8	10.1	-14.8	6.5	-36.1	2.7	-58.5	-
Payroll per Emp. 1st Q. (annualized)	(D)	40,051	-	56,000	39.8	57,783	3.2	52,553	-9.1	41,292	-21.4	-
Annual Payroll ($ mil.)	(D)	5.9	-	13.6	130.5	9.6	-29.4	6.2	-35.3	3.0	-52.4	-
Establishments - 20-49 Emp. Number	13	13	-	14	7.7	11	-21.4	14	27.3	6	-57.1	-53.8
Mid-March Employment	447	420	-6.0	408	-2.9	(D)	-	417	-	204	-51.1	-54.4
1st Quarter Wages (annualized - $ mil.)	41.3	21.6	-47.7	22.0	1.9	(D)	-	25.6	-	18.2	-29.2	-56.0
Payroll per Emp. 1st Q. (annualized)	92,304	51,362	-44.4	53,853	4.8	(D)	-	61,477	-	88,980	44.7	-3.6
Annual Payroll ($ mil.)	33.0	21.4	-35.1	18.8	-12.3	(D)	-	26.2	-	20.3	-22.4	-38.4
Establishments - 50-99 Emp. Number	10	17	70.0	15	-11.8	10	-33.3	9	-10.0	5	-44.4	-50.0
Mid-March Employment	771	1,262	63.7	1,140	-9.7	674	-40.9	679	0.7	364	-46.4	-52.8
1st Quarter Wages (annualized - $ mil.)	59.5	65.2	9.5	95.6	46.7	42.0	-56.1	47.2	12.5	16.9	-64.1	-71.5
Payroll per Emp. 1st Q. (annualized)	77,152	51,626	-33.1	83,860	62.4	62,297	-25.7	69,555	11.7	46,516	-33.1	-39.7
Annual Payroll ($ mil.)	39.8	60.1	51.0	90.9	51.4	61.8	-32.0	64.1	3.7	17.5	-72.7	-55.9
Establishments - 100-249 Emp. Number	5	9	80.0	11	22.2	12	9.1	8	-33.3	5	-37.5	-
Mid-March Employment	788	1,462	85.5	(D)	-	(D)	-	1,430	-	752	-47.4	-4.6
1st Quarter Wages (annualized - $ mil.)	31.1	51.2	64.6	(D)	-	(D)	-	65.9	-	37.4	-43.2	20.3
Payroll per Emp. 1st Q. (annualized)	39,482	35,026	-11.3	(D)	-	(D)	-	46,081	-	49,787	8.0	26.1
Annual Payroll ($ mil.)	26.8	45.5	69.9	(D)	-	(D)	-	69.6	-	36.7	-47.3	36.9
Establishments - 250-499 Emp. Number	3	2	-33.3	3	50.0	2	-33.3	(D)	-	4	-	33.3
Mid-March Employment	785	(D)	-	879	-	(D)	-	(D)	-	1,601	-	103.9
1st Quarter Wages (annualized - $ mil.)	25.2	(D)	-	20.2	-	(D)	-	(D)	-	111.8	-	343.1
Payroll per Emp. 1st Q. (annualized)	32,138	(D)	-	22,999	-	(D)	-	(D)	-	69,826	-	117.3
Annual Payroll ($ mil.)	22.2	(D)	-	22.5	-	(D)	-	(D)	-	131.1	-	489.5
Establishments - 500-999 Emp. Number	3	3	-	4	33.3	4	-	(D)	-	(D)	-	-
Mid-March Employment	(D)	(D)	-	3,155	-	(D)	-	(D)	-	(D)	-	-
1st Quarter Wages (annualized - $ mil.)	(D)	(D)	-	144.4	-	(D)	-	(D)	-	(D)	-	-
Payroll per Emp. 1st Q. (annualized)	(D)	(D)	-	45,777	-	(D)	-	(D)	-	(D)	-	-
Annual Payroll ($ mil.)	(D)	(D)	-	131.6	-	(D)	-	(D)	-	(D)	-	-
Estab. - 1000 or More Emp. Number	2	1	-50.0	1	-	1	-	(D)	-	-	-	-
Mid-March Employment	(D)	(D)	-	(D)	-	(D)	-	(D)	-	-	-	-
1st Quarter Wages (annualized - $ mil.)	(D)	(D)	-	(D)	-	(D)	-	(D)	-	-	-	-
Payroll per Emp. 1st Q. (annualized)	(D)	(D)	-	(D)	-	(D)	-	(D)	-	-	-	-
Annual Payroll ($ mil.)	(D)	(D)	-	(D)	-	(D)	-	(D)	-	-	-	-

Source: *County Business Patterns*, U.S. Department of Commerce, Washington, D.C., for 1988 through 1993. Payroll per employee is calculated using mid-March employment and 1st Quarter wages, annualized. Annual payroll, also shown, may not equal the annualized 1st Quarter wages. Columns headed by a percent sign (%) indicate change from the previous year. *na* stands for not available. The symbol (D) indicates that data are withheld by the source to avoid disclosure of competitive information. A dash (-) indicates that data are not available or cannot be calculated.

ESTABLISHMENTS
Number

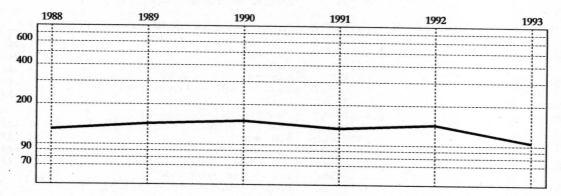

MID-MARCH EMPLOYMENT
Number

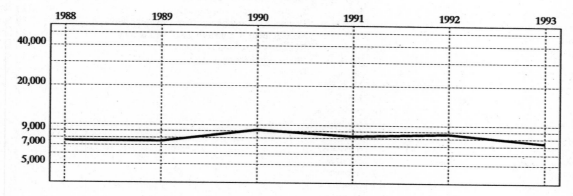

ANNUAL PAYROLL
$ million

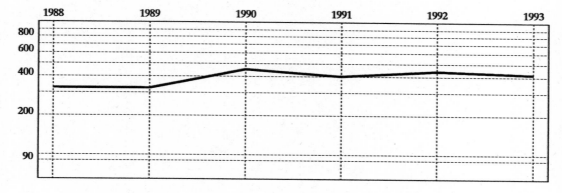

INPUTS AND OUTPUTS FOR SECURITY AND COMMODITY BROKERS - SIC GROUP 62

Economic Sector or Industry Providing Inputs	%	Sector	Economic Sector or Industry Buying Outputs	%	Sector
Security & commodity brokers	21.8	Fin/R.E.	Personal consumption expenditures	35.2	
Computer & data processing services	9.7	Services	Credit agencies other than banks	12.5	Fin/R.E.
Accounting, auditing & bookkeeping	8.2	Services	Insurance carriers	12.3	Fin/R.E.
Air transportation	6.8	Util.	Banking	11.7	Fin/R.E.
Communications, except radio & TV	6.8	Util.	Security & commodity brokers	7.6	Fin/R.E.
Real estate	6.2	Fin/R.E.	S/L Govt. purch., other general government	5.8	S/L Govt
Eating & drinking places	5.4	Trade	Exports	2.8	Foreign
Noncomparable imports	4.0	Foreign	Electric services (utilities)	1.3	Util.
Commercial printing	3.0	Manufg.	Social services, nec	1.1	Services
Detective & protective services	2.7	Services	Real estate	0.9	Fin/R.E.
Banking	2.6	Fin/R.E.	Petroleum refining	0.8	Manufg.
Hotels & lodging places	2.4	Services	State & local government enterprises, nec	0.8	Gov't
U.S. Postal Service	2.4	Gov't	Libraries, vocation education	0.5	Services
Advertising	2.2	Services	Gas production & distribution (utilities)	0.4	Util.
Imports	2.0	Foreign	Colleges, universities, & professional schools	0.3	Services
Petroleum refining	1.7	Manufg.	Communications, except radio & TV	0.3	Util.
Legal services	1.6	Services	Retail trade, except eating & drinking	0.3	Trade
Photofinishing labs, commercial photography	1.5	Services	Child day care services	0.2	Services
Management & consulting services & labs	0.9	Services	Crude petroleum & natural gas	0.2	Mining
Manifold business forms	0.7	Manufg.	Eating & drinking places	0.2	Trade
Motor freight transportation & warehousing	0.7	Util.	Electronic computing equipment	0.2	Manufg.
Maintenance of nonfarm buildings nec	0.6	Constr.	Engineering, architectural, & surveying services	0.2	Services
Sanitary services, steam supply, irrigation	0.6	Util.	Management & consulting services & labs	0.2	Services
Transit & bus transportation	0.5	Util.	Railroads & related services	0.2	Util.
Wholesale trade	0.5	Trade	Business services nec	0.1	Services
Automotive rental & leasing, without drivers	0.4	Services	Drugs	0.1	Manufg.
Electronic computing equipment	0.4	Manufg.			
Insurance carriers	0.4	Fin/R.E.			
Business services nec	0.3	Services			
Photographic equipment & supplies	0.3	Manufg.			
Electrical repair shops	0.2	Services			
Personnel supply services	0.2	Services			
Automotive repair shops & services	0.1	Services			
Business/professional associations	0.1	Services			
Manufacturing industries, nec	0.1	Manufg.			
Paper mills, except building paper	0.1	Manufg.			

Source: Benchmark Input-Output Accounts for the U.S. Economy, 1982, U.S. Department of Commerce, Washington, D.C., July 1991. Data, as reported in the source, are organized by the 1977 SIC structure in use in 1982 but have been matched, as closely as is possible, to the 1987 SIC structure used in this book. Activities with the same percentage are sorted alphabetically by name of activity.

OCCUPATIONS EMPLOYED BY SECURITY AND COMMODITY EXCHANGES AND SERVICES

Occupation	% of Total 1994	Change to 2005	Occupation	% of Total 1994	Change to 2005
Management support workers nec	12.7	77.9	Computer programmers	2.6	30.1
Securities & financial services sales workers	9.1	60.7	Systems analysts	2.6	157.2
Secretaries, ex legal & medical	8.7	46.3	Sales & related workers nec	2.1	60.7
General managers & top executives	7.9	52.5	Data entry keyers, ex composing	2.0	18.6
Brokerage clerks	6.6	-35.7	Receptionists & information clerks	1.8	60.7
General office clerks	5.7	37.0	Clerical support workers nec	1.6	28.5
Financial managers	5.2	60.7	Marketing & sales worker supervisors	1.5	60.7
Clerical supervisors & managers	4.4	64.4	Managers & administrators nec	1.3	60.6
Bookkeeping, accounting, & auditing clerks	4.3	20.5	Professional workers nec	1.2	92.8
Accountants & auditors	2.9	60.7	Computer operators, ex peripheral equipment	1.2	-8.6

Sources: Industry-Occupation Matrix, Bureau of Labor Statistics. These data relate to one or more 3-digit SIC industry groups rather than to a single 4-digit SIC. The change reported for each occupation to the year 2005 is a percent of growth or decline as estimated by the Bureau of Labor Statistics. The abbreviation *nec* stands for not elsewhere classified.

U.S. AND STATE DATA ON INDUSTRY REVENUES AND OTHER ACCOUNTS FOR 1992

State	No. of Estab.	Employ- ment	Payroll ($ mil.)	Revenues ($ mil.)	Empl./ Estab.	Revenue/ Estab. ($)	Payroll/ Estab. ($)	Revenue/ Empl. ($)	Payroll/ Empl. ($)
UNITED STATES	35	6,739	311.8	993.5	193	28,384,743	8,907,514	147,420	46,263
California	7	-	(D)	(D)	(D)	(D)	(D)	(D)	(D)
Illinois	4	2,524	97.7	284.4	631	71,101,500	24,435,500	112,681	38,725
Massachusetts	1	-	(D)	(D)	(D)	(D)	(D)	(D)	(D)
Minnesota	1	-	(D)	(D)	(D)	(D)	(D)	(D)	(D)
Missouri	2	-	(D)	(D)	(D)	(D)	(D)	(D)	(D)
New York	13	3,436	182.6	621.3	264	47,790,538	14,048,923	180,814	53,154
Ohio	1	-	(D)	(D)	(D)	(D)	(D)	(D)	(D)
Pennsylvania	1	-	(D)	(D)	(D)	(D)	(D)	(D)	(D)
Texas	1	-	(D)	(D)	(D)	(D)	(D)	(D)	(D)

Source: 1992 Economic Census, U.S. Department of Commerce, Washington, D.C. This is the only table that shows revenue data as collected by the Bureau of the Census in an Economic Census. The symbol (D) indicates that data are withheld by the source to avoid disclosure of competitive information. A dash (-) indicates that data are not available or cannot be calculated.

ESTABLISHMENTS 1992 - STATE AND REGIONAL CONCENTRATION

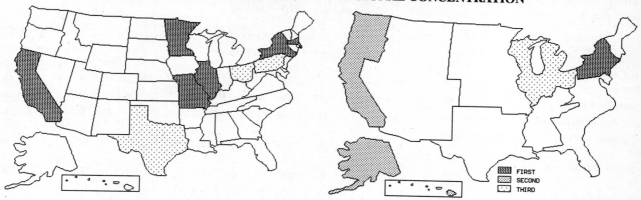

EMPLOYMENT 1992 - STATE AND REGIONAL CONCENTRATION

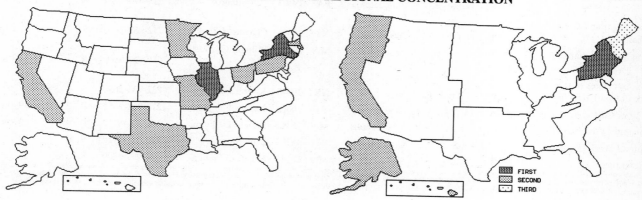

REVENUES 1992 - STATE AND REGIONAL CONCENTRATION

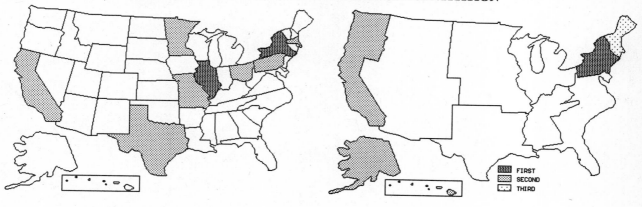

States with the darkest shading indicate those states which have proportionately more establishments, employment, or revenues than would be indicated by the state's population. States with light shading are states with proportionately fewer establishments, less employment, and lower revenues than population distribution. States shaded grey are within 15 percent of the state's population proportion in these categories. States for which no data are available are shown as average (grey). *Regions* are shaded to indicate absolute rank in the category. If no data for the category are available, establishment counts are used to shade the regions. Source of the data is the table on the facing page.

LEADING COMPANIES - SIC 6221 - Commodity Contracts Brokers, Dealers

Number shown: **15**   Total sales/assets ($ mil): **1,034**   Total employment (000): **7.4**

Company Name	Address				CEO Name	Phone	Co. Type	Sales/Assets ($ mil)	Empl. (000)
National Association of Securities Dealers Inc.	1735 K St. N.W.	Washington	DC	20006	Joseph R. Hardiman	202-728-8000	R	332 OR	2.0
American Stock Exchange Inc.	86 Trinity Pl.	New York	NY	10006	Richard F. Syron	212-306-1000	R	144 OR	0.7
Chicago Mercantile Exchange	30 S. Wacker Dr.	Chicago	IL	60606	William J. Brodsky	312-930-1000	R	124 OR	1.0
Chicago Board of Trade	141 W. Jackson Ave.	Chicago	IL	60604	Thomas R. Donovan	312-435-3500	R	109 OR	0.7
Chicago Board Options Exchange Inc.	400 S. LaSalle St.	Chicago	IL	60605	Alger B. Chapman	312-786-5600	R	98 OR	0.9
Chicago Stock Exchange Inc.	440 S. LaSalle St.	Chicago	IL	60605	Homer J. Livingston Jr.	312-663-2222	R	70 OR	0.7
Nasdaq Stock Market Inc.	1735 K St. N.W.	Washington	DC	20006	Joseph R. Hardiman	202-728-8000	S	54 OR	0.3
Philadelphia Stock Exchange Inc.	1900 Market St.	Philadelphia	PA	19103	Nicholas A. Giordano	215-496-5000	R	38 OR	0.6
Coffee, Sugar and Cocoa Exchange Inc.	4 World Trade Ctr.	New York	NY	10048	Charles H. Falk	212-938-2800	R	25 OR*	0.2
Boston Stock Exchange Inc.	1 Boston Pl.	Boston	MA	02108	William G. Morton Jr.	617-723-9500	R	14 OR	<0.1
Citrus Associates of the New York Cotton Exchange Inc.	4 World Trade Ctr.	New York	NY	10048	Joseph J. O'Neill	212-938-2650	R	9 OR	0.1
New York Cotton Exchange	4 World Trade Ctr.	New York	NY	10048	Joseph J. O'Neill	212-938-2650	R	9 OR	0.1
Minneapolis Grain Exchange	400 S. 4th St.	Minneapolis	MN	55415	James H. Lindau	612-338-6212	R	6 OR	<0.1
Cincinnati Stock Exchange	36 E. 4th St.	Cincinnati	OH	45202	Fred Moss	513-621-1410	R	2 OR*	<0.1
Metalsco Inc.	2388 Schuetz Ave.	St. Louis	MO	63146	Sheldon Tauben	314-997-5200	R	1 OR*	<0.1

*Source: Ward's Business Directory of U.S. Private and Public Companies, 1996. Company type codes: P - Public, R - Private, S - Subsidiary, D - Division, J - Joint Venture, A - Affiliate, G - Group. If the dollar values shown are not sales, the following codes apply: TA - Total Assets; OR - Operating Revenues; GB - Gross Billings. * - estimated dollar value. < - less than; na - not available.*

SIC 6280

SECURITY AND COMMODITY SERVICES

The group includes SIC 6282, Investment Advice and SIC 6289, Services Allied With the Exchange of Securities or Commodities, not elsewhere classified.

SIC 6282 includes all establishments that furnish investment advice. Investment information is furnished to companies and individuals concerning securities and commodities on a contract or fee basis. Establishments included in SIC 6280 do not act as brokers and dealers; those who furnish investment advice and also sell securities are classified as SIC 6210. Futures and investment advisory services, investment counseling services, investment research organizations, and managers of mutual funds—on a contract or fee basis—are included.

SIC 6289 includes a variety of services to security or commodity holders, brokers, or dealers, including bondholders protective committees, custodians of securities, exchange clearinghouses for commodities and securities, financial reporting services, quotation services for stocks, royalty owners protective associations, security custodian services, security holders protective committees, and stock transfer agents.

ESTABLISHMENTS, EMPLOYMENT, AND PAYROLL

	1988	1989		1990		1991		1992		1993		% change 88-93
		Value	%	Value	%	Value	%	Value	%	Value	%	
All Establishments	6,344	6,189	-2.4	7,087	14.5	7,954	12.2	11,517	44.8	13,087	13.6	106.3
Mid-March Employment	69,604	67,798	-2.6	75,740	11.7	77,674	2.6	91,846	18.2	119,969	30.6	72.4
1st Quarter Wages (annualized - $ mil.)	4,699.6	4,077.1	-13.2	4,813.8	18.1	4,897.7	1.7	5,859.0	19.6	7,437.9	26.9	58.3
Payroll per Emp. 1st Q. (annualized)	67,519	60,137	-10.9	63,557	5.7	63,055	-0.8	63,792	1.2	61,998	-2.8	-8.2
Annual Payroll ($ mil.)	3,808.3	3,817.3	0.2	4,454.0	16.7	5,062.4	13.7	6,488.7	28.2	9,468.3	45.9	148.6
Establishments - 1-4 Emp. Number	4,553	4,400	-3.4	5,089	15.7	5,738	12.8	8,935	55.7	9,831	10.0	115.9
Mid-March Employment	7,362	7,017	-4.7	8,012	14.2	8,527	6.4	13,152	54.2	14,610	11.1	98.5
1st Quarter Wages (annualized - $ mil.)	278.8	294.2	5.5	308.1	4.7	360.2	16.9	515.3	43.1	609.3	18.3	118.5
Payroll per Emp. 1st Q. (annualized)	37,874	41,926	10.7	38,459	-8.3	42,237	9.8	39,178	-7.2	41,707	6.5	10.1
Annual Payroll ($ mil.)	341.1	364.6	6.9	379.2	4.0	490.2	29.3	709.1	44.6	906.1	27.8	165.6
Establishments - 5-9 Emp. Number	866	863	-0.3	937	8.6	1,116	19.1	1,349	20.9	1,635	21.2	88.8
Mid-March Employment	(D)	5,565	-	6,005	7.9	7,267	21.0	8,709	19.8	10,485	20.4	-
1st Quarter Wages (annualized - $ mil.)	(D)	283.8	-	352.5	24.2	460.6	30.7	593.6	28.9	629.3	6.0	-
Payroll per Emp. 1st Q. (annualized)	(D)	51,002	-	58,699	15.1	63,387	8.0	68,155	7.5	60,016	-11.9	-
Annual Payroll ($ mil.)	(D)	310.7	-	380.6	22.5	511.5	34.4	675.1	32.0	901.2	33.5	-
Establishments - 10-19 Emp. Number	462	464	0.4	540	16.4	546	1.1	634	16.1	788	24.3	70.6
Mid-March Employment	6,111	6,115	0.1	7,153	17.0	7,226	1.0	8,445	16.9	10,652	26.1	74.3
1st Quarter Wages (annualized - $ mil.)	538.3	451.2	-16.2	542.5	20.2	521.0	-4.0	602.2	15.6	774.5	28.6	43.9
Payroll per Emp. 1st Q. (annualized)	88,081	73,794	-16.2	75,843	2.8	72,095	-4.9	71,311	-1.1	72,709	2.0	-17.5
Annual Payroll ($ mil.)	435.9	434.7	-0.3	531.0	22.1	575.7	8.4	724.5	25.8	1,061.4	46.5	143.5
Establishments - 20-49 Emp. Number	263	255	-3.0	293	14.9	327	11.6	350	7.0	505	44.3	92.0
Mid-March Employment	7,863	7,703	-2.0	8,948	16.2	9,647	7.8	10,430	8.1	14,998	43.8	90.7
1st Quarter Wages (annualized - $ mil.)	609.2	566.6	-7.0	723.8	27.8	748.4	3.4	842.4	12.5	1,046.4	24.2	71.8
Payroll per Emp. 1st Q. (annualized)	77,480	73,555	-5.1	80,893	10.0	77,583	-4.1	80,762	4.1	69,771	-13.6	-9.9
Annual Payroll ($ mil.)	484.8	502.3	3.6	632.9	26.0	849.7	34.3	911.5	7.3	1,357.9	49.0	180.1
Establishments - 50-99 Emp. Number	94	94	-	106	12.8	119	12.3	119	-	153	28.6	62.8
Mid-March Employment	6,548	6,412	-2.1	7,322	14.2	7,791	6.4	8,167	4.8	10,518	28.8	60.6
1st Quarter Wages (annualized - $ mil.)	587.7	600.6	2.2	609.3	1.4	635.4	4.3	936.0	47.3	764.1	-18.4	30.0
Payroll per Emp. 1st Q. (annualized)	89,756	93,672	4.4	83,212	-11.2	81,552	-2.0	114,610	40.5	72,649	-36.6	-19.1
Annual Payroll ($ mil.)	423.4	437.6	3.3	504.1	15.2	603.7	19.8	956.5	58.4	840.4	-12.1	98.5
Establishments - 100-249 Emp. Number	66	73	10.6	70	-4.1	63	-10.0	77	22.2	104	35.1	57.6
Mid-March Employment	9,411	10,932	16.2	(D)	-	9,685	-	11,355	17.2	16,176	42.5	71.9
1st Quarter Wages (annualized - $ mil.)	677.7	683.3	0.8	(D)	-	647.1	-	854.8	32.1	1,426.0	66.8	110.4
Payroll per Emp. 1st Q. (annualized)	72,013	62,503	-13.2	(D)	-	66,818	-	75,282	12.7	88,157	17.1	22.4
Annual Payroll ($ mil.)	556.1	662.4	19.1	(D)	-	637.4	-	959.3	50.5	2,042.6	112.9	267.3
Establishments - 250-499 Emp. Number	19	21	10.5	31	47.6	25	-19.4	33	32.0	45	36.4	136.8
Mid-March Employment	6,235	(D)	-	10,682	-	(D)	-	10,951	-	15,582	42.3	149.9
1st Quarter Wages (annualized - $ mil.)	521.4	(D)	-	680.0	-	(D)	-	641.4	-	928.1	44.7	78.0
Payroll per Emp. 1st Q. (annualized)	83,620	(D)	-	63,658	-	(D)	-	58,567	-	59,559	1.7	-28.8
Annual Payroll ($ mil.)	348.5	(D)	-	534.1	-	(D)	-	609.1	-	875.9	43.8	151.3
Establishments - 500-999 Emp. Number	13	14	7.7	16	14.3	14	-12.5	(D)	-	17	-	30.8
Mid-March Employment	8,579	9,240	7.7	10,935	18.3	(D)	-	(D)	-	11,260	-	31.3
1st Quarter Wages (annualized - $ mil.)	598.9	485.2	-19.0	544.7	12.3	(D)	-	(D)	-	608.0	-	1.5
Payroll per Emp. 1st Q. (annualized)	69,805	52,512	-24.8	49,810	-5.1	(D)	-	(D)	-	53,994	-	-22.7
Annual Payroll ($ mil.)	410.8	501.4	22.1	527.1	5.1	(D)	-	(D)	-	566.8	-	38.0
Estab. - 1000 or More Emp. Number	8	5	-37.5	5	-	6	20.0	(D)	-	9	-	12.5
Mid-March Employment	(D)	(D)	-	(D)	-	(D)	-	(D)	-	15,688	-	-
1st Quarter Wages (annualized - $ mil.)	(D)	(D)	-	(D)	-	(D)	-	(D)	-	652.2	-	-
Payroll per Emp. 1st Q. (annualized)	(D)	(D)	-	(D)	-	(D)	-	(D)	-	41,571	-	-
Annual Payroll ($ mil.)	(D)	(D)	-	(D)	-	(D)	-	(D)	-	916.0	-	-

Source: County Business Patterns, U.S. Department of Commerce, Washington, D.C., for 1988 through 1993. Payroll per employee is calculated using mid-March employment and 1st Quarter wages, annualized. Annual payroll, also shown, may not equal the annualized 1st Quarter wages. Columns headed by a percent sign (%) indicate change from the previous year. *na* stands for not available. The symbol (D) indicates that data are withheld by the source to avoid disclosure of competitive information. A dash (-) indicates that data are not available or cannot be calculated.

ESTABLISHMENTS
Number

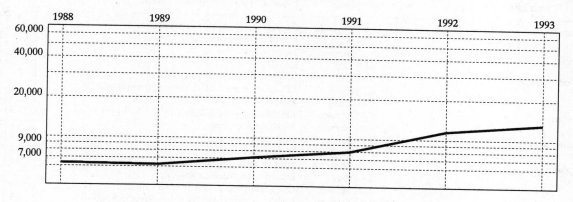

MID-MARCH EMPLOYMENT
Number

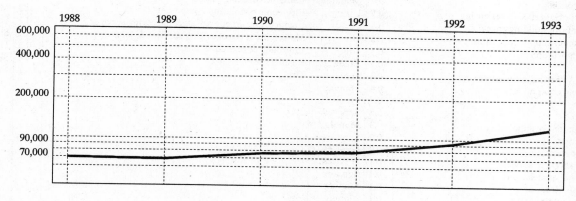

ANNUAL PAYROLL
$ million

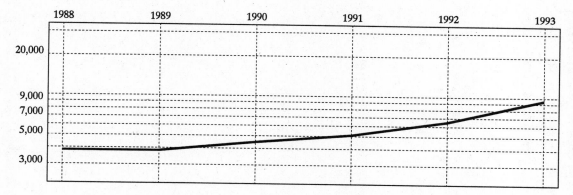

INPUTS AND OUTPUTS FOR SECURITY AND COMMODITY BROKERS - SIC GROUP 62

Economic Sector or Industry Providing Inputs	%	Sector	Economic Sector or Industry Buying Outputs	%	Sector
Security & commodity brokers	21.8	Fin/R.E.	Personal consumption expenditures	35.2	
Computer & data processing services	9.7	Services	Credit agencies other than banks	12.5	Fin/R.E.
Accounting, auditing & bookkeeping	8.2	Services	Insurance carriers	12.3	Fin/R.E.
Air transportation	6.8	Util.	Banking	11.7	Fin/R.E.
Communications, except radio & TV	6.8	Util.	Security & commodity brokers	7.6	Fin/R.E.
Real estate	6.2	Fin/R.E.	S/L Govt. purch., other general government	5.8	S/L Govt
Eating & drinking places	5.4	Trade	Exports	2.8	Foreign
Noncomparable imports	4.0	Foreign	Electric services (utilities)	1.3	Util.
Commercial printing	3.0	Manufg.	Social services, nec	1.1	Services
Detective & protective services	2.7	Services	Real estate	0.9	Fin/R.E.
Banking	2.6	Fin/R.E.	Petroleum refining	0.8	Manufg.
Hotels & lodging places	2.4	Services	State & local government enterprises, nec	0.8	Gov't
U.S. Postal Service	2.4	Gov't	Libraries, vocation education	0.5	Services
Advertising	2.2	Services	Gas production & distribution (utilities)	0.4	Util.
Imports	2.0	Foreign	Colleges, universities, & professional schools	0.3	Services
Petroleum refining	1.7	Manufg.	Communications, except radio & TV	0.3	Util.
Legal services	1.6	Services	Retail trade, except eating & drinking	0.3	Trade
Photofinishing labs, commercial photography	1.5	Services	Child day care services	0.2	Services
Management & consulting services & labs	0.9	Services	Crude petroleum & natural gas	0.2	Mining
Manifold business forms	0.7	Manufg.	Eating & drinking places	0.2	Trade
Motor freight transportation & warehousing	0.7	Util.	Electronic computing equipment	0.2	Manufg.
Maintenance of nonfarm buildings nec	0.6	Constr.	Engineering, architectural, & surveying services	0.2	Services
Sanitary services, steam supply, irrigation	0.6	Util.	Management & consulting services & labs	0.2	Services
Transit & bus transportation	0.5	Util.	Railroads & related services	0.2	Util.
Wholesale trade	0.5	Trade	Business services nec	0.1	Services
Automotive rental & leasing, without drivers	0.4	Services	Drugs	0.1	Manufg.
Electronic computing equipment	0.4	Manufg.			
Insurance carriers	0.4	Fin/R.E.			
Business services nec	0.3	Services			
Photographic equipment & supplies	0.3	Manufg.			
Electrical repair shops	0.2	Services			
Personnel supply services	0.2	Services			
Automotive repair shops & services	0.1	Services			
Business/professional associations	0.1	Services			
Manufacturing industries, nec	0.1	Manufg.			
Paper mills, except building paper	0.1	Manufg.			

Source: Benchmark Input-Output Accounts for the U.S. Economy, 1982, U.S. Department of Commerce, Washington, D.C., July 1991. Data, as reported in the source, are organized by the 1977 SIC structure in use in 1982 but have been matched, as closely as is possible, to the 1987 SIC structure used in this book. Activities with the same percentage are sorted alphabetically by name of activity.

OCCUPATIONS EMPLOYED BY SECURITY AND COMMODITY EXCHANGES AND SERVICES

Occupation	% of Total 1994	Change to 2005	Occupation	% of Total 1994	Change to 2005
Management support workers nec	12.7	77.9	Computer programmers	2.6	30.1
Securities & financial services sales workers	9.1	60.7	Systems analysts	2.6	157.2
Secretaries, ex legal & medical	8.7	46.3	Sales & related workers nec	2.1	60.7
General managers & top executives	7.9	52.5	Data entry keyers, ex composing	2.0	18.6
Brokerage clerks	6.6	-35.7	Receptionists & information clerks	1.8	60.7
General office clerks	5.7	37.0	Clerical support workers nec	1.6	28.5
Financial managers	5.2	60.7	Marketing & sales worker supervisors	1.5	60.7
Clerical supervisors & managers	4.4	64.4	Managers & administrators nec	1.3	60.6
Bookkeeping, accounting, & auditing clerks	4.3	20.5	Professional workers nec	1.2	92.8
Accountants & auditors	2.9	60.7	Computer operators, ex peripheral equipment	1.2	-8.6

Sources: Industry-Occupation Matrix, Bureau of Labor Statistics. These data relate to one or more 3-digit SIC industry groups rather than to a single 4-digit SIC. The change reported for each occupation to the year 2005 is a percent of growth or decline as estimated by the Bureau of Labor Statistics. The abbreviation *nec* stands for not elsewhere classified.

U.S. AND STATE DATA ON INDUSTRY REVENUES AND OTHER ACCOUNTS FOR 1992

State	No. of Estab.	Employ-ment	Payroll ($ mil.)	Revenues ($ mil.)	Empl./ Estab.	Revenue/ Estab. ($)	Payroll/ Estab. ($)	Revenue/ Empl. ($)	Payroll/ Empl. ($)
UNITED STATES	11,905	86,859	6,562.5	17,138.8	7	1,439,629	551,239	197,317	75,553
California	1,741	-	(D)	(D)	(D)	(D)	(D)	(D)	(D)
Colorado	318	3,330	147.6	421.9	10	1,326,780	464,230	126,702	44,332
Florida	697	2,156	131.0	342.7	3	491,742	187,991	158,972	60,775
Georgia	269	1,239	81.9	226.7	5	842,717	304,539	182,963	66,119
Illinois	641	4,528	350.9	1,110.5	7	1,732,505	547,395	245,260	77,491
Indiana	153	756	36.6	89.5	5	584,993	239,092	118,392	48,388
Maryland	239	1,336	82.9	219.2	6	917,285	346,941	164,095	62,065
Massachusetts	498	-	(D)	(D)	(D)	(D)	(D)	(D)	(D)
Michigan	302	986	53.5	129.9	3	430,030	177,036	131,713	54,224
Minnesota	310	-	(D)	(D)	(D)	(D)	(D)	(D)	(D)
Missouri	194	-	(D)	(D)	(D)	(D)	(D)	(D)	(D)
New Jersey	413	7,967	448.9	1,295.9	19	3,137,867	1,086,821	162,663	56,340
New York	1,457	15,855	1,966.7	4,489.5	11	3,081,365	1,349,844	283,163	124,044
North Carolina	174	584	32.7	80.5	3	462,925	187,845	137,926	55,967
Ohio	418	-	(D)	(D)	(D)	(D)	(D)	(D)	(D)
Pennsylvania	476	-	(D)	(D)	(D)	(D)	(D)	(D)	(D)
Tennessee	151	434	37.3	81.5	3	539,728	246,921	187,786	85,910
Texas	691	-	(D)	(D)	(D)	(D)	(D)	(D)	(D)
Virginia	286	1,257	89.7	213.4	4	746,007	313,671	169,736	71,368
Washington	256	1,073	55.2	160.4	4	626,621	215,738	149,501	51,472
Wisconsin	186	1,359	72.3	240.4	7	1,292,366	388,651	176,880	53,193

Source: 1992 Economic Census, U.S. Department of Commerce, Washington, D.C. This is the only table that shows revenue data as collected by the Bureau of the Census in an Economic Census. The symbol (D) indicates that data are withheld by the source to avoid disclosure of competitive information. A dash (-) indicates that data are not available or cannot be calculated.

ESTABLISHMENTS 1992 - STATE AND REGIONAL CONCENTRATION

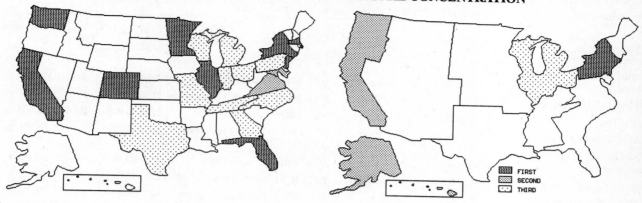

EMPLOYMENT 1992 - STATE AND REGIONAL CONCENTRATION

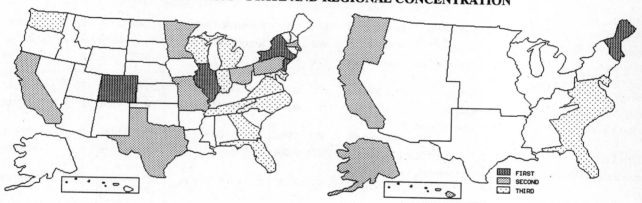

REVENUES 1992 - STATE AND REGIONAL CONCENTRATION

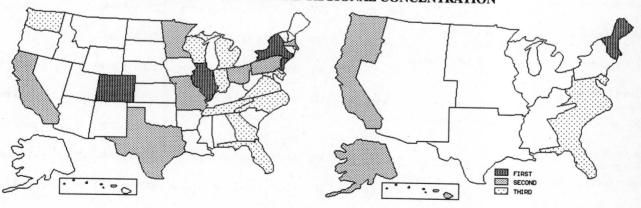

States with the darkest shading indicate those states which have proportionately more establishments, employment, or revenues than would be indicated by the state's population. States with light shading are states with proportionately fewer establishments, less employment, and lower revenues than population distribution. States shaded grey are within 15 percent of the state's population proportion in these categories. States for which no data are available are shown as average (grey). *Regions* are shaded to indicate absolute rank in the category. If no data for the category are available, establishment counts are used to shade the regions. Source of the data is the table on the facing page.

LEADING COMPANIES - SIC 6231 - Security and Commodity Exchanges

Number shown: **100**   Total sales/assets ($ mil): **996,511**   Total employment (000): **474.1**

Company Name	Address				CEO Name	Phone	Co. Type	Sales/Assets ($ mil)	Empl. (000)
Prudential Insurance Company of America	751 Broad St.	Newark	NJ	07102	Arthur F. Ryan	201-802-6000	R	313,660 TA	100.0
J.P. Morgan and Company Inc.	60 Wall St.	New York	NY	10260	Dennis Weatherstone	212-483-2323	P	154,917 TA	15.2
Travelers Inc.	65 E. 55th St.	New York	NY	10022	Sanford I. Weill	212-816-8000	P	115,300 TA	52.0
Equitable Companies Inc.	787 7th Ave.	New York	NY	10019	Richard H. Jenrette	212-554-1234	P	98,991 TA	13.1
Teachers Insurance and Annuity Association	730 3rd Ave.	New York	NY	10017	John H. Biggs	212-490-9000	R	67,483 TA	4.0
CoreStates Financial Corp.	P.O. Box 7618	Philadelphia	PA	19101	Terrence A. Larsen	215-973-3100	P	29,325 TA	13.7
State Street Boston Corp.	P.O. Box 351	Boston	MA	02101	Marshall N. Carter	617-786-3000	P	21,730 TA	11.1
Merrill Lynch and Company Inc.	250 Vesey St.	New York	NY	10281	Daniel P. Tully	212-449-1000	P	18,233 OR	43.8
St. Paul Companies Inc.	385 Washington St.	St. Paul	MN	55102	Douglas W. Leatherdale	612-221-7911	P	17,496 TA	12.6
New England Mutual Life Insurance Co.	501 Boylston St.	Boston	MA	02117	Robert A. Shafto	617-578-2000	R	16,582 TA	3.0
Washington Mutual Bank	1201 3rd Ave.	Seattle	WA	98101	Kerry K. Killinger	206-461-2000	S	15,827 TA	4.7
SunAmerica Inc.	1 SunAmerica Ctr.	Century City	CA	90067	Eli Broad	310-772-6000	P	14,656 TA	4.3
Mutual Life Insurance Company of New York	1740 Broadway	New York	NY	10019	Michael I. Roth	212-708-2000	R	14,166 TA	5.1
Kemper Corp.	1 Kemper Dr.	Long Grove	IL	60049	David B. Mathis	708-540-4700	P	13,154 TA	6.3
ReliaStar Financial Corp.	20 Washington Ave. S.	Minneapolis	MN	55401	John G. Turner	612-372-5432	P	10,367 TA	2.6
AEGON USA Inc.	1111 N. Charles St.	Baltimore	MD	21201	Don Shepard	410-576-4571	S	9,700 TA	5.4
Lehman Brothers Holdings Inc.	3 World Financial Ctr.	New York	NY	10285	Richard S. Fuld Jr.	212-298-2000	P	8,692 OR	9.3
Lehman Brothers Inc.	3 World Financial Ctr.	New York	NY	10285	Richard S. Fuld Jr.	212-298-2000	S	8,692 OR	9.3
USLIFE Corp.	125 Maiden Ln.	New York	NY	10038	Gordon E. Crosby Jr.	212-709-6000	P	7,004 TA	2.2
PaineWebber Group Inc.	1285 Avenue of the Americas	New York	NY	10019	Donald B. Marron	212-713-2000	P	3,964 OR	16.6
Marsh and McLennan Co. Inc.	1166 Avenue of the Americas	New York	NY	10036	A.J.C. Smith	212-345-5000	P	3,435	26.0
PaineWebber Inc.	1285 Ave. of the Amer.	New York	NY	10019	Donald B. Marron	212-713-2000	S	3,364 OR	13.6
American Express Financial Advisors Inc.	IDS Tower 10	Minneapolis	MN	55440	David R. Hubers	612-671-3131	S	3,156 OR	7.7
FMR Corp.	82 Devonshire St.	Boston	MA	02109	Edward C. Johnson III	617-563-7000	R	2,660 OR	14.6
Fund American Enterprises Holdings Inc.	The 1820 House	Norwich	VT	05055	John J. Byrne	802-649-3633	P	1,807 TA	2.1
Kemper Financial Companies Inc.	120 S. LaSalle St.	Chicago	IL	60603	Charles M. Kierscht	312-781-1121	S	1,242 OR	2.8
Kansas City Southern Industries Inc.	114 W. 11th St.	Kansas City	MO	64015	Landon H. Rowland	816-556-0303	P	1,098 OR	8.2
Charles Schwab Corp.	101 Montgomery St.	San Francisco	CA	94104	Charles R. Schwab	415-627-7000	P	965 OR	6.1

Company type codes: P - Public, R - Private, S - Subsidiary, D - Division, J - Joint Venture, A - Affiliate, G - Group. If the dollar values shown are not sales, the following codes apply: TA - Total Assets; OR - Operating Revenues; GB - Gross Billings. * - estimated dollar value. < - less than. *na* - not available.

Continued on next page.

LEADING COMPANIES - SIC 6231 - Security and Commodity Exchanges
Continued

Company Name	Address				CEO Name	Phone	Co. Type	Sales/Assets ($ mil)	Empl. (000)
Charles Schwab Investment Management Inc.	101 Montgomery St.	San Francisco	CA	94104	Charles R. Schwab	415-627-7000	S	965 OR	6.1
Cadence Capital Management Corp.	1 Exchange Pl.	Boston	MA	02109	David B. Breed	617-367-7400	S	940 OR	<0.1
Franklin Resources Inc.	777 Mariners Island	San Mateo	CA	94404	Charles B. Johnson	415-312-3000	P	827 OR	4.1
Piedmont Management Company Inc.	80 Maiden Ln.	New York	NY	10038	Robert M. DeMichele	212-363-4650	P	676 TA	0.2
Kemper Securities Inc.	77 W. Wacker Dr.	Chicago	IL	60606	James R. Boris	312-574-6000	S	674 OR	3.6
Alex. Brown Inc.	135 E. Baltimore St.	Baltimore	MD	21202	A.B. Krongard	410-727-1700	P	628 OR	2.2
Primerica Financial Services Inc.	3120 Breckinridge Blvd	Duluth	GA	30136	Peter M. Dawkins	404-564-6162	S	610 OR*	2.0
Putnam Investments Inc.	1 Post Office Sq.	Boston	MA	02109	Lawrence J. Lasser	617-292-1000	S	610 OR*	2.0
Alliance Capital Management L.P.	1345 Avenue of the Americas	New York	NY	10105	Dave H. Williams	212-969-1000	P	601 OR	1.5
Twentieth Century Companies Inc.	P.O. Box 419200	Kansas City	MO	64141	James E. Stowers Sr.	816-531-5575	R	540 OR*	1.8
Heller Financial Inc.	500 W. Monroe St.	Chicago	IL	60661	Michael Blum	312-441-7000	S	516 OR	1.3
Kemper Financial Services Inc.	120 S. LaSalle St.	Chicago	IL	60603	Charles M. Kierscht	312-781-1121	S	516 OR	0.7
TCW Management Co.	865 S. Figueroa St.	Los Angeles	CA	90017	Marc I. Stern	213-244-0000	S	500 OR	0.5
United Asset Management Corp.	1 International Pl.	Boston	MA	02110	Norton H. Reamer	617-330-8900	P	492 OR	1.9
Piper Jaffray Companies Inc.	222 S. 9th St.	Minneapolis	MN	55402	Addison L. Piper	612-342-6000	P	397 OR	2.7
FCCI Investment Group Inc.	2601 Cattlemen Rd.	Sarasota	FL	34232	Ray Neff	813-955-2811	R	396 OR	0.6
Pax World Management Corp.	224 State St.	Portsmouth	NH	03801	Luther E. Tyson	603-431-8022	R	388 OR	<0.1
Dreyfus Corp.	200 Park Ave.	New York	NY	10166	Howard Stein	212-922-6000	S	386 OR	2.1
PEC Israel Economic Corp.	511 5th Ave.	New York	NY	10017	Frank Klein	212-687-2400	P	384 TA	<0.1
T. Rowe Price Associates Inc.	100 E. Pratt St.	Baltimore	MD	21202	George J. Collins	410-547-2000	P	382 OR	1.8
Legg Mason Inc.	P.O. Box 1476	Baltimore	MD	21202	Raymond A. Mason	410-539-0000	P	372 OR	2.9
Montgomery Asset Management L.P.	600 Montgomery St.	San Francisco	CA	94111	R. Stephen Doyle	415-627-2400	S	313 OR	<0.1
Fenimore Asset Management Inc.	PO Box 310	Cobleskill	NY	12043	Thomas Putnam	518-234-4393	R	310 OR*	<0.1
Compu-Val Investments Inc.	1702 Lovering Ave.	Wilmington	DE	19806	James Kalil	302-652-6767	R	300 OR	<0.1
Tiger Management Corp.	101 Park Ave.	New York	NY	10178	Julian H. Robertson Jr.	212-867-4350	R	300 OR	0.1
Meridian Insurance Group Inc.	P.O. Box 1980	Indianapolis	IN	46206	Norma J. Oman	317-927-8100	P	291 TA	0.5
SEI Corp.	680 E. Swedesford Rd.	Wayne	PA	19087	Alfred P. West Jr.	610-254-1000	P	264 OR	1.2
John Nuveen Co.	333 W. Wacker Dr.	Chicago	IL	60606	Richard J. Franke	312-917-7700	P	220 OR	0.6
Eaton Vance Corp.	24 Federal St.	Boston	MA	02110	M. Dozier Gardner	617-482-8260	P	218 OR	1.0
American Capital Management and Research Inc.	2800 Post Oak Blvd.	Houston	TX	77056	Don Powell	713-993-0500	S	210 OR*	0.7
Hicks, Muse, Tate and Furst Inc.	200 Crescent Ct.	Dallas	TX	75201	Tom Hicks	214-740-7300	R	210 OR*	1.0

Company type codes: P - Public, R - Private, S - Subsidiary, D - Division, J - Joint Venture, A - Affiliate, G - Group. If the dollar values shown are not sales, the following codes apply: TA - Total Assets; OR - Operating Revenues; GB - Gross Billings. * - estimated dollar value. < - less than. *na* - not available.

Continued on next page.

LEADING COMPANIES - SIC 6231 - Security and Commodity Exchanges

Continued

Company Name	Address				CEO Name	Phone	Co. Type	Sales/Assets ($ mil)	Empl. (000)
Janus Capital Corp.	100 Fillmore St.	Denver	CO	80206	Thomas H. Bailey	303-333-3863	S	181 OR	0.5
Delaware Management Company Inc.	1 Commerce Sq.	Philadelphia	PA	19103	Wayne A. Stork	215-988-1200	S	170 OR	0.6
Colonial Group Inc.	1 Financial Ctr.	Boston	MA	02111	C. Herben Emilson	617-426-3750	P	161 OR	0.6
AMRESCO Inc.	1845 Woodall Rogers	Dallas	TX	75201	Richard L. Cravey	214-953-7700	P	157 OR	1.2
Wells Fargo Nikko Investment Advisors	45 Fremont St.	San Francisco	CA	94105	Frederick Grauer	415-597-2000	J	155 OR	0.4
America First Eureka Holdings Inc.	555 California St.	San Francisco	CA	94104	Steve McLin	415-982-3800	S	152 OR	0.5
Interstate/Johnson Lane Inc.	P.O. Box 1012	Charlotte	NC	28201	James H. Morgan	704-379-9000	P	151 OR	1.1
AIM Management Group Inc.	11 Greenway Plz.	Houston	TX	77046	Charles T. Bauer	713-626-1919	R	150 OR*	0.6
Eaton Vance Management	24 Federal St.	Boston	MA	02110	M. Dozier Gardner	617-482-8260	S	150 OR*	0.3
Mesirow Financial Holdings Inc.	350 N. Clark St.	Chicago	IL	60610	Lester A. Morris	312-670-6000	R	150 TA*	0.5
Wellington Management Co.	75 State St.	Boston	MA	02109	Duncan M. McFarland	617-951-5000	R	150 OR*	0.5
Peninsula Asset Management Inc.	1111 3rd Ave. W.	Bradenton	FL	34205	William E. Middlebrook Jr.	813-748-8680	R	140 OR	<0.1
Benham Management International Inc.	1665 Charleston Rd.	Mountain View	CA	94043	James M. Benham	415-965-8300	R	130 OR*	0.5
Pioneer Group Inc.	60 State St.	Boston	MA	02109	John F. Cogan Jr.	617-742-7825	P	129 OR	1.1
Lynch Corp.	8 Sound Shore Dr.	Greenwich	CT	06830	Mario J. Gabelli	203-629-3333	P	127 OR	0.6
Van Kampen American Capital Investment Advisory Corp.	1 Parkview Plz.	Oakbrook Terrace	IL	60181	Don G. Powell	708-684-6000	S	114 OR	<0.1
Southwest Securities Group Inc.	1201 Elm St.	Dallas	TX	75270	Robert A. Buchholz	214-651-1800	P	114 OR	0.5
Butler Capital Corp.	767 5th Ave.	New York	NY	10153	Gilbert Butler	212-980-0606	R	110 OR	0.4
E.M. Warburg, Pincus and Company Inc.	466 Lexington Ave.	New York	NY	10017	Lionel Pincus	212-878-0600	R	100 TA*	0.3
Frank Russell Co.	909 A St.	Tacoma	WA	98402	Michael Phillips	206-572-9500	R	100 OR	1.0
Shott Capital Management	275 Battery St.	San Francisco	CA	94111	George Shott	415-394-7271	R	100 OR	<0.1
S.G.Warburg and Company Inc.	787 7th Ave.	New York	NY	10019	Thomas H. Wyman	212-459-7000	S	100 OR	0.6
Credit Suisse Asset Management Inc.	12 E. 49th St.	New York	NY	10017	Frank Meister	212-238-5800	S	95 OR	<0.1
Kellner, DiLeo and Co.	40 Broad St.	New York	NY	10004	George Kellner	212-440-0100	R	94 OR*	0.3
Blackstone Group L.P.	345 Park Ave.	New York	NY	10154	Stephen A. Schwarzman	212-935-2626	R	92 OR*	0.3
Financial Asset Management Co.	860 Airport Fwy.	Hurst	TX	76054	Sid Lorio	817-485-1800	R	91 OR	<0.1
G.T. Capital Management Inc.	50 California St.	San Francisco	CA	94111	David A. Minella	415-392-6181	S	91 OR*	0.3
James Mitchell and Co.	9710 Scranton Rd.	San Diego	CA	92121	Brian Finneran	619-450-0055	S	91 OR*	0.3
Surewest Financial Corp.	P.O. Box 5102	Sioux Falls	SD	57117	Joe P. Kirby	605-330-7420	R	91 OR*	0.3
Value Line Inc.	711 3rd Ave.	New York	NY	10017	Jean Bernhard Buttner	212-907-1500	P	82	0.4
Julius Baer Investment Management Inc.	330 Madison Ave.	New York	NY	10017	David Bodner	212-297-3600	S	76 OR*	0.3

Company type codes: P - Public, R - Private, S - Subsidiary, D - Division, J - Joint Venture, A - Affiliate, G - Group. If the dollar values shown are not sales, the following codes apply: TA - Total Assets; OR - Operating Revenues; GB - Gross Billings. * - estimated dollar value. < - less than. *na* - not available.

Continued on next page.

LEADING COMPANIES - SIC 6231 - Security and Commodity Exchanges
Continued

Company Name	Address				CEO Name	Phone	Co. Type	Sales/Assets ($ mil)	Empl. (000)
Capital Research and Management Co.	333 S. Hope St.	Los Angeles	CA	90071	R. Michael Shanahan	213-486-9200	S	74 OR*	0.2
Duff and Phelps Corp.	55 E. Monroe St.	Chicago	IL	60603	Francis E. Jeffries	312-263-2610	P	66 OR	0.3
Templeton Worldwide Inc.	500 E. Broward Blvd.	Fort Lauderdale	FL	33394	Chuck E. Johnson	305-764-7390	S	62 OR*	0.3
McLaughlin, Piven, Vogel Inc.	30 Wall St.	New York	NY	10005	J.C. McLaughlin	212-248-0750	R	61 OR*	0.2
Prudential Asset Management Company Inc.	745 Broad St.	Newark	NJ	07101	Richard Yorks	201-802-9617	S	61 OR*	0.2
Putnam Institutional Management	1 Post Office Sq.	Boston	MA	02109	Lawrence J. Lasser	617-292-1000	D	61 OR*	0.2
Feshbach Brothers Ltd.	425 Sherman Ave.	Palo Alto	CA	94306	Kurt Feshbach	415-853-0811	R	60 OR	<0.1
Washington Square Capital Inc.	100 Washington Sq.	Minneapolis	MN	55401	Steven W. Wishart	612-342-3736	S	60 OR	0.1
Fleet Investment Advisors Inc.	100 Westminster St.	Providence	RI	02903	Richard H. Jones	401-278-3318	S	55 OR	0.1
RCM Capital Management of California L.P.	4 Embarcadero Ctr.	San Francisco	CA	94111	Claude Rosenberg	415-954-5474	R	54 OR*	0.2

*Source: Ward's Business Directory of U.S. Private and Public Companies, 1996. Company type codes: P - Public, R - Private, S - Subsidiary, D - Division, J - Joint Venture, A - Affiliate, G - Group. If the dollar values shown are not sales, the following codes apply: TA - Total Assets; OR - Operating Revenues; GB - Gross Billings. * - estimated dollar value. < - less than; na - not available.*

LEADING COMPANIES - SIC 6282 - Investment Advice
Number shown: **33**   Total sales/assets ($ mil): **3,356**   Total employment (000): **8.9**

Company Name	Address				CEO Name	Phone	Co. Type	Sales/Assets ($ mil)	Empl. (000)
Victoria Bankshares Inc.	1 O'Connor Plz.	Victoria	TX	77902	Charles R. Hardlicka	512-573-5151	P	1,746 TA	1.0
Moody's Investors Service	99 Church St.	New York	NY	10007	John Bohn	212-553-0300	S	364	1.3
Rauscher Pierce Refsnes Inc.	700 N. Pearl St.	Dallas	TX	75201	David A. Smith	214-978-0111	S	150 OR	0.9
Kemper Service Co.	811 Main St.	Kansas City	MO	64105	Frank Diaz	816-421-4100	S	150 OR	1.0
Pioneer Group Inc.	60 State St.	Boston	MA	02109	John F. Cogan Jr.	617-742-7825	P	129 OR	1.1
Linsco/Private Ledger Corp.	5935 Cornerstone Ct. W	San Diego	CA	92121	Todd Robinson	619-450-9240	R	95 OR*	0.2
Kemper Clearing Corp.	111 E. Kilbourn Ave.	Milwaukee	WI	53202	Frank V. Geremia	414-225-4100	S	75 OR	0.5
BHC Financial Inc.	1200 One Commerce Sq.	Philadelphia	PA	19103	William T. Spane Jr.	215-636-3000	P	67 OR	0.4
American Stock Transfer and Trust Co.	40 Wall St.	New York	NY	10005	Michael Karfunkel	212-936-5100	R	66 OR*	0.2
Investment Technology Group Inc.	900 3rd Ave.	New York	NY	10022	R. L. Killian Jr.	212-755-6800	P	59 OR	<0.1
ITG Inc.	900 3rd Ave.	New York	NY	10022	R. L. Killian Jr.	212-755-6800	S	59 OR	<0.1

*Company type codes: P - Public, R - Private, S - Subsidiary, D - Division, J - Joint Venture, A - Affiliate, G - Group. If the dollar values shown are not sales, the following codes apply: TA - Total Assets; OR - Operating Revenues; GB - Gross Billings. * - estimated dollar value. < - less than. na - not available.*

Continued on next page.

LEADING COMPANIES - SIC 6282 - Investment Advice

Continued

Company Name	Address				CEO Name	Phone	Co. Type	Sales/Assets ($ mil)	Empl. (000)
Options Clearing Corp.	440 S. LaSalle St.	Chicago	IL	60605	Wayne P. Luthringshausen	312-322-6200	R	53 OR	0.3
Benham Financial Services Inc.	1665 Charleston Rd.	Mountain View	CA	94043	James M. Benham	415-965-8300	S	45 OR*	0.2
EJV Partners L.P.	77 Water St.	New York	NY	10005	Tom Wendel	212-574-1000	R	43 OR*	0.1
Thomson Financial Information	1 State St. Plz.	New York	NY	10004	David Branch	212-943-6700	D	42 OR	0.2
Georgeson and Company Inc.	Wall St. Plz.	New York	NY	10005	William M. Crane	212-440-9800	S	36 OR*	0.2
Sage Clearing Corp.	220 Bush St.	San Francisco	CA	94104	Douglas J. Engmann	415-781-7430	R	35 OR	0.1
Midwest Securities Trust Co.	440 S. LaSalle St.	Chicago	IL	60605	Robert J. McGrail	312-663-2222	S	32 OR	0.3
Coast Fed Services Corp.	19900 Plummer St.	Chatsworth	CA	91311	Bill Moody	818-701-7016	S	30 OR*	0.1
Government Securities Clearing Corp.	55 Water St.	New York	NY	10041	Charles A. Moran	212-412-8400	R	16 OR	<0.1
Philadelphia Depository Trust Co.	1900 Market St.	Philadelphia	PA	19107	Timothy J. Guiheen	215-496-5008	S	13 OR	0.3
Midwest Clearing Corp.	440 S. LaSalle St.	Chicago	IL	60605	Robert J. McGrail	312-663-2222	R	9 OR	<0.1
Keller Enterprises Inc.	888 S.W. 5th Ave.	Portland	OR	97204	Richard Keller	503-228-6200	R	9 OR	<0.1
MBS Clearing Corp.	440 S. LaSalle St.	Chicago	IL	60605	Ronald A. Stewart	312-663-2222	S	7 OR	<0.1
National Quotation Bureau Co.	150 Commerce Rd.	Cedar Grove	NJ	07009	Tom Conoscenti	201-239-6100	S	5 OR	0.1
United Check Clearing Corp.	14276 23rd Ave. N.	Minneapolis	MN	55447	Elloyd A. Hauser	612-559-2225	R	5 OR*	<0.1
Illinois Stock Transfer Co.	223 W.Jackson Bvd.	Chicago	IL	60606	George D. Pearson	312-427-2953	R	4 OR	<0.1
Leland O'Brien Rubenstein Associates Inc.	523 W. 6th St.	Los Angeles	CA	90014	John W. O'Brien	213-488-2700	R	4 OR*	<0.1
Wand Partners L.P.	30 Rockefeller Plz.	New York	NY	10112	Bruce W. Schnitzer	212-632-3795	R	3 OR	<0.1
American Securities Transfer Inc.	1825 Lawrence St.	Denver	CO	80202	Charles R. Harrison	303-234-5300	R	2 OR*	<0.1
Fidelity Transfer Co.	357 S. 200 E.	Salt Lake City	UT	84111	Linda Kener	801-355-7177	R	1 OR*	<0.1
Market Profile Theorems Inc.	1000 2nd Ave.	Seattle	WA	98104	Russell J. Brooks	206-583-0360	R	0 OR	<0.1
International Clearing Systems Inc.	440 S. La Salle St.	Chicago	IL	60605	Wayne P. Luthringshausen	312-322-2086	S	0 OR*	<0.1

Source: Ward's Business Directory of U.S. Private and Public Companies, 1996. Company type codes: P - Public, R - Private, S - Subsidiary, D - Division, J - Joint Venture, A - Affiliate, G - Group. If the dollar values shown are not sales, the following codes apply: TA - Total Assets; OR - Operating Revenues; GB - Gross Billings. * - estimated dollar value. < - less than; *na* - not available.

SIC 6310

LIFE INSURANCE

SIC 6310 includes all establishments primarily engaged in underwriting life insurance. Ownership of these establishments may be by stockholders, policyholders, or other carriers.

The category includes assessment life insurance organizations, benevolent insurance associations, burial insurance societies, cooperative life insurance organizations, fraternal life insurance organizations and protective associations, funeral insurance, legal reserve life insurance companies, life insurance companies and funds, life reinsurance organizations, and reinsurance carriers of life insurance.

ESTABLISHMENTS, EMPLOYMENT, AND PAYROLL

	1988	1989		1990		1991		1992		1993		% change 88-93
		Value	%	Value	%	Value	%	Value	%	Value	%	
All Establishments	14,445	14,330	-0.8	14,057	-1.9	14,461	2.9	14,531	0.5	12,691	-12.7	-12.1
Mid-March Employment	538,287	568,796	5.7	571,775	0.5	616,584	7.8	625,841	1.5	618,304	-1.2	14.9
1st Quarter Wages (annualized - $ mil.)	14,285.8	15,864.8	11.1	16,703.5	5.3	18,702.3	12.0	20,415.7	9.2	20,282.2	-0.7	42.0
Payroll per Emp. 1st Q. (annualized)	26,539	27,892	5.1	29,213	4.7	30,332	3.8	32,621	7.5	32,803	0.6	23.6
Annual Payroll ($ mil.)	13,733.0	14,828.2	8.0	16,272.5	9.7	17,993.8	10.6	19,507.9	8.4	19,716.8	1.1	43.6
Establishments - 1-4 Emp. Number	4,179	4,364	4.4	4,273	-2.1	4,817	12.7	4,811	-0.1	3,463	-28.0	-17.1
Mid-March Employment	8,061	8,636	7.1	8,165	-5.5	8,698	6.5	9,036	3.9	6,907	-23.6	-14.3
1st Quarter Wages (annualized - $ mil.)	257.8	282.8	9.7	318.4	12.6	310.3	-2.5	327.1	5.4	323.3	-1.2	25.4
Payroll per Emp. 1st Q. (annualized)	31,979	32,747	2.4	38,995	19.1	35,677	-8.5	36,201	1.5	46,802	29.3	46.4
Annual Payroll ($ mil.)	338.7	274.2	-19.1	331.0	20.7	301.0	-9.0	303.7	0.9	335.5	10.5	-1.0
Establishments - 5-9 Emp. Number	2,303	2,048	-11.1	2,011	-1.8	1,833	-8.9	1,898	3.5	1,719	-9.4	-25.4
Mid-March Employment	15,884	14,173	-10.8	14,076	-0.7	12,688	-9.9	13,084	3.1	11,799	-9.8	-25.7
1st Quarter Wages (annualized - $ mil.)	446.1	411.7	-7.7	435.2	5.7	402.8	-7.5	454.0	12.7	430.5	-5.2	-3.5
Payroll per Emp. 1st Q. (annualized)	28,087	29,051	3.4	30,920	6.4	31,746	2.7	34,697	9.3	36,489	5.2	29.9
Annual Payroll ($ mil.)	425.0	379.6	-10.7	425.9	12.2	407.2	-4.4	426.9	4.9	391.7	-8.3	-7.8
Establishments - 10-19 Emp. Number	3,422	3,237	-5.4	3,111	-3.9	2,992	-3.8	2,985	-0.2	2,779	-6.9	-18.8
Mid-March Employment	47,056	45,177	-4.0	43,720	-3.2	41,964	-4.0	42,147	0.4	39,754	-5.7	-15.5
1st Quarter Wages (annualized - $ mil.)	1,185.5	1,277.3	7.7	1,268.7	-0.7	1,247.9	-1.6	1,343.7	7.7	1,376.9	2.5	16.1
Payroll per Emp. 1st Q. (annualized)	25,194	28,273	12.2	29,019	2.6	29,737	2.5	31,882	7.2	34,635	8.6	37.5
Annual Payroll ($ mil.)	1,189.9	1,181.2	-0.7	1,238.2	4.8	1,220.3	-1.4	1,297.1	6.3	1,234.2	-4.9	3.7
Establishments - 20-49 Emp. Number	3,051	3,110	1.9	3,020	-2.9	2,979	-1.4	3,065	2.9	3,014	-1.7	-1.2
Mid-March Employment	89,967	90,354	0.4	88,619	-1.9	87,430	-1.3	91,183	4.3	89,355	-2.0	-0.7
1st Quarter Wages (annualized - $ mil.)	2,158.5	2,319.9	7.5	2,404.9	3.7	2,452.6	2.0	2,700.9	10.1	2,816.3	4.3	30.5
Payroll per Emp. 1st Q. (annualized)	23,992	25,675	7.0	27,138	5.7	28,052	3.4	29,621	5.6	31,518	6.4	31.4
Annual Payroll ($ mil.)	2,101.1	2,251.5	7.2	2,378.7	5.7	2,393.8	0.6	2,672.9	11.7	2,659.9	-0.5	26.6
Establishments - 50-99 Emp. Number	867	886	2.2	922	4.1	1,020	10.6	929	-8.9	809	-12.9	-6.7
Mid-March Employment	58,378	60,147	3.0	62,457	3.8	69,867	11.9	63,213	-9.5	56,241	-11.0	-3.7
1st Quarter Wages (annualized - $ mil.)	1,579.1	1,568.3	-0.7	1,650.9	5.3	1,922.3	16.4	1,857.2	-3.4	1,692.9	-8.8	7.2
Payroll per Emp. 1st Q. (annualized)	27,050	26,075	-3.6	26,432	1.4	27,514	4.1	29,381	6.8	30,101	2.5	11.3
Annual Payroll ($ mil.)	1,548.4	1,508.4	-2.6	1,617.0	7.2	1,873.4	15.9	1,808.2	-3.5	1,615.2	-10.7	4.3
Establishments - 100-249 Emp. Number	333	368	10.5	395	7.3	451	14.2	450	-0.2	525	16.7	57.7
Mid-March Employment	50,282	57,513	14.4	60,363	5.0	68,294	13.1	68,720	0.6	80,590	17.3	60.3
1st Quarter Wages (annualized - $ mil.)	1,193.0	1,412.7	18.4	1,557.7	10.3	1,778.9	14.2	2,084.7	17.2	2,337.3	12.1	95.9
Payroll per Emp. 1st Q. (annualized)	23,725	24,563	3.5	25,805	5.1	26,048	0.9	30,336	16.5	29,002	-4.4	22.2
Annual Payroll ($ mil.)	1,168.3	1,364.4	16.8	1,512.9	10.9	1,716.8	13.5	1,982.9	15.5	2,287.6	15.4	95.8
Establishments - 250-499 Emp. Number	137	147	7.3	159	8.2	184	15.7	206	12.0	202	-1.9	47.4
Mid-March Employment	48,505	51,124	5.4	55,890	9.3	64,615	15.6	73,406	13.6	72,585	-1.1	49.6
1st Quarter Wages (annualized - $ mil.)	1,291.0	1,510.5	17.0	1,637.8	8.4	1,876.0	14.5	2,267.7	20.9	2,177.0	-4.0	68.6
Payroll per Emp. 1st Q. (annualized)	26,617	29,545	11.0	29,304	-0.8	29,034	-0.9	30,892	6.4	29,993	-2.9	12.7
Annual Payroll ($ mil.)	1,245.3	1,367.5	9.8	1,567.9	14.7	1,803.4	15.0	2,173.5	20.5	2,173.0	-0.0	74.5
Establishments - 500-999 Emp. Number	83	95	14.5	85	-10.5	101	18.8	110	8.9	105	-4.5	26.5
Mid-March Employment	58,688	65,027	10.8	58,489	-10.1	68,735	17.5	76,901	11.9	74,446	-3.2	26.9
1st Quarter Wages (annualized - $ mil.)	1,498.5	1,627.3	8.6	1,675.6	3.0	2,063.1	23.1	2,346.1	13.7	2,371.4	1.1	58.3
Payroll per Emp. 1st Q. (annualized)	25,533	25,025	-2.0	28,649	14.5	30,015	4.8	30,509	1.6	31,854	4.4	24.8
Annual Payroll ($ mil.)	1,459.8	1,552.0	6.3	1,560.7	0.6	1,943.0	24.5	2,262.6	16.4	2,397.3	6.0	64.2
Estab. - 1000 or More Emp. Number	70	75	7.1	81	8.0	84	3.7	77	-8.3	75	-2.6	7.1
Mid-March Employment	161,466	176,645	9.4	179,996	1.9	194,293	7.9	188,151	-3.2	186,627	-0.8	15.6
1st Quarter Wages (annualized - $ mil.)	4,676.3	5,454.3	16.6	5,754.3	5.5	6,648.3	15.5	7,034.3	5.8	6,756.5	-3.9	44.5
Payroll per Emp. 1st Q. (annualized)	28,961	30,877	6.6	31,969	3.5	34,218	7.0	37,386	9.3	36,203	-3.2	25.0
Annual Payroll ($ mil.)	4,256.5	4,949.4	16.3	5,640.3	14.0	6,335.0	12.3	6,580.3	3.9	6,622.4	0.6	55.6

Source: County Business Patterns, U.S. Department of Commerce, Washington, D.C., for 1988 through 1993. Payroll per employee is calculated using mid-March employment and 1st Quarter wages, annualized. Annual payroll, also shown, may not equal the annualized 1st Quarter wages. Columns headed by a percent sign (%) indicate change from the previous year. na stands for not available. The symbol (D) indicates that data are withheld by the source to avoid disclosure of competitive information. A dash (-) indicates that data are not available or cannot be calculated.

ESTABLISHMENTS
Number

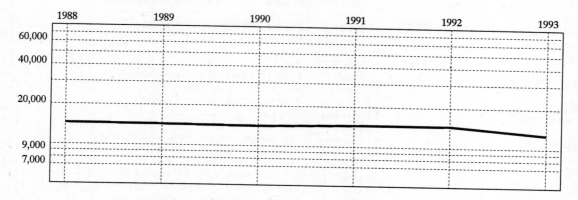

MID-MARCH EMPLOYMENT
Number

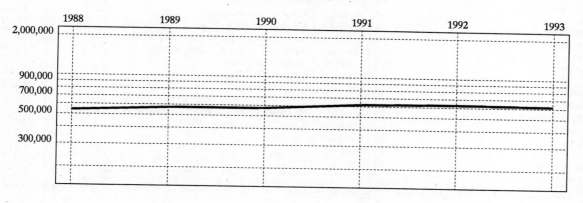

ANNUAL PAYROLL
$ million

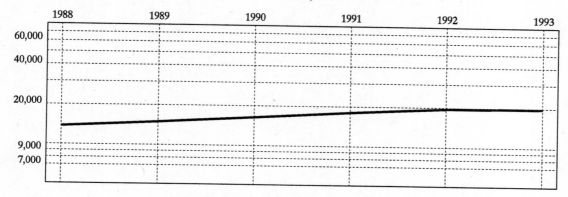

INPUTS AND OUTPUTS FOR INSURANCE CARRIERS - SIC GROUP 63

Economic Sector or Industry Providing Inputs	%	Sector	Economic Sector or Industry Buying Outputs	%	Sector
Insurance agents, brokers, & services	62.9	Fin/R.E.	Personal consumption expenditures	77.1	
Security & commodity brokers	6.8	Fin/R.E.	Owner-occupied dwellings	5.5	Fin/R.E.
Eating & drinking places	4.0	Trade	Real estate	3.6	Fin/R.E.
Real estate	4.0	Fin/R.E.	Banking	0.9	Fin/R.E.
Communications, except radio & TV	3.9	Util.	Federal Government purchases, nondefense	0.9	Fed Govt
Imports	1.8	Foreign	Electric services (utilities)	0.8	Util.
Commercial printing	1.3	Manufg.	Insurance agents, brokers, & services	0.7	Fin/R.E.
Computer & data processing services	1.3	Services	Feed grains	0.6	Agric.
Advertising	1.2	Services	Exports	0.5	Foreign
Hotels & lodging places	1.2	Services	Motor freight transportation & warehousing	0.5	Util.
Legal services	1.2	Services	Retail trade, except eating & drinking	0.5	Trade
Accounting, auditing & bookkeeping	0.9	Services	Credit agencies other than banks	0.4	Fin/R.E.
Banking	0.9	Fin/R.E.	S/L Govt. purch., elem. & secondary education	0.4	S/L Govt
U.S. Postal Service	0.9	Gov't	Sanitary services, steam supply, irrigation	0.4	Util.
Air transportation	0.6	Util.	State & local government enterprises, nec	0.3	Gov't
Credit agencies other than banks	0.6	Fin/R.E.	Water supply & sewage systems	0.3	Util.
Management & consulting services & labs	0.6	Services	Wholesale trade	0.3	Trade
Maintenance of nonfarm buildings nec	0.5	Constr.	Food grains	0.2	Agric.
Manifold business forms	0.5	Manufg.	Meat animals	0.2	Agric.
Motor freight transportation & warehousing	0.5	Util.	Petroleum refining	0.2	Manufg.
Petroleum refining	0.5	Manufg.	Religious organizations	0.2	Services
Photographic equipment & supplies	0.4	Manufg.	Air transportation	0.1	Util.
Transit & bus transportation	0.4	Util.	Arrangement of passenger transportation	0.1	Util.
Business services nec	0.3	Services	Equipment rental & leasing services	0.1	Services
Personnel supply services	0.3	Services	Freight forwarders	0.1	Util.
Wholesale trade	0.3	Trade	Industrial buildings	0.1	Constr.
Automotive rental & leasing, without drivers	0.2	Services	Office buildings	0.1	Constr.
Electric services (utilities)	0.2	Util.	Oil bearing crops	0.1	Agric.
Electronic computing equipment	0.2	Manufg.	Residential 1-unit structures, nonfarm	0.1	Constr.
Detective & protective services	0.1	Services	Transit & bus transportation	0.1	Util.
Electrical repair shops	0.1	Services			
Envelopes	0.1	Manufg.			
Manufacturing industries, nec	0.1	Manufg.			

Source: Benchmark Input-Output Accounts for the U.S. Economy, 1982, U.S. Department of Commerce, Washington, D.C., July 1991. Data, as reported in the source, are organized by the 1977 SIC structure in use in 1982 but have been matched, as closely as is possible, to the 1987 SIC structure used in this book. Activities with the same percentage are sorted alphabetically by name of activity.

OCCUPATIONS EMPLOYED BY LIFE INSURANCE

Occupation	% of Total 1994	Change to 2005	Occupation	% of Total 1994	Change to 2005
Insurance sales workers	19.2	-4.9	Underwriters	2.6	15.3
General office clerks	6.6	-41.4	Managers & administrators nec	2.3	9.8
Insurance policy processing clerks	5.7	4.9	Clerical support workers nec	2.3	-12.1
Insurance claims clerks	4.4	15.3	Marketing & sales worker supervisors	2.3	9.9
Management support workers nec	4.2	31.9	Bookkeeping, accounting, & auditing clerks	2.1	-17.6
Clerical supervisors & managers	3.9	12.4	Adjustment clerks	1.8	25.8
Secretaries, ex legal & medical	3.8	0.1	Accountants & auditors	1.7	26.4
Insurance adjusters, examiners, & investigators	3.6	15.4	Professional workers nec	1.5	64.9
Computer programmers	2.9	-11.0	Claims examiners, insurance	1.5	9.9
Systems analysts	2.7	75.8	Sales & related workers nec	1.2	9.9
General managers & top executives	2.7	4.3	Typists & word processors	1.0	-45.0

Sources: Industry-Occupation Matrix, Bureau of Labor Statistics. These data relate to one or more 3-digit SIC industry groups rather than to a single 4-digit SIC. The change reported for each occupation to the year 2005 is a percent of growth or decline as estimated by the Bureau of Labor Statistics. The abbreviation *nec* stands for not elsewhere classified.

U.S. AND STATE DATA ON INDUSTRY REVENUES AND OTHER ACCOUNTS FOR 1992

State	No. of Estab.	Employ- ment	Payroll ($ mil.)	Revenues ($ mil.)	Empl./ Estab.	Revenue/ Estab. ($)	Payroll/ Estab. ($)	Revenue/ Empl. ($)	Payroll/ Empl. ($)
UNITED STATES	13,424	609,237	19,410.7	378,401.7	45	28,188,449	1,445,970	621,108	31,861
Alabama	306	6,840	200.5	2,736.7	22	8,943,346	655,258	400,097	29,314
Alaska	15	-	(D)	(D)	(D)	(D)	(D)	(D)	(D)
Arizona	199	4,070	114.7	2,045.2	20	10,277,271	576,236	502,500	28,175
Arkansas	123	2,354	58.1	671.3	19	5,457,569	472,195	285,166	24,673
California	1,062	39,186	1,290.6	31,872.8	37	30,012,067	1,215,283	813,373	32,936
Colorado	199	7,551	250.4	5,127.9	38	25,768,337	1,258,327	679,102	33,162
Connecticut	211	46,335	1,856.3	15,173.2	220	71,911,047	8,797,540	327,468	40,062
Delaware	49	1,776	52.7	616.8	36	12,588,020	1,075,367	347,305	29,669
District of Columbia	33	787	31.0	785.8	24	23,812,030	940,788	998,471	39,449
Florida	791	28,311	850.9	12,162.6	36	15,376,182	1,075,748	429,605	30,056
Georgia	479	20,831	592.0	7,984.6	43	16,669,344	1,235,977	383,304	28,421
Hawaii	53	-	(D)	(D)	(D)	(D)	(D)	(D)	(D)
Idaho	42	-	(D)	(D)	(D)	(D)	(D)	(D)	(D)
Illinois	648	30,118	890.1	23,479.2	46	36,233,363	1,373,611	779,574	29,554
Indiana	325	12,608	388.1	13,154.8	39	40,476,458	1,194,191	1,043,373	30,783
Iowa	177	15,184	450.3	5,952.5	86	33,629,983	2,544,124	392,025	29,657
Kansas	169	4,819	141.5	4,417.6	29	26,139,651	837,568	916,705	29,373
Kentucky	220	5,280	161.5	4,434.6	24	20,157,159	734,214	839,882	30,592
Louisiana	345	7,347	202.4	2,958.4	21	8,574,994	586,733	402,664	27,552
Maine	57	4,307	179.4	1,463.2	76	25,670,667	3,148,158	339,733	41,664
Maryland	261	7,323	231.3	5,555.7	28	21,286,387	886,375	758,671	31,591
Massachusetts	296	36,149	1,253.7	21,177.1	122	71,544,105	4,235,314	585,827	34,680
Michigan	337	11,859	351.1	11,524.0	35	34,195,703	1,041,751	971,747	29,604
Minnesota	210	15,157	605.0	11,737.8	72	55,894,276	2,881,014	774,414	39,916
Mississippi	171	3,754	99.8	1,962.3	22	11,475,526	583,713	522,726	26,589
Missouri	294	10,908	330.8	5,666.6	37	19,274,150	1,125,296	519,490	30,330
Montana	36	755	14.8	277.2	21	7,699,750	411,694	367,140	19,630
Nebraska	111	5,307	145.0	2,550.2	48	22,974,829	1,306,261	480,536	27,321
Nevada	39	447	11.0	254.9	11	6,537,026	282,974	570,345	24,689
New Hampshire	65	-	(D)	(D)	(D)	(D)	(D)	(D)	(D)
New Jersey	462	28,172	1,028.1	21,295.1	61	46,093,294	2,225,346	755,896	36,494
New Mexico	61	1,635	34.1	429.6	27	7,043,443	558,475	262,783	20,836
New York	798	63,903	2,070.7	63,992.9	80	80,191,576	2,594,878	1,001,406	32,404
North Carolina	428	12,528	344.2	5,565.8	29	13,004,201	804,157	444,269	27,473
North Dakota	37	612	18.3	373.6	17	10,096,649	494,216	610,418	29,879
Ohio	619	20,260	575.8	15,586.0	33	25,179,309	930,237	769,299	28,421
Oklahoma	149	4,507	115.8	1,649.4	30	11,069,866	777,242	365,966	25,695
Oregon	109	3,199	82.3	1,754.1	29	16,092,413	755,101	548,319	25,729
Pennsylvania	742	40,069	1,239.0	12,881.8	54	17,360,973	1,669,802	321,491	30,921
Rhode Island	53	2,523	60.1	545.5	48	10,292,245	1,133,189	216,207	23,805
South Carolina	242	5,700	155.6	1,410.2	24	5,827,434	643,017	247,410	27,300
South Dakota	40	963	26.0	825.0	24	20,625,975	651,250	856,738	27,051
Tennessee	326	11,906	323.9	6,657.7	37	20,422,503	993,546	559,192	27,204
Texas	1,047	34,862	960.8	19,460.2	33	18,586,625	917,656	558,207	27,560
Utah	75	2,228	49.2	701.7	30	9,356,107	656,653	314,950	22,105
Vermont	43	1,452	48.4	562.5	34	13,081,163	1,126,116	387,390	33,349
Virginia	331	9,922	290.6	7,135.2	30	21,556,541	877,846	719,131	29,285
Washington	203	6,229	183.3	5,921.0	31	29,167,320	903,079	950,548	29,431
West Virginia	90	1,427	34.7	498.0	16	5,532,844	385,378	348,953	24,306
Wisconsin	227	23,092	861.9	13,237.3	102	58,314,247	3,797,048	573,243	37,326
Wyoming	19	-	(D)	(D)	(D)	(D)	(D)	(D)	(D)

Source: 1992 Economic Census, U.S. Department of Commerce, Washington, D.C. This is the only table that shows revenue data as collected by the Bureau of the Census in an Economic Census. The symbol (D) indicates that data are withheld by the source to avoid disclosure of competitive information. A dash (-) indicates that data are not available or cannot be calculated.

ESTABLISHMENTS 1992 - STATE AND REGIONAL CONCENTRATION

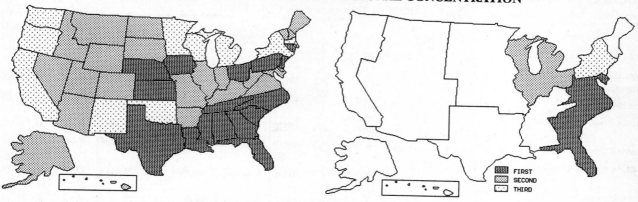

EMPLOYMENT 1992 - STATE AND REGIONAL CONCENTRATION

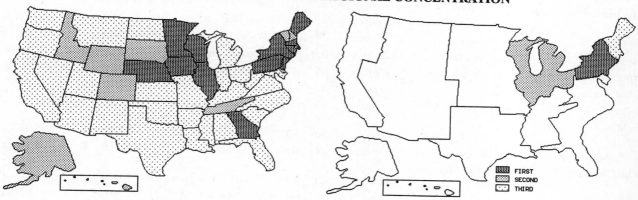

REVENUES 1992 - STATE AND REGIONAL CONCENTRATION

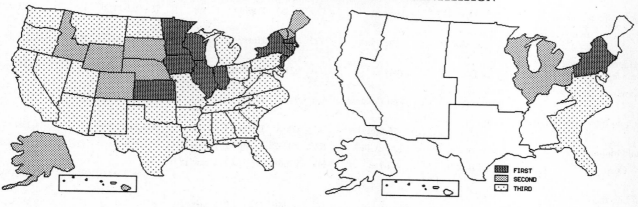

States with the darkest shading indicate those states which have proportionately more establishments, employment, or revenues than would be indicated by the state's population. States with light shading are states with proportionately fewer establishments, less employment, and lower revenues than population distribution. States shaded grey are within 15 percent of the state's population proportion in these categories. States for which no data are available are shown as average (grey). *Regions* are shaded to indicate absolute rank in the category. If no data for the category are available, establishment counts are used to shade the regions. Source of the data is the table on the facing page.

LEADING COMPANIES - SIC 6289 - Security & Commodity Services, nec

Number shown: **100**   Total sales/assets ($ mil): **2,425,588**   Total employment (000): **1,356.1**

Company Name	Address				CEO Name	Phone	Co. Type	Sales/Assets ($ mil)	Empl. (000)
Prudential Insurance Company of America	751 Broad St.	Newark	NJ	07102	Arthur F. Ryan	201-802-6000	R	313,660 TA	100.0
Travelers Inc.	65 E. 55th St.	New York	NY	10022	Sanford I. Weill	212-816-8000	P	115,300 TA	52.0
American International Group Inc.	70 Pine St.	New York	NY	10270	Maurice R. Greenberg	212-770-7000	P	114,346 TA	32.0
Equitable Companies Inc.	787 7th Ave.	New York	NY	10019	Richard H. Jenrette	212-554-1234	P	98,991 TA	13.1
Aetna Life and Casualty Co.	151 Farmington Ave.	Hartford	CT	06156	Ronald E. Compton	203-273-0123	P	94,172 TA	43.1
Northwestern Mutual Life Insurance Co.	720 E. Wisconsin Ave.	Milwaukee	WI	53202	James D. Ericson	414-271-1444	R	87,780 TA	3.3
CIGNA Corp.	P.O. Box 7716	Philadelphia	PA	19192	Wilson H. Taylor	215-761-1000	P	86,102 TA	48.3
ITT Hartford Group Inc.	Hartford Plz.	Hartford	CT	06115	Donald R. Frahm	203-547-5000	S	77,000 TA	22.0
Teachers Insurance and Annuity Association	730 3rd Ave.	New York	NY	10017	John H. Biggs	212-490-9000	R	67,483 TA	4.0
Allstate Corp.	Allstate Plz.	Northbrook	IL	60062	Wayne E. Hedien	708-402-5000	P	59,358 TA	49.0
Allstate Insurance Co.	Allstate Plz.	Northbrook	IL	60062	Wayne E. Hedien	708-402-5000	S	59,358 TA	49.0
New York Life Insurance Co.	51 Madison Ave.	New York	NY	10010	Harry G. Hohn	212-576-7000	R	54,810 TA*	7.5
Sears, Roebuck and Co.	Sears Twr.	Chicago	IL	60684	Edward A. Brennan	312-875-2500	P	54,559	360.0
Loews Corp.	667 Madison Ave.	New York	NY	10021	Laurence A. Tisch	212-545-2000	P	50,336 TA	25.4
Liberty Mutual Insurance Group	175 Berkeley St.	Boston	MA	02117	Gary L. Countryman	617-357-9500	R	50,001 TA	22.0
Lincoln National Corp.	P.O. Box 1110	Fort Wayne	IN	46801	Ian M. Rolland	219-455-2000	P	49,330 TA	9.0
Aetna Life Insurance Co.	151 Farmington Ave.	Hartford	CT	06156	Ronald E. Compton	203-273-0123	S	47,357 TA	24.0
CNA Financial Corp.	CNA Plz.	Chicago	IL	60685	Lawrence A. Tisch	312-822-5000	P	44,320 TA	16.8
Principal Financial Group Inc.	711 High St.	Des Moines	IA	50392	G. David Hurd	515-247-5111	R	44,116 TA	14.8
Principal Mutual Life Insurance Co.	711 High St.	Des Moines	IA	50392	G. David Hurd	515-247-5111	S	44,116 TA	14.8
American General Corp.	P.O. Box 3247	Houston	TX	77253	Harold S. Hook	713-522-1111	P	43,982 TA	12.7
Metropolitan Life Insurance Co.	1 Madison Ave.	New York	NY	10010	Harry Kamen	212-578-2211	R	40,100 TA	55.0
John Hancock Mutual Life Insurance Co.	P.O. Box 111	Boston	MA	02117	Stephen L. Brown	617-572-6000	R	39,146 TA	15.0
Transamerica Corp.	600 Montgomery St.	San Francisco	CA	94111	Frank C. Herringer	415-983-4000	P	36,050 TA	10.7
Household International Inc.	2700 Sanders Rd.	Prospect Heights	IL	60070	Donald C Clark	708-564-5000	P	34,338 TA	15.5
Capital Holding Corp.	P.O. Box 32830	Louisville	KY	40232	Irving W. Bailey II	502-560-2000	P	22,929 TA	9.3
Chubb Corp.	P.O. Box 1615	Warren	NJ	07061	Robert P. Crawford Jr.	908-903-2000	P	20,723 TA	10.0
Aetna Life Insurance and Annuity Co.	151 Farmington Ave.	Hartford	CT	06156	Daniel P. Kearney	203-273-0123	S	19,482 TA	2.7
Merrill Lynch and Company Inc.	250 Vesey St.	New York	NY	10281	Daniel P. Tully	212-449-1000	P	18,233 OR	43.8
Aon Corp.	123 N. Wacker Dr.	Chicago	IL	60606	Patrick G. Ryan	312-701-3000	P	17,922 TA	30.0
Provident Life and Accident Insurance Company of America	1 Fountain Sq.	Chattanooga	TN	37402	J. Harold Chandler	615-755-1011	P	16,892 TA	4.5

Company type codes: P - Public, R - Private, S - Subsidiary, D - Division, J - Joint Venture, A - Affiliate, G - Group. If the dollar values shown are not sales, the following codes apply: TA - Total Assets; OR - Operating Revenues; GB - Gross Billings. * - estimated dollar value. < - less than. *na* - not available.

Continued on next page.

LEADING COMPANIES - SIC 6289 - Security & Commodity Services, nec
Continued

Company Name	Address				CEO Name	Phone	Co. Type	Sales/Assets ($ mil)	Empl. (000)
Provident Life Capital Corp.	1 Fountain Sq.	Chattanooga	TN	37402	J. Harold Chandler	615-755-1011	S	16,892 TA	4.5
New England Mutual Life Insurance Co.	501 Boylston St.	Boston	MA	02117	Robert A. Shafto	617-578-2000	R	16,582 TA	3.0
SAFECO Corp.	SAFECO Plz.	Seattle	WA	98185	Roger H. Eigsti	206-545-5000	P	15,902 TA	7.3
UJB Financial Corp.	P.O. Box 2066	Princeton	NJ	08543	T. Joseph Semrod	609-987-3200	P	15,429 TA	6.1
American Family Life Assurance Co.	1932 Wynnton Rd.	Columbus	GA	31999	Daniel P. Amos	706-323-3431	S	15,323 TA	3.0
Transamerica Insurance Corporation of California	1150 S. Olive St.	Los Angeles	CA	90015	David R. Carpenter	213-742-2111	S	14,950 TA	2.7
Transamerica Occidental Life Insurance Co.	1150 S. Olive St.	Los Angeles	CA	90015	David R. Carpenter	213-742-2111	S	14,950 TA	2.7
SunAmerica Inc.	1 SunAmerica Ctr.	Century City	CA	90067	Eli Broad	310-772-6000	P	14,656 TA	4.3
Mutual Life Insurance Company of New York	1740 Broadway	New York	NY	10019	Michael I. Roth	212-708-2000	R	14,166 TA	5.1
USF and G Corp.	100 Light St.	Baltimore	MD	21202	Norman P. Blake Jr.	410-547-3000	P	13,900 TA	6.5
Kemper Corp.	1 Kemper Dr.	Long Grove	IL	60049	David B. Mathis	708-540-4700	P	13,154 TA	6.3
Conseco Inc.	P.O. Box 1911	Carmel	IN	46032	Stephen C. Hilbert	317-817-6100	P	10,812 TA	3.5
American Financial Corp.	1 E. 4th St.	Cincinnati	OH	45202	Carl H. Lindner	513-579-2121	R	10,550 TA	5.0
ReliaStar Financial Corp.	20 Washington Ave. S.	Minneapolis	MN	55401	John G. Turner	612-372-5432	P	10,367 TA	2.6
Provident Life and Accident Insurance Co.	1 Fountain Sq.	Chattanooga	TN	37402	J. Harold Chandler	615-755-1901	S	10,000 TA	4.5
Guardian Life Insurance Company of America	201 Park Ave. S.	New York	NY	10003	Arthur V. Ferrara	212-598-8000	R	9,871 TA	5.3
AEGON USA Inc.	1111 N. Charles St.	Baltimore	MD	21201	Don Shepard	410-576-4571	S	9,700 TA	5.4
Reliance Group Holdings Inc.	55 E. 52nd St.	New York	NY	10055	Saul P. Steinberg	212-909-1100	P	9,370 TA	9.2
First Colony Corp.	P.O. Box 1280	Lynchburg	VA	24505	Bruce C. Gottwald Jr.	804-845-0911	P	9,269 TA	1.0
General American Life Insurance Co.	P.O. Box 396	St. Louis	MO	63166	Richard Liddy	314-231-1700	R	8,600 TA	5.0
Mutual of Omaha Insurance Co.	Mutual of Omaha Plz.	Omaha	NE	68175	Thomas J. Skutt	402-342-7600	R	8,600 TA	8.9
Minnesota Mutual Life Insurance Co.	400 N. Robert St.	St. Paul	MN	55101	Coleman Bloomfield	612-298-3500	R	8,544 TA	4.0
Torchmark Corp.	2001 3rd Ave. S.	Birmingham	AL	35233	R.K. Richey	205-325-4200	P	8,404 TA	6.3
Western National Corp.	5555 San Felipe Rd.	Houston	TX	77056	Michael J. Poulos	713-888-7800	P	8,321 TA	0.2
Equitable of Iowa Cos.	P.O. Box 1635	Des Moines	IA	50306	Frederick S. Hubbell	515-245-6911	P	7,966 TA	0.5
Lincoln National Life Insurance Co.	1300 S. Clinton St.	Fort Wayne	IN	46802	Robert A. Anker	219-455-2000	S	7,496 TA	3.2
Life Insurance Company of Virginia	6610 W. Broad St.	Richmond	VA	23230	Paul E. Rutledge III	804-281-6000	S	7,297 TA	0.7
Franklin Life Insurance Co.	1 Franklin Sq.	Springfield	IL	62713	Howard C. Humphrey	217-528-2011	S	7,116 TA	1.6
USLIFE Corp.	125 Maiden Ln.	New York	NY	10038	Gordon E. Crosby Jr.	212-709-6000	P	7,004 TA	2.2

Company type codes: P - Public, R - Private, S - Subsidiary, D - Division, J - Joint Venture, A - Affiliate, G - Group. If the dollar values shown are not sales, the following codes apply: TA - Total Assets; OR - Operating Revenues; GB - Gross Billings. * - estimated dollar value. < - less than. *na* - not available.

Continued on next page.

LEADING COMPANIES - SIC 6289 - Security & Commodity Services, nec

Continued

Company Name	Address				CEO Name	Phone	Co. Type	Sales/Assets ($ mil)	Empl. (000)
Kemper Life Insurance Co.	Rte. 22	Long Grove	IL	60049	John B. Scott	708-540-4465	S	7,000 TA	0.4
John Alden Financial Corp.	7300 Corporate Center	Miami	FL	33126	Glendon E. Johnson	305-470-3767	P	6,962 TA	3.7
Jefferson-Pilot Corp.	P.O. Box 21008	Greensboro	NC	27420	David A. Stonecipher	919-691-3000	P	6,140 TA	4.3
Protective Life Corp.	P.O. Box 2606	Birmingham	AL	35202	Drayton Nabers Jr.	205-879-9230	P	6,130 TA	1.1
PFL Life Insurance Co.	4333 Edgewood Rd. N.E.	Cedar Rapids	IA	52499	William L. Busler	319-398-8511	S	6,118 TA	0.3
Penn Mutual Life Insurance Co.	Independence Sq.	Philadelphia	PA	19172	John E. Tait	215-956-8000	R	6,086 TA	1.5
Horace Mann Life Insurance Co.	1 Horace Mann Plz.	Springfield	IL	62715	Paul J. Kardos	217-789-2500	S	6,000 TA*	2.5
American National Insurance Co.	1 Moody Plz.	Galveston	TX	77550	Robert L. Moody	409-763-4661	P	5,961 TA	5.0
Paul Revere Corp.	18 Chestnut St.	Worcester	MA	01608	Charles E. Soule Sr.	508-799-4441	P	5,909 TA	3.4
Nationwide Life Insurance Co.	1 Nationwide Plz.	Columbus	OH	43216	D. Richard McFerson	614-249-7111	S	5,524 TA	3.1
American Life Holding Co.	1400 Des Moines Bldg.	Des Moines	IA	50309	David J. Noble	515-284-7500	P	5,426 TA	0.3
Ameritas Life Insurance Corp.	5900 O St.	Lincoln	NE	68510	Neal E. Tyner	402-467-1122	R	5,399 TA	0.7
Farmers Group Inc.	4680 Wilshire Blvd.	Los Angeles	CA	90010	Leo E. Denlea Jr.	213-932-3200	S	5,344 TA	17.7
MBL Life Assurance Corp.	520 Broad St.	Newark	NJ	07102	Victor H. Palmieri	201-481-8000	R	5,300 TA*	1.0
State Mutual Life Assurance Company of America	440 Lincoln St.	Worcester	MA	01605	John O'Brien	508-855-1000	R	5,198 TA	7.0
Cincinnati Financial Corp.	P.O. Box 145496	Cincinnati	OH	45250	Robert B. Morgan	513-870-2000	P	4,734 TA	2.2
Leucadia National Corp.	315 Park Ave. S.	New York	NY	10010	Joseph S. Steinberg	212-460-1900	P	4,689 TA	4.3
Northwestern National Life Insurance Co.	P.O. Box 20	Minneapolis	MN	55440	John G. Turner	612-372-5432	S	4,638 TA	1.6
Unitrin Inc.	1 E. Wacker Dr.	Chicago	IL	60601	Richard C. Vie	312-661-4600	P	4,570 TA	7.3
Statesman Group Inc.	405 6th Ave.	Des Moines	IA	50309	D.J. Noble	515-284-7500	P	4,491 TA	0.4
Bankers Life Holding Corp.	222 Merchandise Mart	Chicago	IL	60654	Barth T. Murphy	312-396-6000	P	3,929 TA	2.0
Farmers New World Life Insurance Co.	3003 77th Ave.	Mercer Island	WA	98040	Glen W. Vining Jr.	206-232-8400	S	3,886 TA	0.6
Western and Southern Life Insurance Co.	400 Broadway	Cincinnati	OH	45202	John F. Barrett	513-629-1800	R	3,755 TA	4.2
Ohio National Life Insurance Co.	237 William Howard	Cincinnati	OH	45219	David B. O'Maley	513-861-3600	R	3,753 TA	0.5
Life Partners Group Inc.	7887 E. Bellevue Ave.	Englewood	CO	80111	John H. Massey	303-779-1111	P	3,749 TA	0.5
Ohio Casualty Corp.	136 N. 3rd St.	Hamilton	OH	45025	Lauren N. Patch	513-867-3000	P	3,739 TA	4.0
I.C.H. Corp.	P.O. Box 7940	Louisville	KY	40257	Robert Shaw	502-894-2100	P	3,698 TA	1.3
Monumental Life Insurance Co.	2 E. Chase St.	Baltimore	MD	21202	B. Larry Jenkins	410-685-2900	S	3,651 TA	2.1
USLICO Corp.	P.O. Box 3700	Arlington	VA	22203	Daniel J. Callahan III	703-875-3600	P	3,412 TA	0.7
American Express Financial Advisors Inc.	IDS Tower 10	Minneapolis	MN	55440	David R. Hubers	612-671-3131	S	3,156 OR	7.7

Company type codes: P - Public; R - Private; S - Subsidiary; D - Division; J - Joint Venture; A - Affiliate; G - Group. If the dollar values shown are not sales, the following codes apply: TA - Total Assets; OR - Operating Revenues; GB - Gross Billings. * - estimated dollar value. < - less than. *na* - not available.

Continued on next page.

LEADING COMPANIES - SIC 6289 - Security & Commodity Services, nec
Continued

Company Name	Address				CEO Name	Phone	Co. Type	Sales/Assets ($ mil)	Empl. (000)
Horace Mann Educators Corp.	1 Horace Mann Plz.	Springfield	IL	62715	Paul J. Kardos	217-789-2500	P	3,148 TA	2.5
American General Life and Accident Insurance Co.	American General Ctr.	Nashville	TN	37250	James D'Agostino	615-749-1000	S	3,100 TA	7.0
Gulf Life Insurance Co.	American General Ctr.	Nashville	TN	37250	James D'Agostino	615-749-1000	S	3,100 TA	7.9
Life USA Holding Inc.	300 S. Hwy. 169	Minneapolis	MN	55426	Robert W. MacDonald	612-546-7386	P	3,065 TA	0.3
Standard Insurance Co.	P.O. Box 711	Portland	OR	97207	Ronald E. Timpe	503-248-2700	R	3,001 TA	1.1
Federal Kemper Life Assurance Co.	1 Kemper Dr.	Long Grove	IL	60049	John B. Scott	708-320-4500	S	3,000 TA	0.4
National Western Life Insurance Co.	850 E. Anderson Ln.	Austin	TX	78752	Robert L. Moody	512-836-1010	P	2,915 TA	0.2
USG Annuity and Life Co.	700 Locust St.	Des Moines	IA	50309	Jon Newsome	515-282-3230	S	2,873 TA	0.1
Washington National Corp.	300 Tower Pkwy.	Lincolnshire	IL	60069	Robert W. Patin	708-793-3053	P	2,811 TA	1.0
Sentry Insurance, a Mutual Co.	1800 North Point Dr.	Stevens Point	WI	54481	Larry C. Ballard	715-346-6000	R	2,741 TA	4.4

*Source: Ward's Business Directory of U.S. Private and Public Companies, 1996. Company type codes: P - Public, R - Private, S - Subsidiary, D - Division, J - Joint Venture, A - Affiliate, G - Group. If the dollar values shown are not sales, the following codes apply: TA - Total Assets; OR - Operating Revenues; GB - Gross Billings. * - estimated dollar value. < - less than; na - not available.*

FINANCIAL DATA ON INSURANCE

The following 11 tables present information on the employment, structure, and finances of the life insurance industry. Data were obtained from the American Council of Life Insurance, 1001 Pennsylvania Avenue, N.W., Washington, D.C. 20004-2599, and are reproduced by permission. Much more detailed information is available from the council. One table is drawn from the *Statistical Abstract of the United States 1995*.

INCOME OF LIFE INSURANCE COMPANIES

In millions.

Year	Premium receipts				Investment income[2]	Other income[3]	Total income
	Life insurance premiums	Annuity consider-ations	Health insurance premiums[1]	Total premium receipts			
1980	40,829	22,429	29,366	92,624	33,928	4,336	130,888
1981	46,246	27,579	31,803	105,628	39,774	6,464	151,866
1982	50,800	34,644	34,960	120,404	45,532	4,108	170,044
1983	50,265	30,544	38,201	119,010	50,862	6,154	176,026
1984	51,274	42,859	40,671	134,804	59,213	12,092	206,109
1985	60,127	53,899	41,837	155,863	67,952	10,212	234,027
1986	66,213	83,712[4]	44,153	194,078	75,435	12,744	282,257
1987	76,737	88,677	47,549	212,963	82,875	18,460	314,298
1988	73,531	103,278	52,306	229,115	92,042	16,983	338,140
1989	73,290	114,997	56,079	244,366	103,965	18,987	367,318
1990	76,692	129,064	58,254	264,010	111,853	26,337	402,200
1991	79,301	123,590	60,900	263,791	118,984	28,247	411,022
1992	83,868	132,645	65,545	282,058	121,389	23,469	426,916
1993	94,448	156,445	68,658	319,551	124,205	22,594	466,350
1994	96,271	153,850	76,221	326,342	125,999	28,478	480,819

Source: Spectator Year Book and American Council of Life Insurance. *Notes:* Consideration for supplementary contracts with and without life contingencies are included under "Other Income." Prior to 1947, the business of health departments was not included in this series. 1. Includes some premiums for Workers' Compensation and auto and other liability insurance. 2. Beginning with 1951, investment income is net of investment expenses in this series. 3. Beginning in 1975, "Other Income" includes commissions and expense allowance on reinsurance ceded. In 1975, this amounted to $382 million. Beginning in 1992, includes amortization of the Interest Maintenance Reserve (IMR), which amounted to $980 million in 1994. 4. Unusually large increase in annuity premiums in 1986 was due to an NAIC-mandated change in statutory reporting methods.

U.S. LIFE INSURANCE COMPANIES--SUMMARY: 1980 TO 1993

As of December 31 or calendar year, as applicable. Covers domestic and foreign business of U.S. companies.

Item	Unit	1980	1985	1986	1987	1988	1989	1990	1991	1992	1993
U.S. companies	Number	1,958	2,261	2,254	2,337	2,343	2,270	2,195	2,064	1,944	1,840
Sales	Bil. dol.	655	1,530	1,578[1]	1,656	1,716	1,788	2,024	2,014[1]	1,944	1,840
Ordinary	Bil. dol.	461	1,187	1,178	1,267	1,287	1,343	1,368	1,403	1,881	2,130
Group	Bil. dol.	190	342	400[1]	388	428	444	655	611[1]	1,395	1,520
Industrial	Bil. dol.	4	1	(Z)	(Z)	(Z)	(Z)	(Z)	(Z)	1	(Z)
Income	Bil. dol.	130.9	234.0	282.3	314.3	338.1	367.3	402.2	411.0	426.9	466.4
Life insurance premiums	Bil. dol.	40.8	60.1	66.2	76.7	73.5	73.3	76.7	79.3	83.9	94.5
Percent of total	Percent	31.2	25.7	23.5	24.4	21.7	20.0	19.1	19.3	19.7	20.3
Annuity considerations	Bil. dol.	22.4	53.9	83.7	88.7	103.3	115.0	129.1	123.6	132.6	156.4
Health insurance premiums	Bil. dol.	29.4	41.8	44.2	47.6	52.3	56.1	58.2	60.9	65.5	68.7
Investment and other	Bil. dol.	38.3	78.2	88.2	101.3	109.0	122.9	138.2	147.2	144.9	146.8
Disbursements	Bil. dol.	88.2	151.8	186.5	202.3	221.4	246.8	277.1	299.2	305.0	318.9
Payments to policyholders[2][3]	Bil. dol.	59.0	95.7	131.4	144.4	156.8	178.3	200.9	218.6	222.1	231.9
Percent of total	Percent	66.9	63.0	70.5	71.4	70.8	72.2	72.5	73.1	72.8	72.7
Death payments	Bil. dol.	12.9	18.5	19.6	20.7	22.4	23.5	25.5	26.4	28.0	29.8
Matured endowments	Bil. dol.	0.8	0.8	0.8	0.8	0.8	0.8	0.8	0.7	0.7	0.6
Annuity payments	Bil. dol.	7.4	19.7	17.8	20.3	21.9	26.0	28.6	31.8	32.4	36.4
Policy dividends	Bil. dol.	8.1	12.4	12.4	13.0	13.8	14.9	15.7	15.8	15.3	15.8
Surrender values[3]	Bil. dol.	6.4	15.9	49.6	53.7	58.1	73.4	90.2	101.2	100.5	103.1
Disability benefits	Bil. dol.	0.5	0.5	0.5	0.5	0.4	0.5	0.5	0.5	0.6	0.5
Commissions, expenses, etc.[3]	Bil. dol.	27.8	53.1	51.4	54.7	61.3	63.5	70.2	75.1	77.8	80.1
Dividends to stockholders	Bil. dol.	1.4	3.0	3.7	3.3	3.4	5.0	6.0	5.5	5.1	6.9
BALANCE SHEET											
Assets	Bil. dol.	479	826	938	1,045	1,167	1,300	1,408	1,551	1,665	1,839
Government securities	Bil. dol.	33	125	145	151	160	178	211	269	320	384
Corporate securities	Bil. dol.	227	374	433	502	585	664	711	789	863	982
Percent of total assets	Percent	47.4	45.3	46.2	48.1	50.1	51.1	50.5	50.8	51.8	53.4
Bonds	Bil. dol.	180	297	342	406	480	538	583	624	670	730
Stocks	Bil. dol.	47	77	91	97	104	126	128	165	193	252
Mortgages	Bil. dol.	131	172	194	214	233	254	270	265	247	229
Real estate	Bil. dol.	15	29	32	34	37	40	43	47	51	54
Policy loans	Bil. dol.	41	54	54	54	54	57	63	66	72	78
Other	Bil. dol.	32	72	81	90	98	106	110	115	112	112
Interest earned on assets[4]	Percent	8.02	9.63	9.35	9.10	9.03	9.10	8.89	8.63	8.08	7.52
Liabilities[2][5]	Bil. dol.	445	769	873	977	1,092	1,216	1,317	1,445	1,549	1,711
Policy reserves[2]	Bil. dol.	390	665	762	862	969	1,084	1,197	1,305	1,407	1,550
Annuities	Bil. dol.	181	410	489	562	642	730	815	895	960	1,062
Group	Bil. dol.	140	303	356	393	434	474	516	548	560	602
Individual[6]	Bil. dol.	41	107	133	169	208	256	299	347	400	460
Life insurance	Bil. dol.	198	236	252	276	300	324	349	372	402	436
Health insurance	Bil. dol.	11	19	21	24	27	30	33	38	45	52
Asset valuation reserve[7]	Bil. dol.	6	11	15	16	18	19	15	19	21	25
Capital and surplus[2]	Bil. dol.	34	57	64	67	75	84	91	106	115	128

Source: American Council of Life Insurance, Washington, DC, *Life Insurance Fact Book*, biennial; and unpublished data. *Notes:* Z Less than $500 million. 1. Includes Servicemen's Group Life Insurance: $51 billion in 1986 and $167 billion in 1991; as well as federal Employees' Group Life Insurance: $11 billion in 1986. 2. Includes operations of accident and health departments of life insurance companies. 3. Beginning in 1986, data not comparable to prior years due to change in accounting method. 4. Net rate. 5. Includes other obligations not shown separately. 6. Includes reserves for supplementary contracts with and without life contingencies. 7. The asset valuation reserve is carried as a liability in financial statements but functions as surplus.

PURCHASES OF ORDINARY LIFE INSURANCE IN THE UNITED STATES BY STATE

Exclusive of revivals, increases, divided additions and reinsurance acquired. In millions of dollars.

State	In millions						
	1988	1989	1990	1991	1992	1993	1994
Alabama	15,436	18,038	18,370	17,710	17,780	18,305	19,872
Alaska	2,438	1,822	1,904	1,942	1,863	1,932	1,946
Arizona	14,367	13,779	13,547	13,445	13,368	13,769	14,174
Arkansas	7,174	7,401	7,372	8,055	7,824	7,226	9,031
California	122,886	127,828	134,467	126,764	133,867	134,155	135,354
Colorado	16,370	15,630	15,741	15,327	15,770	16,385	16,862
Connecticut	17,134	20,565	19,098	18,345	18,228	19,247	23,904
Delaware	3,700	3,414	3,198	3,303	3,427	3,661	4,013
D.C.	1,893	2,005	3,432	2,565	2,295	2,423	2,170
Florida	51,720	54,637	55,452	55,855	53,997	59,969	61,251
Georgia	30,445	35,264	39,021	36,663	37,190	41,809	36,351
Hawaii	5,252	5,084	5,376	5,540	5,784	5,503	5,718
Idaho	3,915	3,358	3,763	3,670	3,743	3,749	3,801
Illinois	46,364	47,119	52,281	52,714	53,240	56,725	54,234
Indiana	19,786	19,594	26,279	25,704	25,480	28,063	20,685
Iowa	9,997	10,039	10,338	10,483	10,101	10,690	11,520
Kansas	10,271	10,321	10,984	10,854	11,222	11,122	11,625
Kentucky	12,121	11,567	11,593	12,872	12,736	13,066	13,606
Louisiana	20,081	19,349	18,672	17,669	17,002	17,222	18,088
Maine	4,063	3,912	4,533	3,784	3,817	3,738	3,810
Maryland	22,360	22,711	23,478	22,714	23,272	24,284	24,326
Massachusetts	24,325	25,148	25,808	25,856	26,777	27,900	28,046
Michigan	28,515	27,681	28,094	27,809	27,692	29,858	34,040
Minnesota	16,382	17,213	17,567	16,651	17,317	18,431	19,680
Mississippi	8,960	9,384	9,631	9,374	8,731	9,107	10,432
Missouri	19,034	19,345	20,073	19,899	18,714	20,713	21,984
Montana	2,465	2,157	2,365	2,293	2,452	2,584	2,712
Nebraska	7,087	6,550	6,933	6,586	6,522	6,821	7,277
Nevada	4,137	4,381	4,542	4,810	4,922	5,141	5,516
New Hampshire	5,057	5,083	4,906	5,012	4,911	4,957	5,598
New Jersey	36,812	40,215	45,258	42,060	43,634	48,265	44,860
New Mexico	4,989	4,686	4,755	4,497	4,593	4,722	4,963
New York	71,732	76,501	81,699	79,589	79,578	83,529	78,927
North Carolina	27,964	29,197	28,842	27,711	28,569	30,949	33,490
North Dakota	2,345	2,733	2,153	2,275	2,226	2,210	2,189
Ohio	40,645	38,769	48,684	47,920	47,959	52,473	47,605
Oklahoma	11,328	10,950	10,541	9,902	9,606	9,923	10,576
Oregon	9,056	8,805	8,902	9,044	9,000	9,405	10,726
Pennsylvania	44,839	49,696	48,970	48,033	47,012	49,008	47,883
Rhode Island	3,931	4,131	4,496	4,322	4,195	3,982	4,133
South Carolina	17,123	15,334	15,694	15,650	15,341	16,308	17,285
South Dakota	2,764	2,594	2,686	2,727	2,760	2,788	2,759
Tennessee	19,638	21,080	20,232	20,745	20,859	21,626	22,070
Texas	75,852	72,835	70,153	66,698	66,814	68,757	72,358
Utah	7,888	7,565	7,710	7,640	7,453	7,671	7,851
Vermont	1,914	2,016	2,199	2,120	2,038	2,329	2,059
Virginia	25,732	25,482	29,004	27,294	28,182	28,995	28,303
Washington	16,374	16,461	17,528	17,509	17,102	17,596	18,250
West Virginia	4,265	4,110	4,051	3,902	3,815	4,014	4,084
Wisconsin	15,244	15,605	15,655	15,871	15,807	16,722	17,577
Wyoming	1,516	1,575	1,630	1,731	1,548	1,500	1,644
Total U.S.	995,686	1,020,719	1,069,660	1,041,508	1,048,135	1,101,327	1,107,216

Source: American Council of Life insurance. *Notes:* The series includes mass-marketed and monthly debit ordinary insurance. Data include long-term individual credit insurance.

LIFE INSURANCE IN FORCE IN THE UNITED STATES BY STATE 1994

Thousands of policies and millions of dollars.

State	Ordinary		Group		Industrial		Credit		Total amount
	No.	Amount	Master policies	Amount	No.	Amount	No.[1]	Amount	
Alabama	3,031	108,346	16	78,643	4,069	1,470	1,300	3,889	192,349
Alaska	173	13,088	2	11,927	3	5	82	419	25,440
Arizona	1,480	85,522	13	55,172	109	99	671	2,623	143,416
Arkansas	1,544	49,675	8	35,293	223	111	675	1,617	86,697
California	9,898	745,533	75	478,362	847	829	3,361	8,662	1,233,386
Colorado	1,732	105,079	18	71,249	93	106	809	2,374	178,808
Connecticut	1,959	129,433	13	98,730	98	141	519	1,640	229,944
Delaware	484	22,961	3	25,660	115	88	198	758	49,467
D.C.	320	14,674	7	48,077	169	110	142	374	63,235
Florida	6,876	345,963	49	175,181	1,534	1,121	4,708	11,132	533,397
Georgia	4,715	222,253	27	135,962	1,666	958	1,803	6,845	366,018
Hawaii	594	39,577	3	21,294	6	20	296	1,404	62,295
Idaho	465	24,062	2	14,407	19	23	296	1,099	39,590
Illinois	7,818	354,441	49	218,070	1,061	1,123	2,920	9,261	582,895
Indiana	3,700	147,828	30	98,558	548	519	1,419	5,675	252,580
Iowa	2,091	85,757	15	47,441	80	95	735	2,410	135,703
Kansas	1,670	76,960	11	44,194	120	119	637	2,111	123,385
Kentucky	2,358	78,617	15	47,950	573	356	1,223	4,274	123,385
Louisiana	2,809	107,582	18	52,830	2,429	1,020	1,602	4,326	165,758
Maine	615	26,423	4	18,334	39	59	321	1,322	46,138
Maryland	3,053	151,535	12	105,465	763	566	973	4,228	261,794
Massachusetts	3,542	181,346	24	123,320	235	303	977	3,093	308,063
Michigan	4,615	210,495	28	192,409	645	640	2,428	10,913	414,456
Minnesota	2,185	129,006	17	90,756	96	121	908	4,097	223,979
Mississippi	1,454	56,670	13	31,242	457	242	1,118	3,430	91,585
Missouri	3,478	137,112	24	98,161	458	418	1,230	4,281	239,972
Montana	358	18,172	3	11,067	14	14	260	796	30,049
Nebraska	1,136	51,925	6	27,395	45	51	413	1,258	80,630
Nevada	462	30,657	7	15,206	12	19	262	880	46,762
New Hampshire	700	38,593	5	17,039	42	70	229	1,065	56,767
New Jersey	4,446	276,866	46	224,414	592	666	1,132	5,952	507,898
New Mexico	695	34,089	4	25,822	35	30	450	1,523	61,464
New York	9,268	523,612	52	361,171	847	992	2,963	8,677	894,452
North Carolina	5,128	191,570	29	124,334	2,025	1,188	1,849	7,916	325,007
North Dakota	336	19,154	3	10,161	3	5	205	683	30,002
Ohio	6,905	285,897	64	208,732	1,050	1,023	3,013	10,384	506,036
Oklahoma	1,613	67,076	12	42,475	163	136	651	2,345	112,031
Oregon	1,091	66,483	10	46,141	42	46	614	2,604	115,275
Pennsylvania	8,187	359,172	39	219,878	1,610	1,547	3,183	12,886	593,483
Rhode Island	559	27,159	3	17,926	42	45	165	569	45,700
South Carolina	3,026	94,642	15	55,978	1,070	640	1,440	4,721	155,980
South Dakota	423	20,345	4	9,427	3	5	187	690	30,467
Tennessee	3,149	122,912	20	94,183	1,408	669	1,757	6,333	224,097
Texas	8,816	437,724	67	298,981	1,488	1,057	3,961	16,101	753,862
Utah	669	42,257	4	27,188	45	43	431	1,683	71,171
Vermont	340	16,019	2	9,456	16	24	152	577	26,076
Virginia	3,770	176,810	19	148,002	1,137	712	1,551	8,473	333,997
Washington	1,809	116,601	14	82,152	80	82	1,078	4,046	202,881
West Virginia	1,016	29,673	8	23,568	264	181	678	2,196	55,618
Wisconsin	2,845	127,036	19	82,973	178	233	1,166	4,445	214,686
Wyoming	230	10,854	2	6,431	4	6	154	436	17,727
Total U.S.	139,632	6,835,239	951	4,608,746	28,670	20,145	59,293	209,491	11,673,621

Source: American Council of Life Insurance. *Notes:* "Credit" is limited to life insurance on loans of 10 years' or less duration. "Ordinary" and "Group" include credit life insurance on loans of more than 10 years' duration 1. Includes group credit certificates.

LIFE INSURANCE IN FORCE PER HOUSEHOLD BY STATE AND REGION 1994

A "household" is defined by the U.S. Bureau of the Census as consisting of all persons who occupy a housing unit; a "housing unit" is a house, an apartment or other group of rooms, or a single room that is occupied or intended for occupancy as separate living quarters.

State	Amount	State	Amount	State	Amount
Alabama	116,000	Kentucky	90,900	North Dakota	122,100
Alaska	126,100	Louisiana	105,000	Ohio	119,200
Arizona	91,700	Maine	95,900	Oklahoma	89,000
Arkansas	89,200	Maryland	137,200	Oregon	92,500
California	112,300	Massachusetts	136,300	Pennsylvania	126,600
Colorado	121,300	Michigan	113,200	Rhode Island	120,600
Connecticut	183,800	Minnesota	125,700	South Carolina	111,400
Delaware	177,800	Mississippi	93,200	South Dakota	111,000
D.C.	264,300	Missouri	117,700	Tennessee	112,100
Florida	94,800	Montana	91,500	Texas	111,200
Georgia	137,100	Nebraska	127,100	Utah	118,500
Hawaii	157,100	Nevada	80,400	Vermont	117,300
Idaho	95,800	New Hampshire	125,200	Virginia	134,000
Illinois	136,300	New Jersey	172,800	Washington	97,700
Indiana	115,100	New Mexico	98,300	West Virginia	78,500
Iowa	120,500	New York	130,700	Wisconsin	111,600
Kansas	124,300	North Carolina	116,800	Wyoming	98,800

Source: American Council of LIfe Insurance and U.S. Bureau of the Census.

LIFE INSURANCE AND ANNUITY BENEFIT PAYMENTS

In the United States by State, 1994. In thousands of dollars.

	Death payments	Matured endowments	Annuity payments	Disability payments	Surrender values[1]	Policy and contract dividends	Total
Alabama	553,172	7,997	277,783	10,259	493,246	153,081	1,495,538
Alaska	67,431	560	57,635	977	176,521	21,304	324,428
Arizona	384,285	5,531	557,753	7,800	771,139	176,082	1,902,590
Arkansas	249,684	2,898	194,746	4,166	316,760	91,376	859,630
California	3,120,646	44,591	4,008,832	57,703	6,339,728	1,190,431	14,761,931
Colorado	437,155	6,272	537,805	6,982	939,434	194,002	2,121,650
Connecticut	554,240	8,228	1,203,892	11,878	1,187,164	315,148	3,280,550
Delaware	186,212	2,020	104,939	2,266	296,882	86,308	678,627
D.C.	215,608	2,112	141,193	1,070	316,848	56,552	733,383
Florida	1,719,670	29,942	1,958,091	34,059	3,359,128	657,746	7,758,636
Georgia	1,035,966	15,105	472,119	15,088	1,241,581	542,770	3,322,629
Hawaii	133,072	2,365	186,851	4,752	222,171	66,128	615,339
Idaho	101,674	1,290	112,151	2,435	272,558	58,299	548,407
Illinois	1,689,280	38,893	2,368,246	43,377	3,230,673	1,056,088	8,426,557
Indiana	691,865	13,795	627,941	16,230	1,126,342	617,771	3,093,944
Iowa	352,600	9,580	633,565	10,702	741,309	301,052	2,048,808
Kansas	290,871	6,052	345,221	7,209	451,920	192,478	1,293,751
Kentucky	389,053	7,366	401,896	10,030	422,440	168,225	1,399,100
Louisiana	549,400	6,279	343,934	9,059	678,754	159,778	1,747,204
Maine	116,041	4,077	130,230	3,281	163,991	75,435	493,055
Maryland	682,225	12,488	753,282	9,486	967,657	327,521	2,752,959
Massachusetts	770,271	16,347	1,317,319	11,392	2,250,039	587,082	4,952,450
Michigan	1,262,580	19,007	1,476,529	22,006	2,458,536	554,867	5,793,525
Minnesota	462,586	7,925	991,525	10,020	1,655,978	270,434	3,398,468
Mississippi	262,864	3,567	142,675	4,420	302,240	71,733	787,499
Missouri	691,530	12,032	694,329	11,733	1,091,011	292,090	2,792,725
Montana	75,314	1,535	104,165	1,963	152,352	38,405	373,734
Nebraska	197,755	4,276	320,363	5,282	352,085	139,916	1,019,677
Nevada	137,129	1,617	131,476	2,188	238,547	53,683	564,640
New Hampshire	109,043	3,510	152,349	2,100	216,202	90,970	574,174
New Jersey	1,341,366	22,637	1,819,942	25,668	2,175,500	893,580	6,268,693
New Mexico	160,576	2,146	181,087	2,663	201,376	62,605	610,453
New York	2,395,796	47,027	5,006,072	57,499	7,745,763	1,760,269	17,012,426
North Carolina	865,932	14,288	686,107	13,840	1,217,454	402,558	3,200,179
North Dakota	62,748	1,139	97,876	875	170,615	46,975	380,228
Ohio	1,474,372	26,909	2,181,341	36,223	2,593,185	1,032,872	7,344,902
Oklahoma	336,956	4,826	419,772	5,497	481,657	129,421	1,378,129
Oregon	286,984	4,056	568,956	7,744	772,491	121,016	1,761,247
Pennsylvania	1,662,668	41,387	2,145,092	42,807	2,988,145	999,442	7,879,541
Rhode Island	122,446	2,488	150,977	3,339	196,876	80,993	557,119
South Carolina	441,738	9,281	248,179	7,681	154,937	37,001	361,967
South Dakota	70,430	1,933	95,986	1,680	154,937	37,001	361,967
Tennessee	641,259	9,983	569,710	10,277	737,265	221,046	2,189,540
Texas	2,006,392	24,056	1,869,425	28,935	3,034,139	588,626	7,551,573
Utah	161,808	1,741	207,712	2,272	254,060	82,567	710,160
Vermont	61,838	1,862	94,419	1,293	112,282	57,297	328,955
Virginia	928,345	13,421	592,121	12,980	1,055,408	494,563	3,096,838
Washington	462,069	6,381	898,636	28,038	1,277,035	249,799	2,921,958
West Virginia	169,754	5,032	226,056	6,132	192,940	95,243	695,157
Wisconsin	519,526	16,307	909,699	10,834	1,209,308	361,204	3,026,878
Wyoming	43,797	1,008	48,273	512	95,381	22,446	211,417
Total U.S.	31,706,022	555,129	39,756,663	646,703	59,625,726	16,479,588	148,769,831

Source: American Council of Life Insurance. *Notes:* Annuity dividends in this table are included with policy dividends rather than with annuity payments. 1. Beginning with 1994, "Surrender Values" includes annuity withdrawals of funds, which were not included in prior years.

PAYMENTS TO LIFE INSURANCE BENEFICIARIES

In the United States by State, 1994. In thousands of dollars.

State	Ordinary	Group	Industrial	Credit	Total
Alabama	334,087	171,247	27,922	19,916	553,172
Alaska	20,258	45,319	55	1,799	67,431
Arizona	232,219	135,403	2,455	14,208	384,285
Arkansas	158,346	80,816	1,941	8,581	249,684
California	1,875,046	1,180,497	17,042	48,061	3,120,646
Colorado	260,754	164,911	2,683	8,807	437,155
Connecticut	270,073	274,941	3,626	5,600	554,240
Delaware	61,526	117,228	1,651	5,807	186,212
D.C.	45,265	166,543	2,053	1,747	215,608
Florida	1,157,087	470,550	23,125	68,908	1,719,670
Georgia	586,614	401,404	17,436	30,512	1,035,966
Hawaii	73,585	56,184	51	3,252	133,072
Idaho	62,180	35,412	287	3,795	101,674
Illinois	984,354	638,202	31,986	34,738	1,689,280
Indiana	384,165	270,701	13,718	23,281	691,865
Iowa	241,624	100,098	2,884	7,994	352,600
Kansas	182,896	96,395	3,219	8,361	290,871
Kentucky	226,168	136,798	8,479	17,608	389,053
Louisiana	336,929	175,954	19,870	16,647	549,400
Maine	63,530	45,634	1,362	5,515	116,041
Maryland	349,655	296,748	11,848	23,974	682,225
Massachusetts	434,246	317,780	8,628	9,617	770,271
Michigan	531,213	668,063	17,059	46,245	1,262,580
Minnesota	259,010	187,742	3,931	11,903	462,586
Mississippi	167,276	77,671	4,157	13,760	262,864
Missouri	389,246	269,902	10,230	22,152	691,530
Montana	48,652	23,492	253	2,917	75,314
Nebraska	135,598	55,417	1,340	5,400	197,755
Nevada	87,472	44,834	468	4,355	137,129
New Hampshire	66,238	38,523	1,369	2,913	109,043
New Jersey	690,042	605,036	18,689	27,599	1,341,366
New Mexico	83,602	70,932	471	5,571	160,576
New York	1,435,524	871,498	29,028	59,746	2,395,796
North Carolina	532,703	284,345	16,551	32,333	865,932
North Dakota	40,251	20,409	39	2,049	62,748
Ohio	843,313	551,184	30,797	49,078	1,474,372
Oklahoma	208,011	113,038	2,465	13,442	336,956
Oregon	155,782	116,783	1,303	13,116	286,984
Pennsylvania	951,988	596,143	48,598	65,939	1,662,668
Rhode Island	68,567	48,386	1,800	3,693	122,446
South Carolina	272,414	138,724	11,487	19,113	441,738
South Dakota	47,022	19,444	101	3,863	70,430
Tennessee	346,208	251,849	12,834	30,368	641,259
Texas	1,194,413	746,584	13,540	51,855	2,006,392
Utah	84,266	70,800	900	5,842	161,808
Vermont	38,389	20,836	509	2,104	61,838
Virginia	465,818	415,469	13,638	33,420	928,345
Washington	249,155	189,890	1,919	21,105	462,069
West Virginia	84,012	72,208	4,030	9,504	169,754
Wisconsin	309,152	188,070	7,316	14,988	519,526
Wyoming	25,490	16,729	76	1,502	43,797
Total U.S.	18,151,434	12,152,766	457,219	944,603	31,706,022

Source: American Council of Life Insurance.

PREMIUM RECEIPTS OF U.S. LIFE INSURANCE COMPANIES BY STATE 1994

In millions.

State	Life	Annuity	Health	Deposit administration funds	Total
Alabama	1,351	313	817	701	3,182
Alaska	142	69	252	174	637
Arizona	956	654	890	1,242	3,742
Arkansas	702	228	555	349	1,835
California	7,980	5,498	5,871	10,840	30,189
Colorado	1,203	599	1,017	1,772	4,591
Connecticut	1,775	1,126	1,191	2,428	6,520
Delaware	527	455	194	514	1,689
D.C.	247	98	435	1,093	1,872
Florida	4,234	2,431	3,979	4,659	15,303
Georgia	2,601	492	2,165	1,456	6,714
Hawaii	395	239	130	435	1,199
Idaho	304	176	172	293	946
Illinois	4,566	2,560	3,969	6,796	17,891
Indiana	2,115	930	2,079	1,804	6,928
Iowa	1,068	737	1,612	1,153	4,570
Kansas	960	379	1,318	837	3,495
Kentucky	1,099	299	731	673	2,802
Louisiana	1,405	504	1,093	826	3,828
Maine	296	145	296	334	1,071
Maryland	1,588	764	1,044	2,243	5,640
Massachusetts	2,253	1,034	1,305	6,893	11,486
Michigan	3,307	1,956	1,635	4,869	11,767
Minnesota	1,547	1,118	884	2,413	5,963
Mississippi	717	156	663	397	1,933
Missouri	1,858	805	1,529	1,966	6,157
Montana	205	138	214	205	761
Nebraska	619	606	551	612	2,389
Nevada	339	218	364	324	1,244
New Hampshire	368	197	287	361	1,214
New Jersey	3,950	2,086	2,859	3,802	12,698
New Mexico	397	470	299	277	1,444
New York	7,038	3,380	5,487	15,071	30,977
North Carolina	2,633	920	1,895	2,472	7,919
North Dakota	202	151	142	223	717
Ohio	4,631	1,612	2,577	3,957	12,777
Oklahoma	860	398	854	679	2,791
Oregon	789	683	513	1,405	3,390
Pennsylvania	4,351	2,000	2,119	6,440	14,911
Rhode Island	328	200	134	356	1,017
South Carolina	1,217	365	901	645	3,128
South Dakota	229	132	320	223	903
Tennessee	1,690	612	1,498	1,358	5,157
Texas	5,184	2,284	8,501	4,752	20,721
Utah	502	297	357	383	1,539
Vermont	173	88	105	182	549
Virginia	2,330	1,042	2,845	1,807	8,025
Washington	1,257	1,582	850	1,553	5,242
West Virginia	452	198	416	274	1,340
Wisconsin	1,489	942	1,503	2,364	6,298
Wyoming	136	56	128	100	420
Total U.S.	86,563	44,424	71,549	106,986	309,522

Source: American Council of Life Insurance. *Notes:* Data refer to direct premiums collected in each state, without deducting reinsurance ceded, but excluding reinsurance assumed.

MORTGAGES OWNED BY U.S. LIFE INSURANCE COMPANIES BY TYPE AND STATE 1994

In thousands.

State	Farm	Nonfarm	Total
Alabama	34,486	1,459,419	1,493,905
Alaska	1,121	170,446	171,567
Arizona	161,732	2,963,455	3,125,187
Arkansas	259,892	335,686	595,578
California	2,904,916	40,079,626	42,984,542
Colorado	165,255	2,895,319	3,060,574
Connecticut	-	3,029,506	3,029,506
Delaware	16,943	621,044	637,987
District of Columbia	-	3,691,525	3,691,525
Florida	1,297,366	11,364,379	12,661,745
Georgia	124,257	5,717,159	5,841,416
Hawaii	28,380	626,949	655,329
Idaho	180,764	266,686	447,450
Illinois	307,004	11,341,672	11,648,676
Indiana	295,091	2,846,178	3,141,269
Iowa	416,604	910,598	1,327,202
Kansas	145,377	1,206,034	1,351,411
Kentucky	59,711	1,362,144	1,421,855
Louisiana	146,327	1,465,347	1,611,674
Maine	21,054	373,279	394,333
Maryland	21,712	5,975,109	5,996,821
Massachusetts	26,283	7,570,596	7,596,879
Michigan	66,529	5,497,965	5,564,494
Minnesota	225,107	3,245,138	3,470,245
Mississippi	258,603	463,694	722,297
Missouri	178,434	3,513,619	3,692,053
Montana	184,257	134,088	318,345
Nebraska	273,031	503,994	777,025
Nevada	16,482	1,881,152	1,897,634
New Hampshire	-	641,092	641,092
New Jersey	5,929	9,440,618	9,446,547
New Mexico	65,517	626,862	692,379
New York	4,258	15,144,947	15,149,205
North Carolina	73,492	4,257,339	4,330,831
North Dakota	26,974	121,429	148,403
Ohio	91,731	6,165,709	6,257,440
Oklahoma	95,065	564,095	659,160
Oregon	235,246	2,201,925	2,437,171
Pennsylvania	7,047	5,890,277	5,897,324
Rhode Island	-	337,978	337,978
South Carolina	8,018	1,648,364	1,656,382
South Dakota	56,491	55,129	111,620
Tennessee	28,117	2,785,710	2,813,827
Texas	425,273	12,766,242	13,191,515
Utah	11,876	887,799	899,675
Vermont	-	85,565	85,565
Virginia	48,476	8,524,539	8,573,015
Washington	350,292	5,677,807	6,028,099
West Virginia	81,439	228,760	310,199
Wisconsin	65,878	1,475,306	1,541,184
Wyoming	65,004	73,098	138,102
Puerto Rico	-	224,618	224,618
U.S. Territories and Possessions	-	3,603	3,603
Total U.S.	9,562,839	201,340,615	210,903,454
Canada	14,240	4,354,646	4,368,886
Other Foreign	-	60,328	60,328
Grand Total	9,577,079	205,755,589	215,332,668

Source: American Council of Life Insurance.

CHANGE IN LIFE INSURANCE COMPANIES IN BUSINESS IN THE U.S.

Year	In business start of year			New operations	Discontinued	In business year-end			Net changes during year	
	Stock	Mutual	Total			Stock	Mutual	Total		
1980	1,758	137	1,895	155	92	1,823	135	1,958	+	63
1981	1,823	135	1,958	137	104	1,855	136	1,991	+	33
1982	1,855	136	1,991	152	83	1,926	134	2,060	+	69
1983	1,926	134	2,060	137	80	1,985	132	2,117	+	57
1984	1,985	132	2,117	166	90	2,062	131	2,193	+	76
1985	2,062	131	2,193	140	72	2,133	128	2,261	+	68
1986	2,133	128	2,261	89	96	2,128	126	2,254	-	7
1987	2,128	126	2,254	168	85	2,212	125	2,337	+	83
1988	2,212	125	2,337	92	86	2,225	118	2,343	+	6
1989	2,225	118	2,343	111	184	2,153	117	2,270	-	73
1990	2,153	117	2,270	86	161	2,078	117	2,195	-	75
1991	2,078	117	2,195	69	200	1,947	117	2,064	-	131
1992	1,947	117	2,064	79	199	1,835	109	1,944	-	120
1993	1,835	109	1,944	67	167	1,736	108	1,844	-	100
1994	1,736	108	1,844	N.A.	N.A.	N.A.	N.A.	1,770	-	74

Source: American Council of Life Insurance *Notes:* Data for 1993 are revised. The figure for year-end 1994 is preliminary. A change in domicile is reflected in both new and discontinued operations. N.A. stands for not available. 1. Includes seven companies domiciled in Alaska and Hawaii that were started in earlier years.

NUMBER OF PERSONS EMPLOYED IN INSURANCE IN THE UNITED STATES

Year	Home office personnel				Agents, brokers, service personnel	Total
	Life insurance	Health insurance	Other	Total		
1980	531,900	141,900	550,300	1,224,100	463,800	1,687,900
1981	542,200	142,700	552,000	1,236,900	475,800	1,712,700
1982	546,100	142,100	549,100	1,237,300	485,900	1,723,200
1983	539,900	144,800	544,200	1,228,900	498,900	1,727,800
1984	536,700	153,900	549,100	1,239,700	525,000	1,764,700
1985	559,300	170,700	561,600	1,291,600	548,200	1,839,800
1986	578,200	188,100	598,500	1,364,800	579,400	1,944,200
1987	578,000	202,100	634,900	1,415,000	611,800	2,026,800
1988	570,400	216,500	648,500	1,435,400	639,600	2,075,000
1989	550,200	228,100	660,100	1,438,400	651,800	2,090,200
1990	547,500	241,600	673,100	1,462,200	663,300	2,125,500
1991	560,000	258,700	675,900	1,494,600	666,300	2,160,900
1992	550,300	270,100	675,200	1,495,600	656,600	2,152,200
1993	561,800	278,500	678,100	1,518,400	662,100	2,180,500
1994	546,600	286,600	683,400	1,516,600	664,500	2,181,100

Source: U.S. Department of Labor, Bureau of Labor Statistics, *Employment and Earnings,* various issues. *Notes:* Includes only persons on the payroll of insurance establishments that participate in the unemployment insurance program.

SIC 6321

ACCIDENT AND HEALTH INSURANCE

This industry includes organizations that engage in underwriting accident and health insurance. It includes establishments that provide health insurance protection for disability income losses and medical expense coverage on an indemnity basis. Ownership of these establishments may be by stockholders, policyholders, or other carriers. Establishments engaged primarily in providing hospital, medical, and other health services on a service basis or combination of service and indemnity bases are classified under SIC 6324 (see next chapter).

Members of this industry are organizations providing accident and health insurance, assessment associations, disability health insurance providers, fraternal accident and health insurance organizations, health insurance indemnity plans, mutual accident associations, reciprocal interinsurance exchanges for accident and health insurance, mutual sick benefit associations, and reinsurance carriers for these categories.

ESTABLISHMENTS, EMPLOYMENT, AND PAYROLL

	1988	1989 Value	%	1990 Value	%	1991 Value	%	1992 Value	%	1993 Value	%	% change 88-93
All Establishments	1,169	1,077	-7.9	1,067	-0.9	1,385	29.8	1,441	4.0	1,132	-21.4	-3.2
Mid-March Employment	43,967	45,940	4.5	47,878	4.2	55,167	15.2	61,291	11.1	53,925	-12.0	22.6
1st Quarter Wages (annualized - $ mil.)	993.7	1,114.7	12.2	1,194.8	7.2	1,493.2	25.0	1,621.5	8.6	1,465.4	-9.6	47.5
Payroll per Emp. 1st Q. (annualized)	22,601	24,264	7.4	24,954	2.8	27,066	8.5	26,455	-2.3	27,174	2.7	20.2
Annual Payroll ($ mil.)	1,041.5	1,143.7	9.8	1,277.6	11.7	1,501.9	17.6	1,575.4	4.9	1,486.1	-5.7	42.7
Establishments - 1-4 Emp. Number	568	473	-16.7	423	-10.6	649	53.4	731	12.6	474	-35.2	-16.5
Mid-March Employment	(D)	1,044	-	(D)	-	1,254	-	1,488	18.7	949	-36.2	-
1st Quarter Wages (annualized - $ mil.)	(D)	29.7	-	(D)	-	38.2	-	51.9	35.9	41.4	-20.2	-
Payroll per Emp. 1st Q. (annualized)	(D)	28,471	-	(D)	-	30,469	-	34,890	14.5	43,646	25.1	-
Annual Payroll ($ mil.)	(D)	31.9	-	(D)	-	41.9	-	55.9	33.2	41.3	-26.0	-
Establishments - 5-9 Emp. Number	277	268	-3.2	272	1.5	264	-2.9	259	-1.9	228	-12.0	-17.7
Mid-March Employment	1,783	1,766	-1.0	1,786	1.1	1,767	-1.1	1,726	-2.3	1,521	-11.9	-14.7
1st Quarter Wages (annualized - $ mil.)	49.2	53.5	8.7	61.5	14.9	69.9	13.7	70.3	0.5	58.0	-17.4	17.9
Payroll per Emp. 1st Q. (annualized)	27,587	30,285	9.8	34,408	13.6	39,554	15.0	40,707	2.9	38,138	-6.3	38.2
Annual Payroll ($ mil.)	52.5	56.6	7.7	61.3	8.4	66.4	8.3	69.9	5.3	56.6	-19.0	7.8
Establishments - 10-19 Emp. Number	129	127	-1.6	127	-	146	15.0	149	2.1	151	1.3	17.1
Mid-March Employment	(D)	(D)	-	1,638	-	1,934	18.1	1,976	2.2	2,022	2.3	-
1st Quarter Wages (annualized - $ mil.)	(D)	(D)	-	48.0	-	65.5	36.5	68.2	4.2	74.6	9.3	-
Payroll per Emp. 1st Q. (annualized)	(D)	(D)	-	29,287	-	33,853	15.6	34,532	2.0	36,892	6.8	-
Annual Payroll ($ mil.)	(D)	(D)	-	49.8	-	62.7	25.9	65.3	4.2	77.3	18.4	-
Establishments - 20-49 Emp. Number	108	103	-4.6	102	-1.0	159	55.9	135	-15.1	102	-24.4	-5.6
Mid-March Employment	3,279	3,185	-2.9	3,111	-2.3	4,939	58.8	4,249	-14.0	3,091	-27.3	-5.7
1st Quarter Wages (annualized - $ mil.)	88.8	87.9	-0.9	90.5	2.9	159.8	76.6	129.3	-19.1	105.5	-18.4	18.8
Payroll per Emp. 1st Q. (annualized)	27,070	27,611	2.0	29,093	5.4	32,353	11.2	30,422	-6.0	34,118	12.1	26.0
Annual Payroll ($ mil.)	86.5	86.0	-0.6	89.4	3.9	157.5	76.2	127.8	-18.8	107.5	-15.9	24.3
Establishments - 50-99 Emp. Number	36	41	13.9	53	29.3	65	22.6	63	-3.1	69	9.5	91.7
Mid-March Employment	2,595	2,895	11.6	3,614	24.8	4,761	31.7	4,362	-8.4	4,767	9.3	83.7
1st Quarter Wages (annualized - $ mil.)	58.9	66.0	12.0	83.2	26.1	113.7	36.7	120.7	6.2	134.8	11.7	128.8
Payroll per Emp. 1st Q. (annualized)	22,710	22,797	0.4	23,018	1.0	23,884	3.8	27,673	15.9	28,287	2.2	24.6
Annual Payroll ($ mil.)	60.0	67.9	13.1	85.0	25.2	113.7	33.8	113.1	-0.5	138.1	22.1	130.2
Establishments - 100-249 Emp. Number	25	36	44.0	47	30.6	58	23.4	(D)	-	57	-	128.0
Mid-March Employment	4,414	5,697	29.1	7,404	30.0	9,087	22.7	(D)	-	8,633	-	95.6
1st Quarter Wages (annualized - $ mil.)	93.4	129.4	38.6	157.5	21.8	193.1	22.6	(D)	-	196.7	-	110.7
Payroll per Emp. 1st Q. (annualized)	21,153	22,707	7.3	21,275	-6.3	21,253	-0.1	(D)	-	22,786	-	7.7
Annual Payroll ($ mil.)	95.8	123.1	28.5	157.3	27.8	196.8	25.1	(D)	-	200.1	-	108.8
Establishments - 250-499 Emp. Number	12	16	33.3	28	75.0	28	-	32	14.3	37	15.6	208.3
Mid-March Employment	4,210	4,765	13.2	8,983	88.5	9,177	2.2	11,108	21.0	13,474	21.3	220.0
1st Quarter Wages (annualized - $ mil.)	84.2	115.0	36.5	199.2	73.2	215.8	8.3	263.7	22.2	307.3	16.5	264.8
Payroll per Emp. 1st Q. (annualized)	20,009	24,139	20.6	22,179	-8.1	23,515	6.0	23,741	1.0	22,807	-3.9	14.0
Annual Payroll ($ mil.)	85.8	112.0	30.5	208.1	85.7	214.5	3.1	260.6	21.5	308.5	18.4	259.4
Establishments - 500-999 Emp. Number	7	6	-14.3	9	50.0	9	-	9	-	(D)	-	-
Mid-March Employment	4,595	3,848	-16.3	5,870	52.5	5,685	-3.2	6,062	6.6	(D)	-	-
1st Quarter Wages (annualized - $ mil.)	103.4	105.9	2.5	153.8	45.2	143.1	-6.9	239.8	67.5	(D)	-	-
Payroll per Emp. 1st Q. (annualized)	22,504	27,533	22.3	26,198	-4.8	25,172	-3.9	39,550	57.1	(D)	-	-
Annual Payroll ($ mil.)	113.0	102.6	-9.2	199.0	93.9	149.7	-24.8	206.2	37.8	(D)	-	-
Estab. - 1000 or More Emp. Number	7	7	-	6	-14.3	7	16.7	(D)	-	(D)	-	-
Mid-March Employment	(D)	(D)	-	(D)	-	16,563	-	(D)	-	(D)	-	-
1st Quarter Wages (annualized - $ mil.)	(D)	(D)	-	(D)	-	494.1	-	(D)	-	(D)	-	-
Payroll per Emp. 1st Q. (annualized)	(D)	(D)	-	(D)	-	29,829	-	(D)	-	(D)	-	-
Annual Payroll ($ mil.)	(D)	(D)	-	(D)	-	498.6	-	(D)	-	(D)	-	-

Source: County Business Patterns, U.S. Department of Commerce, Washington, D.C., for 1988 through 1993. Payroll per employee is calculated using mid-March employment and 1st Quarter wages, annualized. Annual payroll, also shown, may not equal the annualized 1st Quarter wages. Columns headed by a percent sign (%) indicate change from the previous year. na stands for not available. The symbol (D) indicates that data are withheld by the source to avoid disclosure of competitive information. A dash (-) indicates that data are not available or cannot be calculated.

ESTABLISHMENTS
Number

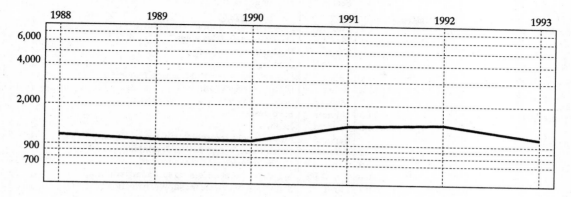

MID-MARCH EMPLOYMENT
Number

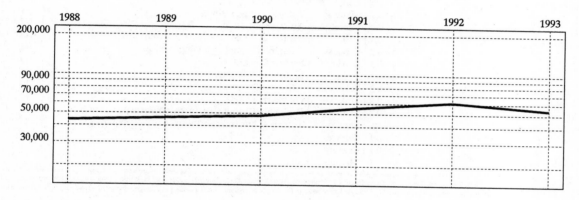

ANNUAL PAYROLL
$ million

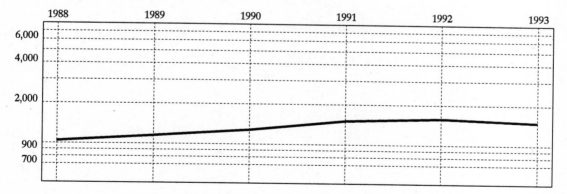

INPUTS AND OUTPUTS FOR INSURANCE CARRIERS - SIC GROUP 63

Economic Sector or Industry Providing Inputs	%	Sector	Economic Sector or Industry Buying Outputs	%	Sector
Insurance agents, brokers, & services	62.9	Fin/R.E.	Personal consumption expenditures	77.1	
Security & commodity brokers	6.8	Fin/R.E.	Owner-occupied dwellings	5.5	Fin/R.E.
Eating & drinking places	4.0	Trade	Real estate	3.6	Fin/R.E.
Real estate	4.0	Fin/R.E.	Banking	0.9	Fin/R.E.
Communications, except radio & TV	3.9	Util.	Federal Government purchases, nondefense	0.9	Fed Govt
Imports	1.8	Foreign	Electric services (utilities)	0.8	Util.
Commercial printing	1.3	Manufg.	Insurance agents, brokers, & services	0.7	Fin/R.E.
Computer & data processing services	1.3	Services	Feed grains	0.6	Agric.
Advertising	1.2	Services	Exports	0.5	Foreign
Hotels & lodging places	1.2	Services	Motor freight transportation & warehousing	0.5	Util.
Legal services	1.2	Services	Retail trade, except eating & drinking	0.5	Trade
Accounting, auditing & bookkeeping	0.9	Services	Credit agencies other than banks	0.4	Fin/R.E.
Banking	0.9	Fin/R.E.	S/L Govt. purch., elem. & secondary education	0.4	S/L Govt
U.S. Postal Service	0.9	Gov't	Sanitary services, steam supply, irrigation	0.4	Util.
Air transportation	0.6	Util.	State & local government enterprises, nec	0.3	Gov't
Credit agencies other than banks	0.6	Fin/R.E.	Water supply & sewage systems	0.3	Util.
Management & consulting services & labs	0.6	Services	Wholesale trade	0.3	Trade
Maintenance of nonfarm buildings nec	0.5	Constr.	Food grains	0.2	Agric.
Manifold business forms	0.5	Manufg.	Meat animals	0.2	Agric.
Motor freight transportation & warehousing	0.5	Util.	Petroleum refining	0.2	Manufg.
Petroleum refining	0.5	Manufg.	Religious organizations	0.2	Services
Photographic equipment & supplies	0.4	Manufg.	Air transportation	0.1	Util.
Transit & bus transportation	0.4	Util.	Arrangement of passenger transportation	0.1	Util.
Business services nec	0.3	Services	Equipment rental & leasing services	0.1	Services
Personnel supply services	0.3	Services	Freight forwarders	0.1	Util.
Wholesale trade	0.3	Trade	Industrial buildings	0.1	Constr.
Automotive rental & leasing, without drivers	0.2	Services	Office buildings	0.1	Constr.
Electric services (utilities)	0.2	Util.	Oil bearing crops	0.1	Agric.
Electronic computing equipment	0.2	Manufg.	Residential 1-unit structures, nonfarm	0.1	Constr.
Detective & protective services	0.1	Services	Transit & bus transportation	0.1	Util.
Electrical repair shops	0.1	Services			
Envelopes	0.1	Manufg.			
Manufacturing industries, nec	0.1	Manufg.			

Source: Benchmark Input-Output Accounts for the U.S. Economy, 1982, U.S. Department of Commerce, Washington, D.C., July 1991. Data, as reported in the source, are organized by the 1977 SIC structure in use in 1982 but have been matched, as closely as is possible, to the 1987 SIC structure used in this book. Activities with the same percentage are sorted alphabetically by name of activity.

OCCUPATIONS EMPLOYED BY MEDICAL SERVICE AND HEALTH INSURANCE

Occupation	% of Total 1994	Change to 2005	Occupation	% of Total 1994	Change to 2005
Insurance adjusters, examiners, & investigators	7.9	16.2	Systems analysts	2.8	77.0
Insurance claims clerks	7.5	10.6	Managers & administrators nec	2.1	10.6
General office clerks	5.6	-5.6	Accountants & auditors	2.0	10.6
Adjustment clerks	5.6	49.4	Registered nurses	2.0	64.7
Insurance policy processing clerks	4.9	10.6	Bookkeeping, accounting, & auditing clerks	1.9	-17.0
Clerical supervisors & managers	4.9	13.2	Sales & related workers nec	1.6	10.6
Secretaries, ex legal & medical	4.3	0.7	Receptionists & information clerks	1.5	10.6
Claims examiners, insurance	4.0	10.6	Mail clerks, ex machine operators, postal service	1.2	-20.3
Insurance sales workers	3.8	-4.3	Health professionals & paraprofessionals nec	1.2	10.6
Clerical support workers nec	3.3	-11.5	Computer operators, ex peripheral equipment	1.2	-37.1
Data entry keyers, ex composing	3.0	-18.3	File clerks	1.2	-44.7
Computer programmers	2.9	-10.4	Correspondence clerks	1.2	-22.5
Management support workers nec	2.9	32.8	Operations research analysts	1.1	44.0
General managers & top executives	2.8	5.0	Underwriters	1.1	37.2

Sources: Industry-Occupation Matrix, Bureau of Labor Statistics. These data relate to one or more 3-digit SIC industry groups rather than to a single 4-digit SIC. The change reported for each occupation to the year 2005 is a percent of growth or decline as estimated by the Bureau of Labor Statistics. The abbreviation *nec* stands for not elsewhere classified.

U.S. AND STATE DATA ON INDUSTRY REVENUES AND OTHER ACCOUNTS FOR 1992

State	No. of Estab.	Employ-ment	Payroll ($ mil.)	Revenues ($ mil.)	Empl./ Estab.	Revenue/ Estab. ($)	Payroll/ Estab. ($)	Revenue/ Empl. ($)	Payroll/ Empl. ($)
UNITED STATES	1,100	53,599	1,466.6	23,446.3	49	21,314,805	1,333,302	437,439	27,363
California	66	1,735	51.1	955.6	26	14,478,515	774,091	550,768	29,447
Colorado	21	183	6.4	87.8	9	4,181,190	305,333	479,809	35,038
Florida	60	1,844	50.1	1,284.4	31	21,405,883	835,200	696,504	27,176
Georgia	19	919	18.8	217.3	48	11,435,895	987,947	236,433	20,425
Illinois	42	6,119	174.5	2,895.9	146	68,949,833	4,155,286	473,262	28,521
Indiana	27	738	22.6	403.3	27	14,938,815	838,704	546,542	30,684
Maryland	17	-	(D)	(D)	(D)	(D)	(D)	(D)	(D)
Massachusetts	23	1,426	46.3	406.8	62	17,687,000	2,012,261	285,274	32,456
Michigan	28	968	24.4	367.0	35	13,105,500	870,607	379,085	25,183
Minnesota	21	872	21.0	240.0	42	11,430,429	1,000,381	275,274	24,092
Missouri	24	530	12.2	272.5	22	11,355,500	508,875	514,211	23,043
New Jersey	19	832	23.0	224.7	44	11,824,579	1,209,947	270,032	27,631
New York	37	1,742	60.1	999.8	47	27,022,595	1,625,595	573,959	34,528
North Carolina	30	1,064	25.9	418.7	35	13,957,767	861,767	393,546	24,298
Ohio	55	4,814	147.5	2,938.1	88	53,419,345	2,681,309	610,317	30,634
Pennsylvania	52	2,417	62.0	706.6	46	13,588,692	1,191,538	292,351	25,635
Tennessee	32	-	(D)	(D)	(D)	(D)	(D)	(D)	(D)
Texas	118	4,466	110.5	2,551.5	38	21,622,695	936,297	571,312	24,739
Virginia	30	580	10.2	267.1	19	8,903,267	340,067	460,514	17,590
Washington	18	218	5.6	128.4	12	7,131,389	313,056	588,830	25,849
Wisconsin	30	4,369	112.3	945.1	146	31,504,367	3,742,167	216,327	25,696

Source: 1992 Economic Census, U.S. Department of Commerce, Washington, D.C. This is the only table that shows revenue data as collected by the Bureau of the Census in an Economic Census. The symbol (D) indicates that data are withheld by the source to avoid disclosure of competitive information. A dash (-) indicates that data are not available or cannot be calculated.

ESTABLISHMENTS 1992 - STATE AND REGIONAL CONCENTRATION

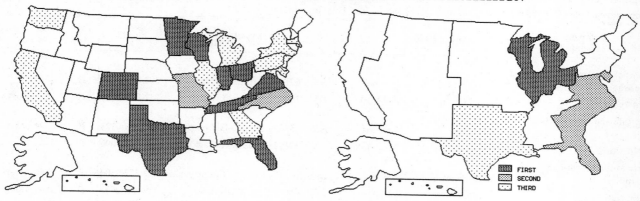

EMPLOYMENT 1992 - STATE AND REGIONAL CONCENTRATION

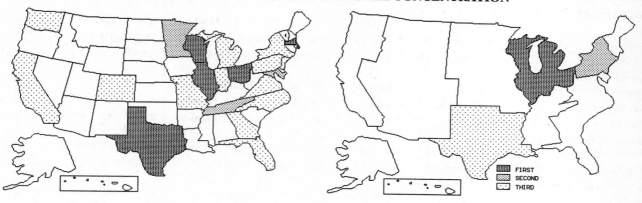

REVENUES 1992 - STATE AND REGIONAL CONCENTRATION

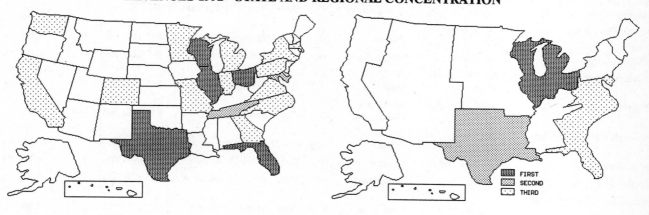

States with the darkest shading indicate those states which have proportionately more establishments, employment, or revenues than would be indicated by the state's population. States with light shading are states with proportionately fewer establishments, less employment, and lower revenues than population distribution. States shaded grey are within 15 percent of the state's population proportion in these categories. States for which no data are available are shown as average (grey). *Regions* are shaded to indicate absolute rank in the category. If no data for the category are available, establishment counts are used to shade the regions. Source of the data is the table on the facing page.

LEADING COMPANIES - SIC 6311 - Life Insurance

Number shown: 100   Total sales/assets ($ mil): **1,159,666**   Total employment (000): **587.1**

Company Name	Address				CEO Name	Phone	Co. Type	Sales/Assets ($ mil)	Empl. (000)
Prudential Insurance Company of America	751 Broad St.	Newark	NJ	07102	Arthur F. Ryan	201-802-6000	R	313,660 TA	100.0
Travelers Inc.	65 E. 55th St.	New York	NY	10022	Sanford I. Weill	212-816-8000	P	115,300 TA	52.0
Aetna Life and Casualty Co.	151 Farmington Ave.	Hartford	CT	06156	Ronald E. Compton	203-273-0123	P	94,172 TA	43.1
CIGNA Corp.	P.O. Box 7716	Philadelphia	PA	19192	Wilson H. Taylor	215-761-1000	P	86,102 TA	48.3
Liberty Mutual Insurance Group	175 Berkeley St.	Boston	MA	02117	Gary L. Countryman	617-357-9500	R	50,001 TA	22.0
Lincoln National Corp.	P.O. Box 1110	Fort Wayne	IN	46801	Ian M. Rolland	219-455-2000	P	49,330 TA	9.0
Aetna Life Insurance Co.	151 Farmington Ave.	Hartford	CT	06156	Ronald E. Compton	203-273-0123	S	47,357 TA	24.0
Principal Financial Group Inc.	711 High St.	Des Moines	IA	50392	G. David Hurd	515-247-5111	R	44,116 TA	14.8
Principal Mutual Life Insurance Co.	711 High St.	Des Moines	IA	50392	G. David Hurd	515-247-5111	S	44,116 TA	14.8
AFLAC Inc.	1932 Wynnton Rd.	Columbus	GA	31999	Daniel P. Amos	706-323-3431	P	20,287 TA	4.0
Aon Corp.	123 N. Wacker Dr.	Chicago	IL	60606	Patrick G. Ryan	312-701-3000	P	17,922 TA	30.0
Provident Life and Accident Insurance Company of America	1 Fountain Sq.	Chattanooga	TN	37402	J. Harold Chandler	615-755-1011	P	16,892 TA	4.5
Provident Life Capital Corp.	1 Fountain Sq.	Chattanooga	TN	37402	J. Harold Chandler	615-755-1011	S	16,892 TA	4.5
SAFECO Corp.	SAFECO Plz.	Seattle	WA	98185	Roger H. Eigsti	206-545-5000	P	15,902 TA	7.3
Transamerica Occidental Life Insurance Co.	1150 S. Olive St.	Los Angeles	CA	90015	David R. Carpenter	213-742-2111	S	14,950 TA	2.7
UNUM Corp.	2211 Congress St.	Portland	ME	04122	James F. Orr III	207-770-2211	P	13,127 TA	7.0
ReliaStar Financial Corp.	20 Washington Ave. S.	Minneapolis	MN	55401	John G. Turner	612-372-5432	P	10,367 TA	2.6
Provident Life and Accident Insurance Co.	1 Fountain Sq.	Chattanooga	TN	37402	J. Harold Chandler	615-755-1901	S	10,000 TA	4.5
Guardian Life Insurance Company of America	201 Park Ave. S.	New York	NY	10003	Arthur V. Ferrara	212-598-8000	R	9,871 TA	5.3
Mutual of Omaha Insurance Co.	Mutual of Omaha Plz.	Omaha	NE	68175	Thomas J. Skutt	402-342-7600	R	8,600 TA	8.9
Torchmark Corp.	2001 3rd Ave. S.	Birmingham	AL	35233	R.K. Richey	205-325-4200	P	8,404 TA	6.3
John Alden Financial Corp.	7300 Corporate Center	Miami	FL	33126	Glendon E. Johnson	305-470-3767	P	6,962 TA	3.7
TIG Holdings Inc.	6300 Canoga Ave.	Woodland Hills	CA	91367	Jon W. Rotenstreich	818-596-5000	P	6,253 TA	3.2
Transamerica Insurance Group	6300 Canoga Ave.	Woodland Hills	CA	91367	Jon W. Rotenstreich	818-596-5000	S	6,253 TA	3.2
Jefferson-Pilot Corp.	P.O. Box 21008	Greensboro	NC	27420	David A. Stonecipher	919-691-3000	P	6,140 TA	4.3
Protective Life Corp.	P.O. Box 2606	Birmingham	AL	35202	Drayton Nabers Jr.	205-879-9230	P	6,130 TA	1.1
American National Insurance Co.	1 Moody Plz.	Galveston	TX	77550	Robert L. Moody	409-763-4661	P	5,961 TA	5.0
Paul Revere Corp.	18 Chestnut St.	Worcester	MA	01608	Charles E. Soule Sr.	508-799-4441	P	5,909 TA	3.4
Utica Mutual Insurance Co.	180 Genesee St.	New Hartford	NY	13413	W. Craig Heston	315-734-2000	R	5,000 TA	1.4
Cincinnati Financial Corp.	P.O. Box 145496	Cincinnati	OH	45250	Robert B. Morgan	513-870-2000	P	4,734 TA	2.2

Company type codes: P - Public, R - Private, S - Subsidiary, D - Division, J - Joint Venture, A - Affiliate, G - Group. If the dollar values shown are not sales, the following codes apply: TA - Total Assets; OR - Operating Revenues; GB - Gross Billings. * - estimated dollar value. < - less than. *na* - not available.

Continued on next page.

LEADING COMPANIES - SIC 6311 - Life Insurance
Continued

Company Name	Address				CEO Name	Phone	Co. Type	Sales/Assets ($ mil)	Empl. (000)
Leucadia National Corp.	315 Park Ave. S.	New York	NY	10010	Joseph S. Steinberg	212-460-1900	P	4,689 TA	4.3
Bankers Life Holding Corp.	222 Merchandise Mart	Chicago	IL	60654	Barth T. Murphy	312-396-6000	P	3,929 TA	2.0
I.C.H. Corp.	P.O. Box 7940	Louisville	KY	40257	Robert Shaw	502-894-2100	P	3,698 TA	1.3
Blue Cross and Blue Shield of Massachusetts Inc.	100 Summer St.	Boston	MA	02110	William C. Van Faasen	617-832-5000	R	3,595 TA	5.8
American General Life and Accident Insurance Co.	American General Ctr.	Nashville	TN	37250	James D'Agostino	615-749-1000	S	3,100 TA	7.0
Gulf Life Insurance Co.	American General Ctr.	Nashville	TN	37250	James D'Agostino	615-749-1000	S	3,100 TA	7.9
Standard Insurance Co.	P.O. Box 711	Portland	OR	97207	Ronald E. Timpe	503-248-2700	R	3,001 TA	1.1
Blue Cross and Blue Shield of Alabama	P.O. Box 995	Birmingham	AL	35298	E. Gene Thrasher	205-988-2100	R	3,000 TA	2.2
Washington National Corp.	300 Tower Pkwy.	Lincolnshire	IL	60069	Robert W. Patin	708-793-3053	P	2,811 TA	1.0
Harcourt General Insurance Cos.	6277 Sea Harbor Dr.	Orlando	FL	32887	Frederick M. Dawson	407-345-2600	S	2,690 TA*	0.6
Blue Cross and Blue Shield of Michigan	600 Lafayette E.	Detroit	MI	48226	Richard E. Whitmer	313-225-9000	R	2,626 TA	6.5
Delphi Financial Group Inc.	P.O. Box 8985	Wilmington	DE	19899	Charles P. O'Brien	302-478-5142	P	2,475 TA	0.5
American Bankers Insurance Group Inc.	11222 Quail Roost Dr.	Miami	FL	33157	R. Kirk Landon	305-253-2244	P	2,432 TA	2.2
Blue Cross of California	P.O. Box 70000	Van Nuys	CA	91470	Leonard D. Schaeffer	818-703-2345	R	2,424 TA	3.6
Bankers Life Insurance Company of Illinois	222 Merchandise Mart	Chicago	IL	60654	Barth T. Murphy	312-396-6000	S	2,239 TA	1.8
Empire Blue Cross and Blue Shield	622 3rd Ave.	New York	NY	10017	G. Robert O'Brien	212-476-1000	R	2,161 TA	7.9
Federated Mutual Insurance Co.	121 E. Park Sq.	Owatonna	MN	55060	Charles I. Buxton II	507-455-5200	R	2,040 TA	2.5
Industrial Indemnity Co.	255 California St.	San Francisco	CA	94111	Robert Whitehead	415-627-5000	R	2,000 TA	1.2
Reliance Standard Life Insurance Co.	2501 Parkway	Philadelphia	PA	19130	Charles P. O'Brien	215-787-4000	S	1,936 TA	0.5
Zenith National Insurance Corp.	21255 Califa St.	Woodland Hills	CA	91367	Stanley R. Zax	818-713-1000	P	1,841 TA	1.5
NAC Reinsurance Corp.	P.O. Box 2568	Greenwich	CT	06836	Ronald Bornhuetter	203-622-5200	S	1,779 TA	0.2
Washington National Insurance Co.	300 Tower Pkwy.	Lincolnshire	IL	60069	Robert Patin	708-793-3000	S	1,700 TA	0.8
Veritus Inc.	120 5th Ave.	Pittsburgh	PA	15222	Eugene J. Barone	412-255-7000	R	1,553 TA	2.8
Blue Cross and Blue Shield of Connecticut Inc.	370 Bassett Rd.	North Haven	CT	06473	John F. Croweak	203-239-4911	R	1,477 TA	2.3
Cuna Mutual Insurance Society	P.O. Box 391	Madison	WI	53701	Richard M. Heins	608-238-5851	R	1,472 TA	5.5
Life Re Corp.	969 High Ridge Rd.	Stamford	CT	06905	Rodney A. Hawes Jr.	203-321-3000	P	1,422 TA	<0.1
Life Reassurance Corporation of America	969 High Ridge Rd.	Stamford	CT	06905	Rodney A. Hawes Jr.	203-321-3000	S	1,422 TA	<0.1
Independent Insurance Group Inc.	1 Independent Dr.	Jacksonville	FL	32276	Wilford C. Lyon Jr.	904-358-5151	P	1,364 TA	4.0

Company type codes: P - Public, R - Private, S - Subsidiary, D - Division, J - Joint Venture, A - Affiliate, G - Group. If the dollar values shown are not sales, the following codes apply: TA - Total Assets; OR - Operating Revenues; GB - Gross Billings. * - estimated dollar value. < - less than. *na* - not available.

Continued on next page.

LEADING COMPANIES - SIC 6311 - Life Insurance

Continued

Company Name	Address				CEO Name	Phone	Co. Type	Sales/Assets ($ mil)	Empl. (000)
Health Care Service Corporation, A Mutual Legal Reserve Co.	233 N. Michigan Ave.	Chicago	IL	60601	S. Martin Hickman	312-938-6000	R	1,314 TA	5.0
Blue Cross and Blue Shield of Virginia	P.O. Box 27401	Richmond	VA	23279	Norwood H. Davis Jr.	804-354-7000	R	1,261 TA	3.9
Blue Cross and Blue Shield of Oregon	P.O. Box 1271	Portland	OR	97207	Richard L. Woolworth	503-225-5221	R	1,230 TA	2.1
Berkshire Life Insurance Co.	700 South St.	Pittsfield	MA	01201	Albert C. Cornelio	413-499-4321	R	1,090 TA	0.3
Pioneer Financial Services Inc.	1750 E. Golf Rd.	Schaumburg	IL	60173	Peter W. Nauert	708-995-0400	P	1,075 TA	1.9
Independent Life and Accident Insurance Co.	1 Independent Dr.	Jacksonville	FL	32276	Jacob F. Bryan	904-358-5151	S	1,074 TA	4.0
Laurentian Capital Corp.	640 Lee Rd.	Wayne	PA	19087	Robert T. Rakich	215-889-7400	P	1,028 TA	0.3
Blue Cross and Blue Shield of New Jersey Inc.	3 Penn Plaza E.	Newark	NJ	07105	William J. Marino	201-466-4000	R	993 TA	3.0
TMG Life Insurance Co.	401 N. Executive Dr.	Brookfield	WI	53008	Ken Evason	414-797-5000	S	980 TA	0.6
Michigan Mutual Insurance Co.	25200 Telegraph Rd.	Southfield	MI	48034	Don Mandich	810-827-7400	R	947 TA	1.2
American Fidelity Group	2000 Classen Blvd.	Oklahoma City	OK	73106	William E. Durrett	405-523-2000	R	944 TA	1.1
Independence Blue Cross	1901 Market St.	Philadelphia	PA	19103	G. Fred DiBona Jr.	215-241-2400	R	939 TA	2.3
Johnson International Inc.	4061 N. Main St.	Racine	WI	53402	Richard G. Jacobs	414-639-6010	R	920 TA	0.7
Golden Rule Financial Corp.	712 Eleventh St.	Lawrenceville	IL	62439	John M. Whelan	618-943-8000	R	896 TA	1.3
Blue Shield of California	P.O. Box 7168	San Francisco	CA	94120	Wayne R. Moon	415-445-5000	R	847 TA	3.4
United Insurance Companies Inc.	4001 McEwen Dr.	Dallas	TX	75244	Ronald L. Jensen	214-960-8497	P	815 TA	0.6
EMPHESYS Financial Group Inc.	1100 Employers Blvd.	Green Bay	WI	54344	William J. Lawson	414-336-1100	P	794 TA	2.2
Capitol American Financial Corp.	1001 Lakeside Ave.	Cleveland	OH	44114	David H. Gunning	216-696-6400	P	793 TA	0.3
Blue Cross and Blue Shield of North Carolina	P.O. Box 2291	Durham	NC	27702	Kenneth C. Otis II	919-489-7431	R	771 TA	2.2
Sedgwick James of Oregon Inc.	111 Columbia St.	Portland	OR	97201	Ronald J. Kutella	503-248-6400	S	770 TA	0.3
Blue Cross and Blue Shield of Maryland Inc.	10455 Mill Run Cir.	Owings Mills	MD	21117	William L. Jews	410-581-3000	R	736 TA	3.9
Blue Cross and Blue Shield of Ohio	2060 E. 9th St.	Cleveland	OH	44115	John Burry Jr.	216-687-7000	R	736 TA	3.0
Wisconsin Physician Service Insurance Corp.	P.O. Box 8190	Madison	WI	53708	James Riordan	608-221-4711	R	650 TA	3.1
Employers Health Insurance Co.	1100 Employers Blvd.	Green Bay	WI	54344	William J. Lawson	414-336-1100	S	644 TA	2.2
Blue Cross and Blue Shield United of Wisconsin	1515 N. River Ctr. Dr.	Milwaukee	WI	53212	Thomas R. Hefty	414-226-5000	R	608 TA	2.4
American Income Holding Inc.	P.O. Box 8985	Wilmington	DE	19899	Bernard Rapoport	302-427-2894	P	605 TA	0.3
American Income Life Insurance Co.	P.O. Box 2608	Waco	TX	76797	Bernard Rapoport	817-751-8600	S	605 TA	0.3
Blue Cross and Blue Shield of Minnesota	P.O. Box 64560	St. Paul	MN	55164	Andrew Czajkowski	612-456-8786	S	573 TA	3.0

Company type codes: P - Public, R - Private, S - Subsidiary, D - Division, J - Joint Venture, A - Affiliate, G - Group. If the dollar values shown are not sales, the following codes apply: TA - Total Assets; OR - Operating Revenues; GB - Gross Billings. * - estimated dollar value. < - less than. *na* - not available.

Continued on next page.

LEADING COMPANIES - SIC 6311 - Life Insurance
Continued

Company Name	Address				CEO Name	Phone	Co. Type	Sales/Assets ($ mil)	Empl. (000)
CSE Insurance Group	P.O. Box 7794	San Francisco	CA	94101	Pierre Jerre	415-495-6800	S	560 TA*	0.2
Business Men's Assurance Company of America	P.O. Box 419458	Kansas City	MO	64141	J. William Sayler	816-753-8000	S	550 TA	0.8
Reliable Life Insurance Co.	231 W. Lockwood Ave.	Webster Groves	MO	63119	Bernal T. Chomeau	314-968-4900	P	531 TA	1.3
Centre Reinsurance Company of New York	1 Chase Manhattan Plz.	New York	NY	10005	Bruce Bunner	212-898-5300	S	523 TA	<0.1
Physicians Mutual Insurance Co.	P.O. Box 3313	Omaha	NE	68131	Robert Reed	402-633-1000	R	505 TA	1.0
Academy Insurance Group Inc.	6600 Peachtree	Atlanta	GA	30328	Pamela Godwin	404-698-7000	S	500 TA	0.1
Academy Life Insurance Co.	6600 Peachtree	Atlanta	GA	30328	Pamela Godwin	404-698-7000	S	500 TA	0.1
Pioneer Life Insurance Company of Illinois	P.O. Box 120	Rockford	IL	61101	Thomas J. Brophy	815-987-5000	S	436 TA	0.6
American Travellers Corp.	3220 Tillman Dr.	Bensalem	PA	19020	John A. Powell	215-244-1600	P	401 TA	0.4
Blue Cross of Washington and Alaska	P.O. Box 327	Seattle	WA	98111	Betty Woods	206-670-4000	R	396 TA	1.2
Boston Mutual Life Insurance Co.	120 Royall St.	Canton	MA	02021	Lawrence J. Finnegan	617-828-7000	R	381 TA	0.3
Blue Cross and Blue Shield of the Rochester Area	150 E. Maine St.	Rochester	NY	14647	Howard Berman	716-454-1700	R	360 TA	2.4
Blue Cross and Blue Shield of Georgia Inc.	P.O. Box 4445	Atlanta	GA	30302	Richard D. Shirk	404-842-8000	R	357 TA	1.8
Blue Cross and Blue Shield of the National Capital Area	550 12th St. S.W.	Washington	DC	20065	Larry C. Glasscock	202-479-8000	S	343 TA	1.8

Source: Ward's Business Directory of U.S. Private and Public Companies, 1996. Company type codes: P - Public, R - Private, S - Subsidiary, D - Division, J - Joint Venture, A - Affiliate, G - Group. If the dollar values shown are not sales, the following codes apply: TA - Total Assets; OR - Operating Revenues; GB - Gross Billings. * - estimated dollar value. < - less than; *na* - not available.

FINANCIAL DATA ON HEALTH INSURANCE

The following table presents additional statistics on health insurance companies drawn from the *Statistical Abstract of the United States 1995*, which is citing the Health Insurance Association of America, 1025 Connecticut Ave., NW, Suite 1200, Washington, DC 10026.

HEALTH INSURANCE--PREMIUM INCOME AND BENEFIT PAYMENTS OF INSURANCE COMPANIES: 1982 TO 1992

In billions of dollars. Includes Puerto Rico and other U.S. outlying areas. Represents premium income of and benefits paid by insurance companies only. Excludes Blue Cross-Blue Shield plans, medical-society sponsored plans, and all other independent plans.

Item	1982	1983	1984	1985	1986	1987	1988	1989	1990	1991	1992
Premiums[1]	58.3	63.2	70.4	75.2	75.5	84.1	98.2	108.0	112.9	116.4	125.0
Group policies[2]	50.0	54.9	60.8	64.4	65.9	74.0	87.6	96.1	100.2	103.0	110.4
Individual and family policies	8.3	8.3	9.6	10.8	9.6	10.1	10.6	11.8	12.7	13.3	14.6
Benefit payments	49.2	51.7	56.0	60.0	64.3	72.5	83.0	89.4	92.5	97.6	104.8
Group policies	44.2	46.9	50.3	53.7	58.9	66.5	76.4	82.2	84.4	88.8	95.2
Individual and family policies	5.0	4.8	5.7	6.3	5.4	5.9	6.6	7.2	8.2	8.8	9.6
Type of coverage:											
Loss of income	5.5	4.9	5.2	5.6	5.6	6.4	6.4	7.2	7.4	7.5	8.3
Medical expense	38.8	41.5	44.1	47.2	50.9	57.4	66.4	72.0	73.8	77.9	82.9
Dental	4.0	4.4	4.9	5.3	5.3	5.9	6.3	6.5	6.4	6.4	7.1
Medical supplement	0.8	1.0	1.8	1.9	2.5	2.8	3.8	3.7	5.0	5.8	6.4

Source: Health Insurance Association of America, Washington, DC, *Source Book of Health Insurance Data*, annual. *Notes:* 1. Earned premiums. 2. Insurance company group premiums and benefit payments include administrative service agreements and minimum premium plans.

SIC 6324

HOSPITAL AND MEDICAL SERVICE PLANS

This industry includes establishments that provide hospital, medical, and other health services to subscribers or members in accordance with prearranged agreements or service plans. The service plans provide benefits to subscribers or members for specified charges. The plans may be through a contract under which a participating hospital or physician agrees to render the covered services without charging any additional fees—or may provide for partial indemnity and service benefits. The industry also includes those separate elements of health maintenance organizations (HMOs) that provide medical insurance. The HMOs themselves are classified under Health Services and are not included in this book.

Dental insurance plans, providing services by contracts with health facilities, group hospitalization plans, hospital and medical service plans, and medical service plans are all included in this industry.

ESTABLISHMENTS, EMPLOYMENT, AND PAYROLL

	1988	1989 Value	%	1990 Value	%	1991 Value	%	1992 Value	%	1993 Value	%	% change 88-93
All Establishments	937	926	-1.2	1,015	9.6	1,196	17.8	1,492	24.7	1,770	18.6	88.9
Mid-March Employment	128,604	135,268	5.2	139,255	2.9	155,974	12.0	172,204	10.4	202,386	17.5	57.4
1st Quarter Wages (annualized - $ mil.)	3,173.4	3,391.6	6.9	3,787.4	11.7	4,397.5	16.1	5,259.4	19.6	6,333.0	20.4	99.6
Payroll per Emp. 1st Q. (annualized)	24,676	25,074	1.6	27,198	8.5	28,194	3.7	30,542	8.3	31,292	2.5	26.8
Annual Payroll ($ mil.)	3,214.9	3,424.5	6.5	3,794.0	10.8	4,425.2	16.6	5,260.2	18.9	6,582.4	25.1	104.7
Establishments - 1-4 Emp. Number	278	266	-4.3	303	13.9	307	1.3	429	39.7	461	7.5	65.8
Mid-March Employment	525	557	6.1	631	13.3	612	-3.0	921	50.5	893	-3.0	70.1
1st Quarter Wages (annualized - $ mil.)	14.8	17.7	19.9	19.7	11.1	19.8	0.5	27.8	40.6	39.5	41.9	167.0
Payroll per Emp. 1st Q. (annualized)	28,168	31,828	13.0	31,220	-1.9	32,340	3.6	30,215	-6.6	44,215	46.3	57.0
Annual Payroll ($ mil.)	55.5	50.3	-9.3	27.5	-45.3	39.7	44.0	38.3	-3.5	60.8	59.0	9.5
Establishments - 5-9 Emp. Number	137	138	0.7	118	-14.5	148	25.4	220	48.6	257	16.8	87.6
Mid-March Employment	(D)	922	-	741	-19.6	983	32.7	1,496	52.2	1,712	14.4	-
1st Quarter Wages (annualized - $ mil.)	(D)	27.1	-	26.7	-1.5	31.9	19.6	48.2	51.1	62.7	30.0	-
Payroll per Emp. 1st Q. (annualized)	(D)	29,380	-	36,000	22.5	32,456	-9.8	32,214	-0.7	36,605	13.6	-
Annual Payroll ($ mil.)	(D)	28.5	-	26.0	-8.9	30.9	18.8	52.9	71.3	67.3	27.2	-
Establishments - 10-19 Emp. Number	121	117	-3.3	139	18.8	172	23.7	183	6.4	216	18.0	78.5
Mid-March Employment	(D)	1,662	-	1,952	17.4	2,391	22.5	2,508	4.9	2,978	18.7	-
1st Quarter Wages (annualized - $ mil.)	(D)	47.1	-	60.0	27.4	68.6	14.4	77.0	12.3	96.8	25.7	-
Payroll per Emp. 1st Q. (annualized)	(D)	28,342	-	30,734	8.4	28,693	-6.6	30,710	7.0	32,520	5.9	-
Annual Payroll ($ mil.)	(D)	45.8	-	60.3	31.5	70.4	16.8	80.1	13.8	102.6	28.1	-
Establishments - 20-49 Emp. Number	146	131	-10.3	154	17.6	219	42.2	241	10.0	280	16.2	91.8
Mid-March Employment	4,537	4,078	-10.1	4,820	18.2	7,231	50.0	7,750	7.2	8,991	16.0	98.2
1st Quarter Wages (annualized - $ mil.)	122.0	105.1	-13.8	135.6	28.9	212.4	56.7	235.3	10.8	295.8	25.7	142.5
Payroll per Emp. 1st Q. (annualized)	26,886	25,782	-4.1	28,126	9.1	29,373	4.4	30,359	3.4	32,894	8.4	22.3
Annual Payroll ($ mil.)	132.8	105.5	-20.6	135.4	28.4	213.8	57.9	240.6	12.5	306.9	27.6	131.2
Establishments - 50-99 Emp. Number	69	77	11.6	95	23.4	91	-4.2	126	38.5	189	50.0	173.9
Mid-March Employment	4,763	5,232	9.8	6,635	26.8	6,513	-1.8	8,814	35.3	13,637	54.7	186.3
1st Quarter Wages (annualized - $ mil.)	116.0	128.1	10.4	168.4	31.5	169.6	0.7	237.1	39.8	404.4	70.6	248.6
Payroll per Emp. 1st Q. (annualized)	24,358	24,476	0.5	25,376	3.7	26,041	2.6	26,897	3.3	29,654	10.3	21.7
Annual Payroll ($ mil.)	117.2	127.9	9.1	176.0	37.6	182.1	3.5	247.6	35.9	456.0	84.2	288.9
Establishments - 100-249 Emp. Number	87	90	3.4	97	7.8	136	40.2	152	11.8	193	27.0	121.8
Mid-March Employment	13,599	13,940	2.5	15,302	9.8	20,971	37.0	24,028	14.6	31,325	30.4	130.3
1st Quarter Wages (annualized - $ mil.)	315.2	328.6	4.3	376.4	14.6	524.5	39.3	674.2	28.6	917.5	36.1	191.1
Payroll per Emp. 1st Q. (annualized)	23,175	23,570	1.7	24,600	4.4	25,010	1.7	28,060	12.2	29,289	4.4	26.4
Annual Payroll ($ mil.)	323.3	321.5	-0.6	386.7	20.3	550.9	42.5	694.7	26.1	962.5	38.6	197.7
Establishments - 250-499 Emp. Number	31	37	19.4	32	-13.5	40	25.0	59	47.5	87	47.5	180.6
Mid-March Employment	10,853	12,974	19.5	10,871	-16.2	13,420	23.4	19,956	48.7	29,505	47.9	171.9
1st Quarter Wages (annualized - $ mil.)	244.7	319.8	30.7	290.9	-9.0	368.0	26.5	620.6	68.6	907.1	46.2	270.7
Payroll per Emp. 1st Q. (annualized)	22,546	24,652	9.3	26,762	8.6	27,425	2.5	31,096	13.4	30,745	-1.1	36.4
Annual Payroll ($ mil.)	246.7	303.7	23.1	273.1	-10.1	369.0	35.1	612.4	66.0	953.1	55.6	286.3
Establishments - 500-999 Emp. Number	32	31	-3.1	39	25.8	44	12.8	41	-6.8	44	7.3	37.5
Mid-March Employment	22,420	21,245	-5.2	26,911	26.7	31,668	17.7	29,969	-5.4	32,322	7.9	44.2
1st Quarter Wages (annualized - $ mil.)	548.7	550.2	0.3	754.8	37.2	912.6	20.9	936.8	2.7	973.7	3.9	77.5
Payroll per Emp. 1st Q. (annualized)	24,472	25,897	5.8	28,049	8.3	28,819	2.7	31,260	8.5	30,126	-3.6	23.1
Annual Payroll ($ mil.)	517.7	551.8	6.6	740.1	34.1	881.9	19.2	947.4	7.4	974.7	2.9	88.3
Estab. - 1000 or More Emp. Number	36	39	8.3	38	-2.6	39	2.6	41	5.1	43	4.9	19.4
Mid-March Employment	69,313	74,658	7.7	71,392	-4.4	72,185	1.1	76,762	6.3	81,023	5.6	16.9
1st Quarter Wages (annualized - $ mil.)	1,742.1	1,867.9	7.2	1,954.9*	4.7	2,090.1	6.9	2,402.4	14.9	2,635.5	9.7	51.3
Payroll per Emp. 1st Q. (annualized)	25,133	25,020	-0.4	27,383	9.4	28,955	5.7	31,297	8.1	32,528	3.9	29.4
Annual Payroll ($ mil.)	1,753.3	1,889.4	7.8	1,968.9	4.2	2,086.5	6.0	2,346.3	12.4	2,698.5	15.0	53.9

Source: County Business Patterns, U.S. Department of Commerce, Washington, D.C., for 1988 through 1993. Payroll per employee is calculated using mid-March employment and 1st Quarter wages, annualized. Annual payroll, also shown, may not equal the annualized 1st Quarter wages. Columns headed by a percent sign (%) indicate change from the previous year. *na* stands for not available. The symbol (D) indicates that data are withheld by the source to avoid disclosure of competitive information. A dash (-) indicates that data are not available or cannot be calculated.

ESTABLISHMENTS
Number

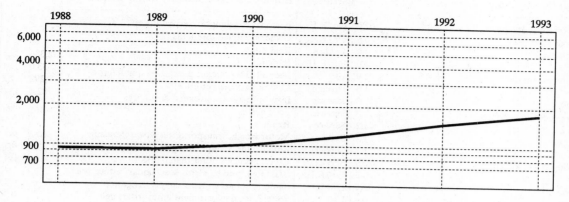

MID-MARCH EMPLOYMENT
Number

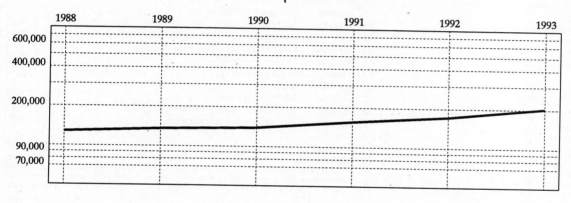

ANNUAL PAYROLL
$ million

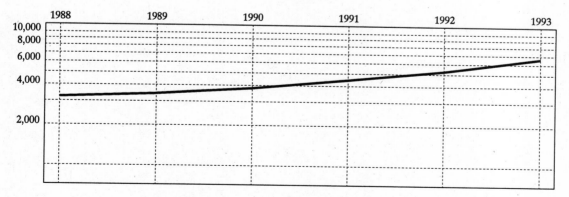

INPUTS AND OUTPUTS FOR INSURANCE CARRIERS - SIC GROUP 63

Economic Sector or Industry Providing Inputs	%	Sector	Economic Sector or Industry Buying Outputs	%	Sector
Insurance agents, brokers, & services	62.9	Fin/R.E.	Personal consumption expenditures	77.1	
Security & commodity brokers	6.8	Fin/R.E.	Owner-occupied dwellings	5.5	Fin/R.E.
Eating & drinking places	4.0	Trade	Real estate	3.6	Fin/R.E.
Real estate	4.0	Fin/R.E.	Banking	0.9	Fin/R.E.
Communications, except radio & TV	3.9	Util.	Federal Government purchases, nondefense	0.9	Fed Govt
Imports	1.8	Foreign	Electric services (utilities)	0.8	Util.
Commercial printing	1.3	Manufg.	Insurance agents, brokers, & services	0.7	Fin/R.E.
Computer & data processing services	1.3	Services	Feed grains	0.6	Agric.
Advertising	1.2	Services	Exports	0.5	Foreign
Hotels & lodging places	1.2	Services	Motor freight transportation & warehousing	0.5	Util.
Legal services	1.2	Services	Retail trade, except eating & drinking	0.5	Trade
Accounting, auditing & bookkeeping	0.9	Services	Credit agencies other than banks	0.4	Fin/R.E.
Banking	0.9	Fin/R.E.	S/L Govt. purch., elem. & secondary education	0.4	S/L Govt
U.S. Postal Service	0.9	Gov't	Sanitary services, steam supply, irrigation	0.4	Util.
Air transportation	0.6	Util.	State & local government enterprises, nec	0.3	Gov't
Credit agencies other than banks	0.6	Fin/R.E.	Water supply & sewage systems	0.3	Util.
Management & consulting services & labs	0.6	Services	Wholesale trade	0.3	Trade
Maintenance of nonfarm buildings nec	0.5	Constr.	Food grains	0.2	Agric.
Manifold business forms	0.5	Manufg.	Meat animals	0.2	Agric.
Motor freight transportation & warehousing	0.5	Util.	Petroleum refining	0.2	Manufg.
Petroleum refining	0.5	Manufg.	Religious organizations	0.2	Services
Photographic equipment & supplies	0.4	Manufg.	Air transportation	0.1	Util.
Transit & bus transportation	0.4	Util.	Arrangement of passenger transportation	0.1	Util.
Business services nec	0.3	Services	Equipment rental & leasing services	0.1	Services
Personnel supply services	0.3	Services	Freight forwarders	0.1	Util.
Wholesale trade	0.3	Trade	Industrial buildings	0.1	Constr.
Automotive rental & leasing, without drivers	0.2	Services	Office buildings	0.1	Constr.
Electric services (utilities)	0.2	Util.	Oil bearing crops	0.1	Agric.
Electronic computing equipment	0.2	Manufg.	Residential 1-unit structures, nonfarm	0.1	Constr.
Detective & protective services	0.1	Services	Transit & bus transportation	0.1	Util.
Electrical repair shops	0.1	Services			
Envelopes	0.1	Manufg.			
Manufacturing industries, nec	0.1	Manufg.			

Source: Benchmark Input-Output Accounts for the U.S. Economy, 1982, U.S. Department of Commerce, Washington, D.C., July 1991. Data, as reported in the source, are organized by the 1977 SIC structure in use in 1982 but have been matched, as closely as is possible, to the 1987 SIC structure used in this book. Activities with the same percentage are sorted alphabetically by name of activity.

OCCUPATIONS EMPLOYED BY MEDICAL SERVICE AND HEALTH INSURANCE

Occupation	% of Total 1994	Change to 2005	Occupation	% of Total 1994	Change to 2005
Insurance adjusters, examiners, & investigators	7.9	16.2	Systems analysts	2.8	77.0
Insurance claims clerks	7.5	10.6	Managers & administrators nec	2.1	10.6
General office clerks	5.6	-5.6	Accountants & auditors	2.0	10.6
Adjustment clerks	5.6	49.4	Registered nurses	2.0	64.7
Insurance policy processing clerks	4.9	10.6	Bookkeeping, accounting, & auditing clerks	1.9	-17.0
Clerical supervisors & managers	4.9	13.2	Sales & related workers nec	1.6	10.6
Secretaries, ex legal & medical	4.3	0.7	Receptionists & information clerks	1.5	10.6
Claims examiners, insurance	4.0	10.6	Mail clerks, ex machine operators, postal service	1.2	-20.3
Insurance sales workers	3.8	-4.3	Health professionals & paraprofessionals nec	1.2	10.6
Clerical support workers nec	3.3	-11.5	Computer operators, ex peripheral equipment	1.2	-37.1
Data entry keyers, ex composing	3.0	-18.3	File clerks	1.2	-44.7
Computer programmers	2.9	-10.4	Correspondence clerks	1.2	-22.5
Management support workers nec	2.9	32.8	Operations research analysts	1.1	44.0
General managers & top executives	2.8	5.0	Underwriters	1.1	37.2

Sources: *Industry-Occupation Matrix*, Bureau of Labor Statistics. These data relate to one or more 3-digit SIC industry groups rather than to a single 4-digit SIC. The change reported for each occupation to the year 2005 is a percent of growth or decline as estimated by the Bureau of Labor Statistics. The abbreviation *nec* stands for not elsewhere classified.

U.S. AND STATE DATA ON INDUSTRY REVENUES AND OTHER ACCOUNTS FOR 1992

State	No. of Estab.	Employ- ment	Payroll ($ mil.)	Revenues ($ mil.)	Empl./ Estab.	Revenue/ Estab. ($)	Payroll/ Estab. ($)	Revenue/ Empl. ($)	Payroll/ Empl. ($)
UNITED STATES	1,746	196,637	6,078.7	124,813.2	113	71,485,208	3,481,474	634,739	30,913
California	251	23,269	796.6	23,231.0	93	92,553,789	3,173,725	998,367	34,235
Colorado	33	2,762	69.5	898.5	84	27,227,152	2,106,394	325,306	25,167
Florida	96	9,529	296.1	4,077.8	99	42,477,396	3,083,958	427,939	31,069
Georgia	30	1,908	58.0	1,271.5	64	42,382,333	1,933,967	666,389	30,408
Illinois	81	8,897	305.8	4,498.2	110	55,533,877	3,775,235	505,591	34,370
Indiana	19	1,737	58.1	1,150.6	91	60,560,211	3,056,579	662,432	33,434
Maryland	36	-	(D)	(D)	(D)	(D)	(D)	(D)	(D)
Massachusetts	53	8,245	278.0	5,367.1	156	101,266,491	5,244,925	650,955	33,715
Michigan	63	9,980	342.8	7,587.7	158	120,438,889	5,441,016	760,286	34,347
Minnesota	32	3,500	110.9	1,158.5	109	36,203,469	3,466,187	331,003	31,691
Missouri	45	4,654	162.1	2,995.6	103	66,569,556	3,601,444	643,668	34,823
New Jersey	50	4,460	148.6	4,091.2	89	81,823,080	2,971,140	917,299	33,309
New York	83	19,718	590.6	13,667.6	238	164,670,470	7,115,277	693,156	29,951
North Carolina	25	2,442	74.6	1,563.8	98	62,551,680	2,984,360	640,373	30,552
Ohio	59	4,916	151.0	2,832.8	83	48,013,780	2,558,949	576,243	30,712
Pennsylvania	75	17,700	533.3	10,017.0	236	133,559,893	7,111,080	565,932	30,132
Tennessee	25	-	(D)	(D)	(D)	(D)	(D)	(D)	(D)
Texas	82	5,582	175.6	3,724.2	68	45,417,268	2,140,866	667,183	31,449
Virginia	46	4,602	142.2	3,017.5	100	65,597,587	3,090,435	655,691	30,891
Washington	50	5,292	151.2	2,721.9	106	54,438,580	3,023,420	514,348	28,566
Wisconsin	52	6,074	134.6	2,153.9	117	41,421,288	2,589,346	354,611	22,168

Source: 1992 Economic Census, U.S. Department of Commerce, Washington, D.C. This is the only table that shows revenue data as collected by the Bureau of the Census in an Economic Census. The symbol (D) indicates that data are withheld by the source to avoid disclosure of competitive information. A dash (-) indicates that data are not available or cannot be calculated.

ESTABLISHMENTS 1992 - STATE AND REGIONAL CONCENTRATION

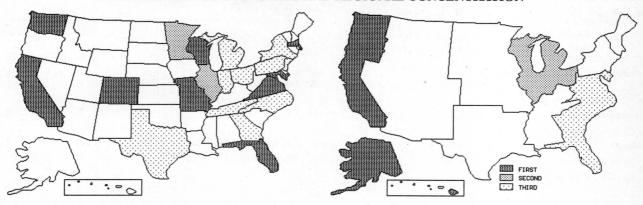

EMPLOYMENT 1992 - STATE AND REGIONAL CONCENTRATION

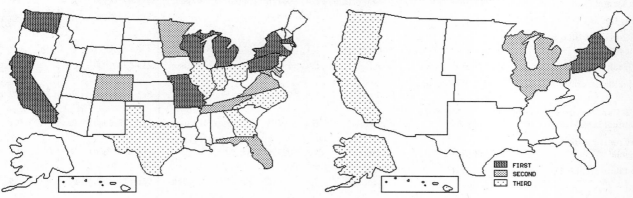

REVENUES 1992 - STATE AND REGIONAL CONCENTRATION

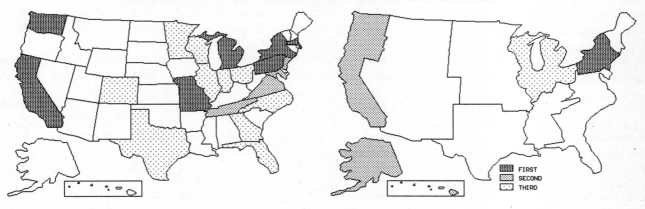

States with the darkest shading indicate those states which have proportionately more establishments, employment, or revenues than would be indicated by the state's population. States with light shading are states with proportionately fewer establishments, less employment, and lower revenues than population distribution. States shaded grey are within 15 percent of the state's population proportion in these categories. States for which no data are available are shown as average (grey). *Regions* are shaded to indicate absolute rank in the category. If no data for the category are available, establishment counts are used to shade the regions. Source of the data is the table on the facing page.

LEADING COMPANIES - SIC 6321 - Accident and Health Insurance

Number shown: **100**   Total sales/assets ($ mil): **64,430**   Total employment (000): **301.6**

Company Name	Address				CEO Name	Phone	Co. Type	Sales/Assets ($ mil)	Empl. (000)
Kaiser Foundation Health Plan Inc.	1 Kaiser Plz.	Oakland	CA	94612	David M. Lawrence	510-271-5910	R	10,762 TA	86.8
Blue Cross and Blue Shield of Massachusetts Inc.	100 Summer St.	Boston	MA	02110	William C. Van Faasen	617-832-5000	R	3,595 TA	5.8
Blue Cross and Blue Shield of Michigan	600 Lafayette E.	Detroit	MI	48226	Richard E. Whitmer	313-225-9000	R	2,626 TA	6.5
Blue Cross of California	P.O. Box 70000	Van Nuys	CA	91470	Leonard D. Schaeffer	818-703-2345	R	2,424 TA	3.6
FHP International Corp.	9900 Talbert Ave.	Fountain Valley	CA	92708	Westcott W. Price III	714-378-5000	P	2,169 TA	14.0
Humana Inc.	P.O. Box 1438	Louisville	KY	40201	David A. Jones	502-580-1000	P	1,957 TA	11.0
Wellpoint Health Networks Inc.	21555 Oxnard St.	Woodland Hills	CA	91367	Leonard D. Schaeffer	818-703-4000	P	1,927 TA	2.7
Delta Dental Plan of California	P.O. Box 7736	San Francisco	CA	94120	William T. Ward	415-972-8300	R	1,800 TA	1.6
Veritus Inc.	120 5th Ave.	Pittsburgh	PA	15222	Eugene J. Barone	412-255-7000	R	1,553 TA	2.8
Blue Cross and Blue Shield of Connecticut Inc.	370 Bassett Rd.	North Haven	CT	06473	John F. Croweak	203-239-4911	R	1,477 TA	2.3
U.S. Healthcare Inc.	P.O. Box 1109	Blue Bell	PA	19422	Leonard Abramson	215-628-4800	P	1,464 TA	4.3
UniHealth America	4100 W. Alameda Ave.	Burbank	CA	91505	Terry Hartshorn	818-566-6300	R	1,379 TA	13.0
Health Care Service Corporation, A Mutual Legal Reserve Co.	233 N. Michigan Ave.	Chicago	IL	60601	S. Martin Hickman	312-938-6000	R	1,314 TA	5.0
Blue Cross and Blue Shield of Virginia	P.O. Box 27401	Richmond	VA	23279	Norwood H. Davis Jr.	804-354-7000	R	1,261 TA	3.9
Foundation Health Corp.	3400 Data Dr.	Rancho Cordova	CA	95670	Daniel D. Crowley	916-631-5000	P	1,235 TA	5.0
Blue Cross and Blue Shield of Oregon	P.O. Box 1271	Portland	OR	97207	Richard L. Woolworth	503-225-5221	R	1,230 TA	2.1
Blue Cross and Blue Shield of Florida Inc.	P.O. Box 44269	Jacksonville	FL	32231	William E. Flaherty	904-791-6111	R	1,173 TA	5.8
PacifiCare Health Systems Inc.	5995 Plaza Dr.	Cypress	CA	90630	Alan R. Hoops	714-952-1121	P	1,105 TA	3.9
Franciscan Health System	1 MacIntyre Dr.	Aston	PA	19014	Ronald R. Aldrich	215-358-3950	R	1,013 OR	12.0
Blue Cross and Blue Shield of New Jersey Inc.	3 Penn Plaza E.	Newark	NJ	07105	William J. Marino	201-466-4000	R	993 TA	3.0
Independence Blue Cross	1901 Market St.	Philadelphia	PA	19103	G. Fred DiBona Jr.	215-241-2400	R	939 TA	2.3
Blue Cross and Blue Shield of Missouri	1831 Chestnut St.	St. Louis	MO	63103	Roy Heimburger	314-923-4444	R	925 TA	1.6
Kaiser Foundation Health Plan of the Northwest	3600 N. Interstate Ave	Portland	OR	97227	Michael Katcher	503-280-2000	S	910 TA*	7.4
Health Systems International Inc.	21600 Oxnard St.	Woodland Hills	CA	91367	Roger Greaves	818-719-6732	P	894 TA	2.7
Blue Cross and Blue Shield of North Carolina	P.O. Box 2291	Durham	NC	27702	Kenneth C. Otis II	919-489-7431	R	771 TA	2.2
FHP Inc.	9900 Talbert Ave.	Fountain Valley	CA	92708	Westcott W. Price III	714-963-7233	S	746 TA	11.0
Blue Cross and Blue Shield of Maryland Inc.	10455 Mill Run Cir.	Owings Mills	MD	21117	William L. Jews	410-581-3000	R	736 TA	3.9

Company type codes: P - Public, R - Private, S - Subsidiary, D - Division, J - Joint Venture, A - Affiliate, G - Group. If the dollar values shown are not sales, the following codes apply: TA - Total Assets; OR - Operating Revenues; GB - Gross Billings. * - estimated dollar value. < - less than. *na* - not available.

Continued on next page.

LEADING COMPANIES - SIC 6321 - Accident and Health Insurance
Continued

Company Name	Address				CEO Name	Phone	Co. Type	Sales/Assets ($ mil)	Empl. (000)
Blue Cross and Blue Shield of Ohio	2060 E. 9th St.	Cleveland	OH	44115	John Burry Jr.	216-687-7000	R	736 TA	3.0
Physician Corporation of America	6101 Blue Lagoon Dr.	Miami	FL	33126	E. Stanley Kardatzke	305-267-6633	P	645 TA	3.6
Blue Cross and Blue Shield United of Wisconsin	1515 N. River Ctr. Dr.	Milwaukee	WI	53212	Thomas R. Hefty	414-226-5000	R	608 TA	2.4
Blue Cross and Blue Shield of Minnesota	P.O. Box 64560	St. Paul	MN	55164	Andrew Czajkowski	612-456-8786	S	573 TA	3.0
United Wisconsin Services Inc.	401 W. Michigan St.	Milwaukee	WI	53203	Thomas R. Hefty	414-226-5756	P	556 TA	1.1
Healthsource Inc.	2 College Park Dr.	Hooksett	NH	03106	Norman C. Payson	603-268-7000	P	424 TA	1.8
Blue Cross of Washington and Alaska	P.O. Box 327	Seattle	WA	98111	Betty Woods	206-670-4000	R	396 TA	1.2
Community Health Plan	1201 Troy-Schenectady	Latham	NY	12110	John Baackes	518-783-1864	R	379 TA	3.0
Blue Cross and Blue Shield of the Rochester Area	150 E. Maine St.	Rochester	NY	14647	Howard Berman	716-454-1700	R	360 TA	2.4
Kaiser Foundation Health Plan of Colorado	10350 E. Dakota Ave.	Denver	CO	80231	R. Michael Alexander	303-344-7200	S	360 TA*	2.9
Blue Cross and Blue Shield of Georgia Inc.	P.O. Box 4445	Atlanta	GA	30302	Richard D. Shirk	404-842-8000	R	357 TA	1.8
RightCHOICE Managed Care Inc.	1831 Chestnut St.	St. Louis	MO	63103	Roy R. Heimburger	314-923-4444	P	354 TA	1.6
Blue Cross and Blue Shield of the National Capital Area	550 12th St. S.W.	Washington	DC	20065	Larry C. Glasscock	202-479-8000	S	343 TA	1.8
Kaiser Foundation Health Plan of the Mid-Atlantic States Inc.	2101 E. Jefferson St.	Rockville	MD	20852	Alan J. Silverstone	301-816-2424	S	340 TA*	2.8
TakeCare Inc.	2300 Clayton Rd.	Concord	CA	94520	Christobel Selecky	510-246-1300	S	336 TA	1.1
Mercy Healthcare Arizona	350 W. Thomas Rd.	Phoenix	AZ	85001	Thomas F. Zenty III	602-285-3000	D	333 TA	3.3
Arkansas Blue Cross and Blue Shield	P.O. Box 2181	Little Rock	AR	72203	Robert L. Shoptaw	501-378-2000	R	333 TA	1.3
Coventry Corp.	53 Century Blvd.	Nashville	TN	37214	Philip Hertik	615-391-2440	P	332 TA	2.8
Blue Cross and Blue Shield of Rhode Island	444 Westminster St.	Providence	RI	02903	Douglas J. McIntosh	401-272-8500	R	282 TA	1.5
Blue Cross and Blue Shield of South Carolina	I-20 and Alpine Rd.	Columbia	SC	29219	M. Edward Sellers	803-788-0222	R	278 TA	3.5
Blue Cross and Blue Shield of Kansas City	P.O. Box 419169	Kansas City	MO	64141	Richard P. Krecker	816-395-2222	R	270 TA	1.1
Mid Atlantic Medical Services Inc.	4 Taft Ct.	Rockville	MD	20850	George T. Jochum	301-294-5140	P	269 TA	0.9
Compcare Health Services Insurance Corp.	P.O. Box 2947	Milwaukee	WI	53201	Jeffrey J. Nohl	414-226-6744	S	253 TA	0.3
ValueRx Pharmacy Program Inc.	1825 S. Woodward Ave.	Bloomfield Hills	MI	48302	Stephen D. Linehan	313-338-4466	S	252 TA	0.6
Westmoreland Health System	532 W. Pittsburgh St.	Greensburg	PA	15601	Joseph J. Peluso	412-832-5040	R	250 TA*	1.8

Company type codes: P - Public, R - Private, S - Subsidiary, D - Division, J - Joint Venture, A - Affiliate, G - Group. If the dollar values shown are not sales, the following codes apply: TA - Total Assets; OR - Operating Revenues; GB - Gross Billings. * - estimated dollar value. < - less than. *na* - not available.

Continued on next page.

LEADING COMPANIES - SIC 6321 - Accident and Health Insurance

Continued

Company Name	Address				CEO Name	Phone	Co. Type	Sales/Assets ($ mil)	Empl. (000)
Blue Cross and Blue Shield of Mississippi	P.O. Box 1043	Jackson	MS	39215	Richard J. Hale	601-932-3704	R	225 TA	1.0
Sierra Health Services Inc.	P.O. Box 15645	Las Vegas	NV	89114	Anthony M. Marlon	702-646-8100	P	223 TA	1.6
Group Health Service of Oklahoma Inc.	P.O. Box 3283	Tulsa	OK	74102	Ralph S. Rhoades	918-560-3500	R	208 TA	0.9
Physicians Health Services Inc.	120 Hawley Ln.	Trumbull	CT	06611	Michael E. Herbert	203-381-6400	P	207 TA	0.5
Blue Cross and Blue Shield of Delaware Inc.	P.O. Box 1991	Wilmington	DE	19899	Robert C. Cole Jr.	302-421-3000	R	206 TA	0.8
Kaiser Foundation Health Plan of Texas	12720 Hillcrest Rd.	Dallas	TX	75230	Sharon Flaherty	214-458-5000	S	205 TA	1.0
ODS Health Plan	315 S.W. 5th Ave.	Portland	OR	97204	A.G. Lindstrand	503-228-6554	S	200 TA	0.3
Constitution HealthCare Inc.	370 Bassett Rd.	North Haven	CT	06473	J.L. Mueller	203-234-2011	R	190 TA	0.2
Sanus Texas Health Plan Inc.	4500 Fuller Dr.	Irving	TX	75038	Steve P. Yerxa	214-650-5500	S	185 TA	0.2
Comprehensive Health Services Inc.	6500 John C. Lodge	Detroit	MI	48202	James W. Patton	313-875-4200	R	180 TA	0.5
Central States Health and Life Company of Omaha	P.O. Box 34350	Omaha	NE	68134	W. Michael Kizer	402-397-1111	R	175 TA	0.6
Oxford Health Plans Inc.	320 Post Rd.	Darien	CT	06820	Stephen F. Wiggins	203-656-1442	P	167 TA	0.4
Louisiana Health Service and Indemnity Co.	P.O. Box 98029	Baton Rouge	LA	70898	P.J. Mills	504-295-3307	R	163 TA	0.7
Blue Cross and Blue Shield of Arizona Inc.	P.O. Box 13466	Phoenix	AZ	85002	Robert B. Bulla	602-864-4100	R	163 TA	0.9
PacifiCare of Oregon	5 Centerpointe Dr.	Lake Oswego	OR	97035	Patrick E. Feyen	503-620-9324	S	162 TA	0.2
HealthPlus of Michigan Inc.	P.O. Box 1700	Flint	MI	48501	Paul A. Fuhs	313-230-2000	R	160 TA*	0.2
Kaiser Foundation Health Plan of Georgia Inc.	3355 Lenox Rd NE #1000	Atlanta	GA	30326	Christopher Binkley	404-233-0555	S	160 TA*	1.4
Physicians Health Services of Connecticut Inc.	120 Hawley Ln.	Trumbull	CT	06611	Michael E. Herbert	203-381-6400	S	160 TA	0.4
Intergroup Healthcare Corp.	1010 N Finance Ctr. Dr	Tucson	AZ	85710	Charles F. Barrett	602-721-4444	P	156 TA	0.6
New Hampshire-Vermont Health Service	3000 Goffs Falls Rd.	Manchester	NH	03111	Joseph L. Marcille	603-695-7000	R	156 TA	0.8
Good Health Plan of Washington	1501 4th Ave.	Seattle	WA	98101	Gerald L. Coe	206-622-6111	S	150 TA	0.3
PCA Health Plans of Florida Inc.	6101 Blue Lagoon Dr.	Miami	FL	33126	Peter Killissanly	305-267-6633	S	150 TA*	1.2
Value Rx Pharmacy Program Inc.	30445 Northwestern Hwy	Farmington	MI	48334	Barry Smith	810-539-0220	S	150 TA	0.3
Delta Dental Plan of New Jersey	P.O. Box 222	Parsippany	NJ	07054	Robert J. Ott	201-334-6300	R	145 TA	0.2
Southeastern Mutual Insurance Co.	9901 Linn Station Rd.	Louisville	KY	40223	James P. Murphy	502-423-2011	R	140 TA*	0.7
Kaiser Foundation Health Plan of North Carolina	3120 Highwoods Blvd.	Raleigh	NC	27604	Theodore M. Carpenter	919-981-6000	S	130 TA*	1.1
Michigan HMO Inc.	1155 Brewery Park Blvd	Detroit	MI	48207	Ronald Dobbins	313-393-0200	R	129 TA	0.2

Company type codes: P - Public, R - Private, S - Subsidiary, D - Division, J - Joint Venture, A - Affiliate, G - Group. If the dollar values shown are not sales, the following codes apply: TA - Total Assets; OR - Operating Revenues; GB - Gross Billings. * - estimated dollar value. < - less than. *na* - not available.

Continued on next page.

LEADING COMPANIES - SIC 6321 - Accident and Health Insurance
Continued

Company Name	Address				CEO Name	Phone	Co. Type	Sales/Assets ($ mil)	Empl. (000)
Maxicare Health Plans Inc.	1149 S. Broadway St.	Los Angeles	CA	90015	Peter J. Ratican	213-765-2000	P	129 TA	0.4
M.D. Enterprises of Connecticut Inc.	6 Devine St.	North Haven	CT	06473	Douglas A. Hayward	203-230-1000	R	125 TA	0.3
Keystone Health Plan Central	P.O. Box 898812	Camp Hill	PA	17089	Joseph Pfister	717-975-7458	S	120 TA	0.1
Humana Health Plan of Ohio Inc.	8044 Montgomery Rd 460	Cincinnati	OH	45236	William Wakefield	513-792-0511	S	110 TA	0.8
Memphis Hospital Service and Surgical Association Inc.	P.O. Box 98	Memphis	TN	38101	Gene Holcomb	901-544-2111	R	110 TA	0.5
Cost Care Inc.	660 Newport Center Dr.	Huntington Beach	CA	92660	Lawrence Goelman	714-729-4655	S	100 TA	0.8
Rocky Mountain HMO Inc.	P.O. Box 60129	Grand Junction	CO	81506	Michael J. Weber	303-244-7760	R	100 TA	0.2
Medica	P.O. Box 9310	Minneapolis	MN	55440	Kaye J. Ehlen	612-992-2900	D	91 TA	0.6
Bisbee-Baldwin Corp.	P.O. Box 1050	Jacksonville	FL	32201	Ron Langley	904-353-6411	R	86 TA*	<0.1
Qual-Med Washington Health Plan Inc. Puget Sound Div.	2331 130th Ave.	Bellevue	WA	98005	Chris Du Laney	206-869-3500	D	85 TA	0.1
Chesapeake Health Plan Inc.	814 Light St.	Baltimore	MD	21230	Leon Kaplan	410-539-8622	S	78 TA	0.2
WellCare Management Group Inc.	P.O. Box 4059	Kingston	NY	12401	Edward A. Ullmann	914-338-4110	P	76 TA	0.4
Group Health Northwest	P.O. Box 204	Spokane	WA	99210	Henry S. Berman	509-838-9100	S	75 TA	0.8
WellCare of New York Inc.	130 Meadow Ave.	Newburgh	NY	12550	Edward Ullmann	914-566-0700	S	74 TA	0.4
Healthsource Maine Inc.	P.O. Box 447	Freeport	ME	04032	Richard M. White	207-865-6161	S	71 TA	0.2
Independent Health Association	511 Farber Lakes Dr.	Williamsville	NY	14221	Frank Colantuono	716-631-3001	R	64 TA*	0.5
American Prepaid Professional Services Inc.	8800 Roswell Rd.	Atlanta	GA	30350	David R. Klock	404-998-8936	S	63 TA	0.2
APPS Dental Inc.	8800 Roswell Rd.	Atlanta	GA	30350	David R. Klock	404-998-8936	P	63 TA	0.2
Total Health Care Inc.	1501 Division St.	Baltimore	MD	21217	Lawrence Peaco	410-383-8300	R	59 TA	0.4
Health New England Inc.	1 Monarch Pl.	Springfield	MA	01144	Richard F. Belloff	413-787-4000	R	56 TA	0.1
Community Care Network Inc.	5251 Viewridge Ct.	San Diego	CA	92123	Jim Buncher	619-278-2273	S	55 TA	0.9

Source: *Ward's Business Directory of U.S. Private and Public Companies*, 1996. Company type codes: P - Public, R - Private, S - Subsidiary, D - Division, J - Joint Venture, A - Affiliate, G - Group. If the dollar values shown are not sales, the following codes apply: TA - Total Assets; OR - Operating Revenues; GB - Gross Billings. * - estimated dollar value. < - less than; *na* - not available.

SIC 6330

FIRE, MARINE, AND CASUALTY INSURANCE

This industry includes all establishments whose primary activity is the underwriting of fire, marine, and casualty insurance. The establishments may be owned by stockholders, policyholders, or other carriers. Specific categories include agricultural insurance (crop and livestock); assessment associations for fire, marine, and casualty insurance; associated factory mutuals for these categories; automobile, boiler, and burglary and theft insurance; contact lens insurance; the Federal Crop Insurance Corporation; insurance carriers for these categories, including mutual insurance; plate glass insurance; property damage insurance; reciprocal interinsurance exchanges for these categories; and workers' compensation insurance.

ESTABLISHMENTS, EMPLOYMENT, AND PAYROLL

	1988	1989 Value	%	1990 Value	%	1991 Value	%	1992 Value	%	1993 Value	%	% change 88-93
All Establishments	16,178	17,330	7.1	18,335	5.8	21,737	18.6	21,722	-0.1	19,055	-12.3	17.8
Mid-March Employment	518,074	524,707	1.3	532,536	1.5	569,584	7.0	584,236	2.6	585,278	0.2	13.0
1st Quarter Wages (annualized - $ mil.)	14,821.0	15,316.5	3.3	17,077.0	11.5	19,288.9	13.0	20,813.1	7.9	21,381.0	2.7	44.3
Payroll per Emp. 1st Q. (annualized)	28,608	29,191	2.0	32,067	9.9	33,865	5.6	35,624	5.2	36,531	2.5	27.7
Annual Payroll ($ mil.)	14,920.0	15,318.0	2.7	16,979.5	10.8	19,115.6	12.6	20,642.2	8.0	21,586.8	4.6	44.7
Establishments - 1-4 Emp. Number	10,473	11,471	9.5	12,714	10.8	15,489	21.8	15,274	-1.4	12,667	-17.1	20.9
Mid-March Employment	19,329	20,846	7.8	22,025	5.7	26,517	20.4	26,150	-1.4	21,072	-19.4	9.0
1st Quarter Wages (annualized - $ mil.)	897.6	835.5	-6.9	1,122.1	34.3	1,220.0	8.7	1,306.5	7.1	1,293.1	-1.0	44.1
Payroll per Emp. 1st Q. (annualized)	46,437	40,080	-13.7	50,944	27.1	46,007	-9.7	49,963	8.6	61,368	22.8	32.2
Annual Payroll ($ mil.)	936.0	919.0	-1.8	1,165.0	26.8	1,287.6	10.5	1,402.5	8.9	1,361.8	-2.9	45.5
Establishments - 5-9 Emp. Number	1,889	1,946	3.0	1,773	-8.9	1,993	12.4	1,997	0.2	1,810	-9.4	-4.2
Mid-March Employment	12,127	12,492	3.0	11,408	-8.7	(D)	-	12,958	-	11,898	-8.2	-1.9
1st Quarter Wages (annualized - $ mil.)	402.7	386.6	-4.0	377.9	-2.3	(D)	-	441.8	-	444.0	0.5	10.3
Payroll per Emp. 1st Q. (annualized)	33,205	30,947	-6.8	33,123	7.0	(D)	-	34,092	-	37,315	9.5	12.4
Annual Payroll ($ mil.)	390.7	381.0	-2.5	367.4	-3.6	(D)	-	449.8	-	456.1	1.4	16.7
Establishments - 10-19 Emp. Number	1,019	1,035	1.6	936	-9.6	1,093	16.8	1,215	11.2	1,244	2.4	22.1
Mid-March Employment	13,924	14,150	1.6	12,805	-9.5	14,818	15.7	16,499	11.3	16,938	2.7	21.6
1st Quarter Wages (annualized - $ mil.)	405.5	404.8	-0.2	389.2	-3.9	479.5	23.2	571.7	19.2	604.5	5.7	49.1
Payroll per Emp. 1st Q. (annualized)	29,121	28,607	-1.8	30,392	6.2	32,358	6.5	34,649	7.1	35,692	3.0	22.6
Annual Payroll ($ mil.)	401.2	410.4	2.3	388.7	-5.3	483.0	24.2	576.2	19.3	624.0	8.3	55.5
Establishments - 20-49 Emp. Number	1,019	1,069	4.9	1,068	-0.1	1,224	14.6	1,230	0.5	1,296	5.4	27.2
Mid-March Employment	31,926	33,875	6.1	33,592	-0.8	38,624	15.0	39,105	1.2	41,904	7.2	31.3
1st Quarter Wages (annualized - $ mil.)	871.7	966.7	10.9	1,057.0	9.3	1,278.7	21.0	1,391.4	8.8	1,482.3	6.5	70.0
Payroll per Emp. 1st Q. (annualized)	27,304	28,537	4.5	31,466	10.3	33,106	5.2	35,580	7.5	35,374	-0.6	29.6
Annual Payroll ($ mil.)	867.9	956.9	10.2	1,032.4	7.9	1,249.3	21.0	1,344.6	7.6	1,496.5	11.3	72.4
Establishments - 50-99 Emp. Number	719	752	4.6	777	3.3	828	6.6	870	5.1	887	2.0	23.4
Mid-March Employment	52,680	54,772	4.0	56,183	2.6	59,729	6.3	62,093	4.0	62,332	0.4	18.3
1st Quarter Wages (annualized - $ mil.)	1,427.6	1,501.6	5.2	1,718.0	14.4	1,938.1	12.8	2,169.4	11.9	2,196.9	1.3	53.9
Payroll per Emp. 1st Q. (annualized)	27,100	27,416	1.2	30,578	11.5	32,448	6.1	34,937	7.7	35,245	0.9	30.1
Annual Payroll ($ mil.)	1,416.4	1,484.1	4.8	1,696.5	14.3	1,895.8	11.7	2,147.5	13.3	2,243.8	4.5	58.4
Establishments - 100-249 Emp. Number	670	658	-1.8	649	-1.4	668	2.9	672	0.6	687	2.2	2.5
Mid-March Employment	102,804	100,007	-2.7	98,699	-1.3	101,837	3.2	103,022	1.2	105,291	2.2	2.4
1st Quarter Wages (annualized - $ mil.)	2,773.5	2,778.2	0.2	2,993.4	7.7	3,268.1	9.2	3,552.1	8.7	3,569.1	0.5	28.7
Payroll per Emp. 1st Q. (annualized)	26,979	27,780	3.0	30,328	9.2	32,092	5.8	34,479	7.4	33,897	-1.7	25.6
Annual Payroll ($ mil.)	2,745.9	2,739.3	-0.2	2,954.6	7.9	3,186.9	7.9	3,449.0	8.2	3,606.1	4.6	31.3
Establishments - 250-499 Emp. Number	201	212	5.5	235	10.8	236	0.4	252	6.8	257	2.0	27.9
Mid-March Employment	72,115	74,993	4.0	83,451	11.3	83,808	0.4	89,255	6.5	90,422	1.3	25.4
1st Quarter Wages (annualized - $ mil.)	1,897.6	2,125.2	12.0	2,553.6	20.2	2,697.0	5.6	3,052.8	13.2	2,979.6	-2.4	57.0
Payroll per Emp. 1st Q. (annualized)	26,314	28,338	7.7	30,600	8.0	32,181	5.2	34,203	6.3	32,952	-3.7	25.2
Annual Payroll ($ mil.)	1,925.0	2,110.4	9.6	2,505.3	18.7	2,650.9	5.8	2,985.0	12.6	3,049.7	2.2	58.4
Establishments - 500-999 Emp. Number	117	116	-0.9	109	-6.0	130	19.3	132	1.5	125	-5.3	6.8
Mid-March Employment	81,380	78,854	-3.1	75,353	-4.4	88,326	17.2	87,958	-0.4	81,683	-7.1	0.4
1st Quarter Wages (annualized - $ mil.)	2,120.9	2,082.4	-1.8	2,176.3	4.5	2,848.1	30.9	2,978.7	4.6	2,815.0	-5.5	32.7
Payroll per Emp. 1st Q. (annualized)	26,061	26,408	1.3	28,881	9.4	32,245	11.6	33,866	5.0	34,462	1.8	32.2
Annual Payroll ($ mil.)	2,147.5	2,066.9	-3.8	2,150.3	4.0	2,833.7	31.8	2,917.2	2.9	2,810.9	-3.6	30.9
Estab. - 1000 or More Emp. Number	71	71	-	74	4.2	76	2.7	80	5.3	82	2.5	15.5
Mid-March Employment	131,789	134,718	2.2	139,020	3.2	(D)	-	147,196	-	153,738	4.4	16.7
1st Quarter Wages (annualized - $ mil.)	4,023.9	4,235.5	5.3	4,689.6	10.7	(D)	-	5,348.8	-	5,996.5	12.1	49.0
Payroll per Emp. 1st Q. (annualized)	30,533	31,440	3.0	33,734	7.3	(D)	-	36,338	-	39,005	7.3	27.7
Annual Payroll ($ mil.)	4,089.3	4,250.0	3.9	4,719.2	11.0	(D)	-	5,370.4	-	5,937.9	10.6	45.2

Source: County Business Patterns, U.S. Department of Commerce, Washington, D.C., for 1988 through 1993. Payroll per employee is calculated using mid-March employment and 1st Quarter wages, annualized. Annual payroll, also shown, may not equal the annualized 1st Quarter wages. Columns headed by a percent sign (%) indicate change from the previous year. *na* stands for not available. The symbol (D) indicates that data are withheld by the source to avoid disclosure of competitive information. A dash (-) indicates that data are not available or cannot be calculated.

ESTABLISHMENTS
Number

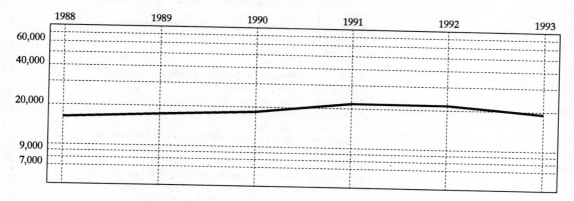

MID-MARCH EMPLOYMENT
Number

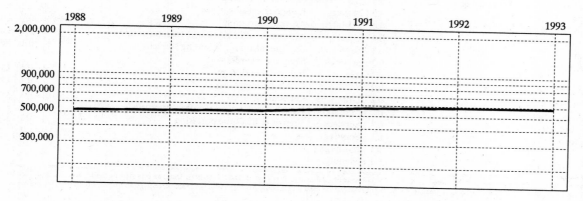

ANNUAL PAYROLL
$ million

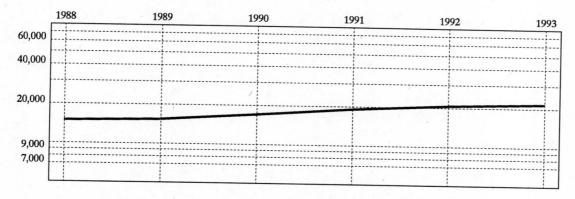

INPUTS AND OUTPUTS FOR INSURANCE CARRIERS - SIC GROUP 63

Economic Sector or Industry Providing Inputs	%	Sector	Economic Sector or Industry Buying Outputs	%	Sector
Insurance agents, brokers, & services	62.9	Fin/R.E.	Personal consumption expenditures	77.1	
Security & commodity brokers	6.8	Fin/R.E.	Owner-occupied dwellings	5.5	Fin/R.E.
Eating & drinking places	4.0	Trade	Real estate	3.6	Fin/R.E.
Real estate	4.0	Fin/R.E.	Banking	0.9	Fin/R.E.
Communications, except radio & TV	3.9	Util.	Federal Government purchases, nondefense	0.9	Fed Govt
Imports	1.8	Foreign	Electric services (utilities)	0.8	Util.
Commercial printing	1.3	Manufg.	Insurance agents, brokers, & services	0.7	Fin/R.E.
Computer & data processing services	1.3	Services	Feed grains	0.6	Agric.
Advertising	1.2	Services	Exports	0.5	Foreign
Hotels & lodging places	1.2	Services	Motor freight transportation & warehousing	0.5	Util.
Legal services	1.2	Services	Retail trade, except eating & drinking	0.5	Trade
Accounting, auditing & bookkeeping	0.9	Services	Credit agencies other than banks	0.4	Fin/R.E.
Banking	0.9	Fin/R.E.	S/L Govt. purch., elem. & secondary education	0.4	S/L Govt
U.S. Postal Service	0.9	Gov't	Sanitary services, steam supply, irrigation	0.4	Util.
Air transportation	0.6	Util.	State & local government enterprises, nec	0.3	Gov't
Credit agencies other than banks	0.6	Fin/R.E.	Water supply & sewage systems	0.3	Util.
Management & consulting services & labs	0.6	Services	Wholesale trade	0.3	Trade
Maintenance of nonfarm buildings nec	0.5	Constr.	Food grains	0.2	Agric.
Manifold business forms	0.5	Manufg.	Meat animals	0.2	Agric.
Motor freight transportation & warehousing	0.5	Util.	Petroleum refining	0.2	Manufg.
Petroleum refining	0.5	Manufg.	Religious organizations	0.2	Services
Photographic equipment & supplies	0.4	Manufg.	Air transportation	0.1	Util.
Transit & bus transportation	0.4	Util.	Arrangement of passenger transportation	0.1	Util.
Business services nec	0.3	Services	Equipment rental & leasing services	0.1	Services
Personnel supply services	0.3	Services	Freight forwarders	0.1	Util.
Wholesale trade	0.3	Trade	Industrial buildings	0.1	Constr.
Automotive rental & leasing, without drivers	0.2	Services	Office buildings	0.1	Constr.
Electric services (utilities)	0.2	Util.	Oil bearing crops	0.1	Agric.
Electronic computing equipment	0.2	Manufg.	Residential 1-unit structures, nonfarm	0.1	Constr.
Detective & protective services	0.1	Services	Transit & bus transportation	0.1	Util.
Electrical repair shops	0.1	Services			
Envelopes	0.1	Manufg.			
Manufacturing industries, nec	0.1	Manufg.			

Source: Benchmark Input-Output Accounts for the U.S. Economy, 1982, U.S. Department of Commerce, Washington, D.C., July 1991. Data, as reported in the source, are organized by the 1977 SIC structure in use in 1982 but have been matched, as closely as is possible, to the 1987 SIC structure used in this book. Activities with the same percentage are sorted alphabetically by name of activity.

OCCUPATIONS EMPLOYED BY FIRE, MARINE, AND CASUALTY INSURANCE

Occupation	% of Total 1994	Change to 2005	Occupation	% of Total 1994	Change to 2005
Insurance adjusters, examiners, & investigators	12.7	17.5	Bookkeeping, accounting, & auditing clerks	2.5	-16.1
Insurance policy processing clerks	7.0	-10.5	File clerks	2.3	-44.0
Underwriters	6.9	11.9	Managers & administrators nec	2.3	11.9
Insurance sales workers	6.7	-3.2	Computer programmers	2.2	-9.3
Clerical supervisors & managers	5.2	4.1	Systems analysts	1.7	79.1
General office clerks	4.9	-4.6	Accountants & auditors	1.4	11.9
Secretaries, ex legal & medical	4.6	1.9	Data entry keyers, ex composing	1.4	-42.2
Claims examiners, insurance	4.5	15.0	Professional workers nec	1.3	34.3
Insurance claims clerks	4.3	0.7	Adjusters & investigators nec	1.2	-10.5
Clerical support workers nec	3.3	-10.5	Lawyers	1.1	14.0
General managers & top executives	2.9	6.2	Billing, cost, & rate clerks	1.1	-16.6
Management support workers nec	2.8	34.3			

Sources: Industry-Occupation Matrix, Bureau of Labor Statistics. These data relate to one or more 3-digit SIC industry groups rather than to a single 4-digit SIC. The change reported for each occupation to the year 2005 is a percent of growth or decline as estimated by the Bureau of Labor Statistics. The abbreviation *nec* stands for not elsewhere classified.

U.S. AND STATE DATA ON INDUSTRY REVENUES AND OTHER ACCOUNTS FOR 1992

State	No. of Estab.	Employ- ment	Payroll ($ mil.)	Revenues ($ mil.)	Empl./ Estab.	Revenue/ Estab. ($)	Payroll/ Estab. ($)	Revenue/ Empl. ($)	Payroll/ Empl. ($)
UNITED STATES	19,002	588,333	21,182.6	258,394.7	31	13,598,290	1,114,758	439,198	36,004
Alabama	495	5,261	184.1	2,812.3	11	5,681,459	371,846	534,560	34,987
Alaska	46	409	20.8	310.5	9	6,750,630	452,804	759,240	50,927
Arizona	284	7,537	245.7	3,247.6	27	11,435,387	865,070	430,894	32,597
Arkansas	130	1,153	37.2	797.6	9	6,135,754	286,485	691,802	32,301
California	2,302	73,370	2,815.6	34,173.4	32	14,845,087	1,223,104	465,768	38,375
Colorado	293	8,569	280.6	3,058.4	29	10,438,389	957,560	356,920	32,742
Connecticut	323	22,617	941.5	9,858.5	70	30,521,653	2,915,003	435,889	41,630
Delaware	38	-	(D)	(D)	(D)	(D)	(D)	(D)	(D)
District of Columbia	17	216	9.5	235.5	13	13,854,118	557,294	1,090,370	43,861
Florida	1,227	22,037	781.3	10,558.7	18	8,605,302	636,726	479,135	35,452
Georgia	521	16,916	579.1	6,362.3	32	12,211,737	1,111,568	376,112	34,235
Hawaii	51	1,427	52.2	696.2	28	13,650,431	1,023,647	487,857	36,584
Idaho	94	1,150	32.6	497.1	12	5,288,766	346,894	432,299	28,355
Illinois	1,059	51,554	2,011.6	25,395.6	49	23,980,730	1,899,524	492,602	39,019
Indiana	435	12,039	384.6	4,567.0	28	10,498,961	884,131	379,354	31,946
Iowa	249	7,222	208.8	2,309.3	29	9,274,149	838,739	319,754	28,918
Kansas	201	6,394	195.6	2,307.3	32	11,478,970	973,254	360,850	30,595
Kentucky	238	2,465	85.2	1,407.9	10	5,915,542	358,189	571,156	34,584
Louisiana	339	5,405	192.8	2,966.7	16	8,751,345	568,705	548,882	35,669
Maine	88	1,771	50.9	595.2	20	6,763,989	578,159	336,099	28,728
Maryland	388	12,238	505.8	5,419.7	32	13,968,232	1,303,665	442,856	41,332
Massachusetts	169	16,995	597.3	7,764.5	101	45,943,716	3,534,408	456,869	35,147
Michigan	620	19,489	685.8	9,802.1	31	15,809,882	1,106,106	502,957	35,188
Minnesota	379	13,876	452.8	5,801.6	37	15,307,726	1,194,821	418,105	32,635
Mississippi	126	2,244	71.5	788.2	18	6,255,627	567,714	351,252	31,877
Missouri	433	10,807	357.7	4,387.0	25	10,131,624	826,067	405,940	33,098
Montana	64	310	9.1	222.3	5	3,473,281	141,984	717,065	29,313
Nebraska	132	4,859	144.8	2,334.0	37	17,681,932	1,096,962	480,349	29,800
Nevada	99	748	30.3	472.2	8	4,770,162	305,687	631,345	40,459
New Hampshire	102	6,209	200.7	1,247.6	61	12,230,951	1,967,863	200,927	32,328
New Jersey	384	27,876	1,090.8	9,927.2	73	25,852,174	2,840,625	356,121	39,130
New Mexico	98	616	22.0	394.4	6	4,024,357	224,020	640,239	35,640
New York	1,288	42,784	1,778.6	24,909.9	33	19,339,985	1,380,914	582,225	41,572
North Carolina	466	10,642	359.7	4,643.3	23	9,964,105	771,959	436,316	33,803
North Dakota	59	-	(D)	(D)	(D)	(D)	(D)	(D)	(D)
Ohio	845	32,242	1,090.5	11,893.3	38	14,074,953	1,290,514	368,877	33,822
Oklahoma	216	5,025	161.5	1,775.7	23	8,220,991	747,903	353,380	32,149
Oregon	298	6,504	216.0	1,980.5	22	6,646,044	724,940	304,508	33,215
Pennsylvania	704	29,791	1,011.6	14,237.8	42	20,224,190	1,436,972	477,924	33,958
Rhode Island	67	3,644	126.3	1,508.2	54	22,511,149	1,885,119	413,899	34,661
South Carolina	189	2,373	81.6	1,969.9	13	10,422,624	431,614	830,121	34,376
South Dakota	63	671	15.5	238.1	11	3,779,873	246,508	354,891	23,145
Tennessee	362	7,192	240.7	3,153.8	20	8,712,204	664,870	438,518	33,465
Texas	1,381	39,591	1,386.8	16,221.8	29	11,746,416	1,004,211	409,735	35,029
Utah	137	1,375	43.9	706.4	10	5,156,328	320,679	513,758	31,951
Vermont	36	591	17.7	315.0	16	8,750,500	490,722	533,025	29,892
Virginia	536	13,049	436.2	4,013.8	24	7,488,461	813,879	307,596	33,431
Washington	446	9,952	347.6	3,431.0	22	7,692,787	779,482	344,753	34,933
West Virginia	77	580	21.1	506.8	8	6,582,338	274,052	873,862	36,383
Wisconsin	383	16,789	511.7	5,509.3	44	14,384,543	1,335,914	328,148	30,476
Wyoming	25	-	(D)	(D)	(D)	(D)	(D)	(D)	(D)

Source: 1992 Economic Census, U.S. Department of Commerce, Washington, D.C. This is the only table that shows revenue data as collected by the Bureau of the Census in an Economic Census. The symbol (D) indicates that data are withheld by the source to avoid disclosure of competitive information. A dash (-) indicates that data are not available or cannot be calculated.

ESTABLISHMENTS 1992 - STATE AND REGIONAL CONCENTRATION

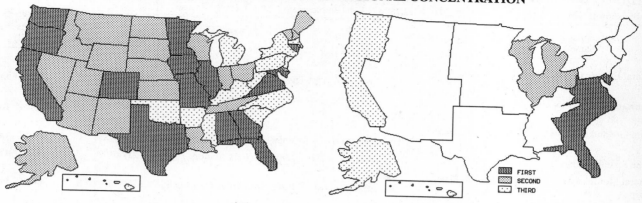

EMPLOYMENT 1992 - STATE AND REGIONAL CONCENTRATION

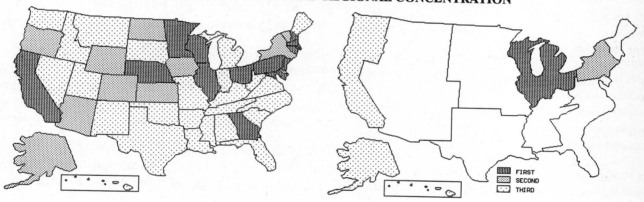

REVENUES 1992 - STATE AND REGIONAL CONCENTRATION

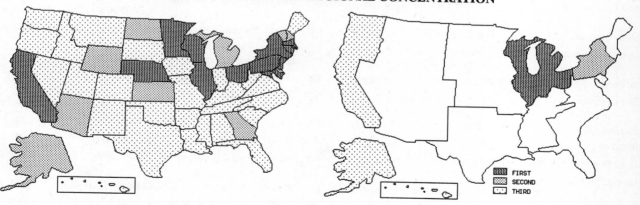

States with the darkest shading indicate those states which have proportionately more establishments, employment, or revenues than would be indicated by the state's population. States with light shading are states with proportionately fewer establishments, less employment, and lower revenues than population distribution. States shaded grey are within 15 percent of the state's population proportion in these categories. States for which no data are available are shown as average (grey). *Regions* are shaded to indicate absolute rank in the category. If no data for the category are available, establishment counts are used to shade the regions. Source of the data is the table on the facing page.

LEADING COMPANIES - SIC 6324 - Hospital and Medical Service Plans

Number shown: **100**   Total sales/assets ($ mil): **1,722,287**   Total employment (000): **1,416.8**

Company Name	Address				CEO Name	Phone	Co. Type	Sales/Assets ($ mil)	Empl. (000)
General Electric Capital Services Inc.	260 Long Ridge Rd.	Stamford	CT	06927	Gary C. Wendt	203-357-6978	S	211,730 TA	25.0
American International Group Inc.	70 Pine St.	New York	NY	10270	Maurice R. Greenberg	212-770-7000	P	114,346 TA	32.0
Aetna Life and Casualty Co.	151 Farmington Ave.	Hartford	CT	06156	Ronald E. Compton	203-273-0123	P	94,172 TA	43.1
Home State Holdings Inc.	1 Harding Rd.	Red Bank	NJ	07701	Robert Abidor	908-219-6600	P	87,221 TA	<0.1
General Motors Acceptance Corp.	3044 W. Grand Blvd.	Detroit	MI	48202	Robert T. O'Connell	313-556-1508	S	80,751 TA	19.3
ITT Hartford Group Inc.	Hartford Plz.	Hartford	CT	06115	Donald R. Frahm	203-547-5000	S	77,000 TA	22.0
Allstate Corp.	Allstate Plz.	Northbrook	IL	60062	Wayne E. Hedien	708-402-5000	P	59,358 TA	49.0
Allstate Insurance Co.	Allstate Plz.	Northbrook	IL	60062	Wayne E. Hedien	708-402-5000	S	59,358 TA	49.0
Sears, Roebuck and Co.	Sears Twr.	Chicago	IL	60684	Edward A. Brennan	312-875-2500	P	54,559	360.0
Loews Corp.	667 Madison Ave.	New York	NY	10021	Laurence A. Tisch	212-545-2000	P	50,336 TA	25.4
Liberty Mutual Insurance Group	175 Berkeley St.	Boston	MA	02117	Gary L. Countryman	617-357-9500	R	50,001 TA	22.0
Lincoln National Corp.	P.O. Box 1110	Fort Wayne	IN	46801	Ian M. Rolland	219-455-2000	P	49,330 TA	9.0
CNA Financial Corp.	CNA Plz.	Chicago	IL	60685	Lawrence A. Tisch	312-822-5000	P	44,320 TA	16.8
Principal Financial Group Inc.	711 High St.	Des Moines	IA	50392	G. David Hurd	515-247-5111	R	44,116 TA	14.8
American General Corp.	P.O. Box 3247	Houston	TX	77253	Harold S. Hook	713-522-1111	P	43,982 TA	12.7
Transamerica Corp.	600 Montgomery St.	San Francisco	CA	94111	Frank C. Herringer	415-983-4000	P	36,050 TA	10.7
Ford Holdings Inc.	The American Rd.	Dearborn	MI	48121	Stanley Seneker	313-322-1639	S	34,755 TA	17.0
General Re Corp.	P.O. Box 10351	Stamford	CT	06904	Ronald E. Ferguson	203-328-5000	P	29,597 TA	3.3
ITT Corp.	1330 Ave. of the Americas	New York	NY	10019	Rand V. Araskog	212-258-1000	P	23,620	110.0
Capital Holding Corp.	P.O. Box 32830	Louisville	KY	40232	Irving W. Bailey II	502-560-2000	P	22,929 TA	9.3
Chubb Corp.	P.O. Box 1615	Warren	NJ	07061	Robert P. Crawford Jr.	908-903-2000	P	20,723 TA	10.0
Berkshire Hathaway Inc.	1440 Kiewit Plz.	Omaha	NE	68131	Warren E. Buffett	402-346-1400	P	19,520 TA	22.0
Continental Casualty Co.	Managment Information	Chicago	IL	60685	Lawrence A. Tisch	312-822-5000	S	19,113 TA	16.8
Xerox Corp.	P.O. Box 1600	Stamford	CT	06904	Paul A. Allaire	203-968-3000	P	17,837	87.6
St. Paul Companies Inc.	385 Washington St.	St. Paul	MN	55102	Douglas W. Leatherdale	612-221-7911	P	17,496 TA	12.6
Continental Corp.	180 Maiden Ln.	New York	NY	10038	John P. Mascotte	212-440-3980	P	16,221 TA	15.0
SAFECO Corp.	SAFECO Plz.	Seattle	WA	98185	Roger H. Eigsti	206-545-5000	P	15,902 TA	7.3
Hartford Fire Insurance Co.	Hartford Plz.	Hartford	CT	06115	Donald R. Frahm	203-547-5000	S	15,415 TA	19.7
Nationwide Mutual Insurance Co.	1 Nationwide Plz.	Columbus	OH	43216	D. Richard McFerson	614-249-7111	R	14,835 TA	32.6
USF and G Corp.	100 Light St.	Baltimore	MD	21202	Norman P. Blake Jr.	410-547-3000	P	13,900 TA	6.5
Kemper Corp.	1 Kemper Dr.	Long Grove	IL	60049	David B. Mathis	708-540-4700	P	13,154 TA	6.3
American Financial Corp.	1 E. 4th St.	Cincinnati	OH	45202	Carl H. Lindner	513-579-2121	R	10,550 TA	5.0
Home Holdings Inc.	59 Maiden Ln.	New York	NY	10038	Lars-Goran Nilsson	212-530-7000	P	10,319 TA	5.5

Company type codes: P - Public, R - Private, S - Subsidiary, D - Division, J - Joint Venture, A - Affiliate, G - Group. If the dollar values shown are not sales, the following codes apply: TA - Total Assets; OR - Operating Revenues; GB - Gross Billings. * - estimated dollar value. < - less than. *na* - not available.

Continued on next page.

LEADING COMPANIES - SIC 6324 - Hospital and Medical Service Plans
Continued

Company Name	Address				CEO Name	Phone	Co. Type	Sales/Assets ($ mil)	Empl. (000)
Aetna Casualty and Surety Co.	151 Farmington Ave.	Hartford	CT	06156	Ronald E. Compton	203-273-0123	S	10,009 TA	10.0
AEGON USA Inc.	1111 N. Charles St.	Baltimore	MD	21201	Don Shepard	410-576-4571	S	9,700 TA	5.4
Reliance Group Holdings Inc.	55 E. 52nd St.	New York	NY	10055	Saul P. Steinberg	212-909-1100	P	9,370 TA	9.2
Deere and Co.	John Deere Rd.	Moline	IL	61265	Hans W. Becherer	309-765-8000	P	9,030	33.0
Mutual of Omaha Insurance Co.	Mutual of Omaha Plz.	Omaha	NE	68175	Thomas J. Skutt	402-342-7600	R	8,600 TA	8.9
Torchmark Corp.	2001 3rd Ave. S.	Birmingham	AL	35233	R.K. Richey	205-325-4200	P	8,404 TA	6.3
United States Fidelity and Guaranty Co.	P.O. Box 1138	Baltimore	MD	21203	Norman P. Blake Jr.	410-547-3000	S	7,820 TA	6.5
Farmers Insurance Exchange	P.O. Box 2478	Los Angeles	CA	90051	Leo E. Denlea Jr.	213-932-3200	S	7,462 TA	17.6
Employers Reinsurance Corp.	P.O. Box 2991	Overland Park	KS	66201	Kaj Ahlmann	913-676-5200	S	7,200 TA	0.7
State Compensation Insurance Fund	P.O. Box 420807	San Francisco	CA	94120	Jack Webb	415-565-1234	R	6,510 TA	6.5
American Re Corp.	555 College Rd. E.	Princeton	NJ	08543	Edward B. Jobe	609-243-4200	P	6,231 TA	1.2
American Re-Insurance Co.	555 College Rd. E.	Princeton	NJ	08543	Edward B. Jobe	609-243-4200	S	6,231 TA	1.2
Jefferson-Pilot Corp.	P.O. Box 21008	Greensboro	NC	27420	David A. Stonecipher	919-691-3000	P	6,140 TA	4.3
Old Republic International Corp.	307 N. Michigan Ave.	Chicago	IL	60601	A.C. Zucaro	312-346-8100	P	6,098 TA	6.1
American National Insurance Co.	1 Moody Plz.	Galveston	TX	77550	Robert L. Moody	409-763-4661	P	5,961 TA	5.0
Halliburton Co.	3600 Lincoln Plz.	Dallas	TX	75201	Thomas H. Cruikshank	214-978-2600	P	5,740	57.2
Allmerica Property and Casualty Companies Inc.	440 Lincoln St.	Worcester	MA	01653	John F. O'Brien	508-855-1000	P	5,409 TA	4.6
General Accident Insurance Company of America	436 Walnut St.	Philadelphia	PA	19106	Walter E. Faren	215-625-1398	S	5,253 TA	5.6
Hanover Insurance Co.	100 North Pkwy.	Worcester	MA	01605	John F. O'Brien	508-853-7200	S	5,100 TA	5.0
Utica Mutual Insurance Co.	180 Genesee St.	New Hartford	NY	13413	W. Craig Heston	315-734-2000	R	5,000 TA	1.4
GEICO Corp.	1 GEICO Plz.	Washington	DC	20076	Olza M. Nicely	301-986-3000	P	4,998 TA	8.2
Cincinnati Financial Corp.	P.O. Box 145496	Cincinnati	OH	45250	Robert B. Morgan	513-870-2000	P	4,734 TA	2.2
Leucadia National Corp.	315 Park Ave. S.	New York	NY	10010	Joseph S. Steinberg	212-460-1900	P	4,689 TA	4.3
Unitrin Inc.	1 E. Wacker Dr.	Chicago	IL	60601	Richard C. Vie	312-661-4600	P	4,570 TA	7.3
American Premier Underwriters Inc.	1 E. 4th St.	Cincinnati	OH	45202	Carl H. Lindner	513-579-6600	P	4,050 TA	5.4
Progressive Corp.	6000 Parkland Blvd.	Mayfield Heights	OH	44124	Peter B. Lewis	216-464-8000	P	4,011 TA	6.1
Ohio Casualty Corp.	136 N. 3rd St.	Hamilton	OH	45025	Lauren N. Patch	513-867-3000	P	3,739 TA	4.0
W.R. Berkley Corp.	P.O. Box 2518	Greenwich	CT	06836	William R. Berkley	203-629-2880	P	3,582 TA	2.6
Transatlantic Holdings Inc.	80 Pine St.	New York	NY	10005	Robert F. Orlich	212-770-2000	P	3,458 TA	0.2
Horace Mann Educators Corp.	1 Horace Mann Plz.	Springfield	IL	62715	Paul J. Kardos	217-789-2500	P	3,148 TA	2.5
Teachers Insurance Co.	1 Horace Mann Plz.	Springfield	IL	62715	Paul J. Kardos	217-789-2500	S	3,140 TA*	2.5

Company type codes: P - Public, R - Private, S - Subsidiary, D - Division, J - Joint Venture, A - Affiliate, G - Group. If the dollar values shown are not sales, the following codes apply: TA - Total Assets; OR - Operating Revenues; GB - Gross Billings. * - estimated dollar value. < - less than. *na* - not available.

Continued on next page.

LEADING COMPANIES - SIC 6324 - Hospital and Medical Service Plans

Continued

Company Name	Address				CEO Name	Phone	Co. Type	Sales/Assets ($ mil)	Empl. (000)
St. Paul Fire and Marine Insurance Co.	385 Washington St.	St. Paul	MN	55102	Douglas W. Leatherdale	612-221-7911	S	2,941 TA	7.3
Standard Fire Insurance Co.	151 Farmington Ave.	Hartford	CT	06156	Ronald E. Compton	203-273-0123	S	2,809 TA	3.9
Sentry Insurance, a Mutual Co.	1800 North Point Dr.	Stevens Point	WI	54481	Larry C. Ballard	715-346-6000	R	2,741 TA	4.4
Lumbermens Mutual Casualty Co.	1 Kemper Dr.	Long Grove	IL	60049	Gerald L. Maatman	708-320-2000	R	2,632 TA	7.0
Government Employees Insurance Co.	5260 Western Ave.	Chevy Chase	MD	20813	Olza M. Nicely	301-986-3000	S	2,387 TA	7.7
Citizens Corp.	440 Lincoln St.	Worcester	MA	01653	John F. O'Brien	508-855-1000	P	2,334 TA	1.8
Citizens Insurance Company of America	645 W. Grand River Ave	Howell	MI	48843	James R. McAuliffe	517-546-2160	S	2,334 TA	1.8
Horace Mann Insurance Co.	1 Horace Mann Plz.	Springfield	IL	62715	Paul J. Kardos	217-789-2500	S	2,320 TA•	2.5
New Jersey Manufacturers Insurance Co.	301 Sullivan Way	West Trenton	NJ	08628	Anthony G. Dickson	609-883-1300	R	2,205 TA	1.6
Nationwide Corp.	1 Nationwide Plz.	Columbus	OH	43216	D. Richard McFerson	614-249-7111	S	2,140 TA	4.4
Orion Capital Corp.	30 Rockefeller Plz.	New York	NY	10112	Alan R. Gruber	212-332-8080	P	2,113 TA	1.5
Argonaut Group Inc.	1800 Avenue of the	Los Angeles	CA	90067	Charles E. Rinsch	310-553-0561	P	2,094 TA	0.6
Federated Mutual Insurance Co.	121 E. Park Sq.	Owatonna	MN	55060	Charles I. Buxton II	507-455-5200	R	2,040 TA	2.5
Argonaut Insurance Co.	250 Middlefield Rd.	Menlo Park	CA	94025	Michael J. Crall	415-326-0900	S	1,960 TA	0.5
Harleysville Mutual Insurance Co.	355 Maple Ave.	Harleysville	PA	19438	Walter R. Bateman II	215-256-5000	R	1,884 TA	2.1
Selective Insurance Group Inc.	40 Wantage Ave.	Branchville	NJ	07890	James W. Entringer	201-948-3000	P	1,867 TA	1.8
Zenith National Insurance Corp.	21255 Califa St.	Woodland Hills	CA	91367	Stanley R. Zax	818-713-1000	P	1,841 TA	1.5
NAC Re Corp.	P.O. Box 2568	Greenwich	CT	06836	Ronald L. Bornhuetter	203-622-5200	P	1,779 TA	0.2
20th Century Industries	6301 Owensmouth Ave.	Woodland Hills	CA	91367	Neil H. Ashley	818-704-3700	P	1,704 TA	2.3
Allendale Mutual Insurance Co.	P.O. Box 7500	Johnston	RI	02919	Shivan S. Subramaniam	401-275-3000	R	1,683 TA	0.1
TIG Insurance Co.	6300 Canoga Ave.	Woodland Hills	CA	91367	Gerald A. Isom	818-596-5000	S	1,600 TA	3.5
National Re Corp.	P.O. Box 10167	Stamford	CT	06904	William D. Warren	203-329-7700	P	1,523 TA	0.3
National Reinsurance Corp.	P.O. Box 10167	Stamford	CT	06904	William D. Warren	203-329-7700	S	1,523 TA	0.3
Cuna Mutual Insurance Society	P.O. Box 391	Madison	WI	53701	Richard M. Heins	608-238-5851	R	1,472 TA	5.5
Independent Insurance Group Inc.	1 Independent Dr.	Jacksonville	FL	32276	Wilford C. Lyon Jr.	904-358-5151	P	1,364 TA	4.0
Signet Star Reinsurance Co.	100 Campus Dr.	Florham Park	NJ	07932	John D. Vollaro	201-301-8000	S	1,300 TA	0.1
Harleysville Group Inc.	355 Maple Ave.	Harleysville	PA	19438	Walter R. Bateman	215-256-5000	P	1,241 TA	2.4
Constitution Reinsurance Corp.	110 William St.	New York	NY	10038	Bard E. Bunaes	212-225-1000	S	1,239 TA	0.2

Company type codes: P - Public, R - Private, S - Subsidiary, D - Division, J - Joint Venture, A - Affiliate, G - Group. If the dollar values shown are not sales, the following codes apply: TA - Total Assets; OR - Operating Revenues; GB - Gross Billings. • - estimated dollar value. < - less than. *na* - not available.

Continued on next page.

LEADING COMPANIES - SIC 6324 - Hospital and Medical Service Plans
Continued

Company Name	Address				CEO Name	Phone	Co. Type	Sales/Assets ($ mil)	Empl. (000)
Motors Insurance Corp.	3044 W. Grand Blvd.	Detroit	MI	48202	Joseph J. Pero	313-556-5000	S	1,189 TA	2.2
Employers Mutual Cos.	P.O. Box 712	Des Moines	IA	50303	Bruce G. Kelley	515-280-2511	R	1,170 TA*	1.6
Zurich Reinsurance Centre Holdings Inc.	1 Chase Manhattan Plz.	New York	NY	10005	Steven M. Gluckstern	212-898-5000	P	1,168 TA	0.2
Zurich Reinsurance Centre Inc.	1 Chase Manhattan Plz.	New York	NY	10005	Steven M. Gluckstern	212-898-5000	S	1,168 TA	0.2
Markel Corp.	4551 Cox Rd.	Glen Allen	VA	23060	Alan I. Kirshner	804-747-0136	P	1,162 TA	0.7
Markel Service Inc.	4551 Cox Rd.	Glen Allen	VA	23060	Alan I. Kirshner	804-747-0136	S	1,162 TA	0.7
Integon Corp.	500 W. 5th St.	Winston-Salem	NC	27152	James T. Lambie	919-770-2000	P	1,152 TA	1.1
SCOR U.S. Corp.	110 William St.	New York	NY	10038	Jerome Karter	212-978-8200	P	1,144 TA	0.2

*Source: Ward's Business Directory of U.S. Private and Public Companies, 1996. Company type codes: P - Public, R - Private, S - Subsidiary, D - Division, J - Joint Venture, A - Affiliate, G - Group. If the dollar values shown are not sales, the following codes apply: TA - Total Assets; OR - Operating Revenues; GB - Gross Billings. * - estimated dollar value. < - less than; na - not available.*

SIC 6350

SURETY INSURANCE

SIC 6350 includes organizations that provide insurance for financial responsibility such as bonding, fidelity, liability, and surety insurance. Specific categories include assessment associations for surety and fidelity insurance; bonding for guaranteeing job completion; bonding of employees; bonding for fidelity or surety, credit and other financial responsibility insurance; fidelity insurance; financial responsibility insurance; liability insurance; mortgage guaranty insurance; reciprocal interinsurance exchanges for these categories; surety insurance; and warranty insurance on homes.

ESTABLISHMENTS, EMPLOYMENT, AND PAYROLL

	1988	1989		1990		1991		1992		1993		% change 88-93
		Value	%	Value	%	Value	%	Value	%	Value	%	
All Establishments	503	566	12.5	586	3.5	777	32.6	801	3.1	594	-25.8	18.1
Mid-March Employment	10,419	14,004	34.4	14,629	4.5	18,636	27.4	17,381	-6.7	11,918	-31.4	14.4
1st Quarter Wages (annualized - $ mil.)	293.1	447.2	52.6	445.7	-0.3	716.9	60.9	709.2	-1.1	545.7	-23.1	86.2
Payroll per Emp. 1st Q. (annualized)	28,133	31,934	13.5	30,466	-4.6	38,470	26.3	40,801	6.1	45,785	12.2	62.7
Annual Payroll ($ mil.)	297.1	441.6	48.6	455.6	3.2	628.6	38.0	662.6	5.4	543.4	-18.0	82.9
Establishments - 1-4 Emp. Number	230	246	7.0	251	2.0	395	57.4	414	4.8	304	-26.6	32.2
Mid-March Employment	457	456	-0.2	446	-2.2	(D)	-	838	-	520	-37.9	13.8
1st Quarter Wages (annualized - $ mil.)	11.7	12.4	6.2	12.5	0.4	(D)	-	28.0	-	19.8	-29.2	69.5
Payroll per Emp. 1st Q. (annualized)	25,619	27,263	6.4	27,973	2.6	(D)	-	33,470	-	38,169	14.0	49.0
Annual Payroll ($ mil.)	13.5	14.6	8.1	13.9	-4.4	(D)	-	34.4	-	23.1	-32.9	71.4
Establishments - 5-9 Emp. Number	86	90	4.7	103	14.4	129	25.2	153	18.6	112	-26.8	30.2
Mid-March Employment	550	600	9.1	659	9.8	(D)	-	988	-	718	-27.3	30.5
1st Quarter Wages (annualized - $ mil.)	15.0	22.3	49.2	21.7	-2.8	(D)	-	35.9	-	26.8	-25.2	79.2
Payroll per Emp. 1st Q. (annualized)	27,215	37,220	36.8	32,923	-11.5	(D)	-	36,287	-	37,354	2.9	37.3
Annual Payroll ($ mil.)	15.5	20.9	34.9	19.8	-5.5	(D)	-	36.2	-	27.6	-23.7	78.2
Establishments - 10-19 Emp. Number	75	93	24.0	81	-12.9	92	13.6	95	3.3	61	-35.8	-18.7
Mid-March Employment	(D)	1,333	-	1,132	-15.1	1,254	10.8	1,291	3.0	810	-37.3	-
1st Quarter Wages (annualized - $ mil.)	(D)	36.3	-	34.0	-6.4	40.2	18.1	44.0	9.4	31.4	-28.5	-
Payroll per Emp. 1st Q. (annualized)	(D)	27,259	-	30,042	10.2	32,041	6.7	34,045	6.3	38,810	14.0	-
Annual Payroll ($ mil.)	(D)	39.5	-	33.9	-14.1	42.1	24.1	46.3	10.1	33.4	-27.9	-
Establishments - 20-49 Emp. Number	76	93	22.4	85	-8.6	110	29.4	95	-13.6	75	-21.1	-1.3
Mid-March Employment	2,249	2,869	27.6	2,662	-7.2	3,591	34.9	3,100	-13.7	2,431	-21.6	8.1
1st Quarter Wages (annualized - $ mil.)	62.5	111.9	79.1	76.5	-31.6	145.9	90.6	132.3	-9.3	110.1	-16.8	76.1
Payroll per Emp. 1st Q. (annualized)	27,794	39,013	40.4	28,739	-26.3	40,616	41.3	42,679	5.1	45,270	6.1	62.9
Annual Payroll ($ mil.)	63.5	113.8	79.1	75.1	-34.0	138.8	84.8	121.0	-12.8	105.3	-13.0	65.7
Establishments - 50-99 Emp. Number	18	18	-	34	88.9	30	-11.8	23	-23.3	21	-8.7	16.7
Mid-March Employment	1,336	1,268	-5.1	2,423	91.1	1,989	-17.9	1,515	-23.8	1,396	-7.9	4.5
1st Quarter Wages (annualized - $ mil.)	42.4	54.0	27.4	75.5	39.7	105.2	39.3	79.5	-24.4	56.9	-28.4	34.2
Payroll per Emp. 1st Q. (annualized)	31,754	42,615	34.2	31,165	-26.9	52,895	69.7	52,491	-0.8	40,774	-22.3	28.4
Annual Payroll ($ mil.)	45.1	50.3	11.6	73.6	46.3	92.4	25.5	69.7	-24.5	54.2	-22.3	20.1
Establishments - 100-249 Emp. Number	11	14	27.3	23	64.3	11	-52.2	14	27.3	12	-14.3	9.1
Mid-March Employment	1,602	2,020	26.1	3,248	60.8	1,615	-50.3	2,103	30.2	1,925	-8.5	20.2
1st Quarter Wages (annualized - $ mil.)	43.5	54.4	24.9	107.8	98.3	86.3	-19.9	140.7	63.0	128.4	-8.7	195.0
Payroll per Emp. 1st Q. (annualized)	27,169	26,921	-0.9	33,197	23.3	53,446	61.0	66,889	25.2	66,697	-0.3	145.5
Annual Payroll ($ mil.)	43.6	54.0	23.9	114.7	112.5	86.5	-24.6	129.3	49.4	133.7	3.4	206.8
Establishments - 250-499 Emp. Number	4	8	100.0	6	-25.0	7	16.7	(D)	-	6	-	50.0
Mid-March Employment	(D)	2,495	-	1,908	-23.5	(D)	-	(D)	-	2,127	-	-
1st Quarter Wages (annualized - $ mil.)	(D)	62.6	-	50.8	-18.9	(D)	-	(D)	-	94.1	-	-
Payroll per Emp. 1st Q. (annualized)	(D)	25,071	-	26,602	6.1	(D)	-	(D)	-	44,233	-	-
Annual Payroll ($ mil.)	(D)	63.9	-	53.0	-17.0	(D)	-	(D)	-	88.6	-	-
Establishments - 500-999 Emp. Number	2	3	50.0	3	-	2	-33.3	(D)	-	3	-	50.0
Mid-March Employment	(D)	(D)	-	2,151	-	(D)	-	(D)	-	1,991	-	-
1st Quarter Wages (annualized - $ mil.)	(D)	(D)	-	66.9	-	(D)	-	(D)	-	78.1	-	-
Payroll per Emp. 1st Q. (annualized)	(D)	(D)	-	31,104	-	(D)	-	(D)	-	39,231	-	-
Annual Payroll ($ mil.)	(D)	(D)	-	71.5	-	(D)	-	(D)	-	77.6	-	-
Estab. - 1000 or More Emp. Number	1	1	-	-	-	1	-	(D)	-	-	-	-
Mid-March Employment	(D)	(D)	-	-	-	(D)	-	(D)	-	-	-	-
1st Quarter Wages (annualized - $ mil.)	(D)	(D)	-	-	-	(D)	-	(D)	-	-	-	-
Payroll per Emp. 1st Q. (annualized)	(D)	(D)	-	(D)	-	(D)	-	(D)	-	-	-	-
Annual Payroll ($ mil.)	(D)	(D)	-	-	-	(D)	-	(D)	-	-	-	-

Source: County Business Patterns, U.S. Department of Commerce, Washington, D.C., for 1988 through 1993. Payroll per employee is calculated using mid-March employment and 1st Quarter wages, annualized. Annual payroll, also shown, may not equal the annualized 1st Quarter wages. Columns headed by a percent sign (%) indicate change from the previous year. na stands for not available. The symbol (D) indicates that data are withheld by the source to avoid disclosure of competitive information. A dash (-) indicates that data are not available or cannot be calculated.

ESTABLISHMENTS
Number

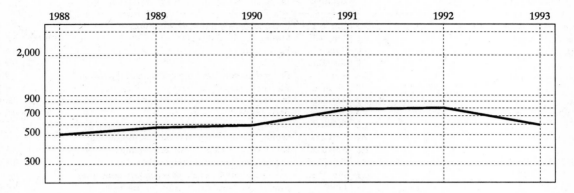

MID-MARCH EMPLOYMENT
Number

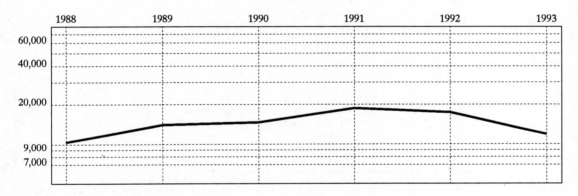

ANNUAL PAYROLL
$ million

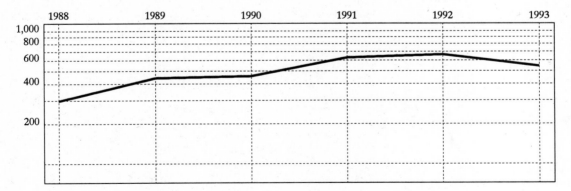

INPUTS AND OUTPUTS FOR INSURANCE CARRIERS - SIC GROUP 63

Economic Sector or Industry Providing Inputs	%	Sector	Economic Sector or Industry Buying Outputs	%	Sector
Insurance agents, brokers, & services	62.9	Fin/R.E.	Personal consumption expenditures	77.1	
Security & commodity brokers	6.8	Fin/R.E.	Owner-occupied dwellings	5.5	Fin/R.E.
Eating & drinking places	4.0	Trade	Real estate	3.6	Fin/R.E.
Real estate	4.0	Fin/R.E.	Banking	0.9	Fin/R.E.
Communications, except radio & TV	3.9	Util.	Federal Government purchases, nondefense	0.9	Fed Govt
Imports	1.8	Foreign	Electric services (utilities)	0.8	Util.
Commercial printing	1.3	Manufg.	Insurance agents, brokers, & services	0.7	Fin/R.E.
Computer & data processing services	1.3	Services	Feed grains	0.6	Agric.
Advertising	1.2	Services	Exports	0.5	Foreign
Hotels & lodging places	1.2	Services	Motor freight transportation & warehousing	0.5	Util.
Legal services	1.2	Services	Retail trade, except eating & drinking	0.5	Trade
Accounting, auditing & bookkeeping	0.9	Services	Credit agencies other than banks	0.4	Fin/R.E.
Banking	0.9	Fin/R.E.	S/L Govt. purch., elem. & secondary education	0.4	S/L Govt
U.S. Postal Service	0.9	Gov't	Sanitary services, steam supply, irrigation	0.4	Util.
Air transportation	0.6	Util.	State & local government enterprises, nec	0.3	Gov't
Credit agencies other than banks	0.6	Fin/R.E.	Water supply & sewage systems	0.3	Util.
Management & consulting services & labs	0.6	Services	Wholesale trade	0.3	Trade
Maintenance of nonfarm buildings nec	0.5	Constr.	Food grains	0.2	Agric.
Manifold business forms	0.5	Manufg.	Meat animals	0.2	Agric.
Motor freight transportation & warehousing	0.5	Util.	Petroleum refining	0.2	Manufg.
Petroleum refining	0.5	Manufg.	Religious organizations	0.2	Services
Photographic equipment & supplies	0.4	Manufg.	Air transportation	0.1	Util.
Transit & bus transportation	0.4	Util.	Arrangement of passenger transportation	0.1	Util.
Business services nec	0.3	Services	Equipment rental & leasing services	0.1	Services
Personnel supply services	0.3	Services	Freight forwarders	0.1	Util.
Wholesale trade	0.3	Trade	Industrial buildings	0.1	Constr.
Automotive rental & leasing, without drivers	0.2	Services	Office buildings	0.1	Constr.
Electric services (utilities)	0.2	Util.	Oil bearing crops	0.1	Agric.
Electronic computing equipment	0.2	Manufg.	Residential 1-unit structures, nonfarm	0.1	Constr.
Detective & protective services	0.1	Services	Transit & bus transportation	0.1	Util.
Electrical repair shops	0.1	Services			
Envelopes	0.1	Manufg.			
Manufacturing industries, nec	0.1	Manufg.			

Source: Benchmark Input-Output Accounts for the U.S. Economy, 1982, U.S. Department of Commerce, Washington, D.C., July 1991. Data, as reported in the source, are organized by the 1977 SIC structure in use in 1982 but have been matched, as closely as is possible, to the 1987 SIC structure used in this book. Activities with the same percentage are sorted alphabetically by name of activity.

OCCUPATIONS EMPLOYED BY PENSION FUNDS AND INSURANCE, NEC

Occupation	% of Total 1994	Change to 2005	Occupation	% of Total 1994	Change to 2005
Title examiners & searchers	11.3	1.8	Insurance sales workers	2.6	10.0
General office clerks	8.3	8.5	Underwriters	2.6	27.2
Secretaries, ex legal & medical	7.0	15.8	Clerical support workers nec	2.4	1.7
General managers & top executives	6.3	20.7	Management support workers nec	2.1	52.7
Clerical supervisors & managers	4.8	30.1	Financial managers	2.0	27.2
Legal assistants, law clerks nec	4.6	57.5	File clerks	2.0	-36.4
Bookkeeping, accounting, & auditing clerks	4.5	-4.6	Accountants & auditors	1.7	27.2
Typists & word processors	4.2	-36.4	Computer programmers	1.7	3.1
Receptionists & information clerks	3.1	27.2	Messengers	1.4	-1.2
Insurance policy processing clerks	3.1	1.8	Marketing & sales worker supervisors	1.3	27.2
Loan & credit clerks	3.0	14.5	Data entry keyers, ex composing	1.2	-6.1
Insurance claims clerks	2.9	16.7	Claims examiners, insurance	1.2	16.0
Insurance adjusters, examiners, & investigators	2.6	33.6	Managers & administrators nec	1.0	27.1

Sources: Industry-Occupation Matrix, Bureau of Labor Statistics. These data relate to one or more 3-digit SIC industry groups rather than to a single 4-digit SIC. The change reported for each occupation to the year 2005 is a percent of growth or decline as estimated by the Bureau of Labor Statistics. The abbreviation *nec* stands for not elsewhere classified.

U.S. AND STATE DATA ON INDUSTRY REVENUES AND OTHER ACCOUNTS FOR 1992

State	No. of Estab.	Employ- ment	Payroll ($ mil.)	Revenues ($ mil.)	Empl./ Estab.	Revenue/ Estab. ($)	Payroll/ Estab. ($)	Revenue/ Empl. ($)	Payroll/ Empl. ($)
UNITED STATES	548	11,167	518.9	4,005.4	20	7,309,053	946,883	358,678	46,467
Alabama	7	-	(D)	(D)	(D)	(D)	(D)	(D)	(D)
Alaska	1	-	(D)	(D)	(D)	(D)	(D)	(D)	(D)
Arizona	15	123	5.5	54.3	8	3,621,067	369,933	441,593	45,114
Arkansas	3	-	(D)	(D)	(D)	(D)	(D)	(D)	(D)
California	97	1,857	82.2	574.7	19	5,925,052	846,969	309,494	44,241
Colorado	12	65	2.0	20.3	5	1,690,000	162,667	312,000	30,031
Connecticut	4	-	(D)	(D)	(D)	(D)	(D)	(D)	(D)
District of Columbia	2	-	(D)	(D)	(D)	(D)	(D)	(D)	(D)
Florida	35	414	12.0	200.0	12	5,714,857	343,657	483,140	29,053
Georgia	17	165	6.2	44.9	10	2,641,118	363,882	272,115	37,491
Hawaii	1	-	(D)	(D)	(D)	(D)	(D)	(D)	(D)
Idaho	1	-	(D)	(D)	(D)	(D)	(D)	(D)	(D)
Illinois	22	488	25.1	291.4	22	13,243,182	1,140,273	597,029	51,406
Indiana	8	42	1.4	13.5	5	1,686,375	179,000	321,214	34,095
Iowa	6	-	(D)	(D)	(D)	(D)	(D)	(D)	(D)
Kansas	9	103	3.4	27.2	11	3,024,778	375,333	264,301	32,796
Kentucky	3	55	1.8	8.6	18	2,875,333	591,667	156,836	32,273
Louisiana	5	-	(D)	(D)	(D)	(D)	(D)	(D)	(D)
Maine	1	-	(D)	(D)	(D)	(D)	(D)	(D)	(D)
Maryland	18	887	34.9	153.8	49	8,546,556	1,936,278	173,436	39,293
Massachusetts	17	-	(D)	(D)	(D)	(D)	(D)	(D)	(D)
Michigan	17	74	2.4	38.1	4	2,243,412	140,412	515,378	32,257
Minnesota	12	-	(D)	(D)	(D)	(D)	(D)	(D)	(D)
Mississippi	1	-	(D)	(D)	(D)	(D)	(D)	(D)	(D)
Missouri	7	60	1.9	20.3	9	2,897,714	274,000	338,067	31,967
Montana	1	-	(D)	(D)	(D)	(D)	(D)	(D)	(D)
Nebraska	5	-	(D)	(D)	(D)	(D)	(D)	(D)	(D)
Nevada	3	-	(D)	(D)	(D)	(D)	(D)	(D)	(D)
New Hampshire	1	-	(D)	(D)	(D)	(D)	(D)	(D)	(D)
New Jersey	20	797	35.5	267.4	40	13,369,200	1,777,150	335,488	44,596
New Mexico	1	-	(D)	(D)	(D)	(D)	(D)	(D)	(D)
New York	39	1,089	117.0	805.5	28	20,654,718	3,000,538	739,701	107,457
North Carolina	17	949	42.0	508.2	56	29,895,941	2,470,294	535,544	44,252
Ohio	17	78	2.6	25.9	5	1,522,412	153,588	331,808	33,474
Oklahoma	2	-	(D)	(D)	(D)	(D)	(D)	(D)	(D)
Oregon	4	21	1.1	6.1	5	1,518,500	271,750	289,238	51,762
Pennsylvania	26	223	12.0	213.5	9	8,211,000	463,038	957,336	53,987
South Carolina	4	8	0.1	1.1	2	278,750	24,000	139,375	12,000
South Dakota	2	-	(D)	(D)	(D)	(D)	(D)	(D)	(D)
Tennessee	9	47	1.5	12.4	5	1,377,556	172,222	263,787	32,979
Texas	37	467	15.6	132.5	13	3,580,027	422,108	283,642	33,443
Utah	4	-	(D)	(D)	(D)	(D)	(D)	(D)	(D)
Virginia	11	246	8.8	74.5	22	6,776,000	799,636	302,992	35,756
Washington	9	113	4.8	32.7	13	3,638,222	535,556	289,770	42,655
Wisconsin	13	981	40.5	60.0	75	4,613,000	3,116,846	61,130	41,304
Wyoming	2	-	(D)	(D)	(D)	(D)	(D)	(D)	(D)

Source: 1992 Economic Census, U.S. Department of Commerce, Washington, D.C. This is the only table that shows revenue data as collected by the Bureau of the Census in an Economic Census. The symbol (D) indicates that data are withheld by the source to avoid disclosure of competitive information. A dash (-) indicates that data are not available or cannot be calculated.

ESTABLISHMENTS 1992 - STATE AND REGIONAL CONCENTRATION

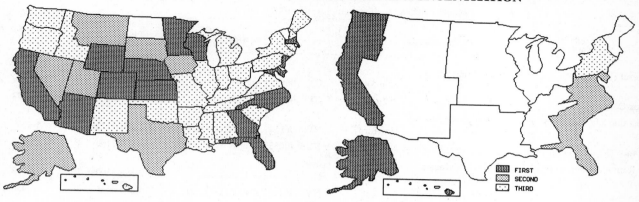

EMPLOYMENT 1992 - STATE AND REGIONAL CONCENTRATION

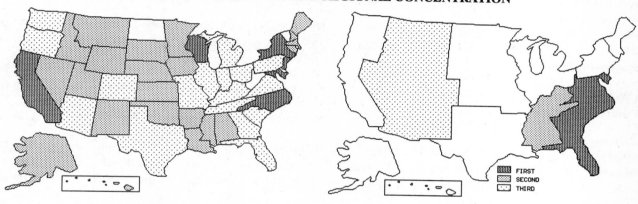

REVENUES 1992 - STATE AND REGIONAL CONCENTRATION

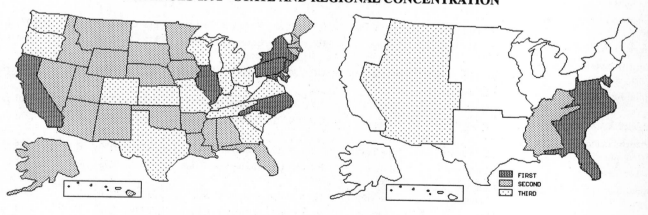

States with the darkest shading indicate those states which have proportionately more establishments, employment, or revenues than would be indicated by the state's population. States with light shading are states with proportionately fewer establishments, less employment, and lower revenues than population distribution. States shaded grey are within 15 percent of the state's population proportion in these categories. States for which no data are available are shown as average (grey). *Regions* are shaded to indicate absolute rank in the category. If no data for the category are available, establishment counts are used to shade the regions. Source of the data is the table on the facing page.

LEADING COMPANIES - SIC 6331 - Fire, Marine, and Casualty Insurance

Number shown: **87**   Total sales/assets ($ mil): **208,863**   Total employment (000): **166.0**

Company Name	Address				CEO Name	Phone	Co. Type	Sales/Assets ($ mil)	Empl. (000)
General Electric Capital Corp.	260 Long Ridge Rd.	Stamford	CT	06927	Gary C. Wendt	203-357-4000	S	117,939 TA	18.6
Xerox Corp.	P.O. Box 1600	Stamford	CT	06904	Paul A. Allaire	203-968-3000	P	17,837	87.6
Aetna Casualty and Surety Co.	151 Farmington Ave.	Hartford	CT	06156	Ronald E. Compton	203-273-0123	S	10,009 TA	10.0
Reliance Group Holdings Inc.	55 E. 52nd St.	New York	NY	10055	Saul P. Steinberg	212-909-1100	P	9,370 TA	9.2
Old Republic International Corp.	307 N. Michigan Ave.	Chicago	IL	60601	A.C. Zucaro	312-346-8100	P	6,098 TA	6.1
MBIA Insurance Corp.	113 King St.	Armonk	NY	10504	David H. Elliott	914-273-4545	P	5,456 TA	0.4
AMBAC Inc.	1 State St. Plz.	New York	NY	10004	Phillip B. Lassiter	212-668-0340	P	4,293 TA	0.6
ADVANTA Corp.	300 Welsh Rd.	Horsham	PA	19044	Dennis Alter	215-657-4000	P	3,113 TA	1.8
Amerin Guaranty Corp.	303 E. Wacker Dr.	Chicago	IL	60601	Gerald L. Friedman	312-540-0078	R	2,500 TA	<0.1
MBIA Municipal Investors Service Corp.	113 King St.	Armonk	NY	10504	Leon J. Karvelis Jr.	914-273-4545	S	2,340 TA*	0.3
FGIC Corp.	115 Broadway	New York	NY	10006	Ann C. Stern	212-312-3000	S	2,300 TA	0.2
Financial Guaranty Insurance Co.	115 Broadway	New York	NY	10006	Stephen Berger	212-312-3000	S	2,300 TA	0.2
Cuna Mutual Insurance Society	P.O. Box 391	Madison	WI	53701	Richard M. Heins	608-238-5851	R	1,472 TA	5.5
GE Capital Mortgage Services Inc.	6601 Six Forks Rd.	Raleigh	NC	27615	Gregory T. Barmore	919-846-4100	S	1,290 TA*	0.8
General Electric Mortgage Insurance Corp.	6601 Six Forks Rd.	Raleigh	NC	27615	Gregory T. Barmore	919-846-4100	S	1,290 TA*	0.8
Markel Corp.	4551 Cox Rd.	Glen Allen	VA	23060	Alan I. Kirshner	804-747-0136	P	1,162 TA	0.7
Markel Service Inc.	4551 Cox Rd.	Glen Allen	VA	23060	Alan I. Kirshner	804-747-0136	S	1,162 TA	0.7
PMI Group Inc.	601 Montgomery St.	San Francisco	CA	94111	W. Roger Haughton	415-788-7878	P	1,117 TA	0.8
Financial Security Assurance Holdings Ltd.	350 Park Ave.	New York	NY	10022	Robert P. Cochran	212-826-0100	P	1,074 TA	0.2
Financial Security Assurance Inc.	350 Park Ave.	New York	NY	10022	Robert P. Cochran	212-826-0100	S	1,074 TA	0.2
Coregis Group Inc.	181 W. Madison St.	Chicago	IL	60602	Courtney C. Smith	312-849-5000	S	1,030 TA*	0.6
Securities Investor Protection Corp.	805 15th St. N.W.	Washington	DC	20005	Theodore H. Focht	202-371-8300	R	817 TA	<0.1
Capital Re Corp.	1325 Avenue of the Americas	New York	NY	10019	Michael E. Satz	212-974-0100	P	810 TA	<0.1
Sedgwick James of Oregon Inc.	111 Columbia St.	Portland	OR	97201	Ronald J. Kutella	503-248-6400	S	770 TA	0.3
Enhance Financial Services Group Inc.	335 Madison Ave.	New York	NY	10017	Daniel J. Gross	212-983-3100	P	765 TA	<0.1
Quaker State Corp.	P.O. Box 989	Oil City	PA	16301	Herbert M. Baum	814-676-7676	P	755	5.4
Capital Reinsurance Co.	1325 Ave. of the Amer.	New York	NY	10019	Michael E. Satz	212-974-0100	S	712 TA	<0.1
MMI Companies Inc.	540 Lake Cook Rd.	Deerfield	IL	60015	B. Frederick Becker	708-940-7550	P	694 TA	0.4
Seaboard Surety Co.	Burnt Mills Rd.	Bedminster	NJ	07921	George Thompson	908-658-3500	S	690 TA*	0.4
Piedmont Management Company Inc.	80 Maiden Ln.	New York	NY	10038	Robert M. DeMichele	212-363-4650	P	676 TA	0.2

Company type codes: P - Public, R - Private, S - Subsidiary, D - Division, J - Joint Venture, A - Affiliate, G - Group. If the dollar values shown are not sales, the following codes apply: TA - Total Assets; OR - Operating Revenues; GB - Gross Billings. * - estimated dollar value. < - less than. *na* - not available.

Continued on next page.

LEADING COMPANIES - SIC 6331 - Fire, Marine, and Casualty Insurance
Continued

Company Name	Address				CEO Name	Phone	Co. Type	Sales/Assets ($ mil)	Empl. (000)
Frontier Insurance Group Inc.	P.O. Box 8000	Rock Hill	NY	12775	Walter A. Rhulen	914-796-2100	P	522 TA	0.4
Executive Risk Inc.	P.O. Box 2002	Simsbury	CT	06070	Roy A. Vander Putten	203-244-8900	P	517 TA	0.2
United Guaranty Residential Insurance Co.	P.O. Box 21367	Greensboro	NC	27420	Charles M. Reid	910-373-0232	S	510 TA*	0.3
Oakwood Homes Corp.	P.O. Box 7386	Greensboro	NC	27417	Nicholas J. St. George	919-855-2400	P	506	3.6
Evanston Insurance Co.	1007 Church St.	Evanston	IL	60201	Paul W. Springman	708-866-2800	S	497 TA	<0.1
Manufacturers Alliance Insurance Co.	925 Chestnut St.	Philadelphia	PA	19107	William M. Loftus	215-629-5000	S	411 TA	0.5
Fidelity and Deposit Company of Maryland	P.O. Box 1227	Baltimore	MD	21203	J.C. Eanes Jr.	410-539-0800	S	342 TA	1.2
Victor O. Schinnerer and Co.	2 Wisconsin Cir.	Chevy Chase	MD	20815	Vince Santorelli	301-961-9800	S	340 TA	0.2
Capital Guaranty Corp.	Steuart Twr.	San Francisco	CA	94105	Michael Djordjevich	415-995-8000	P	334 TA	<0.1
Capital Guaranty Insurance Co.	Steuart Twr.	San Francisco	CA	94105	Michael Djordjevich	415-995-8000	S	334 TA	<0.1
Healthcare Underwriters Mutual Insurance Co.	8 British America Blvd	Latham	NY	12110	Gerald Cassidy	518-786-2700	R	300 TA	<0.1
American International Specialty Lines Insurance Co.	401 Plaza 3	Jersey City	NJ	07311	Thomas Tizzo	201-309-1100	S	250 TA	<0.1
American Bonding Co.	6245 E. Broadway Blvd.	Tucson	AZ	85711	E. Askew	602-747-5555	R	200 TA*	0.1
Acordia of Northwest Indiana Inc.	5730 W. 74th St.	Indianapolis	IN	46278	Douglas L. Cassman	317-290-4100	D	160 TA	0.2
MGIC Investment Corp.	P.O. Box 488	Milwaukee	WI	53201	William H. Lacy	414-347-6480	P	159 TA	1.1
Aon Specialty Group Inc.	123 N. Wacker Dr.	Chicago	IL	60606	Michael Rice	312-701-4538	S	156	0.6
Nobel Insurance Ltd.	3010 L.B.J. Fwy.	Dallas	TX	75234	Jeffry K. Amsbaugh	214-243-1886	P	153 TA	0.3
Shand, Morahan and Company Inc.	1007 Church St.	Evanston	IL	60201	Anthony F. Markel	708-866-2800	S	144 TA	0.2
Exstar Financial Corp.	P.O. Box 678	Solvang	CA	93463	Peter J. O'Shaughnessy	805-688-8013	P	142 TA	<0.1
Amwest Insurance Group Inc.	P.O. Box 4500	Woodland Hills	CA	91365	John E. Savage	818-704-1111	P	141 TA	0.4
Midwest Indemnity Corp.	5550 W. Touhy Ave #400	Skokie	IL	60077	Marvin Silverman	708-982-9800	R	140 TA*	<0.1
P.I.E. Mutual Insurance Co.	1001 Lakeside Ave.	Cleveland	OH	44114	Larry E. Rogers	216-736-8400	R	140 TA	0.1
American Credit Indemnity Co.	100 E. Pratt St.	Baltimore	MD	21202	H. Michael Cushinsky	410-554-0700	S	126 TA	0.3
Intercargo Corp.	1450 E. American Ln.	Schaumburg	IL	60173	James R. Zuhlke	708-517-2990	P	115 TA	0.2
America Service Group Inc.	2 Penns Way	New Castle	DE	19720	Jeffrey A. Reasons	302-322-8200	P	110 OR	1.3
Heritage Life Insurance Co.	30851 Agoura Rd.	Agoura Hills	CA	91301	Edward D. Bostic	818-889-2520	S	105 TA	0.1
Bertholon-Rowland Corp.	16 J St.	New York	NY	10013		212-966-9400	R	100 TA*	<0.1
Kentucky Medical Insurance Co.	303 N. Hurstbourne	Louisville	KY	40222	Steven L. Salman	502-339-5700	P	88 TA	<0.1

Company type codes: P - Public, R - Private, S - Subsidiary, D - Division, J - Joint Venture, A - Affiliate, G - Group. If the dollar values shown are not sales, the following codes apply: TA - Total Assets; OR - Operating Revenues; GB - Gross Billings. * - estimated dollar value. < - less than. *na* - not available.

Continued on next page.

LEADING COMPANIES - SIC 6331 - Fire, Marine, and Casualty Insurance
Continued

Company Name	Address				CEO Name	Phone	Co. Type	Sales/Assets ($ mil)	Empl. (000)
Triad Guaranty Inc.	101 S. Stratford Rd.	Winston-Salem	NC	27104	Darryl W. Thompson	919-723-1282	P	86 TA	<0.1
Pace American Group Inc.	3567 E. Sunrise Dr.	Tucson	AZ	85718	Don H. Pace	602-745-8855	P	81 TA	0.1
MOMED Holding Co.	8630 Delmar Blvd.	St. Louis	MO	63124	Richard V. Bradley	314-872-8000	P	78 TA	<0.1
Enhance Reinsurance Co.	335 Madison Ave.	New York	NY	10017	Wallace O. Sellers	212-983-3100	S	75 TA*	<0.1
Mahoney Group	P.O. Box 15001	Casa Grande	AZ	85230	John W. McEvoy	602-836-7483	R	70 TA	0.1
Wilshire Insurance Co.	P.O. Box 10800	Raleigh	NC	27605	George King	919-833-1600	S	58 TA	<0.1
Roanoke Companies Inc.	1930 Thoreau Dr.	Schaumburg	IL	60173	William D. Sterrett	708-490-9540	R	53 TA	0.2
Monumental General Insurance Group	1111 N. Charles St.	Baltimore	MD	21201	Bart Herbert	410-685-5500	S	48 TA*	0.3
Condor Services Inc.	2361 Rosecrans Ave.	El Segundo	CA	90245	Guy A. Main	310-322-7344	P	40 TA	<0.1
Crusader Insurance Co.	23251 Mulholland Dr.	Woodland Hills	CA	91364	Erwin Cheldin	818-591-9800	S	40 TA	0.1
Homeowners Group Inc.	P.O. Box 9200	Hollywood	FL	33024	Carl Buccellato	305-983-0350	P	39 TA	0.2
American Hole 'n One Inc.	5404 McEver Rd.	Oakwood	GA	30566	Mick Luckhurst	404-967-2922	R	34 TA*	<0.1
Safe Passage International	410 17th St.	Denver	CO	80202	James A. Irwin	303-893-5680	S	30 TA	<0.1
Home Buyers Warranty Corp.	1728 Montreal Cir	Tucker	GA	30084	Gary Mabry	404-982-0669	R	28 TA	<0.1
Property and Casualty Insurance Guaranty Corp.	305 Washington Ave.	Baltimore	MD	21204	Joseph Petr	410-296-1620	R	27 TA*	<0.1
Delta Holding Inc.	P.O. Box 7000	Issaquah	WA	98027	David L. Larson	206-391-2000	R	22 TA	0.2
Credit Card Service Corp.	6860 Commercial Dr.	Springfield	VA	22151	Dave Phillips	703-750-3026	R	15 TA	<0.1
First Security Casualty Co.	30775 Barrington Ave.	Madison Heights	MI	48071	Richard Mazur	810-588-9500	S	13 TA*	<0.1
Delta Management Company Inc.	P.O. Box 7000	Issaquah	WA	98027	David L. Larson	206-391-2000	P	12 TA	0.2
Acstar Holdings Inc.	233 Main St.	New Britain	CT	06050	Henry W. Nozko Jr.	203-224-2000	S	10 TA	<0.1
Acstar Insurance Co.	P.O. Box 2350	New Britain	CT	06050	Henry Nozko Jr.	203-224-2000	S	10 TA	<0.1
Amerinst Insurance Group Inc.	1751 West 47th St.	Chicago	IL	60609	Norman Batchelder	312-523-4416	R	10 TA	<0.1
American Healthcare System	12730 High Bluff Dr.	San Diego	CA	92130	Monroe Trout	619-481-2727	R	6 OR	<0.1
Securities Guaranty Insurance Services Inc.	2677 N. Main St.	Santa Ana	CA	92701	Jim Brooks	714-647-0400	R	6 TA	<0.1
Far West Insurance Co.	6320 Canoga Ave.	Woodland Hills	CA	91367	John E. Savage	818-704-1111	S	5 TA	0.3
J.P. Everhart and Co.	8350 N. Central Expwy.	Dallas	TX	75206	John Everhart	214-691-6911	R	4 TA	<0.1
Freberg Environmental Inc.	1675 Broadway.	Denver	CO	80202	William Freberg	303-571-4235	R	2 TA	<0.1
Commodore Insurance Services Inc.	26300 La Alameda	Mission Viejo	CA	92691	David E. Worden	714-365-0474	R	1 TA*	<0.1
Municipal Mutual Insurance Co.	15721 S. Western Ave.	Gardena	CA	90247	Jame J. Gregg	310-515-6800	R	1 TA*	<0.1

Source: *Ward's Business Directory of U.S. Private and Public Companies*, 1996. Company type codes: P - Public, R - Private, S - Subsidiary, D - Division, J - Joint Venture, A - Affiliate, G - Group. If the dollar values shown are not sales, the following codes apply: TA - Total Assets; OR - Operating Revenues; GB - Gross Billings. * - estimated dollar value. < - less than; *na* - not available.

SIC 6360

TITLE INSURANCE

This industry is made up of establishments engaged primarily in underwriting insurance to protect the owners of real estate and those who lend money on real estate against loss sustained due to a defective title of ownership. Real estate title insurance, title insurance, and title guaranty organizations are included.

ESTABLISHMENTS, EMPLOYMENT, AND PAYROLL

	1988	1989		1990		1991		1992		1993		% change 88-93
		Value	%	Value	%	Value	%	Value	%	Value	%	
All Establishments	3,030	3,162	4.4	3,196	1.1	3,496	9.4	3,560	1.8	2,294	-35.6	-24.3
Mid-March Employment	54,170	56,413	4.1	56,650	0.4	49,399	-12.8	54,042	9.4	40,169	-25.7	-25.8
1st Quarter Wages (annualized - $ mil.)	1,350.8	1,467.1	8.6	1,587.2	8.2	1,379.8	-13.1	1,629.2	18.1	1,277.1	-21.6	-5.5
Payroll per Emp. 1st Q. (annualized)	24,937	26,007	4.3	28,018	7.7	27,932	-0.3	30,147	7.9	31,793	5.5	27.5
Annual Payroll ($ mil.)	1,393.3	1,488.6	6.8	1,574.3	5.8	1,452.8	-7.7	1,749.3	20.4	1,442.0	-17.6	3.5
Establishments - 1-4 Emp. Number	1,027	1,106	7.7	1,210	9.4	1,350	11.6	1,352	0.1	(D)	-	-
Mid-March Employment	(D)	2,550	-	2,782	9.1	(D)	-	3,140	-	(D)	-	-
1st Quarter Wages (annualized - $ mil.)	(D)	56.5	-	75.4	33.4	(D)	-	77.3	-	(D)	-	-
Payroll per Emp. 1st Q. (annualized)	(D)	22,165	-	27,104	22.3	(D)	-	24,614	-	(D)	-	-
Annual Payroll ($ mil.)	(D)	62.3	-	75.5	21.2	(D)	-	90.4	-	(D)	-	-
Establishments - 5-9 Emp. Number	811	840	3.6	798	-5.0	1,040	30.3	1,022	-1.7	636	-37.8	-21.6
Mid-March Employment	5,347	5,510	3.0	5,335	-3.2	7,047	32.1	6,781	-3.8	4,185	-38.3	-21.7
1st Quarter Wages (annualized - $ mil.)	124.6	128.0	2.8	132.5	3.5	166.7	25.9	176.3	5.7	125.2	-29.0	0.5
Payroll per Emp. 1st Q. (annualized)	23,299	23,233	-0.3	24,828	6.9	23,657	-4.7	25,994	9.9	29,920	15.1	28.4
Annual Payroll ($ mil.)	121.8	132.5	8.8	129.5	-2.2	179.2	38.4	197.3	10.1	139.1	-29.5	14.3
Establishments - 10-19 Emp. Number	499	494	-1.0	479	-3.0	521	8.8	541	3.8	357	-34.0	-28.5
Mid-March Employment	6,832	6,750	-1.2	6,528	-3.3	7,062	8.2	7,241	2.5	4,819	-33.4	-29.5
1st Quarter Wages (annualized - $ mil.)	153.9	155.4	1.0	160.2	3.1	181.5	13.2	191.6	5.6	140.5	-26.7	-8.7
Payroll per Emp. 1st Q. (annualized)	22,525	23,023	2.2	24,547	6.6	25,694	4.7	26,465	3.0	29,148	10.1	29.4
Annual Payroll ($ mil.)	157.9	157.4	-0.3	158.2	0.5	190.0	20.1	209.7	10.4	157.4	-25.0	-0.3
Establishments - 20-49 Emp. Number	467	485	3.9	451	-7.0	392	-13.1	420	7.1	322	-23.3	-31.0
Mid-March Employment	13,820	14,516	5.0	14,014	-3.5	11,971	-14.6	13,012	8.7	10,110	-22.3	-26.8
1st Quarter Wages (annualized - $ mil.)	317.1	352.7	11.2	364.1	3.2	320.0	-12.1	366.3	14.5	296.2	-19.1	-6.6
Payroll per Emp. 1st Q. (annualized)	22,944	24,298	5.9	25,982	6.9	26,729	2.9	28,148	5.3	29,295	4.1	27.7
Annual Payroll ($ mil.)	325.6	355.8	9.3	366.5	3.0	333.3	-9.1	403.6	21.1	328.4	-18.6	0.8
Establishments - 50-99 Emp. Number	135	137	1.5	172	25.5	133	-22.7	152	14.3	127	-16.4	-5.9
Mid-March Employment	9,520	9,348	-1.8	11,710	25.3	9,035	-22.8	10,414	15.3	8,434	-19.0	-11.4
1st Quarter Wages (annualized - $ mil.)	237.9	246.7	3.7	330.7	34.0	255.8	-22.7	323.6	26.5	270.9	-16.3	13.9
Payroll per Emp. 1st Q. (annualized)	24,991	26,393	5.6	28,243	7.0	28,312	0.2	31,076	9.8	32,120	3.4	28.5
Annual Payroll ($ mil.)	248.1	244.8	-1.3	323.8	32.2	275.6	-14.9	340.7	23.6	294.2	-13.6	18.6
Establishments - 100-249 Emp. Number	80	85	6.3	72	-15.3	49	-31.9	61	24.5	55	-9.8	-31.3
Mid-March Employment	11,333	11,961	5.5	10,294	-13.9	7,001	-32.0	9,030	29.0	8,158	-9.7	-28.0
1st Quarter Wages (annualized - $ mil.)	317.1	345.5	9.0	326.5	-5.5	228.7	-29.9	315.2	37.8	283.0	-10.2	-10.7
Payroll per Emp. 1st Q. (annualized)	27,977	28,887	3.3	31,716	9.8	32,668	3.0	34,910	6.9	34,688	-0.6	24.0
Annual Payroll ($ mil.)	330.1	355.0	7.5	329.6	-7.2	235.6	-28.5	333.2	41.5	319.6	-4.1	-3.2
Establishments - 250-499 Emp. Number	8	11	37.5	9	-18.2	9	-	(D)	-	6	-	-25.0
Mid-March Employment	2,994	3,661	22.3	2,973	-18.8	(D)	-	(D)	-	2,290	-	-23.5
1st Quarter Wages (annualized - $ mil.)	91.8	119.3	30.0	102.5	-14.1	(D)	-	(D)	-	87.8	-	-4.4
Payroll per Emp. 1st Q. (annualized)	30,647	32,593	6.4	34,476	5.8	(D)	-	(D)	-	38,323	-	25.0
Annual Payroll ($ mil.)	95.0	112.6	18.5	96.2	-14.6	(D)	-	(D)	-	96.6	-	1.6
Establishments - 500-999 Emp. Number	3	4	33.3	5	25.0	2	-60.0	(D)	-	(D)	-	-
Mid-March Employment	(D)	2,117	-	3,014	42.4	(D)	-	(D)	-	(D)	-	-
1st Quarter Wages (annualized - $ mil.)	(D)	62.9	-	95.3	51.5	(D)	-	(D)	-	(D)	-	-
Payroll per Emp. 1st Q. (annualized)	(D)	29,714	-	31,622	6.4	(D)	-	(D)	-	(D)	-	-
Annual Payroll ($ mil.)	(D)	68.2	-	95.0	39.4	(D)	-	(D)	-	(D)	-	-
Estab. - 1000 or More Emp. Number	-	-	-	-	-	-	-	-	-	-	-	-
Mid-March Employment	-	-	-	-	-	-	-	-	-	-	-	-
1st Quarter Wages (annualized - $ mil.)	-	-	-	-	-	-	-	-	-	-	-	-
Payroll per Emp. 1st Q. (annualized)	(D)	(D)	-	(D)	-	(D)	-	-	-	-	-	-
Annual Payroll ($ mil.)	-	-	-	-	-	-	-	-	-	-	-	-

Source: County Business Patterns, U.S. Department of Commerce, Washington, D.C., for 1988 through 1993. Payroll per employee is calculated using mid-March employment and 1st Quarter wages, annualized. Annual payroll, also shown, may not equal the annualized 1st Quarter wages. Columns headed by a percent sign (%) indicate change from the previous year. *na* stands for not available. The symbol (D) indicates that data are withheld by the source to avoid disclosure of competitive information. A dash (-) indicates that data are not available or cannot be calculated.

ESTABLISHMENTS
Number

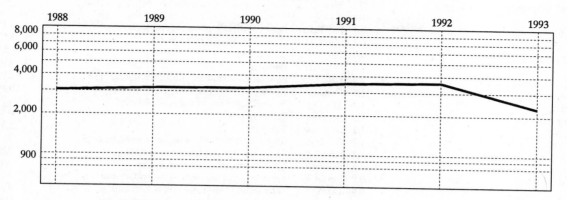

MID-MARCH EMPLOYMENT
Number

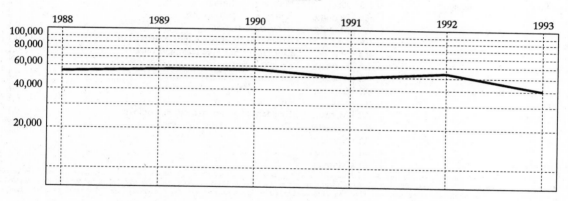

ANNUAL PAYROLL
$ million

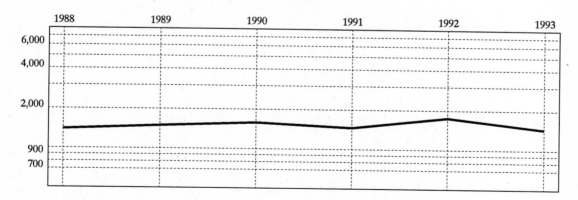

INPUTS AND OUTPUTS FOR INSURANCE CARRIERS - SIC GROUP 63

Economic Sector or Industry Providing Inputs	%	Sector	Economic Sector or Industry Buying Outputs	%	Sector
Insurance agents, brokers, & services	62.9	Fin/R.E.	Personal consumption expenditures	77.1	
Security & commodity brokers	6.8	Fin/R.E.	Owner-occupied dwellings	5.5	Fin/R.E.
Eating & drinking places	4.0	Trade	Real estate	3.6	Fin/R.E.
Real estate	4.0	Fin/R.E.	Banking	0.9	Fin/R.E.
Communications, except radio & TV	3.9	Util.	Federal Government purchases, nondefense	0.9	Fed Govt
Imports	1.8	Foreign	Electric services (utilities)	0.8	Util.
Commercial printing	1.3	Manufg.	Insurance agents, brokers, & services	0.7	Fin/R.E.
Computer & data processing services	1.3	Services	Feed grains	0.6	Agric.
Advertising	1.2	Services	Exports	0.5	Foreign
Hotels & lodging places	1.2	Services	Motor freight transportation & warehousing	0.5	Util.
Legal services	1.2	Services	Retail trade, except eating & drinking	0.5	Trade
Accounting, auditing & bookkeeping	0.9	Services	Credit agencies other than banks	0.4	Fin/R.E.
Banking	0.9	Fin/R.E.	S/L Govt. purch., elem. & secondary education	0.4	S/L Govt
U.S. Postal Service	0.9	Gov't	Sanitary services, steam supply, irrigation	0.4	Util.
Air transportation	0.6	Util.	State & local government enterprises, nec	0.3	Gov't
Credit agencies other than banks	0.6	Fin/R.E.	Water supply & sewage systems	0.3	Util.
Management & consulting services & labs	0.6	Services	Wholesale trade	0.3	Trade
Maintenance of nonfarm buildings nec	0.5	Constr.	Food grains	0.2	Agric.
Manifold business forms	0.5	Manufg.	Meat animals	0.2	Agric.
Motor freight transportation & warehousing	0.5	Util.	Petroleum refining	0.2	Manufg.
Petroleum refining	0.5	Manufg.	Religious organizations	0.2	Services
Photographic equipment & supplies	0.4	Manufg.	Air transportation	0.1	Util.
Transit & bus transportation	0.4	Util.	Arrangement of passenger transportation	0.1	Util.
Business services nec	0.3	Services	Equipment rental & leasing services	0.1	Services
Personnel supply services	0.3	Services	Freight forwarders	0.1	Util.
Wholesale trade	0.3	Trade	Industrial buildings	0.1	Constr.
Automotive rental & leasing, without drivers	0.2	Services	Office buildings	0.1	Constr.
Electric services (utilities)	0.2	Util.	Oil bearing crops	0.1	Agric.
Electronic computing equipment	0.2	Manufg.	Residential 1-unit structures, nonfarm	0.1	Constr.
Detective & protective services	0.1	Services	Transit & bus transportation	0.1	Util.
Electrical repair shops	0.1	Services			
Envelopes	0.1	Manufg.			
Manufacturing industries, nec	0.1	Manufg.			

Source: Benchmark Input-Output Accounts for the U.S. Economy, 1982, U.S. Department of Commerce, Washington, D.C., July 1991. Data, as reported in the source, are organized by the 1977 SIC structure in use in 1982 but have been matched, as closely as is possible, to the 1987 SIC structure used in this book. Activities with the same percentage are sorted alphabetically by name of activity.

OCCUPATIONS EMPLOYED BY PENSION FUNDS AND INSURANCE, NEC

Occupation	% of Total 1994	Change to 2005	Occupation	% of Total 1994	Change to 2005
Title examiners & searchers	11.3	1.8	Insurance sales workers	2.6	10.0
General office clerks	8.3	8.5	Underwriters	2.6	27.2
Secretaries, ex legal & medical	7.0	15.8	Clerical support workers nec	2.4	1.7
General managers & top executives	6.3	20.7	Management support workers nec	2.1	52.7
Clerical supervisors & managers	4.8	30.1	Financial managers	2.0	27.2
Legal assistants, law clerks nec	4.6	57.5	File clerks	2.0	-36.4
Bookkeeping, accounting, & auditing clerks	4.5	-4.6	Accountants & auditors	1.7	27.2
Typists & word processors	4.2	-36.4	Computer programmers	1.7	3.1
Receptionists & information clerks	3.1	27.2	Messengers	1.4	-1.2
Insurance policy processing clerks	3.1	1.8	Marketing & sales worker supervisors	1.3	27.2
Loan & credit clerks	3.0	14.5	Data entry keyers, ex composing	1.2	-6.1
Insurance claims clerks	2.9	16.7	Claims examiners, insurance	1.2	16.0
Insurance adjusters, examiners, & investigators	2.6	33.6	Managers & administrators nec	1.0	27.1

Sources: *Industry-Occupation Matrix*, Bureau of Labor Statistics. These data relate to one or more 3-digit SIC industry groups rather than to a single 4-digit SIC. The change reported for each occupation to the year 2005 is a percent of growth or decline as estimated by the Bureau of Labor Statistics. The abbreviation *nec* stands for not elsewhere classified.

U.S. AND STATE DATA ON INDUSTRY REVENUES AND OTHER ACCOUNTS FOR 1992

State	No. of Estab.	Employ-ment	Payroll ($ mil.)	Revenues ($ mil.)	Empl./ Estab.	Revenue/ Estab. ($)	Payroll/ Estab. ($)	Revenue/ Empl. ($)	Payroll/ Empl. ($)
UNITED STATES	1,532	34,473	1,168.4	4,883.6	23	3,187,701	762,646	141,663	33,892
Alabama	6	70	1.6	4.6	12	774,500	262,667	66,386	22,514
Alaska	4	-	(D)	(D)	(D)	(D)	(D)	(D)	(D)
Arizona	85	1,475	48.3	107.4	17	1,263,753	568,541	72,826	32,763
Arkansas	2	-	(D)	(D)	(D)	(D)	(D)	(D)	(D)
California	426	14,238	516.8	2,098.9	33	4,926,880	1,213,042	147,412	36,294
Colorado	47	755	24.9	52.4	16	1,115,596	529,404	69,448	32,956
Connecticut	15	153	6.5	29.1	10	1,942,667	435,800	190,458	42,725
District of Columbia	5	42	1.7	10.1	8	2,015,400	330,800	239,929	39,381
Florida	153	2,155	61.2	197.6	14	1,291,490	400,000	91,693	28,399
Georgia	11	109	4.9	15.1	10	1,371,727	441,909	138,431	44,596
Hawaii	12	-	(D)	(D)	(D)	(D)	(D)	(D)	(D)
Idaho	5	-	(D)	(D)	(D)	(D)	(D)	(D)	(D)
Illinois	50	-	(D)	(D)	(D)	(D)	(D)	(D)	(D)
Indiana	16	297	8.0	27.0	19	1,686,500	497,500	90,855	26,801
Kansas	12	144	3.7	25.6	12	2,131,667	305,750	177,639	25,479
Kentucky	2	-	(D)	(D)	(D)	(D)	(D)	(D)	(D)
Louisiana	8	107	3.5	20.9	13	2,616,875	435,375	195,654	32,551
Maine	2	-	(D)	(D)	(D)	(D)	(D)	(D)	(D)
Maryland	10	147	4.4	19.4	15	1,939,400	442,000	131,932	30,068
Massachusetts	13	-	(D)	(D)	(D)	(D)	(D)	(D)	(D)
Michigan	38	941	26.4	66.5	25	1,749,000	695,895	70,629	28,102
Minnesota	13	-	(D)	(D)	(D)	(D)	(D)	(D)	(D)
Mississippi	2	-	(D)	(D)	(D)	(D)	(D)	(D)	(D)
Missouri	30	400	13.6	33.0	13	1,099,833	453,567	82,488	34,018
Montana	2	-	(D)	(D)	(D)	(D)	(D)	(D)	(D)
Nebraska	5	-	(D)	(D)	(D)	(D)	(D)	(D)	(D)
Nevada	16	378	11.8	26.4	24	1,650,625	737,875	69,868	31,233
New Hampshire	3	-	(D)	(D)	(D)	(D)	(D)	(D)	(D)
New Jersey	44	348	12.2	50.5	8	1,148,773	276,841	145,247	35,003
New Mexico	7	-	(D)	(D)	(D)	(D)	(D)	(D)	(D)
New York	59	1,132	41.3	175.2	19	2,968,712	699,339	154,730	36,450
North Carolina	31	128	4.5	22.7	4	732,129	144,806	177,313	35,070
Ohio	40	856	25.0	86.9	21	2,173,150	625,625	101,549	29,235
Oklahoma	7	-	(D)	(D)	(D)	(D)	(D)	(D)	(D)
Oregon	68	1,229	34.4	104.7	18	1,539,868	506,088	85,200	28,002
Pennsylvania	68	943	31.6	96.8	14	1,423,779	464,441	102,669	33,491
Rhode Island	6	-	(D)	(D)	(D)	(D)	(D)	(D)	(D)
South Carolina	5	-	(D)	(D)	(D)	(D)	(D)	(D)	(D)
Tennessee	10	191	5.2	18.6	19	1,862,300	515,700	97,503	27,000
Texas	90	2,306	82.9	267.6	26	2,973,344	920,756	116,046	35,936
Utah	5	-	(D)	(D)	(D)	(D)	(D)	(D)	(D)
Vermont	2	-	(D)	(D)	(D)	(D)	(D)	(D)	(D)
Virginia	36	490	15.9	42.8	14	1,189,639	442,806	87,402	32,533
Washington	39	1,466	47.1	141.9	38	3,638,872	1,208,641	96,805	32,153
West Virginia	1	-	(D)	(D)	(D)	(D)	(D)	(D)	(D)
Wisconsin	4	39	1.1	3.5	10	877,250	282,750	89,974	29,000
Wyoming	17	-	(D)	(D)	(D)	(D)	(D)	(D)	(D)

Source: 1992 Economic Census, U.S. Department of Commerce, Washington, D.C. This is the only table that shows revenue data as collected by the Bureau of the Census in an Economic Census. The symbol (D) indicates that data are withheld by the source to avoid disclosure of competitive information. A dash (-) indicates that data are not available or cannot be calculated.

ESTABLISHMENTS 1992 - STATE AND REGIONAL CONCENTRATION

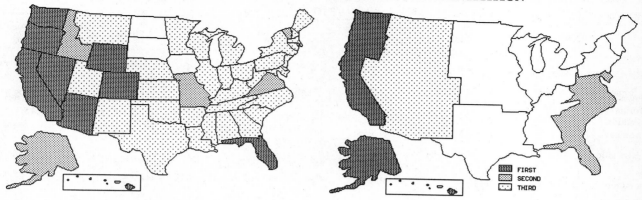

EMPLOYMENT 1992 - STATE AND REGIONAL CONCENTRATION

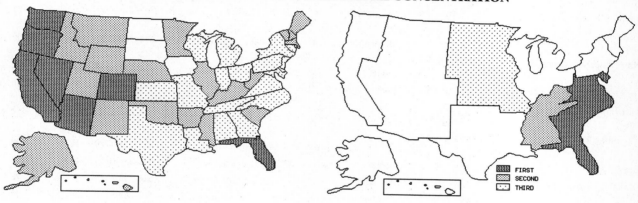

REVENUES 1992 - STATE AND REGIONAL CONCENTRATION

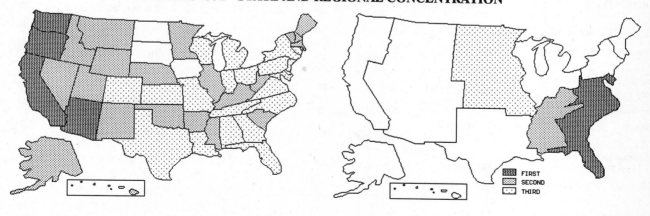

States with the darkest shading indicate those states which have proportionately more establishments, employment, or revenues than would be indicated by the state's population. States with light shading are states with proportionately fewer establishments, less employment, and lower revenues than population distribution. States shaded grey are within 15 percent of the state's population proportion in these categories. States for which no data are available are shown as average (grey). *Regions* are shaded to indicate absolute rank in the category. If no data for the category are available, establishment counts are used to shade the regions. Source of the data is the table on the facing page.

LEADING COMPANIES - SIC 6351 - Surety Insurance

Number shown: **50**   Total sales/assets ($ mil): **32,074**   Total employment (000): **83.5**

Company Name	Address				CEO Name	Phone	Co. Type	Sales/Assets ($ mil)	Empl. (000)
Reliance Group Holdings Inc.	55 E. 52nd St.	New York	NY	10055	Saul P. Steinberg	212-909-1100	P	9,370 TA	9.2
Old Republic International Corp.	307 N. Michigan Ave.	Chicago	IL	60601	A.C. Zucaro	312-346-8100	P	6,098 TA	6.1
Unitrin Inc.	1 E. Wacker Dr.	Chicago	IL	60601	Richard C. Vie	312-661-4600	P	4,570 TA	7.3
Alleghany Corp.	Park Avenue Plz.	New York	NY	10055	John J. Burns Jr.	212-752-1356	P	3,588 TA	9.1
Chicago Title and Trust Co.	111 W. Washington St.	Chicago	IL	60602	Richard P. Toft	312-630-2000	S	1,530 TA*	7.7
First American Financial Corp.	114 E. 5th St.	Santa Ana	CA	92701	Parker S. Kennedy	714-558-3211	P	1,398 TA	10.7
First American Title Insurance Co.	114 E. 5th St.	Santa Ana	CA	92701	Parker S. Kennedy	714-558-3211	S	1,222 TA	8.6
Republic Financial Services Inc.	P.O. Box 660560	Dallas	TX	75266	William A. Bowers	214-559-0300	S	1,000 TA*	1.0
Lawyers Title Corp.	6630 W. Broad St.	Richmond	VA	23230	Charles H. Foster Jr.	804-281-6700	P	526 TA	3.5
Lawyers Title Insurance Corp.	6630 W. Broad St.	Richmond	VA	23230	Charles H. Foster Jr.	804-281-6700	S	474 TA	3.4
Old Republic National Title Insurance Co.	400 2nd Ave. S.	Minneapolis	MN	55401	Dick Cecchettini	612-371-1111	S	400 TA	1.2
Fidelity National Financial Inc.	17911 Von Karman Ave.	Irvine	CA	92714	Frank P. Willey	714-622-5000	P	396 TA	4.7
Victor O. Schinnerer and Co.	2 Wisconsin Cir.	Chevy Chase	MD	20815	Vince Santorelli	301-961-9800	S	340 TA	0.2
Stewart Information Services Corp.	P.O. Box 2029	Houston	TX	77252	Stewart Morris	713-625-8100	P	325 TA	4.2
Old Republic Title Co.	265 Montgomery St.	San Francisco	CA	94104	John Dosa	415-421-9770	R	190 TA*	1.2
Futura Corp.	P.O. Box 7968	Boise	ID	83707	Brent S. Lloyd	208-336-0150	R	100	0.4
Continental Lawyers Title Co.	55 S. Lake Ave.	Pasadena	CA	91101	Edward Zerwekh	818-508-8730	S	78 TA	1.0
ABI Whitehead Insurance	P.O. Box 940967	Maitland	FL	32794	Mark Whitehead	407-660-8180	R	43 TA*	<0.1
Gateway Title Co.	1900 W. Olive Ave.	Burbank	CA	91506	Martin Evans	818-953-2300	R	36 TA*	0.5
Southland Title Corp.	300 E. Magnolia Blvd.	Burbank	CA	91502	David Cronenbold	818-841-0666	R	36 TA	0.3
Utica Fire Insurance Co.	P.O. Box 851	Utica	NY	13503	Frederick E. Bangs	315-736-8211	R	31 TA	<0.1
Alamo Title Insurance of Texas	613 N.W. Loop 410	San Antonio	TX	78216	Don Still	210-377-0881	R	30 TA	<0.1
Attorneys Title Insurance Fund Inc.	P.O. Box 628600	Orlando	FL	32862	Charles J. Kovaleski	407-240-3863	R	30 TA	0.8
Investors Title Co.	P.O. Drawer 2687	Chapel Hill	NC	27514	J. Allen Fine	919-968-2200	P	24 TA	0.1
North Star Title Inc.	5075 Wayzata Blvd.	Minneapolis	MN	55416	Joe Doyle	612-545-1041	S	21 TA*	0.1
California Land Title Comapny of Santa Clara County	1900 Alameda	San Jose	CA	95126	Mike Trudeau	408-296-4500	D	20 TA*	0.1
Investors Title Insurance Co.	121 N. Columbia St.	Chapel Hill	NC	27514	J.A. Fine	919-968-2200	S	17 TA	0.1
Monroe Title Insurance Corp.	47 W. Main St.	Rochester	NY	14614	Dennis W. O'Neill	716-232-2070	R	16 TA	0.3
California Counties Title Co.	209 Fair Oaks Ave.	South Pasadena	CA	91030	James E. Gottwald	818-441-4211	R	16 TA*	0.1
Fremont Indemnity Co.	2020 Santa Monica Blvd	Santa Monica	CA	90404	Hans Coffeng	310-315-3900	S	16 TA*	0.1
Investors Title Co.	3055 Wilshire Blvd.	Los Angeles	CA	90010	Robert Snell	213-380-1080	R	16 TA*	0.1

Company type codes: P - Public, R - Private, S - Subsidiary, D - Division, J - Joint Venture, A - Affiliate, G - Group. If the dollar values shown are not sales, the following codes apply: TA - Total Assets; OR - Operating Revenues; GB - Gross Billings. * - estimated dollar value. < - less than. *na* - not available.

Continued on next page.

LEADING COMPANIES - SIC 6351 - Surety Insurance
Continued

Company Name	Address				CEO Name	Phone	Co. Type	Sales/Assets ($ mil)	Empl. (000)
Diversified Capital Holdings Inc.	4401 N. Atlantic Ave.	Long Beach	CA	90807	Roy E. Hearrean	310-422-0045	R	15 TA	0.2
Northern Counties Title Insurance Co.	888 W. Santa Ana Blvd.	Santa Ana	CA	92701	Roy E. Hearrean	714-973-2119	S	14 TA	0.2
Lawyers Title of Arizona Inc.	40 E. Mitchell Dr.	Phoenix	AZ	85012	Kenneth Pond	602-248-0882	S	12 TA*	0.2
First American Title Insurance Company of Oregon	200 SW Market St. #250	Portland	OR	97201	Chuck O'Rourke	503-222-3651	S	11 TA	0.2
Bay Title and Abstract Inc.	P.O. Box 173	Green Bay	WI	54305	John May	414-431-6100	R	10 TA*	<0.1
Beach Abstract and Guaranty Co.	P.O. Box 2580	Little Rock	AR	72203	George Pitts Jr.	501-376-3301	R	10 OR*	<0.1
Southwest Title and Trust Co.	P.O. Box 1234	Oklahoma City	OK	73101	James Kott	405-236-2861	S	7 TA	0.1
Fidelity National Title Company of Washington	3500 188th St. S.W.	Lynnwood	WA	98037	Chet Hodgson	206-771-3031	S	6 TA	<0.1
Land Title Services Inc.	2323 N. Mayfair Rd.	Wauwatosa	WI	53226	Harve Pollack	414-259-5060	R	6 TA	<0.1
Stewart Title Company of San Diego	7676 Hazard Center Dr.	San Diego	CA	92108	Darrel Delperdang	619-692-1600	S	6 TA	<0.1
Transamerica Title Insurance Co.	801 Civic Center Dr. W	Santa Ana	CA	92702	David R. Porter	714-547-5777	S	6 TA*	<0.1
Florida Title and Guaranty Co.	2958 1st Ave. N.	St. Petersburg	FL	33713	Thomas A. Gregg	813-327-1000	R	3 TA	<0.1
Landata Incorporated of Illinois	2035 S. Arlington	Arlington Heights	IL	60005	Thomas Abbate	708-593-3900	R	3 TA	<0.1
Pacific Title Guaranty Co.	911 Wilshire Blvd.	Los Angeles	CA	90017	Dick Kelley	213-489-3033	R	3 TA	<0.1
Community Title and Escrow Inc.	2402 State St.	Alton	IL	62002	Peggy A. Stillwell	618-466-7755	R	1 OR	<0.1
Landvest Title Associates Inc.	16565 Vanderbilt Dr.	Bonita Springs	FL	33923	Linda Wright	813-992-5252	R	1 TA	<0.1
Ticor Title Agency of San Antonio	10010 San Pedro St.	San Antonio	TX	78216	Jack Rogers	210-340-2921	R	1 TA	<0.1
Title Company Inc.	P.O. Box 445	La Crosse	WI	54602	Michael F. Wille	608-791-2015	R	1 TA	<0.1
Commerce Title Insurance Agency of Florida Inc.	218 Apollo Beach Blvd.	Apollo Beach	FL	33572	Mike Peterson	813-645-4641	R	1 TA*	<0.1

Source: Ward's Business Directory of U.S. Private and Public Companies, 1996. Company type codes: P - Public, R - Private, S - Subsidiary, D - Division, J - Joint Venture, A - Affiliate, G - Group. If the dollar values shown are not sales, the following codes apply: TA - Total Assets; OR - Operating Revenues; GB - Gross Billings. * - estimated dollar value. < - less than; *na* - not available.

SIC 6370

PENSION, HEALTH, AND WELFARE FUNDS

The industry includes organizations primarily engaged in managing pension, retirement, health, and welfare funds. Specific categories include pension funds; union trust funds; union welfare, benefit, and health funds; and welfare pensions.

ESTABLISHMENTS, EMPLOYMENT, AND PAYROLL

	1988	1989		1990		1991		1992		1993		% change 88-93
		Value	%	Value	%	Value	%	Value	%	Value	%	
All Establishments	2,622	5,656	115.7	3,780	-33.2	10,255	171.3	8,459	-17.5	6,027	-28.8	129.9
Mid-March Employment	17,266	26,885	55.7	25,063	-6.8	47,187	88.3	46,693	-1.0	54,405	16.5	215.1
1st Quarter Wages (annualized - $ mil.)	379.8	543.8	43.2	590.9	8.7	983.8	66.5	1,013.5	3.0	1,101.7	8.7	190.0
Payroll per Emp. 1st Q. (annualized)	21,999	20,225	-8.1	23,576	16.6	20,848	-11.6	21,706	4.1	20,249	-6.7	-8.0
Annual Payroll ($ mil.)	407.3	667.0	63.8	632.7	-5.1	1,269.1	100.6	1,214.6	-4.3	1,238.7	2.0	204.2
Establishments - 1-4 Emp. Number	1,731	4,292	147.9	2,554	-40.5	7,829	206.5	6,101	-22.1	3,960	-35.1	128.8
Mid-March Employment	2,915	4,030	38.3	3,603	-10.6	6,102	69.4	6,641	8.8	4,995	-24.8	71.4
1st Quarter Wages (annualized - $ mil.)	55.1	72.8	32.0	74.2	2.0	104.6	40.9	132.0	26.2	104.9	-20.5	90.3
Payroll per Emp. 1st Q. (annualized)	18,916	18,057	-4.5	20,600	14.1	17,143	-16.8	19,877	16.0	21,003	5.7	11.0
Annual Payroll ($ mil.)	92.1	214.9	133.3	129.0	-40.0	433.3	235.8	344.3	-20.5	192.7	-44.0	109.1
Establishments - 5-9 Emp. Number	465	694	49.2	627	-9.7	1,108	76.7	1,086	-2.0	908	-16.4	95.3
Mid-March Employment	3,017	4,607	52.7	4,174	-9.4	7,382	76.9	7,114	-3.6	5,987	-15.8	98.4
1st Quarter Wages (annualized - $ mil.)	66.3	87.2	31.5	89.4	2.5	144.7	61.8	152.9	5.7	134.8	-11.9	103.2
Payroll per Emp. 1st Q. (annualized)	21,981	18,935	-13.9	21,417	13.1	19,596	-8.5	21,499	9.7	22,507	4.7	2.4
Annual Payroll ($ mil.)	68.9	89.7	30.1	94.2	5.0	147.9	57.0	163.1	10.3	140.5	-13.9	103.8
Establishments - 10-19 Emp. Number	262	384	46.6	334	-13.0	721	115.9	700	-2.9	576	-17.7	119.8
Mid-March Employment	3,457	5,019	45.2	4,466	-11.0	9,739	118.1	9,441	-3.1	7,781	-17.6	125.1
1st Quarter Wages (annualized - $ mil.)	72.5	97.5	34.6	93.3	-4.4	189.4	103.1	206.4	9.0	184.9	-10.4	155.1
Payroll per Emp. 1st Q. (annualized)	20,965	19,433	-7.3	20,880	7.4	19,449	-6.9	21,866	12.4	23,760	8.7	13.3
Annual Payroll ($ mil.)	68.7	95.2	38.6	90.6	-4.9	182.3	101.3	210.0	15.2	190.0	-9.5	176.5
Establishments - 20-49 Emp. Number	143	240	67.8	236	-1.7	534	126.3	488	-8.6	406	-16.8	183.9
Mid-March Employment	4,357	7,424	70.4	7,255	-2.3	16,342	125.3	14,867	-9.0	12,474	-16.1	186.3
1st Quarter Wages (annualized - $ mil.)	84.2	135.4	60.7	157.1	16.0	341.4	117.3	301.7	-11.6	278.0	-7.9	230.0
Payroll per Emp. 1st Q. (annualized)	19,334	18,235	-5.7	21,652	18.7	20,891	-3.5	20,291	-2.9	22,283	9.8	15.3
Annual Payroll ($ mil.)	78.0	116.8	49.8	139.3	19.2	306.9	120.4	293.5	-4.4	285.4	-2.8	265.9
Establishments - 50-99 Emp. Number	11	33	200.0	16	-51.5	44	175.0	(D)	-	117	-	963.6
Mid-March Employment	824	2,319	181.4	(D)	-	(D)	-	(D)	-	7,927	-	862.0
1st Quarter Wages (annualized - $ mil.)	21.8	59.6	173.4	(D)	-	(D)	-	(D)	-	160.9	-	637.5
Payroll per Emp. 1st Q. (annualized)	26,481	25,721	-2.9	(D)	-	(D)	-	(D)	-	20,300	-	-23.3
Annual Payroll ($ mil.)	23.2	59.0	154.4	(D)	-	(D)	-	(D)	-	162.1	-	598.3
Establishments - 100-249 Emp. Number	6	8	33.3	9	12.5	16	77.8	31	93.8	47	51.6	683.3
Mid-March Employment	1,112	1,420	27.7	1,638	15.4	2,178	33.0	4,451	104.4	7,197	61.7	547.2
1st Quarter Wages (annualized - $ mil.)	27.5	34.3	24.7	39.7	15.8	55.3	39.2	111.1	100.8	162.3	46.1	489.5
Payroll per Emp. 1st Q. (annualized)	24,759	24,175	-2.4	24,261	0.4	25,399	4.7	24,952	-1.8	22,551	-9.6	-8.9
Annual Payroll ($ mil.)	27.5	34.4	25.5	39.9	15.8	55.0	37.8	110.3	100.6	177.7	61.2	547.5
Establishments - 250-499 Emp. Number	3	4	33.3	2	-50.0	1	-50.0	(D)	-	10	-	233.3
Mid-March Employment	(D)	(D)	-	(D)	-	(D)	-	(D)	-	3,375	-	-
1st Quarter Wages (annualized - $ mil.)	(D)	(D)	-	(D)	-	(D)	-	(D)	-	63.4	-	-
Payroll per Emp. 1st Q. (annualized)	(D)	(D)	-	(D)	-	(D)	-	(D)	-	18,785	-	-
Annual Payroll ($ mil.)	(D)	(D)	-	(D)	-	(D)	-	(D)	-	70.9	-	-
Establishments - 500-999 Emp. Number	1	1	-	1	-	1	-	-	-	(D)	-	-
Mid-March Employment	(D)	(D)	-	(D)	-	(D)	-	-	-	(D)	-	-
1st Quarter Wages (annualized - $ mil.)	(D)	(D)	-	(D)	-	(D)	-	-	-	(D)	-	-
Payroll per Emp. 1st Q. (annualized)	(D)	(D)	-	(D)	-	(D)	-	-	-	(D)	-	-
Annual Payroll ($ mil.)	(D)	(D)	-	(D)	-	(D)	-	-	-	(D)	-	-
Estab. - 1000 or More Emp. Number	-	-	-	1	-	1	-	-	-	(D)	-	-
Mid-March Employment	-	-	-	(D)	-	(D)	-	-	-	(D)	-	-
1st Quarter Wages (annualized - $ mil.)	-	-	-	(D)	-	(D)	-	-	-	(D)	-	-
Payroll per Emp. 1st Q. (annualized)	(D)	(D)	-	(D)	-	(D)	-	-	-	(D)	-	-
Annual Payroll ($ mil.)	-	-	-	(D)	-	(D)	-	-	-	(D)	-	-

Source: County Business Patterns, U.S. Department of Commerce, Washington, D.C., for 1988 through 1993. Payroll per employee is calculated using mid-March employment and 1st Quarter wages, annualized. Annual payroll, also shown, may not equal the annualized 1st Quarter wages. Columns headed by a percent sign (%) indicate change from the previous year. *na* stands for not available. The symbol (D) indicates that data are withheld by the source to avoid disclosure of competitive information. A dash (-) indicates that data are not available or cannot be calculated.

ESTABLISHMENTS
Number

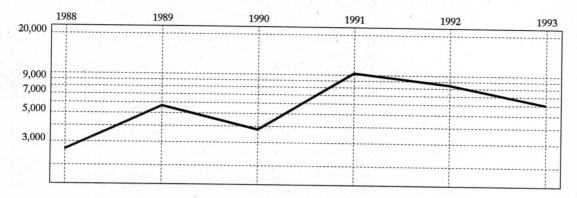

MID-MARCH EMPLOYMENT
Number

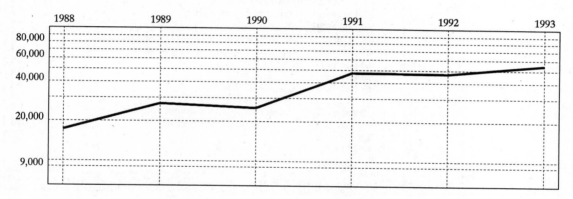

ANNUAL PAYROLL
$ million

INPUTS AND OUTPUTS FOR INSURANCE CARRIERS - SIC GROUP 63

Economic Sector or Industry Providing Inputs	%	Sector	Economic Sector or Industry Buying Outputs	%	Sector
Insurance agents, brokers, & services	62.9	Fin/R.E.	Personal consumption expenditures	77.1	
Security & commodity brokers	6.8	Fin/R.E.	Owner-occupied dwellings	5.5	Fin/R.E.
Eating & drinking places	4.0	Trade	Real estate	3.6	Fin/R.E.
Real estate	4.0	Fin/R.E.	Banking	0.9	Fin/R.E.
Communications, except radio & TV	3.9	Util.	Federal Government purchases, nondefense	0.9	Fed Govt
Imports	1.8	Foreign	Electric services (utilities)	0.8	Util.
Commercial printing	1.3	Manufg.	Insurance agents, brokers, & services	0.7	Fin/R.E.
Computer & data processing services	1.3	Services	Feed grains	0.6	Agric.
Advertising	1.2	Services	Exports	0.5	Foreign
Hotels & lodging places	1.2	Services	Motor freight transportation & warehousing	0.5	Util.
Legal services	1.2	Services	Retail trade, except eating & drinking	0.5	Trade
Accounting, auditing & bookkeeping	0.9	Services	Credit agencies other than banks	0.4	Fin/R.E.
Banking	0.9	Fin/R.E.	S/L Govt. purch., elem. & secondary education	0.4	S/L Govt
U.S. Postal Service	0.9	Gov't	Sanitary services, steam supply, irrigation	0.4	Util.
Air transportation	0.6	Util.	State & local government enterprises, nec	0.3	Gov't
Credit agencies other than banks	0.6	Fin/R.E.	Water supply & sewage systems	0.3	Util.
Management & consulting services & labs	0.6	Services	Wholesale trade	0.3	Trade
Maintenance of nonfarm buildings nec	0.5	Constr.	Food grains	0.2	Agric.
Manifold business forms	0.5	Manufg.	Meat animals	0.2	Agric.
Motor freight transportation & warehousing	0.5	Util.	Petroleum refining	0.2	Manufg.
Petroleum refining	0.5	Manufg.	Religious organizations	0.2	Services
Photographic equipment & supplies	0.4	Manufg.	Air transportation	0.1	Util.
Transit & bus transportation	0.4	Util.	Arrangement of passenger transportation	0.1	Util.
Business services nec	0.3	Services	Equipment rental & leasing services	0.1	Services
Personnel supply services	0.3	Services	Freight forwarders	0.1	Util.
Wholesale trade	0.3	Trade	Industrial buildings	0.1	Constr.
Automotive rental & leasing, without drivers	0.2	Services	Office buildings	0.1	Constr.
Electric services (utilities)	0.2	Util.	Oil bearing crops	0.1	Agric.
Electronic computing equipment	0.2	Manufg.	Residential 1-unit structures, nonfarm	0.1	Constr.
Detective & protective services	0.1	Services	Transit & bus transportation	0.1	Util.
Electrical repair shops	0.1	Services			
Envelopes	0.1	Manufg.			
Manufacturing industries, nec	0.1	Manufg.			

Source: Benchmark Input-Output Accounts for the U.S. Economy, 1982, U.S. Department of Commerce, Washington, D.C., July 1991. Data, as reported in the source, are organized by the 1977 SIC structure in use in 1982 but have been matched, as closely as is possible, to the 1987 SIC structure used in this book. Activities with the same percentage are sorted alphabetically by name of activity.

OCCUPATIONS EMPLOYED BY PENSION FUNDS AND INSURANCE, NEC

Occupation	% of Total 1994	Change to 2005	Occupation	% of Total 1994	Change to 2005
Title examiners & searchers	11.3	1.8	Insurance sales workers	2.6	10.0
General office clerks	8.3	8.5	Underwriters	2.6	27.2
Secretaries, ex legal & medical	7.0	15.8	Clerical support workers nec	2.4	1.7
General managers & top executives	6.3	20.7	Management support workers nec	2.1	52.7
Clerical supervisors & managers	4.8	30.1	Financial managers	2.0	27.2
Legal assistants, law clerks nec	4.6	57.5	File clerks	2.0	-36.4
Bookkeeping, accounting, & auditing clerks	4.5	-4.6	Accountants & auditors	1.7	27.2
Typists & word processors	4.2	-36.4	Computer programmers	1.7	3.1
Receptionists & information clerks	3.1	27.2	Messengers	1.4	-1.2
Insurance policy processing clerks	3.1	1.8	Marketing & sales worker supervisors	1.3	27.2
Loan & credit clerks	3.0	14.5	Data entry keyers, ex composing	1.2	-6.1
Insurance claims clerks	2.9	16.7	Claims examiners, insurance	1.2	16.0
Insurance adjusters, examiners, & investigators	2.6	33.6	Managers & administrators nec	1.0	27.1

Sources: Industry-Occupation Matrix, Bureau of Labor Statistics. These data relate to one or more 3-digit SIC industry groups rather than to a single 4-digit SIC. The change reported for each occupation to the year 2005 is a percent of growth or decline as estimated by the Bureau of Labor Statistics. The abbreviation *nec* stands for not elsewhere classified.

U.S. AND STATE DATA ON INDUSTRY REVENUES AND OTHER ACCOUNTS FOR 1992

State	No. of Estab.	Employ- ment	Payroll ($ mil.)	Revenues ($ mil.)	Empl./ Estab.	Revenue/ Estab. ($)	Payroll/ Estab. ($)	Revenue/ Empl. ($)	Payroll/ Empl. ($)
UNITED STATES	1,491	20,374	596.9	1,379.4	14	925,149	400,348	67,704	29,298
California	245	3,552	114.6	234.5	14	957,331	467,796	66,032	32,266
Colorado	29	953	24.4	68.9	33	2,377,379	840,621	72,344	25,580
Florida	66	-	(D)	(D)	(D)	(D)	(D)	(D)	(D)
Georgia	33	-	(D)	(D)	(D)	(D)	(D)	(D)	(D)
Illinois	80	-	(D)	(D)	(D)	(D)	(D)	(D)	(D)
Indiana	33	618	16.3	32.3	19	978,758	492,485	52,264	26,298
Maryland	30	-	(D)	(D)	(D)	(D)	(D)	(D)	(D)
Massachusetts	39	-	(D)	(D)	(D)	(D)	(D)	(D)	(D)
Michigan	57	-	(D)	(D)	(D)	(D)	(D)	(D)	(D)
Minnesota	29	506	16.7	36.2	17	1,246,655	574,517	71,449	32,927
Missouri	31	-	(D)	(D)	(D)	(D)	(D)	(D)	(D)
New Jersey	49	352	13.8	33.1	7	675,020	282,633	93,966	39,344
New York	99	1,184	37.8	99.5	12	1,004,879	381,364	84,023	31,888
North Carolina	26	-	(D)	(D)	(D)	(D)	(D)	(D)	(D)
Ohio	89	1,590	39.8	99.3	18	1,116,258	447,326	62,482	25,039
Pennsylvania	73	-	(D)	(D)	(D)	(D)	(D)	(D)	(D)
Tennessee	25	-	(D)	(D)	(D)	(D)	(D)	(D)	(D)
Texas	76	813	23.3	48.2	11	634,539	306,092	59,317	28,614
Virginia	43	-	(D)	(D)	(D)	(D)	(D)	(D)	(D)
Washington	36	-	(D)	(D)	(D)	(D)	(D)	(D)	(D)
Wisconsin	41	-	(D)	(D)	(D)	(D)	(D)	(D)	(D)

Source: 1992 Economic Census, U.S. Department of Commerce, Washington, D.C. This is the only table that shows revenue data as collected by the Bureau of the Census in an Economic Census. The symbol (D) indicates that data are withheld by the source to avoid disclosure of competitive information. A dash (-) indicates that data are not available or cannot be calculated.

ESTABLISHMENTS 1992 - STATE AND REGIONAL CONCENTRATION

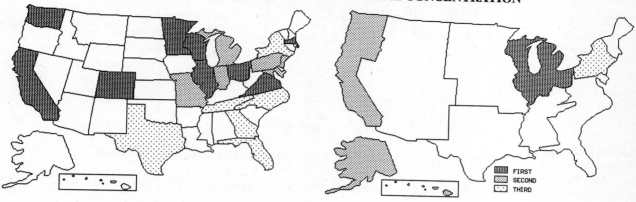

EMPLOYMENT 1992 - STATE AND REGIONAL CONCENTRATION

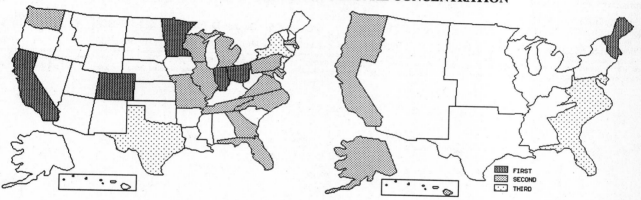

REVENUES 1992 - STATE AND REGIONAL CONCENTRATION

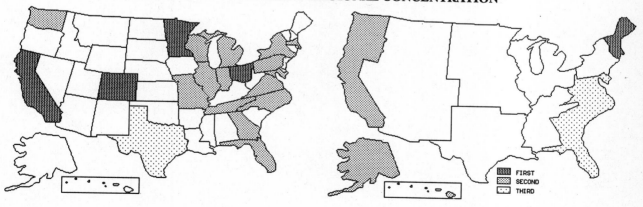

States with the darkest shading indicate those states which have proportionately more establishments, employment, or revenues than would be indicated by the state's population. States with light shading are states with proportionately fewer establishments, less employment, and lower revenues than population distribution. States shaded grey are within 15 percent of the state's population proportion in these categories. States for which no data are available are shown as average (grey). *Regions* are shaded to indicate absolute rank in the category. If no data for the category are available, establishment counts are used to shade the regions. Source of the data is the table on the facing page.

LEADING COMPANIES - SIC 6371 - Pension, Health, and Welfare Funds

Number shown: **9**   Total sales/assets ($ mil): **7,582**   Total employment (000): **4.3**

Company Name	Address				CEO Name	Phone	Co. Type	Sales/Assets ($ mil)	Empl. (000)
Cres Inc.	730 3rd Ave.	New York	NY	10017	John H. Biggs	212-916-4000	R	5,357 TA	4.0
Los Angeles County Employees' Retirement Association	P.O. Box 7060	Pasadena	CA	91109	Marsha Richter	818-564-6000	3	980 TA	0.2
Wyoming Retirement System	1st Fl. East Herschler	Cheyenne	WY	82002	Gerald Fox	307-777-7691	R	480 TA*	<0.1
Hialeah City Employees' Retirement System	501 Palm Ave.	Hialeah	FL	33010	Myles Milander	305-883-8050	3	275 TA	<0.1
Orange County Employees' Retirement System	2942 Daimler St.	Santa Ana	CA	92705	Mary Jean Hackwood	714-975-1962	R	228 TA	<0.1
Employees' Retirement System of the County of Milwaukee	901 N. 9th St.	Milwaukee	WI	53233	Jac R. Amerell	414-278-4242	R	200 TA	<0.1
Mobile Policemen and Firefighter's Pension Fund	P.O. Box 1827	Mobile	AL	36633	Bennett Howard	205-434-7360	3	39 TA	<0.1
Queen City Insurance Agencies Inc.	4785 Eastern Ave.	Cincinnati	OH	45226	Thomas D. Cassady	513-533-1100	R	23 TA	<0.1
SCI Pension Services Inc.	P.O. Box 1326	Cedar Rapids	IA	52406	Donna Sorensen	319-368-2626	S	0 TA	<0.1

Source: Ward's Business Directory of U.S. Private and Public Companies, 1996. Company type codes: P - Public, R - Private, S - Subsidiary, D - Division, J - Joint Venture, A - Affiliate, G - Group. If the dollar values shown are not sales, the following codes apply: TA - Total Assets; OR - Operating Revenues; GB - Gross Billings. * - estimated dollar value. < - less than; *na* - not available.

FINANCIAL DATA ON PENSION FUNDS

The following seven tables present information on various aspects of pension funds. Data were obtained from the American Council of Life Insurance, 1001 Pennsylvania Avenue, N.W., Washington, D.C. 20004-2599, and are reproduced by permission.

NUMBER OF PERSONS COVERED BY MAJOR PENSION AND RETIREMENT PROGRAMS

In the United States. In thousands.

Year	Private plans		Government-administered plans			
	With life insurance companies	Other private plans	Railroad retirement	Federal civilian employees[2]	State and local employees	OASI[2]
1940	695	3,565	1,349	745	1,552	22,900
1945	1,470	5,240	1,846	2,928	2,008	41,070
1950	2,755	7,500	1,881	1,872	2,894	61,506
1955	4,105	12,290	1,876	2,333	3,927	74,887
1960	5,475	17,540	1,654	2,703	5,160	91,496
1965	7,040	21,060	1,661	3,114	6,780	103,827
1970	10,580	25,520	1,633	3,624	8,591	120,014
1975	15,190	30,300[1]	1,564	4,171	11,230	135,744
1976	16,965	N.A.	1,572	4,210	12,290	138,633
1977	19,205	N.A.	1,567	4,292	13,124	141,596
1978	21,615	N.A.	1,580	4,380	13,400[1]	144,260
1979	23,310	N.A.	1,567	4,398	13,680[1]	147,178
1980	26,185	N.A.	1,533	4,460	13,950[1]	153,634
1981	27,665	N.A.	1,483	4,566	14,230[1]	157,569
1982	31,010	N.A.	1,404	4,610	14,504	160,611
1983	32,680	N.A.	1,383	4,683	14,464	161,836
1984	35,570	N.A.	1,362	4,791	14,788	161,986
1985	39,620	N.A.	1,309	4,887	15,235	162,881
1986	45,895	N.A.	1,271	4,938	15,426	164,438
1987	51,015	N.A.	1,243	5,065	15,460	167,077
1988	54,000	N.A.	1,229	5,281	15,864	169,270
1989	59,185	N.A.	1,212	5,499	17,086	171,801
1990	61,990	N.A.	1,184	5,447	16,857	174,143
1991	59,255	N.A.	1,157	5,503	17,502	176,615
1992	58,290	N.A.	1,133	5,475	18,320	179,839
1993	60,680	N.A.	1,107	5,330	N.A.	181,630
1994	64,385	N.A.	1,084	5,340	N.A.	182,179

Source: Compiled by the American Council of Life Insurance. *Notes:* Some data are revised. It is not possible to obtain a total for number of persons covered by pension plans by adding together the figures shown by the year. Each series has been derived separately and there are differences in amount of duplication within each series and among the various series and also differences in definition of "coverage" among the series. Private plans with life insurance companies include persons covered by Keogh plans, tax-deferred annuities and, after 1974, IRA plans. Data for "Other Private Plans," compiled by the Social Security Administration, exclude plans for the self-employed, those having vested benefits but not presently employed at the firm where benefits were accrued, and also exclude an estimated number who have vested benefits from employment other than from their current employment. These data represent various dates during the year, since the fiscal years of the plans are not necessarily the same. Trends from year to year within each series are not affected. The number of persons covered include survivors or dependents of deceased workers and beneficiaries as well as retired workers. Retirement arrangements for members of the armed forces, and provisions for veterans' pensions, are not included. N.A. stands for not available. 1. Estimated. 2. Includes members of the U.S. Civil Service Retirement System, the Tennessee Valley Authority Retirement System, the Foreign Service Retirement System, and the Federal Reserve Employee Retirement System (Board and Bank plans). 3. Includes living workers insured for retirement and/or survivors benefits, including the self-employed, plus dependents of retired workers and survivors of deceased workers who are receiving periodic benefits.

ASSETS AND RESERVES OF MAJOR PENSION AND RETIREMENT PROGRAMS

In the United States. In millions.

Year	Private plans		Government-administered plans			
	With life insurance companies	Other private means	Railroad retirement	Federal civilian employees[1]	State and local employees	Old-age, survivors and disability insurance[2]
1950	5,600	N.A.	2,553	4,344	5,154	13,721
1960	18,850	40,900	3,740	10,790	19,600	22,613
1965	27,350	80,200	3,946	16,516	33,100	19,841
1970	41,175	123,900	4,398	23,922	58,200	38,068
1975	72,210	244,300	3,100	39,248	103,700	44,342
1976	88,990	275,300	3,065	44,089	117,300	41,133
1977	101,520	297,300	2,584	50,832	130,800	35,861
1978	116,555	351,300	2,787	57,677	142,573	31,746
1979	138,515	413,100	2,611	65,914	161,649	30,291
1980	166,850	504,400	2,086	75,802	185,226	26,453
1981	193,210	530,200	1,126	86,867	209,444	24,539
1982	233,790	659,400	460	99,462	245,252	24,778[3]
1983	269,425	800,500	601	114,219	289,731	24,867[3]
1984	313,215	861,100	3,712	129,787	324,369	31,075[3]
1985	373,475	1,093,000	5,109	148,166	373,932	42,163[3]
1986	441,390	1,290,800	6,365	167,606	437,229	46,861
1987	495,420	1,367,000	6,860	185,946	512,854	68,807
1988	562,155	1,421,800	8,031	205,145	577,621	109,762
1989	624,290	1,705,600	8,906	225,963	634,978	162,968
1990	695,700	1,629,100	9,891	247,513	720,803	225,277
1991	745,950	2,055,500	10,655	272,765	783,405	280,747
1992	768,215	2,144,500	11,746	300,555	866,131	331,473
1993	825,375	2,342,100	12,047	330,701	N.A.	378,285
1994	878,460	2,356,400	12,929	358,012	N.A.	436,385

Source: Compiled by the American Council of Life Insurance. *Notes:* Some data are revised. These data are as of various dates during the year, since the fiscal years of the plans are not necessarily the same. Trends from year to year are not affected. N.A. stands for not available. 1. Includes the U.S. Civil Service Retirement System, the Tennessee Valley Retirement System, the Foreign Service Retirement System, and the Federal Reserve Employee Retirement System (Board and Bank plans). 2. Beginning in 1957, assets of Disability Insurance trust Funds are included. Hospital and Supplementary Medical Insurance is not included. 3. Included funds borrowed from the Hospital Insurance Trust Fund.

PENSION FUNDS - DISTRIBUTION OF ASSETS - 1952-1994

In millions.

Calendar year	U.S. government securities	Corporate and foreign bonds	Corporate equities	Mortgages	Open-market paper[1]	Time deposits	Demand deposits and currency	Miscellaneous	Total
1952	2,500	4,600	1,800	200	-	400	300	900	10,700
1955	3,000	7,900	6,100	300	-	700	400	1,300	19,600
1960	2,700	15,700	16,600	1,300	-	1,400	600	2,800	40,900
1965	3,000	22,700	41,200	3,400	-	2,900	900	6,200	80,200
1970	3,000	29,400	67,900	4,200	-	6,300	1,100	11,900	123,900
1975	17,900	41,900	110,800	2,400	9,100	14,500	4,400	43,500	244,300
1976	24,200	40,200	129,000	2,400	11,000	16,700	4,500	47,400	275,300
1977	29,800	44,600	127,300	2,500	11,400	19,700	4,800	57,200	297,300
1978	31,900	53,000	154,000	2,700	11,600	23,700	5,200	69,400	351,300
1979	38,600	63,700	180,500	3,100	16,600	27,900	5,100	77,700	413,100
1980	50,500	77,700	230,600	3,600	22,100	31,900	4,200	83,800	504,400
1981	66,900	83,300	222,600	3,900	31,100	36,500	3,400	82,600	530,200
1982	107,800	95,200	288,700	9,100	19,900	49,400	2,300	87,000	659,400
1983	132,700	107,900	357,200	9,900	23,100	60,900	2,700	106,000	800,500
1984	153,900	123,400	366,900	10,000	26,500	68,000	3,300	109,100	861,100
1985	191,100	155,100	475,200	12,500	29,000	90,000	4,000	136,300	1,093,000
1986	224,300	178,300	564,900	15,500	39,200	109,400	4,300	155,100	1,290,800
1987	242,600	190,100	567,900	13,500	46,600	126,700	5,000	174,800	1,367,000
1988	251,200	203,900	640,700	17,700	51,100	151,300	4,600	101,300	1,421,800
1989	312,600	226,100	776,300	25,100	44,100	188,000	5,800	127,600	1,705,600
1990	323,100	235,500	703,000	23,800	42,700	175,600	5,800	119,600	1,629,100
1991	364,300	275,700	952,900	32,200	39,600	229,100	4,700	157,300	2,055,900
1992	385,300	292,100	1,048,500	35,200	38,200	238,600	4,600	171,600	2,213,800
1993	403,000	309,400	1,216,800	39,000	43,500	244,600	4,600	189,000	2,449,800
1994	380,100	294,500	1,189,200	38,400	41,100	218,700	3,500	185,400	2,350,900

Source: Federal Reserve System. *Notes:* Some data are revised. Details may not add to totals due to rounding. 1. Includes Money Market Fund shares.

PENSION FUNDS - FEDERAL - 1940-1994

In millions.

Year	Persons insured for retirement benefits	Assets[2] (trust funds) (end of year)	Contributions during year[1]			
			Employer	Employee	Self-employed	Total
1940	24.9	2,031	319	319	-	638
1945	40.3	7,121	643	643	-	1,285
1950	59.8	13,721	1,334	1,334	-	2,667
1955	71.4	21,663	2,730	2,664	319	5,713
1960	85.4	22,613	5,632	5,543	701	11,876
1965	95.8	19,841	8,183	7,991	1,032	17,205
1970	108.1	38,068	16,643	16,321	1,774	34,737
1975	122.9	44,342	30,746	30,478	3,036	64,259
1976	125.9	41,133	34,381	34,080	3,133	71,595
1977	128.9	35,861	37,724	37,439	3,548	78,710
1978	133.3	31,746	42,745	42,370	3,768	88,883
1979	137.0	30,291	49,546	49,084	4,404	103,034
1980	139.5	26,453	56,036	55,692	4,983	116,711
1981	142.4	24,539	67,046	66,690	5,628	139,364
1982	1445	24,778[3]	69,702	69,492	6,473	145,667
1983	145.9	24,867[3]	72,314	72,070	5,879	150,263
1984	147.9	31,075[3]	85,647	81,125	7,372	174,145
1985	150.7	42,163[3]	91,801	91,488	8,497	191,785
1986	153.0	46,861	98,964	98,454	9,611	207,029
1987	155.2	68,807	104,781	104,375	11,104	220,260
1988	157.6	109,762	117,728	117,165	14,317	249,209
1989	160.1	162,968	128,832	127,960	14,799	271,591
1990	162.4	225,277	138,686	137,819	17,508	294,013
1991	165.8	280,747	140,751	140,081	20,380	301,212
1992	167.3	331,473	146,353	145,600	18,661	310,614
1993	169.4	378,285	153,154	152,636	15,917	321,707
1994	171.3	436,385	163,104	162,279	19,019	344,402

Source: Social Security Administration. *Notes:* Some data are revised. Data may not add to totals due to rounding. 1. Figures do not include contributions to the hospital and medical insurance programs. 2. Assets do not reflect solely the contributions paid for Social Security by the private economy, less payments and administration costs. For example, prior to 1940, contributions were paid into the government general funds, and an appropriation was then made to a "reserve account" from the general funds, not necessarily equal to the contributions. The OASI trust fund was established in 1940, and from time to time payments from government general funds have been made to this trust fund to cover special items, such as costs of benefits to survivors of certain World War II servicemen. The DI trust fund was established in 1957, and includes certain payments other than regular contributions, such as reimbursement for non-contributory credit for military service. Other payments from government general funds will be made into these funds in the future to cover costs of such items as the special payments to persons 72 and over provided in the Tax Adjustment Act of 1966. The assets shown above do not include funds in the two newest trust funds - the hospital insurance trust fund, effective January 1, 1966, and the supplementary medical insurance trust fund, effective July, 1966. 3. Includes funds borrowed from the Hospital Insurance Trust Fund.

PENSION FUNDS - RAILROAD RETIREMENT SYSTEM - 1930-1994

Thousands of persons and millions of dollars.

Year	Number of persons				Contributions in year[3]			Benefits paid in year			Assets
	Not yet receiving benefits	Retired or disabled	Survivors and dependents	Total	Employers	Employees	Total	Retired or disabled	Survivors and dependents	Total	
1930	[1]	[1]	-	1,400	30	-	30	N.A.	-	N.A.	-
1940	1,205	141	3	1,349	65	65	130	114	-	114	136
1950	1,494	251	136	1,881	273	273	546	254	N.A.	N.A.	2,553
1960	862	384	408	1,654	298	298	596	626	336	962	3,740
1970	650	444	539	1,633	493	467	960	1,108	663	1,771	4,398
1971	595	440	543	1,578	475	450	925	1,200	802	2,002	4,300
1972	586	447	542	1,575	525	475	1,000	1,350	825	2,175	4,100
1973	589	443	550	1,582	540	500	1,040	1,550	1,015	2,565	3,800
1974	585	457	546[2]	1,588	1,201	421	1,622	1,710	1,098	2,808	3,600
1975	532	469	563[2]	1,564	1,209	423	1,632	1,970	1,313	3,283	3,100
1976	541	466	565[2]	1,572	1,325	465	1,790	2,102	1,469	3,571	3,065
1977	534	464	569[2]	1,567	1,457	507	1,964	2,245	1,579	3,824	2,584
1978	553	459	568[2]	1,580	1,520	546	2,066	2,353	1,668	4,021	2,787
1979	545	455	567[2]	1,567	1,732	682	2,414	2,552	1,810	4,362	2,611
1980	518	451	564[2]	1,533	1,845	717	2,562	2,839	2,027	4,866	2,086
1981	477	447	559[2]	1,483	1,971	838	2,809	3,128	2,243	5,371	1,126
1982	404	443	557[2]	1,404	2,193	1,015	3,208	3,421	2,422	5,843	460
1983	393	438	552[2]	1,383	2,169	1,004	3,173	3,565	2,489	6,054	601
1984	386	431	545[2]	1,362	2,548	1,192	3,740	3,623	2,509	6,132	3,712
1985	346	425	538[2]	1,309	2,586	1,278	3,864	3,715	2,555	6,270	5,109
1986	323	418	530[2]	1,271	2,578	1,286	3,864	3,795	2,586	6,381	6,365
1987	308	412	523[2]	1,243	2,537	1,268	3,805	3,919	2,626	6,545	6,860
1988	307	406	516[2]	1,229	2,847	1,456	4,303	4,062	2,678	6,740	8,031
1989	300	402	510[2]	1,212	2,701	1,368	4,069	4,231	2,752	6,983	8,906
1990	287	395	502[2]	1,184	2,676	1,374	4,050	4,421	2,838	7,259	9,891
1991	277	387	493[2]	1,157	2,749	1,415	4,164	4,623	2,947	7,570	10,655
1992	272	379	482[2]	1,133	2,807	1,442	4,249	4,740	3,007	7,747	11,746
1993	267	370	470[2]	1,107	2,750	1,417	4,167	4,844	3,055	7,899	12,047
1994	267	360	457[2]	1,084	2,751	1,430	4,181	4,910	3,094	8,004	12,929

Source: U.S. Railroad Retirement Board. *Notes:* Some data are revised. N.A. stands for not available. 1. Not available separately. 2. Figure includes employee annuitants also receiving benefits as dependents of survivors. 3. Excludes financial interchange transfers from Social Security trust funds.

PENSION FUNDS - STATE AND LOCAL GOVERNMENT - 1950-1992

Thousands of persons and millions of dollars.

Year	Number of persons				Contribution in year			Benefits paid in year			Assets
	Not yet receiving benefits	Retired or disabled	Survivors and dependents	Total	Employers	Employees	Total	Retired or disabled	Survivors and dependents	Total	
1950	2,600	254	40	2,894	510	395	905	274	26	300	5,154
1960	4,500	590	70	5,160	1,725	1,170	2,895	940	75	1,015	19,600
1970	7,300	1,171	120	8,591	4,920	2,975	7,895	2,905	215	3,120	58,200
1971	7,700	1,254	125	9,079	5,495	3,280	8,775	3,372	248	3,620	64,800
1972	8,100	1,333	130	9,563	6,050	3,570	9,620	4,085	250	4,335	73,400
1973	8,300	1,415	135	9,850	6,649	4,166	10,815	4,785	290	5,075	82,700
1974	9,000	1,495	140	10,635	7,821	4,207	12,028	5,495	340	5,835	92,400
1975	9,500	1,585	145	11,230	9,116	4,488	13,604	6,335	390	6,725	103,700
1976	10,450	1,690	150	12,290	10,502	4,808	15,310	7,250	450	7,700	117,300
1977	10,951	1,989	184	13,124	12,369	5,233	17,602	7,965	490	8,455	130,800
1978	11,080[1]	2,120[1]	200[1]	13,400[1]	13,621	5,688	19,309	8,945[1]	605[1]	9,550	142,573
1979	11,210[1]	2,260[1]	210[1]	13,680[1]	15,336	6,069	21,405	10,035[1]	735[1]	10,770	161,649
1980	11,340[1]	2,390[1]	220[1]	13,950[1]	17,532	6,466	23,998	11,307[1]	900[1]	12,207	185,226
1981	11,480[1]	2,520[1]	230[1]	14,230[1]	20,020	7,289	27,309	12,972[1]	858[1]	13,830	209,444
1982	11,607	2,654	244	14,504	21,808	8,123	29,931	14,849	831	15,680	245,252
1983	11,370	2,873	221	14,464	22,956	8,699	31,655	16,750	734	17,484	289,731
1984	11,496	3,051	241	14,788	24,977	8,845	33,822	18,942	872	19,814	324,369
1985	11,842	3,140	253	15,235	27,399	9,479	36,878	21,025	968	21,993	373,932
1986	11,907	3,252	267	15,426	28,599	10,586	39,185	23,408	1,033	24,442	437,229
1987	11,763	3,463	234	15,460	30,384	11,241	41,625	25,045	985	26,030	512,854
1988	12,155	3,438	271	15,864	30,642	11,882	42,524	28,469	1,255	29,724	577,621
1989	12,775	3,834	477	17,086	31,186	12,871	44,057	31,444	1,536	32,980	634,978
1990	12,832	3,726	299	16,857	32,578	13,853	46,431	33,199	1,642	34,841	720,803
1991	13,323	3,821	358	17,502	33,163	16,268	49,431	36,767	2,007	38,774	783,405
1992	13,574	4,354	392	18,320	33,554	16,028	49,582	41,420	2,229	43,649	866,131

Source: Bureau of the Census, U.S. Department of Commerce. *Notes:* Some data are revised. Beneficiaries are as of June 30. Financial data is on a calendar year basis prior to 1977, and on a June 30 fiscal year basis thereafter. Details may not add to totals due to rounding. 1. Estimated.

PENSION FUNDS - FEDERAL CIVILIAN RETIREMENT SYSTEMS - 1991-1994

Thousands of persons and millions of dollars.

	Number of persons receiving benefits				Contributions in year			Benefits paid in year			Assets and re-serves
	Not yet receiving benefits	Retired or disabled	Survivors, depen-dents	Total	Employ-ers	Employ-ees	Total	Age, service and dis-ability	Depen-dents and sur-vivors	Total	
1991											
U.S. Civil Service	3,197	1,629	585	5,411	29,509	4,563	34,072	na	na	32,718	261,576
Federal Reserve System	26	9	1	36	-	3	3	68	7	75	2,748
Foreign Service	9	11	1	21	86	30	116	366	30	396	5,425
Tennessee Valley Authority	22	11	2	35	48	28	76	118	11	129	3,016
Total	3,254	1,660	589	5,503	29,643	4,624	34,267	na	na	33,318	272,765
1992											
U.S. Civil Service	3,160	1,628	594	5,382	31,050	4,713	35,763	27,693	5,065	32,758	288,395
Federal Reserve System	26	10	1	37	-	3	3	83	3	86	2,856
Foreign Service	9	10	2	21	105	36	141	334	36	370	5,999
Tennessee Valley Authority	21	12	2	35	50	30	80	126	12	138	3,305
Total	3,216	1,660	599	5,475	31,205	4,782	35,987	28,236	5,116	33,352	300,555
1993											
U.S. Civil Service	2,949	1,676	607	5,232	32,667	4,703	37,370	29,288	5,377	34,665	317,354
Federal Reserve System	28	12	1	41	-	3	3	83	3	86	2,976
Foreign Service	9	10	2	21	109	35	144	351	38	389	6,662
Tennessee Valley Authority	21	13	2	36	51	34	85	138	13	151	3,709
Total	3,007	1,711	612	5,330	32,827	4,775	37,602	29,860	5,431	35,291	330,701
1994											
U.S. Civil Service	2,933	1,697	613	5,243	4,610	37,044	5,607	36,047	344,256		
Federal Reserve System	27	12	1	40	-	3	3	89	3	92	2,903
Foreign Service	9	10	2	21	113	32	145	363	40	403	7,179
Tennessee Valley Authority	21	13	2	36	53	36	89	140	15	155	3,674
Total	2,990	1,732	618	5,340	32,600	4,681	37,281	31,032	5,665	36,697	358,012

Source: U.S. Office of Personnel Management; Federal Reserve Employee Benefit System; U.S. Department of State; and George B. Buck Consulting Actuaries. *Note:* Some data are revised. na stands for not available.

SIC 6390

INSURANCE CARRIERS, NEC

This industry includes all establishments that provide insurance coverage but are not classified under any of the other insurance categories. The types of organizations included under this SIC include bank deposit insurance providers, deposit or share insurance underwriters, the Federal Deposit Insurance Corporation (FDIC), the Federal Savings and Loan Insurance Corporation (FSLIC) and/or its successor organization (after 1989), health insurance for pets, and warranty insurance on automobiles.

ESTABLISHMENTS, EMPLOYMENT, AND PAYROLL

	1988	1989 Value	%	1990 Value	%	1991 Value	%	1992 Value	%	1993 Value	%	% change 88-93
All Establishments	262	259	-1.1	262	1.2	189	-27.9	211	11.6	162	-23.2	-38.2
Mid-March Employment	6,591	7,596	15.2	7,881	3.8	4,161	-47.2	4,903	17.8	2,891	-41.0	-56.1
1st Quarter Wages (annualized - $ mil.)	169.8	203.2	19.6	218.5	7.6	117.1	-46.4	142.9	22.0	98.9	-30.8	-41.8
Payroll per Emp. 1st Q. (annualized)	25,767	26,749	3.8	27,729	3.7	28,151	1.5	29,151	3.6	34,193	17.3	32.7
Annual Payroll ($ mil.)	170.5	210.2	23.3	226.4	7.7	131.8	-41.8	147.9	12.3	95.7	-35.3	-43.9
Establishments - 1-4 Emp. Number	117	107	-8.5	114	6.5	91	-20.2	100	9.9	(D)	-	-
Mid-March Employment	218	195	-10.6	205	5.1	(D)	-	166	-	(D)	-	-
1st Quarter Wages (annualized - $ mil.)	5.0	5.2	2.2	6.5	26.8	(D)	-	3.8	-	(D)	-	-
Payroll per Emp. 1st Q. (annualized)	23,138	26,441	14.3	31,902	20.7	(D)	-	22,892	-	(D)	-	-
Annual Payroll ($ mil.)	6.2	7.4	19.4	7.9	7.8	(D)	-	4.5	-	(D)	-	-
Establishments - 5-9 Emp. Number	54	49	-9.3	42	-14.3	32	-23.8	36	12.5	22	-38.9	-59.3
Mid-March Employment	(D)	343	-	286	-16.6	225	-21.3	237	5.3	136	-42.6	-
1st Quarter Wages (annualized - $ mil.)	(D)	10.2	-	8.8	-13.5	7.7	-12.0	8.0	2.8	3.3	-58.3	-
Payroll per Emp. 1st Q. (annualized)	(D)	29,679	-	30,797	3.8	34,436	11.8	33,620	-2.4	24,412	-27.4	-
Annual Payroll ($ mil.)	(D)	11.7	-	9.0	-23.1	8.8	-1.8	8.6	-2.3	4.2	-51.9	-
Establishments - 10-19 Emp. Number	43	47	9.3	43	-8.5	24	-44.2	30	25.0	12	-60.0	-72.1
Mid-March Employment	(D)	(D)	-	581	-	322	-44.6	388	20.5	164	-57.7	-
1st Quarter Wages (annualized - $ mil.)	(D)	(D)	-	20.2	-	9.5	-52.7	10.9	13.8	6.2	-43.0	-
Payroll per Emp. 1st Q. (annualized)	(D)	(D)	-	34,775	-	29,652	-14.7	28,010	-5.5	37,756	34.8	-
Annual Payroll ($ mil.)	(D)	(D)	-	22.4	-	9.7	-56.5	11.6	19.0	5.8	-49.6	-
Establishments - 20-49 Emp. Number	30	35	16.7	40	14.3	20	-50.0	21	5.0	19	-9.5	-36.7
Mid-March Employment	906	1,115	23.1	1,279	14.7	624	-51.2	685	9.8	580	-15.3	-36.0
1st Quarter Wages (annualized - $ mil.)	32.0	40.0	25.0	46.9	17.3	20.4	-56.5	30.0	47.0	20.2	-32.5	-36.7
Payroll per Emp. 1st Q. (annualized)	35,302	35,867	1.6	36,669	2.2	32,699	-10.8	43,790	33.9	34,910	-20.3	-1.1
Annual Payroll ($ mil.)	31.2	43.9	40.8	45.5	3.5	19.4	-57.4	27.3	41.0	19.8	-27.7	-36.6
Establishments - 50-99 Emp. Number	7	9	28.6	11	22.2	10	-9.1	13	30.0	12	-7.7	71.4
Mid-March Employment	472	654	38.6	742	13.5	(D)	-	899	-	864	-3.9	83.1
1st Quarter Wages (annualized - $ mil.)	10.6	18.6	75.6	22.2	19.1	(D)	-	25.8	-	21.9	-15.4	106.1
Payroll per Emp. 1st Q. (annualized)	22,475	28,477	26.7	29,881	4.9	(D)	-	28,752	-	25,310	-12.0	12.6
Annual Payroll ($ mil.)	10.2	16.5	61.4	19.9	20.2	(D)	-	27.3	-	22.9	-16.0	123.5
Establishments - 100-249 Emp. Number	4	7	75.0	5	-28.6	9	80.0	7	-22.2	3	-57.1	-25.0
Mid-March Employment	488	1,133	132.2	690	-39.1	1,111	61.0	988	-11.1	463	-53.1	-5.1
1st Quarter Wages (annualized - $ mil.)	15.8	28.7	81.2	23.0	-19.7	21.9	-4.9	23.2	6.1	13.9	-40.0	-11.9
Payroll per Emp. 1st Q. (annualized)	32,434	25,310	-22.0	33,380	31.9	19,723	-40.9	23,522	19.3	30,108	28.0	-7.2
Annual Payroll ($ mil.)	16.0	28.2	76.4	24.5	-13.1	23.6	-3.8	23.7	0.6	12.5	-47.4	-22.0
Establishments - 250-499 Emp. Number	5	3	-40.0	4	33.3	3	-25.0	4	33.3	-	-	-
Mid-March Employment	1,773	(D)	-	1,376	-	(D)	-	1,540	-	-	-	-
1st Quarter Wages (annualized - $ mil.)	37.3	(D)	-	34.0	-	(D)	-	41.2	-	-	-	-
Payroll per Emp. 1st Q. (annualized)	21,013	(D)	-	24,692	-	(D)	-	26,758	-	-	-	-
Annual Payroll ($ mil.)	41.1	(D)	-	38.3	-	(D)	-	44.9	-	-	-	-
Establishments - 500-999 Emp. Number	2	1	-50.0	2	100.0	-	-	-	-	(D)	-	-
Mid-March Employment	(D)	(D)	-	(D)	-	-	-	-	-	(D)	-	-
1st Quarter Wages (annualized - $ mil.)	(D)	(D)	-	(D)	-	(D)	-	-	-	(D)	-	-
Payroll per Emp. 1st Q. (annualized)	(D)	(D)	-	(D)	-	-	-	-	-	(D)	-	-
Annual Payroll ($ mil.)	(D)	(D)	-	(D)	-	-	-	-	-	-	-	-
Estab. - 1000 or More Emp. Number	-	1		1		-	-	-	-	-	-	-
Mid-March Employment	-	(D)	-	(D)	-	-	-	-	-	-	-	-
1st Quarter Wages (annualized - $ mil.)	-	(D)	-	(D)	-	-	-	-	-	-	-	-
Payroll per Emp. 1st Q. (annualized)	(D)	(D)	-	(D)	-	(D)		-	-	-	-	-
Annual Payroll ($ mil.)	-	(D)	-	(D)	-	-	-	-	-	-	-	-

Source: County Business Patterns, U.S. Department of Commerce, Washington, D.C., for 1988 through 1993. Payroll per employee is calculated using mid-March employment and 1st Quarter wages, annualized. Annual payroll, also shown, may not equal the annualized 1st Quarter wages. Columns headed by a percent sign (%) indicate change from the previous year. *na* stands for not available. The symbol (D) indicates that data are withheld by the source to avoid disclosure of competitive information. A dash (-) indicates that data are not available or cannot be calculated.

ESTABLISHMENTS
Number

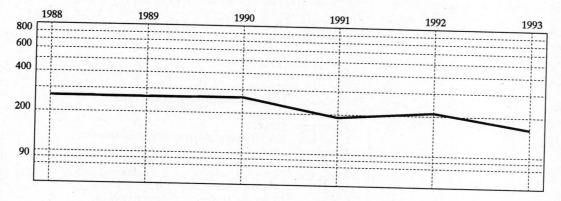

MID-MARCH EMPLOYMENT
Number

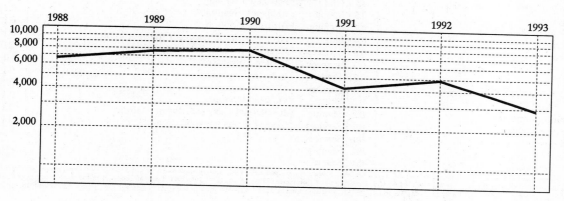

ANNUAL PAYROLL
$ million

INPUTS AND OUTPUTS FOR INSURANCE CARRIERS - SIC GROUP 63

Economic Sector or Industry Providing Inputs	%	Sector	Economic Sector or Industry Buying Outputs	%	Sector
Insurance agents, brokers, & services	62.9	Fin/R.E.	Personal consumption expenditures	77.1	
Security & commodity brokers	6.8	Fin/R.E.	Owner-occupied dwellings	5.5	Fin/R.E.
Eating & drinking places	4.0	Trade	Real estate	3.6	Fin/R.E.
Real estate	4.0	Fin/R.E.	Banking	0.9	Fin/R.E.
Communications, except radio & TV	3.9	Util.	Federal Government purchases, nondefense	0.9	Fed Govt
Imports	1.8	Foreign	Electric services (utilities)	0.8	Util.
Commercial printing	1.3	Manufg.	Insurance agents, brokers, & services	0.7	Fin/R.E.
Computer & data processing services	1.3	Services	Feed grains	0.6	Agric.
Advertising	1.2	Services	Exports	0.5	Foreign
Hotels & lodging places	1.2	Services	Motor freight transportation & warehousing	0.5	Util.
Legal services	1.2	Services	Retail trade, except eating & drinking	0.5	Trade
Accounting, auditing & bookkeeping	0.9	Services	Credit agencies other than banks	0.4	Fin/R.E.
Banking	0.9	Fin/R.E.	S/L Govt. purch., elem. & secondary education	0.4	S/L Govt
U.S. Postal Service	0.9	Gov't	Sanitary services, steam supply, irrigation	0.4	Util.
Air transportation	0.6	Util.	State & local government enterprises, nec	0.3	Gov't
Credit agencies other than banks	0.6	Fin/R.E.	Water supply & sewage systems	0.3	Util.
Management & consulting services & labs	0.6	Services	Wholesale trade	0.3	Trade
Maintenance of nonfarm buildings nec	0.5	Constr.	Food grains	0.2	Agric.
Manifold business forms	0.5	Manufg.	Meat animals	0.2	Agric.
Motor freight transportation & warehousing	0.5	Util.	Petroleum refining	0.2	Manufg.
Petroleum refining	0.5	Manufg.	Religious organizations	0.2	Services
Photographic equipment & supplies	0.4	Manufg.	Air transportation	0.1	Util.
Transit & bus transportation	0.4	Util.	Arrangement of passenger transportation	0.1	Util.
Business services nec	0.3	Services	Equipment rental & leasing services	0.1	Services
Personnel supply services	0.3	Services	Freight forwarders	0.1	Util.
Wholesale trade	0.3	Trade	Industrial buildings	0.1	Constr.
Automotive rental & leasing, without drivers	0.2	Services	Office buildings	0.1	Constr.
Electric services (utilities)	0.2	Util.	Oil bearing crops	0.1	Agric.
Electronic computing equipment	0.2	Manufg.	Residential 1-unit structures, nonfarm	0.1	Constr.
Detective & protective services	0.1	Services	Transit & bus transportation	0.1	Util.
Electrical repair shops	0.1	Services			
Envelopes	0.1	Manufg.			
Manufacturing industries, nec	0.1	Manufg.			

Source: Benchmark Input-Output Accounts for the U.S. Economy, 1982, U.S. Department of Commerce, Washington, D.C., July 1991. Data, as reported in the source, are organized by the 1977 SIC structure in use in 1982 but have been matched, as closely as is possible, to the 1987 SIC structure used in this book. Activities with the same percentage are sorted alphabetically by name of activity.

OCCUPATIONS EMPLOYED BY PENSION FUNDS AND INSURANCE, NEC

Occupation	% of Total 1994	Change to 2005	Occupation	% of Total 1994	Change to 2005
Title examiners & searchers	11.3	1.8	Insurance sales workers	2.6	10.0
General office clerks	8.3	8.5	Underwriters	2.6	27.2
Secretaries, ex legal & medical	7.0	15.8	Clerical support workers nec	2.4	1.7
General managers & top executives	6.3	20.7	Management support workers nec	2.1	52.7
Clerical supervisors & managers	4.8	30.1	Financial managers	2.0	27.2
Legal assistants, law clerks nec	4.6	57.5	File clerks	2.0	-36.4
Bookkeeping, accounting, & auditing clerks	4.5	-4.6	Accountants & auditors	1.7	27.2
Typists & word processors	4.2	-36.4	Computer programmers	1.7	3.1
Receptionists & information clerks	3.1	27.2	Messengers	1.4	-1.2
Insurance policy processing clerks	3.1	1.8	Marketing & sales worker supervisors	1.3	27.2
Loan & credit clerks	3.0	14.5	Data entry keyers, ex composing	1.2	-6.1
Insurance claims clerks	2.9	16.7	Claims examiners, insurance	1.2	16.0
Insurance adjusters, examiners, & investigators	2.6	33.6	Managers & administrators nec	1.0	27.1

Sources: *Industry-Occupation Matrix*, Bureau of Labor Statistics. These data relate to one or more 3-digit SIC industry groups rather than to a single 4-digit SIC. The change reported for each occupation to the year 2005 is a percent of growth or decline as estimated by the Bureau of Labor Statistics. The abbreviation *nec* stands for not elsewhere classified.

U.S. AND STATE DATA ON INDUSTRY REVENUES AND OTHER ACCOUNTS FOR 1992

State	No. of Estab.	Employ-ment	Payroll ($ mil.)	Revenues ($ mil.)	Empl./ Estab.	Revenue/ Estab. ($)	Payroll/ Estab. ($)	Revenue/ Empl. ($)	Payroll/ Empl. ($)
UNITED STATES	134	2,823	95.9	700.7	21	5,229,321	715,567	248,221	33,966
California	13	835	35.8	8.8	64	680,615	2,755,769	10,596	42,904
Colorado	4	110	3.8	9.1	28	2,272,000	947,500	82,618	34,455
Florida	7	-	(D)	(D)	(D)	(D)	(D)	(D)	(D)
Georgia	5	-	(D)	(D)	(D)	(D)	(D)	(D)	(D)
Illinois	7	-	(D)	(D)	(D)	(D)	(D)	(D)	(D)
Maryland	4	-	(D)	(D)	(D)	(D)	(D)	(D)	(D)
Massachusetts	3	-	(D)	(D)	(D)	(D)	(D)	(D)	(D)
Michigan	1	-	(D)	(D)	(D)	(D)	(D)	(D)	(D)
Minnesota	1	-	(D)	(D)	(D)	(D)	(D)	(D)	(D)
Missouri	1	-	(D)	(D)	(D)	(D)	(D)	(D)	(D)
New Jersey	8	388	10.7	46.0	49	5,749,250	1,339,250	118,541	27,613
New York	6	23	0.6	2.0	4	339,500	97,833	88,565	25,522
North Carolina	2	-	(D)	(D)	(D)	(D)	(D)	(D)	(D)
Ohio	7	62	2.5	26.8	9	3,825,143	354,857	431,871	40,065
Pennsylvania	6	-	(D)	(D)	(D)	(D)	(D)	(D)	(D)
Tennessee	2	-	(D)	(D)	(D)	(D)	(D)	(D)	(D)
Texas	11	178	5.7	26.0	16	2,366,273	516,909	146,230	31,944
Virginia	2	-	(D)	(D)	(D)	(D)	(D)	(D)	(D)
Washington	1	-	(D)	(D)	(D)	(D)	(D)	(D)	(D)
Wisconsin	3	-	(D)	(D)	(D)	(D)	(D)	(D)	(D)

Source: 1992 Economic Census, U.S. Department of Commerce, Washington, D.C. This is the only table that shows revenue data as collected by the Bureau of the Census in an Economic Census. The symbol (D) indicates that data are withheld by the source to avoid disclosure of competitive information. A dash (-) indicates that data are not available or cannot be calculated.

ESTABLISHMENTS 1992 - STATE AND REGIONAL CONCENTRATION

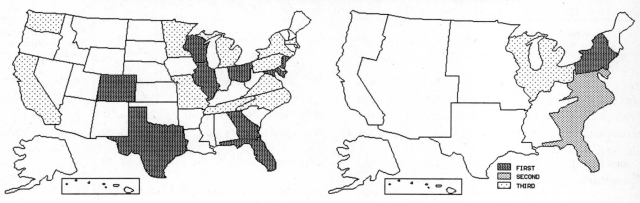

EMPLOYMENT 1992 - STATE AND REGIONAL CONCENTRATION

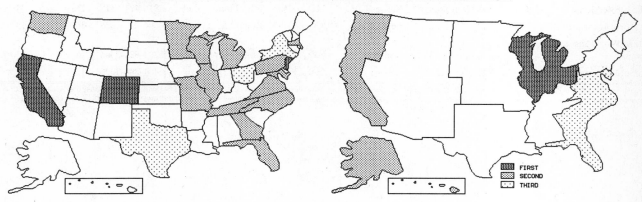

REVENUES 1992 - STATE AND REGIONAL CONCENTRATION

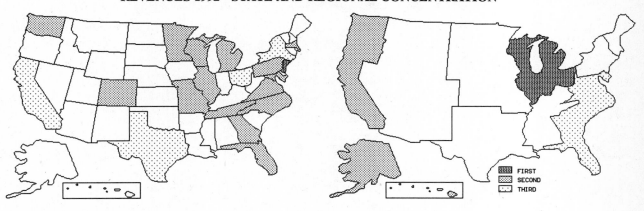

States with the darkest shading indicate those states which have proportionately more establishments, employment, or revenues than would be indicated by the state's population. States with light shading are states with proportionately fewer establishments, less employment, and lower revenues than population distribution. States shaded grey are within 15 percent of the state's population proportion in these categories. States for which no data are available are shown as average (grey). *Regions* are shaded to indicate absolute rank in the category. If no data for the category are available, establishment counts are used to shade the regions. Source of the data is the table on the facing page.

LEADING COMPANIES - SIC 6399 - Insurance Carriers, nec

Number shown: **12**   Total sales/assets ($ mil): **27,521**   Total employment (000): **22.4**

Company Name	Address				CEO Name	Phone	Co. Type	Sales/Assets ($ mil)	Empl. (000)
Federal Deposit Insurance Corp.	550 17th St. N.W.	Washington	DC	20429	Andrew C. Hove Jr.	202-393-8400	R	26,552 TA	21.0
General Star Management Co.	P.O. Box 10354	Stamford	CT	06904	Kevin P. Brooks	203-328-5700	S	360 TA•	0.2
Church Mutual Insurance Co.	3000 Schuster Ln.	Merrill	WI	54452	Dieter H. Nickel	715-536-5577	R	170 TA	0.6
Travel Guard International Inc.	1145 Clark St.	Stevens Point	WI	54481	John M. Noel	715-345-0505	R	120 TA	0.1
American Mutual Share Insurance Corp.	5656 Frantz Rd.	Dublin	OH	43017	Dennis Adams	614-764-1900	R	85 TA	<0.1
California Veterinary Services Inc.	4175 E. La Palma Ave.	Anaheim	CA	92807	Jack Stephens	714-996-2311	R	56 TA	<0.1
Veterinary Pet Insurance Co.	4175 E. La Palma Ave.	Anaheim	CA	92807	Jack Stephens	714-996-2311	S	56 TA	<0.1
Kansas Bankers Surety Co.	611 S. Kansas Ave.	Topeka	KS	66603	Don Towel	913-234-2631	R	54 TA	<0.1
Media/Professional Insurance	2300 Main St.	Kansas City	MO	64108	John Pfannenstiel	816-471-6118	D	34•	0.1
Kirk Horse Insurance Inc.	316 W. High St.	Lexington	KY	40507	Ronald Kirk	606-231-0838	R	13 TA•	<0.1
Western World Insurance Group	48 S. Franklin Tpk.	Ramsey	NJ	07446	Andrew Frazier	201-825-3300	R	13 TA	0.2
Automobile Protection Corp.	15 Dunwoody Pk.	Atlanta	GA	30338	Larry I. Dorfman	404-394-7070	P	8 TA	<0.1

Source: Ward's Business Directory of U.S. Private and Public Companies, 1996. Company type codes: P - Public, R - Private, S - Subsidiary, D - Division, J - Joint Venture, A - Affiliate, G - Group. If the dollar values shown are not sales, the following codes apply: TA - Total Assets; OR - Operating Revenues; GB - Gross Billings. • - estimated dollar value. < - less than; *na* - not available.

SIC 6411

INSURANCE AGENTS, BROKERS, & SERVICE

The industry includes agents and brokers dealing in insurance as well as organizations that offer services to insurance companies and to policyholders. The agents and brokers included in SIC 6410 are primarily engaged in representing one or more insurance carriers. They are independent contractors in the sale or placement of insurance contracts with carriers; they are not employed by the insurance carriers that they represent. The service organizations included here provide services to the insurance industry; however, establishments engaged in searching real estate titles are excluded from this SIC; they are included under SIC 6540 (found later in this book).

In addition to insurance agents and brokers, specific categories of activity included in SIC 6410 are fire insurance underwriters' laboratories, fire loss appraisers, insurance adjusters, advisory services, claim adjusters operating independently, educational services, information bureaus, inspection and investigation services, loss prevention services, medical claims processing services on a fee basis, patrol services, pension and retirement plan consulting services, policyholders' consulting services, professional standards organizations for insurance, rate making organizations for insurance, and report and research services.

ESTABLISHMENTS, EMPLOYMENT, AND PAYROLL

	1988	1989 Value	%	1990 Value	%	1991 Value	%	1992 Value	%	1993 Value	%	% change 88-93
All Establishments	105,133	107,533	2.3	110,834	3.1	112,559	1.6	114,032	1.3	122,292	7.2	16.3
Mid-March Employment	685,969	694,387	1.2	712,305	2.6	678,423	-4.8	641,875	-5.4	656,007	2.2	-4.4
1st Quarter Wages (annualized - $ mil.)	18,080.0	18,595.8	2.9	19,935.0	7.2	19,265.0	-3.4	18,976.2	-1.5	18,864.4	-0.6	4.3
Payroll per Emp. 1st Q. (annualized)	26,357	26,780	1.6	27,987	4.5	28,397	1.5	29,564	4.1	28,756	-2.7	9.1
Annual Payroll ($ mil.)	17,999.2	18,821.4	4.6	20,250.9	7.6	19,581.5	-3.3	19,443.6	-0.7	20,259.4	4.2	12.6
Establishments - 1-4 Emp. Number	75,489	77,596	2.8	80,038	3.1	80,594	0.7	83,835	4.0	90,608	8.1	20.0
Mid-March Employment	139,616	140,486	0.6	146,650	4.4	148,258	1.1	151,890	2.4	163,934	7.9	17.4
1st Quarter Wages (annualized - $ mil.)	2,381.1	2,434.6	2.2	2,679.1	10.0	2,801.0	4.5	2,974.1	6.2	3,152.3	6.0	32.4
Payroll per Emp. 1st Q. (annualized)	17,055	17,330	1.6	18,269	5.4	18,893	3.4	19,580	3.6	19,229	-1.8	12.8
Annual Payroll ($ mil.)	2,685.4	2,753.1	2.5	3,004.9	9.1	3,198.1	6.4	3,350.5	4.8	3,663.7	9.3	36.4
Establishments - 5-9 Emp. Number	16,999	17,040	0.2	17,666	3.7	19,384	9.7	18,107	-6.6	19,247	6.3	13.2
Mid-March Employment	109,524	109,596	0.1	113,731	3.8	124,790	9.7	115,936	-7.1	123,045	6.1	12.3
1st Quarter Wages (annualized - $ mil.)	2,485.7	2,566.8	3.3	2,735.6	6.6	3,148.7	15.1	3,000.6	-4.7	3,126.5	4.2	25.8
Payroll per Emp. 1st Q. (annualized)	22,696	23,421	3.2	24,053	2.7	25,232	4.9	25,882	2.6	25,409	-1.8	12.0
Annual Payroll ($ mil.)	2,561.2	2,676.4	4.5	2,853.8	6.6	3,290.2	15.3	3,163.1	-3.9	3,406.6	7.7	33.0
Establishments - 10-19 Emp. Number	7,385	7,334	-0.7	7,478	2.0	7,541	0.8	7,177	-4.8	7,608	6.0	3.0
Mid-March Employment	97,539	96,953	-0.6	99,375	2.5	99,192	-0.2	94,373	-4.9	100,103	6.1	2.6
1st Quarter Wages (annualized - $ mil.)	2,738.2	2,685.9	-1.9	2,873.4	7.0	3,007.3	4.7	3,037.7	1.0	3,052.9	0.5	11.5
Payroll per Emp. 1st Q. (annualized)	28,073	27,703	-1.3	28,914	4.4	30,318	4.9	32,188	6.2	30,498	-5.2	8.6
Annual Payroll ($ mil.)	2,775.9	2,791.6	0.6	2,988.4	7.1	3,114.8	4.2	3,083.6	-1.0	3,326.4	7.9	19.8
Establishments - 20-49 Emp. Number	3,616	3,813	5.4	3,902	2.3	3,527	-9.6	3,482	-1.3	3,432	-1.4	-5.1
Mid-March Employment	107,341	112,492	4.8	115,595	2.8	103,687	-10.3	103,823	0.1	101,794	-2.0	-5.2
1st Quarter Wages (annualized - $ mil.)	3,318.7	3,482.8	4.9	3,729.0	7.1	3,471.2	-6.9	3,585.9	3.3	3,442.1	-4.0	3.7
Payroll per Emp. 1st Q. (annualized)	30,917	30,960	0.1	32,259	4.2	33,478	3.8	34,539	3.2	33,814	-2.1	9.4
Annual Payroll ($ mil.)	3,285.8	3,524.3	7.3	3,768.8	6.9	3,484.9	-7.5	3,657.8	5.0	3,701.8	1.2	12.7
Establishments - 50-99 Emp. Number	998	1,044	4.6	1,043	-0.1	909	-12.8	866	-4.7	875	1.0	-12.3
Mid-March Employment	67,300	70,455	4.7	70,611	0.2	61,837	-12.4	58,306	-5.7	59,080	1.3	-12.2
1st Quarter Wages (annualized - $ mil.)	2,149.8	2,255.5	4.9	2,363.9	4.8	2,088.4	-11.7	2,092.2	0.2	2,129.0	1.8	-1.0
Payroll per Emp. 1st Q. (annualized)	31,944	32,013	0.2	33,477	4.6	33,772	0.9	35,883	6.2	36,036	0.4	12.8
Annual Payroll ($ mil.)	2,027.7	2,126.6	4.9	2,285.3	7.5	2,018.7	-11.7	2,073.5	2.7	2,196.8	5.9	8.3
Establishments - 100-249 Emp. Number	492	552	12.2	545	-1.3	453	-16.9	451	-0.4	422	-6.4	-14.2
Mid-March Employment	74,564	82,482	10.6	80,761	-2.1	68,524	-15.2	65,601	-4.3	61,765	-5.8	-17.2
1st Quarter Wages (annualized - $ mil.)	2,282.1	2,666.1	16.8	2,742.1	2.8	2,345.7	-14.5	2,401.5	2.4	2,273.3	-5.3	-0.4
Payroll per Emp. 1st Q. (annualized)	30,606	32,324	5.6	33,953	5.0	34,232	0.8	36,607	6.9	36,806	0.5	20.3
Annual Payroll ($ mil.)	2,121.3	2,516.3	18.6	2,600.3	3.3	2,240.0	-13.9	2,300.6	2.7	2,281.4	-0.8	7.6
Establishments - 250-499 Emp. Number	110	107	-2.7	113	5.6	114	0.9	87	-23.7	75	-13.8	-31.8
Mid-March Employment	37,179	35,900	-3.4	37,061	3.2	38,867	4.9	28,253	-27.3	24,933	-11.8	-32.9
1st Quarter Wages (annualized - $ mil.)	1,068.9	1,139.7	6.6	1,238.9	8.7	1,287.5	3.9	1,100.6	-14.5	848.0	-23.0	-20.7
Payroll per Emp. 1st Q. (annualized)	28,750	31,747	10.4	33,430	5.3	33,125	-0.9	38,956	17.6	34,012	-12.7	18.3
Annual Payroll ($ mil.)	1,021.9	1,073.6	5.1	1,185.3	10.4	1,151.8	-2.8	1,012.7	-12.1	826.0	-18.4	-19.2
Establishments - 500-999 Emp. Number	26	32	23.1	31	-3.1	23	-25.8	17	-26.1	16	-5.9	-38.5
Mid-March Employment	17,253	20,651	19.7	20,345	-1.5	15,324	-24.7	11,176	-27.1	9,507	-14.9	-44.9
1st Quarter Wages (annualized - $ mil.)	508.4	604.6	18.9	613.3	1.4	456.6	-25.5	369.8	-19.0	393.6	6.4	-22.6
Payroll per Emp. 1st Q. (annualized)	29,469	29,276	-0.7	30,145	3.0	29,798	-1.2	33,090	11.0	41,406	25.1	40.5
Annual Payroll ($ mil.)	487.5	581.5	19.3	607.1	4.4	423.9	-30.2	363.0	-14.4	368.4	1.5	-24.4
Estab. - 1000 or More Emp. Number	18	15	-16.7	18	20.0	14	-22.2	10	-28.6	9	-10.0	-50.0
Mid-March Employment	35,653	25,372	-28.8	28,176	11.1	17,944	-36.3	12,517	-30.2	11,846	-5.4	-66.8
1st Quarter Wages (annualized - $ mil.)	1,147.0	759.7	-33.8	959.8	26.3	658.5	-31.4	413.8	-37.2	446.6	7.9	-61.1
Payroll per Emp. 1st Q. (annualized)	32,172	29,944	-6.9	34,063	13.8	36,698	7.7	33,061	-9.9	37,701	14.0	17.2
Annual Payroll ($ mil.)	1,032.7	777.9	-24.7	956.9	23.0	659.2	-31.1	438.8	-33.4	488.4	11.3	-52.7

Source: County Business Patterns, U.S. Department of Commerce, Washington, D.C., for 1988 through 1993. Payroll per employee is calculated using mid-March employment and 1st Quarter wages, annualized. Annual payroll, also shown, may not equal the annualized 1st Quarter wages. Columns headed by a percent sign (%) indicate change from the previous year. *na* stands for not available. The symbol (D) indicates that data are withheld by the source to avoid disclosure of competitive information. A dash (-) indicates that data are not available or cannot be calculated.

ESTABLISHMENTS
Number

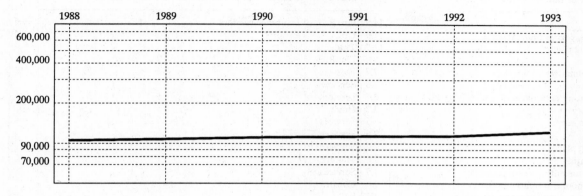

MID-MARCH EMPLOYMENT
Number

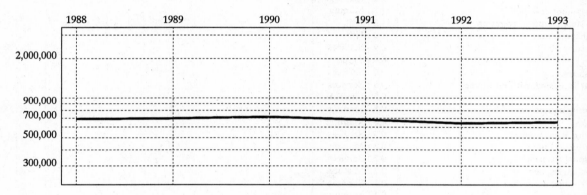

ANNUAL PAYROLL
$ million

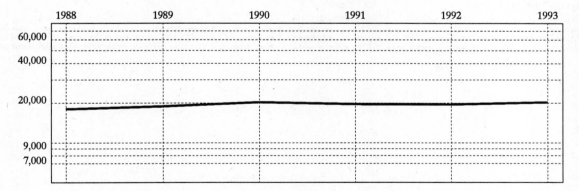

INPUTS AND OUTPUTS FOR INSURANCE AGENTS, BROKERS, & SERVICE - SIC 6411

Economic Sector or Industry Providing Inputs	%	Sector	Economic Sector or Industry Buying Outputs	%	Sector
Real estate	14.9	Fin/R.E.	Insurance carriers	99.6	Fin/R.E.
Communications, except radio & TV	11.9	Util.	Exports	0.4	Foreign
Eating & drinking places	11.7	Trade			
Insurance carriers	8.0	Fin/R.E.			
Noncomparable imports	7.7	Foreign			
Advertising	4.6	Services			
Accounting, auditing & bookkeeping	3.7	Services			
U.S. Postal Service	3.7	Gov't			
Business services nec	3.5	Services			
Legal services	3.5	Services			
Hotels & lodging places	2.6	Services			
Commercial printing	1.8	Manufg.			
Management & consulting services & labs	1.7	Services			
Maintenance of nonfarm buildings nec	1.6	Constr.			
Arrangement of passenger transportation	1.5	Util.			
Manifold business forms	1.5	Manufg.			
Motor freight transportation & warehousing	1.4	Util.			
Air transportation	1.3	Util.			
Computer & data processing services	1.2	Services			
Petroleum refining	1.2	Manufg.			
Photographic equipment & supplies	1.2	Manufg.			
Sanitary services, steam supply, irrigation	1.2	Util.			
Transit & bus transportation	1.0	Util.			
Personnel supply services	0.9	Services			
Wholesale trade	0.8	Trade			
Electrical repair shops	0.6	Services			
Automotive rental & leasing, without drivers	0.5	Services			
Banking	0.5	Fin/R.E.			
Electronic computing equipment	0.5	Manufg.			
Envelopes	0.4	Manufg.			
Automobile parking & car washes	0.3	Services			
Blankbooks & looseleaf binders	0.2	Manufg.			
Business/professional associations	0.2	Services			
Manufacturing industries, nec	0.2	Manufg.			
Automotive repair shops & services	0.1	Services			
Die-cut paper & board	0.1	Manufg.			
Marking devices	0.1	Manufg.			
Membership organizations nec	0.1	Services			
Motor vehicle parts & accessories	0.1	Manufg.			
Periodicals	0.1	Manufg.			
Retail trade, except eating & drinking	0.1	Trade			
Tires & inner tubes	0.1	Manufg.			

Source: Benchmark Input-Output Accounts for the U.S. Economy, 1982, U.S. Department of Commerce, Washington, D.C., July 1991. Data, as reported in the source, are organized by the 1977 SIC structure in use in 1982 but have been matched, as closely as is possible, to the 1987 SIC structure used in this book. Activities with the same percentage are sorted alphabetically by name of activity.

OCCUPATIONS EMPLOYED BY INSURANCE AGENTS, BROKERS, AND SERVICE

Occupation	% of Total 1994	Change to 2005	Occupation	% of Total 1994	Change to 2005
Insurance sales workers	18.3	16.5	Receptionists & information clerks	2.9	10.2
Insurance policy processing clerks	13.5	-11.9	Marketing & sales worker supervisors	2.1	10.2
General managers & top executives	7.6	4.5	Typists & word processors	2.0	-44.9
Insurance adjusters, examiners, & investigators	6.0	25.0	File clerks	1.9	-44.9
General office clerks	6.0	-6.1	Financial managers	1.8	10.2
Secretaries, ex legal & medical	5.7	0.3	Management support workers nec	1.8	10.2
Clerical supervisors & managers	4.5	2.4	Claims examiners, insurance	1.7	25.0
Underwriters	4.5	-11.9	Accountants & auditors	1.0	10.2
Bookkeeping, accounting, & auditing clerks	4.3	-17.4	Clerical support workers nec	1.0	-11.9
Insurance claims clerks	3.0	10.2			

Sources: Industry-Occupation Matrix, Bureau of Labor Statistics. These data relate to one or more 3-digit SIC industry groups rather than to a single 4-digit SIC. The change reported for each occupation to the year 2005 is a percent of growth or decline as estimated by the Bureau of Labor Statistics. The abbreviation *nec* stands for not elsewhere classified.

U.S. AND STATE DATA ON INDUSTRY REVENUES AND OTHER ACCOUNTS FOR 1992

State	No. of Estab.	Employ-ment	Payroll ($ mil.)	Revenues ($ mil.)	Empl./ Estab.	Revenue/ Estab. ($)	Payroll/ Estab. ($)	Revenue/ Empl. ($)	Payroll/ Empl. ($)
UNITED STATES	121,662	635,536	18,921.1	51,705.1	5	424,989	155,522	81,357	29,772
Alabama	1,562	6,925	176.2	555.7	4	355,783	112,784	80,250	25,439
Alaska	203	1,097	37.1	87.3	5	429,842	182,665	79,542	33,802
Arizona	1,874	9,419	252.0	759.6	5	405,324	134,470	80,643	26,754
Arkansas	1,217	4,242	98.4	284.6	3	233,869	80,859	67,095	23,198
California	12,116	69,979	2,393.4	6,429.8	6	530,690	197,541	91,882	34,202
Colorado	2,227	8,623	223.7	645.7	4	289,951	100,445	74,883	25,941
Connecticut	1,561	10,648	389.9	1,029.1	7	659,275	249,751	96,650	36,614
Delaware	301	1,344	36.6	89.4	4	296,907	121,731	66,495	27,263
District of Columbia	132	1,852	78.9	181.6	14	1,375,992	597,356	98,073	42,576
Florida	7,567	39,067	1,031.1	3,131.9	5	413,890	136,257	80,168	26,392
Georgia	3,174	17,882	531.7	1,330.3	6	419,136	167,517	74,395	29,734
Hawaii	375	2,663	79.9	215.8	7	575,491	213,003	81,040	29,995
Idaho	570	2,414	51.4	155.8	4	273,304	90,167	64,533	21,290
Illinois	6,203	34,855	1,096.9	2,922.8	6	471,195	176,831	83,857	31,470
Indiana	2,857	14,127	369.2	1,031.8	5	361,141	129,224	73,036	26,134
Iowa	2,032	7,703	175.1	517.0	4	254,414	86,150	67,113	22,726
Kansas	1,797	7,341	179.3	502.0	4	279,328	99,784	68,377	24,426
Kentucky	1,648	8,274	191.6	555.2	5	336,900	116,274	67,103	23,159
Louisiana	2,183	10,896	259.6	760.1	5	348,186	118,900	69,759	23,821
Maine	519	3,054	80.9	208.7	6	402,164	155,879	68,344	26,490
Maryland	1,994	12,330	393.0	997.7	6	500,344	197,109	80,915	31,876
Massachusetts	2,886	19,886	679.1	1,751.3	7	606,816	235,319	88,066	34,151
Michigan	3,987	20,968	606.3	1,662.1	5	416,867	152,069	79,266	28,915
Minnesota	2,861	12,407	366.5	1,114.0	4	389,391	128,113	89,792	29,542
Mississippi	1,130	4,209	95.8	273.2	4	241,761	84,793	64,906	22,765
Missouri	3,184	14,019	355.1	1,013.2	4	318,206	111,526	72,271	25,330
Montana	621	2,219	46.4	150.1	4	241,721	74,771	67,647	20,925
Nebraska	1,369	4,845	103.1	334.8	4	244,570	75,278	69,106	21,270
Nevada	627	2,703	69.9	188.8	4	301,078	111,544	69,839	25,874
New Hampshire	497	2,731	76.8	198.2	5	398,779	154,445	72,572	28,107
New Jersey	3,225	22,752	826.3	2,117.0	7	656,449	256,226	93,049	36,319
New Mexico	764	3,345	73.6	213.9	4	279,955	96,385	63,942	22,014
New York	7,000	54,300	2,037.8	5,100.0	8	728,570	291,113	93,922	37,528
North Carolina	3,102	12,955	354.2	1,035.7	4	333,875	114,187	79,944	27,341
North Dakota	563	1,490	29.0	100.7	3	178,821	51,430	67,568	19,433
Ohio	5,344	23,576	635.0	1,799.8	4	336,787	118,820	76,340	26,933
Oklahoma	1,806	6,429	139.9	451.4	4	249,955	77,471	70,216	21,763
Oregon	1,537	7,436	205.0	604.5	5	393,295	133,407	81,293	27,575
Pennsylvania	5,136	29,094	921.3	2,467.4	6	480,410	179,376	84,807	31,665
Rhode Island	396	2,224	69.8	184.6	6	466,263	176,227	83,022	31,379
South Carolina	1,422	7,050	173.4	485.5	5	341,390	121,922	68,859	24,592
South Dakota	629	1,775	34.0	107.6	3	171,114	54,038	60,637	19,149
Tennessee	2,307	10,429	285.5	771.0	5	334,188	123,766	73,926	27,378
Texas	8,780	44,461	1,267.8	3,659.2	5	416,764	144,397	82,301	28,515
Utah	837	4,311	109.3	291.9	5	348,760	130,575	67,713	25,352
Vermont	311	1,498	41.1	96.1	5	309,109	132,199	64,174	27,446
Virginia	2,784	14,220	391.5	1,015.9	5	364,897	140,615	71,440	27,530
Washington	2,364	13,099	407.6	957.4	6	405,011	172,408	73,093	31,115
West Virginia	741	3,085	67.7	188.7	4	254,625	91,368	61,159	21,946
Wisconsin	3,037	12,412	311.0	931.5	4	306,716	102,397	75,048	25,055
Wyoming	303	873	15.6	47.7	3	157,422	51,591	54,638	17,906

Source: 1992 Economic Census, U.S. Department of Commerce, Washington, D.C. This is the only table that shows revenue data as collected by the Bureau of the Census in an Economic Census. The symbol (D) indicates that data are withheld by the source to avoid disclosure of competitive information. A dash (-) indicates that data are not available or cannot be calculated.

ESTABLISHMENTS 1992 - STATE AND REGIONAL CONCENTRATION

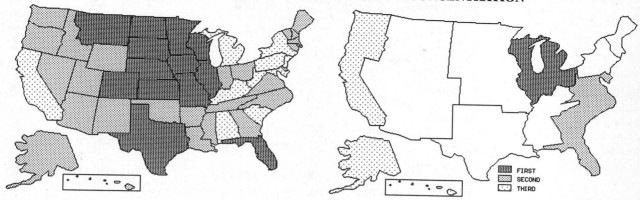

EMPLOYMENT 1992 - STATE AND REGIONAL CONCENTRATION

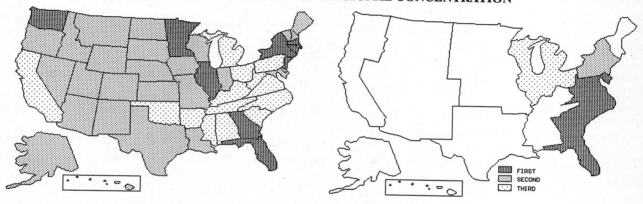

REVENUES 1992 - STATE AND REGIONAL CONCENTRATION

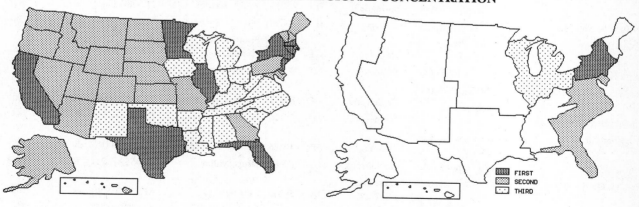

States with the darkest shading indicate those states which have proportionately more establishments, employment, or revenues than would be indicated by the state's population. States with light shading are states with proportionately fewer establishments, less employment, and lower revenues than population distribution. States shaded grey are within 15 percent of the state's population proportion in these categories. States for which no data are available are shown as average (grey). *Regions* are shaded to indicate absolute rank in the category. If no data for the category are available, establishment counts are used to shade the regions. Source of the data is the table on the facing page.

LEADING COMPANIES - SIC 6411 - Insurance Agents, Brokers, & Service

Number shown: **100**   Total sales/assets ($ mil): **64,247**   Total employment (000): **192.8**

Company Name	Address				CEO Name	Phone	Co. Type	Sales/Assets ($ mil)	Empl. (000)
Aon Corp.	123 N. Wacker Dr.	Chicago	IL	60606	Patrick G. Ryan	312-701-3000	P	17,922 TA	30.0
St. Paul Companies Inc.	385 Washington St.	St. Paul	MN	55102	Douglas W. Leatherdale	612-221-7911	P	17,496 TA	12.6
Eli Lilly and Co.	Lilly Corporate Ctr.	Indianapolis	IN	46285	Randall L. Tobias	317-276-2000	P	5,712	24.9
AMBAC Inc.	1 State St. Plz.	New York	NY	10004	Phillip B. Lassiter	212-668-0340	P	4,293 TA	0.6
Marsh and McLennan Companies Inc.	1166 Avenue of the Americas	New York	NY	10036	A.J.C. Smith	212-345-5000	P	3,435	26.0
U.S. Healthcare Inc.	P.O. Box 1109	Blue Bell	PA	19422	Leonard Abramson	215-628-4800	P	1,464 TA	4.3
Equifax Inc.	P.O. Box 4081	Atlanta	GA	30302	C.B. Rogers Jr.	404-885-8000	P	1,422 OR	14.2
Scottsdale Insurance Co.	P.O. Box 4110	Scottsdale	AZ	85261	Vickie Kartchner	602-948-0505	S	900	1.0
Industrial Risk Insurers	85 Woodland St.	Hartford	CT	06105	Gail P. Norstrom Jr.	203-520-7300	R	800 TA	1.1
Poughkeepsie Savings Bank F.S.B.	249 Main Mall	Poughkeepsie	NY	12601	Joseph B. Tockarshewsky	914-431-6200	P	728 TA	0.2
Rollins Hudig Hall Group Inc.	2 World Trade Ctr.	New York	NY	10048	Patrick Ryan	212-441-1000	S	701	13.0
Great Northern Insured Annuity Corp.	P.O. Box 490	Seattle	WA	98111	Patrick E. Welch	206-625-1755	S	699	1.5
Wisconsin Physician Service Insurance Corp.	P.O. Box 8190	Madison	WI	53708	James Riordan	608-221-4711	R	650 TA	3.1
Crawford and Co.	5620 Glenridge Dr. N.E	Atlanta	GA	30342	Dennis A. Smith	404-256-0830	P	588	8.0
American Medical Security Inc.	P.O. Box 19032	Green Bay	WI	54307	Wally Hilliard	414-431-1111	S	585	2.6
Acordia Inc.	120 Monument Cir.	Indianapolis	IN	46204	L. Ben Lytle	317-488-6666	P	412	5.2
Arthur J. Gallagher and Co.	2 Pierce Pl.	Itasca	IL	60143	Robert E. Gallagher	708-773-3800	P	356	3.3
Minet Inc.	220 E. 42nd St.	New York	NY	10017	Alan B. Middleton	212-297-9000	S	328	4.0
Horace Mann Service Corp.	1 Horace Mann Plz.	Springfield	IL	62715	Paul J. Kardos	217-789-2500	S	280•	2.5
AON Risk Services Inc.	123 N. Wacker Dr.	Chicago	IL	60606	Mike O'Halleran	312-701-3000	S	258	1.0
CIGNA RE Corp.	900 Cottage Grove Rd.	Hartford	CT	06152	Francine W. Newman	203-726-6000	S	246	0.1
MetLife Brokerage	214 Carnegie Cir.	Princeton	NJ	08540	Robert Powell	609-243-7100	D	225	0.2
Great Western Life Insurance Co.	8515 E. Orchard Rd.	Englewood	CO	80111	William McCallum	303-689-3000	R	200•	1.8
Employee Benefit Plans Inc.	435 Ford Rd.	Minneapolis	MN	55426	William E. Sagan	612-546-4353	P	184 TA	1.3
Seabury and Smith Inc.	1166 Ave. of the Amer.	New York	NY	10036	Claude Y. Mercier	212-345-4418	S	180•	1.5
CoreSource Inc.	630 Dundee Rd.	Northbrook	IL	60062	Bruce Miller	708-559-8321	R	170•	1.5
Kirke-Van Orsdel Inc.	1776 W. Lakes Pkwy.	West Des Moines	IA	50398	William A. Van Orsdel	515-243-1830	R	160•	1.4
Aon Specialty Group Inc.	123 N. Wacker Dr.	Chicago	IL	60606	Michael Rice	312-701-4538	S	156	0.6
Factory Mutual Engineering Corp.	1151 Boston Prov. Tpk.	Norwood	MA	02062	Paul M. Fitzgerald	617-762-4300	R	155	2.0
Kemper Service Co.	811 Main St.	Kansas City	MO	64105	Frank Diaz	816-421-4100	S	150 OR	1.0
Accordia of Central Florida Inc.	P.O. Box 31666	Tampa	FL	33631	James R. Harper	813-796-6666	S	125	0.1

Company type codes: P - Public, R - Private, S - Subsidiary, D - Division, J - Joint Venture, A - Affiliate, G - Group. If the dollar values shown are not sales, the following codes apply: TA - Total Assets; OR - Operating Revenues; GB - Gross Billings. • - estimated dollar value. < - less than. *na* - not available.

Continued on next page.

LEADING COMPANIES - SIC 6411 - Insurance Agents, Brokers, & Service
Continued

Company Name	Address				CEO Name	Phone	Co. Type	Sales/Assets ($ mil)	Empl. (000)
CRA Managed Care Inc.	321 Union Wharf	Boston	MA	02109	Lois E. Silverman	617-367-2163	P	121	1.9
Southwestern/Great American Inc.	P.O. Box 305140	Nashville	TN	37230	Ralph W. Mosley	615-391-2500	R	120	0.6
Kemper Risk Management Services	1 Kemper Dr.	Long Grove	IL	60049	Frederick G. Mlnchk	708-320-2400	S	107	0.3
National Loss Control Service Corp.	1 Kemper Dr.	Long Grove	IL	60049	Frederick G. Minchk	708-540-2400	S	100	0.4
Willis Faber North America Inc.	P.O. Box 2500	Stoney Creek	NC	27377	Horrace M. Johnson	910-584-0166	S	99 TA•	0.2
Poe and Brown Inc.	P.O. Box 2412	Daytona Beach	FL	32115	J. Hyatt Brown	904-252-9601	P	92	1.0
Gates, McDonald and Co.	P.O. Box 1944	Columbus	OH	43216	David K. Hollingsworth	614-777-3000	S	92•	0.8
Norcal Mutual Insurance Co.	50 Fremont St.	San Francisco	CA	94105	William Newton	415-777-4200	R	91	0.2
Gallagher Bassett Services Inc.	2 Pierce Pl.	Itasca	IL	60143	John G. Campbell	708-773-3800	S	87	1.5
Brakke-Schafnitz Insurance Brokers Inc.	28202 Cabot Rd.	Laguna Niguel	CA	92677	Jim Brakke	714-365-5100	R	85	<0.1
Value Line Inc.	711 3rd Ave.	New York	NY	10017	Jean Bernhard Buttner	212-907-1500	P	82	0.4
E.W. Blanch Holdings Inc.	3500 W. 80th St.	Minneapolis	MN	55431	Edgar W. Blanch Jr.	612-835-3310	P	81	0.6
Gay and Taylor Inc.	Six Concorse Pkwy.	Atlanta	GA	30328	James P. Rippy	404-395-1000	S	72	1.3
AdvaCare Inc.	9696 Skillman Ave.	Dallas	TX	75243	B.J. Rone	214-343-6181	P	71	1.4
Medical Professional Liability Agency Ltd.	2 Depot Plz.	Bedford Hills	NY	10507	Thomas J. Dietz	914-666-0555	S	70	<0.1
First of Michigan Capital Corp.	100 Renaissance Ctr.	Detroit	MI	48243	John G. Martin	313-259-2600	P	63 OR	0.5
E.W. Blanch Company Inc.	3500 W. 80th St.	Minneapolis	MN	55431	Edgar W. Blanch Jr.	612-835-3310	S	62	0.3
MedView Services Inc.	32991 Hamilton Ct.	Farmington Hills	MI	48334	Robert Marks	313-488-5260	S	59•	0.1
National Insurance Group	395 Oyster Point Blvd.	South San Francisco	CA	94080	Mark A. Speizer	415-872-6772	P	55 TA	0.4
Lawrence Agency Corp.	108 Union St.	Schenectady	NY	12305	William J. Mather	518-370-1720	S	55•	0.5
Lawrence Group Inc.	108 Union St.	Schenectady	NY	12305	Lawrence Shore	518-381-9000	R	55•	0.5
Roanoke Companies Inc.	1930 Thoreau Dr.	Schaumburg	IL	60173	William D. Sterrett	708-490-9540	R	53 TA	0.2
H.W. Kaufman Financial Group Inc.	30833 Northwestern Hwy	Southfield	MI	48034	Herbert W. Kaufman	810-932-9000	P	52	0.5
Crop Growers Corp.	P.O. Box 5024	Great Falls	MT	59403	John J. Hemmingson	406-452-8101	P	52	0.2
Crop Growers Insurance Inc.	P.O. Box 5024	Great Falls	MT	59403	John J. Hemmingson	406-452-8101	S	52	0.2
Kaye Insurance Associates L.P.	122 E. 42nd St.	New York	NY	10168	Howard Kaye	212-210-9200	R	51	0.5
Burns and Wilcox Ltd.	P.O. Box 707	Southfield	MI	48037	Herbert W. Kaufman	810-932-9000	S	50	0.4
Louisiana Cos.	P.O. Box 991	Baton Rouge	LA	70821	J.R. Querbes III	504-383-4761	R	50	<0.1
National Insurance Services Inc.	3629 Queen Palm Dr.	Tampa	FL	33619	Carl Giffin	813-626-6111	S	50•	0.4
Norwest Commercial Insurance Services	7401 Metro Blvd.	Minneapolis	MN	55439	David M. Franske	612-921-2701	S	50•	<0.1
United Title Agency of Arizona Inc.	3030 N. Central Ave.	Phoenix	AZ	85012	Milt Farrentelli	602-279-9381	R	46	0.4

Company type codes: P - Public, R - Private, S - Subsidiary, D - Division, J - Joint Venture, A - Affiliate, G - Group. If the dollar values shown are not sales, the following codes apply: TA - Total Assets; OR - Operating Revenues; GB - Gross Billings. • - estimated dollar value. < - less than. *na* - not available.

Continued on next page.

LEADING COMPANIES - SIC 6411 - Insurance Agents, Brokers, & Service

Continued

Company Name	Address				CEO Name	Phone	Co. Type	Sales/Assets ($ mil)	Empl. (000)
Laub Group Inc.	1555 N. Rivercenter Dr	Milwaukee	WI	53212	Raymond H. Laub	414-271-4292	R	45	<0.1
Walter P. Dolle Insurance Agency Inc.	312 Walnut St.	Cincinnati	OH	45202	Robert D. Lang	513-421-6515	R	45	<0.1
Warner Insurance Services Inc.	17-01 Pollitt Dr.	Fair Lawn	NJ	07410	Harvey Krieger	201-794-4800	P	42 TA	0.5
Sedgwick James Inc.	600 Montgomery St.	San Francisco	CA	94111	Donald K. Morford	415-983-5250	S	41•	0.4
National Electronics Warranty Corp.	44873 Falcon Pl.	Sterling	VA	20166	Fred Schaufeld	703-318-7700	R	40	0.2
Proctor Homer Warren Inc.	2100 W. Big Beaver Rd.	Troy	MI	48084	Thomas W. Proctor	313-649-8700	R	40	0.1
Roger Bouchard Insurance Inc.	101 Starcrest Dr.	Clearwater	FL	34625	Richard Bouchard	813-447-6481	R	40	<0.1
Vantage Computer Systems Inc.	100 Great Meadow Rd.	Wethersfield	CT	06109	Robert S. Maltempo	203-721-0694	S	39	0.5
Erisco Inc.	1700 Broadway	New York	NY	10019	Jeremy Davis	212-765-8500	S	36•	0.2
Florida Employers Insurance Service Corp.	2601 Cattlemen Rd.	Sarasota	FL	34232	Ray Neff	813-955-2811	S	36	0.5
Near North Insurance Brokerage Inc.	875 N. Michigan Ave.	Chicago	IL	60611	Michael Segal	312-280-5600	R	35	<0.1
Media/Professional Insurance	2300 Main St.	Kansas City	MO	64108	John Pfannenstiel	816-471-6118	D	34•	0.1
Bland and Co.	12300 Old Tesson Rd.	St. Louis	MO	63128	Steve Mach	314-849-9990	R	30	0.1
John Burnham and Co.	P.O. Box 2910	San Diego	CA	92112	Robert J. Lichter	619-236-1555	R	30 OR•	0.3
Crump Insurance Services Inc.	7557 Rambler Rd.	Dallas	TX	75231	Orville Jones	214-265-2660	S	29	0.3
Herbert H. Landy Insurance Agency Inc.	75 2nd Ave.	Needham	MA	02197	Herbert H. Landy	617-449-7711	R	29	<0.1
United American Healthcare Corp.	1155 Brewery Park Blvd	Detroit	MI	48207	Julius V. Combs	313-393-0200	P	29 OR	0.2
Fox and Lazo Inc.	30 Washington Ave.	Haddonfield	NJ	08033	G. William Fox	609-429-7227	R	27 OR	0.3
Standard Management Corp.	9100 Keystone Crossing	Indianapolis	IN	46240	Ronald D. Hunter	317-574-6200	P	27	<0.1
Hilb Royal Hamilton of Gainesville, Georgia	P.O. Drawer 1058	Gainesville	GA	30503	Joseph T. Wood Jr.	404-536-0161	S	25	<0.1
Hobbs Group Inc.	225 Wyman St.	Waltham	MA	02254	Thomas A. Golub	617-890-1455	S	24	0.2
Robert F. Driver Company Inc.	P.O. Box 670	San Diego	CA	92112	Richard B. Gulley	619-238-1828	R	24	0.2
Piedmont Associates Inc.	5161 Brookhollow Way	Norcross	GA	30071	Joe Buchanan	404-252-0894	R	23•	0.2
Andreini and Co.	220 W. 20th Ave.	San Mateo	CA	94403	David Hoskins	415-573-1111	R	21•	0.2
Holmes Murphy and Associates Inc.	420 Keo Way	Des Moines	IA	50309	Doug Reichardt	515-286-4400	R	21•	0.2
John Mullen and Company Inc.	P.O. Box 2096	Honolulu	HI	96805	John T. Mullen	808-531-9733	R	20•	0.2
Midwest Legal Services Inc.	400 Locust St.	Des Moines	IA	50309	James Brennan	515-246-1200	S	20	<0.1
Riggs, Counselman, Michaels and Downes Inc.	555 Fairmount Ave.	Baltimore	MD	21286	Albert Counselman	410-339-7263	R	20•	0.2

Company type codes: P - Public, R - Private, S - Subsidiary, D - Division, J - Joint Venture, A - Affiliate, G - Group. If the dollar values shown are not sales, the following codes apply: TA - Total Assets; OR - Operating Revenues; GB - Gross Billings. • - estimated dollar value. < - less than. *na* - not available.

Continued on next page.

LEADING COMPANIES - SIC 6411 - Insurance Agents, Brokers, & Service
Continued

Company Name	Address				CEO Name	Phone	Co. Type	Sales/Assets ($ mil)	Empl. (000)
CAPX Corp.	930 Washington Ave.	Miami Beach	FL	33139	Steve Simon	305-673-2700	P	20	<0.1
Tri-City Insurance Brokers Inc.	110 William St.	New York	NY	10038	John G. Hahn	212-732-1360	R	19*	0.2
Anderson and Murison Inc.	P.O. Box 41911	Los Angeles	CA	90041	David Anderson	213-255-2333	R	18	<0.1
AON Re Inc.	123 N. Wacker Dr.	Chicago	IL	60610	Paul R. Davies	312-781-7900	S	18*	0.2
Commerce Insurance Systems Inc.	23200 Chagrin Blvd.	Cleveland	OH	44122	Dennis W. Warnock	216-765-7100	R	18*	<0.1
James D. Collier and Company Inc.	1 Commerce Sq.	Memphis	TN	38103	J. Stuart Collier Jr.	901-529-2900	R	16	<0.1
TriCare Inc.	3353 Peachtree Rd. N.E	Atlanta	GA	30326	Larry G. Gerdes	404-266-7474	P	16	0.1
CyData Inc.	7001 N. Scottsdale Rd.	Scottsdale	AZ	85253	Jim Houtz	602-596-4300	S	15	<0.1
Financial Pacific Insurance Group Inc.	8583 Elder Creek Rd.	Sacramento	CA	95828	Robert C. Goodell	916-381-8067	R	15	<0.1
Acordia Lloyd Insurance Services	160 Spear St.	San Francisco	CA	94105	Gene Totloff	415-541-0404	S	15	0.1

Source: Ward's Business Directory of U.S. Private and Public Companies, 1996. Company type codes: P - Public, R - Private, S - Subsidiary, D - Division, J - Joint Venture, A - Affiliate, G - Group. If the dollar values shown are not sales, the following codes apply: TA - Total Assets; OR - Operating Revenues; GB - Gross Billings. * - estimated dollar value. < - less than; *na* - not available.

LEADING COMPANIES - SIC 6512 - Nonresidential Building Operators
Continued

Company Name	Address				CEO Name	Phone	Co. Type	Sales/Assets ($ mil)	Empl. (000)
Interstate Realty Corp.	88 Union Ave.	Memphis	TN	38103	R. Earl Blankenship	901-528-1000	R	7 OR	<0.1
Barrueta and Associates	1 Thomas Cir. N.W.	Washington	DC	20005	J. Fernando Barrueta	202-775-7000	R	6 OR*	<0.1
Festival Management Group Corp.	3425 McLaughlin Ave.	Los Angeles	CA	90066	Richard Aefa	310-391-1200	R	6 OR	<0.1
Forbes/Cohen Properties	100 Galleria Office	Southfield	MI	48034		810-827-4600	R	6 OR	<0.1

Source: Ward's Business Directory of U.S. Private and Public Companies, 1996. Company type codes: P - Public, R - Private, S - Subsidiary, D - Division, J - Joint Venture, A - Affiliate, G - Group. If the dollar values shown are not sales, the following codes apply: TA - Total Assets; OR - Operating Revenues; GB - Gross Billings. * - estimated dollar value. < - less than; na - not available.

LEADING COMPANIES - SIC 6513 - Apartment Building Operators
Number shown: **99**   Total sales/assets ($ mil): **3,912**   Total employment (000): **60.5**

Company Name	Address				CEO Name	Phone	Co. Type	Sales/Assets ($ mil)	Empl. (000)
Integrated Health Services Inc.	10065 Red Run Blvd.	Owings Mills	MD	21117	Robert N. Elkins	410-998-8400	P	682 OR	21.2
Forest City Enterprises Inc.	10800 Brookpark Rd.	Cleveland	OH	44130	Albert B. Ratner	216-267-1200	P	500 OR	2.3
PM Realty Group	1177 W. Loop S.	Houston	TX	77027	Mike Lutton	713-966-3600	R	430 OR*	3.0
Forest City Rental Properties Corp.	10800 Brookpark Rd.	Cleveland	OH	44130	James Ratner	216-267-1200	S	270 OR*	1.7
A.G. Spanos Construction Inc.	P.O. Box 7126	Stockton	CA	95207	Dean Spanos	209-478-7954	R	234 OR	0.5
Marriott Senior Living Services	1 Marriot Dr.	Bethesda	MD	20814	Paul E. Johnson Jr.	301-380-1780	D	149 OR	3.3
Drever Partners Inc.	4 Embarcadero Ctr.	San Francisco	CA	94111	Michael Masterson	415-433-1773	R	125 OR	0.6
Forum Group Inc.	P.O. Box 40498	Indianapolis	IN	46240	Robert A. Whitman	317-846-0700	P	108 OR	3.8
Shilo Management Corp.	11600 S.W. Barnes Rd.	Portland	OR	97225	Mark S. Hemstreet	503-641-6565	R	94 OR*	2.2
National Housing Partnership Inc.	1225 I St. N.W.	Washington	DC	20005	J. Roderick Heller III	202-347-6247	R	93 OR	4.0
American Baptist Homes of the West	P.O. Box 6669	Oakland	CA	94621	David B. Ferguson	510-635-7600	R	84 OR	1.9
Boykin Management Co.	1500 Terminal Twr.	Cleveland	OH	44113	Robert W. Boykin	216-241-6375	R	75 OR	3.0
Ito Ham U.S.A. Inc.	3190 Corporate Pl.	Hayward	CA	94545	Kinichi Ito	510-887-1612	S	74*	0.2
Senior Campus Living	701 Maiden Choice Ln.	Catonsville	MD	21228	John Erickson	410-242-2880	R	71 OR	1.8
Turnberry Associates	19495 Biscayne Blvd.	North Miami Beach	FL	33180	Donald Soffer	305-937-6200	R	64 OR*	0.3
South West Property Trust Inc.	5949 Sherry Ln.	Dallas	TX	75225	John S. Schneider	214-369-1995	P	59 OR	0.4
CBS Investment Realty Inc.	3033 N. 44th St.	Phoenix	AZ	85018	James Schlesing	602-952-1900	R	56 OR	0.6
Charan Industries Inc.	P.O. Box 74	Garden City	NY	11530	Charles P. Ryan	516-747-6500	R	50 OR	2.0

Company type codes: P - Public, R - Private, S - Subsidiary, D - Division, J - Joint Venture, A - Affiliate, G - Group. If the dollar values shown are not sales, the following codes apply: TA - Total Assets; OR - Operating Revenues; GB - Gross Billings. * - estimated dollar value. < - less than. na - not available.

Continued on next page.

LEADING COMPANIES - SIC 6513 - Apartment Building Operators
Continued

Company Name	Address				CEO Name	Phone	Co. Type	Sales/Assets ($ mil)	Empl. (000)
Great Northwest Management Company Inc.	1525 Park Ave.	Portland	OR	97201	Robert G. Johnson	503-241-1525	R	50 OR	0.1
Wilmac Corp.	P.O. Box 5047	York	PA	17405	Ron Myers	717-854-7857	R	50 OR	1.2
Cynwyd Investments	725 Conshohocken State	Bala Cynwyd	PA	19004	Herbert Kurtz	215-839-4100	R	45 OR	0.2
Bresler and Reiner Inc.	401 M St. S.W.	Washington	DC	20024	Charles S. Bresler	202-488-8800	P	40 OR	0.1
Allen and O'Hara Inc.	P.O. Box 30189	Memphis	TN	38130	Harry S. Hays	901-345-7620	R	36 OR	<0.1
Fetterolf Group Inc.	R.D. 4	Somerset	PA	15501	Donald L. Fetterolf	814-443-4688	R	34 OR	0.5
University City Housing Co.	3418 Sansom St.	Philadelphia	PA	19104	Michael Karp	215-382-2986	R	30 OR*	0.1
Classic Residence by Hyatt	200 W. Madison Ave.	Chicago	IL	60606	Penny Pritzker	312-750-1234	S	27 OR*	0.2
Patterson-Erie Corp.	1250 Tower Ln.	Erie	PA	16505	William L. Patterson Jr.	814-455-8031	R	26 OR	0.6
Koller Enterprises Inc.	1400 S. Hwy. 141	Fenton	MO	63026	A.J. Koller	314-343-9220	R	22	0.1
Hillmark Corporation/Bradbury Suites	P.O. Box 671777	Marietta	GA	30067	R.S. Marks	404-984-0750	R	18 OR*	0.4
Panorama City Corp.	150 Circle Dr.	Lacey	WA	98503	J.T. Quigg	206-456-0111	R	18 OR	0.3
Jonas Equities Inc.	725 Church Ave.	Brooklyn	NY	11218	Terry S. Bernstein	718-871-4840	R	16 OR	<0.1
D.C.G. Development Co.	1-A Lakeview Dr.	Clifton Park	NY	12065	Donald Greene	518-383-0059	R	15 OR	0.1
Highland Management Group Inc.	5290 Villa Way	Edina	MN	55436	Mark Z. Jones II	612-925-1020	R	15 OR*	0.2
Ladha Holdings Inc.	70 John Wesley Dobbs	Atlanta	GA	30303	Shafik Ladha	404-577-3333	R	15 OR	<0.1
Landar Corp.	515 Post Oak Blvd.	Houston	TX	77027	Cecil Holley	713-622-0500	R	15 OR	<0.1
Signature Group L.P.	11400 W. Olympic Blvd.	Los Angeles	CA	90064	Kevin Burnes	310-477-3300	R	14 OR*	0.1
William Lyon Property Management Co.	4490 Von Karmen Ave.	Newport Beach	CA	92660	William Lyon	714-252-9101	S	13 OR*	0.2
Seligman and Associates Inc.	1 Towne Sq.	Southfield	MI	48076	I.R. Seligman	313-352-4440	R	10 OR*	0.2
American Village Corp.	7585 State St. S.E.	Salem	OR	97301	D.D. Decker	503-581-9317	R	8 OR	0.1
Fairfield Properties Inc.	66 Commack Rd.	Commack	NY	11725	Mark Broxmeyer	516-499-6660	R	8 OR*	0.1
R.J. Properties Inc.	7000 Central Pkwy.	Atlanta	GA	30328	J. Robert Love	404-551-0007	S	8 OR*	0.1
Rosenberg Investment Co.	3400 E. Bayaud	Denver	CO	80209	Lawrence R. Rosenberg	303-320-6067	R	8 OR	<0.1
Kuester Properties Inc.	711 E. Morehead St.	Charlotte	NC	28202	Faison Kuester	704-335-1414	R	7 OR*	<0.1
Westminster Capital Inc.	9665 Wilshire Blvd.	Beverly Hills	CA	90212	William Belzberg	310-278-1930	P	7 OR	<0.1
Blankstein Enterprises Inc.	720 N. Old World, 3rd Fl.	Milwaukee	WI	53203	E. Bass	414-271-2697	R	6 OR*	0.1
Hills Community Inc.	7420 Montgomery Rd.	Cincinnati	OH	45236	Stephen Guttman	513-984-0300	R	6 OR*	0.1
Home Leasing Corp.	725 Wedgewood Dr.	Columbus	OH	43228	Debbie Terry	614-272-2800	R	6 OR*	0.1
Mabie and Mintz Inc.	2231 Camino Del Rio	San Diego	CA	92108	T.J. Mintz	619-294-4045	R	6 OR	<0.1

Company type codes: P - Public, R - Private, S - Subsidiary, D - Division, J - Joint Venture, A - Affiliate, G - Group. If the dollar values shown are not sales, the following codes apply: TA - Total Assets; OR - Operating Revenues; GB - Gross Billings. * - estimated dollar value. < - less than. *na* - not available.

Continued on next page.

LEADING COMPANIES - SIC 6513 - Apartment Building Operators
Continued

Company Name	Address				CEO Name	Phone	Co. Type	Sales/Assets ($ mil)	Empl. (000)
NALCO	515 S. Aiken Ave.	Pittsburgh	PA	15232	Linda Beauchamp	412-682-7000	R	6 OR*	0.1
Eaton and Lauth Real Estate Services	P.O. Box 80248	Indianapolis	IN	46280	Robert L. Lauth	317-848-6500	R	5 OR*	<0.1
Pacific Security Cos.	525 Peyton Bldg.	Spokane	WA	99201	Wayne Guthrie	509-624-0183	R	5 OR*	<0.1
Peek Properties	510 University Village	Richardson	TX	75081	Harold Peek	214-783-6040	R	5 OR	<0.1
Southgate Corp.	P.O. Box 396	Newark	OH	43055	John J. O'Neill	614-522-2151	R	5 OR	<0.1
Thomas Yeandle Investment and Construction Co.	20880 Baker Rd.	Castro Valley	CA	94546	Thomas Yeandle	510-537-3920	R	5 OR*	<0.1
Hickok-Dible Co.	9000 W. 64th Ter.	Merriam	KS	66202	William H. Hickok	913-722-3888	R	5 OR	<0.1
Midland Management Co.	P.O. Box 688	Philadelphia	MS	39350	Thomas R. Risher	601-656-4737	R	5 OR	<0.1
Frankfurt Properties Inc.	16500 Lauder Ln.	Dallas	TX	75248	David L. Frankfurt	214-250-3388	R	4 OR*	<0.1
Frauenshuh Cos.	201 S. 7th St.	Minneapolis	MN	55402	David Frauenshuh	612-342-2200	R	4 OR	<0.1
Greystone Communities Inc.	222 W. Las Colinas	Irving	TX	75039	Michael B. Lanahan	214-402-3700	R	4 OR	<0.1
David E. Mazzocco	3151 N.E. Sandy Blvd.	Portland	OR	97232	D.E. Mazzocco	503-234-1058	R	3 OR	<0.1
JLS Realty Management Inc.	1821 Summit Rd.	Cincinnati	OH	45237	John Stalnaker	513-821-1533	R	3 OR	<0.1
John C. Wright and Son	Rte. 1	Purcellville	VA	22132	John R. Wright	703-338-2500	R	3 OR	0.2
McNeil Real Estate Management	13760 Noel Rd.	Dallas	TX	75240	Don Reed	214-448-5800	R	3 OR*	<0.1
Regional Management Inc.	11 E. Fayette St.	Baltimore	MD	21202	Lee Kaufman	410-539-2370	R	3 OR	0.3
Vulcan Development and Management Corp.	P.O. Box 4026	Albany	NY	12204	Mark Simmons	518-270-4711	R	3 OR	<0.1
Walden Management Co.	13601 Preston Rd.	Dallas	TX	75240	Don R. Daseke	214-788-0510	S	3 OR*	0.3
Wheeler/Kolb Management Co.	3525 Mall Blvd.	Duluth	GA	30136	Tom Wheeler	404-476-4801	R	3 OR	<0.1
Arrathoon Trading Co.	108-18 Queens Blvd.	Forest Hills	NY	11375	T. Arrathoon	718-261-2200	R	3 OR	<0.1
Choban Realty Co.	1315 Southview Blvd.	South St. Paul	MN	55075	Michael Choban	612-455-5400	R	3 OR	<0.1
Honer Homes Inc.	304 3rd St. N.E.	Waite Park	MN	56387	Waldemar F. Honer	612-251-7902	R	3 OR	<0.1
Pierce, Pace and Associates	1002 W. Wall Ave.	Midland	TX	79701	Homer E. Pace	915-682-5305	R	3 OR	<0.1
Fidelity Management Co.	2100 W. Loop S. 1255	Houston	TX	77027	J.S. Tuschman	713-626-7200	R	2 OR	<0.1
Millennium III Real Estate Corp.	228 E. 45th St.	New York	NY	10017	Andrew Garr	212-986-9193	R	2 OR	<0.1
Victor Clothing Co.	242 S. Broadway	Los Angeles	CA	90012	I.F. Harter	213-624-0801	R	2	<0.1
Wagner and Truax Company Inc.	2121 N. Causeway Blvd.	Metairie	LA	70001	Dalton L. Truax Jr.	504-830-7300	R	2 OR	<0.1
Westminster Manor Inc.	4100 Jackson Ave.	Austin	TX	78731	Marlene Schaefer	512-454-4711	R	2 OR	<0.1
Worrall-McCarter Inc.	1030 Kapahulu Ave.	Honolulu	HI	96816	Chlois McCarter	808-735-2411	R	2 OR	<0.1
Birtcher Northwest	7690 S.W. Mohawk St.	Tualatin	OR	97062	Mason Frank	503-691-9500	D	1 OR	<0.1
Brigantine Group Inc.	1851 Dalton Ave.	Cincinnati	OH	45214	David Droesch	513-784-1212	R	1 OR	<0.1

Company type codes: P - Public, R - Private, S - Subsidiary, D - Division, J - Joint Venture, A - Affiliate, G - Group. If the dollar values shown are not sales, the following codes apply: TA - Total Assets; OR - Operating Revenues; GB - Gross Billings. * - estimated dollar value. < - less than. *na* - not available.

Continued on next page.

LEADING COMPANIES - SIC 6513 - Apartment Building Operators

Continued

Company Name	Address				CEO Name	Phone	Co. Type	Sales/Assets ($ mil)	Empl. (000)
CMC Management Group Inc.	701 Brickell Ave.	Miami	FL	33133	Esther Ridenhour	305-372-0550	R	1 OR*	<0.1
Coast Properties Ltd.	P.O. Box 104	Kailua Kona	HI	96745	Stathie J. Prattas	808-329-4000	R	1 OR*	<0.1
Decade Properties Inc.	250 Patrick Rd.	Brookfield	WI	53045	Jeffrey Keirheber	414-792-9202	R	1 OR*	<0.1
Duane Larson Construction Co.	201 S. 84th St.	Lincoln	NE	68510	F. Duane Larson	402-489-9655	R	1 OR	<0.1
Hawthorne Management Inc.	212 3rd Ave N.	Minneapolis	MN	55401	Mark Sween	612-339-5693	R	1 OR*	<0.1
Prokop Industries Inc.	6161 Savoy Dr.	Houston	TX	77035	Lester W. Prokop	713-781-2771	R	1 OR*	<0.1
PSI Properties Inc.	5601 Edmond	Waco	TX	76710	M.R. Power	817-772-6031	R	1 OR	<0.1
Sentinel Management Co.	5151 Edina Industrial	Edina	MN	55439	Antonio Bernardi	612-831-5002	R	1 OR*	0.1
SLC Properties	5327 N. Sheridan Rd.	Chicago	IL	60640	Larry Allen	312-878-6333	S	1 OR*	<0.1
Valhal Corp.	55 5th Ave.	New York	NY	10010	Sheldon Stein	212-675-6900	R	1 OR	<0.1
Westchester Investment Co.	8809 Belford Ave.	Los Angeles	CA	90045	Verenice Casas	213-776-0168	R	1 OR	<0.1
Legacy Management and Development Corp.	7151 York Ave. S.	Edina	MN	55435	Roxanne Givens	612-831-1448	R	1 OR	<0.1
Dufner Corbetts Inc.	1 French St.	Hardin	IL	62047	Joan Corbett	618-576-2221	R	1 OR	<0.1
Orchard Mesa Associates	108 N. Greenfield Rd.	Mesa	AZ	85205	John Itter	602-832-7334	R	1 OR*	<0.1
Crown Pointe Div.	2820 S. 80th St.	Omaha	NE	68108	Wally Lee	402-391-7555	D	1 OR	<0.1
Fairlane Rental Properties Inc.	5521 Fairlane Woods Dr	Dearborn	MI	48126	Richard Harb	313-441-5350	R	1 OR*	<0.1
George Pearce Co.	80 S. Lincoln Ave.	Aurora	IL	60505	George F. Pearce	708-897-0541	R	0 OR*	<0.1
Realty Investment Management Inc.	990 Hammond Dr.	Atlanta	GA	30328	Sue Green	404-393-0602	R	0 OR*	<0.1
Tartan West Associates	13643 S.W. Electric	Beaverton	OR	97005	Shirley Wick	503-646-4626	S	0 OR*	<0.1
Mount Carmel Partners	14901 Quorum Dr.	Dallas	TX	75240	Yossi Benvenisti	214-960-6600	R	0 OR	<0.1

Source: Ward's Business Directory of U.S. Private and Public Companies, 1996. Company type codes: P - Public, R - Private, S - Subsidiary, D - Division, J - Joint Venture, A - Affiliate, G - Group. If the dollar values shown are not sales, the following codes apply: TA - Total Assets; OR - Operating Revenues; GB - Gross Billings. * - estimated dollar value. < - less than; *na* - not available.

LEADING COMPANIES - SIC 6514 - Dwelling Operators ex Apartments

Number shown: **19**   Total sales/assets ($ mil): **626**   Total employment (000): **3.9**

Company Name	Address				CEO Name	Phone	Co. Type	Sales/Assets ($ mil)	Empl. (000)
PM Realty Group	1177 W. Loop S.	Houston	TX	77027	Mike Lutton	713-966-3600	R	430 OR*	3.0
Turnberry Associates	19495 Biscayne Blvd.	North Miami Beach	FL	33180	Donald Soffer	305-937-6200	R	64 OR*	0.3
Great Northwest Management Company Inc.	1525 Park Ave.	Portland	OR	97201	Robert G. Johnson	503-241-1525	R	50 OR	0.1
Time Equities Inc.	55 5th Ave.	New York	NY	10003	Robert Kantor	212-206-6000	R	16 OR	<0.1
D.C.G. Development Co.	1-A Lakeview Dr.	Clifton Park	NY	12065	Donald Greene	518-383-0059	R	15 OR	0.1
Gertrude Gardner Inc.	3332 N. Woodlawn Ave.	Metairie	LA	70006	Glenn M. Gardner	504-887-7588	R	13 OR	<0.1
A.W. Perry Inc.	20 Winthrop Sq.	Boston	MA	02110	S. Maxwell Beal	617-542-3164	R	7 OR	<0.1
Gibson Speno Co.	1731 Technology Dr.	San Jose	CA	95110	Drew Gibson	408-436-7100	R	7 OR*	<0.1
Kuester Properties Inc.	711 E. Morehead St.	Charlotte	NC	28202	Faison Kuester	704-335-1414	R	7 OR*	<0.1
Frauenshuh Cos.	201 S. 7th St.	Minneapolis	MN	55402	David Frauenshuh	612-342-2200	R	4 OR*	<0.1
Gallenstein Brothers Inc.	6801 Creek Rd.	Cincinnati	OH	45242	John T. Gallenstein	513-891-0150	R	3 OR	<0.1
JLS Realty Management Inc.	1821 Summit Rd.	Cincinnati	OH	45237	John Stalnaker	513-821-1533	R	3 OR	<0.1
Millennium III Real Estate Corp.	228 E. 45th St.	New York	NY	10017	Andrew Garr	212-986-9193	R	2 OR	<0.1
Brigantine Group Inc.	1851 Dalton Ave.	Cincinnati	OH	45214	David Droesch	513-784-1212	R	1 OR	<0.1
Coast Properties Ltd.	P.O. Box 104	Kailua Kona	HI	96745	Stathie J. Prattas	808-329-4000	R	1 OR*	<0.1
Duane Larson Construction Co.	201 S. 84th St.	Lincoln	NE	68510	F. Duane Larson	402-489-9655	R	1 OR	<0.1
River Market Venture Inc.	509 Delaware St.	Kansas City	MO	64105	Dianna Woolery	816-221-3010	R	1 OR	<0.1
Exclusive Rental Properties Inc.	1406 Shoemaker Rd.	Baltimore	MD	21209	Melanie Sabelhaus	410-296-0900	R	1 OR	<0.1
Seven Cities by the Sea Real Estate Inc.	780 Munras Ave.	Monterey	CA	93940	Donald H. Edgren	408-375-2273	R	0 OR	<0.1

Source: *Ward's Business Directory of U.S. Private and Public Companies*, 1996. Company type codes: P - Public, R - Private, S - Subsidiary, D - Division, J - Joint Venture, A - Affiliate, G - Group. If the dollar values shown are not sales, the following codes apply: TA - Total Assets; OR - Operating Revenues; GB - Gross Billings. * - estimated dollar value. < - less than; *na* - not available.

LEADING COMPANIES - SIC 6515 - Mobile Home Site Operators

Number shown: **8** Total sales/assets ($ mil): **178** Total employment (000): **1.3**

Company Name	Address				CEO Name	Phone	Co. Type	Sales/Assets ($ mil)	Empl. (000)
De Anza Group Inc.	9171 Wilshire Blvd.	Beverly Hills	CA	90210	Michael Gelfand	310-550-1111	R	58 OR*	0.5
Ellenburg Capital Corp.	5550 Macadam Ave. #200	Portland	OR	97201	Gerald D. Ellenburg	503-274-2200	R	52 OR	0.5
Cynwyd Investments	725 Conshohocken State	Bala Cynwyd	PA	19004	Herbert Kurtz	215-839-4100	R	45 OR	0.2
Trailer Mart Inc.	7100 Columbia Rd.	Olmsted Township	OH	44138	Gary J. Brookins	216-235-5300	R	11	<0.1
Thomas Yeandle Investment and Construction Co.	20880 Baker Rd.	Castro Valley	CA	94546	Thomas Yeandle	510-537-3920	R	5 OR*	<0.1
Rancho Carlsbad	5200 El Camino Real	Carlsbad	CA	92008	Ronald S. Schwab	619-438-0332	R	4 OR*	<0.1
Brookwood Park Inc.	6240 Montecito Blvd.	Santa Rosa	CA	95409	E.R. Thomas	707-538-4104	R	2 OR	<0.1
Carey Homes Inc.	3317 Mountain View Dr.	Anchorage	AK	99501	Thomas E. Carey	907-337-9464	R	1	<0.1

Source: Ward's Business Directory of U.S. Private and Public Companies, 1996. Company type codes: P - Public, R - Private, S - Subsidiary, D - Division, J - Joint Venture, A - Affiliate, G - Group. If the dollar values shown are not sales, the following codes apply: TA - Total Assets; OR - Operating Revenues; GB - Gross Billings. * - estimated dollar value. < - less than; *na* - not available.

LEADING COMPANIES - SIC 6519 - Real Property Lessors, nec

Number shown: **44** Total sales/assets ($ mil): **377** Total employment (000): **2.8**

Company Name	Address				CEO Name	Phone	Co. Type	Sales/Assets ($ mil)	Empl. (000)
Horrigan American Inc.	P.O. Box 13428	Reading	PA	19612	Arthur A. Haberberger	215-775-3134	R	100 TA*	0.1
Justice Corp.	19329 U.S. Hwy. 19 N.	Clearwater	FL	34624	Albert N. Justice	813-531-4600	R	75 OR	<0.1
CaliforniaMart	110 E. 9th St.	Los Angeles	CA	90079	Maurice Newman	213-225-6278	R	29 OR	0.3
Peck's Petroleum Inc.	P.O. Box 540	Boaz	AL	35957	Peggy Conn	205-593-4286	R	27*	<0.1
Astrodome USA	P.O. Box 288	Houston	TX	77001	Carl Marsalis	713-799-9500	D	25 OR	1.4
New Mexico and Arizona Land Co.	3033 N. 44th St.	Phoenix	AZ	85018	William A. Pope	602-952-8836	P	21 OR	<0.1
Smithy Braedon ONCOR International	1150 Connecticut Ave.	Washington	DC	20036	James L. Eichberg	202-775-7600	R	10 OR	<0.1
Sports Arenas Inc.	5230 Carroll Canyon Rd	San Diego	CA	92121	Harold S. Elkan	619-587-1060	P	7 OR	0.1
Garrick-Aug Worldwide Ltd.	99 Park Ave.	New York	NY	10016	Charles Aug	212-557-9090	R	7 OR*	<0.1
Marsh Associates Inc.	2448 Park Rd.	Charlotte	NC	28203	D.L. Francis	704-376-0281	R	7 OR	<0.1
Great Northern Iron Ore Properties	P.O. Box 738	South St. Paul	MN	55075	Harry L. Holtz	612-224-2385	P	7 OR	<0.1
Madisonville Realty Co.	630 N. Franklin St.	Madisonville	KY	42431	James L. Beck	502-825-0936	R	6 OR	<0.1

Company type codes: P - Public, R - Private, S - Subsidiary, D - Division, J - Joint Venture, A - Affiliate, G - Group. If the dollar values shown are not sales, the following codes apply: TA - Total Assets; OR - Operating Revenues; GB - Gross Billings. * - estimated dollar value. < - less than. *na* - not available.

Continued on next page.

LEADING COMPANIES - SIC 6519 - Real Property Lessors, nec
Continued

Company Name	Address				CEO Name	Phone	Co. Type	Sales/Assets ($ mil)	Empl. (000)
AmeriCenters Inc.	39209 W. 6 Mile Rd., 111	Livonia	MI	48152	James Blain	313-462-1313	S	5 OR	<0.1
Southern Furniture Exposition Building Inc.	P.O. Box 828	High Point	NC	27261	G. Bruce Miller	919-888-7300	R	5 OR*	<0.1
Hollis and Associates	2257 Larkspur Landing	Larkspur	CA	94939	Peter J. Hollis	415-461-4365	R	4 OR	<0.1
Northco Corp.	1201 Marquette Ave.	Minneapolis	MN	55403	William Bracken	612-332-2212	R	4 OR	<0.1
Jack Brothers and McBurney Inc.	P.O. Box 116	Brawley	CA	92227	Alex C. Jack	619-344-3781	R	3 OR	<0.1
Scannapieco Development Corp.	328 S. Main St.	New Hope	PA	18938	Tom Scannapieco	215-862-5400	R	3 OR*	<0.1
Westwood Management Corp.	5110 Ridgefld Rd.	Bethesda	MD	20816	Laszlo N. Tauber	301-657-2030	R	3 OR	<0.1
Zugsmith/Thind Commercial Real Estate Services Inc.	11812 San Vincente	Los Angeles	CA	90049	Michael Zugsmith	310-447-3500	R	3 OR*	<0.1
United Park City Mines Co.	P.O. Box 1450	Park City	UT	84060	Hank Rothwell	801-649-8011	P	3 OR	<0.1
Metro Office Management Ltd.	620 Herndon Pkwy.	Herndon	VA	22070	Kathlene Buchanan	703-481-9800	R	3 OR	<0.1
Baur Properties	635 Maryville Ctr. Dr.	St. Louis	MO	63141	Edward T. Baur	314-434-3700	R	2 OR	<0.1
Connecticut Commercial Realty	P.O. Box 2089	New London	CT	06320	Robert Zabarsky	203-444-7704	R	2 OR	<0.1
Signature Associates	1 Towne Square	Southfield	MI	48076	Steve Gordon	313-948-9000	R	2 OR	<0.1
Tara Group Inc.	10670 N. Central Expwy	Dallas	TX	75231	Richard D. Morgan	817-265-0838	R	2 OR	<0.1
Four Nines Gold Inc.	877 N. 8th St. W.	Riverton	WY	82501	Bill DeLapp	307-856-9271	S	1 OR	<0.1
Promenade Real Estate Co.	16 E. 52nd St. 14th Fl	New York	NY	10022	Jay D. Lishow	212-758-0430	R	1 OR	<0.1
Peterson Investment Co.	2251 Alvarado St.	San Leandro	CA	94577	Howard Peterson	510-895-0500	R	1 OR*	<0.1
Suite Options Inc.	14004 W. 107th St.	Lenexa	KS	66215	William Jackson	913-451-3300	R	1 OR	<0.1
Teutsch Partners	2001 Western Ave.	Seattle	WA	98121	John Teutsch	206-728-1130	R	1 OR*	<0.1
Lander Energy Co.	309 W. Harmony Rd.	Fort Collins	CO	80526	John H. Ellerby	303-223-5582	P	1 OR	<0.1
TRS Commercial Real Estate Services Inc.	1 Progress Plz.	St. Petersburg	FL	33701	Michael Talmadge	813-824-6777	R	1 OR	<0.1
Riffe Construction Co.	1021 Burning Tree Dr.	Kansas City	MO	64145	Hank Riffe	816-942-6889	R	1 OR	<0.1
Barnes and Tucker Co.	P.O. Box 628	Ebensburg	PA	15931	Allen Wenturine	814-472-4470	R	1 OR	<0.1
HQ International Inc.	1825 I St.	Washington	DC	20006	Gordon McClure	202-429-2000	S	1 OR*	<0.1
Coggins Construction Co.	3939 Glenwood Ave.	Raleigh	NC	27612	Jyles Coggins	919-787-0024	R	1 OR*	<0.1
F.B. Clements and Co.	1815 Madison Ave.	Mankato	MN	56001	Lance Butler	507-625-5641	R	1 OR*	<0.1
GEG Partners	4733 Bethesda Ave.	Bethesda	MD	20814	Brad Eisner	301-656-7193	R	1 OR*	<0.1
New Shawmut Mining Co.	P.O. Box 426	St. Marys	PA	15857	Antonio J. Palumbo	814-834-2891	R	1 OR	<0.1
Calcasieu Real Estate and Oil Company Inc.	3401 Ryan St.	Lake Charles	LA	70605	Arthur Hollins III	318-477-7630	P	0 OR	<0.1
Tyonek Native Corp.	1689 C St.	Anchorage	AK	99501	Seraphim Stephan	907-272-0707	R	0 OR	<0.1

Company type codes: P - Public, R - Private, S - Subsidiary, D - Division, J - Joint Venture, A - Affiliate, G - Group. If the dollar values shown are not sales, the following codes apply: TA - Total Assets; OR - Operating Revenues; GB - Gross Billings. * - estimated dollar value. < - less than. *na* - not available.

Continued on next page.

LEADING COMPANIES - SIC 6519 - Real Property Lessors, nec

Continued

Company Name	Address				CEO Name	Phone	Co. Type	Sales/Assets ($ mil)	Empl. (000)
J. Supple's Sons Planting Co.	29830 Hwy.	Bayou Goula	LA	70788	M.P. Dhlmeyer	504-545-8417	R	0 OR	<0.1
Long Brothers Inc.	P.O. Box 159	Westover	MD	21871	Robert C. Long	410-651-0910	R	0 OR*	<0.1

Source: *Ward's Business Directory of U.S. Private and Public Companies*, 1996. Company type codes: P - Public, R - Private, S - Subsidiary, D - Division, J - Joint Venture, A - Affiliate, G - Group. If the dollar values shown are not sales, the following codes apply: TA - Total Assets; OR - Operating Revenues; GB - Gross Billings. * - estimated dollar value. < - less than; *na* - not available.

SIC 6530

REAL ESTATE AGENTS AND MANAGERS

Establishments in this industry are primarily engaged in renting, buying, selling, managing, and appraising real estate for others. The SIC includes the following types of organizations or activities: agents, appraisers, and brokers for the sale or rental of real estate; buying agents; cemetery management services; condominium managers; cooperative apartment managers; escrow agents; fiduciaries for real estate; housing authorities with operational responsibilities; listing services, including multiple listing, for real estate; real estate auctioneers; and time-sharing services for real estate.

ESTABLISHMENTS, EMPLOYMENT, AND PAYROLL

	1988	1989 Value	%	1990 Value	%	1991 Value	%	1992 Value	%	1993 Value	%	% change 88-93
All Establishments	82,894	70,224	-15.3	72,243	2.9	80,055	10.8	92,086	15.0	110,387	19.9	33.2
Mid-March Employment	616,382	567,121	-8.0	584,669	3.1	581,901	-0.5	637,222	9.5	706,907	10.9	14.7
1st Quarter Wages (annualized - $ mil.)	13,270.1	12,954.4	-2.4	13,291.7	2.6	12,649.6	-4.8	14,173.2	12.0	15,298.7	7.9	15.3
Payroll per Emp. 1st Q. (annualized)	21,529	22,842	6.1	22,734	-0.5	21,738	-4.4	22,242	2.3	21,642	-2.7	0.5
Annual Payroll ($ mil.)	13,504.3	13,169.7	-2.5	13,324.2	1.2	13,108.1	-1.6	14,973.8	14.2	17,025.8	13.7	26.1
Establishments - 1-4 Emp. Number	60,819	50,581	-16.8	51,900	2.6	57,343	10.5	66,863	16.6	81,238	21.5	33.6
Mid-March Employment	97,652	82,946	-15.1	85,469	3.0	93,717	9.7	108,286	15.5	127,699	17.9	30.8
1st Quarter Wages (annualized - $ mil.)	1,877.5	1,552.1	-17.3	1,626.0	4.8	1,696.1	4.3	2,050.8	20.9	2,451.3	19.5	30.6
Payroll per Emp. 1st Q. (annualized)	19,226	18,712	-2.7	19,025	1.7	18,098	-4.9	18,939	4.6	19,196	1.4	-0.2
Annual Payroll ($ mil.)	2,285.3	1,850.7	-19.0	1,894.4	2.4	2,058.0	8.6	2,499.3	21.4	3,234.3	29.4	41.5
Establishments - 5-9 Emp. Number	11,138	9,587	-13.9	9,997	4.3	12,161	21.6	13,253	9.0	15,591	17.6	40.0
Mid-March Employment	71,887	61,953	-13.8	64,806	4.6	78,935	21.8	85,775	8.7	101,110	17.9	40.7
1st Quarter Wages (annualized - $ mil.)	1,451.7	1,282.8	-11.6	1,372.0	7.0	1,706.7	24.4	1,888.3	10.6	2,194.6	16.2	51.2
Payroll per Emp. 1st Q. (annualized)	20,194	20,706	2.5	21,171	2.2	21,622	2.1	22,014	1.8	21,705	-1.4	7.5
Annual Payroll ($ mil.)	1,502.1	1,328.3	-11.6	1,407.3	6.0	1,794.0	27.5	2,011.0	12.1	2,438.0	21.2	62.3
Establishments - 10-19 Emp. Number	5,661	5,053	-10.7	5,176	2.4	5,620	8.6	6,428	14.4	7,596	18.2	34.2
Mid-March Employment	75,879	67,598	-10.9	68,917	2.0	74,707	8.4	85,203	14.0	100,787	18.3	32.8
1st Quarter Wages (annualized - $ mil.)	1,625.8	1,508.0	-7.2	1,597.2	5.9	1,640.2	2.7	1,958.9	19.4	2,305.6	17.7	41.8
Payroll per Emp. 1st Q. (annualized)	21,426	22,308	4.1	23,175	3.9	21,956	-5.3	22,990	4.7	22,876	-0.5	6.8
Annual Payroll ($ mil.)	1,656.5	1,537.1	-7.2	1,578.0	2.7	1,688.8	7.0	2,071.8	22.7	2,510.4	21.2	51.5
Establishments - 20-49 Emp. Number	3,326	3,137	-5.7	3,293	5.0	3,193	-3.0	3,713	16.3	3,993	7.5	20.1
Mid-March Employment	99,962	94,935	-5.0	99,522	4.8	95,479	-4.1	111,179	16.4	118,882	6.9	18.9
1st Quarter Wages (annualized - $ mil.)	2,248.9	2,203.1	-2.0	2,315.9	5.1	2,118.3	-8.5	2,531.2	19.5	2,691.4	6.3	19.7
Payroll per Emp. 1st Q. (annualized)	22,497	23,207	3.2	23,271	0.3	22,186	-4.7	22,767	2.6	22,639	-0.6	0.6
Annual Payroll ($ mil.)	2,247.9	2,194.6	-2.4	2,283.0	4.0	2,141.3	-6.2	2,596.8	21.3	2,877.7	10.8	28.0
Establishments - 50-99 Emp. Number	1,115	1,087	-2.5	1,066	-1.9	1,014	-4.9	1,086	7.1	1,209	11.3	8.4
Mid-March Employment	77,158	74,401	-3.6	73,135	-1.7	68,869	-5.8	74,527	8.2	83,477	12.0	8.2
1st Quarter Wages (annualized - $ mil.)	1,718.3	1,926.0	12.1	1,769.5	-8.1	1,605.5	-9.3	1,777.0	10.7	1,908.1	7.4	11.0
Payroll per Emp. 1st Q. (annualized)	22,270	25,887	16.2	24,195	-6.5	23,312	-3.7	23,843	2.3	22,857	-4.1	2.6
Annual Payroll ($ mil.)	1,678.8	1,899.3	13.1	1,693.6	-10.8	1,573.1	-7.1	1,803.9	14.7	2,014.2	11.7	20.0
Establishments - 100-249 Emp. Number	627	574	-8.5	594	3.5	546	-8.1	564	3.3	567	0.5	-9.6
Mid-March Employment	93,819	85,819	-8.5	88,440	3.1	81,778	-7.5	84,408	3.2	83,654	-0.9	-10.8
1st Quarter Wages (annualized - $ mil.)	2,037.0	2,152.8	5.7	2,084.6	-3.2	1,852.3	-11.1	1,957.5	5.7	1,859.9	-5.0	-8.7
Payroll per Emp. 1st Q. (annualized)	21,712	25,085	15.5	23,571	-6.0	22,650	-3.9	23,191	2.4	22,233	-4.1	2.4
Annual Payroll ($ mil.)	1,988.8	2,106.7	5.9	2,049.6	-2.7	1,858.2	-9.3	1,953.9	5.1	1,960.2	0.3	-1.4
Establishments - 250-499 Emp. Number	152	146	-3.9	155	6.2	120	-22.6	125	4.2	142	13.6	-6.6
Mid-March Employment	49,925	49,751	-0.3	51,944	4.4	40,956	-21.2	43,181	5.4	48,331	11.9	-3.2
1st Quarter Wages (annualized - $ mil.)	1,221.5	1,227.9	0.5	1,233.1	0.4	1,023.3	-17.0	1,117.0	9.2	1,142.1	2.2	-6.5
Payroll per Emp. 1st Q. (annualized)	24,466	24,681	0.9	23,738	-3.8	24,984	5.2	25,868	3.5	23,631	-8.6	-3.4
Annual Payroll ($ mil.)	1,129.1	1,196.1	5.9	1,212.0	1.3	1,002.8	-17.3	1,119.9	11.7	1,196.6	6.8	6.0
Establishments - 500-999 Emp. Number	44	48	9.1	49	2.1	44	-10.2	42	-4.5	42	-	-4.5
Mid-March Employment	(D)	31,156	-	30,891	-0.9	(D)	-	28,006	-	27,350	-2.3	-
1st Quarter Wages (annualized - $ mil.)	(D)	745.5	-	875.0	17.4	(D)	-	578.5	-	503.6	-13.0	-
Payroll per Emp. 1st Q. (annualized)	(D)	23,926	-	28,324	18.4	(D)	-	20,657	-	18,413	-10.9	-
Annual Payroll ($ mil.)	(D)	708.8	-	769.0	8.5	(D)	-	597.6	-	538.2	-9.9	-
Estab. - 1000 or More Emp. Number	12	11	-8.3	13	18.2	14	7.7	12	-14.3	9	-25.0	-25.0
Mid-March Employment	(D)	18,562	-	21,545	16.1	(D)	-	16,657	-	15,617	-6.2	-
1st Quarter Wages (annualized - $ mil.)	(D)	356.3	-	418.4	17.4	(D)	-	314.0	-	242.1	-22.9	-
Payroll per Emp. 1st Q. (annualized)	(D)	19,196	-	19,418	1.2	(D)	-	18,854	-	15,504	-17.8	-
Annual Payroll ($ mil.)	(D)	348.3	-	437.3	25.5	(D)	-	319.6	-	256.2	-19.9	-

Source: County Business Patterns, U.S. Department of Commerce, Washington, D.C., for 1988 through 1993. Payroll per employee is calculated using mid-March employment and 1st Quarter wages, annualized. Annual payroll, also shown, may not equal the annualized 1st Quarter wages. Columns headed by a percent sign (%) indicate change from the previous year. na stands for not available. The symbol (D) indicates that data are withheld by the source to avoid disclosure of competitive information. A dash (-) indicates that data are not available or cannot be calculated.

ESTABLISHMENTS
Number

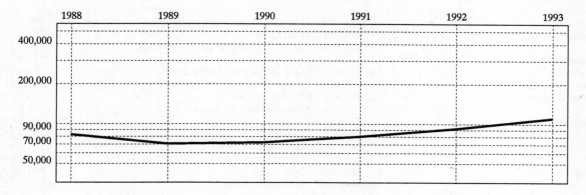

MID-MARCH EMPLOYMENT
Number

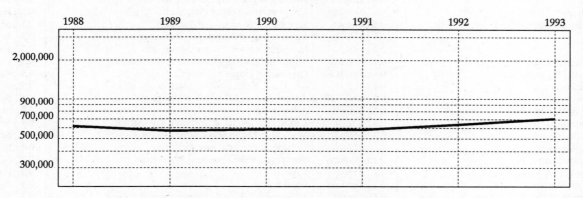

ANNUAL PAYROLL
$ million

INPUTS AND OUTPUTS FOR ALL REAL ESTATE SECTORS - SIC GROUP 65

Economic Sector or Industry Providing Inputs	%	Sector	Economic Sector or Industry Buying Outputs	%	Sector
Real estate	38.6	Fin/R.E.	Personal consumption expenditures	37.6	
Nonfarm residential structure maintenance	12.5	Constr.	Real estate	10.9	Fin/R.E.
Banking	5.6	Fin/R.E.	Retail trade, except eating & drinking	7.4	Trade
Maintenance of nonfarm buildings nec	5.3	Constr.	Hospitals	4.6	Services
Eating & drinking places	4.4	Trade	Gross private fixed investment	4.4	Cap Inv
Insurance carriers	4.3	Fin/R.E.	Owner-occupied dwellings	2.7	Fin/R.E.
Services to dwellings & other buildings	4.2	Services	Wholesale trade	2.7	Trade
Advertising	3.2	Services	Eating & drinking places	1.8	Trade
Maintenance of highways & streets	2.8	Constr.	Religious organizations	1.4	Services
Communications, except radio & TV	2.0	Util.	Banking	1.2	Fin/R.E.
Landscape & horticultural services	1.9	Agric.	Doctors & dentists	1.2	Services
Legal services	1.6	Services	Colleges, universities, & professional schools	1.1	Services
Petroleum refining	1.5	Manufg.	Feed grains	1.1	Agric.
Commercial printing	0.9	Manufg.	Insurance carriers	0.9	Fin/R.E.
Hotels & lodging places	0.7	Services	Legal services	0.9	Services
Management & consulting services & labs	0.7	Services	Meat animals	0.9	Agric.
Accounting, auditing & bookkeeping	0.6	Services	S/L Govt. purch., other general government	0.9	S/L Govt
Business services nec	0.6	Services	Communications, except radio & TV	0.6	Util.
Motor freight transportation & warehousing	0.6	Util.	Hotels & lodging places	0.6	Services
U.S. Postal Service	0.6	Gov't	Amusement & recreation services nec	0.5	Services
Electrical repair shops	0.5	Services	Credit agencies other than banks	0.5	Fin/R.E.
Maintenance of farm service facilities	0.5	Constr.	Elementary & secondary schools	0.5	Services
Wholesale trade	0.5	Trade	Engineering, architectural, & surveying services	0.5	Services
Air transportation	0.4	Util.	Insurance agents, brokers, & services	0.5	Fin/R.E.
Business/professional associations	0.4	Services	Motor freight transportation & warehousing	0.5	Util.
Security & commodity brokers	0.4	Fin/R.E.	Oil bearing crops	0.5	Agric.
Transit & bus transportation	0.4	Util.	S/L Govt. purch., public assistance & relief	0.5	S/L Govt
Arrangement of passenger transportation	0.3	Util.	Accounting, auditing & bookkeeping	0.4	Services
Automotive rental & leasing, without drivers	0.3	Services	Advertising	0.4	Services
Electric services (utilities)	0.3	Util.	Labor, civic, social, & fraternal associations	0.4	Services
Miscellaneous plastics products	0.3	Manufg.	Medical & health services, nec	0.4	Services
Engine electrical equipment	0.2	Manufg.	Nursing & personal care facilities	0.4	Services
Paper mills, except building paper	0.2	Manufg.	Computer & data processing services	0.3	Services
Retail trade, except eating & drinking	0.2	Trade	Exports	0.3	Foreign
Computer & data processing services	0.1	Services	Food grains	0.3	Agric.
Maintenance of farm residential buildings	0.1	Constr.	Management & consulting services & labs	0.3	Services
Nitrogenous & phosphatic fertilizers	0.1	Manufg.	Security & commodity brokers	0.3	Fin/R.E.
Paper coating & glazing	0.1	Manufg.	Water transportation	0.3	Util.
Personnel supply services	0.1	Services	Air transportation	0.2	Util.
Photographic equipment & supplies	0.1	Manufg.	Automotive repair shops & services	0.2	Services
			Beauty & barber shops	0.2	Services
			Business services nec	0.2	Services
			Coal	0.2	Mining
			Crude petroleum & natural gas	0.2	Mining
			Dairy farm products	0.2	Agric.
			Electric services (utilities)	0.2	Util.
			Federal Government purchases, national defense	0.2	Fed Govt
			Federal Government purchases, nondefense	0.2	Fed Govt
			Laundry, dry cleaning, shoe repair	0.2	Services
			Libraries, vocation education	0.2	Services
			Membership organizations nec	0.2	Services
			Social services, nec	0.2	Services
			State & local government enterprises, nec	0.2	Gov't
			Vegetables	0.2	Agric.
			Automobile parking & car washes	0.1	Services
			Child day care services	0.1	Services
			Cotton	0.1	Agric.
			Electronic computing equipment	0.1	Manufg.

Continued on next page.

INPUTS AND OUTPUTS FOR ALL REAL ESTATE SECTORS - SIC GROUP 65 - Continued

Economic Sector or Industry Providing Inputs	%	Sector	Economic Sector or Industry Buying Outputs	%	Sector
			Landscape & horticultural services	0.1	Agric.
			Membership sports & recreation clubs	0.1	Services
			Motion pictures	0.1	Services
			Petroleum & natural gas well drilling	0.1	Constr.
			Portrait, photographic studios	0.1	Services
			Residential care	0.1	Services
			U.S. Postal Service	0.1	Gov't

Source: Benchmark Input-Output Accounts for the U.S. Economy, 1982, U.S. Department of Commerce, Washington, D.C., July 1991. Data, as reported in the source, are organized by the 1977 SIC structure in use in 1982 but have been matched, as closely as is possible, to the 1987 SIC structure used in this book. Activities with the same percentage are sorted alphabetically by name of activity.

OCCUPATIONS EMPLOYED BY REAL ESTATE AGENTS AND MANAGERS

Occupation	% of Total 1994	Change to 2005	Occupation	% of Total 1994	Change to 2005
Maintenance repairers, general utility	11.5	22.6	Guards	3.2	0.3
Property & real estate managers	10.2	31.7	Gardeners & groundskeepers, ex farm	3.2	0.3
Janitors & cleaners, incl maids	9.4	22.6	Brokers, real estate	3.1	11.4
Secretaries, ex legal & medical	7.0	1.4	Real estate clerks	2.5	11.4
Sales agents, real estate	5.8	-0.1	Financial managers	2.1	11.4
General office clerks	5.1	-5.0	Marketing & sales worker supervisors	1.7	11.4
Bookkeeping, accounting, & auditing clerks	5.0	-16.4	Service workers nec	1.3	11.4
Receptionists & information clerks	4.9	33.7	Accountants & auditors	1.3	11.4
General managers & top executives	4.4	5.7	Clerical supervisors & managers	1.3	14.0
Real estate appraisers	3.6	11.4	Typists & word processors	1.1	-44.3

Sources: Industry-Occupation Matrix, Bureau of Labor Statistics. These data relate to one or more 3-digit SIC industry groups rather than to a single 4-digit SIC. The change reported for each occupation to the year 2005 is a percent of growth or decline as estimated by the Bureau of Labor Statistics. The abbreviation nec stands for not elsewhere classified.

U.S. AND STATE DATA ON INDUSTRY REVENUES AND OTHER ACCOUNTS FOR 1992

State	No. of Estab.	Employ- ment	Payroll ($ mil.)	Revenues ($ mil.)	Empl./ Estab.	Revenue/ Estab. ($)	Payroll/ Estab. ($)	Revenue/ Empl. ($)	Payroll/ Empl. ($)
UNITED STATES	106,552	646,561	14,859.5	53,747.0	6	504,421	139,458	83,128	22,982
Alabama	989	4,960	96.7	363.1	5	367,172	97,762	73,212	19,493
Alaska	237	1,176	25.5	102.4	5	432,030	107,447	87,067	21,654
Arizona	2,049	12,841	271.4	971.4	6	474,109	132,448	75,652	21,134
Arkansas	600	3,088	43.9	192.5	5	320,762	73,215	62,324	14,226
California	15,432	93,153	2,370.3	8,212.6	6	532,179	153,596	88,162	25,445
Colorado	2,733	16,451	318.0	1,166.5	6	426,819	116,355	70,907	19,330
Connecticut	1,487	7,885	243.9	1,170.7	5	787,321	164,032	148,478	30,934
Delaware	285	1,189	27.5	133.7	4	469,165	96,593	112,458	23,153
District of Columbia	544	5,876	168.0	465.2	11	855,090	308,783	79,164	28,587
Florida	10,400	58,634	1,112.6	4,515.3	6	434,166	106,982	77,009	18,976
Georgia	2,386	15,958	432.1	1,400.9	7	587,136	181,082	87,787	27,075
Hawaii	1,591	8,832	193.9	733.7	6	461,181	121,881	83,077	21,956
Idaho	463	1,281	23.8	156.0	3	336,937	51,322	121,781	18,550
Illinois	5,027	35,500	979.2	3,315.5	7	659,541	194,790	93,395	27,583
Indiana	1,560	9,053	180.5	671.7	6	430,556	115,722	74,193	19,941
Iowa	733	2,989	58.9	262.5	4	358,181	80,371	87,838	19,710
Kansas	814	5,038	81.6	307.8	6	378,145	100,270	61,098	16,201
Kentucky	785	3,121	51.0	249.3	4	317,583	64,910	79,879	16,326
Louisiana	908	5,633	94.1	329.2	6	362,541	103,607	58,439	16,701
Maine	557	1,949	36.9	155.7	3	279,616	66,321	79,911	18,954
Maryland	2,220	17,256	407.1	1,330.1	8	599,144	183,370	77,080	23,591
Massachusetts	2,390	18,289	522.9	1,533.0	8	641,422	218,767	83,821	28,588
Michigan	2,896	17,458	348.8	1,176.7	6	406,309	120,435	67,400	19,978
Minnesota	1,624	9,816	189.2	779.8	6	480,166	116,520	79,441	19,278
Mississippi	460	1,760	23.8	101.4	4	220,376	51,685	57,598	13,509
Missouri	1,695	9,522	193.3	701.7	6	413,970	114,018	73,690	20,296
Montana	352	910	12.5	89.4	3	254,085	35,608	98,284	13,774
Nebraska	453	2,407	44.9	184.7	5	407,828	99,117	76,754	18,654
Nevada	784	4,418	83.0	341.2	6	435,224	105,893	77,233	18,791
New Hampshire	581	2,377	50.7	194.7	4	335,072	87,196	81,900	21,313
New Jersey	3,325	18,179	436.9	1,839.9	5	553,359	131,411	101,211	24,036
New Mexico	606	2,322	38.8	198.9	4	328,224	64,035	85,661	16,712
New York	10,157	62,036	1,876.4	6,814.8	6	670,947	184,738	109,853	30,247
North Carolina	2,374	11,090	224.2	923.0	5	388,796	94,426	83,228	20,213
North Dakota	165	680	10.4	47.3	4	286,800	62,958	69,591	15,276
Ohio	2,863	21,434	421.9	1,522.3	7	531,712	147,358	71,022	19,683
Oklahoma	883	4,733	88.9	304.9	5	345,256	100,678	64,412	18,783
Oregon	1,327	7,798	133.7	596.3	6	449,376	100,726	76,471	17,141
Pennsylvania	3,134	20,130	438.9	1,621.5	6	517,383	140,041	80,550	21,803
Rhode Island	354	1,780	36.0	145.8	5	411,723	101,794	81,882	20,244
South Carolina	1,287	7,055	132.9	489.4	5	380,256	103,238	69,368	18,833
South Dakota	206	715	10.2	50.2	3	243,738	49,665	70,224	14,309
Tennessee	1,443	9,032	163.6	636.5	6	441,072	113,378	70,468	18,114
Texas	6,778	52,218	1,168.1	3,413.1	8	503,560	172,331	65,363	22,369
Utah	637	3,876	68.8	309.1	6	485,243	108,050	79,747	17,757
Vermont	343	1,132	20.3	88.7	3	258,612	59,044	78,360	17,890
Virginia	2,779	19,721	427.7	1,456.5	7	524,117	153,900	73,856	21,687
Washington	2,716	15,183	314.3	1,293.3	6	476,195	115,707	85,184	20,698
West Virginia	329	976	14.5	82.5	3	250,866	44,061	84,565	14,852
Wisconsin	1,605	7,017	137.9	553.2	4	344,683	85,899	78,840	19,648
Wyoming	206	634	9.5	51.2	3	248,413	45,893	80,715	14,912

Source: 1992 Economic Census, U.S. Department of Commerce, Washington, D.C. This is the only table that shows revenue data as collected by the Bureau of the Census in an Economic Census. The symbol (D) indicates that data are withheld by the source to avoid disclosure of competitive information. A dash (-) indicates that data are not available or cannot be calculated.

ESTABLISHMENTS 1992 - STATE AND REGIONAL CONCENTRATION

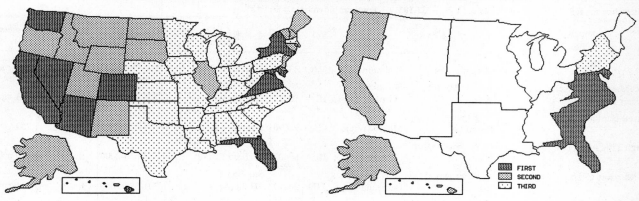

EMPLOYMENT 1992 - STATE AND REGIONAL CONCENTRATION

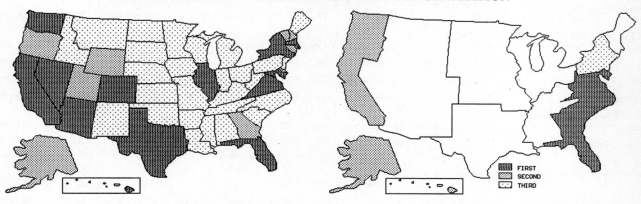

REVENUES 1992 - STATE AND REGIONAL CONCENTRATION

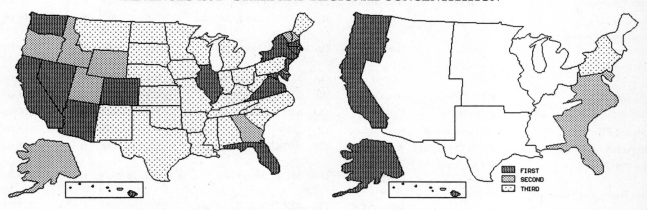

States with the darkest shading indicate those states which have proportionately more establishments, employment, or revenues than would be indicated by the state's population. States with light shading are states with proportionately fewer establishments, less employment, and lower revenues than population distribution. States shaded grey are within 15 percent of the state's population proportion in these categories. States for which no data are available are shown as average (grey). *Regions* are shaded to indicate absolute rank in the category. If no data for the category are available, establishment counts are used to shade the regions. Source of the data is the table on the facing page.

LEADING COMPANIES - SIC 6531 - Real Estate Agents and Managers

Number shown: **100** Total sales/assets ($ mil): **31,108** Total employment (000): **181.0**

Company Name	Address				CEO Name	Phone	Co. Type	Sales/Assets ($ mil)	Empl. (000)
CSX Corp.	901 E. Cary St.	Richmond	VA	23219	John W. Snow	804-782-1400	P	9,608 OR	47.0
ServiceMaster Management Services Inc.	1 ServiceMaster Way.	Downers Grove	IL	60515	Charles W. Stair	708-964-1300	S	1,763 OR	14.0
Coldwell Banker Corp.	27271 Las Ramblas	Mission Viejo	CA	92690	Chandler B. Barton	714-367-1800	R	1,700 OR	2.5
Chicago Title and Trust Co.	111 W. Washington St.	Chicago	IL	60602	Richard P. Toft	312-630-2000	S	1,530 TA*	7.7
Host Marriott Corp.	10400 Fernwood Rd.	Bethesda	MD	20817	Stephen F. Bollenbach	301-380-9000	P	1,354 OR	23.0
Metropolitan Mortgage and Securities Company Inc.	W. 929 Sprague Ave.	Spokane	WA	99204	C. Paul Sandifur Jr.	509-838-3111	R	982 OR	0.3
York Financial Corp.	101 S. George St.	York	PA	17405	Robert W. Pullo	717-846-8777	P	888 TA	0.5
Lennar Corp.	700 N.W. 107th Ave.	Miami	FL	33172	Leonard Miller	305-559-4000	P	818 OR	1.7
Lowe Enterprises Inc.	11777 San Vicente Blvd	Los Angeles	CA	90049	Robert J. Lowe	310-820-6661	R	620 OR*	2.9
Allen Tate Company Inc.	6618 Fairview Rd.	Charlotte	NC	28210	H. Allen Tate Jr.	704-365-6910	R	500 OR*	<0.1
Carlsberg Management Co.	2800 28th St.	Santa Monica	CA	90405	William Geary	310-450-9696	R	500 OR	0.5
Simon Property Group L.P.	P.O. Box 7033	Indianapolis	IN	46207	David Simon	317-636-1600	S	474 OR	4.3
Prudential Summerson-Burrows Realtors	8101 College Blvd.	Overland Park	KS	66210	Rich Henry	913-491-1550	S	392 OR	0.2
Hovnanian Enterprises Inc.	P.O. Box 500	Red Bank	NJ	07701	Kevork S. Hovnanian	908-747-7800	P	387 OR	1.3
Hines Interests L.P.	2800 Post Oak Blvd.	Houston	TX	77056	Jeffrey C. Hines	713-621-8000	R	360 OR*	1.7
Fortune International Realty	2666 Brickell Ave.	Miami	FL	33129	Edgardo Defortuna	305-856-2600	R	345 OR	0.3
Trammell Crow Co.	2001 Ross Ave.	Dallas	TX	75201	J. McDonald Williams	214-979-5100	R	270 OR*	2.5
Stewart Enterprises Inc.	P.O. Drawer 19925	New Orleans	LA	70179	Frank B. Stewart Jr.	504-837-5880	P	254 OR	6.2
Balcor Co.	4849 Golf Rd.	Skokie	IL	60077	Tom E. Meador	708-677-2900	S	240 OR	2.4
Mason-McDuffie Real Estate Inc.	25 Orinda Way	Orinda	CA	94563	David Cobo	510-254-5640	R	236 OR	0.1
Bryant and Associates	3350 Peachtree N.E.	Atlanta	GA	30326	Richard Bryant Jr.	404-262-2828	R	228 OR	<0.1
N.D.C. Inc.	6312 S. 27th St.	Oak Creek	WI	53154	David Ulrich	414-761-2040	R	220 OR*	2.0
Slifer, Smith and Frampton Inc.	230 Bridge St.	Vail	CO	81657	Mark Smith	303-476-2421	R	214 OR	<0.1
Grubb and Ellis Co.	1 Montgomery St.	San Francisco	CA	94104	Wilbert F. Schwartz	415-956-1990	P	202 OR	3.7
North American Title Co.	2185 N. California	Walnut Creek	CA	94596	Dan Wentzel	510-935-5599	R	200 OR*	1.2
Realty One Inc.	6000 Rockside Woods	Independence	OH	44131	Joseph T. Aveni	216-328-2500	R	200 OR	2.0
Florida East Coast Industries Inc.	1650 Prudential Dr.	Jacksonville	FL	32207	W.L. Thornton	904-396-6600	P	200 OR	1.5
Catellus Development Corp.	201 Mission St.	San Francisco	CA	94105	Nelson C. Rising	415-974-4500	P	175 OR	0.2
Trammell Crow Commercial	2001 Ross Ave.	Dallas	TX	75201	J. McDonald Williams	214-979-5100	S	175 OR	2.4
Richard Bowers and Co.	3475 Lenox Rd. N.E.	Atlanta	GA	30326	Richard Bowers	404-816-1600	R	170 OR	<0.1

Company type codes: P - Public, R - Private, S - Subsidiary, D - Division, J - Joint Venture, A - Affiliate, G - Group. If the dollar values shown are not sales, the following codes apply: TA - Total Assets; OR - Operating Revenues; GB - Gross Billings. * - estimated dollar value. < - less than. *na* - not available.

Continued on next page.

LEADING COMPANIES - SIC 6531 - Real Estate Agents and Managers
Continued

Company Name	Address				CEO Name	Phone	Co. Type	Sales/Assets ($ mil)	Empl. (000)
Charles E. Smith Residential Realty L.P.	2345 Crystal Dr.	Arlington	VA	22202	Robert P. Kogod	703-920-8500	S	168 OR	1.2
Capital Realty Group Corp.	14160 Dallas Pkwy.	Dallas	TX	75240	Jeffrey L. Beck	214-770-5600	R	160 OR	1.5
Central Resource Group Inc.	611 5th Ave.	Des Moines	IA	50309	Alfred P. Moore	515-242-2384	S	154 OR	0.8
Alper Holdings USA Inc.	767 3rd Ave.	New York	NY	10017	Nicolas Combele	212-750-0200	R	150 OR*	3.0
CapStar Hotels Inc.	1010 Wisconsin Ave. N	Washington	DC	20007	Paul Whetsell	202-965-4455	R	150 OR	4.0
Charles E. Smith Management Inc.	2345 Crystal Dr.	Arlington	VA	22202	Robert P. Kogod	703-920-8500	R	150 OR	1.4
Hardaway Group Inc.	615 Main St.	Nashville	TN	37206	L.H. Hardway Jr.	615-254-5461	R	150 OR	0.8
Maxim Property Management	2600 Campus Dr.	San Mateo	CA	94403	John H. Pringle	415-570-7800	R	150 OR	0.6
Keyes Company Realtors	1 S.E. 3rd Ave.	Miami	FL	33131	Michael Pappas	305-371-3592	R	140 OR*	1.3
Riverbay Corp.	2049 Bartow Ave.	Bronx	NY	10475	Iris Baez	212-320-3300	R	130 OR	0.8
Mills L.P.	3000 K St. N.W.	Washington	DC	20007	Herbert S. Miller	202-965-3600	S	127 OR	0.7
Adage Inc.	625 Willowbrook Ln.	West Chester	PA	19382	Donald F.U. Goebert	215-430-3900	P	127	0.9
Abrams Industries Inc.	5775-A Glenridge Dr. N	Atlanta	GA	30328	Bernard W. Abrams	404-256-9785	P	124 OR	0.3
Baird and Warner Inc.	200 W. Madison St.	Chicago	IL	60606	Stephen W. Baird	312-368-1855	R	120 OR	1.1
John L. Scott Real Estate	3380 146th Pl. S.E.	Bellevue	WA	98007	J.L. Scott	206-462-5000	R	120 OR	1.3
Kilroy Industries	2250E Imperial Hwy.	El Segundo	CA	90245	John B. Kilroy Jr.	213-772-1193	R	120 OR	0.1
CMT Holding Ltd.	19353 U.S. Highway 19	Clearwater	FL	34624	Richard W. Cope	813-538-5468	R	115 OR	0.4
ConAm Management Corp.	1764 San Diego Ave.	San Diego	CA	92110	Daniel J. Epstein	619-297-6771	R	115 OR	1.7
Peabody Hotel Group	5118 Park Ave.	Memphis	TN	38117	Martin S. Belz	901-762-5400	R	110 OR	2.8
Belz Enterprises	P.O. Box 171199	Memphis	TN	38187	Jack A. Belz	901-767-4780	R	100 OR	3.0
Mego Financial Corp.	4310 Paradise Rd.	Las Vegas	NV	89109	Robert Nederlander	702-737-3700	P	100 TA	0.8
Diamond Parking Inc.	3161 Elliot Ave.	Seattle	WA	98121	Joel Diamond	206-284-6303	R	90 OR	0.7
Muselli Commercial Realtors	805 Wilshire Blvd.	Santa Monica	CA	90401	Vincent C. Muselli	310-458-4100	R	90 OR	<0.1
Arthur J. Rogers and Co.	3170 Des Plaines Ave.	Des Plaines	IL	60016	Arthur J. Rogers	708-297-2200	R	89 OR	0.1
West Shell Inc.	P.O. Box 5390	Cincinnati	OH	45201	Mark Rippe	513-721-4200	R	82 OR	0.8
Robert Martin Co.	100 Clearbrook Rd.	Elmsford	NY	10523	Brad Berger	914-592-4800	R	80 OR	0.1
Slater Realtors	2737 McRae Rd.	Richmond	VA	23235	E.M. Jackson	804-320-1391	R	80 OR	<0.1
Ukpeagvik Inupiat Corp.	P.O. Box 427	Barrow	AK	99723	Ronald Brower	907-852-4460	R	80 OR	0.2
Village Resorts Inc.	3478 Buskirk Ave.	Pleasant Hill	CA	94523	Tom Morrish	510-988-2800	R	80 OR	2.0
Snyder-Hunt Corp.	800 Hethwood Blvd.	Blacksburg	VA	24060	Harry H. Hunt III	703-552-3515	R	77 OR*	0.7
Carr Realty L.P.	1700 Pennsylvania Ave.	Washington	DC	20006	Oliver T. Carr Jr.	202-624-7500	S	76 OR	0.5
Justice Corp.	19329 U.S. Hwy. 19 N.	Clearwater	FL	34624	Albert N. Justice	813-531-4600	R	75 OR	<0.1

Company type codes: P - Public, R - Private, S - Subsidiary, D - Division, J - Joint Venture, A - Affiliate, G - Group. If the dollar values shown are not sales, the following codes apply: TA - Total Assets; OR - Operating Revenues; GB - Gross Billings. * - estimated dollar value. < - less than. *na* - not available.

Continued on next page.

LEADING COMPANIES - SIC 6531 - Real Estate Agents and Managers
Continued

Company Name	Address				CEO Name	Phone	Co. Type	Sales/Assets ($ mil)	Empl. (000)
Macerich Partnership L.P.	P.O. Box 2172	Santa Monica	CA	90407	Arthur M. Coppola	310-394-5333	S	73 OR	0.6
Kevin F. Donohoe Company Inc.	Curtis Ctr.	Philadelphia	PA	19106	Kevin F. Donohoe	215-238-6400	R	71 OR	<0.1
CARTER	1275 Peachtree St. N.E	Atlanta	GA	30367	James B. Carson Jr.	404-888-3000	R	71 OR*	0.7
Habitat Co.	350 W. Hubbard	Chicago	IL	60610	Daniel E. Levin	312-527-5400	R	70 OR	0.6
Mahoney Group	P.O. Box 15001	Casa Grande	AZ	85230	John W. McEvoy	602-836-7483	R	70 TA	0.1
Chicago Capital Consultants Inc.	1919 N. Sheffield	Chicago	IL	60614	Jeffrey B. Gellman	312-296-4900	R	67 OR	<0.1
Cohen-Esrey Real Estate Services Inc.	4435 Main St.	Kansas City	MO	64111	Robert E. Esrey	816-531-8100	R	67 OR*	0.7
Amli Residential Properties L.P.	125 S. Wacker Dr.	Chicago	IL	60606	Gregory T. Mutz	312-984-5037	S	66 OR	0.3
LaSalle Partners Ltd.	11 S. La Salle St.	Chicago	IL	60603	Stuart Scott	312-782-5800	R	66 OR	0.6
Shapell Industries Inc.	8383 Wilshire Blvd.	Beverly Hills	CA	90211	Nathan Shapell	213-655-7330	R	66 OR*	0.3
Marcus and Millichap Co.	2626 Hanover St.	Palo Alto	CA	94304	George M. Marcus	415-494-8900	R	65 OR	0.7
JBG Cos.	1250 Connecticut Ave N	Washington	DC	20036	Lewis Rumford III	202-364-6300	R	64 OR*	0.3
Moore Commercial Co.	390 Grant St.	Denver	CO	80203	Steven D. Miller	303-778-6555	S	62 OR*	<0.1
Shawmut Design and Construction	560 Harrison Ave.	Boston	MA	02118	James S. Ansara	617-338-6200	R	62 OR	<0.1
Fourmidable Group	P.O. Box 9053	Farmington Hills	MI	48333	J. Ronald Slavik	810-488-8400	R	61 OR	0.7
J.W. Charles Financial Services Inc.	980 N. Federal Hwy.	Boca Raton	FL	33432	Joseph M. Hickey	407-338-2600	R	60 OR	0.8
Bauer Blake Biery Inc.	2627 Charlestown Rd.	New Albany	IN	47150	Bernard Bauer	812-945-2356	R	60 OR	<0.1
Real Estate One Inc.	29630 Orchard Lane Rd.	Farmington Hills	MI	48334	R. Elsea	810-851-2600	R	60 OR	0.8
Spaulding and Slye Services L.P.	125 High St.	Boston	MA	02110	James B. Karman	617-523-8000	R	60 OR	0.2
Crescent Real Estate Equities L.P.	777 Main St.	Fort Worth	TX	76102	John C. Goff	817-877-0477	S	58 OR	0.2
Hayman Co.	5700 Crooks Rd.	Troy	MI	48098	Stephen Hayman	313-879-7777	R	56 OR*	0.5
Reckson Operating Partnership L.P.	225 Broadhollow Rd.	Melville	NY	11747	Donald J. Rechler	516-694-6900	S	55 OR	<0.1
Coldwell Banker Relocation Services Inc.	27271 Las Ramblas	Mission Viejo	CA	92691	Stephen C. Roney	714-367-2505	S	55 OR	0.6
J.D. Reece Realtors	7127 W. 110th St.	Overland Park	KS	66210	Jerry D. Reece	913-491-1001	R	55 OR*	0.5
Mall of America Co.	60 E. Broadway	Bloomington	MN	55425	John Wheeler	612-883-8800	R	55 OR	0.5
FRP Properties Inc.	155 E. 21st St.	Jacksonville	FL	32206	John E. Anderson	904-355-1781	P	54 OR	0.6
Bradley Apartment Homes	5444 Westheimer	Houston	TX	77056	Al Bradley Jr.	713-622-5844	R	53 OR	0.3
Comey and Shepherd Inc.	6901 Wooster Pike	Cincinnati	OH	45227	Roy Nelson	513-561-5800	R	52 OR	0.3
Prentiss Properties Limited Inc.	1717 Main St.	Dallas	TX	75201	Michael V. Prentiss	214-761-1440	R	52 OR	0.6
DeWolfe Companies Inc.	271 Lincoln St.	Lexington	MA	02173	Richard B. DeWolfe	617-863-5858	P	52 OR	1.0
Cornish and Carey Residential Inc.	505 Hamilton Ave.	Palo Alto	CA	94301	Rodger Rikard	415-322-4624	R	51 OR	0.9

Company type codes: P - Public, R - Private, S - Subsidiary, D - Division, J - Joint Venture, A - Affiliate, G - Group. If the dollar values shown are not sales, the following codes apply: TA - Total Assets; OR - Operating Revenues; GB - Gross Billings. * - estimated dollar value. < - less than. *na* - not available.

Continued on next page.

LEADING COMPANIES - SIC 6531 - Real Estate Agents and Managers
Continued

Company Name	Address				CEO Name	Phone	Co. Type	Sales/Assets ($ mil)	Empl. (000)
Charter Properties Inc.	129 W. Trade St.	Charlotte	NC	28202	William A. White	704-377-4172	S	50 OR	<0.1
Mooney LeSage and Associates Ltd.	16620 W. Bluemound Rd.	Brookfield	WI	53005	J. Michael Mooney	414-797-9400	R	50 OR	<0.1
Steuart Investment Co.	4646 40th N.W.	Washington	DC	20016	Guy Steuart	202-537-8940	R	50 OR*	0.4
CP L.P.	19500 Hall Rd.	Clinton Township	MI	48038	C.G. Kellogg	810-286-3600	S	48 OR	0.2
Cali Realty L.P.	11 Commerce Dr.	Cranford	NJ	07016	John J. Cali	908-272-8000	S	47 OR	<0.1
Westdale-Better Homes and Gardens	300 E. Beltline N.E.	Grand Rapids	MI	49506	Len Westdale Jr.	616-949-9400	R	46 OR*	0.5
Fostoria Corp.	1375 Euclid Ave.	Cleveland	OH	44115	T.M. Garver	216-771-6105	R	45 OR*	0.4

Source: *Ward's Business Directory of U.S. Private and Public Companies*, 1996. Company type codes: P - Public, R - Private, S - Subsidiary, D - Division, J - Joint Venture, A - Affiliate, G - Group. If the dollar values shown are not sales, the following codes apply: TA - Total Assets; OR - Operating Revenues; GB - Gross Billings. * - estimated dollar value. < - less than; *na* - not available.

FINANCIAL DATA ON REAL ESTATE

The following seven tables present data on real estate sales and on the employment and structure of real estate companies. Data for the first two tables were obtained from the National Association of Realtors, 777 14th Street, N.W., Washington, D.C. 20005 and are reproduced with permission. Much more detailed data are available from the association. Additional tables, dealing with mortgages, are drawn from the *Statistical Abstract of the United States 1995*.

TOTAL SALES: SINGLE-FAMILY, APARTMENT CONDOS AND CO-OPS

Units in thousands.

State	1993	1994	1995	State	1993	1994	1995	State	1993	1994	1995
Alabama	77.9	77.4	74.6	Kentucky	83.3	81.1	78.2	North Dakota	11.8	10.9	10.6
Alaska	NA	NA	NA	Louisiana	49.3	51.4	50.1	Ohio	179.1	186.4	181.4
Arizona	107.9	123.8	122.0	Maine	11.6	13.0	NA	Oklahoma	61.5	59.7	58.1
Arkansas	52.8	52.3	55.3	Maryland	73.4	69.5	59.2	Oregon	58.8	58.1	57.7
California[1]	435.0	482.6	425.4	Massachusetts	66.0	68.7	68.1	Pennsylvania	216.1	216.4	217.2
Colorado	82.1	80.6	76.9	Michigan	170.6	184.2	176.3	Rhode Island	11.0	11.6	11.9
Connecticut	45.9	49.8	51.4	Minnesota	81.8	82.1	78.5	South Carolina	62.2	67.3	69.1
Delaware	9.4	10.4	10.3	Mississippi	43.6	43.5	43.8	South Dakota	13.7	13.2	13.2
District of Columbia	12.3	12.3	11.7	Missouri	106.4	110.2	108.3	Tennessee	120.5	129.8	133.2
Florida	208.9	229.7	220.8	Montana	16.2	15.6	14.8	Texas	258.8	266.9	260.2
Georgia	NA	NA	NA	Nebraska	23.2	23.3	21.0	Utah	31.2	32.4	33.8
Hawaii	12.5	13.1	10.0	Nevada	30.5	32.9	31.9	Vermont	11.0	10.9	9.0
Idaho	23.4	23.1	22.8	New Hampshire	13.6	16.2	NA	Virginia	104.2	99.5	94.0
Illinois	193.9	188.4	181.2	New Jersey	139.0	145.4	138.3	Washington	97.0	101.2	95.5
Indiana	100.8	103.3	100.3	New Mexico	31.0	30.4	28.9	West Virginia	45.7	45.8	44.5
Iowa	53.5	54.3	51.3	New York	143.0	156.3	150.0	Wisconsin	94.6	94.3	93.2
Kansas	53.7	55.7	54.2	North Carolina	185.0	204.1	200.1	Wyoming	10.9	11.0	10.5

Source: Real Estate Outlook Market Trends and Insights, Volume 3, Number 6, June 1996, p. 15. Reproduced by permission. *Notes:* NA stands for not available. 1. Provided by the California Association of Realtors.

APARTMENT CONDOS AND CO-OPS

Year	Unit volume Seasonally Adjusted Annual Rate					Median Sales Price Not seasonally adjusted				
	United States	Northeast	Midwest	South	West	United States	Northeast	Midwest	South	West
1993	401,000	86,000	73,000	131,000	111,000	83,500	99,200	76,400	69,000	103,500
1994	437,000	96,000	75,000	145,000	120,000	87,100	100,100	86,200	69,200	106,600
1995	428,000	99,000	73,000	143,000	113,000	87,700	96,000	90,700	71,000	106,000
1995										
I	406,000	95,000	67,000	137,000	107,000	86,100	95,300	87,800	68,700	108,000
II	413,000	97,000	69,000	140,000	107,000	87,300	95,100	90,000	71,700	104,700
III	444,000	100,000	79,000	147,000	118,000	88,700	97,700	91,600	71,500	105,200
IV	448,000	105,000	78,000	147,000	118,000	88,100	95,500	92,400	71,500	106,800
1996										
Ip	452,000	103,000	74,000	155,000	121,000	88,600	93,500	93,400	71,500	107,900

Source: Real Estate Outlook Market Trends and Insights, Volume 3, Number 6, June 1996, p. 14. Reproduced by permission. *Note:* p Preliminary.

MORTGAGE DEBT OUTSTANDING, BY TYPE OF PROPERTY AND HOLDER

In billions of dollars. As of Dec. 31. Includes Puerto Rico and Guam.

TYPE OF PROPERTY AND HOLDER	1987	1988	1989	1990	1991	1992	1993
Mortgage debt, total	2,990	3,288	3,549	3,764	3,926	4,056	4,215
Residential nonfarm	2,244	2,505	2,715	2,926	3,088	3,259	3,438
One- to four-family homes	1,964	2,208	2,408	2,617	2,781	2,963	3,147
Savings institutions	602	672	669	600	538	490	470
Mortgage pools or trusts[1]	702	790	887	1,044	1,214	1,380	1,494
Government National Mortgage Assoc	309	331	358	392	416	411	405
Federal Home Loan Mortgage Corp.	206	220	266	308	352	402	438
Commercial banks	276	334	390	456	484	508	557
Individuals and others[2]	247	267	319	350	370	383	387
Federal and related agencies	124	134	131	153	163	192	230
Federal National Mortgage Assoc	90	96	91	94	100	124	151
Life insurance companies	13	11	12	13	12	11	9
Five or more units	280	297	306	309	307	295	290
Commercial	659	698	754	759	759	717	697
Farm	88	85	80	78	79	81	81
TYPE OF HOLDER							
Savings institutions	860	925	910	802	705	628	598
Commercial banks	592	674	767	845	876	895	940
Life insurance companies	212	233	254	268	265	247	229
Individuals and others[2]	414	444	502	531	563	575	579
Mortgage pools or trusts[1]	718	812	918	1,079	1,251	1,426	1,551
Government National Mortgage Assoc	318	341	368	404	425	420	414
Federal Home Loan Mortgage Corp	213	226	273	316	359	408	443
Federal National Mortgage Association	140	178	228	300	372	445	496
Farmers Home Administration[3]	(Z)	(Z)	(Z)	(Z)	(Z)	(Z)	(Z)
Federal and related agencies	193	201	198	239	266	286	317
Federal National Mortgage Association	97	103	99	105	112	138	167
Farmers Home Administration[3]	43	42	41	41	42	42	41
Federal Land Banks	34	32	30	29	29	29	28
Federal Home Loan Mortgage Corp	13	17	22	22	27	34	51
Federal Housing and Veterans Admin	6	6	6	9	11	13	12
Government National Mortgage Assoc	(Z)	(Z)	(Z)	(Z)	(Z)	(Z)	(Z)
Resolution Trust Corporation	(X)	(X)	(Z)	33	46	32	17

Source: Board of Governors of the Federal Reserve System, *Federal Reserve Bulletin*, monthly. *Notes:* - Represents zero. X Not applicable. Z Less than $500 million. 1. Outstanding principal balances of mortgage pools backing securities insured or guaranteed by the agency indicated. Includes other pools not shown separately. 2. Includes mortgage companies, real estate investment trusts, State and local retirement funds, noninsured pension funds, State and local credit agencies, credit unions, and finance companies. 3. FmHA-Guaranteed securities sold to the Federal Financing Bank were reallocated from FmHA mortgage pools to FmHA mortgage holdings in 1986 because of accounting changes by the Farmers Home Administration.

VOLUME OF LONG-TERM MORTGAGE LOANS ORIGINATED, BY TYPE OF PROPERTY AND BY LENDER

In billions of dollars. Covers credit extended in primary mortgage markets for financing real estate acquisitions.

Type of Property	1980	1985	1988	1989	1990	1991	1992	1993, by Lender				
								Total[1]	Commercial banks	Mortgage companies	Savings and loan	Life insurance companies
Loans, total	197.2	430.0	673.6	642.3	710.5	793.3	1,124.0	1,238.4	435.6	529.6	189.7	27.0
1-4 family home	133.8	289.8	446.3	452.9	458.4	562.1	893.7	1010.3	259.5	526.5	179.3	0.8
New units	49.1	59.0	85.2	90.4	110.7	120.2	132.4	117.3	45.5	56.0	13.6	0.2
Existing units	84.6	230.8	361.1	362.5	347.7	442.1	761.3	893.0	214.0	470.5	165.7	0.6
Multifamily residential	12.5	31.9	38.2	31.1	32.6	25.5	25.7	32.0	19.1	2.0	6.2	1.5
New units	8.6	10.6	9.0	8.3	6.5	6.1	4.9	4.4	2.0	-	0.3	0.5
Existing units	3.9	21.3	29.2	22.8	26.0	19.4	20.9	27.6	17.1	2.0	5.9	1.0
Nonresidential	35.9	99.4	181.6	150.0	209.5	194.6	184.4	178.5	144.7	1.1	4.2	24.1
Farm properties	15.0	9.0	7.6	8.3	10.0	11.1	20.2	17.6	12.3	-	-	0.6

Source: U.S. Dept. of Housing and Urban Development, monthly and quarterly press releases based on the Survey of Mortgage Lending Activity. *Notes:* - Represents zero. 1. Includes other lenders not shown separately.

MORTGAGE DELINQUENCY AND FORECLOSURE RATES

In percent, except as indicated. Covers one- to four-family residential nonfarm mortgage loans.

Item	1980	1985	1988	1989	1990	1991	1992	1993	1994
Number of mortgage loans outstanding (1,000)	30,033	35,353	41,802	43,571	45,187	45,812	46,887	48,639	(NA)
Delinquency rates:[1]									
Total	5.0	5.8	4.8	4.8	4.7	5.0	4.6	4.2	4.0
Conventional loans	3.1	4.0	2.9	3.1	3.0	3.3	2.9	2.7	2.6
VA loans	5.3	6.6	6.2	6.4	6.4	6.8	6.5	6.3	6.1
FHA loans	6.6	7.5	6.6	6.7	6.7	7.3	7.1	7.1	7.0
Foreclosure rates:[2]									
Total	0.5	1.0	1.2	1.0	0.9	1.0	1.0	1.0	1.0
Conventional loans	0.2	0.7	0.7	0.6	0.7	0.8	0.8	0.8	0.7
VA loans	0.6	1.1	1.6	1.3	1.2	1.3	1.3	1.3	1.4
FHA loans	0.7	1.3	1.8	1.4	1.3	1.4	1.4	1.5	1.5

Source: Mortgage Bankers Association of America, Washington, DC, *National Delinquency Survey*, quarterly. *Notes:* NA Not available. 1. Number of loans delinquent 30 days or more as percentage of mortgage loans serviced in survey. Annual average of quarterly figures. 2. Percentage of loans in the foreclosure process at yearend, not seasonally adjusted.

CHARACTERISTICS OF CONVENTIONAL FIRST MORTGAGE LOANS FOR PURCHASE OF SINGLE-FAMILY HOMES

In percent, except as indicated. Annual averages. Refers to loans originated directly by Savings Association Insurance Fund-insured savings institutions, mortgage bankers, commercial banks, and Federal deposit Insurance Corporation-insured savings banks. Excludes interim construction loans, refinancing loans, junior liens, and federally underwritten loans.

Loan Characteristics	New Homes						Existing Homes					
	1980	1990	1991	1992	1993	1994	1980	1990	1991	1992	1993	1994
Contract interest rate,[1]												
All loans	12.3	9.7	9.0	8.0	7.0	7.3	12.5	9.8	9.1	7.8	6.9	7.3
Fixed-rate loans	(NA)	10.1	9.3	8.3	7.3	7.9	(NA)	10.1	9.4	8.2	7.3	8.0
Adjustable-rate loans[2]	(NA)	8.9	8.1	6.6	5.8	6.5	(NA)	8.9	8.0	6.3	5.5	6.2
Initial fees, charges[3]	2.09	1.98	1.72	1.59	1.29	1.29	1.91	1.74	1.54	1.58	1.19	1.07
Effective interest rate,[4]												
All loans	12.7	10.1	9.3	8.2	7.2	7.5	12.9	10.1	9.3	8.1	7.1	7.5
Fixed-rate loans	(NA)	10.4	9.6	8.5	7.5	8.1	(NA)	10.4	9.7	8.5	7.5	8.2
Adjustable-rate loans[2]	(NA)	9.2	8.4	6.9	5.9	6.6	(NA)	9.2	8.2	6.5	5.7	6.4
Term to maturity (years)	28.1	27.3	26.8	25.6	26.1	27.5	26.9	27.0	26.5	25.4	25.4	27.1
Purchase price ($1,000)	83.2	154.1	155.2	158.1	163.7	170.7	68.3	140.3	145.8	144.1	139.6	136.4
Loan to price ratio	73.2	74.9	75.0	76.6	78.0	78.7	73.5	74.9	74.4	76.5	77.1	80.1
Percent of number of loans with adjustable rates	(NA)	31	25	17	18	41	(NA)	27	22	21	20	39

Source: U.S. Federal Housing Finance Board, annual and monthly press releases. *Notes:* NA Not available. 1. Initial interest rate paid by the borrower as specified in the loan contract. 2. Loans with a contractual provision for periodic adjustments in the contract interest rate. 3. Includes all fees, commissions, discounts, and "points" paid by the borrower, or seller, in order to obtain the loan. Excludes those charges for mortgage, credit, life or property insurance; for property transfer; and for title search and insurance. 4. Contract interest rate plus fees and charges amortized over a 10-year period.

MORTGAGE DELINQUENCY RATES, BY DIVISION: 1990 TO 1994

In percent. Annual average of quarterly figures. Covers one- to four- family residential nonfarm mortgage loans. Represents number of loans delinquent 30 days or more as percentage of loans serviced in survey. Excludes loans in foreclosure.

Year	U.S., total	New England	Middle Atlantic	East North Central	West North Central	South Atlantic	East South Central	West South Central	Mountain	Pacific
1990	4.67	3.53	4.54	5.06	3.82	4.80	6.32	6.45	5.10	3.21
1991	5.01	4.14	5.05	5.20	3.99	5.53	6.69	6.41	5.01	3.45
1992	4.56	4.02	4.86	4.56	3.34	5.05	5.93	5.50	4.12	3.45
1993	4.22	3.54	4.60	4.05	3.18	4.61	5.37	5.01	3.60	3.43
1994	4.09	3.52	4.48	3.69	3.22	4.43	5.13	4.91	3.33	3.56

Source: Mortgage Bankers Association of America, Washington, DC, *National Delinquency Survey*, quarterly.

SIC 6540

TITLE ABSTRACT OFFICES

Title abstract offices are establishments engaged primarily in searching real estate titles. This industry does not include title insurance companies (for these, see SIC 6360). The SIC includes title abstract companies, title and trust companies, title reconveyance companies, and title search companies.

ESTABLISHMENTS, EMPLOYMENT, AND PAYROLL

	1988	1989		1990		1991		1992		1993		% change 88-93
		Value	%	Value	%	Value	%	Value	%	Value	%	
All Establishments	3,113	3,016	-3.1	3,067	1.7	3,529	15.1	4,198	19.0	4,766	13.5	53.1
Mid-March Employment	25,027	23,550	-5.9	23,880	1.4	23,481	-1.7	29,286	24.7	37,536	28.2	50.0
1st Quarter Wages (annualized - $ mil.)	515.4	473.7	-8.1	499.8	5.5	500.9	0.2	654.9	30.7	853.1	30.3	65.5
Payroll per Emp. 1st Q. (annualized)	20,594	20,117	-2.3	20,930	4.0	21,334	1.9	22,361	4.8	22,726	1.6	10.4
Annual Payroll ($ mil.)	536.0	505.3	-5.7	518.0	2.5	558.2	7.7	755.0	35.3	1,047.9	38.8	95.5
Establishments - 1-4 Emp. Number	1,697	1,643	-3.2	1,723	4.9	1,872	8.6	2,363	26.2	2,435	3.0	43.5
Mid-March Employment	3,764	3,512	-6.7	3,698	5.3	3,992	8.0	5,129	28.5	5,034	-1.9	33.7
1st Quarter Wages (annualized - $ mil.)	54.5	52.1	-4.3	59.2	13.6	64.6	9.1	94.5	46.3	92.6	-2.0	70.0
Payroll per Emp. 1st Q. (annualized)	14,468	14,844	2.6	16,011	7.9	16,186	1.1	18,429	13.9	18,394	-0.2	27.1
Annual Payroll ($ mil.)	62.1	57.6	-7.2	65.3	13.5	80.6	23.4	118.4	46.8	128.2	8.2	106.4
Establishments - 5-9 Emp. Number	805	789	-2.0	765	-3.0	1,079	41.0	1,124	4.2	1,323	17.7	64.3
Mid-March Employment	5,250	5,205	-0.9	5,038	-3.2	7,166	42.2	7,332	2.3	8,646	17.9	64.7
1st Quarter Wages (annualized - $ mil.)	88.9	91.8	3.3	93.1	1.5	146.6	57.4	152.4	3.9	176.7	15.9	98.7
Payroll per Emp. 1st Q. (annualized)	16,933	17,638	4.2	18,489	4.8	20,458	10.6	20,783	1.6	20,432	-1.7	20.7
Annual Payroll ($ mil.)	93.8	95.6	2.0	95.5	-0.1	159.7	67.2	176.1	10.3	224.4	27.4	139.3
Establishments - 10-19 Emp. Number	371	360	-3.0	357	-0.8	403	12.9	461	14.4	648	40.6	74.7
Mid-March Employment	4,873	4,742	-2.7	4,648	-2.0	5,231	12.5	6,089	16.4	8,579	40.9	76.1
1st Quarter Wages (annualized - $ mil.)	99.9	99.9	-0.0	99.3	-0.6	115.6	16.4	137.5	19.0	197.5	43.6	97.7
Payroll per Emp. 1st Q. (annualized)	20,502	21,068	2.8	21,360	1.4	22,092	3.4	22,581	2.2	23,019	1.9	12.3
Annual Payroll ($ mil.)	104.0	104.5	0.5	99.4	-4.8	126.3	27.0	158.2	25.3	247.3	56.3	137.8
Establishments - 20-49 Emp. Number	186	175	-5.9	165	-5.7	133	-19.4	195	46.6	283	45.1	52.2
Mid-March Employment	5,308	5,064	-4.6	4,805	-5.1	3,798	-21.0	5,707	50.3	8,511	49.1	60.3
1st Quarter Wages (annualized - $ mil.)	108.2	103.3	-4.5	100.1	-3.1	85.3	-14.8	136.4	59.9	195.9	43.6	81.1
Payroll per Emp. 1st Q. (annualized)	20,379	20,393	0.1	20,832	2.1	22,453	7.8	23,896	6.4	23,015	-3.7	12.9
Annual Payroll ($ mil.)	110.7	108.2	-2.3	101.9	-5.9	95.0	-6.8	154.5	62.7	240.7	55.8	117.4
Establishments - 50-99 Emp. Number	38	34	-10.5	42	23.5	36	-14.3	42	16.7	60	42.9	57.9
Mid-March Employment	2,471	2,329	-5.7	2,839	21.9	2,285	-19.5	2,743	20.0	3,929	43.2	59.0
1st Quarter Wages (annualized - $ mil.)	59.9	48.0	-19.7	57.9	20.6	59.0	1.9	69.0	16.9	106.3	54.1	77.7
Payroll per Emp. 1st Q. (annualized)	24,223	20,627	-14.8	20,410	-1.1	25,836	26.6	25,159	-2.6	27,064	7.6	11.7
Annual Payroll ($ mil.)	61.7	55.7	-9.8	63.2	13.4	61.7	-2.2	75.2	21.8	120.6	60.4	95.5
Establishments - 100-249 Emp. Number	12	13	8.3	13	-	5	-61.5	(D)	-	(D)	-	-
Mid-March Employment	1,673	(D)	-	(D)	-	(D)	-	(D)	-	(D)	-	-
1st Quarter Wages (annualized - $ mil.)	44.9	(D)	-	(D)	-	(D)	-	(D)	-	(D)	-	-
Payroll per Emp. 1st Q. (annualized)	26,812	(D)	-	(D)	-	(D)	-	(D)	-	(D)	-	-
Annual Payroll ($ mil.)	48.6	(D)	-	(D)	-	(D)	-	(D)	-	(D)	-	-
Establishments - 250-499 Emp. Number	3	1	-66.7	1	-	1	-	(D)	-	(D)	-	-
Mid-March Employment	(D)	(D)	-	(D)	-	(D)	-	(D)	-	(D)	-	-
1st Quarter Wages (annualized - $ mil.)	(D)	(D)	-	(D)	-	(D)	-	(D)	-	(D)	-	-
Payroll per Emp. 1st Q. (annualized)	(D)	(D)	-	(D)	-	(D)	-	(D)	-	(D)	-	-
Annual Payroll ($ mil.)	(D)	(D)	-	(D)	-	(D)	-	(D)	-	(D)	-	-
Establishments - 500-999 Emp. Number	1	1	-	1	-	-	-	-	-	(D)	-	-
Mid-March Employment	(D)	(D)	-	(D)	-	-	-	-	-	(D)	-	-
1st Quarter Wages (annualized - $ mil.)	(D)	(D)	-	(D)	-	-	-	-	-	(D)	-	-
Payroll per Emp. 1st Q. (annualized)	(D)	(D)	-	(D)	-	(D)	-	-	-	(D)	-	-
Annual Payroll ($ mil.)	(D)	(D)	-	(D)	-	-	-	-	-	(D)	-	-
Estab. - 1000 or More Emp. Number	-	-	-	-	-	-	-	-	-	-	-	-
Mid-March Employment	-	-	-	-	-	-	-	-	-	-	-	-
1st Quarter Wages (annualized - $ mil.)	-	-	-	-	-	-	-	-	-	-	-	-
Payroll per Emp. 1st Q. (annualized)	(D)	(D)	-	(D)	-	(D)	-	-	-	-	-	-
Annual Payroll ($ mil.)	-	-	-	-	-	-	-	-	-	-	-	-

Source: County Business Patterns, U.S. Department of Commerce, Washington, D.C., for 1988 through 1993. Payroll per employee is calculated using mid-March employment and 1st Quarter wages, annualized. Annual payroll, also shown, may not equal the annualized 1st Quarter wages. Columns headed by a percent sign (%) indicate change from the previous year. *na* stands for not available. The symbol (D) indicates that data are withheld by the source to avoid disclosure of competitive information. A dash (-) indicates that data are not available or cannot be calculated.

ESTABLISHMENTS
Number

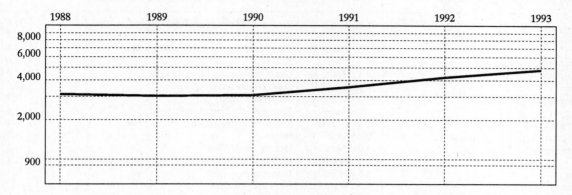

MID-MARCH EMPLOYMENT
Number

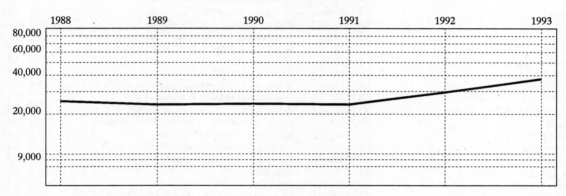

ANNUAL PAYROLL
$ million

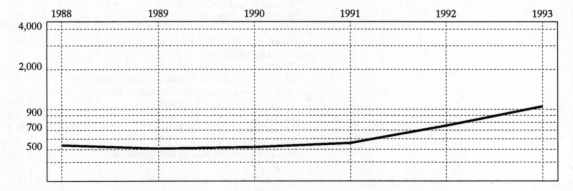

INPUTS AND OUTPUTS FOR ALL REAL ESTATE SECTORS - SIC GROUP 65

Economic Sector or Industry Providing Inputs	%	Sector	Economic Sector or Industry Buying Outputs	%	Sector
Real estate	38.6	Fin/R.E.	Personal consumption expenditures	37.6	
Nonfarm residential structure maintenance	12.5	Constr.	Real estate	10.9	Fin/R.E.
Banking	5.6	Fin/R.E.	Retail trade, except eating & drinking	7.4	Trade
Maintenance of nonfarm buildings nec	5.3	Constr.	Hospitals	4.6	Services
Eating & drinking places	4.4	Trade	Gross private fixed investment	4.4	Cap Inv
Insurance carriers	4.3	Fin/R.E.	Owner-occupied dwellings	2.7	Fin/R.E.
Services to dwellings & other buildings	4.2	Services	Wholesale trade	2.7	Trade
Advertising	3.2	Services	Eating & drinking places	1.8	Trade
Maintenance of highways & streets	2.8	Constr.	Religious organizations	1.4	Services
Communications, except radio & TV	2.0	Util.	Banking	1.2	Fin/R.E.
Landscape & horticultural services	1.9	Agric.	Doctors & dentists	1.2	Services
Legal services	1.6	Services	Colleges, universities, & professional schools	1.1	Services
Petroleum refining	1.5	Manufg.	Feed grains	1.1	Agric.
Commercial printing	0.9	Manufg.	Insurance carriers	0.9	Fin/R.E.
Hotels & lodging places	0.7	Services	Legal services	0.9	Services
Management & consulting services & labs	0.7	Services	Meat animals	0.9	Agric.
Accounting, auditing & bookkeeping	0.6	Services	S/L Govt. purch., other general government	0.9	S/L Govt
Business services nec	0.6	Services	Communications, except radio & TV	0.6	Util.
Motor freight transportation & warehousing	0.6	Util.	Hotels & lodging places	0.6	Services
U.S. Postal Service	0.6	Gov't	Amusement & recreation services nec	0.5	Services
Electrical repair shops	0.5	Services	Credit agencies other than banks	0.5	Fin/R.E.
Maintenance of farm service facilities	0.5	Constr.	Elementary & secondary schools	0.5	Services
Wholesale trade	0.5	Trade	Engineering, architectural, & surveying services	0.5	Services
Air transportation	0.4	Util.	Insurance agents, brokers, & services	0.5	Fin/R.E.
Business/professional associations	0.4	Services	Motor freight transportation & warehousing	0.5	Util.
Security & commodity brokers	0.4	Fin/R.E.	Oil bearing crops	0.5	Agric.
Transit & bus transportation	0.4	Util.	S/L Govt. purch., public assistance & relief	0.5	S/L Govt
Arrangement of passenger transportation	0.3	Util.	Accounting, auditing & bookkeeping	0.4	Services
Automotive rental & leasing, without drivers	0.3	Services	Advertising	0.4	Services
Electric services (utilities)	0.3	Util.	Labor, civic, social, & fraternal associations	0.4	Services
Miscellaneous plastics products	0.3	Manufg.	Medical & health services, nec	0.4	Services
Engine electrical equipment	0.2	Manufg.	Nursing & personal care facilities	0.4	Services
Paper mills, except building paper	0.2	Manufg.	Computer & data processing services	0.3	Services
Retail trade, except eating & drinking	0.2	Trade	Exports	0.3	Foreign
Computer & data processing services	0.1	Services	Food grains	0.3	Agric.
Maintenance of farm residential buildings	0.1	Constr.	Management & consulting services & labs	0.3	Services
Nitrogenous & phosphatic fertilizers	0.1	Manufg.	Security & commodity brokers	0.3	Fin/R.E.
Paper coating & glazing	0.1	Manufg.	Water transportation	0.3	Util.
Personnel supply services	0.1	Services	Air transportation	0.2	Util.
Photographic equipment & supplies	0.1	Manufg.	Automotive repair shops & services	0.2	Services
			Beauty & barber shops	0.2	Services
			Business services nec	0.2	Services
			Coal	0.2	Mining
			Crude petroleum & natural gas	0.2	Mining
			Dairy farm products	0.2	Agric.
			Electric services (utilities)	0.2	Util.
			Federal Government purchases, national defense	0.2	Fed Govt
			Federal Government purchases, nondefense	0.2	Fed Govt
			Laundry, dry cleaning, shoe repair	0.2	Services
			Libraries, vocation education	0.2	Services
			Membership organizations nec	0.2	Services
			Social services, nec	0.2	Services
			State & local government enterprises, nec	0.2	Gov't
			Vegetables	0.2	Agric.
			Automobile parking & car washes	0.1	Services
			Child day care services	0.1	Services
			Cotton	0.1	Agric.
			Electronic computing equipment	0.1	Manufg.

Continued on next page.

INPUTS AND OUTPUTS FOR ALL REAL ESTATE SECTORS - SIC GROUP 65 - Continued

Economic Sector or Industry Providing Inputs	%	Sector	Economic Sector or Industry Buying Outputs	%	Sector
			Landscape & horticultural services	0.1	Agric.
			Membership sports & recreation clubs	0.1	Services
			Motion pictures	0.1	Services
			Petroleum & natural gas well drilling	0.1	Constr.
			Portrait, photographic studios	0.1	Services
			Residential care	0.1	Services
			U.S. Postal Service	0.1	Gov't

Source: Benchmark Input-Output Accounts for the U.S. Economy, 1982, U.S. Department of Commerce, Washington, D.C., July 1991. Data, as reported in the source, are organized by the 1977 SIC structure in use in 1982 but have been matched, as closely as is possible, to the 1987 SIC structure used in this book. Activities with the same percentage are sorted alphabetically by name of activity.

OCCUPATIONS EMPLOYED BY REAL ESTATE NEC

Occupation	% of Total 1994	Change to 2005	Occupation	% of Total 1994	Change to 2005
Gardeners & groundskeepers, ex farm	19.2	-1.4	Janitors & cleaners, incl maids	2.5	-12.0
General office clerks	7.3	-2.4	Typists & word processors	2.3	-40.7
General managers & top executives	7.2	6.7	Marketing & sales worker supervisors	1.9	12.1
Secretaries, ex legal & medical	7.0	2.5	Food preparation & service workers nec	1.8	9.6
Maintenance repairers, general utility	4.5	-1.3	Supervisors, farming, forestry	1.6	9.5
Bookkeeping, accounting, & auditing clerks	4.4	-16.5	Accountants & auditors	1.6	10.7
Sales agents, real estate	4.4	9.7	Guards	1.2	-1.3
Sales & related workers nec	4.1	10.9	Carpenters	1.1	-12.4
Property & real estate managers	3.8	18.1	Service workers nec	1.1	9.5
Receptionists & information clerks	3.4	12.9	Blue collar worker supervisors	1.0	20.1
Financial managers	2.8	11.2			

Sources: Industry-Occupation Matrix, Bureau of Labor Statistics. These data relate to one or more 3-digit SIC industry groups rather than to a single 4-digit SIC. The change reported for each occupation to the year 2005 is a percent of growth or decline as estimated by the Bureau of Labor Statistics. The abbreviation nec stands for not elsewhere classified.

U.S. AND STATE DATA ON INDUSTRY REVENUES AND OTHER ACCOUNTS FOR 1992

State	No. of Estab.	Employ-ment	Payroll ($ mil.)	Revenues ($ mil.)	Empl./ Estab.	Revenue/ Estab. ($)	Payroll/ Estab. ($)	Revenue/ Empl. ($)	Payroll/ Empl. ($)
UNITED STATES	4,716	33,742	880.1	2,337.3	7	495,619	186,622	69,271	26,083
Alabama	62	324	6.3	15.1	5	244,177	100,903	46,725	19,309
Alaska	7	39	1.4	3.2	6	460,857	196,143	82,718	35,205
Arizona	22	148	3.4	7.6	7	347,091	154,045	51,595	22,899
Arkansas	107	607	11.9	26.8	6	250,916	111,402	44,231	19,638
California	284	4,285	137.9	340.4	15	1,198,655	485,736	79,444	32,193
Colorado	61	408	9.3	24.6	7	402,787	152,934	60,221	22,865
Connecticut	25	59	1.6	3.5	2	141,880	65,760	60,119	27,864
Delaware	4	-	(D)	(D)	(D)	(D)	(D)	(D)	(D)
District of Columbia	11	111	2.5	4.6	10	417,636	226,455	41,387	22,441
Florida	305	1,984	47.3	112.9	7	370,134	155,167	56,901	23,854
Georgia	41	212	5.1	12.5	5	304,146	123,512	58,821	23,887
Hawaii	13	532	15.3	25.9	41	1,995,462	1,178,846	48,761	28,806
Idaho	43	413	10.7	26.0	10	605,535	249,791	63,046	26,007
Illinois	232	1,703	40.5	120.2	7	518,198	174,716	70,594	23,802
Indiana	162	1,175	23.6	58.3	7	359,827	145,617	49,610	20,077
Iowa	130	760	14.7	33.0	6	253,554	113,300	43,371	19,380
Kansas	129	635	11.0	29.2	5	226,209	85,163	45,954	17,301
Kentucky	16	80	1.4	5.2	5	325,188	90,125	65,038	18,025
Louisiana	65	381	9.2	21.9	6	336,923	141,231	57,480	24,094
Maine	14	77	2.8	5.9	6	420,643	196,429	76,481	35,714
Maryland	198	1,000	31.8	82.6	5	417,162	160,480	82,598	31,775
Massachusetts	49	233	7.0	17.9	5	364,633	142,143	76,682	29,893
Michigan	103	831	21.4	54.6	8	529,748	207,689	65,661	25,742
Minnesota	162	1,500	38.5	113.0	9	697,469	237,383	75,327	25,637
Mississippi	6	22	0.2	0.8	4	136,000	38,833	37,091	10,591
Missouri	178	1,045	21.4	50.2	6	281,916	120,382	48,020	20,505
Montana	28	183	4.0	10.9	7	387,679	141,107	59,317	21,590
Nebraska	54	177	3.0	8.5	3	157,981	55,926	48,198	17,062
Nevada	25	452	15.3	32.0	18	1,280,640	611,680	70,832	33,832
New Hampshire	20	150	4.8	10.4	8	518,150	242,450	69,087	32,327
New Jersey	146	709	23.4	66.4	5	454,911	160,377	93,677	33,025
New Mexico	44	291	6.9	17.6	7	400,250	156,682	60,519	23,691
New York	385	2,542	74.4	207.3	7	538,569	193,249	81,569	29,269
North Carolina	22	48	1.8	4.9	2	221,273	81,273	101,417	37,250
North Dakota	48	147	2.7	8.1	3	168,604	56,354	55,054	18,401
Ohio	199	1,617	47.7	119.8	8	601,784	239,789	74,060	29,510
Oklahoma	157	1,250	27.9	64.6	8	411,624	178,013	51,700	22,358
Oregon	27	330	8.4	24.6	12	911,222	311,111	74,555	25,455
Pennsylvania	231	1,627	48.7	204.1	7	883,619	211,030	125,455	29,962
Rhode Island	8	42	1.0	3.7	5	458,500	127,250	87,333	24,238
South Carolina	42	119	2.1	5.1	3	122,405	50,381	43,202	17,782
South Dakota	48	157	2.5	7.0	3	145,375	52,688	44,446	16,108
Tennessee	69	304	8.2	18.1	4	262,435	119,029	59,566	27,016
Texas	390	2,633	62.0	181.2	7	464,567	158,992	68,812	23,550
Utah	44	345	9.0	22.4	8	509,000	203,977	64,916	26,014
Vermont	2	-	(D)	(D)	(D)	(D)	(D)	(D)	(D)
Virginia	103	419	12.4	29.8	4	289,019	120,515	71,048	29,625
Washington	46	550	13.5	35.0	12	761,848	293,413	63,718	24,540
West Virginia	3	-	(D)	(D)	(D)	(D)	(D)	(D)	(D)
Wisconsin	137	1,022	22.5	56.3	7	411,197	164,022	55,121	21,987
Wyoming	9	-	(D)	(D)	(D)	(D)	(D)	(D)	(D)

Source: 1992 Economic Census, U.S. Department of Commerce, Washington, D.C. This is the only table that shows revenue data as collected by the Bureau of the Census in an Economic Census. The symbol (D) indicates that data are withheld by the source to avoid disclosure of competitive information. A dash (-) indicates that data are not available or cannot be calculated.

ESTABLISHMENTS 1992 - STATE AND REGIONAL CONCENTRATION

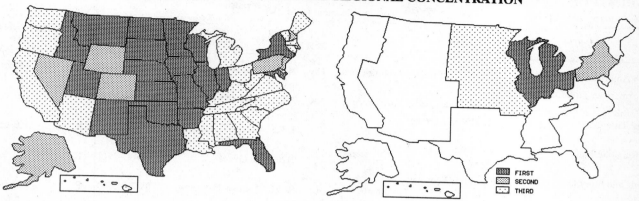

EMPLOYMENT 1992 - STATE AND REGIONAL CONCENTRATION

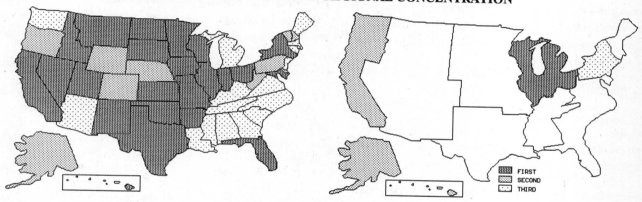

REVENUES 1992 - STATE AND REGIONAL CONCENTRATION

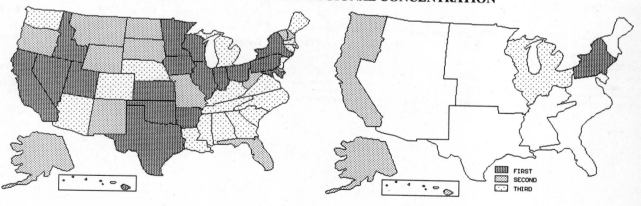

States with the darkest shading indicate those states which have proportionately more establishments, employment, or revenues than would be indicated by the state's population. States with light shading are states with proportionately fewer establishments, less employment, and lower revenues than population distribution. States shaded grey are within 15 percent of the state's population proportion in these categories. States for which no data are available are shown as average (grey). *Regions* are shaded to indicate absolute rank in the category. If no data for the category are available, establishment counts are used to shade the regions. Source of the data is the table on the facing page.

LEADING COMPANIES - SIC 6541 - Title Abstract Offices

Number shown: **20**   Total sales/assets ($ mil): **634**   Total employment (000): **3.9**

Company Name	Address				CEO Name	Phone	Co. Type	Sales/Assets ($ mil)	Empl. (000)
North American Title Co.	2185 N. California	Walnut Creek	CA	94596	Dan Wentzel	510-935-5599	R	200 OR*	1.2
First American Title Company of Alaska Inc.	510 W. Tudor Rd.	Anchorage	AK	99503	Steven Jewett	907-562-0510	S	120 OR	<0.1
World Title Co.	19200 Von Karman Ave.	Irvine	CA	92715	Michael Lowther	818-767-2800	R	100 OR*	0.6
Old Republic Title	101 E. Glenoaks Blvd.	Glendale	CA	91202	Al Gudel	818-247-2917	R	50 OR*	0.3
Koenig and Strey Inc.	3201 Old Glenview Rd.	Wilmette	IL	60091	Thomas E. Koenig	708-729-5050	R	30 OR	0.5
Guardian Title Co.	27271 Las Ramblas	Mission Viejo	CA	92691	Thomas Rutledge	714-367-2115	R	20 OR*	0.1
Monroe Title Insurance Corp.	47 W. Main St.	Rochester	NY	14614	Dennis W. O'Neill	716-232-2070	R	16 TA	0.3
American Title Co.	721 S. Parker Ave.	Orange	CA	92668	John Gondling	714-550-6400	S	16 OR*	0.1
Southwest Land Title Co.	500 N. Akard Rd.	Dallas	TX	75201	William G. Moize	214-720-1020	R	16 OR	0.2
Bay Title and Abstract Inc.	P.O. Box 173	Green Bay	WI	54305	John May	414-431-6100	R	10 TA*	<0.1
Beach Abstract and Guaranty Co.	P.O. Box 2580	Little Rock	AR	72203	George Pitts Jr.	501-376-3301	R	10 OR*	<0.1
Austin Title Co.	1515 S. Capital of Texas Hwy.	Austin	TX	78746	Mickey Blissit	512-306-0988	S	9 OR*	<0.1
Old Republic Title Company of St. Louis	120 S. Central	Clayton	MO	63105	Norman Evilsizer	314-863-0022	S	8 OR*	<0.1
Stewart Fidelity Title Co.	4134 Central Ave.	St. Petersburg	FL	33711	Kevin Hussey	813-327-5775	S	8 OR	<0.1
Old Republic Title Agency Inc.	5255 E. Williams Cir.	Tucson	AZ	85711	Faye Veronda	602-747-2631	R	7 OR*	<0.1
Southwest Title and Trust Co.	P.O. Box 1234	Oklahoma City	OK	73101	James Kott	405-236-2861	S	7 TA	0.1
Landwood Title Co.	1403 N. Tustin Ave.	Santa Ana	CA	92701	Joseph Melodia	714-835-4070	R	4 OR	<0.1
Community Title and Escrow Inc.	2402 State St.	Alton	IL	62002	Peggy A. Stillwell	618-466-7755	R	1 OR	<0.1
American Title and Abstract Inc.	22 W. Pennsylvania Ave	Towson	MD	21204	Gerard J. Zeller Jr.	410-494-1555	R	1 OR*	<0.1
Bartle, McGrane, Duffy and Jones	P.O. Box 484	Troy	NY	12181	Peter B. Jones	518-274-3510	R	1 OR*	<0.1

Source: Ward's Business Directory of U.S. Private and Public Companies, 1996. Company type codes: P - Public, R - Private, S - Subsidiary, D - Division, J - Joint Venture, A - Affiliate, G - Group. If the dollar values shown are not sales, the following codes apply: TA - Total Assets; OR - Operating Revenues; GB - Gross Billings. * - estimated dollar value. < - less than; *na* - not available.

SIC 6552

SUBDIVIDERS AND DEVELOPERS, NEC

Land subdividers and developers are establishments primarily engaged in subdividing real property into lots and in developing the property on their own account. Cemetery subdividers have their own classification—SIC 6553—shown in the next chapter. Establishments primarily engaged in developing lots for others are classified as Construction and are not included in this book.

ESTABLISHMENTS, EMPLOYMENT, AND PAYROLL

	1988	1989 Value	%	1990 Value	%	1991 Value	%	1992 Value	%	1993 Value	%	% change 88-93
All Establishments	10,561	10,605	0.4	10,750	1.4	11,362	5.7	9,172	-19.3	9,400	2.5	-11.0
Mid-March Employment	78,149	82,303	5.3	87,798	6.7	90,033	2.5	75,160	-16.5	57,277	-23.8	-26.7
1st Quarter Wages (annualized - $ mil.)	1,812.0	2,004.9	10.6	2,292.0	14.3	2,293.2	0.1	1,886.1	-17.8	1,511.0	-19.9	-16.6
Payroll per Emp. 1st Q. (annualized)	23,186	24,359	5.1	26,105	7.2	25,470	-2.4	25,095	-1.5	26,381	5.1	13.8
Annual Payroll ($ mil.)	1,934.7	2,111.8	9.2	2,260.1	7.0	2,341.8	3.6	1,987.5	-15.1	1,748.8	-12.0	-9.6
Establishments - 1-4 Emp. Number	7,365	7,303	-0.8	7,351	0.7	7,756	5.5	6,389	-17.6	7,165	12.1	-2.7
Mid-March Employment	(D)	11,177	-	11,595	3.7	12,388	6.8	10,006	-19.2	9,173	-8.3	-
1st Quarter Wages (annualized - $ mil.)	(D)	316.0	-	337.7	6.9	337.6	-0.0	278.4	-17.5	245.5	-11.8	-
Payroll per Emp. 1st Q. (annualized)	(D)	28,276	-	29,125	3.0	27,253	-6.4	27,826	2.1	26,759	-3.8	-
Annual Payroll ($ mil.)	(D)	422.7	-	398.2	-5.8	419.0	5.2	350.9	-16.2	398.2	13.5	-
Establishments - 5-9 Emp. Number	1,614	1,662	3.0	1,635	-1.6	1,747	6.9	1,319	-24.5	1,110	-15.8	-31.2
Mid-March Employment	10,479	10,880	3.8	10,636	-2.2	11,298	6.2	8,637	-23.6	7,156	-17.1	-31.7
1st Quarter Wages (annualized - $ mil.)	256.8	276.4	7.6	277.4	0.4	302.7	9.1	247.2	-18.3	183.1	-25.9	-28.7
Payroll per Emp. 1st Q. (annualized)	24,509	25,404	3.7	26,084	2.7	26,791	2.7	28,622	6.8	25,585	-10.6	4.4
Annual Payroll ($ mil.)	260.6	281.3	7.9	263.3	-6.4	297.9	13.2	250.0	-16.1	200.0	-20.0	-23.3
Establishments - 10-19 Emp. Number	854	852	-0.2	935	9.7	1,050	12.3	783	-25.4	606	-22.6	-29.0
Mid-March Employment	11,285	11,384	0.9	12,479	9.6	13,853	11.0	10,557	-23.8	8,041	-23.8	-28.7
1st Quarter Wages (annualized - $ mil.)	269.1	278.7	3.6	332.8	19.4	391.7	17.7	297.6	-24.0	208.7	-29.9	-22.4
Payroll per Emp. 1st Q. (annualized)	23,846	24,486	2.7	26,672	8.9	28,276	6.0	28,188	-0.3	25,954	-7.9	8.8
Annual Payroll ($ mil.)	280.9	297.4	5.9	322.1	8.3	400.5	24.4	291.3	-27.3	231.9	-20.4	-17.4
Establishments - 20-49 Emp. Number	496	531	7.1	541	1.9	536	-0.9	438	-18.3	345	-21.2	-30.4
Mid-March Employment	14,754	15,776	6.9	16,138	2.3	16,041	-0.6	12,815	-20.1	10,512	-18.0	-28.8
1st Quarter Wages (annualized - $ mil.)	346.1	384.2	11.0	442.4	15.2	425.3	-3.9	340.3	-20.0	290.1	-14.7	-16.2
Payroll per Emp. 1st Q. (annualized)	23,457	24,351	3.8	27,416	12.6	26,514	-3.3	26,551	0.1	27,602	4.0	17.7
Annual Payroll ($ mil.)	348.2	398.8	14.5	418.7	5.0	416.8	-0.5	358.1	-14.1	308.2	-13.9	-11.5
Establishments - 50-99 Emp. Number	140	150	7.1	167	11.3	157	-6.0	141	-10.2	99	-29.8	-29.3
Mid-March Employment	9,631	10,428	8.3	11,378	9.1	(D)	-	9,827	-	6,952	-29.3	-27.8
1st Quarter Wages (annualized - $ mil.)	209.5	268.7	28.2	277.6	3.3	(D)	-	202.6	-	176.2	-13.0	-15.9
Payroll per Emp. 1st Q. (annualized)	21,751	25,763	18.4	24,396	-5.3	(D)	-	20,620	-	25,349	22.9	16.5
Annual Payroll ($ mil.)	211.9	252.9	19.3	268.3	6.1	(D)	-	215.3	-	201.2	-6.6	-5.1
Establishments - 100-249 Emp. Number	69	81	17.4	92	13.6	86	-6.5	77	-10.5	62	-19.5	-10.1
Mid-March Employment	10,524	11,422	8.5	13,566	18.8	12,833	-5.4	11,942	-6.9	9,362	-21.6	-11.0
1st Quarter Wages (annualized - $ mil.)	206.6	259.3	25.5	324.2	25.0	278.5	-14.1	273.9	-1.7	289.5	5.7	40.1
Payroll per Emp. 1st Q. (annualized)	19,631	22,703	15.6	23,902	5.3	21,702	-9.2	22,935	5.7	30,921	34.8	57.5
Annual Payroll ($ mil.)	192.3	249.7	29.9	317.7	27.2	280.2	-11.8	269.5	-3.8	285.5	6.0	48.5
Establishments - 250-499 Emp. Number	18	19	5.6	22	15.8	23	4.5	(D)	-	9	-	-50.0
Mid-March Employment	(D)	(D)	-	7,356	-	(D)	-	(D)	-	2,849	-	-
1st Quarter Wages (annualized - $ mil.)	(D)	(D)	-	189.9	-	(D)	-	(D)	-	56.6	-	-
Payroll per Emp. 1st Q. (annualized)	(D)	(D)	-	25,809	-	(D)	-	(D)	-	19,867	-	-
Annual Payroll ($ mil.)	(D)	(D)	-	164.7	-	(D)	-	(D)	-	58.1	-	-
Establishments - 500-999 Emp. Number	5	7	40.0	7	-	7	-	4	-42.9	(D)	-	-
Mid-March Employment	(D)	(D)	-	4,650	-	4,498	-3.3	2,748	-38.9	(D)	-	-
1st Quarter Wages (annualized - $ mil.)	(D)	(D)	-	109.9	-	111.3	1.3	46.0	-58.6	(D)	-	-
Payroll per Emp. 1st Q. (annualized)	(D)	(D)	-	23,628	-	24,736	4.7	16,757	-32.3	(D)	-	-
Annual Payroll ($ mil.)	(D)	(D)	-	107.1	-	111.2	3.8	50.2	-54.9	(D)	-	-
Estab. - 1000 or More Emp. Number	-	-		-		-		(D)	-	(D)	-	
Mid-March Employment	-	-		-		-		(D)	-	(D)	-	
1st Quarter Wages (annualized - $ mil.)	-	-		-		-		(D)	-	(D)	-	
Payroll per Emp. 1st Q. (annualized)	(D)	(D)	-	(D)	-	(D)	-	(D)	-	(D)	-	
Annual Payroll ($ mil.)	-	-		-		-		(D)	-	(D)	-	

Source: County Business Patterns, U.S. Department of Commerce, Washington, D.C., for 1988 through 1993. Payroll per employee is calculated using mid-March employment and 1st Quarter wages, annualized. Annual payroll, also shown, may not equal the annualized 1st Quarter wages. Columns headed by a percent sign (%) indicate change from the previous year. *na* stands for not available. The symbol (D) indicates that data are withheld by the source to avoid disclosure of competitive information. A dash (-) indicates that data are not available or cannot be calculated.

ESTABLISHMENTS
Number

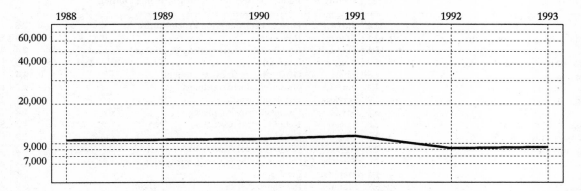

MID-MARCH EMPLOYMENT
Number

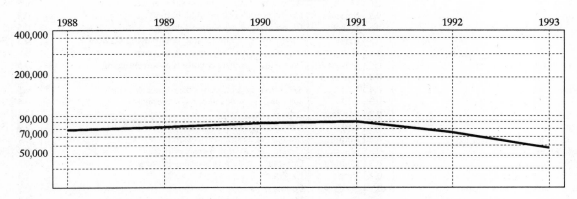

ANNUAL PAYROLL
$ million

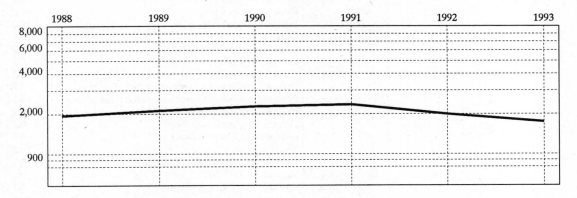

INPUTS AND OUTPUTS FOR ALL REAL ESTATE SECTORS - SIC GROUP 65

Economic Sector or Industry Providing Inputs	%	Sector	Economic Sector or Industry Buying Outputs	%	Sector
Real estate	38.6	Fin/R.E.	Personal consumption expenditures	37.6	
Nonfarm residential structure maintenance	12.5	Constr.	Real estate	10.9	Fin/R.E.
Banking	5.6	Fin/R.E.	Retail trade, except eating & drinking	7.4	Trade
Maintenance of nonfarm buildings nec	5.3	Constr.	Hospitals	4.6	Services
Eating & drinking places	4.4	Trade	Gross private fixed investment	4.4	Cap Inv
Insurance carriers	4.3	Fin/R.E.	Owner-occupied dwellings	2.7	Fin/R.E.
Services to dwellings & other buildings	4.2	Services	Wholesale trade	2.7	Trade
Advertising	3.2	Services	Eating & drinking places	1.8	Trade
Maintenance of highways & streets	2.8	Constr.	Religious organizations	1.4	Services
Communications, except radio & TV	2.0	Util.	Banking	1.2	Fin/R.E.
Landscape & horticultural services	1.9	Agric.	Doctors & dentists	1.2	Services
Legal services	1.6	Services	Colleges, universities, & professional schools	1.1	Services
Petroleum refining	1.5	Manufg.	Feed grains	1.1	Agric.
Commercial printing	0.9	Manufg.	Insurance carriers	0.9	Fin/R.E.
Hotels & lodging places	0.7	Services	Legal services	0.9	Services
Management & consulting services & labs	0.7	Services	Meat animals	0.9	Agric.
Accounting, auditing & bookkeeping	0.6	Services	S/L Govt. purch., other general government	0.9	S/L Govt
Business services nec	0.6	Services	Communications, except radio & TV	0.6	Util.
Motor freight transportation & warehousing	0.6	Util.	Hotels & lodging places	0.6	Services
U.S. Postal Service	0.6	Gov't	Amusement & recreation services nec	0.5	Services
Electrical repair shops	0.5	Services	Credit agencies other than banks	0.5	Fin/R.E.
Maintenance of farm service facilities	0.5	Constr.	Elementary & secondary schools	0.5	Services
Wholesale trade	0.5	Trade	Engineering, architectural, & surveying services	0.5	Services
Air transportation	0.4	Util.	Insurance agents, brokers, & services	0.5	Fin/R.E.
Business/professional associations	0.4	Services	Motor freight transportation & warehousing	0.5	Util.
Security & commodity brokers	0.4	Fin/R.E.	Oil bearing crops	0.5	Agric.
Transit & bus transportation	0.4	Util.	S/L Govt. purch., public assistance & relief	0.5	S/L Govt
Arrangement of passenger transportation	0.3	Util.	Accounting, auditing & bookkeeping	0.4	Services
Automotive rental & leasing, without drivers	0.3	Services	Advertising	0.4	Services
Electric services (utilities)	0.3	Util.	Labor, civic, social, & fraternal associations	0.4	Services
Miscellaneous plastics products	0.3	Manufg.	Medical & health services, nec	0.4	Services
Engine electrical equipment	0.2	Manufg.	Nursing & personal care facilities	0.4	Services
Paper mills, except building paper	0.2	Manufg.	Computer & data processing services	0.3	Services
Retail trade, except eating & drinking	0.2	Trade	Exports	0.3	Foreign
Computer & data processing services	0.1	Services	Food grains	0.3	Agric.
Maintenance of farm residential buildings	0.1	Constr.	Management & consulting services & labs	0.3	Services
Nitrogenous & phosphatic fertilizers	0.1	Manufg.	Security & commodity brokers	0.3	Fin/R.E.
Paper coating & glazing	0.1	Manufg.	Water transportation	0.3	Util.
Personnel supply services	0.1	Services	Air transportation	0.2	Util.
Photographic equipment & supplies	0.1	Manufg.	Automotive repair shops & services	0.2	Services
			Beauty & barber shops	0.2	Services
			Business services nec	0.2	Services
			Coal	0.2	Mining
			Crude petroleum & natural gas	0.2	Mining
			Dairy farm products	0.2	Agric.
			Electric services (utilities)	0.2	Util.
			Federal Government purchases, national defense	0.2	Fed Govt
			Federal Government purchases, nondefense	0.2	Fed Govt
			Laundry, dry cleaning, shoe repair	0.2	Services
			Libraries, vocation education	0.2	Services
			Membership organizations nec	0.2	Services
			Social services, nec	0.2	Services
			State & local government enterprises, nec	0.2	Gov't
			Vegetables	0.2	Agric.
			Automobile parking & car washes	0.1	Services
			Child day care services	0.1	Services
			Cotton	0.1	Agric.
			Electronic computing equipment	0.1	Manufg.

Continued on next page.

INPUTS AND OUTPUTS FOR ALL REAL ESTATE SECTORS - SIC GROUP 65 - Continued

Economic Sector or Industry Providing Inputs	%	Sector	Economic Sector or Industry Buying Outputs	%	Sector
			Landscape & horticultural services	0.1	Agric.
			Membership sports & recreation clubs	0.1	Services
			Motion pictures	0.1	Services
			Petroleum & natural gas well drilling	0.1	Constr.
			Portrait, photographic studios	0.1	Services
			Residential care	0.1	Services
			U.S. Postal Service	0.1	Gov't

Source: Benchmark Input-Output Accounts for the U.S. Economy, 1982, U.S. Department of Commerce, Washington, D.C., July 1991. Data, as reported in the source, are organized by the 1977 SIC structure in use in 1982 but have been matched, as closely as is possible, to the 1987 SIC structure used in this book. Activities with the same percentage are sorted alphabetically by name of activity.

OCCUPATIONS EMPLOYED BY REAL ESTATE NEC

Occupation	% of Total 1994	Change to 2005	Occupation	% of Total 1994	Change to 2005
Gardeners & groundskeepers, ex farm	19.2	-1.4	Janitors & cleaners, incl maids	2.5	-12.0
General office clerks	7.3	-2.4	Typists & word processors	2.3	-40.7
General managers & top executives	7.2	6.7	Marketing & sales worker supervisors	1.9	12.1
Secretaries, ex legal & medical	7.0	2.5	Food preparation & service workers nec	1.8	9.6
Maintenance repairers, general utility	4.5	-1.3	Supervisors, farming, forestry	1.6	9.5
Bookkeeping, accounting, & auditing clerks	4.4	-16.5	Accountants & auditors	1.6	10.7
Sales agents, real estate	4.4	9.7	Guards	1.2	-1.3
Sales & related workers nec	4.1	10.9	Carpenters	1.1	-12.4
Property & real estate managers	3.8	18.1	Service workers nec	1.1	9.5
Receptionists & information clerks	3.4	12.9	Blue collar worker supervisors	1.0	20.1
Financial managers	2.8	11.2			

Sources: Industry-Occupation Matrix, Bureau of Labor Statistics. These data relate to one or more 3-digit SIC industry groups rather than to a single 4-digit SIC. The change reported for each occupation to the year 2005 is a percent of growth or decline as estimated by the Bureau of Labor Statistics. The abbreviation nec stands for not elsewhere classified.

U.S. AND STATE DATA ON INDUSTRY REVENUES AND OTHER ACCOUNTS FOR 1992

State	No. of Estab.	Employ- ment	Payroll ($ mil.)	Revenues ($ mil.)	Empl./ Estab.	Revenue/ Estab. ($)	Payroll/ Estab. ($)	Revenue/ Empl. ($)	Payroll/ Empl. ($)
UNITED STATES	8,848	48,502	1,452.6	9,219.7	5	1,042,009	164,178	190,089	29,950
Alabama	104	355	6.8	44.6	3	428,779	65,750	125,614	19,262
Alaska	19	-	(D)	(D)	(D)	(D)	(D)	(D)	(D)
Arizona	197	1,098	29.3	258.8	6	1,313,761	148,589	235,711	26,659
Arkansas	65	590	12.4	78.9	9	1,213,569	191,231	133,698	21,068
California	1,387	8,763	299.6	1,574.9	6	1,135,440	215,983	179,716	34,186
Colorado	166	676	22.6	158.3	4	953,861	136,006	234,232	33,398
Connecticut	117	265	12.0	73.3	2	626,838	102,308	276,755	45,170
Delaware	33	78	2.0	10.1	2	306,970	61,364	129,872	25,962
District of Columbia	16	46	1.7	18.2	3	1,139,375	104,875	396,304	36,478
Florida	902	6,708	173.2	1,188.8	7	1,317,969	191,979	177,222	25,815
Georgia	317	2,291	68.2	331.3	7	1,045,192	215,101	144,621	29,763
Hawaii	102	877	35.9	306.4	9	3,003,667	351,559	349,343	40,888
Idaho	51	112	3.6	30.7	2	602,784	70,216	274,482	31,973
Illinois	305	1,451	58.8	353.3	5	1,158,354	192,843	243,486	40,535
Indiana	143	616	19.8	143.5	4	1,003,832	138,762	233,032	32,213
Iowa	45	134	3.6	37.3	3	827,911	80,378	278,030	26,993
Kansas	48	198	6.0	66.3	4	1,381,563	125,042	334,924	30,313
Kentucky	82	266	5.9	40.9	3	498,829	71,390	153,774	22,008
Louisiana	89	513	12.4	84.0	6	944,056	139,303	163,784	24,168
Maine	26	30	0.6	7.7	1	296,192	24,692	256,700	21,400
Maryland	206	1,169	39.6	225.7	6	1,095,583	192,136	193,062	33,858
Massachusetts	179	741	19.1	130.9	4	731,324	106,687	176,663	25,772
Michigan	181	800	26.6	109.8	4	606,530	147,133	137,228	33,289
Minnesota	135	501	16.5	104.4	4	773,304	122,333	208,375	32,964
Mississippi	51	373	7.3	33.6	7	658,686	143,549	90,062	19,627
Missouri	188	560	13.8	171.9	3	914,330	73,266	306,954	24,596
Montana	32	200	4.5	20.4	6	638,469	140,063	102,155	22,410
Nebraska	28	45	1.1	13.1	2	467,714	38,571	291,022	24,000
Nevada	113	1,257	44.2	202.0	11	1,787,593	391,062	160,698	35,155
New Hampshire	55	226	7.0	64.4	4	1,170,109	126,764	284,761	30,850
New Jersey	212	1,113	41.3	320.6	5	1,512,448	194,712	288,085	37,088
New Mexico	63	288	8.8	80.7	5	1,281,476	140,063	280,323	30,639
New York	339	1,333	59.5	233.2	4	687,808	175,602	174,919	44,658
North Carolina	319	2,017	45.9	323.9	6	1,015,467	143,824	160,602	22,747
North Dakota	8	-	(D)	(D)	(D)	(D)	(D)	(D)	(D)
Ohio	216	1,539	44.1	309.3	7	1,431,796	204,134	200,954	28,650
Oklahoma	92	264	6.0	38.0	3	412,902	64,967	143,890	22,640
Oregon	117	305	12.4	131.2	3	1,121,726	106,291	430,302	40,774
Pennsylvania	275	1,061	31.1	198.9	4	723,131	112,927	187,428	29,270
Rhode Island	35	90	3.9	18.8	3	537,343	112,486	208,967	43,744
South Carolina	142	1,519	33.2	219.6	11	1,546,718	233,782	144,591	21,855
South Dakota	18	48	1.2	5.0	3	278,056	67,778	104,271	25,417
Tennessee	132	436	11.0	71.2	3	539,742	83,242	163,408	25,202
Texas	645	3,627	92.0	576.4	6	893,611	142,603	158,913	25,360
Utah	64	206	6.5	61.1	3	954,266	100,922	296,471	31,354
Vermont	36	133	3.3	13.0	4	360,611	92,722	97,609	25,098
Virginia	272	1,665	41.8	327.0	6	1,202,272	153,835	196,407	25,131
Washington	295	1,252	37.1	257.7	4	873,712	125,793	205,867	29,640
West Virginia	53	-	(D)	(D)	(D)	(D)	(D)	(D)	(D)
Wisconsin	117	378	11.5	95.7	3	817,684	98,658	253,093	30,537
Wyoming	16	45	0.7	3.4	3	215,250	42,750	76,533	15,200

Source: 1992 Economic Census, U.S. Department of Commerce, Washington, D.C. This is the only table that shows revenue data as collected by the Bureau of the Census in an Economic Census. The symbol (D) indicates that data are withheld by the source to avoid disclosure of competitive information. A dash (-) indicates that data are not available or cannot be calculated.

ESTABLISHMENTS 1992 - STATE AND REGIONAL CONCENTRATION

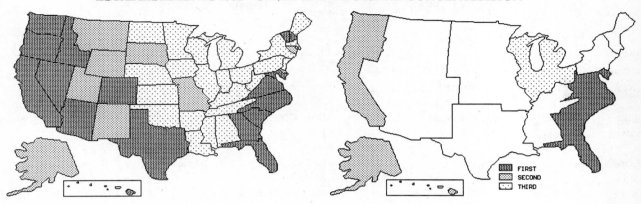

EMPLOYMENT 1992 - STATE AND REGIONAL CONCENTRATION

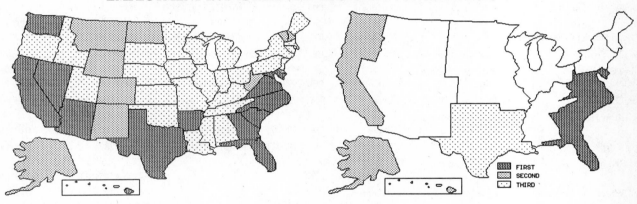

REVENUES 1992 - STATE AND REGIONAL CONCENTRATION

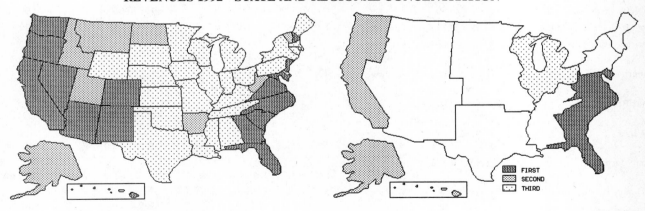

States with the darkest shading indicate those states which have proportionately more establishments, employment, or revenues than would be indicated by the state's population. States with light shading are states with proportionately fewer establishments, less employment, and lower revenues than population distribution. States shaded grey are within 15 percent of the state's population proportion in these categories. States for which no data are available are shown as average (grey). *Regions* are shaded to indicate absolute rank in the category. If no data for the category are available, establishment counts are used to shade the regions. Source of the data is the table on the facing page.

LEADING COMPANIES - SIC 6552 - Subdividers and Developers, nec

Number shown: **100**   Total sales/assets ($ mil): **183,234**   Total employment (000): **681.5**

Company Name	Address				CEO Name	Phone	Co. Type	Sales/Assets ($ mil)	Empl. (000)
Sears, Roebuck and Co.	Sears Twr.	Chicago	IL	60684	Edward A. Brennan	312-875-2500	P	54,559	360.0
Chubb Corp.	P.O. Box 1615	Warren	NJ	07061	Robert P. Crawford Jr.	908-903-2000	P	20,723 TA	10.0
Dominion Resources Inc.	P.O. Box 26532	Richmond	VA	23261	Thomas E. Capps	804-775-5700	P	13,562 TA	12.0
McDonnell Douglas Corp.	P.O. Box 516	St. Louis	MO	63166	Harry C. Stonecipher	314-232-0232	P	13,176	65.8
Weyerhaeuser Co.	33663 Weyerhaeuser	Federal Way	WA	98003	John W. Creighton Jr.	206-924-2345	P	10,398	37.0
Pinnacle West Capital Corp.	P.O. Box 52132	Phoenix	AZ	85072	Richard Snell	602-379-2500	P	6,910 TA	7.4
Reynolds Metals Co.	P.O. Box 27003	Richmond	VA	23261	Richard G. Holder	804-281-2000	P	5,879	29.0
Philip Morris Capital Corp.	800 Westchester Ave.	Rye Brook	NY	10573	Hans G. Storr	914-335-1155	S	5,236 TA	0.1
Cincinnati Gas and Electric Co.	139 E. 4th St.	Cincinnati	OH	45202	Jackson H. Randolph	513-381-2000	P	5,182 TA	4.5
San Diego Gas and Electric Co.	101 Ash St.	San Diego	CA	92101	Thomas A. Page	619-696-2000	P	4,642 TA	4.2
NIPSCO Industries Inc.	5265 Hohman Ave.	Hammond	IN	46320	Gary L. Neale	219-853-5200	P	3,945 TA	4.4
Portland General Corp.	121 S.W. Salmon St.	Portland	OR	97204	Ken L. Harrison	503-464-8820	P	3,559 TA	2.5
Centex Corp.	P.O. Box 19000	Dallas	TX	75219	Laurence E. Hirsch	214-559-6500	P	3,278 OR	6.0
Ritz Carlton Hotel Co.	3414 Peachtree Rd #300	Atlanta	GA	30326	William B. Johnson	404-237-5500	S	3,010 OR	14.0
Liberty Corp.	P.O. Box 789	Greenville	SC	29602	W. Hayne Hipp	803-268-8283	P	2,668 TA	3.3
Galesi Group	Rotterdam Ind Park	Schenectady	NY	12306	F. Galesi	518-356-4445	R	1,720 OR	8.0
United Water Resources Inc.	200 Old Hook Rd.	Harrington Park	NJ	07640	Ronald Dungan	201-784-9434	P	1,457 TA	1.4
Lomas Financial Corp.	P.O. Box 655644	Dallas	TX	75265	Jess Hay	214-879-4000	P	1,078 TA	2.1
Rayonier Inc.	1177 Summer St.	Stamford	CT	06904	Ronald M. Gross	203-348-7000	P	1,069	2.6
Doubletree Hotels Corp.	410 N. 44th St.	Phoenix	AZ	85008	James Grier	602-220-6666	S	1,000 OR	20.0
Alexander and Baldwin Inc.	P.O. Box 3440	Honolulu	HI	96801	John C. Couch	808-525-6611	P	979 OR	3.7
American Fidelity Group	2000 Classen Blvd.	Oklahoma City	OK	73106	William E. Durrett	405-523-2000	R	944 TA	1.1
Southern Union Co.	504 Lavaca St.	Austin	TX	78701	George L. Lindemann	512-477-5852	P	891 TA	1.8
Jupiter Realty Corp.	919 N. Michigan Ave.	Chicago	IL	60611	Andrew Agostini	312-642-6000	R	860 OR*	4.0
NVR Inc.	7601 Lewinsville Rd.	McLean	VA	22102	Dwight C. Schar	703-761-2000	P	821 OR	1.5
Lennar Corp.	700 N.W. 107th Ave.	Miami	FL	33172	Leonard Miller	305-559-4000	P	818 OR	1.7
New Jersey Resources Corp.	P.O. Box 1468	Wall	NJ	07719	Oliver G. Richard III	908-938-1480	P	797 TA	0.8
Lowe Enterprises Inc.	11777 San Vicente Blvd	Los Angeles	CA	90049	Robert J. Lowe	310-820-6661	R	620 OR*	2.9
St. Joe Paper Co.	1650 Prudential Dr.	Jacksonville	FL	32207	Winfred L. Thornton	904-396-6600	P	592	5.0
Richard E. Jacobs Group	25425 Center Ridge Rd.	Cleveland	OH	44145	Martin J. Cleary	216-871-4800	R	560 OR*	2.6
Acceptance Insurance Companies Inc.	222 S. 15th St.	Omaha	NE	68102	Kenneth C. Coon	402-344-8800	P	543 TA	0.8

Company type codes: P - Public, R - Private, S - Subsidiary, D - Division, J - Joint Venture, A - Affiliate, G - Group. If the dollar values shown are not sales, the following codes apply: TA - Total Assets; OR - Operating Revenues; GB - Gross Billings. * - estimated dollar value. < - less than. *na* - not available.

Continued on next page.   338

LEADING COMPANIES - SIC 6552 - Subdividers and Developers, nec
Continued

Company Name	Address				CEO Name	Phone	Co. Type	Sales/Assets ($ mil)	Empl. (000)
Del Webb Corp.	P.O. Box 29040	Phoenix	AZ	85038	Phillip J. Dion	602-808-8000	P	510 OR	1.4
Allen Tate Company Inc.	6618 Fairview Rd.	Charlotte	NC	28210	H. Allen Tate Jr.	704-365-6910	R	500 OR*	<0.1
J.M.B. Properties Co.	900 N. Michigan Ave.	Chicago	IL	60611	Kelly Bergstrom	312-440-4800	R	430 OR*	2.0
Kraus-Anderson Inc.	523 S. 8th St.	Minneapolis	MN	55404	Burton Dahlberg	612-332-1241	R	410 OR	0.5
Hovnanian Enterprises Inc.	P.O. Box 500	Red Bank	NJ	07701	Kevork S. Hovnanian	908-747-7800	P	387 OR	1.3
BUYCO Inc.	827 Fort St.	Honolulu	HI	96813	J.W.A. Buyers	808-536-4461	R	370 OR*	1.7
Hines Interests L.P.	2800 Post Oak Blvd.	Houston	TX	77056	Jeffrey C. Hines	713-621-8000	R	360 OR*	1.7
Helmerich and Payne Inc.	Utica & 21st Sts.	Tulsa	OK	74114	Hans Helmerich	918-742-5531	P	329	1.6
Hahn Property Management Corp.	4350 La Jolla Village	San Diego	CA	92122	John M. Gilchrist	619-546-1001	S	320 OR*	1.5
Mariner Group Inc.	12800 University Dr.	Fort Myers	FL	33907	Robert Taylor	813-481-2011	R	320 OR*	1.5
Gilbert Associates Inc.	P.O. Box 1498	Reading	PA	19603	Timothy S. Cobb	610-775-5900	P	283	3.4
Trammell Crow Co.	2001 Ross Ave.	Dallas	TX	75201	J. McDonald Williams	214-979-5100	R	270 OR*	2.5
Donohoe Companies Inc.	2101 Wisconsin Ave. N	Washington	DC	20007	James A. Donohoe III	202-333-0880	R	248 OR	0.5
A.G. Spanos Construction Inc.	P.O. Box 7126	Stockton	CA	95207	Dean Spanos	209-478-7954	R	234 OR	0.5
Schuler Homes Inc.	828 Fort Street Mall	Honolulu	HI	96813	James K. Schuler	808-521-5661	P	217 OR	<0.1
John Q. Hammons Hotels Inc.	300 John Q. Hammons	Springfield	MO	65806	John Q. Hammons	417-864-6573	P	217 OR	5.8
Sunstates Corp.	4600 Marriott Dr.	Raleigh	NC	27612	Clyde W. Engle	919-781-5611	P	209 OR	2.3
Birtcher Real Estate Ltd.	27611 La Paz Rd.	Laguna Niguel	CA	92656	Michael Voss	714-831-8031	R	200 OR	0.4
Castle and Cooke Homes Inc.	10900 Wilshire 16th Fl	Los Angeles	CA	90024	David H. Murdock	213-879-6600	R	200 OR	0.4
Homart Development Co.	55 W. Monroe St. #3100	Chicago	IL	60603	Michael Gregoire	312-551-5000	S	200 OR	0.9
Florida East Coast Industries Inc.	1650 Prudential Dr.	Jacksonville	FL	32207	W.L. Thornton	904-396-6600	P	200 OR	1.5
MVS Inc.	P.O. Box 5447	Oxnard	CA	93031	Martin V. Smith	805-485-3193	R	190 OR*	0.9
Catellus Development Corp.	201 Mission St.	San Francisco	CA	94105	Nelson C. Rising	415-974-4500	P	175 OR	0.2
Cafaro Co.	2445 Belmont Ave.	Youngstown	OH	44504	Anthony Cafaro	216-747-2661	R	170 OR	0.8
Holtzman and Silverman Cos.	30833 N. Western Hwy.	Farmington Hills	MI	48334	Gilbert Silverman	313-851-9600	R	160 OR*	0.8
Mobil Land Development Corp.	11911 Freedom Dr.	Reston	VA	22090	William Deihl	703-742-6300	S	156 OR	0.4
Mesirow Financial Holdings Inc.	350 N. Clark St.	Chicago	IL	60610	Lester A. Morris	312-670-6000	R	150 TA*	0.5
Paul Semonin Realtors	150 Browenton Pl.	Louisville	KY	40222	George Gans	502-425-4760	R	150 OR*	0.7
Southern Peach Holding Co.	129 Head Ave.	Tallapoosa	GA	30176	George Turner Sr.	404-214-3013	R	146 OR	3.0
Heartland Development Corp.	222 W. Washington Ave.	Madison	WI	53703	Lance W. Ahearn	608-252-0587	S	143 OR	1.5
Mission Viejo Co. *	26137 La Paz Rd.	Mission Viejo	CA	92691	Craig McCallum	714-837-6050	S	134 OR	<0.1

Company type codes: P - Public, R - Private, S - Subsidiary, D - Division, J - Joint Venture, A - Affiliate, G - Group. If the dollar values shown are not sales, the following codes apply: TA - Total Assets; OR - Operating Revenues; GB - Gross Billings. * - estimated dollar value. < - less than. *na* - not available.

Continued on next page.

LEADING COMPANIES - SIC 6552 - Subdividers and Developers, nec
Continued

Company Name	Address				CEO Name	Phone	Co. Type	Sales/Assets ($ mil)	Empl. (000)
Newhall Land and Farming Co.	23823 Valencia Blvd.	Valencia	CA	91355	Thomas L. Lee	805-255-4000	P	134 OR	0.3
AMREP Corp.	10 Columbus Cir.	New York	NY	10019	Anthony B. Gliedman	212-541-7300	P	126 OR	0.7
Kilroy Industries	2250E Imperial Hwy.	El Segundo	CA	90245	John B. Kilroy Jr.	213-772-1193	R	120 OR	0.1
Oriole Homes Corp.	1690 S. Congress Ave.	Delray Beach	FL	33445	Richard D. Levy	407-274-2000	P	120 OR	0.2
Stanley K. Tanger and Co.	P.O. Box 29168	Greensboro	NC	27429	Stanley Tanger	919-274-1666	R	120 OR*	0.6
William A. Hazel Company Inc.	4305 Hazel Park Ct.	Chantilly	VA	22021	John T. Hazel III	703-378-8300	R	120 OR*	0.6
Southern Peach Inc.	129 Head Ave.	Tallapoosa	GA	30176	Bud Jones	404-574-5100	S	117 OR	3.5
Fairfield Communities Inc.	P.O. Box 3375	Little Rock	AR	72202	John W. McConnell	501-664-6000	P	115 OR	1.2
Crown American Corp.	Pasquerilla Plz.	Johnstown	PA	15907	Frank J. Pasquerilla	814-536-4441	R	113 OR	0.4
Farb Companies Ltd.	5847 San Felipe	Houston	TX	77057	Harold Farb	713-954-2100	R	110 OR	0.3
John Wieland Homes Inc.	P.O. Box 87363	Atlanta	GA	30337	John Wieland	404-996-1400	R	110 OR*	0.6
Radnor Corp.	1801 Market St.	Philadelphia	PA	19103	Michael Dingus	215-977-6699	S	110 OR*	<0.1
Triton Group Ltd.	550 W. C St.	San Diego	CA	92101	John C. Stiska	619-231-1818	P	107	0.5
Atlantic Gulf Communities Corp.	2601 S. Bayshore Dr.	Miami	FL	33133	J. Larry Rutherford	305-859-4000	P	106 OR	0.3
CBL and Associates Inc.	6148 Lee Hwy., #300	Chattanooga	TN	37421	Charles B. Lebovitz	615-855-0001	R	105 OR	0.3
Alter Group Ltd.	3000 Glenview Rd.	Wilmette	IL	60091	William A. Alter	708-256-7700	R	100 OR	0.2
Belz Enterprises	P.O. Box 171199	Memphis	TN	38187	Jack A. Belz	901-767-4780	R	100 OR	3.0
Corporex Companies Inc.	50 E. River Center	Covington	KY	41011	William P. Butler	606-292-5500	R	100 OR	0.1
J.C. Nichols Co.	310 Ward Pkwy.	Kansas City	MO	64112	Lynn McCarthy	816-561-3456	R	100 OR*	0.5
LCOR Inc.	300 Berwyn Park Dr.	Berwyn	PA	19312	Eric Eichler	215-251-9100	R	100 OR*	0.5
Stanley Martin Companies Inc.	8000 Towers Cresent Dr	Vienna	VA	22182	Diane C. Basheer	703-760-8100	R	100 OR	0.2
Mego Financial Corp.	4310 Paradise Rd.	Las Vegas	NV	89109	Robert Nederlander	702-737-3700	P	100 TA	0.8
John Buck Co.	200 S. Wacker Dr.	Chicago	IL	60606	John A. Buck	312-993-9800	R	96 OR*	0.5
Shilo Management Corp.	11600 S.W. Barnes Rd.	Portland	OR	97225	Mark S. Hemstreet	503-641-6565	R	94 OR*	2.2
Taubman Company Inc.	P.O. Box 200	Bloomfield Hills	MI	48303	Robert Taubman	313-258-6800	R	93 OR	0.4
Whitebirch Enterprises Inc.	Hwy. 83	Breezy Point	MN	56472	Robert Spizzo	218-562-4204	R	92 OR*	0.4
Pacific Development Inc.	825 N.E. Multnomah St.	Portland	OR	97232	Matt Klein	503-233-4048	S	86 OR	<0.1
Ryan Properties	900 2nd Ave. S.	Minneapolis	MN	55402	James R. Ryan	612-336-1200	R	86 OR	0.1
Davis Building Corp.	3755 E. 82nd St.	Indianapolis	IN	46240	William Blake	317-595-2800	R	84 OR*	0.2
Pan Pacific Development Inc.	2621 Waiwai Loop	Honolulu	HI	96819	T. Metsuneza	808-836-2854	S	83 OR	0.4
Avatar Holdings Inc.	255 Alhambra Cir.	Coral Gables	FL	33134	Lawrence Wilkov	305-442-7000	P	83 OR	1.1

Company type codes: P - Public, R - Private, S - Subsidiary, D - Division, J - Joint Venture, A - Affiliate, G - Group. If the dollar values shown are not sales, the following codes apply: TA - Total Assets; OR - Operating Revenues; GB - Gross Billings. * - estimated dollar value. < - less than. *na* - not available.

Continued on next page.

LEADING COMPANIES - SIC 6552 - Subdividers and Developers, nec
Continued

Company Name	Address				CEO Name	Phone	Co. Type	Sales/Assets ($ mil)	Empl. (000)
Kaiser Resources Inc.	3633 E. Inland Empire	Ontario	CA	91764	Daniel N. Larson	909-483-8500	P	82 TA	<0.1
Robert Martin Co.	100 Clearbrook Rd.	Elmsford	NY	10523	Brad Berger	914-592-4800	R	80 OR	0.1
Van Metre Cos.	5252 Lyngate Ct.	Burke	VA	22015	Richard Rabil	703-425-2600	R	80 OR*	0.4
Malama Pacific Corp.	915 Fort St.	Honolulu	HI	96813	Robert G. Diffley	808-539-7175	S	77 OR	<0.1
Standard Pacific Northern California	3825 Hopyard Rd.	Pleasanton	CA	94566	M.C. Cortney	510-847-8700	S	75 OR	<0.1
Telluride Ski Area Inc.	P.O. Box 11155	Telluride	CO	81435	Ronald D. Allred	303-728-3856	R	75 OR	0.3
Kevin F. Donohoe Company Inc.	Curtis Ctr.	Philadelphia	PA	19106	Kevin F. Donohoe	215-238-6400	R	71 OR	<0.1

Source: *Ward's Business Directory of U.S. Private and Public Companies*, 1996. Company type codes: P - Public, R - Private, S - Subsidiary, D - Division, J - Joint Venture, A - Affiliate, G - Group. If the dollar values shown are not sales, the following codes apply: TA - Total Assets; OR - Operating Revenues; GB - Gross Billings. * - estimated dollar value. < - less than; *na* - not available.

SIC 6553

CEMETERY SUBDIVIDERS AND DEVELOPERS

Establishments in this industry specialize in subdividing real property into cemetery lots and in developing the property for resale on their own account. The SIC includes animal cemetery operation, cemeteries in their real estate operations, cemetery associations, and mausoleum operations.

ESTABLISHMENTS, EMPLOYMENT, AND PAYROLL

	1988	1989 Value	%	1990 Value	%	1991 Value	%	1992 Value	%	1993 Value	%	% change 88-93
All Establishments	4,550	4,572	0.5	4,449	-2.7	5,807	30.5	5,910	1.8	6,327	7.1	39.1
Mid-March Employment	35,300	35,628	0.9	35,244	-1.1	37,835	7.4	38,535	1.9	40,115	4.1	13.6
1st Quarter Wages (annualized - $ mil.)	554.5	580.3	4.7	596.4	2.8	647.1	8.5	701.3	8.4	744.3	6.1	34.2
Payroll per Emp. 1st Q. (annualized)	15,708	16,288	3.7	16,922	3.9	17,103	1.1	18,198	6.4	18,555	2.0	18.1
Annual Payroll ($ mil.)	606.0	625.2	3.2	645.9	3.3	709.1	9.8	765.8	8.0	849.6	10.9	40.2
Establishments - 1-4 Emp. Number	2,733	2,749	0.6	2,644	-3.8	3,799	43.7	3,834	0.9	4,205	9.7	53.9
Mid-March Employment	(D)	4,300	-	4,329	0.7	6,036	39.4	6,270	3.9	6,602	5.3	-
1st Quarter Wages (annualized - $ mil.)	(D)	42.0	-	43.1	2.6	59.0	36.7	64.5	9.3	69.0	7.0	-
Payroll per Emp. 1st Q. (annualized)	(D)	9,768	-	9,960	2.0	9,767	-1.9	10,279	5.2	10,446	1.6	-
Annual Payroll ($ mil.)	(D)	52.9	-	53.6	1.4	74.5	39.1	80.4	7.8	94.4	17.5	-
Establishments - 5-9 Emp. Number	874	883	1.0	840	-4.9	1,009	20.1	1,051	4.2	1,087	3.4	24.4
Mid-March Employment	5,694	5,749	1.0	5,489	-4.5	6,601	20.3	6,809	3.2	7,076	3.9	24.3
1st Quarter Wages (annualized - $ mil.)	75.0	79.1	5.5	79.1	0.0	102.5	29.6	112.0	9.3	112.9	0.8	50.7
Payroll per Emp. 1st Q. (annualized)	13,163	13,753	4.5	14,408	4.8	15,523	7.7	16,448	6.0	15,962	-3.0	21.3
Annual Payroll ($ mil.)	83.6	87.2	4.3	86.9	-0.4	113.7	30.8	120.9	6.4	128.7	6.4	53.9
Establishments - 10-19 Emp. Number	522	511	-2.1	524	2.5	546	4.2	578	5.9	587	1.6	12.5
Mid-March Employment	7,055	7,029	-0.4	7,180	2.1	7,366	2.6	7,836	6.4	7,814	-0.3	10.8
1st Quarter Wages (annualized - $ mil.)	104.7	115.3	10.1	118.3	2.6	127.0	7.3	150.9	18.8	149.8	-0.7	43.1
Payroll per Emp. 1st Q. (annualized)	14,841	16,399	10.5	16,472	0.4	17,236	4.6	19,256	11.7	19,168	-0.5	29.2
Annual Payroll ($ mil.)	115.5	124.0	7.3	127.6	2.9	138.9	8.8	163.3	17.6	166.1	1.7	43.8
Establishments - 20-49 Emp. Number	327	334	2.1	356	6.6	369	3.7	362	-1.9	356	-1.7	8.9
Mid-March Employment	9,827	9,906	0.8	10,441	5.4	10,855	4.0	10,822	-0.3	10,512	-2.9	7.0
1st Quarter Wages (annualized - $ mil.)	166.2	175.0	5.3	193.3	10.4	207.3	7.2	218.6	5.5	215.2	-1.6	29.5
Payroll per Emp. 1st Q. (annualized)	16,912	17,668	4.5	18,514	4.8	19,094	3.1	20,203	5.8	20,469	1.3	21.0
Annual Payroll ($ mil.)	181.9	187.4	3.1	205.6	9.7	220.9	7.5	235.1	6.4	236.9	0.8	30.3
Establishments - 50-99 Emp. Number	71	72	1.4	64	-11.1	68	6.3	69	1.5	69	-	-2.8
Mid-March Employment	4,755	4,764	0.2	4,248	-10.8	(D)	-	4,557	-	4,536	-0.5	-4.6
1st Quarter Wages (annualized - $ mil.)	91.7	94.1	2.6	91.9	-2.3	(D)	-	101.4	-	105.9	4.4	15.4
Payroll per Emp. 1st Q. (annualized)	19,287	19,751	2.4	21,633	9.5	(D)	-	22,255	-	23,337	4.9	21.0
Annual Payroll ($ mil.)	95.9	99.5	3.7	98.8	-0.8	(D)	-	110.6	-	117.9	6.6	22.9
Establishments - 100-249 Emp. Number	21	20	-4.8	17	-15.0	15	-11.8	(D)	-	(D)	-	-
Mid-March Employment	2,988	(D)	-	2,403	-	2,224	-7.4	(D)	-	(D)	-	-
1st Quarter Wages (annualized - $ mil.)	59.0	(D)	-	48.5	-	50.1	3.3	(D)	-	(D)	-	-
Payroll per Emp. 1st Q. (annualized)	19,762	(D)	-	20,198	-	22,549	11.6	(D)	-	(D)	-	-
Annual Payroll ($ mil.)	59.4	(D)	-	51.1	-	50.2	-1.7	(D)	-	(D)	-	-
Establishments - 250-499 Emp. Number	2	3	50.0	4	33.3	1	-75.0	(D)	-	(D)	-	-
Mid-March Employment	(D)	(D)	-	1,154	-	(D)	-	(D)	-	(D)	-	-
1st Quarter Wages (annualized - $ mil.)	(D)	(D)	-	22.2	-	(D)	-	(D)	-	(D)	-	-
Payroll per Emp. 1st Q. (annualized)	(D)	(D)	-	19,220	-	(D)	-	(D)	-	(D)	-	-
Annual Payroll ($ mil.)	(D)	(D)	-	22.4	-	(D)	-	(D)	-	(D)	-	-
Establishments - 500-999 Emp. Number	-	-	-	-	-	-	-	-	-	-	-	-
Mid-March Employment	-	-	-	-	-	-	-	-	-	-	-	-
1st Quarter Wages (annualized - $ mil.)	-	-	-	-	-	-	-	-	-	-	-	-
Payroll per Emp. 1st Q. (annualized)	(D)	(D)	-	(D)	-	(D)	-	-	-	-	-	-
Annual Payroll ($ mil.)	-	-	-	-	-	-	-	-	-	-	-	-
Estab. - 1000 or More Emp. Number	-	-	-	-	-	-	-	-	-	-	-	-
Mid-March Employment	-	-	-	-	-	-	-	-	-	-	-	-
1st Quarter Wages (annualized - $ mil.)	-	-	-	-	-	-	-	-	-	-	-	-
Payroll per Emp. 1st Q. (annualized)	(D)	(D)	-	(D)	-	(D)	-	-	-	-	-	-
Annual Payroll ($ mil.)	-	-	-	-	-	-	-	-	-	-	-	-

Source: County Business Patterns, U.S. Department of Commerce, Washington, D.C., for 1988 through 1993. Payroll per employee is calculated using mid-March employment and 1st Quarter wages, annualized. Annual payroll, also shown, may not equal the annualized 1st Quarter wages. Columns headed by a percent sign (%) indicate change from the previous year. *na* stands for not available. The symbol (D) indicates that data are withheld by the source to avoid disclosure of competitive information. A dash (-) indicates that data are not available or cannot be calculated.

ESTABLISHMENTS
Number

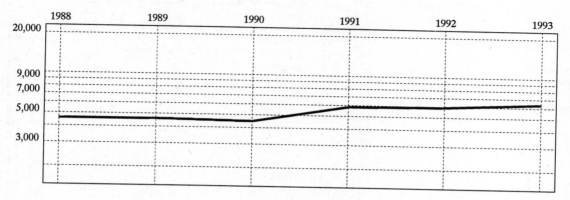

MID-MARCH EMPLOYMENT
Number

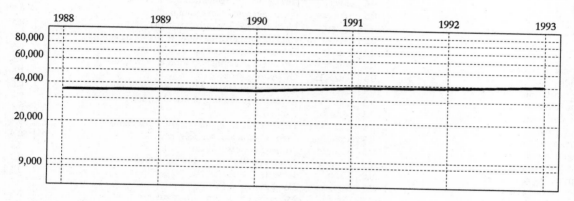

ANNUAL PAYROLL
$ million

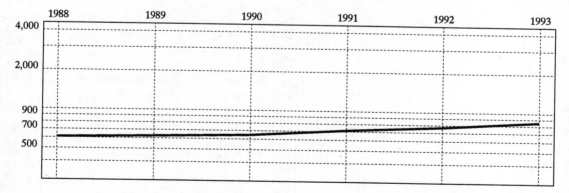

INPUTS AND OUTPUTS FOR ALL REAL ESTATE SECTORS - SIC GROUP 65

Economic Sector or Industry Providing Inputs	%	Sector	Economic Sector or Industry Buying Outputs	%	Sector
Real estate	38.6	Fin/R.E.	Personal consumption expenditures	37.6	
Nonfarm residential structure maintenance	12.5	Constr.	Real estate	10.9	Fin/R.E.
Banking	5.6	Fin/R.E.	Retail trade, except eating & drinking	7.4	Trade
Maintenance of nonfarm buildings nec	5.3	Constr.	Hospitals	4.6	Services
Eating & drinking places	4.4	Trade	Gross private fixed investment	4.4	Cap Inv
Insurance carriers	4.3	Fin/R.E.	Owner-occupied dwellings	2.7	Fin/R.E.
Services to dwellings & other buildings	4.2	Services	Wholesale trade	2.7	Trade
Advertising	3.2	Services	Eating & drinking places	1.8	Trade
Maintenance of highways & streets	2.8	Constr.	Religious organizations	1.4	Services
Communications, except radio & TV	2.0	Util.	Banking	1.2	Fin/R.E.
Landscape & horticultural services	1.9	Agric.	Doctors & dentists	1.2	Services
Legal services	1.6	Services	Colleges, universities, & professional schools	1.1	Services
Petroleum refining	1.5	Manufg.	Feed grains	1.1	Agric.
Commercial printing	0.9	Manufg.	Insurance carriers	0.9	Fin/R.E.
Hotels & lodging places	0.7	Services	Legal services	0.9	Services
Management & consulting services & labs	0.7	Services	Meat animals	0.9	Agric.
Accounting, auditing & bookkeeping	0.6	Services	S/L Govt. purch., other general government	0.9	S/L Govt
Business services nec	0.6	Services	Communications, except radio & TV	0.6	Util.
Motor freight transportation & warehousing	0.6	Util.	Hotels & lodging places	0.6	Services
U.S. Postal Service	0.6	Gov't	Amusement & recreation services nec	0.5	Services
Electrical repair shops	0.5	Services	Credit agencies other than banks	0.5	Fin/R.E.
Maintenance of farm service facilities	0.5	Constr.	Elementary & secondary schools	0.5	Services
Wholesale trade	0.5	Trade	Engineering, architectural, & surveying services	0.5	Services
Air transportation	0.4	Util.	Insurance agents, brokers, & services	0.5	Fin/R.E.
Business/professional associations	0.4	Services	Motor freight transportation & warehousing	0.5	Util.
Security & commodity brokers	0.4	Fin/R.E.	Oil bearing crops	0.5	Agric.
Transit & bus transportation	0.4	Util.	S/L Govt. purch., public assistance & relief	0.5	S/L Govt
Arrangement of passenger transportation	0.3	Util.	Accounting, auditing & bookkeeping	0.4	Services
Automotive rental & leasing, without drivers	0.3	Services	Advertising	0.4	Services
Electric services (utilities)	0.3	Util.	Labor, civic, social, & fraternal associations	0.4	Services
Miscellaneous plastics products	0.3	Manufg.	Medical & health services, nec	0.4	Services
Engine electrical equipment	0.2	Manufg.	Nursing & personal care facilities	0.4	Services
Paper mills, except building paper	0.2	Manufg.	Computer & data processing services	0.3	Services
Retail trade, except eating & drinking	0.2	Trade	Exports	0.3	Foreign
Computer & data processing services	0.1	Services	Food grains	0.3	Agric.
Maintenance of farm residential buildings	0.1	Constr.	Management & consulting services & labs	0.3	Services
Nitrogenous & phosphatic fertilizers	0.1	Manufg.	Security & commodity brokers	0.3	Fin/R.E.
Paper coating & glazing	0.1	Manufg.	Water transportation	0.3	Util.
Personnel supply services	0.1	Services	Air transportation	0.2	Util.
Photographic equipment & supplies	0.1	Manufg.	Automotive repair shops & services	0.2	Services
			Beauty & barber shops	0.2	Services
			Business services nec	0.2	Services
			Coal	0.2	Mining
			Crude petroleum & natural gas	0.2	Mining
			Dairy farm products	0.2	Agric.
			Electric services (utilities)	0.2	Util.
			Federal Government purchases, national defense	0.2	Fed Govt
			Federal Government purchases, nondefense	0.2	Fed Govt
			Laundry, dry cleaning, shoe repair	0.2	Services
			Libraries, vocation education	0.2	Services
			Membership organizations nec	0.2	Services
			Social services, nec	0.2	Services
			State & local government enterprises, nec	0.2	Gov't
			Vegetables	0.2	Agric.
			Automobile parking & car washes	0.1	Services
			Child day care services	0.1	Services
			Cotton	0.1	Agric.
			Electronic computing equipment	0.1	Manufg.

Continued on next page.

INPUTS AND OUTPUTS FOR ALL REAL ESTATE SECTORS - SIC GROUP 65 - Continued

Economic Sector or Industry Providing Inputs	%	Sector	Economic Sector or Industry Buying Outputs	%	Sector
			Landscape & horticultural services	0.1	Agric.
			Membership sports & recreation clubs	0.1	Services
			Motion pictures	0.1	Services
			Petroleum & natural gas well drilling	0.1	Constr.
			Portrait, photographic studios	0.1	Services
			Residential care	0.1	Services
			U.S. Postal Service	0.1	Gov't

Source: Benchmark Input-Output Accounts for the U.S. Economy, 1982, U.S. Department of Commerce, Washington, D.C., July 1991. Data, as reported in the source, are organized by the 1977 SIC structure in use in 1982 but have been matched, as closely as is possible, to the 1987 SIC structure used in this book. Activities with the same percentage are sorted alphabetically by name of activity.

OCCUPATIONS EMPLOYED BY REAL ESTATE NEC

Occupation	% of Total 1994	Change to 2005	Occupation	% of Total 1994	Change to 2005
Gardeners & groundskeepers, ex farm	19.2	-1.4	Janitors & cleaners, incl maids	2.5	-12.0
General office clerks	7.3	-2.4	Typists & word processors	2.3	-40.7
General managers & top executives	7.2	6.7	Marketing & sales worker supervisors	1.9	12.1
Secretaries, ex legal & medical	7.0	2.5	Food preparation & service workers nec	1.8	9.6
Maintenance repairers, general utility	4.5	-1.3	Supervisors, farming, forestry	1.6	9.5
Bookkeeping, accounting, & auditing clerks	4.4	-16.5	Accountants & auditors	1.6	10.7
Sales agents, real estate	4.4	9.7	Guards	1.2	-1.3
Sales & related workers nec	4.1	10.9	Carpenters	1.1	-12.4
Property & real estate managers	3.8	18.1	Service workers nec	1.1	9.5
Receptionists & information clerks	3.4	12.9	Blue collar worker supervisors	1.0	20.1
Financial managers	2.8	11.2			

Sources: Industry-Occupation Matrix, Bureau of Labor Statistics. These data relate to one or more 3-digit SIC industry groups rather than to a single 4-digit SIC. The change reported for each occupation to the year 2005 is a percent of growth or decline as estimated by the Bureau of Labor Statistics. The abbreviation *nec* stands for not elsewhere classified.

U.S. AND STATE DATA ON INDUSTRY REVENUES AND OTHER ACCOUNTS FOR 1992

State	No. of Estab.	Employ-ment	Payroll ($ mil.)	Revenues ($ mil.)	Empl./ Estab.	Revenue/ Estab. ($)	Payroll/ Estab. ($)	Revenue/ Empl. ($)	Payroll/ Empl. ($)
UNITED STATES	6,490	40,102	795.0	2,299.6	6	354,336	122,497	57,345	19,825
Alabama	107	691	9.8	33.4	6	312,252	91,402	48,352	14,153
Alaska	3	-	(D)	(D)	(D)	(D)	(D)	(D)	(D)
Arizona	34	552	9.9	27.1	16	796,265	290,676	49,045	17,904
Arkansas	69	190	2.8	10.7	3	155,174	40,348	56,353	14,653
California	267	3,869	92.8	323.0	14	1,209,682	347,509	83,480	23,982
Colorado	50	434	7.4	20.1	9	402,560	148,680	46,378	17,129
Connecticut	98	435	10.0	28.9	4	294,694	102,510	66,391	23,094
Delaware	20	-	(D)	(D)	(D)	(D)	(D)	(D)	(D)
District of Columbia	7	50	0.9	2.4	7	336,429	132,857	47,100	18,600
Florida	201	3,025	59.8	204.0	15	1,015,070	297,627	67,448	19,776
Georgia	133	861	15.2	57.1	6	429,624	114,338	66,365	17,662
Hawaii	17	453	10.5	23.3	27	1,369,588	616,882	51,397	23,150
Idaho	21	33	0.6	2.5	2	121,048	27,000	77,030	17,182
Illinois	369	1,930	47.7	130.5	5	353,661	129,171	67,617	24,696
Indiana	215	1,262	20.1	51.7	6	240,247	93,712	40,929	15,965
Iowa	154	433	6.6	16.2	3	104,916	42,890	37,314	15,254
Kansas	92	344	5.5	15.2	4	165,554	60,228	44,276	16,108
Kentucky	123	639	10.4	25.7	5	208,602	84,325	40,153	16,232
Louisiana	81	708	9.0	29.8	9	368,222	111,704	42,127	12,780
Maine	63	127	2.1	5.5	2	87,905	33,032	43,606	16,386
Maryland	110	1,301	25.8	63.3	12	575,255	234,982	48,638	19,868
Massachusetts	136	767	19.2	42.6	6	313,037	141,449	55,506	25,081
Michigan	158	1,248	28.1	91.8	8	580,930	178,025	73,547	22,538
Minnesota	144	384	6.3	18.6	3	129,097	44,049	48,411	16,518
Mississippi	43	141	1.9	5.5	3	127,767	43,140	38,965	13,156
Missouri	162	683	10.1	28.1	4	173,167	62,228	41,073	14,760
Montana	28	67	0.9	2.3	2	82,750	33,607	34,582	14,045
Nebraska	60	182	2.6	9.7	3	161,767	43,133	53,330	14,220
Nevada	11	111	3.4	7.3	10	662,182	308,273	65,622	30,550
New Hampshire	29	55	1.0	2.1	2	71,690	33,414	37,800	17,618
New Jersey	204	1,463	38.5	94.5	7	463,353	188,529	64,610	26,288
New Mexico	22	130	1.9	6.3	6	287,318	86,364	48,623	14,615
New York	663	3,607	91.5	238.0	5	358,998	137,964	65,987	25,359
North Carolina	155	810	14.4	43.8	5	282,271	92,632	54,015	17,726
North Dakota	37	-	(D)	(D)	(D)	(D)	(D)	(D)	(D)
Ohio	308	1,920	33.5	96.0	6	311,711	108,623	50,004	17,425
Oklahoma	59	378	5.8	16.8	6	285,559	99,051	44,571	15,460
Oregon	58	322	5.2	20.3	6	350,276	88,845	63,093	16,003
Pennsylvania	671	3,143	54.4	153.0	5	228,034	81,077	48,683	17,309
Rhode Island	34	151	3.6	10.8	4	318,353	104,529	71,682	23,536
South Carolina	101	579	9.6	28.9	6	285,802	94,693	49,855	16,518
South Dakota	30	60	0.7	1.7	2	55,767	22,300	27,883	11,150
Tennessee	131	811	12.6	35.5	6	270,634	96,252	43,715	15,547
Texas	330	2,539	46.7	119.4	8	361,788	141,530	47,022	18,395
Utah	15	97	1.7	6.2	6	413,733	113,000	63,979	17,474
Vermont	57	-	(D)	(D)	(D)	(D)	(D)	(D)	(D)
Virginia	146	1,051	19.1	50.4	7	344,993	131,089	47,925	18,210
Washington	98	682	16.2	46.2	7	471,653	165,327	67,774	23,757
West Virginia	114	460	6.2	21.1	4	184,667	54,404	45,765	13,483
Wisconsin	247	732	10.2	24.5	3	99,016	41,381	33,411	13,963
Wyoming	5	-	(D)	(D)	(D)	(D)	(D)	(D)	(D)

Source: 1992 Economic Census, U.S. Department of Commerce, Washington, D.C. This is the only table that shows revenue data as collected by the Bureau of the Census in an Economic Census. The symbol (D) indicates that data are withheld by the source to avoid disclosure of competitive information. A dash (-) indicates that data are not available or cannot be calculated.

ESTABLISHMENTS 1992 - STATE AND REGIONAL CONCENTRATION

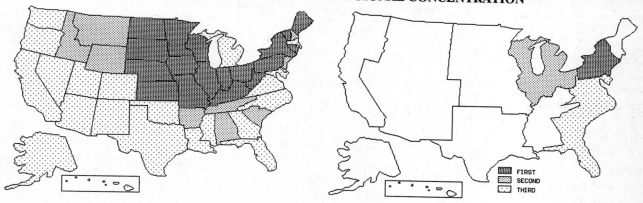

EMPLOYMENT 1992 - STATE AND REGIONAL CONCENTRATION

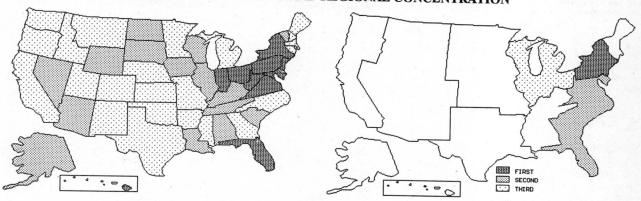

REVENUES 1992 - STATE AND REGIONAL CONCENTRATION

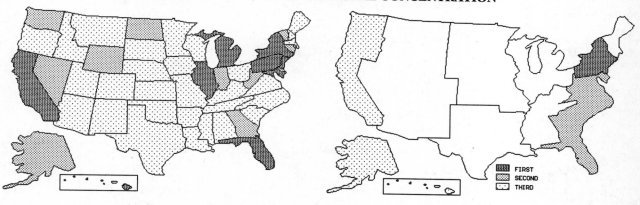

States with the darkest shading indicate those states which have proportionately more establishments, employment, or revenues than would be indicated by the state's population. States with light shading are states with proportionately fewer establishments, less employment, and lower revenues than population distribution. States shaded grey are within 15 percent of the state's population proportion in these categories. States for which no data are available are shown as average (grey). *Regions* are shaded to indicate absolute rank in the category. If no data for the category are available, establishment counts are used to shade the regions. Source of the data is the table on the facing page.

LEADING COMPANIES - SIC 6553 - Cemetery Subdividers and Developers

Number shown: **8**   Total sales/assets ($ mil): **1,252**   Total employment (000): **16.3**

Company Name	Address				CEO Name	Phone	Co. Type	Sales/Assets ($ mil)	Empl. (000)
Service Corporation International	P.O. Box 130548	Houston	TX	77219	Robert L. Waltrip	713-522-5141	P	1,117 OR	15.0
Caballero Woodlawn Funeral Homes and Cemeteries Inc.	P.O. Box 14141A	Miami	FL	33114	Keenan Knopke	305-238-3672	R	53 OR*	0.3
Rose Hills Co.	P.O. Box 110	Whittier	CA	90608	Dennis Poulsen	310-699-0921	R	35 OR*	0.6
MHI Group Inc.	3100 Capital Cir.	Tallahassee	FL	32308	David J. McLaurin	904-385-8883	P	17 OR	0.2
Uniservice Corp.	P.O. Box 11067	Portland	OR	97211	Ellsworth D. Purdy	503-283-1980	R	14 OR	0.2
Cypress Lawn Memorial Park	P.O. Box 397	Colma	CA	94014	Sarafin Mora	415-755-0580	R	9 OR*	<0.1
Parklawn Inc.	P.O. Box 725	Rockville	MD	20848	Robert Maclary	301-881-2151	S	6 OR*	<0.1
Virginia Memorial Garden Inc.	11227 James Madison	King George	VA	22485	Ruth Herrink	703-775-7733	R	1 OR*	<0.1

Source: Ward's Business Directory of U.S. Private and Public Companies, 1996. Company type codes: P - Public, R - Private, S - Subsidiary, D - Division, J - Joint Venture, A - Affiliate, G - Group. If the dollar values shown are not sales, the following codes apply: TA - Total Assets; OR - Operating Revenues; GB - Gross Billings. * - estimated dollar value. < - less than; *na* - not available.

SIC 6710

HOLDING OFFICES

Holding Offices includes SIC 6712, Offices of Bank Holding Companies and SIC 6719, Offices of Holding Companies, not elsewhere classified.

SIC 6712 includes establishments engaged in holding or owning the securities of banks for the sole purpose of exercising some degree of control over the activities of bank companies whose securities they hold. Companies holding securities of banks but which are predominantly operating banks, are classified as banks under the SIC that best fits their operations.

SIC 6719 are establishments that hold the securities of companies other than banks for the sole purpose of exercising some degree of control over the companies whose securities they hold. Companies that hold securities but are predominantly operating companies are classified under the SIC that best fits their operations. This SIC includes holding companies, investment holding companies, personal holding companies—all holding securities of companies other than banks—and public utility holding companies.

ESTABLISHMENTS, EMPLOYMENT, AND PAYROLL

	1988	1989 Value	%	1990 Value	%	1991 Value	%	1992 Value	%	1993 Value	%	% change 88-93
All Establishments	5,564	5,794	4.1	6,241	7.7	6,950	11.4	7,459	7.3	7,944	6.5	42.8
Mid-March Employment	116,615	124,491	6.8	123,470	-0.8	125,745	1.8	137,750	9.5	127,662	-7.3	9.5
1st Quarter Wages (annualized - $ mil.)	5,459.7	5,675.0	3.9	5,785.0	1.9	5,869.8	1.5	6,669.7	13.6	6,626.1	-0.7	21.4
Payroll per Emp. 1st Q. (annualized)	46,818	45,586	-2.6	46,854	2.8	46,680	-0.4	48,419	3.7	51,903	7.2	10.9
Annual Payroll ($ mil.)	4,941.5	5,249.9	6.2	5,429.7	3.4	5,642.7	3.9	6,635.5	17.6	6,986.0	5.3	41.4
Establishments - 1-4 Emp. Number	2,942	3,043	3.4	3,439	13.0	3,937	14.5	4,356	10.6	4,899	12.5	66.5
Mid-March Employment	4,876	4,983	2.2	5,527	10.9	6,050	9.5	6,824	12.8	7,231	6.0	48.3
1st Quarter Wages (annualized - $ mil.)	295.4	285.3	-3.4	321.7	12.7	310.3	-3.5	391.0	26.0	417.5	6.8	41.3
Payroll per Emp. 1st Q. (annualized)	60,575	57,252	-5.5	58,197	1.7	51,297	-11.9	57,304	11.7	57,736	0.8	-4.7
Annual Payroll ($ mil.)	491.3	362.4	-26.2	415.7	14.7	407.8	-1.9	478.7	17.4	571.2	19.3	16.3
Establishments - 5-9 Emp. Number	876	903	3.1	956	5.9	1,075	12.4	1,105	2.8	1,098	-0.6	25.3
Mid-March Employment	5,801	6,002	3.5	6,492	8.2	7,297	12.4	7,465	2.3	7,330	-1.8	26.4
1st Quarter Wages (annualized - $ mil.)	341.3	328.9	-3.6	361.5	9.9	397.5	10.0	437.3	10.0	435.0	-0.5	27.4
Payroll per Emp. 1st Q. (annualized)	58,836	54,804	-6.9	55,677	1.6	54,473	-2.2	58,576	7.5	59,342	1.3	0.9
Annual Payroll ($ mil.)	315.0	318.3	1.0	361.2	13.5	394.6	9.3	472.5	19.7	455.0	-3.7	44.4
Establishments - 10-19 Emp. Number	644	687	6.7	702	2.2	775	10.4	806	4.0	800	-0.7	24.2
Mid-March Employment	8,950	9,332	4.3	9,680	3.7	10,589	9.4	11,020	4.1	11,012	-0.1	23.0
1st Quarter Wages (annualized - $ mil.)	576.1	594.8	3.2	613.7	3.2	609.5	-0.7	706.1	15.8	710.5	0.6	23.3
Payroll per Emp. 1st Q. (annualized)	64,366	63,734	-1.0	63,396	-0.5	57,564	-9.2	64,078	11.3	64,517	0.7	0.2
Annual Payroll ($ mil.)	483.8	549.9	13.7	577.4	5.0	586.2	1.5	710.5	21.2	747.4	5.2	54.5
Establishments - 20-49 Emp. Number	571	609	6.7	610	0.2	627	2.8	634	1.1	621	-2.1	8.8
Mid-March Employment	(D)	18,869	-	18,837	-0.2	19,049	1.1	19,441	2.1	19,224	-1.1	-
1st Quarter Wages (annualized - $ mil.)	(D)	941.7	-	1,054.6	12.0	1,042.0	-1.2	1,110.0	6.5	1,058.0	-4.7	-
Payroll per Emp. 1st Q. (annualized)	(D)	49,907	-	55,984	12.2	54,700	-2.3	57,098	4.4	55,036	-3.6	-
Annual Payroll ($ mil.)	(D)	875.4	-	946.6	8.1	1,016.9	7.4	1,099.4	8.1	1,082.4	-1.5	-
Establishments - 50-99 Emp. Number	288	291	1.0	289	-0.7	284	-1.7	282	-0.7	273	-3.2	-5.2
Mid-March Employment	20,040	19,819	-1.1	19,784	-0.2	19,515	-1.4	19,436	-0.4	18,728	-3.6	-6.5
1st Quarter Wages (annualized - $ mil.)	898.9	897.0	-0.2	915.2	2.0	841.5	-8.1	1,006.0	19.6	1,023.8	1.8	13.9
Payroll per Emp. 1st Q. (annualized)	44,853	45,260	0.9	46,260	2.2	43,119	-6.8	51,760	20.0	54,666	5.6	21.9
Annual Payroll ($ mil.)	771.1	795.8	3.2	787.2	-1.1	805.7	2.4	962.5	19.5	1,011.8	5.1	31.2
Establishments - 100-249 Emp. Number	168	188	11.9	174	-7.4	176	1.1	194	10.2	175	-9.8	4.2
Mid-March Employment	25,831	29,530	14.3	27,216	-7.8	26,833	-1.4	29,570	10.2	26,718	-9.6	3.4
1st Quarter Wages (annualized - $ mil.)	1,091.1	1,278.6	17.2	1,154.1	-9.7	1,151.5	-0.2	1,251.9	8.7	1,334.6	6.6	22.3
Payroll per Emp. 1st Q. (annualized)	42,238	43,299	2.5	42,406	-2.1	42,913	1.2	42,338	-1.3	49,950	18.0	18.3
Annual Payroll ($ mil.)	891.5	1,111.7	24.7	1,086.0	-2.3	1,058.8	-2.5	1,229.9	16.2	1,419.0	15.4	59.2
Establishments - 250-499 Emp. Number	56	54	-3.6	49	-9.3	52	6.1	52	-	54	3.8	-3.6
Mid-March Employment	18,514	19,355	4.5	17,355	-10.3	(D)	-	17,089	-	18,864	10.4	1.9
1st Quarter Wages (annualized - $ mil.)	822.0	726.8	-11.6	714.7	-1.7	(D)	-	821.4	-	836.2	1.8	1.7
Payroll per Emp. 1st Q. (annualized)	44,397	37,549	-15.4	41,183	9.7	(D)	-	48,063	-	44,330	-7.8	-0.2
Annual Payroll ($ mil.)	712.1	701.8	-1.4	657.5	-6.3	(D)	-	812.2	-	856.8	5.5	20.3
Establishments - 500-999 Emp. Number	15	14	-6.7	18	28.6	20	11.1	22	10.0	(D)	-	-
Mid-March Employment	9,404	(D)	-	12,678	-	13,304	4.9	15,283	14.9	(D)	-	-
1st Quarter Wages (annualized - $ mil.)	345.9	(D)	-	431.8	-	497.6	15.2	689.7	38.6	(D)	-	-
Payroll per Emp. 1st Q. (annualized)	36,781	(D)	-	34,062	-	37,400	9.8	45,128	20.7	(D)	-	-
Annual Payroll ($ mil.)	321.7	(D)	-	385.0	-	471.3	22.4	637.8	35.3	(D)	-	-
Estab. - 1000 or More Emp. Number	4	5	25.0	4	-20.0	4	-	8	100.0	(D)	-	-
Mid-March Employment	(D)	(D)	-	5,901	-	(D)	-	11,622	-	(D)	-	-
1st Quarter Wages (annualized - $ mil.)	(D)	(D)	-	217.8	-	(D)	-	256.2	-	(D)	-	-
Payroll per Emp. 1st Q. (annualized)	(D)	(D)	-	36,906	-	(D)	-	22,043	-	(D)	-	-
Annual Payroll ($ mil.)	(D)	(D)	-	213.2	-	(D)	-	231.8	-	(D)	-	-

Source: County Business Patterns, U.S. Department of Commerce. Washington, D.C., for 1988 through 1993. Payroll per employee is calculated using mid-March employment and 1st Quarter wages, annualized. Annual payroll, also shown, may not equal the annualized 1st Quarter wages. Columns headed by a percent sign (%) indicate change from the previous year. *na* stands for not available. The symbol (D) indicates that data are withheld by the source to avoid disclosure of competitive information. A dash (-) indicates that data are not available or cannot be calculated.

ESTABLISHMENTS
Number

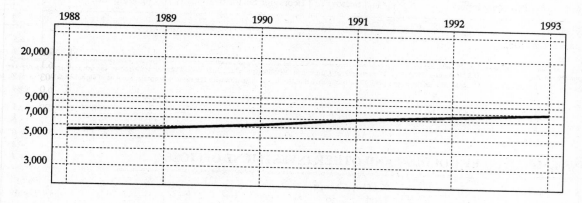

MID-MARCH EMPLOYMENT
Number

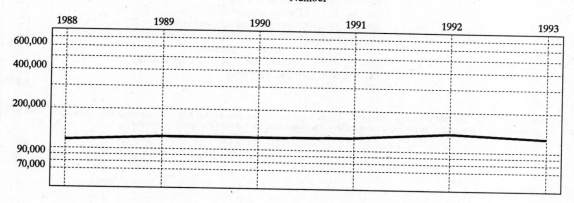

ANNUAL PAYROLL
$ million

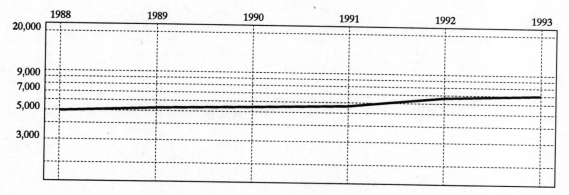

INPUTS AND OUTPUTS FOR HOLDING AND OTHER INVESTMENT OFFICES - SIC GROUP 67

Economic Sector or Industry Providing Inputs	%	Sector	Economic Sector or Industry Buying Outputs	%	Sector
No Input-Output data are available for this industry group.					

Source: Benchmark Input-Output Accounts for the U.S. Economy, 1982, U.S. Department of Commerce, Washington, D.C., July 1991. Data, as reported in the source, are organized by the 1977 SIC structure in use in 1982 but have been matched, as closely as is possible, to the 1987 SIC structure used in this book. Activities with the same percentage are sorted alphabetically by name of activity.

OCCUPATIONS EMPLOYED BY HOLDING AND OTHER INVESTMENT OFFICES

Occupation	% of Total 1994	Change to 2005	Occupation	% of Total 1994	Change to 2005
Secretaries, ex legal & medical	10.7	26.5	Marketing & sales worker supervisors	1.8	39.0
General managers & top executives	10.4	31.8	Securities & financial services sales workers	1.6	39.0
General office clerks	7.7	18.5	Systems analysts	1.5	122.3
Accountants & auditors	6.1	39.0	Clerical support workers nec	1.5	11.2
Financial managers	6.0	39.0	Janitors & cleaners, incl maids	1.5	11.2
Bookkeeping, accounting, & auditing clerks	6.0	4.2	Personnel, training, & labor specialists	1.4	54.8
Management support workers nec	5.5	39.0	Computer programmers	1.2	12.6
Clerical supervisors & managers	4.5	42.2	Maintenance repairers, general utility	1.2	25.1
Professional workers nec	3.4	66.8	Brokerage clerks	1.2	11.2
Receptionists & information clerks	2.2	39.0	Lawyers	1.2	39.0
Managers & administrators nec	2.1	38.9			

Sources: Industry-Occupation Matrix, Bureau of Labor Statistics. These data relate to one or more 3-digit SIC industry groups rather than to a single 4-digit SIC. The change reported for each occupation to the year 2005 is a percent of growth or decline as estimated by the Bureau of Labor Statistics. The abbreviation nec stands for not elsewhere classified.

U.S. AND STATE DATA ON INDUSTRY REVENUES AND OTHER ACCOUNTS FOR 1992

State	No. of Estab.	Employ-ment	Payroll ($ mil.)	Revenues ($ mil.)	Empl./ Estab.	Revenue/ Estab. ($)	Payroll/ Estab. ($)	Revenue/ Empl. ($)	Payroll/ Empl. ($)
UNITED STATES	10,381	108,235	5,934.2	43,634.1	10	4,203,267	571,644	403,142	54,827
Alabama	118	1,265	61.5	319.4	11	2,706,983	521,008	252,509	48,600
Alaska	19	546	12.5	78.4	29	4,124,895	657,000	143,540	22,863
Arizona	100	989	59.8	428.3	10	4,282,810	598,460	433,044	60,512
Arkansas	86	951	44.8	207.1	11	2,408,070	520,802	217,764	47,097
California	807	9,426	543.7	2,473.5	12	3,065,025	673,668	262,410	57,676
Colorado	150	1,840	106.9	756.2	12	5,041,580	712,660	410,998	58,097
Connecticut	216	1,705	130.1	822.1	8	3,806,060	602,116	482,175	76,280
Delaware	970	-	(D)	(D)	(D)	(D)	(D)	(D)	(D)
District of Columbia	30	305	24.6	270.8	10	9,027,033	818,567	887,905	80,515
Florida	499	5,508	249.3	1,144.9	11	2,294,467	499,525	207,868	45,255
Georgia	282	2,376	140.1	531.0	8	1,883,025	496,876	223,490	58,973
Hawaii	51	-	(D)	(D)	(D)	(D)	(D)	(D)	(D)
Idaho	19	-	(D)	(D)	(D)	(D)	(D)	(D)	(D)
Illinois	582	5,688	314.6	3,482.6	10	5,983,763	540,493	612,263	55,304
Indiana	184	1,677	118.2	693.7	9	3,770,228	642,446	413,668	70,489
Iowa	185	587	32.1	260.8	3	1,409,838	173,276	444,327	54,610
Kansas	170	2,175	79.3	547.4	13	3,219,906	466,429	251,671	36,457
Kentucky	116	1,727	93.5	504.3	15	4,347,845	805,784	292,038	54,123
Louisiana	108	917	44.9	631.9	8	5,851,093	415,935	689,115	48,987
Maine	42	237	14.3	46.1	6	1,098,167	340,190	194,612	60,287
Maryland	131	3,018	148.2	426.7	23	3,257,397	1,131,107	141,391	49,097
Massachusetts	221	2,408	115.6	798.4	11	3,612,557	523,213	331,551	48,019
Michigan	264	2,602	124.8	859.0	10	3,253,712	472,754	330,123	47,966
Minnesota	226	1,955	119.7	478.8	9	2,118,730	529,819	244,927	61,248
Mississippi	82	516	20.5	115.1	6	1,403,963	250,500	223,110	39,808
Missouri	275	2,723	141.0	1,433.5	10	5,212,760	512,640	526,445	51,772
Montana	30	169	8.1	57.2	6	1,905,200	268,533	338,201	47,669
Nebraska	124	901	43.1	226.0	7	1,822,266	347,226	250,789	47,787
Nevada	82	498	29.5	237.6	6	2,897,805	359,512	477,149	59,197
New Hampshire	48	1,155	41.9	198.3	24	4,130,708	872,104	171,666	36,243
New Jersey	289	5,474	265.2	1,361.3	19	4,710,381	917,751	248,685	48,453
New Mexico	37	805	36.5	71.7	22	1,937,081	986,568	89,034	45,345
New York	840	9,730	850.1	7,846.5	12	9,341,038	1,011,979	806,421	87,365
North Carolina	139	1,383	81.8	484.9	10	3,488,324	588,230	350,598	59,121
North Dakota	31	83	5.0	31.7	3	1,021,548	161,097	381,542	60,169
Ohio	397	5,821	257.6	1,916.8	15	4,828,277	648,768	329,295	44,247
Oklahoma	119	1,002	43.0	205.2	8	1,724,277	361,756	204,779	42,963
Oregon	80	1,261	54.5	101.5	16	1,268,475	681,662	80,474	43,246
Pennsylvania	398	5,674	336.8	1,493.4	14	3,752,254	846,158	263,200	59,353
Rhode Island	38	194	15.6	81.5	5	2,144,158	411,526	419,990	80,608
South Carolina	92	995	37.1	233.3	11	2,535,565	403,783	234,444	37,335
South Dakota	42	-	(D)	(D)	(D)	(D)	(D)	(D)	(D)
Tennessee	162	1,772	64.3	324.0	11	2,000,056	397,000	182,849	36,295
Texas	750	8,043	486.4	3,005.4	11	4,007,219	648,547	373,668	60,476
Utah	46	241	8.0	60.7	5	1,320,239	173,065	251,996	33,033
Vermont	23	88	4.8	35.5	4	1,544,826	208,261	403,761	54,432
Virginia	215	5,308	227.9	1,901.4	25	8,843,735	1,059,833	358,215	42,928
Washington	138	1,667	107.3	281.4	12	2,039,428	777,188	168,831	64,338
West Virginia	58	260	12.4	100.1	4	1,725,966	213,966	385,023	47,731
Wisconsin	251	2,594	115.5	817.8	10	3,258,259	460,032	315,275	44,513
Wyoming	19	81	1.9	30.9	4	1,627,895	100,842	381,852	23,654

Source: 1992 Economic Census, U.S. Department of Commerce, Washington, D.C. This is the only table that shows revenue data as collected by the Bureau of the Census in an Economic Census. The symbol (D) indicates that data are withheld by the source to avoid disclosure of competitive information. A dash (-) indicates that data are not available or cannot be calculated.

ESTABLISHMENTS 1992 - STATE AND REGIONAL CONCENTRATION

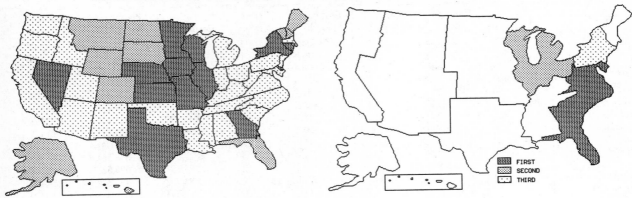

EMPLOYMENT 1992 - STATE AND REGIONAL CONCENTRATION

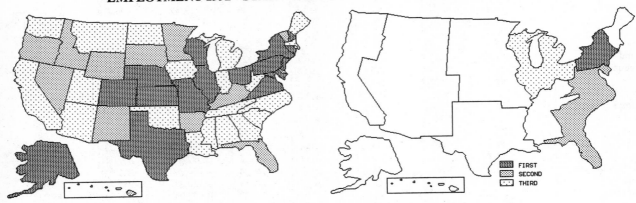

REVENUES 1992 - STATE AND REGIONAL CONCENTRATION

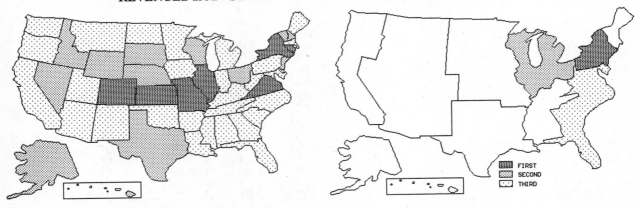

States with the darkest shading indicate those states which have proportionately more establishments, employment, or revenues than would be indicated by the state's population. States with light shading are states with proportionately fewer establishments, less employment, and lower revenues than population distribution. States shaded grey are within 15 percent of the state's population proportion in these categories. States for which no data are available are shown as average (grey). *Regions* are shaded to indicate absolute rank in the category. If no data for the category are available, establishment counts are used to shade the regions. Source of the data is the table on the facing page.

LEADING COMPANIES - SIC 6722 - Management Investment, Open-End

Number shown: **12**   Total sales/assets ($ mil): **575**   Total employment (000): **1.2**

Company Name	Address				CEO Name	Phone	Co. Type	Sales/Assets ($ mil)	Empl. (000)
Capital Associates Inc.	7175 W. Jefferson Ave.	Lakewood	CO	80235	Dennis J. Lacey	303-980-1000	P	155 OR	0.1
Capital Associates International Inc.	7175 W. Jefferson Ave.	Lakewood	CO	80235	Dennis J. Lacey	303-980-1000	S	155 OR	0.1
AIM Equity Funds Inc.	11 Greenway Plz.	Houston	TX	77046	Charles T. Bauer	713-626-1919	S	100 TA*	0.6
SteinRoe Prime Equities	P.O. Box 804058	Chicago	IL	60680	Hans P. Ziegler	312-368-7800	R	90 TA	<0.1
Phoenix Equity Planning Corp.	P.O. Box 2200	Enfield	CT	06083	Phillip McLoughlin	203-253-1000	S	40 TA	0.3
Tripower Resources Inc.	P.O. Box 849	Ardmore	OK	73402	John D. Gibbs	405-226-6700	S	23 TA	<0.1
Selected/Venture Advisers L.P.	124 E. Marcy St.	Santa Fe	NM	87501	Martin H. Proyect	505-983-4335	R	6 TA	<0.1
Managers Funds L.P.	40 Richards Ave.	Norwalk	CT	06854	Robert P. Watson	203-857-5321	R	3 TA*	<0.1
CAI Securities Corp.	7175 W. Jefferson Ave.	Lakewood	CO	80235	Jack Olmstead	303-980-1000	S	1 TA*	<0.1
Snyder Capital Management	350 California St.	San Francisco	CA	94104	Alan Snyder	415-392-3900	R	1 TA*	<0.1
Longleaf Partners Funds	6075 Poplar Ave.	Memphis	TN	38119	Reid Sanders	901-761-2474	R	1 TA*	<0.1
AmTrust Value Fund	P.O. Box 3467	Victoria	TX	77903	Jimmy Baker	512-578-7778	R	0 TA*	<0.1

Source: *Ward's Business Directory of U.S. Private and Public Companies*, 1996. Company type codes: P - Public, R - Private, S - Subsidiary, D - Division, J - Joint Venture, A - Affiliate, G - Group. If the dollar values shown are not sales, the following codes apply: TA - Total Assets; OR - Operating Revenues; GB - Gross Billings. * - estimated dollar value. < - less than; *na* - not available.

LEADING COMPANIES - SIC 6726 - Investment Offices, nec

Number shown: **3**   Total sales/assets ($ mil): **8,047**   Total employment (000): **0.1**

Company Name	Address				CEO Name	Phone	Co. Type	Sales/Assets ($ mil)	Empl. (000)
Voyageur Asset Management	90 S. 7th St.	Minneapolis	MN	55402	John G. Taft	612-376-7000	R	8,000 TA	0.1
Harris and Harris Group Inc.	1 Rockefeller Plz.	New York	NY	10020	Charles E. Harris	212-332-3600	P	32 TA	<0.1
MorAmerica Capital Corp.	101 2nd St. S.E.	Cedar Rapids	IA	52401	Carl Schuettpelz	319-363-8249	3	15 TA	<0.1

Source: *Ward's Business Directory of U.S. Private and Public Companies*, 1996. Company type codes: P - Public, R - Private, S - Subsidiary, D - Division, J - Joint Venture, A - Affiliate, G - Group. If the dollar values shown are not sales, the following codes apply: TA - Total Assets; OR - Operating Revenues; GB - Gross Billings. * - estimated dollar value. < - less than; *na* - not available.

SIC 6732

EDUCATIONAL, RELIGIOUS, ETC. TRUSTS

Educational, religious, and charitable trusts are establishments primarily engaged in the management of funds of trusts and foundations organized for religious, educational, charitable, or nonprofit research purposes. The SIC includes charitable trusts, educational trusts, and religious trusts. The trust operations of not-for-profit research institutes are included under this SIC; the operational activities of such institutes are classified under appropriate Service Industry categories (e.g. business, health, educational, social, or engineering services).

ESTABLISHMENTS, EMPLOYMENT, AND PAYROLL

	1988	1989 Value	%	1990 Value	%	1991 Value	%	1992 Value	%	1993 Value	%	% change 88-93
All Establishments	3,269	3,272	0.1	3,595	9.9	4,391	22.1	4,632	5.5	4,708	1.6	44.0
Mid-March Employment	30,674	37,723	23.0	41,508	10.0	37,000	-10.9	37,048	0.1	36,539	-1.4	19.1
1st Quarter Wages (annualized - $ mil.)	579.2	726.1	25.4	845.9	16.5	799.2	-5.5	881.4	10.3	874.2	-0.8	50.9
Payroll per Emp. 1st Q. (annualized)	18,884	19,248	1.9	20,379	5.9	21,599	6.0	23,791	10.1	23,925	0.6	26.7
Annual Payroll ($ mil.)	610.4	781.3	28.0	897.2	14.8	836.6	-6.8	909.9	8.8	958.0	5.3	56.9
Establishments - 1-4 Emp. Number	2,187	2,123	-2.9	2,360	11.2	3,020	28.0	3,238	7.2	3,257	0.6	48.9
Mid-March Employment	3,986	3,817	-4.2	4,179	9.5	5,105	22.2	5,596	9.6	5,568	-0.5	39.7
1st Quarter Wages (annualized - $ mil.)	81.1	80.3	-1.0	92.4	15.1	115.7	25.3	133.2	15.1	133.2	0.0	64.2
Payroll per Emp. 1st Q. (annualized)	20,343	21,026	3.4	22,105	5.1	22,669	2.6	23,797	5.0	23,917	0.5	17.6
Annual Payroll ($ mil.)	94.6	90.1	-4.7	111.0	23.2	128.6	15.9	147.0	14.3	151.4	2.9	60.0
Establishments - 5-9 Emp. Number	480	490	2.1	530	8.2	629	18.7	667	6.0	702	5.2	46.3
Mid-March Employment	3,157	3,222	2.1	3,485	8.2	4,094	17.5	4,306	5.2	4,526	5.1	43.4
1st Quarter Wages (annualized - $ mil.)	66.3	69.9	5.5	82.0	17.3	100.1	22.1	108.6	8.5	118.9	9.5	79.5
Payroll per Emp. 1st Q. (annualized)	20,992	21,695	3.3	23,527	8.4	24,460	4.0	25,227	3.1	26,278	4.2	25.2
Annual Payroll ($ mil.)	67.8	83.1	22.6	83.4	0.3	101.5	21.8	113.9	12.3	127.3	11.7	87.8
Establishments - 10-19 Emp. Number	295	322	9.2	345	7.1	383	11.0	395	3.1	415	5.1	40.7
Mid-March Employment	3,987	4,302	7.9	4,635	7.7	5,128	10.6	5,293	3.2	5,589	5.6	40.2
1st Quarter Wages (annualized - $ mil.)	76.2	86.9	14.1	96.9	11.5	119.3	23.1	116.0	-2.8	133.5	15.1	75.1
Payroll per Emp. 1st Q. (annualized)	19,119	20,209	5.7	20,909	3.5	23,272	11.3	21,919	-5.8	23,883	9.0	24.9
Annual Payroll ($ mil.)	80.5	90.8	12.8	103.7	14.2	123.2	18.8	123.3	0.1	140.7	14.1	74.8
Establishments - 20-49 Emp. Number	198	214	8.1	223	4.2	255	14.3	234	-8.2	235	0.4	18.7
Mid-March Employment	5,984	6,512	8.8	6,718	3.2	7,084	5.4	6,823	-3.7	7,030	3.0	17.5
1st Quarter Wages (annualized - $ mil.)	111.0	123.4	11.2	142.7	15.6	148.8	4.3	161.4	8.5	173.3	7.4	56.1
Payroll per Emp. 1st Q. (annualized)	18,551	18,952	2.2	21,243	12.1	21,005	-1.1	23,651	12.6	24,652	4.2	32.9
Annual Payroll ($ mil.)	113.6	129.4	14.0	148.7	14.9	157.2	5.8	168.3	7.0	183.5	9.0	61.5
Establishments - 50-99 Emp. Number	68	58	-14.7	67	15.5	51	-23.9	(D)	-	(D)	-	-
Mid-March Employment	(D)	3,898	-	4,457	14.3	3,533	-20.7	(D)	-	(D)	-	-
1st Quarter Wages (annualized - $ mil.)	(D)	72.3	-	82.1	13.6	62.6	-23.8	(D)	-	(D)	-	-
Payroll per Emp. 1st Q. (annualized)	(D)	18,545	-	18,429	-0.6	17,723	-3.8	(D)	-	(D)	-	-
Annual Payroll ($ mil.)	(D)	76.7	-	87.0	13.5	61.4	-29.5	(D)	-	(D)	-	-
Establishments - 100-249 Emp. Number	32	47	46.9	46	-2.1	39	-15.2	32	-17.9	34	6.3	6.3
Mid-March Employment	5,135	7,450	45.1	7,081	-5.0	6,187	-12.6	4,721	-23.7	5,154	9.2	0.4
1st Quarter Wages (annualized - $ mil.)	79.0	117.9	49.3	118.9	0.8	136.4	14.8	118.0	-13.5	134.8	14.2	70.7
Payroll per Emp. 1st Q. (annualized)	15,375	15,824	2.9	16,786	6.1	22,047	31.3	24,995	13.4	26,153	4.6	70.1
Annual Payroll ($ mil.)	80.7	125.5	55.5	122.4	-2.5	143.0	16.9	121.8	-14.8	162.6	33.5	101.4
Establishments - 250-499 Emp. Number	6	12	100.0	17	41.7	11	-35.3	10	-9.1	10	-	66.7
Mid-March Employment	(D)	(D)	-	5,621	-	(D)	-	3,532	-	3,675	4.0	-
1st Quarter Wages (annualized - $ mil.)	(D)	(D)	-	129.1	-	(D)	-	108.3	-	82.3	-23.9	-
Payroll per Emp. 1st Q. (annualized)	(D)	(D)	-	22,967	-	(D)	-	30,651	-	22,408	-26.9	-
Annual Payroll ($ mil.)	(D)	(D)	-	134.6	-	(D)	-	91.7	-	89.0	-2.9	-
Establishments - 500-999 Emp. Number	3	6	100.0	6	-	3	-50.0	(D)	-	(D)	-	-
Mid-March Employment	(D)	(D)	-	(D)	-	(D)	-	(D)	-	(D)	-	-
1st Quarter Wages (annualized - $ mil.)	(D)	(D)	-	(D)	-	(D)	-	(D)	-	(D)	-	-
Payroll per Emp. 1st Q. (annualized)	(D)	(D)	-	(D)	-	(D)	-	(D)	-	(D)	-	-
Annual Payroll ($ mil.)	(D)	(D)	-	(D)	-	(D)	-	(D)	-	(D)	-	-
Estab. - 1000 or More Emp. Number	-	-	-	1	-	-	-	-	-	-	-	-
Mid-March Employment	-	-	-	(D)	-	-	-	-	-	-	-	-
1st Quarter Wages (annualized - $ mil.)	-	-	-	(D)	-	-	-	-	-	-	-	-
Payroll per Emp. 1st Q. (annualized)	(D)	(D)	-	(D)	-	(D)	-	-	-	-	-	-
Annual Payroll ($ mil.)	-	-	-	(D)	-	-	-	-	-	-	-	-

Source: County Business Patterns, U.S. Department of Commerce, Washington, D.C., for 1988 through 1993. Payroll per employee is calculated using mid-March employment and 1st Quarter wages, annualized. Annual payroll, also shown, may not equal the annualized 1st Quarter wages. Columns headed by a percent sign (%) indicate change from the previous year. *na* stands for not available. The symbol (D) indicates that data are withheld by the source to avoid disclosure of competitive information. A dash (-) indicates that data are not available or cannot be calculated.

ESTABLISHMENTS
Number

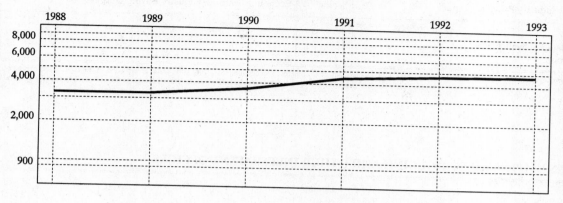

MID-MARCH EMPLOYMENT
Number

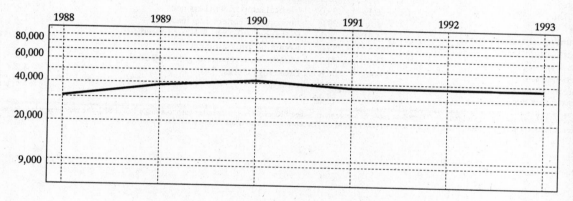

# ANNUAL PAYROLL
$ million

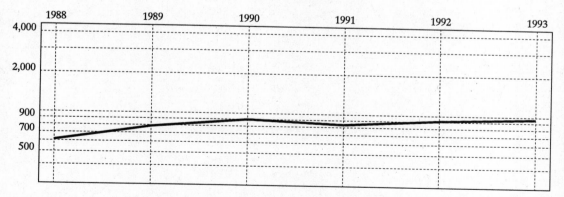

INPUTS AND OUTPUTS FOR HOLDING AND OTHER INVESTMENT OFFICES - SIC GROUP 67

Economic Sector or Industry Providing Inputs	%	Sector	Economic Sector or Industry Buying Outputs	%	Sector
No Input-Output data are available for this industry group.					

Source: Benchmark Input-Output Accounts for the U.S. Economy, 1982, U.S. Department of Commerce, Washington, D.C., July 1991. Data, as reported in the source, are organized by the 1977 SIC structure in use in 1982 but have been matched, as closely as is possible, to the 1987 SIC structure used in this book. Activities with the same percentage are sorted alphabetically by name of activity.

OCCUPATIONS EMPLOYED BY HOLDING AND OTHER INVESTMENT OFFICES

Occupation	% of Total 1994	Change to 2005	Occupation	% of Total 1994	Change to 2005
Secretaries, ex legal & medical	10.7	26.5	Marketing & sales worker supervisors	1.8	39.0
General managers & top executives	10.4	31.8	Securities & financial services sales workers	1.6	39.0
General office clerks	7.7	18.5	Systems analysts	1.5	122.3
Accountants & auditors	6.1	39.0	Clerical support workers nec	1.5	11.2
Financial managers	6.0	39.0	Janitors & cleaners, incl maids	1.5	11.2
Bookkeeping, accounting, & auditing clerks	6.0	4.2	Personnel, training, & labor specialists	1.4	54.8
Management support workers nec	5.5	39.0	Computer programmers	1.2	12.6
Clerical supervisors & managers	4.5	42.2	Maintenance repairers, general utility	1.2	25.1
Professional workers nec	3.4	66.8	Brokerage clerks	1.2	11.2
Receptionists & information clerks	2.2	39.0	Lawyers	1.2	39.0
Managers & administrators nec	2.1	38.9			

Sources: Industry-Occupation Matrix, Bureau of Labor Statistics. These data relate to one or more 3-digit SIC industry groups rather than to a single 4-digit SIC. The change reported for each occupation to the year 2005 is a percent of growth or decline as estimated by the Bureau of Labor Statistics. The abbreviation *nec* stands for not elsewhere classified.

STATE-BY-STATE DATA ON ESTABLISHMENTS, EMPLOYMENT, AND PAYROLL - 1990 AND 1991

State	1990					1991					% Change Empl.
	No. of Estab.	Employ-ment	Pay / Empl.	Payroll ($ mil.)	Pay / Estab.	No. of Estab.	Employ-ment	Pay / Empl.	Payroll ($ mil.)	Pay / Estab.	
Alabama	39	343	11,137	4.2	107,846	49	243	14,765	3.7	74,918	(D)
Alaska	10	30	13,467	0.5	48,700	12	27	19,704	0.5	44,833	(D)
Arizona	34	321	12,361	4.2	123,059	52	289	17,149	4.9	94,077	(D)
Arkansas	26	185	12,346	2.4	92,154	26	129	12,930	1.9	71,577	(D)
California	517	8,402	16,508	148.7	287,640	628	7,965	15,914	133.0	211,791	(D)
Colorado	60	740	19,092	15.0	250,683	88	622	22,514	14.3	162,716	(D)
Connecticut	61	485	24,074	14.0	230,246	71	510	23,027	13.9	195,831	5.2
Delaware	10	21	26,095	0.7	68,700	10	30	22,533	0.8	79,200	42.9
District of Columbia	130	1,618	26,544	43.9	337,962	137	1,945	30,215	59.4	433,832	20.2
Florida	124	1,078	17,273	19.4	156,823	184	1,288	19,425	26.0	141,321	19.5
Georgia	64	419	18,205	8.9	138,359	75	528	17,545	8.9	119,067	26.0
Hawaii	23	282	23,674	6.9	301,522	23	199	19,638	4.3	186,435	(D)
Idaho	9	88	12,455	1.1	120,778	6	78	13,744	1.2	198,167	(D)
Illinois	171	1,316	14,812	21.8	127,643	212	1,502	17,395	27.1	127,939	14.1
Indiana	56	828	18,531	16.3	291,804	75	797	20,949	17.3	230,280	(D)
Iowa	30	571	22,221	13.2	439,000	33	278	21,957	6.0	181,606	(D)
Kansas	25	283	21,470	6.1	244,000	37	271	23,085	6.3	171,324	(D)
Kentucky	33	318	15,082	5.1	153,667	64	324	17,333	5.9	91,594	1.9
Louisiana	35	207	14,628	3.3	93,086	46	180	14,489	2.8	60,543	(D)
Maine	20	90	21,689	2.1	106,150	23	94	22,979	2.6	111,391	4.4
Maryland	75	1,446	19,707	30.2	402,667	77	645	21,259	13.8	179,584	(D)
Massachusetts	135	1,303	48,485	68.0	503,844	156	1,415	48,110	77.7	498,346	8.6
Michigan	72	658	27,021	18.8	260,875	85	765	29,642	23.2	273,271	16.3
Minnesota	75	1,617	17,957	27.6	368,227	89	(D)	-	(D)	-	(D)
Mississippi	25	92	13,174	1.1	42,800	25	58	15,172	0.9	34,960	(D)
Missouri	68	475	16,589	8.5	124,941	82	522	18,084	10.7	129,890	9.9
Montana	15	86	10,744	1.0	64,533	15	(D)	-	(D)	-	-
Nebraska	35	436	17,936	7.8	221,657	48	484	17,537	8.6	179,667	11.0
Nevada	13	18	26,667	0.9	69,462	14	22	35,636	0.8	59,643	22.2
New Hampshire	25	409	13,575	5.3	213,160	28	254	19,559	4.9	176,464	(D)
New Jersey	75	821	25,393	20.6	274,227	95	690	30,719	21.8	229,726	(D)
New Mexico	31	368	16,511	6.2	200,097	35	414	14,763	6.5	185,114	12.5
New York	443	5,871	24,366	146.0	329,670	493	5,272	27,154	144.7	293,582	(D)
North Carolina	71	578	19,142	11.7	164,493	91	581	19,539	12.3	135,297	0.5
North Dakota	11	(D)	-	(D)	-	15	172	11,442	2.7	182,600	-
Ohio	92	772	21,549	15.5	168,261	110	766	17,629	12.9	117,336	(D)
Oklahoma	50	528	19,955	9.7	193,800	56	460	24,913	10.8	193,429	(D)
Oregon	42	246	13,805	3.6	85,571	45	223	17,274	4.0	89,267	(D)
Pennsylvania	181	2,148	15,361	37.2	205,564	203	1,848	18,662	37.3	183,985	(D)
Rhode Island	19	105	19,238	2.1	108,526	21	64	26,125	1.8	86,000	(D)
South Carolina	19	66	26,000	1.9	98,737	39	95	23,326	2.5	62,974	43.9
South Dakota	11	45	16,711	0.8	71,636	9	20	12,600	0.3	28,333	(D)
Tennessee	51	(D)	-	(D)	-	70	337	21,092	7.4	106,314	-
Texas	201	2,309	20,310	57.5	285,965	302	1,915	17,963	35.2	116,483	(D)
Utah	21	109	15,046	1.4	67,619	25	93	15,011	1.3	53,120	(D)
Vermont	13	77	15,584	1.7	129,923	15	76	20,105	2.2	143,933	(D)
Virginia	102	1,003	19,059	19.3	188,784	113	927	21,018	21.4	189,761	(D)
Washington	84	415	15,981	7.3	87,500	106	627	15,279	10.6	99,792	51.1
West Virginia	17	136	13,853	2.1	121,118	20	126	14,349	2.0	98,950	(D)
Wisconsin	38	259	15,954	4.3	113,737	48	283	19,873	5.5	115,063	9.3
Wyoming	8	17	16,235	0.3	34,625	10	24	17,333	0.5	45,300	41.2

Source: County Business Patterns, U.S. Department of Commerce, Washington, D.C., for 1992 and 1993. Employment shown is for mid-March of the year shown. Payroll per employee is calculated by annualizing 1st Quarter payroll (not shown) and then dividing that value by mid-March employment. Dividing total annual payroll (columns 5 and 10) by employment, therefore, will *not* yield the payroll per employee figure (columns 4 and 9). The symbol (D) indicates that data are withheld by the source to avoid disclosure of competitive information. A dash (-) indicates that data are not available or cannot be calculated.

ESTABLISHMENTS 1991 - STATE AND REGIONAL CONCENTRATION

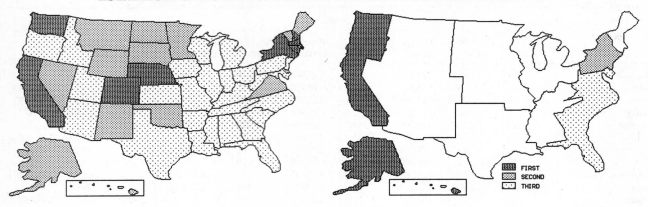

EMPLOYMENT 1991 - STATE AND REGIONAL CONCENTRATION

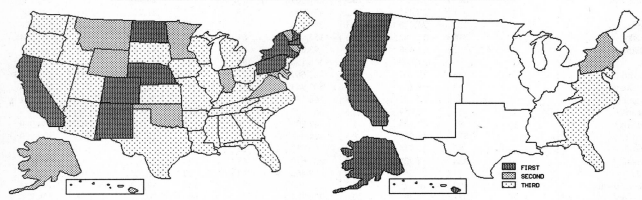

PAYROLL 1991 - STATE AND REGIONAL CONCENTRATION

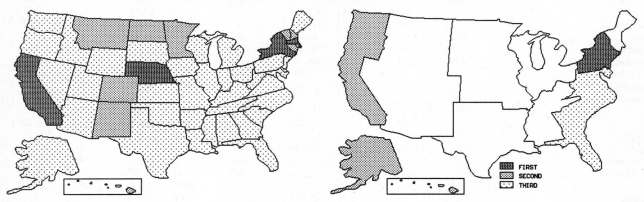

States with the darkest shading indicate those states which have proportionately more establishments, employment, or payrolls than would be indicated by the state's population. States with light shading are states with proportionately fewer establishments, less employment, and lower payrolls than population distribution. States shaded grey are within 15 percent of the state's population proportion in these catego-ries. States for which no data are available are shown as average (grey). *Regions* are shaded to indicate absolute rank in the category. If no data for the category are available, establishment counts are used to shade the regions. Source of the data is the table on the facing page.

LEADING COMPANIES - SIC 6732 - Educational, Religious, etc. Trusts

No company data available for this industry.

SIC 6733

TRUSTS, NEC

The primary activity of establishments classified under SIC 6733 is to manage the funds of trusts and foundations that are organized for purposes other than religious, educational, charitable, or nonprofit research (which are included under SIC 6732, previous chapter). This SIC includes the administration of private estates, personal investment trusts, trusteeships, vacation funds for employees, and other similar trust funds without educational, religious, charitable, or research purposes.

ESTABLISHMENTS, EMPLOYMENT, AND PAYROLL

	1988	1989		1990		1991		1992		1993		% change 88-93
		Value	%	Value	%	Value	%	Value	%	Value	%	
All Establishments	4,521	4,283	-5.3	4,234	-1.1	6,411	51.4	6,060	-5.5	5,648	-6.8	24.9
Mid-March Employment	27,569	25,853	-6.2	23,682	-8.4	25,163	6.3	27,630	9.8	28,135	1.8	2.1
1st Quarter Wages (annualized - $ mil.)	588.7	537.8	-8.7	505.9	-5.9	533.6	5.5	684.4	28.3	625.0	-8.7	6.2
Payroll per Emp. 1st Q. (annualized)	21,355	20,802	-2.6	21,363	2.7	21,206	-0.7	24,770	16.8	22,215	-10.3	4.0
Annual Payroll ($ mil.)	589.1	574.0	-2.6	532.7	-7.2	655.8	23.1	752.9	14.8	712.9	-5.3	21.0
Establishments - 1-4 Emp. Number	3,431	3,229	-5.9	3,174	-1.7	5,305	67.1	4,889	-7.8	4,575	-6.4	33.3
Mid-March Employment	5,492	5,168	-5.9	5,094	-1.4	5,587	9.7	6,130	9.7	5,839	-4.7	6.3
1st Quarter Wages (annualized - $ mil.)	106.1	109.6	3.3	115.1	5.0	103.7	-9.9	120.4	16.0	120.1	-0.2	13.2
Payroll per Emp. 1st Q. (annualized)	19,319	21,207	9.8	22,601	6.6	18,570	-17.8	19,636	5.7	20,575	4.8	6.5
Annual Payroll ($ mil.)	116.6	119.8	2.8	130.1	8.5	224.4	72.5	183.8	-18.1	198.5	8.0	70.3
Establishments - 5-9 Emp. Number	573	541	-5.6	532	-1.7	593	11.5	631	6.4	542	-14.1	-5.4
Mid-March Employment	3,718	3,586	-3.6	3,478	-3.0	3,887	11.8	4,121	6.0	3,537	-14.2	-4.9
1st Quarter Wages (annualized - $ mil.)	67.2	64.7	-3.7	64.3	-0.7	75.8	18.0	92.4	21.8	83.9	-9.2	24.7
Payroll per Emp. 1st Q. (annualized)	18,081	18,055	-0.1	18,483	2.4	19,510	5.6	22,421	14.9	23,707	5.7	31.1
Annual Payroll ($ mil.)	67.7	69.2	2.3	69.8	0.8	76.1	9.0	90.3	18.6	83.1	-8.0	22.7
Establishments - 10-19 Emp. Number	280	270	-3.6	301	11.5	289	-4.0	330	14.2	306	-7.3	9.3
Mid-March Employment	3,777	3,638	-3.7	4,050	11.3	3,777	-6.7	4,415	16.9	4,114	-6.8	8.9
1st Quarter Wages (annualized - $ mil.)	69.8	64.9	-7.1	80.5	24.2	76.6	-4.8	100.6	31.3	104.9	4.3	50.3
Payroll per Emp. 1st Q. (annualized)	18,480	17,826	-3.5	19,882	11.5	20,286	2.0	22,787	12.3	25,509	11.9	38.0
Annual Payroll ($ mil.)	68.9	67.9	-1.4	83.1	22.4	84.2	1.3	109.5	30.0	119.5	9.1	73.4
Establishments - 20-49 Emp. Number	157	167	6.4	167	-	184	10.2	168	-8.7	144	-14.3	-8.3
Mid-March Employment	4,729	5,040	6.6	5,132	1.8	5,643	10.0	5,092	-9.8	4,210	-17.3	-11.0
1st Quarter Wages (annualized - $ mil.)	88.9	98.8	11.2	106.8	8.1	110.0	3.0	111.0	0.9	86.4	-22.2	-2.8
Payroll per Emp. 1st Q. (annualized)	18,789	19,605	4.3	20,812	6.2	19,494	-6.3	21,790	11.8	20,512	-5.9	9.2
Annual Payroll ($ mil.)	83.4	96.5	15.7	108.2	12.1	99.9	-7.7	112.6	12.8	82.5	-26.7	-1.0
Establishments - 50-99 Emp. Number	49	51	4.1	45	-11.8	21	-53.3	(D)	-	(D)	-	-
Mid-March Employment	(D)	3,568	-	3,068	-14.0	1,477	-51.9	(D)	-	(D)	-	-
1st Quarter Wages (annualized - $ mil.)	(D)	84.4	-	64.2	-23.9	43.1	-32.8	(D)	-	(D)	-	-
Payroll per Emp. 1st Q. (annualized)	(D)	23,642	-	20,920	-11.5	29,197	39.6	(D)	-	(D)	-	-
Annual Payroll ($ mil.)	(D)	104.1	-	67.1	-35.5	46.0	-31.4	(D)	-	(D)	-	-
Establishments - 100-249 Emp. Number	22	20	-9.1	11	-45.0	13	18.2	12	-7.7	22	83.3	-
Mid-March Employment	3,073	2,760	-10.2	1,446	-47.6	2,149	48.6	1,903	-11.4	3,730	96.0	21.4
1st Quarter Wages (annualized - $ mil.)	62.0	59.5	-4.1	36.9	-37.9	51.3	38.9	49.4	-3.7	81.4	64.8	31.2
Payroll per Emp. 1st Q. (annualized)	20,182	21,559	6.8	25,535	18.4	23,862	-6.6	25,940	8.7	21,810	-15.9	8.1
Annual Payroll ($ mil.)	64.3	62.5	-2.8	37.4	-40.1	53.2	42.1	50.6	-4.9	83.8	65.7	30.3
Establishments - 250-499 Emp. Number	8	4	-50.0	4	-	4	-	10	150.0	5	-50.0	-37.5
Mid-March Employment	2,869	(D)	-	1,414	-	(D)	-	3,604	-	1,853	-48.6	-35.4
1st Quarter Wages (annualized - $ mil.)	111.0	(D)	-	38.1	-	(D)	-	138.9	-	37.7	-72.8	-66.0
Payroll per Emp. 1st Q. (annualized)	38,706	(D)	-	26,925	-	(D)	-	38,528	-	20,356	-47.2	-47.4
Annual Payroll ($ mil.)	104.2	(D)	-	37.0	-	(D)	-	143.0	-	37.2	-74.0	-64.3
Establishments - 500-999 Emp. Number	1	1	-	-	-	2	-	(D)	-	(D)	-	-
Mid-March Employment	(D)	(D)	-	-	-	(D)	-	(D)	-	(D)	-	-
1st Quarter Wages (annualized - $ mil.)	(D)	(D)	-	-	-	(D)	-	(D)	-	(D)	-	-
Payroll per Emp. 1st Q. (annualized)	(D)	(D)	-	(D)	-	(D)	-	(D)	-	(D)	-	-
Annual Payroll ($ mil.)	(D)	(D)	-	-	-	(D)	-	(D)	-	(D)	-	-
Estab. - 1000 or More Emp. Number	-	-	-	-	-	-	-	-	-	-	-	-
Mid-March Employment	-	-	-	-	-	-	-	-	-	-	-	-
1st Quarter Wages (annualized - $ mil.)	-	-	-	-	-	-	-	-	-	-	-	-
Payroll per Emp. 1st Q. (annualized)	(D)	(D)	-	(D)	-	(D)	-	-	-	-	-	-
Annual Payroll ($ mil.)	-	-	-	-	-	-	-	-	-	-	-	-

Source: County Business Patterns, U.S. Department of Commerce, Washington, D.C., for 1988 through 1993. Payroll per employee is calculated using mid-March employment and 1st Quarter wages, annualized. Annual payroll, also shown, may not equal the annualized 1st Quarter wages. Columns headed by a percent sign (%) indicate change from the previous year. *na* stands for not available. The symbol (D) indicates that data are withheld by the source to avoid disclosure of competitive information. A dash (-) indicates that data are not available or cannot be calculated.

ESTABLISHMENTS
Number

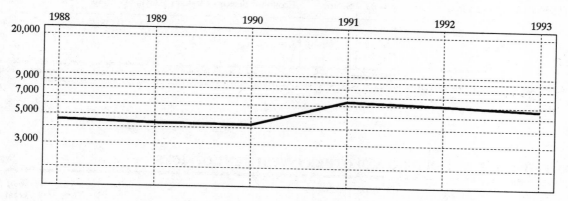

MID-MARCH EMPLOYMENT
Number

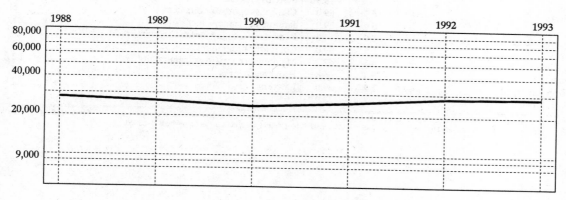

ANNUAL PAYROLL
$ million

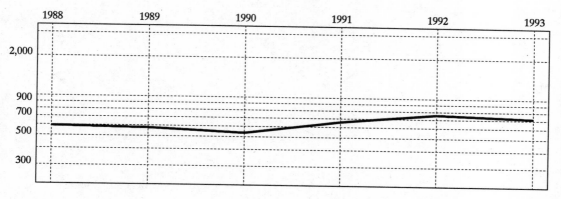

INPUTS AND OUTPUTS FOR HOLDING AND OTHER INVESTMENT OFFICES - SIC GROUP 67

Economic Sector or Industry Providing Inputs	%	Sector	Economic Sector or Industry Buying Outputs	%	Sector
No Input-Output data are available for this industry group.					

Source: Benchmark Input-Output Accounts for the U.S. Economy, 1982, U.S. Department of Commerce, Washington, D.C., July 1991. Data, as reported in the source, are organized by the 1977 SIC structure in use in 1982 but have been matched, as closely as is possible, to the 1987 SIC structure used in this book. Activities with the same percentage are sorted alphabetically by name of activity.

OCCUPATIONS EMPLOYED BY HOLDING AND OTHER INVESTMENT OFFICES

Occupation	% of Total 1994	Change to 2005	Occupation	% of Total 1994	Change to 2005
Secretaries, ex legal & medical	10.7	26.5	Marketing & sales worker supervisors	1.8	39.0
General managers & top executives	10.4	31.8	Securities & financial services sales workers	1.6	39.0
General office clerks	7.7	18.5	Systems analysts	1.5	122.3
Accountants & auditors	6.1	39.0	Clerical support workers nec	1.5	11.2
Financial managers	6.0	39.0	Janitors & cleaners, incl maids	1.5	11.2
Bookkeeping, accounting, & auditing clerks	6.0	4.2	Personnel, training, & labor specialists	1.4	54.8
Management support workers nec	5.5	39.0	Computer programmers	1.2	12.6
Clerical supervisors & managers	4.5	42.2	Maintenance repairers, general utility	1.2	25.1
Professional workers nec	3.4	66.8	Brokerage clerks	1.2	11.2
Receptionists & information clerks	2.2	39.0	Lawyers	1.2	39.0
Managers & administrators nec	2.1	38.9			

Sources: Industry-Occupation Matrix, Bureau of Labor Statistics. These data relate to one or more 3-digit SIC industry groups rather than to a single 4-digit SIC. The change reported for each occupation to the year 2005 is a percent of growth or decline as estimated by the Bureau of Labor Statistics. The abbreviation nec stands for not elsewhere classified.

STATE-BY-STATE DATA ON ESTABLISHMENTS, EMPLOYMENT, AND PAYROLL - 1990 AND 1991

State	1990					1991					% Change Empl.
	No. of Estab.	Employ-ment	Pay / Empl.	Payroll ($ mil.)	Pay / Estab.	No. of Estab.	Employ-ment	Pay / Empl.	Payroll ($ mil.)	Pay / Estab.	
Alabama	46	139	14,763	2.2	48,457	74	240	13,783	3.2	43,703	72.7
Alaska	16	47	24,851	1.0	62,188	22	71	17,915	1.6	73,591	51.1
Arizona	74	688	21,035	14.1	190,743	115	518	20,463	13.1	113,600	(D)
Arkansas	32	187	20,770	3.9	121,812	43	178	19,978	5.6	129,279	(D)
California	771	4,592	20,786	101.9	132,154	1,006	4,045	22,380	97.5	96,896	(D)
Colorado	74	790	17,332	14.1	190,338	87	927	22,179	21.0	241,644	17.3
Connecticut	56	260	26,523	7.8	139,089	96	246	13,902	5.8	60,677	(D)
Delaware	20	144	34,278	4.6	231,650	38	207	29,469	5.9	155,132	43.8
District of Columbia	35	323	29,288	11.3	321,657	56	317	25,110	18.5	330,125	(D)
Florida	191	1,024	19,297	23.2	121,445	313	1,092	20,480	28.7	91,767	6.6
Georgia	58	454	15,859	7.6	131,569	95	325	15,163	10.9	114,537	(D)
Hawaii	44	575	30,991	18.0	408,545	94	309	22,718	8.5	90,351	(D)
Idaho	12	46	15,652	0.8	70,333	19	61	15,934	1.0	50,474	32.6
Illinois	190	1,184	19,145	22.5	118,321	320	1,122	19,590	34.7	108,438	(D)
Indiana	61	212	15,358	4.8	78,426	118	597	18,432	11.9	101,169	181.6
Iowa	34	95	14,021	1.7	50,971	65	122	11,803	1.7	25,492	28.4
Kansas	43	187	12,727	2.9	67,767	104	244	12,852	3.4	32,962	30.5
Kentucky	41	161	14,335	3.3	80,049	55	121	8,033	1.5	27,218	(D)
Louisiana	57	161	14,261	2.3	39,614	63	119	15,496	8.1	128,238	(D)
Maine	14	75	10,987	0.8	59,857	45	80	11,100	0.9	19,822	6.7
Maryland	52	213	15,662	3.2	61,692	154	603	20,829	14.4	93,545	183.1
Massachusetts	217	885	20,176	20.9	96,276	235	828	33,647	31.7	134,991	(D)
Michigan	92	432	19,917	8.8	96,033	218	516	12,000	9.1	41,729	19.4
Minnesota	61	482	19,311	9.8	160,016	99	(D)	-	(D)	-	-
Mississippi	21	59	13,017	1.0	45,667	42	107	10,654	1.2	27,571	81.4
Missouri	73	330	14,655	5.3	71,932	146	763	19,953	17.8	121,781	131.2
Montana	16	84	17,524	1.4	86,812	17	(D)	-	(D)	-	-
Nebraska	31	78	15,231	1.4	46,161	57	151	12,901	2.4	42,491	93.6
Nevada	49	193	14,756	3.2	66,265	54	189	15,090	3.3	60,315	(D)
New Hampshire	18	103	16,117	1.8	99,222	26	93	25,247	2.2	86,192	(D)
New Jersey	65	260	23,292	6.4	98,600	118	361	20,299	8.9	75,220	38.8
New Mexico	21	58	12,828	0.9	41,333	37	148	10,541	2.2	58,703	155.2
New York	285	1,809	38,273	63.3	221,951	366	2,891	31,473	98.8	269,986	59.8
North Carolina	55	285	20,716	5.7	103,364	79	254	19,386	6.1	77,076	(D)
North Dakota	10	(D)	-	(D)	-	20	49	11,102	0.6	31,900	-
Ohio	130	755	13,695	12.0	92,423	223	866	16,841	17.5	78,601	14.7
Oklahoma	132	468	14,205	7.4	56,265	146	660	10,576	8.1	55,788	41.0
Oregon	68	504	15,571	8.2	119,941	87	358	13,933	7.0	80,310	(D)
Pennsylvania	147	1,043	19,333	24.9	169,252	236	795	17,716	31.4	133,051	(D)
Rhode Island	11	50	12,240	0.9	81,000	22	64	16,938	3.0	135,818	28.0
South Carolina	43	120	25,533	3.0	68,930	48	87	19,310	1.8	37,625	(D)
South Dakota	10	46	16,870	0.8	76,600	26	45	10,044	0.5	20,154	(D)
Tennessee	64	(D)	-	(D)	-	69	271	14,568	4.5	64,855	-
Texas	419	2,076	22,911	50.5	120,535	582	2,155	22,283	55.3	94,986	3.8
Utah	17	91	14,066	1.3	77,588	29	77	17,247	1.6	56,379	(D)
Vermont	15	89	24,090	2.1	140,667	30	96	22,417	2.1	70,733	7.9
Virginia	73	446	20,269	10.1	138,438	135	347	17,452	7.8	57,733	(D)
Washington	64	436	23,596	9.0	140,438	141	478	26,787	15.0	106,716	9.6
West Virginia	26	58	8,069	0.6	23,154	38	66	9,455	0.9	24,632	13.8
Wisconsin	71	473	26,554	13.3	187,972	85	288	21,819	6.8	79,847	(D)
Wyoming	9	23	13,217	0.3	31,444	18	43	8,930	0.5	27,222	87.0

Source: County Business Patterns, U.S. Department of Commerce, Washington, D.C., for 1992 and 1993. Employment shown is for mid-March of the year shown. Payroll per employee is calculated by annualizing 1st Quarter payroll (not shown) and then dividing that value by mid-March employment. Dividing total annual payroll (columns 5 and 10) by employment, therefore, will *not* yield the payroll per employee figure (columns 4 and 9). The symbol (D) indicates that data are withheld by the source to avoid disclosure of competitive information. A dash (-) indicates that data are not available or cannot be calculated.

ESTABLISHMENTS 1991 - STATE AND REGIONAL CONCENTRATION

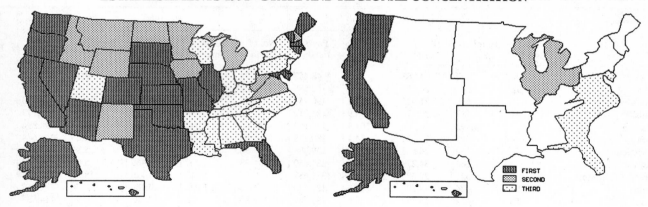

EMPLOYMENT 1991 - STATE AND REGIONAL CONCENTRATION

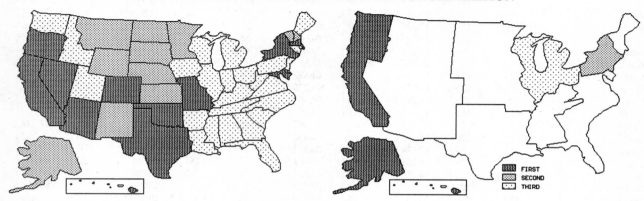

PAYROLL 1991 - STATE AND REGIONAL CONCENTRATION

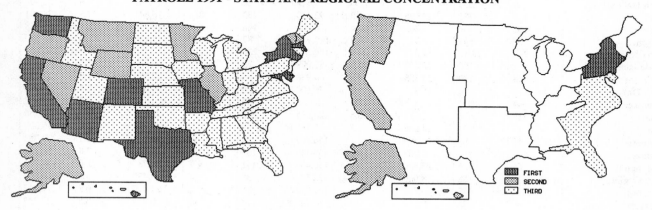

States with the darkest shading indicate those states which have proportionately more establishments, employment, or payrolls than would be indicated by the state's population. States with light shading are states with proportionately fewer establishments, less employment, and lower payrolls than population distribution. States shaded grey are within 15 percent of the state's population proportion in these categories. States for which no data are available are shown as average (grey). *Regions* are shaded to indicate absolute rank in the category. If no data for the category are available, establishment counts are used to shade the regions. Source of the data is the table on the facing page.

LEADING COMPANIES - SIC 6733 - Trusts, nec

Number shown: **1**   Total sales/assets ($ mil): **13,794**   Total employment (000): **9.7**

Company Name	Address				CEO Name	Phone	Co. Type	Sales/Assets ($ mil)	Empl. (000)
Firstar Corp.	777 E. Wisconsin Ave.	Milwaukee	WI	53202	Roger L. Fitzsimonds	414-765-4321	P	13,794 TA	9.7

Source: Ward's Business Directory of U.S. Private and Public Companies, 1996. Company type codes: P - Public, R - Private, S - Subsidiary, D - Division, J - Joint Venture, A - Affiliate, G - Group. If the dollar values shown are not sales, the following codes apply: TA - Total Assets; OR - Operating Revenues; GB - Gross Billings. * - estimated dollar value. < - less than; *na* - not available.

SIC 6792

OIL ROYALTY TRADERS

Establishments in this industry invest in oil and gas royalties or leases; they may own or have only fractional interests in such properties. Activities in this category include buying and selling of oil leases on own account and operation of oil royalty companies.

ESTABLISHMENTS, EMPLOYMENT, AND PAYROLL

	1988	1989		1990		1991		1992		1993		% change 88-93
		Value	%	Value	%	Value	%	Value	%	Value	%	
All Establishments	599	551	-8.0	582	5.6	465	-20.1	603	29.7	774	28.4	29.2
Mid-March Employment	2,758	2,492	-9.6	2,369	-4.9	1,561	-34.1	2,202	41.1	2,621	19.0	-5.0
1st Quarter Wages (annualized - $ mil.)	93.1	78.1	-16.1	76.9	-1.6	55.3	-28.1	86.2	55.8	94.3	9.4	1.3
Payroll per Emp. 1st Q. (annualized)	33,751	31,352	-7.1	32,449	3.5	35,426	9.2	39,128	10.5	35,963	-8.1	6.6
Annual Payroll ($ mil.)	89.5	80.3	-10.3	79.3	-1.3	59.0	-25.6	94.0	59.4	102.5	9.0	14.4
Establishments - 1-4 Emp. Number	462	435	-5.8	469	7.8	390	-16.8	488	25.1	634	29.9	37.2
Mid-March Employment	(D)	801	-	831	3.7	642	-22.7	796	24.0	993	24.7	-
1st Quarter Wages (annualized - $ mil.)	(D)	26.6	-	26.7	0.5	17.7	-33.8	27.8	57.2	30.4	9.6	-
Payroll per Emp. 1st Q. (annualized)	(D)	33,154	-	32,111	-3.1	27,502	-14.4	34,864	26.8	30,626	-12.2	
Annual Payroll ($ mil.)	(D)	24.9	-	26.6	7.0	18.7	-29.8	28.4	51.9	34.5	21.5	-
Establishments - 5-9 Emp. Number	90	80	-11.1	72	-10.0	46	-36.1	70	52.2	(D)	-	-
Mid-March Employment	(D)	515	-	474	-8.0	(D)	-	451	-	(D)	-	-
1st Quarter Wages (annualized - $ mil.)	(D)	18.7	-	17.1	-8.4	(D)	-	17.7	-	(D)	-	-
Payroll per Emp. 1st Q. (annualized)	(D)	36,264	-	36,101	-0.4	(D)	-	39,202	-	(D)	-	-
Annual Payroll ($ mil.)	(D)	18.4	-	16.4	-11.0	(D)	-	18.9	-	(D)	-	-
Establishments - 10-19 Emp. Number	27	23	-14.8	26	13.0	21	-19.2	30	42.9	31	3.3	14.8
Mid-March Employment	(D)	(D)	-	320	-	276	-13.8	405	46.7	433	6.9	-
1st Quarter Wages (annualized - $ mil.)	(D)	(D)	-	11.3	-	12.7	11.7	18.4	45.5	19.5	5.9	-
Payroll per Emp. 1st Q. (annualized)	(D)	(D)	-	35,438	-	45,899	29.5	45,501	-0.9	45,053	-1.0	-
Annual Payroll ($ mil.)	(D)	(D)	-	12.5	-	13.0	3.6	20.2	55.6	20.8	3.2	-
Establishments - 20-49 Emp. Number	15	6	-60.0	11	83.3	6	-45.5	(D)	-	(D)	-	-
Mid-March Employment	407	171	-58.0	328	91.8	160	-51.2	(D)	-	(D)	-	-
1st Quarter Wages (annualized - $ mil.)	13.7	6.1	-55.8	10.2	67.5	6.6	-35.3	(D)	-	(D)	-	-
Payroll per Emp. 1st Q. (annualized)	33,779	35,532	5.2	31,024	-12.7	41,125	32.6	(D)	-	(D)	-	-
Annual Payroll ($ mil.)	13.6	6.8	-50.5	10.8	60.6	8.7	-19.3	(D)	-	(D)	-	-
Establishments - 50-99 Emp. Number	2	4	100.0	2	-50.0	2	-	(D)	-	6	-	200.0
Mid-March Employment	(D)	262	-	(D)	-	(D)	-	(D)	-	361	-	-
1st Quarter Wages (annualized - $ mil.)	(D)	5.8	-	(D)	-	(D)	-	(D)	-	13.3	-	-
Payroll per Emp. 1st Q. (annualized)	(D)	22,000	-	(D)	-	(D)	-	(D)	-	36,931	-	-
Annual Payroll ($ mil.)	(D)	6.1	-	(D)	-	(D)	-	(D)	-	14.4	-	-
Establishments - 100-249 Emp. Number	3	3	-	2	-33.3	-	-	-	-	-	-	-
Mid-March Employment	428	(D)	-	(D)	-	-	-	-	-	-	-	-
1st Quarter Wages (annualized - $ mil.)	10.6	(D)	-	(D)	-	-	-	-	-	-	-	-
Payroll per Emp. 1st Q. (annualized)	24,822	(D)	-	(D)	-	(D)	-	-	-	-	-	-
Annual Payroll ($ mil.)	12.1	(D)	-	(D)	-	-	-	-	-	-	-	-
Establishments - 250-499 Emp. Number	-	-	-	-	-	-	-	-	-	-	-	-
Mid-March Employment	-	-	-	-	-	-	-	-	-	-	-	-
1st Quarter Wages (annualized - $ mil.)	-	-	-	-	-	-	-	-	-	-	-	-
Payroll per Emp. 1st Q. (annualized)	(D)	(D)	-	(D)	-	(D)	-	-	-	-	-	-
Annual Payroll ($ mil.)	-	-	-	-	-	-	-	-	-	-	-	-
Establishments - 500-999 Emp. Number	-	-	-	-	-	-	-	-	-	-	-	-
Mid-March Employment	-	-	-	-	-	-	-	-	-	-	-	-
1st Quarter Wages (annualized - $ mil.)	-	-	-	-	-	-	-	-	-	-	-	-
Payroll per Emp. 1st Q. (annualized)	(D)	(D)	-	(D)	-	(D)	-	-	-	-	-	-
Annual Payroll ($ mil.)	-	-	-	-	-	-	-	-	-	-	-	-
Estab. - 1000 or More Emp. Number	-	-	-	-	-	-	-	-	-	-	-	-
Mid-March Employment	-	-	-	-	-	-	-	-	-	-	-	-
1st Quarter Wages (annualized - $ mil.)	-	-	-	-	-	-	-	-	-	-	-	-
Payroll per Emp. 1st Q. (annualized)	(D)	(D)	-	(D)	-	(D)	-	-	-	-	-	-
Annual Payroll ($ mil.)	-	-	-	-	-	-	-	-	-	-	-	-

Source: County Business Patterns, U.S. Department of Commerce, Washington, D.C., for 1988 through 1993. Payroll per employee is calculated using mid-March employment and 1st Quarter wages, annualized. Annual payroll, also shown, may not equal the annualized 1st Quarter wages. Columns headed by a percent sign (%) indicate change from the previous year. *na* stands for not available. The symbol (D) indicates that data are withheld by the source to avoid disclosure of competitive information. A dash (-) indicates that data are not available or cannot be calculated.

ESTABLISHMENTS
Number

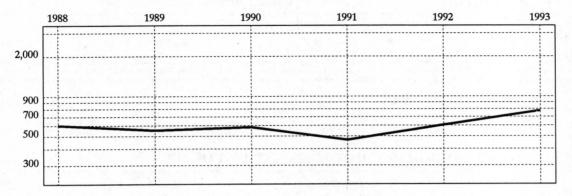

MID-MARCH EMPLOYMENT
Number

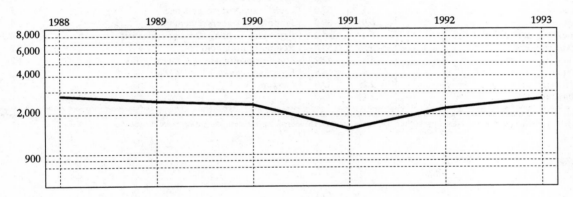

ANNUAL PAYROLL
$ million

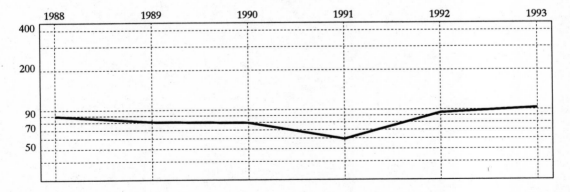

INPUTS AND OUTPUTS FOR HOLDING AND OTHER INVESTMENT OFFICES - SIC GROUP 67

Economic Sector or Industry Providing Inputs	%	Sector	Economic Sector or Industry Buying Outputs	%	Sector
No Input-Output data are available for this industry group.					

Source: Benchmark Input-Output Accounts for the U.S. Economy, 1982, U.S. Department of Commerce, Washington, D.C., July 1991. Data, as reported in the source, are organized by the 1977 SIC structure in use in 1982 but have been matched, as closely as is possible, to the 1987 SIC structure used in this book. Activities with the same percentage are sorted alphabetically by name of activity.

OCCUPATIONS EMPLOYED BY HOLDING AND OTHER INVESTMENT OFFICES

Occupation	% of Total 1994	Change to 2005	Occupation	% of Total 1994	Change to 2005
Secretaries, ex legal & medical	10.7	26.5	Marketing & sales worker supervisors	1.8	39.0
General managers & top executives	10.4	31.8	Securities & financial services sales workers	1.6	39.0
General office clerks	7.7	18.5	Systems analysts	1.5	122.3
Accountants & auditors	6.1	39.0	Clerical support workers nec	1.5	11.2
Financial managers	6.0	39.0	Janitors & cleaners, incl maids	1.5	11.2
Bookkeeping, accounting, & auditing clerks	6.0	4.2	Personnel, training, & labor specialists	1.4	54.8
Management support workers nec	5.5	39.0	Computer programmers	1.2	12.6
Clerical supervisors & managers	4.5	42.2	Maintenance repairers, general utility	1.2	25.1
Professional workers nec	3.4	66.8	Brokerage clerks	1.2	11.2
Receptionists & information clerks	2.2	39.0	Lawyers	1.2	39.0
Managers & administrators nec	2.1	38.9			

Sources: Industry-Occupation Matrix, Bureau of Labor Statistics. These data relate to one or more 3-digit SIC industry groups rather than to a single 4-digit SIC. The change reported for each occupation to the year 2005 is a percent of growth or decline as estimated by the Bureau of Labor Statistics. The abbreviation nec stands for not elsewhere classified.

U.S. AND STATE DATA ON INDUSTRY REVENUES AND OTHER ACCOUNTS FOR 1992

State	No. of Estab.	Employ-ment	Payroll ($ mil.)	Revenues ($ mil.)	Empl./ Estab.	Revenue/ Estab. ($)	Payroll/ Estab. ($)	Revenue/ Empl. ($)	Payroll/ Empl. ($)
UNITED STATES	746	2,228	92.7	686.7	3	920,462	124,311	308,198	41,623
California	38	95	2.6	43.3	3	1,139,079	68,079	455,632	27,232
Colorado	35	94	3.6	37.2	3	1,061,686	103,000	395,309	38,351
Florida	7	14	0.5	2.2	2	315,286	72,857	157,643	36,429
Georgia	5	3	0.2	0.9	1	186,200	32,600	310,333	54,333
Illinois	14	18	1.1	5.7	1	405,857	78,000	315,667	60,667
Indiana	3	-	(D)	(D)	(D)	(D)	(D)	(D)	(D)
Maryland	1	-	(D)	(D)	(D)	(D)	(D)	(D)	(D)
Massachusetts	4	-	(D)	(D)	(D)	(D)	(D)	(D)	(D)
Michigan	11	21	0.6	3.7	2	340,182	52,091	178,190	27,286
Minnesota	4	-	(D)	(D)	(D)	(D)	(D)	(D)	(D)
Missouri	5	-	(D)	(D)	(D)	(D)	(D)	(D)	(D)
New Jersey	2	-	(D)	(D)	(D)	(D)	(D)	(D)	(D)
New York	20	-	(D)	(D)	(D)	(D)	(D)	(D)	(D)
North Carolina	1	-	(D)	(D)	(D)	(D)	(D)	(D)	(D)
Ohio	10	30	1.1	4.1	3	412,300	112,300	137,433	37,433
Pennsylvania	13	-	(D)	(D)	(D)	(D)	(D)	(D)	(D)
Tennessee	1	-	(D)	(D)	(D)	(D)	(D)	(D)	(D)
Texas	307	1,013	46.6	280.5	3	913,697	151,795	276,905	46,003
Virginia	2	-	(D)	(D)	(D)	(D)	(D)	(D)	(D)
Wisconsin	2	-	(D)	(D)	(D)	(D)	(D)	(D)	(D)

Source: 1992 Economic Census, U.S. Department of Commerce, Washington, D.C. This is the only table that shows revenue data as collected by the Bureau of the Census in an Economic Census. The symbol (D) indicates that data are withheld by the source to avoid disclosure of competitive information. A dash (-) indicates that data are not available or cannot be calculated.

ESTABLISHMENTS 1992 - STATE AND REGIONAL CONCENTRATION

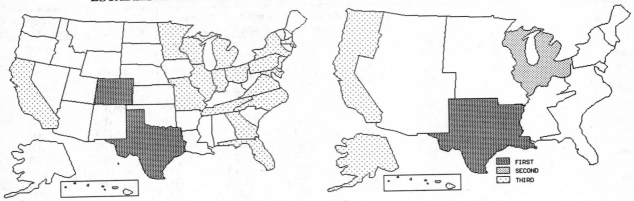

EMPLOYMENT 1992 - STATE AND REGIONAL CONCENTRATION

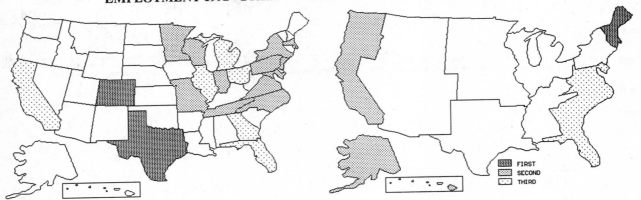

REVENUES 1992 - STATE AND REGIONAL CONCENTRATION

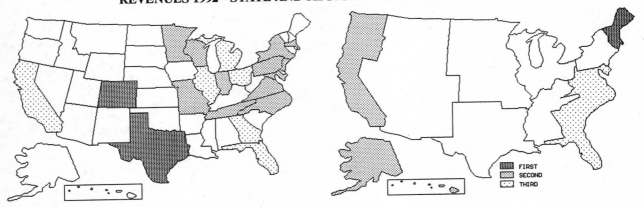

States with the darkest shading indicate those states which have proportionately more establishments, employment, or revenues than would be indicated by the state's population. States with light shading are states with proportionately fewer establishments, less employment, and lower revenues than population distribution. States shaded grey are within 15 percent of the state's population proportion in these categories. States for which no data are available are shown as average (grey). *Regions* are shaded to indicate absolute rank in the category. If no data for the category are available, establishment counts are used to shade the regions. Source of the data is the table on the facing page.

LEADING COMPANIES - SIC 6792 - Oil Royalty Traders

Number shown: **14**   Total sales/assets ($ mil): **100**   Total employment (000): **0.2**

Company Name	Address				CEO Name	Phone	Co. Type	Sales/Assets ($ mil)	Empl. (000)
Tripower Resources Inc.	P.O. Box 849	Ardmore	OK	73402	John D. Gibbs	405-226-6700	S	23 TA	<0.1
Tejon Ranch Co.	P.O. Box 1000	Lebec	CA	93243	Jack Hunt	805-327-8481	P	17	<0.1
Texas Pacific Land Trust	80 Broad St.	New York	NY	10004	George C. Fraser III	212-269-2266	P	15 TA	<0.1
Toreador Royalty Corp.	8117 Preston Rd.	Dallas	TX	75225	Peter R. Vig	214-369-0080	P	8 TA	<0.1
Panhandle Royalty Co.	5400 N.W. Grand Blvd.	Oklahoma City	OK	73112	H.W. Peace II	405-948-1560	P	8 TA	<0.1
Gyrodyne Company of America Inc.	Parkside Ave.	St. James	NY	11780	Dimitri P. Papadakos	516-584-5400	3	7 TA	<0.1
Golden Triangle Royalty and Oil Inc.	P.O. Box 1629	Cisco	TX	76437	Robert Kamon	817-442-2665	P	5 TA	<0.1
Empire Land Corp.	P.O. Box 5902	Metairie	LA	70009	Louis Roussel	504-837-2230	R	4 TA*	<0.1
TPEX Exploration Inc.	999 18th St.	Denver	CO	80202	Timothy L. Hoops	303-295-0344	P	4 TA	<0.1
Tyrex Oil Co.	P.O. Box 2459	Casper	WY	82601	John D. Traut	307-234-4260	P	3 TA	<0.1
Marine Petroleum Trust	P.O. Box 831402	Dallas	TX	75283	R. Ray Bell	214-508-1792	P	3 TA	<0.1
Seven J Stock Farm Inc.	12450 Greenspoint Dr.	Houston	TX	77060	John R. Parten	713-874-2101	R	2*	<0.1
Mountain Laurel Resources Co.	411 Main St.	Mount Hope	WV	25880	Alan T. Law	304-877-9000	R	1 TA	<0.1
Aspen Exploration Corp.	7925 E. Harvard St.	Denver	CO	80231	R.V. Bailey	303-337-3600	P	1	<0.1

Source: Ward's Business Directory of U.S. Private and Public Companies, 1996. Company type codes: P - Public, R - Private, S - Subsidiary, D - Division, J - Joint Venture, A - Affiliate, G - Group. If the dollar values shown are not sales, the following codes apply: TA - Total Assets; OR - Operating Revenues; GB - Gross Billings. * - estimated dollar value. < - less than; *na* - not available.

SIC 6794

PATENT OWNERS AND LESSORS

Patent owners and lessors are engaged primarily in owning or leasing franchises, patents, and copyrights which they, in turn, license to others for use. Activities include the buying and licensing of copyrights; the selling or licensing of franchises; the licensing of music to radio stations; music royalties on sheet music or recorded music; the buying, leasing, and licensing of patents; and the publishing and licensing of performance rights.

ESTABLISHMENTS, EMPLOYMENT, AND PAYROLL

	1988	1989		1990		1991		1992		1993		% change 88-93
		Value	%	Value	%	Value	%	Value	%	Value	%	
All Establishments	847	788	-7.0	861	9.3	864	0.3	1,146	32.6	1,606	40.1	89.6
Mid-March Employment	15,272	14,855	-2.7	15,392	3.6	13,246	-13.9	17,538	32.4	18,363	4.7	20.2
1st Quarter Wages (annualized - $ mil.)	437.5	455.8	4.2	503.7	10.5	426.6	-15.3	586.6	37.5	719.7	22.7	64.5
Payroll per Emp. 1st Q. (annualized)	28,645	30,684	7.1	32,726	6.7	32,207	-1.6	33,448	3.9	39,191	17.2	36.8
Annual Payroll ($ mil.)	448.5	443.3	-1.2	439.8	-0.8	460.7	4.8	636.3	38.1	802.4	26.1	78.9
Establishments - 1-4 Emp. Number	453	435	-4.0	484	11.3	479	-1.0	693	44.7	971	40.1	114.3
Mid-March Employment	(D)	686	-	767	11.8	765	-0.3	1,108	44.8	1,393	25.7	-
1st Quarter Wages (annualized - $ mil.)	(D)	22.1	-	24.0	8.5	24.5	2.1	103.7	323.8	46.7	-54.9	-
Payroll per Emp. 1st Q. (annualized)	(D)	32,198	-	31,244	-3.0	31,984	2.4	93,588	192.6	33,556	-64.1	-
Annual Payroll ($ mil.)	(D)	43.5	-	42.6	-2.3	37.6	-11.6	144.9	285.1	94.0	-35.1	-
Establishments - 5-9 Emp. Number	143	125	-12.6	135	8.0	150	11.1	182	21.3	249	36.8	74.1
Mid-March Employment	(D)	805	-	885	9.9	981	10.8	1,197	22.0	1,623	35.6	-
1st Quarter Wages (annualized - $ mil.)	(D)	25.0	-	33.4	33.6	38.4	14.8	36.1	-5.8	56.1	55.1	-
Payroll per Emp. 1st Q. (annualized)	(D)	31,071	-	37,754	21.5	39,099	3.6	30,195	-22.8	34,543	14.4	-
Annual Payroll ($ mil.)	(D)	24.1	-	30.3	25.5	37.3	23.0	40.4	8.4	65.0	60.9	-
Establishments - 10-19 Emp. Number	123	104	-15.4	115	10.6	113	-1.7	140	23.9	192	37.1	56.1
Mid-March Employment	1,648	1,444	-12.4	1,529	5.9	1,508	-1.4	1,896	25.7	2,503	32.0	51.9
1st Quarter Wages (annualized - $ mil.)	50.5	61.7	22.1	67.5	9.5	52.6	-22.1	68.4	29.9	90.5	32.3	79.1
Payroll per Emp. 1st Q. (annualized)	30,660	42,723	39.3	44,178	3.4	34,907	-21.0	36,059	3.3	36,145	0.2	17.9
Annual Payroll ($ mil.)	47.5	48.1	1.3	54.9	14.0	57.2	4.3	75.5	31.9	102.1	35.4	115.1
Establishments - 20-49 Emp. Number	76	72	-5.3	70	-2.8	73	4.3	85	16.4	131	54.1	72.4
Mid-March Employment	2,267	2,171	-4.2	2,033	-6.4	2,076	2.1	2,525	21.6	3,931	55.7	73.4
1st Quarter Wages (annualized - $ mil.)	75.3	65.9	-12.5	55.5	-15.9	66.9	20.6	85.6	28.0	138.1	61.4	83.3
Payroll per Emp. 1st Q. (annualized)	33,233	30,377	-8.6	27,282	-10.2	32,212	18.1	33,898	5.2	35,138	3.7	5.7
Annual Payroll ($ mil.)	72.4	65.4	-9.7	58.3	-10.8	72.3	24.1	89.1	23.2	146.1	64.0	101.8
Establishments - 50-99 Emp. Number	23	27	17.4	37	37.0	27	-27.0	(D)	-	36	-	56.5
Mid-March Employment	1,505	1,928	28.1	(D)	-	1,739	-	(D)	-	2,334	-	55.1
1st Quarter Wages (annualized - $ mil.)	42.1	54.1	28.4	(D)	-	42.1	-	(D)	-	73.9	-	75.4
Payroll per Emp. 1st Q. (annualized)	27,992	28,048	0.2	(D)	-	24,235	-	(D)	-	31,650	-	13.1
Annual Payroll ($ mil.)	38.9	55.4	42.4	(D)	-	48.0	-	(D)	-	78.0	-	100.4
Establishments - 100-249 Emp. Number	19	17	-10.5	12	-29.4	14	16.7	15	7.1	21	40.0	10.5
Mid-March Employment	2,940	2,607	-11.3	(D)	-	1,952	-	2,206	13.0	3,374	52.9	14.8
1st Quarter Wages (annualized - $ mil.)	86.1	77.3	-10.2	(D)	-	70.6	-	95.8	35.6	143.4	49.7	66.6
Payroll per Emp. 1st Q. (annualized)	29,276	29,645	1.3	(D)	-	36,186	-	43,422	20.0	42,497	-2.1	45.2
Annual Payroll ($ mil.)	85.0	69.0	-18.9	(D)	-	72.0	-	94.8	31.7	159.5	68.3	87.7
Establishments - 250-499 Emp. Number	7	2	-71.4	3	50.0	4	33.3	(D)	-	(D)	-	
Mid-March Employment	2,596	(D)	-	(D)	-	(D)	-	(D)	-	(D)	-	
1st Quarter Wages (annualized - $ mil.)	77.0	(D)	-	(D)	-	(D)	-	(D)	-	(D)	-	
Payroll per Emp. 1st Q. (annualized)	29,644	(D)	-	(D)	-	(D)	-	(D)	-	(D)	-	
Annual Payroll ($ mil.)	93.0	(D)	-	(D)	-	(D)	-	(D)	-	(D)	-	
Establishments - 500-999 Emp. Number	2	5	150.0	3	-40.0	4	33.3	(D)	-	(D)	-	
Mid-March Employment	(D)	(D)	-	(D)	-	(D)	-	(D)	-	(D)	-	
1st Quarter Wages (annualized - $ mil.)	(D)	(D)	-	(D)	-	(D)	-	(D)	-	(D)	-	
Payroll per Emp. 1st Q. (annualized)	(D)	(D)	-	(D)	-	(D)	-	(D)	-	(D)	-	
Annual Payroll ($ mil.)	(D)	(D)	-	(D)	-	(D)	-	(D)	-	(D)	-	
Estab. - 1000 or More Emp. Number	1	1	-	2	100.0	-	-	(D)	-	-	-	
Mid-March Employment	(D)	(D)	-	(D)	-	-	-	(D)	-	-	-	
1st Quarter Wages (annualized - $ mil.)	(D)	(D)	-	(D)	-	-	-	(D)	-	-	-	
Payroll per Emp. 1st Q. (annualized)	(D)	(D)	-	(D)	-	(D)	-	(D)	-	-	-	
Annual Payroll ($ mil.)	(D)	(D)	-	(D)	-	-	-	(D)	-	-	-	

Source: County Business Patterns. U.S. Department of Commerce, Washington, D.C., for 1988 through 1993. Payroll per employee is calculated using mid-March employment and 1st Quarter wages, annualized. Annual payroll, also shown, may not equal the annualized 1st Quarter wages. Columns headed by a percent sign (%) indicate change from the previous year. *na* stands for not available. The symbol (D) indicates that data are withheld by the source to avoid disclosure of competitive information. A dash (-) indicates that data are not available or cannot be calculated.

ESTABLISHMENTS
Number

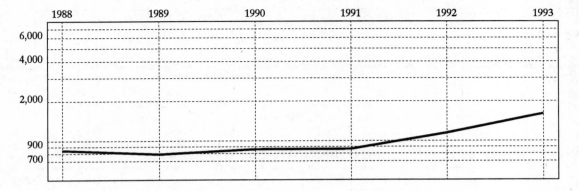

MID-MARCH EMPLOYMENT
Number

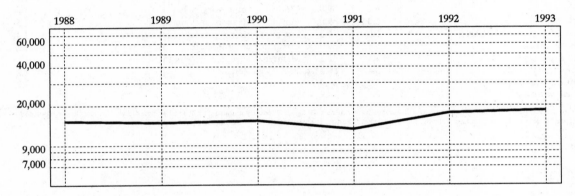

ANNUAL PAYROLL
$ million

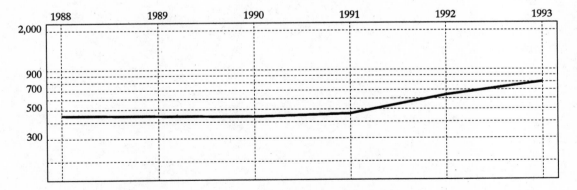

INPUTS AND OUTPUTS FOR HOLDING AND OTHER INVESTMENT OFFICES - SIC GROUP 67

Economic Sector or Industry Providing Inputs	%	Sector	Economic Sector or Industry Buying Outputs	%	Sector
No Input-Output data are available for this industry group.					

Source: Benchmark Input-Output Accounts for the U.S. Economy, 1982, U.S. Department of Commerce, Washington, D.C., July 1991. Data, as reported in the source, are organized by the 1977 SIC structure in use in 1982 but have been matched, as closely as is possible, to the 1987 SIC structure used in this book. Activities with the same percentage are sorted alphabetically by name of activity.

OCCUPATIONS EMPLOYED BY HOLDING AND OTHER INVESTMENT OFFICES

Occupation	% of Total 1994	Change to 2005	Occupation	% of Total 1994	Change to 2005
Secretaries, ex legal & medical	10.7	26.5	Marketing & sales worker supervisors	1.8	39.0
General managers & top executives	10.4	31.8	Securities & financial services sales workers	1.6	39.0
General office clerks	7.7	18.5	Systems analysts	1.5	122.3
Accountants & auditors	6.1	39.0	Clerical support workers nec	1.5	11.2
Financial managers	6.0	39.0	Janitors & cleaners, incl maids	1.5	11.2
Bookkeeping, accounting, & auditing clerks	6.0	4.2	Personnel, training, & labor specialists	1.4	54.8
Management support workers nec	5.5	39.0	Computer programmers	1.2	12.6
Clerical supervisors & managers	4.5	42.2	Maintenance repairers, general utility	1.2	25.1
Professional workers nec	3.4	66.8	Brokerage clerks	1.2	11.2
Receptionists & information clerks	2.2	39.0	Lawyers	1.2	39.0
Managers & administrators nec	2.1	38.9			

Sources: Industry-Occupation Matrix, Bureau of Labor Statistics. These data relate to one or more 3-digit SIC industry groups rather than to a single 4-digit SIC. The change reported for each occupation to the year 2005 is a percent of growth or decline as estimated by the Bureau of Labor Statistics. The abbreviation *nec* stands for not elsewhere classified.

U.S. AND STATE DATA ON INDUSTRY REVENUES AND OTHER ACCOUNTS FOR 1992

State	No. of Estab.	Employ- ment	Payroll ($ mil.)	Revenues ($ mil.)	Empl./ Estab.	Revenue/ Estab. ($)	Payroll/ Estab. ($)	Revenue/ Empl. ($)	Payroll/ Empl. ($)
UNITED STATES	1,514	17,409	689.3	5,412.5	11	3,574,967	455,264	310,902	39,593
California	231	2,832	134.2	924.4	12	4,001,753	580,835	326,414	47,377
Colorado	26	-	(D)	(D)	(D)	(D)	(D)	(D)	(D)
Florida	88	884	25.3	101.8	10	1,156,500	287,182	115,127	28,588
Georgia	45	1,620	30.1	142.1	36	3,157,800	669,800	87,717	18,606
Illinois	63	443	17.4	110.7	7	1,757,254	275,762	249,903	39,217
Indiana	18	-	(D)	(D)	(D)	(D)	(D)	(D)	(D)
Maryland	31	-	(D)	(D)	(D)	(D)	(D)	(D)	(D)
Massachusetts	21	-	(D)	(D)	(D)	(D)	(D)	(D)	(D)
Michigan	56	322	14.9	68.3	6	1,219,518	265,696	212,090	46,208
Minnesota	42	-	(D)	(D)	(D)	(D)	(D)	(D)	(D)
Missouri	29	362	11.3	63.3	12	2,183,414	388,000	174,914	31,083
New Jersey	40	1,527	93.1	652.4	38	16,310,900	2,328,125	427,267	60,986
New York	160	3,032	146.6	1,155.5	19	7,222,031	916,431	381,110	48,360
North Carolina	18	199	7.0	41.7	11	2,315,333	391,056	209,427	35,372
Ohio	48	380	12.3	42.4	8	883,354	256,479	111,582	32,397
Pennsylvania	49	445	15.9	65.6	9	1,338,755	324,163	147,413	35,694
Tennessee	57	550	17.4	108.0	10	1,894,807	305,912	196,371	31,704
Texas	81	986	36.8	170.8	12	2,108,963	454,506	173,252	37,338
Virginia	25	-	(D)	(D)	(D)	(D)	(D)	(D)	(D)
Washington	28	125	4.8	31.0	4	1,106,286	173,179	247,808	38,792
Wisconsin	20	113	3.8	42.5	6	2,123,450	191,450	375,832	33,885

Source: 1992 Economic Census, U.S. Department of Commerce, Washington, D.C. This is the only table that shows revenue data as collected by the Bureau of the Census in an Economic Census. The symbol (D) indicates that data are withheld by the source to avoid disclosure of competitive information. A dash (-) indicates that data are not available or cannot be calculated.

ESTABLISHMENTS 1992 - STATE AND REGIONAL CONCENTRATION

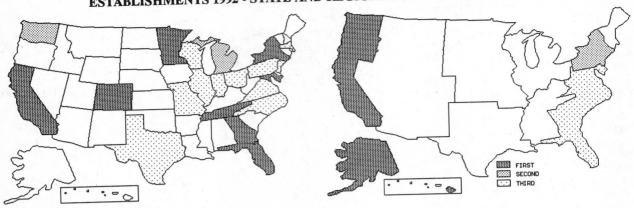

EMPLOYMENT 1992 - STATE AND REGIONAL CONCENTRATION

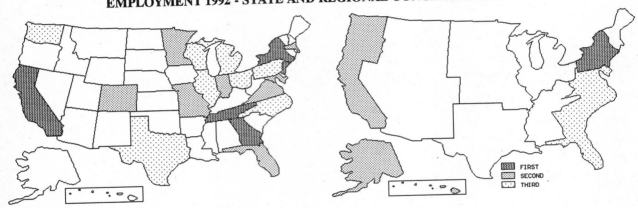

REVENUES 1992 - STATE AND REGIONAL CONCENTRATION

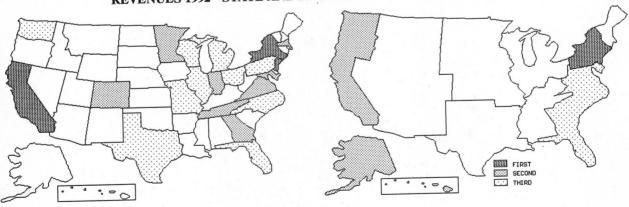

States with the darkest shading indicate those states which have proportionately more establishments, employment, or revenues than would be indicated by the state's population. States with light shading are states with proportionately fewer establishments, less employment, and lower revenues than population distribution. States shaded grey are within 15 percent of the state's population proportion in these categories. States for which no data are available are shown as average (grey). *Regions* are shaded to indicate absolute rank in the category. If no data for the category are available, establishment counts are used to shade the regions. Source of the data is the table on the facing page.

LEADING COMPANIES - SIC 6794 - Patent Owners and Lessors

Number shown: **100**   Total sales/assets ($ mil): **141,654**   Total employment (000): **2,134.2**

Company Name	Address				CEO Name	Phone	Co. Type	Sales/Assets ($ mil)	Empl. (000)
PepsiCo Inc.	700 Anderson Hill Rd.	Purchase	NY	10577	D. Wayne Calloway	914-253-2000	P	28,472	471.0
Carlson Holdings Inc.	P.O. Box 59159	Minneapolis	MN	55459	Curtis Carlson	612-449-1000	R	9,900 OR	33.0
McDonald's Corp.	McDonald's Plz.	Oak Brook	IL	60521	Michael R. Quinlan	708-575-3000	P	8,321	183.0
Burger King Corp.	P.O. Box 020783	Miami	FL	33102	James Adamson	305-378-7011	S	6,700	38.0
IYG Holding Co.	P.O. Box 711	Dallas	TX	75221	Clark J. Matthews II	214-828-7011	S	6,685	30.4
Southland Corp.	P.O. Box 711	Dallas	TX	75221	Clark J. Matthews II	214-828-7011	P	6,685	30.4
National Intergroup Inc.	1220 Senlac Dr.	Carrollton	TX	75006	Abbey J. Butler	214-446-4800	P	5,409	4.1
Tandy Corp.	P.O. Box 17180	Fort Worth	TX	76102	John V. Roach	817-390-3700	P	4,944	47.5
Pizza Hut Inc.	P.O. Box 428	Wichita	KS	67201	Allan Huston	316-681-9000	S	4,129	220.0
Flagstar Companies Inc.	P.O. Box 3800	Spartanburg	SC	29319	Jerome J. Richardson	803-597-8000	P	3,970	123.0
ITT Sheraton Corp.	60 State St.	Boston	MA	02109	John Kapioltas	617-367-3600	S	3,900 OR	8.0
Taco Bell Corp.	17901 Von Karman	Irvine	CA	92714	John E. Martin	714-863-4500	S	2,900	81.0
Turner Broadcasting System Inc.	One CNN Ctr.	Atlanta	GA	30303	R.E. Turner	404-827-1700	P	2,809 OR	6.0
Tandy-Radio Shack	1800 One Tandy Center	Fort Worth	TX	76102	Len Roberts	817-390-3011	D	2,800	30.0
United States Shoe Corp.	1 Eastwood Dr.	Cincinnati	OH	45227	Bannus B. Hudson	513-527-7000	P	2,598	40.0
Domino's Pizza Inc.	P.O. Box 997	Ann Arbor	MI	48106	Thomas Monaghan	313-930-3030	R	2,400	20.0
Kentucky Fried Chicken Corp.	P.O. Box 32070	Louisville	KY	40232	John M. Cranor III	502-456-8300	S	2,300	66.0
Blockbuster Entertainment Corp.	1 Blockbuster Plz.	Fort Lauderdale	FL	33301	H. Wayne Huizenga	305-832-3000	S	2,227 OR	46.0
MicroAge Inc.	2308 S. 55th St.	Tempe	AZ	85282	Jeffrey D. McKeever	602-968-3168	P	2,221 OR	1.7
InaCom Corp.	10810 Farnam Dr.	Omaha	NE	68154	Bill L. Fairfield	402-392-3900	P	1,800	1.9
Hilton Hotels Corp.	9336 Civic Center Dr.	Beverly Hills	CA	90209	Eric M. Hilton	310-278-4321	P	1,506 OR	44.0
Brown Group Inc.	P.O. Box 29	St. Louis	MO	63166	B.A. Bridgewater Jr.	314-854-4000	P	1,462	14.5
Wendy's International Inc.	P.O. Box 256	Dublin	OH	43017	Gordon F. Teter	614-764-3100	P	1,398	44.0
Shoney's Inc.	1727 Elm Hill Pike	Nashville	TN	37210	C. Stephen Lynn	615-391-5201	P	1,166	30.0
CDI Corp.	1717 Arch St.	Philadelphia	PA	19103	Walter R. Garrison	215-569-2200	P	1,098 OR	27.0
Triarc Companies Inc.	900 3rd Ave.	New York	NY	10022	Nelson Peltz	212-230-3000	P	1,063	11.3
Foodmaker Inc.	9330 Balboa Ave.	San Diego	CA	92123	Jack W. Goodall Jr.	619-571-2121	P	1,053	26.2
Jack in the Box Div.	9330 Balboa Ave.	San Diego	CA	92123	Robert J. Nugent	619-571-2121	D	1,026	33.7
UOP	25 E. Algonquin Rd.	Des Plaines	IL	60017	Michael D. Winfield	708-391-2000	J	890•	4.0
Casey's General Stores Inc.	1 Convenience Blvd.	Ankeny	IA	50021	Donald F. Lamberti	515-965-6100	P	731	6.7
General Nutrition Companies Inc.	921 Penn Ave.	Pittsburgh	PA	15222	William E. Watts	412-288-4600	P	628	8.4
CFC Holdings Corp.	1000 Corporate Dr.	Fort Lauderdale	FL	33334	John Carson	305-351-5600	S	610•	9.0
RC/Arby's Corp.	1000 Corporate Dr.	Fort Lauderdale	FL	33334	John Carson	305-351-5600	S	610•	9.0

Company type codes: P - Public, R - Private, S - Subsidiary, D - Division, J - Joint Venture, A - Affiliate, G - Group. If the dollar values shown are not sales, the following codes apply: TA - Total Assets; OR - Operating Revenues; GB - Gross Billings. • - estimated dollar value. < - less than. *na* - not available.

Continued on next page.

LEADING COMPANIES - SIC 6794 - Patent Owners and Lessors

Continued

Company Name	Address				CEO Name	Phone	Co. Type	Sales/Assets ($ mil)	Empl. (000)
Dairy Mart Convenience Stores Inc.	1 Vision Dr.	Enfield	CT	06082	Frank Colaccino	203-741-4444	P	591	5.0
Norrell Corp.	3535 Piedmont Rd. N.E.	Atlanta	GA	30305	C. Douglas Miller	404-240-3000	P	562 OR	1.6
Long John Silver's Inc.	P.O. Box 11988	Lexington	KY	40579	Clyd E. Culp	606-263-6000	S	545	18.2
Midas International Corp.	225 N. Michigan Ave.	Chicago	IL	60601	John R. Moore	312-565-7500	S	543 OR	3.3
CFC Franchising Co.	18831 Von Karman Ave.	Irvine	CA	92715	Kevin Relyea	714-757-7900	S	520 OR	<0.1
Sizzler International Inc.	P.O. Box 92092	Los Angeles	CA	90066	Richard P. Bermingham	310-827-2300	P	488	16.6
Outback Steakhouse Inc.	550 N. Reo St.	Tampa	FL	33609	Chris T. Sullivan	813-282-1225	P	452	8.9
Ryan's Family Steak Houses Inc.	P.O. Box 100	Greer	SC	29652	Charles D. Way	803-879-1000	P	448	15.0
Robert Half International Inc.	2884 Sand Hill Rd.	Menlo Park	CA	94025	Harold M. Messmer Jr.	415-854-9700	P	446 OR	1.6
Crystal Brands Inc.	Crystal Brands Rd.	Southport	CT	06490	Charles J. Campbell	203-254-6200	P	444	3.3
CKE Restaurants Inc.	P.O. Box 4349	Anaheim	CA	92803	Donald E. Doyle	714-774-5796	P	444	12.0
TGI Friday's Inc.	7540 Lyndon B. Johnson	Dallas	TX	75251	Wally Doolin	214-450-5400	S	440*	16.0
Chi-Chi's Inc.	10200 Linn Station Rd.	Louisville	KY	40223	Mohammed Iqbal	502-426-3900	S	433	20.0
VICORP Restaurants Inc.	P.O. Box 16601	Denver	CO	80216	J. Michael Jenkins	303-296-2121	P	413	14.4
Buffets Inc.	10260 Viking Dr.	Eden Prairie	MN	55344	Roe H. Hatlen	612-942-9760	P	410	15.9
Fred's Inc.	4300 New Getwell Rd.	Memphis	TN	38118	Michael J. Hayes	901-365-8880	P	381	4.5
W.S. Badcock Corp.	P.O. Box 497	Mulberry	FL	33860	Wogan S. Badcock III	813-425-4921	R	367 OR	1.2
International Dairy Queen Inc.	7505 Metro Blvd.	Minneapolis	MN	55439	Michael P. Sullivan	612-830-0200	P	341	0.6
Ben Franklin Retail Stores Inc.	P.O. Box 5938	Chicago	IL	60680	John B. Menzer	708-462-6100	P	338 OR	1.3
NPC International Inc.	P.O. Box 62643	Pittsburg	KS	66762	O. Gene Bicknell	316-231-3390	P	337	8.4
Whataburger Inc.	4600 Parkdale Dr.	Corpus Christi	TX	78411	Tom Dobson	512-878-0650	R	330*	10.0
Hospitality Franchise Systems Inc.	P.O. Box 278	Parsippany	NJ	07054	Henry R. Silverman	201-428-9700	P	313 OR	2.1
White Hen Pantry Inc.	660 Industrial Dr.	Elmhurst	IL	60126	Robert G. Robertson	708-833-3100	R	296 OR	0.5
TPI Enterprises Inc.	3950 RCA Blvd.	Palm Beach	FL	33410	J. Gary Sharp	407-691-8800	P	287	10.3
Church's Fried Chicken Inc.	1333 S. Clearview Pkwy	Jefferson	LA	70121	Al Copeland	504-733-4300	S	285	13.0
ShowBiz Pizza Time Inc.	P.O. Box 152077	Irving	TX	75015	Richard M. Frank	214-258-8507	P	268	13.5
Sbarro Inc.	763 Larkfield Rd.	Commack	NY	11725	Anthony Sbarro	516-864-0200	P	265	8.2
DAKA International Inc.	1 Corporate Pl.	Danvers	MA	01923	William H. Baumhauer	508-774-9115	P	250	12.8
Krystal Co.	1 Union Sq.	Chattanooga	TN	37402	Carl Long	615-756-5100	P	248	9.2
Ground Round Restaurants Inc.	35 Braintree Hill	Braintree	MA	02184	Michael P. O'Donnell	617-380-3100	P	244	9.4

Company type codes: P - Public, R - Private, S - Subsidiary, D - Division, J - Joint Venture, A - Affiliate, G - Group. If the dollar values shown are not sales, the following codes apply: TA - Total Assets; OR - Operating Revenues; GB - Gross Billings. * - estimated dollar value. < - less than. *na* - not available.

Continued on next page.

LEADING COMPANIES - SIC 6794 - Patent Owners and Lessors
Continued

Company Name	Address				CEO Name	Phone	Co. Type	Sales/Assets ($ mil)	Empl. (000)
Ground Round Inc.	35 Braintree Hill Park	Braintree	MA	02184	Michael P. O'Donnell	617-380-3100	S	233	10.0
Perkins Restaurant Operating Company L.P.	6075 Poplar Ave.	Memphis	TN	38119	Donald N. Smith	901-766-6400	P	222	7.4
Playboy Enterprises Inc.	680 N. Lake Shore Dr.	Chicago	IL	60611	Christie Hefner	312-751-8000	P	219	0.6
Arby's Inc.	P.O. Box 407008	Fort Lauderdale	FL	33340	Donald L. Pierce	305-351-5100	S	215	9.0
Applebee's International Inc.	4551 W. 107th St.	Overland Park	KS	66207	Abe J. Gustin Jr.	913-967-4000	P	208 OR	8.7
Country Hospitality Corp.	P.O. Box 59159	Minneapolis	MN	55459	Curtis C. Nelson	612-449-1300	S	205 OR	<0.1
Checkers Drive-In Restaurants Inc.	P.O. Box 1079	Clearwater	FL	34617	James E. Mattei	813-441-3500	P	201	8.0
Gymboree Corp.	700 Airport Blvd.	Burlingame	CA	94010	Nancy J. Pedot	415-579-0600	P	188	5.9
Rally's Inc.	10002 Shelbyville Rd.	Louisville	KY	40223	Wayne M. Albritton	502-245-8900	P	186	6.6
Discovery Zone Inc.	205 N. Michigan Ave.	Chicago	IL	60601	Donald F. Flynn	312-616-3800	P	181 OR	14.5
Chart House Enterprises Inc.	115 S. Acacia Ave.	Solana Beach	CA	92075	John M. Creed	619-755-8281	P	175	7.4
Frisch's Restaurants Inc.	2800 Gilbert Ave.	Cincinnati	OH	45206	Craig F. Maier	513-961-2660	P	160	6.3
American Speedy Printing Centers Inc.	2555 Telegraph Rd.	Bloomfield Hills	MI	48302	William McIntyre	313-335-6200	R	157 OR	<0.1
Executive Car Leasing Co.	7807 Santa Monica Blvd	Los Angeles	CA	90046	Sam Goldman	213-654-5000	R	150 OR	0.2
IHOP Corp.	525 N. Brand Blvd.	Glendale	CA	91203	Richard K. Herzer	818-240-6055	P	150 OR	2.2
Ben and Jerry's Homemade Inc.	P.O. Box 240	Waterbury	VT	05676	Robert Holland Jr.	802-244-6957	P	149	0.5
Immunex Corp.	51 University St.	Seattle	WA	98101	Edward V. Fritzky	206-587-0430	P	144	0.8
TCBY Enterprises Inc.	425 W. Capital Ave.	Little Rock	AR	72201	Frank D. Hickingbotham	501-688-8229	P	140	1.1
Signature Foods Inc.	400 Plaza Dr.	Secaucus	NJ	07094	Charles Loccisiano	201-319-9003	P	140	1.5
Valvoline Instant Oil Change Franchising Inc.	P.O. Box 14046	Lexington	KY	40512	Larry Detjen	606-264-7100	S	140 OR	2.5
Southern Industrial Corp.	9009 Regency Square	Jacksonville	FL	32211	David A. Stein	904-725-4122	R	135	0.3
Consolidated Products Inc.	36 S. Pennsylvania St.	Indianapolis	IN	46204	Alan B. Gilman	317-633-4100	P	134	6.5
Mazzio's Corp.	4441 S. 72nd E. Ave.	Tulsa	OK	74145	Craig Bothwell	918-663-8880	R	130 OR*	2.3
Taco Cabana Inc.	262 Losoya St.	San Antonio	TX	78205	Richard Cervera	210-231-8226	P	127	4.7
Uno Restaurant Corp.	100 Charles Park Rd.	West Roxbury	MA	02132	Aaron D. Spencer	617-323-9200	P	124	4.6
Big O Tires Inc.	11755 E. Peakview Ave.	Englewood	CO	80111	Steven P. Cloward	303-790-2800	P	123	0.3
Labor World of America Inc.	8000 N. Federal Hwy.	Boca Raton	FL	33487	Paul Burrell	407-997-5000	S	119 OR	0.1
Uniforce Temporary Personnel Inc.	1335 Jericho Tpk.	New Hyde Park	NY	11040	John Fanning	516-437-3300	P	115 OR	0.2

Company type codes: P - Public, R - Private, S - Subsidiary, D - Division, J - Joint Venture, A - Affiliate, G - Group. If the dollar values shown are not sales, the following codes apply: TA - Total Assets; OR - Operating Revenues; GB - Gross Billings. * - estimated dollar value. < - less than. *na* - not available.

Continued on next page.

LEADING COMPANIES - SIC 6794 - Patent Owners and Lessors

Continued

Company Name	Address				CEO Name	Phone	Co. Type	Sales/Assets ($ mil)	Empl. (000)
O'Charley's Inc.	3038 Sidco Dr.	Nashville	TN	37204	David K. Wachtel	615-256-8500	P	112	3.5
Choice Hotels International Inc.	10750 Columbia Pike	Silver Spring	MD	20901	Robert C. Hazard Jr.	301-593-5600	S	110 OR*	2.2
HQ Network Systems Inc.	120 Montgomery St.	San Francisco	CA	94104	T.J. Tison	415-781-7811	R	110 OR	<0.1
Nursefinders Inc.	1200 Copeland	Arlington	TX	76011	Tim Loncharich	817-460-1181	S	110 OR	0.3
Hungry Howie's Pizza and Subs Inc.	35301 Schoolcraft Rd.	Livonia	MI	48150	Steve Jackson	313-422-1717	R	107 OR	<0.1
Jani-King International Inc.	4950 Keller Springs	Dallas	TX	75248	Jim Cavanaugh	214-991-0900	R	100 OR	4.0
Sonic Corp.	101 Park Ave.	Oklahoma City	OK	73102		405-280-7654	P	100	0.1
El Chico Restaurants Inc.	12200 Stemmons Fwy.	Dallas	TX	75234	Wallace Jones	214-241-5500	P	98	4.1
Boston Chicken Inc.	P.O. Box 4086	Golden	CO	80401	Scott A. Beck	303-278-9500	P	96	2.4

Source: *Ward's Business Directory of U.S. Private and Public Companies*, 1996. Company type codes: P - Public, R - Private, S - Subsidiary, D - Division, J - Joint Venture, A - Affiliate, G - Group. If the dollar values shown are not sales, the following codes apply: TA - Total Assets; OR - Operating Revenues; GB - Gross Billings. * - estimated dollar value. < - less than; *na* - not available.

SIC 6798

REAL ESTATE INVESTMENT TRUSTS

Real estate investment trusts are establishments primarily engaged in closed-end investments in real estate or related mortgage assets. They operate so that they can meet the requirements of the Real Estate Investment Trust Act of 1960 as later amended. This act exempts trusts from corporate income and capital gains taxation, provided that they invest primarily in specified assets, pay out most of their income to shareholders, and meet certain requirements regarding the dispersion of trust ownership. Types of organizations that are included are mortgage trusts and mortgage investment trusts; real estate investment trusts (REITs), realty investment trusts, and realty trusts.

ESTABLISHMENTS, EMPLOYMENT, AND PAYROLL

	1988	1989 Value	%	1990 Value	%	1991 Value	%	1992 Value	%	1993 Value	%	% change 88-93
All Establishments	757	690	-8.9	696	0.9	969	39.2	1,031	6.4	558	-45.9	-26.3
Mid-March Employment	6,696	6,781	1.3	7,448	9.8	6,734	-9.6	7,800	15.8	5,403	-30.7	-19.3
1st Quarter Wages (annualized - $ mil.)	261.5	268.1	2.5	286.9	7.0	257.1	-10.4	286.4	11.4	195.6	-31.7	-25.2
Payroll per Emp. 1st Q. (annualized)	39,047	39,532	1.2	38,523	-2.6	38,172	-0.9	36,724	-3.8	36,205	-1.4	-7.3
Annual Payroll ($ mil.)	234.4	248.9	6.2	258.6	3.9	248.3	-4.0	295.0	18.8	212.8	-27.9	-9.2
Establishments - 1-4 Emp. Number	525	464	-11.6	463	-0.2	742	60.3	795	7.1	408	-48.7	-22.3
Mid-March Employment	902	765	-15.2	797	4.2	1,133	42.2	1,240	9.4	568	-54.2	-37.0
1st Quarter Wages (annualized - $ mil.)	31.8	25.5	-19.8	29.0	13.8	33.5	15.3	39.3	17.3	16.2	-58.6	-49.0
Payroll per Emp. 1st Q. (annualized)	35,282	33,354	-5.5	36,442	9.3	29,546	-18.9	31,668	7.2	28,599	-9.7	-18.9
Annual Payroll ($ mil.)	37.4	30.7	-18.0	30.4	-0.9	36.2	19.1	54.0	49.1	26.3	-51.3	-29.7
Establishments - 5-9 Emp. Number	113	104	-8.0	104	-	101	-2.9	102	1.0	(D)	-	-
Mid-March Employment	742	672	-9.4	676	0.6	647	-4.3	649	0.3	(D)	-	-
1st Quarter Wages (annualized - $ mil.)	29.8	27.0	-9.5	26.4	-2.1	22.5	-14.9	21.8	-3.0	(D)	-	-
Payroll per Emp. 1st Q. (annualized)	40,146	40,125	-0.1	39,036	-2.7	34,726	-11.0	33,578	-3.3	(D)	-	-
Annual Payroll ($ mil.)	27.6	26.2	-5.1	25.8	-1.2	21.1	-18.3	22.1	4.9	(D)	-	-
Establishments - 10-19 Emp. Number	59	52	-11.9	60	15.4	68	13.3	68	-	30	-55.9	-49.2
Mid-March Employment	(D)	677	-	833	23.0	914	9.7	900	-1.5	410	-54.4	-
1st Quarter Wages (annualized - $ mil.)	(D)	23.6	-	36.1	52.8	45.7	26.5	50.8	11.0	21.1	-58.5	-
Payroll per Emp. 1st Q. (annualized)	(D)	34,919	-	43,366	24.2	50,013	15.3	56,391	12.8	51,424	-8.8	-
Annual Payroll ($ mil.)	(D)	22.1	-	33.0	48.9	40.6	23.3	41.8	2.8	23.3	-44.2	-
Establishments - 20-49 Emp. Number	34	41	20.6	38	-7.3	32	-15.8	(D)	-	(D)	-	-
Mid-March Employment	1,093	1,219	11.5	1,158	-5.0	896	-22.6	(D)	-	(D)	-	-
1st Quarter Wages (annualized - $ mil.)	41.5	55.2	33.1	51.7	-6.4	33.3	-35.6	(D)	-	(D)	-	-
Payroll per Emp. 1st Q. (annualized)	37,973	45,316	19.3	44,642	-1.5	37,165	-16.7	(D)	-	(D)	-	-
Annual Payroll ($ mil.)	40.1	47.0	17.4	47.1	0.1	32.6	-30.8	(D)	-	(D)	-	-
Establishments - 50-99 Emp. Number	16	16	-	16	-	15	-6.3	(D)	-	18	-	12.5
Mid-March Employment	(D)	1,107	-	1,038	-6.2	(D)	-	(D)	-	1,085	-	-
1st Quarter Wages (annualized - $ mil.)	(D)	47.0	-	38.4	-18.2	(D)	-	(D)	-	38.8	-	-
Payroll per Emp. 1st Q. (annualized)	(D)	42,446	-	37,037	-12.7	(D)	-	(D)	-	35,779	-	-
Annual Payroll ($ mil.)	(D)	42.9	-	32.0	-25.6	(D)	-	(D)	-	42.8	-	-
Establishments - 100-249 Emp. Number	7	10	42.9	11	10.0	9	-18.2	8	-11.1	9	12.5	28.6
Mid-March Employment	898	1,255	39.8	1,593	26.9	1,417	-11.0	1,428	0.8	1,466	2.7	63.3
1st Quarter Wages (annualized - $ mil.)	37.9	45.9	21.2	58.1	26.5	57.9	-0.4	56.5	-2.4	62.3	10.3	64.5
Payroll per Emp. 1st Q. (annualized)	42,165	36,571	-13.3	36,454	-0.3	40,833	12.0	39,532	-3.2	42,475	7.4	0.7
Annual Payroll ($ mil.)	27.5	39.6	43.7	47.8	20.9	56.0	17.0	57.4	2.6	57.9	0.9	110.4
Establishments - 250-499 Emp. Number	3	3	-	4	33.3	2	-50.0	4	100.0	-	-	-
Mid-March Employment	(D)	1,086	-	1,353	24.6	(D)	-	1,330	-	-	-	-
1st Quarter Wages (annualized - $ mil.)	(D)	43.8	-	47.2	7.6	(D)	-	41.8	-	-	-	-
Payroll per Emp. 1st Q. (annualized)	(D)	40,350	-	34,850	-13.6	(D)	-	31,447	-	-	-	-
Annual Payroll ($ mil.)	(D)	40.4	-	42.5	5.4	(D)	-	42.0	-	-	-	-
Establishments - 500-999 Emp. Number	-	-	-	-	-	-	-	-	-	(D)	-	-
Mid-March Employment	-	-	-	-	-	-	-	-	-	(D)	-	-
1st Quarter Wages (annualized - $ mil.)	-	-	-	-	-	-	-	-	-	(D)	-	-
Payroll per Emp. 1st Q. (annualized)	(D)	(D)	-	(D)	-	(D)	-	-	-	(D)	-	-
Annual Payroll ($ mil.)	-	-	-	-	-	-	-	-	-	(D)	-	-
Estab. - 1000 or More Emp. Number	-	-	-	-	-	-	-	-	-	-	-	-
Mid-March Employment	-	-	-	-	-	-	-	-	-	-	-	-
1st Quarter Wages (annualized - $ mil.)	-	-	-	-	-	-	-	-	-	-	-	-
Payroll per Emp. 1st Q. (annualized)	(D)	(D)	-	(D)	-	(D)	-	-	-	-	-	-
Annual Payroll ($ mil.)	-	-	-	-	-	-	-	-	-	-	-	-

Source: County Business Patterns. U.S. Department of Commerce. Washington, D.C., for 1988 through 1993. Payroll per employee is calculated using mid-March employment and 1st Quarter wages, annualized. Annual payroll, also shown, may not equal the annualized 1st Quarter wages. Columns headed by a percent sign (%) indicate change from the previous year. *na* stands for not available. The symbol (D) indicates that data are withheld by the source to avoid disclosure of competitive information. A dash (-) indicates that data are not available or cannot be calculated.

ESTABLISHMENTS
Number

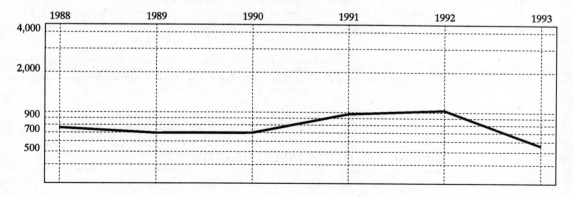

MID-MARCH EMPLOYMENT
Number

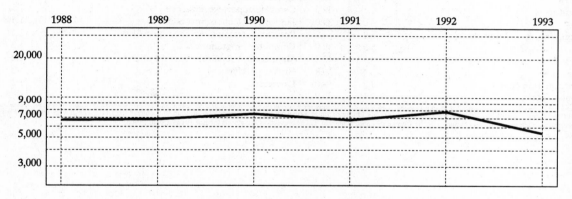

ANNUAL PAYROLL
$ million

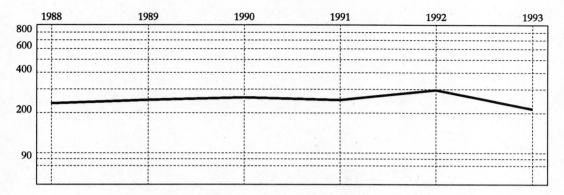

INPUTS AND OUTPUTS FOR HOLDING AND OTHER INVESTMENT OFFICES - SIC GROUP 67

Economic Sector or Industry Providing Inputs	%	Sector	Economic Sector or Industry Buying Outputs	%	Sector
No Input-Output data are available for this industry group.					

Source: *Benchmark Input-Output Accounts for the U.S. Economy, 1982*, U.S. Department of Commerce, Washington, D.C., July 1991. Data, as reported in the source, are organized by the 1977 SIC structure in use in 1982 but have been matched, as closely as is possible, to the 1987 SIC structure used in this book. Activities with the same percentage are sorted alphabetically by name of activity.

OCCUPATIONS EMPLOYED BY HOLDING AND OTHER INVESTMENT OFFICES

Occupation	% of Total 1994	Change to 2005	Occupation	% of Total 1994	Change to 2005
Secretaries, ex legal & medical	10.7	26.5	Marketing & sales worker supervisors	1.8	39.0
General managers & top executives	10.4	31.8	Securities & financial services sales workers	1.6	39.0
General office clerks	7.7	18.5	Systems analysts	1.5	122.3
Accountants & auditors	6.1	39.0	Clerical support workers nec	1.5	11.2
Financial managers	6.0	39.0	Janitors & cleaners, incl maids	1.5	11.2
Bookkeeping, accounting, & auditing clerks	6.0	4.2	Personnel, training, & labor specialists	1.4	54.8
Management support workers nec	5.5	39.0	Computer programmers	1.2	12.6
Clerical supervisors & managers	4.5	42.2	Maintenance repairers, general utility	1.2	25.1
Professional workers nec	3.4	66.8	Brokerage clerks	1.2	11.2
Receptionists & information clerks	2.2	39.0	Lawyers	1.2	39.0
Managers & administrators nec	2.1	38.9			

Sources: *Industry-Occupation Matrix*, Bureau of Labor Statistics. These data relate to one or more 3-digit SIC industry groups rather than to a single 4-digit SIC. The change reported for each occupation to the year 2005 is a percent of growth or decline as estimated by the Bureau of Labor Statistics. The abbreviation *nec* stands for not elsewhere classified.

U.S. AND STATE DATA ON INDUSTRY REVENUES AND OTHER ACCOUNTS FOR 1992

State	No. of Estab.	Employ- ment	Payroll ($ mil.)	Revenues ($ mil.)	Empl./ Estab.	Revenue/ Estab. ($)	Payroll/ Estab. ($)	Revenue/ Empl. ($)	Payroll/ Empl. ($)
UNITED STATES	6,202	24,423	1,225.1	9,750.1	4	1,572,088	197,534	399,217	50,162
California	989	3,545	180.6	942.0	4	952,467	182,646	265,724	50,955
Colorado	128	293	11.5	77.7	2	607,273	90,070	265,294	39,348
Florida	480	1,464	64.6	450.5	3	938,548	134,667	307,721	44,153
Georgia	114	388	12.6	59.0	3	517,325	110,781	151,997	32,549
Illinois	303	1,654	97.2	689.1	5	2,274,376	320,713	416,648	58,752
Indiana	51	188	7.7	40.9	4	802,627	151,353	217,734	41,059
Maryland	106	718	37.2	223.3	7	2,106,283	351,368	310,955	51,873
Massachusetts	176	694	61.6	361.6	4	2,054,653	350,000	521,065	88,761
Michigan	104	362	13.1	103.4	3	994,308	126,163	285,657	36,246
Minnesota	79	-	(D)	(D)	(D)	(D)	(D)	(D)	(D)
Missouri	104	.	(D)	(D)	(D)	(D)	(D)	(D)	(D)
New Jersey	142	537	45.5	174.5	4	1,229,211	320,521	325,043	84,756
New York	600	4,040	250.1	2,056.2	7	3,427,062	416,818	508,970	61,904
North Carolina	101	237	8.9	42.2	2	417,366	87,891	177,865	37,456
Ohio	129	913	31.8	110.3	7	854,806	246,155	120,778	34,780
Pennsylvania	115	515	24.9	81.6	4	709,878	216,313	158,517	48,303
Tennessee	73	-	(D)	(D)	(D)	(D)	(D)	(D)	(D)
Texas	756	2,650	118.8	876.9	4	1,159,970	157,127	330,920	44,826
Virginia	105	366	21.8	152.0	3	1,447,505	207,200	415,268	59,443
Washington	124	336	16.2	60.9	3	491,444	131,000	181,366	48,345
Wisconsin	73	296	6.9	45.7	4	626,096	95,123	154,409	23,459

Source: 1992 Economic Census, U.S. Department of Commerce, Washington, D.C. This is the only table that shows revenue data as collected by the Bureau of the Census in an Economic Census. The symbol (D) indicates that data are withheld by the source to avoid disclosure of competitive information. A dash (-) indicates that data are not available or cannot be calculated.

ESTABLISHMENTS 1992 - STATE AND REGIONAL CONCENTRATION

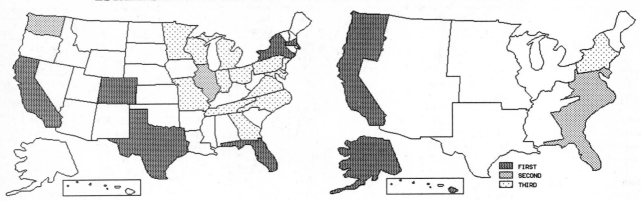

EMPLOYMENT 1992 - STATE AND REGIONAL CONCENTRATION

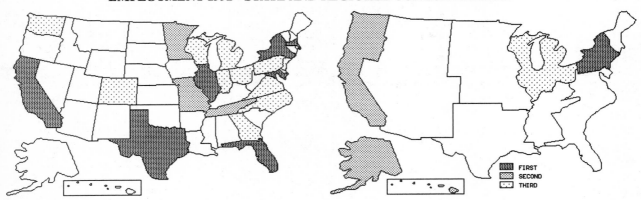

REVENUES 1992 - STATE AND REGIONAL CONCENTRATION

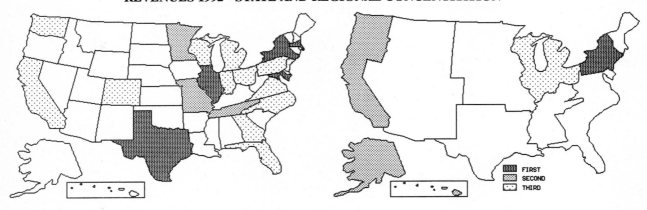

States with the darkest shading indicate those states which have proportionately more establishments, employment, or revenues than would be indicated by the state's population. States with light shading are states with proportionately fewer establishments, less employment, and lower revenues than population distribution. States shaded grey are within 15 percent of the state's population proportion in these categories. States for which no data are available are shown as average (grey). *Regions* are shaded to indicate absolute rank in the category. If no data for the category are available, establishment counts are used to shade the regions. Source of the data is the table on the facing page.

LEADING COMPANIES - SIC 6799 - Investors, nec

Number shown: **100**   Total sales/assets ($ mil): **82,250**   Total employment (000): **94.6**

Company Name	Address				CEO Name	Phone	Co. Type	Sales/Assets ($ mil)	Empl. (000)
Ford Holdings Inc.	The American Rd.	Dearborn	MI	48121	Stanley Seneker	313-322-1639	S	34,755 TA	17.0
SAFECO Corp.	SAFECO Plz.	Seattle	WA	98185	Roger H. Eigsti	206-545-5000	P	15,902 TA	7.3
Pinnacle West Capital Corp.	P.O. Box 52132	Phoenix	AZ	85072	Richard Snell	602-379-2500	P	6,910 TA	7.4
Yucaipa Cos.	10000 Santa Monica	Los Angeles	CA	90067	Ronald W. Burkle	310-789-7200	R	3,930*	30.0
Mission Cos.	18101 Von Karmen Ave.	Irvine	CA	92715	Edward R. Muller	714-752-5588	S	3,291 TA	0.7
Thomas H. Lee Co.	75 State St.	Boston	MA	02109	Thomas H. Lee	617-227-1050	R	1,500 TA	<0.1
American Industrial Partners Management Company Inc.	1 Maritime Plz.	San Francisco	CA	94111	Richard Bingham	415-788-7354	R	1,480 TA*	0.6
Centre Capital Investors L.P.	1 Rockefeller Plz.	New York	NY	10020	Lester Pollack	212-632-6000	R	1,480 TA*	0.6
Pulte Diversified Companies Inc.	33 Bloomfield Hill	Bloomfield Hills	MI	48304	Robert K. Burgess	313-647-2750	S	1,363 OR	2.2
Wingate Partners L.P.	750 N. St. Paul St.	Dallas	TX	75201	Frederick B. Hegi Jr.	214-720-1313	R	1,200 TA	<0.1
Sterling Capital Ltd.	111 S. Calvert St.	Baltimore	MD	21202	Eric Becker	410-385-2200	R	800 TA	<0.1
AIB Real Estate Investment Inc.	5000 Sunset Blvd.	Los Angeles	CA	90027	Huey Yu	213-663-2077	S	740 TA*	0.3
Safeguard Scientifics Inc.	800 Safeguard Bldg.	Wayne	PA	19087	Warren V. Musser	610-293-0600	P	617 TA	2.5
Pulte Financial Companies Inc.	6061 S. Willow Dr.	Greenwood Village	CO	80111	James A. Weissenborn	303-740-3323	S	548 TA	<0.1
Westar Capital	950 S. Coast Dr.	Costa Mesa	CA	92626	George M. Crandell	714-434-5160	R	500 TA	<0.1
Liberty Financial Companies Inc.	600 Atlantic Ave.	Boston	MA	02210	Sam Marnella	617-722-6000	S	490 TA*	0.2
Specialty Foods Corp.	520 Lake Cook Rd.	Deerfield	IL	60015		708-267-3000	R	486 TA	13.0
American Financial Enterprises Inc.	1 E. 4th St.	Cincinnati	OH	45202	Carl H. Lindner	513-579-2172	P	390 TA	<0.1
Berwind Corp.	1500 Market St.	Philadelphia	PA	19102	Graham Berwind Jr.	215-563-2800	R	350*	3.2
Milley and Co.	115 E. Putnam Ave.	Greenwich	CT	06830	Alexander M. Milley	203-661-7800	R	340 TA*	0.1
Riverside Group Inc.	7800 Belfort Pkwy.	Jacksonville	FL	32256	J. Steven Wilson	904-281-2200	P	338 TA	<0.1
Advent International Corp.	101 Federal St.	Boston	MA	02110	Peter A. Brooke	617-951-9400	R	240 TA*	0.1
Hambro International Venture Fund	404 Wyman St.	Waltham	MA	02154	Edwin Goodman	617-523-7767	R	240 TA*	0.1
Code, Hennessy and Simmons L.P.	10 S. Wacker Dr.	Chicago	IL	60606	Andrew Code	312-876-1840	R	237 TA	5.1
Dartfort Partnership	801 Montgomery St #400	San Francisco	CA	94133	Ian R. Wilson	415-982-3019	R	180 TA*	<0.1
Galen Associates	666 3rd Ave.	New York	NY	10017	Bruce F. Wesson	212-818-0240	R	160 TA	<0.1
Sierra Ventures	3000 Sandhill Rd.	Menlo Park	CA	94025	J.M. Drazan	415-854-1000	R	160 TA	<0.1
Heller Equity Capital Corp.	500 W. Monroe St.	Chicago	IL	60661	John M. Goense	312-441-7200	S	150 TA	0.3
Mesirow Financial Holdings Inc.	350 N. Clark St.	Chicago	IL	60610	Lester A. Morris	312-670-6000	R	150 TA*	0.5
Triumph Capital	237 Park Ave.	New York	NY	10017	Michael Nugent	212-551-3636	R	150 TA	<0.1
Bando McGlocklin Capital Corp.	13555 Bishops Ct.	Brookfield	WI	53005	George R. Schonath	414-784-9010	P	131 TA	<0.1
Pioneer Group Inc.	60 State St.	Boston	MA	02109	John F. Cogan Jr.	617-742-7825	P	129 OR	1.1

Company type codes: P - Public, R - Private, S - Subsidiary, D - Division, J - Joint Venture, A - Affiliate, G - Group. If the dollar values shown are not sales, the following codes apply: TA - Total Assets; OR - Operating Revenues; GB - Gross Billings. * - estimated dollar value. < - less than. *na* - not available.

Continued on next page.

LEADING COMPANIES - SIC 6799 - Investors, nec

Continued

Company Name	Address				CEO Name	Phone	Co. Type	Sales/Assets ($ mil)	Empl. (000)
E.M. Warburg, Pincus and Company Inc.	466 Lexington Ave.	New York	NY	10017	Lionel Pincus	212-878-0600	R	100 TA*	0.3
Thompson Clive Inc.	3000 Sand Hill Rd.	Menlo Park	CA	94025	Peter Ziebelman	415-854-0314	S	100 TA	<0.1
Burr, Egan, Deleage and Co.	1 Post Office Sq.	Boston	MA	02109	Bill Egan	617-482-8020	R	98 TA	<0.1
Astra Resources Inc.	1021 Main St.	Houston	TX	77002	Bob Cline	713-750-0055	S	80 TA	0.1
Malaco Records Inc.	3023 W. Northside Dr.	Jackson	MS	39213	Tommy Couch	601-982-4522	R	74 TA*	<0.1
Mattick and Duke Inc.	201 S. Kings Dr.	Charlotte	NC	28204	Mike Mattick	704-333-7237	R	74 TA*	<0.1
EnCap Investment L.L.C.	6688 N. Central Expwy.	Dallas	TX	75206	David B. Miller	214-696-6700	R	71 TA*	<0.1
Paul Revere Investment Management Co.	18 Chestnut St.	Worcester	MA	01608	John Lemery	508-799-4441	S	69 TA	<0.1
Golder, Thoma, Cressey, Rauner Fund IV L.P.	233 S Wacker Dr.	Chicago	IL	60603	Carl D. Thomas	312-853-3322	R	64 TA	<0.1
Kirtland Capital Corp.	2550 SOM Center Rd.	Willoughby Hills	OH	44094	John F. Turbin	216-585-9010	R	64 TA*	<0.1
Berkeley International Capital Corp.	650 California St.	San Francisco	CA	94108	Michael Mayer	415-391-4790	S	61 TA*	<0.1
Canaan Partners	2884 Sand Hill Rd.	Menlo Park	CA	94025	Eric A. Young	415-854-8092	R	61 TA*	<0.1
Equitable Investment Services Inc.	604 Locust St.	Des Moines	IA	50306	Paul R. Schlaak	515-245-6911	S	61 TA*	<0.1
Madison Dearborn Partners Inc.	3 1st National Plz.	Chicago	IL	60602	John A. Canning Jr.	312-732-5400	R	59 TA*	<0.1
Freeman Spogli and Co.	11100 Santa Monica	Los Angeles	CA	90025	Bradford Freeman	310-444-1822	R	58 TA*	<0.1
El Dorado Investment Co.	400 E. Van Buren St.	Phoenix	AZ	85004	Henry B. Sargent	602-252-3441	S	58 TA	<0.1
Healthcare Investment Corp.	379 Thornall St.	Edison	NJ	08837	Wallace H. Steinberg	908-906-4600	R	56 TA*	<0.1
Vietnam Investment Fund Inc.	P.O. Box 150148	San Rafael	CA	94915	Dennis D. Powell	415-455-8500	3	50 TA	<0.1
Carlyle Real Estate L.P.	900 N. Michigan Ave.	Chicago	IL	60611	H. Rigel Barber	312-915-1987	R	50 TA	<0.1
Abrams, Rothman and Company Inc.	1240 Dielman	St. Louis	MO	63132	Lloyd R. Abrams	314-993-3686	R	49 TA*	<0.1
Air Partners L.P.	201 Main St.	Fort Worth	TX	76102	David Bonderman	817-871-4004	R	49 TA*	<0.1
New Enterprise Associates	235 Montgomery St.	San Francisco	CA	94104	C. Richard Kramlick	415-956-1579	R	49 TA*	<0.1
Starwood Capital Group L.P.	3 Pickwick Plz.	Greenwich	CT	06830	Barry Sternlicht	203-861-2100	R	49 TA	<0.1
Venture America Services L.P.	8230 Leesburg Pike	Vienna	VA	22182	James Ball	703-442-4500	R	49 TA*	<0.1
VIP Global Capital Inc.	1360 S. Clarkson St.	Denver	CO	80210	T. Vasko	303-777-0554	R	49 TA*	<0.1
VIP International Inc.	1360 S. Clarkson St.	Denver	CO	80210	T. Vasko	303-777-0554	R	49 TA*	<0.1
Weiss, Peck and Greer	1 New York Plz.	New York	NY	10004	Ron Hoffner	212-908-9500	R	48 TA	0.3
Ampersand Ventures	55 William St.	Wellesley	MA	02181	Richard Charpie	617-239-0700	R	44 TA	0.1
Churchill Capital Inc.	333 S. 7th St.	Minneapolis	MN	55402	Mike Hahn	612-673-6633	R	44 TA*	<0.1
Elfman Venture Partners	650 Dundee Rd.	Northbrook	IL	60062	Rick Elfman	708-571-0606	R	43 TA	<0.1

Company type codes: P - Public, R - Private, S - Subsidiary, D - Division, J - Joint Venture, A - Affiliate, G - Group. If the dollar values shown are not sales, the following codes apply: TA - Total Assets; OR - Operating Revenues; GB - Gross Billings. * - estimated dollar value. < - less than. *na* - not available.

Continued on next page.

LEADING COMPANIES - SIC 6799 - Investors, nec
Continued

Company Name	Address				CEO Name	Phone	Co. Type	Sales/Assets ($ mil)	Empl. (000)
Dominion Ventures Inc.	60 State St.	Boston	MA	02109	Randy Werner	617-367-8575	R	39 TA	<0.1
Capital Resource Partners	175 Portland St.	Boston	MA	02114	Robert Ammernan	617-723-9000	R	37 TA*	<0.1
Exor America Inc.	375 Park Ave.	New York	NY	10152	G. Andrea Botta	212-421-9700	S	37 TA*	<0.1
Interwest Partners	3000 Sand Hill Rd.	Menlo Park	CA	94025	Wallis Hawley	415-854-8585	R	37 TA*	<0.1
Weatherly Private Capital Inc.	20 Exchange Pl.	New York	NY	10005	Thomas A. McFall	212-809-2920	R	37 TA*	<0.1
Winrich Capital Management Inc.	23702 Birtcher Dr.	Lake Forest	CA	92630	Kurt Winrich	714-380-0200	R	37 TA*	<0.1
BancBoston Ventures Inc.	100 Federal St.	Boston	MA	02110	Frederick M. Fritz	617-434-2797	S	35 TA	<0.1
M and I Capital Markets Group Inc.	770 N. Water St.	Milwaukee	WI	53202	John T. Byrnes	414-765-7800	S	34 TA*	<0.1
Merrill Pickard Anderson and Eyre	2480 Sand Hill Rd.	Menlo Park	CA	94025	Steven Merrill	415-854-8600	R	34 TA*	<0.1
Interface Group Massachusetts Inc.	300 1st Ave.	Needham	MA	02194	Sheldon Adelson	617-449-6600	R	33 OR*	0.1
Yeager Wood and Marshall Inc.	630 5th Ave.	New York	NY	10111	George M. Yeager	212-765-5350	R	33 TA*	<0.1
Florida Capital Partners	100 N. Tampa St.	Tampa	FL	33602	John Kirtley	813-222-8000	R	32 TA	<0.1
Shaw Venture Partners	400 S.W. 6th Ave.	Portland	OR	97204	Ralph R. Shaw	503-228-4884	R	30 TA*	<0.1
Prospect Group Inc.	667 Madison Ave.	New York	NY	10021	Gilbert H. Lamphere	212-758-8500	P	30 TA	<0.1
Arete Ventures Inc.	6110 Executive Blvd.	Rockville	MD	20852	Robert W. Shaw	301-881-2555	R	29 TA*	<0.1
Signalert Corp.	150 Great Neck Rd #204	Great Neck	NY	11021	Gerald Appel	516-466-3125	R	29 TA*	<0.1
NAB Asset Corp.	5851 San Felipe St.	Houston	TX	77057	Michael A. Hrebenar	713-952-6800	P	29 TA	<0.1
Institutional Venture Partners	3000 Sand Hill Rd.	Menlo Park	CA	94025		415-854-0132	R	27 TA*	<0.1
Kirshenbaum Investments Inc.	2011 N. Collins Blvd.	Richardson	TX	75080	Myrna Kirshenbaum	214-238-7277	R	27 TA*	<0.1
Sanderling Ventures	2730 Sand Hill Rd.	Menlo Park	CA	94025	Robert McNeil	415-854-9855	R	27 TA*	<0.1
Saugatuck Capital Co.	1 Canterbury Green	Stamford	CT	06901	Frank J. Hawley Jr.	203-348-6669	R	27 TA*	<0.1
Kleiner Perkins Caufield and Byers	4 Embarcadero Ctr.	San Francisco	CA	94111	Thomas Perkins	415-421-3110	R	25 TA	<0.1
Skinner Corp.	1326 5th Ave.	Seattle	WA	98101	Paul W. Skinner	206-623-6480	R	25 TA	0.2
Edelson Technology Partners	300 Tice Blvd.	Woodcliff Lake	NJ	07675	Harry Edelson	201-930-9898	R	25 TA*	<0.1
Catalyst Ventures L.P.	1119 St. Paul St.	Baltimore	MD	21202	John Nehra	410-244-0123	R	24 TA*	<0.1
Advanced Technology Ventures	10 Post Office Sq.	Boston	MA	02109	Albert Paladino	617-423-4050	R	24 TA*	<0.1
Bradford Ventures Ltd.	1212 Ave. of the Americas	New York	NY	10036	Barbara Henagan	212-221-4620	R	24 TA*	<0.1
Camp Investment Group	6631 Amsterdam Way	Wilmington	NC	28405	Rocky Campagna	910-350-0565	R	24 TA*	<0.1
International Daleco Corp.	3333 W. Pacific Coast	Newport Beach	CA	92663	Parker Dale	714-722-0451	R	24 TA*	<0.1
Kilroy Company of Texas Inc.	1221 McKinney St.	Houston	TX	77010	W.S. Kilroy	713-651-0101	R	24 TA	<0.1
McKee and McFarland Inc.	P.O. Box 171133	Memphis	TN	38187	Lewis K. Mckee Jr.	901-332-7700	R	24 TA*	<0.1
Olympic Venture Partners	2420 Carillon Point	Kirkland	WA	98033	George H. Clute	206-889-9192	R	24 TA	<0.1

Company type codes: P - Public, R - Private, S - Subsidiary, D - Division, J - Joint Venture, A - Affiliate, G - Group. If the dollar values shown are not sales, the following codes apply: TA - Total Assets; OR - Operating Revenues; GB - Gross Billings. * - estimated dollar value. < - less than. *na* - not available.

Continued on next page.

LEADING COMPANIES - SIC 6799 - Investors, nec

Continued

Company Name	Address				CEO Name	Phone	Co. Type	Sales/Assets ($ mil)	Empl. (000)
PENMAN Partners	333 W. Wacker Dr.	Chicago	IL	60606	Kelvin J. Pennington	312-444-2763	R	24 TA*	<0.1
Schulweis Realty Inc.	9 W. 57th St.	New York	NY	10019	Harvey Schulweis	212-402-2160	R	24 TA*	<0.1
Sutter Hill Ventures	755 Page Mill Rd.	Palo Alto	CA	94304	Paul M. Wythes	415-493-5600	R	24 TA*	<0.1
KLT Investments Inc.	P.O. Box 410225	Kansas City	MO	64141	John DeStefano	816-556-2200	S	22 TA*	<0.1
Massey Burch Capital Corp.	310 25th Ave. N.	Nashville	TN	37203	Donald M. Johnston	615-329-9448	R	22 TA*	<0.1
FL Management Inc.	240 Madison Ave.	New York	NY	10016	Vincent Lupardi	212-949-7050	R	21 TA	<0.1

Source: *Ward's Business Directory of U.S. Private and Public Companies*, 1996. Company type codes: P - Public, R - Private, S - Subsidiary, D - Division, J - Joint Venture, A - Affiliate, G - Group. If the dollar values shown are not sales, the following codes apply: TA - Total Assets; OR - Operating Revenues; GB - Gross Billings. * - estimated dollar value. < - less than; *na* - not available.

STATE AND COUNTY SUMMARIES

STATE RANKINGS
FINANCE, INSURANCE, AND REAL ESTATE, 1992
Ordered by Population Rank

State	Popul. Rank	Establishments Number	Establishments Rank	Establishments Per Capita Rank	Employment Number	Employment Rank	Employment Per Capita Rank	Revenues ($ 000)	Revenues Rank	Revenues Per Capita Rank	Pay / Employee $	Pay / Employee Rank
California	1	73,264	1	19	768,422	1	20	219,111,871	7	12	33,802	7
New York	2	51,883	2	7	736,114	2	4	346,445,350	1	2	51,456	1
Texas	3	38,157	4	32	397,874	3	27	93,360,908	10	29	29,873	10
Florida	4	39,288	3	5	365,559	5	13	73,904,090	27	27	26,853	27
Pennsylvania	5	22,896	6	44	301,207	6	19	74,992,565	11	17	29,853	11
Illinois	6	27,279	5	21	376,548	4	6	115,885,258	6	6	35,214	6
Ohio	7	22,084	7	40	248,635	7	26	66,597,018	26	20	27,128	26
Michigan	8	16,796	9	49	190,824	10	33	57,950,927	23	18	27,905	23
New Jersey	9	17,936	8	24	227,907	8	9	67,119,276	5	7	35,633	5
North Carolina	10	13,864	12	38	131,369	16	38	29,451,684	29	32	26,651	29
Georgia	11	14,838	10	30	165,396	11	21	38,653,940	12	25	29,760	12
Virginia	12	14,314	11	27	153,252	12	23	38,585,886	18	19	28,184	18
Massachusetts	13	12,691	14	33	216,742	9	5	67,243,075	3	4	37,318	3
Indiana	14	11,397	16	39	121,037	19	30	33,508,336	32	21	26,205	32
Missouri	15	11,823	15	25	130,887	17	17	29,929,028	24	24	27,761	24
Washington	16	13,050	13	13	115,161	20	28	27,208,361	13	28	29,485	13
Tennessee	17	10,192	21	37	101,213	21	34	23,151,652	28	30	26,837	28
Wisconsin	18	11,190	17	28	132,772	14	15	33,309,146	20	15	28,116	20
Maryland	19	10,803	18	29	131,968	15	14	33,100,403	9	14	31,443	9
Minnesota	20	10,610	19	20	124,756	18	11	34,482,844	8	9	32,995	8
Louisiana	21	8,765	23	36	75,249	24	40	14,768,304	40	40	24,492	40
Alabama	22	7,580	25	47	72,553	25	41	16,046,429	37	39	25,359	37
Arizona	23	8,850	22	23	87,929	23	25	15,842,568	22	35	27,938	22
Kentucky	24	6,669	30	50	62,479	28	43	15,463,798	38	36	24,931	38
South Carolina	25	7,170	27	42	62,332	29	42	10,835,569	43	44	23,692	43
Colorado	26	10,509	20	4	98,968	22	10	20,342,234	17	23	28,710	17
Connecticut	27	8,204	24	16	150,374	13	2	47,497,643	2	3	39,472	2
Oklahoma	28	7,037	28	31	59,251	31	39	10,667,092	41	41	24,423	41
Oregon	29	7,324	26	18	64,960	27	29	12,544,111	30	33	26,608	30
Iowa	30	6,931	29	17	70,663	26	18	16,524,806	33	22	26,084	33
Mississippi	31	5,149	32	43	36,933	35	49	6,839,971	48	47	22,516	48
Kansas	32	6,371	31	14	59,313	30	24	18,984,451	36	11	25,400	36
Arkansas	33	4,488	33	46	35,931	37	48	6,084,388	39	48	24,508	39
Utah	34	3,618	37	41	36,186	36	35	5,750,415	42	42	23,962	42
West Virginia	35	3,015	39	51	23,248	44	51	4,414,138	50	49	21,628	50
Nebraska	36	4,321	34	10	48,533	32	8	13,207,003	31	8	26,459	31
New Mexico	37	3,298	38	34	25,824	41	46	3,754,778	46	50	22,889	46
Nevada	38	3,678	36	9	28,366	39	31	6,107,876	35	31	25,579	35
Maine	39	2,528	42	35	23,928	43	36	4,870,870	19	38	28,119	19
Hawaii	40	3,955	35	3	37,200	34	7	8,080,574	21	13	28,021	21
New Hampshire	41	2,571	41	22	28,855	38	16	6,203,119	15	26	29,148	15
Idaho	42	2,408	43	26	17,633	45	45	3,231,052	45	43	23,077	45
Rhode Island	43	1,905	47	45	27,518	40	12	6,429,178	25	16	27,760	25
Montana	44	2,158	45	11	13,630	47	44	2,255,443	49	46	22,188	49
South Dakota	45	2,019	46	8	17,222	46	22	5,455,453	51	10	20,896	51
Delaware	46	2,977	40	1	38,442	33	1	20,425,569	14	1	29,266	14
North Dakota	47	1,843	48	6	12,280	48	37	2,514,313	47	37	22,863	47
Alaska	48	1,073	51	48	8,868	50	47	1,716,836	16	45	29,056	16
D.C.	49	2,182	44	2	25,497	42	3	6,390,672	4	5	37,071	4
Vermont	50	1,458	49	12	12,036	49	32	2,366,360	34	34	25,667	34
Wyoming	51	1,171	50	15	6,527	51	50	1,070,277	44	51	23,262	44

Source: Source: 1992 Economic Census, U.S. Department of Commerce. States with the highest number or ratio in a data field (e.g., number of establishments) have a rank of one (1). Per capita ratio is calculated by dividing a data field of a state by the population of that state in 1992. The ranking by which the table is ordered is shown in bold.

State Rankings, Finance, Insurance, and Real Estate, 1992

Ordered by Establishment Rank

State	Popul. Rank	Establishments Number	Establishments Rank	Establishments Per Capita Rank	Employment Number	Employment Rank	Employment Per Capita Rank	Revenues ($ 000)	Revenues Rank	Revenues Per Capita Rank	Pay / Employee $	Pay / Employee Rank
California	1	73,264	**1**	19	768,422	1	20	219,111,871	7	12	33,802	7
New York	2	51,883	**2**	7	736,114	2	4	346,445,350	1	2	51,456	1
Florida	4	39,288	**3**	5	365,559	5	13	73,904,090	27	27	26,853	27
Texas	3	38,157	**4**	32	397,874	3	27	93,360,908	10	29	29,873	10
Illinois	6	27,279	**5**	21	376,548	4	6	115,885,258	6	6	35,214	6
Pennsylvania	5	22,896	**6**	44	301,207	6	19	74,992,565	11	17	29,853	11
Ohio	7	22,084	**7**	40	248,635	7	26	66,597,018	26	20	27,128	26
New Jersey	9	17,936	**8**	24	227,907	8	9	67,119,276	5	7	35,633	5
Michigan	8	16,796	**9**	49	190,824	10	33	57,950,927	23	18	27,905	23
Georgia	11	14,838	**10**	30	165,396	11	21	38,653,940	12	25	29,760	12
Virginia	12	14,314	**11**	27	153,252	12	23	38,585,886	18	19	28,184	18
North Carolina	10	13,864	**12**	38	131,369	16	38	29,451,684	29	32	26,651	29
Washington	16	13,050	**13**	13	115,161	20	28	27,208,361	13	28	29,485	13
Massachusetts	13	12,691	**14**	33	216,742	9	5	67,243,075	3	4	37,318	3
Missouri	15	11,823	**15**	25	130,887	17	17	29,929,028	24	24	27,761	24
Indiana	14	11,397	**16**	39	121,037	19	30	33,508,336	32	21	26,205	32
Wisconsin	18	11,190	**17**	28	132,772	14	15	33,309,146	20	15	28,116	20
Maryland	19	10,803	**18**	29	131,968	15	14	33,100,403	9	14	31,443	9
Minnesota	20	10,610	**19**	20	124,756	18	11	34,482,844	8	9	32,995	8
Colorado	26	10,509	**20**	4	98,968	22	10	20,342,234	17	23	28,710	17
Tennessee	17	10,192	**21**	37	101,213	21	34	23,151,652	28	30	26,837	28
Arizona	23	8,850	**22**	23	87,929	23	25	15,842,568	22	35	27,938	22
Louisiana	21	8,765	**23**	36	75,249	24	40	14,768,304	40	40	24,492	40
Connecticut	27	8,204	**24**	16	150,374	13	2	47,497,643	2	3	39,472	2
Alabama	22	7,580	**25**	47	72,553	25	41	16,046,429	37	39	25,359	37
Oregon	29	7,324	**26**	18	64,960	27	29	12,544,111	30	33	26,608	30
South Carolina	25	7,170	**27**	42	62,332	29	42	10,835,569	43	44	23,692	43
Oklahoma	28	7,037	**28**	31	59,251	31	39	10,667,092	41	41	24,423	41
Iowa	30	6,931	**29**	17	70,663	26	18	16,524,806	33	22	26,084	33
Kentucky	24	6,669	**30**	50	62,479	28	43	15,463,798	38	36	24,931	38
Kansas	32	6,371	**31**	14	59,313	30	24	18,984,451	36	11	25,400	36
Mississippi	31	5,149	**32**	43	36,933	35	49	6,839,971	48	47	22,516	48
Arkansas	33	4,488	**33**	46	35,931	37	48	6,084,388	39	48	24,508	39
Nebraska	36	4,321	**34**	10	48,533	32	8	13,207,003	31	8	26,459	31
Hawaii	40	3,955	**35**	3	37,200	34	7	8,080,574	21	13	28,021	21
Nevada	38	3,678	**36**	9	28,366	39	31	6,107,876	35	31	25,579	35
Utah	34	3,618	**37**	41	36,186	36	35	5,750,415	42	42	23,962	42
New Mexico	37	3,298	**38**	34	25,824	41	46	3,754,778	46	50	22,889	46
West Virginia	35	3,015	**39**	51	23,248	44	51	4,414,138	50	49	21,628	50
Delaware	46	2,977	**40**	1	38,442	33	1	20,425,569	14	1	29,266	14
New Hampshire	41	2,571	**41**	22	28,855	38	16	6,203,119	15	26	29,148	15
Maine	39	2,528	**42**	35	23,928	43	36	4,870,870	19	38	28,119	19
Idaho	42	2,408	**43**	26	17,633	45	45	3,231,052	45	43	23,077	45
D.C.	49	2,182	**44**	2	25,497	42	3	6,390,672	4	5	37,071	4
Montana	44	2,158	**45**	11	13,630	47	44	2,255,443	49	46	22,188	49
South Dakota	45	2,019	**46**	8	17,222	46	22	5,455,453	51	10	20,896	51
Rhode Island	43	1,905	**47**	45	27,518	40	12	6,429,178	25	16	27,760	25
North Dakota	47	1,843	**48**	6	12,280	48	37	2,514,313	47	37	22,863	47
Vermont	50	1,458	**49**	12	12,036	49	32	2,366,360	34	34	25,667	34
Wyoming	51	1,171	**50**	15	6,527	51	50	1,070,277	44	51	23,262	44
Alaska	48	1,073	**51**	48	8,868	50	47	1,716,836	16	45	29,056	16

Source: Source: 1992 Economic Census, U.S. Department of Commerce. States with the highest number or ratio in a data field (e.g., number of establishments) have a rank of one (1). Per capita ratio is calculated by dividing a data field of a state by the population of that state in 1992. The ranking by which the table is ordered is shown in bold.

State Rankings, Finance, Insurance, and Real Estate, 1992

Ordered by Employment Rank

State	Popul. Rank	Establishments			Employment			Revenues			Pay / Employee	
		Number	Rank	Per Capita Rank	Number	Rank	Per Capita Rank	($ 000)	Rank	Per Capita Rank	$	Rank
California	1	73,264	1	19	768,422	1	20	219,111,871	7	12	33,802	7
New York	2	51,883	2	7	736,114	2	4	346,445,350	1	2	51,456	1
Texas	3	38,157	4	32	397,874	3	27	93,360,908	10	29	29,873	10
Illinois	6	27,279	5	21	376,548	4	6	115,885,258	6	6	35,214	6
Florida	4	39,288	3	5	365,559	5	13	73,904,090	27	27	26,853	27
Pennsylvania	5	22,896	6	44	301,207	6	19	74,992,565	11	17	29,853	11
Ohio	7	22,084	7	40	248,635	7	26	66,597,018	26	20	27,128	26
New Jersey	9	17,936	8	24	227,907	8	9	67,119,276	5	7	27,128	26
Massachusetts	13	12,691	14	33	216,742	9	5	67,243,075	3	4	35,633	5
Michigan	8	16,796	9	49	190,824	10	33	57,950,927	23	18	37,318	3
Georgia	11	14,838	10	30	165,396	11	21	38,653,940	12	25	27,905	23
Virginia	12	14,314	11	27	153,252	12	23	38,585,886	18	19	29,760	12
Connecticut	27	8,204	24	16	150,374	13	2	47,497,643	2	3	28,184	18
Wisconsin	18	11,190	17	28	132,772	14	15	33,309,146	20	15	39,472	2
Maryland	19	10,803	18	29	131,968	15	14	33,100,403	9	14	28,116	20
North Carolina	10	13,864	12	38	131,369	16	38	29,451,684	29	32	31,443	9
Missouri	15	11,823	15	25	130,887	17	17	29,929,028	24	24	26,651	29
Minnesota	20	10,610	19	20	124,756	18	11	34,482,844	8	9	27,761	24
Indiana	14	11,397	16	39	121,037	19	30	33,508,336	32	21	32,995	8
Washington	16	13,050	13	13	115,161	20	28	27,208,361	13	28	26,205	32
Tennessee	17	10,192	21	37	101,213	21	34	23,151,652	28	30	29,485	13
Colorado	26	10,509	20	4	98,968	22	10	20,342,234	17	23	26,837	28
Arizona	23	8,850	22	23	87,929	23	25	15,842,568	22	35	28,710	17
Louisiana	21	8,765	23	36	75,249	24	40	14,768,304	40	40	27,938	22
Alabama	22	7,580	25	47	72,553	25	41	16,046,429	37	39	24,492	40
Iowa	30	6,931	29	17	70,663	26	18	16,524,806	33	22	25,359	37
Oregon	29	7,324	26	18	64,960	27	29	12,544,111	30	33	26,084	33
Kentucky	24	6,669	30	50	62,479	28	43	15,463,798	38	36	26,608	30
South Carolina	25	7,170	27	42	62,332	29	42	10,835,569	43	44	24,931	38
Kansas	32	6,371	31	14	59,313	30	24	18,984,451	36	11	23,692	43
Oklahoma	28	7,037	28	31	59,251	31	39	10,667,092	41	41	25,400	36
Nebraska	36	4,321	34	10	48,533	32	8	13,207,003	31	8	24,423	41
Delaware	46	2,977	40	1	38,442	33	1	20,425,569	14	1	26,459	31
Hawaii	40	3,955	35	3	37,200	34	7	8,080,574	21	13	29,266	14
Mississippi	31	5,149	32	43	36,933	35	49	6,839,971	48	47	28,021	21
Utah	34	3,618	37	41	36,186	36	35	5,750,415	42	42	22,516	48
Arkansas	33	4,488	33	46	35,931	37	48	6,084,388	39	48	23,962	42
New Hampshire	41	2,571	41	22	28,855	38	16	6,203,119	15	26	24,508	39
Nevada	38	3,678	36	9	28,366	39	31	6,107,876	35	31	29,148	15
Rhode Island	43	1,905	47	45	27,518	40	12	6,429,178	25	16	25,579	35
New Mexico	37	3,298	38	34	25,824	41	46	3,754,778	46	50	27,760	25
D.C.	49	2,182	44	2	25,497	42	3	6,390,672	4	5	22,889	46
Maine	39	2,528	42	35	23,928	43	36	4,870,870	19	38	37,071	4
West Virginia	35	3,015	39	51	23,248	44	51	4,414,138	50	49	28,119	19
Idaho	42	2,408	43	26	17,633	45	45	3,231,052	45	43	21,628	50
South Dakota	45	2,019	46	8	17,222	46	22	5,455,453	51	10	23,077	45
Montana	44	2,158	45	11	13,630	47	44	2,255,443	49	46	20,896	51
North Dakota	47	1,843	48	6	12,280	48	37	2,514,313	47	37	22,188	49
Vermont	50	1,458	49	12	12,036	49	32	2,366,360	34	34	22,863	47
Alaska	48	1,073	51	48	8,868	50	47	1,716,836	16	45	25,667	34
Wyoming	51	1,171	50	15	6,527	51	50	1,070,277	44	51	23,262	44

Source: Source: 1992 Economic Census, U.S. Department of Commerce. States with the highest number or ratio in a data field (e.g., number of establishments) have a rank of one (1). Per capita ratio is calculated by dividing a data field of a state by the population of that state in 1992. The ranking by which the table is ordered is shown in bold.

State Rankings, Finance, Insurance, and Real Estate, 1992

Ordered by Revenue Rank

| State | Popul. Rank | Establishments | | | Employment | | | Revenues | | | Pay / Employee | |
		Number	Rank	Per Capita Rank	Number	Rank	Per Capita Rank	($ 000)	Rank	Per Capita Rank	$	Rank
New York	2	51,883	2	7	736,114	2	4	346,445,350	1	2	51,456	1
Connecticut	27	8,204	24	16	150,374	13	2	47,497,643	2	3	39,472	2
Massachusetts	13	12,691	14	33	216,742	9	5	67,243,075	3	4	37,318	3
D.C.	49	2,182	44	2	25,497	42	3	6,390,672	4	5	37,071	4
New Jersey	9	17,936	8	24	227,907	8	9	67,119,276	5	7	35,633	5
Illinois	6	27,279	5	21	376,548	4	6	115,885,258	6	6	35,214	6
California	1	73,264	1	19	768,422	1	20	219,111,871	7	12	33,802	7
Minnesota	20	10,610	19	20	124,756	18	11	34,482,844	8	9	32,995	8
Maryland	19	10,803	18	29	131,968	15	14	33,100,403	9	14	31,443	9
Texas	3	38,157	4	32	397,874	3	27	93,360,908	10	29	29,873	10
Pennsylvania	5	22,896	6	44	301,207	6	19	74,992,565	11	17	29,853	11
Georgia	11	14,838	10	30	165,396	11	21	38,653,940	12	25	29,760	12
Washington	16	13,050	13	13	115,161	20	28	27,208,361	13	28	29,485	13
Delaware	46	2,977	40	1	38,442	33	1	20,425,569	14	1	29,266	14
New Hampshire	41	2,571	41	22	28,855	38	16	6,203,119	15	26	29,148	15
Alaska	48	1,073	51	48	8,868	50	47	1,716,836	16	45	29,056	16
Colorado	26	10,509	20	4	98,968	22	10	20,342,234	17	23	28,710	17
Virginia	12	14,314	11	27	153,252	12	23	38,585,886	18	19	28,184	18
Maine	39	2,528	42	35	23,928	43	36	4,870,870	19	38	28,119	19
Wisconsin	18	11,190	17	28	132,772	14	15	33,309,146	20	15	28,116	20
Hawaii	40	3,955	35	3	37,200	34	7	8,080,574	21	13	28,021	21
Arizona	23	8,850	22	23	87,929	23	25	15,842,568	22	35	27,938	22
Michigan	8	16,796	9	49	190,824	10	33	57,950,927	23	18	27,905	23
Missouri	15	11,823	15	25	130,887	17	17	29,929,028	24	24	27,761	24
Rhode Island	43	1,905	47	45	27,518	40	12	6,429,178	25	16	27,760	25
Ohio	7	22,084	7	40	248,635	7	26	66,597,018	26	20	27,128	26
Florida	4	39,288	3	5	365,559	5	13	73,904,090	27	27	26,853	27
Tennessee	17	10,192	21	37	101,213	21	34	23,151,652	28	30	26,837	28
North Carolina	10	13,864	12	38	131,369	16	38	29,451,684	29	32	26,651	29
Oregon	29	7,324	26	18	64,960	27	29	12,544,111	30	33	26,608	30
Nebraska	36	4,321	34	10	48,533	32	8	13,207,003	31	8	26,459	31
Indiana	14	11,397	16	39	121,037	19	30	33,508,336	32	21	26,205	32
Iowa	30	6,931	29	17	70,663	26	18	16,524,806	33	22	26,084	33
Vermont	50	1,458	49	12	12,036	49	32	2,366,360	34	34	25,667	34
Nevada	38	3,678	36	9	28,366	39	31	6,107,876	35	31	25,579	35
Kansas	32	6,371	31	14	59,313	30	24	18,984,451	36	11	25,400	36
Alabama	22	7,580	25	47	72,553	25	41	16,046,429	37	39	25,359	37
Kentucky	24	6,669	30	50	62,479	28	43	15,463,798	38	36	24,931	38
Arkansas	33	4,488	33	46	35,931	37	48	6,084,388	39	48	24,508	39
Louisiana	21	8,765	23	36	75,249	24	40	14,768,304	40	40	24,492	40
Oklahoma	28	7,037	28	31	59,251	31	39	10,667,092	41	41	24,423	41
Utah	34	3,618	37	41	36,186	36	35	5,750,415	42	42	23,962	42
South Carolina	25	7,170	27	42	62,332	29	42	10,835,569	43	44	23,692	43
Wyoming	51	1,171	50	15	6,527	51	50	1,070,277	44	51	23,262	44
Idaho	42	2,408	43	26	17,633	45	45	3,231,052	45	43	23,077	45
New Mexico	37	3,298	38	34	25,824	41	46	3,754,778	46	50	22,889	46
North Dakota	47	1,843	48	6	12,280	48	37	2,514,313	47	37	22,863	47
Mississippi	31	5,149	32	43	36,933	35	49	6,839,971	48	47	22,516	48
Montana	44	2,158	45	11	13,630	47	44	2,255,443	49	46	22,188	49
West Virginia	35	3,015	39	51	23,248	44	51	4,414,138	50	49	21,628	50
South Dakota	45	2,019	46	8	17,222	46	22	5,455,453	51	10	20,896	51

Source: Source: 1992 Economic Census, U.S. Department of Commerce. States with the highest number or ratio in a data field (e.g., number of establishments) have a rank of one (1). Per capita ratio is calculated by dividing a data field of a state by the population of that state in 1992. The ranking by which the table is ordered is shown in bold.

State Rankings, Finance, Insurance, and Real Estate, 1992

Ordered by Pay / Employee Rank

State	Popul. Rank	Establishments			Employment			Revenues			Pay / Employee	
		Number	Rank	Per Capita Rank	Number	Rank	Per Capita Rank	($ 000)	Rank	Per Capita Rank	$	Rank
New York	2	51,883	2	7	736,114	2	4	346,445,350	1	2	51,456	1
Connecticut	27	8,204	24	16	150,374	13	2	47,497,643	2	3	39,472	2
Massachusetts	13	12,691	14	33	216,742	9	5	67,243,075	3	4	37,318	3
D.C.	49	2,182	44	2	25,497	42	3	6,390,672	4	5	37,071	4
New Jersey	9	17,936	8	24	227,907	8	9	67,119,276	5	7	35,633	5
Illinois	6	27,279	5	21	376,548	4	6	115,885,258	6	6	35,214	6
California	1	73,264	1	19	768,422	1	20	219,111,871	7	12	33,802	7
Minnesota	20	10,610	19	20	124,756	18	11	34,482,844	8	9	32,995	8
Maryland	19	10,803	18	29	131,968	15	14	33,100,403	9	14	31,443	9
Texas	3	38,157	4	32	397,874	3	27	93,360,908	10	29	29,873	10
Pennsylvania	5	22,896	6	44	301,207	6	19	74,992,565	11	17	29,853	11
Georgia	11	14,838	10	30	165,396	11	21	38,653,940	12	25	29,760	12
Washington	16	13,050	13	13	115,161	20	28	27,208,361	13	28	29,485	13
Delaware	46	2,977	40	1	38,442	33	1	20,425,569	14	1	29,266	14
New Hampshire	41	2,571	41	22	28,855	38	16	6,203,119	15	26	29,148	15
Alaska	48	1,073	51	48	8,868	50	47	1,716,836	16	45	29,056	16
Colorado	26	10,509	20	4	98,968	22	10	20,342,234	17	23	28,710	17
Virginia	12	14,314	11	27	153,252	12	23	38,585,886	18	19	28,184	18
Maine	39	2,528	42	35	23,928	43	36	4,870,870	19	38	28,119	19
Wisconsin	18	11,190	17	28	132,772	14	15	33,309,146	20	15	28,116	20
Hawaii	40	3,955	35	3	37,200	34	7	8,080,574	21	13	28,021	21
Arizona	23	8,850	22	23	87,929	23	25	15,842,568	22	35	27,938	22
Michigan	8	16,796	9	49	190,824	10	33	57,950,927	23	18	27,905	23
Missouri	15	11,823	15	25	130,887	17	17	29,929,028	24	24	27,761	24
Rhode Island	43	1,905	47	45	27,518	40	12	6,429,178	25	16	27,760	25
Ohio	7	22,084	7	40	248,635	7	26	66,597,018	26	20	27,128	26
Florida	4	39,288	3	5	365,559	5	13	73,904,090	27	27	26,853	27
Tennessee	17	10,192	21	37	101,213	21	34	23,151,652	28	30	26,837	28
North Carolina	10	13,864	12	38	131,369	16	38	29,451,684	29	32	26,651	29
Oregon	29	7,324	26	18	64,960	27	29	12,544,111	30	33	26,608	30
Nebraska	36	4,321	34	10	48,533	32	8	13,207,003	31	8	26,459	31
Indiana	14	11,397	16	39	121,037	19	30	33,508,336	32	21	26,205	32
Iowa	30	6,931	29	17	70,663	26	18	16,524,806	33	22	26,084	33
Vermont	50	1,458	49	12	12,036	49	32	2,366,360	34	34	25,667	34
Nevada	38	3,678	36	9	28,366	39	31	6,107,876	35	31	25,579	35
Kansas	32	6,371	31	14	59,313	30	24	18,984,451	36	11	25,400	36
Alabama	22	7,580	25	47	72,553	25	41	16,046,429	37	39	25,359	37
Kentucky	24	6,669	30	50	62,479	28	43	15,463,798	38	36	24,931	38
Arkansas	33	4,488	33	46	35,931	37	48	6,084,388	39	48	24,508	39
Louisiana	21	8,765	23	36	75,249	24	40	14,768,304	40	40	24,492	40
Oklahoma	28	7,037	28	31	59,251	31	39	10,667,092	41	41	24,423	41
Utah	34	3,618	37	41	36,186	36	35	5,750,415	42	42	23,962	42
South Carolina	25	7,170	27	42	62,332	29	42	10,835,569	43	44	23,692	43
Wyoming	51	1,171	50	15	6,527	51	50	1,070,277	44	51	23,262	44
Idaho	42	2,408	43	26	17,633	45	45	3,231,052	45	43	23,077	45
New Mexico	37	3,298	38	34	25,824	41	46	3,754,778	46	50	22,889	46
North Dakota	47	1,843	48	6	12,280	48	37	2,514,313	47	37	22,863	47
Mississippi	31	5,149	32	43	36,933	35	49	6,839,971	48	47	22,516	48
Montana	44	2,158	45	11	13,630	47	44	2,255,443	49	46	22,188	49
West Virginia	35	3,015	39	51	23,248	44	51	4,414,138	50	49	21,628	50
South Dakota	45	2,019	46	8	17,222	46	22	5,455,453	51	10	20,896	51

Source: Source: 1992 Economic Census, U.S. Department of Commerce. States with the highest number or ratio in a data field (e.g., number of establishments) have a rank of one (1). Per capita ratio is calculated by dividing a data field of a state by the population of that state in 1992. The ranking by which the table is ordered is shown in bold.

FINANCE, INSURANCE, AND REAL ESTATE BY STATE

SIC	Industry	No. Establishments			Employment		Pay / Employee		Annual Payroll ($ 000)		
		1992	1993	% US	1992	1993	1992	1993	1992	1993	% US
ALABAMA											
60 –	**Finance, insurance, and real estate**	7,621	7,826	1.3	74,907	77,190	24,412	24,783	1,876,879	1,990,826	0.9
6000	Depository institutions	1,542	1,550	1.5	28,718	29,346	22,236	22,526	629,304	652,730	1.1
6010	Central reserve depository	2	1	1.3	-	-	-	-	-	-	-
6020	Commercial banks	1,048	1,076	1.7	23,368	24,514	22,775	22,984	528,360	553,970	1.3
6030	Savings institutions	198	141	0.7	2,563	1,802	20,783	23,703	46,460	41,003	0.5
6060	Credit unions	272	303	2.0	2,471	2,710	18,449	17,446	47,124	49,833	1.7
6090	Functions closely related to banking	22	29	0.6	-	-	-	-	-	-	-
6100	Nondepository institutions	743	789	1.9	5,719	6,488	24,863	22,448	148,964	167,676	0.9
6110	Federal and Federally-sponsored credit	32	38	2.8	114	-	28,491	-	3,287	-	-
6140	Personal credit institutions	497	506	3.0	2,660	2,991	22,716	19,420	59,945	60,174	1.6
6150	Business credit institutions	21	36	0.7	149	-	21,047	-	3,023	-	-
6160	Mortgage bankers and brokers	183	204	1.1	2,771	3,195	27,024	25,142	82,110	98,952	1.1
6200	Security and commodity brokers	222	233	0.7	1,632	1,849	61,615	57,891	101,386	119,192	0.3
6210	Security brokers and dealers	147	156	0.8	1,383	1,533	66,320	63,421	91,555	107,355	0.4
6220	Commodity contracts brokers, dealers	2	5	0.3	-	-	-	-	-	-	-
6230	Security and commodity exchanges	1	-	-	-	-	-	-	-	-	-
6280	Security and commodity services	70	71	0.5	-	-	-	-	-	-	-
6300	Insurance carriers	999	952	2.2	15,951	15,934	30,115	30,910	494,294	502,563	1.0
6310	Life insurance	316	284	2.2	6,816	6,205	27,781	29,080	201,226	179,894	0.9
6321	Accident and health insurance	34	35	3.1	520	842	17,200	19,929	8,578	17,704	1.2
6324	Hospital and medical service plans	22	27	1.5	2,852	2,713	33,049	34,225	90,060	88,872	1.4
6330	Fire, marine, and casualty insurance	522	525	2.8	5,071	5,357	33,987	34,353	177,373	197,277	0.9
6350	Surety insurance	10	7	1.2	-	141	-	36,482	-	5,225	1.0
6360	Title insurance	27	20	0.9	-	-	-	-	-	-	-
6370	Pension, health, and welfare funds	61	51	0.8	262	517	20,947	18,074	6,315	9,029	0.7
6390	Insurance carriers, n.e.c.	3	2	1.2	-	-	-	-	-	-	-
6400	Insurance agents, brokers, and service	1,493	1,560	1.3	7,193	7,349	24,100	24,277	184,377	195,879	1.0
6500	Real estate	2,347	2,456	1.0	13,084	13,518	14,950	15,350	214,190	240,423	0.8
6510	Real estate operators and lessors	991	1,109	1.1	5,062	5,821	12,437	12,840	68,172	80,338	0.9
6530	Real estate agents and managers	848	1,059	1.0	5,296	6,212	17,693	17,355	102,074	127,074	0.7
6540	Title abstract offices	55	60	1.3	292	327	17,301	17,774	5,329	8,152	0.8
6552	Subdividers and developers, n.e.c.	125	111	1.2	797	348	14,058	21,437	11,613	12,322	0.7
6553	Cemetery subdividers and developers	93	99	1.6	703	800	12,848	14,390	9,094	12,034	1.4
6700	Holding and other investment offices	264	276	1.0	2,151	2,170	39,937	50,383	89,621	98,487	0.8
6710	Holding offices	64	83	1.0	1,366	1,319	52,653	68,685	74,569	79,467	1.1
6720	Investment offices	7	3	0.4	35	-	20,000	-	636	-	-
6732	Educational, religious, etc. trusts	50	54	1.1	249	301	14,490	13,635	3,483	4,324	0.5
6733	Trusts, n.e.c.	75	68	1.2	199	-	15,779	-	3,285	-	-
6792	Oil royalty traders	3	8	1.0	15	-	66,933	-	1,281	-	-
6794	Patent owners and lessors	13	11	0.7	120	105	9,467	24,762	1,589	2,988	0.4
6798	Real estate investment trusts	8	1	0.2	12	-	17,000	-	438	-	-
6799	Investors, n.e.c.	37	46	0.9	150	143	27,573	47,357	4,095	5,980	0.5
ALASKA											
60 –	**Finance, insurance, and real estate**	1,102	1,141	0.2	9,047	9,305	29,081	29,363	278,466	299,987	0.1
6000	Depository institutions	194	193	0.2	3,658	3,854	26,318	24,835	98,568	102,184	0.2
6010	Central reserve depository	6	1	1.3	-	-	-	-	-	-	-
6020	Commercial banks	128	117	0.2	2,713	2,775	27,437	24,248	76,397	72,977	0.2
6030	Savings institutions	1	3	0.0	-	-	-	-	-	-	-
6060	Credit unions	51	64	0.4	794	924	23,642	25,208	19,099	24,557	0.8
6090	Functions closely related to banking	8	8	0.2	-	-	-	-	-	-	-

Source: County Business Patterns, 1992/93, CBP-92/93-1, U.S. Department of Commerce, Washington, D.C., April 1995. SIC categories for which data were suppressed or not available for both 1992 and 1993 are *not* displayed. The employment columns represent mid-March employment in the year. Pay per employee is calculated by dividing 1st Quarter payroll, annualized, by mid-March employment. The columns headed "% US" show the state's percentage of the national total for the SIC in 1993; for example, 0.9% for SIC 6030 means that the state had 0.9 percent of the national total establishments (or payroll) in SIC 6030 in 1993. A dash (-) is used to indicate that data are not available or cannot be calculated; *nec* means not elsewhere classified.

Continued on next page.

SIC	Industry	No. Establishments			Employment		Pay / Employee		Annual Payroll ($ 000)		
		1992	1993	% US	1992	1993	1992	1993	1992	1993	% US
ALASKA - [continued]											
6100	Nondepository institutions	46	40	0.1	397	-	33,753	-	15,422	-	-
6140	Personal credit institutions	21	12	0.1	180	43	24,333	25,395	4,473	1,215	0.0
6150	Business credit institutions	4	5	0.1	-	-	-	-	-	-	-
6160	Mortgage bankers and brokers	20	23	0.1	208	232	41,750	46,345	10,633	14,138	0.2
6200	Security and commodity brokers	28	32	0.1	263	289	53,992	50,298	14,212	16,076	0.0
6210	Security brokers and dealers	18	21	0.1	-	255	-	53,161	-	14,835	0.1
6220	Commodity contracts brokers, dealers	1	1	0.1	-	-	-	-	-	-	-
6280	Security and commodity services	9	10	0.1	-	-	-	-	-	-	-
6300	Insurance carriers	107	101	0.2	731	653	45,155	47,663	32,230	30,553	0.1
6310	Life insurance	18	15	0.1	95	94	33,305	38,170	3,169	3,579	0.0
6321	Accident and health insurance	2	1	0.1	-	-	-	-	-	-	-
6324	Hospital and medical service plans	1	1	0.1	-	-	-	-	-	-	-
6330	Fire, marine, and casualty insurance	49	47	0.2	414	395	56,850	56,618	21,189	19,715	0.1
6350	Surety insurance	2	1	0.2	-	-	-	-	-	-	-
6360	Title insurance	12	5	0.2	113	-	33,416	-	4,001	-	-
6370	Pension, health, and welfare funds	23	30	0.5	-	64	-	29,625	-	3,042	0.2
6390	Insurance carriers, n.e.c.	-	1	0.6	-	-	-	-	-	-	-
6400	Insurance agents, brokers, and service	181	195	0.2	991	1,155	34,297	33,482	35,542	41,108	0.2
6500	Real estate	458	501	0.2	2,302	2,525	22,619	25,058	57,641	73,104	0.2
6510	Real estate operators and lessors	170	229	0.2	846	1,335	19,693	29,228	19,856	43,126	0.5
6530	Real estate agents and managers	213	242	0.2	1,107	1,117	25,070	19,993	29,583	27,096	0.2
6540	Title abstract offices	5	6	0.1	35	-	27,771	-	1,127	-	-
6552	Subdividers and developers, n.e.c.	21	19	0.2	184	-	24,522	-	4,534	-	-
6553	Cemetery subdividers and developers	3	2	0.0	-	-	-	-	-	-	-
6700	Holding and other investment offices	84	75	0.3	595	442	26,729	28,851	19,852	15,551	0.1
6710	Holding offices	23	17	0.2	335	157	30,961	36,866	10,937	6,648	0.1
6720	Investment offices	5	5	0.6	18	-	8,889	-	236	-	-
6732	Educational, religious, etc. trusts	12	12	0.3	-	-	-	-	-	-	-
6733	Trusts, n.e.c.	25	19	0.3	-	61	-	27,016	-	2,764	0.4
6794	Patent owners and lessors	1	2	0.1	-	-	-	-	-	-	-
6798	Real estate investment trusts	3	1	0.2	-	-	-	-	-	-	-
6799	Investors, n.e.c.	12	18	0.4	101	-	21,505	-	4,429	-	-
ARIZONA											
60-	**Finance, insurance, and real estate**	9,014	9,275	1.5	90,950	93,443	26,263	26,774	2,457,842	2,700,219	1.2
6000	Depository institutions	1,174	1,009	1.0	26,082	25,818	26,467	26,260	679,243	697,876	1.2
6020	Commercial banks	828	657	1.0	22,938	22,179	26,969	27,505	609,448	628,848	1.5
6030	Savings institutions	133	111	0.6	1,138	718	26,141	21,610	25,505	16,514	0.2
6060	Credit unions	143	154	1.0	1,582	1,899	19,879	18,433	33,252	37,607	1.2
6080	Foreign bank and branches and agencies	1	-	-	-	-	-	-	-	-	-
6090	Functions closely related to banking	68	86	1.8	-	1,022	-	17,061	-	14,904	0.9
6100	Nondepository institutions	581	655	1.6	8,794	9,365	29,206	28,021	275,715	326,492	1.8
6110	Federal and Federally-sponsored credit	5	7	0.5	-	119	-	30,118	-	4,187	0.5
6140	Personal credit institutions	182	179	1.1	1,591	1,469	25,023	21,838	39,026	33,001	0.9
6150	Business credit institutions	69	87	1.8	4,062	3,767	26,023	24,784	106,655	93,297	2.3
6160	Mortgage bankers and brokers	312	379	2.0	3,070	4,010	35,642	33,265	127,148	195,947	2.2
6200	Security and commodity brokers	449	468	1.4	3,105	3,565	52,536	55,448	168,953	215,387	0.5
6210	Security brokers and dealers	232	249	1.3	2,525	3,026	58,123	56,489	151,745	184,563	0.6
6220	Commodity contracts brokers, dealers	8	4	0.3	-	-	-	-	-	-	-
6230	Security and commodity exchanges	1	1	1.0	-	-	-	-	-	-	-
6280	Security and commodity services	206	214	1.6	551	521	28,261	49,797	16,113	29,918	0.3
6300	Insurance carriers	824	710	1.6	15,756	17,249	28,110	30,927	457,156	542,311	1.0
6310	Life insurance	204	180	1.4	3,884	3,753	28,428	30,362	106,884	109,725	0.6
6321	Accident and health insurance	23	17	1.5	280	198	26,786	31,859	6,913	6,368	0.4
6324	Hospital and medical service plans	25	35	2.0	1,557	3,045	25,631	28,796	45,095	91,436	1.4
6330	Fire, marine, and casualty insurance	327	286	1.5	7,511	7,517	29,834	34,146	230,433	250,695	1.2
6350	Surety insurance	16	18	3.0	123	171	29,171	51,930	3,883	6,560	1.2
6360	Title insurance	123	115	5.0	1,797	1,846	25,523	26,132	50,438	64,444	4.5

Source: County Business Patterns, 1992/93, CBP-92/93-1, U.S. Department of Commerce, Washington, D.C., April 1995. SIC categories for which data were suppressed or not available for both 1992 and 1993 are not displayed. The employment columns represent mid-March employment in the year. Pay per employee is calculated by dividing 1st Quarter payroll, annualized, by mid-March employment. The columns headed "% US" show the state's percentage of the national total for the SIC in 1993; for example, 0.9% for SIC 6030 means that the state had 0.9 percent of the national total establishments (or payroll) in SIC 6030 in 1993. A dash (-) is used to indicate that data are not available or cannot be calculated; nec means not elsewhere classified.

Continued on next page.

SIC	Industry	No. Establishments			Employment		Pay / Employee		Annual Payroll ($ 000)		
		1992	1993	% US	1992	1993	1992	1993	1992	1993	% US
ARIZONA - [continued]											
6370	Pension, health, and welfare funds	100	58	1.0	587	719	18,705	16,317	13,217	13,064	1.1
6390	Insurance carriers, n.e.c.	2	-	-	-	-	-	-	-	-	-
6400	Insurance agents, brokers, and service	1,723	1,915	1.6	9,540	10,389	26,811	25,221	275,084	287,059	1.4
6500	Real estate	3,822	4,085	1.7	23,817	23,865	17,363	18,202	447,861	491,545	1.7
6510	Real estate operators and lessors	1,379	1,569	1.5	7,210	7,353	11,691	12,936	94,485	99,892	1.1
6530	Real estate agents and managers	1,722	2,194	2.0	12,314	14,498	20,072	20,256	261,917	339,864	2.0
6540	Title abstract offices	26	24	0.5	214	224	22,056	20,714	4,721	5,672	0.5
6552	Subdividers and developers, n.e.c.	197	223	2.4	1,897	1,394	19,542	24,273	39,971	37,610	2.2
6553	Cemetery subdividers and developers	29	29	0.5	532	356	15,842	18,584	9,199	7,198	0.8
6700	Holding and other investment offices	424	417	1.5	3,025	2,690	38,586	38,452	113,367	107,812	0.9
6710	Holding offices	90	85	1.1	1,544	1,174	52,070	58,617	74,463	69,623	1.0
6720	Investment offices	18	13	1.6	91	34	22,593	26,000	1,953	1,614	0.2
6732	Educational, religious, etc. trusts	60	59	1.3	274	330	18,818	16,885	5,476	5,903	0.6
6733	Trusts, n.e.c.	127	117	2.1	509	487	17,949	19,220	9,729	9,862	1.4
6792	Oil royalty traders	3	2	0.3	6	-	17,333	-	35	-	-
6794	Patent owners and lessors	19	24	1.5	245	167	28,751	27,593	7,252	5,053	0.6
6798	Real estate investment trusts	27	13	2.3	55	-	34,327	-	2,058	-	-
6799	Investors, n.e.c.	54	96	1.9	230	378	40,539	31,672	10,830	13,175	1.0
ARKANSAS											
60 –	**Finance, insurance, and real estate**	4,558	4,681	0.8	37,676	37,613	23,667	24,979	904,583	964,297	0.4
6000	Depository institutions	1,038	1,040	1.0	15,254	15,339	20,602	20,887	321,211	328,752	0.6
6010	Central reserve depository	1	1	1.3	-	-	-	-	-	-	-
6020	Commercial banks	812	835	1.3	13,207	13,420	20,820	20,934	280,710	284,800	0.7
6030	Savings institutions	143	99	0.5	1,433	1,196	18,306	18,953	27,041	26,230	0.3
6060	Credit unions	65	86	0.6	369	407	18,276	20,875	6,955	8,928	0.3
6090	Functions closely related to banking	17	19	0.4	-	-	-	-	-	-	-
6100	Nondepository institutions	148	138	0.3	1,300	1,390	27,705	29,376	36,269	41,625	0.2
6110	Federal and Federally-sponsored credit	1	23	1.7	-	215	-	34,940	-	6,351	0.7
6140	Personal credit institutions	42	21	0.1	431	327	25,002	27,058	10,887	9,174	0.2
6150	Business credit institutions	32	21	0.4	235	63	31,898	26,857	6,397	1,491	0.0
6160	Mortgage bankers and brokers	72	73	0.4	629	785	28,127	29,019	18,949	24,609	0.3
6200	Security and commodity brokers	180	192	0.6	2,005	2,428	71,022	67,341	136,001	157,186	0.4
6210	Security brokers and dealers	119	134	0.7	-	1,866	-	83,106	-	143,933	0.5
6220	Commodity contracts brokers, dealers	4	4	0.3	-	6	-	26,000	-	225	0.0
6280	Security and commodity services	56	54	0.4	-	556	-	14,878	-	13,028	0.1
6300	Insurance carriers	444	355	0.8	5,668	5,169	26,404	27,645	149,651	146,053	0.3
6310	Life insurance	125	127	1.0	2,446	2,262	24,880	25,754	59,845	59,269	0.3
6321	Accident and health insurance	10	7	0.6	-	179	-	23,844	-	4,098	0.3
6324	Hospital and medical service plans	20	20	1.1	-	1,276	-	30,586	-	40,431	0.6
6330	Fire, marine, and casualty insurance	179	126	0.7	1,254	1,085	31,872	33,143	38,742	36,081	0.2
6350	Surety insurance	8	5	0.8	41	-	17,854	-	796	-	-
6360	Title insurance	40	20	0.9	211	108	17,801	16,704	4,455	2,175	0.2
6370	Pension, health, and welfare funds	56	47	0.8	303	231	11,855	12,502	5,252	3,364	0.3
6390	Insurance carriers, n.e.c.	3	2	1.2	26	-	33,846	-	928	-	-
6400	Insurance agents, brokers, and service	1,110	1,224	1.0	3,976	4,502	24,112	22,759	95,961	105,017	0.5
6500	Real estate	1,447	1,541	0.7	7,670	6,950	12,174	14,447	104,372	112,000	0.4
6510	Real estate operators and lessors	588	655	0.6	2,895	2,346	9,445	12,515	30,041	30,385	0.3
6530	Real estate agents and managers	529	635	0.6	3,009	3,129	13,869	13,910	45,008	49,760	0.3
6540	Title abstract offices	101	112	2.3	632	750	16,247	16,501	12,615	16,058	1.5
6552	Subdividers and developers, n.e.c.	60	60	0.6	665	519	13,035	24,470	10,741	12,707	0.7
6553	Cemetery subdividers and developers	65	67	1.1	191	199	12,084	12,101	2,450	2,844	0.3
6700	Holding and other investment offices	186	186	0.7	1,552	1,583	33,691	38,529	52,558	65,601	0.6
6710	Holding offices	51	56	0.7	1,038	1,127	40,004	45,650	42,093	55,156	0.8
6720	Investment offices	8	3	0.4	-	-	-	-	-	-	-
6732	Educational, religious, etc. trusts	30	39	0.8	246	215	20,764	19,628	5,082	4,283	0.4
6733	Trusts, n.e.c.	47	39	0.7	-	128	-	19,500	-	2,624	0.4
6792	Oil royalty traders	4	4	0.5	18	-	20,667	-	370	-	-

Source: County Business Patterns, 1992/93, CBP-92/93-1, U.S. Department of Commerce, Washington, D.C., April 1995. SIC categories for which data were suppressed or not available for both 1992 and 1993 are *not* displayed. The employment columns represent mid-March employment in the year. Pay per employee is calculated by dividing 1st Quarter payroll, annualized, by mid-March employment. The columns headed "% US" show the state's percentage of the national total for the SIC in 1993; for example, 0.9% for SIC 6030 means that the state had 0.9 percent of the national total establishments (or payroll) in SIC 6030 in 1993. A dash (-) is used to indicate that data are not available or cannot be calculated; *nec* means not elsewhere classified.

Continued on next page.

SIC	Industry	No. Establishments			Employment		Pay / Employee		Annual Payroll ($ 000)		
		1992	1993	% US	1992	1993	1992	1993	1992	1993	% US

ARKANSAS - [continued]

SIC	Industry	1992	1993	% US	1992	1993	1992	1993	1992	1993	% US
6794	Patent owners and lessors	2	6	0.4	-	11	-	40,000	-	702	0.1
6798	Real estate investment trusts	2	2	0.4	-	-	-	-	-	-	-
6799	Investors, n.e.c.	35	36	0.7	82	76	26,927	24,737	1,971	2,220	0.2

CALIFORNIA

SIC	Industry	1992	1993	% US	1992	1993	1992	1993	1992	1993	% US
60 –	**Finance, insurance, and real estate**	76,741	75,359	12.4	850,881	832,191	32,771	33,255	27,862,833	28,835,594	12.4
6000	Depository institutions	12,916	11,223	10.9	271,771	255,716	29,183	30,077	7,592,134	7,384,970	12.8
6010	Central reserve depository	12	3	4.0	2,556		36,953	-	92,696		
6020	Commercial banks	7,647	5,971	9.5	181,932	170,083	28,534	29,702	4,961,980	4,685,561	11.1
6030	Savings institutions	3,110	2,913	15.1	62,804	55,180	30,634	29,937	1,796,863	1,642,995	19.9
6060	Credit unions	1,123	1,255	8.2	14,775	17,653	23,739	23,624	356,452	422,371	14.0
6080	Foreign bank and branches and agencies	105	123	21.9	3,530	-	56,468	-	214,382	-	-
6090	Functions closely related to banking	911	955	20.4	6,149	6,779	27,764	34,586	169,254	276,283	16.9
6100	Nondepository institutions	6,713	7,346	17.5	69,372	73,837	37,318	35,497	2,718,085	2,999,207	16.9
6110	Federal and Federally-sponsored credit	39	65	4.7	556	1,216	32,482	48,339	18,431	55,194	6.1
6140	Personal credit institutions	1,970	1,669	9.8	21,966	19,361	31,898	27,280	693,207	533,500	13.9
6150	Business credit institutions	614	684	14.2	9,820	11,539	47,904	48,365	485,971	554,797	13.4
6160	Mortgage bankers and brokers	3,976	4,904	26.5	36,477	41,666	37,923	35,396	1,501,497	1,853,596	21.0
6200	Security and commodity brokers	3,732	4,069	11.9	42,320	44,340	73,841	74,087	3,196,431	3,845,497	9.7
6210	Security brokers and dealers	1,904	2,056	10.5	29,575	29,175	81,755	82,072	2,337,059	2,664,001	9.2
6220	Commodity contracts brokers, dealers	63	70	4.8	336	-	36,048	-	15,671	-	-
6230	Security and commodity exchanges	25	13	12.4	672	-	34,089	-	22,827	-	-
6280	Security and commodity services	1,703	1,923	14.7	11,549	14,514	57,681	59,734	815,950	1,152,265	12.2
6300	Insurance carriers	5,714	4,638	10.6	155,920	154,448	35,769	37,716	5,468,927	5,811,804	11.0
6310	Life insurance	1,154	998	7.9	39,990	37,384	35,528	35,328	1,297,975	1,227,732	6.2
6321	Accident and health insurance	93	64	5.7	1,842	1,157	31,702	34,793	56,967	41,450	2.8
6324	Hospital and medical service plans	226	256	14.5	19,878	25,536	36,578	36,317	691,390	942,143	14.3
6330	Fire, marine, and casualty insurance	2,564	2,266	11.9	69,237	69,286	36,451	39,949	2,535,363	2,785,472	12.9
6350	Surety insurance	118	103	17.3	1,894	2,081	43,611	43,052	85,695	86,781	16.0
6360	Title insurance	583	578	25.2	17,753	13,921	34,395	35,963	634,061	554,126	38.4
6370	Pension, health, and welfare funds	941	358	5.9	5,033	4,443	26,925	32,745	151,705	145,702	11.8
6390	Insurance carriers, n.e.c.	21	13	8.0	246	640	64,911	51,875	13,906	28,323	29.6
6400	Insurance agents, brokers, and service	11,517	11,914	9.7	73,619	70,414	34,507	33,774	2,522,597	2,468,058	12.2
6500	Real estate	32,114	32,288	13.7	197,215	195,572	22,410	21,621	4,581,349	4,516,588	15.2
6510	Real estate operators and lessors	13,760	14,842	14.6	69,795	72,473	17,236	16,968	1,237,451	1,302,854	14.7
6530	Real estate agents and managers	13,058	15,363	13.9	94,500	105,235	24,722	23,507	2,421,905	2,637,657	15.5
6540	Title abstract offices	250	268	5.6	3,518	4,028	29,570	30,736	111,629	139,904	13.4
6552	Subdividers and developers, n.e.c.	1,772	1,351	14.4	15,326	9,445	28,940	30,718	455,837	307,977	17.6
6553	Cemetery subdividers and developers	204	240	3.8	3,384	4,116	23,270	25,236	82,478	115,684	13.6
6700	Holding and other investment offices	3,665	3,589	13.1	32,021	29,996	40,037	41,938	1,343,775	1,404,633	11.9
6710	Holding offices	624	658	8.3	10,627	9,950	54,614	66,246	569,604	689,881	9.9
6720	Investment offices	196	103	12.6	1,856	1,179	68,987	44,872	136,239	71,739	9.7
6732	Educational, religious, etc. trusts	654	668	14.2	7,620	7,092	18,430	18,650	146,960	147,816	15.4
6733	Trusts, n.e.c.	952	904	16.0	4,371	3,986	28,177	22,119	138,835	96,299	13.5
6792	Oil royalty traders	24	39	5.0	95	153	30,653	25,961	3,275	4,362	4.3
6794	Patent owners and lessors	205	242	15.1	2,134	3,090	42,521	42,308	101,075	165,492	20.6
6798	Real estate investment trusts	233	118	21.1	1,704	835	35,911	41,111	60,553	41,874	19.7
6799	Investors, n.e.c.	625	827	16.1	2,990	3,615	44,138	42,535	160,003	182,773	14.5

COLORADO

SIC	Industry	1992	1993	% US	1992	1993	1992	1993	1992	1993	% US
60 –	**Finance, insurance, and real estate**	10,702	11,404	1.9	104,910	110,883	27,986	27,488	2,987,713	3,290,907	1.4
6000	Depository institutions	1,106	1,152	1.1	24,398	26,011	25,388	24,382	608,991	637,145	1.1
6010	Central reserve depository	5	2	2.7	-	-	-	-	-	-	-
6020	Commercial banks	563	587	0.9	15,734	17,229	25,798	25,950	392,911	456,053	1.1
6030	Savings institutions	240	211	1.1	2,580	2,034	25,361	21,231	65,081	41,939	0.5
6060	Credit unions	221	262	1.7	-	3,218	-	16,159	-	53,460	1.8
6080	Foreign bank and branches and agencies	-	1	0.2	-	-	-	-	-	-	-
6090	Functions closely related to banking	77	88	1.9	2,965	2,511	25,504	25,642	76,339	70,093	4.3

Source: County Business Patterns, 1992/93, CBP-92/93-1, U.S. Department of Commerce, Washington, D.C., April 1995. SIC categories for which data were suppressed or not available for both 1992 and 1993 are not displayed. The employment columns represent mid-March employment in the year. Pay per employee is calculated by dividing 1st Quarter payroll, annualized, by mid-March employment. The columns headed "% US" show the state's percentage of the national total for the SIC in 1993; for example, 0.9% for SIC 6030 means that the state had 0.9 percent of the national total establishments (or payroll) in SIC 6030 in 1993. A dash (-) is used to indicate that data are not available or cannot be calculated; nec means not elsewhere classified.

Continued on next page.

SIC	Industry	No. Establishments			Employment		Pay / Employee		Annual Payroll ($ 000)		
		1992	1993	% US	1992	1993	1992	1993	1992	1993	% US
COLORADO - [continued]											
6100	Nondepository institutions	757	851	2.0	9,631	10,761	28,844	30,136	303,364	388,345	2.2
6110	Federal and Federally-sponsored credit	22	24	1.7	-	-	-	-	-	-	-
6140	Personal credit institutions	282	215	1.3	3,149	-	23,510	-	76,192	-	-
6150	Business credit institutions	90	120	2.5	2,752	2,815	29,634	30,133	78,757	82,706	2.0
6160	Mortgage bankers and brokers	342	488	2.6	3,455	4,614	33,605	31,728	142,127	214,969	2.4
6200	Security and commodity brokers	704	711	2.1	8,392	7,941	53,341	54,484	446,668	458,444	1.2
6210	Security brokers and dealers	381	374	1.9	5,989	4,709	57,908	63,365	340,825	306,640	1.1
6220	Commodity contracts brokers, dealers	21	20	1.4	89	86	62,607	58,233	5,925	6,076	0.8
6230	Security and commodity exchanges	1	-	-	-	-	-	-	-	-	-
6280	Security and commodity services	297	316	2.4	2,302	3,146	41,218	41,088	99,370	145,724	1.5
6300	Insurance carriers	952	702	1.6	21,908	23,151	30,861	29,542	663,664	739,993	1.4
6310	Life insurance	214	190	1.5	7,881	9,524	34,586	25,276	256,619	301,320	1.5
6321	Accident and health insurance	32	22	1.9	370	205	32,270	32,917	11,090	6,042	0.4
6324	Hospital and medical service plans	21	34	1.9	2,397	2,759	30,196	31,935	58,614	79,423	1.2
6330	Fire, marine, and casualty insurance	396	285	1.5	8,462	8,230	29,390	34,258	256,539	279,317	1.3
6350	Surety insurance	16	12	2.0	150	65	39,067	38,831	5,894	2,960	0.5
6360	Title insurance	128	61	2.7	1,714	856	26,639	31,206	50,385	34,141	2.4
6370	Pension, health, and welfare funds	134	93	1.5	833	1,408	19,155	24,324	21,340	33,894	2.7
6390	Insurance carriers, n.e.c.	4	5	3.1	-	104	-	28,038	-	2,896	3.0
6400	Insurance agents, brokers, and service	2,001	2,275	1.9	8,375	9,564	25,759	25,564	229,202	266,900	1.3
6500	Real estate	4,576	5,124	2.2	26,063	28,622	17,642	18,187	490,843	572,647	1.9
6510	Real estate operators and lessors	1,491	1,726	1.7	6,640	9,200	13,211	14,319	97,945	146,147	1.6
6530	Real estate agents and managers	2,402	3,029	2.7	16,118	17,586	18,805	19,571	315,975	373,642	2.2
6540	Title abstract offices	53	59	1.2	336	466	18,452	20,258	7,754	11,257	1.1
6552	Subdividers and developers, n.e.c.	153	198	2.1	945	829	31,488	31,595	29,992	29,952	1.7
6553	Cemetery subdividers and developers	45	41	0.6	437	512	13,346	16,758	6,453	9,293	1.1
6700	Holding and other investment offices	550	564	2.1	5,672	4,200	38,454	44,239	220,802	204,397	1.7
6710	Holding offices	117	121	1.5	2,669	2,116	50,855	56,847	137,371	133,223	1.9
6720	Investment offices	29	20	2.5	316	154	38,329	49,844	13,183	8,330	1.1
6732	Educational, religious, etc. trusts	96	105	2.2	655	690	21,435	22,916	14,249	16,031	1.7
6733	Trusts, n.e.c.	103	101	1.8	1,100	311	23,305	15,434	22,247	5,718	0.8
6792	Oil royalty traders	31	43	5.6	102	135	32,549	38,696	3,382	4,545	4.4
6794	Patent owners and lessors	21	37	2.3	267	387	33,318	47,897	9,405	20,440	2.5
6798	Real estate investment trusts	18	9	1.6	59	52	29,559	51,077	1,820	3,345	1.6
6799	Investors, n.e.c.	95	123	2.4	312	328	38,859	30,000	12,609	11,627	0.9
CONNECTICUT											
60 –	**Finance, insurance, and real estate**	8,382	8,402	1.4	158,826	149,232	39,405	40,013	6,240,461	6,330,177	2.7
6000	Depository institutions	1,698	1,643	1.6	32,562	32,331	28,147	27,737	898,376	895,962	1.6
6010	Central reserve depository	10	1	1.3	-	-	-	-	-	-	-
6020	Commercial banks	719	680	1.1	17,197	18,007	28,628	29,167	483,426	518,611	1.2
6030	Savings institutions	689	637	3.3	13,505	12,359	28,032	26,234	368,925	326,347	4.0
6060	Credit unions	252	293	1.9	1,586	1,822	22,429	22,127	36,315	41,610	1.4
6080	Foreign bank and branches and agencies	-	1	0.2	-	-	-	-	-	-	-
6090	Functions closely related to banking	27	30	0.6	-	134	-	50,358	-	8,914	0.5
6100	Nondepository institutions	446	412	1.0	8,606	8,099	54,985	54,139	476,469	435,577	2.5
6110	Federal and Federally-sponsored credit	-	3	0.2	-	-	-	-	-	-	-
6140	Personal credit institutions	172	94	0.6	3,567	3,124	45,663	43,918	162,497	149,639	3.9
6150	Business credit institutions	76	82	1.7	3,050	2,519	74,635	73,169	217,139	163,751	4.0
6160	Mortgage bankers and brokers	189	232	1.3	1,948	-	41,743	-	95,485	-	-
6200	Security and commodity brokers	610	682	2.0	7,195	8,092	89,439	73,905	732,553	854,659	2.2
6210	Security brokers and dealers	282	285	1.5	4,418	4,591	85,601	83,909	429,722	516,535	1.8
6220	Commodity contracts brokers, dealers	16	22	1.5	74	280	63,081	62,614	5,521	66,634	9.2
6230	Security and commodity exchanges	1	1	1.0	-	-	-	-	-	-	-
6280	Security and commodity services	300	372	2.8	2,526	3,221	94,280	60,627	270,851	270,623	2.9
6300	Insurance carriers	779	680	1.6	80,673	70,732	39,588	43,186	3,026,781	3,023,733	5.7
6310	Life insurance	231	201	1.6	46,947	43,381	43,105	44,202	1,882,770	1,871,014	9.5
6321	Accident and health insurance	15	11	1.0	6,388	304	7,338	24,961	49,728	7,848	0.5

Source: County Business Patterns, 1992/93, CBP-92/93-1, U.S. Department of Commerce, Washington, D.C., April 1995. SIC categories for which data were suppressed or not available for both 1992 and 1993 are *not* displayed. The employment columns represent mid-March employment in the year. Pay per employee is calculated by dividing 1st Quarter payroll, annualized, by mid-March employment. The columns headed "% US" show the state's percentage of the national total for the SIC in 1993; for example, 0.9% for SIC 6030 means that the state had 0.9 percent of the national total establishments (or payroll) in SIC 6030 in 1993. A dash (-) is used to indicate that data are not available or cannot be calculated; *nec* means not elsewhere classified.

Continued on next page.

SIC	Industry	No. Establishments			Employment		Pay / Employee		Annual Payroll ($ 000)		
		1992	1993	% US	1992	1993	1992	1993	1992	1993	% US

CONNECTICUT - [continued]

SIC	Industry	1992	1993	% US	1992	1993	1992	1993	1992	1993	% US
6324	Hospital and medical service plans	16	18	1.0	3,268	3,763	33,203	34,535	104,578	148,105	2.3
6330	Fire, marine, and casualty insurance	317	318	1.7	22,516	21,863	42,696	43,900	939,142	949,580	4.4
6350	Surety insurance	9	5	0.8	456	-	63,921	-	23,923	-	-
6360	Title insurance	17	12	0.5	-	162	-	41,086	-	7,199	0.5
6370	Pension, health, and welfare funds	165	112	1.9	743	1,024	15,957	24,309	14,302	31,928	2.6
6390	Insurance carriers, n.e.c.	4	3	1.9	-	-	-	-	-	-	-
6400	Insurance agents, brokers, and service	1,511	1,559	1.3	10,777	10,283	36,171	35,560	402,353	395,723	2.0
6500	Real estate	2,868	2,970	1.3	14,572	15,275	24,887	24,433	405,926	426,935	1.4
6510	Real estate operators and lessors	1,050	1,194	1.2	5,051	5,662	22,118	21,324	119,506	127,317	1.4
6530	Real estate agents and managers	1,308	1,512	1.4	7,598	8,819	27,231	26,474	235,412	270,932	1.6
6540	Title abstract offices	22	27	0.6	54	-	22,963	-	1,580	-	-
6552	Subdividers and developers, n.e.c.	126	120	1.3	739	303	24,390	27,908	19,739	14,776	0.8
6553	Cemetery subdividers and developers	90	94	1.5	416	420	21,269	20,933	9,952	10,301	1.2
6700	Holding and other investment offices	458	445	1.6	3,805	4,177	59,049	53,784	247,944	277,217	2.3
6710	Holding offices	141	144	1.8	2,192	2,108	62,931	62,871	131,098	151,339	2.2
6720	Investment offices	35	20	2.5	224	101	60,554	105,822	24,162	20,593	2.8
6732	Educational, religious, etc. trusts	74	77	1.6	499	709	24,786	24,491	14,913	19,964	2.1
6733	Trusts, n.e.c.	88	96	1.7	335	367	15,606	19,313	5,376	8,130	1.1
6792	Oil royalty traders	4	4	0.5	61	-	62,951	-	4,055	-	-
6794	Patent owners and lessors	23	30	1.9	90	316	24,711	14,392	2,183	5,315	0.7
6798	Real estate investment trusts	15	9	1.6	69	-	36,580	-	4,854	-	-
6799	Investors, n.e.c.	48	64	1.2	290	521	156,966	92,660	44,314	66,169	5.3

DELAWARE

SIC	Industry	1992	1993	% US	1992	1993	1992	1993	1992	1993	% US
60 –	**Finance, insurance, and real estate**	2,885	2,996	0.5	35,402	35,246	29,447	28,488	1,052,791	1,106,792	0.5
6000	Depository institutions	302	317	0.3	18,284	18,438	31,324	28,594	573,222	575,626	1.0
6010	Central reserve depository	1	-	-	-	-	-	-	-	-	-
6020	Commercial banks	210	220	0.4	15,865	17,283	32,745	28,773	516,482	545,331	1.3
6030	Savings institutions	41	38	0.2	-	531	-	27,759	-	14,700	0.2
6060	Credit unions	45	55	0.4	-	-	-	-	-	-	-
6090	Functions closely related to banking	5	3	0.1	1,617	291	20,589	31,601	36,462	9,330	0.6
6100	Nondepository institutions	198	198	0.5	4,181	3,499	24,805	24,979	101,799	97,361	0.5
6110	Federal and Federally-sponsored credit	3	2	0.1	-	-	-	-	-	-	-
6140	Personal credit institutions	77	63	0.4	1,036	-	24,174	-	23,697	-	-
6150	Business credit institutions	52	51	1.1	2,679	2,220	22,526	21,955	58,033	55,090	1.3
6160	Mortgage bankers and brokers	63	77	0.4	436	594	39,688	34,613	18,990	25,142	0.3
6200	Security and commodity brokers	136	107	0.3	778	736	93,162	83,027	77,180	84,169	0.2
6210	Security brokers and dealers	59	41	0.2	-	435	-	94,566	-	43,256	0.1
6220	Commodity contracts brokers, dealers	2	1	0.1	-	-	-	-	-	-	-
6280	Security and commodity services	75	65	0.5	-	-	-	-	-	-	-
6300	Insurance carriers	151	117	0.3	4,592	5,072	28,101	30,935	138,145	160,772	0.3
6310	Life insurance	52	42	0.3	2,066	2,159	28,608	30,105	63,337	66,892	0.3
6321	Accident and health insurance	5	3	0.3	-	-	-	-	-	-	-
6324	Hospital and medical service plans	3	4	0.2	-	-	-	-	-	-	-
6330	Fire, marine, and casualty insurance	40	41	0.2	650	1,563	28,431	31,765	21,780	51,427	0.2
6360	Title insurance	2	4	0.2	-	-	-	-	-	-	-
6370	Pension, health, and welfare funds	47	21	0.3	257	187	20,747	20,749	7,656	3,846	0.3
6390	Insurance carriers, n.e.c.	-	1	0.6	-	-	-	-	-	-	-
6400	Insurance agents, brokers, and service	285	299	0.2	1,783	1,355	31,930	25,821	55,228	38,235	0.2
6500	Real estate	620	650	0.3	3,112	2,817	18,314	19,388	63,447	64,347	0.2
6510	Real estate operators and lessors	281	280	0.3	1,665	1,478	16,802	17,930	30,617	30,924	0.3
6530	Real estate agents and managers	233	296	0.3	1,039	1,119	20,062	21,412	22,772	28,086	0.2
6540	Title abstract offices	2	5	0.1	-	-	-	-	-	-	-
6552	Subdividers and developers, n.e.c.	29	36	0.4	77	92	25,403	19,435	2,833	2,215	0.1
6553	Cemetery subdividers and developers	20	20	0.3	96	90	17,375	17,689	1,873	1,690	0.2
6700	Holding and other investment offices	1,185	1,301	4.7	-	3,200	-	24,320	-	82,429	0.7
6710	Holding offices	954	971	12.2	2,097	2,275	16,319	24,904	27,188	53,802	0.8
6720	Investment offices	47	46	5.6	144	147	27,611	26,721	4,156	3,832	0.5

Source: County Business Patterns, 1992/93, CBP-92/93-1, U.S. Department of Commerce, Washington, D.C., April 1995. SIC categories for which data were suppressed or not available for both 1992 and 1993 are not displayed. The employment columns represent mid-March employment in the year. Pay per employee is calculated by dividing 1st Quarter payroll, annualized, by mid-March employment. The columns headed "% US" show the state's percentage of the national total for the SIC in 1993; for example, 0.9% for SIC 6030 means that the state had 0.9 percent of the national total establishments (or payroll) in SIC 6030 in 1993. A dash (-) is used to indicate that data are not available or cannot be calculated; nec means not elsewhere classified.

Continued on next page.

SIC	Industry	No. Establishments			Employment		Pay / Employee		Annual Payroll ($ 000)		
		1992	1993	% US	1992	1993	1992	1993	1992	1993	% US
DELAWARE - [continued]											
6732	Educational, religious, etc. trusts	15	15	0.3	37	38	29,622	28,737	1,202	1,244	0.1
6733	Trusts, n.e.c.	33	39	0.7	149	232	35,329	29,759	5,503	13,277	1.9
6792	Oil royalty traders	-	3	0.4	-	-	-	-	-	-	-
6794	Patent owners and lessors	37	119	7.4	-	220	-	18,218	-	4,134	0.5
6798	Real estate investment trusts	6	1	0.2	-	-	-	-	-	-	-
6799	Investors, n.e.c.	70	100	1.9	143	-	26,042	-	3,618	-	-
WASHINGTON, D.C.											
60 -	**Finance, insurance, and real estate**	2,363	2,303	0.4	33,259	37,719	40,040	36,785	1,282,618	1,417,310	0.6
6000	Depository institutions	427	425	0.4	6,605	6,010	32,557	31,219	207,320	191,150	0.3
6010	Central reserve depository	1	1	1.3	-	-	-	-	-	-	-
6020	Commercial banks	224	220	0.4	4,548	4,055	34,563	32,965	151,778	135,960	0.3
6030	Savings institutions	82	61	0.3	1,063	695	29,317	30,388	27,165	20,444	0.2
6060	Credit unions	81	99	0.6	731	1,032	23,081	23,702	17,619	25,977	0.9
6080	Foreign bank and branches and agencies	6	5	0.9	-	58	-	45,034	-	2,645	0.1
6090	Functions closely related to banking	33	39	0.8	170	-	26,376	-	5,788	-	-
6100	Nondepository institutions	67	65	0.2	3,097	3,491	85,593	72,712	202,717	217,740	1.2
6110	Federal and Federally-sponsored credit	4	4	0.3	-	-	-	-	-	-	-
6140	Personal credit institutions	25	9	0.1	264	-	27,364	-	7,820	-	-
6150	Business credit institutions	9	20	0.4	-	-	-	-	-	-	-
6160	Mortgage bankers and brokers	26	32	0.2	2,086	595	80,424	41,903	117,856	24,801	0.3
6200	Security and commodity brokers	171	175	0.5	2,204	2,939	86,909	81,964	191,419	248,524	0.6
6210	Security brokers and dealers	97	92	0.5	1,703	2,127	86,910	86,198	147,989	184,014	0.6
6220	Commodity contracts brokers, dealers	2	4	0.3	-	-	-	-	-	-	-
6230	Security and commodity exchanges	4	3	2.9	36	-	76,889	-	2,139	-	-
6280	Security and commodity services	66	76	0.6	460	791	88,157	70,088	40,661	62,551	0.7
6300	Insurance carriers	125	90	0.2	4,269	5,848	39,966	27,727	163,537	167,688	0.3
6310	Life insurance	32	29	0.2	845	1,020	40,918	39,373	35,098	41,948	0.2
6321	Accident and health insurance	6	4	0.4	108	-	57,889	-	3,290	-	-
6324	Hospital and medical service plans	10	11	0.6	-	-	-	-	-	-	-
6330	Fire, marine, and casualty insurance	16	18	0.1	159	216	52,780	55,463	7,777	9,358	0.0
6350	Surety insurance	5	3	0.5	-	-	-	-	-	-	-
6360	Title insurance	9	6	0.3	-	54	-	38,667	-	2,159	0.1
6370	Pension, health, and welfare funds	46	19	0.3	347	2,173	29,787	4,144	10,420	16,444	1.3
6400	Insurance agents, brokers, and service	120	124	0.1	1,668	2,036	40,700	39,250	66,736	83,030	0.4
6500	Real estate	1,180	1,149	0.5	11,282	12,801	23,500	22,248	288,004	317,383	1.1
6510	Real estate operators and lessors	587	589	0.6	4,331	4,227	19,695	18,493	91,025	86,439	1.0
6530	Real estate agents and managers	483	527	0.5	6,397	8,254	25,522	23,958	180,971	221,270	1.3
6540	Title abstract offices	13	9	0.2	98	76	27,061	28,632	2,308	2,236	0.2
6552	Subdividers and developers, n.e.c.	30	14	0.1	147	122	42,531	34,197	6,055	4,106	0.2
6553	Cemetery subdividers and developers	7	6	0.1	48	102	17,500	20,431	929	2,232	0.3
6700	Holding and other investment offices	264	267	1.0	4,046	4,433	37,389	38,793	158,188	185,954	1.6
6710	Holding offices	31	30	0.4	1,280	1,291	48,375	60,211	67,963	85,932	1.2
6720	Investment offices	7	6	0.7	51	58	41,333	57,310	2,285	3,408	0.5
6732	Educational, religious, etc. trusts	139	143	3.0	1,583	1,815	34,921	32,179	56,126	61,489	6.4
6733	Trusts, n.e.c.	56	56	1.0	920	1,050	20,961	18,282	20,803	22,428	3.1
6794	Patent owners and lessors	2	3	0.2	-	-	-	-	-	-	-
6798	Real estate investment trusts	5	5	0.9	-	-	-	-	-	-	-
6799	Investors, n.e.c.	21	22	0.4	126	126	71,619	73,810	7,194	8,251	0.7
FLORIDA											
60 -	**Finance, insurance, and real estate**	39,400	40,583	6.7	375,196	375,856	26,507	27,116	10,116,713	10,574,906	4.6
6000	Depository institutions	5,413	5,188	5.1	103,717	98,403	23,999	25,067	2,410,680	2,356,958	4.1
6010	Central reserve depository	5	3	4.0	-	-	-	-	-	-	-
6020	Commercial banks	3,311	3,216	5.1	72,943	67,690	24,246	25,490	1,706,813	1,582,482	3.8
6030	Savings institutions	1,310	1,100	5.7	20,139	17,621	22,892	23,434	436,276	438,569	5.3
6060	Credit unions	494	522	3.4	6,109	7,171	19,745	18,953	123,170	148,024	4.9
6080	Foreign bank and branches and agencies	36	52	9.3	-	1,879	-	39,619	-	76,223	4.2

Source: County Business Patterns, 1992/93, CBP-92/93-1, U.S. Department of Commerce, Washington, D.C., April 1995. SIC categories for which data were suppressed or not available for both 1992 and 1993 are not displayed. The employment columns represent mid-March employment in the year. Pay per employee is calculated by dividing 1st Quarter payroll, annualized, by mid-March employment. The columns headed "% US" show the state's percentage of the national total for the SIC in 1993; for example, 0.9% for SIC 6030 means that the state had 0.9 percent of the national total establishments (or payroll) in SIC 6030 in 1993. A dash (-) is used to indicate that data are not available or cannot be calculated; nec means not elsewhere classified.

Continued on next page.

SIC	Industry	No. Establishments			Employment		Pay / Employee		Annual Payroll ($ 000)		
		1992	1993	% US	1992	1993	1992	1993	1992	1993	% US
FLORIDA - [continued]											
6090	Functions closely related to banking	251	295	6.3	2,462	-	28,359	-	72,583	-	-
6100	Nondepository institutions	2,427	2,623	6.3	28,865	29,339	29,410	28,239	863,042	892,570	5.0
6110	Federal and Federally-sponsored credit	40	37	2.7	1,287	507	18,315	26,178	32,732	14,093	1.5
6140	Personal credit institutions	869	812	4.8	7,121	6,480	26,406	22,572	189,936	161,685	4.2
6150	Business credit institutions	175	262	5.4	8,676	7,755	31,779	32,199	265,381	236,369	5.7
6160	Mortgage bankers and brokers	1,247	1,506	8.1	11,498	14,594	30,890	28,726	367,061	480,224	5.4
6200	Security and commodity brokers	1,829	1,996	5.8	16,955	19,939	64,292	69,315	1,103,314	1,409,452	3.6
6210	Security brokers and dealers	1,066	1,208	6.2	13,769	15,103	69,530	73,529	946,823	1,104,411	3.8
6220	Commodity contracts brokers, dealers	38	44	3.0	515	356	39,177	41,303	22,239	17,138	2.4
6230	Security and commodity exchanges	4	7	6.7	-	6	-	81,333	-	1,022	0.2
6280	Security and commodity services	695	734	5.6	2,618	4,472	42,484	57,326	132,133	286,822	3.0
6300	Insurance carriers	3,254	2,606	6.0	66,772	65,780	30,707	31,989	2,095,461	2,133,686	4.0
6310	Life insurance	832	743	5.9	26,736	27,882	28,866	30,283	762,446	817,013	4.1
6321	Accident and health insurance	85	64	5.7	1,672	2,262	25,849	25,616	41,566	54,655	3.7
6324	Hospital and medical service plans	89	88	5.0	8,845	9,634	29,457	30,554	272,555	314,737	4.8
6330	Fire, marine, and casualty insurance	1,392	1,232	6.5	22,957	21,781	34,099	36,903	823,928	827,178	3.8
6350	Surety insurance	56	35	5.9	792	393	35,556	32,529	29,286	13,582	2.5
6360	Title insurance	444	165	7.2	3,884	2,348	26,031	24,307	109,379	68,934	4.8
6370	Pension, health, and welfare funds	290	263	4.4	1,204	1,238	37,505	20,598	36,981	28,684	2.3
6390	Insurance carriers, n.e.c.	14	10	6.2	429	230	25,296	35,791	12,275	8,192	8.6
6400	Insurance agents, brokers, and service	6,894	7,591	6.2	37,475	42,085	25,826	25,314	1,012,577	1,167,195	5.8
6500	Real estate	18,006	19,022	8.1	106,104	106,915	17,812	17,597	1,989,938	2,078,340	7.0
6510	Real estate operators and lessors	6,056	6,624	6.5	31,279	32,059	14,591	14,190	480,595	492,426	5.6
6530	Real estate agents and managers	8,344	10,686	9.7	52,717	60,859	18,662	18,197	1,041,268	1,226,282	7.2
6540	Title abstract offices	267	311	6.5	2,057	2,218	20,898	21,235	45,949	55,865	5.3
6552	Subdividers and developers, n.e.c.	851	985	10.5	10,086	8,793	22,600	24,449	221,548	234,301	13.4
6553	Cemetery subdividers and developers	152	180	2.8	2,844	2,777	19,357	19,033	57,853	57,529	6.8
6700	Holding and other investment offices	1,515	1,509	5.5	13,003	10,757	42,930	36,767	598,105	465,368	3.9
6710	Holding offices	383	416	5.2	6,455	5,655	48,724	43,288	298,426	280,558	4.0
6720	Investment offices	83	44	5.4	467	106	44,334	82,491	27,442	26,659	3.6
6732	Educational, religious, etc. trusts	184	181	3.8	1,376	973	22,398	21,316	31,027	22,530	2.4
6733	Trusts, n.e.c.	308	300	5.3	1,678	1,632	27,499	29,522	48,836	48,915	6.9
6792	Oil royalty traders	6	7	0.9	-	14	-	35,429	-	624	0.6
6794	Patent owners and lessors	80	95	5.9	849	749	98,346	28,336	104,358	24,864	3.1
6798	Real estate investment trusts	86	53	9.5	-	387	-	22,584	-	9,748	4.6
6799	Investors, n.e.c.	271	395	7.7	1,437	1,226	30,664	34,480	66,466	50,559	4.0
GEORGIA											
60 –	**Finance, insurance, and real estate**	14,969	15,524	2.6	181,086	178,529	29,690	30,297	5,317,231	5,541,123	2.4
6000	Depository institutions	2,532	2,579	2.5	51,945	50,851	26,419	26,880	1,327,561	1,322,550	2.3
6010	Central reserve depository	7	2	2.7	1,458	-	36,612	-	52,935	-	-
6020	Commercial banks	1,766	1,839	2.9	41,114	41,619	26,516	26,962	1,044,551	1,072,021	2.5
6030	Savings institutions	331	284	1.5	6,075	4,341	22,320	23,007	141,423	100,294	1.2
6060	Credit unions	281	306	2.0	2,162	2,350	20,629	20,480	45,193	50,251	1.7
6080	Foreign bank and branches and agencies	18	15	2.7	247	-	65,036	-	16,050	-	-
6090	Functions closely related to banking	127	132	2.8	750	899	38,453	33,958	26,482	31,905	1.9
6100	Nondepository institutions	1,874	1,970	4.7	15,278	16,994	32,896	32,804	504,278	612,330	3.5
6110	Federal and Federally-sponsored credit	45	44	3.2	-	391	-	43,407	-	15,610	1.7
6140	Personal credit institutions	1,144	1,111	6.5	6,546	6,439	26,293	23,163	168,333	157,168	4.1
6150	Business credit institutions	161	209	4.3	3,293	4,009	39,033	44,508	117,237	161,538	3.9
6160	Mortgage bankers and brokers	482	601	3.2	5,045	6,153	37,748	34,600	205,986	277,916	3.2
6200	Security and commodity brokers	701	727	2.1	5,666	5,988	76,004	77,458	412,074	485,077	1.2
6210	Security brokers and dealers	411	409	2.1	4,338	4,267	84,854	89,144	331,995	379,950	1.3
6220	Commodity contracts brokers, dealers	20	12	0.8	-	-	-	-	-	-	-
6230	Security and commodity exchanges	1	1	1.0	-	-	-	-	-	-	-
6280	Security and commodity services	264	305	2.3	1,106	-	43,960	-	61,199	-	-
6300	Insurance carriers	1,394	1,211	2.8	42,183	44,007	30,735	31,034	1,273,402	1,355,853	2.6
6310	Life insurance	506	450	3.5	19,500	21,136	28,121	29,847	540,919	620,817	3.1

Source: County Business Patterns, 1992/93, CBP-92/93-1, U.S. Department of Commerce, Washington, D.C., April 1995. SIC categories for which data were suppressed or not available for both 1992 and 1993 are not displayed. The employment columns represent mid-March employment in the year. Pay per employee is calculated by dividing 1st Quarter payroll, annualized, by mid-March employment. The columns headed "% US" show the state's percentage of the national total for the SIC in 1993; for example, 0.9% for SIC 6030 means that the state had 0.9 percent of the national total establishments (or payroll) in SIC 6030 in 1993. A dash (-) is used to indicate that data are not available or cannot be calculated; nec means not elsewhere classified.

Continued on next page.

SIC	Industry	No. Establishments			Employment		Pay / Employee		Annual Payroll ($ 000)		
		1992	1993	% US	1992	1993	1992	1993	1992	1993	% US
GEORGIA - [continued]											
6321	Accident and health insurance	31	22	*1.9*	934	1,030	22,090	20,474	19,118	21,567	*1.5*
6324	Hospital and medical service plans	41	35	*2.0*	2,418	2,055	27,055	32,074	63,798	66,440	*1.0*
6330	Fire, marine, and casualty insurance	581	521	*2.7*	17,910	16,650	34,840	35,813	608,698	587,777	*2.7*
6350	Surety insurance	25	17	*2.9*	237	270	46,970	39,467	9,158	10,307	*1.9*
6360	Title insurance	26	14	*0.6*	200	-	37,400	-	7,405	-	-
6370	Pension, health, and welfare funds	172	147	*2.4*	903	2,670	16,447	11,987	19,886	40,676	*3.3*
6390	Insurance carriers, n.e.c.	6	4	*2.5*	-	-	-	-	-	-	-
6400	Insurance agents, brokers, and service	3,035	3,284	*2.7*	19,913	18,598	29,697	29,823	604,341	585,439	*2.9*
6500	Real estate	4,838	5,137	*2.2*	31,616	32,351	22,392	21,240	731,307	772,285	*2.6*
6510	Real estate operators and lessors	1,800	1,992	*2.0*	10,227	9,750	16,505	16,450	179,095	170,916	*1.9*
6530	Real estate agents and managers	1,979	2,561	*2.3*	16,387	19,120	26,489	23,590	435,416	512,437	*3.0*
6540	Title abstract offices	39	45	*0.9*	188	214	25,915	26,561	4,414	5,671	*0.5*
6552	Subdividers and developers, n.e.c.	261	350	*3.7*	2,199	2,241	23,816	24,423	56,766	65,093	*3.7*
6553	Cemetery subdividers and developers	107	122	*1.9*	790	978	15,165	14,793	12,072	15,316	*1.8*
6700	Holding and other investment offices	563	578	*2.1*	12,228	7,455	32,188	42,886	389,472	319,060	*2.7*
6710	Holding offices	210	218	*2.7*	6,329	4,878	46,763	49,152	291,921	229,453	*3.3*
6720	Investment offices	29	25	*3.1*	474	103	28,717	47,728	14,204	7,004	*0.9*
6732	Educational, religious, etc. trusts	81	77	*1.6*	421	614	20,770	23,752	8,954	15,260	*1.6*
6733	Trusts, n.e.c.	84	89	*1.6*	346	465	18,555	16,929	6,932	9,271	*1.3*
6792	Oil royalty traders	3	4	*0.5*	-	7	-	22,286	-	203	*0.2*
6794	Patent owners and lessors	38	46	*2.9*	4,220	683	13,316	43,508	49,440	33,580	*4.2*
6798	Real estate investment trusts	26	14	*2.5*	-	209	-	35,675	-	8,365	*3.9*
6799	Investors, n.e.c.	66	99	*1.9*	281	431	25,011	30,172	7,882	13,668	*1.1*
HAWAII											
60 –	**Finance, insurance, and real estate**	3,983	4,035	*0.7*	40,214	40,358	27,386	27,883	1,122,515	1,202,279	*0.5*
6000	Depository institutions	510	546	*0.5*	11,769	12,447	28,262	29,536	324,877	365,988	*0.6*
6020	Commercial banks	201	253	*0.4*	7,899	8,625	29,866	30,622	227,313	260,176	*0.6*
6030	Savings institutions	173	120	*0.6*	2,472	1,753	26,231	27,192	64,803	51,861	*0.6*
6060	Credit unions	100	135	*0.9*	922	1,249	22,113	23,516	21,143	30,560	*1.0*
6080	Foreign bank and branches and agencies	3	3	*0.5*	24	24	43,667	45,500	1,107	1,123	*0.1*
6090	Functions closely related to banking	33	35	*0.7*	452	796	23,053	31,905	10,511	22,268	*1.4*
6100	Nondepository institutions	268	227	*0.5*	2,229	1,648	36,172	40,743	86,307	82,175	*0.5*
6110	Federal and Federally-sponsored credit	1	1	*0.1*	-	-	-	-	-	-	-
6140	Personal credit institutions	161	97	*0.6*	1,133	431	26,888	27,499	30,307	12,098	*0.3*
6150	Business credit institutions	19	22	*0.5*	113	-	28,673	-	3,401	-	-
6160	Mortgage bankers and brokers	86	106	*0.6*	977	1,077	47,791	47,213	52,360	65,577	*0.7*
6200	Security and commodity brokers	84	81	*0.2*	604	715	63,570	54,495	37,435	39,575	*0.1*
6210	Security brokers and dealers	44	41	*0.2*	517	581	68,124	57,749	32,520	33,235	*0.1*
6220	Commodity contracts brokers, dealers	2	2	*0.1*	-	-	-	-	-	-	-
6280	Security and commodity services	38	38	*0.3*	-	-	-	-	-	-	-
6300	Insurance carriers	301	245	*0.6*	5,130	5,039	27,223	27,727	148,957	158,824	*0.3*
6310	Life insurance	58	52	*0.4*	1,134	1,144	27,838	31,213	30,644	42,247	*0.2*
6321	Accident and health insurance	3	3	*0.3*	-	-	-	-	-	-	-
6324	Hospital and medical service plans	11	12	*0.7*	-	-	-	-	-	-	-
6330	Fire, marine, and casualty insurance	58	51	*0.3*	1,563	1,258	34,119	35,886	54,976	47,158	*0.2*
6350	Surety insurance	4	1	*0.2*	-	-	-	-	-	-	-
6360	Title insurance	13	13	*0.6*	266	291	24,917	22,914	6,324	6,670	*0.5*
6370	Pension, health, and welfare funds	150	112	*1.9*	438	405	16,977	13,264	9,034	8,691	*0.7*
6390	Insurance carriers, n.e.c.	1	-	-	-	-	-	-	-	-	-
6400	Insurance agents, brokers, and service	348	362	*0.3*	2,658	2,839	31,478	30,453	79,717	91,040	*0.4*
6500	Real estate	2,253	2,388	*1.0*	16,246	16,453	22,771	23,019	386,602	412,546	*1.4*
6510	Real estate operators and lessors	640	677	*0.7*	3,629	4,332	21,473	22,596	77,480	104,381	*1.2*
6530	Real estate agents and managers	1,227	1,566	*1.4*	8,557	8,756	21,244	21,502	196,271	211,817	*1.2*
6540	Title abstract offices	3	13	*0.3*	-	542	-	29,004	-	16,436	*1.6*
6552	Subdividers and developers, n.e.c.	132	102	*1.1*	2,638	2,310	27,216	28,168	73,536	66,520	*3.8*
6553	Cemetery subdividers and developers	13	19	*0.3*	334	507	23,461	22,793	7,507	12,632	*1.5*
6700	Holding and other investment offices	210	177	*0.6*	1,388	1,082	33,069	37,601	49,089	44,673	*0.4*

Source: County Business Patterns, 1992/93, CBP-92/93-1, U.S. Department of Commerce, Washington, D.C., April 1995. SIC categories for which data were suppressed or not available for both 1992 and 1993 are *not* displayed. The employment columns represent mid-March employment in the year. Pay per employee is calculated by dividing 1st Quarter payroll, annualized, by mid-March employment. The columns headed "% US" show the state's percentage of the national total for the SIC in 1993; for example, 0.9% for SIC 6030 means that the state had 0.9 percent of the national total establishments (or payroll) in SIC 6030 in 1993. A dash (-) is used to indicate that data are not available or cannot be calculated; *nec* means not elsewhere classified.

Continued on next page.

SIC	Industry	No. Establishments			Employment		Pay / Employee		Annual Payroll ($ 000)		
		1992	1993	% US	1992	1993	1992	1993	1992	1993	% US
HAWAII - [continued]											
6710	Holding offices	38	39	0.5	490	337	45,159	58,255	24,073	21,761	0.3
6720	Investment offices	8	3	0.4	26	7	47,846	18,286	727	160	0.0
6732	Educational, religious, etc. trusts	23	19	0.4	226	214	19,080	22,710	4,764	4,869	0.5
6733	Trusts, n.e.c.	98	70	1.2	382	244	24,021	25,098	9,111	7,183	1.0
6794	Patent owners and lessors	6	5	0.3	-	34	-	13,176	-	527	0.1
6798	Real estate investment trusts	11	6	1.1	-	34	-	52,235	-	1,957	0.9
6799	Investors, n.e.c.	23	33	0.6	162	202	39,605	37,743	7,214	8,109	0.6
IDAHO											
60 –	**Finance, insurance, and real estate**	2,420	2,528	0.4	18,059	18,752	21,602	22,210	401,777	447,122	0.2
6000	Depository institutions	481	485	0.5	7,776	7,443	22,248	23,025	168,081	180,360	0.3
6020	Commercial banks	332	322	0.5	6,650	6,192	22,904	23,871	147,530	156,307	0.4
6030	Savings institutions	44	43	0.2	-	-	-	-	-	-	-
6060	Credit unions	99	117	0.8	762	873	16,152	15,734	11,762	13,606	0.5
6090	Functions closely related to banking	6	3	0.1	-	-	-	-	-	-	-
6100	Nondepository institutions	164	178	0.4	1,043	1,088	25,921	29,438	29,797	33,480	0.2
6110	Federal and Federally-sponsored credit	1	19	1.4	-	-	-	-	-	-	-
6140	Personal credit institutions	87	69	0.4	-	337	-	23,300	-	7,823	0.2
6150	Business credit institutions	27	14	0.3	-	-	-	-	-	-	-
6160	Mortgage bankers and brokers	49	76	0.4	478	575	26,996	32,021	15,699	20,050	0.2
6200	Security and commodity brokers	118	119	0.3	482	531	49,079	45,281	24,087	26,491	0.1
6210	Security brokers and dealers	82	84	0.4	409	432	51,071	48,454	20,829	22,691	0.1
6220	Commodity contracts brokers, dealers	5	5	0.3	17	22	48,706	39,455	893	797	0.1
6280	Security and commodity services	30	30	0.2	54	77	35,556	29,143	2,353	3,003	0.0
6300	Insurance carriers	237	170	0.4	3,099	2,803	22,591	24,978	71,295	70,572	0.1
6310	Life insurance	52	37	0.3	808	568	22,901	24,683	18,443	13,830	0.1
6321	Accident and health insurance	5	5	0.4	-	67	-	20,597	-	1,356	0.1
6324	Hospital and medical service plans	15	16	0.9	-	777	-	27,022	-	21,475	0.3
6330	Fire, marine, and casualty insurance	105	89	0.5	1,156	974	21,215	29,409	24,768	28,528	0.1
6350	Surety insurance	1	-	-	-	-	-	-	-	-	-
6360	Title insurance	34	7	0.3	304	-	20,855	-	7,444	-	-
6370	Pension, health, and welfare funds	22	15	0.2	76	285	13,105	8,449	1,196	2,673	0.2
6390	Insurance carriers, n.e.c.	-	1	0.6	-	-	-	-	-	-	-
6400	Insurance agents, brokers, and service	519	570	0.5	2,109	2,767	20,468	20,572	45,424	61,111	0.3
6500	Real estate	831	935	0.4	3,258	3,889	14,079	14,065	55,248	67,161	0.2
6510	Real estate operators and lessors	248	283	0.3	916	1,099	11,838	11,723	12,141	14,827	0.2
6530	Real estate agents and managers	392	512	0.5	1,224	1,884	13,559	13,376	20,572	31,695	0.2
6540	Title abstract offices	36	41	0.9	481	549	18,528	19,024	11,412	13,192	1.3
6552	Subdividers and developers, n.e.c.	53	62	0.7	184	178	23,239	24,674	4,275	5,541	0.3
6553	Cemetery subdividers and developers	18	23	0.4	42	62	8,857	10,774	448	748	0.1
6700	Holding and other investment offices	67	68	0.2	268	189	20,060	26,222	5,732	5,390	0.0
6710	Holding offices	14	12	0.2	84	27	27,524	54,815	2,448	1,606	0.0
6720	Investment offices	2	4	0.5	-	4	-	15,000	-	84	0.0
6732	Educational, religious, etc. trusts	7	9	0.2	78	17	14,974	16,235	1,260	332	0.0
6733	Trusts, n.e.c.	14	14	0.2	-	53	-	21,585	-	1,175	0.2
6792	Oil royalty traders	1	1	0.1	-	-	-	-	-	-	-
6794	Patent owners and lessors	1	3	0.2	-	-	-	-	-	-	-
6798	Real estate investment trusts	4	4	0.7	-	23	-	19,826	-	283	0.1
6799	Investors, n.e.c.	19	21	0.4	19	57	17,474	19,649	444	1,392	0.1
ILLINOIS											
60 –	**Finance, insurance, and real estate**	27,858	28,491	4.7	402,241	399,475	34,836	34,998	13,794,881	14,481,125	6.2
6000	Depository institutions	4,368	4,461	4.3	116,857	119,663	28,993	27,743	3,295,625	3,449,183	6.0
6010	Central reserve depository	4	5	6.7	-	2,779	-	30,588	-	81,080	9.0
6020	Commercial banks	2,074	2,173	3.5	82,557	86,235	30,668	28,748	2,416,595	2,560,890	6.1
6030	Savings institutions	1,009	916	4.7	22,023	18,878	23,631	24,283	535,298	505,176	6.1
6060	Credit unions	624	739	4.8	-	4,953	-	18,378	-	94,551	3.1
6080	Foreign bank and branches and agencies	42	43	7.7	1,976	2,007	45,587	50,320	93,455	99,289	5.5

Source: County Business Patterns, 1992/93, CBP-92/93-1, U.S. Department of Commerce, Washington, D.C., April 1995. SIC categories for which data were suppressed or not available for both 1992 and 1993 are not displayed. The employment columns represent mid-March employment in the year. Pay per employee is calculated by dividing 1st Quarter payroll, annualized, by mid-March employment. The columns headed "% US" show the state's percentage of the national total for the SIC in 1993; for example, 0.9% for SIC 6030 means that the state had 0.9 percent of the national total establishments (or payroll) in SIC 6030 in 1993. A dash (-) is used to indicate that data are not available or cannot be calculated; nec means not elsewhere classified.

Continued on next page.

SIC	Industry	No. Establishments			Employment		Pay / Employee		Annual Payroll ($ 000)		
		1992	1993	% US	1992	1993	1992	1993	1992	1993	% US
ILLINOIS - [continued]											
6090	Functions closely related to banking	602	584	12.4	4,130	4,811	22,232	21,889	95,320	107,996	6.6
6100	Nondepository institutions	1,684	1,697	4.1	25,278	25,032	36,794	38,750	917,903	1,050,028	5.9
6110	Federal and Federally-sponsored credit	26	45	3.3	137	444	63,153	56,450	7,280	21,165	2.3
6140	Personal credit institutions	750	592	3.5	8,954	9,277	30,552	29,072	294,458	283,362	7.4
6150	Business credit institutions	369	397	8.2	9,258	7,320	43,210	55,015	348,259	370,051	9.0
6160	Mortgage bankers and brokers	512	659	3.6	6,864	7,990	35,783	34,104	264,432	375,386	4.3
6200	Security and commodity brokers	2,323	2,532	7.4	32,550	33,352	76,232	73,239	2,316,412	2,498,620	6.3
6210	Security brokers and dealers	1,089	1,242	6.3	17,003	18,391	104,379	87,859	1,548,911	1,621,711	5.6
6220	Commodity contracts brokers, dealers	484	551	37.5	6,717	-	35,917	-	292,584	-	-
6230	Security and commodity exchanges	25	18	17.1	2,919	-	40,510	-	112,553	-	-
6280	Security and commodity services	642	715	5.5	5,566	5,273	59,247	83,828	337,665	442,284	4.7
6300	Insurance carriers	2,824	2,227	5.1	102,815	102,106	34,216	35,477	3,493,052	3,627,492	6.9
6310	Life insurance	729	592	4.7	35,303	30,515	28,552	31,009	996,484	911,559	4.6
6321	Accident and health insurance	64	40	3.5	3,724	5,706	37,835	24,485	107,227	143,833	9.7
6324	Hospital and medical service plans	84	81	4.6	8,686	7,611	31,559	34,355	301,839	291,199	4.4
6330	Fire, marine, and casualty insurance	1,227	1,018	5.3	48,443	51,144	39,747	40,643	1,901,592	2,077,900	9.6
6350	Surety insurance	26	25	4.2	-	516	-	58,822	-	27,556	5.1
6360	Title insurance	115	80	3.5	2,845	2,630	30,646	35,265	93,979	96,820	6.7
6370	Pension, health, and welfare funds	555	379	6.3	-	3,720	-	18,020	-	72,223	5.8
6390	Insurance carriers, n.e.c.	10	11	6.8	-	264	-	23,379	-	6,298	6.6
6400	Insurance agents, brokers, and service	5,814	6,271	5.1	36,648	37,251	31,771	34,155	1,181,088	1,332,157	6.6
6500	Real estate	9,510	9,967	4.2	63,491	61,325	24,108	23,737	1,633,360	1,618,177	5.5
6510	Real estate operators and lessors	3,463	3,696	3.6	19,949	19,623	19,091	17,944	412,164	382,679	4.3
6530	Real estate agents and managers	4,464	5,239	4.7	35,273	36,352	27,074	26,688	991,848	1,069,199	6.3
6540	Title abstract offices	194	232	4.9	1,378	1,865	19,219	19,213	31,169	46,600	4.4
6552	Subdividers and developers, n.e.c.	325	344	3.7	2,640	1,531	27,177	32,504	84,916	64,660	3.7
6553	Cemetery subdividers and developers	351	374	5.9	1,761	1,898	22,962	24,691	45,320	52,426	6.2
6700	Holding and other investment offices	1,293	1,295	4.7	18,757	15,221	37,806	42,425	690,436	652,839	5.5
6710	Holding offices	370	414	5.2	12,669	9,250	38,674	49,221	458,353	451,063	6.5
6720	Investment offices	53	36	4.4	339	321	48,873	46,567	17,241	12,841	1.7
6732	Educational, religious, etc. trusts	225	227	4.8	1,036	1,153	22,154	20,461	23,714	24,103	2.5
6733	Trusts, n.e.c.	313	246	4.4	1,515	1,819	27,226	24,405	42,188	41,406	5.8
6792	Oil royalty traders	7	15	1.9	14	43	84,286	43,349	1,110	2,699	2.6
6794	Patent owners and lessors	43	55	3.4	887	587	36,627	28,463	34,921	17,447	2.2
6798	Real estate investment trusts	52	29	5.2	804	489	39,294	39,215	32,221	23,182	10.9
6799	Investors, n.e.c.	192	267	5.2	1,357	1,497	49,904	45,878	72,870	78,849	6.3
INDIANA											
60 –	**Finance, insurance, and real estate**	11,618	11,891	2.0	127,170	127,514	25,073	25,996	3,280,421	3,474,690	1.5
6000	Depository institutions	2,561	2,523	2.5	45,721	43,121	21,077	21,720	979,021	921,644	1.6
6010	Central reserve depository	2	1	1.3	-	-	-	-	-	-	-
6020	Commercial banks	1,766	1,712	2.7	36,137	32,507	21,348	22,364	782,555	699,455	1.7
6030	Savings institutions	363	338	1.7	5,527	5,941	20,873	21,120	119,120	132,420	1.6
6060	Credit unions	403	447	2.9	3,713	4,406	18,311	17,764	68,844	83,241	2.8
6090	Functions closely related to banking	26	25	0.5	-	-	-	-	-	-	-
6100	Nondepository institutions	761	746	1.8	9,563	10,796	29,433	30,599	296,007	384,078	2.2
6110	Federal and Federally-sponsored credit	6	52	3.8	-	-	-	-	-	-	-
6140	Personal credit institutions	457	390	2.3	3,947	6,020	24,282	26,459	96,056	162,642	4.2
6150	Business credit institutions	86	49	1.0	-	-	-	-	-	-	-
6160	Mortgage bankers and brokers	204	254	1.4	3,770	4,050	37,133	36,705	154,691	197,094	2.2
6200	Security and commodity brokers	444	476	1.4	3,076	3,699	53,512	57,929	162,838	204,070	0.5
6210	Security brokers and dealers	279	297	1.5	2,637	2,596	57,562	66,260	149,449	165,567	0.6
6220	Commodity contracts brokers, dealers	13	11	0.7	51	75	30,510	27,307	1,433	2,692	0.4
6280	Security and commodity services	151	167	1.3	387	1,027	29,075	39,116	11,949	35,779	0.4
6300	Insurance carriers	1,186	995	2.3	30,160	30,070	29,920	31,872	899,935	1,009,570	1.9
6310	Life insurance	349	294	2.3	12,833	13,081	31,426	33,467	386,662	473,711	2.4
6321	Accident and health insurance	41	29	2.6	-	1,152	-	34,378	-	39,232	2.6
6324	Hospital and medical service plans	16	26	1.5	-	2,436	-	32,906	-	82,014	1.2

Source: County Business Patterns, 1992/93, CBP-92/93-1, U.S. Department of Commerce, Washington, D.C., April 1995. SIC categories for which data were suppressed or not available for both 1992 and 1993 are *not* displayed. The employment columns represent mid-March employment in the year. Pay per employee is calculated by dividing 1st Quarter payroll, annualized, by mid-March employment. The columns headed "% US" show the state's percentage of the national total for the SIC in 1993; for example, 0.9% for SIC 6030 means that the state had 0.9 percent of the national total establishments (or payroll) in SIC 6030 in 1993. A dash (-) is used to indicate that data are not available or cannot be calculated; *nec* means not elsewhere classified.

Continued on next page.

SIC	Industry	No. Establishments			Employment		Pay / Employee		Annual Payroll ($ 000)		
		1992	1993	% US	1992	1993	1992	1993	1992	1993	% US
INDIANA - [continued]											
6330	Fire, marine, and casualty insurance	489	440	2.3	11,590	11,362	30,627	31,413	361,900	368,116	1.7
6350	Surety insurance	12	9	1.5	-	-	-	-	-	-	-
6360	Title insurance	68	39	1.7	-	606	-	23,531	-	17,692	1.2
6370	Pension, health, and welfare funds	202	155	2.6	1,259	1,351	17,106	19,443	23,771	25,301	2.0
6390	Insurance carriers, n.e.c.	3	3	1.9	-	-	-	-	-	-	-
6400	Insurance agents, brokers, and service	2,703	2,907	2.4	13,903	15,100	25,413	25,439	366,556	399,833	2.0
6500	Real estate	3,573	3,859	1.6	20,120	21,378	16,493	16,936	367,525	415,872	1.4
6510	Real estate operators and lessors	1,386	1,579	1.6	6,427	8,107	13,136	13,135	93,247	120,135	1.4
6530	Real estate agents and managers	1,430	1,698	1.5	9,058	9,788	18,133	18,787	177,466	211,192	1.2
6540	Title abstract offices	133	172	3.6	861	1,275	18,039	17,873	17,871	29,233	2.8
6552	Subdividers and developers, n.e.c.	137	156	1.7	1,374	942	22,588	33,002	34,211	33,651	1.9
6553	Cemetery subdividers and developers	194	208	3.3	1,236	1,220	14,676	14,030	19,924	19,909	2.3
6700	Holding and other investment offices	374	366	1.3	3,931	2,835	41,403	39,374	177,518	118,733	1.0
6710	Holding offices	110	103	1.3	2,086	1,094	48,004	58,856	113,044	63,712	0.9
6720	Investment offices	15	12	1.5	338	102	72,615	79,843	20,673	10,119	1.4
6732	Educational, religious, etc. trusts	87	91	1.9	855	889	22,512	24,265	19,841	24,317	2.5
6733	Trusts, n.e.c.	99	95	1.7	381	378	19,759	16,603	7,660	7,926	1.1
6792	Oil royalty traders	1	3	0.4	-	20	-	20,200	-	401	0.4
6794	Patent owners and lessors	14	18	1.1	-	129	-	31,907	-	4,434	0.6
6798	Real estate investment trusts	9	6	1.1	-	20	-	41,000	-	787	0.4
6799	Investors, n.e.c.	32	38	0.7	181	203	44,994	29,084	13,122	7,037	0.6
IOWA											
60 –	**Finance, insurance, and real estate**	6,962	7,029	1.2	73,796	77,598	26,192	26,481	1,897,425	2,084,027	0.9
6000	Depository institutions	1,457	1,486	1.4	22,698	22,693	21,961	22,737	506,900	518,086	0.9
6010	Central reserve depository	5	2	2.7	-	-	-	-	-	-	-
6020	Commercial banks	1,000	990	1.6	18,431	18,236	22,362	23,253	419,409	423,322	1.0
6030	Savings institutions	221	221	1.1	2,421	2,344	21,690	22,983	52,645	55,695	0.7
6060	Credit unions	222	265	1.7	1,536	1,892	16,753	16,643	26,564	32,773	1.1
6080	Foreign bank and branches and agencies	1	1	0.2	-	-	-	-	-	-	-
6090	Functions closely related to banking	8	6	0.1	-	-	-	-	-	-	-
6100	Nondepository institutions	313	266	0.6	4,821	4,866	32,171	35,928	149,325	159,563	0.9
6110	Federal and Federally-sponsored credit	4	32	2.3	14	-	28,857	-	423	-	-
6140	Personal credit institutions	193	128	0.8	1,785	1,525	32,903	43,077	52,966	52,928	1.4
6150	Business credit institutions	63	46	1.0	1,592	-	32,626	-	49,278	-	-
6160	Mortgage bankers and brokers	49	58	0.3	1,426	1,715	30,712	31,466	46,385	54,761	0.6
6200	Security and commodity brokers	374	408	1.2	1,979	2,088	49,556	48,881	95,350	107,676	0.3
6210	Security brokers and dealers	208	238	1.2	1,264	1,408	54,307	59,614	65,662	85,209	0.3
6220	Commodity contracts brokers, dealers	48	49	3.3	217	-	33,954	-	8,611	-	-
6230	Security and commodity exchanges	2	2	1.9	-	-	-	-	-	-	-
6280	Security and commodity services	105	119	0.9	477	-	44,671	-	20,295	-	-
6300	Insurance carriers	684	561	1.3	25,549	27,665	29,970	30,233	727,900	832,342	1.6
6310	Life insurance	200	166	1.3	14,506	15,341	32,070	31,853	426,072	467,264	2.4
6321	Accident and health insurance	19	13	1.1	-	-	-	-	-	-	-
6324	Hospital and medical service plans	33	28	1.6	-	-	-	-	-	-	-
6330	Fire, marine, and casualty insurance	307	247	1.3	7,210	8,694	27,555	28,686	203,051	262,779	1.2
6350	Surety insurance	11	8	1.3	-	864	-	29,968	-	28,981	5.3
6360	Title insurance	4	-	.5	-	-	-	-	-	-	-
6370	Pension, health, and welfare funds	105	96	1.6	-	468	-	16,282	-	9,988	0.8
6390	Insurance carriers, n.e.c.	1	1	0.6	-	-	-	-	-	-	-
6400	Insurance agents, brokers, and service	1,919	2,056	1.7	7,711	8,469	22,834	22,836	179,834	204,268	1.0
6500	Real estate	1,940	1,982	0.8	8,133	8,448	16,461	15,148	138,954	145,698	0.5
6510	Real estate operators and lessors	812	892	0.9	3,135	3,629	14,835	12,747	49,954	51,973	0.6
6530	Real estate agents and managers	683	752	0.7	3,183	3,509	18,154	17,380	57,412	68,428	0.4
6540	Title abstract offices	126	131	2.7	689	742	17,869	17,477	13,221	15,057	1.4
6552	Subdividers and developers, n.e.c.	50	42	0.4	344	191	22,023	16,649	7,481	4,273	0.2
6553	Cemetery subdividers and developers	149	149	2.4	418	373	12,019	12,150	5,472	5,798	0.7
6700	Holding and other investment offices	263	263	1.0	2,453	3,051	34,343	31,207	81,337	107,462	0.9

Source: County Business Patterns, 1992/93, CBP-92/93-1, U.S. Department of Commerce, Washington, D.C., April 1995. SIC categories for which data were suppressed or not available for both 1992 and 1993 are *not* displayed. The employment columns represent mid-March employment in the year. Pay per employee is calculated by dividing 1st Quarter payroll, annualized, by mid-March employment. The columns headed "% US" show the state's percentage of the national total for the SIC in 1993; for example, 0.9% for SIC 6030 means that the state had 0.9 percent of the national total establishments (or payroll) in SIC 6030 in 1993. A dash (-) is used to indicate that data are not available or cannot be calculated; *nec* means not elsewhere classified.

Continued on next page.

SIC	Industry	No. Establishments			Employment		Pay / Employee		Annual Payroll ($ 000)		
		1992	1993	% US	1992	1993	1992	1993	1992	1993	% US
IOWA - [continued]											
6710	Holding offices	95	121	1.5	1,781	1,983	39,331	36,767	65,020	79,433	1.1
6720	Investment offices	19	6	0.7	66	27	22,667	60,000	1,537	1,497	0.2
6732	Educational, religious, etc. trusts	36	39	0.8	254	252	21,622	17,889	5,774	4,891	0.5
6733	Trusts, n.e.c.	62	44	0.8	164	505	14,098	15,311	2,322	12,252	1.7
6792	Oil royalty traders	-	4	0.5	-	-	-	-	-	-	-
6794	Patent owners and lessors	7	13	0.8	67	95	24,716	27,495	1,684	2,604	0.3
6798	Real estate investment trusts	4	3	0.5	14	-	13,143	-	134	-	-
6799	Investors, n.e.c.	28	33	0.6	101	141	29,307	28,482	4,558	5,037	0.4
KANSAS											
60 –	**Finance, insurance, and real estate**	6,500	6,704	1.1	62,947	61,108	24,293	25,341	1,561,871	1,631,594	0.7
6000	Depository institutions	1,272	1,320	1.3	20,157	20,052	21,943	23,239	456,271	484,062	0.8
6010	Central reserve depository	2	1	1.3	-	-	-	-	-	-	-
6020	Commercial banks	930	900	1.4	16,397	15,891	21,631	23,297	370,086	390,724	0.9
6030	Savings institutions	183	205	1.1	2,323	2,590	23,204	24,599	52,887	59,773	0.7
6060	Credit unions	134	190	1.2	1,028	1,231	20,490	16,897	20,869	21,848	0.7
6090	Functions closely related to banking	22	24	0.5	-	-	-	-	-	-	-
6100	Nondepository institutions	381	335	0.8	5,245	5,039	25,604	26,585	137,013	140,139	0.8
6110	Federal and Federally-sponsored credit	32	34	2.5	876	1,070	23,845	25,290	23,629	28,290	3.1
6140	Personal credit institutions	215	147	0.9	1,501	1,104	24,109	22,083	35,918	24,161	0.6
6150	Business credit institutions	37	51	1.1	1,642	1,533	22,787	27,854	36,338	40,376	1.0
6160	Mortgage bankers and brokers	88	102	0.6	1,216	1,332	32,566	29,898	40,814	47,306	0.5
6200	Security and commodity brokers	357	385	1.1	1,616	2,080	47,621	48,450	81,724	109,753	0.3
6210	Security brokers and dealers	201	205	1.0	1,129	1,158	51,061	58,366	61,794	70,318	0.2
6220	Commodity contracts brokers, dealers	29	31	2.1	99	-	22,424	-	2,103	-	-
6230	Security and commodity exchanges	1	3	2.9	-	-	-	-	-	-	-
6280	Security and commodity services	118	146	1.1	374	-	44,310	-	17,274	-	-
6300	Insurance carriers	664	544	1.2	15,515	13,313	27,559	29,353	427,276	395,857	0.8
6310	Life insurance	196	168	1.3	4,229	3,746	26,808	28,178	107,536	100,782	0.5
6321	Accident and health insurance	19	20	1.8	261	171	24,567	30,456	6,173	4,671	0.3
6324	Hospital and medical service plans	33	33	1.9	2,303	2,317	24,016	24,437	58,848	60,686	0.9
6330	Fire, marine, and casualty insurance	264	195	1.0	7,938	6,262	29,327	32,669	231,405	209,212	1.0
6350	Surety insurance	14	9	1.5	176	105	41,727	36,000	6,838	3,929	0.7
6360	Title insurance	26	14	0.6	-	191	-	26,890	-	5,350	0.4
6370	Pension, health, and welfare funds	106	102	1.7	339	513	16,224	18,885	9,564	10,923	0.9
6390	Insurance carriers, n.e.c.	5	3	1.9	-	8	-	26,500	-	304	0.3
6400	Insurance agents, brokers, and service	1,670	1,849	1.5	7,634	7,631	23,084	24,901	176,180	203,853	1.0
6500	Real estate	1,842	1,944	0.8	9,236	9,512	16,295	16,046	157,818	176,849	0.6
6510	Real estate operators and lessors	681	784	0.8	2,896	3,019	13,262	13,721	42,809	46,471	0.5
6530	Real estate agents and managers	761	861	0.8	4,575	5,170	17,729	16,361	82,377	100,157	0.6
6540	Title abstract offices	124	124	2.6	699	625	20,361	19,200	12,959	11,459	1.1
6552	Subdividers and developers, n.e.c.	46	56	0.6	303	304	21,162	29,776	7,480	11,829	0.7
6553	Cemetery subdividers and developers	95	96	1.5	357	389	11,754	14,211	4,564	6,553	0.8
6700	Holding and other investment offices	306	318	1.2	3,460	3,384	34,202	32,767	122,501	117,784	1.0
6710	Holding offices	93	106	1.3	2,281	2,438	37,857	36,788	88,939	93,421	1.3
6720	Investment offices	13	11	1.3	75	17	31,520	39,294	2,621	830	0.1
6732	Educational, religious, etc. trusts	40	45	1.0	291	390	22,900	20,862	6,834	8,526	0.9
6733	Trusts, n.e.c.	85	83	1.5	253	139	14,735	17,871	4,205	4,606	0.6
6792	Oil royalty traders	13	17	2.2	-	23	-	24,522	-	828	0.8
6794	Patent owners and lessors	8	17	1.1	-	287	-	23,289	-	7,324	0.9
6798	Real estate investment trusts	5	1	0.2	-	-	-	-	-	-	-
6799	Investors, n.e.c.	38	37	0.7	307	-	39,570	-	12,132	-	-
KENTUCKY											
60 –	**Finance, insurance, and real estate**	6,703	6,873	1.1	64,128	65,756	25,821	24,699	1,600,838	1,697,530	0.7
6000	Depository institutions	1,523	1,515	1.5	28,121	27,409	21,944	22,386	621,253	619,998	1.1
6010	Central reserve depository	2	1	1.3	-	-	-	-	-	-	-
6020	Commercial banks	1,084	1,084	1.7	23,961	23,427	21,952	22,697	524,905	534,155	1.3

Source: County Business Patterns, 1992/93, CBP-92/93-1, U.S. Department of Commerce, Washington, D.C., April 1995. SIC categories for which data were suppressed or not available for both 1992 and 1993 are *not* displayed. The employment columns represent mid-March employment in the year. Pay per employee is calculated by dividing 1st Quarter payroll, annualized, by mid-March employment. The columns headed "% US" show the state's percentage of the national total for the SIC in 1993; for example, 0.9% for SIC 6030 means that the state had 0.9 percent of the national total establishments (or payroll) in SIC 6030 in 1993. A dash (-) is used to indicate that data are not available or cannot be calculated; *nec* means not elsewhere classified.

Continued on next page.

SIC	Industry	No. Establishments			Employment		Pay / Employee		Annual Payroll ($ 000)		
		1992	1993	% US	1992	1993	1992	1993	1992	1993	% US
KENTUCKY - [continued]											
6030	Savings institutions	253	239	1.2	2,735	2,494	22,587	22,079	65,666	57,263	0.7
6060	Credit unions	160	165	1.1	1,116	1,251	18,932	16,873	22,113	22,373	0.7
6090	Functions closely related to banking	24	26	0.6	-	-	-	-	-	-	-
6100	Nondepository institutions	528	547	1.3	3,832	4,592	29,617	23,030	108,415	119,564	0.7
6110	Federal and Federally-sponsored credit	8	49	3.6	-	353	-	36,737	-	15,221	1.7
6140	Personal credit institutions	366	349	2.1	1,864	2,017	21,021	18,110	39,512	37,973	1.0
6150	Business credit institutions	68	42	0.9	-	868	-	24,083	-	22,186	0.5
6160	Mortgage bankers and brokers	83	106	0.6	977	1,354	34,592	26,109	33,789	44,149	0.5
6200	Security and commodity brokers	211	234	0.7	1,571	1,627	52,117	58,680	90,133	110,137	0.3
6210	Security brokers and dealers	152	164	0.8	1,405	1,343	53,099	59,660	80,720	92,568	0.3
6220	Commodity contracts brokers, dealers	7	5	0.3	16	7	22,250	24,571	361	329	0.0
6280	Security and commodity services	51	64	0.5	145	277	47,421	54,787	9,042	17,226	0.2
6300	Insurance carriers	641	544	1.2	11,255	10,814	28,904	29,669	345,302	330,958	0.6
6310	Life insurance	240	203	1.6	5,232	5,008	27,088	29,432	165,268	149,970	0.8
6321	Accident and health insurance	14	12	1.1	248	279	19,468	20,731	4,853	6,066	0.4
6324	Hospital and medical service plans	31	28	1.6	2,715	2,665	30,147	28,738	77,011	80,488	1.2
6330	Fire, marine, and casualty insurance	266	231	1.2	2,565	2,388	33,238	34,474	83,821	84,113	0.4
6350	Surety insurance	6	5	0.8	82	-	51,854		4,604	-	-
6360	Title insurance	10	7	0.3	-	101	-	21,386	-	2,264	0.2
6370	Pension, health, and welfare funds	61	55	0.9	228	292	16,614	14,288	5,260	5,110	0.4
6390	Insurance carriers, n.e.c.	6	2	1.2	-	-	-	-	-	-	-
6400	Insurance agents, brokers, and service	1,562	1,658	1.4	7,812	8,494	33,137	22,621	178,092	208,696	1.0
6500	Real estate	1,994	2,118	0.9	8,834	9,608	14,498	13,836	138,253	150,495	0.5
6510	Real estate operators and lessors	920	1,037	1.0	3,784	4,699	12,601	11,729	51,364	60,742	0.7
6530	Real estate agents and managers	723	831	0.8	3,258	3,288	16,586	16,781	59,638	62,446	0.4
6540	Title abstract offices	12	17	0.4	51	90	15,686	22,311	918	2,407	0.2
6552	Subdividers and developers, n.e.c.	64	92	1.0	579	778	15,565	13,157	8,008	12,192	0.7
6553	Cemetery subdividers and developers	115	120	1.9	642	734	14,206	13,809	10,309	11,170	1.3
6700	Holding and other investment offices	234	246	0.9	2,619	3,050	48,864	51,507	116,472	151,713	1.3
6710	Holding offices	73	92	1.2	1,945	2,204	56,358	64,323	95,708	132,462	1.9
6720	Investment offices	8	4	0.5	81	8	47,654	17,000	5,010	198	0.0
6732	Educational, religious, etc. trusts	61	64	1.4	334	412	18,515	19,204	6,420	8,643	0.9
6733	Trusts, n.e.c.	50	39	0.7	96	99	22,458	16,202	2,008	3,076	0.4
6792	Oil royalty traders	3	5	0.6	-	-	-	-	-	-	-
6794	Patent owners and lessors	3	5	0.3	-	61	-	25,705	-	2,109	0.3
6798	Real estate investment trusts	2	2	0.4	-	-	-	-	-	-	-
6799	Investors, n.e.c.	28	32	0.6	74	237	41,622	13,603	4,073	4,331	0.3
LOUISIANA											
60 –	**Finance, insurance, and real estate**	8,901	9,095	1.5	78,301	79,918	24,015	23,528	1,905,396	1,971,579	0.8
6000	Depository institutions	1,732	1,763	1.7	28,210	28,917	21,447	21,389	617,428	658,776	1.1
6010	Central reserve depository	2	1	1.3	-	-	-	-	-	-	-
6020	Commercial banks	1,195	1,216	1.9	23,267	24,090	21,765	21,757	522,284	562,385	1.3
6030	Savings institutions	179	154	0.8	2,649	2,204	21,356	21,517	52,290	47,877	0.6
6060	Credit unions	305	344	2.2	1,748	2,066	17,249	16,916	30,617	36,455	1.2
6090	Functions closely related to banking	51	48	1.0	-	-	-	-	-	-	-
6100	Nondepository institutions	1,123	1,144	2.7	5,959	5,823	24,276	21,659	140,092	139,125	0.8
6110	Federal and Federally-sponsored credit	32	33	2.4	248	112	28,742	28,679	7,612	3,358	0.4
6140	Personal credit institutions	912	892	5.2	3,965	3,981	20,829	18,943	86,369	80,979	2.1
6150	Business credit institutions	37	60	1.2	466	259	44,618	22,425	10,316	6,791	0.2
6160	Mortgage bankers and brokers	114	158	0.9	1,217	1,467	27,122	28,398	34,579	47,966	0.5
6200	Security and commodity brokers	291	277	0.8	2,005	2,019	68,475	60,458	131,285	133,472	0.3
6210	Security brokers and dealers	203	182	0.9	1,710	1,632	74,870	68,804	120,919	120,234	0.4
6220	Commodity contracts brokers, dealers	7	4	0.3	-	5	-	16,000	-	105	0.0
6230	Security and commodity exchanges	1	-	-	-	-	-	-	-	-	-
6280	Security and commodity services	77	91	0.7	256	382	29,672	25,382	8,797	13,133	0.1
6300	Insurance carriers	914	802	1.8	15,250	14,594	30,235	31,881	460,058	442,027	0.8
6310	Life insurance	369	323	2.5	7,413	6,841	28,325	29,452	202,732	193,830	1.0

Source: County Business Patterns, 1992/93, CBP-92/93-1, U.S. Department of Commerce, Washington, D.C., April 1995. SIC categories for which data were suppressed or not available for both 1992 and 1993 are *not* displayed. The employment columns represent mid-March employment in the year. Pay per employee is calculated by dividing 1st Quarter payroll, annualized, by mid-March employment. The columns headed "% US" show the state's percentage of the national total for the SIC in 1993; for example, 0.9% for SIC 6030 means that the state had 0.9 percent of the national total establishments (or payroll) in SIC 6030 in 1993. A dash (-) is used to indicate that data are not available or cannot be calculated; *nec* means not elsewhere classified.

Continued on next page.

SIC	Industry	No. Establishments			Employment		Pay / Employee		Annual Payroll ($ 000)		
		1992	1993	% US	1992	1993	1992	1993	1992	1993	% US
LOUISIANA - [continued]											
6321	Accident and health insurance	32	31	2.7	1,018	943	26,515	28,437	27,524	28,170	1.9
6324	Hospital and medical service plans	20	17	1.0	565	676	26,457	25,154	14,804	16,386	0.2
6330	Fire, marine, and casualty insurance	358	317	1.7	5,214	5,193	35,906	38,734	191,664	182,794	0.8
6350	Surety insurance	9	6	1.0	261	150	26,682	34,507	6,659	5,071	0.9
6360	Title insurance	13	11	0.5	111	-	27,892	-	3,539	-	-
6370	Pension, health, and welfare funds	100	94	1.6	503	553	16,374	14,546	9,526	9,519	0.8
6390	Insurance carriers, n.e.c.	3	2	1.2	-	-	-	-	-	-	-
6400	Insurance agents, brokers, and service	2,111	2,168	1.8	10,839	10,934	23,530	23,164	264,176	275,550	1.4
6500	Real estate	2,389	2,587	1.1	13,304	14,065	14,709	13,977	206,859	221,905	0.7
6510	Real estate operators and lessors	1,140	1,360	1.3	5,365	6,415	12,696	11,696	71,658	83,267	0.9
6530	Real estate agents and managers	845	970	0.9	5,263	5,891	15,847	15,298	88,826	100,512	0.6
6540	Title abstract offices	58	72	1.5	306	477	20,810	19,388	7,297	11,659	1.1
6552	Subdividers and developers, n.e.c.	94	92	1.0	962	568	19,306	20,613	18,029	14,415	0.8
6553	Cemetery subdividers and developers	66	71	1.1	702	707	12,028	14,693	8,891	11,638	1.4
6700	Holding and other investment offices	325	339	1.2	1,788	2,737	34,400	28,095	66,354	80,929	0.7
6710	Holding offices	66	75	0.9	1,006	1,550	43,288	34,648	48,022	56,468	0.8
6720	Investment offices	16	11	1.3	87	66	20,598	19,636	1,901	1,271	0.2
6732	Educational, religious, etc. trusts	56	54	1.1	215	220	15,442	17,345	3,406	3,965	0.4
6733	Trusts, n.e.c.	62	68	1.2	136	352	17,382	7,523	2,565	3,346	0.5
6792	Oil royalty traders	39	49	6.3	117	129	34,667	25,736	3,931	4,008	3.9
6794	Patent owners and lessors	7	12	0.7	42	61	29,238	23,607	1,336	1,671	0.2
6798	Real estate investment trusts	6	5	0.9	10	11	17,600	7,273	191	113	0.1
6799	Investors, n.e.c.	59	64	1.2	154	348	30,545	30,437	4,543	10,081	0.8
MAINE											
60 –	**Finance, insurance, and real estate**	2,637	2,624	0.4	24,249	25,206	28,992	30,382	681,691	733,242	0.3
6000	Depository institutions	654	638	0.6	8,826	8,945	21,837	21,521	200,336	202,905	0.4
6010	Central reserve depository	1	1	1.3	-	-	-	-	-	-	-
6020	Commercial banks	370	328	0.5	5,099	4,769	23,030	22,243	121,000	113,768	0.3
6030	Savings institutions	165	165	0.9	2,658	2,647	21,081	22,291	59,205	60,605	0.7
6060	Credit unions	114	136	0.9	-	1,327	-	17,206	-	23,713	0.8
6090	Functions closely related to banking	4	8	0.2	-	-	-	-	-	-	-
6100	Nondepository institutions	67	49	0.1	540	-	25,437	-	14,762	-	-
6110	Federal and Federally-sponsored credit	5	6	0.4	-	-	-	-	-	-	-
6140	Personal credit institutions	36	7	0.0	317	100	21,073	28,800	6,797	3,060	0.1
6150	Business credit institutions	5	7	0.1	-	-	-	-	-	-	-
6160	Mortgage bankers and brokers	21	28	0.2	183	330	31,978	33,358	6,610	15,150	0.2
6200	Security and commodity brokers	87	101	0.3	526	743	62,798	53,690	32,911	41,689	0.1
6210	Security brokers and dealers	47	53	0.3	395	484	67,737	60,950	24,918	29,493	0.1
6220	Commodity contracts brokers, dealers	1	-	-	-	-	-	-	-	-	-
6280	Security and commodity services	38	47	0.4	128	259	48,188	40,124	7,893	12,193	0.1
6300	Insurance carriers	226	200	0.5	7,562	8,040	40,959	45,442	267,125	295,801	0.6
6310	Life insurance	62	50	0.4	4,792	4,515	49,029	58,882	190,019	188,282	1.0
6321	Accident and health insurance	4	2	0.2	-	-	-	-	-	-	-
6324	Hospital and medical service plans	1	5	0.3	-	-	-	-	-	-	-
6330	Fire, marine, and casualty insurance	86	86	0.5	1,259	1,782	29,509	28,249	36,443	53,480	0.2
6350	Surety insurance	2	1	0.2	-	-	-	-	-	-	-
6360	Title insurance	3	2	0.1	-	-	-	-	-	-	-
6370	Pension, health, and welfare funds	68	53	0.9	245	260	10,449	16,723	3,099	4,482	0.4
6400	Insurance agents, brokers, and service	502	500	0.4	3,074	3,078	25,882	25,307	84,712	87,469	0.4
6500	Real estate	978	1,024	0.4	3,142	3,398	17,004	17,157	59,777	67,572	0.2
6510	Real estate operators and lessors	296	366	0.4	896	1,209	16,504	18,088	15,936	22,694	0.3
6530	Real estate agents and managers	488	551	0.5	1,774	1,926	17,560	16,943	34,586	38,830	0.2
6540	Title abstract offices	11	12	0.3	-	74	-	24,919	-	3,201	0.3
6552	Subdividers and developers, n.e.c.	28	22	0.2	126	21	21,905	20,762	3,285	569	0.0
6553	Cemetery subdividers and developers	54	61	1.0	111	152	10,090	9,184	1,750	2,011	0.2
6700	Holding and other investment offices	122	111	0.4	-	-	-	-	-	-	-
6710	Holding offices	34	29	0.4	272	206	52,529	47,320	15,228	10,777	0.2

Source: County Business Patterns, 1992/93, CBP-92/93-1, U.S. Department of Commerce, Washington, D.C., April 1995. SIC categories for which data were suppressed or not available for both 1992 and 1993 are *not* displayed. The employment columns represent mid-March employment in the year. Pay per employee is calculated by dividing 1st Quarter payroll, annualized, by mid-March employment. The columns headed "% US" show the state's percentage of the national total for the SIC in 1993; for example, 0.9% for SIC 6030 means that the state had 0.9 percent of the national total establishments (or payroll) in SIC 6030 in 1993. A dash (-) is used to indicate that data are not available or cannot be calculated; *nec* means not elsewhere classified.

Continued on next page.

SIC	Industry	No. Establishments			Employment		Pay / Employee		Annual Payroll ($ 000)		
		1992	1993	% US	1992	1993	1992	1993	1992	1993	% US
MAINE - [continued]											
6720	Investment offices	5	4	0.5	-	-	-	-	-	-	-
6732	Educational, religious, etc. trusts	23	26	0.6	122	166	18,656	22,627	2,680	4,047	0.4
6733	Trusts, n.e.c.	42	38	0.7	81	-	14,074	-	1,084	-	-
6794	Patent owners and lessors	2	2	0.1	-	-	-	-	-	-	-
6798	Real estate investment trusts	3	2	0.4	-	-	-	-	-	-	-
6799	Investors, n.e.c.	8	10	0.2	42	-	43,905	-	1,874	-	-
MARYLAND											
60 –	**Finance, insurance, and real estate**	11,176	11,346	1.9	141,222	145,683	31,487	31,076	4,444,737	4,797,857	2.1
6000	Depository institutions	2,171	2,175	2.1	43,287	41,233	26,189	26,113	1,100,220	1,120,955	1.9
6010	Central reserve depository	5	1	1.3	477		27,413	-	13,253		-
6020	Commercial banks	1,457	1,461	2.3	31,728	29,481	27,270	27,567	819,962	825,083	2.0
6030	Savings institutions	450	420	2.2	8,473	8,113	23,906	22,786	210,973	212,797	2.6
6060	Credit unions	195	223	1.5	2,350	2,865	20,730	21,449	51,667	64,358	2.1
6090	Functions closely related to banking	60	70	1.5	228		16,228	-	4,008		-
6100	Nondepository institutions	822	897	2.1	10,228	13,150	40,363	33,795	445,247	542,713	3.1
6110	Federal and Federally-sponsored credit	16	15	1.1	268	296	42,433	42,500	10,250	11,213	1.2
6140	Personal credit institutions	319	284	1.7	3,167	3,967	33,276	21,979	115,757	90,640	2.4
6150	Business credit institutions	61	81	1.7	1,257	2,004	40,130	34,848	49,476	77,022	1.9
6160	Mortgage bankers and brokers	416	514	2.8	5,521	6,883	44,443	39,923	269,550	363,789	4.1
6200	Security and commodity brokers	454	472	1.4	5,842	6,374	79,855	71,693	394,726	463,992	1.2
6210	Security brokers and dealers	215	219	1.1	3,628	3,175	101,464	98,540	277,728	288,249	1.0
6220	Commodity contracts brokers, dealers	3	1	0.1	-	-	-	-	-	-	-
6230	Security and commodity exchanges	1	-		-	-	-	-	-	-	-
6280	Security and commodity services	232	251	1.9	-	-	-	-	-	-	-
6300	Insurance carriers	1,103	917	2.1	25,788	27,270	37,180	36,638	935,537	988,291	1.9
6310	Life insurance	276	249	2.0	6,557	7,321	33,400	33,968	203,036	237,707	1.2
6321	Accident and health insurance	29	17	1.5	510	324	29,475	26,062	14,114	7,693	0.5
6324	Hospital and medical service plans	35	36	2.0	3,693	3,838	38,650	35,784	119,456	132,495	2.0
6330	Fire, marine, and casualty insurance	428	411	2.2	12,405	13,569	41,001	39,532	512,621	539,095	2.5
6350	Surety insurance	20	20	3.4	922	926	35,597	39,076	35,597	35,192	6.5
6360	Title insurance	41	19	0.8	279	236	23,656	26,814	7,495	7,090	0.5
6370	Pension, health, and welfare funds	265	160	2.7	1,405	1,027	23,815	24,234	42,501	28,215	2.3
6390	Insurance carriers, n.e.c.	5	5	3.1	-	29	-	29,379	-	804	0.8
6400	Insurance agents, brokers, and service	1,868	1,968	1.6	12,702	12,431	31,299	31,368	406,358	414,638	2.0
6500	Real estate	4,278	4,468	1.9	35,898	35,080	22,510	21,270	850,318	846,806	2.9
6510	Real estate operators and lessors	1,390	1,569	1.5	11,492	11,307	19,337	17,833	232,986	221,598	2.5
6530	Real estate agents and managers	1,958	2,315	2.1	19,053	19,987	23,810	22,508	471,170	505,967	3.0
6540	Title abstract offices	179	217	4.6	851	1,252	28,870	27,776	26,433	42,830	4.1
6552	Subdividers and developers, n.e.c.	229	216	2.3	1,501	1,241	31,443	29,186	50,815	47,493	2.7
6553	Cemetery subdividers and developers	102	106	1.7	1,301	1,261	19,148	18,449	26,835	25,822	3.0
6700	Holding and other investment offices	428	412	1.5	5,349	7,055	34,305	37,669	224,631	280,064	2.4
6710	Holding offices	98	109	1.4	2,636	3,320	37,296	38,065	123,054	131,160	1.9
6720	Investment offices	22	10	1.2	109	53	75,486	104,528	10,431	3,073	0.4
6732	Educational, religious, etc. trusts	86	80	1.7	703	791	23,027	26,650	17,715	22,901	2.4
6733	Trusts, n.e.c.	132	94	1.7	732	952	30,617	28,950	27,264	28,715	4.0
6792	Oil royalty traders	1	1	0.1	-	-	-	-	-	-	-
6794	Patent owners and lessors	22	29	1.8	-	-	-	-	-	-	-
6798	Real estate investment trusts	14	13	2.3	792	-	34,051	-	30,590	-	-
6799	Investors, n.e.c.	37	71	1.4	190	1,360	33,200	45,647	9,236	69,854	5.5
MASSACHUSETTS											
60 –	**Finance, insurance, and real estate**	12,872	13,177	2.2	222,522	225,302	37,624	37,603	8,231,935	8,884,851	3.8
6000	Depository institutions	2,546	2,589	2.5	64,471	62,347	30,624	30,550	1,962,379	1,917,957	3.3
6010	Central reserve depository	4	2	2.7	-	-	-	-	-	-	-
6020	Commercial banks	1,115	1,062	1.7	38,881	36,719	33,633	34,973	1,286,944	1,267,710	3.0
6030	Savings institutions	997	1,045	5.4	19,180	19,460	26,179	23,543	507,970	489,001	5.9
6060	Credit unions	368	414	2.7	3,801	4,147	20,384	19,570	78,486	84,974	2.8

Source: County Business Patterns, 1992/93, CBP-92/93-1, U.S. Department of Commerce, Washington, D.C., April 1995. SIC categories for which data were suppressed or not available for both 1992 and 1993 are *not* displayed. The employment columns represent mid-March employment in the year. Pay per employee is calculated by dividing 1st Quarter payroll, annualized, by mid-March employment. The columns headed "% US" show the state's percentage of the national total for the SIC in 1993; for example, 0.9% for SIC 6030 means that the state had 0.9 percent of the national total establishments (or payroll) in SIC 6030 in 1993. A dash (-) is used to indicate that data are not available or cannot be calculated; *nec* means not elsewhere classified.

Continued on next page.

SIC	Industry	No. Establishments			Employment		Pay / Employee		Annual Payroll ($ 000)		
		1992	1993	% US	1992	1993	1992	1993	1992	1993	% US
MASSACHUSETTS - [continued]											
6080	Foreign bank and branches and agencies	7	8	1.4	-	-	-	-	-	-	-
6090	Functions closely related to banking	54	57	1.2	706	442	37,207	32,235	25,667	14,200	0.9
6100	Nondepository institutions	659	612	1.5	7,635	7,712	34,921	34,447	278,071	331,037	1.9
6110	Federal and Federally-sponsored credit	29	5	0.4	944	-	49,271	-	43,955	-	-
6140	Personal credit institutions	265	169	1.0	2,538	2,350	25,934	25,261	66,714	62,530	1.6
6150	Business credit institutions	86	105	2.2	962	1,496	54,840	50,610	49,095	79,507	1.9
6160	Mortgage bankers and brokers	265	329	1.8	3,167	3,533	31,883	33,679	117,521	176,476	2.0
6200	Security and commodity brokers	799	909	2.6	23,544	24,897	71,396	73,438	1,651,823	1,986,244	5.0
6210	Security brokers and dealers	328	327	1.7	13,207	9,709	72,367	79,480	915,698	800,380	2.8
6220	Commodity contracts brokers, dealers	6	5	0.3	16	-	54,000	-	1,277	-	-
6230	Security and commodity exchanges	4	2	1.9	99	-	55,152	-	5,251	-	-
6280	Security and commodity services	454	574	4.4	10,208	15,118	70,379	69,696	728,900	1,181,969	12.5
6300	Insurance carriers	829	705	1.6	66,335	68,653	37,191	35,297	2,271,878	2,419,341	4.6
6310	Life insurance	311	300	2.4	36,869	40,322	36,277	36,161	1,250,675	1,408,811	7.1
6321	Accident and health insurance	59	22	1.9	6,746	1,270	33,595	35,279	223,458	44,306	3.0
6324	Hospital and medical service plans	17	55	3.1	2,774	9,289	37,327	33,887	104,783	348,256	5.3
6330	Fire, marine, and casualty insurance	188	171	0.9	17,758	16,367	41,665	34,856	626,878	575,014	2.7
6350	Surety insurance	19	16	2.7	168	-	25,762	-	4,205	-	-
6360	Title insurance	18	13	0.6	139	133	42,302	46,256	5,925	6,519	0.5
6370	Pension, health, and welfare funds	205	125	2.1	914	1,127	20,420	20,369	22,872	30,385	2.5
6390	Insurance carriers, n.e.c.	7	3	1.9	953	-	31,601	-	32,469	-	-
6400	Insurance agents, brokers, and service	2,802	2,906	2.4	20,089	19,292	33,152	32,997	681,712	691,111	3.4
6500	Real estate	4,442	4,682	2.0	31,314	32,121	26,598	26,545	873,602	929,136	3.1
6510	Real estate operators and lessors	1,557	1,722	1.7	9,506	10,314	21,543	24,478	216,253	267,567	3.0
6530	Real estate agents and managers	2,071	2,542	2.3	18,118	20,227	29,741	27,853	559,982	615,274	3.6
6540	Title abstract offices	39	54	1.1	189	236	31,958	26,169	7,085	8,263	0.8
6552	Subdividers and developers, n.e.c.	181	174	1.9	1,082	542	30,377	26,030	32,844	17,678	1.0
6553	Cemetery subdividers and developers	121	135	2.1	696	726	19,546	20,639	16,303	17,778	2.1
6700	Holding and other investment offices	770	752	2.7	6,321	9,839	54,836	54,909	355,214	586,923	5.0
6710	Holding offices	141	164	2.1	2,199	2,145	58,114	62,374	139,061	133,339	1.9
6720	Investment offices	52	39	4.8	867	4,144	67,686	63,083	58,079	290,939	39.3
6732	Educational, religious, etc. trusts	158	156	3.3	1,391	1,316	54,505	40,805	61,678	60,939	6.4
6733	Trusts, n.e.c.	219	204	3.6	595	686	27,543	26,531	27,298	25,690	3.6
6792	Oil royalty traders	3	3	0.4	-	4	-	41,000	-	144	0.1
6794	Patent owners and lessors	19	23	1.4	-	272	-	41,456	-	11,249	1.4
6798	Real estate investment trusts	65	42	7.5	580	727	44,421	20,600	29,597	17,282	8.1
6799	Investors, n.e.c.	87	110	2.1	-	536	-	86,881	-	45,675	3.6
MICHIGAN											
60–	**Finance, insurance, and real estate**	17,044	17,328	2.8	198,378	203,010	27,438	26,775	5,580,645	5,863,037	2.5
6000	Depository institutions	3,802	3,918	3.8	71,158	69,852	23,722	22,256	1,681,205	1,653,033	2.9
6010	Central reserve depository	2	1	1.3	-	-	-	-	-	-	-
6020	Commercial banks	2,560	2,572	4.1	53,237	52,469	24,101	22,556	1,270,397	1,252,894	3.0
6030	Savings institutions	555	538	2.8	8,435	7,953	22,702	22,664	205,544	204,836	2.5
6060	Credit unions	634	758	5.0	6,890	8,719	20,377	19,549	145,550	178,654	5.9
6090	Functions closely related to banking	51	48	1.0	-	-	-	-	-	-	-
6100	Nondepository institutions	799	709	1.7	14,178	14,183	33,782	33,901	508,031	535,176	3.0
6110	Federal and Federally-sponsored credit	13	32	2.3	-	243	-	46,288	-	8,290	0.9
6140	Personal credit institutions	323	175	1.0	5,951	4,071	30,867	30,242	184,727	127,347	3.3
6150	Business credit institutions	115	113	2.3	2,092	2,054	50,948	54,715	98,122	98,443	2.4
6160	Mortgage bankers and brokers	335	380	2.1	6,016	7,795	30,905	29,997	221,551	300,413	3.4
6200	Security and commodity brokers	721	766	2.2	5,693	6,385	61,786	59,673	344,831	411,813	1.0
6210	Security brokers and dealers	420	454	2.3	4,737	4,954	64,560	67,253	299,699	346,735	1.2
6220	Commodity contracts brokers, dealers	6	6	0.4	14	12	52,000	55,000	957	1,172	0.2
6280	Security and commodity services	289	301	2.3	937	1,407	48,141	33,484	43,959	63,759	0.7
6300	Insurance carriers	1,659	1,407	3.2	46,007	49,989	32,504	31,660	1,494,513	1,630,728	3.1
6310	Life insurance	374	316	2.5	11,956	11,858	30,940	29,637	352,428	340,539	1.7
6321	Accident and health insurance	53	26	2.3	4,307	964	28,819	26,402	129,710	26,311	1.8

Source: County Business Patterns, 1992/93, CBP-92/93-1, U.S. Department of Commerce, Washington, D.C., April 1995. SIC categories for which data were suppressed or not available for both 1992 and 1993 are *not* displayed. The employment columns represent mid-March employment in the year. Pay per employee is calculated by dividing 1st Quarter payroll, annualized, by mid-March employment. The columns headed "% US" show the state's percentage of the national total for the SIC in 1993; for example, 0.9% for SIC 6030 means that the state had 0.9 percent of the national total establishments (or payroll) in SIC 6030 in 1993. A dash (-) is used to indicate that data are not available or cannot be calculated; *nec* means not elsewhere classified.

Continued on next page.

SIC	Industry	No. Establishments			Employment		Pay / Employee		Annual Payroll ($ 000)		
		1992	1993	% US	1992	1993	1992	1993	1992	1993	% US
MICHIGAN - [continued]											
6324	Hospital and medical service plans	40	67	3.8	5,553	9,875	34,172	34,200	203,211	361,605	5.5
6330	Fire, marine, and casualty insurance	709	633	3.3	20,177	21,539	35,677	35,597	702,775	778,041	3.6
6350	Surety insurance	22	17	2.9	178	79	32,787	32,911	5,751	3,249	0.6
6360	Title insurance	139	100	4.4	2,044	1,721	24,434	24,709	57,728	50,876	3.5
6370	Pension, health, and welfare funds	296	234	3.9	1,498	3,909	19,268	14,043	35,167	66,817	5.4
6390	Insurance carriers, n.e.c.	8	6	3.7	48	35	20,583	29,829	1,105	1,015	1.1
6400	Insurance agents, brokers, and service	3,691	3,894	3.2	19,621	20,967	27,489	26,445	580,413	620,527	3.1
6500	Real estate	5,697	5,972	2.5	33,949	33,436	17,228	17,323	654,339	673,173	2.3
6510	Real estate operators and lessors	2,285	2,415	2.4	12,879	12,705	13,932	14,415	192,991	211,486	2.4
6530	Real estate agents and managers	2,479	2,932	2.7	16,273	17,489	19,125	18,608	349,673	370,320	2.2
6540	Title abstract offices	90	104	2.2	756	893	21,101	20,726	19,045	25,755	2.5
6552	Subdividers and developers, n.e.c.	182	199	2.1	1,306	862	25,721	24,961	37,147	26,833	1.5
6553	Cemetery subdividers and developers	151	159	2.5	1,169	1,328	18,926	20,617	25,313	31,875	3.8
6700	Holding and other investment offices	655	638	2.3	5,514	5,085	37,429	38,575	210,926	219,595	1.9
6710	Holding offices	170	175	2.2	3,245	2,650	43,127	45,816	139,399	134,964	1.9
6720	Investment offices	34	16	2.0	169	76	30,036	28,263	5,398	2,384	0.3
6732	Educational, religious, etc. trusts	101	97	2.1	620	658	27,374	27,696	18,251	18,931	2.0
6733	Trusts, n.e.c.	181	174	3.1	756	764	23,630	25,702	18,776	19,566	2.7
6792	Oil royalty traders	11	8	1.0	58	55	49,655	44,800	2,985	2,909	2.8
6794	Patent owners and lessors	53	54	3.4	321	432	40,498	35,611	14,424	18,590	2.3
6798	Real estate investment trusts	17	10	1.8	86	23	24,140	21,565	2,243	655	0.3
6799	Investors, n.e.c.	66	81	1.6	174	330	29,241	30,194	5,979	11,610	0.9
MINNESOTA											
60 –	**Finance, insurance, and real estate**	10,645	11,182	1.8	127,300	133,603	32,719	33,153	4,134,625	4,532,846	2.0
6000	Depository institutions	1,634	1,679	1.6	35,501	34,972	27,582	27,686	979,377	960,857	1.7
6010	Central reserve depository	3	2	2.7	-	-	-	-	-	-	-
6020	Commercial banks	1,156	1,139	1.8	27,317	27,485	27,933	27,438	756,499	740,143	1.8
6030	Savings institutions	207	206	1.1	3,616	2,749	20,998	33,657	78,778	96,749	1.2
6060	Credit unions	219	288	1.9	-	2,522	-	18,279	-	48,144	1.6
6080	Foreign bank and branches and agencies	1	-	-	-	-	-	-	-	-	-
6090	Functions closely related to banking	47	44	0.9	1,579	-	44,565	-	70,968	-	-
6100	Nondepository institutions	615	589	1.4	9,391	10,472	34,710	35,940	363,102	434,920	2.5
6110	Federal and Federally-sponsored credit	30	48	3.5	1,031	1,501	26,371	41,815	27,068	50,497	5.5
6140	Personal credit institutions	275	186	1.1	2,426	2,352	25,453	24,743	61,507	58,274	1.5
6150	Business credit institutions	92	99	2.1	1,340	1,350	41,961	43,816	70,933	53,592	1.3
6160	Mortgage bankers and brokers	210	253	1.4	4,589	5,252	39,324	37,232	203,113	271,669	3.1
6200	Security and commodity brokers	657	712	2.1	7,295	9,118	67,295	64,599	535,750	634,105	1.6
6210	Security brokers and dealers	300	342	1.7	5,729	6,875	69,369	71,288	395,684	499,157	1.7
6220	Commodity contracts brokers, dealers	32	33	2.2	80	-	42,550	-	3,612	-	-
6230	Security and commodity exchanges	4	2	1.9	103	-	29,476	-	2,831	-	-
6280	Security and commodity services	313	334	2.6	1,377	2,034	63,137	45,345	133,264	128,070	1.4
6300	Insurance carriers	1,032	796	1.8	34,495	36,630	36,201	36,170	1,182,224	1,293,735	2.5
6310	Life insurance	239	197	1.6	14,485	15,940	42,038	41,118	563,666	611,859	3.1
6321	Accident and health insurance	34	22	1.9	-	764	-	25,974	-	18,824	1.3
6324	Hospital and medical service plans	22	35	2.0	-	4,418	-	28,972	-	152,657	2.3
6330	Fire, marine, and casualty insurance	484	380	2.0	14,119	13,489	33,626	34,768	455,427	449,679	2.1
6350	Surety insurance	20	13	2.2	121	54	32,165	35,556	4,333	1,926	0.4
6360	Title insurance	62	35	1.5	1,175	820	27,585	27,385	36,064	28,194	2.0
6370	Pension, health, and welfare funds	161	109	1.8	1,119	1,135	24,154	24,744	25,850	30,302	2.4
6390	Insurance carriers, n.e.c.	4	2	1.2	-	-	-	-	-	-	-
6400	Insurance agents, brokers, and service	2,668	2,973	2.4	12,638	12,381	29,247	29,183	381,166	370,981	1.8
6500	Real estate	3,574	3,957	1.7	20,751	21,648	15,996	17,247	372,961	434,630	1.5
6510	Real estate operators and lessors	1,475	1,658	1.6	8,724	7,983	12,666	14,704	118,448	126,854	1.4
6530	Real estate agents and managers	1,419	1,808	1.6	9,231	10,749	18,136	18,344	184,697	226,981	1.3
6540	Title abstract offices	114	164	3.4	788	1,796	21,107	21,209	20,958	52,157	5.0
6552	Subdividers and developers, n.e.c.	132	142	1.5	954	665	20,700	20,746	25,898	19,634	1.1
6553	Cemetery subdividers and developers	129	145	2.3	320	364	14,550	13,846	5,853	6,371	0.7

Source: County Business Patterns, 1992/93, CBP-92/93-1, U.S. Department of Commerce, Washington, D.C., April 1995. SIC categories for which data were suppressed or not available for both 1992 and 1993 are *not* displayed. The employment columns represent mid-March employment in the year. Pay per employee is calculated by dividing 1st Quarter payroll, annualized, by mid-March employment. The columns headed "% US" show the state's percentage of the national total for the SIC in 1993; for example, 0.9% for SIC 6030 means that the state had 0.9 percent of the national total establishments (or payroll) in SIC 6030 in 1993. A dash (-) is used to indicate that data are not available or cannot be calculated; *nec* means not elsewhere classified.

Continued on next page.

SIC	Industry	No. Establishments			Employment		Pay / Employee		Annual Payroll ($ 000)		
		1992	1993	% US	1992	1993	1992	1993	1992	1993	% US
MINNESOTA - [continued]											
6700	Holding and other investment offices	448	454	1.7	6,373	7,447	58,620	51,959	284,481	351,372	3.0
6710	Holding offices	141	156	2.0	1,973	2,796	56,957	54,974	98,099	145,309	2.1
6720	Investment offices	37	18	2.2	-	-	-	-	-	-	-
6732	Educational, religious, etc. trusts	78	83	1.8	476	501	19,891	23,473	10,360	13,524	1.4
6733	Trusts, n.e.c.	91	87	1.5	312	-	22,385	-	9,245	-	-
6792	Oil royalty traders	-	2	0.3	-	-	-	-	-	-	-
6794	Patent owners and lessors	31	40	2.5	281	1,076	31,160	38,472	9,050	41,628	5.2
6798	Real estate investment trusts	12	4	0.7	-	-	-	-	-	-	-
6799	Investors, n.e.c.	43	63	1.2	112	233	30,714	65,614	3,486	14,109	1.1
MISSISSIPPI											
60 –	**Finance, insurance, and real estate**	5,185	5,312	0.9	37,945	38,627	21,963	22,605	853,007	900,772	0.4
6000	Depository institutions	1,156	1,180	1.1	16,038	16,710	20,426	21,317	337,122	362,497	0.6
6020	Commercial banks	873	910	1.5	13,751	14,048	20,635	21,570	292,208	312,901	0.7
6030	Savings institutions	146	104	0.5	1,668	1,833	20,441	21,999	33,834	35,166	0.4
6060	Credit unions	127	148	1.0	-	784	-	15,796	-	13,523	0.4
6090	Functions closely related to banking	9	18	0.4	-	45	-	10,844	-	907	0.1
6100	Nondepository institutions	653	722	1.7	3,042	3,577	22,322	20,049	69,365	76,559	0.4
6110	Federal and Federally-sponsored credit	29	38	2.8	88	-	28,500	-	2,601	-	-
6140	Personal credit institutions	500	565	3.3	2,256	2,703	21,496	18,482	49,391	52,518	1.4
6150	Business credit institutions	30	28	0.6	137	-	29,985	-	4,387	-	-
6160	Mortgage bankers and brokers	84	88	0.5	508	543	23,228	23,595	12,315	14,968	0.2
6200	Security and commodity brokers	144	152	0.4	737	730	49,346	54,597	33,836	42,116	0.1
6210	Security brokers and dealers	91	90	0.5	567	600	59,647	61,087	31,211	38,672	0.1
6220	Commodity contracts brokers, dealers	5	3	0.2	-	10	-	16,800	-	264	0.0
6280	Security and commodity services	46	59	0.5	138	120	14,986	25,300	2,058	3,180	0.0
6300	Insurance carriers	427	384	0.9	7,283	7,189	26,032	27,799	197,844	203,318	0.4
6310	Life insurance	181	158	1.2	3,378	3,164	25,085	27,349	87,654	85,089	0.4
6321	Accident and health insurance	14	17	1.5	-	-	-	-	-	-	-
6324	Hospital and medical service plans	6	7	0.4	-	-	-	-	-	-	-
6330	Fire, marine, and casualty insurance	149	129	0.7	2,315	2,273	31,110	33,235	73,189	75,182	0.3
6350	Surety insurance	3	1	0.2	-	-	-	-	-	-	-
6360	Title insurance	3	4	0.2	65	-	29,415	-	2,047	-	-
6370	Pension, health, and welfare funds	65	68	1.1	394	-	11,695	-	7,320	-	-
6390	Insurance carriers, n.e.c.	2	-	-	-	-	-	-	-	-	-
6400	Insurance agents, brokers, and service	1,083	1,132	0.9	4,525	4,252	22,375	21,443	105,415	102,363	0.5
6500	Real estate	1,556	1,582	0.7	5,167	4,690	12,358	11,819	69,299	61,705	0.2
6510	Real estate operators and lessors	879	973	1.0	2,528	2,513	10,278	9,901	27,384	25,945	0.3
6530	Real estate agents and managers	468	489	0.4	1,840	1,730	15,150	13,607	30,837	27,510	0.2
6540	Title abstract offices	5	6	0.1	19	69	13,474	11,594	167	986	0.1
6552	Subdividers and developers, n.e.c.	55	57	0.6	236	225	16,017	19,307	4,262	5,012	0.3
6553	Cemetery subdividers and developers	38	46	0.7	144	150	11,417	12,347	1,861	2,066	0.2
6700	Holding and other investment offices	159	154	0.6	778	1,343	47,604	37,412	30,525	46,550	0.4
6710	Holding offices	40	43	0.5	530	853	62,181	45,374	25,260	34,466	0.5
6720	Investment offices	3	3	0.4	5	-	20,000	-	105	-	-
6732	Educational, religious, etc. trusts	30	31	0.7	59	70	15,322	16,629	1,068	1,259	0.1
6733	Trusts, n.e.c.	38	38	0.7	84	-	12,524	-	1,650	-	-
6792	Oil royalty traders	8	10	1.3	-	17	-	14,353	-	243	0.2
6794	Patent owners and lessors	1	3	0.2	-	-	-	-	-	-	-
6798	Real estate investment trusts	4	2	0.4	-	-	-	-	-	-	-
6799	Investors, n.e.c.	27	24	0.5	-	187	-	29,989	-	6,196	0.5
MISSOURI											
60 –	**Finance, insurance, and real estate**	11,989	12,520	2.1	139,267	139,742	27,659	28,063	3,844,516	4,032,465	1.7
6000	Depository institutions	2,092	2,122	2.1	45,290	45,096	22,797	23,340	1,026,874	1,078,702	1.9
6010	Central reserve depository	8	4	5.3	1,930	-	32,953	-	62,476	-	-
6020	Commercial banks	1,423	1,448	2.3	34,551	34,475	22,297	22,971	768,215	804,263	1.9
6030	Savings institutions	417	374	1.9	5,197	4,604	20,632	22,103	107,344	109,929	1.3

Source: County Business Patterns, 1992/93, CBP-92/93-1, U.S. Department of Commerce, Washington, D.C., April 1995. SIC categories for which data were suppressed or not available for both 1992 and 1993 are *not* displayed. The employment columns represent mid-March employment in the year. Pay per employee is calculated by dividing 1st Quarter payroll, annualized, by mid-March employment. The columns headed "% US" show the state's percentage of the national total for the SIC in 1993; for example, 0.9% for SIC 6030 means that the state had 0.9 percent of the national total establishments (or payroll) in SIC 6030 in 1993. A dash (-) is used to indicate that data are not available or cannot be calculated; *nec* means not elsewhere classified.

Continued on next page.

SIC	Industry	No. Establishments			Employment		Pay / Employee		Annual Payroll ($ 000)		
		1992	1993	% US	1992	1993	1992	1993	1992	1993	% US
MISSOURI - [continued]											
6060	Credit unions	186	227	1.5	1,658	-	18,331	-	31,555	-	-
6090	Functions closely related to banking	57	68	1.4	1,938	2,154	31,224	27,929	57,175	63,655	3.9
6100	Nondepository institutions	649	652	1.6	10,521	9,241	33,576	28,892	340,905	304,747	1.7
6110	Federal and Federally-sponsored credit	13	32	2.3	-	238	-	36,084	-	7,055	0.8
6140	Personal credit institutions	351	314	1.8	-	2,381	-	20,840	-	53,140	1.4
6150	Business credit institutions	87	82	1.7	2,198	1,778	50,009	40,983	97,724	62,915	1.5
6160	Mortgage bankers and brokers	182	224	1.2	4,747	4,844	30,845	28,058	155,131	181,637	2.1
6200	Security and commodity brokers	563	593	1.7	9,247	11,390	51,014	52,795	429,574	567,657	1.4
6210	Security brokers and dealers	354	369	1.9	5,738	5,936	61,659	70,759	309,547	356,171	1.2
6220	Commodity contracts brokers, dealers	20	23	1.6	-	-	-	-	-	-	-
6230	Security and commodity exchanges	3	2	1.9	-	-	-	-	-	-	-
6280	Security and commodity services	182	199	1.5	3,361	5,322	33,596	33,283	114,529	206,997	2.2
6300	Insurance carriers	1,258	999	2.3	30,081	31,256	31,531	31,389	921,228	970,295	1.8
6310	Life insurance	332	282	2.2	12,393	12,914	30,845	31,880	353,905	375,203	1.9
6321	Accident and health insurance	32	24	2.1	913	564	27,084	24,433	24,080	13,001	0.9
6324	Hospital and medical service plans	34	50	2.8	3,968	4,930	35,822	32,785	138,823	168,033	2.6
6330	Fire, marine, and casualty insurance	570	416	2.2	10,699	10,941	32,861	32,222	348,618	365,029	1.7
6350	Surety insurance	15	13	2.2	75	59	19,573	29,898	1,597	2,393	0.4
6360	Title insurance	95	62	2.7	1,078	832	22,705	22,471	28,974	23,353	1.6
6370	Pension, health, and welfare funds	172	148	2.5	924	1,013	22,255	20,675	23,747	23,234	1.9
6390	Insurance carriers, n.e.c.	4	4	2.5	18	3	34,889	13,333	751	49	0.1
6400	Insurance agents, brokers, and service	2,940	3,261	2.7	13,942	14,405	25,393	25,716	356,691	386,243	1.9
6500	Real estate	3,938	4,333	1.8	22,177	22,274	16,681	17,248	407,287	452,434	1.5
6510	Real estate operators and lessors	1,609	1,925	1.9	9,584	9,368	14,308	14,046	148,361	150,114	1.7
6530	Real estate agents and managers	1,520	1,809	1.6	9,181	10,135	19,100	20,255	191,048	237,088	1.4
6540	Title abstract offices	154	167	3.5	777	1,121	16,206	17,720	15,262	25,106	2.4
6552	Subdividers and developers, n.e.c.	178	236	2.5	847	845	17,242	17,955	17,258	21,659	1.2
6553	Cemetery subdividers and developers	153	156	2.5	705	746	15,716	14,928	12,150	15,215	1.8
6700	Holding and other investment offices	535	545	2.0	6,192	4,868	40,779	38,996	258,337	216,058	1.8
6710	Holding offices	181	200	2.5	2,963	3,150	50,601	46,908	153,664	168,865	2.4
6720	Investment offices	27	13	1.6	1,267	54	43,713	59,630	55,039	2,390	0.3
6732	Educational, religious, etc. trusts	90	97	2.1	553	697	19,617	22,491	11,846	16,961	1.8
6733	Trusts, n.e.c.	112	94	1.7	719	387	26,275	13,189	18,465	5,769	0.8
6792	Oil royalty traders	3	7	0.9	-	-	-	-	-	-	-
6794	Patent owners and lessors	22	41	2.6	322	289	29,789	37,329	9,565	13,618	1.7
6798	Real estate investment trusts	13	8	1.4	-	-	-	-	-	-	-
6799	Investors, n.e.c.	68	82	1.6	259	263	22,795	23,407	6,838	7,455	0.6
MONTANA											
60 –	**Finance, insurance, and real estate**	2,194	2,261	0.4	14,472	14,591	21,064	21,464	318,847	339,836	0.1
6000	Depository institutions	374	365	0.4	5,764	5,788	21,241	21,274	123,874	126,048	0.2
6010	Central reserve depository	1	1	1.3	-	-	-	-	-	-	-
6020	Commercial banks	212	192	0.3	4,322	4,182	21,988	22,326	95,316	93,762	0.2
6030	Savings institutions	63	64	0.3	646	699	20,545	19,840	14,042	15,269	0.2
6060	Credit unions	91	102	0.7	607	719	15,064	15,677	9,450	11,887	0.4
6090	Functions closely related to banking	7	6	0.1	-	-	-	-	-	-	-
6100	Nondepository institutions	88	80	0.2	604	656	24,682	24,646	16,553	18,423	0.1
6110	Federal and Federally-sponsored credit	-	11	0.8	-	-	-	-	-	-	-
6140	Personal credit institutions	43	31	0.2	243	208	21,679	22,788	5,256	5,299	0.1
6150	Business credit institutions	22	11	0.2	176	-	31,205	-	5,244	-	-
6160	Mortgage bankers and brokers	21	27	0.1	183	273	22,536	21,700	6,023	8,423	0.1
6200	Security and commodity brokers	116	118	0.3	614	615	50,319	52,728	31,355	37,801	0.1
6210	Security brokers and dealers	83	87	0.4	514	531	51,035	54,772	26,690	33,123	0.1
6220	Commodity contracts brokers, dealers	7	8	0.5	22	16	12,545	14,500	290	290	0.0
6280	Security and commodity services	26	23	0.2	78	68	56,256	45,765	4,375	4,388	0.0
6300	Insurance carriers	192	136	0.3	2,164	1,870	20,943	22,761	49,358	46,663	0.1
6310	Life insurance	46	32	0.3	773	731	18,541	19,108	15,087	14,867	0.1
6321	Accident and health insurance	8	6	0.5	-	-	-	-	-	-	-

Source: County Business Patterns, 1992/93, CBP-92/93-1, U.S. Department of Commerce, Washington, D.C., April 1995. SIC categories for which data were suppressed or not available for both 1992 and 1993 are *not* displayed. The employment columns represent mid-March employment in the year. Pay per employee is calculated by dividing 1st Quarter payroll, annualized, by mid-March employment. The columns headed "% US" show the state's percentage of the national total for the SIC in 1993; for example, 0.9% for SIC 6030 means that the state had 0.9 percent of the national total establishments (or payroll) in SIC 6030 in 1993. A dash (-) is used to indicate that data are not available or cannot be calculated; *nec* means not elsewhere classified.

Continued on next page.

SIC	Industry	No. Establishments			Employment		Pay / Employee		Annual Payroll ($ 000)		
		1992	1993	% US	1992	1993	1992	1993	1992	1993	% US
MONTANA - [continued]											
6324	Hospital and medical service plans	8	10	0.6	-	-	-	-	-	-	-
6330	Fire, marine, and casualty insurance	81	63	0.3	331	214	26,985	35,103	9,308	8,726	0.0
6350	Surety insurance	-	1	0.2	-	-	-	-	-	-	-
6360	Title insurance	31	8	0.3	-	-	-	-	-	-	-
6370	Pension, health, and welfare funds	17	16	0.3	-	60	-	13,800	-	1,071	0.1
6390	Insurance carriers, n.e.c.	1	-	-	-	-	-	-	-	-	-
6400	Insurance agents, brokers, and service	552	611	0.5	2,166	2,293	20,205	19,512	45,668	49,547	0.2
6500	Real estate	787	875	0.4	2,586	-	11,350	-	34,196	-	-
6510	Real estate operators and lessors	340	380	0.4	1,166	1,180	10,168	9,512	13,640	14,076	0.2
6530	Real estate agents and managers	308	389	0.4	991	1,086	12,618	12,648	13,888	15,857	0.1
6540	Title abstract offices	25	28	0.6	113	-	15,575	-	2,103	-	-
6552	Subdividers and developers, n.e.c.	22	41	0.4	116	247	5,345	13,506	995	5,442	0.3
6553	Cemetery subdividers and developers	25	29	0.5	63	58	12,190	19,517	881	1,049	0.1
6700	Holding and other investment offices	82	72	0.3	-	528	-	37,280	-	18,157	0.2
6710	Holding offices	26	22	0.3	210	330	39,029	47,721	8,402	14,803	0.2
6720	Investment offices	3	-	-	-	-	-	-	-	-	-
6732	Educational, religious, etc. trusts	18	20	0.4	104	138	13,346	13,362	1,335	1,892	0.2
6733	Trusts, n.e.c.	10	7	0.1	-	-	-	-	-	-	-
6792	Oil royalty traders	5	5	0.6	-	-	-	-	-	-	-
6794	Patent owners and lessors	4	3	0.2	-	-	-	-	-	-	-
6798	Real estate investment trusts	6	2	0.4	-	-	-	-	-	-	-
6799	Investors, n.e.c.	10	12	0.2	28	16	15,857	30,000	517	385	0.0
NEBRASKA											
60 –	**Finance, insurance, and real estate**	4,331	4,421	0.7	51,809	54,691	25,687	25,747	1,353,303	1,453,479	0.6
6000	Depository institutions	935	936	0.9	15,001	15,770	21,841	21,127	342,995	352,612	0.6
6010	Central reserve depository	3	2	2.7	-	-	-	-	-	-	-
6020	Commercial banks	655	659	1.1	11,896	12,696	22,130	21,359	269,364	284,530	0.7
6030	Savings institutions	171	152	0.8	2,027	1,912	19,899	21,144	48,178	45,472	0.6
6060	Credit unions	97	117	0.8	730	919	17,962	16,766	13,215	16,008	0.5
6080	Foreign bank and branches and agencies	1	1	0.2	-	-	-	-	-	-	-
6090	Functions closely related to banking	8	5	0.1	-	-	-	-	-	-	-
6100	Nondepository institutions	181	165	0.4	-	1,430	-	28,582	-	49,152	0.3
6110	Federal and Federally-sponsored credit	2	31	2.3	-	-	-	-	-	-	-
6140	Personal credit institutions	92	62	0.4	536	422	24,649	21,934	13,099	9,344	0.2
6150	Business credit institutions	45	26	0.5	233	-	35,004	-	8,619	-	-
6160	Mortgage bankers and brokers	41	46	0.2	480	622	32,025	29,286	17,741	28,029	0.3
6200	Security and commodity brokers	252	265	0.8	2,860	1,660	43,158	57,460	118,595	92,290	0.2
6210	Security brokers and dealers	153	161	0.8	1,281	1,355	56,496	64,183	68,762	81,855	0.3
6220	Commodity contracts brokers, dealers	16	19	1.3	-	-	-	-	-	-	-
6230	Security and commodity exchanges	-	1	1.0	-	-	-	-	-	-	-
6280	Security and commodity services	80	84	0.6	-	-	-	-	-	-	-
6300	Insurance carriers	385	308	0.7	20,004	22,375	29,159	29,759	580,629	665,596	1.3
6310	Life insurance	126	107	0.8	6,453	7,050	29,124	29,288	185,829	199,772	1.0
6321	Accident and health insurance	24	19	1.7	-	8,731	-	29,131	-	256,227	17.2
6324	Hospital and medical service plans	6	14	0.8	-	1,023	-	32,583	-	30,795	0.5
6330	Fire, marine, and casualty insurance	156	128	0.7	4,249	5,122	28,886	31,097	123,499	164,346	0.8
6350	Surety insurance	8	5	0.8	-	-	-	-	-	-	-
6360	Title insurance	22	14	0.6	-	221	-	23,439	-	6,689	0.5
6370	Pension, health, and welfare funds	36	20	0.3	-	-	-	-	-	-	-
6390	Insurance carriers, n.e.c.	2	1	0.6	-	-	-	-	-	-	-
6400	Insurance agents, brokers, and service	1,283	1,390	1.1	5,199	4,793	21,326	20,317	112,490	103,794	0.5
6500	Real estate	1,105	1,159	0.5	4,952	-	15,275	-	82,548	-	-
6510	Real estate operators and lessors	437	521	0.5	1,757	2,751	11,743	11,472	23,034	34,638	0.4
6530	Real estate agents and managers	442	487	0.4	2,351	2,581	18,829	17,162	46,866	51,912	0.3
6540	Title abstract offices	53	48	1.0	165	171	14,836	16,749	2,887	3,407	0.3
6552	Subdividers and developers, n.e.c.	28	33	0.4	73	132	14,411	14,879	1,193	2,674	0.2
6553	Cemetery subdividers and developers	57	59	0.9	165	160	12,679	13,125	2,092	2,241	0.3

Source: County Business Patterns, 1992/93, CBP-92/93-1, U.S. Department of Commerce, Washington, D.C., April 1995. SIC categories for which data were suppressed or not available for both 1992 and 1993 are *not* displayed. The employment columns represent mid-March employment in the year. Pay per employee is calculated by dividing 1st Quarter payroll, annualized, by mid-March employment. The columns headed "% US" show the state's percentage of the national total for the SIC in 1993; for example, 0.9% for SIC 6030 means that the state had 0.9 percent of the national total establishments (or payroll) in SIC 6030 in 1993. A dash (-) is used to indicate that data are not available or cannot be calculated; *nec* means not elsewhere classified.

Continued on next page.

SIC	Industry	No. Establishments			Employment		Pay / Employee		Annual Payroll ($ 000)		
		1992	1993	% US	1992	1993	1992	1993	1992	1993	% US
NEBRASKA - [continued]											
6700	Holding and other investment offices	188	194	0.7	2,291	2,582	27,462	29,785	66,728	84,018	0.7
6710	Holding offices	77	77	1.0	1,066	1,213	40,537	45,253	47,048	56,515	0.8
6720	Investment offices	9	6	0.7	-	-	-	-	-	-	-
6732	Educational, religious, etc. trusts	45	41	0.9	582	656	15,787	15,799	9,536	11,167	1.2
6733	Trusts, n.e.c.	37	42	0.7	202	76	13,168	17,105	2,508	1,373	0.2
6792	Oil royalty traders	-	1	0.1	-	-	-	-	-	-	-
6794	Patent owners and lessors	1	8	0.5	-	-	-	-	-	-	-
6798	Real estate investment trusts	6	1	0.2	148	-	29,838	-	3,670	-	-
6799	Investors, n.e.c.	9	15	0.3	-	68	-	61,941	-	7,728	0.6
NEVADA											
60 –	**Finance, insurance, and real estate**	3,704	3,753	0.6	30,499	29,894	24,411	24,563	760,095	833,438	0.4
6000	Depository institutions	540	360	0.4	9,654	9,102	23,331	25,064	213,711	223,745	0.4
6020	Commercial banks	361	193	0.3	6,746	6,245	23,933	26,486	147,093	155,793	0.4
6030	Savings institutions	97	94	0.5	1,398	1,491	22,349	22,739	34,413	38,019	0.5
6060	Credit unions	56	57	0.4	807	891	22,820	21,257	18,309	20,036	0.7
6090	Functions closely related to banking	25	16	0.3	703	475	20,097	20,800	13,864	9,897	0.6
6100	Nondepository institutions	260	291	0.7	1,883	2,226	32,081	32,677	64,101	87,818	0.5
6110	Federal and Federally-sponsored credit	1	3	0.2	-	-	-	-	-	-	-
6140	Personal credit institutions	72	81	0.5	393	495	26,636	22,958	10,194	10,804	0.3
6150	Business credit institutions	31	33	0.7	166	-	27,277	-	4,611	-	-
6160	Mortgage bankers and brokers	145	170	0.9	1,309	1,600	34,533	36,072	48,975	72,771	0.8
6200	Security and commodity brokers	135	139	0.4	745	810	59,452	56,647	46,592	54,966	0.1
6210	Security brokers and dealers	65	74	0.4	602	-	66,339	-	39,476	-	-
6220	Commodity contracts brokers, dealers	6	2	0.1	-	-	-	-	-	-	-
6280	Security and commodity services	64	63	0.5	-	-	-	-	-	-	-
6300	Insurance carriers	279	219	0.5	3,075	2,339	28,507	30,794	93,362	77,085	0.1
6310	Life insurance	44	34	0.3	710	386	24,755	26,373	18,668	9,955	0.1
6321	Accident and health insurance	17	13	1.1	278	-	27,683	-	8,555	-	-
6324	Hospital and medical service plans	9	21	1.2	124	-	29,935	-	4,036	-	-
6330	Fire, marine, and casualty insurance	122	98	0.5	838	578	35,322	43,516	31,177	24,742	0.1
6350	Surety insurance	9	5	0.8	49	-	24,000	-	1,601	-	-
6360	Title insurance	29	21	0.9	654	477	27,535	25,954	17,812	15,292	1.1
6370	Pension, health, and welfare funds	46	24	0.4	216	-	21,407	-	6,698	-	-
6390	Insurance carriers, n.e.c.	-	2	1.2	-	-	-	-	-	-	-
6400	Insurance agents, brokers, and service	573	670	0.5	2,403	3,083	23,742	23,512	61,746	80,227	0.4
6500	Real estate	1,668	1,785	0.8	11,164	10,887	18,486	18,505	221,755	259,170	0.9
6510	Real estate operators and lessors	710	821	0.8	4,632	3,982	16,158	13,435	78,592	84,635	1.0
6530	Real estate agents and managers	639	794	0.7	4,071	5,543	17,017	17,946	75,575	114,306	0.7
6540	Title abstract offices	28	24	0.5	492	471	28,024	29,282	16,533	17,975	1.7
6552	Subdividers and developers, n.e.c.	128	120	1.3	1,381	793	26,673	39,697	37,084	38,734	2.2
6553	Cemetery subdividers and developers	8	8	0.1	108	85	27,074	34,729	2,954	2,939	0.3
6700	Holding and other investment offices	242	282	1.0	1,490	1,378	41,216	29,051	56,822	48,680	0.4
6710	Holding offices	72	93	1.2	848	608	50,844	33,539	39,631	25,867	0.4
6720	Investment offices	9	9	1.1	50	33	26,640	88,970	1,174	3,572	0.5
6732	Educational, religious, etc. trusts	17	19	0.4	86	-	22,093	-	1,987	-	-
6733	Trusts, n.e.c.	55	51	0.9	272	341	14,735	11,249	4,697	4,794	0.7
6792	Oil royalty traders	6	2	0.3	41	-	32,390	-	1,466	-	-
6794	Patent owners and lessors	7	22	1.4	20	76	21,000	25,211	355	3,014	0.4
6798	Real estate investment trusts	13	4	0.7	35	-	21,829	-	689	-	-
6799	Investors, n.e.c.	46	77	1.5	117	212	64,821	38,019	5,437	8,580	0.7
NEW HAMPSHIRE											
60 –	**Finance, insurance, and real estate**	2,613	2,672	0.4	29,931	28,705	28,725	26,407	824,824	829,740	0.4
6000	Depository institutions	492	457	0.4	8,620	7,818	26,265	21,261	191,750	180,815	0.3
6020	Commercial banks	323	181	0.3	5,790	2,954	23,534	22,123	121,039	68,664	0.2
6030	Savings institutions	116	216	1.1	2,207	4,076	21,292	20,836	48,511	93,975	1.1
6060	Credit unions	47	54	0.4	585	721	20,991	18,569	13,029	15,377	0.5

Source: County Business Patterns, 1992/93, CBP-92/93-1, U.S. Department of Commerce, Washington, D.C., April 1995. SIC categories for which data were suppressed or not available for both 1992 and 1993 are *not* displayed. The employment columns represent mid-March employment in the year. Pay per employee is calculated by dividing 1st Quarter payroll, annualized, by mid-March employment. The columns headed "% US" show the state's percentage of the national total for the SIC in 1993; for example, 0.9% for SIC 6030 means that the state had 0.9 percent of the national total establishments (or payroll) in SIC 6030 in 1993. A dash (-) is used to indicate that data are not available or cannot be calculated; *nec* means not elsewhere classified.

Continued on next page.

SIC	Industry	No. Establishments			Employment		Pay / Employee		Annual Payroll ($ 000)		
		1992	1993	% US	1992	1993	1992	1993	1992	1993	% US
NEW HAMPSHIRE - [continued]											
6080	Foreign bank and branches and agencies	1	-	-	-	-	-	-	-	-	-
6090	Functions closely related to banking	5	6	0.1	-	67	-	38,030	-	2,799	0.2
6100	Nondepository institutions	122	119	0.3	-	-	-	-	-	-	-
6110	Federal and Federally-sponsored credit	-	2	0.1	-	-	-	-	-	-	-
6140	Personal credit institutions	57	41	0.2	449	317	24,953	25,073	11,158	8,158	0.2
6150	Business credit institutions	11	17	0.4	43	234	47,070	29,197	1,357	6,720	0.2
6160	Mortgage bankers and brokers	50	59	0.3	605	710	28,754	28,146	21,640	31,253	0.4
6200	Security and commodity brokers	123	157	0.5	-	737	-	57,607	-	48,101	0.1
6210	Security brokers and dealers	61	61	0.3	420	-	67,829	-	25,437	-	-
6220	Commodity contracts brokers, dealers	1	1	0.1	-	-	-	-	-	-	-
6280	Security and commodity services	61	95	0.7	137	230	60,204	45,896	9,542	16,626	0.2
6300	Insurance carriers	244	217	0.5	10,588	9,963	31,515	31,204	325,493	320,150	0.6
6310	Life insurance	64	64	0.5	1,792	2,716	25,212	31,000	44,563	79,636	0.4
6321	Accident and health insurance	11	7	0.6	154	-	28,260	-	4,111	-	-
6324	Hospital and medical service plans	6	7	0.4	1,456	-	27,415	-	40,366	-	-
6330	Fire, marine, and casualty insurance	112	102	0.5	6,968	5,383	34,321	32,677	230,763	186,975	0.9
6350	Surety insurance	2	1	0.2	-	-	-	-	-	-	-
6360	Title insurance	4	4	0.2	-	-	-	-	-	-	-
6370	Pension, health, and welfare funds	41	31	0.5	-	361	-	23,535	-	10,162	0.8
6390	Insurance carriers, n.e.c.	2	1	0.6	-	-	-	-	-	-	-
6400	Insurance agents, brokers, and service	477	500	0.4	2,769	2,682	27,158	27,351	78,037	80,902	0.4
6500	Real estate	1,025	1,101	0.5	4,295	4,487	17,498	18,258	85,479	98,480	0.3
6510	Real estate operators and lessors	304	364	0.4	1,275	1,525	16,941	17,377	24,265	30,984	0.3
6530	Real estate agents and managers	491	616	0.6	2,120	2,454	17,787	18,567	42,664	52,968	0.3
6540	Title abstract offices	19	21	0.4	115	185	27,339	23,178	3,403	6,197	0.6
6552	Subdividers and developers, n.e.c.	63	61	0.6	255	263	15,059	18,403	4,391	7,135	0.4
6553	Cemetery subdividers and developers	29	28	0.4	61	57	12,328	12,070	1,064	995	0.1
6700	Holding and other investment offices	128	119	0.4	1,988	1,741	40,312	27,476	70,101	54,551	0.5
6710	Holding offices	34	33	0.4	1,373	1,173	46,179	29,402	49,664	36,235	0.5
6720	Investment offices	6	3	0.4	125	-	21,696	-	3,908	-	-
6732	Educational, religious, etc. trusts	28	26	0.6	270	236	20,341	19,763	5,026	4,547	0.5
6733	Trusts, n.e.c.	31	32	0.6	113	132	18,832	10,727	4,389	2,974	0.4
6794	Patent owners and lessors	1	3	0.2	-	-	-	-	-	-	-
6798	Real estate investment trusts	6	5	0.9	-	93	-	28,000	-	3,134	1.5
6799	Investors, n.e.c.	13	16	0.3	-	40	-	82,800	-	4,825	0.4
NEW JERSEY											
60 –	**Finance, insurance, and real estate**	18,150	18,683	3.1	245,056	245,841	35,222	36,385	8,794,828	9,250,231	4.0
6000	Depository institutions	3,624	3,724	3.6	61,936	60,585	25,642	25,037	1,589,003	1,589,106	2.8
6010	Central reserve depository	2	1	1.3	-	-	-	-	-	-	-
6020	Commercial banks	2,160	2,225	3.6	42,236	43,504	26,032	25,056	1,095,502	1,139,413	2.7
6030	Savings institutions	1,038	1,014	5.2	16,756	14,185	24,108	24,613	406,077	369,291	4.5
6060	Credit unions	311	365	2.4	1,696	2,044	21,804	20,779	36,363	42,634	1.4
6080	Foreign bank and branches and agencies	2	2	0.4	-	-	-	-	-	-	-
6090	Functions closely related to banking	110	113	2.4	739	714	39,334	41,042	28,377	30,621	1.9
6100	Nondepository institutions	989	993	2.4	15,243	15,346	40,625	41,422	635,014	691,192	3.9
6110	Federal and Federally-sponsored credit	7	6	0.4	100	121	35,560	50,975	4,298	6,316	0.7
6140	Personal credit institutions	364	277	1.6	3,434	2,242	35,971	27,459	117,678	67,101	1.7
6150	Business credit institutions	144	186	3.9	3,423	4,613	57,844	54,913	185,733	228,731	5.5
6160	Mortgage bankers and brokers	444	524	2.8	7,986	8,370	36,219	37,589	323,410	389,044	4.4
6200	Security and commodity brokers	1,286	1,273	3.7	25,072	25,379	65,335	68,771	1,578,117	1,773,916	4.5
6210	Security brokers and dealers	821	748	3.8	19,311	17,180	64,255	74,112	1,176,525	1,233,939	4.3
6220	Commodity contracts brokers, dealers	43	45	3.1	401	470	181,885	72,409	94,184	39,056	5.4
6230	Security and commodity exchanges	3	1	1.0	-	-	-	-	-	-	-
6280	Security and commodity services	400	474	3.6	5,136	7,721	60,677	56,711	299,366	500,604	5.3
6300	Insurance carriers	1,458	1,252	2.9	64,985	67,543	37,230	38,494	2,443,083	2,540,101	4.8
6310	Life insurance	481	453	3.6	29,605	30,270	35,911	37,256	1,078,039	1,119,392	5.7
6321	Accident and health insurance	33	24	2.1	1,089	729	30,935	28,247	30,267	20,671	1.4

Source: County Business Patterns, 1992/93, CBP-92/93-1, U.S. Department of Commerce, Washington, D.C., April 1995. SIC categories for which data were suppressed or not available for both 1992 and 1993 are not displayed. The employment columns represent mid-March employment in the year. Pay per employee is calculated by dividing 1st Quarter payroll, annualized, by mid-March employment. The columns headed "% US" show the state's percentage of the national total for the SIC in 1993; for example, 0.9% for SIC 6030 means that the state had 0.9 percent of the national total establishments (or payroll) in SIC 6030 in 1993. A dash (-) is used to indicate that data are not available or cannot be calculated; nec means not elsewhere classified.

Continued on next page.

SIC	Industry	No. Establishments			Employment		Pay / Employee		Annual Payroll ($ 000)		
		1992	1993	% US	1992	1993	1992	1993	1992	1993	% US

NEW JERSEY - [continued]

6324	Hospital and medical service plans	41	41	2.3	3,997	6,972	37,455	37,986	173,222	216,118	3.3
6330	Fire, marine, and casualty insurance	414	387	2.0	26,552	25,980	39,927	41,436	1,023,045	1,067,173	4.9
6350	Surety insurance	22	21	3.5	865	826	46,553	43,177	36,189	35,166	6.5
6360	Title insurance	102	40	1.7	675	343	30,679	36,478	23,533	13,021	0.9
6370	Pension, health, and welfare funds	346	272	4.5	1,975	1,940	23,427	25,161	73,244	54,872	4.4
6390	Insurance carriers, n.e.c.	7	12	7.4	176	483	19,682	27,636	3,599	13,269	13.9
6400	Insurance agents, brokers, and service	3,044	3,174	2.6	25,191	23,811	34,878	34,151	944,214	902,862	4.5
6500	Real estate	7,038	7,497	3.2	38,204	36,312	21,027	22,020	899,033	935,372	3.2
6510	Real estate operators and lessors	3,101	3,488	3.4	15,512	15,411	18,390	18,496	309,209	321,904	3.6
6530	Real estate agents and managers	2,742	3,344	3.0	16,897	17,016	22,624	24,239	425,198	476,310	2.8
6540	Title abstract offices	127	157	3.3	645	805	23,039	24,661	23,271	30,724	2.9
6552	Subdividers and developers, n.e.c.	221	227	2.4	1,655	1,405	28,486	30,389	54,355	57,518	3.3
6553	Cemetery subdividers and developers	186	204	3.2	1,442	1,475	23,828	24,239	37,696	41,587	4.9
6700	Holding and other investment offices	631	691	2.5	8,930	11,299	48,602	50,638	454,847	565,240	4.8
6710	Holding offices	214	255	3.2	6,806	8,040	49,815	49,317	335,046	393,082	5.6
6720	Investment offices	25	19	2.3	144	245	136,194	28,767	31,782	7,653	1.0
6732	Educational, religious, etc. trusts	107	108	2.3	523	489	28,321	30,937	16,547	16,072	1.7
6733	Trusts, n.e.c.	107	103	1.8	359	632	21,415	21,247	10,294	17,677	2.5
6792	Oil royalty traders	1	4	0.5	-	63	-	31,429	-	2,063	2.0
6794	Patent owners and lessors	32	47	2.9	594	1,153	51,502	72,926	29,523	70,065	8.7
6798	Real estate investment trusts	29	13	2.3	-	36	-	44,778	-	1,878	0.9
6799	Investors, n.e.c.	77	135	2.6	-	635	-	82,387	-	54,770	4.3

NEW MEXICO

60 –	**Finance, insurance, and real estate**	3,370	3,458	0.6	26,420	27,983	22,531	21,272	612,530	642,057	0.3
6000	Depository institutions	548	514	0.5	9,861	10,661	20,327	20,648	202,694	224,312	0.4
6020	Commercial banks	417	367	0.6	8,318	8,152	20,667	21,046	173,948	172,551	0.4
6030	Savings institutions	43	41	0.2	675	1,198	18,459	20,875	12,449	26,940	0.3
6060	Credit unions	73	86	0.6	826	1,202	19,041	17,694	15,900	22,470	0.7
6090	Functions closely related to banking	15	20	0.4	42	109	8,190	20,917	397	2,351	0.1
6100	Nondepository institutions	233	265	0.6	-	1,974	-	22,575	-	53,113	0.3
6110	Federal and Federally-sponsored credit	8	9	0.7	-	-	-	-	-	-	-
6140	Personal credit institutions	151	156	0.9	914	949	21,204	19,452	20,198	19,341	0.5
6150	Business credit institutions	17	21	0.4	535	-	51,118	-	22,482	-	-
6160	Mortgage bankers and brokers	54	79	0.4	307	463	33,472	33,857	12,294	22,647	0.3
6200	Security and commodity brokers	125	117	0.3	707	780	58,008	55,051	41,528	46,300	0.1
6210	Security brokers and dealers	83	74	0.4	592	-	62,439	-	34,677	-	-
6220	Commodity contracts brokers, dealers	3	1	0.1	-	-	-	-	-	-	-
6280	Security and commodity services	39	42	0.3	-	-	-	-	-	-	-
6300	Insurance carriers	289	201	0.5	3,995	4,219	24,654	23,208	101,445	98,983	0.2
6310	Life insurance	68	57	0.4	1,659	1,765	20,989	19,483	34,280	32,340	0.2
6321	Accident and health insurance	6	5	0.4	68	48	29,353	16,333	2,588	1,001	0.1
6324	Hospital and medical service plans	12	9	0.5	898	1,435	25,310	24,312	22,230	35,407	0.5
6330	Fire, marine, and casualty insurance	115	94	0.5	616	621	31,253	33,842	20,545	22,312	0.1
6350	Surety insurance	4	1	0.2	26	-	27,846	-	802	-	-
6360	Title insurance	46	8	0.3	545	167	29,306	31,976	16,846	6,453	0.4
6370	Pension, health, and welfare funds	33	25	0.4	140	-	16,086	-	3,186	-	-
6390	Insurance carriers, n.e.c.	1	1	0.6	-	-	-	-	-	-	-
6400	Insurance agents, brokers, and service	672	779	0.6	2,970	3,930	20,248	20,348	65,295	89,714	0.4
6500	Real estate	1,346	1,422	0.6	5,525	5,596	14,546	15,638	89,371	104,175	0.4
6510	Real estate operators and lessors	553	626	0.6	2,105	2,142	12,705	11,755	26,697	27,832	0.3
6530	Real estate agents and managers	537	638	0.6	2,201	2,547	16,234	16,415	40,364	49,859	0.3
6540	Title abstract offices	45	42	0.9	313	314	17,866	25,758	7,046	8,574	0.8
6552	Subdividers and developers, n.e.c.	66	75	0.8	473	468	13,869	22,735	8,064	15,688	0.9
6553	Cemetery subdividers and developers	20	20	0.3	102	109	15,255	15,523	1,658	1,835	0.2
6700	Holding and other investment offices	155	157	0.6	-	814	-	26,717	-	24,601	0.2
6710	Holding offices	35	32	0.4	924	398	47,710	30,181	41,326	12,285	0.2
6720	Investment offices	5	4	0.5	-	-	-	-	-	-	-

Source: County Business Patterns, 1992/93, CBP-92/93-1, U.S. Department of Commerce, Washington, D.C., April 1995. SIC categories for which data were suppressed or not available for both 1992 and 1993 are *not* displayed. The employment columns represent mid-March employment in the year. Pay per employee is calculated by dividing 1st Quarter payroll, annualized, by mid-March employment. The columns headed "% US" show the state's percentage of the national total for the SIC in 1993; for example, 0.9% for SIC 6030 means that the state had 0.9 percent of the national total establishments (or payroll) in SIC 6030 in 1993. A dash (-) is used to indicate that data are not available or cannot be calculated; *nec* means not elsewhere classified.

Continued on next page.

SIC	Industry	No. Establishments			Employment		Pay / Employee		Annual Payroll ($ 000)		
		1992	1993	% US	1992	1993	1992	1993	1992	1993	% US
NEW MEXICO - [continued]											
6732	Educational, religious, etc. trusts	34	34	0.7	393	171	16,702	17,170	6,833	3,179	0.3
6733	Trusts, n.e.c.	38	28	0.5	84	-	20,000	-	1,931	-	-
6792	Oil royalty traders	18	20	2.6	42	43	26,000	27,070	1,100	1,239	1.2
6794	Patent owners and lessors	2	5	0.3	-	-	-	-	-	-	-
6798	Real estate investment trusts	5	3	0.5	22	-	26,000	-	633	-	-
6799	Investors, n.e.c.	13	30	0.6	-	68	-	18,706	-	1,334	0.1
NEW YORK											
60 –	**Finance, insurance, and real estate**	53,356	54,269	8.9	773,424	741,943	55,882	53,099	38,839,247	40,483,465	17.4
6000	Depository institutions	6,805	6,641	6.5	242,926	218,109	44,734	44,950	9,946,359	9,538,406	16.5
6010	Central reserve depository	11	3	4.0	-	-	-	-	-	-	-
6020	Commercial banks	3,875	3,753	6.0	166,719	148,079	47,757	46,302	7,071,171	6,569,450	15.6
6030	Savings institutions	1,526	1,363	7.1	38,276	32,462	23,366	24,693	903,909	833,326	10.1
6060	Credit unions	633	723	4.7	-	-	-	-	-	-	-
6080	Foreign bank and branches and agencies	215	268	47.8	15,092	18,815	61,990	71,467	958,294	1,304,266	72.0
6090	Functions closely related to banking	536	525	11.2	12,694	8,473	61,724	61,251	730,678	536,910	32.8
6100	Nondepository institutions	1,752	1,725	4.1	31,379	31,712	54,045	46,967	1,549,953	1,485,822	8.4
6110	Federal and Federally-sponsored credit	38	32	2.3	1,230	347	31,034	33,153	33,557	11,724	1.3
6140	Personal credit institutions	612	466	2.7	5,490	5,201	52,533	36,527	290,661	177,628	4.6
6150	Business credit institutions	345	416	8.6	15,787	16,639	62,600	59,147	826,972	924,031	22.4
6160	Mortgage bankers and brokers	711	799	4.3	8,525	9,244	43,315	32,255	386,131	355,458	4.0
6200	Security and commodity brokers	5,337	5,793	16.9	132,719	133,855	133,017	118,290	14,447,851	16,561,173	41.9
6210	Security brokers and dealers	3,591	3,843	19.6	108,552	107,345	141,132	124,288	12,001,977	13,119,292	45.4
6220	Commodity contracts brokers, dealers	290	304	20.7	3,100	2,242	65,617	58,719	209,004	164,870	22.8
6230	Security and commodity exchanges	38	30	28.6	3,776	3,819	61,090	68,238	228,459	265,879	64.2
6280	Security and commodity services	1,340	1,610	12.3	17,026	20,446	110,525	102,695	1,987,881	3,010,223	31.8
6300	Insurance carriers	3,345	2,924	6.7	140,561	131,708	37,262	35,835	4,920,428	4,667,572	8.9
6310	Life insurance	890	807	6.4	65,624	55,076	36,744	35,000	2,183,478	1,807,561	9.2
6321	Accident and health insurance	51	37	3.3	2,282	1,844	35,082	31,950	86,709	60,680	4.1
6324	Hospital and medical service plans	75	93	5.3	17,355	19,746	29,658	28,409	511,162	617,226	9.4
6330	Fire, marine, and casualty insurance	1,341	1,285	6.7	42,266	48,196	42,245	39,514	1,723,929	1,909,744	8.8
6350	Surety insurance	48	42	7.1	5,793	895	42,899	112,836	201,882	95,124	17.5
6360	Title insurance	126	63	2.7	1,641	1,147	37,601	44,345	57,140	49,989	3.5
6370	Pension, health, and welfare funds	781	588	9.8	5,139	4,764	23,977	24,209	142,584	126,376	10.2
6390	Insurance carriers, n.e.c.	13	7	4.3	278	34	26,647	14,118	7,591	574	0.6
6400	Insurance agents, brokers, and service	6,713	7,058	5.8	57,259	54,762	37,951	35,147	2,182,216	2,059,121	10.2
6500	Real estate	26,842	27,591	11.7	136,892	139,559	26,099	25,134	3,772,383	3,878,153	13.1
6510	Real estate operators and lessors	14,373	15,650	15.4	62,698	67,440	22,863	21,749	1,511,702	1,599,635	18.0
6530	Real estate agents and managers	8,924	10,413	9.4	59,760	64,163	30,018	28,465	1,866,180	2,019,658	11.9
6540	Title abstract offices	363	400	8.4	2,445	2,843	25,312	25,451	70,947	85,524	8.2
6552	Subdividers and developers, n.e.c.	387	340	3.6	2,148	1,582	32,577	37,727	76,006	70,422	4.0
6553	Cemetery subdividers and developers	613	648	10.2	3,430	3,416	23,348	23,443	94,167	95,623	11.3
6700	Holding and other investment offices	2,351	2,332	8.5	26,334	26,402	58,260	63,862	1,579,527	1,908,312	16.1
6710	Holding offices	591	639	8.0	10,786	12,590	75,166	77,605	821,174	1,089,960	15.6
6720	Investment offices	151	90	11.0	1,597	844	83,081	79,469	133,751	78,296	10.6
6732	Educational, religious, etc. trusts	520	543	11.5	4,946	4,876	30,343	34,988	154,875	196,448	20.5
6733	Trusts, n.e.c.	352	352	6.2	2,939	1,987	29,874	27,312	99,757	74,899	10.5
6792	Oil royalty traders	13	12	1.6	42	43	70,952	65,488	3,051	2,838	2.8
6794	Patent owners and lessors	120	163	10.1	3,132	2,891	39,307	57,588	134,684	181,318	22.6
6798	Real estate investment trusts	65	40	7.2	382	493	79,173	76,300	22,388	30,612	14.4
6799	Investors, n.e.c.	385	479	9.3	1,688	2,549	86,486	81,791	155,297	251,912	20.0
NORTH CAROLINA											
60 –	**Finance, insurance, and real estate**	14,033	14,533	2.4	136,782	141,936	26,507	27,934	3,633,260	4,063,667	1.7
6000	Depository institutions	2,974	3,011	2.9	51,916	53,220	24,620	28,328	1,230,674	1,424,241	2.5
6010	Central reserve depository	1	1	1.3	-	-	-	-	-	-	-
6020	Commercial banks	2,078	2,167	3.5	39,156	42,993	25,979	30,050	979,404	1,212,582	2.9
6030	Savings institutions	532	473	2.4	6,821	6,275	21,002	21,947	138,598	131,576	1.6

Source: County Business Patterns, 1992/93, CBP-92/93-1, U.S. Department of Commerce, Washington, D.C., April 1995. SIC categories for which data were suppressed or not available for both 1992 and 1993 are not displayed. The employment columns represent mid-March employment in the year. Pay per employee is calculated by dividing 1st Quarter payroll, annualized, by mid-March employment. The columns headed "% US" show the state's percentage of the national total for the SIC in 1993; for example, 0.9% for SIC 6030 means that the state had 0.9 percent of the national total establishments (or payroll) in SIC 6030 in 1993. A dash (-) is used to indicate that data are not available or cannot be calculated; nec means not elsewhere classified.

Continued on next page.

SIC	Industry	No. Establishments			Employment		Pay / Employee		Annual Payroll ($ 000)		
		1992	1993	% US	1992	1993	1992	1993	1992	1993	% US
NORTH CAROLINA - [continued]											
6060	Credit unions	294	321	2.1	2,877	3,212	18,190	18,238	52,949	62,108	2.1
6080	Foreign bank and branches and agencies	1	1	0.2	-	-	-	-	-	-	-
6090	Functions closely related to banking	68	47	1.0	-	-	-	-	-	-	-
6100	Nondepository institutions	1,272	1,328	3.2	10,553	13,168	27,958	26,005	297,284	355,621	2.0
6110	Federal and Federally-sponsored credit	86	85	6.2	-	-	-	-	-	-	-
6140	Personal credit institutions	793	749	4.4	4,849	6,007	25,668	20,311	126,686	120,992	3.1
6150	Business credit institutions	65	109	2.3	-	1,319	-	43,527	-	52,343	1.3
6160	Mortgage bankers and brokers	320	379	2.0	3,651	4,752	28,323	28,508	112,659	154,773	1.8
6200	Security and commodity brokers	556	613	1.8	3,725	4,704	60,436	60,742	218,119	305,413	0.8
6210	Security brokers and dealers	366	401	2.0	3,255	3,729	63,112	66,022	198,491	260,114	0.9
6220	Commodity contracts brokers, dealers	3	3	0.2	-	-	-	-	-	-	-
6230	Security and commodity exchanges	3	2	1.9	-	-	-	-	-	-	-
6280	Security and commodity services	179	207	1.6	452	964	42,673	40,718	19,187	44,829	0.5
6300	Insurance carriers	1,272	1,138	2.6	29,425	28,978	30,551	30,361	889,021	914,696	1.7
6310	Life insurance	477	417	3.3	13,720	12,976	28,431	27,838	374,500	371,076	1.9
6321	Accident and health insurance	37	32	2.8	-	1,667	-	22,671	-	38,329	2.6
6324	Hospital and medical service plans	23	25	1.4	-	2,634	-	27,992	-	81,517	1.2
6330	Fire, marine, and casualty insurance	547	497	2.6	10,569	9,887	34,170	34,782	356,645	355,816	1.6
6350	Surety insurance	37	18	3.0	254	978	30,630	43,873	8,082	46,449	8.5
6360	Title insurance	29	47	2.0	939	-	39,480	-	40,076	-	-
6370	Pension, health, and welfare funds	112	100	1.7	566	620	21,293	21,897	16,494	14,944	1.2
6390	Insurance carriers, n.e.c.	2	2	1.2	-	-	-	-	-	-	-
6400	Insurance agents, brokers, and service	2,929	3,074	2.5	12,710	13,604	26,426	26,867	358,297	396,641	2.0
6500	Real estate	4,585	4,950	2.1	23,075	23,688	17,649	17,574	448,334	481,490	1.6
6510	Real estate operators and lessors	1,526	1,827	1.8	7,484	8,071	16,285	14,730	127,903	136,478	1.5
6530	Real estate agents and managers	2,028	2,553	2.3	10,602	12,337	18,148	18,691	216,301	268,405	1.6
6540	Title abstract offices	18	22	0.5	192	65	27,000	33,046	5,443	2,290	0.2
6552	Subdividers and developers, n.e.c.	286	329	3.5	2,295	2,186	20,378	22,399	51,980	54,628	3.1
6553	Cemetery subdividers and developers	138	148	2.3	895	862	16,344	15,499	13,571	14,669	1.7
6700	Holding and other investment offices	432	406	1.5	4,266	3,317	34,500	36,947	154,442	135,987	1.1
6710	Holding offices	109	105	1.3	1,781	1,879	52,552	45,795	94,841	98,037	1.4
6720	Investment offices	18	8	1.0	531	68	22,719	20,882	13,139	1,931	0.3
6732	Educational, religious, etc. trusts	103	95	2.0	698	651	20,006	19,810	15,731	13,208	1.4
6733	Trusts, n.e.c.	95	89	1.6	235	236	18,213	27,525	6,058	5,816	0.8
6794	Patent owners and lessors	16	24	1.5	190	201	29,263	27,104	6,364	7,097	0.9
6798	Real estate investment trusts	16	4	0.7	442	29	20,090	36,414	8,672	703	0.3
6799	Investors, n.e.c.	55	78	1.5	133	251	31,579	36,526	4,894	9,181	0.7
NORTH DAKOTA											
60 –	**Finance, insurance, and real estate**	1,857	1,928	0.3	12,468	13,231	21,942	22,036	284,195	300,455	0.1
6000	Depository institutions	408	412	0.4	5,549	5,834	21,698	22,152	125,789	130,479	0.2
6020	Commercial banks	265	259	0.4	4,244	4,319	22,899	22,679	100,803	99,817	0.2
6030	Savings institutions	63	60	0.3	843	994	18,558	23,002	17,106	21,772	0.3
6060	Credit unions	76	90	0.6	-	502	-	16,088	-	8,439	0.3
6090	Functions closely related to banking	4	3	0.1	-	19	-	17,895	-	451	0.0
6100	Nondepository institutions	82	64	0.2	-	525	-	35,970	-	15,764	0.1
6110	Federal and Federally-sponsored credit	9	21	1.5	-	238	-	41,731	-	7,444	0.8
6140	Personal credit institutions	36	17	0.1	175	124	22,491	26,742	3,914	3,451	0.1
6150	Business credit institutions	26	13	0.3	268	99	26,672	42,222	7,017	2,466	0.1
6160	Mortgage bankers and brokers	11	12	0.1	-	64	-	22,750	-	2,396	0.0
6200	Security and commodity brokers	82	85	0.2	323	358	51,529	48,883	16,791	18,806	0.0
6210	Security brokers and dealers	55	61	0.3	265	-	58,264	-	15,526	-	-
6220	Commodity contracts brokers, dealers	4	5	0.3	-	-	-	-	-	-	-
6280	Security and commodity services	22	19	0.1	-	-	-	-	-	-	-
6300	Insurance carriers	154	125	0.3	2,201	2,302	24,282	25,719	54,191	59,628	0.1
6310	Life insurance	44	38	0.3	523	581	28,979	28,372	15,236	15,855	0.1
6321	Accident and health insurance	8	3	0.3	108	-	22,333	-	2,425	-	-
6324	Hospital and medical service plans	8	9	0.5	-	-	-	-	-	-	-

Source: County Business Patterns, 1992/93, CBP-92/93-1, U.S. Department of Commerce, Washington, D.C., April 1995. SIC categories for which data were suppressed or not available for both 1992 and 1993 are *not* displayed. The employment columns represent mid-March employment in the year. Pay per employee is calculated by dividing 1st Quarter payroll, annualized, by mid-March employment. The columns headed "% US" show the state's percentage of the national total for the SIC in 1993; for example, 0.9% for SIC 6030 means that the state had 0.9 percent of the national total establishments (or payroll) in SIC 6030 in 1993. A dash (-) is used to indicate that data are not available or cannot be calculated; *nec* means not elsewhere classified.

Continued on next page.

SIC	Industry	No. Establishments			Employment		Pay / Employee		Annual Payroll ($ 000)		
		1992	1993	% US	1992	1993	1992	1993	1992	1993	% US
NORTH DAKOTA - [continued]											
6330	Fire, marine, and casualty insurance	80	60	0.3	-	508	-	23,685	-	12,789	0.1
6350	Surety insurance	-	2	0.3	-	-	-	-	-	-	-
6360	Title insurance	3	1	0.0	-	-	-	-	-	-	-
6370	Pension, health, and welfare funds	10	10	0.2	-	-	-	-	-	-	-
6390	Insurance carriers, n.e.c.	-	1	0.6	-	-	-	-	-	-	-
6400	Insurance agents, brokers, and service	519	595	0.5	1,571	1,585	20,835	18,291	35,368	33,553	0.2
6500	Real estate	548	580	0.2	2,019	2,345	13,779	12,631	28,856	32,561	0.1
6510	Real estate operators and lessors	268	306	0.3	934	1,225	9,507	10,942	10,923	15,109	0.2
6530	Real estate agents and managers	167	177	0.2	757	901	18,774	14,801	12,122	13,568	0.1
6540	Title abstract offices	47	47	1.0	136	157	15,412	15,032	2,489	3,082	0.3
6552	Subdividers and developers, n.e.c.	8	11	0.1	42	20	8,286	11,200	592	324	0.0
6553	Cemetery subdividers and developers	35	37	0.6	-	42	-	7,048	-	465	0.1
6700	Holding and other investment offices	63	67	0.2	-	282	-	28,794	-	9,664	0.1
6710	Holding offices	17	22	0.3	85	139	57,176	40,604	4,930	6,114	0.1
6720	Investment offices	1	1	0.1	-	-	-	-	-	-	-
6732	Educational, religious, etc. trusts	14	15	0.3	44	49	14,364	15,265	1,477	1,563	0.2
6733	Trusts, n.e.c.	19	13	0.2	38	-	14,316	-	676	-	-
6792	Oil royalty traders	2	3	0.4	-	-	-	-	-	-	-
6794	Patent owners and lessors	2	5	0.3	-	37	-	23,784	-	999	0.1
6798	Real estate investment trusts	1	2	0.4	-	-	-	-	-	-	-
6799	Investors, n.e.c.	3	5	0.1	-	11	-	5,091	-	96	0.0
OHIO											
60 –	**Finance, insurance, and real estate**	22,378	22,494	3.7	263,580	263,324	26,503	26,247	7,001,691	7,236,221	3.1
6000	Depository institutions	4,971	4,893	4.8	89,773	83,936	24,345	23,965	2,053,675	1,993,075	3.5
6010	Central reserve depository	7	6	8.0	-	-	-	-	-	-	-
6020	Commercial banks	2,989	2,943	4.7	66,181	61,711	25,085	24,665	1,521,199	1,491,461	3.5
6030	Savings institutions	1,217	1,057	5.5	16,965	14,740	22,743	22,774	391,252	341,508	4.1
6060	Credit unions	653	781	5.1	4,433	5,340	17,172	16,812	78,249	95,210	3.2
6080	Foreign bank and branches and agencies	2	-	-	-	-	-	-	-	-	-
6090	Functions closely related to banking	103	106	2.3	787	-	24,518	-	17,412	-	-
6100	Nondepository institutions	1,460	1,366	3.3	17,969	18,593	25,443	23,792	469,158	500,748	2.8
6110	Federal and Federally-sponsored credit	5	56	4.1	-	283	-	27,081	-	11,272	1.2
6140	Personal credit institutions	876	676	4.0	8,564	8,824	23,390	19,094	200,192	169,918	4.4
6150	Business credit institutions	157	134	2.8	4,321	4,126	23,038	25,426	92,699	109,393	2.7
6160	Mortgage bankers and brokers	411	495	2.7	4,926	5,359	31,103	30,097	171,444	210,114	2.4
6200	Security and commodity brokers	937	999	2.9	8,017	9,541	64,416	60,235	519,187	603,488	1.5
6210	Security brokers and dealers	520	518	2.6	6,285	6,644	69,438	69,191	426,897	459,786	1.6
6220	Commodity contracts brokers, dealers	10	12	0.8	37	-	27,351	-	736	-	-
6230	Security and commodity exchanges	1	1	1.0	-	-	-	-	-	-	-
6280	Security and commodity services	400	467	3.6	1,681	2,856	46,644	39,759	90,943	141,994	1.5
6300	Insurance carriers	2,360	1,947	4.4	65,910	67,419	30,171	30,288	2,034,797	2,106,745	4.0
6310	Life insurance	648	556	4.4	20,586	20,228	27,771	29,293	577,180	564,678	2.9
6321	Accident and health insurance	62	59	5.2	909	5,106	24,264	29,975	20,254	152,706	10.3
6324	Hospital and medical service plans	57	57	3.2	7,102	5,005	32,961	30,675	229,657	163,804	2.5
6330	Fire, marine, and casualty insurance	990	877	4.6	32,498	32,423	32,381	31,947	1,075,939	1,106,178	5.1
6350	Surety insurance	19	17	2.9	99	84	27,475	37,048	2,929	3,383	0.6
6360	Title insurance	129	73	3.2	1,693	1,175	26,417	26,614	53,188	37,280	2.6
6370	Pension, health, and welfare funds	425	298	4.9	2,785	3,339	18,805	21,122	66,181	76,202	6.2
6390	Insurance carriers, n.e.c.	13	7	4.3	121	56	37,950	37,571	5,275	2,467	2.6
6400	Insurance agents, brokers, and service	5,034	5,308	4.3	22,948	24,248	27,235	26,001	641,098	678,962	3.4
6500	Real estate	6,767	7,129	3.0	48,867	49,066	16,892	16,693	877,937	932,912	3.1
6510	Real estate operators and lessors	3,005	3,308	3.3	17,792	19,406	13,470	13,357	249,060	280,917	3.2
6530	Real estate agents and managers	2,600	3,000	2.7	23,872	23,930	18,391	18,280	467,179	498,849	2.9
6540	Title abstract offices	154	202	4.2	1,228	1,838	21,564	22,788	31,196	57,174	5.5
6552	Subdividers and developers, n.e.c.	237	241	2.6	2,073	1,867	26,836	25,948	56,901	58,012	3.3
6553	Cemetery subdividers and developers	282	315	5.0	1,867	1,923	16,386	15,786	34,085	35,324	4.2
6700	Holding and other investment offices	806	811	3.0	8,002	8,879	38,329	37,302	316,548	365,362	3.1

Source: County Business Patterns, 1992/93, CBP-92/93-1, U.S. Department of Commerce, Washington, D.C., April 1995. SIC categories for which data were suppressed or not available for both 1992 and 1993 are *not* displayed. The employment columns represent mid-March employment in the year. Pay per employee is calculated by dividing 1st Quarter payroll, annualized, by mid-March employment. The columns headed "% US" show the state's percentage of the national total for the SIC in 1993; for example, 0.9% for SIC 6030 means that the state had 0.9 percent of the national total establishments (or payroll) in SIC 6030 in 1993. A dash (-) is used to indicate that data are not available or cannot be calculated; *nec* means not elsewhere classified.

Continued on next page.

SIC	Industry	No. Establishments			Employment		Pay / Employee		Annual Payroll ($ 000)		
		1992	1993	% US	1992	1993	1992	1993	1992	1993	% US
OHIO - [continued]											
6710	Holding offices	259	289	3.6	5,386	5,261	43,675	45,965	239,911	265,109	3.8
6720	Investment offices	39	18	2.2	236	49	65,831	84,735	14,709	3,164	0.4
6732	Educational, religious, etc. trusts	127	138	2.9	818	998	17,868	20,617	15,943	21,705	2.3
6733	Trusts, n.e.c.	194	180	3.2	591	706	24,095	18,742	13,366	16,489	2.3
6792	Oil royalty traders	8	12	1.6	32	45	21,750	22,311	756	1,456	1.4
6794	Patent owners and lessors	40	51	3.2	399	524	27,779	26,450	11,337	14,451	1.8
6798	Real estate investment trusts	19	15	2.7	163	337	20,515	26,576	5,664	11,512	5.4
6799	Investors, n.e.c.	87	104	2.0	313	959	33,112	28,788	11,371	31,431	2.5
OKLAHOMA											
60 –	**Finance, insurance, and real estate**	7,159	7,512	1.2	63,638	63,874	23,522	23,605	1,548,395	1,577,846	0.7
6000	Depository institutions	1,100	1,159	1.1	22,343	22,897	22,323	22,463	509,707	519,846	0.9
6010	Central reserve depository	2	2	2.7	-	-	-	-	-	-	-
6020	Commercial banks	746	767	1.2	17,572	18,467	22,936	22,819	413,571	424,759	1.0
6030	Savings institutions	180	182	0.9	2,416	1,869	19,361	21,413	46,835	40,474	0.5
6060	Credit unions	120	150	1.0	1,751	1,964	20,715	19,430	35,589	39,411	1.3
6090	Functions closely related to banking	52	58	1.2	-	-	-	-	-	-	-
6100	Nondepository institutions	764	779	1.9	4,251	4,634	22,289	20,856	96,944	108,083	0.6
6110	Federal and Federally-sponsored credit	21	25	1.8	153	178	28,235	30,112	4,490	5,383	0.6
6140	Personal credit institutions	604	587	3.5	2,690	2,645	19,004	17,128	51,303	47,293	1.2
6150	Business credit institutions	34	41	0.8	202	301	28,851	27,575	5,579	10,645	0.3
6160	Mortgage bankers and brokers	92	124	0.7	1,186	1,510	28,040	24,956	35,251	44,713	0.5
6200	Security and commodity brokers	357	348	1.0	1,777	1,765	54,510	62,037	98,066	107,243	0.3
6210	Security brokers and dealers	240	232	1.2	1,432	1,399	60,168	70,330	85,076	92,893	0.3
6220	Commodity contracts brokers, dealers	15	16	1.1	89	50	33,258	41,280	3,195	2,589	0.4
6230	Security and commodity exchanges	1	-	-	-	-	-	-	-	-	-
6280	Security and commodity services	96	100	0.8	240	316	30,883	28,608	9,486	11,761	0.1
6300	Insurance carriers	569	482	1.1	11,796	12,021	28,095	28,482	333,283	347,534	0.7
6310	Life insurance	158	137	1.1	4,738	4,893	24,357	24,965	120,365	125,676	0.6
6321	Accident and health insurance	28	28	2.5	-	1,037	-	24,856	-	26,377	1.8
6324	Hospital and medical service plans	12	20	1.1	-	1,093	-	26,997	-	33,875	0.5
6330	Fire, marine, and casualty insurance	275	206	1.1	5,350	4,482	32,207	34,676	166,807	149,654	0.7
6350	Surety insurance	5	3	0.5	-	-	-	-	-	-	-
6360	Title insurance	9	9	0.4	-	44	-	12,818	-	972	0.1
6370	Pension, health, and welfare funds	71	74	1.2	309	453	18,343	18,737	7,455	10,385	0.8
6390	Insurance carriers, n.e.c.	3	4	2.5	-	-	-	-	-	-	-
6400	Insurance agents, brokers, and service	1,706	1,864	1.5	6,693	6,951	21,678	20,764	153,009	154,784	0.8
6500	Real estate	2,185	2,383	1.0	12,119	11,300	15,827	16,146	201,144	199,819	0.7
6510	Real estate operators and lessors	883	1,069	1.1	3,845	4,133	13,401	13,082	56,478	60,055	0.7
6530	Real estate agents and managers	825	980	0.9	5,886	5,203	17,214	17,500	101,023	95,934	0.6
6540	Title abstract offices	148	156	3.3	1,122	1,331	18,870	20,520	22,915	32,041	3.1
6552	Subdividers and developers, n.e.c.	77	98	1.0	296	260	13,676	19,569	5,679	6,098	0.3
6553	Cemetery subdividers and developers	55	61	1.0	385	368	14,556	13,293	5,905	5,364	0.6
6700	Holding and other investment offices	469	489	1.8	3,596	3,427	30,725	28,551	121,611	116,383	1.0
6710	Holding offices	77	85	1.1	1,647	1,139	34,978	37,910	66,323	58,735	0.8
6720	Investment offices	14	11	1.3	-	35	-	7,543	-	352	0.0
6732	Educational, religious, etc. trusts	53	56	1.2	374	421	28,738	25,083	9,809	9,685	1.0
6733	Trusts, n.e.c.	141	137	2.4	484	515	15,669	16,885	8,289	8,785	1.2
6792	Oil royalty traders	79	97	12.5	256	287	37,500	41,073	9,295	11,584	11.3
6794	Patent owners and lessors	8	10	0.6	458	671	22,079	17,997	10,150	13,849	1.7
6798	Real estate investment trusts	14	7	1.3	24	17	29,500	26,824	683	675	0.3
6799	Investors, n.e.c.	71	83	1.6	306	336	43,359	32,107	14,458	12,673	1.0
OREGON											
60 –	**Finance, insurance, and real estate**	7,409	7,826	1.3	71,571	72,875	25,110	26,713	1,850,498	2,029,648	0.9
6000	Depository institutions	1,223	1,125	1.1	21,630	20,960	22,656	26,792	480,859	553,511	1.0
6010	Central reserve depository	1	2	2.7	-	-	-	-	-	-	-
6020	Commercial banks	780	664	1.1	16,647	15,571	22,401	27,566	360,430	410,792	1.0

Source: County Business Patterns, 1992/93, CBP-92/93-1, U.S. Department of Commerce, Washington, D.C., April 1995. SIC categories for which data were suppressed or not available for both 1992 and 1993 are *not* displayed. The employment columns represent mid-March employment in the year. Pay per employee is calculated by dividing 1st Quarter payroll, annualized, by mid-March employment. The columns headed "% US" show the state's percentage of the national total for the SIC in 1993; for example, 0.9% for SIC 6030 means that the state had 0.9 percent of the national total establishments (or payroll) in SIC 6030 in 1993. A dash (-) is used to indicate that data are not available or cannot be calculated; *nec* means not elsewhere classified.

Continued on next page.

SIC	Industry	No. Establishments			Employment		Pay / Employee		Annual Payroll ($ 000)		
		1992	1993	% US	1992	1993	1992	1993	1992	1993	% US
OREGON - [continued]											
6030	Savings institutions	217	218	1.1	2,605	2,421	25,546	26,113	69,041	62,947	0.8
6060	Credit unions	188	205	1.3	1,986	2,464	20,407	20,289	42,138	51,629	1.7
6080	Foreign bank and branches and agencies	3	3	0.5	-	-	-	-	-	-	-
6090	Functions closely related to banking	34	33	0.7	-	300	-	42,467	-	21,706	1.3
6100	Nondepository institutions	503	540	1.3	4,650	4,934	32,798	32,406	155,882	182,531	1.0
6110	Federal and Federally-sponsored credit	1	12	0.9	-	-	-	-	-	-	-
6140	Personal credit institutions	185	160	0.9	1,274	-	25,994	-	34,769	-	-
6150	Business credit institutions	64	64	1.3	1,032	1,363	35,264	32,942	33,532	46,249	1.1
6160	Mortgage bankers and brokers	244	303	1.6	2,269	2,494	36,300	34,839	86,741	106,891	1.2
6200	Security and commodity brokers	328	359	1.0	3,076	2,814	47,403	58,729	154,619	163,592	0.4
6210	Security brokers and dealers	207	230	1.2	2,537	2,363	47,976	62,223	122,375	142,260	0.5
6220	Commodity contracts brokers, dealers	10	8	0.5	-	10	-	27,200	-	624	0.1
6280	Security and commodity services	110	121	0.9	-	441	-	40,726	-	20,708	0.2
6300	Insurance carriers	725	631	1.4	16,232	16,679	27,699	29,344	466,499	501,841	1.0
6310	Life insurance	118	95	0.7	3,034	3,145	24,956	25,639	75,363	79,317	0.4
6321	Accident and health insurance	22	15	1.3	586	334	23,126	24,060	14,331	7,643	0.5
6324	Hospital and medical service plans	21	33	1.9	2,927	3,668	28,987	27,173	86,147	104,120	1.6
6330	Fire, marine, and casualty insurance	330	289	1.5	7,354	7,145	30,048	34,314	229,826	238,263	1.1
6350	Surety insurance	6	5	0.8	35	27	33,371	35,852	1,194	1,003	0.2
6360	Title insurance	113	78	3.4	1,604	1,333	24,833	26,710	44,553	41,022	2.8
6370	Pension, health, and welfare funds	113	116	1.9	681	1,027	19,695	18,839	14,963	30,473	2.5
6400	Insurance agents, brokers, and service	1,438	1,607	1.3	7,193	8,123	25,325	25,791	192,238	223,908	1.1
6500	Real estate	2,924	3,280	1.4	15,138	16,696	15,233	15,536	255,690	303,334	1.0
6510	Real estate operators and lessors	1,326	1,529	1.5	5,230	6,298	12,954	12,868	71,232	92,263	1.0
6530	Real estate agents and managers	1,198	1,473	1.3	8,149	9,009	16,176	16,513	146,161	173,146	1.0
6540	Title abstract offices	16	31	0.7	165	403	20,024	22,868	4,015	11,586	1.1
6552	Subdividers and developers, n.e.c.	104	149	1.6	555	665	21,564	22,580	14,610	19,995	1.1
6553	Cemetery subdividers and developers	54	61	1.0	321	299	14,816	17,110	5,147	5,479	0.6
6700	Holding and other investment offices	261	277	1.0	2,552	2,502	37,442	38,676	93,271	95,446	0.8
6710	Holding offices	53	61	0.8	1,700	1,432	38,593	51,930	68,072	67,802	1.0
6720	Investment offices	9	9	1.1	-	32	-	32,875	-	1,312	0.2
6732	Educational, religious, etc. trusts	54	62	1.3	290	298	19,738	21,369	6,037	6,503	0.7
6733	Trusts, n.e.c.	73	71	1.3	331	323	55,360	17,845	11,277	6,261	0.9
6792	Oil royalty traders	2	1	0.1	-	-	-	-	-	-	-
6794	Patent owners and lessors	10	17	1.1	53	-	27,170	-	1,478	-	-
6798	Real estate investment trusts	7	2	0.4	-	-	-	-	-	-	-
6799	Investors, n.e.c.	44	54	1.1	103	168	24,117	24,667	2,755	7,124	0.6
PENNSYLVANIA											
60 –	**Finance, insurance, and real estate**	23,600	23,533	3.9	322,177	336,419	28,556	28,014	9,289,898	9,986,674	4.3
6000	Depository institutions	5,686	5,657	5.5	104,618	106,523	24,769	24,322	2,491,924	2,592,919	4.5
6010	Central reserve depository	6	4	5.3	2,069	2,089	31,441	29,605	64,490	63,751	7.1
6020	Commercial banks	3,750	3,727	6.0	82,763	85,961	25,373	24,831	1,996,436	2,113,498	5.0
6030	Savings institutions	992	889	4.6	13,942	11,772	22,096	21,895	310,427	275,753	3.3
6060	Credit unions	763	856	5.6	4,447	5,341	17,967	17,592	82,376	99,084	3.3
6080	Foreign bank and branches and agencies	5	3	0.5	74	-	49,946	-	3,557	-	-
6090	Functions closely related to banking	166	177	3.8	1,317	1,309	26,223	31,034	34,542	38,308	2.3
6100	Nondepository institutions	1,374	1,292	3.1	14,052	15,121	33,015	31,212	488,058	549,056	3.1
6110	Federal and Federally-sponsored credit	46	42	3.1	857	1,101	22,903	28,687	17,879	32,681	3.6
6140	Personal credit institutions	813	668	3.9	5,258	5,459	30,231	26,927	158,079	159,027	4.1
6150	Business credit institutions	106	129	2.7	1,678	2,216	35,502	35,823	59,692	86,337	2.1
6160	Mortgage bankers and brokers	401	449	2.4	6,223	6,344	36,147	33,731	251,360	270,898	3.1
6200	Security and commodity brokers	1,132	1,142	3.3	15,721	16,375	62,396	57,983	1,052,132	1,150,746	2.9
6210	Security brokers and dealers	642	594	3.0	8,165	8,299	79,363	76,186	649,294	665,531	2.3
6220	Commodity contracts brokers, dealers	14	12	0.8	-	-	-	-	-	-	-
6230	Security and commodity exchanges	4	7	6.7	-	-	-	-	-	-	-
6280	Security and commodity services	467	527	4.0	7,125	7,554	43,111	39,233	377,619	463,332	4.9
6300	Insurance carriers	2,540	2,130	4.9	95,578	105,280	30,077	28,614	2,846,233	3,028,053	5.7

Source: County Business Patterns, 1992/93, CBP-92/93-1, U.S. Department of Commerce, Washington, D.C., April 1995. SIC categories for which data were suppressed or not available for both 1992 and 1993 are *not* displayed. The employment columns represent mid-March employment in the year. Pay per employee is calculated by dividing 1st Quarter payroll, annualized, by mid-March employment. The columns headed "% US" show the state's percentage of the national total for the SIC in 1993; for example, 0.9% for SIC 6030 means that the state had 0.9 percent of the national total establishments (or payroll) in SIC 6030 in 1993. A dash (-) is used to indicate that data are not available or cannot be calculated; *nec* means not elsewhere classified.

Continued on next page.

SIC	Industry	No. Establishments			Employment		Pay / Employee		Annual Payroll ($ 000)		
		1992	1993	% US	1992	1993	1992	1993	1992	1993	% US
PENNSYLVANIA - [continued]											
6310	Life insurance	782	741	5.8	41,705	52,233	28,287	26,078	1,112,152	1,328,550	6.7
6321	Accident and health insurance	63	50	4.4	1,428	2,472	25,022	22,924	34,810	59,182	4.0
6324	Hospital and medical service plans	67	70	4.0	17,116	16,295	29,180	28,895	507,726	490,863	7.5
6330	Fire, marine, and casualty insurance	795	722	3.8	29,883	29,509	33,811	33,958	1,007,746	1,008,675	4.7
6350	Surety insurance	47	27	4.5	629	475	53,196	43,672	35,742	24,178	4.4
6360	Title insurance	125	68	3.0	1,088	841	31,033	33,679	37,681	33,844	2.3
6370	Pension, health, and welfare funds	635	444	7.4	3,627	3,405	21,602	20,777	105,778	81,420	6.6
6390	Insurance carriers, n.e.c.	11	5	3.1	47	39	23,660	22,154	1,485	1,214	1.3
6400	Insurance agents, brokers, and service	4,805	5,068	4.1	28,537	29,090	30,197	28,571	901,502	949,175	4.7
6500	Real estate	7,079	7,295	3.1	52,157	49,842	17,462	19,259	980,191	1,072,320	3.6
6510	Real estate operators and lessors	2,593	2,868	2.8	24,699	17,554	13,634	17,048	351,829	334,262	3.8
6530	Real estate agents and managers	2,790	3,193	2.9	18,954	25,946	21,383	20,481	434,441	586,569	3.4
6540	Title abstract offices	221	238	5.0	1,533	1,916	23,298	24,505	46,568	55,655	5.3
6552	Subdividers and developers, n.e.c.	295	287	3.1	1,629	1,233	27,465	27,101	46,439	38,173	2.2
6553	Cemetery subdividers and developers	643	655	10.4	3,133	3,166	16,125	15,299	55,421	55,485	6.5
6700	Holding and other investment offices	934	895	3.3	9,525	11,472	43,962	39,132	435,596	496,534	4.2
6710	Holding offices	268	257	3.2	5,059	7,033	51,747	46,805	269,828	360,873	5.2
6720	Investment offices	45	24	2.9	524	195	111,198	76,903	63,567	18,130	2.4
6732	Educational, religious, etc. trusts	209	210	4.5	1,709	1,726	19,169	18,424	34,021	34,255	3.6
6733	Trusts, n.e.c.	245	225	4.0	985	1,362	20,975	17,894	24,900	28,731	4.0
6792	Oil royalty traders	5	8	1.0	-	29	-	59,034	-	1,817	1.8
6794	Patent owners and lessors	45	58	3.6	469	412	29,586	32,854	14,805	15,690	2.0
6798	Real estate investment trusts	20	20	3.6	-	148	-	53,189	-	8,139	3.8
6799	Investors, n.e.c.	68	90	1.8	394	562	37,310	44,057	14,445	28,457	2.3
RHODE ISLAND											
60–	**Finance, insurance, and real estate**	1,939	2,015	0.3	29,225	26,552	28,142	28,938	827,920	803,658	0.3
6000	Depository institutions	313	319	0.3	8,655	7,873	26,398	25,387	230,400	205,795	0.4
6010	Central reserve depository	1	-	-	-	-	-	-	-	-	-
6020	Commercial banks	157	168	0.3	5,715	5,484	28,037	26,862	161,289	151,536	0.4
6030	Savings institutions	84	72	0.4	2,032	1,457	25,146	22,476	52,162	32,410	0.4
6060	Credit unions	68	73	0.5	-	883	-	19,280	-	18,699	0.6
6090	Functions closely related to banking	3	6	0.1	-	49	-	56,816	-	3,150	0.2
6100	Nondepository institutions	150	154	0.4	-	-	-	-	-	-	-
6110	Federal and Federally-sponsored credit	1	1	0.1	-	-	-	-	-	-	-
6140	Personal credit institutions	70	44	0.3	726	-	33,917	-	20,499	-	-
6150	Business credit institutions	5	13	0.3	-	530	-	45,509	-	19,252	0.5
6160	Mortgage bankers and brokers	70	96	0.5	791	993	21,608	27,734	19,325	33,809	0.4
6200	Security and commodity brokers	83	113	0.3	1,377	1,831	47,834	48,867	63,427	87,227	0.2
6210	Security brokers and dealers	39	44	0.2	1,140	713	42,853	70,485	48,095	48,358	0.2
6220	Commodity contracts brokers, dealers	1	2	0.1	-	-	-	-	-	-	-
6280	Security and commodity services	40	67	0.5	233	-	72,549	-	15,064	-	-
6300	Insurance carriers	174	158	0.4	9,471	8,498	27,869	29,687	269,535	264,435	0.5
6310	Life insurance	60	48	0.4	3,726	2,402	22,201	27,875	86,731	62,784	0.3
6321	Accident and health insurance	5	1	0.1	-	-	-	-	-	-	-
6324	Hospital and medical service plans	2	7	0.4	-	-	-	-	-	-	-
6330	Fire, marine, and casualty insurance	69	71	0.4	3,731	3,933	34,398	31,246	128,496	131,464	0.6
6350	Surety insurance	2	-	-	-	-	-	-	-	-	-
6360	Title insurance	6	6	0.3	-	-	-	-	-	-	-
6370	Pension, health, and welfare funds	30	25	0.4	-	139	-	38,302	-	7,055	0.6
6400	Insurance agents, brokers, and service	382	405	0.3	2,244	2,164	29,783	29,089	73,069	71,638	0.4
6500	Real estate	731	763	0.3	4,203	3,769	17,761	20,016	81,746	84,857	0.3
6510	Real estate operators and lessors	265	300	0.3	1,390	1,503	15,027	22,262	22,542	35,716	0.4
6530	Real estate agents and managers	302	380	0.3	1,927	1,958	20,293	18,165	42,689	39,192	0.2
6540	Title abstract offices	5	7	0.1	35	95	25,486	9,895	993	1,144	0.1
6552	Subdividers and developers, n.e.c.	29	30	0.3	81	51	16,247	41,490	1,400	4,526	0.3
6553	Cemetery subdividers and developers	34	35	0.6	161	141	18,708	20,965	3,637	3,621	0.4
6700	Holding and other investment offices	105	101	0.4	-	-	-	-	-	-	-

Source: County Business Patterns, 1992/93, CBP-92/93-1, U.S. Department of Commerce, Washington, D.C., April 1995. SIC categories for which data were suppressed or not available for both 1992 and 1993 are *not* displayed. The employment columns represent mid-March employment in the year. Pay per employee is calculated by dividing 1st Quarter payroll, annualized, by mid-March employment. The columns headed "% US" show the state's percentage of the national total for the SIC in 1993; for example, 0.9% for SIC 6030 means that the state had 0.9 percent of the national total establishments (or payroll) in SIC 6030 in 1993. A dash (-) is used to indicate that data are not available or cannot be calculated; *nec* means not elsewhere classified.

Continued on next page.

SIC	Industry	No. Establishments			Employment		Pay / Employee		Annual Payroll ($ 000)		
		1992	1993	% US	1992	1993	1992	1993	1992	1993	% US
RHODE ISLAND - [continued]											
6710	Holding offices	23	30	0.4	280	312	56,171	74,359	15,375	20,405	0.3
6720	Investment offices	6	2	0.2	-	-	-	-	-	-	-
6732	Educational, religious, etc. trusts	21	22	0.5	62	88	28,129	25,273	2,037	2,442	0.3
6733	Trusts, n.e.c.	24	23	0.4	84	-	26,000	-	2,522	-	-
6794	Patent owners and lessors	5	5	0.3	94	-	8,213	-	939	-	-
6798	Real estate investment trusts	6	1	0.2	12	-	30,000	-	351	-	-
6799	Investors, n.e.c.	17	17	0.3	100	-	43,040	-	2,753	-	-
SOUTH CAROLINA											
60 –	**Finance, insurance, and real estate**	7,165	7,436	1.2	66,650	67,208	22,693	23,354	1,556,395	1,627,797	0.7
6000	Depository institutions	1,388	1,486	1.4	21,187	21,125	22,289	22,592	476,692	474,850	0.8
6010	Central reserve depository	1	1	1.3	-	-	-	-	-	-	-
6020	Commercial banks	847	947	1.5	14,173	14,349	22,640	23,337	319,818	322,365	0.8
6030	Savings institutions	339	322	1.7	5,157	4,841	21,526	21,227	116,821	111,347	1.3
6060	Credit unions	173	179	1.2	1,679	1,712	21,920	20,598	36,272	36,530	1.2
6080	Foreign bank and branches and agencies	-	1	0.2	-	-	-	-	-	-	-
6090	Functions closely related to banking	28	36	0.8	-	-	-	-	-	-	-
6100	Nondepository institutions	1,148	1,187	2.8	5,775	7,529	24,822	22,849	141,768	185,365	1.0
6110	Federal and Federally-sponsored credit	18	26	1.9	-	-	-	-	-	-	-
6140	Personal credit institutions	914	917	5.4	3,715	4,397	22,053	18,262	81,520	83,876	2.2
6150	Business credit institutions	31	44	0.9	-	-	-	-	-	-	-
6160	Mortgage bankers and brokers	173	200	1.1	1,321	2,398	29,463	28,716	38,869	78,115	0.9
6200	Security and commodity brokers	231	260	0.8	1,298	1,475	57,270	60,198	72,786	90,598	0.2
6210	Security brokers and dealers	160	187	1.0	1,158	1,265	59,261	64,101	66,560	83,428	0.3
6220	Commodity contracts brokers, dealers	5	4	0.3	-	11	-	16,727	-	212	0.0
6280	Security and commodity services	66	69	0.5	-	199	-	37,789	-	6,958	0.1
6300	Insurance carriers	580	538	1.2	13,891	14,044	26,145	27,473	360,797	378,905	0.7
6310	Life insurance	251	238	1.9	6,701	6,466	26,326	27,071	174,582	169,097	0.9
6321	Accident and health insurance	18	32	2.8	-	-	-	-	-	-	-
6324	Hospital and medical service plans	12	13	0.7	-	-	-	-	-	-	-
6330	Fire, marine, and casualty insurance	224	198	1.0	2,253	2,225	36,609	39,094	81,127	87,057	0.4
6350	Surety insurance	15	7	1.2	45	9	14,489	12,889	662	167	0.0
6360	Title insurance	10	9	0.4	40	41	34,600	31,707	1,412	1,392	0.1
6370	Pension, health, and welfare funds	42	38	0.6	241	250	25,577	12,400	5,201	3,059	0.2
6390	Insurance carriers, n.e.c.	1	1	0.6	-	-	-	-	-	-	-
6400	Insurance agents, brokers, and service	1,346	1,416	1.2	7,343	7,250	22,806	24,356	179,565	195,411	1.0
6500	Real estate	2,259	2,347	1.0	13,608	14,267	15,784	15,264	239,038	248,683	0.8
6510	Real estate operators and lessors	653	753	0.7	2,808	4,255	13,705	11,099	41,832	53,470	0.6
6530	Real estate agents and managers	1,058	1,303	1.2	7,103	7,817	16,500	17,046	131,965	150,168	0.9
6540	Title abstract offices	37	39	0.8	109	118	17,358	16,169	2,122	2,382	0.2
6552	Subdividers and developers, n.e.c.	131	126	1.3	1,902	1,426	15,880	18,502	34,365	29,397	1.7
6553	Cemetery subdividers and developers	85	93	1.5	506	638	16,103	13,843	8,322	12,031	1.4
6700	Holding and other investment offices	203	191	0.7	3,337	1,277	20,270	31,868	77,589	43,745	0.4
6710	Holding offices	64	65	0.8	2,893	892	20,456	36,807	67,322	34,348	0.5
6720	Investment offices	10	5	0.6	32	-	24,500	-	839	-	-
6732	Educational, religious, etc. trusts	40	37	0.8	116	-	21,552	-	2,627	-	-
6733	Trusts, n.e.c.	40	37	0.7	123	119	14,732	10,655	3,040	2,031	0.3
6792	Oil royalty traders	-	1	0.1	-	-	-	-	-	-	-
6794	Patent owners and lessors	9	10	0.6	-	19	-	48,842	-	1,074	0.1
6798	Real estate investment trusts	6	3	0.5	-	-	-	-	-	-	-
6799	Investors, n.e.c.	24	32	0.6	113	106	14,442	21,472	1,756	2,679	0.2
SOUTH DAKOTA											
60 –	**Finance, insurance, and real estate**	2,025	2,099	0.3	17,537	17,669	20,542	20,707	363,003	375,302	0.2
6000	Depository institutions	442	452	0.4	9,257	9,027	20,710	20,996	190,945	189,615	0.3
6020	Commercial banks	317	312	0.5	8,253	7,951	21,021	21,411	171,854	170,715	0.4
6030	Savings institutions	65	63	0.3	580	558	19,634	19,082	11,792	9,960	0.1
6060	Credit unions	60	75	0.5	424	-	16,123	-	7,299	-	-

Source: County Business Patterns, 1992/93, CBP-92/93-1, U.S. Department of Commerce, Washington, D.C., April 1995. SIC categories for which data were suppressed or not available for both 1992 and 1993 are *not* displayed. The employment columns represent mid-March employment in the year. Pay per employee is calculated by dividing 1st Quarter payroll, annualized, by mid-March employment. The columns headed "% US" show the state's percentage of the national total for the SIC in 1993; for example, 0.9% for SIC 6030 means that the state had 0.9 percent of the national total establishments (or payroll) in SIC 6030 in 1993. A dash (-) is used to indicate that data are not available or cannot be calculated; *nec* means not elsewhere classified.

Continued on next page.

SIC	Industry	No. Establishments			Employment		Pay / Employee		Annual Payroll ($ 000)		
		1992	1993	% US	1992	1993	1992	1993	1992	1993	% US
SOUTH DAKOTA - [continued]											
6090	Functions closely related to banking	-	1	0.0	-	-	-	-	-	-	-
6100	Nondepository institutions	76	72	0.2	1,229	1,253	20,426	20,935	24,461	25,076	0.1
6110	Federal and Federally-sponsored credit	2	15	1.1	-	-	-	-	-	-	-
6140	Personal credit institutions	38	21	0.1	-	438	-	18,886	-	8,850	0.2
6150	Business credit institutions	23	19	0.4	737	589	18,084	14,750	12,553	8,064	0.2
6160	Mortgage bankers and brokers	13	17	0.1	-	-	-	-	-	-	-
6200	Security and commodity brokers	89	103	0.3	-	542	-	38,362	-	21,563	0.1
6210	Security brokers and dealers	55	61	0.3	-	380	-	44,516	-	17,956	0.1
6220	Commodity contracts brokers, dealers	11	11	0.7	-	30	-	31,333	-	881	0.1
6280	Security and commodity services	23	31	0.2	-	132	-	22,242	-	2,726	0.0
6300	Insurance carriers	169	138	0.3	2,487	2,379	24,397	24,368	62,650	60,058	0.1
6310	Life insurance	45	37	0.3	957	878	26,997	24,943	25,676	23,059	0.1
6321	Accident and health insurance	9	8	0.7	116	-	22,310	-	2,428	-	-
6324	Hospital and medical service plans	12	12	0.7	134	168	27,313	25,119	3,396	4,245	0.1
6330	Fire, marine, and casualty insurance	74	61	0.3	701	656	22,037	22,890	15,615	15,833	0.1
6350	Surety insurance	3	2	0.3	-	-	-	-	-	-	-
6360	Title insurance	8	1	0.0	35	-	13,829	-	708	-	-
6370	Pension, health, and welfare funds	15	14	0.2	-	71	-	17,915	-	1,895	0.2
6390	Insurance carriers, n.e.c.	2	3	1.9	-	-	-	-	-	-	-
6400	Insurance agents, brokers, and service	596	631	0.5	1,680	1,861	19,102	19,512	33,550	39,227	0.2
6500	Real estate	578	629	0.3	1,994	2,105	11,541	12,196	26,366	30,218	0.1
6510	Real estate operators and lessors	258	301	0.3	961	931	10,123	10,453	10,649	11,489	0.1
6530	Real estate agents and managers	200	220	0.2	644	894	12,932	13,329	9,460	13,074	0.1
6540	Title abstract offices	46	48	1.0	158	173	14,608	14,913	2,666	3,189	0.3
6552	Subdividers and developers, n.e.c.	18	24	0.3	110	63	11,164	15,619	1,816	1,806	0.1
6553	Cemetery subdividers and developers	30	32	0.5	55	44	9,600	10,455	679	626	0.1
6700	Holding and other investment offices	73	72	0.3	-	-	-	-	-	-	-
6710	Holding offices	23	25	0.3	217	118	29,806	23,458	3,869	3,099	0.0
6720	Investment offices	4	2	0.2	-	-	-	-	-	-	-
6732	Educational, religious, etc. trusts	11	12	0.3	-	40	-	10,000	-	440	0.0
6733	Trusts, n.e.c.	17	13	0.2	-	24	-	13,000	-	337	0.0
6792	Oil royalty traders	1	-	-	-	-	-	-	-	-	-
6794	Patent owners and lessors	3	6	0.4	-	250	-	13,024	-	3,662	0.5
6799	Investors, n.e.c.	11	11	0.2	16	13	21,500	36,308	421	442	0.0
TENNESSEE											
60 –	**Finance, insurance, and real estate**	10,277	10,450	1.7	107,154	105,422	27,231	27,255	2,961,408	2,992,833	1.3
6000	Depository institutions	2,215	2,222	2.2	35,579	36,708	24,538	24,886	849,748	897,366	1.6
6010	Central reserve depository	3	4	5.3	419	410	23,045	23,649	9,774	10,068	1.1
6020	Commercial banks	1,577	1,578	2.5	28,665	28,860	25,236	25,610	705,553	719,077	1.7
6030	Savings institutions	266	207	1.1	3,829	3,213	23,510	22,519	79,789	71,619	0.9
6060	Credit unions	321	385	2.5	2,189	2,927	19,114	20,687	43,685	65,544	2.2
6090	Functions closely related to banking	47	48	1.0	477	1,298	17,040	24,518	10,936	31,058	1.9
6100	Nondepository institutions	944	887	2.1	7,883	7,951	27,503	27,371	206,469	227,618	1.3
6110	Federal and Federally-sponsored credit	3	51	3.7	-	-	-	-	-	-	-
6140	Personal credit institutions	605	492	2.9	4,097	3,680	24,891	22,593	97,824	85,919	2.2
6150	Business credit institutions	100	76	1.6	1,784	-	20,854	-	40,165	-	-
6160	Mortgage bankers and brokers	224	266	1.4	1,964	2,493	38,980	36,059	66,528	94,748	1.1
6200	Security and commodity brokers	438	448	1.3	3,790	4,156	68,438	69,655	269,582	330,649	0.8
6210	Security brokers and dealers	271	276	1.4	3,326	3,527	71,747	72,474	229,790	274,019	0.9
6220	Commodity contracts brokers, dealers	22	15	1.0	-	-	-	-	-	-	-
6230	Security and commodity exchanges	2	1	1.0	-	-	-	-	-	-	-
6280	Security and commodity services	139	156	1.2	370	549	43,168	53,399	32,427	47,883	0.5
6300	Insurance carriers	1,000	850	1.9	24,012	23,179	28,325	30,247	700,358	700,689	1.3
6310	Life insurance	340	300	2.4	12,216	11,550	27,549	28,176	345,079	328,049	1.7
6321	Accident and health insurance	39	30	2.7	844	522	21,692	27,326	19,581	14,687	1.0
6324	Hospital and medical service plans	16	33	1.9	2,585	2,915	25,075	30,285	68,839	87,004	1.3
6330	Fire, marine, and casualty insurance	428	363	1.9	7,207	7,202	32,639	34,455	238,449	245,838	1.1

Source: County Business Patterns, 1992/93, CBP-92/93-1, U.S. Department of Commerce, Washington, D.C., April 1995. SIC categories for which data were suppressed or not available for both 1992 and 1993 are *not* displayed. The employment columns represent mid-March employment in the year. Pay per employee is calculated by dividing 1st Quarter payroll, annualized, by mid-March employment. The columns headed "% US" show the state's percentage of the national total for the SIC in 1993; for example, 0.9% for SIC 6030 means that the state had 0.9 percent of the national total establishments (or payroll) in SIC 6030 in 1993. A dash (-) is used to indicate that data are not available or cannot be calculated; *nec* means not elsewhere classified.

Continued on next page.

SIC	Industry	No. Establishments			Employment		Pay / Employee		Annual Payroll ($ 000)		
		1992	1993	% US	1992	1993	1992	1993	1992	1993	% US
TENNESSEE - [continued]											
6350	Surety insurance	14	10	1.7	86	45	35,860	96,178	3,182	4,424	0.8
6360	Title insurance	41	28	1.2	278	308	20,590	32,026	7,408	8,094	0.6
6370	Pension, health, and welfare funds	113	81	1.3	717	622	21,010	16,611	16,319	12,145	1.0
6390	Insurance carriers, n.e.c.	4	4	2.5	12	15	41,000	29,867	311	440	0.5
6400	Insurance agents, brokers, and service	2,162	2,316	1.9	11,325	10,630	28,788	27,437	336,971	315,577	1.6
6500	Real estate	3,112	3,309	1.4	18,077	18,670	16,930	16,710	332,348	361,180	1.2
6510	Real estate operators and lessors	1,259	1,412	1.4	6,452	6,916	15,486	15,268	100,115	114,539	1.3
6530	Real estate agents and managers	1,270	1,532	1.4	8,780	10,015	17,986	17,778	171,610	207,637	1.2
6540	Title abstract offices	62	69	1.4	283	406	21,088	20,010	7,936	12,619	1.2
6552	Subdividers and developers, n.e.c.	136	141	1.5	773	560	20,279	17,579	22,567	14,230	0.8
6553	Cemetery subdividers and developers	132	126	2.0	893	762	14,078	13,323	13,074	11,037	1.3
6700	Holding and other investment offices	394	406	1.5	5,954	3,620	37,923	32,581	237,906	130,935	1.1
6710	Holding offices	123	134	1.7	3,601	2,034	39,742	37,784	148,317	83,086	1.2
6720	Investment offices	18	9	1.1	105	10	52,267	75,600	5,312	972	0.1
6732	Educational, religious, etc. trusts	64	61	1.3	1,275	468	33,710	12,915	48,522	6,664	0.7
6733	Trusts, n.e.c.	70	68	1.2	258	228	15,411	23,439	4,583	5,605	0.8
6792	Oil royalty traders	-	1	0.1	-	-	-	-	-	-	-
6794	Patent owners and lessors	41	61	3.8	391	629	34,721	30,410	14,450	23,911	3.0
6798	Real estate investment trusts	6	5	0.9	-	-	-	-	-	-	-
6799	Investors, n.e.c.	49	62	1.2	-	212	-	44,151	-	9,761	0.8
TEXAS											
60 –	**Finance, insurance, and real estate**	38,733	39,705	6.5	433,033	426,356	28,379	28,523	12,615,245	12,948,459	5.6
6000	Depository institutions	5,004	4,818	4.7	121,689	113,149	26,005	25,254	3,122,934	2,907,355	5.0
6010	Central reserve depository	10	5	6.7	-	-	-	-	-	-	-
6020	Commercial banks	2,810	2,606	4.2	95,617	87,747	26,296	25,530	2,470,374	2,244,544	5.3
6030	Savings institutions	806	643	3.3	12,572	9,266	27,704	29,470	336,520	302,190	3.7
6060	Credit unions	860	1,023	6.7	8,908	10,942	19,344	19,258	181,517	222,636	7.4
6080	Foreign bank and branches and agencies	21	21	3.7	-	430	-	60,530	-	28,573	1.6
6090	Functions closely related to banking	490	518	11.0	2,283	-	22,080	-	50,209	-	-
6100	Nondepository institutions	2,896	3,006	7.2	32,598	36,085	29,528	28,018	1,025,526	1,178,553	6.6
6110	Federal and Federally-sponsored credit	82	145	10.5	1,229	1,661	25,471	29,898	32,322	49,902	5.5
6140	Personal credit institutions	1,616	1,452	8.5	13,761	14,733	25,084	21,612	355,821	339,281	8.8
6150	Business credit institutions	357	395	8.2	4,152	5,211	35,951	32,809	153,122	183,791	4.5
6160	Mortgage bankers and brokers	778	998	5.4	13,191	14,437	32,608	32,612	477,237	604,898	6.9
6200	Security and commodity brokers	1,964	2,031	5.9	18,245	19,878	71,153	73,059	1,341,313	1,523,306	3.9
6210	Security brokers and dealers	1,266	1,271	6.5	12,797	13,391	81,026	81,741	1,043,716	1,131,253	3.9
6220	Commodity contracts brokers, dealers	51	49	3.3	141	-	69,106	-	8,901	-	-
6230	Security and commodity exchanges	3	3	2.9	-	-	-	-	-	-	-
6280	Security and commodity services	628	705	5.4	5,215	6,269	46,847	54,191	280,790	368,747	3.9
6300	Insurance carriers	3,735	3,130	7.1	90,479	88,218	29,541	30,993	2,761,005	2,845,605	5.4
6310	Life insurance	1,129	976	7.7	36,254	33,865	27,305	28,025	986,382	964,822	4.9
6321	Accident and health insurance	105	125	11.0	2,906	3,999	25,963	26,612	77,568	117,558	7.9
6324	Hospital and medical service plans	83	75	4.2	4,906	5,561	27,823	30,069	144,400	172,333	2.6
6330	Fire, marine, and casualty insurance	1,595	1,428	7.5	38,333	38,601	32,619	34,421	1,306,129	1,388,459	6.4
6350	Surety insurance	45	37	6.2	640	505	39,269	36,570	21,871	19,007	3.5
6360	Title insurance	308	219	9.5	3,948	3,460	30,216	32,694	131,653	128,299	8.9
6370	Pension, health, and welfare funds	412	247	4.1	2,586	1,948	19,666	22,386	68,601	47,245	3.8
6390	Insurance carriers, n.e.c.	21	16	9.9	366	271	29,934	26,804	10,258	7,662	8.0
6400	Insurance agents, brokers, and service	8,164	8,847	7.2	44,690	45,282	26,568	26,722	1,255,128	1,303,635	6.4
6500	Real estate	14,345	15,095	6.4	101,999	99,620	19,830	19,524	2,114,556	2,151,457	7.3
6510	Real estate operators and lessors	5,750	6,640	6.5	33,107	33,006	15,983	15,726	558,577	573,089	6.5
6530	Real estate agents and managers	5,937	6,942	6.3	52,466	56,428	21,633	21,213	1,165,347	1,315,142	7.7
6540	Title abstract offices	359	383	8.0	2,437	3,181	20,336	21,867	58,278	80,480	7.7
6552	Subdividers and developers, n.e.c.	604	667	7.1	5,894	4,279	27,259	26,460	167,154	128,760	7.4
6553	Cemetery subdividers and developers	288	317	5.0	2,612	2,555	16,760	16,986	46,620	47,002	5.5
6700	Holding and other investment offices	2,541	2,692	9.8	18,648	17,831	41,647	37,236	794,168	757,983	6.4
6710	Holding offices	523	561	7.1	8,771	6,895	54,541	49,813	473,205	377,356	5.4

Source: County Business Patterns, 1992/93, CBP-92/93-1, U.S. Department of Commerce, Washington, D.C., April 1995. SIC categories for which data were suppressed or not available for both 1992 and 1993 are *not* displayed. The employment columns represent mid-March employment in the year. Pay per employee is calculated by dividing 1st Quarter payroll, annualized, by mid-March employment. The columns headed "% US" show the state's percentage of the national total for the SIC in 1993; for example, 0.9% for SIC 6030 means that the state had 0.9 percent of the national total establishments (or payroll) in SIC 6030 in 1993. A dash (-) is used to indicate that data are not available or cannot be calculated; *nec* means not elsewhere classified.

Continued on next page.

SIC	Industry	No. Establishments			Employment		Pay / Employee		Annual Payroll ($ 000)		
		1992	1993	% US	1992	1993	1992	1993	1992	1993	% US
TEXAS - [continued]											
6720	Investment offices	96	73	8.9	874	338	46,947	46,710	37,988	16,519	2.2
6732	Educational, religious, etc. trusts	317	313	6.6	2,261	2,323	18,335	19,728	43,098	49,367	5.2
6733	Trusts, n.e.c.	561	539	9.5	2,251	3,049	24,464	24,956	60,602	78,076	11.0
6792	Oil royalty traders	278	338	43.7	1,053	1,120	39,347	36,632	49,176	45,592	44.5
6794	Patent owners and lessors	59	88	5.5	603	1,016	32,405	30,402	23,070	38,467	4.8
6798	Real estate investment trusts	94	39	7.0	826	414	34,058	22,551	29,734	10,750	5.1
6799	Investors, n.e.c.	498	720	14.0	1,636	2,643	36,142	37,927	62,115	119,245	9.5
UTAH											
60 –	**Finance, insurance, and real estate**	3,669	4,012	0.7	35,682	38,774	23,001	22,850	845,528	984,699	0.4
6000	Depository institutions	685	734	0.7	11,679	12,237	23,437	22,797	269,810	300,600	0.5
6010	Central reserve depository	2	1	1.3	-	-	-	-	-	-	-
6020	Commercial banks	438	457	0.7	8,803	9,143	24,418	23,997	209,747	231,055	0.5
6030	Savings institutions	42	35	0.2	-	489	-	24,262	-	14,612	0.2
6060	Credit unions	194	228	1.5	1,980	2,329	17,582	17,163	36,389	44,574	1.5
6090	Functions closely related to banking	9	13	0.3	-	-	-	-	-	-	--
6100	Nondepository institutions	317	334	0.8	4,340	4,828	23,917	23,759	116,147	153,765	0.9
6110	Federal and Federally-sponsored credit	1	1	0.1	-	-	-	-	-	-	-
6140	Personal credit institutions	146	111	0.7	1,086	-	22,365	-	23,390	-	-
6150	Business credit institutions	36	36	0.7	1,661	1,699	18,040	17,737	27,668	31,863	0.8
6160	Mortgage bankers and brokers	127	185	1.0	1,528	2,288	31,128	28,360	62,998	97,069	1.1
6200	Security and commodity brokers	177	185	0.5	1,151	1,369	44,441	42,738	51,428	61,727	0.2
6210	Security brokers and dealers	90	94	0.5	943	1,010	49,056	49,442	46,107	51,141	0.2
6220	Commodity contracts brokers, dealers	4	3	0.2	-	-	-	-	-	-	-
6230	Security and commodity exchanges	1	1	1.0	-	-	-	-	-	-	-
6280	Security and commodity services	79	87	0.7	-	-	-	-	-	-	-
6300	Insurance carriers	368	280	0.6	6,272	5,908	24,876	25,035	156,552	154,596	0.3
6310	Life insurance	80	69	0.5	2,410	2,291	23,972	22,308	53,988	49,531	0.3
6321	Accident and health insurance	11	14	1.2	628	447	26,815	24,376	17,412	11,179	0.8
6324	Hospital and medical service plans	15	15	0.8	941	1,274	21,615	23,636	21,271	34,433	0.5
6330	Fire, marine, and casualty insurance	161	135	0.7	1,250	1,297	30,499	31,278	38,728	43,838	0.2
6350	Surety insurance	9	4	0.7	-	27	-	29,333	-	796	0.1
6360	Title insurance	57	11	0.5	489	-	20,818	-	13,642	-	-
6370	Pension, health, and welfare funds	32	30	0.5	462	432	22,814	24,639	9,763	10,562	0.9
6390	Insurance carriers, n.e.c.	2	2	1.2	-	-	-	-	-	-	-
6400	Insurance agents, brokers, and service	737	869	0.7	3,965	4,872	24,033	23,516	98,318	129,295	0.6
6500	Real estate	1,218	1,447	0.6	7,117	8,294	15,301	15,773	120,583	143,070	0.5
6510	Real estate operators and lessors	435	520	0.5	2,067	2,520	11,834	12,989	26,725	35,404	0.4
6530	Real estate agents and managers	549	750	0.7	3,700	4,954	16,219	15,338	63,938	84,332	0.5
6540	Title abstract offices	35	48	1.0	285	468	20,533	17,957	8,213	12,005	1.1
6552	Subdividers and developers, n.e.c.	62	89	0.9	533	221	20,203	40,633	11,688	7,777	0.4
6553	Cemetery subdividers and developers	16	16	0.3	93	84	14,452	17,476	1,645	1,851	0.2
6700	Holding and other investment offices	161	156	0.6	691	711	24,359	29,226	17,388	20,919	0.2
6710	Holding offices	31	35	0.4	253	253	32,332	47,589	8,039	11,392	0.2
6720	Investment offices	8	3	0.4	-	-	-	-	-	-	-
6732	Educational, religious, etc. trusts	26	22	0.5	100	-	14,960	-	1,599	-	-
6733	Trusts, n.e.c.	41	34	0.6	135	136	13,985	13,588	2,081	2,090	0.3
6792	Oil royalty traders	2	4	0.5	-	-	-	-	-	-	-
6794	Patent owners and lessors	3	12	0.7	-	109	-	27,376	-	2,865	0.4
6798	Real estate investment trusts	7	3	0.5	-	-	-	-	-	-	-
6799	Investors, n.e.c.	28	40	0.8	-	121	-	22,281	-	3,218	0.3
VERMONT											
60 –	**Finance, insurance, and real estate**	1,496	1,519	0.2	13,056	12,353	26,588	26,276	344,337	333,349	0.1
6000	Depository institutions	321	335	0.3	5,244	4,951	22,709	22,309	117,897	108,320	0.2
6020	Commercial banks	231	227	0.4	4,146	3,514	22,522	22,341	93,613	75,308	0.2
6030	Savings institutions	39	49	0.3	824	1,077	24,437	23,094	19,061	25,430	0.3
6060	Credit unions	51	58	0.4	274	-	20,336	-	5,223	-	-

Source: County Business Patterns, 1992/93, CBP-92/93-1, U.S. Department of Commerce, Washington, D.C., April 1995. SIC categories for which data were suppressed or not available for both 1992 and 1993 are *not* displayed. The employment columns represent mid-March employment in the year. Pay per employee is calculated by dividing 1st Quarter payroll, annualized, by mid-March employment. The columns headed "% US" show the state's percentage of the national total for the SIC in 1993; for example, 0.9% for SIC 6030 means that the state had 0.9 percent of the national total establishments (or payroll) in SIC 6030 in 1993. A dash (-) is used to indicate that data are not available or cannot be calculated; *nec* means not elsewhere classified.

Continued on next page.

SIC	Industry	No. Establishments			Employment		Pay / Employee		Annual Payroll ($ 000)		
		1992	1993	% US	1992	1993	1992	1993	1992	1993	% US
VERMONT - [continued]											
6090	Functions closely related to banking	-	1	0.0	-	-	-	-	-	-	-
6100	Nondepository institutions	42	44	0.1	-	-	-	-	-	-	-
6110	Federal and Federally-sponsored credit	3	5	0.4	-	-	-	-	-	-	-
6140	Personal credit institutions	13	4	0.0	-	-	-	-	-	-	-
6150	Business credit institutions	4	6	0.1	-	22	-	25,818	-	700	0.0
6160	Mortgage bankers and brokers	21	28	0.2	186	257	31,806	25,759	5,517	8,426	0.1
6200	Security and commodity brokers	59	56	0.2	390	336	55,990	56,988	24,102	20,092	0.1
6210	Security brokers and dealers	29	27	0.1	283	252	59,208	63,556	16,762	16,264	0.1
6220	Commodity contracts brokers, dealers	1	1	0.1	-	-	-	-	-	-	-
6280	Security and commodity services	27	28	0.2	96	-	47,792	-	7,193	-	-
6300	Insurance carriers	130	110	0.3	2,318	2,630	33,983	34,479	71,141	86,383	0.2
6310	Life insurance	46	35	0.3	1,459	1,534	38,733	39,450	48,552	53,710	0.3
6321	Accident and health insurance	8	6	0.5	76	-	27,947	-	1,917	-	-
6324	Hospital and medical service plans	-	2	0.1	-	-	-	-	-	-	-
6330	Fire, marine, and casualty insurance	43	39	0.2	652	634	26,865	27,388	18,698	18,768	0.1
6350	Surety insurance	2	-	-	-	-	-	-	-	-	-
6360	Title insurance	3	3	0.1	10	11	22,400	33,091	342	316	0.0
6370	Pension, health, and welfare funds	28	24	0.4	-	69	-	34,029	-	2,554	0.2
6400	Insurance agents, brokers, and service	294	316	0.3	1,735	1,537	27,145	25,317	49,676	41,738	0.2
6500	Real estate	594	592	0.3	1,888	2,007	16,983	17,224	33,183	36,637	0.1
6510	Real estate operators and lessors	152	158	0.2	583	545	19,513	19,831	10,386	9,714	0.1
6530	Real estate agents and managers	277	330	0.3	949	1,284	16,354	16,592	16,428	23,389	0.1
6540	Title abstract offices	2	2	0.0	-	-	-	-	-	-	-
6552	Subdividers and developers, n.e.c.	31	39	0.4	106	117	17,245	17,915	2,290	2,743	0.2
6553	Cemetery subdividers and developers	58	59	0.9	52	-	6,538	-	668	-	-
6700	Holding and other investment offices	54	65	0.2	-	-	-	-	-	-	-
6710	Holding offices	13	29	0.4	707	341	36,260	32,798	25,202	14,854	0.2
6732	Educational, religious, etc. trusts	12	13	0.3	-	81	-	18,519	-	2,193	0.2
6733	Trusts, n.e.c.	20	15	0.3	83	69	24,482	16,928	2,180	1,142	0.2
6794	Patent owners and lessors	-	1	0.1	-	-	-	-	-	-	-
6798	Real estate investment trusts	1	-	-	-	-	-	-	-	-	-
6799	Investors, n.e.c.	6	6	0.1	-	-	-	-	-	-	-
VIRGINIA											
60 –	**Finance, insurance, and real estate**	14,544	14,699	2.4	159,631	158,963	28,039	29,454	4,580,449	4,961,700	2.1
6000	Depository institutions	3,073	3,004	2.9	50,449	51,144	24,045	25,561	1,207,776	1,324,557	2.3
6010	Central reserve depository	2	2	2.7	-	-	-	-	-	-	-
6020	Commercial banks	2,158	2,171	3.5	37,276	37,976	24,019	25,950	886,155	973,232	2.3
6030	Savings institutions	526	386	2.0	6,173	5,262	25,003	23,903	137,860	135,615	1.6
6060	Credit unions	319	373	2.4	5,421	6,024	20,617	21,690	126,369	143,278	4.8
6080	Foreign bank and branches and agencies	1	-	-	-	-	-	-	-	-	-
6090	Functions closely related to banking	67	71	1.5	-	-	-	-	-	-	-
6100	Nondepository institutions	1,098	1,082	2.6	14,900	14,534	34,678	38,642	537,783	607,104	3.4
6110	Federal and Federally-sponsored credit	23	42	3.1	1,211	-	24,687	-	30,869	-	-
6140	Personal credit institutions	490	382	2.2	3,463	2,781	24,691	21,979	88,208	63,288	1.6
6150	Business credit institutions	88	87	1.8	1,621	-	31,487	-	55,559	-	-
6160	Mortgage bankers and brokers	479	567	3.1	8,550	6,482	40,815	34,581	360,281	299,628	3.4
6200	Security and commodity brokers	602	684	2.0	4,918	5,412	59,209	59,465	323,697	385,421	1.0
6210	Security brokers and dealers	297	347	1.8	3,498	3,904	65,344	61,766	238,153	280,109	1.0
6220	Commodity contracts brokers, dealers	9	7	0.5	-	-	-	-	-	-	-
6230	Security and commodity exchanges	2	2	1.9	-	-	-	-	-	-	-
6280	Security and commodity services	288	328	2.5	1,387	-	44,484	-	83,874	-	-
6300	Insurance carriers	1,402	1,197	2.7	30,409	28,551	30,479	31,527	940,157	915,386	1.7
6310	Life insurance	367	312	2.5	10,213	9,398	29,672	29,312	294,530	278,087	1.4
6321	Accident and health insurance	45	36	3.2	811	585	20,099	25,121	16,213	14,487	1.0
6324	Hospital and medical service plans	44	47	2.7	4,573	5,306	31,278	33,312	139,725	179,340	2.7
6330	Fire, marine, and casualty insurance	604	543	2.8	13,041	11,973	32,090	33,633	437,023	407,981	1.9
6350	Surety insurance	14	11	1.9	-	88	-	36,409	-	3,462	0.6

Source: County Business Patterns, 1992/93, CBP-92/93-1, U.S. Department of Commerce, Washington, D.C., April 1995. SIC categories for which data were suppressed or not available for both 1992 and 1993 are *not* displayed. The employment columns represent mid-March employment in the year. Pay per employee is calculated by dividing 1st Quarter payroll, annualized, by mid-March employment. The columns headed "% US" show the state's percentage of the national total for the SIC in 1993; for example, 0.9% for SIC 6030 means that the state had 0.9 percent of the national total establishments (or payroll) in SIC 6030 in 1993. A dash (-) is used to indicate that data are not available or cannot be calculated; *nec* means not elsewhere classified.

Continued on next page.

SIC	Industry	No. Establishments			Employment		Pay / Employee		Annual Payroll ($ 000)		
		1992	1993	% US	1992	1993	1992	1993	1992	1993	% US
VIRGINIA - [continued]											
6360	Title insurance	137	88	3.8	797	557	27,829	30,377	24,136	17,849	1.2
6370	Pension, health, and welfare funds	179	156	2.6	720	638	19,706	15,950	17,605	13,183	1.1
6390	Insurance carriers, n.e.c.	3	3	1.9	-	5	-	38,400		737	0.8
6400	Insurance agents, brokers, and service	2,514	2,779	2.3	12,222	13,581	27,277	27,017	339,215	385,829	1.9
6500	Real estate	5,267	5,377	2.3	36,719	35,821	19,441	19,870	758,955	809,671	2.7
6510	Real estate operators and lessors	1,836	1,934	1.9	12,824	10,809	16,154	15,834	217,335	190,705	2.2
6530	Real estate agents and managers	2,367	2,858	2.6	18,261	21,484	20,669	21,647	412,358	529,438	3.1
6540	Title abstract offices	102	110	2.3	373	587	24,043	26,228	10,665	18,405	1.8
6552	Subdividers and developers, n.e.c.	282	274	2.9	2,545	1,739	25,625	23,372	60,105	47,704	2.7
6553	Cemetery subdividers and developers	134	143	2.3	1,033	1,121	17,588	15,772	18,662	20,914	2.5
6700	Holding and other investment offices	559	546	2.0	7,616	7,346	37,629	42,789	293,779	338,362	2.9
6710	Holding offices	174	172	2.2	5,636	5,227	41,357	48,543	235,712	248,296	3.6
6720	Investment offices	21	12	1.5	83	14	27,084	48,857	3,139	943	0.1
6732	Educational, religious, etc. trusts	130	132	2.8	971	925	23,061	27,347	23,820	28,693	3.0
6733	Trusts, n.e.c.	128	105	1.9	457	301	16,656	15,110	9,253	6,240	0.9
6792	Oil royalty traders	1	4	0.5	-	3	-	5,333	-	21	0.0
6794	Patent owners and lessors	17	28	1.7	-	203	-	35,941	-	8,956	1.1
6798	Real estate investment trusts	16	13	2.3	-	328	-	18,402	-	5,634	2.6
6799	Investors, n.e.c.	51	77	1.5	237	334	55,038	49,976	12,205	39,548	3.1
WASHINGTON											
60 –	**Finance, insurance, and real estate**	13,177	13,739	2.3	125,837	125,305	28,465	29,325	3,646,961	3,768,288	1.6
6000	Depository institutions	2,058	2,073	2.0	41,157	37,884	27,184	27,288	1,128,435	991,160	1.7
6010	Central reserve depository	3	2	2.7	298	-	36,832	-	10,498	-	-
6020	Commercial banks	1,214	1,151	1.8	28,848	22,554	26,638	25,267	768,754	581,904	1.4
6030	Savings institutions	462	488	2.5	7,435	9,163	31,689	34,069	243,134	256,418	3.1
6060	Credit unions	273	323	2.1	3,766	4,871	21,268	20,520	81,094	103,949	3.4
6080	Foreign bank and branches and agencies	6	9	1.6	153	-	44,026	-	7,240	-	-
6090	Functions closely related to banking	98	100	2.1	657	855	25,796	38,330	17,611	31,438	1.9
6100	Nondepository institutions	884	989	2.4	7,355	8,412	35,870	35,487	280,481	359,363	2.0
6110	Federal and Federally-sponsored credit	2	14	1.0	-	-	-	-	-	-	-
6140	Personal credit institutions	309	238	1.4	2,073	1,695	27,917	24,972	58,181	42,799	1.1
6150	Business credit institutions	84	106	2.2	822	-	55,270	-	34,408	-	-
6160	Mortgage bankers and brokers	479	627	3.4	4,299	5,594	36,246	35,821	183,148	269,054	3.1
6200	Security and commodity brokers	649	706	2.1	5,074	5,374	59,289	66,403	304,566	354,578	0.9
6210	Security brokers and dealers	405	420	2.1	3,883	4,081	66,476	71,347	262,751	284,884	1.0
6220	Commodity contracts brokers, dealers	11	14	1.0	17	25	48,471	41,600	787	1,104	0.2
6280	Security and commodity services	228	271	2.1	1,162	1,265	35,756	50,972	40,503	68,450	0.7
6300	Insurance carriers	1,028	872	2.0	25,877	25,301	31,443	35,019	787,694	853,761	1.6
6310	Life insurance	231	192	1.5	6,577	6,436	32,310	35,735	197,930	212,400	1.1
6321	Accident and health insurance	23	16	1.4	370	338	30,616	29,325	10,722	9,903	0.7
6324	Hospital and medical service plans	39	51	2.9	4,709	5,097	20,730	30,104	95,965	153,685	2.3
6330	Fire, marine, and casualty insurance	489	445	2.3	10,950	9,753	36,442	38,873	377,233	359,004	1.7
6350	Surety insurance	18	10	1.7	-	136	-	38,647		5,835	1.1
6360	Title insurance	71	45	2.0	2,001	1,596	29,661	31,935	69,079	57,909	4.0
6370	Pension, health, and welfare funds	148	111	1.8	943	1,262	26,350	25,223	26,666	32,014	2.6
6390	Insurance carriers, n.e.c.	3	-	-	-	-	-	-	-	-	-
6400	Insurance agents, brokers, and service	2,229	2,426	2.0	12,300	13,636	30,939	30,467	375,191	429,905	2.1
6500	Real estate	5,783	6,151	2.6	29,481	30,575	17,708	17,632	571,293	611,824	2.1
6510	Real estate operators and lessors	2,493	2,771	2.7	9,516	10,872	13,398	13,503	145,432	165,596	1.9
6530	Real estate agents and managers	2,395	2,793	2.5	15,923	16,760	18,768	19,270	319,926	366,309	2.2
6540	Title abstract offices	39	45	0.9	538	625	22,171	23,328	13,408	16,121	1.5
6552	Subdividers and developers, n.e.c.	290	346	3.7	1,400	1,637	29,069	24,706	43,814	45,860	2.6
6553	Cemetery subdividers and developers	90	96	1.5	642	635	21,439	20,882	15,513	15,063	1.8
6700	Holding and other investment offices	524	500	1.8	4,101	3,469	40,294	35,691	181,967	143,885	1.2
6710	Holding offices	113	96	1.2	2,019	1,718	54,595	45,185	120,950	89,717	1.3
6720	Investment offices	32	17	2.1	165	52	39,467	38,154	6,809	2,603	0.4
6732	Educational, religious, etc. trusts	96	92	2.0	578	541	18,035	20,399	10,736	12,282	1.3

Source: County Business Patterns, 1992/93, CBP-92/93-1, U.S. Department of Commerce, Washington, D.C., April 1995. SIC categories for which data were suppressed or not available for both 1992 and 1993 are *not* displayed. The employment columns represent mid-March employment in the year. Pay per employee is calculated by dividing 1st Quarter payroll, annualized, by mid-March employment. The columns headed "% US" show the state's percentage of the national total for the SIC in 1993; for example, 0.9% for SIC 6030 means that the state had 0.9 percent of the national total establishments (or payroll) in SIC 6030 in 1993. A dash (-) is used to indicate that data are not available or cannot be calculated; *nec* means not elsewhere classified.

Continued on next page.

SIC	Industry	No. Establishments			Employment		Pay / Employee		Annual Payroll ($ 000)		
		1992	1993	% State	1992	1993	1992	1993	1992	1993	% State
LAUDERDALE, AL											
60 –	**Finance, insurance, and real estate**	180	185	2.4	1,166	1,103	23,084	24,189	27,273	27,366	1.4
6000	Depository institutions	41	39	2.5	516	519	21,403	23,013	11,064	11,428	1.8
6020	Commercial banks	26	25	2.3	397	399	22,519	24,331	8,831	9,317	1.7
6030	Savings institutions	9	8	5.7	87	85	22,519	24,331	8,831	9,317	1.7
6060	Credit unions	6	6	2.0	32	35	17,793	19,906	1,633	1,548	3.8
6100	Nondepository institutions	14	17	2.2	45	74	17,375	15,543	600	563	1.1
6140	Personal credit institutions	10	13	2.6	41	64	24,000	17,568	1,122	1,343	0.8
6160	Mortgage bankers and brokers	4	4	2.0	4	10	23,902	16,312	965	1,046	1.7
6200	Security and commodity brokers	6	4	1.7	58	30	25,000	25,600	157	297	0.3
6210	Security brokers and dealers	5	4	2.6	-	30	46,345	66,533	3,038	2,809	2.4
6300	Insurance carriers	28	23	2.4	197	185	-	66,533	-	2,809	2.6
6310	Life insurance	10	8	2.8	152	136	32,041	32,541	6,374	5,723	1.1
6330	Fire, marine, and casualty insurance	13	12	2.3	37	-	32,000	32,059	4,821	4,069	2.3
6400	Insurance agents, brokers, and service	42	41	2.6	184	148	32,000	-	1,253	-	-
6500	Real estate	46	58	2.4	153	145	21,522	24,081	3,849	3,876	2.0
6510	Real estate operators and lessors	17	26	2.3	54	71	11,085	12,607	1,774	2,157	0.9
6530	Real estate agents and managers	18	26	2.5	40	52	9,481	10,254	477	815	1.0
6700	Holding and other investment offices	3	3	1.1	13	2	13,900	11,923	599	831	0.7
							10,462	14,000	52	30	0.0
LAWRENCE, AL											
60 –	**Finance, insurance, and real estate**	19	17	0.2	158	105	13,646	15,886	2,465	1,869	0.1
6000	Depository institutions	8	7	0.5	94	80	12,766	13,900	1,187	1,211	0.2
6400	Insurance agents, brokers, and service	4	3	0.2	4	6	12,000	10,000	58	68	0.0
6500	Real estate	2	3	0.1	-	4	-	8,000	-	63	0.0
LEE, AL											
60 –	**Finance, insurance, and real estate**	158	166	2.1	1,381	1,401	16,130	17,028	23,613	24,666	1.2
6000	Depository institutions	26	28	1.8	466	543	20,197	20,449	9,610	10,605	1.6
6100	Nondepository institutions	19	17	2.2	122	49	13,148	19,102	1,516	1,018	0.6
6140	Personal credit institutions	12	13	2.6	59	-	17,220	-	1,027	-	-
6200	Security and commodity brokers	5	4	1.7	14	-	33,714	-	600	-	-
6300	Insurance carriers	14	10	1.1	177	134	20,723	24,657	4,048	3,577	0.7
6310	Life insurance	6	3	1.1	130	96	21,200	24,042	3,079	2,464	1.4
6400	Insurance agents, brokers, and service	25	26	1.7	71	75	18,930	17,440	1,356	1,440	0.7
6500	Real estate	66	79	3.2	478	584	10,050	10,863	5,446	7,045	2.9
6510	Real estate operators and lessors	31	43	3.9	106	253	8,642	8,838	911	2,438	3.0
6530	Real estate agents and managers	22	32	3.0	175	326	11,474	12,417	2,494	4,541	3.6
6700	Holding and other investment offices	3	2	0.7	53	-	18,340	-	1,037	-	-
LIMESTONE, AL											
60 –	**Finance, insurance, and real estate**	68	76	1.0	299	356	20,482	17,382	6,207	6,763	0.3
6000	Depository institutions	13	12	0.8	124	122	19,968	21,377	2,589	2,644	0.4
6020	Commercial banks	7	9	0.8	97	-	20,412	-	2,144	-	-
6100	Nondepository institutions	9	12	1.5	25	31	18,240	18,194	467	661	0.4
6300	Insurance carriers	9	8	0.8	41	-	20,878	-	950	-	-
6400	Insurance agents, brokers, and service	14	18	1.2	41	46	34,829	18,087	1,145	1,022	0.5
6500	Real estate	19	22	0.9	55	111	10,109	8,937	715	1,014	0.4
6510	Real estate operators and lessors	11	10	0.9	44	47	9,364	8,426	433	430	0.5
6530	Real estate agents and managers	5	9	0.8	8	57	14,000	5,754	143	337	0.3
LOWNDES, AL											
60 –	**Finance, insurance, and real estate**	9	11	0.1	50	61	24,160	25,639	1,248	1,363	0.1
6500	Real estate	3	3	0.1	6	8	4,667	5,000	35	40	0.0
6510	Real estate operators and lessors	2	3	0.3	-	8	-	5,000	-	40	0.0

Source: County Business Patterns, 1992/93, CBP-92/93-1, U.S. Department of Commerce, Washington, D.C., April 1995. SIC categories for which data were suppressed or not available for both 1992 and 1993 are not displayed. The employment columns represent mid-March employment in the year. Pay per employee is calculated by dividing 1st Quarter payroll, annualized, by mid-March employment. The columns headed "% State" show the county's percentage of the state total for the SIC in 1993; for example, 0.9% for SIC 6030 means that the county had 0.9 percent of the state's total establishments (or payroll) in SIC 6030 in 1993. A dash (-) is used to indicate that data are not available or cannot be calculated; nec means not elsewhere classified.

SIC	Industry	No. Establishments			Employment		Pay / Employee		Annual Payroll ($ 000)		
		1992	1993	% State	1992	1993	1992	1993	1992	1993	% State

MACON, AL

SIC	Industry	1992	1993	% State	1992	1993	1992	1993	1992	1993	% State
60 –	**Finance, insurance, and real estate**	14	16	0.2	104	140	19,731	15,771	2,076	2,343	0.1
6000	Depository institutions	4	5	0.3	70	88	22,000	19,000	1,527	1,747	0.3
6500	Real estate	6	8	0.3	22	-	12,000	-	265	-	-
6510	Real estate operators and lessors	5	6	0.5	-	39	-	6,564	-	296	0.4

MADISON, AL

SIC	Industry	1992	1993	% State	1992	1993	1992	1993	1992	1993	% State
60 –	**Finance, insurance, and real estate**	559	576	7.4	3,843	3,977	23,242	22,009	90,395	93,280	4.7
6000	Depository institutions	92	98	6.3	1,561	1,614	22,106	21,643	34,335	34,916	5.3
6020	Commercial banks	60	69	6.4	946	1,098	23,044	23,166	21,609	25,392	4.6
6030	Savings institutions	17	8	5.7	175	41	21,097	26,146	3,701	1,298	3.2
6060	Credit unions	14	18	5.9	-	472	-	17,720	-	8,118	16.3
6090	Functions closely related to banking	1	3	10.3	-	3	-	20,000	-	108	-
6100	Nondepository institutions	55	61	7.7	260	297	26,046	22,586	7,341	8,498	5.1
6140	Personal credit institutions	30	32	6.3	158	162	23,797	18,593	3,709	3,126	5.2
6160	Mortgage bankers and brokers	21	25	12.3	93	122	29,978	26,885	3,389	4,889	4.9
6200	Security and commodity brokers	20	18	7.7	168	173	70,952	58,243	10,760	11,168	9.4
6210	Security brokers and dealers	15	16	10.3	159	-	73,384	-	10,402	-	-
6280	Security and commodity services	5	2	2.8	9	-	28,000	-	358	-	-
6300	Insurance carriers	59	62	6.5	472	477	30,492	30,063	14,685	14,444	2.9
6310	Life insurance	18	16	5.6	264	257	25,864	27,160	7,224	6,978	3.9
6330	Fire, marine, and casualty insurance	29	36	6.9	107	131	34,542	35,328	3,968	4,757	2.4
6370	Pension, health, and welfare funds	4	5	9.8	-	19	-	6,526	-	154	1.7
6400	Insurance agents, brokers, and service	99	101	6.5	307	313	20,756	20,204	6,251	6,456	3.3
6500	Real estate	218	222	9.0	1,006	995	14,179	13,717	15,706	15,662	6.5
6510	Real estate operators and lessors	93	102	9.2	351	397	13,880	13,773	5,178	6,032	7.5
6530	Real estate agents and managers	79	96	9.1	497	533	15,034	13,944	8,287	8,623	6.8
6552	Subdividers and developers, n.e.c.	19	13	11.7	87	42	11,632	12,286	1,184	731	5.9
6553	Cemetery subdividers and developers	6	5	5.1	13	12	7,077	8,000	112	124	1.0
6700	Holding and other investment offices	16	14	5.1	69	108	15,826	13,889	1,317	2,136	2.2

MARENGO, AL

SIC	Industry	1992	1993	% State	1992	1993	1992	1993	1992	1993	% State
60 –	**Finance, insurance, and real estate**	32	33	0.4	236	253	19,542	20,553	5,160	5,684	0.3
6000	Depository institutions	9	7	0.5	158	159	17,266	18,465	2,950	3,251	0.5
6020	Commercial banks	7	7	0.7	155	159	17,213	18,465	2,927	3,251	0.6
6100	Nondepository institutions	5	6	0.8	11	14	29,455	23,714	324	354	0.2
6300	Insurance carriers	6	7	0.7	46	57	26,000	28,842	1,429	1,748	0.3
6400	Insurance agents, brokers, and service	3	3	0.2	15	11	21,333	19,273	330	203	0.1
6500	Real estate	9	10	0.4	6	12	7,333	6,333	127	128	0.1
6510	Real estate operators and lessors	7	7	0.6	4	5	9,000	10,400	119	77	0.1

MARION, AL

SIC	Industry	1992	1993	% State	1992	1993	1992	1993	1992	1993	% State
60 –	**Finance, insurance, and real estate**	37	38	0.5	295	294	17,885	18,966	5,613	5,702	0.3
6000	Depository institutions	13	13	0.8	221	223	17,575	19,085	4,095	4,237	0.6
6400	Insurance agents, brokers, and service	10	10	0.6	21	24	21,333	16,500	486	542	0.3
6500	Real estate	8	9	0.4	16	16	8,500	9,750	135	159	0.1
6510	Real estate operators and lessors	5	6	0.5	11	9	8,364	11,111	84	104	0.1

MARSHALL, AL

SIC	Industry	1992	1993	% State	1992	1993	1992	1993	1992	1993	% State
60 –	**Finance, insurance, and real estate**	147	148	1.9	787	869	20,147	21,017	16,712	17,549	0.9
6000	Depository institutions	32	32	2.1	436	443	19,752	20,813	8,213	8,511	1.3
6020	Commercial banks	24	24	2.2	395	409	20,010	21,183	7,559	7,947	1.4
6030	Savings institutions	5	4	2.8	16	-	17,500	-	236	-	-
6060	Credit unions	3	3	1.0	25	-	17,120	-	418	-	-
6100	Nondepository institutions	16	18	2.3	56	69	19,429	21,855	1,353	1,799	1.1
6140	Personal credit institutions	10	13	2.6	-	50	-	21,920	-	1,222	2.0
6280	Security and commodity services	1	3	4.2	-	3	-	12,000	-	159	-
6300	Insurance carriers	16	15	1.6	111	159	28,973	24,830	3,763	3,375	0.7
6310	Life insurance	3	3	1.1	74	74	26,432	26,108	2,416	1,842	1.0

Source: County Business Patterns, 1992/93, CBP-92/93-1, U.S. Department of Commerce, Washington, D.C., April 1995. SIC categories for which data were suppressed or not available for both 1992 and 1993 are *not* displayed. The employment columns represent mid-March employment in the year. Pay per employee is calculated by dividing 1st Quarter payroll, annualized, by mid-March employment. The columns headed "% State" show the county's percentage of the state total for the SIC in 1993; for example, 0.9% for SIC 6030 means that the county had 0.9 percent of the state's total establishments (or payroll) in SIC 6030 in 1993. A dash (-) is used to indicate that data are not available or cannot be calculated; *nec* means not elsewhere classified.

Continued on next page.

SIC	Industry	No. Establishments			Employment		Pay / Employee		Annual Payroll ($ 000)		
		1992	1993	% State	1992	1993	1992	1993	1992	1993	% State
MARSHALL, AL - [continued]											
6400	Insurance agents, brokers, and service	26	30	1.9	69	76	19,768	20,053	1,333	1,577	0.8
6500	Real estate	51	47	1.9	98	107	10,612	13,159	1,334	1,601	0.7
6510	Real estate operators and lessors	18	20	1.8	43	45	8,930	9,333	407	442	0.6
6530	Real estate agents and managers	24	23	2.2	38	40	12,632	16,700	722	768	0.6
MOBILE, AL											
60 –	**Finance, insurance, and real estate**	741	765	9.8	6,211	6,569	23,840	23,812	153,839	166,516	8.4
6000	Depository institutions	131	136	8.8	2,089	2,086	21,790	22,297	44,304	45,470	7.0
6020	Commercial banks	68	68	6.3	1,634	1,639	22,952	23,900	36,278	37,798	6.8
6030	Savings institutions	28	23	16.3	309	262	17,294	17,069	5,333	4,501	11.0
6060	Credit unions	26	34	11.2	121	155	19,769	15,948	2,405	2,792	5.6
6090	Functions closely related to banking	9	11	37.9	25	30	11,200	13,200	288	379	-
6100	Nondepository institutions	80	75	9.5	441	498	24,590	22,137	11,431	12,106	7.2
6140	Personal credit institutions	57	48	9.5	354	387	23,164	19,576	8,262	7,771	12.9
6200	Security and commodity brokers	25	29	12.4	214	287	73,178	52,488	14,707	16,747	14.1
6210	Security brokers and dealers	19	19	12.2	199	208	77,327	62,385	14,261	14,532	13.5
6280	Security and commodity services	6	8	11.3	15	-	18,133	-	446	-	-
6300	Insurance carriers	92	81	8.5	985	965	28,573	30,674	30,482	28,663	5.7
6310	Life insurance	28	28	9.9	612	601	26,196	26,423	16,757	15,139	8.4
6330	Fire, marine, and casualty insurance	43	38	7.2	199	191	37,025	43,916	7,565	8,300	4.2
6360	Title insurance	8	7	35.0	84	-	18,095	-	1,757	-	-
6370	Pension, health, and welfare funds	7	4	7.8	8	-	14,500	-	160	-	-
6400	Insurance agents, brokers, and service	142	158	10.1	808	938	23,559	23,740	20,086	23,024	11.8
6500	Real estate	234	252	10.3	1,230	1,262	15,587	16,666	20,795	27,764	11.5
6510	Real estate operators and lessors	98	105	9.5	535	527	13,929	12,941	7,843	7,240	9.0
6530	Real estate agents and managers	89	122	11.5	375	570	16,128	19,200	7,468	11,771	9.3
6540	Title abstract offices	3	6	10.0	28	63	20,571	25,651	694	2,525	31.0
6552	Subdividers and developers, n.e.c.	6	8	7.2	32	-	25,500	-	549	-	-
6553	Cemetery subdividers and developers	8	10	10.1	99	-	12,323	-	1,232	-	-
6710	Holding offices	5	11	13.3	27	-	78,667	-	1,750	-	-
6732	Educational, religious, etc. trusts	5	5	9.3	8	17	14,500	15,765	179	214	4.9
6733	Trusts, n.e.c.	6	4	5.9	17	8	15,765	10,500	279	102	-
6792	Oil royalty traders	2	4	50.0	-	82	-	15,268	-	1,028	-
6794	Patent owners and lessors	3	2	18.2	18	-	6,444	-	110	-	-
6799	Investors, n.e.c.	8	6	13.0	18	-	21,778	-	395	-	-
MONROE, AL											
60 –	**Finance, insurance, and real estate**	35	37	0.5	206	216	17,670	17,185	3,857	4,035	0.2
6000	Depository institutions	12	13	0.8	127	128	17,953	17,656	2,472	2,474	0.4
6020	Commercial banks	9	10	0.9	115	-	18,470	-	2,358	-	-
6140	Personal credit institutions	3	3	0.6	-	21	-	12,000	-	268	0.4
6400	Insurance agents, brokers, and service	9	6	0.4	43	15	13,767	16,533	625	277	0.1
6500	Real estate	7	9	0.4	13	24	10,769	6,500	131	160	0.1
6510	Real estate operators and lessors	3	4	0.4	5	-	9,600	-	50	-	-
6530	Real estate agents and managers	2	3	0.3	-	15	-	5,600	-	81	0.1
MONTGOMERY, AL											
60 –	**Finance, insurance, and real estate**	571	582	7.4	7,957	8,602	26,417	25,007	221,683	237,572	11.9
6000	Depository institutions	76	75	4.8	2,083	2,065	22,735	23,485	47,292	49,248	7.5
6020	Commercial banks	49	48	4.5	1,760	1,739	23,634	24,605	41,332	42,797	7.7
6060	Credit unions	18	22	7.3	289	304	17,467	17,526	5,269	6,059	12.2
6100	Nondepository institutions	55	57	7.2	1,178	1,482	24,954	20,699	31,410	36,328	21.7
6140	Personal credit institutions	32	31	6.1	-	218	-	20,661	-	4,631	7.7
6160	Mortgage bankers and brokers	18	20	9.8	912	1,247	25,430	20,465	25,196	31,057	31.4
6200	Security and commodity brokers	32	30	12.9	318	326	65,233	64,699	21,731	25,165	21.1
6210	Security brokers and dealers	18	20	12.8	213	219	74,310	74,557	16,322	19,706	18.4
6300	Insurance carriers	71	70	7.4	1,845	1,844	33,309	28,976	62,980	56,462	11.2
6310	Life insurance	27	24	8.5	476	420	28,235	29,552	13,894	11,612	6.5

Source: County Business Patterns, 1992/93, CBP-92/93-1, U.S. Department of Commerce, Washington, D.C., April 1995. SIC categories for which data were suppressed or not available for both 1992 and 1993 are not displayed. The employment columns represent mid-March employment in the year. Pay per employee is calculated by dividing 1st Quarter payroll, annualized, by mid-March employment. The columns headed "% State" show the county's percentage of the state total for the SIC in 1993; for example, 0.9% for SIC 6030 means that the county had 0.9 percent of the state's total establishments (or payroll) in SIC 6030 in 1993. A dash (-) is used to indicate that data are not available or cannot be calculated; nec means not elsewhere classified.

Continued on next page.

SIC	Industry	No. Establishments			Employment		Pay / Employee		Annual Payroll ($ 000)		
		1992	1993	% State	1992	1993	1992	1993	1992	1993	% State
MONTGOMERY, AL - [continued]											
6330	Fire, marine, and casualty insurance	29	30	5.7	1,169	1,196	35,411	28,207	41,459	36,930	18.7
6370	Pension, health, and welfare funds	4	4	7.8	-	131	-	26,992	-	4,242	47.0
6400	Insurance agents, brokers, and service	116	122	7.8	721	1,005	25,847	25,887	21,427	29,418	15.0
6500	Real estate	200	202	8.2	1,643	1,618	14,600	16,949	28,094	30,396	12.6
6510	Real estate operators and lessors	96	106	9.6	741	513	12,011	11,314	9,677	6,416	8.0
6530	Real estate agents and managers	59	76	7.2	543	1,043	19,116	19,958	11,658	22,616	17.8
6540	Title abstract offices	4	4	6.7	33	33	11,152	11,152	526	638	7.8
6552	Subdividers and developers, n.e.c.	17	11	9.9	43	19	24,930	17,474	992	562	4.6
6553	Cemetery subdividers and developers	5	3	3.0	53	10	12,830	10,400	651	105	0.9
6700	Holding and other investment offices	21	25	9.1	169	-	51,053	-	8,749	-	-
6710	Holding offices	5	6	7.2	102	97	70,980	57,814	7,305	7,789	9.8
6732	Educational, religious, etc. trusts	5	7	13.0	19	81	17,263	5,926	367	519	12.0
6733	Trusts, n.e.c.	6	5	7.4	27	28	19,556	23,286	664	747	
MORGAN, AL											
60 –	**Finance, insurance, and real estate**	213	210	2.7	1,833	1,706	20,744	21,667	38,618	38,984	2.0
6000	Depository institutions	41	40	2.6	803	816	19,422	20,319	15,772	16,552	2.5
6020	Commercial banks	25	24	2.2	613	629	19,850	20,719	12,132	12,776	2.3
6100	Nondepository institutions	31	31	3.9	234	232	22,957	19,724	4,910	5,133	3.1
6140	Personal credit institutions	22	22	4.3	113	120	31,186	22,233	3,047	2,582	4.3
6200	Security and commodity brokers	5	5	2.1	21	23	58,857	42,261	1,057	1,183	1.0
6300	Insurance carriers	28	26	2.7	416	322	26,106	31,416	11,255	10,517	2.1
6310	Life insurance	9	8	2.8	338	247	25,314	30,915	8,739	8,008	4.5
6400	Insurance agents, brokers, and service	39	38	2.4	116	122	19,000	18,689	2,436	2,605	1.3
6500	Real estate	65	67	2.7	186	172	12,774	12,953	2,595	2,849	1.2
6510	Real estate operators and lessors	36	37	3.3	96	97	11,625	10,557	1,056	1,220	1.5
6530	Real estate agents and managers	19	24	2.3	48	-	15,250	-	838	-	-
6700	Holding and other investment offices	4	3	1.1	57	19	6,667	11,158	593	145	0.1
PERRY, AL											
60 –	**Finance, insurance, and real estate**	17	16	0.2	91	95	17,407	16,842	1,648	1,709	0.1
6000	Depository institutions	4	4	0.3	58	62	19,034	17,935	1,148	1,185	0.2
6020	Commercial banks	4	4	0.4	58	62	19,034	17,935	1,148	1,185	0.2
6400	Insurance agents, brokers, and service	4	4	0.3	9	8	15,556	17,500	144	159	0.1
PICKENS, AL											
60 –	**Finance, insurance, and real estate**	31	31	0.4	205	195	16,215	17,292	3,295	3,309	0.2
6100	Nondepository institutions	3	1	0.1	3	-	16,000	-	73	-	-
6300	Insurance carriers	4	2	0.2	11	-	21,091	-	246	-	-
6330	Fire, marine, and casualty insurance	4	2	0.4	11	-	21,091	-	246	-	-
6400	Insurance agents, brokers, and service	4	5	0.3	14	-	7,429	-	98	-	-
6500	Real estate	5	6	0.2	7	8	7,429	9,000	60	81	0.0
PIKE, AL											
60 –	**Finance, insurance, and real estate**	57	56	0.7	479	567	20,209	18,709	9,747	11,410	0.6
6000	Depository institutions	11	11	0.7	257	249	19,798	19,952	4,590	4,948	0.8
6100	Nondepository institutions	5	5	0.6	23	22	19,652	22,000	488	488	0.3
6300	Insurance carriers	7	7	0.7	68	72	21,000	22,278	1,777	1,812	0.4
6400	Insurance agents, brokers, and service	11	11	0.7	57	76	21,404	20,789	1,319	1,973	1.0
6500	Real estate	19	18	0.7	-	37	-	11,027	-	386	0.2
6510	Real estate operators and lessors	7	7	0.6	11	-	11,273	-	103	-	-
6530	Real estate agents and managers	10	9	0.8	13	19	7,692	12,211	99	157	0.1
6700	Holding and other investment offices	3	4	1.4	-	111	-	14,090	-	1,803	1.8
RANDOLPH, AL											
60 –	**Finance, insurance, and real estate**	33	31	0.4	171	170	21,942	21,671	4,061	3,819	0.2
6000	Depository institutions	10	10	0.6	93	96	23,355	22,875	2,300	2,158	0.3
6020	Commercial banks	9	10	0.9	-	96	-	22,875	-	2,158	0.4

Source: County Business Patterns, 1992/93, CBP-92/93-1, U.S. Department of Commerce, Washington, D.C., April 1995. SIC categories for which data were suppressed or not available for both 1992 and 1993 are *not* displayed. The employment columns represent mid-March employment in the year. Pay per employee is calculated by dividing 1st Quarter payroll, annualized, by mid-March employment. The columns headed "% State" show the county's percentage of the state total for the SIC in 1993; for example, 0.9% for SIC 6030 means that the county had 0.9 percent of the state's total establishments (or payroll) in SIC 6030 in 1993. A dash (-) is used to indicate that data are not available or cannot be calculated; *nec* means not elsewhere classified.

Continued on next page.

SIC	Industry	No. Establishments			Employment		Pay / Employee		Annual Payroll ($ 000)		
		1992	1993	% State	1992	1993	1992	1993	1992	1993	% State
RANDOLPH, AL - [continued]											
6100	Nondepository institutions	4	3	0.4	14	8	10,286	22,000	149	173	0.1
6140	Personal credit institutions	3	3	0.6	-	8		22,000	-	173	0.3
6300	Insurance carriers	4	4	0.4	40	39	27,300	25,026	1,237	1,121	0.2
6400	Insurance agents, brokers, and service	7	7	0.4	12	15	14,000	11,200	180	181	0.1
6500	Real estate	8	7	0.3	12	12	14,667	14,000	195	186	0.1
6530	Real estate agents and managers	3	4	0.4	5	9	10,400	16,444	74	116	0.1
RUSSELL, AL											
60 −	**Finance, insurance, and real estate**	66	66	0.8	431	408	18,172	18,696	8,148	7,788	0.4
6000	Depository institutions	15	14	0.9	231	213	18,338	20,150	4,200	4,279	0.7
6020	Commercial banks	10	12	1.1	179	-	17,810		3,188		-
6100	Nondepository institutions	6	7	0.9	-	17	-	18,118	-	365	0.2
6300	Insurance carriers	6	6	0.6	76	69	26,474	24,928	2,247	1,782	0.4
6400	Insurance agents, brokers, and service	9	11	0.7	34	34	14,824	15,882	515	519	0.3
6500	Real estate	29	28	1.1	73	75	11,342	10,240	924	843	0.4
6510	Real estate operators and lessors	6	10	0.9	10	30	12,400	9,467	134	323	0.4
6530	Real estate agents and managers	16	15	1.4	34	26	12,588	12,308	535	343	0.3
ST. CLAIR, AL											
60 −	**Finance, insurance, and real estate**	49	53	0.7	315	317	23,340	21,666	7,534	7,863	0.4
6000	Depository institutions	18	18	1.2	209	229	22,737	19,738	4,818	5,159	0.8
6400	Insurance agents, brokers, and service	6	6	0.4	-	13	-	16,923	-	219	0.1
6500	Real estate	16	18	0.7	34	31	14,353	14,323	563	527	0.2
6510	Real estate operators and lessors	7	4	0.4	23	9	12,696	14,667	299	152	0.2
6530	Real estate agents and managers	6	11	1.0	8	20	17,500	14,600	166	335	0.3
SHELBY, AL											
60 −	**Finance, insurance, and real estate**	175	176	2.2	1,510	1,753	26,705	24,748	41,496	48,389	2.4
6000	Depository institutions	28	29	1.9	324	323	20,580	21,337	6,770	7,095	1.1
6020	Commercial banks	23	24	2.2	307	308	20,873	21,597	6,537	6,745	1.2
6100	Nondepository institutions	8	10	1.3	41	243	29,951	25,136	1,262	7,916	4.7
6140	Personal credit institutions	4	5	1.0	40	-	30,600	-	1,216	-	-
6160	Mortgage bankers and brokers	4	4	2.0	1	-	4,000	-	46	-	-
6200	Security and commodity brokers	8	10	4.3	20	24	85,000	78,333	1,554	1,981	1.7
6300	Insurance carriers	24	23	2.4	80	337	38,600	25,092	3,001	9,097	1.8
6310	Life insurance	9	7	2.5	41	23	45,171	55,130	1,748	1,083	0.6
6330	Fire, marine, and casualty insurance	11	11	2.1	28	-	33,714	-	950	-	-
6400	Insurance agents, brokers, and service	45	47	3.0	406	324	24,808	24,148	10,675	8,504	4.3
6500	Real estate	50	47	1.9	405	438	20,800	18,776	8,652	7,227	3.0
6510	Real estate operators and lessors	15	20	1.8	35	50	15,657	16,400	633	1,419	1.8
6530	Real estate agents and managers	18	19	1.8	324	341	22,099	18,674	7,233	4,696	3.7
6552	Subdividers and developers, n.e.c.	4	4	3.6	20	37	9,600	23,892	194	877	7.1
6553	Cemetery subdividers and developers	2	4	4.0	-	10	-	15,200	-	235	2.0
6700	Holding and other investment offices	12	10	3.6	234	64	39,077	62,500	9,582	6,569	6.7
6710	Holding offices	7	6	7.2	230	-	39,530	-	9,501	-	-
SUMTER, AL											
60 −	**Finance, insurance, and real estate**	14	14	0.2	92	97	18,435	19,093	1,797	1,876	0.1
6000	Depository institutions	4	4	0.3	53	57	18,642	19,579	1,013	1,114	0.2
6510	Real estate operators and lessors	5	5	0.5	-	14	-	8,286	-	133	0.2
TALLADEGA, AL											
60 −	**Finance, insurance, and real estate**	92	95	1.2	708	652	18,915	19,663	14,567	13,469	0.7
6000	Depository institutions	21	20	1.3	365	346	17,490	19,121	6,988	6,643	1.0
6020	Commercial banks	13	12	1.1	269	249	18,171	19,968	5,288	4,846	0.9
6100	Nondepository institutions	15	15	1.9	-	53	-	20,830	-	1,093	0.7
6140	Personal credit institutions	13	13	2.6	49	-	17,388	-	904	-	-
6300	Insurance carriers	12	11	1.2	81	75	25,037	28,000	2,396	2,254	0.4

Source: County Business Patterns, 1992/93, CBP-92/93-1, U.S. Department of Commerce, Washington, D.C., April 1995. SIC categories for which data were suppressed or not available for both 1992 and 1993 are not displayed. The employment columns represent mid-March employment in the year. Pay per employee is calculated by dividing 1st Quarter payroll, annualized, by mid-March employment. The columns headed "% State" show the county's percentage of the state total for the SIC in 1993; for example, 0.9% for SIC 6030 means that the county had 0.9 percent of the state's total establishments (or payroll) in SIC 6030 in 1993. A dash (-) is used to indicate that data are not available or cannot be calculated; nec means not elsewhere classified.

Continued on next page.

SIC	Industry	No. Establishments			Employment		Pay / Employee		Annual Payroll ($ 000)		
		1992	1993	% State	1992	1993	1992	1993	1992	1993	% State
TALLADEGA, AL - [continued]											
6400	Insurance agents, brokers, and service	15	17	*1.1*	62	60	21,290	18,267	1,229	1,225	*0.6*
6500	Real estate	23	26	*1.1*	79	70	18,937	15,314	1,558	1,373	*0.6*
6510	Real estate operators and lessors	6	8	*0.7*	20	19	13,800	13,053	309	306	*0.4*
6530	Real estate agents and managers	12	15	*1.4*	35	35	30,400	20,457	1,071	925	*0.7*
6553	Cemetery subdividers and developers	3	3	*3.0*	16	16	7,250	6,750	132	142	*1.2*
6700	Holding and other investment offices	5	6	*2.2*	67	48	18,866	17,333	1,368	881	*0.9*
TALLAPOOSA, AL											
60 –	**Finance, insurance, and real estate**	56	59	*0.8*	380	464	24,432	19,552	9,428	8,759	*0.4*
6000	Depository institutions	12	12	*0.8*	217	229	22,894	19,389	4,864	4,450	*0.7*
6200	Security and commodity brokers	1	3	*1.3*	-	2	-	14,000	-	79	*0.1*
6210	Security brokers and dealers	1	3	*1.9*	-	2	-	14,000	-	79	*0.1*
6300	Insurance carriers	4	6	*0.6*	-	113	-	19,292	-	1,571	*0.3*
6400	Insurance agents, brokers, and service	12	11	*0.7*	30	31	19,200	15,484	600	580	*0.3*
6500	Real estate	18	17	*0.7*	-	30	-	11,600	-	387	*0.2*
6510	Real estate operators and lessors	10	8	*0.7*	14	17	7,429	8,706	168	169	*0.2*
6530	Real estate agents and managers	6	8	*0.8*	8	-	15,500	-	172	-	-
TUSCALOOSA, AL											
60 –	**Finance, insurance, and real estate**	278	287	*3.7*	2,303	2,277	20,259	22,284	48,995	55,008	*2.8*
6000	Depository institutions	55	56	*3.6*	741	773	22,170	23,281	16,935	18,778	*2.9*
6020	Commercial banks	29	30	*2.8*	530	524	23,419	24,412	12,422	12,932	*2.3*
6060	Credit unions	14	15	*5.0*	123	153	19,122	19,712	2,531	3,195	*6.4*
6100	Nondepository institutions	25	28	*3.5*	124	128	20,258	16,656	2,424	2,037	*1.2*
6140	Personal credit institutions	17	18	*3.6*	99	94	19,717	16,043	1,868	1,517	*2.5*
6160	Mortgage bankers and brokers	7	7	*3.4*	-	20	-	23,600	-	376	*0.4*
6200	Security and commodity brokers	9	11	*4.7*	35	40	42,286	28,200	1,554	2,043	*1.7*
6210	Security brokers and dealers	5	6	*3.8*	31	35	45,548	29,714	1,467	1,929	*1.8*
6280	Security and commodity services	4	5	*7.0*	4	5	17,000	17,600	87	114	
6300	Insurance carriers	28	30	*3.2*	303	300	26,284	28,240	8,411	8,945	*1.8*
6310	Life insurance	10	12	*4.2*	187	228	27,936	26,912	5,405	6,348	*3.5*
6330	Fire, marine, and casualty insurance	14	15	*2.9*	-	57	-	34,667	-	2,164	*1.1*
6400	Insurance agents, brokers, and service	47	45	*2.9*	246	278	24,504	25,525	6,983	8,425	*4.3*
6500	Real estate	100	104	*4.2*	696	618	13,529	14,000	10,065	9,886	*4.1*
6510	Real estate operators and lessors	41	47	*4.2*	209	166	11,502	12,458	2,742	2,519	*3.1*
6530	Real estate agents and managers	39	44	*4.2*	371	367	14,404	14,354	5,527	6,018	*4.7*
6540	Title abstract offices	3	5	*8.3*	-	20	-	21,600	-	634	*7.8*
6552	Subdividers and developers, n.e.c.	4	3	*2.7*	17	17	14,353	15,059	306	99	*0.8*
6553	Cemetery subdividers and developers	2	5	*5.1*	-	48	-	13,083	-	616	*5.1*
6700	Holding and other investment offices	14	13	*4.7*	158	140	17,899	37,600	2,623	4,894	*5.0*
6732	Educational, religious, etc. trusts	6	5	*9.3*	95	67	16,884	19,821	1,323	1,441	*33.3*
6733	Trusts, n.e.c.	4	4	*5.9*	51	-	11,373	-	612	-	
WALKER, AL											
60 –	**Finance, insurance, and real estate**	88	92	*1.2*	803	801	21,086	22,507	18,146	18,836	*0.9*
6000	Depository institutions	27	27	*1.7*	425	432	19,981	20,176	8,684	8,749	*1.3*
6020	Commercial banks	22	22	*2.0*	-	335	-	20,442	-	6,869	*1.2*
6100	Nondepository institutions	5	5	*0.6*	41	-	15,024	-	665	-	-
6140	Personal credit institutions	5	5	*1.0*	41	-	15,024	-	665	-	-
6300	Insurance carriers	14	13	*1.4*	174	173	25,494	27,145	5,080	4,956	*1.0*
6310	Life insurance	4	4	*1.4*	142	-	24,986	-	4,093	-	-
6400	Insurance agents, brokers, and service	13	14	*0.9*	52	57	23,231	22,526	1,466	1,577	*0.8*
6500	Real estate	22	23	*0.9*	94	79	16,426	16,304	1,579	1,434	*0.6*
6510	Real estate operators and lessors	11	11	*1.0*	39	38	11,692	12,947	467	501	*0.6*
6530	Real estate agents and managers	7	8	*0.8*	36	28	24,000	19,286	890	550	*0.4*
6700	Holding and other investment offices	7	8	*2.9*	17	27	37,412	43,259	672	1,176	*1.2*

Source: County Business Patterns, 1992/93, CBP-92/93-1, U.S. Department of Commerce, Washington, D.C., April 1995. SIC categories for which data were suppressed or not available for both 1992 and 1993 are *not* displayed. The employment columns represent mid-March employment in the year. Pay per employee is calculated by dividing 1st Quarter payroll, annualized, by mid-March employment. The columns headed "% State" show the county's percentage of the state total for the SIC in 1993; for example, *0.9% for SIC 6030 means that the county had 0.9 percent of the state's total establishments* (or payroll) in SIC 6030 in 1993. A dash (-) is used to indicate that data are not available or cannot be calculated; *nec* means not elsewhere classified.

SIC	Industry	No. Establishments			Employment		Pay / Employee		Annual Payroll ($ 000)		
		1992	1993	% State	1992	1993	1992	1993	1992	1993	% State
WASHINGTON, AL											
60 –	**Finance, insurance, and real estate**	13	11	0.1	93	109	22,710	16,404	2,184	1,599	0.1
6000	Depository institutions	7	7	0.5	72	97	14,833	16,330	1,201	1,415	0.2
6500	Real estate	3	2	0.1	5	-	16,800	-	89	-	-
WILCOX, AL											
60 –	**Finance, insurance, and real estate**	17	16	0.2	88	103	16,409	16,738	1,525	1,794	0.1
6000	Depository institutions	5	5	0.3	71	75	16,676	16,480	1,216	1,262	0.2
6400	Insurance agents, brokers, and service	3	3	0.2	-	12	-	17,333	-	188	0.1
6500	Real estate	7	5	0.2	5	-	7,200	-	38	-	-
6510	Real estate operators and lessors	6	4	0.4	-	4	-	5,000	-	20	0.0
WINSTON, AL											
60 –	**Finance, insurance, and real estate**	27	30	0.4	210	256	15,714	14,625	3,622	4,229	0.2
6000	Depository institutions	8	8	0.5	141	176	14,553	13,705	2,312	2,630	0.4
6400	Insurance agents, brokers, and service	8	8	0.5	19	19	18,105	18,947	359	380	0.2
6500	Real estate	4	6	0.2	8	9	11,500	9,333	109	191	0.1

Source: County Business Patterns, 1992/93, CBP-92/93-1, U.S. Department of Commerce, Washington, D.C., April 1995. SIC categories for which data were suppressed or not available for both 1992 and 1993 are *not* displayed. The employment columns represent mid-March employment in the year. Pay per employee is calculated by dividing 1st Quarter payroll, annualized, by mid-March employment. The columns headed "% State" show the county's percentage of the state total for the SIC in 1993; for example, 0.9% for SIC 6030 means that the county had 0.9 percent of the state's total establishments (or payroll) in SIC 6030 in 1993. A dash (-) is used to indicate that data are not available or cannot be calculated; *nec* means not elsewhere classified.

ALASKA

SIC	Industry	No. Establishments			Employment		Pay / Employee		Annual Payroll ($ 000)		
		1992	1993	% State	1992	1993	1992	1993	1992	1993	% State
ALEUTIANS EAST BOROUGH, AK											
60 –	**Finance, insurance, and real estate**	3	3	0.3	-	13	-	10,154	-	156	0.1
ALEUTIANS WEST BOROUGH, AK											
60 –	**Finance, insurance, and real estate**	5	4	0.4	-	-	-	-	-	-	-
ANCHORAGE, AK											
60 –	**Finance, insurance, and real estate**	607	624	54.7	5,911	6,133	30,801	31,208	191,497	209,833	69.9
6000	Depository institutions	78	71	36.8	2,413	2,540	26,801	24,461	66,585	67,519	66.1
6020	Commercial banks	49	37	31.6	1,829	1,864	27,729	23,618	52,533	48,366	66.3
6060	Credit unions	23	28	43.8	566	637	24,269	26,700	13,824	17,883	72.8
6090	Functions closely related to banking	6	6	75.0	18	39	12,222	28,205	228	1,270	-
6100	Nondepository institutions	33	31	77.5	312	-	36,077	-	13,016	-	-
6200	Security and commodity brokers	22	23	71.9	-	245	-	50,122	-	13,555	84.3
6210	Security brokers and dealers	14	15	71.4	175	213	63,771	53,239	11,103	12,395	83.6
6300	Insurance carriers	74	73	72.3	647	600	44,828	47,380	26,781	27,374	89.6
6310	Life insurance	14	12	80.0	90	-	34,178	-	3,065	-	-
6330	Fire, marine, and casualty insurance	36	34	72.3	392	-	53,827	-	18,483	-	-
6360	Title insurance	4	2	40.0	70	-	35,143	-	2,486	-	-
6400	Insurance agents, brokers, and service	110	119	61.0	651	747	36,332	36,059	24,445	28,095	68.3
6500	Real estate	248	269	53.7	1,261	1,470	22,503	27,646	31,923	46,111	63.1
6510	Real estate operators and lessors	82	105	45.9	376	654	19,894	34,208	9,202	24,338	56.4
6530	Real estate agents and managers	121	145	59.9	634	770	23,621	21,938	16,587	19,944	73.6
6552	Subdividers and developers, n.e.c.	12	13	68.4	147	-	25,741	-	3,722	-	-
6700	Holding and other investment offices	40	36	48.0	381	-	31,801	-	15,482	-	-
6710	Holding offices	16	8	47.1	294	85	31,619	48,753	9,940	4,993	75.1
6732	Educational, religious, etc. trusts	8	8	66.7	14	-	28,286	-	469	-	-
6733	Trusts, n.e.c.	9	9	47.4	23	-	29,913	-	1,064	-	-
BETHEL, AK											
60 –	**Finance, insurance, and real estate**	11	12	1.1	82	114	16,488	18,491	1,434	1,899	0.6
6000	Depository institutions	3	3	1.6	21	-	23,810	-	531	-	-
6500	Real estate	5	4	0.8	-	29	-	18,621	-	627	0.9
6510	Real estate operators and lessors	4	4	1.7	43	29	13,860	18,621	680	627	1.5
6700	Holding and other investment offices	2	4	5.3	-	52	-	16,000	-	495	3.2
BRISTOL BAY, AK											
60 –	**Finance, insurance, and real estate**	2	3	0.3	-	15	-	18,933	-	282	0.1
DENALI BOROUGH, AK											
60 –	**Finance, insurance, and real estate**	1	1	0.1	-	-	-	-	-	-	-
DILLINGHAM, AK											
60 –	**Finance, insurance, and real estate**	9	10	0.9	62	61	12,839	14,295	849	985	0.3
6500	Real estate	3	5	1.0	7	-	9,143	-	76	-	-
6700	Holding and other investment offices	4	3	4.0	-	27	-	2,963	-	71	0.5
FAIRBANKS NORTH STAR, AK											
60 –	**Finance, insurance, and real estate**	152	158	13.8	918	946	26,675	23,573	25,840	25,317	8.4
6000	Depository institutions	31	34	17.6	369	379	27,144	26,575	9,962	10,214	10.0
6020	Commercial banks	18	15	12.8	250	208	30,304	24,635	7,416	5,783	7.9
6100	Nondepository institutions	4	3	7.5	22	13	26,000	29,846	653	357	-

Source: County Business Patterns, 1992/93, CBP-92/93-1, U.S. Department of Commerce, Washington, D.C., April 1995. SIC categories for which data were suppressed or not available for both 1992 and 1993 are *not* displayed. The employment columns represent mid-March employment in the year. Pay per employee is calculated by dividing 1st Quarter payroll, annualized, by mid-March employment. The columns headed "% State" show the county's percentage of the state total for the SIC in 1993; for example, 0.9% for SIC 6030 means that the county had 0.9 percent of the state's total establishments (or payroll) in SIC 6030 in 1993. A dash (-) is used to indicate that data are not available or cannot be calculated; *nec* means not elsewhere classified.

Continued on next page.

SIC	Industry	No. Establishments			Employment		Pay / Employee		Annual Payroll ($ 000)		
		1992	1993	% State	1992	1993	1992	1993	1992	1993	% State
FAIRBANKS NORTH STAR, AK - [continued]											
6280	Security and commodity services	-	3	30.0	-	2	-	20,000	-	81	-
6300	Insurance carriers	16	14	13.9	36	29	54,889	52,552	2,865	1,890	6.2
6400	Insurance agents, brokers, and service	26	27	13.8	105	124	27,200	26,935	3,034	3,587	8.7
6500	Real estate	64	68	13.6	356	365	21,775	16,132	8,048	7,847	10.7
6510	Real estate operators and lessors	28	30	13.1	157	-	19,414	-	3,403	-	-
6530	Real estate agents and managers	29	32	13.2	176	183	24,591	14,601	4,140	4,006	14.8
6552	Subdividers and developers, n.e.c.	3	3	15.8	13	-	13,846	-	183	-	-
HAINES, AK											
60 –	**Finance, insurance, and real estate**	6	5	0.4	-	23	-	15,304	-	431	0.1
JUNEAU, AK											
60 –	**Finance, insurance, and real estate**	69	68	6.0	491	485	30,501	29,872	15,784	16,413	5.5
6000	Depository institutions	14	16	8.3	200	205	23,320	24,195	4,881	5,461	5.3
6020	Commercial banks	8	9	7.7	98	110	23,755	23,273	2,469	2,906	4.0
6300	Insurance carriers	4	1	1.0	12	-	58,667	-	1,045	-	-
6400	Insurance agents, brokers, and service	9	8	4.1	53	45	34,113	39,022	1,666	1,681	4.1
6500	Real estate	35	35	7.0	139	135	27,770	22,341	3,671	3,542	4.8
6510	Real estate operators and lessors	20	22	9.6	83	99	22,747	24,525	1,678	2,803	6.5
6530	Real estate agents and managers	8	13	5.4	30	36	45,200	16,333	1,309	739	2.7
KENAI PENINSULA, AK											
60 –	**Finance, insurance, and real estate**	59	57	5.0	329	316	20,049	22,025	7,415	7,814	2.6
6000	Depository institutions	12	12	6.2	140	146	21,629	21,479	3,176	3,393	3.3
6400	Insurance agents, brokers, and service	12	12	6.2	74	91	29,622	26,022	2,627	2,483	6.0
6500	Real estate	28	25	5.0	78	64	10,667	13,812	1,033	1,287	1.8
6510	Real estate operators and lessors	8	10	4.4	20	-	11,600	-	405	-	-
6530	Real estate agents and managers	16	14	5.8	49	28	11,102	13,143	539	489	1.8
KETCHIKAN GATEWAY, AK											
60 –	**Finance, insurance, and real estate**	39	42	3.7	261	238	30,651	30,605	7,884	6,913	2.3
6000	Depository institutions	10	9	4.7	134	135	33,881	35,081	4,000	4,179	4.1
6020	Commercial banks	5	5	4.3	100	118	37,880	36,983	3,268	3,828	5.2
6060	Credit unions	4	4	6.3	-	17	-	21,882	-	351	1.4
6400	Insurance agents, brokers, and service	6	7	3.6	34	45	40,941	31,733	1,179	1,484	3.6
6500	Real estate	16	22	4.4	37	50	19,892	19,280	801	1,066	1.5
6510	Real estate operators and lessors	7	10	4.4	9	21	20,000	16,000	199	374	0.9
6530	Real estate agents and managers	8	12	5.0	20	29	22,200	21,655	492	692	2.6
KODIAK ISLAND, AK											
60 –	**Finance, insurance, and real estate**	20	21	1.8	106	111	25,509	25,477	2,803	3,016	1.0
6000	Depository institutions	4	6	3.1	43	66	25,209	24,848	1,142	1,758	1.7
6020	Commercial banks	4	4	3.4	43	-	25,209	-	1,142	-	-
6400	Insurance agents, brokers, and service	3	3	1.5	17	16	32,706	34,000	600	605	1.5
6500	Real estate	8	10	2.0	19	-	18,105	-	278	-	-
6510	Real estate operators and lessors	3	7	3.1	8	-	21,500	-	156	-	-
6530	Real estate agents and managers	3	3	1.2	8	7	14,000	20,000	70	140	0.5
LAKE AND PENINSULA BOROUGH, AK											
60 –	**Finance, insurance, and real estate**	2	2	0.2	-	-	-	-	-	-	-
MATANUSKA-SUSITNA, AK											
60 –	**Finance, insurance, and real estate**	42	48	4.2	212	229	24,943	25,991	5,853	6,878	2.3
6000	Depository institutions	9	10	5.2	98	117	21,551	21,915	2,296	2,814	2.8

Source: County Business Patterns, 1992/93, CBP-92/93-1, U.S. Department of Commerce, Washington, D.C., April 1995. SIC categories for which data were suppressed or not available for both 1992 and 1993 are *not* displayed. The employment columns represent mid-March employment in the year. Pay per employee is calculated by dividing 1st Quarter payroll, annualized, by mid-March employment. The columns headed "% State" show the county's percentage of the state total for the SIC in 1993; for example, 0.9% for SIC 6030 means that the county had 0.9 percent of the state's total establishments (or payroll) in SIC 6030 in 1993. A dash (-) is used to indicate that data are not available or cannot be calculated; *nec* means not elsewhere classified.

Continued on next page.

SIC	Industry	No. Establishments			Employment		Pay / Employee		Annual Payroll ($ 000)		
		1992	1993	% State	1992	1993	1992	1993	1992	1993	% State
MATANUSKA-SUSITNA, AK - [continued]											
6400	Insurance agents, brokers, and service	6	8	*4.1*	22	35	27,273	25,943	635	998	*2.4*
6500	Real estate	19	23	*4.6*	53	63	18,868	19,429	1,142	1,727	*2.4*
6530	Real estate agents and managers	15	15	*6.2*	41	42	14,829	17,143	645	747	*2.8*
NOME, AK											
60 –	**Finance, insurance, and real estate**	10	10	*0.9*	65	69	20,246	27,072	1,313	1,966	*0.7*
6500	Real estate	5	5	*1.0*	29	42	13,793	23,905	438	1,007	*1.4*
6510	Real estate operators and lessors	2	5	*2.2*	-	42	-	23,905	-	1,007	*2.3*
NORTH SLOPE, AK											
60 –	**Finance, insurance, and real estate**	3	3	*0.3*	172	153	34,116	42,431	6,617	6,632	*2.2*
NORTH WEST ARTIC, AK											
60 –	**Finance, insurance, and real estate**	3	4	*0.4*	-	-	-	-	-	-	-
PRINCE OF WALES-OUTER KETCHIKAN, AK											
60 –	**Finance, insurance, and real estate**	5	4	*0.4*	50	21	20,480	20,952	1,689	443	*0.1*
6000	Depository institutions	4	4	*2.1*	-	21	-	20,952	-	443	*0.4*
6020	Commercial banks	3	4	*3.4*	-	21	-	20,952	-	443	*0.6*
SITKA, AK											
60 –	**Finance, insurance, and real estate**	16	18	*1.6*	80	82	22,800	23,951	2,280	2,682	*0.9*
6500	Real estate	7	8	*1.6*	21	21	17,714	19,619	438	484	*0.7*
6510	Real estate operators and lessors	4	5	*2.2*	12	13	15,000	19,077	249	308	*0.7*
6530	Real estate agents and managers	3	3	*1.2*	9	8	21,333	20,500	189	176	*0.6*
SKAGWAY-YAKUTATANGOON, AK											
60 –	**Finance, insurance, and real estate**	4	5	*0.4*	14	28	13,714	18,429	248	605	*0.2*
SOUTHEAST FAIRBANKS, AK											
60 –	**Finance, insurance, and real estate**	6	7	*0.6*	19	29	15,158	22,483	287	660	*0.2*
6700	Holding and other investment offices	2	3	*4.0*	-	4	-	14,000	-	64	*0.4*
VALDEZ-CORDOVA, AK											
60 –	**Finance, insurance, and real estate**	10	14	*1.2*	52	85	24,538	27,529	1,299	2,420	*0.8*
6500	Real estate	3	6	*1.2*	9	18	28,889	24,444	237	551	*0.8*
WADE HAMPTON, AK											
60 –	**Finance, insurance, and real estate**	1	1	*0.1*	-	-	-	-	-	-	-
WRANGELL-PETERSBURG, AK											
60 –	**Finance, insurance, and real estate**	7	7	*0.6*	41	-	25,951	-	1,097	-	-
YUKON-KOYUKUK, AK											
60 –	**Finance, insurance, and real estate**	9	9	*0.8*	-	49	-	17,306	-	951	*0.3*
6500	Real estate	1	3	*0.6*	-	25	-	12,000	-	350	*0.5*
6510	Real estate operators and lessors	1	3	*1.3*	-	25	-	12,000	-	350	*0.8*
6700	Holding and other investment offices	7	5	*6.7*	24	-	21,167	-	512	-	-

Source: County Business Patterns, 1992/93, CBP-92/93-1, U.S. Department of Commerce, Washington, D.C., April 1995. SIC categories for which data were suppressed or not available for both 1992 and 1993 are *not* displayed. The employment columns represent mid-March employment in the year. Pay per employee is calculated by dividing 1st Quarter payroll, annualized, by mid-March employment. The columns headed "% State" show the county's percentage of the state total for the SIC in 1993; for example, 0.9% for SIC 6030 means that the county had 0.9 percent of the state's total establishments (or payroll) in SIC 6030 in 1993. A dash (-) is used to indicate that data are not available or cannot be calculated; *nec* means not elsewhere classified.

ARIZONA

SIC	Industry	No. Establishments			Employment		Pay / Employee		Annual Payroll ($ 000)		
		1992	1993	% State	1992	1993	1992	1993	1992	1993	% State
APACHE, AZ											
60 –	**Finance, insurance, and real estate**	34	33	0.4	146	117	14,603	17,299	2,248	2,171	0.1
6400	Insurance agents, brokers, and service	5	6	0.3	22	-	10,909	-	248	-	-
6500	Real estate	19	16	0.4	67	-	12,537	-	939	-	-
6530	Real estate agents and managers	5	5	0.2	10	11	15,600	12,000	204	183	0.1
COCHISE, AZ											
60 –	**Finance, insurance, and real estate**	167	186	2.0	748	970	15,401	13,984	11,921	14,411	0.5
6000	Depository institutions	29	25	2.5	276	243	18,754	19,868	5,102	4,967	0.7
6020	Commercial banks	20	16	2.4	223	182	19,767	22,242	4,329	4,095	0.7
6100	Nondepository institutions	5	10	1.5	-	60	-	15,400	-	883	0.3
6140	Personal credit institutions	3	6	3.4	-	52	-	7,769	-	306	0.9
6160	Mortgage bankers and brokers	2	4	1.1	-	8	-	65,000	-	577	0.3
6280	Security and commodity services	6	1	0.5	9	-	13,333	-	128	-	-
6300	Insurance carriers	9	8	1.1	50	181	21,520	9,083	1,177	1,747	0.3
6400	Insurance agents, brokers, and service	30	35	1.8	82	105	11,707	10,933	1,047	1,208	0.4
6500	Real estate	81	101	2.5	296	363	10,338	12,220	3,462	4,996	1.0
6510	Real estate operators and lessors	36	44	2.8	130	150	7,138	6,533	998	1,112	1.1
6530	Real estate agents and managers	32	47	2.1	73	158	9,644	14,456	895	2,603	0.8
6700	Holding and other investment offices	6	4	1.0	14	-	16,286	-	219	-	-
COCONINO, AZ											
60 –	**Finance, insurance, and real estate**	210	220	2.4	1,505	893	13,813	20,421	23,586	21,081	0.8
6000	Depository institutions	25	21	2.1	274	228	19,839	21,877	5,612	5,090	0.7
6020	Commercial banks	19	15	2.3	218	169	20,349	23,408	4,592	3,986	0.6
6060	Credit unions	6	6	3.9	56	59	17,857	17,492	1,020	1,104	2.9
6100	Nondepository institutions	12	14	2.1	53	54	34,491	32,148	2,195	2,380	0.7
6140	Personal credit institutions	4	5	2.8	-	21	-	23,238	-	550	1.7
6160	Mortgage bankers and brokers	7	9	2.4	31	33	44,129	37,818	1,641	1,830	0.9
6210	Security brokers and dealers	4	5	2.0	-	12	-	52,667	-	589	0.3
6300	Insurance carriers	16	15	2.1	110	86	22,982	30,884	2,817	2,683	0.5
6360	Title insurance	6	4	3.5	66	-	21,152	-	1,588	-	-
6400	Insurance agents, brokers, and service	38	44	2.3	115	139	18,087	16,748	2,031	2,589	0.9
6500	Real estate	106	113	2.8	915	356	8,857	14,697	9,890	6,866	1.4
6510	Real estate operators and lessors	40	42	2.7	147	140	11,320	14,143	2,067	2,572	2.6
6530	Real estate agents and managers	48	64	2.9	715	197	7,994	15,046	6,603	3,939	1.2
6552	Subdividers and developers, n.e.c.	7	6	2.7	13	-	21,846	-	649	-	-
6700	Holding and other investment offices	6	6	1.4	16	-	20,250	-	379	-	-
GILA, AZ											
60 –	**Finance, insurance, and real estate**	60	59	0.6	242	256	17,802	18,516	4,595	4,829	0.2
6000	Depository institutions	12	10	1.0	92	79	22,174	24,354	2,119	1,945	0.3
6300	Insurance carriers	5	5	0.7	22	-	27,636	-	743	-	-
6400	Insurance agents, brokers, and service	11	11	0.6	43	43	15,907	19,814	628	727	0.3
6500	Real estate	28	28	0.7	83	105	11,229	10,819	1,058	1,163	0.2
6510	Real estate operators and lessors	12	13	0.8	39	66	6,462	8,000	266	481	0.5
6530	Real estate agents and managers	8	10	0.5	11	-	13,818	-	183	-	-
6552	Subdividers and developers, n.e.c.	1	3	1.3	-	2	-	8,000	-	11	0.0
6700	Holding and other investment offices	2	3	0.7	-	2	-	10,000	-	12	0.0

Source: County Business Patterns, 1992/93, CBP-92/93-1, U.S. Department of Commerce, Washington, D.C., April 1995. SIC categories for which data were suppressed or not available for both 1992 and 1993 are *not* displayed. The employment columns represent mid-March employment in the year. Pay per employee is calculated by dividing 1st Quarter payroll, annualized, by mid-March employment. The columns headed "% State" show the county's percentage of the state total for the SIC in 1993; for example, 0.9% for SIC 6030 means that the county had 0.9 percent of the state's total establishments (or payroll) in SIC 6030 in 1993. A dash (-) is used to indicate that data are not available or cannot be calculated; *nec* means not elsewhere classified.

SIC	Industry	No. Establishments			Employment		Pay / Employee		Annual Payroll ($ 000)		
		1992	1993	% State	1992	1993	1992	1993	1992	1993	% State
GRAHAM, AZ											
60 –	**Finance, insurance, and real estate**	35	35	0.4	143	165	22,937	18,182	3,091	3,367	0.1
6000	Depository institutions	7	5	0.5	69	63	28,116	24,952	1,615	1,597	0.2
6400	Insurance agents, brokers, and service	6	8	0.4	16	-	12,750	-	221	-	-
6510	Real estate operators and lessors	5	9	0.6	9	27	5,333	5,778	62	176	0.2
6530	Real estate agents and managers	5	3	0.1	15	-	5,067	-	81	-	-
6700	Holding and other investment offices	3	3	0.7	13	29	44,615	16,828	589	611	0.6
GREENLEE, AZ											
60 –	**Finance, insurance, and real estate**	5	5	0.1	-	-	-	-	-	-	-
LA PAZ, AZ											
60 –	**Finance, insurance, and real estate**	23	27	0.3	129	-	13,271	-	1,658	-	-
6400	Insurance agents, brokers, and service	4	5	0.3	8	-	16,500	-	126	-	-
6500	Real estate	11	16	0.4	74	79	11,676	10,987	805	895	0.2
6530	Real estate agents and managers	4	6	0.3	17	29	13,412	8,000	221	266	0.1
MARICOPA, AZ											
60 –	**Finance, insurance, and real estate**	5,835	5,932	64.0	70,822	73,981	27,838	28,169	2,021,473	2,229,837	82.6
6000	Depository institutions	716	596	59.1	21,033	21,180	27,452	26,921	565,306	581,987	83.4
6020	Commercial banks	515	392	59.7	19,102	18,784	27,791	27,922	521,056	537,639	85.5
6030	Savings institutions	86	73	65.8	780	503	27,851	21,773	18,203	11,641	70.5
6060	Credit unions	73	76	49.4	913	1,021	21,227	20,380	20,498	21,985	58.5
6090	Functions closely related to banking	42	54	62.8	238	872	22,824	15,968	5,549	10,719	71.9
6100	Nondepository institutions	408	455	69.5	7,931	8,178	29,292	28,658	248,264	283,237	86.8
6150	Business credit institutions	56	70	80.5	4,024	3,666	26,009	25,077	105,619	91,692	98.3
6160	Mortgage bankers and brokers	223	266	70.2	2,596	3,282	36,092	34,564	108,733	161,098	82.2
6200	Security and commodity brokers	323	334	71.4	2,433	2,810	54,053	57,862	137,063	177,642	82.5
6210	Security brokers and dealers	163	167	67.1	1,965	2,399	59,601	57,407	121,709	149,369	80.9
6280	Security and commodity services	151	162	75.7	-	393	-	61,272	-	27,367	91.5
6300	Insurance carriers	583	488	68.7	13,666	14,793	28,304	31,368	395,458	470,337	86.7
6310	Life insurance	160	143	79.4	3,284	3,101	29,104	31,254	91,457	93,278	85.0
6321	Accident and health insurance	17	14	82.4	262	-	25,420	-	6,154	-	-
6324	Hospital and medical service plans	19	25	71.4	1,193	-	25,019	-	33,478	-	-
6330	Fire, marine, and casualty insurance	220	198	69.2	7,178	7,256	29,418	33,716	216,057	238,503	95.1
6360	Title insurance	68	66	57.4	1,073	1,163	27,146	27,756	31,822	45,827	71.1
6370	Pension, health, and welfare funds	79	27	46.6	539	-	19,228	-	12,369	-	-
6400	Insurance agents, brokers, and service	1,171	1,308	68.3	7,367	8,036	28,820	26,884	230,526	236,906	82.5
6500	Real estate	2,338	2,468	60.4	15,868	16,615	18,977	19,647	327,110	364,592	74.2
6510	Real estate operators and lessors	803	912	58.1	4,488	4,358	12,946	14,228	65,280	64,520	64.6
6530	Real estate agents and managers	1,086	1,382	63.0	8,679	10,924	21,572	21,165	198,710	262,979	77.4
6540	Title abstract offices	10	6	25.0	85	69	24,800	19,478	1,975	1,999	35.2
6552	Subdividers and developers, n.e.c.	118	123	55.2	1,326	1,000	19,759	27,148	28,476	29,438	78.3
6553	Cemetery subdividers and developers	13	12	41.4	272	230	19,103	18,435	5,692	4,534	63.0
6710	Holding offices	67	57	67.1	1,181	848	59,224	64,340	63,810	56,134	80.6
6732	Educational, religious, etc. trusts	35	32	54.2	182	181	20,374	20,243	3,837	3,754	63.6
6733	Trusts, n.e.c.	79	73	62.4	296	280	19,311	21,357	6,162	6,307	64.0
6792	Oil royalty traders	3	2	100.0	6	-	17,333	-	35	-	-
6794	Patent owners and lessors	14	18	75.0	-	134	-	31,045	-	4,362	86.3
6799	Investors, n.e.c.	38	67	69.8	174	311	43,310	31,395	8,505	10,478	79.5
MOHAVE, AZ											
60 –	**Finance, insurance, and real estate**	236	238	2.6	1,151	1,218	19,552	19,714	23,639	30,378	1.1
6000	Depository institutions	26	23	2.3	320	280	20,900	23,457	6,436	6,739	1.0
6020	Commercial banks	20	17	2.6	291	245	21,086	24,310	5,871	6,144	1.0
6100	Nondepository institutions	18	19	2.9	90	212	26,356	18,000	2,604	8,218	2.5
6160	Mortgage bankers and brokers	16	16	4.2	-	201	-	17,871	-	7,979	4.1
6200	Security and commodity brokers	7	9	1.9	-	20	-	21,600	-	478	0.2
6300	Insurance carriers	15	9	1.3	76	64	23,474	27,938	2,001	1,925	0.4

Source: County Business Patterns, 1992/93, CBP-92/93-1, U.S. Department of Commerce, Washington, D.C., April 1995. SIC categories for which data were suppressed or not available for both 1992 and 1993 are not displayed. The employment columns represent mid-March employment in the year. Pay per employee is calculated by dividing 1st Quarter payroll, annualized, by mid-March employment. The columns headed "% State" show the county's percentage of the state total for the SIC in 1993; for example, 0.9% for SIC 6030 means that the county had 0.9 percent of the state's total establishments (or payroll) in SIC 6030 in 1993. A dash (-) is used to indicate that data are not available or cannot be calculated; nec means not elsewhere classified.

Continued on next page.

SIC	Industry	No. Establishments			Employment		Pay / Employee		Annual Payroll ($ 000)		
		1992	1993	% State	1992	1993	1992	1993	1992	1993	% State
MOHAVE, AZ - [continued]											
6400	Insurance agents, brokers, and service	44	55	2.9	203	243	19,468	22,733	4,463	6,017	2.1
6500	Real estate	119	117	2.9	433	380	16,453	15,137	7,573	6,854	1.4
6510	Real estate operators and lessors	26	23	1.5	68	-	10,824	-	789	-	-
6530	Real estate agents and managers	61	75	3.4	237	245	16,506	15,543	4,361	4,809	1.4
6552	Subdividers and developers, n.e.c.	9	14	6.3	35	50	16,343	21,520	607	1,156	3.1
6553	Cemetery subdividers and developers	2	4	13.8	-	18	-	14,667	-	252	3.5
6700	Holding and other investment offices	7	6	1.4	-	19	-	6,947	-	147	0.1
NAVAJO, AZ											
60 -	**Finance, insurance, and real estate**	91	92	1.0	419	-	15,198	-	6,561	-	-
6000	Depository institutions	21	19	1.9	161	140	18,683	20,914	2,765	3,071	0.4
6020	Commercial banks	18	16	2.4	152	130	19,000	21,538	2,642	2,925	0.5
6060	Credit unions	3	3	1.9	9	10	13,333	12,800	123	146	0.4
6300	Insurance carriers	9	8	1.1	43	-	20,744	-	947	-	-
6400	Insurance agents, brokers, and service	24	22	1.1	58	71	15,103	16,394	1,014	1,349	0.5
6500	Real estate	33	36	0.9	141	108	9,702	10,481	1,608	1,462	0.3
6510	Real estate operators and lessors	11	13	0.8	104	62	8,692	9,677	963	733	0.7
6530	Real estate agents and managers	17	20	0.9	24	35	13,667	12,914	461	650	0.2
6552	Subdividers and developers, n.e.c.	3	3	1.3	11	11	6,909	7,273	82	79	0.2
PIMA, AZ											
60 -	**Finance, insurance, and real estate**	1,580	1,677	18.1	11,997	11,497	22,896	23,655	288,820	306,039	11.3
6000	Depository institutions	205	182	18.0	2,711	2,464	23,259	23,729	66,086	65,343	9.4
6020	Commercial banks	116	96	14.6	1,827	1,643	23,888	26,344	46,586	48,271	7.7
6060	Credit unions	35	37	24.0	433	522	18,189	15,418	8,415	9,072	24.1
6100	Nondepository institutions	93	116	17.7	-	657	-	26,417	-	26,744	8.2
6140	Personal credit institutions	39	40	22.3	-	218	-	19,229	-	4,203	12.7
6150	Business credit institutions	6	10	11.5	-	35	-	22,400	-	860	0.9
6160	Mortgage bankers and brokers	48	66	17.4	284	404	36,479	30,644	12,205	21,681	11.1
6200	Security and commodity brokers	76	91	19.4	549	608	50,616	49,362	28,159	33,136	15.4
6210	Security brokers and dealers	43	50	20.1	486	536	54,576	53,910	27,066	31,111	16.9
6280	Security and commodity services	33	41	19.2	63	72	20,063	15,500	1,093	2,025	6.8
6300	Insurance carriers	134	126	17.7	1,550	1,818	27,528	30,634	47,348	56,396	10.4
6360	Title insurance	10	11	9.6	320	310	25,150	24,348	9,329	9,026	14.0
6400	Insurance agents, brokers, and service	283	299	15.6	1,138	1,101	20,770	20,276	24,064	24,193	8.4
6500	Real estate	697	773	18.9	4,440	4,262	15,992	16,176	74,757	80,973	16.5
6510	Real estate operators and lessors	287	321	20.5	1,500	1,641	10,251	11,559	17,072	20,826	20.8
6530	Real estate agents and managers	298	396	18.0	2,047	2,378	20,256	19,026	42,552	54,422	16.0
6552	Subdividers and developers, n.e.c.	33	33	14.8	362	90	18,298	15,511	6,679	1,815	4.8
6553	Cemetery subdividers and developers	5	5	17.2	209	87	12,440	22,069	2,874	2,188	30.4
6700	Holding and other investment offices	90	89	21.3	757	-	25,363	-	20,246	-	-
6710	Holding offices	16	19	22.4	321	284	25,296	43,972	8,409	11,427	16.4
6732	Educational, religious, etc. trusts	14	15	25.4	-	95	-	13,347	-	1,365	23.1
6733	Trusts, n.e.c.	29	26	22.2	116	109	17,414	18,202	2,116	2,107	21.4
6794	Patent owners and lessors	5	6	25.0	-	33	-	13,576	-	691	13.7
6798	Real estate investment trusts	6	4	30.8	-	9	-	64,000	-	491	-
6799	Investors, n.e.c.	9	14	14.6	40	39	40,900	45,333	2,159	2,142	16.3
PINAL, AZ											
60 -	**Finance, insurance, and real estate**	145	148	1.6	868	853	18,659	19,137	16,267	17,587	0.7
6000	Depository institutions	29	27	2.7	255	231	21,349	24,069	5,363	5,690	0.8
6020	Commercial banks	23	20	3.0	221	182	21,955	25,780	4,632	4,727	0.8
6100	Nondepository institutions	4	4	0.6	-	32	-	15,375	-	566	0.2
6300	Insurance carriers	12	12	1.7	60	55	26,467	28,145	1,673	1,803	0.3
6400	Insurance agents, brokers, and service	21	23	1.2	158	193	33,696	30,259	5,365	6,578	2.3

Source: County Business Patterns, 1992/93, CBP-92/93-1, U.S. Department of Commerce, Washington, D.C., April 1995. SIC categories for which data were suppressed or not available for both 1992 and 1993 are *not* displayed. The employment columns represent mid-March employment in the year. Pay per employee is calculated by dividing 1st Quarter payroll, annualized, by mid-March employment. The columns headed "% State" show the county's percentage of the state total for the SIC in 1993; for example, 0.9% for SIC 6030 means that the county had 0.9 percent of the state's total establishments (or payroll) in SIC 6030 in 1993. A dash (-) is used to indicate that data are not available or cannot be calculated; *nec* means not elsewhere classified.

Continued on next page.

SIC	Industry	No. Establishments			Employment		Pay / Employee		Annual Payroll ($ 000)		
		1992	1993	% State	1992	1993	1992	1993	1992	1993	% State
PINAL, AZ - [continued]											
6500	Real estate	71	73	1.8	339	302	8,260	7,391	2,758	2,264	0.5
6510	Real estate operators and lessors	38	48	3.1	193	224	5,492	6,321	1,052	1,481	1.5
6530	Real estate agents and managers	20	23	1.0	71	-	10,254	-	661	-	-
SANTA CRUZ, AZ											
60 –	**Finance, insurance, and real estate**	70	77	0.8	-	285	-	18,358	-	5,529	0.2
6000	Depository institutions	11	13	1.3	68	95	38,765	25,768	1,547	2,370	0.3
6020	Commercial banks	7	7	1.1	64	85	40,500	27,953	1,493	2,283	0.4
6090	Functions closely related to banking	4	6	7.0	4	10	11,000	7,200	54	87	0.6
6400	Insurance agents, brokers, and service	12	11	0.6	46	39	17,043	17,128	819	768	0.3
6500	Real estate	41	44	1.1	123	119	13,431	12,941	2,206	1,711	0.3
6510	Real estate operators and lessors	16	23	1.5	38	69	9,263	13,043	695	964	1.0
6530	Real estate agents and managers	16	17	0.8	55	-	13,673	-	921	-	-
6552	Subdividers and developers, n.e.c.	3	3	1.3	5	-	7,200	-	43	-	-
YAVAPAI, AZ											
60 –	**Finance, insurance, and real estate**	301	329	3.5	1,260	1,417	19,114	19,404	25,245	30,583	1.1
6000	Depository institutions	41	34	3.4	385	324	21,423	24,198	8,119	7,887	1.1
6020	Commercial banks	33	29	4.4	317	284	21,691	25,141	6,720	7,172	1.1
6100	Nondepository institutions	20	22	3.4	84	129	19,762	19,442	2,040	3,042	0.9
6160	Mortgage bankers and brokers	11	13	3.4	54	73	22,074	26,466	1,475	2,400	1.2
6200	Security and commodity brokers	15	16	3.4	54	63	40,889	42,603	2,132	2,572	1.2
6210	Security brokers and dealers	7	9	3.6	33	38	56,364	60,947	1,767	2,199	1.2
6280	Security and commodity services	8	7	3.3	21	25	16,571	14,720	365	373	1.2
6300	Insurance carriers	18	17	2.4	71	95	27,380	19,453	2,000	2,611	0.5
6400	Insurance agents, brokers, and service	38	48	2.5	153	212	13,098	13,528	2,081	3,130	1.1
6500	Real estate	157	181	4.4	474	560	15,122	16,114	7,998	10,421	2.1
6510	Real estate operators and lessors	41	53	3.4	117	208	9,538	16,135	1,450	2,739	2.7
6530	Real estate agents and managers	82	102	4.6	256	267	16,297	15,850	4,290	5,545	1.6
6552	Subdividers and developers, n.e.c.	15	22	9.9	43	73	28,279	17,918	1,480	1,991	5.3
6553	Cemetery subdividers and developers	3	3	10.3	14	-	10,000	-	147	-	-
6700	Holding and other investment offices	12	11	2.6	39	34	21,846	21,294	875	920	0.9
YUMA, AZ											
60 –	**Finance, insurance, and real estate**	221	217	2.3	1,241	1,282	18,785	18,103	23,165	25,509	0.9
6000	Depository institutions	39	41	4.1	336	408	21,833	21,735	7,238	9,280	1.3
6020	Commercial banks	29	27	4.1	292	288	23,027	23,681	6,585	7,034	1.1
6090	Functions closely related to banking	4	5	5.8	-	15	-	8,533	-	181	1.2
6100	Nondepository institutions	13	9	1.4	94	31	20,383	29,290	2,089	1,117	0.3
6140	Personal credit institutions	8	4	2.2	78	-	18,821	-	1,652	-	-
6200	Security and commodity brokers	8	4	0.9	15	39	29,600	20,410	314	394	0.2
6210	Security brokers and dealers	4	3	1.2	9	-	43,111	-	246	-	-
6280	Security and commodity services	4	1	0.5	6	-	9,333	-	68	-	-
6300	Insurance carriers	13	11	1.5	73	75	28,548	27,840	2,093	2,258	0.4
6400	Insurance agents, brokers, and service	36	39	2.0	131	150	19,756	17,520	2,451	2,863	1.0
6500	Real estate	107	104	2.5	533	528	13,659	12,652	7,415	8,268	1.7
6510	Real estate operators and lessors	50	50	3.2	286	274	9,860	10,161	2,891	2,868	2.9
6530	Real estate agents and managers	40	44	2.0	104	121	15,038	14,149	1,774	2,970	0.9
6700	Holding and other investment offices	5	9	2.2	59	51	28,203	24,314	1,565	1,329	1.2

Source: County Business Patterns, 1992/93, CBP-92/93-1, U.S. Department of Commerce, Washington, D.C., April 1995. SIC categories for which data were suppressed or not available for both 1992 and 1993 are *not* displayed. The employment columns represent mid-March employment in the year. Pay per employee is calculated by dividing 1st Quarter payroll, annualized, by mid-March employment. The columns headed "% State" show the county's percentage of the state total for the SIC in 1993; for example, 0.9% for SIC 6030 means that the county had 0.9 percent of the state's total establishments (or payroll) in SIC 6030 in 1993. A dash (-) is used to indicate that data are not available or cannot be calculated; *nec* means not elsewhere classified.

ARKANSAS

SIC	Industry	No. Establishments			Employment		Pay / Employee		Annual Payroll ($ 000)		
		1992	1993	% State	1992	1993	1992	1993	1992	1993	% State
ARKANSAS, AR											
60–	**Finance, insurance, and real estate**	41	39	0.8	303	302	19,578	23,483	6,731	6,478	0.7
6000	Depository institutions	11	11	1.1	222	223	19,405	18,960	4,769	4,628	1.4
6020	Commercial banks	11	11	1.3	222	223	19,405	18,960	4,769	4,628	1.6
6400	Insurance agents, brokers, and service	11	11	0.9	38	36	15,789	15,333	595	578	0.6
6510	Real estate operators and lessors	4	3	0.5	5	2	12,000	16,000	47	25	0.1
6530	Real estate agents and managers	3	5	0.8	9	–	15,111	–	146	–	–
ASHLEY, AR											
60–	**Finance, insurance, and real estate**	29	32	0.7	276	228	20,377	23,754	5,213	4,854	0.5
6000	Depository institutions	10	11	1.1	142	163	22,817	25,227	2,735	3,383	1.0
6020	Commercial banks	10	10	1.2	142	–	22,817	–	2,735	–	–
6400	Insurance agents, brokers, and service	9	11	0.9	32	35	14,375	13,943	576	597	0.6
6510	Real estate operators and lessors	3	3	0.5	4	4	11,000	7,000	31	30	0.1
BAXTER, AR											
60–	**Finance, insurance, and real estate**	70	75	1.6	354	378	20,678	20,053	7,920	8,101	0.8
6000	Depository institutions	11	11	1.1	188	188	22,021	20,404	4,392	4,102	1.2
6200	Security and commodity brokers	5	5	2.6	14	–	68,857	–	1,013	–	–
6300	Insurance carriers	7	6	1.7	35	36	24,000	29,667	844	–	–
6400	Insurance agents, brokers, and service	14	20	1.6	–	42	–	15,524	–	706	0.7
6500	Real estate	32	31	2.0	82	96	10,146	8,833	1,004	973	0.9
6510	Real estate operators and lessors	8	8	1.2	15	28	10,933	8,143	196	222	0.7
6530	Real estate agents and managers	18	19	3.0	41	47	8,195	8,426	405	451	0.9
6540	Title abstract offices	3	2	1.8	19	–	14,737	–	338	–	–
BENTON, AR											
60–	**Finance, insurance, and real estate**	212	218	4.7	1,922	1,991	18,914	21,943	41,098	43,467	4.5
6000	Depository institutions	41	40	3.8	900	835	19,644	22,017	18,731	17,811	5.4
6020	Commercial banks	31	32	3.8	816	756	19,696	22,550	16,825	16,290	5.7
6100	Nondepository institutions	5	4	2.9	74	42	24,270	22,571	1,948	1,035	2.5
6200	Security and commodity brokers	9	10	5.2	47	49	52,000	48,980	2,263	2,490	1.6
6300	Insurance carriers	23	10	2.8	67	28	17,194	30,143	2,699	934	0.6
6330	Fire, marine, and casualty insurance	13	7	5.6	27	–	25,037	–	739	–	–
6400	Insurance agents, brokers, and service	50	54	4.4	307	348	19,244	19,586	6,806	6,266	6.0
6500	Real estate	75	88	5.7	499	649	12,818	19,606	7,633	13,217	11.8
6510	Real estate operators and lessors	31	32	4.9	79	–	13,215	–	1,170	–	–
6530	Real estate agents and managers	28	43	6.8	202	216	9,782	9,833	2,173	2,494	5.0
6540	Title abstract offices	3	3	2.7	91	107	14,725	14,841	1,557	1,937	12.1
6700	Holding and other investment offices	9	12	6.5	28	40	34,857	39,300	1,018	1,714	2.6
6710	Holding offices	2	5	8.9	–	29	–	47,724	–	1,457	2.6
6733	Trusts, n.e.c.	5	2	5.1	2	–	22,000	–	47	–	–
BOONE, AR											
60–	**Finance, insurance, and real estate**	61	59	1.3	313	330	18,326	19,552	6,196	6,762	0.7
6000	Depository institutions	13	12	1.2	195	190	20,574	23,263	4,274	4,333	1.3
6400	Insurance agents, brokers, and service	14	15	1.2	44	46	15,818	14,609	706	735	0.7
6500	Real estate	28	27	1.8	60	83	9,800	9,783	783	1,054	0.9
6510	Real estate operators and lessors	10	9	1.4	23	–	6,435	–	141	–	–
6530	Real estate agents and managers	14	15	2.4	16	33	11,250	8,970	226	323	0.6

Source: County Business Patterns, 1992/93, CBP-92/93-1, U.S. Department of Commerce, Washington, D.C., April 1995. SIC categories for which data were suppressed or not available for both 1992 and 1993 are *not* displayed. The employment columns represent mid-March employment in the year. Pay per employee is calculated by dividing 1st Quarter payroll, annualized, by mid-March employment. The columns headed "% State" show the county's percentage of the state total for the SIC in 1993; for example, 0.9% for SIC 6030 means that the county had 0.9 percent of the state's total establishments (or payroll) in SIC 6030 in 1993. A dash (-) is used to indicate that data are not available or cannot be calculated; *nec* means not elsewhere classified.

SIC	Industry	No. Establishments			Employment		Pay / Employee		Annual Payroll ($ 000)		
		1992	1993	% State	1992	1993	1992	1993	1992	1993	% State
BRADLEY, AR											
60 –	**Finance, insurance, and real estate**	17	17	*0.4*	131	127	19,176	17,984	2,597	2,328	*0.2*
6000	Depository institutions	7	6	*0.6*	104	98	20,346	19,224	2,104	1,845	*0.6*
6500	Real estate	5	5	*0.3*	9	12	5,778	4,667	53	58	*0.1*
CALHOUN, AR											
60 –	**Finance, insurance, and real estate**	3	3	*0.1*	-	-	-	-	-	-	-
CARROLL, AR											
60 –	**Finance, insurance, and real estate**	39	41	*0.9*	181	239	21,370	20,435	4,474	5,381	*0.6*
6000	Depository institutions	10	10	*1.0*	110	156	21,636	20,256	2,904	3,454	*1.1*
6400	Insurance agents, brokers, and service	11	12	*1.0*	20	26	16,200	14,462	370	464	*0.4*
6500	Real estate	12	14	*0.9*	33	40	15,515	15,200	603	806	*0.7*
6510	Real estate operators and lessors	1	3	*0.5*	-	1	-	12,000	-	25	*0.1*
6530	Real estate agents and managers	7	8	*1.3*	8	14	11,000	9,429	107	150	*0.3*
CHICOT, AR											
60 –	**Finance, insurance, and real estate**	25	25	*0.5*	133	131	18,586	19,450	2,494	2,551	*0.3*
6000	Depository institutions	6	6	*0.6*	90	90	21,067	19,689	1,797	1,809	*0.6*
6020	Commercial banks	6	6	*0.7*	90	90	21,067	19,689	1,797	1,809	*0.6*
6400	Insurance agents, brokers, and service	3	4	*0.3*	8	-	10,000	-	73	-	-
6500	Real estate	11	11	*0.7*	15	13	5,067	4,923	60	90	*0.1*
6510	Real estate operators and lessors	6	6	*0.9*	8	7	5,500	5,143	36	42	*0.1*
CLARK, AR											
60 –	**Finance, insurance, and real estate**	46	50	*1.1*	275	317	17,178	16,013	5,307	6,049	*0.6*
6000	Depository institutions	14	13	*1.3*	166	171	17,349	15,953	3,212	3,193	*1.0*
6020	Commercial banks	11	10	*1.2*	158	158	17,266	16,405	3,065	3,037	*1.1*
6400	Insurance agents, brokers, and service	10	11	*0.9*	36	44	17,556	13,727	662	752	*0.7*
6500	Real estate	16	16	*1.0*	-	51	-	8,314	-	546	*0.5*
6510	Real estate operators and lessors	8	9	*1.4*	17	17	8,471	8,941	160	189	*0.6*
6530	Real estate agents and managers	4	4	*0.6*	8	12	13,000	8,667	107	123	*0.2*
6700	Holding and other investment offices	5	5	*2.7*	-	37	-	24,649	-	1,109	*1.7*
CLAY, AR											
60 –	**Finance, insurance, and real estate**	30	28	*0.6*	153	142	16,863	16,901	2,607	2,715	*0.3*
6000	Depository institutions	9	8	*0.8*	108	98	18,000	18,204	1,960	1,861	*0.6*
6020	Commercial banks	6	6	*0.7*	74	-	18,811	-	1,379	-	-
6030	Savings institutions	3	2	*2.0*	34	-	16,235	-	581	-	-
6400	Insurance agents, brokers, and service	8	7	*0.6*	23	26	15,826	15,077	399	448	*0.4*
6500	Real estate	9	11	*0.7*	12	-	9,000	-	105	-	-
6540	Title abstract offices	2	3	*2.7*	-	5	-	13,600	-	71	*0.4*
6553	Cemetery subdividers and developers	5	5	*7.5*	6	6	5,333	4,667	45	47	*1.7*
CLEBURNE, AR											
60 –	**Finance, insurance, and real estate**	38	39	*0.8*	283	185	12,000	15,200	3,711	3,109	*0.3*
6000	Depository institutions	13	13	*1.3*	121	124	15,603	16,000	1,926	2,062	*0.6*
6020	Commercial banks	13	13	*1.6*	121	124	15,603	16,000	1,926	2,062	*0.7*
6400	Insurance agents, brokers, and service	8	10	*0.8*	15	29	12,800	15,724	196	551	*0.5*
6500	Real estate	12	13	*0.8*	126	19	7,365	10,526	1,189	277	*0.2*
6510	Real estate operators and lessors	4	4	*0.6*	6	-	6,000	-	25	-	-
6530	Real estate agents and managers	3	8	*1.3*	-	14	-	12,571	-	209	*0.4*
CLEVELAND, AR											
60 –	**Finance, insurance, and real estate**	6	6	*0.1*	26	22	14,308	17,091	384	382	*0.0*

Source: County Business Patterns, 1992/93, CBP-92/93-1, U.S. Department of Commerce, Washington, D.C., April 1995. SIC categories for which data were suppressed or not available for both 1992 and 1993 are *not* displayed. The employment columns represent mid-March employment in the year. Pay per employee is calculated by dividing 1st Quarter payroll, annualized, by mid-March employment. The columns headed "% State" show the county's percentage of the state total for the SIC in 1993; for example, 0.9% for SIC 6030 means that the county had 0.9 percent of the state's total establishments (or payroll) in SIC 6030 in 1993. A dash (-) is used to indicate that data are not available or cannot be calculated; *nec* means not elsewhere classified.

SIC	Industry	No. Establishments			Employment		Pay / Employee		Annual Payroll ($ 000)		
		1992	1993	% State	1992	1993	1992	1993	1992	1993	% State
COLUMBIA, AR											
60 –	**Finance, insurance, and real estate**	38	36	0.8	234	238	20,103	19,311	4,992	4,838	0.5
6000	Depository institutions	13	13	1.3	174	177	19,586	19,751	3,547	3,522	1.1
6400	Insurance agents, brokers, and service	8	8	0.7	27	29	17,333	16,276	571	517	0.5
6500	Real estate	6	6	0.4	8	11	11,000	12,727	116	142	0.1
6510	Real estate operators and lessors	3	2	0.3	7	-	7,429	-	43	-	-
6700	Holding and other investment offices	5	4	2.2	7	7	48,000	24,571	343	252	0.4
CONWAY, AR											
60 –	**Finance, insurance, and real estate**	20	21	0.4	108	113	16,444	16,850	1,853	1,841	0.2
6000	Depository institutions	9	9	0.9	80	85	18,300	17,647	1,489	1,419	0.4
6400	Insurance agents, brokers, and service	8	8	0.7	24	23	10,167	15,478	288	334	0.3
6500	Real estate	2	4	0.3	-	5	-	9,600	-	88	0.1
CRAIGHEAD, AR											
60 –	**Finance, insurance, and real estate**	147	159	3.4	1,048	1,044	23,084	22,743	24,187	25,066	2.6
6000	Depository institutions	31	32	3.1	522	510	20,207	20,400	10,726	11,221	3.4
6020	Commercial banks	23	27	3.2	416	-	21,010	-	8,773	-	-
6030	Savings institutions	8	5	5.1	106	-	17,057	-	1,953	-	-
6100	Nondepository institutions	6	4	2.9	70	41	38,686	40,780	2,206	1,598	3.8
6200	Security and commodity brokers	8	7	3.6	42	43	64,857	55,814	2,226	2,582	1.6
6210	Security brokers and dealers	5	5	3.7	36	-	71,000	-	2,117	-	-
6280	Security and commodity services	3	2	3.7	6	-	28,000	-	109	-	-
6300	Insurance carriers	17	17	4.8	116	123	29,207	31,057	3,774	3,875	2.7
6310	Life insurance	8	7	5.5	75	84	27,840	28,762	2,433	2,301	3.9
6400	Insurance agents, brokers, and service	36	41	3.3	101	112	23,842	23,679	2,490	2,423	2.3
6500	Real estate	43	52	3.4	150	195	12,107	12,738	2,125	2,969	2.7
6510	Real estate operators and lessors	25	29	4.4	77	84	10,753	11,714	946	1,068	3.5
6530	Real estate agents and managers	7	12	1.9	9	44	8,000	11,273	89	727	1.5
6540	Title abstract offices	4	4	3.6	35	40	16,457	16,800	651	808	5.0
6700	Holding and other investment offices	6	6	3.2	47	20	12,766	15,600	640	398	0.6
CRAWFORD, AR											
60 –	**Finance, insurance, and real estate**	43	51	1.1	229	263	20,472	19,194	4,927	5,401	0.6
6000	Depository institutions	14	14	1.3	153	175	22,797	20,617	3,702	3,843	1.2
6400	Insurance agents, brokers, and service	9	10	0.8	18	23	10,889	12,348	211	288	0.3
6500	Real estate	15	21	1.4	51	58	12,157	12,690	645	829	0.7
6510	Real estate operators and lessors	5	8	1.2	17	27	11,294	9,630	163	244	0.8
6530	Real estate agents and managers	6	8	1.3	17	-	14,353	-	271	-	-
CRITTENDEN, AR											
60 –	**Finance, insurance, and real estate**	73	73	1.6	520	546	21,477	22,110	10,897	11,414	1.2
6000	Depository institutions	19	20	1.9	291	300	21,223	22,293	6,125	6,259	1.9
6020	Commercial banks	14	15	1.8	205	-	22,088	-	4,458	-	-
6300	Insurance carriers	8	5	1.4	69	59	20,522	19,661	1,394	1,058	0.7
6310	Life insurance	3	3	2.4	61	-	21,574	-	1,283	-	-
6400	Insurance agents, brokers, and service	13	14	1.1	30	40	16,533	16,600	556	739	0.7
6500	Real estate	28	28	1.8	120	123	23,100	24,098	2,577	2,797	2.5
6510	Real estate operators and lessors	12	15	2.3	41	93	15,220	26,495	616	1,860	6.1
6530	Real estate agents and managers	8	9	1.4	55	12	31,345	7,000	1,214	138	0.3
CROSS, AR											
60 –	**Finance, insurance, and real estate**	31	31	0.7	268	188	14,821	18,319	3,923	3,535	0.4
6000	Depository institutions	11	11	1.1	140	151	21,600	19,788	2,904	3,083	0.9
6500	Real estate	11	10	0.6	106	15	6,000	9,067	721	140	0.1
6530	Real estate agents and managers	4	3	0.5	-	2	-	6,000	-	21	0.0

Source: County Business Patterns, 1992/93, CBP-92/93-1, U.S. Department of Commerce, Washington, D.C., April 1995. SIC categories for which data were suppressed or not available for both 1992 and 1993 are not displayed. The employment columns represent mid-March employment in the year. Pay per employee is calculated by dividing 1st Quarter payroll, annualized, by mid-March employment. The columns headed "% State" show the county's percentage of the state total for the SIC in 1993; for example, 0.9% for SIC 6030 means that the county had 0.9 percent of the state's total establishments (or payroll) in SIC 6030 in 1993. A dash (-) is used to indicate that data are not available or cannot be calculated; nec means not elsewhere classified.

SIC	Industry	No. Establishments			Employment		Pay / Employee		Annual Payroll ($ 000)		
		1992	1993	% State	1992	1993	1992	1993	1992	1993	% State
DALLAS, AR											
60–	**Finance, insurance, and real estate**	12	12	0.3	82	85	15,415	16,518	1,512	1,626	0.2
6000	Depository institutions	6	6	0.6	64	75	17,750	17,067	1,373	1,478	0.4
6400	Insurance agents, brokers, and service	2	3	0.2	-	6	-	17,333	-	122	0.1
6500	Real estate	3	3	0.2	11	4	1,818	5,000	24	26	0.0
DESHA, AR											
60–	**Finance, insurance, and real estate**	37	36	0.8	219	195	15,452	16,574	3,756	3,443	0.4
6000	Depository institutions	10	10	1.0	139	114	17,899	20,105	2,685	2,420	0.7
6020	Commercial banks	10	10	1.2	139	114	17,899	20,105	2,685	2,420	0.8
6400	Insurance agents, brokers, and service	9	9	0.7	32	-	16,500	-	677	-	-
6500	Real estate	16	16	1.0	-	46	-	8,000	-	418	0.4
6510	Real estate operators and lessors	10	10	1.5	32	-	3,500	-	131	-	-
6530	Real estate agents and managers	4	4	0.6	11	10	18,909	20,800	213	254	0.5
DREW, AR											
60–	**Finance, insurance, and real estate**	21	22	0.5	148	152	21,054	23,184	2,863	2,926	0.3
6400	Insurance agents, brokers, and service	5	8	0.7	16	-	17,750	-	286	-	-
6500	Real estate	10	9	0.6	21	24	10,857	10,000	271	270	0.2
6510	Real estate operators and lessors	6	4	0.6	6	-	10,000	-	83	-	-
6530	Real estate agents and managers	2	4	0.6	-	13	-	12,615	-	178	0.4
FAULKNER, AR											
60–	**Finance, insurance, and real estate**	91	106	2.3	517	542	17,238	18,435	9,657	11,448	1.2
6000	Depository institutions	21	22	2.1	302	294	18,013	19,170	5,575	6,137	1.9
6020	Commercial banks	15	17	2.0	256	249	18,406	20,000	4,789	5,421	1.9
6100	Nondepository institutions	5	5	3.6	12	18	16,000	14,889	182	315	0.8
6200	Security and commodity brokers	4	5	2.6	9	-	52,000	-	609	-	-
6300	Insurance carriers	10	8	2.3	36	34	21,111	27,294	905	911	0.6
6400	Insurance agents, brokers, and service	22	31	2.5	76	104	13,368	12,538	1,031	1,428	1.4
6500	Real estate	29	34	2.2	82	81	12,634	13,975	1,355	1,659	1.5
6530	Real estate agents and managers	12	16	2.5	27	39	13,630	12,410	604	890	1.8
FRANKLIN, AR											
60–	**Finance, insurance, and real estate**	18	19	0.4	126	123	25,397	21,691	3,113	2,932	0.3
6500	Real estate	7	6	0.4	-	7	-	9,143	-	66	0.1
FULTON, AR											
60–	**Finance, insurance, and real estate**	13	13	0.3	78	70	16,462	17,829	1,269	1,366	0.1
6000	Depository institutions	4	4	0.4	49	50	22,204	20,800	1,060	1,046	0.3
6020	Commercial banks	4	4	0.5	49	50	22,204	20,800	1,060	1,046	0.4
6400	Insurance agents, brokers, and service	5	4	0.3	9	8	13,778	15,000	128	122	0.1
6500	Real estate	4	5	0.3	20	12	3,600	7,333	81	198	0.2
GARLAND, AR											
60–	**Finance, insurance, and real estate**	176	187	4.0	1,540	1,506	17,673	18,290	28,657	29,751	3.1
6000	Depository institutions	29	29	2.8	435	455	20,138	18,769	9,023	9,381	2.9
6020	Commercial banks	22	21	2.5	418	429	19,923	18,648	8,599	8,836	3.1
6100	Nondepository institutions	7	7	5.1	14	14	16,571	16,000	255	182	0.4
6160	Mortgage bankers and brokers	3	4	5.5	7	8	20,571	18,500	166	146	0.6
6200	Security and commodity brokers	7	9	4.7	51	50	53,412	65,920	2,824	3,492	2.2
6210	Security brokers and dealers	6	9	6.7	-	50	-	65,920	-	3,492	2.4
6300	Insurance carriers	16	14	3.9	123	83	25,431	26,506	2,752	2,456	1.7
6310	Life insurance	4	3	2.4	59	50	30,576	25,520	1,650	1,269	2.1
6370	Pension, health, and welfare funds	3	2	4.3	29	-	13,655	-	238	-	-
6400	Insurance agents, brokers, and service	37	41	3.3	91	98	22,286	24,735	2,613	2,664	2.5
6500	Real estate	73	79	5.1	816	794	12,461	13,335	11,015	11,335	10.1

Source: County Business Patterns, 1992/93, CBP-92/93-1, U.S. Department of Commerce, Washington, D.C., April 1995. SIC categories for which data were suppressed or not available for both 1992 and 1993 are *not* displayed. The employment columns represent mid-March employment in the year. Pay per employee is calculated by dividing 1st Quarter payroll, annualized, by mid-March employment. The columns headed "% State" show the county's percentage of the state total for the SIC in 1993; for example, 0.9% for SIC 6030 means that the county had 0.9 percent of the state's total establishments (or payroll) in SIC 6030 in 1993. A dash (-) is used to indicate that data are not available or cannot be calculated; *nec* means not elsewhere classified.

Continued on next page.

SIC	Industry	No. Establishments			Employment		Pay / Employee		Annual Payroll ($ 000)		
		1992	1993	% State	1992	1993	1992	1993	1992	1993	% State
GARLAND, AR - [continued]											
6510	Real estate operators and lessors	19	24	3.7	52	-	10,231	-	787	-	-
6530	Real estate agents and managers	46	48	7.6	665	576	11,609	11,611	7,857	7,286	14.6
6700	Holding and other investment offices	7	8	4.3	10	12	17,600	22,667	175	241	0.4
GRANT, AR											
60 –	**Finance, insurance, and real estate**	11	12	0.3	70	75	17,314	17,707	1,231	1,410	0.1
6000	Depository institutions	5	5	0.5	59	62	17,763	18,323	1,054	1,189	0.4
GREENE, AR											
60 –	**Finance, insurance, and real estate**	47	47	1.0	294	283	21,469	22,558	5,929	5,985	0.6
6000	Depository institutions	8	8	0.8	159	163	24,050	22,380	3,338	3,396	1.0
6020	Commercial banks	7	8	1.0	-	163	-	22,380	-	3,396	1.2
6300	Insurance carriers	7	4	1.1	49	-	13,714	-	430	-	-
6400	Insurance agents, brokers, and service	14	16	1.3	29	43	31,034	33,581	1,031	1,133	1.1
6500	Real estate	14	14	0.9	-	30	-	11,733	-	450	0.4
6510	Real estate operators and lessors	5	6	0.9	5	7	6,400	6,857	45	75	0.2
6530	Real estate agents and managers	4	5	0.8	2	10	10,000	10,800	44	127	0.3
HEMPSTEAD, AR											
60 –	**Finance, insurance, and real estate**	28	29	0.6	195	209	22,995	19,656	4,140	4,211	0.4
6000	Depository institutions	9	8	0.8	137	141	24,876	22,411	2,986	3,177	1.0
6400	Insurance agents, brokers, and service	5	6	0.5	21	-	19,810	-	422	-	-
6510	Real estate operators and lessors	6	7	1.1	24	30	18,667	8,400	458	280	0.9
6530	Real estate agents and managers	3	4	0.6	3	6	13,333	10,667	50	60	0.1
HOT SPRING, AR											
60 –	**Finance, insurance, and real estate**	30	31	0.7	207	197	14,184	15,330	3,205	3,482	0.4
6000	Depository institutions	8	9	0.9	125	135	16,416	16,030	2,325	2,542	0.8
6400	Insurance agents, brokers, and service	10	11	0.9	25	22	10,080	10,909	253	209	0.2
6500	Real estate	6	5	0.3	37	26	10,270	15,692	378	455	0.4
6700	Holding and other investment offices	3	3	1.6	9	7	10,667	12,000	59	73	0.1
HOWARD, AR											
60 –	**Finance, insurance, and real estate**	20	21	0.4	64	107	16,500	19,215	1,134	2,105	0.2
6000	Depository institutions	6	7	0.7	40	80	16,800	20,950	781	1,729	0.5
6400	Insurance agents, brokers, and service	8	9	0.7	19	21	16,421	15,619	286	312	0.3
6500	Real estate	5	5	0.3	-	6	-	8,667	-	64	0.1
INDEPENDENCE, AR											
60 –	**Finance, insurance, and real estate**	54	55	1.2	291	292	17,759	18,548	5,435	5,814	0.6
6000	Depository institutions	18	18	1.7	173	182	18,867	19,604	3,425	3,630	1.1
6020	Commercial banks	15	15	1.8	164	-	18,829	-	3,320	-	-
6200	Security and commodity brokers	3	3	1.6	8	7	36,500	26,286	319	203	0.1
6210	Security brokers and dealers	2	3	2.2	-	7	-	26,286	-	203	0.1
6400	Insurance agents, brokers, and service	12	13	1.1	37	40	19,892	19,600	772	870	0.8
6500	Real estate	16	17	1.1	68	53	11,471	12,226	798	862	0.8
6510	Real estate operators and lessors	6	7	1.1	13	-	4,308	-	60	-	-
6530	Real estate agents and managers	6	7	1.1	43	24	13,116	15,833	442	345	0.7
IZARD, AR											
60 –	**Finance, insurance, and real estate**	24	23	0.5	131	127	13,863	13,386	1,962	1,948	0.2
6000	Depository institutions	8	7	0.7	59	58	17,288	17,517	1,068	1,140	0.3
6020	Commercial banks	7	7	0.8	-	58	-	17,517	-	1,140	0.4
6400	Insurance agents, brokers, and service	4	4	0.3	25	23	14,560	16,696	419	460	0.4

Source: County Business Patterns, 1992/93, CBP-92/93-1, U.S. Department of Commerce, Washington, D.C., April 1995. SIC categories for which data were suppressed or not available for both 1992 and 1993 are not displayed. The employment columns represent mid-March employment in the year. Pay per employee is calculated by dividing 1st Quarter payroll, annualized, by mid-March employment. The columns headed "% State" show the county's percentage of the state total for the SIC in 1993; for example, 0.9% for SIC 6030 means that the county had 0.9 percent of the state's total establishments (or payroll) in SIC 6030 in 1993. A dash (-) is used to indicate that data are not available or cannot be calculated; nec means not elsewhere classified.

Continued on next page.

SIC	Industry	No. Establishments			Employment		Pay / Employee		Annual Payroll ($ 000)		
		1992	1993	% State	1992	1993	1992	1993	1992	1993	% State
IZARD, AR - [continued]											
6500	Real estate	12	12	0.8	47	46	9,191	6,522	475	348	0.3
6510	Real estate operators and lessors	3	2	0.3	7	-	6,286	-	52	-	-
6530	Real estate agents and managers	7	9	1.4	36	38	9,667	6,526	386	286	0.6
JACKSON, AR											
60 –	**Finance, insurance, and real estate**	39	38	0.8	165	161	16,873	18,658	3,204	3,222	0.3
6000	Depository institutions	10	10	1.0	94	95	18,766	19,663	2,002	2,065	0.6
6400	Insurance agents, brokers, and service	11	11	0.9	27	-	16,889	-	398	-	-
6500	Real estate	11	11	0.7	-	28	-	12,143	-	495	0.4
6510	Real estate operators and lessors	5	6	0.9	17	-	9,176	-	152	-	-
6530	Real estate agents and managers	2	3	0.5	-	6	-	18,667	-	127	0.3
6700	Holding and other investment offices	5	4	2.2	5	-	10,400	-	39	-	-
JEFFERSON, AR											
60 –	**Finance, insurance, and real estate**	143	143	3.1	1,320	1,339	18,748	19,053	24,912	25,446	2.6
6000	Depository institutions	36	36	3.5	735	741	20,827	20,707	14,730	14,484	4.4
6020	Commercial banks	27	27	3.2	667	680	20,828	20,841	13,788	13,257	4.7
6100	Nondepository institutions	6	3	2.2	25	-	15,200	-	396	-	-
6200	Security and commodity brokers	3	4	2.1	10	11	32,000	46,182	409	548	0.3
6300	Insurance carriers	14	13	3.7	73	79	29,808	25,570	2,103	1,951	1.3
6310	Life insurance	4	6	4.7	-	62	-	22,581	-	1,382	2.3
6330	Fire, marine, and casualty insurance	6	4	3.2	13	-	23,692	-	324	-	-
6400	Insurance agents, brokers, and service	34	39	3.2	107	128	21,645	21,531	2,595	3,037	2.9
6500	Real estate	42	43	2.8	356	356	10,697	11,169	4,217	4,258	3.8
6510	Real estate operators and lessors	17	17	2.6	97	191	10,722	11,079	1,105	2,056	6.8
6530	Real estate agents and managers	18	19	3.0	233	138	10,163	10,290	2,662	1,704	3.4
6700	Holding and other investment offices	8	5	2.7	14	-	31,429	-	462	-	-
JOHNSON, AR											
60 –	**Finance, insurance, and real estate**	25	28	0.6	146	162	20,000	18,420	3,785	3,171	0.3
6000	Depository institutions	7	7	0.7	87	100	20,276	17,600	2,175	1,907	0.6
6400	Insurance agents, brokers, and service	7	8	0.7	29	-	17,517	-	376	-	-
6500	Real estate	11	12	0.8	30	-	21,600	-	1,234	-	-
6510	Real estate operators and lessors	4	5	0.8	-	17	-	25,412	-	543	1.8
6530	Real estate agents and managers	4	4	0.6	-	6	-	10,667	-	98	0.2
LAFAYETTE, AR											
60 –	**Finance, insurance, and real estate**	11	10	0.2	76	75	16,474	21,920	1,342	1,482	0.2
6000	Depository institutions	4	4	0.4	-	49	-	25,551	-	1,124	0.3
6020	Commercial banks	4	4	0.5	-	49	-	25,551	-	1,124	0.4
6400	Insurance agents, brokers, and service	3	3	0.2	10	-	8,800	-	82	-	-
LAWRENCE, AR											
60 –	**Finance, insurance, and real estate**	24	27	0.6	125	144	18,048	16,750	2,403	2,528	0.3
6000	Depository institutions	11	11	1.1	92	109	21,217	18,826	2,059	2,140	0.7
6400	Insurance agents, brokers, and service	8	8	0.7	18	-	10,667	-	217	-	-
6500	Real estate	4	6	0.4	-	16	-	7,000	-	121	0.1
6510	Real estate operators and lessors	1	3	0.5	-	4	-	6,000	-	24	0.1
LEE, AR											
60 –	**Finance, insurance, and real estate**	14	13	0.3	58	56	19,793	17,143	1,155	1,157	0.1
6400	Insurance agents, brokers, and service	4	3	0.2	10	-	15,600	-	163	-	-
6500	Real estate	4	5	0.3	4	5	8,000	7,200	33	42	0.0
LINCOLN, AR											
60 –	**Finance, insurance, and real estate**	9	9	0.2	54	53	16,296	21,208	1,008	1,110	0.1

Source: County Business Patterns, 1992/93, CBP-92/93-1, U.S. Department of Commerce, Washington, D.C., April 1995. SIC categories for which data were suppressed or not available for both 1992 and 1993 are not displayed. The employment columns represent mid-March employment in the year. Pay per employee is calculated by dividing 1st Quarter payroll, annualized, by mid-March employment. The columns headed "% State" show the county's percentage of the state total for the SIC in 1993; for example, 0.9% for SIC 6030 means that the county had 0.9 percent of the state's total establishments (or payroll) in SIC 6030 in 1993. A dash (-) is used to indicate that data are not available or cannot be calculated; nec means not elsewhere classified.

SIC	Industry	No. Establishments			Employment		Pay / Employee		Annual Payroll ($ 000)		
		1992	1993	% State	1992	1993	1992	1993	1992	1993	% State
LITTLE RIVER, AR											
60 –	**Finance, insurance, and real estate**	18	18	0.4	93	115	16,559	17,843	1,647	2,042	0.2
6000	Depository institutions	7	6	0.6	55	71	17,964	20,563	1,042	1,395	0.4
6500	Real estate	6	7	0.5	-	15	-	6,667	-	128	0.1
6510	Real estate operators and lessors	4	5	0.8	4	-	5,000	-	20	-	-
LOGAN, AR											
60 –	**Finance, insurance, and real estate**	34	38	0.8	182	182	15,824	16,901	3,038	3,235	0.3
6000	Depository institutions	12	11	1.1	130	126	17,262	18,667	2,381	2,406	0.7
6020	Commercial banks	9	8	1.0	122	117	17,508	19,111	2,268	2,290	0.8
6400	Insurance agents, brokers, and service	9	12	1.0	19	20	19,789	16,600	364	400	0.4
6500	Real estate	9	9	0.6	25	15	7,840	8,800	217	150	0.1
6510	Real estate operators and lessors	4	2	0.3	15	-	6,400	-	111	-	-
6530	Real estate agents and managers	3	5	0.8	6	7	8,000	8,000	46	65	0.1
LONOKE, AR											
60 –	**Finance, insurance, and real estate**	39	48	1.0	250	249	17,296	18,040	4,862	5,136	0.5
6000	Depository institutions	14	14	1.3	183	176	18,885	19,068	3,813	3,858	1.2
6400	Insurance agents, brokers, and service	10	16	1.3	26	36	12,308	14,556	339	552	0.5
6500	Real estate	9	14	0.9	19	29	10,526	10,621	222	417	0.4
6510	Real estate operators and lessors	3	3	0.5	7	7	6,857	8,000	69	29	0.1
6530	Real estate agents and managers	3	7	1.1	-	13	-	10,154	-	233	0.5
MADISON, AR											
60 –	**Finance, insurance, and real estate**	13	13	0.3	63	67	15,492	16,358	1,082	1,197	0.1
6000	Depository institutions	5	5	0.5	48	53	17,167	17,434	901	1,011	0.3
6020	Commercial banks	4	5	0.6	-	53	-	17,434	-	1,011	0.4
6400	Insurance agents, brokers, and service	3	3	0.2	-	7	-	13,714	-	99	0.1
6500	Real estate	4	4	0.3	7	-	6,857	-	74	-	-
MARION, AR											
60 –	**Finance, insurance, and real estate**	22	20	0.4	89	101	14,427	15,644	1,454	1,658	0.2
6000	Depository institutions	8	7	0.7	64	72	15,125	17,222	1,054	1,175	0.4
6400	Insurance agents, brokers, and service	3	4	0.3	8	12	15,500	13,000	143	171	0.2
6500	Real estate	10	9	0.6	-	17	-	10,824	-	312	0.3
6530	Real estate agents and managers	5	6	0.9	6	-	12,667	-	98	-	-
MILLER, AR											
60 –	**Finance, insurance, and real estate**	57	52	1.1	487	513	20,665	22,214	10,463	11,319	1.2
6000	Depository institutions	12	12	1.2	294	303	21,619	22,257	6,755	6,974	2.1
6300	Insurance carriers	14	13	3.7	98	111	25,429	26,486	2,578	2,728	1.9
6310	Life insurance	4	5	3.9	71	83	28,169	31,663	1,938	2,454	4.1
6400	Insurance agents, brokers, and service	11	10	0.8	28	33	20,429	27,758	562	1,052	1.0
6500	Real estate	14	12	0.8	43	53	8,930	11,849	398	412	0.4
6510	Real estate operators and lessors	7	8	1.2	26	-	5,385	-	176	-	-
6530	Real estate agents and managers	4	2	0.3	6	-	8,667	-	45	-	-
MISSISSIPPI, AR											
60 –	**Finance, insurance, and real estate**	88	91	1.9	509	562	17,807	20,028	9,686	11,830	1.2
6000	Depository institutions	23	23	2.2	311	340	16,926	16,859	5,429	5,842	1.8
6020	Commercial banks	15	18	2.2	233	-	17,099	-	4,066	-	-
6300	Insurance carriers	4	4	1.1	11	10	22,909	27,600	263	268	0.2
6400	Insurance agents, brokers, and service	24	26	2.1	61	71	16,197	14,141	1,021	1,105	1.1
6500	Real estate	31	30	1.9	95	77	9,516	10,442	1,066	934	0.8
6510	Real estate operators and lessors	16	16	2.4	54	65	7,926	8,308	474	597	2.0
6530	Real estate agents and managers	9	10	1.6	28	6	7,429	12,000	195	102	0.2

Source: County Business Patterns, 1992/93, CBP-92/93-1, U.S. Department of Commerce, Washington, D.C., April 1995. SIC categories for which data were suppressed or not available for both 1992 and 1993 are not displayed. The employment columns represent mid-March employment in the year. Pay per employee is calculated by dividing 1st Quarter payroll, annualized, by mid-March employment. The columns headed "% State" show the county's percentage of the state total for the SIC in 1993; for example, 0.9% for SIC 6030 means that the county had 0.9 percent of the state's total establishments (or payroll) in SIC 6030 in 1993. A dash (-) is used to indicate that data are not available or cannot be calculated; nec means not elsewhere classified.

SIC	Industry	No. Establishments			Employment		Pay / Employee		Annual Payroll ($ 000)		
		1992	1993	% State	1992	1993	1992	1993	1992	1993	% State
MONROE, AR											
60 –	**Finance, insurance, and real estate**	20	18	0.4	96	120	17,458	18,733	1,909	2,174	0.2
6000	Depository institutions	5	5	0.5	60	63	19,400	20,000	1,304	1,353	0.4
6400	Insurance agents, brokers, and service	6	6	0.5	10	8	17,600	19,000	177	168	0.2
6510	Real estate operators and lessors	6	4	0.6	16	-	11,500	-	194	-	-
MONTGOMERY, AR											
60 –	**Finance, insurance, and real estate**	5	6	0.1	29	32	14,759	14,250	500	530	0.1
NEVADA, AR											
60 –	**Finance, insurance, and real estate**	6	9	0.2	47	52	20,851	19,077	1,028	1,061	0.1
NEWTON, AR											
60 –	**Finance, insurance, and real estate**	3	3	0.1	-	-	-	-	-	-	-
OUACHITA, AR											
60 –	**Finance, insurance, and real estate**	42	44	0.9	217	290	17,235	18,993	3,938	5,824	0.6
6000	Depository institutions	19	18	1.7	147	151	18,803	17,245	2,778	2,946	0.9
6020	Commercial banks	13	13	1.6	115	122	18,574	16,721	2,160	2,293	0.8
6300	Insurance carriers	4	2	0.6	17	-	11,294	-	190	-	-
6400	Insurance agents, brokers, and service	7	11	0.9	26	37	13,692	15,351	429	701	0.7
6500	Real estate	7	8	0.5	15	-	12,000	-	194	-	-
6510	Real estate operators and lessors	4	4	0.6	6	-	7,333	-	58	-	-
PERRY, AR											
60 –	**Finance, insurance, and real estate**	3	3	0.1	-	-	-	-	-	-	-
PHILLIPS, AR											
60 –	**Finance, insurance, and real estate**	35	38	0.8	257	250	16,732	18,080	4,516	4,717	0.5
6000	Depository institutions	7	7	0.7	154	152	19,247	20,316	3,122	3,147	1.0
6020	Commercial banks	7	7	0.8	154	152	19,247	20,316	3,122	3,147	1.1
6400	Insurance agents, brokers, and service	6	6	0.5	29	28	20,276	21,571	624	632	0.6
6500	Real estate	18	20	1.3	67	65	9,433	10,338	668	728	0.6
6510	Real estate operators and lessors	10	11	1.7	47	45	8,000	9,511	399	465	1.5
6530	Real estate agents and managers	3	5	0.8	5	7	12,800	11,429	84	100	0.2
PIKE, AR											
60 –	**Finance, insurance, and real estate**	14	14	0.3	95	96	15,537	16,292	1,697	1,775	0.2
6000	Depository institutions	5	5	0.5	71	79	17,465	17,114	1,449	1,548	0.5
6020	Commercial banks	5	5	0.6	71	79	17,465	17,114	1,449	1,548	0.5
POINSETT, AR											
60 –	**Finance, insurance, and real estate**	38	35	0.7	250	248	18,352	16,306	5,211	4,653	0.5
6000	Depository institutions	11	12	1.2	130	144	18,000	17,083	2,703	2,872	0.9
6400	Insurance agents, brokers, and service	10	10	0.8	26	-	8,615	-	238	-	-
6500	Real estate	12	11	0.7	30	42	17,600	12,476	666	695	0.6
6510	Real estate operators and lessors	6	7	1.1	22	37	15,818	12,108	457	613	2.0
POLK, AR											
60 –	**Finance, insurance, and real estate**	21	24	0.5	119	170	13,513	16,682	2,343	2,816	0.3
6000	Depository institutions	7	7	0.7	61	-	17,377	-	1,729	-	-
6400	Insurance agents, brokers, and service	4	5	0.4	38	-	10,211	-	402	-	-
6500	Real estate	9	12	0.8	-	15	-	6,667	-	145	0.1
6510	Real estate operators and lessors	4	4	0.6	3	6	2,667	3,333	28	36	0.1
6530	Real estate agents and managers	3	5	0.8	4	4	12,000	12,000	48	69	0.1

Source: County Business Patterns, 1992/93, CBP-92/93-1, U.S. Department of Commerce, Washington, D.C., April 1995. SIC categories for which data were suppressed or not available for both 1992 and 1993 are not displayed. The employment columns represent mid-March employment in the year. Pay per employee is calculated by dividing 1st Quarter payroll, annualized, by mid-March employment. The columns headed "% State" show the county's percentage of the state total for the SIC in 1993; for example, 0.9% for SIC 6030 means that the county had 0.9 percent of the state's total establishments (or payroll) in SIC 6030 in 1993. A dash (-) is used to indicate that data are not available or cannot be calculated; nec means not elsewhere classified.

SIC	Industry	No. Establishments			Employment		Pay / Employee		Annual Payroll ($ 000)		
		1992	1993	% State	1992	1993	1992	1993	1992	1993	% State
POPE, AR											
60 –	**Finance, insurance, and real estate**	88	100	2.1	555	547	19,027	19,846	10,287	11,231	1.2
6000	Depository institutions	26	23	2.2	279	269	18,452	18,216	4,724	4,953	1.5
6020	Commercial banks	22	20	2.4	255	253	18,855	18,482	4,445	4,729	1.7
6360	Title insurance	3	1	5.0	32	-	11,125	-	359	-	-
6400	Insurance agents, brokers, and service	20	28	2.3	58	76	15,586	14,474	961	1,196	1.1
6500	Real estate	26	36	2.3	66	81	9,758	11,160	704	1,063	0.9
6510	Real estate operators and lessors	8	11	1.7	10	20	8,400	9,000	88	180	0.6
6530	Real estate agents and managers	10	17	2.7	44	39	10,091	12,615	465	612	1.2
6540	Title abstract offices	1	4	3.6	-	12	-	14,000	-	211	1.3
6552	Subdividers and developers, n.e.c.	3	2	3.3	3	-	4,000		21	-	-
PRAIRIE, AR											
60 –	**Finance, insurance, and real estate**	10	11	0.2	51	53	15,451	15,623	936	970	0.1
6000	Depository institutions	5	6	0.6	-	44	-	16,727	-	832	0.3
6020	Commercial banks	5	6	0.7	-	44	-	16,727	-	832	0.3
6400	Insurance agents, brokers, and service	3	3	0.2	6	-	10,667	-	109	-	-
PULASKI, AR											
60 –	**Finance, insurance, and real estate**	1,172	1,180	25.2	14,709	14,308	30,403	32,686	437,234	467,945	48.5
6000	Depository institutions	177	190	18.3	2,945	2,797	23,746	25,454	69,343	68,955	21.0
6020	Commercial banks	128	141	16.9	2,382	2,234	24,163	25,449	56,350	53,128	18.7
6030	Savings institutions	22	12	12.1	241	191	20,830	22,827	5,605	5,000	19.1
6060	Credit unions	22	30	34.9	143	-	19,552	-	2,869	-	-
6090	Functions closely related to banking	4	6	31.6	-	133	-	28,632	-	4,313	-
6140	Personal credit institutions	18	7	33.3	252	196	26,048	29,490	6,584	5,871	64.0
6160	Mortgage bankers and brokers	34	39	53.4	481	639	29,979	28,782	14,405	20,595	83.7
6200	Security and commodity brokers	75	74	38.5	1,488	1,890	78,374	70,808	109,471	126,046	80.2
6210	Security brokers and dealers	43	43	32.1	1,319	1,378	83,685	92,049	95,814	114,434	79.5
6300	Insurance carriers	172	158	44.5	4,189	3,957	27,773	28,228	113,982	115,181	78.9
6310	Life insurance	71	72	56.7	1,776	1,608	25,070	25,256	43,464	42,783	72.2
6330	Fire, marine, and casualty insurance	61	48	38.1	904	829	33,712	32,893	28,805	27,140	75.2
6370	Pension, health, and welfare funds	15	14	29.8	111	72	12,432	17,389	1,371	1,511	44.9
6400	Insurance agents, brokers, and service	288	298	24.3	1,385	1,518	36,254	32,598	45,737	48,612	46.3
6500	Real estate	335	343	22.3	2,964	2,156	12,758	16,330	41,955	38,986	34.8
6510	Real estate operators and lessors	131	149	22.7	1,552	669	8,644	14,284	14,200	9,785	32.2
6530	Real estate agents and managers	134	150	23.6	939	1,213	17,887	16,768	18,847	22,492	45.2
6540	Title abstract offices	17	17	15.2	131	155	20,641	20,955	3,599	4,556	28.4
6552	Subdividers and developers, n.e.c.	17	12	20.0	191	31	14,010	27,742	3,030	615	4.8
6553	Cemetery subdividers and developers	11	13	19.4	65	86	15,508	13,907	1,041	1,356	47.7
6700	Holding and other investment offices	65	63	33.9	762	915	36,499	37,705	27,612	35,970	54.8
6710	Holding offices	23	24	42.9	528	696	41,008	42,879	22,055	30,991	56.2
6720	Investment offices	4	-	-	13	-	69,846		583	-	-
6732	Educational, religious, etc. trusts	15	17	43.6	141	167	18,383	19,545	2,577	3,234	75.5
6733	Trusts, n.e.c.	13	11	28.2	54	-	20,296	-	1,080	-	-
RANDOLPH, AR											
60 –	**Finance, insurance, and real estate**	21	22	0.5	114	121	20,912	21,157	2,821	2,923	0.3
6000	Depository institutions	7	7	0.7	80	85	23,700	22,306	2,220	2,294	0.7
6400	Insurance agents, brokers, and service	5	5	0.4	10	10	19,200	18,800	201	211	0.2
6510	Real estate operators and lessors	1	4	0.6	-	5	-	4,000	-	25	0.1
6530	Real estate agents and managers	3	2	0.3	4	-	4,000	-	18	-	-
ST. FRANCIS, AR											
60 –	**Finance, insurance, and real estate**	44	43	0.9	234	269	19,333	19,152	4,791	5,324	0.6
6000	Depository institutions	13	12	1.2	139	153	18,906	17,673	2,639	2,736	0.8
6400	Insurance agents, brokers, and service	13	12	1.0	26	-	15,692	-	450	-	-

Source: County Business Patterns, 1992/93, CBP-92/93-1, U.S. Department of Commerce, Washington, D.C., April 1995. SIC categories for which data were suppressed or not available for both 1992 and 1993 are *not* displayed. The employment columns represent mid-March employment in the year. Pay per employee is calculated by dividing 1st Quarter payroll, annualized, by mid-March employment. The columns headed "% State" show the county's percentage of the state total for the SIC in 1993; for example, 0.9% for SIC 6030 means that the county had 0.9 percent of the state's total establishments (or payroll) in SIC 6030 in 1993. A dash (-) is used to indicate that data are not available or cannot be calculated; *nec* means not elsewhere classified.

Continued on next page.

SIC	Industry	No. Establishments			Employment		Pay / Employee		Annual Payroll ($ 000)		
		1992	1993	% State	1992	1993	1992	1993	1992	1993	% State
ST. FRANCIS, AR - [continued]											
6500	Real estate	13	14	0.9	23	30	9,043	8,667	248	271	0.2
6510	Real estate operators and lessors	5	6	0.9	-	16	-	5,750	-	80	0.3
6530	Real estate agents and managers	5	5	0.8	9	6	10,667	12,000	95	66	0.1
SALINE, AR											
60 –	**Finance, insurance, and real estate**	72	77	1.6	381	400	17,606	15,390	7,089	7,201	0.7
6000	Depository institutions	13	14	1.3	198	213	20,283	16,695	4,075	3,863	1.2
6060	Credit unions	4	4	4.7	12	13	16,333	14,769	206	213	2.4
6300	Insurance carriers	6	5	1.4	27	-	17,037	-	517	-	-
6330	Fire, marine, and casualty insurance	4	3	2.4	-	19	-	22,947	-	492	1.4
6400	Insurance agents, brokers, and service	22	24	2.0	67	81	15,164	13,383	1,242	1,309	1.2
6500	Real estate	28	32	2.1	82	79	11,659	10,987	1,015	1,280	1.1
6510	Real estate operators and lessors	10	14	2.1	24	-	9,500	-	209	-	-
6530	Real estate agents and managers	8	14	2.2	16	23	15,000	13,391	310	631	1.3
SCOTT, AR											
60 –	**Finance, insurance, and real estate**	13	13	0.3	97	97	13,567	16,536	1,488	1,566	0.2
6000	Depository institutions	5	5	0.5	79	80	14,228	17,650	1,282	1,368	0.4
6500	Real estate	5	4	0.3	-	8	-	8,000	-	78	0.1
6530	Real estate agents and managers	3	3	0.5	5	-	5,600	-	34	-	-
SEARCY, AR											
60 –	**Finance, insurance, and real estate**	6	6	0.1	38	33	16,105	16,848	632	586	0.1
SEBASTIAN, AR											
60 –	**Finance, insurance, and real estate**	268	269	5.7	2,045	2,082	22,081	24,148	47,276	56,773	5.9
6000	Depository institutions	46	48	4.6	933	902	19,786	20,208	19,508	21,171	6.4
6020	Commercial banks	31	32	3.8	673	702	21,058	20,325	14,946	15,697	5.5
6100	Nondepository institutions	7	7	5.1	33	44	27,394	23,273	1,266	1,019	2.4
6160	Mortgage bankers and brokers	4	4	5.5	4	8	29,000	16,000	478	149	0.6
6200	Security and commodity brokers	15	13	6.8	67	73	42,925	45,589	2,923	3,226	2.1
6210	Security brokers and dealers	13	9	6.7	-	62	-	51,548	-	3,076	2.1
6280	Security and commodity services	2	4	7.4	-	11	-	12,000	-	150	1.2
6300	Insurance carriers	27	21	5.9	136	102	24,647	30,471	3,223	2,782	1.9
6330	Fire, marine, and casualty insurance	17	11	8.7	52	42	30,846	35,429	1,639	1,467	4.1
6400	Insurance agents, brokers, and service	72	81	6.6	281	313	20,840	19,540	6,106	6,616	6.3
6500	Real estate	86	85	5.5	280	336	14,014	14,202	4,320	5,963	5.3
6510	Real estate operators and lessors	43	46	7.0	158	190	12,304	13,011	2,083	2,809	9.2
6530	Real estate agents and managers	26	30	4.7	47	91	17,277	16,791	1,061	1,975	4.0
6540	Title abstract offices	5	4	3.6	46	40	17,391	13,500	818	900	5.6
6552	Subdividers and developers, n.e.c.	3	2	3.3	10	-	16,800	-	168	-	-
6553	Cemetery subdividers and developers	3	2	3.0	10	-	13,600	-	137	-	-
6700	Holding and other investment offices	15	14	7.5	315	312	31,060	43,910	9,930	15,996	24.4
SEVIER, AR											
60 –	**Finance, insurance, and real estate**	19	19	0.4	196	111	19,408	21,586	3,722	2,324	0.2
6000	Depository institutions	8	8	0.8	82	86	21,561	23,116	1,658	1,817	0.6
6400	Insurance agents, brokers, and service	7	8	0.7	-	17	-	17,412	-	384	0.4
6500	Real estate	3	3	0.2	-	8	-	14,000	-	123	0.1
SHARP, AR											
60 –	**Finance, insurance, and real estate**	33	32	0.7	160	166	15,875	16,000	2,749	2,909	0.3
6000	Depository institutions	10	10	1.0	102	109	18,353	18,128	1,955	2,021	0.6
6400	Insurance agents, brokers, and service	4	4	0.3	14	-	11,429	-	175	-	-
6500	Real estate	16	15	1.0	39	40	10,564	11,300	515	625	0.6
6530	Real estate agents and managers	11	9	1.4	28	27	9,857	10,963	348	376	0.8

Source: County Business Patterns, 1992/93, CBP-92/93-1, U.S. Department of Commerce, Washington, D.C., April 1995. SIC categories for which data were suppressed or not available for both 1992 and 1993 are *not* displayed. The employment columns represent mid-March employment in the year. Pay per employee is calculated by dividing 1st Quarter payroll, annualized, by mid-March employment. The columns headed "% State" show the county's percentage of the state total for the SIC in 1993; for example, 0.9% for SIC 6030 means that the county had 0.9 percent of the state's total establishments (or payroll) in SIC 6030 in 1993. A dash (-) is used to indicate that data are not available or cannot be calculated; *nec* means not elsewhere classified.

SIC	Industry	No. Establishments			Employment		Pay / Employee		Annual Payroll ($ 000)		
		1992	1993	% State	1992	1993	1992	1993	1992	1993	% State
STONE, AR											
60 –	**Finance, insurance, and real estate**	10	9	0.2	56	52	13,714	16,154	782	1,042	0.1
6400	Insurance agents, brokers, and service	6	5	0.4	17	-	10,588	-	181	-	-
6500	Real estate	2	3	0.2	-	7	-	8,571	-	96	0.1
UNION, AR											
60 –	**Finance, insurance, and real estate**	101	100	2.1	688	766	21,192	21,295	14,939	16,579	1.7
6000	Depository institutions	18	19	1.8	346	406	22,139	20,433	7,495	8,795	2.7
6300	Insurance carriers	16	14	3.9	84	138	24,143	21,420	2,362	2,812	1.9
6310	Life insurance	3	3	2.4	63	71	24,381	28,056	1,717	1,878	3.2
6400	Insurance agents, brokers, and service	20	22	1.8	69	68	20,928	21,059	1,559	1,598	1.5
6500	Real estate	25	27	1.8	105	77	10,933	13,143	1,483	1,078	1.0
6510	Real estate operators and lessors	14	14	2.1	65	33	7,815	7,515	742	281	0.9
6530	Real estate agents and managers	5	7	1.1	14	17	16,000	15,765	240	254	0.5
6540	Title abstract offices	3	3	2.7	20	-	16,000	-	403	-	-
6700	Holding and other investment offices	14	11	5.9	44	-	17,455	-	620	-	-
6733	Trusts, n.e.c.	5	3	7.7	3	2	17,333	6,000	94	41	1.6
6799	Investors, n.e.c.	5	4	11.1	19	-	11,579		220	-	-
VAN BUREN, AR											
60 –	**Finance, insurance, and real estate**	29	27	0.6	304	209	12,184	16,383	4,231	3,614	0.4
6000	Depository institutions	9	8	0.8	84	81	14,143	15,160	1,330	1,340	0.4
6020	Commercial banks	8	8	1.0	-	81	-	15,160	-	1,340	0.5
6400	Insurance agents, brokers, and service	6	8	0.7	13	-	12,308	-	187	-	-
6500	Real estate	10	8	0.5	200	106	10,560	16,453	2,438	1,792	1.6
WASHINGTON, AR											
60 –	**Finance, insurance, and real estate**	270	285	6.1	1,838	1,824	25,267	24,711	46,542	47,552	4.9
6000	Depository institutions	56	49	4.7	838	751	20,616	19,787	16,405	15,547	4.7
6020	Commercial banks	42	40	4.8	737	655	20,944	19,847	14,488	13,610	4.8
6030	Savings institutions	10	6	6.1	82	76	17,902	18,474	1,486	1,438	5.5
6100	Nondepository institutions	11	10	7.2	72	85	30,611	23,106	2,213	2,089	5.0
6140	Personal credit institutions	4	4	19.0	57	65	26,596	19,815	1,573	1,525	16.6
6150	Business credit institutions	4	3	14.3	6	7	86,000	52,000	372	210	14.1
6160	Mortgage bankers and brokers	3	2	2.7	9	-	19,111	-	268	-	-
6200	Security and commodity brokers	14	13	6.8	149	157	56,859	62,981	8,770	10,108	6.4
6210	Security brokers and dealers	8	8	6.0	125	137	64,096	65,606	8,100	9,317	6.5
6280	Security and commodity services	6	5	9.3	24	20	19,167	45,000	670	791	6.1
6300	Insurance carriers	26	22	6.2	141	127	28,709	30,583	4,151	3,877	2.7
6330	Fire, marine, and casualty insurance	13	12	9.5	54	58	33,481	34,690	1,838	2,085	5.8
6370	Pension, health, and welfare funds	5	3	6.4	12	-	26,000	-	413	-	-
6400	Insurance agents, brokers, and service	58	65	5.3	197	253	18,782	19,273	4,514	5,759	5.5
6500	Real estate	96	113	7.3	362	360	14,254	13,800	4,958	5,596	5.0
6510	Real estate operators and lessors	48	57	8.7	170	139	12,706	11,281	2,140	1,581	5.2
6530	Real estate agents and managers	38	46	7.2	139	176	17,324	15,614	2,126	3,209	6.4
6553	Cemetery subdividers and developers	4	5	7.5	6	8	6,000	8,500	37	88	3.1
6700	Holding and other investment offices	9	13	7.0	79	91	70,633	50,901	5,531	4,576	7.0
6733	Trusts, n.e.c.	3	4	10.3	-	4	-	26,000	-	48	1.8
WHITE, AR											
60 –	**Finance, insurance, and real estate**	91	96	2.1	503	511	15,618	16,524	8,661	9,176	1.0
6000	Depository institutions	26	26	2.5	284	286	18,930	18,685	5,653	5,642	1.7
6020	Commercial banks	22	22	2.6	277	277	19,090	18,975	5,564	5,545	1.9
6060	Credit unions	4	4	4.7	7	9	12,571	9,778	89	97	1.1
6300	Insurance carriers	3	4	1.1	-	24	-	4,833	-	176	0.1
6370	Pension, health, and welfare funds	3	4	8.5	-	24	-	4,833	-	176	5.2
6400	Insurance agents, brokers, and service	28	31	2.5	65	84	12,062	16,143	889	1,575	1.5

Source: County Business Patterns, 1992/93, CBP-92/93-1, U.S. Department of Commerce, Washington, D.C., April 1995. SIC categories for which data were suppressed or not available for both 1992 and 1993 are not displayed. The employment columns represent mid-March employment in the year. Pay per employee is calculated by dividing 1st Quarter payroll, annualized, by mid-March employment. The columns headed "% State" show the county's percentage of the state total for the SIC in 1993; for example, 0.9% for SIC 6030 means that the county had 0.9 percent of the state's total establishments (or payroll) in SIC 6030 in 1993. A dash (-) is used to indicate that data are not available or cannot be calculated; nec means not elsewhere classified.

Continued on next page.

SIC	Industry	No. Establishments			Employment		Pay / Employee		Annual Payroll ($ 000)		
		1992	1993	% State	1992	1993	1992	1993	1992	1993	% State
WHITE, AR - [continued]											
6500	Real estate	30	29	*1.9*	85	99	9,224	8,606	1,007	1,116	*1.0*
6510	Real estate operators and lessors	14	16	*2.4*	34	-	8,824	-	372	-	-
6530	Real estate agents and managers	11	10	*1.6*	26	24	8,462	9,333	237	253	*0.5*
WOODRUFF, AR											
60 –	**Finance, insurance, and real estate**	12	11	*0.2*	57	65	20,912	19,385	1,363	1,461	*0.2*
6000	Depository institutions	4	4	*0.4*	45	47	22,400	21,957	1,199	1,232	*0.4*
6020	Commercial banks	4	4	*0.5*	45	47	22,400	21,957	1,199	1,232	*0.4*
6400	Insurance agents, brokers, and service	4	3	*0.2*	8	-	21,500	-	140	-	-
6500	Real estate	4	4	*0.3*	4	-	3,000	-	24	-	-
YELL, AR											
60 –	**Finance, insurance, and real estate**	24	22	*0.5*	132	135	18,545	16,652	2,804	2,612	*0.3*
6000	Depository institutions	7	7	*0.7*	96	92	19,000	17,783	2,183	2,018	*0.6*
6400	Insurance agents, brokers, and service	6	7	*0.6*	13	22	11,077	10,182	153	201	*0.2*
6530	Real estate agents and managers	3	3	*0.5*	3	4	10,667	11,000	56	65	*0.1*

Source: County Business Patterns, 1992/93, CBP-92/93-1, U.S. Department of Commerce, Washington, D.C., April 1995. SIC categories for which data were suppressed or not available for both 1992 and 1993 are *not* displayed. The employment columns represent mid-March employment in the year. Pay per employee is calculated by dividing 1st Quarter payroll, annualized, by mid-March employment. The columns headed "% State" show the county's percentage of the state total for the SIC in 1993; for example, 0.9% for SIC 6030 means that the county had 0.9 percent of the state's total establishments (or payroll) in SIC 6030 in 1993. A dash (-) is used to indicate that data are not available or cannot be calculated; *nec* means not elsewhere classified.

CALIFORNIA

SIC	Industry	No. Establishments			Employment		Pay / Employee		Annual Payroll ($ 000)		
		1992	1993	% State	1992	1993	1992	1993	1992	1993	% State
ALAMEDA, CA											
60 –	**Finance, insurance, and real estate**	3,135	3,118	*4.1*	29,912	30,666	28,282	28,203	838,600	900,022	*3.1*
6000	Depository institutions	489	455	*4.1*	10,721	10,468	27,022	26,247	276,845	268,901	*3.6*
6020	Commercial banks	243	195	*3.3*	5,933	5,808	24,970	23,489	139,865	132,446	*2.8*
6030	Savings institutions	141	138	*4.7*	4,063	3,539	30,952	31,834	120,019	109,751	*6.7*
6060	Credit unions	65	78	*6.2*	558	755	23,412	23,857	13,605	18,248	*4.3*
6090	Functions closely related to banking	40	44	*4.6*	167	366	16,383	20,929	3,356	8,456	*3.1*
6100	Nondepository institutions	264	268	*3.6*	2,052	2,056	38,823	36,333	80,524	89,433	*3.0*
6140	Personal credit institutions	96	76	*4.6*	856	802	30,589	26,793	24,405	25,277	*4.7*
6150	Business credit institutions	28	28	*4.1*	319	275	52,765	52,902	14,250	13,548	*2.4*
6160	Mortgage bankers and brokers	133	163	*3.3*	809	978	42,897	39,517	39,829	50,577	*2.7*
6200	Security and commodity brokers	93	111	*2.7*	1,041	1,134	63,143	54,466	57,797	65,850	*1.7*
6210	Security brokers and dealers	47	52	*2.5*	672	640	57,601	60,294	36,852	41,739	*1.6*
6300	Insurance carriers	260	210	*4.5*	4,856	4,701	29,066	32,574	146,197	165,283	*2.8*
6310	Life insurance	42	33	*3.3*	741	647	29,020	31,190	20,095	18,785	*1.5*
6321	Accident and health insurance	6	4	*6.3*	20	35	39,600	54,514	2,586	1,762	*4.3*
6324	Hospital and medical service plans	9	14	*5.5*	473	765	39,577	28,068	17,244	33,315	*3.5*
6330	Fire, marine, and casualty insurance	104	93	*4.1*	2,437	2,226	26,695	33,750	67,044	72,985	*2.6*
6360	Title insurance	32	42	*7.3*	669	639	35,785	35,750	25,368	25,245	*4.6*
6370	Pension, health, and welfare funds	63	19	*5.3*	490	353	20,049	28,986	12,161	11,275	*7.7*
6400	Insurance agents, brokers, and service	431	478	*4.0*	2,155	2,537	31,586	31,696	71,275	82,911	*3.4*
6500	Real estate	1,435	1,435	*4.4*	7,699	7,989	19,298	18,594	154,455	157,470	*3.5*
6510	Real estate operators and lessors	694	752	*5.1*	3,846	4,278	14,998	15,464	60,940	69,441	*5.3*
6530	Real estate agents and managers	562	596	*3.9*	2,979	3,125	22,026	20,934	67,471	69,802	*2.6*
6540	Title abstract offices	23	21	*7.8*	180	163	29,000	30,773	5,295	5,742	*4.1*
6552	Subdividers and developers, n.e.c.	50	43	*3.2*	278	200	34,460	30,300	10,439	6,062	*2.0*
6553	Cemetery subdividers and developers	10	10	*4.2*	176	178	28,614	24,180	4,998	4,766	*4.1*
6700	Holding and other investment offices	146	144	*4.0*	912	1,356	34,518	37,690	30,213	51,162	*3.6*
6710	Holding offices	23	26	*4.0*	277	719	46,253	48,506	12,557	33,524	*4.9*
6720	Investment offices	7	4	*3.9*	27	5	30,370	16,800	706	72	*0.1*
6732	Educational, religious, etc. trusts	39	39	*5.8*	281	205	15,502	16,878	3,958	3,718	*2.5*
6733	Trusts, n.e.c.	50	40	*4.4*	89	230	15,101	32,209	1,833	8,474	*8.8*
6794	Patent owners and lessors	8	7	*2.9*	48	-	37,750	-	1,838	-	-
6799	Investors, n.e.c.	14	24	*2.9*	132	111	63,273	20,144	7,136	2,444	*1.3*
ALPINE, CA											
60 –	**Finance, insurance, and real estate**	2	2	*0.0*	-	-	-	-	-	-	-
AMADOR, CA											
60 –	**Finance, insurance, and real estate**	75	69	*0.1*	486	471	17,506	17,461	8,463	8,170	*0.0*
6000	Depository institutions	18	17	*0.2*	151	172	20,185	18,070	2,913	3,114	*0.0*
6020	Commercial banks	11	10	*0.2*	117	136	20,855	17,853	2,275	2,408	*0.1*
6200	Security and commodity brokers	4	5	*0.1*	8	-	14,500	-	109	-	-
6300	Insurance carriers	9	5	*0.1*	166	127	20,602	21,638	3,626	2,674	*0.0*
6400	Insurance agents, brokers, and service	14	14	*0.1*	-	64	-	16,938	-	1,177	*0.0*
6500	Real estate	29	26	*0.1*	118	100	10,475	11,600	1,207	986	*0.0*
6510	Real estate operators and lessors	10	11	*0.1*	52	58	9,538	7,931	483	457	*0.0*
6530	Real estate agents and managers	3	9	*0.1*	-	27	-	11,704	-	334	*0.0*
6552	Subdividers and developers, n.e.c.	5	5	*0.4*	15	-	6,133	-	98	-	-

Source: County Business Patterns, 1992/93, CBP-92/93-1, U.S. Department of Commerce, Washington, D.C., April 1995. SIC categories for which data were suppressed or not available for both 1992 and 1993 are *not* displayed. The employment columns represent mid-March employment in the year. Pay per employee is calculated by dividing 1st Quarter payroll, annualized, by mid-March employment. The columns headed "% State" show the county's percentage of the state total for the SIC in 1993; for example, 0.9% for SIC 6030 means that the county had 0.9 percent of the state's total establishments (or payroll) in SIC 6030 in 1993. A dash (-) is used to indicate that data are not available or cannot be calculated; *nec* means not elsewhere classified.

SIC	Industry	No. Establishments			Employment		Pay / Employee		Annual Payroll ($ 000)		
		1992	1993	% State	1992	1993	1992	1993	1992	1993	% State
BUTTE, CA											
60 –	**Finance, insurance, and real estate**	393	401	0.5	2,836	2,845	20,568	20,458	58,812	59,521	0.2
6000	Depository institutions	72	65	0.6	1,037	976	21,527	20,463	20,431	18,869	0.3
6020	Commercial banks	43	40	0.7	738	752	22,130	20,856	15,218	14,301	0.3
6030	Savings institutions	17	13	0.4	224	152	20,607	19,447	3,815	3,133	0.2
6100	Nondepository institutions	26	27	0.4	140	116	34,771	30,448	4,891	4,180	0.1
6160	Mortgage bankers and brokers	16	16	0.3	85	59	38,447	31,458	3,253	2,370	0.1
6200	Security and commodity brokers	20	26	0.6	82	103	40,049	41,709	3,610	4,670	0.1
6210	Security brokers and dealers	14	18	0.9	69	69	44,754	52,580	3,349	3,865	0.1
6280	Security and commodity services	4	8	0.4	-	34	-	19,647	-	805	0.1
6300	Insurance carriers	28	26	0.6	429	375	24,233	25,771	10,305	9,311	0.2
6330	Fire, marine, and casualty insurance	14	17	0.8	39	40	49,641	47,100	1,912	2,008	0.1
6400	Insurance agents, brokers, and service	77	84	0.7	290	369	22,055	27,024	7,025	10,371	0.4
6500	Real estate	161	162	0.5	834	878	12,878	11,895	12,002	11,689	0.3
6510	Real estate operators and lessors	63	72	0.5	179	320	9,698	8,738	2,095	3,201	0.2
6530	Real estate agents and managers	71	77	0.5	532	369	12,752	13,138	7,448	5,341	0.2
6552	Subdividers and developers, n.e.c.	9	11	0.8	24	-	22,500		821	-	-
6700	Holding and other investment offices	9	11	0.3	24	28	13,500	11,571	548	431	0.0
CALAVERAS, CA											
60 –	**Finance, insurance, and real estate**	71	68	0.1	325	348	20,935	20,471	6,340	7,213	0.0
6000	Depository institutions	12	11	0.1	150	149	19,280	20,483	2,746	2,984	0.0
6300	Insurance carriers	11	7	0.2	66	-	31,091	-	1,719	-	-
6400	Insurance agents, brokers, and service	6	12	0.1	-	57	-	21,825	-	1,294	0.1
6500	Real estate	35	34	0.1	67	105	14,149	18,248	976	1,944	0.0
6510	Real estate operators and lessors	5	7	0.0	14	25	22,286	17,920	372	514	0.0
6530	Real estate agents and managers	23	23	0.1	29	47	11,448	21,447	321	596	0.0
6552	Subdividers and developers, n.e.c.	4	4	0.3	20	33	12,600	13,939	240	834	0.3
COLUSA, CA											
60 –	**Finance, insurance, and real estate**	29	27	0.0	154	166	16,649	17,566	2,589	2,946	0.0
6000	Depository institutions	10	9	0.1	81	79	14,074	15,342	1,073	1,207	0.0
6500	Real estate	10	10	0.0	36	37	15,222	17,189	579	684	0.0
6510	Real estate operators and lessors	6	7	0.0	11	22	10,909	15,455	144	350	0.0
CONTRA COSTA, CA											
60 –	**Finance, insurance, and real estate**	2,873	2,787	3.7	31,159	34,196	34,561	34,802	1,065,006	1,231,943	4.3
6000	Depository institutions	735	494	4.4	12,980	14,110	33,305	34,985	417,744	485,009	6.6
6020	Commercial banks	566	331	5.5	11,074	12,201	34,369	36,493	366,845	434,467	9.3
6030	Savings institutions	109	107	3.7	1,524	1,523	26,945	26,295	40,072	42,229	2.6
6060	Credit unions	42	42	3.3	283	323	26,375	22,068	7,942	6,933	1.6
6090	Functions closely related to banking	16	14	1.5	-	63	-	19,111	-	1,380	0.5
6100	Nondepository institutions	281	344	4.7	2,695	3,195	40,784	35,050	117,059	137,008	4.6
6140	Personal credit institutions	61	54	3.2	532	490	32,526	24,710	16,950	12,186	2.3
6150	Business credit institutions	25	23	3.4	263	154	41,171	36,026	9,379	6,054	1.1
6160	Mortgage bankers and brokers	191	265	5.4	1,892	2,550	43,099	36,960	90,386	118,564	6.4
6200	Security and commodity brokers	154	168	4.1	793	935	59,435	70,794	47,054	61,986	1.6
6210	Security brokers and dealers	75	76	3.7	572	600	66,762	83,267	36,519	44,095	1.7
6280	Security and commodity services	76	87	4.5	-	332	-	48,747	-	17,779	1.5
6300	Insurance carriers	253	213	4.6	5,575	6,257	37,131	36,267	199,245	227,952	3.9
6310	Life insurance	54	56	5.6	2,581	3,633	38,404	35,043	94,665	125,089	10.2
6330	Fire, marine, and casualty insurance	111	87	3.8	1,508	1,175	34,570	39,047	49,061	45,757	1.6
6350	Surety insurance	5	6	5.8	-	197	-	32,264	-	6,661	7.7
6360	Title insurance	38	40	6.9	774	619	37,039	37,073	30,112	25,841	4.7
6370	Pension, health, and welfare funds	36	16	4.5	191	112	29,634	35,500	5,363	3,840	2.6
6400	Insurance agents, brokers, and service	386	435	3.7	2,646	2,497	31,952	32,790	86,993	88,984	3.6
6500	Real estate	984	1,047	3.2	5,617	6,130	25,481	22,688	145,554	156,169	3.5
6510	Real estate operators and lessors	357	410	2.8	1,461	1,629	17,051	14,880	25,648	27,600	2.1
6530	Real estate agents and managers	453	551	3.6	3,111	3,839	26,971	24,130	83,307	103,487	3.9

Source: County Business Patterns, 1992/93, CBP-92/93-1, U.S. Department of Commerce, Washington, D.C., April 1995. SIC categories for which data were suppressed or not available for both 1992 and 1993 are not displayed. The employment columns represent mid-March employment in the year. Pay per employee is calculated by dividing 1st Quarter payroll, annualized, by mid-March employment. The columns headed "% State" show the county's percentage of the state total for the SIC in 1993; for example, 0.9% for SIC 6030 means that the county had 0.9 percent of the state's total establishments (or payroll) in SIC 6030 in 1993. A dash (-) is used to indicate that data are not available or cannot be calculated; nec means not elsewhere classified.

Continued on next page.

SIC	Industry	No. Establishments			Employment		Pay / Employee		Annual Payroll ($ 000)		
		1992	1993	% State	1992	1993	1992	1993	1992	1993	% State
CONTRA COSTA, CA - [continued]											
6540	Title abstract offices	14	12	4.5	133	–	27,368	–	4,765	–	–
6552	Subdividers and developers, n.e.c.	61	54	4.0	553	333	33,873	37,826	19,447	13,945	4.5
6553	Cemetery subdividers and developers	13	12	5.0	174	164	29,563	26,976	5,457	5,002	4.3
6700	Holding and other investment offices	72	79	2.2	598	848	63,759	71,094	35,987	63,975	4.6
6710	Holding offices	12	14	2.1	329	466	91,514	106,361	26,710	51,765	7.5
6720	Investment offices	6	4	3.9	62	–	56,065	–	4,264	–	–
6732	Educational, religious, etc. trusts	14	11	1.6	74	–	12,270	–	1,202	–	–
6733	Trusts, n.e.c.	18	20	2.2	66	59	27,394	25,085	1,853	1,483	1.5
6794	Patent owners and lessors	3	7	2.9	21	122	26,857	36,033	705	5,279	3.2
6798	Real estate investment trusts	5	1	0.8	7	–	13,143	–	68	–	–
6799	Investors, n.e.c.	13	22	2.7	36	–	28,111	–	967	–	–
DEL NORTE, CA											
60 –	**Finance, insurance, and real estate**	40	36	0.0	160	157	16,125	17,962	2,741	2,796	0.0
6000	Depository institutions	11	10	0.1	86	87	16,744	18,253	1,525	1,481	0.0
6020	Commercial banks	5	5	0.1	52	62	15,154	18,065	861	1,127	0.0
6500	Real estate	19	17	0.1	35	33	10,171	12,848	388	388	0.0
6510	Real estate operators and lessors	7	7	0.0	5	6	12,000	6,667	73	67	0.0
6530	Real estate agents and managers	9	7	0.0	12	7	8,333	9,714	86	71	0.0
EL DORADO, CA											
60 –	**Finance, insurance, and real estate**	302	312	0.4	2,154	2,028	19,146	19,418	44,533	43,448	0.2
6000	Depository institutions	45	43	0.4	583	508	18,655	19,402	10,692	10,110	0.1
6020	Commercial banks	22	19	0.3	371	303	18,059	18,917	6,393	5,699	0.1
6030	Savings institutions	18	19	0.7	179	172	19,933	20,930	3,737	3,851	0.2
6100	Nondepository institutions	20	28	0.4	91	101	29,451	25,584	3,575	3,431	0.1
6140	Personal credit institutions	3	3	0.2	17	–	16,235	–	298	–	–
6160	Mortgage bankers and brokers	17	24	0.5	74	81	32,486	28,099	3,277	3,152	0.2
6300	Insurance carriers	22	19	0.4	464	448	22,414	22,116	11,198	10,470	0.2
6360	Title insurance	6	8	1.4	73	64	26,137	28,188	1,840	1,912	0.3
6400	Insurance agents, brokers, and service	44	48	0.4	122	145	21,180	23,338	2,746	3,992	0.2
6500	Real estate	157	157	0.5	821	774	16,877	16,517	15,354	14,488	0.3
6510	Real estate operators and lessors	50	54	0.4	247	220	14,834	12,455	3,734	2,791	0.2
6530	Real estate agents and managers	68	74	0.5	389	431	14,211	15,258	6,516	7,172	0.3
6552	Subdividers and developers, n.e.c.	15	16	1.2	71	35	23,268	30,629	1,993	1,808	0.6
FRESNO, CA											
60 –	**Finance, insurance, and real estate**	1,444	1,432	1.9	13,974	13,831	25,174	24,479	349,775	349,555	1.2
6000	Depository institutions	231	206	1.8	3,723	3,749	21,259	21,607	74,909	76,675	1.0
6020	Commercial banks	136	117	2.0	2,507	2,663	21,109	21,989	50,579	55,202	1.2
6030	Savings institutions	56	45	1.5	788	599	22,741	21,643	15,853	11,603	0.7
6060	Credit unions	20	26	2.1	352	411	20,784	20,876	7,493	8,972	2.1
6090	Functions closely related to banking	19	18	1.9	76	76	13,053	11,895	984	898	0.3
6100	Nondepository institutions	131	152	2.1	942	1,002	33,592	29,194	31,588	36,757	1.2
6110	Federal and Federally-sponsored credit	1	5	7.7	–	66	–	40,182	–	2,666	4.8
6140	Personal credit institutions	53	46	2.8	330	321	26,352	24,835	9,010	7,846	1.5
6150	Business credit institutions	18	18	2.6	124	76	29,290	32,579	3,529	2,614	0.5
6160	Mortgage bankers and brokers	56	81	1.7	469	536	39,693	29,978	18,223	23,521	1.3
6200	Security and commodity brokers	51	57	1.4	369	391	65,214	56,123	22,907	21,911	0.6
6210	Security brokers and dealers	25	26	1.3	313	337	74,083	62,588	21,733	20,970	0.8
6300	Insurance carriers	162	137	3.0	3,263	3,400	27,119	27,689	88,940	96,045	1.7
6310	Life insurance	37	34	3.4	1,004	1,056	24,355	25,777	24,156	26,419	2.2
6330	Fire, marine, and casualty insurance	75	63	2.8	1,542	1,455	28,939	28,918	45,127	43,739	1.6
6360	Title insurance	12	12	2.1	330	335	30,048	31,522	10,444	11,100	2.0
6370	Pension, health, and welfare funds	26	18	5.0	–	387	–	21,674	–	8,747	6.0
6400	Insurance agents, brokers, and service	318	344	2.9	1,968	1,864	28,907	27,833	58,007	55,160	2.2
6500	Real estate	491	477	1.5	2,935	2,890	18,201	16,965	55,770	49,413	1.1
6510	Real estate operators and lessors	233	232	1.6	1,181	1,302	15,052	14,452	17,402	17,664	1.4

*Source: County Business Patterns, 1992/93, CBP-92/93-1, U.S. Department of Commerce, Washington, D.C., April 1995. SIC categories for which data were suppressed or not available for both 1992 and 1993 are *not* displayed. The employment columns represent mid-March employment in the year. Pay per employee is calculated by dividing 1st Quarter payroll, annualized, by mid-March employment. The columns headed "% State" show the county's percentage of the state total for the SIC in 1993; for example, 0.9% for SIC 6030 means that the county had 0.9 percent of the state's total establishments (or payroll) in SIC 6030 in 1993. A dash (-) is used to indicate that data are not available or cannot be calculated; *nec* means not elsewhere classified.*

Continued on next page.

SIC	Industry	No. Establishments			Employment		Pay / Employee		Annual Payroll ($ 000)		
		1992	1993	% State	1992	1993	1992	1993	1992	1993	% State
FRESNO, CA - [continued]											
6530	Real estate agents and managers	170	204	1.3	1,239	1,318	19,144	18,000	25,394	24,798	0.9
6552	Subdividers and developers, n.e.c.	30	30	2.2	154	120	16,519	17,833	3,032	2,463	0.8
6553	Cemetery subdividers and developers	5	5	2.1	112	103	33,143	30,524	3,288	3,070	2.7
6710	Holding offices	12	13	2.0	157	62	48,994	43,161	7,746	3,490	0.5
6720	Investment offices	3	-	-	20	-	27,400	-	371	-	-
6732	Educational, religious, etc. trusts	8	9	1.3	-	372	-	14,591	-	6,688	4.5
6733	Trusts, n.e.c.	21	18	2.0	-	48	-	21,333	-	1,083	1.1
6799	Investors, n.e.c.	7	10	1.2	-	17	-	38,588	-	623	0.3
GLENN, CA											
60 –	**Finance, insurance, and real estate**	33	35	0.0	150	150	17,493	18,293	2,649	2,817	0.0
6000	Depository institutions	7	7	0.1	61	58	18,098	20,897	1,046	1,168	0.0
6400	Insurance agents, brokers, and service	9	14	0.1	-	55	-	16,800	-	986	0.0
6500	Real estate	11	10	0.0	31	15	10,323	4,267	312	69	0.0
6510	Real estate operators and lessors	6	5	0.0	18	11	4,222	2,545	66	29	0.0
6530	Real estate agents and managers	4	5	0.0	5	4	8,800	9,000	46	40	0.0
HUMBOLDT, CA											
60 –	**Finance, insurance, and real estate**	251	265	0.4	1,625	1,677	18,986	18,693	32,567	34,346	0.1
6000	Depository institutions	48	45	0.4	662	641	18,526	18,964	12,019	12,265	0.2
6020	Commercial banks	28	25	0.4	465	448	17,781	18,929	7,935	8,588	0.2
6030	Savings institutions	7	7	0.2	72	65	21,278	21,169	1,483	999	0.1
6060	Credit unions	13	13	1.0	125	128	19,712	17,969	2,601	2,678	0.6
6100	Nondepository institutions	11	13	0.2	56	49	27,857	29,469	1,787	1,744	0.1
6140	Personal credit institutions	3	4	0.2	9	-	25,333	-	241	-	-
6200	Security and commodity brokers	9	7	0.2	48	50	65,500	44,480	2,620	2,705	0.1
6300	Insurance carriers	11	8	0.2	105	81	26,552	31,802	2,923	2,719	0.0
6330	Fire, marine, and casualty insurance	7	5	0.2	26	21	31,846	44,381	885	928	0.0
6400	Insurance agents, brokers, and service	50	54	0.5	182	200	20,000	21,680	4,135	5,066	0.2
6500	Real estate	112	127	0.4	388	409	13,258	13,751	6,094	6,136	0.1
6510	Real estate operators and lessors	56	59	0.4	142	218	13,380	13,890	2,501	2,971	0.2
6530	Real estate agents and managers	37	53	0.3	126	114	9,873	9,719	1,192	1,293	0.0
6552	Subdividers and developers, n.e.c.	8	7	0.5	-	9	-	29,333	-	503	0.2
6700	Holding and other investment offices	10	11	0.3	184	247	12,565	12,097	2,989	3,711	0.3
IMPERIAL, CA											
60 –	**Finance, insurance, and real estate**	164	165	0.2	1,149	1,193	18,865	18,126	21,172	22,669	0.1
6000	Depository institutions	35	33	0.3	561	538	21,419	19,822	10,999	10,464	0.1
6020	Commercial banks	20	17	0.3	437	388	22,124	21,464	8,621	7,853	0.2
6100	Nondepository institutions	11	11	0.1	62	50	24,452	28,160	1,523	1,563	0.1
6160	Mortgage bankers and brokers	1	3	0.1	-	3	-	30,667	-	156	0.0
6300	Insurance carriers	12	10	0.2	50	44	26,000	28,364	1,431	1,411	0.0
6400	Insurance agents, brokers, and service	34	38	0.3	140	126	20,343	21,587	2,967	2,747	0.1
6500	Real estate	67	68	0.2	274	391	11,766	13,043	3,477	5,980	0.1
6510	Real estate operators and lessors	39	42	0.3	127	186	8,630	13,054	1,173	2,643	0.2
6530	Real estate agents and managers	19	21	0.1	78	159	10,564	14,289	934	2,882	0.1
6552	Subdividers and developers, n.e.c.	3	3	0.2	-	14	-	7,143	-	123	0.0
INYO, CA											
60 –	**Finance, insurance, and real estate**	40	37	0.0	167	153	17,940	17,725	2,934	3,065	0.0
6000	Depository institutions	7	6	0.1	88	71	17,136	17,352	1,166	1,190	0.0
6300	Insurance carriers	3	4	0.1	11	-	25,091	-	304	-	-
6400	Insurance agents, brokers, and service	9	9	0.1	19	19	12,421	16,421	230	314	0.0
6500	Real estate	17	15	0.0	36	46	19,000	15,043	872	954	0.0
6510	Real estate operators and lessors	6	8	0.1	12	-	16,333	-	197	-	-
6530	Real estate agents and managers	7	5	0.0	7	-	6,857	-	58	-	-

Source: County Business Patterns, 1992/93, CBP-92/93-1, U.S. Department of Commerce, Washington, D.C., April 1995. SIC categories for which data were suppressed or not available for both 1992 and 1993 are *not* displayed. The employment columns represent mid-March employment in the year. Pay per employee is calculated by dividing 1st Quarter payroll, annualized, by mid-March employment. The columns headed "% State" show the county's percentage of the state total for the SIC in 1993; for example, 0.9% for SIC 6030 means that the county had 0.9 percent of the state's total establishments (or payroll) in SIC 6030 in 1993. A dash (-) is used to indicate that data are not available or cannot be calculated; *nec* means not elsewhere classified.

SIC	Industry	No. Establishments			Employment		Pay / Employee		Annual Payroll ($ 000)		
		1992	1993	% State	1992	1993	1992	1993	1992	1993	% State
KERN, CA											
60 –	**Finance, insurance, and real estate**	868	858	1.1	6,567	6,097	23,476	23,074	157,381	143,494	0.5
6000	Depository institutions	167	148	1.3	2,597	2,270	21,972	20,645	157,381	143,494	0.5
6020	Commercial banks	111	94	1.6	1,826	1,410	21,643	20,235	55,959	45,513	0.6
6030	Savings institutions	20	18	0.6	221	252	28,308	25,841	38,755	27,212	0.6
6060	Credit unions	31	31	2.5	516	571	21,085	20,196	6,136	6,716	0.4
6090	Functions closely related to banking	5	5	0.5	34	37	11,882	7,784	10,610	11,302	2.7
6100	Nondepository institutions	70	78	1.1	457	516	32,709	29,186	458	283	0.1
6140	Personal credit institutions	32	30	1.8	-	164	-	24,415	16,164	18,807	0.6
6160	Mortgage bankers and brokers	34	41	0.8	284	330	35,831	31,491	-	3,953	0.7
6200	Security and commodity brokers	26	25	0.6	-	178	-	49,438	11,500	14,154	0.8
6210	Security brokers and dealers	17	17	0.8	143	160	51,860	53,400	-	9,215	0.2
6280	Security and commodity services	9	8	0.4	-	18	-	14,222	7,951	9,011	0.3
6300	Insurance carriers	57	51	1.1	574	547	29,617	31,612	-	204	0.0
6310	Life insurance	13	11	1.1	167	156	22,659	25,692	17,076	16,979	0.3
6330	Fire, marine, and casualty insurance	29	23	1.0	93	79	40,602	43,291	3,590	3,720	0.3
6360	Title insurance	5	6	1.0	276	247	31,768	33,393	3,879	3,614	0.1
6370	Pension, health, and welfare funds	7	6	1.7	-	21	-	14,667	8,797	7,977	1.4
6400	Insurance agents, brokers, and service	185	190	1.6	674	662	24,421	23,293	-	350	0.2
6500	Real estate	329	334	1.0	1,861	1,836	16,619	18,013	16,447	15,480	0.6
6510	Real estate operators and lessors	141	142	1.0	793	644	13,549	15,075	32,781	34,301	0.8
6530	Real estate agents and managers	141	161	1.0	780	968	17,308	18,570	12,276	12,017	0.9
6552	Subdividers and developers, n.e.c.	16	16	1.2	53	81	31,170	21,877	13,633	16,538	0.6
6553	Cemetery subdividers and developers	5	6	2.5	72	75	22,611	20,053	1,737	1,757	0.6
6700	Holding and other investment offices	33	31	0.9	232	-	42,103	-	1,552	1,376	1.2
6732	Educational, religious, etc. trusts	5	6	0.9	13	14	13,538	16,857	10,339	-	-
6733	Trusts, n.e.c.	9	7	0.8	25	22	11,840	11,636	172	210	0.1
6792	Oil royalty traders	4	4	10.3	5	-	40,800	-	323	337	0.3
6799	Investors, n.e.c.	8	6	0.7	-	9	-	132,889	149	-	-
									-	416	0.2
KINGS, CA											
60 –	**Finance, insurance, and real estate**	123	120	0.2	648	727	19,741	18,669	13,572	15,222	0.1
6000	Depository institutions	22	21	0.2	311	319	18,354	16,539	13,572	15,222	0.1
6020	Commercial banks	13	12	0.2	218	219	19,229	16,895	5,342	5,370	0.1
6060	Credit unions	5	5	0.4	72	74	16,278	16,973	3,940	3,736	0.1
6100	Nondepository institutions	11	12	0.2	56	66	30,000	29,212	1,078	1,322	0.3
6140	Personal credit institutions	7	7	0.4	29	-	27,862	-	1,822	2,499	0.1
6160	Mortgage bankers and brokers	2	3	0.1	-	23	-	31,478	775	-	-
6200	Security and commodity brokers	4	3	0.1	13	-	27,385	-	-	1,321	0.1
6300	Insurance carriers	8	6	0.1	40	24	24,400	29,333	452	-	-
6400	Insurance agents, brokers, and service	21	22	0.2	90	125	24,400	25,632	1,097	701	0.0
6500	Real estate	54	54	0.2	129	174	13,953	11,862	2,453	3,735	0.2
6510	Real estate operators and lessors	32	29	0.2	82	96	11,220	10,167	2,341	2,447	0.1
6530	Real estate agents and managers	16	22	0.1	19	-	13,053	-	1,085	977	0.1
6700	Holding and other investment offices	3	2	0.1	9	-	8,444	-	306	-	-
									65	-	-
LAKE, CA											
60 –	**Finance, insurance, and real estate**	96	99	0.1	654	712	20,165	20,146	13,575	15,016	0.1
6000	Depository institutions	25	21	0.2	231	224	22,303	22,982	13,575	15,016	0.1
6020	Commercial banks	13	13	0.2	151	172	22,808	24,209	5,254	5,244	0.1
6100	Nondepository institutions	3	3	0.0	2	-	22,000	-	3,373	4,219	0.1
6200	Security and commodity brokers	3	3	0.1	2	-	10,000	-	44	-	-
6300	Insurance carriers	8	8	0.2	284	-	21,577	-	23	-	-
6400	Insurance agents, brokers, and service	9	12	0.1	23	50	16,870	19,520	6,475	-	-
6500	Real estate	43	48	0.1	105	180	12,381	12,489	392	1,020	0.0
									1,185	2,428	0.1

Source: County Business Patterns, 1992/93, CBP-92/93-1, U.S. Department of Commerce, Washington, D.C., April 1995. SIC categories for which data were suppressed or not available for both 1992 and 1993 are not displayed. The employment columns represent mid-March employment in the year. Pay per employee is calculated by dividing 1st Quarter payroll, annualized, by mid-March employment. The columns headed "% State" show the county's percentage of the state total for the SIC in 1993; for example, 0.9% for SIC 6030 means that the county had 0.9 percent of the state's total establishments (or payroll) in SIC 6030 in 1993. A dash (-) is used to indicate that data are not available or cannot be calculated; nec means not elsewhere classified.

Continued on next page.

SIC	Industry	No. Establishments			Employment		Pay / Employee		Annual Payroll ($ 000)		
		1992	1993	% State	1992	1993	1992	1993	1992	1993	% State
LAKE, CA - [continued]											
6510	Real estate operators and lessors	16	24	0.2	31	72	12,387	7,611	351	564	0.0
6530	Real estate agents and managers	14	18	0.1	26	79	12,308	14,228	348	1,235	0.0
6700	Holding and other investment offices	5	4	0.1	7	6	22,286	24,667	202	262	0.0
LASSEN, CA											
60 –	**Finance, insurance, and real estate**	38	37	0.0	183	166	15,956	19,229	3,164	3,321	0.0
6000	Depository institutions	9	9	0.1	93	90	17,075	19,422	1,593	1,760	0.0
6020	Commercial banks	5	6	0.1	66	74	17,152	19,838	1,115	1,466	0.0
6300	Insurance carriers	6	4	0.1	21	11	26,095	31,636	573	345	0.0
6400	Insurance agents, brokers, and service	6	7	0.1	24	19	11,500	15,789	284	266	0.0
6500	Real estate	11	11	0.0	28	24	9,571	8,500	328	260	0.0
6530	Real estate agents and managers	5	5	0.0	11	9	10,182	6,222	119	85	0.0
LOS ANGELES, CA											
60 –	**Finance, insurance, and real estate**	21,264	20,792	27.6	279,891	261,081	34,984	35,825	9,782,275	9,805,700	34.0
6000	Depository institutions	3,262	2,844	25.3	98,559	84,316	30,787	31,484	2,921,949	2,580,728	34.9
6020	Commercial banks	1,748	1,339	22.4	65,379	53,313	29,577	29,979	1,863,425	1,478,299	31.6
6030	Savings institutions	836	760	26.1	23,232	19,829	31,654	30,246	676,747	588,376	35.8
6060	Credit unions	255	299	23.8	3,707	-	25,962	-	100,034	-	-
6080	Foreign bank and branches and agencies	73	91	74.0	2,739	3,134	59,244	64,294	174,799	221,275	-
6090	Functions closely related to banking	341	354	37.1	-	2,979	-	38,986	-	147,609	53.4
6100	Nondepository institutions	1,719	1,823	24.8	19,886	19,207	37,375	38,154	763,762	777,975	25.9
6110	Federal and Federally-sponsored credit	4	4	6.2	56	321	45,071	66,741	2,299	19,835	35.9
6140	Personal credit institutions	507	402	24.1	7,620	5,573	34,727	33,090	268,150	178,513	33.5
6150	Business credit institutions	194	227	33.2	2,610	3,829	45,493	44,240	108,824	165,580	29.8
6160	Mortgage bankers and brokers	973	1,178	24.0	9,457	9,454	37,413	37,747	380,894	412,876	22.3
6200	Security and commodity brokers	1,039	1,144	28.1	13,220	14,349	86,844	80,171	1,224,600	1,493,144	38.8
6210	Security brokers and dealers	535	591	28.7	9,247	9,499	95,656	88,564	858,330	983,371	36.9
6220	Commodity contracts brokers, dealers	20	25	35.7	124	-	40,968	-	5,166	-	-
6230	Security and commodity exchanges	9	4	30.8	275	-	24,320	-	6,623	-	-
6280	Security and commodity services	460	521	27.1	3,520	4,674	71,176	64,681	353,154	500,696	43.5
6300	Insurance carriers	1,316	1,064	22.9	49,543	50,329	37,522	40,363	1,791,917	2,019,633	34.8
6310	Life insurance	347	303	30.4	16,098	13,824	36,950	37,738	552,640	489,589	39.9
6321	Accident and health insurance	23	16	25.0	905	579	29,357	21,589	26,395	12,680	30.6
6324	Hospital and medical service plans	41	59	23.0	6,293	9,590	42,258	40,599	231,466	407,830	43.3
6330	Fire, marine, and casualty insurance	596	512	22.6	20,059	20,675	36,473	42,286	739,410	875,843	31.4
6350	Surety insurance	33	32	31.1	799	888	45,927	45,937	37,939	38,953	44.9
6360	Title insurance	48	42	7.3	3,679	2,866	41,807	41,421	148,558	124,610	22.5
6370	Pension, health, and welfare funds	215	92	25.7	1,514	1,297	27,495	32,318	47,326	42,711	29.3
6390	Insurance carriers, n.e.c.	9	7	53.8	171	610	37,754	52,839	7,162	27,403	96.8
6400	Insurance agents, brokers, and service	2,987	3,068	25.8	23,715	21,465	38,869	36,987	900,623	821,525	33.3
6500	Real estate	9,653	9,570	29.6	58,960	57,022	23,941	23,264	1,470,109	1,398,716	31.0
6510	Real estate operators and lessors	4,551	4,928	33.2	22,673	22,702	19,110	18,725	446,980	456,142	35.0
6530	Real estate agents and managers	3,560	4,133	26.9	27,493	29,885	26,671	25,829	763,365	801,014	30.4
6540	Title abstract offices	30	36	13.4	997	1,221	34,752	33,661	35,337	46,504	33.2
6552	Subdividers and developers, n.e.c.	481	344	25.5	3,485	1,938	28,357	30,871	103,699	63,814	20.7
6553	Cemetery subdividers and developers	43	62	25.8	991	1,210	26,503	21,967	28,063	28,158	24.3
6700	Holding and other investment offices	1,223	1,211	33.7	13,363	11,395	42,244	46,271	568,628	558,783	39.8
6710	Holding offices	222	240	36.5	5,137	3,534	53,214	83,935	246,369	267,214	38.7
6720	Investment offices	63	31	30.1	705	397	62,026	50,065	45,824	31,116	43.4
6732	Educational, religious, etc. trusts	193	202	30.2	3,126	3,055	21,280	18,662	69,362	63,567	43.0
6733	Trusts, n.e.c.	283	278	30.8	1,648	1,533	41,650	19,961	79,686	35,525	36.9
6792	Oil royalty traders	6	11	28.2	32	37	21,125	21,730	644	910	20.9
6794	Patent owners and lessors	88	104	43.0	876	1,078	47,781	49,087	48,702	81,697	49.4
6798	Real estate investment trusts	102	48	40.7	910	408	38,141	50,137	34,069	23,843	56.9
6799	Investors, n.e.c.	204	286	34.6	712	1,345	33,809	35,994	31,790	53,981	29.5

Source: County Business Patterns, 1992/93, CBP-92/93-1, U.S. Department of Commerce, Washington, D.C., April 1995. SIC categories for which data were suppressed or not available for both 1992 and 1993 are *not* displayed. The employment columns represent mid-March employment in the year. Pay per employee is calculated by dividing 1st Quarter payroll, annualized, by mid-March employment. The columns headed "% State" show the county's percentage of the state total for the SIC in 1993; for example, 0.9% for SIC 6030 means that the county had 0.9 percent of the state's total establishments (or payroll) in SIC 6030 in 1993. A dash (-) is used to indicate that data are not available or cannot be calculated; *nec* means not elsewhere classified.

SIC	Industry	No. Establishments			Employment		Pay / Employee		Annual Payroll ($ 000)		
		1992	1993	% State	1992	1993	1992	1993	1992	1993	% State
MADERA, CA											
60–	**Finance, insurance, and real estate**	125	131	0.2	611	667	19,830	18,513	12,177	13,406	0.0
6000	Depository institutions	23	20	0.2	285	279	18,821	18,151	4,984	5,064	0.1
6020	Commercial banks	12	11	0.2	215	212	18,047	19,038	3,790	4,039	0.1
6100	Nondepository institutions	8	7	0.1	24	53	32,500	16,453	737	907	0.1
6160	Mortgage bankers and brokers	3	3	0.1	7	4	42,857	31,000	224	190	0.0
6200	Security and commodity brokers	2	4	0.1	-	6	-	10,667	-	54	0.0
6300	Insurance carriers	11	11	0.2	91	70	25,934	32,800	2,462	2,372	0.0
6360	Title insurance	5	5	0.9	76	60	24,105	27,667	1,901	1,796	0.3
6400	Insurance agents, brokers, and service	19	26	0.2	55	56	20,727	21,571	1,264	1,180	0.0
6500	Real estate	59	58	0.2	132	173	13,394	11,954	1,918	2,588	0.1
6510	Real estate operators and lessors	5	7	0.0	17	12	17,647	16,000	321	173	0.0
6530	Real estate agents and managers	41	43	0.3	76	136	12,789	11,235	1,059	1,594	0.1
6552	Subdividers and developers, n.e.c.	8	5	0.4	33	-	13,576	-	481	-	-
6700	Holding and other investment offices	3	5	0.1	-	30	-	25,867	-	1,241	0.1
MARIN, CA											
60–	**Finance, insurance, and real estate**	1,073	1,114	1.5	10,100	9,886	40,370	37,788	412,421	391,547	1.4
6000	Depository institutions	112	111	1.0	1,733	1,681	24,662	24,326	43,188	39,707	0.5
6020	Commercial banks	63	59	1.0	1,292	1,251	24,598	23,332	31,321	27,449	0.6
6030	Savings institutions	43	42	1.4	420	390	24,971	27,867	11,389	11,363	0.7
6100	Nondepository institutions	69	85	1.2	522	601	41,893	35,967	26,514	27,436	0.9
6140	Personal credit institutions	14	9	0.5	92	48	33,261	35,500	3,069	1,668	0.3
6150	Business credit institutions	10	16	2.3	67	82	27,403	34,683	2,271	3,323	0.6
6160	Mortgage bankers and brokers	44	59	1.2	362	471	46,829	36,238	21,127	22,433	1.2
6200	Security and commodity brokers	83	99	2.4	539	677	81,217	85,507	51,787	63,283	1.6
6210	Security brokers and dealers	31	32	1.6	267	263	74,951	57,278	19,117	16,384	0.6
6280	Security and commodity services	48	67	3.5	250	414	90,288	103,440	30,863	46,899	4.1
6300	Insurance carriers	76	53	1.1	3,652	3,253	56,941	48,832	189,165	158,705	2.7
6310	Life insurance	11	9	0.9	874	711	42,481	45,018	34,183	31,036	2.5
6330	Fire, marine, and casualty insurance	41	30	1.3	2,588	2,443	62,912	49,302	146,140	121,746	4.4
6360	Title insurance	9	8	1.4	121	-	38,083	-	4,624	-	-
6400	Insurance agents, brokers, and service	170	183	1.5	789	896	32,243	34,625	27,725	31,617	1.3
6500	Real estate	468	501	1.6	2,306	2,322	20,985	20,084	53,018	51,952	1.2
6510	Real estate operators and lessors	215	226	1.5	1,068	1,061	14,659	13,576	18,281	15,242	1.2
6530	Real estate agents and managers	192	244	1.6	970	1,102	24,981	24,036	24,845	30,315	1.1
6552	Subdividers and developers, n.e.c.	20	19	1.4	102	44	31,843	36,636	3,367	2,103	0.7
6553	Cemetery subdividers and developers	3	3	1.3	22	17	22,000	28,235	459	475	0.4
6700	Holding and other investment offices	91	78	2.2	-	383	-	28,606	-	13,011	0.9
6710	Holding offices	11	12	1.8	153	-	15,242	-	2,381	-	-
6720	Investment offices	7	2	1.9	58	-	15,172	-	922	-	-
6732	Educational, religious, etc. trusts	18	18	2.7	130	140	18,554	26,800	2,675	3,986	2.7
6733	Trusts, n.e.c.	16	15	1.7	31	25	26,452	27,040	826	812	0.8
6794	Patent owners and lessors	9	8	3.3	32	28	42,750	39,714	1,901	1,148	0.7
6798	Real estate investment trusts	6	3	2.5	-	10	-	34,400	-	585	1.4
6799	Investors, n.e.c.	17	19	2.3	43	44	72,093	50,545	3,406	3,468	1.9
MARIPOSA, CA											
60–	**Finance, insurance, and real estate**	22	20	0.0	117	120	19,077	20,200	2,387	2,501	0.0
6300	Insurance carriers	3	2	0.0	10	-	20,400	-	255	-	-
6400	Insurance agents, brokers, and service	4	4	0.0	-	20	-	21,200	-	348	0.0
6500	Real estate	8	7	0.0	-	35	-	13,257	-	574	0.0
6530	Real estate agents and managers	4	4	0.0	24	31	13,833	14,194	370	537	0.0
MENDOCINO, CA											
60–	**Finance, insurance, and real estate**	180	178	0.2	1,038	1,021	17,881	18,656	20,040	21,015	0.1
6000	Depository institutions	31	29	0.3	443	429	19,016	20,625	8,953	9,450	0.1
6020	Commercial banks	14	20	0.3	175	346	15,726	20,624	2,912	7,559	0.2
6030	Savings institutions	13	5	0.2	238	48	21,462	22,500	5,450	1,220	0.1

Source: County Business Patterns, 1992/93, CBP-92/93-1, U.S. Department of Commerce, Washington, D.C., April 1995. SIC categories for which data were suppressed or not available for both 1992 and 1993 are *not* displayed. The employment columns represent mid-March employment in the year. Pay per employee is calculated by dividing 1st Quarter payroll, annualized, by mid-March employment. The columns headed "% State" show the county's percentage of the state total for the SIC in 1993; for example, 0.9% for SIC 6030 means that the county had 0.9 percent of the state's total establishments (or payroll) in SIC 6030 in 1993. A dash (-) is used to indicate that data are not available or cannot be calculated; *nec* means not elsewhere classified.

Continued on next page.

SIC	Industry	No. Establishments			Employment		Pay / Employee		Annual Payroll ($ 000)		
		1992	1993	% State	1992	1993	1992	1993	1992	1993	% State
MENDOCINO, CA - [continued]											
6060	Credit unions	4	4	0.3	30	35	18,800	18,057	591	671	0.2
6100	Nondepository institutions	9	11	0.1	18	-	25,111	-	577	-	-
6160	Mortgage bankers and brokers	6	8	0.2	6	15	14,000	16,267	145	262	0.0
6200	Security and commodity brokers	5	4	0.1	24	-	56,500	-	1,350	-	-
6210	Security brokers and dealers	5	4	0.2	24	-	56,500	-	1,350	-	-
6300	Insurance carriers	18	12	0.3	136	104	23,471	26,923	3,406	3,168	0.1
6330	Fire, marine, and casualty insurance	5	3	0.1	-	9	-	36,889	-	351	0.0
6360	Title insurance	9	5	0.9	73	-	23,452	-	1,754	-	-
6400	Insurance agents, brokers, and service	31	34	0.3	96	116	19,917	18,724	1,885	2,184	0.1
6500	Real estate	82	83	0.3	311	309	10,264	9,851	3,775	4,035	0.1
6510	Real estate operators and lessors	34	39	0.3	117	148	9,231	9,270	1,253	1,825	0.1
6530	Real estate agents and managers	35	39	0.3	136	156	10,618	9,949	1,704	2,093	0.1
6552	Subdividers and developers, n.e.c.	3	3	0.2	5	-	11,200	-	35	-	-
6700	Holding and other investment offices	4	5	0.1	10	9	3,200	12,889	94	68	0.0
MERCED, CA											
60–	**Finance, insurance, and real estate**	250	239	0.3	2,352	1,988	17,524	23,465	42,475	45,694	0.2
6000	Depository institutions	45	42	0.4	588	605	19,728	20,820	11,591	11,701	0.2
6020	Commercial banks	30	27	0.5	408	420	18,755	19,010	8,071	7,627	0.2
6060	Credit unions	6	7	0.6	92	105	24,696	24,990	2,117	2,433	0.6
6100	Nondepository institutions	18	17	0.2	67	81	32,657	31,951	2,058	2,766	0.1
6140	Personal credit institutions	11	9	0.5	-	38	-	25,263	-	942	0.2
6160	Mortgage bankers and brokers	5	7	0.1	20	-	44,600	-	855	-	-
6200	Security and commodity brokers	7	8	0.2	25	30	70,880	55,600	1,842	1,865	0.0
6300	Insurance carriers	18	18	0.4	985	652	14,185	29,417	14,337	17,875	0.3
6330	Fire, marine, and casualty insurance	8	10	0.4	-	567	-	30,279	-	15,593	0.6
6360	Title insurance	5	5	0.9	69	58	23,304	26,276	1,748	1,747	0.3
6370	Pension, health, and welfare funds	3	1	0.3	10	-	15,600	-	298	-	-
6400	Insurance agents, brokers, and service	47	46	0.4	247	218	24,227	23,890	6,037	5,437	0.2
6500	Real estate	111	103	0.3	416	395	13,106	13,458	6,184	5,935	0.1
6510	Real estate operators and lessors	59	59	0.4	145	160	9,434	9,175	1,451	1,513	0.1
6530	Real estate agents and managers	35	35	0.2	169	139	14,746	15,712	2,865	2,573	0.1
6552	Subdividers and developers, n.e.c.	4	4	0.3	-	45	-	6,044	-	310	0.1
6700	Holding and other investment offices	4	5	0.1	24	7	10,333	13,143	426	115	0.0
MODOC, CA											
60–	**Finance, insurance, and real estate**	17	15	0.0	61	80	16,459	15,100	1,135	1,166	0.0
6400	Insurance agents, brokers, and service	3	3	0.0	11	8	20,727	30,000	188	197	0.0
6500	Real estate	7	6	0.0	16	-	15,750	-	320	-	-
MONO, CA											
60–	**Finance, insurance, and real estate**	56	63	0.1	517	524	12,766	15,076	5,805	6,508	0.0
6000	Depository institutions	4	3	0.0	68	-	10,765	-	518	-	-
6020	Commercial banks	4	3	0.1	68	-	10,765	-	518	-	-
6400	Insurance agents, brokers, and service	3	4	0.0	9	7	8,889	15,429	91	148	0.0
6500	Real estate	44	53	0.2	424	469	12,670	14,380	4,731	5,364	0.1
6510	Real estate operators and lessors	5	6	0.0	59	-	13,763	-	862	-	-
6530	Real estate agents and managers	32	44	0.3	336	413	11,976	13,908	3,195	4,248	0.2
MONTEREY, CA											
60–	**Finance, insurance, and real estate**	773	769	1.0	5,059	7,547	26,291	22,687	137,188	182,023	0.6
6000	Depository institutions	124	112	1.0	1,611	1,658	22,555	22,072	36,641	35,040	0.5
6020	Commercial banks	69	60	1.0	1,116	1,114	21,473	21,239	23,937	22,767	0.5
6030	Savings institutions	35	32	1.1	337	349	27,490	25,169	9,475	8,366	0.9
6060	Credit unions	17	17	1.4	150	184	20,000	22,043	3,117	3,833	0.0
6090	Functions closely related to banking	3	3	0.3	8	11	13,500	8,727	112	74	0.0
6100	Nondepository institutions	53	62	0.8	253	2,708	32,174	17,120	8,708	54,660	1.8
6160	Mortgage bankers and brokers	30	40	0.8	136	-	36,706	-	5,594	-	-

Source: County Business Patterns, 1992/93, CBP-92/93-1, U.S. Department of Commerce, Washington, D.C., April 1995. SIC categories for which data were suppressed or not available for both 1992 and 1993 are *not* displayed. The employment columns represent mid-March employment in the year. Pay per employee is calculated by dividing 1st Quarter payroll, annualized, by mid-March employment. The columns headed "% State" show the county's percentage of the state total for the SIC in 1993; for example, 0.9% for SIC 6030 means that the county had 0.9 percent of the state's total establishments (or payroll) in SIC 6030 in 1993. A dash (-) is used to indicate that data are not available or cannot be calculated; *nec* means not elsewhere classified.

Continued on next page.

SIC	Industry	No. Establishments			Employment		Pay / Employee		Annual Payroll ($ 000)		
		1992	1993	% State	1992	1993	1992	1993	1992	1993	% State
MONTEREY, CA - [continued]											
6200	Security and commodity brokers	39	44	1.1	265	263	77,509	71,787	19,630	19,532	0.5
6210	Security brokers and dealers	20	21	1.0	233	228	84,412	78,614	18,409	18,127	0.7
6280	Security and commodity services	18	23	1.2	32	35	27,250	27,314	1,220	1,405	0.1
6300	Insurance carriers	57	41	0.9	706	730	38,317	37,847	24,931	26,093	0.4
6310	Life insurance	8	4	0.4	78	159	27,590	24,000	2,169	4,155	0.3
6330	Fire, marine, and casualty insurance	18	15	0.7	272	283	52,059	50,488	11,603	11,846	0.4
6360	Title insurance	15	13	2.2	284	236	29,915	33,508	8,676	8,505	1.5
6400	Insurance agents, brokers, and service	124	131	1.1	403	486	26,094	27,185	11,637	13,814	0.6
6500	Real estate	322	334	1.0	1,564	1,525	16,118	15,620	28,282	27,510	0.6
6510	Real estate operators and lessors	153	170	1.1	772	872	14,301	13,688	11,920	13,241	1.0
6530	Real estate agents and managers	122	144	0.9	506	560	18,925	16,693	10,621	9,676	0.4
6552	Subdividers and developers, n.e.c.	15	15	1.1	113	74	21,381	31,081	3,377	4,056	1.3
6710	Holding offices	7	4	0.6	101	-	10,574	-	1,452	-	-
6732	Educational, religious, etc. trusts	11	9	1.3	25	20	17,920	23,600	487	549	0.4
6733	Trusts, n.e.c.	16	14	1.5	40	61	15,800	10,164	612	1,031	1.1
6798	Real estate investment trusts	3	1	0.8	8	-	25,500	-	105	-	-
NAPA, CA											
60 –	**Finance, insurance, and real estate**	296	293	0.4	2,217	1,870	29,041	31,600	58,945	58,219	0.2
6000	Depository institutions	51	46	0.4	812	495	25,729	29,018	15,851	14,068	0.2
6020	Commercial banks	30	26	0.4	664	362	26,711	31,403	12,922	11,180	0.2
6030	Savings institutions	14	12	0.4	106	87	22,491	24,046	2,168	2,012	0.1
6060	Credit unions	7	8	0.6	42	46	18,381	19,652	761	876	0.2
6100	Nondepository institutions	19	21	0.3	-	68	-	31,471	-	2,669	0.1
6140	Personal credit institutions	8	7	0.4	27	-	24,889	-	652	-	-
6160	Mortgage bankers and brokers	9	13	0.3	24	39	30,833	33,231	815	1,861	0.1
6200	Security and commodity brokers	15	16	0.4	87	71	55,954	66,592	5,142	5,383	0.1
6210	Security brokers and dealers	11	9	0.4	79	62	58,076	66,129	4,783	4,766	0.2
6280	Security and commodity services	4	7	0.4	8	9	35,000	69,778	359	617	0.1
6300	Insurance carriers	20	13	0.3	132	72	32,182	38,722	4,929	2,800	0.0
6360	Title insurance	5	3	0.5	79	-	31,139	-	2,966	-	-
6370	Pension, health, and welfare funds	6	-	-	6	-	4,000	-	248	-	-
6400	Insurance agents, brokers, and service	37	39	0.3	428	469	43,794	45,211	16,577	19,897	0.8
6500	Real estate	129	134	0.4	574	587	16,383	16,361	9,710	19,897	0.8
6510	Real estate operators and lessors	60	65	0.4	332	339	9,675	10,289	3,680	3,557	0.3
6530	Real estate agents and managers	51	58	0.4	159	195	26,717	24,677	4,000	4,738	0.2
6552	Subdividers and developers, n.e.c.	6	6	0.4	39	-	13,231	-	496	-	-
6553	Cemetery subdividers and developers	3	3	1.3	30	27	26,267	28,296	872	904	0.8
6700	Holding and other investment offices	24	22	0.6	71	-	30,141		2,480	-	-
6710	Holding offices	6	4	0.6	-	36	-	64,889	-	1,229	0.2
6732	Educational, religious, etc. trusts	3	4	0.6	9	-	25,333	-	229	-	-
6733	Trusts, n.e.c.	6	7	0.8	6	7	16,667	15,429	117	135	0.1
NEVADA, CA											
60 –	**Finance, insurance, and real estate**	203	201	0.3	2,031	1,490	20,041	21,842	38,279	34,453	0.1
6000	Depository institutions	35	31	0.3	503	540	25,487	21,726	11,694	12,133	0.2
6020	Commercial banks	19	16	0.3	394	425	27,401	23,125	9,761	10,199	0.2
6030	Savings institutions	13	13	0.4	100	-	18,280	-	1,775	-	-
6100	Nondepository institutions	16	18	0.2	49	90	40,653	31,156	2,024	2,630	0.1
6140	Personal credit institutions	2	4	0.2	-	18	-	28,444	-	576	0.1
6160	Mortgage bankers and brokers	13	14	0.3	39	72	41,436	31,833	-	576	0.1
6200	Security and commodity brokers	8	11	0.3	31	42	46,710	51,524	1,632	2,054	0.1
6210	Security brokers and dealers	4	7	0.3	-	27	-	66,667	1,620	2,178	0.1
6280	Security and commodity services	4	4	0.2	-	15	-	24,267	-	1,830	0.1
6300	Insurance carriers	17	11	0.2	319	321	20,627	22,642	-	348	0.0
6360	Title insurance	8	4	0.7	96	-	24,750	-	8,556	7,620	0.1
6400	Insurance agents, brokers, and service	24	25	0.2	128	93	22,688	29,677	2,793	-	-
6500	Real estate	95	98	0.3	976	367	15,057	15,063	3,112	2,981	0.1
									10,910	6,609	0.1

Source: County Business Patterns, 1992/93, CBP-92/93-1, U.S. Department of Commerce, Washington, D.C., April 1995. SIC categories for which data were suppressed or not available for both 1992 and 1993 are *not* displayed. The employment columns represent mid-March employment in the year. Pay per employee is calculated by dividing 1st Quarter payroll, annualized, by mid-March employment. The columns headed "% State" show the county's percentage of the state total for the SIC in 1993; for example, 0.9% for SIC 6030 means that the county had 0.9 percent of the state's total establishments (or payroll) in SIC 6030 in 1993. A dash (-) is used to indicate that data are not available or cannot be calculated; *nec* means not elsewhere classified.

Continued on next page.

SIC	Industry	No. Establishments			Employment		Pay / Employee		Annual Payroll ($ 000)		
		1992	1993	% State	1992	1993	1992	1993	1992	1993	% State
NEVADA, CA - [continued]											
6510	Real estate operators and lessors	29	29	0.2	755	92	14,803	11,435	7,594	1,094	0.1
6530	Real estate agents and managers	46	56	0.4	142	178	13,183	13,348	1,892	2,744	0.1
6540	Title abstract offices	1	6	2.2	-	87	-	23,402	-	2,574	1.8
6552	Subdividers and developers, n.e.c.	8	6	0.4	29	-	24,552	-	375	-	-
6700	Holding and other investment offices	8	7	0.2	25	37	10,560	7,784	363	302	0.0
ORANGE, CA											
60 –	**Finance, insurance, and real estate**	8,019	8,046	10.7	108,063	107,230	33,233	32,953	3,615,324	3,760,461	13.0
6000	Depository institutions	1,067	963	8.6	25,629	25,035	28,411	27,297	701,117	682,750	9.2
6020	Commercial banks	551	452	7.6	15,288	15,178	26,132	25,585	394,703	373,344	8.0
6030	Savings institutions	327	318	10.9	7,735	7,291	33,586	31,284	235,213	238,286	14.5
6060	Credit unions	102	108	8.6	1,406	1,750	23,943	22,510	36,239	39,892	9.4
6100	Nondepository institutions	1,027	1,151	15.7	11,142	12,855	38,216	35,880	464,872	548,496	18.3
6140	Personal credit institutions	261	238	14.3	2,956	3,260	35,177	30,609	100,348	106,739	20.0
6150	Business credit institutions	101	124	18.1	1,091	1,349	40,326	45,835	50,804	60,927	11.0
6160	Mortgage bankers and brokers	643	784	16.0	6,775	8,237	39,738	36,331	304,467	380,096	20.5
6200	Security and commodity brokers	422	449	11.0	4,859	4,613	55,676	56,948	269,783	327,753	8.5
6210	Security brokers and dealers	208	231	11.2	2,744	2,799	65,437	65,706	170,213	192,286	7.2
6220	Commodity contracts brokers, dealers	6	7	10.0	15	-	22,400	-	483	-	-
6280	Security and commodity services	204	210	10.9	1,994	1,792	43,621	43,779	97,262	134,412	11.7
6300	Insurance carriers	655	563	12.1	24,327	24,778	37,435	38,264	907,781	937,724	16.1
6310	Life insurance	142	129	12.9	5,953	5,918	43,069	40,721	216,542	207,495	16.9
6321	Accident and health insurance	12	9	14.1	287	266	37,380	52,632	10,357	13,815	33.3
6324	Hospital and medical service plans	22	31	12.1	2,652	3,323	39,923	34,781	110,601	128,216	13.6
6330	Fire, marine, and casualty insurance	343	314	13.9	12,740	12,928	34,218	37,521	451,415	483,231	17.3
6350	Surety insurance	20	16	15.5	294	-	42,585	-	13,368	-	-
6360	Title insurance	26	23	4.0	1,805	1,450	39,883	42,629	85,669	73,504	13.3
6370	Pension, health, and welfare funds	85	37	10.3	589	526	28,971	30,745	19,566	17,434	12.0
6400	Insurance agents, brokers, and service	1,381	1,402	11.8	10,252	8,830	34,503	34,741	352,273	314,743	12.8
6500	Real estate	3,057	3,088	9.6	27,019	25,442	26,119	25,953	723,564	705,377	15.6
6510	Real estate operators and lessors	1,131	1,212	8.2	7,063	7,477	19,524	20,738	140,506	154,511	11.9
6530	Real estate agents and managers	1,333	1,659	10.8	13,847	14,955	27,204	25,045	392,927	409,738	15.5
6540	Title abstract offices	12	16	6.0	262	418	32,962	32,507	9,488	15,130	10.8
6552	Subdividers and developers, n.e.c.	249	164	12.1	4,194	2,201	32,685	41,425	134,447	91,171	29.6
6553	Cemetery subdividers and developers	8	16	6.7	175	368	25,463	68,685	4,731	33,119	28.6
6700	Holding and other investment offices	353	371	10.3	3,941	4,737	38,586	35,210	150,263	187,366	13.3
6710	Holding offices	88	84	12.8	1,522	1,812	60,066	40,252	86,826	91,253	13.2
6720	Investment offices	17	11	10.7	120	88	20,367	39,455	2,769	3,683	5.1
6732	Educational, religious, etc. trusts	42	40	6.0	1,024	686	11,250	16,315	11,415	11,347	7.7
6733	Trusts, n.e.c.	74	98	10.8	262	691	20,122	25,470	5,417	14,152	14.7
6792	Oil royalty traders	5	7	17.9	9	10	26,222	29,200	261	306	7.0
6794	Patent owners and lessors	30	36	14.9	572	854	44,706	44,899	25,510	41,011	24.8
6798	Real estate investment trusts	24	14	11.9	86	64	56,884	73,000	4,730	4,445	10.6
6799	Investors, n.e.c.	47	78	9.4	143	463	36,531	35,931	5,770	18,553	10.2
PLACER, CA											
60 –	**Finance, insurance, and real estate**	528	524	0.7	4,100	4,544	23,506	21,879	101,544	107,557	0.4
6000	Depository institutions	87	79	0.7	1,395	1,303	24,616	22,717	34,532	28,486	0.4
6020	Commercial banks	44	43	0.7	952	928	23,097	21,711	22,428	18,190	0.4
6030	Savings institutions	35	27	0.9	394	313	28,802	26,211	11,046	8,944	0.5
6100	Nondepository institutions	53	62	0.8	403	513	35,117	30,495	15,810	19,323	0.6
6140	Personal credit institutions	20	19	1.1	194	-	29,670	-	6,044	-	-
6160	Mortgage bankers and brokers	31	41	0.8	204	317	40,647	35,041	9,667	14,212	0.8
6200	Security and commodity brokers	18	18	0.4	52	62	41,231	47,355	2,469	3,462	0.1
6300	Insurance carriers	37	37	0.8	400	415	32,530	33,966	13,034	14,890	0.3
6310	Life insurance	4	5	0.5	55	55	41,891	42,545	2,276	2,199	0.2
6330	Fire, marine, and casualty insurance	18	17	0.8	149	186	36,081	39,505	5,513	7,422	0.3
6360	Title insurance	10	11	1.9	148	120	28,541	28,433	3,850	3,946	0.7

Source: County Business Patterns, 1992/93, CBP-92/93-1, U.S. Department of Commerce, Washington, D.C., April 1995. SIC categories for which data were suppressed or not available for both 1992 and 1993 are *not* displayed. The employment columns represent mid-March employment in the year. Pay per employee is calculated by dividing 1st Quarter payroll, annualized, by mid-March employment. The columns headed "% State" show the county's percentage of the state total for the SIC in 1993; for example, 0.9% for SIC 6030 means that the county had 0.9 percent of the state's total establishments (or payroll) in SIC 6030 in 1993. A dash (-) is used to indicate that data are not available or cannot be calculated; *nec* means not elsewhere classified.

Continued on next page.

SIC	Industry	No. Establishments			Employment		Pay / Employee		Annual Payroll ($ 000)		
		1992	1993	% State	1992	1993	1992	1993	1992	1993	% State
PLACER, CA - [continued]											
6370	Pension, health, and welfare funds	5	2	0.6	48	-	23,083	-	1,395	-	-
6400	Insurance agents, brokers, and service	74	73	0.6	256	244	21,125	22,787	6,032	6,467	0.3
6500	Real estate	243	240	0.7	1,513	1,885	16,137	15,357	26,565	31,387	0.7
6510	Real estate operators and lessors	71	78	0.5	532	985	12,549	9,913	6,850	10,901	0.8
6530	Real estate agents and managers	125	139	0.9	718	765	16,134	19,069	12,929	15,966	0.6
6552	Subdividers and developers, n.e.c.	13	12	0.9	21	-	38,476	-	1,045	-	-
PLUMAS, CA											
60 -	**Finance, insurance, and real estate**	50	54	0.1	264	244	16,333	18,082	4,567	4,861	0.0
6000	Depository institutions	11	11	0.1	123	127	20,130	20,283	2,472	2,481	0.0
6300	Insurance carriers	4	3	0.1	18	-	19,556	-	369	-	-
6400	Insurance agents, brokers, and service	8	10	0.1	-	19	-	15,789	-	320	0.0
6500	Real estate	25	28	0.1	96	85	12,750	15,247	1,430	1,785	0.0
6510	Real estate operators and lessors	8	7	0.0	37	27	12,649	12,593	486	500	0.0
6530	Real estate agents and managers	11	15	0.1	22	-	12,000	-	364	-	-
6552	Subdividers and developers, n.e.c.	3	4	0.3	17	15	14,824	20,533	333	477	0.2
RIVERSIDE, CA											
60 -	**Finance, insurance, and real estate**	2,213	2,143	2.8	16,835	17,675	23,272	23,341	393,799	449,709	1.6
6000	Depository institutions	342	318	2.8	5,059	5,006	20,750	21,046	101,292	103,885	1.4
6020	Commercial banks	173	145	2.4	3,377	3,246	19,093	20,281	61,819	60,805	1.3
6030	Savings institutions	107	107	3.7	1,323	1,348	24,450	22,516	30,889	33,346	2.0
6060	Credit unions	18	18	1.4	219	252	21,699	22,905	4,943	6,039	1.4
6090	Functions closely related to banking	43	48	5.0	139	160	24,374	21,250	3,630	3,695	1.3
6100	Nondepository institutions	222	238	3.2	1,661	2,336	30,485	30,861	51,019	94,663	3.2
6140	Personal credit institutions	60	56	3.4	289	303	30,547	20,264	8,787	5,890	1.1
6150	Business credit institutions	11	14	2.0	73	155	28,548	30,090	2,404	4,977	0.9
6160	Mortgage bankers and brokers	147	165	3.4	1,290	1,846	30,657	32,633	39,641	82,836	4.5
6200	Security and commodity brokers	91	87	2.1	501	522	61,469	61,272	30,552	33,810	0.9
6210	Security brokers and dealers	56	54	2.6	401	421	70,324	69,976	27,522	30,836	1.2
6280	Security and commodity services	34	33	1.7	-	101	-	24,990	-	2,974	0.3
6300	Insurance carriers	151	117	2.5	1,925	1,503	27,572	31,729	53,774	51,851	0.9
6310	Life insurance	26	21	2.1	358	294	21,665	25,020	7,272	7,440	0.6
6330	Fire, marine, and casualty insurance	75	69	3.0	401	413	40,778	40,881	16,608	17,745	0.6
6360	Title insurance	19	11	1.9	936	617	25,949	30,496	24,777	21,821	3.9
6370	Pension, health, and welfare funds	21	9	2.5	101	97	21,901	29,856	2,193	2,829	1.9
6400	Insurance agents, brokers, and service	324	315	2.6	1,267	1,170	24,562	26,315	32,882	33,058	1.3
6500	Real estate	1,018	1,012	3.1	5,944	6,921	18,570	16,974	112,690	124,363	2.8
6510	Real estate operators and lessors	361	397	2.7	1,734	1,786	14,399	13,884	25,728	26,849	2.1
6530	Real estate agents and managers	480	548	3.6	2,557	3,748	19,571	17,412	53,360	69,553	2.6
6540	Title abstract offices	3	4	1.5	-	45	-	23,644	-	1,171	0.8
6552	Subdividers and developers, n.e.c.	68	51	3.8	1,255	1,267	21,399	19,886	25,308	25,470	8.3
6553	Cemetery subdividers and developers	5	6	2.5	68	75	16,118	15,467	1,201	1,228	1.1
6710	Holding offices	12	11	1.7	55	70	46,109	49,886	2,750	3,809	0.6
6720	Investment offices	4	1	1.0	44	-	19,909	-	819	-	-
6732	Educational, religious, etc. trusts	10	9	1.3	30	28	22,133	24,857	646	909	0.6
6733	Trusts, n.e.c.	17	14	1.5	33	42	17,455	18,190	646	781	0.8
6799	Investors, n.e.c.	14	10	1.2	-	42	-	28,857	-	1,171	0.6
SACRAMENTO, CA											
60 -	**Finance, insurance, and real estate**	2,781	2,762	3.7	35,869	34,685	27,954	27,900	996,379	1,032,205	3.6
6000	Depository institutions	424	376	3.4	9,460	8,967	25,411	24,704	219,523	222,672	3.0
6020	Commercial banks	216	168	2.8	5,686	5,761	24,979	24,327	132,573	138,574	3.0
6030	Savings institutions	106	98	3.4	2,283	1,558	29,020	29,630	54,530	48,577	3.0
6060	Credit unions	70	75	6.0	1,285	1,486	21,650	22,218	27,994	33,234	7.9
6090	Functions closely related to banking	31	35	3.7	-	162	-	13,556	-	2,287	0.8
6100	Nondepository institutions	286	320	4.4	2,922	3,406	34,074	28,830	99,064	120,341	4.0
6110	Federal and Federally-sponsored credit	2	4	6.2	-	319	-	41,768	-	12,906	23.4

Source: County Business Patterns, 1992/93, CBP-92/93-1, U.S. Department of Commerce, Washington, D.C., April 1995. SIC categories for which data were suppressed or not available for both 1992 and 1993 are *not* displayed. The employment columns represent mid-March employment in the year. Pay per employee is calculated by dividing 1st Quarter payroll, annualized, by mid-March employment. The columns headed "% State" show the county's percentage of the state total for the SIC in 1993; for example, 0.9% for SIC 6030 means that the county had 0.9 percent of the state's total establishments (or payroll) in SIC 6030 in 1993. A dash (-) is used to indicate that data are not available or cannot be calculated; *nec* means not elsewhere classified.

Continued on next page.

SIC	Industry	No. Establishments			Employment		Pay / Employee		Annual Payroll ($ 000)		
		1992	1993	% State	1992	1993	1992	1993	1992	1993	% State
SACRAMENTO, CA - [continued]											
6140	Personal credit institutions	93	76	4.6	857	810	24,653	20,074	19,816	16,234	3.0
6150	Business credit institutions	18	24	3.5	341	189	40,235	37,439	13,436	7,677	1.4
6160	Mortgage bankers and brokers	172	216	4.4	1,709	2,088	37,613	29,471	65,333	83,524	4.5
6200	Security and commodity brokers	102	120	2.9	872	871	58,317	56,804	52,352	53,018	1.4
6210	Security brokers and dealers	49	64	3.1	584	652	72,616	63,595	40,728	43,385	1.6
6220	Commodity contracts brokers, dealers	3	2	2.9	16	-	27,750	-	422	-	-
6280	Security and commodity services	50	54	2.8	272		29,412	-	11,202	-	-
6300	Insurance carriers	293	267	5.8	10,709	9,922	32,743	35,128	354,181	351,969	6.1
6310	Life insurance	70	60	6.0	1,523	1,051	27,945	31,661	31,231	31,279	2.5
6321	Accident and health insurance	4	6	9.4	10	66	18,800	11,333	158	941	2.3
6324	Hospital and medical service plans	23	28	10.9	2,789	2,919	34,851	34,142	101,520	96,482	10.2
6330	Fire, marine, and casualty insurance	135	123	5.4	5,565	5,293	33,573	36,939	194,815	201,234	7.2
6350	Surety insurance	9	4	3.9	48	19	34,167	37,053	1,791	786	0.9
6360	Title insurance	12	20	3.5	622	417	29,994	33,228	19,965	16,305	2.9
6370	Pension, health, and welfare funds	40	26	7.3	152	157	23,447	30,420	4,701	4,942	3.4
6400	Insurance agents, brokers, and service	519	522	4.4	3,316	3,178	30,733	28,473	101,966	96,162	3.9
6500	Real estate	1,064	1,063	3.3	7,887	7,291	17,457	18,335	141,981	145,448	3.2
6510	Real estate operators and lessors	415	423	2.9	2,856	1,788	12,286	14,016	33,259	25,798	2.0
6530	Real estate agents and managers	449	543	3.5	3,792	4,761	19,623	18,305	79,114	95,637	3.6
6540	Title abstract offices	30	31	11.6	335	372	25,075	33,376	9,674	14,743	10.5
6552	Subdividers and developers, n.e.c.	72	41	3.0	409	191	27,081	29,089	10,870	5,484	1.8
6553	Cemetery subdividers and developers	14	14	5.8	159	173	20,428	19,908	3,287	3,581	3.1
6700	Holding and other investment offices	90	89	2.5	-	998	-	23,303	-	39,702	2.8
6710	Holding offices	7	10	1.5	188	193	49,319	10,093	14,182	15,227	2.2
6720	Investment offices	5	1	1.0	61	-	22,230	-	907	-	-
6732	Educational, religious, etc. trusts	18	23	3.4	68	-	24,647	-	1,899	-	-
6733	Trusts, n.e.c.	35	25	2.8	114	117	22,070	22,462	2,364	2,995	3.1
6794	Patent owners and lessors	11	9	3.7	125	72	18,496	27,167	3,026	3,320	2.0
SAN BENITO, CA											
60 –	**Finance, insurance, and real estate**	54	53	0.1	290	308	20,207	19,468	5,965	6,353	0.0
6000	Depository institutions	7	8	0.1	125	126	21,376	21,556	2,328	2,526	0.0
6100	Nondepository institutions	4	4	0.1	2	-	12,000	-	42	-	-
6300	Insurance carriers	7	4	0.1	42	19	26,000	31,158	1,128	599	0.0
6360	Title insurance	3	2	0.3	31	-	29,548	-	962	-	-
6400	Insurance agents, brokers, and service	10	9	0.1	61	61	20,197	23,869	1,578	1,912	0.1
6500	Real estate	26	25	0.1	60	89	14,000	12,360	889	1,098	0.0
6510	Real estate operators and lessors	8	8	0.1	25	-	9,440	-	229	-	-
6530	Real estate agents and managers	13	14	0.1	23	-	15,652	-	512	-	-
SAN BERNARDINO, CA											
60 –	**Finance, insurance, and real estate**	2,273	2,187	2.9	17,533	17,487	26,116	25,436	443,449	465,745	1.6
6000	Depository institutions	351	349	3.1	5,003	5,708	24,290	23,367	113,756	125,354	1.7
6020	Commercial banks	163	146	2.4	3,006	3,322	22,597	21,695	65,094	68,072	1.5
6030	Savings institutions	91	91	3.1	1,318	1,443	30,055	27,678	34,094	39,140	2.4
6060	Credit unions	39	55	4.4	288	691	20,014	23,716	6,011	12,729	3.0
6090	Functions closely related to banking	55	57	6.0	-	252	-	19,746	-	5,413	2.0
6100	Nondepository institutions	328	330	4.5	2,747	2,744	29,881	28,939	82,714	94,752	3.2
6140	Personal credit institutions	112	88	5.3	921	623	26,849	24,398	24,427	14,802	2.8
6150	Business credit institutions	12	16	2.3	85	-	39,859	-	3,365	-	-
6160	Mortgage bankers and brokers	198	224	4.6	1,667	1,951	31,263	29,146	52,599	72,972	3.9
6200	Security and commodity brokers	57	62	1.5	272	273	52,662	49,055	14,435	14,924	0.4
6210	Security brokers and dealers	29	34	1.7	189	222	60,317	50,559	11,412	12,535	0.5
6280	Security and commodity services	26	27	1.4	75	-	36,107	-	2,807	-	-
6300	Insurance carriers	190	144	3.1	3,354	2,569	30,244	32,399	97,076	87,141	1.5
6310	Life insurance	26	24	2.4	544	477	25,912	27,044	13,876	12,422	1.0
6330	Fire, marine, and casualty insurance	103	88	3.9	1,154	1,125	39,508	35,502	41,768	44,558	1.6
6350	Surety insurance	2	3	2.9	-	45	-	44,711	-	974	1.1

Source: County Business Patterns, 1992/93, CBP-92/93-1, U.S. Department of Commerce, Washington, D.C., April 1995. SIC categories for which data were suppressed or not available for both 1992 and 1993 are not displayed. The employment columns represent mid-March employment in the year. Pay per employee is calculated by dividing 1st Quarter payroll, annualized, by mid-March employment. The columns headed "% State" show the county's percentage of the state total for the SIC in 1993; for example, 0.9% for SIC 6030 means that the county had 0.9 percent of the state's total establishments (or payroll) in SIC 6030 in 1993. A dash (-) is used to indicate that data are not available or cannot be calculated; nec means not elsewhere classified.

Continued on next page.

SIC	Industry	No. Establishments			Employment		Pay / Employee		Annual Payroll ($ 000)		
		1992	1993	% State	1992	1993	1992	1993	1992	1993	% State
SAN BERNARDINO, CA - [continued]											
6360	Title insurance	11	15	2.6	770	730	28,218	29,962	20,641	23,970	4.3
6370	Pension, health, and welfare funds	21	5	1.4	85	9	18,400	30,667	1,142	308	0.2
6400	Insurance agents, brokers, and service	390	390	3.3	1,999	1,833	28,652	26,595	55,403	51,411	2.1
6500	Real estate	891	842	2.6	3,785	3,811	18,060	18,760	67,819	77,212	1.7
6510	Real estate operators and lessors	341	365	2.5	1,265	1,296	12,961	13,370	16,574	19,514	1.5
6530	Real estate agents and managers	407	442	2.9	1,577	2,145	21,608	21,598	33,726	49,096	1.9
6540	Title abstract offices	4	6	2.2	-	128	-	25,156	-	3,652	2.6
6552	Subdividers and developers, n.e.c.	32	12	0.9	250	54	18,480	24,963	4,206	1,275	0.4
6553	Cemetery subdividers and developers	9	10	4.2	194	186	14,887	17,462	2,806	3,396	2.9
6700	Holding and other investment offices	58	63	1.8	263	449	29,186	23,109	7,870	11,328	0.8
6710	Holding offices	12	11	1.7	137	195	39,416	27,918	5,408	5,434	0.8
6720	Investment offices	3	1	1.0	7	-	56,571	-	275	-	-
6732	Educational, religious, etc. trusts	15	17	2.5	42	76	16,381	12,842	747	1,128	0.8
6733	Trusts, n.e.c.	17	19	2.1	53	-	11,774	-	628	-	-
6794	Patent owners and lessors	2	4	1.7	-	52	-	36,077	-	1,932	1.2
6799	Investors, n.e.c.	7	11	1.3	8	66	9,500	18,606	390	1,822	1.0
SAN DIEGO, CA											
60 –	**Finance, insurance, and real estate**	7,131	6,975	9.3	69,835	66,960	28,375	28,265	2,025,813	1,976,879	6.9
6000	Depository institutions	1,021	944	8.4	20,108	19,813	26,251	25,664	529,180	496,798	6.7
6020	Commercial banks	539	459	7.7	12,785	12,518	25,530	24,163	327,992	297,334	6.3
6030	Savings institutions	275	278	9.5	4,827	4,493	29,625	30,482	144,213	127,961	7.8
6060	Credit unions	111	114	9.1	2,055	2,143	23,918	23,703	47,272	50,133	11.9
6090	Functions closely related to banking	92	91	9.5	421	605	20,684	27,299	9,111	19,682	7.1
6100	Nondepository institutions	581	633	8.6	8,917	6,310	33,698	32,910	313,623	249,192	8.3
6140	Personal credit institutions	170	135	8.1	3,851	1,376	29,599	26,564	113,362	34,476	6.5
6150	Business credit institutions	39	40	5.8	411	322	45,557	23,689	19,229	7,376	1.3
6160	Mortgage bankers and brokers	364	456	9.3	4,626	4,603	36,038	35,431	179,598	206,956	11.2
6200	Security and commodity brokers	381	385	9.5	3,067	3,014	60,413	68,362	187,002	224,713	5.8
6210	Security brokers and dealers	199	193	9.4	2,372	2,262	63,894	72,065	147,814	169,219	6.4
6220	Commodity contracts brokers, dealers	9	11	15.7	46	59	47,565	35,797	3,351	4,244	-
6280	Security and commodity services	167	180	9.4	640	693	49,175	59,048	35,698	51,249	4.4
6300	Insurance carriers	402	346	7.5	9,124	8,968	31,069	33,512	285,689	300,267	5.2
6310	Life insurance	102	90	9.0	3,138	2,683	30,394	31,065	90,201	75,994	6.2
6321	Accident and health insurance	14	6	9.4	103	36	29,010	32,444	3,168	1,274	3.1
6324	Hospital and medical service plans	18	19	7.4	308	1,036	27,442	30,201	9,465	31,457	3.3
6330	Fire, marine, and casualty insurance	201	184	8.1	3,960	3,966	31,792	35,625	127,646	140,697	5.1
6350	Surety insurance	13	12	11.7	150	134	34,987	36,209	5,958	3,979	4.6
6360	Title insurance	17	14	2.4	1,291	984	31,610	34,537	43,975	42,314	7.6
6370	Pension, health, and welfare funds	36	21	5.9	174	129	27,034	35,752	5,192	4,552	3.1
6400	Insurance agents, brokers, and service	987	978	8.2	4,879	5,236	30,477	31,670	151,863	174,066	7.1
6500	Real estate	3,286	3,315	10.3	19,626	20,908	20,280	19,291	418,508	431,650	9.6
6510	Real estate operators and lessors	1,363	1,488	10.0	6,783	7,429	17,208	15,367	116,894	120,150	9.2
6530	Real estate agents and managers	1,332	1,619	10.5	9,423	11,682	20,444	20,489	208,973	259,761	9.8
6540	Title abstract offices	10	11	4.1	124	137	23,226	26,277	3,146	3,986	2.8
6552	Subdividers and developers, n.e.c.	205	151	11.2	1,703	1,096	32,420	32,854	57,021	37,510	12.2
6553	Cemetery subdividers and developers	15	17	7.1	384	527	16,396	16,509	6,608	7,993	6.9
6700	Holding and other investment offices	338	318	8.9	2,175	1,922	27,978	30,196	61,181	63,219	4.5
6710	Holding offices	57	68	10.3	556	441	43,518	42,458	24,465	20,084	2.9
6720	Investment offices	10	6	5.8	31	-	22,968	-	769	-	-
6732	Educational, religious, etc. trusts	63	66	9.9	570	477	12,575	13,283	7,273	7,394	5.0
6733	Trusts, n.e.c.	92	78	8.6	422	271	17,555	17,387	6,894	5,063	5.3
6794	Patent owners and lessors	18	24	9.9	241	484	34,888	30,372	8,814	15,902	9.6
6798	Real estate investment trusts	15	4	3.4	79	-	33,215	-	2,236	-	-
6799	Investors, n.e.c.	66	67	8.1	239	225	40,301	53,280	9,824	12,134	6.6

Source: County Business Patterns, 1992/93, CBP-92/93-1, U.S. Department of Commerce, Washington, D.C., April 1995. SIC categories for which data were suppressed or not available for both 1992 and 1993 are *not* displayed. The employment columns represent mid-March employment in the year. Pay per employee is calculated by dividing 1st Quarter payroll, annualized, by mid-March employment. The columns headed "% State" show the county's percentage of the state total for the SIC in 1993; for example, 0.9% for SIC 6030 means that the county had 0.9 percent of the state's total establishments (or payroll) in SIC 6030 in 1993. A dash (-) is used to indicate that data are not available or cannot be calculated; *nec* means not elsewhere classified.

SIC	Industry	No. Establishments			Employment		Pay / Employee		Annual Payroll ($ 000)		
		1992	1993	% State	1992	1993	1992	1993	1992	1993	% State
SAN FRANCISCO, CA											
60 –	**Finance, insurance, and real estate**	5,032	4,554	6.0	74,458	73,720	48,145	52,575	3,478,308	3,845,805	13.3
6000	Depository institutions	1,769	1,270	11.3	28,963	28,616	39,654	47,426	1,046,553	1,191,417	16.1
6020	Commercial banks	1,510	1,009	16.9	22,928	23,294	39,625	48,007	820,593	945,960	20.2
6030	Savings institutions	157	142	4.9	3,036	2,267	37,789	36,349	103,753	85,676	5.2
6080	Foreign bank and branches and agencies	26	29	23.6	735	566	47,788	63,647	36,767	36,535	-
6090	Functions closely related to banking	42	51	5.3	385	600	45,309	68,127	15,052	42,094	15.2
6100	Nondepository institutions	188	211	2.9	2,995	2,775	51,845	62,659	157,883	167,314	5.6
6110	Federal and Federally-sponsored credit	4	-	-	30	-	27,867	-	861	-	-
6140	Personal credit institutions	34	28	1.7	402	363	45,662	45,576	17,211	16,039	3.0
6150	Business credit institutions	41	45	6.6	1,767	1,686	58,275	72,403	108,106	109,379	19.7
6160	Mortgage bankers and brokers	104	138	2.8	774	726	42,000	48,573	30,010	41,896	2.3
6200	Security and commodity brokers	468	508	12.5	9,828	10,398	90,114	95,294	882,657	1,095,564	28.5
6210	Security brokers and dealers	255	268	13.0	8,031	7,637	92,291	97,980	719,489	848,033	31.8
6230	Security and commodity exchanges	10	5	38.5	352	-	38,170	-	13,617	-	-
6280	Security and commodity services	196	232	12.1	1,402	-	92,374	-	147,784	-	-
6300	Insurance carriers	311	260	5.6	11,659	11,894	42,451	43,600	476,375	514,715	8.9
6310	Life insurance	88	66	6.6	2,410	2,268	36,362	34,804	81,982	73,214	6.0
6330	Fire, marine, and casualty insurance	100	104	4.6	6,251	6,460	42,574	45,147	263,293	304,766	10.9
6350	Surety insurance	12	7	6.8	325	128	48,615	46,688	15,360	6,553	7.6
6360	Title insurance	29	36	6.2	499	428	39,351	45,000	21,088	20,409	3.7
6370	Pension, health, and welfare funds	65	32	8.9	294	585	43,932	47,966	12,334	25,072	17.2
6400	Insurance agents, brokers, and service	419	432	3.6	5,159	5,342	46,793	46,538	231,638	248,804	10.1
6500	Real estate	1,497	1,528	4.7	11,573	10,940	30,657	29,510	360,323	337,008	7.5
6510	Real estate operators and lessors	775	820	5.5	4,263	3,429	21,519	24,204	94,973	85,783	6.6
6530	Real estate agents and managers	520	651	4.2	6,448	7,295	36,653	31,969	237,565	244,391	9.3
6552	Subdividers and developers, n.e.c.	60	44	3.3	292	156	32,397	36,872	9,072	5,832	1.9
6700	Holding and other investment offices	352	325	9.1	3,201	2,759	63,254	68,729	236,351	225,130	16.0
6710	Holding offices	59	59	9.0	1,031	1,284	73,234	95,536	92,045	142,465	20.7
6720	Investment offices	32	19	18.4	325	127	154,954	95,748	52,694	18,358	25.6
6732	Educational, religious, etc. trusts	91	90	13.5	690	615	27,965	30,068	19,708	20,968	14.2
6733	Trusts, n.e.c.	76	70	7.7	291	211	27,093	31,052	8,115	5,420	5.6
6794	Patent owners and lessors	8	7	2.9	60	125	43,800	48,256	3,222	4,632	2.8
6798	Real estate investment trusts	17	12	10.2	300	56	35,507	49,857	11,207	5,174	12.4
6799	Investors, n.e.c.	62	66	8.0	493	335	72,763	61,875	48,746	27,873	15.3
SAN JOAQUIN, CA											
60 –	**Finance, insurance, and real estate**	940	914	1.2	9,301	9,080	24,442	25,059	229,860	232,286	0.8
6000	Depository institutions	153	145	1.3	4,082	3,684	24,974	25,789	99,010	91,053	1.2
6020	Commercial banks	73	66	1.1	1,769	1,757	22,496	22,304	39,088	37,423	0.8
6030	Savings institutions	51	42	1.4	2,142	1,675	27,111	30,123	56,285	48,356	2.9
6060	Credit unions	15	24	1.9	123	200	25,789	22,580	2,795	4,328	1.0
6090	Functions closely related to banking	14	13	1.4	48	52	18,833	16,308	842	946	0.3
6100	Nondepository institutions	82	89	1.2	515	514	30,718	28,887	16,066	16,936	0.6
6140	Personal credit institutions	39	31	1.9	199	157	24,724	23,541	5,021	3,785	0.7
6150	Business credit institutions	7	3	0.4	72	-	20,333	-	2,185	-	-
6160	Mortgage bankers and brokers	36	51	1.0	244	281	38,672	30,833	8,860	10,612	0.6
6200	Security and commodity brokers	30	26	0.6	180	165	56,511	54,618	9,368	9,260	0.2
6210	Security brokers and dealers	17	12	0.6	161	133	60,000	62,256	8,737	8,332	0.3
6300	Insurance carriers	100	72	1.6	1,368	1,581	24,213	26,302	34,777	43,918	0.8
6310	Life insurance	17	13	1.3	520	582	20,254	20,749	10,052	11,289	0.9
6324	Hospital and medical service plans	5	8	3.1	-	471	-	26,828	-	14,606	1.6
6330	Fire, marine, and casualty insurance	38	33	1.5	171	162	38,994	40,198	7,025	7,246	0.3
6360	Title insurance	14	12	2.1	297	195	28,135	31,467	8,819	6,317	1.1
6370	Pension, health, and welfare funds	23	6	1.7	-	171	-	24,702	-	4,460	3.1
6400	Insurance agents, brokers, and service	176	176	1.5	870	826	25,209	25,584	22,718	22,419	0.9
6500	Real estate	376	382	1.2	2,183	2,172	19,124	19,538	44,999	44,935	1.0
6510	Real estate operators and lessors	154	159	1.1	463	509	12,924	12,094	5,974	6,872	0.5
6530	Real estate agents and managers	157	184	1.2	1,355	1,423	19,758	21,394	29,440	31,801	1.2

Source: *County Business Patterns, 1992/93,* CBP-92/93-1, U.S. Department of Commerce, Washington, D.C., April 1995. SIC categories for which data were suppressed or not available for both 1992 and 1993 are *not* displayed. The employment columns represent mid-March employment in the year. Pay per employee is calculated by dividing 1st Quarter payroll, annualized, by mid-March employment. The columns headed "% State" show the county's percentage of the state total for the SIC in 1993; for example, 0.9% for SIC 6030 means that the county had 0.9 percent of the state's total establishments (or payroll) in SIC 6030 in 1993. A dash (-) is used to indicate that data are not available or cannot be calculated; *nec* means not elsewhere classified.

Continued on next page.

SIC	Industry	No. Establishments			Employment		Pay / Employee		Annual Payroll ($ 000)		
		1992	1993	% State	1992	1993	1992	1993	1992	1993	% State

SAN JOAQUIN, CA - [continued]

SIC	Industry	1992	1993	% State	1992	1993	1992	1993	1992	1993	% State
6540	Title abstract offices	6	6	2.2	108	95	22,593	28,379	2,613	2,955	2.1
6552	Subdividers and developers, n.e.c.	26	23	1.7	112	67	29,750	24,060	3,583	1,726	0.6
6553	Cemetery subdividers and developers	8	9	3.8	75	78	22,667	19,590	1,779	1,580	1.4
6732	Educational, religious, etc. trusts	4	5	0.7	37	84	19,784	18,857	771	1,932	1.3
6733	Trusts, n.e.c.	6	4	0.4	28	18	16,714	18,222	651	194	0.2

SAN LUIS OBISPO, CA

SIC	Industry	1992	1993	% State	1992	1993	1992	1993	1992	1993	% State
60 –	**Finance, insurance, and real estate**	506	512	0.7	3,127	3,143	23,133	22,110	72,630	72,498	0.3
6000	Depository institutions	92	88	0.8	1,477	1,420	22,269	21,417	31,710	30,804	0.4
6020	Commercial banks	59	54	0.9	1,128	1,054	21,528	21,241	23,641	22,668	0.5
6030	Savings institutions	22	24	0.8	231	238	27,567	24,168	5,733	5,964	0.4
6100	Nondepository institutions	37	36	0.5	180	171	32,622	28,936	6,751	6,102	0.2
6140	Personal credit institutions	5	4	0.2	12	16	26,000	12,750	339	277	0.1
6150	Business credit institutions	5	2	0.3	41	-	30,732	-	1,286	-	-
6160	Mortgage bankers and brokers	26	28	0.6	126	134	33,968	28,836	5,116	5,080	0.3
6200	Security and commodity brokers	23	27	0.7	75	94	66,133	42,213	4,316	5,137	0.1
6210	Security brokers and dealers	12	16	0.8	62	72	75,677	49,667	3,961	4,512	0.2
6280	Security and commodity services	10	11	0.6	13	22	20,615	17,818	351	625	0.1
6300	Insurance carriers	37	30	0.6	276	235	33,014	34,911	8,772	7,514	0.1
6310	Life insurance	7	4	0.4	35	59	35,314	35,119	889	1,770	0.1
6330	Fire, marine, and casualty insurance	20	19	0.8	37	31	47,676	52,903	1,849	1,612	0.1
6360	Title insurance	6	5	0.9	187	-	29,497	-	5,325	-	-
6370	Pension, health, and welfare funds	4	2	0.6	17	-	35,059	-	709	-	-
6400	Insurance agents, brokers, and service	73	88	0.7	267	335	26,951	25,815	7,190	8,834	0.4
6500	Real estate	229	227	0.7	811	804	14,654	15,224	13,424	12,744	0.3
6510	Real estate operators and lessors	93	99	0.7	295	305	10,264	10,321	3,708	3,378	0.3
6530	Real estate agents and managers	103	114	0.7	381	430	17,155	17,042	6,852	7,807	0.3
6552	Subdividers and developers, n.e.c.	10	6	0.4	-	16	-	27,000	-	477	0.2
6700	Holding and other investment offices	15	16	0.4	41	84	10,244	12,762	467	1,363	0.1
6732	Educational, religious, etc. trusts	4	3	0.4	10	4	11,600	19,000	107	116	0.1
6733	Trusts, n.e.c.	5	7	0.8	21	-	7,238	-	145	-	-

SAN MATEO, CA

SIC	Industry	1992	1993	% State	1992	1993	1992	1993	1992	1993	% State
60 –	**Finance, insurance, and real estate**	2,128	2,138	2.8	26,948	25,985	33,920	34,704	928,690	939,609	3.3
6000	Depository institutions	276	250	2.2	4,757	4,511	27,437	29,419	125,525	121,678	1.6
6020	Commercial banks	129	104	1.7	2,369	2,263	21,540	20,224	47,900	43,629	0.9
6030	Savings institutions	103	96	3.3	1,909	1,707	34,684	41,783	65,270	63,135	3.8
6060	Credit unions	36	38	3.0	449	442	28,454	29,638	11,826	12,314	2.9
6090	Functions closely related to banking	8	12	1.3	30	99	16,800	25,414	529	2,600	0.9
6100	Nondepository institutions	168	188	2.6	2,565	3,518	51,707	45,168	151,062	175,723	5.9
6140	Personal credit institutions	41	37	2.2	-	234	-	20,872	-	5,129	1.0
6150	Business credit institutions	31	31	4.5	2,019	2,786	55,988	49,153	128,520	148,429	26.8
6160	Mortgage bankers and brokers	95	120	2.4	334	498	36,455	34,289	15,945	22,165	1.2
6200	Security and commodity brokers	126	160	3.9	2,512	2,356	40,869	46,093	104,230	110,089	2.9
6210	Security brokers and dealers	41	53	2.6	597	517	55,471	76,735	31,150	35,328	1.3
6220	Commodity contracts brokers, dealers	3	5	7.1	-	13	-	55,077	-	737	-
6280	Security and commodity services	81	102	5.3	1,883	1,826	36,064	37,354	71,833	74,024	6.4
6300	Insurance carriers	185	145	3.1	4,095	4,583	35,227	36,051	136,820	166,524	2.9
6310	Life insurance	30	28	2.8	916	888	26,258	22,613	25,196	19,839	1.6
6330	Fire, marine, and casualty insurance	70	62	2.7	1,846	2,273	40,752	42,744	65,558	97,987	3.5
6350	Surety insurance	6	4	3.9	104	46	41,769	50,435	4,884	2,689	3.1
6360	Title insurance	22	33	5.7	590	449	34,034	36,071	21,063	17,107	3.1
6370	Pension, health, and welfare funds	51	10	2.8	264	181	36,470	31,912	9,256	5,081	3.5
6400	Insurance agents, brokers, and service	335	342	2.9	2,796	2,208	40,595	35,817	108,734	83,183	3.4
6500	Real estate	864	879	2.7	8,173	7,184	25,180	24,914	208,758	189,830	4.2
6510	Real estate operators and lessors	350	398	2.7	1,994	2,761	18,923	19,264	39,546	57,634	4.4
6530	Real estate agents and managers	382	430	2.8	5,339	3,864	26,502	28,836	139,002	115,207	4.4
6552	Subdividers and developers, n.e.c.	44	31	2.3	392	265	39,612	28,589	17,206	8,977	2.9

Source: County Business Patterns, 1992/93, CBP-92/93-1, U.S. Department of Commerce, Washington, D.C., April 1995. SIC categories for which data were suppressed or not available for both 1992 and 1993 are not displayed. The employment columns represent mid-March employment in the year. Pay per employee is calculated by dividing 1st Quarter payroll, annualized, by mid-March employment. The columns headed "% State" show the county's percentage of the state total for the SIC in 1993; for example, 0.9% for SIC 6030 means that the county had 0.9 percent of the state's total establishments (or payroll) in SIC 6030 in 1993. A dash (-) is used to indicate that data are not available or cannot be calculated; nec means not elsewhere classified.

Continued on next page.

SIC	Industry	No. Establishments			Employment		Pay / Employee		Annual Payroll ($ 000)		
		1992	1993	% State	1992	1993	1992	1993	1992	1993	% State
SAN MATEO, CA - [continued]											
6553	Cemetery subdividers and developers	12	11	4.6	204	286	24,980	23,510	6,285	7,684	6.6
6700	Holding and other investment offices	163	163	4.5	1,585	1,010	44,096	55,152	76,430	68,757	4.9
6710	Holding offices	29	29	4.4	269	376	49,770	53,809	12,622	23,200	3.4
6720	Investment offices	16	10	9.7	253	58	74,751	18,759	21,892	1,206	1.7
6732	Educational, religious, etc. trusts	12	11	1.6	55	53	48,218	51,321	2,732	2,904	2.0
6733	Trusts, n.e.c.	36	33	3.7	590	80	21,146	46,100	12,444	3,776	3.9
6794	Patent owners and lessors	6	6	2.5	40	25	43,400	46,400	1,817	1,160	0.7
6798	Real estate investment trusts	9	5	4.2	30	-	57,600	-	1,540	-	-
6799	Investors, n.e.c.	52	66	8.0	342	389	53,778	65,337	22,932	35,238	19.3
SANTA BARBARA, CA											
60 –	**Finance, insurance, and real estate**	971	996	1.3	8,248	8,342	28,044	27,206	226,946	232,826	0.8
6000	Depository institutions	160	143	1.3	2,910	2,520	25,100	24,476	66,406	60,229	0.8
6020	Commercial banks	98	85	1.4	2,000	1,908	23,304	24,505	47,340	45,783	1.0
6030	Savings institutions	38	35	1.2	654	363	33,015	28,099	14,310	9,845	0.6
6060	Credit unions	20	19	1.5	245	236	19,053	19,186	4,538	4,392	1.0
6090	Functions closely related to banking	4	4	0.4	11	13	15,636	15,077	218	209	0.1
6100	Nondepository institutions	62	72	1.0	493	656	35,708	32,726	18,651	21,398	0.7
6140	Personal credit institutions	20	21	1.3	306	374	37,020	34,321	11,371	12,228	2.3
6160	Mortgage bankers and brokers	35	47	1.0	145	244	31,366	28,230	5,627	7,746	0.4
6200	Security and commodity brokers	61	69	1.7	547	642	60,614	56,100	32,283	36,683	1.0
6210	Security brokers and dealers	29	35	1.7	409	384	64,822	75,240	24,937	28,340	1.1
6300	Insurance carriers	76	64	1.4	625	581	37,990	38,017	22,424	20,665	0.4
6310	Life insurance	10	7	0.7	247	242	43,174	36,645	9,050	7,987	0.7
6324	Hospital and medical service plans	10	5	2.0	-	52	-	39,077	-	1,950	0.2
6330	Fire, marine, and casualty insurance	37	36	1.6	83	95	47,904	44,547	3,848	4,112	0.1
6360	Title insurance	11	11	1.9	197	174	33,909	37,057	7,188	6,104	1.1
6370	Pension, health, and welfare funds	7	5	1.4	19	18	19,158	28,222	321	512	0.4
6400	Insurance agents, brokers, and service	131	136	1.1	1,025	826	32,550	34,005	34,672	29,114	1.2
6500	Real estate	421	448	1.4	2,413	2,863	17,877	17,270	45,582	55,821	1.2
6510	Real estate operators and lessors	197	222	1.5	833	1,370	14,459	14,307	12,608	21,792	1.7
6530	Real estate agents and managers	165	205	1.3	1,198	1,350	19,359	18,939	24,378	29,053	1.1
6552	Subdividers and developers, n.e.c.	18	14	1.0	134	105	22,866	25,905	3,045	3,583	1.2
6720	Investment offices	4	3	2.9	3	-	144,000	-	581	-	-
6732	Educational, religious, etc. trusts	9	10	1.5	89	67	24,135	26,925	1,829	1,800	1.2
6733	Trusts, n.e.c.	20	23	2.5	52	78	23,923	23,128	1,043	2,312	2.4
6799	Investors, n.e.c.	10	13	1.6	18	50	41,778	33,840	568	1,615	0.9
SANTA CLARA, CA											
60 –	**Finance, insurance, and real estate**	3,839	3,869	5.1	32,030	32,078	30,133	29,368	978,589	997,951	3.5
6000	Depository institutions	563	525	4.7	9,657	9,898	25,711	25,526	237,906	245,599	3.3
6020	Commercial banks	305	260	4.4	6,737	6,740	25,259	24,904	160,880	158,917	3.4
6030	Savings institutions	153	151	5.2	1,871	1,764	26,792	27,170	47,965	47,804	2.9
6060	Credit unions	68	70	5.6	887	1,227	27,441	26,579	25,057	33,955	8.0
6100	Nondepository institutions	373	429	5.8	3,419	3,751	35,062	32,724	131,487	146,367	4.9
6140	Personal credit institutions	92	77	4.6	918	606	22,937	23,340	20,619	13,511	2.5
6150	Business credit institutions	23	31	4.5	188	235	35,191	40,698	7,067	11,010	2.0
6160	Mortgage bankers and brokers	255	321	6.5	2,227	2,910	39,734	34,034	100,044	121,846	6.6
6200	Security and commodity brokers	166	182	4.5	1,666	1,702	63,258	63,215	99,472	106,140	2.8
6210	Security brokers and dealers	79	81	3.9	1,364	1,039	67,856	72,100	84,668	76,364	2.9
6220	Commodity contracts brokers, dealers	3	4	5.7	-	6	-	30,000	-	194	-
6280	Security and commodity services	84	97	5.0	-	657	-	49,467	-	29,582	2.6
6300	Insurance carriers	353	268	5.8	4,661	3,880	37,415	38,332	175,550	157,301	2.7
6310	Life insurance	52	43	4.3	948	758	36,460	38,142	32,041	31,409	2.6
6321	Accident and health insurance	7	2	3.1	39	-	33,026	-	1,382	-	-
6324	Hospital and medical service plans	5	5	2.0	236	-	28,169	-	9,115	-	-
6330	Fire, marine, and casualty insurance	143	126	5.6	1,830	1,626	41,447	42,654	74,315	68,704	2.5
6350	Surety insurance	9	4	3.9	-	16	-	45,000	-	462	0.5

Source: County Business Patterns, 1992/93, CBP-92/93-1, U.S. Department of Commerce, Washington, D.C., April 1995. SIC categories for which data were suppressed or not available for both 1992 and 1993 are *not* displayed. The employment columns represent mid-March employment in the year. Pay per employee is calculated by dividing 1st Quarter payroll, annualized, by mid-March employment. The columns headed "% State" show the county's percentage of the state total for the SIC in 1993; for example, 0.9% for SIC 6030 means that the county had 0.9 percent of the state's total establishments (or payroll) in SIC 6030 in 1993. A dash (-) is used to indicate that data are not available or cannot be calculated; *nec* means not elsewhere classified.

Continued on next page.

SIC	Industry	No. Establishments			Employment		Pay / Employee		Annual Payroll ($ 000)		
		1992	1993	% State	1992	1993	1992	1993	1992	1993	% State
SANTA CLARA, CA - [continued]											
6360	Title insurance	56	71	12.3	1,293	1,076	36,201	32,788	48,235	39,615	7.1
6370	Pension, health, and welfare funds	78	17	4.7	273	172	27,897	36,977	9,104	6,429	4.4
6400	Insurance agents, brokers, and service	560	607	5.1	2,968	2,642	28,628	31,067	86,495	87,228	3.5
6500	Real estate	1,654	1,690	5.2	8,534	9,290	22,546	20,811	203,259	211,454	4.7
6510	Real estate operators and lessors	682	720	4.9	3,251	4,018	18,423	16,099	62,024	67,601	5.2
6530	Real estate agents and managers	713	886	5.8	4,064	4,555	23,283	23,891	98,078	122,397	4.6
6540	Title abstract offices	25	18	6.7	249	298	34,394	29,611	9,250	9,327	6.7
6552	Subdividers and developers, n.e.c.	73	54	4.0	337	184	36,831	31,826	15,189	6,479	2.1
6553	Cemetery subdividers and developers	4	6	2.5	144	232	27,750	21,776	4,100	5,410	4.7
6700	Holding and other investment offices	161	158	4.4	883	701	35,176	39,030	36,199	35,577	2.5
6710	Holding offices	24	19	2.9	262	179	41,466	42,279	11,538	9,211	1.3
6720	Investment offices	8	5	4.9	65	15	26,831	55,200	2,147	826	1.2
6732	Educational, religious, etc. trusts	25	28	4.2	145	147	25,545	28,626	4,135	4,720	3.2
6733	Trusts, n.e.c.	47	41	4.5	167	133	21,701	21,143	6,712	6,143	6.4
6794	Patent owners and lessors	5	6	2.5	18	33	30,889	46,909	739	1,898	1.1
6799	Investors, n.e.c.	35	52	6.3	109	173	57,798	56,555	6,881	12,042	6.6
SANTA CRUZ, CA											
60 –	**Finance, insurance, and real estate**	548	559	0.7	3,488	3,701	23,407	22,858	85,401	93,155	0.3
6000	Depository institutions	80	80	0.7	1,225	1,351	20,744	20,669	25,809	27,434	0.4
6020	Commercial banks	43	41	0.7	833	929	19,717	19,910	16,690	17,625	0.4
6030	Savings institutions	27	28	1.0	272	287	23,176	22,927	6,499	6,893	0.4
6060	Credit unions	8	8	0.6	-	124	-	20,258	-	2,595	0.6
6090	Functions closely related to banking	2	3	0.3	-	11	-	30,545	-	321	0.1
6100	Nondepository institutions	42	46	0.6	177	216	31,277	30,722	7,629	9,381	0.3
6140	Personal credit institutions	8	7	0.4	35	-	28,571	-	1,029	-	-
6150	Business credit institutions	2	4	0.6	-	6	-	18,667	-	195	0.0
6160	Mortgage bankers and brokers	30	34	0.7	113	182	33,204	30,857	5,685	8,427	0.5
6200	Security and commodity brokers	17	18	0.4	71	88	46,873	40,045	3,637	4,909	0.1
6210	Security brokers and dealers	8	12	0.6	60	83	53,067	41,108	3,471	4,730	0.2
6280	Security and commodity services	9	6	0.3	11	5	13,091	22,400	166	179	0.0
6300	Insurance carriers	37	28	0.6	292	221	30,000	35,041	8,025	8,090	0.1
6330	Fire, marine, and casualty insurance	14	12	0.5	54	-	39,037	-	2,151	-	-
6360	Title insurance	11	10	1.7	140	-	35,143	-	4,609	-	-
6370	Pension, health, and welfare funds	6	1	0.3	56	-	15,571		491	-	-
6400	Insurance agents, brokers, and service	89	88	0.7	341	440	26,076	28,273	8,181	12,600	0.5
6500	Real estate	258	275	0.9	1,156	1,139	18,052	16,130	21,632	21,496	0.5
6510	Real estate operators and lessors	101	113	0.8	477	590	12,956	14,576	6,863	9,059	0.7
6530	Real estate agents and managers	122	140	0.9	438	478	18,767	17,632	8,160	10,219	0.4
6552	Subdividers and developers, n.e.c.	13	15	1.1	26	31	29,692	22,968	842	1,337	0.4
6553	Cemetery subdividers and developers	4	4	1.7	46	27	10,174	17,037	516	480	0.4
6700	Holding and other investment offices	25	24	0.7	226	246	39,150	32,341	10,488	9,245	0.7
6732	Educational, religious, etc. trusts	11	11	1.6	39	52	11,795	11,385	515	574	0.4
6733	Trusts, n.e.c.	5	4	0.4	15	10	20,000	16,400	301	216	0.2
SHASTA, CA											
60 –	**Finance, insurance, and real estate**	360	353	0.5	1,958	1,976	21,301	20,308	42,779	41,502	0.1
6000	Depository institutions	48	50	0.4	664	706	21,482	22,040	14,107	14,111	0.2
6020	Commercial banks	31	30	0.5	517	554	21,834	22,065	11,124	11,181	0.2
6030	Savings institutions	10	10	0.3	113	97	20,991	25,155	2,402	2,045	0.1
6060	Credit unions	7	9	0.7	34	-	17,765	-	581	-	-
6100	Nondepository institutions	35	33	0.4	224	171	31,339	26,129	6,711	5,545	0.2
6140	Personal credit institutions	12	10	0.6	50	43	25,440	26,884	1,218	1,073	0.2
6160	Mortgage bankers and brokers	23	23	0.5	174	128	33,034	25,875	5,493	4,472	0.2
6200	Security and commodity brokers	12	13	0.3	55	45	40,945	51,911	2,403	2,758	0.1
6300	Insurance carriers	31	26	0.6	253	184	25,866	26,783	7,032	4,635	0.1
6360	Title insurance	10	7	1.2	165	106	26,279	25,811	4,452	2,444	0.4
6370	Pension, health, and welfare funds	3	4	1.1	9	8	21,333	21,000	532	157	0.1

Source: County Business Patterns, 1992/93, CBP-92/93-1, U.S. Department of Commerce, Washington, D.C., April 1995. SIC categories for which data were suppressed or not available for both 1992 and 1993 are not displayed. The employment columns represent mid-March employment in the year. Pay per employee is calculated by dividing 1st Quarter payroll, annualized, by mid-March employment. The columns headed "% State" show the county's percentage of the state total for the SIC in 1993; for example, 0.9% for SIC 6030 means that the county had 0.9 percent of the state's total establishments (or payroll) in SIC 6030 in 1993. A dash (-) is used to indicate that data are not available or cannot be calculated; nec means not elsewhere classified.

Continued on next page.

SIC	Industry	No. Establishments			Employment		Pay / Employee		Annual Payroll ($ 000)		
		1992	1993	% State	1992	1993	1992	1993	1992	1993	% State
SHASTA, CA - [continued]											
6400	Insurance agents, brokers, and service	80	75	0.6	205	206	21,171	19,359	4,215	4,081	0.2
6500	Real estate	147	149	0.5	530	634	12,294	12,669	7,297	9,122	0.2
6510	Real estate operators and lessors	69	71	0.5	204	285	9,765	7,677	2,178	2,412	0.2
6530	Real estate agents and managers	52	55	0.4	178	209	13,326	14,909	2,489	3,264	0.1
6552	Subdividers and developers, n.e.c.	14	16	1.2	39	-	12,923	-	940	-	-
6700	Holding and other investment offices	7	7	0.2	27	30	28,593	27,200	1,014	1,250	0.1
6733	Trusts, n.e.c.	4	2	0.2	13	-	22,769	-	470	-	-
SIERRA, CA											
60 –	**Finance, insurance, and real estate**	4	3	0.0	11	7	18,182	19,429	171	156	0.0
SISKIYOU, CA											
60 –	**Finance, insurance, and real estate**	103	94	0.1	657	449	14,192	16,722	9,055	8,335	0.0
6000	Depository institutions	28	26	0.2	276	245	16,362	17,731	4,444	4,510	0.1
6300	Insurance carriers	9	4	0.1	46	28	20,261	22,286	1,024	655	0.0
6400	Insurance agents, brokers, and service	17	18	0.2	50	63	12,320	15,111	630	1,010	0.0
6500	Real estate	40	39	0.1	249	93	9,671	11,183	2,003	1,306	0.0
6510	Real estate operators and lessors	17	20	0.1	61	58	10,295	11,655	800	839	0.1
6530	Real estate agents and managers	16	15	0.1	28	-	10,286	-	352	-	-
6700	Holding and other investment offices	3	3	0.1	8	7	13,500	11,429	74	88	0.0
SOLANO, CA											
60 –	**Finance, insurance, and real estate**	586	595	0.8	3,786	4,036	21,473	20,905	83,026	91,141	0.3
6000	Depository institutions	96	95	0.8	1,388	1,347	19,922	20,537	27,669	28,798	0.4
6020	Commercial banks	55	51	0.9	843	805	21,338	21,610	17,953	18,187	0.4
6030	Savings institutions	20	19	0.7	211	159	19,583	21,384	4,122	3,302	0.2
6060	Credit unions	14	18	1.4	311	351	16,695	18,348	5,255	6,866	1.6
6090	Functions closely related to banking	7	7	0.7	23	32	14,783	13,375	339	443	0.2
6100	Nondepository institutions	64	62	0.8	409	403	34,866	30,521	14,230	14,528	0.5
6140	Personal credit institutions	29	26	1.6	166	-	30,265	-	4,991	-	-
6160	Mortgage bankers and brokers	35	34	0.7	243	257	38,008	34,101	9,239	10,954	0.6
6210	Security brokers and dealers	9	7	0.3	46	-	43,913	-	1,892	-	-
6280	Security and commodity services	5	6	0.3	-	10	-	23,200	-	221	0.0
6300	Insurance carriers	42	35	0.8	403	808	26,998	23,733	11,440	20,203	0.3
6310	Life insurance	5	6	0.6	66	427	25,818	16,393	1,625	6,722	0.5
6330	Fire, marine, and casualty insurance	19	16	0.7	78	184	31,744	35,870	2,429	7,203	0.3
6360	Title insurance	13	12	2.1	237	-	26,160	-	6,860	-	-
6400	Insurance agents, brokers, and service	88	94	0.8	243	231	22,486	18,996	5,496	4,755	0.2
6500	Real estate	265	285	0.9	1,112	1,042	15,784	15,881	18,570	17,553	0.4
6510	Real estate operators and lessors	88	110	0.7	342	438	13,123	12,146	4,432	5,889	0.5
6530	Real estate agents and managers	131	151	1.0	506	492	16,767	16,772	9,177	8,388	0.3
6552	Subdividers and developers, n.e.c.	13	14	1.0	126	49	17,175	25,796	2,201	1,150	0.4
6553	Cemetery subdividers and developers	3	3	1.3	31	27	20,516	22,963	665	649	0.6
6700	Holding and other investment offices	15	10	0.3	168	155	17,762	16,774	3,243	3,072	0.2
6733	Trusts, n.e.c.	5	4	0.4	-	20	-	10,800	-	204	0.2
SONOMA, CA											
60 –	**Finance, insurance, and real estate**	1,160	1,112	1.5	12,001	12,341	30,110	31,763	367,200	411,293	1.4
6000	Depository institutions	162	157	1.4	2,438	2,358	25,618	26,054	59,258	63,176	0.9
6020	Commercial banks	83	78	1.3	1,627	1,458	23,383	24,091	35,791	35,037	0.7
6030	Savings institutions	56	55	1.9	661	702	31,449	30,980	19,759	23,538	1.4
6060	Credit unions	16	18	1.4	128	181	24,844	23,337	3,249	4,263	1.0
6090	Functions closely related to banking	7	6	0.6	22	17	20,182	20,000	459	338	0.1
6100	Nondepository institutions	95	120	1.6	1,358	1,475	39,876	35,520	53,754	70,263	2.3
6140	Personal credit institutions	18	19	1.1	83	84	31,373	21,714	2,458	1,668	0.3
6160	Mortgage bankers and brokers	72	94	1.9	1,246	1,337	40,671	36,760	50,232	67,026	3.6
6200	Security and commodity brokers	50	56	1.4	256	273	56,109	54,066	15,889	18,380	0.5
6210	Security brokers and dealers	24	30	1.5	205	232	61,463	57,724	13,519	16,389	0.6

Source: County Business Patterns, 1992/93, CBP-92/93-1, U.S. Department of Commerce, Washington, D.C., April 1995. SIC categories for which data were suppressed or not available for both 1992 and 1993 are not displayed. The employment columns represent mid-March employment in the year. Pay per employee is calculated by dividing 1st Quarter payroll, annualized, by mid-March employment. The columns headed "% State" show the county's percentage of the state total for the SIC in 1993; for example, 0.9% for SIC 6030 means that the county had 0.9 percent of the state's total establishments (or payroll) in SIC 6030 in 1993. A dash (-) is used to indicate that data are not available or cannot be calculated; nec means not elsewhere classified.

Continued on next page.

SIC	Industry	No. Establishments			Employment		Pay / Employee		Annual Payroll ($ 000)		
		1992	1993	% State	1992	1993	1992	1993	1992	1993	% State
SONOMA, CA - [continued]											
6280	Security and commodity services	26	26	1.4	51	41	34,588	33,366	2,370	1,991	0.2
6300	Insurance carriers	134	76	1.6	4,603	4,805	33,588	38,674	163,040	178,649	3.1
6310	Life insurance	10	11	1.1	578	559	37,640	42,877	19,419	18,896	1.5
6330	Fire, marine, and casualty insurance	38	36	1.6	3,460	3,682	34,348	38,815	127,707	139,169	5.0
6360	Title insurance	26	20	3.5	379	232	26,438	30,017	10,870	8,015	1.4
6400	Insurance agents, brokers, and service	188	185	1.6	1,125	1,122	28,267	27,626	32,161	33,397	1.4
6500	Real estate	483	466	1.4	1,750	1,634	19,838	20,218	34,577	33,241	0.7
6510	Real estate operators and lessors	179	187	1.3	686	608	15,965	16,539	9,607	9,713	0.7
6530	Real estate agents and managers	237	245	1.6	826	880	21,046	21,527	16,661	18,856	0.7
6552	Subdividers and developers, n.e.c.	30	22	1.6	51	36	30,667	30,333	2,724	1,216	0.4
6710	Holding offices	5	3	0.5	-	5	-	118,400	-	536	0.1
6732	Educational, religious, etc. trusts	13	14	2.1	311	376	8,977	8,234	3,211	3,254	2.2
6733	Trusts, n.e.c.	16	19	2.1	32	21	16,250	18,667	854	980	1.0
6799	Investors, n.e.c.	5	6	0.7	4	9	88,000	22,222	173	329	0.2
STANISLAUS, CA											
60 –	**Finance, insurance, and real estate**	711	695	0.9	4,991	5,126	22,446	23,172	114,462	127,752	0.4
6000	Depository institutions	119	111	1.0	1,540	1,660	21,101	19,735	31,608	33,012	0.4
6020	Commercial banks	68	57	1.0	1,085	1,134	20,962	18,977	22,345	21,675	0.5
6030	Savings institutions	30	29	1.0	287	312	22,913	22,564	6,061	7,102	0.4
6060	Credit unions	11	13	1.0	117	150	18,701	21,360	2,191	3,275	0.8
6090	Functions closely related to banking	10	12	1.3	51	64	19,373	15,562	1,011	960	0.3
6100	Nondepository institutions	80	88	1.2	611	573	33,597	33,166	20,467	23,179	0.8
6140	Personal credit institutions	27	24	1.4	136	100	27,765	29,480	3,555	2,453	0.5
6160	Mortgage bankers and brokers	41	53	1.1	366	364	33,344	32,187	12,767	16,927	0.9
6200	Security and commodity brokers	26	23	0.6	156	198	44,282	40,747	7,407	9,289	0.2
6210	Security brokers and dealers	15	15	0.7	140	188	47,429	42,191	7,155	9,171	0.3
6280	Security and commodity services	11	8	0.4	16	10	16,750	13,600	252	118	0.0
6300	Insurance carriers	63	45	1.0	888	860	26,423	27,591	24,637	24,152	0.4
6330	Fire, marine, and casualty insurance	29	23	1.0	106	99	36,113	41,939	4,123	4,216	0.2
6360	Title insurance	10	10	1.7	299	220	29,659	32,618	9,534	7,487	1.4
6400	Insurance agents, brokers, and service	130	135	1.1	435	601	18,198	24,992	8,105	14,984	0.6
6500	Real estate	267	271	0.8	1,164	1,093	14,045	15,016	17,735	18,987	0.4
6510	Real estate operators and lessors	115	123	0.8	564	565	11,248	12,135	7,201	8,423	0.6
6530	Real estate agents and managers	88	126	0.8	326	400	17,301	16,860	6,209	7,513	0.3
6552	Subdividers and developers, n.e.c.	18	13	1.0	125	100	18,944	23,000	2,225	2,503	0.8
6553	Cemetery subdividers and developers	6	7	2.9	27	28	18,667	18,286	533	538	0.5
6700	Holding and other investment offices	26	22	0.6	197	141	22,173	26,865	4,503	4,149	0.3
6732	Educational, religious, etc. trusts	5	6	0.9	-	24	-	10,333	-	261	0.2
6733	Trusts, n.e.c.	14	10	1.1	-	26	-	11,538	-	463	0.5
6799	Investors, n.e.c.	3	3	0.4	5	-	31,200	-	164	-	-
SUTTER, CA											
60 –	**Finance, insurance, and real estate**	150	152	0.2	875	906	20,114	20,071	17,510	18,691	0.1
6000	Depository institutions	22	23	0.2	338	353	19,207	20,487	6,884	7,313	0.1
6020	Commercial banks	12	11	0.2	217	223	20,092	18,978	4,408	4,576	0.1
6030	Savings institutions	6	7	0.2	55	67	18,255	23,881	1,137	1,462	0.1
6100	Nondepository institutions	16	19	0.3	73	97	46,247	44,124	2,599	4,113	0.1
6140	Personal credit institutions	6	6	0.4	-	24	-	27,667	-	683	0.1
6160	Mortgage bankers and brokers	8	10	0.2	33	57	61,697	51,298	1,306	2,832	0.2
6300	Insurance carriers	12	9	0.2	93	-	29,591	-	2,837	-	-
6360	Title insurance	3	1	0.2	67	-	24,179	-	1,705	-	-
6400	Insurance agents, brokers, and service	24	23	0.2	81	98	18,469	17,184	1,464	1,821	0.1
6500	Real estate	70	71	0.2	266	289	12,075	11,045	3,427	3,476	0.1

Source: County Business Patterns, 1992/93, CBP-92/93-1, U.S. Department of Commerce, Washington, D.C., April 1995. SIC categories for which data were suppressed or not available for both 1992 and 1993 are *not* displayed. The employment columns represent mid-March employment in the year. Pay per employee is calculated by dividing 1st Quarter payroll, annualized, by mid-March employment. The columns headed "% State" show the county's percentage of the state total for the SIC in 1993; for example, 0.9% for SIC 6030 means that the county had 0.9 percent of the state's total establishments (or payroll) in SIC 6030 in 1993. A dash (-) is used to indicate that data are not available or cannot be calculated; *nec* means not elsewhere classified.

Continued on next page.

SIC	Industry	No. Establishments			Employment		Pay / Employee		Annual Payroll ($ 000)		
		1992	1993	% State	1992	1993	1992	1993	1992	1993	% State
SUTTER, CA - [continued]											
6510	Real estate operators and lessors	24	30	0.2	56	-	8,357	-	458	-	-
6530	Real estate agents and managers	40	40	0.3	185	218	13,146	10,881	2,592	2,543	0.1
6700	Holding and other investment offices	4	5	0.1	-	20	-	7,600	-	170	0.0
TEHAMA, CA											
60 –	**Finance, insurance, and real estate**	90	79	0.1	558	638	18,029	19,969	9,967	10,661	0.0
6000	Depository institutions	14	13	0.1	197	222	19,431	19,387	3,381	3,842	0.1
6020	Commercial banks	9	9	0.2	170	198	20,000	19,677	2,908	3,539	0.1
6100	Nondepository institutions	4	3	0.0	14	36	19,714	31,889	359	1,157	0.0
6300	Insurance carriers	10	6	0.1	210	220	21,010	25,636	4,658	3,967	0.1
6400	Insurance agents, brokers, and service	19	18	0.2	50	47	13,840	15,915	700	772	0.0
6500	Real estate	39	35	0.1	83	107	8,434	7,065	721	788	0.0
6510	Real estate operators and lessors	20	19	0.1	58	76	7,448	6,737	445	541	0.0
6530	Real estate agents and managers	17	14	0.1	23	-	10,087	-	238	-	-
TRINITY, CA											
60 –	**Finance, insurance, and real estate**	17	16	0.0	72	60	17,778	17,733	1,384	1,081	0.0
6000	Depository institutions	5	5	0.0	43	33	17,953	19,273	810	501	0.0
6400	Insurance agents, brokers, and service	3	3	0.0	8	-	14,500	-	118	-	-
6500	Real estate	6	6	0.0	15	15	20,267	17,867	322	369	0.0
TULARE, CA											
60 –	**Finance, insurance, and real estate**	436	436	0.6	3,930	3,838	23,008	22,817	95,816	90,833	0.3
6000	Depository institutions	78	70	0.6	1,139	1,151	21,830	22,269	24,300	23,877	0.3
6020	Commercial banks	50	44	0.7	914	903	22,197	23,322	19,886	19,470	0.4
6030	Savings institutions	14	11	0.4	108	-	22,185	-	2,172	-	-
6060	Credit unions	7	8	0.6	-	116	-	20,414	-	2,384	0.6
6100	Nondepository institutions	48	50	0.7	304	349	30,303	25,524	9,887	10,998	0.4
6160	Mortgage bankers and brokers	13	16	0.3	85	120	39,388	31,100	4,402	5,848	0.3
6200	Security and commodity brokers	11	8	0.2	58	60	50,897	45,067	3,016	3,344	0.1
6210	Security brokers and dealers	9	8	0.4	-	60	-	45,067	-	3,344	0.1
6300	Insurance carriers	43	37	0.8	1,383	1,167	25,316	27,362	39,338	32,471	0.6
6310	Life insurance	7	5	0.5	-	443	-	21,887	-	8,983	0.7
6330	Fire, marine, and casualty insurance	20	17	0.8	553	502	30,467	31,530	22,283	16,613	0.6
6360	Title insurance	12	12	2.1	231	174	28,294	30,736	6,539	5,697	1.0
6370	Pension, health, and welfare funds	4	3	0.8	-	48	-	22,083	-	1,178	0.8
6400	Insurance agents, brokers, and service	96	105	0.9	445	444	22,867	22,279	9,889	10,291	0.4
6500	Real estate	146	148	0.5	549	616	12,284	11,201	8,214	8,528	0.2
6510	Real estate operators and lessors	59	54	0.4	240	316	9,183	7,000	2,692	2,975	0.2
6530	Real estate agents and managers	61	78	0.5	249	237	15,647	16,388	3,893	4,398	0.2
6552	Subdividers and developers, n.e.c.	11	15	1.1	29	63	8,000	12,762	1,136	1,112	0.4
6732	Educational, religious, etc. trusts	3	3	0.4	2	4	30,000	25,000	82	133	0.1
6733	Trusts, n.e.c.	5	5	0.6	30	4	6,533	18,000	218	80	0.1
TUOLUMNE, CA											
60 –	**Finance, insurance, and real estate**	119	123	0.2	690	661	18,342	19,516	13,338	14,738	0.1
6000	Depository institutions	21	20	0.2	266	265	17,699	18,581	4,672	5,744	0.1
6020	Commercial banks	14	13	0.2	196	200	17,449	17,800	3,362	4,384	0.1
6030	Savings institutions	7	7	0.2	70	65	18,400	20,985	1,310	1,360	0.1
6100	Nondepository institutions	7	7	0.1	28	26	23,714	24,308	892	882	0.0
6160	Mortgage bankers and brokers	5	6	0.1	18	-	21,778	-	598	-	-
6300	Insurance carriers	6	6	0.1	135	132	22,074	23,212	3,360	3,156	0.1
6400	Insurance agents, brokers, and service	16	18	0.2	84	74	22,190	24,324	1,945	1,941	0.1
6500	Real estate	65	65	0.2	167	154	12,335	12,753	2,011	2,385	0.1
6510	Real estate operators and lessors	18	21	0.1	69	56	7,072	10,143	534	874	0.1
6530	Real estate agents and managers	37	37	0.2	58	-	13,793	-	715	-	-

Source: County Business Patterns, 1992/93, CBP-92/93-1, U.S. Department of Commerce, Washington, D.C., April 1995. SIC categories for which data were suppressed or not available for both 1992 and 1993 are *not* displayed. The employment columns represent mid-March employment in the year. Pay per employee is calculated by dividing 1st Quarter payroll, annualized, by mid-March employment. The columns headed "% State" show the county's percentage of the state total for the SIC in 1993; for example, 0.9% for SIC 6030 means that the county had 0.9 percent of the state's total establishments (or payroll) in SIC 6030 in 1993. A dash (-) is used to indicate that data are not available or cannot be calculated; *nec* means not elsewhere classified.

SIC	Industry	No. Establishments			Employment		Pay / Employee		Annual Payroll ($ 000)		
		1992	1993	% State	1992	1993	1992	1993	1992	1993	% State
VENTURA, CA											
60–	**Finance, insurance, and real estate**	1,375	1,369	1.8	11,306	11,253	27,372	26,360	297,976	294,344	1.0
6000	Depository institutions	220	205	1.8	3,313	3,310	24,130	21,144	76,682	69,327	0.9
6020	Commercial banks	117	104	1.7	2,240	2,221	24,027	20,674	52,282	44,369	0.9
6030	Savings institutions	69	65	2.2	738	712	25,247	22,455	16,779	16,342	1.0
6060	Credit unions	20	23	1.8	263	308	21,217	20,052	5,561	6,378	1.5
6090	Functions closely related to banking	14	13	1.4	72	69	26,556	27,652	2,060	2,238	0.8
6100	Nondepository institutions	137	146	2.0	604	775	32,245	28,335	21,269	26,601	0.9
6140	Personal credit institutions	45	40	2.4	288	259	29,139	23,985	7,958	5,642	1.1
6150	Business credit institutions	9	8	1.2	22	-	37,273	-	859	-	-
6160	Mortgage bankers and brokers	82	96	2.0	291	430	35,010	29,963	12,353	17,966	1.0
6200	Security and commodity brokers	62	71	1.7	443	545	47,810	44,037	21,559	27,022	0.7
6210	Security brokers and dealers	32	36	1.8	286	306	58,308	61,778	16,544	20,896	0.8
6280	Security and commodity services	30	34	1.8	157	-	28,688	-	5,015	-	-
6300	Insurance carriers	96	81	1.7	2,789	2,550	35,563	39,475	86,304	84,033	1.4
6310	Life insurance	17	14	1.4	316	265	27,519	27,758	8,456	6,852	0.6
6330	Fire, marine, and casualty insurance	50	43	1.9	1,061	1,010	32,893	33,549	35,216	32,352	1.2
6360	Title insurance	9	9	1.6	342	298	36,772	38,644	12,471	14,839	2.7
6370	Pension, health, and welfare funds	12	4	1.1	59	-	23,254	-	1,556	-	-
6400	Insurance agents, brokers, and service	264	274	2.3	840	863	27,652	26,851	24,886	25,390	1.0
6500	Real estate	543	547	1.7	2,989	2,918	19,053	16,861	58,391	54,051	1.2
6510	Real estate operators and lessors	187	201	1.4	1,070	1,157	13,574	14,292	16,272	17,921	1.4
6530	Real estate agents and managers	277	312	2.0	1,337	1,526	21,418	18,433	28,837	31,386	1.2
6540	Title abstract offices	2	3	1.1	-	5	-	24,800	-	144	0.1
6552	Subdividers and developers, n.e.c.	24	25	1.9	419	188	23,074	19,596	9,552	3,770	1.2
6553	Cemetery subdividers and developers	3	4	1.7	30	42	20,133	17,333	644	797	0.7
6700	Holding and other investment offices	50	42	1.2	318	284	28,491	25,676	8,498	7,467	0.5
6710	Holding offices	5	8	1.2	77	36	40,831	51,111	2,570	1,740	0.3
6732	Educational, religious, etc. trusts	10	7	1.0	76	65	19,105	16,862	1,504	1,182	0.8
6733	Trusts, n.e.c.	15	11	1.2	52	40	24,769	24,100	1,110	1,022	1.1
6799	Investors, n.e.c.	9	7	0.8	35	11	18,057	22,909	474	288	0.2
YOLO, CA											
60–	**Finance, insurance, and real estate**	297	287	0.4	2,726	3,260	22,468	24,466	73,652	87,533	0.3
6000	Depository institutions	48	41	0.4	1,236	1,185	23,188	24,810	38,666	32,804	0.4
6020	Commercial banks	24	21	0.4	620	395	18,071	19,959	11,362	7,475	0.2
6100	Nondepository institutions	11	10	0.1	85	85	39,624	46,541	3,614	3,993	0.1
6140	Personal credit institutions	4	3	0.2	12	-	26,000	-	306	-	-
6200	Security and commodity brokers	7	9	0.2	37	44	32,432	29,909	1,262	1,545	0.0
6300	Insurance carriers	24	21	0.5	421	399	26,005	25,083	11,602	10,511	0.2
6330	Fire, marine, and casualty insurance	8	7	0.3	52	50	36,231	35,600	1,834	1,665	0.1
6360	Title insurance	7	8	1.4	85	119	27,718	29,311	2,466	3,517	0.6
6400	Insurance agents, brokers, and service	34	39	0.3	156	713	28,872	31,989	4,810	23,159	0.9
6500	Real estate	157	152	0.5	744	790	15,242	14,299	12,454	14,268	0.3
6510	Real estate operators and lessors	76	81	0.5	386	467	13,181	12,702	5,428	6,478	0.5
6530	Real estate agents and managers	50	51	0.3	202	-	15,188	-	3,424	-	-
6552	Subdividers and developers, n.e.c.	11	15	1.1	70	-	23,886	-	1,900	-	-
6732	Educational, religious, etc. trusts	3	4	0.6	13	15	30,154	28,000	416	426	0.3
6733	Trusts, n.e.c.	6	5	0.6	13	13	16,308	14,154	222	187	0.2
YUBA, CA											
60–	**Finance, insurance, and real estate**	76	73	0.1	621	591	19,440	19,614	11,998	11,684	0.0
6000	Depository institutions	13	12	0.1	157	161	20,357	19,280	3,029	3,098	0.0
6020	Commercial banks	6	6	0.1	119	124	20,336	19,452	2,341	2,421	0.1
6300	Insurance carriers	10	5	0.1	298	246	19,839	21,089	5,810	5,218	0.1
6360	Title insurance	3	2	0.3	36	-	33,000	-	972	-	-
6400	Insurance agents, brokers, and service	19	22	0.2	54	73	24,667	24,603	1,470	1,775	0.1
6500	Real estate	26	29	0.1	89	101	13,079	12,158	1,033	1,308	0.0

Source: County Business Patterns, 1992/93, CBP-92/93-1, U.S. Department of Commerce, Washington, D.C., April 1995. SIC categories for which data were suppressed or not available for both 1992 and 1993 are *not* displayed. The employment columns represent mid-March employment in the year. Pay per employee is calculated by dividing 1st Quarter payroll, annualized, by mid-March employment. The columns headed "% State" show the county's percentage of the state total for the SIC in 1993; for example, 0.9% for SIC 6030 means that the county had 0.9 percent of the state's total establishments (or payroll) in SIC 6030 in 1993. A dash (-) is used to indicate that data are not available or cannot be calculated; *nec* means not elsewhere classified.

Continued on next page.

SIC	Industry	No. Establishments			Employment		Pay / Employee		Annual Payroll ($ 000)		
		1992	1993	% State	1992	1993	1992	1993	1992	1993	% State

YUBA, CA - [continued]

SIC	Industry	No. Establishments			Employment		Pay / Employee		Annual Payroll ($ 000)		
6510	Real estate operators and lessors	11	14	0.1	27	50	6,815	9,600	136	487	0.0
6530	Real estate agents and managers	10	9	0.1	22	-	16,545	-	353	-	-
6700	Holding and other investment offices	3	2	0.1	16	-	22,500	-	558	-	-

Source: County Business Patterns, 1992/93, CBP-92/93-1, U.S. Department of Commerce, Washington, D.C., April 1995. SIC categories for which data were suppressed or not available for both 1992 and 1993 are not displayed. The employment columns represent mid-March employment in the year. Pay per employee is calculated by dividing 1st Quarter payroll, annualized, by mid-March employment. The columns headed "% State" show the county's percentage of the state total for the SIC in 1993; for example, 0.9% for SIC 6030 means that the county had 0.9 percent of the state's total establishments (or payroll) in SIC 6030 in 1993. A dash (-) is used to indicate that data are not available or cannot be calculated; nec means not elsewhere classified.

COLORADO

SIC	Industry	No. Establishments			Employment		Pay / Employee		Annual Payroll ($ 000)		
		1992	1993	% State	1992	1993	1992	1993	1992	1993	% State
ADAMS, CO											
60 –	**Finance, insurance, and real estate**	453	477	4.2	2,709	3,259	23,009	20,551	63,951	72,208	2.2
6000	Depository institutions	47	57	4.9	771	1,097	20,939	20,058	15,905	23,524	3.7
6020	Commercial banks	18	24	4.1	523	742	20,184	23,671	10,257	18,844	4.1
6030	Savings institutions	13	11	5.2	126	-	24,825	-	3,169	-	-
6060	Credit unions	10	17	6.5	-	240	-	11,950	-	2,988	5.6
6100	Nondepository institutions	43	39	4.6	414	394	23,285	22,467	10,338	10,785	2.8
6140	Personal credit institutions	28	18	8.4	297	-	22,734	-	6,727	-	-
6160	Mortgage bankers and brokers	12	20	4.1	96	161	28,083	26,460	3,438	6,145	2.9
6280	Security and commodity services	7	8	2.5	18	20	22,222	23,000	395	443	0.3
6300	Insurance carriers	61	42	6.0	426	339	27,793	27,599	13,179	9,414	1.3
6310	Life insurance	7	7	3.7	82	55	31,220	36,509	2,953	1,882	0.6
6370	Pension, health, and welfare funds	13	14	15.1	54	109	13,481	15,450	1,383	1,807	5.3
6400	Insurance agents, brokers, and service	107	123	5.4	310	339	20,877	21,027	6,977	7,660	2.9
6500	Real estate	173	191	3.7	705	966	13,759	11,466	10,348	13,821	2.4
6510	Real estate operators and lessors	81	76	4.4	405	645	13,037	8,781	5,245	6,771	4.6
6530	Real estate agents and managers	76	105	3.5	240	300	15,500	17,280	4,202	6,689	1.8
6552	Subdividers and developers, n.e.c.	2	3	1.5	-	5	-	11,200	-	107	0.4
6553	Cemetery subdividers and developers	4	4	9.8	-	16	-	10,750	-	227	2.4
6700	Holding and other investment offices	10	11	2.0	57	96	139,368	82,375	6,595	6,346	3.1
6710	Holding offices	3	3	2.5	-	81	-	94,321	-	5,990	4.5
ALAMOSA, CO											
60 –	**Finance, insurance, and real estate**	32	31	0.3	193	214	20,539	17,850	3,484	3,802	0.1
6000	Depository institutions	6	6	0.5	111	125	21,766	20,480	2,118	2,293	0.4
6400	Insurance agents, brokers, and service	13	14	0.6	57	59	20,211	15,119	939	1,034	0.4
6500	Real estate	10	9	0.2	17	-	15,294	-	250	-	-
6510	Real estate operators and lessors	3	4	0.2	7	-	14,857	-	107	-	-
6530	Real estate agents and managers	5	5	0.2	7	12	13,143	10,333	121	145	0.0
ARAPAHOE, CO											
60 –	**Finance, insurance, and real estate**	1,681	1,805	15.8	23,861	26,070	31,634	29,119	742,506	877,474	26.7
6000	Depository institutions	141	140	12.2	4,283	4,085	28,336	25,342	119,237	107,090	16.8
6020	Commercial banks	67	64	10.9	1,175	1,403	25,944	25,542	29,217	35,634	7.8
6030	Savings institutions	35	31	14.7	518	338	28,548	29,337	14,556	9,334	22.3
6090	Functions closely related to banking	16	18	20.5	2,087	-	26,890	-	54,998	-	-
6100	Nondepository institutions	175	199	23.4	3,798	4,506	27,890	31,324	111,344	159,105	41.0
6140	Personal credit institutions	72	61	28.4	1,446	-	22,445	-	34,880	-	-
6150	Business credit institutions	19	24	20.0	1,471	1,417	29,066	29,157	38,766	37,951	45.9
6160	Mortgage bankers and brokers	80	111	22.7	868	1,304	35,143	33,666	37,414	69,151	32.2
6200	Security and commodity brokers	115	118	16.6	1,927	2,259	53,158	50,199	86,275	109,075	23.8
6210	Security brokers and dealers	66	67	17.9	1,486	1,413	58,444	60,008	70,558	80,092	26.1
6280	Security and commodity services	49	50	15.8	441	-	35,347	-	15,717	-	-
6300	Insurance carriers	214	187	26.6	7,605	8,663	34,125	25,381	248,574	284,228	38.4
6310	Life insurance	53	51	26.8	3,906	5,138	36,219	18,807	131,691	161,570	53.6
6330	Fire, marine, and casualty insurance	97	82	28.8	2,412	2,561	33,950	36,245	80,466	91,305	32.7
6360	Title insurance	19	7	11.5	308	-	26,896	-	8,349	-	-
6370	Pension, health, and welfare funds	24	29	31.2	426	354	21,455	22,712	9,591	8,571	25.3
6400	Insurance agents, brokers, and service	325	368	16.2	1,636	-	33,770	-	56,093	-	-
6500	Real estate	605	683	13.3	3,568	3,590	20,028	20,874	78,755	89,008	15.5
6510	Real estate operators and lessors	180	210	12.2	832	966	15,668	16,170	15,604	19,468	13.3
6530	Real estate agents and managers	320	425	14.0	2,206	2,332	21,146	22,302	50,102	60,379	16.2

Source: *County Business Patterns, 1992/93*, CBP-92/93-1, U.S. Department of Commerce, Washington, D.C., April 1995. SIC categories for which data were suppressed or not available for both 1992 and 1993 are *not* displayed. The employment columns represent mid-March employment in the year. Pay per employee is calculated by dividing 1st Quarter payroll, annualized, by mid-March employment. The columns headed "% State" show the county's percentage of the state total for the SIC in 1993; for example, 0.9% for SIC 6030 means that the county had 0.9 percent of the state's total establishments (or payroll) in SIC 6030 in 1993. A dash (-) is used to indicate that data are not available or cannot be calculated; *nec* means not elsewhere classified.

Continued on next page.

SIC	Industry	No. Establishments			Employment		Pay / Employee		Annual Payroll ($ 000)		
		1992	1993	% State	1992	1993	1992	1993	1992	1993	% State
ARAPAHOE, CO - [continued]											
6540	Title abstract offices	1	3	5.1	-	4	-	23,000	-	126	1.1
6552	Subdividers and developers, n.e.c.	25	29	14.6	175	275	34,034	25,600	5,840	8,605	28.7
6553	Cemetery subdividers and developers	4	4	9.8	-	12	-	13,667	-	168	1.8
6700	Holding and other investment offices	99	103	18.3	-	985	-	49,385	-	63,886	31.3
6710	Holding offices	25	27	22.3	455	482	38,646	53,602	18,557	38,151	28.6
6720	Investment offices	4	5	25.0	8	-	29,000	-	291	-	-
6732	Educational, religious, etc. trusts	8	7	6.7	48	29	17,833	24,552	933	708	4.4
6733	Trusts, n.e.c.	15	20	19.8	35	46	17,029	13,739	634	984	17.2
6792	Oil royalty traders	5	7	16.3	5	-	38,400	-	451	-	-
6794	Patent owners and lessors	11	15	40.5	165	312	35,612	52,256	6,052	17,941	87.8
6798	Real estate investment trusts	6	2	22.2	23	-	48,348	-	989	-	-
6799	Investors, n.e.c.	21	19	15.4	92	52	28,217	31,846	2,813	2,307	19.8
ARCHULETA, CO											
60 –	**Finance, insurance, and real estate**	24	27	0.2	245	178	16,441	18,382	4,390	3,315	0.1
6000	Depository institutions	4	4	0.3	-	49	-	18,776	-	998	0.2
6400	Insurance agents, brokers, and service	2	6	0.3	-	15	-	9,600	-	169	0.1
6500	Real estate	15	17	0.3	192	114	16,104	19,368	3,414	2,148	0.4
6510	Real estate operators and lessors	4	5	0.3	9	-	15,111	-	135	-	-
6530	Real estate agents and managers	8	11	0.4	152	85	16,132	19,906	2,750	1,545	0.4
BACA, CO											
60 –	**Finance, insurance, and real estate**	11	11	0.1	40	44	15,500	15,091	633	726	0.0
6500	Real estate	5	5	0.1	7	7	7,429	8,000	55	59	0.0
BENT, CO											
60 –	**Finance, insurance, and real estate**	6	9	0.1	-	44	-	19,091	-	991	0.0
6000	Depository institutions	2	3	0.3	-	38	-	20,737	-	936	0.1
BOULDER, CO											
60 –	**Finance, insurance, and real estate**	750	832	7.3	4,618	5,028	24,104	23,558	121,577	140,360	4.3
6000	Depository institutions	68	75	6.5	1,548	1,587	22,568	23,340	33,683	37,872	5.9
6020	Commercial banks	37	40	6.8	1,228	1,189	23,814	25,359	27,576	30,725	6.7
6060	Credit unions	14	16	6.1	202	257	15,921	17,198	3,355	4,456	8.3
6100	Nondepository institutions	52	68	8.0	408	479	28,520	31,967	14,684	22,509	5.8
6140	Personal credit institutions	14	10	4.7	114	66	20,982	23,879	2,399	1,787	-
6150	Business credit institutions	5	14	11.7	8	83	34,500	23,084	340	2,389	2.9
6160	Mortgage bankers and brokers	29	44	9.0	283	330	31,618	35,818	11,886	18,333	8.5
6200	Security and commodity brokers	61	76	10.7	267	317	52,584	46,965	14,381	18,276	4.0
6210	Security brokers and dealers	32	34	9.1	207	222	59,923	56,991	11,770	14,111	4.6
6220	Commodity contracts brokers, dealers	3	5	25.0	10	-	53,200	-	649	-	-
6300	Insurance carriers	50	37	5.3	233	270	24,790	24,830	6,327	7,263	1.0
6324	Hospital and medical service plans	-	3	8.8	-	26	-	13,077	-	417	0.5
6360	Title insurance	8	5	8.2	74	55	22,270	30,618	1,862	2,638	7.7
6370	Pension, health, and welfare funds	12	8	8.6	83	119	14,120	14,017	1,445	1,138	3.4
6400	Insurance agents, brokers, and service	140	156	6.9	449	532	19,804	21,203	11,614	13,801	5.2
6500	Real estate	339	385	7.5	1,435	1,543	16,410	16,342	27,403	31,027	5.4
6510	Real estate operators and lessors	125	133	7.7	537	646	12,946	13,170	8,600	10,052	6.9
6530	Real estate agents and managers	167	222	7.3	734	824	17,869	17,951	14,600	17,965	4.8
6552	Subdividers and developers, n.e.c.	10	21	10.6	34	39	38,000	29,538	1,364	1,631	5.4
6553	Cemetery subdividers and developers	3	5	12.2	15	25	16,533	23,200	278	685	7.4
6700	Holding and other investment offices	40	35	6.2	278	300	44,906	26,707	13,485	9,612	4.7
6732	Educational, religious, etc. trusts	13	11	10.5	127	135	20,409	20,800	2,634	2,782	17.4
6733	Trusts, n.e.c.	5	6	5.9	57	40	17,895	11,300	1,139	531	9.3
6799	Investors, n.e.c.	9	8	6.5	-	43	-	40,000	-	1,568	13.5

Source: County Business Patterns, 1992/93, CBP-92/93-1, U.S. Department of Commerce, Washington, D.C., April 1995. SIC categories for which data were suppressed or not available for both 1992 and 1993 are *not* displayed. The employment columns represent mid-March employment in the year. Pay per employee is calculated by dividing 1st Quarter payroll, annualized, by mid-March employment. The columns headed "% State" show the county's percentage of the state total for the SIC in 1993; for example, 0.9% for SIC 6030 means that the county had 0.9 percent of the state's total establishments (or payroll) in SIC 6030 in 1993. A dash (-) is used to indicate that data are not available or cannot be calculated; *nec* means not elsewhere classified.

SIC	Industry	No. Establishments			Employment		Pay / Employee		Annual Payroll ($ 000)		
		1992	1993	% State	1992	1993	1992	1993	1992	1993	% State
CHAFFEE, CO											
60 –	**Finance, insurance, and real estate**	36	40	0.4	170	186	15,176	19,247	2,722	3,656	0.1
6000	Depository institutions	6	7	0.6	109	119	17,174	21,479	1,915	2,457	0.4
6020	Commercial banks	3	3	0.5	38	54	23,684	28,000	936	1,587	0.3
6030	Savings institutions	3	3	1.4	71	-	13,690	-	979	-	-
6400	Insurance agents, brokers, and service	9	12	0.5	23	-	18,087	-	429	-	-
6500	Real estate	18	19	0.4	34	42	7,529	9,619	334	479	0.1
6510	Real estate operators and lessors	5	7	0.4	5	9	8,000	8,444	62	114	0.1
6530	Real estate agents and managers	6	8	0.3	11	20	9,091	9,600	122	201	0.1
CHEYENNE, CO											
60 –	**Finance, insurance, and real estate**	4	4	0.0	43	49	17,116	17,061	841	962	0.0
CLEAR CREEK, CO											
60 –	**Finance, insurance, and real estate**	21	19	0.2	62	-	15,806	-	1,023	-	-
6400	Insurance agents, brokers, and service	3	4	0.2	6	-	15,333	-	108	-	-
6500	Real estate	13	11	0.2	23	-	11,652	-	282	-	-
6510	Real estate operators and lessors	5	4	0.2	13	-	6,462	-	97	-	-
6530	Real estate agents and managers	6	6	0.2	6	7	18,000	12,000	117	61	0.0
CONEJOS, CO											
60 –	**Finance, insurance, and real estate**	4	6	0.1	44	45	15,182	13,956	701	748	0.0
COSTILLA, CO											
60 –	**Finance, insurance, and real estate**	1	2	0.0	-	-	-	-	-	-	-
CROWLEY, CO											
60 –	**Finance, insurance, and real estate**	3	4	0.0	-	-	-	-	-	-	-
CUSTER, CO											
60 –	**Finance, insurance, and real estate**	10	11	0.1	36	54	18,111	14,148	705	980	0.0
6500	Real estate	6	7	0.1	14	22	11,714	8,909	227	362	0.1
6530	Real estate agents and managers	6	7	0.2	14	22	11,714	8,909	227	362	0.1
DELTA, CO											
60 –	**Finance, insurance, and real estate**	44	45	0.4	232	269	17,897	19,390	4,807	5,322	0.2
6000	Depository institutions	11	12	1.0	128	136	19,906	23,500	2,824	3,026	0.5
6020	Commercial banks	6	6	1.0	101	105	19,525	25,029	2,220	2,349	0.5
6100	Nondepository institutions	3	3	0.4	11	-	30,909	-	537	-	-
6400	Insurance agents, brokers, and service	11	13	0.6	38	-	13,895	-	571	-	-
6500	Real estate	15	16	0.3	42	58	11,714	11,448	595	740	0.1
6530	Real estate agents and managers	6	9	0.3	13	33	12,615	12,606	211	438	0.1
DENVER, CO											
60 –	**Finance, insurance, and real estate**	2,472	2,447	21.5	34,061	35,995	33,155	32,494	1,151,908	1,228,145	37.3
6000	Depository institutions	219	214	18.6	7,094	8,351	28,284	26,578	198,707	216,383	34.0
6020	Commercial banks	88	88	15.0	4,788	5,947	30,700	28,497	142,309	174,517	38.3
6030	Savings institutions	51	38	18.0	-	296	-	18,824	-	5,427	12.9
6060	Credit unions	49	56	21.4	619	795	21,525	14,803	13,098	12,436	23.3
6090	Functions closely related to banking	29	28	31.8	810	294	22,528	25,837	19,895	8,403	12.0
6100	Nondepository institutions	168	182	21.4	2,641	2,873	30,828	30,669	91,288	104,540	26.9
6140	Personal credit institutions	41	24	11.2	371	-	23,213	-	9,361	-	-
6150	Business credit institutions	29	43	35.8	918	1,001	28,449	29,730	26,556	30,253	36.6
6160	Mortgage bankers and brokers	95	113	23.2	1,343	1,579	34,591	31,995	55,109	65,774	30.6
6200	Security and commodity brokers	230	234	32.9	4,522	4,237	58,337	59,520	273,420	279,214	60.9
6210	Security brokers and dealers	110	113	30.2	3,028	2,340	63,398	68,161	198,830	172,771	56.3
6220	Commodity contracts brokers, dealers	4	3	15.0	48	-	75,250	-	3,722	-	-
6280	Security and commodity services	116	118	37.3	1,446	-	47,178	-	70,868	-	-
6300	Insurance carriers	230	170	24.2	6,434	7,131	33,521	33,575	210,063	242,594	32.8

Source: County Business Patterns, 1992/93, CBP-92/93-1, U.S. Department of Commerce, Washington, D.C., April 1995. SIC categories for which data were suppressed or not available for both 1992 and 1993 *are not* displayed. The employment columns represent mid-March employment in the year. Pay per employee is calculated by dividing 1st Quarter payroll, annualized, by mid-March employment. The columns headed "% State" show the county's percentage of the state total for the SIC in 1993; for example, 0.9% for SIC 6030 means that the county had 0.9 percent of the state's total establishments (or payroll) in SIC 6030 in 1993. A dash (-) is used to indicate that data are not available or cannot be calculated; *nec* means not elsewhere classified.

Continued on next page.

SIC	Industry	No. Establishments			Employment		Pay / Employee		Annual Payroll ($ 000)		
		1992	1993	% State	1992	1993	1992	1993	1992	1993	% State
DENVER, CO - [continued]											
6310	Life insurance	83	70	36.8	2,814	3,137	34,530	33,571	92,431	103,845	34.5
6321	Accident and health insurance	6	4	18.2	-	114	-	21,439	-	2,003	33.2
6324	Hospital and medical service plans	10	15	44.1	-	1,563	-	36,033	-	54,953	69.2
6330	Fire, marine, and casualty insurance	63	50	17.5	1,315	1,302	31,991	31,862	42,956	43,202	15.5
6360	Title insurance	17	10	16.4	545	377	30,576	32,531	18,540	16,601	48.6
6370	Pension, health, and welfare funds	43	14	15.1	118	-	20,712	-	5,819	-	-
6400	Insurance agents, brokers, and service	358	377	16.6	1,999	2,417	30,997	34,555	63,973	86,587	32.4
6500	Real estate	1,016	1,058	20.6	7,863	9,088	20,621	21,379	170,899	206,297	36.0
6510	Real estate operators and lessors	427	478	27.7	1,933	3,649	13,968	17,524	29,486	66,635	45.6
6530	Real estate agents and managers	477	541	17.9	5,193	5,182	22,335	23,896	120,510	132,265	35.4
6540	Title abstract offices	4	8	13.6	47	138	24,340	23,275	1,149	3,624	32.2
6552	Subdividers and developers, n.e.c.	31	20	10.1	310	-	34,103	-	10,889	-	-
6700	Holding and other investment offices	203	205	36.3	3,250	1,841	40,629	47,920	130,917	90,502	44.3
6710	Holding offices	40	41	33.9	1,638	1,089	52,005	58,777	85,396	65,095	48.9
6720	Investment offices	13	6	30.0	265	80	29,977	64,200	8,343	5,593	67.1
6732	Educational, religious, etc. trusts	36	44	41.9	221	276	28,181	25,014	6,270	7,023	43.8
6733	Trusts, n.e.c.	37	33	32.7	783	92	25,681	18,174	16,650	1,901	33.2
6792	Oil royalty traders	17	22	51.2	-	87	-	41,333	-	3,153	69.4
6799	Investors, n.e.c.	37	46	37.4	126	129	40,952	29,643	5,241	4,570	39.3
DOLORES, CO											
60 –	**Finance, insurance, and real estate**	3	3	0.0	-	-	-	-	-	-	-
DOUGLAS, CO											
60 –	**Finance, insurance, and real estate**	151	178	1.6	719	865	24,501	24,199	17,910	21,804	0.7
6000	Depository institutions	12	16	1.4	165	192	25,406	25,333	4,015	4,736	0.7
6020	Commercial banks	9	12	2.0	151	175	25,589	25,509	3,662	4,327	0.9
6100	Nondepository institutions	7	9	1.1	15	19	17,867	29,895	357	699	0.2
6160	Mortgage bankers and brokers	5	5	1.0	-	10	-	15,600	-	180	0.1
6200	Security and commodity brokers	10	11	1.5	-	24	-	24,833	-	653	0.1
6210	Security brokers and dealers	5	5	1.3	11	11	34,182	46,545	356	525	0.2
6280	Security and commodity services	4	6	1.9	9	13	5,333	6,462	74	128	0.1
6300	Insurance carriers	16	10	1.4	83	79	28,723	30,886	2,566	2,471	0.3
6400	Insurance agents, brokers, and service	25	37	1.6	67	96	34,328	28,667	2,042	2,917	1.1
6500	Real estate	79	90	1.8	365	446	21,556	21,426	7,940	10,138	1.8
6510	Real estate operators and lessors	14	21	1.2	39	-	9,949	-	412	-	-
6530	Real estate agents and managers	45	63	2.1	140	251	12,457	15,028	2,747	5,667	1.5
6700	Holding and other investment offices	2	5	0.9	-	9	-	17,333	-	190	0.1
EAGLE, CO											
60 –	**Finance, insurance, and real estate**	199	206	1.8	1,497	1,683	19,706	20,511	27,552	33,159	1.0
6000	Depository institutions	12	12	1.0	187	195	31,701	31,877	4,974	5,333	0.8
6100	Nondepository institutions	7	9	1.1	20	-	13,400	-	497	-	-
6160	Mortgage bankers and brokers	7	9	1.8	20	-	13,400	-	497	-	-
6400	Insurance agents, brokers, and service	11	10	0.4	32	38	28,375	38,737	1,148	1,354	0.5
6500	Real estate	156	162	3.2	1,212	1,372	17,337	17,796	19,464	23,908	4.2
6510	Real estate operators and lessors	13	20	1.2	206	133	16,680	15,038	3,233	1,923	1.3
6530	Real estate agents and managers	115	122	4.0	772	1,170	16,352	17,019	11,582	18,572	5.0
6552	Subdividers and developers, n.e.c.	9	12	6.1	54	59	26,222	38,576	1,750	3,039	10.1
ELBERT, CO											
60 –	**Finance, insurance, and real estate**	8	9	0.1	46	40	13,130	16,100	659	731	0.0
6400	Insurance agents, brokers, and service	2	3	0.1	-	9	-	13,778	-	106	0.0
EL PASO, CO											
60 –	**Finance, insurance, and real estate**	1,063	1,165	10.2	9,584	8,841	21,328	23,612	211,453	216,259	6.6
6000	Depository institutions	98	103	8.9	1,971	1,812	21,001	21,667	42,382	39,814	6.2
6020	Commercial banks	39	41	7.0	1,258	1,019	21,816	25,225	27,991	25,972	5.7

Source: County Business Patterns, 1992/93, CBP-92/93-1, U.S. Department of Commerce, Washington, D.C., April 1995. SIC categories for which data were suppressed or not available for both 1992 and 1993 are *not* displayed. The employment columns represent mid-March employment in the year. Pay per employee is calculated by dividing 1st Quarter payroll, annualized, by mid-March employment. The columns headed "% State" show the county's percentage of the state total for the SIC in 1993; for example, 0.9% for SIC 6030 means that the county had 0.9 percent of the state's total establishments (or payroll) in SIC 6030 in 1993. A dash (-) is used to indicate that data are not available or cannot be calculated; *nec* means not elsewhere classified.

Continued on next page.

SIC	Industry	No. Establishments			Employment		Pay / Employee		Annual Payroll ($ 000)		
		1992	1993	% State	1992	1993	1992	1993	1992	1993	% State
EL PASO, CO - [continued]											
6030	Savings institutions	12	13	6.2	150	142	25,867	19,746	4,159	3,122	7.4
6060	Credit unions	28	31	11.8	533	597	17,636	16,650	9,481	9,893	18.5
6090	Functions closely related to banking	19	18	20.5	30	54	22,267	15,037	751	827	1.2
6100	Nondepository institutions	77	85	10.0	729	760	31,298	31,363	24,753	29,562	7.6
6140	Personal credit institutions	36	34	15.8	225	-	24,516	-	5,573	-	-
6150	Business credit institutions	6	8	6.7	196	164	44,122	51,000	8,921	7,882	9.5
6160	Mortgage bankers and brokers	28	42	8.6	252	348	32,587	29,598	9,917	16,496	7.7
6200	Security and commodity brokers	74	82	11.5	403	440	47,792	49,109	19,406	21,206	4.6
6210	Security brokers and dealers	45	49	13.1	337	330	52,285	58,388	17,453	18,470	6.0
6280	Security and commodity services	28	32	10.1	-	110	-	21,273	-	2,732	1.9
6300	Insurance carriers	112	72	10.3	3,472	2,703	20,560	25,154	69,276	65,071	8.8
6310	Life insurance	26	22	11.6	375	465	24,544	25,557	9,601	11,307	3.8
6330	Fire, marine, and casualty insurance	47	32	11.2	2,229	1,414	20,285	27,174	48,868	42,531	15.2
6360	Title insurance	14	7	11.5	195	147	24,985	26,857	5,431	5,293	15.5
6370	Pension, health, and welfare funds	18	6	6.5	57	46	14,456	24,957	867	727	2.1
6400	Insurance agents, brokers, and service	205	229	10.1	725	931	19,123	21,302	15,592	19,070	7.1
6500	Real estate	451	545	10.6	1,989	2,016	15,005	15,897	34,370	36,916	6.4
6510	Real estate operators and lessors	149	168	9.7	617	589	11,669	12,475	8,469	8,219	5.6
6530	Real estate agents and managers	245	347	11.5	1,111	1,364	16,976	16,610	20,729	26,002	7.0
6552	Subdividers and developers, n.e.c.	14	21	10.6	73	-	17,205	-	1,306	-	-
6700	Holding and other investment offices	46	49	8.7	295	179	19,810	23,330	5,674	4,620	2.3
6710	Holding offices	8	9	7.4	30	23	32,267	32,000	1,031	789	0.6
6720	Investment offices	3	2	10.0	16	-	15,500	-	162	-	-
6732	Educational, religious, etc. trusts	12	16	15.2	75	86	22,507	24,837	1,748	2,193	13.7
6733	Trusts, n.e.c.	7	7	6.9	59	36	19,458	10,111	729	311	5.4
6799	Investors, n.e.c.	6	11	8.9	-	21	-	34,286	-	1,014	8.7
FREMONT, CO											
60 –	**Finance, insurance, and real estate**	48	45	0.4	272	272	18,794	20,824	5,450	5,876	0.2
6000	Depository institutions	10	9	0.8	159	156	22,642	23,385	3,504	3,543	0.6
6020	Commercial banks	5	6	1.0	135	141	23,200	24,454	3,047	3,349	0.7
6400	Insurance agents, brokers, and service	11	11	0.5	40	39	16,600	28,410	905	1,084	0.4
6500	Real estate	19	18	0.4	57	67	8,982	10,030	649	891	0.2
6530	Real estate agents and managers	8	9	0.3	26	22	6,462	9,091	196	287	0.1
6700	Holding and other investment offices	3	3	0.5	9	5	6,222	4,800	136	104	0.1
GARFIELD, CO											
60 –	**Finance, insurance, and real estate**	92	108	0.9	661	690	21,604	22,928	14,158	15,984	0.5
6000	Depository institutions	15	15	1.3	185	199	23,827	24,925	3,977	5,049	0.8
6100	Nondepository institutions	3	3	0.4	-	20	-	20,800	-	410	0.1
6160	Mortgage bankers and brokers	3	3	0.6	-	20	-	20,800	-	410	0.2
6200	Security and commodity brokers	4	5	0.7	84	81	38,952	41,877	2,634	2,726	0.6
6400	Insurance agents, brokers, and service	19	25	1.1	62	85	22,000	19,388	1,558	2,067	0.8
6500	Real estate	44	56	1.1	233	269	13,511	14,335	4,037	4,569	0.8
6510	Real estate operators and lessors	13	18	1.0	65	136	11,138	11,265	1,144	1,844	1.3
6530	Real estate agents and managers	22	32	1.1	148	111	13,568	15,856	2,294	2,037	0.5
6552	Subdividers and developers, n.e.c.	3	5	2.5	16	22	21,750	25,636	500	682	2.3
GILPIN, CO											
60 –	**Finance, insurance, and real estate**	5	5	0.0	103	7	12,000	18,857	1,669	183	0.0
GRAND, CO											
60 –	**Finance, insurance, and real estate**	44	47	0.4	342	399	14,994	14,346	5,011	5,903	0.2
6000	Depository institutions	5	5	0.4	-	50	-	21,840	-	1,116	0.2

Source: County Business Patterns, 1992/93, CBP-92/93-1, U.S. Department of Commerce, Washington, D.C., April 1995. SIC categories for which data were suppressed or not available for both 1992 and 1993 are *not* displayed. The employment columns represent mid-March employment in the year. Pay per employee is calculated by dividing 1st Quarter payroll, annualized, by mid-March employment. The columns headed "% State" show the county's percentage of the state total for the SIC in 1993; for example, 0.9% for SIC 6030 means that the county had 0.9 percent of the state's total establishments (or payroll) in SIC 6030 in 1993. A dash (-) is used to indicate that data are not available or cannot be calculated; *nec* means not elsewhere classified.

Continued on next page.

SIC	Industry	No. Establishments			Employment		Pay / Employee		Annual Payroll ($ 000)		
		1992	1993	% State	1992	1993	1992	1993	1992	1993	% State
GRAND, CO - [continued]											
6500	Real estate	33	34	0.7	267	320	13,678	12,975	3,487	4,188	0.7
6510	Real estate operators and lessors	5	8	0.5	7	-	8,571	-	64	-	-
6530	Real estate agents and managers	21	24	0.8	223	258	13,561	12,884	2,721	3,283	0.9
GUNNISON, CO											
60 –	**Finance, insurance, and real estate**	54	65	0.6	439	525	15,872	14,202	6,919	8,049	0.2
6000	Depository institutions	5	7	0.6	73	86	23,781	22,698	1,661	1,989	0.3
6020	Commercial banks	3	3	0.5	-	67	-	23,224	-	1,535	0.3
6400	Insurance agents, brokers, and service	6	8	0.4	14	-	16,571	-	232	-	-
6500	Real estate	40	46	0.9	338	410	13,929	11,922	4,434	4,984	0.9
6510	Real estate operators and lessors	3	7	0.4	14	-	17,429	-	193	-	-
6530	Real estate agents and managers	29	36	1.2	311	372	13,865	11,860	4,040	4,263	1.1
HINSDALE, CO											
60 –	**Finance, insurance, and real estate**	5	6	0.1	18	21	17,111	18,857	330	431	0.0
HUERFANO, CO											
60 –	**Finance, insurance, and real estate**	15	16	0.1	42	42	13,429	12,857	631	596	0.0
6400	Insurance agents, brokers, and service	4	4	0.2	10	-	15,200	-	136	-	-
6500	Real estate	7	8	0.2	-	14	-	7,143	-	122	0.0
6530	Real estate agents and managers	3	3	0.1	-	3	-	4,000	-	18	0.0
JACKSON, CO											
60 –	**Finance, insurance, and real estate**	2	2	0.0	-	-	-	-	-	-	-
JEFFERSON, CO											
60 –	**Finance, insurance, and real estate**	1,174	1,298	11.4	8,532	9,018	25,439	24,840	224,869	239,506	7.3
6000	Depository institutions	118	117	10.2	2,257	2,350	27,573	25,379	57,889	59,124	9.3
6020	Commercial banks	57	57	9.7	1,570	1,549	28,899	28,227	40,555	41,660	9.1
6030	Savings institutions	29	25	11.8	407	333	26,467	20,120	11,046	7,275	17.3
6060	Credit unions	27	28	10.7	267	328	22,007	18,085	6,114	6,300	11.8
6090	Functions closely related to banking	4	7	8.0	-	140	-	23,457	-	3,889	5.5
6100	Nondepository institutions	80	107	12.6	725	854	32,044	27,635	24,203	29,126	7.5
6140	Personal credit institutions	35	29	13.5	430	337	27,498	26,326	10,921	8,427	-
6150	Business credit institutions	12	16	13.3	57	106	25,895	22,717	1,884	2,966	3.6
6160	Mortgage bankers and brokers	32	61	12.5	235	405	42,009	30,153	11,341	17,600	8.2
6200	Security and commodity brokers	86	65	9.1	745	217	35,791	37,014	32,485	8,826	1.9
6210	Security brokers and dealers	48	28	7.5	602	112	34,419	40,250	25,918	4,781	1.6
6220	Commodity contracts brokers, dealers	8	4	20.0	25	10	53,600	25,600	1,369	290	4.8
6280	Security and commodity services	29	33	10.4	118	95	39,017	34,400	5,196	3,755	2.6
6300	Insurance carriers	112	88	12.5	933	1,281	29,869	33,917	25,785	40,131	5.4
6310	Life insurance	19	18	9.5	383	363	31,561	36,275	9,879	11,915	4.0
6330	Fire, marine, and casualty insurance	62	47	16.5	258	-	31,752	-	7,951	-	-
6360	Title insurance	17	7	11.5	180	-	26,511	-	5,287	-	-
6370	Pension, health, and welfare funds	9	11	11.8	71	71	19,437	17,408	1,483	1,113	3.3
6400	Insurance agents, brokers, and service	266	320	14.1	1,432	1,322	24,478	23,879	38,129	34,725	13.0
6500	Real estate	468	536	10.5	2,152	2,461	15,805	16,390	37,693	48,303	8.4
6510	Real estate operators and lessors	138	173	10.0	703	814	11,903	11,705	8,943	10,487	7.2
6530	Real estate agents and managers	255	322	10.6	1,127	1,276	17,807	19,028	21,803	30,490	8.2
6552	Subdividers and developers, n.e.c.	18	22	11.1	34	-	19,647	-	838	-	-
6553	Cemetery subdividers and developers	5	4	9.8	129	-	13,891	-	2,041	-	-
6700	Holding and other investment offices	44	55	9.8	288	-	27,722	-	8,685	-	-
6710	Holding offices	12	12	9.9	113	98	39,717	49,265	4,746	4,524	3.4
KIOWA, CO											
60 –	**Finance, insurance, and real estate**	3	2	0.0	-	-	-	-	-	-	-

Source: County Business Patterns, 1992/93, CBP-92/93-1, U.S. Department of Commerce, Washington, D.C., April 1995. SIC categories for which data were suppressed or not available for both 1992 and 1993 are not displayed. The employment columns represent mid-March employment in the year. Pay per employee is calculated by dividing 1st Quarter payroll, annualized, by mid-March employment. The columns headed "% State" show the county's percentage of the state total for the SIC in 1993; for example, 0.9% for SIC 6030 means that the county had 0.9 percent of the state's total establishments (or payroll) in SIC 6030 in 1993. A dash (-) is used to indicate that data are not available or cannot be calculated; nec means not elsewhere classified.

SIC	Industry	No. Establishments			Employment		Pay / Employee		Annual Payroll ($ 000)		
		1992	1993	% State	1992	1993	1992	1993	1992	1993	% State
KIT CARSON, CO											
60 –	**Finance, insurance, and real estate**	24	24	0.2	93	102	21,505	20,157	2,139	2,348	0.1
6000	Depository institutions	6	6	0.5	55	63	26,473	24,254	1,555	1,559	0.2
6400	Insurance agents, brokers, and service	10	11	0.5	16	-	11,250	-	191	-	-
6500	Real estate	4	4	0.1	10	10	13,600	15,200	165	202	0.0
LAKE, CO											
60 –	**Finance, insurance, and real estate**	17	17	0.1	57	53	15,439	15,547	923	919	0.0
6000	Depository institutions	4	4	0.3	20	-	24,400	-	518	-	-
6400	Insurance agents, brokers, and service	3	4	0.2	13	15	11,077	14,400	164	218	0.1
6500	Real estate	8	8	0.2	-	15	-	8,267	-	104	0.0
6530	Real estate agents and managers	5	5	0.2	14	10	6,571	4,800	87	47	0.0
LA PLATA, CO											
60 –	**Finance, insurance, and real estate**	110	127	1.1	672	658	17,744	17,605	11,957	14,423	0.4
6000	Depository institutions	9	10	0.9	252	182	18,016	19,802	3,757	4,849	0.8
6100	Nondepository institutions	5	5	0.6	-	17	-	28,471	-	707	0.2
6200	Security and commodity brokers	5	5	0.7	51	42	39,608	52,762	1,973	2,709	0.6
6400	Insurance agents, brokers, and service	15	22	1.0	78	114	9,333	9,895	740	1,576	0.6
6500	Real estate	71	82	1.6	253	299	14,403	13,833	4,338	4,554	0.8
6510	Real estate operators and lessors	19	24	1.4	55	85	12,582	11,153	748	976	0.7
6530	Real estate agents and managers	41	50	1.7	148	175	13,351	13,463	2,368	2,519	0.7
6552	Subdividers and developers, n.e.c.	6	6	3.0	16	-	26,500	-	649	-	-
6700	Holding and other investment offices	4	3	0.5	-	4	-	4,000	-	28	0.0
LARIMER, CO											
60 –	**Finance, insurance, and real estate**	509	546	4.8	3,028	3,022	20,851	22,056	65,234	71,036	2.2
6000	Depository institutions	40	43	3.7	1,075	1,148	23,260	22,697	23,632	23,751	3.7
6020	Commercial banks	21	24	4.1	790	857	22,106	22,688	16,975	19,174	4.2
6030	Savings institutions	14	12	5.7	192	181	32,438	26,696	5,162	2,936	7.0
6100	Nondepository institutions	32	40	4.7	266	259	21,774	26,842	7,296	10,633	2.7
6140	Personal credit institutions	11	9	4.2	54	66	21,407	17,091	1,206	1,056	-
6160	Mortgage bankers and brokers	14	25	5.1	196	170	21,551	30,588	5,617	8,851	4.1
6200	Security and commodity brokers	33	33	4.6	116	112	42,207	51,857	4,938	5,352	1.2
6210	Security brokers and dealers	19	21	5.6	85	93	54,447	59,828	4,629	4,878	1.6
6220	Commodity contracts brokers, dealers	3	3	15.0	-	7	-	14,286	-	265	4.4
6280	Security and commodity services	11	9	2.8	-	12	-	12,000	-	209	0.1
6300	Insurance carriers	45	29	4.1	305	208	24,315	30,923	7,910	6,203	0.8
6310	Life insurance	6	7	3.7	80	75	26,200	32,320	2,098	2,108	0.7
6360	Title insurance	7	5	8.2	100	47	21,160	22,043	2,389	1,231	3.6
6400	Insurance agents, brokers, and service	113	130	5.7	286	354	20,252	17,808	5,678	7,572	2.8
6500	Real estate	221	253	4.9	873	877	14,163	15,503	14,004	15,873	2.8
6510	Real estate operators and lessors	88	96	5.6	431	380	13,290	11,358	6,604	5,340	3.7
6530	Real estate agents and managers	106	143	4.7	371	467	14,005	18,561	5,888	9,456	2.5
6552	Subdividers and developers, n.e.c.	8	11	5.6	18	29	34,667	20,690	376	777	2.6
6700	Holding and other investment offices	25	18	3.2	107	64	17,495	23,500	1,776	1,652	0.8
6710	Holding offices	5	1	0.8	33	-	19,030	-	424	-	-
6732	Educational, religious, etc. trusts	6	4	3.8	34	26	12,353	12,615	411	366	2.3
6733	Trusts, n.e.c.	9	7	6.9	32	24	17,875	19,833	605	488	8.5
LAS ANIMAS, CO											
60 –	**Finance, insurance, and real estate**	25	24	0.2	136	115	14,088	17,843	2,062	2,362	0.1
6000	Depository institutions	4	5	0.4	86	72	15,674	22,111	1,460	1,744	0.3
6400	Insurance agents, brokers, and service	8	8	0.4	21	-	12,571	-	272	-	-
6500	Real estate	8	8	0.2	17	18	8,471	8,444	164	225	0.0

Source: County Business Patterns, 1992/93, CBP-92/93-1, U.S. Department of Commerce, Washington, D.C., April 1995. SIC categories for which data were suppressed or not available for both 1992 and 1993 are *not* displayed. The employment columns represent mid-March employment in the year. Pay per employee is calculated by dividing 1st Quarter payroll, annualized, by mid-March employment. The columns headed "% State" show the county's percentage of the state total for the SIC in 1993; for example, 0.9% for SIC 6030 means that the county had 0.9 percent of the state's total establishments (or payroll) in SIC 6030 in 1993. A dash (-) is used to indicate that data are not available or cannot be calculated; *nec* means not elsewhere classified.

SIC	Industry	No. Establishments			Employment		Pay / Employee		Annual Payroll ($ 000)		
		1992	1993	% State	1992	1993	1992	1993	1992	1993	% State
LINCOLN, CO											
60 –	**Finance, insurance, and real estate**	8	7	0.1	54	50	19,185	19,200	1,092	1,114	0.0
6000	Depository institutions	3	3	0.3	-	40	-	21,500	-	1,011	0.2
6400	Insurance agents, brokers, and service	3	3	0.1	6	-	7,333	-	45	-	-
LOGAN, CO											
60 –	**Finance, insurance, and real estate**	46	46	0.4	252	261	23,937	27,847	6,193	6,551	0.2
6000	Depository institutions	9	8	0.7	133	144	22,586	21,944	3,058	3,274	0.5
6020	Commercial banks	5	4	0.7	83	92	23,566	22,391	1,936	1,900	0.4
6400	Insurance agents, brokers, and service	16	17	0.7	65	68	28,492	42,529	1,818	2,031	0.8
6500	Real estate	13	14	0.3	20	18	9,000	8,000	199	169	0.0
6510	Real estate operators and lessors	8	9	0.5	10	11	10,800	9,091	117	125	0.1
6530	Real estate agents and managers	3	5	0.2	6	7	6,667	6,286	46	44	0.0
MESA, CO											
60 –	**Finance, insurance, and real estate**	220	239	2.1	1,186	1,338	21,349	21,468	26,691	32,200	1.0
6000	Depository institutions	35	38	3.3	500	558	21,472	21,520	10,625	12,735	2.0
6020	Commercial banks	18	20	3.4	353	397	22,584	22,821	8,003	9,984	2.2
6030	Savings institutions	7	6	2.8	77	-	19,740	-	1,379	-	-
6060	Credit unions	10	11	4.2	70	81	17,771	18,074	1,243	1,528	2.9
6100	Nondepository institutions	16	15	1.8	118	106	32,881	26,000	4,673	4,870	1.3
6140	Personal credit institutions	7	5	2.3	60	-	34,600	-	1,816	-	-
6160	Mortgage bankers and brokers	7	8	1.6	-	56	-	30,000	-	3,718	1.7
6280	Security and commodity services	4	3	0.9	12	-	38,667	-	457	-	-
6300	Insurance carriers	13	12	1.7	50	56	26,800	29,143	1,391	1,644	0.2
6310	Life insurance	4	3	1.6	-	35	-	28,571	-	944	0.3
6400	Insurance agents, brokers, and service	54	59	2.6	182	221	15,736	20,814	3,015	4,455	1.7
6500	Real estate	86	97	1.9	285	348	13,782	13,529	4,305	5,322	0.9
6510	Real estate operators and lessors	22	28	1.6	112	152	12,500	9,816	1,453	1,612	1.1
6530	Real estate agents and managers	53	64	2.1	119	165	14,487	14,497	1,983	2,701	0.7
MINERAL, CO											
60 –	**Finance, insurance, and real estate**	2	2	0.0	-	-	-	-	-	-	-
MOFFAT, CO											
60 –	**Finance, insurance, and real estate**	22	23	0.2	103	107	20,699	22,654	2,169	2,370	0.1
6000	Depository institutions	6	5	0.4	62	61	20,323	24,328	1,172	1,338	0.2
6400	Insurance agents, brokers, and service	5	6	0.3	11	-	19,273	-	247	-	-
6500	Real estate	8	10	0.2	20	28	14,400	12,571	298	363	0.1
6530	Real estate agents and managers	4	6	0.2	7	7	12,571	10,857	96	96	0.0
MONTEZUMA, CO											
60 –	**Finance, insurance, and real estate**	35	38	0.3	234	263	16,479	15,985	4,477	5,687	0.2
6000	Depository institutions	8	8	0.7	146	141	18,932	18,780	3,149	3,305	0.5
6400	Insurance agents, brokers, and service	8	10	0.4	30	40	11,200	14,500	466	759	0.3
6500	Real estate	14	15	0.3	-	70	-	9,314	-	790	0.1
6510	Real estate operators and lessors	5	6	0.3	29	-	7,724	-	230	-	-
6530	Real estate agents and managers	8	8	0.3	13	-	16,000	-	232	-	-
MONTROSE, CO											
60 –	**Finance, insurance, and real estate**	67	73	0.6	386	423	19,886	20,643	8,047	8,981	0.3
6000	Depository institutions	11	13	1.1	149	167	22,738	23,880	3,389	3,620	0.6
6020	Commercial banks	8	8	1.4	133	141	23,248	25,390	3,082	3,184	0.7
6160	Mortgage bankers and brokers	3	3	0.6	17	-	8,706	-	154	-	-
6400	Insurance agents, brokers, and service	20	18	0.8	53	56	18,264	17,357	1,058	1,017	0.4

Source: County Business Patterns, 1992/93, CBP-92/93-1, U.S. Department of Commerce, Washington, D.C., April 1995. SIC categories for which data were suppressed or not available for both 1992 and 1993 are *not* displayed. The employment columns represent mid-March employment in the year. Pay per employee is calculated by dividing 1st Quarter payroll, annualized, by mid-March employment. The columns headed "% State" show the county's percentage of the state total for the SIC in 1993; for example, 0.9% for SIC 6030 means that the county had 0.9 percent of the state's total establishments (or payroll) in SIC 6030 in 1993. A dash (-) is used to indicate that data are not available or cannot be calculated; *nec* means not elsewhere classified.

Continued on next page.

SIC	Industry	No. Establishments			Employment		Pay / Employee		Annual Payroll ($ 000)		
		1992	1993	% State	1992	1993	1992	1993	1992	1993	% State
MONTROSE, CO - [continued]											
6500	Real estate	25	32	0.6	80	101	11,900	12,356	1,161	1,574	0.3
6510	Real estate operators and lessors	9	11	0.6	35	39	7,200	8,615	284	425	0.3
6530	Real estate agents and managers	11	17	0.6	31	42	13,161	11,429	525	504	0.1
MORGAN, CO											
60 –	**Finance, insurance, and real estate**	51	59	0.5	262	265	20,840	20,830	5,714	5,998	0.2
6000	Depository institutions	13	14	1.2	149	153	23,436	22,379	3,636	3,558	0.6
6020	Commercial banks	7	7	1.2	122	124	24,295	22,935	3,095	2,955	0.6
6100	Nondepository institutions	4	4	0.5	13	15	25,846	24,800	323	363	0.1
6400	Insurance agents, brokers, and service	11	17	0.7	46	62	16,609	17,677	846	1,343	0.5
6500	Real estate	12	17	0.3	29	-	8,276	-	242	-	-
6510	Real estate operators and lessors	4	8	0.5	16	12	3,000	4,667	51	76	0.1
6530	Real estate agents and managers	8	8	0.3	13	13	14,769	18,154	191	276	0.1
6700	Holding and other investment offices	4	4	0.7	-	6	-	46,000	-	287	0.1
OTERO, CO											
60 –	**Finance, insurance, and real estate**	39	42	0.4	228	261	17,702	14,835	4,555	4,254	0.1
6000	Depository institutions	13	14	1.2	127	157	20,819	18,191	3,030	3,177	0.5
6020	Commercial banks	8	10	1.7	104	141	20,192	19,064	2,468	2,993	0.7
6400	Insurance agents, brokers, and service	8	11	0.5	18	-	10,667	-	211	-	-
6500	Real estate	8	9	0.2	39	41	10,051	8,293	414	346	0.1
6510	Real estate operators and lessors	1	3	0.2	-	20	-	10,600	-	218	0.1
6530	Real estate agents and managers	7	6	0.2	-	21	-	6,095	-	128	0.0
OURAY, CO											
60 –	**Finance, insurance, and real estate**	9	13	0.1	46	-	15,391	-	845	-	-
6530	Real estate agents and managers	3	7	0.2	8	8	15,000	10,500	105	161	0.0
PARK, CO											
60 –	**Finance, insurance, and real estate**	5	10	0.1	16	18	17,000	16,000	418	604	0.0
6500	Real estate	3	7	0.1	-	8	-	22,000	-	409	0.1
PHILLIPS, CO											
60 –	**Finance, insurance, and real estate**	16	15	0.1	59	76	15,254	17,105	1,308	1,430	0.0
6000	Depository institutions	7	6	0.5	44	62	17,091	18,452	1,149	1,240	0.2
6020	Commercial banks	4	3	0.5	33	52	17,818	18,538	966	1,044	0.2
6500	Real estate	3	3	0.1	7	6	6,286	6,667	49	41	0.0
PITKIN, CO											
60 –	**Finance, insurance, and real estate**	168	185	1.6	1,390	1,262	21,338	21,255	28,517	27,229	0.8
6000	Depository institutions	7	7	0.6	176	160	26,227	32,375	4,342	4,560	0.7
6100	Nondepository institutions	10	14	1.6	57	30	34,456	32,800	1,971	1,426	0.4
6280	Security and commodity services	5	4	1.3	2	3	20,000	16,000	78	82	0.1
6400	Insurance agents, brokers, and service	7	10	0.4	39	47	31,795	33,787	1,356	1,783	0.7
6500	Real estate	120	134	2.6	1,062	983	18,810	18,014	19,002	18,006	3.1
6510	Real estate operators and lessors	20	31	1.8	66	120	21,455	14,267	1,343	1,940	1.3
6530	Real estate agents and managers	80	94	3.1	931	831	18,221	17,723	16,062	14,612	3.9
6552	Subdividers and developers, n.e.c.	5	6	3.0	21	12	33,143	64,000	688	665	2.2
6700	Holding and other investment offices	12	12	2.1	23	26	27,652	27,077	549	708	0.3
6732	Educational, religious, etc. trusts	4	4	3.8	13	13	32,308	31,077	337	398	2.5
6733	Trusts, n.e.c.	3	3	3.0	4	6	19,000	14,667	61	67	1.2
PROWERS, CO											
60 –	**Finance, insurance, and real estate**	42	41	0.4	217	209	18,544	17,665	4,188	3,931	0.1
6000	Depository institutions	10	10	0.9	132	115	19,515	20,730	2,644	2,558	0.4
6020	Commercial banks	5	5	0.9	114	99	20,877	22,061	2,440	2,347	0.5
6400	Insurance agents, brokers, and service	12	14	0.6	44	50	11,909	11,840	623	630	0.2

Source: County Business Patterns, 1992/93, CBP-92/93-1, U.S. Department of Commerce, Washington, D.C., April 1995. SIC categories for which data were suppressed or not available for both 1992 and 1993 are not displayed. The employment columns represent mid-March employment in the year. Pay per employee is calculated by dividing 1st Quarter payroll, annualized, by mid-March employment. The columns headed "% State" show the county's percentage of the state total for the SIC in 1993; for example, 0.9% for SIC 6030 means that the county had 0.9 percent of the state's total establishments (or payroll) in SIC 6030 in 1993. A dash (-) is used to indicate that data are not available or cannot be calculated; nec means not elsewhere classified.

Continued on next page.

SIC	Industry	No. Establishments			Employment		Pay / Employee		Annual Payroll ($ 000)		
		1992	1993	% State	1992	1993	1992	1993	1992	1993	% State
PROWERS, CO - [continued]											
6500	Real estate	13	12	0.2	19	17	17,895	13,176	220	206	0.0
6510	Real estate operators and lessors	5	6	0.3	9	8	8,889	9,500	89	107	0.1
6530	Real estate agents and managers	6	5	0.2	8	-	30,000	-	111	-	-
PUEBLO, CO											
60 –	**Finance, insurance, and real estate**	223	236	2.1	1,447	1,540	25,496	22,766	38,809	38,776	1.2
6000	Depository institutions	34	39	3.4	621	563	20,277	20,654	13,285	14,715	2.3
6020	Commercial banks	13	15	2.6	402	335	19,881	22,507	8,668	10,458	2.3
6030	Savings institutions	6	5	2.4	45	-	28,178	-	1,241	-	-
6060	Credit unions	15	19	7.3	174	-	19,149	-	3,376	-	-
6100	Nondepository institutions	20	14	1.6	102	82	21,451	24,000	2,236	2,399	0.6
6140	Personal credit institutions	13	9	4.2	47	-	22,213	-	1,038	-	-
6160	Mortgage bankers and brokers	4	4	0.8	-	30	-	30,000	-	1,148	0.5
6200	Security and commodity brokers	8	7	1.0	-	49	-	66,204	-	2,320	0.5
6210	Security brokers and dealers	6	4	1.1	-	40	-	80,300	-	2,299	0.7
6280	Security and commodity services	2	3	0.9	-	9	-	3,556	-	21	0.0
6300	Insurance carriers	21	19	2.7	99	240	25,495	17,933	2,565	3,827	0.5
6310	Life insurance	4	4	2.1	52	83	22,846	22,458	1,239	1,616	0.5
6400	Insurance agents, brokers, and service	62	63	2.8	199	206	17,487	16,408	3,512	3,805	1.4
6500	Real estate	74	86	1.7	305	277	12,092	12,130	3,860	3,801	0.7
6510	Real estate operators and lessors	40	43	2.5	187	165	9,604	9,527	1,919	1,755	1.2
6530	Real estate agents and managers	27	35	1.2	59	69	13,424	13,333	917	1,094	0.3
6700	Holding and other investment offices	4	8	1.4	-	123	-	58,341	-	7,909	3.9
RIO BLANCO, CO											
60 –	**Finance, insurance, and real estate**	12	12	0.1	61	61	20,721	19,607	1,296	1,280	0.0
6000	Depository institutions	4	4	0.3	44	43	21,727	20,651	968	934	0.1
6400	Insurance agents, brokers, and service	3	3	0.1	9	8	17,778	17,500	147	152	0.1
6500	Real estate	5	5	0.1	8	10	18,500	16,800	181	194	0.0
RIO GRANDE, CO											
60 –	**Finance, insurance, and real estate**	29	31	0.3	160	163	15,825	15,877	2,800	2,807	0.1
6000	Depository institutions	6	6	0.5	74	69	18,432	20,870	1,504	1,598	0.3
6400	Insurance agents, brokers, and service	6	6	0.3	14	16	14,286	11,500	205	176	0.1
6500	Real estate	14	16	0.3	58	63	8,690	8,381	542	591	0.1
6510	Real estate operators and lessors	6	6	0.3	40	44	8,400	8,727	371	424	0.3
6530	Real estate agents and managers	6	7	0.2	-	12	-	8,333	-	115	0.0
ROUTT, CO											
60 –	**Finance, insurance, and real estate**	80	85	0.7	1,019	971	16,950	18,822	15,053	15,246	0.5
6000	Depository institutions	6	6	0.5	102	128	24,314	23,250	2,346	2,791	0.4
6100	Nondepository institutions	3	5	0.6	6	8	40,667	30,500	277	406	0.1
6160	Mortgage bankers and brokers	3	5	1.0	6	8	40,667	30,500	277	406	0.2
6400	Insurance agents, brokers, and service	14	17	0.7	48	94	29,333	16,894	1,560	1,794	0.7
6500	Real estate	48	50	1.0	809	701	14,769	15,013	9,653	8,119	1.4
6510	Real estate operators and lessors	2	3	0.2	-	2	-	12,000	-	35	0.0
6530	Real estate agents and managers	35	41	1.4	793	696	14,704	14,822	9,291	7,872	2.1
SAGUACHE, CO											
60 –	**Finance, insurance, and real estate**	5	6	0.1	24	28	18,167	28,571	511	556	0.0
SAN JUAN, CO											
60 –	**Finance, insurance, and real estate**	1	1	0.0	-	-	-	-	-	-	-
SAN MIGUEL, CO											
60 –	**Finance, insurance, and real estate**	40	56	0.5	296	449	19,973	20,543	6,995	9,690	0.3

Source: County Business Patterns, 1992/93, CBP-92/93-1, U.S. Department of Commerce, Washington, D.C., April 1995. SIC categories for which data were suppressed or not available for both 1992 and 1993 are *not* displayed. The employment columns represent mid-March employment in the year. Pay per employee is calculated by dividing 1st Quarter payroll, annualized, by mid-March employment. The columns headed "% State" show the county's percentage of the state total for the SIC in 1993; for example, 0.9% for SIC 6030 means that the county had 0.9 percent of the state's total establishments (or payroll) in SIC 6030 in 1993. A dash (-) is used to indicate that data are not available or cannot be calculated; *nec* means not elsewhere classified.

Continued on next page.

SIC	Industry	No. Establishments			Employment		Pay / Employee		Annual Payroll ($ 000)		
		1992	1993	% State	1992	1993	1992	1993	1992	1993	% State
SAN MIGUEL, CO - [continued]											
6500	Real estate	33	47	0.9	236	361	20,119	19,845	5,587	7,520	1.3
6530	Real estate agents and managers	23	35	1.2	210	316	16,000	16,152	3,776	5,202	1.4
6552	Subdividers and developers, n.e.c.	3	5	2.5	10	11	92,000	104,364	1,090	1,316	4.4
SEDGWICK, CO											
60 –	**Finance, insurance, and real estate**	9	8	0.1	37	-	16,432	-	693	-	-
6000	Depository institutions	4	4	0.3	31	-	18,323	-	604	-	-
6400	Insurance agents, brokers, and service	2	3	0.1	-	5	-	4,800	-	30	0.0
SUMMIT, CO											
60 –	**Finance, insurance, and real estate**	147	163	1.4	1,044	1,199	18,149	20,520	19,561	23,194	0.7
6000	Depository institutions	5	5	0.4	113	122	34,407	28,426	3,490	3,312	0.5
6020	Commercial banks	5	5	0.9	113	122	34,407	28,426	3,490	3,312	0.7
6100	Nondepository institutions	5	5	0.6	17	31	20,000	34,194	749	1,087	0.3
6160	Mortgage bankers and brokers	5	5	1.0	17	31	20,000	34,194	749	1,087	0.5
6300	Insurance carriers	3	-	-	12	-	23,000	-	383	-	-
6360	Title insurance	3	-	-	12	-	23,000	-	383	-	-
6400	Insurance agents, brokers, and service	10	12	0.5	24	67	20,500	19,403	534	1,519	0.6
6500	Real estate	118	137	2.7	852	964	15,479	18,983	13,565	16,766	2.9
6510	Real estate operators and lessors	12	17	1.0	33	81	9,091	15,901	470	1,698	1.2
6530	Real estate agents and managers	86	107	3.5	711	840	16,096	18,686	11,260	13,318	3.6
6552	Subdividers and developers, n.e.c.	5	11	5.6	4	-	47,000	-	466	-	-
TELLER, CO											
60 –	**Finance, insurance, and real estate**	39	45	0.4	177	216	15,435	15,704	3,420	4,361	0.1
6000	Depository institutions	4	4	0.3	70	74	15,486	16,270	1,263	1,378	0.2
6400	Insurance agents, brokers, and service	4	5	0.2	6	33	10,000	16,727	78	731	0.3
6500	Real estate	24	31	0.6	75	79	13,707	13,165	1,305	1,585	0.3
6510	Real estate operators and lessors	8	7	0.4	15	14	12,000	10,000	170	180	0.1
6530	Real estate agents and managers	12	20	0.7	30	63	20,800	14,159	879	1,375	0.4
WASHINGTON, CO											
60 –	**Finance, insurance, and real estate**	10	10	0.1	59	54	23,051	20,370	1,339	1,134	0.0
6000	Depository institutions	6	6	0.5	47	43	26,723	23,163	1,235	1,029	0.2
6020	Commercial banks	3	3	0.5	39	35	30,462	26,171	1,157	948	0.2
WELD, CO											
60 –	**Finance, insurance, and real estate**	248	271	2.4	3,380	3,560	27,659	31,022	100,156	108,882	3.3
6000	Depository institutions	34	39	3.4	589	643	21,250	21,804	12,527	13,711	2.2
6020	Commercial banks	22	24	4.1	506	541	21,146	22,240	10,637	11,715	2.6
6030	Savings institutions	7	7	3.3	39	-	24,308	-	994	-	-
6060	Credit unions	5	6	2.3	44	62	19,727	20,903	896	1,253	2.3
6100	Nondepository institutions	12	17	2.0	89	94	26,517	27,106	2,543	3,285	0.8
6140	Personal credit institutions	5	5	2.3	25	-	18,880	-	500	-	-
6160	Mortgage bankers and brokers	3	10	2.0	6	44	27,333	24,273	258	1,592	0.7
6310	Life insurance	3	3	1.6	97	99	43,588	43,313	4,180	4,135	1.4
6400	Insurance agents, brokers, and service	61	69	3.0	175	225	17,554	17,671	4,511	5,718	2.1
6500	Real estate	95	108	2.1	332	364	11,904	13,264	4,816	5,732	1.0
6510	Real estate operators and lessors	49	60	3.5	151	-	9,589	-	1,564	-	-
6530	Real estate agents and managers	37	45	1.5	127	135	13,449	16,741	2,099	2,469	0.7
6700	Holding and other investment offices	12	10	1.8	105	96	28,495	32,208	3,301	3,412	1.7
6799	Investors, n.e.c.	4	1	0.8	7	-	9,714	-	73	-	-
YUMA, CO											
60 –	**Finance, insurance, and real estate**	24	22	0.2	122	121	23,672	21,124	2,687	2,459	0.1

Source: County Business Patterns, 1992/93, CBP-92/93-1, U.S. Department of Commerce, Washington, D.C., April 1995. SIC categories for which data were suppressed or not available for both 1992 and 1993 are not displayed. The employment columns represent mid-March employment in the year. Pay per employee is calculated by dividing 1st Quarter payroll, annualized, by mid-March employment. The columns headed "% State" show the county's percentage of the state total for the SIC in 1993; for example, 0.9% for SIC 6030 means that the county had 0.9 percent of the state's total establishments (or payroll) in SIC 6030 in 1993. A dash (-) is used to indicate that data are not available or cannot be calculated; nec means not elsewhere classified.

Continued on next page.

SIC	Industry	No. Establishments			Employment		Pay / Employee		Annual Payroll ($ 000)		
		1992	1993	% State	1992	1993	1992	1993	1992	1993	% State
YUMA, CO - [continued]											
6000	Depository institutions	9	9	0.8	84	80	25,476	22,250	1,880	1,642	0.3
6020	Commercial banks	5	5	0.9	68	64	28,294	24,250	1,655	1,406	0.3
6400	Insurance agents, brokers, and service	7	6	0.3	18	-	14,222	-	273	-	-

Source: County Business Patterns, 1992/93, CBP-92/93-1, U.S. Department of Commerce, Washington, D.C., April 1995. SIC categories for which data were suppressed or not available for both 1992 and 1993 are not displayed. The employment columns represent mid-March employment in the year. Pay per employee is calculated by dividing 1st Quarter payroll, annualized, by mid-March employment. The columns headed "% State" show the county's percentage of the state total for the SIC in 1993; for example, 0.9% for SIC 6030 means that the county had 0.9 percent of the state's total establishments (or payroll) in SIC 6030 in 1993. A dash (-) is used to indicate that data are not available or cannot be calculated; nec means not elsewhere classified.

CONNECTICUT

SIC	Industry	No. Establishments			Employment		Pay / Employee		Annual Payroll ($ 000)		
		1992	1993	% State	1992	1993	1992	1993	1992	1993	% State
FAIRFIELD, CT											
60 –	**Finance, insurance, and real estate**	2,792	2,820	33.6	35,014	35,285	54,468	49,496	1,949,777	2,055,378	32.5
6000	Depository institutions	464	445	27.1	8,799	9,100	30,618	30,456	245,040	282,016	31.5
6020	Commercial banks	264	224	32.9	5,027	5,208	29,585	31,035	141,541	161,824	31.2
6030	Savings institutions	130	146	22.9	3,466	3,471	31,888	29,542	93,580	104,769	32.1
6100	Nondepository institutions	178	179	43.4	6,383	5,842	61,429	57,843	387,594	329,134	75.6
6140	Personal credit institutions	46	31	33.0	2,824	2,586	50,660	47,722	142,560	133,811	89.4
6150	Business credit institutions	50	57	69.5	2,616	2,121	78,209	74,455	193,809	141,532	86.4
6160	Mortgage bankers and brokers	77	90	38.8	924	1,135	47,459	49,861	50,611	53,777	-
6200	Security and commodity brokers	361	411	60.3	3,829	4,603	115,265	82,464	522,897	611,782	71.6
6210	Security brokers and dealers	145	163	57.2	2,188	2,280	105,320	95,872	292,580	351,769	68.1
6280	Security and commodity services	194	226	60.8	1,414	2,044	130,475	70,190	199,315	192,542	71.1
6300	Insurance carriers	183	157	23.1	4,952	5,602	60,470	57,217	260,560	316,938	10.5
6310	Life insurance	63	57	28.4	2,129	2,094	34,610	37,830	76,083	81,606	4.4
6330	Fire, marine, and casualty insurance	72	74	23.3	2,361	2,629	85,203	79,296	161,226	193,117	20.3
6360	Title insurance	7	5	41.7	57	60	43,018	40,533	2,686	2,608	36.2
6400	Insurance agents, brokers, and service	402	421	27.0	2,971	2,941	43,728	43,282	131,405	137,053	34.6
6500	Real estate	962	973	32.8	4,961	4,535	30,779	30,590	170,265	165,439	38.8
6510	Real estate operators and lessors	331	354	29.6	1,280	1,196	26,950	25,130	39,067	34,669	27.2
6530	Real estate agents and managers	468	551	36.4	2,894	3,050	33,909	33,107	108,015	118,404	43.7
6540	Title abstract offices	11	12	44.4	31	37	25,935	25,405	1,115	1,307	-
6552	Subdividers and developers, n.e.c.	41	31	25.8	356	115	27,697	30,157	11,117	7,114	48.1
6553	Cemetery subdividers and developers	17	19	20.2	135	137	23,674	23,971	3,432	3,621	35.2
6700	Holding and other investment offices	235	228	51.2	2,608	2,530	66,544	59,165	189,891	195,479	70.5
6710	Holding offices	85	89	61.8	1,713	1,155	61,658	65,676	97,940	93,730	61.9
6720	Investment offices	25	13	65.0	159	76	73,384	119,579	19,480	16,912	82.1
6732	Educational, religious, etc. trusts	24	26	33.8	250	367	33,008	31,913	9,341	13,030	65.3
6733	Trusts, n.e.c.	24	32	33.3	114	215	22,667	21,879	2,731	5,407	66.5
6792	Oil royalty traders	4	4	100.0	61	-	62,951	-	4,055	-	-
6799	Investors, n.e.c.	34	46	71.9	239	470	163,096	91,217	37,374	59,230	89.5
HARTFORD, CT											
60 –	**Finance, insurance, and real estate**	2,393	2,405	28.6	88,754	79,605	37,236	40,141	3,230,590	3,202,327	50.6
6000	Depository institutions	458	442	26.9	12,346	11,784	28,685	28,723	360,108	337,767	37.7
6020	Commercial banks	175	178	26.2	7,757	8,115	29,644	30,725	232,142	243,324	46.9
6030	Savings institutions	187	152	23.9	3,870	2,887	27,900	24,849	111,052	76,517	23.4
6060	Credit unions	86	104	35.5	689	759	22,653	22,213	16,193	17,355	41.7
6100	Nondepository institutions	118	108	26.2	1,302	1,312	40,270	53,259	58,027	65,899	15.1
6140	Personal credit institutions	51	22	23.4	250	-	29,952	-	7,222	-	-
6150	Business credit institutions	18	17	20.7	381	348	54,877	70,345	21,093	20,893	12.8
6160	Mortgage bankers and brokers	49	68	29.3	671	787	35,821	51,375	29,712	39,772	-
6200	Security and commodity brokers	125	142	20.8	2,655	2,664	59,031	60,811	165,460	191,711	22.4
6210	Security brokers and dealers	64	65	22.8	1,665	1,730	63,695	67,147	97,900	122,648	23.7
6300	Insurance carriers	312	280	41.2	63,122	53,633	38,903	43,014	2,334,057	2,266,014	74.9
6310	Life insurance	106	92	45.8	36,924	34,427	45,014	45,675	1,524,516	1,515,678	81.0
6321	Accident and health insurance	7	5	45.5	6,324	273	7,113	22,212	48,102	5,599	71.3
6324	Hospital and medical service plans	5	8	44.4	457	726	31,457	32,176	13,591	28,447	19.2
6330	Fire, marine, and casualty insurance	129	124	39.0	18,542	17,394	37,862	39,287	716,872	687,595	72.4
6360	Title insurance	7	5	41.7	91	-	41,670	-	3,742	-	-
6370	Pension, health, and welfare funds	48	41	36.6	238	499	21,815	20,024	6,054	16,779	52.6
6400	Insurance agents, brokers, and service	480	507	32.5	3,972	3,757	35,470	35,475	146,858	142,094	35.9
6500	Real estate	800	828	27.9	4,771	5,336	24,595	24,154	131,174	138,904	32.5

Source: County Business Patterns, 1992/93, CBP-92/93-1, U.S. Department of Commerce, Washington, D.C., April 1995. SIC categories for which data were suppressed or not available for both 1992 and 1993 are *not* displayed. The employment columns represent mid-March employment in the year. Pay per employee is calculated by dividing 1st Quarter payroll, annualized, by mid-March employment. The columns headed "% State" show the county's percentage of the state total for the SIC in 1993; for example, 0.9% for SIC 6030 means that the county had 0.9 percent of the state's total establishments (or payroll) in SIC 6030 in 1993. A dash (-) is used to indicate that data are not available or cannot be calculated; *nec* means not elsewhere classified.

Continued on next page.

SIC	Industry	No. Establishments			Employment		Pay / Employee		Annual Payroll ($ 000)		
		1992	1993	% State	1992	1993	1992	1993	1992	1993	% State
HARTFORD, CT - [continued]											
6510	Real estate operators and lessors	326	354	*29.6*	1,956	2,145	22,910	25,156	45,140	50,713	*39.8*
6530	Real estate agents and managers	355	401	*26.5*	2,353	3,019	25,958	23,300	73,212	80,777	*29.8*
6540	Title abstract offices	3	5	*18.5*	9	7	17,333	13,714	146	137	*-*
6552	Subdividers and developers, n.e.c.	43	46	*38.3*	141	82	27,348	31,171	3,855	4,950	*33.5*
6553	Cemetery subdividers and developers	13	15	*16.0*	67	70	20,537	21,486	1,546	1,802	*17.5*
6710	Holding offices	30	30	*20.8*	222	756	59,694	54,709	14,055	42,822	*28.3*
6732	Educational, religious, etc. trusts	16	17	*22.1*	33	62	23,515	30,000	818	1,858	*9.3*
6733	Trusts, n.e.c.	23	22	*22.9*	70	-	8,114	-	519	-	*-*
6794	Patent owners and lessors	5	9	*30.0*	-	79	-	28,658	-	2,706	*50.9*
6799	Investors, n.e.c.	7	10	*15.6*	40	-	115,600	-	6,079	-	*-*
LITCHFIELD, CT											
60 –	**Finance, insurance, and real estate**	318	289	*3.4*	2,125	1,986	26,359	25,680	60,476	54,636	*0.9*
6000	Depository institutions	90	86	*5.2*	1,193	1,217	23,923	21,791	29,057	26,753	*3.0*
6020	Commercial banks	43	41	*6.0*	564	582	24,163	22,557	13,842	12,759	*2.5*
6030	Savings institutions	40	39	*6.1*	604	610	23,934	21,193	14,751	13,495	*4.1*
6060	Credit unions	7	6	*2.0*	25	25	18,240	18,560	464	499	*1.2*
6100	Nondepository institutions	7	3	*0.7*	23	-	30,087	-	476	-	*-*
6200	Security and commodity brokers	15	14	*2.1*	50	-	35,760	-	2,281	-	*-*
6210	Security brokers and dealers	8	4	*1.4*	17	-	44,941	-	879	-	*-*
6400	Insurance agents, brokers, and service	66	61	*3.9*	352	310	33,148	31,613	13,149	10,535	*2.7*
6500	Real estate	106	99	*3.3*	338	260	21,444	18,523	8,478	6,075	*1.4*
6510	Real estate operators and lessors	30	31	*2.6*	101	74	22,059	11,514	2,592	1,181	*0.9*
6530	Real estate agents and managers	48	51	*3.4*	165	144	22,497	21,444	4,379	3,699	*1.4*
6552	Subdividers and developers, n.e.c.	3	5	*4.2*	3	-	10,667	-	31	-	*-*
6553	Cemetery subdividers and developers	9	10	*10.6*	35	37	20,457	20,108	858	923	*9.0*
6732	Educational, religious, etc. trusts	6	5	*6.5*	23	-	24,696	-	588	-	*-*
6733	Trusts, n.e.c.	5	-	*-*	7	-	16,000	-	39	-	*-*
MIDDLESEX, CT											
60 –	**Finance, insurance, and real estate**	292	291	*3.5*	7,476	7,221	37,892	37,776	283,619	289,017	*4.6*
6000	Depository institutions	78	75	*4.6*	764	869	27,927	27,171	21,064	24,425	*2.7*
6020	Commercial banks	28	27	*4.0*	276	278	22,855	21,799	5,909	6,972	*1.3*
6030	Savings institutions	46	41	*6.4*	474	559	31,046	30,211	14,830	16,723	*5.1*
6060	Credit unions	4	7	*2.4*	14	32	22,286	20,750	325	730	*1.8*
6140	Personal credit institutions	7	3	*3.2*	81	-	24,988	-	2,316	-	*-*
6280	Security and commodity services	4	5	*1.3*	6	-	24,667	-	135	-	*-*
6330	Fire, marine, and casualty insurance	14	15	*4.7*	69	-	45,623	-	3,029	-	*-*
6400	Insurance agents, brokers, and service	59	63	*4.0*	485	382	35,315	28,063	15,523	11,615	*2.9*
6500	Real estate	100	103	*3.5*	378	436	17,450	15,193	7,091	7,633	*1.8*
6510	Real estate operators and lessors	36	39	*3.3*	205	252	16,566	14,460	3,583	3,972	*3.1*
6530	Real estate agents and managers	44	53	*3.5*	140	169	18,914	16,450	2,781	3,356	*1.2*
6552	Subdividers and developers, n.e.c.	3	4	*3.3*	3	5	21,333	15,200	76	118	*0.8*
6553	Cemetery subdividers and developers	7	7	*7.4*	11	10	12,727	12,400	186	187	*1.8*
NEW HAVEN, CT											
60 –	**Finance, insurance, and real estate**	1,821	1,828	*21.8*	20,196	19,454	28,515	29,066	581,248	588,051	*9.3*
6000	Depository institutions	389	378	*23.0*	6,643	6,240	26,730	25,921	177,546	157,922	*17.6*
6020	Commercial banks	146	143	*21.0*	2,779	2,773	27,093	25,356	71,781	67,854	*13.1*
6030	Savings institutions	164	148	*23.2*	3,384	3,067	26,665	26,691	94,199	80,645	*24.7*
6060	Credit unions	65	78	*26.6*	304	377	23,750	22,663	6,952	8,263	*19.9*
6100	Nondepository institutions	105	89	*21.6*	683	738	32,814	32,748	24,167	31,019	*7.1*
6140	Personal credit institutions	54	32	*34.0*	363	-	25,653	-	9,266	-	*-*
6160	Mortgage bankers and brokers	45	51	*22.0*	285	403	40,379	38,094	13,318	22,469	*-*
6200	Security and commodity brokers	65	72	*10.6*	446	533	72,251	73,741	30,536	34,391	*4.0*
6210	Security brokers and dealers	36	34	*11.9*	395	431	77,053	84,733	28,264	30,509	*5.9*
6300	Insurance carriers	195	157	*23.1*	6,427	5,630	29,634	32,001	183,016	184,474	*6.1*
6400	Insurance agents, brokers, and service	356	358	*23.0*	2,263	2,193	30,618	29,638	73,262	72,813	*18.4*

Source: County Business Patterns, 1992/93, CBP-92/93-1, U.S. Department of Commerce, Washington, D.C., April 1995. SIC categories for which data were suppressed or not available for both 1992 and 1993 are *not* displayed. The employment columns represent mid-March employment in the year. Pay per employee is calculated by dividing 1st Quarter payroll, annualized, by mid-March employment. The columns headed "% State" show the county's percentage of the state total for the SIC in 1993; for example, 0.9% for SIC 6030 means that the county had 0.9 percent of the state's total establishments (or payroll) in SIC 6030 in 1993. A dash (-) is used to indicate that data are not available or cannot be calculated; *nec* means not elsewhere classified.

Continued on next page.

SIC	Industry	No. Establishments			Employment		Pay / Employee		Annual Payroll ($ 000)		
		1992	1993	% State	1992	1993	1992	1993	1992	1993	% State
NEW HAVEN, CT - [continued]											
6500	Real estate	638	699	23.5	3,276	3,801	19,437	20,308	71,745	90,050	21.1
6510	Real estate operators and lessors	228	303	25.4	1,088	1,542	17,776	15,883	20,752	28,512	22.4
6530	Real estate agents and managers	288	338	22.4	1,744	2,061	20,798	23,546	41,318	55,995	20.7
6540	Title abstract offices	5	4	14.8	11	9	20,000	25,333	241	264	-
6552	Subdividers and developers, n.e.c.	25	22	18.3	198	69	16,000	23,188	3,549	1,680	11.4
6553	Cemetery subdividers and developers	28	27	28.7	122	120	20,230	19,533	2,962	2,826	27.4
6710	Holding offices	19	19	13.2	223	161	70,960	87,180	15,048	13,481	8.9
6732	Educational, religious, etc. trusts	12	14	18.2	24	42	12,000	12,381	317	546	2.7
6733	Trusts, n.e.c.	27	31	32.3	127	71	14,142	24,507	1,841	1,868	23.0
NEW LONDON, CT											
60 –	**Finance, insurance, and real estate**	419	429	5.1	3,179	3,446	26,566	26,559	86,327	91,549	1.4
6000	Depository institutions	119	122	7.4	1,760	1,921	24,775	23,202	43,066	43,686	4.9
6020	Commercial banks	31	40	5.9	444	731	24,081	25,040	10,617	19,120	3.7
6030	Savings institutions	65	55	8.6	1,036	919	26,174	22,507	26,198	18,205	5.6
6100	Nondepository institutions	17	16	3.9	-	83	-	24,530	-	3,222	0.7
6140	Personal credit institutions	8	4	4.3	34	-	18,000	-	667	-	-
6160	Mortgage bankers and brokers	8	11	4.7	-	55	-	23,491	-	2,220	-
6200	Security and commodity brokers	21	20	2.9	-	104	-	90,962	-	7,630	0.9
6210	Security brokers and dealers	16	12	4.2	-	82	-	103,220	-	6,638	1.3
6280	Security and commodity services	5	8	2.2	-	22	-	45,273	-	992	0.4
6300	Insurance carriers	32	29	4.3	-	408	-	37,294	-	14,165	0.5
6310	Life insurance	7	6	3.0	-	221	-	38,860	-	7,328	0.4
6330	Fire, marine, and casualty insurance	22	20	6.3	197	-	33,726	-	6,790	-	-
6400	Insurance agents, brokers, and service	78	80	5.1	356	360	27,596	25,489	10,525	10,178	2.6
6500	Real estate	142	149	5.0	491	543	19,014	19,116	10,677	11,803	2.8
6510	Real estate operators and lessors	50	58	4.9	219	202	18,922	16,792	4,773	3,788	3.0
6530	Real estate agents and managers	60	69	4.6	193	281	17,699	20,399	3,888	6,492	2.4
6540	Title abstract offices	1	3	11.1	-	4	-	13,000	-	63	-
6552	Subdividers and developers, n.e.c.	7	8	6.7	24	25	28,167	22,880	707	611	4.1
6553	Cemetery subdividers and developers	7	7	7.4	31	31	25,419	20,387	758	725	7.0
6700	Holding and other investment offices	10	13	2.9	-	27	-	25,333	-	865	0.3
6733	Trusts, n.e.c.	2	4	4.2	-	4	-	12,000	-	90	1.1
TOLLAND, CT											
60 –	**Finance, insurance, and real estate**	201	192	2.3	1,128	1,145	22,879	21,432	26,263	26,323	0.4
6000	Depository institutions	54	48	2.9	546	522	21,788	19,992	12,176	11,446	1.3
6020	Commercial banks	18	13	1.9	165	-	22,861	-	3,586	-	-
6030	Savings institutions	33	33	5.2	366	382	21,541	20,052	8,352	8,410	2.6
6060	Credit unions	3	2	0.7	15	-	16,000	-	238	-	-
6400	Insurance agents, brokers, and service	39	37	2.4	202	191	27,109	27,937	5,982	6,225	1.6
6500	Real estate	76	75	2.5	210	-	15,905	-	3,973	-	-
6510	Real estate operators and lessors	33	33	2.8	134	153	16,388	18,196	2,415	2,834	2.2
6530	Real estate agents and managers	31	35	2.3	56	67	13,643	23,045	985	1,703	0.6
6553	Cemetery subdividers and developers	3	3	3.2	5	5	8,000	8,000	55	53	0.5
6700	Holding and other investment offices	13	10	2.2	111	-	24,360	-	1,639	-	-
WINDHAM, CT											
60 –	**Finance, insurance, and real estate**	146	148	1.8	954	1,090	22,063	22,077	22,161	22,896	0.4
6000	Depository institutions	46	47	2.9	511	678	19,624	21,032	10,319	11,947	1.3
6020	Commercial banks	14	14	2.1	185	-	21,405	-	4,008	-	-
6030	Savings institutions	24	23	3.6	305	464	18,597	21,397	5,963	7,583	2.3
6060	Credit unions	8	10	3.4	21	-	18,857	-	348	-	-
6100	Nondepository institutions	7	6	1.5	23	-	23,304	-	620	-	-
6160	Mortgage bankers and brokers	3	4	1.7	-	11	-	9,455	-	347	-
6200	Security and commodity brokers	8	10	1.5	-	58	-	14,483	-	968	0.1
6210	Security brokers and dealers	5	3	1.1	-	6	-	50,667	-	325	0.1
6280	Security and commodity services	3	7	1.9	-	52	-	10,308	-	643	0.2

Source: County Business Patterns, 1992/93, CBP-92/93-1, U.S. Department of Commerce, Washington, D.C., April 1995. SIC categories for which data were suppressed or not available for both 1992 and 1993 are *not* displayed. The employment columns represent mid-March employment in the year. Pay per employee is calculated by dividing 1st Quarter payroll, annualized, by mid-March employment. The columns headed "% State" show the county's percentage of the state total for the SIC in 1993; for example, 0.9% for SIC 6030 means that the county had 0.9 percent of the state's total establishments (or payroll) in SIC 6030 in 1993. A dash (-) is used to indicate that data are not available or cannot be calculated; *nec* means not elsewhere classified.

Continued on next page.

SIC	Industry	No. Establishments			Employment		Pay / Employee		Annual Payroll ($ 000)		
		1992	1993	% State	1992	1993	1992	1993	1992	1993	% State
WINDHAM, CT - [continued]											
6400	Insurance agents, brokers, and service	31	32	2.1	176	149	31,955	33,960	5,649	5,210	1.3
6500	Real estate	44	44	1.5	147	-	16,435	-	2,523	-	-
6510	Real estate operators and lessors	16	22	1.8	68	98	16,294	15,878	1,184	1,648	1.3
6530	Real estate agents and managers	14	14	0.9	53	28	16,604	17,143	834	506	0.2
6553	Cemetery subdividers and developers	6	6	6.4	10	10	12,400	12,000	155	164	1.6

Source: County Business Patterns, 1992/93, CBP-92/93-1, U.S. Department of Commerce, Washington, D.C., April 1995. SIC categories for which data were suppressed or not available for both 1992 and 1993 are *not* displayed. The employment columns represent mid-March employment in the year. Pay per employee is calculated by dividing 1st Quarter payroll, annualized, by mid-March employment. The columns headed "% State" show the county's percentage of the state total for the SIC in 1993; for example, 0.9% for SIC 6030 means that the county had 0.9 percent of the state's total establishments (or payroll) in SIC 6030 in 1993. A dash (-) is used to indicate that data are not available or cannot be calculated; *nec* means not elsewhere classified.

DELAWARE

SIC	Industry	No. Establishments			Employment		Pay / Employee		Annual Payroll ($ 000)		
		1992	1993	% State	1992	1993	1992	1993	1992	1993	% State
KENT, DE											
60–	**Finance, insurance, and real estate**	239	248	8.3	1,728	2,514	30,285	25,497	51,035	63,656	5.8
6000	Depository institutions	36	38	12.0	390	937	22,062	13,567	8,352	13,591	2.4
6020	Commercial banks	28	29	13.2	321	845	22,941	13,335	6,976	12,062	2.2
6100	Nondepository institutions	23	26	13.1	382	555	17,246	18,530	6,903	10,828	11.1
6140	Personal credit institutions	14	13	20.6	56	54	23,786	25,037	1,266	1,379	-
6160	Mortgage bankers and brokers	5	8	10.4	-	82	-	35,756	-	3,258	13.0
6300	Insurance carriers	21	22	18.8	333	477	27,195	31,321	9,505	12,986	8.1
6330	Fire, marine, and casualty insurance	7	10	24.4	-	260	-	33,662	-	7,087	13.8
6400	Insurance agents, brokers, and service	59	60	20.1	216	216	32,574	27,296	6,602	6,697	17.5
6500	Real estate	76	80	12.3	272	226	12,941	13,929	3,982	3,620	5.6
6510	Real estate operators and lessors	38	39	13.9	103	124	14,874	13,516	1,694	1,943	6.3
6530	Real estate agents and managers	23	31	10.5	54	87	15,926	15,264	961	1,494	5.3
6553	Cemetery subdividers and developers	4	4	20.0	-	8	-	10,500	-	94	5.6
NEW CASTLE, DE											
60–	**Finance, insurance, and real estate**	2,350	2,435	81.3	31,623	30,282	29,884	29,535	955,075	993,898	89.8
6000	Depository institutions	212	225	71.0	16,606	15,867	32,280	30,578	536,090	532,903	92.6
6020	Commercial banks	136	144	65.5	14,310	14,861	33,900	30,792	481,770	505,009	92.6
6030	Savings institutions	37	33	86.8	539	510	28,267	28,533	15,294	14,534	98.9
6090	Functions closely related to banking	4	3	100.0	-	291	-	31,601	-	9,330	100.0
6100	Nondepository institutions	165	158	79.8	3,757	2,898	25,531	26,141	93,801	85,114	87.4
6140	Personal credit institutions	58	44	69.8	958	582	24,213	26,680	21,931	14,433	-
6150	Business credit institutions	47	45	88.2	2,378	1,806	23,632	23,825	53,651	49,174	89.3
6160	Mortgage bankers and brokers	56	65	84.4	-	506	-	33,929	-	21,450	85.3
6200	Security and commodity brokers	125	98	91.6	687	648	80,588	68,463	62,480	68,579	81.5
6210	Security brokers and dealers	51	36	87.8	438	354	93,817	69,299	34,651	27,842	64.4
6280	Security and commodity services	73	62	95.4	-	294	-	67,456	-	40,737	-
6300	Insurance carriers	122	92	78.6	4,217	4,582	28,253	30,919	127,861	147,480	91.7
6310	Life insurance	40	33	78.6	1,935	2,014	28,899	30,542	59,876	63,419	94.8
6400	Insurance agents, brokers, and service	181	195	65.2	1,377	933	32,404	25,929	43,458	25,532	66.8
6500	Real estate	379	385	59.2	2,382	2,079	19,102	20,723	49,963	50,326	78.2
6510	Real estate operators and lessors	185	166	59.3	1,340	1,107	16,761	18,482	23,706	23,206	75.0
6530	Real estate agents and managers	136	176	59.5	802	813	21,102	23,808	18,420	22,648	80.6
6552	Subdividers and developers, n.e.c.	19	18	50.0	54	55	27,185	19,855	2,420	1,617	73.0
6553	Cemetery subdividers and developers	12	12	60.0	81	69	19,062	20,870	1,722	1,516	89.7
6700	Holding and other investment offices	1,158	1,275	98.0	-	3,146	-	24,187	-	80,111	97.2
6710	Holding offices	939	958	98.7	2,038	2,244	15,884	24,758	25,236	52,260	97.1
6798	Real estate investment trusts	5	1	100.0	5	-	6,400	-	21	-	-
SUSSEX, DE											
60–	**Finance, insurance, and real estate**	296	313	10.4	2,051	2,450	21,999	18,617	46,681	49,238	4.4
6000	Depository institutions	54	54	17.0	1,288	1,634	21,795	17,946	28,780	29,132	5.1
6020	Commercial banks	46	47	21.4	1,234	1,577	21,906	18,016	27,736	28,260	5.2
6100	Nondepository institutions	10	14	7.1	42	46	28,571	29,565	1,095	1,419	1.5
6140	Personal credit institutions	5	6	9.5	22	-	23,455	-	500	-	-
6160	Mortgage bankers and brokers	2	4	5.2	-	6	-	76,667	-	434	1.7
6300	Insurance carriers	8	3	2.6	42	13	20,000	22,154	779	306	0.2
6330	Fire, marine, and casualty insurance	4	1	2.4	14	-	18,857	-	271	-	-
6400	Insurance agents, brokers, and service	45	44	14.7	190	206	27,768	23,786	5,168	6,006	15.7
6500	Real estate	165	185	28.5	458	512	17,406	16,375	9,502	10,401	16.2

Source: County Business Patterns, 1992/93, CBP-92/93-1, U.S. Department of Commerce, Washington, D.C., April 1995. SIC categories for which data were suppressed or not available for both 1992 and 1993 are *not* displayed. The employment columns represent mid-March employment in the year. Pay per employee is calculated by dividing 1st Quarter payroll, annualized, by mid-March employment. The columns headed "% State" show the county's percentage of the state total for the SIC in 1993; for example, 0.9% for SIC 6030 means that the county had 0.9 percent of the state's total establishments (or payroll) in SIC 6030 in 1993. A dash (-) is used to indicate that data are not available or cannot be calculated; *nec* means not elsewhere classified.

Continued on next page.

SIC	Industry	No. Establishments			Employment		Pay / Employee		Annual Payroll ($ 000)		
		1992	1993	% State	1992	1993	1992	1993	1992	1993	% State
SUSSEX, DE - [continued]											
6510	Real estate operators and lessors	58	75	26.8	222	247	17,946	17,668	5,217	5,775	18.7
6530	Real estate agents and managers	74	89	30.1	183	219	16,721	14,959	3,391	3,944	14.0
6553	Cemetery subdividers and developers	4	4	20.0	-	13	-	5,231	-	80	4.7

Source: County Business Patterns, 1992/93, CBP-92/93-1, U.S. Department of Commerce, Washington, D.C., April 1995. SIC categories for which data were suppressed or not available for both 1992 and 1993 are *not* displayed. The employment columns represent mid-March employment in the year. Pay per employee is calculated by dividing 1st Quarter payroll, annualized, by mid-March employment. The columns headed "% State" show the county's percentage of the state total for the SIC in 1993; for example, 0.9% for SIC 6030 means that the county had 0.9 percent of the state's total establishments (or payroll) in SIC 6030 in 1993. A dash (-) is used to indicate that data are not available or cannot be calculated; *nec* means not elsewhere classified.

WASHINGTON, D.C.

Source: County Business Patterns, 1992/93, CBP-92/93-1, U.S. Department of Commerce, Washington, D.C., April 1995.

SIC	Industry	No. Establishments			Employment		Pay / Employee		Annual Payroll ($ 000)		
		1992	1993	% State	1992	1993	1992	1993	1992	1993	% State
WASHINGTON, D.C.											
60 –	**Finance, insurance, and real estate**	2,363	2,303	100.0	33,259	37,719	40,040	36,785	1,282,618	1,417,310	100.0
6000	Depository institutions	427	425	100.0	6,605	6,010	32,557	31,219	207,320	191,150	100.0
6020	Commercial banks	224	220	100.0	4,548	4,055	34,563	32,965	151,778	135,960	100.0
6030	Savings institutions	82	61	100.0	1,063	695	29,317	30,388	27,165	20,444	100.0
6060	Credit unions	81	99	100.0	731	1,032	23,081	23,702	17,619	25,977	100.0
6080	Foreign bank and branches and agencies	6	5	100.0	-	58		45,034		2,645	100.0
6090	Functions closely related to banking	33	39	100.0	170	-	26,376		5,788		
6100	Nondepository institutions	67	65	100.0	3,097	3,491	85,593	72,712	202,717	217,740	100.0
6140	Personal credit institutions	25	9	100.0	264	-	27,364	-	7,820	-	-
6160	Mortgage bankers and brokers	26	32	100.0	2,086	595	80,424	41,903	117,856	24,801	100.0
6200	Security and commodity brokers	171	175	100.0	2,204	2,939	86,909	81,964	191,419	248,524	100.0
6210	Security brokers and dealers	97	92	100.0	1,703	2,127	86,910	86,198	147,989	184,014	100.0
6230	Security and commodity exchanges	4	3	100.0	36	-	76,889		2,139		
6280	Security and commodity services	66	76	100.0	460	791	88,157	70,088	40,661	62,551	100.0
6300	Insurance carriers	125	90	100.0	4,269	5,848	39,966	27,727	163,537	167,688	100.0
6310	Life insurance	32	29	100.0	845	1,020	40,918	39,373	35,098	41,948	100.0
6321	Accident and health insurance	6	4	100.0	108	-	57,889	-	3,290	-	-
6330	Fire, marine, and casualty insurance	16	18	100.0	159	216	52,780	55,463	7,777	9,358	100.0
6360	Title insurance	9	6	100.0	-	54	-	38,667	-	2,159	100.0
6370	Pension, health, and welfare funds	46	19	100.0	347	2,173	29,787	4,144	10,420	16,444	100.0
6400	Insurance agents, brokers, and service	120	124	100.0	1,668	2,036	40,700	39,250	66,736	83,030	100.0
6500	Real estate	1,180	1,149	100.0	11,282	12,801	23,500	22,248	288,004	317,383	100.0
6510	Real estate operators and lessors	587	589	100.0	4,331	4,227	19,695	18,493	91,025	86,439	100.0
6530	Real estate agents and managers	483	527	100.0	6,397	8,254	25,522	23,958	180,971	221,270	100.0
6540	Title abstract offices	13	9	100.0	98	76	27,061	28,632	2,308	2,236	100.0
6552	Subdividers and developers, n.e.c.	30	14	100.0	147	122	42,531	34,197	6,055	4,106	100.0
6553	Cemetery subdividers and developers	7	6	100.0	48	102	17,500	20,431	929	2,232	100.0
6700	Holding and other investment offices	264	267	100.0	4,046	4,433	37,389	38,793	158,188	185,954	100.0
6710	Holding offices	31	30	100.0	1,280	1,291	48,375	60,211	67,963	85,932	100.0
6720	Investment offices	7	6	100.0	51	58	41,333	57,310	2,285	3,408	100.0
6732	Educational, religious, etc. trusts	139	143	100.0	1,583	1,815	34,921	32,179	56,126	61,489	100.0
6733	Trusts, n.e.c.	56	56	100.0	920	1,050	20,961	18,282	20,803	22,428	100.0
6799	Investors, n.e.c.	21	22	100.0	126	126	71,619	73,810	7,194	8,251	100.0

Source: County Business Patterns, 1992/93, CBP-92/93-1, U.S. Department of Commerce, Washington, D.C., April 1995. SIC categories for which data were suppressed or not available for both 1992 and 1993 are *not* displayed. The employment columns represent mid-March employment in the year. Pay per employee is calculated by dividing 1st Quarter payroll, annualized, by mid-March employment. The columns headed "% State" show the county's percentage of the state total for the SIC in 1993; for example, 0.9% for SIC 6030 means that the county had 0.9 percent of the state's total establishments (or payroll) in SIC 6030 in 1993. A dash (-) is used to indicate that data are not available or cannot be calculated; *nec* means not elsewhere classified.

SIC	Industry	No. Establishments			Employment		Pay / Employee		Annual Payroll ($ 000)		
		1992	1993	% State	1992	1993	1992	1993	1992	1993	% State
ORANGE, FL - [continued]											
6200	Security and commodity brokers	110	117	5.9	931	1,073	64,339	65,059	56,825	70,826	5.0
6210	Security brokers and dealers	58	63	5.2	735	811	72,397	77,085	49,226	60,994	5.5
6300	Insurance carriers	245	210	8.1	7,499	7,176	33,596	29,153	244,824	215,371	10.1
6310	Life insurance	80	73	9.8	3,204	2,875	31,322	27,279	95,727	81,570	10.0
6321	Accident and health insurance	9	8	12.5	75	112	31,467	28,964	2,579	3,236	5.9
6324	Hospital and medical service plans	6	8	9.1	330	355	31,176	30,772	10,551	11,732	3.7
6330	Fire, marine, and casualty insurance	96	95	7.7	3,093	3,281	30,805	30,481	103,880	99,352	12.0
6360	Title insurance	20	16	9.7	631	492	29,040	30,528	19,599	17,740	25.7
6370	Pension, health, and welfare funds	25	7	2.7	122	-	196,820	-	11,099	-	-
6400	Insurance agents, brokers, and service	446	468	6.2	3,158	3,336	28,142	26,550	96,825	101,426	8.7
6500	Real estate	929	973	5.1	7,743	7,255	21,722	20,729	177,544	168,852	8.1
6510	Real estate operators and lessors	323	339	5.1	2,132	1,942	15,871	14,855	36,394	30,729	6.2
6530	Real estate agents and managers	389	521	4.9	4,348	4,473	22,330	20,046	104,125	100,903	8.2
6540	Title abstract offices	19	21	6.8	178	212	20,674	21,849	4,114	5,111	9.1
6552	Subdividers and developers, n.e.c.	54	61	6.2	458	401	47,275	55,112	19,653	25,236	10.8
6553	Cemetery subdividers and developers	5	10	5.6	174	213	19,793	23,437	3,445	6,265	10.9
6700	Holding and other investment offices	74	76	5.0	475	468	42,400	45,009	18,165	20,134	4.3
6710	Holding offices	21	23	5.5	298	317	51,034	52,416	13,486	14,860	5.3
6732	Educational, religious, etc. trusts	13	13	7.2	40	37	20,400	24,541	878	1,027	4.6
6733	Trusts, n.e.c.	18	14	4.7	72	51	30,778	25,961	1,923	1,812	3.7
6794	Patent owners and lessors	5	5	5.3	35	24	31,886	13,667	643	489	2.0
6798	Real estate investment trusts	4	1	1.9	12	-	17,333	-	349	-	-
6799	Investors, n.e.c.	6	16	4.1	10	-	16,000	-	184	-	-
OSCEOLA, FL											
60 –	**Finance, insurance, and real estate**	247	266	0.7	2,262	2,544	17,729	18,858	43,954	52,570	0.5
6000	Depository institutions	36	31	0.6	574	460	17,645	19,226	9,687	9,148	0.4
6020	Commercial banks	24	21	0.7	385	287	16,405	20,028	6,096	5,904	0.4
6100	Nondepository institutions	7	12	0.5	21	-	26,667	-	562	-	-
6140	Personal credit institutions	3	5	0.6	11	20	28,000	20,000	244	481	0.3
6160	Mortgage bankers and brokers	1	5	0.3	-	6	-	8,667	-	312	0.1
6300	Insurance carriers	20	15	0.6	110	73	31,855	37,425	3,602	2,613	0.1
6310	Life insurance	3	4	0.5	-	39	-	32,513	-	1,105	0.1
6360	Title insurance	6	2	1.2	54	-	24,519	-	1,334	-	-
6400	Insurance agents, brokers, and service	33	40	0.5	173	159	24,532	25,107	4,534	4,119	0.4
6500	Real estate	146	157	0.8	1,376	1,742	15,669	17,470	25,430	34,085	1.6
6510	Real estate operators and lessors	40	45	0.7	204	169	11,647	15,148	2,928	2,410	0.5
6530	Real estate agents and managers	76	101	0.9	968	1,552	16,769	17,634	19,659	31,088	2.5
6552	Subdividers and developers, n.e.c.	7	5	0.5	55	-	20,218	-	708	-	-
6700	Holding and other investment offices	4	8	0.5	-	75	-	16,533	-	1,239	0.3
6799	Investors, n.e.c.	3	5	1.3	3	-	10,667	-	84	-	-
PALM BEACH, FL											
60 –	**Finance, insurance, and real estate**	3,729	3,927	9.7	29,435	29,780	32,444	32,475	951,743	1,028,101	9.7
6000	Depository institutions	473	448	8.6	6,827	6,500	25,366	26,641	165,401	169,742	7.2
6020	Commercial banks	240	233	7.2	3,970	3,417	26,921	27,093	102,113	88,371	5.6
6030	Savings institutions	197	181	16.5	2,578	2,630	22,748	26,411	55,796	69,430	15.8
6060	Credit unions	22	23	4.4	194	318	23,546	21,358	4,538	7,245	4.9
6090	Functions closely related to banking	14	11	3.7	85	135	36,329	32,148	2,954	4,696	-
6100	Nondepository institutions	163	204	7.8	1,087	1,152	31,003	30,844	36,978	45,281	5.1
6140	Personal credit institutions	39	36	4.4	385	233	25,943	25,047	10,222	5,935	3.7
6150	Business credit institutions	19	25	9.5	136	178	36,118	33,101	5,277	6,928	2.9
6160	Mortgage bankers and brokers	99	140	9.3	469	720	33,586	31,939	18,114	31,562	6.6
6200	Security and commodity brokers	275	321	16.1	2,902	3,120	70,197	81,281	204,992	253,950	18.0
6210	Security brokers and dealers	156	197	16.3	2,421	2,687	75,665	85,658	183,622	220,824	20.0
6220	Commodity contracts brokers, dealers	6	9	20.5	150	45	18,907	28,000	1,479	1,970	11.5
6280	Security and commodity services	107	115	15.7	320	388	54,900	57,144	19,651	31,156	10.9
6300	Insurance carriers	234	191	7.3	2,573	2,353	37,141	36,813	93,280	83,930	3.9

Source: County Business Patterns, 1992/93, CBP-92/93-1, U.S. Department of Commerce, Washington, D.C., April 1995. SIC categories for which data were suppressed or not available for both 1992 and 1993 are not displayed. The employment columns represent mid-March employment in the year. Pay per employee is calculated by dividing 1st Quarter payroll, annualized, by mid-March employment. The columns headed "% State" show the county's percentage of the state total for the SIC in 1993; for example, 0.9% for SIC 6030 means that the county had 0.9 percent of the state's total establishments (or payroll) in SIC 6030 in 1993. A dash (-) is used to indicate that data are not available or cannot be calculated; nec means not elsewhere classified.

Continued on next page.

SIC	Industry	No. Establishments			Employment		Pay / Employee		Annual Payroll ($ 000)		
		1992	1993	% State	1992	1993	1992	1993	1992	1993	% State
PALM BEACH, FL - [continued]											
6310	Life insurance	60	56	7.5	1,245	1,214	36,302	35,147	39,300	39,198	4.8
6330	Fire, marine, and casualty insurance	102	93	7.5	818	783	39,956	44,404	34,525	34,971	4.2
6360	Title insurance	38	16	9.7	283	155	28,792	30,555	8,518	5,108	7.4
6370	Pension, health, and welfare funds	10	13	4.9	-	56	-	22,786	-	1,457	5.1
6400	Insurance agents, brokers, and service	608	663	8.7	2,991	3,495	30,594	31,602	94,680	118,117	10.1
6500	Real estate	1,771	1,889	9.9	10,853	11,475	20,141	19,730	229,242	246,348	11.9
6510	Real estate operators and lessors	467	523	7.9	2,381	2,898	18,308	15,805	45,232	50,481	10.3
6530	Real estate agents and managers	950	1,212	11.3	6,385	7,647	19,983	19,616	135,839	159,962	13.0
6540	Title abstract offices	16	28	9.0	130	139	29,631	26,187	3,156	4,901	8.8
6552	Subdividers and developers, n.e.c.	74	93	9.4	1,252	654	22,233	37,774	26,162	27,774	11.9
6553	Cemetery subdividers and developers	9	9	5.0	115	111	16,626	16,396	2,745	2,173	3.8
6700	Holding and other investment offices	197	207	13.7	2,047	1,628	65,249	47,742	121,828	106,681	22.9
6710	Holding offices	43	57	13.7	1,049	1,023	95,847	56,770	86,365	78,536	28.0
6720	Investment offices	15	9	20.5	128	9	51,812	162,667	9,255	7,388	27.7
6732	Educational, religious, etc. trusts	28	30	16.6	487	268	25,610	20,194	11,284	5,727	25.4
6733	Trusts, n.e.c.	32	30	10.0	125	92	36,192	41,957	4,703	3,856	7.9
6794	Patent owners and lessors	8	11	11.6	72	63	19,667	23,365	1,422	2,388	9.6
6798	Real estate investment trusts	9	4	7.5	47	-	38,894		1,715	-	-
6799	Investors, n.e.c.	47	61	15.4	128	152	42,094	42,447	6,031	7,477	14.8
PASCO, FL											
60 –	**Finance, insurance, and real estate**	538	543	1.3	3,786	3,615	18,775	20,077	71,611	73,739	0.7
6000	Depository institutions	114	105	2.0	1,083	1,386	19,398	20,323	20,533	26,872	1.1
6020	Commercial banks	82	72	2.2	895	1,161	19,571	20,799	17,053	22,610	1.4
6030	Savings institutions	28	27	2.5	174	191	18,207	18,052	3,009	3,654	0.8
6060	Credit unions	3	3	0.6	-	29	-	15,724	-	507	0.3
6090	Functions closely related to banking	1	3	1.0	-	5	-	23,200	-	101	-
6100	Nondepository institutions	19	20	0.8	75	66	26,827	29,273	2,207	2,098	0.2
6160	Mortgage bankers and brokers	8	10	0.7	15	-	42,667	-	749	-	-
6200	Security and commodity brokers	17	19	1.0	137	149	54,686	56,081	7,948	8,803	0.6
6210	Security brokers and dealers	13	14	1.2	131	140	56,519	58,943	7,817	8,571	0.8
6280	Security and commodity services	4	5	0.7	6	9	14,667	11,556	131	232	0.1
6300	Insurance carriers	41	27	1.0	224	402	37,768	24,995	8,447	10,601	0.5
6360	Title insurance	11	4	2.4	42	-	19,333	-	851	-	-
6370	Pension, health, and welfare funds	3	1	0.4	24	-	20,833	-	235	-	-
6400	Insurance agents, brokers, and service	114	127	1.7	604	661	13,404	13,253	9,114	10,546	0.9
6500	Real estate	229	237	1.2	1,653	938	14,388	16,094	23,135	14,450	0.7
6510	Real estate operators and lessors	86	96	1.4	330	426	10,861	17,587	3,594	6,349	1.3
6530	Real estate agents and managers	76	107	1.0	1,071	379	14,768	13,446	14,916	5,412	0.4
6540	Title abstract offices	6	7	2.3	24	29	17,000	18,069	524	571	1.0
6552	Subdividers and developers, n.e.c.	19	20	2.0	65	62	18,523	17,871	1,301	1,178	0.5
6553	Cemetery subdividers and developers	3	3	1.7	77	-	18,961	-	1,469	-	-
6700	Holding and other investment offices	4	8	0.5	10	13	23,200	16,923	227	369	0.1
PINELLAS, FL											
60 –	**Finance, insurance, and real estate**	2,707	2,736	6.7	24,380	24,173	24,858	25,595	634,746	664,189	6.3
6000	Depository institutions	377	362	7.0	5,009	5,499	22,099	21,602	105,807	119,453	5.1
6020	Commercial banks	238	222	6.9	3,325	3,331	22,076	22,259	67,944	71,529	4.5
6030	Savings institutions	93	97	8.8	1,390	1,852	22,374	20,475	32,072	41,162	9.4
6060	Credit unions	32	29	5.6	254	244	19,118	17,967	4,819	4,810	3.2
6090	Functions closely related to banking	13	14	4.7	-	72	-	32,500	-	1,952	-
6100	Nondepository institutions	158	158	6.0	1,970	2,093	29,795	28,682	60,063	56,754	6.4
6140	Personal credit institutions	54	49	6.0	908	517	21,256	17,694	19,227	9,454	5.8
6150	Business credit institutions	11	15	5.7	124	-	29,097	-	3,831	-	-
6160	Mortgage bankers and brokers	83	93	6.2	907	1,496	38,739	32,075	36,157	43,762	9.1
6200	Security and commodity brokers	162	160	8.0	2,538	2,597	48,325	52,481	137,547	161,765	11.5
6210	Security brokers and dealers	96	95	7.9	2,257	2,287	48,658	54,242	122,055	143,602	13.0
6280	Security and commodity services	63	65	8.9	273	310	46,256	39,484	15,289	18,163	6.3

Source: County Business Patterns, 1992/93, CBP-92/93-1, U.S. Department of Commerce, Washington, D.C., April 1995. SIC categories for which data were suppressed or not available for both 1992 and 1993 are *not* displayed. The employment columns represent mid-March employment in the year. Pay per employee is calculated by dividing 1st Quarter payroll, annualized, by mid-March employment. The columns headed "% State" show the county's percentage of the state total for the SIC in 1993; for example, 0.9% for SIC 6030 means that the county had 0.9 percent of the state's total establishments (or payroll) in SIC 6030 in 1993. A dash (-) is used to indicate that data are not available or cannot be calculated; *nec* means not elsewhere classified.

Continued on next page.

SIC	Industry	No. Establishments			Employment		Pay / Employee		Annual Payroll ($ 000)		
		1992	1993	% State	1992	1993	1992	1993	1992	1993	% State
PINELLAS, FL - [continued]											
6300	Insurance carriers	235	183	7.0	3,515	2,833	28,616	31,037	104,075	88,342	4.1
6310	Life insurance	33	28	3.8	975	958	26,219	29,954	27,062	26,861	3.3
6321	Accident and health insurance	4	2	3.1	15	-	19,467	-	317	-	-
6324	Hospital and medical service plans	6	3	3.4	148	-	26,081	-	3,453	-	-
6330	Fire, marine, and casualty insurance	133	109	8.8	1,752	1,481	32,306	34,679	57,942	51,346	6.2
6360	Title insurance	37	14	8.5	244	197	24,918	17,503	6,718	5,110	7.4
6370	Pension, health, and welfare funds	16	23	8.7	62	101	26,581	19,327	1,215	2,418	8.4
6400	Insurance agents, brokers, and service	478	545	7.2	2,490	2,757	25,182	24,911	67,851	77,734	6.7
6500	Real estate	1,190	1,220	6.4	7,590	7,277	15,280	15,565	119,606	123,339	5.9
6510	Real estate operators and lessors	444	470	7.1	2,807	2,675	12,962	13,412	36,838	39,103	7.9
6530	Real estate agents and managers	550	683	6.4	3,417	3,927	15,915	16,818	56,097	71,102	5.8
6540	Title abstract offices	12	12	3.9	114	60	19,579	16,400	2,391	1,240	2.2
6552	Subdividers and developers, n.e.c.	40	31	3.1	498	405	18,739	15,151	9,121	7,189	3.1
6553	Cemetery subdividers and developers	15	15	8.3	311	200	17,582	20,260	5,900	4,484	7.8
6700	Holding and other investment offices	101	102	6.8	1,045	785	31,721	35,949	37,974	30,721	6.6
6710	Holding offices	28	35	8.4	340	399	55,400	49,664	19,228	21,695	7.7
6720	Investment offices	5	3	6.8	91	5	18,989	7,200	1,847	40	0.2
6732	Educational, religious, etc. trusts	12	9	5.0	92	40	16,913	17,300	1,288	740	3.3
6733	Trusts, n.e.c.	25	22	7.3	331	80	19,190	22,800	10,139	2,257	4.6
6794	Patent owners and lessors	9	10	10.5	113	95	19,469	20,253	2,245	2,423	9.7
6799	Investors, n.e.c.	14	18	4.6	67	114	33,134	33,544	3,036	3,407	6.7
POLK, FL											
60 –	**Finance, insurance, and real estate**	860	848	2.1	9,670	9,400	21,921	25,374	221,482	239,127	2.3
6000	Depository institutions	152	142	2.7	2,376	2,127	19,646	19,827	45,461	43,794	1.9
6020	Commercial banks	111	102	3.2	1,871	1,604	20,263	20,082	36,408	33,459	2.1
6030	Savings institutions	20	19	1.7	367	359	17,995	19,298	6,886	7,264	1.7
6060	Credit unions	17	17	3.3	131	151	16,092	19,311	2,078	2,967	2.0
6090	Functions closely related to banking	4	4	1.4	7	13	8,000	8,923	89	104	-
6100	Nondepository institutions	57	56	2.1	279	298	24,645	21,906	7,051	8,286	0.9
6140	Personal credit institutions	32	30	3.7	156	-	23,487	-	3,582	-	-
6160	Mortgage bankers and brokers	20	22	1.5	73	117	22,082	19,966	1,815	3,863	0.8
6200	Security and commodity brokers	28	31	1.6	186	178	56,774	75,034	9,623	9,878	0.7
6210	Security brokers and dealers	18	17	1.4	167	158	61,988	82,962	9,437	9,577	0.9
6280	Security and commodity services	10	14	1.9	19	20	10,947	12,400	186	301	0.1
6300	Insurance carriers	80	63	2.4	3,598	3,100	26,173	37,288	103,542	109,598	5.1
6310	Life insurance	25	19	2.6	554	440	24,491	30,827	14,610	12,042	1.5
6330	Fire, marine, and casualty insurance	44	35	2.8	2,982	-	26,685	-	87,919	-	-
6370	Pension, health, and welfare funds	5	4	1.5	39	-	13,231	-	366	-	-
6400	Insurance agents, brokers, and service	178	187	2.5	966	1,536	21,458	20,557	23,027	36,403	3.1
6500	Real estate	347	355	1.9	2,208	2,012	14,366	13,980	31,750	30,277	1.5
6510	Real estate operators and lessors	156	177	2.7	790	867	11,367	12,360	9,089	11,997	2.4
6530	Real estate agents and managers	106	137	1.3	436	488	19,817	15,836	8,293	8,435	0.7
6540	Title abstract offices	6	6	1.9	60	32	31,133	24,750	1,772	935	1.7
6552	Subdividers and developers, n.e.c.	30	25	2.5	515	566	12,854	14,163	6,353	7,464	3.2
6553	Cemetery subdividers and developers	2	3	1.7	-	55	-	15,127	-	887	1.5
6710	Holding offices	3	1	0.2	3	-	26,667	-	65	-	-
PUTNAM, FL											
60 –	**Finance, insurance, and real estate**	94	95	0.2	498	480	17,398	16,517	8,607	8,327	0.1
6000	Depository institutions	21	20	0.4	277	256	19,769	18,625	5,262	4,833	0.2
6020	Commercial banks	14	13	0.4	157	131	20,943	18,809	2,925	2,327	0.1
6100	Nondepository institutions	9	10	0.4	27	34	21,185	19,765	651	641	0.1
6300	Insurance carriers	6	2	0.1	26	-	19,538	-	545	-	-
6400	Insurance agents, brokers, and service	22	26	0.3	85	96	16,188	15,375	1,358	1,619	0.1

Source: County Business Patterns, 1992/93, CBP-92/93-1, U.S. Department of Commerce, Washington, D.C., April 1995. SIC categories for which data were suppressed or not available for both 1992 and 1993 are not displayed. The employment columns represent mid-March employment in the year. Pay per employee is calculated by dividing 1st Quarter payroll, annualized, by mid-March employment. The columns headed "% State" show the county's percentage of the state total for the SIC in 1993; for example, 0.9% for SIC 6030 means that the county had 0.9 percent of the state's total establishments (or payroll) in SIC 6030 in 1993. A dash (-) is used to indicate that data are not available or cannot be calculated; nec means not elsewhere classified.

Continued on next page.

SIC	Industry	No. Establishments			Employment		Pay / Employee		Annual Payroll ($ 000)		
		1992	1993	% State	1992	1993	1992	1993	1992	1993	% State
PUTNAM, FL - [continued]											
6500	Real estate	33	34	0.2	77	79	8,831	8,354	733	806	0.0
6510	Real estate operators and lessors	11	10	0.2	29	-	4,690	-	170	-	-
6530	Real estate agents and managers	13	17	0.2	22	28	9,636	8,571	236	257	0.0
ST. JOHNS, FL											
60-	**Finance, insurance, and real estate**	229	248	0.6	1,073	1,198	20,809	20,935	22,320	26,657	0.3
6000	Depository institutions	28	28	0.5	325	379	19,508	21,414	6,391	7,895	0.3
6020	Commercial banks	23	24	0.7	-	363	-	21,609	-	7,605	0.5
6100	Nondepository institutions	9	10	0.4	18	17	24,444	19,765	364	421	0.0
6160	Mortgage bankers and brokers	6	5	0.3	11	9	28,000	20,000	232	260	0.1
6200	Security and commodity brokers	12	14	0.7	56	54	58,857	62,444	2,665	3,491	0.2
6300	Insurance carriers	17	12	0.5	43	36	31,628	32,333	1,431	1,861	0.1
6310	Life insurance	4	3	0.4	18	20	24,667	20,400	439	415	0.1
6400	Insurance agents, brokers, and service	35	38	0.5	105	121	23,695	27,537	2,201	2,777	0.2
6500	Real estate	121	139	0.7	501	572	15,864	14,748	8,769	9,913	0.5
6510	Real estate operators and lessors	34	29	0.4	148	100	14,946	16,400	2,320	1,970	0.4
6530	Real estate agents and managers	66	95	0.9	264	369	16,424	14,266	4,600	6,163	0.5
6552	Subdividers and developers, n.e.c.	9	9	0.9	52	87	18,077	15,678	1,305	1,405	0.6
6700	Holding and other investment offices	7	7	0.5	25	19	18,240	17,053	499	299	0.1
6710	Holding offices	2	3	0.7	-	1	-	12,000	-	37	0.0
ST. LUCIE, FL											
60-	**Finance, insurance, and real estate**	312	318	0.8	2,427	2,390	21,674	22,495	52,340	54,219	0.5
6000	Depository institutions	49	50	1.0	942	1,028	23,338	25,432	21,564	24,830	1.1
6020	Commercial banks	33	32	1.0	610	689	23,534	26,833	14,195	16,973	1.1
6030	Savings institutions	11	12	1.1	285	-	22,161	-	6,359	-	-
6100	Nondepository institutions	20	21	0.8	78	109	20,000	19,743	1,897	2,510	0.3
6140	Personal credit institutions	8	9	1.1	29	-	20,276	-	588	-	-
6160	Mortgage bankers and brokers	10	10	0.7	41	61	48,960	48,444	1,104	796	0.1
6200	Security and commodity brokers	7	5	0.3	25	18	48,960	48,444	1,104	796	0.1
6300	Insurance carriers	34	28	1.1	193	197	33,098	30,457	6,278	6,119	0.3
6310	Life insurance	8	7	0.9	99	103	33,172	30,563	3,042	2,957	0.4
6400	Insurance agents, brokers, and service	66	69	0.9	226	216	18,761	18,981	4,506	4,642	0.4
6500	Real estate	128	135	0.7	921	778	17,125	16,000	15,114	12,897	0.6
6510	Real estate operators and lessors	37	39	0.6	349	353	14,521	14,584	5,174	5,108	1.0
6530	Real estate agents and managers	61	83	0.8	465	328	18,022	17,854	7,661	6,171	0.5
6552	Subdividers and developers, n.e.c.	8	8	0.8	66	-	27,152	-	1,687	-	-
6700	Holding and other investment offices	8	10	0.7	42	44	34,190	46,545	1,877	2,425	0.5
SANTA ROSA, FL											
60-	**Finance, insurance, and real estate**	144	156	0.4	675	774	15,473	15,721	11,552	13,128	0.1
6000	Depository institutions	25	28	0.5	257	282	18,210	17,277	4,652	4,808	0.2
6020	Commercial banks	20	24	0.7	218	253	18,037	17,107	3,811	4,194	0.3
6060	Credit unions	3	4	0.8	-	29	-	18,759	-	614	0.4
6100	Nondepository institutions	9	8	0.3	25	-	18,720	-	545	-	-
6140	Personal credit institutions	4	4	0.5	14	20	22,000	13,800	328	251	0.2
6300	Insurance carriers	10	6	0.2	36	-	43,778	-	1,638	-	-
6400	Insurance agents, brokers, and service	26	26	0.3	66	68	15,939	19,412	1,074	1,470	0.1
6500	Real estate	70	82	0.4	285	351	9,137	11,123	3,591	4,723	0.2
6510	Real estate operators and lessors	13	20	0.3	43	-	7,070	-	368	-	-
6530	Real estate agents and managers	34	48	0.4	158	223	11,089	10,924	2,299	2,935	0.2
6552	Subdividers and developers, n.e.c.	7	12	1.2	63	-	6,159	-	700	-	-
6700	Holding and other investment offices	2	4	0.3	-	6	-	31,333	-	185	0.0
SARASOTA, FL											
60-	**Finance, insurance, and real estate**	1,157	1,221	3.0	7,833	7,423	25,981	27,842	202,654	208,785	2.0
6000	Depository institutions	186	160	3.1	2,665	2,039	22,826	25,085	60,961	47,336	2.0
6020	Commercial banks	120	104	3.2	1,970	1,595	23,697	26,184	45,117	37,007	2.3

Source: County Business Patterns, 1992/93, CBP-92/93-1, U.S. Department of Commerce, Washington, D.C., April 1995. SIC categories for which data were suppressed or not available for both 1992 and 1993 are *not* displayed. The employment columns represent mid-March employment in the year. Pay per employee is calculated by dividing 1st Quarter payroll, annualized, by mid-March employment. The columns headed "% State" show the county's percentage of the state total for the SIC in 1993; for example, 0.9% for SIC 6030 means that the county had 0.9 percent of the state's total establishments (or payroll) in SIC 6030 in 1993. A dash (-) is used to indicate that data are not available or cannot be calculated; *nec* means not elsewhere classified.

Continued on next page.

SIC	Industry	No. Establishments			Employment		Pay / Employee		Annual Payroll ($ 000)		
		1992	1993	% State	1992	1993	1992	1993	1992	1993	% State
SARASOTA, FL - [continued]											
6030	Savings institutions	59	47	4.3	664	367	20,367	22,005	15,288	8,794	2.0
6060	Credit unions	4	6	1.1	24	68	21,167	17,529	447	1,418	1.0
6090	Functions closely related to banking	3	3	1.0	7	9	16,571	12,889	109	117	-
6100	Nondepository institutions	57	62	2.4	-	204	-	22,608	-	6,251	0.7
6140	Personal credit institutions	18	13	1.6	104	67	22,000	16,597	2,230	1,269	0.8
6150	Business credit institutions	2	3	1.1	-	4	-	39,000	-	143	0.1
6160	Mortgage bankers and brokers	36	46	3.1	136	133	25,500	25,143	3,956	4,839	1.0
6200	Security and commodity brokers	89	94	4.7	682	731	61,255	74,966	42,149	47,663	3.4
6210	Security brokers and dealers	57	58	4.8	634	668	64,019	74,317	40,461	43,319	3.9
6280	Security and commodity services	31	36	4.9	-	63	-	81,841	-	4,344	1.5
6300	Insurance carriers	91	71	2.7	872	575	32,986	36,452	26,352	22,380	1.0
6310	Life insurance	17	15	2.0	267	264	32,584	36,273	8,567	9,522	1.2
6330	Fire, marine, and casualty insurance	46	38	3.1	380	174	37,263	46,782	11,540	8,664	1.0
6360	Title insurance	18	8	4.8	127	90	24,157	20,044	3,188	2,138	3.1
6370	Pension, health, and welfare funds	4	6	2.3	4	3	16,000	34,667	310	643	2.2
6400	Insurance agents, brokers, and service	167	186	2.5	702	1,052	26,137	28,080	18,285	36,518	3.1
6500	Real estate	518	592	3.1	2,342	2,674	16,487	15,819	39,284	44,913	2.2
6510	Real estate operators and lessors	124	150	2.3	475	890	13,347	12,449	6,581	11,730	2.4
6530	Real estate agents and managers	286	391	3.7	1,366	1,535	15,654	16,724	21,850	26,955	2.2
6540	Title abstract offices	6	6	1.9	29	26	20,000	19,077	633	514	0.9
6552	Subdividers and developers, n.e.c.	29	35	3.6	261	151	24,077	24,768	6,030	4,224	1.8
6553	Cemetery subdividers and developers	4	5	2.8	73	70	19,068	17,371	1,402	1,280	2.2
6700	Holding and other investment offices	48	55	3.6	319	-	28,088	-	8,946	-	-
6710	Holding offices	10	11	2.6	104	48	57,423	23,917	5,653	994	0.4
6732	Educational, religious, etc. trusts	7	4	2.2	140	10	9,686	40,000	1,231	408	1.8
6733	Trusts, n.e.c.	12	20	6.7	28	45	29,143	22,311	1,083	1,332	2.7
6799	Investors, n.e.c.	9	10	2.5	24	14	14,000	14,857	371	217	0.4
SEMINOLE, FL											
60 –	**Finance, insurance, and real estate**	843	891	2.2	5,321	5,623	25,029	25,197	136,919	156,949	1.5
6000	Depository institutions	99	98	1.9	1,298	1,302	22,370	23,982	27,551	32,038	1.4
6020	Commercial banks	59	64	2.0	733	816	20,993	23,235	14,236	18,574	1.2
6030	Savings institutions	23	17	1.5	471	397	25,418	27,224	11,661	11,925	2.7
6060	Credit unions	9	8	1.5	61	68	17,311	16,824	1,107	1,213	0.8
6090	Functions closely related to banking	8	9	3.1	33	21	18,788	14,857	547	326	-
6100	Nondepository institutions	88	99	3.8	398	481	32,050	27,035	13,017	18,108	2.0
6140	Personal credit institutions	24	26	3.2	116	128	31,345	21,656	3,359	2,778	1.7
6150	Business credit institutions	5	4	1.5	-	9	-	74,667	-	682	0.3
6160	Mortgage bankers and brokers	53	69	4.6	253	344	33,328	27,791	8,747	14,648	3.1
6200	Security and commodity brokers	24	37	1.9	127	-	33,039	-	4,359	-	-
6210	Security brokers and dealers	10	15	1.2	113	-	30,938	-	3,076	-	-
6280	Security and commodity services	12	20	2.7	11	-	60,727	-	1,192	-	-
6300	Insurance carriers	91	72	2.8	645	705	34,419	35,245	22,492	24,680	1.2
6310	Life insurance	24	18	2.4	233	221	27,845	31,566	6,716	6,452	0.8
6330	Fire, marine, and casualty insurance	42	37	3.0	251	377	44,558	39,618	11,358	14,806	1.8
6360	Title insurance	15	7	4.2	101	49	26,337	24,735	2,641	1,653	2.4
6370	Pension, health, and welfare funds	6	5	1.9	-	23	-	20,522	-	476	1.7
6400	Insurance agents, brokers, and service	184	201	2.6	1,144	1,348	27,294	25,697	33,472	40,688	3.5
6500	Real estate	333	353	1.9	1,523	1,558	18,555	18,493	29,951	30,519	1.5
6510	Real estate operators and lessors	74	98	1.5	346	497	13,376	12,290	4,673	6,527	1.3
6530	Real estate agents and managers	169	210	2.0	788	848	19,183	20,297	15,833	19,053	1.6
6540	Title abstract offices	8	9	2.9	44	47	17,909	23,149	1,089	1,224	2.2
6552	Subdividers and developers, n.e.c.	20	26	2.6	113	-	31,965	-	4,282	-	-
6700	Holding and other investment offices	21	29	1.9	121	128	24,826	37,312	3,708	6,221	1.3

Source: County Business Patterns, 1992/93, CBP-92/93-1, U.S. Department of Commerce, Washington, D.C., April 1995. SIC categories for which data were suppressed or not available for both 1992 and 1993 are not displayed. The employment columns represent mid-March employment in the year. Pay per employee is calculated by dividing 1st Quarter payroll, annualized, by mid-March employment. The columns headed "% State" show the county's percentage of the state total for the SIC in 1993; for example, 0.9% for SIC 6030 means that the county had 0.9 percent of the state's total establishments (or payroll) in SIC 6030 in 1993. A dash (-) is used to indicate that data are not available or cannot be calculated; nec means not elsewhere classified.

Continued on next page.

SIC	Industry	No. Establishments			Employment		Pay / Employee		Annual Payroll ($ 000)		
		1992	1993	% State	1992	1993	1992	1993	1992	1993	% State
SEMINOLE, FL - [continued]											
6710	Holding offices	2	6	1.4	-	8	-	27,000	-	599	0.2
6794	Patent owners and lessors	6	6	6.3	45	34	33,956	54,353	2,152	1,852	7.4
6799	Investors, n.e.c.	5	6	1.5	34	-	24,471	-	735	-	-
SUMTER, FL											
60 –	**Finance, insurance, and real estate**	31	36	0.1	128	103	14,906	17,670	1,886	1,900	0.0
6000	Depository institutions	6	6	0.1	65	50	16,862	18,720	1,041	921	0.0
6500	Real estate	17	19	0.1	41	31	8,683	13,935	365	433	0.0
6510	Real estate operators and lessors	11	10	0.2	22	19	8,000	15,158	214	278	0.1
6530	Real estate agents and managers	4	7	0.1	8	-	7,000	-	63	-	-
SUWANNEE, FL											
60 –	**Finance, insurance, and real estate**	42	42	0.1	266	234	17,383	18,256	4,466	4,169	0.0
6000	Depository institutions	10	7	0.1	149	113	19,275	23,115	2,676	2,239	0.1
6020	Commercial banks	6	3	0.1	81	39	19,556	19,897	1,351	787	0.0
6400	Insurance agents, brokers, and service	11	12	0.2	45	45	17,600	17,600	812	819	0.1
6500	Real estate	17	16	0.1	38	40	6,526	6,700	269	401	0.0
6510	Real estate operators and lessors	6	6	0.1	21	21	4,952	4,952	109	125	0.0
6530	Real estate agents and managers	9	7	0.1	-	8	-	8,000	-	167	0.0
6700	Holding and other investment offices	1	3	0.2	-	2	-	8,000	-	15	0.0
6710	Holding offices	1	3	0.7	-	2	-	8,000	-	15	0.0
TAYLOR, FL											
60 –	**Finance, insurance, and real estate**	23	27	0.1	188	192	16,149	16,146	3,286	3,548	0.0
6000	Depository institutions	6	6	0.1	135	140	18,252	18,286	2,633	2,720	0.1
6500	Real estate	7	8	0.0	27	24	9,926	11,000	302	418	0.0
6510	Real estate operators and lessors	3	4	0.1	12	-	8,333	-	106	-	-
6530	Real estate agents and managers	2	3	0.0	-	10	-	7,600	-	161	0.0
UNION, FL											
60 –	**Finance, insurance, and real estate**	8	6	0.0	39	35	16,923	18,629	693	721	0.0
VOLUSIA, FL											
60 –	**Finance, insurance, and real estate**	996	999	2.5	6,025	6,122	20,615	21,045	124,574	135,942	1.3
6000	Depository institutions	158	133	2.6	1,952	1,779	22,701	24,926	41,198	40,804	1.7
6020	Commercial banks	123	112	3.5	1,718	1,621	23,350	25,379	36,830	37,172	2.3
6030	Savings institutions	28	14	1.3	195	115	18,421	22,539	3,752	3,022	0.7
6100	Nondepository institutions	52	57	2.2	244	298	24,770	21,946	6,240	8,501	1.0
6160	Mortgage bankers and brokers	24	28	1.9	136	164	24,676	25,439	3,583	5,941	1.2
6200	Security and commodity brokers	26	28	1.4	185	188	47,070	44,574	9,280	9,794	0.7
6210	Security brokers and dealers	16	15	1.2	173	169	49,110	47,834	9,102	9,412	0.9
6280	Security and commodity services	10	13	1.8	12	19	17,667	15,579	178	382	0.1
6300	Insurance carriers	74	61	2.3	565	510	30,499	32,275	17,549	16,822	0.8
6310	Life insurance	18	14	1.9	230	196	23,635	28,449	5,781	5,236	0.6
6330	Fire, marine, and casualty insurance	38	33	2.7	176	-	35,523	-	6,582	-	-
6360	Title insurance	6	4	2.4	-	32	-	22,250	-	821	1.2
6400	Insurance agents, brokers, and service	153	170	2.2	663	831	22,190	24,698	15,678	23,455	2.0
6500	Real estate	516	534	2.8	2,352	2,474	13,595	12,721	33,530	35,548	1.7
6510	Real estate operators and lessors	161	172	2.6	721	860	10,613	10,851	8,631	10,941	2.2
6530	Real estate agents and managers	267	320	3.0	1,136	1,390	13,669	12,777	16,711	19,818	1.6
6540	Title abstract offices	6	6	1.9	53	65	18,491	20,492	1,095	1,500	2.7
6552	Subdividers and developers, n.e.c.	24	21	2.1	107	57	21,346	21,754	1,517	1,441	0.6
6553	Cemetery subdividers and developers	11	12	6.7	126	99	18,349	17,859	2,105	1,781	3.1
6700	Holding and other investment offices	16	16	1.1	-	42	-	26,571	-	1,018	0.2

Source: County Business Patterns, 1992/93, CBP-92/93-1, U.S. Department of Commerce, Washington, D.C., April 1995. SIC categories for which data were suppressed or not available for both 1992 and 1993 are *not* displayed. The employment columns represent mid-March employment in the year. Pay per employee is calculated by dividing 1st Quarter payroll, annualized, by mid-March employment. The columns headed "% State" show the county's percentage of the state total for the SIC in 1993; for example, 0.9% for SIC 6030 means that the county had 0.9 percent of the state's total establishments (or payroll) in SIC 6030 in 1993. A dash (-) is used to indicate that data are not available or cannot be calculated; *nec* means not elsewhere classified.

Continued on next page.

SIC	Industry	No. Establishments			Employment		Pay / Employee		Annual Payroll ($ 000)		
		1992	1993	% State	1992	1993	1992	1993	1992	1993	% State
VOLUSIA, FL - [continued]											
6710	Holding offices	3	2	0.5	13	-	27,385	-	370	-	-
6732	Educational, religious, etc. trusts	2	3	1.7	-	3	-	29,333	-	102	0.5
6733	Trusts, n.e.c.	6	5	1.7	-	5	-	9,600	-	136	0.3
WAKULLA, FL											
60-	**Finance, insurance, and real estate**	19	20	0.0	88	95	21,409	16,589	1,747	1,700	0.0
6000	Depository institutions	5	4	0.1	58	63	26,276	18,921	1,352	1,219	0.1
6400	Insurance agents, brokers, and service	4	7	0.1	-	11	-	14,182	-	182	0.0
6500	Real estate	8	9	0.0	14	21	12,000	10,857	215	299	0.0
6530	Real estate agents and managers	2	5	0.0	-	14	-	9,714	-	202	0.0
WALTON, FL											
60-	**Finance, insurance, and real estate**	70	78	0.2	578	415	14,913	15,219	9,382	7,668	0.1
6000	Depository institutions	8	10	0.2	72	101	17,944	20,594	1,295	2,054	0.1
6020	Commercial banks	3	5	0.2	35	43	19,429	23,256	721	883	0.1
6100	Nondepository institutions	2	3	0.1	-	8	-	23,500	-	269	0.0
6200	Security and commodity brokers	3	2	0.1	4	-	26,000	-	190	-	-
6300	Insurance carriers	3	3	0.1	4	-	42,000	-	211	-	-
6400	Insurance agents, brokers, and service	4	5	0.1	15	20	15,467	15,800	243	357	0.0
6500	Real estate	49	54	0.3	473	273	13,945	12,029	7,182	4,438	0.2
6510	Real estate operators and lessors	7	10	0.2	7	15	13,143	10,400	148	249	0.1
6530	Real estate agents and managers	30	37	0.3	437	251	13,785	12,064	6,549	3,974	0.3
6552	Subdividers and developers, n.e.c.	5	7	0.7	9	7	19,556	14,286	154	215	0.1
WASHINGTON, FL											
60-	**Finance, insurance, and real estate**	21	18	0.0	69	68	17,159	17,353	1,326	1,217	0.0
6000	Depository institutions	4	3	0.1	32	21	19,000	19,810	627	380	0.0
6400	Insurance agents, brokers, and service	5	5	0.1	-	23	-	16,522	-	391	0.0
6500	Real estate	9	7	0.0	16	21	11,500	11,429	227	301	0.0
6510	Real estate operators and lessors	5	2	0.0	7	-	10,286	-	88	-	-

Source: County Business Patterns, 1992/93, CBP-92/93-1, U.S. Department of Commerce, Washington, D.C., April 1995. SIC categories for which data were suppressed or not available for both 1992 and 1993 are *not* displayed. The employment columns represent mid-March employment in the year. Pay per employee is calculated by dividing 1st Quarter payroll, annualized, by mid-March employment. The columns headed "% State" show the county's percentage of the state total for the SIC in 1993; for example, 0.9% for SIC 6030 means that the county had 0.9 percent of the state's total establishments (or payroll) in SIC 6030 in 1993. A dash (-) is used to indicate that data are not available or cannot be calculated; *nec* means not elsewhere classified.

GEORGIA

SIC	Industry	No. Establishments			Employment		Pay / Employee		Annual Payroll ($ 000)		
		1992	1993	% State	1992	1993	1992	1993	1992	1993	% State
APPLING, GA											
60 –	**Finance, insurance, and real estate**	17	17	0.1	116	122	18,897	18,459	2,126	2,248	0.0
6000	Depository institutions	3	3	0.1	75	83	21,653	19,807	1,576	1,656	0.1
6100	Nondepository institutions	5	4	0.2	-	15	-	24,800	-	338	0.1
6140	Personal credit institutions	4	4	0.4	-	15	-	24,800	-	338	0.2
6400	Insurance agents, brokers, and service	7	7	0.2	22	22	10,364	10,364	235	234	0.0
6500	Real estate	2	3	0.1	-	2	-	4,000	-	20	0.0
ATKINSON, GA											
60 –	**Finance, insurance, and real estate**	9	11	0.1	41	-	19,415	-	851	-	-
6400	Insurance agents, brokers, and service	3	3	0.1	7	-	13,143	-	99	-	-
BACON, GA											
60 –	**Finance, insurance, and real estate**	15	17	0.1	96	108	17,458	18,444	1,851	1,969	0.0
6000	Depository institutions	3	3	0.1	66	76	18,788	20,105	1,427	1,513	0.1
6100	Nondepository institutions	4	4	0.2	11	-	14,909	-	152	-	-
6140	Personal credit institutions	4	4	0.4	11	-	14,909	-	152	-	-
6400	Insurance agents, brokers, and service	5	5	0.2	15	13	11,733	12,308	188	188	0.0
6500	Real estate	2	3	0.1	-	2	-	26,000	-	45	0.0
BAKER, GA											
60 –	**Finance, insurance, and real estate**	1	1	0.0	-	-	-	-	-	-	-
BALDWIN, GA											
60 –	**Finance, insurance, and real estate**	58	61	0.4	482	397	20,000	20,252	9,407	8,202	0.1
6000	Depository institutions	15	12	0.5	249	263	22,988	21,262	5,500	5,573	0.4
6020	Commercial banks	8	8	0.4	208	-	23,385	-	4,748	-	-
6100	Nondepository institutions	14	13	0.7	53	45	19,547	20,089	1,152	912	0.1
6140	Personal credit institutions	11	9	0.8	45	32	16,978	18,000	887	585	0.4
6400	Insurance agents, brokers, and service	9	13	0.4	39	39	14,154	14,872	606	654	0.1
6500	Real estate	14	14	0.3	34	36	10,353	10,556	453	478	0.1
6510	Real estate operators and lessors	8	7	0.4	20	21	9,000	10,095	267	242	0.1
6530	Real estate agents and managers	3	5	0.2	8	-	11,500	-	103	-	-
BANKS, GA											
60 –	**Finance, insurance, and real estate**	2	3	0.0	-	-	-	-	-	-	-
BARROW, GA											
60 –	**Finance, insurance, and real estate**	40	38	0.2	332	307	18,747	20,261	6,752	6,305	0.1
6000	Depository institutions	7	7	0.3	232	214	17,276	17,458	4,126	3,934	0.3
6100	Nondepository institutions	9	8	0.4	43	36	27,907	39,222	1,363	1,124	0.2
6400	Insurance agents, brokers, and service	7	7	0.2	23	26	17,739	18,154	552	575	0.1
6500	Real estate	14	13	0.3	28	27	11,714	12,889	408	399	0.1
6510	Real estate operators and lessors	8	9	0.5	18	23	12,000	11,304	224	263	0.2
BARTOW, GA											
60 –	**Finance, insurance, and real estate**	88	97	0.6	482	475	20,822	20,817	10,356	10,686	0.2
6000	Depository institutions	15	16	0.6	261	218	21,732	20,661	5,733	4,893	0.4
6020	Commercial banks	10	11	0.6	217	203	21,014	20,493	4,655	4,435	0.4
6100	Nondepository institutions	13	15	0.8	43	47	20,930	29,106	819	1,507	0.2
6140	Personal credit institutions	10	10	0.9	31	26	19,484	22,462	522	600	0.4
6200	Security and commodity brokers	3	3	0.4	4	6	17,000	20,000	75	212	0.0

*Source: County Business Patterns, 1992/93, CBP-92/93-1, U.S. Department of Commerce, Washington, D.C., April 1995. SIC categories for which data were suppressed or not available for both 1992 and 1993 are *not* displayed. The employment columns represent mid-March employment in the year. Pay per employee is calculated by dividing 1st Quarter payroll, annualized, by mid-March employment. The columns headed "% State" show the county's percentage of the state total for the SIC in 1993; for example, 0.9% for SIC 6030 means that the county had 0.9 percent of the state's total establishments (or payroll) in SIC 6030 in 1993. A dash (-) is used to indicate that data are not available or cannot be calculated; *nec* means not elsewhere classified.*

Continued on next page.

SIC	Industry	No. Establishments			Employment		Pay / Employee		Annual Payroll ($ 000)		
		1992	1993	% State	1992	1993	1992	1993	1992	1993	% State
BARTOW, GA - [continued]											
6300	Insurance carriers	7	6	0.5	18	19	43,333	49,053	854	782	0.1
6400	Insurance agents, brokers, and service	20	23	0.7	63	59	19,556	20,881	1,294	1,317	0.2
6500	Real estate	26	29	0.6	62	96	12,710	9,333	921	1,124	0.1
6510	Real estate operators and lessors	8	10	0.5	24	-	10,500	-	254	-	-
6530	Real estate agents and managers	11	14	0.5	24	60	12,833	8,467	325	572	0.1
6700	Holding and other investment offices	4	5	0.9	31	30	19,226	27,867	660	851	0.3
BEN HILL, GA											
60 –	**Finance, insurance, and real estate**	35	37	0.2	235	250	19,762	21,216	5,191	5,354	0.1
6000	Depository institutions	6	5	0.2	-	79	-	25,418	-	1,943	0.1
6020	Commercial banks	5	5	0.3	-	79	-	25,418	-	1,943	0.2
6100	Nondepository institutions	6	7	0.4	33	34	15,758	15,765	573	597	0.1
6140	Personal credit institutions	6	6	0.5	33	-	15,758	-	573	-	-
6400	Insurance agents, brokers, and service	9	8	0.2	23	31	15,130	18,065	361	505	0.1
6500	Real estate	10	12	0.2	60	60	14,467	13,400	941	832	0.1
6510	Real estate operators and lessors	7	9	0.5	54	54	15,333	14,074	897	786	0.5
6530	Real estate agents and managers	3	3	0.1	6	6	6,667	7,333	44	46	0.0
BERRIEN, GA											
60 –	**Finance, insurance, and real estate**	26	27	0.2	205	242	20,820	18,744	4,479	4,841	0.1
6000	Depository institutions	9	10	0.4	78	80	18,821	17,850	1,560	1,599	0.1
6020	Commercial banks	7	7	0.4	-	75	-	18,347	-	1,500	0.1
6100	Nondepository institutions	4	4	0.2	18	55	16,000	5,745	297	323	0.1
6500	Real estate	4	4	0.1	8	4	9,500	8,000	60	22	0.0
BIBB, GA											
60 –	**Finance, insurance, and real estate**	451	449	2.9	8,056	7,266	25,576	26,933	202,162	191,752	3.5
6000	Depository institutions	70	72	2.8	1,014	1,137	20,552	21,963	20,868	22,850	1.7
6020	Commercial banks	44	45	2.4	775	865	21,110	22,553	16,028	17,576	1.6
6100	Nondepository institutions	54	58	2.9	627	648	23,049	23,895	15,717	15,763	2.6
6140	Personal credit institutions	43	46	4.1	-	231	-	22,961	-	5,496	3.5
6160	Mortgage bankers and brokers	6	8	1.3	86	-	51,814	-	5,424	-	-
6200	Security and commodity brokers	16	17	2.3	111	123	73,009	73,854	7,303	8,876	1.8
6210	Security brokers and dealers	11	13	3.2	106	113	75,962	79,363	7,235	8,751	2.3
6280	Security and commodity services	5	4	1.3	5	10	10,400	11,600	68	125	-
6300	Insurance carriers	62	56	4.6	4,750	4,090	27,778	28,932	127,355	115,842	8.5
6310	Life insurance	29	24	5.3	1,150	864	22,842	25,935	24,886	20,652	3.3
6330	Fire, marine, and casualty insurance	22	22	4.2	3,541	3,190	29,530	29,779	101,409	93,756	16.0
6400	Insurance agents, brokers, and service	87	98	3.0	454	378	27,031	21,196	11,707	8,300	1.4
6500	Real estate	147	134	2.6	847	681	14,966	19,806	13,200	14,424	1.9
6510	Real estate operators and lessors	59	53	2.7	210	218	11,543	10,679	2,989	2,413	1.4
6530	Real estate agents and managers	66	67	2.6	410	380	18,839	25,684	7,988	10,118	2.0
6552	Subdividers and developers, n.e.c.	5	8	2.3	28	-	9,857	-	255	-	-
6553	Cemetery subdividers and developers	5	4	3.3	43	52	13,581	15,462	556	821	5.4
6700	Holding and other investment offices	15	14	2.4	253	209	22,735	30,258	6,012	5,697	1.8
6732	Educational, religious, etc. trusts	4	5	6.5	11	14	18,909	15,714	190	208	1.4
6733	Trusts, n.e.c.	6	5	5.6	13	-	17,538	-	258	-	-
BLECKLEY, GA											
60 –	**Finance, insurance, and real estate**	13	13	0.1	75	72	20,747	21,833	1,607	1,529	0.0
6000	Depository institutions	3	3	0.1	-	49	-	24,082	-	1,156	0.1
6100	Nondepository institutions	4	4	0.2	15	-	16,267	-	268	-	-
6140	Personal credit institutions	3	3	0.3	14	-	17,143	-	266	-	-
6400	Insurance agents, brokers, and service	4	4	0.1	10	9	14,800	13,778	158	144	0.0

Source: County Business Patterns, 1992/93, CBP-92/93-1, U.S. Department of Commerce, Washington, D.C., April 1995. SIC categories for which data were suppressed or not available for both 1992 and 1993 are *not* displayed. The employment columns represent mid-March employment in the year. Pay per employee is calculated by dividing 1st Quarter payroll, annualized, by mid-March employment. The columns headed "% State" show the county's percentage of the state total for the SIC in 1993; for example, 0.9% for SIC 6030 means that the county had 0.9 percent of the state's total establishments (or payroll) in SIC 6030 in 1993. A dash (-) is used to indicate that data are not available or cannot be calculated; *nec* means not elsewhere classified.

SIC	Industry	No. Establishments			Employment		Pay / Employee		Annual Payroll ($ 000)		
		1992	1993	% State	1992	1993	1992	1993	1992	1993	% State
BRANTLEY, GA											
60 –	Finance, insurance, and real estate	4	5	0.0	31	–	17,806	–	500	–	–
BROOKS, GA											
60 –	Finance, insurance, and real estate	20	21	0.1	104	105	17,077	17,829	1,908	1,999	0.0
6000	Depository institutions	8	8	0.3	68	70	17,235	19,029	1,276	1,315	0.1
6400	Insurance agents, brokers, and service	3	3	0.1	11	8	19,273	21,500	195	186	0.0
6500	Real estate	4	4	0.1	–	6	–	6,000	–	19	0.0
6510	Real estate operators and lessors	3	3	0.2	5	–	4,000	–	29	–	–
BRYAN, GA											
60 –	Finance, insurance, and real estate	15	19	0.1	101	107	17,703	20,822	2,079	2,528	0.0
6400	Insurance agents, brokers, and service	4	5	0.2	6	10	11,333	7,600	80	93	0.0
6500	Real estate	5	7	0.1	15	14	13,333	16,571	263	324	0.0
BULLOCH, GA											
60 –	Finance, insurance, and real estate	79	79	0.5	691	597	20,857	21,079	15,387	13,178	0.2
6000	Depository institutions	18	16	0.6	284	224	19,662	21,411	5,701	4,860	0.4
6020	Commercial banks	15	14	0.8	274	–	19,825	–	5,550	–	–
6060	Credit unions	3	2	0.7	10	–	15,200	–	151	–	–
6100	Nondepository institutions	14	15	0.8	74	107	25,784	16,710	2,271	1,967	0.3
6140	Personal credit institutions	11	12	1.1	45	–	23,111	–	992	–	–
6300	Insurance carriers	7	8	0.7	99	91	29,293	34,110	3,097	3,095	0.2
6310	Life insurance	5	5	1.1	–	89	–	33,618	–	2,909	0.5
6500	Real estate	25	24	0.5	59	64	9,220	10,562	663	920	0.1
6510	Real estate operators and lessors	12	11	0.6	–	24	–	5,167	–	353	0.2
6530	Real estate agents and managers	12	12	0.5	25	–	11,040	–	386	–	–
BURKE, GA											
60 –	Finance, insurance, and real estate	25	25	0.2	–	–	–	–	–	–	–
6000	Depository institutions	10	10	0.4	102	114	18,314	16,316	1,992	1,972	0.1
6140	Personal credit institutions	3	3	0.3	–	13	–	18,769	–	246	0.2
BUTTS, GA											
60 –	Finance, insurance, and real estate	23	26	0.2	99	121	20,889	18,017	2,084	2,190	0.0
6100	Nondepository institutions	3	3	0.2	9	9	20,444	20,000	154	165	0.0
6140	Personal credit institutions	3	3	0.3	9	9	20,444	20,000	154	165	0.1
6400	Insurance agents, brokers, and service	4	6	0.2	15	15	13,067	15,200	179	225	0.0
6500	Real estate	11	13	0.3	24	27	12,667	16,148	343	513	0.1
6510	Real estate operators and lessors	8	10	0.5	21	25	13,905	17,120	315	477	0.3
6530	Real estate agents and managers	2	3	0.1	–	2	–	4,000	–	36	0.0
CALHOUN, GA											
60 –	Finance, insurance, and real estate	10	9	0.1	77	71	14,701	19,155	1,208	1,282	0.0
6000	Depository institutions	3	2	0.1	40	–	21,200	–	854	–	–
6020	Commercial banks	3	2	0.1	40	–	21,200	–	854	–	–
CAMDEN, GA											
60 –	Finance, insurance, and real estate	52	57	0.4	218	246	16,202	15,691	3,476	4,004	0.1
6000	Depository institutions	12	14	0.5	114	125	19,018	19,072	2,075	2,402	0.2
6100	Nondepository institutions	5	5	0.3	15	14	19,733	16,571	291	244	0.0
6200	Security and commodity brokers	3	2	0.3	3	–	8,000	–	31	–	–
6400	Insurance agents, brokers, and service	7	9	0.3	16	21	14,000	12,762	221	282	0.0
6500	Real estate	21	25	0.5	63	79	11,111	9,165	726	822	0.1
6510	Real estate operators and lessors	10	12	0.6	40	–	9,300	–	395	–	–
6530	Real estate agents and managers	6	11	0.4	9	25	11,111	10,400	106	296	0.1

Source: County Business Patterns, 1992/93, CBP-92/93-1, U.S. Department of Commerce, Washington, D.C., April 1995. SIC categories for which data were suppressed or not available for both 1992 and 1993 are not displayed. The employment columns represent mid-March employment in the year. Pay per employee is calculated by dividing 1st Quarter payroll, annualized, by mid-March employment. The columns headed "% State" show the county's percentage of the state total for the SIC in 1993; for example, 0.9% for SIC 6030 means that the county had 0.9 percent of the state's total establishments (or payroll) in SIC 6030 in 1993. A dash (-) is used to indicate that data are not available or cannot be calculated; nec means not elsewhere classified.

SIC	Industry	No. Establishments			Employment		Pay / Employee		Annual Payroll ($ 000)		
		1992	1993	% State	1992	1993	1992	1993	1992	1993	% State
CANDLER, GA											
60 –	**Finance, insurance, and real estate**	15	13	0.1	84	64	15,857	15,688	1,433	1,043	0.0
6400	Insurance agents, brokers, and service	6	5	0.2	13	13	10,769	12,308	140	153	0.0
CARROLL, GA											
60 –	**Finance, insurance, and real estate**	125	135	0.9	1,047	942	19,591	19,762	21,219	19,276	0.3
6000	Depository institutions	30	31	1.2	601	481	18,037	18,204	10,999	8,804	0.7
6100	Nondepository institutions	21	22	1.1	72	79	18,111	20,000	1,383	1,697	0.3
6140	Personal credit institutions	15	17	1.5	58	66	16,000	17,758	989	1,215	0.8
6200	Security and commodity brokers	5	6	0.8	-	7	-	25,143	-	243	0.1
6300	Insurance carriers	13	7	0.6	107	95	27,103	27,958	3,415	2,821	0.2
6310	Life insurance	3	2	0.4	68	-	33,059	-	2,746	-	-
6400	Insurance agents, brokers, and service	22	28	0.9	139	143	25,784	24,112	3,449	3,595	0.6
6500	Real estate	33	41	0.8	103	137	14,058	14,599	1,491	2,116	0.3
6510	Real estate operators and lessors	14	15	0.8	57	37	13,263	12,324	770	423	0.2
6530	Real estate agents and managers	13	20	0.8	33	72	18,424	16,111	641	1,148	0.2
6553	Cemetery subdividers and developers	3	2	1.6	9	-	5,333	-	44	-	-
CATOOSA, GA											
60 –	**Finance, insurance, and real estate**	41	43	0.3	300	319	23,640	22,470	6,747	6,689	0.1
6000	Depository institutions	13	13	0.5	179	187	26,190	25,947	4,234	4,211	0.3
6060	Credit unions	3	3	1.0	4	8	17,000	19,000	100	105	0.2
6400	Insurance agents, brokers, and service	7	10	0.3	21	23	21,524	18,957	431	475	0.1
6500	Real estate	16	15	0.3	51	65	14,667	10,646	728	774	0.1
6510	Real estate operators and lessors	6	4	0.2	7	-	12,571	-	106	-	-
6530	Real estate agents and managers	8	10	0.4	42	55	15,429	10,691	602	687	0.1
CHARLTON, GA											
60 –	**Finance, insurance, and real estate**	9	9	0.1	59	54	12,339	14,222	734	744	0.0
6400	Insurance agents, brokers, and service	3	3	0.1	7	-	8,000	-	82	-	-
6500	Real estate	3	3	0.1	17	15	5,647	7,467	130	94	0.0
CHATHAM, GA											
60 –	**Finance, insurance, and real estate**	561	577	3.7	5,121	4,735	25,493	24,849	126,928	125,128	2.3
6000	Depository institutions	107	108	4.2	1,176	1,212	21,524	22,921	24,061	27,687	2.1
6020	Commercial banks	64	68	3.7	937	1,035	22,374	24,205	20,360	24,592	2.3
6060	Credit unions	24	22	7.2	131	65	19,206	16,554	1,939	1,139	2.3
6100	Nondepository institutions	58	61	3.1	-	292	-	22,863	-	6,754	1.1
6140	Personal credit institutions	44	42	3.8	197	222	23,797	19,730	4,437	4,439	2.8
6150	Business credit institutions	1	3	1.4	-	9	-	20,889	-	182	0.1
6160	Mortgage bankers and brokers	11	16	2.7	48	61	30,833	34,557	1,617	2,133	0.8
6200	Security and commodity brokers	26	29	4.0	224	232	52,089	56,966	12,997	16,406	3.4
6210	Security brokers and dealers	17	19	4.6	196	200	53,388	59,860	11,200	15,067	4.0
6280	Security and commodity services	9	10	3.3	28	32	43,000	38,875	1,797	1,339	-
6300	Insurance carriers	58	55	4.5	1,182	915	24,995	26,256	29,471	23,656	1.7
6310	Life insurance	21	19	4.2	436	328	27,028	27,110	11,427	9,601	1.5
6330	Fire, marine, and casualty insurance	21	21	4.0	564	519	27,113	26,451	15,272	12,560	2.1
6370	Pension, health, and welfare funds	11	11	7.5	126	43	8,159	13,953	1,372	695	1.7
6400	Insurance agents, brokers, and service	99	110	3.3	704	641	30,659	25,123	20,957	17,237	2.9
6500	Real estate	186	185	3.6	1,339	1,221	20,102	18,002	25,261	24,172	3.1
6510	Real estate operators and lessors	80	84	4.2	429	406	14,685	13,744	6,705	6,625	3.9
6530	Real estate agents and managers	72	86	3.4	562	626	17,452	16,569	10,236	11,502	2.2
6540	Title abstract offices	4	4	8.9	7	8	17,143	19,000	148	171	3.0
6700	Holding and other investment offices	26	29	5.0	217	222	40,903	35,495	7,616	9,216	2.9
6710	Holding offices	7	10	4.6	122	132	57,672	45,697	5,512	7,671	3.3
6732	Educational, religious, etc. trusts	5	5	6.5	41	28	12,683	17,714	502	499	3.3
6733	Trusts, n.e.c.	8	8	9.0	22	39	18,727	18,667	448	274	3.0

Source: County Business Patterns, 1992/93, CBP-92/93-1, U.S. Department of Commerce, Washington, D.C., April 1995. SIC categories for which data were suppressed or not available for both 1992 and 1993 are *not* displayed. The employment columns represent mid-March employment in the year. Pay per employee is calculated by dividing 1st Quarter payroll, annualized, by mid-March employment. The columns headed "% State" show the county's percentage of the state total for the SIC in 1993; for example, 0.9% for SIC 6030 means that the county had 0.9 percent of the state's total establishments (or payroll) in SIC 6030 in 1993. A dash (-) is used to indicate that data are not available or cannot be calculated; *nec* means not elsewhere classified.

SIC	Industry	No. Establishments			Employment		Pay / Employee		Annual Payroll ($ 000)		
		1992	1993	% State	1992	1993	1992	1993	1992	1993	% State
CHATTAHOOCHEE, GA											
60–	**Finance, insurance, and real estate**	5	5	0.0	66	-	10,545	-	693	-	-
CHATTOOGA, GA											
60–	**Finance, insurance, and real estate**	17	17	0.1	137	142	19,212	17,352	2,808	2,877	0.1
6000	Depository institutions	5	6	0.2	102	106	19,686	17,811	2,168	2,232	0.2
6400	Insurance agents, brokers, and service	7	7	0.2	18	21	21,778	16,190	378	336	0.1
CHEROKEE, GA											
60–	**Finance, insurance, and real estate**	119	123	0.8	1,043	620	14,098	20,406	15,610	14,572	0.3
6000	Depository institutions	25	21	0.8	735	332	14,177	22,000	9,678	7,553	0.6
6020	Commercial banks	18	16	0.9	675	292	13,440	22,781	8,321	6,825	0.6
6030	Savings institutions	4	2	0.7	56	-	23,357	-	1,306	-	-
6100	Nondepository institutions	15	15	0.8	113	70	9,593	23,371	1,323	2,040	0.3
6160	Mortgage bankers and brokers	6	6	1.0	79	37	7,139	28,000	748	1,432	0.5
6300	Insurance carriers	8	6	0.5	15	10	34,133	44,800	585	477	0.0
6400	Insurance agents, brokers, and service	25	30	0.9	67	76	13,851	19,526	1,017	1,595	0.3
6500	Real estate	42	47	0.9	104	100	15,962	14,760	2,756	2,566	0.3
6510	Real estate operators and lessors	6	8	0.4	20	32	12,000	7,500	785	285	0.2
6530	Real estate agents and managers	19	28	1.1	50	42	19,680	15,810	1,340	874	0.2
6552	Subdividers and developers, n.e.c.	9	8	2.3	20	15	12,000	22,133	384	1,070	1.6
6553	Cemetery subdividers and developers	2	3	2.5	-	11	-	21,818	-	337	2.2
CLARKE, GA											
60–	**Finance, insurance, and real estate**	254	271	1.7	1,747	1,631	22,983	24,383	41,889	41,737	0.8
6000	Depository institutions	40	39	1.5	583	504	20,151	22,048	11,943	11,167	0.8
6020	Commercial banks	32	32	1.7	543	473	20,545	22,182	11,346	10,478	1.0
6100	Nondepository institutions	26	31	1.6	164	187	27,024	24,791	4,815	5,013	0.8
6140	Personal credit institutions	18	19	1.7	127	136	25,260	23,735	3,149	3,341	2.1
6160	Mortgage bankers and brokers	8	11	1.8	37	-	33,081	-	1,666	-	-
6200	Security and commodity brokers	15	16	2.2	90	91	65,156	59,956	5,908	6,445	1.3
6210	Security brokers and dealers	8	8	2.0	75	72	73,813	70,556	5,545	5,942	1.6
6280	Security and commodity services	7	8	2.6	15	19	21,867	19,789	363	503	-
6300	Insurance carriers	22	22	1.8	287	281	28,892	33,139	8,720	9,082	0.7
6310	Life insurance	13	13	2.9	254	243	28,220	32,971	7,573	7,710	1.2
6400	Insurance agents, brokers, and service	49	50	1.5	221	220	22,860	21,309	5,200	4,862	0.8
6500	Real estate	96	107	2.1	379	318	11,145	12,377	4,643	4,479	0.6
6510	Real estate operators and lessors	49	49	2.5	244	168	9,311	11,429	2,412	2,094	1.2
6530	Real estate agents and managers	29	50	2.0	90	133	14,844	13,955	1,610	2,200	0.4
6552	Subdividers and developers, n.e.c.	4	5	1.4	10	-	13,200	-	126	-	-
6553	Cemetery subdividers and developers	3	2	1.6	13	-	14,154	-	187	-	-
6700	Holding and other investment offices	6	6	1.0	23	30	23,478	20,933	660	689	0.2
CLAY, GA											
60–	**Finance, insurance, and real estate**	2	2	0.0	-	-	-	-	-	-	-
CLAYTON, GA											
60–	**Finance, insurance, and real estate**	293	294	1.9	1,628	2,509	21,688	20,603	37,451	52,900	1.0
6000	Depository institutions	59	58	2.2	617	659	23,449	23,077	14,321	14,876	1.1
6020	Commercial banks	41	41	2.2	441	458	25,578	25,293	10,920	10,889	1.0
6030	Savings institutions	9	7	2.5	109	-	18,752	-	2,106	-	-
6060	Credit unions	6	8	2.6	-	102	-	16,706	-	1,943	3.9
6100	Nondepository institutions	40	30	1.5	216	249	24,926	19,663	5,421	5,017	0.8
6140	Personal credit institutions	28	20	1.8	116	-	25,241	-	2,683	-	-
6160	Mortgage bankers and brokers	9	9	1.5	78	95	25,077	25,263	2,269	2,620	0.9
6200	Security and commodity brokers	4	5	0.7	5	5	27,200	16,000	129	106	0.0
6300	Insurance carriers	21	23	1.9	90	702	34,400	25,145	3,365	17,078	1.3
6310	Life insurance	2	4	0.9	-	80	-	54,950	-	3,319	0.5
6400	Insurance agents, brokers, and service	64	67	2.0	193	314	21,492	13,287	4,782	5,128	0.9

Source: County Business Patterns, 1992/93, CBP-92/93-1, U.S. Department of Commerce, Washington, D.C., April 1995. SIC categories for which data were suppressed or not available for both 1992 and 1993 are not displayed. The employment columns represent mid-March employment in the year. Pay per employee is calculated by dividing 1st Quarter payroll, annualized, by mid-March employment. The columns headed "% State" show the county's percentage of the state total for the SIC in 1993; for example, 0.9% for SIC 6030 means that the county had 0.9 percent of the state's total establishments (or payroll) in SIC 6030 in 1993. A dash (-) is used to indicate that data are not available or cannot be calculated; nec means not elsewhere classified.

Continued on next page.

SIC	Industry	No. Establishments			Employment		Pay / Employee		Annual Payroll ($ 000)		
		1992	1993	% State	1992	1993	1992	1993	1992	1993	% State
CLAYTON, GA - [continued]											
6500	Real estate	97	102	2.0	448	484	14,768	15,157	7,218	7,701	1.0
6510	Real estate operators and lessors	47	52	2.6	231	201	12,831	13,493	3,133	3,040	1.8
6530	Real estate agents and managers	37	39	1.5	165	224	16,436	13,768	3,124	3,300	0.6
6552	Subdividers and developers, n.e.c.	4	7	2.0	12	-	14,000	-	149	-	-
6700	Holding and other investment offices	8	9	1.6	59	96	24,746	24,458	2,215	2,994	0.9
CLINCH, GA											
60 -	**Finance, insurance, and real estate**	4	4	0.0	-	-	-	-	-	-	-
COBB, GA											
60 -	**Finance, insurance, and real estate**	1,339	1,382	8.9	14,088	15,537	30,185	30,344	436,606	508,926	9.2
6000	Depository institutions	171	170	6.6	2,544	2,381	27,673	28,192	66,050	70,161	5.3
6020	Commercial banks	116	120	6.5	1,551	1,760	24,812	25,609	36,786	45,788	4.3
6030	Savings institutions	24	21	7.4	601	295	14,908	22,658	7,608	7,254	7.2
6090	Functions closely related to banking	17	19	14.4	203	240	71,054	56,467	12,915	15,174	47.6
6100	Nondepository institutions	195	198	10.1	1,678	2,313	42,598	37,667	71,799	97,157	15.9
6140	Personal credit institutions	70	66	5.9	384	-	31,281	-	11,365	-	-
6150	Business credit institutions	33	29	13.9	331	693	64,302	43,215	19,983	29,417	18.2
6160	Mortgage bankers and brokers	88	100	16.6	954	1,118	39,841	35,073	40,192	51,078	18.4
6200	Security and commodity brokers	65	76	10.5	356	503	45,899	53,710	18,988	29,243	6.0
6210	Security brokers and dealers	34	31	7.6	258	280	43,209	51,314	10,166	14,813	3.9
6300	Insurance carriers	138	110	9.1	2,671	2,864	30,275	30,638	80,276	89,247	6.6
6310	Life insurance	53	46	10.2	1,645	1,837	24,491	29,224	42,866	52,708	8.5
6324	Hospital and medical service plans	3	-	-	19	-	25,684	-	474	-	-
6330	Fire, marine, and casualty insurance	59	49	9.4	857	999	38,651	33,221	31,394	35,249	6.0
6370	Pension, health, and welfare funds	15	12	8.2	57	-	14,877	-	981	-	-
6400	Insurance agents, brokers, and service	268	294	9.0	1,447	1,578	29,205	29,815	46,753	50,346	8.6
6500	Real estate	435	458	8.9	3,855	4,557	23,577	23,156	96,659	123,208	16.0
6510	Real estate operators and lessors	154	152	7.6	1,352	1,778	19,781	17,242	28,195	30,039	17.6
6530	Real estate agents and managers	180	258	10.1	2,059	2,447	25,193	27,382	55,081	83,760	16.3
6540	Title abstract offices	4	6	13.3	72	71	29,444	29,239	1,503	1,572	27.7
6552	Subdividers and developers, n.e.c.	33	30	8.6	116	135	31,103	32,296	4,919	6,431	9.9
6553	Cemetery subdividers and developers	8	8	6.6	48	125	13,500	11,392	797	1,261	8.2
6700	Holding and other investment offices	62	68	11.8	1,427	1,101	34,657	37,203	52,537	39,563	12.4
6710	Holding offices	30	30	13.8	1,279	814	33,317	36,005	43,796	26,127	11.4
6732	Educational, religious, etc. trusts	4	4	5.2	6	-	14,000	-	110	-	-
6733	Trusts, n.e.c.	4	6	6.7	17	-	27,765	-	437	-	-
6794	Patent owners and lessors	9	12	26.1	56	101	36,429	35,287	2,139	4,008	11.9
6798	Real estate investment trusts	2	3	21.4	-	58	-	59,655	-	3,828	45.8
6799	Investors, n.e.c.	5	9	9.1	-	14	-	17,143	-	449	3.3
COFFEE, GA											
60 -	**Finance, insurance, and real estate**	53	58	0.4	366	399	20,415	20,130	7,797	7,837	0.1
6000	Depository institutions	16	17	0.7	195	189	23,077	25,481	4,384	4,361	0.3
6100	Nondepository institutions	9	10	0.5	44	46	20,182	19,913	907	1,023	0.2
6400	Insurance agents, brokers, and service	13	13	0.4	-	43	-	13,209	-	736	0.1
6500	Real estate	11	13	0.3	38	43	9,263	8,465	376	362	0.0
6510	Real estate operators and lessors	6	9	0.5	17	35	7,529	9,029	133	301	0.2
6530	Real estate agents and managers	3	4	0.2	5	8	8,800	6,000	55	61	0.0
COLQUITT, GA											
60 -	**Finance, insurance, and real estate**	72	66	0.4	349	348	21,811	22,759	7,725	7,520	0.1
6000	Depository institutions	9	11	0.4	-	156	-	26,590	-	3,568	0.3
6020	Commercial banks	6	8	0.4	-	153	-	26,954	-	3,544	0.3
6060	Credit unions	3	3	1.0	3	3	9,333	8,000	28	24	0.0
6100	Nondepository institutions	13	11	0.6	53	48	29,585	23,333	1,684	1,031	0.2
6140	Personal credit institutions	10	9	0.8	45	-	29,511	-	1,433	-	-
6200	Security and commodity brokers	5	7	1.0	13	12	21,538	20,000	402	439	0.1

Source: County Business Patterns, 1992/93, CBP-92/93-1, U.S. Department of Commerce, Washington, D.C., April 1995. SIC categories for which data were suppressed or not available for both 1992 and 1993 are *not* displayed. The employment columns represent mid-March employment in the year. Pay per employee is calculated by dividing 1st Quarter payroll, annualized, by mid-March employment. The columns headed "% State" show the county's percentage of the state total for the SIC in 1993; for example, 0.9% for SIC 6030 means that the county had 0.9 percent of the state's total establishments (or payroll) in SIC 6030 in 1993. A dash (-) is used to indicate that data are not available or cannot be calculated; *nec* means not elsewhere classified.

Continued on next page.

SIC	Industry	No. Establishments			Employment		Pay / Employee		Annual Payroll ($ 000)		
		1992	1993	% State	1992	1993	1992	1993	1992	1993	% State
COLQUITT, GA - [continued]											
6210	Security brokers and dealers	4	7	*1.7*	-	12	-	20,000	-	439	*0.1*
6370	Pension, health, and welfare funds	3	1	*0.7*	4	-	45,000	-	88	-	-
6400	Insurance agents, brokers, and service	15	15	*0.5*	63	55	17,079	17,673	1,097	1,096	*0.2*
6500	Real estate	20	18	*0.4*	60	-	7,467	-	477	-	-
6510	Real estate operators and lessors	11	10	*0.5*	38	23	6,211	8,000	286	204	*0.1*
6530	Real estate agents and managers	6	5	*0.2*	18	-	9,778	-	159	-	-
6700	Holding and other investment offices	4	3	*0.5*	28	-	25,286	-	681	-	-
COLUMBIA, GA											
60 –	**Finance, insurance, and real estate**	110	135	*0.9*	668	697	18,323	20,247	14,549	17,106	*0.3*
6000	Depository institutions	14	18	*0.7*	151	185	18,013	18,811	2,904	3,829	*0.3*
6100	Nondepository institutions	10	23	*1.2*	58	149	24,207	21,262	1,871	4,396	*0.7*
6140	Personal credit institutions	3	7	*0.6*	11	-	17,091	-	196	-	-
6160	Mortgage bankers and brokers	6	15	*2.5*	41	124	28,293	22,516	1,610	3,966	*1.4*
6300	Insurance carriers	16	12	*1.0*	274	132	16,949	28,030	5,831	4,122	*0.3*
6310	Life insurance	7	5	*1.1*	121	108	22,843	26,889	3,528	3,273	*0.5*
6330	Fire, marine, and casualty insurance	6	7	*1.3*	-	24	-	33,167	-	849	*0.1*
6400	Insurance agents, brokers, and service	26	32	*1.0*	60	78	21,467	16,410	1,458	1,539	*0.3*
6500	Real estate	39	45	*0.9*	113	145	17,204	15,476	2,130	2,715	*0.4*
6510	Real estate operators and lessors	6	7	*0.4*	7	16	19,429	10,250	145	190	*0.1*
6530	Real estate agents and managers	17	29	*1.1*	53	89	21,132	17,618	1,177	1,849	*0.4*
6552	Subdividers and developers, n.e.c.	5	7	*2.0*	8	-	6,500	-	82	-	-
COOK, GA											
60 –	**Finance, insurance, and real estate**	20	19	*0.1*	183	194	15,410	16,701	2,954	2,997	*0.1*
6000	Depository institutions	6	6	*0.2*	66	71	19,939	21,859	1,375	1,495	*0.1*
6100	Nondepository institutions	3	3	*0.2*	-	12	-	27,667	-	297	*0.0*
6140	Personal credit institutions	3	3	*0.3*	-	12	-	27,667	-	297	*0.2*
6400	Insurance agents, brokers, and service	6	6	*0.2*	11	-	17,818	-	205	-	-
6500	Real estate	3	2	*0.0*	7	-	12,000	-	75	-	-
COWETA, GA											
60 –	**Finance, insurance, and real estate**	95	93	*0.6*	462	453	22,104	23,647	10,481	11,278	*0.2*
6000	Depository institutions	22	23	*0.9*	270	264	22,637	24,439	5,986	6,482	*0.5*
6060	Credit unions	2	3	*1.0*	-	6	-	10,000	-	63	*0.1*
6100	Nondepository institutions	13	15	*0.8*	-	51	-	15,451	-	881	*0.1*
6160	Mortgage bankers and brokers	4	5	*0.8*	5	11	27,200	21,091	163	320	*0.1*
6300	Insurance carriers	4	4	*0.3*	16	-	27,750	-	447	-	-
6400	Insurance agents, brokers, and service	19	17	*0.5*	68	65	22,647	28,246	1,552	1,885	*0.3*
6500	Real estate	35	32	*0.6*	61	63	17,836	19,810	1,510	1,579	*0.2*
6510	Real estate operators and lessors	5	7	*0.4*	17	17	18,353	19,294	299	322	*0.2*
6530	Real estate agents and managers	18	20	*0.8*	26	35	11,538	21,943	574	1,119	*0.2*
CRAWFORD, GA											
60 –	**Finance, insurance, and real estate**	3	5	*0.0*	-	26	-	16,769	-	417	*0.0*
CRISP, GA											
60 –	**Finance, insurance, and real estate**	47	48	*0.3*	293	288	16,765	18,208	5,316	5,690	*0.1*
6000	Depository institutions	11	10	*0.4*	138	142	18,435	19,155	2,817	2,957	*0.2*
6100	Nondepository institutions	8	8	*0.4*	33	-	23,030	-	704	-	-
6140	Personal credit institutions	7	7	*0.6*	-	21	-	18,476	-	377	*0.2*
6500	Real estate	15	16	*0.3*	55	55	9,309	10,255	532	624	*0.1*
6510	Real estate operators and lessors	9	11	*0.6*	36	-	7,000	-	275	-	-
6530	Real estate agents and managers	2	3	*0.1*	-	2	-	8,000	-	15	*0.0*

Source: County Business Patterns, 1992/93, CBP-92/93-1, U.S. Department of Commerce, Washington, D.C., April 1995. SIC categories for which data were suppressed or not available for both 1992 and 1993 are *not* displayed. The employment columns represent mid-March employment in the year. Pay per employee is calculated by dividing 1st Quarter payroll, annualized, by mid-March employment. The columns headed "% State" show the county's percentage of the state total for the SIC in 1993; for example, 0.9% for SIC 6030 means that the county had 0.9 percent of the state's total establishments (or payroll) in SIC 6030 in 1993. A dash (-) is used to indicate that data are not available or cannot be calculated; *nec* means not elsewhere classified.

SIC	Industry	No. Establishments			Employment		Pay / Employee		Annual Payroll ($ 000)		
		1992	1993	% State	1992	1993	1992	1993	1992	1993	% State
DADE, GA											
60 –	**Finance, insurance, and real estate**	10	9	*0.1*	68	81	17,941	17,383	1,334	1,536	*0.0*
6400	Insurance agents, brokers, and service	5	4	*0.1*	7	8	12,571	11,500	97	100	*0.0*
DAWSON, GA											
60 –	**Finance, insurance, and real estate**	9	10	*0.1*	53	64	19,019	17,062	1,031	1,176	*0.0*
6400	Insurance agents, brokers, and service	3	3	*0.1*	8	-	13,500	-	106	-	-
6500	Real estate	2	3	*0.1*	-	5	-	13,600	-	51	*0.0*
DECATUR, GA											
60 –	**Finance, insurance, and real estate**	55	49	*0.3*	383	351	18,141	21,265	7,498	7,607	*0.1*
6000	Depository institutions	7	7	*0.3*	125	122	19,808	19,311	2,488	2,441	*0.2*
6020	Commercial banks	4	4	*0.2*	95	92	20,337	19,652	1,898	1,819	*0.2*
6100	Nondepository institutions	11	11	*0.6*	96	102	22,792	26,627	2,440	2,726	*0.4*
6400	Insurance agents, brokers, and service	16	16	*0.5*	50	39	12,000	15,897	646	623	*0.1*
6500	Real estate	12	11	*0.2*	60	32	10,133	6,500	619	209	*0.0*
6510	Real estate operators and lessors	8	7	*0.4*	54	24	10,222	3,500	574	67	*0.0*
6530	Real estate agents and managers	2	4	*0.2*	-	8	-	15,500	-	142	*0.0*
DE KALB, GA											
60 –	**Finance, insurance, and real estate**	1,754	1,791	*11.5*	25,925	23,659	29,850	30,251	761,309	754,235	*13.6*
6000	Depository institutions	242	245	*9.5*	4,309	4,306	28,439	26,968	113,544	107,145	*8.1*
6020	Commercial banks	131	148	*8.0*	2,105	2,859	30,537	26,787	56,487	74,274	*6.9*
6030	Savings institutions	48	33	*11.6*	1,497	868	26,442	29,991	41,477	18,657	*18.6*
6060	Credit unions	31	34	*11.1*	349	379	22,407	22,744	8,320	9,047	*18.0*
6100	Nondepository institutions	195	223	*11.3*	3,233	3,280	39,291	35,546	118,647	130,131	*21.3*
6140	Personal credit institutions	71	71	*6.4*	818	885	34,846	28,868	27,735	31,807	*20.2*
6150	Business credit institutions	36	50	*23.9*	1,236	979	46,832	48,486	49,649	41,642	*25.8*
6160	Mortgage bankers and brokers	84	101	*16.8*	1,175	1,416	34,543	30,774	41,192	56,670	*20.4*
6210	Security brokers and dealers	46	32	*7.8*	274	238	62,642	54,908	17,963	14,687	*3.9*
6280	Security and commodity services	26	32	*10.5*	85	159	36,000	37,660	3,807	8,114	-
6300	Insurance carriers	225	204	*16.8*	7,225	7,811	35,758	32,488	255,307	268,440	*19.8*
6310	Life insurance	83	71	*15.8*	3,038	3,279	36,359	33,815	113,200	119,367	*19.2*
6321	Accident and health insurance	3	5	*22.7*	-	102	-	29,098	-	3,182	*14.8*
6330	Fire, marine, and casualty insurance	94	87	*16.7*	3,782	3,677	35,726	35,005	129,435	134,302	*22.8*
6350	Surety insurance	4	3	*17.6*	77	67	34,078	33,075	2,318	2,084	*20.2*
6370	Pension, health, and welfare funds	32	30	*20.4*	180	-	19,844	-	3,485	-	-
6400	Insurance agents, brokers, and service	348	363	*11.1*	2,622	2,768	32,696	31,480	90,426	95,665	*16.3*
6500	Real estate	600	619	*12.0*	4,943	4,432	21,763	21,254	117,787	101,033	*13.1*
6510	Real estate operators and lessors	203	230	*11.5*	1,249	1,254	17,275	17,872	23,564	24,259	*14.2*
6530	Real estate agents and managers	277	334	*13.0*	3,277	2,984	23,747	22,188	83,077	70,624	*13.8*
6540	Title abstract offices	6	4	*8.9*	36	30	26,222	32,000	1,035	1,040	*18.3*
6552	Subdividers and developers, n.e.c.	25	31	*8.9*	138	102	21,043	35,843	2,747	3,561	*5.5*
6553	Cemetery subdividers and developers	4	5	*4.1*	72	54	10,889	13,704	781	666	*4.3*
6700	Holding and other investment offices	64	67	*11.6*	2,981	538	13,338	47,465	34,051	23,877	*7.5*
6710	Holding offices	20	22	*10.1*	190	279	54,505	66,380	10,301	16,190	*7.1*
6732	Educational, religious, etc. trusts	12	10	*13.0*	41	26	18,537	23,077	775	645	*4.2*
6733	Trusts, n.e.c.	8	11	*12.4*	37	-	25,622	-	981	-	-
6794	Patent owners and lessors	7	7	*15.2*	-	111	-	24,865	-	3,246	*9.7*
DODGE, GA											
60 –	**Finance, insurance, and real estate**	32	29	*0.2*	242	184	15,603	20,043	4,027	4,122	*0.1*
6000	Depository institutions	9	9	*0.3*	127	131	18,047	17,466	2,472	2,547	*0.2*
6100	Nondepository institutions	4	5	*0.3*	23	-	12,174	-	280	-	-
6140	Personal credit institutions	4	5	*0.5*	23	-	12,174	-	280	-	-
6400	Insurance agents, brokers, and service	11	10	*0.3*	21	23	17,143	15,304	341	370	*0.1*
6500	Real estate	2	3	*0.1*	-	7	-	6,857	-	63	*0.0*

Source: *County Business Patterns, 1992/93,* CBP-92/93-1, U.S. Department of Commerce, Washington, D.C., April 1995. SIC categories for which data were suppressed or not available for both 1992 and 1993 are *not* displayed. The employment columns represent mid-March employment in the year. Pay per employee is calculated by dividing 1st Quarter payroll, annualized, by mid-March employment. The columns headed "% State" show the county's percentage of the state total for the SIC in 1993; for example, 0.9% for SIC 6030 means that the county had 0.9 percent of the state's total establishments (or payroll) in SIC 6030 in 1993. A dash (-) is used to indicate that data are not available or cannot be calculated; *nec* means not elsewhere classified.

SIC	Industry	No. Establishments			Employment		Pay / Employee		Annual Payroll ($ 000)		
		1992	1993	% State	1992	1993	1992	1993	1992	1993	% State
DOOLY, GA											
60 –	**Finance, insurance, and real estate**	16	16	0.1	108	104	20,815	24,308	2,224	2,265	0.0
DOUGHERTY, GA											
60 –	**Finance, insurance, and real estate**	267	277	1.8	2,067	1,922	23,327	25,253	48,930	46,080	0.8
6000	Depository institutions	37	38	1.5	760	690	21,384	22,974	15,396	14,104	1.1
6020	Commercial banks	25	26	1.4	614	538	22,358	23,190	12,864	10,973	1.0
6060	Credit unions	6	8	2.6	-	126	-	22,254	-	2,548	5.1
6100	Nondepository institutions	35	37	1.9	177	226	20,633	30,142	3,691	6,556	1.1
6140	Personal credit institutions	33	32	2.9	-	139	-	19,338	-	2,779	1.8
6200	Security and commodity brokers	8	7	1.0	48	50	52,667	53,360	2,564	2,716	0.6
6300	Insurance carriers	43	37	3.1	480	316	26,233	31,228	13,072	9,315	0.7
6310	Life insurance	17	15	3.3	418	249	24,593	30,265	10,498	6,928	1.1
6330	Fire, marine, and casualty insurance	14	15	2.9	42	-	37,333	-	1,709	-	-
6370	Pension, health, and welfare funds	9	5	3.4	4	15	6,000	7,733	251	224	0.6
6400	Insurance agents, brokers, and service	56	64	1.9	202	238	22,020	20,202	4,799	5,110	0.9
6500	Real estate	77	85	1.7	310	284	16,800	13,746	5,634	4,041	0.5
6510	Real estate operators and lessors	31	43	2.2	153	121	20,026	11,405	3,242	1,443	0.8
6530	Real estate agents and managers	33	36	1.4	102	126	16,588	17,048	1,861	2,221	0.4
6552	Subdividers and developers, n.e.c.	4	3	0.9	13	-	11,077	-	169	-	-
6700	Holding and other investment offices	11	9	1.6	90	118	39,289	39,186	3,774	4,238	1.3
6710	Holding offices	4	4	1.8	84	101	41,190	42,812	3,554	3,979	1.7
6733	Trusts, n.e.c.	6	5	5.6	-	17	-	17,647	-	259	2.8
DOUGLAS, GA											
60 –	**Finance, insurance, and real estate**	98	110	0.7	604	735	25,517	26,460	22,718	24,351	0.4
6000	Depository institutions	24	26	1.0	300	293	20,387	21,338	6,103	6,558	0.5
6020	Commercial banks	18	19	1.0	251	237	20,335	20,759	4,989	4,780	0.4
6100	Nondepository institutions	11	15	0.8	-	208	-	37,385	-	12,423	2.0
6200	Security and commodity brokers	3	3	0.4	3	-	12,000	-	60	-	-
6300	Insurance carriers	9	7	0.6	33	33	41,697	59,273	1,506	1,595	0.1
6400	Insurance agents, brokers, and service	20	19	0.6	83	99	19,952	17,616	1,699	1,911	0.3
6500	Real estate	29	38	0.7	80	96	14,500	15,250	1,198	1,618	0.2
6510	Real estate operators and lessors	12	15	0.8	51	57	10,353	10,035	547	648	0.4
6530	Real estate agents and managers	10	17	0.7	16	24	21,750	21,833	415	657	0.1
6552	Subdividers and developers, n.e.c.	1	3	0.9	-	8	-	30,000	-	169	0.3
EARLY, GA											
60 –	**Finance, insurance, and real estate**	15	19	0.1	93	117	18,323	16,786	1,868	2,170	0.0
6000	Depository institutions	5	5	0.2	63	63	18,984	17,143	1,288	1,240	0.1
6100	Nondepository institutions	4	5	0.3	-	17	-	13,176	-	206	0.0
6400	Insurance agents, brokers, and service	4	4	0.1	13	15	18,769	21,333	309	343	0.1
EFFINGHAM, GA											
60 –	**Finance, insurance, and real estate**	22	23	0.1	87	93	18,161	18,151	1,623	1,795	0.0
6000	Depository institutions	6	5	0.2	49	50	21,551	23,200	1,082	1,212	0.1
6100	Nondepository institutions	2	3	0.2	-	12	-	11,000	-	136	0.0
6400	Insurance agents, brokers, and service	5	4	0.1	-	10	-	20,000	-	210	0.0
6500	Real estate	9	11	0.2	18	21	9,111	9,333	183	237	0.0
6510	Real estate operators and lessors	3	2	0.1	7	-	6,857	-	50	-	-
6530	Real estate agents and managers	3	8	0.3	3	14	9,333	9,429	32	164	0.0
ELBERT, GA											
60 –	**Finance, insurance, and real estate**	27	28	0.2	207	211	20,019	17,725	4,409	4,775	0.1
6000	Depository institutions	8	9	0.3	127	125	18,583	14,592	2,502	2,618	0.2
6100	Nondepository institutions	5	4	0.2	16	14	27,500	33,429	320	353	0.1

Source: County Business Patterns, 1992/93, CBP-92/93-1, U.S. Department of Commerce, Washington, D.C., April 1995. SIC categories for which data were suppressed or not available for both 1992 and 1993 are not displayed. The employment columns represent mid-March employment in the year. Pay per employee is calculated by dividing 1st Quarter payroll, annualized, by mid-March employment. The columns headed "% State" show the county's percentage of the state total for the SIC in 1993; for example, 0.9% for SIC 6030 means that the county had 0.9 percent of the state's total establishments (or payroll) in SIC 6030 in 1993. A dash (-) is used to indicate that data are not available or cannot be calculated; nec means not elsewhere classified.

Continued on next page.

SIC	Industry	No. Establishments			Employment		Pay / Employee		Annual Payroll ($ 000)		
		1992	1993	% State	1992	1993	1992	1993	1992	1993	% State
ELBERT, GA - [continued]											
6140	Personal credit institutions	5	4	0.4	16	14	27,500	33,429	320	353	0.2
6500	Real estate	6	7	0.1	7	9	8,571	8,000	72	82	0.0
6510	Real estate operators and lessors	4	4	0.2	6	6	9,333	8,667	55	53	0.0
EMANUEL, GA											
60 –	**Finance, insurance, and real estate**	33	32	0.2	257	238	18,272	19,008	4,839	4,619	0.1
6000	Depository institutions	5	4	0.2	137	125	17,577	17,568	2,436	2,365	0.2
6020	Commercial banks	5	4	0.2	137	125	17,577	17,568	2,436	2,365	0.2
6100	Nondepository institutions	6	6	0.3	17	15	17,882	20,000	325	348	0.1
6500	Real estate	8	6	0.1	14	10	7,143	7,200	81	71	0.0
6510	Real estate operators and lessors	3	2	0.1	3	-	4,000	-	12	-	-
EVANS, GA											
60 –	**Finance, insurance, and real estate**	16	16	0.1	85	92	18,965	18,435	1,617	1,643	0.0
6400	Insurance agents, brokers, and service	6	6	0.2	12	14	13,000	13,143	190	194	0.0
6500	Real estate	3	3	0.1	5	8	4,000	4,500	25	23	0.0
FANNIN, GA											
60 –	**Finance, insurance, and real estate**	22	22	0.1	126	143	16,286	17,007	2,136	2,626	0.0
6000	Depository institutions	5	5	0.2	65	71	18,831	19,211	1,237	1,464	0.1
6020	Commercial banks	4	5	0.3	-	71	-	19,211	-	1,464	0.1
6100	Nondepository institutions	3	3	0.2	-	17	-	12,706	-	191	0.0
6140	Personal credit institutions	3	3	0.3	-	17	-	12,706	-	191	0.1
6400	Insurance agents, brokers, and service	9	8	0.2	27	28	16,741	14,000	480	424	0.1
6500	Real estate	4	4	0.1	6	-	8,000	-	41	-	-
FAYETTE, GA											
60 –	**Finance, insurance, and real estate**	127	147	0.9	746	889	24,772	24,441	19,830	27,291	0.5
6000	Depository institutions	21	26	1.0	310	386	26,813	26,114	8,453	12,638	1.0
6020	Commercial banks	13	16	0.9	244	301	23,328	23,508	5,005	7,281	0.7
6100	Nondepository institutions	12	12	0.6	65	75	38,646	39,520	2,582	4,156	0.7
6140	Personal credit institutions	6	3	0.3	15	-	27,467	-	379	-	-
6160	Mortgage bankers and brokers	6	7	1.2	50	67	42,000	41,851	2,203	3,970	1.4
6200	Security and commodity brokers	5	5	0.7	11	10	28,364	49,200	460	564	0.1
6300	Insurance carriers	10	8	0.7	-	85	-	33,553	-	2,914	0.2
6330	Fire, marine, and casualty insurance	7	6	1.2	17	-	58,824	-	1,058	-	-
6400	Insurance agents, brokers, and service	27	32	1.0	109	127	16,587	16,945	1,892	2,422	0.4
6500	Real estate	48	60	1.2	176	198	16,523	15,051	3,743	4,349	0.6
6510	Real estate operators and lessors	12	15	0.8	72	41	17,611	15,317	1,818	923	0.5
6530	Real estate agents and managers	21	38	1.5	58	136	15,241	14,912	1,039	3,006	0.6
6700	Holding and other investment offices	4	4	0.7	-	8	-	26,000	-	248	0.1
FLOYD, GA											
60 –	**Finance, insurance, and real estate**	154	153	1.0	1,338	1,447	23,623	25,545	31,496	37,537	0.7
6000	Depository institutions	27	30	1.2	546	536	22,813	23,567	11,943	11,821	0.9
6020	Commercial banks	21	23	1.3	420	398	23,619	24,935	9,287	8,967	0.8
6100	Nondepository institutions	18	16	0.8	-	50	-	20,960	-	1,246	0.2
6140	Personal credit institutions	15	14	1.3	54	-	19,630	-	1,068	-	-
6300	Insurance carriers	20	18	1.5	314	294	30,701	32,027	10,377	9,957	0.7
6310	Life insurance	9	9	2.0	283	263	31,237	32,243	9,390	8,711	1.4
6370	Pension, health, and welfare funds	3	3	2.0	11	-	6,182	-	182	-	-
6400	Insurance agents, brokers, and service	49	45	1.4	163	182	22,724	22,396	3,998	4,283	0.7
6500	Real estate	35	36	0.7	232	202	14,293	13,129	2,844	3,193	0.4
6510	Real estate operators and lessors	7	10	0.5	99	119	12,566	11,462	1,176	1,623	0.9
6530	Real estate agents and managers	17	22	0.9	101	75	15,248	15,627	1,106	1,160	0.2

Source: County Business Patterns, 1992/93, CBP-92/93-1, U.S. Department of Commerce, Washington, D.C., April 1995. SIC categories for which data were suppressed or not available for both 1992 and 1993 are *not* displayed. The employment columns represent mid-March employment in the year. Pay per employee is calculated by dividing 1st Quarter payroll, annualized, by mid-March employment. The columns headed "% State" show the county's percentage of the state total for the SIC in 1993; for example, 0.9% for SIC 6030 means that the county had 0.9 percent of the state's total establishments (or payroll) in SIC 6030 in 1993. A dash (-) is used to indicate that data are not available or cannot be calculated; *nec* means not elsewhere classified.

SIC	Industry	No. Establishments			Employment		Pay / Employee		Annual Payroll ($ 000)		
		1992	1993	% State	1992	1993	1992	1993	1992	1993	% State
FORSYTH, GA											
60 –	**Finance, insurance, and real estate**	63	71	0.5	395	336	22,157	22,702	8,310	8,886	0.2
6000	Depository institutions	12	13	0.5	190	177	22,968	22,531	4,143	4,626	0.3
6140	Personal credit institutions	4	4	0.4	-	15	-	18,933	-	381	0.2
6160	Mortgage bankers and brokers	4	3	0.5	11	-	36,000	-	484	-	-
6300	Insurance carriers	4	2	0.2	55	-	17,382	-	560	-	-
6400	Insurance agents, brokers, and service	15	15	0.5	56	45	21,429	21,867	1,157	969	0.2
6500	Real estate	19	29	0.6	-	61	-	17,049	-	1,397	0.2
6510	Real estate operators and lessors	5	7	0.4	13	19	19,077	14,526	296	410	0.2
6530	Real estate agents and managers	7	17	0.7	19	29	14,737	16,828	281	571	0.1
6700	Holding and other investment offices	3	2	0.3	3	-	6,667	-	18	-	-
FRANKLIN, GA											
60 –	**Finance, insurance, and real estate**	32	30	0.2	190	194	20,926	23,299	4,173	4,369	0.1
6000	Depository institutions	10	10	0.4	131	133	20,855	23,248	2,925	3,003	0.2
6020	Commercial banks	10	10	0.5	131	133	20,855	23,248	2,925	3,003	0.3
6100	Nondepository institutions	4	4	0.2	13	16	26,462	33,500	332	449	0.1
6400	Insurance agents, brokers, and service	9	9	0.3	-	27	-	25,630	-	717	0.1
6500	Real estate	8	6	0.1	21	-	10,095	-	223	-	-
6510	Real estate operators and lessors	3	3	0.2	5	-	4,800	-	24	-	-
6530	Real estate agents and managers	3	3	0.1	-	12	-	14,000	-	168	0.0
FULTON, GA											
60 –	**Finance, insurance, and real estate**	3,025	3,166	20.4	65,287	63,741	36,477	37,858	2,268,908	2,388,269	43.1
6000	Depository institutions	410	414	16.1	18,602	18,023	33,326	34,126	584,265	563,774	42.6
6020	Commercial banks	259	253	13.8	15,640	14,895	33,451	34,247	488,336	456,803	42.6
6030	Savings institutions	46	40	14.1	808	713	22,277	22,648	17,966	16,601	16.6
6060	Credit unions	49	57	18.6	436	493	27,422	26,361	11,763	13,306	26.5
6080	Foreign bank and branches and agencies	11	11	73.3	173	231	62,058	58,926	10,716	14,709	-
6100	Nondepository institutions	284	309	15.7	4,238	5,040	37,860	39,403	158,972	212,853	34.8
6140	Personal credit institutions	94	82	7.4	1,431	1,427	34,300	28,919	48,778	41,188	26.2
6150	Business credit institutions	58	74	35.4	1,080	1,692	34,467	48,262	36,431	72,425	44.8
6160	Mortgage bankers and brokers	121	151	25.1	1,699	1,920	42,999	39,396	72,520	99,206	35.7
6200	Security and commodity brokers	301	305	42.0	3,802	3,884	87,837	90,680	309,564	360,380	74.3
6210	Security brokers and dealers	166	165	40.3	2,850	2,785	100,011	105,304	248,003	284,640	74.9
6220	Commodity contracts brokers, dealers	8	5	41.7	84	16	57,476	38,000	3,861	716	-
6280	Security and commodity services	124	135	44.3	779	1,083	46,624	53,850	43,901	75,024	-
6300	Insurance carriers	308	275	22.7	15,041	14,682	31,575	32,714	449,745	456,980	33.7
6310	Life insurance	130	115	25.6	8,108	8,350	26,651	27,544	199,053	216,236	34.8
6321	Accident and health insurance	9	10	45.5	370	-	20,573	-	7,660	-	-
6324	Hospital and medical service plans	9	11	31.4	977	-	31,492	-	30,228	-	-
6330	Fire, marine, and casualty insurance	100	102	19.6	5,262	4,462	39,720	42,100	200,532	178,307	30.3
6350	Surety insurance	8	8	47.1	67	186	34,149	41,484	2,005	7,494	72.7
6360	Title insurance	11	8	57.1	132	118	41,727	44,203	5,377	4,641	-
6370	Pension, health, and welfare funds	39	21	14.3	119	92	29,109	43,348	4,660	3,857	9.5
6400	Insurance agents, brokers, and service	459	511	15.6	6,645	6,092	35,621	39,469	236,408	243,310	41.6
6500	Real estate	1,065	1,151	22.4	11,085	11,758	29,393	26,319	316,418	342,748	44.4
6510	Real estate operators and lessors	351	390	19.6	2,741	2,125	20,101	21,935	56,126	50,345	29.5
6530	Real estate agents and managers	481	638	24.9	6,783	8,450	33,954	27,535	215,431	259,198	50.6
6540	Title abstract offices	6	8	17.8	27	53	28,593	24,377	608	1,375	24.2
6552	Subdividers and developers, n.e.c.	66	86	24.6	881	870	27,882	27,775	27,145	26,820	41.2
6553	Cemetery subdividers and developers	13	17	13.9	203	253	20,552	18,245	4,234	4,752	31.0
6700	Holding and other investment offices	182	181	31.3	4,233	2,739	41,249	55,201	161,734	146,427	45.9
6710	Holding offices	63	63	28.9	1,967	1,772	64,834	65,363	113,068	105,978	46.2
6720	Investment offices	16	9	36.0	147	50	46,204	45,120	8,425	4,165	59.5
6732	Educational, religious, etc. trusts	26	26	33.8	194	162	21,505	24,914	4,312	3,942	25.8

Source: County Business Patterns, 1992/93, CBP-92/93-1, U.S. Department of Commerce, Washington, D.C., April 1995. SIC categories for which data were suppressed or not available for both 1992 and 1993 are *not* displayed. The employment columns represent mid-March employment in the year. Pay per employee is calculated by dividing 1st Quarter payroll, annualized, by mid-March employment. The columns headed "% State" show the county's percentage of the state total for the SIC in 1993; for example, 0.9% for SIC 6030 means that the county had 0.9 percent of the state's total establishments (or payroll) in SIC 6030 in 1993. A dash (-) is used to indicate that data are not available or cannot be calculated; *nec* means not elsewhere classified.

Continued on next page.

SIC	Industry	No. Establishments			Employment		Pay / Employee		Annual Payroll ($ 000)		
		1992	1993	% State	1992	1993	1992	1993	1992	1993	% State
FULTON, GA - [continued]											
6733	Trusts, n.e.c.	18	21	23.6	131	294	23,206	14,721	3,162	5,760	62.1
6794	Patent owners and lessors	14	15	32.6	1,655	369	16,331	54,276	25,333	21,896	65.2
6799	Investors, n.e.c.	25	40	40.4	92	78	39,348	47,949	4,300	3,897	28.5
GILMER, GA											
60 –	**Finance, insurance, and real estate**	29	30	0.2	206	253	17,340	13,455	3,479	3,678	0.1
6000	Depository institutions	3	5	0.2	106	109	20,528	18,936	2,151	2,138	0.2
6100	Nondepository institutions	4	5	0.3	-	12	-	22,333	-	284	0.0
6400	Insurance agents, brokers, and service	7	7	0.2	24	19	17,667	15,789	333	322	0.1
6500	Real estate	14	13	0.3	40	113	11,500	6,832	556	934	0.1
6530	Real estate agents and managers	5	10	0.4	3	109	6,667	6,826	20	901	0.2
GLASCOCK, GA											
60 –	**Finance, insurance, and real estate**	3	2	0.0	-	-	-	-	-	-	-
GLYNN, GA											
60 –	**Finance, insurance, and real estate**	187	198	1.3	1,328	1,379	20,419	20,580	27,705	30,098	0.5
6000	Depository institutions	35	36	1.4	591	603	21,712	22,600	12,804	14,462	1.1
6020	Commercial banks	21	22	1.2	368	356	22,413	25,404	7,922	9,720	0.9
6100	Nondepository institutions	14	16	0.8	54	52	18,593	20,846	1,212	1,437	0.2
6140	Personal credit institutions	11	11	1.0	44	39	17,000	19,077	866	915	0.6
6160	Mortgage bankers and brokers	3	5	0.8	10	13	25,600	26,154	346	522	0.2
6300	Insurance carriers	12	16	1.3	163	165	25,031	25,576	4,070	4,352	0.3
6310	Life insurance	6	8	1.8	-	150	-	23,387	-	3,586	0.6
6400	Insurance agents, brokers, and service	36	36	1.1	135	127	23,437	22,331	2,843	2,857	0.5
6500	Real estate	79	85	1.7	325	383	12,246	12,658	4,475	5,114	0.7
6510	Real estate operators and lessors	33	33	1.7	133	134	9,594	11,373	1,447	1,388	0.8
6530	Real estate agents and managers	29	42	1.6	127	180	14,929	13,667	1,996	2,746	0.5
GORDON, GA											
60 –	**Finance, insurance, and real estate**	47	47	0.3	305	-	19,213	-	6,221	-	-
6000	Depository institutions	7	7	0.3	187	184	19,979	20,109	3,989	3,999	0.3
6100	Nondepository institutions	7	6	0.3	22	15	16,364	22,133	360	366	0.1
6140	Personal credit institutions	7	6	0.5	22	15	16,364	22,133	360	366	0.2
6400	Insurance agents, brokers, and service	15	16	0.5	56	55	19,929	20,291	1,107	1,118	0.2
6500	Real estate	13	14	0.3	27	27	14,074	15,111	447	565	0.1
6510	Real estate operators and lessors	3	3	0.2	4	-	6,000	-	26	-	-
6530	Real estate agents and managers	8	10	0.4	21	-	16,000	-	401	-	-
GRADY, GA											
60 –	**Finance, insurance, and real estate**	33	35	0.2	182	186	19,560	19,441	3,291	3,307	0.1
6000	Depository institutions	9	9	0.3	114	115	22,877	22,922	2,278	2,257	0.2
6100	Nondepository institutions	8	7	0.4	22	23	21,818	21,043	475	481	0.1
6400	Insurance agents, brokers, and service	7	10	0.3	32	-	11,375	-	421	-	-
6500	Real estate	7	8	0.2	-	19	-	6,526	-	117	0.0
6530	Real estate agents and managers	3	2	0.1	5	-	7,200	-	31	-	-
GREENE, GA											
60 –	**Finance, insurance, and real estate**	22	23	0.1	333	397	13,646	12,554	5,260	5,567	0.1
6000	Depository institutions	8	7	0.3	110	124	15,709	13,097	1,949	1,882	0.1
6020	Commercial banks	8	7	0.4	110	124	15,709	13,097	1,949	1,882	0.2
6400	Insurance agents, brokers, and service	4	4	0.1	16	12	14,500	14,333	220	178	0.0
GWINNETT, GA											
60 –	**Finance, insurance, and real estate**	843	937	6.0	10,413	10,198	31,237	32,177	342,198	334,885	6.0
6000	Depository institutions	133	131	5.1	1,421	1,545	23,620	24,707	33,777	35,778	2.7
6020	Commercial banks	92	96	5.2	1,042	1,143	24,702	25,533	25,386	28,727	2.7
6030	Savings institutions	26	20	7.0	308	317	21,714	24,328	7,225	5,812	5.8

Source: County Business Patterns, 1992/93, CBP-92/93-1, U.S. Department of Commerce, Washington, D.C., April 1995. SIC categories for which data were suppressed or not available for both 1992 and 1993 are not displayed. The employment columns represent mid-March employment in the year. Pay per employee is calculated by dividing 1st Quarter payroll, annualized, by mid-March employment. The columns headed "% State" show the county's percentage of the state total for the SIC in 1993; for example, 0.9% for SIC 6030 means that the county had 0.9 percent of the state's total establishments (or payroll) in SIC 6030 in 1993. A dash (-) is used to indicate that data are not available or cannot be calculated; nec means not elsewhere classified.

Continued on next page.

SIC	Industry	No. Establishments			Employment		Pay / Employee		Annual Payroll ($ 000)		
		1992	1993	% State	1992	1993	1992	1993	1992	1993	% State
GWINNETT, GA - [continued]											
6060	Credit unions	9	8	2.6	--	34	--	21,882	--	787	1.6
6090	Functions closely related to banking	6	6	4.5	--	51	--	10,431	--	450	1.4
6100	Nondepository institutions	85	94	4.8	663	640	30,824	33,831	21,150	24,483	4.0
6140	Personal credit institutions	43	40	3.6	342	188	29,287	20,872	9,019	3,919	2.5
6150	Business credit institutions	9	12	5.7	65	196	44,000	50,551	2,281	9,314	5.8
6160	Mortgage bankers and brokers	31	41	6.8	251	255	28,924	30,651	9,599	11,249	4.0
6280	Security and commodity services	12	11	3.6	18	27	20,444	34,667	346	911	--
6300	Insurance carriers	93	92	7.6	4,435	4,938	33,400	36,438	152,472	175,155	12.9
6310	Life insurance	20	21	4.7	1,663	1,883	32,002	36,302	52,362	62,762	10.1
6330	Fire, marine, and casualty insurance	58	52	10.0	2,638	2,684	34,928	39,216	93,930	99,563	16.9
6370	Pension, health, and welfare funds	11	15	10.2	111	348	19,243	15,552	5,506	11,940	29.4
6400	Insurance agents, brokers, and service	214	248	7.6	1,398	1,505	31,293	30,544	44,077	49,396	8.4
6500	Real estate	264	313	6.1	1,284	1,096	22,461	24,646	34,188	33,506	4.3
6510	Real estate operators and lessors	71	77	3.9	346	364	19,179	20,143	7,521	7,365	4.3
6530	Real estate agents and managers	106	177	6.9	680	571	22,682	26,515	17,915	18,874	3.7
6540	Title abstract offices	5	4	8.9	25	25	20,960	25,920	586	853	15.0
6552	Subdividers and developers, n.e.c.	18	39	11.1	87	107	36,138	32,336	3,855	5,185	8.0
6553	Cemetery subdividers and developers	4	5	4.1	43	23	9,116	15,652	406	729	4.8
6700	Holding and other investment offices	17	30	5.2	1,155	425	42,268	32,414	54,702	14,535	4.6
6710	Holding offices	10	18	8.3	1,126	395	42,043	32,395	53,291	13,171	5.7
HABERSHAM, GA											
60 –	**Finance, insurance, and real estate**	52	49	0.3	387	395	22,801	20,861	8,758	8,391	0.2
6000	Depository institutions	17	18	0.7	266	302	22,075	18,556	5,779	5,679	0.4
6100	Nondepository institutions	8	6	0.3	26	19	19,231	25,053	412	430	0.1
6400	Insurance agents, brokers, and service	10	11	0.3	28	31	17,857	17,548	493	555	0.1
6500	Real estate	10	8	0.2	23	15	11,826	10,400	298	194	0.0
6510	Real estate operators and lessors	6	3	0.2	15	--	8,800	--	160	--	--
6530	Real estate agents and managers	3	4	0.2	--	8	--	10,000	--	103	0.0
HALL, GA											
60 –	**Finance, insurance, and real estate**	200	215	1.4	2,462	2,352	23,690	25,792	62,022	64,995	1.2
6000	Depository institutions	24	27	1.0	1,009	963	25,816	27,535	27,534	28,199	2.1
6100	Nondepository institutions	37	40	2.0	244	216	18,934	22,630	4,748	5,087	0.8
6140	Personal credit institutions	30	29	2.6	205	145	16,332	20,607	3,429	3,006	1.9
6200	Security and commodity brokers	8	8	1.1	28	27	74,429	86,519	1,989	2,496	0.5
6300	Insurance carriers	25	23	1.9	824	733	22,223	22,941	19,502	16,990	1.3
6310	Life insurance	4	5	1.1	175	99	28,000	40,202	5,352	3,783	0.6
6330	Fire, marine, and casualty insurance	13	14	2.7	623	617	19,910	19,851	13,109	12,637	2.1
6400	Insurance agents, brokers, and service	40	47	1.4	143	166	24,615	25,807	4,097	4,965	0.8
6500	Real estate	61	64	1.2	199	192	15,779	14,521	3,468	3,519	0.5
6510	Real estate operators and lessors	18	25	1.3	41	38	12,976	13,053	583	646	0.4
6530	Real estate agents and managers	26	32	1.2	92	115	17,652	16,487	1,843	2,392	0.5
6553	Cemetery subdividers and developers	5	4	3.3	--	37	--	10,595	--	447	2.9
6700	Holding and other investment offices	5	6	1.0	15	55	40,000	55,200	684	3,739	1.2
6710	Holding offices	2	3	1.4	--	51	--	57,882	--	2,913	1.3
HANCOCK, GA											
60 –	**Finance, insurance, and real estate**	4	5	0.0	82	81	14,195	16,741	1,358	1,410	0.0
HARALSON, GA											
60 –	**Finance, insurance, and real estate**	12	21	0.1	88	134	21,136	17,701	2,277	2,963	0.1
6000	Depository institutions	8	13	0.5	76	121	22,526	18,083	2,135	2,783	0.2
6500	Real estate	1	3	0.1	--	3	--	4,000	--	17	0.0

Source: County Business Patterns, 1992/93, CBP-92/93-1, U.S. Department of Commerce, Washington, D.C., April 1995. SIC categories for which data were suppressed or not available for both 1992 and 1993 are not displayed. The employment columns represent mid-March employment in the year. Pay per employee is calculated by dividing 1st Quarter payroll, annualized, by mid-March employment. The columns headed "% State" show the county's percentage of the state total for the SIC in 1993; for example, 0.9% for SIC 6030 means that the county had 0.9 percent of the state's total establishments (or payroll) in SIC 6030 in 1993. A dash (-) is used to indicate that data are not available or cannot be calculated; nec means not elsewhere classified.

SIC	Industry	No. Establishments			Employment		Pay / Employee		Annual Payroll ($ 000)		
		1992	1993	% State	1992	1993	1992	1993	1992	1993	% State
HARRIS, GA											
60 –	**Finance, insurance, and real estate**	12	14	*0.1*	221	263	14,733	14,616	3,735	4,103	*0.1*
6400	Insurance agents, brokers, and service	3	4	*0.1*	-	4	-	7,000	-	47	*0.0*
6500	Real estate	2	3	*0.1*	-	22	-	7,273	-	193	*0.0*
HART, GA											
60 –	**Finance, insurance, and real estate**	21	21	*0.1*	120	111	19,733	20,973	2,481	2,397	*0.0*
6000	Depository institutions	3	3	*0.1*	57	51	20,140	20,471	1,212	1,049	*0.1*
6020	Commercial banks	3	3	*0.2*	57	51	20,140	20,471	1,212	1,049	*0.1*
6400	Insurance agents, brokers, and service	6	6	*0.2*	25	-	18,720	-	485	-	-
6500	Real estate	6	6	*0.1*	16	15	7,000	8,533	120	165	*0.0*
6510	Real estate operators and lessors	3	4	*0.2*	6	-	4,667	-	32	-	-
HEARD, GA											
60 –	**Finance, insurance, and real estate**	4	4	*0.0*	28	-	21,429	-	695	-	-
6000	Depository institutions	2	3	*0.1*	-	25	-	24,160	-	917	*0.1*
HENRY, GA											
60 –	**Finance, insurance, and real estate**	90	96	*0.6*	518	530	23,012	24,702	12,485	14,235	*0.3*
6000	Depository institutions	21	21	*0.8*	225	221	22,578	27,385	5,372	5,970	*0.5*
6020	Commercial banks	16	16	*0.9*	206	199	21,087	25,447	4,467	4,947	*0.5*
6100	Nondepository institutions	8	9	*0.5*	58	-	27,517	-	1,604	-	-
6140	Personal credit institutions	5	6	*0.5*	28	-	12,714	-	326	-	-
6160	Mortgage bankers and brokers	3	3	*0.5*	30	-	41,333	-	1,278	-	-
6400	Insurance agents, brokers, and service	18	21	*0.6*	80	86	37,200	34,140	2,902	3,404	*0.6*
6500	Real estate	36	40	*0.8*	136	160	12,706	13,625	2,039	2,440	*0.3*
6510	Real estate operators and lessors	12	15	*0.8*	69	92	11,072	11,174	806	944	*0.6*
6530	Real estate agents and managers	17	18	*0.7*	23	40	18,957	15,200	594	955	*0.2*
HOUSTON, GA											
60 –	**Finance, insurance, and real estate**	154	163	*1.0*	874	962	19,918	19,410	18,182	19,670	*0.4*
6000	Depository institutions	33	31	*1.2*	515	499	19,876	20,665	10,138	10,124	*0.8*
6020	Commercial banks	21	20	*1.1*	-	281	-	19,302	-	5,145	*0.5*
6100	Nondepository institutions	18	21	*1.1*	65	71	22,215	21,127	1,471	1,687	*0.3*
6140	Personal credit institutions	15	17	*1.5*	52	54	21,769	20,815	1,151	1,212	*0.8*
6200	Security and commodity brokers	7	9	*1.2*	17	19	19,765	23,579	417	546	*0.1*
6210	Security brokers and dealers	3	5	*1.2*	12	13	22,000	29,231	319	446	*0.1*
6280	Security and commodity services	4	4	*1.3*	5	6	14,400	11,333	98	100	-
6400	Insurance agents, brokers, and service	28	30	*0.9*	102	112	18,824	20,321	2,168	2,352	*0.4*
6500	Real estate	54	61	*1.2*	128	210	14,312	12,267	2,293	3,212	*0.4*
6510	Real estate operators and lessors	16	24	*1.2*	38	92	10,105	11,000	492	1,057	*0.6*
6530	Real estate agents and managers	32	30	*1.2*	78	56	15,128	13,571	1,338	935	*0.2*
IRWIN, GA											
60 –	**Finance, insurance, and real estate**	9	8	*0.1*	62	60	15,097	14,733	1,089	1,077	*0.0*
6000	Depository institutions	4	3	*0.1*	53	-	15,472	-	940	-	-
6020	Commercial banks	4	3	*0.2*	53	-	15,472	-	940	-	-
JACKSON, GA											
60 –	**Finance, insurance, and real estate**	39	35	*0.2*	213	241	19,887	19,054	4,256	4,600	*0.1*
6000	Depository institutions	10	10	*0.4*	159	178	21,057	19,753	3,344	3,601	*0.3*
6020	Commercial banks	10	10	*0.5*	159	178	21,057	19,753	3,344	3,601	*0.3*
6100	Nondepository institutions	7	6	*0.3*	16	18	19,250	23,778	279	326	*0.1*
6140	Personal credit institutions	6	6	*0.5*	-	18	-	23,778	-	326	*0.2*
6400	Insurance agents, brokers, and service	10	9	*0.3*	24	-	17,500	-	425	-	-

Source: County Business Patterns, 1992/93, CBP-92/93-1, U.S. Department of Commerce, Washington, D.C., April 1995. SIC categories for which data were suppressed or not available for both 1992 and 1993 are *not* displayed. The employment columns represent mid-March employment in the year. Pay per employee is calculated by dividing 1st Quarter payroll, annualized, by mid-March employment. The columns headed "% State" show the county's percentage of the state total for the SIC in 1993; for example, 0.9% for SIC 6030 means that the county had 0.9 percent of the state's total establishments (or payroll) in SIC 6030 in 1993. A dash (-) is used to indicate that data are not available or cannot be calculated; *nec* means not elsewhere classified.

Continued on next page.

SIC	Industry	No. Establishments			Employment		Pay / Employee		Annual Payroll ($ 000)		
		1992	1993	% State	1992	1993	1992	1993	1992	1993	% State
JACKSON, GA - [continued]											
6500	Real estate	12	9	0.2	14	22	11,429	12,545	208	267	0.0
6510	Real estate operators and lessors	4	5	0.3	3	14	6,667	10,857	38	168	0.1
6552	Subdividers and developers, n.e.c.	5	2	0.6	6	-	12,667	-	76	-	-
JASPER, GA											
60 –	**Finance, insurance, and real estate**	12	13	0.1	75	73	15,573	16,329	1,190	1,302	0.0
6400	Insurance agents, brokers, and service	3	5	0.2	8	11	12,000	11,636	86	117	0.0
6500	Real estate	4	3	0.1	27	-	9,778	-	274	-	-
JEFF DAVIS, GA											
60 –	**Finance, insurance, and real estate**	21	19	0.1	82	83	15,317	15,952	1,291	1,364	0.0
6000	Depository institutions	5	5	0.2	51	56	16,549	16,500	902	962	0.1
6100	Nondepository institutions	4	4	0.2	10	-	23,200	-	228	-	-
6400	Insurance agents, brokers, and service	8	8	0.2	16	12	9,250	12,000	138	140	0.0
6500	Real estate	4	2	0.0	5	-	6,400	-	23	-	-
JEFFERSON, GA											
60 –	**Finance, insurance, and real estate**	21	21	0.1	137	169	18,540	16,024	2,727	3,091	0.1
6000	Depository institutions	8	8	0.3	103	106	19,573	19,283	1,962	1,979	0.1
6020	Commercial banks	8	8	0.4	103	106	19,573	19,283	1,962	1,979	0.2
6100	Nondepository institutions	3	3	0.2	15	-	13,067	-	374	-	-
6140	Personal credit institutions	3	3	0.3	15	-	13,067	-	374	-	-
6400	Insurance agents, brokers, and service	5	5	0.2	-	13	-	20,308	-	265	0.0
6500	Real estate	4	4	0.1	6	33	10,667	6,061	138	227	0.0
JENKINS, GA											
60 –	**Finance, insurance, and real estate**	8	8	0.1	54	58	17,111	16,345	955	1,044	0.0
6400	Insurance agents, brokers, and service	3	3	0.1	7	9	14,286	10,667	96	96	0.0
JOHNSON, GA											
60 –	**Finance, insurance, and real estate**	7	7	0.0	39	43	13,128	12,186	582	597	0.0
JONES, GA											
60 –	**Finance, insurance, and real estate**	13	12	0.1	43	-	18,605	-	916	-	-
6500	Real estate	8	7	0.1	15	18	20,533	22,222	408	572	0.1
6510	Real estate operators and lessors	4	5	0.3	3	-	6,667	-	56	-	-
LAMAR, GA											
60 –	**Finance, insurance, and real estate**	13	13	0.1	131	157	20,214	19,541	2,808	3,500	0.1
6100	Nondepository institutions	3	4	0.2	10	20	12,800	19,800	134	469	0.1
6140	Personal credit institutions	3	3	0.3	10	-	12,800	-	134	-	-
LANIER, GA											
60 –	**Finance, insurance, and real estate**	5	5	0.0	58	58	20,828	17,379	1,294	1,188	0.0
LAURENS, GA											
60 –	**Finance, insurance, and real estate**	77	84	0.5	475	474	22,131	20,869	10,909	10,327	0.2
6000	Depository institutions	18	19	0.7	218	226	20,954	21,522	4,687	5,097	0.4
6100	Nondepository institutions	11	17	0.9	62	74	27,161	17,514	1,886	1,503	0.2
6140	Personal credit institutions	9	10	0.9	-	52	-	13,615	-	741	0.5
6300	Insurance carriers	7	5	0.4	70	52	35,829	34,846	2,295	1,605	0.1
6400	Insurance agents, brokers, and service	22	23	0.7	55	-	14,545	-	842	-	-
6500	Real estate	16	18	0.4	52	57	13,385	14,596	888	954	0.1
6510	Real estate operators and lessors	9	8	0.4	42	26	13,143	8,000	690	274	0.2
6530	Real estate agents and managers	1	6	0.2	-	26	-	22,154	-	592	0.1

Source: County Business Patterns, 1992/93, CBP-92/93-1, U.S. Department of Commerce, Washington, D.C., April 1995. SIC categories for which data were suppressed or not available for both 1992 and 1993 are *not* displayed. The employment columns represent mid-March employment in the year. Pay per employee is calculated by dividing 1st Quarter payroll, annualized, by mid-March employment. The columns headed "% State" show the county's percentage of the state total for the SIC in 1993; for example, 0.9% for SIC 6030 means that the county had 0.9 percent of the state's total establishments (or payroll) in SIC 6030 in 1993. A dash (-) is used to indicate that data are not available or cannot be calculated; *nec* means not elsewhere classified.

SIC	Industry	No. Establishments			Employment		Pay / Employee		Annual Payroll ($ 000)		
		1992	1993	% State	1992	1993	1992	1993	1992	1993	% State
LEE, GA											
60 –	**Finance, insurance, and real estate**	3	4	0.0	-	-	-	-	-	-	-
LIBERTY, GA											
60 –	**Finance, insurance, and real estate**	57	64	0.4	369	396	18,005	15,869	7,574	7,838	0.1
6000	Depository institutions	10	11	0.4	175	196	19,771	16,612	3,983	3,821	0.3
6030	Savings institutions	2	3	1.1	-	18	-	13,556	-	255	0.3
6100	Nondepository institutions	4	2	0.1	14	-	38,857	-	480	-	-
6400	Insurance agents, brokers, and service	12	15	0.5	35	38	13,600	12,000	509	537	0.1
6500	Real estate	25	31	0.6	133	139	14,887	15,309	2,377	3,068	0.4
6510	Real estate operators and lessors	8	13	0.7	28	-	7,000	-	209	-	-
6530	Real estate agents and managers	13	16	0.6	82	89	14,976	15,056	1,329	1,472	0.3
6700	Holding and other investment offices	3	2	0.3	8	-	10,500	-	114	-	-
LINCOLN, GA											
60 –	**Finance, insurance, and real estate**	6	6	0.0	-	-	-	-	-	-	-
6400	Insurance agents, brokers, and service	3	3	0.1	-	6	-	37,333	-	201	0.0
LONG, GA											
60 –	**Finance, insurance, and real estate**	1	1	0.0	-	-	-	-	-	-	-
LOWNDES, GA											
60 –	**Finance, insurance, and real estate**	190	197	1.3	1,235	1,492	19,048	17,633	24,927	27,195	0.5
6000	Depository institutions	30	33	1.3	447	475	20,617	20,488	9,457	9,709	0.7
6020	Commercial banks	21	23	1.3	363	391	20,408	20,409	7,527	7,688	0.7
6100	Nondepository institutions	27	29	1.5	111	107	21,658	22,467	2,320	2,510	0.4
6140	Personal credit institutions	24	24	2.2	105	96	21,905	21,958	2,170	2,118	1.3
6200	Security and commodity brokers	4	5	0.7	-	27	-	60,296	-	1,607	0.3
6210	Security brokers and dealers	3	5	1.2	-	27	-	60,296	-	1,607	0.4
6300	Insurance carriers	17	16	1.3	242	166	20,281	26,795	5,576	4,510	0.3
6310	Life insurance	9	9	2.0	169	156	21,799	25,128	4,233	4,005	0.6
6400	Insurance agents, brokers, and service	37	36	1.1	128	121	16,938	17,388	2,157	2,489	0.4
6500	Real estate	72	73	1.4	276	578	11,188	9,433	3,508	5,753	0.7
6510	Real estate operators and lessors	33	35	1.8	153	108	9,255	12,037	1,481	1,137	0.7
6530	Real estate agents and managers	27	28	1.1	83	429	14,361	8,625	1,344	4,008	0.8
6552	Subdividers and developers, n.e.c.	5	8	2.3	10	-	14,400	-	313	-	-
6700	Holding and other investment offices	3	5	0.9	-	18	-	30,000	-	617	0.2
LUMPKIN, GA											
60 –	**Finance, insurance, and real estate**	18	20	0.1	150	153	20,640	20,889	3,199	3,404	0.1
6000	Depository institutions	3	4	0.2	92	79	18,609	19,949	1,724	1,461	0.1
6020	Commercial banks	2	4	0.2	-	79	-	19,949	-	1,461	0.1
6100	Nondepository institutions	2	3	0.2	-	4	-	8,000	-	49	0.0
6140	Personal credit institutions	2	3	0.3	-	4	-	8,000	-	49	0.0
6500	Real estate	7	6	0.1	31	34	14,323	13,647	506	550	0.1
6530	Real estate agents and managers	5	5	0.2	29	-	15,172	-	499	-	-
MCDUFFIE, GA											
60 –	**Finance, insurance, and real estate**	37	35	0.2	267	265	20,449	19,426	5,573	5,296	0.1
6000	Depository institutions	10	10	0.4	176	183	20,159	19,301	3,567	3,595	0.3
6100	Nondepository institutions	7	7	0.4	44	28	19,727	17,429	911	507	0.1
6400	Insurance agents, brokers, and service	5	6	0.2	9	26	21,778	17,385	203	465	0.1
6500	Real estate	9	6	0.1	26	17	12,769	10,353	350	183	0.0
6530	Real estate agents and managers	5	3	0.1	15	7	14,667	9,714	225	91	0.0
MCINTOSH, GA											
60 –	**Finance, insurance, and real estate**	7	9	0.1	-	57	-	34,175	-	1,746	0.0
6500	Real estate	3	4	0.1	8	-	5,000	-	42	-	-

Source: County Business Patterns, 1992/93, CBP-92/93-1, U.S. Department of Commerce, Washington, D.C., April 1995. SIC categories for which data were suppressed or not available for both 1992 and 1993 are *not* displayed. The employment columns represent mid-March employment in the year. Pay per employee is calculated by dividing 1st Quarter payroll, annualized, by mid-March employment. The columns headed "% State" show the county's percentage of the state total for the SIC in 1993; for example, 0.9% for SIC 6030 means that the county had 0.9 percent of the state's total establishments (or payroll) in SIC 6030 in 1993. A dash (-) is used to indicate that data are not available or cannot be calculated; *nec* means not elsewhere classified.

SIC	Industry	No. Establishments			Employment		Pay / Employee		Annual Payroll ($ 000)		
		1992	1993	% State	1992	1993	1992	1993	1992	1993	% State
MACON, GA											
60 –	**Finance, insurance, and real estate**	20	22	*0.1*	81	88	15,506	15,364	1,291	1,314	*0.0*
6000	Depository institutions	5	5	*0.2*	40	40	18,300	19,100	747	754	*0.1*
6100	Nondepository institutions	4	4	*0.2*	15	-	15,200	-	223	-	-
6140	Personal credit institutions	4	4	*0.4*	15	-	15,200	-	223	-	-
6400	Insurance agents, brokers, and service	5	6	*0.2*	15	17	11,733	10,824	184	239	*0.0*
6500	Real estate	5	5	*0.1*	-	10	-	10,000	-	55	*0.0*
MADISON, GA											
60 –	**Finance, insurance, and real estate**	11	11	*0.1*	66	70	14,727	14,743	1,292	1,253	*0.0*
6400	Insurance agents, brokers, and service	3	3	*0.1*	3	4	13,333	10,000	36	62	*0.0*
MARION, GA											
60 –	**Finance, insurance, and real estate**	2	2	*0.0*	-	-	-	-	-	-	-
MERIWETHER, GA											
60 –	**Finance, insurance, and real estate**	23	24	*0.2*	138	141	19,449	19,887	2,590	2,820	*0.1*
6000	Depository institutions	9	9	*0.3*	99	99	21,131	20,323	2,083	2,064	*0.2*
6020	Commercial banks	9	9	*0.5*	99	99	21,131	20,323	2,083	2,064	*0.2*
6100	Nondepository institutions	6	6	*0.3*	-	17	-	25,176	-	363	*0.1*
6400	Insurance agents, brokers, and service	6	6	*0.2*	16	21	13,250	16,000	126	363	*0.1*
6500	Real estate	2	3	*0.1*	-	4	-	7,000	-	30	*0.0*
MILLER, GA											
60 –	**Finance, insurance, and real estate**	5	5	*0.0*	41	44	20,488	19,364	880	896	*0.0*
MITCHELL, GA											
60 –	**Finance, insurance, and real estate**	32	36	*0.2*	196	189	18,224	18,201	3,556	3,694	*0.1*
6000	Depository institutions	7	7	*0.3*	122	114	20,459	20,842	2,404	2,490	*0.2*
6100	Nondepository institutions	5	7	*0.4*	-	24	-	22,333	-	592	*0.1*
6400	Insurance agents, brokers, and service	7	10	*0.3*	24	27	14,167	14,370	375	444	*0.1*
6500	Real estate	11	11	*0.2*	19	-	6,947		141	-	-
6510	Real estate operators and lessors	7	6	*0.3*	15	12	6,400	5,000	107	71	*0.0*
6530	Real estate agents and managers	3	3	*0.1*	-	9	-	5,333	-	57	*0.0*
MONROE, GA											
60 –	**Finance, insurance, and real estate**	17	15	*0.1*	83	83	17,831	17,928	1,478	1,564	*0.0*
6000	Depository institutions	4	4	*0.2*	53	52	21,283	21,769	1,142	1,181	*0.1*
6100	Nondepository institutions	5	3	*0.2*	-	6	-	17,333	-	106	*0.0*
6140	Personal credit institutions	4	3	*0.3*	7	6	18,286	17,333	113	106	*0.1*
6400	Insurance agents, brokers, and service	6	6	*0.2*	17	-	11,059	-	199	-	-
MONTGOMERY, GA											
60 –	**Finance, insurance, and real estate**	11	10	*0.1*	61	61	17,967	19,148	1,173	1,229	*0.0*
6100	Nondepository institutions	4	4	*0.2*	11	-	20,000	-	214	-	-
6140	Personal credit institutions	4	4	*0.4*	11	-	20,000	-	214	-	-
6400	Insurance agents, brokers, and service	5	4	*0.1*	-	7	-	8,571	-	79	*0.0*
MORGAN, GA											
60 –	**Finance, insurance, and real estate**	21	21	*0.1*	143	200	18,210	22,520	2,623	4,422	*0.1*
6000	Depository institutions	6	5	*0.2*	87	146	19,172	21,808	1,631	3,160	*0.2*
6020	Commercial banks	6	5	*0.3*	87	146	19,172	21,808	1,631	3,160	*0.3*
6100	Nondepository institutions	4	5	*0.3*	24	22	16,167	36,727	376	656	*0.1*
6400	Insurance agents, brokers, and service	3	3	*0.1*	20	19	23,000	21,684	499	512	*0.1*
6500	Real estate	5	5	*0.1*	5	6	8,800	10,000	57	54	*0.0*
6510	Real estate operators and lessors	3	3	*0.2*	3	-	10,667	-	45	-	-

Source: County Business Patterns, 1992/93, CBP-92/93-1, U.S. Department of Commerce, Washington, D.C., April 1995. SIC categories for which data were suppressed or not available for both 1992 and 1993 are *not* displayed. The employment columns represent mid-March employment in the year. Pay per employee is calculated by dividing 1st Quarter payroll, annualized, by mid-March employment. The columns headed "% State" show the county's percentage of the state total for the SIC in 1993; for example, 0.9% for SIC 6030 means that the county had 0.9 percent of the state's total establishments (or payroll) in SIC 6030 in 1993. A dash (-) is used to indicate that data are not available or cannot be calculated; *nec* means not elsewhere classified.

SIC	Industry	No. Establishments			Employment		Pay / Employee		Annual Payroll ($ 000)		
		1992	1993	% State	1992	1993	1992	1993	1992	1993	% State
MURRAY, GA											
60 –	**Finance, insurance, and real estate**	32	25	0.2	351	194	16,764	18,639	5,837	3,640	0.1
6000	Depository institutions	9	9	0.3	114	117	23,579	21,026	2,809	2,622	0.2
6100	Nondepository institutions	4	4	0.2	-	15	-	21,333	-	281	0.0
6300	Insurance carriers	3	2	0.2	13	-	8,615	-	224	-	-
6400	Insurance agents, brokers, and service	6	4	0.1	17	17	25,176	25,647	449	434	0.1
6500	Real estate	8	5	0.1	188	10	12,234	9,600	2,025	94	0.0
MUSCOGEE, GA											
60 –	**Finance, insurance, and real estate**	480	503	3.2	6,539	6,906	27,094	25,520	182,411	188,177	3.4
6000	Depository institutions	69	75	2.9	1,385	1,377	22,117	22,568	30,107	31,399	2.4
6020	Commercial banks	53	56	3.0	1,265	1,244	22,776	23,186	28,188	29,138	2.7
6100	Nondepository institutions	68	68	3.5	474	436	24,540	22,046	10,896	10,689	1.7
6140	Personal credit institutions	46	43	3.9	241	264	23,519	18,258	5,536	5,193	3.3
6150	Business credit institutions	5	3	1.4	-	5	-	31,200	-	165	0.1
6160	Mortgage bankers and brokers	15	22	3.7	80	167	39,800	27,760	3,231	5,331	1.9
6200	Security and commodity brokers	19	20	2.8	-	153	-	59,294	-	9,528	2.0
6210	Security brokers and dealers	11	12	2.9	139	135	58,561	64,119	8,288	9,011	2.4
6280	Security and commodity services	7	8	2.6	14	18	34,000	23,111	335	517	-
6300	Insurance carriers	48	39	3.2	1,349	3,116	26,028	25,561	34,552	84,943	6.3
6310	Life insurance	17	14	3.1	316	1,772	24,165	28,779	8,079	56,098	9.0
6400	Insurance agents, brokers, and service	95	102	3.1	1,708	-	29,365	-	50,642	-	-
6500	Real estate	159	177	3.4	1,178	921	14,930	15,049	19,523	14,638	1.9
6510	Real estate operators and lessors	81	96	4.8	714	450	14,118	14,853	11,545	7,310	4.3
6530	Real estate agents and managers	55	71	2.8	361	427	17,219	15,447	6,585	6,617	1.3
6552	Subdividers and developers, n.e.c.	4	4	1.1	27	-	10,222	-	297	-	-
6553	Cemetery subdividers and developers	3	4	3.3	-	37	-	12,541	-	591	3.9
6700	Holding and other investment offices	21	20	3.5	266	431	84,872	49,782	27,097	25,136	7.9
6710	Holding offices	8	7	3.2	234	280	93,043	64,043	25,515	21,030	9.2
6732	Educational, religious, etc. trusts	5	3	3.9	14	-	20,857	-	276	-	-
6733	Trusts, n.e.c.	3	3	3.4	5	3	6,400	14,667	26	84	0.9
NEWTON, GA											
60 –	**Finance, insurance, and real estate**	53	54	0.3	358	376	21,788	18,117	7,775	7,773	0.1
6000	Depository institutions	9	10	0.4	234	242	18,256	15,322	4,502	4,100	0.3
6140	Personal credit institutions	6	6	0.5	32	32	32,625	25,125	953	1,018	0.6
6400	Insurance agents, brokers, and service	14	13	0.4	-	41	-	17,073	-	968	0.2
6500	Real estate	19	18	0.4	40	43	33,800	22,698	1,071	928	0.1
6510	Real estate operators and lessors	7	9	0.5	14	-	16,286	-	231	-	-
6530	Real estate agents and managers	8	6	0.2	-	13	-	11,077	-	162	0.0
OCONEE, GA											
60 –	**Finance, insurance, and real estate**	20	30	0.2	109	144	19,156	17,167	2,307	2,597	0.0
6000	Depository institutions	6	6	0.2	90	91	21,022	23,077	1,931	2,059	0.2
6020	Commercial banks	6	6	0.3	90	91	21,022	23,077	1,931	2,059	0.2
6400	Insurance agents, brokers, and service	7	11	0.3	16	-	11,000	-	175	-	-
6500	Real estate	7	12	0.2	3	39	6,667	5,436	201	311	0.0
6510	Real estate operators and lessors	2	6	0.3	-	31	-	4,903	-	242	0.1
6530	Real estate agents and managers	3	6	0.2	3	8	6,667	7,500	24	69	0.0
OGLETHORPE, GA											
60 –	**Finance, insurance, and real estate**	2	2	0.0	-	-	-	-	-	-	-
PAULDING, GA											
60 –	**Finance, insurance, and real estate**	34	41	0.3	181	180	24,972	19,733	4,340	3,846	0.1
6100	Nondepository institutions	5	6	0.3	9	15	16,889	12,800	164	234	0.0

Source: County Business Patterns, 1992/93, CBP-92/93-1, U.S. Department of Commerce, Washington, D.C., April 1995. SIC categories for which data were suppressed or not available for both 1992 and 1993 are *not* displayed. The employment columns represent mid-March employment in the year. Pay per employee is calculated by dividing 1st Quarter payroll, annualized, by mid-March employment. The columns headed "% State" show the county's percentage of the state total for the SIC in 1993; for example, 0.9% for SIC 6030 means that the county had 0.9 percent of the state's total establishments (or payroll) in SIC 6030 in 1993. A dash (-) is used to indicate that data are not available or cannot be calculated; *nec* means not elsewhere classified.

Continued on next page.

SIC	Industry	No. Establishments			Employment		Pay / Employee		Annual Payroll ($ 000)		
		1992	1993	% State	1992	1993	1992	1993	1992	1993	% State
PAULDING, GA - [continued]											
6500	Real estate	9	12	0.2	27	20	18,963	16,200	624	411	0.1
6510	Real estate operators and lessors	2	3	0.2	-	4	-	13,000	-	71	0.0
6530	Real estate agents and managers	4	5	0.2	3	6	8,000	11,333	20	89	0.0
PEACH, GA											
60 –	**Finance, insurance, and real estate**	28	29	0.2	185	191	19,114	19,812	3,853	4,192	0.1
6100	Nondepository institutions	4	4	0.2	12	11	17,000	17,818	199	204	0.0
6140	Personal credit institutions	4	4	0.4	12	11	17,000	17,818	199	204	0.1
6400	Insurance agents, brokers, and service	7	8	0.2	59	58	24,542	23,586	1,470	1,464	0.3
6500	Real estate	12	11	0.2	28	24	11,571	13,833	397	352	0.0
6510	Real estate operators and lessors	6	6	0.3	12	14	9,000	7,714	110	111	0.1
6530	Real estate agents and managers	2	5	0.2	-	10	-	22,400	-	241	0.0
PICKENS, GA											
60 –	**Finance, insurance, and real estate**	27	30	0.2	195	295	19,836	17,356	4,000	6,414	0.1
6000	Depository institutions	5	5	0.2	123	130	20,163	20,062	2,667	3,491	0.3
6400	Insurance agents, brokers, and service	7	6	0.2	18	18	25,778	21,333	392	378	0.1
6500	Real estate	12	16	0.3	34	134	18,000	13,970	698	2,320	0.3
6530	Real estate agents and managers	3	9	0.4	8	93	19,000	14,882	154	1,716	0.3
6552	Subdividers and developers, n.e.c.	3	4	1.1	2	33	4,000	12,000	11	475	0.7
PIERCE, GA											
60 –	**Finance, insurance, and real estate**	21	16	0.1	113	90	19,009	18,222	2,201	1,773	0.0
6000	Depository institutions	5	4	0.2	67	51	20,836	18,824	1,448	1,083	0.1
6100	Nondepository institutions	3	3	0.2	-	16	-	22,000	-	358	0.1
6400	Insurance agents, brokers, and service	6	6	0.2	16	16	17,000	16,250	257	265	0.0
6500	Real estate	6	3	0.1	12	7	8,333	9,714	101	67	0.0
6510	Real estate operators and lessors	4	1	0.1	9	-	7,111	-	65	-	-
PIKE, GA											
60 –	**Finance, insurance, and real estate**	8	9	0.1	51	57	19,059	16,982	961	1,034	0.0
POLK, GA											
60 –	**Finance, insurance, and real estate**	52	53	0.3	270	248	16,948	18,548	4,573	4,668	0.1
6000	Depository institutions	11	13	0.5	173	154	20,879	22,545	3,523	3,430	0.3
6100	Nondepository institutions	7	8	0.4	23	17	10,783	17,176	251	280	0.0
6140	Personal credit institutions	5	5	0.5	21	15	10,476	18,133	222	242	0.2
6400	Insurance agents, brokers, and service	16	16	0.5	30	34	14,533	12,471	442	423	0.1
6500	Real estate	15	13	0.3	32	33	6,750	10,788	287	475	0.1
6530	Real estate agents and managers	8	4	0.2	8	5	7,500	13,600	82	94	0.2
PULASKI, GA											
60 –	**Finance, insurance, and real estate**	14	15	0.1	109	110	14,422	15,164	1,776	1,881	0.0
6100	Nondepository institutions	3	4	0.2	7	-	18,857	-	167	-	-
6400	Insurance agents, brokers, and service	5	6	0.2	14	13	16,571	17,538	248	241	0.0
PUTNAM, GA											
60 –	**Finance, insurance, and real estate**	15	15	0.1	106	92	20,604	20,652	2,396	2,340	0.0
6100	Nondepository institutions	3	3	0.2	-	12	-	28,000	-	382	0.1
6140	Personal credit institutions	3	3	0.3	-	12	-	28,000	-	382	0.2
6400	Insurance agents, brokers, and service	3	3	0.1	8	-	12,000	-	106	-	-
6500	Real estate	6	6	0.1	15	12	10,667	13,000	164	186	0.0
6530	Real estate agents and managers	4	3	0.1	-	9	-	12,889	-	139	0.0
QUITMAN, GA											
60 –	**Finance, insurance, and real estate**	3	4	0.0	-	5	-	16,000	-	89	0.0

Source: County Business Patterns, 1992/93, CBP-92/93-1, U.S. Department of Commerce, Washington, D.C., April 1995. SIC categories for which data were suppressed or not available for both 1992 and 1993 are *not* displayed. The employment columns represent mid-March employment in the year. Pay per employee is calculated by dividing 1st Quarter payroll, annualized, by mid-March employment. The columns headed "% State" show the county's percentage of the state total for the SIC in 1993; for example, 0.9% for SIC 6030 means that the county had 0.9 percent of the state's total establishments (or payroll) in SIC 6030 in 1993. A dash (-) is used to indicate that data are not available or cannot be calculated; *nec* means not elsewhere classified.

SIC	Industry	No. Establishments			Employment		Pay / Employee		Annual Payroll ($ 000)		
		1992	1993	% State	1992	1993	1992	1993	1992	1993	% State
RABUN, GA											
60 –	**Finance, insurance, and real estate**	28	30	0.2	170	145	19,129	20,193	3,190	3,138	0.1
6000	Depository institutions	4	4	0.2	103	94	21,670	22,085	2,196	2,037	0.2
6400	Insurance agents, brokers, and service	4	4	0.1	10	10	20,400	19,200	209	228	0.0
6500	Real estate	16	18	0.4	50	34	10,560	10,118	523	539	0.1
6530	Real estate agents and managers	9	13	0.5	41	31	9,951	10,452	388	468	0.1
RANDOLPH, GA											
60 –	**Finance, insurance, and real estate**	12	12	0.1	64	64	19,812	15,875	1,245	1,123	0.0
6400	Insurance agents, brokers, and service	5	4	0.1	10	8	11,600	11,500	107	117	0.0
6500	Real estate	2	3	0.1	-	4	-	15,000	-	66	0.0
6510	Real estate operators and lessors	1	3	0.2	-	4	-	15,000	-	66	0.0
RICHMOND, GA											
60 –	**Finance, insurance, and real estate**	429	419	2.7	4,080	3,691	23,258	24,251	93,942	92,572	1.7
6000	Depository institutions	73	74	2.9	1,210	980	20,559	22,094	24,888	21,383	1.6
6020	Commercial banks	43	41	2.2	799	737	20,010	23,951	15,912	16,899	1.6
6060	Credit unions	11	14	4.6	79	103	16,962	17,398	1,386	2,048	4.1
6140	Personal credit institutions	45	39	3.5	169	166	20,947	15,663	3,474	2,781	1.8
6150	Business credit institutions	3	3	1.4	5	-	12,800	-	64	-	-
6160	Mortgage bankers and brokers	11	16	2.7	88	98	33,227	33,592	3,097	3,256	1.2
6200	Security and commodity brokers	15	18	2.5	103	132	75,689	60,515	7,450	8,034	1.7
6210	Security brokers and dealers	9	10	2.4	92	102	78,000	74,667	7,050	7,575	2.0
6280	Security and commodity services	6	8	2.6	11	30	56,364	12,400	400	459	-
6300	Insurance carriers	42	32	2.6	951	799	23,588	22,889	19,980	17,882	1.3
6310	Life insurance	16	11	2.4	264	224	25,303	28,232	6,157	5,975	1.0
6330	Fire, marine, and casualty insurance	15	13	2.5	-	121	-	26,446	-	3,086	0.5
6370	Pension, health, and welfare funds	5	4	2.7	5	-	5,600	-	28	-	-
6400	Insurance agents, brokers, and service	73	79	2.4	316	360	23,962	21,222	7,705	8,672	1.5
6500	Real estate	150	148	2.9	968	874	15,244	16,165	15,704	17,104	2.2
6510	Real estate operators and lessors	66	78	3.9	507	601	14,193	15,175	7,501	10,907	6.4
6530	Real estate agents and managers	64	60	2.3	303	205	19,525	18,829	6,863	4,961	1.0
6552	Subdividers and developers, n.e.c.	4	5	1.4	111	-	8,541	-	527	-	-
6553	Cemetery subdividers and developers	3	3	2.5	25	56	12,800	13,000	362	731	4.8
6700	Holding and other investment offices	15	9	1.6	153	97	58,954	95,546	9,472	8,743	2.7
ROCKDALE, GA											
60 –	**Finance, insurance, and real estate**	121	116	0.7	570	479	21,340	23,499	11,981	12,896	0.2
6000	Depository institutions	20	21	0.8	214	217	25,252	26,396	4,909	5,932	0.4
6020	Commercial banks	13	15	0.8	166	184	27,108	27,304	3,861	4,973	0.5
6030	Savings institutions	4	3	1.1	39	-	19,179	-	898	-	-
6100	Nondepository institutions	11	11	0.6	38	-	21,053	-	708	-	-
6140	Personal credit institutions	8	7	0.6	27	31	21,481	13,161	537	590	0.4
6200	Security and commodity brokers	6	4	0.6	7	6	50,857	54,667	407	379	0.1
6300	Insurance carriers	13	9	0.7	38	29	26,947	33,379	1,072	1,060	0.1
6370	Pension, health, and welfare funds	2	3	2.0	-	1	-	32,000	-	66	0.2
6400	Insurance agents, brokers, and service	28	29	0.9	94	89	24,681	23,101	2,315	2,190	0.4
6500	Real estate	40	41	0.8	100	98	15,960	13,837	1,913	2,184	0.3
6510	Real estate operators and lessors	11	12	0.6	44	35	12,273	14,286	629	533	0.3
6530	Real estate agents and managers	21	23	0.9	45	51	18,756	13,412	906	1,161	0.2
6552	Subdividers and developers, n.e.c.	3	4	1.1	-	5	-	16,800	-	365	0.6
6700	Holding and other investment offices	3	1	0.2	79	-	8,405	-	657	-	-
SCHLEY, GA											
60 –	**Finance, insurance, and real estate**	3	3	0.0	-	-	-	-	-	-	-

Source: County Business Patterns, 1992/93, CBP-92/93-1, U.S. Department of Commerce, Washington, D.C., April 1995. SIC categories for which data were suppressed or not available for both 1992 and 1993 are not displayed. The employment columns represent mid-March employment in the year. Pay per employee is calculated by dividing 1st Quarter payroll, annualized, by mid-March employment. The columns headed "% State" show the county's percentage of the state total for the SIC in 1993; for example, 0.9% for SIC 6030 means that the county had 0.9 percent of the state's total establishments (or payroll) in SIC 6030 in 1993. A dash (-) is used to indicate that data are not available or cannot be calculated; nec means not elsewhere classified.

SIC	Industry	No. Establishments			Employment		Pay / Employee		Annual Payroll ($ 000)		
		1992	1993	% State	1992	1993	1992	1993	1992	1993	% State
SCREVEN, GA											
60 –	**Finance, insurance, and real estate**	18	19	0.1	89	97	16,404	17,196	1,580	1,802	0.0
6000	Depository institutions	4	4	0.2	57	61	18,456	18,361	1,163	1,248	0.1
6100	Nondepository institutions	6	8	0.4	18	20	15,333	20,000	269	390	0.1
6140	Personal credit institutions	4	5	0.5	9	10	21,333	24,400	173	230	0.1
6400	Insurance agents, brokers, and service	5	4	0.1	11	11	10,909	11,273	128	134	0.0
6500	Real estate	3	3	0.1	3	5	4,000	4,800	20	30	0.0
6530	Real estate agents and managers	3	2	0.1	3	-	4,000	-	20	-	-
SEMINOLE, GA											
60 –	**Finance, insurance, and real estate**	12	12	0.1	97	76	15,959	16,421	1,646	1,528	0.0
6000	Depository institutions	3	3	0.1	72	51	17,111	17,804	1,331	1,198	0.1
6400	Insurance agents, brokers, and service	4	5	0.2	12	14	9,000	10,286	118	151	0.0
SPALDING, GA											
60 –	**Finance, insurance, and real estate**	103	101	0.7	721	1,097	21,537	17,232	15,968	21,085	0.4
6000	Depository institutions	15	14	0.5	278	309	21,424	20,078	5,748	6,489	0.5
6020	Commercial banks	10	10	0.5	226	251	21,912	20,239	4,677	5,235	0.5
6100	Nondepository institutions	15	13	0.7	83	116	23,133	40,448	1,935	5,997	1.0
6300	Insurance carriers	16	15	1.2	190	515	24,884	9,887	5,302	5,400	0.4
6310	Life insurance	9	9	2.0	176	166	23,386	24,337	4,689	4,332	0.7
6400	Insurance agents, brokers, and service	22	22	0.7	68	60	16,882	16,933	1,059	1,035	0.2
6500	Real estate	30	33	0.6	86	82	12,744	12,732	1,224	1,251	0.2
6510	Real estate operators and lessors	14	15	0.8	53	-	11,774	-	660	-	-
6530	Real estate agents and managers	14	17	0.7	28	27	14,571	14,370	440	511	0.1
STEPHENS, GA											
60 –	**Finance, insurance, and real estate**	27	30	0.2	241	249	41,494	46,201	7,772	8,799	0.2
6000	Depository institutions	6	7	0.3	124	125	22,355	21,568	2,876	2,933	0.2
6140	Personal credit institutions	3	3	0.3	10	11	24,400	23,636	210	220	0.1
6500	Real estate	6	8	0.2	-	14	-	12,571	-	242	0.0
6510	Real estate operators and lessors	1	4	0.2	-	9	-	14,222	-	135	0.1
STEWART, GA											
60 –	**Finance, insurance, and real estate**	7	7	0.0	36	35	15,222	16,914	552	630	0.0
SUMTER, GA											
60 –	**Finance, insurance, and real estate**	55	48	0.3	395	330	20,618	21,927	8,052	7,531	0.1
6000	Depository institutions	8	7	0.3	199	154	19,859	20,883	3,614	3,371	0.3
6020	Commercial banks	8	7	0.4	199	154	19,859	20,883	3,614	3,371	0.3
6100	Nondepository institutions	11	10	0.5	33	27	16,606	20,444	591	635	0.1
6400	Insurance agents, brokers, and service	13	12	0.4	44	45	17,273	16,533	815	738	0.1
6500	Real estate	16	13	0.3	41	24	12,780	10,000	454	293	0.0
6510	Real estate operators and lessors	10	11	0.6	28	-	11,714	-	278	-	-
6530	Real estate agents and managers	4	2	0.1	3	-	10,667	-	58	-	-
TALBOT, GA											
60 –	**Finance, insurance, and real estate**	3	2	0.0	-	-	-	-	-	-	-
TALIAFERRO, GA											
60 –	**Finance, insurance, and real estate**	1	1	0.0	-	-	-	-	-	-	-
TATTNALL, GA											
60 –	**Finance, insurance, and real estate**	20	21	0.1	181	149	16,619	17,154	3,303	2,760	0.0
6000	Depository institutions	8	8	0.3	112	121	18,500	17,950	2,269	2,395	0.2
6100	Nondepository institutions	3	4	0.2	6	7	18,000	16,571	111	115	0.0

Source: County Business Patterns, 1992/93, CBP-92/93-1, U.S. Department of Commerce, Washington, D.C., April 1995. SIC categories for which data were suppressed or not available for both 1992 and 1993 are not displayed. The employment columns represent mid-March employment in the year. Pay per employee is calculated by dividing 1st Quarter payroll, annualized, by mid-March employment. The columns headed "% State" show the county's percentage of the state total for the SIC in 1993; for example, 0.9% for SIC 6030 means that the county had 0.9 percent of the state's total establishments (or payroll) in SIC 6030 in 1993. A dash (-) is used to indicate that data are not available or cannot be calculated; nec means not elsewhere classified.

Continued on next page.

SIC	Industry	No. Establishments			Employment		Pay / Employee		Annual Payroll ($ 000)		
		1992	1993	% State	1992	1993	1992	1993	1992	1993	% State
TATTNALL, GA - [continued]											
6140	Personal credit institutions	3	4	0.4	6	7	18,000	16,571	111	115	0.1
6400	Insurance agents, brokers, and service	6	6	0.2	-	16	-	14,750	-	219	0.0
6500	Real estate	2	3	0.1	-	5	-	6,400	-	31	0.0
TAYLOR, GA											
60 –	**Finance, insurance, and real estate**	14	14	0.1	56	61	20,286	19,672	1,325	1,347	0.0
6400	Insurance agents, brokers, and service	3	3	0.1	4	7	8,000	11,429	104	94	0.0
6500	Real estate	4	4	0.1	3	4	13,333	9,000	39	45	0.0
TELFAIR, GA											
60 –	**Finance, insurance, and real estate**	18	18	0.1	131	125	18,015	17,312	2,484	2,399	0.0
6000	Depository institutions	5	5	0.2	66	65	18,121	18,031	1,324	1,366	0.1
6020	Commercial banks	5	5	0.3	66	65	18,121	18,031	1,324	1,366	0.1
6500	Real estate	4	4	0.1	8	11	8,000	6,545	75	64	0.0
6510	Real estate operators and lessors	4	4	0.2	8	11	8,000	6,545	75	64	0.0
TERRELL, GA											
60 –	**Finance, insurance, and real estate**	11	11	0.1	84	89	19,190	18,876	1,794	1,806	0.0
6000	Depository institutions	3	3	0.1	60	-	18,467	-	1,325	-	-
6020	Commercial banks	3	3	0.2	60	-	18,467	-	1,325	-	-
6400	Insurance agents, brokers, and service	4	4	0.1	12	14	19,333	18,000	198	248	0.0
THOMAS, GA											
60 –	**Finance, insurance, and real estate**	91	97	0.6	573	589	20,356	21,908	12,256	12,962	0.2
6000	Depository institutions	16	19	0.7	208	238	23,365	24,218	4,629	5,297	0.4
6020	Commercial banks	13	16	0.9	164	196	24,878	25,082	3,744	4,304	0.4
6100	Nondepository institutions	10	9	0.5	36	35	17,778	18,857	638	644	0.1
6140	Personal credit institutions	9	9	0.8	34	35	18,235	18,857	630	644	0.4
6200	Security and commodity brokers	4	6	0.8	18	20	34,667	41,200	684	913	0.2
6210	Security brokers and dealers	3	3	0.7	-	15	-	48,000	-	714	0.2
6280	Security and commodity services	1	3	1.0	-	5	-	20,800	-	199	-
6300	Insurance carriers	6	6	0.5	125	102	22,848	26,314	3,363	2,675	0.2
6310	Life insurance	5	6	1.3	-	102	-	26,314	-	2,675	0.4
6400	Insurance agents, brokers, and service	22	24	0.7	89	107	17,079	17,308	1,727	2,342	0.4
6500	Real estate	26	27	0.5	72	72	10,667	12,222	863	825	0.1
6510	Real estate operators and lessors	13	16	0.8	46	53	9,565	11,925	469	514	0.3
6700	Holding and other investment offices	7	6	1.0	25	15	15,840	16,000	352	266	0.1
6733	Trusts, n.e.c.	4	3	3.4	10	2	12,000	4,000	80	10	0.1
TIFT, GA											
60 –	**Finance, insurance, and real estate**	92	96	0.6	386	581	19,886	19,484	8,198	11,565	0.2
6000	Depository institutions	12	17	0.7	179	252	22,726	23,206	4,098	5,452	0.4
6100	Nondepository institutions	14	13	0.7	60	68	22,733	25,235	1,434	2,051	0.3
6300	Insurance carriers	6	4	0.3	23	45	19,130	18,489	660	793	0.1
6400	Insurance agents, brokers, and service	23	26	0.8	49	68	15,673	13,824	826	1,071	0.2
6500	Real estate	32	30	0.6	66	133	11,394	11,489	817	1,676	0.2
6510	Real estate operators and lessors	18	17	0.9	-	95	-	11,663	-	1,211	0.7
6530	Real estate agents and managers	11	11	0.4	17	-	15,529	-	359	-	-
TOOMBS, GA											
60 –	**Finance, insurance, and real estate**	46	46	0.3	263	271	23,878	23,365	6,109	6,445	0.1
6000	Depository institutions	12	10	0.4	162	142	20,469	19,296	3,218	2,938	0.2
6100	Nondepository institutions	6	7	0.4	18	18	16,667	18,444	354	303	0.0
6400	Insurance agents, brokers, and service	13	14	0.4	43	44	13,581	15,091	664	851	0.1

Source: County Business Patterns, 1992/93, CBP-92/93-1, U.S. Department of Commerce, Washington, D.C., April 1995. SIC categories for which data were suppressed or not available for both 1992 and 1993 are *not* displayed. The employment columns represent mid-March employment in the year. Pay per employee is calculated by dividing 1st Quarter payroll, annualized, by mid-March employment. The columns headed "% State" show the county's percentage of the state total for the SIC in 1993; for example, 0.9% for SIC 6030 means that the county had 0.9 percent of the state's total establishments (or payroll) in SIC 6030 in 1993. A dash (-) is used to indicate that data are not available or cannot be calculated; *nec* means not elsewhere classified.

Continued on next page.

SIC	Industry	No. Establishments			Employment		Pay / Employee		Annual Payroll ($ 000)		
		1992	1993	% State	1992	1993	1992	1993	1992	1993	% State
TOOMBS, GA - [continued]											
6500	Real estate	13	12	0.2	-	64	--	39,250	-	2,262	0.3
6510	Real estate operators and lessors	5	6	0.3	-	18	-	63,778	-	476	0.3
6530	Real estate agents and managers	3	2	0.1	3	-	8,000	-	41	-	-
TOWNS, GA											
60 –	**Finance, insurance, and real estate**	15	16	0.1	73	89	16,548	13,573	1,362	1,369	0.0
6500	Real estate	8	7	0.1	18	8	12,222	13,000	235	142	0.0
TREUTLEN, GA											
60 –	**Finance, insurance, and real estate**	7	7	0.0	34	34	15,412	16,118	700	756	0.0
TROUP, GA											
60 –	**Finance, insurance, and real estate**	106	105	0.7	789	777	26,935	24,885	20,470	20,031	0.4
6000	Depository institutions	18	20	0.8	365	396	24,811	23,101	9,161	9,226	0.7
6100	Nondepository institutions	20	18	0.9	67	55	26,209	25,818	1,754	1,424	0.2
6140	Personal credit institutions	17	15	1.4	50	47	27,840	25,787	1,199	1,163	0.7
6210	Security brokers and dealers	3	3	0.7	19	-	34,737	-	759	-	-
6300	Insurance carriers	9	7	0.6	119	91	26,185	30,418	3,373	2,863	0.2
6400	Insurance agents, brokers, and service	20	20	0.6	104	98	22,346	24,776	2,412	2,616	0.4
6500	Real estate	28	30	0.6	87	80	12,828	12,750	1,225	1,301	0.2
6510	Real estate operators and lessors	17	19	1.0	46	39	11,043	12,000	551	584	0.3
6530	Real estate agents and managers	7	9	0.4	25	-	16,000	-	458	-	-
TURNER, GA											
60 –	**Finance, insurance, and real estate**	13	12	0.1	71	68	19,437	17,118	1,665	1,412	0.0
6400	Insurance agents, brokers, and service	5	5	0.2	11	11	9,818	9,455	195	198	0.0
6500	Real estate	3	3	0.1	4	4	8,000	9,000	33	36	0.0
6510	Real estate operators and lessors	2	3	0.2	-	4	-	9,000	-	36	0.0
TWIGGS, GA											
60 –	**Finance, insurance, and real estate**	3	3	0.0	-	-	-	-	-	-	-
UNION, GA											
60 –	**Finance, insurance, and real estate**	22	22	0.1	158	160	19,013	17,500	3,346	3,669	0.1
6100	Nondepository institutions	3	2	0.1	6	-	24,000	-	82	-	-
6500	Real estate	8	10	0.2	11	15	8,364	6,933	105	121	0.0
6530	Real estate agents and managers	4	6	0.2	7	-	10,286	-	85	-	-
UPSON, GA											
60 –	**Finance, insurance, and real estate**	39	37	0.2	223	231	20,520	18,355	4,646	4,614	0.1
6000	Depository institutions	7	7	0.3	128	142	23,312	16,817	3,010	2,718	0.2
6100	Nondepository institutions	9	9	0.5	25	-	19,680	-	608	-	-
6400	Insurance agents, brokers, and service	12	11	0.3	41	41	19,415	21,463	809	857	0.1
6500	Real estate	9	8	0.2	-	16	-	9,500	-	200	0.0
6530	Real estate agents and managers	3	4	0.2	3	3	17,333	10,667	36	42	0.0
WALKER, GA											
60 –	**Finance, insurance, and real estate**	62	66	0.4	401	373	20,100	19,925	8,169	8,136	0.1
6000	Depository institutions	16	16	0.6	229	207	19,721	20,135	4,679	4,501	0.3
6020	Commercial banks	10	10	0.5	171	172	19,626	20,442	3,544	3,686	0.3
6100	Nondepository institutions	11	10	0.5	32	32	18,125	21,000	624	730	0.1
6400	Insurance agents, brokers, and service	17	19	0.6	63	75	23,810	22,080	1,698	1,974	0.3
6500	Real estate	13	17	0.3	48	55	13,333	14,473	632	771	0.1
6510	Real estate operators and lessors	6	7	0.4	12	-	11,333	-	135	-	-
6530	Real estate agents and managers	4	5	0.2	12	11	17,333	10,182	230	112	0.0
6553	Cemetery subdividers and developers	3	4	3.3	24	30	12,333	15,600	267	395	2.6

Source: County Business Patterns, 1992/93, CBP-92/93-1, U.S. Department of Commerce, Washington, D.C., April 1995. SIC categories for which data were suppressed or not available for both 1992 and 1993 are *not* displayed. The employment columns represent mid-March employment in the year. Pay per employee is calculated by dividing 1st Quarter payroll, annualized, by mid-March employment. The columns headed "% State" show the county's percentage of the state total for the SIC in 1993; for example, 0.9% for SIC 6030 means that the county had 0.9 percent of the state's total establishments (or payroll) in SIC 6030 in 1993. A dash (-) is used to indicate that data are not available or cannot be calculated; *nec* means not elsewhere classified.

SIC	Industry	No. Establishments			Employment		Pay / Employee		Annual Payroll ($ 000)		
		1992	1993	% State	1992	1993	1992	1993	1992	1993	% State
WALTON, GA											
60 –	**Finance, insurance, and real estate**	57	58	0.4	379	333	19,704	21,526	7,959	8,046	0.1
6000	Depository institutions	11	11	0.4	174	173	22,368	22,960	4,040	4,336	0.3
6020	Commercial banks	11	11	0.6	174	173	22,368	22,960	4,040	4,336	0.4
6100	Nondepository institutions	9	9	0.5	34	22	10,706	16,909	369	397	0.1
6400	Insurance agents, brokers, and service	13	15	0.5	-	39	-	19,692	-	954	0.2
6500	Real estate	19	18	0.4	69	47	8,406	8,851	707	469	0.1
6510	Real estate operators and lessors	9	10	0.5	23	34	11,304	9,294	273	343	0.2
6530	Real estate agents and managers	6	6	0.2	10	-	8,000	-	62	-	-
WARE, GA											
60 –	**Finance, insurance, and real estate**	73	78	0.5	506	521	20,964	21,152	10,729	11,339	0.2
6000	Depository institutions	17	17	0.7	226	233	20,708	20,446	4,438	4,487	0.3
6140	Personal credit institutions	9	9	0.8	-	30	-	20,667	-	646	0.4
6300	Insurance carriers	5	6	0.5	81	81	20,840	21,778	1,838	1,873	0.1
6400	Insurance agents, brokers, and service	19	20	0.6	76	71	20,211	20,620	1,411	1,478	0.3
6500	Real estate	19	21	0.4	51	73	11,686	15,342	727	1,273	0.2
6510	Real estate operators and lessors	5	8	0.4	14	13	11,143	12,308	159	192	0.1
6530	Real estate agents and managers	7	9	0.4	23	33	10,783	13,333	291	459	0.1
WARREN, GA											
60 –	**Finance, insurance, and real estate**	6	4	0.0	27	19	16,444	15,789	524	370	0.0
WASHINGTON, GA											
60 –	**Finance, insurance, and real estate**	32	31	0.2	166	158	21,518	18,861	3,452	3,383	0.1
6000	Depository institutions	6	6	0.2	98	99	20,163	19,192	1,999	2,110	0.2
6100	Nondepository institutions	7	6	0.3	24	21	24,833	18,667	552	462	0.1
6400	Insurance agents, brokers, and service	6	7	0.2	22	21	22,364	20,000	511	515	0.1
6500	Real estate	10	8	0.2	13	11	14,462	9,818	247	170	0.0
6510	Real estate operators and lessors	5	5	0.3	6	6	16,000	7,333	156	105	0.1
6530	Real estate agents and managers	4	3	0.1	6	5	14,667	12,800	89	65	0.0
WAYNE, GA											
60 –	**Finance, insurance, and real estate**	28	29	0.2	159	153	16,528	18,222	2,706	2,726	0.0
6000	Depository institutions	7	7	0.3	76	85	17,053	19,435	1,290	1,651	0.1
6100	Nondepository institutions	7	6	0.3	40	20	19,900	26,400	832	455	0.1
6140	Personal credit institutions	6	6	0.5	-	20	-	26,400	-	455	0.3
6400	Insurance agents, brokers, and service	8	10	0.3	28	42	13,714	12,762	401	535	0.1
6500	Real estate	6	5	0.1	15	-	10,133	-	183	-	-
6530	Real estate agents and managers	2	3	0.1	-	4	-	7,000	-	22	0.0
WEBSTER, GA											
60 –	**Finance, insurance, and real estate**	2	2	0.0	-	-	-	-	-	-	-
WHEELER, GA											
60 –	**Finance, insurance, and real estate**	4	3	0.0	-	-	-	-	-	-	-
WHITE, GA											
60 –	**Finance, insurance, and real estate**	30	29	0.2	248	276	17,919	15,464	4,723	4,049	0.1
6000	Depository institutions	6	6	0.2	97	94	20,247	24,511	2,037	2,485	0.2
6020	Commercial banks	5	6	0.3	-	94	-	24,511	-	2,485	0.2
6400	Insurance agents, brokers, and service	5	5	0.2	14	12	10,000	11,000	129	159	0.0
6500	Real estate	16	15	0.3	125	101	17,248	13,545	2,472	1,245	0.2
6530	Real estate agents and managers	10	11	0.4	-	64	-	12,188	-	892	0.2
WHITFIELD, GA											
60 –	**Finance, insurance, and real estate**	164	152	1.0	1,185	1,120	21,752	23,132	27,788	29,212	0.5
6000	Depository institutions	20	20	0.8	518	391	20,772	24,143	11,256	11,990	0.9
6100	Nondepository institutions	28	25	1.3	127	119	22,898	24,000	3,067	2,984	0.5

Source: County Business Patterns, 1992/93, CBP-92/93-1, U.S. Department of Commerce, Washington, D.C., April 1995. SIC categories for which data were suppressed or not available for both 1992 and 1993 are *not* displayed. The employment columns represent mid-March employment in the year. Pay per employee is calculated by dividing 1st Quarter payroll, annualized, by mid-March employment. The columns headed "% State" show the county's percentage of the state total for the SIC in 1993; for example, 0.9% for SIC 6030 means that the county had 0.9 percent of the state's total establishments (or payroll) in SIC 6030 in 1993. A dash (-) is used to indicate that data are not available or cannot be calculated; *nec* means not elsewhere classified.

Continued on next page.

SIC	Industry	No. Establishments			Employment		Pay / Employee		Annual Payroll ($ 000)		
		1992	1993	% State	1992	1993	1992	1993	1992	1993	% State
WHITFIELD, GA - [continued]											
6140	Personal credit institutions	21	19	*1.7*	100	76	20,000	19,684	1,850	1,525	*1.0*
6160	Mortgage bankers and brokers	5	4	*0.7*	22	-	36,000	-	1,073	-	-
6200	Security and commodity brokers	6	4	*0.6*	18	18	49,111	61,556	1,003	1,071	*0.2*
6210	Security brokers and dealers	5	4	*1.0*	-	18	-	61,556	-	1,071	*0.3*
6300	Insurance carriers	14	14	*1.2*	52	59	45,385	49,898	2,714	2,673	*0.2*
6370	Pension, health, and welfare funds	4	5	*3.4*	8	-	17,500	-	137	-	-
6400	Insurance agents, brokers, and service	34	34	*1.0*	111	125	26,811	25,664	3,434	3,600	*0.6*
6500	Real estate	53	47	*0.9*	135	159	15,200	14,868	2,454	2,666	*0.3*
6510	Real estate operators and lessors	32	26	*1.3*	69	79	13,623	13,114	1,059	1,020	*0.6*
6530	Real estate agents and managers	14	17	*0.7*	33	36	17,333	17,667	640	795	*0.2*
6700	Holding and other investment offices	9	8	*1.4*	224	249	17,125	16,016	3,860	4,228	*1.3*
6710	Holding offices	5	4	*1.8*	207	234	17,237	15,897	3,453	3,560	*1.6*
WILCOX, GA											
60 –	**Finance, insurance, and real estate**	11	10	*0.1*	52	43	17,077	20,279	1,036	963	*0.0*
6000	Depository institutions	8	8	*0.3*	47	-	17,957	-	980	-	-
WILKES, GA											
60 –	**Finance, insurance, and real estate**	17	19	*0.1*	92	98	20,522	19,020	1,943	2,021	*0.0*
6000	Depository institutions	3	3	*0.1*	56	60	23,500	21,333	1,354	1,372	*0.1*
6100	Nondepository institutions	5	5	*0.3*	13	13	20,923	20,923	286	302	*0.0*
6400	Insurance agents, brokers, and service	5	7	*0.2*	16	16	16,250	16,500	262	302	*0.1*
WILKINSON, GA											
60 –	**Finance, insurance, and real estate**	8	8	*0.1*	57	61	20,702	18,098	1,219	1,188	*0.0*
6000	Depository institutions	5	5	*0.2*	51	53	21,020	18,491	1,101	1,047	*0.1*
WORTH, GA											
60 –	**Finance, insurance, and real estate**	25	24	*0.2*	136	129	19,559	18,822	2,957	2,876	*0.1*
6000	Depository institutions	6	4	*0.2*	71	68	21,239	21,765	1,542	1,599	*0.1*
6020	Commercial banks	6	4	*0.2*	71	68	21,239	21,765	1,542	1,599	*0.1*
6100	Nondepository institutions	5	4	*0.2*	18	12	16,889	16,667	296	174	*0.0*
6140	Personal credit institutions	5	4	*0.4*	18	12	16,889	16,667	296	174	*0.1*
6400	Insurance agents, brokers, and service	6	6	*0.2*	39	-	20,000	-	1,027	-	-
6500	Real estate	8	9	*0.2*	8	11	8,500	4,364	92	81	*0.0*
6510	Real estate operators and lessors	5	6	*0.3*	5	6	6,400	6,000	33	32	*0.0*

Source: County Business Patterns, 1992/93, CBP-92/93-1, U.S. Department of Commerce, Washington, D.C., April 1995. SIC categories for which data were suppressed or not available for both 1992 and 1993 are *not* displayed. The employment columns represent mid-March employment in the year. Pay per employee is calculated by dividing 1st Quarter payroll, annualized, by mid-March employment. The columns headed "% State" show the county's percentage of the state total for the SIC in 1993; for example, 0.9% for SIC 6030 means that the county had 0.9 percent of the state's total establishments (or payroll) in SIC 6030 in 1993. A dash (-) is used to indicate that data are not available or cannot be calculated; *nec* means not elsewhere classified.

HAWAII

SIC	Industry	No. Establishments			Employment		Pay / Employee		Annual Payroll ($ 000)		
		1992	1993	% State	1992	1993	1992	1993	1992	1993	% State
HAWAII, HI											
60 –	**Finance, insurance, and real estate**	399	388	9.6	3,119	3,243	24,235	24,736	76,079	82,311	6.8
6000	Depository institutions	59	63	11.5	659	825	21,724	23,137	14,450	18,241	5.0
6020	Commercial banks	22	28	11.1	346	366	20,647	22,481	7,260	8,336	3.2
6030	Savings institutions	21	14	11.7	108	-	21,074	-	2,431	-	-
6060	Credit unions	13	18	13.3	-	231	-	21,143	-	4,962	16.2
6100	Nondepository institutions	29	22	9.7	220	97	31,364	43,052	6,249	4,613	5.6
6160	Mortgage bankers and brokers	7	10	9.4	47	58	66,383	52,897	2,392	3,564	5.4
6200	Security and commodity brokers	7	7	8.6	29	-	83,586	-	2,253	-	-
6300	Insurance carriers	14	10	4.1	83	77	25,446	28,623	2,429	2,195	1.4
6330	Fire, marine, and casualty insurance	5	3	5.9	25	-	43,520	-	1,220	-	-
6400	Insurance agents, brokers, and service	36	34	9.4	158	159	25,215	25,308	3,859	4,214	4.6
6500	Real estate	241	241	10.1	1,914	2,004	23,331	23,595	45,367	49,436	12.0
6530	Real estate agents and managers	133	148	9.5	919	642	22,538	19,421	20,247	13,651	6.4
6700	Holding and other investment offices	13	11	6.2	56	-	21,357	-	1,472	-	-
HONOLULU, HI											
60 –	**Finance, insurance, and real estate**	2,998	3,052	75.6	32,448	32,322	28,348	29,057	940,080	1,006,425	83.7
6000	Depository institutions	368	387	70.9	10,376	10,760	29,229	30,625	940,080	1,006,425	83.7
6020	Commercial banks	141	179	70.8	7,074	7,753	30,993	31,602	210,121	241,008	92.6
6030	Savings institutions	125	86	71.7	2,195	1,501	26,850	27,909	58,678	45,809	88.3
6060	Credit unions	73	92	68.1	730	840	22,471	24,171	17,067	21,431	70.1
6080	Foreign bank and branches and agencies	3	3	100.0	24	24	43,667	45,500	1,107	1,123	100.0
6090	Functions closely related to banking	26	27	77.1	353	642	21,654	33,072	7,929	19,221	86.3
6100	Nondepository institutions	186	167	73.6	1,620	1,368	36,605	41,181	66,966	69,433	84.5
6160	Mortgage bankers and brokers	56	74	69.8	705	893	47,296	47,901	41,037	55,419	84.5
6210	Security brokers and dealers	33	31	75.6	451	519	68,266	57,156	28,436	28,682	86.3
6280	Security and commodity services	35	34	89.5	81	127	38,025	41,102	4,772	6,229	-
6300	Insurance carriers	270	219	89.4	4,957	4,886	27,177	27,622	143,601	154,055	97.0
6370	Pension, health, and welfare funds	146	109	97.3	437	403	16,998	13,300	9,022	8,649	99.5
6400	Insurance agents, brokers, and service	280	295	81.5	2,381	2,553	32,277	31,353	72,988	84,234	92.5
6500	Real estate	1,640	1,760	73.7	11,150	11,032	23,196	23,550	273,055	286,249	69.4
6510	Real estate operators and lessors	510	535	79.0	2,492	2,577	22,575	23,246	55,697	62,672	60.0
6530	Real estate agents and managers	856	1,127	72.0	6,101	6,323	21,910	22,321	146,667	161,975	76.5
6552	Subdividers and developers, n.e.c.	94	70	68.6	1,547	1,331	26,924	28,322	43,091	38,727	58.2
6553	Cemetery subdividers and developers	9	11	57.9	-	276	-	20,217	-	6,297	49.8
6700	Holding and other investment offices	177	150	84.7	1,245	943	34,368	39,919	45,888	41,532	93.0
6710	Holding offices	38	37	94.9	490	-	45,159	-	24,073	-	-
6720	Investment offices	7	3	100.0	-	7	-	18,286	-	160	100.0
6732	Educational, religious, etc. trusts	18	15	78.9	198	186	19,051	23,161	4,303	4,331	89.0
6733	Trusts, n.e.c.	79	56	80.0	301	-	23,243	-	6,866	-	-
6794	Patent owners and lessors	6	5	100.0	-	34	-	13,176	-	527	100.0
6799	Investors, n.e.c.	19	28	84.8	155	-	41,058	-	7,150	-	-
KAUAI, HI											
60 –	**Finance, insurance, and real estate**	177	179	4.4	-	-	-	-	-	-	-
6000	Depository institutions	29	36	6.6	248	319	19,419	22,182	4,992	7,132	1.9
6020	Commercial banks	15	18	7.1	170	171	18,588	20,772	3,298	3,601	1.4
6030	Savings institutions	9	6	5.0	45	36	21,689	27,444	1,010	965	1.9
6060	Credit unions	5	12	8.9	33	112	20,606	22,643	684	2,566	8.4
6100	Nondepository institutions	24	14	6.2	195	45	31,385	33,600	5,353	1,419	1.7
6160	Mortgage bankers and brokers	10	8	7.5	96	25	38,000	38,400	2,942	899	1.4

Source: County Business Patterns, 1992/93, CBP-92/93-1, U.S. Department of Commerce, Washington, D.C., April 1995. SIC categories for which data were suppressed or not available for both 1992 and 1993 are *not* displayed. The employment columns represent mid-March employment in the year. Pay per employee is calculated by dividing 1st Quarter payroll, annualized, by mid-March employment. The columns headed "% State" show the county's percentage of the state total for the SIC in 1993; for example, 0.9% for SIC 6030 means that the county had 0.9 percent of the state's total establishments (or payroll) in SIC 6030 in 1993. A dash (-) is used to indicate that data are not available or cannot be calculated; *nec* means not elsewhere classified.

Continued on next page.

SIC	Industry	No. Establishments			Employment		Pay / Employee		Annual Payroll ($ 000)		
		1992	1993	% State	1992	1993	1992	1993	1992	1993	% State
KAUAI, HI - [continued]											
6300	Insurance carriers	5	6	2.4	35	-	22,286	-	847	-	-
6400	Insurance agents, brokers, and service	14	13	3.6	44	51	26,364	15,686	1,115	870	1.0
6500	Real estate	95	101	4.2	-	779	-	22,300	-	19,328	4.7
6510	Real estate operators and lessors	19	21	3.1	179	-	16,067	-	2,899	-	-
6530	Real estate agents and managers	53	69	4.4	428	359	13,421	20,869	6,322	8,185	3.9
MAUI, HI											
60 –	**Finance, insurance, and real estate**	408	415	10.3	3,166	3,533	22,946	21,926	73,630	83,065	6.9
6000	Depository institutions	54	60	11.0	486	543	20,996	22,004	10,533	12,023	3.3
6020	Commercial banks	23	28	11.1	309	335	20,595	21,863	6,634	7,231	2.8
6030	Savings institutions	18	14	11.7	124	-	21,419	-	2,684	-	-
6060	Credit unions	9	13	9.6	-	66	-	24,970	-	1,601	5.2
6100	Nondepository institutions	29	24	10.6	194	138	42,825	37,101	7,739	6,710	8.2
6160	Mortgage bankers and brokers	13	14	13.2	129	101	51,008	40,040	5,989	5,695	8.7
6300	Insurance carriers	12	9	3.7	55	-	37,236	-	2,080	-	-
6400	Insurance agents, brokers, and service	18	20	5.5	75	76	22,293	20,895	1,755	1,722	1.9
6500	Real estate	276	286	12.0	2,258	2,638	20,843	20,573	48,497	57,533	13.9
6510	Real estate operators and lessors	50	50	7.4	707	1,038	22,263	23,087	15,878	26,079	25.0
6530	Real estate agents and managers	185	222	14.2	1,109	1,432	19,528	18,978	23,035	28,006	13.2
6552	Subdividers and developers, n.e.c.	13	9	8.8	372	-	22,892	-	8,504	-	-
6700	Holding and other investment offices	14	11	6.2	-	68	-	23,471	-	1,602	3.6
6732	Educational, religious, etc. trusts	5	3	15.8	28	-	19,286	-	461	-	-
6733	Trusts, n.e.c.	5	4	5.7	29	-	29,793	-	785	-	-

Source: County Business Patterns, 1992/93, CBP-92/93-1, U.S. Department of Commerce, Washington, D.C., April 1995. SIC categories for which data were suppressed or not available for both 1992 and 1993 are *not* displayed. The employment columns represent mid-March employment in the year. Pay per employee is calculated by dividing 1st Quarter payroll, annualized, by mid-March employment. The columns headed "% State" show the county's percentage of the state total for the SIC in 1993; for example, 0.9% for SIC 6030 means that the county had 0.9 percent of the state's total establishments (or payroll) in SIC 6030 in 1993. A dash (-) is used to indicate that data are not available or cannot be calculated; *nec* means not elsewhere classified.

IDAHO

SIC	Industry	No. Establishments			Employment		Pay / Employee		Annual Payroll ($ 000)		
		1992	1993	% State	1992	1993	1992	1993	1992	1993	% State
ADA, ID											
60 –	**Finance, insurance, and real estate**	725	770	30.5	8,031	8,520	24,364	24,791	199,697	223,371	50.0
6000	Depository institutions	107	118	24.3	3,857	3,661	24,155	25,470	89,391	95,237	52.8
6020	Commercial banks	69	79	24.5	3,457	3,254	24,810	26,320	82,799	88,248	56.5
6060	Credit unions	24	26	22.2	290	302	17,076	16,689	4,006	4,239	31.2
6100	Nondepository institutions	54	71	39.9	478	585	29,372	31,658	16,229	19,477	58.2
6140	Personal credit institutions	28	25	36.2	128	133	28,188	24,602	3,478	3,171	40.5
6150	Business credit institutions	4	7	50.0	20	18	21,000	34,444	476	985	-
6160	Mortgage bankers and brokers	22	39	51.3	330	434	30,339	33,705	12,275	15,321	76.4
6200	Security and commodity brokers	38	39	32.8	229	258	59,459	50,341	13,544	13,854	52.3
6210	Security brokers and dealers	25	23	27.4	194	213	60,412	52,207	11,295	11,407	50.3
6300	Insurance carriers	96	77	45.3	1,429	1,495	25,450	24,658	36,201	37,578	53.2
6310	Life insurance	33	23	62.2	567	337	21,728	23,739	12,399	7,955	57.5
6330	Fire, marine, and casualty insurance	45	39	43.8	324	332	30,407	32,735	9,925	11,559	40.5
6370	Pension, health, and welfare funds	7	3	20.0	26	-	12,308	-	335	-	-
6400	Insurance agents, brokers, and service	163	168	29.5	732	846	22,885	24,567	17,631	21,939	35.9
6500	Real estate	244	270	28.9	1,206	1,541	15,111	15,512	23,038	30,071	44.8
6510	Real estate operators and lessors	72	75	26.5	236	291	13,322	14,405	3,508	5,235	35.3
6530	Real estate agents and managers	102	145	28.3	412	840	15,291	14,281	8,381	14,949	47.2
6540	Title abstract offices	7	8	19.5	196	195	20,714	20,656	5,298	5,371	40.7
6552	Subdividers and developers, n.e.c.	26	30	48.4	55	86	28,800	28,279	2,100	3,177	57.3
6553	Cemetery subdividers and developers	1	3	13.0	-	12	-	12,000	-	221	29.5
6700	Holding and other investment offices	20	24	35.3	76	92	19,895	26,870	1,550	2,658	49.3
6733	Trusts, n.e.c.	6	6	42.9	28	-	16,429	-	407	-	-
ADAMS, ID											
60 –	**Finance, insurance, and real estate**	7	7	0.3	16	-	13,250	-	238	-	-
6500	Real estate	3	4	0.4	-	8	-	14,000	-	125	0.2
BANNOCK, ID											
60 –	**Finance, insurance, and real estate**	154	153	6.1	1,649	1,507	18,139	22,447	30,786	34,760	7.8
6000	Depository institutions	34	33	6.8	370	365	19,730	20,559	7,475	8,501	4.7
6020	Commercial banks	20	19	5.9	245	234	20,571	21,846	5,133	5,953	3.8
6100	Nondepository institutions	13	11	6.2	58	63	23,517	28,952	1,283	1,549	4.6
6140	Personal credit institutions	8	6	8.7	37	34	18,811	20,000	671	691	8.8
6200	Security and commodity brokers	7	7	5.9	35	49	42,400	30,857	1,469	1,927	7.3
6210	Security brokers and dealers	4	6	7.1	25	-	56,800	-	1,417	-	-
6280	Security and commodity services	3	1	3.3	10	-	6,400	-	52	-	-
6300	Insurance carriers	23	18	10.6	868	669	17,447	25,979	15,172	16,326	23.1
6330	Fire, marine, and casualty insurance	9	9	10.1	735	565	16,060	26,535	11,809	13,993	49.1
6400	Insurance agents, brokers, and service	24	28	4.9	83	105	16,289	16,457	1,345	1,752	2.9
6500	Real estate	45	50	5.3	221	239	13,647	15,046	3,638	4,355	6.5
6510	Real estate operators and lessors	14	15	5.3	57	-	9,825	-	595	-	-
6530	Real estate agents and managers	22	28	5.5	68	77	12,882	12,831	1,020	1,258	4.0
6700	Holding and other investment offices	8	6	8.8	14	17	18,000	16,706	404	350	6.5
BEAR LAKE, ID											
60 –	**Finance, insurance, and real estate**	9	9	0.4	77	85	11,636	10,071	1,005	1,067	0.2
6000	Depository institutions	3	3	0.6	39	34	14,051	13,294	541	511	0.3
6020	Commercial banks	3	3	0.9	39	34	14,051	13,294	541	511	0.3

Source: County Business Patterns, 1992/93, CBP-92/93-1, U.S. Department of Commerce, Washington, D.C., April 1995. SIC categories for which data were suppressed or not available for both 1992 and 1993 are *not* displayed. The employment columns represent mid-March employment in the year. Pay per employee is calculated by dividing 1st Quarter payroll, annualized, by mid-March employment. The columns headed "% State" show the county's percentage of the state total for the SIC in 1993; for example, 0.9% for SIC 6030 means that the county had 0.9 percent of the state's total establishments (or payroll) in SIC 6030 in 1993. A dash (-) is used to indicate that data are not available or cannot be calculated; *nec* means not elsewhere classified.

SIC	Industry	No. Establishments			Employment		Pay / Employee		Annual Payroll ($ 000)		
		1992	1993	% State	1992	1993	1992	1993	1992	1993	% State
BENEWAH, ID											
60 –	**Finance, insurance, and real estate**	17	17	0.7	71	62	13,014	15,097	1,032	1,036	0.2
6000	Depository institutions	4	4	0.8	31	31	17,290	18,065	613	609	0.3
6400	Insurance agents, brokers, and service	5	6	1.1	-	16	-	9,250	-	162	0.3
6500	Real estate	6	7	0.7	20	15	11,200	15,200	247	265	0.4
BINGHAM, ID											
60 –	**Finance, insurance, and real estate**	45	41	1.6	188	188	18,128	19,064	3,498	3,694	0.8
6000	Depository institutions	14	15	3.1	111	119	18,162	17,378	1,867	1,985	1.1
6020	Commercial banks	7	7	2.2	84	85	18,238	17,835	1,290	1,325	0.8
6100	Nondepository institutions	5	3	1.7	22	18	28,000	31,111	638	564	1.7
6400	Insurance agents, brokers, and service	9	10	1.8	26	37	15,846	18,811	552	840	1.4
6500	Real estate	11	10	1.1	18	11	4,222	12,000	105	135	0.2
6530	Real estate agents and managers	4	6	1.2	2	6	10,000	16,667	28	99	0.3
BLAINE, ID											
60 –	**Finance, insurance, and real estate**	93	105	4.2	413	405	20,484	18,736	9,163	9,351	2.1
6000	Depository institutions	10	8	1.6	92	60	24,304	24,400	2,215	1,525	0.8
6100	Nondepository institutions	6	11	6.2	-	14	-	17,714	-	456	1.4
6300	Insurance carriers	4	1	0.6	33	-	18,061	-	675	-	-
6400	Insurance agents, brokers, and service	6	11	1.9	-	55	-	19,273	-	1,265	2.1
6500	Real estate	54	59	6.3	211	247	17,024	14,818	4,445	4,703	7.0
6510	Real estate operators and lessors	7	15	5.3	8	-	12,500	-	155	-	-
6530	Real estate agents and managers	31	38	7.4	102	186	21,725	14,667	2,324	3,575	11.3
6552	Subdividers and developers, n.e.c.	3	3	4.8	-	1	-	52,000	-	108	1.9
6700	Holding and other investment offices	9	9	13.2	28	11	21,429	24,364	372	296	5.5
BOISE, ID											
60 –	**Finance, insurance, and real estate**	3	3	0.1	-	6	-	4,000	-	36	0.0
6500	Real estate	2	3	0.3	-	6	-	4,000	-	36	0.1
BONNER, ID											
60 –	**Finance, insurance, and real estate**	73	80	3.2	376	400	16,372	16,950	6,711	7,659	1.7
6000	Depository institutions	11	9	1.9	116	101	21,517	23,644	2,484	2,279	1.3
6020	Commercial banks	8	6	1.9	107	93	21,981	24,129	2,321	2,127	1.4
6100	Nondepository institutions	3	4	2.2	4	-	11,000	-	57	-	-
6200	Security and commodity brokers	6	6	5.0	6	9	21,333	33,778	217	233	0.9
6400	Insurance agents, brokers, and service	7	9	1.6	-	63	-	15,619	-	1,202	2.0
6500	Real estate	42	50	5.3	208	221	12,981	13,810	3,072	3,767	5.6
6510	Real estate operators and lessors	12	12	4.2	58	65	21,724	21,662	1,195	1,454	9.8
6530	Real estate agents and managers	24	32	6.3	140	143	9,257	10,210	1,697	2,014	6.4
6552	Subdividers and developers, n.e.c.	4	4	6.5	2	-	6,000	-	36	-	-
BONNEVILLE, ID											
60 –	**Finance, insurance, and real estate**	182	181	7.2	1,118	1,173	21,546	21,555	24,877	27,993	6.3
6000	Depository institutions	38	38	7.8	543	566	19,396	20,212	10,679	12,540	7.0
6020	Commercial banks	25	26	8.1	387	408	21,147	21,951	8,193	9,889	6.3
6100	Nondepository institutions	16	17	9.6	117	128	26,667	26,062	3,151	3,457	10.3
6140	Personal credit institutions	10	10	14.5	69	64	24,232	24,500	1,633	1,552	19.8
6200	Security and commodity brokers	9	9	7.6	51	61	50,588	45,311	2,549	3,005	11.3
6400	Insurance agents, brokers, and service	39	47	8.2	193	222	23,212	20,631	4,803	5,246	8.6
6500	Real estate	61	57	6.1	145	161	11,310	12,075	1,910	2,445	3.6
6510	Real estate operators and lessors	17	20	7.1	40	53	9,000	8,528	408	536	3.6
6530	Real estate agents and managers	32	33	6.4	64	89	11,625	13,124	941	1,533	4.8
6552	Subdividers and developers, n.e.c.	3	2	3.2	10	-	8,800	-	113	-	-

Source: County Business Patterns, 1992/93, CBP-92/93-1, U.S. Department of Commerce, Washington, D.C., April 1995. SIC categories for which data were suppressed or not available for both 1992 and 1993 are *not* displayed. The employment columns represent mid-March employment in the year. Pay per employee is calculated by dividing 1st Quarter payroll, annualized, by mid-March employment. The columns headed "% State" show the county's percentage of the state total for the SIC in 1993; for example, 0.9% for SIC 6030 means that the county had 0.9 percent of the state's total establishments (or payroll) in SIC 6030 in 1993. A dash (-) is used to indicate that data are not available or cannot be calculated; *nec* means not elsewhere classified.

SIC	Industry	No. Establishments			Employment		Pay / Employee		Annual Payroll ($ 000)		
		1992	1993	% State	1992	1993	1992	1993	1992	1993	% State
BOUNDARY, ID											
60 –	**Finance, insurance, and real estate**	15	16	0.6	63	56	14,159	15,000	986	935	0.2
6500	Real estate	7	9	1.0	18	-	9,333	-	196	-	-
6530	Real estate agents and managers	3	6	1.2	3	11	9,333	10,182	35	130	0.4
BUTTE, ID											
60 –	**Finance, insurance, and real estate**	4	4	0.2	17	14	15,765	17,714	267	269	0.1
CAMAS, ID											
60 –	**Finance, insurance, and real estate**	1	1	0.0	-	-	-	-	-	-	-
CANYON, ID											
60 –	**Finance, insurance, and real estate**	145	159	6.3	916	977	20,135	20,639	19,523	21,868	4.9
6000	Depository institutions	33	34	7.0	340	346	20,776	21,376	7,296	8,416	4.7
6020	Commercial banks	16	16	5.0	238	227	20,370	21,586	4,812	5,439	3.5
6100	Nondepository institutions	11	9	5.1	84	76	24,810	30,211	2,092	2,083	6.2
6140	Personal credit institutions	8	5	7.2	43	-	17,116	-	789	-	-
6300	Insurance carriers	13	11	6.5	134	112	27,761	29,536	3,940	3,290	4.7
6400	Insurance agents, brokers, and service	41	42	7.4	110	158	14,000	16,506	1,681	3,144	5.1
6500	Real estate	38	53	5.7	208	264	13,673	13,333	3,038	3,728	5.6
6510	Real estate operators and lessors	16	23	8.1	167	193	13,916	12,207	2,421	2,438	16.4
6530	Real estate agents and managers	15	27	5.3	21	42	13,905	13,905	334	675	2.1
CARIBOU, ID											
60 –	**Finance, insurance, and real estate**	13	13	0.5	-	-	-	-	-	-	-
6400	Insurance agents, brokers, and service	4	4	0.7	9	-	12,444	-	116	-	-
6500	Real estate	4	5	0.5	9	10	8,444	10,000	119	144	0.2
CASSIA, ID											
60 –	**Finance, insurance, and real estate**	42	39	1.5	224	226	17,929	18,496	4,568	5,091	1.1
6000	Depository institutions	13	15	3.1	128	127	18,250	18,551	2,575	2,877	1.6
6020	Commercial banks	9	9	2.8	115	112	18,122	18,143	2,360	2,610	1.7
6140	Personal credit institutions	3	2	2.9	8	-	20,500	-	166	-	-
6400	Insurance agents, brokers, and service	7	7	1.2	24	54	11,167	15,259	267	1,147	1.9
6500	Real estate	14	10	1.1	50	26	15,120	11,538	1,016	328	0.5
6510	Real estate operators and lessors	4	3	1.1	-	11	-	6,182	-	85	0.6
6530	Real estate agents and managers	8	6	1.2	12	-	17,333	-	226	-	-
CLARK, ID											
60 –	**Finance, insurance, and real estate**	3	3	0.1	8	-	10,500	-	85	-	-
CLEARWATER, ID											
60 –	**Finance, insurance, and real estate**	15	15	0.6	60	73	13,067	11,397	829	939	0.2
6000	Depository institutions	6	6	1.2	38	37	15,579	16,000	603	638	0.4
6400	Insurance agents, brokers, and service	5	5	0.9	19	28	8,842	7,429	198	259	0.4
6500	Real estate	4	4	0.4	3	8	8,000	4,000	28	42	0.1
CUSTER, ID											
60 –	**Finance, insurance, and real estate**	7	7	0.3	-	25	-	15,360	-	433	0.1
6000	Depository institutions	3	3	0.6	22	18	16,000	18,444	345	346	0.2
ELMORE, ID											
60 –	**Finance, insurance, and real estate**	35	38	1.5	183	195	13,858	14,133	2,694	2,995	0.7
6000	Depository institutions	9	9	1.9	93	89	17,247	17,753	1,611	1,662	0.9
6020	Commercial banks	4	4	1.2	51	-	19,137	-	952	-	-
6300	Insurance carriers	3	-	-	10	-	16,800	-	236	-	-

Source: County Business Patterns, 1992/93, CBP-92/93-1, U.S. Department of Commerce, Washington, D.C., April 1995. SIC categories for which data were suppressed or not available for both 1992 and 1993 are not displayed. The employment columns represent mid-March employment in the year. Pay per employee is calculated by dividing 1st Quarter payroll, annualized, by mid-March employment. The columns headed "% State" show the county's percentage of the state total for the SIC in 1993; for example, 0.9% for SIC 6030 means that the county had 0.9 percent of the state's total establishments (or payroll) in SIC 6030 in 1993. A dash (-) is used to indicate that data are not available or cannot be calculated; nec means not elsewhere classified.

Continued on next page.

SIC	Industry	No. Establishments			Employment		Pay / Employee		Annual Payroll ($ 000)		
		1992	1993	% State	1992	1993	1992	1993	1992	1993	% State
ELMORE, ID - [continued]											
6400	Insurance agents, brokers, and service	10	15	2.6	17	41	9,647	12,976	197	595	1.0
6500	Real estate	8	8	0.9	51	55	6,510	7,491	385	428	0.6
6530	Real estate agents and managers	5	7	1.4	12	-	11,333	-	158	-	-
FRANKLIN, ID											
60 –	**Finance, insurance, and real estate**	10	10	0.4	-	-	-	-	-	-	-
6400	Insurance agents, brokers, and service	3	3	0.5	7	9	11,429	11,111	97	102	0.2
6500	Real estate	4	4	0.4	9	11	8,444	10,182	79	123	0.2
FREMONT, ID											
60 –	**Finance, insurance, and real estate**	11	10	0.4	-	67	-	14,746	-	1,101	0.2
6000	Depository institutions	4	4	0.8	28	28	18,286	17,714	499	540	0.3
6400	Insurance agents, brokers, and service	5	4	0.7	8	-	13,000	-	140	-	-
GEM, ID											
60 –	**Finance, insurance, and real estate**	17	17	0.7	64	65	14,250	15,200	1,017	1,100	0.2
6400	Insurance agents, brokers, and service	6	6	1.1	12	15	8,667	10,133	118	173	0.3
6500	Real estate	4	4	0.4	8	8	11,500	13,000	98	105	0.2
GOODING, ID											
60 –	**Finance, insurance, and real estate**	18	16	0.6	81	68	15,753	14,588	1,310	1,126	0.3
6000	Depository institutions	6	5	1.0	46	-	20,261	-	896	-	-
6020	Commercial banks	6	5	1.6	46	-	20,261	-	896	-	-
6400	Insurance agents, brokers, and service	6	6	1.1	19	19	11,368	11,368	216	240	0.4
6500	Real estate	3	4	0.4	-	10	-	5,600	-	92	0.1
IDAHO, ID											
60 –	**Finance, insurance, and real estate**	21	19	0.8	120	106	12,500	13,547	1,626	1,689	0.4
6000	Depository institutions	8	8	1.6	64	62	14,438	14,129	1,020	1,074	0.6
6400	Insurance agents, brokers, and service	7	5	0.9	37	-	8,432	-	296	-	-
6500	Real estate	3	4	0.4	8	16	12,000	12,250	134	233	0.3
JEFFERSON, ID											
60 –	**Finance, insurance, and real estate**	17	17	0.7	86	66	17,674	17,455	1,223	1,305	0.3
6000	Depository institutions	4	5	1.0	35	-	20,571	-	714	-	-
6020	Commercial banks	4	4	1.2	35	38	20,571	20,211	714	816	0.5
6400	Insurance agents, brokers, and service	4	4	0.7	6	11	14,667	16,364	109	170	0.3
6500	Real estate	6	7	0.7	35	14	15,429	7,429	238	200	0.3
6553	Cemetery subdividers and developers	2	4	17.4	-	6	-	4,667	-	33	4.4
JEROME, ID											
60 –	**Finance, insurance, and real estate**	17	15	0.6	69	63	16,406	18,921	1,162	1,314	0.3
6000	Depository institutions	5	5	1.0	44	39	18,000	19,282	753	793	0.4
6400	Insurance agents, brokers, and service	4	5	0.9	-	18	-	16,889	-	268	0.4
6500	Real estate	4	3	0.3	6	-	7,333	-	111	-	-
KOOTENAI, ID											
60 –	**Finance, insurance, and real estate**	203	234	9.3	1,065	1,136	25,007	21,109	25,023	27,051	6.1
6000	Depository institutions	30	27	5.6	463	341	27,421	23,367	9,913	8,689	4.8
6020	Commercial banks	26	21	6.5	449	319	27,786	23,900	9,513	7,934	5.1
6100	Nondepository institutions	13	16	9.0	-	60	-	23,667	-	1,830	5.5
6140	Personal credit institutions	6	6	8.7	-	23	-	25,043	-	535	6.8
6200	Security and commodity brokers	8	9	7.6	37	40	47,459	53,800	1,807	2,481	9.4
6300	Insurance carriers	15	13	7.6	102	68	21,333	17,471	2,664	1,422	2.0
6370	Pension, health, and welfare funds	5	4	26.7	41	-	14,732	-	614	-	-
6400	Insurance agents, brokers, and service	39	43	7.5	105	224	23,886	19,304	2,542	4,765	7.8
6500	Real estate	92	116	12.4	290	370	20,883	16,800	6,388	7,146	10.6
6510	Real estate operators and lessors	25	26	9.2	72	-	9,167	-	903	-	-

Source: County Business Patterns, 1992/93, CBP-92/93-1, U.S. Department of Commerce, Washington, D.C., April 1995. SIC categories for which data were suppressed or not available for both 1992 and 1993 are not displayed. The employment columns represent mid-March employment in the year. Pay per employee is calculated by dividing 1st Quarter payroll, annualized, by mid-March employment. The columns headed "% State" show the county's percentage of the state total for the SIC in 1993; for example, 0.9% for SIC 6030 means that the county had 0.9 percent of the state's total establishments (or payroll) in SIC 6030 in 1993. A dash (-) is used to indicate that data are not available or cannot be calculated; nec means not elsewhere classified.

Continued on next page.

SIC	Industry	No. Establishments			Employment		Pay / Employee		Annual Payroll ($ 000)		
		1992	1993	% State	1992	1993	1992	1993	1992	1993	% State
KOOTENAI, ID - [continued]											
6530	Real estate agents and managers	44	73	14.3	107	167	17,234	14,587	2,255	3,041	9.6
6552	Subdividers and developers, n.e.c.	7	13	21.0	34	-	59,059	-	1,174	-	-
6700	Holding and other investment offices	6	10	14.7	-	33	-	21,576	-	718	13.3
LATAH, ID											
60 –	**Finance, insurance, and real estate**	58	66	2.6	285	297	16,126	15,811	5,024	5,588	1.2
6000	Depository institutions	16	13	2.7	153	141	17,647	18,043	2,832	2,916	1.6
6020	Commercial banks	11	10	3.1	131	-	17,191	-	2,370	-	-
6300	Insurance carriers	6	5	2.9	9	10	16,889	13,200	168	145	0.2
6330	Fire, marine, and casualty insurance	6	5	5.6	9	10	16,889	13,200	168	145	0.5
6400	Insurance agents, brokers, and service	11	15	2.6	-	57	-	12,982	-	940	1.5
6500	Real estate	23	29	3.1	70	83	13,314	12,964	1,088	1,370	2.0
6510	Real estate operators and lessors	15	17	6.0	55	50	13,527	12,640	824	756	5.1
6530	Real estate agents and managers	6	11	2.1	9	-	8,000	-	141	-	-
LEMHI, ID											
60 –	**Finance, insurance, and real estate**	11	12	0.5	50	44	16,480	15,273	815	706	0.2
6000	Depository institutions	4	3	0.6	32	-	19,250	-	606	-	-
6400	Insurance agents, brokers, and service	3	5	0.9	5	8	12,800	10,000	66	85	0.1
6500	Real estate	2	3	0.3	-	10	-	11,600	-	79	0.1
6510	Real estate operators and lessors	1	3	1.1	-	10	-	11,600	-	79	0.5
LEWIS, ID											
60 –	**Finance, insurance, and real estate**	7	8	0.3	33	33	13,333	13,455	456	480	0.1
6000	Depository institutions	5	5	1.0	-	27	-	14,667	-	429	0.2
LINCOLN, ID											
60 –	**Finance, insurance, and real estate**	3	3	0.1	8	11	17,500	14,182	134	167	0.0
MADISON, ID											
60 –	**Finance, insurance, and real estate**	33	34	1.3	166	170	14,940	15,247	3,073	3,522	0.8
6000	Depository institutions	7	9	1.9	82	95	16,780	17,221	1,900	2,412	1.3
6020	Commercial banks	5	5	1.6	-	73	-	17,479	-	2,059	1.3
6100	Nondepository institutions	5	3	1.7	24	-	19,500	-	466	-	-
6400	Insurance agents, brokers, and service	6	7	1.2	14	23	18,571	16,174	306	432	0.7
6500	Real estate	10	12	1.3	36	36	4,778	5,222	202	230	0.3
6510	Real estate operators and lessors	6	9	3.2	12	30	5,333	4,267	80	165	1.1
6530	Real estate agents and managers	4	3	0.6	24	6	4,500	10,000	122	65	0.2
MINIDOKA, ID											
60 –	**Finance, insurance, and real estate**	16	15	0.6	79	73	18,076	18,082	1,420	1,427	0.3
6000	Depository institutions	6	6	1.2	56	53	19,071	21,057	1,056	1,174	0.7
6400	Insurance agents, brokers, and service	7	6	1.1	18	16	18,444	11,750	323	232	0.4
NEZ PERCE, ID											
60 –	**Finance, insurance, and real estate**	99	102	4.0	848	997	23,623	24,879	21,034	25,295	5.7
6000	Depository institutions	19	21	4.3	212	233	22,623	24,515	4,784	5,826	3.2
6020	Commercial banks	11	10	3.1	140	123	23,314	27,154	3,079	3,158	2.0
6100	Nondepository institutions	7	5	2.8	39	20	20,000	28,600	836	551	1.6
6200	Security and commodity brokers	9	6	5.0	26	22	34,000	44,182	929	1,106	4.2
6300	Insurance carriers	9	9	5.3	243	255	25,119	26,259	6,298	7,237	10.3
6400	Insurance agents, brokers, and service	23	27	4.7	242	378	25,207	25,111	6,581	8,896	14.6
6500	Real estate	29	31	3.3	76	79	13,895	15,747	1,293	1,549	2.3
6510	Real estate operators and lessors	13	12	4.2	-	27	-	9,926	-	291	2.0
6530	Real estate agents and managers	11	15	2.9	32	43	16,250	18,326	649	1,038	3.3
6700	Holding and other investment offices	3	3	4.4	10	10	31,200	11,600	313	130	2.4

Source: County Business Patterns, 1992/93, CBP-92/93-1, U.S. Department of Commerce, Washington, D.C., April 1995. SIC categories for which data were suppressed or not available for both 1992 and 1993 are *not* displayed. The employment columns represent mid-March employment in the year. Pay per employee is calculated by dividing 1st Quarter payroll, annualized, by mid-March employment. The columns headed "% State" show the county's percentage of the state total for the SIC in 1993; for example, 0.9% for SIC 6030 means that the county had 0.9 percent of the state's total establishments (or payroll) in SIC 6030 in 1993. A dash (-) is used to indicate that data are not available or cannot be calculated; *nec* means not elsewhere classified.

SIC	Industry	No. Establishments			Employment		Pay / Employee		Annual Payroll ($ 000)		
		1992	1993	% State	1992	1993	1992	1993	1992	1993	% State
ONEIDA, ID											
60-	**Finance, insurance, and real estate**	5	5	0.2	80	79	14,500	14,734	1,217	1,266	0.3
OWYHEE, ID											
60-	**Finance, insurance, and real estate**	10	9	0.4	-	41	-	14,146	-	618	0.1
6500	Real estate	5	5	0.5	13	13	6,462	7,692	110	121	0.2
PAYETTE, ID											
60-	**Finance, insurance, and real estate**	27	27	1.1	198	188	17,879	17,574	3,958	3,502	0.8
6000	Depository institutions	5	4	0.8	54	-	19,037	-	1,068	-	-
6020	Commercial banks	5	4	1.2	54	-	19,037	-	1,068	-	-
6300	Insurance carriers	3	2	1.2	21	-	18,476	-	427	-	-
6400	Insurance agents, brokers, and service	5	7	1.2	-	33	-	20,121	-	746	1.2
6500	Real estate	10	10	1.1	11	22	5,455	7,273	248	190	0.3
6530	Real estate agents and managers	5	7	1.4	5	12	5,600	10,333	208	151	0.5
POWER, ID											
60-	**Finance, insurance, and real estate**	10	11	0.4	-	-	-	-	-	-	-
6000	Depository institutions	3	4	0.8	24	-	17,000	-	394	-	-
6020	Commercial banks	3	3	0.9	24	-	17,000	-	394	-	-
6400	Insurance agents, brokers, and service	4	4	0.7	4	5	7,000	4,800	27	23	0.0
SHOSHONE, ID											
60-	**Finance, insurance, and real estate**	34	29	1.1	145	127	14,234	16,409	2,214	2,243	0.5
6000	Depository institutions	11	7	1.4	69	-	14,957	-	1,170	-	-
6400	Insurance agents, brokers, and service	6	7	1.2	15	18	17,867	20,000	243	319	0.5
6500	Real estate	14	13	1.4	49	55	10,041	10,473	563	689	1.0
6510	Real estate operators and lessors	6	7	2.5	23	-	12,870	-	321	-	-
TETON, ID											
60-	**Finance, insurance, and real estate**	7	7	0.3	24	30	13,333	12,933	338	450	0.1
6500	Real estate	3	3	0.3	4	5	7,000	5,600	29	63	0.1
TWIN FALLS, ID											
60-	**Finance, insurance, and real estate**	149	147	5.8	820	812	21,371	23,690	18,316	20,190	4.5
6000	Depository institutions	26	29	6.0	332	333	23,325	26,342	7,694	8,901	4.9
6020	Commercial banks	17	18	5.6	270	260	22,415	25,123	6,297	7,218	4.6
6030	Savings institutions	6	5	11.6	51	58	31,059	35,724	1,285	1,505	-
6060	Credit unions	3	6	5.1	11	15	9,818	11,200	112	178	1.3
6100	Nondepository institutions	12	12	6.7	53	66	28,453	28,606	1,570	1,900	5.7
6140	Personal credit institutions	7	6	8.7	24	-	21,667	-	530	-	-
6160	Mortgage bankers and brokers	2	3	3.9	-	17	-	27,059	-	585	2.9
6200	Security and commodity brokers	11	10	8.4	28	26	41,286	43,077	1,430	1,239	4.7
6300	Insurance carriers	17	12	7.1	89	64	22,472	24,750	2,167	1,576	2.2
6330	Fire, marine, and casualty insurance	9	8	9.0	19	16	34,105	38,250	613	601	2.1
6400	Insurance agents, brokers, and service	35	33	5.8	177	179	21,582	22,547	3,785	4,434	7.3
6500	Real estate	44	48	5.1	136	137	9,353	11,971	1,616	1,996	3.0
6510	Real estate operators and lessors	16	18	6.4	67	56	7,463	11,857	666	775	5.2
6530	Real estate agents and managers	23	24	4.7	37	57	10,811	11,298	566	855	2.7
6553	Cemetery subdividers and developers	3	4	17.4	-	17	-	12,706	-	196	26.2
6700	Holding and other investment offices	4	3	4.4	5	7	4,800	28,000	54	144	2.7
VALLEY, ID											
60-	**Finance, insurance, and real estate**	29	35	1.4	99	118	12,646	12,339	1,664	1,929	0.4
6000	Depository institutions	4	4	0.8	34	-	16,941	-	638	-	-
6400	Insurance agents, brokers, and service	4	5	0.9	11	14	15,636	12,857	186	212	0.3
6500	Real estate	17	22	2.4	45	66	9,600	10,000	739	927	1.4
6510	Real estate operators and lessors	2	3	1.1	-	2	-	22,000	-	71	0.5
6530	Real estate agents and managers	10	12	2.3	20	22	8,000	11,455	228	258	0.8

Source: County Business Patterns, 1992/93, CBP-92/93-1, U.S. Department of Commerce, Washington, D.C., April 1995. SIC categories for which data were suppressed or not available for both 1992 and 1993 are *not* displayed. The employment columns represent mid-March employment in the year. Pay per employee is calculated by dividing 1st Quarter payroll, annualized, by mid-March employment. The columns headed "% State" show the county's percentage of the state total for the SIC in 1993; for example, 0.9% for SIC 6030 means that the county had 0.9 percent of the state's total establishments (or payroll) in SIC 6030 in 1993. A dash (-) is used to indicate that data are not available or cannot be calculated; *nec* means not elsewhere classified.

Continued on next page.

SIC	Industry	No. Establishments			Employment		Pay / Employee		Annual Payroll ($ 000)		
		1992	1993	% State	1992	1993	1992	1993	1992	1993	% State
VALLEY, ID - [continued]											
6540	Title abstract offices	2	3	7.3	-	27	-	11,259	-	528	4.0
6552	Subdividers and developers, n.e.c.	3	4	6.5	2	15	4,000	4,000	53	70	1.3
6700	Holding and other investment offices	2	3	4.4	-	2	-	8,000	-	32	0.6
WASHINGTON, ID											
60 –	**Finance, insurance, and real estate**	18	18	0.7	92	94	11,348	11,191	1,097	1,093	0.2
6000	Depository institutions	5	4	0.8	41	-	17,171	-	695	-	-
6020	Commercial banks	5	4	1.2	41	-	17,171	-	695	-	-
6400	Insurance agents, brokers, and service	5	6	1.1	14	20	8,000	10,000	113	219	0.4
6500	Real estate	5	6	0.6	28	35	5,143	4,229	195	152	0.2
6530	Real estate agents and managers	3	5	1.0	26	-	4,923	-	181	-	-

Source: County Business Patterns, 1992/93, CBP-92/93-1, U.S. Department of Commerce, Washington, D.C., April 1995. SIC categories for which data were suppressed or not available for both 1992 and 1993 are *not* displayed. The employment columns represent mid-March employment in the year. Pay per employee is calculated by dividing 1st Quarter payroll, annualized, by mid-March employment. The columns headed "% State" show the county's percentage of the state total for the SIC in 1993; for example, 0.9% for SIC 6030 means that the county had 0.9 percent of the state's total establishments (or payroll) in SIC 6030 in 1993. A dash (-) is used to indicate that data are not available or cannot be calculated; *nec* means not elsewhere classified.

ILLINOIS

SIC	Industry	No. Establishments			Employment		Pay / Employee		Annual Payroll ($ 000)		
		1992	1993	% State	1992	1993	1992	1993	1992	1993	% State
ADAMS, IL											
60 –	**Finance, insurance, and real estate**	158	175	0.6	1,109	1,272	19,953	18,874	23,215	25,825	0.2
6000	Depository institutions	40	39	0.9	522	521	18,138	17,674	10,031	9,782	0.3
6020	Commercial banks	25	23	1.1	431	425	19,378	18,532	8,846	8,391	0.3
6030	Savings institutions	5	5	0.5	59	54	11,525	15,852	744	909	0.2
6060	Credit unions	10	11	1.5	32	42	13,625	11,333	441	482	0.5
6100	Nondepository institutions	7	7	0.4	33	44	23,152	18,909	698	668	0.1
6200	Security and commodity brokers	12	11	0.4	-	47	-	61,277	-	3,211	0.1
6210	Security brokers and dealers	8	9	0.7	39	-	65,128	-	2,390	-	-
6300	Insurance carriers	16	15	0.7	263	256	22,266	23,250	5,625	5,772	0.2
6310	Life insurance	5	4	0.7	72	66	29,333	33,515	2,110	1,808	0.2
6400	Insurance agents, brokers, and service	47	50	0.8	118	115	18,915	18,991	2,204	2,318	0.2
6500	Real estate	33	48	0.5	111	119	8,216	8,773	1,189	1,404	0.1
6510	Real estate operators and lessors	14	24	0.6	62	63	7,097	7,683	515	586	0.2
6530	Real estate agents and managers	10	16	0.3	15	24	9,067	10,000	194	372	0.0
6540	Title abstract offices	3	3	1.3	12	-	13,333	-	187	-	-
6553	Cemetery subdividers and developers	4	5	1.3	20	-	8,000	-	231	-	-
6700	Holding and other investment offices	3	5	0.4	-	170	-	11,224	-	2,670	0.4
ALEXANDER, IL											
60 –	**Finance, insurance, and real estate**	12	12	0.0	90	69	19,333	19,246	1,564	1,055	0.0
BOND, IL											
60 –	**Finance, insurance, and real estate**	38	40	0.1	194	239	17,876	18,996	3,721	4,745	0.0
6000	Depository institutions	12	11	0.2	133	143	16,722	16,867	2,442	2,499	0.1
6540	Title abstract offices	1	3	1.3	-	6	-	7,333	-	64	0.1
BOONE, IL											
60 –	**Finance, insurance, and real estate**	60	62	0.2	311	340	17,325	17,200	5,940	6,774	0.0
6000	Depository institutions	14	14	0.3	219	229	18,027	18,847	4,354	4,780	0.1
6020	Commercial banks	8	8	0.4	147	159	19,810	20,629	3,122	3,565	0.1
6400	Insurance agents, brokers, and service	15	16	0.3	-	45	-	12,444	-	594	0.0
6500	Real estate	23	25	0.3	-	52	-	13,923	-	1,098	0.1
6510	Real estate operators and lessors	9	8	0.2	25	25	16,480	16,000	449	466	0.1
6530	Real estate agents and managers	7	9	0.2	10	-	12,000	-	134	-	-
BROWN, IL											
60 –	**Finance, insurance, and real estate**	16	16	0.1	92	86	22,087	18,698	1,856	1,930	0.0
6000	Depository institutions	5	5	0.1	55	53	18,909	19,925	1,043	1,045	0.0
6400	Insurance agents, brokers, and service	5	5	0.1	-	9	-	16,889	-	145	0.0
BUREAU, IL											
60 –	**Finance, insurance, and real estate**	82	79	0.3	508	556	18,315	20,827	10,120	10,595	0.1
6000	Depository institutions	25	25	0.6	360	405	18,778	22,222	7,491	7,972	0.2
6020	Commercial banks	20	18	0.8	328	317	19,305	22,473	7,025	7,077	0.3
6100	Nondepository institutions	4	3	0.2	13	-	21,538	-	247	-	-
6200	Security and commodity brokers	4	4	0.2	-	5	-	31,200	-	235	0.0
6210	Security brokers and dealers	3	2	0.2	7	-	17,143	-	147	-	-

Source: *County Business Patterns, 1992/93*, CBP-92/93-1, U.S. Department of Commerce, Washington, D.C., April 1995. SIC categories for which data were suppressed or not available for both 1992 and 1993 are *not* displayed. The employment columns represent mid-March employment in the year. Pay per employee is calculated by dividing 1st Quarter payroll, annualized, by mid-March employment. The columns headed "% State" show the county's percentage of the state total for the SIC in 1993; for example, 0.9% for SIC 6030 means that the county had 0.9 percent of the state's total establishments (or payroll) in SIC 6030 in 1993. A dash (-) is used to indicate that data are not available or cannot be calculated; *nec* means not elsewhere classified.

Continued on next page.

SIC	Industry	No. Establishments			Employment		Pay / Employee		Annual Payroll ($ 000)		
		1992	1993	% State	1992	1993	1992	1993	1992	1993	% State
BUREAU, IL - [continued]											
6400	Insurance agents, brokers, and service	23	24	0.4	82	89	19,073	18,697	1,599	1,612	0.1
6530	Real estate agents and managers	4	4	0.1	9	10	16,444	16,000	157	125	0.0
6700	Holding and other investment offices	3	3	0.2	2	4	4,000	4,000	9	15	0.0
CALHOUN, IL											
60 –	**Finance, insurance, and real estate**	7	9	0.0	56	57	18,929	19,368	1,160	1,253	0.0
CARROLL, IL											
60 –	**Finance, insurance, and real estate**	36	37	0.1	237	266	19,122	15,925	4,200	4,664	0.0
6000	Depository institutions	15	15	0.3	162	175	20,938	17,874	3,250	3,311	0.1
6020	Commercial banks	11	11	0.5	137	150	20,964	17,813	2,843	2,879	0.1
6400	Insurance agents, brokers, and service	10	12	0.2	26	-	12,308	-	308	-	
CASS, IL											
60 –	**Finance, insurance, and real estate**	24	24	0.1	173	168	17,618	18,381	3,398	3,490	0.0
6000	Depository institutions	8	8	0.2	123	123	18,341	18,894	2,442	2,570	0.1
CHAMPAIGN, IL											
60 –	**Finance, insurance, and real estate**	370	382	1.3	3,029	3,129	22,930	22,816	70,711	73,044	0.5
6000	Depository institutions	68	75	1.7	1,319	1,346	23,609	22,098	30,690	29,535	0.9
6020	Commercial banks	38	42	1.9	1,003	1,077	25,627	23,484	24,798	24,927	1.0
6030	Savings institutions	15	9	1.0	166	-	18,361	-	3,483	-	-
6060	Credit unions	13	22	3.0	-	161	-	16,099	-	2,708	2.9
6100	Nondepository institutions	25	15	0.9	105	101	27,124	33,624	2,825	3,080	0.3
6140	Personal credit institutions	20	9	1.5	63	-	18,222	-	1,191	-	-
6160	Mortgage bankers and brokers	2	3	0.5	-	22	-	29,455	-	920	0.2
6200	Security and commodity brokers	22	25	1.0	93	134	44,387	38,687	4,342	5,564	0.2
6210	Security brokers and dealers	10	10	0.8	51	61	48,863	50,164	2,676	3,136	0.2
6220	Commodity contracts brokers, dealers	4	6	1.1	15	-	26,667	-	405	-	-
6280	Security and commodity services	8	8	1.1	27	54	45,778	30,889	1,261	1,907	0.4
6300	Insurance carriers	31	23	1.0	458	386	21,895	23,472	10,080	9,537	0.3
6310	Life insurance	9	7	1.2	227	107	27,859	29,047	5,783	2,830	0.3
6330	Fire, marine, and casualty insurance	14	9	0.9	-	132	-	24,242	-	3,412	0.2
6400	Insurance agents, brokers, and service	82	96	1.5	354	354	25,186	28,441	9,594	9,763	0.7
6500	Real estate	130	140	1.4	629	739	17,056	17,272	11,477	14,152	0.9
6510	Real estate operators and lessors	53	60	1.6	232	335	18,259	14,675	3,908	5,297	1.4
6530	Real estate agents and managers	51	70	1.3	301	375	16,757	19,669	5,571	8,288	0.8
6552	Subdividers and developers, n.e.c.	7	3	0.9	17	-	16,235	-	261	44	0.1
6553	Cemetery subdividers and developers	3	3	0.8	1	-	4,000	-	32	-	-
6700	Holding and other investment offices	12	8	0.6	71	69	23,493	17,043	1,703	1,413	0.2
6710	Holding offices	5	4	1.0	28	33	34,571	21,818	985	897	0.2
CHRISTIAN, IL											
60 –	**Finance, insurance, and real estate**	65	63	0.2	533	505	19,152	20,261	10,185	10,355	0.1
6000	Depository institutions	19	21	0.5	289	265	20,789	23,487	5,804	6,028	0.2
6020	Commercial banks	14	16	0.7	253	238	21,328	24,353	5,095	5,577	0.2
6400	Insurance agents, brokers, and service	26	26	0.4	88	102	15,318	14,078	1,514	1,533	0.1
6530	Real estate agents and managers	3	4	0.1	10	13	12,400	13,231	136	191	0.0
CLARK, IL											
60 –	**Finance, insurance, and real estate**	28	27	0.1	211	190	17,175	18,168	3,652	3,665	0.0
6000	Depository institutions	8	8	0.2	122	117	18,721	18,564	2,366	2,368	0.1
6400	Insurance agents, brokers, and service	12	13	0.2	-	35	-	13,486	-	467	0.0
CLAY, IL											
60 –	**Finance, insurance, and real estate**	26	28	0.1	258	261	16,977	16,552	4,451	4,609	0.0
6000	Depository institutions	7	7	0.2	113	111	18,407	20,108	2,235	2,385	0.1
6500	Real estate	5	6	0.1	-	118	-	13,017	-	1,652	0.1

Source: County Business Patterns, 1992/93, CBP-92/93-1, U.S. Department of Commerce, Washington, D.C., April 1995. SIC categories for which data were suppressed or not available for both 1992 and 1993 are *not* displayed. The employment columns represent mid-March employment in the year. Pay per employee is calculated by dividing 1st Quarter payroll, annualized, by mid-March employment. The columns headed "% State" show the county's percentage of the state total for the SIC in 1993; for example, 0.9% for SIC 6030 means that the county had 0.9 percent of the state's total establishments (or payroll) in SIC 6030 in 1993. A dash (-) is used to indicate that data are not available or cannot be calculated; *nec* means not elsewhere classified.

SIC	Industry	No. Establishments			Employment		Pay / Employee		Annual Payroll ($ 000)		
		1992	1993	% State	1992	1993	1992	1993	1992	1993	% State
CLINTON, IL											
60 –	**Finance, insurance, and real estate**	57	58	0.2	411	411	14,988	15,406	6,961	7,078	0.0
6000	Depository institutions	18	18	0.4	224	234	19,054	18,855	4,875	4,855	0.1
6020	Commercial banks	13	13	0.6	197	209	19,553	19,215	4,454	4,415	0.2
6500	Real estate	13	13	0.1	117	105	7,658	8,533	1,026	1,117	0.1
6510	Real estate operators and lessors	5	5	0.1	101	91	7,723	8,220	882	837	0.2
6530	Real estate agents and managers	4	3	0.1	4	4	5,000	6,000	28	29	0.0
COLES, IL											
60 –	**Finance, insurance, and real estate**	110	104	0.4	778	748	18,535	17,663	15,396	13,787	0.1
6000	Depository institutions	31	29	0.7	413	412	19,680	17,214	8,416	7,312	0.2
6020	Commercial banks	19	18	0.8	348	332	20,034	16,928	7,183	5,790	0.2
6030	Savings institutions	5	5	0.5	42	56	21,238	21,429	962	1,228	0.2
6060	Credit unions	7	6	0.8	23	24	11,478	11,333	271	294	0.3
6100	Nondepository institutions	6	5	0.3	-	13	-	20,923	-	275	0.0
6140	Personal credit institutions	5	5	0.8	-	13	-	20,923	-	275	0.1
6210	Security brokers and dealers	5	3	0.2	18	-	30,000	-	635	-	-
6300	Insurance carriers	11	7	0.3	181	154	19,249	18,701	3,788	2,863	0.1
6400	Insurance agents, brokers, and service	27	29	0.5	72	88	14,500	16,909	1,186	1,624	0.1
6500	Real estate	25	25	0.3	66	62	11,879	12,645	921	938	0.1
6510	Real estate operators and lessors	10	11	0.3	38	26	10,105	8,923	394	285	0.1
6530	Real estate agents and managers	11	11	0.2	19	24	12,842	13,500	310	380	0.0
6540	Title abstract offices	2	3	1.3	-	12	-	19,000	-	273	0.6
6700	Holding and other investment offices	4	5	0.4	8	-	15,500	-	143	-	-
COOK, IL											
60 –	**Finance, insurance, and real estate**	13,822	14,048	49.3	245,454	240,605	39,906	39,453	9,479,761	9,826,697	67.9
6000	Depository institutions	1,750	1,718	38.5	69,065	69,240	34,233	32,323	2,256,017	2,320,113	67.3
6020	Commercial banks	514	513	23.6	47,183	47,904	37,535	34,382	1,646,526	1,699,683	66.4
6030	Savings institutions	453	434	47.4	13,362	11,143	24,867	26,145	341,234	321,714	63.7
6090	Functions closely related to banking	525	496	84.9	3,530	4,267	22,622	21,979	82,591	97,156	90.0
6100	Nondepository institutions	745	808	47.6	12,041	14,622	43,661	41,586	531,567	652,581	62.1
6140	Personal credit institutions	286	225	38.0	4,429	-	32,960	-	166,289	-	-
6150	Business credit institutions	140	190	47.9	3,418	3,891	63,757	65,036	192,745	223,307	60.3
6160	Mortgage bankers and brokers	296	385	58.4	4,114	5,019	37,438	33,960	165,797	233,914	62.3
6200	Security and commodity brokers	1,501	1,615	63.8	28,446	28,733	78,893	75,568	2,065,002	2,209,291	88.4
6210	Security brokers and dealers	619	728	58.6	13,952	15,022	113,410	93,306	1,354,483	1,395,231	86.0
6220	Commodity contracts brokers, dealers	392	438	79.5	6,478	6,803	35,808	39,213	278,667	316,443	-
6230	Security and commodity exchanges	20	16	88.9	2,910	-	40,393	-	111,720	-	-
6280	Security and commodity services	401	430	60.1	4,800	4,323	61,813	92,125	296,991	398,057	90.0
6300	Insurance carriers	1,267	980	44.0	55,624	53,387	37,542	36,601	2,041,046	1,989,006	54.8
6310	Life insurance	353	281	47.5	17,892	15,008	28,758	29,892	518,332	435,616	47.8
6321	Accident and health insurance	29	21	52.5	3,516	4,044	36,771	21,434	97,587	91,215	63.4
6324	Hospital and medical service plans	46	51	63.0	7,052	5,737	34,074	37,899	267,603	241,705	83.0
6330	Fire, marine, and casualty insurance	529	454	44.6	23,323	24,130	46,519	43,865	1,026,667	1,077,583	51.9
6350	Surety insurance	17	14	56.0	249	-	50,747	-	12,122	-	-
6360	Title insurance	47	34	42.5	1,951	1,828	34,536	40,000	71,367	75,642	78.1
6370	Pension, health, and welfare funds	236	119	31.4	1,460	2,044	24,589	18,935	44,063	39,607	54.8
6390	Insurance carriers, n.e.c.	5	6	54.5	173	-	17,480	-	3,026	-	-
6400	Insurance agents, brokers, and service	2,198	2,370	37.8	18,298	19,674	37,947	41,208	682,480	837,902	62.9
6500	Real estate	5,579	5,746	57.7	44,668	41,796	26,547	26,193	1,241,604	1,193,651	73.8
6510	Real estate operators and lessors	2,238	2,287	61.9	13,486	12,567	20,620	19,592	300,920	266,475	69.6
6530	Real estate agents and managers	2,668	3,105	59.3	26,768	26,670	29,116	28,727	798,200	829,742	77.6
6540	Title abstract offices	39	54	23.3	416	599	25,692	22,290	12,523	17,459	37.5
6552	Subdividers and developers, n.e.c.	171	174	50.6	1,572	998	31,692	36,513	54,263	43,330	67.0
6553	Cemetery subdividers and developers	81	89	23.8	925	934	30,495	34,420	31,631	35,415	67.6
6700	Holding and other investment offices	758	785	60.6	13,825	10,275	36,685	45,076	501,163	475,900	72.9
6710	Holding offices	204	236	57.0	9,231	5,877	34,701	51,296	304,274	305,446	67.7
6720	Investment offices	34	21	58.3	257	230	58,879	50,261	15,506	9,880	76.9

Source: County Business Patterns, 1992/93, CBP-92/93-1, U.S. Department of Commerce, Washington, D.C., April 1995. SIC categories for which data were suppressed or not available for both 1992 and 1993 are *not* displayed. The employment columns represent mid-March employment in the year. Pay per employee is calculated by dividing 1st Quarter payroll, annualized, by mid-March employment. The columns headed "% State" show the county's percentage of the state total for the SIC in 1993; for example, 0.9% for SIC 6030 means that the county had 0.9 percent of the state's total establishments (or payroll) in SIC 6030 in 1993. A dash (-) is used to indicate that data are not available or cannot be calculated; *nec* means not elsewhere classified.

Continued on next page.

SIC	Industry	No. Establishments			Employment		Pay / Employee		Annual Payroll ($ 000)		
		1992	1993	% State	1992	1993	1992	1993	1992	1993	% State
COOK, IL - [continued]											
6732	Educational, religious, etc. trusts	145	143	63.0	717	654	24,441	25,535	18,609	17,588	73.0
6733	Trusts, n.e.c.	141	139	56.5	720	1,412	32,633	27,428	23,473	35,796	86.5
6792	Oil royalty traders	2	4	26.7	-	11	-	64,000	-	772	28.6
6794	Patent owners and lessors	24	30	54.5	737	331	40,011	36,266	31,071	12,021	68.9
6798	Real estate investment trusts	39	22	75.9	766	480	39,953	39,775	31,025	23,052	99.4
6799	Investors, n.e.c.	146	189	70.8	1,293	1,280	50,688	49,144	69,997	71,332	90.5
CRAWFORD, IL											
60 –	**Finance, insurance, and real estate**	45	47	0.2	369	342	19,111	19,310	7,289	6,850	0.0
6000	Depository institutions	12	12	0.3	219	224	21,041	19,554	4,614	4,347	0.1
6200	Security and commodity brokers	3	3	0.1	-	6	-	51,333	-	360	0.0
6400	Insurance agents, brokers, and service	10	12	0.2	51	58	14,510	15,862	842	1,064	0.1
6530	Real estate agents and managers	5	5	0.1	7	8	13,714	13,500	108	116	0.0
6540	Title abstract offices	3	3	1.3	-	20	-	11,600	-	291	0.6
CUMBERLAND, IL											
60 –	**Finance, insurance, and real estate**	11	10	0.0	64	58	17,562	16,828	1,143	1,204	0.0
DE KALB, IL											
60 –	**Finance, insurance, and real estate**	136	159	0.6	1,060	1,173	22,374	23,216	25,405	25,750	0.2
6000	Depository institutions	30	31	0.7	668	767	23,102	23,630	14,913	16,478	0.5
6020	Commercial banks	23	23	1.1	607	706	24,402	24,204	13,976	15,434	0.6
6030	Savings institutions	4	4	0.4	44	34	7,455	15,882	601	598	0.1
6100	Nondepository institutions	3	6	0.4	13	8	18,154	24,500	245	312	0.0
6200	Security and commodity brokers	6	9	0.4	-	21	-	48,190	-	1,276	0.1
6210	Security brokers and dealers	4	5	0.4	14	-	59,429	-	1,015	-	-
6280	Security and commodity services	1	3	0.4	-	6	-	4,667	-	40	0.0
6300	Insurance carriers	9	8	0.4	72	69	27,778	30,435	2,048	1,746	0.0
6400	Insurance agents, brokers, and service	29	42	0.7	102	117	26,000	23,932	2,328	2,686	0.2
6500	Real estate	51	55	0.6	168	161	13,881	15,180	2,441	2,780	0.2
6510	Real estate operators and lessors	16	24	0.6	80	101	15,650	16,119	1,185	1,749	0.5
6530	Real estate agents and managers	25	23	0.4	69	51	12,174	13,333	952	834	0.1
6700	Holding and other investment offices	8	8	0.6	-	30	-	18,533	-	472	0.1
6732	Educational, religious, etc. trusts	5	4	1.8	-	12	-	14,000	-	165	0.7
DE WITT, IL											
60 –	**Finance, insurance, and real estate**	25	28	0.1	159	151	19,270	21,828	3,299	3,538	0.0
6000	Depository institutions	8	8	0.2	110	99	20,800	24,202	2,491	2,561	0.1
6020	Commercial banks	6	5	0.2	-	85	-	22,400	-	2,137	0.1
6700	Holding and other investment offices	3	4	0.3	7	8	11,429	12,000	82	135	0.0
DOUGLAS, IL											
60 –	**Finance, insurance, and real estate**	30	29	0.1	197	191	20,832	23,246	4,134	4,326	0.0
6000	Depository institutions	8	9	0.2	113	115	21,664	23,130	2,384	2,419	0.1
6020	Commercial banks	6	6	0.3	-	107	-	23,589	-	2,285	0.1
6400	Insurance agents, brokers, and service	10	11	0.2	54	53	19,556	21,132	1,124	1,230	0.1
6510	Real estate operators and lessors	4	2	0.1	7	-	20,000	-	134	-	-
DU PAGE, IL											
60 –	**Finance, insurance, and real estate**	2,384	2,531	8.9	33,321	35,168	30,273	32,050	1,031,727	1,187,990	8.2
6000	Depository institutions	252	263	5.9	6,319	6,543	23,723	24,862	152,907	171,169	5.0
6020	Commercial banks	105	115	5.3	3,690	3,772	22,717	25,182	87,371	95,828	3.7
6030	Savings institutions	103	98	10.7	2,050	2,153	25,251	24,137	51,695	59,597	11.8
6060	Credit unions	32	34	4.6	337	365	24,688	26,016	8,485	9,667	10.2
6100	Nondepository institutions	224	235	13.8	6,465	4,354	24,325	29,776	166,416	157,081	15.0
6140	Personal credit institutions	76	65	11.0	1,836	1,644	27,564	24,394	59,395	43,155	15.2
6150	Business credit institutions	38	37	9.3	3,327	1,141	18,403	32,926	52,008	37,953	10.3
6160	Mortgage bankers and brokers	103	133	20.2	1,267	1,569	35,195	33,124	53,392	75,973	20.2

Source: County Business Patterns, 1992/93, CBP-92/93-1, U.S. Department of Commerce, Washington, D.C., April 1995. SIC categories for which data were suppressed or not available for both 1992 and 1993 are *not* displayed. The employment columns represent mid-March employment in the year. Pay per employee is calculated by dividing 1st Quarter payroll, annualized, by mid-March employment. The columns headed "% State" show the county's percentage of the state total for the SIC in 1993; for example, 0.9% for SIC 6030 means that the county had 0.9 percent of the state's total establishments (or payroll) in SIC 6030 in 1993. A dash (-) is used to indicate that data are not available or cannot be calculated; *nec* means not elsewhere classified.

Continued on next page.

SIC	Industry	No. Establishments			Employment		Pay / Employee		Annual Payroll ($ 000)		
		1992	1993	% State	1992	1993	1992	1993	1992	1993	% State
DU PAGE, IL - [continued]											
6200	Security and commodity brokers	199	233	9.2	1,488	1,797	58,772	65,019	94,033	110,937	4.4
6210	Security brokers and dealers	89	106	8.5	1,058	1,323	62,771	65,666	68,532	82,454	5.1
6220	Commodity contracts brokers, dealers	34	44	8.0	36	101	59,222	56,198	4,861	7,363	-
6280	Security and commodity services	68	83	11.6	354	373	48,023	65,115	19,119	21,120	4.8
6300	Insurance carriers	317	283	12.7	7,734	9,662	33,685	33,600	247,470	329,819	9.1
6310	Life insurance	102	98	16.6	2,936	3,629	35,157	37,528	89,556	128,153	14.1
6321	Accident and health insurance	8	6	15.0	104	-	85,462	-	7,043	-	-
6324	Hospital and medical service plans	7	11	13.6	84	-	23,190	-	3,042	-	-
6330	Fire, marine, and casualty insurance	125	119	11.7	3,923	4,740	33,459	31,257	131,389	158,769	7.6
6350	Surety insurance	7	9	36.0	67	-	35,701	-	2,475	-	-
6360	Title insurance	10	11	13.8	172	-	25,698	-	5,019	-	-
6370	Pension, health, and welfare funds	56	29	7.7	431	376	19,258	26,766	8,911	10,216	14.1
6400	Insurance agents, brokers, and service	518	560	8.9	4,582	4,439	33,180	34,498	157,138	163,441	12.3
6500	Real estate	766	845	8.5	5,317	5,904	24,771	24,705	146,784	169,301	10.5
6510	Real estate operators and lessors	185	220	6.0	1,288	1,619	19,239	19,012	26,815	33,013	8.6
6530	Real estate agents and managers	441	562	10.7	3,364	3,925	26,962	27,023	97,233	122,886	11.5
6540	Title abstract offices	12	14	6.0	119	181	19,092	20,000	2,487	4,520	9.7
6552	Subdividers and developers, n.e.c.	37	26	7.6	223	126	34,439	32,603	11,107	6,763	10.5
6553	Cemetery subdividers and developers	8	7	1.9	87	49	19,448	25,469	1,945	1,649	3.1
6700	Holding and other investment offices	100	104	8.0	1,003	-	54,086	-	51,224	-	-
6710	Holding offices	33	37	8.9	699	684	65,436	71,000	40,073	39,930	8.9
6720	Investment offices	6	4	11.1	34	-	16,471	-	781	-	-
6732	Educational, religious, etc. trusts	10	11	4.8	53	61	23,245	25,311	1,257	1,362	5.7
6733	Trusts, n.e.c.	23	11	4.5	126	-	29,778	-	5,222	-	-
6794	Patent owners and lessors	8	12	21.8	47	-	21,872	-	1,429	-	-
6799	Investors, n.e.c.	14	25	9.4	23	128	40,348	31,406	1,490	5,171	6.6
EDGAR, IL											
60 –	**Finance, insurance, and real estate**	31	33	0.1	252	252	17,587	18,206	4,645	5,093	0.0
6000	Depository institutions	12	12	0.3	200	206	18,720	19,126	3,982	4,385	0.1
6530	Real estate agents and managers	2	4	0.1	-	5	-	5,600	-	44	0.0
EDWARDS, IL											
60 –	**Finance, insurance, and real estate**	15	15	0.1	123	123	12,585	13,691	1,827	1,877	0.0
6500	Real estate	6	6	0.1	61	57	6,754	7,930	543	560	0.0
EFFINGHAM, IL											
60 –	**Finance, insurance, and real estate**	78	78	0.3	707	458	16,537	18,253	11,945	8,752	0.1
6000	Depository institutions	16	15	0.3	281	301	18,577	17,767	5,507	5,673	0.2
6020	Commercial banks	10	10	0.5	233	252	19,159	18,206	4,696	4,879	0.2
6030	Savings institutions	3	3	0.3	41	-	16,683	-	742	-	-
6060	Credit unions	3	2	0.3	7	-	10,286	-	69	-	-
6100	Nondepository institutions	3	3	0.2	9	9	16,444	19,556	172	180	0.0
6140	Personal credit institutions	3	3	0.5	9	9	16,444	19,556	172	180	0.1
6400	Insurance agents, brokers, and service	24	26	0.4	61	60	17,639	18,933	1,112	1,150	0.1
6530	Real estate agents and managers	10	12	0.2	26	24	9,385	10,333	254	251	0.0
FAYETTE, IL											
60 –	**Finance, insurance, and real estate**	29	30	0.1	174	172	19,655	20,326	3,618	3,690	0.0
6000	Depository institutions	9	8	0.2	125	118	18,336	19,119	2,472	2,487	0.1
6020	Commercial banks	8	8	0.4	-	118	-	19,119	-	2,487	0.1
6510	Real estate operators and lessors	5	6	0.2	5	9	8,000	7,111	50	65	0.0
FORD, IL											
60 –	**Finance, insurance, and real estate**	38	36	0.1	170	162	17,271	18,988	3,085	3,241	0.0

Source: County Business Patterns, 1992/93, CBP-92/93-1, U.S. Department of Commerce, Washington, D.C., April 1995. SIC categories for which data were suppressed or not available for both 1992 and 1993 are *not* displayed. The employment columns represent mid-March employment in the year. Pay per employee is calculated by dividing 1st Quarter payroll, annualized, by mid-March employment. The columns headed "% State" show the county's percentage of the state total for the SIC in 1993; for example, 0.9% for SIC 6030 means that the county had 0.9 percent of the state's total establishments (or payroll) in SIC 6030 in 1993. A dash (-) is used to indicate that data are not available or cannot be calculated; *nec* means not elsewhere classified.

Continued on next page.

SIC	Industry	No. Establishments			Employment		Pay / Employee		Annual Payroll ($ 000)		
		1992	1993	% State	1992	1993	1992	1993	1992	1993	% State
FORD, IL - [continued]											
6000	Depository institutions	14	13	0.3	132	122	18,606	20,426	2,553	2,624	0.1
6020	Commercial banks	9	10	0.5	113	116	19,115	20,724	2,220	2,542	0.1
6530	Real estate agents and managers	4	5	0.1	5	6	6,400	6,667	37	43	0.0
FRANKLIN, IL											
60 –	**Finance, insurance, and real estate**	51	57	0.2	406	352	17,547	17,955	7,277	6,750	0.0
6000	Depository institutions	13	10	0.2	291	206	17,485	16,621	5,045	3,528	0.1
6400	Insurance agents, brokers, and service	20	22	0.4	60	57	13,667	13,544	858	868	0.1
6510	Real estate operators and lessors	3	4	0.1	3	-	12,000	-	52	-	-
6530	Real estate agents and managers	4	5	0.1	6	7	7,333	6,857	58	68	0.0
FULTON, IL											
60 –	**Finance, insurance, and real estate**	68	68	0.2	327	333	18,459	19,495	6,005	6,378	0.0
6000	Depository institutions	25	24	0.5	233	232	19,863	21,552	4,427	4,711	0.1
6020	Commercial banks	18	18	0.8	210	210	20,590	22,419	4,110	4,402	0.2
6030	Savings institutions	7	6	0.7	23	22	13,217	13,273	317	309	0.1
6400	Insurance agents, brokers, and service	26	25	0.4	55	49	14,327	14,367	833	773	0.1
6510	Real estate operators and lessors	4	6	0.2	3	25	25,333	10,720	93	300	0.1
6530	Real estate agents and managers	6	6	0.1	16	7	8,750	9,714	148	86	0.0
GALLATIN, IL											
60 –	**Finance, insurance, and real estate**	6	8	0.0	34	-	15,882	-	555	-	-
GREENE, IL											
60 –	**Finance, insurance, and real estate**	24	26	0.1	140	127	14,486	16,913	2,098	2,138	0.0
6000	Depository institutions	5	6	0.1	105	90	16,648	20,933	1,794	1,816	0.1
6020	Commercial banks	5	5	0.2	105	-	16,648	-	1,794	-	-
6400	Insurance agents, brokers, and service	7	10	0.2	11	18	9,091	8,000	106	165	0.0
GRUNDY, IL											
60 –	**Finance, insurance, and real estate**	74	76	0.3	518	563	17,012	16,739	9,643	10,780	0.1
6000	Depository institutions	17	17	0.4	304	348	18,750	17,322	6,148	7,040	0.2
6020	Commercial banks	10	10	0.5	253	291	19,621	18,172	5,421	6,107	0.2
6400	Insurance agents, brokers, and service	16	22	0.4	-	50	-	14,240	-	830	0.1
6500	Real estate	27	25	0.3	128	135	11,438	12,622	1,673	1,869	0.1
6510	Real estate operators and lessors	9	9	0.2	34	-	10,235	-	404	-	-
6530	Real estate agents and managers	14	11	0.2	57	58	8,982	7,379	544	475	0.0
HAMILTON, IL											
60 –	**Finance, insurance, and real estate**	14	14	0.0	71	84	16,845	16,952	1,304	1,462	0.0
HANCOCK, IL											
60 –	**Finance, insurance, and real estate**	43	40	0.1	223	235	17,973	16,936	4,069	4,212	0.0
6000	Depository institutions	15	14	0.3	162	172	19,062	17,628	3,183	3,355	0.1
6400	Insurance agents, brokers, and service	22	21	0.3	50	50	14,240	14,880	770	751	0.1
HARDIN, IL											
60 –	**Finance, insurance, and real estate**	5	5	0.0	39	40	10,667	11,100	548	518	0.0
HENDERSON, IL											
60 –	**Finance, insurance, and real estate**	15	13	0.0	88	102	16,545	14,824	1,609	1,672	0.0
6000	Depository institutions	6	6	0.1	61	72	21,049	18,389	1,412	1,462	0.0
HENRY, IL											
60 –	**Finance, insurance, and real estate**	97	97	0.3	623	628	21,066	20,656	13,600	13,483	0.1
6000	Depository institutions	26	27	0.6	381	384	21,627	21,104	8,393	8,268	0.2
6020	Commercial banks	18	19	0.9	326	327	21,926	21,333	7,268	7,094	0.3
6100	Nondepository institutions	3	4	0.2	24	-	29,167	-	683	-	-

Source: County Business Patterns, 1992/93, CBP-92/93-1, U.S. Department of Commerce, Washington, D.C., April 1995. SIC categories for which data were suppressed or not available for both 1992 and 1993 are not displayed. The employment columns represent mid-March employment in the year. Pay per employee is calculated by dividing 1st Quarter payroll, annualized, by mid-March employment. The columns headed "% State" show the county's percentage of the state total for the SIC in 1993; for example, 0.9% for SIC 6030 means that the county had 0.9 percent of the state's total establishments (or payroll) in SIC 6030 in 1993. A dash (-) is used to indicate that data are not available or cannot be calculated; nec means not elsewhere classified.

Continued on next page.

SIC	Industry	No. Establishments			Employment		Pay / Employee		Annual Payroll ($ 000)		
		1992	1993	% State	1992	1993	1992	1993	1992	1993	% State
HENRY, IL - [continued]											
6400	Insurance agents, brokers, and service	36	34	0.5	122	121	21,279	19,273	2,639	2,523	0.2
6510	Real estate operators and lessors	1	4	0.1	-	5	-	8,000	-	40	0.0
6530	Real estate agents and managers	13	12	0.2	33	30	12,000	13,200	549	578	0.1
IROQUOIS, IL											
60 –	**Finance, insurance, and real estate**	65	67	0.2	360	361	19,544	19,224	7,463	7,461	0.1
6000	Depository institutions	21	21	0.5	235	239	20,153	19,464	5,209	5,251	0.2
6020	Commercial banks	15	15	0.7	194	200	19,814	19,040	4,261	4,388	0.2
6400	Insurance agents, brokers, and service	27	27	0.4	77	76	17,403	18,789	1,194	1,320	0.1
6530	Real estate agents and managers	5	5	0.1	14	8	15,429	6,500	240	69	0.0
6700	Holding and other investment offices	-	4	0.3	-	3	-	1,333	-	32	0.0
JACKSON, IL											
60 –	**Finance, insurance, and real estate**	137	149	0.5	882	1,052	18,259	18,354	16,807	20,287	0.1
6000	Depository institutions	24	25	0.6	390	387	15,374	16,010	6,302	6,736	0.2
6020	Commercial banks	16	16	0.7	289	287	15,917	16,655	4,825	5,106	0.2
6030	Savings institutions	4	4	0.4	58	58	13,931	14,138	832	965	0.2
6100	Nondepository institutions	6	6	0.4	35	34	22,629	25,882	816	921	0.1
6140	Personal credit institutions	6	6	1.0	35	34	22,629	25,882	816	921	0.3
6200	Security and commodity brokers	10	11	0.4	40	47	60,200	51,064	2,241	2,482	0.1
6210	Security brokers and dealers	10	9	0.7	40	-	60,200	-	2,241	-	
6300	Insurance carriers	9	10	0.4	96	165	21,833	23,467	2,121	3,800	0.1
6310	Life insurance	3	4	0.7	53	120	27,019	25,767	1,410	2,908	0.3
6400	Insurance agents, brokers, and service	35	33	0.5	106	90	22,943	22,533	2,516	2,197	0.2
6500	Real estate	44	51	0.5	193	245	10,674	11,053	2,393	3,262	0.2
6510	Real estate operators and lessors	23	26	0.7	103	119	10,369	10,689	1,174	1,357	0.4
6530	Real estate agents and managers	16	19	0.4	72	105	10,667	9,143	866	1,142	0.1
6700	Holding and other investment offices	9	13	1.0	22	84	14,545	14,571	418	889	0.1
JASPER, IL											
60 –	**Finance, insurance, and real estate**	21	21	0.1	136	137	16,529	17,226	2,366	2,515	0.0
6000	Depository institutions	4	4	0.1	96	93	18,625	19,097	1,913	1,905	0.1
6400	Insurance agents, brokers, and service	7	9	0.1	-	25	-	15,200	-	372	0.0
6530	Real estate agents and managers	3	3	0.1	8	-	6,500	-	93	-	-
JEFFERSON, IL											
60 –	**Finance, insurance, and real estate**	92	86	0.3	537	586	21,266	23,788	11,482	13,390	0.1
6000	Depository institutions	16	14	0.3	294	279	19,837	19,527	5,824	5,466	0.2
6100	Nondepository institutions	5	5	0.3	18	85	20,444	34,729	297	2,212	0.2
6200	Security and commodity brokers	5	5	0.2	-	27	-	52,444	-	1,431	0.1
6300	Insurance carriers	19	12	0.5	95	59	24,421	28,678	2,466	1,742	0.0
6310	Life insurance	4	4	0.7	55	-	24,436	-	1,399	-	-
6400	Insurance agents, brokers, and service	25	25	0.4	-	58	-	19,724	-	1,213	0.1
6500	Real estate	20	21	0.2	53	61	16,453	15,541	912	999	0.1
6510	Real estate operators and lessors	9	9	0.2	15	25	12,800	12,000	212	325	0.1
6530	Real estate agents and managers	6	9	0.2	22	23	20,364	22,087	465	535	0.1
6700	Holding and other investment offices	2	4	0.3	-	17	-	20,000	-	327	0.1
6710	Holding offices	1	4	1.0	-	17	-	20,000	-	327	0.1
JERSEY, IL											
60 –	**Finance, insurance, and real estate**	22	23	0.1	141	147	17,901	19,510	2,412	2,662	0.0
6000	Depository institutions	4	4	0.1	103	103	18,641	19,340	1,765	1,763	0.1
6020	Commercial banks	4	4	0.2	103	103	18,641	19,340	1,765	1,763	0.1
6530	Real estate agents and managers	4	6	0.1	4	-	7,000	-	34	-	-

Source: County Business Patterns, 1992/93, CBP-92/93-1, U.S. Department of Commerce, Washington, D.C., April 1995. SIC categories for which data were suppressed or not available for both 1992 and 1993 are *not* displayed. The employment columns represent mid-March employment in the year. Pay per employee is calculated by dividing 1st Quarter payroll, annualized, by mid-March employment. The columns headed "% State" show the county's percentage of the state total for the SIC in 1993; for example, 0.9% for SIC 6030 means that the county had 0.9 percent of the state's total establishments (or payroll) in SIC 6030 in 1993. A dash (-) is used to indicate that data are not available or cannot be calculated; *nec* means not elsewhere classified.

SIC	Industry	No. Establishments			Employment		Pay / Employee		Annual Payroll ($ 000)		
		1992	1993	% State	1992	1993	1992	1993	1992	1993	% State
JO DAVIESS, IL											
60 –	**Finance, insurance, and real estate**	59	56	0.2	690	340	13,635	17,176	11,648	6,658	0.0
6000	Depository institutions	17	17	0.4	201	210	20,159	20,076	4,360	4,690	0.1
6400	Insurance agents, brokers, and service	14	16	0.3	39	-	13,949	-	561	-	0.1
6500	Real estate	21	18	0.2	429	71	10,601	13,239	6,473	1,214	0.1
6510	Real estate operators and lessors	7	3	0.1	-	5	-	11,200	-	78	0.0
6530	Real estate agents and managers	8	8	0.2	-	51	-	15,373	-	982	0.1
6540	Title abstract offices	2	3	1.3	-	8	-	11,000	-	109	0.2
6553	Cemetery subdividers and developers	2	4	1.1	-	7	-	1,714	-	45	0.1
JOHNSON, IL											
60 –	**Finance, insurance, and real estate**	12	13	0.0	53	57	17,585	17,333	1,055	1,107	0.0
6000	Depository institutions	3	3	0.1	-	34	-	22,941	-	895	0.0
6400	Insurance agents, brokers, and service	6	7	0.1	-	13	-	9,231	-	126	0.0
KANE, IL											
60 –	**Finance, insurance, and real estate**	693	698	2.4	10,089	10,238	22,522	23,221	234,322	267,919	1.9
6000	Depository institutions	107	118	2.6	3,057	4,314	23,515	21,573	71,867	107,451	3.1
6020	Commercial banks	50	64	2.9	2,225	3,713	23,468	22,029	52,004	94,798	3.7
6030	Savings institutions	27	19	2.1	706	437	24,385	18,151	17,216	9,170	1.8
6060	Credit unions	24	31	4.2	96	140	21,000	21,429	2,120	3,098	3.3
6090	Functions closely related to banking	5	4	0.7	-	24	-	14,333	-	385	0.4
6100	Nondepository institutions	44	36	2.1	180	281	31,689	28,555	6,796	10,743	1.0
6140	Personal credit institutions	30	22	3.7	135	122	25,215	25,016	3,495	2,994	1.1
6160	Mortgage bankers and brokers	10	10	1.5	-	120	-	26,167	-	5,704	1.5
6200	Security and commodity brokers	29	37	1.5	74	82	47,622	62,244	4,242	5,856	0.2
6210	Security brokers and dealers	18	20	1.6	62	60	51,806	61,000	3,705	4,216	0.3
6300	Insurance carriers	83	63	2.8	4,804	3,415	20,520	23,478	101,570	88,019	2.4
6310	Life insurance	15	13	2.2	3,206	2,278	22,866	21,464	76,100	57,669	6.3
6330	Fire, marine, and casualty insurance	37	27	2.7	1,241	811	15,707	31,556	19,688	24,269	1.2
6360	Title insurance	5	3	3.8	85	-	23,294	-	2,317	-	-
6370	Pension, health, and welfare funds	26	19	5.0	272	246	13,956	13,089	3,465	3,469	4.8
6400	Insurance agents, brokers, and service	164	174	2.8	736	834	29,929	29,995	21,472	25,573	1.9
6500	Real estate	245	248	2.5	1,158	1,223	18,263	18,639	24,713	26,621	1.6
6510	Real estate operators and lessors	70	76	2.1	621	700	17,230	17,680	12,507	13,525	3.5
6530	Real estate agents and managers	123	133	2.5	417	379	20,470	18,586	8,713	8,534	0.8
6540	Title abstract offices	7	8	3.4	25	75	16,960	20,800	626	2,072	4.4
6552	Subdividers and developers, n.e.c.	13	21	6.1	26	43	21,231	32,372	1,196	1,760	2.7
6553	Cemetery subdividers and developers	8	8	2.1	29	26	13,379	16,308	476	676	1.3
6700	Holding and other investment offices	21	22	1.7	80	89	54,450	39,955	3,662	3,656	0.6
6710	Holding offices	5	6	1.4	17	-	117,412	-	1,645	-	-
6732	Educational, religious, etc. trusts	5	4	1.8	15	18	16,800	14,667	311	315	1.3
6733	Trusts, n.e.c.	3	4	1.6	15	-	45,333	-	236	-	-
KANKAKEE, IL											
60 –	**Finance, insurance, and real estate**	201	217	0.8	1,721	1,758	19,277	19,552	34,054	36,506	0.3
6000	Depository institutions	56	65	1.5	777	814	19,377	19,877	15,903	17,194	0.5
6020	Commercial banks	23	31	1.4	489	566	19,231	19,859	9,764	11,919	0.5
6030	Savings institutions	11	5	0.5	174	-	20,529	-	3,767	-	-
6060	Credit unions	18	23	3.1	91	110	18,813	17,200	1,753	1,940	2.1
6090	Functions closely related to banking	4	6	1.0	23	-	16,000	-	619	-	-
6100	Nondepository institutions	12	9	0.5	-	36	-	17,222	-	636	0.1
6140	Personal credit institutions	9	6	1.0	29	28	16,138	15,286	467	386	0.1
6200	Security and commodity brokers	10	11	0.4	-	38	-	71,474	-	2,851	0.1
6210	Security brokers and dealers	6	6	0.5	32	-	74,625	-	2,352	-	-
6280	Security and commodity services	3	4	0.6	-	5	-	21,600	-	60	0.0
6300	Insurance carriers	13	12	0.5	490	441	19,118	19,374	8,692	8,632	0.2
6400	Insurance agents, brokers, and service	53	51	0.8	135	161	13,837	15,429	2,031	2,697	0.2
6500	Real estate	53	63	0.6	235	240	14,349	12,483	3,861	3,657	0.2

Source: County Business Patterns, 1992/93, CBP-92/93-1, U.S. Department of Commerce, Washington, D.C., April 1995. SIC categories for which data were suppressed or not available for both 1992 and 1993 are not displayed. The employment columns represent mid-March employment in the year. Pay per employee is calculated by dividing 1st Quarter payroll, annualized, by mid-March employment. The columns headed "% State" show the county's percentage of the state total for the SIC in 1993; for example, 0.9% for SIC 6030 means that the county had 0.9 percent of the state's total establishments (or payroll) in SIC 6030 in 1993. A dash (-) is used to indicate that data are not available or cannot be calculated; nec means not elsewhere classified.

Continued on next page.

SIC	Industry	No. Establishments			Employment		Pay / Employee		Annual Payroll ($ 000)		
		1992	1993	% State	1992	1993	1992	1993	1992	1993	% State
KANKAKEE, IL - [continued]											
6510	Real estate operators and lessors	18	25	0.7	90	155	14,400	10,813	1,696	2,046	0.5
6530	Real estate agents and managers	21	31	0.6	97	60	13,361	13,533	1,345	1,014	0.1
6552	Subdividers and developers, n.e.c.	2	3	0.9	-	5	-	32,800	-	171	0.3
6700	Holding and other investment offices	4	6	0.5	10	28	30,400	29,714	386	839	0.1
KENDALL, IL											
60 –	**Finance, insurance, and real estate**	50	45	0.2	310	343	18,632	17,889	6,585	7,153	0.0
6000	Depository institutions	11	11	0.2	205	222	18,263	18,468	4,397	4,505	0.1
6500	Real estate	22	17	0.2	-	51	-	9,804	-	572	0.0
6510	Real estate operators and lessors	4	5	0.1	19	-	8,211	-	167	-	-
6530	Real estate agents and managers	13	11	0.2	25	29	11,520	11,172	359	367	0.0
KNOX, IL											
60 –	**Finance, insurance, and real estate**	112	109	0.4	712	621	18,657	18,235	13,273	11,922	0.1
6000	Depository institutions	29	32	0.7	390	362	19,723	18,773	7,527	7,192	0.2
6020	Commercial banks	15	15	0.7	236	248	22,034	20,258	5,121	5,148	0.2
6210	Security brokers and dealers	3	3	0.2	18	-	57,111	-	968	-	-
6300	Insurance carriers	13	9	0.4	107	-	16,150	-	1,846	-	-
6400	Insurance agents, brokers, and service	26	27	0.4	85	92	16,471	17,696	1,465	1,684	0.1
6500	Real estate	26	29	0.3	72	94	10,667	9,660	831	1,058	0.1
6510	Real estate operators and lessors	10	11	0.3	34	46	9,412	9,565	337	523	0.1
6530	Real estate agents and managers	10	12	0.2	18	-	12,000	-	237	-	-
6700	Holding and other investment offices	5	2	0.2	10	-	10,400	-	67	-	-
LAKE, IL											
60 –	**Finance, insurance, and real estate**	1,434	1,524	5.3	17,254	17,301	39,952	39,620	671,909	709,363	4.9
6000	Depository institutions	154	166	3.7	3,454	3,344	24,359	23,602	80,695	82,466	2.4
6020	Commercial banks	85	92	4.2	2,717	2,506	24,362	23,765	62,365	61,907	2.4
6030	Savings institutions	27	26	2.8	370	421	27,795	29,226	10,284	12,496	2.5
6060	Credit unions	27	28	3.8	319	373	21,229	17,491	6,876	7,310	7.7
6090	Functions closely related to banking	15	19	3.3	48	-	18,500	-	1,170	-	-
6100	Nondepository institutions	207	220	13.0	3,251	3,290	48,780	46,778	141,067	154,114	14.7
6140	Personal credit institutions	38	34	5.7	684	722	49,632	40,765	30,173	25,391	9.0
6150	Business credit institutions	138	143	36.0	-	2,129	-	50,170	-	104,086	28.1
6160	Mortgage bankers and brokers	29	43	6.5	-	439	-	40,219	-	24,637	6.6
6200	Security and commodity brokers	174	193	7.6	772	786	66,876	65,221	59,252	67,153	2.7
6210	Security brokers and dealers	89	106	8.5	559	609	68,064	64,466	40,420	50,063	3.1
6220	Commodity contracts brokers, dealers	28	33	6.0	56	64	70,571	48,062	5,543	5,781	-
6280	Security and commodity services	51	53	7.4	152	113	62,237	79,009	12,963	11,289	2.6
6300	Insurance carriers	120	103	4.6	5,822	5,670	37,333	42,105	213,399	230,651	6.4
6310	Life insurance	20	14	2.4	2,422	1,373	36,188	48,720	81,868	50,514	5.5
6330	Fire, marine, and casualty insurance	65	62	6.1	3,135	3,138	39,784	41,663	125,837	138,587	6.7
6360	Title insurance	6	5	6.3	118	-	19,424	-	2,376	-	-
6370	Pension, health, and welfare funds	24	18	4.7	103	-	19,883	-	2,201	-	-
6400	Insurance agents, brokers, and service	239	264	4.2	-	1,165	-	33,452	-	40,801	3.1
6500	Real estate	479	514	5.2	1,778	2,052	21,690	22,805	46,193	57,135	3.5
6510	Real estate operators and lessors	143	161	4.4	583	635	18,676	19,345	11,938	14,085	3.7
6530	Real estate agents and managers	242	297	5.7	829	1,186	21,549	24,374	21,361	34,437	3.2
6540	Title abstract offices	6	8	3.4	77	95	15,013	18,484	1,251	2,386	5.1
6552	Subdividers and developers, n.e.c.	21	21	6.1	131	80	34,656	30,150	6,362	4,524	7.0
6553	Cemetery subdividers and developers	20	19	5.1	42	52	22,857	27,154	1,007	1,474	2.8
6700	Holding and other investment offices	58	61	4.7	831	-	79,095	-	52,388	-	-
6710	Holding offices	23	23	5.6	777	411	82,255	67,182	50,276	22,770	5.0
6720	Investment offices	2	5	13.9	-	24	-	25,667	-	509	4.0

Source: County Business Patterns, 1992/93, CBP-92/93-1, U.S. Department of Commerce, Washington, D.C., April 1995. SIC categories for which data were suppressed or not available for both 1992 and 1993 are *not* displayed. The employment columns represent mid-March employment in the year. Pay per employee is calculated by dividing 1st Quarter payroll, annualized, by mid-March employment. The columns headed "% State" show the county's percentage of the state total for the SIC in 1993; for example, 0.9% for SIC 6030 means that the county had 0.9 percent of the state's total establishments (or payroll) in SIC 6030 in 1993. A dash (-) is used to indicate that data are not available or cannot be calculated; *nec* means not elsewhere classified.

Continued on next page.

SIC	Industry	No. Establishments			Employment		Pay / Employee		Annual Payroll ($ 000)		
		1992	1993	% State	1992	1993	1992	1993	1992	1993	% State
LAKE, IL - [continued]											
6732	Educational, religious, etc. trusts	9	10	4.4	20	-	32,200	-	562	-	-
6733	Trusts, n.e.c.	5	5	2.0	22	-	18,000	-	332	-	-
6799	Investors, n.e.c.	11	11	4.1	10	-	75,200	-	847	-	-
LA SALLE, IL											
60 –	**Finance, insurance, and real estate**	266	257	0.9	1,793	1,616	18,688	19,121	35,893	32,963	0.2
6000	Depository institutions	73	79	1.8	890	963	20,216	19,323	19,096	20,252	0.6
6020	Commercial banks	42	42	1.9	653	656	20,564	20,159	13,794	14,058	0.5
6030	Savings institutions	15	13	1.4	170	186	22,259	20,473	4,470	4,490	0.9
6100	Nondepository institutions	16	8	0.5	-	24	-	20,333	-	570	0.1
6140	Personal credit institutions	13	6	1.0	67	-	15,045	-	1,079	-	-
6200	Security and commodity brokers	14	12	0.5	-	42	-	31,905	-	1,480	0.1
6210	Security brokers and dealers	11	9	0.7	37	35	36,216	36,343	1,623	1,408	0.1
6300	Insurance carriers	27	18	0.8	209	136	21,053	28,912	4,344	3,281	0.1
6310	Life insurance	8	7	1.2	101	105	29,545	32,571	2,818	2,708	0.3
6370	Pension, health, and welfare funds	5	3	0.8	60	-	5,467	-	331	-	-
6400	Insurance agents, brokers, and service	71	75	1.2	225	234	17,120	16,376	4,188	4,266	0.3
6500	Real estate	55	56	0.6	161	180	10,037	12,756	1,928	2,675	0.2
6510	Real estate operators and lessors	16	16	0.4	-	46	-	9,391	-	475	0.1
6530	Real estate agents and managers	21	22	0.4	74	86	9,676	11,907	984	1,258	0.1
6553	Cemetery subdividers and developers	14	14	3.7	-	32	-	8,875	-	345	0.7
6700	Holding and other investment offices	10	9	0.7	183	37	14,689	10,919	3,026	439	0.1
LAWRENCE, IL											
60 –	**Finance, insurance, and real estate**	27	27	0.1	1,094	1,128	22,834	21,904	25,397	26,272	0.2
6020	Commercial banks	5	5	0.2	-	68	-	18,765	-	1,509	0.1
LEE, IL											
60 –	**Finance, insurance, and real estate**	66	71	0.2	550	571	19,142	18,886	11,064	12,160	0.1
6000	Depository institutions	15	17	0.4	210	267	20,762	21,423	4,499	6,001	0.2
6020	Commercial banks	11	12	0.6	182	234	22,220	22,017	4,181	5,415	0.2
6300	Insurance carriers	5	4	0.2	114	-	27,895	-	3,191	-	-
6400	Insurance agents, brokers, and service	15	20	0.3	66	-	16,303	-	1,152	-	-
6500	Real estate	22	22	0.2	138	140	11,710	12,343	1,917	2,069	0.1
6510	Real estate operators and lessors	4	5	0.1	25	31	9,280	9,161	235	304	0.1
6530	Real estate agents and managers	14	13	0.2	97	90	12,041	11,911	1,444	1,464	0.1
6700	Holding and other investment offices	3	3	0.2	9	-	7,556	-	59	-	-
6732	Educational, religious, etc. trusts	3	3	1.3	9	-	7,556	-	59	-	-
LIVINGSTON, IL											
60 –	**Finance, insurance, and real estate**	90	90	0.3	483	472	19,627	19,915	10,542	10,338	0.1
6000	Depository institutions	18	20	0.4	322	317	19,528	20,959	6,778	7,282	0.2
6020	Commercial banks	12	15	0.7	270	288	19,793	21,014	5,739	6,331	0.2
6100	Nondepository institutions	4	3	0.2	-	8	-	41,500	-	231	0.0
6400	Insurance agents, brokers, and service	33	36	0.6	98	106	18,571	16,038	2,313	2,060	0.2
6530	Real estate agents and managers	6	10	0.2	6	10	8,000	10,000	56	140	0.0
LOGAN, IL											
60 –	**Finance, insurance, and real estate**	85	88	0.3	590	589	19,044	19,246	11,573	12,044	0.1
6000	Depository institutions	20	23	0.5	217	222	21,143	20,414	4,690	4,812	0.1
6020	Commercial banks	15	20	0.9	181	204	20,088	20,569	3,796	4,437	0.2
6300	Insurance carriers	11	5	0.2	229	219	19,651	21,187	4,666	4,781	0.1
6400	Insurance agents, brokers, and service	25	29	0.5	77	87	13,558	14,667	1,055	1,465	0.1
6500	Real estate	20	25	0.3	-	50	-	8,880	-	481	0.0

Source: County Business Patterns, 1992/93, CBP-92/93-1, U.S. Department of Commerce, Washington, D.C., April 1995. SIC categories for which data were suppressed or not available for both 1992 and 1993 are not displayed. The employment columns represent mid-March employment in the year. Pay per employee is calculated by dividing 1st Quarter payroll, annualized, by mid-March employment. The columns headed "% State" show the county's percentage of the state total for the SIC in 1993; for example, 0.9% for SIC 6030 means that the county had 0.9 percent of the state's total establishments (or payroll) in SIC 6030 in 1993. A dash (-) is used to indicate that data are not available or cannot be calculated; nec means not elsewhere classified.

Continued on next page.

SIC	Industry	No. Establishments			Employment		Pay / Employee		Annual Payroll ($ 000)		
		1992	1993	% State	1992	1993	1992	1993	1992	1993	% State
LOGAN, IL - [continued]											
6510	Real estate operators and lessors	10	13	0.4	29	-	11,862	-	347	-	-
6530	Real estate agents and managers	7	8	0.2	11	13	6,182	7,385	90	102	0.0
6700	Holding and other investment offices	6	3	0.2	15	-	21,600	-	302	-	-
MCDONOUGH, IL											
60 -	**Finance, insurance, and real estate**	63	68	0.2	503	539	16,684	16,089	10,131	9,217	0.1
6000	Depository institutions	14	15	0.3	225	237	18,702	18,127	5,846	4,601	0.1
6200	Security and commodity brokers	3	4	0.2	-	8	-	40,000	-	290	0.0
6400	Insurance agents, brokers, and service	20	21	0.3	60	63	15,800	15,937	1,145	1,229	0.1
6500	Real estate	14	18	0.2	135	158	10,578	9,873	1,404	1,646	0.1
6510	Real estate operators and lessors	7	10	0.3	113	130	10,619	10,400	1,168	1,402	0.4
6530	Real estate agents and managers	4	6	0.1	16	-	10,750	-	161	-	-
6700	Holding and other investment offices	4	4	0.3	43	-	13,860	-	590	-	-
MCHENRY, IL											
60 -	**Finance, insurance, and real estate**	348	365	1.3	2,312	2,385	23,182	22,108	57,927	58,794	0.4
6000	Depository institutions	72	63	1.4	1,253	1,122	22,072	20,791	28,752	23,858	0.7
6020	Commercial banks	35	35	1.6	826	836	23,884	22,536	19,402	18,946	0.7
6030	Savings institutions	28	19	2.1	389	250	18,807	15,536	8,769	4,296	0.9
6100	Nondepository institutions	18	24	1.4	91	111	31,780	25,946	3,482	4,584	0.4
6140	Personal credit institutions	7	9	1.5	26	35	22,923	21,486	628	811	0.3
6160	Mortgage bankers and brokers	8	12	1.8	57	66	36,632	28,788	2,641	3,518	0.9
6200	Security and commodity brokers	17	17	0.7	-	49	-	59,265	-	3,298	0.1
6300	Insurance carriers	33	23	1.0	133	123	23,188	25,008	3,590	3,426	0.1
6360	Title insurance	6	5	6.3	85	-	20,235	-	2,082	-	-
6370	Pension, health, and welfare funds	5	3	0.8	5	-	4,800		40	-	-
6400	Insurance agents, brokers, and service	79	102	1.6	353	410	23,989	23,249	9,166	10,141	0.8
6500	Real estate	119	126	1.3	399	492	17,283	16,837	7,991	10,469	0.6
6510	Real estate operators and lessors	20	24	0.6	59	132	12,271	13,788	947	1,847	0.5
6530	Real estate agents and managers	65	75	1.4	201	242	18,149	16,612	4,235	5,852	0.5
6540	Title abstract offices	3	5	2.2	33	30	15,152	19,733	545	735	1.6
6552	Subdividers and developers, n.e.c.	10	12	3.5	27	39	19,407	20,308	545	921	1.4
6553	Cemetery subdividers and developers	8	9	2.4	29	39	22,483	20,000	713	786	1.5
6700	Holding and other investment offices	10	10	0.8	-	78		34,923	-	3,018	0.5
6710	Holding offices	4	4	1.0	20	-	84,600	-	1,545	-	-
MCLEAN, IL											
60 -	**Finance, insurance, and real estate**	314	318	1.1	16,162	17,342	33,842	39,161	603,258	658,223	4.5
6000	Depository institutions	64	66	1.5	1,472	1,831	22,821	22,250	35,624	41,999	1.2
6020	Commercial banks	36	41	1.9	687	1,089	23,790	21,557	17,215	23,485	0.9
6030	Savings institutions	12	9	1.0	729	688	22,524	23,785	17,606	17,581	3.5
6060	Credit unions	15	16	2.2	-	54	-	16,667	-	933	1.0
6210	Security brokers and dealers	10	10	0.8	53	62	162,340	69,226	5,736	4,722	0.3
6310	Life insurance	18	13	2.2	1,289	1,220	34,622	39,682	46,942	46,825	5.1
6370	Pension, health, and welfare funds	2	5	1.3	-	102	-	1,804	-	82	0.1
6400	Insurance agents, brokers, and service	89	86	1.4	3,075	2,057	29,610	32,482	100,469	72,209	5.4
6510	Real estate operators and lessors	33	40	1.1	114	-	12,246	-	1,499	-	-
6530	Real estate agents and managers	30	37	0.7	172	185	20,140	19,243	3,251	3,291	0.3
6553	Cemetery subdividers and developers	6	6	1.6	31	30	21,806	18,533	703	700	1.3
MACON, IL											
60 -	**Finance, insurance, and real estate**	247	259	0.9	2,295	2,655	23,386	21,915	54,052	58,792	0.4
6000	Depository institutions	49	67	1.5	1,035	1,187	19,358	19,053	20,396	24,427	0.7
6020	Commercial banks	22	30	1.4	585	860	20,280	19,921	11,876	18,594	0.7
6030	Savings institutions	8	6	0.7	116	-	18,897	-	2,240	-	-
6060	Credit unions	15	23	3.1	-	185	-	16,649	-	3,293	3.5
6100	Nondepository institutions	15	9	0.5	120	74	19,600	26,216	2,446	1,886	0.2
6200	Security and commodity brokers	11	12	0.5	81	78	61,679	60,821	4,572	4,752	0.2

Source: County Business Patterns, 1992/93, CBP-92/93-1, U.S. Department of Commerce, Washington, D.C., April 1995. SIC categories for which data were suppressed or not available for both 1992 and 1993 are *not* displayed. The employment columns represent mid-March employment in the year. Pay per employee is calculated by dividing 1st Quarter payroll, annualized, by mid-March employment. The columns headed "% State" show the county's percentage of the state total for the SIC in 1993; for example, 0.9% for SIC 6030 means that the county had 0.9 percent of the state's total establishments (or payroll) in SIC 6030 in 1993. A dash (-) is used to indicate that data are not available or cannot be calculated; *nec* means not elsewhere classified.

Continued on next page.

SIC	Industry	No. Establishments			Employment		Pay / Employee		Annual Payroll ($ 000)		
		1992	1993	% State	1992	1993	1992	1993	1992	1993	% State
MACON, IL - [continued]											
6210	Security brokers and dealers	7	10	0.8	69	-	67,478	-	4,231	-	-
6300	Insurance carriers	23	17	0.8	506	515	31,407	35,138	15,300	16,891	0.5
6310	Life insurance	6	6	1.0	77	-	26,130	-	1,981	-	-
6400	Insurance agents, brokers, and service	84	92	1.5	246	264	20,488	21,530	5,329	5,338	0.4
6500	Real estate	56	57	0.6	232	534	14,707	9,468	4,142	5,377	0.3
6510	Real estate operators and lessors	25	29	0.8	75	382	11,253	7,560	1,362	2,940	0.8
6530	Real estate agents and managers	21	23	0.4	101	133	17,347	13,985	1,935	2,123	0.2
6700	Holding and other investment offices	9	5	0.4	75	3	25,920	16,000	1,867	121	0.0
MACOUPIN, IL											
60 –	**Finance, insurance, and real estate**	86	84	0.3	509	-	17,917	-	9,795	-	-
6000	Depository institutions	24	24	0.5	338	354	18,438	18,362	6,626	6,764	0.2
6020	Commercial banks	19	19	0.9	311	324	18,997	18,815	6,272	6,315	0.2
6030	Savings institutions	5	5	0.5	27	30	12,000	13,467	354	449	0.1
6400	Insurance agents, brokers, and service	31	33	0.5	63	70	18,095	17,886	1,213	1,289	0.1
6500	Real estate	20	18	0.2	57	-	17,053	-	1,069	-	-
6510	Real estate operators and lessors	5	9	0.2	19	24	12,000	10,333	230	262	0.1
6530	Real estate agents and managers	5	4	0.1	9	11	18,667	17,091	218	260	0.0
6553	Cemetery subdividers and developers	4	3	0.8	9	-	5,778	-	64	-	-
MADISON, IL											
60 –	**Finance, insurance, and real estate**	492	497	1.7	4,141	3,628	20,893	20,606	88,316	78,733	0.5
6000	Depository institutions	99	107	2.4	1,645	1,717	21,267	19,825	34,838	36,188	1.0
6020	Commercial banks	55	59	2.7	1,237	1,321	21,882	20,273	26,638	28,577	1.1
6030	Savings institutions	18	15	1.6	216	170	21,944	21,600	4,959	3,861	0.8
6100	Nondepository institutions	23	14	0.8	76	59	20,105	20,949	1,600	1,575	0.1
6140	Personal credit institutions	19	11	1.9	60	-	19,000	-	1,221	-	-
6200	Security and commodity brokers	25	26	1.0	80	70	32,300	43,143	2,655	3,182	0.1
6210	Security brokers and dealers	18	18	1.4	66	58	35,091	48,552	2,364	2,940	0.2
6280	Security and commodity services	7	8	1.1	14	12	19,143	17,000	291	242	0.1
6300	Insurance carriers	55	45	2.0	720	728	27,289	29,110	20,486	20,046	0.6
6310	Life insurance	7	7	1.2	88	83	29,636	29,735	2,649	2,344	0.3
6330	Fire, marine, and casualty insurance	35	27	2.7	574	594	27,157	29,535	15,898	16,552	0.8
6400	Insurance agents, brokers, and service	144	156	2.5	390	366	14,626	15,749	6,048	6,542	0.5
6500	Real estate	130	139	1.4	1,148	596	17,836	12,322	21,080	8,452	0.5
6510	Real estate operators and lessors	46	48	1.3	837	211	19,560	11,716	16,609	2,782	0.7
6530	Real estate agents and managers	53	62	1.2	156	203	12,897	11,901	2,165	2,701	0.3
6540	Title abstract offices	5	6	2.6	60	98	14,000	14,286	967	1,753	3.8
6552	Subdividers and developers, n.e.c.	4	6	1.7	13	24	14,154	7,667	195	139	0.2
6553	Cemetery subdividers and developers	15	16	4.3	60	60	13,933	14,533	882	997	1.9
6700	Holding and other investment offices	15	10	0.8	-	92	-	23,522	-	2,748	0.4
6710	Holding offices	5	4	1.0	12	-	29,333	-	339	-	-
MARION, IL											
60 –	**Finance, insurance, and real estate**	96	92	0.3	633	655	20,727	20,171	13,638	14,105	0.1
6000	Depository institutions	17	23	0.5	282	323	20,028	18,514	5,584	6,267	0.2
6020	Commercial banks	13	18	0.8	258	296	20,124	18,527	5,086	5,683	0.2
6100	Nondepository institutions	6	5	0.3	15	-	18,133	-	297	-	-
6140	Personal credit institutions	5	4	0.7	-	13	-	21,231	-	320	0.1
6300	Insurance carriers	12	8	0.4	168	171	23,857	25,450	4,393	4,611	0.1
6400	Insurance agents, brokers, and service	27	31	0.5	65	83	16,677	17,253	1,118	1,558	0.1
6500	Real estate	20	17	0.2	58	50	10,690	11,840	744	756	0.0
6510	Real estate operators and lessors	6	4	0.1	11	9	9,455	11,556	158	129	0.0
6530	Real estate agents and managers	9	10	0.2	26	23	9,692	10,609	267	319	0.0

Source: County Business Patterns, 1992/93, CBP-92/93-1, U.S. Department of Commerce, Washington, D.C., April 1995. SIC categories for which data were suppressed or not available for both 1992 and 1993 are *not* displayed. The employment columns represent mid-March employment in the year. Pay per employee is calculated by dividing 1st Quarter payroll, annualized, by mid-March employment. The columns headed "% State" show the county's percentage of the state total for the SIC in 1993; for example, 0.9% for SIC 6030 means that the county had 0.9 percent of the state's total establishments (or payroll) in SIC 6030 in 1993. A dash (-) is used to indicate that data are not available or cannot be calculated; *nec* means not elsewhere classified.

SIC	Industry	No. Establishments			Employment		Pay / Employee		Annual Payroll ($ 000)		
		1992	1993	% State	1992	1993	1992	1993	1992	1993	% State
MARSHALL, IL											
60–	**Finance, insurance, and real estate**	31	30	0.1	-	-	-	-	-	-	-
6000	Depository institutions	8	8	0.2	88	89	23,045	23,730	2,184	2,246	0.1
6400	Insurance agents, brokers, and service	11	12	0.2	25	-	11,040	-	319	-	-
MASON, IL											
60–	**Finance, insurance, and real estate**	32	32	0.1	158	169	19,418	17,609	2,869	2,894	0.0
6000	Depository institutions	9	9	0.2	112	118	22,429	21,186	2,328	2,419	0.1
6400	Insurance agents, brokers, and service	14	15	0.2	-	34	-	11,412	-	384	0.0
MASSAC, IL											
60–	**Finance, insurance, and real estate**	19	18	0.1	94	108	18,468	18,481	1,936	2,208	0.0
6000	Depository institutions	6	5	0.1	71	76	20,507	21,316	1,607	1,654	0.0
6020	Commercial banks	3	3	0.1	61	-	22,295	-	1,523	-	-
6400	Insurance agents, brokers, and service	7	6	0.1	-	15	-	12,533	-	279	0.0
6530	Real estate agents and managers	3	2	0.0	2	-	8,000	-	25	-	-
MENARD, IL											
60–	**Finance, insurance, and real estate**	22	24	0.1	127	113	18,992	16,920	1,956	2,064	0.0
6000	Depository institutions	8	7	0.2	98	80	21,184	19,350	1,579	1,620	0.0
6020	Commercial banks	8	7	0.3	98	80	21,184	19,350	1,579	1,620	0.1
6400	Insurance agents, brokers, and service	7	9	0.1	16	-	10,750	-	186	-	-
MERCER, IL											
60–	**Finance, insurance, and real estate**	35	36	0.1	146	154	16,274	15,896	2,497	2,671	0.0
6000	Depository institutions	10	12	0.3	104	108	16,385	16,222	1,797	1,939	0.1
6020	Commercial banks	8	8	0.4	-	96	-	16,917	-	1,797	0.1
6400	Insurance agents, brokers, and service	14	13	0.2	30	-	9,333	-	354	-	-
MONROE, IL											
60–	**Finance, insurance, and real estate**	50	52	0.2	297	291	17,764	16,619	5,294	6,020	0.0
6000	Depository institutions	10	12	0.3	193	193	16,891	16,850	3,303	3,984	0.1
6200	Security and commodity brokers	4	4	0.2	-	10	-	34,000	-	458	0.0
6400	Insurance agents, brokers, and service	16	19	0.3	43	-	23,163	-	900	-	-
6530	Real estate agents and managers	5	6	0.1	10	-	12,000	-	124	-	-
MONTGOMERY, IL											
60–	**Finance, insurance, and real estate**	71	73	0.3	501	429	14,459	18,238	7,376	7,965	0.1
6000	Depository institutions	23	22	0.5	388	314	15,103	19,439	5,784	5,873	0.2
6020	Commercial banks	16	16	0.7	354	286	15,198	19,790	5,286	5,405	0.2
6030	Savings institutions	4	4	0.4	28	-	15,143	-	434	-	-
6060	Credit unions	3	2	0.3	6	-	9,333	-	64	-	-
6100	Nondepository institutions	4	3	0.2	8	-	12,500	-	152	-	-
6400	Insurance agents, brokers, and service	16	20	0.3	47	51	9,872	10,510	478	583	0.0
6510	Real estate operators and lessors	4	5	0.1	5	5	6,400	8,000	66	264	0.1
6530	Real estate agents and managers	8	9	0.2	17	17	9,647	9,412	148	167	0.0
MORGAN, IL											
60–	**Finance, insurance, and real estate**	75	81	0.3	912	911	22,018	22,674	20,363	20,927	0.1
6000	Depository institutions	20	19	0.4	317	316	20,909	22,215	6,625	6,845	0.2
6020	Commercial banks	14	14	0.6	252	-	20,968	-	5,173	-	-
6100	Nondepository institutions	4	4	0.2	15	16	17,333	20,500	290	256	0.0
6200	Security and commodity brokers	3	3	0.1	15	12	35,733	56,333	553	612	0.0
6210	Security brokers and dealers	3	3	0.2	15	12	35,733	56,333	553	612	0.0
6300	Insurance carriers	13	14	0.6	394	409	25,766	25,242	10,231	10,445	0.3
6370	Pension, health, and welfare funds	6	6	1.6	61	59	14,230	15,661	878	915	1.3

Source: County Business Patterns, 1992/93, CBP-92/93-1, U.S. Department of Commerce, Washington, D.C., April 1995. SIC categories for which data were suppressed or not available for both 1992 and 1993 are not displayed. The employment columns represent mid-March employment in the year. Pay per employee is calculated by dividing 1st Quarter payroll, annualized, by mid-March employment. The columns headed "% State" show the county's percentage of the state total for the SIC in 1993; for example, 0.9% for SIC 6030 means that the county had 0.9 percent of the state's total establishments (or payroll) in SIC 6030 in 1993. A dash (-) is used to indicate that data are not available or cannot be calculated; nec means not elsewhere classified.

Continued on next page.

SIC	Industry	No. Establishments			Employment		Pay / Employee		Annual Payroll ($ 000)		
		1992	1993	% State	1992	1993	1992	1993	1992	1993	% State
MORGAN, IL - [continued]											
6400	Insurance agents, brokers, and service	17	19	0.3	70	75	18,286	15,947	1,342	1,525	0.1
6510	Real estate operators and lessors	8	9	0.2	36	30	14,222	16,667	640	677	0.2
6530	Real estate agents and managers	4	6	0.1	6	8	6,000	6,000	39	66	0.0
MOULTRIE, IL											
60 –	**Finance, insurance, and real estate**	20	19	0.1	113	115	20,354	20,800	2,285	2,236	0.0
6000	Depository institutions	7	6	0.1	85	81	19,200	21,037	1,749	1,690	0.0
6020	Commercial banks	7	6	0.3	85	81	19,200	21,037	1,749	1,690	0.0
6400	Insurance agents, brokers, and service	7	7	0.1	-	20	-	28,600	-	415	0.1
OGLE, IL											
60 –	**Finance, insurance, and real estate**	91	98	0.3	456	732	19,246	22,639	9,793	18,644	0.1
6000	Depository institutions	24	25	0.6	317	341	21,312	20,798	7,295	7,264	0.2
6020	Commercial banks	13	13	0.6	256	264	21,453	22,000	5,931	5,858	0.2
6030	Savings institutions	6	6	0.7	-	57		17,333	-	1,120	0.2
6060	Credit unions	4	5	0.7	17	-	15,059		258	-	-
6400	Insurance agents, brokers, and service	29	35	0.6	71	78	13,239	13,795	1,239	1,337	0.1
6510	Real estate operators and lessors	4	6	0.2	7	10	5,714	9,200	56	131	0.0
6530	Real estate agents and managers	8	11	0.2	15	14	12,000	12,286	194	230	0.0
6553	Cemetery subdividers and developers	8	7	1.9	3	-	2,667	-	34	-	-
6700	Holding and other investment offices	3	4	0.3	6	-	21,333	-	133	-	-
PEORIA, IL											
60 –	**Finance, insurance, and real estate**	523	520	1.8	6,278	5,987	26,876	27,879	153,029	168,195	1.2
6000	Depository institutions	83	86	1.9	1,815	2,139	21,964	25,135	39,672	51,683	1.5
6020	Commercial banks	43	46	2.1	1,153	1,460	21,336	24,871	25,382	35,226	1.4
6060	Credit unions	17	19	2.6	363	-	26,623	-	8,863	-	-
6100	Nondepository institutions	39	30	1.8	1,080	215	21,804	25,284	12,155	5,494	0.5
6140	Personal credit institutions	25	17	2.9	549	133	20,474	17,474	5,428	2,446	0.9
6150	Business credit institutions	5	4	1.0	33	-	39,030	-	1,035	-	-
6160	Mortgage bankers and brokers	9	8	1.2	498	51	22,129	34,902	5,692	2,027	0.5
6200	Security and commodity brokers	27	24	0.9	187	186	70,310	64,731	13,547	13,482	0.5
6210	Security brokers and dealers	16	11	0.9	167	160	76,814	70,850	13,140	12,430	0.8
6300	Insurance carriers	81	63	2.8	1,726	1,853	35,386	32,555	55,609	59,647	1.6
6310	Life insurance	29	26	4.4	824	910	31,893	32,119	24,204	27,111	3.0
6330	Fire, marine, and casualty insurance	32	24	2.4	800	774	40,685	36,114	29,076	28,921	1.4
6370	Pension, health, and welfare funds	17	11	2.9	68	-	21,000	-	1,515	-	-
6400	Insurance agents, brokers, and service	157	172	2.7	732	732	22,814	21,858	17,160	16,590	1.2
6500	Real estate	108	118	1.2	581	636	17,281	17,862	10,583	12,166	0.8
6510	Real estate operators and lessors	43	50	1.4	146	193	14,603	19,503	2,337	4,029	1.1
6530	Real estate agents and managers	50	54	1.0	365	331	18,137	17,631	6,803	6,249	0.6
6553	Cemetery subdividers and developers	9	11	2.9	53	-	17,811	-	907	-	-
6700	Holding and other investment offices	28	27	2.1	157	226	27,720	35,345	4,303	9,133	1.4
6710	Holding offices	4	6	1.4	52	107	44,462	54,280	2,572	7,272	1.6
6732	Educational, religious, etc. trusts	10	9	4.0	58	56	19,103	21,143	792	866	3.6
6733	Trusts, n.e.c.	9	7	2.8	43	57	16,837	15,368	752	670	1.6
6799	Investors, n.e.c.	4	5	1.9	-	6	-	20,000	-	325	0.4
PERRY, IL											
60 –	**Finance, insurance, and real estate**	37	36	0.1	211	222	18,882	21,225	4,170	4,959	0.0
6000	Depository institutions	8	8	0.2	155	145	19,665	18,979	3,172	2,917	0.1
6020	Commercial banks	5	5	0.2	146	141	20,055	19,092	3,066	2,863	0.1
6400	Insurance agents, brokers, and service	12	12	0.2	20	-	10,600	-	250	-	-
6500	Real estate	11	12	0.1	21	-	25,714	-	543	-	-

Source: County Business Patterns, 1992/93, CBP-92/93-1, U.S. Department of Commerce, Washington, D.C., April 1995. SIC categories for which data were suppressed or not available for both 1992 and 1993 are *not* displayed. The employment columns represent mid-March employment in the year. Pay per employee is calculated by dividing 1st Quarter payroll, annualized, by mid-March employment. The columns headed "% State" show the county's percentage of the state total for the SIC in 1993; for example, 0.9% for SIC 6030 means that the county had 0.9 percent of the state's total establishments (or payroll) in SIC 6030 in 1993. A dash (-) is used to indicate that data are not available or cannot be calculated; *nec* means not elsewhere classified.

SIC	Industry	No. Establishments			Employment		Pay / Employee		Annual Payroll ($ 000)		
		1992	1993	% State	1992	1993	1992	1993	1992	1993	% State
PIATT, IL											
60 –	**Finance, insurance, and real estate**	29	29	0.1	202	203	15,941	16,591	3,670	3,887	0.0
6000	Depository institutions	14	10	0.2	169	126	15,858	17,302	2,919	2,368	0.1
6020	Commercial banks	11	7	0.3	163	120	15,951	17,467	2,832	2,277	0.1
PIKE, IL											
60 –	**Finance, insurance, and real estate**	42	40	0.1	181	181	18,696	16,884	3,923	3,567	0.0
6000	Depository institutions	12	12	0.3	127	128	19,244	18,094	2,940	2,739	0.1
POPE, IL											
60 –	**Finance, insurance, and real estate**	3	2	0.0	-	-	-	-	-	-	-
PULASKI, IL											
60 –	**Finance, insurance, and real estate**	11	9	0.0	44	-	13,182	-	692	-	-
6400	Insurance agents, brokers, and service	2	3	0.0	-	6	-	15,333	-	88	0.0
PUTNAM, IL											
60 –	**Finance, insurance, and real estate**	10	9	0.0	50	-	19,600	-	1,018	-	-
RANDOLPH, IL											
60 –	**Finance, insurance, and real estate**	60	58	0.2	366	367	19,770	18,332	6,802	6,958	0.0
6000	Depository institutions	20	20	0.4	275	263	21,425	20,487	5,475	5,582	0.2
6020	Commercial banks	11	11	0.5	195	180	19,569	19,422	3,637	3,549	0.1
6510	Real estate operators and lessors	6	6	0.2	7	-	4,571	-	34	-	-
RICHLAND, IL											
60 –	**Finance, insurance, and real estate**	30	31	0.1	199	193	24,261	26,756	4,553	4,625	0.0
6000	Depository institutions	7	7	0.2	112	115	26,107	29,809	2,534	2,611	0.1
ROCK ISLAND, IL											
60 –	**Finance, insurance, and real estate**	294	300	1.1	4,377	4,383	26,466	25,231	120,789	115,896	0.8
6000	Depository institutions	67	71	1.6	1,242	1,346	22,068	20,363	27,430	28,817	0.8
6020	Commercial banks	40	43	2.0	960	986	22,833	21,473	21,911	22,306	0.9
6060	Credit unions	20	22	3.0	228	312	18,982	16,821	4,337	5,510	5.8
6100	Nondepository institutions	16	15	0.9	165	142	33,673	34,761	5,945	5,610	0.5
6140	Personal credit institutions	11	11	1.9	139	115	34,129	37,391	5,150	4,979	1.8
6200	Security and commodity brokers	10	14	0.6	-	69	-	49,623	-	4,165	0.2
6300	Insurance carriers	37	35	1.6	1,475	2,169	27,466	29,291	46,044	63,774	1.8
6310	Life insurance	8	10	1.7	1,042	1,832	25,228	29,098	31,323	52,087	5.7
6330	Fire, marine, and casualty insurance	12	8	0.8	-	283	-	32,975	-	10,312	0.5
6400	Insurance agents, brokers, and service	63	61	1.0	228	209	23,930	21,397	5,842	5,103	0.4
6500	Real estate	90	93	0.9	428	391	15,589	14,527	7,984	7,275	0.4
6510	Real estate operators and lessors	45	47	1.3	226	231	13,327	13,143	3,502	3,613	0.9
6530	Real estate agents and managers	26	34	0.6	120	85	19,900	18,024	2,890	1,959	0.2
6540	Title abstract offices	4	6	2.6	43	52	16,372	15,385	898	1,296	2.8
6553	Cemetery subdividers and developers	4	5	1.3	18	-	14,000	-	299	-	-
6700	Holding and other investment offices	10	11	0.8	-	57	-	19,930	-	1,152	0.2
6732	Educational, religious, etc. trusts	3	4	1.8	17	-	10,118	-	161	-	-
ST. CLAIR, IL											
60 –	**Finance, insurance, and real estate**	443	458	1.6	3,113	3,158	21,999	20,827	69,818	69,583	0.5
6000	Depository institutions	76	84	1.9	1,278	1,388	20,172	18,643	25,838	26,803	0.8
6020	Commercial banks	48	52	2.4	1,044	1,113	20,716	19,597	21,618	22,218	0.9
6030	Savings institutions	10	10	1.1	114	115	15,158	15,130	1,770	2,024	0.4
6060	Credit unions	15	19	2.6	105	139	21,524	15,194	2,267	2,317	2.5
6090	Functions closely related to banking	3	3	0.5	15	21	10,933	10,095	183	244	0.2
6100	Nondepository institutions	31	29	1.7	153	201	23,085	22,030	3,963	5,238	0.5
6140	Personal credit institutions	21	20	3.4	86	90	21,860	17,289	1,897	1,629	0.6
6160	Mortgage bankers and brokers	7	9	1.4	62	111	25,484	25,874	1,972	3,609	1.0

Source: County Business Patterns, 1992/93, CBP-92/93-1, U.S. Department of Commerce, Washington, D.C., April 1995. SIC categories for which data were suppressed or not available for both 1992 and 1993 are *not* displayed. The employment columns represent mid-March employment in the year. Pay per employee is calculated by dividing 1st Quarter payroll, annualized, by mid-March employment. The columns headed "% State" show the county's percentage of the state total for the SIC in 1993; for example, 0.9% for SIC 6030 means that the county had 0.9 percent of the state's total establishments (or payroll) in SIC 6030 in 1993. A dash (-) is used to indicate that data are not available or cannot be calculated; *nec* means not elsewhere classified.

Continued on next page.

SIC	Industry	No. Establishments			Employment		Pay / Employee		Annual Payroll ($ 000)		
		1992	1993	% State	1992	1993	1992	1993	1992	1993	% State
ST. CLAIR, IL - [continued]											
6200	Security and commodity brokers	27	29	1.1	111	182	55,604	40,286	6,206	7,577	0.3
6210	Security brokers and dealers	14	16	1.3	93	79	63,613	64,506	5,800	5,210	0.3
6280	Security and commodity services	13	13	1.8	18	103	14,222	21,709	406	2,367	0.5
6300	Insurance carriers	57	39	1.8	311	301	25,106	24,611	7,228	7,661	0.2
6310	Life insurance	16	10	1.7	182	196	23,758	23,816	4,236	4,535	0.5
6370	Pension, health, and welfare funds	12	10	2.6	-	14	-	10,000	-	408	0.6
6400	Insurance agents, brokers, and service	110	124	2.0	323	350	17,300	16,297	5,892	6,295	0.5
6500	Real estate	123	137	1.4	586	526	14,928	15,817	10,167	9,409	0.6
6510	Real estate operators and lessors	38	57	1.5	153	199	14,431	13,769	2,424	2,959	0.8
6530	Real estate agents and managers	54	59	1.1	238	225	16,067	15,058	4,270	3,878	0.4
6552	Subdividers and developers, n.e.c.	10	11	3.2	90	26	8,533	23,692	910	735	1.1
6553	Cemetery subdividers and developers	8	7	1.9	47	-	21,532	-	1,112	-	-
6700	Holding and other investment offices	19	16	1.2	351	210	30,929	31,924	10,524	6,600	1.0
6710	Holding offices	3	4	1.0	131	-	38,687	-	5,067	-	-
6733	Trusts, n.e.c.	12	8	3.3	211	-	27,033	-	5,359	-	-
SALINE, IL											
60 –	**Finance, insurance, and real estate**	57	54	0.2	533	557	16,773	17,429	9,689	10,293	0.1
6000	Depository institutions	16	15	0.3	238	223	16,437	18,170	4,079	4,026	0.1
6100	Nondepository institutions	4	4	0.2	16	-	14,750	-	298	-	-
6400	Insurance agents, brokers, and service	17	17	0.3	42	-	13,905	-	606	-	-
6500	Real estate	12	12	0.1	-	60	-	6,800	-	425	0.0
6510	Real estate operators and lessors	2	3	0.1	-	6	-	22,667	-	143	0.0
6530	Real estate agents and managers	4	4	0.1	21	45	4,000	3,467	95	123	0.0
6540	Title abstract offices	3	2	0.9	8	-	11,500	-	95	-	-
SANGAMON, IL											
60 –	**Finance, insurance, and real estate**	482	492	1.7	7,908	7,710	25,825	27,997	196,620	209,489	1.4
6000	Depository institutions	78	89	2.0	1,899	1,921	23,056	26,074	43,095	46,382	1.3
6020	Commercial banks	47	61	2.8	1,611	1,688	23,655	26,931	37,066	41,834	1.6
6030	Savings institutions	14	11	1.2	168	110	22,048	23,273	3,928	2,380	0.5
6100	Nondepository institutions	24	24	1.4	336	387	29,262	31,762	8,779	14,094	1.3
6160	Mortgage bankers and brokers	7	8	1.2	264	292	30,636	36,233	6,968	12,175	3.2
6200	Security and commodity brokers	21	21	0.8	109	102	50,202	62,157	5,522	6,361	0.3
6210	Security brokers and dealers	14	11	0.9	99	88	52,202	68,909	5,349	5,992	0.4
6300	Insurance carriers	85	71	3.2	4,162	3,728	28,328	30,477	108,702	106,545	2.9
6310	Life insurance	24	18	3.0	2,027	1,622	25,472	25,785	49,854	44,326	4.9
6330	Fire, marine, and casualty insurance	30	25	2.5	1,730	1,697	33,054	36,641	49,437	51,767	2.5
6400	Insurance agents, brokers, and service	124	121	1.9	659	628	21,147	22,115	15,581	15,644	1.2
6500	Real estate	125	141	1.4	596	546	13,483	15,136	9,950	9,785	0.6
6510	Real estate operators and lessors	55	66	1.8	214	237	12,037	12,726	2,860	3,410	0.9
6530	Real estate agents and managers	44	55	1.0	259	188	13,328	17,766	4,556	4,010	0.4
6540	Title abstract offices	5	4	1.7	46	46	18,957	19,304	1,032	1,215	2.6
6552	Subdividers and developers, n.e.c.	6	8	2.3	26	56	9,385	13,143	431	834	1.3
6553	Cemetery subdividers and developers	5	5	1.3	16	15	15,000	15,733	250	253	0.5
6700	Holding and other investment offices	24	25	1.9	-	398	-	28,553	-	10,678	1.6
6710	Holding offices	12	14	3.4	110	302	42,618	35,762	4,388	10,276	2.3
6732	Educational, religious, etc. trusts	3	5	2.2	16	87	17,500	5,793	252	338	1.4
6733	Trusts, n.e.c.	7	3	1.2	19	5	13,474	3,200	235	11	0.0
SCHUYLER, IL											
60 –	**Finance, insurance, and real estate**	9	9	0.0	54	54	16,222	15,481	984	964	0.0
6400	Insurance agents, brokers, and service	4	4	0.1	13	-	12,615	-	161	-	-
SCOTT, IL											
60 –	**Finance, insurance, and real estate**	13	12	0.0	61	65	17,639	15,323	1,143	1,098	0.0
6020	Commercial banks	3	3	0.1	-	42	-	19,048	-	889	0.0
6400	Insurance agents, brokers, and service	5	4	0.1	-	16	-	10,000	-	175	0.0

Source: County Business Patterns, 1992/93, CBP-92/93-1, U.S. Department of Commerce, Washington, D.C., April 1995. SIC categories for which data were suppressed or not available for both 1992 and 1993 are *not* displayed. The employment columns represent mid-March employment in the year. Pay per employee is calculated by dividing 1st Quarter payroll, annualized, by mid-March employment. The columns headed "% State" show the county's percentage of the state total for the SIC in 1993; for example, 0.9% for SIC 6030 means that the county had 0.9 percent of the state's total establishments (or payroll) in SIC 6030 in 1993. A dash (-) is used to indicate that data are not available or cannot be calculated; *nec* means not elsewhere classified.

SIC	Industry	No. Establishments			Employment		Pay / Employee		Annual Payroll ($ 000)		
		1992	1993	% State	1992	1993	1992	1993	1992	1993	% State
SHELBY, IL											
60 –	**Finance, insurance, and real estate**	44	45	0.2	220	225	18,964	19,644	4,122	4,576	0.0
6000	Depository institutions	16	16	0.4	148	145	19,514	21,186	2,806	3,107	0.1
6020	Commercial banks	13	13	0.6	134	134	19,373	20,627	2,522	2,801	0.1
6030	Savings institutions	3	3	0.3	14	11	20,857	28,000	284	306	0.1
6200	Security and commodity brokers	2	3	0.1	-	6	-	9,333	-	67	0.0
6400	Insurance agents, brokers, and service	15	15	0.2	-	48	-	21,583	-	1,063	0.1
6530	Real estate agents and managers	4	4	0.1	4	5	12,000	12,800	57	72	0.0
STARK, IL											
60 –	**Finance, insurance, and real estate**	16	16	0.1	103	81	26,757	26,815	2,708	1,598	0.0
6000	Depository institutions	4	5	0.1	60	60	15,267	15,533	1,116	1,120	0.0
6020	Commercial banks	4	4	0.2	60	-	15,267	-	1,116	-	-
STEPHENSON, IL											
60 –	**Finance, insurance, and real estate**	119	121	0.4	1,982	1,977	24,809	25,139	48,625	49,683	0.3
6000	Depository institutions	22	23	0.5	406	399	21,281	22,055	8,747	8,666	0.3
6020	Commercial banks	16	16	0.7	338	331	22,260	23,009	7,530	7,401	0.3
6100	Nondepository institutions	4	5	0.3	14	15	32,286	27,733	373	392	0.0
6200	Security and commodity brokers	4	6	0.2	13	12	82,462	59,000	794	842	0.0
6210	Security brokers and dealers	4	5	0.4	13	-	82,462	-	794	-	-
6300	Insurance carriers	17	16	0.7	1,284	1,241	26,090	26,214	32,690	32,136	0.9
6400	Insurance agents, brokers, and service	37	38	0.6	88	106	21,227	17,019	1,826	1,954	0.1
6500	Real estate	28	25	0.3	105	94	12,267	12,511	1,438	1,502	0.1
6510	Real estate operators and lessors	7	5	0.1	20	25	10,600	11,040	229	316	0.1
6530	Real estate agents and managers	14	14	0.3	35	28	12,686	10,857	415	404	0.0
6700	Holding and other investment offices	7	8	0.6	72	110	32,667	38,764	2,757	4,191	0.6
TAZEWELL, IL											
60 –	**Finance, insurance, and real estate**	213	212	0.7	1,970	1,936	20,317	21,081	42,913	43,276	0.3
6000	Depository institutions	51	54	1.2	763	772	20,529	20,456	17,235	16,560	0.5
6020	Commercial banks	30	32	1.5	538	547	19,955	21,287	12,128	12,188	0.5
6030	Savings institutions	15	14	1.5	-	148	-	19,054	-	2,984	0.6
6060	Credit unions	5	8	1.1	-	77	-	17,247	-	1,388	1.5
6100	Nondepository institutions	9	4	0.2	27	15	21,481	27,467	442	313	0.0
6200	Security and commodity brokers	8	12	0.5	20	27	33,400	29,333	792	1,021	0.0
6210	Security brokers and dealers	5	8	0.6	-	24	-	31,833	-	981	0.1
6300	Insurance carriers	22	17	0.8	646	643	23,944	24,292	15,591	15,624	0.4
6330	Fire, marine, and casualty insurance	11	9	0.9	470	464	23,311	24,198	10,996	11,184	0.5
6400	Insurance agents, brokers, and service	72	73	1.2	236	234	18,424	19,573	5,151	5,272	0.4
6500	Real estate	46	48	0.5	262	225	11,389	14,204	3,383	4,014	0.2
6510	Real estate operators and lessors	12	13	0.4	58	30	8,690	11,333	444	496	0.1
6530	Real estate agents and managers	26	27	0.5	151	154	14,066	15,870	2,384	2,855	0.3
6553	Cemetery subdividers and developers	4	4	1.1	7	-	2,857	-	42	-	-
6700	Holding and other investment offices	5	4	0.3	16	20	19,500	21,000	319	472	0.1
UNION, IL											
60 –	**Finance, insurance, and real estate**	24	24	0.1	142	116	16,620	17,655	2,621	2,748	0.0
6000	Depository institutions	9	9	0.2	114	82	16,070	16,829	1,937	1,914	0.1
6020	Commercial banks	6	6	0.3	107	74	16,000	16,919	1,805	1,760	0.1
6400	Insurance agents, brokers, and service	9	8	0.1	15	23	10,667	11,652	288	392	0.0
VERMILION, IL											
60 –	**Finance, insurance, and real estate**	186	182	0.6	1,426	1,450	19,919	20,695	30,879	32,729	0.2
6000	Depository institutions	47	50	1.1	645	643	18,288	17,928	12,109	12,840	0.4
6020	Commercial banks	22	24	1.1	495	485	18,764	18,441	9,566	10,127	0.4
6060	Credit unions	17	19	2.6	91	99	15,121	15,030	1,319	1,596	1.7
6100	Nondepository institutions	10	6	0.4	34	27	19,647	15,111	728	459	0.0
6140	Personal credit institutions	8	6	1.0	-	27	-	15,111	-	459	0.2

Source: County Business Patterns, 1992/93, CBP-92/93-1, U.S. Department of Commerce, Washington, D.C., April 1995. SIC categories for which data were suppressed or not available for both 1992 and 1993 are not displayed. The employment columns represent mid-March employment in the year. Pay per employee is calculated by dividing 1st Quarter payroll, annualized, by mid-March employment. The columns headed "% State" show the county's percentage of the state total for the SIC in 1993; for example, 0.9% for SIC 6030 means that the county had 0.9 percent of the state's total establishments (or payroll) in SIC 6030 in 1993. A dash (-) is used to indicate that data are not available or cannot be calculated; nec means not elsewhere classified.

Continued on next page.

SIC	Industry	No. Establishments			Employment		Pay / Employee		Annual Payroll ($ 000)		
		1992	1993	% State	1992	1993	1992	1993	1992	1993	% State
VERMILION, IL - [continued]											
6200	Security and commodity brokers	4	4	0.2	18	17	40,000	51,765	786	987	0.0
6210	Security brokers and dealers	4	4	0.3	18	17	40,000	51,765	786	987	0.1
6300	Insurance carriers	16	12	0.5	220	214	22,982	23,533	4,974	5,313	0.1
6400	Insurance agents, brokers, and service	46	48	0.8	273	307	20,850	25,629	7,361	8,605	0.6
6500	Real estate	54	53	0.5	220	226	18,036	16,867	4,312	4,065	0.3
6510	Real estate operators and lessors	22	25	0.7	120	82	18,367	10,439	2,297	797	0.2
6530	Real estate agents and managers	18	14	0.3	49	35	21,224	18,629	1,007	682	0.1
6540	Title abstract offices	4	4	1.7	24	22	12,833	15,273	338	379	0.8
6553	Cemetery subdividers and developers	6	9	2.4	-	87	-	22,621	-	2,156	4.1
6700	Holding and other investment offices	9	9	0.7	16	16	31,500	29,750	609	460	0.1
6710	Holding offices	4	5	1.2	-	10	-	42,800	-	397	0.1
WABASH, IL											
60 –	**Finance, insurance, and real estate**	24	23	0.1	184	170	18,739	19,694	3,760	3,782	0.0
6000	Depository institutions	9	9	0.2	138	129	19,246	18,419	2,770	2,628	0.1
6020	Commercial banks	6	6	0.3	125	116	19,680	18,931	2,551	2,413	0.1
6400	Insurance agents, brokers, and service	6	5	0.1	16	16	18,250	19,000	358	385	0.0
WARREN, IL											
60 –	**Finance, insurance, and real estate**	39	32	0.1	264	211	17,288	17,062	4,606	3,744	0.0
6000	Depository institutions	10	7	0.2	190	129	16,884	16,496	3,275	2,296	0.1
6200	Security and commodity brokers	5	5	0.2	-	9	-	11,556	-	103	0.0
6280	Security and commodity services	3	3	0.4	1	-	8,000	-	14	-	-
6400	Insurance agents, brokers, and service	11	9	0.1	30	33	14,933	12,727	449	474	0.0
6530	Real estate agents and managers	2	3	0.1	-	4	-	20,000	-	89	0.0
WASHINGTON, IL											
60 –	**Finance, insurance, and real estate**	29	31	0.1	175	193	17,760	16,974	3,143	3,363	0.0
6000	Depository institutions	10	10	0.2	124	130	18,935	17,785	2,383	2,506	0.1
6400	Insurance agents, brokers, and service	12	11	0.2	-	45	-	18,578	-	716	0.1
6510	Real estate operators and lessors	2	3	0.1	-	4	-	3,000	-	35	0.0
WAYNE, IL											
60 –	**Finance, insurance, and real estate**	30	26	0.1	165	141	17,358	17,135	2,626	2,492	0.0
6000	Depository institutions	6	5	0.1	118	97	20,034	19,918	2,114	1,959	0.1
6400	Insurance agents, brokers, and service	12	11	0.2	-	28	-	11,286	-	331	0.0
6530	Real estate agents and managers	4	3	0.1	5	-	7,200	-	39	-	-
WHITE, IL											
60 –	**Finance, insurance, and real estate**	33	36	0.1	177	187	25,333	23,166	4,231	4,245	0.0
6000	Depository institutions	6	6	0.1	94	101	28,723	25,109	2,316	2,365	0.1
6020	Commercial banks	6	6	0.3	94	101	28,723	25,109	2,316	2,365	0.1
6400	Insurance agents, brokers, and service	12	14	0.2	25	-	21,600	-	579	-	-
6510	Real estate operators and lessors	5	5	0.1	11	11	4,727	5,091	53	55	0.0
WHITESIDE, IL											
60 –	**Finance, insurance, and real estate**	121	133	0.5	924	854	17,857	18,913	16,525	16,714	0.1
6000	Depository institutions	21	22	0.5	511	533	20,407	18,904	10,093	10,225	0.3
6020	Commercial banks	12	12	0.6	368	407	21,620	17,975	7,823	7,675	0.3
6060	Credit unions	6	6	0.8	-	28	-	16,857	-	477	0.5
6100	Nondepository institutions	5	6	0.4	25	-	28,640	-	850	-	-
6140	Personal credit institutions	3	4	0.7	-	15	-	24,000	-	326	0.1
6200	Security and commodity brokers	7	9	0.4	-	30	-	47,200	-	1,408	0.1
6210	Security brokers and dealers	3	5	0.4	16	24	72,250	55,833	927	1,343	0.1
6280	Security and commodity services	4	4	0.6	-	6	-	12,667	-	65	0.0
6300	Insurance carriers	13	14	0.6	62	-	10,774	-	662	-	-
6400	Insurance agents, brokers, and service	33	36	0.6	137	130	14,131	15,231	2,043	2,091	0.2
6500	Real estate	39	43	0.4	164	87	9,268	11,908	1,852	1,216	0.1

Source: County Business Patterns, 1992/93, CBP-92/93-1, U.S. Department of Commerce, Washington, D.C., April 1995. SIC categories for which data were suppressed or not available for both 1992 and 1993 are *not* displayed. The employment columns represent mid-March employment in the year. Pay per employee is calculated by dividing 1st Quarter payroll, annualized, by mid-March employment. The columns headed "% State" show the county's percentage of the state total for the SIC in 1993; for example, 0.9% for SIC 6030 means that the county had 0.9 percent of the state's total establishments (or payroll) in SIC 6030 in 1993. A dash (-) is used to indicate that data are not available or cannot be calculated; *nec* means not elsewhere classified.

Continued on next page.

SIC	Industry	No. Establishments			Employment		Pay / Employee		Annual Payroll ($ 000)		
		1992	1993	% State	1992	1993	1992	1993	1992	1993	% State
WHITESIDE, IL - [continued]											
6510	Real estate operators and lessors	16	16	0.4	64	30	10,500	11,067	619	313	0.1
6530	Real estate agents and managers	12	19	0.4	22	-	8,000	-	229	-	-
6553	Cemetery subdividers and developers	3	4	1.1	11	9	13,455	18,667	171	182	0.3
6700	Holding and other investment offices	3	3	0.2	-	2	-	10,000	-	25	0.0
WILL, IL											
60 –	**Finance, insurance, and real estate**	520	560	2.0	4,192	4,195	21,452	21,863	97,064	100,505	0.7
6000	Depository institutions	90	99	2.2	1,993	2,051	19,815	19,899	42,056	43,665	1.3
6020	Commercial banks	40	55	2.5	1,393	1,486	20,327	20,878	28,855	31,641	1.2
6030	Savings institutions	26	19	2.1	499	430	19,214	17,767	11,275	10,076	2.0
6060	Credit unions	14	18	2.4	81	90	17,284	16,756	1,419	1,243	1.3
6090	Functions closely related to banking	9	7	1.2	-	45	-	14,222	-	705	0.7
6100	Nondepository institutions	30	33	1.9	156	187	22,692	20,941	3,787	5,103	0.5
6140	Personal credit institutions	22	21	3.5	133	142	23,218	21,352	3,149	3,101	1.1
6210	Security brokers and dealers	15	17	1.4	53	55	45,962	47,927	2,466	2,789	0.2
6220	Commodity contracts brokers, dealers	3	4	0.7	6	-	4,000	-	86	-	-
6280	Security and commodity services	8	9	1.3	30	16	25,733	35,500	1,011	560	0.1
6300	Insurance carriers	63	42	1.9	835	587	22,596	27,550	19,126	16,025	0.4
6310	Life insurance	5	4	0.7	109	99	28,697	31,596	2,900	2,715	0.3
6330	Fire, marine, and casualty insurance	29	19	1.9	367	292	28,033	32,055	10,879	9,995	0.5
6370	Pension, health, and welfare funds	20	17	4.5	204	-	11,961	-	1,985	-	-
6400	Insurance agents, brokers, and service	136	157	2.5	452	484	26,956	26,612	13,816	15,658	1.2
6500	Real estate	161	186	1.9	548	652	15,460	13,840	9,988	11,205	0.7
6510	Real estate operators and lessors	36	44	1.2	124	139	13,419	12,374	1,803	2,114	0.6
6530	Real estate agents and managers	88	108	2.1	338	399	14,722	12,361	5,758	6,244	0.6
6540	Title abstract offices	-	6	2.6	-	43	-	20,000	-	943	2.0
6552	Subdividers and developers, n.e.c.	7	17	4.9	15	37	26,400	26,486	577	1,326	2.1
6553	Cemetery subdividers and developers	8	9	2.4	28	33	18,000	16,000	573	565	1.1
6700	Holding and other investment offices	12	12	0.9	116	-	34,000	-	4,501	-	-
6710	Holding offices	3	3	0.7	74	112	41,027	39,321	3,619	3,671	0.8
6733	Trusts, n.e.c.	5	4	1.6	5	-	12,000	-	82	-	-
WILLIAMSON, IL											
60 –	**Finance, insurance, and real estate**	116	113	0.4	1,094	1,030	17,795	18,396	21,579	21,197	0.1
6000	Depository institutions	19	20	0.4	247	250	16,988	16,912	4,395	4,300	0.1
6020	Commercial banks	13	13	0.6	209	215	16,938	16,763	3,680	3,623	0.1
6100	Nondepository institutions	6	6	0.4	-	17	-	25,882	-	814	0.1
6300	Insurance carriers	13	9	0.4	154	512	19,766	19,234	3,070	11,075	0.3
6400	Insurance agents, brokers, and service	41	44	0.7	476	123	18,126	16,000	8,976	2,141	0.2
6500	Real estate	30	26	0.3	111	111	10,883	13,045	1,413	1,723	0.1
6510	Real estate operators and lessors	14	9	0.2	85	77	10,118	11,065	878	852	0.2
6530	Real estate agents and managers	11	11	0.2	18	17	13,778	14,118	415	326	0.0
6700	Holding and other investment offices	5	3	0.2	84	-	19,143	-	2,855	-	-
WINNEBAGO, IL											
60 –	**Finance, insurance, and real estate**	592	578	2.0	5,981	5,447	22,689	25,294	133,665	147,349	1.0
6000	Depository institutions	85	88	2.0	1,589	1,634	22,120	21,559	33,525	36,448	1.1
6020	Commercial banks	39	37	1.7	957	968	21,266	21,347	19,988	20,998	0.8
6030	Savings institutions	17	17	1.9	437	423	22,865	20,823	8,888	9,693	1.9
6060	Credit unions	23	28	3.8	114	145	17,053	15,200	1,955	2,271	2.4
6090	Functions closely related to banking	6	6	1.0	81	98	35,309	36,245	2,694	3,486	3.2
6100	Nondepository institutions	41	30	1.8	242	236	26,083	35,203	6,716	7,582	0.7
6140	Personal credit institutions	26	16	2.7	113	-	21,381	-	2,543	-	-
6160	Mortgage bankers and brokers	12	13	2.0	122	132	30,459	47,212	3,986	5,400	1.4
6200	Security and commodity brokers	35	42	1.7	187	321	65,433	43,688	11,066	14,904	0.6
6210	Security brokers and dealers	21	25	2.0	160	222	73,100	58,342	10,286	13,967	0.9
6280	Security and commodity services	13	17	2.4	-	99	-	10,828	-	937	0.2
6300	Insurance carriers	87	69	3.1	1,663	1,030	16,794	27,173	26,236	29,592	0.8

Source: County Business Patterns, 1992/93, CBP-92/93-1, U.S. Department of Commerce, Washington, D.C., April 1995. SIC categories for which data were suppressed or not available for both 1992 and 1993 are *not* displayed. The employment columns represent mid-March employment in the year. Pay per employee is calculated by dividing 1st Quarter payroll, annualized, by mid-March employment. The columns headed "% State" show the county's percentage of the state total for the SIC in 1993; for example, 0.9% for SIC 6030 means that the county had 0.9 percent of the state's total establishments (or payroll) in SIC 6030 in 1993. A dash (-) is used to indicate that data are not available or cannot be calculated; *nec* means not elsewhere classified.

Continued on next page.

SIC	Industry	No. Establishments			Employment		Pay / Employee		Annual Payroll ($ 000)		
		1992	1993	% State	1992	1993	1992	1993	1992	1993	% State
WINNEBAGO, IL - [continued]											
6310	Life insurance	27	19	3.2	1,138	506	14,007	29,510	14,069	14,008	1.5
6330	Fire, marine, and casualty insurance	24	19	1.9	179	249	29,318	28,177	5,341	7,353	0.4
6370	Pension, health, and welfare funds	30	28	7.4	117	-	11,179	-	1,528	-	-
6400	Insurance agents, brokers, and service	138	146	2.3	698	595	24,246	23,509	16,952	14,652	1.1
6500	Real estate	170	171	1.7	887	902	15,770	16,173	16,893	18,963	1.2
6510	Real estate operators and lessors	67	67	1.8	264	236	12,909	12,915	3,575	3,352	0.9
6530	Real estate agents and managers	68	77	1.5	359	463	16,279	16,562	7,263	9,405	0.9
6540	Title abstract offices	3	5	2.2	-	106	-	21,283	-	3,390	7.3
6552	Subdividers and developers, n.e.c.	6	11	3.2	73	22	16,219	20,364	1,464	1,474	2.3
6553	Cemetery subdividers and developers	10	10	2.7	79	74	16,608	15,514	1,372	1,329	2.5
6700	Holding and other investment offices	36	32	2.5	715	729	32,403	32,444	22,277	25,208	3.9
6710	Holding offices	14	9	2.2	665	658	34,051	33,860	21,635	23,554	5.2
6733	Trusts, n.e.c.	15	13	5.3	-	37	-	9,081	-	360	0.9
WOODFORD, IL											
60 –	**Finance, insurance, and real estate**	53	48	0.2	244	231	20,967	20,831	5,322	5,042	0.0
6000	Depository institutions	15	15	0.3	147	145	22,531	21,655	3,413	3,315	0.1
6020	Commercial banks	8	10	0.5	99	117	24,323	23,761	2,514	2,955	0.1
6100	Nondepository institutions	3	3	0.2	-	11	-	31,636	-	295	0.0
6400	Insurance agents, brokers, and service	21	20	0.3	50	50	13,840	15,600	811	858	0.1

Source: County Business Patterns, 1992/93, CBP-92/93-1, U.S. Department of Commerce, Washington, D.C., April 1995. SIC categories for which data were suppressed or not available for both 1992 and 1993 are *not* displayed. The employment columns represent mid-March employment in the year. Pay per employee is calculated by dividing 1st Quarter payroll, annualized, by mid-March employment. The columns headed "% State" show the county's percentage of the state total for the SIC in 1993; for example, 0.9% for SIC 6030 means that the county had 0.9 percent of the state's total establishments (or payroll) in SIC 6030 in 1993. A dash (-) is used to indicate that data are not available or cannot be calculated; *nec* means not elsewhere classified.

INDIANA

SIC	Industry	No. Establishments			Employment		Pay / Employee		Annual Payroll ($ 000)		
		1992	1993	% State	1992	1993	1992	1993	1992	1993	% State
ADAMS, IN											
60 –	**Finance, insurance, and real estate**	53	56	0.5	280	302	17,943	17,815	5,527	4,984	0.1
6000	Depository institutions	16	17	0.7	177	196	19,164	18,592	3,647	3,048	0.3
6020	Commercial banks	11	11	0.6	157	174	19,720	19,195	3,338	2,715	0.4
6300	Insurance carriers	3	3	0.3	8	8	8,000	9,000	70	77	0.0
6330	Fire, marine, and casualty insurance	3	3	0.7	8	8	8,000	9,000	70	77	0.0
6400	Insurance agents, brokers, and service	17	18	0.6	49	50	15,592	17,440	912	1,000	0.3
6530	Real estate agents and managers	6	8	0.5	3	10	9,333	12,000	69	103	0.0
ALLEN, IN											
60 –	**Finance, insurance, and real estate**	789	814	6.8	12,634	13,493	31,884	32,301	395,056	383,076	11.0
6000	Depository institutions	136	142	5.6	3,149	3,901	22,825	24,360	71,994	60,366	6.5
6020	Commercial banks	84	84	4.9	2,500	3,152	24,029	26,269	60,161	47,021	6.7
6060	Credit unions	36	40	8.9	-	566	-	16,657	-	9,972	12.0
6100	Nondepository institutions	57	61	8.2	1,315	1,385	39,580	34,628	56,617	66,327	17.3
6140	Personal credit institutions	30	28	7.2	152	155	19,289	16,335	3,122	2,455	1.5
6150	Business credit institutions	4	4	8.2	69	-	27,246	-	1,874	-	-
6160	Mortgage bankers and brokers	22	28	11.0	1,092	1,217	43,245	37,108	51,613	63,380	32.2
6200	Security and commodity brokers	45	41	8.6	-	671	-	49,317	-	26,392	12.9
6210	Security brokers and dealers	25	20	6.7	195	-	69,026	-	13,497	-	-
6280	Security and commodity services	19	20	12.0	-	470	-	46,060	-	14,384	40.2
6300	Insurance carriers	88	83	8.3	4,616	4,609	35,156	37,541	153,235	151,159	15.0
6310	Life insurance	28	23	7.8	3,398	3,826	36,518	37,583	116,285	121,698	25.7
6321	Accident and health insurance	6	1	3.4	335	-	16,776	-	6,403	-	-
6330	Fire, marine, and casualty insurance	39	41	9.3	553	435	44,817	40,469	22,503	17,645	4.8
6370	Pension, health, and welfare funds	10	10	6.5	188	-	14,681	-	2,624	-	-
6400	Insurance agents, brokers, and service	193	206	7.1	1,330	1,321	30,821	34,074	39,328	37,976	9.5
6500	Real estate	243	258	6.7	1,354	1,308	15,583	15,156	22,742	23,797	5.7
6510	Real estate operators and lessors	90	102	6.5	458	451	14,279	12,763	6,990	6,720	5.6
6530	Real estate agents and managers	105	122	7.2	648	603	15,451	16,809	10,362	11,777	5.6
6540	Title abstract offices	5	7	4.1	-	83	-	20,337	-	2,217	7.6
6552	Subdividers and developers, n.e.c.	9	13	8.3	31	60	20,516	14,333	984	1,335	4.0
6553	Cemetery subdividers and developers	8	11	5.3	83	111	13,108	12,468	1,329	1,660	8.3
6732	Educational, religious, etc. trusts	12	10	11.0	55	-	11,200	-	708	-	-
6733	Trusts, n.e.c.	7	5	5.3	22	-	36,182	-	783	-	-
BARTHOLOMEW, IN											
60 –	**Finance, insurance, and real estate**	166	171	1.4	1,977	2,534	29,060	28,189	59,109	73,389	2.1
6000	Depository institutions	32	31	1.2	523	565	25,300	26,896	12,657	14,282	1.5
6020	Commercial banks	20	19	1.1	288	311	30,625	32,849	8,043	9,060	1.3
6100	Nondepository institutions	10	12	1.6	35	35	19,543	19,771	663	750	0.2
6200	Security and commodity brokers	9	9	1.9	58	105	61,655	74,933	3,302	7,744	3.8
6210	Security brokers and dealers	4	4	1.3	51	-	64,392	-	2,983	-	-
6280	Security and commodity services	5	5	3.0	7	-	41,714	-	319	-	-
6300	Insurance carriers	23	19	1.9	427	824	31,869	27,956	13,420	23,639	2.3
6310	Life insurance	4	4	1.4	66	-	30,545	-	1,774	-	-
6370	Pension, health, and welfare funds	6	6	3.9	-	20	-	5,400	-	128	0.5
6400	Insurance agents, brokers, and service	31	38	1.3	601	665	20,672	21,353	13,036	14,526	3.6
6500	Real estate	51	51	1.3	248	272	17,161	17,559	4,797	5,490	1.3
6510	Real estate operators and lessors	24	26	1.6	113	127	14,195	15,118	1,793	2,196	1.8
6530	Real estate agents and managers	18	18	1.1	69	78	21,971	20,154	1,717	1,930	0.9

Source: County Business Patterns, 1992/93, CBP-92/93-1, U.S. Department of Commerce, Washington, D.C., April 1995. SIC categories for which data were suppressed or not available for both 1992 and 1993 are *not* displayed. The employment columns represent mid-March employment in the year. Pay per employee is calculated by dividing 1st Quarter payroll, annualized, by mid-March employment. The columns headed "% State" show the county's percentage of the state total for the SIC in 1993; for example, 0.9% for SIC 6030 means that the county had 0.9 percent of the state's total establishments (or payroll) in SIC 6030 in 1993. A dash (-) is used to indicate that data are not available or cannot be calculated; *nec* means not elsewhere classified.

Continued on next page.

SIC	Industry	No. Establishments			Employment		Pay / Employee		Annual Payroll ($ 000)		
		1992	1993	% State	1992	1993	1992	1993	1992	1993	% State
BARTHOLOMEW, IN - [continued]											
6540	Title abstract offices	3	3	1.7	23	20	13,739	15,600	353	353	1.2
6700	Holding and other investment offices	10	11	3.0	85	68	113,788	83,294	11,234	6,958	5.9
6733	Trusts, n.e.c.	4	6	6.3	5	--	4,000	-	20	-	-
BENTON, IN											
60 –	**Finance, insurance, and real estate**	22	21	0.2	133	149	18,947	16,993	2,483	2,802	0.1
6000	Depository institutions	7	7	0.3	94	105	20,255	16,876	1,748	1,889	0.2
6400	Insurance agents, brokers, and service	8	8	0.3	18	20	15,778	15,000	329	366	0.1
BLACKFORD, IN											
60 –	**Finance, insurance, and real estate**	22	23	0.2	154	151	15,922	18,066	2,666	2,781	0.1
6000	Depository institutions	10	10	0.4	107	99	15,402	17,495	1,726	1,699	0.2
6400	Insurance agents, brokers, and service	5	5	0.2	17	18	11,529	13,333	218	255	0.1
BOONE, IN											
60 –	**Finance, insurance, and real estate**	76	84	0.7	523	561	18,264	21,005	10,440	11,745	0.3
6000	Depository institutions	14	17	0.7	160	186	20,875	26,086	3,025	4,193	0.5
6100	Nondepository institutions	5	2	0.3	16	--	19,500	-	1,023	-	-
6200	Security and commodity brokers	4	6	1.3	--	16	-	23,750	-	557	0.3
6400	Insurance agents, brokers, and service	23	27	0.9	69	70	18,435	20,629	1,368	1,498	0.4
6500	Real estate	24	26	0.7	95	99	9,642	9,535	1,033	1,042	0.3
6510	Real estate operators and lessors	8	7	0.4	15	--	11,200	-	183	-	-
6530	Real estate agents and managers	8	14	0.8	21	27	10,095	13,333	216	378	0.2
6540	Title abstract offices	3	3	1.7	13	18	16,923	16,000	267	322	1.1
BROWN, IN											
60 –	**Finance, insurance, and real estate**	18	20	0.2	62	71	15,935	15,718	1,083	1,227	0.0
6000	Depository institutions	5	5	0.2	31	32	16,000	16,000	549	599	0.1
6400	Insurance agents, brokers, and service	3	3	0.1	19	15	17,053	23,467	338	335	0.1
6500	Real estate	10	12	0.3	12	24	14,000	10,500	196	293	0.1
6530	Real estate agents and managers	5	6	0.4	7	--	11,429	-	94	-	-
CARROLL, IN											
60 –	**Finance, insurance, and real estate**	28	32	0.3	244	189	18,541	15,852	4,575	3,371	0.1
6000	Depository institutions	9	9	0.4	135	129	17,748	15,628	2,439	2,139	0.2
6400	Insurance agents, brokers, and service	9	10	0.3	38	37	22,526	20,000	838	794	0.2
6500	Real estate	7	10	0.3	65	18	17,785	9,111	1,171	331	0.1
6510	Real estate operators and lessors	3	4	0.3	6	7	5,333	5,714	38	108	0.1
CASS, IN											
60 –	**Finance, insurance, and real estate**	65	64	0.5	458	471	20,131	20,433	9,542	9,176	0.3
6000	Depository institutions	19	19	0.8	299	290	18,916	19,200	5,838	5,057	0.5
6020	Commercial banks	12	12	0.7	242	233	18,182	18,249	4,708	3,757	0.5
6100	Nondepository institutions	5	5	0.7	17	15	13,647	16,800	231	229	0.1
6200	Security and commodity brokers	3	3	0.6	15	--	57,333	-	946	-	-
6300	Insurance carriers	3	2	0.2	11	--	50,909	-	454	-	-
6400	Insurance agents, brokers, and service	14	15	0.5	66	68	16,061	23,294	1,139	1,485	0.4
6500	Real estate	17	16	0.4	44	56	13,364	11,000	600	772	0.2
6510	Real estate operators and lessors	8	7	0.4	12	13	7,000	6,769	93	103	0.1
6530	Real estate agents and managers	5	4	0.2	14	12	16,571	15,667	219	273	0.1
6700	Holding and other investment offices	4	4	1.1	6	8	44,000	54,000	334	382	0.3
CLARK, IN											
60 –	**Finance, insurance, and real estate**	135	148	1.2	980	1,297	19,857	20,580	21,511	24,753	0.7
6000	Depository institutions	42	37	1.5	560	827	21,564	23,008	13,799	15,003	1.6
6020	Commercial banks	31	27	1.6	482	745	21,726	23,350	12,069	13,083	1.9
6100	Nondepository institutions	11	11	1.5	40	71	23,500	13,465	982	1,290	0.3
6140	Personal credit institutions	7	8	2.1	24	61	23,000	10,492	590	925	0.6

Source: County Business Patterns, 1992/93, CBP-92/93-1, U.S. Department of Commerce, Washington, D.C., April 1995. SIC categories for which data were suppressed or not available for both 1992 and 1993 are *not* displayed. The employment columns represent mid-March employment in the year. Pay per employee is calculated by dividing 1st Quarter payroll, annualized, by mid-March employment. The columns headed "% State" show the county's percentage of the state total for the SIC in 1993; for example, 0.9% for SIC 6030 means that the county had 0.9 percent of the state's total establishments (or payroll) in SIC 6030 in 1993. A dash (-) is used to indicate that data are not available or cannot be calculated; *nec* means not elsewhere classified.

Continued on next page.

SIC	Industry	No. Establishments			Employment		Pay / Employee		Annual Payroll ($ 000)		
		1992	1993	% State	1992	1993	1992	1993	1992	1993	% State
CLARK, IN - [continued]											
6160	Mortgage bankers and brokers	3	3	1.2	14	10	26,000	31,600	356	365	0.2
6300	Insurance carriers	12	10	1.0	59	56	32,610	30,357	1,965	1,942	0.2
6330	Fire, marine, and casualty insurance	8	8	1.8	26	-	41,692		1,128	-	-
6400	Insurance agents, brokers, and service	21	30	1.0	62	63	18,452	16,190	1,025	1,171	0.3
6500	Real estate	45	55	1.4	236	257	11,831	11,704	2,987	3,636	0.9
6510	Real estate operators and lessors	26	32	2.0	150	150	10,187	10,400	1,533	1,958	1.6
6530	Real estate agents and managers	12	13	0.8	64	80	15,625	13,450	1,145	1,190	0.6
CLAY, IN											
60 –	**Finance, insurance, and real estate**	38	39	0.3	241	246	17,245	17,870	4,511	4,785	0.1
6000	Depository institutions	13	13	0.5	173	183	17,434	18,120	3,322	3,570	0.4
6300	Insurance carriers	2	3	0.3	-	10		20,400	-	196	0.0
6400	Insurance agents, brokers, and service	11	11	0.4	31	31	16,258	16,000	577	593	0.1
6500	Real estate	9	8	0.2	18	16	8,000	13,000	137	215	0.1
6530	Real estate agents and managers	3	2	0.1	3	-	10,667		27	-	-
CLINTON, IN											
60 –	**Finance, insurance, and real estate**	60	64	0.5	359	371	16,836	16,194	6,412	6,213	0.2
6000	Depository institutions	14	16	0.6	235	259	16,834	16,124	3,990	3,991	0.4
6100	Nondepository institutions	4	3	0.4	16	10	17,500	24,400	294	289	0.1
6400	Insurance agents, brokers, and service	13	17	0.6	33	30	17,212	19,200	608	708	0.2
6500	Real estate	20	21	0.5	41	53	10,049	9,434	536	731	0.2
6510	Real estate operators and lessors	10	11	0.7	15	26	8,533	6,462	137	195	0.2
6530	Real estate agents and managers	5	5	0.3	9	8	6,222	16,000	115	137	0.1
CRAWFORD, IN											
60 –	**Finance, insurance, and real estate**	13	14	0.1	57	59	20,421	20,542	1,150	1,189	0.0
6000	Depository institutions	7	7	0.3	46	48	20,261	20,333	909	917	0.1
6020	Commercial banks	7	7	0.4	46	48	20,261	20,333	909	917	0.1
DAVIESS, IN											
60 –	**Finance, insurance, and real estate**	50	54	0.5	308	296	18,935	21,243	6,383	6,290	0.2
6000	Depository institutions	17	18	0.7	226	197	19,628	22,924	4,772	4,375	0.5
6100	Nondepository institutions	3	3	0.4	-	20		25,400	-	370	0.1
6400	Insurance agents, brokers, and service	11	11	0.4	37	38	12,541	12,842	484	592	0.1
6500	Real estate	15	18	0.5	22	25	11,091	9,280	282	294	0.1
6510	Real estate operators and lessors	4	5	0.3	-	7		4,571		39	0.0
6530	Real estate agents and managers	7	7	0.4	11	8	10,182	9,000	101	85	0.0
6553	Cemetery subdividers and developers	3	4	1.9	6	7	15,333	13,714	116	127	0.6
DEARBORN, IN											
60 –	**Finance, insurance, and real estate**	74	79	0.7	500	478	18,336	16,870	9,870	9,154	0.3
6000	Depository institutions	23	22	0.9	294	280	18,871	16,329	5,707	4,978	0.5
6020	Commercial banks	14	14	0.8	191	173	19,916	16,185	3,824	2,879	0.4
6030	Savings institutions	4	4	1.2	92	99	17,913	17,091	1,783	2,007	1.5
6060	Credit unions	5	4	0.9	11	8	8,727	10,000	100	92	0.1
6300	Insurance carriers	7	5	0.5	24	20	17,333	15,200	419	310	0.0
6400	Insurance agents, brokers, and service	15	17	0.6	70	70	24,514	22,571	1,960	1,826	0.5
6500	Real estate	25	31	0.8	101	102	13,030	14,039	1,580	1,781	0.4
6510	Real estate operators and lessors	9	8	0.5	20	21	7,000	7,238	164	195	0.2
6530	Real estate agents and managers	11	15	0.9	56	41	17,071	12,098	1,125	600	0.3
6540	Title abstract offices	-	3	1.7	-	13		10,462	-	192	0.7
DECATUR, IN											
60 –	**Finance, insurance, and real estate**	40	37	0.3	260	244	18,600	20,197	4,947	5,414	0.2
6000	Depository institutions	8	8	0.3	146	150	20,384	19,387	2,953	3,088	0.3
6100	Nondepository institutions	2	3	0.4	-	12		26,667	-	373	0.1
6300	Insurance carriers	3	2	0.2	18	-	13,556		336	-	-

Source: County Business Patterns, 1992/93, CBP-92/93-1, U.S. Department of Commerce, Washington, D.C., April 1995. SIC categories for which data were suppressed or not available for both 1992 and 1993 are not displayed. The employment columns represent mid-March employment in the year. Pay per employee is calculated by dividing 1st Quarter payroll, annualized, by mid-March employment. The columns headed "% State" show the county's percentage of the state total for the SIC in 1993; for example, 0.9% for SIC 6030 means that the county had 0.9 percent of the state's total establishments (or payroll) in SIC 6030 in 1993. A dash (-) is used to indicate that data are not available or cannot be calculated; nec means not elsewhere classified.

Continued on next page.

SIC	Industry	No. Establishments			Employment		Pay / Employee		Annual Payroll ($ 000)		
		1992	1993	% State	1992	1993	1992	1993	1992	1993	% State
STEUBEN, IN											
60 –	**Finance, insurance, and real estate**	54	51	0.4	271	268	17,978	19,328	5,469	4,675	0.1
6000	Depository institutions	16	16	0.6	179	169	19,061	20,994	3,676	2,799	0.3
6020	Commercial banks	11	11	0.6	148	135	19,378	22,252	3,080	2,177	0.3
6400	Insurance agents, brokers, and service	11	10	0.3	25	22	14,880	17,818	386	425	0.1
6500	Real estate	19	20	0.5	45	51	13,689	14,196	855	905	0.2
6510	Real estate operators and lessors	9	8	0.5	19	20	12,842	14,400	446	391	0.3
6530	Real estate agents and managers	6	8	0.5	13	19	13,538	12,000	207	265	0.1
SULLIVAN, IN											
60 –	**Finance, insurance, and real estate**	40	37	0.3	213	212	14,329	15,434	3,179	3,549	0.1
6000	Depository institutions	11	11	0.4	118	120	17,593	19,367	2,210	2,335	0.3
6400	Insurance agents, brokers, and service	8	9	0.3	29	30	13,241	11,867	387	384	0.1
6500	Real estate	15	13	0.3	24	32	10,167	8,125	276	281	0.1
6510	Real estate operators and lessors	3	3	0.2	-	5	-	10,400	-	57	0.0
6530	Real estate agents and managers	8	7	0.4	10	18	5,200	6,000	88	117	0.1
SWITZERLAND, IN											
60 –	**Finance, insurance, and real estate**	10	10	0.1	53	51	15,698	17,412	897	968	0.0
6400	Insurance agents, brokers, and service	3	3	0.1	9	11	10,667	7,636	86	69	0.0
TIPPECANOE, IN											
60 –	**Finance, insurance, and real estate**	299	303	2.5	3,924	3,792	24,845	29,182	103,835	110,701	3.2
6000	Depository institutions	61	56	2.2	1,081	921	20,740	22,436	22,554	22,013	2.4
6020	Commercial banks	41	38	2.2	820	723	20,615	22,351	16,943	16,962	2.4
6030	Savings institutions	11	9	2.7	128	149	23,031	26,228	3,125	3,945	3.0
6060	Credit unions	9	9	2.0	133	49	19,308	12,163	2,486	1,106	1.3
6100	Nondepository institutions	21	19	2.5	-	130	-	24,585	-	3,209	0.8
6140	Personal credit institutions	13	11	2.8	59	61	16,949	14,295	1,122	918	0.6
6200	Security and commodity brokers	15	16	3.4	70	72	48,514	45,889	3,169	3,595	1.8
6210	Security brokers and dealers	6	9	3.0	-	52	-	58,231	-	3,260	2.0
6280	Security and commodity services	8	6	3.6	19	-	22,526	-	312	-	-
6300	Insurance carriers	24	20	2.0	1,930	1,875	29,791	37,510	59,877	65,144	6.5
6400	Insurance agents, brokers, and service	66	69	2.4	242	246	20,628	21,122	7,619	7,306	1.8
6500	Real estate	109	120	3.1	497	543	13,586	14,556	7,780	9,353	2.2
6510	Real estate operators and lessors	49	57	3.6	191	227	10,827	12,705	2,431	3,141	2.6
6530	Real estate agents and managers	38	47	2.8	170	188	16,635	14,319	3,090	3,308	1.6
6552	Subdividers and developers, n.e.c.	7	8	5.1	100	90	14,000	17,778	1,708	2,018	6.0
6553	Cemetery subdividers and developers	8	6	2.9	24	-	15,833	-	468	-	-
6700	Holding and other investment offices	3	3	0.8	-	5	-	12,800	-	81	0.1
TIPTON, IN											
60 –	**Finance, insurance, and real estate**	24	25	0.2	153	176	17,046	14,636	2,775	2,798	0.1
6000	Depository institutions	4	4	0.2	98	119	18,082	13,244	1,824	1,810	0.2
6300	Insurance carriers	3	3	0.3	15	10	17,333	16,400	274	113	0.0
6330	Fire, marine, and casualty insurance	3	3	0.7	15	10	17,333	16,400	274	113	0.0
6400	Insurance agents, brokers, and service	6	7	0.2	-	24	-	15,500	-	387	0.1
6500	Real estate	8	8	0.2	14	16	8,000	10,250	132	164	0.0
6510	Real estate operators and lessors	2	4	0.3	-	9	-	9,333	-	75	0.1
UNION, IN											
60 –	**Finance, insurance, and real estate**	13	13	0.1	83	90	17,301	16,444	1,580	1,650	0.0
6000	Depository institutions	4	4	0.2	60	66	19,867	18,848	1,267	1,358	0.1
6400	Insurance agents, brokers, and service	4	4	0.1	10	10	10,800	12,800	125	137	0.0
6500	Real estate	5	5	0.1	13	14	10,462	7,714	188	155	0.0

Source: County Business Patterns, 1992/93, CBP-92/93-1, U.S. Department of Commerce, Washington, D.C., April 1995. SIC categories for which data were suppressed or not available for both 1992 and 1993 are *not* displayed. The employment columns represent mid-March employment in the year. Pay per employee is calculated by dividing 1st Quarter payroll, annualized, by mid-March employment. The columns headed "% State" show the county's percentage of the state total for the SIC in 1993; for example, 0.9% for SIC 6030 means that the county had 0.9 percent of the state's total establishments (or payroll) in SIC 6030 in 1993. A dash (-) is used to indicate that data are not available or cannot be calculated; *nec* means not elsewhere classified.

SIC	Industry	No. Establishments			Employment		Pay / Employee		Annual Payroll ($ 000)		
		1992	1993	% State	1992	1993	1992	1993	1992	1993	% State
VANDERBURGH, IN											
60 –	**Finance, insurance, and real estate**	467	464	3.9	5,315	5,280	23,250	26,180	126,870	143,842	4.1
6000	Depository institutions	78	82	3.3	1,778	1,817	20,182	21,270	37,185	43,831	4.8
6020	Commercial banks	44	44	2.6	1,293	1,296	20,421	21,929	27,268	32,108	4.6
6030	Savings institutions	23	23	6.8	383	387	19,091	19,959	7,713	9,163	6.9
6060	Credit unions	11	15	3.4	102	134	21,255	18,687	2,204	2,560	3.1
6100	Nondepository institutions	45	46	6.2	1,260	1,263	26,276	32,231	34,133	40,794	10.6
6200	Security and commodity brokers	24	20	4.2	153	186	58,824	70,903	9,294	10,903	5.3
6210	Security brokers and dealers	16	13	4.4	140	151	63,629	86,225	9,198	10,743	6.5
6280	Security and commodity services	8	7	4.2	13	35	7,077	4,800	96	160	0.4
6300	Insurance carriers	54	45	4.5	479	408	29,603	34,157	14,028	13,547	1.3
6310	Life insurance	16	16	5.4	238	199	28,790	33,648	6,800	6,178	1.3
6330	Fire, marine, and casualty insurance	29	21	4.8	122	94	31,180	34,979	3,627	3,337	0.9
6400	Insurance agents, brokers, and service	100	104	3.6	582	574	25,230	26,585	15,439	16,412	4.1
6500	Real estate	149	154	4.0	1,002	951	15,277	13,943	15,867	14,855	3.6
6510	Real estate operators and lessors	76	77	4.9	559	477	12,959	11,757	7,460	6,099	5.1
6530	Real estate agents and managers	53	60	3.5	299	384	18,047	15,823	5,690	6,732	3.2
6540	Title abstract offices	3	5	2.9	46	50	17,565	17,440	969	1,004	3.4
6552	Subdividers and developers, n.e.c.	4	4	2.6	8	2	7,000	18,000	80	245	0.7
6553	Cemetery subdividers and developers	3	7	3.4	34	38	23,647	17,579	782	725	3.6
6710	Holding offices	4	6	5.8	9	57	21,778	48,842	196	3,026	4.7
6732	Educational, religious, etc. trusts	3	3	3.3	3	–	21,333	–	57	–	
6733	Trusts, n.e.c.	6	1	1.1	33	–	24,848	–	296	–	
VERMILLION, IN											
60 –	**Finance, insurance, and real estate**	18	20	0.2	127	117	15,118	16,410	2,002	2,029	0.1
6000	Depository institutions	6	7	0.3	96	89	14,917	17,258	1,483	1,606	0.2
6400	Insurance agents, brokers, and service	5	5	0.2	10	10	15,200	16,800	165	199	0.0
VIGO, IN											
60 –	**Finance, insurance, and real estate**	215	212	1.8	1,885	1,893	20,798	21,215	39,171	40,044	1.2
6000	Depository institutions	39	41	1.6	903	949	18,405	19,098	17,357	19,027	2.1
6020	Commercial banks	24	25	1.5	685	729	18,698	19,457	13,472	14,948	2.1
6030	Savings institutions	8	8	2.4	158	162	18,835	18,988	2,997	3,125	2.4
6060	Credit unions	7	8	1.8	60	58	13,933	14,897	888	954	1.1
6100	Nondepository institutions	15	13	1.7	76	85	25,474	24,282	1,932	1,956	0.5
6140	Personal credit institutions	15	13	3.3	76	85	25,474	24,282	1,932	1,956	1.2
6200	Security and commodity brokers	7	7	1.5	–	50	–	68,320	–	3,218	1.6
6210	Security brokers and dealers	5	6	2.0	44	–	60,636	–	2,803	–	–
6300	Insurance carriers	42	22	2.2	304	206	31,816	15,767	7,906	3,285	0.3
6310	Life insurance	5	4	1.4	97	78	20,577	21,590	2,054	1,695	0.4
6330	Fire, marine, and casualty insurance	12	12	2.7	93	–	66,409	–	3,677	–	–
6370	Pension, health, and welfare funds	22	5	3.2	–	97	–	6,268	–	776	3.1
6400	Insurance agents, brokers, and service	41	48	1.7	142	205	20,423	36,312	2,700	5,375	1.3
6500	Real estate	60	70	1.8	352	359	13,193	14,440	5,784	6,523	1.6
6510	Real estate operators and lessors	30	34	2.2	95	154	11,874	13,169	1,175	2,326	1.9
6530	Real estate agents and managers	23	28	1.6	188	150	15,894	16,347	3,585	3,180	1.5
6540	Title abstract offices	3	4	2.3	39	–	8,513	–	543	–	–
6700	Holding and other investment offices	10	10	2.7	60	–	11,333	–	606	–	–
6710	Holding offices	3	1	1.0	5	–	29,600	–	130	–	–
6799	Investors, n.e.c.	4	4	10.5	28	–	9,714	–	264	–	–
WABASH, IN											
60 –	**Finance, insurance, and real estate**	81	87	0.7	406	447	17,389	17,387	7,368	7,517	0.2
6000	Depository institutions	24	24	1.0	230	235	18,452	20,409	4,257	4,200	0.5
6020	Commercial banks	15	15	0.9	158	154	18,911	21,766	2,988	2,562	0.4
6400	Insurance agents, brokers, and service	19	17	0.6	73	72	15,178	16,111	1,142	1,240	0.3
6500	Real estate	30	38	1.0	66	74	11,394	12,270	956	1,111	0.3

Source: County Business Patterns, 1992/93, CBP-92/93-1, U.S. Department of Commerce, Washington, D.C., April 1995. SIC categories for which data were suppressed or not available for both 1992 and 1993 are *not* displayed. The employment columns represent mid-March employment in the year. Pay per employee is calculated by dividing 1st Quarter payroll, annualized, by mid-March employment. The columns headed "% State" show the county's percentage of the state total for the SIC in 1993; for example, 0.9% for SIC 6030 means that the county had 0.9 percent of the state's total establishments (or payroll) in SIC 6030 in 1993. A dash (-) is used to indicate that data are not available or cannot be calculated; *nec* means not elsewhere classified.

Continued on next page.

SIC	Industry	No. Establishments			Employment		Pay / Employee		Annual Payroll ($ 000)		
		1992	1993	% State	1992	1993	1992	1993	1992	1993	% State
WABASH, IN - [continued]											
6510	Real estate operators and lessors	12	20	1.3	19	34	14,526	11,176	361	436	0.4
6530	Real estate agents and managers	9	12	0.7	22	23	9,818	13,217	311	385	0.2
6540	Title abstract offices	3	3	1.7	17	15	11,294	13,333	203	238	0.8
WARREN, IN											
60 –	**Finance, insurance, and real estate**	15	15	0.1	96	100	12,917	13,560	1,311	1,255	0.0
6000	Depository institutions	5	5	0.2	-	39	-	14,872	-	573	0.1
6400	Insurance agents, brokers, and service	3	3	0.1	-	13	-	14,769	-	177	0.0
6500	Real estate	6	6	0.2	50	-	10,800	-	548	-	-
WARRICK, IN											
60 –	**Finance, insurance, and real estate**	65	65	0.5	332	340	18,229	19,024	6,282	6,970	0.2
6000	Depository institutions	21	20	0.8	206	218	20,291	19,908	4,225	4,559	0.5
6020	Commercial banks	12	12	0.7	126	138	18,603	20,058	2,419	2,961	0.4
6200	Security and commodity brokers	2	3	0.6	-	10	-	44,000	-	421	0.2
6400	Insurance agents, brokers, and service	15	16	0.6	39	38	11,795	12,211	-	529	0.1
6500	Real estate	21	20	0.5	59	45	10,169	11,111	479	670	0.2
6510	Real estate operators and lessors	7	5	0.3	18	10	7,111	10,800	722	116	0.1
6530	Real estate agents and managers	7	8	0.5	16	21	12,500	11,619	151	342	0.2
6540	Title abstract offices	3	3	1.7	10	-	10,800	-	219	-	-
6553	Cemetery subdividers and developers	2	3	1.4	-	1	-	4,000	160	28	0.1
WASHINGTON, IN											
60 –	**Finance, insurance, and real estate**	34	34	0.3	179	146	16,022	19,096	2,911	2,945	0.1
6000	Depository institutions	9	9	0.4	101	81	14,733	19,704	1,411	1,620	0.2
6400	Insurance agents, brokers, and service	12	12	0.4	36	30	10,222	16,133	442	527	0.1
6500	Real estate	10	11	0.3	25	-	8,160	-	211	-	-
6510	Real estate operators and lessors	4	5	0.3	13	16	8,615	7,250	118	131	0.1
6530	Real estate agents and managers	2	4	0.2	-	7	-	6,857	-	60	0.0
WAYNE, IN											
60 –	**Finance, insurance, and real estate**	160	157	1.3	1,303	1,280	19,045	19,447	25,295	26,875	0.8
6000	Depository institutions	43	46	1.8	578	554	18,955	19,155	11,343	11,787	1.3
6020	Commercial banks	27	27	1.6	436	379	19,367	20,549	8,726	8,423	1.2
6030	Savings institutions	7	7	2.1	113	126	18,655	16,762	2,201	2,533	1.9
6060	Credit unions	9	12	2.7	29	49	13,931	14,531	416	831	1.0
6100	Nondepository institutions	17	11	1.5	87	48	19,494	15,583	1,665	771	0.2
6140	Personal credit institutions	14	9	2.3	76	-	18,632	-	1,389	-	-
6300	Insurance carriers	16	13	1.3	313	305	20,882	23,895	6,307	7,105	0.7
6310	Life insurance	7	7	2.4	287	293	21,143	23,904	5,816	6,807	1.4
6370	Pension, health, and welfare funds	4	1	0.6	11	-	8,000	-	82	-	-
6400	Insurance agents, brokers, and service	27	30	1.0	101	105	20,079	20,190	2,183	2,333	0.6
6500	Real estate	45	47	1.2	195	242	13,210	12,545	2,785	3,616	0.9
6510	Real estate operators and lessors	15	19	1.2	75	171	10,133	11,930	815	2,263	1.9
6530	Real estate agents and managers	17	17	1.0	34	28	14,588	17,571	520	702	0.3
6553	Cemetery subdividers and developers	5	7	3.4	13	20	18,769	10,600	248	261	1.3
WELLS, IN											
60 –	**Finance, insurance, and real estate**	44	50	0.4	238	259	19,445	19,830	4,667	4,706	0.1
6000	Depository institutions	10	10	0.4	153	158	19,739	19,949	2,939	2,738	0.3
6020	Commercial banks	7	7	0.4	138	141	19,913	20,766	2,686	2,485	0.4
6400	Insurance agents, brokers, and service	10	10	0.3	25	26	21,280	20,308	566	593	0.1
6500	Real estate	20	25	0.6	49	67	16,082	16,299	836	1,004	0.2
6510	Real estate operators and lessors	9	10	0.6	19	30	10,947	12,800	267	281	0.2
6530	Real estate agents and managers	6	11	0.6	18	27	24,000	17,333	335	505	0.2

Source: County Business Patterns, 1992/93, CBP-92/93-1, U.S. Department of Commerce, Washington, D.C., April 1995. SIC categories for which data were suppressed or not available for both 1992 and 1993 are *not* displayed. The employment columns represent mid-March employment in the year. Pay per employee is calculated by dividing 1st Quarter payroll, annualized, by mid-March employment. The columns headed "% State" show the county's percentage of the state total for the SIC in 1993; for example, 0.9% for SIC 6030 means that the county had 0.9 percent of the state's total establishments (or payroll) in SIC 6030 in 1993. A dash (-) is used to indicate that data are not available or cannot be calculated; *nec* means not elsewhere classified.

SIC	Industry	No. Establishments			Employment		Pay / Employee		Annual Payroll ($ 000)		
		1992	1993	% State	1992	1993	1992	1993	1992	1993	% State
WHITE, IN											
60 –	**Finance, insurance, and real estate**	52	50	*0.4*	273	268	20,015	23,075	6,119	5,078	*0.1*
6000	Depository institutions	14	14	*0.6*	167	173	19,617	23,214	3,523	2,663	*0.3*
6200	Security and commodity brokers	3	3	*0.6*	3	-	12,000	-	31	-	-
6400	Insurance agents, brokers, and service	17	19	*0.7*	54	54	19,333	17,037	1,176	986	*0.2*
6500	Real estate	13	12	*0.3*	28	21	18,286	30,476	788	812	*0.2*
6510	Real estate operators and lessors	5	5	*0.3*	7	-	24,571	-	278	-	-
6530	Real estate agents and managers	2	4	*0.2*	-	8	-	54,500	-	563	*0.3*
WHITLEY, IN											
60 –	**Finance, insurance, and real estate**	52	56	*0.5*	317	406	18,902	23,320	6,117	8,084	*0.2*
6000	Depository institutions	16	14	*0.6*	218	244	18,587	25,639	3,969	4,678	*0.5*
6020	Commercial banks	11	9	*0.5*	190	220	19,305	26,909	3,554	4,329	*0.6*
6300	Insurance carriers	6	5	*0.5*	13	6	18,462	18,667	260	96	*0.0*
6400	Insurance agents, brokers, and service	12	16	*0.6*	35	50	24,457	21,440	732	1,023	*0.3*
6500	Real estate	14	16	*0.4*	44	96	16,273	19,583	1,007	2,121	*0.5*
6510	Real estate operators and lessors	3	5	*0.3*	4	-	5,000	-	20	-	-
6530	Real estate agents and managers	6	9	*0.5*	30	35	19,467	17,829	852	713	*0.3*

Source: County Business Patterns, 1992/93, CBP-92/93-1, U.S. Department of Commerce, Washington, D.C., April 1995. SIC categories for which data were suppressed or not available for both 1992 and 1993 are *not* displayed. The employment columns represent mid-March employment in the year. Pay per employee is calculated by dividing 1st Quarter payroll, annualized, by mid-March employment. The columns headed "% State" show the county's percentage of the state total for the SIC in 1993; for example, 0.9% for SIC 6030 means that the county had 0.9 percent of the state's total establishments (or payroll) in SIC 6030 in 1993. A dash (-) is used to indicate that data are not available or cannot be calculated; *nec* means not elsewhere classified.

IOWA

SIC	Industry	No. Establishments			Employment		Pay / Employee		Annual Payroll ($ 000)		
		1992	1993	% State	1992	1993	1992	1993	1992	1993	% State
ADAIR, IA											
60 –	**Finance, insurance, and real estate**	17	16	0.2	-	-	-	-	-	-	-
6000	Depository institutions	6	6	0.4	58	61	24,552	24,393	1,528	1,682	0.3
6020	Commercial banks	6	6	0.6	58	61	24,552	24,393	1,528	1,682	0.4
6400	Insurance agents, brokers, and service	3	4	0.2	9	10	29,778	28,000	216	241	0.1
6500	Real estate	6	5	0.3	-	10	-	4,400		50	0.0
ADAMS, IA											
60 –	**Finance, insurance, and real estate**	12	14	0.2	59	60	16,542	16,000	1,020	1,007	0.0
6000	Depository institutions	4	4	0.3	45	-	17,156	-	824	-	-
6400	Insurance agents, brokers, and service	5	5	0.2	-	13	-	14,462	-	177	0.1
6500	Real estate	2	4	0.2	-	5	-	4,800	-	25	0.0
ALLAMAKEE, IA											
60 –	**Finance, insurance, and real estate**	33	33	0.5	151	155	19,841	18,581	3,080	3,411	0.2
6000	Depository institutions	7	7	0.5	103	101	23,573	22,653	2,456	2,610	0.5
6020	Commercial banks	7	6	0.6	103	-	23,573		2,456	-	-
6400	Insurance agents, brokers, and service	9	10	0.5	20	26	9,400	13,231	186	381	0.2
6500	Real estate	13	13	0.7	13	20	13,846	8,800	227	320	0.2
6510	Real estate operators and lessors	5	5	0.6	-	8	-	6,000	-	132	0.3
6553	Cemetery subdividers and developers	6	6	4.0	4	-	3,000	-	32	-	-
APPANOOSE, IA											
60 –	**Finance, insurance, and real estate**	24	24	0.3	131	167	16,458	23,066	2,296	3,651	0.2
6000	Depository institutions	7	7	0.5	82	83	19,122	20,241	1,698	1,749	0.3
6400	Insurance agents, brokers, and service	8	8	0.4	24	25	10,167	11,200	255	287	0.1
6500	Real estate	6	5	0.3	14	14	11,429	14,000	147	172	0.1
AUDUBON, IA											
60 –	**Finance, insurance, and real estate**	17	18	0.3	76	82	16,684	17,220	1,256	1,417	0.1
6000	Depository institutions	5	5	0.3	55	55	19,564	20,218	1,063	1,109	0.2
6020	Commercial banks	5	5	0.5	55	55	19,564	20,218	1,063	1,109	0.3
6400	Insurance agents, brokers, and service	6	5	0.2	-	11	-	13,818	-	162	0.1
6500	Real estate	4	6	0.3	9	-	8,444	-	78	-	-
6510	Real estate operators and lessors	1	3	0.3	-	3	-	4,000	-	12	0.0
BENTON, IA											
60 –	**Finance, insurance, and real estate**	51	52	0.7	233	247	19,090	17,765	4,760	4,802	0.2
6000	Depository institutions	17	16	1.1	151	157	21,351	20,739	3,497	3,486	0.7
6400	Insurance agents, brokers, and service	18	21	1.0	42	53	15,810	11,774	691	724	0.4
6500	Real estate	12	11	0.6	25	24	12,000	12,000	344	318	0.2
6530	Real estate agents and managers	2	4	0.5	-	9	-	9,778	-	90	0.1
BLACK HAWK, IA											
60 –	**Finance, insurance, and real estate**	287	298	4.2	2,585	2,558	22,550	22,980	59,784	61,699	3.0
6000	Depository institutions	54	56	3.8	932	928	22,601	23,694	21,482	22,364	4.3
6020	Commercial banks	33	33	3.3	629	641	22,550	23,607	14,259	15,496	3.7
6100	Nondepository institutions	18	17	6.4	554	560	23,560	22,064	14,027	13,304	8.3
6140	Personal credit institutions	12	10	7.8	-	53	-	17,736	-	929	1.8
6200	Security and commodity brokers	16	19	4.7	107	123	36,598	33,431	3,807	4,101	3.8
6210	Security brokers and dealers	9	11	4.6	75	56	43,253	55,357	3,056	2,990	3.5
6300	Insurance carriers	29	20	3.6	287	197	25,394	27,452	6,641	5,570	0.7

Source: County Business Patterns, 1992/93, CBP-92/93-1, U.S. Department of Commerce, Washington, D.C., April 1995. SIC categories for which data were suppressed or not available for both 1992 and 1993 are *not* displayed. The employment columns represent mid-March employment in the year. Pay per employee is calculated by dividing 1st Quarter payroll, annualized, by mid-March employment. The columns headed "% State" show the county's percentage of the state total for the SIC in 1993; for example, 0.9% for SIC 6030 means that the county had 0.9 percent of the state's total establishments (or payroll) in SIC 6030 in 1993. A dash (-) is used to indicate that data are not available or cannot be calculated; *nec* means not elsewhere classified.

Continued on next page.

SIC	Industry	No. Establishments			Employment		Pay / Employee		Annual Payroll ($ 000)		
		1992	1993	% State	1992	1993	1992	1993	1992	1993	% State
BLACK HAWK, IA - [continued]											
6310	Life insurance	10	7	4.2	168	122	26,333	27,574	4,349	3,576	0.8
6330	Fire, marine, and casualty insurance	9	5	2.0	77	55	20,416	19,273	1,077	615	0.2
6400	Insurance agents, brokers, and service	69	78	3.8	286	284	20,559	22,521	6,222	7,096	3.5
6500	Real estate	88	98	4.9	308	360	14,442	14,911	4,729	6,070	4.2
6510	Real estate operators and lessors	39	46	5.2	129	161	14,481	12,472	1,910	2,056	4.0
6530	Real estate agents and managers	38	43	5.7	105	144	13,829	17,667	1,652	2,894	4.2
6700	Holding and other investment offices	13	10	3.8	111	106	23,820	29,774	2,876	3,194	3.0
BOONE, IA											
60 –	**Finance, insurance, and real estate**	44	51	0.7	273	268	16,864	16,866	4,527	4,510	0.2
6000	Depository institutions	11	12	0.8	161	173	18,932	19,191	2,961	3,220	0.6
6020	Commercial banks	6	6	0.6	104	107	19,962	20,112	1,991	2,038	0.5
6200	Security and commodity brokers	3	4	1.0	-	7	-	13,714	-	109	0.1
6400	Insurance agents, brokers, and service	17	21	1.0	68	55	15,529	13,673	1,083	809	0.4
6500	Real estate	12	13	0.7	36	-	9,444	-	327	-	-
6510	Real estate operators and lessors	8	9	1.0	21	16	4,952	5,250	89	86	0.2
BREMER, IA											
60 –	**Finance, insurance, and real estate**	70	63	0.9	1,126	1,257	25,332	25,123	29,303	29,722	1.4
6000	Depository institutions	15	15	1.0	209	190	20,459	18,989	4,500	3,821	0.7
6020	Commercial banks	12	13	1.3	191	-	20,733	-	4,106	-	-
6210	Security brokers and dealers	3	3	1.3	-	13	-	21,846	-	316	0.4
6400	Insurance agents, brokers, and service	24	21	1.0	54	49	18,148	20,082	1,090	1,074	0.5
6500	Real estate	10	11	0.6	-	25	-	16,000	-	556	0.4
6510	Real estate operators and lessors	4	4	0.4	4	-	12,000	-	47	-	-
6530	Real estate agents and managers	5	6	0.8	8	-	30,000	-	237	-	-
6700	Holding and other investment offices	3	1	0.4	9	-	16,444	-	95	-	-
BUCHANAN, IA											
60 –	**Finance, insurance, and real estate**	55	53	0.8	246	238	18,602	19,361	4,674	5,029	0.2
6000	Depository institutions	14	15	1.0	145	141	20,690	21,418	3,087	3,292	0.6
6020	Commercial banks	10	10	1.0	133	128	21,143	22,094	2,907	3,086	0.7
6300	Insurance carriers	9	6	1.1	27	21	28,741	37,143	737	827	0.1
6370	Pension, health, and welfare funds	5	3	3.1	1	-	4,000	-	44	-	-
6400	Insurance agents, brokers, and service	16	18	0.9	41	51	12,683	11,294	578	633	0.3
6500	Real estate	11	11	0.6	15	19	10,400	8,211	173	198	0.1
6510	Real estate operators and lessors	6	5	0.6	6	6	7,333	3,333	47	49	0.1
6530	Real estate agents and managers	2	3	0.4	-	6	-	6,000	-	36	0.1
BUENA VISTA, IA											
60 –	**Finance, insurance, and real estate**	67	67	1.0	360	365	19,900	21,074	7,784	8,345	0.4
6000	Depository institutions	18	18	1.2	222	213	21,027	22,742	5,338	5,493	1.1
6020	Commercial banks	11	12	1.2	147	-	20,299	-	3,660	-	-
6200	Security and commodity brokers	6	7	1.7	29	35	25,517	24,914	792	1,022	0.9
6210	Security brokers and dealers	4	4	1.7	-	22	-	34,909	-	870	1.0
6400	Insurance agents, brokers, and service	17	18	0.9	48	51	12,667	13,255	607	851	0.4
6500	Real estate	19	17	0.9	34	34	11,176	13,529	438	527	0.4
6510	Real estate operators and lessors	9	8	0.9	15	17	5,600	6,824	98	118	0.2
6530	Real estate agents and managers	5	5	0.7	9	8	20,000	30,000	211	280	0.4
BUTLER, IA											
60 –	**Finance, insurance, and real estate**	29	27	0.4	149	161	15,034	17,540	2,783	2,622	0.1
6000	Depository institutions	10	10	0.7	93	111	18,495	19,459	2,184	1,975	0.4
6020	Commercial banks	10	10	1.0	93	111	18,495	19,459	2,184	1,975	0.5
6400	Insurance agents, brokers, and service	13	13	0.6	40	35	8,500	13,943	407	452	0.2
6553	Cemetery subdividers and developers	3	1	0.7	4	-	4,000	-	13	-	-

Source: County Business Patterns, 1992/93, CBP-92/93-1, U.S. Department of Commerce, Washington, D.C., April 1995. SIC categories for which data were suppressed or not available for both 1992 and 1993 are not displayed. The employment columns represent mid-March employment in the year. Pay per employee is calculated by dividing 1st Quarter payroll, annualized, by mid-March employment. The columns headed "% State" show the county's percentage of the state total for the SIC in 1993; for example, 0.9% for SIC 6030 means that the county had 0.9 percent of the state's total establishments (or payroll) in SIC 6030 in 1993. A dash (-) is used to indicate that data are not available or cannot be calculated; nec means not elsewhere classified.

SIC	Industry	No. Establishments			Employment		Pay / Employee		Annual Payroll ($ 000)		
		1992	1993	% State	1992	1993	1992	1993	1992	1993	% State
CALHOUN, IA											
60 –	**Finance, insurance, and real estate**	31	32	0.5	142	154	17,887	18,831	2,757	2,891	0.1
6000	Depository institutions	10	8	0.5	98	88	19,755	20,591	2,098	1,826	0.4
6400	Insurance agents, brokers, and service	13	15	0.7	23	31	13,913	14,194	370	462	0.2
6500	Real estate	5	5	0.3	-	8	-	5,500	-	41	0.0
6530	Real estate agents and managers	3	2	0.3	6	-	4,667	-	30	-	-
CARROLL, IA											
60 –	**Finance, insurance, and real estate**	66	69	1.0	351	714	20,171	16,992	8,093	13,444	0.6
6000	Depository institutions	15	15	1.0	179	191	23,173	25,257	4,854	5,049	1.0
6200	Security and commodity brokers	5	5	1.2	17	18	34,353	31,111	652	701	0.7
6300	Insurance carriers	5	4	0.7	20	-	7,200	-	130	-	-
6400	Insurance agents, brokers, and service	20	23	1.1	56	63	16,786	16,698	1,047	1,090	0.5
6500	Real estate	14	15	0.8	-	20	-	10,400	-	270	0.2
6510	Real estate operators and lessors	5	7	0.8	6	10	7,333	13,200	92	186	0.4
6530	Real estate agents and managers	7	7	0.9	26	-	13,692	-	364	-	-
CASS, IA											
60 –	**Finance, insurance, and real estate**	44	48	0.7	203	206	18,443	17,942	3,750	4,082	0.2
6000	Depository institutions	10	10	0.7	105	103	21,029	22,990	2,323	2,504	0.5
6200	Security and commodity brokers	3	4	1.0	-	8	-	39,000	-	383	0.4
6300	Insurance carriers	3	3	0.5	6	-	13,333	-	84	-	-
6400	Insurance agents, brokers, and service	17	21	1.0	61	66	13,311	11,091	743	786	0.4
6500	Real estate	9	9	0.5	20	16	9,600	10,750	193	286	0.2
6510	Real estate operators and lessors	3	3	0.3	7	5	12,000	10,400	62	94	0.2
6553	Cemetery subdividers and developers	3	3	2.0	5	-	5,600	-	39	-	-
CEDAR, IA											
60 –	**Finance, insurance, and real estate**	32	32	0.5	182	193	20,396	19,648	3,957	4,129	0.2
6000	Depository institutions	10	10	0.7	134	136	19,284	19,294	2,820	2,970	0.6
6400	Insurance agents, brokers, and service	10	11	0.5	30	37	26,133	21,838	806	841	0.4
6500	Real estate	8	7	0.4	11	9	9,091	8,444	109	103	0.1
6510	Real estate operators and lessors	4	4	0.4	6	5	8,000	6,400	49	33	0.1
CERRO GORDO, IA											
60 –	**Finance, insurance, and real estate**	144	138	2.0	1,057	1,038	22,085	23,383	24,664	24,089	1.2
6000	Depository institutions	31	32	2.2	339	349	21,180	24,917	9,298	8,189	1.6
6020	Commercial banks	14	15	1.5	266	270	22,677	26,459	8,077	6,761	1.6
6100	Nondepository institutions	9	6	2.3	38	33	22,316	24,606	784	742	0.5
6140	Personal credit institutions	5	3	2.3	17	18	14,353	12,444	233	176	0.3
6200	Security and commodity brokers	7	9	2.2	-	32	-	44,625	-	1,638	1.5
6210	Security brokers and dealers	3	5	2.1	25	-	49,600	-	1,250	-	-
6280	Security and commodity services	2	3	2.5	-	1	-	12,000	-	17	-
6300	Insurance carriers	14	6	1.1	413	-	22,344	-	8,657	-	-
6400	Insurance agents, brokers, and service	42	42	2.0	101	106	26,495	25,849	2,503	2,540	1.2
6500	Real estate	39	41	2.1	100	107	9,880	9,981	1,072	1,219	0.8
6510	Real estate operators and lessors	19	20	2.2	59	51	6,915	7,608	435	373	0.7
6530	Real estate agents and managers	12	15	2.0	26	43	12,308	10,698	365	614	0.9
CHEROKEE, IA											
60 –	**Finance, insurance, and real estate**	39	40	0.6	194	177	17,216	19,932	3,486	3,560	0.2
6000	Depository institutions	11	11	0.7	113	103	21,558	24,350	2,463	2,529	0.5
6300	Insurance carriers	4	3	0.5	12	3	8,333	4,000	107	24	0.0
6400	Insurance agents, brokers, and service	12	17	0.8	36	53	13,000	13,962	514	725	0.4
6500	Real estate	9	6	0.3	27	10	9,333	12,400	272	132	0.1
6530	Real estate agents and managers	4	3	0.4	-	6	-	10,667	-	61	0.1

Source: County Business Patterns, 1992/93, CBP-92/93-1, U.S. Department of Commerce, Washington, D.C., April 1995. SIC categories for which data were suppressed or not available for both 1992 and 1993 are not displayed. The employment columns represent mid-March employment in the year. Pay per employee is calculated by dividing 1st Quarter payroll, annualized, by mid-March employment. The columns headed "% State" show the county's percentage of the state total for the SIC in 1993; for example, 0.9% for SIC 6030 means that the county had 0.9 percent of the state's total establishments (or payroll) in SIC 6030 in 1993. A dash (-) is used to indicate that data are not available or cannot be calculated; nec means not elsewhere classified.

SIC	Industry	No. Establishments			Employment		Pay / Employee		Annual Payroll ($ 000)		
		1992	1993	% State	1992	1993	1992	1993	1992	1993	% State
CHICKASAW, IA											
60 –	**Finance, insurance, and real estate**	35	30	0.4	151	130	16,636	21,323	3,027	3,071	0.1
6000	Depository institutions	9	9	0.6	92	78	19,739	25,949	2,229	2,304	0.4
6400	Insurance agents, brokers, and service	11	9	0.4	36	32	12,667	16,750	559	543	0.3
6500	Real estate	9	9	0.5	12	13	8,667	7,692	107	110	0.1
6530	Real estate agents and managers	4	3	0.4	5	5	6,400	4,800	33	25	0.0
CLARKE, IA											
60 –	**Finance, insurance, and real estate**	19	22	0.3	89	88	18,247	20,136	1,683	2,211	0.1
6000	Depository institutions	5	5	0.3	65	63	19,692	21,968	1,242	1,692	0.3
6400	Insurance agents, brokers, and service	8	11	0.5	17	19	16,000	17,053	345	420	0.2
6500	Real estate	5	6	0.3	-	6	-	10,667	-	99	0.1
6510	Real estate operators and lessors	1	3	0.3	-	3	-	10,667	-	43	0.1
6530	Real estate agents and managers	3	3	0.4	5	3	12,000	10,667	60	56	0.1
CLAY, IA											
60 –	**Finance, insurance, and real estate**	56	56	0.8	441	339	16,971	22,029	7,673	7,037	0.3
6000	Depository institutions	12	11	0.7	227	209	20,758	25,895	4,737	4,709	0.9
6100	Nondepository institutions	3	2	0.8	4	-	32,000	-	98	-	-
6200	Security and commodity brokers	5	5	1.2	-	11	-	33,091	-	560	0.5
6300	Insurance carriers	4	2	0.4	10	-	17,200	-	159	-	-
6330	Fire, marine, and casualty insurance	4	2	0.8	10	-	17,200	-	159	-	-
6400	Insurance agents, brokers, and service	14	18	0.9	78	42	11,333	14,762	868	682	0.3
6500	Real estate	16	17	0.9	27	36	16,741	11,111	447	466	0.3
6510	Real estate operators and lessors	4	6	0.7	7	-	2,857	-	18	-	-
6530	Real estate agents and managers	7	10	1.3	10	20	32,800	13,400	243	333	0.5
CLAYTON, IA											
60 –	**Finance, insurance, and real estate**	54	54	0.8	217	230	20,111	19,409	4,726	5,042	0.2
6000	Depository institutions	13	13	0.9	136	156	25,176	22,897	3,805	4,103	0.8
6400	Insurance agents, brokers, and service	20	20	1.0	35	36	14,057	13,333	474	510	0.2
6500	Real estate	16	15	0.8	32	22	8,375	10,364	274	248	0.2
6510	Real estate operators and lessors	3	2	0.2	6	-	7,333	-	17	-	-
6530	Real estate agents and managers	3	3	0.4	-	9	-	12,000	-	113	0.2
6553	Cemetery subdividers and developers	8	9	6.0	5	-	4,000	-	34	-	-
CLINTON, IA											
60 –	**Finance, insurance, and real estate**	116	117	1.7	788	739	21,665	19,302	16,301	14,301	0.7
6000	Depository institutions	25	25	1.7	382	365	18,942	20,219	7,197	7,072	1.4
6020	Commercial banks	12	12	1.2	252	244	19,460	21,869	4,832	4,813	1.1
6200	Security and commodity brokers	7	8	2.0	14	15	22,286	25,600	331	407	0.4
6210	Security brokers and dealers	4	5	2.1	8	9	32,500	36,000	271	336	0.4
6300	Insurance carriers	8	8	1.4	172	164	21,209	22,341	3,795	3,811	0.5
6370	Pension, health, and welfare funds	3	3	3.1	-	1	-	4,000	-	48	0.5
6400	Insurance agents, brokers, and service	27	29	1.4	71	71	16,958	18,028	1,371	1,358	0.7
6500	Real estate	42	43	2.2	117	109	10,325	10,569	1,355	1,336	0.9
6510	Real estate operators and lessors	22	19	2.1	71	51	9,634	7,922	759	433	0.8
6530	Real estate agents and managers	11	15	2.0	11	26	6,545	11,385	102	406	0.6
6553	Cemetery subdividers and developers	6	6	4.0	18	-	11,333	-	227	-	-
CRAWFORD, IA											
60 –	**Finance, insurance, and real estate**	45	43	0.6	203	216	19,251	19,019	3,952	4,151	0.2
6000	Depository institutions	14	13	0.9	129	120	21,395	23,500	2,722	2,691	0.5
6020	Commercial banks	10	10	1.0	109	112	22,826	24,143	2,397	2,580	0.6
6400	Insurance agents, brokers, and service	16	14	0.7	43	56	17,395	11,929	769	732	0.4

Source: County Business Patterns, 1992/93, CBP-92/93-1, U.S. Department of Commerce, Washington, D.C., April 1995. SIC categories for which data were suppressed or not available for both 1992 and 1993 are *not* displayed. The employment columns represent mid-March employment in the year. Pay per employee is calculated by dividing 1st Quarter payroll, annualized, by mid-March employment. The columns headed "% State" show the county's percentage of the state total for the SIC in 1993; for example, 0.9% for SIC 6030 means that the county had 0.9 percent of the state's total establishments (or payroll) in SIC 6030 in 1993. A dash (-) is used to indicate that data are not available or cannot be calculated; *nec* means not elsewhere classified.

Continued on next page.

SIC	Industry	No. Establishments			Employment		Pay / Employee		Annual Payroll ($ 000)		
		1992	1993	% State	1992	1993	1992	1993	1992	1993	% State
CRAWFORD, IA - [continued]											
6500	Real estate	11	12	0.6	14	14	6,000	6,571	97	144	0.1
6510	Real estate operators and lessors	4	5	0.6	8	8	6,500	7,000	52	61	0.1
6530	Real estate agents and managers	3	3	0.4	2	2	4,000	6,000	15	51	0.1
DALLAS, IA											
60 –	**Finance, insurance, and real estate**	54	55	0.8	363	329	20,298	24,012	6,874	7,274	0.3
6000	Depository institutions	16	16	1.1	164	170	24,829	23,647	3,694	3,534	0.7
6400	Insurance agents, brokers, and service	19	21	1.0	83	91	17,831	15,956	1,606	1,459	0.7
6500	Real estate	11	10	0.5	72	30	7,833	25,867	509	592	0.4
6510	Real estate operators and lessors	5	6	0.7	9	12	16,444	43,333	180	320	0.6
6530	Real estate agents and managers	3	2	0.3	35	-	4,914	-	90	-	-
DAVIS, IA											
60 –	**Finance, insurance, and real estate**	10	11	0.2	68	58	17,000	17,586	1,224	1,174	0.1
6400	Insurance agents, brokers, and service	4	4	0.2	13	12	20,308	20,333	271	256	0.1
DECATUR, IA											
60 –	**Finance, insurance, and real estate**	11	14	0.2	58	62	19,517	13,097	1,121	921	0.0
6000	Depository institutions	4	4	0.3	46	46	22,174	14,348	998	753	0.1
6400	Insurance agents, brokers, and service	4	6	0.3	9	12	11,556	11,333	110	149	0.1
6500	Real estate	3	4	0.2	3	4	2,667	4,000	13	19	0.0
DELAWARE, IA											
60 –	**Finance, insurance, and real estate**	31	28	0.4	152	148	18,158	18,730	2,964	3,070	0.1
6000	Depository institutions	6	5	0.3	84	77	20,286	17,714	1,814	1,619	0.3
6020	Commercial banks	6	5	0.5	84	77	20,286	17,714	1,814	1,619	0.4
6330	Fire, marine, and casualty insurance	3	1	0.4	6	-	9,333	-	61	-	-
6400	Insurance agents, brokers, and service	9	11	0.5	31	31	13,935	15,226	465	498	0.2
6500	Real estate	7	5	0.3	17	10	10,588	14,400	205	176	0.1
DES MOINES, IA											
60 –	**Finance, insurance, and real estate**	107	107	1.5	770	675	18,374	20,071	14,771	14,874	0.7
6000	Depository institutions	21	22	1.5	322	336	22,112	21,571	7,134	7,389	1.4
6020	Commercial banks	9	9	0.9	243	248	23,720	22,726	5,701	5,744	1.4
6100	Nondepository institutions	5	3	1.1	12	9	17,667	24,000	210	155	0.1
6300	Insurance carriers	13	12	2.1	65	73	24,246	26,301	1,588	2,019	0.2
6310	Life insurance	3	2	1.2	29	-	28,414	-	860	-	-
6330	Fire, marine, and casualty insurance	3	3	1.2	-	9	-	28,000	-	264	0.1
6400	Insurance agents, brokers, and service	26	30	1.5	71	77	19,155	20,779	1,349	1,496	0.7
6500	Real estate	34	34	1.7	219	146	8,420	12,027	2,004	1,932	1.3
6510	Real estate operators and lessors	14	16	1.8	113	56	5,451	9,643	602	502	1.0
6530	Real estate agents and managers	13	11	1.5	70	56	11,543	14,214	937	941	1.4
DICKINSON, IA											
60 –	**Finance, insurance, and real estate**	62	67	1.0	272	377	15,794	14,621	4,589	7,326	0.4
6000	Depository institutions	12	12	0.8	105	111	22,895	22,703	2,440	2,523	0.5
6400	Insurance agents, brokers, and service	10	10	0.5	36	29	14,000	16,552	460	501	0.2
6500	Real estate	31	36	1.8	101	217	9,584	9,696	1,204	3,855	2.6
6510	Real estate operators and lessors	12	13	1.5	34	-	7,412	-	272	-	-
6530	Real estate agents and managers	12	20	2.7	25	186	12,640	10,215	331	3,438	5.0
6552	Subdividers and developers, n.e.c.	4	1	2.4	5	-	11,200	-	103	-	-
DUBUQUE, IA											
60 –	**Finance, insurance, and real estate**	226	226	3.2	1,511	1,746	22,176	20,589	33,615	38,149	1.8
6000	Depository institutions	47	52	3.5	867	907	21,236	21,791	18,192	20,503	4.0
6020	Commercial banks	26	26	2.6	617	615	23,164	24,280	13,602	14,839	3.5
6100	Nondepository institutions	8	6	2.3	23	21	21,217	18,476	517	411	0.3
6140	Personal credit institutions	8	6	4.7	23	21	21,217	18,476	517	411	0.8

Source: County Business Patterns, 1992/93, CBP-92/93-1, U.S. Department of Commerce, Washington, D.C., April 1995. SIC categories for which data were suppressed or not available for both 1992 and 1993 are not displayed. The employment columns represent mid-March employment in the year. Pay per employee is calculated by dividing 1st Quarter payroll, annualized, by mid-March employment. The columns headed "% State" show the county's percentage of the state total for the SIC in 1993; for example, 0.9% for SIC 6030 means that the county had 0.9 percent of the state's total establishments (or payroll) in SIC 6030 in 1993. A dash (-) is used to indicate that data are not available or cannot be calculated; nec means not elsewhere classified.

Continued on next page.

SIC	Industry	No. Establishments			Employment		Pay / Employee		Annual Payroll ($ 000)		
		1992	1993	% State	1992	1993	1992	1993	1992	1993	% State
DUBUQUE, IA - [continued]											
6200	Security and commodity brokers	12	15	3.7	61	88	56,262	35,682	2,672	2,737	2.5
6210	Security brokers and dealers	10	12	5.0	-	75	-	40,800	-	2,645	3.1
6280	Security and commodity services	2	3	2.5	-	13	-	6,154	-	92	-
6300	Insurance carriers	28	19	3.4	157	199	22,446	20,643	3,534	3,925	0.5
6310	Life insurance	6	7	4.2	28	60	36,571	22,000	817	1,196	0.3
6330	Fire, marine, and casualty insurance	11	8	3.2	21	17	19,810	20,235	459	376	0.1
6400	Insurance agents, brokers, and service	53	57	2.8	221	213	22,045	22,723	5,612	5,561	2.7
6500	Real estate	65	71	3.6	163	309	13,301	11,055	2,709	4,369	3.0
6510	Real estate operators and lessors	29	37	4.1	90	230	10,267	9,583	1,004	2,553	4.9
6530	Real estate agents and managers	23	25	3.3	45	-	16,178	-	943	-	-
6700	Holding and other investment offices	13	6	2.3	19	9	32,211	32,444	379	643	0.6
6710	Holding offices	6	6	5.0	-	9	-	32,444	-	643	0.8
EMMET, IA											
60 –	**Finance, insurance, and real estate**	24	26	0.4	120	120	15,367	16,600	2,084	2,231	0.1
6000	Depository institutions	6	8	0.5	64	71	17,875	18,535	1,265	1,453	0.3
6020	Commercial banks	4	4	0.4	-	53	-	19,925	-	1,165	0.3
6400	Insurance agents, brokers, and service	6	9	0.4	14	21	17,143	15,619	237	329	0.2
6500	Real estate	7	7	0.4	19	-	7,789	-	158	-	-
6510	Real estate operators and lessors	3	4	0.4	8	11	6,000	5,818	56	65	0.1
FAYETTE, IA											
60 –	**Finance, insurance, and real estate**	46	45	0.6	242	245	18,298	16,865	4,732	4,530	0.2
6000	Depository institutions	13	13	0.9	165	157	19,345	18,268	3,534	3,226	0.6
6400	Insurance agents, brokers, and service	17	20	1.0	40	49	16,000	12,163	587	646	0.3
6500	Real estate	9	7	0.4	20	23	8,600	7,826	179	183	0.1
6530	Real estate agents and managers	4	3	0.4	4	6	5,000	4,667	25	28	0.0
FLOYD, IA											
60 –	**Finance, insurance, and real estate**	39	39	0.6	232	217	20,155	21,806	4,412	4,628	0.2
6000	Depository institutions	8	8	0.5	135	133	23,259	22,737	2,680	2,839	0.5
6400	Insurance agents, brokers, and service	14	17	0.8	45	42	16,089	18,667	740	813	0.4
6500	Real estate	11	10	0.5	33	27	5,818	7,704	232	238	0.2
6530	Real estate agents and managers	3	4	0.5	9	10	9,778	11,200	98	111	0.2
6553	Cemetery subdividers and developers	3	3	2.0	7	-	2,857	-	47	-	-
FRANKLIN, IA											
60 –	**Finance, insurance, and real estate**	39	39	0.6	116	120	18,103	17,467	2,436	2,529	0.1
6000	Depository institutions	9	9	0.6	67	67	20,358	20,537	1,428	1,495	0.3
6200	Security and commodity brokers	3	3	0.7	-	8	-	20,000	-	360	0.3
6400	Insurance agents, brokers, and service	8	9	0.4	19	19	21,895	17,895	342	349	0.2
6500	Real estate	15	14	0.7	18	19	8,667	8,211	242	212	0.1
6510	Real estate operators and lessors	7	6	0.7	-	8	-	5,500	-	67	0.1
6530	Real estate agents and managers	3	4	0.5	3	4	8,000	7,000	21	27	0.0
6553	Cemetery subdividers and developers	3	3	2.0	5	-	5,600	-	34	-	-
FREMONT, IA											
60 –	**Finance, insurance, and real estate**	15	16	0.2	76	82	23,789	21,805	1,897	1,899	0.1
6000	Depository institutions	9	9	0.6	56	64	26,357	22,812	1,579	1,525	0.3
6400	Insurance agents, brokers, and service	6	7	0.3	20	18	16,600	18,222	318	374	0.2
GREENE, IA											
60 –	**Finance, insurance, and real estate**	24	24	0.3	160	156	21,950	22,308	3,521	3,447	0.2
6000	Depository institutions	8	8	0.5	107	109	25,121	23,780	2,672	2,531	0.5
6400	Insurance agents, brokers, and service	8	11	0.5	28	38	16,857	16,211	488	652	0.3
6500	Real estate	5	3	0.2	9	-	12,000	-	106	-	-

Source: County Business Patterns, 1992/93, CBP-92/93-1, U.S. Department of Commerce, Washington, D.C., April 1995. SIC categories for which data were suppressed or not available for both 1992 and 1993 are *not* displayed. The employment columns represent mid-March employment in the year. Pay per employee is calculated by dividing 1st Quarter payroll, annualized, by mid-March employment. The columns headed "% State" show the county's percentage of the state total for the SIC in 1993; for example, 0.9% for SIC 6030 means that the county had 0.9 percent of the state's total establishments (or payroll) in SIC 6030 in 1993. A dash (-) is used to indicate that data are not available or cannot be calculated; *nec* means not elsewhere classified.

SIC	Industry	No. Establishments			Employment		Pay / Employee		Annual Payroll ($ 000)		
		1992	1993	% State	1992	1993	1992	1993	1992	1993	% State
GRUNDY, IA											
60 –	**Finance, insurance, and real estate**	23	25	0.4	131	147	20,641	21,279	2,958	3,083	0.1
6000	Depository institutions	9	9	0.6	107	122	22,766	23,148	2,665	2,716	0.5
6400	Insurance agents, brokers, and service	6	8	0.4	5	8	10,400	9,000	55	81	0.0
6510	Real estate operators and lessors	1	3	0.3	-	2	-	2,000	-	41	0.1
GUTHRIE, IA											
60 –	**Finance, insurance, and real estate**	35	33	0.5	172	148	15,535	18,892	2,760	2,990	0.1
6000	Depository institutions	7	7	0.5	74	75	20,000	20,000	1,586	1,578	0.3
6400	Insurance agents, brokers, and service	14	13	0.6	38	37	18,105	16,000	659	681	0.3
6500	Real estate	10	8	0.4	45	18	6,489	14,222	230	286	0.2
6530	Real estate agents and managers	2	5	0.7	-	12	-	18,000	-	242	0.4
HAMILTON, IA											
60 –	**Finance, insurance, and real estate**	31	30	0.4	206	215	22,427	21,247	4,879	4,829	0.2
6000	Depository institutions	10	11	0.7	149	158	21,718	20,051	3,313	3,219	0.6
6300	Insurance carriers	3	1	0.2	6	-	8,000	-	71	-	-
6400	Insurance agents, brokers, and service	8	8	0.4	27	29	16,296	16,414	580	556	0.3
6500	Real estate	6	7	0.4	7	15	18,857	13,600	139	197	0.1
6510	Real estate operators and lessors	3	3	0.3	2	3	10,000	8,000	22	24	0.0
HANCOCK, IA											
60 –	**Finance, insurance, and real estate**	37	37	0.5	156	152	18,487	16,789	2,733	2,658	0.1
6000	Depository institutions	11	10	0.7	89	82	19,730	20,000	1,854	1,794	0.3
6020	Commercial banks	11	10	1.0	89	82	19,730	20,000	1,854	1,794	0.4
6400	Insurance agents, brokers, and service	13	13	0.6	23	19	11,478	10,737	267	258	0.1
6510	Real estate operators and lessors	3	6	0.7	6	29	4,667	6,345	30	186	0.4
HARDIN, IA											
60 –	**Finance, insurance, and real estate**	61	59	0.8	294	288	19,102	20,389	5,866	6,122	0.3
6000	Depository institutions	17	17	1.1	187	188	20,385	21,468	4,039	4,211	0.8
6400	Insurance agents, brokers, and service	13	15	0.7	46	47	17,652	17,447	806	911	0.4
6500	Real estate	22	20	1.0	40	32	9,600	9,500	384	318	0.2
6510	Real estate operators and lessors	3	3	0.3	2	4	6,000	7,000	14	25	0.0
6530	Real estate agents and managers	9	9	1.2	21	-	10,667	-	207	-	-
HARRISON, IA											
60 –	**Finance, insurance, and real estate**	44	40	0.6	161	174	16,025	15,540	2,657	2,791	0.1
6000	Depository institutions	10	10	0.7	82	92	19,268	19,870	1,635	1,865	0.4
6400	Insurance agents, brokers, and service	14	18	0.9	35	44	17,029	14,636	598	678	0.3
6500	Real estate	13	11	0.6	33	-	6,182	-	237	-	-
6510	Real estate operators and lessors	8	7	0.8	27	30	5,333	6,000	163	190	0.4
6700	Holding and other investment offices	3	-	-	3	-	28,000	-	85	-	-
6710	Holding offices	3	-	-	3	-	28,000	-	85	-	-
HENRY, IA											
60 –	**Finance, insurance, and real estate**	47	45	0.6	228	253	18,053	16,806	4,136	4,306	0.2
6000	Depository institutions	9	9	0.6	114	124	20,246	18,968	2,313	2,414	0.5
6200	Security and commodity brokers	3	3	0.7	-	19	-	28,000	-	589	0.5
6300	Insurance carriers	4	1	0.2	11	-	13,818	-	109	-	-
6400	Insurance agents, brokers, and service	11	12	0.6	26	32	14,154	16,625	369	524	0.3
6500	Real estate	17	16	0.8	44	60	5,909	5,733	339	436	0.3
6510	Real estate operators and lessors	8	8	0.9	19	36	2,947	4,111	62	170	0.3
6530	Real estate agents and managers	5	7	0.9	18	-	8,222	-	183	-	-
HOWARD, IA											
60 –	**Finance, insurance, and real estate**	26	24	0.3	122	110	17,246	18,655	2,229	2,161	0.1
6400	Insurance agents, brokers, and service	9	9	0.4	-	21	-	14,095	-	301	0.1

Source: County Business Patterns, 1992/93, CBP-92/93-1, U.S. Department of Commerce, Washington, D.C., April 1995. SIC categories for which data were suppressed or not available for both 1992 and 1993 are *not* displayed. The employment columns represent mid-March employment in the year. Pay per employee is calculated by dividing 1st Quarter payroll, annualized, by mid-March employment. The columns headed "% State" show the county's percentage of the state total for the SIC in 1993; for example, 0.9% for SIC 6030 means that the county had 0.9 percent of the state's total establishments (or payroll) in SIC 6030 in 1993. A dash (-) is used to indicate that data are not available or cannot be calculated; *nec* means not elsewhere classified.

Continued on next page.

SIC	Industry	No. Establishments			Employment		Pay / Employee		Annual Payroll ($ 000)		
		1992	1993	% State	1992	1993	1992	1993	1992	1993	% State
HOWARD, IA - [continued]											
6500	Real estate	10	9	0.5	13	15	8,923	13,600	136	221	0.2
6510	Real estate operators and lessors	3	4	0.4	1	4	4,000	3,000	8	15	0.0
6530	Real estate agents and managers	4	3	0.4	8	-	5,000	-	47	-	-
HUMBOLDT, IA											
60-	**Finance, insurance, and real estate**	22	21	0.3	128	132	21,875	22,545	2,622	2,771	0.1
6000	Depository institutions	4	5	0.3	72	73	20,111	22,466	1,468	1,544	0.3
6400	Insurance agents, brokers, and service	7	7	0.3	29	28	27,034	26,000	544	571	0.3
6530	Real estate agents and managers	3	4	0.5	6	13	30,000	14,769	178	191	0.3
IDA, IA											
60-	**Finance, insurance, and real estate**	23	24	0.3	121	120	20,132	20,767	2,344	2,391	0.1
6000	Depository institutions	7	7	0.5	83	82	24,096	25,317	1,833	1,947	0.4
6400	Insurance agents, brokers, and service	6	6	0.3	12	13	9,000	9,231	131	99	0.0
6500	Real estate	7	8	0.4	18	20	11,111	10,800	223	243	0.2
6510	Real estate operators and lessors	3	4	0.4	-	11	-	4,727	-	47	0.1
IOWA, IA											
60-	**Finance, insurance, and real estate**	33	32	0.5	145	140	18,234	21,429	2,949	3,642	0.2
6000	Depository institutions	7	7	0.5	75	72	24,213	26,278	2,034	2,051	0.4
6400	Insurance agents, brokers, and service	13	13	0.6	32	30	10,625	12,533	422	493	0.2
6500	Real estate	6	6	0.3	21	14	9,143	12,286	190	148	0.1
JACKSON, IA											
60-	**Finance, insurance, and real estate**	43	40	0.6	244	256	17,541	16,750	4,362	4,409	0.2
6000	Depository institutions	11	11	0.7	161	165	20,472	20,048	3,264	3,336	0.6
6020	Commercial banks	11	11	1.1	161	165	20,472	20,048	3,264	3,336	0.8
6400	Insurance agents, brokers, and service	15	13	0.6	42	55	10,952	8,291	508	487	0.2
6500	Real estate	11	10	0.5	20	16	7,600	8,750	180	166	0.1
6510	Real estate operators and lessors	5	4	0.4	6	4	3,333	5,000	23	19	0.0
6530	Real estate agents and managers	3	3	0.4	5	3	5,600	5,333	42	33	0.0
JASPER, IA											
60-	**Finance, insurance, and real estate**	76	75	1.1	429	403	26,359	24,784	9,762	8,463	0.4
6000	Depository institutions	19	19	1.3	239	236	19,916	20,136	4,686	4,728	0.9
6100	Nondepository institutions	4	4	1.5	21	21	52,952	41,143	710	598	0.4
6400	Insurance agents, brokers, and service	27	23	1.1	73	51	28,603	38,039	1,495	1,345	0.7
6500	Real estate	18	21	1.1	28	44	8,143	10,636	260	543	0.4
6510	Real estate operators and lessors	11	10	1.1	14	-	5,143	-	89	-	-
6530	Real estate agents and managers	6	9	1.2	9	12	12,444	18,333	123	260	0.4
6700	Holding and other investment offices	4	4	1.5	-	6	-	10,000	-	149	0.1
JEFFERSON, IA											
60-	**Finance, insurance, and real estate**	67	72	1.0	312	285	25,026	28,604	7,886	8,188	0.4
6000	Depository institutions	9	8	0.5	124	115	23,613	27,861	2,606	2,892	0.6
6020	Commercial banks	4	3	0.3	105	99	25,752	28,646	2,399	2,558	0.6
6200	Security and commodity brokers	24	26	6.4	68	73	30,588	39,452	2,476	3,200	3.0
6210	Security brokers and dealers	3	11	4.6	-	20	-	67,800	-	1,595	1.9
6220	Commodity contracts brokers, dealers	6	6	12.2	19	22	28,421	40,909	872	931	-
6280	Security and commodity services	8	9	7.6	26	31	18,308	20,129	580	674	-
6400	Insurance agents, brokers, and service	9	9	0.4	22	19	17,455	19,158	526	444	0.2
6500	Real estate	18	19	1.0	46	-	12,261	-	866	-	-
6510	Real estate operators and lessors	7	6	0.7	27	19	10,815	11,158	578	277	0.5
6530	Real estate agents and managers	7	11	1.5	-	13	-	12,000	-	130	0.2
6700	Holding and other investment offices	5	8	3.0	-	29	-	39,034	-	1,024	1.0

Source: County Business Patterns, 1992/93, CBP-92/93-1, U.S. Department of Commerce, Washington, D.C., April 1995. SIC categories for which data were suppressed or not available for both 1992 and 1993 are not displayed. The employment columns represent mid-March employment in the year. Pay per employee is calculated by dividing 1st Quarter payroll, annualized, by mid-March employment. The columns headed "% State" show the county's percentage of the state total for the SIC in 1993; for example, 0.9% for SIC 6030 means that the county had 0.9 percent of the state's total establishments (or payroll) in SIC 6030 in 1993. A dash (-) is used to indicate that data are not available or cannot be calculated; nec means not elsewhere classified.

SIC	Industry	No. Establishments			Employment		Pay / Employee		Annual Payroll ($ 000)		
		1992	1993	% State	1992	1993	1992	1993	1992	1993	% State
JOHNSON, IA											
60–	**Finance, insurance, and real estate**	196	195	2.8	1,545	1,650	24,942	23,290	36,011	38,624	1.9
6000	Depository institutions	30	29	2.0	701	732	22,802	22,738	15,919	16,727	3.2
6020	Commercial banks	21	21	2.1	588	622	23,694	23,479	13,893	14,536	3.4
6100	Nondepository institutions	4	5	1.9	22	25	31,636	19,040	795	693	0.4
6200	Security and commodity brokers	10	10	2.5	-	37	-	65,189	-	2,393	2.2
6210	Security brokers and dealers	9	7	2.9	36	34	92,444	70,000	2,235	2,349	2.8
6280	Security and commodity services	1	3	2.5	-	3	-	10,667	-	44	-
6300	Insurance carriers	17	9	1.6	41	57	16,780	13,333	733	835	0.1
6310	Life insurance	5	2	1.2	21	-	16,952	-	365	-	-
6330	Fire, marine, and casualty insurance	9	5	2.0	19	16	16,000	18,750	333	332	0.1
6400	Insurance agents, brokers, and service	43	51	2.5	308	353	26,156	24,567	6,847	7,644	3.7
6500	Real estate	86	85	4.3	307	307	23,049	21,160	6,505	7,086	4.9
6510	Real estate operators and lessors	43	40	4.5	150	113	13,760	32,673	2,211	3,168	6.1
6530	Real estate agents and managers	30	35	4.7	113	114	16,956	15,298	2,251	2,437	3.6
6540	Title abstract offices	4	3	2.3	21	26	51,429	23,692	1,007	886	5.9
6700	Holding and other investment offices	5	6	2.3	128	139	20,656	21,353	2,944	3,246	3.0
JONES, IA											
60–	**Finance, insurance, and real estate**	39	36	0.5	219	200	22,411	16,120	4,502	3,508	0.2
6000	Depository institutions	13	12	0.8	171	146	25,380	18,082	3,879	2,888	0.6
6020	Commercial banks	8	8	0.8	106	104	18,906	18,885	2,130	2,192	0.5
6400	Insurance agents, brokers, and service	14	13	0.6	21	26	14,476	12,154	348	309	0.2
6500	Real estate	6	6	0.3	13	12	9,846	9,667	144	157	0.1
KEOKUK, IA											
60–	**Finance, insurance, and real estate**	26	24	0.3	139	145	19,137	19,338	2,865	3,085	0.1
6000	Depository institutions	9	9	0.6	96	99	21,833	22,384	2,198	2,396	0.5
6400	Insurance agents, brokers, and service	12	9	0.4	-	31	-	13,548	-	500	0.2
6500	Real estate	4	5	0.3	8	-	9,000	-	81	-	-
KOSSUTH, IA											
60–	**Finance, insurance, and real estate**	48	52	0.7	327	343	22,532	23,172	7,679	8,124	0.4
6000	Depository institutions	15	14	0.9	124	130	21,806	19,692	3,195	2,945	0.6
6020	Commercial banks	12	11	1.1	114	-	22,421	-	2,975	-	-
6200	Security and commodity brokers	4	4	1.0	-	7	-	33,714	-	248	0.2
6400	Insurance agents, brokers, and service	11	14	0.7	24	26	11,500	12,308	343	380	0.2
6500	Real estate	12	13	0.7	16	14	7,250	7,714	118	126	0.1
6510	Real estate operators and lessors	5	6	0.7	7	-	3,429	-	30	-	-
6530	Real estate agents and managers	4	4	0.5	-	3	-	6,667	-	31	0.0
6700	Holding and other investment offices	3	4	1.5	5	-	11,200	-	54	-	-
LEE, IA											
60–	**Finance, insurance, and real estate**	88	83	1.2	498	491	21,173	20,358	10,777	9,265	0.4
6000	Depository institutions	25	24	1.6	280	292	23,071	23,151	5,956	5,927	1.1
6020	Commercial banks	12	10	1.0	228	225	21,895	20,942	4,988	4,549	1.1
6030	Savings institutions	3	4	1.8	-	48	-	38,917	-	1,197	2.1
6060	Credit unions	10	10	3.8	-	19	-	9,474	-	181	0.6
6100	Nondepository institutions	3	1	0.4	7	-	18,857	-	157	-	-
6140	Personal credit institutions	3	1	0.8	7	-	18,857	-	157	-	-
6200	Security and commodity brokers	7	6	1.5	-	15	-	42,933	-	723	0.7
6210	Security brokers and dealers	5	4	1.7	11	-	51,273	-	670	-	-
6400	Insurance agents, brokers, and service	28	27	1.3	81	86	16,198	16,186	1,515	1,518	0.7
6500	Real estate	20	21	1.1	72	73	10,833	12,877	843	893	0.6
6510	Real estate operators and lessors	7	10	1.1	41	46	8,195	7,652	342	425	0.8
6530	Real estate agents and managers	9	8	1.1	15	12	12,800	27,667	238	208	0.3
6540	Title abstract offices	3	3	2.3	15	15	16,267	17,067	255	260	1.7

Source: County Business Patterns, 1992/93, CBP-92/93-1, U.S. Department of Commerce, Washington, D.C., April 1995. SIC categories for which data were suppressed or not available for both 1992 and 1993 are not displayed. The employment columns represent mid-March employment in the year. Pay per employee is calculated by dividing 1st Quarter payroll, annualized, by mid-March employment. The columns headed "% State" show the county's percentage of the state total for the SIC in 1993; for example, 0.9% for SIC 6030 means that the county had 0.9 percent of the state's total establishments (or payroll) in SIC 6030 in 1993. A dash (-) is used to indicate that data are not available or cannot be calculated; nec means not elsewhere classified.

SIC	Industry	No. Establishments			Employment		Pay / Employee		Annual Payroll ($ 000)		
		1992	1993	% State	1992	1993	1992	1993	1992	1993	% State

LINN, IA

SIC	Industry	1992	1993	% State	1992	1993	1992	1993	1992	1993	% State
60 –	**Finance, insurance, and real estate**	466	486	6.9	5,569	5,917	27,214	26,828	147,760	166,882	8.0
6000	Depository institutions	77	79	5.3	1,496	1,504	21,473	20,495	32,386	33,652	6.5
6020	Commercial banks	42	41	4.1	1,135	1,104	22,425	21,688	25,022	26,100	6.2
6030	Savings institutions	12	12	5.4	123	-	22,764	-	3,237	-	-
6060	Credit unions	20	24	9.1	219	248	15,854	16,129	3,719	4,220	12.9
6090	Functions closely related to banking	3	2	33.3	19	-	21,053	-	408	-	-
6100	Nondepository institutions	26	21	7.9	370	373	32,141	27,668	11,268	10,319	6.5
6160	Mortgage bankers and brokers	7	7	12.1	57	57	63,158	56,912	3,051	3,308	6.0
6200	Security and commodity brokers	30	35	8.6	296	320	51,162	52,325	13,448	14,624	13.6
6210	Security brokers and dealers	14	18	7.6	91	217	49,934	64,479	4,531	11,929	14.0
6300	Insurance carriers	59	60	10.7	1,285	1,378	25,833	27,303	32,409	38,395	4.6
6310	Life insurance	24	20	12.0	632	611	23,538	25,630	15,339	15,961	3.4
6330	Fire, marine, and casualty insurance	21	22	8.9	552	669	27,326	27,617	14,171	19,297	7.3
6370	Pension, health, and welfare funds	9	12	12.5	39	-	15,897	-	806	-	-
6400	Insurance agents, brokers, and service	115	113	5.5	377	384	27,926	22,812	11,611	9,699	4.7
6500	Real estate	134	142	7.2	736	707	18,408	16,107	14,289	14,629	10.0
6510	Real estate operators and lessors	57	61	6.8	287	300	15,805	15,187	4,619	5,770	11.1
6530	Real estate agents and managers	54	66	8.8	209	319	18,756	14,784	4,799	6,225	9.1
6552	Subdividers and developers, n.e.c.	7	5	11.9	-	7	-	37,143	-	489	11.4
6553	Cemetery subdividers and developers	5	6	4.0	-	42	-	23,333	-	1,233	21.3
6700	Holding and other investment offices	25	36	13.7	1,009	1,251	34,811	34,436	32,349	45,564	42.4
6710	Holding offices	6	16	13.2	964	1,209	34,701	34,369	29,860	43,834	55.2
6732	Educational, religious, etc. trusts	4	6	15.4	7	10	27,429	24,400	220	255	5.2
6733	Trusts, n.e.c.	4	2	4.5	14	-	8,000	-	96	-	-
6794	Patent owners and lessors	-	3	23.1	-	11	-	13,091	-	140	5.4
6799	Investors, n.e.c.	7	6	18.2	15	12	75,467	25,333	1,683	377	7.5

LOUISA, IA

SIC	Industry	1992	1993	% State	1992	1993	1992	1993	1992	1993	% State
60 –	**Finance, insurance, and real estate**	24	23	0.3	106	105	18,226	18,476	1,893	1,915	0.1
6000	Depository institutions	6	6	0.4	76	76	21,789	21,842	1,599	1,593	0.3
6400	Insurance agents, brokers, and service	9	8	0.4	12	14	12,000	12,571	156	187	0.1
6510	Real estate operators and lessors	3	4	0.4	3	6	6,667	4,000	20	25	0.0

LUCAS, IA

SIC	Industry	1992	1993	% State	1992	1993	1992	1993	1992	1993	% State
60 –	**Finance, insurance, and real estate**	16	15	0.2	106	111	25,887	25,622	2,274	2,497	0.1
6000	Depository institutions	4	4	0.3	65	74	19,877	19,081	1,304	1,442	0.3
6020	Commercial banks	4	4	0.4	65	74	19,877	19,081	1,304	1,442	0.3
6400	Insurance agents, brokers, and service	6	6	0.3	24	23	48,333	45,739	698	766	0.4
6500	Real estate	3	2	0.1	6	-	8,000	-	51	-	-

LYON, IA

SIC	Industry	1992	1993	% State	1992	1993	1992	1993	1992	1993	% State
60 –	**Finance, insurance, and real estate**	24	24	0.3	118	122	19,458	18,885	2,341	2,358	0.1
6000	Depository institutions	10	10	0.7	87	93	21,701	20,688	1,928	1,928	0.4
6400	Insurance agents, brokers, and service	8	10	0.5	19	22	13,895	14,545	268	346	0.2

MADISON, IA

SIC	Industry	1992	1993	% State	1992	1993	1992	1993	1992	1993	% State
60 –	**Finance, insurance, and real estate**	20	23	0.3	116	122	17,207	18,590	2,233	2,614	0.1
6000	Depository institutions	6	6	0.4	79	60	19,392	19,533	1,735	1,272	0.2
6400	Insurance agents, brokers, and service	6	7	0.3	14	18	14,857	13,333	286	272	0.1
6500	Real estate	4	6	0.3	13	11	11,692	12,364	142	211	0.1

MAHASKA, IA

SIC	Industry	1992	1993	% State	1992	1993	1992	1993	1992	1993	% State
60 –	**Finance, insurance, and real estate**	48	48	0.7	275	264	22,720	21,515	6,658	5,875	0.3
6000	Depository institutions	8	8	0.5	162	168	23,284	22,048	3,875	3,545	0.7
6020	Commercial banks	5	5	0.5	134	138	24,149	22,522	3,309	2,901	0.7
6030	Savings institutions	3	3	1.4	28	30	19,143	19,867	566	644	1.2
6200	Security and commodity brokers	3	3	0.7	-	10	-	56,800	-	611	0.6
6210	Security brokers and dealers	2	3	1.3	-	10	-	56,800	-	611	0.7

Source: County Business Patterns, 1992/93, CBP-92/93-1, U.S. Department of Commerce, Washington, D.C., April 1995. SIC categories for which data were suppressed or not available for both 1992 and 1993 are not displayed. The employment columns represent mid-March employment in the year. Pay per employee is calculated by dividing 1st Quarter payroll, annualized, by mid-March employment. The columns headed "% State" show the county's percentage of the state total for the SIC in 1993; for example, 0.9% for SIC 6030 means that the county had 0.9 percent of the state's total establishments (or payroll) in SIC 6030 in 1993. A dash (-) is used to indicate that data are not available or cannot be calculated; nec means not elsewhere classified.

Continued on next page.

SIC	Industry	No. Establishments			Employment		Pay / Employee		Annual Payroll ($ 000)		
		1992	1993	% State	1992	1993	1992	1993	1992	1993	% State
MAHASKA, IA - [continued]											
6300	Insurance carriers	5	2	0.4	15	-	20,533	-	359	-	-
6400	Insurance agents, brokers, and service	14	17	0.8	34	35	16,118	14,971	657	578	0.3
6500	Real estate	14	15	0.8	38	33	11,579	9,576	469	475	0.3
6510	Real estate operators and lessors	5	6	0.7	21	17	13,333	7,294	279	151	0.3
6530	Real estate agents and managers	6	5	0.7	8	5	9,500	10,400	83	100	0.1
MARION, IA											
60 –	**Finance, insurance, and real estate**	53	50	0.7	292	273	19,315	22,095	6,638	7,423	0.4
6000	Depository institutions	12	12	0.8	192	183	18,417	21,115	4,045	4,494	0.9
6020	Commercial banks	7	7	0.7	119	119	18,689	18,790	2,611	2,696	0.6
6400	Insurance agents, brokers, and service	16	17	0.8	50	48	20,000	21,583	1,108	1,156	0.6
6500	Real estate	15	14	0.7	28	26	12,143	11,846	446	557	0.4
6510	Real estate operators and lessors	4	6	0.7	4	6	3,000	8,000	97	159	0.3
6530	Real estate agents and managers	8	6	0.8	17	-	14,353	-	207	-	-
MARSHALL, IA											
60 –	**Finance, insurance, and real estate**	88	88	1.3	498	539	20,120	20,438	10,329	11,203	0.5
6000	Depository institutions	21	21	1.4	314	324	21,096	21,667	6,475	7,000	1.4
6020	Commercial banks	12	12	1.2	237	244	21,688	22,180	4,969	5,335	1.3
6030	Savings institutions	5	5	2.3	40	41	21,500	22,634	897	981	1.8
6060	Credit unions	4	4	1.5	37	39	16,865	17,436	609	684	2.1
6100	Nondepository institutions	5	5	1.9	18	24	21,111	22,000	440	489	0.3
6200	Security and commodity brokers	5	4	1.0	12	-	45,667	-	649	-	-
6300	Insurance carriers	8	8	1.4	27	25	20,000	14,560	569	372	0.0
6330	Fire, marine, and casualty insurance	4	4	1.6	12	-	19,667	-	260	-	-
6400	Insurance agents, brokers, and service	22	22	1.1	44	51	21,455	22,431	1,041	1,165	0.6
6500	Real estate	24	25	1.3	78	99	12,103	10,545	1,122	1,350	0.9
6510	Real estate operators and lessors	10	10	1.1	28	42	7,000	8,095	184	363	0.7
6530	Real estate agents and managers	7	8	1.1	24	27	12,833	12,296	452	501	0.7
6540	Title abstract offices	3	3	2.3	9	10	20,444	16,400	195	203	1.3
6700	Holding and other investment offices	3	3	1.1	5	-	8,000	-	33	-	-
MILLS, IA											
60 –	**Finance, insurance, and real estate**	17	17	0.2	109	99	18,936	22,303	2,150	2,193	0.1
6000	Depository institutions	6	6	0.4	84	77	20,952	24,312	1,818	1,843	0.4
6400	Insurance agents, brokers, and service	3	4	0.2	-	9	-	20,889	-	195	0.1
6500	Real estate	7	7	0.4	16	13	7,250	11,385	130	155	0.1
6530	Real estate agents and managers	3	3	0.4	8	4	4,500	14,000	43	55	0.1
MITCHELL, IA											
60 –	**Finance, insurance, and real estate**	22	27	0.4	141	143	17,589	19,692	2,883	3,068	0.1
6000	Depository institutions	6	6	0.4	97	99	19,175	20,646	2,245	2,313	0.4
6400	Insurance agents, brokers, and service	9	12	0.6	27	22	10,963	15,455	326	364	0.2
6500	Real estate	4	5	0.3	4	5	11,000	9,600	46	50	0.0
MONONA, IA											
60 –	**Finance, insurance, and real estate**	19	20	0.3	138	129	18,928	19,783	2,461	2,401	0.1
6000	Depository institutions	10	9	0.6	102	92	21,137	22,913	2,001	1,932	0.4
6400	Insurance agents, brokers, and service	4	4	0.2	-	23	-	13,391	-	315	0.2
6500	Real estate	4	6	0.3	14	-	4,857	-	77	-	-
MONROE, IA											
60 –	**Finance, insurance, and real estate**	10	11	0.2	-	-	-	-	-	-	-
6400	Insurance agents, brokers, and service	4	5	0.2	11	11	9,818	13,091	132	205	0.1
6500	Real estate	3	3	0.2	4	4	3,000	4,000	17	17	0.0

Source: County Business Patterns, 1992/93, CBP-92/93-1, U.S. Department of Commerce, Washington, D.C., April 1995. SIC categories for which data were suppressed or not available for both 1992 and 1993 are not displayed. The employment columns represent mid-March employment in the year. Pay per employee is calculated by dividing 1st Quarter payroll, annualized, by mid-March employment. The columns headed "% State" show the county's percentage of the state total for the SIC in 1993; for example, 0.9% for SIC 6030 means that the county had 0.9 percent of the state's total establishments (or payroll) in SIC 6030 in 1993. A dash (-) is used to indicate that data are not available or cannot be calculated; nec means not elsewhere classified.

SIC	Industry	No. Establishments			Employment		Pay / Employee		Annual Payroll ($ 000)		
		1992	1993	% State	1992	1993	1992	1993	1992	1993	% State
MONTGOMERY, IA											
60 –	**Finance, insurance, and real estate**	32	30	*0.4*	143	142	22,238	23,972	3,118	3,078	*0.1*
6000	Depository institutions	8	8	*0.5*	90	85	21,733	25,365	2,005	1,860	*0.4*
6200	Security and commodity brokers	5	4	*1.0*	7	7	18,857	28,000	143	194	*0.2*
6210	Security brokers and dealers	4	4	*1.7*	-	7	-	28,000	-	194	*0.2*
6300	Insurance carriers	3	2	*0.4*	9	-	31,556	-	224	-	-
6400	Insurance agents, brokers, and service	8	9	*0.4*	17	23	22,588	14,087	331	389	*0.2*
6500	Real estate	7	6	*0.3*	-	11	-	10,909	-	138	*0.1*
6510	Real estate operators and lessors	3	3	*0.3*	8	-	10,000	-	87	-	-
MUSCATINE, IA											
60 –	**Finance, insurance, and real estate**	81	78	*1.1*	552	496	21,638	21,411	12,089	11,041	*0.5*
6000	Depository institutions	19	21	*1.4*	272	277	22,294	22,022	6,158	6,244	*1.2*
6020	Commercial banks	14	14	*1.4*	246	245	22,943	22,759	5,684	5,670	*1.3*
6100	Nondepository institutions	5	3	*1.1*	-	9	-	17,333	-	153	*0.1*
6140	Personal credit institutions	4	2	*1.6*	12	-	20,667	-	212	-	-
6300	Insurance carriers	3	3	*0.5*	20	22	23,600	22,364	447	465	*0.1*
6330	Fire, marine, and casualty insurance	3	3	*1.2*	20	22	23,600	22,364	447	465	*0.2*
6400	Insurance agents, brokers, and service	21	22	*1.1*	67	74	25,373	23,784	1,496	1,736	*0.8*
6500	Real estate	23	21	*1.1*	52	78	18,077	14,872	1,256	1,381	*0.9*
6510	Real estate operators and lessors	9	8	*0.9*	26	49	20,000	15,020	717	887	*1.7*
6530	Real estate agents and managers	9	10	*1.3*	13	16	16,000	13,500	219	236	*0.3*
6700	Holding and other investment offices	8	6	*2.3*	124	-	18,774	-	2,292	-	-
O'BRIEN, IA											
60 –	**Finance, insurance, and real estate**	41	41	*0.6*	263	267	20,152	20,989	5,353	5,670	*0.3*
6000	Depository institutions	13	13	*0.9*	142	143	21,944	23,748	3,242	3,349	*0.6*
6400	Insurance agents, brokers, and service	15	17	*0.8*	66	71	16,485	16,620	1,150	1,325	*0.6*
6500	Real estate	8	7	*0.4*	30	33	8,933	9,333	295	340	*0.2*
6510	Real estate operators and lessors	4	3	*0.3*	8	-	10,000	-	73	-	-
OSCEOLA, IA											
60 –	**Finance, insurance, and real estate**	21	23	*0.3*	100	105	18,640	17,714	1,720	1,808	*0.1*
6000	Depository institutions	7	7	*0.5*	68	69	22,118	20,870	1,342	1,368	*0.3*
6400	Insurance agents, brokers, and service	8	9	*0.4*	-	20	-	11,800	-	230	*0.1*
6500	Real estate	4	5	*0.3*	6	-	8,000	-	50	-	-
PAGE, IA											
60 –	**Finance, insurance, and real estate**	39	36	*0.5*	225	217	22,880	22,986	5,341	5,161	*0.2*
6000	Depository institutions	11	11	*0.7*	157	153	23,389	24,288	3,842	3,900	*0.8*
6020	Commercial banks	6	6	*0.6*	140	136	24,343	24,912	3,554	3,557	*0.8*
6400	Insurance agents, brokers, and service	10	10	*0.5*	27	31	16,296	13,935	560	564	*0.3*
6500	Real estate	11	9	*0.5*	18	20	7,333	6,800	145	138	*0.1*
6510	Real estate operators and lessors	5	5	*0.6*	8	10	4,500	3,200	41	39	*0.1*
PALO ALTO, IA											
60 –	**Finance, insurance, and real estate**	32	31	*0.4*	135	141	23,496	23,064	3,128	3,116	*0.1*
6000	Depository institutions	9	9	*0.6*	88	94	25,864	25,532	2,297	2,341	*0.5*
6020	Commercial banks	9	9	*0.9*	88	94	25,864	25,532	2,297	2,341	*0.6*
6400	Insurance agents, brokers, and service	8	10	*0.5*	14	21	24,286	18,476	311	335	*0.2*
6500	Real estate	10	9	*0.5*	12	13	15,333	10,769	191	144	*0.1*
6530	Real estate agents and managers	4	3	*0.4*	5	5	12,000	12,000	69	60	*0.1*
PLYMOUTH, IA											
60 –	**Finance, insurance, and real estate**	52	52	*0.7*	340	361	21,529	21,119	7,895	8,396	*0.4*
6000	Depository institutions	13	14	*0.9*	154	173	26,364	23,723	4,608	4,867	*0.9*
6020	Commercial banks	11	10	*1.0*	-	142	-	24,366	-	4,196	*1.0*
6200	Security and commodity brokers	4	5	*1.2*	7	-	39,429	-	314	-	-
6220	Commodity contracts brokers, dealers	2	3	*6.1*	-	8	-	23,500	-	194	-

Source: County Business Patterns, 1992/93, CBP-92/93-1, U.S. Department of Commerce, Washington, D.C., April 1995. SIC categories for which data were suppressed or not available for both 1992 and 1993 are not displayed. The employment columns represent mid-March employment in the year. Pay per employee is calculated by dividing 1st Quarter payroll, annualized, by mid-March employment. The columns headed "% State" show the county's percentage of the state total for the SIC in 1993; for example, 0.9% for SIC 6030 means that the county had 0.9 percent of the state's total establishments (or payroll) in SIC 6030 in 1993. A dash (-) is used to indicate that data are not available or cannot be calculated; nec means not elsewhere classified.

Continued on next page.

SIC	Industry	No. Establishments			Employment		Pay / Employee		Annual Payroll ($ 000)		
		1992	1993	% State	1992	1993	1992	1993	1992	1993	% State
PLYMOUTH, IA - [continued]											
6400	Insurance agents, brokers, and service	17	19	0.9	41	48	10,829	12,000	459	549	0.3
6500	Real estate	12	11	0.6	27	28	7,704	7,571	245	237	0.2
6553	Cemetery subdividers and developers	3	3	2.0	3	3	2,667	2,667	11	12	0.2
POCAHONTAS, IA											
60 –	**Finance, insurance, and real estate**	24	22	0.3	122	124	17,639	21,774	2,304	2,576	0.1
6000	Depository institutions	7	6	0.4	93	89	20,043	26,157	1,966	2,194	0.4
6400	Insurance agents, brokers, and service	11	10	0.5	-	20	-	11,400	-	243	0.1
6500	Real estate	4	4	0.2	7	-	8,571	-	67	-	-
POLK, IA											
60 –	**Finance, insurance, and real estate**	1,144	1,157	16.5	32,704	34,751	31,289	31,712	975,711	1,093,310	52.5
6000	Depository institutions	134	145	9.8	4,152	4,010	23,906	25,947	96,639	100,849	19.5
6020	Commercial banks	62	63	6.4	3,227	3,050	23,902	26,450	74,992	76,660	18.1
6030	Savings institutions	31	35	15.8	421	425	24,409	26,654	9,816	12,157	21.8
6060	Credit unions	33	42	15.8	-	336	-	17,655	-	6,171	18.8
6090	Functions closely related to banking	4	2	33.3	75	-	26,507	-	1,991	-	-
6100	Nondepository institutions	106	98	36.8	3,109	3,255	35,359	41,004	104,858	118,940	74.5
6140	Personal credit institutions	64	40	31.3	1,179	1,067	39,712	53,987	41,082	44,548	84.2
6150	Business credit institutions	18	29	63.0	1,125	1,126	32,046	34,387	35,465	37,904	-
6160	Mortgage bankers and brokers	20	28	48.3	788	-	33,665	-	27,774	-	-
6200	Security and commodity brokers	73	78	19.1	610	698	63,305	57,095	37,447	43,639	40.5
6210	Security brokers and dealers	30	41	17.2	364	437	73,132	69,767	24,650	31,967	37.5
6220	Commodity contracts brokers, dealers	10	8	16.3	91	73	42,330	35,945	4,323	4,237	-
6280	Security and commodity services	33	29	24.4	155	188	52,542	35,851	8,474	7,435	-
6300	Insurance carriers	197	184	32.8	19,123	20,572	31,935	32,125	572,564	653,997	78.6
6310	Life insurance	84	76	45.8	11,762	12,216	33,967	33,783	361,278	393,617	84.2
6330	Fire, marine, and casualty insurance	70	69	27.9	4,675	6,244	30,225	30,498	146,069	202,117	76.9
6400	Insurance agents, brokers, and service	261	290	14.1	2,259	2,837	30,553	29,740	70,593	90,761	44.4
6500	Real estate	309	300	15.1	2,749	2,384	21,881	19,950	59,474	49,699	34.1
6510	Real estate operators and lessors	148	168	18.8	929	1,003	22,700	15,980	22,644	18,336	35.3
6530	Real estate agents and managers	116	109	14.5	1,404	1,171	22,470	22,938	27,989	25,911	37.9
6540	Title abstract offices	2	4	3.1	-	119	-	23,630	-	3,085	20.5
6552	Subdividers and developers, n.e.c.	12	11	26.2	198	76	19,071	21,158	4,542	2,037	47.7
6553	Cemetery subdividers and developers	6	4	2.7	44	-	13,273	-	557	-	-
6700	Holding and other investment offices	58	59	22.4	472	-	48,305	-	23,279	-	-
6710	Holding offices	17	21	17.4	330	273	60,061	57,363	20,220	14,102	17.8
6720	Investment offices	6	1	16.7	33	-	15,515	-	537	-	-
6732	Educational, religious, etc. trusts	11	12	30.8	22	26	20,364	15,385	382	445	9.1
6733	Trusts, n.e.c.	14	13	29.5	44	414	18,636	16,010	911	11,046	90.2
6799	Investors, n.e.c.	4	7	21.2	8	-	30,500	-	254	-	-
POTTAWATTAMIE, IA											
60 –	**Finance, insurance, and real estate**	136	137	1.9	1,306	1,271	22,573	21,410	28,033	28,781	1.4
6000	Depository institutions	33	35	2.4	505	495	19,350	19,103	9,652	9,940	1.9
6020	Commercial banks	24	24	2.4	459	437	19,599	18,847	8,802	8,685	2.1
6100	Nondepository institutions	6	6	2.3	28	20	23,143	27,800	550	808	0.5
6300	Insurance carriers	8	6	1.1	60	20	18,200	33,800	1,065	721	0.1
6330	Fire, marine, and casualty insurance	5	3	1.2	43	-	17,395	-	774	-	-
6400	Insurance agents, brokers, and service	37	35	1.7	322	318	27,217	29,157	8,391	9,088	4.4
6500	Real estate	41	40	2.0	197	225	12,995	12,516	2,833	3,251	2.2
6510	Real estate operators and lessors	18	15	1.7	84	58	11,762	10,690	1,047	703	1.4
6530	Real estate agents and managers	15	19	2.5	56	92	16,786	13,348	1,036	1,538	2.2
6553	Cemetery subdividers and developers	4	4	2.7	37	-	10,378	-	429	-	-
6710	Holding offices	3	5	4.1	-	15	-	48,533	-	589	0.7

Source: County Business Patterns, 1992/93, CBP-92/93-1, U.S. Department of Commerce, Washington, D.C., April 1995. SIC categories for which data were suppressed or not available for both 1992 and 1993 are *not* displayed. The employment columns represent mid-March employment in the year. Pay per employee is calculated by dividing 1st Quarter payroll, annualized, by mid-March employment. The columns headed "% State" show the county's percentage of the state total for the SIC in 1993; for example, 0.9% for SIC 6030 means that the county had 0.9 percent of the state's total establishments (or payroll) in SIC 6030 in 1993. A dash (-) is used to indicate that data are not available or cannot be calculated; *nec* means not elsewhere classified.

SIC	Industry	No. Establishments			Employment		Pay / Employee		Annual Payroll ($ 000)		
		1992	1993	% State	1992	1993	1992	1993	1992	1993	% State
POWESHIEK, IA											
60 –	**Finance, insurance, and real estate**	42	46	*0.7*	757	895	24,983	22,163	19,759	26,521	*1.3*
6000	Depository institutions	11	11	*0.7*	130	136	33,815	25,500	4,130	3,878	*0.7*
6020	Commercial banks	8	9	*0.9*	103	-	36,777	-	3,207	-	*-*
6400	Insurance agents, brokers, and service	12	13	*0.6*	-	35	-	19,771	-	881	*0.4*
6500	Real estate	10	13	*0.7*	-	24	-	10,833	-	310	*0.2*
6510	Real estate operators and lessors	5	5	*0.6*	11	-	11,273	-	138	-	*-*
6530	Real estate agents and managers	2	6	*0.8*	-	7	-	4,000	-	32	*0.0*
RINGGOLD, IA											
60 –	**Finance, insurance, and real estate**	11	10	*0.1*	54	48	14,815	15,583	863	721	*0.0*
6020	Commercial banks	3	2	*0.2*	28	-	20,143	-	618	-	*-*
6400	Insurance agents, brokers, and service	5	5	*0.2*	13	13	7,385	7,385	107	113	*0.1*
SAC, IA											
60 –	**Finance, insurance, and real estate**	37	37	*0.5*	165	168	18,036	18,952	2,988	3,149	*0.2*
6000	Depository institutions	13	13	*0.9*	100	109	23,440	22,349	2,433	2,448	*0.5*
6400	Insurance agents, brokers, and service	11	12	*0.6*	42	39	12,667	16,718	455	575	*0.3*
6500	Real estate	10	11	*0.6*	19	-	4,421	-	88	-	*-*
6510	Real estate operators and lessors	3	6	*0.7*	11	12	2,545	2,333	28	29	*0.1*
6530	Real estate agents and managers	3	1	*0.1*	2	-	2,000	-	7	-	*-*
6540	Title abstract offices	2	3	*2.3*	-	5	-	9,600	-	80	*0.5*
SCOTT, IA											
60 –	**Finance, insurance, and real estate**	369	379	*5.4*	3,523	3,928	24,028	25,651	87,747	103,944	*5.0*
6000	Depository institutions	53	59	*4.0*	1,180	1,155	20,732	24,516	24,760	25,170	*4.9*
6020	Commercial banks	30	31	*3.1*	885	766	19,281	25,467	17,825	16,704	*3.9*
6100	Nondepository institutions	24	20	*7.5*	180	154	24,378	26,494	4,728	4,464	*2.8*
6140	Personal credit institutions	16	11	*8.6*	141	-	21,333	-	2,923	-	*-*
6160	Mortgage bankers and brokers	7	8	*13.8*	-	63	-	33,524	-	2,345	*4.3*
6200	Security and commodity brokers	19	20	*4.9*	161	183	60,124	61,770	9,775	11,366	*10.6*
6210	Security brokers and dealers	14	14	*5.9*	146	153	62,740	68,732	9,090	10,342	*12.1*
6300	Insurance carriers	45	33	*5.9*	982	1,048	26,033	29,294	26,247	32,527	*3.9*
6310	Life insurance	15	12	*7.2*	344	406	13,174	13,399	4,455	5,232	*1.1*
6330	Fire, marine, and casualty insurance	19	14	*5.7*	213	195	29,258	29,538	6,435	5,874	*2.2*
6400	Insurance agents, brokers, and service	101	110	*5.4*	484	443	21,570	23,711	10,905	11,372	*5.6*
6500	Real estate	108	118	*6.0*	500	861	17,424	15,345	10,227	16,321	*11.2*
6510	Real estate operators and lessors	52	55	*6.2*	241	426	12,664	7,915	3,759	4,539	*8.7*
6530	Real estate agents and managers	36	51	*6.8*	203	376	22,621	22,798	5,279	10,203	*14.9*
6540	Title abstract offices	3	2	*1.5*	9	-	22,667	-	246	-	*-*
6552	Subdividers and developers, n.e.c.	3	5	*11.9*	14	16	20,286	23,500	418	563	*13.2*
6553	Cemetery subdividers and developers	3	4	*2.7*	10	33	11,200	20,000	134	739	*12.7*
6700	Holding and other investment offices	19	19	*7.2*	36	84	39,000	31,429	1,105	2,724	*2.5*
6710	Holding offices	8	9	*7.4*	-	46	-	50,783	-	2,465	*3.1*
6720	Investment offices	3	1	*16.7*	5	-	18,400	-	141	-	*-*
6733	Trusts, n.e.c.	4	3	*6.8*	-	25	-	5,280	-	68	*0.6*
SHELBY, IA											
60 –	**Finance, insurance, and real estate**	33	34	*0.5*	171	188	20,257	19,489	3,562	3,720	*0.2*
6000	Depository institutions	12	12	*0.8*	111	118	21,009	20,712	2,424	2,532	*0.5*
6020	Commercial banks	9	9	*0.9*	97	104	21,814	21,077	2,185	2,309	*0.5*
6400	Insurance agents, brokers, and service	12	11	*0.5*	27	29	13,333	12,966	368	380	*0.2*
6500	Real estate	5	5	*0.3*	10	14	22,000	15,143	239	234	*0.2*
SIOUX, IA											
60 –	**Finance, insurance, and real estate**	67	71	*1.0*	396	413	18,091	17,346	7,729	7,782	*0.4*
6000	Depository institutions	19	19	*1.3*	244	260	21,426	19,662	5,641	5,521	*1.1*
6020	Commercial banks	15	14	*1.4*	-	231	-	20,225	-	5,068	*1.2*
6030	Savings institutions	4	5	*2.3*	-	29	-	15,172	-	453	*0.8*

Source: County Business Patterns, 1992/93, CBP-92/93-1, U.S. Department of Commerce, Washington, D.C., April 1995. SIC categories for which data were suppressed or not available for both 1992 and 1993 are not displayed. The employment columns represent mid-March employment in the year. Pay per employee is calculated by dividing 1st Quarter payroll, annualized, by mid-March employment. The columns headed "% State" show the county's percentage of the state total for the SIC in 1993; for example, 0.9% for SIC 6030 means that the county had 0.9 percent of the state's total establishments (or payroll) in SIC 6030 in 1993. A dash (-) is used to indicate that data are not available or cannot be calculated; nec means not elsewhere classified.

Continued on next page.

SIC	Industry	No. Establishments			Employment		Pay / Employee		Annual Payroll ($ 000)		
		1992	1993	% State	1992	1993	1992	1993	1992	1993	% State
SIOUX, IA - [continued]											
6200	Security and commodity brokers	3	6	*1.5*	5	-	16,800	-	80	-	-
6220	Commodity contracts brokers, dealers	3	5	*10.2*	5	10	16,800	16,400	80	167	-
6300	Insurance carriers	3	3	*0.5*	-	15	-	14,133	-	233	*0.0*
6400	Insurance agents, brokers, and service	29	26	*1.3*	89	81	11,236	12,593	1,063	1,080	*0.5*
6500	Real estate	11	14	*0.7*	21	24	9,333	9,667	251	285	*0.2*
6530	Real estate agents and managers	4	7	*0.9*	9	10	8,444	9,200	85	116	*0.2*
6553	Cemetery subdividers and developers	2	3	*2.0*	-	3	-	2,667	-	13	*0.2*
STORY, IA											
60 –	**Finance, insurance, and real estate**	150	151	*2.1*	1,144	1,142	20,115	20,140	23,325	24,193	*1.2*
6000	Depository institutions	31	33	*2.2*	481	479	20,990	19,758	10,287	9,863	*1.9*
6020	Commercial banks	23	24	*2.4*	325	341	21,305	19,988	6,988	7,121	*1.7*
6030	Savings institutions	6	3	*1.4*	-	53	-	22,038	-	1,191	*2.1*
6060	Credit unions	2	6	*2.3*	-	85	-	17,412	-	1,551	*4.7*
6100	Nondepository institutions	7	3	*1.1*	51	19	17,176	10,526	907	154	*0.1*
6140	Personal credit institutions	6	3	*2.3*	-	19	-	10,526	-	154	*0.3*
6200	Security and commodity brokers	6	8	*2.0*	23	-	40,000	-	919	-	-
6300	Insurance carriers	9	11	*2.0*	156	152	24,974	27,474	3,527	3,959	*0.5*
6310	Life insurance	3	3	*1.8*	-	91	-	28,264	-	2,375	*0.5*
6330	Fire, marine, and casualty insurance	4	4	*1.6*	22	-	27,091	-	605	-	-
6400	Insurance agents, brokers, and service	40	38	*1.8*	115	125	18,330	18,944	2,314	2,456	*1.2*
6500	Real estate	51	54	*2.7*	298	341	11,933	14,006	4,080	5,630	*3.9*
6510	Real estate operators and lessors	17	23	*2.6*	39	92	10,667	15,087	479	1,700	*3.3*
6530	Real estate agents and managers	26	25	*3.3*	230	217	11,983	12,276	3,131	3,058	*4.5*
6700	Holding and other investment offices	6	4	*1.5*	20	-	78,000	-	1,291	-	-
TAMA, IA											
60 –	**Finance, insurance, and real estate**	32	34	*0.5*	251	245	17,721	18,661	4,601	4,841	*0.2*
6000	Depository institutions	13	13	*0.9*	108	103	24,556	26,097	2,607	2,448	*0.5*
6400	Insurance agents, brokers, and service	8	11	*0.5*	27	33	13,778	12,485	428	436	*0.2*
TAYLOR, IA											
60 –	**Finance, insurance, and real estate**	18	18	*0.3*	66	68	19,333	19,294	1,156	1,180	*0.1*
6000	Depository institutions	5	5	*0.3*	-	45	-	23,556	-	917	*0.2*
6020	Commercial banks	4	4	*0.4*	34	-	27,176	-	821	-	-
6400	Insurance agents, brokers, and service	6	7	*0.3*	11	13	8,000	9,538	98	130	*0.1*
6500	Real estate	6	6	*0.3*	12	10	10,667	12,800	108	133	*0.1*
UNION, IA											
60 –	**Finance, insurance, and real estate**	31	31	*0.4*	146	155	22,384	20,103	3,014	3,055	*0.1*
6000	Depository institutions	6	6	*0.4*	89	96	27,461	23,167	2,146	2,125	*0.4*
6400	Insurance agents, brokers, and service	5	6	*0.3*	14	16	12,857	14,000	199	236	*0.1*
6500	Real estate	16	15	*0.8*	27	27	7,111	7,852	209	227	*0.2*
6510	Real estate operators and lessors	3	5	*0.6*	9	-	4,889	-	46	-	-
6530	Real estate agents and managers	10	8	*1.1*	14	11	8,286	8,000	121	93	*0.1*
VAN BUREN, IA											
60 –	**Finance, insurance, and real estate**	21	20	*0.3*	74	72	17,135	18,056	1,471	1,336	*0.1*
6000	Depository institutions	8	8	*0.5*	53	50	19,774	21,440	1,204	1,065	*0.2*
6020	Commercial banks	8	8	*0.8*	53	50	19,774	21,440	1,204	1,065	*0.3*
6400	Insurance agents, brokers, and service	6	5	*0.2*	-	13	-	12,000	-	163	*0.1*
6500	Real estate	6	6	*0.3*	6	-	9,333	-	69	-	-
6553	Cemetery subdividers and developers	3	3	*2.0*	-	-	-	-	9	12	*0.2*
WAPELLO, IA											
60 –	**Finance, insurance, and real estate**	74	77	*1.1*	382	395	18,220	19,494	7,605	8,509	*0.4*
6000	Depository institutions	17	18	*1.2*	200	236	19,180	20,356	4,091	5,111	*1.0*
6020	Commercial banks	9	8	*0.8*	162	173	19,926	22,405	3,669	4,045	*1.0*

Source: County Business Patterns, 1992/93, CBP-92/93-1, U.S. Department of Commerce, Washington, D.C., April 1995. SIC categories for which data were suppressed or not available for both 1992 and 1993 are *not* displayed. The employment columns represent mid-March employment in the year. Pay per employee is calculated by dividing 1st Quarter payroll, annualized, by mid-March employment. The columns headed "% State" show the county's percentage of the state total for the SIC in 1993; for example, 0.9% for SIC 6030 means that the county had 0.9 percent of the state's total establishments (or payroll) in SIC 6030 in 1993. A dash (-) is used to indicate that data are not available or cannot be calculated; *nec* means not elsewhere classified.

Continued on next page.

SIC	Industry	No. Establishments			Employment		Pay / Employee		Annual Payroll ($ 000)		
		1992	1993	% State	1992	1993	1992	1993	1992	1993	% Sta
WAPELLO, IA - [continued]											
6030	Savings institutions	3	3	1.4	24	11	16,500	17,818	234	214	0.4
6060	Credit unions	5	7	2.6	14	52	15,143	14,077	188	852	2.6
6100	Nondepository institutions	7	6	2.3	47	22	15,489	21,273	926	389	0.2
6300	Insurance carriers	8	7	1.2	-	40	-	21,300	-	1,186	0.1
6400	Insurance agents, brokers, and service	13	15	0.7	41	44	19,512	19,727	831	921	0.5
6500	Real estate	25	27	1.4	49	44	7,265	7,545	412	495	0.3
6510	Real estate operators and lessors	12	12	1.3	23	-	5,391	-	161	-	-
6530	Real estate agents and managers	10	13	1.7	15	19	9,067	8,000	140	222	0.3
6700	Holding and other investment offices	3	2	0.8	5	-	10,400	-	24	-	-
WARREN, IA											
60 –	**Finance, insurance, and real estate**	53	57	0.8	255	274	18,086	17,796	5,092	5,435	0.3
6000	Depository institutions	10	12	0.8	151	149	18,834	19,329	2,896	2,937	0.6
6400	Insurance agents, brokers, and service	15	19	0.9	54	65	16,148	14,585	1,173	1,279	0.6
6500	Real estate	20	21	1.1	41	51	12,390	12,235	606	772	0.5
6510	Real estate operators and lessors	11	9	1.0	14	12	7,714	10,333	147	142	0.3
6530	Real estate agents and managers	5	7	0.9	16	20	15,500	13,600	300	389	0.6
WASHINGTON, IA											
60 –	**Finance, insurance, and real estate**	49	49	0.7	226	221	18,973	21,068	4,741	4,810	0.2
6000	Depository institutions	12	12	0.8	140	134	20,286	23,612	3,179	3,204	0.6
6200	Security and commodity brokers	5	5	1.2	7	7	30,857	37,714	267	298	0.3
6400	Insurance agents, brokers, and service	16	15	0.7	40	41	14,200	13,756	607	613	0.3
6500	Real estate	12	12	0.6	23	22	7,652	7,818	233	244	0.2
6510	Real estate operators and lessors	4	6	0.7	3	7	5,333	4,000	39	55	0.1
6530	Real estate agents and managers	4	3	0.4	6	3	3,333	8,000	25	22	0.0
6540	Title abstract offices	3	3	2.3	12	12	10,333	10,000	155	167	1.1
WAYNE, IA											
60 –	**Finance, insurance, and real estate**	14	13	0.2	61	60	16,000	17,267	995	1,066	0.1
6400	Insurance agents, brokers, and service	5	4	0.2	-	8	-	17,000	-	123	0.1
WEBSTER, IA											
60 –	**Finance, insurance, and real estate**	105	106	1.5	554	586	20,282	21,638	12,037	11,649	0.6
6000	Depository institutions	17	17	1.1	297	340	21,751	23,318	6,963	6,267	1.2
6020	Commercial banks	11	11	1.1	217	243	22,802	24,938	5,354	4,532	1.1
6100	Nondepository institutions	8	3	1.1	13	8	18,154	22,000	230	182	0.1
6280	Security and commodity services	5	4	3.4	5	4	20,000	15,000	86	90	-
6300	Insurance carriers	6	4	0.7	27	23	19,111	24,870	522	577	0.1
6400	Insurance agents, brokers, and service	32	37	1.8	97	89	18,227	17,978	1,704	1,611	0.8
6500	Real estate	31	33	1.7	87	101	11,402	11,287	1,090	1,244	0.9
6510	Real estate operators and lessors	12	14	1.6	30	58	9,600	9,241	286	450	0.9
6530	Real estate agents and managers	12	15	2.0	37	30	12,649	12,400	509	486	0.7
6553	Cemetery subdividers and developers	3	3	2.0	11	-	10,182	-	153	-	-
WINNEBAGO, IA											
60 –	**Finance, insurance, and real estate**	38	37	0.5	183	190	19,563	19,158	3,572	3,804	0.2
6000	Depository institutions	9	9	0.6	123	128	21,854	21,906	2,817	2,971	0.6
6200	Security and commodity brokers	3	3	0.7	3	5	10,667	10,400	34	55	0.1
6400	Insurance agents, brokers, and service	12	11	0.5	27	24	11,556	13,333	294	335	0.2
6500	Real estate	7	8	0.4	15	20	9,600	8,400	145	169	0.1
6510	Real estate operators and lessors	3	4	0.4	3	4	2,667	3,000	9	13	0.0
6700	Holding and other investment offices	4	4	1.5	5	-	24,000	-	102	-	-
WINNESHIEK, IA											
60 –	**Finance, insurance, and real estate**	45	46	0.7	226	239	21,947	19,715	4,827	4,913	0.2
6000	Depository institutions	7	7	0.5	145	149	22,179	22,685	3,381	3,488	0.7
6100	Nondepository institutions	2	3	1.1	-	17	-	23,294	-	322	0.2

Source: County Business Patterns, 1992/93, CBP-92/93-1, U.S. Department of Commerce, Washington, D.C., April 1995. SIC categories for which data were suppressed or not available for both 1992 a 1993 are *not* displayed. The employment columns represent mid-March employment in the year. Pay per employee is calculated by dividing 1st Quarter payroll, annualized, by mid-March employme The columns headed "% State" show the county's percentage of the state total for the SIC in 1993; for example, 0.9% for SIC 6030 means that the county had 0.9 percent of the state's total establishme (or payroll) in SIC 6030 in 1993. A dash (-) is used to indicate that data are not available or cannot be calculated; *nec* means not elsewhere classified.

Continued on next page.

SIC	Industry	No. Establishments			Employment		Pay / Employee		Annual Payroll ($ 000)		
		1992	1993	% State	1992	1993	1992	1993	1992	1993	% State
WINNESHIEK, IA - [continued]											
6200	Security and commodity brokers	3	3	0.7	8	9	24,000	27,556	232	310	0.3
6210	Security brokers and dealers	3	2	0.8	8	-	24,000	-	232	-	-
6400	Insurance agents, brokers, and service	16	17	0.8	33	33	13,333	12,121	481	472	0.2
6500	Real estate	14	14	0.7	20	-	26,200	-	251	-	-
6510	Real estate operators and lessors	4	5	0.6	6	-	4,667	-	33	-	-
6530	Real estate agents and managers	5	4	0.5	9	6	28,889	12,000	103	57	0.1
6553	Cemetery subdividers and developers	4	4	2.7	-	2	-	12,000	-	47	0.8
WOODBURY, IA											
60 –	**Finance, insurance, and real estate**	256	263	3.7	2,192	2,369	22,878	23,065	51,662	55,086	2.6
6000	Depository institutions	38	42	2.8	823	827	21,293	22,960	18,607	19,597	3.8
6020	Commercial banks	25	26	2.6	634	624	22,694	24,417	15,169	15,640	3.7
6100	Nondepository institutions	16	11	4.1	70	64	23,314	24,375	1,578	1,259	0.8
6140	Personal credit institutions	13	8	6.3	54	41	18,370	16,976	987	730	1.4
6200	Security and commodity brokers	13	17	4.2	176	138	34,091	41,594	5,637	6,242	5.8
6210	Security brokers and dealers	12	13	5.5	-	123	-	45,659	-	6,116	7.2
6280	Security and commodity services	1	4	3.4	-	15	-	8,267	-	126	-
6300	Insurance carriers	38	36	6.4	473	645	28,195	25,060	13,957	16,195	1.9
6310	Life insurance	12	13	7.8	213	355	32,300	27,290	6,351	9,987	2.1
6400	Insurance agents, brokers, and service	70	69	3.4	192	227	21,729	21,004	4,433	5,036	2.5
6500	Real estate	70	75	3.8	418	438	15,665	14,521	6,431	6,277	4.3
6510	Real estate operators and lessors	35	41	4.6	226	233	17,628	16,378	3,522	3,294	6.3
6530	Real estate agents and managers	22	27	3.6	104	170	13,038	11,412	1,558	2,204	3.2
6540	Title abstract offices	3	4	3.1	21	-	20,762	-	537	-	-
6700	Holding and other investment offices	11	13	4.9	40	30	23,400	35,333	1,019	480	0.4
WORTH, IA											
60 –	**Finance, insurance, and real estate**	19	21	0.3	81	82	16,593	18,293	1,247	1,455	0.1
6000	Depository institutions	8	7	0.5	56	52	18,286	22,154	920	1,077	0.2
6400	Insurance agents, brokers, and service	4	6	0.3	9	13	11,111	8,308	101	121	0.1
6500	Real estate	4	5	0.3	-	9	-	9,778	-	98	0.1
WRIGHT, IA											
60 –	**Finance, insurance, and real estate**	49	47	0.7	275	253	18,575	18,119	4,730	4,524	0.2
6000	Depository institutions	14	12	0.8	153	132	23,895	25,000	3,309	3,099	0.6
6020	Commercial banks	11	9	0.9	145	124	24,331	25,290	3,175	2,930	0.7
6200	Security and commodity brokers	1	3	0.7	-	1	-	4,000	-	20	0.0
6400	Insurance agents, brokers, and service	17	18	0.9	100	80	12,240	11,850	1,114	1,028	0.5
6500	Real estate	15	13	0.7	18	-	10,889	-	274	-	-
6510	Real estate operators and lessors	11	10	1.1	8	28	7,500	4,714	99	141	0.3

Source: County Business Patterns, 1992/93, CBP-92/93-1, U.S. Department of Commerce, Washington, D.C., April 1995. SIC categories for which data were suppressed or not available for both 1992 and 1993 are *not* displayed. The employment columns represent mid-March employment in the year. Pay per employee is calculated by dividing 1st Quarter payroll, annualized, by mid-March employment. The columns headed "% State" show the county's percentage of the state total for the SIC in 1993; for example, 0.9% for SIC 6030 means that the county had 0.9 percent of the state's total establishments (or payroll) in SIC 6030 in 1993. A dash (-) is used to indicate that data are not available or cannot be calculated; *nec* means not elsewhere classified.

KANSAS

SIC	Industry	No. Establishments			Employment		Pay / Employee		Annual Payroll ($ 000)		
		1992	1993	% State	1992	1993	1992	1993	1992	1993	% State
ALLEN, KS											
60 –	**Finance, insurance, and real estate**	34	34	0.5	176	172	18,750	17,674	3,261	3,104	0.2
6000	Depository institutions	10	9	0.7	106	104	22,679	22,077	2,356	2,322	0.5
6400	Insurance agents, brokers, and service	10	15	0.8	39	42	11,179	11,905	471	517	0.3
6500	Real estate	7	6	0.3	16	18	6,750	6,222	105	114	0.1
6510	Real estate operators and lessors	3	3	0.4	8	9	2,500	2,222	15	20	0.0
6700	Holding and other investment offices	3	2	0.6	5	-	4,800	-	17	-	-
ANDERSON, KS											
60 –	**Finance, insurance, and real estate**	17	16	0.2	76	108	18,684	14,741	1,594	1,767	0.1
6000	Depository institutions	8	7	0.5	59	86	20,475	15,907	1,362	1,529	0.3
6400	Insurance agents, brokers, and service	4	5	0.3	-	18	-	11,333	-	215	0.1
6500	Real estate	3	2	0.1	3	-	13,333	-	40	-	-
ATCHISON, KS											
60 –	**Finance, insurance, and real estate**	41	42	0.6	179	214	22,279	20,505	3,871	4,343	0.3
6000	Depository institutions	9	10	0.8	107	115	24,935	20,243	2,518	2,462	0.5
6020	Commercial banks	7	7	0.8	-	108	-	20,741	-	2,372	0.6
6400	Insurance agents, brokers, and service	11	12	0.6	24	28	19,167	12,571	372	422	0.2
6500	Real estate	12	11	0.6	24	30	9,500	8,400	281	273	0.2
6510	Real estate operators and lessors	5	5	0.6	7	10	8,571	7,200	85	77	0.2
6530	Real estate agents and managers	2	3	0.3	-	13	-	8,000	-	105	0.1
6700	Holding and other investment offices	3	3	0.9	4	4	19,000	13,000	79	63	0.1
BARBER, KS											
60 –	**Finance, insurance, and real estate**	23	21	0.3	82	92	15,220	17,174	1,632	1,821	0.1
6000	Depository institutions	9	9	0.7	54	72	19,407	19,389	1,376	1,614	0.3
6020	Commercial banks	9	9	1.0	54	72	19,407	19,389	1,376	1,614	0.4
6400	Insurance agents, brokers, and service	6	6	0.3	16	9	8,750	14,667	132	133	0.1
6500	Real estate	7	6	0.3	-	11	-	4,727	-	74	0.0
BARTON, KS											
60 –	**Finance, insurance, and real estate**	83	89	1.3	471	476	21,945	23,353	10,875	10,476	0.6
6000	Depository institutions	17	19	1.4	248	250	21,935	21,056	5,657	5,674	1.2
6200	Security and commodity brokers	5	5	1.3	10	9	69,200	88,889	690	752	0.7
6300	Insurance carriers	9	8	1.5	32	35	18,750	20,343	675	617	0.2
6370	Pension, health, and welfare funds	3	3	2.9	7	-	10,857	-	121	-	-
6400	Insurance agents, brokers, and service	31	33	1.8	110	119	16,073	15,328	2,023	2,215	1.1
6500	Real estate	17	20	1.0	60	54	20,200	12,444	1,313	542	0.3
6510	Real estate operators and lessors	7	9	1.1	12	25	6,333	7,200	78	167	0.4
6530	Real estate agents and managers	6	9	1.0	38	-	24,842	-	1,069	-	-
6700	Holding and other investment offices	3	4	1.3	-	9	-	204,889	-	676	0.6
BOURBON, KS											
60 –	**Finance, insurance, and real estate**	38	40	0.6	742	722	20,469	23,003	13,761	15,073	0.9
6000	Depository institutions	7	7	0.5	102	104	21,373	21,423	2,162	2,298	0.5
6300	Insurance carriers	5	3	0.6	247	-	25,198	-	6,787	-	-
6400	Insurance agents, brokers, and service	10	13	0.7	312	313	19,795	21,291	4,137	4,641	2.3
6500	Real estate	10	12	0.6	71	14	4,056	11,714	236	224	0.1
6510	Real estate operators and lessors	5	7	0.9	7	6	11,429	9,333	78	82	0.2

Source: County Business Patterns, 1992/93, CBP-92/93-1, U.S. Department of Commerce, Washington, D.C., April 1995. SIC categories for which data were suppressed or not available for both 1992 and 1993 are *not* displayed. The employment columns represent mid-March employment in the year. Pay per employee is calculated by dividing 1st Quarter payroll, annualized, by mid-March employment. The columns headed "% State" show the county's percentage of the state total for the SIC in 1993; for example, 0.9% for SIC 6030 means that the county had 0.9 percent of the state's total establishments (or payroll) in SIC 6030 in 1993. A dash (-) is used to indicate that data are not available or cannot be calculated; *nec* means not elsewhere classified.

SIC	Industry	No. Establishments			Employment		Pay / Employee		Annual Payroll ($ 000)		
		1992	1993	% State	1992	1993	1992	1993	1992	1993	% State
BROWN, KS											
60 –	**Finance, insurance, and real estate**	29	25	0.4	143	149	17,594	15,383	2,539	2,528	0.2
6000	Depository institutions	7	5	0.4	103	93	19,806	19,656	2,033	2,014	0.4
6020	Commercial banks	7	5	0.6	103	93	19,806	19,656	2,033	2,014	0.5
6300	Insurance carriers	3	1	0.2	10	-	17,200	-	174	-	-
6400	Insurance agents, brokers, and service	10	10	0.5	-	20	-	11,200	-	251	0.1
6500	Real estate	6	6	0.3	12	8	5,667	7,500	71	72	0.0
BUTLER, KS											
60 –	**Finance, insurance, and real estate**	86	94	1.4	561	573	19,316	20,042	11,664	12,631	0.8
6000	Depository institutions	30	32	2.4	373	400	20,525	20,760	8,228	8,791	1.8
6020	Commercial banks	20	20	2.2	291	308	20,948	20,766	6,588	6,792	1.7
6400	Insurance agents, brokers, and service	24	29	1.6	82	92	17,902	20,391	1,654	1,833	0.9
6500	Real estate	22	23	1.2	70	55	12,114	11,564	877	942	0.5
6510	Real estate operators and lessors	7	9	1.1	10	12	6,800	12,333	49	166	0.4
6530	Real estate agents and managers	10	11	1.3	26	20	14,308	8,400	423	422	0.4
6540	Title abstract offices	3	3	2.4	23	23	14,435	13,913	335	354	3.1
CHASE, KS											
60 –	**Finance, insurance, and real estate**	8	6	0.1	-	-	-	-	-	-	-
6500	Real estate	2	3	0.2	-	3	-	12,000	-	42	0.0
CHAUTAUQUA, KS											
60 –	**Finance, insurance, and real estate**	5	6	0.1	36	38	14,778	16,842	578	694	0.0
CHEROKEE, KS											
60 –	**Finance, insurance, and real estate**	25	26	0.4	144	154	21,417	19,143	3,026	3,076	0.2
6000	Depository institutions	9	9	0.7	99	103	26,061	22,951	2,517	2,461	0.5
6020	Commercial banks	9	9	1.0	99	103	26,061	22,951	2,517	2,461	0.6
6400	Insurance agents, brokers, and service	10	9	0.5	32	-	12,750	-	408	-	-
6500	Real estate	6	7	0.4	13	15	7,385	6,933	101	110	0.1
6510	Real estate operators and lessors	3	3	0.4	5	8	8,800	7,000	53	58	0.1
CHEYENNE, KS											
60 –	**Finance, insurance, and real estate**	10	9	0.1	50	-	18,800	-	1,134	-	-
6400	Insurance agents, brokers, and service	5	5	0.3	5	5	6,400	5,600	30	32	0.0
CLARK, KS											
60 –	**Finance, insurance, and real estate**	9	9	0.1	47	56	20,340	17,143	1,185	1,280	0.1
6000	Depository institutions	4	4	0.3	34	38	24,588	20,947	1,049	1,100	0.2
CLAY, KS											
60 –	**Finance, insurance, and real estate**	18	18	0.3	91	96	16,659	17,000	1,753	1,751	0.1
6000	Depository institutions	6	7	0.5	72	79	18,278	18,278	1,513	1,525	0.3
6020	Commercial banks	4	4	0.4	-	63	-	18,667	-	1,326	0.3
6400	Insurance agents, brokers, and service	5	6	0.3	9	-	7,556	-	65	-	-
6500	Real estate	4	4	0.2	4	6	13,000	9,333	53	63	0.0
CLOUD, KS											
60 –	**Finance, insurance, and real estate**	29	28	0.4	179	151	16,291	19,126	3,161	3,209	0.2
6000	Depository institutions	11	11	0.8	131	108	15,908	19,852	2,265	2,365	0.5
6020	Commercial banks	9	9	1.0	127	-	15,969	-	2,245	-	-
6400	Insurance agents, brokers, and service	7	7	0.4	20	19	11,200	7,158	163	158	0.1
6500	Real estate	5	5	0.3	11	8	12,000	13,500	140	121	0.1
6530	Real estate agents and managers	3	3	0.3	6	-	16,667	-	102	-	-

Source: County Business Patterns, 1992/93, CBP-92/93-1, U.S. Department of Commerce, Washington, D.C., April 1995. SIC categories for which data were suppressed or not available for both 1992 and 1993 are *not* displayed. The employment columns represent mid-March employment in the year. Pay per employee is calculated by dividing 1st Quarter payroll, annualized, by mid-March employment. The columns headed "% State" show the county's percentage of the state total for the SIC in 1993; for example, 0.9% for SIC 6030 means that the county had 0.9 percent of the state's total establishments (or payroll) in SIC 6030 in 1993. A dash (-) is used to indicate that data are not available or cannot be calculated; *nec* means not elsewhere classified.

SIC	Industry	No. Establishments			Employment		Pay / Employee		Annual Payroll ($ 000)		
		1992	1993	% State	1992	1993	1992	1993	1992	1993	% Stat
COFFEY, KS											
60 –	**Finance, insurance, and real estate**	18	21	0.3	-	-	-	-	-	-	-
6400	Insurance agents, brokers, and service	3	6	0.3	-	9	-	15,111	-	143	0.1
6500	Real estate	6	6	0.3	-	6	-	5,333	-	31	0.0
6530	Real estate agents and managers	3	3	0.3	6	3	9,333	9,333	64	19	0.0
COMANCHE, KS											
60 –	**Finance, insurance, and real estate**	8	9	0.1	-	-	-	-	-	-	-
COWLEY, KS											
60 –	**Finance, insurance, and real estate**	64	67	1.0	454	425	18,167	19,454	8,258	8,618	0.5
6000	Depository institutions	20	22	1.7	271	271	21,830	22,022	5,904	6,078	1.3
6020	Commercial banks	13	13	1.4	194	202	22,660	22,356	4,442	4,573	1.2
6200	Security and commodity brokers	6	6	1.6	26	18	6,462	13,778	207	297	0.3
6300	Insurance carriers	5	2	0.4	50	-	13,680	-	442	-	-
6400	Insurance agents, brokers, and service	15	20	1.1	54	62	15,259	16,839	964	1,129	0.6
6500	Real estate	11	11	0.6	38	43	11,053	11,814	448	552	0.3
6510	Real estate operators and lessors	3	3	0.4	13	11	8,308	16,364	103	178	0.4
6530	Real estate agents and managers	5	7	0.8	12	-	5,333	-	77	-	-
6700	Holding and other investment offices	4	4	1.3	-	7	-	12,000	-	139	0.1
CRAWFORD, KS											
60 –	**Finance, insurance, and real estate**	90	84	1.3	483	466	19,296	18,979	9,624	9,416	0.6
6000	Depository institutions	18	20	1.5	273	259	21,319	20,587	5,884	5,677	1.2
6020	Commercial banks	14	14	1.6	195	197	21,251	21,340	4,348	4,520	1.2
6100	Nondepository institutions	4	2	0.6	12	-	14,667	-	179	-	-
6140	Personal credit institutions	4	1	0.7	12	-	14,667	-	179	-	-
6200	Security and commodity brokers	3	4	1.0	-	15	-	49,333	-	702	0.6
6300	Insurance carriers	7	2	0.4	51	-	24,941	-	1,280	-	-
6370	Pension, health, and welfare funds	3	-	-	2	-	10,000	-	20	-	-
6400	Insurance agents, brokers, and service	25	26	1.4	67	70	14,149	13,943	1,004	1,122	0.6
6500	Real estate	31	28	1.4	64	71	7,875	6,873	635	606	0.3
6510	Real estate operators and lessors	8	13	1.7	10	25	5,200	6,880	73	235	0.5
6530	Real estate agents and managers	16	12	1.4	32	29	7,875	6,069	262	202	0.2
DECATUR, KS											
60 –	**Finance, insurance, and real estate**	15	16	0.2	50	57	17,120	18,175	1,208	1,144	0.1
6000	Depository institutions	5	6	0.5	-	40	-	23,200	-	974	0.2
6400	Insurance agents, brokers, and service	6	6	0.3	7	10	12,000	8,800	93	110	0.1
6500	Real estate	3	4	0.2	9	7	5,778	2,857	57	60	0.0
DICKINSON, KS											
60 –	**Finance, insurance, and real estate**	54	55	0.8	240	249	20,983	18,843	5,282	5,173	0.3
6000	Depository institutions	17	16	1.2	158	164	23,443	19,756	3,868	3,638	0.8
6300	Insurance carriers	4	4	0.7	25	-	22,560	-	614	-	-
6400	Insurance agents, brokers, and service	14	14	0.8	26	29	15,846	17,379	405	488	0.2
6500	Real estate	14	15	0.8	25	27	8,640	8,593	249	291	0.2
6510	Real estate operators and lessors	6	8	1.0	9	12	4,889	4,333	59	79	0.2
6530	Real estate agents and managers	3	3	0.3	7	7	8,571	11,429	63	77	0.1
DONIPHAN, KS											
60 –	**Finance, insurance, and real estate**	13	16	0.2	74	72	17,784	19,889	1,602	1,722	0.1
6000	Depository institutions	8	9	0.7	60	66	18,400	20,970	1,369	1,667	0.3
6400	Insurance agents, brokers, and service	2	4	0.2	-	3	-	8,000	-	29	0.0
6500	Real estate	2	3	0.2	-	3	-	8,000	-	26	0.0

Source: County Business Patterns, 1992/93, CBP-92/93-1, U.S. Department of Commerce, Washington, D.C., April 1995. SIC categories for which data were suppressed or not available for both 1992 and 1993 are not displayed. The employment columns represent mid-March employment in the year. Pay per employee is calculated by dividing 1st Quarter payroll, annualized, by mid-March employment. The columns headed "% State" show the county's percentage of the state total for the SIC in 1993; for example, 0.9% for SIC 6030 means that the county had 0.9 percent of the state's total establishments (or payroll) in SIC 6030 in 1993. A dash (-) is used to indicate that data are not available or cannot be calculated; nec means not elsewhere classified.

SIC	Industry	No. Establishments			Employment		Pay / Employee		Annual Payroll ($ 000)		
		1992	1993	% State	1992	1993	1992	1993	1992	1993	% State
DOUGLAS, KS											
60 –	**Finance, insurance, and real estate**	157	170	2.5	1,453	1,667	18,502	19,693	30,572	36,044	2.2
6000	Depository institutions	24	27	2.0	423	508	21,712	23,535	9,107	11,929	2.5
6020	Commercial banks	15	12	1.3	322	368	23,416	25,348	7,460	9,940	2.5
6030	Savings institutions	6	9	4.4	91	123	16,747	19,740	1,522	1,779	3.0
6060	Credit unions	3	6	3.2	10	17	12,000	11,765	125	210	1.0
6200	Security and commodity brokers	13	14	3.6	-	41	-	30,634	-	1,523	1.4
6210	Security brokers and dealers	7	8	3.9	-	30	-	38,533	-	1,384	2.0
6280	Security and commodity services	6	6	4.1	-	11	-	9,091	-	139	-
6300	Insurance carriers	6	8	1.5	23	-	22,261	-	561	-	-
6400	Insurance agents, brokers, and service	34	34	1.8	97	90	20,206	21,289	2,212	2,680	1.3
6500	Real estate	66	75	3.9	286	258	12,671	13,984	4,374	4,956	2.8
6510	Real estate operators and lessors	27	35	4.5	130	106	9,138	12,830	1,254	1,683	3.6
6530	Real estate agents and managers	28	34	3.9	99	123	16,162	13,789	2,142	2,396	2.4
6700	Holding and other investment offices	6	5	1.6	110	127	24,327	21,984	2,779	2,922	2.5
EDWARDS, KS											
60 –	**Finance, insurance, and real estate**	9	8	0.1	53	61	21,660	19,672	1,191	1,234	0.1
6000	Depository institutions	5	5	0.4	46	53	23,217	20,981	1,109	1,149	0.2
ELK, KS											
60 –	**Finance, insurance, and real estate**	12	9	0.1	-	-	-	-	-	-	-
6000	Depository institutions	4	2	0.2	21	-	24,000	-	400	-	-
6020	Commercial banks	4	2	0.2	21	-	24,000	-	400	-	-
6400	Insurance agents, brokers, and service	3	2	0.1	4	-	10,000	-	46	-	-
6500	Real estate	3	3	0.2	3	2	6,667	8,000	28	36	0.0
ELLIS, KS											
60 –	**Finance, insurance, and real estate**	82	83	1.2	457	432	20,245	20,194	9,377	9,020	0.6
6000	Depository institutions	17	16	1.2	240	204	21,700	22,176	5,056	4,626	1.0
6020	Commercial banks	13	12	1.3	208	166	21,885	23,639	4,460	3,977	1.0
6300	Insurance carriers	9	6	1.1	29	18	17,931	23,778	570	369	0.1
6330	Fire, marine, and casualty insurance	5	4	2.1	13	-	23,077	-	330	-	-
6400	Insurance agents, brokers, and service	22	27	1.5	80	107	21,350	18,542	1,748	2,053	1.0
6500	Real estate	22	23	1.2	58	60	12,897	11,333	715	780	0.4
6510	Real estate operators and lessors	13	12	1.5	30	-	11,067	-	387	-	-
6530	Real estate agents and managers	7	10	1.2	24	26	9,167	12,000	256	369	0.4
6700	Holding and other investment offices	6	7	2.2	21	25	13,524	14,080	303	343	0.3
6733	Trusts, n.e.c.	3	3	3.6	4	-	7,000	-	29	-	-
ELLSWORTH, KS											
60 –	**Finance, insurance, and real estate**	15	17	0.3	79	79	13,671	16,304	1,124	1,342	0.1
6000	Depository institutions	6	7	0.5	59	61	15,864	19,016	976	1,193	0.2
6500	Real estate	4	4	0.2	6	4	4,000	5,000	26	26	0.0
FINNEY, KS											
60 –	**Finance, insurance, and real estate**	84	85	1.3	515	540	23,744	23,793	11,929	13,801	0.8
6000	Depository institutions	14	15	1.1	200	273	26,660	24,029	5,149	7,011	1.4
6020	Commercial banks	10	10	1.1	186	209	26,882	26,354	4,713	5,396	1.4
6100	Nondepository institutions	3	3	0.9	83	-	20,193	-	1,718	-	-
6200	Security and commodity brokers	5	8	2.1	38	44	21,158	23,000	900	1,355	1.2
6300	Insurance carriers	7	5	0.9	28	-	33,286	-	941	-	-
6400	Insurance agents, brokers, and service	20	17	0.9	74	60	25,297	25,200	1,586	1,394	0.7
6500	Real estate	32	34	1.7	87	87	17,425	16,782	1,530	1,540	0.9
6510	Real estate operators and lessors	10	11	1.4	37	41	17,946	17,463	679	757	1.6
6530	Real estate agents and managers	17	19	2.2	41	41	17,268	15,415	671	671	0.7

Source: County Business Patterns, 1992/93, CBP-92/93-1, U.S. Department of Commerce, Washington, D.C., April 1995. SIC categories for which data were suppressed or not available for both 1992 and 1993 are not displayed. The employment columns represent mid-March employment in the year. Pay per employee is calculated by dividing 1st Quarter payroll, annualized, by mid-March employment. The columns headed "% State" show the county's percentage of the state total for the SIC in 1993; for example, 0.9% for SIC 6030 means that the county had 0.9 percent of the state's total establishments (or payroll) in SIC 6030 in 1993. A dash (-) is used to indicate that data are not available or cannot be calculated; nec means not elsewhere classified.

Continued on next page.

SIC	Industry	No. Establishments			Employment		Pay / Employee		Annual Payroll ($ 000)		
		1992	1993	% State	1992	1993	1992	1993	1992	1993	% State
FINNEY, KS - [continued]											
6540	Title abstract offices	2	3	2.4	-	5	-	22,400	-	111	1.0
6700	Holding and other investment offices	3	3	0.9	5	-	19,200	-	105	-	-
6733	Trusts, n.e.c.	3	3	3.6	5	-	19,200	-	105	-	-
FORD, KS											
60 –	**Finance, insurance, and real estate**	74	75	1.1	402	389	22,687	22,272	9,261	9,076	0.6
6000	Depository institutions	18	19	1.4	225	228	24,569	23,667	5,810	5,474	1.1
6020	Commercial banks	13	13	1.4	170	173	24,565	24,277	4,356	4,161	1.1
6370	Pension, health, and welfare funds	4	4	3.9	22	-	20,545		173	-	-
6400	Insurance agents, brokers, and service	22	23	1.2	66	73	15,576	15,123	1,031	1,179	0.6
6500	Real estate	17	19	1.0	49	46	11,755	12,696	688	655	0.4
6510	Real estate operators and lessors	8	10	1.3	16	15	11,000	10,933	189	189	0.4
6530	Real estate agents and managers	6	7	0.8	17	-	13,882		274	-	-
FRANKLIN, KS											
60 –	**Finance, insurance, and real estate**	32	35	0.5	245	229	20,833	25,083	5,304	5,716	0.4
6000	Depository institutions	10	9	0.7	192	178	21,896	22,517	4,284	4,232	0.9
6400	Insurance agents, brokers, and service	15	16	0.9	30	25	15,600	16,800	574	563	0.3
6500	Real estate	4	6	0.3	7	10	10,857	9,600	83	103	0.1
GEARY, KS											
60 –	**Finance, insurance, and real estate**	59	62	0.9	374	368	17,358	17,022	6,861	6,824	0.4
6000	Depository institutions	11	11	0.8	184	186	17,978	16,645	3,517	3,421	0.7
6020	Commercial banks	6	5	0.6	159	156	18,893	17,564	3,204	3,061	0.8
6100	Nondepository institutions	5	5	1.5	-	25	-	17,920	-	388	0.3
6140	Personal credit institutions	3	3	2.0	19	-	21,684	-	400	-	-
6300	Insurance carriers	4	5	0.9	17	-	18,118	-	310	-	-
6400	Insurance agents, brokers, and service	11	12	0.6	36	34	16,222	15,765	576	559	0.3
6500	Real estate	22	24	1.2	66	63	12,061	12,063	869	886	0.5
6510	Real estate operators and lessors	14	16	2.0	34	-	14,588	-	571	-	-
6530	Real estate agents and managers	6	7	0.8	25	16	10,240	10,000	233	157	0.2
6700	Holding and other investment offices	4	4	1.3	43	-	13,488	-	761	-	-
GOVE, KS											
60 –	**Finance, insurance, and real estate**	11	11	0.2	45	-	18,844	-	1,095	-	-
6000	Depository institutions	3	6	0.5	33	-	21,455	-	967	-	-
6020	Commercial banks	3	3	0.3	33	-	21,455	-	967	-	-
6400	Insurance agents, brokers, and service	4	4	0.2	3	4	6,667	9,000	22	36	0.0
GRAHAM, KS											
60 –	**Finance, insurance, and real estate**	10	10	0.1	69	66	17,739	18,000	1,332	1,328	0.1
6000	Depository institutions	5	5	0.4	57	56	19,439	19,214	1,219	1,221	0.3
GRANT, KS											
60 –	**Finance, insurance, and real estate**	13	15	0.2	102	96	19,490	19,750	2,034	2,121	0.1
6000	Depository institutions	4	5	0.4	-	73	-	21,370	-	1,725	0.4
6400	Insurance agents, brokers, and service	3	6	0.3	-	11	-	14,909	-	197	0.1
GRAY, KS											
60 –	**Finance, insurance, and real estate**	16	16	0.2	205	193	25,659	26,321	5,509	5,461	0.3
GREELEY, KS											
60 –	**Finance, insurance, and real estate**	7	8	0.1	21	-	20,000	-	405	-	-
6400	Insurance agents, brokers, and service	3	3	0.2	3	3	13,333	12,000	44	46	0.0
6500	Real estate	2	3	0.2	-	3	-	5,333	-	21	0.0

Source: County Business Patterns, 1992/93, CBP-92/93-1, U.S. Department of Commerce, Washington, D.C., April 1995. SIC categories for which data were suppressed or not available for both 1992 and 1993 are *not* displayed. The employment columns represent mid-March employment in the year. Pay per employee is calculated by dividing 1st Quarter payroll, annualized, by mid-March employment. The columns headed "% State" show the county's percentage of the state total for the SIC in 1993; for example, 0.9% for SIC 6030 means that the county had 0.9 percent of the state's total establishments (or payroll) in SIC 6030 in 1993. A dash (-) is used to indicate that data are not available or cannot be calculated; *nec* means not elsewhere classified.

SIC	Industry	No. Establishments			Employment		Pay / Employee		Annual Payroll ($ 000)		
		1992	1993	% State	1992	1993	1992	1993	1992	1993	% State
SHERIDAN, KS											
60–	**Finance, insurance, and real estate**	11	10	0.1	55	52	27,418	27,000	1,630	1,642	0.1
6000	Depository institutions	4	4	0.3	39	39	31,179	28,923	1,412	1,441	0.3
6400	Insurance agents, brokers, and service	4	4	0.2	11	–	21,455	–	163	–	–
SHERMAN, KS											
60–	**Finance, insurance, and real estate**	21	20	0.3	118	129	23,966	21,581	3,079	2,777	0.2
6000	Depository institutions	4	4	0.3	96	96	24,875	22,917	2,558	2,118	0.4
6020	Commercial banks	4	4	0.4	96	96	24,875	22,917	2,558	2,118	0.5
6500	Real estate	8	7	0.4	6	11	10,667	8,364	76	90	0.1
6530	Real estate agents and managers	4	3	0.3	3	3	6,667	8,000	26	25	0.0
SMITH, KS											
60–	**Finance, insurance, and real estate**	11	9	0.1	75	77	15,840	16,052	1,413	1,510	0.1
6000	Depository institutions	5	5	0.4	67	72	17,075	16,611	1,358	1,454	0.3
6020	Commercial banks	5	5	0.6	67	72	17,075	16,611	1,358	1,454	0.4
6400	Insurance agents, brokers, and service	3	1	0.1	4	–	3,000	–	17	–	–
6500	Real estate	3	3	0.2	4	–	8,000	–	38	–	–
STAFFORD, KS											
60–	**Finance, insurance, and real estate**	15	16	0.2	69	71	19,362	20,620	1,468	1,636	0.1
6000	Depository institutions	6	6	0.5	55	56	21,309	23,357	1,286	1,463	0.3
6020	Commercial banks	6	6	0.7	55	56	21,309	23,357	1,286	1,463	0.4
6400	Insurance agents, brokers, and service	4	5	0.3	5	7	13,600	10,857	72	78	0.0
STANTON, KS											
60–	**Finance, insurance, and real estate**	1	2	0.0	–	–	–	–	–	–	–
STEVENS, KS											
60–	**Finance, insurance, and real estate**	7	9	0.1	54	68	20,889	19,765	1,172	1,379	0.1
6400	Insurance agents, brokers, and service	3	4	0.2	–	9	–	13,333	–	129	0.1
SUMNER, KS											
60–	**Finance, insurance, and real estate**	46	48	0.7	254	259	20,472	20,463	5,446	5,735	0.4
6000	Depository institutions	14	14	1.1	187	190	22,888	23,116	4,439	4,632	1.0
6400	Insurance agents, brokers, and service	20	21	1.1	37	45	13,405	13,067	515	664	0.3
6500	Real estate	9	9	0.5	24	13	11,833	12,000	329	210	0.1
6530	Real estate agents and managers	2	3	0.3	–	5	–	10,400	–	54	0.1
THOMAS, KS											
60–	**Finance, insurance, and real estate**	34	28	0.4	256	134	19,562	20,478	3,558	2,886	0.2
6000	Depository institutions	7	5	0.4	152	52	20,763	19,615	1,696	963	0.2
6200	Security and commodity brokers	6	4	1.0	24	–	12,333	–	288	–	–
6280	Security and commodity services	4	2	1.4	20	–	5,400	–	88	–	–
6400	Insurance agents, brokers, and service	9	10	0.5	20	25	14,600	13,440	341	466	0.2
6500	Real estate	6	6	0.3	17	21	11,765	11,619	229	254	0.1
6530	Real estate agents and managers	3	3	0.3	–	8	–	11,000	–	84	0.1
TREGO, KS											
60–	**Finance, insurance, and real estate**	10	10	0.1	37	42	16,324	19,333	740	895	0.1
6000	Depository institutions	3	3	0.2	27	28	18,667	23,429	619	741	0.2
6400	Insurance agents, brokers, and service	4	4	0.2	6	9	11,333	12,000	85	112	0.1
6500	Real estate	3	3	0.2	4	5	8,000	9,600	36	42	0.0
WABAUNSEE, KS											
60–	**Finance, insurance, and real estate**	11	11	0.2	54	55	16,370	16,291	958	1,013	0.1
6000	Depository institutions	5	5	0.4	–	46	–	17,391	–	905	0.2
6020	Commercial banks	5	5	0.6	–	46	–	17,391	–	905	0.2

Source: County Business Patterns, 1992/93, CBP-92/93-1, U.S. Department of Commerce, Washington, D.C., April 1995. SIC categories for which data were suppressed or not available for both 1992 and 1993 are *not* displayed. The employment columns represent mid-March employment in the year. Pay per employee is calculated by dividing 1st Quarter payroll, annualized, by mid-March employment. The columns headed "% State" show the county's percentage of the state total for the SIC in 1993; for example, 0.9% for SIC 6030 means that the county had 0.9 percent of the state's total establishments (or payroll) in SIC 6030 in 1993. A dash (-) is used to indicate that data are not available or cannot be calculated; *nec* means not elsewhere classified.

SIC	Industry	No. Establishments			Employment		Pay / Employee		Annual Payroll ($ 000)		
		1992	1993	% State	1992	1993	1992	1993	1992	1993	% State
WALLACE, KS											
60 –	**Finance, insurance, and real estate**	4	2	0.0	6	-	9,333	-	72	-	-
WASHINGTON, KS											
60 –	**Finance, insurance, and real estate**	22	23	0.3	102	108	16,902	16,704	2,003	2,204	0.1
6000	Depository institutions	8	8	0.6	76	83	19,105	18,410	1,682	1,834	0.4
6020	Commercial banks	8	8	0.9	76	83	19,105	18,410	1,682	1,834	0.5
6400	Insurance agents, brokers, and service	6	8	0.4	19	19	12,211	13,053	263	334	0.2
6500	Real estate	7	7	0.4	-	6	-	4,667	-	36	0.0
6553	Cemetery subdividers and developers	4	4	4.2	3	3	2,667	2,667	13	11	0.2
WICHITA, KS											
60 –	**Finance, insurance, and real estate**	9	8	0.1	34	-	17,765	-	661	-	-
6400	Insurance agents, brokers, and service	3	3	0.2	-	7	-	10,286	-	78	0.0
WILSON, KS											
60 –	**Finance, insurance, and real estate**	17	17	0.3	83	85	20,723	19,200	2,129	1,985	0.1
6000	Depository institutions	5	5	0.4	63	63	22,540	21,587	1,778	1,633	0.3
6400	Insurance agents, brokers, and service	6	7	0.4	6	-	34,667	-	251	-	-
6500	Real estate	4	4	0.2	-	8	-	4,500	-	39	0.0
WOODSON, KS											
60 –	**Finance, insurance, and real estate**	11	13	0.2	40	-	17,000	-	693	-	-
6000	Depository institutions	4	4	0.3	28	28	21,571	15,857	611	473	0.1
6020	Commercial banks	4	4	0.4	28	28	21,571	15,857	611	473	0.1
6400	Insurance agents, brokers, and service	2	3	0.2	-	5	-	5,600	-	22	0.0
6500	Real estate	3	4	0.2	6	7	7,333	7,429	45	63	0.0
WYANDOTTE, KS											
60 –	**Finance, insurance, and real estate**	225	230	3.4	2,344	2,317	16,985	17,806	41,912	43,055	2.6
6000	Depository institutions	53	60	4.5	1,110	1,144	21,261	21,073	24,215	24,629	5.1
6020	Commercial banks	29	29	3.2	976	975	21,172	21,526	21,329	21,323	5.5
6030	Savings institutions	5	5	2.4	60	-	27,867		1,672	-	-
6060	Credit unions	15	21	11.1	-	94	-	17,702	-	1,656	7.6
6100	Nondepository institutions	19	14	4.2	97	74	20,784	31,514	2,215	1,946	1.4
6140	Personal credit institutions	16	9	6.1	77	50	19,688	36,160	1,666	1,446	6.0
6200	Security and commodity brokers	3	4	1.0	45	6	3,911	46,000	204	257	0.2
6300	Insurance carriers	16	13	2.4	522	424	8,774	11,358	5,209	5,538	1.4
6310	Life insurance	4	5	3.0	500	415	8,568	11,200	4,581	5,334	5.3
6330	Fire, marine, and casualty insurance	7	2	1.0	13	-	14,769	-	198	-	-
6400	Insurance agents, brokers, and service	32	37	2.0	108	113	16,037	14,407	1,924	1,900	0.9
6500	Real estate	93	96	4.9	373	464	13,769	12,672	5,491	6,395	3.6
6510	Real estate operators and lessors	44	50	6.4	128	236	9,938	10,627	1,468	2,706	5.8
6530	Real estate agents and managers	31	33	3.8	148	153	15,486	13,542	2,225	2,021	2.0
6540	Title abstract offices	3	5	4.0	27	27	17,185	18,815	551	673	5.9
6552	Subdividers and developers, n.e.c.	3	3	5.4	9	20	10,667	12,800	106	319	2.7
6553	Cemetery subdividers and developers	6	5	5.2	56	28	16,571	19,143	980	676	10.3
6700	Holding and other investment offices	9	6	1.9	89	92	28,899	24,087	2,654	2,390	2.0

Source: County Business Patterns, 1992/93, CBP-92/93-1, U.S. Department of Commerce, Washington, D.C., April 1995. SIC categories for which data were suppressed or not available for both 1992 and 1993 are *not* displayed. The employment columns represent mid-March employment in the year. Pay per employee is calculated by dividing 1st Quarter payroll, annualized, by mid-March employment. The columns headed "% State" show the county's percentage of the state total for the SIC in 1993; for example, 0.9% for SIC 6030 means that the county had 0.9 percent of the state's total establishments (or payroll) in SIC 6030 in 1993. A dash (-) is used to indicate that data are not available or cannot be calculated; *nec* means not elsewhere classified.

KENTUCKY

SIC	Industry	No. Establishments			Employment		Pay / Employee		Annual Payroll ($ 000)		
		1992	1993	% State	1992	1993	1992	1993	1992	1993	% State
ADAIR, KY											
60 –	**Finance, insurance, and real estate**	20	20	0.3	94	90	17,191	17,333	1,812	1,745	0.1
6000	Depository institutions	7	7	0.5	63	63	21,016	19,492	1,406	1,396	0.2
6400	Insurance agents, brokers, and service	4	5	0.3	8	8	14,500	19,500	134	167	0.1
6500	Real estate	6	5	0.2	12	9	4,667	7,111	133	72	0.0
6510	Real estate operators and lessors	3	3	0.3	8	-	6,500		52	-	-
ALLEN, KY											
60 –	**Finance, insurance, and real estate**	9	13	0.2	112	105	22,321	23,086	2,447	2,544	0.1
6000	Depository institutions	3	4	0.3	80	77	18,900	18,805	1,510	1,503	0.2
6400	Insurance agents, brokers, and service	5	5	0.3	-	24	-	38,500	-	947	0.5
ANDERSON, KY											
60 –	**Finance, insurance, and real estate**	14	17	0.2	89	110	21,393	22,400	2,098	2,276	0.1
6000	Depository institutions	3	3	0.2	63	70	25,460	28,914	1,731	1,749	0.3
6500	Real estate	3	4	0.2	7	10	8,571	8,000	70	78	0.1
BALLARD, KY											
60 –	**Finance, insurance, and real estate**	12	13	0.2	84	80	17,571	18,950	1,685	1,806	0.1
6000	Depository institutions	6	6	0.4	63	57	18,984	20,561	1,353	1,462	0.2
6400	Insurance agents, brokers, and service	3	5	0.3	5	-	15,200	-	93	-	-
BARREN, KY											
60 –	**Finance, insurance, and real estate**	61	62	0.9	351	379	21,527	19,873	7,522	7,544	0.4
6000	Depository institutions	14	14	0.9	205	219	20,312	17,242	4,098	3,997	0.6
6100	Nondepository institutions	5	5	0.9	22	23	16,545	19,652	420	451	0.4
6400	Insurance agents, brokers, and service	13	13	0.8	50	50	18,880	17,440	979	934	0.4
6500	Real estate	18	19	0.9	36	48	6,889	8,667	319	597	0.4
6510	Real estate operators and lessors	9	9	0.9	24	-	6,000	-	209	-	-
6530	Real estate agents and managers	5	8	1.0	7	8	9,714	9,000	68	201	0.3
BATH, KY											
60 –	**Finance, insurance, and real estate**	15	16	0.2	73	78	22,575	20,769	1,410	1,469	0.1
6000	Depository institutions	6	6	0.4	53	54	21,434	21,407	1,021	1,062	0.2
6020	Commercial banks	6	6	0.6	53	54	21,434	21,407	1,021	1,062	0.2
6400	Insurance agents, brokers, and service	4	4	0.2	-	10	-	15,600	-	110	0.1
6500	Real estate	3	4	0.2	6	-	7,333	-	47	-	-
BELL, KY											
60 –	**Finance, insurance, and real estate**	34	38	0.6	306	293	19,856	21,324	6,399	6,438	0.4
6000	Depository institutions	13	17	1.1	199	202	19,176	19,287	3,907	4,115	0.7
6030	Savings institutions	6	6	2.5	68	73	19,529	20,438	1,479	1,614	2.8
6300	Insurance carriers	3	3	0.6	55	-	25,455	-	1,588	-	-
6400	Insurance agents, brokers, and service	8	9	0.5	-	17	-	16,000	-	305	0.1
6500	Real estate	7	6	0.3	18	16	14,000	13,500	246	214	0.1
BOONE, KY											
60 –	**Finance, insurance, and real estate**	134	128	1.9	739	701	20,926	22,984	16,021	16,040	0.9
6000	Depository institutions	32	32	2.1	302	311	21,603	22,971	6,693	6,399	1.0
6020	Commercial banks	25	27	2.5	268	291	21,791	23,505	5,968	6,065	1.1
6030	Savings institutions	7	5	2.1	34	20	20,118	15,200	725	334	0.6
6100	Nondepository institutions	10	12	2.2	69	81	13,681	15,605	943	1,328	1.1

Source: County Business Patterns, 1992/93, CBP-92/93-1, U.S. Department of Commerce, Washington, D.C., April 1995. SIC categories for which data were suppressed or not available for both 1992 and 1993 are *not* displayed. The employment columns represent mid-March employment in the year. Pay per employee is calculated by dividing 1st Quarter payroll, annualized, by mid-March employment. The columns headed "% State" show the county's percentage of the state total for the SIC in 1993; for example, 0.9% for SIC 6030 means that the county had 0.9 percent of the state's total establishments (or payroll) in SIC 6030 in 1993. A dash (-) is used to indicate that data are not available or cannot be calculated; *nec* means not elsewhere classified.

Continued on next page.

SIC	Industry	No. Establishments			Employment		Pay / Employee		Annual Payroll ($ 000)		
		1992	1993	% State	1992	1993	1992	1993	1992	1993	% State
BOONE, KY - [continued]											
6140	Personal credit institutions	8	8	2.3	-	57	-	13,263	-	730	1.9
6300	Insurance carriers	19	16	2.9	82	87	30,634	30,989	2,417	2,715	0.8
6310	Life insurance	5	4	2.0	51	-	23,765	-	1,164	-	-
6330	Fire, marine, and casualty insurance	11	9	3.9	-	33	-	36,848	-	1,298	1.5
6400	Insurance agents, brokers, and service	25	24	1.4	88	83	29,182	36,289	2,866	3,248	1.6
6500	Real estate	42	40	1.9	181	125	13,238	13,248	2,565	1,814	1.2
6510	Real estate operators and lessors	26	24	2.3	104	98	14,385	12,408	1,511	1,222	2.0
6530	Real estate agents and managers	11	13	1.6	67	-	11,463	-	786	-	-
6700	Holding and other investment offices	5	4	1.6	-	14	-	24,286	-	536	0.4
BOURBON, KY											
60 –	**Finance, insurance, and real estate**	30	28	0.4	176	169	20,523	20,284	3,719	3,474	0.2
6100	Nondepository institutions	4	4	0.7	11	10	17,818	20,400	225	229	0.2
6300	Insurance carriers	3	2	0.4	2	-	54,000	-	123	-	-
6400	Insurance agents, brokers, and service	11	11	0.7	-	33	-	19,758	-	898	0.4
6500	Real estate	8	7	0.3	16	16	9,250	10,000	166	205	0.1
6553	Cemetery subdividers and developers	3	3	2.5	-	6	-	8,667	-	64	0.6
BOYD, KY											
60 –	**Finance, insurance, and real estate**	109	111	1.6	859	915	23,367	20,953	20,613	20,694	1.2
6000	Depository institutions	28	30	2.0	489	509	21,832	20,417	11,211	11,401	1.8
6020	Commercial banks	16	18	1.7	399	412	21,794	20,049	9,031	9,011	1.7
6030	Savings institutions	5	5	2.1	50	54	22,080	22,519	1,263	1,442	2.5
6060	Credit unions	7	7	4.2	40	43	21,900	21,302	917	948	4.2
6100	Nondepository institutions	7	6	1.1	62	70	18,258	16,000	1,167	1,116	0.9
6140	Personal credit institutions	6	6	1.7	-	70	-	16,000	-	1,116	2.9
6200	Security and commodity brokers	3	7	3.0	28	39	65,000	36,410	1,874	2,222	2.0
6210	Security brokers and dealers	3	7	4.3	28	39	65,000	36,410	1,874	2,222	2.4
6300	Insurance carriers	4	4	0.7	34	37	36,000	40,108	1,214	1,282	0.4
6400	Insurance agents, brokers, and service	24	20	1.2	93	97	38,194	33,237	3,210	3,075	1.5
6500	Real estate	40	41	1.9	144	155	11,056	9,316	1,837	1,504	1.0
6510	Real estate operators and lessors	21	19	1.8	82	87	9,707	7,724	866	578	1.0
6530	Real estate agents and managers	12	15	1.8	30	40	16,667	12,800	525	588	0.9
6553	Cemetery subdividers and developers	6	6	5.0	28	-	10,000	-	427	-	-
6700	Holding and other investment offices	3	3	1.2	9	8	8,444	11,000	100	94	0.1
BOYLE, KY											
60 –	**Finance, insurance, and real estate**	55	51	0.7	438	395	21,397	23,848	9,647	9,052	0.5
6000	Depository institutions	14	13	0.9	241	211	21,046	23,621	4,906	4,443	0.7
6020	Commercial banks	9	9	0.8	214	190	21,196	24,084	4,349	4,006	0.7
6100	Nondepository institutions	5	6	1.1	24	29	23,500	24,414	574	767	0.6
6300	Insurance carriers	3	3	0.6	72	76	30,000	26,421	2,249	2,035	0.6
6310	Life insurance	3	3	1.5	72	76	30,000	26,421	2,249	2,035	1.4
6400	Insurance agents, brokers, and service	14	13	0.8	-	37	-	16,432	-	727	0.3
6500	Real estate	16	13	0.6	50	33	12,000	16,606	695	496	0.3
6510	Real estate operators and lessors	3	4	0.4	-	12	-	20,000	-	201	0.3
6530	Real estate agents and managers	7	6	0.7	15	11	17,867	13,455	271	152	0.2
BRACKEN, KY											
60 –	**Finance, insurance, and real estate**	7	7	0.1	39	40	16,513	16,100	642	671	0.0
6400	Insurance agents, brokers, and service	3	3	0.2	5	5	8,800	9,600	49	56	0.0
BREATHITT, KY											
60 –	**Finance, insurance, and real estate**	14	14	0.2	125	180	23,616	16,022	3,013	3,032	0.2
6400	Insurance agents, brokers, and service	2	3	0.2	-	6	-	13,333	-	76	0.0
6500	Real estate	4	3	0.1	6	5	8,667	10,400	53	54	0.0

Source: County Business Patterns, 1992/93, CBP-92/93-1, U.S. Department of Commerce, Washington, D.C., April 1995. SIC categories for which data were suppressed or not available for both 1992 and 1993 are not displayed. The employment columns represent mid-March employment in the year. Pay per employee is calculated by dividing 1st Quarter payroll, annualized, by mid-March employment. The columns headed "% State" show the county's percentage of the state total for the SIC in 1993; for example, 0.9% for SIC 6030 means that the county had 0.9 percent of the state's total establishments (or payroll) in SIC 6030 in 1993. A dash (-) is used to indicate that data are not available or cannot be calculated; nec means not elsewhere classified.

SIC	Industry	No. Establishments			Employment		Pay / Employee		Annual Payroll ($ 000)		
		1992	1993	% State	1992	1993	1992	1993	1992	1993	% State
BRECKINRIDGE, KY											
60 –	**Finance, insurance, and real estate**	21	21	0.3	131	135	15,359	15,467	2,374	2,512	0.1
6000	Depository institutions	9	9	0.6	103	101	16,777	17,386	2,084	2,130	0.3
6400	Insurance agents, brokers, and service	6	6	0.4	-	13	-	11,077	-	161	0.1
6500	Real estate	4	4	0.2	7	-	6,857	-	46	-	-
BULLITT, KY											
60 –	**Finance, insurance, and real estate**	51	53	0.8	248	270	18,597	15,822	5,162	4,965	0.3
6000	Depository institutions	6	6	0.4	146	155	19,973	18,219	3,161	3,176	0.5
6100	Nondepository institutions	1	4	0.7	-	17		8,941	-	233	0.2
6300	Insurance carriers	6	4	0.7	13	5	30,154	44,800	393	257	0.1
6400	Insurance agents, brokers, and service	11	13	0.8	-	31	-	12,129	-	414	0.2
6500	Real estate	25	26	1.2	61	62	10,754	11,226	811	885	0.6
6510	Real estate operators and lessors	7	7	0.7	19	22	6,947	6,727	145	132	0.2
6530	Real estate agents and managers	7	13	1.6	11	16	16,364	13,500	213	401	0.6
BUTLER, KY											
60 –	**Finance, insurance, and real estate**	10	11	0.2	77	83	21,403	17,157	1,704	1,490	0.1
CALDWELL, KY											
60 –	**Finance, insurance, and real estate**	17	15	0.2	128	133	21,125	20,541	3,174	3,161	0.2
6000	Depository institutions	5	5	0.3	97	101	20,907	20,594	2,454	2,463	0.4
6100	Nondepository institutions	4	3	0.5	12	9	26,333	19,111	303	189	0.2
6140	Personal credit institutions	4	3	0.9	12	9	26,333	19,111	303	189	0.5
CALLOWAY, KY											
60 –	**Finance, insurance, and real estate**	56	61	0.9	385	337	20,468	19,929	10,538	7,417	0.4
6000	Depository institutions	12	11	0.7	199	198	21,769	20,202	6,019	4,247	0.7
6020	Commercial banks	9	7	0.6	179	173	21,989	20,254	5,610	3,769	0.7
6100	Nondepository institutions	3	3	0.5	11	12	19,636	20,667	189	209	0.2
6400	Insurance agents, brokers, and service	22	22	1.3	63	63	13,460	14,540	1,057	1,210	0.6
6500	Real estate	14	18	0.8	26	40	6,000	7,200	211	270	0.2
6510	Real estate operators and lessors	8	9	0.9	11	22	6,545	8,545	106	152	0.3
6530	Real estate agents and managers	4	6	0.7	4	9	10,000	6,222	52	66	0.1
6553	Cemetery subdividers and developers	1	3	2.5	-	9	-	4,889	-	52	0.5
CAMPBELL, KY											
60 –	**Finance, insurance, and real estate**	123	126	1.8	798	784	28,687	24,276	22,869	22,551	1.3
6000	Depository institutions	34	36	2.4	338	289	23,195	19,502	7,794	6,463	1.0
6020	Commercial banks	20	23	2.1	215	183	21,284	19,148	4,470	4,042	0.8
6100	Nondepository institutions	4	3	0.5	21	-	23,048	-	385	-	-
6140	Personal credit institutions	4	3	0.9	21	-	23,048	-	385	-	-
6300	Insurance carriers	13	11	2.0	99	107	17,899	22,355	2,025	2,180	0.7
6330	Fire, marine, and casualty insurance	5	4	1.7	16	-	29,750	-	477	-	-
6400	Insurance agents, brokers, and service	20	20	1.2	93	119	25,333	20,874	2,506	2,830	1.4
6500	Real estate	46	49	2.3	135	145	13,659	13,931	2,028	2,395	1.6
6510	Real estate operators and lessors	20	18	1.7	72	81	12,278	11,753	920	1,014	1.7
6530	Real estate agents and managers	22	24	2.9	-	42	-	16,667	-	906	1.5
6700	Holding and other investment offices	6	6	2.4	112	103	76,750	59,728	8,131	8,315	5.5
CARLISLE, KY											
60 –	**Finance, insurance, and real estate**	8	8	0.1	50	53	15,280	15,321	808	872	0.1
CARROLL, KY											
60 –	**Finance, insurance, and real estate**	16	15	0.2	-	62	-	19,290	-	1,197	0.1

Source: County Business Patterns, 1992/93, CBP-92/93-1, U.S. Department of Commerce, Washington, D.C., April 1995. SIC categories for which data were suppressed or not available for both 1992 and 1993 are *not* displayed. The employment columns represent mid-March employment in the year. Pay per employee is calculated by dividing 1st Quarter payroll, annualized, by mid-March employment. The columns headed "% State" show the county's percentage of the state total for the SIC in 1993; for example, 0.9% for SIC 6030 means that the county had 0.9 percent of the state's total establishments (or payroll) in SIC 6030 in 1993. A dash (-) is used to indicate that data are not available or cannot be calculated; *nec* means not elsewhere classified.

Continued on next page.

SIC	Industry	No. Establishments			Employment		Pay / Employee		Annual Payroll ($ 000)		
		1992	1993	% State	1992	1993	1992	1993	1992	1993	% State
CARROLL, KY - [continued]											
6000	Depository institutions	3	3	0.2	33	-	21,939	-	602	-	-
6400	Insurance agents, brokers, and service	7	6	0.4	-	15	-	14,933	-	243	0.1
6500	Real estate	5	5	0.2	9	9	4,889	4,889	65	49	0.0
CARTER, KY											
60 –	**Finance, insurance, and real estate**	27	30	0.4	228	188	14,737	17,681	3,384	3,421	0.2
6000	Depository institutions	8	8	0.5	128	131	22,938	20,214	2,904	2,668	0.4
6500	Real estate	7	9	0.4	9	26	10,222	7,692	134	229	0.2
6530	Real estate agents and managers	4	6	0.7	5	5	10,400	12,800	63	103	0.2
CASEY, KY											
60 –	**Finance, insurance, and real estate**	13	13	0.2	64	63	17,062	18,603	1,238	1,326	0.1
6400	Insurance agents, brokers, and service	4	4	0.2	15	10	10,667	16,000	170	180	0.1
CHRISTIAN, KY											
60 –	**Finance, insurance, and real estate**	123	135	2.0	943	915	20,174	20,520	18,682	18,634	1.1
6000	Depository institutions	24	28	1.8	495	522	18,707	20,375	8,452	9,868	1.6
6020	Commercial banks	14	16	1.5	345	328	19,884	22,610	5,987	6,393	1.2
6030	Savings institutions	3	5	2.1	-	88	-	20,136	-	2,017	3.5
6100	Nondepository institutions	18	17	3.1	92	92	19,043	17,304	1,695	1,724	1.4
6300	Insurance carriers	10	9	1.7	141	84	25,390	24,810	3,703	1,914	0.6
6310	Life insurance	5	5	2.5	103	62	22,330	23,419	2,365	1,420	0.9
6400	Insurance agents, brokers, and service	20	22	1.3	86	79	27,535	21,671	2,478	1,995	1.0
6500	Real estate	45	49	2.3	103	109	9,786	9,908	1,121	1,216	0.8
6510	Real estate operators and lessors	34	35	3.4	69	71	9,333	9,577	708	741	1.2
6530	Real estate agents and managers	8	12	1.4	26	-	10,154	-	296	-	-
CLARK, KY											
60 –	**Finance, insurance, and real estate**	48	46	0.7	304	239	20,697	21,473	6,612	5,071	0.3
6000	Depository institutions	10	9	0.6	191	131	22,262	24,366	4,285	3,101	0.5
6400	Insurance agents, brokers, and service	14	11	0.7	30	32	9,067	8,125	262	270	0.1
6500	Real estate	17	17	0.8	41	35	13,561	10,057	547	403	0.3
6510	Real estate operators and lessors	8	9	0.9	19	16	13,684	8,250	268	161	0.3
6530	Real estate agents and managers	6	6	0.7	9	12	16,889	12,000	134	151	0.2
6700	Holding and other investment offices	2	3	1.2	-	5	-	14,400	-	100	0.1
CLAY, KY											
60 –	**Finance, insurance, and real estate**	17	17	0.2	143	140	14,350	14,486	2,380	2,463	0.1
6100	Nondepository institutions	4	4	0.7	20	27	11,800	12,296	276	401	0.3
6400	Insurance agents, brokers, and service	3	4	0.2	7	12	12,571	10,000	110	161	0.1
6500	Real estate	4	4	0.2	7	5	4,571	6,400	39	42	0.0
CLINTON, KY											
60 –	**Finance, insurance, and real estate**	10	10	0.1	52	54	17,538	18,741	961	1,076	0.1
6400	Insurance agents, brokers, and service	5	6	0.4	15	15	22,400	24,533	336	371	0.2
CRITTENDEN, KY											
60 –	**Finance, insurance, and real estate**	13	14	0.2	69	70	16,580	15,257	1,131	1,176	0.1
6000	Depository institutions	3	3	0.2	43	-	19,814	-	813	-	-
6400	Insurance agents, brokers, and service	4	5	0.3	15	15	13,600	15,467	219	244	0.1
6500	Real estate	3	4	0.2	7	8	3,429	3,000	28	34	0.0
CUMBERLAND, KY											
60 –	**Finance, insurance, and real estate**	9	10	0.1	56	57	18,786	18,456	1,043	1,114	0.1
6400	Insurance agents, brokers, and service	3	3	0.2	6	6	16,000	15,333	90	105	0.1

Source: County Business Patterns, 1992/93, CBP-92/93-1, U.S. Department of Commerce, Washington, D.C., April 1995. SIC categories for which data were suppressed or not available for both 1992 and 1993 are not displayed. The employment columns represent mid-March employment in the year. Pay per employee is calculated by dividing 1st Quarter payroll, annualized, by mid-March employment. The columns headed "% State" show the county's percentage of the state total for the SIC in 1993; for example, 0.9% for SIC 6030 means that the county had 0.9 percent of the state's total establishments (or payroll) in SIC 6030 in 1993. A dash (-) is used to indicate that data are not available or cannot be calculated; nec means not elsewhere classified.

SIC	Industry	No. Establishments			Employment		Pay / Employee		Annual Payroll ($ 000)		
		1992	1993	% State	1992	1993	1992	1993	1992	1993	% State
DAVIESS, KY											
60 –	**Finance, insurance, and real estate**	214	204	3.0	1,806	1,865	24,651	24,442	43,267	47,902	2.8
6000	Depository institutions	54	53	3.5	685	758	18,996	20,881	12,823	14,544	2.3
6020	Commercial banks	27	26	2.4	484	473	19,116	21,463	8,940	9,948	1.9
6030	Savings institutions	11	12	5.0	106	183	21,057	22,251	2,257	2,886	5.0
6100	Nondepository institutions	18	18	3.3	415	463	34,911	29,460	14,342	16,667	13.9
6140	Personal credit institutions	14	12	3.4	-	66	-	15,939	-	1,125	3.0
6200	Security and commodity brokers	7	6	2.6	30	27	70,133	74,074	2,029	2,224	2.0
6210	Security brokers and dealers	7	6	3.7	30	27	70,133	74,074	2,029	2,224	2.4
6300	Insurance carriers	27	25	4.6	198	206	28,747	33,398	6,035	6,826	2.1
6310	Life insurance	8	8	3.9	134	140	24,657	28,429	3,544	3,937	2.6
6330	Fire, marine, and casualty insurance	11	11	4.8	51	50	40,392	42,960	2,094	2,262	2.7
6370	Pension, health, and welfare funds	5	3	5.5	-	-	-	-	-	34	0.7
6400	Insurance agents, brokers, and service	43	41	2.5	151	151	21,854	20,503	3,158	3,131	1.5
6500	Real estate	58	56	2.6	321	251	17,782	14,550	4,660	4,051	2.7
6510	Real estate operators and lessors	36	36	3.5	180	172	11,867	12,326	2,473	2,327	3.8
6530	Real estate agents and managers	12	15	1.8	48	49	20,000	19,347	863	998	1.6
6553	Cemetery subdividers and developers	3	3	2.5	13	-	19,077	-	321	-	
6700	Holding and other investment offices	7	5	2.0	6	9	36,000	54,222	220	459	0.3
6733	Trusts, n.e.c.	4	2	5.1	2	-	12,000	-	65	-	
EDMONSON, KY											
60 –	**Finance, insurance, and real estate**	7	5	0.1	52	54	13,308	13,926	817	869	0.1
ELLIOTT, KY											
60 –	**Finance, insurance, and real estate**	5	5	0.1	33	31	18,667	16,903	550	527	0.0
ESTILL, KY											
60 –	**Finance, insurance, and real estate**	14	12	0.2	88	98	16,000	16,163	1,550	1,642	0.1
6000	Depository institutions	4	4	0.3	60	71	16,533	16,056	1,048	1,155	0.2
6100	Nondepository institutions	3	2	0.4	12	-	15,333	-	232	-	-
6140	Personal credit institutions	3	2	0.6	12	-	15,333	-	232	-	-
6400	Insurance agents, brokers, and service	3	3	0.2	12	-	17,667	-	249	-	-
6500	Real estate	4	3	0.1	4	4	5,000	18,000	21	29	0.0
FAYETTE, KY											
60 –	**Finance, insurance, and real estate**	791	796	11.6	7,742	8,663	30,924	26,197	204,918	230,744	13.6
6000	Depository institutions	116	104	6.9	2,182	2,663	25,861	28,318	54,052	69,092	11.1
6020	Commercial banks	80	69	6.4	1,918	2,346	26,202	29,439	47,408	61,854	11.6
6030	Savings institutions	14	13	5.4	114	135	21,930	20,681	2,860	3,280	5.7
6060	Credit unions	15	16	9.7	135	171	22,874	17,684	3,166	3,287	14.7
6090	Functions closely related to banking	7	6	23.1	15	11	38,933	48,364	618	671	-
6100	Nondepository institutions	63	63	11.5	382	414	28,806	25,797	11,330	12,365	10.3
6140	Personal credit institutions	37	32	9.2	221	243	23,330	18,403	4,966	4,680	12.3
6160	Mortgage bankers and brokers	20	24	22.6	143	105	36,000	39,886	5,806	5,627	12.7
6200	Security and commodity brokers	33	31	13.2	241	249	52,813	61,703	13,378	17,236	15.6
6210	Security brokers and dealers	23	18	11.0	225	216	55,129	62,111	12,778	14,835	16.0
6300	Insurance carriers	101	96	17.6	2,102	1,938	25,855	27,707	65,163	55,552	16.8
6310	Life insurance	35	28	13.8	1,227	990	23,746	27,596	39,469	28,091	18.7
6330	Fire, marine, and casualty insurance	46	45	19.5	455	417	32,009	34,091	15,494	14,644	17.4
6400	Insurance agents, brokers, and service	169	179	10.8	1,048	1,124	70,885	26,559	28,489	31,972	15.3
6500	Real estate	271	283	13.4	1,560	1,791	14,779	13,963	24,709	27,589	18.3
6510	Real estate operators and lessors	115	131	12.6	444	799	15,640	12,621	7,511	11,142	18.3
6530	Real estate agents and managers	119	130	15.6	613	557	15,863	16,704	10,458	10,655	17.1
6552	Subdividers and developers, n.e.c.	10	14	15.2	299	324	9,940	12,272	3,319	4,043	33.2
6553	Cemetery subdividers and developers	5	5	4.2	56	109	16,000	14,899	956	1,683	15.1
6700	Holding and other investment offices	35	37	15.0	193	370	34,611	34,962	6,625	12,889	8.5

Source: County Business Patterns, 1992/93, CBP-92/93-1, U.S. Department of Commerce, Washington, D.C., April 1995. SIC categories for which data were suppressed or not available for both 1992 and 1993 are *not* displayed. The employment columns represent mid-March employment in the year. Pay per employee is calculated by dividing 1st Quarter payroll, annualized, by mid-March employment. The columns headed "% State" show the county's percentage of the state total for the SIC in 1993; for example, 0.9% for SIC 6030 means that the county had 0.9 percent of the state's total establishments (or payroll) in SIC 6030 in 1993. A dash (-) is used to indicate that data are not available or cannot be calculated; *nec* means not elsewhere classified.

Continued on next page.

SIC	Industry	No. Establishments			Employment		Pay / Employee		Annual Payroll ($ 000)		
		1992	1993	% State	1992	1993	1992	1993	1992	1993	% State
FAYETTE, KY - [continued]											
6710	Holding offices	9	15	*16.3*	-	230	-	41,791	-	9,327	*7.0*
6732	Educational, religious, etc. trusts	7	8	*12.5*	97	96	21,237	21,708	2,108	1,760	*20.4*
6733	Trusts, n.e.c.	9	6	*15.4*	26	11	54,769	46,909	1,093	1,108	*36.0*
FLEMING, KY											
60 –	**Finance, insurance, and real estate**	24	22	*0.3*	134	133	15,134	15,549	2,102	2,304	*0.1*
6400	Insurance agents, brokers, and service	7	8	*0.5*	18	30	8,667	12,000	151	406	*0.2*
6500	Real estate	4	4	*0.2*	2	4	10,000	8,000	30	39	*0.0*
FLOYD, KY											
60 –	**Finance, insurance, and real estate**	42	40	*0.6*	381	425	18,310	19,266	7,218	8,784	*0.5*
6000	Depository institutions	10	10	*0.7*	262	254	18,183	19,165	4,874	4,869	*0.8*
6100	Nondepository institutions	3	3	*0.5*	15	22	16,533	16,182	268	416	*0.3*
6140	Personal credit institutions	3	3	*0.9*	15	22	16,533	16,182	268	416	*1.1*
6400	Insurance agents, brokers, and service	8	8	*0.5*	22	21	17,818	14,857	398	402	*0.2*
6500	Real estate	16	14	*0.7*	42	74	12,286	17,946	614	1,647	*1.1*
6530	Real estate agents and managers	3	3	*0.4*	5	-	12,000	-	60	-	-
FRANKLIN, KY											
60 –	**Finance, insurance, and real estate**	91	92	*1.3*	857	876	20,359	22,274	18,454	19,716	*1.2*
6000	Depository institutions	20	21	*1.4*	412	432	20,214	21,694	9,073	9,167	*1.5*
6020	Commercial banks	11	11	*1.0*	-	258	-	24,667	-	5,867	*1.1*
6100	Nondepository institutions	7	6	*1.1*	21	29	22,857	14,621	469	416	*0.3*
6140	Personal credit institutions	7	6	*1.7*	21	29	22,857	14,621	469	416	*1.1*
6300	Insurance carriers	13	11	*2.0*	221	235	21,176	24,715	4,728	5,878	*1.8*
6310	Life insurance	4	3	*1.5*	178	174	20,809	22,345	3,742	3,845	*2.6*
6370	Pension, health, and welfare funds	3	3	*5.5*	25	25	21,280	24,160	550	663	*13.0*
6400	Insurance agents, brokers, and service	23	26	*1.6*	109	81	19,963	19,259	2,307	1,643	*0.8*
6500	Real estate	23	21	*1.0*	59	59	8,814	10,373	571	717	*0.5*
6510	Real estate operators and lessors	15	13	*1.3*	33	33	7,758	11,030	303	396	*0.7*
6530	Real estate agents and managers	6	5	*0.6*	13	13	8,308	9,538	116	147	*0.2*
FULTON, KY											
60 –	**Finance, insurance, and real estate**	21	20	*0.3*	118	114	16,712	17,333	2,117	2,084	*0.1*
6000	Depository institutions	9	9	*0.6*	89	93	16,404	16,043	1,629	1,661	*0.3*
6400	Insurance agents, brokers, and service	5	5	*0.3*	-	10	-	14,800	-	123	*0.1*
6500	Real estate	3	3	*0.1*	5	3	4,800	9,333	41	37	*0.0*
GALLATIN, KY											
60 –	**Finance, insurance, and real estate**	5	4	*0.1*	19	21	22,105	14,286	403	311	*0.0*
GARRARD, KY											
60 –	**Finance, insurance, and real estate**	12	14	*0.2*	35	33	19,771	21,576	758	767	*0.0*
6400	Insurance agents, brokers, and service	2	4	*0.2*	-	5	-	10,400	-	54	*0.0*
6500	Real estate	6	6	*0.3*	6	4	10,000	9,000	61	62	*0.0*
6530	Real estate agents and managers	3	5	*0.6*	3	-	6,667	-	18	-	-
GRANT, KY											
60 –	**Finance, insurance, and real estate**	28	29	*0.4*	179	160	17,520	16,725	3,317	2,989	*0.2*
6000	Depository institutions	13	14	*0.9*	128	128	18,094	16,875	2,643	2,426	*0.4*
6400	Insurance agents, brokers, and service	6	6	*0.4*	17	-	12,706	-	200	-	-
6500	Real estate	4	6	*0.3*	10	6	8,400	13,333	88	115	*0.1*
GRAVES, KY											
60 –	**Finance, insurance, and real estate**	51	58	*0.8*	385	369	18,255	18,927	7,286	7,025	*0.4*
6000	Depository institutions	11	12	*0.8*	192	211	17,604	17,915	3,630	3,898	*0.6*
6020	Commercial banks	5	8	*0.7*	-	176	-	17,955	-	3,263	*0.6*
6030	Savings institutions	5	2	*0.8*	88	-	18,591	-	1,825	-	-

Source: County Business Patterns, 1992/93, CBP-92/93-1, U.S. Department of Commerce, Washington, D.C., April 1995. SIC categories for which data were suppressed or not available for both 1992 and 1993 are not displayed. The employment columns represent mid-March employment in the year. Pay per employee is calculated by dividing 1st Quarter payroll, annualized, by mid-March employment. The columns headed "% State" show the county's percentage of the state total for the SIC in 1993; for example, 0.9% for SIC 6030 means that the county had 0.9 percent of the state's total establishments (or payroll) in SIC 6030 in 1993. A dash (-) is used to indicate that data are not available or cannot be calculated; nec means not elsewhere classified.

Continued on next page.

SIC	Industry	No. Establishments			Employment		Pay / Employee		Annual Payroll ($ 000)		
		1992	1993	% State	1992	1993	1992	1993	1992	1993	% State
GRAVES, KY - [continued]											
6100	Nondepository institutions	6	4	0.7	-	12	-	24,667	-	300	0.3
6140	Personal credit institutions	5	4	1.1	-	12	-	24,667	-	300	0.8
6200	Security and commodity brokers	3	4	1.7	8	24	19,000	35,000	201	692	0.6
6300	Insurance carriers	3	2	0.4	27	-	29,333	-	766	-	-
6400	Insurance agents, brokers, and service	12	11	0.7	-	40	-	23,500	-	764	0.4
6500	Real estate	15	24	1.1	75	56	13,333	9,429	1,073	711	0.5
6530	Real estate agents and managers	9	11	1.3	55	22	11,127	16,364	709	345	0.6
GRAYSON, KY											
60 –	**Finance, insurance, and real estate**	34	36	0.5	198	208	16,687	15,365	3,580	3,477	0.2
6000	Depository institutions	11	11	0.7	121	119	19,405	18,420	2,626	2,425	0.4
6400	Insurance agents, brokers, and service	11	12	0.7	34	35	13,882	11,314	437	429	0.2
6500	Real estate	9	10	0.5	33	43	10,182	10,419	381	458	0.3
6510	Real estate operators and lessors	4	4	0.4	8	-	12,500	-	100	-	-
6530	Real estate agents and managers	3	5	0.6	3	29	8,000	10,345	30	336	0.5
GREEN, KY											
60 –	**Finance, insurance, and real estate**	17	18	0.3	98	97	16,041	15,052	1,633	1,631	0.1
6000	Depository institutions	6	6	0.4	67	68	17,731	17,588	1,306	1,335	0.2
6400	Insurance agents, brokers, and service	5	7	0.4	14	15	21,143	12,000	243	205	0.1
6500	Real estate	5	5	0.2	-	14	-	6,000	-	91	0.1
6510	Real estate operators and lessors	3	3	0.3	5	-	9,600	-	55	-	-
GREENUP, KY											
60 –	**Finance, insurance, and real estate**	37	36	0.5	286	274	19,441	19,066	5,531	5,411	0.3
6000	Depository institutions	16	15	1.0	168	156	18,452	17,974	2,838	2,901	0.5
6300	Insurance carriers	4	3	0.6	69	68	25,449	25,588	1,933	1,699	0.5
6400	Insurance agents, brokers, and service	9	9	0.5	31	32	16,516	16,000	567	604	0.3
6500	Real estate	8	9	0.4	18	18	10,667	9,333	193	207	0.1
6510	Real estate operators and lessors	5	6	0.6	10	10	9,600	8,400	92	93	0.2
HANCOCK, KY											
60 –	**Finance, insurance, and real estate**	10	10	0.1	54	-	13,037	-	893	-	-
6000	Depository institutions	4	4	0.3	40	42	14,400	14,857	773	813	0.1
6500	Real estate	4	3	0.1	-	10	-	6,400	-	66	0.0
6510	Real estate operators and lessors	3	3	0.3	-	10	-	6,400	-	66	0.1
HARDIN, KY											
60 –	**Finance, insurance, and real estate**	148	159	2.3	966	1,081	20,447	19,604	20,448	21,749	1.3
6000	Depository institutions	38	37	2.4	557	542	20,661	21,218	12,101	11,774	1.9
6020	Commercial banks	26	24	2.2	385	345	20,197	22,110	8,037	7,657	1.4
6100	Nondepository institutions	13	12	2.2	65	88	22,708	15,545	1,501	1,378	1.2
6140	Personal credit institutions	10	11	3.2	51	-	21,490	-	1,144	-	-
6200	Security and commodity brokers	7	8	3.4	19	21	16,421	24,190	311	511	0.5
6210	Security brokers and dealers	4	5	3.0	-	15	-	30,400	-	459	0.5
6280	Security and commodity services	3	3	4.7	-	6	-	8,667	-	52	0.3
6300	Insurance carriers	8	9	1.7	84	105	32,429	29,219	2,174	3,080	0.9
6400	Insurance agents, brokers, and service	33	31	1.9	92	117	17,435	14,940	2,059	1,968	0.9
6500	Real estate	46	57	2.7	89	169	12,629	13,231	1,333	2,695	1.8
6510	Real estate operators and lessors	16	25	2.4	30	87	11,600	14,667	367	1,430	2.4
6530	Real estate agents and managers	25	27	3.2	38	70	12,842	11,257	624	956	1.5
6700	Holding and other investment offices	3	5	2.0	60	39	16,733	19,590	969	343	0.2
HARLAN, KY											
60 –	**Finance, insurance, and real estate**	34	33	0.5	236	261	20,407	17,180	4,790	4,726	0.3
6000	Depository institutions	7	7	0.5	96	102	19,125	18,078	1,887	2,003	0.3
6100	Nondepository institutions	6	5	0.9	28	38	17,000	12,526	521	606	0.5
6140	Personal credit institutions	6	5	1.4	28	38	17,000	12,526	521	606	1.6

Source: County Business Patterns, 1992/93, CBP-92/93-1, U.S. Department of Commerce, Washington, D.C., April 1995. SIC categories for which data were suppressed or not available for both 1992 and 1993 are not displayed. The employment columns represent mid-March employment in the year. Pay per employee is calculated by dividing 1st Quarter payroll, annualized, by mid-March employment. The columns headed "% State" show the county's percentage of the state total for the SIC in 1993; for example, 0.9% for SIC 6030 means that the county had 0.9 percent of the state's total establishments (or payroll) in SIC 6030 in 1993. A dash (-) is used to indicate that data are not available or cannot be calculated; nec means not elsewhere classified.

Continued on next page.

SIC	Industry	No. Establishments			Employment		Pay / Employee		Annual Payroll ($ 000)		
		1992	1993	% State	1992	1993	1992	1993	1992	1993	% State
HARLAN, KY - [continued]											
6400	Insurance agents, brokers, and service	6	6	0.4	32	30	16,625	15,067	556	509	0.2
6500	Real estate	11	10	0.5	40	49	12,800	10,286	573	406	0.3
6510	Real estate operators and lessors	7	5	0.5	31	19	13,290	9,474	385	189	0.3
HARRISON, KY											
60−	**Finance, insurance, and real estate**	28	29	0.4	172	181	14,860	15,006	2,745	2,878	0.2
6000	Depository institutions	9	9	0.6	111	116	18,162	18,103	2,155	2,244	0.4
6400	Insurance agents, brokers, and service	6	6	0.4	19	20	11,158	14,000	246	300	0.1
6500	Real estate	10	11	0.5	33	36	6,788	6,556	244	236	0.2
6510	Real estate operators and lessors	3	5	0.5	2	-	14,000	-	30	-	-
6530	Real estate agents and managers	5	4	0.5	-	13	-	5,538	-	75	0.1
HART, KY											
60−	**Finance, insurance, and real estate**	17	16	0.2	126	105	16,667	19,124	2,063	1,937	0.1
6000	Depository institutions	6	6	0.4	87	85	16,322	19,435	1,482	1,557	0.3
6400	Insurance agents, brokers, and service	6	7	0.4	14	13	16,857	19,692	262	278	0.1
HENDERSON, KY											
60−	**Finance, insurance, and real estate**	86	84	1.2	572	553	16,713	17,027	9,788	10,098	0.6
6000	Depository institutions	14	14	0.9	256	264	16,969	16,773	4,443	4,784	0.8
6100	Nondepository institutions	7	7	1.3	39	40	23,487	24,400	947	1,030	0.9
6200	Security and commodity brokers	4	3	1.3	11	12	52,727	57,333	592	628	0.6
6300	Insurance carriers	9	8	1.5	57	86	24,982	14,140	1,336	1,231	0.4
6370	Pension, health, and welfare funds	4	3	5.5	29	61	22,345	8,852	546	511	10.0
6400	Insurance agents, brokers, and service	19	21	1.3	75	72	15,413	16,944	1,300	1,382	0.7
6500	Real estate	30	28	1.3	132	74	8,030	10,919	1,076	951	0.6
6530	Real estate agents and managers	17	12	1.4	98	-	6,776	-	674	-	-
6700	Holding and other investment offices	3	3	1.2	2	5	40,000	16,000	94	92	0.1
HENRY, KY											
60−	**Finance, insurance, and real estate**	18	17	0.2	125	125	16,416	16,224	2,125	2,152	0.1
6000	Depository institutions	4	4	0.3	98	101	18,245	17,822	1,825	1,919	0.3
6020	Commercial banks	4	4	0.4	98	101	18,245	17,822	1,825	1,919	0.4
6400	Insurance agents, brokers, and service	7	7	0.4	-	16	-	11,250	-	176	0.1
6500	Real estate	6	6	0.3	7	8	5,714	6,000	63	57	0.0
6530	Real estate agents and managers	4	4	0.5	4	-	7,000	-	44	-	-
HICKMAN, KY											
60−	**Finance, insurance, and real estate**	11	10	0.1	56	55	12,857	13,455	765	863	0.1
6000	Depository institutions	3	3	0.2	31	32	16,903	17,375	575	663	0.1
6020	Commercial banks	2	3	0.3	-	32	-	17,375	-	663	0.1
6400	Insurance agents, brokers, and service	4	3	0.2	8	8	10,500	9,000	85	87	0.0
HOPKINS, KY											
60−	**Finance, insurance, and real estate**	104	103	1.5	946	708	22,465	21,554	20,532	14,599	0.9
6000	Depository institutions	25	26	1.7	304	310	16,934	17,768	5,420	5,877	0.9
6020	Commercial banks	19	19	1.8	265	269	17,208	18,156	4,676	5,067	0.9
6100	Nondepository institutions	13	11	2.0	165	128	11,976	15,438	2,226	1,992	1.7
6140	Personal credit institutions	10	8	2.3	48	52	19,833	22,231	1,031	1,168	3.1
6150	Business credit institutions	3	2	4.8	117	-	8,752	-	1,195	-	-
6300	Insurance carriers	9	6	1.1	239	28	29,490	31,143	6,724	748	0.2
6400	Insurance agents, brokers, and service	23	24	1.4	117	121	31,692	32,595	2,937	3,020	1.4
6500	Real estate	27	29	1.4	96	87	22,125	10,391	1,804	917	0.6
6510	Real estate operators and lessors	17	20	1.9	60	68	11,133	9,235	542	613	1.0
6530	Real estate agents and managers	8	9	1.1	34	19	42,353	14,526	1,244	304	0.5

Source: County Business Patterns, 1992/93, CBP-92/93-1, U.S. Department of Commerce, Washington, D.C., April 1995. SIC categories for which data were suppressed or not available for both 1992 and 1993 are *not* displayed. The employment columns represent mid-March employment in the year. Pay per employee is calculated by dividing 1st Quarter payroll, annualized, by mid-March employment. The columns headed "% State" show the county's percentage of the state total for the SIC in 1993; for example, 0.9% for SIC 6030 means that the county had 0.9 percent of the state's total establishments (or payroll) in SIC 6030 in 1993. A dash (-) is used to indicate that data are not available or cannot be calculated; *nec* means not elsewhere classified.

SIC	Industry	No. Establishments			Employment		Pay / Employee		Annual Payroll ($ 000)		
		1992	1993	% State	1992	1993	1992	1993	1992	1993	% State
JACKSON, KY											
60 –	**Finance, insurance, and real estate**	7	6	0.1	39	44	16,615	15,182	758	773	0.0
JEFFERSON, KY											
60 –	**Finance, insurance, and real estate**	1,707	1,779	25.9	25,629	26,288	28,526	29,343	738,933	807,315	47.6
6000	Depository institutions	300	298	19.7	9,310	8,333	24,706	25,399	227,078	215,649	34.8
6020	Commercial banks	185	182	16.8	8,015	7,156	24,544	25,597	192,111	186,675	34.9
6030	Savings institutions	48	49	20.5	719	658	28,156	27,185	21,339	17,680	30.9
6060	Credit unions	57	57	34.5	342	368	17,883	17,359	6,427	6,767	30.2
6100	Nondepository institutions	125	143	26.1	1,114	1,734	33,899	26,111	36,445	52,348	43.8
6110	Federal and Federally-sponsored credit	1	9	18.4	-	182	-	42,857	-	9,573	62.9
6140	Personal credit institutions	66	60	17.2	457	474	24,998	21,932	11,657	10,764	28.3
6150	Business credit institutions	19	21	50.0	-	316	-	31,835	-	11,361	51.2
6160	Mortgage bankers and brokers	38	53	50.0	373	762	37,748	22,336	13,461	20,650	46.8
6200	Security and commodity brokers	74	81	34.6	972	993	53,667	60,483	58,796	71,172	64.6
6210	Security brokers and dealers	40	42	25.6	846	766	53,716	61,285	50,333	56,329	60.9
6300	Insurance carriers	240	201	36.9	6,265	6,395	30,374	30,248	198,059	203,666	61.5
6310	Life insurance	100	77	37.9	2,157	2,174	28,571	30,473	74,025	70,983	47.3
6321	Accident and health insurance	6	5	41.7	233	253	18,575	18,324	4,432	5,069	83.6
6324	Hospital and medical service plans	13	10	35.7	2,264	2,188	31,019	29,565	65,835	67,807	84.2
6330	Fire, marine, and casualty insurance	89	89	38.5	1,384	1,579	35,691	33,495	47,061	54,293	64.5
6370	Pension, health, and welfare funds	19	11	20.0	75	-	20,427	-	2,886	-	-
6400	Insurance agents, brokers, and service	378	421	25.4	3,190	3,573	22,989	25,602	79,209	99,564	47.7
6500	Real estate	503	545	25.7	3,224	3,482	17,092	16,546	59,792	62,949	41.8
6510	Real estate operators and lessors	212	244	23.5	1,383	1,407	13,767	13,669	19,981	20,971	34.5
6530	Real estate agents and managers	202	233	28.0	1,392	1,511	19,399	19,486	30,276	31,920	51.1
6540	Title abstract offices	6	9	52.9	-	59	-	24,407	-	1,512	62.8
6552	Subdividers and developers, n.e.c.	23	38	41.3	88	238	22,409	11,832	1,912	3,465	28.4
6553	Cemetery subdividers and developers	12	14	11.7	200	251	20,460	17,705	4,364	4,745	42.5
6700	Holding and other investment offices	84	87	35.4	1,531	1,752	59,407	62,986	78,565	100,904	66.5
6710	Holding offices	23	28	30.4	1,288	1,367	64,901	76,527	69,325	93,937	70.9
6732	Educational, religious, etc. trusts	29	28	43.8	131	152	24,366	21,158	3,250	3,501	40.5
6733	Trusts, n.e.c.	9	10	25.6	14	41	11,429	12,780	230	1,162	37.8
6799	Investors, n.e.c.	13	16	50.0	-	180	-	9,333	-	1,935	44.7
JESSAMINE, KY											
60 –	**Finance, insurance, and real estate**	28	31	0.5	272	288	15,074	14,986	4,362	4,963	0.3
6000	Depository institutions	8	8	0.5	151	130	17,404	18,554	2,644	2,513	0.4
6400	Insurance agents, brokers, and service	6	5	0.3	9	10	15,556	17,200	149	191	0.1
6500	Real estate	11	14	0.7	105	141	11,086	10,950	1,372	1,978	1.3
6510	Real estate operators and lessors	4	7	0.7	18	65	9,111	9,846	200	762	1.3
JOHNSON, KY											
60 –	**Finance, insurance, and real estate**	23	21	0.3	279	280	16,703	16,257	4,734	4,612	0.3
6000	Depository institutions	7	7	0.5	164	200	16,976	14,620	2,910	3,021	0.5
6400	Insurance agents, brokers, and service	6	6	0.4	29	-	14,759	-	448	-	-
6500	Real estate	5	4	0.2	26	8	7,846	8,000	198	61	0.0
6510	Real estate operators and lessors	4	3	0.3	24	-	7,667	-	172	-	-
KENTON, KY											
60 –	**Finance, insurance, and real estate**	261	275	4.0	2,711	2,586	28,633	22,189	77,442	63,224	3.7
6000	Depository institutions	71	67	4.4	1,099	785	22,741	21,916	25,778	18,511	3.0
6020	Commercial banks	36	40	3.7	663	568	24,603	23,099	16,097	13,472	2.5
6030	Savings institutions	26	18	7.5	381	169	21,039	20,024	9,008	4,335	7.6
6100	Nondepository institutions	17	19	3.5	452	460	50,566	20,339	18,774	9,693	8.1
6140	Personal credit institutions	6	6	1.7	-	26	-	19,231	-	521	1.4
6210	Security brokers and dealers	4	5	3.0	35	-	54,400	-	1,712	-	-
6300	Insurance carriers	25	25	4.6	251	354	35,602	28,181	9,612	9,612	2.9
6310	Life insurance	8	10	4.9	136	269	27,941	24,283	4,023	6,255	4.2

Source: County Business Patterns, 1992/93, CBP-92/93-1, U.S. Department of Commerce, Washington, D.C., April 1995. SIC categories for which data were suppressed or not available for both 1992 and 1993 are *not* displayed. The employment columns represent mid-March employment in the year. Pay per employee is calculated by dividing 1st Quarter payroll, annualized, by mid-March employment. The columns headed "% State" show the county's percentage of the state total for the SIC in 1993; for example, 0.9% for SIC 6030 means that the county had 0.9 percent of the state's total establishments (or payroll) in SIC 6030 in 1993. A dash (-) is used to indicate that data are not available or cannot be calculated; *nec* means not elsewhere classified.

Continued on next page.

SIC	Industry	No. Establishments			Employment		Pay / Employee		Annual Payroll ($ 000)		
		1992	1993	% State	1992	1993	1992	1993	1992	1993	% State
KENTON, KY - [continued]											
6330	Fire, marine, and casualty insurance	11	11	4.8	57	–	37,263	–	2,262	–	–
6400	Insurance agents, brokers, and service	51	53	3.2	236	228	21,542	20,386	5,651	6,056	2.9
6500	Real estate	82	92	4.3	456	566	19,237	16,544	9,622	11,306	7.5
6510	Real estate operators and lessors	38	50	4.8	198	356	17,313	12,427	3,654	4,934	8.1
6530	Real estate agents and managers	25	28	3.4	164	144	22,683	23,333	4,350	4,078	6.5
6540	Title abstract offices	4	5	29.4	10	16	15,600	20,000	196	557	23.1
6552	Subdividers and developers, n.e.c.	7	5	5.4	46	26	19,478	34,615	713	1,284	10.5
6553	Cemetery subdividers and developers	4	4	3.3	25	24	14,880	15,000	453	453	4.1
6700	Holding and other investment offices	8	11	4.5	169	147	27,148	29,959	5,819	5,523	3.6
6710	Holding offices	3	8	8.7	113	125	30,230	34,112	4,694	5,340	4.0
KNOTT, KY											
60 –	**Finance, insurance, and real estate**	6	6	0.1	34	35	26,353	27,200	967	1,035	0.1
6400	Insurance agents, brokers, and service	3	3	0.2	6	6	20,667	20,000	131	133	0.1
KNOX, KY											
60 –	**Finance, insurance, and real estate**	26	26	0.4	198	210	17,354	17,467	3,641	3,941	0.2
6000	Depository institutions	9	9	0.6	134	136	18,060	18,382	2,588	2,716	0.4
6400	Insurance agents, brokers, and service	6	6	0.4	25	20	12,480	14,200	324	325	0.2
6500	Real estate	6	6	0.3	13	21	8,308	6,667	112	111	0.1
LARUE, KY											
60 –	**Finance, insurance, and real estate**	18	19	0.3	89	100	18,607	17,920	1,715	1,920	0.1
6000	Depository institutions	7	7	0.5	69	70	19,594	20,400	1,359	1,464	0.2
6400	Insurance agents, brokers, and service	8	9	0.5	16	27	17,750	12,889	335	438	0.2
6500	Real estate	3	3	0.1	4	3	5,000	5,333	21	18	0.0
LAUREL, KY											
60 –	**Finance, insurance, and real estate**	47	49	0.7	385	407	16,997	16,295	7,302	8,151	0.5
6000	Depository institutions	10	10	0.7	228	226	17,333	17,434	4,163	4,212	0.7
6100	Nondepository institutions	5	5	0.9	–	24	–	17,333	–	459	0.4
6140	Personal credit institutions	3	4	1.1	14	–	16,571	–	210	–	–
6300	Insurance carriers	4	3	0.6	–	4	–	13,000	–	48	0.0
6400	Insurance agents, brokers, and service	8	11	0.7	46	64	18,087	16,125	1,291	1,562	0.7
6500	Real estate	13	12	0.6	56	69	8,714	7,130	512	573	0.4
6510	Real estate operators and lessors	2	5	0.5	–	37	–	7,243	–	317	0.5
6530	Real estate agents and managers	6	6	0.7	35	–	7,771	–	278	–	–
6700	Holding and other investment offices	6	6	2.4	12	–	42,667	–	553	–	–
LAWRENCE, KY											
60 –	**Finance, insurance, and real estate**	10	13	0.2	82	82	17,268	17,902	1,482	1,453	0.1
6000	Depository institutions	4	4	0.3	56	53	16,429	16,302	927	907	0.1
6500	Real estate	–	3	0.1	–	5	–	14,400	–	53	0.0
LEE, KY											
60 –	**Finance, insurance, and real estate**	10	9	0.1	56	51	15,929	18,353	949	1,095	0.1
6500	Real estate	5	5	0.2	11	10	7,273	7,200	72	72	0.0
LESLIE, KY											
60 –	**Finance, insurance, and real estate**	5	5	0.1	38	–	21,474	–	910	–	–
LETCHER, KY											
60 –	**Finance, insurance, and real estate**	26	21	0.3	209	176	16,785	16,795	4,050	3,469	0.2
6400	Insurance agents, brokers, and service	12	8	0.5	–	23	–	11,478	–	287	0.1
6500	Real estate	4	2	0.1	62	–	11,871	–	1,076	–	–
6510	Real estate operators and lessors	4	2	0.2	62	–	11,871	–	1,076	–	–

Source: County Business Patterns, 1992/93, CBP-92/93-1, U.S. Department of Commerce, Washington, D.C., April 1995. SIC categories for which data were suppressed or not available for both 1992 and 1993 are not displayed. The employment columns represent mid-March employment in the year. Pay per employee is calculated by dividing 1st Quarter payroll, annualized, by mid-March employment. The columns headed "% State" show the county's percentage of the state total for the SIC in 1993; for example, 0.9% for SIC 6030 means that the county had 0.9 percent of the state's total establishments (or payroll) in SIC 6030 in 1993. A dash (-) is used to indicate that data are not available or cannot be calculated; nec means not elsewhere classified.

SIC	Industry	No. Establishments			Employment		Pay / Employee		Annual Payroll ($ 000)		
		1992	1993	% State	1992	1993	1992	1993	1992	1993	% State
LEWIS, KY											
60 –	**Finance, insurance, and real estate**	10	8	*0.1*	81	105	16,543	12,533	1,507	1,420	*0.1*
6000	Depository institutions	6	2	*0.1*	71	-	17,465	-	1,407	-	-
6020	Commercial banks	6	2	*0.2*	71	-	17,465	-	1,407	-	-
6500	Real estate	2	3	*0.1*	-	4	-	4,000	-	13	*0.0*
LINCOLN, KY											
60 –	**Finance, insurance, and real estate**	17	18	*0.3*	273	189	13,568	22,201	3,588	4,041	*0.2*
6100	Nondepository institutions	3	3	*0.5*	16	8	20,000	23,500	236	204	*0.2*
6400	Insurance agents, brokers, and service	4	5	*0.3*	15	18	12,533	14,000	203	252	*0.1*
6500	Real estate	4	5	*0.2*	4	3	5,000	10,667	22	54	*0.0*
LIVINGSTON, KY											
60 –	**Finance, insurance, and real estate**	7	8	*0.1*	44	38	16,000	17,158	721	635	*0.0*
LOGAN, KY											
60 –	**Finance, insurance, and real estate**	46	44	*0.6*	228	232	17,649	17,603	4,288	4,927	*0.3*
6000	Depository institutions	13	12	*0.8*	142	145	21,155	20,000	3,057	3,043	*0.5*
6100	Nondepository institutions	4	4	*0.7*	14	16	23,429	22,000	330	383	*0.3*
6400	Insurance agents, brokers, and service	10	11	*0.7*	31	31	12,903	13,935	509	456	*0.2*
6500	Real estate	13	12	*0.6*	29	32	4,966	5,000	174	166	*0.1*
6510	Real estate operators and lessors	9	8	*0.8*	27	29	4,741	4,690	149	139	*0.2*
6530	Real estate agents and managers	3	3	*0.4*	1	-	8,000	-	17	-	-
LYON, KY											
60 –	**Finance, insurance, and real estate**	13	13	*0.2*	50	56	17,040	14,429	905	1,058	*0.1*
6400	Insurance agents, brokers, and service	4	4	*0.2*	11	13	10,909	10,769	127	140	*0.1*
6510	Real estate operators and lessors	1	3	*0.3*	-	14	-	18,857	-	422	*0.7*
MCCRACKEN, KY											
60 –	**Finance, insurance, and real estate**	170	165	*2.4*	1,138	1,181	23,406	23,367	25,417	26,976	*1.6*
6000	Depository institutions	31	35	*2.3*	589	645	23,844	24,347	12,589	13,933	*2.2*
6020	Commercial banks	21	24	*2.2*	505	583	24,879	24,954	11,124	12,849	*2.4*
6100	Nondepository institutions	17	12	*2.2*	86	69	27,302	21,043	1,830	1,500	*1.3*
6140	Personal credit institutions	13	8	*2.3*	68	44	23,176	17,818	1,307	696	*1.8*
6200	Security and commodity brokers	7	7	*3.0*	22	26	72,000	72,154	1,332	1,940	*1.8*
6210	Security brokers and dealers	7	7	*4.3*	22	26	72,000	72,154	1,332	1,940	*2.1*
6300	Insurance carriers	15	11	*2.0*	115	110	23,930	28,036	2,973	3,258	*1.0*
6310	Life insurance	7	5	*2.5*	101	-	22,297	-	2,319	-	-
6400	Insurance agents, brokers, and service	33	38	*2.3*	147	142	18,177	18,310	2,790	2,896	*1.4*
6500	Real estate	60	55	*2.6*	161	171	11,528	10,503	1,966	2,076	*1.4*
6510	Real estate operators and lessors	35	35	*3.4*	85	128	10,071	10,688	936	1,461	*2.4*
6530	Real estate agents and managers	18	14	*1.7*	53	26	13,585	9,077	726	263	*0.4*
6553	Cemetery subdividers and developers	4	4	*3.3*	-	17	-	11,294	-	222	*2.0*
6700	Holding and other investment offices	7	7	*2.8*	18	18	76,667	60,222	1,937	1,373	*0.9*
6710	Holding offices	4	4	*4.3*	14	13	94,286	76,923	1,852	1,280	*1.0*
MCCREARY, KY											
60 –	**Finance, insurance, and real estate**	7	8	*0.1*	65	72	17,723	16,167	1,257	1,332	*0.1*
MCLEAN, KY											
60 –	**Finance, insurance, and real estate**	11	13	*0.2*	63	70	18,921	17,886	1,325	1,439	*0.1*
6000	Depository institutions	5	5	*0.3*	50	54	19,520	19,037	1,089	1,164	*0.2*
MADISON, KY											
60 –	**Finance, insurance, and real estate**	97	93	*1.4*	636	504	19,063	18,778	12,267	9,627	*0.6*
6000	Depository institutions	26	24	*1.6*	383	267	21,201	22,022	8,113	5,700	*0.9*
6100	Nondepository institutions	6	8	*1.5*	-	28	-	18,857	-	536	*0.4*
6300	Insurance carriers	9	5	*0.9*	31	-	32,129	-	940	-	-

Source: County Business Patterns, 1992/93, CBP-92/93-1, U.S. Department of Commerce, Washington, D.C., April 1995. SIC categories for which data were suppressed or not available for both 1992 and 1993 are *not* displayed. The employment columns represent mid-March employment in the year. Pay per employee is calculated by dividing 1st Quarter payroll, annualized, by mid-March employment. The columns headed "% State" show the county's percentage of the state total for the SIC in 1993; for example, 0.9% for SIC 6030 means that the county had 0.9 percent of the state's total establishments (or payroll) in SIC 6030 in 1993. A dash (-) is used to indicate that data are not available or cannot be calculated; *nec* means not elsewhere classified.

Continued on next page.

SIC	Industry	No. Establishments			Employment		Pay / Employee		Annual Payroll ($ 000)		
		1992	1993	% State	1992	1993	1992	1993	1992	1993	% State
MADISON, KY - [continued]											
6400	Insurance agents, brokers, and service	17	18	1.1	62	60	14,516	14,200	925	951	0.5
6500	Real estate	34	33	1.6	114	110	10,667	10,291	1,335	1,284	0.9
6510	Real estate operators and lessors	13	15	1.4	52	51	10,615	9,961	601	609	1.0
6530	Real estate agents and managers	13	14	1.7	36	37	11,667	11,784	447	470	0.8
MAGOFFIN, KY											
60 –	**Finance, insurance, and real estate**	6	6	0.1	41	–	17,268	–	979	–	–
MARION, KY											
60 –	**Finance, insurance, and real estate**	18	21	0.3	140	134	18,029	18,716	2,331	2,566	0.2
6000	Depository institutions	6	7	0.5	92	87	19,913	20,000	1,648	1,842	0.3
6100	Nondepository institutions	2	3	0.5	–	9	–	30,222	–	172	0.1
6400	Insurance agents, brokers, and service	4	5	0.3	–	28	–	11,429	–	337	0.2
6500	Real estate	6	6	0.3	11	10	15,636	17,600	173	215	0.1
6510	Real estate operators and lessors	–	3	0.3	–	2	–	22,000	–	82	0.1
MARSHALL, KY											
60 –	**Finance, insurance, and real estate**	38	40	0.6	338	349	19,065	19,358	6,575	6,905	0.4
6000	Depository institutions	11	11	0.7	205	208	19,122	20,577	3,927	4,101	0.7
6200	Security and commodity brokers	3	3	1.3	5	–	8,000	–	82	–	–
6400	Insurance agents, brokers, and service	11	12	0.7	81	85	24,543	23,200	2,053	2,292	1.1
6500	Real estate	10	12	0.6	32	43	4,625	5,302	172	263	0.2
6510	Real estate operators and lessors	6	7	0.7	28	32	4,429	4,625	139	158	0.3
MARTIN, KY											
60 –	**Finance, insurance, and real estate**	8	6	0.1	71	72	13,465	13,944	1,000	1,122	0.1
MASON, KY											
60 –	**Finance, insurance, and real estate**	39	37	0.5	271	306	17,417	17,490	4,747	5,452	0.3
6000	Depository institutions	10	10	0.7	130	167	19,385	16,934	2,328	2,842	0.5
6100	Nondepository institutions	4	5	0.9	24	23	15,000	18,435	384	510	0.4
6300	Insurance carriers	3	2	0.4	55	–	14,618	–	932	–	–
6400	Insurance agents, brokers, and service	9	10	0.6	32	50	11,500	13,840	415	735	0.4
6500	Real estate	10	7	0.3	20	15	11,800	13,333	257	222	0.1
6510	Real estate operators and lessors	3	3	0.3	–	6	–	17,333	–	116	0.2
MEADE, KY											
60 –	**Finance, insurance, and real estate**	18	22	0.3	161	159	15,652	14,818	2,485	2,492	0.1
6000	Depository institutions	8	8	0.5	126	119	17,016	15,563	2,080	1,952	0.3
6400	Insurance agents, brokers, and service	5	5	0.3	21	21	12,381	14,095	272	290	0.1
6500	Real estate	5	8	0.4	14	–	8,286	–	133	–	–
6530	Real estate agents and managers	4	4	0.5	–	14	–	10,857	–	176	0.3
MENIFEE, KY											
60 –	**Finance, insurance, and real estate**	4	4	0.1	13	–	14,769	–	173	–	–
MERCER, KY											
60 –	**Finance, insurance, and real estate**	28	28	0.4	158	152	16,127	15,105	2,354	2,504	0.1
6000	Depository institutions	9	9	0.6	75	63	22,933	22,857	1,388	1,493	0.2
6400	Insurance agents, brokers, and service	10	10	0.6	27	–	15,556	–	445	–	–
6500	Real estate	6	7	0.3	49	52	6,367	6,846	406	440	0.3
6510	Real estate operators and lessors	2	3	0.3	–	3	–	9,333	–	21	0.0
6530	Real estate agents and managers	3	3	0.4	13	–	5,846	–	120	–	–
METCALFE, KY											
60 –	**Finance, insurance, and real estate**	12	12	0.2	53	59	15,698	13,288	953	853	0.1
6500	Real estate	3	3	0.1	2	2	12,000	12,000	32	32	0.0

Source: County Business Patterns, 1992/93, CBP-92/93-1, U.S. Department of Commerce, Washington, D.C., April 1995. SIC categories for which data were suppressed or not available for both 1992 and 1993 are not displayed. The employment columns represent mid-March employment in the year. Pay per employee is calculated by dividing 1st Quarter payroll, annualized, by mid-March employment. The columns headed "% State" show the county's percentage of the state total for the SIC in 1993; for example, 0.9% for SIC 6030 means that the county had 0.9 percent of the state's total establishments (or payroll) in SIC 6030 in 1993. A dash (-) is used to indicate that data are not available or cannot be calculated; nec means not elsewhere classified.

SIC	Industry	No. Establishments			Employment		Pay / Employee		Annual Payroll ($ 000)		
		1992	1993	% State	1992	1993	1992	1993	1992	1993	% State
MONROE, KY											
60 –	**Finance, insurance, and real estate**	12	14	0.2	84	81	17,286	19,210	1,541	1,572	0.1
6000	Depository institutions	5	5	0.3	62	62	18,710	20,323	1,228	1,240	0.2
6020	Commercial banks	5	5	0.5	62	62	18,710	20,323	1,228	1,240	0.2
6400	Insurance agents, brokers, and service	5	7	0.4	20	-	13,800	-	297	-	-
MONTGOMERY, KY											
60 –	**Finance, insurance, and real estate**	32	35	0.5	219	243	18,100	18,222	3,930	4,257	0.3
6000	Depository institutions	10	10	0.7	160	165	19,625	21,358	3,083	3,315	0.5
6100	Nondepository institutions	3	3	0.5	16	-	17,750	-	281	-	-
6140	Personal credit institutions	3	3	0.9	16	-	17,750	-	281	-	-
6400	Insurance agents, brokers, and service	8	8	0.5	26	30	12,769	12,800	388	407	0.2
6500	Real estate	9	12	0.6	-	25	-	7,040	-	189	0.1
6510	Real estate operators and lessors	5	7	0.7	8	-	5,000	-	41	-	-
6530	Real estate agents and managers	3	4	0.5	4	5	13,000	12,800	60	74	0.1
MORGAN, KY											
60 –	**Finance, insurance, and real estate**	8	10	0.1	85	101	19,200	21,228	1,676	2,177	0.1
6400	Insurance agents, brokers, and service	3	3	0.2	14	14	18,571	33,143	266	343	0.2
MUHLENBERG, KY											
60 –	**Finance, insurance, and real estate**	33	35	0.5	269	265	17,502	18,551	4,848	5,408	0.3
6000	Depository institutions	9	8	0.5	183	177	18,776	18,757	3,404	3,622	0.6
6100	Nondepository institutions	3	3	0.5	12	10	17,333	18,400	230	195	0.2
6140	Personal credit institutions	3	3	0.9	12	10	17,333	18,400	230	195	0.5
6400	Insurance agents, brokers, and service	9	9	0.5	40	47	16,200	18,894	751	1,014	0.5
6500	Real estate	5	9	0.4	18	24	6,000	9,500	79	260	0.2
6530	Real estate agents and managers	1	4	0.5	-	8	-	7,000	-	85	0.1
6700	Holding and other investment offices	3	2	0.8	5	-	4,800	-	30	-	-
NELSON, KY											
60 –	**Finance, insurance, and real estate**	47	49	0.7	244	296	18,344	16,324	4,839	5,479	0.3
6000	Depository institutions	11	11	0.7	144	148	19,417	19,351	2,992	3,187	0.5
6100	Nondepository institutions	5	5	0.9	19	25	19,158	16,160	378	408	0.3
6400	Insurance agents, brokers, and service	11	11	0.7	34	43	10,941	11,256	377	494	0.2
6500	Real estate	16	19	0.9	26	67	9,077	7,881	347	806	0.5
6510	Real estate operators and lessors	11	11	1.1	18	50	9,556	6,880	196	540	0.9
NICHOLAS, KY											
60 –	**Finance, insurance, and real estate**	9	11	0.2	-	40	-	16,600	-	806	0.0
6400	Insurance agents, brokers, and service	3	4	0.2	7	5	9,714	12,000	66	145	0.1
6500	Real estate	2	3	0.1	-	6	-	7,333	-	56	0.0
OHIO, KY											
60 –	**Finance, insurance, and real estate**	20	20	0.3	124	136	16,129	15,118	2,105	2,178	0.1
6000	Depository institutions	9	8	0.5	100	83	17,200	16,819	1,808	1,435	0.2
6020	Commercial banks	9	8	0.7	100	83	17,200	16,819	1,808	1,435	0.3
6400	Insurance agents, brokers, and service	4	7	0.4	10	-	13,200	-	140	-	-
6500	Real estate	4	3	0.1	-	7	-	6,857	-	54	0.0
OLDHAM, KY											
60 –	**Finance, insurance, and real estate**	33	41	0.6	173	199	18,220	23,457	3,353	5,399	0.3
6000	Depository institutions	6	8	0.5	-	83	-	29,928	-	2,737	0.4
6400	Insurance agents, brokers, and service	10	10	0.6	21	38	12,952	22,526	323	1,094	0.5
6500	Real estate	13	19	0.9	42	72	12,857	16,667	599	1,423	0.9
6510	Real estate operators and lessors	6	9	0.9	13	-	9,538	-	160	-	-
6530	Real estate agents and managers	5	8	1.0	-	50	-	19,520	-	1,144	1.8

Source: County Business Patterns, 1992/93, CBP-92/93-1, U.S. Department of Commerce, Washington, D.C., April 1995. SIC categories for which data were suppressed or not available for both 1992 and 1993 are not displayed. The employment columns represent mid-March employment in the year. Pay per employee is calculated by dividing 1st Quarter payroll, annualized, by mid-March employment. The columns headed "% State" show the county's percentage of the state total for the SIC in 1993; for example, 0.9% for SIC 6030 means that the county had 0.9 percent of the state's total establishments (or payroll) in SIC 6030 in 1993. A dash (-) is used to indicate that data are not available or cannot be calculated; nec means not elsewhere classified.

SIC	Industry	No. Establishments			Employment		Pay / Employee		Annual Payroll ($ 000)		
		1992	1993	% State	1992	1993	1992	1993	1992	1993	% State
OWEN, KY											
60 –	**Finance, insurance, and real estate**	11	12	0.2	75	80	16,160	18,000	1,270	1,517	0.1
6000	Depository institutions	4	4	0.3	61	56	16,984	20,500	1,043	1,153	0.2
6020	Commercial banks	4	4	0.4	61	56	16,984	20,500	1,043	1,153	0.2
6400	Insurance agents, brokers, and service	3	3	0.2	4	7	7,000	6,286	33	46	0.0
OWSLEY, KY											
60 –	**Finance, insurance, and real estate**	4	4	0.1	16	15	17,500	21,333	290	321	0.0
PENDLETON, KY											
60 –	**Finance, insurance, and real estate**	19	18	0.3	81	83	13,037	14,458	1,063	1,267	0.1
6000	Depository institutions	9	10	0.7	56	61	15,571	17,115	878	1,109	0.2
6020	Commercial banks	6	7	0.6	47	44	16,170	17,455	683	778	0.1
6400	Insurance agents, brokers, and service	4	4	0.2	13	-	9,538	-	121	-	-
6500	Real estate	4	3	0.1	-	10	-	4,000	-	52	0.0
PERRY, KY											
60 –	**Finance, insurance, and real estate**	39	37	0.5	286	294	22,210	20,531	6,868	6,253	0.4
6000	Depository institutions	9	9	0.6	148	148	18,892	20,216	3,191	3,447	0.6
6100	Nondepository institutions	7	7	1.3	36	55	18,333	12,727	727	726	0.6
6400	Insurance agents, brokers, and service	5	5	0.3	37	-	16,649	-	598	-	-
6500	Real estate	13	9	0.4	33	24	20,727	21,167	687	485	0.3
6510	Real estate operators and lessors	8	6	0.6	-	20	-	23,800	-	454	0.7
6530	Real estate agents and managers	4	3	0.4	-	4	-	8,000	-	31	0.0
PIKE, KY											
60 –	**Finance, insurance, and real estate**	82	90	1.3	873	838	19,858	23,695	18,504	22,006	1.3
6000	Depository institutions	26	26	1.7	553	457	18,958	23,440	11,036	10,849	1.7
6300	Insurance carriers	5	7	1.3	65	82	39,754	40,293	2,802	4,050	1.2
6310	Life insurance	3	3	1.5	-	72	-	41,444	-	3,655	2.4
6400	Insurance agents, brokers, and service	20	24	1.4	138	143	19,217	20,895	2,602	2,946	1.4
6500	Real estate	22	26	1.2	85	109	12,235	13,248	1,346	2,634	1.8
6510	Real estate operators and lessors	10	13	1.3	53	69	13,660	14,841	999	1,066	1.8
6530	Real estate agents and managers	6	9	1.1	8	23	8,000	8,696	77	410	0.7
POWELL, KY											
60 –	**Finance, insurance, and real estate**	12	12	0.2	60	59	17,600	15,119	1,081	968	0.1
6400	Insurance agents, brokers, and service	4	4	0.2	9	11	13,778	12,364	130	139	0.1
6500	Real estate	2	3	0.1	-	3	-	8,000	-	33	0.0
PULASKI, KY											
60 –	**Finance, insurance, and real estate**	90	99	1.4	557	656	19,397	19,890	11,229	12,478	0.7
6000	Depository institutions	17	17	1.1	320	328	17,612	19,171	5,700	5,701	0.9
6020	Commercial banks	13	13	1.2	286	295	17,706	19,227	5,052	5,011	0.9
6030	Savings institutions	4	4	1.7	34	33	16,824	18,667	648	690	1.2
6100	Nondepository institutions	14	14	2.6	49	63	23,510	21,333	1,203	1,329	1.1
6300	Insurance carriers	5	4	0.7	52	44	34,538	47,636	1,865	1,528	0.5
6400	Insurance agents, brokers, and service	23	24	1.4	70	75	18,629	17,920	1,375	1,501	0.7
6500	Real estate	25	34	1.6	52	131	9,538	10,565	565	1,786	1.2
6510	Real estate operators and lessors	8	13	1.3	7	28	14,857	9,571	122	339	0.6
6530	Real estate agents and managers	12	18	2.2	20	83	8,400	11,952	217	1,302	2.1
ROBERTSON, KY											
60 –	**Finance, insurance, and real estate**	6	6	0.1	-	22	-	11,818	-	272	0.0
ROCKCASTLE, KY											
60 –	**Finance, insurance, and real estate**	9	9	0.1	73	80	15,014	15,300	1,248	1,348	0.1
6400	Insurance agents, brokers, and service	3	3	0.2	8	11	16,500	13,818	158	176	0.1

Source: County Business Patterns, 1992/93, CBP-92/93-1, U.S. Department of Commerce, Washington, D.C., April 1995. SIC categories for which data were suppressed or not available for both 1992 and 1993 are *not* displayed. The employment columns represent mid-March employment in the year. Pay per employee is calculated by dividing 1st Quarter payroll, annualized, by mid-March employment. The columns headed "% State" show the county's percentage of the state total for the SIC in 1993; for example, 0.9% for SIC 6030 means that the county had 0.9 percent of the state's total establishments (or payroll) in SIC 6030 in 1993. A dash (-) is used to indicate that data are not available or cannot be calculated; *nec* means not elsewhere classified.

SIC	Industry	No. Establishments			Employment		Pay / Employee		Annual Payroll ($ 000)		
		1992	1993	% State	1992	1993	1992	1993	1992	1993	% State
ROWAN, KY											
60 –	**Finance, insurance, and real estate**	25	26	0.4	152	-	23,000	-	3,472	-	-
6000	Depository institutions	6	6	0.4	86	98	22,093	16,082	2,075	1,762	0.3
6400	Insurance agents, brokers, and service	6	7	0.4	23	21	16,000	16,000	366	373	0.2
6500	Real estate	9	9	0.4	13	20	5,846	10,800	93	230	0.2
6510	Real estate operators and lessors	6	7	0.7	10	-	6,800	-	84	-	-
RUSSELL, KY											
60 –	**Finance, insurance, and real estate**	27	25	0.4	143	158	15,301	14,987	2,354	2,596	0.2
6000	Depository institutions	8	8	0.5	84	100	18,048	17,280	1,668	1,878	0.3
6100	Nondepository institutions	3	4	0.7	7	8	17,143	14,500	108	155	0.1
6140	Personal credit institutions	3	4	1.1	7	8	17,143	14,500	108	155	0.4
6400	Insurance agents, brokers, and service	8	7	0.4	19	20	11,368	10,000	226	225	0.1
6500	Real estate	8	6	0.3	33	30	10,182	10,800	352	338	0.2
6530	Real estate agents and managers	5	2	0.2	26	-	10,154	-	278	-	-
SCOTT, KY											
60 –	**Finance, insurance, and real estate**	39	41	0.6	240	218	17,700	19,670	4,472	4,394	0.3
6000	Depository institutions	7	7	0.5	144	128	20,694	23,469	3,092	2,962	0.5
6100	Nondepository institutions	3	5	0.9	9	12	22,222	18,667	213	274	0.2
6400	Insurance agents, brokers, and service	11	9	0.5	24	23	16,000	15,304	399	371	0.2
6500	Real estate	14	15	0.7	55	51	9,600	10,039	573	578	0.4
6510	Real estate operators and lessors	4	4	0.4	30	-	6,667	-	230	-	-
6530	Real estate agents and managers	7	9	1.1	15	19	13,867	13,684	215	238	0.4
SHELBY, KY											
60 –	**Finance, insurance, and real estate**	43	47	0.7	320	433	21,638	20,887	7,012	9,559	0.6
6000	Depository institutions	10	10	0.7	177	239	21,107	23,096	3,783	5,617	0.9
6100	Nondepository institutions	4	3	0.5	-	15	-	23,467	-	486	0.4
6400	Insurance agents, brokers, and service	10	11	0.7	27	33	16,444	15,879	456	526	0.3
6500	Real estate	16	19	0.9	51	98	9,725	7,918	664	961	0.6
6510	Real estate operators and lessors	4	6	0.6	20	49	5,800	5,469	148	271	0.4
6530	Real estate agents and managers	8	9	1.1	19	23	14,316	9,913	389	221	0.4
SIMPSON, KY											
60 –	**Finance, insurance, and real estate**	27	26	0.4	168	168	19,048	18,238	3,310	3,219	0.2
6000	Depository institutions	8	8	0.5	116	117	19,483	19,419	2,310	2,372	0.4
6400	Insurance agents, brokers, and service	6	6	0.4	19	-	24,421	-	464	-	-
6500	Real estate	9	10	0.5	22	24	9,273	10,500	241	285	0.2
6510	Real estate operators and lessors	3	5	0.5	9	13	13,333	12,000	143	149	0.2
SPENCER, KY											
60 –	**Finance, insurance, and real estate**	10	8	0.1	-	-	-	-	-	-	-
TAYLOR, KY											
60 –	**Finance, insurance, and real estate**	37	39	0.6	236	233	24,915	22,970	5,977	5,498	0.3
6000	Depository institutions	5	5	0.3	108	100	22,556	21,320	2,506	2,344	0.4
6100	Nondepository institutions	6	7	1.3	21	22	21,714	21,636	455	499	0.4
6400	Insurance agents, brokers, and service	12	14	0.8	30	35	14,267	13,943	505	596	0.3
6500	Real estate	7	10	0.5	26	29	6,000	6,483	175	306	0.2
6510	Real estate operators and lessors	4	5	0.5	9	12	8,000	7,333	72	110	0.2
TODD, KY											
60 –	**Finance, insurance, and real estate**	17	18	0.3	80	82	19,100	16,683	1,287	1,277	0.1
6000	Depository institutions	9	9	0.6	65	66	19,077	16,667	1,044	1,024	0.2
6400	Insurance agents, brokers, and service	5	7	0.4	11	-	16,727	-	162	-	-

Source: County Business Patterns, 1992/93, CBP-92/93-1, U.S. Department of Commerce, Washington, D.C., April 1995. SIC categories for which data were suppressed or not available for both 1992 and 1993 are *not* displayed. The employment columns represent mid-March employment in the year. Pay per employee is calculated by dividing 1st Quarter payroll, annualized, by mid-March employment. The columns headed "% State" show the county's percentage of the state total for the SIC in 1993; for example, 0.9% for SIC 6030 means that the county had 0.9 percent of the state's total establishments (or payroll) in SIC 6030 in 1993. A dash (-) is used to indicate that data are not available or cannot be calculated; *nec* means not elsewhere classified.

SIC	Industry	No. Establishments			Employment		Pay / Employee		Annual Payroll ($ 000)		
		1992	1993	% State	1992	1993	1992	1993	1992	1993	% State
TRIGG, KY											
60 –	**Finance, insurance, and real estate**	15	15	*0.2*	119	93	17,983	17,419	2,287	1,745	*0.1*
6000	Depository institutions	3	3	*0.2*	71	56	19,324	17,786	1,394	1,127	*0.2*
6400	Insurance agents, brokers, and service	3	3	*0.2*	-	8	-	24,500	-	214	*0.1*
6500	Real estate	7	7	*0.3*	12	-	6,667	-	103	-	-
6530	Real estate agents and managers	5	5	*0.6*	-	10	-	8,400	-	102	*0.2*
TRIMBLE, KY											
60 –	**Finance, insurance, and real estate**	7	7	*0.1*	-	46	-	18,783	-	934	*0.1*
6400	Insurance agents, brokers, and service	3	3	*0.2*	8	8	16,000	15,500	134	124	*0.1*
UNION, KY											
60 –	**Finance, insurance, and real estate**	24	24	*0.3*	149	126	17,047	22,984	2,711	2,868	*0.2*
6000	Depository institutions	11	10	*0.7*	117	97	17,915	24,454	2,266	2,406	*0.4*
6400	Insurance agents, brokers, and service	6	7	*0.4*	17	15	14,118	14,933	236	264	*0.1*
6500	Real estate	3	3	*0.1*	6	6	4,667	4,667	25	28	*0.0*
WARREN, KY											
60 –	**Finance, insurance, and real estate**	169	176	*2.6*	1,362	1,408	56,162	25,102	32,198	35,936	*2.1*
6000	Depository institutions	27	28	*1.8*	537	531	21,125	19,759	11,420	11,125	*1.8*
6020	Commercial banks	17	17	*1.6*	417	391	18,149	20,399	7,942	8,480	*1.6*
6030	Savings institutions	5	5	*2.1*	68	77	29,000	21,766	1,649	1,725	*3.0*
6060	Credit unions	5	6	*3.6*	52	63	34,692	13,333	1,829	920	*4.1*
6140	Personal credit institutions	13	12	*3.4*	50	47	19,120	20,085	794	853	*2.2*
6200	Security and commodity brokers	14	15	*6.4*	50	50	54,800	57,440	2,637	2,772	*2.5*
6210	Security brokers and dealers	14	15	*9.1*	50	50	54,800	57,440	2,637	2,772	*3.0*
6300	Insurance carriers	24	21	*3.9*	256	231	29,797	33,645	7,875	7,257	*2.2*
6310	Life insurance	12	10	*4.9*	188	192	27,787	32,458	5,239	5,708	*3.8*
6330	Fire, marine, and casualty insurance	10	8	*3.5*	50	-	34,800	-	1,842	-	-
6400	Insurance agents, brokers, and service	34	36	*2.2*	194	234	248,742	24,684	4,589	6,433	*3.1*
6500	Real estate	50	52	*2.5*	212	195	10,585	10,831	2,332	2,524	*1.7*
6510	Real estate operators and lessors	31	32	*3.1*	133	142	9,504	9,324	1,417	1,510	*2.5*
6530	Real estate agents and managers	14	19	*2.3*	51	-	14,902	-	664	-	-
WASHINGTON, KY											
60 –	**Finance, insurance, and real estate**	14	14	*0.2*	74	80	17,243	18,100	1,504	1,633	*0.1*
6000	Depository institutions	5	5	*0.3*	54	58	19,185	20,552	1,249	1,366	*0.2*
6400	Insurance agents, brokers, and service	4	5	*0.3*	-	16	-	13,750	-	228	*0.1*
6500	Real estate	4	4	*0.2*	6	6	6,000	6,000	37	39	*0.0*
WAYNE, KY											
60 –	**Finance, insurance, and real estate**	16	18	*0.3*	121	124	21,983	20,387	2,509	2,394	*0.1*
6100	Nondepository institutions	3	4	*0.7*	-	18	-	12,889	-	247	*0.2*
6140	Personal credit institutions	3	4	*1.1*	-	18	-	12,889	-	247	*0.7*
6400	Insurance agents, brokers, and service	5	5	*0.3*	18	19	12,889	13,263	228	245	*0.1*
6500	Real estate	3	4	*0.2*	7	8	6,286	6,000	49	54	*0.0*
WEBSTER, KY											
60 –	**Finance, insurance, and real estate**	24	24	*0.3*	164	171	16,463	15,649	2,741	2,929	*0.2*
6000	Depository institutions	10	10	*0.7*	125	128	17,952	17,031	2,297	2,387	*0.4*
6400	Insurance agents, brokers, and service	10	9	*0.5*	-	27	-	13,333	-	384	*0.2*
6500	Real estate	3	5	*0.2*	10	16	5,200	8,500	56	158	*0.1*
WHITLEY, KY											
60 –	**Finance, insurance, and real estate**	55	59	*0.9*	472	496	17,119	20,008	8,659	10,992	*0.6*
6000	Depository institutions	16	16	*1.1*	282	286	16,936	16,895	5,154	5,288	*0.9*
6100	Nondepository institutions	3	4	*0.7*	-	19	-	14,526	-	375	*0.3*
6300	Insurance carriers	3	3	*0.6*	70	66	25,829	24,667	1,807	1,632	*0.5*
6310	Life insurance	3	3	*1.5*	70	66	25,829	24,667	1,807	1,632	*1.1*

Source: County Business Patterns, 1992/93, CBP-92/93-1, U.S. Department of Commerce, Washington, D.C., April 1995. SIC categories for which data were suppressed or not available for both 1992 and 1993 are *not* displayed. The employment columns represent mid-March employment in the year. Pay per employee is calculated by dividing 1st Quarter payroll, annualized, by mid-March employment. The columns headed "% State" show the county's percentage of the state total for the SIC in 1993; for example, 0.9% for SIC 6030 means that the county had 0.9 percent of the state's total establishments (or payroll) in SIC 6030 in 1993. A dash (-) is used to indicate that data are not available or cannot be calculated; *nec* means not elsewhere classified.

Continued on next page.

SIC	Industry	No. Establishments			Employment		Pay / Employee		Annual Payroll ($ 000)		
		1992	1993	% State	1992	1993	1992	1993	1992	1993	% State
WHITLEY, KY - [continued]											
6400	Insurance agents, brokers, and service	15	15	0.9	50	50	13,200	13,680	698	759	0.4
6500	Real estate	16	17	0.8	50	40	8,240	13,800	498	958	0.6
6510	Real estate operators and lessors	8	11	1.1	27	26	12,444	11,538	415	686	1.1
6530	Real estate agents and managers	5	4	0.5	6	-	7,333	-	43	-	-
WOLFE, KY											
60 -	**Finance, insurance, and real estate**	2	2	0.0	-	-	-	-	-	-	-
WOODFORD, KY											
60 -	**Finance, insurance, and real estate**	38	40	0.6	209	209	19,751	19,349	4,653	4,178	0.2
6000	Depository institutions	6	6	0.4	121	133	22,446	23,308	2,861	3,049	0.5
6020	Commercial banks	6	6	0.6	121	133	22,446	23,308	2,861	3,049	0.6
6100	Nondepository institutions	2	3	0.5	-	5	-	16,000	-	174	0.1
6400	Insurance agents, brokers, and service	10	12	0.7	27	34	13,037	12,471	387	465	0.2
6500	Real estate	17	16	0.8	48	34	15,500	10,588	1,084	404	0.3
6510	Real estate operators and lessors	6	9	0.9	23	20	16,522	12,200	459	275	0.5
6530	Real estate agents and managers	4	7	0.8	3	14	13,333	8,286	68	129	0.2

Source: County Business Patterns, 1992/93, CBP-92/93-1, U.S. Department of Commerce, Washington, D.C., April 1995. SIC categories for which data were suppressed or not available for both 1992 and 1993 are *not* displayed. The employment columns represent mid-March employment in the year. Pay per employee is calculated by dividing 1st Quarter payroll, annualized, by mid-March employment. The columns headed "% State" show the county's percentage of the state total for the SIC in 1993; for example, 0.9% for SIC 6030 means that the county had 0.9 percent of the state's total establishments (or payroll) in SIC 6030 in 1993. A dash (-) is used to indicate that data are not available or cannot be calculated; *nec* means not elsewhere classified.

LOUISIANA

SIC	Industry	No. Establishments			Employment		Pay / Employee		Annual Payroll ($ 000)		
		1992	1993	% State	1992	1993	1992	1993	1992	1993	% State
ACADIA, LA											
60–	**Finance, insurance, and real estate**	78	79	0.9	500	476	17,584	18,370	9,503	9,033	0.5
6000	Depository institutions	18	18	1.0	298	299	17,302	18,783	5,297	5,688	0.9
6020	Commercial banks	12	12	1.0	259	260	17,375	18,523	4,595	4,857	0.9
6100	Nondepository institutions	16	18	1.6	44	47	20,909	19,404	931	810	0.6
6400	Insurance agents, brokers, and service	21	20	0.9	83	75	13,735	14,773	1,506	1,455	0.5
6500	Real estate	14	14	0.5	-	22	-	14,000	-	227	0.1
6510	Real estate operators and lessors	7	8	0.6	11	11	10,909	18,909	98	136	0.2
6530	Real estate agents and managers	4	5	0.5	7	-	10,286	-	81	-	-
ALLEN, LA											
60–	**Finance, insurance, and real estate**	31	32	0.4	146	170	16,027	15,976	2,500	2,568	0.1
6000	Depository institutions	10	10	0.6	67	84	17,493	15,762	1,220	1,345	0.2
6060	Credit unions	3	3	0.9	7	9	10,286	9,333	76	84	0.2
6100	Nondepository institutions	5	6	0.5	-	24	-	11,167	-	249	0.2
6140	Personal credit institutions	4	6	0.7	19	24	12,421	11,167	228	249	0.3
6400	Insurance agents, brokers, and service	5	6	0.3	17	23	19,059	23,478	371	407	0.1
6500	Real estate	7	7	0.3	7	-	8,000	-	54	-	-
6510	Real estate operators and lessors	4	4	0.3	4	4	9,000	9,000	35	36	0.0
ASCENSION, LA											
60–	**Finance, insurance, and real estate**	97	95	1.0	668	692	24,976	24,173	15,371	16,574	0.8
6000	Depository institutions	21	21	1.2	248	256	20,419	17,938	5,286	5,792	0.9
6020	Commercial banks	13	13	1.1	221	228	20,760	17,860	4,803	5,257	0.9
6060	Credit unions	8	8	2.3	27	28	17,630	18,571	483	535	1.5
6100	Nondepository institutions	22	20	1.7	108	80	16,111	17,550	1,632	1,450	1.0
6140	Personal credit institutions	20	18	2.0	105	-	15,924	-	1,558	-	-
6300	Insurance carriers	10	9	1.1	137	147	43,766	42,803	4,037	4,425	1.0
6400	Insurance agents, brokers, and service	22	21	1.0	80	97	16,950	17,237	1,727	1,983	0.7
6510	Real estate operators and lessors	7	9	0.7	23	27	9,043	8,000	192	307	0.4
6530	Real estate agents and managers	4	7	0.7	9	-	10,667	-	105	-	-
ASSUMPTION, LA											
60–	**Finance, insurance, and real estate**	17	19	0.2	129	129	16,620	17,798	2,704	2,671	0.1
6400	Insurance agents, brokers, and service	7	6	0.3	-	33	-	17,939	-	754	0.3
6500	Real estate	4	6	0.2	11	20	9,091	10,600	121	235	0.1
AVOYELLES, LA											
60–	**Finance, insurance, and real estate**	71	69	0.8	711	667	17,840	17,547	12,896	11,524	0.6
6000	Depository institutions	12	12	0.7	166	172	18,699	18,372	3,417	3,920	0.6
6100	Nondepository institutions	14	14	1.2	83	40	22,940	17,500	1,905	688	0.5
6140	Personal credit institutions	12	10	1.1	-	32	-	16,625	-	485	0.6
6310	Life insurance	3	3	0.9	51	-	17,412	-	958	-	-
6400	Insurance agents, brokers, and service	24	21	1.0	77	75	13,403	14,400	1,102	1,179	0.4
6510	Real estate operators and lessors	12	14	1.0	28	-	8,143	-	245	-	-
BEAUREGARD, LA											
60–	**Finance, insurance, and real estate**	47	49	0.5	290	320	24,193	18,838	6,687	6,894	0.3
6000	Depository institutions	11	11	0.6	104	111	18,500	17,766	1,982	2,078	0.3
6020	Commercial banks	7	7	0.6	86	92	16,605	15,783	1,579	1,662	0.3
6100	Nondepository institutions	7	7	0.6	-	18	-	20,222	-	389	0.3
6300	Insurance carriers	5	5	0.6	69	130	26,609	21,200	1,733	3,451	0.8

Source: County Business Patterns, 1992/93, CBP-92/93-1, U.S. Department of Commerce, Washington, D.C., April 1995. SIC categories for which data were suppressed or not available for both 1992 and 1993 are *not* displayed. The employment columns represent mid-March employment in the year. Pay per employee is calculated by dividing 1st Quarter payroll, annualized, by mid-March employment. The columns headed "% State" show the county's percentage of the state total for the SIC in 1993; for example, 0.9% for SIC 6030 means that the county had 0.9 percent of the state's total establishments (or payroll) in SIC 6030 in 1993. A dash (-) is used to indicate that data are not available or cannot be calculated; *nec* means not elsewhere classified.

Continued on next page.

SIC	Industry	No. Establishments			Employment		Pay / Employee		Annual Payroll ($ 000)		
		1992	1993	% State	1992	1993	1992	1993	1992	1993	% State
BEAUREGARD, LA - [continued]											
6400	Insurance agents, brokers, and service	11	12	0.6	80	33	30,700	13,333	2,244	421	0.2
6500	Real estate	10	12	0.5	14	-	18,857	-	181	-	-
6510	Real estate operators and lessors	2	4	0.3	-	4	-	4,000	-	91	0.1
6530	Real estate agents and managers	5	6	0.6	7	13	25,714	12,308	102	172	0.2
BIENVILLE, LA											
60 -	**Finance, insurance, and real estate**	24	26	0.3	142	145	20,310	19,890	3,533	2,964	0.2
6000	Depository institutions	6	6	0.3	77	78	19,117	18,667	1,591	1,581	0.2
6020	Commercial banks	6	6	0.5	77	78	19,117	18,667	1,591	1,581	0.3
6400	Insurance agents, brokers, and service	7	8	0.4	24	36	24,833	22,333	614	749	0.3
6500	Real estate	7	7	0.3	10	9	6,400	6,222	58	57	0.0
6510	Real estate operators and lessors	3	3	0.2	3	-	8,000	-	22	-	-
6553	Cemetery subdividers and developers	2	3	4.2	-	4	-	3,000	-	12	0.1
BOSSIER, LA											
60 -	**Finance, insurance, and real estate**	129	124	1.4	950	892	17,604	19,471	18,053	19,734	1.0
6000	Depository institutions	26	26	1.5	397	416	18,428	19,875	8,333	8,947	1.4
6020	Commercial banks	20	20	1.6	265	260	17,962	20,123	5,687	5,952	1.1
6100	Nondepository institutions	12	13	1.1	49	-	22,041	-	1,094	-	-
6200	Security and commodity brokers	3	3	1.1	5	-	8,800	-	48	-	-
6300	Insurance carriers	19	13	1.6	230	48	18,296	28,667	4,077	1,481	0.3
6310	Life insurance	6	3	0.9	54	-	20,000	-	973	-	-
6400	Insurance agents, brokers, and service	25	24	1.1	116	114	18,448	18,000	2,304	2,233	0.8
6500	Real estate	39	39	1.5	143	152	12,643	13,579	2,050	2,583	1.2
6510	Real estate operators and lessors	20	23	1.7	94	102	12,000	10,902	1,244	1,336	1.6
6530	Real estate agents and managers	13	14	1.4	38	-	11,579	-	421	-	-
6700	Holding and other investment offices	5	6	1.8	10	-	12,800	-	147	-	-
CADDO, LA											
60 -	**Finance, insurance, and real estate**	658	651	7.2	5,391	5,049	22,313	23,035	120,870	117,394	6.0
6000	Depository institutions	101	108	6.1	1,884	1,738	20,117	21,922	35,852	37,406	5.7
6020	Commercial banks	66	68	5.6	1,657	1,486	20,478	22,404	31,522	32,303	5.7
6060	Credit unions	29	34	9.9	182	208	15,560	17,423	3,012	3,818	10.5
6100	Nondepository institutions	75	68	5.9	468	451	22,718	21,588	12,156	11,066	8.0
6140	Personal credit institutions	59	51	5.7	338	334	21,432	20,790	8,410	7,447	9.2
6160	Mortgage bankers and brokers	13	14	8.9	99	-	26,667	-	3,007	-	-
6200	Security and commodity brokers	28	23	8.3	156	160	56,897	54,525	8,802	8,843	6.6
6210	Security brokers and dealers	21	17	9.3	145	135	59,890	62,548	8,587	8,523	7.1
6280	Security and commodity services	6	6	6.6	-	25	-	11,200	-	320	2.4
6300	Insurance carriers	77	72	9.0	1,102	992	28,189	28,093	29,827	26,603	6.0
6310	Life insurance	46	45	13.9	833	772	27,227	25,130	22,136	20,019	10.3
6324	Hospital and medical service plans	4	4	23.5	-	25	-	29,440	-	563	3.4
6330	Fire, marine, and casualty insurance	20	16	5.0	182	130	35,692	47,969	5,735	4,481	2.5
6370	Pension, health, and welfare funds	5	4	4.3	57	60	17,754	20,267	1,085	1,344	14.1
6400	Insurance agents, brokers, and service	156	156	7.2	811	686	22,392	23,773	20,007	17,420	6.3
6500	Real estate	180	176	6.8	881	902	13,376	14,058	12,329	13,097	5.9
6510	Real estate operators and lessors	80	90	6.6	318	384	10,654	10,167	3,379	3,979	4.8
6530	Real estate agents and managers	64	57	5.9	385	331	14,992	16,713	5,961	5,772	5.7
6540	Title abstract offices	8	10	13.9	34	73	24,235	20,767	1,004	1,743	14.9
6552	Subdividers and developers, n.e.c.	12	13	14.1	47	63	17,532	20,698	929	1,089	7.6
6553	Cemetery subdividers and developers	4	5	7.0	54	51	8,667	8,314	495	496	4.3
6700	Holding and other investment offices	41	48	14.2	89	120	21,079	24,067	1,897	2,959	3.7
6732	Educational, religious, etc. trusts	4	4	7.4	10	11	20,800	22,182	218	258	6.5
6733	Trusts, n.e.c.	11	15	22.1	31	46	16,129	12,435	518	693	20.7
6792	Oil royalty traders	11	14	28.6	16	-	24,750	-	372	-	-
6799	Investors, n.e.c.	8	10	15.6	15	21	22,400	19,619	331	353	3.5

Source: County Business Patterns, 1992/93, CBP-92/93-1, U.S. Department of Commerce, Washington, D.C., April 1995. SIC categories for which data were suppressed or not available for both 1992 and 1993 are not displayed. The employment columns represent mid-March employment in the year. Pay per employee is calculated by dividing 1st Quarter payroll, annualized, by mid-March employment. The columns headed "% State" show the county's percentage of the state total for the SIC in 1993; for example, 0.9% for SIC 6030 means that the county had 0.9 percent of the state's total establishments (or payroll) in SIC 6030 in 1993. A dash (-) is used to indicate that data are not available or cannot be calculated; nec means not elsewhere classified.

SIC	Industry	No. Establishments			Employment		Pay / Employee		Annual Payroll ($ 000)		
		1992	1993	% State	1992	1993	1992	1993	1992	1993	% State
CALCASIEU, LA											
60 –	**Finance, insurance, and real estate**	382	397	*4.4*	2,875	2,873	20,710	21,129	62,610	65,899	*3.3*
6000	Depository institutions	78	79	*4.5*	1,277	1,273	19,070	20,528	24,939	28,756	*4.4*
6020	Commercial banks	52	52	*4.3*	1,083	1,074	19,162	21,274	21,365	25,012	*4.4*
6140	Personal credit institutions	34	32	*3.6*	139	164	20,719	17,927	2,907	2,904	*3.6*
6200	Security and commodity brokers	12	13	*4.7*	68	62	64,118	65,935	4,228	4,510	*3.4*
6300	Insurance carriers	42	35	*4.4*	332	222	24,940	29,676	8,686	6,694	*1.5*
6310	Life insurance	14	10	*3.1*	236	143	21,966	24,056	5,359	3,731	*1.9*
6400	Insurance agents, brokers, and service	72	81	*3.7*	339	380	22,608	22,368	8,870	9,659	*3.5*
6500	Real estate	124	135	*5.2*	539	581	12,920	11,373	7,729	7,559	*3.4*
6510	Real estate operators and lessors	58	67	*4.9*	225	319	12,587	10,031	3,123	3,600	*4.3*
6530	Real estate agents and managers	45	53	*5.5*	173	197	15,491	13,503	2,915	3,019	*3.0*
6540	Title abstract offices	2	3	*4.2*	-	38	-	12,947	-	646	*5.5*
6552	Subdividers and developers, n.e.c.	6	5	*5.4*	12	9	10,333	12,889	132	153	*1.1*
6553	Cemetery subdividers and developers	5	4	*5.6*	74	18	9,135	7,778	750	120	*1.0*
6700	Holding and other investment offices	15	13	*3.8*	164	164	28,415	32,024	4,823	5,124	*6.3*
6799	Investors, n.e.c.	3	4	*6.3*	10	-	34,400	-	347	-	-
CALDWELL, LA											
60 –	**Finance, insurance, and real estate**	15	13	*0.1*	87	81	16,414	19,753	1,645	1,928	*0.1*
6000	Depository institutions	4	4	*0.2*	68	63	17,118	19,365	1,354	1,460	*0.2*
6500	Real estate	5	5	*0.2*	6	-	4,667	-	28	-	-
CAMERON, LA											
60 –	**Finance, insurance, and real estate**	12	12	*0.1*	76	-	16,632	-	1,165	-	-
6400	Insurance agents, brokers, and service	3	3	*0.1*	7	9	13,143	12,000	90	87	*0.0*
CATAHOULA, LA											
60 –	**Finance, insurance, and real estate**	16	14	*0.2*	92	83	17,435	19,422	1,740	1,659	*0.1*
6000	Depository institutions	6	6	*0.3*	62	59	17,548	20,678	1,155	1,230	*0.2*
6020	Commercial banks	6	6	*0.5*	62	59	17,548	20,678	1,155	1,230	*0.2*
6100	Nondepository institutions	3	2	*0.2*	8	-	24,000	-	190	-	-
6140	Personal credit institutions	3	2	*0.2*	8	-	24,000	-	190	-	-
6400	Insurance agents, brokers, and service	4	4	*0.2*	11	11	13,455	13,455	166	178	*0.1*
CLAIBORNE, LA											
60 –	**Finance, insurance, and real estate**	21	21	*0.2*	-	122	-	15,279	-	2,236	*0.1*
6000	Depository institutions	5	5	*0.3*	64	76	15,562	16,211	1,132	1,494	*0.2*
6100	Nondepository institutions	4	5	*0.4*	9	11	15,556	12,000	145	167	*0.1*
6140	Personal credit institutions	4	5	*0.6*	9	11	15,556	12,000	145	167	*0.2*
6400	Insurance agents, brokers, and service	6	6	*0.3*	28	24	16,857	15,500	472	461	*0.2*
6500	Real estate	4	4	*0.2*	6	-	11,333	-	65	-	-
6510	Real estate operators and lessors	3	3	*0.2*	-	3	-	9,333	-	25	*0.0*
CONCORDIA, LA											
60 –	**Finance, insurance, and real estate**	23	20	*0.2*	136	166	18,647	17,229	2,562	3,250	*0.2*
6100	Nondepository institutions	4	5	*0.4*	16	14	12,500	14,000	185	171	*0.1*
6140	Personal credit institutions	4	4	*0.4*	16	-	12,500	-	185	-	-
6400	Insurance agents, brokers, and service	8	7	*0.3*	19	23	17,895	14,087	332	357	*0.1*
DE SOTO, LA											
60 –	**Finance, insurance, and real estate**	55	52	*0.6*	225	252	17,707	17,460	4,194	4,548	*0.2*
6000	Depository institutions	13	13	*0.7*	123	133	18,016	17,955	2,392	2,607	*0.4*
6020	Commercial banks	11	11	*0.9*	117	-	18,427	-	2,367	-	-
6100	Nondepository institutions	8	7	*0.6*	26	18	12,154	15,778	364	316	*0.2*
6140	Personal credit institutions	8	6	*0.7*	26	-	12,154	-	364	-	-

Source: County Business Patterns, 1992/93, CBP-92/93-1, U.S. Department of Commerce, Washington, D.C., April 1995. SIC categories for which data were suppressed or not available for both 1992 and 1993 are *not* displayed. The employment columns represent mid-March employment in the year. Pay per employee is calculated by dividing 1st Quarter payroll, annualized, by mid-March employment. The columns headed "% State" show the county's percentage of the state total for the SIC in 1993; for example, 0.9% for SIC 6030 means that the county had 0.9 percent of the state's total establishments (or payroll) in SIC 6030 in 1993. A dash (-) is used to indicate that data are not available or cannot be calculated; *nec* means not elsewhere classified.

Continued on next page.

SIC	Industry	No. Establishments			Employment		Pay / Employee		Annual Payroll ($ 000)		
		1992	1993	% State	1992	1993	1992	1993	1992	1993	% State
DE SOTO, LA - [continued]											
6400	Insurance agents, brokers, and service	8	9	0.4	17	34	9,412	6,588	177	215	0.1
6510	Real estate operators and lessors	15	13	1.0	27	-	25,185	-	655	-	-
6700	Holding and other investment offices	4	3	0.9	7	8	12,000	11,500	61	76	0.1
EAST BATON ROUGE, LA											
60 –	**Finance, insurance, and real estate**	1,153	1,198	13.2	12,718	13,309	24,775	23,838	317,362	338,879	17.2
6000	Depository institutions	184	183	10.4	3,927	3,930	23,407	22,013	88,832	92,809	14.1
6020	Commercial banks	132	133	10.9	3,050	3,327	24,550	22,409	75,478	80,075	14.2
6030	Savings institutions	17	10	6.5	421	88	18,964	22,591	4,199	2,379	5.0
6060	Credit unions	30	35	10.2	350	418	19,737	18,555	6,950	8,083	22.2
6090	Functions closely related to banking	5	5	10.4	106	97	20,302	22,804	2,205	2,272	-
6100	Nondepository institutions	160	172	15.0	875	924	23,054	21,784	22,214	23,756	17.1
6110	Federal and Federally-sponsored credit	4	2	6.1	11	-	26,182	-	289	-	-
6140	Personal credit institutions	127	133	14.9	721	709	22,791	20,220	18,297	17,430	21.5
6160	Mortgage bankers and brokers	22	28	17.7	114	159	23,649	27,899	3,042	5,014	10.5
6200	Security and commodity brokers	48	46	16.6	291	333	62,777	59,375	17,762	20,507	15.4
6210	Security brokers and dealers	30	25	13.7	244	234	66,066	75,282	15,527	16,818	14.0
6280	Security and commodity services	18	21	23.1	47	99	45,702	21,778	2,235	3,689	28.1
6300	Insurance carriers	150	133	16.6	3,485	3,453	26,856	26,873	94,678	92,404	20.9
6310	Life insurance	47	43	13.3	1,303	1,211	25,501	26,375	32,514	31,343	16.2
6321	Accident and health insurance	10	11	35.5	801	776	25,573	28,036	21,275	23,660	84.0
6324	Hospital and medical service plans	6	4	23.5	490	531	26,106	23,540	12,423	12,452	76.0
6330	Fire, marine, and casualty insurance	58	54	17.0	598	740	36,027	30,724	23,297	21,033	11.5
6370	Pension, health, and welfare funds	21	15	16.0	110	75	11,855	11,680	1,137	951	10.0
6400	Insurance agents, brokers, and service	269	281	13.0	1,434	1,815	27,174	25,155	38,085	50,466	18.3
6500	Real estate	290	335	12.9	1,791	1,790	14,140	13,093	26,671	28,731	12.9
6510	Real estate operators and lessors	120	153	11.3	684	785	12,515	12,158	9,244	10,877	13.1
6530	Real estate agents and managers	124	150	15.5	670	840	14,251	12,233	10,721	12,483	12.4
6540	Title abstract offices	6	7	9.7	13	31	27,077	19,613	325	889	7.6
6552	Subdividers and developers, n.e.c.	11	16	17.4	183	14	19,541	88,857	2,825	2,143	14.9
6553	Cemetery subdividers and developers	5	4	5.6	176	115	11,795	14,643	1,985	2,065	17.7
6700	Holding and other investment offices	45	42	12.4	299	552	45,418	24,942	16,346	15,700	19.4
6710	Holding offices	9	12	16.0	184	444	54,717	24,486	13,208	13,211	23.4
6720	Investment offices	3	-	-	9	-	14,222	-	177	-	-
6732	Educational, religious, etc. trusts	7	7	13.0	16	14	20,750	25,714	320	379	9.6
6733	Trusts, n.e.c.	14	10	14.7	34	50	21,647	10,640	874	513	15.3
6799	Investors, n.e.c.	4	5	7.8	23	-	50,783	-	694	-	-
EAST CARROLL, LA											
60 –	**Finance, insurance, and real estate**	11	11	0.1	66	65	18,545	18,954	1,298	1,355	0.1
6100	Nondepository institutions	5	4	0.3	10	-	13,600	-	132	-	-
6140	Personal credit institutions	3	2	0.2	7	-	10,286	-	68	-	-
6400	Insurance agents, brokers, and service	3	3	0.1	-	12	-	19,000	-	212	0.1
EAST FELICIANA, LA											
60 –	**Finance, insurance, and real estate**	19	19	0.2	156	128	16,436	16,344	2,761	2,381	0.1
6000	Depository institutions	7	7	0.4	90	89	16,933	16,360	1,603	1,689	0.3
6400	Insurance agents, brokers, and service	6	6	0.3	18	16	12,222	16,750	254	317	0.1
EVANGELINE, LA											
60 –	**Finance, insurance, and real estate**	55	58	0.6	305	376	15,200	14,340	4,923	5,770	0.3
6000	Depository institutions	14	14	0.8	164	240	18,634	15,900	3,311	4,063	0.6
6020	Commercial banks	11	11	0.9	147	217	19,646	16,903	3,135	3,940	0.7
6100	Nondepository institutions	9	11	1.0	36	39	15,889	15,385	636	657	0.5
6400	Insurance agents, brokers, and service	13	15	0.7	36	36	9,778	9,222	323	371	0.1

Source: County Business Patterns, 1992/93, CBP-92/93-1, U.S. Department of Commerce, Washington, D.C., April 1995. SIC categories for which data were suppressed or not available for both 1992 and 1993 are *not* displayed. The employment columns represent mid-March employment in the year. Pay per employee is calculated by dividing 1st Quarter payroll, annualized, by mid-March employment. The columns headed "% State" show the county's percentage of the state total for the SIC in 1993; for example, 0.9% for SIC 6030 means that the county had 0.9 percent of the state's total establishments (or payroll) in SIC 6030 in 1993. A dash (-) is used to indicate that data are not available or cannot be calculated; *nec* means not elsewhere classified.

Continued on next page.

SIC	Industry	No. Establishments			Employment		Pay / Employee		Annual Payroll ($ 000)		
		1992	1993	% State	1992	1993	1992	1993	1992	1993	% State
EVANGELINE, LA - [continued]											
6500	Real estate	14	15	0.6	42	-	4,762	-	230	-	-
6510	Real estate operators and lessors	8	10	0.7	19	-	6,316	-	131	-	-
6530	Real estate agents and managers	3	3	0.3	-	4	-	2,000	-	13	0.0
FRANKLIN, LA											
60 –	**Finance, insurance, and real estate**	36	41	0.5	235	213	17,549	14,967	4,304	3,881	0.2
6000	Depository institutions	8	9	0.5	111	109	19,315	18,385	2,324	2,349	0.4
6020	Commercial banks	8	8	0.7	111	-	19,315	-	2,324	-	-
6100	Nondepository institutions	8	9	0.8	46	26	22,435	19,077	971	471	0.3
6400	Insurance agents, brokers, and service	12	13	0.6	40	46	12,600	10,696	541	574	0.2
6500	Real estate	5	7	0.3	7	9	10,857	10,222	87	181	0.1
GRANT, LA											
60 –	**Finance, insurance, and real estate**	10	11	0.1	-	-	-	-	-	-	-
6400	Insurance agents, brokers, and service	3	3	0.1	-	5	-	8,000	-	45	0.0
6500	Real estate	3	2	0.1	3	-	8,000	-	32	-	-
IBERIA, LA											
60 –	**Finance, insurance, and real estate**	154	144	1.6	952	967	19,092	20,054	18,781	19,404	1.0
6000	Depository institutions	43	36	2.0	471	510	18,718	18,800	8,722	9,261	1.4
6060	Credit unions	8	6	1.7	-	14	-	5,714	-	80	0.2
6100	Nondepository institutions	22	22	1.9	72	-	19,389	-	1,399	-	-
6140	Personal credit institutions	22	22	2.5	72	-	19,389	-	1,399	-	-
6300	Insurance carriers	12	11	1.4	148	110	26,000	37,782	3,909	3,897	0.9
6400	Insurance agents, brokers, and service	33	33	1.5	127	129	18,677	18,543	2,761	2,670	1.0
6500	Real estate	38	38	1.5	122	136	10,590	9,912	1,416	1,517	0.7
6510	Real estate operators and lessors	21	23	1.7	78	85	8,872	9,129	800	930	1.1
6530	Real estate agents and managers	7	7	0.7	11	-	8,727	-	130	-	-
6553	Cemetery subdividers and developers	5	6	8.5	-	32	-	6,375	-	189	1.6
IBERVILLE, LA											
60 –	**Finance, insurance, and real estate**	49	50	0.5	280	278	20,171	20,201	5,882	5,981	0.3
6000	Depository institutions	17	17	1.0	207	217	21,546	21,493	4,574	4,742	0.7
6020	Commercial banks	12	12	1.0	180	186	21,711	22,129	4,006	4,122	0.7
6100	Nondepository institutions	11	11	1.0	30	26	14,933	15,846	515	532	0.4
6140	Personal credit institutions	9	9	1.0	26	-	15,538	-	456	-	-
6400	Insurance agents, brokers, and service	6	5	0.2	12	10	10,667	13,200	124	158	0.1
6500	Real estate	11	10	0.4	25	17	17,280	6,588	425	147	0.1
6510	Real estate operators and lessors	8	7	0.5	20	11	18,200	2,545	342	68	0.1
6530	Real estate agents and managers	3	3	0.3	5	6	13,600	14,000	83	79	0.1
6700	Holding and other investment offices	1	3	0.9	-	3	-	16,000	-	62	0.1
JACKSON, LA											
60 –	**Finance, insurance, and real estate**	27	27	0.3	-	140	-	17,400	-	2,791	0.1
6000	Depository institutions	6	6	0.3	75	71	20,960	21,014	1,741	1,815	0.3
6100	Nondepository institutions	7	6	0.5	19	21	19,368	15,810	345	308	0.2
6140	Personal credit institutions	7	6	0.7	19	21	19,368	15,810	345	308	0.4
6400	Insurance agents, brokers, and service	6	6	0.3	-	32	-	12,250	-	404	0.1
6500	Real estate	6	7	0.3	6	-	8,000	-	48	-	-
6530	Real estate agents and managers	3	1	0.1	3	-	8,000	-	24	-	-
JEFFERSON, LA											
60 –	**Finance, insurance, and real estate**	1,172	1,232	13.5	11,101	10,990	24,912	24,845	279,013	288,653	14.6
6000	Depository institutions	156	159	9.0	2,309	2,450	20,172	20,256	48,396	52,862	8.0
6020	Commercial banks	82	82	6.7	1,761	1,881	20,661	20,940	37,740	42,077	7.5
6030	Savings institutions	33	32	20.8	404	387	19,525	19,349	8,209	7,889	16.5
6060	Credit unions	28	33	9.6	118	138	16,746	16,029	2,054	2,318	6.4
6090	Functions closely related to banking	13	12	25.0	26	44	12,615	12,273	393	578	-

Source: County Business Patterns, 1992/93, CBP-92/93-1, U.S. Department of Commerce, Washington, D.C., April 1995. SIC categories for which data were suppressed or not available for both 1992 and 1993 are not displayed. The employment columns represent mid-March employment in the year. Pay per employee is calculated by dividing 1st Quarter payroll, annualized, by mid-March employment. The columns headed "% State" show the county's percentage of the state total for the SIC in 1993; for example, 0.9% for SIC 6030 means that the county had 0.9 percent of the state's total establishments (or payroll) in SIC 6030 in 1993. A dash (-) is used to indicate that data are not available or cannot be calculated; nec means not elsewhere classified.

Continued on next page.

SIC	Industry	No. Establishments			Employment		Pay / Employee		Annual Payroll ($ 000)		
		1992	1993	% State	1992	1993	1992	1993	1992	1993	% State
JEFFERSON, LA - [continued]											
6100	Nondepository institutions	119	127	*11.1*	721	762	26,080	22,420	19,557	20,339	*14.6*
6140	Personal credit institutions	84	75	*8.4*	527	553	25,040	20,514	12,983	11,841	*14.6*
6150	Business credit institutions	7	13	*21.7*	22	-	36,545	-	867	-	*-*
6160	Mortgage bankers and brokers	27	38	*24.1*	165	178	28,145	27,416	5,547	6,905	*14.4*
6210	Security brokers and dealers	15	11	*6.0*	69	70	65,797	73,600	4,516	5,744	*4.8*
6300	Insurance carriers	163	147	*18.3*	2,484	2,435	35,214	35,915	86,917	84,210	*19.1*
6310	Life insurance	54	50	*15.5*	1,055	1,019	32,557	35,474	33,726	33,438	*17.3*
6321	Accident and health insurance	7	5	*16.1*	-	42	-	37,143	-	1,480	*5.3*
6324	Hospital and medical service plans	4	4	*23.5*	-	80	-	29,550	-	1,949	*11.9*
6330	Fire, marine, and casualty insurance	75	67	*21.1*	1,145	1,139	38,243	37,124	43,765	42,018	*23.0*
6370	Pension, health, and welfare funds	13	16	*17.0*	69	77	18,957	16,468	1,494	1,521	*16.0*
6400	Insurance agents, brokers, and service	351	369	*17.0*	2,391	2,073	25,862	26,427	59,179	60,121	*21.8*
6500	Real estate	310	355	*13.7*	2,703	2,735	16,167	16,048	45,883	49,269	*22.2*
6510	Real estate operators and lessors	122	162	*11.9*	891	791	15,044	14,756	13,608	13,137	*15.8*
6530	Real estate agents and managers	138	161	*16.6*	1,339	1,623	16,311	16,143	22,901	28,548	*28.4*
6540	Title abstract offices	11	16	*22.2*	47	130	18,383	17,600	1,371	3,326	*28.5*
6552	Subdividers and developers, n.e.c.	9	8	*8.7*	110	61	22,655	25,705	2,715	1,760	*12.2*
6553	Cemetery subdividers and developers	4	5	*7.0*	134	130	13,493	16,646	1,883	2,448	*21.0*
6700	Holding and other investment offices	40	39	*11.5*	312	343	38,141	38,262	12,867	14,011	*17.3*
6710	Holding offices	7	9	*12.0*	206	231	45,087	43,117	10,134	10,716	*19.0*
6733	Trusts, n.e.c.	4	5	*7.4*	15	11	16,800	37,455	222	387	*11.6*
6794	Patent owners and lessors	5	8	*66.7*	-	51	-	26,431	-	1,537	*92.0*
JEFFERSON DAVIS, LA											
60 –	**Finance, insurance, and real estate**	54	55	*0.6*	340	324	17,282	18,296	5,680	5,747	*0.3*
6000	Depository institutions	16	17	*1.0*	222	213	17,604	18,648	3,663	3,857	*0.6*
6020	Commercial banks	14	14	*1.2*	-	205	-	19,044	-	3,782	*0.7*
6060	Credit unions	2	3	*0.9*	-	8	-	8,500	-	75	*0.2*
6100	Nondepository institutions	10	9	*0.8*	37	27	18,595	18,667	533	460	*0.3*
6400	Insurance agents, brokers, and service	15	13	*0.6*	50	50	15,040	15,680	764	767	*0.3*
6500	Real estate	9	12	*0.5*	22	26	9,636	8,923	217	238	*0.1*
6510	Real estate operators and lessors	3	7	*0.5*	-	12	-	9,667	-	127	*0.2*
6530	Real estate agents and managers	4	4	*0.4*	7	-	10,857	-	75	-	*-*
LAFAYETTE, LA											
60 –	**Finance, insurance, and real estate**	499	528	*5.8*	3,143	3,730	25,366	22,402	81,481	88,059	*4.5*
6000	Depository institutions	74	77	*4.4*	1,007	1,048	21,414	20,744	21,858	23,719	*3.6*
6020	Commercial banks	50	52	*4.3*	799	806	21,947	20,868	17,539	18,692	*3.3*
6030	Savings institutions	9	8	*5.2*	147	166	20,735	22,819	3,302	3,828	*8.0*
6060	Credit unions	13	14	*4.1*	-	55	-	16,655	-	989	*2.7*
6090	Functions closely related to banking	2	3	*6.3*	-	21	-	10,286	-	210	*-*
6100	Nondepository institutions	48	51	*4.5*	237	306	22,481	19,712	5,496	6,692	*4.8*
6140	Personal credit institutions	36	37	*4.1*	193	229	23,254	20,070	4,636	4,764	*5.9*
6150	Business credit institutions	5	6	*10.0*	30	56	16,667 ·	16,000	494	1,048	*15.4*
6160	Mortgage bankers and brokers	5	7	*4.4*	10	-	21,600	-	207	-	*-*
6200	Security and commodity brokers	31	31	*11.2*	147	160	64,354	62,475	9,482	10,200	*7.6*
6210	Security brokers and dealers	27	27	*14.8*	143	155	65,622	64,000	9,386	10,098	*8.4*
6280	Security and commodity services	3	4	*4.4*	-	5	-	15,200	-	102	*0.8*
6300	Insurance carriers	51	49	*6.1*	537	596	32,536	30,215	18,038	18,036	*4.1*
6310	Life insurance	22	21	*6.5*	424	408	30,849	31,892	13,489	12,999	*6.7*
6330	Fire, marine, and casualty insurance	18	16	*5.0*	-	78	-	42,872	-	3,373	*1.8*
6370	Pension, health, and welfare funds	5	7	*7.4*	-	73	-	4,932	-	469	*4.9*
6400	Insurance agents, brokers, and service	128	131	*6.0*	509	498	24,558	24,755	12,560	12,289	*4.5*
6500	Real estate	150	165	*6.4*	628	822	13,197	11,976	9,894	11,998	*5.4*
6510	Real estate operators and lessors	79	93	*6.8*	387	564	11,938	9,794	5,200	6,289	*7.6*
6530	Real estate agents and managers	47	64	*6.6*	175	229	16,457	16,472	3,830	4,829	*4.8*
6540	Title abstract offices	3	4	*5.6*	7	7	19,429	45,714	130	622	*5.3*
6700	Holding and other investment offices	17	24	*7.1*	78	300	65,538	18,707	4,153	5,125	*6.3*

Source: County Business Patterns, 1992/93, CBP-92/93-1, U.S. Department of Commerce, Washington, D.C., April 1995. SIC categories for which data were suppressed or not available for both 1992 and 1993 are *not* displayed. The employment columns represent mid-March employment in the year. Pay per employee is calculated by dividing 1st Quarter payroll, annualized, by mid-March employment. The columns headed "% State" show the county's percentage of the state total for the SIC in 1993; for example, 0.9% for SIC 6030 means that the county had 0.9 percent of the state's total establishments (or payroll) in SIC 6030 in 1993. A dash (-) is used to indicate that data are not available or cannot be calculated; *nec* means not elsewhere classified.

Continued on next page.

SIC	Industry	No. Establishments			Employment		Pay / Employee		Annual Payroll ($ 000)		
		1992	1993	% State	1992	1993	1992	1993	1992	1993	% State
LAFAYETTE, LA - [continued]											
6710	Holding offices	2	4	5.3	-	58	-	64,138	-	3,096	5.5
6732	Educational, religious, etc. trusts	3	3	5.6	16	16	20,000	20,750	328	324	8.2
6733	Trusts, n.e.c.	3	9	13.2	-	192	-	1,062	-	228	6.8
LAFOURCHE, LA											
60 –	**Finance, insurance, and real estate**	151	147	1.6	988	971	17,579	18,064	18,700	18,324	0.9
6000	Depository institutions	52	52	2.9	548	557	16,080	15,583	9,488	9,356	1.4
6020	Commercial banks	44	44	3.6	462	472	16,286	15,678	8,192	8,360	1.5
6100	Nondepository institutions	23	19	1.7	78	88	23,333	19,864	1,805	1,795	1.3
6140	Personal credit institutions	20	18	2.0	71	-	22,028	-	1,613	-	-
6300	Insurance carriers	11	8	1.0	95	87	24,379	33,471	2,626	2,637	0.6
6310	Life insurance	5	5	1.5	85	-	23,953	-	2,320	-	-
6330	Fire, marine, and casualty insurance	6	3	0.9	10	-	28,000	-	306	-	-
6400	Insurance agents, brokers, and service	35	36	1.7	154	157	20,597	20,510	3,413	3,411	1.2
6500	Real estate	24	26	1.0	96	68	8,875	7,294	918	603	0.3
6510	Real estate operators and lessors	13	15	1.1	73	-	8,822	-	644	-	-
6530	Real estate agents and managers	4	9	0.9	10	30	7,600	4,133	90	146	0.1
LA SALLE, LA											
60 –	**Finance, insurance, and real estate**	20	20	0.2	143	157	14,657	17,070	2,430	2,790	0.1
6000	Depository institutions	8	8	0.5	93	97	13,806	15,258	1,503	1,611	0.2
6020	Commercial banks	8	8	0.7	93	97	13,806	15,258	1,503	1,611	0.3
6100	Nondepository institutions	4	4	0.3	12	-	12,333	-	156	-	-
6140	Personal credit institutions	4	3	0.3	12	9	12,333	14,667	156	130	0.2
6400	Insurance agents, brokers, and service	4	6	0.3	16	24	17,250	19,000	333	488	0.2
LINCOLN, LA											
60 –	**Finance, insurance, and real estate**	104	107	1.2	936	980	19,932	19,433	19,212	19,498	1.0
6000	Depository institutions	21	22	1.2	282	278	19,277	19,568	5,819	4,997	0.8
6020	Commercial banks	16	17	1.4	241	234	19,220	19,453	4,941	4,040	0.7
6100	Nondepository institutions	15	15	1.3	46	65	19,478	21,538	1,201	1,421	1.0
6400	Insurance agents, brokers, and service	26	26	1.2	121	139	16,992	16,489	2,284	2,713	1.0
6500	Real estate	26	27	1.0	96	110	8,708	8,945	809	1,082	0.5
6510	Real estate operators and lessors	11	11	0.8	54	70	9,259	8,400	475	736	0.9
6530	Real estate agents and managers	11	12	1.2	29	31	7,724	10,968	231	286	0.3
6700	Holding and other investment offices	3	4	1.2	93	-	7,785	-	835	-	-
LIVINGSTON, LA											
60 –	**Finance, insurance, and real estate**	58	57	0.6	343	378	18,321	18,720	6,663	7,803	0.4
6000	Depository institutions	15	15	0.9	231	262	19,273	19,282	4,616	5,458	0.8
6100	Nondepository institutions	8	9	0.8	31	31	23,226	22,710	756	731	0.5
6140	Personal credit institutions	8	9	1.0	31	31	23,226	22,710	756	731	0.9
6400	Insurance agents, brokers, and service	18	17	0.8	42	48	12,381	11,583	580	635	0.2
6500	Real estate	12	11	0.4	26	23	5,077	6,087	119	272	0.1
6510	Real estate operators and lessors	4	3	0.2	11	12	2,545	7,000	27	71	0.1
6530	Real estate agents and managers	4	5	0.5	8	8	3,500	3,500	24	175	0.2
6552	Subdividers and developers, n.e.c.	3	2	2.2	6	-	10,667	-	56	-	-
MADISON, LA											
60 –	**Finance, insurance, and real estate**	24	25	0.3	154	134	15,091	13,701	2,456	2,053	0.1
6000	Depository institutions	4	4	0.2	60	60	16,800	17,267	1,156	1,208	0.2
6020	Commercial banks	4	4	0.3	60	60	16,800	17,267	1,156	1,208	0.2
6400	Insurance agents, brokers, and service	5	5	0.2	10	9	10,000	11,111	113	108	0.0
6500	Real estate	10	9	0.3	49	49	7,673	6,122	336	325	0.1

Source: County Business Patterns, 1992/93, CBP-92/93-1, U.S. Department of Commerce, Washington, D.C., April 1995. SIC categories for which data were suppressed or not available for both 1992 and 1993 are not displayed. The employment columns represent mid-March employment in the year. Pay per employee is calculated by dividing 1st Quarter payroll, annualized, by mid-March employment. The columns headed "% State" show the county's percentage of the state total for the SIC in 1993; for example, 0.9% for SIC 6030 means that the county had 0.9 percent of the state's total establishments (or payroll) in SIC 6030 in 1993. A dash (-) is used to indicate that data are not available or cannot be calculated; nec means not elsewhere classified.

SIC	Industry	No. Establishments			Employment		Pay / Employee		Annual Payroll ($ 000)		
		1992	1993	% State	1992	1993	1992	1993	1992	1993	% State
MOREHOUSE, LA											
60–	**Finance, insurance, and real estate**	45	55	*0.6*	225	231	19,982	21,818	4,869	5,244	*0.3*
6000	Depository institutions	8	9	*0.5*	101	128	23,881	25,281	2,695	3,252	*0.5*
6100	Nondepository institutions	13	13	*1.1*	54	35	17,704	16,114	950	644	*0.5*
6400	Insurance agents, brokers, and service	9	14	*0.6*	19	21	13,053	12,762	275	286	*0.1*
6500	Real estate	8	13	*0.5*	14	16	7,143	8,750	130	148	*0.1*
6510	Real estate operators and lessors	4	7	*0.5*	9	8	8,889	6,000	87	55	*0.1*
NATCHITOCHES, LA											
60–	**Finance, insurance, and real estate**	79	82	*0.9*	427	386	17,283	18,632	7,902	8,404	*0.4*
6000	Depository institutions	14	13	*0.7*	182	201	20,198	19,005	3,596	4,042	*0.6*
6020	Commercial banks	10	10	*0.8*	153	170	19,869	19,247	2,995	3,420	*0.6*
6100	Nondepository institutions	13	11	*1.0*	88	-	9,318	-	973	-	-
6300	Insurance carriers	2	3	*0.4*	-	36	-	10,222	-	748	*0.2*
6400	Insurance agents, brokers, and service	15	14	*0.6*	47	45	14,468	15,467	683	747	*0.3*
6500	Real estate	30	34	*1.3*	54	57	7,481	7,930	445	530	*0.2*
6510	Real estate operators and lessors	16	23	*1.7*	30	-	7,867	-	261	-	-
6530	Real estate agents and managers	9	9	*0.9*	16	18	8,250	8,444	145	164	*0.2*
ORLEANS, LA											
60–	**Finance, insurance, and real estate**	1,074	1,073	*11.8*	14,881	15,093	29,926	27,171	432,299	436,973	*22.2*
6000	Depository institutions	195	208	*11.8*	5,830	5,962	26,769	26,344	156,514	167,384	*25.4*
6020	Commercial banks	86	100	*8.2*	4,387	4,666	27,964	27,544	124,189	138,353	*24.6*
6030	Savings institutions	33	27	*17.5*	803	638	24,468	22,821	18,635	14,858	*31.0*
6060	Credit unions	56	63	*18.3*	306	342	17,556	17,193	5,237	6,028	*16.5*
6100	Nondepository institutions	84	72	*6.3*	772	-	38,218	-	18,763	-	-
6140	Personal credit institutions	62	48	*5.4*	257	209	20,918	20,306	5,627	4,330	*5.3*
6150	Business credit institutions	6	8	*13.3*	288	-	59,583	-	6,825	-	-
6160	Mortgage bankers and brokers	12	16	*10.1*	216	232	31,037	32,845	5,996	8,115	*16.9*
6200	Security and commodity brokers	53	45	*16.2*	907	856	83,713	65,958	70,818	65,599	*49.1*
6210	Security brokers and dealers	35	27	*14.8*	819	745	88,171	68,639	65,879	58,877	*49.0*
6220	Commodity contracts brokers, dealers	4	2	*50.0*	20	-	24,200	-	548	-	-
6280	Security and commodity services	12	16	*17.6*	67	-	47,940	-	4,378	-	-
6300	Insurance carriers	116	99	*12.3*	2,238	2,112	33,966	32,697	70,005	66,455	*15.0*
6310	Life insurance	55	42	*13.0*	1,598	1,416	34,370	34,192	48,232	44,791	*23.1*
6321	Accident and health insurance	4	3	*9.7*	66	-	19,152	-	1,412	-	-
6330	Fire, marine, and casualty insurance	33	31	*9.8*	395	316	38,815	39,228	15,092	12,510	*6.8*
6370	Pension, health, and welfare funds	20	19	*20.2*	91	117	21,978	21,949	2,382	3,236	*34.0*
6400	Insurance agents, brokers, and service	196	197	*9.1*	1,460	1,432	29,249	28,385	45,512	41,857	*15.2*
6500	Real estate	359	380	*14.7*	3,365	3,737	16,590	15,664	60,368	64,996	*29.3*
6510	Real estate operators and lessors	159	188	*13.8*	1,160	1,707	15,072	13,120	18,787	24,140	*29.0*
6530	Real estate agents and managers	142	159	*16.4*	1,633	1,646	16,424	16,644	29,242	29,906	*29.8*
6540	Title abstract offices	4	4	*5.6*	104	102	24,385	22,627	2,556	2,479	*21.3*
6552	Subdividers and developers, n.e.c.	23	16	*17.4*	205	76	22,146	28,895	4,488	3,727	*25.9*
6553	Cemetery subdividers and developers	9	11	*15.5*	150	206	14,933	20,583	2,597	4,741	*40.7*
6700	Holding and other investment offices	68	70	*20.6*	296	509	30,176	30,672	10,137	17,324	*21.4*
6710	Holding offices	18	18	*24.0*	102	161	46,863	50,012	5,665	8,299	*14.7*
6732	Educational, religious, etc. trusts	13	14	*25.9*	75	90	18,613	20,000	1,427	1,730	*43.6*
6733	Trusts, n.e.c.	8	8	*11.8*	16	-	27,000	-	461	-	-
6792	Oil royalty traders	6	11	*22.4*	-	41	-	25,951	-	1,589	*39.6*
6799	Investors, n.e.c.	17	14	*21.9*	42	150	24,952	22,080	1,086	3,663	*36.3*
OUACHITA, LA											
60–	**Finance, insurance, and real estate**	423	425	*4.7*	5,463	5,570	26,325	29,759	150,784	153,462	*7.8*
6000	Depository institutions	63	67	*3.8*	1,104	1,147	22,228	22,392	26,133	27,900	*4.2*
6020	Commercial banks	50	50	*4.1*	1,017	1,049	22,474	22,806	24,365	26,025	*4.6*
6100	Nondepository institutions	60	64	*5.6*	742	841	25,191	25,836	19,389	21,923	*15.8*
6140	Personal credit institutions	49	50	*5.6*	183	184	20,743	16,913	4,115	3,444	*4.3*
6200	Security and commodity brokers	15	13	*4.7*	61	57	72,656	62,386	3,681	3,260	*2.4*

Source: County Business Patterns, 1992/93, CBP-92/93-1, U.S. Department of Commerce, Washington, D.C., April 1995. SIC categories for which data were suppressed or not available for both 1992 and 1993 are not displayed. The employment columns represent mid-March employment in the year. Pay per employee is calculated by dividing 1st Quarter payroll, annualized, by mid-March employment. The columns headed "% State" show the county's percentage of the state total for the SIC in 1993; for example, 0.9% for SIC 6030 means that the county had 0.9 percent of the state's total establishments (or payroll) in SIC 6030 in 1993. A dash (-) is used to indicate that data are not available or cannot be calculated; nec means not elsewhere classified.

Continued on next page.

SIC	Industry	No. Establishments			Employment		Pay / Employee		Annual Payroll ($ 000)		
		1992	1993	% State	1992	1993	1992	1993	1992	1993	% State
OUACHITA, LA - [continued]											
6210	Security brokers and dealers	11	8	4.4	53	49	79,472	68,163	3,452	3,002	2.5
6300	Insurance carriers	48	37	4.6	2,596	2,581	32,091	39,287	87,907	85,190	19.3
6400	Insurance agents, brokers, and service	76	85	3.9	287	307	18,704	20,782	6,157	7,661	2.8
6500	Real estate	146	147	5.7	638	600	10,608	10,573	6,761	6,813	3.1
6510	Real estate operators and lessors	101	105	7.7	415	404	9,234	10,436	3,761	4,280	5.1
6530	Real estate agents and managers	32	37	3.8	180	175	12,800	11,223	2,241	2,292	2.3
6732	Educational, religious, etc. trusts	4	3	5.6	12	14	13,667	14,286	189	225	5.7
6733	Trusts, n.e.c.	3	1	1.5	2	-	8,000	-	19	-	-
PLAQUEMINES, LA											
60 –	**Finance, insurance, and real estate**	47	46	0.5	308	257	24,390	18,490	7,076	5,376	0.3
6000	Depository institutions	10	10	0.6	95	128	18,821	19,969	2,027	2,776	0.4
6100	Nondepository institutions	6	6	0.5	23	25	12,000	11,040	284	295	0.2
6140	Personal credit institutions	6	6	0.7	23	25	12,000	11,040	284	295	0.4
6300	Insurance carriers	5	3	0.4	67	-	35,701	-	1,882	-	-
6400	Insurance agents, brokers, and service	10	11	0.5	85	45	28,471	17,600	2,323	862	0.3
6500	Real estate	16	16	0.6	38	-	16,737	-	560	-	-
6510	Real estate operators and lessors	7	9	0.7	13	-	26,769	-	279	-	-
6530	Real estate agents and managers	3	7	0.7	-	14	-	10,571	-	359	0.4
POINTE COUPEE, LA											
60 –	**Finance, insurance, and real estate**	30	35	0.4	170	176	20,141	20,568	3,484	3,585	0.2
6000	Depository institutions	10	11	0.6	122	119	22,525	25,008	2,845	2,848	0.4
6020	Commercial banks	10	10	0.8	122	-	22,525	-	2,845	-	-
6400	Insurance agents, brokers, and service	10	9	0.4	32	28	16,500	16,000	483	487	0.2
6500	Real estate	7	10	0.4	11	19	5,818	4,211	73	114	0.1
6530	Real estate agents and managers	3	4	0.4	6	9	6,000	3,556	44	54	0.1
RAPIDES, LA											
60 –	**Finance, insurance, and real estate**	300	301	3.3	1,893	1,956	22,434	22,898	43,184	45,963	2.3
6000	Depository institutions	61	64	3.6	649	681	20,709	19,683	13,128	14,243	2.2
6020	Commercial banks	39	43	3.5	528	547	21,818	21,170	11,197	12,365	2.2
6060	Credit unions	18	18	5.2	97	-	16,660	-	1,633	-	-
6090	Functions closely related to banking	4	3	6.3	24	-	12,667	-	298	-	-
6100	Nondepository institutions	40	44	3.8	163	189	20,564	17,714	3,530	3,340	2.4
6140	Personal credit institutions	32	34	3.8	123	155	18,634	15,277	2,409	2,244	2.8
6200	Security and commodity brokers	7	8	2.9	25	27	75,680	80,593	2,025	2,059	1.5
6300	Insurance carriers	38	37	4.6	293	331	27,358	26,743	8,524	8,677	2.0
6310	Life insurance	17	15	4.6	239	252	25,573	26,444	6,397	6,352	3.3
6330	Fire, marine, and casualty insurance	16	18	5.7	-	52	-	37,846	-	2,032	1.1
6400	Insurance agents, brokers, and service	81	73	3.4	374	391	24,995	23,325	9,538	10,187	3.7
6500	Real estate	59	63	2.4	299	250	13,926	13,040	4,124	3,875	1.7
6510	Real estate operators and lessors	25	25	1.8	133	118	11,910	11,424	1,522	1,605	1.9
6530	Real estate agents and managers	23	30	3.1	101	88	16,911	14,455	1,541	1,608	1.6
6540	Title abstract offices	3	6	8.3	10	-	9,200	-	105	-	-
6700	Holding and other investment offices	14	12	3.5	90	87	25,067	53,195	2,315	3,582	4.4
6710	Holding offices	7	3	4.0	71	-	28,282	-	2,076	-	-
6732	Educational, religious, etc. trusts	5	6	11.1	15	-	13,867	-	219	-	-
RED RIVER, LA											
60 –	**Finance, insurance, and real estate**	16	14	0.2	77	76	18,545	19,526	1,497	1,570	0.1
6100	Nondepository institutions	3	2	0.2	4	-	15,000	-	70	-	-
6140	Personal credit institutions	3	2	0.2	4	-	15,000	-	70	-	-
6400	Insurance agents, brokers, and service	5	5	0.2	17	18	16,235	17,778	288	373	0.1
6500	Real estate	4	3	0.1	3	3	9,333	9,333	26	24	0.0

Source: County Business Patterns, 1992/93, CBP-92/93-1, U.S. Department of Commerce, Washington, D.C., April 1995. SIC categories for which data were suppressed or not available for both 1992 and 1993 are *not* displayed. The employment columns represent mid-March employment in the year. Pay per employee is calculated by dividing 1st Quarter payroll, annualized, by mid-March employment. The columns headed "% State" show the county's percentage of the state total for the SIC in 1993; for example, 0.9% for SIC 6030 means that the county had 0.9 percent of the state's total establishments (or payroll) in SIC 6030 in 1993. A dash (-) is used to indicate that data are not available or cannot be calculated; *nec* means not elsewhere classified.

SIC	Industry	No. Establishments			Employment		Pay / Employee		Annual Payroll ($ 000)		
		1992	1993	% State	1992	1993	1992	1993	1992	1993	% State
RICHLAND, LA											
60–	**Finance, insurance, and real estate**	30	32	0.4	192	205	18,083	19,707	3,939	4,204	0.2
6000	Depository institutions	7	7	0.4	122	133	19,902	19,098	2,869	3,015	0.5
6100	Nondepository institutions	7	7	0.6	-	20		12,000		238	0.2
6140	Personal credit institutions	5	5	0.6	13	-	11,692	-	145	-	-
6400	Insurance agents, brokers, and service	8	9	0.4	32	33	19,125	31,030	617	719	0.3
6500	Real estate	6	9	0.3	14	19	10,000	12,421	166	232	0.1
SABINE, LA											
60–	**Finance, insurance, and real estate**	26	26	0.3	186	192	17,226	20,458	3,503	3,737	0.2
6100	Nondepository institutions	8	8	0.7	19	-	14,947	-	288		
6140	Personal credit institutions	8	8	0.9	19	-	14,947	-	288		
6300	Insurance carriers	4	3	0.4	-	5	-	62,400	-	312	0.1
6400	Insurance agents, brokers, and service	3	4	0.2	14	15	21,429	20,267	334	323	0.1
6500	Real estate	3	3	0.1	-	3	-	16,000		53	0.0
ST. BERNARD, LA											
60–	**Finance, insurance, and real estate**	73	71	0.8	510	564	17,271	17,525	9,483	10,624	0.5
6000	Depository institutions	28	29	1.6	377	384	17,326	18,458	6,835	7,514	1.1
6020	Commercial banks	22	22	1.8	345	348	17,368	18,218	6,238	6,739	1.2
6060	Credit unions	3	3	0.9	17	16	15,529	17,250	274	283	0.8
6100	Nondepository institutions	5	4	0.3	20	-	20,800	-	412	-	-
6140	Personal credit institutions	5	4	0.4	20	-	20,800	-	412	-	-
6400	Insurance agents, brokers, and service	15	15	0.7	51	64	12,157	12,438	750	919	0.3
6500	Real estate	19	20	0.8	49	96	17,878	14,792	1,110	1,580	0.7
6510	Real estate operators and lessors	11	13	1.0	32	41	21,500	16,098	835	773	0.9
6530	Real estate agents and managers	4	3	0.3	-	11	-	9,091	-	109	0.1
6552	Subdividers and developers, n.e.c.	3	2	2.2	7	-	9,714	-	119	-	-
ST. CHARLES, LA											
60–	**Finance, insurance, and real estate**	58	60	0.7	294	313	19,728	19,540	6,541	6,606	0.3
6000	Depository institutions	22	24	1.4	192	213	18,229	18,103	3,891	4,100	0.6
6020	Commercial banks	14	14	1.2	148	162	17,703	18,420	2,955	3,106	0.6
6100	Nondepository institutions	5	3	0.3	-	10	-	14,800	-	165	0.1
6140	Personal credit institutions	5	3	0.3	-	10	-	14,800	-	165	0.2
6300	Insurance carriers	5	5	0.6	19	-	50,947	-	1,002	-	-
6400	Insurance agents, brokers, and service	10	11	0.5	25	26	21,280	21,231	766	736	0.3
6500	Real estate	14	16	0.6	39	-	13,436	-	766	-	-
6510	Real estate operators and lessors	4	6	0.4	10	-	8,800	-	611	-	-
6530	Real estate agents and managers	8	9	0.9	17	-	17,882	-	329	-	-
ST. HELENA, LA											
60–	**Finance, insurance, and real estate**	8	8	0.1	-	-	-	-	-	-	-
ST. JAMES, LA											
60–	**Finance, insurance, and real estate**	36	35	0.4	230	238	18,243	16,622	4,461	4,474	0.2
6000	Depository institutions	14	16	0.9	158	169	19,190	16,497	3,160	3,128	0.5
6100	Nondepository institutions	7	5	0.4	28	24	13,000	16,667	379	408	0.3
6140	Personal credit institutions	7	5	0.6	28	24	13,000	16,667	379	408	0.5
6400	Insurance agents, brokers, and service	11	10	0.5	39	38	19,692	19,263	815	823	0.3
6500	Real estate	4	4	0.2	5	7	6,400	5,143	107	115	0.1
ST. JOHN THE BAPTIST, LA											
60–	**Finance, insurance, and real estate**	49	49	0.5	385	495	23,917	21,883	8,113	10,450	0.5
6000	Depository institutions	12	13	0.7	168	191	18,952	17,194	3,192	3,720	0.6
6020	Commercial banks	9	9	0.7	147	167	19,429	17,916	2,850	3,380	0.6
6100	Nondepository institutions	7	6	0.5	23	18	23,130	26,667	503	428	0.3

Source: County Business Patterns, 1992/93, CBP-92/93-1, U.S. Department of Commerce, Washington, D.C., April 1995. SIC categories for which data were suppressed or not available for both 1992 and 1993 are *not* displayed. The employment columns represent mid-March employment in the year. Pay per employee is calculated by dividing 1st Quarter payroll, annualized, by mid-March employment. The columns headed "% State" show the county's percentage of the state total for the SIC in 1993; for example, 0.9% for SIC 6030 means that the county had 0.9 percent of the state's total establishments (or payroll) in SIC 6030 in 1993. A dash (-) is used to indicate that data are not available or cannot be calculated; *nec* means not elsewhere classified.

Continued on next page.

SIC	Industry	No. Establishments			Employment		Pay / Employee		Annual Payroll ($ 000)		
		1992	1993	% State	1992	1993	1992	1993	1992	1993	% State
ST. JOHN THE BAPTIST, LA - [continued]											
6140	Personal credit institutions	7	6	0.7	23	18	23,130	26,667	503	428	0.5
6400	Insurance agents, brokers, and service	15	13	0.6	61	68	18,361	16,353	926	966	0.4
6500	Real estate	8	12	0.5	88	195	31,091	23,918	1,888	3,898	1.8
ST. LANDRY, LA											
60 –	**Finance, insurance, and real estate**	138	141	1.6	977	1,035	17,138	15,915	19,318	19,843	1.0
6000	Depository institutions	33	33	1.9	433	448	18,180	17,938	9,280	9,475	1.4
6020	Commercial banks	25	25	2.1	360	369	18,233	17,886	7,800	7,877	1.4
6100	Nondepository institutions	20	20	1.7	95	106	18,947	19,132	1,970	2,219	1.6
6300	Insurance carriers	10	6	0.7	114	92	14,842	16,000	1,891	1,916	0.4
6310	Life insurance	3	3	0.9	84	-	13,333	-	1,280	-	-
6400	Insurance agents, brokers, and service	35	41	1.9	233	281	15,794	12,783	4,303	4,587	1.7
6500	Real estate	35	38	1.5	88	-	8,455	-	896	-	-
6510	Real estate operators and lessors	23	28	2.1	70	82	6,971	9,073	618	933	1.1
6530	Real estate agents and managers	7	8	0.8	10	12	19,200	11,000	201	150	0.1
ST. MARTIN, LA											
60 –	**Finance, insurance, and real estate**	59	55	0.6	382	350	15,801	18,046	6,725	6,807	0.3
6000	Depository institutions	17	16	0.9	188	179	18,298	18,927	3,770	3,776	0.6
6020	Commercial banks	14	13	1.1	177	166	18,169	18,699	3,553	3,505	0.6
6140	Personal credit institutions	9	9	1.0	43	-	19,907	-	1,022	-	-
6400	Insurance agents, brokers, and service	17	17	0.8	56	61	16,786	17,836	947	1,121	0.4
6500	Real estate	10	9	0.3	74	58	5,514	7,655	498	492	0.2
6510	Real estate operators and lessors	4	7	0.5	13	-	10,154	-	122	-	-
6530	Real estate agents and managers	4	2	0.2	55	-	4,364	-	337	-	-
ST. MARY, LA											
60 –	**Finance, insurance, and real estate**	124	126	1.4	870	762	18,570	19,029	17,867	16,057	0.8
6000	Depository institutions	31	32	1.8	424	426	17,123	18,103	8,543	8,827	1.3
6020	Commercial banks	22	22	1.8	338	306	16,615	17,542	6,860	6,340	1.1
6030	Savings institutions	6	6	3.9	-	111	-	19,784	-	2,353	4.9
6060	Credit unions	3	4	1.2	-	9	-	16,444	-	134	0.4
6100	Nondepository institutions	17	16	1.4	48	49	23,417	30,122	1,036	1,059	0.8
6140	Personal credit institutions	15	15	1.7	45	-	23,467	-	948	-	-
6400	Insurance agents, brokers, and service	26	24	1.1	120	122	19,900	20,230	2,552	2,709	1.0
6500	Real estate	42	45	1.7	201	108	15,363	11,481	3,401	1,704	0.8
6510	Real estate operators and lessors	25	32	2.4	67	86	16,358	11,442	1,111	1,393	1.7
6700	Holding and other investment offices	4	5	1.5	-	46	-	19,130	-	933	1.2
ST. TAMMANY, LA											
60 –	**Finance, insurance, and real estate**	274	298	3.3	1,675	1,971	24,186	24,396	43,025	50,276	2.6
6000	Depository institutions	57	53	3.0	590	679	19,288	19,617	12,190	13,194	2.0
6020	Commercial banks	42	42	3.5	536	615	19,209	19,499	11,091	11,813	2.1
6030	Savings institutions	9	5	3.2	31	41	24,000	24,683	781	1,048	2.2
6060	Credit unions	6	6	1.7	23	23	14,783	13,739	318	333	0.9
6100	Nondepository institutions	26	30	2.6	76	104	36,368	25,462	2,277	3,120	2.2
6140	Personal credit institutions	17	21	2.4	52	73	32,769	16,055	1,238	1,306	1.6
6200	Security and commodity brokers	11	12	4.3	41	66	53,756	62,545	2,188	3,791	2.8
6210	Security brokers and dealers	5	7	3.8	-	56	-	70,429	-	3,423	2.8
6280	Security and commodity services	5	5	5.5	-	10	-	18,400	-	368	2.8
6300	Insurance carriers	23	23	2.9	108	138	40,222	40,783	4,849	5,534	1.3
6310	Life insurance	5	5	1.5	-	67	-	39,701	-	2,253	1.2
6400	Insurance agents, brokers, and service	67	75	3.5	424	467	21,179	25,011	10,604	13,003	4.7
6500	Real estate	79	93	3.6	370	420	17,730	16,695	6,870	8,316	3.7
6510	Real estate operators and lessors	22	30	2.2	43	84	13,302	14,333	568	1,299	1.6
6530	Real estate agents and managers	39	49	5.1	118	152	23,627	22,184	3,072	3,875	3.9

Source: County Business Patterns, 1992/93, CBP-92/93-1, U.S. Department of Commerce, Washington, D.C., April 1995. SIC categories for which data were suppressed or not available for both 1992 and 1993 are *not* displayed. The employment columns represent mid-March employment in the year. Pay per employee is calculated by dividing 1st Quarter payroll, annualized, by mid-March employment. The columns headed "% State" show the county's percentage of the state total for the SIC in 1993; for example, 0.9% for SIC 6030 means that the county had 0.9 percent of the state's total establishments (or payroll) in SIC 6030 in 1993. A dash (-) is used to indicate that data are not available or cannot be calculated; *nec* means not elsewhere classified.

Continued on next page.

SIC	Industry	No. Establishments			Employment		Pay / Employee		Annual Payroll ($ 000)		
		1992	1993	% State	1992	1993	1992	1993	1992	1993	% State
ST. TAMMANY, LA - [continued]											
6540	Title abstract offices	1	3	4.2	-	11	-	8,000	-	129	1.1
6552	Subdividers and developers, n.e.c.	7	10	10.9	161	173	12,795	13,572	2,291	3,007	20.9
6700	Holding and other investment offices	11	12	3.5	66	97	64,848	37,814	4,047	3,318	4.1
TANGIPAHOA, LA											
60 –	**Finance, insurance, and real estate**	159	160	1.8	864	896	21,792	20,554	18,526	19,788	1.0
6000	Depository institutions	35	34	1.9	444	468	19,901	20,932	8,986	9,595	1.5
6020	Commercial banks	27	27	2.2	395	412	19,676	20,806	7,947	8,446	1.5
6100	Nondepository institutions	27	29	2.5	77	89	19,065	21,483	1,505	3,055	2.2
6140	Personal credit institutions	20	22	2.5	61	66	16,590	17,212	1,044	1,392	1.7
6160	Mortgage bankers and brokers	3	4	2.5	-	14	-	36,286	-	1,357	2.8
6300	Insurance carriers	14	10	1.2	103	94	28,388	33,617	3,134	3,168	0.7
6310	Life insurance	6	5	1.5	85	-	25,129	-	2,294	-	-
6400	Insurance agents, brokers, and service	36	36	1.7	118	119	16,237	15,798	2,191	2,172	0.8
6500	Real estate	41	42	1.6	105	106	28,000	8,717	2,041	972	0.4
6510	Real estate operators and lessors	19	19	1.4	47	52	8,851	9,077	423	474	0.6
6530	Real estate agents and managers	15	17	1.8	47	-	52,681	-	1,553	-	-
TENSAS, LA											
60 –	**Finance, insurance, and real estate**	10	10	0.1	62	71	20,194	17,577	1,404	1,485	0.1
TERREBONNE, LA											
60 –	**Finance, insurance, and real estate**	207	212	2.3	1,349	1,365	19,626	19,036	26,891	28,365	1.4
6000	Depository institutions	46	46	2.6	645	603	17,203	17,433	11,129	11,156	1.7
6020	Commercial banks	36	36	3.0	593	559	17,518	17,875	10,442	10,673	1.9
6030	Savings institutions	5	4	2.6	40	-	14,000	-	534	-	-
6060	Credit unions	5	6	1.7	12	-	12,333	-	153	-	-
6100	Nondepository institutions	27	25	2.2	-	98	-	18,857	-	2,088	1.5
6140	Personal credit institutions	20	22	2.5	78	-	23,436	-	1,755	-	-
6160	Mortgage bankers and brokers	3	2	1.3	12	-	25,333	-	182	-	-
6300	Insurance carriers	15	17	2.1	181	201	27,558	27,821	5,326	5,999	1.4
6370	Pension, health, and welfare funds	1	4	4.3	-	20	-	5,800	-	101	1.1
6400	Insurance agents, brokers, and service	48	47	2.2	195	203	25,969	24,197	5,331	5,835	2.1
6500	Real estate	65	68	2.6	211	238	10,995	9,798	2,390	2,393	1.1
6510	Real estate operators and lessors	37	45	3.3	128	189	10,844	8,063	1,433	1,499	1.8
6530	Real estate agents and managers	16	16	1.6	48	42	12,583	14,571	670	710	0.7
6540	Title abstract offices	2	3	4.2	-	2	-	68,000	-	124	1.1
UNION, LA											
60 –	**Finance, insurance, and real estate**	23	24	0.3	194	204	15,608	16,020	3,096	3,201	0.2
6000	Depository institutions	6	6	0.3	108	107	15,889	17,720	1,764	1,833	0.3
6020	Commercial banks	6	6	0.5	108	107	15,889	17,720	1,764	1,833	0.3
6100	Nondepository institutions	3	4	0.3	7	8	20,571	17,000	142	117	0.1
6400	Insurance agents, brokers, and service	4	4	0.2	-	22	-	6,364	-	145	0.1
6500	Real estate	7	8	0.3	20	-	15,400	-	250	-	-
VERMILION, LA											
60 –	**Finance, insurance, and real estate**	74	77	0.8	476	460	18,479	19,200	9,558	9,713	0.5
6000	Depository institutions	26	25	1.4	298	275	19,034	19,593	6,219	5,993	0.9
6020	Commercial banks	21	21	1.7	275	256	19,229	19,047	5,858	5,608	1.0
6100	Nondepository institutions	13	14	1.2	41	40	19,220	19,000	757	785	0.6
6300	Insurance carriers	4	4	0.5	14	48	34,857	26,167	428	1,389	0.3
6400	Insurance agents, brokers, and service	19	21	1.0	69	65	14,087	11,323	1,070	750	0.3
6500	Real estate	9	10	0.4	-	14	-	7,714	-	129	0.1
6510	Real estate operators and lessors	3	3	0.2	5	-	7,200	-	35	-	-
6530	Real estate agents and managers	5	6	0.6	6	8	9,333	8,000	73	85	0.1

*Source: County Business Patterns, 1992/93, CBP-92/93-1, U.S. Department of Commerce, Washington, D.C., April 1995. SIC categories for which data were suppressed or not available for both 1992 and 1993 are *not* displayed. The employment columns represent mid-March employment in the year. Pay per employee is calculated by dividing 1st Quarter payroll, annualized, by mid-March employment. The columns headed "% State" show the county's percentage of the state total for the SIC in 1993; for example, 0.9% for SIC 6030 means that the county had 0.9 percent of the state's total establishments (or payroll) in SIC 6030 in 1993. A dash (-) is used to indicate that data are not available or cannot be calculated; *nec* means not elsewhere classified.

SIC	Industry	No. Establishments			Employment		Pay / Employee		Annual Payroll ($ 000)		
		1992	1993	% State	1992	1993	1992	1993	1992	1993	% State
VERNON, LA											
60 –	**Finance, insurance, and real estate**	65	73	0.8	395	403	14,349	14,988	6,214	6,940	0.4
6000	Depository institutions	10	9	0.5	163	172	16,344	16,860	2,805	2,875	0.4
6100	Nondepository institutions	15	20	1.7	68	65	14,176	18,954	1,183	1,772	1.3
6140	Personal credit institutions	10	15	1.7	49	44	12,653	16,000	830	932	1.2
6160	Mortgage bankers and brokers	4	4	2.5	18	-	18,667	-	333	-	-
6300	Insurance carriers	4	3	0.4	22	-	22,909	-	456	-	-
6400	Insurance agents, brokers, and service	13	14	0.6	47	52	15,830	14,769	821	864	0.3
6500	Real estate	23	26	1.0	95	100	8,337	9,120	949	1,186	0.5
6510	Real estate operators and lessors	15	18	1.3	75	83	8,587	8,723	763	943	1.1
6530	Real estate agents and managers	5	7	0.7	10	-	7,600	-	84	-	-
WASHINGTON, LA											
60 –	**Finance, insurance, and real estate**	66	64	0.7	393	443	15,949	16,226	7,316	8,087	0.4
6000	Depository institutions	20	21	1.2	213	223	16,038	16,143	4,020	4,238	0.6
6100	Nondepository institutions	11	13	1.1	-	52	-	14,231	-	1,219	0.9
6140	Personal credit institutions	10	12	1.3	36	-	17,222	-	705	-	-
6300	Insurance carriers	4	4	0.5	58	63	20,966	21,778	1,405	1,421	0.3
6400	Insurance agents, brokers, and service	23	19	0.9	78	69	12,615	15,884	1,070	1,061	0.4
6500	Real estate	6	5	0.2	7	-	4,000	-	27	-	-
WEBSTER, LA											
60 –	**Finance, insurance, and real estate**	77	78	0.9	419	431	18,606	19,026	8,108	8,202	0.4
6000	Depository institutions	19	19	1.1	204	205	20,608	21,405	4,486	4,439	0.7
6020	Commercial banks	14	13	1.1	188	171	20,426	21,193	4,096	3,626	0.6
6100	Nondepository institutions	18	18	1.6	59	44	17,559	14,364	1,011	664	0.5
6400	Insurance agents, brokers, and service	20	22	1.0	89	106	17,258	16,943	1,563	1,684	0.6
6500	Real estate	13	11	0.4	33	-	9,576	-	303	-	-
6510	Real estate operators and lessors	7	5	0.4	10	-	6,000	-	59	-	-
6530	Real estate agents and managers	5	6	0.6	-	32	-	7,250	-	259	0.3
WEST BATON ROUGE, LA											
60 –	**Finance, insurance, and real estate**	16	15	0.2	123	93	15,805	22,452	2,343	2,300	0.1
6400	Insurance agents, brokers, and service	4	5	0.2	13	13	16,000	17,846	309	324	0.1
6500	Real estate	4	4	0.2	39	12	8,205	16,000	361	191	0.1
6510	Real estate operators and lessors	4	4	0.3	39	12	8,205	16,000	361	191	0.2
WEST CARROLL, LA											
60 –	**Finance, insurance, and real estate**	13	18	0.2	70	73	15,086	15,562	1,018	1,138	0.1
6400	Insurance agents, brokers, and service	4	4	0.2	10	10	14,800	15,200	150	163	0.1
6500	Real estate	2	5	0.2	-	7	-	5,143	-	43	0.0
6510	Real estate operators and lessors	2	3	0.2	-	6	-	5,333	-	35	0.0
WEST FELICIANA, LA											
60 –	**Finance, insurance, and real estate**	8	9	0.1	60	68	15,000	14,765	1,008	1,077	0.1
6000	Depository institutions	3	3	0.2	53	58	16,151	16,414	964	1,012	0.2
6400	Insurance agents, brokers, and service	2	3	0.1	-	4	-	9,000	-	55	0.0
WINN, LA											
60 –	**Finance, insurance, and real estate**	19	20	0.2	134	138	16,269	16,870	2,351	2,505	0.1
6300	Insurance carriers	3	3	0.4	32	-	18,125	-	645	-	-
6400	Insurance agents, brokers, and service	8	8	0.4	-	41	-	14,829	-	650	0.2
6500	Real estate	4	5	0.2	13	12	6,154	8,667	88	110	0.0

Source: County Business Patterns, 1992/93, CBP-92/93-1, U.S. Department of Commerce, Washington, D.C., April 1995. SIC categories for which data were suppressed or not available for both 1992 and 1993 are *not* displayed. The employment columns represent mid-March employment in the year. Pay per employee is calculated by dividing 1st Quarter payroll, annualized, by mid-March employment. The columns headed "% State" show the county's percentage of the state total for the SIC in 1993; for example, 0.9% for SIC 6030 means that the county had 0.9 percent of the state's total establishments (or payroll) in SIC 6030 in 1993. A dash (-) is used to indicate that data are not available or cannot be calculated; *nec* means not elsewhere classified.

MAINE

SIC	Industry	No. Establishments			Employment		Pay / Employee		Annual Payroll ($ 000)		
		1992	1993	% State	1992	1993	1992	1993	1992	1993	% State
ANDROSCOGGIN, ME											
60–	**Finance, insurance, and real estate**	222	221	8.4	2,135	2,078	21,418	21,875	49,785	48,697	6.6
6000	Depository institutions	57	59	9.2	920	865	19,457	18,303	18,914	15,889	7.8
6020	Commercial banks	27	25	7.6	375	263	21,675	17,551	8,390	5,059	4.4
6030	Savings institutions	16	16	9.7	380	292	18,505	22,068	7,597	6,257	10.3
6100	Nondepository institutions	6	4	8.2	39	29	25,846	34,897	1,081	1,229	-
6200	Security and commodity brokers	8	9	8.9	15	28	29,333	34,429	635	1,113	2.7
6300	Insurance carriers	24	16	8.0	620	586	21,497	24,205	13,585	14,128	4.8
6330	Fire, marine, and casualty insurance	9	8	9.3	82	462	25,463	24,234	1,949	11,061	20.7
6400	Insurance agents, brokers, and service	38	39	7.8	272	284	31,132	29,732	9,198	9,250	10.6
6500	Real estate	78	84	8.2	236	256	14,847	16,375	4,311	5,727	8.5
6510	Real estate operators and lessors	30	38	10.4	100	131	10,200	9,221	1,080	1,585	7.0
6530	Real estate agents and managers	28	27	4.9	102	76	18,902	27,474	2,566	2,788	7.2
6553	Cemetery subdividers and developers	12	13	21.3	20	-	12,400		330		-
6700	Holding and other investment offices	11	10	9.0	33	30	32,727	27,600	2,061	1,361	-
6733	Trusts, n.e.c.	3	3	7.9	7	-	25,714	-	128		
AROOSTOOK, ME											
60–	**Finance, insurance, and real estate**	174	170	6.5	971	922	18,122	19,675	18,059	19,649	2.7
6000	Depository institutions	60	54	8.5	534	499	17,131	17,259	9,139	9,649	4.8
6020	Commercial banks	32	25	7.6	336	280	17,821	17,800	5,744	5,816	5.1
6030	Savings institutions	15	15	9.1	102	103	15,882	17,010	1,782	1,896	3.1
6200	Security and commodity brokers	3	3	3.0	6	-	10,667	-	57	-	-
6300	Insurance carriers	8	7	3.5	102	118	28,706	32,339	2,945	3,781	1.3
6370	Pension, health, and welfare funds	3	2	3.8	10	-	2,400	-	45	-	-
6400	Insurance agents, brokers, and service	37	37	7.4	162	161	21,111	21,714	3,518	3,675	4.2
6500	Real estate	58	63	6.2	132	121	10,394	14,281	1,639	1,971	2.9
6510	Real estate operators and lessors	28	31	8.5	71	67	11,775	15,940	1,033	1,186	5.2
6530	Real estate agents and managers	23	28	5.1	53	51	8,830	12,784	502	740	1.9
6553	Cemetery subdividers and developers	4	4	6.6	3	3	2,667	2,667	45	45	2.2
6700	Holding and other investment offices	4	3	2.7	-	3	-	6,667	-	50	-
CUMBERLAND, ME											
60–	**Finance, insurance, and real estate**	793	816	31.1	12,115	12,915	37,339	39,360	411,984	454,717	62.0
6000	Depository institutions	142	137	21.5	2,614	2,594	26,043	25,798	69,876	69,550	34.3
6020	Commercial banks	81	70	21.3	1,724	1,616	28,487	27,965	69,876	69,550	40.5
6030	Savings institutions	31	30	18.2	647	635	21,601	22,576	49,982	46,035	25.5
6100	Nondepository institutions	32	30	61.2	-	271	-	36,649	14,761	15,470	-
6140	Personal credit institutions	15	6	85.7	149	-	28,188	-	-	12,963	-
6160	Mortgage bankers and brokers	14	19	67.9	110	146	32,545	43,288	4,098	9,201	60.7
6200	Security and commodity brokers	39	45	44.6	386	536	70,611	57,985	26,472	32,231	77.3
6210	Security brokers and dealers	22	23	43.4	300	348	74,200	66,782	20,182	22,967	77.9
6280	Security and commodity services	16	22	46.8	-	188	-	41,702	-	9,264	76.0
6300	Insurance carriers	114	101	50.5	6,300	6,821	44,471	48,501	237,140	261,088	88.3
6310	Life insurance	34	27	54.0	4,031	4,076	53,566	61,306	170,745	173,210	92.0
6330	Fire, marine, and casualty insurance	40	42	48.8	882	1,120	31,837	29,557	27,282	35,663	66.7
6370	Pension, health, and welfare funds	30	21	39.6	121	142	9,025	21,296	1,549	2,658	59.3
6400	Insurance agents, brokers, and service	139	147	29.4	1,078	1,061	29,618	28,652	31,460	35,744	40.9
6500	Real estate	288	320	31.3	1,281	1,473	21,137	21,784	29,180	35,482	52.5
6510	Real estate operators and lessors	82	117	32.0	327	551	22,789	23,441	7,703	12,527	55.2
6530	Real estate agents and managers	154	179	32.5	813	850	20,654	20,809	18,382	20,296	52.3
6540	Title abstract offices	6	5	41.7	15	-	18,400	-	322	-	-

Source: County Business Patterns, 1992/93, CBP-92/93-1, U.S. Department of Commerce, Washington, D.C., April 1995. SIC categories for which data were suppressed or not available for both 1992 and 1993 are *not* displayed. The employment columns represent mid-March employment in the year. Pay per employee is calculated by dividing 1st Quarter payroll, annualized, by mid-March employment. The columns headed "% State" show the county's percentage of the state total for the SIC in 1993; for example, 0.9% for SIC 6030 means that the county had 0.9 percent of the state's total establishments (or payroll) in SIC 6030 in 1993. A dash (-) is used to indicate that data are not available or cannot be calculated; *nec* means not elsewhere classified.

Continued on next page.

SIC	Industry	No. Establishments			Employment		Pay / Employee		Annual Payroll ($ 000)		
		1992	1993	% State	1992	1993	1992	1993	1992	1993	% State
CUMBERLAND, ME - [continued]											
6552	Subdividers and developers, n.e.c.	11	7	31.8	38	5	31,579	28,800	1,245	243	42.7
6553	Cemetery subdividers and developers	7	7	11.5	21	27	12,952	8,889	335	336	16.7
6700	Holding and other investment offices	38	35	31.5	190	-	51,789	-	9,336	-	-
6710	Holding offices	10	12	41.4	98	98	72,327	61,020	6,513	6,379	59.2
6720	Investment offices	3	2	50.0	12	-	11,000	-	169	-	-
6732	Educational, religious, etc. trusts	4	5	19.2	9	15	28,889	24,000	275	365	9.0
6733	Trusts, n.e.c.	10	10	26.3	13	-	15,692	-	211	-	-
6799	Investors, n.e.c.	6	3	30.0	40	-	45,800	-	1,861	-	-
FRANKLIN, ME											
60 –	**Finance, insurance, and real estate**	75	64	2.4	427	479	20,600	17,762	10,483	8,907	1.2
6000	Depository institutions	21	21	3.3	163	205	20,294	19,746	3,135	4,046	2.0
6030	Savings institutions	11	11	6.7	111	127	21,910	21,858	2,326	2,604	4.3
6300	Insurance carriers	4	3	1.5	-	10	-	7,600	-	49	0.0
6400	Insurance agents, brokers, and service	14	10	2.0	88	102	30,955	24,314	4,501	2,826	3.2
6500	Real estate	29	27	2.6	125	152	16,960	12,211	2,138	1,941	2.9
6510	Real estate operators and lessors	8	6	1.6	9	-	8,889	-	103	-	-
6530	Real estate agents and managers	15	19	3.4	107	143	18,206	12,503	1,937	1,839	4.7
HANCOCK, ME											
60 –	**Finance, insurance, and real estate**	118	122	4.6	724	762	19,762	20,320	14,776	15,955	2.2
6000	Depository institutions	27	27	4.2	418	421	21,608	23,867	9,067	9,688	4.8
6020	Commercial banks	19	19	5.8	355	358	22,254	24,771	7,928	8,442	7.4
6400	Insurance agents, brokers, and service	22	23	4.6	153	124	18,980	24,419	3,354	3,348	3.8
6500	Real estate	51	51	5.0	88	143	10,818	7,077	1,091	1,430	2.1
6510	Real estate operators and lessors	11	14	3.8	20	29	11,400	9,241	227	342	1.5
6530	Real estate agents and managers	25	27	4.9	52	94	9,154	5,319	442	721	1.9
6552	Subdividers and developers, n.e.c.	3	1	4.5	4	-	39,000	-	248	-	-
6553	Cemetery subdividers and developers	4	6	9.8	2	2	4,000	4,000	34	58	2.9
6700	Holding and other investment offices	16	17	15.3	-	57	-	13,333	-	870	-
6732	Educational, religious, etc. trusts	5	6	23.1	14	23	17,143	17,565	291	466	11.5
6733	Trusts, n.e.c.	7	7	18.4	24	15	9,833	14,667	227	236	-
KENNEBEC, ME											
60 –	**Finance, insurance, and real estate**	231	236	9.0	1,850	1,811	20,830	21,191	42,410	44,263	6.0
6000	Depository institutions	68	65	10.2	1,033	1,096	19,597	18,876	22,677	25,014	12.3
6020	Commercial banks	38	32	9.8	646	628	19,988	18,357	14,533	14,915	13.1
6030	Savings institutions	9	9	5.5	215	242	20,335	20,926	5,029	5,589	9.2
6060	Credit unions	21	23	16.9	172	-	17,209	-	3,115	-	-
6100	Nondepository institutions	6	2	4.1	69	-	26,087	-	1,981	-	-
6200	Security and commodity brokers	11	11	10.9	36	-	35,667	-	1,335	-	-
6210	Security brokers and dealers	5	6	11.3	28	-	39,571	-	1,086	-	-
6280	Security and commodity services	6	5	10.6	8	9	22,000	23,111	249	322	2.6
6300	Insurance carriers	20	19	9.5	192	126	20,667	30,571	4,077	3,889	1.3
6310	Life insurance	6	5	10.0	87	-	22,713	-	1,899	-	-
6330	Fire, marine, and casualty insurance	9	9	10.5	102	-	19,333	-	2,101	-	-
6370	Pension, health, and welfare funds	5	5	9.4	3	-	6,667	-	77	-	-
6400	Insurance agents, brokers, and service	44	47	9.4	227	229	24,035	23,371	5,692	5,806	6.6
6500	Real estate	72	79	7.7	244	219	16,311	16,073	4,940	4,342	6.4
6510	Real estate operators and lessors	22	29	7.9	51	74	18,275	17,297	1,219	1,520	6.7
6530	Real estate agents and managers	35	43	7.8	116	131	17,690	15,298	2,505	2,559	6.6
6552	Subdividers and developers, n.e.c.	3	3	13.6	49	1	10,286	8,000	791	6	1.1
6553	Cemetery subdividers and developers	3	3	4.9	6	-	12,000	-	80	-	-
6700	Holding and other investment offices	10	13	11.7	49	-	36,816	-	1,708	-	-
6733	Trusts, n.e.c.	5	6	15.8	19	-	20,421	-	383	-	-

Source: County Business Patterns, 1992/93, CBP-92/93-1, U.S. Department of Commerce, Washington, D.C., April 1995. SIC categories for which data were suppressed or not available for both 1992 and 1993 are not displayed. The employment columns represent mid-March employment in the year. Pay per employee is calculated by dividing 1st Quarter payroll, annualized, by mid-March employment. The columns headed "% State" show the county's percentage of the state total for the SIC in 1993; for example, 0.9% for SIC 6030 means that the county had 0.9 percent of the state's total establishments (or payroll) in SIC 6030 in 1993. A dash (-) is used to indicate that data are not available or cannot be calculated; nec means not elsewhere classified.

SIC	Industry	No. Establishments			Employment		Pay / Employee		Annual Payroll ($ 000)		
		1992	1993	% State	1992	1993	1992	1993	1992	1993	% State
KNOX, ME											
60 –	**Finance, insurance, and real estate**	76	76	2.9	395	443	21,833	20,804	9,270	10,008	1.4
6000	Depository institutions	20	20	3.1	218	234	19,009	20,154	4,480	5,075	2.5
6020	Commercial banks	14	14	4.3	169	180	19,314	20,044	3,562	3,927	3.5
6300	Insurance carriers	4	4	2.0	16	-	32,500	-	567	-	-
6400	Insurance agents, brokers, and service	15	12	2.4	110	111	28,655	22,414	3,246	2,722	3.1
6500	Real estate	28	32	3.1	-	52	-	16,231	-	997	1.5
6530	Real estate agents and managers	15	22	4.0	19	38	17,053	17,789	330	784	2.0
6700	Holding and other investment offices	6	4	3.6	7	6	11,429	8,667	99	75	-
LINCOLN, ME											
60 –	**Finance, insurance, and real estate**	62	58	2.2	416	403	19,702	19,404	9,374	9,375	1.3
6000	Depository institutions	17	16	2.5	198	205	19,702	19,404	9,374	9,375	1.3
6020	Commercial banks	12	12	3.7	158	165	18,707	18,010	4,006	4,396	2.2
6030	Savings institutions	4	4	2.4	-	40	18,785	17,915	3,213	3,513	3.1
6400	Insurance agents, brokers, and service	16	15	3.0	76	80	-	18,400	-	883	1.5
6510	Real estate operators and lessors	1	4	1.1	-	12	23,474	21,100	1,915	1,897	2.2
6530	Real estate agents and managers	8	13	2.4	49	20	-	2,000	-	65	0.3
6700	Holding and other investment offices	5	4	3.6	69	70	10,857	14,400	472	442	1.1
							19,304	19,257	1,645	1,584	-
OXFORD, ME											
60 –	**Finance, insurance, and real estate**	82	82	3.1	516	601	20,829	20,539	11,143	12,749	1.7
6000	Depository institutions	24	25	3.9	275	365	22,429	21,841	6,185	7,464	3.7
6020	Commercial banks	13	11	3.4	-	159	-	18,340	-	2,713	2.4
6030	Savings institutions	10	10	6.1	145	161	26,703	27,180	3,688	4,046	6.7
6060	Credit unions	1	4	2.9	-	45	-	15,111	-	705	3.0
6300	Insurance carriers	5	5	2.5	10	-	49,200	-	517	-	-
6400	Insurance agents, brokers, and service	16	15	3.0	81	81	22,222	19,802	1,985	2,115	2.4
6500	Real estate	32	35	3.4	94	113	15,702	13,699	1,605	1,796	2.7
6510	Real estate operators and lessors	10	12	3.3	50	48	16,000	16,417	867	966	4.3
6530	Real estate agents and managers	15	20	3.6	31	58	17,419	12,759	613	808	2.1
6553	Cemetery subdividers and developers	3	3	4.9	-	7	-	2,857	-	22	1.1
PENOBSCOT, ME											
60 –	**Finance, insurance, and real estate**	297	286	10.9	2,026	2,053	22,855	23,314	49,157	50,470	6.9
6000	Depository institutions	75	74	11.6	1,002	964	21,633	20,544	22,658	20,902	10.3
6020	Commercial banks	46	40	12.2	579	499	22,694	20,537	13,252	10,733	9.4
6060	Credit unions	16	17	12.5	-	177	-	16,859	-	2,881	12.1
6100	Nondepository institutions	6	6	12.2	32	131	22,375	22,840	772	3,887	-
6200	Security and commodity brokers	11	16	15.8	55	96	55,564	48,542	3,054	4,652	11.2
6210	Security brokers and dealers	8	9	17.0	42	-	60,667	-	2,575	-	-
6280	Security and commodity services	3	6	12.8	13	-	39,077	-	479	-	-
6300	Insurance carriers	19	18	9.0	164	169	30,049	37,444	4,894	6,082	2.1
6310	Life insurance	5	5	10.0	88	122	31,500	37,016	2,844	4,334	2.3
6330	Fire, marine, and casualty insurance	11	12	14.0	61	-	33,311	-	2,000	-	-
6370	Pension, health, and welfare funds	3	1	1.9	15	-	8,267	-	50	-	-
6400	Insurance agents, brokers, and service	60	59	11.8	338	348	18,757	20,000	7,130	7,150	8.2
6500	Real estate	112	104	10.2	309	291	14,628	14,832	5,111	4,665	6.9
6510	Real estate operators and lessors	41	42	11.5	98	93	15,592	16,645	1,472	1,476	6.5
6530	Real estate agents and managers	57	56	10.2	163	179	14,380	13,899	2,598	2,836	7.3
6553	Cemetery subdividers and developers	2	3	4.9	-	16	-	15,500	-	316	15.7
6700	Holding and other investment offices	14	9	8.1	126	54	40,222	51,926	5,538	3,132	-
6710	Holding offices	5	3	10.3	95	-	46,358	-	4,867	-	-
PISCATAQUIS, ME											
60 –	**Finance, insurance, and real estate**	27	27	1.0	117	113	15,863	16,637	1,973	1,975	0.3
6000	Depository institutions	8	9	1.4	62	72	16,839	16,500	1,100	1,223	0.6
6400	Insurance agents, brokers, and service	5	5	1.0	23	22	24,174	24,000	585	554	0.6

Source: County Business Patterns, 1992/93, CBP-92/93-1, U.S. Department of Commerce, Washington, D.C., April 1995. SIC categories for which data were suppressed or not available for both 1992 and 1993 are *not* displayed. The employment columns represent mid-March employment in the year. Pay per employee is calculated by dividing 1st Quarter payroll, annualized, by mid-March employment. The columns headed "% State" show the county's percentage of the state total for the SIC in 1993; for example, 0.9% for SIC 6030 means that the county had 0.9 percent of the state's total establishments (or payroll) in SIC 6030 in 1993. A dash (-) is used to indicate that data are not available or cannot be calculated; *nec* means not elsewhere classified.

Continued on next page.

SIC	Industry	No. Establishments			Employment		Pay / Employee		Annual Payroll ($ 000)		
		1992	1993	% State	1992	1993	1992	1993	1992	1993	% State
PISCATAQUIS, ME - [continued]											
6500	Real estate	13	13	1.3	-	19	-	8,632	-	198	0.3
6510	Real estate operators and lessors	5	5	1.4	11	-	7,273	-	80	-	
6530	Real estate agents and managers	7	7	1.3	12	9	7,667	7,556	106	88	0.2
SAGADAHOC, ME											
60 –	**Finance, insurance, and real estate**	43	39	1.5	238	242	20,790	21,256	5,090	5,562	0.8
6000	Depository institutions	12	12	1.9	155	158	19,794	21,519	3,255	3,611	1.8
6030	Savings institutions	4	4	2.4	65	70	22,215	23,257	1,465	1,692	2.8
6060	Credit unions	3	3	2.2	54	53	18,667	20,830	1,078	1,150	4.8
6400	Insurance agents, brokers, and service	8	7	1.4	40	43	24,000	22,884	932	948	1.1
6510	Real estate operators and lessors	5	5	1.4	3	13	17,333	14,769	58	205	0.9
6530	Real estate agents and managers	11	9	1.6	28	24	20,429	15,000	549	496	1.3
SOMERSET, ME											
60 –	**Finance, insurance, and real estate**	68	66	2.5	349	407	20,034	20,462	7,241	8,607	1.2
6000	Depository institutions	23	24	3.8	213	217	19,662	19,963	4,090	4,413	2.2
6020	Commercial banks	12	11	3.4	76	65	15,000	15,138	1,292	1,323	1.2
6400	Insurance agents, brokers, and service	17	15	3.0	70	115	25,371	24,487	2,118	2,886	3.3
6510	Real estate operators and lessors	6	9	2.5	25	28	8,960	8,714	231	303	1.3
6530	Real estate agents and managers	11	13	2.4	20	24	14,000	12,833	266	359	0.9
WALDO, ME											
60 –	**Finance, insurance, and real estate**	35	32	1.2	135	132	16,593	17,121	2,366	2,557	0.3
6000	Depository institutions	9	9	1.4	56	60	19,786	19,000	1,078	1,260	0.6
6020	Commercial banks	6	6	1.8	-	38	-	19,053	-	843	0.7
6400	Insurance agents, brokers, and service	10	9	1.8	46	45	18,609	18,133	903	885	1.0
6500	Real estate	13	10	1.0	30	-	8,133		349	-	-
6510	Real estate operators and lessors	4	2	0.5	7	-	8,000		63	-	-
6530	Real estate agents and managers	5	5	0.9	6	16	4,000	13,500	50	239	0.6
WASHINGTON, ME											
60 –	**Finance, insurance, and real estate**	46	43	1.6	297	267	19,569	20,255	5,561	5,329	0.7
6000	Depository institutions	18	17	2.7	200	198	20,860	21,131	3,798	3,880	1.9
6020	Commercial banks	11	10	3.0	-	71	-	18,028	-	1,191	1.0
6400	Insurance agents, brokers, and service	12	11	2.2	57	35	20,421	26,171	1,272	1,063	1.2
6500	Real estate	12	12	1.2	29	-	10,621		311	-	-
6510	Real estate operators and lessors	4	3	0.8	18	-	11,556		187	-	-
6530	Real estate agents and managers	8	9	1.6	11	21	9,091	9,143	124	235	0.6
YORK, ME											
60 –	**Finance, insurance, and real estate**	288	286	10.9	1,538	1,578	19,490	19,795	33,019	34,422	4.7
6000	Depository institutions	73	69	10.8	765	792	20,591	20,116	16,878	16,845	8.3
6020	Commercial banks	41	37	11.3	327	331	20,171	18,864	6,813	7,007	6.2
6030	Savings institutions	22	22	13.3	324	334	21,988	22,359	7,928	7,553	12.5
6060	Credit unions	10	10	7.4	114	127	17,825	17,480	2,137	2,285	9.6
6200	Security and commodity brokers	5	7	6.9	9	-	21,778	-	197	-	-
6300	Insurance carriers	19	17	8.5	112	113	19,643	26,584	2,352	3,318	1.1
6330	Fire, marine, and casualty insurance	8	7	8.1	-	56	-	25,571	-	1,618	3.0
6400	Insurance agents, brokers, and service	49	49	9.8	253	237	24,791	24,878	6,903	6,600	7.5
6500	Real estate	133	135	13.2	365	377	13,732	13,061	6,045	6,249	9.2
6510	Real estate operators and lessors	31	42	11.5	96	122	11,792	15,738	1,438	2,005	8.8
6530	Real estate agents and managers	71	74	13.4	192	192	13,958	13,417	3,144	3,600	14.6
6552	Subdividers and developers, n.e.c.	7	3	13.6	24	5	26,667	13,600	734	83	25.9
6553	Cemetery subdividers and developers	13	14	23.0	37	58	7,676	6,207	461	520	

Source: County Business Patterns, 1992/93, CBP-92/93-1, U.S. Department of Commerce, Washington, D.C., April 1995. SIC categories for which data were suppressed or not available for both 1992 and 1993 are *not* displayed. The employment columns represent mid-March employment in the year. Pay per employee is calculated by dividing 1st Quarter payroll, annualized, by mid-March employment. The columns headed "% State" show the county's percentage of the state total for the SIC in 1993; for example, 0.9% for SIC 6030 means that the county had 0.9 percent of the state's total establishments (or payroll) in SIC 6030 in 1993. A dash (-) is used to indicate that data are not available or cannot be calculated; *nec* means not elsewhere classified.

Continued on next page.

SIC	Industry	No. Establishments			Employment		Pay / Employee		Annual Payroll ($ 000)		
		1992	1993	% State	1992	1993	1992	1993	1992	1993	% State
YORK, ME - [continued]											
6700	Holding and other investment offices	8	8	7.2	-	36	-	10,889	-	233	-
6710	Holding offices	3	4	13.8	-	33	-	11,273	-	213	2.0
6733	Trusts, n.e.c.	3	3	7.9	2	-	4,000	-	7	-	-

Source: County Business Patterns, 1992/93, CBP-92/93-1, U.S. Department of Commerce, Washington, D.C., April 1995. SIC categories for which data were suppressed or not available for both 1992 and 1993 are *not* displayed. The employment columns represent mid-March employment in the year. Pay per employee is calculated by dividing 1st Quarter payroll, annualized, by mid-March employment. The columns headed "% State" show the county's percentage of the state total for the SIC in 1993; for example, 0.9% for SIC 6030 means that the county had 0.9 percent of the state's total establishments (or payroll) in SIC 6030 in 1993. A dash (-) is used to indicate that data are not available or cannot be calculated; *nec* means not elsewhere classified.

MARYLAND

SIC	Industry	No. Establishments			Employment		Pay / Employee		Annual Payroll ($ 000)		
		1992	1993	% State	1992	1993	1992	1993	1992	1993	% State
ALLEGANY, MD											
60–	**Finance, insurance, and real estate**	151	150	*1.3*	1,011	1,024	21,084	21,359	21,819	23,783	*0.5*
6000	Depository institutions	48	51	*2.3*	501	548	17,948	18,504	9,498	11,653	*1.0*
6020	Commercial banks	29	26	*1.8*	303	293	18,627	19,823	5,846	6,852	*0.8*
6100	Nondepository institutions	11	5	*0.6*	70	-	16,000	-	1,182	-	-
6210	Security brokers and dealers	6	5	*2.3*	26	-	51,231	-	1,604	-	-
6300	Insurance carriers	16	16	*1.7*	108	117	26,963	22,974	2,732	2,586	*0.3*
6310	Life insurance	8	6	*2.4*	80	91	26,950	21,758	1,936	2,049	*0.9*
6370	Pension, health, and welfare funds	2	3	*1.9*	-	5	-	4,000	-	36	*0.1*
6400	Insurance agents, brokers, and service	27	27	*1.4*	146	137	33,041	34,131	4,390	4,507	*1.1*
6500	Real estate	39	41	*0.9*	151	151	12,185	10,305	1,935	1,744	*0.2*
6510	Real estate operators and lessors	17	18	*1.1*	43	77	15,163	11,636	679	859	*0.4*
6530	Real estate agents and managers	13	15	*0.6*	71	32	10,761	10,000	819	411	*0.1*
6553	Cemetery subdividers and developers	7	7	*6.6*	34	-	10,941	-	401	-	-
ANNE ARUNDEL, MD											
60–	**Finance, insurance, and real estate**	842	890	*7.8*	7,426	7,933	27,800	26,965	214,558	232,071	*4.8*
6000	Depository institutions	187	188	*8.6*	2,787	3,117	23,881	21,852	66,625	69,137	*6.2*
6020	Commercial banks	122	123	*8.4*	1,924	2,261	24,310	22,820	47,154	50,475	*6.1*
6030	Savings institutions	39	38	*9.0*	608	615	24,533	19,434	14,571	13,785	*6.5*
6090	Functions closely related to banking	4	6	*8.6*	6	-	36,667	-	247	-	-
6100	Nondepository institutions	73	83	*9.3*	585	592	39,795	36,676	25,180	28,246	*5.2*
6140	Personal credit institutions	32	27	*9.5*	240	120	34,050	19,900	8,242	2,794	*3.1*
6150	Business credit institutions	6	9	*11.1*	-	63	-	34,794	-	2,559	*3.3*
6160	Mortgage bankers and brokers	34	47	*9.1*	329	409	43,720	41,888	16,074	22,893	*6.3*
6210	Security brokers and dealers	18	16	*7.3*	170	160	52,494	63,400	9,364	11,262	*3.9*
6300	Insurance carriers	93	80	*8.7*	1,388	1,197	32,798	33,113	47,608	42,499	*4.3*
6310	Life insurance	17	17	*6.8*	322	394	32,758	33,726	10,255	14,136	*5.9*
6330	Fire, marine, and casualty insurance	52	49	*11.9*	931	729	34,780	33,822	34,828	26,409	*4.9*
6400	Insurance agents, brokers, and service	127	137	*7.0*	535	524	30,445	29,046	15,938	16,016	*3.9*
6500	Real estate	302	348	*7.8*	1,579	1,834	20,866	22,401	36,151	47,198	*5.6*
6510	Real estate operators and lessors	61	81	*5.2*	469	539	15,804	17,536	8,203	9,619	*4.3*
6530	Real estate agents and managers	163	203	*8.8*	741	996	21,053	22,402	17,292	26,278	*5.2*
6540	Title abstract offices	23	32	*14.7*	104	164	36,308	32,512	3,312	5,728	*13.4*
6552	Subdividers and developers, n.e.c.	19	22	*10.2*	70	54	21,314	34,815	1,724	3,185	*6.7*
6553	Cemetery subdividers and developers	4	8	*7.5*	77	79	20,416	25,772	1,576	2,308	*8.9*
6700	Holding and other investment offices	23	20	*4.9*	325	395	34,732	38,734	11,762	15,288	*5.5*
6710	Holding offices	6	8	*7.3*	272	-	34,779	-	10,093	-	-
BALTIMORE, MD											
60–	**Finance, insurance, and real estate**	1,947	1,969	*17.4*	27,421	26,548	30,441	29,567	825,650	822,024	*17.1*
6000	Depository institutions	355	348	*16.0*	6,211	5,736	24,628	23,656	146,500	139,746	*12.5*
6020	Commercial banks	219	217	*14.9*	4,648	4,065	25,797	25,358	111,180	103,450	*12.5*
6030	Savings institutions	104	98	*23.3*	1,138	1,191	21,529	19,238	26,076	25,016	*11.8*
6060	Credit unions	26	29	*13.0*	385	468	20,062	20,179	8,327	10,542	*16.4*
6090	Functions closely related to banking	5	4	*5.7*	-	12	-	21,333	-	738	-
6100	Nondepository institutions	172	190	*21.2*	3,031	3,230	34,539	31,775	116,925	119,189	*22.0*
6140	Personal credit institutions	74	70	*24.6*	1,279	-	24,378	-	42,880	-	-
6150	Business credit institutions	16	23	*28.4*	1,025	1,315	40,343	38,002	39,977	55,369	*71.9*
6160	Mortgage bankers and brokers	79	94	*18.3*	721	830	44,316	38,308	33,873	42,720	*11.7*
6200	Security and commodity brokers	80	79	*16.7*	1,198	1,046	52,508	39,824	56,575	50,552	*10.9*
6210	Security brokers and dealers	33	32	*14.6*	-	339	-	72,755	-	24,834	*8.6*

Source: County Business Patterns, 1992/93, CBP-92/93-1, U.S. Department of Commerce, Washington, D.C., April 1995. SIC categories for which data were suppressed or not available for both 1992 and 1993 are *not* displayed. The employment columns represent mid-March employment in the year. Pay per employee is calculated by dividing 1st Quarter payroll, annualized, by mid-March employment. The columns headed "% State" show the county's percentage of the state total for the SIC in 1993; for example, 0.9% for SIC 6030 means that the county had 0.9 percent of the state's total establishments (or payroll) in SIC 6030 in 1993. A dash (-) is used to indicate that data are not available or cannot be calculated; *nec* means not elsewhere classified.

Continued on next page.

SIC	Industry	No. Establishments			Employment		Pay / Employee		Annual Payroll ($ 000)		
		1992	1993	% State	1992	1993	1992	1993	1992	1993	% State
BALTIMORE, MD - [continued]											
6280	Security and commodity services	46	47	18.7	801	707	31,556	24,034	30,205	25,718	-
6300	Insurance carriers	240	208	22.7	6,584	6,301	36,813	35,966	223,432	217,771	22.0
6310	Life insurance	65	58	23.3	1,597	1,363	32,441	34,365	48,528	43,838	18.4
6321	Accident and health insurance	7	5	29.4	91	-	31,033	-	2,710	-	-
6330	Fire, marine, and casualty insurance	98	90	21.9	1,795	1,843	35,822	35,499	64,349	68,770	12.8
6370	Pension, health, and welfare funds	48	37	23.1	280	253	29,157	25,344	10,579	7,139	25.3
6400	Insurance agents, brokers, and service	443	464	23.6	3,398	3,172	34,035	35,072	115,259	111,333	26.9
6500	Real estate	587	612	13.7	5,277	5,530	20,193	20,498	116,842	127,293	15.0
6510	Real estate operators and lessors	199	236	15.0	2,236	2,663	19,073	19,163	44,214	53,244	24.0
6530	Real estate agents and managers	257	301	13.0	2,061	2,149	20,751	21,022	45,707	51,876	10.3
6540	Title abstract offices	22	29	13.4	125	215	26,240	29,414	3,409	7,471	17.4
6552	Subdividers and developers, n.e.c.	28	28	13.0	275	211	25,062	29,611	9,645	9,312	19.6
6553	Cemetery subdividers and developers	15	14	13.2	292	292	16,356	15,658	5,611	5,339	20.7
6700	Holding and other investment offices	61	60	14.6	661	-	27,522	-	22,991	-	-
6710	Holding offices	17	17	15.6	439	433	27,426	28,517	13,816	13,921	10.6
6732	Educational, religious, etc. trusts	16	13	16.3	64	-	24,125	-	1,571	-	-
6733	Trusts, n.e.c.	10	9	9.6	23	-	17,739	-	549	-	-
6794	Patent owners and lessors	6	5	17.2	74	111	20,270	18,054	1,868	2,455	-
6799	Investors, n.e.c.	8	13	18.3	58	-	45,517	-	5,064	-	-
CALVERT, MD											
60-	**Finance, insurance, and real estate**	86	100	0.9	329	400	19,793	21,600	7,664	9,966	0.2
6000	Depository institutions	13	16	0.7	112	147	22,071	23,946	2,671	3,555	0.3
6020	Commercial banks	11	12	0.8	-	127	-	23,811	-	3,001	0.4
6100	Nondepository institutions	4	4	0.4	16	-	33,250	-	551	-	-
6300	Insurance carriers	5	5	0.5	50	27	13,200	26,519	832	772	0.1
6400	Insurance agents, brokers, and service	18	21	1.1	-	47	-	20,000	-	1,153	0.3
6500	Real estate	45	51	1.1	102	165	17,882	18,182	2,402	3,554	0.4
6510	Real estate operators and lessors	6	6	0.4	13	6	18,154	19,333	266	198	0.1
6530	Real estate agents and managers	25	31	1.3	51	112	16,157	18,500	1,168	2,010	0.4
6540	Title abstract offices	5	5	2.3	21	26	28,571	22,154	712	857	2.0
6552	Subdividers and developers, n.e.c.	4	5	2.3	-	12	-	13,667	-	397	0.8
CAROLINE, MD											
60-	**Finance, insurance, and real estate**	44	45	0.4	239	244	24,469	27,803	6,114	7,088	0.1
6000	Depository institutions	14	14	0.6	116	-	21,172	-	2,648	-	-
6300	Insurance carriers	4	1	0.1	4	-	14,000	-	123	-	-
6400	Insurance agents, brokers, and service	8	11	0.6	30	-	24,000	-	676	-	-
6500	Real estate	15	16	0.4	50	37	12,320	15,676	678	687	0.1
6530	Real estate agents and managers	5	7	0.3	-	9	-	14,667	-	113	0.0
CARROLL, MD											
60-	**Finance, insurance, and real estate**	225	237	2.1	1,506	1,604	20,016	19,875	31,519	36,037	0.8
6000	Depository institutions	51	50	2.3	765	796	20,204	19,402	16,116	16,300	1.5
6020	Commercial banks	43	44	3.0	722	755	20,349	19,539	15,319	15,496	1.9
6100	Nondepository institutions	6	9	1.0	-	33	-	25,212	-	842	0.2
6140	Personal credit institutions	4	5	1.8	-	18	-	24,000	-	367	0.4
6300	Insurance carriers	21	18	2.0	119	149	24,437	21,128	2,877	3,366	0.3
6310	Life insurance	3	4	1.6	-	93	-	20,258	-	2,060	0.9
6370	Pension, health, and welfare funds	6	3	1.9	23	-	14,783	-	298	-	-
6400	Insurance agents, brokers, and service	57	55	2.8	167	182	20,120	19,780	3,734	4,337	1.0
6500	Real estate	84	97	2.2	234	243	19,949	20,379	4,692	6,761	0.8
6510	Real estate operators and lessors	24	29	1.8	87	70	21,977	19,086	1,438	1,928	0.9
6530	Real estate agents and managers	33	44	1.9	83	123	18,169	18,634	1,718	3,418	0.7

Source: County Business Patterns, 1992/93, CBP-92/93-1, U.S. Department of Commerce, Washington, D.C., April 1995. SIC categories for which data were suppressed or not available for both 1992 and 1993 are *not* displayed. The employment columns represent mid-March employment in the year. Pay per employee is calculated by dividing 1st Quarter payroll, annualized, by mid-March employment. The columns headed "% State" show the county's percentage of the state total for the SIC in 1993; for example, 0.9% for SIC 6030 means that the county had 0.9 percent of the state's total establishments (or payroll) in SIC 6030 in 1993. A dash (-) is used to indicate that data are not available or cannot be calculated; *nec* means not elsewhere classified.

Continued on next page.

SIC	Industry	No. Establishments			Employment		Pay / Employee		Annual Payroll ($ 000)		
		1992	1993	% State	1992	1993	1992	1993	1992	1993	% State
CARROLL, MD - [continued]											
6540	Title abstract offices	7	9	*4.1*	22	24	28,909	39,167	775	988	*2.3*
6552	Subdividers and developers, n.e.c.	1	4	*1.9*	-	4	-	16,000	-	56	*0.1*
6553	Cemetery subdividers and developers	7	10	*9.4*	22	22	18,364	14,545	389	367	*1.4*
CECIL, MD											
60 –	**Finance, insurance, and real estate**	94	96	*0.8*	529	544	23,259	21,441	12,702	12,431	*0.3*
6000	Depository institutions	20	21	*1.0*	271	277	19,336	19,827	5,530	6,114	*0.5*
6020	Commercial banks	16	16	*1.1*	226	225	19,628	20,124	4,715	5,102	*0.6*
6100	Nondepository institutions	4	3	*0.3*	15	-	24,800	-	392	-	-
6300	Insurance carriers	3	2	*0.2*	17	-	13,882		753	-	-
6400	Insurance agents, brokers, and service	23	22	*1.1*	71	80	23,155	24,550	1,867	2,017	*0.5*
6500	Real estate	38	42	*0.9*	106	110	35,849	24,218	3,138	2,792	*0.3*
6510	Real estate operators and lessors	9	16	*1.0*	21	25	40,571	46,400	695	693	*0.3*
6530	Real estate agents and managers	14	16	*0.7*	59	54	43,593	18,593	1,986	1,414	*0.3*
6540	Title abstract offices	3	3	*1.4*	14	15	15,143	16,267	259	331	*0.8*
6552	Subdividers and developers, n.e.c.	5	5	*2.3*	7	-	16,571	-	128	-	-
6553	Cemetery subdividers and developers	3	2	*1.9*	2	-	10,000		34	-	-
6700	Holding and other investment offices	4	5	*1.2*	-	52	-	19,846	-	1,020	*0.4*
CHARLES, MD											
60 –	**Finance, insurance, and real estate**	189	186	*1.6*	1,209	1,230	24,807	24,354	31,731	36,001	*0.8*
6000	Depository institutions	44	43	*2.0*	519	543	23,083	21,738	12,388	13,157	*1.2*
6020	Commercial banks	32	32	*2.2*	341	345	22,229	20,510	7,619	7,467	*0.9*
6100	Nondepository institutions	20	21	*2.3*	153	180	41,752	34,978	5,999	8,240	*1.5*
6160	Mortgage bankers and brokers	11	9	*1.8*	123	125	45,333	43,072	5,192	7,275	*2.0*
6310	Life insurance	3	3	*1.2*	62	84	28,000	25,571	1,620	2,174	*0.9*
6400	Insurance agents, brokers, and service	39	41	*2.1*	123	123	21,528	22,992	3,566	3,812	*0.9*
6500	Real estate	67	65	*1.5*	325	271	17,969	20,251	6,768	7,128	*0.8*
6510	Real estate operators and lessors	11	14	*0.9*	25	-	19,520		534	-	-
6530	Real estate agents and managers	39	46	*2.0*	230	203	17,600	20,473	4,684	5,532	*1.1*
6540	Title abstract offices	5	3	*1.4*	13	14	28,308	20,857	410	509	*1.2*
DORCHESTER, MD											
60 –	**Finance, insurance, and real estate**	53	56	*0.5*	246	260	19,480	18,754	5,697	5,971	*0.1*
6000	Depository institutions	15	15	*0.7*	126	129	18,571	18,636	2,808	2,974	*0.3*
6400	Insurance agents, brokers, and service	13	16	*0.8*	46	58	26,783	23,310	1,524	1,743	*0.4*
6500	Real estate	20	22	*0.5*	42	47	10,286	10,043	489	618	*0.1*
6510	Real estate operators and lessors	5	8	*0.5*	15	23	3,200	5,913	83	206	*0.1*
6530	Real estate agents and managers	14	11	*0.5*	-	16	-	18,750	-	365	*0.1*
FREDERICK, MD											
60 –	**Finance, insurance, and real estate**	349	370	*3.3*	7,449	8,623	29,211	32,967	231,496	288,981	*6.0*
6000	Depository institutions	77	81	*3.7*	2,654	2,698	22,374	22,102	61,948	65,289	*5.8*
6100	Nondepository institutions	27	31	*3.5*	1,026	1,061	42,324	38,850	51,387	48,938	*9.0*
6160	Mortgage bankers and brokers	14	14	*2.7*	965	935	43,465	41,360	49,574	46,147	*12.7*
6210	Security brokers and dealers	7	8	*3.7*	70	-	52,800		3,323	-	-
6300	Insurance carriers	37	35	*3.8*	2,453	2,378	30,324	38,298	77,166	86,153	*8.7*
6310	Life insurance	7	7	*2.8*	-	200	-	31,260	-	5,643	*2.4*
6370	Pension, health, and welfare funds	8	6	*3.8*	-	36	-	15,778	-	277	*1.0*
6400	Insurance agents, brokers, and service	55	58	*2.9*	425	328	28,198	23,098	12,290	8,955	*2.2*
6500	Real estate	134	146	*3.3*	556	608	19,799	15,671	12,039	11,341	*1.3*
6510	Real estate operators and lessors	40	49	*3.1*	135	262	13,600	10,443	2,136	2,804	*1.3*
6530	Real estate agents and managers	60	74	*3.2*	229	239	22,620	20,485	5,646	6,085	*1.2*
6540	Title abstract offices	6	8	*3.7*	32	53	24,250	20,226	863	1,398	*3.3*
6552	Subdividers and developers, n.e.c.	8	7	*3.2*	35	13	33,486	28,308	1,190	432	*0.9*
6700	Holding and other investment offices	6	6	*1.5*	-	89	-	14,921	-	1,355	*0.5*

Source: County Business Patterns, 1992/93, CBP-92/93-1, U.S. Department of Commerce, Washington, D.C., April 1995. SIC categories for which data were suppressed or not available for both 1992 and 1993 are *not* displayed. The employment columns represent mid-March employment in the year. Pay per employee is calculated by dividing 1st Quarter payroll, annualized, by mid-March employment. The columns headed "% State" show the county's percentage of the state total for the SIC in 1993; for example, 0.9% for SIC 6030 means that the county had 0.9 percent of the state's total establishments (or payroll) in SIC 6030 in 1993. A dash (-) is used to indicate that data are not available or cannot be calculated; *nec* means not elsewhere classified.

SIC	Industry	No. Establishments			Employment		Pay / Employee		Annual Payroll ($ 000)		
		1992	1993	% State	1992	1993	1992	1993	1992	1993	% State
GARRETT, MD											
60 –	**Finance, insurance, and real estate**	57	54	*0.5*	475	426	17,962	17,531	8,424	8,087	*0.2*
6000	Depository institutions	18	18	*0.8*	304	325	18,355	17,723	5,463	6,133	*0.5*
6400	Insurance agents, brokers, and service	10	10	*0.5*	41	36	20,585	23,000	851	984	*0.2*
6500	Real estate	21	21	*0.5*	72	50	14,444	13,680	926	770	*0.1*
6510	Real estate operators and lessors	3	4	*0.3*	11	12	4,000	3,333	44	47	*0.0*
6530	Real estate agents and managers	12	13	*0.6*	38	29	12,947	15,172	489	436	*0.1*
HARFORD, MD											
60 –	**Finance, insurance, and real estate**	326	335	*3.0*	1,951	2,163	21,962	22,561	45,805	52,693	*1.1*
6000	Depository institutions	71	70	*3.2*	871	884	18,930	19,991	17,942	18,648	*1.7*
6020	Commercial banks	49	50	*3.4*	474	514	19,173	19,743	10,064	10,877	*1.3*
6060	Credit unions	7	6	*2.7*	208	222	21,269	23,351	4,725	5,138	*8.0*
6100	Nondepository institutions	14	18	*2.0*	68	85	35,235	31,718	2,091	3,547	*0.7*
6140	Personal credit institutions	6	7	*2.5*	-	27	-	19,407	-	559	*0.6*
6160	Mortgage bankers and brokers	6	8	*1.6*	39	-	44,308	-	1,385	-	-
6200	Security and commodity brokers	19	19	*4.0*	59	-	42,508	-	2,153	-	-
6210	Security brokers and dealers	6	8	*3.7*	32	-	66,125	-	1,640	-	-
6280	Security and commodity services	13	11	*4.4*	27	28	14,519	11,571	513	469	-
6300	Insurance carriers	24	21	*2.3*	219	351	31,452	30,587	7,296	10,407	*1.1*
6310	Life insurance	5	6	*2.4*	56	199	31,071	28,161	1,576	4,623	*1.9*
6400	Insurance agents, brokers, and service	62	61	*3.1*	210	208	20,114	22,135	4,703	5,160	*1.2*
6500	Real estate	131	137	*3.1*	517	567	19,853	19,160	11,309	12,559	*1.5*
6510	Real estate operators and lessors	38	45	*2.9*	203	219	14,778	13,571	3,544	3,134	*1.4*
6530	Real estate agents and managers	56	71	*3.1*	188	230	20,915	19,426	4,196	5,416	*1.1*
6540	Title abstract offices	3	6	*2.8*	12	29	31,667	26,759	474	855	*2.0*
6552	Subdividers and developers, n.e.c.	13	10	*4.6*	33	-	39,152	-	1,527	-	-
6553	Cemetery subdividers and developers	7	4	*3.8*	62	-	23,161	-	1,111	-	-
6700	Holding and other investment offices	5	9	*2.2*	7	-	11,429	-	311	-	-
HOWARD, MD											
60 –	**Finance, insurance, and real estate**	566	545	*4.8*	6,265	7,003	34,892	30,227	221,040	236,199	*4.9*
6000	Depository institutions	81	80	*3.7*	1,186	1,266	23,767	22,670	28,221	29,679	*2.6*
6020	Commercial banks	63	62	*4.2*	1,019	1,148	24,813	23,439	25,881	27,667	*3.4*
6030	Savings institutions	13	12	*2.9*	151	83	17,907	13,735	2,140	1,283	*0.6*
6060	Credit unions	5	6	*2.7*	16	35	12,500	18,629	200	729	*1.1*
6100	Nondepository institutions	52	60	*6.7*	887	1,209	40,618	33,846	38,835	52,711	*9.7*
6140	Personal credit institutions	12	12	*4.2*	-	238	-	25,412	-	6,827	*7.5*
6150	Business credit institutions	7	9	*11.1*	-	112	-	36,357	-	3,669	*4.8*
6160	Mortgage bankers and brokers	33	39	*7.6*	760	859	41,479	35,856	34,861	42,215	*11.6*
6200	Security and commodity brokers	23	24	*5.1*	147	-	40,027	-	5,629	-	-
6210	Security brokers and dealers	9	10	*4.6*	96	60	54,625	65,667	4,832	3,796	*1.3*
6300	Insurance carriers	74	66	*7.2*	1,143	1,045	33,806	32,777	36,089	33,730	*3.4*
6310	Life insurance	18	21	*8.4*	331	412	43,069	34,883	11,183	11,398	*4.8*
6330	Fire, marine, and casualty insurance	28	28	*6.8*	463	406	35,335	34,315	15,491	15,006	*2.8*
6400	Insurance agents, brokers, and service	94	94	*4.8*	532	475	29,248	27,933	16,406	16,276	*3.9*
6500	Real estate	220	200	*4.5*	2,267	1,882	39,479	21,622	88,559	49,214	*5.8*
6510	Real estate operators and lessors	55	49	*3.1*	747	430	25,349	17,098	17,599	7,347	*3.3*
6530	Real estate agents and managers	94	106	*4.6*	1,123	1,087	49,485	20,714	55,938	27,678	*5.5*
6540	Title abstract offices	13	20	*9.2*	74	174	26,216	26,253	2,485	6,458	*15.1*
6552	Subdividers and developers, n.e.c.	27	19	*8.8*	152	162	57,737	36,222	7,864	7,268	*15.3*
6553	Cemetery subdividers and developers	5	5	*4.7*	74	27	16,757	13,630	1,194	437	*1.7*
6700	Holding and other investment offices	19	19	*4.6*	-	1,032	-	47,779	-	49,976	*17.8*
6710	Holding offices	5	5	*4.6*	8	12	160,500	149,000	2,087	2,210	*1.7*
6732	Educational, religious, etc. trusts	4	3	*3.8*	20	-	16,000	-	426	-	-
6733	Trusts, n.e.c.	5	2	*2.1*	6	-	34,667	-	388	-	-

Source: *County Business Patterns, 1992/93*, CBP-92/93-1, U.S. Department of Commerce, Washington, D.C., April 1995. SIC categories for which data were suppressed or not available for both 1992 and 1993 are *not* displayed. The employment columns represent mid-March employment in the year. Pay per employee is calculated by dividing 1st Quarter payroll, annualized, by mid-March employment. The columns headed "% State" show the county's percentage of the state total for the SIC in 1993; for example, 0.9% for SIC 6030 means that the county had 0.9 percent of the state's total establishments (or payroll) in SIC 6030 in 1993. A dash (-) is used to indicate that data are not available or cannot be calculated; *nec* means not elsewhere classified.

SIC	Industry	No. Establishments			Employment		Pay / Employee		Annual Payroll ($ 000)		
		1992	1993	% State	1992	1993	1992	1993	1992	1993	% State
KENT, MD											
60 –	**Finance, insurance, and real estate**	52	48	*0.4*	296	292	21,432	24,205	6,164	6,595	*0.1*
6000	Depository institutions	16	15	*0.7*	171	175	20,585	21,623	3,600	3,448	*0.3*
6400	Insurance agents, brokers, and service	11	10	*0.5*	46	46	22,696	26,609	1,121	1,205	*0.3*
6500	Real estate	19	18	*0.4*	48	30	11,000	12,933	466	427	*0.1*
6510	Real estate operators and lessors	3	4	*0.3*	5	-	8,000	-	57	-	-
6530	Real estate agents and managers	11	13	*0.6*	27	21	13,333	10,476	275	257	*0.1*
MONTGOMERY, MD											
60 –	**Finance, insurance, and real estate**	2,558	2,657	*23.4*	34,154	33,718	30,523	31,529	1,055,827	1,150,835	*24.0*
6000	Depository institutions	400	400	*18.4*	5,806	5,078	24,267	27,916	147,050	149,578	*13.3*
6020	Commercial banks	264	268	*18.3*	3,797	3,156	22,763	27,369	86,774	81,640	*9.9*
6030	Savings institutions	95	85	*20.2*	1,551	1,351	28,067	31,138	49,101	53,895	*25.3*
6060	Credit unions	37	40	*17.9*	-	460	-	24,600	-	11,942	*18.6*
6090	Functions closely related to banking	3	7	*10.0*	-	111	-	17,982	-	2,101	-
6100	Nondepository institutions	188	219	*24.4*	1,624	1,967	44,869	41,141	79,376	107,778	*19.9*
6140	Personal credit institutions	34	36	*12.7*	217	244	27,760	19,246	6,187	4,926	*5.4*
6150	Business credit institutions	15	14	*17.3*	63	-	22,095	-	1,180	-	-
6160	Mortgage bankers and brokers	138	168	*32.7*	1,343	1,653	48,724	44,649	71,993	101,263	*27.8*
6200	Security and commodity brokers	137	143	*30.3*	1,274	2,036	62,973	54,481	75,630	113,232	*24.4*
6210	Security brokers and dealers	62	63	*28.8*	995	-	65,483	-	55,293	-	-
6280	Security and commodity services	74	79	*31.5*	-	1,233	-	53,035	-	62,490	-
6300	Insurance carriers	201	184	*20.1*	5,153	5,422	41,314	36,193	191,992	191,960	*19.4*
6310	Life insurance	53	38	*15.3*	989	1,047	39,648	32,416	36,300	32,040	*13.5*
6321	Accident and health insurance	7	4	*23.5*	135	73	35,674	37,096	3,589	2,578	*33.5*
6324	Hospital and medical service plans	9	8	*22.2*	495	432	43,612	47,231	20,883	20,774	*15.7*
6330	Fire, marine, and casualty insurance	89	89	*21.7*	3,328	3,597	43,022	36,649	127,119	128,214	*23.8*
6370	Pension, health, and welfare funds	33	37	*23.1*	175	232	19,017	25,759	3,306	6,528	*23.1*
6400	Insurance agents, brokers, and service	373	398	*20.2*	3,825	3,440	30,695	31,560	122,480	121,565	*29.3*
6500	Real estate	1,123	1,181	*26.4*	13,770	12,710	22,924	23,267	332,636	334,957	*39.6*
6510	Real estate operators and lessors	363	383	*24.4*	3,319	2,594	22,997	19,272	79,679	56,999	*25.7*
6530	Real estate agents and managers	551	673	*29.1*	9,293	9,248	22,240	23,865	216,426	247,894	*49.0*
6540	Title abstract offices	37	44	*20.3*	212	300	34,245	30,027	7,323	10,476	*24.5*
6552	Subdividers and developers, n.e.c.	64	58	*26.9*	470	476	33,574	29,109	16,945	16,440	*34.6*
6553	Cemetery subdividers and developers	8	10	*9.4*	96	83	23,917	24,771	3,538	2,514	*9.7*
6700	Holding and other investment offices	124	119	*28.9*	2,429	2,804	36,940	41,819	95,098	122,545	*43.8*
6710	Holding offices	26	27	*24.8*	891	1,403	42,981	44,080	39,914	63,183	*48.2*
6720	Investment offices	7	2	*20.0*	16	-	53,500	-	1,429	-	-
6732	Educational, religious, etc. trusts	20	24	*30.0*	72	152	18,944	41,526	1,894	6,224	*27.2*
6733	Trusts, n.e.c.	31	20	*21.3*	561	739	33,932	31,231	19,285	23,356	*81.3*
6794	Patent owners and lessors	8	12	*41.4*	23	-	37,391	-	1,112	-	-
6798	Real estate investment trusts	10	7	*53.8*	786	-	33,944		28,129	-	-
6799	Investors, n.e.c.	19	26	*36.6*	51	295	31,922	47,539	2,225	17,270	*24.7*
PRINCE GEORGE'S, MD											
60 –	**Finance, insurance, and real estate**	1,277	1,291	*11.4*	12,335	12,043	25,348	24,449	320,611	321,276	*6.7*
6000	Depository institutions	286	285	*13.1*	5,109	4,911	23,053	22,948	116,515	113,506	*10.1*
6020	Commercial banks	174	166	*11.4*	3,390	3,021	23,680	23,293	77,403	67,737	*8.2*
6030	Savings institutions	55	54	*12.9*	1,039	991	21,987	21,808	23,726	24,791	*11.7*
6060	Credit unions	29	38	*17.0*	610	772	22,098	24,689	14,162	19,115	*29.7*
6090	Functions closely related to banking	26	27	*38.6*	62	127	17,290	13,071	1,140	1,863	-
6100	Nondepository institutions	107	110	*12.3*	1,002	992	38,291	32,327	42,127	40,803	*7.5*
6140	Personal credit institutions	51	37	*13.0*	435	332	28,359	21,651	11,822	6,980	*7.7*
6160	Mortgage bankers and brokers	49	67	*13.0*	495	621	45,059	38,499	25,975	32,781	*9.0*
6210	Security brokers and dealers	9	13	*5.9*	55	59	52,000	43,390	2,319	2,345	*0.8*
6300	Insurance carriers	118	99	*10.8*	1,380	1,187	30,904	31,447	40,937	38,168	*3.9*
6310	Life insurance	29	32	*12.9*	712	668	27,787	28,353	18,640	18,291	*7.7*
6330	Fire, marine, and casualty insurance	45	41	*10.0*	314	299	45,834	46,328	14,518	14,350	*2.7*
6370	Pension, health, and welfare funds	32	21	*13.1*	339	106	23,823	19,774	7,211	2,428	*8.6*

Source: County Business Patterns, 1992/93, CBP-92/93-1, U.S. Department of Commerce, Washington, D.C., April 1995. SIC categories for which data were suppressed or not available for both 1992 and 1993 are *not* displayed. The employment columns represent mid-March employment in the year. Pay per employee is calculated by dividing 1st Quarter payroll, annualized, by mid-March employment. The columns headed "% State" show the county's percentage of the state total for the SIC in 1993; for example, 0.9% for SIC 6030 means that the county had 0.9 percent of the state's total establishments (or payroll) in SIC 6030 in 1993. A dash (-) is used to indicate that data are not available or cannot be calculated; *nec* means not elsewhere classified.

Continued on next page.

SIC	Industry	No. Establishments			Employment		Pay / Employee		Annual Payroll ($ 000)		
		1992	1993	% State	1992	1993	1992	1993	1992	1993	% State
PRINCE GEORGE'S, MD - [continued]											
6400	Insurance agents, brokers, and service	186	201	10.2	803	884	27,895	28,403	24,490	27,495	6.6
6500	Real estate	502	516	11.5	3,777	3,689	21,091	20,067	85,421	86,146	10.2
6510	Real estate operators and lessors	173	206	13.1	1,424	1,660	17,447	18,089	26,402	34,202	15.4
6530	Real estate agents and managers	225	251	10.8	1,535	1,591	22,205	20,935	36,205	38,421	7.6
6540	Title abstract offices	33	29	13.4	129	107	23,876	26,093	4,126	4,324	10.1
6552	Subdividers and developers, n.e.c.	18	17	7.9	152	70	31,289	32,171	4,834	3,114	6.6
6553	Cemetery subdividers and developers	7	7	6.6	230	250	24,870	22,256	5,503	5,892	22.8
6700	Holding and other investment offices	40	48	11.7	164	245	29,854	25,029	5,560	8,162	2.9
6710	Holding offices	10	16	14.7	75	111	46,667	38,811	3,674	6,070	4.6
6732	Educational, religious, etc. trusts	6	6	7.5	28	29	13,571	13,655	394	411	1.8
6733	Trusts, n.e.c.	18	18	19.1	41	57	15,024	12,772	778	1,116	3.9
QUEEN ANNE'S, MD											
60 –	**Finance, insurance, and real estate**	61	65	0.6	289	265	19,862	19,970	5,902	5,880	0.1
6000	Depository institutions	14	13	0.6	121	125	21,620	22,368	2,737	2,913	0.3
6020	Commercial banks	13	13	0.9	-	125	-	22,368	-	2,913	0.4
6400	Insurance agents, brokers, and service	11	15	0.8	43	58	23,442	20,069	1,132	1,178	0.3
6500	Real estate	30	33	0.7	108	71	14,556	15,042	1,484	1,416	0.2
6530	Real estate agents and managers	14	20	0.9	34	-	15,529	-	601	-	-
ST. MARY'S, MD											
60 –	**Finance, insurance, and real estate**	102	109	1.0	563	584	20,135	17,589	11,463	11,399	0.2
6000	Depository institutions	24	26	1.2	287	290	17,937	17,352	5,562	5,333	0.5
6020	Commercial banks	17	17	1.2	217	221	18,452	17,792	4,430	4,257	0.5
6100	Nondepository institutions	5	6	0.7	32	-	27,875	-	992	-	-
6300	Insurance carriers	6	3	0.3	9	-	27,111	-	274	-	-
6400	Insurance agents, brokers, and service	20	25	1.3	64	84	21,812	18,905	1,399	1,562	0.4
6500	Real estate	41	45	1.0	165	172	21,891	15,116	3,159	3,003	0.4
6510	Real estate operators and lessors	13	15	1.0	90	100	13,556	13,280	1,413	1,395	0.6
6530	Real estate agents and managers	17	21	0.9	30	37	19,067	11,676	645	545	0.1
6540	Title abstract offices	3	4	1.8	8	10	66,500	37,200	241	338	0.8
6700	Holding and other investment offices	6	3	0.7	6	4	7,333	12,000	77	48	0.0
6733	Trusts, n.e.c.	4	2	2.1	1	-	4,000	-	25	-	-
SOMERSET, MD											
60 –	**Finance, insurance, and real estate**	27	31	0.3	153	170	16,732	20,424	3,088	3,526	0.1
6000	Depository institutions	10	10	0.5	104	-	18,115	-	2,323	-	-
6020	Commercial banks	10	10	0.7	104	-	18,115	-	2,323	-	-
6500	Real estate	9	11	0.2	21	24	8,571	9,167	215	236	0.0
6510	Real estate operators and lessors	4	4	0.3	7	9	6,286	6,222	73	63	0.0
TALBOT, MD											
60 –	**Finance, insurance, and real estate**	139	144	1.3	588	675	29,905	27,881	16,860	20,045	0.4
6000	Depository institutions	19	19	0.9	189	203	34,603	31,409	5,487	5,933	0.5
6100	Nondepository institutions	4	5	0.6	32	-	25,250	-	827	-	-
6200	Security and commodity brokers	10	10	2.1	31	31	93,935	83,742	2,149	2,624	0.6
6210	Security brokers and dealers	8	6	2.7	-	27	-	93,778	-	2,528	0.9
6280	Security and commodity services	2	4	1.6	-	4	-	16,000	-	96	-
6300	Insurance carriers	13	9	1.0	88	102	26,591	28,510	2,490	3,208	0.3
6400	Insurance agents, brokers, and service	19	21	1.1	72	90	30,444	26,756	2,327	2,581	0.6
6500	Real estate	67	71	1.6	154	186	14,675	15,075	3,029	3,680	0.4
6510	Real estate operators and lessors	18	26	1.7	53	96	12,000	13,167	897	1,595	0.7
6530	Real estate agents and managers	32	37	1.6	62	66	16,323	17,333	1,423	1,633	0.3
6540	Title abstract offices	3	2	0.9	14	-	6,286	-	149	-	-

Source: County Business Patterns, 1992/93, CBP-92/93-1, U.S. Department of Commerce, Washington, D.C., April 1995. SIC categories for which data were suppressed or not available for both 1992 and 1993 are not displayed. The employment columns represent mid-March employment in the year. Pay per employee is calculated by dividing 1st Quarter payroll, annualized, by mid-March employment. The columns headed "% State" show the county's percentage of the state total for the SIC in 1993; for example, 0.9% for SIC 6030 means that the county had 0.9 percent of the state's total establishments (or payroll) in SIC 6030 in 1993. A dash (-) is used to indicate that data are not available or cannot be calculated; nec means not elsewhere classified.

Continued on next page.

SIC	Industry	No. Establishments			Employment		Pay / Employee		Annual Payroll ($ 000)		
		1992	1993	% State	1992	1993	1992	1993	1992	1993	% State
TALBOT, MD - [continued]											
6552	Subdividers and developers, n.e.c.	4	4	1.9	3	6	24,000	18,667	83	107	0.2
6700	Holding and other investment offices	7	9	2.2	22	-	24,182	-	551	-	-
6733	Trusts, n.e.c.	3	4	4.3	6	-	20,667	-	153	-	-
WASHINGTON, MD											
60-	**Finance, insurance, and real estate**	251	249	2.2	3,865	3,544	20,863	21,857	74,190	79,487	1.7
6000	Depository institutions	71	66	3.0	2,753	2,128	19,664	20,216	47,351	42,428	3.8
6020	Commercial banks	52	49	3.4	2,549	1,957	19,865	19,951	43,597	38,561	4.7
6030	Savings institutions	14	11	2.6	164	126	16,805	25,175	2,987	2,960	1.4
6060	Credit unions	5	6	2.7	40	45	18,600	17,867	767	907	1.4
6100	Nondepository institutions	13	15	1.7	52	354	23,462	23,492	1,297	10,348	1.9
6140	Personal credit institutions	9	8	2.8	37	-	22,162	-	828	-	-
6200	Security and commodity brokers	7	11	2.3	35	-	69,486	-	2,569	-	-
6300	Insurance carriers	31	26	2.8	487	419	25,216	27,924	11,923	11,855	1.2
6310	Life insurance	10	10	4.0	189	234	26,243	28,530	4,682	6,610	2.8
6330	Fire, marine, and casualty insurance	11	12	2.9	167	175	25,557	26,949	4,598	5,057	0.9
6400	Insurance agents, brokers, and service	44	44	2.2	210	252	26,571	25,810	5,605	6,583	1.6
6500	Real estate	80	79	1.8	308	328	13,403	13,427	4,562	4,818	0.6
6510	Real estate operators and lessors	33	36	2.3	124	188	13,710	12,638	1,573	2,246	1.0
6530	Real estate agents and managers	30	30	1.3	113	-	13,097	-	1,742	-	-
6552	Subdividers and developers, n.e.c.	3	5	2.3	4	14	17,000	10,571	95	216	0.5
6553	Cemetery subdividers and developers	7	7	6.6	55	67	14,836	15,045	997	1,104	4.3
6700	Holding and other investment offices	5	8	1.9	20	-	43,000	-	883	-	-
WICOMICO, MD											
60-	**Finance, insurance, and real estate**	191	188	1.7	1,909	1,871	22,873	22,303	45,117	46,525	1.0
6000	Depository institutions	48	49	2.3	946	905	23,416	19,394	22,958	20,394	1.8
6020	Commercial banks	36	37	2.5	369	387	20,531	20,672	8,053	8,292	1.0
6030	Savings institutions	6	6	1.4	550	486	25,920	18,947	14,566	11,727	5.5
6060	Credit unions	6	6	2.7	27	32	11,852	10,750	339	375	0.6
6100	Nondepository institutions	16	17	1.9	88	125	32,091	26,336	2,949	3,505	0.6
6140	Personal credit institutions	10	12	4.2	57	81	26,175	19,111	1,568	1,546	1.7
6160	Mortgage bankers and brokers	3	4	0.8	20	-	55,000	-	1,154	-	-
6200	Security and commodity brokers	8	6	1.3	33	-	43,879	-	1,443	-	-
6280	Security and commodity services	3	2	0.8	4	-	13,000	-	51	-	-
6300	Insurance carriers	20	22	2.4	277	327	25,314	27,853	6,617	8,947	0.9
6310	Life insurance	8	9	3.6	176	221	25,591	28,833	4,340	6,013	2.5
6330	Fire, marine, and casualty insurance	6	8	1.9	-	95	-	25,516	-	2,463	0.5
6400	Insurance agents, brokers, and service	41	42	2.1	246	233	24,862	24,893	6,194	6,227	1.5
6500	Real estate	53	47	1.1	309	229	12,220	16,332	4,306	4,687	0.6
6510	Real estate operators and lessors	21	14	0.9	109	52	8,807	13,308	1,105	789	0.4
6530	Real estate agents and managers	19	29	1.3	97	147	18,845	18,639	1,999	3,544	0.7
6553	Cemetery subdividers and developers	3	3	2.8	23	-	12,870	-	289	-	-
6700	Holding and other investment offices	5	5	1.2	10	-	33,600	-	650	-	-
WORCESTER, MD											
60-	**Finance, insurance, and real estate**	178	179	1.6	1,281	1,068	18,729	19,127	26,392	24,690	0.5
6000	Depository institutions	35	37	1.7	259	256	19,042	19,484	5,120	5,149	0.5
6020	Commercial banks	32	34	2.3	247	243	19,239	19,802	4,934	4,975	0.6
6100	Nondepository institutions	5	7	0.8	37	-	44,000	-	1,360	-	-
6400	Insurance agents, brokers, and service	21	18	0.9	80	72	26,600	25,111	2,350	2,098	0.5
6500	Real estate	108	111	2.5	676	681	17,077	17,022	13,435	15,109	1.8
6510	Real estate operators and lessors	22	27	1.7	124	115	10,839	14,678	2,033	3,339	1.5
6530	Real estate agents and managers	71	78	3.4	529	556	18,775	17,633	11,096	11,628	2.3
6540	Title abstract offices	4	4	1.8	5	-	12,000	-	80	-	-

Source: County Business Patterns, 1992/93, CBP-92/93-1, U.S. Department of Commerce, Washington, D.C., April 1995. SIC categories for which data were suppressed or not available for both 1992 and 1993 are not displayed. The employment columns represent mid-March employment in the year. Pay per employee is calculated by dividing 1st Quarter payroll, annualized, by mid-March employment. The columns headed "% State" show the county's percentage of the state total for the SIC in 1993; for example, 0.9% for SIC 6030 means that the county had 0.9 percent of the state's total establishments (or payroll) in SIC 6030 in 1993. A dash (-) is used to indicate that data are not available or cannot be calculated; nec means not elsewhere classified.

SIC	Industry	No. Establishments			Employment		Pay / Employee		Annual Payroll ($ 000)		
		1992	1993	% State	1992	1993	1992	1993	1992	1993	% State
BALTIMORE CITY, MD											
60 –	**Finance, insurance, and real estate**	1,411	1,352	*11.9*	29,733	33,451	42,378	39,413	1,214,904	1,356,267	*28.3*
6000	Depository institutions	254	260	*12.0*	11,119	10,464	35,612	35,271	363,159	384,591	*34.3*
6020	Commercial banks	145	153	*10.5*	9,472	8,769	37,203	37,401	320,113	341,655	*41.4*
6030	Savings institutions	57	53	*12.6*	882	863	29,646	25,687	24,271	23,420	*11.0*
6060	Credit unions	28	30	*13.5*	-	328	-	17,817		6,147	*9.6*
6100	Nondepository institutions	92	86	*9.6*	1,444	3,130	51,011	31,035	71,416	110,969	*20.4*
6140	Personal credit institutions	48	35	*12.3*	602	1,625	63,037	24,911	37,108	42,349	*46.7*
6160	Mortgage bankers and brokers	29	36	*7.0*	617	1,258	41,323	36,668	25,283	58,327	*16.0*
6200	Security and commodity brokers	81	87	*18.4*	2,642	2,563	108,719	104,520	227,860	261,162	*56.3*
6210	Security brokers and dealers	44	40	*18.3*	1,732	1,512	140,674	139,032	169,405	178,719	*62.0*
6280	Security and commodity services	35	47	*18.7*	895	1,051	48,304	54,870	58,034	82,443	*-*
6300	Insurance carriers	169	102	*11.1*	6,143	8,034	42,592	40,654	277,081	330,282	*33.4*
6310	Life insurance	39	29	*11.6*	1,309	2,184	39,853	39,614	50,253	84,925	*35.7*
6330	Fire, marine, and casualty insurance	30	33	*8.0*	3,185	4,023	50,527	46,407	172,891	189,337	*35.1*
6370	Pension, health, and welfare funds	74	21	*13.1*	406	319	25,714	26,031	15,140	8,572	*30.4*
6400	Insurance agents, brokers, and service	159	169	*8.6*	1,513	1,840	38,200	36,143	56,319	66,618	*16.1*
6500	Real estate	543	558	*12.5*	5,284	5,465	21,727	20,979	115,677	120,668	*14.2*
6510	Real estate operators and lessors	266	286	*18.2*	2,199	2,108	16,680	17,059	39,871	39,646	*17.9*
6530	Real estate agents and managers	201	219	*9.5*	2,418	2,928	26,199	23,807	60,507	68,814	*13.6*
6540	Title abstract offices	9	16	*7.4*	62	94	25,097	22,043	1,758	2,578	*6.0*
6552	Subdividers and developers, n.e.c.	17	18	*8.3*	211	124	21,934	25,806	5,107	3,709	*7.8*
6553	Cemetery subdividers and developers	14	13	*12.3*	245	208	19,069	17,615	4,715	3,995	*15.5*
6700	Holding and other investment offices	101	81	*19.7*	1,079	1,419	39,481	33,700	69,569	47,032	*16.8*
6710	Holding offices	19	17	*15.6*	426	709	49,850	36,976	42,080	26,287	*20.0*
6720	Investment offices	8	5	*50.0*	75	-	94,133	-	8,648	-	*-*
6732	Educational, religious, etc. trusts	29	24	*30.0*	454	524	25,313	24,000	12,246	14,005	*61.2*
6733	Trusts, n.e.c.	36	22	*23.4*	64	112	22,938	26,607	4,927	3,195	*11.1*

*Source: County Business Patterns, 1992/93, CBP-92/93-1, U.S. Department of Commerce, Washington, D.C., April 1995. SIC categories for which data were suppressed or not available for both 1992 and 1993 are *not* displayed. The employment columns represent mid-March employment in the year. Pay per employee is calculated by dividing 1st Quarter payroll, annualized, by mid-March employment. The columns headed "% State" show the county's percentage of the state total for the SIC in 1993; for example, 0.9% for SIC 6030 means that the county had 0.9 percent of the state's total establishments (or payroll) in SIC 6030 in 1993. A dash (-) is used to indicate that data are not available or cannot be calculated; *nec* means not elsewhere classified.*

MASSACHUSETTS

SIC	Industry	No. Establishments			Employment		Pay / Employee		Annual Payroll ($ 000)		
		1992	1993	% State	1992	1993	1992	1993	1992	1993	% State
BARNSTABLE, MA											
60 –	**Finance, insurance, and real estate**	522	533	4.0	3,297	3,720	25,423	24,190	85,720	97,518	1.1
6000	Depository institutions	112	110	4.2	1,264	1,412	22,187	22,348	29,361	32,189	1.7
6020	Commercial banks	54	50	4.7	647	703	21,694	22,469	15,294	17,549	1.4
6030	Savings institutions	53	58	5.6	568	-	23,063	-	13,408	-	-
6060	Credit unions	5	1	0.2	49	-	18,531	-	659	-	-
6100	Nondepository institutions	22	21	3.4	88	124	36,500	25,484	3,667	4,602	1.4
6160	Mortgage bankers and brokers	11	14	4.3	39	95	39,282	28,505	1,844	4,113	2.3
6200	Security and commodity brokers	25	27	3.0	259	187	55,058	64,556	10,580	12,150	0.6
6210	Security brokers and dealers	15	13	4.0	245	163	57,322	71,067	10,334	11,584	1.4
6280	Security and commodity services	10	14	2.4	14	24	15,429	20,333	246	566	0.0
6300	Insurance carriers	13	14	2.0	228	218	26,035	32,477	6,226	6,874	0.3
6310	Life insurance	6	5	1.7	177	170	25,785	34,494	4,706	5,410	0.4
6370	Pension, health, and welfare funds	3	5	4.0	-	8	-	8,500	-	165	0.5
6400	Insurance agents, brokers, and service	105	104	3.6	558	566	28,968	27,682	17,140	17,246	2.5
6500	Real estate	221	232	5.0	825	1,066	18,090	16,390	17,296	21,242	2.3
6510	Real estate operators and lessors	43	57	3.3	201	258	19,522	16,016	4,815	4,927	1.8
6530	Real estate agents and managers	134	158	6.2	475	779	18,291	16,252	9,737	15,451	2.5
6540	Title abstract offices	5	7	13.0	6	15	12,000	22,133	215	366	4.4
6552	Subdividers and developers, n.e.c.	9	7	4.0	14	-	21,429	-	406	-	-
6700	Holding and other investment offices	24	25	3.3	75	147	17,067	20,272	1,450	3,215	0.5
6710	Holding offices	3	2	1.2	8	-	33,000	-	213	-	-
6732	Educational, religious, etc. trusts	4	5	3.2	9	-	26,222	-	273	-	-
6733	Trusts, n.e.c.	13	12	5.9	53	-	12,453	-	811	-	-
BERKSHIRE, MA											
60 –	**Finance, insurance, and real estate**	257	244	1.9	2,700	3,144	30,476	25,642	77,188	76,963	0.9
6000	Depository institutions	69	67	2.6	1,014	1,087	24,974	22,329	25,386	24,854	1.3
6020	Commercial banks	22	21	2.0	337	355	24,795	22,175	8,003	7,735	0.6
6030	Savings institutions	31	28	2.7	580	584	25,655	24,267	15,324	14,709	3.0
6060	Credit unions	16	18	4.3	97	148	21,526	15,054	2,059	2,410	2.8
6100	Nondepository institutions	9	5	0.8	53	-	23,245	-	1,226	-	-
6200	Security and commodity brokers	11	10	1.1	73	61	39,123	50,033	2,897	2,918	0.1
6300	Insurance carriers	13	8	1.1	684	1,168	50,263	30,195	27,684	29,421	1.2
6400	Insurance agents, brokers, and service	50	51	1.8	418	347	29,378	29,706	12,873	10,957	1.6
6500	Real estate	89	91	1.9	394	387	11,584	13,271	5,423	6,099	0.7
6510	Real estate operators and lessors	31	35	2.0	90	78	9,022	15,385	1,032	1,345	0.5
6530	Real estate agents and managers	36	52	2.0	236	295	10,932	12,488	3,056	4,395	0.7
6552	Subdividers and developers, n.e.c.	7	1	0.6	20	-	27,200	-	600	-	-
6700	Holding and other investment offices	16	12	1.6	64	-	25,750	-	1,699	-	-
6799	Investors, n.e.c.	2	3	2.7	-	13	-	35,385	-	421	0.9
BRISTOL, MA											
60 –	**Finance, insurance, and real estate**	822	819	6.2	7,177	7,682	23,630	23,827	171,201	190,935	2.1
6000	Depository institutions	211	212	8.2	2,945	2,921	21,369	19,755	65,138	63,496	3.3
6020	Commercial banks	69	58	5.5	1,045	805	22,094	20,641	22,992	17,491	1.4
6030	Savings institutions	96	100	9.6	1,423	1,521	22,505	21,005	34,115	36,342	7.4
6100	Nondepository institutions	43	30	4.9	321	296	24,436	28,122	7,635	10,043	3.0
6140	Personal credit institutions	27	14	8.3	186	104	19,290	21,269	3,405	2,605	4.2
6160	Mortgage bankers and brokers	10	13	4.0	83	177	35,614	31,367	2,784	7,023	4.0
6200	Security and commodity brokers	16	19	2.1	55	61	79,345	71,607	4,034	4,233	0.2
6210	Security brokers and dealers	11	9	2.8	47	48	87,404	86,250	3,706	3,941	0.5

Source: County Business Patterns, 1992/93, CBP-92/93-1, U.S. Department of Commerce, Washington, D.C., April 1995. SIC categories for which data were suppressed or not available for both 1992 and 1993 are *not* displayed. The employment columns represent mid-March employment in the year. Pay per employee is calculated by dividing 1st Quarter payroll, annualized, by mid-March employment. The columns headed "% State" show the county's percentage of the state total for the SIC in 1993; for example, 0.9% for SIC 6030 means that the county had 0.9 percent of the state's total establishments (or payroll) in SIC 6030 in 1993. A dash (-) is used to indicate that data are not available or cannot be calculated; *nec* means not elsewhere classified.

Continued on next page.

714

SIC	Industry	No. Establishments			Employment		Pay / Employee		Annual Payroll ($ 000)		
		1992	1993	% State	1992	1993	1992	1993	1992	1993	% State
BRISTOL, MA - [continued]											
6280	Security and commodity services	5	10	1.7	8	13	32,000	17,538	328	292	0.0
6300	Insurance carriers	43	41	5.8	1,680	2,114	26,140	28,412	42,387	55,986	2.3
6310	Life insurance	19	18	6.0	-	470	-	35,455	-	14,161	1.0
6330	Fire, marine, and casualty insurance	12	10	5.8	1,157	1,537	23,682	26,327	27,850	39,253	6.8
6400	Insurance agents, brokers, and service	214	221	7.6	1,034	1,050	26,344	25,295	27,084	28,814	4.2
6500	Real estate	269	273	5.8	1,070	1,130	20,321	20,736	23,498	25,809	2.8
6510	Real estate operators and lessors	113	116	6.7	444	482	14,649	13,909	7,131	7,317	2.7
6530	Real estate agents and managers	97	121	4.8	419	493	27,885	28,665	11,980	15,044	2.4
6552	Subdividers and developers, n.e.c.	15	18	10.3	38	74	21,789	19,189	900	2,036	11.5
6553	Cemetery subdividers and developers	14	14	10.4	90	73	12,000	13,644	1,171	1,126	6.3
6732	Educational, religious, etc. trusts	4	3	1.9	15	13	8,000	7,692	119	90	0.1
6733	Trusts, n.e.c.	8	8	3.9	17	18	17,176	15,556	288	296	1.2
DUKES, MA											
60 –	**Finance, insurance, and real estate**	52	53	0.4	276	291	26,522	24,454	7,790	7,938	0.1
6400	Insurance agents, brokers, and service	8	9	0.3	47	47	34,894	35,234	1,487	1,621	0.2
6500	Real estate	26	24	0.5	-	55	-	19,345	-	1,283	0.1
6530	Real estate agents and managers	20	18	0.7	36	37	20,333	18,162	908	714	0.1
6700	Holding and other investment offices	2	3	0.4	-	5	-	31,200	-	171	0.0
ESSEX, MA											
60 –	**Finance, insurance, and real estate**	1,219	1,274	9.7	12,130	11,941	29,050	27,630	363,923	356,190	4.0
6000	Depository institutions	280	284	11.0	5,156	4,592	26,618	22,713	139,310	107,781	5.6
6020	Commercial banks	134	103	9.7	2,146	1,423	25,331	20,562	54,489	30,524	2.4
6030	Savings institutions	100	123	11.8	2,673	2,768	28,597	24,364	78,034	69,351	14.2
6060	Credit unions	41	52	12.6	323	382	18,638	18,691	6,333	7,495	8.8
6090	Functions closely related to banking	5	6	10.5	14	19	30,286	24,211	454	411	2.9
6100	Nondepository institutions	72	70	11.4	732	933	36,317	30,864	29,593	42,810	12.9
6110	Federal and Federally-sponsored credit	4	-	-	47	-	23,915	-	1,039	-	-
6140	Personal credit institutions	28	15	8.9	122	115	25,443	19,409	3,346	2,389	3.8
6150	Business credit institutions	8	9	8.6	70	68	96,686	68,588	5,193	4,431	5.6
6160	Mortgage bankers and brokers	31	45	13.7	492	747	31,659	29,216	19,996	35,910	20.3
6200	Security and commodity brokers	38	50	5.5	142	232	58,394	53,431	9,151	13,158	0.7
6210	Security brokers and dealers	12	14	4.3	86	130	69,395	65,046	6,452	8,356	1.0
6280	Security and commodity services	25	34	5.9	53	-	43,094	-	2,624	-	-
6300	Insurance carriers	61	55	7.8	2,840	2,672	32,985	33,168	90,828	85,004	3.5
6310	Life insurance	25	22	7.3	999	933	24,993	26,448	24,872	23,369	1.7
6330	Fire, marine, and casualty insurance	14	12	7.0	1,095	1,027	38,711	39,529	41,012	38,934	6.8
6400	Insurance agents, brokers, and service	288	301	10.4	1,409	1,549	30,637	31,651	48,343	54,353	7.9
6500	Real estate	424	459	9.8	1,622	1,671	22,015	20,809	38,767	40,089	4.3
6510	Real estate operators and lessors	157	176	10.2	478	523	19,556	18,707	9,624	10,749	4.0
6530	Real estate agents and managers	197	242	9.5	868	1,047	22,885	21,834	22,462	26,205	4.3
6540	Title abstract offices	4	5	9.3	-	11	-	39,273	-	730	8.8
6552	Subdividers and developers, n.e.c.	14	16	9.2	66	31	33,758	18,452	2,116	851	4.8
6553	Cemetery subdividers and developers	12	14	10.4	54	57	18,296	19,088	1,233	1,262	7.1
6710	Holding offices	6	10	6.1	116	91	37,966	49,714	4,524	3,963	3.0
6732	Educational, religious, etc. trusts	10	9	5.8	26	42	32,154	30,476	876	1,299	2.1
6733	Trusts, n.e.c.	19	19	9.3	24	27	20,333	27,259	562	873	3.4
6798	Real estate investment trusts	8	4	9.5	-	9	-	21,778	-	190	1.1
6799	Investors, n.e.c.	5	4	3.6	21	-	45,143	-	1,048	-	-
FRANKLIN, MA											
60 –	**Finance, insurance, and real estate**	96	99	0.8	1,408	1,049	18,864	20,663	29,235	23,151	0.3
6000	Depository institutions	27	31	1.2	321	339	19,838	19,953	6,845	6,903	0.4
6020	Commercial banks	12	10	0.9	142	-	20,479	-	3,158	-	-
6030	Savings institutions	12	17	1.6	165	217	19,830	22,194	3,479	4,796	1.0
6060	Credit unions	3	4	1.0	14	-	13,429	-	208	-	-
6400	Insurance agents, brokers, and service	25	23	0.8	118	117	23,254	20,957	3,097	2,894	0.4

Source: County Business Patterns, 1992/93, CBP-92/93-1, U.S. Department of Commerce, Washington, D.C., April 1995. SIC categories for which data were suppressed or not available for both 1992 and 1993 are *not* displayed. The employment columns represent mid-March employment in the year. Pay per employee is calculated by dividing 1st Quarter payroll, annualized, by mid-March employment. The columns headed "% State" show the county's percentage of the state total for the SIC in 1993; for example, 0.9% for SIC 6030 means that the county had 0.9 percent of the state's total establishments (or payroll) in SIC 6030 in 1993. A dash (-) is used to indicate that data are not available or cannot be calculated; *nec* means not elsewhere classified.

Continued on next page.

SIC	Industry	No. Establishments			Employment		Pay / Employee		Annual Payroll ($ 000)		
		1992	1993	% State	1992	1993	1992	1993	1992	1993	% State
FRANKLIN, MA - [continued]											
6500	Real estate	33	33	0.7	-	70	-	13,429	-	1,082	0.1
6510	Real estate operators and lessors	11	11	0.6	12	31	14,333	14,581	196	479	0.2
6530	Real estate agents and managers	14	14	0.6	32	27	16,875	12,593	638	411	0.1
6553	Cemetery subdividers and developers	6	6	4.4	14	-	4,000	-	89	-	-
HAMPDEN, MA											
60 –	**Finance, insurance, and real estate**	882	898	6.8	22,852	22,343	29,108	28,646	666,273	725,563	8.2
6000	Depository institutions	194	209	8.1	3,222	3,015	24,272	22,030	76,996	70,823	3.7
6020	Commercial banks	76	87	8.2	1,322	1,334	26,163	21,241	31,005	30,992	2.4
6030	Savings institutions	81	89	8.5	1,575	1,418	23,517	23,464	39,144	34,996	7.2
6060	Credit unions	33	30	7.2	313	257	20,652	18,459	6,724	4,762	5.6
6090	Functions closely related to banking	4	3	5.3	12	6	9,333	11,333	123	73	0.5
6100	Nondepository institutions	43	30	4.9	473	386	33,463	34,560	16,999	14,584	4.4
6160	Mortgage bankers and brokers	13	13	4.0	116	82	42,517	42,195	4,841	4,097	2.3
6200	Security and commodity brokers	30	40	4.4	350	437	58,994	56,659	20,407	24,940	1.3
6210	Security brokers and dealers	19	18	5.5	310	315	63,535	61,613	19,368	20,511	2.6
6280	Security and commodity services	10	22	3.8	-	122	-	43,869	-	4,429	0.4
6300	Insurance carriers	74	66	9.4	15,816	15,542	30,436	30,099	481,443	539,974	22.3
6330	Fire, marine, and casualty insurance	13	12	7.0	1,084	-	34,325	-	35,124	-	-
6370	Pension, health, and welfare funds	18	12	9.6	-	69	-	23,594	-	1,790	5.9
6400	Insurance agents, brokers, and service	250	244	8.4	1,413	1,276	26,420	27,502	37,591	38,626	5.6
6500	Real estate	274	285	6.1	1,536	1,582	19,802	18,655	31,284	31,998	3.4
6510	Real estate operators and lessors	116	126	7.3	605	634	18,453	15,893	11,066	10,567	3.9
6530	Real estate agents and managers	110	133	5.2	748	814	19,850	19,956	15,606	17,782	2.9
6552	Subdividers and developers, n.e.c.	8	8	4.6	73	39	32,822	35,385	2,388	1,580	8.9
6553	Cemetery subdividers and developers	11	13	9.6	64	71	19,938	18,423	1,382	1,475	8.3
6710	Holding offices	3	7	4.3	-	60	-	34,400	-	3,556	2.7
6733	Trusts, n.e.c.	4	5	2.5	-	6	-	10,000	-	82	0.3
HAMPSHIRE, MA											
60 –	**Finance, insurance, and real estate**	223	238	1.8	1,363	1,373	23,985	21,597	36,651	35,494	0.4
6000	Depository institutions	45	58	2.2	597	692	22,218	18,902	13,985	15,096	0.8
6020	Commercial banks	15	22	2.1	145	283	20,772	17,300	3,240	5,814	0.5
6030	Savings institutions	25	29	2.8	432	363	22,898	20,044	10,389	8,319	1.7
6060	Credit unions	4	7	1.7	-	46	-	19,739	-	963	1.1
6400	Insurance agents, brokers, and service	47	47	1.6	254	254	27,449	26,614	7,604	7,644	1.1
6500	Real estate	101	103	2.2	335	292	16,752	17,192	6,482	5,994	0.6
6510	Real estate operators and lessors	39	44	2.6	192	149	16,354	17,799	3,540	2,875	1.1
6530	Real estate agents and managers	44	47	1.8	110	122	17,273	16,885	2,294	2,391	0.4
6552	Subdividers and developers, n.e.c.	4	4	2.3	-	6	-	21,333	-	529	3.0
6553	Cemetery subdividers and developers	7	7	5.2	11	14	13,455	12,571	182	198	1.1
6733	Trusts, n.e.c.	4	5	2.5	4	-	13,000	-	86	-	-
MIDDLESEX, MA											
60 –	**Finance, insurance, and real estate**	2,937	2,999	22.8	35,037	35,258	29,223	30,073	1,053,139	1,141,779	12.9
6000	Depository institutions	561	572	22.1	13,067	12,855	25,316	26,488	330,172	339,520	17.7
6020	Commercial banks	267	246	23.2	6,222	5,455	24,445	26,130	146,083	139,323	11.0
6030	Savings institutions	208	220	21.1	4,376	4,995	25,479	23,903	111,826	124,536	25.5
6060	Credit unions	77	95	22.9	-	862	-	20,631	-	18,716	22.0
6100	Nondepository institutions	181	165	27.0	2,794	1,761	29,654	38,826	83,984	87,615	26.5
6110	Federal and Federally-sponsored credit	6	1	20.0	222	-	21,874	-	3,545	-	-
6140	Personal credit institutions	66	42	24.9	712	-	25,961	-	18,502	-	-
6150	Business credit institutions	29	33	31.4	384	349	43,458	48,539	16,468	15,960	20.1
6160	Mortgage bankers and brokers	77	89	27.1	1,475	987	28,998	38,849	45,399	60,478	34.3
6200	Security and commodity brokers	135	154	16.9	897	1,242	56,437	43,662	58,470	67,354	3.4
6210	Security brokers and dealers	35	42	12.8	372	380	59,785	59,305	22,275	24,989	3.1
6280	Security and commodity services	99	112	19.5	525	862	54,065	36,766	36,065	42,365	3.6
6300	Insurance carriers	170	130	18.4	5,353	6,401	35,699	34,513	185,123	225,206	9.3

Source: County Business Patterns, 1992/93, CBP-92/93-1, U.S. Department of Commerce, Washington, D.C., April 1995. SIC categories for which data were suppressed or not available for both 1992 and 1993 are *not* displayed. The employment columns represent mid-March employment in the year. Pay per employee is calculated by dividing 1st Quarter payroll, annualized, by mid-March employment. The columns headed "% State" show the county's percentage of the state total for the SIC in 1993; for example, 0.9% for SIC 6030 means that the county had 0.9 percent of the state's total establishments (or payroll) in SIC 6030 in 1993. A dash (-) is used to indicate that data are not available or cannot be calculated; *nec* means not elsewhere classified.

Continued on next page.

SIC	Industry	No. Establishments			Employment		Pay / Employee		Annual Payroll ($ 000)		
		1992	1993	% State	1992	1993	1992	1993	1992	1993	% State
MIDDLESEX, MA - [continued]											
6310	Life insurance	65	64	21.3	1,321	1,507	35,455	35,403	42,030	48,090	3.4
6330	Fire, marine, and casualty insurance	36	35	20.5	2,657	2,873	37,877	35,674	93,123	99,850	17.4
6370	Pension, health, and welfare funds	48	12	9.6	162	67	14,123	32,836	4,370	1,999	6.6
6400	Insurance agents, brokers, and service	652	680	23.4	5,033	4,949	31,155	30,856	165,674	166,991	24.2
6500	Real estate	1,031	1,094	23.4	6,540	6,558	24,431	24,496	178,342	186,689	20.1
6510	Real estate operators and lessors	377	415	24.1	2,259	2,163	19,288	18,772	47,518	44,601	16.7
6530	Real estate agents and managers	489	613	24.1	3,382	4,126	27,973	27,281	108,022	131,884	21.4
6540	Title abstract offices	4	6	11.1	28	21	36,286	36,000	1,111	1,094	13.2
6552	Subdividers and developers, n.e.c.	44	38	21.8	338	80	26,272	31,800	8,454	3,459	19.6
6553	Cemetery subdividers and developers	11	12	8.9	149	157	25,691	25,529	5,056	5,187	29.2
6700	Holding and other investment offices	201	198	26.3	1,227	1,223	37,627	41,926	45,317	55,461	9.4
6710	Holding offices	34	39	23.8	507	379	46,178	60,422	20,197	23,963	18.0
6720	Investment offices	10	7	17.9	35	-	61,143	-	2,014	-	-
6732	Educational, religious, etc. trusts	57	54	34.6	320	374	25,462	27,433	9,132	10,751	17.6
6733	Trusts, n.e.c.	50	49	24.0	133	203	21,594	22,581	3,424	5,070	19.7
6794	Patent owners and lessors	9	10	43.5	-	108	-	39,852	-	4,409	39.2
6798	Real estate investment trusts	14	10	23.8	50	-	64,960	-	3,621	-	-
6799	Investors, n.e.c.	22	26	23.6	98	73	40,571	63,890	4,018	4,837	10.6
NANTUCKET, MA											
60 –	**Finance, insurance, and real estate**	31	31	0.2	200	220	28,980	27,836	6,380	6,710	0.1
6400	Insurance agents, brokers, and service	4	4	0.1	28	27	42,429	37,778	1,119	1,214	0.2
6500	Real estate	19	18	0.4	87	91	24,598	29,934	2,580	2,645	0.3
6530	Real estate agents and managers	15	13	0.5	79	83	24,608	31,711	2,351	2,469	0.4
6700	Holding and other investment offices	3	3	0.4	5	-	33,600	-	69	-	-
NORFOLK, MA											
60 –	**Finance, insurance, and real estate**	1,545	1,579	12.0	28,392	30,875	31,202	30,456	924,206	1,003,227	11.3
6000	Depository institutions	266	263	10.2	11,019	10,921	28,411	28,915	334,910	337,273	17.6
6020	Commercial banks	135	132	12.4	8,486	8,421	29,512	30,335	274,896	273,886	21.6
6030	Savings institutions	97	97	9.3	2,312	2,252	24,626	23,892	54,254	57,700	11.8
6060	Credit unions	31	31	7.5	-	232	-	25,034	-	5,027	5.9
6090	Functions closely related to banking	3	3	5.3	-	16	-	45,000	-	660	4.6
6100	Nondepository institutions	92	99	16.2	-	1,952	-	29,436	-	63,991	19.3
6140	Personal credit institutions	27	26	15.4	451	1,095	28,914	23,847	12,923	27,009	43.2
6150	Business credit institutions	10	13	12.4	-	105	-	52,267	-	4,740	6.0
6160	Mortgage bankers and brokers	50	59	17.9	469	752	32,171	34,388	17,749	31,708	18.0
6200	Security and commodity brokers	80	91	10.0	1,265	-	44,180	-	55,591	-	-
6210	Security brokers and dealers	30	29	8.9	-	286	-	82,238	-	28,546	3.6
6280	Security and commodity services	48	61	10.6	984	352	32,573	31,807	32,114	13,136	1.1
6300	Insurance carriers	143	115	16.3	8,383	9,398	34,524	32,506	287,951	296,135	12.2
6310	Life insurance	50	43	14.3	2,361	3,509	34,963	32,761	79,737	101,645	7.2
6330	Fire, marine, and casualty insurance	32	34	19.9	3,070	3,185	34,258	31,533	106,692	104,217	18.1
6350	Surety insurance	4	6	37.5	-	73	-	39,452	-	3,073	-
6400	Insurance agents, brokers, and service	355	377	13.0	2,083	2,158	33,771	32,356	75,494	81,646	11.8
6500	Real estate	512	552	11.8	4,010	4,344	23,231	23,780	100,569	123,140	13.3
6510	Real estate operators and lessors	173	179	10.4	1,384	1,405	22,477	22,984	33,339	38,975	14.6
6530	Real estate agents and managers	230	320	12.6	2,036	2,667	23,110	24,138	50,812	76,802	12.5
6540	Title abstract offices	2	6	11.1	-	54	-	28,222	-	1,753	21.2
6552	Subdividers and developers, n.e.c.	20	19	10.9	183	86	30,536	26,372	5,879	2,556	14.5
6553	Cemetery subdividers and developers	15	18	13.3	112	124	18,821	21,387	2,342	2,684	15.1
6700	Holding and other investment offices	95	81	10.8	613	1,453	51,869	36,663	34,700	58,530	10.0
6710	Holding offices	10	20	12.2	78	-	55,949	-	4,012	-	-
6720	Investment offices	7	2	5.1	32	-	13,000	-	537	-	-
6732	Educational, religious, etc. trusts	13	13	8.3	309	318	68,155	58,604	23,066	22,701	37.3
6733	Trusts, n.e.c.	32	23	11.3	80	66	18,800	15,758	2,735	1,620	6.3

Source: County Business Patterns, 1992/93, CBP-92/93-1, U.S. Department of Commerce, Washington, D.C., April 1995. SIC categories for which data were suppressed or not available for both 1992 and 1993 are *not* displayed. The employment columns represent mid-March employment in the year. Pay per employee is calculated by dividing 1st Quarter payroll, annualized, by mid-March employment. The columns headed "% State" show the county's percentage of the state total for the SIC in 1993; for example, 0.9% for SIC 6030 means that the county had 0.9 percent of the state's total establishments (or payroll) in SIC 6030 in 1993. A dash (-) is used to indicate that data are not available or cannot be calculated; *nec* means not elsewhere classified.

Continued on next page.

SIC	Industry	No. Establishments			Employment		Pay / Employee		Annual Payroll ($ 000)		
		1992	1993	% State	1992	1993	1992	1993	1992	1993	% State
NORFOLK, MA - [continued]											
						36		54,333		1,566	13.9
6794	Patent owners and lessors	2	3	13.0	-	13	-	7,692	-	106	0.6
6798	Real estate investment trusts	10	6	14.3	-	56	39,127	67,214	1,982	4,572	10.0
6799	Investors, n.e.c.	15	13	11.8	55						
PLYMOUTH, MA											
60 –	**Finance, insurance, and real estate**	721	755	5.7	8,639	8,695	26,432	26,344	225,688	254,469	2.9
6000	Depository institutions	155	156	6.0	2,691	2,672	23,951	23,091	60,017	64,531	3.4
6020	Commercial banks	53	54	5.1	784	1,082	26,026	24,373	20,187	26,899	2.1
6030	Savings institutions	79	80	7.7	1,407	1,136	23,673	23,025	29,954	28,114	5.7
6060	Credit unions	23	22	5.3	500	454	21,480	20,203	9,876	9,518	11.2
6100	Nondepository institutions	39	42	6.9	270	370	33,881	24,595	10,168	12,364	3.7
6140	Personal credit institutions	14	11	6.5	91	-	27,780	-	2,480	-	-
6150	Business credit institutions	5	5	4.8	9	-	26,667	-	277	-	-
6160	Mortgage bankers and brokers	18	26	7.9	162	278	38,173	25,194	7,215	10,269	5.8
6200	Security and commodity brokers	25	30	3.3	398	538	41,156	41,100	15,542	24,290	1.2
6210	Security brokers and dealers	11	13	4.0	168	139	68,571	90,734	8,668	12,191	1.5
6280	Security and commodity services	13	16	2.8	226	-	20,991	-	6,737	-	-
6300	Insurance carriers	45	41	5.8	3,159	3,212	26,339	27,661	82,037	100,130	4.1
6330	Fire, marine, and casualty insurance	9	9	5.3	794	-	29,300	-	19,467	-	-
6370	Pension, health, and welfare funds	12	10	8.0	53	179	14,340	20,626	772	6,301	20.7
6400	Insurance agents, brokers, and service	207	209	7.2	1,107	990	29,973	29,014	33,394	30,683	4.4
6500	Real estate	228	257	5.5	931	828	21,899	20,246	22,729	20,493	2.2
6510	Real estate operators and lessors	53	73	4.2	215	262	23,553	22,305	5,481	6,736	2.5
6530	Real estate agents and managers	118	151	5.9	505	471	22,210	18,837	12,457	11,279	1.8
6540	Title abstract offices	4	5	9.3	16	22	29,000	29,091	579	762	9.2
6552	Subdividers and developers, n.e.c.	10	13	7.5	34	57	26,353	20,772	907	1,140	6.4
6553	Cemetery subdividers and developers	8	10	7.4	13	14	15,692	15,143	251	391	2.2
6700	Holding and other investment offices	22	20	2.7	83	85	19,229	21,365	1,801	1,978	0.3
6732	Educational, religious, etc. trusts	5	5	3.2	-	26	-	11,692	-	366	0.6
6733	Trusts, n.e.c.	11	10	4.9	17	24	18,588	16,000	392	369	1.4
SUFFOLK, MA											
60 –	**Finance, insurance, and real estate**	2,359	2,429	18.4	83,690	80,078	51,624	53,638	4,089,361	4,381,612	49.3
6000	Depository institutions	309	322	12.4	18,474	17,072	43,397	45,156	764,394	737,607	38.5
6020	Commercial banks	161	170	16.0	15,779	14,811	44,289	47,515	659,912	663,959	52.4
6030	Savings institutions	79	72	6.9	1,582	1,364	39,424	27,109	66,199	42,953	8.8
6060	Credit unions	31	41	9.9	-	485	-	23,777	-	13,050	15.4
6090	Functions closely related to banking	30	30	52.6	449	-	38,441	-	16,714	-	-
6100	Nondepository institutions	77	81	13.2	-	1,169	-	42,703	-	64,213	19.4
6110	Federal and Federally-sponsored credit	6	-	-	340	-	86,894	-	27,389	-	-
6140	Personal credit institutions	24	14	8.3	-	219	-	28,566	-	7,250	11.6
6150	Business credit institutions	24	30	28.6	406	694	62,236	50,184	23,302	41,686	52.4
6160	Mortgage bankers and brokers	23	36	10.9	173	256	40,370	34,516	11,460	15,184	8.6
6200	Security and commodity brokers	395	430	47.3	19,835	21,148	75,162	77,650	1,456,669	1,774,199	89.3
6210	Security brokers and dealers	179	171	52.3	11,446	7,999	73,226	81,593	805,822	672,940	84.1
6230	Security and commodity exchanges	4	2	100.0	99	-	55,152	-	5,251	-	-
6280	Security and commodity services	206	256	44.6	8,276	13,089	78,108	75,384	644,819	1,097,870	92.9
6300	Insurance carriers	177	148	21.0	21,621	17,527	45,968	46,334	832,004	742,954	30.7
6310	Life insurance	62	62	20.7	12,107	10,960	42,496	49,033	457,440	459,453	32.6
6330	Fire, marine, and casualty insurance	46	36	21.1	6,776	4,082	54,499	42,900	270,465	176,887	30.8
6360	Title insurance	10	9	69.2	116	-	43,103	-	4,993	-	-
6370	Pension, health, and welfare funds	43	27	21.6	325	469	28,554	23,352	9,058	14,504	47.7
6400	Insurance agents, brokers, and service	320	339	11.7	3,987	4,399	45,718	43,464	165,542	192,532	27.9
6500	Real estate	822	842	18.0	12,228	12,505	33,795	33,754	409,714	428,632	46.1
6510	Real estate operators and lessors	292	324	18.8	2,910	3,654	26,827	34,957	78,472	126,140	47.1
6530	Real estate agents and managers	405	468	18.4	8,520	8,595	36,447	33,459	305,651	294,851	47.9
6552	Subdividers and developers, n.e.c.	36	26	14.9	252	98	40,143	28,653	9,956	3,328	18.8
6553	Cemetery subdividers and developers	12	14	10.4	110	117	23,855	26,325	3,020	3,609	20.3

Source: County Business Patterns, 1992/93, CBP-92/93-1, U.S. Department of Commerce, Washington, D.C., April 1995. SIC categories for which data were suppressed or not available for both 1992 and 1993 are *not* displayed. The employment columns represent mid-March employment in the year. Pay per employee is calculated by dividing 1st Quarter payroll, annualized, by mid-March employment. The columns headed "% State" show the county's percentage of the state total for the SIC in 1993; for example, 0.9% for SIC 6030 means that the county had 0.9 percent of the state's total establishments (or payroll) in SIC 6030 in 1993. A dash (-) is used to indicate that data are not available or cannot be calculated; *nec* means not elsewhere classified.

Continued on next page.

SIC	Industry	No. Establishments			Employment		Pay / Employee		Annual Payroll ($ 000)		
		1992	1993	% State	1992	1993	1992	1993	1992	1993	% State
SUFFOLK, MA - [continued]											
6700	Holding and other investment offices	246	258	*34.3*	3,573	6,113	66,315	65,293	239,064	432,833	*73.7*
6710	Holding offices	53	57	*34.8*	1,205	1,287	66,158	68,535	92,811	85,685	*64.3*
6720	Investment offices	26	25	*64.1*	772	3,211	71,782	73,208	54,766	264,154	*90.8*
6732	Educational, religious, etc. trusts	49	49	*31.4*	619	415	70,061	47,711	26,088	22,193	*36.4*
6733	Trusts, n.e.c.	55	56	*27.5*	238	246	40,689	40,293	17,740	15,686	*61.1*
6798	Real estate investment trusts	18	11	*26.2*	441	-	47,102	-	24,256	-	-
6799	Investors, n.e.c.	35	51	*46.4*	-	318	-	108,239		31,532	*69.0*
WORCESTER, MA											
60 –	**Finance, insurance, and real estate**	1,206	1,225	*9.3*	15,361	18,632	31,766	29,993	495,180	583,261	*6.6*
6000	Depository institutions	299	287	*11.1*	4,455	4,498	23,892	23,477	108,768	110,700	*5.8*
6020	Commercial banks	107	99	*9.3*	1,668	1,768	24,947	27,079	43,597	47,543	*3.8*
6030	Savings institutions	128	124	*11.9*	1,999	2,044	24,394	21,951	48,835	49,647	*10.2*
6100	Nondepository institutions	69	63	*10.3*	517	658	29,493	38,073	16,457	28,572	*8.6*
6140	Personal credit institutions	34	25	*14.8*	334	263	28,503	27,057	9,458	9,460	*15.1*
6150	Business credit institutions	5	10	*9.5*	30	258	33,333	50,775	1,016	12,147	*15.3*
6160	Mortgage bankers and brokers	27	28	*8.5*	146	137	31,479	35,299	5,842	6,965	*3.9*
6200	Security and commodity brokers	35	45	*5.0*	-	297	-	52,377		16,633	*0.8*
6210	Security brokers and dealers	10	10	*3.1*	185	184	67,114	68,565	12,300	13,411	*1.7*
6280	Security and commodity services	25	35	*6.1*	-	113	-	26,018	-	3,222	*0.3*
6300	Insurance carriers	78	75	*10.6*	5,646	9,865	41,345	33,025	217,593	325,334	*13.4*
6310	Life insurance	36	38	*12.7*	3,935	7,186	46,890	34,761	168,843	239,949	*17.0*
6330	Fire, marine, and casualty insurance	20	17	*9.9*	1,061	1,952	30,730	29,789	31,186	65,321	*11.4*
6400	Insurance agents, brokers, and service	277	297	*10.2*	2,600	1,563	28,717	29,162	85,270	55,890	*8.1*
6500	Real estate	393	418	*8.9*	1,622	1,541	18,042	19,289	34,516	33,900	*3.6*
6510	Real estate operators and lessors	147	158	*9.2*	697	657	16,430	16,274	13,495	12,353	*4.6*
6530	Real estate agents and managers	162	191	*7.5*	672	670	18,863	21,887	14,008	15,555	*2.5*
6540	Title abstract offices	15	17	*31.5*	56	82	27,714	22,244	2,516	2,764	*33.5*
6552	Subdividers and developers, n.e.c.	13	23	*13.2*	54	55	16,222	25,455	951	1,552	*8.8*
6553	Cemetery subdividers and developers	21	22	*16.3*	63	76	15,873	14,947	1,208	1,416	*8.0*
6700	Holding and other investment offices	54	39	*5.2*	305	-	49,023	-	18,607	-	-
6710	Holding offices	20	17	*10.4*	212	155	58,717	59,871	14,111	9,179	*6.9*
6732	Educational, religious, etc. trusts	5	5	*3.2*	17	-	27,765	-	498	-	-
6733	Trusts, n.e.c.	13	9	*4.4*	10	13	26,000	11,385	809	492	*1.9*

Source: County Business Patterns, 1992/93, CBP-92/93-1, U.S. Department of Commerce, Washington, D.C., April 1995. SIC categories for which data were suppressed or not available for both 1992 and 1993 are *not* displayed. The employment columns represent mid-March employment in the year. Pay per employee is calculated by dividing 1st Quarter payroll, annualized, by mid-March employment. The columns headed "% State" show the county's percentage of the state total for the SIC in 1993; for example, 0.9% for SIC 6030 means that the county had 0.9 percent of the state's total establishments (or payroll) in SIC 6030 in 1993. A dash (-) is used to indicate that data are not available or cannot be calculated; *nec* means not elsewhere classified.

MICHIGAN

SIC	Industry	No. Establishments			Employment		Pay / Employee		Annual Payroll ($ 000)		
		1992	1993	% State	1992	1993	1992	1993	1992	1993	% State
ALCONA, MI											
60–	**Finance, insurance, and real estate**	9	10	0.1	-	29	-	11,448	-	396	0.0
6000	Depository institutions	4	4	0.1	20	-	13,400	-	263	-	-
6400	Insurance agents, brokers, and service	3	4	0.1	-	5	-	14,400	-	97	0.0
ALGER, MI											
60–	**Finance, insurance, and real estate**	17	20	0.1	85	86	15,529	15,302	1,386	1,412	0.0
6000	Depository institutions	11	11	0.3	67	67	15,045	14,567	1,057	1,013	0.1
6500	Real estate	1	3	0.1	-	2	-	8,000	-	33	0.0
6530	Real estate agents and managers	1	3	0.1	-	2	-	8,000	-	33	0.0
ALLEGAN, MI											
60–	**Finance, insurance, and real estate**	115	122	0.7	751	666	17,726	18,438	13,273	14,040	0.2
6000	Depository institutions	43	45	1.1	445	428	18,274	16,710	7,556	7,787	0.5
6020	Commercial banks	30	33	1.3	281	257	17,181	15,907	4,600	4,420	0.4
6300	Insurance carriers	5	3	0.2	-	20	-	33,400	-	701	0.0
6400	Insurance agents, brokers, and service	32	34	0.9	112	126	21,964	23,460	2,602	3,450	0.6
6500	Real estate	31	35	0.6	143	70	9,930	13,657	1,563	1,641	0.2
6510	Real estate operators and lessors	13	14	0.6	107	-	9,570	-	1,141	-	-
6530	Real estate agents and managers	14	18	0.6	31	24	6,839	10,667	289	862	0.2
ALPENA, MI											
60–	**Finance, insurance, and real estate**	66	66	0.4	448	515	19,804	18,214	9,843	10,256	0.2
6000	Depository institutions	21	21	0.5	228	224	18,439	17,500	4,155	4,297	0.3
6020	Commercial banks	12	11	0.4	140	126	18,686	17,429	2,516	2,368	0.2
6300	Insurance carriers	9	7	0.5	52	46	27,308	26,957	1,461	1,389	0.1
6400	Insurance agents, brokers, and service	13	16	0.4	95	115	17,979	15,791	1,766	1,942	0.3
6500	Real estate	14	14	0.2	23	80	8,696	7,800	250	771	0.1
6530	Real estate agents and managers	11	10	0.3	19	71	9,053	7,437	207	589	0.2
6700	Holding and other investment offices	5	5	0.8	-	40	-	29,200	-	1,288	0.6
ANTRIM, MI											
60–	**Finance, insurance, and real estate**	41	43	0.2	167	172	15,569	12,767	2,790	2,703	0.0
6000	Depository institutions	14	14	0.4	83	78	19,133	14,462	1,590	1,298	0.1
6500	Real estate	18	20	0.3	64	75	11,562	9,813	801	939	0.1
6510	Real estate operators and lessors	3	4	0.2	2	-	10,000	-	42	-	-
6530	Real estate agents and managers	12	15	0.5	59	72	11,661	9,611	675	875	0.2
ARENAC, MI											
60–	**Finance, insurance, and real estate**	28	26	0.2	145	143	15,614	11,916	2,353	2,277	0.0
6000	Depository institutions	10	9	0.2	107	101	16,636	12,832	1,853	1,863	0.1
6020	Commercial banks	7	6	0.2	94	87	17,191	12,690	1,672	1,654	0.1
6400	Insurance agents, brokers, and service	7	8	0.2	25	24	16,160	13,333	403	315	0.1
6530	Real estate agents and managers	3	5	0.2	4	-	6,000	-	27	-	-
BARAGA, MI											
60–	**Finance, insurance, and real estate**	15	16	0.1	76	76	18,684	20,684	1,442	1,567	0.0
6000	Depository institutions	5	5	0.1	42	-	21,333	-	868	-	-
6020	Commercial banks	4	4	0.2	-	37	-	22,054	-	851	0.1
6400	Insurance agents, brokers, and service	6	6	0.2	12	15	20,000	26,933	287	336	0.1

Source: County Business Patterns, 1992/93, CBP-92/93-1, U.S. Department of Commerce, Washington, D.C., April 1995. SIC categories for which data were suppressed or not available for both 1992 and 1993 are *not* displayed. The employment columns represent mid-March employment in the year. Pay per employee is calculated by dividing 1st Quarter payroll, annualized, by mid-March employment. The columns headed "% State" show the county's percentage of the state total for the SIC in 1993; for example, 0.9% for SIC 6030 means that the county had 0.9 percent of the state's total establishments (or payroll) in SIC 6030 in 1993. A dash (-) is used to indicate that data are not available or cannot be calculated; *nec* means not elsewhere classified.

SIC	Industry	No. Establishments 1992	1993	% State	Employment 1992	1993	Pay / Employee 1992	1993	Annual Payroll ($ 000) 1992	1993	% State
BARRY, MI											
60 –	**Finance, insurance, and real estate**	56	50	0.3	584	590	19,260	24,108	12,274	13,812	0.2
6000	Depository institutions	13	13	0.3	172	187	18,558	17,968	3,385	3,586	0.2
6020	Commercial banks	7	6	0.2	127	130	18,457	18,769	2,420	2,508	0.2
6030	Savings institutions	3	3	0.6	31	41	20,129	15,805	726	806	0.4
6060	Credit unions	3	4	0.5	14	16	16,000	17,000	239	272	0.2
6400	Insurance agents, brokers, and service	20	16	0.4	61	62	15,344	16,194	944	1,047	0.2
6500	Real estate	15	13	0.2	34	22	10,118	9,818	405	315	0.0
6510	Real estate operators and lessors	5	4	0.2	16	-	8,500	-	154	-	-
6530	Real estate agents and managers	8	8	0.3	16	15	12,000	10,400	189	199	0.1
BAY, MI											
60 –	**Finance, insurance, and real estate**	193	193	1.1	1,554	1,616	19,776	21,059	34,771	34,869	0.6
6000	Depository institutions	57	61	1.6	983	1,062	18,336	19,122	21,770	20,165	1.2
6020	Commercial banks	40	41	1.6	742	742	19,084	18,323	14,461	13,014	1.0
6100	Nondepository institutions	6	4	0.6	86	36	20,326	29,889	1,793	1,170	0.2
6140	Personal credit institutions	3	-	-	52	-	16,154	-	887	-	-
6200	Security and commodity brokers	9	11	1.4	47	48	38,468	56,167	2,217	3,079	0.7
6210	Security brokers and dealers	7	8	1.8	-	46	-	58,435	-	3,039	0.9
6280	Security and commodity services	2	3	1.0	-	2	-	4,000	-	40	0.1
6300	Insurance carriers	13	11	0.8	95	89	34,611	34,697	3,006	2,750	0.2
6310	Life insurance	4	5	1.6	-	39	-	39,077	-	1,185	0.3
6330	Fire, marine, and casualty insurance	5	4	0.6	50	-	32,800	-	1,571	-	-
6400	Insurance agents, brokers, and service	43	40	1.0	151	161	22,040	22,484	3,337	3,719	0.6
6500	Real estate	59	59	1.0	187	174	13,176	12,345	2,551	2,796	0.4
6510	Real estate operators and lessors	31	32	1.3	104	78	9,654	10,308	939	918	0.4
6530	Real estate agents and managers	17	19	0.6	28	35	14,143	12,914	547	658	0.2
6553	Cemetery subdividers and developers	4	5	3.1	-	19	-	15,368	-	354	1.1
6700	Holding and other investment offices	6	7	1.1	5	46	14,400	23,826	97	1,190	0.5
BENZIE, MI											
60 –	**Finance, insurance, and real estate**	26	26	0.2	128	147	18,781	16,054	2,692	2,711	0.0
6000	Depository institutions	7	8	0.2	77	87	21,610	18,023	1,812	1,819	0.1
6020	Commercial banks	7	7	0.3	77	-	21,610	-	1,812	-	-
6400	Insurance agents, brokers, and service	8	8	0.2	19	26	16,842	13,385	336	393	0.1
6500	Real estate	10	10	0.2	-	34	-	13,059	-	499	0.1
6530	Real estate agents and managers	6	6	0.2	12	12	9,333	9,667	156	145	0.0
BERRIEN, MI											
60 –	**Finance, insurance, and real estate**	331	327	1.9	2,634	2,600	23,831	25,549	63,265	66,190	1.1
6000	Depository institutions	89	91	2.3	1,073	1,082	19,940	19,937	22,980	23,107	1.4
6020	Commercial banks	60	63	2.4	766	749	19,227	19,621	16,228	16,093	1.3
6030	Savings institutions	14	12	2.2	144	141	22,194	20,511	3,169	3,022	1.5
6060	Credit unions	15	16	2.1	163	192	21,301	20,750	3,583	3,992	2.2
6200	Security and commodity brokers	7	9	1.2	-	32	-	55,750	-	1,695	0.4
6210	Security brokers and dealers	5	5	1.1	-	26	-	59,846	-	1,404	0.4
6280	Security and commodity services	2	4	1.3	-	6	-	38,000	-	291	0.5
6300	Insurance carriers	20	13	0.9	122	99	31,508	35,152	4,105	3,537	0.2
6310	Life insurance	5	4	1.3	58	56	25,586	26,429	1,543	1,260	0.4
6330	Fire, marine, and casualty insurance	9	8	1.3	44	-	47,182	-	2,160	-	-
6400	Insurance agents, brokers, and service	80	87	2.2	279	250	22,165	22,560	6,165	6,265	1.0
6500	Real estate	117	110	1.8	399	436	13,564	14,706	7,159	7,887	1.2
6510	Real estate operators and lessors	47	40	1.7	134	195	10,567	10,810	1,702	2,361	1.1
6530	Real estate agents and managers	53	62	2.1	196	188	13,878	16,149	3,313	3,621	1.0
6552	Subdividers and developers, n.e.c.	2	4	2.0	-	11	-	33,818	-	381	1.4
6733	Trusts, n.e.c.	6	6	3.4	27	28	5,185	4,714	147	124	0.6

Source: County Business Patterns, 1992/93, CBP-92/93-1, U.S. Department of Commerce, Washington, D.C., April 1995. SIC categories for which data were suppressed or not available for both 1992 and 1993 are *not* displayed. The employment columns represent mid-March employment in the year. Pay per employee is calculated by dividing 1st Quarter payroll, annualized, by mid-March employment. The columns headed "% State" show the county's percentage of the state total for the SIC in 1993; for example, 0.9% for SIC 6030 means that the county had 0.9 percent of the state's total establishments (or payroll) in SIC 6030 in 1993. A dash (-) is used to indicate that data are not available or cannot be calculated; *nec* means not elsewhere classified.

SIC	Industry	No. Establishments			Employment		Pay / Employee		Annual Payroll ($ 000)		
		1992	1993	% State	1992	1993	1992	1993	1992	1993	% State
BRANCH, MI											
60 –	**Finance, insurance, and real estate**	75	74	0.4	532	391	19,481	19,325	10,668	8,196	0.1
6000	Depository institutions	21	22	0.6	253	252	18,925	17,540	4,971	4,734	0.3
6020	Commercial banks	14	15	0.6	206	194	18,718	16,660	4,019	3,494	0.3
6300	Insurance carriers	9	8	0.6	39	35	30,872	30,971	1,290	1,142	0.1
6330	Fire, marine, and casualty insurance	5	4	0.6	27	-	32,148	-	912	-	-
6400	Insurance agents, brokers, and service	16	16	0.4	47	47	16,255	18,723	787	909	0.1
6500	Real estate	23	24	0.4	49	46	14,122	14,348	780	838	0.1
6510	Real estate operators and lessors	10	9	0.4	15	22	8,533	17,273	159	460	0.2
6530	Real estate agents and managers	9	11	0.4	23	14	17,739	10,571	440	211	0.1
CALHOUN, MI											
60 –	**Finance, insurance, and real estate**	224	227	1.3	3,907	4,223	29,234	32,077	122,403	134,006	2.3
6000	Depository institutions	62	61	1.6	567	729	19,210	19,407	11,915	15,280	0.9
6020	Commercial banks	31	30	1.2	264	396	17,924	19,566	5,136	8,110	0.6
6030	Savings institutions	13	13	2.4	134	136	17,433	17,765	2,646	2,825	1.4
6060	Credit unions	18	18	2.4	169	197	22,627	20,223	4,133	4,345	2.4
6100	Nondepository institutions	2	3	0.4	-	13	-	16,615	-	384	0.1
6200	Security and commodity brokers	7	7	0.9	-	39	-	54,872	-	2,476	0.6
6210	Security brokers and dealers	6	7	1.5	43	39	51,814	54,872	2,242	2,476	0.7
6300	Insurance carriers	27	21	1.5	2,639	2,652	31,271	36,985	88,374	93,281	5.7
6400	Insurance agents, brokers, and service	56	60	1.5	171	198	25,474	22,485	4,192	4,736	0.8
6500	Real estate	58	62	1.0	217	278	13,253	12,086	3,390	4,159	0.6
6510	Real estate operators and lessors	20	18	0.7	109	108	12,294	10,852	1,518	1,512	0.7
6530	Real estate agents and managers	31	36	1.2	76	142	13,632	12,141	1,323	1,998	0.5
6700	Holding and other investment offices	12	13	2.0	260	314	43,046	41,592	12,063	13,690	6.2
CASS, MI											
60 –	**Finance, insurance, and real estate**	63	62	0.4	301	334	18,977	18,970	6,417	7,359	0.1
6000	Depository institutions	19	19	0.5	144	174	18,250	19,034	2,699	3,476	0.2
6020	Commercial banks	13	14	0.5	110	149	18,400	18,926	2,094	2,969	0.2
6400	Insurance agents, brokers, and service	19	17	0.4	48	41	16,917	15,805	832	804	0.1
6500	Real estate	20	20	0.3	57	66	12,561	9,697	937	804	0.1
6530	Real estate agents and managers	9	9	0.3	13	24	13,846	8,500	211	223	0.1
CHARLEVOIX, MI											
60 –	**Finance, insurance, and real estate**	57	61	0.4	296	330	16,905	17,333	5,527	6,210	0.1
6000	Depository institutions	18	21	0.5	150	173	19,973	19,861	3,052	3,287	0.2
6200	Security and commodity brokers	1	4	0.5	-	3	-	16,000	-	68	0.0
6400	Insurance agents, brokers, and service	12	13	0.3	36	54	20,444	20,963	822	1,319	0.2
6500	Real estate	20	20	0.3	84	89	10,238	10,022	1,110	1,258	0.2
6510	Real estate operators and lessors	4	2	0.1	7	-	6,286	-	54	-	-
6530	Real estate agents and managers	13	17	0.6	62	83	9,226	10,506	734	1,198	0.3
CHEBOYGAN, MI											
60 –	**Finance, insurance, and real estate**	46	49	0.3	235	224	16,749	17,196	4,399	4,509	0.1
6000	Depository institutions	18	17	0.4	152	140	18,079	18,914	2,856	2,836	0.2
6400	Insurance agents, brokers, and service	8	11	0.3	38	39	17,474	16,308	723	701	0.1
6500	Real estate	15	16	0.3	32	33	10,750	11,758	538	705	0.1
6510	Real estate operators and lessors	4	4	0.2	7	-	4,571	-	44	-	-
6530	Real estate agents and managers	8	10	0.3	14	20	11,429	10,800	244	346	0.1
CHIPPEWA, MI											
60 –	**Finance, insurance, and real estate**	67	66	0.4	395	421	16,365	16,238	7,010	7,488	0.1
6000	Depository institutions	23	24	0.6	266	279	16,917	16,129	4,695	4,880	0.3
6020	Commercial banks	12	13	0.5	180	174	17,800	18,322	3,366	3,414	0.3
6400	Insurance agents, brokers, and service	16	12	0.3	48	43	13,500	14,419	695	711	0.1

Source: County Business Patterns, 1992/93, CBP-92/93-1, U.S. Department of Commerce, Washington, D.C., April 1995. SIC categories for which data were suppressed or not available for both 1992 and 1993 are not displayed. The employment columns represent mid-March employment in the year. Pay per employee is calculated by dividing 1st Quarter payroll, annualized, by mid-March employment. The columns headed "% State" show the county's percentage of the state total for the SIC in 1993; for example, 0.9% for SIC 6030 means that the county had 0.9 percent of the state's total establishments (or payroll) in SIC 6030 in 1993. A dash (-) is used to indicate that data are not available or cannot be calculated; nec means not elsewhere classified.

Continued on next page.

SIC	Industry	No. Establishments			Employment		Pay / Employee		Annual Payroll ($ 000)		
		1992	1993	% State	1992	1993	1992	1993	1992	1993	% State
CHIPPEWA, MI - [continued]											
6500	Real estate	23	25	0.4	68	87	12,647	12,598	1,106	1,263	0.2
6510	Real estate operators and lessors	8	10	0.4	17	39	9,647	14,359	219	574	0.3
6530	Real estate agents and managers	8	11	0.4	19	29	10,526	10,207	248	354	0.1
CLARE, MI											
60 –	**Finance, insurance, and real estate**	47	46	0.3	200	213	14,420	15,324	3,254	3,483	0.1
6000	Depository institutions	12	12	0.3	139	151	15,396	17,113	2,266	2,551	0.2
6400	Insurance agents, brokers, and service	14	16	0.4	26	-	14,769	-	453	-	-
6500	Real estate	15	17	0.3	29	-	9,793	-	391	-	-
6510	Real estate operators and lessors	5	3	0.1	14	-	6,857	-	113	-	-
6530	Real estate agents and managers	5	11	0.4	11	19	14,545	5,684	223	222	0.1
CLINTON, MI											
60 –	**Finance, insurance, and real estate**	58	60	0.3	351	372	18,336	18,634	6,632	7,528	0.1
6000	Depository institutions	16	16	0.4	198	220	18,444	18,036	3,577	4,308	0.3
6020	Commercial banks	12	11	0.4	-	171	-	18,620	-	3,494	0.3
6300	Insurance carriers	5	6	0.4	12	16	16,667	17,500	253	367	0.0
6370	Pension, health, and welfare funds	3	3	1.3	-	3	-	2,667	-	42	0.1
6400	Insurance agents, brokers, and service	14	16	0.4	58	64	22,759	21,750	1,418	1,416	0.2
6500	Real estate	17	18	0.3	49	57	10,694	12,702	659	946	0.1
6510	Real estate operators and lessors	5	7	0.3	23	29	9,217	12,966	295	471	0.2
6530	Real estate agents and managers	9	7	0.2	21	22	12,571	13,636	313	421	0.1
6553	Cemetery subdividers and developers	2	4	2.5	-	6	-	8,000	-	54	0.2
6700	Holding and other investment offices	3	2	0.3	1	-	12,000	-	22	-	-
CRAWFORD, MI											
60 –	**Finance, insurance, and real estate**	16	19	0.1	114	121	15,860	16,562	1,888	2,123	0.0
6000	Depository institutions	7	7	0.2	93	89	15,656	16,899	1,474	1,537	0.1
6400	Insurance agents, brokers, and service	5	6	0.2	-	17	-	18,118	-	299	0.0
6500	Real estate	3	5	0.1	6	-	14,667	-	109	-	-
DELTA, MI											
60 –	**Finance, insurance, and real estate**	76	74	0.4	564	536	19,738	21,448	11,333	11,523	0.2
6000	Depository institutions	21	21	0.5	324	314	18,543	20,102	6,083	6,314	0.4
6020	Commercial banks	11	12	0.5	198	241	18,707	20,365	3,713	4,856	0.4
6300	Insurance carriers	8	6	0.4	81	79	29,728	29,165	2,327	2,255	0.1
6400	Insurance agents, brokers, and service	18	20	0.5	64	65	19,438	18,954	1,332	1,234	0.2
6500	Real estate	24	22	0.4	82	67	10,000	12,179	946	979	0.1
6510	Real estate operators and lessors	9	7	0.3	33	-	8,727	-	262	-	-
6530	Real estate agents and managers	10	11	0.4	28	21	7,143	12,762	250	304	0.1
DICKINSON, MI											
60 –	**Finance, insurance, and real estate**	62	60	0.3	349	360	18,819	18,567	6,778	7,082	0.1
6000	Depository institutions	16	16	0.4	182	219	18,703	18,137	3,570	4,218	0.3
6020	Commercial banks	12	12	0.5	157	171	18,955	19,135	3,132	3,443	0.3
6300	Insurance carriers	9	7	0.5	16	20	35,500	32,400	599	641	0.0
6400	Insurance agents, brokers, and service	13	16	0.4	62	70	18,839	18,400	1,085	1,286	0.2
6500	Real estate	17	16	0.3	41	36	10,244	9,000	533	366	0.1
6510	Real estate operators and lessors	7	6	0.2	21	21	5,905	7,810	154	169	0.1
6530	Real estate agents and managers	7	8	0.3	9	12	12,444	10,667	134	159	0.0
EATON, MI											
60 –	**Finance, insurance, and real estate**	144	151	0.9	777	851	21,745	21,382	18,054	19,674	0.3
6000	Depository institutions	36	35	0.9	308	347	21,169	21,141	6,752	7,825	0.5
6020	Commercial banks	20	19	0.7	114	123	17,018	15,805	2,014	2,037	0.2
6030	Savings institutions	7	7	1.3	72	81	23,833	23,111	1,638	1,904	0.9
6060	Credit unions	9	9	1.2	122	143	23,475	24,615	3,100	3,884	2.2
6100	Nondepository institutions	3	3	0.4	-	14	-	31,714	-	384	0.1

Source: County Business Patterns, 1992/93, CBP-92/93-1, U.S. Department of Commerce, Washington, D.C., April 1995. SIC categories for which data were suppressed or not available for both 1992 and 1993 are not displayed. The employment columns represent mid-March employment in the year. Pay per employee is calculated by dividing 1st Quarter payroll, annualized, by mid-March employment. The columns headed "% State" show the county's percentage of the state total for the SIC in 1993; for example, 0.9% for SIC 6030 means that the county had 0.9 percent of the state's total establishments (or payroll) in SIC 6030 in 1993. A dash (-) is used to indicate that data are not available or cannot be calculated; nec means not elsewhere classified.

Continued on next page.

SIC	Industry	No. Establishments			Employment		Pay / Employee		Annual Payroll ($ 000)		
		1992	1993	% State	1992	1993	1992	1993	1992	1993	% State
EATON, MI - [continued]											
6300	Insurance carriers	10	11	0.8	151	134	32,371	34,955	5,065	4,963	0.3
6330	Fire, marine, and casualty insurance	6	6	0.9	115	-	36,243	-	4,296	-	-
6400	Insurance agents, brokers, and service	34	36	0.9	92	88	19,261	20,773	1,878	1,986	0.3
6500	Real estate	57	59	1.0	203	254	15,507	13,480	3,731	3,957	0.6
6510	Real estate operators and lessors	19	21	0.9	99	133	12,404	12,602	1,266	1,556	0.7
6530	Real estate agents and managers	29	30	1.0	86	97	19,674	13,979	2,160	1,895	0.5
EMMET, MI											
60 –	**Finance, insurance, and real estate**	93	98	0.6	485	547	20,289	18,479	10,698	12,045	0.2
6000	Depository institutions	20	21	0.5	197	236	23,228	19,814	4,544	5,226	0.3
6020	Commercial banks	17	17	0.7	186	201	23,591	20,358	4,345	4,612	0.4
6210	Security brokers and dealers	3	3	0.7	9	-	21,333	-	250	-	-
6300	Insurance carriers	3	4	0.3	12	28	41,333	25,143	513	738	0.0
6400	Insurance agents, brokers, and service	17	17	0.4	57	54	19,649	18,667	1,190	1,360	0.2
6500	Real estate	39	42	0.7	144	161	12,278	13,193	2,578	2,697	0.4
6510	Real estate operators and lessors	9	10	0.4	14	18	9,429	13,333	150	203	0.1
6530	Real estate agents and managers	27	28	1.0	115	134	12,383	12,746	1,977	2,219	0.6
6700	Holding and other investment offices	8	9	1.4	43	51	24,837	18,196	987	1,010	0.5
GENESEE, MI											
60 –	**Finance, insurance, and real estate**	638	663	3.8	5,747	6,139	22,908	22,905	139,731	156,965	2.7
6000	Depository institutions	136	136	3.5	2,812	2,777	22,057	20,941	62,958	65,825	4.0
6020	Commercial banks	94	96	3.7	2,208	2,153	22,513	21,065	49,869	52,153	4.2
6030	Savings institutions	18	17	3.2	160	163	17,475	18,307	2,858	3,246	1.6
6060	Credit unions	24	23	3.0	444	461	21,441	21,293	10,231	10,426	5.8
6100	Nondepository institutions	24	26	3.7	237	302	28,624	26,503	7,332	8,988	1.7
6140	Personal credit institutions	9	9	5.1	132	-	26,394	-	3,822	-	-
6160	Mortgage bankers and brokers	13	15	3.9	-	152	-	23,974	-	4,605	1.5
6200	Security and commodity brokers	25	25	3.3	193	226	51,461	50,265	9,921	11,714	2.8
6210	Security brokers and dealers	18	18	4.0	186	180	50,796	60,022	9,341	11,080	3.2
6280	Security and commodity services	7	7	2.3	7	46	69,143	12,087	580	634	1.0
6300	Insurance carriers	67	55	3.9	684	765	27,275	30,248	20,219	23,984	1.5
6310	Life insurance	16	12	3.8	242	192	21,355	22,958	5,248	4,550	1.3
6330	Fire, marine, and casualty insurance	35	28	4.4	318	257	32,868	37,354	10,945	9,908	1.3
6360	Title insurance	6	2	2.0	92	-	25,652	-	3,262	-	-
6400	Insurance agents, brokers, and service	143	163	4.2	627	724	21,729	21,514	15,593	19,005	3.1
6500	Real estate	225	241	4.0	1,039	1,085	14,753	15,617	17,309	20,338	3.0
6510	Real estate operators and lessors	91	105	4.3	465	469	14,873	13,825	7,101	7,181	3.4
6530	Real estate agents and managers	100	112	3.8	373	436	14,574	16,083	6,763	8,248	2.2
6552	Subdividers and developers, n.e.c.	4	7	3.5	11	13	12,727	14,462	155	366	1.4
6553	Cemetery subdividers and developers	6	10	6.3	110	135	17,091	17,689	2,188	2,869	9.0
6700	Holding and other investment offices	18	17	2.7	155	260	34,219	28,600	6,399	7,111	3.2
GLADWIN, MI											
60 –	**Finance, insurance, and real estate**	26	27	0.2	159	162	20,805	20,173	2,950	2,990	0.1
6000	Depository institutions	8	8	0.2	78	68	16,564	16,176	1,123	1,143	0.1
6400	Insurance agents, brokers, and service	5	6	0.2	32	-	21,125	-	794	-	-
6500	Real estate	11	12	0.2	-	56	-	23,857	-	983	0.1
6530	Real estate agents and managers	5	9	0.3	30	22	37,067	7,636	796	161	0.0
GOGEBIC, MI											
60 –	**Finance, insurance, and real estate**	47	44	0.3	334	288	11,437	15,222	4,060	4,387	0.1
6000	Depository institutions	10	9	0.2	117	118	17,709	17,424	2,148	2,214	0.1
6300	Insurance carriers	7	5	0.4	28	30	21,143	19,867	603	513	0.0
6400	Insurance agents, brokers, and service	13	13	0.3	24	-	17,000	-	518	-	-

Source: County Business Patterns, 1992/93, CBP-92/93-1, U.S. Department of Commerce, Washington, D.C., April 1995. SIC categories for which data were suppressed or not available for both 1992 and 1993 are *not* displayed. The employment columns represent mid-March employment in the year. Pay per employee is calculated by dividing 1st Quarter payroll, annualized, by mid-March employment. The columns headed "% State" show the county's percentage of the state total for the SIC in 1993; for example, 0.9% for SIC 6030 means that the county had 0.9 percent of the state's total establishments (or payroll) in SIC 6030 in 1993. A dash (-) is used to indicate that data are not available or cannot be calculated; *nec* means not elsewhere classified.

Continued on next page.

SIC	Industry	No. Establishments			Employment		Pay / Employee		Annual Payroll ($ 000)		
		1992	1993	% State	1992	1993	1992	1993	1992	1993	% State
GOGEBIC, MI - [continued]											
6500	Real estate	14	14	0.2	158	84	2,987	7,429	395	503	0.1
6510	Real estate operators and lessors	6	8	0.3	7	29	6,857	8,966	44	179	0.1
6530	Real estate agents and managers	7	6	0.2	27	55	10,519	6,618	195	324	0.1
GRAND TRAVERSE, MI											
60 –	**Finance, insurance, and real estate**	236	227	1.3	1,756	1,866	25,674	25,861	45,545	52,216	0.9
6000	Depository institutions	53	51	1.3	762	795	22,047	21,892	16,646	18,381	1.1
6020	Commercial banks	36	34	1.3	596	618	23,248	22,595	13,184	14,633	1.2
6100	Nondepository institutions	15	11	1.6	87	73	25,977	22,959	2,322	2,448	0.5
6140	Personal credit institutions	4	2	1.1	40	-	25,400	-	1,019	-	-
6150	Business credit institutions	4	2	1.8	14	-	35,429		298	-	-
6160	Mortgage bankers and brokers	7	7	1.8	33	43	22,667	19,070	1,005	1,602	0.5
6200	Security and commodity brokers	16	18	2.3	120	125	61,133	60,288	6,711	8,041	2.0
6210	Security brokers and dealers	12	14	3.1	115	122	63,374	61,508	6,643	7,992	2.3
6280	Security and commodity services	4	4	1.3	5	3	9,600	10,667	68	49	0.1
6300	Insurance carriers	30	27	1.9	272	314	30,912	32,713	8,372	10,699	0.7
6310	Life insurance	5	3	0.9	-	27	-	34,815	-	748	0.2
6324	Hospital and medical service plans	2	4	6.0	-	37	-	31,027	-	1,272	0.4
6330	Fire, marine, and casualty insurance	13	10	1.6	182	190	33,912	37,221	5,805	7,773	1.0
6360	Title insurance	3	3	3.0	18	22	17,556	17,455	467	531	1.0
6370	Pension, health, and welfare funds	6	7	3.0	10	38	21,600	19,158	341	375	0.6
6400	Insurance agents, brokers, and service	38	42	1.1	194	208	23,876	24,250	5,201	5,861	0.9
6500	Real estate	69	67	1.1	287	309	16,195	16,492	5,460	5,899	0.9
6510	Real estate operators and lessors	16	17	0.7	43	56	16,372	10,357	751	656	0.3
6530	Real estate agents and managers	37	40	1.4	136	222	20,412	16,306	3,126	3,885	1.0
6552	Subdividers and developers, n.e.c.	4	3	1.5	58	2	7,172	6,000	650	18	0.1
GRATIOT, MI											
60 –	**Finance, insurance, and real estate**	63	63	0.4	426	451	18,207	17,055	7,694	7,706	0.1
6000	Depository institutions	19	20	0.5	279	294	20,703	19,279	5,672	5,566	0.3
6020	Commercial banks	17	17	0.7	-	273	-	19,546	-	5,215	0.4
6200	Security and commodity brokers	3	2	0.3	10	-	29,600	-	348	-	-
6400	Insurance agents, brokers, and service	21	20	0.5	52	67	17,923	15,522	890	1,034	0.2
6500	Real estate	15	16	0.3	69	75	4,580	4,587	388	442	0.1
6510	Real estate operators and lessors	6	6	0.2	11	13	9,455	10,462	140	180	0.1
6530	Real estate agents and managers	6	7	0.2	9	9	12,444	9,333	127	117	0.0
HILLSDALE, MI											
60 –	**Finance, insurance, and real estate**	61	62	0.4	335	347	16,454	16,334	6,022	6,141	0.1
6000	Depository institutions	19	20	0.5	210	213	15,924	15,775	3,610	3,696	0.2
6020	Commercial banks	16	16	0.6	198	194	16,061	16,289	3,382	3,417	0.3
6400	Insurance agents, brokers, and service	18	19	0.5	55	62	18,255	18,516	1,073	1,326	0.2
6500	Real estate	18	16	0.3	39	50	7,179	8,240	410	455	0.1
6510	Real estate operators and lessors	6	3	0.1	12	-	4,667	-	67	-	-
6530	Real estate agents and managers	10	12	0.4	13	36	9,231	7,778	214	319	0.1
HOUGHTON, MI											
60 –	**Finance, insurance, and real estate**	67	67	0.4	592	574	20,108	19,429	12,163	11,761	0.2
6000	Depository institutions	21	19	0.5	404	372	21,188	20,925	8,646	8,138	0.5
6300	Insurance carriers	7	6	0.4	50	50	19,200	17,040	1,176	999	0.1
6330	Fire, marine, and casualty insurance	4	4	0.6	33	-	16,242	-	657	-	-
6400	Insurance agents, brokers, and service	17	19	0.5	66	67	19,939	20,179	1,191	1,284	0.2
6500	Real estate	16	16	0.3	41	60	9,659	8,133	447	619	0.1
6530	Real estate agents and managers	4	3	0.1	8	2	12,000	8,000	120	24	0.0

Source: County Business Patterns, 1992/93, CBP-92/93-1, U.S. Department of Commerce, Washington, D.C., April 1995. SIC categories for which data were suppressed or not available for both 1992 and 1993 are not displayed. The employment columns represent mid-March employment in the year. Pay per employee is calculated by dividing 1st Quarter payroll, annualized, by mid-March employment. The columns headed "% State" show the county's percentage of the state total for the SIC in 1993; for example, 0.9% for SIC 6030 means that the county had 0.9 percent of the state's total establishments (or payroll) in SIC 6030 in 1993. A dash (-) is used to indicate that data are not available or cannot be calculated; nec means not elsewhere classified.

SIC	Industry	No. Establishments			Employment		Pay / Employee		Annual Payroll ($ 000)		
		1992	1993	% State	1992	1993	1992	1993	1992	1993	% State
HURON, MI											
60 –	**Finance, insurance, and real estate**	83	78	0.5	485	388	17,105	19,505	8,679	7,512	0.1
6000	Depository institutions	27	26	0.7	254	255	18,724	20,486	4,925	5,160	0.3
6020	Commercial banks	21	20	0.8	226	225	19,257	21,209	4,495	4,687	0.4
6300	Insurance carriers	7	6	0.4	24	13	9,333	4,000	220	64	0.0
6370	Pension, health, and welfare funds	3	4	1.7	3	-	8,000	-	29	-	-
6400	Insurance agents, brokers, and service	28	30	0.8	73	77	14,247	16,156	1,153	1,362	0.2
6500	Real estate	15	11	0.2	107	26	14,467	16,615	1,523	364	0.1
6530	Real estate agents and managers	4	6	0.2	5	10	35,200	22,800	98	133	0.0
INGHAM, MI											
60 –	**Finance, insurance, and real estate**	729	714	4.1	10,996	10,824	28,953	28,045	320,198	321,706	5.5
6000	Depository institutions	126	138	3.5	2,685	2,868	27,176	23,782	70,312	72,350	4.4
6020	Commercial banks	83	97	3.8	1,898	2,120	28,457	23,498	50,665	53,197	4.2
6060	Credit unions	22	23	3.0	491	490	22,428	24,906	11,314	11,958	6.7
6100	Nondepository institutions	34	32	4.5	292	275	29,644	34,065	9,508	10,372	1.9
6140	Personal credit institutions	12	10	5.7	126	104	24,540	27,308	3,354	2,939	2.3
6160	Mortgage bankers and brokers	15	17	4.5	110	117	33,418	38,120	4,484	5,798	1.9
6200	Security and commodity brokers	39	36	4.7	278	278	58,619	59,827	14,263	16,509	4.0
6210	Security brokers and dealers	26	23	5.1	241	217	63,469	71,189	12,911	14,911	4.3
6280	Security and commodity services	13	13	4.3	37	61	27,027	19,410	1,352	1,598	2.5
6300	Insurance carriers	100	90	6.4	4,487	4,421	34,237	33,569	155,563	152,003	9.3
6310	Life insurance	25	21	6.6	1,738	1,593	38,838	36,038	63,138	54,589	16.0
6330	Fire, marine, and casualty insurance	36	37	5.8	1,624	1,650	30,640	29,593	54,781	55,953	7.2
6360	Title insurance	3	4	4.0	88	93	68,182	23,742	4,095	2,664	5.2
6370	Pension, health, and welfare funds	22	17	7.3	-	198	-	21,838	-	4,919	7.4
6400	Insurance agents, brokers, and service	170	157	4.0	988	842	32,158	29,900	32,321	29,345	4.7
6500	Real estate	219	224	3.8	2,009	1,851	13,852	15,311	30,671	32,424	4.8
6510	Real estate operators and lessors	96	105	4.3	775	495	10,952	15,871	9,194	8,895	4.2
6530	Real estate agents and managers	91	98	3.3	1,091	1,237	15,098	13,979	18,475	20,409	5.5
6552	Subdividers and developers, n.e.c.	13	15	7.5	56	64	28,000	37,375	1,502	2,364	8.8
6710	Holding offices	8	5	2.9	74	23	33,784	32,174	2,758	897	0.7
6732	Educational, religious, etc. trusts	10	10	10.3	30	29	23,067	21,517	683	603	3.2
6733	Trusts, n.e.c.	12	10	5.7	20	19	24,200	22,316	489	441	2.3
IONIA, MI											
60 –	**Finance, insurance, and real estate**	70	75	0.4	517	547	18,228	18,750	9,490	10,894	0.2
6000	Depository institutions	24	26	0.7	248	296	19,516	17,392	4,960	5,821	0.4
6020	Commercial banks	18	19	0.7	225	230	19,929	17,670	4,609	4,713	0.4
6400	Insurance agents, brokers, and service	20	21	0.5	68	77	18,235	18,701	1,218	1,708	0.3
6500	Real estate	18	21	0.4	57	62	9,193	10,710	616	766	0.1
6510	Real estate operators and lessors	5	7	0.3	30	34	9,200	10,235	322	400	0.2
6530	Real estate agents and managers	10	10	0.3	23	19	10,087	10,526	267	254	0.1
6553	Cemetery subdividers and developers	3	3	1.9	4	4	4,000	3,000	27	23	0.1
IOSCO, MI											
60 –	**Finance, insurance, and real estate**	53	50	0.3	336	325	16,869	17,182	5,903	5,811	0.1
6000	Depository institutions	17	16	0.4	214	212	16,075	17,245	3,593	3,723	0.2
6020	Commercial banks	9	9	0.3	141	117	17,277	19,111	2,571	2,348	0.2
6300	Insurance carriers	4	2	0.1	24	-	30,667	-	645	-	-
6400	Insurance agents, brokers, and service	13	12	0.3	44	43	18,273	16,558	744	706	0.1
6500	Real estate	15	17	0.3	40	45	11,600	11,200	567	688	0.1
6530	Real estate agents and managers	10	11	0.4	22	25	11,091	11,040	314	362	0.1
IRON, MI											
60 –	**Finance, insurance, and real estate**	26	27	0.2	151	161	17,086	16,646	2,755	2,679	0.0
6000	Depository institutions	11	11	0.3	101	103	16,792	17,243	1,834	1,799	0.1

Source: County Business Patterns, 1992/93, CBP-92/93-1, U.S. Department of Commerce, Washington, D.C., April 1995. SIC categories for which data were suppressed or not available for both 1992 and 1993 are not displayed. The employment columns represent mid-March employment in the year. Pay per employee is calculated by dividing 1st Quarter payroll, annualized, by mid-March employment. The columns headed "% State" show the county's percentage of the state total for the SIC in 1993; for example, 0.9% for SIC 6030 means that the county had 0.9 percent of the state's total establishments (or payroll) in SIC 6030 in 1993. A dash (-) is used to indicate that data are not available or cannot be calculated; nec means not elsewhere classified.

Continued on next page.

SIC	Industry	No. Establishments			Employment		Pay / Employee		Annual Payroll ($ 000)		
		1992	1993	% State	1992	1993	1992	1993	1992	1993	% State
IRON, MI - [continued]											
6020	Commercial banks	7	7	0.3	75	82	18,827	17,317	1,533	1,473	0.1
6500	Real estate	7	7	0.1	-	11	-	18,545	-	238	0.0
6530	Real estate agents and managers	3	2	0.1	3	-	6,667	-	35	-	
ISABELLA, MI											
60 –	**Finance, insurance, and real estate**	97	107	0.6	784	805	15,148	16,889	13,847	15,235	0.3
6000	Depository institutions	26	26	0.7	274	276	18,467	19,522	5,137	5,498	0.3
6020	Commercial banks	20	20	0.8	218	228	19,450	19,825	4,330	4,660	0.4
6300	Insurance carriers	5	7	0.5	39	91	27,795	22,154	1,216	1,923	0.1
6400	Insurance agents, brokers, and service	24	27	0.7	80	90	16,400	17,289	2,059	2,491	0.4
6500	Real estate	32	37	0.6	360	312	9,122	10,321	4,098	3,787	0.6
6510	Real estate operators and lessors	12	13	0.5	43	33	10,605	11,879	507	507	0.2
6530	Real estate agents and managers	11	17	0.6	305	273	8,813	9,963	3,430	3,140	0.8
6552	Subdividers and developers, n.e.c.	1	3	1.5	-	-	-	-	-	18	0.1
JACKSON, MI											
60 –	**Finance, insurance, and real estate**	252	266	1.5	1,908	1,788	24,008	24,383	45,106	44,717	0.8
6000	Depository institutions	74	73	1.9	1,018	869	22,318	21,220	21,425	18,128	1.1
6020	Commercial banks	45	45	1.7	557	522	24,819	23,249	12,826	11,235	0.9
6030	Savings institutions	13	12	2.2	-	147	-	20,027	-	3,151	1.5
6060	Credit unions	14	16	2.1	177	200	20,633	16,800	3,709	3,742	2.1
6100	Nondepository institutions	3	5	0.7	33	39	24,485	23,795	789	851	0.2
6200	Security and commodity brokers	7	6	0.8	48	49	52,917	66,449	2,564	3,443	0.8
6210	Security brokers and dealers	7	6	1.3	48	49	52,917	66,449	2,564	3,443	1.0
6300	Insurance carriers	33	27	1.9	209	201	23,541	26,607	4,965	5,622	0.3
6310	Life insurance	6	5	1.6	56	67	28,571	27,701	1,507	1,546	0.5
6330	Fire, marine, and casualty insurance	9	4	0.6	81	59	30,519	34,441	2,498	2,060	0.3
6370	Pension, health, and welfare funds	13	15	6.4	61	47	10,885	13,447	734	1,092	1.6
6400	Insurance agents, brokers, and service	50	58	1.5	220	255	29,164	29,224	7,189	8,486	1.4
6500	Real estate	68	81	1.4	281	294	16,897	16,381	4,458	4,502	0.7
6510	Real estate operators and lessors	31	37	1.5	158	195	17,316	14,564	2,136	2,154	1.0
6530	Real estate agents and managers	31	37	1.3	92	79	17,087	21,063	1,818	1,421	0.4
6553	Cemetery subdividers and developers	3	4	2.5	14	16	20,000	17,500	318	363	1.1
6700	Holding and other investment offices	17	16	2.5	99	81	36,929	41,432	3,716	3,685	1.7
KALAMAZOO, MI											
60 –	**Finance, insurance, and real estate**	495	521	3.0	7,205	6,762	26,096	24,154	188,321	171,949	2.9
6000	Depository institutions	104	126	3.2	3,605	3,056	25,399	24,260	94,257	75,186	4.5
6020	Commercial banks	73	84	3.3	3,269	2,618	25,537	24,863	86,271	65,627	5.2
6030	Savings institutions	19	20	3.7	232	219	25,241	20,694	5,717	4,880	2.4
6140	Personal credit institutions	12	7	4.0	79	30	26,430	24,933	2,088	782	0.6
6160	Mortgage bankers and brokers	11	14	3.7	209	289	25,799	22,367	5,611	7,059	2.3
6200	Security and commodity brokers	30	31	4.0	193	239	63,668	42,393	9,474	10,067	2.4
6210	Security brokers and dealers	18	19	4.2	167	210	69,461	43,848	8,711	9,109	2.6
6280	Security and commodity services	12	12	4.0	26	29	26,462	31,862	763	958	1.5
6300	Insurance carriers	43	39	2.8	630	724	27,683	28,884	17,551	21,406	1.3
6310	Life insurance	11	8	2.5	278	215	24,446	27,888	6,997	5,905	1.7
6330	Fire, marine, and casualty insurance	16	17	2.7	142	-	34,563	-	4,993	-	-
6360	Title insurance	5	2	2.0	62	-	30,774	-	1,289	-	-
6370	Pension, health, and welfare funds	6	6	2.6	-	195	-	26,256	-	5,520	8.3
6400	Insurance agents, brokers, and service	108	113	2.9	716	655	25,246	26,406	21,128	20,963	3.4
6500	Real estate	164	168	2.8	1,399	1,449	17,252	16,516	24,985	25,684	3.8
6510	Real estate operators and lessors	74	66	2.7	880	938	16,768	16,333	14,621	15,805	7.5
6530	Real estate agents and managers	68	89	3.0	354	467	17,638	17,139	6,946	9,131	2.5

Source: County Business Patterns, 1992/93, CBP-92/93-1, U.S. Department of Commerce, Washington, D.C., April 1995. SIC categories for which data were suppressed or not available for both 1992 and 1993 are *not* displayed. The employment columns represent mid-March employment in the year. Pay per employee is calculated by dividing 1st Quarter payroll, annualized, by mid-March employment. The columns headed "% State" show the county's percentage of the state total for the SIC in 1993; for example, 0.9% for SIC 6030 means that the county had 0.9 percent of the state's total establishments (or payroll) in SIC 6030 in 1993. A dash (-) is used to indicate that data are not available or cannot be calculated; *nec* means not elsewhere classified.

Continued on next page.

SIC	Industry	No. Establishments			Employment		Pay / Employee		Annual Payroll ($ 000)		
		1992	1993	% State	1992	1993	1992	1993	1992	1993	% State
KALAMAZOO, MI - [continued]											
6700	Holding and other investment offices	15	19	3.0	287	291	51,094	29,086	11,001	9,112	4.1
6710	Holding offices	5	7	4.0	208	-	57,538	-	8,313	-	-
6732	Educational, religious, etc. trusts	4	4	4.1	51	-	34,275	-	1,822	-	-
KALKASKA, MI											
60 –	**Finance, insurance, and real estate**	17	18	0.1	62	78	14,839	14,000	1,013	1,241	0.0
6400	Insurance agents, brokers, and service	7	7	0.2	23	-	15,130	-	366	-	-
6500	Real estate	4	5	0.1	9	13	10,667	8,000	117	135	0.0
6530	Real estate agents and managers	3	3	0.1	-	11	-	8,727	-	118	0.0
KENT, MI											
60 –	**Finance, insurance, and real estate**	1,245	1,274	7.4	14,828	14,997	26,773	26,225	403,094	421,050	7.2
6000	Depository institutions	222	233	5.9	3,852	4,755	21,806	22,753	86,970	117,576	7.1
6020	Commercial banks	158	160	6.2	3,301	4,038	22,056	23,340	75,417	102,527	8.2
6060	Credit unions	46	52	6.9	406	580	18,345	17,841	7,515	10,756	6.0
6100	Nondepository institutions	84	76	10.7	900	901	26,800	27,503	26,321	28,817	5.4
6140	Personal credit institutions	37	21	12.0	407	245	25,494	27,739	11,037	7,404	5.8
6160	Mortgage bankers and brokers	35	38	10.0	428	544	27,402	25,765	13,034	17,649	5.9
6200	Security and commodity brokers	57	55	7.2	491	544	61,450	59,875	29,332	34,055	8.3
6210	Security brokers and dealers	32	37	8.1	428	461	65,308	64,469	26,520	30,697	8.9
6280	Security and commodity services	24	17	5.6	62	83	35,613	34,361	2,707	3,312	5.2
6300	Insurance carriers	147	134	9.5	4,084	4,065	31,416	29,245	121,534	115,905	7.1
6310	Life insurance	46	38	12.0	919	985	25,597	22,745	21,262	21,846	6.4
6330	Fire, marine, and casualty insurance	61	55	8.7	2,530	2,317	34,900	32,109	80,953	71,096	9.1
6370	Pension, health, and welfare funds	23	27	11.5	234	-	20,615	-	5,167	-	-
6400	Insurance agents, brokers, and service	309	327	8.4	1,887	1,954	28,725	28,852	55,081	61,608	9.9
6500	Real estate	372	399	6.7	2,460	2,405	15,353	14,874	42,562	41,822	6.2
6510	Real estate operators and lessors	163	171	7.1	1,295	1,266	14,094	12,780	19,834	18,351	8.7
6530	Real estate agents and managers	147	179	6.1	800	955	16,610	17,634	15,591	19,791	5.3
6552	Subdividers and developers, n.e.c.	14	16	8.0	102	38	24,235	19,263	2,729	826	3.1
6553	Cemetery subdividers and developers	11	12	7.5	90	106	13,644	12,340	1,256	1,227	3.8
6700	Holding and other investment offices	54	50	7.8	1,154	373	33,300	44,847	41,294	21,267	9.7
6710	Holding offices	20	17	9.7	1,001	239	35,317	44,435	38,166	11,914	8.8
6732	Educational, religious, etc. trusts	10	11	11.3	73	59	17,699	15,932	1,327	1,112	5.9
6733	Trusts, n.e.c.	15	13	7.5	39	15	19,385	31,733	867	517	2.6
6799	Investors, n.e.c.	2	4	4.9	-	10	-	29,600	-	273	2.4
KEWEENAW, MI											
60 –	**Finance, insurance, and real estate**	3	3	0.0	-	8	-	10,500	-	95	0.0
LAKE, MI											
60 –	**Finance, insurance, and real estate**	10	11	0.1	56	57	16,429	16,281	1,058	1,180	0.0
6400	Insurance agents, brokers, and service	3	3	0.1	10	12	20,400	17,667	268	291	0.0
LAPEER, MI											
60 –	**Finance, insurance, and real estate**	93	95	0.5	645	624	17,984	18,647	12,807	12,652	0.2
6000	Depository institutions	24	27	0.7	295	341	18,075	17,232	5,634	6,212	0.4
6020	Commercial banks	20	21	0.8	277	296	17,603	16,878	5,136	5,236	0.4
6030	Savings institutions	4	4	0.7	18	-	25,333	-	498	-	-
6100	Nondepository institutions	3	2	0.3	50	-	14,480	-	843	-	-
6300	Insurance carriers	6	4	0.3	-	64	-	28,625	-	1,951	0.1
6360	Title insurance	3	2	2.0	24	-	22,000	-	696	-	-
6400	Insurance agents, brokers, and service	21	24	0.6	97	96	21,567	18,583	2,376	2,010	0.3
6500	Real estate	34	34	0.6	67	98	13,373	12,857	1,246	1,582	0.2
6510	Real estate operators and lessors	9	8	0.3	20	-	12,600	-	289	-	-
6530	Real estate agents and managers	16	24	0.8	30	64	12,800	14,125	546	1,104	0.3

Source: County Business Patterns, 1992/93, CBP-92/93-1, U.S. Department of Commerce, Washington, D.C., April 1995. SIC categories for which data were suppressed or not available for both 1992 and 1993 are not displayed. The employment columns represent mid-March employment in the year. Pay per employee is calculated by dividing 1st Quarter payroll, annualized, by mid-March employment. The columns headed "% State" show the county's percentage of the state total for the SIC in 1993; for example, 0.9% for SIC 6030 means that the county had 0.9 percent of the state's total establishments (or payroll) in SIC 6030 in 1993. A dash (-) is used to indicate that data are not available or cannot be calculated; nec means not elsewhere classified.

SIC	Industry	No. Establishments			Employment		Pay / Employee		Annual Payroll ($ 000)		
		1992	1993	% State	1992	1993	1992	1993	1992	1993	% State
LEELANAU, MI											
60 –	**Finance, insurance, and real estate**	37	36	0.2	104	114	17,615	15,965	2,210	2,336	0.0
6000	Depository institutions	6	7	0.2	-	27	-	17,481	-	505	0.0
6400	Insurance agents, brokers, and service	7	7	0.2	25	31	23,520	21,806	738	816	0.1
6500	Real estate	17	16	0.3	34	37	11,765	9,514	499	521	0.1
6510	Real estate operators and lessors	2	4	0.2	-	10	-	12,000	-	186	0.1
6530	Real estate agents and managers	12	12	0.4	22	27	10,727	8,593	260	335	0.1
6700	Holding and other investment offices	4	3	0.5	8	-	12,000	-	210	-	-
LENAWEE, MI											
60 –	**Finance, insurance, and real estate**	147	153	0.9	1,149	1,099	20,536	20,710	26,417	24,641	0.4
6000	Depository institutions	38	32	0.8	635	598	18,702	19,084	11,819	11,249	0.7
6020	Commercial banks	29	27	1.0	540	508	18,681	19,583	9,455	9,558	0.8
6100	Nondepository institutions	5	5	0.7	73	21	20,274	31,619	1,530	486	0.1
6300	Insurance carriers	12	10	0.7	104	106	31,615	32,679	3,094	3,571	0.2
6370	Pension, health, and welfare funds	3	3	1.3	-	-	-	-	28	-	-
6400	Insurance agents, brokers, and service	39	46	1.2	192	193	24,771	22,881	7,456	5,915	1.0
6500	Real estate	48	54	0.9	121	146	10,545	12,055	1,480	2,171	0.3
6510	Real estate operators and lessors	15	16	0.7	36	-	8,222	-	335	-	-
6530	Real estate agents and managers	27	32	1.1	66	82	11,394	11,122	807	1,229	0.3
LIVINGSTON, MI											
60 –	**Finance, insurance, and real estate**	174	183	1.1	2,198	2,299	25,030	26,573	57,002	62,569	1.1
6000	Depository institutions	36	40	1.0	478	495	17,766	21,786	9,392	10,231	0.6
6020	Commercial banks	26	30	1.2	385	403	18,244	23,017	7,790	8,494	0.7
6100	Nondepository institutions	8	9	1.3	38	-	28,526	-	1,302	-	-
6160	Mortgage bankers and brokers	5	6	1.6	26	27	28,923	30,222	981	1,043	0.3
6200	Security and commodity brokers	4	3	0.4	13	-	8,000	-	95	-	-
6300	Insurance carriers	11	9	0.6	1,165	-	30,438	-	34,689	-	-
6400	Insurance agents, brokers, and service	39	43	1.1	283	381	23,972	21,449	7,146	10,398	1.7
6500	Real estate	68	72	1.2	200	209	14,160	15,636	4,146	4,653	0.7
6510	Real estate operators and lessors	20	22	0.9	47	60	11,660	14,800	772	1,057	0.5
6530	Real estate agents and managers	32	41	1.4	91	138	15,868	16,145	1,844	2,854	0.8
6552	Subdividers and developers, n.e.c.	3	3	1.5	-	-	-	-	-	60	0.2
6700	Holding and other investment offices	8	7	1.1	21	-	12,381	-	232	-	-
6710	Holding offices	4	3	1.7	5	3	22,400	21,333	93	91	0.1
LUCE, MI											
60 –	**Finance, insurance, and real estate**	12	12	0.1	138	142	14,406	12,930	2,033	2,050	0.0
6400	Insurance agents, brokers, and service	6	6	0.2	15	15	17,067	18,133	268	291	0.0
MACKINAC, MI											
60 –	**Finance, insurance, and real estate**	20	20	0.1	102	112	14,824	14,500	1,548	1,615	0.0
6000	Depository institutions	9	10	0.3	71	74	16,338	16,216	1,123	1,236	0.1
6020	Commercial banks	9	9	0.3	71	-	16,338	-	1,123	-	-
6400	Insurance agents, brokers, and service	2	3	0.1	-	11	-	16,727	-	180	0.0
6500	Real estate	7	7	0.1	18	27	10,222	8,889	251	199	0.0
6530	Real estate agents and managers	3	3	0.1	11	23	8,000	8,870	141	158	0.0
MACOMB, MI											
60 –	**Finance, insurance, and real estate**	1,118	1,165	6.7	8,965	10,640	22,339	19,425	212,840	243,128	4.1
6000	Depository institutions	241	251	6.4	3,804	3,217	19,607	18,902	73,143	68,308	4.1
6020	Commercial banks	150	144	5.6	2,720	2,148	19,538	18,367	51,185	44,603	3.6
6030	Savings institutions	45	47	8.7	636	479	19,925	22,021	13,112	12,094	5.9
6060	Credit unions	46	60	7.9	448	590	19,571	18,319	8,846	11,611	6.5
6100	Nondepository institutions	57	47	6.6	528	572	27,348	29,748	15,620	20,594	3.8
6140	Personal credit institutions	28	13	7.4	265	159	21,887	25,535	6,024	3,927	3.1
6150	Business credit institutions	-	5	4.4	-	90	-	31,111	-	2,789	2.8
6160	Mortgage bankers and brokers	26	28	7.4	263	323	32,852	31,443	9,570	13,863	4.6

Source: County Business Patterns, 1992/93, CBP-92/93-1, U.S. Department of Commerce, Washington, D.C., April 1995. SIC categories for which data were suppressed or not available for both 1992 and 1993 are not displayed. The employment columns represent mid-March employment in the year. Pay per employee is calculated by dividing 1st Quarter payroll, annualized, by mid-March employment. The columns headed "% State" show the county's percentage of the state total for the SIC in 1993; for example, 0.9% for SIC 6030 means that the county had 0.9 percent of the state's total establishments (or payroll) in SIC 6030 in 1993. A dash (-) is used to indicate that data are not available or cannot be calculated; nec means not elsewhere classified.

Continued on next page.

SIC	Industry	No. Establishments			Employment		Pay / Employee		Annual Payroll ($ 000)		
		1992	1993	% State	1992	1993	1992	1993	1992	1993	% State

MACOMB, MI - [continued]

SIC	Industry	1992	1993	% State	1992	1993	1992	1993	1992	1993	% State
6210	Security brokers and dealers	15	18	4.0	75	84	62,667	65,095	4,358	5,977	1.7
6300	Insurance carriers	115	102	7.2	1,311	3,280	29,288	16,416	42,156	65,138	4.0
6310	Life insurance	12	10	3.2	350	253	21,886	27,225	7,887	6,627	1.9
6330	Fire, marine, and casualty insurance	68	52	8.2	579	492	39,793	46,935	23,980	24,832	3.2
6360	Title insurance	4	4	4.0	164	-	20,415	-	5,034	-	-
6370	Pension, health, and welfare funds	22	29	12.4	144	2,294	14,222	7,942	2,625	26,564	39.8
6400	Insurance agents, brokers, and service	229	251	6.4	1,316	1,329	25,778	24,202	38,741	37,316	6.0
6500	Real estate	408	442	7.4	1,737	1,920	15,604	15,194	31,422	35,978	5.3
6510	Real estate operators and lessors	194	199	8.2	939	1,065	13,534	13,777	14,714	17,060	8.1
6530	Real estate agents and managers	150	195	6.7	560	663	17,421	15,228	10,818	12,805	3.5
6540	Title abstract offices	3	4	3.8	41	35	18,732	19,886	1,278	1,219	4.7
6552	Subdividers and developers, n.e.c.	10	19	9.5	18	31	24,667	24,645	760	1,553	5.8
6553	Cemetery subdividers and developers	10	8	5.0	95	94	23,368	26,851	2,353	2,681	8.4
6700	Holding and other investment offices	34	37	5.8	149	176	37,315	35,727	5,875	7,636	3.5
6710	Holding offices	8	7	4.0	69	98	50,551	43,592	3,620	4,519	3.3
6732	Educational, religious, etc. trusts	4	3	3.1	15	16	22,667	19,250	340	311	1.6
6733	Trusts, n.e.c.	10	12	6.9	29	13	22,897	21,846	773	710	3.6
6794	Patent owners and lessors	8	11	20.4	33	-	30,303	-	1,069	-	-

MANISTEE, MI

SIC	Industry	1992	1993	% State	1992	1993	1992	1993	1992	1993	% State
60 –	**Finance, insurance, and real estate**	45	43	0.2	265	224	15,834	16,643	4,118	3,941	0.1
6000	Depository institutions	17	17	0.4	171	160	17,123	15,925	2,916	2,590	0.2
6020	Commercial banks	11	11	0.4	139	128	17,986	16,531	2,449	2,117	0.2
6400	Insurance agents, brokers, and service	9	12	0.3	26	40	22,000	22,400	594	901	0.1
6500	Real estate	11	10	0.2	39	-	10,051	-	300	-	-
6530	Real estate agents and managers	4	4	0.1	23	3	9,565	8,000	131	33	0.0
6553	Cemetery subdividers and developers	3	3	1.9	-	7	-	15,429	-	130	0.4
6700	Holding and other investment offices	3	1	0.2	7	-	3,429	-	34	-	-

MARQUETTE, MI

SIC	Industry	1992	1993	% State	1992	1993	1992	1993	1992	1993	% State
60 –	**Finance, insurance, and real estate**	132	139	0.8	1,091	1,221	18,544	18,962	21,933	23,286	0.4
6000	Depository institutions	38	41	1.0	642	674	17,383	18,605	11,137	12,140	0.7
6020	Commercial banks	28	32	1.2	534	568	17,558	18,944	9,187	10,523	0.8
6200	Security and commodity brokers	5	8	1.0	-	23	-	57,217	-	1,335	0.3
6300	Insurance carriers	13	10	0.7	87	84	29,563	32,190	3,582	2,697	0.2
6310	Life insurance	3	3	0.9	-	35	-	34,743	-	1,115	0.3
6330	Fire, marine, and casualty insurance	5	4	0.6	11	-	44,364	-	547	-	-
6370	Pension, health, and welfare funds	4	2	0.9	13	-	9,846	-	1,014	-	-
6400	Insurance agents, brokers, and service	32	31	0.8	135	138	20,326	20,667	2,865	2,923	0.5
6500	Real estate	39	44 ·	0.7	202	292	13,287	11,822	3,098	3,896	0.6
6510	Real estate operators and lessors	21	22	0.9	132	211	12,121	10,199	1,776	2,382	1.1
6530	Real estate agents and managers	10	18	0.6	45	68	17,867	16,235	921	1,174	0.3
6553	Cemetery subdividers and developers	3	3	1.9	5	-	15,200	-	138	-	-
6700	Holding and other investment offices	4	3	0.5	4	-	16,000	-	128	-	-

MASON, MI

SIC	Industry	1992	1993	% State	1992	1993	1992	1993	1992	1993	% State
60 –	**Finance, insurance, and real estate**	60	58	0.3	292	290	16,027	18,786	5,121	6,099	0.1
6000	Depository institutions	14	14	0.4	168	154	14,119	17,455	2,605	2,807	0.2
6020	Commercial banks	9	9	0.3	133	126	13,985	18,508	2,148	2,394	0.2
6400	Insurance agents, brokers, and service	21	20	0.5	50	51	16,960	17,098	929	1,038	0.2
6500	Real estate	18	18	0.3	35	44	12,114	11,455	482	619	0.1
6510	Real estate operators and lessors	6	7	0.3	6	-	6,000	-	86	-	-
6530	Real estate agents and managers	8	8	0.3	20	20	13,400	13,200	329	357	0.1

MECOSTA, MI

SIC	Industry	1992	1993	% State	1992	1993	1992	1993	1992	1993	% State
60 –	**Finance, insurance, and real estate**	67	69	0.4	346	334	16,728	17,485	6,820	7,167	0.1
6000	Depository institutions	17	18	0.5	172	179	15,302	16,514	3,231	3,054	0.2
6020	Commercial banks	14	14	0.5	-	150	-	16,480	-	2,537	0.2

Source: County Business Patterns, 1992/93, CBP-92/93-1, U.S. Department of Commerce, Washington, D.C., April 1995. SIC categories for which data were suppressed or not available for both 1992 and 1993 are *not* displayed. The employment columns represent mid-March employment in the year. Pay per employee is calculated by dividing 1st Quarter payroll, annualized, by mid-March employment. The columns headed "% State" show the county's percentage of the state total for the SIC in 1993; for example, 0.9% for SIC 6030 means that the county had 0.9 percent of the state's total establishments (or payroll) in SIC 6030 in 1993. A dash (-) is used to indicate that data are not available or cannot be calculated; *nec* means not elsewhere classified.

Continued on next page.

SIC	Industry	No. Establishments 1992	1993	% State	Employment 1992	1993	Pay / Employee 1992	1993	Annual Payroll ($ 000) 1992	1993	% State
MECOSTA, MI - [continued]											
6200	Security and commodity brokers	4	4	0.5	20	-	48,400	-	1,003	-	-
6210	Security brokers and dealers	4	4	0.9	20	-	48,400	-	1,003	-	-
6400	Insurance agents, brokers, and service	11	14	0.4	42	51	10,952	14,196	500	812	0.1
6500	Real estate	28	29	0.5	89	86	14,112	13,163	1,615	2,215	0.3
6510	Real estate operators and lessors	7	6	0.2	14	-	16,000	-	206	-	-
6530	Real estate agents and managers	18	21	0.7	38	39	13,158	11,692	539	556	0.2
6700	Holding and other investment offices	3	3	0.5	3	-	9,333	-	13	10	0.0
MENOMINEE, MI											
60 -	**Finance, insurance, and real estate**	44	39	0.2	254	273	18,976	16,718	4,593	4,643	0.1
6000	Depository institutions	14	15	0.4	141	151	19,092	16,874	2,525	2,748	0.2
6020	Commercial banks	9	9	0.3	122	126	19,738	17,333	2,218	2,369	0.2
6300	Insurance carriers	5	4	0.3	24	-	28,167	-	611	-	-
6400	Insurance agents, brokers, and service	11	10	0.3	52	51	20,923	14,745	1,113	760	0.1
6500	Real estate	11	8	0.1	25	20	8,320	11,400	183	176	0.0
6530	Real estate agents and managers	2	3	0.1	-	3	-	10,667	-	28	0.0
6540	Title abstract offices	3	2	1.9	8	-	9,500	-	70	-	-
MIDLAND, MI											
60 -	**Finance, insurance, and real estate**	128	129	0.7	874	887	28,256	26,525	24,973	25,199	0.4
6000	Depository institutions	31	30	0.8	460	443	21,383	21,815	10,036	9,630	0.6
6020	Commercial banks	22	21	0.8	315	289	22,286	22,519	6,477	5,850	0.5
6210	Security brokers and dealers	5	6	1.3	33	31	55,758	70,452	1,830	2,147	0.6
6300	Insurance carriers	13	11	0.8	96	102	43,750	41,176	4,177	4,940	0.3
6370	Pension, health, and welfare funds	3	2	0.9	-	-	-	-	24	-	-
6400	Insurance agents, brokers, and service	22	24	0.6	82	87	46,732	28,506	3,339	2,911	0.5
6500	Real estate	45	48	0.8	156	164	17,538	21,634	3,347	3,442	0.5
6510	Real estate operators and lessors	20	21	0.9	56	67	12,929	11,761	908	936	0.4
6530	Real estate agents and managers	16	18	0.6	58	54	17,931	16,889	1,320	1,184	0.3
6540	Title abstract offices	3	3	2.9	16	19	31,500	22,947	552	560	2.2
6700	Holding and other investment offices	9	8	1.3	44	58	50,182	24,690	2,207	2,102	1.0
6733	Trusts, n.e.c.	4	4	2.3	8	-	14,500	-	132	-	-
MISSAUKEE, MI											
60 -	**Finance, insurance, and real estate**	16	16	0.1	84	79	17,476	19,190	1,741	1,648	0.0
6000	Depository institutions	4	4	0.1	-	46	-	19,043	-	848	0.1
6020	Commercial banks	4	4	0.2	-	46	-	19,043	-	848	0.1
6400	Insurance agents, brokers, and service	5	6	0.2	24	27	16,667	18,815	564	663	0.1
6500	Real estate	6	6	0.1	10	6	8,800	22,000	221	137	0.0
6510	Real estate operators and lessors	3	3	0.1	-	3	-	37,333	-	102	0.0
MONROE, MI											
60 -	**Finance, insurance, and real estate**	185	181	1.0	1,211	1,080	19,267	19,330	23,280	21,741	0.4
6000	Depository institutions	56	56	1.4	668	612	20,994	20,529	12,902	11,897	0.7
6020	Commercial banks	38	38	1.5	526	458	21,719	22,210	10,550	9,167	0.7
6030	Savings institutions	11	10	1.9	90	-	18,533	-	1,436	-	-
6060	Credit unions	7	8	1.1	52	-	17,923	-	916	-	-
6200	Security and commodity brokers	2	5	0.7	-	6	-	25,333	-	171	0.0
6300	Insurance carriers	10	9	0.6	92	81	22,435	26,568	2,078	2,284	0.1
6370	Pension, health, and welfare funds	4	3	1.3	27	4	13,926	33,000	230	179	0.3
6400	Insurance agents, brokers, and service	48	49	1.3	169	181	18,201	19,249	3,367	3,973	0.6
6500	Real estate	64	58	1.0	232	182	10,310	10,615	2,942	2,887	0.4
6510	Real estate operators and lessors	30	29	1.2	145	116	7,972	10,276	1,527	1,705	0.8
6530	Real estate agents and managers	21	24	0.8	37	41	10,162	8,683	526	665	0.2

Source: County Business Patterns, 1992/93, CBP-92/93-1, U.S. Department of Commerce, Washington, D.C., April 1995. SIC categories for which data were suppressed or not available for both 1992 and 1993 are *not* displayed. The employment columns represent mid-March employment in the year. Pay per employee is calculated by dividing 1st Quarter payroll, annualized, by mid-March employment. The columns headed "% State" show the county's percentage of the state total for the SIC in 1993; for example, 0.9% for SIC 6030 means that the county had 0.9 percent of the state's total establishments (or payroll) in SIC 6030 in 1993. A dash (-) is used to indicate that data are not available or cannot be calculated; *nec* means not elsewhere classified.

Continued on next page.

SIC	Industry	No. Establishments			Employment		Pay / Employee		Annual Payroll ($ 000)		
		1992	1993	% State	1992	1993	1992	1993	1992	1993	% State
MONROE, MI - [continued]											
6540	Title abstract offices	3	2	1.9	18	–	22,222	–	420	–	–
6552	Subdividers and developers, n.e.c.	3	–	–	8	–	20,500	–	160	–	–
6553	Cemetery subdividers and developers	3	3	1.9	18	–	11,111	–	218	–	–
MONTCALM, MI											
60 –	**Finance, insurance, and real estate**	80	83	0.5	412	438	18,155	17,616	7,834	8,403	0.1
6000	Depository institutions	28	28	0.7	265	279	17,328	17,921	4,821	5,320	0.3
6020	Commercial banks	21	22	0.9	221	236	17,774	18,576	4,121	4,674	0.4
6060	Credit unions	6	6	0.8	–	43	–	14,326	–	646	0.4
6300	Insurance carriers	7	4	0.3	27	25	23,259	18,720	681	598	0.0
6400	Insurance agents, brokers, and service	26	32	0.8	75	94	17,440	16,085	1,344	1,638	0.3
6500	Real estate	15	16	0.3	36	31	11,111	11,226	475	451	0.1
6510	Real estate operators and lessors	5	7	0.3	11	15	4,364	7,200	77	121	0.1
6530	Real estate agents and managers	9	8	0.3	24	14	13,833	16,571	387	322	0.1
MONTMORENCY, MI											
60 –	**Finance, insurance, and real estate**	18	17	0.1	84	90	13,619	12,800	1,203	1,322	0.0
6000	Depository institutions	6	6	0.2	41	43	17,756	16,372	730	762	0.0
6400	Insurance agents, brokers, and service	5	5	0.1	16	18	14,500	13,556	267	339	0.1
6500	Real estate	7	6	0.1	27	29	6,815	7,034	206	221	0.0
MUSKEGON, MI											
60 –	**Finance, insurance, and real estate**	243	248	1.4	1,594	1,692	21,355	22,071	35,595	41,058	0.7
6000	Depository institutions	58	64	1.6	739	747	19,832	20,102	13,777	15,199	0.9
6020	Commercial banks	32	36	1.4	549	536	19,964	20,761	10,034	11,168	0.9
6100	Nondepository institutions	11	4	0.6	51	18	15,529	21,111	1,009	508	0.1
6140	Personal credit institutions	7	1	0.6	35	–	14,171	–	565	–	–
6200	Security and commodity brokers	9	10	1.3	45	43	52,978	54,791	2,628	2,288	0.6
6300	Insurance carriers	23	21	1.5	202	230	29,861	30,191	6,523	7,283	0.4
6310	Life insurance	5	5	1.6	78	99	28,974	27,152	2,199	2,250	0.7
6360	Title insurance	3	2	2.0	28	–	20,571	–	690	–	–
6400	Insurance agents, brokers, and service	57	59	1.5	222	259	22,072	20,618	5,335	5,903	1.0
6500	Real estate	81	84	1.4	324	372	15,531	15,301	6,054	7,803	1.2
6510	Real estate operators and lessors	35	38	1.6	127	193	9,512	10,943	1,350	2,175	1.0
6530	Real estate agents and managers	32	39	1.3	95	96	15,242	14,583	1,769	2,019	0.5
6700	Holding and other investment offices	4	6	0.9	11	23	22,182	70,261	269	2,074	0.9
6710	Holding offices	1	3	1.7	–	20	–	78,400	–	2,020	1.5
NEWAYGO, MI											
60 –	**Finance, insurance, and real estate**	44	46	0.3	302	310	20,397	19,252	6,397	6,315	0.1
6000	Depository institutions	9	10	0.3	112	114	19,607	18,912	2,216	2,251	0.1
6200	Security and commodity brokers	4	4	0.5	5	6	16,000	16,667	68	105	0.0
6400	Insurance agents, brokers, and service	12	13	0.3	96	45	27,500	17,867	2,668	900	0.1
6500	Real estate	13	14	0.2	63	42	9,778	10,571	789	630	0.1
6530	Real estate agents and managers	6	10	0.3	25	21	8,960	9,905	323	310	0.1
OAKLAND, MI											
60 –	**Finance, insurance, and real estate**	3,594	3,714	21.4	54,687	58,435	30,619	30,355	1,739,386	1,948,975	33.2
6000	Depository institutions	457	462	11.8	12,522	13,128	26,748	24,914	341,673	367,246	22.2
6020	Commercial banks	308	296	11.5	8,318	9,488	26,710	25,259	234,168	267,377	21.3
6030	Savings institutions	74	81	15.1	2,297	2,347	25,806	25,929	66,212	72,292	35.3
6060	Credit unions	66	77	10.2	963	1,251	23,132	20,627	22,083	26,757	15.0
6090	Functions closely related to banking	9	8	16.7	944	42	33,068	18,095	19,210	820	–
6100	Nondepository institutions	252	266	37.5	6,870	8,832	35,568	35,679	268,520	355,243	66.4
6140	Personal credit institutions	61	51	29.1	1,332	2,046	28,931	32,266	39,724	69,860	54.9
6150	Business credit institutions	37	47	41.6	1,260	1,201	56,498	62,595	66,722	63,788	64.8
6160	Mortgage bankers and brokers	148	165	43.4	4,271	5,584	31,491	31,111	161,591	221,161	73.6
6200	Security and commodity brokers	207	222	29.0	1,973	2,278	71,645	66,980	137,655	169,907	41.3

Source: County Business Patterns, 1992/93, CBP-92/93-1, U.S. Department of Commerce, Washington, D.C., April 1995. SIC categories for which data were suppressed or not available for both 1992 and 1993 are *not* displayed. The employment columns represent mid-March employment in the year. Pay per employee is calculated by dividing 1st Quarter payroll, annualized, by mid-March employment. The columns headed "% State" show the county's percentage of the state total for the SIC in 1993; for example, 0.9% for SIC 6030 means that the county had 0.9 percent of the state's total establishments (or payroll) in SIC 6030 in 1993. A dash (-) is used to indicate that data are not available or cannot be calculated; *nec* means not elsewhere classified.

Continued on next page.

SIC	Industry	No. Establishments			Employment		Pay / Employee		Annual Payroll ($ 000)		
		1992	1993	% State	1992	1993	1992	1993	1992	1993	% State
OAKLAND, MI - [continued]											
6210	Security brokers and dealers	94	99	21.8	1,574	1,661	76,313	77,132	118,983	134,703	38.8
6280	Security and commodity services	112	120	39.9	399	606	53,233	40,271	18,622	35,119	55.1
6300	Insurance carriers	416	372	26.4	14,916	16,067	32,817	32,140	478,636	527,724	32.4
6310	Life insurance	128	106	33.5	5,053	5,463	33,118	30,752	157,995	160,764	47.2
6330	Fire, marine, and casualty insurance	174	171	27.0	4,638	5,554	36,469	33,766	160,557	190,912	24.5
6350	Surety insurance	12	10	58.8	-	61	-	35,410	-	2,433	74.9
6360	Title insurance	23	24	24.0	756	720	22,841	27,956	19,596	21,951	43.1
6370	Pension, health, and welfare funds	50	34	14.5	396	355	27,434	27,718	10,896	10,672	16.0
6400	Insurance agents, brokers, and service	761	787	20.2	5,187	5,370	31,334	30,985	178,540	188,194	30.3
6500	Real estate	1,338	1,438	24.1	11,626	11,069	21,223	21,173	276,731	267,707	39.8
6510	Real estate operators and lessors	523	559	23.1	3,381	3,105	16,295	16,799	59,509	64,105	30.3
6530	Real estate agents and managers	596	746	25.4	7,047	7,173	22,915	22,207	182,168	175,939	47.5
6540	Title abstract offices	9	14	13.5	225	238	23,804	23,479	5,899	6,769	26.3
6552	Subdividers and developers, n.e.c.	58	56	28.1	442	275	31,837	36,131	15,253	11,207	41.8
6553	Cemetery subdividers and developers	16	17	10.7	159	229	26,818	29,432	5,044	7,972	25.0
6700	Holding and other investment offices	155	157	24.6	1,183	1,187	37,403	39,528	46,638	57,440	26.2
6710	Holding offices	36	46	26.3	617	653	43,417	45,960	27,964	36,514	27.1
6720	Investment offices	14	5	31.3	67	8	39,463	74,500	2,111	705	29.6
6732	Educational, religious, etc. trusts	11	12	12.4	46	53	41,565	42,868	1,956	2,506	13.2
6733	Trusts, n.e.c.	40	38	21.8	194	130	15,237	7,354	2,918	1,467	7.5
6794	Patent owners and lessors	15	14	25.9	121	212	45,058	40,547	6,423	10,204	54.9
6798	Real estate investment trusts	7	3	30.0	-	4	-	15,000	-	71	10.8
6799	Investors, n.e.c.	21	30	37.0	68	91	22,176	36,615	2,458	4,327	37.3
OCEANA, MI											
60 –	**Finance, insurance, and real estate**	33	37	0.2	170	178	16,376	16,360	2,736	2,993	0.1
6000	Depository institutions	9	10	0.3	108	118	18,481	17,424	1,770	1,984	0.1
6020	Commercial banks	7	7	0.3	-	103	-	17,204	-	1,692	0.1
6400	Insurance agents, brokers, and service	10	12	0.3	33	37	14,545	16,541	495	590	0.1
6500	Real estate	9	12	0.2	15	20	8,533	6,800	282	305	0.0
OGEMAW, MI											
60 –	**Finance, insurance, and real estate**	33	32	0.2	119	167	16,303	15,569	2,213	3,319	0.1
6000	Depository institutions	11	11	0.3	83	116	17,831	17,069	1,583	2,320	0.1
6400	Insurance agents, brokers, and service	6	7	0.2	-	25	-	15,520	-	668	0.1
6500	Real estate	15	12	0.2	18	24	11,556	9,000	291	311	0.0
6510	Real estate operators and lessors	8	1	0.0	7	-	7,429	-	50	-	-
6530	Real estate agents and managers	4	8	0.3	4	14	7,000	5,143	60	121	0.0
ONTONAGON, MI											
60 –	**Finance, insurance, and real estate**	15	16	0.1	-	90	-	17,244	-	1,764	0.0
6000	Depository institutions	7	7	0.2	65	58	17,600	17,931	1,255	1,263	0.1
6400	Insurance agents, brokers, and service	5	6	0.2	-	28	-	17,714	-	486	0.1
6500	Real estate	3	3	0.1	4	4	3,000	4,000	11	15	0.0
OSCEOLA, MI											
60 –	**Finance, insurance, and real estate**	29	30	0.2	154	147	15,299	15,075	2,511	2,323	0.0
6000	Depository institutions	12	13	0.3	107	108	16,411	14,926	1,815	1,662	0.1
6020	Commercial banks	10	10	0.4	-	104	-	15,154	-	1,626	0.1
6060	Credit unions	2	3	0.4	-	4	-	9,000	-	36	0.0
6400	Insurance agents, brokers, and service	10	11	0.3	33	-	14,545	-	506	-	-
6500	Real estate	4	4	0.1	-	7	-	14,286	-	126	0.0
OSCODA, MI											
60 –	**Finance, insurance, and real estate**	15	14	0.1	54	58	12,963	11,655	697	708	0.0

Source: County Business Patterns, 1992/93, CBP-92/93-1, U.S. Department of Commerce, Washington, D.C., April 1995. SIC categories for which data were suppressed or not available for both 1992 and 1993 are *not* displayed. The employment columns represent mid-March employment in the year. Pay per employee is calculated by dividing 1st Quarter payroll, annualized, by mid-March employment. The columns headed "% State" show the county's percentage of the state total for the SIC in 1993; for example, 0.9% for SIC 6030 means that the county had 0.9 percent of the state's total establishments (or payroll) in SIC 6030 in 1993. A dash (-) is used to indicate that data are not available or cannot be calculated; *nec* means not elsewhere classified.

Continued on next page.

SIC	Industry	No. Establishments			Employment		Pay / Employee		Annual Payroll ($ 000)		
		1992	1993	% State	1992	1993	1992	1993	1992	1993	% State
OSCODA, MI - [continued]											
6000	Depository institutions	5	5	0.1	29	-	14,207	-	390	-	-
6500	Real estate	8	7	0.1	-	16	-	8,500	-	160	0.0
6530	Real estate agents and managers	3	4	0.1	-	4	-	7,000	-	30	0.0
OTSEGO, MI											
60 –	**Finance, insurance, and real estate**	50	50	0.3	250	262	20,864	18,763	5,972	5,804	0.1
6000	Depository institutions	11	11	0.3	132	138	20,939	17,913	2,851	2,705	0.2
6300	Insurance carriers	5	4	0.3	42	41	23,333	25,854	1,159	1,210	0.1
6400	Insurance agents, brokers, and service	10	11	0.3	34	36	20,588	17,000	829	868	0.1
6500	Real estate	19	21	0.4	31	37	15,355	12,216	809	661	0.1
6510	Real estate operators and lessors	3	4	0.2	4	4	11,000	10,000	46	97	0.0
6530	Real estate agents and managers	12	14	0.5	16	27	11,750	12,296	297	440	0.1
OTTAWA, MI											
60 –	**Finance, insurance, and real estate**	313	322	1.9	2,291	2,427	24,410	25,823	51,720	63,452	1.1
6000	Depository institutions	77	80	2.0	1,292	1,369	21,752	25,744	23,369	32,648	2.0
6020	Commercial banks	59	57	2.2	1,180	1,234	22,458	26,778	21,613	30,236	2.4
6030	Savings institutions	7	8	1.5	69	69	13,333	16,754	1,039	1,236	0.6
6060	Credit unions	11	15	2.0	43	66	15,907	15,818	717	1,176	0.7
6100	Nondepository institutions	8	6	0.8	49	68	25,224	19,588	1,256	1,560	0.3
6140	Personal credit institutions	6	3	1.7	-	41	-	13,854	-	734	0.6
6160	Mortgage bankers and brokers	2	3	0.8	-	27	-	28,296	-	826	0.3
6200	Security and commodity brokers	22	25	3.3	147	156	42,476	48,231	6,142	7,569	1.8
6210	Security brokers and dealers	13	17	3.7	71	86	45,803	55,953	3,587	5,081	1.5
6300	Insurance carriers	27	20	1.4	120	50	27,267	38,800	3,614	2,214	0.1
6330	Fire, marine, and casualty insurance	15	13	2.1	32	32	39,500	44,875	1,474	1,622	0.2
6370	Pension, health, and welfare funds	4	4	1.7	3	-	25,333	-	285	-	-
6400	Insurance agents, brokers, and service	70	75	1.9	300	356	26,200	24,674	8,620	9,835	1.6
6500	Real estate	98	106	1.8	324	370	15,333	15,211	6,254	7,254	1.1
6510	Real estate operators and lessors	27	35	1.4	85	88	17,741	19,864	1,901	2,058	1.0
6530	Real estate agents and managers	48	57	1.9	186	234	13,548	12,632	3,094	4,175	1.1
6552	Subdividers and developers, n.e.c.	7	8	4.0	13	-	16,308	-	289	-	-
6700	Holding and other investment offices	11	10	1.6	59	58	71,864	38,276	2,465	2,372	1.1
6710	Holding offices	3	4	2.3	-	9	-	140,444	-	1,273	0.9
PRESQUE ISLE, MI											
60 –	**Finance, insurance, and real estate**	25	24	0.1	124	125	17,806	15,616	2,175	2,196	0.0
6000	Depository institutions	9	9	0.2	77	76	16,831	15,526	1,296	1,307	0.1
6020	Commercial banks	4	4	0.2	43	36	15,070	15,111	654	664	0.1
6300	Insurance carriers	3	1	0.1	5	-	13,600	-	78	-	-
6400	Insurance agents, brokers, and service	7	9	0.2	32	37	23,250	17,514	669	745	0.1
6500	Real estate	4	3	0.1	-	8	-	10,500	-	113	0.0
6530	Real estate agents and managers	4	3	0.1	-	8	-	10,500	-	113	0.0
ROSCOMMON, MI											
60 –	**Finance, insurance, and real estate**	51	52	0.3	223	236	13,632	12,525	3,146	3,406	0.1
6000	Depository institutions	11	11	0.3	130	137	15,354	12,584	1,853	1,894	0.1
6400	Insurance agents, brokers, and service	15	16	0.4	46	-	13,391	-	677	-	-
6500	Real estate	22	23	0.4	38	49	9,474	11,510	548	631	0.1
6510	Real estate operators and lessors	5	3	0.1	7	3	5,143	9,333	38	34	0.0
6530	Real estate agents and managers	14	16	0.5	17	31	10,588	12,000	315	467	0.1
6540	Title abstract offices	3	3	2.9	14	15	10,286	10,933	195	118	0.5
SAGINAW, MI											
60 –	**Finance, insurance, and real estate**	369	371	2.1	3,639	3,667	23,217	22,939	84,120	89,020	1.5
6000	Depository institutions	105	115	2.9	1,446	1,542	20,326	19,294	30,461	32,893	2.0
6020	Commercial banks	57	61	2.4	929	951	20,590	18,616	19,325	20,018	1.6
6030	Savings institutions	22	23	4.3	-	247	-	17,312	-	4,870	2.4

Source: County Business Patterns, 1992/93, CBP-92/93-1, U.S. Department of Commerce, Washington, D.C., April 1995. SIC categories for which data were suppressed or not available for both 1992 and 1993 are *not* displayed. The employment columns represent mid-March employment in the year. Pay per employee is calculated by dividing 1st Quarter payroll, annualized, by mid-March employment. The columns headed "% State" show the county's percentage of the state total for the SIC in 1993; for example, 0.9% for SIC 6030 means that the county had 0.9 percent of the state's total establishments (or payroll) in SIC 6030 in 1993. A dash (-) is used to indicate that data are not available or cannot be calculated; *nec* means not elsewhere classified.

Continued on next page.

SIC	Industry	No. Establishments			Employment		Pay / Employee		Annual Payroll ($ 000)		
		1992	1993	% State	1992	1993	1992	1993	1992	1993	% State
SAGINAW, MI - [continued]											
6060	Credit unions	25	31	4.1	260	344	23,462	22,593	6,372	8,005	4.5
6100	Nondepository institutions	15	9	1.3	162	133	22,272	27,820	3,775	3,839	0.7
6140	Personal credit institutions	12	6	3.4	118	91	23,085	29,407	2,821	2,785	2.2
6200	Security and commodity brokers	19	20	2.6	136	150	61,735	64,347	7,628	9,132	2.2
6210	Security brokers and dealers	13	10	2.2	125	117	64,640	74,803	7,291	8,239	2.4
6280	Security and commodity services	6	9	3.0	11	32	28,727	27,875	337	877	1.4
6300	Insurance carriers	46	41	2.9	1,005	1,002	28,056	26,475	26,275	26,806	1.6
6310	Life insurance	14	12	3.8	464	408	27,267	27,245	11,417	11,276	3.3
6330	Fire, marine, and casualty insurance	19	15	2.4	392	378	32,714	31,058	11,759	11,890	1.5
6400	Insurance agents, brokers, and service	86	90	2.3	375	380	21,888	22,053	8,576	8,950	1.4
6500	Real estate	90	89	1.5	481	425	12,441	12,744	6,655	6,549	1.0
6510	Real estate operators and lessors	41	44	1.8	250	254	10,576	10,772	3,012	3,307	1.6
6530	Real estate agents and managers	35	38	1.3	140	117	11,886	12,239	1,801	1,660	0.4
6552	Subdividers and developers, n.e.c.	3	1	0.5	-	-	-	-	26	-	-
6553	Cemetery subdividers and developers	3	2	1.3	47	-	19,915	-	1,010	-	-
6700	Holding and other investment offices	8	7	1.1	34	35	20,706	19,657	750	851	0.4
6733	Trusts, n.e.c.	3	5	2.9	7	-	13,143		99	-	-
ST. CLAIR, MI											
60 –	**Finance, insurance, and real estate**	217	216	1.2	1,818	1,815	21,932	22,550	41,890	41,545	0.7
6000	Depository institutions	54	59	1.5	834	1,001	18,988	18,781	15,070	18,427	1.1
6020	Commercial banks	41	40	1.6	639	742	19,624	19,660	11,775	14,118	1.1
6100	Nondepository institutions	9	5	0.7	59	9	19,797	10,222	1,211	211	0.0
6140	Personal credit institutions	9	3	1.7	59	-	19,797	-	1,211	-	-
6200	Security and commodity brokers	3	4	0.5	22	23	52,909	58,609	1,203	1,534	0.4
6210	Security brokers and dealers	3	4	0.9	22	23	52,909	58,609	1,203	1,534	0.4
6300	Insurance carriers	22	18	1.3	204	201	29,627	30,269	6,790	6,641	0.4
6310	Life insurance	5	3	0.9	128	112	25,219	25,143	3,432	2,963	0.9
6330	Fire, marine, and casualty insurance	11	10	1.6	55	52	43,636	48,154	2,688	2,916	0.4
6400	Insurance agents, brokers, and service	48	50	1.3	168	199	22,571	22,392	3,981	4,638	0.7
6500	Real estate	69	70	1.2	346	294	14,821	16,735	6,273	6,092	0.9
6510	Real estate operators and lessors	22	28	1.2	152	126	10,474	11,841	1,800	1,761	0.8
6530	Real estate agents and managers	30	35	1.2	96	119	16,167	18,286	1,785	2,696	0.7
6540	Title abstract offices	4	3	2.9	63	40	17,841	16,800	1,282	863	3.4
6700	Holding and other investment offices	12	10	1.6	185	88	36,432	59,409	7,362	4,002	1.8
6710	Holding offices	7	6	3.4	169	80	37,846	60,050	6,820	3,679	2.7
ST. JOSEPH, MI											
60 –	**Finance, insurance, and real estate**	91	100	0.6	559	586	20,358	19,986	10,764	11,611	0.2
6000	Depository institutions	31	38	1.0	367	411	20,632	20,350	6,699	7,746	0.5
6020	Commercial banks	21	25	1.0	-	313	-	20,613	-	5,673	0.5
6060	Credit unions	3	6	0.8	5	-	4,000	-	20	-	-
6300	Insurance carriers	4	1	0.1	11	-	18,909	-	232	-	-
6400	Insurance agents, brokers, and service	24	27	0.7	82	90	16,976	16,444	1,606	1,699	0.3
6500	Real estate	25	27	0.5	73	70	20,986	17,314	1,474	1,489	0.2
6510	Real estate operators and lessors	9	7	0.3	35	-	19,429	-	633	-	-
6530	Real estate agents and managers	10	16	0.5	18	36	14,000	11,556	290	514	0.1
SANILAC, MI											
60 –	**Finance, insurance, and real estate**	69	72	0.4	383	397	16,950	16,816	7,039	7,255	0.1
6000	Depository institutions	20	19	0.5	256	260	17,719	16,708	4,728	4,770	0.3
6400	Insurance agents, brokers, and service	21	24	0.6	62	70	17,677	16,171	1,169	1,277	0.2
6500	Real estate	20	21	0.4	38	39	13,368	9,949	591	458	0.1
6510	Real estate operators and lessors	5	5	0.2	10	9	7,600	6,222	69	61	0.0
6530	Real estate agents and managers	11	13	0.4	22	27	11,636	11,407	346	377	0.1

Source: County Business Patterns, 1992/93, CBP-92/93-1, U.S. Department of Commerce, Washington, D.C., April 1995. SIC categories for which data were suppressed or not available for both 1992 and 1993 are *not* displayed. The employment columns represent mid-March employment in the year. Pay per employee is calculated by dividing 1st Quarter payroll, annualized, by mid-March employment. The columns headed "% State" show the county's percentage of the state total for the SIC in 1993; for example, 0.9% for SIC 6030 means that the county had 0.9 percent of the state's total establishments (or payroll) in SIC 6030 in 1993. A dash (-) is used to indicate that data are not available or cannot be calculated; *nec* means not elsewhere classified.

SIC	Industry	No. Establishments			Employment		Pay / Employee		Annual Payroll ($ 000)		
		1992	1993	% State	1992	1993	1992	1993	1992	1993	% State
SCHOOLCRAFT, MI											
60–	**Finance, insurance, and real estate**	14	16	0.1	99	108	15,960	17,593	1,612	1,835	0.0
6000	Depository institutions	5	5	0.1	72	76	14,944	17,263	1,100	1,216	0.1
6400	Insurance agents, brokers, and service	4	3	0.1	10	-	28,800	-	300	-	-
6530	Real estate agents and managers	3	3	0.1	10	2	9,600	16,000	124	59	0.0
SHIAWASSEE, MI											
60–	**Finance, insurance, and real estate**	91	94	0.5	577	610	22,593	20,885	13,130	14,930	0.3
6000	Depository institutions	29	29	0.7	349	366	18,246	16,240	6,791	6,955	0.4
6020	Commercial banks	21	21	0.8	284	296	18,155	16,716	5,533	5,873	0.5
6200	Security and commodity brokers	4	4	0.5	9	9	69,333	83,111	594	683	0.2
6300	Insurance carriers	6	5	0.4	31	22	20,387	26,364	686	624	0.0
6400	Insurance agents, brokers, and service	25	29	0.7	98	115	17,510	15,791	1,819	2,289	0.4
6500	Real estate	23	23	0.4	47	52	13,872	12,000	689	1,002	0.1
6510	Real estate operators and lessors	8	6	0.2	18	10	7,778	8,800	147	107	0.1
6530	Real estate agents and managers	11	13	0.4	17	30	21,882	14,133	340	765	0.2
6553	Cemetery subdividers and developers	3	3	1.9	11	12	11,273	9,333	159	124	0.4
TUSCOLA, MI											
60–	**Finance, insurance, and real estate**	76	76	0.4	399	388	16,341	18,247	7,268	7,267	0.1
6000	Depository institutions	30	31	0.8	278	276	16,317	17,507	4,852	5,036	0.3
6020	Commercial banks	23	23	0.9	242	232	16,678	18,052	4,334	4,429	0.4
6030	Savings institutions	3	3	0.6	15	15	14,933	17,067	249	277	0.1
6060	Credit unions	4	5	0.7	21	29	13,143	13,379	269	330	0.2
6100	Nondepository institutions	3	2	0.3	17	-	13,647	-	356	-	-
6400	Insurance agents, brokers, and service	29	28	0.7	73	69	18,356	20,232	1,457	1,377	0.2
6500	Real estate	11	13	0.2	21	28	8,000	12,000	258	426	0.1
6510	Real estate operators and lessors	3	3	0.1	4	4	12,000	11,000	45	44	0.0
6530	Real estate agents and managers	4	6	0.2	5	9	12,800	12,889	127	124	0.0
VAN BUREN, MI											
60–	**Finance, insurance, and real estate**	92	92	0.5	535	507	15,850	17,041	9,632	9,271	0.2
6000	Depository institutions	28	27	0.7	308	284	16,922	19,070	5,850	5,736	0.3
6020	Commercial banks	20	20	0.8	261	243	17,165	19,588	5,102	5,026	0.4
6030	Savings institutions	5	4	0.7	32	26	16,750	15,231	548	450	0.2
6060	Credit unions	3	3	0.4	15	15	13,067	17,333	200	260	0.1
6300	Insurance carriers	5	2	0.1	13	-	16,615	-	239	-	-
6400	Insurance agents, brokers, and service	27	30	0.8	95	127	15,747	16,409	1,739	2,140	0.3
6500	Real estate	29	30	0.5	106	79	11,396	9,316	1,451	883	0.1
6510	Real estate operators and lessors	12	11	0.5	-	31	-	8,129	-	287	0.1
6530	Real estate agents and managers	14	17	0.6	26	-	6,000	-	261	-	-
WASHTENAW, MI											
60–	**Finance, insurance, and real estate**	616	637	3.7	5,890	5,948	24,622	24,646	154,237	163,823	2.8
6000	Depository institutions	125	124	3.2	2,198	2,026	22,646	23,019	49,649	47,141	2.9
6020	Commercial banks	87	84	3.3	1,526	1,310	22,189	23,866	33,476	30,214	2.4
6030	Savings institutions	27	27	5.0	507	494	24,110	22,534	12,612	12,364	6.0
6060	Credit unions	11	13	1.7	165	222	22,376	19,099	3,561	4,563	2.6
6100	Nondepository institutions	28	31	4.4	349	370	30,407	29,016	13,220	14,384	2.7
6140	Personal credit institutions	7	7	4.0	160	114	26,675	27,965	4,088	3,290	2.6
6150	Business credit institutions	5	4	3.5	47	38	44,255	39,474	2,330	2,009	2.0
6160	Mortgage bankers and brokers	16	18	4.7	142	201	30,028	27,085	6,802	8,519	2.8
6200	Security and commodity brokers	34	36	4.7	227	213	62,044	68,732	15,564	17,770	4.3
6210	Security brokers and dealers	15	18	4.0	-	160	-	76,400	-	13,413	3.9
6280	Security and commodity services	17	15	5.0	86	-	69,070	-	8,381	-	-
6300	Insurance carriers	47	45	3.2	375	383	27,755	29,911	11,473	11,993	0.7
6310	Life insurance	7	7	2.2	94	115	24,596	32,522	2,371	3,430	1.0
6330	Fire, marine, and casualty insurance	24	22	3.5	138	127	38,058	40,252	5,257	5,537	0.7
6360	Title insurance	5	4	4.0	81	80	21,975	22,850	2,703	2,118	4.2

Source: County Business Patterns, 1992/93, CBP-92/93-1, U.S. Department of Commerce, Washington, D.C., April 1995. SIC categories for which data were suppressed or not available for both 1992 and 1993 are *not* displayed. The employment columns represent mid-March employment in the year. Pay per employee is calculated by dividing 1st Quarter payroll, annualized, by mid-March employment. The columns headed "% State" show the county's percentage of the state total for the SIC in 1993; for example, 0.9% for SIC 6030 means that the county had 0.9 percent of the state's total establishments (or payroll) in SIC 6030 in 1993. A dash (-) is used to indicate that data are not available or cannot be calculated; *nec* means not elsewhere classified.

Continued on next page.

SIC	Industry	No. Establishments			Employment		Pay / Employee		Annual Payroll ($ 000)		
		1992	1993	% State	1992	1993	1992	1993	1992	1993	% State
WASHTENAW, MI - [continued]											
6370	Pension, health, and welfare funds	10	11	4.7	-	61	-	12,721	-	876	1.3
6400	Insurance agents, brokers, and service	98	109	2.8	439	602	24,310	23,449	12,814	17,581	2.8
6500	Real estate	256	261	4.4	1,770	1,730	17,853	18,044	32,843	34,841	5.2
6510	Real estate operators and lessors	92	97	4.0	497	511	14,881	13,800	7,078	7,332	3.5
6530	Real estate agents and managers	125	139	4.7	1,127	1,121	19,372	19,879	23,139	25,157	6.8
6540	Title abstract offices	3	3	2.9	20	19	16,000	17,895	314	361	1.4
6552	Subdividers and developers, n.e.c.	10	9	4.5	41	35	11,122	20,457	493	867	3.2
6553	Cemetery subdividers and developers	7	8	5.0	34	34	17,176	17,412	645	691	2.2
6710	Holding offices	7	7	4.0	66	98	76,788	41,020	4,588	4,693	3.5
6732	Educational, religious, etc. trusts	6	6	6.2	76	78	31,895	33,487	2,317	2,624	13.9
6733	Trusts, n.e.c.	6	7	4.0	54	26	7,481	13,077	451	488	2.5
6794	Patent owners and lessors	4	5	9.3	-	35	-	23,314	-	381	2.0
WAYNE, MI											
60–	**Finance, insurance, and real estate**	2,383	2,323	13.4	44,047	42,423	31,747	29,871	1,395,901	1,346,473	23.0
6000	Depository institutions	635	642	16.4	18,078	15,613	27,771	24,199	483,164	393,639	23.8
6020	Commercial banks	390	376	14.6	13,496	11,755	29,062	24,426	371,986	300,931	24.0
6030	Savings institutions	97	90	16.7	1,589	1,413	24,078	23,708	40,294	37,258	18.2
6060	Credit unions	114	140	18.5	1,518	1,794	21,362	21,075	32,568	39,903	22.3
6100	Nondepository institutions	120	84	11.8	2,985	1,405	39,086	31,470	114,962	47,860	8.9
6140	Personal credit institutions	68	26	14.9	2,253	831	36,879	28,813	83,509	23,819	18.7
6150	Business credit institutions	15	16	14.2	411	215	55,942	45,079	19,256	9,381	9.5
6160	Mortgage bankers and brokers	36	41	10.8	319	358	33,028	29,520	12,136	14,645	4.9
6200	Security and commodity brokers	97	102	13.3	1,294	1,525	60,022	55,570	78,412	89,900	21.8
6210	Security brokers and dealers	64	59	13.0	1,157	1,215	59,938	62,347	71,937	78,006	22.5
6280	Security and commodity services	32	43	14.3	136	310	60,853	29,006	6,456	11,894	18.7
6300	Insurance carriers	236	179	12.7	11,831	12,608	34,993	35,163	413,925	468,904	28.8
6310	Life insurance	48	45	14.2	1,965	1,760	26,532	26,014	51,698	47,391	13.9
6330	Fire, marine, and casualty insurance	88	86	13.6	4,861	5,669	41,521	39,812	189,935	231,831	29.8
6360	Title insurance	11	10	10.0	253	206	21,929	24,078	8,338	8,026	15.8
6400	Insurance agents, brokers, and service	351	364	9.3	2,774	3,283	33,590	30,534	94,891	103,008	16.6
6500	Real estate	815	832	13.9	5,059	4,925	17,098	17,804	92,889	101,003	15.0
6510	Real estate operators and lessors	384	430	17.8	2,164	2,239	13,018	14,926	30,507	39,087	18.5
6530	Real estate agents and managers	329	340	11.6	2,108	2,088	18,590	20,356	40,988	46,154	12.5
6540	Title abstract offices	6	11	10.6	23	110	21,739	19,273	892	4,164	16.2
6552	Subdividers and developers, n.e.c.	15	13	6.5	258	123	32,961	7,902	8,487	1,266	4.7
6553	Cemetery subdividers and developers	24	25	15.7	318	336	21,308	24,548	7,780	9,721	30.5
6700	Holding and other investment offices	126	115	18.0	851	1,144	46,848	47,741	41,088	58,395	26.6
6710	Holding offices	36	39	22.3	406	698	64,956	59,393	25,913	45,672	33.8
6720	Investment offices	6	2	12.5	40	-	34,900	-	1,950	-	-
6732	Educational, religious, etc. trusts	23	21	21.6	153	172	24,758	26,256	4,429	4,258	22.5
6733	Trusts, n.e.c.	32	27	15.5	77	139	20,779	25,094	1,788	2,065	10.6
6794	Patent owners and lessors	11	10	18.5	71	77	56,225	42,494	4,127	4,451	23.9
6798	Real estate investment trusts	5	3	30.0	-	8	-	10,500	-	90	13.7
6799	Investors, n.e.c.	9	9	11.1	24	21	26,167	31,619	559	674	5.8
WEXFORD, MI											
60–	**Finance, insurance, and real estate**	60	59	0.3	369	335	19,187	18,149	7,017	6,667	0.1
6000	Depository institutions	15	16	0.4	207	205	19,014	18,459	3,788	3,894	0.2
6020	Commercial banks	13	13	0.5	-	180	-	18,711	-	3,466	0.3
6300	Insurance carriers	6	3	0.2	29	-	16,276	-	465	-	-
6370	Pension, health, and welfare funds	3	1	0.4	4	-	10,000	-	12	-	-
6400	Insurance agents, brokers, and service	20	19	0.5	62	60	22,065	21,933	1,482	1,436	0.2
6500	Real estate	15	18	0.3	41	44	17,659	9,727	765	774	0.1
6510	Real estate operators and lessors	5	5	0.2	20	18	10,400	9,333	204	171	0.1
6530	Real estate agents and managers	7	9	0.3	17	25	28,000	9,760	528	521	0.1

*Source: County Business Patterns, 1992/93, CBP-92/93-1, U.S. Department of Commerce, Washington, D.C., April 1995. SIC categories for which data were suppressed or not available for both 1992 and 1993 are *not* displayed. The employment columns represent mid-March employment in the year. Pay per employee is calculated by dividing 1st Quarter payroll, annualized, by mid-March employment. The columns headed "% State" show the county's percentage of the state total for the SIC in 1993; for example, 0.9% for SIC 6030 means that the county had 0.9 percent of the state's total establishments (or payroll) in SIC 6030 in 1993. A dash (-) is used to indicate that data are not available or cannot be calculated; nec means not elsewhere classified.*

MINNESOTA

SIC	Industry	No. Establishments			Employment		Pay / Employee		Annual Payroll ($ 000)		
		1992	1993	% State	1992	1993	1992	1993	1992	1993	% State
AITKIN, MN											
60 –	**Finance, insurance, and real estate**	23	27	0.2	111	140	16,468	14,457	2,006	2,631	0.1
6000	Depository institutions	5	5	0.3	63	75	18,286	17,493	1,235	1,671	0.2
6400	Insurance agents, brokers, and service	5	6	0.2	16	-	13,000	-	224	-	-
6500	Real estate	10	13	0.3	-	41	-	9,268	-	522	0.1
6530	Real estate agents and managers	6	11	0.6	4	-	21,000	-	136	-	-
ANOKA, MN											
60 –	**Finance, insurance, and real estate**	357	388	3.5	2,033	2,152	20,944	19,407	44,413	47,453	1.0
6000	Depository institutions	46	52	3.1	614	669	22,150	21,782	13,779	14,717	1.5
6020	Commercial banks	27	29	2.5	476	475	22,739	22,863	10,856	10,847	1.5
6060	Credit unions	9	13	4.5	59	92	21,627	16,739	1,326	1,640	3.4
6100	Nondepository institutions	44	39	6.6	222	330	31,387	21,394	7,385	8,440	1.9
6140	Personal credit institutions	29	19	10.2	126	212	25,651	14,132	3,478	2,434	4.2
6150	Business credit institutions	3	5	5.1	-	19	-	15,579	-	329	0.6
6160	Mortgage bankers and brokers	10	15	5.9	90	99	40,089	38,061	3,665	5,677	2.1
6200	Security and commodity brokers	10	9	1.3	13	15	32,615	46,133	447	500	0.1
6210	Security brokers and dealers	2	5	1.5	-	8	-	29,000	-	246	0.0
6280	Security and commodity services	7	4	1.2	-	7	-	65,714	-	254	0.2
6300	Insurance carriers	31	12	1.5	254	-	34,063	-	5,347	-	-
6330	Fire, marine, and casualty insurance	22	11	2.9	189	-	38,349	-	3,371	-	-
6400	Insurance agents, brokers, and service	94	118	4.0	262	411	17,771	20,642	7,024	8,988	2.4
6500	Real estate	126	152	3.8	628	663	12,510	14,112	10,045	13,139	3.0
6510	Real estate operators and lessors	58	61	3.7	314	243	9,949	11,226	3,525	3,199	2.5
6530	Real estate agents and managers	44	70	3.9	138	291	11,855	13,045	2,147	4,405	1.9
6540	Title abstract offices	3	9	5.5	-	77	-	25,455	-	2,686	5.1
6552	Subdividers and developers, n.e.c.	4	8	5.6	101	42	17,624	17,619	2,427	2,687	13.7
6700	Holding and other investment offices	6	6	1.3	40	-	10,600	-	386	-	-
BECKER, MN											
60 –	**Finance, insurance, and real estate**	62	62	0.6	341	319	17,689	19,072	6,250	6,305	0.1
6000	Depository institutions	10	9	0.5	170	163	20,235	22,405	3,553	3,555	0.4
6020	Commercial banks	10	9	0.8	170	163	20,235	22,405	3,553	3,555	0.5
6200	Security and commodity brokers	3	4	0.6	5	-	22,400	-	155	-	-
6400	Insurance agents, brokers, and service	19	17	0.6	48	45	14,667	14,400	719	744	0.2
6500	Real estate	22	25	0.6	82	85	11,415	11,718	1,015	1,287	0.3
6510	Real estate operators and lessors	5	7	0.4	29	-	15,034	-	425	-	-
6530	Real estate agents and managers	13	14	0.8	42	46	7,810	7,565	353	360	0.2
BELTRAMI, MN											
60 –	**Finance, insurance, and real estate**	54	56	0.5	344	364	18,384	17,571	6,530	6,856	0.2
6000	Depository institutions	13	13	0.8	207	207	17,662	18,628	3,816	4,050	0.4
6200	Security and commodity brokers	3	3	0.4	6	6	19,333	16,000	126	101	0.0
6400	Insurance agents, brokers, and service	17	17	0.6	48	58	18,667	16,000	936	961	0.3
6500	Real estate	13	15	0.4	-	52	-	12,462	-	845	0.2
6530	Real estate agents and managers	3	9	0.5	6	35	15,333	10,400	102	504	0.2
6700	Holding and other investment offices	4	4	0.9	31	-	28,903	-	738	-	-
BENTON, MN											
60 –	**Finance, insurance, and real estate**	28	28	0.3	113	113	18,018	22,938	2,442	2,676	0.1
6000	Depository institutions	4	5	0.3	60	59	18,133	22,644	1,349	1,300	0.1
6300	Insurance carriers	3	2	0.3	8	-	19,000	-	163	-	-

Source: County Business Patterns, 1992/93, CBP-92/93-1, U.S. Department of Commerce, Washington, D.C., April 1995. SIC categories for which data were suppressed or not available for both 1992 and 1993 are *not* displayed. The employment columns represent mid-March employment in the year. Pay per employee is calculated by dividing 1st Quarter payroll, annualized, by mid-March employment. The columns headed "% State" show the county's percentage of the state total for the SIC in 1993; for example, 0.9% for SIC 6030 means that the county had 0.9 percent of the state's total establishments (or payroll) in SIC 6030 in 1993. A dash (-) is used to indicate that data are not available or cannot be calculated; *nec* means not elsewhere classified.

Continued on next page.

SIC	Industry	No. Establishments			Employment		Pay / Employee		Annual Payroll ($ 000)		
		1992	1993	% State	1992	1993	1992	1993	1992	1993	% State
REDWOOD, MN - [continued]											
6500	Real estate	17	19	0.5	26	28	5,077	4,286	165	137	0.0
6510	Real estate operators and lessors	8	12	0.7	13	18	4,308	3,778	61	82	0.1
6530	Real estate agents and managers	5	4	0.2	6	5	6,000	7,200	39	39	0.0
RENVILLE, MN											
60 –	**Finance, insurance, and real estate**	48	46	0.4	251	241	20,558	20,880	5,597	5,368	0.1
6000	Depository institutions	13	11	0.7	136	132	22,206	21,606	3,274	3,026	0.3
6400	Insurance agents, brokers, and service	19	19	0.6	48	56	17,000	15,571	889	953	0.3
6500	Real estate	6	7	0.2	-	17		15,529	-	314	0.1
6510	Real estate operators and lessors	3	4	0.2	8	-	1,500	-	12	-	-
RICE, MN											
60 –	**Finance, insurance, and real estate**	96	98	0.9	519	586	20,925	20,717	11,552	12,634	0.3
6000	Depository institutions	18	18	1.1	283	300	22,799	22,387	6,320	6,742	0.7
6100	Nondepository institutions	7	5	0.8	23	43	30,435	25,860	719	1,094	0.3
6200	Security and commodity brokers	6	7	1.0	-	16		28,250	-	548	0.1
6400	Insurance agents, brokers, and service	21	23	0.8	64	87	18,938	18,667	1,256	1,441	0.4
6500	Real estate	31	38	1.0	63	71	11,111	12,056	1,068	1,122	0.3
6510	Real estate operators and lessors	10	12	0.7	20	-	8,800	-	213	-	-
6530	Real estate agents and managers	12	18	1.0	21	-	15,619	-	385	-	-
ROCK, MN											
60 –	**Finance, insurance, and real estate**	34	35	0.3	338	357	23,704	25,378	8,349	8,650	0.2
6000	Depository institutions	10	10	0.6	88	96	20,955	19,792	2,004	1,842	0.2
6020	Commercial banks	10	10	0.9	88	96	20,955	19,792	2,004	1,842	0.2
6500	Real estate	8	8	0.2	18	18	5,556	5,111	102	104	0.0
6510	Real estate operators and lessors	5	5	0.3	10	11	4,000	3,273	39	41	0.0
ROSEAU, MN											
60 –	**Finance, insurance, and real estate**	22	23	0.2	134	142	18,000	17,380	2,774	2,250	0.0
6000	Depository institutions	5	5	0.3	88	87	21,364	22,621	2,222	1,715	0.2
6020	Commercial banks	5	5	0.4	88	87	21,364	22,621	2,222	1,715	0.2
6400	Insurance agents, brokers, and service	8	9	0.3	22	-	12,364	-	275	-	-
6500	Real estate	6	7	0.2	10	27	10,000	4,444	113	151	0.0
6510	Real estate operators and lessors	3	4	0.2	-	21		2,667	-	73	0.1
ST. LOUIS, MN											
60 –	**Finance, insurance, and real estate**	430	438	3.9	2,912	2,940	21,397	21,607	63,353	66,691	1.5
6000	Depository institutions	81	88	5.2	1,229	1,257	20,967	20,150	26,661	27,842	2.9
6020	Commercial banks	47	45	4.0	924	894	22,069	20,904	20,834	21,170	2.9
6030	Savings institutions	10	10	4.9	132	145	21,788	24,634	3,218	3,466	3.6
6100	Nondepository institutions	27	19	3.2	147	115	24,463	26,052	3,539	3,733	0.9
6160	Mortgage bankers and brokers	10	9	3.6	72	73	27,889	26,411	1,969	2,602	1.0
6200	Security and commodity brokers	23	27	3.8	141	158	52,652	65,367	7,523	9,370	1.5
6210	Security brokers and dealers	16	17	5.0	121	126	56,595	65,651	6,935	8,006	1.6
6300	Insurance carriers	37	29	3.6	248	220	26,855	28,527	6,178	5,969	0.5
6310	Life insurance	9	8	4.1	115	103	27,896	27,845	3,124	2,907	0.5
6330	Fire, marine, and casualty insurance	15	12	3.2	-	68		35,176	-	2,056	0.5
6400	Insurance agents, brokers, and service	126	139	4.7	384	408	20,573	20,627	7,847	8,289	2.2
6500	Real estate	117	113	2.9	697	678	12,528	12,378	9,747	9,452	2.2
6510	Real estate operators and lessors	47	51	3.1	320	245	12,100	12,033	3,996	2,976	2.3
6530	Real estate agents and managers	49	50	2.8	289	346	11,806	12,104	3,663	4,488	2.0
6540	Title abstract offices	4	4	2.4	45	55	16,889	15,564	1,278	1,472	2.8
6553	Cemetery subdividers and developers	9	8	5.5	-	32		12,500	-	516	8.1
6733	Trusts, n.e.c.	4	4	4.6	-	9		20,000	-	199	-
6799	Investors, n.e.c.	6	7	11.1	17	-	14,588	-	314	-	-

Source: County Business Patterns, 1992/93, CBP-92/93-1, U.S. Department of Commerce, Washington, D.C., April 1995. SIC categories for which data were suppressed or not available for both 1992 and 1993 are *not* displayed. The employment columns represent mid-March employment in the year. Pay per employee is calculated by dividing 1st Quarter payroll, annualized, by mid-March employment. The columns headed "% State" show the county's percentage of the state total for the SIC in 1993; for example, 0.9% for SIC 6030 means that the county had 0.9 percent of the state's total establishments (or payroll) in SIC 6030 in 1993. A dash (-) is used to indicate that data are not available or cannot be calculated; *nec* means not elsewhere classified.

SIC	Industry	No. Establishments			Employment		Pay / Employee		Annual Payroll ($ 000)		
		1992	1993	% State	1992	1993	1992	1993	1992	1993	% State
SCOTT, MN											
60 –	**Finance, insurance, and real estate**	105	101	0.9	541	523	20,481	20,214	11,673	11,202	0.2
6000	Depository institutions	18	16	1.0	295	284	20,529	20,915	6,152	6,285	0.7
6100	Nondepository institutions	3	3	0.5	7	7	22,286	25,143	169	152	0.0
6300	Insurance carriers	8	3	0.4	44	-	12,364	-	553	-	-
6400	Insurance agents, brokers, and service	24	26	0.9	57	61	17,965	18,820	1,247	1,478	0.4
6500	Real estate	48	49	1.2	112	127	22,250	13,827	2,624	2,103	0.5
6510	Real estate operators and lessors	15	16	1.0	24	34	20,333	17,882	677	621	0.5
6530	Real estate agents and managers	20	23	1.3	49	55	24,163	13,164	928	876	0.4
6540	Title abstract offices	2	3	1.8	-	13	-	21,846	-	425	0.8
SHERBURNE, MN											
60 –	**Finance, insurance, and real estate**	55	60	0.5	409	433	20,333	20,573	8,919	9,755	0.2
6000	Depository institutions	13	13	0.8	283	306	22,233	22,497	6,719	7,293	0.8
6020	Commercial banks	10	10	0.9	273	-	22,579	-	6,582	-	-
6200	Security and commodity brokers	3	2	0.3	6	-	24,000	-	176	-	-
6400	Insurance agents, brokers, and service	11	14	0.5	33	39	17,818	17,436	644	764	0.2
6500	Real estate	24	27	0.7	73	70	15,781	14,000	1,260	1,302	0.3
6510	Real estate operators and lessors	3	4	0.2	2	5	6,000	16,800	30	123	0.1
6530	Real estate agents and managers	11	16	0.9	36	47	15,111	11,574	597	690	0.3
6540	Title abstract offices	2	3	1.8	-	17	-	20,235	-	452	0.9
SIBLEY, MN											
60 –	**Finance, insurance, and real estate**	29	30	0.3	125	131	20,192	21,313	2,778	3,026	0.1
6000	Depository institutions	8	8	0.5	86	93	23,814	24,387	2,201	2,460	0.3
6400	Insurance agents, brokers, and service	8	9	0.3	16	18	11,500	12,000	201	229	0.1
6500	Real estate	8	8	0.2	13	10	10,462	8,000	199	150	0.0
6530	Real estate agents and managers	4	2	0.1	10	-	11,200	-	114	-	-
6553	Cemetery subdividers and developers	2	3	2.1	-	2	-	4,000	-	12	0.2
STEARNS, MN											
60 –	**Finance, insurance, and real estate**	297	301	2.7	2,083	2,217	21,120	21,295	46,482	51,442	1.1
6000	Depository institutions	48	52	3.1	915	996	23,454	21,373	22,459	22,772	2.4
6020	Commercial banks	33	33	2.9	695	741	23,586	21,987	17,040	17,257	2.3
6030	Savings institutions	12	11	5.3	-	134	-	23,701	-	3,502	3.6
6060	Credit unions	2	8	2.8	-	121	-	15,041	-	2,013	4.2
6100	Nondepository institutions	18	14	2.4	167	-	22,036	-	3,919	-	-
6140	Personal credit institutions	13	8	4.3	119	90	18,521	11,422	2,415	1,176	2.0
6200	Security and commodity brokers	10	12	1.7	49	173	75,429	41,526	3,284	7,434	1.2
6210	Security brokers and dealers	5	8	2.3	-	170	-	42,071	-	7,398	1.5
6280	Security and commodity services	4	3	0.9	3	-	14,667	-	54	-	-
6300	Insurance carriers	31	23	2.9	191	229	26,325	22,568	5,136	5,681	0.4
6310	Life insurance	7	4	2.0	74	77	31,027	25,506	2,249	2,472	0.4
6330	Fire, marine, and casualty insurance	18	15	3.9	103	99	24,660	25,010	2,554	2,658	0.6
6400	Insurance agents, brokers, and service	88	97	3.3	324	273	11,617	15,868	4,005	4,660	1.3
6500	Real estate	95	99	2.5	392	391	14,082	15,028	6,714	7,451	1.7
6510	Real estate operators and lessors	39	43	2.6	100	104	8,160	9,500	975	1,077	0.8
6530	Real estate agents and managers	42	47	2.6	226	234	13,805	14,991	3,896	4,538	2.0
6540	Title abstract offices	4	4	2.4	41	42	27,902	24,952	1,468	1,704	3.3
6552	Subdividers and developers, n.e.c.	3	2	1.4	3	-	57,333	-	102	-	-
6700	Holding and other investment offices	7	4	0.9	45	-	18,756	-	965	-	-
STEELE, MN											
60 –	**Finance, insurance, and real estate**	64	67	0.6	1,699	1,989	32,593	31,781	54,268	55,882	1.2
6000	Depository institutions	17	18	1.1	174	183	22,115	22,142	3,874	4,199	0.4

Source: County Business Patterns, 1992/93, CBP-92/93-1, U.S. Department of Commerce, Washington, D.C., April 1995. SIC categories for which data were suppressed or not available for both 1992 and 1993 are not displayed. The employment columns represent mid-March employment in the year. Pay per employee is calculated by dividing 1st Quarter payroll, annualized, by mid-March employment. The columns headed "% State" show the county's percentage of the state total for the SIC in 1993; for example, 0.9% for SIC 6030 means that the county had 0.9 percent of the state's total establishments (or payroll) in SIC 6030 in 1993. A dash (-) is used to indicate that data are not available or cannot be calculated; nec means not elsewhere classified.

Continued on next page.

SIC	Industry	No. Establishments			Employment		Pay / Employee		Annual Payroll ($ 000)		
		1992	1993	% State	1992	1993	1992	1993	1992	1993	% State
STEELE, MN - [continued]											
6020	Commercial banks	12	12	1.1	145	146	23,421	22,411	3,373	3,434	0.5
6510	Real estate operators and lessors	4	4	0.2	5	-	6,400	-	44	-	-
6553	Cemetery subdividers and developers	3	3	2.1	-	4	-	4,000	-	30	0.5
STEVENS, MN											
60–	**Finance, insurance, and real estate**	31	38	0.3	164	192	19,098	19,458	3,273	3,467	0.1
6000	Depository institutions	7	8	0.5	100	117	19,640	20,103	2,094	2,236	0.2
6400	Insurance agents, brokers, and service	8	12	0.4	26	37	24,615	20,541	616	671	0.2
6500	Real estate	10	13	0.3	-	22	-	7,091	-	161	0.0
6510	Real estate operators and lessors	6	9	0.5	11	-	7,273	-	78	-	-
SWIFT, MN											
60–	**Finance, insurance, and real estate**	25	31	0.3	129	138	19,411	16,261	2,618	2,649	0.1
6000	Depository institutions	9	9	0.5	94	96	23,872	18,750	2,343	2,158	0.2
6500	Real estate	5	9	0.2	16	17	7,000	9,412	111	169	0.0
6510	Real estate operators and lessors	1	5	0.3	-	6	-	8,667	-	49	0.0
TODD, MN											
60–	**Finance, insurance, and real estate**	37	39	0.3	188	233	17,255	17,253	3,541	3,972	0.1
6000	Depository institutions	8	8	0.5	116	128	20,690	21,375	2,569	2,627	0.3
6400	Insurance agents, brokers, and service	15	15	0.5	39	-	14,051	-	634	-	-
6500	Real estate	10	13	0.3	20	43	9,400	8,372	231	365	0.1
6530	Real estate agents and managers	5	8	0.4	7	17	6,286	7,765	42	112	0.0
TRAVERSE, MN											
60–	**Finance, insurance, and real estate**	11	14	0.1	62	59	19,161	16,678	1,246	1,108	0.0
6000	Depository institutions	4	4	0.2	53	45	20,906	18,844	1,157	959	0.1
6400	Insurance agents, brokers, and service	4	6	0.2	-	11	-	10,909	-	125	0.0
6500	Real estate	2	4	0.1	-	3	-	5,333	-	24	0.0
WABASHA, MN											
60–	**Finance, insurance, and real estate**	31	37	0.3	175	198	18,766	19,192	3,648	3,920	0.1
6000	Depository institutions	8	10	0.6	127	145	21,165	21,159	3,011	3,152	0.3
6400	Insurance agents, brokers, and service	11	12	0.4	17	-	11,529	-	195	-	-
6500	Real estate	9	10	0.3	26	31	13,385	15,742	384	493	0.1
6530	Real estate agents and managers	4	5	0.3	5	-	6,400	-	35	-	-
WADENA, MN											
60–	**Finance, insurance, and real estate**	25	30	0.3	154	140	16,779	16,629	3,004	3,119	0.1
6000	Depository institutions	7	8	0.5	111	90	18,883	19,778	2,498	2,533	0.3
6500	Real estate	7	8	0.2	13	17	7,385	5,412	110	127	0.0
6510	Real estate operators and lessors	3	4	0.2	1	3	4,000	2,667	8	10	0.0
WASECA, MN											
60–	**Finance, insurance, and real estate**	29	32	0.3	216	219	19,444	21,096	4,243	4,541	0.1
6000	Depository institutions	10	9	0.5	114	118	21,474	23,864	2,481	2,629	0.3
6400	Insurance agents, brokers, and service	10	12	0.4	18	19	18,000	15,579	315	327	0.1
6500	Real estate	4	6	0.2	8	11	7,500	5,455	57	88	0.0
WASHINGTON, MN											
60–	**Finance, insurance, and real estate**	233	262	2.3	2,104	2,267	35,814	30,495	65,359	69,482	1.5
6000	Depository institutions	26	28	1.7	444	485	24,604	24,561	10,548	11,705	1.2
6020	Commercial banks	23	23	2.0	-	454	-	24,634	-	10,983	1.5
6100	Nondepository institutions	9	9	1.5	17	-	19,294	-	648	-	-
6160	Mortgage bankers and brokers	6	7	2.8	9	-	19,111	-	484	-	-
6200	Security and commodity brokers	16	15	2.1	218	177	63,119	39,751	10,758	6,811	1.1
6300	Insurance carriers	24	15	1.9	923	-	40,438	-	31,795	-	-
6400	Insurance agents, brokers, and service	63	70	2.4	183	187	47,716	29,326	6,120	5,361	1.4

Source: County Business Patterns, 1992/93, CBP-92/93-1, U.S. Department of Commerce, Washington, D.C., April 1995. SIC categories for which data were suppressed or not available for both 1992 and 1993 are *not* displayed. The employment columns represent mid-March employment in the year. Pay per employee is calculated by dividing 1st Quarter payroll, annualized, by mid-March employment. The columns headed "% State" show the county's percentage of the state total for the SIC in 1993; for example, 0.9% for SIC 6030 means that the county had 0.9 percent of the state's total establishments (or payroll) in SIC 6030 in 1993. A dash (-) is used to indicate that data are not available or cannot be calculated; *nec* means not elsewhere classified.

Continued on next page.

SIC	Industry	No. Establishments			Employment		Pay / Employee		Annual Payroll ($ 000)		
		1992	1993	% State	1992	1993	1992	1993	1992	1993	% State
WASHINGTON, MN - [continued]											
6500	Real estate	84	111	2.8	272	425	12,588	15,144	4,497	8,197	1.9
6510	Real estate operators and lessors	28	34	2.1	72	125	10,222	9,152	935	1,347	1.1
6530	Real estate agents and managers	42	62	3.4	148	207	13,324	16,947	2,523	4,137	1.8
6540	Title abstract offices	3	10	6.1	22	85	18,182	19,012	648	2,595	5.0
6700	Holding and other investment offices	11	14	3.1	47	124	18,298	37,903	993	5,519	1.6
WATONWAN, MN											
60 –	**Finance, insurance, and real estate**	28	28	0.3	146	151	17,397	15,974	2,661	2,690	0.1
6000	Depository institutions	11	11	0.7	104	113	19,692	16,850	2,123	2,152	0.2
6400	Insurance agents, brokers, and service	9	9	0.3	26	26	12,308	13,538	364	394	0.1
6500	Real estate	4	4	0.1	12	6	9,667	4,667	118	33	0.0
WILKIN, MN											
60 –	**Finance, insurance, and real estate**	18	20	0.2	86	77	18,558	21,766	1,609	1,764	0.0
6000	Depository institutions	6	6	0.4	59	53	20,407	23,094	1,225	1,273	0.1
6400	Insurance agents, brokers, and service	6	6	0.2	13	-	13,538	-	178	-	-
6500	Real estate	3	5	0.1	4	5	6,000	10,400	27	148	0.0
WINONA, MN											
60 –	**Finance, insurance, and real estate**	85	87	0.8	494	565	21,360	21,862	11,072	11,857	0.3
6000	Depository institutions	14	14	0.8	302	340	21,735	22,412	6,571	6,397	0.7
6100	Nondepository institutions	4	7	1.2	11	-	27,636	-	279	-	-
6150	Business credit institutions	2	3	3.0	-	4	-	37,000	-	126	0.2
6200	Security and commodity brokers	2	3	0.4	-	8	-	63,000	-	694	0.1
6400	Insurance agents, brokers, and service	25	27	0.9	72	86	26,222	24,186	2,072	2,295	0.6
6500	Real estate	31	30	0.8	78	82	12,051	12,146	1,206	1,242	0.3
6510	Real estate operators and lessors	16	18	1.1	35	-	10,971	-	473	-	-
6530	Real estate agents and managers	8	7	0.4	20	20	12,400	13,600	317	305	0.1
6700	Holding and other investment offices	3	3	0.7	6	15	19,333	32,000	130	514	0.1
WRIGHT, MN											
60 –	**Finance, insurance, and real estate**	113	125	1.1	590	636	18,922	19,119	12,185	13,656	0.3
6000	Depository institutions	22	23	1.4	335	369	22,866	22,255	7,719	8,506	0.9
6200	Security and commodity brokers	3	4	0.6	-	5	-	18,400	-	124	0.0
6300	Insurance carriers	8	4	0.5	12	13	7,000	13,846	144	221	0.0
6400	Insurance agents, brokers, and service	35	42	1.4	112	100	17,357	18,840	2,563	2,228	0.6
6500	Real estate	39	47	1.2	93	123	10,065	11,024	1,226	2,266	0.5
6510	Real estate operators and lessors	17	20	1.2	48	-	8,167	-	417	-	-
6530	Real estate agents and managers	14	19	1.1	27	52	13,185	9,615	479	768	0.3
YELLOW MEDICINE, MN											
60 –	**Finance, insurance, and real estate**	28	29	0.3	152	146	16,184	17,534	2,607	2,696	0.1
6000	Depository institutions	10	10	0.6	107	102	18,206	19,686	2,082	2,095	0.2
6400	Insurance agents, brokers, and service	7	11	0.4	18	-	12,222	-	227	-	-
6500	Real estate	7	7	0.2	14	13	5,714	5,538	79	71	0.0
6510	Real estate operators and lessors	5	5	0.3	13	-	5,231	-	64	-	-

Source: County Business Patterns, 1992/93, CBP-92/93-1, U.S. Department of Commerce, Washington, D.C., April 1995. SIC categories for which data were suppressed or not available for both 1992 and 1993 are *not* displayed. The employment columns represent mid-March employment in the year. Pay per employee is calculated by dividing 1st Quarter payroll, annualized, by mid-March employment. The columns headed "% State" show the county's percentage of the state total for the SIC in 1993; for example, *0.9%* for SIC 6030 means that the county had 0.9 percent of the state's total establishments (or payroll) in SIC 6030 in 1993. A dash (-) is used to indicate that data are not available or cannot be calculated; *nec* means not elsewhere classified.

MISSISSIPPI

SIC	Industry	No. Establishments			Employment		Pay / Employee		Annual Payroll ($ 000)		
		1992	1993	% State	1992	1993	1992	1993	1992	1993	% State
ADAMS, MS											
60 –	**Finance, insurance, and real estate**	90	93	1.8	471	490	20,722	20,906	10,212	11,421	1.3
6000	Depository institutions	19	20	1.7	207	212	20,812	21,585	4,379	4,837	1.3
6020	Commercial banks	12	12	1.3	164	168	21,732	22,738	3,558	4,224	1.3
6030	Savings institutions	3	2	1.9	27	-	19,556	-	564	-	-
6060	Credit unions	4	5	3.4	16	-	13,500	-	257	-	-
6100	Nondepository institutions	11	13	1.8	-	48	-	14,833	-	739	1.0
6140	Personal credit institutions	8	10	1.8	-	43	-	14,512	-	633	1.2
6160	Mortgage bankers and brokers	3	3	3.4	2	5	26,000	17,600	114	106	0.7
6200	Security and commodity brokers	4	3	2.0	9	6	62,667	114,000	600	627	1.5
6210	Security brokers and dealers	4	3	3.3	9	6	62,667	114,000	600	627	1.6
6300	Insurance carriers	8	9	2.3	88	86	26,455	26,326	2,452	2,418	1.2
6400	Insurance agents, brokers, and service	15	13	1.1	48	-	19,583	-	1,010	-	-
6500	Real estate	31	33	2.1	83	86	11,952	13,209	1,122	1,809	2.9
6510	Real estate operators and lessors	19	17	1.7	52	-	12,231	-	723	-	-
6530	Real estate agents and managers	8	13	2.7	15	26	11,733	14,308	192	919	3.3
ALCORN, MS											
60 –	**Finance, insurance, and real estate**	71	69	1.3	426	493	21,484	22,264	10,756	12,201	1.4
6000	Depository institutions	13	14	1.2	174	173	22,069	23,630	3,905	3,964	1.1
6100	Nondepository institutions	18	18	2.5	120	140	20,633	18,743	2,746	3,321	4.3
6140	Personal credit institutions	15	17	3.0	112	-	20,857	-	2,582	-	-
6400	Insurance agents, brokers, and service	11	9	0.8	37	-	29,189	-	1,008	-	-
6500	Real estate	24	23	1.5	64	58	9,750	9,379	612	595	1.0
6510	Real estate operators and lessors	13	16	1.6	23	28	10,087	9,714	224	281	1.1
6530	Real estate agents and managers	7	4	0.8	22	20	10,545	11,000	240	218	0.8
AMITE, MS											
60 –	**Finance, insurance, and real estate**	10	10	0.2	44	46	17,000	16,957	757	795	0.1
6500	Real estate	3	3	0.2	-	2	-	6,000	6	24	0.0
ATTALA, MS											
60 –	**Finance, insurance, and real estate**	33	33	0.6	184	162	19,957	20,691	4,138	4,014	0.4
6000	Depository institutions	6	7	0.6	100	105	22,520	20,267	2,517	2,624	0.7
6100	Nondepository institutions	7	8	1.1	30	30	18,000	18,933	585	612	0.8
6140	Personal credit institutions	7	7	1.2	30	-	18,000	-	585	-	-
6300	Insurance carriers	4	3	0.8	-	-	-	-	-	40	0.0
6370	Pension, health, and welfare funds	2	3	4.4	-	-	-	-	-	40	-
6400	Insurance agents, brokers, and service	9	9	0.8	22	-	26,000	-	691	-	-
6500	Real estate	6	5	0.3	4	4	5,000	5,000	23	21	0.0
BENTON, MS											
60 –	**Finance, insurance, and real estate**	6	5	0.1	20	-	14,400	-	300	-	-
BOLIVAR, MS											
60 –	**Finance, insurance, and real estate**	83	82	1.5	455	591	17,451	14,822	8,281	8,736	1.0
6000	Depository institutions	21	21	1.8	214	338	18,841	14,083	4,064	4,442	1.2
6020	Commercial banks	17	17	1.9	199	322	18,573	13,863	3,664	4,088	1.3
6100	Nondepository institutions	9	9	1.2	23	28	21,913	17,286	511	537	0.7
6140	Personal credit institutions	6	7	1.2	19	-	18,316	-	361	-	-
6200	Security and commodity brokers	3	4	2.6	4	8	23,000	26,000	146	250	0.6
6400	Insurance agents, brokers, and service	18	17	1.5	140	60	15,314	15,000	2,221	927	0.9

Source: County Business Patterns, 1992/93, CBP-92/93-1, U.S. Department of Commerce, Washington, D.C., April 1995. SIC categories for which data were suppressed or not available for both 1992 and 1993 are *not* displayed. The employment columns represent mid-March employment in the year. Pay per employee is calculated by dividing 1st Quarter payroll, annualized, by mid-March employment. The columns headed "% State" show the county's percentage of the state total for the SIC in 1993; for example, 0.9% for SIC 6030 means that the county had 0.9 percent of the state's total establishments (or payroll) in SIC 6030 in 1993. A dash (-) is used to indicate that data are not available or cannot be calculated; *nec* means not elsewhere classified.

Continued on next page.

SIC	Industry	No. Establishments			Employment		Pay / Employee		Annual Payroll ($ 000)		
		1992	1993	% State	1992	1993	1992	1993	1992	1993	% State
BOLIVAR, MS - [continued]											
6500	Real estate	25	24	*1.5*	35	36	7,429	7,333	267	266	*0.4*
6510	Real estate operators and lessors	16	20	*2.1*	-	31	-	6,452	-	197	*0.8*
6530	Real estate agents and managers	7	4	*0.8*	13	5	7,692	12,800	93	69	*0.3*
CALHOUN, MS											
60 –	**Finance, insurance, and real estate**	24	24	*0.5*	77	81	15,896	18,074	1,307	1,454	*0.2*
6020	Commercial banks	6	6	*0.7*	41	-	17,268	-	765	-	-
6100	Nondepository institutions	5	5	*0.7*	17	-	21,412	-	394	-	-
6400	Insurance agents, brokers, and service	4	5	*0.4*	10	8	11,600	12,500	109	106	*0.1*
6500	Real estate	7	6	*0.4*	6	6	4,000	4,000	26	24	*0.0*
6510	Real estate operators and lessors	6	6	*0.6*	5	6	4,000	4,000	22	24	*0.1*
CARROLL, MS											
60 –	**Finance, insurance, and real estate**	9	9	*0.2*	-	22	-	14,182	-	355	*0.0*
6000	Depository institutions	3	3	*0.3*	-	15	-	17,867	-	310	*0.1*
6020	Commercial banks	3	3	*0.3*	-	15	-	17,867	-	310	*0.1*
6500	Real estate	4	4	*0.3*	5	-	4,800	-	24	-	-
CHICKASAW, MS											
60 –	**Finance, insurance, and real estate**	32	30	*0.6*	109	117	15,450	18,017	1,852	2,006	*0.2*
6000	Depository institutions	6	7	*0.6*	65	69	17,600	19,884	1,280	1,376	*0.4*
6020	Commercial banks	6	7	*0.8*	65	69	17,600	19,884	1,280	1,376	*0.4*
6400	Insurance agents, brokers, and service	10	8	*0.7*	16	24	11,750	16,333	208	287	*0.3*
6500	Real estate	10	10	*0.6*	11	10	5,455	5,600	62	62	*0.1*
6510	Real estate operators and lessors	9	10	*1.0*	-	10	-	5,600	-	62	*0.2*
CHOCTAW, MS											
60 –	**Finance, insurance, and real estate**	8	7	*0.1*	-	-	-	-	-	-	-
CLAIBORNE, MS											
60 –	**Finance, insurance, and real estate**	8	9	*0.2*	56	-	17,643	-	1,147	-	-
CLARKE, MS											
60 –	**Finance, insurance, and real estate**	17	19	*0.4*	138	152	20,145	19,605	3,037	3,230	*0.4*
6000	Depository institutions	8	8	*0.7*	116	119	20,069	20,471	2,524	2,623	*0.7*
6020	Commercial banks	8	7	*0.8*	116	-	20,069	-	2,524	-	-
6400	Insurance agents, brokers, and service	5	4	*0.4*	11	14	18,909	16,000	272	328	*0.3*
CLAY, MS											
60 –	**Finance, insurance, and real estate**	34	36	*0.7*	165	171	18,545	16,959	2,942	3,055	*0.3*
6000	Depository institutions	8	9	*0.8*	105	103	17,219	19,767	1,904	2,126	*0.6*
6020	Commercial banks	5	7	*0.8*	90	-	17,511	-	1,678	-	-
6100	Nondepository institutions	6	6	*0.8*	-	18	-	18,000	-	322	*0.4*
6140	Personal credit institutions	6	6	*1.1*	-	18	-	18,000	-	322	*0.6*
6400	Insurance agents, brokers, and service	5	5	*0.4*	17	18	40,235	20,222	508	456	*0.4*
6500	Real estate	14	13	*0.8*	18	26	6,444	4,308	131	120	*0.2*
6510	Real estate operators and lessors	5	7	*0.7*	8	-	4,500	-	40	-	-
6530	Real estate agents and managers	8	5	*1.0*	-	15	-	2,667	-	49	*0.2*
COAHOMA, MS											
60 –	**Finance, insurance, and real estate**	76	85	*1.6*	426	449	21,765	21,292	9,341	9,881	*1.1*
6000	Depository institutions	17	16	*1.4*	232	225	21,241	22,169	4,807	5,088	*1.4*
6020	Commercial banks	13	12	*1.3*	223	216	21,596	22,574	4,689	4,970	*1.6*
6100	Nondepository institutions	5	5	*0.7*	17	-	27,059	-	474	-	-
6140	Personal credit institutions	3	3	*0.5*	-	10	-	24,000	-	256	*0.5*
6200	Security and commodity brokers	3	3	*2.0*	-	12	-	30,000	-	665	*1.6*
6400	Insurance agents, brokers, and service	15	16	*1.4*	54	56	25,778	24,786	1,401	1,413	*1.4*

Source: County Business Patterns, 1992/93, CBP-92/93-1, U.S. Department of Commerce, Washington, D.C., April 1995. SIC categories for which data were suppressed or not available for both 1992 and 1993 are *not* displayed. The employment columns represent mid-March employment in the year. Pay per employee is calculated by dividing 1st Quarter payroll, annualized, by mid-March employment. The columns headed "% State" show the county's percentage of the state total for the SIC in 1993; for example, 0.9% for SIC 6030 means that the county had 0.9 percent of the state's total establishments (or payroll) in SIC 6030 in 1993. A dash (-) is used to indicate that data are not available or cannot be calculated; *nec* means not elsewhere classified.

Continued on next page.

SIC	Industry	No. Establishments			Employment		Pay / Employee		Annual Payroll ($ 000)		
		1992	1993	% State	1992	1993	1992	1993	1992	1993	% State
COAHOMA, MS - [continued]											
6500	Real estate	31	42	2.7	62	86	11,419	9,349	706	836	1.4
6510	Real estate operators and lessors	20	26	2.7	-	48	-	7,750	-	409	1.6
6530	Real estate agents and managers	10	13	2.7	24	37	18,333	11,459	430	404	1.5
COPIAH, MS											
60 –	**Finance, insurance, and real estate**	35	33	0.6	167	153	18,443	19,529	3,057	2,962	0.3
6000	Depository institutions	14	13	1.1	116	111	19,414	19,964	2,312	2,264	0.6
6020	Commercial banks	13	13	1.4	-	111	-	19,964	-	2,264	0.7
6100	Nondepository institutions	7	7	1.0	18	19	18,444	17,895	337	356	0.5
6140	Personal credit institutions	7	7	1.2	18	19	18,444	17,895	337	356	0.7
6400	Insurance agents, brokers, and service	6	7	0.6	19	14	12,842	22,286	240	252	0.2
6500	Real estate	3	3	0.2	5	6	4,000	4,667	29	25	0.0
6510	Real estate operators and lessors	3	3	0.3	5	6	4,000	4,667	29	25	0.1
COVINGTON, MS											
60 –	**Finance, insurance, and real estate**	23	23	0.4	135	110	15,644	16,909	1,992	1,889	0.2
6000	Depository institutions	9	8	0.7	86	80	15,302	17,450	1,306	1,405	0.4
6100	Nondepository institutions	3	4	0.6	32	14	16,750	16,286	421	212	0.3
6140	Personal credit institutions	3	4	0.7	32	14	16,750	16,286	421	212	0.4
6400	Insurance agents, brokers, and service	6	6	0.5	12	12	18,333	18,333	233	246	0.2
6500	Real estate	5	5	0.3	5	4	8,000	4,000	32	26	0.0
6510	Real estate operators and lessors	3	5	0.5	-	4	-	4,000	-	26	0.1
DE SOTO, MS											
60 –	**Finance, insurance, and real estate**	107	110	2.1	565	590	21,848	19,559	11,834	12,011	1.3
6000	Depository institutions	29	30	2.5	319	317	19,749	22,360	6,485	7,062	1.9
6100	Nondepository institutions	18	19	2.6	64	126	25,500	13,429	1,589	1,979	2.6
6140	Personal credit institutions	12	13	2.3	47	102	22,809	10,549	1,013	1,094	2.1
6160	Mortgage bankers and brokers	6	6	6.8	17	24	32,941	25,667	576	885	5.9
6330	Fire, marine, and casualty insurance	3	1	0.8	10	-	42,000	-	329	-	-
6400	Insurance agents, brokers, and service	20	25	2.2	68	71	21,882	20,901	1,623	1,587	1.6
6500	Real estate	31	31	2.0	62	61	28,065	13,574	1,084	938	1.5
6510	Real estate operators and lessors	10	12	1.2	19	30	61,895	10,933	564	321	1.2
6530	Real estate agents and managers	12	15	3.1	21	23	11,810	15,130	296	454	1.7
FORREST, MS											
60 –	**Finance, insurance, and real estate**	227	238	4.5	1,778	1,790	19,701	21,855	35,337	38,851	4.3
6000	Depository institutions	48	48	4.1	975	1,028	18,905	22,611	18,132	21,495	5.9
6020	Commercial banks	31	30	3.3	-	432	-	19,009	-	8,009	2.6
6100	Nondepository institutions	29	33	4.6	144	151	20,806	24,132	2,697	3,227	4.2
6140	Personal credit institutions	20	24	4.2	82	116	21,512	16,793	1,824	2,066	3.9
6160	Mortgage bankers and brokers	6	6	6.8	27	20	19,556	51,000	449	631	4.2
6210	Security brokers and dealers	7	6	6.7	30	34	53,200	46,941	1,435	1,751	4.5
6300	Insurance carriers	24	22	5.7	168	149	23,000	25,987	4,162	4,115	2.0
6310	Life insurance	9	8	5.1	129	117	20,806	23,556	2,882	2,852	3.4
6330	Fire, marine, and casualty insurance	11	11	8.5	22	19	29,455	32,000	710	586	0.8
6400	Insurance agents, brokers, and service	44	50	4.4	154	162	21,948	19,901	3,670	3,428	3.3
6500	Real estate	68	73	4.6	291	255	14,832	12,173	4,170	3,989	6.5
6510	Real estate operators and lessors	39	39	4.0	104	86	12,731	10,000	1,390	984	3.8
6530	Real estate agents and managers	21	31	6.3	137	165	18,423	13,358	2,284	2,963	10.8
FRANKLIN, MS											
60 –	**Finance, insurance, and real estate**	7	8	0.2	-	-	-	-	-	-	-
6500	Real estate	2	3	0.2	-	1	-	4,000	-	10	0.0

Source: County Business Patterns, 1992/93, CBP-92/93-1, U.S. Department of Commerce, Washington, D.C., April 1995. SIC categories for which data were suppressed or not available for both 1992 and 1993 are not displayed. The employment columns represent mid-March employment in the year. Pay per employee is calculated by dividing 1st Quarter payroll, annualized, by mid-March employment. The columns headed "% State" show the county's percentage of the state total for the SIC in 1993; for example, 0.9% for SIC 6030 means that the county had 0.9 percent of the state's total establishments (or payroll) in SIC 6030 in 1993. A dash (-) is used to indicate that data are not available or cannot be calculated; nec means not elsewhere classified.

SIC	Industry	No. Establishments			Employment		Pay / Employee		Annual Payroll ($ 000)		
		1992	1993	% State	1992	1993	1992	1993	1992	1993	% State
GEORGE, MS											
60–	**Finance, insurance, and real estate**	26	22	0.4	118	107	17,932	18,280	2,251	2,202	0.2
6000	Depository institutions	8	6	0.5	85	80	19,624	19,400	1,795	1,780	0.5
6100	Nondepository institutions	3	3	0.4	11	-	22,545	-	255	-	-
6400	Insurance agents, brokers, and service	9	8	0.7	15	12	10,933	12,333	157	156	0.2
6500	Real estate	4	4	0.3	4	4	4,000	5,000	22	17	0.0
GREENE, MS											
60–	**Finance, insurance, and real estate**	9	9	0.2	-	-	-	-	-	-	-
6500	Real estate	3	4	0.3	2	5	6,000	10,400	33	43	0.1
GRENADA, MS											
60–	**Finance, insurance, and real estate**	63	70	1.3	482	538	21,402	21,784	10,360	11,786	1.3
6000	Depository institutions	12	14	1.2	369	-	21,225	-	8,063	-	-
6100	Nondepository institutions	15	13	1.8	50	61	17,120	17,639	944	1,099	1.4
6400	Insurance agents, brokers, and service	5	5	0.4	17	-	16,941	-	294	-	-
6500	Real estate	27	32	2.0	33	54	6,061	5,630	205	360	0.6
6510	Real estate operators and lessors	22	23	2.4	27	-	5,481	-	150	-	-
6530	Real estate agents and managers	3	7	1.4	4	8	9,000	6,500	40	92	0.3
6700	Holding and other investment offices	2	3	1.9	-	12	-	49,333	-	613	1.3
HANCOCK, MS											
60–	**Finance, insurance, and real estate**	59	61	1.1	249	261	16,627	16,751	4,434	4,655	0.5
6000	Depository institutions	15	15	1.3	99	98	16,606	16,245	1,728	1,867	0.5
6020	Commercial banks	11	13	1.4	84	-	16,571	-	1,482	-	-
6100	Nondepository institutions	3	5	0.7	6	11	22,000	16,364	121	201	0.3
6300	Insurance carriers	5	4	1.0	-	9	-	11,556	-	49	0.0
6400	Insurance agents, brokers, and service	10	9	0.8	31	-	17,935	-	638	-	-
6500	Real estate	25	26	1.6	99	112	14,667	15,500	1,620	1,686	2.7
6510	Real estate operators and lessors	10	10	1.0	36	36	7,222	7,444	309	305	1.2
6530	Real estate agents and managers	10	14	2.9	34	-	8,588	-	340	-	-
HARRISON, MS											
60–	**Finance, insurance, and real estate**	362	383	7.2	2,536	2,677	19,128	18,932	53,794	60,665	6.7
6000	Depository institutions	72	74	6.3	1,199	1,335	17,992	17,921	25,616	28,651	7.9
6020	Commercial banks	46	49	5.4	873	980	18,460	18,841	19,555	22,443	7.2
6060	Credit unions	11	15	10.1	197	-	16,569	-	4,070	-	-
6100	Nondepository institutions	37	47	6.5	151	197	24,106	19,736	3,741	3,883	5.1
6140	Personal credit institutions	31	35	6.2	131	168	23,420	17,405	3,146	2,950	5.6
6200	Security and commodity brokers	15	10	6.6	67	59	50,030	52,339	3,214	3,770	9.0
6210	Security brokers and dealers	11	6	6.7	62	51	49,419	58,588	3,073	3,650	9.4
6280	Security and commodity services	4	4	6.8	5	8	57,600	12,500	141	120	3.8
6300	Insurance carriers	24	25	6.5	293	275	24,997	28,015	7,205	7,151	3.5
6310	Life insurance	11	10	6.3	212	177	20,264	23,096	4,310	3,828	4.5
6400	Insurance agents, brokers, and service	83	85	7.5	281	290	25,196	19,103	7,402	9,218	9.0
6500	Real estate	127	136	8.6	540	460	10,126	11,609	6,538	6,583	10.7
6510	Real estate operators and lessors	62	77	7.9	211	264	10,104	10,712	2,251	3,087	11.9
6530	Real estate agents and managers	50	52	10.6	269	186	10,052	12,989	3,423	3,412	12.4
6552	Subdividers and developers, n.e.c.	1	3	5.3	-	2	-	10,000	-	32	0.6
6553	Cemetery subdividers and developers	2	3	6.5	-	7	-	10,286	-	51	2.5
6700	Holding and other investment offices	4	6	3.9	5	61	14,400	19,607	78	1,409	3.0
HINDS, MS											
60–	**Finance, insurance, and real estate**	956	966	18.2	10,996	11,177	27,352	27,975	299,712	310,379	34.5
6000	Depository institutions	140	144	12.2	2,875	3,220	23,841	24,412	69,444	74,247	20.5
6020	Commercial banks	88	96	10.5	2,476	2,498	23,963	25,717	60,434	64,664	20.7
6030	Savings institutions	18	11	10.6	270	562	24,637	20,292	6,259	6,343	18.0
6060	Credit unions	29	31	20.9	116	-	20,172	-	2,498	-	-
6090	Functions closely related to banking	4	6	33.3	8	-	19,500	-	179	-	-

Source: *County Business Patterns, 1992/93*, CBP-92/93-1, U.S. Department of Commerce, Washington, D.C., April 1995. SIC categories for which data were suppressed or not available for both 1992 and 1993 are *not* displayed. The employment columns represent mid-March employment in the year. Pay per employee is calculated by dividing 1st Quarter payroll, annualized, by mid-March employment. The columns headed "% State" show the county's percentage of the state total for the SIC in 1993; for example, 0.9% for SIC 6030 means that the county had 0.9 percent of the state's total establishments (or payroll) in SIC 6030 in 1993. A dash (-) is used to indicate that data are not available or cannot be calculated; *nec* means not elsewhere classified.

Continued on next page.

SIC	Industry	No. Establishments			Employment		Pay / Employee		Annual Payroll ($ 000)		
		1992	1993	% State	1992	1993	1992	1993	1992	1993	% State
HINDS, MS - [continued]											
6100	Nondepository institutions	92	94	13.0	792	855	24,682	23,181	20,447	21,839	28.5
6140	Personal credit institutions	57	56	9.9	395	445	25,144	22,715	10,639	10,948	20.8
6150	Business credit institutions	5	7	25.0	28	-	31,143	-	821	-	-
6160	Mortgage bankers and brokers	25	26	29.5	350	347	23,177	21,971	8,381	8,711	58.2
6200	Security and commodity brokers	41	51	33.6	340	436	70,141	65,560	21,141	28,619	68.0
6210	Security brokers and dealers	22	26	28.9	313	377	73,738	70,154	20,173	26,637	68.9
6280	Security and commodity services	19	24	40.7	27	-	28,444	-	968	-	-
6300	Insurance carriers	138	113	29.4	3,688	3,551	28,367	29,233	106,330	102,635	50.5
6310	Life insurance	66	48	30.4	1,598	1,367	26,493	28,418	42,046	37,562	44.1
6330	Fire, marine, and casualty insurance	40	36	27.9	1,753	1,754	30,410	31,756	54,338	55,116	73.3
6370	Pension, health, and welfare funds	19	19	27.9	-	175	-	19,589	-	4,235	-
6400	Insurance agents, brokers, and service	221	228	20.1	1,521	1,290	28,358	26,915	44,184	38,909	38.0
6500	Real estate	272	284	18.0	1,094	1,046	14,022	13,824	16,351	16,035	26.0
6510	Real estate operators and lessors	144	172	17.7	487	580	10,793	11,124	5,430	7,100	27.4
6530	Real estate agents and managers	86	89	18.2	451	364	17,171	16,495	8,567	6,735	24.5
6552	Subdividers and developers, n.e.c.	12	15	26.3	36	54	17,444	20,444	496	1,093	21.8
6553	Cemetery subdividers and developers	5	5	10.9	34	-	19,529	-	809	-	-
6700	Holding and other investment offices	46	46	29.9	-	643	-	37,306	-	22,431	48.2
6710	Holding offices	11	8	18.6	259	455	56,772	43,323	10,605	17,508	50.8
6720	Investment offices	3	3	100.0	5	-	20,000	-	105	-	-
6732	Educational, religious, etc. trusts	7	7	22.6	12	-	21,000	-	342	-	-
6733	Trusts, n.e.c.	12	11	28.9	39	68	12,000	10,118	864	814	-
6792	Oil royalty traders	3	7	70.0	5	11	14,400	16,000	87	178	73.3
6799	Investors, n.e.c.	7	8	33.3	24	-	39,833	-	986	-	-
HOLMES, MS											
60 -	**Finance, insurance, and real estate**	24	27	0.5	132	137	17,667	20,642	2,274	2,561	0.3
6000	Depository institutions	9	9	0.8	94	94	21,149	26,723	1,897	2,085	0.6
6020	Commercial banks	9	9	1.0	94	94	21,149	26,723	1,897	2,085	0.7
6400	Insurance agents, brokers, and service	6	6	0.5	21	-	11,429	-	260	-	-
6500	Real estate	9	11	0.7	17	24	6,118	4,500	117	227	0.4
6510	Real estate operators and lessors	6	8	0.8	9	-	7,556	-	75	-	-
HUMPHREYS, MS											
60 -	**Finance, insurance, and real estate**	16	15	0.3	118	122	22,271	18,918	2,407	2,491	0.3
6000	Depository institutions	5	5	0.4	89	97	25,798	20,577	2,026	2,167	0.6
6400	Insurance agents, brokers, and service	4	2	0.2	10	-	14,800	-	124	-	-
6500	Real estate	4	5	0.3	9	11	7,556	8,000	74	93	0.2
ISSAQUENA, MS											
60 -	**Finance, insurance, and real estate**	4	3	0.1	-	2	-	10,000	-	26	0.0
6500	Real estate	3	1	0.1	1	-	4,000	-	14	-	-
ITAWAMBA, MS											
60 -	**Finance, insurance, and real estate**	18	20	0.4	70	78	15,829	17,846	1,149	1,210	0.1
6400	Insurance agents, brokers, and service	4	6	0.5	12	16	19,333	17,000	234	282	0.3
6500	Real estate	7	7	0.4	7	10	5,714	4,800	45	50	0.1
6510	Real estate operators and lessors	6	6	0.6	6	-	6,000	-	44	-	-
JACKSON, MS											
60 -	**Finance, insurance, and real estate**	183	189	3.6	1,252	1,246	14,121	14,196	21,246	22,279	2.5
6000	Depository institutions	46	49	4.2	434	487	17,788	17,807	9,019	10,481	2.9
6020	Commercial banks	26	28	3.1	338	348	17,586	16,897	6,830	7,203	2.3
6030	Savings institutions	11	9	8.7	67	-	20,657	-	1,737	-	-
6060	Credit unions	9	12	8.1	29	-	13,517	-	452	-	-
6100	Nondepository institutions	18	19	2.6	90	78	21,244	15,590	2,079	1,286	1.7
6300	Insurance carriers	16	13	3.4	277	271	9,747	9,638	4,152	4,740	2.3
6370	Pension, health, and welfare funds	7	6	8.8	243	-	6,453	-	2,723	-	-

Source: County Business Patterns, 1992/93, CBP-92/93-1, U.S. Department of Commerce, Washington, D.C., April 1995. SIC categories for which data were suppressed or not available for both 1992 and 1993 are *not* displayed. The employment columns represent mid-March employment in the year. Pay per employee is calculated by dividing 1st Quarter payroll, annualized, by mid-March employment. The columns headed "% State" show the county's percentage of the state total for the SIC in 1993; for example, 0.9% for SIC 6030 means that the county had 0.9 percent of the state's total establishments (or payroll) in SIC 6030 in 1993. A dash (-) is used to indicate that data are not available or cannot be calculated; *nec* means not elsewhere classified.

Continued on next page.

SIC	Industry	No. Establishments			Employment		Pay / Employee		Annual Payroll ($ 000)		
		1992	1993	% State	1992	1993	1992	1993	1992	1993	% State
JACKSON, MS - [continued]											
6400	Insurance agents, brokers, and service	37	39	3.4	195	201	13,846	13,512	2,966	2,827	2.8
6500	Real estate	59	61	3.9	241	175	10,423	10,903	2,764	2,473	4.0
6510	Real estate operators and lessors	19	22	2.3	94	-	9,191	-	872	-	-
6530	Real estate agents and managers	34	36	7.4	77	62	11,221	11,097	867	934	3.4
6710	Holding offices	-	3	7.0	-	22	-	10,545	-	225	0.7
JASPER, MS											
60 –	**Finance, insurance, and real estate**	22	20	0.4	92	88	19,348	16,364	1,406	1,399	0.2
6000	Depository institutions	7	7	0.6	49	-	19,673	-	941	-	-
6100	Nondepository institutions	3	4	0.6	-	7	-	20,571	-	156	0.2
6140	Personal credit institutions	3	4	0.7	-	7	-	20,571	-	156	0.3
6400	Insurance agents, brokers, and service	5	5	0.4	11	27	8,727	10,222	103	292	0.3
6500	Real estate	4	3	0.2	5	4	3,200	3,000	16	12	0.0
JEFFERSON, MS											
60 –	**Finance, insurance, and real estate**	6	4	0.1	20	-	14,400	-	310	-	-
JEFFERSON DAVIS, MS											
60 –	**Finance, insurance, and real estate**	15	17	0.3	57	57	16,702	15,930	927	945	0.1
6100	Nondepository institutions	2	3	0.4	-	9	-	16,000	-	156	0.2
6140	Personal credit institutions	2	3	0.5	-	9	-	16,000	-	156	0.3
6400	Insurance agents, brokers, and service	4	5	0.4	7	-	12,571	-	92	-	-
6500	Real estate	3	3	0.2	4	4	5,000	5,000	20	20	0.0
6510	Real estate operators and lessors	3	3	0.3	4	4	5,000	5,000	20	20	0.1
JONES, MS											
60 –	**Finance, insurance, and real estate**	108	108	2.0	534	598	19,648	20,448	11,186	12,458	1.4
6000	Depository institutions	31	30	2.5	315	320	19,911	19,838	6,331	6,515	1.8
6020	Commercial banks	23	23	2.5	246	-	20,114	-	4,842	-	-
6100	Nondepository institutions	15	20	2.8	50	105	19,280	19,962	951	2,173	2.8
6140	Personal credit institutions	12	16	2.8	44	93	19,091	20,043	814	1,916	3.6
6300	Insurance carriers	8	7	1.8	34	-	37,412	-	1,525	-	-
6400	Insurance agents, brokers, and service	27	28	2.5	76	83	17,947	17,542	1,558	1,643	1.6
6500	Real estate	23	21	1.3	57	54	10,456	15,185	699	750	1.2
6510	Real estate operators and lessors	12	13	1.3	28	-	9,143	-	321	-	-
6530	Real estate agents and managers	7	7	1.4	13	12	8,308	14,333	136	160	0.6
KEMPER, MS											
60 –	**Finance, insurance, and real estate**	9	9	0.2	52	55	13,692	13,236	769	787	0.1
6000	Depository institutions	4	4	0.3	38	41	15,263	14,537	620	647	0.2
6020	Commercial banks	4	4	0.4	38	41	15,263	14,537	620	647	0.2
LAFAYETTE, MS											
60 –	**Finance, insurance, and real estate**	62	68	1.3	316	316	15,620	17,190	5,601	5,837	0.6
6000	Depository institutions	15	15	1.3	128	127	15,406	17,575	2,087	2,253	0.6
6140	Personal credit institutions	8	8	1.4	23	31	18,609	17,548	439	575	1.1
6300	Insurance carriers	4	3	0.8	61	52	18,230	22,692	1,489	1,375	0.7
6400	Insurance agents, brokers, and service	14	15	1.3	35	34	16,800	18,824	683	679	0.7
6500	Real estate	17	23	1.5	62	61	11,484	8,590	691	608	1.0
6510	Real estate operators and lessors	13	18	1.8	57	58	12,140	8,690	669	555	2.1
6530	Real estate agents and managers	3	4	0.8	5	-	4,000	-	20	-	-
LAMAR, MS											
60 –	**Finance, insurance, and real estate**	25	23	0.4	108	136	15,741	14,294	1,846	2,433	0.3

Source: County Business Patterns, 1992/93, CBP-92/93-1, U.S. Department of Commerce, Washington, D.C., April 1995. SIC categories for which data were suppressed or not available for both 1992 and 1993 are not displayed. The employment columns represent mid-March employment in the year. Pay per employee is calculated by dividing 1st Quarter payroll, annualized, by mid-March employment. The columns headed "% State" show the county's percentage of the state total for the SIC in 1993; for example, 0.9% for SIC 6030 means that the county had 0.9 percent of the state's total establishments (or payroll) in SIC 6030 in 1993. A dash (-) is used to indicate that data are not available or cannot be calculated; nec means not elsewhere classified.

Continued on next page.

SIC	Industry	No. Establishments			Employment		Pay / Employee		Annual Payroll ($ 000)		
		1992	1993	% State	1992	1993	1992	1993	1992	1993	% State
LAMAR, MS - [continued]											
6400	Insurance agents, brokers, and service	6	5	0.4	16	-	14,500	-	206	-	-
6500	Real estate	11	10	0.6	20	33	10,200	9,697	283	605	1.0
6510	Real estate operators and lessors	7	6	0.6	7	-	10,286		73		
LAUDERDALE, MS											
60 –	**Finance, insurance, and real estate**	186	189	3.6	1,412	1,341	21,184	21,721	32,117	30,300	3.4
6000	Depository institutions	36	40	3.4	436	480	19,248	18,883	8,814	9,448	2.6
6020	Commercial banks	27	30	3.3	354	418	19,107	18,986	7,161	8,217	2.6
6100	Nondepository institutions	29	26	3.6	146	214	22,329	18,056	3,563	4,176	5.5
6140	Personal credit institutions	22	21	3.7	122	119	22,066	19,798	2,906	2,437	4.6
6200	Security and commodity brokers	6	7	4.6	20	22	61,200	44,909	1,260	1,291	3.1
6300	Insurance carriers	13	16	4.2	219	207	23,324	25,449	5,593	5,292	2.6
6310	Life insurance	9	10	6.3	202	190	23,188	25,768	5,147	4,840	5.7
6400	Insurance agents, brokers, and service	31	34	3.0	108	121	28,000	27,736	2,972	3,047	3.0
6500	Real estate	59	55	3.5	457	129	18,004	11,349	9,189	1,705	2.8
6510	Real estate operators and lessors	32	32	3.3	156	69	11,487	10,609	1,807	953	3.7
6530	Real estate agents and managers	22	20	4.1	285	44	21,853	11,909	7,167	551	2.0
6700	Holding and other investment offices	12	11	7.1	26	168	26,000	30,500	726	5,341	11.5
LAWRENCE, MS											
60 –	**Finance, insurance, and real estate**	14	12	0.2	68	66	15,706	16,848	1,096	1,101	0.1
6400	Insurance agents, brokers, and service	5	4	0.4	13	16	15,077	13,500	187	203	0.2
6500	Real estate	3	3	0.2	8	7	5,000	6,857	45	47	0.1
6510	Real estate operators and lessors	1	3	0.3	-	7	-	6,857	-	47	0.2
LEAKE, MS											
60 –	**Finance, insurance, and real estate**	26	26	0.5	143	139	22,322	26,561	3,029	3,053	0.3
6000	Depository institutions	8	8	0.7	101	96	24,990	30,542	2,409	2,353	0.6
6100	Nondepository institutions	5	6	0.8	18	-	20,222	-	334	-	-
6140	Personal credit institutions	5	6	1.1	18	-	20,222	-	334	-	-
6400	Insurance agents, brokers, and service	3	4	0.4	9	11	14,667	13,091	123	155	0.2
6500	Real estate	6	6	0.4	7	7	9,714	9,714	68	67	0.1
6510	Real estate operators and lessors	6	6	0.6	7	7	9,714	9,714	68	67	0.3
LEE, MS											
60 –	**Finance, insurance, and real estate**	173	181	3.4	1,642	1,692	22,385	24,903	40,162	43,318	4.8
6000	Depository institutions	22	23	1.9	784	845	24,449	25,709	21,716	23,478	6.5
6020	Commercial banks	17	17	1.9	-	818	-	25,643	-	22,908	7.3
6060	Credit unions	4	5	3.4	6	-	7,333	-	44	-	-
6100	Nondepository institutions	32	33	4.6	197	186	23,228	23,548	4,626	4,409	5.8
6140	Personal credit institutions	27	27	4.8	179	168	23,084	22,000	4,134	3,687	7.0
6200	Security and commodity brokers	7	5	3.3	18	16	42,444	48,000	788	790	1.9
6210	Security brokers and dealers	4	4	4.4	14	-	51,143	-	738	-	-
6300	Insurance carriers	25	26	6.8	283	311	26,431	31,871	8,095	9,343	4.6
6310	Life insurance	13	15	9.5	241	277	26,224	31,220	6,946	8,255	9.7
6400	Insurance agents, brokers, and service	38	41	3.6	121	95	21,851	25,179	2,567	2,501	2.4
6500	Real estate	44	46	2.9	229	213	8,472	12,150	2,076	2,363	3.8
6510	Real estate operators and lessors	27	30	3.1	105	158	6,590	10,228	733	1,336	5.1
6530	Real estate agents and managers	11	14	2.9	42	-	14,762	-	702	-	-
6700	Holding and other investment offices	5	7	4.5	10	26	18,400	14,308	294	434	0.9
LEFLORE, MS											
60 –	**Finance, insurance, and real estate**	80	87	1.6	466	483	20,026	21,822	9,875	10,947	1.2
6000	Depository institutions	16	16	1.4	166	173	21,398	21,711	3,850	3,788	1.0
6100	Nondepository institutions	13	15	2.1	62	64	20,645	22,125	1,264	1,498	2.0
6140	Personal credit institutions	7	9	1.6	31	43	17,032	14,419	522	684	1.3
6300	Insurance carriers	6	6	1.6	96	120	25,167	28,600	2,696	3,660	1.8
6400	Insurance agents, brokers, and service	14	16	1.4	77	66	20,831	21,394	1,530	1,449	1.4

Source: County Business Patterns, 1992/93, CBP-92/93-1, U.S. Department of Commerce, Washington, D.C., April 1995. SIC categories for which data were suppressed or not available for both 1992 and 1993 are not displayed. The employment columns represent mid-March employment in the year. Pay per employee is calculated by dividing 1st Quarter payroll, annualized, by mid-March employment. The columns headed "% State" show the county's percentage of the state total for the SIC in 1993; for example, 0.9% for SIC 6030 means that the county had 0.9 percent of the state's total establishments (or payroll) in SIC 6030 in 1993. A dash (-) is used to indicate that data are not available or cannot be calculated; nec means not elsewhere classified.

Continued on next page.

SIC	Industry	No. Establishments			Employment		Pay / Employee		Annual Payroll ($ 000)		
		1992	1993	% State	1992	1993	1992	1993	1992	1993	% State
LEFLORE, MS - [continued]											
6500	Real estate	27	28	1.8	58	52	6,828	8,385	443	460	0.7
6510	Real estate operators and lessors	20	22	2.3	38	46	6,842	6,087	279	316	1.2
6530	Real estate agents and managers	5	5	1.0	19	-	6,947	-	155	-	-
LINCOLN, MS											
60 –	**Finance, insurance, and real estate**	63	58	1.1	312	298	18,282	18,403	5,795	5,807	0.6
6000	Depository institutions	14	11	0.9	158	150	20,810	21,013	3,358	3,266	0.9
6100	Nondepository institutions	12	13	1.8	46	65	17,565	14,462	767	897	1.2
6140	Personal credit institutions	9	11	1.9	39	-	15,487	-	586	-	-
6300	Insurance carriers	6	5	1.3	20	20	22,800	21,800	502	479	0.2
6400	Insurance agents, brokers, and service	14	14	1.2	51	34	15,216	17,529	783	764	0.7
6500	Real estate	13	11	0.7	27	21	9,630	10,667	264	253	0.4
6510	Real estate operators and lessors	8	7	0.7	14	-	6,000	-	88	-	-
6530	Real estate agents and managers	3	3	0.6	7	5	17,714	16,000	121	85	0.3
LOWNDES, MS											
60 –	**Finance, insurance, and real estate**	162	169	3.2	855	834	19,251	20,763	16,501	17,127	1.9
6000	Depository institutions	30	36	3.1	380	397	20,326	22,549	7,402	7,489	2.1
6020	Commercial banks	19	21	2.3	311	332	20,656	23,120	6,025	6,094	1.9
6100	Nondepository institutions	16	14	1.9	65	83	19,692	15,133	1,293	1,309	1.7
6140	Personal credit institutions	15	14	2.5	-	83	-	15,133	-	1,309	2.5
6200	Security and commodity brokers	7	9	5.9	24	20	30,667	18,000	733	928	2.2
6210	Security brokers and dealers	7	6	6.7	24	-	30,667	-	733	-	-
6300	Insurance carriers	29	31	8.1	148	129	22,541	26,233	3,301	3,696	1.8
6310	Life insurance	7	6	3.8	109	78	22,312	23,692	2,331	1,712	2.0
6370	Pension, health, and welfare funds	15	19	27.9	-	31	-	8,903	-	825	-
6400	Insurance agents, brokers, and service	30	33	2.9	93	93	18,495	19,828	1,963	2,126	2.1
6500	Real estate	45	39	2.5	135	96	10,963	11,375	1,561	1,187	1.9
6510	Real estate operators and lessors	24	18	1.8	83	47	10,506	10,298	901	499	1.9
6530	Real estate agents and managers	15	16	3.3	45	48	11,378	12,583	552	559	2.0
6700	Holding and other investment offices	5	7	4.5	10	16	18,400	26,750	248	392	0.8
MADISON, MS											
60 –	**Finance, insurance, and real estate**	131	143	2.7	1,196	1,311	30,418	31,146	32,387	38,455	4.3
6000	Depository institutions	22	23	1.9	220	277	20,745	24,895	4,618	7,066	1.9
6100	Nondepository institutions	11	13	1.8	97	90	33,402	24,356	2,906	1,996	2.6
6140	Personal credit institutions	7	8	1.4	57	-	28,842	-	1,051	-	-
6300	Insurance carriers	16	20	5.2	381	442	27,969	29,566	10,157	14,187	7.0
6330	Fire, marine, and casualty insurance	8	10	7.8	-	262	-	32,412	-	9,398	12.5
6400	Insurance agents, brokers, and service	31	35	3.1	123	139	25,463	27,396	3,380	4,533	4.4
6500	Real estate	43	43	2.7	194	192	12,660	15,646	2,837	2,502	4.1
6510	Real estate operators and lessors	16	23	2.4	75	91	12,800	18,593	1,216	1,108	4.3
6530	Real estate agents and managers	22	16	3.3	40	-	13,700	-	692	-	-
MARION, MS											
60 –	**Finance, insurance, and real estate**	38	41	0.8	279	208	18,853	18,038	5,336	4,323	0.5
6000	Depository institutions	14	11	0.9	215	142	20,260	19,352	4,392	3,235	0.9
6020	Commercial banks	9	7	0.8	178	-	20,697	-	3,699	-	-
6100	Nondepository institutions	5	8	1.1	17	26	20,235	17,538	352	478	0.6
6140	Personal credit institutions	5	8	1.4	17	26	20,235	17,538	352	478	0.9
6400	Insurance agents, brokers, and service	9	11	1.0	25	20	11,680	12,800	302	334	0.3
6500	Real estate	10	11	0.7	22	20	12,182	14,600	290	276	0.4
MARSHALL, MS											
60 –	**Finance, insurance, and real estate**	25	27	0.5	162	190	19,901	18,821	3,676	4,036	0.4
6000	Depository institutions	8	8	0.7	111	134	19,964	17,791	2,509	2,678	0.7
6020	Commercial banks	8	8	0.9	111	134	19,964	17,791	2,509	2,678	0.9

Source: County Business Patterns, 1992/93, CBP-92/93-1, U.S. Department of Commerce, Washington, D.C., April 1995. SIC categories for which data were suppressed or not available for both 1992 and 1993 are not displayed. The employment columns represent mid-March employment in the year. Pay per employee is calculated by dividing 1st Quarter payroll, annualized, by mid-March employment. The columns headed "% State" show the county's percentage of the state total for the SIC in 1993; for example, 0.9% for SIC 6030 means that the county had 0.9 percent of the state's total establishments (or payroll) in SIC 6030 in 1993. A dash (-) is used to indicate that data are not available or cannot be calculated; nec means not elsewhere classified.

Continued on next page.

SIC	Industry	No. Establishments			Employment		Pay / Employee		Annual Payroll ($ 000)		
		1992	1993	% State	1992	1993	1992	1993	1992	1993	% State
MARSHALL, MS - [continued]											
6100	Nondepository institutions	3	5	0.7	6	14	21,333	20,000	129	294	0.4
6500	Real estate	7	7	0.4	19	12	17,684	20,667	406	358	0.6
6510	Real estate operators and lessors	3	4	0.4	3	-	4,000	-	13	-	-
MONROE, MS											
60 –	**Finance, insurance, and real estate**	69	72	1.4	380	411	20,484	21,771	8,254	9,113	1.0
6000	Depository institutions	23	23	1.9	174	195	19,862	22,215	3,582	4,183	1.2
6020	Commercial banks	18	18	2.0	155	175	20,387	22,743	3,238	3,799	1.2
6140	Personal credit institutions	10	14	2.5	-	42	-	20,190	-	852	1.6
6400	Insurance agents, brokers, and service	13	15	1.3	49	47	14,857	15,830	794	821	0.8
6500	Real estate	15	13	0.8	-	19	-	11,579	-	238	0.4
6510	Real estate operators and lessors	9	11	1.1	9	-	6,667	-	69	-	-
6530	Real estate agents and managers	5	1	0.2	8	-	13,000	-	111	-	-
MONTGOMERY, MS											
60 –	**Finance, insurance, and real estate**	24	23	0.4	129	121	19,008	16,694	2,938	2,325	0.3
6000	Depository institutions	7	7	0.6	77	78	20,727	18,872	1,927	1,712	0.5
6100	Nondepository institutions	8	9	1.2	29	-	15,172	-	501	-	-
6140	Personal credit institutions	5	6	1.1	21	20	15,810	15,200	360	356	0.7
6400	Insurance agents, brokers, and service	5	5	0.4	-	13	-	9,231	-	122	0.1
NESHOBA, MS											
60 –	**Finance, insurance, and real estate**	42	45	0.8	349	372	14,430	17,075	5,584	6,757	0.8
6000	Depository institutions	19	20	1.7	167	209	17,126	18,584	2,959	3,940	1.1
6100	Nondepository institutions	5	6	0.8	18	-	24,222	-	448	-	-
6300	Insurance carriers	2	3	0.8	-	1	-	4,000	-	48	0.0
6400	Insurance agents, brokers, and service	7	6	0.5	-	10	-	14,000	-	153	0.1
6500	Real estate	7	8	0.5	-	130	-	14,400	-	2,122	3.4
NEWTON, MS											
60 –	**Finance, insurance, and real estate**	24	25	0.5	131	132	20,183	24,242	2,592	2,915	0.3
6000	Depository institutions	6	7	0.6	88	-	21,955	-	1,896	-	-
6100	Nondepository institutions	8	7	1.0	21	22	20,571	19,818	386	385	0.5
6400	Insurance agents, brokers, and service	5	5	0.4	15	18	16,000	16,000	273	330	0.3
6500	Real estate	5	5	0.3	7	7	5,714	4,571	37	36	0.1
6510	Real estate operators and lessors	2	5	0.5	-	7	-	4,571	-	36	0.1
NOXUBEE, MS											
60 –	**Finance, insurance, and real estate**	13	13	0.2	80	89	15,850	14,697	1,305	1,442	0.2
6000	Depository institutions	5	5	0.4	61	70	15,672	14,171	1,003	1,124	0.3
6020	Commercial banks	5	5	0.5	61	70	15,672	14,171	1,003	1,124	0.4
6100	Nondepository institutions	3	3	0.4	11	11	21,455	21,455	214	215	0.3
6140	Personal credit institutions	3	3	0.5	11	11	21,455	21,455	214	215	0.4
OKTIBBEHA, MS											
60 –	**Finance, insurance, and real estate**	70	72	1.4	382	407	19,958	21,140	7,316	8,306	0.9
6000	Depository institutions	18	19	1.6	248	251	23,500	25,275	5,335	5,640	1.6
6020	Commercial banks	15	16	1.8	232	233	23,914	26,026	5,060	5,352	1.7
6100	Nondepository institutions	8	9	1.2	29	-	18,207	-	533	-	-
6140	Personal credit institutions	6	7	1.2	-	34	-	15,529	-	510	1.0
6200	Security and commodity brokers	3	4	2.6	4	6	18,000	26,000	119	198	0.5
6300	Insurance carriers	4	2	0.5	11	-	32,000	-	343	-	-
6330	Fire, marine, and casualty insurance	4	2	1.6	11	-	32,000	-	343	-	-
6400	Insurance agents, brokers, and service	12	12	1.1	22	27	10,000	14,667	262	442	0.4

Source: County Business Patterns, 1992/93, CBP-92/93-1, U.S. Department of Commerce, Washington, D.C., April 1995. SIC categories for which data were suppressed or not available for both 1992 and 1993 are *not* displayed. The employment columns represent mid-March employment in the year. Pay per employee is calculated by dividing 1st Quarter payroll, annualized, by mid-March employment. The columns headed "% State" show the county's percentage of the state total for the SIC in 1993; for example, 0.9% for SIC 6030 means that the county had 0.9 percent of the state's total establishments (or payroll) in SIC 6030 in 1993. A dash (-) is used to indicate that data are not available or cannot be calculated; *nec* means not elsewhere classified.

Continued on next page.

SIC	Industry	No. Establishments			Employment		Pay / Employee		Annual Payroll ($ 000)		
		1992	1993	% State	1992	1993	1992	1993	1992	1993	% State
OKTIBBEHA, MS - [continued]											
6500	Real estate	25	26	1.6	68	82	9,176	11,317	724	1,216	2.0
6510	Real estate operators and lessors	13	13	1.3	45	-	7,111	-	370	-	-
6530	Real estate agents and managers	6	10	2.0	8	34	6,000	13,529	56	516	1.9
PANOLA, MS											
60 –	**Finance, insurance, and real estate**	44	44	0.8	252	274	19,905	21,358	5,678	6,291	0.7
6000	Depository institutions	11	11	0.9	151	165	20,424	20,752	3,369	3,593	1.0
6100	Nondepository institutions	8	9	1.2	-	32	-	20,375	-	734	1.0
6140	Personal credit institutions	8	9	1.6	-	32	-	20,375	-	734	1.4
6400	Insurance agents, brokers, and service	9	9	0.8	35	-	18,286	-	679	-	-
6500	Real estate	13	13	0.8	13	14	9,231	8,857	136	132	0.2
6510	Real estate operators and lessors	10	10	1.0	10	10	6,000	5,600	63	63	0.2
PEARL RIVER, MS											
60 –	**Finance, insurance, and real estate**	50	55	1.0	188	210	15,617	15,981	3,504	3,817	0.4
6000	Depository institutions	7	10	0.8	102	114	14,784	14,737	1,897	1,940	0.5
6100	Nondepository institutions	11	13	1.8	24	35	19,167	15,200	530	588	0.8
6140	Personal credit institutions	8	11	1.9	19	-	17,263	-	404	-	-
6300	Insurance carriers	4	4	1.0	11	-	37,455	-	426	-	-
6400	Insurance agents, brokers, and service	9	12	1.1	20	28	10,600	16,857	227	528	0.5
6500	Real estate	15	14	0.9	26	20	12,000	6,400	351	175	0.3
6510	Real estate operators and lessors	4	6	0.6	4	-	8,000	-	33	-	-
6530	Real estate agents and managers	8	7	1.4	13	12	5,538	8,000	87	109	0.4
PERRY, MS											
60 –	**Finance, insurance, and real estate**	10	9	0.2	58	62	18,759	17,226	1,203	1,277	0.1
PIKE, MS											
60 –	**Finance, insurance, and real estate**	81	84	1.6	442	455	18,244	15,578	8,390	7,793	0.9
6000	Depository institutions	20	19	1.6	237	223	18,768	19,013	4,435	4,705	1.3
6020	Commercial banks	16	15	1.6	222	207	19,045	19,536	4,218	4,399	1.4
6100	Nondepository institutions	12	14	1.9	35	50	18,629	15,760	705	897	1.2
6140	Personal credit institutions	9	11	1.9	32	44	19,000	15,273	625	777	1.5
6200	Security and commodity brokers	1	3	2.0	-	3	-	16,000	-	80	0.2
6300	Insurance carriers	7	7	1.8	-	24	-	23,667	-	575	0.3
6400	Insurance agents, brokers, and service	12	13	1.1	36	40	16,000	13,700	580	565	0.6
6500	Real estate	24	24	1.5	103	111	17,282	7,604	1,907	916	1.5
6510	Real estate operators and lessors	14	16	1.6	50	60	6,560	5,333	341	355	1.4
6700	Holding and other investment offices	5	4	2.6	4	4	15,000	13,000	63	55	0.1
PONTOTOC, MS											
60 –	**Finance, insurance, and real estate**	26	23	0.4	132	136	18,212	18,765	2,520	2,553	0.3
6000	Depository institutions	6	6	0.5	91	96	19,033	19,625	1,842	1,898	0.5
6100	Nondepository institutions	6	6	0.8	17	17	18,353	18,824	283	302	0.4
6140	Personal credit institutions	6	6	1.1	17	17	18,353	18,824	283	302	0.6
6400	Insurance agents, brokers, and service	9	7	0.6	18	17	18,444	19,059	364	330	0.3
6500	Real estate	5	4	0.3	6	6	4,667	4,000	31	23	0.0
PRENTISS, MS											
60 –	**Finance, insurance, and real estate**	35	39	0.7	190	169	15,221	18,864	3,227	3,281	0.4
6000	Depository institutions	9	10	0.8	114	91	17,333	25,363	2,294	2,345	0.6
6100	Nondepository institutions	4	5	0.7	14	16	16,571	16,250	245	282	0.4
6140	Personal credit institutions	3	5	0.9	-	16	-	16,250	-	282	0.5
6400	Insurance agents, brokers, and service	7	9	0.8	26	33	15,692	13,091	411	458	0.4

Source: County Business Patterns, 1992/93, CBP-92/93-1, U.S. Department of Commerce, Washington, D.C., April 1995. SIC categories for which data were suppressed or not available for both 1992 and 1993 are *not* displayed. The employment columns represent mid-March employment in the year. Pay per employee is calculated by dividing 1st Quarter payroll, annualized, by mid-March employment. The columns headed "% State" show the county's percentage of the state total for the SIC in 1993; for example, 0.9% for SIC 6030 means that the county had 0.9 percent of the state's total establishments (or payroll) in SIC 6030 in 1993. A dash (-) is used to indicate that data are not available or cannot be calculated; *nec* means not elsewhere classified.

Continued on next page.

SIC	Industry	No. Establishments			Employment		Pay / Employee		Annual Payroll ($ 000)		
		1992	1993	% State	1992	1993	1992	1993	1992	1993	% State
PRENTISS, MS - [continued]											
6500	Real estate	13	15	0.9	-	29	-	6,483	-	196	0.3
6510	Real estate operators and lessors	12	12	1.2	30	27	7,200	5,630	232	146	0.6
6530	Real estate agents and managers	-	3	0.6	-	2	-	18,000	-	50	0.2
QUITMAN, MS											
60 -	**Finance, insurance, and real estate**	15	16	0.3	79	90	24,304	19,511	1,824	1,937	0.2
6000	Depository institutions	6	6	0.5	-	59	-	19,254	-	1,182	0.3
6020	Commercial banks	6	6	0.7	-	59	-	19,254	-	1,182	0.4
6400	Insurance agents, brokers, and service	3	3	0.3	6	6	21,333	20,000	130	231	0.2
6500	Real estate	3	3	0.2	5	5	4,000	4,800	20	21	0.0
RANKIN, MS											
60 -	**Finance, insurance, and real estate**	194	194	3.7	2,148	1,864	21,521	24,459	46,296	48,022	5.3
6000	Depository institutions	37	36	3.1	575	325	18,790	21,785	8,247	7,282	2.0
6020	Commercial banks	28	29	3.2	555	310	18,948	22,026	7,899	6,992	2.2
6100	Nondepository institutions	20	22	3.0	73	91	20,877	21,714	1,668	3,099	4.0
6140	Personal credit institutions	12	14	2.5	-	42	-	22,571	-	1,042	2.0
6160	Mortgage bankers and brokers	6	7	8.0	29	-	22,621	-	741	-	
6200	Security and commodity brokers	6	5	3.3	75	10	8,160	10,800	494	80	0.2
6300	Insurance carriers	24	20	5.2	1,009	998	24,440	27,780	26,217	28,386	14.0
6330	Fire, marine, and casualty insurance	11	9	7.0	108	-	35,000	-	3,994	-	
6400	Insurance agents, brokers, and service	44	46	4.1	209	194	22,411	24,412	5,556	5,098	5.0
6500	Real estate	57	61	3.9	169	223	12,994	12,395	2,481	3,147	5.1
6510	Real estate operators and lessors	27	27	2.8	55	70	10,909	13,314	656	985	3.8
6530	Real estate agents and managers	20	24	4.9	97	130	12,948	11,169	1,349	1,590	5.8
6552	Subdividers and developers, n.e.c.	4	8	14.0	9	-	24,000	-	272	-	-
6700	Holding and other investment offices	6	4	2.6	38	23	46,000	52,348	1,633	930	2.0
SCOTT, MS											
60 -	**Finance, insurance, and real estate**	38	41	0.8	252	254	19,905	19,087	5,015	5,290	0.6
6000	Depository institutions	10	10	0.8	171	174	21,591	20,207	3,625	3,787	1.0
6100	Nondepository institutions	7	9	1.2	22	-	21,818	-	463	-	-
6140	Personal credit institutions	3	6	1.1	13	18	22,462	22,667	306	455	0.9
6400	Insurance agents, brokers, and service	8	12	1.1	26	-	16,308	-	432	-	-
6500	Real estate	10	9	0.6	16	13	8,750	10,462	139	134	0.2
SHARKEY, MS											
60 -	**Finance, insurance, and real estate**	10	13	0.2	44	44	20,636	17,909	933	873	0.1
SIMPSON, MS											
60 -	**Finance, insurance, and real estate**	38	40	0.8	148	167	17,378	17,701	2,933	3,208	0.4
6000	Depository institutions	13	13	1.1	104	113	19,731	19,788	2,283	2,388	0.7
6020	Commercial banks	10	10	1.1	99	106	19,879	20,000	2,185	2,270	0.7
6100	Nondepository institutions	5	6	0.8	8	15	15,500	15,733	164	263	0.3
6140	Personal credit institutions	5	5	0.9	8	-	15,500	-	164	-	-
6400	Insurance agents, brokers, and service	10	9	0.8	25	27	12,800	13,630	383	412	0.4
6500	Real estate	8	9	0.6	10	9	6,400	8,444	79	96	0.2
SMITH, MS											
60 -	**Finance, insurance, and real estate**	12	13	0.2	82	80	14,927	15,850	1,249	1,360	0.2
6000	Depository institutions	4	4	0.3	70	70	16,229	17,314	1,172	1,360	0.4
6020	Commercial banks	4	4	0.4	70	70	16,229	17,314	1,172	1,281	0.4
6400	Insurance agents, brokers, and service	5	5	0.4	11	8	7,636	6,000	69	58	0.1
6500	Real estate	3	4	0.3	1	2	4,000	4,000	8	21	0.0

Source: County Business Patterns, 1992/93, CBP-92/93-1, U.S. Department of Commerce, Washington, D.C., April 1995. SIC categories for which data were suppressed or not available for both 1992 and 1993 are *not* displayed. The employment columns represent mid-March employment in the year. Pay per employee is calculated by dividing 1st Quarter payroll, annualized, by mid-March employment. The columns headed "% State" show the county's percentage of the state total for the SIC in 1993; for example, 0.9% for SIC 6030 means that the county had 0.9 percent of the state's total establishments (or payroll) in SIC 6030 in 1993. A dash (-) is used to indicate that data are not available or cannot be calculated; *nec* means not elsewhere classified.

SIC	Industry	No. Establishments			Employment		Pay / Employee		Annual Payroll ($ 000)		
		1992	1993	% State	1992	1993	1992	1993	1992	1993	% State
STONE, MS											
60 –	**Finance, insurance, and real estate**	15	16	*0.3*	93	96	14,452	15,542	1,620	1,757	*0.2*
6000	Depository institutions	6	5	*0.4*	76	75	15,632	16,373	1,434	1,498	*0.4*
6400	Insurance agents, brokers, and service	3	2	*0.2*	11	-	11,273	-	128	-	-
6500	Real estate	5	7	*0.4*	-	6	-	6,000	-	35	*0.1*
SUNFLOWER, MS											
60 –	**Finance, insurance, and real estate**	56	53	*1.0*	257	263	16,280	17,034	4,591	5,400	*0.6*
6000	Depository institutions	13	14	*1.2*	151	153	16,662	18,458	2,788	3,453	*1.0*
6020	Commercial banks	11	11	*1.2*	-	144	-	18,778	-	3,315	*1.1*
6100	Nondepository institutions	6	7	*1.0*	21	22	20,000	19,273	390	388	*0.5*
6400	Insurance agents, brokers, and service	12	11	*1.0*	37	37	16,757	15,135	625	620	*0.6*
6500	Real estate	20	15	*0.9*	34	34	10,118	10,353	365	369	*0.6*
6510	Real estate operators and lessors	12	12	*1.2*	24	30	12,167	11,067	303	347	*1.3*
6530	Real estate agents and managers	3	2	*0.4*	5	-	6,400	-	44	-	-
TALLAHATCHIE, MS											
60 –	**Finance, insurance, and real estate**	12	13	*0.2*	72	65	17,000	18,708	1,245	1,260	*0.1*
6000	Depository institutions	5	5	*0.4*	53	47	17,283	20,511	944	985	*0.3*
6020	Commercial banks	5	5	*0.5*	53	47	17,283	20,511	944	985	*0.3*
6400	Insurance agents, brokers, and service	4	5	*0.4*	15	15	14,133	13,067	209	209	*0.2*
TATE, MS											
60 –	**Finance, insurance, and real estate**	31	35	*0.7*	156	164	20,923	21,634	3,213	3,547	*0.4*
6000	Depository institutions	7	6	*0.5*	93	92	21,333	21,783	2,047	2,150	*0.6*
6400	Insurance agents, brokers, and service	10	10	*0.9*	31	-	21,032	-	511	-	-
6500	Real estate	6	10	*0.6*	6	9	6,667	5,333	40	49	*0.1*
6510	Real estate operators and lessors	3	4	*0.4*	3	5	5,333	4,000	16	20	*0.1*
6530	Real estate agents and managers	2	6	*1.2*	-	4	-	7,000	-	29	*0.1*
TIPPAH, MS											
60 –	**Finance, insurance, and real estate**	30	32	*0.6*	-	209	-	14,144	-	3,435	*0.4*
6000	Depository institutions	9	9	*0.8*	126	127	18,349	17,165	2,401	2,618	*0.7*
6100	Nondepository institutions	3	4	*0.6*	11	-	17,091	-	188	-	-
6140	Personal credit institutions	3	4	*0.7*	11	-	17,091	-	188	-	-
6400	Insurance agents, brokers, and service	6	6	*0.5*	-	18	-	12,000	-	246	*0.2*
6500	Real estate	10	11	*0.7*	10	45	4,000	4,178	40	216	*0.4*
TISHOMINGO, MS											
60 –	**Finance, insurance, and real estate**	30	28	*0.5*	160	163	16,300	16,123	2,676	2,777	*0.3*
6000	Depository institutions	16	14	*1.2*	126	132	17,873	16,758	2,304	2,378	*0.7*
6100	Nondepository institutions	2	3	*0.4*	-	8	-	18,500	-	133	*0.2*
6140	Personal credit institutions	2	3	*0.5*	-	8	-	18,500	-	133	*0.3*
6400	Insurance agents, brokers, and service	4	4	*0.4*	9	-	12,444	-	129	-	-
6500	Real estate	6	5	*0.3*	15	10	6,133	9,200	98	77	*0.1*
TUNICA, MS											
60 –	**Finance, insurance, and real estate**	12	11	*0.2*	77	61	17,714	13,574	1,096	968	*0.1*
6000	Depository institutions	4	3	*0.3*	59	-	18,644	-	832	-	-
6500	Real estate	4	4	*0.3*	-	7	-	5,714	-	37	*0.1*
6510	Real estate operators and lessors	4	4	*0.4*	-	7	-	5,714	-	37	*0.1*
UNION, MS											
60 –	**Finance, insurance, and real estate**	30	28	*0.5*	174	173	17,885	18,983	3,081	3,286	*0.4*
6000	Depository institutions	5	5	*0.4*	120	118	19,633	20,644	2,296	2,375	*0.7*
6400	Insurance agents, brokers, and service	7	8	*0.7*	21	22	18,857	20,545	415	456	*0.4*

Source: County Business Patterns, 1992/93, CBP-92/93-1, U.S. Department of Commerce, Washington, D.C., April 1995. SIC categories for which data were suppressed or not available for both 1992 and 1993 are *not* displayed. The employment columns represent mid-March employment in the year. Pay per employee is calculated by dividing 1st Quarter payroll, annualized, by mid-March employment. The columns headed "% State" show the county's percentage of the state total for the SIC in 1993; for example, 0.9% for SIC 6030 means that the county had 0.9 percent of the state's total establishments (or payroll) in SIC 6030 in 1993. A dash (-) is used to indicate that data are not available or cannot be calculated; *nec* means not elsewhere classified.

Continued on next page.

SIC	Industry	No. Establishments			Employment		Pay / Employee		Annual Payroll ($ 000)		
		1992	1993	% State	1992	1993	1992	1993	1992	1993	% State
UNION, MS - [continued]											
6500	Real estate	12	9	0.6	16	12	5,750	6,333	88	88	0.1
6510	Real estate operators and lessors	8	8	0.8	11	-	6,545	-	74	-	-
6530	Real estate agents and managers	4	1	0.2	5	-	4,000	-	14	-	-
WALTHALL, MS											
60 –	**Finance, insurance, and real estate**	13	12	0.2	79	81	16,962	15,407	1,287	1,343	0.1
6000	Depository institutions	4	4	0.3	57	60	19,368	17,067	1,050	1,073	0.3
6400	Insurance agents, brokers, and service	2	3	0.3	-	11	-	10,182	-	154	0.2
6500	Real estate	4	3	0.2	5	-	4,000	-	20	-	-
WARREN, MS											
60 –	**Finance, insurance, and real estate**	101	102	1.9	562	597	19,338	18,901	9,986	11,082	1.2
6000	Depository institutions	25	28	2.4	341	352	19,413	20,670	5,974	7,076	2.0
6020	Commercial banks	18	19	2.1	302	309	19,603	21,036	5,217	6,199	2.0
6100	Nondepository institutions	12	11	1.5	-	56	-	11,714	-	628	0.8
6140	Personal credit institutions	9	8	1.4	36	50	20,000	11,600	662	567	1.1
6200	Security and commodity brokers	3	4	2.6	-	7	-	50,857	-	379	0.9
6300	Insurance carriers	7	5	1.3	16	19	17,250	20,211	296	428	0.2
6400	Insurance agents, brokers, and service	19	20	1.8	70	75	21,314	20,693	1,486	1,473	1.4
6500	Real estate	31	30	1.9	79	76	12,000	9,316	1,004	738	1.2
6510	Real estate operators and lessors	16	20	2.1	48	54	13,250	8,889	684	486	1.9
6530	Real estate agents and managers	9	9	1.8	22	21	10,182	10,476	221	250	0.9
6700	Holding and other investment offices	4	4	2.6	9	12	40,000	29,333	194	360	0.8
WASHINGTON, MS											
60 –	**Finance, insurance, and real estate**	147	145	2.7	806	757	17,340	18,135	14,745	14,279	1.6
6000	Depository institutions	31	31	2.6	334	299	18,539	20,455	6,254	6,385	1.8
6020	Commercial banks	25	24	2.6	286	254	18,671	21,402	5,417	5,641	1.8
6100	Nondepository institutions	17	18	2.5	60	83	21,133	16,482	1,224	1,309	1.7
6140	Personal credit institutions	11	12	2.1	-	71	-	14,310	-	956	1.8
6160	Mortgage bankers and brokers	4	3	3.4	7	5	18,857	16,000	105	76	0.5
6200	Security and commodity brokers	4	2	1.3	20	-	19,600	-	458	-	-
6300	Insurance carriers	8	10	2.6	107	101	21,607	25,465	2,794	2,663	1.3
6400	Insurance agents, brokers, and service	25	25	2.2	111	105	17,117	16,914	1,937	1,853	1.8
6500	Real estate	57	55	3.5	154	146	10,234	10,630	1,763	1,676	2.7
6510	Real estate operators and lessors	30	39	4.0	92	96	11,957	11,458	1,151	1,172	4.5
6530	Real estate agents and managers	14	13	2.7	29	38	10,345	9,263	351	398	1.4
6552	Subdividers and developers, n.e.c.	4	-	-	4	-	7,000	-	28	-	-
6553	Cemetery subdividers and developers	3	3	6.5	16	12	6,250	8,333	114	106	5.1
6700	Holding and other investment offices	5	4	2.6	20	-	16,800	-	315	-	-
WAYNE, MS											
60 –	**Finance, insurance, and real estate**	21	22	0.4	125	131	16,800	17,374	2,263	2,538	0.3
6000	Depository institutions	5	5	0.4	79	80	17,013	17,350	1,452	1,487	0.4
6400	Insurance agents, brokers, and service	6	7	0.6	23	25	13,913	14,880	367	421	0.4
6500	Real estate	4	4	0.3	4	6	5,000	5,333	22	88	0.1
WEBSTER, MS											
60 –	**Finance, insurance, and real estate**	15	16	0.3	68	68	15,706	15,529	1,105	1,112	0.1
6000	Depository institutions	5	5	0.4	47	45	17,447	17,333	808	781	0.2
6020	Commercial banks	5	5	0.5	47	45	17,447	17,333	808	781	0.2
6100	Nondepository institutions	2	3	0.4	-	7	-	20,000	-	137	0.2
6140	Personal credit institutions	2	3	0.5	-	7	-	20,000	-	137	0.3
6400	Insurance agents, brokers, and service	3	3	0.3	-	9	-	12,000	-	168	0.2
6500	Real estate	5	5	0.3	6	7	4,000	4,000	24	26	0.0
6510	Real estate operators and lessors	5	4	0.4	6	-	4,000	-	24	-	-

Source: County Business Patterns, 1992/93, CBP-92/93-1, U.S. Department of Commerce, Washington, D.C., April 1995. SIC categories for which data were suppressed or not available for both 1992 and 1993 are *not* displayed. The employment columns represent mid-March employment in the year. Pay per employee is calculated by dividing 1st Quarter payroll, annualized, by mid-March employment. The columns headed "% State" show the county's percentage of the state total for the SIC in 1993; for example, 0.9% for SIC 6030 means that the county had 0.9 percent of the state's total establishments (or payroll) in SIC 6030 in 1993. A dash (-) is used to indicate that data are not available or cannot be calculated; *nec* means not elsewhere classified.

SIC	Industry	No. Establishments			Employment		Pay / Employee		Annual Payroll ($ 000)		
		1992	1993	% State	1992	1993	1992	1993	1992	1993	% State
WILKINSON, MS											
60 –	**Finance, insurance, and real estate**	14	15	*0.3*	58	57	19,034	18,456	1,195	1,183	*0.1*
6400	Insurance agents, brokers, and service	3	3	*0.3*	11	11	14,909	13,091	159	153	*0.1*
6500	Real estate	6	7	*0.4*	4	5	4,000	4,000	56	56	*0.1*
6510	Real estate operators and lessors	3	4	*0.4*	3	3	4,000	4,000	12	14	*0.1*
WINSTON, MS											
60 –	**Finance, insurance, and real estate**	47	39	*0.7*	329	330	20,742	21,152	7,188	7,443	*0.8*
6000	Depository institutions	11	12	*1.0*	113	104	18,336	20,923	2,174	2,294	*0.6*
6020	Commercial banks	7	9	*1.0*	85	-	18,118	-	1,656	-	-
6400	Insurance agents, brokers, and service	7	7	*0.6*	21	-	12,571	-	289	-	-
6500	Real estate	21	10	*0.6*	123	128	9,528	16,531	1,402	1,672	*2.7*
6510	Real estate operators and lessors	20	6	*0.6*	122	-	9,541	-	1,394	-	-
YALOBUSHA, MS											
60 –	**Finance, insurance, and real estate**	19	20	*0.4*	104	109	14,962	15,560	1,642	1,632	*0.2*
6000	Depository institutions	7	7	*0.6*	77	82	16,468	16,732	1,344	1,341	*0.4*
6020	Commercial banks	7	7	*0.8*	77	82	16,468	16,732	1,344	1,341	*0.4*
6400	Insurance agents, brokers, and service	4	4	*0.4*	-	13	-	12,615	-	161	*0.2*
6500	Real estate	6	7	*0.4*	7	-	5,143	-	39	-	-
6510	Real estate operators and lessors	4	4	*0.4*	-	5	-	5,600	-	25	*0.1*
YAZOO, MS											
60 –	**Finance, insurance, and real estate**	32	33	*0.6*	169	189	23,361	21,566	3,600	3,842	*0.4*
6000	Depository institutions	10	11	*0.9*	102	121	28,078	25,025	2,489	2,738	*0.8*
6020	Commercial banks	10	10	*1.1*	102	-	28,078	-	2,489	-	-
6100	Nondepository institutions	5	5	*0.7*	20	-	19,800	-	383	-	-
6400	Insurance agents, brokers, and service	5	7	*0.6*	22	23	20,182	21,391	464	542	*0.5*
6500	Real estate	10	9	*0.6*	22	24	10,364	7,667	238	181	*0.3*
6510	Real estate operators and lessors	7	7	*0.7*	14	-	11,143	-	165	-	-
6530	Real estate agents and managers	3	2	*0.4*	8	-	9,000	-	73	-	-

Source: County Business Patterns, 1992/93, CBP-92/93-1, U.S. Department of Commerce, Washington, D.C., April 1995. SIC categories for which data were suppressed or not available for both 1992 and 1993 are *not* displayed. The employment columns represent mid-March employment in the year. Pay per employee is calculated by dividing 1st Quarter payroll, annualized, by mid-March employment. The columns headed "% State" show the county's percentage of the state total for the SIC in 1993; for example, 0.9% for SIC 6030 means that the county had 0.9 percent of the state's total establishments (or payroll) in SIC 6030 in 1993. A dash (-) is used to indicate that data are not available or cannot be calculated; *nec* means not elsewhere classified.

MISSOURI

SIC	Industry	No. Establishments			Employment		Pay / Employee		Annual Payroll ($ 000)		
		1992	1993	% State	1992	1993	1992	1993	1992	1993	% State
ADAIR, MO											
60 –	**Finance, insurance, and real estate**	48	55	0.4	258	257	17,333	16,778	4,619	4,791	0.1
6000	Depository institutions	9	9	0.4	150	157	15,680	15,643	2,504	2,677	0.2
6100	Nondepository institutions	2	3	0.5	-	12	-	24,667	-	288	0.1
6300	Insurance carriers	4	3	0.3	27	-	24,741	-	779	-	-
6400	Insurance agents, brokers, and service	10	13	0.4	-	39	-	15,487	-	749	0.2
6500	Real estate	18	20	0.5	40	31	17,200	9,161	523	340	0.1
6510	Real estate operators and lessors	5	7	0.4	15	13	17,067	8,615	262	106	0.1
6530	Real estate agents and managers	9	9	0.5	21	15	19,238	9,867	234	203	0.1
6700	Holding and other investment offices	3	4	0.7	5	4	4,000	5,000	35	26	0.0
ANDREW, MO											
60 –	**Finance, insurance, and real estate**	20	23	0.2	71	76	14,817	13,789	1,089	1,220	0.0
6000	Depository institutions	5	5	0.2	36	40	17,444	15,100	648	631	0.1
6020	Commercial banks	5	5	0.3	36	40	17,444	15,100	648	631	0.1
6400	Insurance agents, brokers, and service	3	5	0.2	6	10	14,667	12,400	101	137	0.0
6500	Real estate	9	10	0.2	25	25	12,000	12,640	292	436	0.1
6510	Real estate operators and lessors	3	4	0.2	9	10	3,556	5,200	43	53	0.0
ATCHISON, MO											
60 –	**Finance, insurance, and real estate**	21	23	0.2	100	99	16,600	14,263	1,718	1,624	0.0
6000	Depository institutions	5	5	0.2	58	57	21,172	16,912	1,250	1,116	0.1
6020	Commercial banks	5	5	0.3	58	57	21,172	16,912	1,250	1,116	0.1
6400	Insurance agents, brokers, and service	10	12	0.4	-	25	-	11,040	-	329	0.1
6500	Real estate	4	4	0.1	8	-	5,500	-	55	-	-
AUDRAIN, MO											
60 –	**Finance, insurance, and real estate**	68	67	0.5	297	303	16,700	17,056	5,311	5,416	0.1
6000	Depository institutions	14	17	0.8	164	172	20,415	20,023	3,468	3,601	0.3
6020	Commercial banks	11	13	0.9	-	136	-	21,059	-	2,997	0.4
6100	Nondepository institutions	4	3	0.5	20	14	16,200	27,429	332	310	0.1
6400	Insurance agents, brokers, and service	24	22	0.7	51	55	10,196	10,109	549	593	0.2
6500	Real estate	18	17	0.4	33	33	10,667	10,545	444	459	0.1
6510	Real estate operators and lessors	7	6	0.3	7	7	9,143	6,857	71	56	0.0
6553	Cemetery subdividers and developers	3	3	1.9	5	5	4,800	4,800	28	28	0.2
6700	Holding and other investment offices	4	4	0.7	2	2	6,000	8,000	19	21	0.0
6732	Educational, religious, etc. trusts	3	3	3.1	2	-	6,000	-	18	-	-
BARRY, MO											
60 –	**Finance, insurance, and real estate**	54	60	0.5	305	309	16,643	16,155	4,927	5,322	0.1
6000	Depository institutions	15	14	0.7	226	194	18,460	19,649	3,951	3,912	0.4
6300	Insurance carriers	3	3	0.3	8	9	9,500	10,222	99	98	0.0
6330	Fire, marine, and casualty insurance	3	3	0.7	8	9	9,500	10,222	99	98	0.0
6400	Insurance agents, brokers, and service	16	17	0.5	-	33	-	11,515	-	415	0.1
6500	Real estate	15	20	0.5	29	41	7,586	6,927	236	422	0.1
6510	Real estate operators and lessors	7	11	0.6	15	17	3,200	3,059	43	141	0.1
6530	Real estate agents and managers	4	3	0.2	5	-	9,600	-	50	-	-
6552	Subdividers and developers, n.e.c.	2	4	1.7	-	8	-	9,500	-	100	0.5
6700	Holding and other investment offices	3	4	0.7	5	-	9,600	-	39	-	-

Source: County Business Patterns, 1992/93, CBP-92/93-1, U.S. Department of Commerce, Washington, D.C., April 1995. SIC categories for which data were suppressed or not available for both 1992 and 1993 are *not* displayed. The employment columns represent mid-March employment in the year. Pay per employee is calculated by dividing 1st Quarter payroll, annualized, by mid-March employment. The columns headed "% State" show the county's percentage of the state total for the SIC in 1993; for example, 0.9% for SIC 6030 means that the county had 0.9 percent of the state's total establishments (or payroll) in SIC 6030 in 1993. A dash (-) is used to indicate that data are not available or cannot be calculated; *nec* means not elsewhere classified.

SIC	Industry	No. Establishments			Employment		Pay / Employee		Annual Payroll ($ 000)		
		1992	1993	% State	1992	1993	1992	1993	1992	1993	% State
BARTON, MO											
60 –	**Finance, insurance, and real estate**	25	25	0.2	162	180	15,259	14,822	2,780	3,226	0.1
6000	Depository institutions	10	9	0.4	83	81	19,566	18,914	1,751	1,688	0.2
6400	Insurance agents, brokers, and service	6	7	0.2	-	17	-	11,059	-	193	0.0
6500	Real estate	5	5	0.1	23	28	1,565	3,286	128	122	0.0
BATES, MO											
60 –	**Finance, insurance, and real estate**	30	31	0.2	181	164	17,392	15,732	3,246	2,840	0.1
6000	Depository institutions	12	12	0.6	131	110	19,481	17,745	2,607	2,157	0.2
6020	Commercial banks	12	12	0.8	131	110	19,481	17,745	2,607	2,157	0.3
6300	Insurance carriers	3	1	0.1	11	-	11,273	-	108	-	-
6330	Fire, marine, and casualty insurance	3	1	0.2	11	-	11,273	-	108	-	-
6400	Insurance agents, brokers, and service	9	11	0.3	27	37	12,889	12,432	409	496	0.1
6500	Real estate	3	3	0.1	8	-	11,000	-	94	-	-
6700	Holding and other investment offices	1	3	0.6	-	3	-	6,667	-	31	0.0
BENTON, MO											
60 –	**Finance, insurance, and real estate**	31	32	0.3	121	125	17,950	18,400	2,390	2,480	0.1
6000	Depository institutions	5	5	0.2	74	76	20,919	21,158	1,590	1,681	0.2
6020	Commercial banks	5	5	0.3	74	76	20,919	21,158	1,590	1,681	0.2
6400	Insurance agents, brokers, and service	10	9	0.3	16	17	11,750	10,588	219	237	0.1
6500	Real estate	13	15	0.3	28	29	13,857	16,138	514	499	0.1
6530	Real estate agents and managers	5	4	0.2	14	3	11,714	10,667	178	50	0.0
BOLLINGER, MO											
60 –	**Finance, insurance, and real estate**	14	14	0.1	58	47	12,552	13,617	661	658	0.0
6000	Depository institutions	5	4	0.2	-	33	-	15,030	-	510	0.0
6020	Commercial banks	5	4	0.3	-	33	-	15,030	-	510	0.1
6400	Insurance agents, brokers, and service	4	5	0.2	6	-	10,667	-	60	-	-
6500	Real estate	3	3	0.1	5	6	13,600	10,667	73	80	0.0
BOONE, MO											
60 –	**Finance, insurance, and real estate**	294	311	2.5	5,119	5,119	26,882	29,679	145,780	157,313	3.9
6000	Depository institutions	38	43	2.0	875	869	19,643	19,066	18,104	18,784	1.7
6020	Commercial banks	29	33	2.3	760	760	19,821	19,179	15,973	16,546	2.1
6030	Savings institutions	5	5	1.3	51	-	17,804	-	955	-	-
6060	Credit unions	4	4	1.8	64	61	19,000	18,754	1,176	1,185	-
6100	Nondepository institutions	17	17	2.6	72	87	23,000	20,368	1,785	1,874	0.6
6140	Personal credit institutions	11	11	3.5	47	56	25,021	20,000	1,214	1,202	2.3
6200	Security and commodity brokers	11	11	1.9	46	37	21,130	44,757	1,109	1,587	0.3
6210	Security brokers and dealers	8	9	2.4	32	-	26,000	-	951	-	-
6300	Insurance carriers	38	30	3.0	3,108	3,079	32,564	36,456	106,491	113,571	11.7
6310	Life insurance	15	12	4.3	264	250	26,485	30,288	7,194	7,615	2.0
6330	Fire, marine, and casualty insurance	16	14	3.4	2,805	2,817	33,278	36,997	98,233	105,469	28.9
6400	Insurance agents, brokers, and service	67	75	2.3	489	528	21,808	24,485	11,108	13,110	3.4
6500	Real estate	111	122	2.8	480	468	10,767	12,675	6,190	7,107	1.6
6510	Real estate operators and lessors	50	61	3.2	235	226	7,336	9,628	1,963	2,555	1.7
6530	Real estate agents and managers	42	44	2.4	142	167	14,930	12,240	2,621	2,410	1.0
6552	Subdividers and developers, n.e.c.	7	13	5.5	31	-	13,548	-	492	-	-
6700	Holding and other investment offices	12	13	2.4	49	51	15,347	16,157	993	1,280	0.6
6710	Holding offices	4	5	2.5	36	-	18,333	-	884	-	-
6732	Educational, religious, etc. trusts	3	4	4.1	2	-	6,000	-	46	-	-
BUCHANAN, MO											
60 –	**Finance, insurance, and real estate**	221	215	1.7	1,987	2,031	20,560	19,525	41,455	41,679	1.0
6000	Depository institutions	43	44	2.1	657	684	19,756	20,404	13,481	14,360	1.3
6020	Commercial banks	24	24	1.7	567	576	19,922	20,722	11,444	11,966	1.5
6030	Savings institutions	6	5	1.3	47	51	20,340	21,725	1,083	1,278	1.2
6100	Nondepository institutions	16	14	2.1	-	64	-	21,375	-	1,284	0.4

Source: County Business Patterns, 1992/93, CBP-92/93-1, U.S. Department of Commerce, Washington, D.C., April 1995. SIC categories for which data were suppressed or not available for both 1992 and 1993 are not displayed. The employment columns represent mid-March employment in the year. Pay per employee is calculated by dividing 1st Quarter payroll, annualized, by mid-March employment. The columns headed "% State" show the county's percentage of the state total for the SIC in 1993; for example, 0.9% for SIC 6030 means that the county had 0.9 percent of the state's total establishments (or payroll) in SIC 6030 in 1993. A dash (-) is used to indicate that data are not available or cannot be calculated; nec means not elsewhere classified.

Continued on next page.

SIC	Industry	No. Establishments			Employment		Pay / Employee		Annual Payroll ($ 000)		
		1992	1993	% State	1992	1993	1992	1993	1992	1993	% State
BUCHANAN, MO - [continued]											
6200	Security and commodity brokers	5	5	0.8	-	31	-	60,645	-	1,741	0.3
6300	Insurance carriers	28	27	2.7	681	714	23,001	21,838	15,486	16,972	1.7
6310	Life insurance	7	7	2.5	-	56	-	21,786	-	1,085	0.3
6330	Fire, marine, and casualty insurance	12	10	2.4	-	649	-	22,077	-	15,833	4.3
6370	Pension, health, and welfare funds	9	10	6.8	9	9	7,111	4,889	59	54	0.2
6400	Insurance agents, brokers, and service	58	60	1.8	134	124	20,358	19,097	2,630	2,520	0.7
6500	Real estate	56	56	1.3	363	380	11,658	10,958	4,146	4,376	1.0
6510	Real estate operators and lessors	25	27	1.4	205	142	10,049	10,225	1,962	1,503	1.0
6530	Real estate agents and managers	19	22	1.2	66	115	14,121	12,243	942	1,581	0.7
6700	Holding and other investment offices	15	9	1.7	78	34	35,077	9,647	3,175	426	0.2
6733	Trusts, n.e.c.	5	3	3.2	2	-	6,000	-	135	-	-
6799	Investors, n.e.c.	3	3	3.7	-	7	-	10,857	-	67	0.9
BUTLER, MO											
60 –	**Finance, insurance, and real estate**	66	70	0.6	410	433	18,585	18,661	8,188	8,450	0.2
6000	Depository institutions	14	16	0.8	251	243	19,076	19,506	4,760	4,882	0.5
6020	Commercial banks	10	12	0.8	211	202	19,223	19,545	4,004	4,055	0.5
6100	Nondepository institutions	5	5	0.8	28	37	17,571	13,730	517	534	0.5
6300	Insurance carriers	6	4	0.4	-	44	-	26,000	-	1,217	0.1
6400	Insurance agents, brokers, and service	22	25	0.8	56	69	17,000	15,942	997	1,150	0.3
6500	Real estate	15	16	0.4	29	32	9,793	9,875	406	388	0.1
6510	Real estate operators and lessors	2	3	0.2	-	5	-	11,200	-	53	0.0
6530	Real estate agents and managers	5	7	0.4	6	10	10,000	7,600	66	83	0.0
6540	Title abstract offices	4	4	2.4	14	-	11,143	-	207	-	-
CALDWELL, MO											
60 –	**Finance, insurance, and real estate**	16	15	0.1	72	68	14,444	14,059	1,167	1,286	0.0
6000	Depository institutions	6	5	0.2	50	43	16,960	18,047	949	1,068	0.1
6400	Insurance agents, brokers, and service	4	4	0.1	-	6	-	8,667	-	56	0.0
6500	Real estate	5	5	0.1	13	-	9,231	-	142	-	-
CALLAWAY, MO											
60 –	**Finance, insurance, and real estate**	39	42	0.3	244	253	17,000	17,107	4,929	5,164	0.1
6000	Depository institutions	15	15	0.7	172	175	17,256	17,646	3,460	3,542	0.3
6020	Commercial banks	11	11	0.8	124	128	19,258	18,938	2,725	2,734	0.3
6030	Savings institutions	4	4	1.1	48	47	12,083	14,128	735	808	0.7
6400	Insurance agents, brokers, and service	11	11	0.3	25	29	11,200	10,345	309	330	0.1
6500	Real estate	8	10	0.2	29	37	14,621	14,595	466	858	0.2
6510	Real estate operators and lessors	2	3	0.2	-	7	-	16,000	-	113	0.1
6530	Real estate agents and managers	2	4	0.2	-	19	-	15,158	-	366	0.2
CAMDEN, MO											
60 –	**Finance, insurance, and real estate**	88	91	0.7	588	563	16,020	16,909	11,212	11,157	0.3
6000	Depository institutions	16	16	0.8	246	250	18,049	18,416	4,728	5,242	0.5
6020	Commercial banks	12	12	0.8	219	222	18,484	18,757	4,289	4,763	0.6
6030	Savings institutions	4	4	1.1	27	28	14,519	15,714	439	479	0.4
6200	Security and commodity brokers	3	4	0.7	6	9	108,667	90,222	600	866	0.2
6210	Security brokers and dealers	3	4	1.1	6	9	108,667	90,222	600	866	0.2
6400	Insurance agents, brokers, and service	20	19	0.6	75	63	12,107	15,746	997	1,035	0.3
6500	Real estate	43	49	1.1	236	238	12,847	12,891	4,175	3,988	0.9
6510	Real estate operators and lessors	11	12	0.6	17	22	9,647	13,455	191	242	0.2
6530	Real estate agents and managers	20	28	1.5	175	168	12,411	11,690	3,186	2,771	1.2
6540	Title abstract offices	3	4	2.4	23	34	13,217	14,706	405	596	2.4
6552	Subdividers and developers, n.e.c.	4	4	1.7	16	14	20,750	22,000	360	354	1.6

Source: County Business Patterns, 1992/93, CBP-92/93-1, U.S. Department of Commerce, Washington, D.C., April 1995. SIC categories for which data were suppressed or not available for both 1992 and 1993 are not displayed. The employment columns represent mid-March employment in the year. Pay per employee is calculated by dividing 1st Quarter payroll, annualized, by mid-March employment. The columns headed "% State" show the county's percentage of the state total for the SIC in 1993; for example, 0.9% for SIC 6030 means that the county had 0.9 percent of the state's total establishments (or payroll) in SIC 6030 in 1993. A dash (-) is used to indicate that data are not available or cannot be calculated; nec means not elsewhere classified.

SIC	Industry	No. Establishments			Employment		Pay / Employee		Annual Payroll ($ 000)		
		1992	1993	% State	1992	1993	1992	1993	1992	1993	% State
CAPE GIRARDEAU, MO											
60 –	**Finance, insurance, and real estate**	187	192	1.5	1,448	1,339	18,704	21,440	26,471	29,217	0.7
6000	Depository institutions	23	24	1.1	600	571	19,967	18,746	11,501	11,512	1.1
6020	Commercial banks	20	21	1.5	-	555	-	18,732	-	11,178	1.4
6100	Nondepository institutions	9	9	1.4	133	81	18,346	22,568	2,510	1,841	0.6
6140	Personal credit institutions	6	7	2.2	103	-	17,709	-	1,876	-	-
6200	Security and commodity brokers	8	8	1.3	32	34	34,625	38,353	1,084	1,375	0.2
6300	Insurance carriers	17	14	1.4	77	87	24,779	34,345	1,952	2,722	0.3
6330	Fire, marine, and casualty insurance	9	6	1.4	-	18	-	33,111	-	623	0.2
6400	Insurance agents, brokers, and service	54	69	2.1	143	303	15,552	23,617	2,442	6,485	1.7
6500	Real estate	62	57	1.3	387	182	11,504	12,220	4,530	2,772	0.6
6510	Real estate operators and lessors	29	24	1.2	306	89	10,928	10,022	2,980	1,014	0.7
6530	Real estate agents and managers	25	27	1.5	47	68	13,106	14,059	904	1,338	0.6
6552	Subdividers and developers, n.e.c.	4	4	1.7	22	-	10,182	-	232	-	-
6700	Holding and other investment offices	14	11	2.0	76	81	39,105	30,914	2,452	2,510	1.2
6710	Holding offices	4	3	1.5	57	67	48,772	34,149	2,232	2,283	1.4
6733	Trusts, n.e.c.	5	3	3.2	11	-	11,273	-	154	-	-
CARROLL, MO											
60 –	**Finance, insurance, and real estate**	23	25	0.2	112	109	17,893	18,092	2,488	2,077	0.1
6000	Depository institutions	9	10	0.5	76	84	21,105	20,333	1,667	1,784	0.2
6020	Commercial banks	6	7	0.5	58	66	22,138	20,121	1,299	1,372	0.2
6030	Savings institutions	3	3	0.8	18	18	17,778	21,111	368	412	0.4
6500	Real estate	7	10	0.2	15	12	16,533	7,333	639	119	0.0
6530	Real estate agents and managers	1	4	0.2	-	2	-	6,000	-	12	0.0
CARTER, MO											
60 –	**Finance, insurance, and real estate**	6	8	0.1	31	45	17,677	15,556	536	775	0.0
CASS, MO											
60 –	**Finance, insurance, and real estate**	102	111	0.9	623	635	17,246	17,449	11,802	12,665	0.3
6000	Depository institutions	24	24	1.1	324	311	17,185	17,929	5,735	5,867	0.5
6020	Commercial banks	19	20	1.4	286	-	17,161	-	5,094	-	-
6100	Nondepository institutions	4	4	0.6	16	27	22,250	16,000	363	433	0.1
6330	Fire, marine, and casualty insurance	4	4	1.0	-	6	-	28,000	-	159	0.0
6400	Insurance agents, brokers, and service	23	26	0.8	73	73	16,548	18,356	1,470	1,476	0.4
6500	Real estate	40	47	1.1	174	199	15,701	15,055	3,246	4,078	0.9
6510	Real estate operators and lessors	18	24	1.2	55	75	15,345	12,267	934	1,180	0.8
6530	Real estate agents and managers	12	14	0.8	28	27	13,286	13,926	346	489	0.2
CEDAR, MO											
60 –	**Finance, insurance, and real estate**	19	21	0.2	109	105	15,119	20,038	2,053	2,032	0.1
6000	Depository institutions	5	5	0.2	74	70	17,081	24,171	1,647	1,594	0.1
6400	Insurance agents, brokers, and service	7	8	0.2	-	21	-	14,095	-	308	0.1
6500	Real estate	5	7	0.2	11	-	7,636	-	83	-	-
6530	Real estate agents and managers	2	3	0.2	-	7	-	6,857	-	54	0.0
CHARITON, MO											
60 –	**Finance, insurance, and real estate**	29	30	0.2	127	130	14,677	14,215	1,997	1,943	0.0
6000	Depository institutions	8	8	0.4	77	80	17,818	15,950	1,497	1,358	0.1
6020	Commercial banks	8	8	0.6	77	80	17,818	15,950	1,497	1,358	0.2
6400	Insurance agents, brokers, and service	8	11	0.3	15	20	4,800	5,400	81	111	0.0
6500	Real estate	7	7	0.2	19	17	7,579	8,000	160	160	0.0
CHRISTIAN, MO											
60 –	**Finance, insurance, and real estate**	60	65	0.5	317	335	15,710	15,737	5,457	5,424	0.1
6000	Depository institutions	15	15	0.7	224	230	18,357	17,722	4,415	3,938	0.4
6330	Fire, marine, and casualty insurance	5	3	0.7	11	8	20,000	23,500	214	205	0.1
6400	Insurance agents, brokers, and service	12	15	0.5	-	25	-	15,200	-	432	0.1

Source: County Business Patterns, 1992/93, CBP-92/93-1, U.S. Department of Commerce, Washington, D.C., April 1995. SIC categories for which data were suppressed or not available for both 1992 and 1993 are *not* displayed. The employment columns represent mid-March employment in the year. Pay per employee is calculated by dividing 1st Quarter payroll, annualized, by mid-March employment. The columns headed "% State" show the county's percentage of the state total for the SIC in 1993; for example, 0.9% for SIC 6030 means that the county had 0.9 percent of the state's total establishments (or payroll) in SIC 6030 in 1993. A dash (-) is used to indicate that data are not available or cannot be calculated; *nec* means not elsewhere classified.

Continued on next page.

SIC	Industry	No. Establishments			Employment		Pay / Employee		Annual Payroll ($ 000)		
		1992	1993	% State	1992	1993	1992	1993	1992	1993	% State
CHRISTIAN, MO - [continued]											
6500	Real estate	23	27	0.6	49	64	5,878	7,688	357	613	0.1
6510	Real estate operators and lessors	11	14	0.7	26	28	4,308	6,143	129	199	0.1
6530	Real estate agents and managers	10	10	0.6	17	21	5,647	7,429	111	232	0.1
CLARK, MO											
60 –	**Finance, insurance, and real estate**	14	15	0.1	65	79	13,846	11,241	933	965	0.0
6000	Depository institutions	5	5	0.2	48	56	14,500	12,429	718	744	0.1
6500	Real estate	5	6	0.1	7	13	7,429	4,923	58	62	0.0
6510	Real estate operators and lessors	2	3	0.2	-	8	-	2,000	-	13	0.0
CLAY, MO											
60 –	**Finance, insurance, and real estate**	347	367	2.9	3,351	2,904	28,320	19,942	87,100	62,614	1.6
6000	Depository institutions	60	59	2.8	1,011	782	16,969	20,046	17,461	16,314	1.5
6020	Commercial banks	38	39	2.7	833	559	16,677	20,544	14,060	11,528	1.4
6030	Savings institutions	15	11	2.9	155	148	18,065	18,595	2,890	3,207	2.9
6100	Nondepository institutions	31	35	5.4	933	875	51,288	21,344	39,123	19,304	6.3
6140	Personal credit institutions	14	13	4.1	106	-	22,264	-	2,525	-	-
6160	Mortgage bankers and brokers	14	16	7.1	-	73	-	28,384	-	3,411	1.9
6200	Security and commodity brokers	11	13	2.2	43	-	43,814	-	1,263	-	-
6300	Insurance carriers	31	24	2.4	202	180	24,119	23,756	5,177	4,418	0.5
6310	Life insurance	4	4	1.4	114	115	19,333	17,217	2,257	1,949	0.5
6330	Fire, marine, and casualty insurance	19	15	3.6	52	39	38,231	43,897	2,008	1,801	0.5
6360	Title insurance	5	2	3.2	34	-	19,765	-	879	-	-
6400	Insurance agents, brokers, and service	86	93	2.9	226	225	23,611	18,702	4,602	4,939	1.3
6500	Real estate	117	127	2.9	880	746	18,141	15,796	17,605	13,655	3.0
6510	Real estate operators and lessors	38	44	2.3	326	374	18,466	14,118	6,384	6,204	4.1
6530	Real estate agents and managers	49	67	3.7	392	263	18,633	16,973	8,163	4,885	2.1
6540	Title abstract offices	4	4	2.4	13	22	12,923	16,364	200	433	1.7
6552	Subdividers and developers, n.e.c.	12	9	3.8	87	-	18,345	-	1,803	-	-
6700	Holding and other investment offices	11	16	2.9	56	-	32,786	-	1,869	-	-
6733	Trusts, n.e.c.	3	4	4.3	-	3	-	18,667	-	115	2.0
CLINTON, MO											
60 –	**Finance, insurance, and real estate**	26	35	0.3	193	218	18,114	16,037	3,811	3,948	0.1
6000	Depository institutions	9	9	0.4	131	137	20,366	19,007	2,944	2,908	0.3
6020	Commercial banks	6	6	0.4	72	73	21,500	19,452	1,633	1,535	0.2
6030	Savings institutions	3	3	0.8	59	64	18,983	18,500	1,311	1,373	1.2
6400	Insurance agents, brokers, and service	7	10	0.3	-	32	-	14,500	-	482	0.1
6500	Real estate	6	13	0.3	20	37	6,600	7,243	141	365	0.1
6530	Real estate agents and managers	3	6	0.3	5	11	7,200	4,000	37	64	0.0
COLE, MO											
60 –	**Finance, insurance, and real estate**	191	198	1.6	2,468	2,414	22,875	25,478	60,162	63,984	1.6
6000	Depository institutions	34	43	2.0	639	751	21,421	20,842	15,136	17,417	1.6
6020	Commercial banks	20	24	1.7	532	582	21,226	21,065	12,542	13,799	1.7
6030	Savings institutions	7	8	2.1	84	91	22,810	21,055	2,015	2,088	1.9
6060	Credit unions	7	11	4.8	23	78	20,870	18,923	579	1,530	-
6100	Nondepository institutions	13	11	1.7	149	121	25,208	30,876	3,716	3,257	1.1
6140	Personal credit institutions	10	8	2.5	-	74	-	22,649	-	1,714	3.2
6200	Security and commodity brokers	5	6	1.0	29	30	61,379	74,400	1,647	1,938	0.3
6210	Security brokers and dealers	5	6	1.6	29	30	61,379	74,400	1,647	1,938	0.5
6300	Insurance carriers	31	25	2.5	321	353	26,804	28,215	9,022	10,150	1.0
6310	Life insurance	11	9	3.2	128	156	24,688	25,385	3,343	3,967	1.1
6330	Fire, marine, and casualty insurance	12	6	1.4	108	89	28,481	29,258	3,135	2,810	0.8
6400	Insurance agents, brokers, and service	49	50	1.5	722	530	23,163	31,917	17,985	17,376	4.5
6500	Real estate	49	53	1.2	169	177	13,988	14,576	2,570	3,065	0.7
6510	Real estate operators and lessors	23	27	1.4	79	80	12,101	12,700	1,029	1,157	0.8

Source: County Business Patterns, 1992/93, CBP-92/93-1, U.S. Department of Commerce, Washington, D.C., April 1995. SIC categories for which data were suppressed or not available for both 1992 and 1993 are not displayed. The employment columns represent mid-March employment in the year. Pay per employee is calculated by dividing 1st Quarter payroll, annualized, by mid-March employment. The columns headed "% State" show the county's percentage of the state total for the SIC in 1993; for example, 0.9% for SIC 6030 means that the county had 0.9 percent of the state's total establishments (or payroll) in SIC 6030 in 1993. A dash (-) is used to indicate that data are not available or cannot be calculated; nec means not elsewhere classified.

Continued on next page.

SIC	Industry	No. Establishments			Employment		Pay / Employee		Annual Payroll ($ 000)		
		1992	1993	% State	1992	1993	1992	1993	1992	1993	% State
COLE, MO - [continued]											
6530	Real estate agents and managers	13	17	0.9	50	53	13,440	14,943	699	909	0.4
6553	Cemetery subdividers and developers	4	3	1.9	-	10	-	12,000	-	141	0.9
6700	Holding and other investment offices	10	10	1.8	439	452	21,731	23,071	10,086	10,781	5.0
COOPER, MO											
60 –	**Finance, insurance, and real estate**	26	27	0.2	123	123	17,691	18,179	2,270	2,235	0.1
6000	Depository institutions	8	8	0.4	72	73	21,278	21,425	1,518	1,597	0.1
6400	Insurance agents, brokers, and service	7	7	0.2	14	16	11,143	10,250	157	148	0.0
6500	Real estate	6	7	0.2	12	13	9,000	7,692	159	173	0.0
6530	Real estate agents and managers	1	3	0.2	-	6	-	8,000	-	49	0.0
CRAWFORD, MO											
60 –	**Finance, insurance, and real estate**	27	30	0.2	159	170	15,648	15,365	2,699	2,949	0.1
6000	Depository institutions	7	8	0.4	106	115	17,849	17,287	1,992	2,169	0.2
6020	Commercial banks	7	8	0.6	106	115	17,849	17,287	1,992	2,169	0.3
6500	Real estate	11	13	0.3	36	33	9,333	10,545	391	449	0.1
6510	Real estate operators and lessors	5	5	0.3	16	12	9,500	11,333	169	166	0.1
6530	Real estate agents and managers	2	4	0.2	-	7	-	8,000	-	63	0.0
DADE, MO											
60 –	**Finance, insurance, and real estate**	12	13	0.1	49	55	12,571	12,145	680	758	0.0
6400	Insurance agents, brokers, and service	3	4	0.1	-	9	-	10,667	-	95	0.0
6500	Real estate	5	5	0.1	7	8	5,143	4,500	36	37	0.0
DALLAS, MO											
60 –	**Finance, insurance, and real estate**	20	20	0.2	95	94	16,716	15,319	1,689	1,645	0.0
6000	Depository institutions	5	5	0.2	66	67	20,909	18,030	1,466	1,382	0.1
6400	Insurance agents, brokers, and service	5	7	0.2	10	-	10,400	-	111	-	-
6500	Real estate	8	7	0.2	-	10	-	5,200	-	68	0.0
6510	Real estate operators and lessors	4	4	0.2	9	6	1,778	3,333	18	17	0.0
DAVIESS, MO											
60 –	**Finance, insurance, and real estate**	15	16	0.1	93	97	14,839	13,237	1,430	1,400	0.0
6000	Depository institutions	5	5	0.2	54	58	19,259	15,172	1,091	1,007	0.1
6400	Insurance agents, brokers, and service	5	5	0.2	8	-	4,000	-	39	-	-
6500	Real estate	3	4	0.1	-	22	-	10,182	-	272	0.1
DE KALB, MO											
60 –	**Finance, insurance, and real estate**	15	15	0.1	286	290	21,203	21,297	6,249	6,220	0.2
DENT, MO											
60 –	**Finance, insurance, and real estate**	29	28	0.2	154	161	18,935	21,043	2,864	3,215	0.1
6000	Depository institutions	8	6	0.3	100	102	22,520	25,098	2,211	2,379	0.2
6300	Insurance carriers	3	3	0.3	7	-	23,429	-	98	-	-
6400	Insurance agents, brokers, and service	6	5	0.2	18	16	15,111	20,000	281	288	0.1
6500	Real estate	9	12	0.3	19	35	8,211	9,829	199	459	0.1
6530	Real estate agents and managers	5	6	0.3	11	22	4,727	6,364	84	129	0.1
6700	Holding and other investment offices	3	2	0.4	10	-	7,200	-	75	-	-
DOUGLAS, MO											
60 –	**Finance, insurance, and real estate**	15	14	0.1	64	68	16,375	17,353	1,059	1,151	0.0
6000	Depository institutions	5	5	0.2	49	54	17,714	19,037	857	985	0.1
6400	Insurance agents, brokers, and service	5	5	0.2	10	10	13,200	11,600	150	131	0.0
6500	Real estate	4	4	0.1	-	4	-	9,000	-	35	0.0

Source: County Business Patterns, 1992/93, CBP-92/93-1, U.S. Department of Commerce, Washington, D.C., April 1995. SIC categories for which data were suppressed or not available for both 1992 and 1993 are *not* displayed. The employment columns represent mid-March employment in the year. Pay per employee is calculated by dividing 1st Quarter payroll, annualized, by mid-March employment. The columns headed "% State" show the county's percentage of the state total for the SIC in 1993; for example, 0.9% for SIC 6030 means that the county had 0.9 percent of the state's total establishments (or payroll) in SIC 6030 in 1993. A dash (-) is used to indicate that data are not available or cannot be calculated; *nec* means not elsewhere classified.

SIC	Industry	No. Establishments			Employment		Pay / Employee		Annual Payroll ($ 000)		
		1992	1993	% State	1992	1993	1992	1993	1992	1993	% State
DUNKLIN, MO											
60 –	**Finance, insurance, and real estate**	71	73	0.6	391	399	16,051	15,519	6,692	6,929	0.2
6000	Depository institutions	18	18	0.8	225	224	18,667	18,321	4,453	4,541	0.4
6020	Commercial banks	14	14	1.0	212	210	18,943	18,533	4,272	4,320	0.5
6100	Nondepository institutions	4	5	0.8	22	32	14,364	15,500	349	546	0.2
6400	Insurance agents, brokers, and service	24	24	0.7	58	53	16,276	14,943	941	854	0.2
6500	Real estate	20	23	0.5	80	87	8,100	7,724	785	827	0.2
6510	Real estate operators and lessors	8	12	0.6	5	-	7,200	-	105	-	-
6530	Real estate agents and managers	5	6	0.3	41	56	6,927	7,143	333	473	0.2
6553	Cemetery subdividers and developers	3	4	2.6	-	9	-	8,000	-	83	0.5
FRANKLIN, MO											
60 –	**Finance, insurance, and real estate**	155	159	1.3	807	854	19,633	19,874	17,971	19,785	0.5
6000	Depository institutions	34	34	1.6	490	504	18,343	18,905	10,732	11,269	1.0
6020	Commercial banks	26	26	1.8	421	439	18,603	19,153	9,485	10,034	1.2
6030	Savings institutions	8	8	2.1	69	65	16,754	17,231	1,247	1,235	1.1
6100	Nondepository institutions	3	5	0.8	11	-	29,091	-	298	-	-
6140	Personal credit institutions	2	4	1.3	-	18	-	11,778	-	254	0.5
6200	Security and commodity brokers	6	5	0.8	-	31	-	52,903	-	1,632	0.3
6210	Security brokers and dealers	6	5	1.4	-	31	-	52,903	-	1,632	0.5
6300	Insurance carriers	10	10	1.0	58	56	22,966	30,286	1,435	1,670	0.2
6400	Insurance agents, brokers, and service	42	40	1.2	102	111	16,902	15,892	1,776	1,918	0.5
6500	Real estate	56	61	1.4	104	126	13,077	12,127	1,706	2,482	0.5
6510	Real estate operators and lessors	17	18	0.9	22	18	9,818	7,111	338	172	0.1
6530	Real estate agents and managers	21	33	1.8	34	71	11,176	10,366	467	1,041	0.4
6552	Subdividers and developers, n.e.c.	5	5	2.1	6	15	18,000	7,733	174	632	2.9
GASCONADE, MO											
60 –	**Finance, insurance, and real estate**	25	28	0.2	108	123	11,778	13,626	1,359	1,851	0.0
6000	Depository institutions	9	9	0.4	73	77	12,329	13,143	1,005	1,129	0.1
6300	Insurance carriers	3	3	0.3	9	9	6,667	8,000	64	72	0.0
6330	Fire, marine, and casualty insurance	3	3	0.7	9	9	6,667	8,000	64	72	0.0
6400	Insurance agents, brokers, and service	5	8	0.2	-	25	-	18,560	-	453	0.1
6500	Real estate	7	8	0.2	-	12	-	10,667	-	197	0.0
6530	Real estate agents and managers	2	4	0.2	-	7	-	12,000	-	104	0.0
GENTRY, MO											
60 –	**Finance, insurance, and real estate**	21	17	0.1	72	63	14,778	16,000	1,246	1,098	0.0
6000	Depository institutions	4	4	0.2	46	40	18,435	19,900	1,015	870	0.1
6020	Commercial banks	4	4	0.3	46	40	18,435	19,900	1,015	870	0.1
6300	Insurance carriers	3	1	0.1	3	-	6,667	-	24	-	-
6400	Insurance agents, brokers, and service	8	8	0.2	14	14	10,857	10,857	143	143	0.0
6500	Real estate	6	4	0.1	9	-	4,889	-	64	-	-
6510	Real estate operators and lessors	3	1	0.1	4	-	4,000	-	14	-	-
GREENE, MO											
60 –	**Finance, insurance, and real estate**	675	715	5.7	5,482	5,760	19,302	19,403	110,803	119,613	3.0
6000	Depository institutions	84	93	4.4	2,139	2,073	18,246	19,190	40,164	40,956	3.8
6020	Commercial banks	46	49	3.4	1,444	1,468	19,981	20,569	29,144	29,911	3.7
6030	Savings institutions	27	26	7.0	623	468	14,215	15,256	9,654	8,415	7.7
6100	Nondepository institutions	43	46	7.1	344	337	24,477	24,546	8,186	7,928	2.6
6140	Personal credit institutions	23	26	8.3	189	180	24,508	21,156	4,696	4,075	7.7
6150	Business credit institutions	1	3	3.7	-	15	-	18,400	-	306	0.5
6160	Mortgage bankers and brokers	14	17	7.6	139	142	25,727	29,493	3,256	3,547	2.0
6200	Security and commodity brokers	25	31	5.2	105	166	40,610	40,145	4,725	7,039	1.2
6210	Security brokers and dealers	17	21	5.7	93	111	41,591	49,802	4,357	6,005	1.7
6280	Security and commodity services	8	10	5.0	12	55	33,000	20,655	368	1,034	0.5
6300	Insurance carriers	70	50	5.0	921	1,038	23,492	23,495	22,112	25,020	2.6
6310	Life insurance	24	21	7.4	272	314	24,485	25,223	6,370	7,458	2.0

Source: County Business Patterns, 1992/93, CBP-92/93-1, U.S. Department of Commerce, Washington, D.C., April 1995. SIC categories for which data were suppressed or not available for both 1992 and 1993 are not displayed. The employment columns represent mid-March employment in the year. Pay per employee is calculated by dividing 1st Quarter payroll, annualized, by mid-March employment. The columns headed "% State" show the county's percentage of the state total for the SIC in 1993; for example, 0.9% for SIC 6030 means that the county had 0.9 percent of the state's total establishments (or payroll) in SIC 6030 in 1993. A dash (-) is used to indicate that data are not available or cannot be calculated; nec means not elsewhere classified.

Continued on next page.

SIC	Industry	No. Establishments			Employment		Pay / Employee		Annual Payroll ($ 000)		
		1992	1993	% State	1992	1993	1992	1993	1992	1993	% State
GREENE, MO - [continued]									13,027	13,559	*3.7*
6330	Fire, marine, and casualty insurance	29	18	*4.3*	534	546	23,738	23,678	284	1,336	*5.8*
6370	Pension, health, and welfare funds	6	7	*4.7*	21	71	9,143	13,465	17,431	18,087	*4.7*
6400	Insurance agents, brokers, and service	199	222	*6.8*	815	828	20,344	20,502	17,300	19,813	*4.4*
6500	Real estate	237	257	*5.9*	1,123	1,282	13,485	11,710	4,843	6,269	*4.2*
6510	Real estate operators and lessors	111	139	*7.2*	386	606	11,171	9,432	10,208	12,323	*5.2*
6530	Real estate agents and managers	91	93	*5.1*	607	613	14,801	13,866	1,199	633	*2.9*
6552	Subdividers and developers, n.e.c.	11	16	*6.8*	66	21	15,273	17,524	384	388	*2.6*
6553	Cemetery subdividers and developers	6	6	*3.8*	31	29	9,290	9,931	885	770	*0.4*
6700	Holding and other investment offices	17	16	*2.9*	35	36	21,143	18,667	-	590	*0.3*
6710	Holding offices	4	4	*2.0*	-	10	-	44,800	-	124	*0.7*
6732	Educational, religious, etc. trusts	5	6	*6.2*	-	10	-	12,000	19	32	*0.6*
6733	Trusts, n.e.c.	3	3	*3.2*	5	12	3,200	2,667			
GRUNDY, MO											
60 –	**Finance, insurance, and real estate**	32	34	*0.3*	139	127	18,504	19,685	2,730	2,753	*0.1*
6000	Depository institutions	8	7	*0.3*	94	75	18,638	19,840	1,786	1,705	*0.2*
6400	Insurance agents, brokers, and service	11	11	*0.3*	-	25	-	11,200	-	307	*0.1*
6500	Real estate	10	12	*0.3*	12	-	7,333	-	103	-	*-*
6510	Real estate operators and lessors	3	5	*0.3*	3	6	4,000	4,667	12	24	*0.0*
6530	Real estate agents and managers	5	5	*0.3*	8	13	9,000	13,846	78	194	*0.1*
HARRISON, MO											
60 –	**Finance, insurance, and real estate**	24	24	*0.2*	118	115	14,881	15,270	1,741	1,767	*0.0*
6000	Depository institutions	8	8	*0.4*	83	84	17,542	16,762	1,416	1,416	*0.1*
6020	Commercial banks	7	8	*0.6*	-	84	-	16,762	-	1,416	*0.2*
6400	Insurance agents, brokers, and service	6	6	*0.2*	11	13	12,000	14,154	148	171	*0.0*
6510	Real estate operators and lessors	2	3	*0.2*	-	6	-	2,667	-	16	*0.0*
6530	Real estate agents and managers	4	4	*0.2*	10	5	8,000	14,400	78	74	*0.0*
HENRY, MO											
60 –	**Finance, insurance, and real estate**	50	51	*0.4*	214	214	18,112	17,813	4,298	4,113	*0.1*
6000	Depository institutions	15	15	*0.7*	116	119	17,000	15,294	2,068	2,062	*0.2*
6400	Insurance agents, brokers, and service	17	15	*0.5*	59	58	21,831	23,586	1,451	1,390	*0.4*
6500	Real estate	12	14	*0.3*	22	19	12,000	9,474	419	231	*0.1*
6510	Real estate operators and lessors	4	7	*0.4*	4	7	7,000	6,286	33	43	*0.0*
6530	Real estate agents and managers	5	5	*0.3*	6	-	12,667	-	80	-	*-*
HICKORY, MO											
60 –	**Finance, insurance, and real estate**	17	16	*0.1*	61	40	10,820	8,600	674	382	*0.0*
6500	Real estate	10	10	*0.2*	16	16	2,500	3,000	51	52	*0.0*
6552	Subdividers and developers, n.e.c.	2	4	*1.7*	-	4	-	4,000	-	16	*0.1*
HOLT, MO											
60 –	**Finance, insurance, and real estate**	16	17	*0.1*	67	66	15,463	16,303	1,247	1,326	*0.0*
6000	Depository institutions	6	6	*0.3*	45	44	16,889	17,182	966	1,023	*0.1*
6020	Commercial banks	6	6	*0.4*	45	44	16,889	17,182	966	1,023	*0.1*
6400	Insurance agents, brokers, and service	6	7	*0.2*	8	8	15,500	17,000	124	139	*0.0*
HOWARD, MO											
60 –	**Finance, insurance, and real estate**	14	14	*0.1*	67	76	17,552	15,947	1,356	1,444	*0.0*
6000	Depository institutions	5	5	*0.2*	53	59	19,925	17,898	1,215	1,273	*0.1*
6020	Commercial banks	5	5	*0.3*	53	59	19,925	17,898	1,215	1,273	*0.2*
6400	Insurance agents, brokers, and service	6	6	*0.2*	9	10	9,333	9,200	96	102	*0.0*
HOWELL, MO											
60 –	**Finance, insurance, and real estate**	60	66	*0.5*	323	359	19,666	17,760	6,826	6,979	*0.2*
6000	Depository institutions	11	11	*0.5*	192	176	20,500	20,500	4,044	3,952	*0.4*
6100	Nondepository institutions	2	3	*0.5*	-	21	-	10,667	-	209	*0.1*

Source: County Business Patterns, 1992/93, CBP-92/93-1, U.S. Department of Commerce, Washington, D.C., April 1995. SIC categories for which data were suppressed or not available for both 1992 and 1993 are not displayed. The employment columns represent mid-March employment in the year. Pay per employee is calculated by dividing 1st Quarter payroll, annualized, by mid-March employment. The columns headed "% State" show the county's percentage of the state total for the SIC in 1993; for example, 0.9% for SIC 6030 means that the county had 0.9 percent of the state's total establishments (or payroll) in SIC 6030 in 1993. A dash (-) is used to indicate that data are not available or cannot be calculated; nec means not elsewhere classified.

Continued on next page.

SIC	Industry	No. Establishments			Employment		Pay / Employee		Annual Payroll ($ 000)		
		1992	1993	% State	1992	1993	1992	1993	1992	1993	% State
HOWELL, MO - [continued]											
6300	Insurance carriers	3	3	0.3	19	-	33,474	-	703	-	-
6330	Fire, marine, and casualty insurance	3	3	0.7	19	-	33,474	-	703	-	-
6400	Insurance agents, brokers, and service	22	26	0.8	41	48	18,537	16,750	772	851	0.2
6500	Real estate	19	20	0.5	54	97	10,593	9,196	792	1,203	0.3
6510	Real estate operators and lessors	9	9	0.5	23	64	7,826	7,188	232	512	0.3
6530	Real estate agents and managers	5	7	0.4	7	8	11,429	16,000	89	155	0.1
IRON, MO											
60 –	**Finance, insurance, and real estate**	19	19	0.2	89	91	13,708	13,890	1,300	1,432	0.0
6000	Depository institutions	7	6	0.3	66	58	16,061	15,310	1,138	972	0.1
6400	Insurance agents, brokers, and service	4	4	0.1	6	6	10,000	9,333	60	67	0.0
6500	Real estate	8	8	0.2	17	-	5,882	-	102	-	-
6510	Real estate operators and lessors	3	3	0.2	7	5	2,857	3,200	17	25	0.0
6530	Real estate agents and managers	2	3	0.2	-	5	-	4,000	-	17	0.0
JACKSON, MO											
60 –	**Finance, insurance, and real estate**	1,673	1,702	13.6	31,676	32,869	30,462	29,943	961,207	1,073,698	26.6
6000	Depository institutions	248	247	11.6	8,880	8,852	24,962	26,428	218,807	237,714	22.0
6020	Commercial banks	134	140	9.7	6,827	6,617	24,224	26,021	166,298	171,057	21.3
6030	Savings institutions	51	39	10.4	770	537	21,512	22,473	13,222	14,115	12.8
6100	Nondepository institutions	126	118	18.1	-	2,008	-	27,892	-	82,638	27.1
6140	Personal credit institutions	68	62	19.7	588	425	28,048	21,826	17,095	9,779	18.4
6150	Business credit institutions	18	17	20.7	100	101	53,160	36,238	8,203	3,847	6.1
6160	Mortgage bankers and brokers	36	39	17.4	599	1,482	33,763	29,063	27,688	69,012	38.0
6200	Security and commodity brokers	91	99	16.7	3,432	5,267	41,598	38,223	146,972	237,820	41.9
6210	Security brokers and dealers	53	54	14.6	980	913	68,143	72,276	69,210	78,152	21.9
6280	Security and commodity services	27	31	15.6	-	4,279	-	31,039	-	157,074	75.9
6300	Insurance carriers	209	186	18.6	8,353	8,588	33,039	30,522	257,718	257,463	26.5
6310	Life insurance	54	44	15.6	4,198	4,216	33,327	30,082	123,849	116,327	31.0
6321	Accident and health insurance	8	5	20.8	440	24	29,773	27,500	12,387	674	5.2
6324	Hospital and medical service plans	16	23	46.0	1,991	2,421	33,804	32,720	65,895	82,350	49.0
6330	Fire, marine, and casualty insurance	83	68	16.3	1,302	1,413	34,025	30,706	43,546	44,211	12.1
6360	Title insurance	11	11	17.7	227	274	25,780	24,540	6,678	8,004	34.3
6370	Pension, health, and welfare funds	30	32	21.6	165	237	28,000	22,245	4,421	5,829	25.1
6400	Insurance agents, brokers, and service	349	374	11.5	3,009	3,259	30,781	29,764	89,521	100,937	26.1
6500	Real estate	550	587	13.5	4,112	3,825	19,398	20,757	81,563	87,671	19.4
6510	Real estate operators and lessors	256	291	15.1	1,858	1,613	17,341	21,232	31,361	33,549	22.3
6530	Real estate agents and managers	206	244	13.5	1,730	1,724	21,593	20,984	38,641	40,312	17.0
6540	Title abstract offices	6	7	4.2	50	174	17,680	21,632	949	4,307	17.2
6552	Subdividers and developers, n.e.c.	27	28	11.9	120	119	13,567	15,529	2,148	3,208	14.8
6553	Cemetery subdividers and developers	10	13	8.3	162	189	19,284	17,545	3,326	6,249	41.1
6700	Holding and other investment offices	99	88	16.1	2,583	989	42,496	52,368	113,265	66,617	30.8
6710	Holding offices	34	30	15.0	643	744	53,033	58,769	40,065	57,537	34.1
6732	Educational, religious, etc. trusts	12	13	13.4	114	154	34,912	36,701	4,498	6,235	36.8
6733	Trusts, n.e.c.	28	26	27.7	453	53	33,042	18,491	14,205	1,109	19.2
6799	Investors, n.e.c.	12	11	13.4	61	12	33,574	21,333	2,296	282	3.8
JASPER, MO											
60 –	**Finance, insurance, and real estate**	198	233	1.9	1,350	1,403	19,508	19,193	27,762	27,799	0.7
6000	Depository institutions	39	39	1.8	635	655	21,317	21,166	13,157	13,808	1.3
6020	Commercial banks	30	30	2.1	588	602	21,796	21,781	12,396	12,981	1.6
6100	Nondepository institutions	5	6	0.9	-	24	-	24,833	-	814	0.3
6200	Security and commodity brokers	11	12	2.0	49	50	38,694	46,640	2,177	2,427	0.4
6300	Insurance carriers	22	15	1.5	214	131	21,028	23,389	4,727	2,927	0.3
6310	Life insurance	7	6	2.1	112	69	22,786	22,783	2,584	1,309	0.3
6330	Fire, marine, and casualty insurance	10	6	1.4	35	-	26,629	-	1,008	-	-
6400	Insurance agents, brokers, and service	54	57	1.7	168	186	18,548	18,258	3,188	3,334	0.9
6500	Real estate	60	93	2.1	216	259	12,056	11,166	2,729	3,364	0.7

Source: County Business Patterns, 1992/93, CBP-92/93-1, U.S. Department of Commerce, Washington, D.C., April 1995. SIC categories for which data were suppressed or not available for both 1992 and 1993 are not displayed. The employment columns represent mid-March employment in the year. Pay per employee is calculated by dividing 1st Quarter payroll, annualized, by mid-March employment. The columns headed "% State" show the county's percentage of the state total for the SIC in 1993; for example, 0.9% for SIC 6030 means that the county had 0.9 percent of the state's total establishments (or payroll) in SIC 6030 in 1993. A dash (-) is used to indicate that data are not available or cannot be calculated; nec means not elsewhere classified.

Continued on next page.

SIC	Industry	No. Establishments			Employment		Pay / Employee		Annual Payroll ($ 000)		
		1992	1993	% State	1992	1993	1992	1993	1992	1993	% Sta
JASPER, MO - [continued]											
6510	Real estate operators and lessors	28	54	2.8	96	137	10,292	8,438	1,072	1,456	1.0
6530	Real estate agents and managers	22	27	1.5	76	73	11,789	13,315	848	963	0.4
6552	Subdividers and developers, n.e.c.	2	5	2.1	-	5	-	7,200	-	51	0.2
6700	Holding and other investment offices	7	11	2.0	-	98	-	8,000	-	1,125	0.5
JEFFERSON, MO											
60-	**Finance, insurance, and real estate**	209	211	1.7	1,076	1,076	18,654	17,929	21,839	21,758	0.5
6000	Depository institutions	35	38	1.8	532	523	18,038	17,797	9,385	9,175	0.9
6020	Commercial banks	27	29	2.0	466	454	18,120	18,194	8,191	8,070	1.0
6030	Savings institutions	5	5	1.3	55	55	19,273	17,018	1,100	989	0.9
6060	Credit unions	3	4	1.8	11	14	8,364	8,000	94	116	
6100	Nondepository institutions	10	9	1.4	41	40	18,537	12,300	788	543	0.2
6140	Personal credit institutions	7	7	2.2	29	-	20,000	-	584	-	
6300	Insurance carriers	16	11	1.1	96	52	30,250	33,000	2,892	1,837	0.2
6310	Life insurance	4	3	1.1	43	31	37,302	31,355	1,456	1,008	0.3
6400	Insurance agents, brokers, and service	49	50	1.5	130	141	15,323	15,489	2,262	2,596	0.7
6500	Real estate	93	96	2.2	264	307	15,924	16,013	5,806	6,927	1.5
6510	Real estate operators and lessors	36	43	2.2	69	121	10,667	14,314	867	2,030	1.4
6530	Real estate agents and managers	30	35	1.9	74	71	14,378	15,606	1,241	1,501	0.6
6552	Subdividers and developers, n.e.c.	10	9	3.8	21	-	18,667		461	-	
6553	Cemetery subdividers and developers	3	7	4.5	16	16	9,000	7,750	138	145	1.0
JOHNSON, MO											
60-	**Finance, insurance, and real estate**	67	71	0.6	350	340	18,080	18,071	6,532	6,726	0.2
6000	Depository institutions	16	16	0.8	192	205	21,062	20,117	4,249	4,513	0.4
6020	Commercial banks	13	13	0.9	162	174	21,605	21,034	3,678	3,951	0.5
6100	Nondepository institutions	3	3	0.5	8	5	27,500	21,600	182	132	0.0
6140	Personal credit institutions	3	3	1.0	8	5	27,500	21,600	182	132	0.2
6300	Insurance carriers	6	1	0.1	18	-	13,333	-	250	-	-
6400	Insurance agents, brokers, and service	15	22	0.7	43	60	13,395	13,933	594	775	0.2
6500	Real estate	21	24	0.6	71	57	9,972	9,684	814	633	0.1
6510	Real estate operators and lessors	7	11	0.6	35	-	4,686	-	181	-	-
6530	Real estate agents and managers	4	6	0.3	7	10	23,429	22,800	199	276	0.1
6553	Cemetery subdividers and developers	4	4	2.6	13	-	7,077	-	98	-	-
KNOX, MO											
60-	**Finance, insurance, and real estate**	9	10	0.1	53	56	14,113	13,214	745	749	0.0
6500	Real estate	3	4	0.1	2	2	6,000	6,000	14	15	0.0
LACLEDE, MO											
60-	**Finance, insurance, and real estate**	50	57	0.5	339	320	18,065	16,762	7,146	5,492	0.1
6000	Depository institutions	8	10	0.5	217	207	16,719	18,667	3,603	3,861	0.4
6300	Insurance carriers	4	1	0.1	10	-	14,000	-	636	-	-
6400	Insurance agents, brokers, and service	16	20	0.6	37	57	11,351	10,947	487	633	0.2
6500	Real estate	17	21	0.5	36	39	11,667	9,949	455	493	0.1
6510	Real estate operators and lessors	7	10	0.5	15	20	8,533	9,400	143	213	0.1
6530	Real estate agents and managers	5	7	0.4	6	-	21,333	-	165	-	-
LAFAYETTE, MO											
60-	**Finance, insurance, and real estate**	65	66	0.5	363	369	15,835	16,553	6,658	6,585	0.2
6000	Depository institutions	18	18	0.8	197	200	17,604	18,800	4,122	3,971	0.4
6020	Commercial banks	15	15	1.0	179	180	17,274	18,622	3,693	3,517	0.4
6030	Savings institutions	3	3	0.8	18	20	20,889	20,400	429	454	0.4
6400	Insurance agents, brokers, and service	25	29	0.9	72	89	13,667	12,584	1,085	1,230	0.3

Source: County Business Patterns, 1992/93, CBP-92/93-1, U.S. Department of Commerce, Washington, D.C., April 1995. SIC categories for which data were suppressed or not available for both 1992 a 1993 are *not* displayed. The employment columns represent mid-March employment in the year. Pay per employee is calculated by dividing 1st Quarter payroll, annualized, by mid-March employment. The columns headed "% State" show the county's percentage of the state total for the SIC in 1993; for example, 0.9% for SIC 6030 means that the county had 0.9 percent of the state's total establishment (or payroll) in SIC 6030 in 1993. A dash (-) is used to indicate that data are not available or cannot be calculated; *nec* means not elsewhere classified.

Continued on next page.

SIC	Industry	No. Establishments			Employment		Pay / Employee		Annual Payroll ($ 000)		
		1992	1993	% State	1992	1993	1992	1993	1992	1993	% State
LAFAYETTE, MO - [continued]											
6500	Real estate	14	13	0.3	56	47	10,500	10,128	629	579	0.1
6510	Real estate operators and lessors	7	4	0.2	20	8	8,800	9,000	199	72	0.0
6530	Real estate agents and managers	1	4	0.2	-	10	-	6,800	-	102	0.0
LAWRENCE, MO											
60 –	**Finance, insurance, and real estate**	45	44	0.4	214	228	15,028	16,561	3,195	3,866	0.1
6000	Depository institutions	12	13	0.6	131	145	16,214	17,214	1,959	2,520	0.2
6400	Insurance agents, brokers, and service	13	13	0.4	34	39	13,294	13,231	528	565	0.1
6500	Real estate	16	15	0.3	36	30	7,889	7,200	302	279	0.1
6510	Real estate operators and lessors	6	7	0.4	18	12	4,000	4,333	71	86	0.1
6530	Real estate agents and managers	7	6	0.3	11	-	15,636	-	181	-	-
LEWIS, MO											
60 –	**Finance, insurance, and real estate**	21	36	0.3	115	117	16,243	14,667	2,153	2,062	0.1
6000	Depository institutions	8	8	0.4	73	74	18,740	15,946	1,602	1,323	0.1
6400	Insurance agents, brokers, and service	6	6	0.2	-	10	-	9,600	-	124	0.0
6500	Real estate	5	20	0.5	10	-	4,800	-	55	-	-
6510	Real estate operators and lessors	4	19	1.0	-	12	-	5,333	-	84	0.1
LINCOLN, MO											
60 –	**Finance, insurance, and real estate**	40	44	0.4	209	219	18,450	17,242	4,671	4,473	0.1
6000	Depository institutions	11	11	0.5	144	146	20,194	18,959	3,672	3,287	0.3
6300	Insurance carriers	3	4	0.4	12	13	18,000	16,923	236	199	0.0
6400	Insurance agents, brokers, and service	11	13	0.4	24	28	15,167	13,143	380	507	0.1
6500	Real estate	15	16	0.4	29	32	12,690	13,125	383	480	0.1
6510	Real estate operators and lessors	3	6	0.3	3	-	4,000	-	12	-	-
6530	Real estate agents and managers	8	8	0.4	18	16	13,556	15,500	256	291	0.1
LINN, MO											
60 –	**Finance, insurance, and real estate**	37	36	0.3	190	169	17,368	17,775	3,557	2,793	0.1
6000	Depository institutions	11	11	0.5	121	115	19,041	19,513	2,405	2,155	0.2
6400	Insurance agents, brokers, and service	12	12	0.4	22	22	13,455	13,273	337	340	0.1
6500	Real estate	9	7	0.2	13	13	6,769	6,769	103	98	0.0
6510	Real estate operators and lessors	2	3	0.2	-	5	-	2,400	-	12	0.0
6530	Real estate agents and managers	3	2	0.1	4	-	5,000	-	18	-	-
LIVINGSTON, MO											
60 –	**Finance, insurance, and real estate**	41	40	0.3	255	252	17,820	20,032	5,206	5,573	0.1
6000	Depository institutions	6	6	0.3	144	154	17,250	18,649	3,068	3,529	0.3
6300	Insurance carriers	9	7	0.7	44	24	17,636	24,333	692	585	0.1
6370	Pension, health, and welfare funds	4	3	2.0	18	-	12,667	-	130	6	0.0
6400	Insurance agents, brokers, and service	13	15	0.5	32	36	17,125	16,889	575	602	0.2
6500	Real estate	7	7	0.2	17	20	8,235	7,000	168	163	0.0
6510	Real estate operators and lessors	5	4	0.2	-	9	-	3,111	-	28	0.0
MCDONALD, MO											
60 –	**Finance, insurance, and real estate**	17	19	0.2	108	111	19,259	18,919	2,046	1,799	0.0
6000	Depository institutions	7	7	0.3	93	87	20,516	21,793	1,841	1,530	0.1
6020	Commercial banks	7	7	0.5	93	87	20,516	21,793	1,841	1,530	0.2
6400	Insurance agents, brokers, and service	4	7	0.2	5	11	5,600	10,909	31	144	0.0
6500	Real estate	4	5	0.1	-	13	-	6,462	-	125	0.0
MACON, MO											
60 –	**Finance, insurance, and real estate**	34	35	0.3	181	189	18,829	19,132	3,379	3,463	0.1
6000	Depository institutions	8	8	0.4	121	126	23,669	23,810	2,767	2,878	0.3
6400	Insurance agents, brokers, and service	10	10	0.3	19	20	7,789	8,400	193	182	0.0
6500	Real estate	12	13	0.3	-	28	-	7,286	-	207	0.0

Source: County Business Patterns, 1992/93, CBP-92/93-1, U.S. Department of Commerce, Washington, D.C., April 1995. SIC categories for which data were suppressed or not available for both 1992 and 1993 are *not* displayed. The employment columns represent mid-March employment in the year. Pay per employee is calculated by dividing 1st Quarter payroll, annualized, by mid-March employment. The columns headed "% State" show the county's percentage of the state total for the SIC in 1993; for example, 0.9% for SIC 6030 means that the county had 0.9 percent of the state's total establishments (or payroll) in SIC 6030 in 1993. A dash (-) is used to indicate that data are not available or cannot be calculated; *nec* means not elsewhere classified.

Continued on next page.

SIC	Industry	No. Establishments			Employment		Pay / Employee		Annual Payroll ($ 000)		
		1992	1993	% State	1992	1993	1992	1993	1992	1993	% State
MACON, MO - [continued]											
6510	Real estate operators and lessors	3	4	0.2	10	8	6,800	10,000	68	81	0.1
6530	Real estate agents and managers	4	3	0.2	-	7	-	4,571	-	37	0.0
6553	Cemetery subdividers and developers	3	3	1.9	5	2	2,400	4,000	15	14	0.1
MADISON, MO											
60 –	**Finance, insurance, and real estate**	16	16	0.1	116	-	15,310	-	1,778	-	-
6000	Depository institutions	8	8	0.4	91	104	15,560	15,154	1,421	1,586	0.1
6400	Insurance agents, brokers, and service	6	6	0.2	-	20	-	15,600	-	346	0.1
MARIES, MO											
60 –	**Finance, insurance, and real estate**	11	13	0.1	51	54	18,353	21,111	990	1,175	0.0
6400	Insurance agents, brokers, and service	4	4	0.1	6	5	8,667	6,400	43	45	0.0
MARION, MO											
60 –	**Finance, insurance, and real estate**	80	78	0.6	354	340	15,797	17,447	5,876	6,000	0.1
6000	Depository institutions	15	17	0.8	144	146	15,750	18,795	2,490	2,652	0.2
6020	Commercial banks	4	5	0.3	88	87	16,318	18,621	1,577	1,639	0.2
6030	Savings institutions	7	7	1.9	51	51	15,529	20,863	868	959	0.9
6060	Credit unions	4	5	2.2	5	8	8,000	7,500	45	54	-
6300	Insurance carriers	7	3	0.3	43	-	17,767	-	734	-	-
6310	Life insurance	3	1	0.4	34	-	18,824	-	629	-	-
6400	Insurance agents, brokers, and service	31	31	1.0	55	63	12,873	12,000	897	964	0.2
6500	Real estate	18	19	0.4	34	-	11,412	-	534	-	-
6510	Real estate operators and lessors	6	5	0.3	8	7	11,000	16,571	176	107	0.1
6530	Real estate agents and managers	6	10	0.6	7	13	13,143	9,538	101	136	0.1
6553	Cemetery subdividers and developers	3	3	1.9	16	18	9,500	9,778	176	194	1.3
MERCER, MO											
60 –	**Finance, insurance, and real estate**	9	9	0.1	-	-	-	-	-	-	-
6400	Insurance agents, brokers, and service	3	4	0.1	7	7	10,286	10,286	71	94	0.0
MILLER, MO											
60 –	**Finance, insurance, and real estate**	49	59	0.5	284	286	16,394	18,336	5,137	7,518	0.2
6000	Depository institutions	11	11	0.5	120	122	22,633	20,689	2,787	2,661	0.2
6400	Insurance agents, brokers, and service	10	10	0.3	24	27	13,000	11,704	332	377	0.1
6500	Real estate	24	34	0.8	124	127	10,613	15,370	1,838	3,981	0.9
6510	Real estate operators and lessors	4	4	0.2	7	12	6,286	9,333	63	127	0.1
6530	Real estate agents and managers	11	19	1.1	98	96	7,224	16,875	1,043	2,446	1.0
6540	Title abstract offices	2	3	1.8	-	12	-	11,000	-	155	0.6
6552	Subdividers and developers, n.e.c.	4	6	2.5	12	4	41,333	21,000	626	251	1.2
MISSISSIPPI, MO											
60 –	**Finance, insurance, and real estate**	17	18	0.1	96	96	17,208	21,583	1,825	1,963	0.0
6000	Depository institutions	4	5	0.2	65	72	19,446	24,222	1,390	1,597	0.1
6400	Insurance agents, brokers, and service	7	9	0.3	21	21	11,810	14,286	286	335	0.1
MONITEAU, MO											
60 –	**Finance, insurance, and real estate**	21	24	0.2	108	106	17,852	17,925	2,028	2,093	0.1
6000	Depository institutions	9	9	0.4	85	81	20,376	21,136	1,837	1,863	0.2
6400	Insurance agents, brokers, and service	6	8	0.2	12	14	9,667	8,000	118	138	0.0
6510	Real estate operators and lessors	3	3	0.2	-	4	-	4,000	-	16	0.0
MONROE, MO											
60 –	**Finance, insurance, and real estate**	15	17	0.1	68	69	20,176	19,942	1,379	1,391	0.0

Source: County Business Patterns, 1992/93, CBP-92/93-1, U.S. Department of Commerce, Washington, D.C., April 1995. SIC categories for which data were suppressed or not available for both 1992 and 1993 are *not* displayed. The employment columns represent mid-March employment in the year. Pay per employee is calculated by dividing 1st Quarter payroll, annualized, by mid-March employment. The columns headed "% State" show the county's percentage of the state total for the SIC in 1993; for example, 0.9% for SIC 6030 means that the county had 0.9 percent of the state's total establishments (or payroll) in SIC 6030 in 1993. A dash (-) is used to indicate that data are not available or cannot be calculated; *nec* means not elsewhere classified.

Continued on next page.

SIC	Industry	No. Establishments			Employment		Pay / Employee		Annual Payroll ($ 000)		
		1992	1993	% State	1992	1993	1992	1993	1992	1993	% State
MONROE, MO - [continued]											
6000	Depository institutions	5	5	0.2	53	53	21,358	20,755	1,097	1,077	0.1
6300	Insurance carriers	3	1	0.1	4	-	8,000	-	37	-	-
6500	Real estate	4	6	0.1	-	6	-	13,333	-	92	0.0
MONTGOMERY, MO											
60 –	**Finance, insurance, and real estate**	23	23	0.2	131	143	18,137	17,650	2,470	2,668	0.1
6000	Depository institutions	7	7	0.3	87	94	17,471	17,404	1,601	1,716	0.2
6020	Commercial banks	7	7	0.5	87	94	17,471	17,404	1,601	1,716	0.2
6400	Insurance agents, brokers, and service	6	7	0.2	-	19	-	24,421	-	505	0.1
6500	Real estate	6	6	0.1	10	15	7,200	6,933	75	129	0.0
MORGAN, MO											
60 –	**Finance, insurance, and real estate**	31	31	0.2	117	111	14,256	14,486	1,923	1,910	0.0
6000	Depository institutions	7	6	0.3	77	71	15,896	17,014	1,449	1,460	0.1
6400	Insurance agents, brokers, and service	5	6	0.2	7	7	18,286	13,143	103	95	0.0
6510	Real estate operators and lessors	6	7	0.4	5	6	8,000	4,667	44	27	0.0
6530	Real estate agents and managers	8	7	0.4	15	12	13,067	13,000	208	170	0.1
NEW MADRID, MO											
60 –	**Finance, insurance, and real estate**	30	29	0.2	193	169	16,580	17,136	3,464	3,184	0.1
6000	Depository institutions	10	11	0.5	111	115	19,964	19,235	2,375	2,359	0.2
6400	Insurance agents, brokers, and service	10	10	0.3	24	23	11,333	13,217	278	329	0.1
NEWTON, MO											
60 –	**Finance, insurance, and real estate**	79	82	0.7	366	417	16,077	17,487	6,629	7,687	0.2
6000	Depository institutions	17	17	0.8	184	200	18,304	18,500	3,570	3,900	0.4
6100	Nondepository institutions	3	5	0.8	17	19	24,706	26,947	449	476	0.2
6200	Security and commodity brokers	3	2	0.3	8	-	21,500	-	222	-	-
6210	Security brokers and dealers	3	2	0.5	8	-	21,500	-	222	-	-
6400	Insurance agents, brokers, and service	24	25	0.8	54	72	12,963	19,889	837	1,352	0.4
6500	Real estate	29	28	0.6	67	68	9,254	8,176	789	737	0.2
6510	Real estate operators and lessors	13	14	0.7	-	35	-	4,914	-	224	0.1
6530	Real estate agents and managers	6	6	0.3	14	13	7,429	10,154	147	184	0.1
6553	Cemetery subdividers and developers	4	4	2.6	4	4	3,000	4,000	22	26	0.2
NODAWAY, MO											
60 –	**Finance, insurance, and real estate**	41	44	0.4	224	296	19,143	18,081	4,081	5,298	0.1
6000	Depository institutions	10	10	0.5	143	141	20,168	21,163	2,633	3,197	0.3
6300	Insurance carriers	4	3	0.3	-	84	-	13,905	-	756	0.1
6400	Insurance agents, brokers, and service	10	15	0.5	22	25	21,273	16,320	392	449	0.1
6500	Real estate	14	14	0.3	43	-	13,860	-	668	-	-
6510	Real estate operators and lessors	6	8	0.4	13	15	6,462	6,133	95	108	0.1
6530	Real estate agents and managers	4	4	0.2	20	21	23,000	16,952	525	413	0.2
OREGON, MO											
60 –	**Finance, insurance, and real estate**	14	16	0.1	59	71	16,881	15,099	1,080	1,110	0.0
6000	Depository institutions	4	4	0.2	43	52	19,535	16,462	891	889	0.1
6400	Insurance agents, brokers, and service	6	7	0.2	8	9	10,500	9,333	91	82	0.0
6500	Real estate	4	5	0.1	8	10	9,000	13,200	98	139	0.0
OSAGE, MO											
60 –	**Finance, insurance, and real estate**	17	15	0.1	83	85	19,325	19,765	1,716	1,854	0.0
6000	Depository institutions	7	7	0.3	66	70	21,879	22,114	1,566	1,705	0.2
6020	Commercial banks	7	7	0.5	66	70	21,879	22,114	1,566	1,705	0.2
6500	Real estate	5	3	0.1	8	6	7,000	7,333	57	49	0.0

Source: County Business Patterns, 1992/93, CBP-92/93-1, U.S. Department of Commerce, Washington, D.C., April 1995. SIC categories for which data were suppressed or not available for both 1992 and 1993 are not displayed. The employment columns represent mid-March employment in the year. Pay per employee is calculated by dividing 1st Quarter payroll, annualized, by mid-March employment. The columns headed "% State" show the county's percentage of the state total for the SIC in 1993; for example, 0.9% for SIC 6030 means that the county had 0.9 percent of the state's total establishments (or payroll) in SIC 6030 in 1993. A dash (-) is used to indicate that data are not available or cannot be calculated; nec means not elsewhere classified.

SIC	Industry	No. Establishments			Employment		Pay / Employee		Annual Payroll ($ 000)		
		1992	1993	% State	1992	1993	1992	1993	1992	1993	% State
OZARK, MO											
60 –	**Finance, insurance, and real estate**	14	13	0.1	128	88	8,656	18,773	1,216	1,867	0.0
6400	Insurance agents, brokers, and service	3	4	0.1	-	6	-	13,333	-	84	0.0
6500	Real estate	5	5	0.1	74	-	2,000	-	221	-	-
PEMISCOT, MO											
60 –	**Finance, insurance, and real estate**	26	27	0.2	147	176	21,551	19,341	3,550	3,559	0.1
6000	Depository institutions	9	9	0.4	104	102	22,423	18,157	2,646	2,205	0.2
6400	Insurance agents, brokers, and service	11	11	0.3	32	34	24,125	28,235	825	1,061	0.3
6500	Real estate	3	4	0.1	6	-	9,333	-	62	-	-
PERRY, MO											
60 –	**Finance, insurance, and real estate**	33	34	0.3	223	218	23,265	23,321	4,501	4,783	0.1
6000	Depository institutions	8	8	0.4	138	137	19,855	21,693	2,678	2,858	0.3
6400	Insurance agents, brokers, and service	9	9	0.3	44	39	26,636	16,308	950	771	0.2
6500	Real estate	10	11	0.3	25	21	9,280	11,048	266	259	0.1
6530	Real estate agents and managers	3	5	0.3	3	7	8,000	9,143	25	72	0.0
6700	Holding and other investment offices	2	3	0.6	-	11	-	91,273	-	646	0.3
PETTIS, MO											
60 –	**Finance, insurance, and real estate**	91	97	0.8	604	551	17,073	17,459	10,315	10,622	0.3
6000	Depository institutions	21	22	1.0	370	335	16,011	16,239	5,802	5,863	0.5
6020	Commercial banks	18	18	1.2	301	323	16,651	16,396	5,356	5,684	0.7
6300	Insurance carriers	7	4	0.4	53	36	23,774	27,556	1,265	1,008	0.1
6400	Insurance agents, brokers, and service	27	28	0.9	83	71	19,373	20,620	1,346	1,440	0.4
6500	Real estate	27	33	0.8	61	73	8,197	7,781	554	646	0.1
6510	Real estate operators and lessors	15	20	1.0	39	48	6,359	6,167	275	328	0.2
6530	Real estate agents and managers	8	11	0.6	11	-	10,909	-	138	-	-
PHELPS, MO											
60 –	**Finance, insurance, and real estate**	67	68	0.5	378	380	18,730	17,853	7,012	7,486	0.2
6000	Depository institutions	16	16	0.8	214	208	20,879	18,769	4,167	4,351	0.4
6020	Commercial banks	11	11	0.8	170	172	21,976	19,116	3,422	3,611	0.4
6100	Nondepository institutions	4	3	0.5	10	10	18,000	16,800	193	190	0.1
6140	Personal credit institutions	3	3	1.0	-	10	-	16,800	-	190	0.4
6300	Insurance carriers	3	4	0.4	11	20	22,182	20,600	263	415	0.0
6330	Fire, marine, and casualty insurance	3	3	0.7	11	-	22,182	-	263	-	-
6400	Insurance agents, brokers, and service	21	22	0.7	53	57	17,208	17,684	929	1,088	0.3
6500	Real estate	18	17	0.4	48	43	9,917	11,442	607	522	0.1
6510	Real estate operators and lessors	5	7	0.4	21	14	7,810	8,000	221	121	0.1
6530	Real estate agents and managers	10	9	0.5	13	-	5,846	-	102	-	-
PIKE, MO											
60 –	**Finance, insurance, and real estate**	30	31	0.2	160	166	18,300	18,675	3,427	3,224	0.1
6000	Depository institutions	9	9	0.4	103	107	21,087	21,383	2,564	2,325	0.2
6400	Insurance agents, brokers, and service	7	9	0.3	17	23	13,647	11,826	246	312	0.1
6500	Real estate	8	7	0.2	25	20	11,200	13,400	338	282	0.1
PLATTE, MO											
60 –	**Finance, insurance, and real estate**	125	139	1.1	899	905	23,746	27,275	21,942	25,761	0.6
6000	Depository institutions	27	24	1.1	424	398	21,028	25,126	9,653	9,971	0.9
6020	Commercial banks	21	19	1.3	286	259	18,503	16,618	5,491	4,695	0.6
6200	Security and commodity brokers	11	12	2.0	212	201	34,642	41,891	6,654	8,445	1.5
6310	Life insurance	3	2	0.7	31	-	27,484	-	774	-	-
6400	Insurance agents, brokers, and service	27	32	1.0	56	90	22,500	21,511	1,363	2,175	0.6

Source: County Business Patterns, 1992/93, CBP-92/93-1, U.S. Department of Commerce, Washington, D.C., April 1995. SIC categories for which data were suppressed or not available for both 1992 and 1993 are not displayed. The employment columns represent mid-March employment in the year. Pay per employee is calculated by dividing 1st Quarter payroll, annualized, by mid-March employment. The columns headed "% State" show the county's percentage of the state total for the SIC in 1993; for example, 0.9% for SIC 6030 means that the county had 0.9 percent of the state's total establishments (or payroll) in SIC 6030 in 1993. A dash (-) is used to indicate that data are not available or cannot be calculated; nec means not elsewhere classified.

Continued on next page.

SIC	Industry	No. Establishments			Employment		Pay / Employee		Annual Payroll ($ 000)		
		1992	1993	% State	1992	1993	1992	1993	1992	1993	% State
PLATTE, MO - [continued]											
6500	Real estate	47	60	*1.4*	127	134	11,276	12,060	1,748	2,180	*0.5*
6510	Real estate operators and lessors	23	28	*1.5*	74	76	9,676	10,263	793	914	*0.6*
6530	Real estate agents and managers	17	21	*1.2*	43	47	13,395	14,043	718	933	*0.4*
POLK, MO											
60 –	**Finance, insurance, and real estate**	36	32	*0.3*	210	222	14,305	14,288	3,352	3,612	*0.1*
6000	Depository institutions	9	9	*0.4*	143	148	16,112	16,838	2,566	2,772	*0.3*
6300	Insurance carriers	3	1	*0.1*	3	-	9,333	-	42	-	-
6400	Insurance agents, brokers, and service	12	11	*0.3*	38	34	7,263	8,235	277	309	*0.1*
6500	Real estate	9	8	*0.2*	19	21	7,579	7,429	188	193	*0.0*
6510	Real estate operators and lessors	5	5	*0.3*	7	-	2,857	-	43	-	-
PULASKI, MO											
60 –	**Finance, insurance, and real estate**	54	59	*0.5*	300	310	16,133	16,465	5,100	5,097	*0.1*
6000	Depository institutions	15	17	*0.8*	208	213	17,288	17,991	3,830	3,671	*0.3*
6020	Commercial banks	9	9	*0.6*	150	147	18,747	19,483	2,912	2,653	*0.3*
6090	Functions closely related to banking	3	5	*7.4*	-	17	-	10,353	-	201	*0.3*
6200	Security and commodity brokers	2	4	*0.7*	-	4	-	9,000	-	41	*0.0*
6400	Insurance agents, brokers, and service	13	16	*0.5*	27	28	10,222	12,857	326	448	*0.1*
6500	Real estate	22	17	*0.4*	52	46	11,923	10,087	624	526	*0.1*
6510	Real estate operators and lessors	9	7	*0.4*	19	16	10,316	8,500	193	139	*0.1*
6530	Real estate agents and managers	10	9	*0.5*	21	-	14,286	-	305	-	-
PUTNAM, MO											
60 –	**Finance, insurance, and real estate**	15	14	*0.1*	78	81	11,846	12,790	993	1,132	*0.0*
6000	Depository institutions	3	3	*0.1*	51	-	15,294	-	832	-	-
6020	Commercial banks	3	3	*0.2*	51	-	15,294	-	832	-	-
6400	Insurance agents, brokers, and service	5	4	*0.1*	9	9	7,111	5,333	64	56	*0.0*
6500	Real estate	6	6	*0.1*	-	21	-	6,476	-	135	*0.0*
6530	Real estate agents and managers	1	3	*0.2*	-	14	-	4,857	-	82	*0.0*
RALLS, MO											
60 –	**Finance, insurance, and real estate**	10	9	*0.1*	45	45	23,111	20,178	1,087	1,113	*0.0*
6500	Real estate	3	3	*0.1*	7	7	6,286	6,857	45	57	*0.0*
RANDOLPH, MO											
60 –	**Finance, insurance, and real estate**	47	47	*0.4*	517	365	17,702	18,608	9,272	7,095	*0.2*
6000	Depository institutions	13	14	*0.7*	147	145	19,701	20,662	2,868	2,988	*0.3*
6300	Insurance carriers	5	3	*0.3*	23	-	15,478	-	370	-	-
6400	Insurance agents, brokers, and service	13	14	*0.4*	44	49	12,273	14,204	538	715	*0.2*
6500	Real estate	8	11	*0.3*	28	33	15,857	14,061	478	561	*0.1*
RAY, MO											
60 –	**Finance, insurance, and real estate**	22	23	*0.2*	139	124	19,281	19,645	2,784	2,675	*0.1*
6000	Depository institutions	9	9	*0.4*	106	95	21,321	20,042	2,282	2,050	*0.2*
6400	Insurance agents, brokers, and service	3	4	*0.1*	9	6	5,333	7,333	48	59	*0.0*
6500	Real estate	7	8	*0.2*	15	-	14,400	-	218	-	-
6510	Real estate operators and lessors	1	3	*0.2*	-	10	-	5,200	-	61	*0.0*
6530	Real estate agents and managers	3	2	*0.1*	5	-	4,800	-	22	-	-
REYNOLDS, MO											
60 –	**Finance, insurance, and real estate**	8	11	*0.1*	25	34	8,160	13,294	316	517	*0.0*
6500	Real estate	2	5	*0.1*	-	10	-	13,600	-	137	*0.0*
RIPLEY, MO											
60 –	**Finance, insurance, and real estate**	18	18	*0.1*	87	94	17,701	16,298	1,627	1,631	*0.0*
6000	Depository institutions	8	8	*0.4*	67	75	20,896	18,560	1,428	1,477	*0.1*
6400	Insurance agents, brokers, and service	5	5	*0.2*	12	13	7,333	7,385	94	95	*0.0*

Source: County Business Patterns, 1992/93, CBP-92/93-1, U.S. Department of Commerce, Washington, D.C., April 1995. SIC categories for which data were suppressed or not available for both 1992 and 1993 are *not* displayed. The employment columns represent mid-March employment in the year. Pay per employee is calculated by dividing 1st Quarter payroll, annualized, by mid-March employment. The columns headed "% State" show the county's percentage of the state total for the SIC in 1993; for example, 0.9% for SIC 6030 means that the county had 0.9 percent of the state's total establishments (or payroll) in SIC 6030 in 1993. A dash (-) is used to indicate that data are not available or cannot be calculated; *nec* means not elsewhere classified.

SIC	Industry	No. Establishments			Employment		Pay / Employee		Annual Payroll ($ 000)		
		1992	1993	% State	1992	1993	1992	1993	1992	1993	% State
ST. CHARLES, MO											
60 –	**Finance, insurance, and real estate**	367	403	*3.2*	2,069	2,151	20,613	20,880	44,676	48,385	*1.2*
6000	Depository institutions	48	49	*2.3*	707	683	18,806	20,047	13,266	12,888	*1.2*
6020	Commercial banks	35	36	*2.5*	569	539	19,466	21,247	10,946	10,565	*1.3*
6030	Savings institutions	10	9	*2.4*	117	117	15,761	14,940	1,896	1,825	*1.7*
6060	Credit unions	3	4	*1.8*	21	27	17,905	18,222	424	498	*-*
6100	Nondepository institutions	22	27	*4.1*	125	168	26,752	24,500	4,185	5,854	*1.9*
6160	Mortgage bankers and brokers	7	12	*5.4*	56	82	31,643	27,805	2,418	4,046	*2.2*
6200	Security and commodity brokers	23	24	*4.0*	76	-	35,579	-	2,813	-	*-*
6210	Security brokers and dealers	14	16	*4.3*	57	55	40,140	41,891	2,290	2,596	*0.7*
6280	Security and commodity services	9	8	*4.0*	19	-	21,895	-	523	-	*-*
6300	Insurance carriers	50	42	*4.2*	333	326	27,459	30,319	9,067	9,119	*0.9*
6310	Life insurance	10	10	*3.5*	137	156	29,985	37,000	3,365	4,758	*1.3*
6330	Fire, marine, and casualty insurance	28	22	*5.3*	76	87	27,316	29,379	2,155	2,604	*0.7*
6360	Title insurance	9	6	*9.7*	117	79	24,718	18,430	3,484	1,618	*6.9*
6400	Insurance agents, brokers, and service	87	113	*3.5*	271	335	18,258	17,887	5,361	6,487	*1.7*
6500	Real estate	129	143	*3.3*	504	509	16,087	14,436	9,025	9,826	*2.2*
6510	Real estate operators and lessors	58	61	*3.2*	231	217	14,719	10,157	3,922	3,053	*2.0*
6530	Real estate agents and managers	50	60	*3.3*	153	193	15,974	16,290	2,837	4,276	*1.8*
6540	Title abstract offices	6	6	*3.6*	40	41	19,200	21,463	857	1,105	*4.4*
6552	Subdividers and developers, n.e.c.	4	12	*5.1*	-	52	-	19,769	-	1,139	*5.3*
ST. CLAIR, MO											
60 –	**Finance, insurance, and real estate**	14	16	*0.1*	77	80	12,987	12,150	1,041	1,032	*0.0*
6000	Depository institutions	4	4	*0.2*	47	55	16,681	13,745	822	797	*0.1*
6020	Commercial banks	4	4	*0.3*	47	55	16,681	13,745	822	797	*0.1*
6400	Insurance agents, brokers, and service	4	5	*0.2*	8	7	10,000	11,429	84	83	*0.0*
STE. GENEVIEVE, MO											
60 –	**Finance, insurance, and real estate**	27	29	*0.2*	-	-	-	-	-	-	*-*
6000	Depository institutions	7	7	*0.3*	96	102	17,958	18,196	1,758	1,845	*0.2*
6020	Commercial banks	7	7	*0.5*	96	102	17,958	18,196	1,758	1,845	*0.2*
6400	Insurance agents, brokers, and service	6	6	*0.2*	21	21	11,810	13,333	347	389	*0.1*
6500	Real estate	10	11	*0.3*	19	20	8,421	8,600	192	215	*0.0*
6510	Real estate operators and lessors	5	6	*0.3*	7	9	4,000	4,000	41	51	*0.0*
ST. FRANCOIS, MO											
60 –	**Finance, insurance, and real estate**	86	85	*0.7*	596	580	15,993	17,124	10,321	10,575	*0.3*
6000	Depository institutions	18	20	*0.9*	309	303	17,036	17,518	5,551	5,564	*0.5*
6020	Commercial banks	14	15	*1.0*	259	248	16,077	16,452	4,375	4,268	*0.5*
6100	Nondepository institutions	6	6	*0.9*	23	32	19,478	14,625	514	429	*0.1*
6300	Insurance carriers	6	4	*0.4*	47	51	20,596	20,157	1,021	1,025	*0.1*
6310	Life insurance	4	3	*1.1*	44	-	21,818	-	1,006	-	*-*
6400	Insurance agents, brokers, and service	22	22	*0.7*	51	65	11,373	14,154	805	1,026	*0.3*
6500	Real estate	28	28	*0.6*	126	111	10,635	11,063	1,504	1,536	*0.3*
6510	Real estate operators and lessors	12	12	*0.6*	75	25	9,120	6,720	708	209	*0.1*
6530	Real estate agents and managers	8	10	*0.6*	17	52	12,941	12,231	239	732	*0.3*
6553	Cemetery subdividers and developers	3	2	*1.3*	4	-	7,000	-	39	-	*-*
ST. LOUIS, MO											
60 –	**Finance, insurance, and real estate**	3,017	3,144	*25.1*	40,180	38,426	29,766	30,745	1,226,539	1,209,913	*30.0*
6000	Depository institutions	338	330	*15.6*	8,114	7,978	23,932	24,015	191,286	196,198	*18.2*
6020	Commercial banks	190	183	*12.6*	5,055	4,941	24,356	24,189	118,697	120,700	*15.0*
6030	Savings institutions	99	87	*23.3*	1,534	1,427	25,969	27,434	40,525	41,500	*37.8*
6100	Nondepository institutions	208	227	*34.8*	5,851	4,315	33,764	32,929	189,892	149,119	*48.9*
6140	Personal credit institutions	109	89	*28.3*	1,336	879	27,246	22,562	35,643	20,608	*38.8*
6150	Business credit institutions	31	37	*45.1*	836	678	57,301	67,162	42,347	36,774	*58.5*
6160	Mortgage bankers and brokers	66	101	*45.1*	3,673	2,758	30,792	27,817	111,754	91,737	*50.5*
6200	Security and commodity brokers	213	218	*36.8*	1,812	1,980	58,093	63,083	107,203	127,213	*22.4*

Source: County Business Patterns, 1992/93, CBP-92/93-1, U.S. Department of Commerce, Washington, D.C., April 1995. SIC categories for which data were suppressed or not available for both 1992 and 1993 are *not* displayed. The employment columns represent mid-March employment in the year. Pay per employee is calculated by dividing 1st Quarter payroll, annualized, by mid-March employment. The columns headed "% State" show the county's percentage of the state total for the SIC in 1993; for example, 0.9% for SIC 6030 means that the county had 0.9 percent of the state's total establishments (or payroll) in SIC 6030 in 1993. A dash (-) is used to indicate that data are not available or cannot be calculated; *nec* means not elsewhere classified.

Continued on next page.

SIC	Industry	No. Establishments			Employment		Pay / Employee		Annual Payroll ($ 000)		
		1992	1993	% State	1992	1993	1992	1993	1992	1993	% State
ST. LOUIS, MO - [continued]											
6210	Security brokers and dealers	109	106	28.7	1,234	1,304	65,180	73,331	81,057	92,291	25.9
6280	Security and commodity services	102	111	55.8	575	-	43,151	-	25,904	-	-
6300	Insurance carriers	373	280	28.0	10,081	10,351	31,817	31,549	312,511	327,948	33.8
6310	Life insurance	121	101	35.8	5,243	5,432	29,199	31,492	149,577	161,636	43.1
6330	Fire, marine, and casualty insurance	159	105	25.2	3,838	3,626	36,822	33,895	133,678	129,234	35.4
6360	Title insurance	26	25	40.3	399	385	24,982	23,034	12,117	11,648	49.9
6370	Pension, health, and welfare funds	44	25	16.9	395	346	22,420	22,451	10,046	8,563	36.9
6400	Insurance agents, brokers, and service	711	809	24.8	3,503	3,538	30,876	32,512	109,826	117,927	30.5
6500	Real estate	993	1,087	25.1	7,606	7,523	18,717	19,284	153,147	166,487	36.8
6510	Real estate operators and lessors	372	451	23.4	3,326	3,324	14,296	14,396	50,344	55,506	37.0
6530	Real estate agents and managers	464	552	30.5	3,389	3,721	22,402	23,188	81,689	97,037	40.9
6540	Title abstract offices	7	7	4.2	99	130	18,869	22,062	2,133	3,511	14.0
6552	Subdividers and developers, n.e.c.	30	39	16.5	209	123	25,301	25,593	5,129	4,097	18.9
6553	Cemetery subdividers and developers	24	23	14.7	193	181	20,580	21,392	4,368	4,551	29.9
6700	Holding and other investment offices	173	186	34.1	1,546	1,730	42,039	40,828	66,698	78,330	36.3
6710	Holding offices	63	78	39.0	1,007	1,122	48,874	45,184	47,576	55,441	32.8
6720	Investment offices	15	9	69.2	-	46	-	54,696	-	1,561	65.3
6732	Educational, religious, etc. trusts	19	21	21.6	-	114	-	31,193	-	3,913	23.1
6733	Trusts, n.e.c.	25	18	19.1	111	109	18,018	15,890	2,210	2,118	36.7
6794	Patent owners and lessors	12	22	53.7	173	223	39,260	37,274	7,125	10,712	78.7
6798	Real estate investment trusts	4	3	37.5	11	-	45,455	-	275	-	-
6799	Investors, n.e.c.	25	34	41.5	63	-	22,222	-	1,988	-	-
SALINE, MO											
60–	**Finance, insurance, and real estate**	46	49	0.4	228	236	17,298	15,847	4,068	4,006	0.1
6000	Depository institutions	10	10	0.5	133	132	20,030	18,606	2,690	2,549	0.2
6100	Nondepository institutions	3	2	0.3	9	-	17,778	-	157	-	-
6300	Insurance carriers	4	1	0.1	15	-	16,000	-	238	-	-
6400	Insurance agents, brokers, and service	14	17	0.5	-	35	-	12,229	-	480	0.1
6500	Real estate	13	17	0.4	33	51	7,758	6,118	309	450	0.1
6510	Real estate operators and lessors	7	8	0.4	-	14	-	4,571	-	84	0.1
6530	Real estate agents and managers	3	5	0.3	3	29	10,667	6,207	52	256	0.1
SCHUYLER, MO											
60–	**Finance, insurance, and real estate**	6	6	0.0	32	28	18,500	14,429	539	415	0.0
SCOTLAND, MO											
60–	**Finance, insurance, and real estate**	18	20	0.2	71	65	13,746	16,923	927	1,010	0.0
6000	Depository institutions	4	4	0.2	40	40	18,900	19,900	697	728	0.1
6400	Insurance agents, brokers, and service	6	8	0.2	14	13	6,286	9,231	101	123	0.0
6500	Real estate	4	4	0.1	6	5	5,333	5,600	32	29	0.0
SCOTT, MO											
60–	**Finance, insurance, and real estate**	77	78	0.6	458	464	21,057	21,319	9,334	10,778	0.3
6000	Depository institutions	18	18	0.8	255	257	19,514	18,864	4,944	5,373	0.5
6100	Nondepository institutions	7	6	0.9	28	-	36,143	-	854	-	-
6300	Insurance carriers	7	7	0.7	69	52	22,319	30,308	1,481	1,974	0.2
6330	Fire, marine, and casualty insurance	3	3	0.7	8	-	34,500	-	300	-	-
6400	Insurance agents, brokers, and service	19	21	0.6	59	70	22,847	21,086	1,184	1,526	0.4
6500	Real estate	21	23	0.5	33	34	11,636	10,235	479	413	0.1
6510	Real estate operators and lessors	12	12	0.6	11	10	10,182	5,600	121	77	0.1
SHANNON, MO											
60–	**Finance, insurance, and real estate**	6	5	0.0	-	37	-	15,459	-	921	0.0
6000	Depository institutions	3	3	0.1	33	-	14,909	-	802	-	-
6020	Commercial banks	3	3	0.2	33	-	14,909	-	802	-	-

Source: County Business Patterns, 1992/93, CBP-92/93-1, U.S. Department of Commerce, Washington, D.C., April 1995. SIC categories for which data were suppressed or not available for both 1992 and 1993 are *not* displayed. The employment columns represent mid-March employment in the year. Pay per employee is calculated by dividing 1st Quarter payroll, annualized, by mid-March employment. The columns headed "% State" show the county's percentage of the state total for the SIC in 1993; for example, 0.9% for SIC 6030 means that the county had 0.9 percent of the state's total establishments (or payroll) in SIC 6030 in 1993. A dash (-) is used to indicate that data are not available or cannot be calculated; *nec* means not elsewhere classified.

SIC	Industry	No. Establishments			Employment		Pay / Employee		Annual Payroll ($ 000)		
		1992	1993	% State	1992	1993	1992	1993	1992	1993	% State
SHELBY, MO											
60 –	**Finance, insurance, and real estate**	18	19	0.2	86	92	15,581	17,043	1,385	1,555	0.0
6000	Depository institutions	5	5	0.2	52	50	18,923	20,720	1,014	1,044	0.1
6400	Insurance agents, brokers, and service	6	6	0.2	14	15	9,143	10,400	142	167	0.0
6500	Real estate	4	5	0.1	11	17	3,636	3,294	46	67	0.0
STODDARD, MO											
60 –	**Finance, insurance, and real estate**	65	57	0.5	243	238	20,016	18,941	4,949	4,859	0.1
6000	Depository institutions	15	16	0.8	138	143	21,246	22,126	2,930	3,150	0.3
6020	Commercial banks	12	13	0.9	130	135	21,662	22,519	2,810	3,024	0.4
6200	Security and commodity brokers	4	3	0.5	7	-	21,143	-	178	-	-
6300	Insurance carriers	4	4	0.4	16	10	17,500	12,800	305	281	0.0
6400	Insurance agents, brokers, and service	20	19	0.6	33	38	27,515	13,895	632	660	0.2
6500	Real estate	17	14	0.3	33	30	10,667	10,533	505	423	0.1
6510	Real estate operators and lessors	7	6	0.3	16	11	7,500	6,182	201	85	0.1
6530	Real estate agents and managers	8	6	0.3	8	-	7,500	-	99	-	-
STONE, MO											
60 –	**Finance, insurance, and real estate**	51	53	0.4	250	246	13,264	14,374	4,370	4,404	0.1
6000	Depository institutions	11	10	0.5	84	83	22,429	19,373	1,880	1,813	0.2
6400	Insurance agents, brokers, and service	10	12	0.4	39	-	14,769	-	674	-	-
6500	Real estate	27	29	0.7	124	134	6,677	11,075	1,777	2,122	0.5
6510	Real estate operators and lessors	5	7	0.4	13	-	6,462	-	199	-	-
6530	Real estate agents and managers	14	17	0.9	62	78	7,419	9,026	765	1,438	0.6
SULLIVAN, MO											
60 –	**Finance, insurance, and real estate**	11	9	0.1	-	-	-	-	-	-	-
6500	Real estate	5	3	0.1	3	3	8,000	6,667	32	23	0.0
TANEY, MO											
60 –	**Finance, insurance, and real estate**	100	130	1.0	511	652	14,231	14,859	9,528	14,222	0.4
6000	Depository institutions	17	20	0.9	209	175	17,837	17,326	3,146	3,612	0.3
6020	Commercial banks	11	12	0.8	173	136	18,682	18,588	2,652	2,938	0.4
6030	Savings institutions	6	6	1.6	36	-	13,778	-	494	-	-
6200	Security and commodity brokers	2	3	0.5	-	10	-	40,400	-	466	0.1
6210	Security brokers and dealers	1	3	0.8	-	10	-	40,400	-	466	0.1
6400	Insurance agents, brokers, and service	15	16	0.5	52	71	21,538	15,549	1,267	1,282	0.3
6500	Real estate	59	86	2.0	198	364	8,424	12,484	3,935	7,829	1.7
6510	Real estate operators and lessors	13	22	1.1	36	96	9,778	11,708	1,308	1,968	1.3
6530	Real estate agents and managers	29	43	2.4	93	228	8,516	13,404	1,192	4,375	1.8
6552	Subdividers and developers, n.e.c.	10	19	8.1	58	40	7,172	9,100	1,248	1,469	6.8
6700	Holding and other investment offices	5	3	0.6	27	-	13,778	-	726	-	-
TEXAS, MO											
60 –	**Finance, insurance, and real estate**	32	34	0.3	183	229	13,377	11,633	3,112	3,271	0.1
6000	Depository institutions	10	10	0.5	134	172	15,104	12,814	2,634	2,706	0.3
6400	Insurance agents, brokers, and service	11	13	0.4	25	32	9,600	10,125	272	382	0.1
6500	Real estate	10	11	0.3	-	25	-	5,440	-	183	0.0
6510	Real estate operators and lessors	6	6	0.3	9	17	5,778	2,824	54	48	0.0
VERNON, MO											
60 –	**Finance, insurance, and real estate**	41	38	0.3	511	515	15,969	17,802	9,201	10,077	0.2
6000	Depository institutions	13	11	0.5	339	324	18,761	22,420	7,196	7,813	0.7
6200	Security and commodity brokers	3	3	0.5	5	7	23,200	26,286	184	224	0.0
6400	Insurance agents, brokers, and service	13	12	0.4	140	159	7,200	6,440	1,120	1,293	0.3

Source: County Business Patterns, 1992/93, CBP-92/93-1, U.S. Department of Commerce, Washington, D.C., April 1995. SIC categories for which data were suppressed or not available for both 1992 and 1993 are not displayed. The employment columns represent mid-March employment in the year. Pay per employee is calculated by dividing 1st Quarter payroll, annualized, by mid-March employment. The columns headed "% State" show the county's percentage of the state total for the SIC in 1993; for example, 0.9% for SIC 6030 means that the county had 0.9 percent of the state's total establishments (or payroll) in SIC 6030 in 1993. A dash (-) is used to indicate that data are not available or cannot be calculated; nec means not elsewhere classified.

Continued on next page.

SIC	Industry	No. Establishments			Employment		Pay / Employee		Annual Payroll ($ 000)		
		1992	1993	% State	1992	1993	1992	1993	1992	1993	% State
VERNON, MO - [continued]											
6500	Real estate	8	8	0.2	12	14	11,000	10,857	134	264	0.1
6510	Real estate operators and lessors	3	1	0.1	4	-	13,000	-	51	-	-
6530	Real estate agents and managers	5	5	0.3	8	6	10,000	4,000	83	102	0.0
WARREN, MO											
60 –	**Finance, insurance, and real estate**	31	36	0.3	296	321	14,973	14,480	4,668	5,206	0.1
6000	Depository institutions	7	7	0.3	72	72	21,056	19,000	1,587	1,505	0.1
6400	Insurance agents, brokers, and service	8	10	0.3	-	19	-	18,526	-	475	0.1
6500	Real estate	10	12	0.3	15	42	9,067	7,905	133	395	0.1
6510	Real estate operators and lessors	4	4	0.2	7	12	8,571	5,667	67	72	0.0
6530	Real estate agents and managers	2	4	0.2	-	23	-	9,739	-	277	0.1
WASHINGTON, MO											
60 –	**Finance, insurance, and real estate**	17	19	0.2	88	89	16,364	17,393	1,505	1,648	0.0
6000	Depository institutions	7	7	0.3	71	73	19,042	19,836	1,419	1,545	0.1
6400	Insurance agents, brokers, and service	3	4	0.1	9	6	4,889	4,667	38	38	0.0
6500	Real estate	5	5	0.1	-	4	-	7,000	-	37	0.0
6700	Holding and other investment offices	2	3	0.6	-	6	-	7,333	-	28	0.0
WAYNE, MO											
60 –	**Finance, insurance, and real estate**	20	16	0.1	88	77	12,955	11,844	1,235	1,027	0.0
6000	Depository institutions	8	5	0.2	67	49	14,567	14,367	1,063	777	0.1
6400	Insurance agents, brokers, and service	7	8	0.2	9	23	5,778	6,957	54	192	0.0
6500	Real estate	3	3	0.1	-	5	-	9,600	-	58	0.0
WEBSTER, MO											
60 –	**Finance, insurance, and real estate**	33	38	0.3	183	189	15,781	15,069	3,213	3,462	0.1
6000	Depository institutions	8	8	0.4	134	132	17,313	15,970	2,580	2,581	0.2
6400	Insurance agents, brokers, and service	9	10	0.3	19	20	11,789	12,200	234	257	0.1
6500	Real estate	11	17	0.4	18	28	8,667	11,714	201	440	0.1
6510	Real estate operators and lessors	2	7	0.4	-	5	-	5,600	-	72	0.0
6530	Real estate agents and managers	5	7	0.4	8	-	5,500	-	57	-	-
WORTH, MO											
60 –	**Finance, insurance, and real estate**	8	9	0.1	-	-	-	-	-	-	-
6400	Insurance agents, brokers, and service	4	4	0.1	6	7	8,000	6,857	48	50	0.0
WRIGHT, MO											
60 –	**Finance, insurance, and real estate**	30	36	0.3	145	139	19,559	17,755	2,840	2,435	0.1
6000	Depository institutions	8	8	0.4	103	86	21,165	19,767	2,151	1,640	0.2
6300	Insurance carriers	3	1	0.1	7	-	12,571	-	81	-	-
6400	Insurance agents, brokers, and service	8	14	0.4	16	24	13,250	13,500	245	347	0.1
6500	Real estate	8	9	0.2	12	16	9,667	5,500	99	97	0.0
ST. LOUIS CITY, MO											
60 –	**Finance, insurance, and real estate**	935	953	7.6	22,254	23,113	35,057	36,415	703,945	769,055	19.1
6000	Depository institutions	148	156	7.4	8,435	8,686	28,858	28,992	227,861	248,386	23.0
6020	Commercial banks	65	66	4.6	5,924	6,422	27,402	28,486	151,168	178,581	22.2
6030	Savings institutions	27	26	7.0	323	296	20,173	18,081	6,404	5,815	5.3
6060	Credit unions	31	36	15.9	374	421	19,829	19,021	7,683	8,268	-
6140	Personal credit institutions	27	18	5.7	205	154	32,390	22,312	6,548	4,917	9.3
6150	Business credit institutions	14	12	14.6	342	209	27,661	31,311	9,245	6,172	9.8
6160	Mortgage bankers and brokers	12	15	6.7	90	194	33,911	28,969	3,467	7,528	4.1
6200	Security and commodity brokers	55	56	9.4	3,100	3,231	61,170	72,709	140,312	161,298	28.4
6210	Security brokers and dealers	36	38	10.3	2,922	3,128	61,996	72,999	132,151	154,623	43.4
6300	Insurance carriers	121	114	11.4	4,603	5,266	35,114	35,211	152,575	174,206	18.0
6310	Life insurance	37	33	11.7	1,357	1,697	37,244	42,579	42,100	57,526	15.3
6330	Fire, marine, and casualty insurance	26	24	5.8	811	1,029	35,413	32,762	28,353	35,005	9.6

Source: County Business Patterns, 1992/93, CBP-92/93-1, U.S. Department of Commerce, Washington, D.C., April 1995. SIC categories for which data were suppressed or not available for both 1992 and 1993 are *not* displayed. The employment columns represent mid-March employment in the year. Pay per employee is calculated by dividing 1st Quarter payroll, annualized, by mid-March employment. The columns headed "% State" show the county's percentage of the state total for the SIC in 1993; for example, 0.9% for SIC 6030 means that the county had 0.9 percent of the state's total establishments (or payroll) in SIC 6030 in 1993. A dash (-) is used to indicate that data are not available or cannot be calculated; *nec* means not elsewhere classified.

Continued on next page.

SIC	Industry	No. Establishments			Employment		Pay / Employee		Annual Payroll ($ 000)		
		1992	1993	% State	1992	1993	1992	1993	1992	1993	% State
ST. LOUIS CITY, MO - [continued]											
6370	Pension, health, and welfare funds	41	38	25.7	207	-	20,560	-	5,676	-	-
6400	Insurance agents, brokers, and service	158	166	5.1	1,518	1,515	30,909	29,861	46,216	47,560	12.3
6500	Real estate	326	342	7.9	2,919	3,077	18,509	21,231	61,517	75,119	16.6
6510	Real estate operators and lessors	174	195	10.1	1,469	1,327	17,459	14,119	30,708	24,424	16.3
6530	Real estate agents and managers	118	129	7.1	1,335	1,584	19,380	26,919	28,191	46,422	19.6
6552	Subdividers and developers, n.e.c.	12	11	4.7	36	84	21,111	22,905	864	1,837	8.5
6553	Cemetery subdividers and developers	3	3	1.9	33	-	24,606	-	867	-	-
6700	Holding and other investment offices	65	69	12.7	665	655	70,346	54,418	45,965	36,352	16.8
6710	Holding offices	24	25	12.5	520	430	83,800	70,437	42,237	30,927	18.3
6732	Educational, religious, etc. trusts	14	16	16.5	-	99	-	19,556	-	1,555	9.2
6733	Trusts, n.e.c.	13	14	14.9	27	-	19,556	-	726	-	
6794	Patent owners and lessors	1	3	7.3	-	29	-	39,034	-	1,386	10.2
6799	Investors, n.e.c.	8	9	11.0	-	52	-	22,385	-	1,251	16.8

Source: County Business Patterns, 1992/93, CBP-92/93-1, U.S. Department of Commerce, Washington, D.C., April 1995. SIC categories for which data were suppressed or not available for both 1992 and 1993 are *not* displayed. The employment columns represent mid-March employment in the year. Pay per employee is calculated by dividing 1st Quarter payroll, annualized, by mid-March employment. The columns headed "% State" show the county's percentage of the state total for the SIC in 1993; for example, 0.9% for SIC 6030 means that the county had 0.9 percent of the state's total establishments (or payroll) in SIC 6030 in 1993. A dash (-) is used to indicate that data are not available or cannot be calculated; *nec* means not elsewhere classified.

MONTANA

SIC	Industry	No. Establishments			Employment		Pay / Employee		Annual Payroll ($ 000)		
		1992	1993	% State	1992	1993	1992	1993	1992	1993	% State
BEAVERHEAD, MT											
60–	**Finance, insurance, and real estate**	24	27	1.2	99	107	18,747	20,262	2,107	2,286	0.7
6000	Depository institutions	4	4	1.1	52	59	22,615	22,441	1,346	1,434	1.1
6400	Insurance agents, brokers, and service	7	9	1.5	19	21	13,895	15,238	295	266	0.5
6500	Real estate	9	10	1.1	19	19	11,368	12,421	235	320	-
6530	Real estate agents and managers	4	5	1.3	4	8	5,000	7,000	36	86	0.5
BIG HORN, MT											
60–	**Finance, insurance, and real estate**	17	16	0.7	97	81	15,876	17,235	1,596	1,310	0.4
6000	Depository institutions	3	3	0.8	48	50	18,833	21,280	871	921	0.7
6400	Insurance agents, brokers, and service	7	7	1.1	18	22	13,333	12,000	259	294	0.6
6500	Real estate	7	6	0.7	31	9	12,774	7,556	466	95	-
BLAINE, MT											
60–	**Finance, insurance, and real estate**	14	11	0.5	87	82	18,759	17,512	1,758	1,773	0.5
6000	Depository institutions	4	3	0.8	37	29	22,270	21,103	858	683	0.5
6020	Commercial banks	4	3	1.6	37	29	22,270	21,103	858	683	0.7
6500	Real estate	5	2	0.2	39	-	16,205	-	682	-	-
BROADWATER, MT											
60–	**Finance, insurance, and real estate**	8	8	0.4	24	24	21,500	19,500	532	528	0.2
6500	Real estate	3	2	0.2	2	-	8,000	-	15	-	-
CARBON, MT											
60–	**Finance, insurance, and real estate**	16	16	0.7	68	74	17,235	17,135	1,269	1,331	0.4
6000	Depository institutions	4	4	1.1	40	-	19,000	-	793	-	-
6400	Insurance agents, brokers, and service	2	3	0.5	-	12	-	28,000	-	299	0.6
6500	Real estate	7	8	0.9	12	17	6,667	5,882	169	132	-
CARTER, MT											
60–	**Finance, insurance, and real estate**	3	3	0.1	-	-	-	-	-	-	-
CASCADE, MT											
60–	**Finance, insurance, and real estate**	239	240	10.6	1,770	1,751	22,357	23,219	40,955	45,505	13.4
6000	Depository institutions	35	30	8.2	465	417	20,929	22,139	10,111	9,450	7.5
6020	Commercial banks	16	13	6.8	258	208	23,519	24,154	6,385	5,172	5.5
6060	Credit unions	11	10	9.8	114	120	13,263	16,267	1,565	2,065	17.4
6100	Nondepository institutions	13	12	15.0	122	197	17,279	18,234	2,806	3,736	20.3
6140	Personal credit institutions	6	6	19.4	37	-	18,486	-	715	-	-
6160	Mortgage bankers and brokers	3	4	14.8	-	136	-	16,147	-	2,306	27.4
6200	Security and commodity brokers	14	14	11.9	121	123	55,207	60,878	6,997	10,224	27.0
6210	Security brokers and dealers	10	8	9.2	112	106	59,000	67,170	6,933	9,624	29.1
6300	Insurance carriers	29	26	19.1	326	275	18,945	23,898	6,604	7,181	15.4
6310	Life insurance	6	6	18.8	43	-	25,023	-	1,064	-	-
6330	Fire, marine, and casualty insurance	15	15	23.8	91	68	22,374	35,471	2,035	3,094	35.5
6370	Pension, health, and welfare funds	3	3	18.8	19	15	2,105	3,733	118	74	6.9
6400	Insurance agents, brokers, and service	54	67	11.0	386	397	27,917	21,773	10,095	8,727	17.6
6500	Real estate	84	79	9.0	280	259	7,971	9,869	2,494	2,948	-
6510	Real estate operators and lessors	41	39	10.3	92	125	8,478	9,408	915	1,347	9.6

Source: County Business Patterns, 1992/93, CBP-92/93-1, U.S. Department of Commerce, Washington, D.C., April 1995. SIC categories for which data were suppressed or not available for both 1992 and 1993 are *not* displayed. The employment columns represent mid-March employment in the year. Pay per employee is calculated by dividing 1st Quarter payroll, annualized, by mid-March employment. The columns headed "% State" show the county's percentage of the state total for the SIC in 1993; for example, 0.9% for SIC 6030 means that the county had 0.9 percent of the state's total establishments (or payroll) in SIC 6030 in 1993. A dash (-) is used to indicate that data are not available or cannot be calculated; *nec* means not elsewhere classified.

Continued on next page.

SIC	Industry	No. Establishments			Employment		Pay / Employee		Annual Payroll ($ 000)		
		1992	1993	% State	1992	1993	1992	1993	1992	1993	% State
CASCADE, MT - [continued]											
6530	Real estate agents and managers	32	34	8.7	160	112	7,600	8,607	1,299	1,051	6.6
6553	Cemetery subdividers and developers	3	3	10.3	-	12	-	13,667	-	200	19.1
6710	Holding offices	5	3	13.6	14	-	29,714	-	428	-	-
CHOUTEAU, MT											
60 –	**Finance, insurance, and real estate**	13	14	0.6	81	72	21,185	21,889	1,529	1,450	0.4
6000	Depository institutions	4	3	0.8	-	41	-	25,951	-	858	0.7
6020	Commercial banks	4	3	1.6	-	41	-	25,951	-	858	0.9
6400	Insurance agents, brokers, and service	6	7	1.1	21	18	25,143	22,000	453	468	0.9
CUSTER, MT											
60 –	**Finance, insurance, and real estate**	36	36	1.6	184	176	21,739	22,636	4,306	4,265	1.3
6000	Depository institutions	6	6	1.6	90	90	22,578	22,089	2,097	2,087	1.7
6020	Commercial banks	3	3	1.6	81	81	23,358	22,716	1,959	1,924	2.1
6400	Insurance agents, brokers, and service	12	12	2.0	40	31	18,500	19,097	930	729	1.5
6500	Real estate	9	9	1.0	14	10	8,000	7,600	108	89	-
DANIELS, MT											
60 –	**Finance, insurance, and real estate**	4	6	0.3	37	37	17,081	17,730	651	722	0.2
DAWSON, MT											
60 –	**Finance, insurance, and real estate**	31	26	1.1	187	132	14,888	16,273	2,724	2,199	0.6
6000	Depository institutions	7	8	2.2	69	81	20,290	17,728	1,454	1,408	1.1
6020	Commercial banks	3	3	1.6	59	63	21,627	19,937	1,323	1,226	1.3
6400	Insurance agents, brokers, and service	6	8	1.3	14	-	30,000	-	418	-	-
6500	Real estate	13	8	0.9	89	26	8,494	5,846	634	173	-
6510	Real estate operators and lessors	8	6	1.6	74	-	6,054	-	499	-	-
DEER LODGE, MT											
60 –	**Finance, insurance, and real estate**	19	17	0.8	159	90	16,025	13,956	1,527	1,214	0.4
6000	Depository institutions	7	5	1.4	87	48	22,069	17,500	1,046	842	0.7
6400	Insurance agents, brokers, and service	5	7	1.1	10	15	16,000	14,667	162	218	0.4
6500	Real estate	4	3	0.3	54	-	7,630	-	246	-	-
FALLON, MT											
60 –	**Finance, insurance, and real estate**	8	8	0.4	54	40	9,926	14,500	576	619	0.2
6400	Insurance agents, brokers, and service	3	4	0.7	27	12	5,481	13,333	163	170	0.3
FERGUS, MT											
60 –	**Finance, insurance, and real estate**	29	27	1.2	180	176	19,689	19,909	3,569	3,446	1.0
6000	Depository institutions	9	7	1.9	123	106	22,114	22,000	2,708	2,308	1.8
6400	Insurance agents, brokers, and service	8	10	1.6	15	22	15,467	15,091	227	338	0.7
6500	Real estate	6	6	0.7	23	-	9,043	-	211	-	-
FLATHEAD, MT											
60 –	**Finance, insurance, and real estate**	203	227	10.0	1,194	1,350	18,858	19,321	25,739	30,637	9.0
6000	Depository institutions	27	26	7.1	501	506	21,341	20,174	10,831	10,769	8.5
6020	Commercial banks	12	11	5.7	351	341	21,083	20,152	6,958	6,858	7.3
6100	Nondepository institutions	9	11	13.8	32	47	26,125	31,745	1,697	2,652	14.4
6140	Personal credit institutions	3	3	9.7	9	7	19,556	32,000	169	268	5.1
6150	Business credit institutions	1	4	36.4	-	11	-	21,818	-	194	-
6160	Mortgage bankers and brokers	4	4	14.8	-	29	-	35,448	-	2,190	26.0
6200	Security and commodity brokers	13	11	9.3	45	33	34,400	51,030	1,529	2,017	5.3
6280	Security and commodity services	3	3	13.0	10	7	16,000	24,000	166	190	4.3
6300	Insurance carriers	12	12	8.8	64	35	19,312	18,057	1,360	848	1.8
6330	Fire, marine, and casualty insurance	7	7	11.1	30	-	23,200	-	776	-	-
6400	Insurance agents, brokers, and service	44	47	7.7	195	178	17,087	21,843	3,872	4,870	9.8
6500	Real estate	91	111	12.7	339	537	12,578	13,460	5,912	9,065	-

Source: County Business Patterns, 1992/93, CBP-92/93-1, U.S. Department of Commerce, Washington, D.C., April 1995. SIC categories for which data were suppressed or not available for both 1992 and 1993 are *not* displayed. The employment columns represent mid-March employment in the year. Pay per employee is calculated by dividing 1st Quarter payroll, annualized, by mid-March employment. The columns headed "% State" show the county's percentage of the state total for the SIC in 1993; for example, 0.9% for SIC 6030 means that the county had 0.9 percent of the state's total establishments (or payroll) in SIC 6030 in 1993. A dash (-) is used to indicate that data are not available or cannot be calculated; *nec* means not elsewhere classified.

Continued on next page.

SIC	Industry	No. Establishments			Employment		Pay / Employee		Annual Payroll ($ 000)		
		1992	1993	% State	1992	1993	1992	1993	1992	1993	% State
FLATHEAD, MT - [continued]											
6510	Real estate operators and lessors	32	33	8.7	111	53	11,856	5,585	2,060	569	4.0
6530	Real estate agents and managers	46	62	15.9	169	247	10,911	12,049	2,394	2,969	18.7
6540	Title abstract offices	3	4	14.3	-	62	-	18,710	-	1,346	-
6552	Subdividers and developers, n.e.c.	2	8	19.5	-	170	-	14,188	-	4,001	73.5
6553	Cemetery subdividers and developers	2	3	10.3	-	5	-	76,800	-	179	17.1
6700	Holding and other investment offices	7	9	12.5	18	14	33,778	68,000	538	416	2.3
GALLATIN, MT											
60 –	**Finance, insurance, and real estate**	170	185	8.2	833	882	25,479	24,744	22,816	24,672	7.3
6000	Depository institutions	17	16	4.4	315	294	19,835	19,918	6,528	6,255	5.0
6020	Commercial banks	11	10	5.2	266	239	20,707	21,172	5,738	5,434	5.8
6200	Security and commodity brokers	14	13	11.0	86	76	72,000	65,737	6,271	6,159	16.3
6300	Insurance carriers	7	9	6.6	38	31	37,684	34,968	1,312	1,042	2.2
6400	Insurance agents, brokers, and service	46	43	7.0	147	130	17,279	18,892	2,965	2,519	5.1
6500	Real estate	73	90	10.3	201	242	15,821	12,430	3,715	3,946	-
6510	Real estate operators and lessors	23	31	8.2	64	72	7,125	8,833	535	896	6.4
6530	Real estate agents and managers	38	49	12.6	114	118	20,561	12,746	2,278	1,659	10.5
GARFIELD, MT											
60 –	**Finance, insurance, and real estate**	1	1	0.0	-	-	-	-	-	-	-
GLACIER, MT											
60 –	**Finance, insurance, and real estate**	16	15	0.7	113	121	18,336	18,843	2,271	2,931	0.9
6000	Depository institutions	6	5	1.4	53	49	18,717	18,776	1,033	897	0.7
6020	Commercial banks	3	3	1.6	42	-	19,238	-	836	-	-
6400	Insurance agents, brokers, and service	4	5	0.8	22	-	18,364	-	416	-	-
GRANITE, MT											
60 –	**Finance, insurance, and real estate**	3	3	0.1	-	-	-	-	-	-	-
HILL, MT											
60 –	**Finance, insurance, and real estate**	47	44	1.9	214	196	18,598	18,122	4,073	3,744	1.1
6000	Depository institutions	10	9	2.5	102	91	20,510	20,484	2,138	1,931	1.5
6020	Commercial banks	6	4	2.1	83	58	22,602	24,069	1,906	1,452	1.5
6200	Security and commodity brokers	4	2	1.7	11	-	48,000	-	514	-	-
6210	Security brokers and dealers	4	2	2.3	11	-	48,000	-	514	-	-
6400	Insurance agents, brokers, and service	13	13	2.1	40	43	13,600	14,419	595	641	1.3
6500	Real estate	15	18	2.1	38	44	10,000	8,182	406	383	-
6510	Real estate operators and lessors	6	11	2.9	11	37	8,000	7,892	138	308	2.2
6530	Real estate agents and managers	6	7	1.8	10	7	7,600	9,714	90	75	0.5
JEFFERSON, MT											
60 –	**Finance, insurance, and real estate**	12	14	0.6	36	39	16,222	13,333	552	555	0.2
6000	Depository institutions	3	3	0.8	-	23	-	17,739	-	403	0.3
6500	Real estate	6	7	0.8	7	10	16,000	6,000	114	57	-
6510	Real estate operators and lessors	3	3	0.8	5	-	9,600	-	41	-	-
6530	Real estate agents and managers	2	3	0.8	-	4	-	4,000	-	15	0.1
JUDITH BASIN, MT											
60 –	**Finance, insurance, and real estate**	4	5	0.2	-	16	-	21,750	-	390	0.1
LAKE, MT											
60 –	**Finance, insurance, and real estate**	38	47	2.1	221	257	19,964	17,572	4,528	4,869	1.4
6000	Depository institutions	8	9	2.5	150	153	21,893	20,183	3,303	3,228	2.6
6400	Insurance agents, brokers, and service	9	10	1.6	40	49	15,400	16,898	628	895	1.8

Source: County Business Patterns, 1992/93, CBP-92/93-1, U.S. Department of Commerce, Washington, D.C., April 1995. SIC categories for which data were suppressed or not available for both 1992 and 1993 are not displayed. The employment columns represent mid-March employment in the year. Pay per employee is calculated by dividing 1st Quarter payroll, annualized, by mid-March employment. The columns headed "% State" show the county's percentage of the state total for the SIC in 1993; for example, 0.9% for SIC 6030 means that the county had 0.9 percent of the state's total establishments (or payroll) in SIC 6030 in 1993. A dash (-) is used to indicate that data are not available or cannot be calculated; nec means not elsewhere classified.

Continued on next page.

SIC	Industry	No. Establishments			Employment		Pay / Employee		Annual Payroll ($ 000)		
		1992	1993	% State	1992	1993	1992	1993	1992	1993	% State
LAKE, MT - [continued]											
6500	Real estate	17	23	2.6	24	40	13,667	10,500	403	576	-
6510	Real estate operators and lessors	5	5	1.3	6	-	13,333	-	97	-	-
6530	Real estate agents and managers	9	15	3.9	8	21	7,500	7,238	93	208	1.3
LEWIS AND CLARK, MT											
60 –	**Finance, insurance, and real estate**	152	151	6.7	1,545	1,520	22,633	23,279	38,000	39,495	11.6
6000	Depository institutions	28	26	7.1	445	441	22,454	21,959	10,351	10,242	8.1
6020	Commercial banks	11	10	5.2	197	192	21,523	22,167	4,369	4,269	4.6
6100	Nondepository institutions	7	7	8.8	80	76	20,900	22,263	1,762	1,844	10.0
6140	Personal credit institutions	4	5	16.1	25	-	22,400	-	547	-	-
6200	Security and commodity brokers	7	7	5.9	-	22	-	58,182	-	1,427	3.8
6280	Security and commodity services	3	2	8.7	9	-	18,667	-	173	-	-
6300	Insurance carriers	22	15	11.0	688	650	25,081	26,308	19,528	19,331	41.4
6330	Fire, marine, and casualty insurance	12	10	15.9	108	-	34,222	-	3,669	-	-
6400	Insurance agents, brokers, and service	31	34	5.6	125	155	21,120	21,703	2,623	4,068	8.2
6500	Real estate	51	57	6.5	144	159	11,500	11,799	1,920	2,193	-
6510	Real estate operators and lessors	27	31	8.2	93	96	10,882	9,417	1,040	951	6.8
6530	Real estate agents and managers	16	19	4.9	28	36	13,571	13,556	517	694	4.4
6553	Cemetery subdividers and developers	3	3	10.3	6	4	11,333	17,000	73	82	7.8
6700	Holding and other investment offices	6	5	6.9	-	17	-	22,824	-	390	2.1
LIBERTY, MT											
60 –	**Finance, insurance, and real estate**	6	5	0.2	21	15	20,952	18,667	747	376	0.1
LINCOLN, MT											
60 –	**Finance, insurance, and real estate**	29	30	1.3	113	144	17,664	17,667	2,321	2,569	0.8
6000	Depository institutions	6	6	1.6	64	79	21,188	22,937	1,449	1,608	1.3
6400	Insurance agents, brokers, and service	5	7	1.1	-	23	-	18,435	-	497	1.0
6500	Real estate	17	17	1.9	27	42	7,852	7,333	361	464	-
6510	Real estate operators and lessors	8	8	2.1	12	17	5,333	5,882	134	116	0.8
6530	Real estate agents and managers	5	6	1.5	5	12	13,600	8,000	81	170	1.1
MCCONE, MT											
60 –	**Finance, insurance, and real estate**	4	5	0.2	14	15	13,143	13,333	242	277	0.1
MADISON, MT											
60 –	**Finance, insurance, and real estate**	11	12	0.5	59	63	17,356	18,349	966	1,187	0.3
6400	Insurance agents, brokers, and service	4	5	0.8	-	18	-	9,111	-	189	0.4
6500	Real estate	5	5	0.6	5	-	9,600	-	57	-	-
6530	Real estate agents and managers	3	3	0.8	3	4	13,333	7,000	45	36	0.2
MEAGHER, MT											
60 –	**Finance, insurance, and real estate**	4	4	0.2	-	-	-	-	-	-	-
MINERAL, MT											
60 –	**Finance, insurance, and real estate**	5	6	0.3	-	17	-	14,353	-	257	0.1
MISSOULA, MT											
60 –	**Finance, insurance, and real estate**	252	269	11.9	1,617	1,675	21,116	22,101	35,303	38,454	11.3
6000	Depository institutions	28	31	8.5	551	578	20,740	20,768	11,528	12,216	9.7
6020	Commercial banks	14	13	6.8	348	334	22,402	22,503	7,431	7,189	7.7
6060	Credit unions	6	9	8.8	-	99	-	15,838	-	1,630	13.7
6140	Personal credit institutions	10	6	19.4	50	-	21,680	-	1,131	-	-
6160	Mortgage bankers and brokers	4	5	18.5	-	21	-	21,714	-	553	6.6
6200	Security and commodity brokers	11	10	8.5	74	78	38,919	38,872	2,865	3,482	9.2
6210	Security brokers and dealers	9	10	11.5	-	78	-	38,872	-	3,482	10.5
6300	Insurance carriers	26	21	15.4	165	135	19,394	24,356	3,480	3,450	7.4
6310	Life insurance	6	4	12.5	79	51	17,165	20,471	1,374	1,051	7.1

Source: County Business Patterns, 1992/93, CBP-92/93-1, U.S. Department of Commerce, Washington, D.C., April 1995. SIC categories for which data were suppressed or not available for both 1992 and 1993 are not displayed. The employment columns represent mid-March employment in the year. Pay per employee is calculated by dividing 1st Quarter payroll, annualized, by mid-March employment. The columns headed "% State" show the county's percentage of the state total for the SIC in 1993; for example, 0.9% for SIC 6030 means that the county had 0.9 percent of the state's total establishments (or payroll) in SIC 6030 in 1993. A dash (-) is used to indicate that data are not available or cannot be calculated; nec means not elsewhere classified.

Continued on next page.

SIC	Industry	No. Establishments			Employment		Pay / Employee		Annual Payroll ($ 000)		
		1992	1993	% State	1992	1993	1992	1993	1992	1993	% State
MISSOULA, MT - [continued]											
6330	Fire, marine, and casualty insurance	11	9	*14.3*	29	21	32,276	45,333	1,026	939	*10.8*
6370	Pension, health, and welfare funds	4	6	*37.5*	34	-	12,471	-	607		
6400	Insurance agents, brokers, and service	67	72	*11.8*	273	286	22,198	20,727	6,597	7,028	*14.2*
6500	Real estate	92	112	*12.8*	346	393	11,156	12,346	4,717	5,976	
6510	Real estate operators and lessors	32	41	*10.8*	139	158	10,072	9,367	1,659	1,776	*12.6*
6530	Real estate agents and managers	44	55	*14.1*	173	191	11,931	14,660	2,469	3,420	*21.6*
6552	Subdividers and developers, n.e.c.	6	10	*24.4*	1	-	4,000	-	78	-	-
6700	Holding and other investment offices	11	9	*12.5*	113	-	39,221	-	3,884	-	-
MUSSELSHELL, MT											
60 –	**Finance, insurance, and real estate**	7	8	*0.4*	32	44	11,125	12,909	403	627	*0.2*
6500	Real estate	3	4	*0.5*	4	-	5,000	-	32	-	-
PARK, MT											
60 –	**Finance, insurance, and real estate**	31	33	*1.5*	133	101	21,474	17,782	2,635	2,163	*0.6*
6000	Depository institutions	4	3	*0.8*	83	50	22,892	20,160	1,673	1,128	*0.9*
6400	Insurance agents, brokers, and service	6	7	*1.1*	16	19	16,250	13,684	317	312	*0.6*
6500	Real estate	15	18	*2.1*	19	20	7,579	6,600	155	227	-
6510	Real estate operators and lessors	8	11	*2.9*	8	-	7,000	-	64	-	-
6530	Real estate agents and managers	5	6	*1.5*	6	-	6,000	-	42	-	-
PETROLEUM, MT											
60 –	**Finance, insurance, and real estate**	1	1	*0.0*	-	-	-	-	-	-	-
PHILLIPS, MT											
60 –	**Finance, insurance, and real estate**	7	7	*0.3*	57	61	18,456	18,689	1,105	1,201	*0.4*
6000	Depository institutions	3	3	*0.8*	46	50	18,435	18,080	891	931	*0.7*
PONDERA, MT											
60 –	**Finance, insurance, and real estate**	22	17	*0.8*	123	66	18,211	21,455	2,318	1,551	*0.5*
6000	Depository institutions	6	4	*1.1*	55	36	24,436	27,333	1,378	1,020	*0.8*
6400	Insurance agents, brokers, and service	5	5	*0.8*	10	-	17,200	-	160	-	-
6500	Real estate	8	6	*0.7*	46	8	9,217	8,000	472	85	-
POWDER RIVER, MT											
60 –	**Finance, insurance, and real estate**	4	4	*0.2*	14	17	20,000	17,412	289	321	*0.1*
POWELL, MT											
60 –	**Finance, insurance, and real estate**	18	14	*0.6*	56	53	16,429	15,547	1,073	929	*0.3*
6400	Insurance agents, brokers, and service	7	5	*0.8*	10	9	12,000	12,000	101	119	*0.2*
6500	Real estate	6	5	*0.6*	9	7	8,000	9,714	80	73	-
6510	Real estate operators and lessors	3	3	*0.8*	3	-	5,333	-	16	-	-
PRAIRIE, MT											
60 –	**Finance, insurance, and real estate**	4	4	*0.2*	19	18	25,474	26,222	469	449	*0.1*
RAVALLI, MT											
60 –	**Finance, insurance, and real estate**	60	69	*3.1*	296	333	15,365	15,075	4,634	5,411	*1.6*
6000	Depository institutions	9	9	*2.5*	170	167	17,506	17,844	2,815	2,953	*2.3*
6020	Commercial banks	5	5	*2.6*	140	134	17,000	17,642	2,466	2,557	*2.7*
6400	Insurance agents, brokers, and service	15	15	*2.5*	45	56	15,911	15,571	804	962	*1.9*
6500	Real estate	30	38	*4.3*	52	88	10,538	9,591	641	1,070	-
6510	Real estate operators and lessors	7	8	*2.1*	28	36	10,714	8,111	282	309	*2.2*
6530	Real estate agents and managers	15	25	*6.4*	14	48	11,143	11,167	254	684	*4.3*

Source: County Business Patterns, 1992/93, CBP-92/93-1, U.S. Department of Commerce, Washington, D.C., April 1995. SIC categories for which data were suppressed or not available for both 1992 and 1993 are *not* displayed. The employment columns represent mid-March employment in the year. Pay per employee is calculated by dividing 1st Quarter payroll, annualized, by mid-March employment. The columns headed "% State" show the county's percentage of the state total for the SIC in 1993; for example, 0.9% for SIC 6030 means that the county had 0.9 percent of the state's total establishments (or payroll) in SIC 6030 in 1993. A dash (-) is used to indicate that data are not available or cannot be calculated; *nec* means not elsewhere classified.

SIC	Industry	No. Establishments			Employment		Pay / Employee		Annual Payroll ($ 000)		
		1992	1993	% State	1992	1993	1992	1993	1992	1993	% State
RICHLAND, MT											
60–	**Finance, insurance, and real estate**	27	22	*1.0*	131	126	19,450	20,000	2,646	2,594	*0.8*
6000	Depository institutions	6	6	*1.6*	72	75	22,000	20,640	1,665	1,679	*1.3*
6200	Security and commodity brokers	4	4	*3.4*	8	7	28,500	39,429	238	292	*0.8*
6400	Insurance agents, brokers, and service	8	6	*1.0*	22	-	15,818	-	343	-	-
6500	Real estate	5	4	*0.5*	15	10	8,000	10,400	119	103	-
ROOSEVELT, MT											
60–	**Finance, insurance, and real estate**	19	17	*0.8*	100	99	16,480	16,485	1,889	1,866	*0.5*
6000	Depository institutions	7	7	*1.9*	79	77	17,165	17,403	1,589	1,555	*1.2*
6400	Insurance agents, brokers, and service	8	8	*1.3*	17	-	14,824	-	238	-	-
ROSEBUD, MT											
60–	**Finance, insurance, and real estate**	12	12	*0.5*	105	100	19,314	20,520	2,071	2,442	*0.7*
6000	Depository institutions	4	4	*1.1*	42	42	21,048	22,095	838	878	*0.7*
6020	Commercial banks	4	4	*2.1*	42	42	21,048	22,095	838	878	*0.9*
6400	Insurance agents, brokers, and service	3	3	*0.5*	-	9	-	13,778	-	125	*0.3*
6500	Real estate	4	5	*0.6*	56	49	19,000	20,408	1,123	1,439	-
SANDERS, MT											
60–	**Finance, insurance, and real estate**	13	19	*0.8*	49	63	15,265	14,413	860	1,048	*0.3*
6400	Insurance agents, brokers, and service	3	4	*0.7*	-	11	-	8,364	-	82	*0.2*
6500	Real estate	7	11	*1.3*	9	-	5,333	-	62	-	-
6510	Real estate operators and lessors	3	4	*1.1*	3	-	8,000	-	27	-	-
6530	Real estate agents and managers	2	4	*1.0*	-	7	-	10,286	-	97	*0.6*
SHERIDAN, MT											
60–	**Finance, insurance, and real estate**	12	13	*0.6*	63	66	18,667	19,091	1,297	1,378	*0.4*
6000	Depository institutions	4	4	*1.1*	40	42	21,100	21,905	979	1,044	*0.8*
6400	Insurance agents, brokers, and service	5	5	*0.8*	17	17	16,706	17,176	269	280	*0.6*
SILVER BOW, MT											
60–	**Finance, insurance, and real estate**	82	85	*3.8*	481	499	27,435	26,549	12,642	13,012	*3.8*
6000	Depository institutions	16	20	*5.5*	173	212	19,977	20,660	3,496	4,060	*3.2*
6020	Commercial banks	5	6	*3.1*	110	122	21,927	23,803	2,418	2,514	*2.7*
6060	Credit unions	8	10	*9.8*	-	59	-	15,051	-	926	*7.8*
6200	Security and commodity brokers	4	3	*2.5*	-	25	-	60,160	-	1,659	*4.4*
6210	Security brokers and dealers	3	3	*3.4*	-	25	-	60,160	-	1,659	*5.0*
6400	Insurance agents, brokers, and service	17	19	*3.1*	-	40	-	16,400	-	753	*1.5*
6500	Real estate	30	34	*3.9*	71	78	16,169	16,564	1,091	1,304	-
6510	Real estate operators and lessors	18	21	*5.5*	43	50	11,535	12,400	539	728	*5.2*
6530	Real estate agents and managers	6	8	*2.1*	8	-	40,000	-	131	-	-
6553	Cemetery subdividers and developers	3	3	*10.3*	11	8	13,455	15,000	172	157	*15.0*
STILLWATER, MT											
60–	**Finance, insurance, and real estate**	10	9	*0.4*	63	57	16,762	19,368	1,367	1,589	*0.5*
SWEET GRASS, MT											
60–	**Finance, insurance, and real estate**	7	7	*0.3*	-	47	-	19,404	-	839	*0.2*
6000	Depository institutions	3	3	*0.8*	28	37	19,143	22,595	591	767	*0.6*
6500	Real estate	3	4	*0.5*	5	10	6,400	7,600	43	72	-
TETON, MT											
60–	**Finance, insurance, and real estate**	19	18	*0.8*	76	78	16,579	15,385	1,456	1,434	*0.4*
6500	Real estate	6	5	*0.6*	11	10	7,636	5,200	71	38	-

Source: County Business Patterns, 1992/93, CBP-92/93-1, U.S. Department of Commerce, Washington, D.C., April 1995. SIC categories for which data were suppressed or not available for both 1992 and 1993 are *not* displayed. The employment columns represent mid-March employment in the year. Pay per employee is calculated by dividing 1st Quarter payroll, annualized, by mid-March employment. The columns headed "% State" show the county's percentage of the state total for the SIC in 1993; for example, 0.9% for SIC 6030 means that the county had 0.9 percent of the state's total establishments (or payroll) in SIC 6030 in 1993. A dash (-) is used to indicate that data are not available or cannot be calculated; *nec* means not elsewhere classified.

SIC	Industry	No. Establishments			Employment		Pay / Employee		Annual Payroll ($ 000)		
		1992	1993	% State	1992	1993	1992	1993	1992	1993	% State
TOOLE, MT											
60 –	**Finance, insurance, and real estate**	13	12	0.5	85	75	21,129	19,413	1,845	1,484	0.4
6000	Depository institutions	6	5	1.4	65	53	21,908	19,698	1,447	1,141	0.9
TREASURE, MT											
60 –	**Finance, insurance, and real estate**	2	1	0.0	-	-	-	-	-	-	-
VALLEY, MT											
60 –	**Finance, insurance, and real estate**	25	23	1.0	151	132	17,801	17,606	2,662	2,440	0.7
6000	Depository institutions	7	5	1.4	91	79	18,681	18,785	1,739	1,532	1.2
6400	Insurance agents, brokers, and service	10	9	1.5	22	20	11,818	17,000	259	306	0.6
6500	Real estate	4	6	0.7	-	21	-	9,333	-	255	-
6510	Real estate operators and lessors	4	6	1.6	-	21	-	9,333	-	255	1.8
WHEATLAND, MT											
60 –	**Finance, insurance, and real estate**	7	7	0.3	29	27	12,414	12,296	385	342	0.1
6500	Real estate	3	3	0.3	7	7	5,714	5,714	40	40	-
WIBAUX, MT											
60 –	**Finance, insurance, and real estate**	4	7	0.3	13	11	13,231	21,091	188	220	0.1
6400	Insurance agents, brokers, and service	1	3	0.5	-	1	-	4,000	-	10	0.0
YELLOWSTONE, MT											
60 –	**Finance, insurance, and real estate**	370	374	16.5	3,231	3,288	22,014	22,526	72,998	77,901	22.9
6000	Depository institutions	43	48	13.2	1,129	1,242	23,479	23,816	26,248	29,185	23.2
6020	Commercial banks	20	21	10.9	895	973	24,299	25,225	21,715	23,555	25.1
6030	Savings institutions	7	7	10.9	89	-	24,584	-	1,965	-	-
6060	Credit unions	14	17	16.7	-	137	-	16,175	-	2,351	19.8
6100	Nondepository institutions	21	18	22.5	161	162	32,646	26,988	5,283	5,432	29.5
6140	Personal credit institutions	10	6	19.4	65	54	28,492	27,704	1,833	1,775	33.5
6150	Business credit institutions	5	3	27.3	50	-	34,080	-	1,654	-	-
6160	Mortgage bankers and brokers	6	8	29.6	46	77	36,957	24,260	1,796	2,784	33.1
6200	Security and commodity brokers	29	28	23.7	169	190	53,941	53,537	9,172	10,218	27.0
6210	Security brokers and dealers	22	22	25.3	152	181	57,816	55,691	8,798	10,061	30.4
6220	Commodity contracts brokers, dealers	3	3	37.5	-	6	-	12,000	-	123	42.4
6280	Security and commodity services	4	3	13.0	-	3	-	6,667	-	34	0.8
6300	Insurance carriers	49	36	26.5	752	677	18,367	18,239	14,836	13,459	28.8
6310	Life insurance	24	18	56.3	563	569	16,256	16,710	10,207	10,754	72.3
6330	Fire, marine, and casualty insurance	13	9	14.3	29	-	27,310	-	926	-	-
6400	Insurance agents, brokers, and service	91	105	17.2	409	461	19,433	20,529	8,165	10,261	20.7
6500	Real estate	118	126	14.4	484	450	10,785	12,213	6,019	6,730	-
6510	Real estate operators and lessors	55	59	15.5	220	233	10,382	9,854	2,391	2,579	18.3
6530	Real estate agents and managers	41	58	14.9	137	170	13,810	14,235	2,354	3,073	19.4
6552	Subdividers and developers, n.e.c.	6	3	7.3	83	-	2,747	-	255	-	-
6553	Cemetery subdividers and developers	2	3	10.3	-	9	-	25,333	-	239	22.8
6700	Holding and other investment offices	19	13	18.1	127	106	25,732	24,830	3,275	2,616	14.4
6710	Holding offices	7	3	13.6	60	27	27,333	34,074	1,890	979	6.6

Source: County Business Patterns, 1992/93, CBP-92/93-1, U.S. Department of Commerce, Washington, D.C., April 1995. SIC categories for which data were suppressed or not available for both 1992 and 1993 are *not* displayed. The employment columns represent mid-March employment in the year. Pay per employee is calculated by dividing 1st Quarter payroll, annualized, by mid-March employment. The columns headed "% State" show the county's percentage of the state total for the SIC in 1993; for example, 0.9% for SIC 6030 means that the county had 0.9 percent of the state's total establishments (or payroll) in SIC 6030 in 1993. A dash (-) is used to indicate that data are not available or cannot be calculated; *nec* means not elsewhere classified.

NEBRASKA

SIC	Industry	No. Establishments			Employment		Pay / Employee		Annual Payroll ($ 000)		
		1992	1993	% State	1992	1993	1992	1993	1992	1993	% State
ADAMS, NE											
60 –	**Finance, insurance, and real estate**	85	81	1.8	394	362	18,619	20,442	7,206	7,518	0.5
6000	Depository institutions	12	13	1.4	193	207	20,332	20,329	3,845	4,290	1.2
6020	Commercial banks	8	8	1.2	173	180	20,624	21,111	3,453	3,850	1.4
6030	Savings institutions	4	4	2.6	20	-	17,800	-	392	-	-
6200	Security and commodity brokers	5	5	1.9	12	-	63,667	-	742	-	-
6300	Insurance carriers	5	4	1.3	4	-	34,000	-	155	-	-
6400	Insurance agents, brokers, and service	28	26	1.9	69	74	17,391	16,378	1,123	1,176	1.1
6500	Real estate	31	29	2.5	96	58	9,042	11,931	963	764	-
6510	Real estate operators and lessors	15	16	3.1	34	-	9,176	-	359	-	-
6530	Real estate agents and managers	10	9	1.8	49	20	8,408	14,800	421	265	0.5
6540	Title abstract offices	3	3	6.3	9	7	12,000	16,000	118	124	3.6
ANTELOPE, NE											
60 –	**Finance, insurance, and real estate**	19	19	0.4	86	90	19,070	16,800	1,688	1,633	0.1
6000	Depository institutions	7	7	0.7	55	61	21,818	18,951	1,283	1,253	0.4
6020	Commercial banks	7	7	1.1	55	61	21,818	18,951	1,283	1,253	0.4
6400	Insurance agents, brokers, and service	5	7	0.5	-	14	-	7,714	-	138	0.1
6500	Real estate	3	2	0.2	3	-	5,333	-	15	-	-
BANNER, NE											
60 –	**Finance, insurance, and real estate**	1	1	0.0	-	-	-	-	-	-	-
BLAINE, NE											
60 –	**Finance, insurance, and real estate**	1	1	0.0	-	-	-	-	-	-	-
BOONE, NE											
60 –	**Finance, insurance, and real estate**	18	16	0.4	85	86	18,071	17,953	1,856	1,859	0.1
6000	Depository institutions	7	7	0.7	66	67	18,970	19,284	1,599	1,646	0.5
6400	Insurance agents, brokers, and service	4	5	0.4	4	7	7,000	6,286	30	40	0.0
6500	Real estate	4	2	0.2	7	-	10,857	-	71	-	-
BOX BUTTE, NE											
60 –	**Finance, insurance, and real estate**	34	39	0.9	199	212	20,482	20,302	4,410	4,657	0.3
6000	Depository institutions	10	10	1.1	144	150	20,889	21,333	3,283	3,371	1.0
6020	Commercial banks	5	5	0.8	117	123	21,812	22,146	2,767	2,819	1.0
6400	Insurance agents, brokers, and service	11	12	0.9	25	29	22,720	18,621	623	687	0.7
6500	Real estate	9	13	1.1	17	23	9,647	7,478	156	223	-
6530	Real estate agents and managers	3	6	1.2	5	-	16,000	-	73	-	-
BOYD, NE											
60 –	**Finance, insurance, and real estate**	9	10	0.2	-	35	-	18,743	-	852	0.1
6000	Depository institutions	4	5	0.5	27	26	20,000	22,154	699	740	0.2
6020	Commercial banks	4	5	0.8	27	26	20,000	22,154	699	740	0.3
6500	Real estate	3	2	0.2	5	-	12,800	-	67	-	-
BROWN, NE											
60 –	**Finance, insurance, and real estate**	10	10	0.2	-	51	-	20,784	-	1,228	0.1

Source: County Business Patterns, 1992/93, CBP-92/93-1, U.S. Department of Commerce, Washington, D.C., April 1995. SIC categories for which data were suppressed or not available for both 1992 and 1993 are *not* displayed. The employment columns represent mid-March employment in the year. Pay per employee is calculated by dividing 1st Quarter payroll, annualized, by mid-March employment. The columns headed "% State" show the county's percentage of the state total for the SIC in 1993; for example, 0.9% for SIC 6030 means that the county had 0.9 percent of the state's total establishments (or payroll) in SIC 6030 in 1993. A dash (-) is used to indicate that data are not available or cannot be calculated; *nec* means not elsewhere classified.

Continued on next page.

SIC	Industry	No. Establishments			Employment		Pay / Employee		Annual Payroll ($ 000)		
		1992	1993	% State	1992	1993	1992	1993	1992	1993	% State
BROWN, NE - [continued]											
6000	Depository institutions	3	3	0.3	35	39	22,057	21,231	934	994	0.3
6020	Commercial banks	3	3	0.5	35	39	22,057	21,231	934	994	0.3
6400	Insurance agents, brokers, and service	5	6	0.4	11	-	18,909	-	206	-	-
BUFFALO, NE											
60 -	**Finance, insurance, and real estate**	106	104	2.4	525	630	18,690	16,844	10,397	11,668	0.8
6000	Depository institutions	22	22	2.4	270	360	18,400	14,544	5,275	5,882	1.7
6020	Commercial banks	13	15	2.3	224	325	18,643	14,302	4,425	5,278	1.9
6030	Savings institutions	4	3	2.0	29	17	19,862	19,765	619	355	0.8
6060	Credit unions	4	4	3.4	-	18	-	14,000	-	249	1.6
6100	Nondepository institutions	5	3	1.8	19	-	34,526	-	531	-	-
6200	Security and commodity brokers	8	11	4.2	18	-	48,444	-	997	-	-
6300	Insurance carriers	7	5	1.6	28	31	16,714	23,871	490	608	0.1
6400	Insurance agents, brokers, and service	30	31	2.2	88	98	17,136	16,163	1,639	1,747	1.7
6500	Real estate	28	28	2.4	97	92	12,495	12,913	1,283	1,345	
6510	Real estate operators and lessors	14	13	2.5	33	31	9,818	10,581	365	395	1.1
6530	Real estate agents and managers	8	11	2.3	48	48	12,750	12,750	605	628	1.2
6700	Holding and other investment offices	6	4	2.1	5	6	25,600	22,000	182	167	0.2
BURT, NE											
60 -	**Finance, insurance, and real estate**	18	19	0.4	95	102	19,032	16,235	1,742	1,811	0.1
6000	Depository institutions	6	7	0.7	64	70	20,688	17,371	1,283	1,382	0.4
6020	Commercial banks	6	7	1.1	64	70	20,688	17,371	1,283	1,382	0.5
6400	Insurance agents, brokers, and service	4	4	0.3	16	16	15,750	15,000	253	261	0.3
6500	Real estate	5	5	0.4	-	10	-	3,600	-	43	-
BUTLER, NE											
60 -	**Finance, insurance, and real estate**	17	16	0.4	73	74	18,027	18,216	1,247	1,356	0.1
6000	Depository institutions	7	7	0.7	59	61	20,068	19,934	1,117	1,197	0.3
6020	Commercial banks	7	7	1.1	59	61	20,068	19,934	1,117	1,197	0.4
6400	Insurance agents, brokers, and service	6	6	0.4	-	10	-	12,000	-	145	0.1
6500	Real estate	3	3	0.3	2	3	4,000	4,000	12	14	-
CASS, NE											
60 -	**Finance, insurance, and real estate**	41	43	1.0	192	226	17,438	16,460	3,585	4,191	0.3
6000	Depository institutions	13	12	1.3	125	142	19,808	19,042	2,606	3,073	0.9
6020	Commercial banks	12	12	1.8	-	142	-	19,042	-	3,073	1.1
6400	Insurance agents, brokers, and service	9	13	0.9	14	24	5,143	4,500	78	121	0.1
6500	Real estate	12	11	0.9	36	40	9,333	9,600	385	435	
6530	Real estate agents and managers	5	5	1.0	25	8	10,560	21,500	303	148	0.3
6700	Holding and other investment offices	2	3	1.5	-	9	-	13,778	-	126	0.1
CEDAR, NE											
60 -	**Finance, insurance, and real estate**	22	21	0.5	105	104	19,505	19,231	1,995	1,997	0.1
6000	Depository institutions	7	7	0.7	76	71	22,842	24,113	1,726	1,712	0.5
6020	Commercial banks	7	7	1.1	76	71	22,842	24,113	1,726	1,712	0.6
6400	Insurance agents, brokers, and service	8	8	0.6	13	18	11,385	9,111	159	181	0.2
6500	Real estate	6	6	0.5	-	15	-	8,267	-	104	-
6530	Real estate agents and managers	4	4	0.8	6	-	24,667	-	94	-	-
CHASE, NE											
60 -	**Finance, insurance, and real estate**	11	12	0.3	66	73	23,515	22,521	1,552	1,598	0.1
6000	Depository institutions	4	4	0.4	46	54	24,783	22,815	1,199	1,254	0.4
6020	Commercial banks	4	4	0.6	46	54	24,783	22,815	1,199	1,254	0.4

Source: County Business Patterns, 1992/93, CBP-92/93-1, U.S. Department of Commerce, Washington, D.C., April 1995. SIC categories for which data were suppressed or not available for both 1992 and 1993 are not displayed. The employment columns represent mid-March employment in the year. Pay per employee is calculated by dividing 1st Quarter payroll, annualized, by mid-March employment. The columns headed "% State" show the county's percentage of the state total for the SIC in 1993; for example, 0.9% for SIC 6030 means that the county had 0.9 percent of the state's total establishments (or payroll) in SIC 6030 in 1993. A dash (-) is used to indicate that data are not available or cannot be calculated; nec means not elsewhere classified.

SIC	Industry	No. Establishments			Employment		Pay / Employee		Annual Payroll ($ 000)		
		1992	1993	% State	1992	1993	1992	1993	1992	1993	% State
CHERRY, NE											
60 –	**Finance, insurance, and real estate**	15	16	*0.4*	81	76	19,556	16,263	1,573	1,286	*0.1*
6000	Depository institutions	6	6	*0.6*	57	54	21,333	16,000	1,201	915	*0.3*
CHEYENNE, NE											
60 –	**Finance, insurance, and real estate**	33	31	*0.7*	143	155	16,364	15,458	2,377	2,512	*0.2*
6000	Depository institutions	8	8	*0.9*	83	95	20,723	18,821	1,744	1,818	*0.5*
6200	Security and commodity brokers	4	4	*1.5*	7	5	21,143	26,400	146	140	*0.2*
6400	Insurance agents, brokers, and service	10	12	*0.9*	19	-	12,000	-	240	-	-
6500	Real estate	7	5	*0.4*	13	11	8,308	6,909	110	86	-
CLAY, NE											
60 –	**Finance, insurance, and real estate**	19	19	*0.4*	81	85	17,086	17,129	1,513	1,685	*0.1*
6000	Depository institutions	7	7	*0.7*	51	52	21,647	21,769	1,226	1,356	*0.4*
6400	Insurance agents, brokers, and service	6	7	*0.5*	-	20	-	9,800	-	196	*0.2*
6500	Real estate	5	4	*0.3*	7	-	6,857	-	52	-	-
COLFAX, NE											
60 –	**Finance, insurance, and real estate**	22	22	*0.5*	-	-	-	-	-	-	-
6000	Depository institutions	7	7	*0.7*	80	91	23,350	21,099	1,910	1,867	*0.5*
6020	Commercial banks	7	7	*1.1*	80	91	23,350	21,099	1,910	1,867	*0.7*
CUMING, NE											
60 –	**Finance, insurance, and real estate**	25	28	*0.6*	156	169	19,462	19,479	3,151	3,485	*0.2*
6000	Depository institutions	10	10	*1.1*	115	118	21,357	22,576	2,563	2,769	*0.8*
6400	Insurance agents, brokers, and service	9	10	*0.7*	22	26	10,000	9,077	231	295	*0.3*
6500	Real estate	3	4	*0.3*	7	12	7,429	7,333	74	132	-
CUSTER, NE											
60 –	**Finance, insurance, and real estate**	37	39	*0.9*	160	159	19,625	19,874	3,131	3,290	*0.2*
6000	Depository institutions	12	12	*1.3*	102	99	23,059	23,152	2,386	2,414	*0.7*
6400	Insurance agents, brokers, and service	13	13	*0.9*	28	29	12,143	12,966	348	418	*0.4*
6500	Real estate	8	9	*0.8*	17	19	4,941	4,842	87	99	-
6530	Real estate agents and managers	5	6	*1.2*	7	9	6,286	5,333	44	48	*0.1*
DAKOTA, NE											
60 –	**Finance, insurance, and real estate**	29	25	*0.6*	515	600	26,221	25,760	15,495	18,234	*1.3*
6000	Depository institutions	8	8	*0.9*	90	111	22,311	20,577	2,375	2,225	*0.6*
6530	Real estate agents and managers	4	4	*0.8*	40	35	8,900	8,914	383	347	*0.7*
DAWES, NE											
60 –	**Finance, insurance, and real estate**	18	20	*0.5*	92	97	13,391	13,113	1,318	1,460	*0.1*
6000	Depository institutions	5	5	*0.5*	67	71	15,701	15,549	1,147	1,265	*0.4*
6500	Real estate	5	8	*0.7*	6	-	3,333	-	25	-	-
6530	Real estate agents and managers	2	5	*1.0*	-	5	-	4,000	-	37	*0.1*
DAWSON, NE											
60 –	**Finance, insurance, and real estate**	65	61	*1.4*	316	306	18,785	19,150	5,772	6,065	*0.4*
6000	Depository institutions	18	18	*1.9*	195	199	20,841	20,442	3,851	4,006	*1.1*
6100	Nondepository institutions	5	3	*1.8*	14	10	23,714	22,800	281	196	*0.4*
6400	Insurance agents, brokers, and service	25	26	*1.9*	78	78	13,179	13,897	1,043	1,211	*1.2*
6500	Real estate	11	10	*0.9*	17	-	10,353	-	170	-	-
6510	Real estate operators and lessors	7	6	*1.2*	7	8	5,143	8,000	38	72	*0.2*
DEUEL, NE											
60 –	**Finance, insurance, and real estate**	6	6	*0.1*	-	-	-	-	-	-	-

Source: County Business Patterns, 1992/93, CBP-92/93-1, U.S. Department of Commerce, Washington, D.C., April 1995. SIC categories for which data were suppressed or not available for both 1992 and 1993 are *not* displayed. The employment columns represent mid-March employment in the year. Pay per employee is calculated by dividing 1st Quarter payroll, annualized, by mid-March employment. The columns headed "% State" show the county's percentage of the state total for the SIC in 1993; for example, 0.9% for SIC 6030 means that the county had 0.9 percent of the state's total establishments (or payroll) in SIC 6030 in 1993. A dash (-) is used to indicate that data are not available or cannot be calculated; *nec* means not elsewhere classified.

SIC	Industry	No. Establishments			Employment		Pay / Employee		Annual Payroll ($ 000)		
		1992	1993	% State	1992	1993	1992	1993	1992	1993	% State
DIXON, NE											
60 –	**Finance, insurance, and real estate**	12	11	*0.2*	56	64	13,286	12,438	799	802	*0.1*
6000	Depository institutions	5	5	*0.5*	44	-	15,545	-	741	-	-
6020	Commercial banks	5	5	*0.8*	44	-	15,545		741	-	-
6400	Insurance agents, brokers, and service	5	4	*0.3*	-	14	-	5,143	-	70	*0.1*
DODGE, NE											
60 –	**Finance, insurance, and real estate**	81	81	*1.8*	470	471	19,813	19,618	9,489	9,990	*0.7*
6000	Depository institutions	20	20	*2.1*	256	273	20,891	19,604	5,443	5,883	*1.7*
6020	Commercial banks	14	14	*2.1*	229	243	21,869	20,247	5,028	5,372	*1.9*
6300	Insurance carriers	7	3	*1.0*	25	11	21,600	21,455	480	263	*0.0*
6330	Fire, marine, and casualty insurance	3	1	*0.8*	11	-	14,182	-	178	-	-
6400	Insurance agents, brokers, and service	22	30	*2.2*	94	95	15,745	17,516	1,594	1,846	*1.8*
6500	Real estate	24	22	*1.9*	78	74	15,744	17,568	1,310	1,270	-
6530	Real estate agents and managers	12	10	*2.1*	46	35	20,522	27,314	903	758	*1.5*
DOUGLAS, NE											
60 –	**Finance, insurance, and real estate**	1,324	1,361	*30.8*	28,356	29,436	28,664	28,486	809,889	855,395	*58.9*
6000	Depository institutions	181	185	*19.8*	5,545	5,993	23,770	22,614	139,268	143,728	*40.8*
6020	Commercial banks	83	91	*13.8*	4,024	4,392	24,093	23,630	97,544	106,134	*37.3*
6030	Savings institutions	53	43	*28.3*	860	964	20,735	19,876	23,214	24,512	*53.9*
6140	Personal credit institutions	39	25	*40.3*	288	238	25,778	22,252	7,246	5,258	*56.3*
6150	Business credit institutions	5	15	*57.7*	-	106	-	30,075		3,349	-
6160	Mortgage bankers and brokers	23	24	*52.2*	306	378	36,327	31,587	12,883	18,246	*65.1*
6200	Security and commodity brokers	95	101	*38.1*	2,294	1,065	42,422	62,915	91,629	60,556	*65.6*
6210	Security brokers and dealers	55	56	*34.8*	799	881	60,025	69,031	43,769	52,727	*64.4*
6220	Commodity contracts brokers, dealers	5	6	*31.6*	18	22	50,000	39,273	840	862	-
6280	Security and commodity services	35	39	*46.4*	1,477	162	32,807	32,864	47,020	6,967	-
6300	Insurance carriers	176	142	*46.1*	13,270	15,136	30,449	30,154	394,301	452,538	*68.0*
6310	Life insurance	63	47	*43.9*	2,919	3,155	32,171	31,157	88,812	90,028	*45.1*
6330	Fire, marine, and casualty insurance	59	58	*45.3*	1,313	2,071	32,363	32,191	39,217	69,625	*42.4*
6360	Title insurance	8	8	*57.1*	124	-	21,290	-	3,467	-	-
6370	Pension, health, and welfare funds	26	7	*35.0*	205	164	30,810	33,293	7,504	5,599	-
6400	Insurance agents, brokers, and service	377	404	*29.1*	2,531	1,883	26,775	27,002	67,631	53,366	*51.4*
6500	Real estate	350	377	*32.5*	2,569	2,835	17,901	16,171	49,186	54,114	-
6510	Real estate operators and lessors	147	177	*34.0*	975	1,096	13,071	12,310	13,829	15,197	*43.9*
6530	Real estate agents and managers	150	167	*34.3*	1,274	1,551	21,984	18,525	29,126	34,486	*66.4*
6540	Title abstract offices	3	4	*8.3*	-	42	-	20,952		1,052	*30.9*
6552	Subdividers and developers, n.e.c.	11	16	*48.5*	23	85	29,043	17,600	709	2,159	*80.7*
6553	Cemetery subdividers and developers	7	8	*13.6*	70	59	18,800	20,203	1,248	1,180	*52.7*
6700	Holding and other investment offices	76	84	*43.3*	1,310	1,521	29,227	30,509	38,868	52,402	*62.4*
6710	Holding offices	29	29	*37.7*	651	655	43,275	51,847	28,930	35,263	*62.4*
6732	Educational, religious, etc. trusts	18	17	*41.5*	204	229	10,314	10,952	2,193	2,703	*24.2*
6733	Trusts, n.e.c.	11	18	*42.9*	30	-	19,067	-	647	-	-
DUNDY, NE											
60 –	**Finance, insurance, and real estate**	6	6	*0.1*	19	20	25,263	18,800	468	367	*0.0*
FILLMORE, NE											
60 –	**Finance, insurance, and real estate**	23	21	*0.5*	153	126	16,837	21,175	2,563	2,762	*0.2*
6000	Depository institutions	8	8	*0.9*	95	92	21,347	23,087	1,996	2,085	*0.6*
6020	Commercial banks	8	8	*1.2*	95	92	21,347	23,087	1,996	2,085	*0.7*
6400	Insurance agents, brokers, and service	7	8	*0.6*	28	28	14,571	17,143	444	620	*0.6*
6500	Real estate	8	5	*0.4*	30	6	4,667	10,667	123	57	-
FRANKLIN, NE											
60 –	**Finance, insurance, and real estate**	12	11	*0.2*	53	50	13,962	14,160	868	887	*0.1*

Source: County Business Patterns, 1992/93, CBP-92/93-1, U.S. Department of Commerce, Washington, D.C., April 1995. SIC categories for which data were suppressed or not available for both 1992 and 1993 are *not* displayed. The employment columns represent mid-March employment in the year. Pay per employee is calculated by dividing 1st Quarter payroll, annualized, by mid-March employment. The columns headed "% State" show the county's percentage of the state total for the SIC in 1993; for example, 0.9% for SIC 6030 means that the county had 0.9 percent of the state's total establishments (or payroll) in SIC 6030 in 1993. A dash (-) is used to indicate that data are not available or cannot be calculated; *nec* means not elsewhere classified.

Continued on next page.

SIC	Industry	No. Establishments			Employment		Pay / Employee		Annual Payroll ($ 000)		
		1992	1993	% State	1992	1993	1992	1993	1992	1993	% State
FRANKLIN, NE - [continued]											
6000	Depository institutions	4	3	0.3	35	21	17,143	16,381	721	396	0.1
6020	Commercial banks	4	3	0.5	35	21	17,143	16,381	721	396	0.1
6400	Insurance agents, brokers, and service	6	5	0.4	15	-	8,533	-	135	-	-
FRONTIER, NE											
60 –	**Finance, insurance, and real estate**	4	4	0.1	-	-	-	-	-	-	-
FURNAS, NE											
60 –	**Finance, insurance, and real estate**	17	19	0.4	85	92	15,765	16,478	1,560	1,709	0.1
6000	Depository institutions	6	6	0.6	62	66	18,839	19,455	1,381	1,486	0.4
6400	Insurance agents, brokers, and service	8	8	0.6	19	-	8,211	-	155	-	-
6500	Real estate	3	3	0.3	4	5	4,000	4,800	24	25	-
GAGE, NE											
60 –	**Finance, insurance, and real estate**	67	63	1.4	300	284	19,933	18,493	5,604	5,540	0.4
6000	Depository institutions	19	16	1.7	183	154	21,486	20,260	3,434	3,180	0.9
6020	Commercial banks	14	11	1.7	156	129	22,513	21,023	2,950	2,760	1.0
6300	Insurance carriers	4	4	1.3	9	-	8,889	-	77	-	-
6400	Insurance agents, brokers, and service	19	19	1.4	42	43	11,333	11,535	496	551	0.5
6500	Real estate	15	17	1.5	36	56	12,556	10,071	483	626	-
6510	Real estate operators and lessors	2	5	1.0	-	34	-	11,765	-	437	1.3
6530	Real estate agents and managers	8	9	1.8	19	14	17,053	8,000	348	127	0.2
6553	Cemetery subdividers and developers	3	3	5.1	-	8	-	6,500	-	62	2.8
6710	Holding offices	2	3	3.9	-	10	-	16,400	-	174	0.3
GARDEN, NE											
60 –	**Finance, insurance, and real estate**	8	7	0.2	34	29	15,765	18,621	635	709	0.0
6000	Depository institutions	3	3	0.3	26	25	18,462	19,840	592	661	0.2
6020	Commercial banks	3	3	0.5	26	25	18,462	19,840	592	661	0.2
6400	Insurance agents, brokers, and service	3	3	0.2	2	-	8,000	-	19	-	-
GARFIELD, NE											
60 –	**Finance, insurance, and real estate**	5	6	0.1	-	-	-	-	-	-	-
GOSPER, NE											
60 –	**Finance, insurance, and real estate**	7	7	0.2	-	-	-	-	-	-	-
6400	Insurance agents, brokers, and service	4	4	0.3	22	-	13,455	-	301	-	-
GRANT, NE											
60 –	**Finance, insurance, and real estate**	2	2	0.0	-	-	-	-	-	-	-
GREELEY, NE											
60 –	**Finance, insurance, and real estate**	6	6	0.1	32	-	21,875	-	713	-	-
6000	Depository institutions	3	3	0.3	-	25	-	26,400	-	696	0.2
6020	Commercial banks	3	3	0.5	-	25	-	26,400	-	696	0.2
HALL, NE											
60 –	**Finance, insurance, and real estate**	156	167	3.8	1,216	1,296	19,891	20,849	24,927	28,238	1.9
6000	Depository institutions	24	26	2.8	359	370	20,591	20,670	7,646	8,682	2.5
6020	Commercial banks	15	17	2.6	250	255	21,424	21,663	5,488	6,399	2.2
6030	Savings institutions	6	6	3.9	96	101	18,833	18,614	1,924	2,025	4.5
6060	Credit unions	3	3	2.6	13	14	17,538	17,429	234	258	1.6
6100	Nondepository institutions	7	9	5.5	34	48	29,765	28,917	899	1,072	2.2
6140	Personal credit institutions	5	6	9.7	-	26	-	19,385	-	531	5.7
6200	Security and commodity brokers	9	11	4.2	16	21	51,000	48,762	844	1,196	1.3
6280	Security and commodity services	3	3	3.6	4	4	12,000	9,000	48	42	-
6300	Insurance carriers	14	15	4.9	485	539	18,375	19,896	8,776	10,400	1.6
6310	Life insurance	7	9	8.4	466	523	18,112	19,771	8,344	10,044	5.0

Source: County Business Patterns, 1992/93, CBP-92/93-1, U.S. Department of Commerce, Washington, D.C., April 1995. SIC categories for which data were suppressed or not available for both 1992 and 1993 are not displayed. The employment columns represent mid-March employment in the year. Pay per employee is calculated by dividing 1st Quarter payroll, annualized, by mid-March employment. The columns headed "% State" show the county's percentage of the state total for the SIC in 1993; for example, 0.9% for SIC 6030 means that the county had 0.9 percent of the state's total establishments (or payroll) in SIC 6030 in 1993. A dash (-) is used to indicate that data are not available or cannot be calculated; nec means not elsewhere classified.

Continued on next page.

SIC	Industry	No. Establishments			Employment		Pay / Employee		Annual Payroll ($ 000)		
		1992	1993	% State	1992	1993	1992	1993	1992	1993	% State
HALL, NE - [continued]											
6400	Insurance agents, brokers, and service	52	54	3.9	188	195	19,298	20,821	4,021	4,658	4.5
6500	Real estate	41	44	3.8	109	94	14,239	13,106	1,855	1,279	-
6510	Real estate operators and lessors	18	22	4.2	49	-	8,000	-	453	-	-
6530	Real estate agents and managers	18	19	3.9	46	48	19,304	16,250	975	786	1.5
6700	Holding and other investment offices	9	8	4.1	25	29	35,040	32,552	886	951	1.1
HAMILTON, NE											
60 –	**Finance, insurance, and real estate**	23	26	0.6	96	126	20,708	15,810	2,280	2,320	0.2
6000	Depository institutions	6	6	0.6	67	80	23,164	17,150	1,769	1,640	0.5
6020	Commercial banks	6	6	0.9	67	80	23,164	17,150	1,769	1,640	0.6
6400	Insurance agents, brokers, and service	9	10	0.7	22	23	12,545	14,435	311	366	0.4
6500	Real estate	8	9	0.8	7	-	22,857	-	200	-	-
6530	Real estate agents and managers	3	4	0.8	-	9	-	19,111	-	173	0.3
HARLAN, NE											
60 –	**Finance, insurance, and real estate**	7	7	0.2	40	36	21,000	20,444	896	755	0.1
6000	Depository institutions	4	4	0.4	35	31	23,314	22,839	867	722	0.2
6020	Commercial banks	4	4	0.6	35	31	23,314	22,839	867	722	0.3
HAYES, NE											
60 –	**Finance, insurance, and real estate**	4	4	0.1	-	9	-	18,222	-	144	0.0
HITCHCOCK, NE											
60 –	**Finance, insurance, and real estate**	7	7	0.2	47	46	19,574	21,217	1,081	1,146	0.1
6000	Depository institutions	3	3	0.3	16	15	19,500	20,267	450	458	0.1
6020	Commercial banks	3	3	0.5	16	15	19,500	20,267	450	458	0.2
HOLT, NE											
60 –	**Finance, insurance, and real estate**	36	38	0.9	178	182	19,393	16,989	3,685	3,387	0.2
6000	Depository institutions	10	10	1.1	109	116	20,917	17,793	2,474	2,328	0.7
6400	Insurance agents, brokers, and service	11	13	0.9	32	34	9,750	9,529	329	374	0.4
6500	Real estate	11	12	1.0	22	21	16,364	7,619	378	208	-
6530	Real estate agents and managers	5	7	1.4	16	13	19,750	6,462	335	120	0.2
HOOKER, NE											
60 –	**Finance, insurance, and real estate**	2	2	0.0	-	-	-	-	-	-	-
HOWARD, NE											
60 –	**Finance, insurance, and real estate**	13	16	0.4	53	57	19,774	19,158	904	990	0.1
6000	Depository institutions	7	6	0.6	46	32	21,130	21,250	828	524	0.1
6500	Real estate	1	3	0.3	-	-	-	-	-	13	-
JEFFERSON, NE											
60 –	**Finance, insurance, and real estate**	21	22	0.5	103	111	14,563	14,811	1,873	1,959	0.1
6000	Depository institutions	7	7	0.7	69	68	18,899	20,353	1,626	1,667	0.5
6400	Insurance agents, brokers, and service	6	6	0.4	11	15	7,273	8,000	87	117	0.1
6500	Real estate	6	6	0.5	-	23	-	4,522	-	136	-
6530	Real estate agents and managers	3	3	0.6	15	-	4,000	-	81	-	-
JOHNSON, NE											
60 –	**Finance, insurance, and real estate**	15	15	0.3	70	67	18,400	19,104	1,258	1,251	0.1
6000	Depository institutions	7	6	0.6	59	47	20,136	21,957	1,066	1,003	0.3
6400	Insurance agents, brokers, and service	5	6	0.4	8	17	11,000	13,882	179	234	0.2
6500	Real estate	3	3	0.3	3	3	4,000	4,000	13	14	-

Source: County Business Patterns, 1992/93, CBP-92/93-1, U.S. Department of Commerce, Washington, D.C., April 1995. SIC categories for which data were suppressed or not available for both 1992 and 1993 are *not* displayed. The employment columns represent mid-March employment in the year. Pay per employee is calculated by dividing 1st Quarter payroll, annualized, by mid-March employment. The columns headed "% State" show the county's percentage of the state total for the SIC in 1993; for example, 0.9% for SIC 6030 means that the county had 0.9 percent of the state's total establishments (or payroll) in SIC 6030 in 1993. A dash (-) is used to indicate that data are not available or cannot be calculated; *nec* means not elsewhere classified.

SIC	Industry	No. Establishments			Employment		Pay / Employee		Annual Payroll ($ 000)		
		1992	1993	% State	1992	1993	1992	1993	1992	1993	% State
KEARNEY, NE											
60–	**Finance, insurance, and real estate**	12	11	*0.2*	83	81	18,361	19,951	1,776	1,819	*0.1*
6000	Depository institutions	4	4	*0.4*	59	62	20,542	21,161	1,397	1,463	*0.4*
6020	Commercial banks	4	4	*0.6*	59	62	20,542	21,161	1,397	1,463	*0.5*
6400	Insurance agents, brokers, and service	6	4	*0.3*	-	12	-	20,667		300	*0.3*
KEITH, NE											
60–	**Finance, insurance, and real estate**	32	29	*0.7*	153	177	20,392	18,486	3,140	3,352	*0.2*
6000	Depository institutions	8	9	*1.0*	109	141	21,541	18,014	2,371	2,546	*0.7*
6400	Insurance agents, brokers, and service	10	11	*0.8*	26	23	13,385	16,522	345	435	*0.4*
6500	Real estate	8	5	*0.4*	9	6	18,222	7,333	103	66	-
6510	Real estate operators and lessors	5	2	*0.4*	4	-	28,000	-	46	-	-
6530	Real estate agents and managers	3	3	*0.6*	5	-	10,400	-	57	-	-
KEYA PAHA, NE											
60–	**Finance, insurance, and real estate**	1	1	*0.0*	-	-	-	-	-	-	-
KIMBALL, NE											
60–	**Finance, insurance, and real estate**	7	7	*0.2*	57	56	18,737	19,071	1,089	1,120	*0.1*
6000	Depository institutions	3	3	*0.3*	49	44	19,673	21,273	939	953	*0.3*
6020	Commercial banks	3	3	*0.5*	49	44	19,673	21,273	939	953	*0.3*
KNOX, NE											
60–	**Finance, insurance, and real estate**	28	29	*0.7*	115	119	16,800	17,546	2,006	2,079	*0.1*
6000	Depository institutions	9	9	*1.0*	65	69	24,185	24,464	1,650	1,694	*0.5*
6500	Real estate	5	5	*0.4*	12	12	7,333	9,000	86	103	-
LANCASTER, NE											
60–	**Finance, insurance, and real estate**	646	672	*15.2*	10,031	10,412	25,557	27,385	266,279	289,708	*19.9*
6000	Depository institutions	103	107	*11.4*	2,078	1,902	21,546	23,531	46,414	44,512	*12.6*
6020	Commercial banks	56	55	*8.3*	1,384	1,305	21,396	22,562	29,260	30,109	*10.6*
6030	Savings institutions	27	26	*17.1*	585	434	22,817	28,618	15,088	11,342	*24.9*
6100	Nondepository institutions	31	27	*16.4*	176	182	25,636	26,659	4,925	5,565	*11.3*
6140	Personal credit institutions	19	14	*22.6*	100	68	23,560	20,235	2,457	1,480	*15.8*
6150	Business credit institutions	4	3	*11.5*	13	-	34,769	-	449	-	-
6160	Mortgage bankers and brokers	8	9	*19.6*	63	88	27,048	30,318	2,019	3,197	*11.4*
6200	Security and commodity brokers	45	46	*17.4*	320	339	52,912	52,189	16,702	19,064	*20.7*
6210	Security brokers and dealers	33	33	*20.5*	299	290	55,237	57,338	16,184	17,966	*21.9*
6280	Security and commodity services	12	12	*14.3*	21	-	19,810	-	518	-	-
6300	Insurance carriers	89	77	*25.0*	5,400	5,624	27,148	29,514	150,937	166,035	*24.9*
6310	Life insurance	37	32	*29.9*	2,754	2,823	27,251	28,060	77,208	80,468	*40.3*
6330	Fire, marine, and casualty insurance	32	29	*22.7*	2,442	2,540	27,708	31,082	69,916	78,136	*47.5*
6360	Title insurance	4	2	*14.3*	93	-	15,914	-	1,663	-	-
6370	Pension, health, and welfare funds	7	6	*30.0*	-	9	-	17,333	-	178	-
6400	Insurance agents, brokers, and service	157	179	*12.9*	593	661	22,597	21,222	13,058	14,291	*13.8*
6500	Real estate	183	196	*16.9*	834	905	14,043	14,077	13,425	14,912	-
6510	Real estate operators and lessors	90	108	*20.7*	343	460	11,872	11,061	4,440	5,653	*16.3*
6530	Real estate agents and managers	68	74	*15.2*	406	383	15,990	17,034	7,555	7,907	*15.2*
6552	Subdividers and developers, n.e.c.	9	8	*24.2*	18	19	8,222	13,263	224	278	*10.4*
6553	Cemetery subdividers and developers	3	3	*5.1*	22	-	15,091	-	348	-	-
6700	Holding and other investment offices	38	40	*20.6*	630	799	29,263	31,384	20,818	25,329	*30.1*
6710	Holding offices	16	16	*20.8*	271	391	41,151	43,141	13,261	16,282	*28.8*
6732	Educational, religious, etc. trusts	11	11	*26.8*	338	387	19,905	19,318	6,894	8,087	*72.4*
6733	Trusts, n.e.c.	8	6	*14.3*	15	9	15,733	24,889	222	224	*16.3*
LINCOLN, NE											
60–	**Finance, insurance, and real estate**	90	91	*2.1*	411	435	19,474	19,770	8,389	8,861	*0.6*
6000	Depository institutions	20	20	*2.1*	230	240	19,043	20,000	4,508	4,834	*1.4*
6020	Commercial banks	14	14	*2.1*	197	209	19,371	20,249	3,909	4,249	*1.5*

Source: County Business Patterns, 1992/93, CBP-92/93-1, U.S. Department of Commerce, Washington, D.C., April 1995. SIC categories for which data were suppressed or not available for both 1992 and 1993 are *not* displayed. The employment columns represent mid-March employment in the year. Pay per employee is calculated by dividing 1st Quarter payroll, annualized, by mid-March employment. The columns headed "% State" show the county's percentage of the state total for the SIC in 1993; for example, 0.9% for SIC 6030 means that the county had 0.9 percent of the state's total establishments (or payroll) in SIC 6030 in 1993. A dash (-) is used to indicate that data are not available or cannot be calculated; *nec* means not elsewhere classified.

Continued on next page.

SIC	Industry	No. Establishments			Employment		Pay / Employee		Annual Payroll ($ 000)		
		1992	1993	% State	1992	1993	1992	1993	1992	1993	% State
LINCOLN, NE - [continued]											
6100	Nondepository institutions	6	6	3.6	-	37	-	24,649	-	585	1.2
6140	Personal credit institutions	3	3	4.8	13	9	23,077	20,000	329	237	2.5
6300	Insurance carriers	3	3	1.0	4	4	33,000	47,000	128	176	0.0
6400	Insurance agents, brokers, and service	32	30	2.2	75	76	17,493	17,368	1,486	1,672	1.6
6500	Real estate	22	25	2.2	-	61	-	12,131	-	910	-
6510	Real estate operators and lessors	7	8	1.5	12	21	15,000	10,095	192	237	0.7
6530	Real estate agents and managers	12	12	2.5	25	28	14,240	12,714	415	468	0.9
LOGAN, NE											
60 –	**Finance, insurance, and real estate**	2	2	0.0	-	-	-	-	-	-	-
LOUP, NE											
60 –	**Finance, insurance, and real estate**	1	1	0.0	-	-	-	-	-	-	-
MADISON, NE											
60 –	**Finance, insurance, and real estate**	106	110	2.5	605	630	22,255	20,413	13,488	13,318	0.9
6000	Depository institutions	18	19	2.0	214	225	20,243	18,756	4,587	4,460	1.3
6020	Commercial banks	11	12	1.8	180	189	21,356	19,471	4,077	3,922	1.4
6030	Savings institutions	3	3	2.0	26	27	15,385	16,444	416	437	1.0
6060	Credit unions	4	4	3.4	8	9	11,000	10,667	94	101	0.6
6100	Nondepository institutions	3	4	2.4	21	-	33,714	-	599	-	-
6200	Security and commodity brokers	7	6	2.3	16	14	37,500	38,286	594	787	0.9
6300	Insurance carriers	7	7	2.3	56	57	38,786	33,895	2,208	2,072	0.3
6400	Insurance agents, brokers, and service	35	37	2.7	141	142	16,284	15,296	2,406	2,630	2.5
6500	Real estate	30	33	2.8	103	112	9,903	9,964	1,020	1,168	-
6510	Real estate operators and lessors	11	16	3.1	17	24	4,941	6,667	100	205	0.6
6530	Real estate agents and managers	14	13	2.7	62	65	12,323	12,554	758	806	1.6
MERRICK, NE											
60 –	**Finance, insurance, and real estate**	23	25	0.6	83	85	15,036	19,482	1,371	1,563	0.1
6000	Depository institutions	8	8	0.9	64	63	16,188	22,476	1,142	1,307	0.4
6400	Insurance agents, brokers, and service	6	7	0.5	12	14	14,000	12,857	158	176	0.2
6500	Real estate	6	7	0.6	5	5	5,600	6,400	50	58	-
6510	Real estate operators and lessors	4	3	0.6	4	4	5,000	5,000	22	20	0.1
MORRILL, NE											
60 –	**Finance, insurance, and real estate**	12	12	0.3	50	53	17,840	18,717	959	995	0.1
6000	Depository institutions	3	3	0.3	31	30	18,839	22,267	601	641	0.2
6020	Commercial banks	3	3	0.5	31	30	18,839	22,267	601	641	0.2
6400	Insurance agents, brokers, and service	4	4	0.3	11	13	16,000	14,769	217	239	0.2
NANCE, NE											
60 –	**Finance, insurance, and real estate**	10	10	0.2	54	56	16,741	16,357	1,141	1,204	0.1
6000	Depository institutions	3	3	0.3	39	40	19,179	19,200	991	1,056	0.3
6020	Commercial banks	3	3	0.5	39	40	19,179	19,200	991	1,056	0.4
6500	Real estate	4	4	0.3	-	4	-	4,000	-	26	-
NEMAHA, NE											
60 –	**Finance, insurance, and real estate**	18	19	0.4	84	85	18,667	18,729	1,633	1,762	0.1
6000	Depository institutions	6	6	0.6	59	61	19,186	19,607	1,214	1,302	0.4
6400	Insurance agents, brokers, and service	4	5	0.4	10	9	10,000	16,444	118	152	0.1
6500	Real estate	5	5	0.4	7	-	26,286	-	148	-	-
6530	Real estate agents and managers	1	3	0.6	-	3	-	14,667	-	68	0.1
NUCKOLLS, NE											
60 –	**Finance, insurance, and real estate**	17	16	0.4	85	89	19,576	18,697	1,797	1,787	0.1
6000	Depository institutions	6	5	0.5	63	65	20,063	19,077	1,385	1,360	0.4
6400	Insurance agents, brokers, and service	7	6	0.4	13	14	17,846	17,714	193	210	0.2

Source: County Business Patterns, 1992/93, CBP-92/93-1, U.S. Department of Commerce, Washington, D.C., April 1995. SIC categories for which data were suppressed or not available for both 1992 and 1993 are not displayed. The employment columns represent mid-March employment in the year. Pay per employee is calculated by dividing 1st Quarter payroll, annualized, by mid-March employment. The columns headed "% State" show the county's percentage of the state total for the SIC in 1993; for example, 0.9% for SIC 6030 means that the county had 0.9 percent of the state's total establishments (or payroll) in SIC 6030 in 1993. A dash (-) is used to indicate that data are not available or cannot be calculated; nec means not elsewhere classified.

SIC	Industry	No. Establishments			Employment		Pay / Employee		Annual Payroll ($ 000)		
		1992	1993	% State	1992	1993	1992	1993	1992	1993	% State
OTOE, NE											
60 –	**Finance, insurance, and real estate**	33	34	*0.8*	201	212	21,373	19,208	4,221	4,444	*0.3*
6000	Depository institutions	11	11	*1.2*	142	143	22,254	19,105	3,009	2,971	*0.8*
6300	Insurance carriers	4	1	*0.3*	7	-	10,286	-	86	-	-
6400	Insurance agents, brokers, and service	8	10	*0.7*	30	39	16,400	15,179	503	628	*0.6*
6500	Real estate	5	6	*0.5*	6	8	26,667	29,000	192	222	-
PAWNEE, NE											
60 –	**Finance, insurance, and real estate**	9	8	*0.2*	-	28	-	19,143	-	646	*0.0*
6000	Depository institutions	6	4	*0.4*	31	21	18,323	22,667	750	582	*0.2*
6020	Commercial banks	6	4	*0.6*	31	21	18,323	22,667	750	582	*0.2*
PERKINS, NE											
60 –	**Finance, insurance, and real estate**	12	12	*0.3*	43	-	18,047	-	813	-	-
6000	Depository institutions	4	4	*0.4*	28	19	23,143	16,842	681	342	*0.1*
6400	Insurance agents, brokers, and service	5	5	*0.4*	8	10	10,000	9,200	89	99	*0.1*
PHELPS, NE											
60 –	**Finance, insurance, and real estate**	34	36	*0.8*	192	226	18,354	17,434	4,163	4,355	*0.3*
6000	Depository institutions	7	7	*0.7*	107	107	22,467	23,103	2,741	2,787	*0.8*
6200	Security and commodity brokers	5	4	*1.5*	6	7	9,333	20,000	83	170	*0.2*
6400	Insurance agents, brokers, and service	12	12	*0.9*	53	63	10,038	9,270	561	574	*0.6*
6500	Real estate	5	7	*0.6*	11	-	4,364	-	116	-	-
6700	Holding and other investment offices	3	3	*1.5*	-	27	-	16,741	-	469	*0.6*
PIERCE, NE											
60 –	**Finance, insurance, and real estate**	16	13	*0.3*	73	72	21,753	18,333	1,572	1,469	*0.1*
6000	Depository institutions	5	4	*0.4*	47	47	26,298	21,277	1,209	1,122	*0.3*
6020	Commercial banks	4	4	*0.6*	-	47	-	21,277	-	1,122	*0.4*
6400	Insurance agents, brokers, and service	8	7	*0.5*	19	-	13,684	-	274	-	-
PLATTE, NE											
60 –	**Finance, insurance, and real estate**	80	93	*2.1*	480	549	22,075	20,758	12,874	12,097	*0.8*
6000	Depository institutions	22	23	*2.5*	300	319	21,133	20,489	6,536	6,820	*1.9*
6020	Commercial banks	12	13	*2.0*	201	212	22,965	22,491	4,605	4,697	*1.7*
6030	Savings institutions	6	6	*3.9*	59	62	21,288	19,226	1,409	1,494	*3.3*
6060	Credit unions	4	4	*3.4*	40	45	11,700	12,800	522	629	*3.9*
6100	Nondepository institutions	4	4	*2.4*	36	-	38,222	-	3,227	-	-
6200	Security and commodity brokers	7	9	*3.4*	13	17	32,923	38,118	453	810	*0.9*
6210	Security brokers and dealers	5	6	*3.7*	-	14	-	44,571	-	783	*1.0*
6300	Insurance carriers	5	3	*1.0*	12	-	17,667	-	217	-	-
6400	Insurance agents, brokers, and service	23	28	*2.0*	73	86	20,658	19,907	1,639	1,805	*1.7*
6500	Real estate	19	26	*2.2*	46	78	15,913	13,641	802	1,130	-
6510	Real estate operators and lessors	7	13	*2.5*	10	-	13,600	-	151	-	-
6530	Real estate agents and managers	9	12	*2.5*	24	22	19,167	15,636	493	389	*0.7*
POLK, NE											
60 –	**Finance, insurance, and real estate**	14	12	*0.3*	85	79	14,729	14,430	1,360	1,300	*0.1*
6000	Depository institutions	6	6	*0.6*	66	66	17,394	15,879	1,259	1,194	*0.3*
RED WILLOW, NE											
60 –	**Finance, insurance, and real estate**	40	40	*0.9*	182	204	23,626	19,196	4,322	4,021	*0.3*
6000	Depository institutions	12	12	*1.3*	122	135	25,607	20,119	3,161	2,851	*0.8*
6020	Commercial banks	7	7	*1.1*	107	120	27,252	20,867	2,919	2,620	*0.9*
6300	Insurance carriers	3	2	*0.6*	3	-	4,000	-	23	-	-
6400	Insurance agents, brokers, and service	13	17	*1.2*	18	34	16,222	11,176	308	365	*0.4*

Source: County Business Patterns, 1992/93, CBP-92/93-1, U.S. Department of Commerce, Washington, D.C., April 1995. SIC categories for which data were suppressed or not available for both 1992 and 1993 are *not* displayed. The employment columns represent mid-March employment in the year. Pay per employee is calculated by dividing 1st Quarter payroll, annualized, by mid-March employment. The columns headed "% State" show the county's percentage of the state total for the SIC in 1993; for example, 0.9% for SIC 6030 means that the county had 0.9 percent of the state's total establishments (or payroll) in SIC 6030 in 1993. A dash (-) is used to indicate that data are not available or cannot be calculated; *nec* means not elsewhere classified.

Continued on next page.

SIC	Industry	No. Establishments			Employment		Pay / Employee		Annual Payroll ($ 000)		
		1992	1993	% State	1992	1993	1992	1993	1992	1993	% State
RED WILLOW, NE - [continued]											
6500	Real estate	8	6	0.5	21	18	9,143	10,000	214	195	-
6510	Real estate operators and lessors	4	4	0.8	12	-	7,333	-	102	-	-
6530	Real estate agents and managers	3	2	0.4	7	-	13,143	-	92	-	-
RICHARDSON, NE											
60 –	**Finance, insurance, and real estate**	24	25	0.6	123	132	15,122	15,091	1,960	2,041	0.1
6000	Depository institutions	8	8	0.9	94	104	16,511	15,654	1,591	1,634	0.5
6500	Real estate	7	7	0.6	-	9	-	7,556	-	78	-
6510	Real estate operators and lessors	2	4	0.8	-	5	-	5,600	-	31	0.1
6530	Real estate agents and managers	3	1	0.2	4	-	8,000	-	35	-	-
ROCK, NE											
60 –	**Finance, insurance, and real estate**	4	4	0.1	13	14	21,231	18,857	274	295	0.0
SALINE, NE											
60 –	**Finance, insurance, and real estate**	31	30	0.7	206	173	14,252	17,595	3,096	3,185	0.2
6000	Depository institutions	11	10	1.1	159	117	14,189	19,282	2,326	2,354	0.7
6400	Insurance agents, brokers, and service	13	14	1.0	30	-	12,133	-	395	-	-
6500	Real estate	4	4	0.3	-	15	-	15,200	-	244	-
SARPY, NE											
60 –	**Finance, insurance, and real estate**	146	149	3.4	1,086	1,278	21,565	23,809	24,283	33,152	2.3
6000	Depository institutions	31	31	3.3	422	484	19,962	17,545	7,886	9,429	2.7
6020	Commercial banks	22	21	3.2	277	316	20,173	16,456	5,362	5,748	2.0
6140	Personal credit institutions	5	4	6.5	29	-	23,034	-	718	-	-
6200	Security and commodity brokers	11	9	3.4	26	22	22,308	17,818	688	576	0.6
6300	Insurance carriers	9	9	2.9	234	-	33,863	-	9,154	-	-
6400	Insurance agents, brokers, and service	30	40	2.9	73	83	18,521	23,904	1,581	2,278	2.2
6500	Real estate	57	53	4.6	171	190	16,655	15,179	2,917	3,139	-
6510	Real estate operators and lessors	22	21	4.0	66	75	11,091	10,560	812	941	2.7
6530	Real estate agents and managers	25	27	5.5	70	90	23,943	19,778	1,640	1,855	3.6
SAUNDERS, NE											
60 –	**Finance, insurance, and real estate**	40	39	0.9	211	188	20,512	19,638	4,873	4,241	0.3
6000	Depository institutions	16	16	1.7	123	118	22,602	21,797	3,143	3,041	0.9
6400	Insurance agents, brokers, and service	10	11	0.8	24	25	13,500	13,280	349	364	0.4
6530	Real estate agents and managers	4	5	1.0	8	-	23,000	-	244	-	-
SCOTTS BLUFF, NE											
60 –	**Finance, insurance, and real estate**	98	97	2.2	568	630	19,486	20,616	11,551	15,409	1.1
6000	Depository institutions	18	19	2.0	263	271	20,030	21,299	5,378	5,462	1.5
6020	Commercial banks	14	14	2.1	252	255	20,286	21,867	5,206	5,246	1.8
6100	Nondepository institutions	5	6	3.6	100	134	23,760	23,373	2,489	5,744	11.7
6200	Security and commodity brokers	3	4	1.5	14	26	42,286	37,846	684	962	1.0
6300	Insurance carriers	7	3	1.0	28	-	16,000	-	411	-	-
6330	Fire, marine, and casualty insurance	3	-	-	8	-	12,000	-	65	-	-
6400	Insurance agents, brokers, and service	32	31	2.2	86	95	16,744	16,800	1,547	1,691	1.6
6500	Real estate	30	31	2.7	75	87	12,107	11,218	1,004	1,099	-
6510	Real estate operators and lessors	11	13	2.5	22	-	9,091	-	224	-	-
6530	Real estate agents and managers	14	14	2.9	43	48	13,674	11,583	604	652	1.3
6700	Holding and other investment offices	3	3	1.5	2	-	18,000	-	38	-	-
SEWARD, NE											
60 –	**Finance, insurance, and real estate**	31	32	0.7	194	200	18,825	18,700	4,375	4,660	0.3
6000	Depository institutions	10	9	1.0	139	135	18,504	19,111	3,175	3,214	0.9
6020	Commercial banks	6	6	0.9	129	127	19,194	19,685	3,071	3,129	1.1
6300	Insurance carriers	3	2	0.6	7	-	10,286	-	76	-	-

Source: County Business Patterns, 1992/93, CBP-92/93-1, U.S. Department of Commerce, Washington, D.C., April 1995. SIC categories for which data were suppressed or not available for both 1992 and 1993 are *not* displayed. The employment columns represent mid-March employment in the year. Pay per employee is calculated by dividing 1st Quarter payroll, annualized, by mid-March employment. The columns headed "% State" show the county's percentage of the state total for the SIC in 1993; for example, 0.9% for SIC 6030 means that the county had 0.9 percent of the state's total establishments (or payroll) in SIC 6030 in 1993. A dash (-) is used to indicate that data are not available or cannot be calculated; *nec* means not elsewhere classified.

Continued on next page.

SIC	Industry	No. Establishments			Employment		Pay / Employee		Annual Payroll ($ 000)		
		1992	1993	% State	1992	1993	1992	1993	1992	1993	% State
SEWARD, NE - [continued]											
6400	Insurance agents, brokers, and service	7	10	0.7	25	31	19,200	17,161	461	555	0.5
6500	Real estate	8	9	0.8	18	28	16,444	11,571	333	409	-
6530	Real estate agents and managers	4	4	0.8	12	13	20,000	19,077	281	295	0.6
SHERIDAN, NE											
60 –	**Finance, insurance, and real estate**	12	10	0.2	102	72	18,471	19,111	1,688	1,572	0.1
6000	Depository institutions	5	3	0.3	89	60	19,820	20,800	1,571	1,415	0.4
6020	Commercial banks	5	3	0.5	89	60	19,820	20,800	1,571	1,415	0.5
6400	Insurance agents, brokers, and service	5	5	0.4	11	-	9,091	-	102	-	-
SHERMAN, NE											
60 –	**Finance, insurance, and real estate**	7	7	0.2	37	-	14,703	-	685	-	-
6000	Depository institutions	3	3	0.3	27	-	17,333	-	609	-	-
6020	Commercial banks	3	3	0.5	27	-	17,333	-	609	-	-
SIOUX, NE											
60 –	**Finance, insurance, and real estate**	2	2	0.0	-	-	-	-	-	-	-
STANTON, NE											
60 –	**Finance, insurance, and real estate**	11	11	0.2	45	41	14,844	16,683	888	867	0.1
6000	Depository institutions	3	3	0.3	27	28	18,074	18,571	720	761	0.2
6020	Commercial banks	3	3	0.5	27	28	18,074	18,571	720	761	0.3
6400	Insurance agents, brokers, and service	4	3	0.2	9	7	12,444	9,714	122	65	0.1
6500	Real estate	3	5	0.4	-	6	-	16,000	-	41	-
THAYER, NE											
60 –	**Finance, insurance, and real estate**	22	20	0.5	166	164	13,325	13,659	2,495	2,670	0.2
6000	Depository institutions	9	9	1.0	89	92	17,573	17,957	1,755	1,933	0.5
6400	Insurance agents, brokers, and service	6	6	0.4	-	18	-	12,222	-	241	0.2
6500	Real estate	6	4	0.3	56	-	7,357	-	499	-	-
THOMAS, NE											
60 –	**Finance, insurance, and real estate**	2	3	0.1	-	-	-	-	-	-	-
THURSTON, NE											
60 –	**Finance, insurance, and real estate**	10	10	0.2	-	56	-	21,857	-	1,237	0.1
6400	Insurance agents, brokers, and service	4	3	0.2	5	3	4,000	5,333	17	18	0.0
VALLEY, NE											
60 –	**Finance, insurance, and real estate**	15	14	0.3	75	82	21,867	18,537	1,663	1,659	0.1
6000	Depository institutions	5	5	0.5	49	58	27,429	21,241	1,357	1,344	0.4
6400	Insurance agents, brokers, and service	5	6	0.4	12	-	13,333	-	159	-	-
WASHINGTON, NE											
60 –	**Finance, insurance, and real estate**	30	34	0.8	255	718	13,035	13,772	3,742	9,690	0.7
6000	Depository institutions	5	5	0.5	90	94	18,089	21,532	1,738	1,996	0.6
6400	Insurance agents, brokers, and service	12	15	1.1	40	-	8,300	-	335	-	-
6500	Real estate	10	11	0.9	116	-	9,931	-	1,415	-	-
6530	Real estate agents and managers	6	7	1.4	6	-	16,667	-	169	-	-
WAYNE, NE											
60 –	**Finance, insurance, and real estate**	22	23	0.5	107	331	20,075	13,051	2,394	4,483	0.3
6000	Depository institutions	7	8	0.9	76	299	23,421	12,843	1,906	3,927	1.1
6400	Insurance agents, brokers, and service	9	9	0.6	14	-	9,143	-	182	-	-

Source: County Business Patterns, 1992/93, CBP-92/93-1, U.S. Department of Commerce, Washington, D.C., April 1995. SIC categories for which data were suppressed or not available for both 1992 and 1993 are *not* displayed. The employment columns represent mid-March employment in the year. Pay per employee is calculated by dividing 1st Quarter payroll, annualized, by mid-March employment. The columns headed "% State" show the county's percentage of the state total for the SIC in 1993; for example, 0.9% for SIC 6030 means that the county had 0.9 percent of the state's total establishments (or payroll) in SIC 6030 in 1993. A dash (-) is used to indicate that data are not available or cannot be calculated; *nec* means not elsewhere classified.

SIC	Industry	No. Establishments			Employment		Pay / Employee		Annual Payroll ($ 000)		
		1992	1993	% State	1992	1993	1992	1993	1992	1993	% State
WEBSTER, NE											
60 –	**Finance, insurance, and real estate**	5	6	0.1	-	-	-	-	-	-	-
6000	Depository institutions	3	3	0.3	-	31	-	19,871	-	776	0.2
6020	Commercial banks	3	3	0.5	-	31	-	19,871	-	776	0.3
WHEELER, NE											
60 –	**Finance, insurance, and real estate**	2	2	0.0	-	-	-	-	-	-	-
YORK, NE											
60 –	**Finance, insurance, and real estate**	54	51	1.2	300	297	18,200	17,212	6,020	6,075	0.4
6000	Depository institutions	14	12	1.3	199	200	18,131	15,920	3,435	3,497	1.0
6100	Nondepository institutions	3	3	1.8	7	-	35,429	-	232	-	-
6200	Security and commodity brokers	6	6	2.3	7	-	22,857	-	207	-	-
6400	Insurance agents, brokers, and service	15	15	1.1	49	47	13,224	13,277	677	672	0.6
6500	Real estate	10	11	0.9	24	22	8,000	9,091	357	213	-
6530	Real estate agents and managers	3	4	0.8	10	11	4,400	8,000	54	83	0.2

Source: County Business Patterns, 1992/93, CBP-92/93-1, U.S. Department of Commerce, Washington, D.C., April 1995. SIC categories for which data were suppressed or not available for both 1992 and 1993 are *not* displayed. The employment columns represent mid-March employment in the year. Pay per employee is calculated by dividing 1st Quarter payroll, annualized, by mid-March employment. The columns headed "% State" show the county's percentage of the state total for the SIC in 1993; for example, 0.9% for SIC 6030 means that the county had 0.9 percent of the state's total establishments (or payroll) in SIC 6030 in 1993. A dash (-) is used to indicate that data are not available or cannot be calculated; *nec* means not elsewhere classified.

NEVADA

SIC	Industry	No. Establishments			Employment		Pay / Employee		Annual Payroll ($ 000)		
		1992	1993	% State	1992	1993	1992	1993	1992	1993	% State
CHURCHILL, NV											
60 –	**Finance, insurance, and real estate**	41	40	1.1	169	148	19,266	18,784	3,395	3,073	0.4
6000	Depository institutions	7	6	1.7	78	63	23,487	21,206	1,835	1,489	0.7
6020	Commercial banks	4	3	1.6	59	-	26,169	-	1,512	-	-
6400	Insurance agents, brokers, and service	9	11	1.6	30	26	13,600	18,154	414	501	0.6
6500	Real estate	22	20	1.1	49	-	14,612	-	842	-	-
6510	Real estate operators and lessors	12	11	1.3	-	24	-	5,167	-	164	0.2
6530	Real estate agents and managers	8	7	0.9	18	-	10,667	-	199	-	-
CLARK, NV											
60 –	**Finance, insurance, and real estate**	2,153	2,185	58.2	20,176	20,031	24,804	25,029	510,999	580,009	69.6
6000	Depository institutions	306	206	57.2	6,438	6,435	23,083	24,915	143,734	157,591	70.4
6020	Commercial banks	207	112	58.0	4,730	4,730	23,073	25,754	102,166	116,010	74.5
6030	Savings institutions	49	50	53.2	922	994	22,655	22,978	23,091	25,085	66.0
6060	Credit unions	32	33	57.9	594	-	24,054	-	14,066	-	-
6090	Functions closely related to banking	17	11	68.8	192	-	22,375	-	4,379	-	-
6100	Nondepository institutions	177	195	67.0	1,396	1,628	32,415	32,980	47,390	65,196	74.2
6140	Personal credit institutions	51	54	66.7	307	341	27,583	21,279	8,127	7,426	68.7
6150	Business credit institutions	19	22	66.7	100	76	28,080	23,000	2,961	1,976	-
6160	Mortgage bankers and brokers	99	118	69.4	983	1,211	34,507	36,902	36,165	55,693	76.5
6200	Security and commodity brokers	65	67	48.2	-	488	-	55,615	-	32,853	59.8
6210	Security brokers and dealers	33	39	52.7	361	425	63,512	56,979	22,830	27,692	-
6280	Security and commodity services	28	26	41.3	72	-	27,556	-	3,781	-	-
6300	Insurance carriers	182	146	66.7	1,781	1,498	28,761	31,378	54,849	51,284	66.5
6310	Life insurance	34	26	76.5	624	303	24,801	27,591	16,610	8,109	81.5
6321	Accident and health insurance	14	9	69.2	269	-	27,836	-	8,350	-	-
6324	Hospital and medical service plans	4	17	81.0	43	-	35,349	-	1,741	-	-
6330	Fire, marine, and casualty insurance	81	65	66.3	315	266	41,003	49,128	13,951	13,318	53.8
6360	Title insurance	12	15	71.4	352	-	27,523	-	9,499	-	-
6370	Pension, health, and welfare funds	30	8	33.3	-	51	-	27,843	-	1,561	-
6400	Insurance agents, brokers, and service	318	373	55.7	1,391	1,847	24,152	23,424	36,766	48,508	60.5
6500	Real estate	951	1,020	57.1	7,606	7,197	19,926	19,779	160,580	190,669	73.6
6510	Real estate operators and lessors	411	472	57.5	3,146	2,648	17,386	12,906	57,512	63,726	75.3
6530	Real estate agents and managers	356	450	56.7	2,464	3,520	18,174	19,802	48,027	78,718	68.9
6552	Subdividers and developers, n.e.c.	73	73	60.8	1,243	658	26,932	41,805	32,887	33,752	87.1
6553	Cemetery subdividers and developers	4	3	37.5	85	61	27,624	38,820	2,370	2,311	78.6
6700	Holding and other investment offices	149	173	61.3	1,095	-	40,281	-	39,969	-	-
6710	Holding offices	51	59	63.4	724	546	49,552	32,059	31,652	21,893	84.6
6720	Investment offices	9	6	66.7	50	-	26,640	-	1,174	-	-
6732	Educational, religious, etc. trusts	6	9	47.4	69	65	19,652	21,846	1,347	1,556	-
6733	Trusts, n.e.c.	29	21	41.2	126	105	14,603	12,152	1,807	1,390	29.0
6799	Investors, n.e.c.	27	52	67.5	57	-	31,439	-	2,036	-	-
DOUGLAS, NV											
60 –	**Finance, insurance, and real estate**	136	144	3.8	1,010	915	17,846	18,221	19,214	18,358	2.2
6000	Depository institutions	17	11	3.1	150	102	24,720	24,588	3,528	2,417	1.1
6020	Commercial banks	12	6	3.1	123	76	25,789	26,000	2,967	1,898	1.2
6400	Insurance agents, brokers, and service	14	16	2.4	-	51	-	18,353	-	1,081	1.3
6500	Real estate	85	96	5.4	722	671	13,512	14,456	10,741	10,720	4.1
6510	Real estate operators and lessors	22	35	4.3	83	91	17,301	12,088	1,473	1,392	1.6
6530	Real estate agents and managers	40	48	6.0	552	518	11,790	13,429	7,215	7,315	6.4

Source: County Business Patterns, 1992/93, CBP-92/93-1, U.S. Department of Commerce, Washington, D.C., April 1995. SIC categories for which data were suppressed or not available for both 1992 and 1993 are *not* displayed. The employment columns represent mid-March employment in the year. Pay per employee is calculated by dividing 1st Quarter payroll, annualized, by mid-March employment. The columns headed "% State" show the county's percentage of the state total for the SIC in 1993; for example, 0.9% for SIC 6030 means that the county had 0.9 percent of the state's total establishments (or payroll) in SIC 6030 in 1993. A dash (-) is used to indicate that data are not available or cannot be calculated; *nec* means not elsewhere classified.

Continued on next page.

SIC	Industry	No. Establishments			Employment		Pay / Employee		Annual Payroll ($ 000)		
		1992	1993	% State	1992	1993	1992	1993	1992	1993	% State
SUSSEX, NJ											
60 –	**Finance, insurance, and real estate**	203	201	1.1	2,194	2,250	26,244	27,093	62,695	64,166	0.7
6000	Depository institutions	59	56	1.5	558	524	20,151	20,260	11,477	11,438	0.7
6020	Commercial banks	47	44	2.0	495	459	20,267	20,453	10,194	10,017	0.9
6030	Savings institutions	12	12	1.2	63	65	19,238	18,892	1,283	1,421	0.4
6400	Insurance agents, brokers, and service	40	43	1.4	178	169	33,551	34,911	6,169	6,941	0.8
6500	Real estate	73	80	1.1	227	302	15,084	16,000	4,205	5,993	0.6
6510	Real estate operators and lessors	17	24	0.7	31	52	23,097	17,231	895	968	0.3
6530	Real estate agents and managers	32	40	1.2	138	195	12,087	14,954	2,066	3,766	0.8
6540	Title abstract offices	7	7	4.5	23	42	18,783	19,429	537	1,013	3.3
6552	Subdividers and developers, n.e.c.	4	2	0.9	8	-	15,000	-	137	-	-
6553	Cemetery subdividers and developers	6	7	3.4	15	-	12,533	-	225	-	-
UNION, NJ											
60 –	**Finance, insurance, and real estate**	1,190	1,254	6.7	12,485	11,895	30,200	30,213	396,566	386,745	4.2
6000	Depository institutions	216	220	5.9	4,385	3,615	26,041	24,662	110,995	90,176	5.7
6020	Commercial banks	105	107	4.8	2,598	2,600	26,403	25,598	61,367	68,015	6.0
6030	Savings institutions	64	63	6.2	1,236	724	22,848	22,939	28,565	15,994	4.3
6060	Credit unions	40	45	12.3	-	266	-	20,857	-	5,707	13.4
6090	Functions closely related to banking	6	5	4.4	-	25	-	17,600	-	460	1.5
6100	Nondepository institutions	65	65	6.5	777	797	39,609	37,310	34,539	36,237	5.2
6140	Personal credit institutions	23	19	6.9	124	99	27,032	25,414	3,416	2,595	3.9
6150	Business credit institutions	9	13	7.0	52	81	55,538	44,049	2,963	3,341	1.5
6160	Mortgage bankers and brokers	31	33	6.3	595	617	40,867	38,334	27,631	30,301	7.8
6200	Security and commodity brokers	45	53	4.2	336	339	60,833	62,383	19,705	24,449	1.4
6210	Security brokers and dealers	22	25	3.3	188	218	90,383	80,183	15,546	19,831	1.6
6280	Security and commodity services	21	28	5.9	145	121	23,283	30,314	4,105	4,618	0.9
6300	Insurance carriers	97	84	6.7	1,994	2,261	37,765	40,833	78,059	88,204	3.5
6310	Life insurance	23	21	4.6	554	791	36,830	38,908	19,671	25,849	2.3
6321	Accident and health insurance	3	2	8.3	21	-	23,619	-	504	-	-
6330	Fire, marine, and casualty insurance	20	20	5.2	1,151	1,124	39,868	41,288	46,087	48,231	4.5
6360	Title insurance	9	2	5.0	65	-	33,908	-	2,651	-	-
6370	Pension, health, and welfare funds	37	36	13.2	136	300	33,118	45,213	7,240	12,233	22.3
6400	Insurance agents, brokers, and service	211	224	7.1	1,449	1,490	34,396	34,972	53,813	57,788	6.4
6500	Real estate	510	566	7.5	2,566	2,505	20,098	21,763	59,735	67,160	7.2
6510	Real estate operators and lessors	258	288	8.3	1,240	1,100	17,103	17,484	23,988	22,518	7.0
6530	Real estate agents and managers	154	193	5.8	790	952	23,878	26,008	20,345	28,531	6.0
6540	Title abstract offices	5	7	4.5	-	54	-	23,037	-	2,786	9.1
6552	Subdividers and developers, n.e.c.	27	50	22.0	119	201	17,445	20,517	2,501	6,791	11.8
6553	Cemetery subdividers and developers	12	15	7.4	204	188	22,569	26,468	4,854	5,923	14.2
6710	Holding offices	9	10	3.9	405	463	19,654	13,719	10,478	7,151	1.8
6732	Educational, religious, etc. trusts	7	6	5.6	29	28	30,897	35,143	1,062	1,019	6.3
6733	Trusts, n.e.c.	11	11	10.7	41	281	20,098	23,530	1,483	8,139	46.0
WARREN, NJ											
60 –	**Finance, insurance, and real estate**	154	149	0.8	857	845	23,659	22,466	20,857	20,236	0.2
6000	Depository institutions	52	52	1.4	474	449	21,030	20,071	9,745	9,982	0.6
6020	Commercial banks	38	38	1.7	390	371	21,651	20,291	7,968	8,460	0.7
6030	Savings institutions	9	9	0.9	69	-	19,304	-	1,385	-	-
6060	Credit unions	5	5	1.4	15	-	12,800	-	392	-	-
6100	Nondepository institutions	6	3	0.3	12	-	21,333	-	329	-	-
6400	Insurance agents, brokers, and service	32	31	1.0	115	185	32,174	27,676	3,573	5,157	0.6
6500	Real estate	55	58	0.8	144	159	14,528	15,472	2,598	2,876	0.3
6510	Real estate operators and lessors	19	17	0.5	39	55	18,974	15,927	1,034	1,046	0.3
6530	Real estate agents and managers	19	25	0.7	75	-	13,760	-	1,150	-	-
6540	Title abstract offices	4	4	2.5	5	-	24,800	-	141	-	-
6553	Cemetery subdividers and developers	11	11	5.4	17	16	7,765	9,000	198	211	0.5

Source: County Business Patterns, 1992/93, CBP-92/93-1, U.S. Department of Commerce, Washington, D.C., April 1995. SIC categories for which data were suppressed or not available for both 1992 and 1993 are *not* displayed. The employment columns represent mid-March employment in the year. Pay per employee is calculated by dividing 1st Quarter payroll, annualized, by mid-March employment. The columns headed "% State" show the county's percentage of the state total for the SIC in 1993; for example, 0.9% for SIC 6030 means that the county had 0.9 percent of the state's total establishments (or payroll) in SIC 6030 in 1993. A dash (-) is used to indicate that data are not available or cannot be calculated; *nec* means not elsewhere classified.

NEW MEXICO

SIC	Industry	No. Establishments			Employment		Pay / Employee		Annual Payroll ($ 000)		
		1992	1993	% State	1992	1993	1992	1993	1992	1993	% State
BERNALILLO, NM											
60 –	**Finance, insurance, and real estate**	1,392	1,446	41.8	13,581	15,374	25,235	22,248	345,600	366,507	57.1
6000	Depository institutions	165	150	29.2	4,105	4,865	21,238	21,517	87,640	108,213	48.2
6020	Commercial banks	128	106	28.9	3,483	3,445	21,627	21,816	75,523	76,336	44.2
6030	Savings institutions	10	9	22.0	161	-	16,497	-	2,809	-	-
6060	Credit unions	19	24	27.9	430	-	20,781	-	9,006	-	-
6090	Functions closely related to banking	8	11	55.0	31	-	8,516	-	302	-	-
6100	Nondepository institutions	102	119	44.9	1,276	1,393	37,411	23,793	44,766	40,386	76.0
6140	Personal credit institutions	54	52	33.3	497	514	23,115	21,136	11,884	11,505	59.5
6160	Mortgage bankers and brokers	36	52	65.8	-	390	-	34,595	-	19,617	86.6
6200	Security and commodity brokers	60	56	47.9	-	477	-	48,369	-	24,238	52.3
6210	Security brokers and dealers	35	33	44.6	342	391	65,404	52,512	19,156	21,073	-
6280	Security and commodity services	25	23	54.8	-	86	-	29,535	-	3,165	-
6300	Insurance carriers	169	126	62.7	2,552	3,834	24,475	22,828	66,782	88,300	89.2
6321	Accident and health insurance	6	5	100.0	68	48	29,353	16,333	2,588	1,001	100.0
6330	Fire, marine, and casualty insurance	65	47	50.0	474	484	28,498	30,612	14,475	15,882	71.2
6350	Surety insurance	4	1	100.0	26	-	27,846	-	802	-	-
6360	Title insurance	16	5	62.5	271	-	31,144	-	10,045	-	-
6400	Insurance agents, brokers, and service	286	351	45.1	1,387	1,896	22,125	21,591	33,137	46,756	52.1
6500	Real estate	546	581	40.9	2,633	2,591	15,300	15,923	42,416	47,007	45.1
6510	Real estate operators and lessors	250	283	45.2	1,196	1,103	13,759	12,540	15,905	14,825	53.3
6530	Real estate agents and managers	203	253	39.7	1,051	1,259	15,825	17,792	18,053	25,966	52.1
6540	Title abstract offices	6	6	14.3	51	-	28,314	-	1,756	-	-
6552	Subdividers and developers, n.e.c.	32	26	34.7	137	106	19,358	23,509	3,022	3,084	19.7
6553	Cemetery subdividers and developers	5	5	25.0	58	-	16,000	-	945	-	-
6700	Holding and other investment offices	62	61	38.9	1,195	-	41,182	-	46,279	-	-
6710	Holding offices	22	20	62.5	834	189	51,132	47,407	39,825	9,052	73.7
6732	Educational, religious, etc. trusts	12	13	38.2	276	68	17,551	17,471	4,961	1,263	39.7
6733	Trusts, n.e.c.	14	11	39.3	31	20	20,129	21,600	539	481	-
6799	Investors, n.e.c.	4	10	33.3	11	-	10,545	-	132	-	-
CATRON, NM											
60 –	**Finance, insurance, and real estate**	2	3	0.1	-	3	-	6,667	-	78	0.0
6500	Real estate	2	3	0.2	-	3	-	6,667	-	78	0.1
6530	Real estate agents and managers	1	3	0.5	-	3	-	6,667	-	78	0.2
CHAVES, NM											
60 –	**Finance, insurance, and real estate**	157	152	4.4	896	774	21,049	19,716	20,431	17,684	2.8
6000	Depository institutions	28	24	4.7	401	391	20,878	20,399	8,154	8,228	3.7
6020	Commercial banks	19	14	3.8	263	238	22,753	21,361	5,490	4,861	2.8
6100	Nondepository institutions	11	10	3.8	-	42	-	15,905	-	697	1.3
6140	Personal credit institutions	8	7	4.5	32	35	16,875	14,057	525	497	2.6
6200	Security and commodity brokers	6	6	5.1	25	26	48,320	53,846	1,607	1,762	3.8
6300	Insurance carriers	8	5	2.5	172	45	26,465	26,222	5,445	1,192	1.2
6400	Insurance agents, brokers, and service	30	30	3.9	73	102	16,164	15,490	1,413	1,713	1.9
6500	Real estate	60	61	4.3	146	136	12,575	11,441	2,022	2,750	2.6
6510	Real estate operators and lessors	29	31	5.0	70	71	12,514	10,310	894	1,140	4.1
6530	Real estate agents and managers	25	27	4.2	59	-	12,407	-	904	-	-
6792	Oil royalty traders	10	11	55.0	30	22	21,200	21,636	726	539	43.5

Source: County Business Patterns, 1992/93, CBP-92/93-1, U.S. Department of Commerce, Washington, D.C., April 1995. SIC categories for which data were suppressed or not available for both 1992 and 1993 are *not* displayed. The employment columns represent mid-March employment in the year. Pay per employee is calculated by dividing 1st Quarter payroll, annualized, by mid-March employment. The columns headed "% State" show the county's percentage of the state total for the SIC in 1993; for example, 0.9% for SIC 6030 means that the county had 0.9 percent of the state's total establishments (or payroll) in SIC 6030 in 1993. A dash (-) is used to indicate that data are not available or cannot be calculated; *nec* means not elsewhere classified.

SIC	Industry	No. Establishments			Employment		Pay / Employee		Annual Payroll ($ 000)		
		1992	1993	% State	1992	1993	1992	1993	1992	1993	% State
CIBOLA, NM											
60 –	**Finance, insurance, and real estate**	26	26	0.8	154	137	19,740	18,482	2,873	2,755	0.4
6000	Depository institutions	7	7	1.4	82	76	20,000	17,474	1,408	1,376	0.6
6020	Commercial banks	7	6	1.6	82	-	20,000	-	1,408	-	-
6400	Insurance agents, brokers, and service	8	8	1.0	30	-	24,800	-	793	-	-
6500	Real estate	8	8	0.6	-	23	-	13,565	-	392	0.4
6510	Real estate operators and lessors	6	6	1.0	20	-	7,000	-	152	-	-
COLFAX, NM											
60 –	**Finance, insurance, and real estate**	36	38	1.1	217	214	17,032	17,196	3,843	3,658	0.6
6000	Depository institutions	13	14	2.7	112	118	18,821	20,915	2,252	2,388	1.1
6020	Commercial banks	11	11	3.0	-	116	-	21,069	-	2,355	1.4
6400	Insurance agents, brokers, and service	9	9	1.2	41	38	20,390	15,474	825	618	0.7
6500	Real estate	10	12	0.8	27	27	10,222	10,074	207	217	0.2
6510	Real estate operators and lessors	1	4	0.6	-	3	-	5,333	-	26	0.1
6530	Real estate agents and managers	5	7	1.1	7	-	4,571	-	38	-	-
CURRY, NM											
60 –	**Finance, insurance, and real estate**	84	85	2.5	688	697	17,291	16,970	12,572	12,108	1.9
6000	Depository institutions	20	19	3.7	410	406	18,332	17,576	7,926	7,131	3.2
6020	Commercial banks	15	14	3.8	303	296	19,776	18,514	6,335	5,428	3.1
6100	Nondepository institutions	8	9	3.4	35	54	23,200	18,074	848	992	1.9
6400	Insurance agents, brokers, and service	19	20	2.6	73	100	17,863	16,160	1,261	1,538	1.7
6500	Real estate	28	29	2.0	124	96	9,387	11,083	1,222	1,379	1.3
6510	Real estate operators and lessors	12	11	1.8	24	43	10,667	12,744	268	623	2.2
6530	Real estate agents and managers	6	14	2.2	43	41	12,558	7,805	551	414	0.8
DE BACA, NM											
60 –	**Finance, insurance, and real estate**	5	4	0.1	-	20	-	15,200	-	363	0.1
6500	Real estate	3	2	0.1	2	-	6,000	-	28	-	-
DONA ANA, NM											
60 –	**Finance, insurance, and real estate**	286	301	8.7	1,891	1,735	19,848	19,901	40,109	36,480	5.7
6000	Depository institutions	41	41	8.0	740	786	20,638	20,967	16,172	16,307	7.3
6020	Commercial banks	33	31	8.4	623	576	21,297	23,153	14,163	13,298	7.7
6060	Credit unions	2	3	3.5	-	119	-	13,815	-	1,853	8.2
6100	Nondepository institutions	21	22	8.3	172	112	19,047	21,107	3,493	2,613	4.9
6140	Personal credit institutions	16	18	11.5	-	94	-	19,149	-	1,930	10.0
6200	Security and commodity brokers	9	10	8.5	49	-	57,878	-	2,796	-	-
6300	Insurance carriers	25	19	9.5	284	106	24,000	24,566	6,846	2,575	2.6
6370	Pension, health, and welfare funds	7	4	16.0	70	-	16,743	-	316	-	-
6400	Insurance agents, brokers, and service	53	66	8.5	224	269	18,000	17,145	4,551	4,990	5.6
6500	Real estate	130	135	9.5	396	379	11,990	11,905	5,658	5,715	5.5
6510	Real estate operators and lessors	59	73	11.7	160	192	8,950	9,521	1,499	2,075	7.5
6530	Real estate agents and managers	48	51	8.0	126	143	14,222	13,762	2,100	2,406	4.8
6540	Title abstract offices	4	2	4.8	37	-	17,838	-	920	-	-
6552	Subdividers and developers, n.e.c.	7	4	5.3	33	-	10,788	-	431	-	-
6700	Holding and other investment offices	7	8	5.1	26	-	21,231	-	593	-	-
EDDY, NM											
60 –	**Finance, insurance, and real estate**	99	100	2.9	792	681	20,515	20,458	15,469	14,227	2.2
6000	Depository institutions	18	21	4.1	339	360	21,959	21,656	6,768	7,371	3.3
6020	Commercial banks	13	13	3.5	316	330	22,228	22,376	6,466	6,929	4.0
6100	Nondepository institutions	8	6	2.3	33	17	14,788	20,471	532	368	0.7
6140	Personal credit institutions	8	6	3.8	33	17	14,788	20,471	532	368	1.9
6200	Security and commodity brokers	5	4	3.4	19	-	32,000	-	630	-	-
6300	Insurance carriers	6	4	2.0	135	-	25,393	-	2,887	-	-
6400	Insurance agents, brokers, and service	25	27	3.5	147	190	18,585	18,000	2,577	3,522	3.9
6500	Real estate	31	31	2.2	102	65	10,784	11,323	1,657	1,362	1.3

Source: County Business Patterns, 1992/93, CBP-92/93-1, U.S. Department of Commerce, Washington, D.C., April 1995. SIC categories for which data were suppressed or not available for both 1992 and 1993 are not displayed. The employment columns represent mid-March employment in the year. Pay per employee is calculated by dividing 1st Quarter payroll, annualized, by mid-March employment. The columns headed "% State" show the county's percentage of the state total for the SIC in 1993; for example, 0.9% for SIC 6030 means that the county had 0.9 percent of the state's total establishments (or payroll) in SIC 6030 in 1993. A dash (-) is used to indicate that data are not available or cannot be calculated; nec means not elsewhere classified.

Continued on next page.

SIC	Industry	No. Establishments			Employment		Pay / Employee		Annual Payroll ($ 000)		
		1992	1993	% State	1992	1993	1992	1993	1992	1993	% State
EDDY, NM - [continued]											
6510	Real estate operators and lessors	19	18	2.9	48	-	9,417	-	446	-	-
6530	Real estate agents and managers	8	11	1.7	13	-	5,538	-	83	-	-
6700	Holding and other investment offices	6	7	4.5	17	20	26,353	35,600	418	697	2.8
6792	Oil royalty traders	3	4	20.0	-	14	-	38,857	-	552	44.6
GRANT, NM											
60 –	**Finance, insurance, and real estate**	52	51	1.5	278	257	15,468	16,996	4,661	4,673	0.7
6000	Depository institutions	12	12	2.3	156	163	19,282	18,552	3,134	2,978	1.3
6020	Commercial banks	8	8	2.2	131	136	19,969	19,882	2,782	2,698	1.6
6100	Nondepository institutions	2	3	1.1	-	6	-	18,000	-	159	0.3
6140	Personal credit institutions	2	3	1.9	-	6	-	18,000	-	159	0.8
6400	Insurance agents, brokers, and service	14	12	1.5	61	51	11,934	14,431	755	783	0.9
6500	Real estate	21	22	1.5	44	-	7,273	-	465	-	-
6510	Real estate operators and lessors	3	6	1.0	3	5	12,000	12,800	42	93	0.3
6530	Real estate agents and managers	12	12	1.9	23	-	7,826	-	243	-	-
GUADALUPE, NM											
60 –	**Finance, insurance, and real estate**	5	6	0.2	-	21	-	14,286	-	310	0.0
HARDING, NM											
60 –	**Finance, insurance, and real estate**	2	2	0.1	-	-	-	-	-	-	-
HIDALGO, NM											
60 –	**Finance, insurance, and real estate**	8	8	0.2	-	-	-	-	-	-	-
LEA, NM											
60 –	**Finance, insurance, and real estate**	97	91	2.6	538	506	17,383	19,478	9,287	9,920	1.5
6000	Depository institutions	25	22	4.3	284	263	17,310	20,091	4,895	5,213	2.3
6020	Commercial banks	18	16	4.4	264	241	17,409	20,183	4,564	4,794	2.8
6100	Nondepository institutions	4	5	1.9	13	24	18,462	12,333	276	368	0.7
6400	Insurance agents, brokers, and service	24	27	3.5	81	112	20,494	19,964	1,561	2,239	2.5
6500	Real estate	29	22	1.5	98	51	12,571	12,392	1,179	656	0.6
6510	Real estate operators and lessors	12	10	1.6	28	19	14,714	9,895	349	205	0.7
6530	Real estate agents and managers	12	11	1.7	18	-	19,111	-	353	-	-
6700	Holding and other investment offices	6	8	5.1	13	21	23,385	28,190	301	514	2.1
6792	Oil royalty traders	3	3	15.0	5	-	24,800	-	108	-	-
LINCOLN, NM											
60 –	**Finance, insurance, and real estate**	62	61	1.8	336	322	17,631	16,708	6,081	5,771	0.9
6000	Depository institutions	12	12	2.3	117	132	20,034	18,273	2,312	2,453	1.1
6020	Commercial banks	8	8	2.2	99	112	20,202	18,179	1,960	2,054	1.2
6400	Insurance agents, brokers, and service	7	9	1.2	98	79	21,429	21,418	1,972	1,849	2.1
6500	Real estate	37	36	2.5	105	105	11,429	11,314	1,475	1,394	1.3
6510	Real estate operators and lessors	10	8	1.3	-	19	-	8,000	-	184	0.7
6530	Real estate agents and managers	23	26	4.1	60	77	12,133	10,701	898	946	1.9
LOS ALAMOS, NM											
60 –	**Finance, insurance, and real estate**	36	32	0.9	360	346	20,978	24,543	7,539	8,300	1.3
6000	Depository institutions	9	7	1.4	251	261	22,183	25,533	5,481	6,248	2.8
6400	Insurance agents, brokers, and service	9	9	1.2	52	32	19,923	27,500	1,156	1,010	1.1
6500	Real estate	15	12	0.8	-	42	-	12,095	-	570	0.5
6510	Real estate operators and lessors	9	7	1.1	33	22	9,697	11,636	308	273	1.0
6530	Real estate agents and managers	4	5	0.8	8	20	7,500	12,600	60	297	0.6
LUNA, NM											
60 –	**Finance, insurance, and real estate**	22	22	0.6	169	167	16,757	17,701	2,823	2,913	0.5
6000	Depository institutions	6	6	1.2	120	121	18,067	18,810	2,104	2,220	1.0
6400	Insurance agents, brokers, and service	3	3	0.4	16	-	16,250	-	284	-	-

Source: County Business Patterns, 1992/93, CBP-92/93-1, U.S. Department of Commerce, Washington, D.C., April 1995. SIC categories for which data were suppressed or not available for both 1992 and 1993 are not displayed. The employment columns represent mid-March employment in the year. Pay per employee is calculated by dividing 1st Quarter payroll, annualized, by mid-March employment. The columns headed "% State" show the county's percentage of the state total for the SIC in 1993; for example, 0.9% for SIC 6030 means that the county had 0.9 percent of the state's total establishments (or payroll) in SIC 6030 in 1993. A dash (-) is used to indicate that data are not available or cannot be calculated; nec means not elsewhere classified.

Continued on next page.

SIC	Industry	No. Establishments			Employment		Pay / Employee		Annual Payroll ($ 000)		
		1992	1993	% State	1992	1993	1992	1993	1992	1993	% State
LUNA, NM - [continued]											
6500	Real estate	9	11	0.8	20	20	11,200	12,000	232	265	0.3
6510	Real estate operators and lessors	3	4	0.6	13	10	11,077	11,200	125	109	0.4
6530	Real estate agents and managers	6	6	0.9	7	-	11,429	-	107	-	-
MCKINLEY, NM											
60 -	**Finance, insurance, and real estate**	54	52	1.5	363	377	17,091	18,302	7,328	7,457	1.2
6000	Depository institutions	13	12	2.3	181	178	18,895	19,685	3,642	3,561	1.6
6100	Nondepository institutions	3	6	2.3	14	31	20,000	18,194	320	728	1.4
6400	Insurance agents, brokers, and service	13	10	1.3	51	45	17,412	22,844	1,484	1,109	1.2
6500	Real estate	22	20	1.4	79	82	11,443	12,244	1,051	1,126	1.1
6510	Real estate operators and lessors	11	10	1.6	45	-	10,667	-	547	-	-
6530	Real estate agents and managers	8	7	1.1	24	51	10,167	11,216	281	618	1.2
MORA, NM											
60 -	**Finance, insurance, and real estate**	3	3	0.1	5	5	12,000	12,800	62	65	0.0
6000	Depository institutions	3	3	0.6	5	5	12,000	12,800	62	65	0.0
OTERO, NM											
60 -	**Finance, insurance, and real estate**	83	86	2.5	480	533	16,425	15,677	8,660	9,298	1.4
6000	Depository institutions	13	14	2.7	262	277	17,344	17,069	4,910	5,213	2.3
6020	Commercial banks	6	6	1.6	177	186	16,701	16,215	3,315	3,410	2.0
6100	Nondepository institutions	8	10	3.8	22	-	20,909	-	494	-	-
6140	Personal credit institutions	7	8	5.1	-	27	-	18,963	-	505	2.6
6400	Insurance agents, brokers, and service	18	22	2.8	61	93	14,492	12,989	1,084	1,406	1.6
6500	Real estate	34	34	2.4	103	120	12,505	11,667	1,364	1,641	1.6
6510	Real estate operators and lessors	14	17	2.7	47	55	11,319	10,400	508	658	2.4
6530	Real estate agents and managers	15	14	2.2	39	-	11,692	-	488	-	-
QUAY, NM											
60 -	**Finance, insurance, and real estate**	23	27	0.8	169	160	15,740	17,900	3,229	3,155	0.5
6000	Depository institutions	7	8	1.6	86	91	20,372	22,813	2,175	2,343	1.0
6020	Commercial banks	4	4	1.1	71	72	20,732	24,111	1,898	1,989	1.2
6500	Real estate	8	10	0.7	53	46	9,358	9,565	601	429	0.4
6530	Real estate agents and managers	1	3	0.5	-	3	-	8,000	-	30	0.1
RIO ARRIBA, NM											
60 -	**Finance, insurance, and real estate**	33	33	1.0	234	210	17,368	19,124	4,378	4,138	0.6
6000	Depository institutions	8	7	1.4	155	145	17,187	18,400	2,669	2,683	1.2
6020	Commercial banks	8	7	1.9	155	145	17,187	18,400	2,669	2,683	1.6
6100	Nondepository institutions	3	2	0.8	9	-	19,556	-	148	-	-
6400	Insurance agents, brokers, and service	9	9	1.2	33	30	22,545	20,533	890	725	0.8
6500	Real estate	10	11	0.8	34	21	10,353	13,714	487	356	0.3
6510	Real estate operators and lessors	3	3	0.5	8	1	6,500	4,000	74	14	0.1
ROOSEVELT, NM											
60 -	**Finance, insurance, and real estate**	21	26	0.8	126	127	16,857	15,937	2,193	2,232	0.3
6400	Insurance agents, brokers, and service	8	8	1.0	23	-	12,174	-	311	-	-
6500	Real estate	6	11	0.8	11	14	11,273	6,571	116	98	0.1
6510	Real estate operators and lessors	3	6	1.0	3	6	6,667	7,333	20	48	0.2
SANDOVAL, NM											
60 -	**Finance, insurance, and real estate**	69	67	1.9	462	381	17,853	21,480	8,876	8,687	1.4
6000	Depository institutions	17	12	2.3	135	94	17,719	17,915	2,400	1,750	0.8
6020	Commercial banks	13	9	2.5	116	85	17,690	18,588	2,213	1,640	1.0
6300	Insurance carriers	5	1	0.5	35	-	19,886	-	382	-	-
6400	Insurance agents, brokers, and service	12	15	1.9	36	67	22,111	27,940	1,038	2,178	2.4

Source: County Business Patterns, 1992/93, CBP-92/93-1, U.S. Department of Commerce, Washington, D.C., April 1995. SIC categories for which data were suppressed or not available for both 1992 and 1993 are *not* displayed. The employment columns represent mid-March employment in the year. Pay per employee is calculated by dividing 1st Quarter payroll, annualized, by mid-March employment. The columns headed "% State" show the county's percentage of the state total for the SIC in 1993; for example, 0.9% for SIC 6030 means that the county had 0.9 percent of the state's total establishments (or payroll) in SIC 6030 in 1993. A dash (-) is used to indicate that data are not available or cannot be calculated; *nec* means not elsewhere classified.

Continued on next page.

SIC	Industry	No. Establishments			Employment		Pay / Employee		Annual Payroll ($ 000)		
		1992	1993	% State	1992	1993	1992	1993	1992	1993	% State
SANDOVAL, NM - [continued]											
6500	Real estate	29	35	2.5	241	209	17,461	20,440	4,904	4,344	4.2
6510	Real estate operators and lessors	8	9	1.4	16	18	10,750	11,778	225	246	0.9
6530	Real estate agents and managers	11	16	2.5	194	83	18,062	20,145	3,895	1,391	2.8
SAN JUAN, NM											
60 –	**Finance, insurance, and real estate**	133	134	3.9	946	1,019	22,448	20,298	19,685	21,005	3.3
6000	Depository institutions	28	27	5.3	500	456	18,912	18,044	9,758	8,538	3.8
6020	Commercial banks	21	19	5.2	456	407	18,982	18,025	8,971	7,642	4.4
6100	Nondepository institutions	13	14	5.3	36	72	23,222	15,944	887	1,290	2.4
6200	Security and commodity brokers	5	2	1.7	21	-	42,286	-	868	-	-
6210	Security brokers and dealers	5	2	2.7	21	-	42,286	-	868	-	-
6300	Insurance carriers	7	6	3.0	138	-	41,362	-	3,002	-	-
6400	Insurance agents, brokers, and service	31	32	4.1	142	138	20,873	19,942	3,274	3,201	3.6
6500	Real estate	45	49	3.4	104	304	12,346	23,224	1,794	6,206	6.0
6510	Real estate operators and lessors	23	24	3.8	53	97	9,811	9,567	631	1,137	4.1
6530	Real estate agents and managers	14	17	2.7	28	78	18,429	13,333	737	1,401	2.8
6540	Title abstract offices	-	3	7.1	-	27	-	108,148	-	1,356	15.8
6700	Holding and other investment offices	4	4	2.5	5	-	20,000	-	102	-	-
SAN MIGUEL, NM											
60 –	**Finance, insurance, and real estate**	37	39	1.1	231	235	16,433	18,349	4,341	4,637	0.7
6000	Depository institutions	9	8	1.6	104	105	17,192	19,619	1,893	2,102	0.9
6100	Nondepository institutions	5	5	1.9	13	13	21,538	25,231	334	276	0.5
6140	Personal credit institutions	5	5	3.2	13	13	21,538	25,231	334	276	1.4
6400	Insurance agents, brokers, and service	5	7	0.9	22	-	14,364	-	344	-	-
6500	Real estate	13	14	1.0	-	35	-	9,829	-	570	0.5
6510	Real estate operators and lessors	5	3	0.5	6	6	11,333	5,333	77	33	0.1
6530	Real estate agents and managers	3	5	0.8	15	-	12,000	-	381	-	-
SANTA FE, NM											
60 –	**Finance, insurance, and real estate**	356	370	10.7	2,378	2,568	23,960	25,288	63,971	77,068	12.0
6000	Depository institutions	41	37	7.2	662	673	22,441	22,003	14,650	14,641	6.5
6020	Commercial banks	30	25	6.8	544	539	21,963	21,900	11,913	11,383	6.6
6100	Nondepository institutions	26	33	12.5	69	-	27,246	-	2,336	-	-
6140	Personal credit institutions	13	14	9.0	40	-	22,600	-	885	-	-
6160	Mortgage bankers and brokers	11	17	21.5	-	58	-	30,966	-	2,484	11.0
6200	Security and commodity brokers	22	22	18.8	130	154	77,077	86,857	10,404	14,490	31.3
6210	Security brokers and dealers	15	11	14.9	-	85	-	96,047	-	5,845	-
6280	Security and commodity services	7	11	26.2	-	69	-	75,536	-	8,645	-
6300	Insurance carriers	23	12	6.0	364	-	23,923	-	9,405	-	-
6360	Title insurance	3	-	-	91	-	27,033	-	3,211	-	-
6400	Insurance agents, brokers, and service	50	58	7.4	188	417	21,830	23,722	4,616	11,177	12.5
6500	Real estate	158	174	12.2	808	852	17,891	19,019	17,649	22,935	22.0
6510	Real estate operators and lessors	47	56	8.9	210	245	15,600	14,857	3,411	4,074	14.6
6530	Real estate agents and managers	79	93	14.6	319	441	23,724	19,628	9,535	11,455	23.0
6540	Title abstract offices	2	3	7.1	-	15	-	15,733	-	501	5.8
6552	Subdividers and developers, n.e.c.	12	16	21.3	241	140	12,183	25,457	3,771	6,671	42.5
6700	Holding and other investment offices	36	34	21.7	157	311	18,803	20,219	4,911	8,757	35.6
6710	Holding offices	5	5	15.6	-	174	-	11,356	-	2,226	18.1
6732	Educational, religious, etc. trusts	12	13	38.2	46	-	18,870	-	937	-	-
6733	Trusts, n.e.c.	13	8	28.6	39	36	22,872	19,889	1,006	805	-
SIERRA, NM											
60 –	**Finance, insurance, and real estate**	25	25	0.7	101	134	16,911	16,687	1,625	2,556	0.4
6000	Depository institutions	7	7	1.4	63	88	18,476	19,591	1,106	1,971	0.9
6400	Insurance agents, brokers, and service	3	4	0.5	-	14	-	14,857	-	239	0.3

Source: County Business Patterns, 1992/93, CBP-92/93-1, U.S. Department of Commerce, Washington, D.C., April 1995. SIC categories for which data were suppressed or not available for both 1992 and 1993 are not displayed. The employment columns represent mid-March employment in the year. Pay per employee is calculated by dividing 1st Quarter payroll, annualized, by mid-March employment. The columns headed "% State" show the county's percentage of the state total for the SIC in 1993; for example, 0.9% for SIC 6030 means that the county had 0.9 percent of the state's total establishments (or payroll) in SIC 6030 in 1993. A dash (-) is used to indicate that data are not available or cannot be calculated; nec means not elsewhere classified.

Continued on next page.

SIC	Industry	No. Establishments			Employment		Pay / Employee		Annual Payroll ($ 000)		
		1992	1993	% State	1992	1993	1992	1993	1992	1993	% State
SIERRA, NM - [continued]											
6500	Real estate	10	11	0.8	14	25	9,143	7,840	129	235	0.2
6510	Real estate operators and lessors	4	5	0.8	4	-	5,000	-	21	-	-
6530	Real estate agents and managers	4	5	0.8	7	7	9,143	10,286	56	74	0.1
SOCORRO, NM											
60 –	**Finance, insurance, and real estate**	19	22	0.6	113	107	14,336	14,430	1,639	1,663	0.3
6000	Depository institutions	4	3	0.6	68	-	19,118	-	1,290	-	-
6020	Commercial banks	4	3	0.8	68	-	19,118	-	1,290	-	-
6400	Insurance agents, brokers, and service	4	6	0.8	14	-	8,286	-	127	-	-
6510	Real estate operators and lessors	4	6	1.0	6	11	1,333	2,909	32	39	0.1
6530	Real estate agents and managers	4	3	0.5	11	-	5,091	-	30	-	-
TAOS, NM											
60 –	**Finance, insurance, and real estate**	68	69	2.0	346	343	15,214	15,335	5,190	5,530	0.9
6000	Depository institutions	10	10	1.9	126	114	18,730	20,632	2,438	2,497	1.1
6200	Security and commodity brokers	2	3	2.6	-	11	-	10,909	-	190	0.4
6400	Insurance agents, brokers, and service	8	8	1.0	38	31	18,737	17,032	749	621	0.7
6500	Real estate	44	45	3.2	170	179	11,906	12,000	1,807	2,124	2.0
6510	Real estate operators and lessors	11	15	2.4	15	44	9,867	10,364	124	370	1.3
6530	Real estate agents and managers	26	24	3.8	119	104	12,034	12,231	1,112	1,038	2.1
6540	Title abstract offices	3	3	7.1	28	-	11,714	-	339	-	-
TORRANCE, NM											
60 –	**Finance, insurance, and real estate**	10	10	0.3	38	32	13,895	13,750	569	482	0.1
6400	Insurance agents, brokers, and service	2	3	0.4	-	11	-	15,636	-	193	0.2
UNION, NM											
60 –	**Finance, insurance, and real estate**	9	9	0.3	63	81	19,429	14,864	1,263	1,317	0.2
6000	Depository institutions	2	3	0.6	-	58	-	17,379	-	1,107	0.5
6020	Commercial banks	2	3	0.8	-	58	-	17,379	-	1,107	0.6
6400	Insurance agents, brokers, and service	4	4	0.5	9	-	11,111	-	107	-	-
VALENCIA, NM											
60 –	**Finance, insurance, and real estate**	56	58	1.7	384	379	16,708	16,158	6,674	6,354	1.0
6000	Depository institutions	13	11	2.1	217	220	17,401	18,000	4,011	3,803	1.7
6100	Nondepository institutions	5	8	3.0	14	17	19,143	17,882	269	369	0.7
6140	Personal credit institutions	5	8	5.1	14	17	19,143	17,882	269	369	1.9
6300	Insurance carriers	6	3	1.5	66	-	14,727	-	1,019	-	-
6400	Insurance agents, brokers, and service	10	12	1.5	-	37	-	13,730	-	560	0.6
6500	Real estate	20	22	1.5	59	97	17,356	11,010	958	1,320	1.3
6510	Real estate operators and lessors	4	5	0.8	17	41	9,647	4,683	181	223	0.8
6530	Real estate agents and managers	10	10	1.6	14	15	24,286	10,400	261	198	0.4
6540	Title abstract offices	3	3	7.1	23	30	18,609	18,267	414	670	7.8
6552	Subdividers and developers, n.e.c.	2	4	5.3	-	11	-	15,636	-	229	1.5

Source: County Business Patterns, 1992/93, CBP-92/93-1, U.S. Department of Commerce, Washington, D.C., April 1995. SIC categories for which data were suppressed or not available for both 1992 and 1993 are *not* displayed. The employment columns represent mid-March employment in the year. Pay per employee is calculated by dividing 1st Quarter payroll, annualized, by mid-March employment. The columns headed "% State" show the county's percentage of the state total for the SIC in 1993; for example, 0.9% for SIC 6030 means that the county had 0.9 percent of the state's total establishments (or payroll) in SIC 6030 in 1993. A dash (-) is used to indicate that data are not available or cannot be calculated; *nec* means not elsewhere classified.

NEW YORK

SIC	Industry	No. Establishments			Employment		Pay / Employee		Annual Payroll ($ 000)		
		1992	1993	% State	1992	1993	1992	1993	1992	1993	% State
ALBANY, NY											
60 –	**Finance, insurance, and real estate**	906	946	1.7	17,389	17,050	28,068	27,133	509,716	523,644	1.3
6000	Depository institutions	168	169	2.5	3,735	3,848	24,813	25,040	98,389	111,567	1.2
6020	Commercial banks	109	113	3.0	2,417	2,599	26,185	26,790	69,537	82,194	1.3
6030	Savings institutions	38	33	2.4	1,074	907	22,101	21,036	23,250	21,376	2.6
6100	Nondepository institutions	63	65	3.8	788	809	29,041	27,466	23,811	24,434	1.6
6140	Personal credit institutions	30	26	5.6	278	251	27,122	23,474	7,663	6,300	3.5
6150	Business credit institutions	4	4	1.0	162	–	30,272	–	4,869	–	–
6160	Mortgage bankers and brokers	28	34	4.3	284	369	31,042	29,539	9,446	12,348	3.5
6200	Security and commodity brokers	47	54	0.9	807	872	63,945	58,505	56,933	64,448	0.4
6210	Security brokers and dealers	30	32	0.8	692	717	68,162	62,003	51,443	56,213	0.4
6280	Security and commodity services	17	22	1.4	115	155	38,574	42,323	5,490	8,235	0.3
6300	Insurance carriers	127	122	4.2	7,809	7,784	26,256	25,036	200,418	207,558	4.4
6310	Life insurance	48	37	4.6	3,184	2,038	24,575	27,492	74,673	57,382	3.2
6330	Fire, marine, and casualty insurance	47	51	4.0	2,151	2,313	28,984	28,477	64,097	66,998	3.5
6370	Pension, health, and welfare funds	16	17	2.9	75	106	31,467	14,981	1,679	1,701	1.3
6400	Insurance agents, brokers, and service	171	193	2.7	1,478	1,359	28,514	28,012	45,467	43,702	2.1
6500	Real estate	301	312	1.1	2,053	2,040	17,066	17,059	39,589	40,668	1.0
6510	Real estate operators and lessors	163	170	1.1	1,253	1,204	14,043	13,787	19,233	18,900	1.2
6530	Real estate agents and managers	89	120	1.2	545	715	23,464	21,807	14,083	18,229	0.9
6540	Title abstract offices	7	5	1.3	53	41	21,509	24,293	1,914	1,755	2.1
6552	Subdividers and developers, n.e.c.	7	4	1.2	31	20	23,226	23,000	1,037	429	0.6
6553	Cemetery subdividers and developers	10	10	1.5	65	58	17,969	18,621	1,212	1,273	1.3
6700	Holding and other investment offices	29	31	1.3	719	338	53,814	74,817	45,109	31,267	1.6
6733	Trusts, n.e.c.	6	8	2.3	–	24	–	13,667	–	324	0.4
ALLEGANY, NY											
60 –	**Finance, insurance, and real estate**	66	63	0.1	277	277	16,939	15,408	5,010	5,101	0.0
6000	Depository institutions	22	21	0.3	148	152	15,351	14,684	2,385	2,668	0.0
6020	Commercial banks	18	17	0.5	124	127	15,258	14,929	2,002	2,294	0.0
6400	Insurance agents, brokers, and service	12	12	0.2	56	57	22,071	19,439	1,314	1,338	0.1
6500	Real estate	26	26	0.1	46	–	12,435	–	733	–	–
6510	Real estate operators and lessors	9	11	0.1	17	–	14,353	–	297	–	–
6530	Real estate agents and managers	7	6	0.1	10	6	9,200	11,333	126	110	0.0
6553	Cemetery subdividers and developers	6	6	0.9	–	7	–	4,000	–	67	0.1
6700	Holding and other investment offices	4	3	0.1	–	3	–	5,333	–	10	0.0
BRONX, NY											
60 –	**Finance, insurance, and real estate**	2,532	2,568	4.7	11,939	12,027	22,698	22,130	278,191	284,339	0.7
6000	Depository institutions	196	189	2.8	2,252	2,102	23,503	22,588	53,000	50,288	0.5
6020	Commercial banks	88	85	2.3	1,185	1,081	26,039	25,073	30,275	27,572	0.4
6030	Savings institutions	39	38	2.8	849	729	18,163	17,948	15,279	13,934	1.7
6090	Functions closely related to banking	65	63	12.0	205	279	30,537	24,502	7,079	8,389	1.6
6100	Nondepository institutions	18	13	0.8	54	46	30,074	33,826	1,781	1,515	0.1
6140	Personal credit institutions	5	5	1.1	24	–	29,667	–	864	–	–
6200	Security and commodity brokers	18	13	0.2	36	31	44,556	55,355	1,885	1,631	0.0
6300	Insurance carriers	55	48	1.6	1,534	1,503	33,802	34,379	48,337	48,563	1.0
6310	Life insurance	11	10	1.2	891	912	30,599	32,759	25,480	27,531	1.5
6330	Fire, marine, and casualty insurance	27	25	1.9	555	520	39,777	37,408	20,212	18,628	1.0
6370	Pension, health, and welfare funds	15	13	2.2	–	71	–	33,014	–	2,404	1.9
6400	Insurance agents, brokers, and service	95	98	1.4	278	284	19,741	19,479	6,146	6,349	0.3
6500	Real estate	2,105	2,175	7.9	7,444	7,677	20,449	19,962	161,662	170,204	4.4

Source: County Business Patterns, 1992/93, CBP-92/93-1, U.S. Department of Commerce, Washington, D.C., April 1995. SIC categories for which data were suppressed or not available for both 1992 and 1993 are *not* displayed. The employment columns represent mid-March employment in the year. Pay per employee is calculated by dividing 1st Quarter payroll, annualized, by mid-March employment. The columns headed "% State" show the county's percentage of the state total for the SIC in 1993; for example, 0.9% for SIC 6030 means that the county had 0.9 percent of the state's total establishments (or payroll) in SIC 6030 in 1993. A dash (-) is used to indicate that data are not available or cannot be calculated; *nec* means not elsewhere classified.

Continued on next page.

SIC	Industry	No. Establishments			Employment		Pay / Employee		Annual Payroll ($ 000)		
		1992	1993	% State	1992	1993	1992	1993	1992	1993	% State
BRONX, NY - [continued]											
6510	Real estate operators and lessors	1,464	1,651	*10.5*	3,523	4,955	16,551	18,532	62,293	101,038	*6.3*
6530	Real estate agents and managers	448	489	*4.7*	3,052	2,334	24,784	21,933	79,804	57,698	*2.9*
6540	Title abstract offices	5	7	*1.8*	19	26	31,579	28,769	641	833	*1.0*
6552	Subdividers and developers, n.e.c.	19	14	*4.1*	136	23	20,765	26,609	2,898	781	*1.1*
6553	Cemetery subdividers and developers	3	4	*0.6*	320	325	27,212	26,622	9,544	9,661	*10.1*
6700	Holding and other investment offices	45	32	*1.4*	341	384	15,460	12,875	5,380	5,789	*0.3*
6732	Educational, religious, etc. trusts	6	6	*1.1*	36	45	23,889	19,289	842	929	*0.5*
6733	Trusts, n.e.c.	18	13	*3.7*	27	25	15,704	13,440	407	405	*0.5*
6798	Real estate investment trusts	4	3	*7.5*	5	-	13,600	-	75	-	-
6799	Investors, n.e.c.	10	2	*0.4*	10	-	8,400	-	90	-	-
BROOME, NY											
60 –	**Finance, insurance, and real estate**	410	398	*0.7*	3,994	4,190	23,811	22,719	97,728	97,145	*0.2*
6000	Depository institutions	88	86	*1.3*	1,338	1,281	21,175	20,962	31,045	27,546	*0.3*
6020	Commercial banks	48	48	*1.3*	609	535	21,077	19,918	15,335	11,375	*0.2*
6100	Nondepository institutions	14	17	*1.0*	117	128	30,667	27,219	3,471	3,601	*0.2*
6140	Personal credit institutions	8	8	*1.7*	49	62	31,184	25,613	1,494	1,349	*0.8*
6160	Mortgage bankers and brokers	6	9	*1.1*	68	66	30,294	28,727	1,977	2,252	*0.6*
6200	Security and commodity brokers	21	21	*0.4*	140	178	54,486	42,090	7,051	9,040	*0.1*
6210	Security brokers and dealers	15	16	*0.4*	131	171	57,557	43,205	6,954	8,898	*0.1*
6280	Security and commodity services	6	4	*0.2*	9	7	9,778	14,857	97	116	*0.0*
6300	Insurance carriers	49	47	*1.6*	1,440	1,676	24,408	23,148	34,317	36,653	*0.8*
6310	Life insurance	16	15	*1.9*	667	840	29,547	29,371	18,996	22,236	*1.2*
6330	Fire, marine, and casualty insurance	18	20	*1.6*	189	214	25,757	27,626	5,095	4,896	*0.3*
6400	Insurance agents, brokers, and service	88	86	*1.2*	415	387	24,733	25,344	11,681	10,975	*0.5*
6500	Real estate	132	126	*0.5*	464	501	15,336	13,421	7,730	7,779	*0.2*
6510	Real estate operators and lessors	63	68	*0.4*	208	284	13,846	11,493	3,009	3,557	*0.2*
6530	Real estate agents and managers	37	35	*0.3*	125	146	17,504	16,548	2,501	2,993	*0.1*
6540	Title abstract offices	4	4	*1.0*	22	24	12,909	13,500	333	343	*0.4*
6553	Cemetery subdividers and developers	16	17	*2.6*	44	-	16,273	-	887	-	-
6700	Holding and other investment offices	18	15	*0.6*	80	39	37,800	52,205	2,433	1,551	*0.1*
6732	Educational, religious, etc. trusts	12	11	*2.0*	-	23	-	15,304	-	368	*0.2*
CATTARAUGUS, NY											
60 –	**Finance, insurance, and real estate**	146	146	*0.3*	793	851	19,087	19,239	16,407	18,037	*0.0*
6000	Depository institutions	37	39	*0.6*	401	423	17,446	17,712	8,007	8,474	*0.1*
6020	Commercial banks	28	28	*0.7*	348	364	17,828	18,022	7,174	7,517	*0.1*
6060	Credit unions	9	11	*1.5*	53	59	14,943	15,797	833	957	-
6100	Nondepository institutions	6	4	*0.2*	-	19	-	23,158	-	496	*0.0*
6140	Personal credit institutions	4	2	*0.4*	8	-	21,000	-	170	-	-
6200	Security and commodity brokers	3	3	*0.1*	-	16	-	59,750	-	1,000	*0.0*
6210	Security brokers and dealers	3	3	*0.1*	-	16	-	59,750	-	1,000	*0.0*
6300	Insurance carriers	13	11	*0.4*	107	146	25,869	25,836	2,693	3,692	*0.1*
6400	Insurance agents, brokers, and service	36	40	*0.6*	104	107	20,231	19,402	2,217	2,338	*0.1*
6500	Real estate	51	49	*0.2*	150	140	12,853	11,686	2,066	2,037	*0.1*
6510	Real estate operators and lessors	18	18	*0.1*	45	34	8,089	7,294	373	267	*0.0*
6530	Real estate agents and managers	10	12	*0.1*	35	56	14,286	13,071	520	957	*0.0*
6553	Cemetery subdividers and developers	17	15	*2.3*	-	20	-	5,200	-	164	*0.2*
CAYUGA, NY											
60 –	**Finance, insurance, and real estate**	106	109	*0.2*	854	995	19,316	18,714	17,014	19,459	*0.0*
6000	Depository institutions	21	22	*0.3*	341	350	18,534	20,023	6,472	7,035	*0.1*
6020	Commercial banks	9	14	*0.4*	83	-	19,229	-	1,557	-	-
6060	Credit unions	3	3	*0.4*	-	11	-	13,455	-	169	-
6100	Nondepository institutions	5	4	*0.2*	51	48	31,922	26,750	1,440	1,327	*0.1*
6200	Security and commodity brokers	3	3	*0.1*	-	4	-	29,000	-	127	*0.0*
6300	Insurance carriers	8	8	*0.3*	259	345	17,838	18,087	4,825	6,534	*0.1*
6400	Insurance agents, brokers, and service	29	32	*0.5*	108	113	21,593	20,814	2,526	2,536	*0.1*

Source: County Business Patterns, 1992/93, CBP-92/93-1, U.S. Department of Commerce, Washington, D.C., April 1995. SIC categories for which data were suppressed or not available for both 1992 and 1993 are *not* displayed. The employment columns represent mid-March employment in the year. Pay per employee is calculated by dividing 1st Quarter payroll, annualized, by mid-March employment. The columns headed "% State" show the county's percentage of the state total for the SIC in 1993; for example, 0.9% for SIC 6030 means that the county had 0.9 percent of the state's total establishments (or payroll) in SIC 6030 in 1993. A dash (-) is used to indicate that data are not available or cannot be calculated; *nec* means not elsewhere classified.

Continued on next page.

SIC	Industry	No. Establishments			Employment		Pay / Employee		Annual Payroll ($ 000)		
		1992	1993	% State	1992	1993	1992	1993	1992	1993	% State
CAYUGA, NY - [continued]											
6500	Real estate	35	36	0.1	80	129	14,900	11,473	1,336	1,714	0.0
6510	Real estate operators and lessors	11	16	0.1	29	93	16,828	11,140	523	1,163	0.1
6530	Real estate agents and managers	11	9	0.1	33	10	14,788	7,200	502	72	0.0
6553	Cemetery subdividers and developers	8	9	1.4	8	-	6,500	-	110	-	-
6700	Holding and other investment offices	4	3	0.1	5	-	24,000	-	135	-	-
CHAUTAUQUA, NY											
60 –	**Finance, insurance, and real estate**	250	250	0.5	1,286	1,377	20,019	19,341	29,634	32,255	0.1
6000	Depository institutions	66	67	1.0	551	549	17,735	16,459	12,868	13,623	0.1
6020	Commercial banks	43	43	1.1	436	430	18,982	16,940	11,317	11,825	0.2
6100	Nondepository institutions	12	11	0.6	40	39	22,800	20,923	1,007	1,106	0.1
6160	Mortgage bankers and brokers	4	3	0.4	13	-	15,692	-	283	-	-
6200	Security and commodity brokers	10	9	0.2	48	49	45,833	47,755	2,251	2,391	0.0
6210	Security brokers and dealers	6	5	0.1	43	42	47,256	51,238	2,089	2,188	0.0
6280	Security and commodity services	3	4	0.2	-	7	-	26,857	-	203	0.0
6300	Insurance carriers	18	16	0.5	132	204	24,818	22,412	3,348	4,123	0.1
6330	Fire, marine, and casualty insurance	8	9	0.7	-	22	-	37,818	-	778	0.0
6400	Insurance agents, brokers, and service	64	64	0.9	280	267	23,886	24,060	6,584	6,919	0.3
6500	Real estate	68	70	0.3	210	245	10,914	12,098	2,845	3,540	0.1
6510	Real estate operators and lessors	25	29	0.2	72	116	11,111	9,828	975	1,332	0.1
6530	Real estate agents and managers	27	25	0.2	94	74	9,277	11,243	1,156	1,049	0.1
6540	Title abstract offices	1	3	0.8	-	25	-	24,960	-	626	0.7
6553	Cemetery subdividers and developers	11	10	1.5	-	28	-	11,714	-	413	0.4
6700	Holding and other investment offices	12	13	0.6	25	24	24,160	20,000	731	553	0.0
6710	Holding offices	8	8	1.3	15	-	30,133	-	573	-	-
6732	Educational, religious, etc. trusts	3	3	0.6	-	8	-	19,500	-	171	0.1
CHEMUNG, NY											
60 –	**Finance, insurance, and real estate**	138	142	0.3	1,298	1,355	24,616	23,191	31,650	33,541	0.1
6000	Depository institutions	39	40	0.6	562	584	22,263	20,473	12,043	12,663	0.1
6020	Commercial banks	17	18	0.5	309	313	23,146	20,064	7,042	7,235	0.1
6030	Savings institutions	10	10	0.7	178	192	22,831	22,604	3,682	4,044	0.5
6060	Credit unions	12	12	1.7	75	79	17,280	16,911	1,319	1,384	-
6200	Security and commodity brokers	9	9	0.2	79	75	45,215	43,893	3,616	3,790	0.0
6300	Insurance carriers	12	14	0.5	341	334	25,267	25,784	8,411	8,210	0.2
6330	Fire, marine, and casualty insurance	5	6	0.5	-	18	-	46,444	-	896	0.0
6400	Insurance agents, brokers, and service	27	26	0.4	118	117	32,339	29,368	3,409	3,266	0.2
6500	Real estate	45	45	0.2	184	224	15,239	14,554	3,512	4,101	0.1
6510	Real estate operators and lessors	20	24	0.2	82	158	14,098	15,063	1,248	2,949	0.2
6530	Real estate agents and managers	14	13	0.1	73	44	16,274	12,727	1,743	749	0.0
CHENANGO, NY											
60 –	**Finance, insurance, and real estate**	101	92	0.2	993	1,208	20,951	19,748	21,714	25,160	0.1
6000	Depository institutions	20	20	0.3	467	457	19,675	22,792	10,301	10,830	0.1
6100	Nondepository institutions	3	2	0.1	30	-	25,867	-	777	-	-
6300	Insurance carriers	8	10	0.3	-	532	-	17,120	-	10,019	0.2
6400	Insurance agents, brokers, and service	31	26	0.4	101	88	26,772	26,682	2,356	2,235	0.1
6500	Real estate	36	32	0.1	82	118	11,463	8,949	1,064	1,165	0.0
6510	Real estate operators and lessors	9	9	0.1	37	85	16,000	9,976	641	836	0.1
6530	Real estate agents and managers	11	10	0.1	18	-	8,000	-	156	-	-
6553	Cemetery subdividers and developers	11	12	1.9	-	14	-	4,000	-	125	0.1
CLINTON, NY											
60 –	**Finance, insurance, and real estate**	150	149	0.3	902	868	20,758	19,332	20,027	20,006	0.0
6000	Depository institutions	38	37	0.6	403	353	19,454	17,881	8,904	8,661	0.1
6020	Commercial banks	18	19	0.5	185	187	18,941	17,048	4,574	4,955	0.1
6060	Credit unions	10	10	1.4	45	-	16,622	-	737	-	-
6200	Security and commodity brokers	4	4	0.1	19	22	48,632	41,091	938	1,076	0.0

Source: County Business Patterns, 1992/93, CBP-92/93-1, U.S. Department of Commerce, Washington, D.C., April 1995. SIC categories for which data were suppressed or not available for both 1992 and 1993 are not displayed. The employment columns represent mid-March employment in the year. Pay per employee is calculated by dividing 1st Quarter payroll, annualized, by mid-March employment. The columns headed "% State" show the county's percentage of the state total for the SIC in 1993; for example, 0.9% for SIC 6030 means that the county had 0.9 percent of the state's total establishments (or payroll) in SIC 6030 in 1993. A dash (-) is used to indicate that data are not available or cannot be calculated; nec means not elsewhere classified.

Continued on next page.

SIC	Industry	No. Establishments			Employment		Pay / Employee		Annual Payroll ($ 000)		
		1992	1993	% State	1992	1993	1992	1993	1992	1993	% State
CLINTON, NY - [continued]											
6300	Insurance carriers	14	12	0.4	100	126	23,480	22,476	2,638	2,818	0.1
6310	Life insurance	3	3	0.4	-	65	-	24,862	-	1,560	0.1
6370	Pension, health, and welfare funds	7	6	1.0	43	-	16,372	-	858	-	-
6400	Insurance agents, brokers, and service	34	35	0.5	168	176	24,952	24,068	4,244	4,528	0.2
6500	Real estate	55	55	0.2	163	171	13,276	12,538	2,350	2,524	0.1
6510	Real estate operators and lessors	25	27	0.2	93	97	13,849	12,454	1,359	1,323	0.1
6530	Real estate agents and managers	17	19	0.2	43	53	10,605	12,302	522	799	0.0
6553	Cemetery subdividers and developers	6	5	0.8	-	7	-	7,429	-	82	0.1
COLUMBIA, NY											
60 -	**Finance, insurance, and real estate**	93	97	0.2	562	642	21,915	18,293	12,743	14,958	0.0
6000	Depository institutions	22	23	0.3	314	355	19,045	17,870	6,567	7,565	0.1
6400	Insurance agents, brokers, and service	21	22	0.3	123	127	33,236	22,740	3,637	4,608	0.2
6500	Real estate	36	38	0.1	77	110	14,805	12,291	1,360	1,451	0.0
6510	Real estate operators and lessors	7	10	0.1	15	23	13,067	11,478	174	285	0.0
6530	Real estate agents and managers	14	17	0.2	25	63	14,400	10,159	427	522	0.0
6553	Cemetery subdividers and developers	7	7	1.1	8	7	2,000	2,286	47	47	0.0
6700	Holding and other investment offices	9	9	0.4	30	23	24,400	25,739	724	597	0.0
CORTLAND, NY											
60 -	**Finance, insurance, and real estate**	76	72	0.1	554	540	19,495	19,444	11,459	11,330	0.0
6000	Depository institutions	17	17	0.3	319	309	18,345	18,084	5,874	5,828	0.1
6020	Commercial banks	10	11	0.3	181	-	20,619	-	3,646	-	-
6330	Fire, marine, and casualty insurance	5	4	0.3	43	-	30,047	-	1,324	-	-
6400	Insurance agents, brokers, and service	16	17	0.2	76	84	17,632	17,762	1,996	2,120	0.1
6500	Real estate	31	27	0.1	68	48	13,706	9,750	997	527	0.0
6510	Real estate operators and lessors	17	14	0.1	36	35	9,556	10,400	406	379	0.0
6530	Real estate agents and managers	3	4	0.0	13	4	22,769	12,000	290	56	0.0
6553	Cemetery subdividers and developers	8	9	1.4	-	9	-	6,222	-	92	0.1
DELAWARE, NY											
60 -	**Finance, insurance, and real estate**	109	108	0.2	631	618	18,174	19,055	11,814	12,872	0.0
6000	Depository institutions	23	24	0.4	332	320	19,398	19,750	6,348	6,456	0.1
6020	Commercial banks	19	19	0.5	-	228	-	19,947	-	4,638	0.1
6300	Insurance carriers	7	6	0.2	-	46	-	22,000	-	1,074	0.0
6400	Insurance agents, brokers, and service	27	26	0.4	105	98	22,781	23,224	2,682	2,944	0.1
6500	Real estate	44	46	0.2	131	134	6,962	8,836	1,277	1,410	0.0
6510	Real estate operators and lessors	13	10	0.1	28	40	9,000	11,800	454	518	0.0
6530	Real estate agents and managers	14	17	0.2	63	61	7,048	8,787	542	661	0.0
6540	Title abstract offices	3	3	0.8	6	6	6,667	6,000	45	43	0.1
6552	Subdividers and developers, n.e.c.	1	3	0.9	-	6	-	11,333	-	48	0.1
6553	Cemetery subdividers and developers	11	12	1.9	27	21	2,667	3,429	140	129	0.1
6700	Holding and other investment offices	3	3	0.1	9	-	29,333	-	208	-	-
DUTCHESS, NY											
60 -	**Finance, insurance, and real estate**	543	572	1.1	4,365	4,404	25,787	25,510	116,300	120,358	0.3
6000	Depository institutions	109	108	1.6	1,899	1,867	22,978	22,224	44,620	42,706	0.4
6020	Commercial banks	61	61	1.6	796	782	21,618	21,550	17,783	17,828	0.3
6030	Savings institutions	36	35	2.6	668	676	26,257	24,160	17,906	16,127	1.9
6060	Credit unions	12	12	1.7	435	409	20,432	20,313	8,931	8,751	-
6100	Nondepository institutions	27	26	1.5	154	248	25,091	25,048	4,150	7,349	0.5
6160	Mortgage bankers and brokers	14	13	1.6	108	192	23,889	26,396	2,831	6,110	1.7
6200	Security and commodity brokers	24	30	0.5	161	185	75,602	61,903	11,587	13,154	0.1
6210	Security brokers and dealers	10	14	0.4	132	166	85,091	66,867	10,524	12,854	0.1
6280	Security and commodity services	14	16	1.0	29	19	32,414	18,526	1,063	300	0.0
6300	Insurance carriers	44	41	1.4	510	495	29,498	31,014	14,921	14,817	0.3
6310	Life insurance	8	8	1.0	260	273	26,569	27,956	6,878	7,723	0.4
6330	Fire, marine, and casualty insurance	21	21	1.6	152	139	33,868	34,705	5,028	4,515	0.2

Source: County Business Patterns, 1992/93, CBP-92/93-1, U.S. Department of Commerce, Washington, D.C., April 1995. SIC categories for which data were suppressed or not available for both 1992 and 1993 are not displayed. The employment columns represent mid-March employment in the year. Pay per employee is calculated by dividing 1st Quarter payroll, annualized, by mid-March employment. The columns headed "% State" show the county's percentage of the state total for the SIC in 1993; for example, 0.9% for SIC 6030 means that the county had 0.9 percent of the state's total establishments (or payroll) in SIC 6030 in 1993. A dash (-) is used to indicate that data are not available or cannot be calculated; nec means not elsewhere classified.

Continued on next page.

SIC	Industry	No. Establishments			Employment		Pay / Employee		Annual Payroll ($ 000)		
		1992	1993	% State	1992	1993	1992	1993	1992	1993	% State
DUTCHESS, NY - [continued]											
6370	Pension, health, and welfare funds	9	9	1.5	64	-	24,438	-	1,561	-	-
6400	Insurance agents, brokers, and service	100	103	1.5	697	676	26,755	28,166	19,857	20,268	1.0
6500	Real estate	216	241	0.9	883	873	20,512	20,124	19,330	19,983	0.5
6510	Real estate operators and lessors	89	114	0.7	355	441	19,718	18,440	7,273	9,133	0.6
6530	Real estate agents and managers	77	100	1.0	373	343	21,373	21,528	8,220	8,267	0.4
6540	Title abstract offices	8	10	2.5	39	52	27,385	28,538	1,151	1,875	2.2
6553	Cemetery subdividers and developers	13	15	2.3	38	-	14,526	-	656	-	-
6700	Holding and other investment offices	23	23	1.0	61	60	17,770	20,467	1,835	2,081	0.1
6710	Holding offices	3	4	0.6	-	22	-	21,818	-	490	0.0
6733	Trusts, n.e.c.	4	3	0.9	-	5	-	23,200	-	86	0.1
ERIE, NY											
60 –	**Finance, insurance, and real estate**	1,817	1,898	3.5	28,038	27,084	26,756	26,348	759,482	760,369	1.9
6000	Depository institutions	322	338	5.1	10,903	10,032	26,199	25,325	287,484	256,329	2.7
6020	Commercial banks	200	203	5.4	9,642	8,769	26,428	26,037	254,811	228,898	3.5
6030	Savings institutions	30	26	1.9	-	182	-	26,286	-	5,002	0.6
6060	Credit unions	86	103	14.2	355	477	13,938	14,323	5,152	7,231	-
6090	Functions closely related to banking	5	4	0.8	395	-	38,461	-	16,040	-	-
6100	Nondepository institutions	122	121	7.0	2,329	2,337	28,938	27,680	71,507	75,657	5.1
6140	Personal credit institutions	66	47	10.1	537	455	22,994	22,057	12,488	10,324	5.8
6150	Business credit institutions	13	24	5.8	65	298	37,477	36,859	2,709	12,953	1.4
6160	Mortgage bankers and brokers	43	49	6.1	1,727	1,584	30,464	27,568	56,310	52,374	14.7
6200	Security and commodity brokers	80	92	1.6	1,148	1,043	51,530	52,552	56,368	55,889	0.3
6210	Security brokers and dealers	41	45	1.2	731	662	68,602	69,166	47,523	46,125	0.4
6280	Security and commodity services	37	47	2.9	413	381	21,608	23,685	8,749	9,764	0.3
6300	Insurance carriers	195	187	6.4	5,251	5,845	30,047	28,483	152,761	172,199	3.7
6310	Life insurance	51	49	6.1	1,249	1,581	32,112	28,612	37,340	41,640	2.3
6330	Fire, marine, and casualty insurance	93	91	7.1	1,865	1,784	33,177	31,720	59,775	60,202	3.2
6350	Surety insurance	5	7	16.7	24	-	32,500	-	664	-	-
6360	Title insurance	4	3	4.8	148	145	25,838	31,200	3,442	3,906	7.8
6370	Pension, health, and welfare funds	27	23	3.9	224	384	20,839	22,062	5,296	10,006	7.9
6390	Insurance carriers, n.e.c.	4	1	14.3	40	-	23,000	-	860	-	-
6400	Insurance agents, brokers, and service	439	441	6.2	2,994	2,676	24,659	24,033	76,761	71,072	3.5
6500	Real estate	591	660	2.4	4,330	4,116	17,252	17,893	79,796	82,919	2.1
6510	Real estate operators and lessors	287	349	2.2	1,776	2,064	17,236	15,731	32,191	35,087	2.2
6530	Real estate agents and managers	209	249	2.4	2,023	1,718	16,753	20,033	36,279	39,562	2.0
6540	Title abstract offices	7	8	2.0	70	78	19,143	18,103	1,497	1,591	1.9
6552	Subdividers and developers, n.e.c.	17	19	5.6	59	62	31,458	25,419	1,941	2,249	3.2
6553	Cemetery subdividers and developers	25	29	4.5	161	171	18,658	19,485	3,725	3,643	3.8
6710	Holding offices	28	26	4.1	270	253	38,815	58,972	12,576	21,392	2.0
6720	Investment offices	5	1	1.1	32	-	45,500	-	1,146	-	-
6732	Educational, religious, etc. trusts	15	14	2.6	75	64	18,187	20,938	1,382	1,251	0.6
6733	Trusts, n.e.c.	7	5	1.4	47	-	26,213	-	794	-	-
6794	Patent owners and lessors	2	3	1.8	-	25	-	27,040	-	688	0.4
6799	Investors, n.e.c.	6	8	1.7	31	41	53,548	73,854	2,339	4,561	1.8
ESSEX, NY											
60 –	**Finance, insurance, and real estate**	79	77	0.1	384	379	18,583	17,150	7,033	7,214	0.0
6000	Depository institutions	20	20	0.3	190	193	18,295	16,249	3,291	3,459	0.0
6020	Commercial banks	16	16	0.4	148	144	19,081	17,056	2,576	2,746	0.0
6400	Insurance agents, brokers, and service	25	23	0.3	95	81	18,526	19,654	1,822	1,760	0.1
6500	Real estate	27	26	0.1	81	91	15,062	13,451	1,244	1,300	0.0
6510	Real estate operators and lessors	8	7	0.0	24	43	16,833	14,419	446	614	0.0
6530	Real estate agents and managers	8	12	0.1	30	35	13,467	13,029	420	524	0.0
6553	Cemetery subdividers and developers	5	4	0.6	-	2	-	4,000	-	13	0.0
6700	Holding and other investment offices	3	3	0.1	12	-	16,333	-	197	-	-

Source: County Business Patterns, 1992/93, CBP-92/93-1, U.S. Department of Commerce, Washington, D.C., April 1995. SIC categories for which data were suppressed or not available for both 1992 and 1993 are *not* displayed. The employment columns represent mid-March employment in the year. Pay per employee is calculated by dividing 1st Quarter payroll, annualized, by mid-March employment. The columns headed "% State" show the county's percentage of the state total for the SIC in 1993; for example, 0.9% for SIC 6030 means that the county had 0.9 percent of the state's total establishments (or payroll) in SIC 6030 in 1993. A dash (-) is used to indicate that data are not available or cannot be calculated; *nec* means not elsewhere classified.

SIC	Industry	No. Establishments			Employment		Pay / Employee		Annual Payroll ($ 000)		
		1992	1993	% State	1992	1993	1992	1993	1992	1993	% State
FRANKLIN, NY											
60 –	**Finance, insurance, and real estate**	89	88	0.2	410	447	15,980	16,107	7,058	8,048	0.0
6000	Depository institutions	21	21	0.3	234	239	16,154	16,301	4,050	4,523	0.0
6020	Commercial banks	14	14	0.4	159	163	15,497	15,730	2,677	2,989	0.0
6100	Nondepository institutions	4	4	0.2	10	-	28,000	-	280	-	-
6400	Insurance agents, brokers, and service	20	21	0.3	81	80	18,469	16,950	1,528	1,509	0.1
6500	Real estate	39	39	0.1	79	108	10,532	13,296	1,016	1,531	0.0
6510	Real estate operators and lessors	10	10	0.1	22	59	13,455	14,508	355	734	0.0
6530	Real estate agents and managers	11	16	0.2	14	29	13,714	11,448	216	461	0.0
6540	Title abstract offices	3	3	0.8	-	7	-	11,429	-	92	0.1
6553	Cemetery subdividers and developers	9	8	1.2	5	-	9,600	-	73	-	-
FULTON, NY											
60 –	**Finance, insurance, and real estate**	69	74	0.1	415	426	20,569	18,657	9,177	9,541	0.0
6000	Depository institutions	21	21	0.3	233	228	17,579	17,140	4,153	4,640	0.0
6020	Commercial banks	15	15	0.4	158	151	17,316	16,848	2,761	3,021	0.0
6030	Savings institutions	3	3	0.2	51	52	17,412	17,231	917	1,110	0.1
6060	Credit unions	3	3	0.4	24	25	19,667	18,720	475	509	-
6100	Nondepository institutions	3	3	0.2	13	-	39,077	-	725	-	-
6140	Personal credit institutions	3	3	0.6	13	-	39,077	-	725	-	-
6300	Insurance carriers	3	5	0.2	-	27	-	17,333	-	544	0.0
6400	Insurance agents, brokers, and service	17	17	0.2	93	78	23,140	23,333	2,548	2,338	0.1
6500	Real estate	20	21	0.1	-	39	-	11,385	-	533	0.0
6510	Real estate operators and lessors	5	6	0.0	7	15	12,571	11,200	146	189	0.0
6530	Real estate agents and managers	7	7	0.1	18	19	9,333	11,789	191	255	0.0
6700	Holding and other investment offices	3	5	0.2	-	25	-	7,360	-	151	0.0
GENESEE, NY											
60 –	**Finance, insurance, and real estate**	95	96	0.2	549	585	20,087	21,901	11,892	13,029	0.0
6000	Depository institutions	20	22	0.3	205	205	18,439	19,434	3,850	3,881	0.0
6020	Commercial banks	13	14	0.4	143	150	18,154	19,493	2,661	2,949	0.0
6300	Insurance carriers	6	7	0.2	81	135	31,160	27,763	2,343	3,592	0.1
6400	Insurance agents, brokers, and service	27	28	0.4	101	103	18,851	18,641	1,965	2,067	0.1
6500	Real estate	37	35	0.1	136	110	13,794	15,309	2,158	1,991	0.1
6510	Real estate operators and lessors	14	16	0.1	61	54	10,426	15,852	816	985	0.1
6530	Real estate agents and managers	10	10	0.1	23	35	17,739	15,314	417	668	0.0
6540	Title abstract offices	3	2	0.5	25	-	17,600	-	488	-	-
6553	Cemetery subdividers and developers	7	6	0.9	5	7	5,600	3,429	44	40	0.0
GREENE, NY											
60 –	**Finance, insurance, and real estate**	71	70	0.1	454	470	17,233	17,838	8,426	9,215	0.0
6000	Depository institutions	18	18	0.3	193	199	19,130	18,432	3,829	4,051	0.0
6400	Insurance agents, brokers, and service	16	16	0.2	84	86	17,571	21,116	1,882	2,059	0.1
6510	Real estate operators and lessors	11	9	0.1	26	17	14,769	12,471	311	244	0.0
6530	Real estate agents and managers	12	15	0.1	38	65	14,526	12,308	533	938	0.0
6553	Cemetery subdividers and developers	5	4	0.6	11	-	5,091	-	63	-	-
HAMILTON, NY											
60 –	**Finance, insurance, and real estate**	7	8	0.0	23	60	17,913	7,000	427	545	0.0
6500	Real estate	2	3	0.0	-	3	-	6,667	-	65	0.0
HERKIMER, NY											
60 –	**Finance, insurance, and real estate**	97	101	0.2	729	780	19,122	21,010	14,749	17,204	0.0
6000	Depository institutions	26	27	0.4	333	349	18,018	17,089	5,883	6,608	0.1
6020	Commercial banks	19	19	0.5	279	284	18,380	17,394	4,974	5,526	0.1
6030	Savings institutions	5	5	0.4	-	44	-	15,909	-	707	0.1
6060	Credit unions	2	3	0.4	-	21	-	15,429	-	375	0.1
6100	Nondepository institutions	3	2	0.1	14	-	26,000	-	366	-	-
6300	Insurance carriers	5	6	0.2	-	97	-	28,041	-	2,652	0.1

Source: County Business Patterns, 1992/93, CBP-92/93-1, U.S. Department of Commerce, Washington, D.C., April 1995. SIC categories for which data were suppressed or not available for both 1992 and 1993 are *not* displayed. The employment columns represent mid-March employment in the year. Pay per employee is calculated by dividing 1st Quarter payroll, annualized, by mid-March employment. The columns headed "% State" show the county's percentage of the state total for the SIC in 1993; for example, 0.9% for SIC 6030 means that the county had 0.9 percent of the state's total establishments (or payroll) in SIC 6030 in 1993. A dash (-) is used to indicate that data are not available or cannot be calculated; *nec* means not elsewhere classified.

Continued on next page.

SIC	Industry	No. Establishments			Employment		Pay / Employee		Annual Payroll ($ 000)		
		1992	1993	% State	1992	1993	1992	1993	1992	1993	% State
HERKIMER, NY - [continued]											
6400	Insurance agents, brokers, and service	21	22	0.3	95	100	21,895	21,880	2,156	2,294	0.1
6500	Real estate	39	41	0.1	221	222	17,792	23,207	4,917	5,337	0.1
6510	Real estate operators and lessors	12	17	0.1	58	83	8,138	8,675	458	837	0.1
JEFFERSON, NY											
60 –	**Finance, insurance, and real estate**	219	222	0.4	1,290	1,377	19,991	19,535	27,567	29,348	0.1
6000	Depository institutions	56	59	0.9	602	633	17,482	16,354	12,215	11,955	0.1
6020	Commercial banks	41	43	1.1	438	437	17,352	16,192	8,945	8,366	0.1
6030	Savings institutions	7	7	0.5	133	143	19,218	17,958	2,893	2,825	0.3
6060	Credit unions	8	9	1.2	31	53	11,871	13,358	377	764	-
6100	Nondepository institutions	6	4	0.2	38	22	24,000	26,000	946	632	0.0
6300	Insurance carriers	14	15	0.5	181	252	28,884	26,619	5,066	6,967	0.1
6330	Fire, marine, and casualty insurance	5	7	0.5	-	111	-	27,027	-	3,120	0.2
6400	Insurance agents, brokers, and service	46	46	0.7	216	189	20,148	19,005	4,359	4,076	0.2
6500	Real estate	84	88	0.3	219	249	10,904	11,695	2,798	3,206	0.1
6510	Real estate operators and lessors	36	43	0.3	115	157	10,991	9,987	1,403	1,736	0.1
6530	Real estate agents and managers	18	15	0.1	38	29	9,684	14,483	462	488	0.0
6540	Title abstract offices	3	3	0.8	13	14	25,231	42,000	435	514	0.6
6553	Cemetery subdividers and developers	25	24	3.7	-	39	-	4,821	-	311	0.3
6700	Holding and other investment offices	5	4	0.2	9	7	12,444	21,143	127	156	0.0
KINGS, NY											
60 –	**Finance, insurance, and real estate**	4,086	4,081	7.5	22,052	22,693	25,282	26,386	567,048	632,105	1.6
6000	Depository institutions	378	375	5.6	7,338	7,402	24,726	28,225	178,069	215,539	2.3
6020	Commercial banks	150	144	3.8	2,788	3,131	30,595	34,581	79,599	107,203	1.6
6030	Savings institutions	133	130	9.5	4,161	3,795	20,511	23,506	87,320	95,320	11.4
6060	Credit unions	9	15	2.1	87	-	23,080	-	1,973	-	-
6090	Functions closely related to banking	84	84	16.0	298	353	29,383	24,850	9,118	10,232	1.9
6100	Nondepository institutions	70	63	3.7	373	358	26,520	41,542	11,483	27,696	1.9
6140	Personal credit institutions	25	17	3.6	119	65	26,387	33,908	3,873	2,216	1.2
6150	Business credit institutions	5	6	1.4	87	-	29,057	-	2,184	-	-
6160	Mortgage bankers and brokers	39	39	4.9	167	235	25,293	25,481	5,406	8,068	2.3
6200	Security and commodity brokers	43	47	0.8	466	494	69,082	46,308	30,259	31,546	0.2
6210	Security brokers and dealers	27	30	0.8	226	243	69,894	60,724	14,178	13,119	0.1
6220	Commodity contracts brokers, dealers	3	5	1.6	-	27	-	34,519	-	816	0.5
6280	Security and commodity services	12	11	0.7	-	224	-	32,089	-	17,554	0.6
6300	Insurance carriers	130	121	4.1	2,127	2,334	46,669	49,810	95,008	99,793	2.1
6310	Life insurance	45	45	5.6	1,463	1,724	45,635	48,615	58,998	67,377	3.7
6330	Fire, marine, and casualty insurance	54	53	4.1	506	483	56,680	60,505	28,927	29,077	1.5
6370	Pension, health, and welfare funds	26	18	3.1	143	115	23,720	26,400	6,800	3,003	2.4
6400	Insurance agents, brokers, and service	299	306	4.3	1,136	1,127	23,602	22,910	28,048	28,846	1.4
6500	Real estate	3,108	3,118	11.3	9,893	10,255	18,984	18,614	204,699	208,994	5.4
6510	Real estate operators and lessors	1,932	2,111	13.5	4,975	5,486	15,943	15,992	86,391	95,427	6.0
6530	Real estate agents and managers	880	944	9.1	3,619	4,180	20,387	20,424	78,947	91,942	4.6
6540	Title abstract offices	21	25	6.3	178	190	26,944	28,021	5,640	6,474	7.6
6552	Subdividers and developers, n.e.c.	18	18	5.3	315	143	35,695	35,217	12,014	5,314	7.5
6553	Cemetery subdividers and developers	6	6	0.9	298	234	31,383	30,410	11,208	9,323	9.7
6710	Holding offices	15	15	2.3	60	82	48,133	33,024	2,562	3,063	0.3
6732	Educational, religious, etc. trusts	14	12	2.2	40	44	17,400	16,727	771	831	0.4
6733	Trusts, n.e.c.	14	14	4.0	26	149	14,462	27,973	427	4,634	6.2
6799	Investors, n.e.c.	6	2	0.4	36	-	12,111	-	440	-	-
LEWIS, NY											
60 –	**Finance, insurance, and real estate**	44	46	0.1	211	201	15,299	14,547	3,657	3,204	0.0
6000	Depository institutions	10	12	0.2	93	93	14,323	14,538	1,475	1,316	0.0
6020	Commercial banks	8	9	0.2	-	82	-	14,634	-	1,151	0.0
6400	Insurance agents, brokers, and service	10	10	0.1	62	-	20,194	-	1,445	-	-

Source: County Business Patterns, 1992/93, CBP-92/93-1, U.S. Department of Commerce, Washington, D.C., April 1995. SIC categories for which data were suppressed or not available for both 1992 and 1993 are not displayed. The employment columns represent mid-March employment in the year. Pay per employee is calculated by dividing 1st Quarter payroll, annualized, by mid-March employment. The columns headed "% State" show the county's percentage of the state total for the SIC in 1993; for example, 0.9% for SIC 6030 means that the county had 0.9 percent of the state's total establishments (or payroll) in SIC 6030 in 1993. A dash (-) is used to indicate that data are not available or cannot be calculated; nec means not elsewhere classified.

Continued on next page.

SIC	Industry	No. Establishments			Employment		Pay / Employee		Annual Payroll ($ 000)		
		1992	1993	% State	1992	1993	1992	1993	1992	1993	% State
LEWIS, NY - [continued]											
6500	Real estate	21	23	0.1	-	59	-	9,424	-	632	0.0
6510	Real estate operators and lessors	4	7	0.0	5	41	3,200	10,634	17	464	0.0
6530	Real estate agents and managers	4	2	0.0	6	-	3,333	-	25	-	-
LIVINGSTON, NY											
60 -	**Finance, insurance, and real estate**	87	84	0.2	384	415	19,583	20,260	8,012	8,831	0.0
6000	Depository institutions	22	23	0.3	168	173	16,714	16,116	3,093	3,324	0.0
6020	Commercial banks	18	19	0.5	146	152	16,795	16,211	2,731	2,961	0.0
6300	Insurance carriers	3	4	0.1	33	-	29,212	-	1,041	-	-
6400	Insurance agents, brokers, and service	23	22	0.3	84	78	22,952	23,538	1,804	1,813	0.1
6500	Real estate	36	31	0.1	82	84	16,537	11,762	1,566	1,224	0.0
6510	Real estate operators and lessors	10	11	0.1	25	30	13,280	10,933	376	346	0.0
6530	Real estate agents and managers	9	10	0.1	17	23	20,471	18,435	401	551	0.0
6540	Title abstract offices	4	3	0.8	22	-	20,545	-	513	-	-
6553	Cemetery subdividers and developers	8	7	1.1	7	-	2,857	-	68	-	-
MADISON, NY											
60 -	**Finance, insurance, and real estate**	102	107	0.2	580	557	20,345	20,144	12,784	12,174	0.0
6000	Depository institutions	22	22	0.3	308	319	20,584	19,285	6,459	6,557	0.1
6020	Commercial banks	14	12	0.3	186	185	21,548	19,914	4,038	3,931	0.1
6030	Savings institutions	5	7	0.5	-	116	-	19,517	-	2,401	0.3
6060	Credit unions	3	3	0.4	-	18	-	11,333	-	225	-
6300	Insurance carriers	4	5	0.2	21	24	17,143	16,500	368	505	0.0
6400	Insurance agents, brokers, and service	21	20	0.3	119	82	23,832	27,415	3,223	2,344	0.1
6500	Real estate	47	51	0.2	100	101	14,560	14,891	1,663	1,747	0.0
6510	Real estate operators and lessors	17	20	0.1	35	48	12,914	13,750	433	693	0.0
6530	Real estate agents and managers	8	11	0.1	25	26	16,960	18,769	573	518	0.0
6540	Title abstract offices	4	4	1.0	12	12	21,333	21,000	339	357	0.4
6552	Subdividers and developers, n.e.c.	3	3	0.9	6	-	8,667	-	63	-	-
6553	Cemetery subdividers and developers	10	12	1.9	7	7	6,857	6,857	95	104	0.1
6700	Holding and other investment offices	2	3	0.1	-	2	-	6,000	-	60	0.0
MONROE, NY											
60 -	**Finance, insurance, and real estate**	1,484	1,479	2.7	20,498	20,196	27,968	28,687	579,269	610,008	1.5
6000	Depository institutions	271	269	4.1	7,922	7,565	26,860	26,626	204,952	197,675	2.1
6020	Commercial banks	170	164	4.4	5,472	4,966	27,052	27,588	144,161	134,650	2.0
6030	Savings institutions	69	64	4.7	2,193	2,233	27,318	25,804	56,121	55,567	6.7
6060	Credit unions	30	37	5.1	-	346	-	19,064	-	7,209	-
6090	Functions closely related to banking	2	4	0.8	-	20	-	10,600	-	249	0.0
6100	Nondepository institutions	97	98	5.7	951	929	31,605	29,042	30,617	29,595	2.0
6140	Personal credit institutions	43	36	7.7	407	363	30,133	24,331	11,057	8,206	4.6
6150	Business credit institutions	14	15	3.6	-	86	-	46,744	-	3,639	0.4
6160	Mortgage bankers and brokers	38	47	5.9	479	480	31,031	29,433	16,130	17,750	5.0
6200	Security and commodity brokers	89	96	1.7	1,046	1,157	64,956	58,669	71,437	82,357	0.5
6210	Security brokers and dealers	44	42	1.1	659	709	67,514	64,102	42,209	48,515	0.4
6280	Security and commodity services	44	54	3.4	387	448	60,599	50,071	29,218	33,842	1.1
6300	Insurance carriers	158	128	4.4	3,522	3,776	31,783	33,434	114,154	126,350	2.7
6310	Life insurance	45	39	4.8	941	1,026	32,701	35,290	28,863	32,421	1.8
6330	Fire, marine, and casualty insurance	76	66	5.1	1,190	1,232	34,047	33,370	41,554	41,964	2.2
6370	Pension, health, and welfare funds	22	14	2.4	119	-	21,176	-	3,888	-	-
6400	Insurance agents, brokers, and service	284	296	4.2	1,806	1,754	28,569	29,888	54,296	56,667	2.8
6500	Real estate	528	543	2.0	4,366	4,502	18,292	18,008	84,397	90,070	2.3
6510	Real estate operators and lessors	256	284	1.8	1,952	2,184	14,768	15,053	31,682	37,286	2.3
6530	Real estate agents and managers	201	226	2.2	2,078	2,027	20,928	19,998	43,636	44,070	2.2
6540	Title abstract offices	6	8	2.0	120	190	29,000	28,547	3,827	5,647	6.6
6552	Subdividers and developers, n.e.c.	13	9	2.6	39	26	20,513	20,462	1,532	1,138	1.6
6553	Cemetery subdividers and developers	14	15	2.3	73	75	20,110	22,720	1,794	1,925	2.0
6710	Holding offices	16	13	2.0	161	55	35,230	50,109	6,011	3,306	0.3

Source: County Business Patterns, 1992/93, CBP-92/93-1, U.S. Department of Commerce, Washington, D.C., April 1995. SIC categories for which data were suppressed or not available for both 1992 and 1993 are *not* displayed. The employment columns represent mid-March employment in the year. Pay per employee is calculated by dividing 1st Quarter payroll, annualized, by mid-March employment. The columns headed "% State" show the county's percentage of the state total for the SIC in 1993; for example, 0.9% for SIC 6030 means that the county had 0.9 percent of the state's total establishments (or payroll) in SIC 6030 in 1993. A dash (-) is used to indicate that data are not available or cannot be calculated; *nec* means not elsewhere classified.

Continued on next page.

SIC	Industry	No. Establishments			Employment		Pay / Employee		Annual Payroll ($ 000)		
		1992	1993	% State	1992	1993	1992	1993	1992	1993	% State
MONROE, NY - [continued]											
6732	Educational, religious, etc. trusts	14	12	2.2	496	61	7,468	18,885	3,654	1,406	0.7
6733	Trusts, n.e.c.	9	8	2.3	84	-	29,000	-	2,149	-	-
6794	Patent owners and lessors	3	3	1.8	-	57	-	48,772	-	3,471	1.9
6799	Investors, n.e.c.	10	11	2.3	90	46	62,044	68,957	5,647	3,510	1.4
MONTGOMERY, NY											
60–	**Finance, insurance, and real estate**	79	82	0.2	691	712	16,984	17,360	13,518	14,301	0.0
6000	Depository institutions	23	23	0.3	403	422	16,516	15,915	7,507	7,865	0.1
6020	Commercial banks	13	13	0.3	223	235	15,713	15,898	4,230	4,602	0.1
6300	Insurance carriers	5	4	0.1	77	86	21,247	24,884	1,796	2,091	0.0
6400	Insurance agents, brokers, and service	20	19	0.3	112	96	18,143	17,500	2,585	1,811	0.1
6500	Real estate	28	31	0.1	-	82	-	9,805	-	977	0.0
6510	Real estate operators and lessors	6	7	0.0	16	18	7,500	5,556	118	94	0.0
6530	Real estate agents and managers	4	10	0.1	4	20	24,000	14,200	125	333	0.0
6553	Cemetery subdividers and developers	14	13	2.0	24	-	4,833	-	189	-	-
NASSAU, NY											
60–	**Finance, insurance, and real estate**	4,699	4,799	8.8	52,555	53,229	32,269	33,414	1,743,970	1,952,798	4.8
6000	Depository institutions	541	540	8.1	16,966	14,739	26,663	29,094	448,151	437,987	4.6
6020	Commercial banks	318	324	8.6	9,627	9,311	28,610	28,832	266,756	274,410	4.2
6030	Savings institutions	183	177	13.0	6,171	4,969	24,126	30,483	153,484	150,189	18.0
6060	Credit unions	25	28	3.9	-	253	-	22,545	-	9,900	-
6090	Functions closely related to banking	14	11	2.1	557	206	24,273	15,456	16,109	3,488	0.6
6100	Nondepository institutions	254	261	15.1	3,848	4,097	31,573	31,502	129,086	150,282	10.1
6140	Personal credit institutions	43	36	7.7	442	1,036	31,973	30,008	13,113	30,578	17.2
6150	Business credit institutions	53	60	14.4	921	1,284	33,993	30,249	28,590	43,484	4.7
6160	Mortgage bankers and brokers	145	164	20.5	1,763	1,777	34,217	33,279	70,707	76,217	21.4
6200	Security and commodity brokers	280	314	5.4	2,835	3,976	69,902	58,050	209,109	286,040	1.7
6210	Security brokers and dealers	181	181	4.7	2,521	3,595	73,985	59,885	193,421	266,233	2.0
6220	Commodity contracts brokers, dealers	14	17	5.6	108	57	21,370	45,123	2,820	2,927	1.8
6230	Security and commodity exchanges	1	3	10.0	-	5	-	58,400	-	299	0.1
6280	Security and commodity services	81	113	7.0	205	319	45,190	39,674	12,513	16,581	0.6
6300	Insurance carriers	404	334	11.4	10,055	9,830	36,593	36,528	353,585	353,248	7.6
6310	Life insurance	102	101	12.5	3,226	3,338	37,777	36,429	112,324	114,157	6.3
6321	Accident and health insurance	3	5	13.5	94	198	30,723	64,303	3,464	14,180	23.4
6324	Hospital and medical service plans	7	7	7.5	312	304	33,256	33,197	10,836	9,279	1.5
6330	Fire, marine, and casualty insurance	170	154	12.0	5,443	5,245	36,398	36,210	192,535	191,594	10.0
6360	Title insurance	19	7	11.1	244	149	39,295	60,617	10,015	6,838	13.7
6370	Pension, health, and welfare funds	93	54	9.2	631	545	25,033	25,490	18,697	15,353	12.1
6400	Insurance agents, brokers, and service	1,037	1,093	15.5	9,083	9,367	30,818	30,376	307,162	316,069	15.3
6500	Real estate	2,025	2,090	7.6	8,623	8,746	24,435	24,964	238,268	257,080	6.6
6510	Real estate operators and lessors	918	1,012	6.5	3,345	3,826	22,013	21,441	83,067	93,514	5.8
6530	Real estate agents and managers	779	959	9.2	3,810	3,977	25,802	27,360	108,081	128,772	6.4
6540	Title abstract offices	47	60	15.0	327	527	31,939	29,070	12,691	19,020	22.2
6552	Subdividers and developers, n.e.c.	36	27	7.9	169	130	35,172	25,785	6,227	4,228	6.0
6553	Cemetery subdividers and developers	13	17	2.6	288	285	29,389	30,933	10,107	10,608	11.1
6700	Holding and other investment offices	155	161	6.9	-	2,033	-	56,057	-	134,602	7.1
6710	Holding offices	45	49	7.7	427	1,484	82,333	58,208	28,301	111,842	10.3
6720	Investment offices	12	5	5.6	50	13	21,280	44,615	1,001	407	0.5
6732	Educational, religious, etc. trusts	18	24	4.4	89	81	33,978	26,222	3,302	2,457	1.3
6733	Trusts, n.e.c.	22	23	6.5	61	47	27,344	26,553	1,450	1,488	2.0
6794	Patent owners and lessors	11	9	5.5	205	189	53,912	40,233	9,731	8,330	4.6
6798	Real estate investment trusts	7	5	12.5	32	23	37,000	49,913	1,129	1,076	3.5
6799	Investors, n.e.c.	24	44	9.2	99	119	47,192	118,286	4,886	8,090	3.2

Source: County Business Patterns, 1992/93, CBP-92/93-1, U.S. Department of Commerce, Washington, D.C., April 1995. SIC categories for which data were suppressed or not available for both 1992 and 1993 are *not* displayed. The employment columns represent mid-March employment in the year. Pay per employee is calculated by dividing 1st Quarter payroll, annualized, by mid-March employment. The columns headed "% State" show the county's percentage of the state total for the SIC in 1993; for example, 0.9% for SIC 6030 means that the county had 0.9 percent of the state's total establishments (or payroll) in SIC 6030 in 1993. A dash (-) is used to indicate that data are not available or cannot be calculated; *nec* means not elsewhere classified.

SIC	Industry	No. Establishments			Employment		Pay / Employee		Annual Payroll ($ 000)		
		1992	1993	% State	1992	1993	1992	1993	1992	1993	% State
NEW YORK, NY											
60 –	**Finance, insurance, and real estate**	18,122	18,464	*34.0*	434,826	405,456	77,246	73,704	29,063,156	30,310,124	*74.9*
6000	Depository institutions	1,409	1,297	*19.5*	129,417	115,034	60,459	62,201	6,991,054	6,800,812	*71.3*
6020	Commercial banks	707	604	*16.1*	95,405	82,189	61,635	61,808	5,082,068	4,749,459	*72.3*
6030	Savings institutions	175	124	*9.1*	4,311	3,478	28,904	32,005	131,181	113,323	*13.6*
6080	Foreign bank and branches and agencies	207	256	*95.5*	14,966	18,555	62,273	71,759	954,637	1,290,731	*99.0*
6090	Functions closely related to banking	249	242	*46.1*	9,984	6,288	70,647	73,391	648,956	475,337	*88.5*
6100	Nondepository institutions	374	373	*21.6*	15,608	12,054	75,433	64,443	1,018,578	733,718	*49.4*
6110	Federal and Federally-sponsored credit	8	2	*6.3*	72	-	174,778	-	6,969	-	*-*
6140	Personal credit institutions	70	44	*9.4*	1,737	925	106,892	87,641	187,524	68,309	*38.5*
6150	Business credit institutions	167	196	*47.1*	12,261	9,877	67,702	64,468	688,251	607,399	*65.7*
6160	Mortgage bankers and brokers	112	123	*15.4*	1,419	914	100,772	54,963	130,187	48,539	*13.7*
6200	Security and commodity brokers	4,017	4,369	*75.4*	120,942	120,283	139,794	124,877	13,659,939	15,582,262	*94.1*
6210	Security brokers and dealers	2,851	3,120	*81.2*	99,433	97,013	147,802	130,639	11,354,851	12,354,957	*94.2*
6220	Commodity contracts brokers, dealers	243	249	*81.9*	2,894	2,072	67,574	59,915	200,748	156,875	*95.2*
6230	Security and commodity exchanges	34	23	*76.7*	3,771	3,807	61,052	68,172	227,915	265,063	*99.7*
6280	Security and commodity services	835	975	*60.6*	14,612	17,388	121,020	112,901	1,858,034	2,804,552	*93.2*
6300	Insurance carriers	689	558	*19.1*	62,072	52,239	46,286	44,377	2,593,296	2,262,651	*48.5*
6310	Life insurance	184	158	*19.6*	30,066	21,380	47,226	44,351	1,236,592	883,782	*48.9*
6321	Accident and health insurance	11	8	*21.6*	-	161	-	60,795	-	9,478	*15.6*
6324	Hospital and medical service plans	18	22	*23.7*	-	8,506	-	33,663	-	312,501	*50.6*
6330	Fire, marine, and casualty insurance	171	172	*13.4*	14,862	19,480	55,200	47,051	756,950	897,436	*47.0*
6350	Surety insurance	21	13	*31.0*	5,614	767	42,202	125,272	193,982	89,989	*94.6*
6360	Title insurance	13	12	*19.0*	582	351	47,519	54,553	22,974	22,318	*44.6*
6370	Pension, health, and welfare funds	260	171	*29.1*	1,980	1,589	25,103	26,376	58,598	46,813	*37.0*
6390	Insurance carriers, n.e.c.	4	1	*14.3*	173	-	22,890	-	4,285	-	*-*
6400	Insurance agents, brokers, and service	959	1,036	*14.7*	20,374	18,996	52,265	49,066	1,032,969	968,687	*47.0*
6500	Real estate	9,102	9,262	*33.6*	64,816	65,594	32,151	30,493	2,150,586	2,170,440	*56.0*
6510	Real estate operators and lessors	5,320	5,616	*35.9*	31,598	32,609	27,982	26,082	920,684	912,554	*57.0*
6530	Real estate agents and managers	3,080	3,508	*33.7*	30,342	31,956	36,663	34,471	1,135,593	1,200,774	*59.5*
6540	Title abstract offices	20	22	*5.5*	172	241	28,628	30,705	5,841	9,742	*11.4*
6552	Subdividers and developers, n.e.c.	103	69	*20.3*	638	718	45,442	53,554	28,593	42,974	*61.0*
6553	Cemetery subdividers and developers	5	14	*2.2*	39	59	29,538	20,746	1,116	1,415	*1.5*
6700	Holding and other investment offices	1,390	1,397	*59.9*	18,280	17,644	67,898	74,756	1,248,803	1,485,897	*77.9*
6710	Holding offices	328	342	*53.5*	7,201	6,750	88,170	103,425	616,466	762,824	*70.0*
6720	Investment offices	103	68	*75.6*	1,332	777	93,724	83,495	125,316	75,815	*96.8*
6732	Educational, religious, etc. trusts	322	353	*65.0*	3,323	3,979	37,240	38,578	126,485	177,059	*90.1*
6733	Trusts, n.e.c.	178	190	*54.0*	1,611	1,136	34,135	33,408	63,548	56,281	*75.1*
6792	Oil royalty traders	9	8	*66.7*	26	28	63,692	58,000	2,092	1,959	*69.0*
6794	Patent owners and lessors	79	102	*62.6*	2,782	2,428	38,723	62,188	119,671	162,570	*89.7*
6798	Real estate investment trusts	34	24	*60.0*	252	456	109,762	79,702	19,134	29,320	*95.8*
6799	Investors, n.e.c.	246	303	*63.3*	1,212	2,072	102,832	84,434	133,782	219,170	*87.0*
NIAGARA, NY											
60 –	**Finance, insurance, and real estate**	305	306	*0.6*	1,965	1,949	20,289	20,809	41,212	42,870	*0.1*
6000	Depository institutions	84	89	*1.3*	932	903	20,502	22,392	18,720	19,473	*0.2*
6020	Commercial banks	44	46	*1.2*	538	478	17,903	17,113	10,331	9,758	*0.1*
6100	Nondepository institutions	12	8	*0.5*	69	57	17,217	17,965	1,169	954	*0.1*
6200	Security and commodity brokers	8	8	*0.1*	48	45	46,917	46,844	2,388	2,374	*0.0*
6300	Insurance carriers	30	27	*0.9*	183	185	25,836	22,422	4,462	4,372	*0.1*
6330	Fire, marine, and casualty insurance	17	13	*1.0*	65	36	28,554	39,222	1,974	1,515	*0.1*
6370	Pension, health, and welfare funds	5	6	*1.0*	3	3	53,333	32,000	126	426	*0.3*
6400	Insurance agents, brokers, and service	63	67	*0.9*	314	323	20,089	20,669	7,140	8,036	*0.4*
6500	Real estate	100	100	*0.4*	410	379	13,707	14,755	6,678	6,486	*0.2*
6510	Real estate operators and lessors	51	54	*0.3*	215	214	12,651	12,561	3,304	3,364	*0.2*
6530	Real estate agents and managers	31	33	*0.3*	130	110	13,815	16,982	2,066	2,016	*0.1*
6552	Subdividers and developers, n.e.c.	2	3	*0.9*	-	3	-	16,000	-	31	*0.0*

Source: County Business Patterns, 1992/93, CBP-92/93-1, U.S. Department of Commerce, Washington, D.C., April 1995. SIC categories for which data were suppressed or not available for both 1992 and 1993 are not displayed. The employment columns represent mid-March employment in the year. Pay per employee is calculated by dividing 1st Quarter payroll, annualized, by mid-March employment. The columns headed "% State" show the county's percentage of the state total for the SIC in 1993; for example, 0.9% for SIC 6030 means that the county had 0.9 percent of the state's total establishments (or payroll) in SIC 6030 in 1993. A dash (-) is used to indicate that data are not available or cannot be calculated; nec means not elsewhere classified.

Continued on next page.

SIC	Industry	No. Establishments			Employment		Pay / Employee		Annual Payroll ($ 000)		
		1992	1993	% State	1992	1993	1992	1993	1992	1993	% State
NIAGARA, NY - [continued]											
6553	Cemetery subdividers and developers	9	9	1.4	41	-	17,268	-	789	-	-
6700	Holding and other investment offices	8	7	0.3	9	57	73,778	13,825	655	1,175	0.1
6710	Holding offices	2	3	0.5	-	54	-	9,852	-	871	0.1
ONEIDA, NY											
60 –	**Finance, insurance, and real estate**	455	482	0.9	9,662	10,974	20,374	19,271	195,709	219,025	0.5
6000	Depository institutions	85	97	1.5	2,015	2,946	19,200	18,185	37,675	53,321	0.6
6020	Commercial banks	46	53	1.4	1,122	2,072	18,720	18,025	19,898	37,295	0.6
6030	Savings institutions	19	21	1.5	568	621	19,472	20,039	11,637	11,829	1.4
6100	Nondepository institutions	17	13	0.8	329	365	19,574	17,556	5,977	6,641	0.4
6140	Personal credit institutions	14	9	1.9	-	352	-	17,398	-	6,298	3.5
6160	Mortgage bankers and brokers	2	4	0.5	-	13	-	21,846	-	343	0.1
6200	Security and commodity brokers	18	23	0.4	121	158	50,017	41,165	6,162	7,283	0.0
6210	Security brokers and dealers	6	5	0.1	70	85	67,714	61,082	4,730	5,614	0.0
6280	Security and commodity services	12	18	1.1	51	73	25,725	17,973	1,432	1,669	0.1
6300	Insurance carriers	60	55	1.9	6,108	6,292	20,346	19,585	123,682	127,574	2.7
6330	Fire, marine, and casualty insurance	24	23	1.8	1,934	1,921	26,647	25,385	50,198	50,339	2.6
6370	Pension, health, and welfare funds	12	12	2.0	92	100	15,826	15,800	1,731	2,010	1.6
6400	Insurance agents, brokers, and service	99	110	1.6	505	485	24,222	20,701	12,117	10,861	0.5
6500	Real estate	163	172	0.6	554	590	14,975	14,088	9,289	9,344	0.2
6510	Real estate operators and lessors	61	77	0.5	223	312	12,753	11,603	2,778	4,018	0.3
6530	Real estate agents and managers	54	58	0.6	152	147	15,868	16,054	2,830	2,610	0.1
6540	Title abstract offices	5	5	1.3	75	68	24,587	24,588	1,959	1,736	2.0
6553	Cemetery subdividers and developers	29	31	4.8	59	63	9,559	10,476	827	952	1.0
6700	Holding and other investment offices	13	11	0.5	30	-	29,200	-	807	-	-
ONONDAGA, NY											
60 –	**Finance, insurance, and real estate**	1,073	1,090	2.0	20,590	17,659	27,386	27,000	563,874	508,347	1.3
6000	Depository institutions	176	184	2.8	4,368	3,442	22,079	20,231	100,226	78,889	0.8
6020	Commercial banks	105	140	3.7	2,803	2,938	22,554	20,564	65,930	68,810	1.0
6030	Savings institutions	44	13	1.0	1,350	193	21,695	18,301	30,170	3,981	0.5
6060	Credit unions	25	31	4.3	-	311	-	18,289	-	6,098	-
6100	Nondepository institutions	75	66	3.8	806	881	28,774	27,378	23,701	29,907	2.0
6140	Personal credit institutions	44	30	6.4	310	-	26,439	-	8,194	-	-
6150	Business credit institutions	8	9	2.2	234	238	26,598	33,899	6,521	8,876	1.0
6160	Mortgage bankers and brokers	21	26	3.3	252	339	33,444	26,985	8,738	14,230	4.0
6200	Security and commodity brokers	44	49	0.8	536	570	60,313	59,782	32,034	36,081	0.2
6210	Security brokers and dealers	24	23	0.6	445	449	62,166	61,942	27,447	30,097	0.2
6280	Security and commodity services	20	26	1.6	91	121	51,253	51,769	4,587	5,984	0.2
6300	Insurance carriers	165	159	5.4	9,860	8,029	28,752	29,370	272,098	244,683	5.2
6310	Life insurance	41	34	4.2	3,953	2,301	28,071	30,714	96,691	71,835	4.0
6330	Fire, marine, and casualty insurance	74	75	5.8	3,707	3,460	31,513	30,508	120,258	113,168	5.9
6360	Title insurance	4	2	3.2	100	-	27,040	-	2,516	-	-
6370	Pension, health, and welfare funds	29	32	5.4	273	366	22,315	22,262	6,329	9,498	7.5
6400	Insurance agents, brokers, and service	237	245	3.5	1,696	1,742	27,281	25,520	49,375	46,894	2.3
6500	Real estate	347	361	1.3	2,806	2,645	22,981	20,918	68,739	58,740	1.5
6510	Real estate operators and lessors	160	166	1.1	905	799	12,354	13,752	12,880	12,044	0.8
6530	Real estate agents and managers	121	141	1.4	1,567	1,679	30,259	24,284	49,264	42,322	2.1
6540	Title abstract offices	11	15	3.8	99	81	17,616	24,148	1,973	2,323	2.7
6552	Subdividers and developers, n.e.c.	17	12	3.5	106	18	18,189	25,111	2,178	675	1.0
6553	Cemetery subdividers and developers	19	22	3.4	65	61	16,308	16,984	1,149	1,188	1.2
6710	Holding offices	9	7	1.1	125	-	33,696	-	4,093	-	-
6720	Investment offices	3	-	-	8	-	29,000	-	291	-	-
6732	Educational, religious, etc. trusts	6	6	1.1	-	28	-	18,000	-	544	0.3
6733	Trusts, n.e.c.	5	5	1.4	1	1	8,000	8,000	24	33	0.0

Source: County Business Patterns, 1992/93, CBP-92/93-1, U.S. Department of Commerce, Washington, D.C., April 1995. SIC categories for which data were suppressed or not available for both 1992 and 1993 are *not* displayed. The employment columns represent mid-March employment in the year. Pay per employee is calculated by dividing 1st Quarter payroll, annualized, by mid-March employment. The columns headed "% State" show the county's percentage of the state total for the SIC in 1993; for example, 0.9% for SIC 6030 means that the county had 0.9 percent of the state's total establishments (or payroll) in SIC 6030 in 1993. A dash (-) is used to indicate that data are not available or cannot be calculated; *nec* means not elsewhere classified.

SIC	Industry	No. Establishments			Employment		Pay / Employee		Annual Payroll ($ 000)		
		1992	1993	% State	1992	1993	1992	1993	1992	1993	% State
ONTARIO, NY											
60 –	**Finance, insurance, and real estate**	157	155	0.3	1,074	1,045	20,819	21,872	24,260	25,171	0.1
6000	Depository institutions	31	31	0.5	606	576	18,686	19,410	12,227	12,058	0.1
6020	Commercial banks	20	20	0.5	425	396	19,134	19,636	8,729	8,431	0.1
6030	Savings institutions	5	5	0.4	152	146	17,684	19,014	2,963	3,010	0.4
6060	Credit unions	6	6	0.8	29	34	17,379	18,471	535	617	
6100	Nondepository institutions	6	5	0.3	-	38	-	24,947	-	1,314	0.1
6140	Personal credit institutions	4	3	0.6	15	-	27,733	-	409	-	-
6200	Security and commodity brokers	7	8	0.1	41	-	37,854	-	1,822	-	-
6210	Security brokers and dealers	3	4	0.1	17	-	50,118	-	945	-	-
6280	Security and commodity services	4	4	0.2	24	24	29,167	30,333	877	965	0.0
6300	Insurance carriers	13	12	0.4	70	90	24,000	27,022	1,758	2,294	0.0
6400	Insurance agents, brokers, and service	37	37	0.5	141	138	26,468	25,420	3,851	3,758	0.2
6500	Real estate	62	60	0.2	185	148	15,286	16,081	3,301	2,967	0.1
6510	Real estate operators and lessors	24	25	0.2	56	73	16,071	19,452	974	1,550	0.1
6530	Real estate agents and managers	19	22	0.2	52	-	15,077	-	1,058	-	-
6540	Title abstract offices	4	1	0.3	49	-	19,510	-	992	-	-
ORANGE, NY											
60 –	**Finance, insurance, and real estate**	609	614	1.1	5,523	5,854	23,236	23,006	136,458	146,204	0.4
6000	Depository institutions	123	119	1.8	1,949	1,974	20,530	20,478	46,717	48,326	0.5
6020	Commercial banks	79	74	2.0	1,280	1,282	20,131	20,041	31,912	32,623	0.5
6030	Savings institutions	39	35	2.6	648	613	21,469	21,618	14,462	14,116	1.7
6060	Credit unions	5	10	1.4	21	79	15,810	18,734	343	1,587	-
6100	Nondepository institutions	29	29	1.7	231	238	36,208	33,076	8,221	8,691	0.6
6140	Personal credit institutions	16	11	2.4	124	-	24,548	-	3,251	-	-
6160	Mortgage bankers and brokers	10	14	1.8	94	150	52,936	30,907	4,562	6,038	1.7
6200	Security and commodity brokers	25	27	0.5	96	106	41,042	50,566	4,280	5,200	0.0
6210	Security brokers and dealers	11	11	0.3	64	67	50,875	65,433	3,634	4,352	0.0
6280	Security and commodity services	12	15	0.9	31	-	21,161	-	594	-	-
6300	Insurance carriers	55	51	1.7	1,881	2,106	24,289	24,251	45,757	51,817	1.1
6310	Life insurance	17	16	2.0	387	508	27,421	31,740	10,545	14,195	0.8
6400	Insurance agents, brokers, and service	119	135	1.9	500	526	25,608	23,779	12,962	13,291	0.6
6500	Real estate	249	243	0.9	844	882	19,877	18,844	17,739	18,148	0.5
6510	Real estate operators and lessors	84	97	0.6	380	298	19,053	16,255	7,617	5,544	0.3
6530	Real estate agents and managers	96	106	1.0	280	465	19,086	19,656	5,701	9,500	0.5
6540	Title abstract offices	13	18	4.5	63	78	30,159	24,974	2,018	2,220	2.6
6552	Subdividers and developers, n.e.c.	11	6	1.8	20	5	21,200	7,200	391	93	0.1
6553	Cemetery subdividers and developers	15	14	2.2	39	34	20,103	18,235	810	727	0.8
6700	Holding and other investment offices	9	10	0.4	22	22	34,000	37,455	782	731	0.0
ORLEANS, NY											
60 –	**Finance, insurance, and real estate**	52	49	0.1	570	448	17,298	20,643	10,948	9,628	0.0
6000	Depository institutions	13	13	0.2	438	309	16,612	21,359	8,269	6,830	0.1
6030	Savings institutions	5	5	0.4	378	248	16,656	22,871	7,289	5,805	0.7
6400	Insurance agents, brokers, and service	13	14	0.2	46	-	21,304	-	997	-	-
6500	Real estate	18	16	0.1	50	30	15,120	12,400	844	481	0.0
6510	Real estate operators and lessors	5	5	0.0	-	10	-	8,000	-	104	0.0
6530	Real estate agents and managers	5	4	0.0	9	5	19,111	15,200	228	118	0.0
6540	Title abstract offices	3	2	0.5	26	-	16,923	-	499	-	-
6553	Cemetery subdividers and developers	4	4	0.6	3	4	4,000	4,000	18	21	0.0
OSWEGO, NY											
60 –	**Finance, insurance, and real estate**	150	150	0.3	796	763	17,201	17,279	13,979	14,473	0.0
6000	Depository institutions	36	37	0.6	366	377	16,765	17,294	6,457	7,221	0.1
6020	Commercial banks	13	16	0.4	114	143	13,930	14,266	1,770	2,541	0.0
6030	Savings institutions	15	12	0.9	213	187	17,690	19,358	4,013	3,784	0.5
6060	Credit unions	8	9	1.2	39	47	20,000	18,298	674	896	
6300	Insurance carriers	13	14	0.5	78	52	28,923	30,308	1,903	1,496	0.0

Source: County Business Patterns, 1992/93, CBP-92/93-1, U.S. Department of Commerce, Washington, D.C., April 1995. SIC categories for which data were suppressed or not available for both 1992 and 1993 are *not* displayed. The employment columns represent mid-March employment in the year. Pay per employee is calculated by dividing 1st Quarter payroll, annualized, by mid-March employment. The columns headed "% State" show the county's percentage of the state total for the SIC in 1993; for example, 0.9% for SIC 6030 means that the county had 0.9 percent of the state's total establishments (or payroll) in SIC 6030 in 1993. A dash (-) is used to indicate that data are not available or cannot be calculated; *nec* means not elsewhere classified.

Continued on next page.

SIC	Industry	No. Establishments			Employment		Pay / Employee		Annual Payroll ($ 000)		
		1992	1993	% State	1992	1993	1992	1993	1992	1993	% State
OSWEGO, NY - [continued]											
6370	Pension, health, and welfare funds	6	7	1.2	28	17	28,286	30,824	592	494	0.4
6400	Insurance agents, brokers, and service	36	34	0.5	163	157	19,190	18,981	3,140	3,302	0.2
6500	Real estate	59	60	0.2	165	165	10,206	11,127	1,989	2,169	0.1
6510	Real estate operators and lessors	23	26	0.2	90	103	8,178	9,553	811	1,044	0.1
6530	Real estate agents and managers	10	16	0.2	17	29	11,059	15,724	292	573	0.0
6540	Title abstract offices	6	5	1.3	28	-	13,857	-	415	-	-
6553	Cemetery subdividers and developers	12	12	1.9	-	12	-	6,000	-	185	0.2
OTSEGO, NY											
60–	**Finance, insurance, and real estate**	117	120	0.2	1,356	1,444	18,558	20,069	29,842	32,829	0.1
6000	Depository institutions	27	28	0.4	367	366	21,232	22,197	7,322	7,936	0.1
6210	Security brokers and dealers	6	6	0.2	16	20	64,750	61,600	1,161	1,454	0.0
6300	Insurance carriers	7	8	0.3	703	784	16,051	18,551	15,538	17,330	0.4
6400	Insurance agents, brokers, and service	26	27	0.4	105	111	26,019	24,649	3,121	3,333	0.2
6500	Real estate	47	47	0.2	73	64	9,699	9,688	830	814	0.0
6510	Real estate operators and lessors	14	12	0.1	34	24	10,588	9,500	297	268	0.0
6530	Real estate agents and managers	13	12	0.1	-	12	-	10,333	-	153	0.0
6553	Cemetery subdividers and developers	18	22	3.4	21	-	4,952	-	256	-	-
PUTNAM, NY											
60–	**Finance, insurance, and real estate**	139	148	0.3	803	868	26,999	25,622	22,614	25,685	0.1
6000	Depository institutions	26	25	0.4	297	298	25,455	22,899	7,705	7,629	0.1
6020	Commercial banks	15	15	0.4	147	158	27,238	22,430	4,221	4,170	0.1
6030	Savings institutions	7	6	0.4	130	123	23,015	22,797	2,962	2,959	0.4
6100	Nondepository institutions	6	5	0.3	81	-	33,037	-	2,892	-	-
6300	Insurance carriers	7	8	0.3	69	-	37,217	-	2,516	-	-
6330	Fire, marine, and casualty insurance	3	4	0.3	-	31	-	37,677	-	1,356	0.1
6400	Insurance agents, brokers, and service	26	26	0.4	112	106	30,000	28,491	3,525	3,425	0.2
6500	Real estate	67	76	0.3	207	224	20,773	18,375	4,765	4,902	0.1
6510	Real estate operators and lessors	16	23	0.1	19	52	12,000	19,308	336	1,229	0.1
6530	Real estate agents and managers	34	42	0.4	105	101	22,743	18,772	2,659	2,239	0.1
6540	Title abstract offices	5	5	1.3	17	22	22,118	20,364	478	516	0.6
6553	Cemetery subdividers and developers	4	4	0.6	39	-	21,026	-	834	-	-
QUEENS, NY											
60–	**Finance, insurance, and real estate**	3,635	3,646	6.7	30,924	28,549	31,296	33,302	906,161	926,782	2.3
6000	Depository institutions	511	485	7.3	13,701	10,240	37,518	35,017	450,940	349,984	3.7
6020	Commercial banks	232	207	5.5	8,579	5,193	46,872	46,010	333,692	215,676	3.3
6030	Savings institutions	169	163	12.0	4,445	4,144	21,156	21,347	98,154	101,381	12.2
6060	Credit unions	36	37	5.1	200	-	28,520	-	5,676	-	-
6080	Foreign bank and branches and agencies	6	9	3.4	-	253	-	50,292	-	13,116	1.0
6090	Functions closely related to banking	65	68	13.0	345	427	25,101	28,487	9,764	13,487	2.5
6100	Nondepository institutions	69	72	4.2	989	3,300	46,843	61,743	38,072	175,590	11.8
6200	Security and commodity brokers	42	47	0.8	405	400	47,891	56,160	19,431	21,692	0.1
6210	Security brokers and dealers	31	30	0.8	383	267	49,034	62,172	18,680	16,578	0.1
6220	Commodity contracts brokers, dealers	1	3	1.0	-	4	-	16,000	-	27	0.0
6280	Security and commodity services	7	12	0.7	8	129	18,000	44,961	199	5,076	0.2
6300	Insurance carriers	203	166	5.7	3,792	2,222	31,507	40,653	116,529	80,596	1.7
6310	Life insurance	39	38	4.7	2,699	1,384	28,333	38,387	73,874	43,173	2.4
6321	Accident and health insurance	3	2	5.4	4	-	17,000	-	77	-	-
6330	Fire, marine, and casualty insurance	83	70	5.4	617	-	49,802	-	29,105	-	-
6360	Title insurance	5	1	1.6	17	-	31,765	-	533	-	-
6370	Pension, health, and welfare funds	73	53	9.0	455	414	25,644	26,599	12,940	11,073	8.8
6400	Insurance agents, brokers, and service	303	321	4.5	1,294	1,564	25,555	22,166	34,489	37,317	1.8
6500	Real estate	2,450	2,508	9.1	9,929	10,357	22,197	22,488	231,529	253,413	6.5
6510	Real estate operators and lessors	1,370	1,469	9.4	4,687	4,731	19,957	20,226	96,367	104,571	6.5
6530	Real estate agents and managers	832	978	9.4	4,096	5,057	24,182	24,216	103,786	129,329	6.4
6540	Title abstract offices	16	16	4.0	162	178	22,938	23,708	3,772	4,987	5.8

Source: County Business Patterns, 1992/93, CBP-92/93-1, U.S. Department of Commerce, Washington, D.C., April 1995. SIC categories for which data were suppressed or not available for both 1992 and 1993 are *not* displayed. The employment columns represent mid-March employment in the year. Pay per employee is calculated by dividing 1st Quarter payroll, annualized, by mid-March employment. The columns headed "% State" show the county's percentage of the state total for the SIC in 1993; for example, 0.9% for SIC 6030 means that the county had 0.9 percent of the state's total establishments (or payroll) in SIC 6030 in 1993. A dash (-) is used to indicate that data are not available or cannot be calculated; *nec* means not elsewhere classified.

Continued on next page.

SIC	Industry	No. Establishments			Employment		Pay / Employee		Annual Payroll ($ 000)		
		1992	1993	% State	1992	1993	1992	1993	1992	1993	% State
CARTERET, NC - [continued]											
6510	Real estate operators and lessors	25	26	*1.4*	172	75	15,372	10,240	2,850	914	*0.7*
6530	Real estate agents and managers	43	58	*2.3*	172	226	12,233	12,850	2,583	3,623	*1.3*
6552	Subdividers and developers, n.e.c.	4	4	*1.2*	7	8	10,857	14,000	101	196	*0.4*
CASWELL, NC											
60 –	**Finance, insurance, and real estate**	11	10	*0.1*	-	39	-	21,538	-	769	*0.0*
6000	Depository institutions	4	4	*0.1*	20	18	15,000	18,222	284	342	*0.0*
CATAWBA, NC											
60 –	**Finance, insurance, and real estate**	247	255	*1.8*	1,713	1,685	21,457	22,419	38,522	38,798	*1.0*
6000	Depository institutions	58	59	*2.0*	762	812	20,924	21,606	16,646	17,934	*1.3*
6020	Commercial banks	34	34	*1.6*	487	523	22,144	23,449	11,285	11,981	*1.0*
6030	Savings institutions	17	18	*3.8*	242	255	18,860	18,259	4,792	5,316	*4.0*
6100	Nondepository institutions	23	26	*2.0*	110	104	25,345	22,115	2,888	2,373	*0.7*
6140	Personal credit institutions	18	20	*2.7*	74	84	24,000	20,238	1,861	1,766	*1.5*
6160	Mortgage bankers and brokers	3	3	*0.8*	-	14	-	28,000	-	497	*0.3*
6200	Security and commodity brokers	8	11	*1.8*	47	44	47,745	44,545	2,092	2,275	*0.7*
6300	Insurance carriers	23	16	*1.4*	253	145	24,142	32,193	6,337	4,647	*0.5*
6310	Life insurance	12	5	*1.2*	219	98	21,900	29,020	4,987	2,784	*0.8*
6400	Insurance agents, brokers, and service	60	62	*2.0*	238	307	21,513	22,502	5,604	6,582	*1.7*
6500	Real estate	69	73	*1.5*	284	251	14,887	16,064	4,795	4,775	*1.0*
6510	Real estate operators and lessors	29	27	*1.5*	158	110	11,722	12,182	2,127	1,677	*1.2*
6530	Real estate agents and managers	27	39	*1.5*	73	116	20,384	19,517	1,729	2,610	*1.0*
6700	Holding and other investment offices	6	8	*2.0*	19	22	17,053	16,545	160	212	*0.2*
CHATHAM, NC											
60 –	**Finance, insurance, and real estate**	48	50	*0.3*	276	285	17,275	18,919	5,299	5,820	*0.1*
6000	Depository institutions	16	16	*0.5*	109	110	18,899	21,273	2,180	2,304	*0.2*
6020	Commercial banks	11	11	*0.5*	77	78	20,052	22,410	1,611	1,673	*0.1*
6400	Insurance agents, brokers, and service	12	13	*0.4*	31	32	16,516	18,000	643	670	*0.2*
6500	Real estate	15	16	*0.3*	96	99	13,917	14,828	1,501	1,772	*0.4*
CHEROKEE, NC											
60 –	**Finance, insurance, and real estate**	32	38	*0.3*	175	186	19,246	19,763	3,501	4,309	*0.1*
6000	Depository institutions	13	12	*0.4*	101	106	19,089	19,547	1,912	2,495	*0.2*
6020	Commercial banks	8	8	*0.4*	77	87	18,545	18,391	1,488	2,070	*0.2*
6400	Insurance agents, brokers, and service	6	8	*0.3*	32	34	23,750	26,471	766	899	*0.2*
6500	Real estate	9	14	*0.3*	26	29	10,154	9,103	469	477	*0.1*
6510	Real estate operators and lessors	5	7	*0.4*	19	21	10,316	9,143	296	326	*0.2*
6530	Real estate agents and managers	3	6	*0.2*	6	7	9,333	9,714	170	146	*0.1*
CHOWAN, NC											
60 –	**Finance, insurance, and real estate**	23	21	*0.1*	136	128	17,647	20,562	2,431	2,726	*0.1*
6000	Depository institutions	6	7	*0.2*	56	60	19,786	21,933	1,112	1,373	*0.1*
6030	Savings institutions	2	3	*0.6*	-	22	-	22,909	-	557	*0.4*
6400	Insurance agents, brokers, and service	6	5	*0.2*	20	19	16,800	16,421	305	320	*0.1*
6500	Real estate	5	4	*0.1*	12	6	7,000	8,000	84	72	*0.0*
CLAY, NC											
60 –	**Finance, insurance, and real estate**	13	15	*0.1*	64	70	16,438	17,714	1,765	1,946	*0.0*
6000	Depository institutions	4	4	*0.1*	-	25	-	18,720	-	513	*0.0*
6020	Commercial banks	4	4	*0.2*	-	25	-	18,720	-	513	*0.0*
6400	Insurance agents, brokers, and service	2	3	*0.1*	-	14	-	24,286	-	354	*0.1*
6500	Real estate	7	8	*0.2*	30	31	9,867	13,935	990	1,079	*0.2*

Source: County Business Patterns, 1992/93, CBP-92/93-1, U.S. Department of Commerce, Washington, D.C., April 1995. SIC categories for which data were suppressed or not available for both 1992 and 1993 are *not* displayed. The employment columns represent mid-March employment in the year. Pay per employee is calculated by dividing 1st Quarter payroll, annualized, by mid-March employment. The columns headed "% State" show the county's percentage of the state total for the SIC in 1993; for example, 0.9% for SIC 6030 means that the county had 0.9 percent of the state's total establishments (or payroll) in SIC 6030 in 1993. A dash (-) is used to indicate that data are not available or cannot be calculated; *nec* means not elsewhere classified.

SIC	Industry	No. Establishments			Employment		Pay / Employee		Annual Payroll ($ 000)		
		1992	1993	% State	1992	1993	1992	1993	1992	1993	% State
CLEVELAND, NC											
60 –	**Finance, insurance, and real estate**	138	138	0.9	885	882	21,247	20,649	19,728	20,145	0.5
6000	Depository institutions	38	37	1.2	412	435	21,650	19,844	9,497	9,826	0.7
6020	Commercial banks	22	23	1.1	258	274	20,264	20,613	5,418	6,574	0.5
6030	Savings institutions	10	9	1.9	124	130	25,677	19,108	3,646	2,746	2.1
6060	Credit unions	6	5	1.6	30	31	16,933	16,129	433	506	0.8
6100	Nondepository institutions	15	14	1.1	57	60	24,140	20,200	1,291	1,245	0.4
6200	Security and commodity brokers	6	7	1.1	16	16	39,000	36,000	714	733	0.2
6300	Insurance carriers	15	14	1.2	83	85	35,614	37,129	2,595	3,019	0.3
6310	Life insurance	4	4	1.0	70	75	36,514	37,440	2,098	2,657	0.7
6330	Fire, marine, and casualty insurance	6	4	0.8	12	-	33,000	-	454	-	-
6370	Pension, health, and welfare funds	5	6	6.0	1	-	4,000	-	43	-	-
6400	Insurance agents, brokers, and service	21	21	0.7	93	99	22,538	24,081	2,500	2,792	0.7
6500	Real estate	37	40	0.8	219	176	12,548	11,227	2,895	2,159	0.4
6510	Real estate operators and lessors	18	22	1.2	157	110	11,949	9,964	1,941	1,183	0.9
6530	Real estate agents and managers	14	16	0.6	39	-	13,231	-	605	-	-
6700	Holding and other investment offices	6	5	1.2	5	11	16,800	25,091	236	371	0.3
6733	Trusts, n.e.c.	4	2	2.2	1	-	8,000	-	193	-	-
COLUMBUS, NC											
60 –	**Finance, insurance, and real estate**	70	70	0.5	715	727	32,778	25,684	20,875	19,693	0.5
6000	Depository institutions	25	25	0.8	541	431	32,192	20,464	15,598	9,099	0.6
6020	Commercial banks	19	20	0.9	-	389	-	20,607	-	8,210	0.7
6100	Nondepository institutions	6	4	0.3	39	-	21,846	-	911	-	-
6400	Insurance agents, brokers, and service	20	20	0.7	61	71	15,869	15,493	1,048	1,240	0.3
6500	Real estate	11	13	0.3	21	-	13,333	-	347	-	-
6530	Real estate agents and managers	5	5	0.2	10	7	16,800	28,571	198	213	0.1
CRAVEN, NC											
60 –	**Finance, insurance, and real estate**	162	157	1.1	1,055	912	18,142	20,184	21,029	20,348	0.5
6000	Depository institutions	37	36	1.2	426	418	18,582	19,388	8,008	8,299	0.6
6020	Commercial banks	24	25	1.2	279	266	19,814	22,045	5,414	5,760	0.5
6030	Savings institutions	7	5	1.1	-	31	-	16,516	-	584	0.4
6060	Credit unions	5	6	1.9	102	121	15,804	14,281	1,725	1,955	3.1
6100	Nondepository institutions	16	15	1.1	80	105	22,550	20,952	2,128	2,541	0.7
6140	Personal credit institutions	13	12	1.6	56	-	21,643	-	1,211	-	-
6200	Security and commodity brokers	7	9	1.5	19	-	56,211	-	1,150	-	-
6210	Security brokers and dealers	4	6	1.5	17	-	62,118	-	1,133	-	-
6280	Security and commodity services	3	3	1.4	2	2	6,000	12,000	17	36	0.1
6300	Insurance carriers	12	10	0.9	61	38	26,098	39,684	1,632	1,584	0.2
6400	Insurance agents, brokers, and service	31	33	1.1	114	121	20,596	19,504	2,683	2,796	0.7
6500	Real estate	56	52	1.1	347	200	12,334	13,460	5,277	3,380	0.7
6510	Real estate operators and lessors	14	15	0.8	34	49	13,412	11,429	443	610	0.4
6530	Real estate agents and managers	22	28	1.1	248	94	12,435	18,170	3,865	2,166	0.8
6552	Subdividers and developers, n.e.c.	7	8	2.4	40	-	12,200	-	647	-	-
6700	Holding and other investment offices	3	2	0.5	8	-	16,500	-	151	-	-
CUMBERLAND, NC											
60 –	**Finance, insurance, and real estate**	535	552	3.8	3,235	3,586	20,863	20,514	70,716	80,043	2.0
6000	Depository institutions	84	81	2.7	1,066	1,073	18,649	19,702	19,979	20,995	1.5
6020	Commercial banks	55	55	2.5	787	741	19,639	21,371	15,343	15,679	1.3
6030	Savings institutions	7	7	1.5	62	64	18,710	19,062	1,141	1,196	0.9
6060	Credit unions	10	13	4.0	167	192	15,880	16,000	2,841	3,151	5.1
6090	Functions closely related to banking	12	6	12.8	50	76	12,240	13,316	654	969	-
6100	Nondepository institutions	59	66	5.0	368	504	29,011	23,167	12,010	12,387	3.5
6140	Personal credit institutions	34	34	4.5	212	330	25,585	18,267	5,547	5,464	4.5
6150	Business credit institutions	3	7	6.4	13	-	15,385	-	185	-	-
6160	Mortgage bankers and brokers	19	23	6.1	116	134	34,793	32,507	5,155	5,604	3.6
6200	Security and commodity brokers	21	20	3.3	117	109	33,162	35,780	4,351	4,172	1.4

Source: *County Business Patterns, 1992/93*, CBP-92/93-1, U.S. Department of Commerce, Washington, D.C., April 1995. SIC categories for which data were suppressed or not available for both 1992 and 1993 are *not* displayed. The employment columns represent mid-March employment in the year. Pay per employee is calculated by dividing 1st Quarter payroll, annualized, by mid-March employment. The columns headed "% State" show the county's percentage of the state total for the SIC in 1993; for example, 0.9% for SIC 6030 means that the county had 0.9 percent of the state's total establishments (or payroll) in SIC 6030 in 1993. A dash (-) is used to indicate that data are not available or cannot be calculated; *nec* means not elsewhere classified.

Continued on next page.

SIC	Industry	No. Establishments			Employment		Pay / Employee		Annual Payroll ($ 000)		
		1992	1993	% State	1992	1993	1992	1993	1992	1993	% State
CUMBERLAND, NC - [continued]											
6210	Security brokers and dealers	9	9	2.2	79	90	42,329	39,511	3,795	3,712	1.4
6300	Insurance carriers	47	48	4.2	538	518	25,777	28,371	14,049	14,522	1.6
6310	Life insurance	24	23	5.5	449	408	21,710	24,000	9,790	9,653	2.6
6370	Pension, health, and welfare funds	1	4	4.0	-	8	-	13,000	-	103	0.7
6400	Insurance agents, brokers, and service	115	116	3.8	317	360	18,032	17,789	6,065	6,805	1.7
6500	Real estate	198	212	4.3	703	996	15,488	15,100	12,165	20,234	4.2
6510	Real estate operators and lessors	82	96	5.3	250	555	15,808	14,465	4,030	12,321	9.0
6530	Real estate agents and managers	81	95	3.7	324	342	14,679	16,363	5,398	6,033	2.2
6552	Subdividers and developers, n.e.c.	7	12	3.6	31	59	16,258	14,169	692	1,188	2.2
6553	Cemetery subdividers and developers	5	6	4.1	36	33	14,111	13,818	529	554	3.8
6710	Holding offices	4	1	1.0	102	-	21,529	-	1,668	-	-
CURRITUCK, NC											
60 –	**Finance, insurance, and real estate**	18	19	0.1	68	97	22,529	20,000	1,459	2,165	0.1
6510	Real estate operators and lessors	1	3	0.2	-	10	-	5,600	-	56	0.0
6530	Real estate agents and managers	6	9	0.4	18	-	13,333	-	254	-	-
DARE, NC											
60 –	**Finance, insurance, and real estate**	128	130	0.9	758	742	15,942	18,458	13,548	15,467	0.4
6000	Depository institutions	21	23	0.8	173	181	20,555	22,851	3,543	3,748	0.3
6020	Commercial banks	17	19	0.9	155	164	20,903	23,146	3,222	3,407	0.3
6100	Nondepository institutions	6	9	0.7	-	27	-	37,185	-	1,356	0.4
6400	Insurance agents, brokers, and service	13	13	0.4	60	57	19,533	18,947	1,392	1,324	0.3
6500	Real estate	86	82	1.7	503	476	12,930	15,664	7,641	8,980	1.9
6510	Real estate operators and lessors	7	10	0.5	107	28	2,579	10,571	379	506	0.4
6530	Real estate agents and managers	62	67	2.6	338	435	15,882	15,982	6,197	8,272	3.1
6552	Subdividers and developers, n.e.c.	4	3	0.9	19	8	19,789	15,000	403	101	0.2
DAVIDSON, NC											
60 –	**Finance, insurance, and real estate**	151	161	1.1	1,047	984	20,027	21,667	19,862	22,304	0.5
6000	Depository institutions	41	40	1.3	568	569	20,965	22,566	10,200	13,224	0.9
6020	Commercial banks	30	30	1.4	419	445	20,993	23,236	7,162	10,175	0.8
6100	Nondepository institutions	10	8	0.6	34	39	27,529	15,897	820	626	0.2
6140	Personal credit institutions	7	5	0.7	-	32	-	14,875	-	419	0.3
6400	Insurance agents, brokers, and service	33	35	1.1	131	133	25,649	24,932	3,211	3,341	0.8
6500	Real estate	56	67	1.4	275	225	13,280	16,533	4,372	4,228	0.9
6510	Real estate operators and lessors	24	38	2.1	52	73	7,308	9,918	482	873	0.6
6530	Real estate agents and managers	20	25	1.0	180	130	12,444	19,262	3,033	2,763	1.0
DAVIE, NC											
60 –	**Finance, insurance, and real estate**	30	30	0.2	131	132	21,679	22,455	2,865	3,035	0.1
6000	Depository institutions	11	12	0.4	85	90	21,835	23,556	1,842	2,000	0.1
6020	Commercial banks	7	8	0.4	59	-	20,542	-	1,203	-	-
6100	Nondepository institutions	3	4	0.3	8	9	25,000	20,444	186	209	0.1
6400	Insurance agents, brokers, and service	6	5	0.2	23	21	20,696	21,333	528	522	0.1
6500	Real estate	6	5	0.1	11	7	17,455	7,429	178	134	0.0
DUPLIN, NC											
60 –	**Finance, insurance, and real estate**	53	56	0.4	232	222	18,776	20,180	4,693	4,974	0.1
6000	Depository institutions	21	23	0.8	140	129	19,600	20,589	2,619	2,666	0.2
6020	Commercial banks	17	19	0.9	122	116	19,672	20,828	2,269	2,383	0.2
6100	Nondepository institutions	4	4	0.3	16	18	26,000	29,556	423	518	0.1
6400	Insurance agents, brokers, and service	13	15	0.5	54	55	18,148	20,000	1,368	1,563	0.4
6500	Real estate	11	11	0.2	18	-	8,444	-	156	-	-
6553	Cemetery subdividers and developers	3	3	2.0	5	-	11,200	-	55	-	-

Source: County Business Patterns, 1992/93, CBP-92/93-1, U.S. Department of Commerce, Washington, D.C., April 1995. SIC categories for which data were suppressed or not available for both 1992 and 1993 are not displayed. The employment columns represent mid-March employment in the year. Pay per employee is calculated by dividing 1st Quarter payroll, annualized, by mid-March employment. The columns headed "% State" show the county's percentage of the state total for the SIC in 1993; for example, 0.9% for SIC 6030 means that the county had 0.9 percent of the state's total establishments (or payroll) in SIC 6030 in 1993. A dash (-) is used to indicate that data are not available or cannot be calculated; nec means not elsewhere classified.

SIC	Industry	No. Establishments			Employment		Pay / Employee		Annual Payroll ($ 000)		
		1992	1993	% State	1992	1993	1992	1993	1992	1993	% State
DURHAM, NC											
60 –	**Finance, insurance, and real estate**	444	450	3.1	4,494	4,615	27,764	27,886	126,499	125,554	3.1
6000	Depository institutions	88	86	2.9	1,429	1,590	24,745	26,423	34,977	39,234	2.8
6020	Commercial banks	66	63	2.9	1,241	1,288	24,503	27,102	30,125	33,286	2.7
6030	Savings institutions	12	13	2.7	114	221	32,561	25,430	3,466	4,395	3.3
6060	Credit unions	6	6	1.9	61	68	16,852	18,588	1,138	1,275	2.1
6090	Functions closely related to banking	4	4	8.5	13	13	16,308	16,923	248	278	-
6100	Nondepository institutions	31	34	2.6	149	171	28,000	26,012	4,706	5,884	1.7
6140	Personal credit institutions	20	21	2.8	66	85	21,273	16,094	1,430	1,434	1.2
6160	Mortgage bankers and brokers	11	13	3.4	83	86	33,349	35,814	3,276	4,450	2.9
6200	Security and commodity brokers	18	18	2.9	186	460	55,720	33,357	10,314	11,131	3.6
6210	Security brokers and dealers	14	12	3.0	177	444	57,243	33,387	9,916	10,391	4.0
6280	Security and commodity services	4	6	2.9	9	16	25,778	32,500	398	740	1.7
6300	Insurance carriers	47	41	3.6	1,560	1,243	30,277	34,008	44,407	41,295	4.5
6310	Life insurance	22	19	4.6	933	761	26,915	33,740	24,888	25,355	6.8
6370	Pension, health, and welfare funds	4	3	3.0	-	1	-	20,000	-	50	0.3
6400	Insurance agents, brokers, and service	83	83	2.7	337	346	27,632	27,861	9,794	11,031	2.8
6500	Real estate	163	173	3.5	774	701	21,674	17,997	20,175	15,059	3.1
6510	Real estate operators and lessors	51	57	3.1	268	236	18,522	17,441	5,107	4,734	3.5
6530	Real estate agents and managers	82	102	4.0	325	357	19,668	19,922	7,306	8,479	3.2
6552	Subdividers and developers, n.e.c.	9	6	1.8	26	36	19,385	15,222	1,071	724	1.3
6553	Cemetery subdividers and developers	6	6	4.1	43	53	15,721	11,396	683	717	4.9
6700	Holding and other investment offices	14	15	3.7	59	104	26,373	22,731	2,126	1,920	1.4
6732	Educational, religious, etc. trusts	6	8	8.4	-	16	-	27,500	-	423	3.2
6733	Trusts, n.e.c.	4	3	3.4	21	23	22,667	24,522	515	592	10.2
EDGECOMBE, NC											
60 –	**Finance, insurance, and real estate**	110	110	0.8	730	866	21,315	21,035	16,073	18,563	0.5
6000	Depository institutions	23	22	0.7	161	168	20,422	20,595	3,221	3,574	0.3
6020	Commercial banks	16	15	0.7	130	136	20,677	20,676	2,595	2,876	0.2
6030	Savings institutions	3	3	0.6	-	18	-	24,889	-	493	0.4
6060	Credit unions	4	4	1.2	-	14	-	14,286	-	205	0.3
6100	Nondepository institutions	10	13	1.0	42	61	21,524	19,869	937	1,226	0.3
6140	Personal credit institutions	8	10	1.3	-	45	-	19,556	-	861	0.7
6200	Security and commodity brokers	3	4	0.7	17	-	51,529	-	744	-	-
6210	Security brokers and dealers	3	4	1.0	17	-	51,529	-	744	-	-
6300	Insurance carriers	7	5	0.4	53	-	17,660	-	1,008	-	-
6400	Insurance agents, brokers, and service	23	26	0.8	75	125	20,373	24,064	1,787	3,161	0.8
6500	Real estate	38	37	0.7	227	221	8,899	11,511	2,885	2,762	0.6
6510	Real estate operators and lessors	20	19	1.0	160	167	5,225	10,132	1,640	1,894	1.4
6530	Real estate agents and managers	12	14	0.5	40	38	19,900	18,211	834	690	0.3
6700	Holding and other investment offices	6	3	0.7	155	-	38,761	-	5,491	-	-
FORSYTH, NC											
60 –	**Finance, insurance, and real estate**	665	751	5.2	9,262	11,194	28,645	29,020	268,489	340,182	8.4
6000	Depository institutions	133	140	4.6	4,115	4,714	26,813	29,926	109,136	140,249	9.8
6020	Commercial banks	83	97	4.5	2,461	4,256	27,876	30,964	68,343	130,484	10.8
6030	Savings institutions	30	19	4.0	270	-	27,170	-	7,599	-	-
6060	Credit unions	15	19	5.9	-	213	-	22,498	-	5,082	8.2
6100	Nondepository institutions	62	66	5.0	1,127	1,881	20,358	20,147	24,216	40,498	11.4
6140	Personal credit institutions	35	33	4.4	-	855	-	19,050	-	16,291	13.5
6160	Mortgage bankers and brokers	20	23	6.1	315	412	20,483	22,573	7,838	11,779	7.6
6200	Security and commodity brokers	39	40	6.5	298	367	64,255	72,992	21,129	25,937	8.5
6210	Security brokers and dealers	20	23	5.7	244	316	68,918	76,620	18,195	22,732	8.7
6300	Insurance carriers	67	69	6.1	1,951	2,396	32,394	30,254	61,406	79,783	8.7
6310	Life insurance	26	26	6.2	1,516	1,722	30,396	24,929	39,889	48,665	13.1
6330	Fire, marine, and casualty insurance	25	24	4.8	135	155	27,881	32,619	4,238	5,424	1.5
6370	Pension, health, and welfare funds	4	8	8.0	-	100	-	29,560	-	2,016	13.5
6400	Insurance agents, brokers, and service	151	163	5.3	749	746	30,969	32,177	23,940	24,690	6.2

Source: County Business Patterns, 1992/93, CBP-92/93-1, U.S. Department of Commerce, Washington, D.C., April 1995. SIC categories for which data were suppressed or not available for both 1992 and 1993 are *not* displayed. The employment columns represent mid-March employment in the year. Pay per employee is calculated by dividing 1st Quarter payroll, annualized, by mid-March employment. The columns headed "% State" show the county's percentage of the state total for the SIC in 1993; for example, 0.9% for SIC 6030 means that the county had 0.9 percent of the state's total establishments (or payroll) in SIC 6030 in 1993. A dash (-) is used to indicate that data are not available or cannot be calculated; *nec* means not elsewhere classified.

Continued on next page.

SIC	Industry	No. Establishments			Employment		Pay / Employee		Annual Payroll ($ 000)		
		1992	1993	% State	1992	1993	1992	1993	1992	1993	% State
FORSYTH, NC - [continued]											
6500	Real estate	187	250	5.1	712	956	18,287	16,151	14,748	18,013	3.7
6510	Real estate operators and lessors	54	119	6.5	178	396	16,854	16,323	3,425	6,519	4.8
6530	Real estate agents and managers	88	109	4.3	383	500	18,402	16,176	8,055	10,075	3.8
6552	Subdividers and developers, n.e.c.	15	10	3.0	41	5	21,756	16,000	1,223	381	0.7
6553	Cemetery subdividers and developers	7	7	4.7	61	52	20,525	14,615	1,131	899	6.1
6700	Holding and other investment offices	26	23	5.7	310	134	43,445	53,463	13,914	11,012	8.1
6710	Holding offices	7	7	6.7	202	-	49,683	-	10,318	-	-
6732	Educational, religious, etc. trusts	4	3	3.2	21	21	29,714	34,286	646	749	5.7
6733	Trusts, n.e.c.	6	5	5.6	45	49	35,644	29,061	1,662	1,450	24.9
6794	Patent owners and lessors	3	3	12.5	-	3	-	41,333	-	1,430	20.1
6799	Investors, n.e.c.	4	4	5.1	28	18	27,286	22,000	701	554	6.0
FRANKLIN, NC											
60 –	**Finance, insurance, and real estate**	27	25	0.2	146	137	19,096	20,905	2,793	2,788	0.1
6000	Depository institutions	8	9	0.3	68	69	18,765	21,101	1,369	1,403	0.1
6100	Nondepository institutions	3	3	0.2	12	-	17,000	-	214	-	-
6400	Insurance agents, brokers, and service	6	5	0.2	27	26	29,037	31,538	610	677	0.2
6500	Real estate	10	7	0.1	39	28	13,436	11,286	600	436	0.1
6510	Real estate operators and lessors	4	2	0.1	4	-	8,000	-	35	-	-
6530	Real estate agents and managers	3	4	0.2	-	23	-	12,870	-	412	0.2
GASTON, NC											
60 –	**Finance, insurance, and real estate**	263	250	1.7	1,751	1,812	21,738	22,115	38,282	41,291	1.0
6000	Depository institutions	66	65	2.2	779	795	21,012	22,546	16,549	17,923	1.3
6020	Commercial banks	46	47	2.2	634	656	20,126	22,732	12,874	14,734	1.2
6030	Savings institutions	14	12	2.5	112	97	25,714	24,206	2,991	2,496	1.9
6060	Credit unions	6	6	1.9	33	42	22,061	15,810	684	693	1.1
6100	Nondepository institutions	31	29	2.2	137	151	23,533	20,848	3,174	3,299	0.9
6140	Personal credit institutions	21	18	2.4	104	108	23,077	17,778	2,292	1,898	1.6
6150	Business credit institutions	2	4	3.7	-	18	-	29,556	-	512	1.0
6160	Mortgage bankers and brokers	8	7	1.8	-	25	-	27,840	-	889	0.6
6200	Security and commodity brokers	10	12	2.0	22	21	32,182	29,333	685	937	0.3
6300	Insurance carriers	24	23	2.0	168	208	34,167	32,346	5,457	6,763	0.7
6310	Life insurance	9	9	2.2	132	122	31,455	35,410	3,741	4,176	1.1
6400	Insurance agents, brokers, and service	54	54	1.8	238	246	24,689	23,675	5,643	5,959	1.5
6500	Real estate	71	58	1.2	349	321	14,602	13,495	5,413	4,884	1.0
6510	Real estate operators and lessors	24	24	1.3	102	124	16,863	15,032	1,777	2,066	1.5
6530	Real estate agents and managers	32	29	1.1	171	173	11,368	12,763	2,296	2,392	0.9
6700	Holding and other investment offices	7	9	2.2	58	70	18,138	21,429	1,361	1,526	1.1
GATES, NC											
60 –	**Finance, insurance, and real estate**	5	5	0.0	-	38	-	18,421	-	782	0.0
GRAHAM, NC											
60 –	**Finance, insurance, and real estate**	7	7	0.0	-	36	-	21,444	-	682	0.0
6500	Real estate	3	3	0.1	4	7	2,000	14,286	34	34	0.0
GRANVILLE, NC											
60 –	**Finance, insurance, and real estate**	55	58	0.4	227	234	18,907	20,564	4,618	4,734	0.1
6000	Depository institutions	15	16	0.5	145	138	20,248	22,406	3,024	2,909	0.2
6020	Commercial banks	11	11	0.5	128	115	19,938	23,165	2,700	2,449	0.2
6100	Nondepository institutions	4	5	0.4	13	13	18,769	26,154	248	316	0.1
6400	Insurance agents, brokers, and service	10	12	0.4	21	35	14,095	13,143	306	500	0.1
6500	Real estate	23	23	0.5	35	-	12,000	-	489	-	-

Source: County Business Patterns, 1992/93, CBP-92/93-1, U.S. Department of Commerce, Washington, D.C., April 1995. SIC categories for which data were suppressed or not available for both 1992 and 1993 are *not* displayed. The employment columns represent mid-March employment in the year. Pay per employee is calculated by dividing 1st Quarter payroll, annualized, by mid-March employment. The columns headed "% State" show the county's percentage of the state total for the SIC in 1993; for example, 0.9% for SIC 6030 means that the county had 0.9 percent of the state's total establishments (or payroll) in SIC 6030 in 1993. A dash (-) is used to indicate that data are not available or cannot be calculated; *nec* means not elsewhere classified.

Continued on next page.

SIC	Industry	No. Establishments			Employment		Pay / Employee		Annual Payroll ($ 000)		
		1992	1993	% State	1992	1993	1992	1993	1992	1993	% State
GRANVILLE, NC - [continued]											
6510	Real estate operators and lessors	9	11	0.6	7	18	10,857	10,444	110	217	0.2
6530	Real estate agents and managers	7	7	0.3	17	11	14,588	10,182	264	135	0.1
6552	Subdividers and developers, n.e.c.	1	3	0.9	-	12	-	5,667	-	78	0.1
GREENE, NC											
60 -	**Finance, insurance, and real estate**	15	15	0.1	45	-	16,711	-	832	-	-
6000	Depository institutions	6	6	0.2	28	-	17,714	-	496	-	-
6020	Commercial banks	5	5	0.2	-	24	-	18,333	-	457	0.0
6400	Insurance agents, brokers, and service	4	4	0.1	8	7	14,000	13,143	193	207	0.1
GUILFORD, NC											
60 -	**Finance, insurance, and real estate**	1,119	1,163	8.0	14,399	15,319	26,822	25,996	374,477	406,199	10.0
6000	Depository institutions	182	190	6.3	3,892	3,999	23,316	24,748	83,815	89,665	6.3
6020	Commercial banks	130	146	6.7	2,914	2,884	23,407	26,129	63,965	67,910	5.6
6030	Savings institutions	28	15	3.2	747	854	22,806	20,974	13,779	15,475	11.8
6100	Nondepository institutions	101	119	9.0	955	1,517	27,987	25,535	27,591	42,316	11.9
6140	Personal credit institutions	48	52	6.9	365	406	24,241	22,857	9,481	10,937	9.0
6160	Mortgage bankers and brokers	40	52	13.7	382	866	25,937	23,409	11,316	23,131	14.9
6200	Security and commodity brokers	54	57	9.3	414	444	68,396	56,775	25,680	26,436	8.7
6210	Security brokers and dealers	31	29	7.2	335	329	75,869	67,951	22,779	22,866	8.8
6300	Insurance carriers	132	112	9.8	4,813	5,024	30,789	27,498	140,956	140,720	15.4
6310	Life insurance	59	44	10.6	3,245	3,396	32,092	27,124	97,503	92,401	24.9
6330	Fire, marine, and casualty insurance	46	44	8.9	901	929	30,681	30,816	27,230	29,609	8.3
6360	Title insurance	6	6	12.8	57	-	34,105	-	2,311	-	-
6370	Pension, health, and welfare funds	12	11	11.0	127	117	23,811	25,162	4,027	3,749	25.1
6400	Insurance agents, brokers, and service	253	270	8.8	1,085	1,215	28,317	29,389	32,499	38,144	9.6
6500	Real estate	346	370	7.5	2,888	2,775	18,472	18,316	54,150	57,636	12.0
6510	Real estate operators and lessors	130	163	8.9	1,488	1,409	17,911	15,923	27,419	25,500	18.7
6530	Real estate agents and managers	159	183	7.2	1,028	1,197	18,459	19,519	20,106	27,063	10.1
6540	Title abstract offices	1	3	13.6	-	4	-	8,000	-	30	1.3
6552	Subdividers and developers, n.e.c.	18	13	4.0	96	146	42,667	32,082	3,444	4,659	8.5
6553	Cemetery subdividers and developers	5	4	2.7	150	19	12,853	16,421	998	285	1.9
6700	Holding and other investment offices	48	42	10.3	-	333	-	30,631	-	10,807	7.9
6710	Holding offices	9	8	7.6	144	143	34,833	41,594	5,749	7,285	7.4
6732	Educational, religious, etc. trusts	11	11	11.6	109	153	15,046	11,216	1,458	1,743	13.2
6733	Trusts, n.e.c.	16	12	13.5	62	23	8,129	99,304	1,209	1,202	20.7
HALIFAX, NC											
60 -	**Finance, insurance, and real estate**	99	99	0.7	507	553	19,755	19,450	10,789	11,208	0.3
6000	Depository institutions	27	28	0.9	225	259	20,302	22,162	4,700	5,717	0.4
6020	Commercial banks	17	19	0.9	146	152	20,740	25,289	3,136	3,591	0.3
6100	Nondepository institutions	12	12	0.9	71	64	20,845	16,438	1,594	1,022	0.3
6310	Life insurance	4	3	0.7	23	23	18,609	18,087	473	441	0.1
6400	Insurance agents, brokers, and service	22	25	0.8	100	119	21,880	19,395	2,506	2,577	0.6
6500	Real estate	28	23	0.5	73	68	10,301	10,294	886	797	0.2
6510	Real estate operators and lessors	10	7	0.4	34	29	9,882	9,931	384	326	0.2
6530	Real estate agents and managers	9	12	0.5	16	33	10,000	9,818	215	379	0.1
HARNETT, NC											
60 -	**Finance, insurance, and real estate**	90	87	0.6	560	551	17,907	17,532	10,075	10,288	0.3
6000	Depository institutions	26	26	0.9	254	257	19,811	19,829	4,927	5,227	0.4
6020	Commercial banks	20	20	0.9	192	184	19,625	19,935	3,646	3,739	0.3
6100	Nondepository institutions	7	6	0.5	24	19	24,833	27,368	562	483	0.1
6400	Insurance agents, brokers, and service	21	20	0.7	85	85	19,906	20,847	1,916	2,085	0.5
6500	Real estate	26	25	0.5	159	146	11,597	10,603	1,951	1,708	0.4

Source: County Business Patterns, 1992/93, CBP-92/93-1, U.S. Department of Commerce, Washington, D.C., April 1995. SIC categories for which data were suppressed or not available for both 1992 and 1993 are *not* displayed. The employment columns represent mid-March employment in the year. Pay per employee is calculated by dividing 1st Quarter payroll, annualized, by mid-March employment. The columns headed "% State" show the county's percentage of the state total for the SIC in 1993; for example, 0.9% for SIC 6030 means that the county had 0.9 percent of the state's total establishments (or payroll) in SIC 6030 in 1993. A dash (-) is used to indicate that data are not available or cannot be calculated; *nec* means not elsewhere classified.

Continued on next page.

SIC	Industry	No. Establishments			Employment		Pay / Employee		Annual Payroll ($ 000)		
		1992	1993	% State	1992	1993	1992	1993	1992	1993	% State
HARNETT, NC - [continued]											
6510	Real estate operators and lessors	11	11	0.6	69	47	9,449	9,532	636	497	0.4
6530	Real estate agents and managers	8	8	0.3	84	90	12,095	11,333	1,105	1,093	0.4
6700	Holding and other investment offices	4	4	1.0	-	20	-	10,000	-	259	0.2
HAYWOOD, NC											
60 –	**Finance, insurance, and real estate**	81	85	· 0.6	529	521	18,881	19,493	10,838	11,437	0.3
6000	Depository institutions	17	18	0.6	282	276	19,135	20,000	5,963	6,326	0.4
6020	Commercial banks	12	12	0.6	-	106	-	21,132	-	2,248	0.2
6030	Savings institutions	3	3	0.6	157	153	18,726	19,451	3,444	3,730	2.8
6060	Credit unions	2	3	0.9	-	17	-	17,882	-	348	0.6
6140	Personal credit institutions	8	8	1.1	-	40	-	17,300	-	709	0.6
6280	Security and commodity services	1	3	1.4	-	2	-	12,000	-	35	0.1
6400	Insurance agents, brokers, and service	16	15	0.5	70	65	20,629	17,908	1,500	1,427	0.4
6500	Real estate	30	29	0.6	75	80	11,413	11,050	937	1,032	0.2
6510	Real estate operators and lessors	6	10	0.5	18	30	7,556	7,467	132	312	0.2
6530	Real estate agents and managers	16	15	0.6	44	45	13,818	14,311	655	693	0.3
6552	Subdividers and developers, n.e.c.	4	3	0.9	7	5	8,571	3,200	74	24	0.0
HENDERSON, NC											
60 –	**Finance, insurance, and real estate**	133	133	0.9	699	778	21,734	21,383	16,552	18,174	0.4
6000	Depository institutions	25	28	0.9	287	327	18,927	18,226	5,539	6,078	0.4
6020	Commercial banks	20	22	1.0	257	286	19,175	18,350	4,997	5,326	0.4
6030	Savings institutions	3	3	0.6	-	18	-	24,000	-	436	0.3
6060	Credit unions	2	3	0.9	-	23	-	12,174	-	316	0.5
6100	Nondepository institutions	14	14	1.1	135	130	23,911	23,785	3,274	3,313	0.9
6140	Personal credit institutions	10	10	1.3	86	78	23,674	23,436	2,053	1,816	1.5
6200	Security and commodity brokers	10	10	1.6	38	32	50,105	71,250	1,908	2,198	0.7
6300	Insurance carriers	10	9	0.8	52	58	29,538	27,793	1,641	1,785	0.2
6310	Life insurance	3	2	0.5	34	-	26,000	-	904	-	-
6400	Insurance agents, brokers, and service	27	26	0.8	103	99	19,340	21,899	2,548	2,593	0.7
6500	Real estate	42	41	0.8	78	127	13,026	11,339	1,374	2,033	0.4
6510	Real estate operators and lessors	9	12	0.7	13	63	7,077	6,159	117	647	0.5
6530	Real estate agents and managers	22	24	0.9	44	53	16,182	17,434	829	1,144	0.4
6700	Holding and other investment offices	5	5	1.2	6	5	14,000	16,800	268	174	0.1
HERTFORD, NC											
60 –	**Finance, insurance, and real estate**	45	41	0.3	176	186	17,227	16,774	3,045	3,284	0.1
6000	Depository institutions	12	11	0.4	105	104	17,905	19,231	1,807	2,047	0.1
6020	Commercial banks	8	7	0.3	78	77	19,333	21,143	1,489	1,676	0.1
6100	Nondepository institutions	8	7	0.5	25	30	19,200	16,933	493	533	0.1
6400	Insurance agents, brokers, and service	9	9	0.3	25	30	16,640	12,533	492	408	0.1
6500	Real estate	12	11	0.2	18	19	10,889	9,684	225	216	0.0
6510	Real estate operators and lessors	3	2	0.1	6	-	13,333	-	90	-	-
6530	Real estate agents and managers	6	6	0.2	8	-	9,500	-	110	-	-
HOKE, NC											
60 –	**Finance, insurance, and real estate**	24	24	0.2	84	106	17,048	15,774	1,470	1,609	0.0
6000	Depository institutions	7	6	0.2	53	53	17,736	18,113	942	948	0.1
6100	Nondepository institutions	3	3	0.2	9	-	17,778	-	160	-	-
6400	Insurance agents, brokers, and service	7	7	0.2	-	16	-	17,500	-	298	0.1
6500	Real estate	6	7	0.1	8	9	8,000	9,778	94	93	0.0
6510	Real estate operators and lessors	3	4	0.2	4	4	3,000	4,000	13	17	0.0
HYDE, NC											
60 –	**Finance, insurance, and real estate**	11	9	0.1	86	85	17,023	17,600	1,543	1,664	0.0

Source: County Business Patterns, 1992/93, CBP-92/93-1, U.S. Department of Commerce, Washington, D.C., April 1995. SIC categories for which data were suppressed or not available for both 1992 and 1993 are not displayed. The employment columns represent mid-March employment in the year. Pay per employee is calculated by dividing 1st Quarter payroll, annualized, by mid-March employment. The columns headed "% State" show the county's percentage of the state total for the SIC in 1993; for example, 0.9% for SIC 6030 means that the county had 0.9 percent of the state's total establishments (or payroll) in SIC 6030 in 1993. A dash (-) is used to indicate that data are not available or cannot be calculated; nec means not elsewhere classified.

SIC	Industry	No. Establishments			Employment		Pay / Employee		Annual Payroll ($ 000)		
		1992	1993	% State	1992	1993	1992	1993	1992	1993	% State
IREDELL, NC											
60 –	**Finance, insurance, and real estate**	169	178	*1.2*	892	910	22,713	24,286	21,041	21,901	*0.5*
6000	Depository institutions	43	41	*1.4*	430	426	20,893	23,005	9,091	9,227	*0.6*
6020	Commercial banks	30	30	*1.4*	302	321	20,517	22,766	6,409	6,604	*0.5*
6100	Nondepository institutions	19	18	*1.4*	114	148	29,404	23,595	3,335	3,768	*1.1*
6140	Personal credit institutions	14	13	*1.7*	-	79	-	18,228	-	1,544	*1.3*
6210	Security brokers and dealers	7	8	*2.0*	15	16	60,267	66,250	900	1,049	*0.4*
6300	Insurance carriers	13	15	*1.3*	52	55	20,385	24,800	1,414	1,554	*0.2*
6370	Pension, health, and welfare funds	5	5	*5.0*	8	7	5,500	6,286	247	169	*1.1*
6400	Insurance agents, brokers, and service	38	41	*1.3*	139	131	27,137	26,595	3,532	3,657	*0.9*
6500	Real estate	46	50	*1.0*	136	120	15,735	14,567	2,693	1,943	*0.4*
6510	Real estate operators and lessors	17	18	*1.0*	47	45	21,362	17,778	1,579	797	*0.6*
6530	Real estate agents and managers	21	28	*1.1*	60	60	11,133	11,667	635	899	*0.3*
JACKSON, NC											
60 –	**Finance, insurance, and real estate**	53	52	*0.4*	232	242	18,966	18,579	4,634	4,975	*0.1*
6000	Depository institutions	13	13	*0.4*	103	99	19,728	21,172	2,104	1,967	*0.1*
6020	Commercial banks	9	9	*0.4*	71	68	20,338	22,176	1,479	1,397	*0.1*
6400	Insurance agents, brokers, and service	10	11	*0.4*	44	49	23,000	21,633	1,099	1,218	*0.3*
6500	Real estate	25	24	*0.5*	62	79	15,355	12,405	989	1,389	*0.3*
6510	Real estate operators and lessors	3	7	*0.4*	4	17	7,000	11,529	41	222	*0.2*
6530	Real estate agents and managers	12	14	*0.5*	40	56	15,600	11,857	653	997	*0.4*
JOHNSTON, NC											
60 –	**Finance, insurance, and real estate**	144	143	*1.0*	695	760	19,568	21,711	14,184	18,271	*0.4*
6000	Depository institutions	40	42	*1.4*	341	372	20,645	24,914	7,306	9,346	*0.7*
6020	Commercial banks	30	32	*1.5*	287	318	20,753	25,296	6,167	7,813	*0.6*
6100	Nondepository institutions	11	12	*0.9*	37	48	17,405	19,500	679	899	*0.3*
6300	Insurance carriers	6	5	*0.4*	34	55	31,647	28,727	1,193	1,759	*0.2*
6400	Insurance agents, brokers, and service	33	32	*1.0*	125	119	14,816	17,613	2,077	2,215	*0.6*
6500	Real estate	48	47	*0.9*	109	132	10,899	11,000	1,430	2,803	*0.6*
6510	Real estate operators and lessors	16	17	*0.9*	31	32	7,226	9,125	294	353	*0.3*
6530	Real estate agents and managers	18	21	*0.8*	39	69	11,590	10,261	561	957	*0.4*
6552	Subdividers and developers, n.e.c.	4	5	*1.5*	24	24	17,500	18,167	428	613	*1.1*
6553	Cemetery subdividers and developers	1	3	*2.0*	-	7	-	2,286	-	22	*0.1*
JONES, NC											
60 –	**Finance, insurance, and real estate**	5	5	*0.0*	-	20	-	21,000	-	429	*0.0*
LEE, NC											
60 –	**Finance, insurance, and real estate**	108	102	*0.7*	545	559	22,943	22,433	13,245	14,025	*0.3*
6000	Depository institutions	21	19	*0.6*	302	312	23,762	25,090	7,205	8,797	*0.6*
6020	Commercial banks	13	11	*0.5*	219	223	25,553	27,229	5,539	6,993	*0.6*
6100	Nondepository institutions	7	7	*0.5*	31	20	34,710	23,200	1,167	424	*0.1*
6300	Insurance carriers	6	4	*0.4*	-	15	-	29,867	-	562	*0.1*
6400	Insurance agents, brokers, and service	26	26	*0.8*	81	77	21,481	21,922	2,000	1,690	*0.4*
6500	Real estate	42	42	*0.8*	102	123	11,529	9,659	1,446	1,518	*0.3*
6510	Real estate operators and lessors	18	21	*1.1*	50	55	10,480	7,345	593	511	*0.4*
6530	Real estate agents and managers	16	16	*0.6*	41	53	12,976	12,000	675	806	*0.3*
LENOIR, NC											
60 –	**Finance, insurance, and real estate**	125	131	*0.9*	847	714	25,743	24,146	21,520	17,590	*0.4*
6000	Depository institutions	27	29	*1.0*	327	308	20,954	23,078	6,770	7,249	*0.5*
6020	Commercial banks	17	23	*1.1*	210	247	20,933	24,632	4,257	6,254	*0.5*
6100	Nondepository institutions	13	16	*1.2*	77	71	28,831	19,380	2,207	1,446	*0.4*
6140	Personal credit institutions	11	11	*1.5*	-	63	-	19,365	-	1,288	*1.1*
6200	Security and commodity brokers	4	6	*1.0*	19	-	90,947	-	1,628	-	*-*
6210	Security brokers and dealers	4	5	*1.2*	19	-	90,947	-	1,628	-	*-*
6300	Insurance carriers	12	13	*1.1*	201	72	34,169	39,556	7,092	3,258	*0.4*

Source: County Business Patterns, 1992/93, CBP-92/93-1, U.S. Department of Commerce, Washington, D.C., April 1995. SIC categories for which data were suppressed or not available for both 1992 and 1993 are *not* displayed. The employment columns represent mid-March employment in the year. Pay per employee is calculated by dividing 1st Quarter payroll, annualized, by mid-March employment. The columns headed "% State" show the county's percentage of the state total for the SIC in 1993; for example, 0.9% for SIC 6030 means that the county had 0.9 percent of the state's total establishments (or payroll) in SIC 6030 in 1993. A dash (-) is used to indicate that data are not available or cannot be calculated; *nec* means not elsewhere classified.

Continued on next page.

SIC	Industry	No. Establishments			Employment		Pay / Employee		Annual Payroll ($ 000)		
		1992	1993	% State	1992	1993	1992	1993	1992	1993	% State
LENOIR, NC - [continued]											
6310	Life insurance	6	6	1.4	187	57	34,225	41,193	6,604	2,689	0.7
6400	Insurance agents, brokers, and service	36	36	1.2	121	135	21,157	21,630	2,453	2,675	0.7
6500	Real estate	29	28	0.6	94	96	15,617	9,667	1,269	1,038	0.2
6510	Real estate operators and lessors	11	14	0.8	48	-	13,833	-	451	-	-
6530	Real estate agents and managers	10	10	0.4	28	45	16,286	8,622	502	475	0.2
6700	Holding and other investment offices	4	3	0.7	8	-	13,500	-	101	-	-
LINCOLN, NC											
60 –	**Finance, insurance, and real estate**	69	69	0.5	331	342	22,018	22,246	7,309	8,027	0.2
6000	Depository institutions	18	18	0.6	204	201	21,686	21,791	4,239	4,380	0.3
6020	Commercial banks	13	13	0.6	161	160	21,839	21,675	3,169	3,303	0.3
6100	Nondepository institutions	5	5	0.4	18	18	19,556	20,444	367	397	0.1
6400	Insurance agents, brokers, and service	14	13	0.4	34	38	23,647	16,421	724	700	0.2
6500	Real estate	25	25	0.5	56	65	17,071	18,400	1,193	1,515	0.3
6510	Real estate operators and lessors	9	8	0.4	12	-	5,667	-	111	-	-
6530	Real estate agents and managers	13	14	0.5	38	43	22,105	23,814	1,007	1,293	0.5
MCDOWELL, NC											
60 –	**Finance, insurance, and real estate**	45	46	0.3	197	189	18,761	20,698	3,943	4,190	0.1
6000	Depository institutions	10	8	0.3	106	98	20,717	23,143	2,199	2,136	0.1
6020	Commercial banks	6	5	0.2	77	70	21,558	25,371	1,688	1,575	0.1
6300	Insurance carriers	4	5	0.4	-	13	-	24,308	-	338	0.0
6400	Insurance agents, brokers, and service	12	11	0.4	35	35	19,200	19,657	713	735	0.2
6500	Real estate	14	17	0.3	27	25	9,333	8,000	309	423	0.1
6510	Real estate operators and lessors	5	7	0.4	5	9	4,800	7,111	28	75	0.1
6530	Real estate agents and managers	4	6	0.2	5	7	6,400	5,143	96	105	0.0
MACON, NC											
60 –	**Finance, insurance, and real estate**	51	58	0.4	250	235	20,816	21,719	5,208	5,345	0.1
6000	Depository institutions	13	14	0.5	148	144	19,135	21,806	2,760	2,903	0.2
6020	Commercial banks	10	10	0.5	-	76	-	22,158	-	1,662	0.1
6400	Insurance agents, brokers, and service	10	12	0.4	44	50	18,818	21,200	1,003	1,353	0.3
6500	Real estate	21	26	0.5	39	33	28,821	19,636	878	780	0.2
6510	Real estate operators and lessors	3	4	0.2	2	2	20,000	20,000	42	53	0.0
6530	Real estate agents and managers	16	20	0.8	32	29	28,875	16,966	750	629	0.2
MADISON, NC											
60 –	**Finance, insurance, and real estate**	15	18	0.1	51	51	17,725	17,961	867	972	0.0
6000	Depository institutions	6	6	0.2	-	32	-	18,750	-	617	0.0
6400	Insurance agents, brokers, and service	4	4	0.1	12	10	17,000	19,600	188	210	0.1
6500	Real estate	3	6	0.1	2	-	8,000	-	20	-	-
6530	Real estate agents and managers	1	4	0.2	-	2	-	6,000	-	41	0.0
MARTIN, NC											
60 –	**Finance, insurance, and real estate**	40	38	0.3	176	177	18,932	19,593	3,389	3,459	0.1
6000	Depository institutions	15	14	0.5	92	93	18,913	20,473	1,826	1,869	0.1
6020	Commercial banks	11	10	0.5	74	73	19,189	21,205	1,469	1,528	0.1
6100	Nondepository institutions	5	4	0.3	21	18	19,048	20,222	393	346	0.1
6300	Insurance carriers	4	2	0.2	12	-	19,333	-	229	-	-
6400	Insurance agents, brokers, and service	10	12	0.4	46	52	19,652	18,077	876	950	0.2
6500	Real estate	4	5	0.1	3	5	9,333	9,600	38	60	0.0
MECKLENBURG, NC											
60 –	**Finance, insurance, and real estate**	1,966	2,113	14.5	35,485	37,628	33,139	36,233	1,149,389	1,351,977	33.3
6000	Depository institutions	296	307	10.2	12,050	13,146	31,814	39,295	364,028	455,452	32.0
6020	Commercial banks	222	228	10.5	10,213	12,096	34,214	40,494	329,369	429,171	35.4
6030	Savings institutions	25	25	5.3	301	329	22,086	23,198	7,576	8,541	6.5
6060	Credit unions	29	35	10.9	-	262	-	21,282	-	5,873	9.5

Source: County Business Patterns, 1992/93, CBP-92/93-1, U.S. Department of Commerce, Washington, D.C., April 1995. SIC categories for which data were suppressed or not available for both 1992 and 1993 are *not* displayed. The employment columns represent mid-March employment in the year. Pay per employee is calculated by dividing 1st Quarter payroll, annualized, by mid-March employment. The columns headed "% State" show the county's percentage of the state total for the SIC in 1993; for example, 0.9% for SIC 6030 means that the county had 0.9 percent of the state's total establishments (or payroll) in SIC 6030 in 1993. A dash (-) is used to indicate that data are not available or cannot be calculated; *nec* means not elsewhere classified.

Continued on next page.

SIC	Industry	No. Establishments			Employment		Pay / Employee		Annual Payroll ($ 000)		
		1992	1993	% State	1992	1993	1992	1993	1992	1993	% State
MECKLENBURG, NC - [continued]											
6090	Functions closely related to banking	19	17	36.2	921	-	14,228	-	12,933	-	-
6100	Nondepository institutions	207	220	16.6	3,878	4,161	31,493	31,026	117,424	126,571	35.6
6140	Personal credit institutions	88	73	9.7	1,376	1,251	30,715	22,395	42,218	28,017	23.2
6150	Business credit institutions	29	46	42.2	785	811	41,676	47,596	25,442	33,964	64.9
6160	Mortgage bankers and brokers	87	99	26.1	1,715	2,060	27,468	29,691	49,724	62,738	40.5
6200	Security and commodity brokers	96	118	19.2	1,084	1,675	77,970	75,100	75,958	137,532	45.0
6210	Security brokers and dealers	62	72	18.0	985	1,170	78,891	86,219	71,088	111,339	42.8
6300	Insurance carriers	277	259	22.8	9,639	9,320	31,875	32,514	300,433	316,625	34.6
6310	Life insurance	111	108	25.9	3,209	3,114	26,367	29,517	83,577	93,522	25.2
6330	Fire, marine, and casualty insurance	112	103	20.7	5,752	5,455	35,955	35,641	199,942	204,697	57.5
6350	Surety insurance	11	8	44.4	60	64	34,800	39,500	2,349	2,506	5.4
6360	Title insurance	4	8	17.0	38	34	36,421	31,765	1,242	1,059	-
6370	Pension, health, and welfare funds	23	18	18.0	104	107	24,923	21,981	3,114	2,470	16.5
6400	Insurance agents, brokers, and service	382	410	13.3	2,268	2,514	32,995	34,285	79,497	89,769	22.6
6500	Real estate	609	699	14.1	4,471	4,809	24,032	23,902	112,018	122,576	25.5
6510	Real estate operators and lessors	213	248	13.6	1,269	1,464	26,112	19,462	31,550	29,907	21.9
6530	Real estate agents and managers	278	376	14.7	1,996	2,509	23,966	24,287	52,726	68,174	25.4
6540	Title abstract offices	5	5	22.7	163	30	25,423	32,533	4,144	1,050	45.9
6552	Subdividers and developers, n.e.c.	40	44	13.4	748	716	22,674	31,765	17,804	20,823	38.1
6553	Cemetery subdividers and developers	9	9	6.1	76	61	18,316	20,852	1,433	1,335	9.1
6710	Holding offices	25	36	34.3	780	981	63,636	45,256	52,472	56,521	57.7
6720	Investment offices	10	4	50.0	493	-	23,619	-	12,572	-	-
6732	Educational, religious, etc. trusts	12	9	9.5	69	50	38,377	44,000	2,842	2,172	16.4
6733	Trusts, n.e.c.	14	15	16.9	36	44	18,667	19,364	963	897	15.4
6794	Patent owners and lessors	5	7	29.2	118	132	32,271	27,576	4,373	3,543	49.9
MITCHELL, NC											
60 –	**Finance, insurance, and real estate**	19	18	0.1	119	106	20,874	22,264	2,499	2,443	0.1
6000	Depository institutions	7	7	0.2	53	56	23,472	22,143	1,210	1,236	0.1
6400	Insurance agents, brokers, and service	3	4	0.1	36	-	21,667	-	824	-	-
6500	Real estate	5	5	0.1	-	10	-	20,000	-	221	0.0
MONTGOMERY, NC											
60 –	**Finance, insurance, and real estate**	37	35	0.2	189	205	21,418	23,844	3,804	4,377	0.1
6000	Depository institutions	16	16	0.5	142	141	24,732	27,461	3,020	3,204	0.2
6100	Nondepository institutions	4	3	0.2	-	15	-	20,533	-	326	0.1
6140	Personal credit institutions	3	3	0.4	13	15	18,154	20,533	268	326	0.3
6400	Insurance agents, brokers, and service	10	7	0.2	22	-	9,636	-	298	-	-
6500	Real estate	5	7	0.1	10	26	4,000	17,231	60	560	0.1
MOORE, NC											
60 –	**Finance, insurance, and real estate**	138	130	0.9	788	794	21,756	21,814	18,603	18,706	0.5
6000	Depository institutions	41	38	1.3	345	339	20,452	22,714	7,283	7,379	0.5
6020	Commercial banks	28	25	1.2	242	228	20,298	23,088	5,134	4,910	0.4
6100	Nondepository institutions	6	5	0.4	-	15	-	22,667	-	375	0.1
6200	Security and commodity brokers	11	10	1.6	35	34	50,743	57,529	2,222	2,759	0.9
6210	Security brokers and dealers	6	6	1.5	28	28	61,429	66,286	2,120	2,619	1.0
6280	Security and commodity services	5	4	1.9	7	6	8,000	16,667	102	140	0.3
6300	Insurance carriers	7	3	0.3	11	-	37,091	-	456	-	-
6400	Insurance agents, brokers, and service	25	25	0.8	113	91	21,982	23,341	2,624	2,312	0.6
6500	Real estate	46	48	1.0	264	296	18,697	15,635	5,488	5,166	1.1
6510	Real estate operators and lessors	7	7	0.4	38	10	15,158	7,600	581	87	0.1
6530	Real estate agents and managers	19	32	1.3	49	119	21,061	19,529	1,243	2,463	0.9
NASH, NC											
60 –	**Finance, insurance, and real estate**	162	172	1.2	1,831	1,760	23,399	26,177	44,587	44,157	1.1
6000	Depository institutions	39	47	1.6	1,011	1,127	22,971	27,020	25,659	29,307	2.1
6020	Commercial banks	27	36	1.7	742	830	23,375	29,451	19,882	24,053	2.0

Source: County Business Patterns, 1992/93, CBP-92/93-1, U.S. Department of Commerce, Washington, D.C., April 1995. SIC categories for which data were suppressed or not available for both 1992 and 1993 are not displayed. The employment columns represent mid-March employment in the year. Pay per employee is calculated by dividing 1st Quarter payroll, annualized, by mid-March employment. The columns headed "% State" show the county's percentage of the state total for the SIC in 1993; for example, 0.9% for SIC 6030 means that the county had 0.9 percent of the state's total establishments (or payroll) in SIC 6030 in 1993. A dash (-) is used to indicate that data are not available or cannot be calculated; nec means not elsewhere classified.

Continued on next page.

SIC	Industry	No. Establishments			Employment		Pay / Employee		Annual Payroll ($ 000)		
		1992	1993	% State	1992	1993	1992	1993	1992	1993	% State
NASH, NC - [continued]											
6100	Nondepository institutions	13	10	0.8	50	49	23,040	20,816	1,091	1,130	0.3
6140	Personal credit institutions	8	6	0.8	-	30	-	18,800	-	714	0.6
6200	Security and commodity brokers	8	10	1.6	-	62	-	46,710	-	2,782	0.9
6210	Security brokers and dealers	6	4	1.0	39	32	67,897	76,250	2,699	2,343	0.9
6280	Security and commodity services	2	6	2.9	-	30	-	15,200	-	439	1.0
6300	Insurance carriers	21	17	1.5	224	252	32,179	29,968	6,583	6,445	0.7
6310	Life insurance	10	8	1.9	203	-	28,552	-	5,457	-	-
6400	Insurance agents, brokers, and service	33	39	1.3	103	102	18,835	20,784	2,006	2,287	0.6
6500	Real estate	42	45	0.9	160	164	12,975	11,854	2,247	2,150	0.4
6510	Real estate operators and lessors	15	16	0.9	33	-	11,758	-	443	-	-
6530	Real estate agents and managers	14	26	1.0	57	76	12,982	14,684	905	1,225	0.5
6552	Subdividers and developers, n.e.c.	4	2	0.6	41	-	12,000	-	436	-	-
6700	Holding and other investment offices	6	4	1.0	-	4	-	22,000	-	56	0.0
NEW HANOVER, NC											
60 –	**Finance, insurance, and real estate**	405	430	3.0	2,654	2,824	21,919	22,941	61,638	70,566	1.7
6000	Depository institutions	75	75	2.5	874	946	22,389	23,104	19,114	21,696	1.5
6020	Commercial banks	52	50	2.3	637	627	21,940	23,190	13,706	14,578	1.2
6030	Savings institutions	12	13	2.7	171	241	25,661	25,095	4,190	5,707	4.3
6100	Nondepository institutions	35	41	3.1	204	311	25,196	24,772	5,477	9,375	2.6
6160	Mortgage bankers and brokers	14	18	4.7	120	196	24,900	27,429	3,290	6,990	4.5
6200	Security and commodity brokers	12	20	3.3	105	107	45,067	48,561	4,476	5,556	1.8
6210	Security brokers and dealers	9	15	3.7	98	100	46,653	50,360	4,301	5,190	2.0
6280	Security and commodity services	3	5	2.4	7	7	22,857	22,857	175	366	0.8
6300	Insurance carriers	35	28	2.5	282	241	27,560	31,386	8,180	7,518	0.8
6310	Life insurance	16	11	2.6	201	191	24,060	28,105	4,967	4,986	1.3
6330	Fire, marine, and casualty insurance	11	12	2.4	-	23	-	61,217	-	1,344	0.4
6400	Insurance agents, brokers, and service	76	79	2.6	265	332	22,838	23,687	6,823	8,753	2.2
6500	Real estate	161	178	3.6	843	866	15,426	16,554	15,164	17,304	3.6
6510	Real estate operators and lessors	42	50	2.7	204	239	14,510	12,653	3,492	3,787	2.8
6530	Real estate agents and managers	72	97	3.8	269	341	14,632	15,331	4,256	6,338	2.4
6552	Subdividers and developers, n.e.c.	12	19	5.8	253	234	16,458	20,803	4,990	5,767	10.6
6553	Cemetery subdividers and developers	4	6	4.1	-	44	-	20,091	-	834	5.7
6700	Holding and other investment offices	11	9	2.2	81	21	23,506	12,571	2,404	364	0.3
NORTHAMPTON, NC											
60 –	**Finance, insurance, and real estate**	14	14	0.1	54	56	16,963	26,643	946	1,548	0.0
6000	Depository institutions	6	6	0.2	32	34	17,750	34,235	508	1,164	0.1
6020	Commercial banks	6	6	0.3	32	34	17,750	34,235	508	1,164	0.1
6500	Real estate	3	4	0.1	6	10	8,667	8,800	128	115	0.0
ONSLOW, NC											
60 –	**Finance, insurance, and real estate**	208	222	1.5	1,184	1,341	16,176	15,254	20,241	22,424	0.6
6000	Depository institutions	48	40	1.3	520	486	16,323	17,531	8,933	8,499	0.6
6020	Commercial banks	27	25	1.2	278	265	17,784	18,989	4,975	4,721	0.4
6060	Credit unions	9	9	2.8	176	182	13,841	15,143	2,788	3,069	4.9
6100	Nondepository institutions	13	14	1.1	60	78	22,133	19,538	1,465	1,599	0.4
6140	Personal credit institutions	9	9	1.2	47	63	21,362	16,190	1,085	926	0.8
6280	Security and commodity services	9	5	2.4	16	12	8,250	8,333	140	120	0.3
6400	Insurance agents, brokers, and service	33	37	1.2	160	167	17,725	17,174	2,975	3,337	0.8
6500	Real estate	90	106	2.1	372	557	13,376	10,959	5,308	7,507	1.6
6510	Real estate operators and lessors	36	41	2.2	183	183	13,792	12,765	2,226	2,261	1.7
6530	Real estate agents and managers	37	54	2.1	129	341	13,767	9,806	2,301	4,273	1.6
6552	Subdividers and developers, n.e.c.	4	7	2.1	8	-	12,500	-	131	-	-

Source: County Business Patterns, 1992/93, CBP-92/93-1, U.S. Department of Commerce, Washington, D.C., April 1995. SIC categories for which data were suppressed or not available for both 1992 and 1993 are *not* displayed. The employment columns represent mid-March employment in the year. Pay per employee is calculated by dividing 1st Quarter payroll, annualized, by mid-March employment. The columns headed "% State" show the county's percentage of the state total for the SIC in 1993; for example, 0.9% for SIC 6030 means that the county had 0.9 percent of the state's total establishments (or payroll) in SIC 6030 in 1993. A dash (-) is used to indicate that data are not available or cannot be calculated; *nec* means not elsewhere classified.

SIC	Industry	No. Establishments			Employment		Pay / Employee		Annual Payroll ($ 000)		
		1992	1993	% State	1992	1993	1992	1993	1992	1993	% State
ORANGE, NC											
60–	**Finance, insurance, and real estate**	172	179	1.2	2,841	2,870	25,625	26,902	77,780	83,590	2.1
6000	Depository institutions	39	41	1.4	491	473	19,739	22,097	9,680	9,704	0.7
6020	Commercial banks	28	34	1.6	358	366	19,095	23,213	6,717	7,579	0.6
6100	Nondepository institutions	3	4	0.3	-	16	-	39,250	-	934	0.3
6200	Security and commodity brokers	8	4	0.7	53	-	63,623	-	3,304	-	-
6400	Insurance agents, brokers, and service	25	29	0.9	199	195	22,111	28,472	5,432	6,036	1.5
6500	Real estate	80	84	1.7	262	234	16,031	18,547	4,871	4,773	1.0
6510	Real estate operators and lessors	29	28	1.5	124	103	14,323	13,786	1,848	1,594	1.2
6530	Real estate agents and managers	39	46	1.8	106	119	16,528	20,807	2,612	2,886	1.1
6552	Subdividers and developers, n.e.c.	6	7	2.1	26	6	22,923	66,667	241	260	0.5
6700	Holding and other investment offices	12	11	2.7	-	74	-	38,432	-	3,297	2.4
PAMLICO, NC											
60–	**Finance, insurance, and real estate**	13	13	0.1	53	-	16,000	-	864	-	-
6500	Real estate	5	6	0.1	8	9	8,000	13,333	62	137	0.0
6530	Real estate agents and managers	3	4	0.2	4	-	10,000	-	35	-	-
PASQUOTANK, NC											
60–	**Finance, insurance, and real estate**	73	74	0.5	399	434	20,261	19,935	8,446	9,456	0.2
6000	Depository institutions	15	15	0.5	188	184	21,106	23,304	4,089	4,224	0.3
6020	Commercial banks	10	10	0.5	140	135	22,086	26,222	3,230	3,441	0.3
6100	Nondepository institutions	6	9	0.7	22	28	22,545	23,714	522	624	0.2
6300	Insurance carriers	7	5	0.4	66	64	20,242	19,750	1,363	1,404	0.2
6400	Insurance agents, brokers, and service	18	16	0.5	65	60	21,046	19,600	1,356	1,502	0.4
6500	Real estate	23	26	0.5	43	86	10,419	9,070	623	1,145	0.2
6510	Real estate operators and lessors	14	16	0.9	35	66	9,486	8,788	464	873	0.6
6530	Real estate agents and managers	5	7	0.3	5	9	17,600	10,667	93	128	0.0
PENDER, NC											
60–	**Finance, insurance, and real estate**	38	39	0.3	154	160	16,701	17,000	2,814	3,094	0.1
6000	Depository institutions	9	8	0.3	68	65	18,176	20,123	1,250	1,372	0.1
6500	Real estate	23	25	0.5	74	79	13,135	11,949	1,248	1,313	0.3
6530	Real estate agents and managers	11	18	0.7	28	47	16,429	12,170	542	803	0.3
PERQUIMANS, NC											
60–	**Finance, insurance, and real estate**	11	11	0.1	48	57	15,083	13,825	776	834	0.0
6000	Depository institutions	4	4	0.1	20	26	23,800	19,385	444	494	0.0
PERSON, NC											
60–	**Finance, insurance, and real estate**	39	40	0.3	193	180	17,306	18,711	3,592	3,743	0.1
6000	Depository institutions	10	10	0.3	94	97	19,830	19,588	1,850	2,125	0.1
6100	Nondepository institutions	6	6	0.5	22	27	18,364	15,852	433	462	0.1
6400	Insurance agents, brokers, and service	7	9	0.3	31	29	15,355	18,897	636	675	0.2
6500	Real estate	9	9	0.2	33	22	11,758	16,727	452	330	0.1
6530	Real estate agents and managers	3	4	0.2	8	-	15,500	-	154	-	-
6700	Holding and other investment offices	2	3	0.7	-	1	-	24,000	-	33	0.0
PITT, NC											
60–	**Finance, insurance, and real estate**	245	251	1.7	1,568	1,582	21,089	22,508	32,943	39,111	1.0
6000	Depository institutions	58	57	1.9	754	734	21,199	24,289	14,758	18,930	1.3
6020	Commercial banks	44	45	2.1	631	641	21,946	24,917	12,574	17,093	1.4
6030	Savings institutions	8	7	1.5	53	52	22,113	23,615	1,283	1,196	0.9
6060	Credit unions	5	5	1.6	-	41	-	15,317	-	641	1.0
6100	Nondepository institutions	25	26	2.0	140	157	28,600	26,369	4,008	4,416	1.2
6140	Personal credit institutions	15	16	2.1	64	92	26,812	21,696	1,828	2,371	2.0
6200	Security and commodity brokers	7	9	1.5	43	38	39,721	53,474	1,975	2,318	0.8
6210	Security brokers and dealers	6	6	1.5	-	37	-	54,811	-	2,308	0.9
6280	Security and commodity services	1	3	1.4	-	1	-	4,000	-	10	0.0

Source: County Business Patterns, 1992/93, CBP-92/93-1, U.S. Department of Commerce, Washington, D.C., April 1995. SIC categories for which data were suppressed or not available for both 1992 and 1993 are *not* displayed. The employment columns represent mid-March employment in the year. Pay per employee is calculated by dividing 1st Quarter payroll, annualized, by mid-March employment. The columns headed "% State" show the county's percentage of the state total for the SIC in 1993; for example, 0.9% for SIC 6030 means that the county had 0.9 percent of the state's total establishments (or payroll) in SIC 6030 in 1993. A dash (-) is used to indicate that data are not available or cannot be calculated; *nec* means not elsewhere classified.

Continued on next page.

SIC	Industry	No. Establishments			Employment		Pay / Employee		Annual Payroll ($ 000)		
		1992	1993	% State	1992	1993	1992	1993	1992	1993	% State
PITT, NC - [continued]											
6300	Insurance carriers	18	15	1.3	136	130	27,118	27,754	3,596	3,589	0.4
6310	Life insurance	8	5	1.2	77	75	21,143	23,733	1,334	1,582	0.4
6400	Insurance agents, brokers, and service	45	48	1.6	150	170	19,520	19,247	2,942	3,602	0.9
6500	Real estate	81	90	1.8	274	308	12,730	11,636	4,216	4,998	1.0
6510	Real estate operators and lessors	29	35	1.9	102	111	12,510	10,270	1,316	1,280	0.9
6530	Real estate agents and managers	31	40	1.6	113	126	14,513	14,889	2,055	2,223	0.8
6552	Subdividers and developers, n.e.c.	8	10	3.0	42	64	8,095	7,250	567	1,395	2.6
6553	Cemetery subdividers and developers	4	4	2.7	6	5	20,000	20,000	101	96	0.7
6700	Holding and other investment offices	10	6	1.5	-	45	-	25,422	-	1,258	0.9
POLK, NC											
60 –	**Finance, insurance, and real estate**	36	38	0.3	121	120	20,463	24,533	3,736	3,335	0.1
6000	Depository institutions	7	7	0.2	67	63	21,672	23,175	1,334	1,390	0.1
6200	Security and commodity brokers	3	5	0.8	-	13	-	55,692	-	746	0.2
6400	Insurance agents, brokers, and service	7	7	0.2	-	18	-	24,444	-	814	0.2
6500	Real estate	16	16	0.3	25	23	11,840	12,348	336	334	0.1
6510	Real estate operators and lessors	2	4	0.2	-	6	-	8,667	-	64	0.0
6530	Real estate agents and managers	10	11	0.4	17	-	14,824		268	-	-
6700	Holding and other investment offices	3	3	0.7	-	3	-	12,000	-	51	0.0
RANDOLPH, NC											
60 –	**Finance, insurance, and real estate**	131	140	1.0	793	937	21,084	20,277	17,559	19,725	0.5
6000	Depository institutions	42	41	1.4	466	478	21,605	22,251	10,177	10,773	0.8
6020	Commercial banks	30	29	1.3	334	341	20,323	20,305	7,184	7,436	0.6
6030	Savings institutions	9	9	1.9	111	115	26,414	28,870	2,643	2,937	2.2
6100	Nondepository institutions	12	10	0.8	-	48	-	21,417	-	1,047	0.3
6200	Security and commodity brokers	5	5	0.8	-	13	-	31,692	-	337	0.1
6210	Security brokers and dealers	4	4	1.0	10	-	31,200	-	320	-	-
6300	Insurance carriers	11	13	1.1	68	161	25,000	17,615	1,855	2,606	0.3
6310	Life insurance	2	3	0.7	-	43	-	22,512	-	1,099	0.3
6330	Fire, marine, and casualty insurance	6	7	1.4	-	11	-	69,091	-	757	0.2
6370	Pension, health, and welfare funds	3	3	3.0	31	107	10,581	10,355	515	750	5.0
6400	Insurance agents, brokers, and service	32	34	1.1	79	86	18,835	19,070	1,620	1,794	0.5
6500	Real estate	26	33	0.7	117	145	16,752	16,552	2,277	3,112	0.6
6510	Real estate operators and lessors	8	13	0.7	-	82	-	18,098	-	1,875	1.4
6530	Real estate agents and managers	12	14	0.5	39	32	16,000	13,625	595	637	0.2
6700	Holding and other investment offices	3	4	1.0	5	6	14,400	8,000	82	56	0.0
RICHMOND, NC											
60 –	**Finance, insurance, and real estate**	70	67	0.5	388	338	19,103	20,746	7,637	6,871	0.2
6000	Depository institutions	20	19	0.6	165	163	18,958	20,049	3,149	3,355	0.2
6020	Commercial banks	13	13	0.6	106	104	19,208	21,154	2,045	2,160	0.2
6100	Nondepository institutions	10	9	0.7	45	55	21,778	20,945	997	982	0.3
6300	Insurance carriers	6	3	0.3	84	-	25,381	-	2,251	-	-
6400	Insurance agents, brokers, and service	17	13	0.4	-	35	-	14,743	-	504	0.1
6500	Real estate	14	18	0.4	45	-	8,444	-	399	-	-
6510	Real estate operators and lessors	6	7	0.4	-	23	-	10,261	-	245	0.2
6530	Real estate agents and managers	7	8	0.3	17	11	8,235	9,818	139	112	0.0
6700	Holding and other investment offices	2	4	1.0	-	6	-	7,333	-	38	0.0
ROBESON, NC											
60 –	**Finance, insurance, and real estate**	129	130	0.9	1,036	1,271	21,143	33,847	24,417	43,202	1.1
6000	Depository institutions	32	33	1.1	674	859	23,009	40,992	16,717	34,117	2.4
6020	Commercial banks	23	23	1.1	586	756	23,495	44,032	14,907	32,133	2.6
6100	Nondepository institutions	17	16	1.2	74	72	19,351	19,722	1,447	1,495	0.4
6300	Insurance carriers	11	10	0.9	108	141	22,407	24,426	2,632	3,790	0.4
6310	Life insurance	5	6	1.4	96	-	20,792	-	2,163	-	-
6400	Insurance agents, brokers, and service	36	37	1.2	105	122	17,219	17,443	2,773	2,813	0.7

Source: County Business Patterns, 1992/93, CBP-92/93-1, U.S. Department of Commerce, Washington, D.C., April 1995. SIC categories for which data were suppressed or not available for both 1992 and 1993 are *not* displayed. The employment columns represent mid-March employment in the year. Pay per employee is calculated by dividing 1st Quarter payroll, annualized, by mid-March employment. The columns headed "% State" show the county's percentage of the state total for the SIC in 1993; for example, 0.9% for SIC 6030 means that the county had 0.9 percent of the state's total establishments (or payroll) in SIC 6030 in 1993. A dash (-) is used to indicate that data are not available or cannot be calculated; *nec* means not elsewhere classified.

Continued on next page.

SIC	Industry	No. Establishments			Employment		Pay / Employee		Annual Payroll ($ 000)		
		1992	1993	% State	1992	1993	1992	1993	1992	1993	% State
ROBESON, NC - [continued]											
6500	Real estate	28	30	0.6	61	72	9,508	9,889	692	857	0.2
6510	Real estate operators and lessors	15	20	1.1	39	39	7,487	7,590	327	360	0.3
6530	Real estate agents and managers	10	8	0.3	17	-	14,588	-	310	-	-
ROCKINGHAM, NC											
60 –	**Finance, insurance, and real estate**	118	121	0.8	831	678	16,529	20,879	13,558	14,734	0.4
6000	Depository institutions	32	32	1.1	365	361	22,663	23,380	7,986	8,232	0.6
6020	Commercial banks	24	24	1.1	304	299	22,750	23,264	6,576	6,660	0.5
6100	Nondepository institutions	15	16	1.2	65	74	24,492	22,649	1,500	1,636	0.5
6140	Personal credit institutions	10	10	1.3	42	49	22,286	21,878	840	883	0.7
6200	Security and commodity brokers	6	4	0.7	192	-	3,083	-	451	-	-
6210	Security brokers and dealers	6	3	0.7	192	-	3,083	-	451	-	-
6300	Insurance carriers	9	8	0.7	42	-	21,333	-	991	-	-
6400	Insurance agents, brokers, and service	22	26	0.8	66	92	18,667	22,087	1,498	2,356	0.6
6500	Real estate	34	34	0.7	101	104	11,406	8,885	1,132	1,019	0.2
6510	Real estate operators and lessors	10	10	0.5	35	28	11,657	11,429	370	348	0.3
6530	Real estate agents and managers	13	20	0.8	33	60	11,758	7,333	363	499	0.2
6552	Subdividers and developers, n.e.c.	3	2	0.6	3	-	10,667	-	47	-	-
6553	Cemetery subdividers and developers	3	2	1.4	12	-	14,333	-	193	-	-
ROWAN, NC											
60 –	**Finance, insurance, and real estate**	175	176	1.2	1,078	1,181	22,646	22,527	24,733	26,976	0.7
6000	Depository institutions	46	46	1.5	530	451	22,709	23,681	11,478	10,702	0.8
6020	Commercial banks	31	32	1.5	396	323	21,616	23,183	8,095	7,312	0.6
6030	Savings institutions	9	8	1.7	105	96	28,533	27,625	2,885	2,849	2.2
6060	Credit unions	6	6	1.9	29	32	16,552	16,875	498	541	0.9
6100	Nondepository institutions	11	13	1.0	44	92	24,455	17,913	1,045	2,020	0.6
6140	Personal credit institutions	9	9	1.2	-	47	-	16,766	-	799	0.7
6210	Security brokers and dealers	5	6	1.5	13	16	60,000	75,000	976	1,163	0.4
6300	Insurance carriers	22	17	1.5	168	175	25,214	28,937	4,269	4,817	0.5
6310	Life insurance	7	6	1.4	134	133	25,701	29,113	3,367	3,577	1.0
6330	Fire, marine, and casualty insurance	8	6	1.2	-	25	-	34,240	-	834	0.2
6370	Pension, health, and welfare funds	3	3	3.0	2	-	16,000	-	58	-	-
6400	Insurance agents, brokers, and service	40	42	1.4	120	133	15,833	15,789	2,262	2,384	0.6
6500	Real estate	45	44	0.9	123	169	17,333	13,988	2,303	3,047	0.6
6510	Real estate operators and lessors	24	22	1.2	68	102	11,118	9,843	834	1,205	0.9
6530	Real estate agents and managers	14	17	0.7	36	-	25,667	-	1,022	-	-
6553	Cemetery subdividers and developers	4	3	2.0	14	-	28,571	-	419	-	-
RUTHERFORD, NC											
60 –	**Finance, insurance, and real estate**	92	86	0.6	540	446	18,733	19,632	10,205	8,881	0.2
6000	Depository institutions	24	24	0.8	197	200	21,442	22,020	4,185	4,353	0.3
6020	Commercial banks	21	22	1.0	171	-	21,614	-	3,578	-	-
6100	Nondepository institutions	7	7	0.5	28	30	25,857	27,067	712	764	0.2
6400	Insurance agents, brokers, and service	23	24	0.8	82	92	17,951	14,304	1,471	1,358	0.3
6500	Real estate	30	26	0.5	209	107	14,450	14,243	3,162	1,643	0.3
6510	Real estate operators and lessors	11	7	0.4	49	13	5,388	7,385	312	92	0.1
6530	Real estate agents and managers	9	15	0.6	-	85	-	15,576	-	1,440	0.5
6553	Cemetery subdividers and developers	3	2	1.4	8	-	9,500	-	77	-	-
SAMPSON, NC											
60 –	**Finance, insurance, and real estate**	71	74	0.5	284	292	17,690	19,521	5,397	6,173	0.2
6000	Depository institutions	22	22	0.7	159	154	17,610	20,675	2,887	3,432	0.2
6020	Commercial banks	17	17	0.8	123	119	18,244	20,739	2,344	2,710	0.2
6100	Nondepository institutions	10	11	0.8	37	49	20,649	19,918	803	998	0.3
6140	Personal credit institutions	7	7	0.9	25	-	18,240	-	491	-	-
6300	Insurance carriers	4	3	0.3	6	-	26,000	-	168	-	-
6400	Insurance agents, brokers, and service	19	21	0.7	48	53	15,500	14,717	839	929	0.2

Source: County Business Patterns, 1992/93, CBP-92/93-1, U.S. Department of Commerce, Washington, D.C., April 1995. SIC categories for which data were suppressed or not available for both 1992 and 1993 are *not* displayed. The employment columns represent mid-March employment in the year. Pay per employee is calculated by dividing 1st Quarter payroll, annualized, by mid-March employment. The columns headed "% State" show the county's percentage of the state total for the SIC in 1993; for example, 0.9% for SIC 6030 means that the county had 0.9 percent of the state's total establishments (or payroll) in SIC 6030 in 1993. A dash (-) is used to indicate that data are not available or cannot be calculated; *nec* means not elsewhere classified.

Continued on next page.

SIC	Industry	No. Establishments			Employment		Pay / Employee		Annual Payroll ($ 000)		
		1992	1993	% State	1992	1993	1992	1993	1992	1993	% State
SAMPSON, NC - [continued]											
6500	Real estate	13	13	0.3	27	-	8,741	-	272	-	-
6510	Real estate operators and lessors	4	4	0.2	11	-	10,182	-	122	-	-
6530	Real estate agents and managers	4	7	0.3	7	14	9,143	8,571	79	118	0.0
SCOTLAND, NC											
60 –	**Finance, insurance, and real estate**	57	55	0.4	287	366	20,167	16,448	5,935	6,016	0.1
6000	Depository institutions	17	15	0.5	141	127	18,894	21,102	2,418	2,393	0.2
6020	Commercial banks	7	6	0.3	111	88	18,955	19,909	1,952	1,597	0.1
6030	Savings institutions	5	6	1.3	-	29	-	25,793	-	637	0.5
6060	Credit unions	5	3	0.9	-	10	-	18,000	-	159	0.3
6100	Nondepository institutions	7	8	0.6	28	38	24,714	17,158	709	657	0.2
6400	Insurance agents, brokers, and service	12	12	0.4	52	128	23,538	11,188	1,458	1,601	0.4
6500	Real estate	17	16	0.3	56	42	12,000	11,333	775	646	0.1
6510	Real estate operators and lessors	7	6	0.3	-	25	-	13,120	-	445	0.3
6530	Real estate agents and managers	6	8	0.3	29	-	12,966	-	409	-	-
STANLY, NC											
60 –	**Finance, insurance, and real estate**	82	78	0.5	417	433	20,240	19,880	8,487	9,088	0.2
6000	Depository institutions	27	25	0.8	264	250	20,485	20,656	5,337	5,141	0.4
6020	Commercial banks	19	17	0.8	188	169	19,936	21,136	3,710	3,521	0.3
6100	Nondepository institutions	9	8	0.6	24	18	27,167	20,000	619	364	0.1
6300	Insurance carriers	8	7	0.6	27	-	29,037	-	756	-	-
6400	Insurance agents, brokers, and service	17	17	0.6	57	63	17,544	18,984	1,167	1,409	0.4
6500	Real estate	18	18	0.4	37	80	9,730	15,150	397	1,573	0.3
6510	Real estate operators and lessors	4	5	0.3	4	9	6,000	6,222	40	91	0.1
6530	Real estate agents and managers	8	8	0.3	14	-	8,857	-	128	-	-
6552	Subdividers and developers, n.e.c.	3	3	0.9	7	-	6,286	-	73	-	-
STOKES, NC											
60 –	**Finance, insurance, and real estate**	23	25	0.2	113	109	20,531	20,073	2,387	2,333	0.1
6000	Depository institutions	9	9	0.3	89	76	20,989	20,684	1,839	1,668	0.1
6400	Insurance agents, brokers, and service	8	8	0.3	-	27	-	16,296	-	459	0.1
6500	Real estate	4	6	0.1	1	-	8,000	-	36	-	-
6530	Real estate agents and managers	2	4	0.2	-	1	-	16,000	-	59	0.0
SURRY, NC											
60 –	**Finance, insurance, and real estate**	98	102	0.7	628	668	21,140	22,144	13,498	14,478	0.4
6000	Depository institutions	25	25	0.8	403	428	22,591	23,822	8,731	9,270	0.7
6020	Commercial banks	17	19	0.9	272	-	23,971	-	6,064	-	-
6100	Nondepository institutions	10	10	0.8	45	-	19,111	-	1,170	-	-
6300	Insurance carriers	2	3	0.3	-	12	-	20,000	-	266	0.0
6400	Insurance agents, brokers, and service	33	32	1.0	107	117	20,673	20,957	2,361	2,487	0.6
6500	Real estate	24	30	0.6	53	56	12,679	10,786	719	832	0.2
6510	Real estate operators and lessors	8	12	0.7	20	26	11,200	8,769	240	305	0.2
6530	Real estate agents and managers	7	14	0.5	16	22	15,250	13,273	262	398	0.1
6700	Holding and other investment offices	3	1	0.2	8	-	15,000	-	161	-	-
SWAIN, NC											
60 –	**Finance, insurance, and real estate**	11	11	0.1	-	44	-	17,909	-	809	0.0
6500	Real estate	3	4	0.1	5	4	4,000	4,000	24	27	0.0
TRANSYLVANIA, NC											
60 –	**Finance, insurance, and real estate**	45	49	0.3	426	333	15,596	19,724	7,765	6,653	0.2
6000	Depository institutions	10	11	0.4	122	121	18,164	19,471	2,263	1,764	0.1
6020	Commercial banks	4	6	0.3	52	61	18,615	20,721	977	1,148	0.1

Source: County Business Patterns, 1992/93, CBP-92/93-1, U.S. Department of Commerce, Washington, D.C., April 1995. SIC categories for which data were suppressed or not available for both 1992 and 1993 are *not* displayed. The employment columns represent mid-March employment in the year. Pay per employee is calculated by dividing 1st Quarter payroll, annualized, by mid-March employment. The columns headed "% State" show the county's percentage of the state total for the SIC in 1993; for example, 0.9% for SIC 6030 means that the county had 0.9 percent of the state's total establishments (or payroll) in SIC 6030 in 1993. A dash (-) is used to indicate that data are not available or cannot be calculated; *nec* means not elsewhere classified.

Continued on next page.

SIC	Industry	No. Establishments			Employment		Pay / Employee		Annual Payroll ($ 000)		
		1992	1993	% State	1992	1993	1992	1993	1992	1993	% State
TRANSYLVANIA, NC - [continued]											
6400	Insurance agents, brokers, and service	6	7	0.2	28	36	17,714	15,000	543	592	0.1
6500	Real estate	20	23	0.5	254	159	13,197	18,918	4,084	3,580	0.7
6530	Real estate agents and managers	13	16	0.6	227	126	13,093	17,111	3,664	2,399	0.9
TYRRELL, NC											
60 –	**Finance, insurance, and real estate**	3	3	0.0	-	-	-	-	-	-	-
UNION, NC											
60 –	**Finance, insurance, and real estate**	125	133	0.9	985	990	25,182	25,451	25,068	25,982	0.6
6000	Depository institutions	33	35	1.2	686	672	22,845	23,536	15,564	15,728	1.1
6100	Nondepository institutions	15	14	1.1	64	69	26,750	25,333	1,847	2,274	0.6
6140	Personal credit institutions	10	10	1.3	36	38	26,000	22,842	948	893	0.7
6300	Insurance carriers	8	9	0.8	58	80	47,379	43,950	2,916	3,678	0.4
6400	Insurance agents, brokers, and service	29	28	0.9	81	69	23,259	18,493	1,911	1,390	0.4
6500	Real estate	34	40	0.8	67	74	18,149	18,432	1,280	1,591	0.3
6510	Real estate operators and lessors	13	18	1.0	17	40	12,941	14,800	253	673	0.5
6530	Real estate agents and managers	13	17	0.7	29	25	15,172	18,880	475	544	0.2
6552	Subdividers and developers, n.e.c.	2	5	1.5	-	9	-	33,333	-	374	0.7
VANCE, NC											
60 –	**Finance, insurance, and real estate**	74	73	0.5	302	298	19,974	20,859	6,587	7,032	0.2
6000	Depository institutions	12	12	0.4	126	121	17,397	20,992	2,266	2,662	0.2
6020	Commercial banks	7	7	0.3	101	97	17,663	21,979	1,809	2,231	0.2
6100	Nondepository institutions	9	10	0.8	45	43	21,689	18,419	942	894	0.3
6140	Personal credit institutions	9	10	1.3	45	43	21,689	18,419	942	894	0.7
6400	Insurance agents, brokers, and service	14	13	0.4	50	50	20,560	21,360	1,355	1,439	0.4
6500	Real estate	35	34	0.7	66	73	18,424	16,384	1,350	1,385	0.3
6510	Real estate operators and lessors	15	17	0.9	40	44	9,600	11,727	443	704	0.5
6530	Real estate agents and managers	9	14	0.5	14	25	23,429	22,560	347	542	0.2
WAKE, NC											
60 –	**Finance, insurance, and real estate**	1,401	1,437	9.9	18,071	16,638	26,225	28,132	474,683	489,766	12.1
6000	Depository institutions	232	231	7.7	5,622	4,485	20,867	25,478	108,498	113,257	8.0
6020	Commercial banks	164	173	8.0	3,638	3,522	23,362	26,535	85,355	92,120	7.6
6030	Savings institutions	31	23	4.9	1,085	257	11,388	22,957	7,807	5,345	4.1
6060	Credit unions	32	32	10.0	630	689	20,648	21,068	13,314	15,396	24.8
6090	Functions closely related to banking	5	3	6.4	269	17	25,874	23,294	2,022	396	-
6100	Nondepository institutions	114	117	8.8	943	1,357	34,515	31,629	33,122	43,993	12.4
6140	Personal credit institutions	47	43	5.7	323	627	27,926	22,526	8,781	10,529	8.7
6160	Mortgage bankers and brokers	60	68	17.9	565	617	35,483	34,438	20,823	25,777	16.7
6200	Security and commodity brokers	70	74	12.1	462	553	67,913	56,007	29,981	35,275	11.5
6210	Security brokers and dealers	40	34	8.5	410	427	72,527	65,845	28,273	32,254	12.4
6280	Security and commodity services	28	40	19.3	52	126	31,538	22,667	1,669	3,021	6.7
6300	Insurance carriers	182	162	14.2	5,322	4,895	30,564	30,479	165,644	156,168	17.1
6310	Life insurance	57	51	12.2	1,397	751	29,924	29,161	40,814	24,992	6.7
6330	Fire, marine, and casualty insurance	81	74	14.9	2,773	2,494	30,132	30,946	86,675	77,943	21.9
6350	Surety insurance	4	2	11.1	57	-	21,263	-	1,212	-	-
6370	Pension, health, and welfare funds	19	15	15.0	197	-	23,736	-	4,974	-	-
6400	Insurance agents, brokers, and service	281	303	9.9	1,432	1,339	25,101	25,323	37,115	36,770	9.3
6500	Real estate	468	502	10.1	3,000	3,039	20,789	21,137	68,981	73,105	15.2
6510	Real estate operators and lessors	155	176	9.6	777	736	15,568	15,082	12,865	12,967	9.5
6530	Real estate agents and managers	227	277	10.8	1,833	2,112	22,510	23,159	45,008	55,406	20.6
6552	Subdividers and developers, n.e.c.	31	32	9.7	195	76	26,359	24,316	6,160	2,431	4.5
6553	Cemetery subdividers and developers	7	9	6.1	76	103	18,842	17,786	1,401	1,798	12.3

Source: County Business Patterns, 1992/93, CBP-92/93-1, U.S. Department of Commerce, Washington, D.C., April 1995. SIC categories for which data were suppressed or not available for both 1992 and 1993 are *not* displayed. The employment columns represent mid-March employment in the year. Pay per employee is calculated by dividing 1st Quarter payroll, annualized, by mid-March employment. The columns headed "% State" show the county's percentage of the state total for the SIC in 1993; for example, 0.9% for SIC 6030 means that the county had 0.9 percent of the state's total establishments (or payroll) in SIC 6030 in 1993. A dash (-) is used to indicate that data are not available or cannot be calculated; *nec* means not elsewhere classified.

Continued on next page.

SIC	Industry	No. Establishments			Employment		Pay / Employee		Annual Payroll ($ 000)		
		1992	1993	% State	1992	1993	1992	1993	1992	1993	% State
WAKE, NC - [continued]											
6710	Holding offices	13	9	8.6	71	97	105,183	112,495	6,496	8,896	9.1
6732	Educational, religious, etc. trusts	19	18	18.9	261	258	18,605	20,419	5,054	5,386	40.8
6733	Trusts, n.e.c.	11	11	12.4	-	16	-	21,500	-	240	4.1
WARREN, NC											
60 –	**Finance, insurance, and real estate**	14	13	0.1	54	50	18,074	20,160	991	985	0.0
6000	Depository institutions	4	4	0.1	31	30	20,645	22,800	629	646	0.0
6400	Insurance agents, brokers, and service	4	4	0.1	12	12	12,667	16,000	165	178	0.0
6500	Real estate	3	2	0.0	4	-	9,000	-	51	-	-
WASHINGTON, NC											
60 –	**Finance, insurance, and real estate**	20	20	0.1	95	102	18,316	18,824	1,725	1,945	0.0
6000	Depository institutions	8	9	0.3	58	72	19,034	19,611	1,098	1,393	0.1
6020	Commercial banks	6	6	0.3	-	42	-	20,857	-	837	0.1
6100	Nondepository institutions	5	4	0.3	22	15	17,091	18,400	379	302	0.1
6400	Insurance agents, brokers, and service	4	4	0.1	13	13	17,846	16,308	217	222	0.1
6500	Real estate	3	3	0.1	2	2	14,000	10,000	31	28	0.0
WATAUGA, NC											
60 –	**Finance, insurance, and real estate**	93	98	0.7	578	546	19,003	18,205	13,110	11,138	0.3
6000	Depository institutions	13	13	0.4	170	168	20,447	21,524	3,458	3,673	0.3
6100	Nondepository institutions	6	6	0.5	12	10	35,000	22,400	440	251	0.1
6140	Personal credit institutions	3	2	0.3	6	-	52,000	-	319	-	-
6160	Mortgage bankers and brokers	2	3	0.8	-	4	-	15,000	-	75	0.0
6400	Insurance agents, brokers, and service	16	17	0.6	93	107	23,527	24,449	2,558	2,924	0.7
6500	Real estate	47	52	1.1	283	241	13,965	12,382	4,555	3,692	0.8
6510	Real estate operators and lessors	13	14	0.8	99	58	13,010	11,724	1,439	818	0.6
6530	Real estate agents and managers	25	32	1.3	75	169	13,013	12,615	1,118	2,578	1.0
6700	Holding and other investment offices	3	4	1.0	-	13	-	19,077	-	343	0.3
WAYNE, NC											
60 –	**Finance, insurance, and real estate**	190	188	1.3	1,197	1,205	21,387	21,597	28,493	29,374	0.7
6000	Depository institutions	42	43	1.4	511	502	22,990	22,932	11,541	12,140	0.9
6020	Commercial banks	26	28	1.3	328	334	23,232	24,754	7,143	8,869	0.7
6030	Savings institutions	10	8	1.7	130	107	23,323	20,897	3,240	2,231	1.7
6100	Nondepository institutions	18	18	1.4	97	98	23,010	20,694	2,099	2,099	0.6
6140	Personal credit institutions	15	15	2.0	72	86	20,500	17,907	1,435	1,505	1.2
6300	Insurance carriers	14	10	0.9	104	74	24,808	21,838	2,561	1,830	0.2
6310	Life insurance	7	4	1.0	95	60	22,358	17,667	2,222	1,177	0.3
6400	Insurance agents, brokers, and service	56	54	1.8	358	379	19,609	21,784	9,208	10,272	2.6
6500	Real estate	56	57	1.2	117	141	14,462	15,574	2,694	2,572	0.5
6510	Real estate operators and lessors	21	24	1.3	48	52	12,167	15,923	1,190	884	0.6
6530	Real estate agents and managers	25	27	1.1	52	74	16,538	16,270	1,125	1,368	0.5
WILKES, NC											
60 –	**Finance, insurance, and real estate**	69	75	0.5	945	1,022	20,618	22,168	20,019	23,148	0.6
6000	Depository institutions	18	20	0.7	740	745	19,135	21,396	14,106	16,352	1.1
6200	Security and commodity brokers	5	6	1.0	11	13	42,545	37,538	474	538	0.2
6300	Insurance carriers	7	7	0.6	58	92	27,724	25,435	1,752	2,081	0.2
6310	Life insurance	3	4	1.0	51	-	28,078	-	1,538	-	-
6330	Fire, marine, and casualty insurance	4	3	0.6	7	-	25,143	-	214	-	-
6400	Insurance agents, brokers, and service	14	15	0.5	58	63	24,759	23,810	1,801	1,894	0.5
6500	Real estate	16	19	0.4	46	59	21,130	23,186	1,057	1,391	0.3
6510	Real estate operators and lessors	5	6	0.3	6	13	10,000	10,154	68	134	0.1
6530	Real estate agents and managers	5	9	0.4	10	22	11,600	20,364	121	535	0.2

Source: County Business Patterns, 1992/93, CBP-92/93-1, U.S. Department of Commerce, Washington, D.C., April 1995. SIC categories for which data were suppressed or not available for both 1992 and 1993 are *not* displayed. The employment columns represent mid-March employment in the year. Pay per employee is calculated by dividing 1st Quarter payroll, annualized, by mid-March employment. The columns headed "% State" show the county's percentage of the state total for the SIC in 1993; for example, 0.9% for SIC 6030 means that the county had 0.9 percent of the state's total establishments (or payroll) in SIC 6030 in 1993. A dash (-) is used to indicate that data are not available or cannot be calculated; *nec* means not elsewhere classified.

SIC	Industry	No. Establishments			Employment		Pay / Employee		Annual Payroll ($ 000)		
		1992	1993	% State	1992	1993	1992	1993	1992	1993	% State

WILSON, NC

SIC	Industry	1992	1993	% State	1992	1993	1992	1993	1992	1993	% State
60 –	**Finance, insurance, and real estate**	137	143	*1.0*	1,543	1,811	32,187	31,490	39,452	48,647	*1.2*
6000	Depository institutions	35	39	*1.3*	1,171	1,422	34,439	33,691	29,447	38,991	*2.7*
6020	Commercial banks	27	28	*1.3*	1,125	1,116	35,143	36,362	28,627	36,007	*3.0*
6030	Savings institutions	6	8	*1.7*	-	284	-	24,380	-	2,572	*2.0*
6060	Credit unions	1	3	*0.9*	-	22	-	18,364	-	412	*0.7*
6100	Nondepository institutions	16	13	*1.0*	60	58	25,600	17,241	1,476	971	*0.3*
6200	Security and commodity brokers	5	5	*0.8*	-	31	-	69,032	-	2,427	*0.8*
6210	Security brokers and dealers	4	4	*1.0*	35	-	64,343	-	2,413	-	-
6300	Insurance carriers	7	9	*0.8*	72	89	27,667	25,933	2,140	2,273	*0.2*
6310	Life insurance	3	4	*1.0*	-	79	-	24,253	-	1,819	*0.5*
6400	Insurance agents, brokers, and service	36	35	*1.1*	90	106	20,267	20,415	2,035	2,032	*0.5*
6500	Real estate	35	39	*0.8*	108	104	13,148	14,385	1,632	1,906	*0.4*
6510	Real estate operators and lessors	9	10	*0.5*	31	-	8,645	-	331	-	-
6530	Real estate agents and managers	21	26	*1.0*	53	55	12,075	14,691	744	1,060	*0.4*
6700	Holding and other investment offices	3	3	*0.7*	-	1	-	12,000	-	47	*0.0*

YADKIN, NC

SIC	Industry	1992	1993	% State	1992	1993	1992	1993	1992	1993	% State
60 –	**Finance, insurance, and real estate**	27	25	*0.2*	197	113	14,843	22,336	3,053	2,519	*0.1*
6000	Depository institutions	8	8	*0.3*	72	66	21,056	24,121	1,493	1,495	*0.1*
6300	Insurance carriers	3	1	*0.1*	4	-	18,000	-	73	-	-
6400	Insurance agents, brokers, and service	8	9	*0.3*	30	30	17,200	20,133	561	678	*0.2*
6500	Real estate	5	4	*0.1*	-	6	-	12,667	-	74	*0.0*

YANCEY, NC

SIC	Industry	1992	1993	% State	1992	1993	1992	1993	1992	1993	% State
60 –	**Finance, insurance, and real estate**	20	23	*0.2*	74	90	17,027	15,289	1,373	1,669	*0.0*
6000	Depository institutions	5	5	*0.2*	34	36	20,824	20,000	681	742	*0.1*
6400	Insurance agents, brokers, and service	5	5	*0.2*	17	19	16,000	16,211	300	316	*0.1*
6500	Real estate	7	10	*0.2*	15	26	9,600	7,846	264	463	*0.1*
6510	Real estate operators and lessors	3	3	*0.2*	4	4	5,000	5,000	21	21	*0.0*

Source: County Business Patterns, 1992/93, CBP-92/93-1, U.S. Department of Commerce, Washington, D.C., April 1995. SIC categories for which data were suppressed or not available for both 1992 and 1993 are *not* displayed. The employment columns represent mid-March employment in the year. Pay per employee is calculated by dividing 1st Quarter payroll, annualized, by mid-March employment. The columns headed "% State" show the county's percentage of the state total for the SIC in 1993; for example, 0.9% for SIC 6030 means that the county had 0.9 percent of the state's total establishments (or payroll) in SIC 6030 in 1993. A dash (-) is used to indicate that data are not available or cannot be calculated; *nec* means not elsewhere classified.

NORTH DAKOTA

SIC	Industry	No. Establishments			Employment		Pay / Employee		Annual Payroll ($ 000)		
		1992	1993	% State	1992	1993	1992	1993	1992	1993	% State
ADAMS, ND											
60 –	**Finance, insurance, and real estate**	12	11	0.6	-	36	-	17,222	-	685	0.2
6000	Depository institutions	7	6	1.5	34	24	17,647	20,167	590	532	0.4
BARNES, ND											
60 –	**Finance, insurance, and real estate**	28	30	1.6	139	-	21,554	-	3,130	-	-
6000	Depository institutions	7	7	1.7	90	90	23,022	25,867	2,157	2,423	1.9
6400	Insurance agents, brokers, and service	11	13	2.2	27	29	14,963	16,828	430	532	1.6
6500	Real estate	7	8	1.4	7	-	7,429	-	62	-	-
6510	Real estate operators and lessors	2	3	1.0	-	4	-	4,000	-	18	0.1
6553	Cemetery subdividers and developers	4	4	10.8	2	1	4,000	4,000	18	17	3.7
BENSON, ND											
60 –	**Finance, insurance, and real estate**	12	13	0.7	46	53	18,783	19,094	1,033	1,187	0.4
6000	Depository institutions	4	4	1.0	-	21	-	25,714	-	599	0.5
BILLINGS, ND											
60 –	**Finance, insurance, and real estate**	1	1	0.1	-	-	-	-	-	-	-
BOTTINEAU, ND											
60 –	**Finance, insurance, and real estate**	25	28	1.5	95	105	17,979	19,619	1,853	2,087	0.7
6000	Depository institutions	9	9	2.2	64	66	20,875	25,152	1,460	1,640	1.3
6400	Insurance agents, brokers, and service	5	7	1.2	9	-	14,222	-	142	-	-
6500	Real estate	7	9	1.6	13	20	7,692	3,800	95	121	0.4
6510	Real estate operators and lessors	4	7	2.3	8	-	5,500	-	46	-	-
BOWMAN, ND											
60 –	**Finance, insurance, and real estate**	10	9	0.5	66	59	18,545	20,475	1,219	1,261	0.4
6400	Insurance agents, brokers, and service	4	4	0.7	10	-	14,000	-	164	-	-
BURKE, ND											
60 –	**Finance, insurance, and real estate**	13	13	0.7	-	38	-	14,526	-	669	0.2
6000	Depository institutions	4	4	1.0	-	25	-	18,400	-	567	0.4
6020	Commercial banks	4	4	1.5	-	25	-	18,400	-	567	0.6
6500	Real estate	5	5	0.9	6	7	5,333	4,571	27	35	0.1
BURLEIGH, ND											
60 –	**Finance, insurance, and real estate**	227	234	12.1	1,317	1,364	23,547	24,176	32,245	35,177	11.7
6000	Depository institutions	32	34	8.3	529	545	26,087	24,668	12,434	12,555	9.6
6020	Commercial banks	16	19	7.3	398	433	28,442	25,931	9,928	10,230	10.2
6030	Savings institutions	6	4	6.7	72	-	18,778	-	1,282	-	-
6060	Credit unions	9	10	11.1	-	63	-	15,873	-	1,033	12.2
6100	Nondepository institutions	8	9	14.1	31	34	17,935	23,765	782	1,067	6.8
6140	Personal credit institutions	5	3	17.6	18	15	24,889	29,067	453	438	12.7
6200	Security and commodity brokers	11	15	17.6	66	75	52,182	49,973	3,555	3,978	21.2
6210	Security brokers and dealers	9	12	19.7	-	70	-	52,457	-	3,866	-
6300	Insurance carriers	22	18	14.4	167	191	27,665	30,157	4,692	6,501	10.9
6310	Life insurance	7	6	15.8	54	54	40,444	38,148	2,183	2,069	13.0
6330	Fire, marine, and casualty insurance	9	7	11.7	67	-	25,612	-	1,748	-	-
6400	Insurance agents, brokers, and service	68	73	12.3	191	207	20,356	19,961	4,727	4,801	14.3
6500	Real estate	72	71	12.2	276	253	11,435	13,771	3,550	3,719	11.4
6510	Real estate operators and lessors	36	39	12.7	153	113	11,111	10,407	1,852	1,227	8.1

Source: County Business Patterns, 1992/93, CBP-92/93-1, U.S. Department of Commerce, Washington, D.C., April 1995. SIC categories for which data were suppressed or not available for both 1992 and 1993 are *not* displayed. The employment columns represent mid-March employment in the year. Pay per employee is calculated by dividing 1st Quarter payroll, annualized, by mid-March employment. The columns headed "% State" show the county's percentage of the state total for the SIC in 1993; for example, 0.9% for SIC 6030 means that the county had 0.9 percent of the state's total establishments (or payroll) in SIC 6030 in 1993. A dash (-) is used to indicate that data are not available or cannot be calculated; *nec* means not elsewhere classified.

Continued on next page.

SIC	Industry	No. Establishments			Employment		Pay / Employee		Annual Payroll ($ 000)		
		1992	1993	% State	1992	1993	1992	1993	1992	1993	% State
BURLEIGH, ND - [continued]											
6530	Real estate agents and managers	26	24	*13.6*	65	118	14,277	17,559	1,061	2,185	*16.1*
6553	Cemetery subdividers and developers	3	3	*8.1*	8	-	7,500	-	93	-	-
6700	Holding and other investment offices	14	14	*20.9*	57	59	27,158	27,119	2,505	2,556	*26.4*
CASS, ND											
60 –	**Finance, insurance, and real estate**	399	414	*21.5*	4,686	5,120	25,169	24,444	120,185	127,027	*42.3*
6000	Depository institutions	61	55	*13.3*	1,450	1,629	22,099	22,824	33,602	35,641	*27.3*
6020	Commercial banks	38	30	*11.6*	911	915	23,816	23,366	22,069	21,074	*21.1*
6030	Savings institutions	9	9	*15.0*	485	643	19,596	23,048	10,622	13,598	*62.5*
6100	Nondepository institutions	23	18	*28.1*	170	162	29,788	38,938	5,237	5,988	*38.0*
6140	Personal credit institutions	11	7	*41.2*	96	82	26,250	27,659	2,518	2,386	*69.1*
6200	Security and commodity brokers	25	24	*28.2*	142	159	54,338	51,245	7,421	8,491	*45.2*
6210	Security brokers and dealers	14	14	*23.0*	112	124	64,464	63,806	6,862	8,231	-
6280	Security and commodity services	11	10	*52.6*	30	35	16,533	6,743	559	260	-
6300	Insurance carriers	55	48	*38.4*	1,669	1,768	24,580	25,536	41,382	44,604	*74.8*
6310	Life insurance	27	25	*65.8*	401	456	26,594	26,395	10,908	11,425	*72.1*
6330	Fire, marine, and casualty insurance	18	15	*25.0*	122	-	26,918	-	3,307		-
6400	Insurance agents, brokers, and service	94	114	*19.2*	554	430	26,968	24,177	16,343	13,242	*39.5*
6500	Real estate	125	135	*23.3*	639	860	21,296	15,991	12,596	14,555	*44.7*
6510	Real estate operators and lessors	60	64	*20.9*	229	387	11,144	15,959	3,971	6,766	*44.8*
6530	Real estate agents and managers	49	55	*31.1*	329	421	27,429	16,067	6,482	6,684	*49.3*
6552	Subdividers and developers, n.e.c.	4	7	*63.6*	-	15	-	12,000	-	247	*76.2*
6553	Cemetery subdividers and developers	5	5	*13.5*	12	-	24,667	-	209	-	-
6700	Holding and other investment offices	16	20	*29.9*	62	112	57,226	37,679	3,604	4,506	*46.6*
6710	Holding offices	5	7	*31.8*	-	59	-	54,169	-	3,366	*55.1*
CAVALIER, ND											
60 –	**Finance, insurance, and real estate**	22	22	*1.1*	88	82	19,818	21,366	1,851	1,909	*0.6*
6000	Depository institutions	5	5	*1.2*	52	49	24,308	25,714	1,264	1,355	*1.0*
6400	Insurance agents, brokers, and service	10	10	*1.7*	22	20	15,818	16,400	472	444	*1.3*
6500	Real estate	4	4	*0.7*	5	4	5,600	7,000	28	30	*0.1*
DICKEY, ND											
60 –	**Finance, insurance, and real estate**	13	14	*0.7*	63	66	18,794	19,273	1,408	1,446	*0.5*
6000	Depository institutions	5	5	*1.2*	49	51	21,388	22,353	1,278	1,298	*1.0*
6400	Insurance agents, brokers, and service	5	6	*1.0*	10	11	11,600	9,818	111	124	*0.4*
6500	Real estate	3	3	*0.5*	4	4	5,000	6,000	19	24	*0.1*
DIVIDE, ND											
60 –	**Finance, insurance, and real estate**	12	12	*0.6*	53	52	12,302	13,923	785	829	*0.3*
6400	Insurance agents, brokers, and service	3	3	*0.5*	5	5	15,200	14,400	60	73	*0.2*
6500	Real estate	5	5	*0.9*	14	-	4,571	-	73	-	-
6510	Real estate operators and lessors	3	3	*1.0*	-	6	-	3,333	-	21	*0.1*
DUNN, ND											
60 –	**Finance, insurance, and real estate**	6	7	*0.4*	31	31	21,161	18,194	651	570	*0.2*
6000	Depository institutions	3	3	*0.7*	28	27	22,714	20,000	632	546	*0.4*
EDDY, ND											
60 –	**Finance, insurance, and real estate**	5	5	*0.3*	24	23	12,667	13,913	308	348	*0.1*
EMMONS, ND											
60 –	**Finance, insurance, and real estate**	13	12	*0.6*	56	52	17,143	18,231	1,036	1,043	*0.3*
6000	Depository institutions	5	6	*1.5*	35	40	20,686	21,300	858	945	*0.7*
6020	Commercial banks	3	3	*1.2*	-	34	-	23,765	-	901	*0.9*

Source: County Business Patterns, 1992/93, CBP-92/93-1, U.S. Department of Commerce, Washington, D.C., April 1995. SIC categories for which data were suppressed or not available for both 1992 and 1993 are *not* displayed. The employment columns represent mid-March employment in the year. Pay per employee is calculated by dividing 1st Quarter payroll, annualized, by mid-March employment. The columns headed "% State" show the county's percentage of the state total for the SIC in 1993; for example, 0.9% for SIC 6030 means that the county had 0.9 percent of the state's total establishments (or payroll) in SIC 6030 in 1993. A dash (-) is used to indicate that data are not available or cannot be calculated; *nec* means not elsewhere classified.

Continued on next page.

SIC	Industry	No. Establishments			Employment		Pay / Employee		Annual Payroll ($ 000)		
		1992	1993	% State	1992	1993	1992	1993	1992	1993	% State
EMMONS, ND - [continued]											
6060	Credit unions	1	3	3.3	-	6	-	7,333	-	44	0.5
6400	Insurance agents, brokers, and service	3	3	0.5	9	7	14,222	9,143	70	65	0.2
6500	Real estate	3	2	0.3	8	-	11,000	-	87	-	-
FOSTER, ND											
60 –	**Finance, insurance, and real estate**	17	17	0.9	51	36	15,843	17,556	880	547	0.2
6400	Insurance agents, brokers, and service	6	7	1.2	11	13	14,909	10,154	155	193	0.6
6500	Real estate	6	6	1.0	6	-	5,333	-	36	-	-
6510	Real estate operators and lessors	3	3	1.0	4	4	3,000	3,000	12	16	0.1
GOLDEN VALLEY, ND											
60 –	**Finance, insurance, and real estate**	6	7	0.4	-	-	-	-	-	-	-
GRAND FORKS, ND											
60 –	**Finance, insurance, and real estate**	164	162	8.4	1,157	1,183	20,812	21,856	25,554	26,274	8.7
6000	Depository institutions	27	33	8.0	452	496	20,274	21,677	9,840	11,010	8.4
6020	Commercial banks	16	17	6.6	378	391	21,471	22,322	8,717	8,933	8.9
6100	Nondepository institutions	9	6	9.4	87	72	27,862	42,167	2,410	1,779	11.3
6140	Personal credit institutions	6	2	11.8	18	-	16,000	-	283	-	-
6200	Security and commodity brokers	12	8	9.4	40	41	50,900	50,049	2,076	2,292	12.2
6210	Security brokers and dealers	8	5	8.2	-	32	-	55,625	-	2,111	-
6300	Insurance carriers	15	13	10.4	136	131	25,265	25,924	3,448	3,580	6.0
6330	Fire, marine, and casualty insurance	6	7	11.7	71	73	20,451	22,301	1,610	1,831	14.3
6400	Insurance agents, brokers, and service	43	45	7.6	141	155	23,234	19,277	3,056	3,209	9.6
6500	Real estate	53	54	9.3	290	281	12,014	12,327	4,415	4,217	13.0
6510	Real estate operators and lessors	24	26	8.5	137	123	8,438	10,049	1,286	1,303	8.6
6530	Real estate agents and managers	20	22	12.4	123	136	15,707	14,412	2,344	2,338	17.2
6700	Holding and other investment offices	4	3	4.5	-	7	-	24,000	-	187	1.9
GRANT, ND											
60 –	**Finance, insurance, and real estate**	8	8	0.4	41	47	16,683	15,319	751	804	0.3
6000	Depository institutions	3	3	0.7	27	34	20,444	17,176	617	662	0.5
6020	Commercial banks	3	3	1.2	27	34	20,444	17,176	617	662	0.7
GRIGGS, ND											
60 –	**Finance, insurance, and real estate**	7	9	0.5	63	93	27,873	24,602	1,491	1,852	0.6
6000	Depository institutions	4	4	1.0	53	82	30,717	25,854	1,376	1,714	1.3
6020	Commercial banks	4	4	1.5	53	82	30,717	25,854	1,376	1,714	1.7
HETTINGER, ND											
60 –	**Finance, insurance, and real estate**	15	16	0.8	56	-	15,643	-	960	-	-
6020	Commercial banks	3	3	1.2	33	-	17,939	-	657	-	-
6400	Insurance agents, brokers, and service	7	8	1.3	10	8	8,000	9,500	85	91	0.3
6500	Real estate	3	3	0.5	5	-	4,800	-	42	-	-
KIDDER, ND											
60 –	**Finance, insurance, and real estate**	9	9	0.5	38	39	18,947	19,179	812	833	0.3
6400	Insurance agents, brokers, and service	4	4	0.7	7	8	10,286	10,500	87	93	0.3
LA MOURE, ND											
60 –	**Finance, insurance, and real estate**	17	17	0.9	92	104	17,391	17,577	1,768	1,781	0.6
6000	Depository institutions	8	8	1.9	67	75	18,567	17,920	1,432	1,415	1.1
6020	Commercial banks	5	5	1.9	49	57	17,224	17,404	976	1,060	1.1
6060	Credit unions	3	3	3.3	18	18	22,222	19,556	456	355	4.2

Source: County Business Patterns, 1992/93, CBP-92/93-1, U.S. Department of Commerce, Washington, D.C., April 1995. SIC categories for which data were suppressed or not available for both 1992 and 1993 are *not* displayed. The employment columns represent mid-March employment in the year. Pay per employee is calculated by dividing 1st Quarter payroll, annualized, by mid-March employment. The columns headed "% State" show the county's percentage of the state total for the SIC in 1993; for example, 0.9% for SIC 6030 means that the county had 0.9 percent of the state's total establishments (or payroll) in SIC 6030 in 1993. A dash (-) is used to indicate that data are not available or cannot be calculated; *nec* means not elsewhere classified.

Continued on next page.

SIC	Industry	No. Establishments			Employment		Pay / Employee		Annual Payroll ($ 000)		
		1992	1993	% State	1992	1993	1992	1993	1992	1993	% State
LA MOURE, ND - [continued]											
6400	Insurance agents, brokers, and service	4	4	0.7	-	11	-	5,091	-	57	0.2
6500	Real estate	3	3	0.5	4	-	3,000	-	12	-	-
6510	Real estate operators and lessors	3	3	1.0	4	-	3,000	-	12	-	-
LOGAN, ND											
60–	**Finance, insurance, and real estate**	7	6	0.3	-	30	-	15,333	-	669	0.2
6000	Depository institutions	3	3	0.7	26	26	20,308	17,077	628	641	0.5
6500	Real estate	3	2	0.3	10	-	5,200	-	54	-	-
MCHENRY, ND											
60–	**Finance, insurance, and real estate**	22	21	1.1	71	75	15,099	13,333	1,203	1,112	0.4
6000	Depository institutions	8	8	1.9	49	-	18,122	-	987	-	-
6020	Commercial banks	7	7	2.7	-	45	-	17,067	-	899	0.9
6400	Insurance agents, brokers, and service	6	5	0.8	-	14	-	6,000	-	104	0.3
6500	Real estate	6	7	1.2	9	9	4,889	5,778	48	60	0.2
MCINTOSH, ND											
60–	**Finance, insurance, and real estate**	13	13	0.7	61	59	15,541	15,729	1,047	1,024	0.3
6400	Insurance agents, brokers, and service	4	4	0.7	9	7	3,556	6,286	28	36	0.1
6500	Real estate	3	3	0.5	5	5	4,800	6,400	30	28	0.1
MCKENZIE, ND											
60–	**Finance, insurance, and real estate**	10	9	0.5	69	70	19,942	20,914	1,319	1,467	0.5
6000	Depository institutions	5	5	1.2	59	61	20,814	22,426	1,195	1,359	1.0
MCLEAN, ND											
60–	**Finance, insurance, and real estate**	21	25	1.3	111	134	17,261	15,075	2,173	2,241	0.7
6000	Depository institutions	9	8	1.9	89	82	18,966	18,878	1,938	1,733	1.3
6020	Commercial banks	6	5	1.9	77	68	20,260	19,941	1,797	1,545	1.5
6300	Insurance carriers	3	2	1.6	10	-	7,200	-	76	-	-
6330	Fire, marine, and casualty insurance	3	2	3.3	10	-	7,200	-	76	-	-
6400	Insurance agents, brokers, and service	4	9	1.5	6	17	19,333	9,176	110	142	0.4
6500	Real estate	5	5	0.9	6	-	6,667	-	49	-	-
6510	Real estate operators and lessors	4	4	1.3	-	16	-	3,750	-	60	0.4
MERCER, ND											
60–	**Finance, insurance, and real estate**	19	20	1.0	88	94	17,318	15,915	1,766	1,632	0.5
6000	Depository institutions	7	7	1.7	70	74	18,971	17,243	1,538	1,380	1.1
6400	Insurance agents, brokers, and service	6	7	1.2	8	9	6,500	6,667	89	106	0.3
MORTON, ND											
60–	**Finance, insurance, and real estate**	46	43	2.2	257	265	17,261	21,328	4,762	5,265	1.8
6000	Depository institutions	12	13	3.2	118	130	20,373	24,923	2,616	3,052	2.3
6020	Commercial banks	6	7	2.7	98	110	21,102	25,891	2,271	2,666	2.7
6400	Insurance agents, brokers, and service	15	16	2.7	-	51	-	7,765	-	434	1.3
6500	Real estate	12	10	1.7	37	-	5,730	-	311	-	-
6510	Real estate operators and lessors	9	7	2.3	27	10	4,148	10,800	194	129	0.9
MOUNTRAIL, ND											
60–	**Finance, insurance, and real estate**	18	18	0.9	104	111	16,500	19,207	1,900	2,319	0.8
6000	Depository institutions	5	5	1.2	47	-	22,468	-	1,129	-	-
6020	Commercial banks	4	4	1.5	-	39	-	28,205	-	1,101	1.1
6400	Insurance agents, brokers, and service	6	8	1.3	10	14	11,600	10,286	164	198	0.6
NELSON, ND											
60–	**Finance, insurance, and real estate**	20	23	1.2	64	64	22,375	17,312	2,050	1,562	0.5
6020	Commercial banks	6	6	2.3	47	47	28,596	21,362	1,946	1,427	1.4

Source: County Business Patterns, 1992/93, CBP-92/93-1, U.S. Department of Commerce, Washington, D.C., April 1995. SIC categories for which data were suppressed or not available for both 1992 and 1993 are *not* displayed. The employment columns represent mid-March employment in the year. Pay per employee is calculated by dividing 1st Quarter payroll, annualized, by mid-March employment. The columns headed "% State" show the county's percentage of the state total for the SIC in 1993; for example, 0.9% for SIC 6030 means that the county had 0.9 percent of the state's total establishments (or payroll) in SIC 6030 in 1993. A dash (-) is used to indicate that data are not available or cannot be calculated; *nec* means not elsewhere classified.

Continued on next page.

SIC	Industry	No. Establishments			Employment		Pay / Employee		Annual Payroll ($ 000)		
		1992	1993	% State	1992	1993	1992	1993	1992	1993	% State
NELSON, ND - [continued]											
6400	Insurance agents, brokers, and service	4	5	0.8	6	6	5,333	6,000	36	51	0.2
6500	Real estate	6	8	1.4	6	7	2,667	3,429	24	37	0.1
6510	Real estate operators and lessors	4	5	1.6	6	7	2,667	3,429	19	28	0.2
OLIVER, ND											
60 –	**Finance, insurance, and real estate**	2	3	0.2	-	-	-	-	-	-	-
PEMBINA, ND											
60 –	**Finance, insurance, and real estate**	28	27	1.4	112	117	20,929	22,803	2,481	2,642	0.9
6000	Depository institutions	8	9	2.2	77	86	22,234	24,047	1,876	2,110	1.6
6400	Insurance agents, brokers, and service	7	9	1.5	12	17	23,333	19,765	294	341	1.0
6500	Real estate	6	7	1.2	5	-	9,600	-	56	-	-
6553	Cemetery subdividers and developers	3	3	8.1	-	-	-	-	8	9	1.9
PIERCE, ND											
60 –	**Finance, insurance, and real estate**	14	15	0.8	68	78	17,765	18,667	1,351	1,569	0.5
6000	Depository institutions	3	3	0.7	-	30	-	21,867	-	675	0.5
6400	Insurance agents, brokers, and service	4	4	0.7	9	9	9,778	9,778	90	87	0.3
6500	Real estate	5	5	0.9	3	4	12,000	8,000	41	41	0.1
RAMSEY, ND											
60 –	**Finance, insurance, and real estate**	34	38	2.0	195	243	18,831	17,169	3,895	4,462	1.5
6000	Depository institutions	11	11	2.7	127	138	20,661	20,986	2,772	3,093	2.4
6020	Commercial banks	8	8	3.1	100	106	21,640	21,925	2,294	2,504	2.5
6400	Insurance agents, brokers, and service	10	11	1.8	27	30	16,148	15,733	450	529	1.6
6500	Real estate	9	11	1.9	26	63	6,615	5,397	179	403	1.2
6510	Real estate operators and lessors	6	10	3.3	15	-	4,000	-	61	-	-
RANSOM, ND											
60 –	**Finance, insurance, and real estate**	21	21	1.1	96	104	17,958	19,577	1,748	1,940	0.6
6000	Depository institutions	4	5	1.2	67	70	20,239	21,714	1,381	1,537	1.2
6400	Insurance agents, brokers, and service	8	9	1.5	12	17	9,000	8,706	109	145	0.4
RENVILLE, ND											
60 –	**Finance, insurance, and real estate**	11	13	0.7	-	28	-	13,857	-	403	0.1
6000	Depository institutions	4	5	1.2	-	21	-	14,667	-	319	0.2
6400	Insurance agents, brokers, and service	3	5	0.8	3	3	18,667	18,667	56	59	0.2
6500	Real estate	3	3	0.5	4	4	5,000	6,000	21	25	0.1
RICHLAND, ND											
60 –	**Finance, insurance, and real estate**	37	41	2.1	197	226	20,345	19,823	4,182	4,343	1.4
6000	Depository institutions	12	12	2.9	103	113	23,689	22,407	2,575	2,590	2.0
6020	Commercial banks	7	7	2.7	78	87	26,359	23,080	2,167	2,037	2.0
6400	Insurance agents, brokers, and service	7	10	1.7	15	17	22,933	17,176	357	305	0.9
6500	Real estate	13	15	2.6	57	76	8,982	9,000	551	719	2.2
6510	Real estate operators and lessors	3	8	2.6	7	64	11,429	7,750	90	509	3.4
6530	Real estate agents and managers	6	5	2.8	41	-	7,415	-	304	-	-
ROLETTE, ND											
60 –	**Finance, insurance, and real estate**	15	18	0.9	70	72	18,457	18,111	1,379	1,424	0.5
6000	Depository institutions	5	5	1.2	51	51	20,784	20,784	1,113	1,130	0.9
6400	Insurance agents, brokers, and service	4	7	1.2	10	-	17,600	-	183	-	-
6500	Real estate	4	4	0.7	8	-	5,500	-	48	-	-
SARGENT, ND											
60 –	**Finance, insurance, and real estate**	13	13	0.7	-	50	-	13,040	-	1,103	0.4
6400	Insurance agents, brokers, and service	5	5	0.8	6	-	10,000	-	63	-	-
6500	Real estate	3	3	0.5	4	-	3,000	-	13	-	-

Source: County Business Patterns, 1992/93, CBP-92/93-1, U.S. Department of Commerce, Washington, D.C., April 1995. SIC categories for which data were suppressed or not available for both 1992 and 1993 are *not* displayed. The employment columns represent mid-March employment in the year. Pay per employee is calculated by dividing 1st Quarter payroll, annualized, by mid-March employment. The columns headed "% State" show the county's percentage of the state total for the SIC in 1993; for example, 0.9% for SIC 6030 means that the county had 0.9 percent of the state's total establishments (or payroll) in SIC 6030 in 1993. A dash (-) is used to indicate that data are not available or cannot be calculated; *nec* means not elsewhere classified.

SIC	Industry	No. Establishments			Employment		Pay / Employee		Annual Payroll ($ 000)		
		1992	1993	% State	1992	1993	1992	1993	1992	1993	% State
SHERIDAN, ND											
60 –	**Finance, insurance, and real estate**	7	7	0.4	31	33	12,129	13,939	449	493	0.2
6500	Real estate	4	4	0.7	-	8	-	4,000	- -	32	0.1
SIOUX, ND											
60 –	**Finance, insurance, and real estate**	1	1	0.1	-	-	-	-	-	-	-
STARK, ND											
60 –	**Finance, insurance, and real estate**	65	75	3.9	263	271	21,293	19,100	5,745	5,596	1.9
6000	Depository institutions	10	10	2.4	140	137	22,886	19,679	3,447	3,029	2.3
6020	Commercial banks	6	6	2.3	105	102	24,229	18,941	2,795	2,287	2.3
6300	Insurance carriers	3	2	1.6	6	-	14,667	-	88	-	-
6400	Insurance agents, brokers, and service	23	28	4.7	39	47	15,385	12,766	606	672	2.0
6500	Real estate	22	28	4.8	56	56	9,429	8,357	587	605	1.9
6510	Real estate operators and lessors	9	11	3.6	34	-	7,647	-	292	-	-
6530	Real estate agents and managers	8	15	8.5	12	16	11,667	6,250	158	145	1.1
6540	Title abstract offices	3	2	4.3	8	-	13,000	-	113	-	-
STEELE, ND											
60 –	**Finance, insurance, and real estate**	9	9	0.5	37	39	16,324	15,179	855	884	0.3
6000	Depository institutions	3	3	0.7	27	28	18,815	17,143	666	690	0.5
6020	Commercial banks	3	3	1.2	27	28	18,815	17,143	666	690	0.7
6400	Insurance agents, brokers, and service	3	3	0.5	6	6	14,000	16,000	169	163	0.5
STUTSMAN, ND											
60 –	**Finance, insurance, and real estate**	57	63	3.3	349	384	22,476	23,135	8,447	9,027	3.0
6000	Depository institutions	10	10	2.4	159	154	20,704	21,870	3,466	3,532	2.7
6020	Commercial banks	7	7	2.7	99	92	21,131	21,913	2,180	2,057	2.1
6200	Security and commodity brokers	4	4	4.7	-	10	-	50,800	-	461	2.5
6300	Insurance carriers	6	6	4.8	56	58	21,643	26,345	1,239	1,426	2.4
6400	Insurance agents, brokers, and service	17	17	2.9	75	76	24,427	25,684	1,898	1,923	5.7
6500	Real estate	15	21	3.6	29	63	13,793	9,333	531	715	2.2
6530	Real estate agents and managers	6	7	4.0	12	23	15,333	10,435	208	242	1.8
TOWNER, ND											
60 –	**Finance, insurance, and real estate**	21	21	1.1	78	77	15,231	15,948	1,196	1,185	0.4
6000	Depository institutions	7	6	1.5	47	43	19,064	21,302	891	880	0.7
6300	Insurance carriers	3	1	0.8	4	-	12,000	-	48	-	-
6400	Insurance agents, brokers, and service	4	6	1.0	-	8	-	13,500	-	115	0.3
6500	Real estate	6	6	1.0	20	-	7,200	-	148	-	-
6510	Real estate operators and lessors	5	5	1.6	-	22	-	6,545	-	124	0.8
TRAILL, ND											
60 –	**Finance, insurance, and real estate**	33	34	1.8	137	139	19,942	19,971	2,703	2,857	1.0
6000	Depository institutions	7	8	1.9	81	87	20,938	19,724	1,787	1,936	1.5
6400	Insurance agents, brokers, and service	10	12	2.0	20	23	26,600	24,174	338	413	1.2
6500	Real estate	8	9	1.6	10	10	6,800	8,000	76	93	0.3
6510	Real estate operators and lessors	4	5	1.6	5	6	8,000	9,333	46	67	0.4
WALSH, ND											
60 –	**Finance, insurance, and real estate**	47	42	2.2	199	197	21,246	21,746	4,029	4,263	1.4
6000	Depository institutions	8	7	1.7	116	112	22,793	24,786	2,575	2,675	2.1
6400	Insurance agents, brokers, and service	14	15	2.5	22	24	19,273	15,667	388	424	1.3
6500	Real estate	17	12	2.1	24	23	5,500	6,783	121	161	0.5
6510	Real estate operators and lessors	12	7	2.3	17	-	4,706	-	66	-	-
6530	Real estate agents and managers	2	3	1.7	-	6	-	10,000	-	81	0.6

Source: County Business Patterns, 1992/93, CBP-92/93-1, U.S. Department of Commerce, Washington, D.C., April 1995. SIC categories for which data were suppressed or not available for both 1992 and 1993 are *not* displayed. The employment columns represent mid-March employment in the year. Pay per employee is calculated by dividing 1st Quarter payroll, annualized, by mid-March employment. The columns headed "% State" show the county's percentage of the state total for the SIC in 1993; for example, 0.9% for SIC 6030 means that the county had 0.9 percent of the state's total establishments (or payroll) in SIC 6030 in 1993. A dash (-) is used to indicate that data are not available or cannot be calculated; *nec* means not elsewhere classified.

SIC	Industry	No. Establishments			Employment		Pay / Employee		Annual Payroll ($ 000)		
		1992	1993	% State	1992	1993	1992	1993	1992	1993	% State
WARD, ND											
60 –	**Finance, insurance, and real estate**	149	152	7.9	917	903	19,459	20,483	18,183	19,447	6.5
6000	Depository institutions	23	25	6.1	428	434	21,738	21,207	9,306	9,476	7.3
6020	Commercial banks	9	9	3.5	304	305	24,092	22,636	7,175	6,969	7.0
6030	Savings institutions	5	6	10.0	54	51	15,778	20,235	935	1,106	5.1
6060	Credit unions	9	10	11.1	70	78	16,114	16,256	1,196	1,401	16.6
6100	Nondepository institutions	7	5	7.8	100	69	23,520	31,768	2,006	2,093	13.3
6140	Personal credit institutions	3	2	11.8	11	-	22,182	-	255	-	-
6200	Security and commodity brokers	9	13	15.3	23	34	39,826	32,118	969	1,449	7.7
6300	Insurance carriers	15	13	10.4	47	50	27,915	30,800	1,401	1,591	2.7
6400	Insurance agents, brokers, and service	45	44	7.4	111	113	16,180	16,743	1,979	1,972	5.9
6500	Real estate	44	46	7.9	197	190	10,071	12,421	2,382	2,683	8.2
6510	Real estate operators and lessors	20	22	7.2	68	-	8,059	-	648	-	-
6530	Real estate agents and managers	19	22	12.4	89	95	11,416	13,263	1,064	1,353	10.0
6700	Holding and other investment offices	6	6	9.0	11	13	16,364	16,615	1,064	183	1.9
6733	Trusts, n.e.c.	3	2	15.4	5	-	5,600	-	11	-	-
WELLS, ND											
60 –	**Finance, insurance, and real estate**	21	24	1.2	91	111	16,747	17,261	1,674	1,885	0.6
6000	Depository institutions	6	6	1.5	61	76	21,311	21,316	1,412	1,509	1.2
6500	Real estate	7	7	1.2	11	11	5,091	4,727	60	70	0.2
6510	Real estate operators and lessors	3	3	1.0	7	6	2,286	1,333	15	20	0.1
WILLIAMS, ND											
60 –	**Finance, insurance, and real estate**	54	63	3.3	380	401	17,758	18,683	6,657	7,043	2.3
6000	Depository institutions	11	11	2.7	222	213	19,369	22,535	4,310	4,668	3.6
6020	Commercial banks	5	5	1.9	161	154	19,677	23,091	3,172	3,400	3.4
6200	Security and commodity brokers	4	5	5.9	-	8	-	29,500	-	334	1.8
6210	Security brokers and dealers	3	5	8.2	-	8	-	29,500	-	334	-
6300	Insurance carriers	3	2	1.6	8	-	16,000	-	140	-	-
6400	Insurance agents, brokers, and service	14	20	3.4	50	64	17,520	15,188	988	979	2.9
6500	Real estate	18	21	3.6	76	101	10,211	10,139	592	639	2.0
6530	Real estate agents and managers	7	6	3.4	40	52	11,600	12,846	256	293	2.2
6700	Holding and other investment offices	3	3	4.5	5	3	11,200	6,667	41	84	0.9

Source: County Business Patterns, 1992/93, CBP-92/93-1, U.S. Department of Commerce, Washington, D.C., April 1995. SIC categories for which data were suppressed or not available for both 1992 and 1993 are *not* displayed. The employment columns represent mid-March employment in the year. Pay per employee is calculated by dividing 1st Quarter payroll, annualized, by mid-March employment. The columns headed "% State" show the county's percentage of the state total for the SIC in 1993; for example, 0.9% for SIC 6030 means that the county had 0.9 percent of the state's total establishments (or payroll) in SIC 6030 in 1993. A dash (-) is used to indicate that data are not available or cannot be calculated; *nec* means not elsewhere classified.

OHIO

SIC	Industry	No. Establishments			Employment		Pay / Employee		Annual Payroll ($ 000)		
		1992	1993	% State	1992	1993	1992	1993	1992	1993	% State
ADAMS, OH											
60 –	**Finance, insurance, and real estate**	32	29	0.1	141	142	18,014	17,268	2,473	2,559	0.0
6000	Depository institutions	10	10	0.2	101	105	19,564	18,019	1,910	1,973	0.1
6500	Real estate	6	6	0.1	5	6	9,600	9,333	56	60	0.0
ALLEN, OH											
60 –	**Finance, insurance, and real estate**	236	238	1.1	1,676	1,806	18,547	18,368	32,252	34,496	0.5
6000	Depository institutions	60	58	1.2	760	807	20,895	20,986	15,980	16,793	0.8
6020	Commercial banks	35	41	1.4	538	654	20,677	21,407	11,148	13,640	0.9
6030	Savings institutions	13	3	0.3	153	69	22,954	24,986	3,572	1,796	0.5
6060	Credit unions	12	14	1.8	69	84	18,029	14,429	1,260	1,357	1.4
6100	Nondepository institutions	18	15	1.1	61	107	27,213	14,804	1,769	1,607	0.3
6140	Personal credit institutions	14	11	1.6	51	96	25,961	12,833	1,395	1,215	0.7
6160	Mortgage bankers and brokers	4	4	0.8	10	11	33,600	32,000	374	392	0.2
6200	Security and commodity brokers	8	10	1.0	21	55	31,810	29,891	763	1,821	0.3
6210	Security brokers and dealers	4	6	1.2	9	22	62,667	65,455	642	1,606	0.3
6280	Security and commodity services	4	4	0.9	12	33	8,667	6,182	121	215	0.2
6300	Insurance carriers	19	15	0.8	216	211	21,056	22,616	4,503	4,540	0.2
6330	Fire, marine, and casualty insurance	11	8	0.9	105	97	21,638	20,907	2,483	2,270	0.2
6400	Insurance agents, brokers, and service	60	65	1.2	216	229	18,741	16,821	4,662	4,609	0.7
6500	Real estate	66	69	1.0	386	381	9,637	10,131	3,891	4,452	0.5
6510	Real estate operators and lessors	39	38	1.1	236	272	7,932	8,794	1,956	2,589	0.9
6530	Real estate agents and managers	22	24	0.8	117	75	11,009	13,227	1,394	1,297	0.3
6700	Holding and other investment offices	5	6	0.7	16	16	35,000	32,750	684	674	0.2
ASHLAND, OH											
60 –	**Finance, insurance, and real estate**	84	85	0.4	1,046	517	30,015	18,004	14,025	9,173	0.1
6000	Depository institutions	23	25	0.5	243	260	17,827	18,108	4,342	4,655	0.2
6020	Commercial banks	14	14	0.5	183	183	19,257	20,459	3,518	3,718	0.2
6030	Savings institutions	5	5	0.5	49	58	13,551	13,724	680	767	0.2
6060	Credit unions	4	6	0.8	11	19	13,091	8,842	144	170	0.2
6100	Nondepository institutions	7	6	0.4	-	31	-	25,548	-	883	0.2
6140	Personal credit institutions	4	2	0.3	11	-	17,818	-	218	-	-
6400	Insurance agents, brokers, and service	20	20	0.4	66	68	29,697	26,588	1,638	1,696	0.2
6500	Real estate	25	26	0.4	88	133	11,182	6,015	766	759	0.1
6510	Real estate operators and lessors	11	12	0.4	58	59	4,276	4,000	250	248	0.1
6530	Real estate agents and managers	9	10	0.3	19	22	34,947	9,455	402	327	0.1
6553	Cemetery subdividers and developers	4	3	1.0	9	-	6,667	-	101	-	-
ASHTABULA, OH											
60 –	**Finance, insurance, and real estate**	168	163	0.7	848	870	18,047	18,671	16,388	16,587	0.2
6000	Depository institutions	53	49	1.0	507	508	18,619	19,748	9,619	9,639	0.5
6020	Commercial banks	27	22	0.7	263	245	20,517	21,420	5,314	4,910	0.3
6030	Savings institutions	15	15	1.4	195	211	17,190	19,090	3,566	3,907	1.1
6060	Credit unions	11	12	1.5	49	52	14,122	14,538	739	822	0.9
6100	Nondepository institutions	7	5	0.4	-	31	-	14,968	-	504	0.1
6140	Personal credit institutions	5	4	0.6	20	-	17,400	-	395	-	-
6200	Security and commodity brokers	5	5	0.5	-	17	-	41,647	-	683	0.1
6300	Insurance carriers	8	5	0.3	56	52	19,643	17,692	1,411	890	0.0
6400	Insurance agents, brokers, and service	39	45	0.8	104	129	23,346	20,868	2,665	3,073	0.5
6500	Real estate	49	48	0.7	113	118	9,912	11,356	1,295	1,709	0.2
6510	Real estate operators and lessors	25	25	0.8	45	48	7,467	6,833	385	491	0.2

Source: County Business Patterns, 1992/93, CBP-92/93-1, U.S. Department of Commerce, Washington, D.C., April 1995. SIC categories for which data were suppressed or not available for both 1992 and 1993 are *not* displayed. The employment columns represent mid-March employment in the year. Pay per employee is calculated by dividing 1st Quarter payroll, annualized, by mid-March employment. The columns headed "% State" show the county's percentage of the state total for the SIC in 1993; for example, 0.9% for SIC 6030 means that the county had 0.9 percent of the state's total establishments (or payroll) in SIC 6030 in 1993. A dash (-) is used to indicate that data are not available or cannot be calculated; *nec* means not elsewhere classified.

Continued on next page.

SIC	Industry	No. Establishments			Employment		Pay / Employee		Annual Payroll ($ 000)		
		1992	1993	% State	1992	1993	1992	1993	1992	1993	% State
ASHTABULA, OH - [continued]											
6530	Real estate agents and managers	15	19	0.6	44	51	11,636	14,353	621	846	0.2
6700	Holding and other investment offices	7	6	0.7	22	15	7,091	5,867	166	89	0.0
6732	Educational, religious, etc. trusts	4	4	2.9	9	-	7,111	-	72	-	-
ATHENS, OH											
60 –	**Finance, insurance, and real estate**	87	91	0.4	541	534	16,584	17,903	9,599	10,290	0.1
6000	Depository institutions	25	25	0.5	342	328	16,655	18,915	5,873	6,193	0.3
6020	Commercial banks	20	21	0.7	284	286	16,592	18,797	4,863	5,332	0.4
6100	Nondepository institutions	2	3	0.2	-	7	-	22,286	-	212	0.0
6300	Insurance carriers	3	3	0.2	-	18	-	18,889	-	361	0.0
6400	Insurance agents, brokers, and service	18	17	0.3	71	75	23,775	21,333	1,912	2,002	0.3
6500	Real estate	32	36	0.5	76	85	9,158	10,306	852	1,127	0.1
6510	Real estate operators and lessors	25	26	0.8	70	70	9,257	9,771	761	817	0.3
6530	Real estate agents and managers	3	5	0.2	3	9	10,667	16,000	56	196	0.0
AUGLAIZE, OH											
60 –	**Finance, insurance, and real estate**	80	84	0.4	405	476	18,548	17,370	7,775	8,642	0.1
6000	Depository institutions	25	23	0.5	212	233	20,472	19,845	4,030	4,311	0.2
6020	Commercial banks	18	21	0.7	181	-	20,840	-	3,446	-	-
6300	Insurance carriers	8	7	0.4	-	44	-	19,273	-	1,070	0.1
6400	Insurance agents, brokers, and service	19	20	0.4	72	82	20,611	18,049	1,806	1,833	0.3
6500	Real estate	19	25	0.4	48	57	6,500	7,509	388	557	0.1
6510	Real estate operators and lessors	5	6	0.2	12	14	5,333	6,857	96	108	0.0
6530	Real estate agents and managers	7	10	0.3	14	22	7,143	9,455	103	322	0.1
6553	Cemetery subdividers and developers	5	6	1.9	15	19	6,400	5,684	126	116	0.3
BELMONT, OH											
60 –	**Finance, insurance, and real estate**	125	133	0.6	749	1,173	17,672	16,477	13,441	20,679	0.3
6000	Depository institutions	33	42	0.9	427	638	19,354	17,317	8,108	11,520	0.6
6020	Commercial banks	22	29	1.0	299	502	19,679	17,673	5,622	8,952	0.6
6100	Nondepository institutions	5	3	0.2	-	23	-	11,130	-	264	0.1
6140	Personal credit institutions	4	2	0.3	12	-	26,000	-	324	-	-
6300	Insurance carriers	10	11	0.6	56	219	24,429	19,525	1,333	4,626	0.2
6400	Insurance agents, brokers, and service	42	40	0.8	110	104	16,000	16,423	2,032	1,997	0.3
6500	Real estate	33	34	0.5	138	182	10,551	10,901	1,563	2,207	0.2
6510	Real estate operators and lessors	17	17	0.5	61	94	13,443	13,362	877	1,387	0.5
6530	Real estate agents and managers	10	12	0.4	54	67	5,926	6,627	363	508	0.1
6553	Cemetery subdividers and developers	4	5	1.6	21	21	14,286	13,524	307	312	0.9
BROWN, OH											
60 –	**Finance, insurance, and real estate**	41	41	0.2	396	376	15,717	15,830	6,765	6,453	0.1
6000	Depository institutions	16	16	0.3	154	280	15,636	16,943	2,610	4,912	0.2
6400	Insurance agents, brokers, and service	9	9	0.2	28	-	14,857	-	607	-	-
6500	Real estate	13	14	0.2	-	55	-	11,127	-	735	0.1
6510	Real estate operators and lessors	5	7	0.2	10	16	5,200	10,000	51	155	0.1
6530	Real estate agents and managers	6	6	0.2	32	-	10,000	-	435	-	-
BUTLER, OH											
60 –	**Finance, insurance, and real estate**	480	477	2.1	6,546	6,771	26,576	24,357	183,292	187,754	2.6
6000	Depository institutions	112	113	2.3	1,364	1,395	21,994	20,568	28,490	29,470	1.5
6020	Commercial banks	65	69	2.3	873	983	21,347	22,128	18,010	22,014	1.5
6030	Savings institutions	27	21	2.0	398	249	24,894	18,378	8,512	5,104	1.5
6100	Nondepository institutions	29	25	1.8	186	248	23,849	20,032	4,936	5,235	1.0
6140	Personal credit institutions	23	17	2.5	119	110	21,244	15,745	2,568	1,572	0.9
6150	Business credit institutions	2	4	3.0	-	69	-	20,638	-	1,719	1.6
6160	Mortgage bankers and brokers	3	4	0.8	61	69	28,984	26,261	2,101	1,944	0.9
6200	Security and commodity brokers	15	14	1.4	24	16	14,167	19,000	459	363	0.1
6210	Security brokers and dealers	7	7	1.4	16	10	12,250	21,600	210	277	0.1

Source: County Business Patterns, 1992/93, CBP-92/93-1, U.S. Department of Commerce, Washington, D.C., April 1995. SIC categories for which data were suppressed or not available for both 1992 and 1993 are *not* displayed. The employment columns represent mid-March employment in the year. Pay per employee is calculated by dividing 1st Quarter payroll, annualized, by mid-March employment. The columns headed "% State" show the county's percentage of the state total for the SIC in 1993; for example, 0.9% for SIC 6030 means that the county had 0.9 percent of the state's total establishments (or payroll) in SIC 6030 in 1993. A dash (-) is used to indicate that data are not available or cannot be calculated; *nec* means not elsewhere classified.

Continued on next page.

SIC	Industry	No. Establishments			Employment		Pay / Employee		Annual Payroll ($ 000)		
		1992	1993	% State	1992	1993	1992	1993	1992	1993	% State
BUTLER, OH - [continued]											
6280	Security and commodity services	8	7	1.5	8	6	18,000	14,667	249	86	0.1
6300	Insurance carriers	48	39	2.0	3,918	3,824	30,077	27,367	127,734	124,294	5.9
6310	Life insurance	10	6	1.1	372	-	33,000	-	12,287	-	
6400	Insurance agents, brokers, and service	111	121	2.3	342	406	22,971	27,596	8,783	11,415	1.7
6500	Real estate	148	150	2.1	615	684	14,901	16,158	9,821	12,394	1.3
6510	Real estate operators and lessors	60	61	1.8	187	337	11,465	14,849	2,229	5,448	1.9
6530	Real estate agents and managers	55	67	2.2	240	182	15,483	17,077	3,752	4,125	0.8
6552	Subdividers and developers, n.e.c.	11	13	5.4	75	107	17,707	17,757	1,585	1,357	2.3
6553	Cemetery subdividers and developers	7	7	2.2	47	41	17,191	13,854	766	704	2.0
6700	Holding and other investment offices	17	15	1.8	97	198	44,619	20,465	3,069	4,583	1.3
6710	Holding offices	6	7	2.4	66	160	54,424	20,000	2,484	3,445	1.3
CARROLL, OH											
60 –	**Finance, insurance, and real estate**	28	26	0.1	96	102	15,542	15,882	1,498	1,622	0.0
6000	Depository institutions	10	9	0.2	-	65	-	16,554	-	1,086	0.1
6020	Commercial banks	10	9	0.3	-	65	-	16,554	-	1,086	0.1
6400	Insurance agents, brokers, and service	6	6	0.1	12	13	16,667	16,308	222	241	0.0
6500	Real estate	8	6	0.1	11	12	6,545	7,000	102	63	0.0
6510	Real estate operators and lessors	4	3	0.1	5	3	7,200	8,000	27	29	0.0
6530	Real estate agents and managers	4	3	0.1	6	9	6,000	6,667	75	34	0.0
CHAMPAIGN, OH											
60 –	**Finance, insurance, and real estate**	50	55	0.2	351	374	19,772	17,508	7,024	6,852	0.1
6000	Depository institutions	21	21	0.4	254	270	22,630	19,407	5,691	5,422	0.3
6400	Insurance agents, brokers, and service	14	13	0.2	48	51	14,250	13,020	687	757	0.1
6500	Real estate	12	16	0.2	-	29	-	6,069	-	221	0.0
6510	Real estate operators and lessors	7	10	0.3	13	21	5,538	6,857	87	174	0.1
CLARK, OH											
60 –	**Finance, insurance, and real estate**	198	198	0.9	1,935	1,472	20,041	19,636	41,293	28,934	0.4
6000	Depository institutions	45	48	1.0	530	602	18,143	18,698	10,304	11,806	0.6
6020	Commercial banks	30	30	1.0	431	455	17,633	18,514	8,122	8,835	0.6
6030	Savings institutions	6	5	0.5	64	63	20,062	17,905	1,434	1,323	0.4
6060	Credit unions	9	13	1.7	35	84	20,914	20,286	748	1,648	1.7
6100	Nondepository institutions	20	12	0.9	545	254	14,429	15,150	9,590	2,429	0.5
6160	Mortgage bankers and brokers	6	4	0.8	457	189	12,788	15,661	7,727	1,582	0.8
6300	Insurance carriers	16	13	0.7	253	158	26,482	32,506	7,760	4,924	0.2
6310	Life insurance	4	4	0.7	109	53	21,835	28,075	2,440	1,348	0.2
6400	Insurance agents, brokers, and service	50	52	1.0	341	196	28,422	22,082	8,527	4,853	0.7
6500	Real estate	54	60	0.8	228	231	15,351	12,502	3,713	3,491	0.4
6510	Real estate operators and lessors	24	29	0.9	105	123	9,905	9,138	1,098	1,261	0.4
6530	Real estate agents and managers	19	23	0.8	49	61	16,653	17,049	859	1,292	0.3
CLERMONT, OH											
60 –	**Finance, insurance, and real estate**	181	176	0.8	1,680	1,709	22,010	23,871	39,314	42,180	0.6
6000	Depository institutions	44	45	0.9	425	512	19,529	21,633	9,847	10,666	0.5
6020	Commercial banks	30	30	1.0	313	382	19,157	22,094	7,137	7,781	0.5
6030	Savings institutions	13	12	1.1	-	120	-	20,933	-	2,761	0.8
6060	Credit unions	1	3	0.4	-	10	-	12,400	-	124	0.1
6100	Nondepository institutions	14	9	0.7	157	190	21,987	14,737	3,735	3,339	0.7
6300	Insurance carriers	17	14	0.7	432	544	29,157	30,794	12,728	16,943	0.8
6400	Insurance agents, brokers, and service	33	36	0.7	246	103	19,089	18,408	4,816	2,023	0.3
6500	Real estate	66	67	0.9	350	319	14,000	13,743	5,122	5,107	0.5
6510	Real estate operators and lessors	30	30	0.9	214	191	9,570	11,016	2,447	2,414	0.9
6530	Real estate agents and managers	27	27	0.9	78	-	14,821	-	1,110	-	
6552	Subdividers and developers, n.e.c.	6	6	2.5	-	22	-	29,273	-	581	1.0

Source: County Business Patterns, 1992/93, CBP-92/93-1, U.S. Department of Commerce, Washington, D.C., April 1995. SIC categories for which data were suppressed or not available for both 1992 and 1993 are not displayed. The employment columns represent mid-March employment in the year. Pay per employee is calculated by dividing 1st Quarter payroll, annualized, by mid-March employment. The columns headed "% State" show the county's percentage of the state total for the SIC in 1993; for example, 0.9% for SIC 6030 means that the county had 0.9 percent of the state's total establishments (or payroll) in SIC 6030 in 1993. A dash (-) is used to indicate that data are not available or cannot be calculated; nec means not elsewhere classified.

SIC	Industry	No. Establishments			Employment		Pay / Employee		Annual Payroll ($ 000)		
		1992	1993	% State	1992	1993	1992	1993	1992	1993	% State
CLINTON, OH											
60 –	**Finance, insurance, and real estate**	66	66	0.3	577	512	19,390	21,039	12,238	12,257	0.2
6000	Depository institutions	19	18	0.4	258	272	21,163	23,647	5,652	6,356	0.3
6020	Commercial banks	13	12	0.4	183	192	22,448	24,354	3,906	4,355	0.3
6100	Nondepository institutions	4	4	0.3	108	122	22,074	19,377	1,983	2,393	0.5
6200	Security and commodity brokers	2	3	0.3	-	3	-	17,333	-	67	0.0
6400	Insurance agents, brokers, and service	13	12	0.2	-	59	-	21,966	-	1,376	0.2
6500	Real estate	25	25	0.4	154	54	9,636	10,370	1,665	795	0.1
6510	Real estate operators and lessors	8	8	0.2	17	16	8,706	10,250	173	184	0.1
6530	Real estate agents and managers	11	10	0.3	126	21	10,095	13,143	1,410	447	0.1
6553	Cemetery subdividers and developers	5	6	1.9	10	-	4,400	-	62	-	-
COLUMBIANA, OH											
60 –	**Finance, insurance, and real estate**	168	176	0.8	1,297	1,222	18,079	16,926	23,358	21,703	0.3
6000	Depository institutions	58	59	1.2	671	747	16,984	16,734	12,060	13,001	0.7
6020	Commercial banks	40	41	1.4	512	576	17,305	17,097	9,324	10,198	0.7
6030	Savings institutions	15	14	1.3	154	156	16,052	15,897	2,672	2,631	0.8
6060	Credit unions	3	4	0.5	5	15	12,800	11,467	64	172	0.2
6100	Nondepository institutions	8	7	0.5	-	56	-	11,857	-	693	0.1
6140	Personal credit institutions	6	4	0.6	31	-	17,806	-	575	-	-
6300	Insurance carriers	12	12	0.6	104	103	21,231	21,165	2,340	2,267	0.1
6400	Insurance agents, brokers, and service	41	47	0.9	150	159	17,013	18,289	2,821	2,931	0.4
6500	Real estate	41	45	0.6	191	137	11,037	9,431	2,321	1,536	0.2
6510	Real estate operators and lessors	15	16	0.5	136	68	10,912	6,294	1,552	531	0.2
6530	Real estate agents and managers	15	20	0.7	30	47	9,867	11,489	376	651	0.1
6553	Cemetery subdividers and developers	7	8	2.5	18	-	13,778	-	293	-	-
6700	Holding and other investment offices	5	2	0.2	130	-	27,292	-	2,123	-	-
COSHOCTON, OH											
60 –	**Finance, insurance, and real estate**	48	48	0.2	267	294	16,644	17,224	4,950	5,021	0.1
6000	Depository institutions	12	12	0.2	152	168	16,368	17,857	2,549	2,900	0.1
6020	Commercial banks	7	8	0.3	-	139	-	18,273	-	2,371	0.2
6100	Nondepository institutions	5	6	0.4	19	-	20,000	-	382	-	-
6140	Personal credit institutions	4	5	0.7	-	27	-	12,296	-	348	0.2
6200	Security and commodity brokers	5	4	0.4	12	9	23,333	32,444	299	286	0.0
6300	Insurance carriers	4	2	0.1	41	-	18,049	-	895	-	-
6400	Insurance agents, brokers, and service	11	13	0.2	29	42	15,586	14,476	462	654	0.1
6500	Real estate	9	10	0.1	-	14	-	9,429	-	136	0.0
6510	Real estate operators and lessors	4	5	0.2	5	6	8,000	14,000	41	78	0.0
6530	Real estate agents and managers	3	3	0.1	4	-	7,000	-	29	-	-
CRAWFORD, OH											
60 –	**Finance, insurance, and real estate**	79	82	0.4	576	451	19,035	18,687	11,221	8,988	0.1
6000	Depository institutions	23	24	0.5	304	294	19,132	18,789	5,896	5,930	0.3
6020	Commercial banks	13	13	0.4	173	171	18,405	18,386	3,305	3,462	0.2
6100	Nondepository institutions	4	3	0.2	-	21	-	12,762	-	210	0.0
6140	Personal credit institutions	4	3	0.4	-	21	-	12,762	-	210	0.1
6400	Insurance agents, brokers, and service	24	28	0.5	61	58	19,016	18,966	1,166	1,262	0.2
6500	Real estate	18	19	0.3	46	47	6,783	8,170	405	423	0.0
6510	Real estate operators and lessors	10	11	0.3	20	25	6,600	7,360	121	184	0.1
6530	Real estate agents and managers	5	5	0.2	16	11	6,500	10,545	175	129	0.0
6553	Cemetery subdividers and developers	3	3	1.0	10	11	7,600	7,636	109	110	0.3
CUYAHOGA, OH											
60 –	**Finance, insurance, and real estate**	3,647	3,654	16.2	60,635	54,587	29,810	28,918	1,709,941	1,658,717	22.9
6000	Depository institutions	704	668	13.7	22,637	14,401	29,121	28,819	542,466	411,032	20.6
6020	Commercial banks	317	259	8.8	17,127	9,287	30,406	29,776	408,106	278,567	18.7
6030	Savings institutions	221	205	19.4	3,885	3,318	24,872	28,239	93,448	87,943	25.8
6060	Credit unions	119	153	19.6	577	766	13,608	14,277	7,816	11,528	12.1

Source: County Business Patterns, 1992/93, CBP-92/93-1, U.S. Department of Commerce, Washington, D.C., April 1995. SIC categories for which data were suppressed or not available for both 1992 and 1993 are *not* displayed. The employment columns represent mid-March employment in the year. Pay per employee is calculated by dividing 1st Quarter payroll, annualized, by mid-March employment. The columns headed "% State" show the county's percentage of the state total for the SIC in 1993; for example, 0.9% for SIC 6030 means that the county had 0.9 percent of the state's total establishments (or payroll) in SIC 6030 in 1993. A dash (-) is used to indicate that data are not available or cannot be calculated; *nec* means not elsewhere classified.

Continued on next page.

SIC	Industry	No. Establishments			Employment		Pay / Employee		Annual Payroll ($ 000)		
		1992	1993	% State	1992	1993	1992	1993	1992	1993	% State
CUYAHOGA, OH - [continued]											
6100	Nondepository institutions	261	235	17.2	2,261	2,813	28,858	26,082	69,607	85,586	17.1
6140	Personal credit institutions	140	94	13.9	1,073	1,109	23,676	17,385	25,071	18,597	10.9
6150	Business credit institutions	28	38	28.4	118	-	48,508	-	4,624	-	-
6160	Mortgage bankers and brokers	89	100	20.2	1,011	1,236	32,233	28,382	38,272	47,719	22.7
6200	Security and commodity brokers	192	202	20.2	2,166	2,389	72,981	73,991	154,822	170,610	28.3
6210	Security brokers and dealers	91	86	16.6	1,813	1,837	74,180	82,903	132,496	141,337	30.7
6300	Insurance carriers	444	368	18.9	13,064	12,919	33,814	32,424	445,343	455,730	21.6
6310	Life insurance	142	125	22.5	3,644	3,266	30,639	29,522	108,294	91,046	16.1
6321	Accident and health insurance	9	10	16.9	343	906	19,965	24,415	4,832	23,335	15.3
6324	Hospital and medical service plans	9	11	19.3	2,062	2,075	34,033	32,118	69,536	74,032	45.2
6330	Fire, marine, and casualty insurance	168	157	17.9	5,623	5,413	38,647	37,114	214,261	229,502	20.7
6350	Surety insurance	5	4	23.5	25	-	29,280	-	743	-	-
6360	Title insurance	21	11	15.1	686	593	25,510	25,875	19,350	18,835	50.5
6370	Pension, health, and welfare funds	82	48	16.1	655	636	25,576	25,843	26,606	17,527	23.0
6390	Insurance carriers, n.e.c.	4	2	28.6	14	-	23,143	-	1,198	-	-
6400	Insurance agents, brokers, and service	706	763	14.4	4,272	5,520	32,691	29,808	143,227	176,110	25.9
6500	Real estate	1,197	1,266	17.8	14,106	14,387	18,437	17,859	268,423	280,976	30.1
6510	Real estate operators and lessors	547	608	18.4	3,682	5,630	14,935	15,231	53,709	90,179	32.1
6530	Real estate agents and managers	479	561	18.7	8,731	7,606	18,789	18,282	170,280	151,791	30.4
6540	Title abstract offices	22	30	14.9	323	450	25,139	25,387	9,559	14,516	25.4
6552	Subdividers and developers, n.e.c.	41	35	14.5	437	372	36,320	36,968	16,195	15,990	27.6
6553	Cemetery subdividers and developers	20	23	7.3	285	306	20,435	21,333	7,112	8,074	22.9
6700	Holding and other investment offices	135	143	17.6	1,367	1,337	41,419	35,031	60,251	51,511	14.1
6710	Holding offices	50	54	18.7	798	711	51,078	40,056	44,370	31,819	12.0
6720	Investment offices	6	3	16.7	44	-	50,636	-	1,940	-	-
6732	Educational, religious, etc. trusts	20	24	17.4	215	294	12,577	17,524	2,567	5,268	24.3
6733	Trusts, n.e.c.	22	24	13.3	97	99	37,485	35,515	4,295	3,333	20.2
6794	Patent owners and lessors	5	8	15.7	129	-	33,395	-	3,991	-	-
6798	Real estate investment trusts	3	5	33.3	-	81	-	39,012	-	3,587	31.2
6799	Investors, n.e.c.	23	23	22.1	-	70	-	34,400	-	3,805	12.1
DARKE, OH											
60 -	**Finance, insurance, and real estate**	98	96	0.4	607	666	19,947	16,961	11,891	12,051	0.2
6000	Depository institutions	30	30	0.6	372	381	20,602	18,121	7,433	6,783	0.3
6020	Commercial banks	24	25	0.8	312	330	21,346	18,327	6,386	5,829	0.4
6100	Nondepository institutions	5	5	0.4	14	20	19,429	15,600	315	331	0.1
6200	Security and commodity brokers	4	5	0.5	-	21	-	17,524	-	593	0.1
6300	Insurance carriers	5	4	0.2	26	25	17,231	18,240	479	466	0.0
6400	Insurance agents, brokers, and service	33	34	0.6	147	171	18,803	15,041	2,668	3,120	0.5
6500	Real estate	19	18	0.3	-	48	-	14,250	-	758	0.1
6510	Real estate operators and lessors	4	6	0.2	8	-	16,500	-	165	-	-
6530	Real estate agents and managers	9	8	0.3	17	-	5,882	-	111	-	-
DEFIANCE, OH											
60 -	**Finance, insurance, and real estate**	68	65	0.3	499	490	22,389	22,702	10,756	11,640	0.2
6000	Depository institutions	19	20	0.4	332	330	21,494	21,939	6,831	7,468	0.4
6020	Commercial banks	12	13	0.4	185	179	23,092	19,218	3,765	3,676	0.2
6100	Nondepository institutions	3	3	0.2	-	19	-	15,158	-	286	0.1
6300	Insurance carriers	5	4	0.2	-	34	-	21,647	-	808	0.0
6400	Insurance agents, brokers, and service	17	18	0.3	68	68	22,824	27,353	1,625	1,811	0.3
6500	Real estate	20	16	0.2	-	28	-	12,143	-	417	0.0
6510	Real estate operators and lessors	7	4	0.1	14	-	7,714	-	132	-	-
6530	Real estate agents and managers	11	10	0.3	23	19	13,913	13,684	357	337	0.1
DELAWARE, OH											
60 -	**Finance, insurance, and real estate**	135	136	0.6	1,035	1,266	18,613	24,550	16,439	33,543	0.5
6000	Depository institutions	23	26	0.5	248	846	17,742	26,629	4,432	23,476	1.2
6020	Commercial banks	16	19	0.6	214	-	18,037	-	3,857	-	-

Source: County Business Patterns, 1992/93, CBP-92/93-1, U.S. Department of Commerce, Washington, D.C., April 1995. SIC categories for which data were suppressed or not available for both 1992 and 1993 are *not* displayed. The employment columns represent mid-March employment in the year. Pay per employee is calculated by dividing 1st Quarter payroll, annualized, by mid-March employment. The columns headed "% State" show the county's percentage of the state total for the SIC in 1993; for example, 0.9% for SIC 6030 means that the county had 0.9 percent of the state's total establishments (or payroll) in SIC 6030 in 1993. A dash (-) is used to indicate that data are not available or cannot be calculated; *nec* means not elsewhere classified.

Continued on next page.

SIC	Industry	No. Establishments			Employment		Pay / Employee		Annual Payroll ($ 000)		
		1992	1993	% State	1992	1993	1992	1993	1992	1993	% State
DELAWARE, OH - [continued]											
6030	Savings institutions	4	4	0.4	31	-	16,129	-	534	-	-
6060	Credit unions	3	3	0.4	3	3	13,333	13,333	41	44	0.0
6100	Nondepository institutions	6	8	0.6	-	36	-	34,556	-	1,510	0.3
6140	Personal credit institutions	3	3	0.4	10	16	19,600	14,750	194	277	0.2
6200	Security and commodity brokers	2	5	0.5	-	11	-	32,727	-	419	0.1
6300	Insurance carriers	17	8	0.4	335	85	19,176	9,976	3,502	894	0.0
6400	Insurance agents, brokers, and service	31	32	0.6	194	107	22,969	29,196	4,299	3,330	0.5
6500	Real estate	52	53	0.7	184	169	16,174	16,734	3,255	3,634	0.4
6510	Real estate operators and lessors	23	28	0.8	95	109	16,295	15,963	1,525	2,023	0.7
6530	Real estate agents and managers	20	20	0.7	51	48	17,098	19,667	1,197	1,335	0.3
6552	Subdividers and developers, n.e.c.	3	2	0.8	7	-	21,714	-	124	-	-
6700	Holding and other investment offices	4	4	0.5	-	12	-	12,333	-	280	0.1
ERIE, OH											
60 –	**Finance, insurance, and real estate**	158	168	0.7	910	974	20,980	19,076	19,088	19,464	0.3
6000	Depository institutions	31	33	0.7	380	420	20,032	19,495	7,410	7,671	0.4
6020	Commercial banks	22	24	0.8	342	356	20,538	19,764	6,824	6,488	0.4
6030	Savings institutions	6	4	0.4	33	28	16,727	17,857	545	460	0.1
6060	Credit unions	3	5	0.6	5	36	7,200	18,111	41	723	0.8
6100	Nondepository institutions	9	6	0.4	50	33	20,960	13,212	1,223	587	0.1
6200	Security and commodity brokers	7	9	0.9	26	30	52,154	34,533	1,116	1,162	0.2
6280	Security and commodity services	3	3	0.6	-	4	-	10,000	-	45	0.0
6300	Insurance carriers	18	13	0.7	115	114	25,426	26,561	2,657	2,696	0.1
6310	Life insurance	5	4	0.7	69	71	25,043	24,394	1,473	1,441	0.3
6400	Insurance agents, brokers, and service	37	44	0.8	124	129	23,710	20,713	3,044	3,493	0.5
6500	Real estate	51	56	0.8	193	200	14,176	13,680	3,093	3,290	0.4
6510	Real estate operators and lessors	25	28	0.8	73	91	12,000	12,088	945	1,155	0.4
6530	Real estate agents and managers	18	21	0.7	86	92	14,977	15,609	1,472	1,792	0.4
6552	Subdividers and developers, n.e.c.	2	3	1.2	-	4	-	17,000	-	178	0.3
6700	Holding and other investment offices	5	7	0.9	22	48	21,636	10,083	545	565	0.2
FAIRFIELD, OH											
60 –	**Finance, insurance, and real estate**	157	167	0.7	1,013	1,098	21,477	20,324	21,336	23,245	0.3
6000	Depository institutions	32	34	0.7	363	373	21,994	21,866	7,209	7,796	0.4
6020	Commercial banks	24	24	0.8	285	284	20,660	20,380	5,137	5,437	0.4
6030	Savings institutions	6	6	0.6	-	79	-	27,797	-	2,174	0.6
6060	Credit unions	2	4	0.5	-	10	-	17,200	-	185	0.2
6100	Nondepository institutions	10	10	0.7	-	60	-	25,600	-	2,364	0.5
6140	Personal credit institutions	7	5	0.7	30	-	18,133	-	556	-	-
6200	Security and commodity brokers	4	4	0.4	20	-	57,600	-	1,111	-	-
6210	Security brokers and dealers	4	4	0.8	20	-	57,600	-	1,111	-	-
6300	Insurance carriers	10	13	0.7	82	198	23,122	32,465	2,001	5,966	0.3
6310	Life insurance	3	3	0.5	63	-	20,762	-	1,316	-	-
6330	Fire, marine, and casualty insurance	5	8	0.9	-	136	-	36,000	-	4,526	0.4
6400	Insurance agents, brokers, and service	41	39	0.7	240	114	29,000	15,368	6,195	1,898	0.3
6500	Real estate	54	64	0.9	216	283	8,926	8,254	2,544	3,001	0.3
6510	Real estate operators and lessors	15	24	0.7	58	158	8,000	6,354	593	1,180	0.4
6530	Real estate agents and managers	20	28	0.9	66	73	14,424	15,671	1,199	1,464	0.3
6552	Subdividers and developers, n.e.c.	3	2	0.8	44	-	6,000	-	318	-	-
6553	Cemetery subdividers and developers	5	7	2.2	8	16	3,500	2,250	42	58	0.2
FAYETTE, OH											
60 –	**Finance, insurance, and real estate**	50	50	0.2	241	241	19,668	20,863	4,999	5,342	0.1
6000	Depository institutions	11	11	0.2	98	103	16,653	17,592	1,753	1,917	0.1
6100	Nondepository institutions	7	7	0.5	37	39	24,757	25,846	910	1,097	0.2
6200	Security and commodity brokers	3	3	0.3	10	-	29,200	-	351	-	-
6400	Insurance agents, brokers, and service	13	12	0.2	-	37	-	19,027	-	711	0.1

Source: County Business Patterns, 1992/93, CBP-92/93-1, U.S. Department of Commerce, Washington, D.C., April 1995. SIC categories for which data were suppressed or not available for both 1992 and 1993 are not displayed. The employment columns represent mid-March employment in the year. Pay per employee is calculated by dividing 1st Quarter payroll, annualized, by mid-March employment. The columns headed "% State" show the county's percentage of the state total for the SIC in 1993; for example, 0.9% for SIC 6030 means that the county had 0.9 percent of the state's total establishments (or payroll) in SIC 6030 in 1993. A dash (-) is used to indicate that data are not available or cannot be calculated; nec means not elsewhere classified.

Continued on next page.

SIC	Industry	No. Establishments			Employment		Pay / Employee		Annual Payroll ($ 000)		
		1992	1993	% State	1992	1993	1992	1993	1992	1993	% State
FAYETTE, OH - [continued]											
6500	Real estate	12	11	0.2	-	21	-	7,429	-	184	0.0
6510	Real estate operators and lessors	5	4	0.1	-	13	-	7,385	-	112	0.0
6530	Real estate agents and managers	6	6	0.2	7	-	7,429	-	61	-	-
FRANKLIN, OH											
60 –	**Finance, insurance, and real estate**	2,798	2,853	12.7	53,351	56,799	29,342	29,521	1,569,601	1,736,284	24.0
6000	Depository institutions	446	438	9.0	12,124	13,258	27,270	28,454	325,666	381,791	19.2
6020	Commercial banks	285	283	9.6	10,046	11,031	28,205	29,573	279,040	330,161	22.1
6030	Savings institutions	96	88	8.3	1,050	1,215	22,872	20,550	23,689	23,747	7.0
6060	Credit unions	46	50	6.4	536	-	17,739	-	9,284	-	-
6090	Functions closely related to banking	16	16	15.1	-	474	-	29,671	-	15,498	-
6100	Nondepository institutions	233	249	18.2	6,094	6,742	25,288	23,066	148,677	173,401	34.6
6140	Personal credit institutions	123	103	15.2	2,155	2,163	23,410	19,841	49,531	46,593	27.4
6150	Business credit institutions	27	34	25.4	2,578	2,683	22,216	19,168	51,381	52,480	48.0
6160	Mortgage bankers and brokers	80	111	22.4	1,335	1,896	34,457	32,259	47,256	74,324	35.4
6200	Security and commodity brokers	142	161	16.1	1,826	2,351	69,522	56,795	119,972	143,653	23.8
6210	Security brokers and dealers	79	86	16.6	1,573	1,677	75,911	65,589	111,047	113,687	24.7
6300	Insurance carriers	364	320	16.4	19,683	20,224	31,286	31,430	615,571	632,512	30.0
6310	Life insurance	91	85	15.3	5,591	5,725	31,607	33,854	178,792	183,342	32.5
6321	Accident and health insurance	20	17	28.8	423	1,803	27,376	31,809	11,729	54,655	35.8
6324	Hospital and medical service plans	12	15	26.3	1,594	833	36,866	28,447	56,081	23,833	14.5
6330	Fire, marine, and casualty insurance	147	134	15.3	11,265	10,738	31,006	30,660	346,573	337,997	30.6
6360	Title insurance	19	16	21.9	125	130	31,168	33,508	4,511	4,244	11.4
6370	Pension, health, and welfare funds	65	42	14.1	517	903	18,971	25,931	11,752	24,507	32.2
6400	Insurance agents, brokers, and service	557	586	11.0	3,469	3,646	32,986	32,845	111,411	116,614	17.2
6500	Real estate	928	973	13.6	8,900	8,617	18,969	18,674	179,698	181,419	19.4
6510	Real estate operators and lessors	395	443	13.4	3,660	2,544	15,577	15,571	60,069	43,387	15.4
6530	Real estate agents and managers	371	444	14.8	4,006	5,315	20,654	19,150	88,886	115,453	23.1
6540	Title abstract offices	24	28	13.9	228	271	23,351	23,882	5,811	8,331	14.6
6552	Subdividers and developers, n.e.c.	45	32	13.3	468	336	28,034	29,155	13,078	10,471	18.0
6553	Cemetery subdividers and developers	14	17	5.4	127	127	22,236	22,520	2,811	3,273	9.3
6700	Holding and other investment offices	115	113	13.9	1,085	1,800	43,064	48,122	60,512	99,119	27.1
6710	Holding offices	35	35	12.1	604	1,015	56,225	63,168	47,152	74,092	27.9
6720	Investment offices	11	6	33.3	31	15	30,323	22,400	1,357	328	10.4
6732	Educational, religious, etc. trusts	15	17	12.3	79	102	31,038	36,784	2,902	3,997	18.4
6733	Trusts, n.e.c.	26	23	12.8	113	65	13,274	16,000	1,392	1,043	6.3
6798	Real estate investment trusts	3	1	6.7	131	-	18,962	-	2,385	-	-
6799	Investors, n.e.c.	12	20	19.2	66	478	53,636	27,498	3,433	14,967	47.6
FULTON, OH											
60 –	**Finance, insurance, and real estate**	74	71	0.3	438	645	17,671	20,316	10,400	15,350	0.2
6000	Depository institutions	27	24	0.5	296	280	18,405	19,414	5,808	5,772	0.3
6020	Commercial banks	22	19	0.6	242	225	18,893	20,213	4,859	4,825	0.3
6030	Savings institutions	5	5	0.5	54	55	16,222	16,145	949	947	0.3
6100	Nondepository institutions	3	3	0.2	8	-	19,000	-	181	-	-
6400	Insurance agents, brokers, and service	26	24	0.5	84	72	19,143	18,778	1,632	1,655	0.2
6500	Real estate	11	13	0.2	40	54	6,100	8,000	254	466	0.0
6510	Real estate operators and lessors	3	4	0.1	16	-	3,750	-	68	-	-
6530	Real estate agents and managers	6	8	0.3	17	38	9,176	9,474	149	380	0.1
GALLIA, OH											
60 –	**Finance, insurance, and real estate**	44	50	0.2	289	293	18,256	17,543	5,971	6,448	0.1
6000	Depository institutions	10	10	0.2	183	180	17,486	16,867	3,699	3,896	0.2
6400	Insurance agents, brokers, and service	10	11	0.2	43	47	22,326	20,936	1,133	1,296	0.2

Source: County Business Patterns, 1992/93, CBP-92/93-1, U.S. Department of Commerce, Washington, D.C., April 1995. SIC categories for which data were suppressed or not available for both 1992 and 1993 are not displayed. The employment columns represent mid-March employment in the year. Pay per employee is calculated by dividing 1st Quarter payroll, annualized, by mid-March employment. The columns headed "% State" show the county's percentage of the state total for the SIC in 1993; for example, 0.9% for SIC 6030 means that the county had 0.9 percent of the state's total establishments (or payroll) in SIC 6030 in 1993. A dash (-) is used to indicate that data are not available or cannot be calculated; nec means not elsewhere classified.

Continued on next page.

SIC	Industry	No. Establishments			Employment		Pay / Employee		Annual Payroll ($ 000)		
		1992	1993	% State	1992	1993	1992	1993	1992	1993	% State
GALLIA, OH - [continued]											
6500	Real estate	17	20	0.3	38	36	17,263	14,444	634	586	0.1
6510	Real estate operators and lessors	11	11	0.3	26	24	16,154	14,667	392	361	0.1
6530	Real estate agents and managers	5	6	0.2	-	11	-	14,545	-	176	0.0
GEAUGA, OH											
60 –	**Finance, insurance, and real estate**	133	131	0.6	608	674	19,493	18,724	12,755	13,845	0.2
6000	Depository institutions	30	30	0.6	284	301	19,986	19,309	5,732	5,880	0.3
6020	Commercial banks	19	18	0.6	199	208	21,186	20,231	4,186	4,321	0.3
6100	Nondepository institutions	3	6	0.4	-	30	-	18,133	-	633	0.1
6160	Mortgage bankers and brokers	1	3	0.6	-	4	-	14,000	-	114	0.1
6200	Security and commodity brokers	4	4	0.4	-	14	-	14,571	-	250	0.0
6280	Security and commodity services	4	4	0.9	-	14	-	14,571	-	250	0.2
6300	Insurance carriers	11	5	0.3	60	26	24,600	32,000	1,409	835	0.0
6400	Insurance agents, brokers, and service	33	35	0.7	80	97	18,150	17,031	1,699	1,827	0.3
6500	Real estate	47	45	0.6	166	192	16,747	16,667	3,317	3,869	0.4
6510	Real estate operators and lessors	14	13	0.4	27	38	11,852	12,947	438	617	0.2
6530	Real estate agents and managers	22	24	0.8	63	86	17,016	14,744	1,326	1,567	0.3
6540	Title abstract offices	2	3	1.5	-	18	-	28,222	-	502	0.9
6700	Holding and other investment offices	5	6	0.7	3	14	37,333	26,857	276	551	0.2
6710	Holding offices	3	6	2.1	1	14	40,000	26,857	195	551	0.2
GREENE, OH											
60 –	**Finance, insurance, and real estate**	202	216	1.0	1,333	1,373	21,857	20,192	31,436	31,702	0.4
6000	Depository institutions	50	50	1.0	709	735	19,526	18,873	12,821	12,649	0.6
6020	Commercial banks	28	30	1.0	295	327	20,515	20,208	4,677	4,835	0.3
6100	Nondepository institutions	10	10	0.7	54	64	26,444	26,562	2,376	2,908	0.6
6140	Personal credit institutions	8	7	1.0	-	44	-	19,273	-	733	0.4
6200	Security and commodity brokers	14	13	1.3	40	36	60,100	55,444	3,658	3,652	0.6
6300	Insurance carriers	9	10	0.5	-	79	-	20,810	-	1,993	0.1
6400	Insurance agents, brokers, and service	39	46	0.9	115	125	21,287	21,920	2,674	3,031	0.4
6500	Real estate	76	82	1.2	282	317	15,220	15,672	5,044	6,590	0.7
6510	Real estate operators and lessors	30	34	1.0	152	183	15,316	14,929	2,694	3,002	1.1
6530	Real estate agents and managers	32	35	1.2	81	83	15,802	16,771	1,395	1,877	0.4
6552	Subdividers and developers, n.e.c.	2	5	2.1	-	15	-	20,800	-	851	1.5
6553	Cemetery subdividers and developers	4	4	1.3	9	-	6,222	-	69	-	-
6700	Holding and other investment offices	4	5	0.6	-	17	-	47,294	-	879	0.2
GUERNSEY, OH											
60 –	**Finance, insurance, and real estate**	56	59	0.3	439	485	17,002	16,619	8,121	8,803	0.1
6000	Depository institutions	14	14	0.3	242	259	18,215	18,703	4,224	5,086	0.3
6020	Commercial banks	10	9	0.3	152	147	18,579	21,007	2,578	2,809	0.2
6100	Nondepository institutions	5	5	0.4	18	-	19,556	-	397	-	-
6300	Insurance carriers	6	4	0.2	51	-	22,275	-	1,476	-	-
6330	Fire, marine, and casualty insurance	4	3	0.3	-	15	-	28,800	-	539	0.0
6400	Insurance agents, brokers, and service	10	13	0.2	26	-	17,538	-	619	-	-
6500	Real estate	18	19	0.3	89	118	8,000	8,169	954	1,255	0.1
6510	Real estate operators and lessors	7	8	0.2	16	16	7,500	9,500	133	214	0.1
6530	Real estate agents and managers	6	5	0.2	11	-	13,455	-	276	-	-
HAMILTON, OH											
60 –	**Finance, insurance, and real estate**	2,555	2,479	11.0	33,549	34,817	29,018	28,520	1,002,717	1,011,409	14.0
6000	Depository institutions	498	468	9.6	9,334	8,893	26,736	26,679	251,282	215,721	10.8
6020	Commercial banks	251	257	8.7	6,164	6,139	27,909	28,772	167,933	151,529	10.2
6030	Savings institutions	171	132	12.5	2,100	1,680	25,493	21,331	58,999	39,115	11.5
6060	Credit unions	60	67	8.6	559	605	20,716	19,835	11,437	11,838	12.4
6100	Nondepository institutions	164	149	10.9	1,843	2,424	32,341	30,117	64,507	82,332	16.4
6140	Personal credit institutions	78	58	8.6	1,134	1,373	27,958	26,462	33,433	33,127	19.5
6160	Mortgage bankers and brokers	63	72	14.5	522	601	38,084	33,364	23,243	30,623	14.6

Source: County Business Patterns, 1992/93, CBP-92/93-1, U.S. Department of Commerce, Washington, D.C., April 1995. SIC categories for which data were suppressed or not available for both 1992 and 1993 are *not* displayed. The employment columns represent mid-March employment in the year. Pay per employee is calculated by dividing 1st Quarter payroll, annualized, by mid-March employment. The columns headed "% State" show the county's percentage of the state total for the SIC in 1993; for example, 0.9% for SIC 6030 means that the county had 0.9 percent of the state's total establishments (or payroll) in SIC 6030 in 1993. A dash (-) is used to indicate that data are not available or cannot be calculated; nec means not elsewhere classified.

Continued on next page.

SIC	Industry	No. Establishments			Employment		Pay / Employee		Annual Payroll ($ 000)		
		1992	1993	% State	1992	1993	1992	1993	1992	1993	% State
HAMILTON, OH - [continued]											
6200	Security and commodity brokers	132	136	*13.6*	1,434	1,840	60,335	56,402	93,436	110,347	*18.3*
6210	Security brokers and dealers	76	64	*12.4*	978	1,072	63,239	62,545	62,513	69,319	*15.1*
6300	Insurance carriers	344	241	*12.4*	10,025	10,805	29,533	30,808	288,269	328,531	*15.6*
6310	Life insurance	105	93	*16.7*	4,839	5,635	26,222	28,464	124,444	151,346	*26.8*
6321	Accident and health insurance	5	10	*16.9*	22	-	36,000	-	697	-	-
6324	Hospital and medical service plans	10	9	*15.8*	1,684	-	34,487	-	57,691	-	-
6330	Fire, marine, and casualty insurance	126	94	*10.7*	2,875	2,489	33,764	35,683	91,208	91,388	*8.3*
6350	Surety insurance	5	3	*17.6*	23	-	21,043	-	545	-	-
6360	Title insurance	11	6	*8.2*	95	51	31,705	25,804	3,600	1,542	*4.1*
6370	Pension, health, and welfare funds	79	25	*8.4*	483	381	19,884	20,735	9,930	8,993	*11.8*
6390	Insurance carriers, n.e.c.	3	1	*14.3*	4	-	34,000	-	154		-
6400	Insurance agents, brokers, and service	485	496	*9.3*	2,849	2,765	29,968	27,456	88,952	85,953	*12.7*
6500	Real estate	796	840	*11.8*	6,090	6,390	18,237	18,136	118,731	135,118	*14.5*
6510	Real estate operators and lessors	339	368	*11.1*	2,548	2,484	12,590	12,762	33,469	34,039	*12.1*
6530	Real estate agents and managers	324	378	*12.6*	2,807	3,179	22,092	20,497	66,800	74,878	*15.0*
6540	Title abstract offices	12	14	*6.9*	89	156	26,202	28,769	3,071	6,750	*11.8*
6552	Subdividers and developers, n.e.c.	31	44	*18.3*	189	338	32,381	29,420	5,284	13,534	*23.3*
6553	Cemetery subdividers and developers	24	30	*9.5*	240	230	19,900	19,861	5,445	5,489	*15.5*
6700	Holding and other investment offices	128	142	*17.5*	878	1,103	47,813	27,594	44,992	36,088	*9.9*
6710	Holding offices	36	48	*16.6*	471	492	56,637	33,341	29,633	18,255	*6.9*
6720	Investment offices	3	-	-	52	-	79,462	-	4,799		-
6732	Educational, religious, etc. trusts	23	24	*17.4*	193	215	17,181	17,656	3,951	4,374	*20.2*
6733	Trusts, n.e.c.	37	48	*26.7*	70	296	80,057	20,324	3,641	8,232	*49.9*
6799	Investors, n.e.c.	15	14	*13.5*	41	59	17,659	49,085	923	4,142	*13.2*
HANCOCK, OH											
60 –	**Finance, insurance, and real estate**	146	155	*0.7*	1,295	1,225	25,174	23,079	32,656	30,658	*0.4*
6000	Depository institutions	40	34	*0.7*	589	498	23,273	20,956	12,830	9,751	*0.5*
6020	Commercial banks	26	26	*0.9*	394	450	22,619	21,609	8,032	8,849	*0.6*
6100	Nondepository institutions	11	10	*0.7*	175	174	24,914	21,977	4,747	4,360	*0.9*
6140	Personal credit institutions	6	6	*0.9*	56	-	25,643	-	1,412	-	-
6210	Security brokers and dealers	3	3	*0.6*	-	17	-	120,000	-	1,955	*0.4*
6300	Insurance carriers	13	13	*0.7*	144	126	24,056	21,968	3,482	3,054	*0.1*
6310	Life insurance	4	3	*0.5*	78	65	26,564	24,492	2,025	1,604	*0.3*
6400	Insurance agents, brokers, and service	34	37	*0.7*	109	115	21,468	22,643	2,726	3,157	*0.5*
6500	Real estate	40	52	*0.7*	232	267	12,931	15,041	3,668	4,846	*0.5*
6510	Real estate operators and lessors	24	32	*1.0*	89	108	8,584	10,889	1,230	1,610	*0.6*
6530	Real estate agents and managers	13	13	*0.4*	136	122	15,147	17,705	2,322	2,634	*0.5*
HARDIN, OH											
60 –	**Finance, insurance, and real estate**	41	39	*0.2*	200	227	18,200	15,930	3,721	3,719	*0.1*
6000	Depository institutions	16	17	*0.3*	137	148	18,102	17,324	2,530	2,607	*0.1*
6020	Commercial banks	10	13	*0.4*	104	118	17,615	17,254	1,898	2,094	*0.1*
6030	Savings institutions	3	1	*0.1*	28	-	22,143	-	601	-	-
6060	Credit unions	3	3	*0.4*	5	-	5,600	-	31	-	-
6400	Insurance agents, brokers, and service	14	14	*0.3*	34	54	16,118	11,704	590	712	*0.1*
6500	Real estate	6	5	*0.1*	7	6	8,571	7,333	65	40	*0.0*
6510	Real estate operators and lessors	5	3	*0.1*	5	-	11,200	-	60	-	-
HARRISON, OH											
60 –	**Finance, insurance, and real estate**	23	23	*0.1*	171	178	19,462	10,607	2,921	1,885	*0.0*
6020	Commercial banks	4	6	*0.2*	32	-	17,125	-	490	-	-
6500	Real estate	13	11	*0.2*	114	117	20,211	6,769	1,996	830	*0.1*
6510	Real estate operators and lessors	9	6	*0.2*	95	77	23,158	7,532	1,888	637	*0.2*

Source: County Business Patterns, 1992/93, CBP-92/93-1, U.S. Department of Commerce, Washington, D.C., April 1995. SIC categories for which data were suppressed or not available for both 1992 and 1993 are *not* displayed. The employment columns represent mid-March employment in the year. Pay per employee is calculated by dividing 1st Quarter payroll, annualized, by mid-March employment. The columns headed "% State" show the county's percentage of the state total for the SIC in 1993; for example, 0.9% for SIC 6030 means that the county had 0.9 percent of the state's total establishments (or payroll) in SIC 6030 in 1993. A dash (-) is used to indicate that data are not available or cannot be calculated; *nec* means not elsewhere classified.

SIC	Industry	No. Establishments			Employment		Pay / Employee		Annual Payroll ($ 000)		
		1992	1993	% State	1992	1993	1992	1993	1992	1993	% State
HENRY, OH											
60–	**Finance, insurance, and real estate**	53	49	0.2	271	293	17,609	17,666	5,521	5,997	0.1
6000	Depository institutions	17	14	0.3	147	132	17,224	17,273	2,635	2,404	0.1
6300	Insurance carriers	5	5	0.3	33	58	16,606	17,586	622	1,168	0.1
6400	Insurance agents, brokers, and service	20	18	0.3	44	56	17,727	16,000	999	997	0.1
6500	Real estate	6	7	0.1	-	25	-	6,400	-	196	0.0
6530	Real estate agents and managers	2	3	0.1	-	7	-	7,429	-	75	0.0
HIGHLAND, OH											
60–	**Finance, insurance, and real estate**	67	66	0.3	358	380	20,581	21,158	6,916	7,464	0.1
6000	Depository institutions	20	20	0.4	217	231	23,429	22,667	4,612	4,982	0.2
6020	Commercial banks	11	11	0.4	155	171	23,794	22,199	3,101	3,515	0.2
6400	Insurance agents, brokers, and service	19	19	0.4	39	48	24,923	27,917	730	905	0.1
6500	Real estate	20	19	0.3	62	57	9,613	11,158	750	749	0.1
6510	Real estate operators and lessors	8	8	0.2	29	28	5,793	7,286	254	260	0.1
6530	Real estate agents and managers	8	8	0.3	23	24	14,957	16,833	395	451	0.1
HOCKING, OH											
60–	**Finance, insurance, and real estate**	23	24	0.1	155	167	15,716	15,545	2,569	2,789	0.0
6000	Depository institutions	7	7	0.1	98	109	16,776	16,661	1,606	1,797	0.1
6400	Insurance agents, brokers, and service	8	8	0.2	14	23	24,000	16,696	521	545	0.1
6500	Real estate	5	6	0.1	25	8	4,640	6,000	62	74	0.0
HOLMES, OH											
60–	**Finance, insurance, and real estate**	32	32	0.1	278	292	19,209	18,671	5,118	5,564	0.1
6000	Depository institutions	14	14	0.3	183	203	18,426	17,261	3,281	3,482	0.2
6400	Insurance agents, brokers, and service	7	8	0.2	35	40	35,543	31,800	1,088	1,345	0.2
6500	Real estate	4	4	0.1	-	10	-	10,400	-	152	0.0
6700	Holding and other investment offices	3	3	0.4	26	27	10,923	10,815	285	318	0.1
HURON, OH											
60–	**Finance, insurance, and real estate**	92	94	0.4	570	570	19,684	20,491	11,557	11,560	0.2
6000	Depository institutions	26	26	0.5	345	364	20,336	21,330	6,862	7,280	0.4
6020	Commercial banks	19	18	0.6	284	269	18,901	20,045	5,483	5,164	0.3
6100	Nondepository institutions	5	5	0.4	48	-	20,167	-	830	-	-
6140	Personal credit institutions	3	3	0.4	-	17	-	11,765	-	241	0.1
6300	Insurance carriers	7	5	0.3	28	19	21,286	24,211	650	437	0.0
6400	Insurance agents, brokers, and service	23	23	0.4	78	82	18,462	18,829	1,747	1,749	0.3
6500	Real estate	26	27	0.4	57	65	14,596	11,631	1,014	933	0.1
6510	Real estate operators and lessors	15	16	0.5	34	40	5,059	4,700	327	200	0.1
6530	Real estate agents and managers	7	8	0.3	11	12	14,545	10,667	154	265	0.1
6700	Holding and other investment offices	2	4	0.5	-	3	-	152,000	-	386	0.1
JACKSON, OH											
60–	**Finance, insurance, and real estate**	50	48	0.2	1,124	1,156	19,206	17,433	21,708	21,657	0.3
6000	Depository institutions	15	16	0.3	148	154	19,189	19,065	3,173	3,613	0.2
6020	Commercial banks	11	11	0.4	-	136	-	19,235	-	3,274	0.2
6400	Insurance agents, brokers, and service	15	16	0.3	46	44	24,522	23,545	1,179	1,215	0.2
6500	Real estate	7	6	0.1	-	11	-	11,273	-	144	0.0
JEFFERSON, OH											
60–	**Finance, insurance, and real estate**	127	138	0.6	1,047	1,297	16,611	17,446	18,226	23,674	0.3
6000	Depository institutions	43	43	0.9	582	749	15,766	16,908	9,118	12,263	0.6
6020	Commercial banks	32	33	1.1	522	693	16,169	17,281	8,370	11,522	0.8
6100	Nondepository institutions	6	6	0.4	26	39	24,000	16,410	618	657	0.1
6140	Personal credit institutions	6	6	0.9	26	39	24,000	16,410	618	657	0.4
6300	Insurance carriers	9	10	0.5	105	128	25,638	22,406	2,631	3,605	0.2
6310	Life insurance	4	4	0.7	88	96	26,409	24,583	2,290	2,442	0.4
6400	Insurance agents, brokers, and service	35	35	0.7	94	90	18,468	19,822	2,089	2,066	0.3

*Source: County Business Patterns, 1992/93, CBP-92/93-1, U.S. Department of Commerce, Washington, D.C., April 1995. SIC categories for which data were suppressed or not available for both 1992 and 1993 are *not* displayed. The employment columns represent mid-March employment in the year. Pay per employee is calculated by dividing 1st Quarter payroll, annualized, by mid-March employment. The columns headed "% State" show the county's percentage of the state total for the SIC in 1993; for example, 0.9% for SIC 6030 means that the county had 0.9 percent of the state's total establishments (or payroll) in SIC 6030 in 1993. A dash (-) is used to indicate that data are not available or cannot be calculated; *nec* means not elsewhere classified.*

Continued on next page.

SIC	Industry	No. Establishments			Employment		Pay / Employee		Annual Payroll ($ 000)		
		1992	1993	% State	1992	1993	1992	1993	1992	1993	% State
JEFFERSON, OH - [continued]											
6500	Real estate	30	37	0.5	219	254	10,046	10,378	2,529	2,850	0.3
6510	Real estate operators and lessors	13	16	0.5	167	206	8,958	9,340	1,738	2,056	0.7
6530	Real estate agents and managers	8	13	0.4	13	-	11,077	-	182	-	-
KNOX, OH											
60-	**Finance, insurance, and real estate**	79	85	0.4	509	585	16,212	16,957	8,552	9,985	0.1
6000	Depository institutions	17	17	0.3	297	321	16,822	19,053	5,092	5,726	0.3
6020	Commercial banks	10	10	0.3	238	258	16,941	19,674	4,118	4,652	0.3
6100	Nondepository institutions	5	5	0.4	-	12	-	26,333	-	346	0.1
6140	Personal credit institutions	3	2	0.3	7	-	26,286	-	206	-	-
6200	Security and commodity brokers	3	1	0.1	9	-	28,889	-	214	-	-
6210	Security brokers and dealers	3	1	0.2	9	-	28,889	-	214	-	-
6300	Insurance carriers	5	5	0.3	41	46	11,024	10,522	510	569	0.0
6400	Insurance agents, brokers, and service	20	20	0.4	51	62	18,039	16,645	1,045	1,150	0.2
6500	Real estate	27	34	0.5	74	113	9,459	10,124	835	1,399	0.1
6510	Real estate operators and lessors	11	15	0.5	25	57	5,600	8,702	168	509	0.2
6530	Real estate agents and managers	10	13	0.4	41	-	12,585	-	605	-	-
6553	Cemetery subdividers and developers	4	4	1.3	8	8	5,500	4,500	54	53	0.2
LAKE, OH											
60-	**Finance, insurance, and real estate**	426	426	1.9	2,927	2,860	20,398	21,372	62,168	62,676	0.9
6000	Depository institutions	109	99	2.0	1,310	1,235	19,982	21,723	26,519	26,264	1.3
6020	Commercial banks	54	45	1.5	954	884	21,602	24,014	20,644	20,256	1.4
6030	Savings institutions	34	31	2.9	268	256	16,358	16,609	4,592	4,543	1.3
6100	Nondepository institutions	24	22	1.6	98	148	31,469	21,459	4,238	3,689	0.7
6140	Personal credit institutions	16	13	1.9	73	111	31,616	17,766	2,003	1,755	1.0
6160	Mortgage bankers and brokers	8	8	1.6	25	-	31,040	-	2,235	-	-
6200	Security and commodity brokers	16	17	1.7	-	83	-	52,482	-	4,554	0.8
6210	Security brokers and dealers	7	7	1.4	-	58	-	68,621	-	4,069	0.9
6280	Security and commodity services	9	10	2.1	20	25	14,800	15,040	349	485	0.3
6300	Insurance carriers	32	29	1.5	377	333	23,809	23,459	9,340	7,953	0.4
6310	Life insurance	6	5	0.9	250	186	23,824	23,376	5,975	4,169	0.7
6330	Fire, marine, and casualty insurance	17	17	1.9	55	65	34,255	35,077	2,101	2,506	0.2
6370	Pension, health, and welfare funds	4	3	1.0	39	-	8,718	-	415	-	-
6400	Insurance agents, brokers, and service	103	104	2.0	311	323	21,531	21,152	7,126	7,145	1.1
6500	Real estate	128	144	2.0	636	685	11,497	12,958	8,791	10,510	1.1
6510	Real estate operators and lessors	65	70	2.1	334	326	8,874	9,877	3,494	3,750	1.3
6530	Real estate agents and managers	40	56	1.9	117	195	17,470	16,656	2,471	3,644	0.7
6540	Title abstract offices	9	12	5.9	58	74	17,448	21,568	1,233	2,174	3.8
6552	Subdividers and developers, n.e.c.	6	4	1.7	100	89	9,680	9,079	992	928	1.6
6700	Holding and other investment offices	13	10	1.2	126	-	31,937	-	3,068	-	-
6794	Patent owners and lessors	3	2	3.9	58	-	20,759	-	1,304	-	-
LAWRENCE, OH											
60-	**Finance, insurance, and real estate**	59	65	0.3	582	585	20,268	19,569	12,449	14,082	0.2
6000	Depository institutions	19	21	0.4	208	440	18,288	20,164	4,284	10,120	0.5
6020	Commercial banks	9	10	0.3	-	370	-	21,081	-	8,952	0.6
6030	Savings institutions	7	7	0.7	52	52	17,000	15,846	914	891	0.3
6060	Credit unions	3	4	0.5	-	18	-	13,778	-	277	0.3
6100	Nondepository institutions	9	7	0.5	283	58	22,883	20,207	6,476	2,392	0.5
6400	Insurance agents, brokers, and service	17	19	0.4	58	56	17,448	17,786	1,167	1,125	0.2
6500	Real estate	9	13	0.2	-	22	-	11,091	-	320	0.0
6510	Real estate operators and lessors	3	6	0.2	7	14	9,143	9,143	82	153	0.1
6530	Real estate agents and managers	3	5	0.2	12	6	17,333	16,000	204	109	0.0

Source: County Business Patterns, 1992/93, CBP-92/93-1, U.S. Department of Commerce, Washington, D.C., April 1995. SIC categories for which data were suppressed or not available for both 1992 and 1993 are not displayed. The employment columns represent mid-March employment in the year. Pay per employee is calculated by dividing 1st Quarter payroll, annualized, by mid-March employment. The columns headed "% State" show the county's percentage of the state total for the SIC in 1993; for example, 0.9% for SIC 6030 means that the county had 0.9 percent of the state's total establishments (or payroll) in SIC 6030 in 1993. A dash (-) is used to indicate that data are not available or cannot be calculated; nec means not elsewhere classified.

SIC	Industry	No. Establishments			Employment		Pay / Employee		Annual Payroll ($ 000)		
		1992	1993	% State	1992	1993	1992	1993	1992	1993	% State
LICKING, OH											
60 –	**Finance, insurance, and real estate**	207	212	0.9	4,017	3,665	27,591	31,926	106,690	108,819	1.5
6000	Depository institutions	53	53	1.1	693	673	28,635	24,386	14,334	14,374	0.7
6020	Commercial banks	34	34	1.2	546	521	30,864	25,228	11,397	11,336	0.8
6030	Savings institutions	12	12	1.1	92	102	22,217	23,529	1,924	2,137	0.6
6060	Credit unions	7	7	0.9	55	50	17,236	17,360	1,013	901	0.9
6100	Nondepository institutions	9	11	0.8	37	74	23,351	14,486	977	1,360	0.3
6140	Personal credit institutions	7	7	1.0	-	64	-	13,875	-	931	0.5
6200	Security and commodity brokers	5	4	0.4	20	-	57,800	-	1,079	-	-
6210	Security brokers and dealers	5	4	0.8	20	-	57,800	-	1,079	-	-
6300	Insurance carriers	31	21	1.1	2,326	-	32,316	-	78,508	-	-
6310	Life insurance	8	7	1.3	-	140	-	30,486	-	3,833	0.7
6400	Insurance agents, brokers, and service	47	57	1.1	146	166	22,658	20,578	3,063	3,503	0.5
6500	Real estate	52	58	0.8	336	347	12,762	13,671	4,813	5,548	0.6
6510	Real estate operators and lessors	17	18	0.5	157	79	10,904	11,544	1,917	1,098	0.4
6530	Real estate agents and managers	25	35	1.2	136	242	15,000	14,512	2,235	4,184	0.8
6700	Holding and other investment offices	10	8	1.0	459	53	13,516	14,792	3,916	712	0.2
6732	Educational, religious, etc. trusts	3	2	1.4	22	-	8,364	-	194	-	-
LOGAN, OH											
60 –	**Finance, insurance, and real estate**	79	78	0.3	446	459	19,166	18,031	8,402	8,401	0.1
6000	Depository institutions	27	27	0.6	281	291	19,060	18,378	5,314	5,173	0.3
6020	Commercial banks	20	20	0.7	191	195	18,094	18,462	3,377	3,587	0.2
6100	Nondepository institutions	4	4	0.3	15	20	28,800	21,200	399	472	0.1
6400	Insurance agents, brokers, and service	20	20	0.4	68	62	16,471	16,774	1,103	1,078	0.2
6500	Real estate	22	21	0.3	-	50	-	12,080	-	723	0.1
6510	Real estate operators and lessors	13	11	0.3	28	30	12,143	12,800	365	388	0.1
6530	Real estate agents and managers	6	8	0.3	10	14	10,800	9,429	126	170	0.0
LORAIN, OH											
60 –	**Finance, insurance, and real estate**	443	458	2.0	3,671	3,598	19,472	19,827	78,231	80,224	1.1
6000	Depository institutions	129	130	2.7	2,007	1,956	19,049	19,683	41,036	41,861	2.1
6020	Commercial banks	80	84	2.9	1,087	1,101	18,285	18,372	20,293	21,503	1.4
6030	Savings institutions	24	19	1.8	794	722	20,892	22,648	19,060	18,338	5.4
6100	Nondepository institutions	22	21	1.5	101	120	22,535	18,400	2,331	2,699	0.5
6140	Personal credit institutions	16	13	1.9	81	90	22,074	16,711	1,804	1,446	0.9
6200	Security and commodity brokers	14	16	1.6	60	64	32,000	36,812	2,024	2,436	0.4
6210	Security brokers and dealers	11	13	2.5	52	54	35,385	41,778	1,943	2,354	0.5
6280	Security and commodity services	3	3	0.6	8	10	10,000	10,000	81	82	0.1
6300	Insurance carriers	38	30	1.5	252	175	26,032	28,137	7,930	4,669	0.2
6310	Life insurance	7	5	0.9	102	107	20,980	27,028	2,330	2,688	0.5
6330	Fire, marine, and casualty insurance	18	16	1.8	53	-	34,717	-	1,965	-	-
6370	Pension, health, and welfare funds	9	8	2.7	46	23	19,826	13,739	593	141	0.2
6400	Insurance agents, brokers, and service	90	94	1.8	301	340	20,199	18,365	6,159	7,358	1.1
6500	Real estate	136	151	2.1	907	890	15,577	16,454	15,378	17,791	1.9
6510	Real estate operators and lessors	69	76	2.3	217	-	11,373	-	2,502	-	-
6530	Real estate agents and managers	43	54	1.8	488	459	13,639	14,336	7,258	7,490	1.5
6540	Title abstract offices	3	7	3.5	4	-	17,000	-	83	-	-
6552	Subdividers and developers, n.e.c.	5	9	3.7	119	113	30,319	30,690	3,873	3,944	6.8
6553	Cemetery subdividers and developers	5	4	1.3	33	23	19,636	23,652	716	589	1.7
6700	Holding and other investment offices	14	16	2.0	43	53	53,116	46,415	3,373	3,410	0.9
6710	Holding offices	4	10	3.5	14	-	106,000	-	2,316	-	-
6799	Investors, n.e.c.	3	1	1.0	16	-	30,250	-	733	-	-
LUCAS, OH											
60 –	**Finance, insurance, and real estate**	973	946	4.2	9,614	9,317	26,173	25,372	263,961	252,251	3.5
6000	Depository institutions	204	201	4.1	3,367	3,120	26,721	24,400	84,614	77,442	3.9
6020	Commercial banks	121	117	4.0	2,652	2,489	27,042	25,848	68,905	63,969	4.3
6030	Savings institutions	38	34	3.2	381	341	29,123	19,050	8,017	7,045	2.1

Source: County Business Patterns, 1992/93, CBP-92/93-1, U.S. Department of Commerce, Washington, D.C., April 1995. SIC categories for which data were suppressed or not available for both 1992 and 1993 are not displayed. The employment columns represent mid-March employment in the year. Pay per employee is calculated by dividing 1st Quarter payroll, annualized, by mid-March employment. The columns headed "% State" show the county's percentage of the state total for the SIC in 1993; for example, 0.9% for SIC 6030 means that the county had 0.9 percent of the state's total establishments (or payroll) in SIC 6030 in 1993. A dash (-) is used to indicate that data are not available or cannot be calculated; nec means not elsewhere classified.

Continued on next page.

SIC	Industry	No. Establishments			Employment		Pay / Employee		Annual Payroll ($ 000)		
		1992	1993	% State	1992	1993	1992	1993	1992	1993	% State
LUCAS, OH - [continued]											
6100	Nondepository institutions	58	49	3.6	351	374	27,123	22,021	9,678	8,584	1.7
6140	Personal credit institutions	39	28	4.1	231	239	22,372	16,017	4,987	3,771	2.2
6160	Mortgage bankers and brokers	18	20	4.0	-	134	-	32,776	-	4,781	2.3
6200	Security and commodity brokers	49	49	4.9	385	444	59,751	57,622	22,348	26,319	4.4
6210	Security brokers and dealers	24	24	4.6	305	354	67,554	65,469	20,485	22,723	4.9
6280	Security and commodity services	23	23	4.9	75	-	31,307	-	1,793	-	-
6300	Insurance carriers	95	83	4.3	2,325	1,908	27,143	27,484	74,176	53,099	2.5
6310	Life insurance	31	23	4.1	988	651	25,178	26,974	35,329	16,074	2.8
6330	Fire, marine, and casualty insurance	39	33	3.8	230	174	33,026	37,678	7,761	6,638	0.6
6360	Title insurance	5	3	4.1	154	-	25,065	-	4,878	-	-
6370	Pension, health, and welfare funds	15	17	5.7	94	-	13,021	-	1,671	-	-
6400	Insurance agents, brokers, and service	248	263	5.0	1,155	1,299	25,198	24,619	30,960	36,572	5.4
6500	Real estate	276	257	3.6	1,824	1,771	16,849	16,784	34,506	35,963	3.9
6510	Real estate operators and lessors	131	124	3.7	792	612	15,399	13,346	12,624	9,094	3.2
6530	Real estate agents and managers	106	112	3.7	780	925	17,108	18,837	15,161	20,747	4.2
6540	Title abstract offices	2	4	2.0	-	52	-	24,231	-	2,497	4.4
6552	Subdividers and developers, n.e.c.	13	8	3.3	108	69	21,630	15,130	3,183	1,568	2.7
6553	Cemetery subdividers and developers	6	7	2.2	100	111	19,040	16,360	2,045	2,053	5.8
6700	Holding and other investment offices	43	44	5.4	207	401	29,894	30,663	7,679	14,272	3.9
6710	Holding offices	9	11	3.8	41	166	29,171	38,096	2,518	7,875	3.0
6720	Investment offices	3	1	5.6	25	-	38,240	-	944	-	-
6732	Educational, religious, etc. trusts	7	9	6.5	25	68	21,760	13,471	673	951	4.4
6733	Trusts, n.e.c.	13	6	3.3	45	10	22,044	16,000	804	155	0.9
6794	Patent owners and lessors	5	5	9.8	61	93	35,279	26,581	2,263	2,620	18.1
6798	Real estate investment trusts	1	3	20.0	-	1	-	140,000	-	363	3.2
6799	Investors, n.e.c.	4	8	7.7	-	60		35,000	-	2,193	7.0
MADISON, OH											
60 -	**Finance, insurance, and real estate**	53	51	0.2	174	209	15,931	15,177	2,881	3,277	0.0
6000	Depository institutions	12	13	0.3	95	92	16,968	17,826	1,622	1,624	0.1
6400	Insurance agents, brokers, and service	18	15	0.3	41	39	17,951	19,897	765	777	0.1
6500	Real estate	16	18	0.3	-	62	-	7,677	-	537	0.1
6510	Real estate operators and lessors	8	9	0.3	17	38	6,588	6,316	122	249	0.1
6530	Real estate agents and managers	5	6	0.2	10	21	14,800	10,476	161	272	0.1
MAHONING, OH											
60 -	**Finance, insurance, and real estate**	524	527	2.3	6,684	5,364	20,451	21,827	140,811	121,861	1.7
6000	Depository institutions	116	119	2.4	3,115	2,557	19,813	19,456	64,444	52,179	2.6
6020	Commercial banks	68	67	2.3	1,877	1,774	18,321	20,144	34,062	34,754	2.3
6030	Savings institutions	27	26	2.5	1,151	667	22,346	18,231	28,736	15,434	4.5
6100	Nondepository institutions	41	33	2.4	241	259	22,423	19,320	5,663	5,330	1.1
6140	Personal credit institutions	30	23	3.4	142	142	25,493	20,423	3,608	2,949	1.7
6160	Mortgage bankers and brokers	11	10	2.0	99	117	18,020	17,983	2,055	2,381	1.1
6200	Security and commodity brokers	15	19	1.9	153	204	46,797	54,510	6,823	10,720	1.8
6210	Security brokers and dealers	10	13	2.5	147	199	48,109	55,638	6,675	10,492	2.3
6280	Security and commodity services	4	6	1.3	6	5	14,667	9,600	101	228	0.2
6300	Insurance carriers	61	56	2.9	1,044	978	21,655	24,499	22,885	23,988	1.1
6310	Life insurance	22	19	3.4	423	354	24,823	26,147	10,381	9,051	1.6
6330	Fire, marine, and casualty insurance	22	19	2.2	99	106	33,899	34,906	3,732	4,027	0.4
6370	Pension, health, and welfare funds	11	12	4.0	-	218	-	15,229	-	3,157	4.1
6400	Insurance agents, brokers, and service	128	131	2.5	661	570	30,638	27,930	19,564	16,345	2.4
6500	Real estate	143	152	2.1	1,372	712	12,647	12,303	19,135	10,134	1.1
6510	Real estate operators and lessors	69	85	2.6	397	382	8,987	8,921	3,984	3,656	1.3
6530	Real estate agents and managers	46	47	1.6	835	200	14,228	12,820	13,044	3,355	0.7
6540	Title abstract offices	4	5	2.5	9	34	16,889	39,059	248	1,486	2.6
6552	Subdividers and developers, n.e.c.	4	3	1.2	19	3	9,684	56,000	165	115	0.2
6553	Cemetery subdividers and developers	10	12	3.8	77	93	15,065	13,892	1,320	1,522	4.3
6700	Holding and other investment offices	20	17	2.1	98	84	22,490	30,571	2,297	3,165	0.9

Source: County Business Patterns, 1992/93, CBP-92/93-1, U.S. Department of Commerce, Washington, D.C., April 1995. SIC categories for which data were suppressed or not available for both 1992 and 1993 are not displayed. The employment columns represent mid-March employment in the year. Pay per employee is calculated by dividing 1st Quarter payroll, annualized, by mid-March employment. The columns headed "% State" show the county's percentage of the state total for the SIC in 1993; for example, 0.9% for SIC 6030 means that the county had 0.9 percent of the state's total establishments (or payroll) in SIC 6030 in 1993. A dash (-) is used to indicate that data are not available or cannot be calculated; nec means not elsewhere classified.

Continued on next page.

SIC	Industry	No. Establishments			Employment		Pay / Employee		Annual Payroll ($ 000)		
		1992	1993	% State	1992	1993	1992	1993	1992	1993	% State
MAHONING, OH - [continued]											
6710	Holding offices	8	8	2.8	46	54	38,348	42,074	1,844	2,868	1.1
6732	Educational, religious, etc. trusts	4	4	2.9	26	-	10,308	-	249	-	
6733	Trusts, n.e.c.	3	3	1.7	3	5	12,000	5,600	23	16	0.1
MARION, OH											
60 –	**Finance, insurance, and real estate**	121	118	0.5	686	719	19,009	19,638	13,703	14,692	0.2
6000	Depository institutions	34	33	0.7	325	326	18,843	17,485	5,906	6,043	0.3
6020	Commercial banks	21	19	0.6	257	250	19,051	17,744	4,778	4,773	0.3
6030	Savings institutions	7	7	0.7	-	45	-	18,400	-	816	0.2
6060	Credit unions	6	7	0.9	-	31	-	14,065	-	454	0.5
6100	Nondepository institutions	6	5	0.4	-	21	-	16,000	-	365	0.1
6140	Personal credit institutions	5	5	0.7	-	21	-	16,000	-	365	0.2
6200	Security and commodity brokers	5	3	0.3	14	-	89,714	-	1,120	-	-
6300	Insurance carriers	13	10	0.5	85	87	19,388	22,943	2,066	1,940	0.1
6310	Life insurance	3	3	0.5	68	69	18,882	21,855	1,683	1,535	0.3
6400	Insurance agents, brokers, and service	25	28	0.5	80	90	13,400	14,178	1,187	1,319	0.2
6500	Real estate	35	36	0.5	100	109	10,560	11,890	1,216	1,559	0.2
6510	Real estate operators and lessors	20	21	0.6	54	75	6,741	7,307	448	587	0.2
6530	Real estate agents and managers	6	10	0.3	16	23	15,250	26,957	266	801	0.2
6553	Cemetery subdividers and developers	4	4	1.3	19	-	7,789	-	176	-	-
MEDINA, OH											
60 –	**Finance, insurance, and real estate**	197	206	0.9	2,270	2,680	26,481	24,967	80,476	81,604	1.1
6000	Depository institutions	48	46	0.9	530	535	17,479	18,602	9,549	9,806	0.5
6020	Commercial banks	30	29	1.0	388	403	18,567	19,246	7,266	7,530	0.5
6140	Personal credit institutions	7	7	1.0	-	52	-	16,846	-	931	0.5
6280	Security and commodity services	4	5	1.1	9	7	14,222	13,143	124	427	0.3
6400	Insurance agents, brokers, and service	42	44	0.8	194	179	20,557	18,860	4,301	4,483	0.7
6500	Real estate	61	70	1.0	-	202	-	14,396	-	3,671	0.4
6510	Real estate operators and lessors	16	19	0.6	34	45	10,235	11,733	449	583	0.2
6530	Real estate agents and managers	26	36	1.2	71	85	13,465	14,024	1,147	1,569	0.3
6540	Title abstract offices	8	9	4.5	48	55	16,667	17,455	936	1,203	2.1
6553	Cemetery subdividers and developers	4	4	1.3	15	-	11,733	-	185	-	-
6700	Holding and other investment offices	12	9	1.1	121	56	36,595	64,857	6,341	5,482	1.5
6710	Holding offices	8	6	2.1	112	-	38,714	-	5,789	-	-
MEIGS, OH											
60 –	**Finance, insurance, and real estate**	21	20	0.1	-	125	-	13,184	-	1,956	0.0
6000	Depository institutions	7	6	0.1	96	76	14,250	14,421	1,497	1,392	0.1
6020	Commercial banks	7	6	0.2	96	76	14,250	14,421	1,497	1,392	0.1
6500	Real estate	4	4	0.1	6	4	10,667	16,000	58	45	0.0
MERCER, OH											
60 –	**Finance, insurance, and real estate**	69	74	0.3	666	692	22,829	22,780	14,011	15,494	0.2
6000	Depository institutions	25	26	0.5	262	298	23,221	23,141	5,330	6,015	0.3
6020	Commercial banks	20	20	0.7	219	255	24,712	24,157	4,651	5,313	0.4
6400	Insurance agents, brokers, and service	23	23	0.4	83	69	22,651	25,101	1,986	1,672	0.2
6500	Real estate	9	14	0.2	-	22	-	14,000	-	417	0.0
6510	Real estate operators and lessors	2	7	0.2	-	7	-	18,286	-	162	0.1
6530	Real estate agents and managers	3	5	0.2	6	-	8,000	-	88	-	-
MIAMI, OH											
60 –	**Finance, insurance, and real estate**	153	156	0.7	1,341	1,352	21,748	22,379	29,405	31,145	0.4
6000	Depository institutions	40	41	0.8	526	539	22,433	22,004	10,966	11,319	0.6
6020	Commercial banks	26	26	0.9	331	324	24,024	23,506	7,250	7,363	0.5
6030	Savings institutions	11	11	1.0	187	204	19,936	20,098	3,591	3,787	1.1
6060	Credit unions	3	4	0.5	8	11	15,000	13,091	125	169	0.2
6100	Nondepository institutions	9	12	0.9	36	47	25,333	20,000	1,039	1,147	0.2

Source: County Business Patterns, 1992/93, CBP-92/93-1, U.S. Department of Commerce, Washington, D.C., April 1995. SIC categories for which data were suppressed or not available for both 1992 and 1993 are *not* displayed. The employment columns represent mid-March employment in the year. Pay per employee is calculated by dividing 1st Quarter payroll, annualized, by mid-March employment. The columns headed "% State" show the county's percentage of the state total for the SIC in 1993; for example, 0.9% for SIC 6030 means that the county had 0.9 percent of the state's total establishments (or payroll) in SIC 6030 in 1993. A dash (-) is used to indicate that data are not available or cannot be calculated; *nec* means not elsewhere classified.

Continued on next page.

SIC	Industry	No. Establishments			Employment		Pay / Employee		Annual Payroll ($ 000)		
		1992	1993	% State	1992	1993	1992	1993	1992	1993	% State
MIAMI, OH - [continued]											
6300	Insurance carriers	10	9	0.5	95	149	25,811	31,624	2,645	4,745	0.2
6310	Life insurance	5	3	0.5	71	-	26,423	-	2,027	-	-
6330	Fire, marine, and casualty insurance	4	4	0.5	-	74	-	30,000	-	2,059	0.2
6400	Insurance agents, brokers, and service	43	38	0.7	174	122	23,333	21,148	4,028	2,647	0.4
6500	Real estate	44	49	0.7	172	183	11,372	10,842	2,072	2,333	0.3
6510	Real estate operators and lessors	15	21	0.6	86	125	8,744	9,472	855	1,251	0.4
6530	Real estate agents and managers	22	21	0.7	56	37	14,500	15,892	875	752	0.2
6553	Cemetery subdividers and developers	3	3	1.0	-	20	-	10,400	-	264	0.7
MONROE, OH											
60 –	**Finance, insurance, and real estate**	22	23	0.1	94	-	16,043	-	1,610	-	-
6000	Depository institutions	6	8	0.2	56	79	15,857	15,139	973	1,299	0.1
6400	Insurance agents, brokers, and service	5	8	0.2	10	16	22,000	16,000	223	256	0.0
6500	Real estate	4	4	0.1	3	4	6,667	3,000	25	19	0.0
MONTGOMERY, OH											
60 –	**Finance, insurance, and real estate**	1,211	1,239	5.5	13,226	14,774	26,588	26,790	362,655	426,109	5.9
6000	Depository institutions	224	228	4.7	4,543	4,885	23,047	24,521	99,988	117,486	5.9
6020	Commercial banks	140	139	4.7	3,517	3,705	23,519	24,909	78,229	87,413	5.9
6030	Savings institutions	49	42	4.0	679	657	23,140	27,604	15,105	20,285	5.9
6100	Nondepository institutions	94	88	6.4	1,317	939	27,465	33,529	36,584	37,228	7.4
6140	Personal credit institutions	55	41	6.1	458	384	23,764	18,917	10,596	7,138	4.2
6150	Business credit institutions	5	7	5.2	186	262	14,817	50,504	2,998	16,375	15.0
6160	Mortgage bankers and brokers	34	39	7.9	673	293	33,480	37,502	22,990	13,711	6.5
6200	Security and commodity brokers	54	55	5.5	598	741	68,227	55,379	44,832	51,621	8.6
6210	Security brokers and dealers	22	20	3.9	364	410	84,066	64,429	30,782	29,311	6.4
6280	Security and commodity services	32	34	7.3	234	-	43,590	-	14,050	-	-
6300	Insurance carriers	125	118	6.1	1,916	2,659	23,595	25,410	49,914	71,921	3.4
6310	Life insurance	37	32	5.8	703	832	23,744	26,663	17,719	22,346	4.0
6321	Accident and health insurance	5	7	11.9	39	132	24,103	22,061	1,109	4,068	2.7
6324	Hospital and medical service plans	4	5	8.8	92	343	27,087	32,478	2,582	11,542	7.0
6330	Fire, marine, and casualty insurance	53	49	5.6	908	1,017	23,137	22,521	23,340	24,087	2.2
6360	Title insurance	7	5	6.8	103	78	28,427	29,692	3,865	3,586	9.6
6370	Pension, health, and welfare funds	18	20	6.7	70	257	16,343	23,767	1,294	6,292	8.3
6400	Insurance agents, brokers, and service	260	284	5.4	-	1,230	-	24,989	-	34,295	5.1
6500	Real estate	405	424	5.9	3,071	3,135	19,822	17,823	61,130	62,374	6.7
6510	Real estate operators and lessors	182	198	6.0	1,178	1,308	16,346	14,358	18,817	21,231	7.6
6530	Real estate agents and managers	168	193	6.4	1,543	1,559	21,887	20,536	33,604	34,447	6.9
6540	Title abstract offices	13	14	6.9	116	146	23,862	19,315	3,487	4,300	7.5
6552	Subdividers and developers, n.e.c.	8	8	3.3	52	33	42,000	18,667	1,900	765	1.3
6553	Cemetery subdividers and developers	9	9	2.9	101	89	16,713	18,472	1,960	1,600	4.5
6700	Holding and other investment offices	46	39	4.8	565	1,159	51,179	41,629	34,916	50,101	13.7
6710	Holding offices	18	18	6.2	450	1,002	49,244	44,287	28,631	46,314	17.5
6720	Investment offices	6	3	16.7	53	-	100,830	-	4,365	-	-
6732	Educational, religious, etc. trusts	8	9	6.5	36	-	26,333	-	1,028	-	-
6733	Trusts, n.e.c.	5	1	0.6	9	-	29,333	-	289	-	-
MORGAN, OH											
60 –	**Finance, insurance, and real estate**	22	22	0.1	96	102	13,417	13,294	1,315	1,375	0.0
6000	Depository institutions	7	7	0.1	75	84	15,147	14,429	1,143	1,210	0.1
6020	Commercial banks	6	7	0.2	-	84	-	14,429	-	1,210	0.1
6400	Insurance agents, brokers, and service	7	7	0.1	12	12	9,667	10,000	118	116	0.0
6500	Real estate	4	4	0.1	6	6	4,000	4,000	25	28	0.0
6510	Real estate operators and lessors	4	3	0.1	6	-	4,000	-	25	-	-

Source: County Business Patterns, 1992/93, CBP-92/93-1, U.S. Department of Commerce, Washington, D.C., April 1995. SIC categories for which data were suppressed or not available for both 1992 and 1993 are *not* displayed. The employment columns represent mid-March employment in the year. Pay per employee is calculated by dividing 1st Quarter payroll, annualized, by mid-March employment. The columns headed "% State" show the county's percentage of the state total for the SIC in 1993; for example, 0.9% for SIC 6030 means that the county had 0.9 percent of the state's total establishments (or payroll) in SIC 6030 in 1993. A dash (-) is used to indicate that data are not available or cannot be calculated; *nec* means not elsewhere classified.

SIC	Industry	No. Establishments			Employment		Pay / Employee		Annual Payroll ($ 000)		
		1992	1993	% State	1992	1993	1992	1993	1992	1993	% State
MORROW, OH											
60 –	**Finance, insurance, and real estate**	26	25	0.1	102	99	10,941	11,636	1,201	1,327	0.0
6000	Depository institutions	7	7	0.1	-	44	-	14,364	-	667	0.0
6400	Insurance agents, brokers, and service	6	6	0.1	-	16	-	12,250	-	213	0.0
6500	Real estate	13	12	0.2	-	39	-	8,308	-	447	0.0
6510	Real estate operators and lessors	7	8	0.2	12	16	4,667	6,000	55	109	0.0
6530	Real estate agents and managers	5	3	0.1	10	22	6,800	10,182	70	316	0.1
MUSKINGUM, OH											
60 –	**Finance, insurance, and real estate**	149	147	0.7	969	977	20,384	22,043	19,295	21,679	0.3
6000	Depository institutions	34	34	0.7	451	461	22,315	21,093	9,419	9,617	0.5
6020	Commercial banks	17	25	0.8	246	365	23,187	22,225	5,014	8,073	0.5
6100	Nondepository institutions	14	13	1.0	61	72	17,967	13,333	1,012	1,230	0.2
6140	Personal credit institutions	8	7	1.0	-	38	-	17,789	-	805	0.5
6160	Mortgage bankers and brokers	3	2	0.4	11	-	4,364	-	60	-	-
6200	Security and commodity brokers	6	6	0.6	31	41	55,226	67,902	1,762	2,277	0.4
6300	Insurance carriers	17	15	0.8	135	116	21,185	25,655	2,670	3,001	0.1
6310	Life insurance	3	4	0.7	89	79	19,596	24,658	1,515	1,920	0.3
6370	Pension, health, and welfare funds	3	1	0.3	-	-	-	-	11	-	-
6400	Insurance agents, brokers, and service	33	33	0.6	141	138	17,957	21,594	2,890	3,140	0.5
6500	Real estate	41	41	0.6	146	135	9,726	13,511	1,480	1,962	0.2
6510	Real estate operators and lessors	22	23	0.7	93	94	7,269	12,851	748	1,274	0.5
6530	Real estate agents and managers	15	14	0.5	34	-	14,471	-	485	-	-
6700	Holding and other investment offices	4	5	0.6	4	14	17,000	20,571	62	452	0.1
NOBLE, OH											
60 –	**Finance, insurance, and real estate**	10	10	0.0	70	87	21,314	19,724	1,633	1,779	0.0
6000	Depository institutions	3	4	0.1	55	65	21,309	18,462	1,298	1,356	0.1
OTTAWA, OH											
60 –	**Finance, insurance, and real estate**	95	91	0.4	603	488	16,033	16,770	9,859	8,876	0.1
6000	Depository institutions	18	16	0.3	199	198	20,563	20,202	4,000	3,936	0.2
6020	Commercial banks	12	12	0.4	155	155	19,948	19,561	3,134	3,076	0.2
6400	Insurance agents, brokers, and service	32	29	0.5	87	79	16,230	15,038	1,419	1,354	0.2
6500	Real estate	38	40	0.6	261	120	12,950	14,433	3,580	2,208	0.2
6510	Real estate operators and lessors	12	18	0.5	35	56	12,914	13,643	401	805	0.3
6530	Real estate agents and managers	19	18	0.6	184	-	11,870	-	2,260	-	-
PAULDING, OH											
60 –	**Finance, insurance, and real estate**	21	21	0.1	134	125	13,731	14,944	1,978	2,045	0.0
6000	Depository institutions	7	7	0.1	70	71	16,743	17,014	1,250	1,301	0.1
6400	Insurance agents, brokers, and service	9	10	0.2	42	-	14,095	-	620	-	-
6500	Real estate	3	3	0.0	-	20	-	3,800	-	90	0.0
PERRY, OH											
60 –	**Finance, insurance, and real estate**	27	28	0.1	166	171	15,976	17,754	2,878	3,297	0.0
6000	Depository institutions	10	10	0.2	121	124	16,364	18,097	2,152	2,336	0.1
6400	Insurance agents, brokers, and service	9	11	0.2	23	23	16,696	19,130	425	582	0.1
6500	Real estate	4	4	0.1	6	7	6,667	6,286	43	60	0.0
PICKAWAY, OH											
60 –	**Finance, insurance, and real estate**	67	72	0.3	320	342	16,125	16,234	5,616	6,220	0.1
6000	Depository institutions	16	15	0.3	166	148	15,976	17,568	2,654	2,623	0.1
6020	Commercial banks	13	12	0.4	157	139	16,025	17,698	2,515	2,476	0.2
6100	Nondepository institutions	5	6	0.4	19	39	22,947	16,000	553	849	0.2
6400	Insurance agents, brokers, and service	18	21	0.4	59	70	17,831	17,771	1,191	1,410	0.2

Source: County Business Patterns, 1992/93, CBP-92/93-1, U.S. Department of Commerce, Washington, D.C., April 1995. SIC categories for which data were suppressed or not available for both 1992 and 1993 are not displayed. The employment columns represent mid-March employment in the year. Pay per employee is calculated by dividing 1st Quarter payroll, annualized, by mid-March employment. The columns headed "% State" show the county's percentage of the state total for the SIC in 1993; for example, 0.9% for SIC 6030 means that the county had 0.9 percent of the state's total establishments (or payroll) in SIC 6030 in 1993. A dash (-) is used to indicate that data are not available or cannot be calculated; nec means not elsewhere classified.

Continued on next page.

SIC	Industry	No. Establishments			Employment		Pay / Employee		Annual Payroll ($ 000)		
		1992	1993	% State	1992	1993	1992	1993	1992	1993	% State
PICKAWAY, OH - [continued]											
6500	Real estate	22	26	0.4	52	64	6,769	7,312	499	713	0.1
6510	Real estate operators and lessors	11	15	0.5	30	37	6,000	6,811	193	297	0.1
6530	Real estate agents and managers	6	6	0.2	8	7	10,000	10,286	112	176	0.0
PIKE, OH											
60 –	**Finance, insurance, and real estate**	21	21	0.1	197	206	15,066	15,612	3,275	3,304	0.0
6000	Depository institutions	7	7	0.1	116	114	15,931	18,000	1,909	2,110	0.1
6500	Real estate	5	5	0.1	-	55	-	10,182	-	571	0.1
PORTAGE, OH											
60 –	**Finance, insurance, and real estate**	202	204	0.9	1,526	1,441	18,626	17,963	29,189	28,836	0.4
6000	Depository institutions	47	47	1.0	389	871	17,563	18,076	6,963	17,604	0.9
6020	Commercial banks	27	28	1.0	236	729	18,136	17,800	4,330	14,686	1.0
6030	Savings institutions	16	14	1.3	120	122	17,933	19,377	2,225	2,500	0.7
6060	Credit unions	4	5	0.6	33	20	12,121	20,200	408	418	0.4
6200	Security and commodity brokers	6	9	0.9	-	34	-	30,235	-	1,105	0.2
6300	Insurance carriers	13	8	0.4	81	-	27,309	-	2,564	-	-
6400	Insurance agents, brokers, and service	52	51	1.0	157	162	20,153	20,988	3,153	3,535	0.5
6500	Real estate	72	78	1.1	335	293	11,690	12,560	4,205	3,846	0.4
6510	Real estate operators and lessors	43	47	1.4	231	197	11,636	11,878	2,782	2,466	0.9
6530	Real estate agents and managers	21	22	0.7	71	67	11,099	13,552	864	843	0.2
6540	Title abstract offices	4	5	2.5	13	22	17,538	16,182	278	423	0.7
6700	Holding and other investment offices	5	4	0.5	9	13	61,778	50,462	454	657	0.2
PREBLE, OH											
60 –	**Finance, insurance, and real estate**	50	50	0.2	279	296	18,710	18,338	5,420	5,572	0.1
6000	Depository institutions	19	19	0.4	169	176	21,018	20,955	3,426	3,563	0.2
6020	Commercial banks	16	16	0.5	158	165	21,570	21,261	3,268	3,371	0.2
6030	Savings institutions	3	2	0.2	11	-	13,091	-	158	-	-
6400	Insurance agents, brokers, and service	14	14	0.3	41	51	16,488	15,686	805	956	0.1
6500	Real estate	12	13	0.2	49	46	10,857	10,522	682	622	0.1
6510	Real estate operators and lessors	3	4	0.1	6	7	6,000	14,857	109	157	0.1
6530	Real estate agents and managers	7	6	0.2	-	28	-	10,857	-	372	0.1
6553	Cemetery subdividers and developers	2	3	1.0	-	11	-	6,909	-	93	0.3
PUTNAM, OH											
60 –	**Finance, insurance, and real estate**	51	52	0.2	289	308	17,121	17,623	4,753	5,304	0.1
6000	Depository institutions	18	18	0.4	191	182	19,539	20,857	3,388	3,553	0.2
6300	Insurance carriers	4	2	0.1	12	-	14,333	-	194	-	-
6400	Insurance agents, brokers, and service	18	19	0.4	52	53	13,615	15,925	783	852	0.1
6500	Real estate	9	11	0.2	-	58	-	9,310	-	662	0.1
6510	Real estate operators and lessors	8	9	0.3	27	-	6,222	-	210	-	-
RICHLAND, OH											
60 –	**Finance, insurance, and real estate**	274	278	1.2	2,547	2,479	23,645	23,669	62,193	61,605	0.9
6000	Depository institutions	70	67	1.4	934	761	19,996	18,586	18,503	14,767	0.7
6020	Commercial banks	42	39	1.3	576	530	19,826	19,713	11,196	10,800	0.7
6030	Savings institutions	19	18	1.7	294	157	21,537	16,713	6,331	2,827	0.8
6060	Credit unions	9	10	1.3	64	74	14,438	14,486	976	1,140	1.2
6100	Nondepository institutions	16	15	1.1	100	94	22,280	17,319	2,369	1,868	0.4
6140	Personal credit institutions	11	10	1.5	76	68	22,316	14,588	1,763	1,045	0.6
6200	Security and commodity brokers	8	7	0.7	47	48	61,617	67,000	2,842	3,076	0.5
6300	Insurance carriers	41	32	1.6	924	1,021	30,242	31,068	29,060	32,750	1.6
6310	Life insurance	7	5	0.9	106	90	23,321	29,644	2,639	2,479	0.4
6330	Fire, marine, and casualty insurance	19	17	1.9	765	862	31,106	31,128	24,260	28,129	2.5
6360	Title insurance	4	3	4.1	34	-	37,529	-	1,533	-	-
6370	Pension, health, and welfare funds	9	6	2.0	15	24	16,800	21,000	453	317	0.4
6400	Insurance agents, brokers, and service	59	65	1.2	214	205	23,907	22,595	5,496	4,947	0.7

Source: County Business Patterns, 1992/93, CBP-92/93-1, U.S. Department of Commerce, Washington, D.C., April 1995. SIC categories for which data were suppressed or not available for both 1992 and 1993 are *not* displayed. The employment columns represent mid-March employment in the year. Pay per employee is calculated by dividing 1st Quarter payroll, annualized, by mid-March employment. The columns headed "% State" show the county's percentage of the state total for the SIC in 1993; for example, 0.9% for SIC 6030 means that the county had 0.9 percent of the state's total establishments (or payroll) in SIC 6030 in 1993. A dash (-) is used to indicate that data are not available or cannot be calculated; *nec* means not elsewhere classified.

Continued on next page.

SIC	Industry	No. Establishments			Employment		Pay / Employee		Annual Payroll ($ 000)		
		1992	1993	% State	1992	1993	1992	1993	1992	1993	% State
RICHLAND, OH - [continued]											
6500	Real estate	74	85	1.2	305	341	10,177	9,091	3,661	3,912	0.4
6510	Real estate operators and lessors	36	46	1.4	177	101	9,808	7,525	1,780	924	0.3
6530	Real estate agents and managers	22	25	0.8	64	199	12,438	9,588	1,129	2,364	0.5
6552	Subdividers and developers, n.e.c.	2	3	1.2	-	2	-	14,000	-	103	0.2
6553	Cemetery subdividers and developers	7	7	2.2	40	36	8,800	10,000	409	431	1.2
6700	Holding and other investment offices	6	7	0.9	23	9	11,304	26,222	262	285	0.1
ROSS, OH											
60 –	**Finance, insurance, and real estate**	101	105	0.5	544	506	18,118	18,443	10,419	10,265	0.1
6000	Depository institutions	23	24	0.5	206	206	16,117	17,165	3,458	3,770	0.2
6020	Commercial banks	15	16	0.5	175	180	16,503	17,378	2,998	3,282	0.2
6100	Nondepository institutions	8	10	0.7	-	47	-	22,979	-	1,304	0.3
6140	Personal credit institutions	3	4	0.6	15	-	20,800	-	365	-	-
6200	Security and commodity brokers	2	5	0.5	-	12	-	69,333	-	848	0.1
6300	Insurance carriers	9	5	0.3	82	37	27,561	32,432	2,271	1,241	0.1
6400	Insurance agents, brokers, and service	24	29	0.5	66	78	19,394	14,974	1,431	1,378	0.2
6500	Real estate	31	29	0.4	136	122	11,000	12,066	1,669	1,666	0.2
6510	Real estate operators and lessors	15	16	0.5	55	-	9,673	-	617	-	-
6530	Real estate agents and managers	11	7	0.2	18	24	16,222	17,833	359	456	0.1
6700	Holding and other investment offices	4	3	0.4	11	4	2,909	11,000	60	58	0.0
SANDUSKY, OH											
60 –	**Finance, insurance, and real estate**	100	104	0.5	728	779	17,308	20,883	13,886	16,869	0.2
6000	Depository institutions	26	26	0.5	400	416	18,970	19,067	7,674	7,986	0.4
6020	Commercial banks	18	18	0.6	327	327	19,131	19,792	6,274	6,436	0.4
6300	Insurance carriers	8	7	0.4	37	29	17,189	18,483	631	536	0.0
6400	Insurance agents, brokers, and service	37	42	0.8	146	148	15,562	16,432	2,406	2,763	0.4
6500	Real estate	19	21	0.3	52	57	9,308	10,386	547	649	0.1
6510	Real estate operators and lessors	11	12	0.4	33	33	10,545	13,091	370	448	0.2
6530	Real estate agents and managers	4	4	0.1	5	6	8,800	10,000	50	75	0.0
6553	Cemetery subdividers and developers	4	5	1.6	14	18	6,571	5,556	127	126	0.4
6700	Holding and other investment offices	5	3	0.4	79	116	13,823	35,793	2,087	4,312	1.2
6710	Holding offices	2	3	1.0	-	116	-	35,793	-	4,312	1.6
SCIOTO, OH											
60 –	**Finance, insurance, and real estate**	109	112	0.5	726	899	18,601	17,651	13,164	16,595	0.2
6000	Depository institutions	28	28	0.6	371	370	20,420	20,292	6,963	7,483	0.4
6020	Commercial banks	18	18	0.6	253	253	19,304	19,368	4,127	4,634	0.3
6100	Nondepository institutions	4	4	0.3	-	17	-	19,529	-	344	0.1
6300	Insurance carriers	11	10	0.5	136	223	18,824	20,269	2,664	4,629	0.2
6400	Insurance agents, brokers, and service	34	40	0.8	106	118	18,792	17,932	2,035	2,341	0.3
6500	Real estate	27	25	0.4	85	161	8,706	6,534	862	1,451	0.2
6510	Real estate operators and lessors	15	15	0.5	48	86	7,333	7,581	399	749	0.3
6530	Real estate agents and managers	8	7	0.2	25	14	10,720	11,714	258	220	0.0
6553	Cemetery subdividers and developers	3	2	0.6	12	-	10,000	-	160	-	-
6700	Holding and other investment offices	4	3	0.4	8	-	10,000	-	68	-	-
SENECA, OH											
60 –	**Finance, insurance, and real estate**	110	118	0.5	507	523	17,893	17,369	9,692	10,296	0.1
6000	Depository institutions	30	31	0.6	255	312	17,553	15,885	4,311	5,249	0.3
6020	Commercial banks	21	22	0.7	197	228	17,929	16,456	3,392	3,946	0.3
6100	Nondepository institutions	7	3	0.2	52	13	21,231	29,538	1,158	486	0.1
6400	Insurance agents, brokers, and service	34	35	0.7	96	91	21,375	22,769	2,541	2,683	0.4
6500	Real estate	28	36	0.5	64	61	8,000	7,803	581	617	0.1
6510	Real estate operators and lessors	14	17	0.5	27	23	9,333	8,870	265	241	0.1

Source: County Business Patterns, 1992/93, CBP-92/93-1, U.S. Department of Commerce, Washington, D.C., April 1995. SIC categories for which data were suppressed or not available for both 1992 and 1993 are not displayed. The employment columns represent mid-March employment in the year. Pay per employee is calculated by dividing 1st Quarter payroll, annualized, by mid-March employment. The columns headed "% State" show the county's percentage of the state total for the SIC in 1993; for example, 0.9% for SIC 6030 means that the county had 0.9 percent of the state's total establishments (or payroll) in SIC 6030 in 1993. A dash (-) is used to indicate that data are not available or cannot be calculated; nec means not elsewhere classified.

Continued on next page.

SIC	Industry	No. Establishments			Employment		Pay / Employee		Annual Payroll ($ 000)		
		1992	1993	% State	1992	1993	1992	1993	1992	1993	% State
SENECA, OH - [continued]											
6530	Real estate agents and managers	9	14	0.5	16	29	8,000	8,276	141	339	0.1
6553	Cemetery subdividers and developers	3	3	1.0	-	8	-	3,000	-	31	0.1
6700	Holding and other investment offices	4	5	0.6	5	-	17,600	-	86	-	-
SHELBY, OH											
60 –	**Finance, insurance, and real estate**	70	73	0.3	396	400	21,343	20,910	8,659	8,419	0.1
6000	Depository institutions	25	25	0.5	286	271	21,734	23,395	6,114	6,279	0.3
6020	Commercial banks	18	20	0.7	222	223	22,973	24,682	4,936	5,275	0.4
6030	Savings institutions	4	2	0.2	52	-	15,692	-	910	-	-
6100	Nondepository institutions	2	3	0.2	-	25	-	8,640	-	218	0.0
6400	Insurance agents, brokers, and service	25	24	0.5	59	56	15,797	17,929	1,100	1,089	0.2
6500	Real estate	13	16	0.2	-	40	-	8,000	-	361	0.0
6510	Real estate operators and lessors	6	8	0.2	11	22	6,545	4,727	84	125	0.0
6530	Real estate agents and managers	6	8	0.3	17	18	15,529	12,000	273	236	0.0
STARK, OH											
60 –	**Finance, insurance, and real estate**	741	747	3.3	6,012	5,897	23,500	22,748	148,013	140,580	1.9
6000	Depository institutions	160	163	3.3	1,930	2,106	20,864	21,466	42,876	45,208	2.3
6020	Commercial banks	98	93	3.2	1,195	1,370	20,365	20,199	26,449	26,932	1.8
6030	Savings institutions	33	31	2.9	576	531	23,597	27,751	13,989	15,262	4.5
6100	Nondepository institutions	52	50	3.7	400	418	23,580	21,196	9,755	9,966	2.0
6140	Personal credit institutions	35	26	3.8	232	230	23,638	18,748	5,338	4,240	2.5
6160	Mortgage bankers and brokers	14	20	4.0	162	176	23,679	24,773	4,292	5,472	2.6
6200	Security and commodity brokers	31	31	3.1	131	188	51,450	45,660	7,044	9,144	1.5
6210	Security brokers and dealers	22	18	3.5	113	118	56,956	59,729	6,754	7,508	1.6
6280	Security and commodity services	9	13	2.8	18	70	16,889	21,943	290	1,636	1.2
6300	Insurance carriers	79	76	3.9	1,718	1,260	29,807	25,546	52,639	35,394	1.7
6310	Life insurance	20	13	2.3	568	308	25,577	22,325	14,572	6,789	1.2
6330	Fire, marine, and casualty insurance	36	36	4.1	884	653	34,136	28,239	30,741	21,319	1.9
6370	Pension, health, and welfare funds	15	20	6.7	92	124	24,565	20,903	2,719	2,949	3.9
6400	Insurance agents, brokers, and service	199	195	3.7	714	696	22,622	23,017	16,586	18,161	2.7
6500	Real estate	190	207	2.9	969	1,023	13,329	14,612	14,002	16,736	1.8
6510	Real estate operators and lessors	71	91	2.8	242	523	11,421	12,069	3,036	5,931	2.1
6530	Real estate agents and managers	81	82	2.7	540	336	13,319	17,298	7,921	7,643	1.5
6540	Title abstract offices	4	6	3.0	31	40	10,710	19,600	359	1,011	1.8
6552	Subdividers and developers, n.e.c.	7	9	3.7	49	22	20,408	43,455	1,199	1,258	2.2
6553	Cemetery subdividers and developers	18	19	6.0	87	102	11,632	10,627	1,107	893	2.5
6700	Holding and other investment offices	30	25	3.1	150	206	30,453	40,466	5,111	5,971	1.6
6710	Holding offices	8	9	3.1	38	95	54,947	45,221	2,328	3,081	1.2
6732	Educational, religious, etc. trusts	5	5	3.6	30	21	14,800	26,857	456	567	2.6
6733	Trusts, n.e.c.	10	5	2.8	20	-	14,200	-	397	-	-
SUMMIT, OH											
60 –	**Finance, insurance, and real estate**	1,088	1,077	4.8	10,442	10,471	26,688	26,954	278,285	298,196	4.1
6000	Depository institutions	219	213	4.4	3,610	3,237	22,089	22,343	76,546	72,035	3.6
6020	Commercial banks	124	117	4.0	2,670	2,218	23,097	23,607	59,485	51,901	3.5
6030	Savings institutions	56	53	5.0	693	705	19,648	21,237	12,748	15,234	4.5
6060	Credit unions	30	32	4.1	217	274	18,138	15,839	3,933	4,411	4.6
6090	Functions closely related to banking	9	11	10.4	30	40	17,333	16,300	380	489	-
6100	Nondepository institutions	68	64	4.7	427	-	25,864	-	12,152	-	-
6140	Personal credit institutions	38	28	4.1	269	260	20,283	17,538	5,720	4,710	2.8
6160	Mortgage bankers and brokers	23	33	6.7	135	215	36,741	28,781	5,735	9,381	4.5
6200	Security and commodity brokers	55	62	6.2	417	422	65,707	63,251	27,558	29,959	5.0
6210	Security brokers and dealers	27	28	5.4	338	332	71,290	74,373	24,323	26,849	5.8
6280	Security and commodity services	28	34	7.3	79	90	41,823	22,222	3,235	3,110	2.2
6300	Insurance carriers	148	117	6.0	2,341	2,353	26,572	28,287	62,706	66,682	3.2
6310	Life insurance	35	31	5.6	763	821	21,594	22,358	16,141	17,645	3.1
6330	Fire, marine, and casualty insurance	68	56	6.4	1,037	1,125	32,305	34,091	33,969	38,623	3.5

Source: County Business Patterns, 1992/93, CBP-92/93-1, U.S. Department of Commerce, Washington, D.C., April 1995. SIC categories for which data were suppressed or not available for both 1992 and 1993 are not displayed. The employment columns represent mid-March employment in the year. Pay per employee is calculated by dividing 1st Quarter payroll, annualized, by mid-March employment. The columns headed "% State" show the county's percentage of the state total for the SIC in 1993; for example, 0.9% for SIC 6030 means that the county had 0.9 percent of the state's total establishments (or payroll) in SIC 6030 in 1993. A dash (-) is used to indicate that data are not available or cannot be calculated; nec means not elsewhere classified.

Continued on next page.

SIC	Industry	No. Establishments			Employment		Pay / Employee		Annual Payroll ($ 000)		
		1992	1993	% State	1992	1993	1992	1993	1992	1993	% State
SUMMIT, OH - [continued]											
6360	Title insurance	10	4	5.5	176	-	25,409	-	5,194	-	-
6370	Pension, health, and welfare funds	27	20	6.7	211	216	16,171	20,593	3,086	4,761	6.2
6400	Insurance agents, brokers, and service	253	263	5.0	994	1,057	26,249	23,917	27,350	27,865	4.1
6500	Real estate	307	316	4.4	1,869	2,121	18,164	18,821	37,590	47,199	5.1
6510	Real estate operators and lessors	111	119	3.6	559	650	14,633	13,797	8,846	9,548	3.4
6530	Real estate agents and managers	125	149	5.0	752	1,019	19,335	20,707	16,407	25,885	5.2
6540	Title abstract offices	18	21	10.4	121	212	17,355	20,943	2,253	5,518	9.7
6552	Subdividers and developers, n.e.c.	12	12	5.0	182	100	28,176	31,440	5,182	3,692	6.4
6553	Cemetery subdividers and developers	12	13	4.1	131	140	17,160	16,200	2,433	2,535	7.2
6700	Holding and other investment offices	35	39	4.8	767	773	48,934	51,312	33,598	39,228	10.7
6710	Holding offices	14	16	5.5	708	710	51,147	53,735	32,192	37,091	14.0
6732	Educational, religious, etc. trusts	4	4	2.9	11	11	26,182	22,182	257	243	1.1
6733	Trusts, n.e.c.	8	8	4.4	8	6	6,500	8,000	162	505	3.1
6794	Patent owners and lessors	5	5	9.8	31	39	18,065	26,769	774	1,234	8.5
TRUMBULL, OH											
60 –	**Finance, insurance, and real estate**	349	349	1.6	2,740	2,669	16,702	18,910	49,505	51,121	0.7
6000	Depository institutions	86	90	1.8	1,330	1,471	18,063	19,845	25,440	27,068	1.4
6020	Commercial banks	56	56	1.9	850	938	16,329	17,996	15,213	16,135	1.1
6030	Savings institutions	21	20	1.9	364	364	20,429	25,264	7,504	7,651	2.2
6060	Credit unions	9	14	1.8	116	169	23,345	18,438	2,723	3,282	3.4
6100	Nondepository institutions	25	20	1.5	119	111	22,017	18,883	2,744	2,296	0.5
6140	Personal credit institutions	20	14	2.1	103	92	20,427	15,000	2,115	1,360	0.8
6280	Security and commodity services	3	4	0.9	-	10	-	11,200	-	166	0.1
6300	Insurance carriers	24	15	0.8	123	103	26,699	31,379	3,409	3,078	0.1
6370	Pension, health, and welfare funds	4	3	1.0	6	3	11,333	13,333	58	51	0.1
6400	Insurance agents, brokers, and service	81	84	1.6	310	301	18,658	18,937	6,964	6,682	1.0
6500	Real estate	109	114	1.6	768	560	10,333	12,350	8,807	8,365	0.9
6510	Real estate operators and lessors	49	55	1.7	187	174	16,449	11,356	3,300	2,199	0.8
6530	Real estate agents and managers	38	40	1.3	527	317	8,000	13,338	4,835	5,180	1.0
6540	Title abstract offices	4	8	4.0	14	32	8,000	11,000	151	486	0.9
6552	Subdividers and developers, n.e.c.	4	5	2.1	5	12	6,400	9,000	56	197	0.3
6553	Cemetery subdividers and developers	6	6	1.9	24	25	16,333	10,080	334	303	0.9
6700	Holding and other investment offices	16	17	2.1	61	94	17,836	25,319	1,128	2,601	0.7
6710	Holding offices	4	5	1.7	12	-	31,667	-	396	-	-
TUSCARAWAS, OH											
60 –	**Finance, insurance, and real estate**	160	158	0.7	927	973	18,688	18,664	17,561	18,686	0.3
6000	Depository institutions	40	41	0.8	503	535	19,427	19,282	9,545	10,113	0.5
6020	Commercial banks	30	32	1.1	415	439	20,154	20,018	8,079	8,509	0.6
6030	Savings institutions	6	5	0.5	39	42	20,000	20,095	827	910	0.3
6060	Credit unions	4	4	0.5	49	54	12,816	12,667	639	694	0.7
6100	Nondepository institutions	10	12	0.9	-	54	-	24,074	-	1,376	0.3
6140	Personal credit institutions	6	7	1.0	23	37	25,391	16,973	610	670	0.4
6160	Mortgage bankers and brokers	3	3	0.6	11	-	43,636	-	509	-	-
6300	Insurance carriers	9	6	0.3	45	17	21,511	39,059	1,035	527	0.0
6310	Life insurance	4	2	0.4	35	-	18,286	-	663	-	-
6400	Insurance agents, brokers, and service	48	48	0.9	125	141	23,776	22,355	3,138	3,436	0.5
6500	Real estate	45	41	0.6	198	165	9,212	10,715	2,065	2,209	0.2
6510	Real estate operators and lessors	23	18	0.5	123	87	6,309	7,862	841	750	0.3
6530	Real estate agents and managers	12	16	0.5	52	66	14,077	14,242	840	1,242	0.2
6553	Cemetery subdividers and developers	5	5	1.6	5	-	8,000	-	46	-	-
6700	Holding and other investment offices	3	3	0.4	5	-	4,000	-	16	-	-
UNION, OH											
60 –	**Finance, insurance, and real estate**	46	47	0.2	221	206	18,136	18,621	4,242	4,402	0.1
6000	Depository institutions	15	13	0.3	-	134	-	20,537	-	3,048	0.2
6020	Commercial banks	9	8	0.3	103	97	17,670	17,856	1,984	1,998	0.1

Source: County Business Patterns, 1992/93, CBP-92/93-1, U.S. Department of Commerce, Washington, D.C., April 1995. SIC categories for which data were suppressed or not available for both 1992 and 1993 are *not* displayed. The employment columns represent mid-March employment in the year. Pay per employee is calculated by dividing 1st Quarter payroll, annualized, by mid-March employment. The columns headed "% State" show the county's percentage of the state total for the SIC in 1993; for example, 0.9% for SIC 6030 means that the county had 0.9 percent of the state's total establishments (or payroll) in SIC 6030 in 1993. A dash (-) is used to indicate that data are not available or cannot be calculated; *nec* means not elsewhere classified.

Continued on next page.

SIC	Industry	No. Establishments			Employment		Pay / Employee		Annual Payroll ($ 000)		
		1992	1993	% State	1992	1993	1992	1993	1992	1993	% State
UNION, OH - [continued]											
6400	Insurance agents, brokers, and service	11	15	0.3	-	37	-	17,405	-	659	0.1
6500	Real estate	10	11	0.2	-	16	-	8,500	-	199	0.0
6510	Real estate operators and lessors	5	6	0.2	-	11	-	5,091	-	64	0.0
6530	Real estate agents and managers	4	5	0.2	6	5	13,333	16,000	99	135	0.0
VAN WERT, OH											
60 –	**Finance, insurance, and real estate**	45	49	0.2	729	760	25,953	28,700	18,638	21,840	0.3
6000	Depository institutions	15	16	0.3	154	157	19,143	21,656	3,208	2,787	0.1
6020	Commercial banks	11	12	0.4	128	-	18,469	-	2,500	-	-
6100	Nondepository institutions	4	3	0.2	-	17	-	12,941	-	206	0.0
6400	Insurance agents, brokers, and service	13	15	0.3	38	38	13,895	14,211	567	595	0.1
6500	Real estate	5	5	0.1	9	6	11,556	14,000	117	97	0.0
VINTON, OH											
60 –	**Finance, insurance, and real estate**	7	7	0.0	-	83	-	19,904	-	2,058	0.0
WARREN, OH											
60 –	**Finance, insurance, and real estate**	164	160	0.7	1,012	1,232	24,292	18,474	25,554	23,631	0.3
6000	Depository institutions	55	52	1.1	469	605	25,245	14,638	11,982	8,711	0.4
6020	Commercial banks	39	40	1.4	314	537	22,624	13,907	6,429	7,197	0.5
6100	Nondepository institutions	8	8	0.6	111	122	31,459	31,213	3,306	3,630	0.7
6140	Personal credit institutions	5	3	0.4	-	89	-	21,708	-	1,801	1.1
6300	Insurance carriers	17	16	0.8	86	101	21,767	23,604	2,162	2,811	0.1
6310	Life insurance	4	4	0.7	57	70	20,632	22,629	1,253	1,987	0.4
6370	Pension, health, and welfare funds	5	2	0.7	7	-	4,000	-	139	-	-
6400	Insurance agents, brokers, and service	38	39	0.7	140	135	22,886	24,030	3,491	3,472	0.5
6500	Real estate	42	42	0.6	154	213	12,961	10,216	2,149	2,587	0.3
6510	Real estate operators and lessors	17	14	0.4	88	139	9,773	7,568	837	1,176	0.4
6530	Real estate agents and managers	21	24	0.8	60	69	17,667	15,130	1,066	1,206	0.2
WASHINGTON, OH											
60 –	**Finance, insurance, and real estate**	163	133	0.6	1,091	945	14,511	17,024	16,186	16,835	0.2
6000	Depository institutions	36	34	0.7	654	570	13,896	16,646	8,989	9,326	0.5
6020	Commercial banks	29	27	0.9	603	520	13,506	16,469	8,025	8,297	0.6
6100	Nondepository institutions	8	7	0.5	56	63	24,143	19,111	1,357	1,263	0.3
6200	Security and commodity brokers	3	4	0.4	-	15	-	26,400	-	458	0.1
6300	Insurance carriers	15	10	0.5	-	38	-	21,158	-	734	0.0
6370	Pension, health, and welfare funds	8	5	1.7	9	10	10,667	9,600	260	45	0.1
6400	Insurance agents, brokers, and service	25	31	0.6	104	102	19,500	19,451	2,279	2,600	0.4
6500	Real estate	65	39	0.5	171	115	7,649	10,852	1,316	1,424	0.2
6510	Real estate operators and lessors	40	24	0.7	106	81	6,113	7,753	611	732	0.3
6530	Real estate agents and managers	19	12	0.4	48	-	7,250	-	282	-	-
6700	Holding and other investment offices	11	8	1.0	57	42	20,140	22,952	1,121	1,030	0.3
6733	Trusts, n.e.c.	7	4	2.2	10	1	6,000	4,000	40	42	0.3
WAYNE, OH											
60 –	**Finance, insurance, and real estate**	188	194	0.9	1,531	1,663	20,314	21,263	30,700	35,986	0.5
6000	Depository institutions	57	57	1.2	798	820	18,266	19,922	14,836	15,795	0.8
6020	Commercial banks	38	38	1.3	499	515	17,547	18,625	8,848	9,426	0.6
6030	Savings institutions	11	11	1.0	274	276	20,015	23,203	5,636	5,985	1.8
6060	Credit unions	8	8	1.0	25	29	13,440	11,724	352	384	0.4
6100	Nondepository institutions	6	10	0.7	32	36	16,875	16,556	628	756	0.2
6140	Personal credit institutions	4	6	0.9	-	27	-	12,593	-	455	0.3
6200	Security and commodity brokers	8	8	0.8	23	20	41,043	40,400	776	805	0.1
6210	Security brokers and dealers	6	8	1.5	-	20	-	40,400	-	805	0.2
6300	Insurance carriers	19	14	0.7	354	359	26,836	25,270	8,054	8,609	0.4
6310	Life insurance	5	4	0.7	35	40	23,086	22,900	647	775	0.1
6330	Fire, marine, and casualty insurance	8	7	0.8	296	318	27,959	25,610	7,015	7,764	0.7

Source: County Business Patterns, 1992/93, CBP-92/93-1, U.S. Department of Commerce, Washington, D.C., April 1995. SIC categories for which data were suppressed or not available for both 1992 and 1993 are not displayed. The employment columns represent mid-March employment in the year. Pay per employee is calculated by dividing 1st Quarter payroll, annualized, by mid-March employment. The columns headed "% State" show the county's percentage of the state total for the SIC in 1993; for example, 0.9% for SIC 6030 means that the county had 0.9 percent of the state's total establishments (or payroll) in SIC 6030 in 1993. A dash (-) is used to indicate that data are not available or cannot be calculated; nec means not elsewhere classified.

Continued on next page.

SIC	Industry	No. Establishments			Employment		Pay / Employee		Annual Payroll ($ 000)		
		1992	1993	% State	1992	1993	1992	1993	1992	1993	% State
WAYNE, OH - [continued]											
6370	Pension, health, and welfare funds	4	3	1.0	-	1	-	12,000	-	70	0.1
6400	Insurance agents, brokers, and service	43	44	0.8	136	156	21,647	21,462	3,393	3,949	0.6
6500	Real estate	47	53	0.7	172	258	13,279	18,465	2,621	5,651	0.6
6510	Real estate operators and lessors	20	23	0.7	57	123	12,070	24,553	811	3,364	1.2
6530	Real estate agents and managers	21	25	0.8	100	119	14,240	13,042	1,599	2,057	0.4
6700	Holding and other investment offices	8	8	1.0	16	14	19,500	31,143	392	421	0.1
WILLIAMS, OH											
60 –	**Finance, insurance, and real estate**	58	56	0.2	360	365	19,844	18,849	7,505	7,657	0.1
6000	Depository institutions	25	24	0.5	246	238	18,179	18,387	4,625	4,589	0.2
6020	Commercial banks	18	17	0.6	205	196	18,634	19,000	3,939	3,873	0.3
6400	Insurance agents, brokers, and service	13	11	0.2	50	40	30,000	32,200	1,622	1,627	0.2
6500	Real estate	13	15	0.2	25	44	17,920	8,455	460	446	0.0
6510	Real estate operators and lessors	4	5	0.2	4	14	5,000	5,714	23	74	0.0
6530	Real estate agents and managers	9	9	0.3	21	30	20,381	9,733	437	367	0.1
WOOD, OH											
60 –	**Finance, insurance, and real estate**	203	224	1.0	1,437	1,536	22,903	22,073	33,709	35,571	0.5
6000	Depository institutions	62	62	1.3	661	679	21,422	20,837	13,593	13,725	0.7
6020	Commercial banks	41	40	1.4	468	488	21,513	20,205	9,526	9,426	0.6
6030	Savings institutions	12	12	1.1	157	155	21,885	23,535	3,432	3,627	1.1
6100	Nondepository institutions	6	4	0.3	23	23	22,087	27,478	560	824	0.2
6200	Security and commodity brokers	9	14	1.4	-	58	-	41,379	-	2,578	0.4
6300	Insurance carriers	21	14	0.7	206	177	30,311	32,429	6,503	5,494	0.3
6310	Life insurance	3	3	0.5	89	86	29,708	34,047	2,595	2,834	0.5
6330	Fire, marine, and casualty insurance	11	7	0.8	59	53	30,983	32,679	2,076	1,895	0.2
6400	Insurance agents, brokers, and service	39	50	0.9	146	168	25,068	22,357	3,749	3,991	0.6
6500	Real estate	57	71	1.0	321	362	15,178	13,591	5,685	6,345	0.7
6510	Real estate operators and lessors	28	39	1.2	213	263	16,225	13,506	4,074	4,478	1.6
6530	Real estate agents and managers	19	23	0.8	85	75	11,435	11,893	1,091	1,082	0.2
6552	Subdividers and developers, n.e.c.	3	4	1.7	4	3	19,000	18,667	69	229	0.4
6700	Holding and other investment offices	8	9	1.1	41	69	50,634	33,449	2,167	2,614	0.7
6733	Trusts, n.e.c.	3	3	1.7	1	-	4,000	-	31	-	-
WYANDOT, OH											
60 –	**Finance, insurance, and real estate**	42	44	0.2	218	204	18,018	20,451	3,847	4,357	0.1
6000	Depository institutions	15	14	0.3	159	150	18,843	20,907	2,872	3,225	0.2
6020	Commercial banks	11	12	0.4	144	-	18,944	-	2,603	-	-
6300	Insurance carriers	4	1	0.1	10	-	13,600	-	145	-	-
6400	Insurance agents, brokers, and service	14	19	0.4	23	27	20,870	21,333	403	508	0.1
6500	Real estate	8	8	0.1	-	20	-	11,400	-	282	0.0
6530	Real estate agents and managers	5	4	0.1	15	-	12,533	-	249	-	-

Source: County Business Patterns, 1992/93, CBP-92/93-1, U.S. Department of Commerce, Washington, D.C., April 1995. SIC categories for which data were suppressed or not available for both 1992 and 1993 are not displayed. The employment columns represent mid-March employment in the year. Pay per employee is calculated by dividing 1st Quarter payroll, annualized, by mid-March employment. The columns headed "% State" show the county's percentage of the state total for the SIC in 1993; for example, 0.9% for SIC 6030 means that the county had 0.9 percent of the state's total establishments (or payroll) in SIC 6030 in 1993. A dash (-) is used to indicate that data are not available or cannot be calculated; nec means not elsewhere classified.

OKLAHOMA

SIC	Industry	No. Establishments			Employment		Pay / Employee		Annual Payroll ($ 000)		
		1992	1993	% State	1992	1993	1992	1993	1992	1993	% State
ADAIR, OK											
60 –	**Finance, insurance, and real estate**	17	18	0.2	79	87	17,063	17,517	1,620	1,760	0.1
6000	Depository institutions	4	4	0.3	54	54	17,630	18,519	1,165	1,232	0.2
6020	Commercial banks	4	4	0.5	54	54	17,630	18,519	1,165	1,232	0.3
6100	Nondepository institutions	4	5	0.6	-	11	-	19,273	-	218	0.2
6400	Insurance agents, brokers, and service	3	4	0.2	-	9	-	12,444	-	96	0.1
6500	Real estate	5	5	0.2	12	13	15,000	15,385	192	214	0.1
ALFALFA, OK											
60 –	**Finance, insurance, and real estate**	15	16	0.2	78	82	16,154	16,927	1,299	1,391	0.1
6000	Depository institutions	7	7	0.6	65	69	16,985	17,333	1,142	1,199	0.2
6020	Commercial banks	7	7	0.9	65	69	16,985	17,333	1,142	1,199	0.3
6400	Insurance agents, brokers, and service	5	6	0.3	9	7	10,222	14,857	91	103	0.1
6500	Real estate	2	3	0.1	-	6	-	14,667	-	89	0.0
ATOKA, OK											
60 –	**Finance, insurance, and real estate**	11	12	0.2	73	92	18,027	14,565	1,306	1,596	0.1
6400	Insurance agents, brokers, and service	6	6	0.3	-	10	-	8,400	-	92	0.1
BEAVER, OK											
60 –	**Finance, insurance, and real estate**	9	8	0.1	54	52	18,370	17,000	947	898	0.1
6000	Depository institutions	5	5	0.4	44	42	17,545	17,048	776	747	0.1
BECKHAM, OK											
60 –	**Finance, insurance, and real estate**	38	38	0.5	201	202	18,269	19,327	4,050	3,984	0.3
6000	Depository institutions	9	9	0.8	114	113	19,193	19,681	2,376	2,219	0.4
6400	Insurance agents, brokers, and service	8	10	0.5	24	24	14,667	15,833	393	416	0.3
6500	Real estate	16	13	0.5	48	48	10,417	9,167	548	491	0.2
6510	Real estate operators and lessors	10	11	1.0	39	-	7,897	-	379	-	-
BLAINE, OK											
60 –	**Finance, insurance, and real estate**	26	26	0.3	150	128	17,600	17,781	2,837	2,448	0.2
6000	Depository institutions	8	7	0.6	117	78	18,974	20,872	2,366	1,746	0.3
6020	Commercial banks	6	7	0.9	-	78	-	20,872	-	1,746	0.4
6400	Insurance agents, brokers, and service	8	8	0.4	18	-	12,222	-	256	-	-
6500	Real estate	8	7	0.3	-	8	-	13,500	-	115	0.1
6540	Title abstract offices	4	4	2.6	9	6	14,667	16,667	117	95	0.3
BRYAN, OK											
60 –	**Finance, insurance, and real estate**	42	49	0.7	323	323	17,932	17,796	6,323	6,443	0.4
6000	Depository institutions	10	10	0.9	188	204	20,000	18,451	4,144	4,336	0.8
6100	Nondepository institutions	9	10	1.3	39	32	13,949	18,625	606	618	0.6
6400	Insurance agents, brokers, and service	8	15	0.8	29	36	18,897	18,111	569	686	0.4
6500	Real estate	11	12	0.5	58	-	12,483	-	718	-	-
6510	Real estate operators and lessors	4	5	0.5	24	17	11,167	9,882	246	150	0.2
6530	Real estate agents and managers	3	5	0.5	7	-	4,571	-	38	-	-
CADDO, OK											
60 –	**Finance, insurance, and real estate**	38	41	0.5	233	260	22,043	18,923	5,860	5,463	0.3
6000	Depository institutions	14	14	1.2	157	161	24,510	22,460	4,384	3,719	0.7

Source: County Business Patterns, 1992/93, CBP-92/93-1, U.S. Department of Commerce, Washington, D.C., April 1995. SIC categories for which data were suppressed or not available for both 1992 and 1993 are *not* displayed. The employment columns represent mid-March employment in the year. Pay per employee is calculated by dividing 1st Quarter payroll, annualized, by mid-March employment. The columns headed "% State" show the county's percentage of the state total for the SIC in 1993; for example, 0.9% for SIC 6030 means that the county had 0.9 percent of the state's total establishments (or payroll) in SIC 6030 in 1993. A dash (-) is used to indicate that data are not available or cannot be calculated; *nec* means not elsewhere classified.

Continued on next page.

SIC	Industry	No. Establishments			Employment		Pay / Employee		Annual Payroll ($ 000)		
		1992	1993	% State	1992	1993	1992	1993	1992	1993	% State
CADDO, OK - [continued]											
6400	Insurance agents, brokers, and service	10	11	0.6	19	20	8,842	8,600	168	249	0.2
6500	Real estate	8	10	0.4	24	49	9,000	6,367	281	431	0.2
6510	Real estate operators and lessors	3	5	0.5	13	36	8,308	5,444	159	297	0.5
CANADIAN, OK											
60 –	**Finance, insurance, and real estate**	111	114	1.5	-	866	-	16,291	-	15,590	1.0
6000	Depository institutions	23	23	2.0	341	337	20,012	20,439	7,306	7,044	1.4
6020	Commercial banks	15	15	2.0	252	251	20,762	20,829	5,497	5,281	1.2
6030	Savings institutions	5	5	2.7	29	-	15,724	-	611	-	-
6060	Credit unions	3	3	2.0	60	-	18,933	-	1,198	-	-
6100	Nondepository institutions	5	4	0.5	103	76	26,680	22,632	2,673	1,843	1.7
6400	Insurance agents, brokers, and service	27	27	1.4	94	108	9,745	9,370	993	1,112	0.7
6500	Real estate	39	45	1.9	267	318	11,745	11,057	3,525	4,273	2.1
6510	Real estate operators and lessors	15	20	1.9	103	114	10,718	8,842	1,187	1,141	1.9
6530	Real estate agents and managers	14	18	1.8	120	170	10,567	10,800	1,457	2,191	2.3
6552	Subdividers and developers, n.e.c.	3	3	3.1	5	-	20,800	-	144	-	-
6700	Holding and other investment offices	8	7	1.4	40	-	7,700	-	410	-	-
CARTER, OK											
60 –	**Finance, insurance, and real estate**	122	134	1.8	-	857	-	22,427	-	19,202	1.2
6000	Depository institutions	14	15	1.3	314	340	22,331	21,212	7,597	7,013	1.3
6020	Commercial banks	10	11	1.4	296	315	22,784	21,943	7,326	6,740	1.6
6100	Nondepository institutions	21	23	3.0	62	67	16,258	15,522	1,027	1,176	1.1
6140	Personal credit institutions	19	20	3.4	-	56	-	16,357	-	1,022	2.2
6160	Mortgage bankers and brokers	2	3	2.4	-	11	-	11,273	-	154	0.3
6200	Security and commodity brokers	7	7	2.0	-	15	-	26,133	-	468	0.4
6300	Insurance carriers	10	8	1.7	67	64	13,791	18,188	1,001	1,548	0.4
6330	Fire, marine, and casualty insurance	4	2	1.0	21	-	14,667	-	270	-	-
6400	Insurance agents, brokers, and service	25	31	1.7	86	99	20,000	19,879	1,816	1,877	1.2
6500	Real estate	23	27	1.1	79	74	9,519	11,351	801	971	0.5
6510	Real estate operators and lessors	12	16	1.5	41	38	6,049	7,368	257	303	0.5
6530	Real estate agents and managers	5	6	0.6	7	8	9,143	14,000	67	167	0.2
6700	Holding and other investment offices	22	23	4.7	208	198	35,885	33,354	6,626	6,149	5.3
CHEROKEE, OK											
60 –	**Finance, insurance, and real estate**	49	54	0.7	233	346	16,326	16,162	4,305	6,020	0.4
6000	Depository institutions	6	10	0.9	138	247	17,014	16,421	2,781	4,366	0.8
6020	Commercial banks	4	7	0.9	-	233	-	16,549	-	4,125	1.0
6100	Nondepository institutions	11	12	1.5	25	29	10,880	11,310	293	342	0.3
6200	Security and commodity brokers	3	3	0.9	-	6	-	60,000	-	369	0.3
6400	Insurance agents, brokers, and service	9	12	0.6	25	-	12,160	-	311	-	-
6500	Real estate	16	16	0.7	33	37	12,848	12,757	464	539	0.3
6510	Real estate operators and lessors	4	5	0.5	6	-	9,333	-	63	-	-
6530	Real estate agents and managers	6	7	0.7	11	13	9,818	8,923	110	168	0.2
6552	Subdividers and developers, n.e.c.	1	3	3.1	-	8	-	17,000	-	133	2.2
CHOCTAW, OK											
60 –	**Finance, insurance, and real estate**	26	26	0.3	128	116	16,562	18,310	2,213	2,052	0.1
6000	Depository institutions	4	4	0.3	63	66	25,143	23,939	1,667	1,437	0.3
6020	Commercial banks	4	4	0.5	63	66	25,143	23,939	1,667	1,437	0.3
6100	Nondepository institutions	7	8	1.0	26	26	8,308	10,154	219	302	0.3
6140	Personal credit institutions	7	7	1.2	26	-	8,308	-	219	-	-
6500	Real estate	3	4	0.2	9	4	7,556	13,000	57	61	0.0
CIMARRON, OK											
60 –	**Finance, insurance, and real estate**	7	6	0.1	-	42	-	13,429	-	683	0.0

Source: County Business Patterns, 1992/93, CBP-92/93-1, U.S. Department of Commerce, Washington, D.C., April 1995. SIC categories for which data were suppressed or not available for both 1992 and 1993 are not displayed. The employment columns represent mid-March employment in the year. Pay per employee is calculated by dividing 1st Quarter payroll, annualized, by mid-March employment. The columns headed "% State" show the county's percentage of the state total for the SIC in 1993; for example, 0.9% for SIC 6030 means that the county had 0.9 percent of the state's total establishments (or payroll) in SIC 6030 in 1993. A dash (-) is used to indicate that data are not available or cannot be calculated; nec means not elsewhere classified.

SIC	Industry	No. Establishments			Employment		Pay / Employee		Annual Payroll ($ 000)		
		1992	1993	% State	1992	1993	1992	1993	1992	1993	% State
CLEVELAND, OK											
60 –	**Finance, insurance, and real estate**	272	313	*4.2*	1,920	1,825	18,058	18,374	36,961	36,676	*2.3*
6000	Depository institutions	30	35	*3.0*	602	607	20,645	20,422	13,276	12,575	*2.4*
6020	Commercial banks	20	23	*3.0*	553	542	21,071	20,908	12,482	11,416	*2.7*
6030	Savings institutions	6	5	*2.7*	38	30	16,105	16,667	632	518	*1.3*
6060	Credit unions	4	6	*4.0*	11	-	14,909	-	162	-	-
6100	Nondepository institutions	18	17	*2.2*	70	89	18,514	16,809	1,579	1,714	*1.6*
6140	Personal credit institutions	14	13	*2.2*	-	55	-	12,655	-	839	*1.8*
6160	Mortgage bankers and brokers	3	3	*2.4*	28	-	21,857		822	-	-
6200	Security and commodity brokers	8	10	*2.9*	22	19	35,818	48,421	885	1,225	*1.1*
6300	Insurance carriers	15	14	*2.9*	93	31	30,710	38,968	2,662	1,303	*0.4*
6400	Insurance agents, brokers, and service	55	67	*3.6*	177	212	18,554	19,906	3,407	4,909	*3.2*
6500	Real estate	137	159	*6.7*	832	728	13,442	13,396	11,525	10,973	*5.5*
6510	Real estate operators and lessors	59	68	*6.4*	321	300	10,779	9,773	4,039	3,175	*5.3*
6530	Real estate agents and managers	50	70	*7.1*	350	275	14,297	12,975	4,407	3,652	*3.8*
6540	Title abstract offices	4	6	*3.8*	86	94	22,651	22,894	2,023	2,459	*7.7*
6553	Cemetery subdividers and developers	3	5	*8.2*	3	12	5,333	8,333	18	104	*1.9*
6700	Holding and other investment offices	9	11	*2.2*	124	139	22,871	25,468	3,627	3,977	*3.4*
6792	Oil royalty traders	1	3	*3.1*	-	3	-	14,667	-	66	*0.6*
COAL, OK											
60 –	**Finance, insurance, and real estate**	3	4	*0.1*	-	-	-	-	-	-	-
COMANCHE, OK											
60 –	**Finance, insurance, and real estate**	268	279	*3.7*	1,828	1,646	16,470	15,915	27,540	27,759	*1.8*
6000	Depository institutions	33	33	*2.8*	857	678	16,560	16,920	12,233	12,208	*2.3*
6020	Commercial banks	19	19	*2.5*	493	515	17,176	17,934	9,322	9,858	*2.3*
6030	Savings institutions	5	3	*1.6*	273	-	15,780	-	1,317	-	-
6060	Credit unions	6	7	*4.7*	-	112	-	14,679	-	1,772	*4.5*
6100	Nondepository institutions	49	55	*7.1*	219	227	16,274	14,026	3,813	3,539	*3.3*
6140	Personal credit institutions	45	48	*8.2*	209	209	15,866	13,512	3,499	2,983	*6.3*
6160	Mortgage bankers and brokers	3	6	*4.8*	-	18	-	20,000	-	554	*1.2*
6200	Security and commodity brokers	12	9	*2.6*	38	38	32,947	40,737	1,326	1,442	*1.3*
6210	Security brokers and dealers	9	7	*3.0*	36	-	34,222	-	1,300	-	-
6280	Security and commodity services	3	2	*2.0*	2	-	10,000	-	26	-	-
6300	Insurance carriers	15	13	*2.7*	62	54	44,129	33,704	1,803	1,761	*0.5*
6310	Life insurance	4	3	*2.2*	28	31	22,286	27,613	639	903	*0.7*
6400	Insurance agents, brokers, and service	50	52	*2.8*	136	140	15,176	15,543	2,265	2,341	*1.5*
6500	Real estate	103	110	*4.6*	480	462	11,717	10,944	5,531	5,783	*2.9*
6510	Real estate operators and lessors	41	54	*5.1*	144	266	9,750	8,797	1,636	2,703	*4.5*
6530	Real estate agents and managers	44	46	*4.7*	217	131	13,991	12,672	2,639	2,010	*2.1*
6552	Subdividers and developers, n.e.c.	8	7	*7.1*	50	19	5,680	9,474	292	176	*2.9*
6700	Holding and other investment offices	6	7	*1.4*	36	47	18,778	20,000	569	685	*0.6*
COTTON, OK											
60 –	**Finance, insurance, and real estate**	7	7	*0.1*	-	-	-	-	-	-	-
6400	Insurance agents, brokers, and service	3	3	*0.2*	-	6	-	14,667	-	78	*0.1*
CRAIG, OK											
60 –	**Finance, insurance, and real estate**	28	28	*0.4*	164	177	18,634	18,893	3,156	3,497	*0.2*
6000	Depository institutions	6	8	*0.7*	101	117	19,446	19,795	1,993	2,324	*0.4*
6020	Commercial banks	5	5	*0.7*	-	109	-	20,110	-	2,196	*0.5*
6100	Nondepository institutions	4	3	*0.4*	15	-	18,667	-	316	-	-
6400	Insurance agents, brokers, and service	7	8	*0.4*	16	18	17,250	15,333	268	260	*0.2*
6500	Real estate	10	8	*0.3*	-	28	-	15,429	-	551	*0.3*
6510	Real estate operators and lessors	3	4	*0.4*	2	-	4,000	-	20	-	-

Source: County Business Patterns, 1992/93, CBP-92/93-1, U.S. Department of Commerce, Washington, D.C., April 1995. SIC categories for which data were suppressed or not available for both 1992 and 1993 are *not* displayed. The employment columns represent mid-March employment in the year. Pay per employee is calculated by dividing 1st Quarter payroll, annualized, by mid-March employment. The columns headed "% State" show the county's percentage of the state total for the SIC in 1993; for example, 0.9% for SIC 6030 means that the county had 0.9 percent of the state's total establishments (or payroll) in SIC 6030 in 1993. A dash (-) is used to indicate that data are not available or cannot be calculated; *nec* means not elsewhere classified.

SIC	Industry	No. Establishments			Employment		Pay / Employee		Annual Payroll ($ 000)		
		1992	1993	% State	1992	1993	1992	1993	1992	1993	% State
CREEK, OK											
60 –	**Finance, insurance, and real estate**	87	92	1.2	556	551	18,252	18,817	10,921	10,919	0.7
6000	Depository institutions	14	15	1.3	317	324	20,278	20,259	6,433	6,745	1.3
6100	Nondepository institutions	20	20	2.6	56	51	14,071	15,137	807	783	0.7
6140	Personal credit institutions	17	16	2.7	52	-	14,308	-	756	-	-
6160	Mortgage bankers and brokers	3	3	2.4	4	-	11,000	-	51	-	-
6300	Insurance carriers	4	2	0.4	7	-	26,286	-	214	-	-
6330	Fire, marine, and casualty insurance	3	1	0.5	7	-	26,286	-	203	-	-
6400	Insurance agents, brokers, and service	19	24	1.3	47	64	15,745	14,250	792	1,009	0.7
6500	Real estate	20	20	0.8	80	57	12,500	14,596	1,585	939	0.5
6510	Real estate operators and lessors	8	9	0.8	22	18	9,091	10,889	248	218	0.4
6530	Real estate agents and managers	5	6	0.6	19	17	11,158	12,471	215	203	0.2
6540	Title abstract offices	3	3	1.9	14	-	18,571	-	289	-	-
6700	Holding and other investment offices	9	9	1.8	-	49	-	18,122	-	980	0.8
6710	Holding offices	3	3	3.5	6	-	45,333	-	368	-	-
CUSTER, OK											
60 –	**Finance, insurance, and real estate**	80	88	1.2	395	405	19,423	18,449	8,137	8,234	0.5
6000	Depository institutions	17	17	1.5	212	205	23,000	21,307	4,901	4,686	0.9
6020	Commercial banks	11	11	1.4	183	176	24,568	22,500	4,506	4,284	1.0
6100	Nondepository institutions	11	12	1.5	39	46	20,000	19,565	829	879	0.8
6140	Personal credit institutions	8	9	1.5	25	-	17,440	-	486	-	-
6400	Insurance agents, brokers, and service	22	22	1.2	71	71	16,169	15,437	1,085	1,083	0.7
6500	Real estate	23	28	1.2	48	52	9,417	10,077	529	625	0.3
6510	Real estate operators and lessors	13	19	1.8	23	-	7,826	-	245	-	-
6530	Real estate agents and managers	6	6	0.6	13	13	8,615	8,615	109	176	0.2
DELAWARE, OK											
60 –	**Finance, insurance, and real estate**	36	36	0.5	194	206	17,113	16,175	3,456	3,518	0.2
6000	Depository institutions	8	8	0.7	98	108	23,102	19,370	2,225	2,061	0.4
6400	Insurance agents, brokers, and service	5	5	0.3	22	11	22,545	20,364	528	242	0.2
6500	Real estate	16	19	0.8	62	80	7,548	11,450	621	1,112	0.6
6510	Real estate operators and lessors	5	5	0.5	14	9	7,429	8,000	221	93	0.2
6530	Real estate agents and managers	7	9	0.9	22	55	10,000	9,018	257	624	0.7
DEWEY, OK											
60 –	**Finance, insurance, and real estate**	10	10	0.1	67	73	20,836	19,726	1,461	1,546	0.1
6000	Depository institutions	5	5	0.4	56	58	23,143	23,034	1,364	1,440	0.3
6020	Commercial banks	5	5	0.7	56	58	23,143	23,034	1,364	1,440	0.3
ELLIS, OK											
60 –	**Finance, insurance, and real estate**	9	9	0.1	53	53	16,755	17,962	925	966	0.1
6000	Depository institutions	3	3	0.3	40	41	18,400	19,707	762	814	0.2
6020	Commercial banks	3	3	0.4	40	41	18,400	19,707	762	814	0.2
GARFIELD, OK											
60 –	**Finance, insurance, and real estate**	165	166	2.2	1,019	979	20,416	20,613	22,008	20,964	1.3
6000	Depository institutions	22	24	2.1	369	404	23,263	21,743	8,565	9,307	1.8
6020	Commercial banks	15	16	2.1	301	325	24,545	22,806	7,375	7,895	1.9
6100	Nondepository institutions	19	18	2.3	81	84	24,049	19,810	1,904	1,792	1.7
6140	Personal credit institutions	16	15	2.6	53	53	19,925	15,623	1,092	864	1.8
6200	Security and commodity brokers	12	10	2.9	-	23	-	77,217	-	1,627	1.5
6210	Security brokers and dealers	5	4	1.7	13	-	81,231	-	1,501	-	-
6300	Insurance carriers	13	14	2.9	44	124	20,545	22,065	879	2,441	0.7
6310	Life insurance	4	5	3.6	15	68	30,667	29,706	391	1,731	1.4
6330	Fire, marine, and casualty insurance	5	5	2.4	7	-	32,000	-	229	-	-
6400	Insurance agents, brokers, and service	33	35	1.9	172	114	17,605	17,825	3,608	2,417	1.6
6500	Real estate	56	56	2.3	198	213	11,354	12,657	2,560	2,931	1.5
6510	Real estate operators and lessors	25	28	2.6	88	94	8,545	8,000	895	844	1.4

Source: County Business Patterns, 1992/93, CBP-92/93-1, U.S. Department of Commerce, Washington, D.C., April 1995. SIC categories for which data were suppressed or not available for both 1992 and 1993 are not displayed. The employment columns represent mid-March employment in the year. Pay per employee is calculated by dividing 1st Quarter payroll, annualized, by mid-March employment. The columns headed "% State" show the county's percentage of the state total for the SIC in 1993; for example, 0.9% for SIC 6030 means that the county had 0.9 percent of the state's total establishments (or payroll) in SIC 6030 in 1993. A dash (-) is used to indicate that data are not available or cannot be calculated; nec means not elsewhere classified.

Continued on next page.

SIC	Industry	No. Establishments			Employment		Pay / Employee		Annual Payroll ($ 000)		
		1992	1993	% State	1992	1993	1992	1993	1992	1993	% State
GARFIELD, OK - [continued]											
6530	Real estate agents and managers	20	20	2.0	71	88	12,113	15,364	993	1,450	1.5
6700	Holding and other investment offices	10	9	1.8	-	17	-	28,941	-	449	0.4
6799	Investors, n.e.c.	3	5	6.0	-	12	-	37,333	-	406	3.2
GARVIN, OK											
60 –	**Finance, insurance, and real estate**	58	52	0.7	258	240	19,922	19,083	5,387	5,178	0.3
6000	Depository institutions	13	13	1.1	153	159	20,392	20,629	3,542	3,810	0.7
6100	Nondepository institutions	10	7	0.9	-	24	-	18,667	-	447	0.4
6200	Security and commodity brokers	3	3	0.9	9	8	30,222	27,500	256	268	0.2
6400	Insurance agents, brokers, and service	16	17	0.9	33	-	14,424	-	524	-	-
6500	Real estate	11	10	0.4	17	12	9,412	10,667	166	148	0.1
6510	Real estate operators and lessors	4	5	0.5	4	5	8,000	8,000	32	40	0.1
6540	Title abstract offices	3	3	1.9	6	-	15,333	-	109	-	-
GRADY, OK											
60 –	**Finance, insurance, and real estate**	65	66	0.9	433	397	17,533	18,317	8,061	8,171	0.5
6000	Depository institutions	16	17	1.5	287	260	18,578	18,738	5,512	5,397	1.0
6020	Commercial banks	13	14	1.8	235	252	20,494	18,730	5,268	5,265	1.2
6030	Savings institutions	3	3	1.6	52	8	9,923	19,000	244	132	0.3
6100	Nondepository institutions	9	10	1.3	24	26	15,500	15,846	398	436	0.4
6200	Security and commodity brokers	4	4	1.1	8	9	30,000	28,444	248	303	0.3
6300	Insurance carriers	5	4	0.8	28	23	18,286	24,348	598	609	0.2
6400	Insurance agents, brokers, and service	11	13	0.7	33	30	14,303	19,467	522	612	0.4
6500	Real estate	16	15	0.6	44	36	12,727	13,556	642	673	0.3
6510	Real estate operators and lessors	6	5	0.5	-	8	-	8,500	-	110	0.2
6700	Holding and other investment offices	4	3	0.6	9	13	11,556	7,692	141	141	0.1
GRANT, OK											
60 –	**Finance, insurance, and real estate**	16	16	0.2	83	84	18,940	20,952	1,879	1,969	0.1
6000	Depository institutions	8	8	0.7	70	68	20,457	23,000	1,713	1,760	0.3
6020	Commercial banks	7	8	1.0	-	68	-	23,000	-	1,760	0.4
6400	Insurance agents, brokers, and service	3	3	0.2	8	-	10,500	-	85	-	-
6500	Real estate	3	3	0.1	2	5	20,000	19,200	65	101	0.1
GREER, OK											
60 –	**Finance, insurance, and real estate**	9	10	0.1	62	-	15,419	-	966	-	-
6000	Depository institutions	4	4	0.3	54	-	16,074	-	875	-	-
6020	Commercial banks	4	4	0.5	54	-	16,074	-	875	-	-
6400	Insurance agents, brokers, and service	3	5	0.3	-	7	-	9,143	-	74	0.0
HARMON, OK											
60 –	**Finance, insurance, and real estate**	7	7	0.1	-	50	-	13,920	-	1,098	0.1
HARPER, OK											
60 –	**Finance, insurance, and real estate**	7	9	0.1	-	-	-	-	-	-	-
6400	Insurance agents, brokers, and service	3	4	0.2	5	8	10,400	8,500	43	79	0.1
6500	Real estate	2	3	0.1	-	4	-	13,000	-	54	0.0
HASKELL, OK											
60 –	**Finance, insurance, and real estate**	8	9	0.1	-	-	-	-	-	-	-
6400	Insurance agents, brokers, and service	3	4	0.2	9	10	13,778	12,800	131	145	0.1
6500	Real estate	3	3	0.1	6	-	16,667	-	124	-	-
HUGHES, OK											
60 –	**Finance, insurance, and real estate**	19	21	0.3	99	106	15,111	15,396	1,624	1,738	0.1
6000	Depository institutions	4	4	0.3	75	72	16,320	17,611	1,288	1,356	0.3
6020	Commercial banks	4	4	0.5	75	72	16,320	17,611	1,288	1,356	0.3

Source: County Business Patterns, 1992/93, CBP-92/93-1, U.S. Department of Commerce, Washington, D.C., April 1995. SIC categories for which data were suppressed or not available for both 1992 and 1993 are *not* displayed. The employment columns represent mid-March employment in the year. Pay per employee is calculated by dividing 1st Quarter payroll, annualized, by mid-March employment. The columns headed "% State" show the county's percentage of the state total for the SIC in 1993; for example, 0.9% for SIC 6030 means that the county had 0.9 percent of the state's total establishments (or payroll) in SIC 6030 in 1993. A dash (-) is used to indicate that data are not available or cannot be calculated; *nec* means not elsewhere classified.

Continued on next page.

SIC	Industry	No. Establishments			Employment		Pay / Employee		Annual Payroll ($ 000)		
		1992	1993	% State	1992	1993	1992	1993	1992	1993	% State
HUGHES, OK - [continued]											
6400	Insurance agents, brokers, and service	6	5	0.3	13	14	10,462	11,143	155	153	0.1
6500	Real estate	5	6	0.3	5	8	15,200	13,000	116	112	0.1
6700	Holding and other investment offices	2	3	0.6	-	5	-	10,400	-	54	0.0
JACKSON, OK											
60 –	**Finance, insurance, and real estate**	60	60	0.8	351	331	22,621	16,640	7,461	7,102	0.5
6000	Depository institutions	9	11	0.9	158	201	26,557	16,000	3,326	4,443	0.9
6100	Nondepository institutions	14	13	1.7	77	43	17,351	18,698	1,399	838	0.8
6400	Insurance agents, brokers, and service	11	12	0.6	25	25	14,880	15,040	416	479	0.3
6510	Real estate operators and lessors	10	13	1.2	24	32	7,833	10,500	239	394	0.7
6530	Real estate agents and managers	7	6	0.6	11	6	8,364	7,333	103	44	0.0
JEFFERSON, OK											
60 –	**Finance, insurance, and real estate**	13	15	0.2	72	68	17,611	17,824	1,315	1,426	0.1
6000	Depository institutions	5	4	0.3	57	48	20,211	20,167	1,202	1,159	0.2
6020	Commercial banks	5	4	0.5	57	48	20,211	20,167	1,202	1,159	0.3
6400	Insurance agents, brokers, and service	2	3	0.2	-	2	-	8,000	-	24	0.0
JOHNSTON, OK											
60 –	**Finance, insurance, and real estate**	7	8	0.1	-	61	-	8,787	-	548	0.0
6500	Real estate	2	3	0.1	-	4	-	9,000	-	30	0.0
KAY, OK											
60 –	**Finance, insurance, and real estate**	107	122	1.6	-	826	-	20,823	-	17,648	1.1
6000	Depository institutions	22	26	2.2	541	471	20,909	22,633	11,296	10,870	2.1
6100	Nondepository institutions	15	16	2.1	148	135	15,351	17,452	2,255	2,195	2.0
6140	Personal credit institutions	11	11	1.9	48	-	14,667	-	682	-	-
6300	Insurance carriers	7	7	1.5	-	15	-	39,733	-	598	0.2
6400	Insurance agents, brokers, and service	27	33	1.8	88	89	17,045	17,438	1,451	1,617	1.0
6500	Real estate	29	33	1.4	-	87	-	9,701	-	952	0.5
6510	Real estate operators and lessors	10	11	1.0	28	-	7,000	-	205	-	-
6530	Real estate agents and managers	10	13	1.3	15	13	8,800	8,615	115	120	0.1
6553	Cemetery subdividers and developers	5	5	8.2	13	-	10,154	-	151	-	-
KINGFISHER, OK											
60 –	**Finance, insurance, and real estate**	35	33	0.4	305	292	19,384	17,260	5,880	5,298	0.3
6000	Depository institutions	13	10	0.9	223	190	20,969	19,789	4,442	3,909	0.8
6400	Insurance agents, brokers, and service	12	12	0.6	-	36	-	12,000	-	482	0.3
6500	Real estate	5	7	0.3	-	39	-	8,308	-	377	0.2
6530	Real estate agents and managers	3	5	0.5	7	-	9,143	-	152	-	-
KIOWA, OK											
60 –	**Finance, insurance, and real estate**	26	24	0.3	108	112	16,481	16,429	1,889	2,268	0.1
6000	Depository institutions	8	8	0.7	80	83	19,250	18,602	1,621	1,952	0.4
6020	Commercial banks	8	8	1.0	80	83	19,250	18,602	1,621	1,952	0.5
6400	Insurance agents, brokers, and service	11	9	0.5	16	18	6,250	7,556	107	134	0.1
6500	Real estate	4	3	0.1	6	6	12,000	12,667	79	76	0.0
LATIMER, OK											
60 –	**Finance, insurance, and real estate**	17	18	0.2	-	70	-	13,943	-	1,026	0.1
6000	Depository institutions	3	2	0.2	43	-	15,349	-	711	-	-
6020	Commercial banks	3	2	0.3	43	-	15,349	-	711	-	-
6100	Nondepository institutions	4	4	0.5	-	10	-	12,800	-	122	0.1
6400	Insurance agents, brokers, and service	3	4	0.2	4	6	7,000	6,667	32	37	0.0
6500	Real estate	4	4	0.2	8	-	11,500	-	85	-	-

Source: County Business Patterns, 1992/93, CBP-92/93-1, U.S. Department of Commerce, Washington, D.C., April 1995. SIC categories for which data were suppressed or not available for both 1992 and 1993 are *not* displayed. The employment columns represent mid-March employment in the year. Pay per employee is calculated by dividing 1st Quarter payroll, annualized, by mid-March employment. The columns headed "% State" show the county's percentage of the state total for the SIC in 1993; for example, 0.9% for SIC 6030 means that the county had 0.9 percent of the state's total establishments (or payroll) in SIC 6030 in 1993. A dash (-) is used to indicate that data are not available or cannot be calculated; *nec* means not elsewhere classified.

SIC	Industry	No. Establishments			Employment		Pay / Employee		Annual Payroll ($ 000)		
		1992	1993	% State	1992	1993	1992	1993	1992	1993	% State
LE FLORE, OK											
60 –	**Finance, insurance, and real estate**	63	67	*0.9*	304	325	18,474	17,625	6,115	6,389	*0.4*
6000	Depository institutions	11	12	*1.0*	187	199	20,920	19,337	4,322	4,292	*0.8*
6100	Nondepository institutions	14	12	*1.5*	-	36	-	15,444	-	584	*0.5*
6400	Insurance agents, brokers, and service	16	18	*1.0*	40	38	12,900	11,684	544	497	*0.3*
6500	Real estate	16	18	*0.8*	34	-	13,647	-	487	-	*-*
6510	Real estate operators and lessors	5	7	*0.7*	6	5	10,000	12,000	60	67	*0.1*
6530	Real estate agents and managers	6	6	*0.6*	5	8	8,800	9,000	45	64	*0.1*
6700	Holding and other investment offices	2	4	*0.8*	-	8	-	13,500	-	204	*0.2*
LINCOLN, OK											
60 –	**Finance, insurance, and real estate**	34	32	*0.4*	544	511	24,772	25,636	14,065	13,478	*0.9*
6000	Depository institutions	16	14	*1.2*	186	183	20,108	20,415	4,257	3,928	*0.8*
6020	Commercial banks	13	11	*1.4*	173	166	20,439	20,964	4,035	3,678	*0.9*
6530	Real estate agents and managers	6	4	*0.4*	-	5	-	8,800	-	43	*0.0*
LOGAN, OK											
60 –	**Finance, insurance, and real estate**	37	35	*0.5*	162	156	18,370	18,410	3,124	3,135	*0.2*
6000	Depository institutions	9	9	*0.8*	97	93	19,464	19,613	1,959	1,953	*0.4*
6100	Nondepository institutions	6	6	*0.8*	10	11	12,800	11,273	125	119	*0.1*
6140	Personal credit institutions	6	6	*1.0*	10	11	12,800	11,273	125	119	*0.3*
6400	Insurance agents, brokers, and service	9	9	*0.5*	24	-	16,000	-	370	-	*-*
6500	Real estate	7	6	*0.3*	21	19	12,952	15,368	354	360	*0.2*
LOVE, OK											
60 –	**Finance, insurance, and real estate**	10	13	*0.2*	131	114	22,931	16,947	2,523	1,965	*0.1*
6400	Insurance agents, brokers, and service	1	3	*0.2*	-	5	-	4,000	-	26	*0.0*
6500	Real estate	4	5	*0.2*	-	63	-	17,905	-	1,078	*0.5*
MCCLAIN, OK											
60 –	**Finance, insurance, and real estate**	27	27	*0.4*	180	197	16,956	15,228	3,226	3,738	*0.2*
6000	Depository institutions	6	6	*0.5*	126	139	18,476	16,317	2,418	2,945	*0.6*
6400	Insurance agents, brokers, and service	12	12	*0.6*	31	34	13,935	14,353	487	479	*0.3*
6500	Real estate	5	6	*0.3*	17	-	12,235	-	230	-	*-*
MCCURTAIN, OK											
60 –	**Finance, insurance, and real estate**	40	44	*0.6*	271	275	17,373	17,280	5,177	5,289	*0.3*
6000	Depository institutions	9	10	*0.9*	179	184	20,335	19,283	4,046	4,026	*0.8*
6100	Nondepository institutions	8	9	*1.2*	-	27	-	12,000	-	323	*0.3*
6400	Insurance agents, brokers, and service	13	16	*0.9*	34	37	11,176	11,459	403	470	*0.3*
6500	Real estate	8	8	*0.3*	21	-	13,143	-	301	-	*-*
6510	Real estate operators and lessors	5	5	*0.5*	9	10	5,778	7,600	54	74	*0.1*
MCINTOSH, OK											
60 –	**Finance, insurance, and real estate**	25	25	*0.3*	134	125	13,493	14,208	2,227	2,567	*0.2*
6000	Depository institutions	4	5	*0.4*	80	77	16,350	16,935	1,667	2,076	*0.4*
6400	Insurance agents, brokers, and service	9	10	*0.5*	-	23	-	10,087	-	230	*0.1*
6500	Real estate	10	7	*0.3*	34	20	8,118	8,800	299	176	*0.1*
6530	Real estate agents and managers	2	4	*0.4*	-	14	-	8,000	-	100	*0.1*
MAJOR, OK											
60 –	**Finance, insurance, and real estate**	14	15	*0.2*	69	64	26,493	22,250	1,789	1,529	*0.1*
6000	Depository institutions	5	5	*0.4*	50	-	32,000	-	1,549	-	*-*
6400	Insurance agents, brokers, and service	7	8	*0.4*	-	18	-	10,444	-	194	*0.1*
MARSHALL, OK											
60 –	**Finance, insurance, and real estate**	21	25	*0.3*	121	120	13,388	15,700	1,760	2,142	*0.1*
6000	Depository institutions	3	3	*0.3*	73	76	18,027	18,737	1,459	1,476	*0.3*
6020	Commercial banks	3	3	*0.4*	73	76	18,027	18,737	1,459	1,476	*0.3*

Source: County Business Patterns, 1992/93, CBP-92/93-1, U.S. Department of Commerce, Washington, D.C., April 1995. SIC categories for which data were suppressed or not available for both 1992 and 1993 are *not* displayed. The employment columns represent mid-March employment in the year. Pay per employee is calculated by dividing 1st Quarter payroll, annualized, by mid-March employment. The columns headed "% State" show the county's percentage of the state total for the SIC in 1993; for example, 0.9% for SIC 6030 means that the county had 0.9 percent of the state's total establishments (or payroll) in SIC 6030 in 1993. A dash (-) is used to indicate that data are not available or cannot be calculated; *nec* means not elsewhere classified.

Continued on next page.

SIC	Industry	No. Establishments			Employment		Pay / Employee		Annual Payroll ($ 000)		
		1992	1993	% State	1992	1993	1992	1993	1992	1993	% State
MARSHALL, OK - [continued]											
6400	Insurance agents, brokers, and service	7	8	0.4	-	19	-	10,737	-	360	0.2
6500	Real estate	9	11	0.5	30	18	5,467	11,111	142	235	0.1
6530	Real estate agents and managers	5	6	0.6	6	8	6,000	6,500	43	113	0.1
MAYES, OK											
60 –	**Finance, insurance, and real estate**	42	41	0.5	257	240	17,992	17,783	4,884	4,707	0.3
6000	Depository institutions	10	11	0.9	173	159	19,376	18,717	3,474	3,207	0.6
6020	Commercial banks	8	8	1.0	-	144	-	19,139	-	2,964	0.7
6100	Nondepository institutions	6	7	0.9	12	11	17,667	20,364	192	249	0.2
6400	Insurance agents, brokers, and service	8	9	0.5	26	29	12,308	13,517	367	490	0.3
6500	Real estate	15	12	0.5	42	-	12,857	-	578	-	-
6510	Real estate operators and lessors	7	5	0.5	21	13	8,381	7,385	168	97	0.2
6530	Real estate agents and managers	5	5	0.5	9	14	10,667	7,714	88	125	0.1
MURRAY, OK											
60 –	**Finance, insurance, and real estate**	16	17	0.2	88	84	17,182	19,476	1,636	1,779	0.1
6000	Depository institutions	5	5	0.4	61	59	18,689	21,763	1,251	1,380	0.3
6400	Insurance agents, brokers, and service	6	7	0.4	14	14	11,714	13,143	182	195	0.1
MUSKOGEE, OK											
60 –	**Finance, insurance, and real estate**	135	144	1.9	1,071	1,206	19,638	20,030	20,202	23,707	1.5
6000	Depository institutions	23	27	2.3	544	714	20,750	20,997	11,632	14,239	2.7
6020	Commercial banks	13	16	2.1	363	563	20,320	20,973	8,060	12,108	2.9
6100	Nondepository institutions	23	25	3.2	66	85	17,636	15,012	1,083	1,183	1.1
6200	Security and commodity brokers	3	4	1.1	-	14	-	44,286	-	638	0.6
6210	Security brokers and dealers	3	4	1.7	-	14	-	44,286	-	638	0.7
6300	Insurance carriers	16	12	2.5	49	94	28,245	25,106	1,483	2,107	0.6
6330	Fire, marine, and casualty insurance	8	5	2.4	12	-	29,000	-	400	-	-
6370	Pension, health, and welfare funds	4	4	5.4	5	50	17,600	19,600	159	860	8.3
6400	Insurance agents, brokers, and service	27	30	1.6	107	104	16,150	18,923	1,800	2,020	1.3
6500	Real estate	35	35	1.5	255	162	14,416	11,111	2,315	1,890	0.9
6510	Real estate operators and lessors	16	19	1.8	69	115	8,348	7,409	649	1,026	1.7
6530	Real estate agents and managers	12	12	1.2	126	20	19,302	13,400	940	296	0.3
6700	Holding and other investment offices	8	11	2.2	-	33	-	34,545	-	1,630	1.4
6710	Holding offices	3	4	4.7	34	24	35,059	41,000	1,188	1,436	2.4
NOBLE, OK											
60 –	**Finance, insurance, and real estate**	23	22	0.3	124	118	17,419	18,203	2,429	2,534	0.2
6000	Depository institutions	6	6	0.5	89	88	20,090	20,273	2,036	2,097	0.4
6400	Insurance agents, brokers, and service	9	9	0.5	19	-	11,789	-	224	-	-
6500	Real estate	7	5	0.2	-	7	-	14,857	-	145	0.1
6510	Real estate operators and lessors	4	2	0.2	4	-	5,000	-	35	-	-
NOWATA, OK											
60 –	**Finance, insurance, and real estate**	18	18	0.2	88	90	23,227	22,089	2,168	1,841	0.1
6400	Insurance agents, brokers, and service	5	5	0.3	-	10	-	10,800	-	123	0.1
6500	Real estate	6	6	0.3	21	24	28,571	26,667	538	556	0.3
6700	Holding and other investment offices	3	2	0.4	2	-	102,000	-	248	-	-
OKFUSKEE, OK											
60 –	**Finance, insurance, and real estate**	11	13	0.2	70	71	25,886	25,239	1,527	1,609	0.1
6000	Depository institutions	3	3	0.3	47	48	21,191	20,417	1,122	1,164	0.2
6020	Commercial banks	3	3	0.4	47	48	21,191	20,417	1,122	1,164	0.3
6400	Insurance agents, brokers, and service	2	4	0.2	-	4	-	18,000	-	77	0.0
6500	Real estate	3	3	0.1	8	7	10,000	10,857	85	93	0.0

Source: County Business Patterns, 1992/93, CBP-92/93-1, U.S. Department of Commerce, Washington, D.C., April 1995. SIC categories for which data were suppressed or not available for both 1992 and 1993 are *not* displayed. The employment columns represent mid-March employment in the year. Pay per employee is calculated by dividing 1st Quarter payroll, annualized, by mid-March employment. The columns headed "% State" show the county's percentage of the state total for the SIC in 1993; for example, 0.9% for SIC 6030 means that the county had 0.9 percent of the state's total establishments (or payroll) in SIC 6030 in 1993. A dash (-) is used to indicate that data are not available or cannot be calculated; *nec* means not elsewhere classified.

SIC	Industry	No. Establishments			Employment		Pay / Employee		Annual Payroll ($ 000)		
		1992	1993	% State	1992	1993	1992	1993	1992	1993	% State
OKLAHOMA, OK											
60–	**Finance, insurance, and real estate**	2,022	2,128	28.3	21,696	21,705	25,635	25,798	569,235	581,279	36.8
6000	Depository institutions	215	241	20.8	6,197	6,481	23,868	24,582	149,535	151,121	29.1
6020	Commercial banks	118	131	17.1	4,196	4,573	24,876	25,121	102,430	104,755	24.7
6030	Savings institutions	44	41	22.5	814	688	20,226	23,302	19,928	18,012	44.5
6060	Credit unions	34	45	30.0	772	791	22,782	21,659	16,957	16,785	42.6
6140	Personal credit institutions	104	102	17.4	700	865	21,383	18,936	15,009	17,331	36.6
6160	Mortgage bankers and brokers	41	51	41.1	658	808	27,976	24,723	19,217	23,579	52.7
6200	Security and commodity brokers	132	120	34.5	796	785	58,246	60,586	46,779	51,722	48.2
6210	Security brokers and dealers	82	71	30.6	605	617	66,314	66,632	39,168	43,454	46.8
6220	Commodity contracts brokers, dealers	6	6	37.5	-	24	-	60,333	-	1,700	65.7
6280	Security and commodity services	42	43	43.0	132	144	37,697	34,722	6,184	6,568	55.8
6300	Insurance carriers	256	220	45.6	5,591	5,346	28,392	27,445	154,099	150,360	43.3
6310	Life insurance	79	68	49.6	2,448	2,541	24,735	26,125	64,496	68,063	54.2
6330	Fire, marine, and casualty insurance	109	82	39.8	2,512	1,567	33,237	31,931	72,923	49,310	32.9
6360	Title insurance	6	8	88.9	123	-	21,886	-	3,070	-	-
6370	Pension, health, and welfare funds	34	33	44.6	114	181	16,561	19,779	2,952	4,549	43.8
6400	Insurance agents, brokers, and service	470	519	27.8	2,477	2,361	25,780	24,161	68,579	62,311	40.3
6500	Real estate	630	694	29.1	3,870	3,732	16,126	17,580	66,173	71,987	36.0
6510	Real estate operators and lessors	279	353	33.0	1,221	1,517	14,208	14,186	18,852	23,676	39.4
6530	Real estate agents and managers	233	282	28.8	1,909	1,617	17,134	19,540	33,952	33,796	35.2
6540	Title abstract offices	23	29	18.6	281	418	18,605	22,842	5,434	11,301	35.3
6552	Subdividers and developers, n.e.c.	23	19	19.4	56	51	14,143	23,529	952	1,350	22.1
6553	Cemetery subdividers and developers	10	11	18.0	165	129	14,012	13,519	2,343	1,864	34.8
6700	Holding and other investment offices	155	168	34.4	1,077	1,141	33,010	37,714	42,469	47,392	40.7
6710	Holding offices	16	19	22.4	487	508	32,616	41,583	18,032	24,604	41.9
6720	Investment offices	8	7	63.6	26	32	10,923	6,625	341	251	71.3
6732	Educational, religious, etc. trusts	16	15	26.8	55	66	22,982	20,545	1,243	1,173	12.1
6733	Trusts, n.e.c.	42	42	30.7	98	124	19,918	18,323	1,924	2,320	26.4
6799	Investors, n.e.c.	30	35	42.2	205	139	43,005	45,468	11,142	7,043	55.6
OKMULGEE, OK											
60–	**Finance, insurance, and real estate**	63	62	0.8	360	337	19,200	21,068	6,835	7,040	0.4
6000	Depository institutions	12	13	1.1	217	215	21,917	24,484	4,663	5,076	1.0
6020	Commercial banks	7	7	0.9	190	185	22,526	25,405	4,112	4,409	1.0
6030	Savings institutions	2	3	1.6	-	7	-	13,714	-	112	0.3
6060	Credit unions	3	3	2.0	-	23	-	20,348	-	555	1.4
6100	Nondepository institutions	14	13	1.7	-	24	-	18,167	-	390	0.4
6140	Personal credit institutions	14	13	2.2	-	24	-	18,167	-	390	0.8
6200	Security and commodity brokers	2	3	0.9	-	10	-	45,200	-	495	0.5
6210	Security brokers and dealers	2	3	1.3	-	10	-	45,200	-	495	0.5
6300	Insurance carriers	3	3	0.6	16	-	14,500	-	240	-	-
6400	Insurance agents, brokers, and service	14	14	0.8	38	-	13,053	-	543	-	-
6500	Real estate	13	10	0.4	43	35	11,442	9,600	440	358	0.2
6510	Real estate operators and lessors	4	3	0.3	15	-	8,533	-	112	-	-
6530	Real estate agents and managers	3	5	0.5	6	10	9,333	8,800	63	93	0.1
6540	Title abstract offices	3	1	0.6	16	-	15,750	-	197	-	-
6700	Holding and other investment offices	5	6	1.2	-	6	-	8,667	-	72	0.1
6733	Trusts, n.e.c.	2	3	2.2	-	3	-	6,667	-	18	0.2
OSAGE, OK											
60–	**Finance, insurance, and real estate**	29	37	0.5	187	196	20,107	20,653	3,740	4,236	0.3
6000	Depository institutions	8	10	0.9	77	86	25,351	26,093	2,007	2,343	0.5
6400	Insurance agents, brokers, and service	10	12	0.6	28	26	21,429	22,154	472	453	0.3
6510	Real estate operators and lessors	4	5	0.5	10	9	10,400	12,444	99	109	0.2
6530	Real estate agents and managers	1	4	0.4	-	2	-	8,000	-	45	0.0

Source: County Business Patterns, 1992/93, CBP-92/93-1, U.S. Department of Commerce, Washington, D.C., April 1995. SIC categories for which data were suppressed or not available for both 1992 and 1993 are *not* displayed. The employment columns represent mid-March employment in the year. Pay per employee is calculated by dividing 1st Quarter payroll, annualized, by mid-March employment. The columns headed "% State" show the county's percentage of the state total for the SIC in 1993; for example, 0.9% for SIC 6030 means that the county had 0.9 percent of the state's total establishments (or payroll) in SIC 6030 in 1993. A dash (-) is used to indicate that data are not available or cannot be calculated; *nec* means not elsewhere classified.

SIC	Industry	No. Establishments			Employment		Pay / Employee		Annual Payroll ($ 000)		
		1992	1993	% State	1992	1993	1992	1993	1992	1993	% State
OTTAWA, OK											
60 –	**Finance, insurance, and real estate**	62	68	0.9	397	426	16,544	17,080	7,740	7,965	0.5
6000	Depository institutions	14	15	1.3	210	206	15,752	16,738	3,633	3,865	0.7
6020	Commercial banks	10	10	1.3	159	157	15,270	16,510	2,733	2,856	0.7
6100	Nondepository institutions	9	9	1.2	24	-	15,167	-	401	-	-
6140	Personal credit institutions	9	9	1.5	24	-	15,167	-	401	-	-
6300	Insurance carriers	5	3	0.6	-	11	-	35,273	-	330	0.1
6330	Fire, marine, and casualty insurance	4	3	1.5	10	11	42,800	35,273	514	330	0.2
6400	Insurance agents, brokers, and service	11	12	0.6	59	65	15,932	17,969	1,422	913	0.6
6500	Real estate	19	24	1.0	81	100	12,099	12,880	1,174	1,764	0.9
6510	Real estate operators and lessors	6	9	0.8	26	46	14,154	14,261	468	966	1.6
6530	Real estate agents and managers	8	9	0.9	41	39	11,122	11,590	519	575	0.6
PAWNEE, OK											
60 –	**Finance, insurance, and real estate**	16	18	0.2	107	104	17,570	18,462	2,037	2,135	0.1
6000	Depository institutions	6	7	0.6	87	85	19,356	20,329	1,848	1,941	0.4
6500	Real estate	3	3	0.1	7	6	10,286	12,667	75	77	0.0
PAYNE, OK											
60 –	**Finance, insurance, and real estate**	142	144	1.9	754	804	16,928	16,184	13,618	13,768	0.9
6000	Depository institutions	22	22	1.9	399	410	18,266	18,556	7,666	8,115	1.6
6020	Commercial banks	13	13	1.7	329	340	18,468	19,129	6,504	7,012	1.7
6100	Nondepository institutions	12	11	1.4	33	38	20,121	17,474	699	734	0.7
6200	Security and commodity brokers	9	9	2.6	16	17	32,750	14,588	594	264	0.2
6210	Security brokers and dealers	6	7	3.0	14	-	36,286	-	578	-	-
6280	Security and commodity services	3	2	2.0	2	-	8,000	-	16	-	-
6300	Insurance carriers	6	3	0.6	7	-	30,286	-	257	-	-
6400	Insurance agents, brokers, and service	38	40	2.1	96	113	16,167	13,558	1,625	1,482	1.0
6500	Real estate	49	53	2.2	190	210	11,200	11,714	2,460	2,612	1.3
6510	Real estate operators and lessors	20	25	2.3	101	79	10,297	9,873	1,159	848	1.4
6530	Real estate agents and managers	22	20	2.0	76	102	12,474	13,725	1,112	1,459	1.5
6553	Cemetery subdividers and developers	3	4	6.6	-	6	-	9,333	-	68	1.3
6700	Holding and other investment offices	6	6	1.2	13	-	30,462	-	317	-	-
PITTSBURG, OK											
60 –	**Finance, insurance, and real estate**	88	87	1.2	501	502	14,850	16,637	8,857	9,159	0.6
6000	Depository institutions	10	11	0.9	238	233	15,714	17,133	4,764	4,698	0.9
6020	Commercial banks	7	7	0.9	225	221	15,840	17,376	4,607	4,534	1.1
6100	Nondepository institutions	19	19	2.4	50	51	16,720	17,490	878	1,003	0.9
6200	Security and commodity brokers	4	4	1.1	-	8	-	32,000	-	279	0.3
6210	Security brokers and dealers	4	4	1.7	-	8	-	32,000	-	279	0.3
6300	Insurance carriers	7	6	1.2	24	25	19,833	22,880	596	596	0.2
6400	Insurance agents, brokers, and service	17	19	1.0	65	72	15,815	15,000	1,023	1,124	0.7
6500	Real estate	25	24	1.0	80	99	8,600	9,495	1,026	1,052	0.5
6510	Real estate operators and lessors	9	8	0.7	26	23	7,385	5,565	448	139	0.2
6530	Real estate agents and managers	8	12	1.2	27	49	9,037	9,878	280	566	0.6
PONTOTOC, OK											
60 –	**Finance, insurance, and real estate**	77	76	1.0	421	417	18,480	18,293	7,529	7,708	0.5
6000	Depository institutions	12	13	1.1	249	251	18,908	18,789	4,624	4,809	0.9
6020	Commercial banks	8	8	1.0	203	205	19,054	18,380	3,774	3,787	0.9
6100	Nondepository institutions	16	14	1.8	49	44	15,918	16,364	703	668	0.6
6140	Personal credit institutions	15	14	2.4	-	44	-	16,364	-	668	1.4
6400	Insurance agents, brokers, and service	21	19	1.0	67	59	16,716	19,593	1,045	1,145	0.7
6500	Real estate	17	21	0.9	30	37	11,200	10,811	365	448	0.2

Source: County Business Patterns, 1992/93, CBP-92/93-1, U.S. Department of Commerce, Washington, D.C., April 1995. SIC categories for which data were suppressed or not available for both 1992 and 1993 are *not* displayed. The employment columns represent mid-March employment in the year. Pay per employee is calculated by dividing 1st Quarter payroll, annualized, by mid-March employment. The columns headed "% State" show the county's percentage of the state total for the SIC in 1993; for example, 0.9% for SIC 6030 means that the county had 0.9 percent of the state's total establishments (or payroll) in SIC 6030 in 1993. A dash (-) is used to indicate that data are not available or cannot be calculated; *nec* means not elsewhere classified.

Continued on next page.

SIC	Industry	No. Establishments			Employment		Pay / Employee		Annual Payroll ($ 000)		
		1992	1993	% State	1992	1993	1992	1993	1992	1993	% State
PONTOTOC, OK - [continued]											
6510	Real estate operators and lessors	7	10	0.9	14	-	11,714	-	158	-	-
6530	Real estate agents and managers	7	9	0.9	-	14	-	7,143	-	121	0.1
6700	Holding and other investment offices	6	5	1.0	16	15	11,500	10,667	161	165	0.1
POTTAWATOMIE, OK											
60 –	**Finance, insurance, and real estate**	108	113	1.5	590	612	17,010	18,137	10,342	11,204	0.7
6000	Depository institutions	16	17	1.5	306	312	17,203	17,795	5,349	5,487	1.1
6020	Commercial banks	10	10	1.3	279	280	17,204	17,729	4,859	4,863	1.1
6100	Nondepository institutions	20	17	2.2	71	52	13,070	16,692	958	918	0.8
6200	Security and commodity brokers	6	7	2.0	-	15	-	53,600	-	731	0.7
6210	Security brokers and dealers	4	4	1.7	15	10	37,600	77,600	689	693	0.7
6280	Security and commodity services	2	3	3.0	-	5	-	5,600	-	38	0.3
6300	Insurance carriers	3	4	0.8	-	20	-	25,800	-	530	0.2
6400	Insurance agents, brokers, and service	27	26	1.4	60	74	15,400	14,162	1,053	1,153	0.7
6500	Real estate	32	36	1.5	112	116	10,607	12,034	1,298	1,652	0.8
6510	Real estate operators and lessors	15	20	1.9	33	49	10,061	12,327	481	723	1.2
6530	Real estate agents and managers	12	12	1.2	43	38	11,163	10,842	416	511	0.5
6700	Holding and other investment offices	4	6	1.2	12	23	73,333	39,826	675	733	0.6
PUSHMATAHA, OK											
60 –	**Finance, insurance, and real estate**	12	13	0.2	88	100	14,773	15,160	1,685	2,001	0.1
6000	Depository institutions	3	3	0.3	52	54	17,923	18,148	1,261	1,403	0.3
6020	Commercial banks	3	3	0.4	52	54	17,923	18,148	1,261	1,403	0.3
6400	Insurance agents, brokers, and service	5	5	0.3	-	12	-	7,333	-	79	0.1
ROGER MILLS, OK											
60 –	**Finance, insurance, and real estate**	6	5	0.1	-	-	-	-	-	-	-
ROGERS, OK											
60 –	**Finance, insurance, and real estate**	74	81	1.1	553	491	23,139	20,024	11,732	9,753	0.6
6000	Depository institutions	13	12	1.0	286	209	24,545	23,081	6,392	4,621	0.9
6020	Commercial banks	9	8	1.0	-	135	-	22,548	-	3,255	0.8
6030	Savings institutions	4	4	2.2	-	74	-	24,054	-	1,366	3.4
6100	Nondepository institutions	6	5	0.6	16	16	16,750	17,750	267	326	0.3
6140	Personal credit institutions	6	5	0.9	16	16	16,750	17,750	267	326	0.7
6400	Insurance agents, brokers, and service	23	24	1.3	70	64	12,971	14,500	988	1,040	0.7
6500	Real estate	26	32	1.3	85	143	17,271	13,706	1,672	2,277	1.1
6510	Real estate operators and lessors	10	14	1.3	24	69	14,333	8,290	416	745	1.2
6530	Real estate agents and managers	10	14	1.4	28	46	19,000	17,304	633	868	0.9
SEMINOLE, OK											
60 –	**Finance, insurance, and real estate**	44	46	0.6	199	273	15,417	15,502	3,286	4,560	0.3
6000	Depository institutions	9	8	0.7	114	107	16,596	17,607	2,051	1,973	0.4
6100	Nondepository institutions	7	7	0.9	14	15	16,857	17,333	222	231	0.2
6140	Personal credit institutions	7	7	1.2	14	15	16,857	17,333	222	231	0.5
6400	Insurance agents, brokers, and service	13	14	0.8	37	35	12,108	13,257	473	503	0.3
6500	Real estate	11	13	0.5	25	-	10,560	-	310	-	-
6510	Real estate operators and lessors	7	7	0.7	13	12	9,231	11,000	129	140	0.2
6530	Real estate agents and managers	2	4	0.4	-	6	-	10,000	-	75	0.1
SEQUOYAH, OK											
60 –	**Finance, insurance, and real estate**	51	51	0.7	263	261	15,711	15,433	4,369	4,706	0.3
6000	Depository institutions	8	9	0.8	122	121	16,721	16,595	2,129	2,328	0.4
6100	Nondepository institutions	19	20	2.6	58	76	18,621	14,316	1,111	1,169	1.1
6140	Personal credit institutions	18	19	3.2	57	-	18,667	-	1,094	-	-
6400	Insurance agents, brokers, and service	8	9	0.5	21	24	16,571	16,167	362	402	0.3

Source: County Business Patterns, 1992/93, CBP-92/93-1, U.S. Department of Commerce, Washington, D.C., April 1995. SIC categories for which data were suppressed or not available for both 1992 and 1993 are not displayed. The employment columns represent mid-March employment in the year. Pay per employee is calculated by dividing 1st Quarter payroll, annualized, by mid-March employment. The columns headed "% State" show the county's percentage of the state total for the SIC in 1993; for example, 0.9% for SIC 6030 means that the county had 0.9 percent of the state's total establishments (or payroll) in SIC 6030 in 1993. A dash (-) is used to indicate that data are not available or cannot be calculated; nec means not elsewhere classified.

Continued on next page.

SIC	Industry	No. Establishments			Employment		Pay / Employee		Annual Payroll ($ 000)		
		1992	1993	% State	1992	1993	1992	1993	1992	1993	% State
SEQUOYAH, OK - [continued]											
6500	Real estate	11	9	0.4	55	35	10,109	13,714	657	722	0.4
6510	Real estate operators and lessors	4	3	0.3	23	10	9,217	20,800	204	221	0.4
6530	Real estate agents and managers	3	3	0.3	14	12	12,000	9,667	242	215	0.2
STEPHENS, OK											
60 –	**Finance, insurance, and real estate**	84	86	1.1	717	788	18,321	17,711	13,678	14,572	0.9
6000	Depository institutions	20	22	1.9	311	340	22,392	21,506	7,231	6,910	1.3
6020	Commercial banks	15	15	2.0	279	306	23,097	22,157	6,762	6,332	1.5
6100	Nondepository institutions	14	15	1.9	-	56	-	20,286	-	1,230	1.1
6140	Personal credit institutions	11	10	1.7	39	-	24,308	-	640	-	-
6200	Security and commodity brokers	4	3	0.9	9	-	55,556	-	418	-	-
6300	Insurance carriers	3	4	0.8	-	77	-	15,377	-	1,524	0.4
6400	Insurance agents, brokers, and service	19	18	1.0	112	92	15,821	19,304	1,862	1,850	1.2
6500	Real estate	18	16	0.7	73	96	13,863	12,750	1,091	1,470	0.7
6510	Real estate operators and lessors	6	5	0.5	25	33	13,280	13,455	495	568	0.9
6530	Real estate agents and managers	8	7	0.7	13	35	7,077	7,200	101	309	0.3
6700	Holding and other investment offices	6	8	1.6	110	-	7,418	-	1,272	-	-
TEXAS, OK											
60 –	**Finance, insurance, and real estate**	33	37	0.5	229	237	21,450	21,840	6,199	6,529	0.4
6000	Depository institutions	6	6	0.5	142	144	20,451	20,944	3,456	3,469	0.7
6200	Security and commodity brokers	4	3	0.9	-	5	-	33,600	-	188	0.2
6400	Insurance agents, brokers, and service	12	15	0.8	33	38	17,333	15,263	598	662	0.4
6500	Real estate	7	8	0.3	16	-	12,250	-	203	-	-
6510	Real estate operators and lessors	3	3	0.3	-	6	-	5,333	-	31	0.1
6530	Real estate agents and managers	3	4	0.4	3	4	10,667	9,000	33	38	0.0
TILLMAN, OK											
60 –	**Finance, insurance, and real estate**	17	18	0.2	116	116	18,379	19,172	2,167	2,480	0.2
6000	Depository institutions	5	5	0.4	93	96	20,559	20,375	1,925	2,142	0.4
6020	Commercial banks	5	5	0.7	93	96	20,559	20,375	1,925	2,142	0.5
6400	Insurance agents, brokers, and service	6	7	0.4	8	9	9,000	8,889	82	94	0.1
6500	Real estate	3	3	0.1	8	6	8,000	12,000	65	72	0.0
TULSA, OK											
60 –	**Finance, insurance, and real estate**	1,568	1,632	21.7	18,961	19,013	26,797	27,228	528,565	536,935	34.0
6000	Depository institutions	202	203	17.5	4,242	4,384	25,955	26,575	109,405	115,190	22.2
6020	Commercial banks	108	102	13.3	3,248	3,357	27,490	28,305	88,863	92,952	21.9
6030	Savings institutions	29	29	15.9	329	315	22,711	24,127	7,402	7,393	18.3
6060	Credit unions	39	46	30.7	532	584	20,271	18,692	10,430	11,758	29.8
6090	Functions closely related to banking	26	26	44.8	133	128	19,218	23,188	2,710	3,087	-
6100	Nondepository institutions	144	147	18.9	-	1,148	-	24,815	-	32,812	30.4
6110	Federal and Federally-sponsored credit	3	3	12.0	-	28	-	38,143	-	835	15.5
6140	Personal credit institutions	99	84	14.3	723	521	22,490	19,555	16,360	10,368	21.9
6150	Business credit institutions	11	19	46.3	59	149	33,627	29,101	1,939	5,441	51.1
6160	Mortgage bankers and brokers	27	40	32.3	283	450	34,120	28,658	10,558	16,121	36.1
6200	Security and commodity brokers	76	77	22.1	573	601	61,368	72,506	34,385	37,276	34.8
6210	Security brokers and dealers	50	48	20.7	477	489	66,616	82,315	30,239	32,952	35.5
6300	Insurance carriers	146	130	27.0	5,542	5,745	28,150	29,782	162,669	171,390	49.3
6310	Life insurance	50	47	34.3	1,959	2,107	23,902	23,267	48,442	51,259	40.8
6330	Fire, marine, and casualty insurance	64	52	25.2	2,618	2,489	31,254	36,773	87,013	85,815	57.3
6370	Pension, health, and welfare funds	17	15	20.3	137	-	22,891	-	3,298	-	-
6400	Insurance agents, brokers, and service	376	395	21.2	1,646	1,849	25,623	24,790	41,748	47,585	30.7
6500	Real estate	490	548	23.0	3,697	3,378	18,192	19,428	70,120	69,206	34.6
6510	Real estate operators and lessors	180	215	20.1	1,113	912	17,272	18,219	20,334	17,945	29.9
6530	Real estate agents and managers	233	282	28.8	2,147	2,081	17,900	19,702	38,686	41,580	43.3
6540	Title abstract offices	10	11	7.1	196	225	23,816	22,382	5,153	6,231	19.4
6552	Subdividers and developers, n.e.c.	17	24	24.5	61	44	22,361	26,091	2,177	1,265	20.7

Source: *County Business Patterns, 1992/93*, CBP-92/93-1, U.S. Department of Commerce, Washington, D.C., April 1995. SIC categories for which data were suppressed or not available for both 1992 and 1993 are *not* displayed. The employment columns represent mid-March employment in the year. Pay per employee is calculated by dividing 1st Quarter payroll, annualized, by mid-March employment. The columns headed "% State" show the county's percentage of the state total for the SIC in 1993; for example, 0.9% for SIC 6030 means that the county had 0.9 percent of the state's total establishments (or payroll) in SIC 6030 in 1993. A dash (-) is used to indicate that data are not available or cannot be calculated; *nec* means not elsewhere classified.

Continued on next page.

SIC	Industry	No. Establishments			Employment		Pay / Employee		Annual Payroll ($ 000)		
		1992	1993	% State	1992	1993	1992	1993	1992	1993	% State
TULSA, OK - [continued]											
6553	Cemetery subdividers and developers	6	6	9.8	97	115	20,948	15,826	2,246	2,042	38.1
6700	Holding and other investment offices	129	127	26.0	1,318	1,093	34,765	25,134	50,298	40,335	34.7
6710	Holding offices	28	26	30.6	661	231	41,507	45,870	33,629	21,459	36.5
6720	Investment offices	4	1	9.1	9	-	16,444	-	293	-	-
6732	Educational, religious, etc. trusts	14	17	30.4	33	67	24,121	17,552	679	1,003	10.4
6733	Trusts, n.e.c.	27	29	21.2	80	90	32,150	30,444	2,941	2,526	28.8
6792	Oil royalty traders	21	24	24.7	104	101	41,615	39,129	4,292	4,251	36.7
6799	Investors, n.e.c.	24	24	28.9	68	-	50,353	-	2,303	-	-
WAGONER, OK											
60-	**Finance, insurance, and real estate**	30	33	0.4	154	154	18,208	17,273	3,058	3,207	0.2
6000	Depository institutions	7	8	0.7	82	79	22,146	20,658	1,971	1,916	0.4
6400	Insurance agents, brokers, and service	9	8	0.4	18	21	9,333	8,571	190	201	0.1
6500	Real estate	10	13	0.5	46	46	16,000	16,435	829	992	0.5
6510	Real estate operators and lessors	2	3	0.3	-	14	-	11,429	-	190	0.3
6530	Real estate agents and managers	4	5	0.5	9	7	19,111	24,571	199	196	0.2
WASHINGTON, OK											
60-	**Finance, insurance, and real estate**	104	112	1.5	-	832	-	24,255	-	20,383	1.3
6000	Depository institutions	10	10	0.9	346	420	28,543	21,486	9,992	9,438	1.8
6100	Nondepository institutions	7	7	0.9	-	23	-	16,696	-	395	0.4
6140	Personal credit institutions	7	7	1.2	-	23	-	16,696	-	395	0.8
6200	Security and commodity brokers	11	11	3.2	-	42	-	95,714	-	2,450	2.3
6210	Security brokers and dealers	6	6	2.6	-	28	-	127,429	-	1,700	1.8
6280	Security and commodity services	4	5	5.0	-	14	-	32,286	-	750	6.4
6300	Insurance carriers	5	9	1.9	-	17	-	44,235	-	1,079	0.3
6400	Insurance agents, brokers, and service	22	22	1.2	88	108	19,727	18,333	2,541	2,589	1.7
6500	Real estate	36	40	1.7	125	142	15,616	14,704	2,393	2,440	1.2
6510	Real estate operators and lessors	13	17	1.6	68	32	15,412	12,125	1,029	459	0.8
6530	Real estate agents and managers	15	17	1.7	31	88	14,065	13,409	650	1,321	1.4
6552	Subdividers and developers, n.e.c.	-	3	3.1	-	4	-	9,000	-	41	0.7
6700	Holding and other investment offices	13	13	2.7	-	80	-	24,150	-	1,992	1.7
6710	Holding offices	2	3	3.5	-	37	-	26,595	-	945	1.6
6799	Investors, n.e.c.	2	3	3.6	-	5	-	20,800	-	140	1.1
WASHITA, OK											
60-	**Finance, insurance, and real estate**	17	18	0.2	111	104	14,162	15,962	1,733	1,775	0.1
6000	Depository institutions	8	8	0.7	94	85	12,553	15,059	1,320	1,418	0.3
6400	Insurance agents, brokers, and service	4	5	0.3	9	11	12,444	11,273	134	132	0.1
WOODS, OK											
60-	**Finance, insurance, and real estate**	26	27	0.4	209	180	14,048	15,756	3,329	3,147	0.2
6000	Depository institutions	6	5	0.4	123	111	17,854	18,559	2,584	2,302	0.4
6020	Commercial banks	6	5	0.7	123	111	17,854	18,559	2,584	2,302	0.5
6400	Insurance agents, brokers, and service	9	10	0.5	21	19	10,667	11,579	231	228	0.1
6500	Real estate	8	8	0.3	56	33	4,143	3,636	189	147	0.1
6510	Real estate operators and lessors	5	5	0.5	-	8	-	4,500	-	68	0.1
WOODWARD, OK											
60-	**Finance, insurance, and real estate**	38	37	0.5	217	282	23,465	20,922	5,841	6,399	0.4
6000	Depository institutions	6	6	0.5	103	144	27,340	22,583	3,167	3,371	0.6
6100	Nondepository institutions	4	4	0.5	20	26	30,000	26,308	605	659	0.6
6200	Security and commodity brokers	3	3	0.9	-	7	-	72,000	-	502	0.5
6210	Security brokers and dealers	3	3	1.3	-	7	-	72,000	-	502	0.5
6300	Insurance carriers	5	2	0.4	16	-	9,500	-	128	-	-

Source: County Business Patterns, 1992/93, CBP-92/93-1, U.S. Department of Commerce, Washington, D.C., April 1995. SIC categories for which data were suppressed or not available for both 1992 and 1993 are *not* displayed. The employment columns represent mid-March employment in the year. Pay per employee is calculated by dividing 1st Quarter payroll, annualized, by mid-March employment. The columns headed "% State" show the county's percentage of the state total for the SIC in 1993; for example, 0.9% for SIC 6030 means that the county had 0.9 percent of the state's total establishments (or payroll) in SIC 6030 in 1993. A dash (-) is used to indicate that data are not available or cannot be calculated; *nec* means not elsewhere classified.

Continued on next page.

SIC	Industry	No. Establishments			Employment		Pay / Employee		Annual Payroll ($ 000)		
		1992	1993	% State	1992	1993	1992	1993	1992	1993	% State
WOODWARD, OK - [continued]											
6400	Insurance agents, brokers, and service	10	13	0.7	48	72	16,833	13,889	1,102	1,359	0.9
6500	Real estate	9	8	0.3	20	22	17,200	16,000	402	401	0.2
6510	Real estate operators and lessors	4	3	0.3	9	11	11,556	11,636	133	130	0.2

Source: County Business Patterns, 1992/93, CBP-92/93-1, U.S. Department of Commerce, Washington, D.C., April 1995. SIC categories for which data were suppressed or not available for both 1992 and 1993 are *not* displayed. The employment columns represent mid-March employment in the year. Pay per employee is calculated by dividing 1st Quarter payroll, annualized, by mid-March employment. The columns headed "% State" show the county's percentage of the state total for the SIC in 1993; for example, 0.9% for SIC 6030 means that the county had 0.9 percent of the state's total establishments (or payroll) in SIC 6030 in 1993. A dash (-) is used to indicate that data are not available or cannot be calculated; *nec* means not elsewhere classified.

OREGON

SIC	Industry	No. Establishments			Employment		Pay / Employee		Annual Payroll ($ 000)		
		1992	1993	% State	1992	1993	1992	1993	1992	1993	% State
BAKER, OR											
60 –	**Finance, insurance, and real estate**	37	40	0.5	179	176	18,771	18,750	3,385	3,445	0.2
6000	Depository institutions	7	6	0.5	97	81	19,588	21,333	1,799	1,758	0.3
6400	Insurance agents, brokers, and service	13	12	0.7	39	-	20,000	-	869	-	-
6500	Real estate	10	14	0.4	18	30	9,556	10,133	200	312	0.1
6510	Real estate operators and lessors	1	3	0.2	-	9	-	13,778	-	97	0.1
6530	Real estate agents and managers	7	9	0.6	14	21	8,857	8,571	147	210	0.1
BENTON, OR											
60 –	**Finance, insurance, and real estate**	185	214	2.7	1,055	998	15,462	17,507	17,605	20,611	1.0
6000	Depository institutions	25	27	2.4	345	320	19,084	19,238	6,433	6,484	1.2
6020	Commercial banks	14	15	2.3	218	178	17,560	18,404	3,847	3,603	0.9
6030	Savings institutions	6	6	2.8	31	-	29,806	-	644	-	-
6060	Credit unions	5	5	2.4	96	107	19,083	18,542	1,942	2,051	4.0
6100	Nondepository institutions	5	6	1.1	-	14	-	73,429	-	864	0.5
6200	Security and commodity brokers	12	13	3.6	-	37	-	48,432	-	2,196	1.3
6210	Security brokers and dealers	7	6	2.6	-	32	-	54,625	-	2,150	1.5
6280	Security and commodity services	5	7	5.8	3	5	5,333	8,800	16	46	0.2
6300	Insurance carriers	11	7	1.1	57	38	22,175	27,053	1,259	1,201	0.2
6330	Fire, marine, and casualty insurance	6	4	1.4	22	-	22,545	-	392	-	-
6360	Title insurance	5	3	3.8	35	-	21,943	-	867	-	-
6400	Insurance agents, brokers, and service	26	30	1.9	90	112	19,022	16,964	1,893	2,282	1.0
6500	Real estate	102	126	3.8	504	461	8,651	11,124	5,078	7,003	2.3
6510	Real estate operators and lessors	49	56	3.7	214	216	7,963	8,981	1,697	2,063	2.2
6530	Real estate agents and managers	41	58	3.9	262	220	8,748	12,509	2,770	4,195	2.4
6552	Subdividers and developers, n.e.c.	4	7	4.7	7	12	20,000	17,667	235	442	2.2
6553	Cemetery subdividers and developers	4	4	6.6	5	-	12,000	-	60	-	-
6700	Holding and other investment offices	4	5	1.8	-	16	-	27,500	-	581	0.6
CLACKAMAS, OR											
60 –	**Finance, insurance, and real estate**	676	723	9.2	4,274	5,354	24,608	23,532	118,109	137,744	6.8
6000	Depository institutions	105	97	8.6	958	1,070	19,766	20,740	19,574	23,089	4.2
6020	Commercial banks	65	54	8.1	712	762	18,876	19,675	13,712	15,495	3.8
6030	Savings institutions	24	24	11.0	136	167	23,059	27,066	3,570	4,744	7.5
6100	Nondepository institutions	72	80	14.8	501	858	31,385	27,590	19,073	29,245	16.0
6140	Personal credit institutions	25	26	16.3	188	195	29,574	28,369	5,289	5,666	-
6150	Business credit institutions	5	3	4.7	28	-	32,429	-	953	-	-
6160	Mortgage bankers and brokers	42	49	16.2	285	379	32,477	36,021	12,831	18,843	17.6
6200	Security and commodity brokers	26	31	8.6	128	165	52,219	40,291	8,270	7,925	4.8
6210	Security brokers and dealers	15	17	7.4	56	89	47,786	35,910	3,161	4,105	2.9
6220	Commodity contracts brokers, dealers	3	3	37.5	6	5	60,667	33,600	383	312	50.0
6280	Security and commodity services	8	11	9.1	66	71	55,212	46,254	4,726	3,508	16.9
6300	Insurance carriers	73	65	10.3	1,103	1,387	29,588	30,151	36,375	43,645	8.7
6310	Life insurance	12	10	10.5	113	178	35,504	25,573	3,896	3,816	4.8
6324	Hospital and medical service plans	1	4	12.1	-	484	-	25,983	-	15,225	14.6
6330	Fire, marine, and casualty insurance	41	31	10.7	544	530	33,654	36,898	21,071	17,786	7.5
6360	Title insurance	10	13	16.7	87	116	23,034	28,966	2,296	4,918	12.0
6370	Pension, health, and welfare funds	9	7	6.0	-	79	-	22,481	-	1,900	6.2
6400	Insurance agents, brokers, and service	120	140	8.7	523	560	29,446	20,171	16,502	11,452	5.1
6500	Real estate	258	286	8.7	926	1,157	14,281	13,179	15,292	18,483	6.1
6510	Real estate operators and lessors	112	137	9.0	298	579	11,570	9,568	3,453	6,289	6.8
6530	Real estate agents and managers	108	124	8.4	538	526	15,279	16,624	9,548	10,981	6.3

Source: County Business Patterns, 1992/93, CBP-92/93-1, U.S. Department of Commerce, Washington, D.C., April 1995. SIC categories for which data were suppressed or not available for both 1992 and 1993 are *not* displayed. The employment columns represent mid-March employment in the year. Pay per employee is calculated by dividing 1st Quarter payroll, annualized, by mid-March employment. The columns headed "% State" show the county's percentage of the state total for the SIC in 1993; for example, 0.9% for SIC 6030 means that the county had 0.9 percent of the state's total establishments (or payroll) in SIC 6030 in 1993. A dash (-) is used to indicate that data are not available or cannot be calculated; *nec* means not elsewhere classified.

Continued on next page.

SIC	Industry	No. Establishments			Employment		Pay / Employee		Annual Payroll ($ 000)		
		1992	1993	% State	1992	1993	1992	1993	1992	1993	% State
CLACKAMAS, OR - [continued]											
6552	Subdividers and developers, n.e.c.	11	18	*12.1*	33	-	22,061	-	1,177	-	-
6710	Holding offices	6	7	*11.5*	76	98	22,105	41,918	1,474	2,404	*3.5*
6732	Educational, religious, etc. trusts	4	4	*6.5*	30	32	7,467	10,500	295	310	*4.8*
6733	Trusts, n.e.c.	3	4	*5.6*	-	3	-	18,667	-	77	*1.2*
CLATSOP, OR											
60 –	**Finance, insurance, and real estate**	85	86	*1.1*	394	409	15,442	15,687	6,573	7,131	*0.4*
6000	Depository institutions	19	16	*1.4*	169	155	17,846	18,039	3,031	2,921	*0.5*
6020	Commercial banks	12	10	*1.5*	137	121	18,277	18,116	2,502	2,358	*0.6*
6100	Nondepository institutions	3	5	*0.9*	-	14	-	19,143	-	396	*0.2*
6300	Insurance carriers	6	4	*0.6*	27	-	24,444	-	731	-	-
6400	Insurance agents, brokers, and service	14	16	*1.0*	38	46	20,842	20,348	841	916	*0.4*
6500	Real estate	39	39	*1.2*	148	163	9,081	9,988	1,583	2,011	*0.7*
6510	Real estate operators and lessors	22	20	*1.3*	94	52	7,489	7,923	914	510	*0.6*
6530	Real estate agents and managers	16	16	*1.1*	49	92	11,102	9,826	570	1,159	*0.7*
6700	Holding and other investment offices	2	4	*1.4*	-	11	-	17,091	-	202	*0.2*
COLUMBIA, OR											
60 –	**Finance, insurance, and real estate**	47	46	*0.6*	248	241	16,887	17,311	4,483	4,703	*0.2*
6000	Depository institutions	16	14	*1.2*	144	143	17,111	16,951	2,559	2,553	*0.5*
6020	Commercial banks	10	8	*1.2*	79	72	17,468	16,222	1,347	1,160	*0.3*
6300	Insurance carriers	4	3	*0.5*	14	-	24,571	-	390	-	-
6400	Insurance agents, brokers, and service	11	13	*0.8*	39	47	16,410	15,574	691	859	*0.4*
6500	Real estate	12	15	*0.5*	39	42	9,128	13,048	391	750	*0.2*
6530	Real estate agents and managers	4	7	*0.5*	10	12	10,400	15,667	141	225	*0.1*
COOS, OR											
60 –	**Finance, insurance, and real estate**	115	121	*1.5*	705	666	19,926	20,835	15,154	14,607	*0.7*
6000	Depository institutions	37	33	*2.9*	394	359	20,325	21,259	8,631	7,552	*1.4*
6020	Commercial banks	30	25	*3.8*	350	306	20,777	22,118	7,880	6,691	*1.6*
6140	Personal credit institutions	4	2	*1.3*	12	-	17,333	-	254	-	-
6300	Insurance carriers	8	7	*1.1*	39	16	28,718	41,750	1,220	758	*0.2*
6360	Title insurance	3	2	*2.6*	28	-	21,143	-	667	-	-
6400	Insurance agents, brokers, and service	20	22	*1.4*	71	78	20,845	17,795	1,382	1,428	*0.6*
6500	Real estate	40	48	*1.5*	147	160	12,190	14,175	1,920	2,679	*0.9*
6510	Real estate operators and lessors	16	20	*1.3*	66	61	9,818	11,344	668	892	*1.0*
6530	Real estate agents and managers	20	22	*1.5*	67	72	14,507	16,500	1,067	1,359	*0.8*
CROOK, OR											
60 –	**Finance, insurance, and real estate**	23	24	*0.3*	107	110	15,215	15,018	1,555	1,764	*0.1*
6000	Depository institutions	6	6	*0.5*	56	60	16,429	16,467	913	1,025	*0.2*
6400	Insurance agents, brokers, and service	3	5	*0.3*	16	-	19,500	-	324	-	-
6500	Real estate	8	7	*0.2*	19	14	9,684	4,286	119	93	*0.0*
6510	Real estate operators and lessors	4	3	*0.2*	7	7	4,571	2,857	36	25	*0.0*
6530	Real estate agents and managers	2	4	*0.3*	-	7	-	5,714	-	68	*0.0*
CURRY, OR											
60 –	**Finance, insurance, and real estate**	56	62	*0.8*	227	245	19,172	18,547	4,366	4,582	*0.2*
6000	Depository institutions	11	11	*1.0*	115	132	18,957	16,424	2,157	2,252	*0.4*
6400	Insurance agents, brokers, and service	8	11	*0.7*	-	39	-	23,590	-	1,030	*0.5*
6500	Real estate	32	34	*1.0*	57	67	16,140	13,493	913	959	*0.3*
6510	Real estate operators and lessors	10	11	*0.7*	12	-	6,333	-	95	-	-
6530	Real estate agents and managers	15	17	*1.2*	21	32	17,524	11,375	430	444	*0.3*
DESCHUTES, OR											
60 –	**Finance, insurance, and real estate**	258	296	*3.8*	2,033	2,390	21,131	21,496	47,277	56,042	*2.8*
6000	Depository institutions	37	34	*3.0*	468	428	22,274	26,738	11,268	10,593	*1.9*
6020	Commercial banks	30	24	*3.6*	393	340	23,593	28,306	10,015	8,138	*2.0*

Source: County Business Patterns, 1992/93, CBP-92/93-1, U.S. Department of Commerce, Washington, D.C., April 1995. SIC categories for which data were suppressed or not available for both 1992 and 1993 are not displayed. The employment columns represent mid-March employment in the year. Pay per employee is calculated by dividing 1st Quarter payroll, annualized, by mid-March employment. The columns headed "% State" show the county's percentage of the state total for the SIC in 1993; for example, 0.9% for SIC 6030 means that the county had 0.9 percent of the state's total establishments (or payroll) in SIC 6030 in 1993. A dash (-) is used to indicate that data are not available or cannot be calculated; nec means not elsewhere classified.

Continued on next page.

SIC	Industry	No. Establishments			Employment		Pay / Employee		Annual Payroll ($ 000)		
		1992	1993	% State	1992	1993	1992	1993	1992	1993	% State
DESCHUTES, OR - [continued]											
6030	Savings institutions	4	6	2.8	36	50	17,556	19,760	724	1,485	2.4
6060	Credit unions	3	3	1.5	39	-	13,333	-	529	-	-
6100	Nondepository institutions	21	26	4.8	69	109	40,638	33,541	3,376	5,337	2.9
6160	Mortgage bankers and brokers	11	16	5.3	29	66	51,448	38,000	1,675	3,986	3.7
6200	Security and commodity brokers	11	14	3.9	64	69	67,562	65,275	3,951	4,683	2.9
6300	Insurance carriers	22	19	3.0	210	135	23,352	27,319	5,696	3,923	0.8
6330	Fire, marine, and casualty insurance	12	11	3.8	-	24	-	40,000	-	960	0.4
6360	Title insurance	4	-	-	99	-	21,091	-	2,314	-	-
6400	Insurance agents, brokers, and service	41	50	3.1	-	228	-	20,632	-	4,799	2.1
6500	Real estate	119	141	4.3	1,055	1,407	16,269	16,267	19,615	25,910	8.5
6510	Real estate operators and lessors	32	34	2.2	88	102	7,955	7,725	818	820	0.9
6530	Real estate agents and managers	66	89	6.0	831	1,137	16,881	15,697	15,656	18,939	10.9
6540	Title abstract offices	1	3	9.7	-	74	-	20,757	-	2,125	18.3
6552	Subdividers and developers, n.e.c.	6	10	6.7	61	92	28,590	29,348	2,194	3,987	19.9
6700	Holding and other investment offices	7	12	4.3	-	14	-	35,143	-	797	0.8
DOUGLAS, OR											
60 –	**Finance, insurance, and real estate**	169	174	2.2	794	804	19,038	20,090	15,397	15,717	0.8
6000	Depository institutions	33	30	2.7	366	362	19,858	19,072	6,779	6,757	1.2
6020	Commercial banks	27	24	3.6	325	316	20,234	19,165	6,072	5,890	1.4
6100	Nondepository institutions	10	10	1.9	29	28	20,276	23,714	817	788	0.4
6140	Personal credit institutions	4	4	2.5	17	-	19,059	-	336	-	-
6160	Mortgage bankers and brokers	2	4	1.3	-	6	-	28,667	-	181	0.2
6300	Insurance carriers	8	5	0.8	18	10	40,000	49,600	838	523	0.1
6400	Insurance agents, brokers, and service	34	35	2.2	125	133	19,392	18,586	2,591	2,710	1.2
6500	Real estate	78	85	2.6	236	251	13,051	12,733	3,284	3,599	1.2
6510	Real estate operators and lessors	31	35	2.3	105	98	12,267	11,837	1,075	1,011	1.1
6530	Real estate agents and managers	38	43	2.9	70	-	11,429	-	851	-	-
6540	Title abstract offices	2	3	9.7	-	60	-	18,067	-	1,487	12.8
GILLIAM, OR											
60 –	**Finance, insurance, and real estate**	4	4	0.1	11	14	16,727	14,286	177	179	0.0
GRANT, OR											
60 –	**Finance, insurance, and real estate**	12	18	0.2	59	71	17,085	15,268	1,058	1,219	0.1
6000	Depository institutions	6	6	0.5	-	47	-	16,000	-	769	0.1
6400	Insurance agents, brokers, and service	4	7	0.4	14	16	19,429	13,750	289	257	0.1
6500	Real estate	2	5	0.2	-	8	-	14,000	-	193	0.1
HARNEY, OR											
60 –	**Finance, insurance, and real estate**	14	13	0.2	55	56	14,036	13,786	759	815	0.0
6000	Depository institutions	4	4	0.4	34	35	15,765	15,657	515	564	0.1
6400	Insurance agents, brokers, and service	5	5	0.3	8	10	15,500	11,200	142	149	0.1
6500	Real estate	5	4	0.1	13	11	8,615	10,182	102	102	0.0
HOOD RIVER, OR											
60 –	**Finance, insurance, and real estate**	43	42	0.5	187	185	13,925	15,070	2,799	3,279	0.2
6000	Depository institutions	10	9	0.8	75	62	18,453	19,742	1,373	1,418	0.3
6020	Commercial banks	7	6	0.9	61	-	19,213	-	1,163	-	-
6500	Real estate	22	22	0.7	78	90	8,000	8,356	714	850	0.3
6510	Real estate operators and lessors	6	8	0.5	16	-	4,750	-	73	-	-
6530	Real estate agents and managers	9	11	0.7	18	34	10,222	10,118	201	318	0.2
JACKSON, OR											
60 –	**Finance, insurance, and real estate**	398	424	5.4	2,403	2,705	22,548	22,254	54,612	66,585	3.3
6000	Depository institutions	61	63	5.6	763	920	21,636	21,900	16,053	21,055	3.8
6020	Commercial banks	43	40	6.0	581	481	21,281	23,692	11,596	10,797	2.6
6030	Savings institutions	15	16	7.3	168	333	23,595	21,610	4,257	8,670	13.8

Source: County Business Patterns, 1992/93, CBP-92/93-1, U.S. Department of Commerce, Washington, D.C., April 1995. SIC categories for which data were suppressed or not available for both 1992 and 1993 are *not* displayed. The employment columns represent mid-March employment in the year. Pay per employee is calculated by dividing 1st Quarter payroll, annualized, by mid-March employment. The columns headed "% State" show the county's percentage of the state total for the SIC in 1993; for example, 0.9% for SIC 6030 means that the county had 0.9 percent of the state's total establishments (or payroll) in SIC 6030 in 1993. A dash (-) is used to indicate that data are not available or cannot be calculated; *nec* means not elsewhere classified.

Continued on next page.

SIC	Industry	No. Establishments			Employment		Pay / Employee		Annual Payroll ($ 000)		
		1992	1993	% State	1992	1993	1992	1993	1992	1993	% State
JACKSON, OR - [continued]											
6100	Nondepository institutions	25	29	5.4	207	245	24,232	25,959	5,266	8,155	4.5
6140	Personal credit institutions	14	11	6.9	107	-	24,897	-	2,690	-	-
6160	Mortgage bankers and brokers	9	15	5.0	-	122	-	25,049	-	3,640	3.4
6200	Security and commodity brokers	20	20	5.6	158	180	53,494	58,000	8,798	9,250	5.7
6300	Insurance carriers	48	46	7.3	341	241	24,915	21,461	8,011	8,428	1.7
6310	Life insurance	5	2	2.1	36	-	24,222	-	873	-	-
6330	Fire, marine, and casualty insurance	16	16	5.5	35	-	37,029	-	1,431	-	-
6370	Pension, health, and welfare funds	20	24	20.7	74	46	17,297	13,304	1,601	3,147	10.3
6400	Insurance agents, brokers, and service	62	74	4.6	286	320	17,860	17,375	5,207	6,288	2.8
6500	Real estate	163	177	5.4	586	709	15,065	14,748	9,920	11,222	3.7
6510	Real estate operators and lessors	77	91	6.0	264	332	10,894	10,205	3,379	3,955	4.3
6530	Real estate agents and managers	63	76	5.2	180	244	17,111	17,328	3,479	4,606	2.7
6552	Subdividers and developers, n.e.c.	4	5	3.4	7	6	12,571	17,333	89	134	0.7
6700	Holding and other investment offices	19	15	5.4	62	90	28,645	22,889	1,357	2,187	2.3
6732	Educational, religious, etc. trusts	3	3	4.8	-	7	-	16,000	-	99	1.5
6733	Trusts, n.e.c.	12	6	8.5	23	-	25,043	-	398	-	-
JEFFERSON, OR											
60 –	**Finance, insurance, and real estate**	22	23	0.3	85	91	17,129	17,055	1,482	2,694	0.1
6400	Insurance agents, brokers, and service	5	6	0.4	22	-	20,182	-	480	-	-
6500	Real estate	11	11	0.3	15	18	5,867	3,778	89	85	0.0
6510	Real estate operators and lessors	6	8	0.5	10	11	5,600	4,364	62	61	0.1
6530	Real estate agents and managers	3	3	0.2	3	7	6,667	2,857	20	24	0.0
JOSEPHINE, OR											
60 –	**Finance, insurance, and real estate**	122	126	1.6	681	730	19,166	19,096	14,210	17,119	0.8
6000	Depository institutions	25	23	2.0	317	329	21,741	20,146	7,255	6,669	1.2
6020	Commercial banks	16	13	2.0	206	195	20,971	22,523	4,458	3,996	1.0
6100	Nondepository institutions	6	9	1.7	-	27	-	20,741	-	839	0.5
6160	Mortgage bankers and brokers	5	7	2.3	20	-	19,000	-	446	-	-
6300	Insurance carriers	8	7	1.1	20	-	42,400	-	1,018	-	-
6400	Insurance agents, brokers, and service	24	25	1.6	93	97	18,538	20,536	1,950	2,094	0.9
6500	Real estate	53	57	1.7	205	246	11,785	10,602	2,633	4,798	1.6
6510	Real estate operators and lessors	20	23	1.5	48	63	8,167	8,762	459	2,418	2.6
6530	Real estate agents and managers	24	26	1.8	129	150	12,403	10,453	1,756	1,900	1.1
6552	Subdividers and developers, n.e.c.	2	3	2.0	-	2	-	12,000	-	25	0.1
6700	Holding and other investment offices	3	1	0.4	9	-	6,667	-	62	-	-
KLAMATH, OR											
60 –	**Finance, insurance, and real estate**	113	111	1.4	695	720	20,616	22,128	15,312	15,427	0.8
6000	Depository institutions	19	18	1.6	251	312	20,908	22,256	5,460	6,790	1.2
6020	Commercial banks	10	9	1.4	148	159	21,919	23,472	3,316	3,340	0.8
6100	Nondepository institutions	5	3	0.6	66	-	24,303	-	1,663	-	-
6300	Insurance carriers	10	7	1.1	55	62	25,018	25,032	1,385	1,742	0.3
6400	Insurance agents, brokers, and service	20	24	1.5	126	113	19,937	17,558	2,758	2,323	1.0
6500	Real estate	52	54	1.6	158	177	17,873	21,966	3,174	2,987	1.0
6510	Real estate operators and lessors	20	22	1.4	51	64	7,922	9,938	544	712	0.8
6530	Real estate agents and managers	21	22	1.5	48	50	10,583	10,880	687	737	0.4
6552	Subdividers and developers, n.e.c.	4	6	4.0	-	19	-	106,737	-	1,011	5.1
LAKE, OR											
60 –	**Finance, insurance, and real estate**	12	10	0.1	42	-	16,857	-	690	-	-
6000	Depository institutions	3	3	0.3	25	24	16,000	15,333	366	367	0.1
6020	Commercial banks	3	2	0.3	25	-	16,000	-	366	-	-
6400	Insurance agents, brokers, and service	4	5	0.3	-	17	-	12,235	-	217	0.1

Source: County Business Patterns, 1992/93, CBP-92/93-1, U.S. Department of Commerce, Washington, D.C., April 1995. SIC categories for which data were suppressed or not available for both 1992 and 1993 are *not* displayed. The employment columns represent mid-March employment in the year. Pay per employee is calculated by dividing 1st Quarter payroll, annualized, by mid-March employment. The columns headed "% State" show the county's percentage of the state total for the SIC in 1993; for example, 0.9% for SIC 6030 means that the county had 0.9 percent of the state's total establishments (or payroll) in SIC 6030 in 1993. A dash (-) is used to indicate that data are not available or cannot be calculated; *nec* means not elsewhere classified.

SIC	Industry	No. Establishments			Employment		Pay / Employee		Annual Payroll ($ 000)		
		1992	1993	% State	1992	1993	1992	1993	1992	1993	% State
LANE, OR											
	LANE, OR	724	768	9.8	4,742	4,865	20,971	22,879	106,077	116,413	5.7
60–	**Finance, insurance, and real estate**	105	103	9.2	1,497	1,539	21,927	22,519	33,656	35,103	6.3
6000	Depository institutions	63	62	9.3	988	995	21,854	22,689	21,793	22,302	5.4
6020	Commercial banks	26	27	13.2	349	393	20,676	20,397	7,535	8,223	15.9
6060	Credit unions	44	42	7.8	247	258	31,449	28,930	7,628	8,435	4.6
6100	Nondepository institutions	21	21	6.9	87	112	41,011	32,821	3,337	4,628	4.3
6160	Mortgage bankers and brokers	39	41	11.4	232	241	39,483	51,369	9,609	10,322	6.3
6200	Security and commodity brokers	21	26	11.3	183	214	44,000	56,430	8,551	9,980	7.0
6210	Security brokers and dealers	17	15	12.4	-	27	-	11,259	-	342	1.7
6280	Security and commodity services	65	65	10.3	592	641	26,020	26,034	16,929	16,117	3.2
6300	Insurance carriers	12	13	13.7	87	88	25,379	27,455	2,270	2,507	3.2
6310	Life insurance	37	34	11.8	160	174	35,100	38,161	5,547	6,540	2.7
6330	Fire, marine, and casualty insurance	6	3	3.8	92	-	22,217	-	2,488	-	-
6360	Title insurance	5	11	9.5	11	-	9,455	-	507	-	-
6370	Pension, health, and welfare funds	153	170	10.6	696	900	24,724	24,916	19,577	24,825	11.1
6400	Insurance agents, brokers, and service	292	324	9.9	1,415	1,226	11,172	13,148	17,222	20,076	6.6
6500	Real estate	129	138	9.0	664	581	11,229	11,387	7,975	7,355	8.0
6510	Real estate operators and lessors	129	160	10.9	678	577	11,021	14,586	8,226	9,993	5.8
6530	Real estate agents and managers	1	4	12.9	-	7	-	20,000	-	1,283	11.1
6540	Title abstract offices	5	13	8.7	6	48	6,667	16,000	57	1,227	6.1
6552	Subdividers and developers, n.e.c.	6	6	9.8	-	12	-	14,667	-	179	3.3
6553	Cemetery subdividers and developers	26	23	8.3	63	60	20,190	26,267	1,456	1,535	1.6
6700	Holding and other investment offices	3	6	9.8	27	-	26,815	-	839	-	-
6710	Holding offices	3	2	22.2	6	-	9,333	-	82	-	-
6720	Investment offices	5	5	8.1	14	13	13,143	16,923	193	225	3.5
6732	Educational, religious, etc. trusts	8	8	11.3	6	5	9,333	8,800	86	66	1.1
6733	Trusts, n.e.c.	5	1	1.9	8	-	28,500	-	233	-	-
6799	Investors, n.e.c.										
LINCOLN, OR											
60–	**Finance, insurance, and real estate**	118	127	1.6	625	670	17,549	16,931	12,071	12,254	0.6
6000	Depository institutions	24	21	1.9	265	258	20,815	19,984	5,734	5,185	0.9
6020	Commercial banks	18	15	2.3	238	230	21,630	20,296	5,344	4,730	1.2
6300	Insurance carriers	8	2	0.3	40	-	31,000	-	1,375	-	-
6400	Insurance agents, brokers, and service	17	22	1.4	57	86	21,333	24,651	1,471	2,405	1.1
6500	Real estate	64	77	2.3	248	300	10,081	10,200	2,841	3,562	1.2
6510	Real estate operators and lessors	19	22	1.4	89	70	7,281	7,314	728	570	0.6
6530	Real estate agents and managers	33	48	3.3	122	211	10,426	10,237	1,407	2,495	1.4
6552	Subdividers and developers, n.e.c.	2	3	2.0	-	3	-	12,000	-	119	0.6
LINN, OR											
60–	**Finance, insurance, and real estate**	144	140	1.8	828	838	19,686	20,711	17,482	18,914	0.9
6000	Depository institutions	30	29	2.6	348	353	19,253	20,215	6,874	7,119	1.3
6020	Commercial banks	20	18	2.7	232	216	18,345	19,167	4,368	4,312	1.0
6030	Savings institutions	5	5	2.3	47	53	23,234	25,660	1,061	1,075	1.7
6060	Credit unions	5	6	2.9	69	84	19,594	19,476	1,445	1,732	3.4
6100	Nondepository institutions	6	5	0.9	21	18	24,762	28,222	562	538	0.3
6300	Insurance carriers	16	12	1.9	71	52	23,211	24,846	1,810	1,499	0.3
6360	Title insurance	7	3	3.8	36	-	21,556	-	897	-	-
6400	Insurance agents, brokers, and service	39	41	2.6	261	280	22,268	23,443	6,329	7,526	3.4
6500	Real estate	44	46	1.4	98	116	10,327	11,586	1,229	1,562	0.5
6510	Real estate operators and lessors	27	26	1.7	61	60	7,016	9,400	434	613	0.7
6530	Real estate agents and managers	10	14	1.0	23	-	15,478	-	498	-	-
6553	Cemetery subdividers and developers	3	4	6.6	6	-	13,333	-	91	-	-
MALHEUR, OR											
60–	**Finance, insurance, and real estate**	50	53	0.7	297	243	18,586	19,753	5,958	5,284	0.3
6000	Depository institutions	11	9	0.8	106	80	19,962	19,700	2,101	1,667	0.3
6020	Commercial banks	7	5	0.8	79	50	19,443	19,840	1,528	1,017	0.2

Source: County Business Patterns, 1992/93, CBP-92/93-1, U.S. Department of Commerce, Washington, D.C., April 1995. SIC categories for which data were suppressed or not available for both 1992 and 1993 are *not* displayed. The employment columns represent mid-March employment in the year. Pay per employee is calculated by dividing 1st Quarter payroll, annualized, by mid-March employment. The columns headed "% State" show the county's percentage of the state total for the SIC in 1993; for example, 0.9% for SIC 6030 means that the county had 0.9 percent of the state's total establishments (or payroll) in SIC 6030 in 1993. A dash (-) is used to indicate that data are not available or cannot be calculated; *nec* means not elsewhere classified.

Continued on next page.

SIC	Industry	No. Establishments			Employment		Pay / Employee		Annual Payroll ($ 000)		
		1992	1993	% State	1992	1993	1992	1993	1992	1993	% State
MALHEUR, OR - [continued]											
6400	Insurance agents, brokers, and service	16	19	1.2	97	89	19,629	19,101	2,191	1,957	0.9
6500	Real estate	17	17	0.5	35	47	14,857	10,383	664	588	0.2
6510	Real estate operators and lessors	9	10	0.7	19	-	10,526	-	253	-	-
6530	Real estate agents and managers	6	6	0.4	7	9	22,286	8,889	145	83	0.0
6700	Holding and other investment offices	1	4	1.4	-	4	-	23,000	-	108	0.1
MARION, OR											
60 –	**Finance, insurance, and real estate**	594	644	8.2	6,243	6,760	25,387	28,231	170,296	193,023	9.5
6000	Depository institutions	89	88	7.8	1,231	1,292	21,478	24,059	26,628	30,582	5.5
6020	Commercial banks	62	53	8.0	1,033	909	22,238	23,740	22,769	22,374	5.4
6030	Savings institutions	14	21	9.6	106	215	16,302	27,460	2,043	4,647	7.4
6100	Nondepository institutions	44	51	9.4	345	355	24,383	25,713	8,951	10,201	5.6
6160	Mortgage bankers and brokers	25	34	11.2	108	129	21,593	25,054	2,710	4,479	4.2
6200	Security and commodity brokers	30	32	8.9	106	120	43,623	50,233	4,751	6,123	3.7
6210	Security brokers and dealers	18	20	8.7	92	99	47,174	57,051	4,451	5,780	4.1
6280	Security and commodity services	11	12	9.9	-	21	-	18,095	-	343	1.7
6300	Insurance carriers	63	50	7.9	3,160	3,319	30,814	35,707	105,197	115,908	23.1
6310	Life insurance	11	5	5.3	184	129	27,043	29,054	5,192	3,551	4.5
6330	Fire, marine, and casualty insurance	31	29	10.0	-	2,758	-	38,073	-	99,144	41.6
6360	Title insurance	7	2	2.6	166	-	24,072	-	4,392	-	-
6400	Insurance agents, brokers, and service	120	131	8.2	439	489	21,531	20,671	10,485	10,609	4.7
6500	Real estate	232	272	8.3	910	1,120	11,991	12,375	12,769	17,257	5.7
6510	Real estate operators and lessors	117	143	9.4	424	535	7,717	8,022	3,646	5,308	5.8
6530	Real estate agents and managers	87	111	7.5	423	479	15,981	14,363	7,926	9,314	5.4
6552	Subdividers and developers, n.e.c.	7	7	4.7	20	39	12,400	22,462	468	501	2.5
6553	Cemetery subdividers and developers	7	6	9.8	18	18	16,000	14,222	284	278	5.1
6700	Holding and other investment offices	16	20	7.2	52	65	24,538	32,677	1,515	2,343	2.5
6710	Holding offices	3	3	4.9	-	4	-	67,000	-	239	0.4
6794	Patent owners and lessors	3	3	17.6	26	-	26,000	-	706	-	-
6799	Investors, n.e.c.	4	6	11.1	9	-	21,778	-	186	-	-
MORROW, OR											
60 –	**Finance, insurance, and real estate**	11	11	0.1	51	57	18,510	17,614	994	1,068	0.1
6000	Depository institutions	4	4	0.4	-	39	-	18,359	-	670	0.1
6020	Commercial banks	4	4	0.6	-	39	-	18,359	-	670	0.2
6400	Insurance agents, brokers, and service	3	4	0.2	-	14	-	16,000	-	336	0.2
6500	Real estate	3	3	0.1	5	4	10,400	16,000	56	62	0.0
MULTNOMAH, OR											
60 –	**Finance, insurance, and real estate**	1,988	2,078	26.6	33,111	32,543	28,553	31,170	940,573	1,022,546	50.4
6000	Depository institutions	302	256	22.8	10,164	9,106	24,844	33,503	237,992	284,985	51.5
6020	Commercial banks	168	125	18.8	7,884	7,168	24,342	34,643	177,661	219,408	53.4
6030	Savings institutions	51	43	19.7	1,227	674	28,619	29,733	35,110	19,842	31.5
6060	Credit unions	61	66	32.2	707	-	22,535	-	16,555	-	-
6090	Functions closely related to banking	19	18	54.5	-	247	-	47,822	-	20,578	94.8
6100	Nondepository institutions	145	140	25.9	1,902	1,813	37,359	38,500	68,279	75,918	41.6
6140	Personal credit institutions	51	38	23.8	295	231	26,875	25,680	9,215	7,574	-
6150	Business credit institutions	25	33	51.6	450	396	41,049	53,465	15,588	19,841	42.9
6160	Mortgage bankers and brokers	67	69	22.8	1,157	1,186	38,596	36,000	43,461	48,503	45.4
6200	Security and commodity brokers	107	116	32.3	2,092	1,733	48,006	63,398	106,141	109,118	66.7
6210	Security brokers and dealers	68	68	29.6	1,795	1,503	47,374	65,544	83,571	95,463	67.1
6300	Insurance carriers	213	203	32.2	7,895	8,637	27,198	26,928	217,772	240,586	47.9
6310	Life insurance	55	47	49.5	2,414	2,519	24,230	25,151	57,890	62,278	78.5
6321	Accident and health insurance	10	7	46.7	224	200	19,393	19,280	4,269	3,508	45.9
6324	Hospital and medical service plans	7	13	39.4	2,187	2,562	29,586	28,123	65,489	69,833	67.1
6330	Fire, marine, and casualty insurance	73	66	22.8	2,053	2,042	29,750	29,471	60,379	61,390	25.8
6360	Title insurance	18	21	26.9	605	722	29,574	29,471	19,943	22,531	54.9
6400	Insurance agents, brokers, and service	367	404	25.1	2,712	3,105	30,929	33,516	86,146	108,236	48.3

Source: County Business Patterns, 1992/93, CBP-92/93-1, U.S. Department of Commerce, Washington, D.C., April 1995. SIC categories for which data were suppressed or not available for both 1992 and 1993 are *not* displayed. The employment columns represent mid-March employment in the year. Pay per employee is calculated by dividing 1st Quarter payroll, annualized, by mid-March employment. The columns headed "% State" show the county's percentage of the state total for the SIC in 1993; for example, 0.9% for SIC 6030 means that the county had 0.9 percent of the state's total establishments (or payroll) in SIC 6030 in 1993. A dash (-) is used to indicate that data are not available or cannot be calculated; *nec* means not elsewhere classified.

Continued on next page.

SIC	Industry	No. Establishments			Employment		Pay / Employee		Annual Payroll ($ 000)		
		1992	1993	% State	1992	1993	1992	1993	1992	1993	% State
MULTNOMAH, OR - [continued]											
6500	Real estate	741	834	25.4	5,880	6,369	18,341	18,508	114,943	132,357	43.6
6510	Real estate operators and lessors	376	447	29.2	1,913	2,366	17,213	17,243	33,606	45,604	49.4
6530	Real estate agents and managers	282	350	23.8	3,480	3,828	18,777	18,781	69,993	80,289	46.4
6552	Subdividers and developers, n.e.c.	25	25	16.8	124	96	29,226	33,500	3,809	4,294	21.5
6553	Cemetery subdividers and developers	5	7	11.5	101	78	17,030	25,231	1,952	2,062	37.6
6710	Holding offices	20	20	32.8	892	914	46,350	61,698	41,714	49,558	73.1
6720	Investment offices	3	5	55.6	15	-	50,933	-	896	-	-
6732	Educational, religious, etc. trusts	28	31	50.0	162	196	22,469	22,816	3,849	4,569	70.3
6733	Trusts, n.e.c.	31	33	46.5	240	244	70,333	18,033	9,582	5,040	80.5
6794	Patent owners and lessors	3	8	47.1	-	174	-	16,000	-	3,495	-
POLK, OR											
60 –	**Finance, insurance, and real estate**	69	74	0.9	252	270	16,873	18,430	4,340	5,201	0.3
6000	Depository institutions	13	13	1.2	97	108	19,918	19,741	1,854	1,970	0.4
6020	Commercial banks	9	8	1.2	-	80	-	20,100	-	1,540	0.4
6030	Savings institutions	4	5	2.3	-	28	-	18,714	-	430	0.7
6300	Insurance carriers	5	4	0.6	17	-	26,824	-	503	-	-
6400	Insurance agents, brokers, and service	18	16	1.0	48	42	16,750	19,905	907	925	0.4
6500	Real estate	29	39	1.2	83	103	11,373	14,058	939	1,605	0.5
6510	Real estate operators and lessors	11	19	1.2	39	64	12,103	13,938	508	871	0.9
6530	Real estate agents and managers	12	17	1.2	32	32	9,250	12,000	247	478	0.3
SHERMAN, OR											
60 –	**Finance, insurance, and real estate**	3	3	0.0	8	8	8,000	9,000	68	80	0.0
TILLAMOOK, OR											
60 –	**Finance, insurance, and real estate**	42	43	0.5	200	181	14,360	15,890	3,066	3,045	0.2
6000	Depository institutions	9	9	0.8	89	78	17,303	19,333	1,549	1,466	0.3
6300	Insurance carriers	3	2	0.3	17	-	20,235	-	383	-	-
6360	Title insurance	3	2	2.6	17	-	20,235	-	383	-	-
6400	Insurance agents, brokers, and service	7	7	0.4	23	-	12,870	-	309	-	-
6500	Real estate	20	24	0.7	59	69	8,271	9,333	620	813	0.3
6510	Real estate operators and lessors	6	7	0.5	17	-	4,471	-	93	-	-
6530	Real estate agents and managers	14	15	1.0	42	41	9,810	11,317	527	596	0.3
UMATILLA, OR											
60 –	**Finance, insurance, and real estate**	120	118	1.5	918	631	18,397	17,369	20,026	11,475	0.6
6000	Depository institutions	28	22	2.0	313	264	20,805	20,682	6,424	5,423	1.0
6020	Commercial banks	22	16	2.4	290	241	21,131	20,963	6,043	5,022	1.2
6300	Insurance carriers	13	11	1.7	44	54	23,727	19,407	1,114	991	0.2
6400	Insurance agents, brokers, and service	32	33	2.1	118	143	15,424	14,769	1,876	2,511	1.1
6500	Real estate	37	43	1.3	94	134	9,191	8,119	984	1,244	0.4
6510	Real estate operators and lessors	23	28	1.8	56	94	8,857	7,362	546	764	0.8
UNION, OR											
60 –	**Finance, insurance, and real estate**	48	48	0.6	202	189	16,297	17,820	3,449	3,473	0.2
6000	Depository institutions	11	10	0.9	102	92	17,059	19,087	1,828	1,726	0.3
6020	Commercial banks	6	5	0.8	70	-	18,400	-	1,354	-	-
6200	Security and commodity brokers	4	4	1.1	8	9	37,000	32,889	312	313	0.2
6300	Insurance carriers	4	3	0.5	-	5	-	40,000	-	209	0.0
6400	Insurance agents, brokers, and service	12	11	0.7	34	38	19,059	19,368	609	789	0.4
6500	Real estate	16	20	0.6	44	45	6,182	8,444	315	436	0.1
6510	Real estate operators and lessors	8	9	0.6	21	-	4,762	-	93	-	-
6530	Real estate agents and managers	4	9	0.6	10	24	7,200	9,333	83	225	0.1

Source: County Business Patterns, 1992/93, CBP-92/93-1, U.S. Department of Commerce, Washington, D.C., April 1995. SIC categories for which data were suppressed or not available for both 1992 and 1993 are *not* displayed. The employment columns represent mid-March employment in the year. Pay per employee is calculated by dividing 1st Quarter payroll, annualized, by mid-March employment. The columns headed "% State" show the county's percentage of the state total for the SIC in 1993; for example, 0.9% for SIC 6030 means that the county had 0.9 percent of the state's total establishments (or payroll) in SIC 6030 in 1993. A dash (-) is used to indicate that data are not available or cannot be calculated; *nec* means not elsewhere classified.

SIC	Industry	No. Establishments			Employment		Pay / Employee		Annual Payroll ($ 000)		
		1992	1993	% State	1992	1993	1992	1993	1992	1993	% State
WALLOWA, OR											
60 –	**Finance, insurance, and real estate**	21	24	0.3	78	80	16,718	15,200	1,282	1,394	0.1
6000	Depository institutions	5	5	0.4	-	43	-	16,651	-	781	0.1
6400	Insurance agents, brokers, and service	7	7	0.4	19	-	15,789	-	310	-	-
6500	Real estate	8	11	0.3	15	14	17,067	10,000	247	232	0.1
6510	Real estate operators and lessors	3	3	0.2	4	-	7,000	-	29	-	-
6530	Real estate agents and managers	4	7	0.5	8	10	20,500	11,600	150	197	0.1
WASCO, OR											
60 –	**Finance, insurance, and real estate**	60	59	0.8	219	285	20,548	19,396	4,706	5,510	0.3
6000	Depository institutions	12	11	1.0	114	146	21,263	20,822	2,355	2,707	0.5
6020	Commercial banks	9	8	1.2	105	134	21,676	21,463	2,210	2,531	0.6
6100	Nondepository institutions	3	3	0.6	-	10	-	49,200	-	481	0.3
6300	Insurance carriers	4	1	0.2	6	-	34,667	-	143	-	-
6400	Insurance agents, brokers, and service	20	21	1.3	46	65	18,174	16,677	886	1,240	0.6
6500	Real estate	18	21	0.6	36	60	11,778	12,133	602	831	0.3
6510	Real estate operators and lessors	10	12	0.8	17	39	6,118	7,487	192	322	0.3
6530	Real estate agents and managers	4	6	0.4	7	9	12,571	21,778	144	189	0.1
WASHINGTON, OR											
60 –	**Finance, insurance, and real estate**	896	946	12.1	8,561	8,298	23,929	24,574	213,885	233,959	11.5
6000	Depository institutions	126	118	10.5	2,305	2,434	21,423	22,508	51,703	65,849	11.9
6020	Commercial banks	74	68	10.2	1,855	1,970	20,694	21,202	39,515	53,755	13.1
6030	Savings institutions	35	35	16.1	282	295	26,709	30,983	8,434	7,720	12.3
6060	Credit unions	12	11	5.4	152	156	21,632	23,641	3,521	4,133	8.0
6090	Functions closely related to banking	4	4	12.1	-	13	-	14,462	-	241	1.1
6100	Nondepository institutions	84	102	18.9	1,088	1,046	32,007	31,033	35,334	37,445	20.5
6140	Personal credit institutions	29	27	16.9	304	177	26,697	23,887	8,456	4,031	-
6150	Business credit institutions	9	14	21.9	279	481	32,158	28,058	8,371	14,290	30.9
6160	Mortgage bankers and brokers	44	61	20.1	437	388	39,359	37,979	18,000	19,124	17.9
6210	Security brokers and dealers	19	22	9.6	74	87	42,108	49,379	3,045	4,484	3.2
6280	Security and commodity services	18	19	15.7	-	41	-	12,878	-	755	3.6
6300	Insurance carriers	107	94	14.9	2,228	1,802	26,009	30,735	57,349	56,034	11.2
6310	Life insurance	13	11	11.6	160	175	25,850	29,486	4,067	5,709	7.2
6330	Fire, marine, and casualty insurance	64	54	18.7	1,762	1,330	25,140	31,158	44,208	41,287	17.3
6360	Title insurance	13	18	23.1	122	153	22,885	26,222	3,180	4,052	9.9
6400	Insurance agents, brokers, and service	176	199	12.4	676	732	24,142	23,672	17,453	18,908	8.4
6500	Real estate	336	362	11.0	1,848	1,860	15,701	15,763	34,731	37,499	12.4
6510	Real estate operators and lessors	136	148	9.7	497	612	15,517	14,268	8,429	9,459	10.3
6530	Real estate agents and managers	144	163	11.1	1,004	975	15,673	16,931	18,457	20,976	12.1
6552	Subdividers and developers, n.e.c.	19	39	26.2	200	236	14,760	14,186	4,063	6,135	30.7
6553	Cemetery subdividers and developers	3	5	8.2	48	32	13,750	20,500	807	674	12.3
6700	Holding and other investment offices	25	27	9.7	288	279	45,000	33,649	13,201	12,460	13.1
6710	Holding offices	10	10	16.4	214	167	51,308	37,772	10,184	7,841	11.6
6732	Educational, religious, etc. trusts	4	4	6.5	31	-	32,129	-	986	-	-
6733	Trusts, n.e.c.	4	3	4.2	13	-	14,462	-	224	-	-
WHEELER, OR											
60 –	**Finance, insurance, and real estate**	3	3	0.0	19	-	9,053	-	150	-	-
YAMHILL, OR											
60 –	**Finance, insurance, and real estate**	127	130	1.7	983	935	20,688	22,083	21,072	21,582	1.1
6000	Depository institutions	22	19	1.7	243	227	19,095	19,965	4,905	4,535	0.8
6020	Commercial banks	14	11	1.7	171	146	18,947	19,096	3,407	2,799	0.7
6100	Nondepository institutions	5	9	1.7	-	17	-	24,235	-	566	0.3
6200	Security and commodity brokers	4	4	1.1	-	10	-	44,800	-	615	0.4
6300	Insurance carriers	9	5	0.8	188	-	30,468	-	5,762	-	-
6400	Insurance agents, brokers, and service	26	30	1.9	238	148	12,471	17,243	2,679	3,276	1.5
6500	Real estate	56	57	1.7	144	207	14,222	12,483	2,340	3,074	1.0

Source: County Business Patterns, 1992/93, CBP-92/93-1, U.S. Department of Commerce, Washington, D.C., April 1995. SIC categories for which data were suppressed or not available for both 1992 and 1993 are not displayed. The employment columns represent mid-March employment in the year. Pay per employee is calculated by dividing 1st Quarter payroll, annualized, by mid-March employment. The columns headed "% State" show the county's percentage of the state total for the SIC in 1993; for example, 0.9% for SIC 6030 means that the county had 0.9 percent of the state's total establishments (or payroll) in SIC 6030 in 1993. A dash (-) is used to indicate that data are not available or cannot be calculated; nec means not elsewhere classified.

Continued on next page.

SIC	Industry	No. Establishments			Employment		Pay / Employee		Annual Payroll ($ 000)		
		1992	1993	% State	1992	1993	1992	1993	1992	1993	% State
YAMHILL, OR - [continued]											
6510	Real estate operators and lessors	30	33	2.2	88	150	12,364	9,600	1,113	1,533	1.7
6530	Real estate agents and managers	15	18	1.2	21	37	16,762	20,757	479	1,052	0.6
6700	Holding and other investment offices	5	6	2.2	147	-	29,306	-	4,505	-	-

Source: County Business Patterns, 1992/93, CBP-92/93-1, U.S. Department of Commerce, Washington, D.C., April 1995. SIC categories for which data were suppressed or not available for both 1992 and 1993 are not displayed. The employment columns represent mid-March employment in the year. Pay per employee is calculated by dividing 1st Quarter payroll, annualized, by mid-March employment. The columns headed "% State" show the county's percentage of the state total for the SIC in 1993; for example, 0.9% for SIC 6030 means that the county had 0.9 percent of the state's total establishments (or payroll) in SIC 6030 in 1993. A dash (-) is used to indicate that data are not available or cannot be calculated; nec means not elsewhere classified.

PENNSYLVANIA

SIC	Industry	No. Establishments			Employment		Pay / Employee		Annual Payroll ($ 000)		
		1992	1993	% State	1992	1993	1992	1993	1992	1993	% State
ADAMS, PA											
60 –	**Finance, insurance, and real estate**	114	100	0.4	826	664	18,150	19,211	16,423	13,806	0.1
6000	Depository institutions	37	27	0.5	509	312	16,770	18,667	9,492	6,044	0.2
6300	Insurance carriers	8	7	0.3	46	72	30,261	29,889	1,557	2,467	0.1
6400	Insurance agents, brokers, and service	24	24	0.5	123	130	22,341	21,046	3,002	3,159	0.3
6500	Real estate	38	36	0.5	121	132	11,570	11,879	1,467	1,658	0.2
6510	Real estate operators and lessors	11	11	0.4	56	52	10,929	13,615	516	673	0.2
6530	Real estate agents and managers	10	12	0.4	26	40	14,000	13,300	470	607	0.1
6540	Title abstract offices	4	4	1.7	10	18	10,000	8,222	135	182	0.3
6553	Cemetery subdividers and developers	8	8	1.2	20	-	9,200	-	214	-	-
ALLEGHENY, PA											
60 –	**Finance, insurance, and real estate**	3,308	3,280	13.9	54,617	55,797	30,998	31,998	1,731,986	1,881,835	18.8
6000	Depository institutions	616	623	11.0	20,897	20,740	28,380	30,688	562,964	613,746	23.7
6020	Commercial banks	337	348	9.3	17,481	17,783	29,545	31,867	484,485	543,141	25.7
6030	Savings institutions	163	136	15.3	2,412	1,924	22,633	24,131	55,415	46,991	17.0
6060	Credit unions	95	118	13.8	388	506	14,969	15,652	6,061	8,522	8.6
6090	Functions closely related to banking	17	18	10.2	142	-	18,282	-	2,487	-	-
6100	Nondepository institutions	233	205	15.9	2,233	2,336	32,632	30,341	77,274	74,011	13.5
6110	Federal and Federally-sponsored credit	11	2	4.8	73	-	21,096	-	1,530	-	-
6140	Personal credit institutions	128	96	14.4	918	837	26,741	23,751	24,507	20,370	12.8
6150	Business credit institutions	27	32	24.8	321	-	39,352	-	12,099	-	-
6160	Mortgage bankers and brokers	65	73	16.3	899	1,049	37,362	32,507	38,468	37,049	13.7
6200	Security and commodity brokers	173	170	14.9	3,090	2,172	72,114	64,087	244,335	202,486	17.6
6210	Security brokers and dealers	83	81	13.6	1,327	-	92,781	-	123,108	-	-
6280	Security and commodity services	86	88	16.7	1,742	762	56,641	47,444	119,968	104,842	22.6
6300	Insurance carriers	432	331	15.5	12,620	12,585	29,647	29,832	375,990	373,373	12.3
6310	Life insurance	136	128	17.3	5,328	5,896	26,492	24,626	140,349	143,911	10.8
6330	Fire, marine, and casualty insurance	129	112	15.5	3,309	2,678	34,194	36,013	113,012	98,184	9.7
6350	Surety insurance	13	6	22.2	134	-	39,433	-	4,497	-	-
6370	Pension, health, and welfare funds	121	56	12.6	717	483	21,021	26,186	27,931	13,878	17.0
6400	Insurance agents, brokers, and service	601	643	12.7	3,941	4,269	29,413	28,749	119,293	130,946	13.8
6500	Real estate	1,064	1,117	15.3	8,617	8,295	19,946	22,415	190,965	196,986	18.4
6510	Real estate operators and lessors	436	511	17.8	2,548	2,640	15,397	16,444	41,583	48,406	14.5
6530	Real estate agents and managers	433	477	14.9	4,298	4,202	22,142	24,611	101,013	107,847	18.4
6540	Title abstract offices	16	18	7.6	552	801	24,254	28,974	20,644	23,206	41.7
6552	Subdividers and developers, n.e.c.	50	46	16.0	267	208	27,146	33,019	8,721	7,297	19.1
6553	Cemetery subdividers and developers	52	55	8.4	450	435	19,067	20,497	9,189	9,604	17.3
6700	Holding and other investment offices	171	171	19.1	2,303	3,947	39,211	37,097	111,137	193,114	38.9
6710	Holding offices	43	48	18.7	1,009	2,612	55,275	43,695	71,240	157,299	43.6
6732	Educational, religious, etc. trusts	45	48	22.9	843	836	10,904	11,589	10,258	11,011	32.1
6733	Trusts, n.e.c.	48	40	17.8	202	281	23,050	24,626	6,211	8,031	28.0
6794	Patent owners and lessors	10	15	25.9	91	118	45,582	38,475	3,498	3,976	25.3
ARMSTRONG, PA											
60 –	**Finance, insurance, and real estate**	105	115	0.5	620	621	16,594	16,857	10,921	11,470	0.1
6000	Depository institutions	38	37	0.7	395	390	16,506	17,856	6,930	7,309	0.3
6020	Commercial banks	30	29	0.8	365	360	16,592	18,000	6,472	6,827	0.3
6100	Nondepository institutions	3	3	0.2	15	18	21,867	17,333	300	353	0.1
6140	Personal credit institutions	3	3	0.4	15	18	21,867	17,333	300	353	0.2
6300	Insurance carriers	14	10	0.5	49	48	9,388	14,083	481	676	0.0
6400	Insurance agents, brokers, and service	26	35	0.7	75	88	22,827	16,818	1,802	1,875	0.2

Source: County Business Patterns, 1992/93, CBP-92/93-1, U.S. Department of Commerce, Washington, D.C., April 1995. SIC categories for which data were suppressed or not available for both 1992 and 1993 are *not* displayed. The employment columns represent mid-March employment in the year. Pay per employee is calculated by dividing 1st Quarter payroll, annualized, by mid-March employment. The columns headed "% State" show the county's percentage of the state total for the SIC in 1993; for example, 0.9% for SIC 6030 means that the county had 0.9 percent of the state's total establishments (or payroll) in SIC 6030 in 1993. A dash (-) is used to indicate that data are not available or cannot be calculated; *nec* means not elsewhere classified.

Continued on next page.

SIC	Industry	No. Establishments			Employment		Pay / Employee		Annual Payroll ($ 000)		
		1992	1993	% State	1992	1993	1992	1993	1992	1993	% State
ARMSTRONG, PA - [continued]											
6500	Real estate	20	24	0.3	64	58	9,562	9,310	666	681	0.1
6510	Real estate operators and lessors	8	9	0.3	37	36	6,054	8,111	244	330	0.1
6530	Real estate agents and managers	5	7	0.2	9	-	9,778	-	100	-	
6553	Cemetery subdividers and developers	6	7	1.1	-	15	-	12,267	-	207	0.4
6700	Holding and other investment offices	4	6	0.7	22	19	29,818	26,105	742	576	0.1
BEAVER, PA											
60 –	**Finance, insurance, and real estate**	263	265	1.1	1,823	1,774	20,149	20,327	38,035	37,568	0.4
6000	Depository institutions	90	92	1.6	888	833	18,982	18,564	16,699	15,660	0.6
6020	Commercial banks	52	53	1.4	622	527	19,646	18,391	11,613	9,894	0.5
6030	Savings institutions	15	15	1.7	124	132	19,774	22,758	2,699	2,885	1.0
6100	Nondepository institutions	15	11	0.9	62	56	23,613	22,857	1,590	1,531	0.3
6200	Security and commodity brokers	4	4	0.4	28	27	79,714	89,481	2,137	2,315	0.2
6210	Security brokers and dealers	4	4	0.7	28	27	79,714	89,481	2,137	2,315	0.3
6300	Insurance carriers	21	19	0.9	344	340	19,895	20,765	6,813	6,844	0.2
6310	Life insurance	8	8	1.1	314	315	20,140	19,505	6,264	6,148	0.5
6400	Insurance agents, brokers, and service	59	58	1.1	200	194	19,560	20,433	4,665	4,580	0.5
6500	Real estate	70	77	1.1	287	315	18,355	18,235	5,975	6,472	0.6
6510	Real estate operators and lessors	27	28	1.0	122	140	19,213	18,171	2,635	2,695	0.8
6530	Real estate agents and managers	29	33	1.0	-	108	-	16,926	-	2,055	0.4
6552	Subdividers and developers, n.e.c.	-	3	1.0	-	3	-	38,667	-	309	0.8
6553	Cemetery subdividers and developers	11	10	1.5	66	60	19,879	19,733	1,392	1,288	2.3
6700	Holding and other investment offices	4	4	0.4	14	9	11,143	14,667	156	166	0.0
BEDFORD, PA											
60 –	**Finance, insurance, and real estate**	70	64	0.3	422	428	17,355	17,187	7,499	8,074	0.1
6000	Depository institutions	25	25	0.4	231	247	17,489	17,360	4,326	4,658	0.2
6300	Insurance carriers	6	4	0.2	55	50	19,345	19,120	1,001	1,016	0.0
6330	Fire, marine, and casualty insurance	3	3	0.4	51	-	19,843	-	943	-	-
6400	Insurance agents, brokers, and service	16	14	0.3	54	54	19,037	17,926	1,206	1,267	0.1
6500	Real estate	20	18	0.2	73	68	13,041	12,412	700	821	0.1
6510	Real estate operators and lessors	5	7	0.2	31	30	22,452	18,667	405	562	0.2
6530	Real estate agents and managers	6	4	0.1	31	25	5,935	7,200	162	140	0.0
6553	Cemetery subdividers and developers	8	7	1.1	11	13	6,545	8,000	100	119	0.2
BERKS, PA											
60 –	**Finance, insurance, and real estate**	588	602	2.6	8,189	8,290	30,701	29,177	240,228	244,326	2.4
6000	Depository institutions	148	149	2.6	3,805	3,109	31,013	24,106	103,319	77,551	3.0
6020	Commercial banks	110	102	2.7	3,454	2,461	31,398	24,447	94,056	60,331	2.9
6030	Savings institutions	16	22	2.5	161	-	23,652	-	3,593	-	-
6060	Credit unions	19	23	2.7	-	152	-	20,184	-	3,216	3.2
6100	Nondepository institutions	33	33	2.6	247	283	32,761	30,163	8,028	9,818	1.8
6160	Mortgage bankers and brokers	10	12	2.7	107	114	40,673	32,561	4,215	5,385	2.0
6200	Security and commodity brokers	23	23	2.0	201	190	75,741	70,589	15,499	15,558	1.4
6210	Security brokers and dealers	12	9	1.5	139	127	75,137	76,535	10,052	10,956	1.6
6280	Security and commodity services	11	14	2.7	62	63	77,097	58,603	5,447	4,602	1.0
6300	Insurance carriers	56	55	2.6	2,251	2,670	30,427	30,617	70,545	76,590	2.5
6310	Life insurance	15	16	2.2	757	676	23,281	32,775	18,778	17,208	1.3
6330	Fire, marine, and casualty insurance	12	14	1.9	1,387	-	34,959	-	48,341	-	-
6360	Title insurance	3	2	2.9	44	-	33,000	-	1,562	-	-
6370	Pension, health, and welfare funds	20	20	4.5	-	62	-	9,290	-	2,157	2.6
6400	Insurance agents, brokers, and service	118	120	2.4	640	621	27,888	29,230	17,662	19,653	2.1
6500	Real estate	183	201	2.8	775	793	17,966	18,880	14,924	17,387	1.6
6510	Real estate operators and lessors	58	62	2.2	270	330	15,230	19,552	4,729	6,985	2.1
6530	Real estate agents and managers	64	86	2.7	252	260	20,317	18,954	5,020	6,045	1.0
6540	Title abstract offices	7	7	2.9	51	54	23,529	24,148	1,296	1,475	2.7
6552	Subdividers and developers, n.e.c.	9	9	3.1	53	31	33,962	30,710	1,841	1,214	3.2
6553	Cemetery subdividers and developers	32	35	5.3	105	118	11,276	11,322	1,379	1,649	3.0

Source: County Business Patterns, 1992/93, CBP-92/93-1, U.S. Department of Commerce, Washington, D.C., April 1995. SIC categories for which data were suppressed or not available for both 1992 and 1993 are not displayed. The employment columns represent mid-March employment in the year. Pay per employee is calculated by dividing 1st Quarter payroll, annualized, by mid-March employment. The columns headed "% State" show the county's percentage of the state total for the SIC in 1993; for example, 0.9% for SIC 6030 means that the county had 0.9 percent of the state's total establishments (or payroll) in SIC 6030 in 1993. A dash (-) is used to indicate that data are not available or cannot be calculated; nec means not elsewhere classified.

Continued on next page.

SIC	Industry	No. Establishments			Employment		Pay / Employee		Annual Payroll ($ 000)		
		1992	1993	% State	1992	1993	1992	1993	1992	1993	% State
BERKS, PA - [continued]											
6700	Holding and other investment offices	27	21	2.3	270	624	36,385	48,263	10,251	27,769	5.6
6710	Holding offices	9	9	3.5	222	566	37,856	49,470	8,526	25,732	7.1
6732	Educational, religious, etc. trusts	4	4	1.9	-	24	-	25,500	-	729	2.1
6733	Trusts, n.e.c.	8	5	2.2	9	-	18,222	-	188	-	-
BLAIR, PA											
60 –	**Finance, insurance, and real estate**	238	257	1.1	2,261	2,529	20,495	20,332	47,119	52,957	0.5
6000	Depository institutions	69	75	1.3	1,167	1,158	20,668	21,116	23,151	24,227	0.9
6020	Commercial banks	44	50	1.3	971	969	21,343	21,779	19,562	20,467	1.0
6030	Savings institutions	13	12	1.3	129	123	20,403	20,390	2,817	2,893	1.0
6060	Credit unions	11	12	1.4	63	-	11,619	-	739	-	-
6100	Nondepository institutions	11	11	0.9	55	-	23,127	-	1,277	-	-
6140	Personal credit institutions	9	8	1.2	-	48	-	20,667	-	1,081	0.7
6200	Security and commodity brokers	9	10	0.9	59	68	61,424	51,882	3,974	3,962	0.3
6210	Security brokers and dealers	6	6	1.0	53	52	64,528	58,923	3,652	3,408	0.5
6280	Security and commodity services	3	4	0.8	6	16	34,000	29,000	322	554	0.1
6300	Insurance carriers	27	26	1.2	271	414	25,845	23,758	7,042	9,653	0.3
6310	Life insurance	9	9	1.2	190	345	25,579	21,959	4,885	7,228	0.5
6330	Fire, marine, and casualty insurance	11	11	1.5	-	60	-	37,067	-	2,302	0.2
6370	Pension, health, and welfare funds	3	3	0.7	6	-	3,333	-	22	-	-
6400	Insurance agents, brokers, and service	59	66	1.3	215	260	19,014	17,954	4,472	5,017	0.5
6500	Real estate	60	68	0.9	487	563	12,559	13,400	7,031	8,602	0.8
6510	Real estate operators and lessors	20	32	1.1	82	94	11,951	10,681	1,060	1,106	0.3
6530	Real estate agents and managers	22	21	0.7	301	403	13,515	14,243	4,886	6,526	1.1
6553	Cemetery subdividers and developers	14	13	2.0	60	-	13,133	-	840	-	-
6700	Holding and other investment offices	3	1	0.1	7	-	16,571	-	172	-	-
BRADFORD, PA											
60 –	**Finance, insurance, and real estate**	101	100	0.4	737	748	21,938	21,021	15,939	15,599	0.2
6000	Depository institutions	39	38	0.7	358	372	17,251	17,000	6,322	6,309	0.2
6020	Commercial banks	30	30	0.8	319	336	17,492	17,095	5,732	5,709	0.3
6100	Nondepository institutions	5	5	0.4	52	50	28,154	27,440	1,242	1,309	0.2
6400	Insurance agents, brokers, and service	30	28	0.6	142	106	24,732	18,566	3,026	2,307	0.2
6510	Real estate operators and lessors	8	8	0.3	16	-	12,000	-	259	-	-
6553	Cemetery subdividers and developers	6	5	0.8	7	-	9,714	-	94	-	-
BUCKS, PA											
60 –	**Finance, insurance, and real estate**	1,166	1,180	5.0	9,922	10,653	27,381	26,546	291,284	325,591	3.3
6000	Depository institutions	234	235	4.2	2,820	3,221	22,604	22,220	63,679	75,001	2.9
6020	Commercial banks	159	156	4.2	2,019	2,413	23,087	22,677	46,428	56,746	2.7
6030	Savings institutions	54	53	6.0	568	500	21,120	21,168	11,967	11,383	4.1
6060	Credit unions	12	16	1.9	196	265	22,041	18,717	4,380	5,470	5.5
6090	Functions closely related to banking	9	10	5.6	37	43	22,054	30,419	904	1,402	3.7
6100	Nondepository institutions	97	92	7.1	902	967	32,887	32,802	36,779	42,383	7.7
6140	Personal credit institutions	46	38	5.7	372	232	25,247	22,724	9,848	5,297	3.3
6160	Mortgage bankers and brokers	44	48	10.7	510	667	37,067	36,156	25,618	34,813	12.9
6200	Security and commodity brokers	61	57	5.0	224	264	55,804	55,515	15,333	22,249	1.9
6210	Security brokers and dealers	26	26	4.4	158	184	66,228	69,000	12,932	19,533	2.9
6280	Security and commodity services	35	31	5.9	66	80	30,848	24,500	2,401	2,716	0.6
6300	Insurance carriers	103	86	4.0	2,269	2,390	31,924	30,867	73,304	73,291	2.4
6310	Life insurance	24	19	2.6	1,505	851	31,833	35,079	46,882	27,499	2.1
6321	Accident and health insurance	3	4	8.0	340	-	23,753	-	8,198	-	-
6330	Fire, marine, and casualty insurance	28	25	3.5	81	74	81,284	83,784	6,739	6,721	0.7
6360	Title insurance	13	8	11.8	40	-	37,100	-	1,647	-	-
6370	Pension, health, and welfare funds	32	29	6.5	301	-	26,977	-	9,558	-	-
6400	Insurance agents, brokers, and service	260	272	5.4	1,115	1,172	28,997	26,959	35,854	40,544	4.3
6500	Real estate	375	394	5.4	2,249	2,199	21,321	20,688	52,151	54,453	5.1
6510	Real estate operators and lessors	112	129	4.5	662	617	17,807	16,506	13,120	12,785	3.8

Source: County Business Patterns, 1992/93, CBP-92/93-1, U.S. Department of Commerce, Washington, D.C., April 1995. SIC categories for which data were suppressed or not available for both 1992 and 1993 are not displayed. The employment columns represent mid-March employment in the year. Pay per employee is calculated by dividing 1st Quarter payroll, annualized, by mid-March employment. The columns headed "% State" show the county's percentage of the state total for the SIC in 1993; for example, 0.9% for SIC 6030 means that the county had 0.9 percent of the state's total establishments (or payroll) in SIC 6030 in 1993. A dash (-) is used to indicate that data are not available or cannot be calculated; nec means not elsewhere classified.

Continued on next page.

SIC	Industry	No. Establishments			Employment		Pay / Employee		Annual Payroll ($ 000)		
		1992	1993	% State	1992	1993	1992	1993	1992	1993	% State
BUCKS, PA - [continued]											
6530	Real estate agents and managers	169	196	6.1	1,136	1,226	22,187	21,752	27,182	30,773	5.2
6540	Title abstract offices	23	32	13.4	129	158	26,357	23,772	3,632	5,327	9.6
6552	Subdividers and developers, n.e.c.	14	11	3.8	38	45	37,158	37,244	1,429	1,742	4.6
6553	Cemetery subdividers and developers	21	21	3.2	180	153	21,689	20,967	4,169	3,707	6.7
6700	Holding and other investment offices	36	43	4.8	343	-	38,041	-	14,184	-	-
6710	Holding offices	16	11	4.3	241	232	45,295	41,207	12,003	10,632	2.9
6732	Educational, religious, etc. trusts	6	7	3.3	66	106	15,212	19,132	1,013	2,043	6.0
6733	Trusts, n.e.c.	9	12	5.3	23	69	36,522	8,000	908	537	1.9
BUTLER, PA											
60 –	**Finance, insurance, and real estate**	282	295	1.3	1,991	1,779	22,107	21,075	44,987	38,970	0.4
6000	Depository institutions	78	79	1.4	702	695	19,385	19,597	13,149	13,396	0.5
6020	Commercial banks	50	52	1.4	573	568	20,503	20,725	11,201	11,483	0.5
6030	Savings institutions	12	11	1.2	81	74	15,358	15,459	1,293	1,168	0.4
6060	Credit unions	16	16	1.9	48	53	12,833	13,283	655	745	0.8
6100	Nondepository institutions	21	19	1.5	130	106	18,185	21,245	2,358	2,529	0.5
6140	Personal credit institutions	16	14	2.1	89	82	21,348	23,073	1,877	2,013	1.3
6200	Security and commodity brokers	6	6	0.5	21	26	60,762	54,308	994	1,230	0.1
6300	Insurance carriers	25	19	0.9	619	404	28,110	25,693	18,717	10,883	0.4
6310	Life insurance	4	3	0.4	58	57	25,172	29,965	1,442	1,527	0.1
6330	Fire, marine, and casualty insurance	13	9	1.2	532	320	29,293	26,212	16,863	8,979	0.9
6370	Pension, health, and welfare funds	7	7	1.6	-	27	-	10,519	-	377	0.5
6400	Insurance agents, brokers, and service	65	77	1.5	199	210	20,764	20,800	4,258	4,659	0.5
6500	Real estate	78	87	1.2	277	291	15,105	14,969	4,414	5,003	0.5
6510	Real estate operators and lessors	36	39	1.4	150	143	14,080	14,601	2,105	2,323	0.7
6530	Real estate agents and managers	24	29	0.9	88	114	17,682	15,158	1,757	2,024	0.3
6540	Title abstract offices	3	4	1.7	9	8	25,333	31,500	215	300	0.5
6553	Cemetery subdividers and developers	15	14	2.1	30	-	9,600	-	337	-	-
6700	Holding and other investment offices	9	8	0.9	43	47	24,465	23,489	1,097	1,270	0.3
CAMBRIA, PA											
60 –	**Finance, insurance, and real estate**	284	292	1.2	4,575	4,465	19,917	19,757	92,776	95,036	1.0
6000	Depository institutions	99	103	1.8	1,388	1,444	19,669	18,873	27,357	28,295	1.1
6020	Commercial banks	68	71	1.9	1,124	1,158	19,577	19,022	21,994	22,961	1.1
6030	Savings institutions	16	16	1.8	184	194	20,717	19,608	3,899	3,832	1.4
6060	Credit unions	15	16	1.9	80	92	18,550	15,435	1,464	1,502	1.5
6100	Nondepository institutions	13	10	0.8	48	-	23,917	-	1,320	-	-
6200	Security and commodity brokers	7	9	0.8	-	44	-	72,455	-	3,478	0.3
6210	Security brokers and dealers	5	6	1.0	35	-	69,486	-	2,482	-	-
6300	Insurance carriers	27	28	1.3	1,658	1,611	17,163	16,968	29,298	29,924	1.0
6310	Life insurance	12	11	1.5	1,522	-	16,786	-	26,316	-	-
6330	Fire, marine, and casualty insurance	11	13	1.8	106	89	18,415	26,247	2,209	2,700	0.3
6400	Insurance agents, brokers, and service	68	67	1.3	305	315	24,302	21,397	7,892	8,149	0.9
6500	Real estate	61	66	0.9	952	812	19,151	20,483	17,612	17,852	1.7
6510	Real estate operators and lessors	26	30	1.0	833	702	20,034	21,487	15,829	15,833	4.7
6530	Real estate agents and managers	19	17	0.5	68	50	14,941	18,400	999	1,041	0.2
6552	Subdividers and developers, n.e.c.	1	4	1.4	-	14	-	8,000	-	200	0.5
6553	Cemetery subdividers and developers	11	12	1.8	-	44	-	11,545	-	675	1.2
6700	Holding and other investment offices	8	8	0.9	168	178	33,595	32,809	6,235	5,968	1.2
6710	Holding offices	3	3	1.2	-	172	-	33,302	-	5,849	1.6
CAMERON, PA											
60 –	**Finance, insurance, and real estate**	6	5	0.0	51	51	14,353	14,039	814	825	0.0
CARBON, PA											
60 –	**Finance, insurance, and real estate**	83	78	0.3	519	634	20,902	16,215	10,552	10,527	0.1
6000	Depository institutions	29	28	0.5	333	419	20,384	14,530	6,493	6,406	0.2
6020	Commercial banks	20	19	0.5	289	374	21,135	14,385	5,759	5,655	0.3

Source: County Business Patterns, 1992/93, CBP-92/93-1, U.S. Department of Commerce, Washington, D.C., April 1995. SIC categories for which data were suppressed or not available for both 1992 and 1993 are not displayed. The employment columns represent mid-March employment in the year. Pay per employee is calculated by dividing 1st Quarter payroll, annualized, by mid-March employment. The columns headed "% State" show the county's percentage of the state total for the SIC in 1993; for example, 0.9% for SIC 6030 means that the county had 0.9 percent of the state's total establishments (or payroll) in SIC 6030 in 1993. A dash (-) is used to indicate that data are not available or cannot be calculated; nec means not elsewhere classified.

Continued on next page.

SIC	Industry	No. Establishments			Employment		Pay / Employee		Annual Payroll ($ 000)		
		1992	1993	% State	1992	1993	1992	1993	1992	1993	% State
CARBON, PA - [continued]											
6030	Savings institutions	6	6	0.7	-	37	-	15,892	-	634	0.2
6060	Credit unions	3	3	0.4	-	8	-	15,000	-	117	0.1
6400	Insurance agents, brokers, and service	16	18	0.4	46	57	22,870	21,123	1,017	1,211	0.1
6500	Real estate	31	27	0.4	83	-	14,361	-	1,226	-	-
6510	Real estate operators and lessors	6	4	0.1	10	7	14,800	9,714	156	70	0.0
6530	Real estate agents and managers	12	13	0.4	45	60	19,022	11,733	845	746	0.1
CENTRE, PA											
60 –	**Finance, insurance, and real estate**	248	259	1.1	1,973	2,055	23,092	23,251	45,014	48,546	0.5
6000	Depository institutions	62	67	1.2	851	906	21,946	23,024	17,657	20,508	0.8
6020	Commercial banks	44	48	1.3	591	623	21,090	20,655	12,086	12,712	0.6
6140	Personal credit institutions	9	7	1.0	31	22	23,355	18,727	739	526	0.3
6200	Security and commodity brokers	21	23	2.0	123	104	49,008	48,115	5,761	5,007	0.4
6210	Security brokers and dealers	12	12	2.0	57	49	56,070	56,653	2,988	2,873	0.4
6280	Security and commodity services	9	11	2.1	66	55	42,909	40,509	2,773	2,134	0.5
6300	Insurance carriers	19	19	0.9	142	270	27,606	24,385	3,911	6,598	0.2
6310	Life insurance	7	7	0.9	74	143	28,865	30,182	2,062	4,286	0.3
6330	Fire, marine, and casualty insurance	4	6	0.8	-	13	-	37,846	-	481	0.0
6370	Pension, health, and welfare funds	6	5	1.1	40	-	25,700	-	1,037	-	-
6400	Insurance agents, brokers, and service	58	59	1.2	224	199	23,661	19,518	5,504	4,055	0.4
6500	Real estate	70	74	1.0	472	431	15,305	17,262	8,046	8,471	0.8
6510	Real estate operators and lessors	38	39	1.4	282	203	13,929	15,113	4,191	3,620	1.1
6530	Real estate agents and managers	21	28	0.9	163	207	17,767	19,575	3,066	4,380	0.7
6553	Cemetery subdividers and developers	6	5	0.8	16	-	8,250	-	203	-	-
6733	Trusts, n.e.c.	3	3	1.3	6	-	23,333	-	104	-	-
CHESTER, PA											
60 –	**Finance, insurance, and real estate**	912	898	3.8	13,761	14,951	31,843	32,416	466,524	555,178	5.6
6000	Depository institutions	194	166	2.9	2,398	2,359	26,754	24,841	61,389	59,447	2.3
6020	Commercial banks	129	119	3.2	1,541	1,684	26,437	24,637	41,197	42,400	2.0
6030	Savings institutions	42	27	3.0	689	495	28,331	25,689	16,404	12,931	4.7
6060	Credit unions	19	17	2.0	135	-	21,126	-	2,780	-	-
6100	Nondepository institutions	67	71	5.5	1,172	1,362	33,652	35,451	41,247	51,537	9.4
6150	Business credit institutions	11	13	10.1	584	709	36,630	40,000	21,510	27,411	31.7
6160	Mortgage bankers and brokers	36	41	9.1	325	496	31,015	32,613	11,889	20,016	7.4
6200	Security and commodity brokers	60	57	5.0	3,159	3,502	33,384	31,653	133,691	147,009	12.8
6280	Security and commodity services	37	42	8.0	2,766	3,239	31,278	29,934	104,999	131,333	28.3
6300	Insurance carriers	94	90	4.2	3,234	3,176	34,428	33,404	106,715	105,033	3.5
6310	Life insurance	18	21	2.8	2,508	2,450	33,660	32,860	77,947	76,340	5.7
6330	Fire, marine, and casualty insurance	35	33	4.6	464	450	42,534	40,000	19,207	19,439	1.9
6360	Title insurance	11	5	7.4	58	34	36,828	28,941	2,379	1,059	3.1
6370	Pension, health, and welfare funds	24	25	5.6	109	94	20,183	20,681	3,515	2,836	3.5
6400	Insurance agents, brokers, and service	184	195	3.8	1,303	1,634	34,130	35,283	49,081	86,945	9.2
6500	Real estate	278	283	3.9	2,141	2,480	24,021	27,110	54,359	74,605	7.0
6510	Real estate operators and lessors	80	97	3.4	1,000	1,001	21,052	19,524	21,494	22,746	6.8
6530	Real estate agents and managers	124	133	4.2	742	1,165	24,933	32,872	19,445	40,264	6.9
6540	Title abstract offices	10	10	4.2	79	41	22,734	31,415	2,355	2,760	5.0
6552	Subdividers and developers, n.e.c.	25	25	8.7	92	151	47,000	38,331	4,109	6,176	16.2
6553	Cemetery subdividers and developers	13	13	2.0	87	122	19,356	18,984	1,812	2,572	4.6
6710	Holding offices	11	13	5.1	198	318	96,000	103,459	17,013	27,361	7.6
6732	Educational, religious, etc. trusts	5	7	3.3	15	44	17,600	23,909	271	1,090	3.2
6733	Trusts, n.e.c.	10	7	3.1	57	3	20,772	25,333	1,118	197	0.7
CLARION, PA											
60 –	**Finance, insurance, and real estate**	73	73	0.3	449	483	19,278	21,880	8,441	10,561	0.1
6000	Depository institutions	22	22	0.4	221	226	15,837	16,478	3,571	3,940	0.2
6020	Commercial banks	16	16	0.4	193	195	15,876	16,677	3,094	3,415	0.2
6200	Security and commodity brokers	3	4	0.4	-	19	-	32,632	-	606	0.1

Source: County Business Patterns, 1992/93, CBP-92/93-1, U.S. Department of Commerce, Washington, D.C., April 1995. SIC categories for which data were suppressed or not available for both 1992 and 1993 are not displayed. The employment columns represent mid-March employment in the year. Pay per employee is calculated by dividing 1st Quarter payroll, annualized, by mid-March employment. The columns headed "% State" show the county's percentage of the state total for the SIC in 1993; for example, 0.9% for SIC 6030 means that the county had 0.9 percent of the state's total establishments (or payroll) in SIC 6030 in 1993. A dash (-) is used to indicate that data are not available or cannot be calculated; nec means not elsewhere classified.

Continued on next page.

SIC	Industry	No. Establishments			Employment		Pay / Employee		Annual Payroll ($ 000)		
		1992	1993	% State	1992	1993	1992	1993	1992	1993	% State
CLARION, PA - [continued]											
6400	Insurance agents, brokers, and service	21	20	0.4	103	104	23,728	25,885	2,043	2,333	0.2
6500	Real estate	19	21	0.3	56	54	14,357	14,889	892	925	0.1
6510	Real estate operators and lessors	8	9	0.3	-	33	-	19,273	-	696	0.2
6530	Real estate agents and managers	5	4	0.1	20	-	10,200	-	240	-	-
6553	Cemetery subdividers and developers	5	6	0.9	6	-	4,000	-	37	-	-
CLEARFIELD, PA											
60 –	**Finance, insurance, and real estate**	114	112	0.5	958	955	19,678	19,451	19,500	19,387	0.2
6000	Depository institutions	38	37	0.7	542	546	18,155	18,850	10,012	10,565	0.4
6020	Commercial banks	31	31	0.8	513	517	18,448	19,048	9,602	10,126	0.5
6030	Savings institutions	3	3	0.3	14	-	16,857	-	248	-	-
6060	Credit unions	4	3	0.4	15	-	9,333	-	162	-	-
6100	Nondepository institutions	4	3	0.2	16	10	21,250	23,600	339	240	0.0
6140	Personal credit institutions	4	3	0.4	16	10	21,250	23,600	339	240	0.2
6300	Insurance carriers	12	11	0.5	109	162	25,872	21,728	2,932	3,680	0.1
6310	Life insurance	4	4	0.5	101	153	24,950	20,863	2,447	3,274	0.2
6330	Fire, marine, and casualty insurance	4	5	0.7	8	-	37,500	-	329	-	-
6370	Pension, health, and welfare funds	4	2	0.5	-	-	-	-	156	-	-
6400	Insurance agents, brokers, and service	28	29	0.6	110	123	25,164	21,691	2,771	2,866	0.3
6500	Real estate	26	25	0.3	165	100	17,018	16,720	3,111	1,813	0.2
6510	Real estate operators and lessors	9	11	0.4	29	34	14,069	13,647	380	514	0.2
6530	Real estate agents and managers	11	10	0.3	44	56	14,000	19,286	702	1,147	0.2
6553	Cemetery subdividers and developers	4	4	0.6	-	10	-	12,800	-	152	0.3
CLINTON, PA											
60 –	**Finance, insurance, and real estate**	51	50	0.2	245	300	17,469	16,480	4,459	4,968	0.0
6000	Depository institutions	18	18	0.3	124	144	15,387	15,194	2,062	2,141	0.1
6020	Commercial banks	12	12	0.3	93	107	15,441	15,065	1,525	1,488	0.1
6300	Insurance carriers	5	4	0.2	30	45	30,133	28,533	875	1,164	0.0
6400	Insurance agents, brokers, and service	15	14	0.3	43	41	18,698	18,634	814	862	0.1
6500	Real estate	9	11	0.2	40	62	10,900	8,129	478	637	0.1
6510	Real estate operators and lessors	4	5	0.2	-	38	-	6,842	-	331	0.1
6530	Real estate agents and managers	3	3	0.1	13	-	12,923	-	172	-	-
COLUMBIA, PA											
60 –	**Finance, insurance, and real estate**	114	118	0.5	730	672	16,088	17,095	12,774	12,664	0.1
6000	Depository institutions	33	33	0.6	407	395	15,165	16,628	6,869	6,761	0.3
6140	Personal credit institutions	2	3	0.4	-	7	-	20,571	-	201	0.1
6300	Insurance carriers	11	10	0.5	81	64	30,420	29,562	2,402	2,065	0.1
6370	Pension, health, and welfare funds	3	4	0.9	-	1	-	4,000	-	130	0.2
6400	Insurance agents, brokers, and service	31	35	0.7	94	95	15,191	15,832	1,621	1,753	0.2
6500	Real estate	33	33	0.5	129	105	10,419	12,000	1,542	1,763	0.2
6510	Real estate operators and lessors	7	10	0.3	47	48	12,681	15,583	702	1,136	0.3
6530	Real estate agents and managers	12	10	0.3	49	-	7,673	-	426	-	-
6540	Title abstract offices	4	2	0.8	8	-	14,500	-	136	-	-
6552	Subdividers and developers, n.e.c.	2	3	1.0	-	13	-	6,154	-	102	0.3
6553	Cemetery subdividers and developers	6	7	1.1	-	18	-	8,000	-	188	0.3
CRAWFORD, PA											
60 –	**Finance, insurance, and real estate**	137	131	0.6	772	779	21,953	21,438	16,993	18,231	0.2
6000	Depository institutions	42	37	0.7	366	353	23,639	21,892	7,879	7,833	0.3
6020	Commercial banks	30	26	0.7	299	289	26,154	23,931	7,012	6,936	0.3
6100	Nondepository institutions	9	8	0.6	36	-	27,444	-	966	-	-
6140	Personal credit institutions	8	7	1.0	-	25	-	20,800	-	509	0.3
6300	Insurance carriers	9	6	0.3	75	67	23,040	26,746	2,255	1,854	0.1
6400	Insurance agents, brokers, and service	31	31	0.6	106	101	17,698	19,168	1,902	2,205	0.2
6500	Real estate	37	41	0.6	87	116	10,897	11,931	1,400	2,538	0.2
6510	Real estate operators and lessors	17	16	0.6	45	68	13,067	14,294	978	2,036	0.6

Source: County Business Patterns, 1992/93, CBP-92/93-1, U.S. Department of Commerce, Washington, D.C., April 1995. SIC categories for which data were suppressed or not available for both 1992 and 1993 are not displayed. The employment columns represent mid-March employment in the year. Pay per employee is calculated by dividing 1st Quarter payroll, annualized, by mid-March employment. The columns headed "% State" show the county's percentage of the state total for the SIC in 1993; for example, 0.9% for SIC 6030 means that the county had 0.9 percent of the state's total establishments (or payroll) in SIC 6030 in 1993. A dash (-) is used to indicate that data are not available or cannot be calculated; nec means not elsewhere classified.

Continued on next page.

SIC	Industry	No. Establishments			Employment		Pay / Employee		Annual Payroll ($ 000)		
		1992	1993	% State	1992	1993	1992	1993	1992	1993	% State
CRAWFORD, PA - [continued]											
6530	Real estate agents and managers	11	16	0.5	22	31	8,000	7,484	193	277	0.0
6553	Cemetery subdividers and developers	7	7	1.1	16	-	9,250	-	191	-	-
6700	Holding and other investment offices	5	4	0.4	72	-	22,056	-	1,379	-	-
CUMBERLAND, PA											
60 –	**Finance, insurance, and real estate**	512	523	2.2	11,111	11,154	24,781	25,336	286,206	298,109	3.0
6000	Depository institutions	112	115	2.0	1,590	1,584	20,088	19,753	32,409	32,197	1.2
6020	Commercial banks	70	73	2.0	1,184	1,171	21,139	20,557	24,739	24,196	1.1
6030	Savings institutions	21	18	2.0	207	183	15,478	16,044	3,588	3,430	1.2
6060	Credit unions	21	24	2.8	199	230	18,633	18,609	4,082	4,571	4.6
6100	Nondepository institutions	48	45	3.5	310	348	35,948	28,494	11,142	11,731	2.1
6160	Mortgage bankers and brokers	19	20	4.5	164	202	45,366	33,010	7,236	8,568	3.2
6200	Security and commodity brokers	20	22	1.9	104	168	67,654	57,333	6,749	9,448	0.8
6210	Security brokers and dealers	16	16	2.7	97	123	71,835	73,854	6,678	8,929	1.3
6280	Security and commodity services	4	6	1.1	7	45	9,714	12,178	71	519	0.1
6300	Insurance carriers	76	71	3.3	7,531	7,452	24,344	25,497	191,784	198,824	6.6
6330	Fire, marine, and casualty insurance	25	24	3.3	1,284	1,233	29,545	30,462	38,766	39,460	3.9
6400	Insurance agents, brokers, and service	117	121	2.4	926	911	29,784	29,379	28,167	28,200	3.0
6500	Real estate	125	135	1.9	563	629	18,636	17,978	12,033	13,915	1.3
6510	Real estate operators and lessors	34	43	1.5	171	194	12,304	12,639	2,450	3,224	1.0
6530	Real estate agents and managers	60	66	2.1	294	333	21,946	20,360	7,289	8,143	1.4
6540	Title abstract offices	4	5	2.1	6	16	26,667	26,000	221	454	0.8
6552	Subdividers and developers, n.e.c.	12	14	4.9	27	28	21,481	21,857	718	912	2.4
6553	Cemetery subdividers and developers	7	7	1.1	53	58	17,736	18,069	980	1,182	2.1
6733	Trusts, n.e.c.	5	5	2.2	-	5	-	32,800	-	169	0.6
DAUPHIN, PA											
60 –	**Finance, insurance, and real estate**	540	533	2.3	9,462	9,462	26,625	25,916	244,705	255,934	2.6
6000	Depository institutions	124	127	2.2	2,883	3,186	24,101	23,525	67,134	77,573	3.0
6020	Commercial banks	88	89	2.4	2,143	2,333	24,493	23,959	49,857	56,727	2.7
6060	Credit unions	14	17	2.0	363	477	25,245	21,208	8,813	12,058	12.2
6100	Nondepository institutions	39	32	2.5	286	256	31,790	31,078	9,282	8,291	1.5
6140	Personal credit institutions	26	21	3.1	215	178	27,293	25,236	5,937	4,492	2.8
6200	Security and commodity brokers	24	25	2.2	147	138	60,980	50,696	8,849	9,024	0.8
6210	Security brokers and dealers	15	15	2.5	116	110	67,655	57,200	7,592	7,665	1.2
6280	Security and commodity services	9	10	1.9	31	28	36,000	25,143	1,257	1,359	0.3
6300	Insurance carriers	75	68	3.2	4,632	4,105	28,261	28,567	125,565	118,866	3.9
6310	Life insurance	19	15	2.0	395	325	24,071	26,585	9,757	8,739	0.7
6321	Accident and health insurance	3	3	6.0	25	-	23,840	-	711	-	-
6324	Hospital and medical service plans	3	2	2.9	1,909	-	24,972	-	42,337	-	-
6330	Fire, marine, and casualty insurance	29	29	4.0	2,183	2,108	32,290	29,996	69,859	64,107	6.4
6360	Title insurance	3	1	1.5	16	-	31,250	-	610	-	-
6370	Pension, health, and welfare funds	16	17	3.8	80	-	16,700	-	1,326	-	-
6400	Insurance agents, brokers, and service	112	118	2.3	679	945	24,677	23,403	16,316	24,057	2.5
6500	Real estate	146	146	2.0	732	739	18,126	17,478	14,078	14,759	1.4
6510	Real estate operators and lessors	59	65	2.3	299	416	16,348	15,490	5,545	7,056	2.1
6530	Real estate agents and managers	49	59	1.8	206	230	20,563	22,313	4,425	6,145	1.0
6540	Title abstract offices	4	4	1.7	16	17	31,500	21,176	385	399	0.7
6552	Subdividers and developers, n.e.c.	9	2	0.7	114	-	20,421	-	2,129	-	-
6553	Cemetery subdividers and developers	15	16	2.4	63	-	11,238	-	924	-	-
6700	Holding and other investment offices	20	17	1.9	103	93	33,592	32,430	3,481	3,364	0.7
6710	Holding offices	4	3	1.2	52	39	42,308	38,974	2,140	1,731	0.5
6732	Educational, religious, etc. trusts	8	7	3.3	31	30	30,839	34,533	1,080	1,085	3.2
6733	Trusts, n.e.c.	5	5	2.2	11	-	16,364	-	188	-	-

Source: County Business Patterns, 1992/93, CBP-92/93-1, U.S. Department of Commerce, Washington, D.C., April 1995. SIC categories for which data were suppressed or not available for both 1992 and 1993 are *not* displayed. The employment columns represent mid-March employment in the year. Pay per employee is calculated by dividing 1st Quarter payroll, annualized, by mid-March employment. The columns headed "% State" show the county's percentage of the state total for the SIC in 1993; for example, 0.9% for SIC 6030 means that the county had 0.9 percent of the state's total establishments (or payroll) in SIC 6030 in 1993. A dash (-) is used to indicate that data are not available or cannot be calculated; *nec* means not elsewhere classified.

SIC	Industry	No. Establishments			Employment		Pay / Employee		Annual Payroll ($ 000)		
		1992	1993	% State	1992	1993	1992	1993	1992	1993	% State
DELAWARE, PA											
60 –	**Finance, insurance, and real estate**	1,273	1,276	5.4	16,450	15,949	32,911	32,578	567,755	574,816	5.8
6000	Depository institutions	244	237	4.2	3,762	3,752	23,613	22,539	84,869	86,942	3.4
6020	Commercial banks	147	144	3.9	2,754	2,829	23,608	23,000	61,798	66,698	3.2
6030	Savings institutions	63	55	6.2	770	566	24,265	20,671	17,832	13,176	4.8
6060	Credit unions	25	27	3.2	173	282	19,723	18,723	3,718	4,392	4.4
6090	Functions closely related to banking	9	10	5.6	65	-	26,462	-	1,521	-	-
6100	Nondepository institutions	55	54	4.2	880	883	37,136	32,276	35,415	38,613	7.0
6140	Personal credit institutions	30	25	3.7	253	236	29,818	26,186	7,282	6,382	4.0
6150	Business credit institutions	4	5	3.9	63	-	41,968		2,521		
6160	Mortgage bankers and brokers	21	23	5.1	564	589	39,879	33,739	25,612	29,899	11.0
6200	Security and commodity brokers	79	89	7.8	758	930	92,417	69,475	85,863	96,389	8.4
6210	Security brokers and dealers	39	37	6.2	287	-	134,718	-	44,858	-	
6280	Security and commodity services	38	50	9.5	-	520	-	52,485	-	58,590	12.6
6300	Insurance carriers	170	142	6.7	5,541	5,672	34,244	36,159	191,933	196,996	6.5
6310	Life insurance	51	50	6.7	1,674	1,996	36,779	33,878	58,036	63,749	4.8
6321	Accident and health insurance	7	6	12.0	114	-	28,912	-	2,485	-	-
6324	Hospital and medical service plans	4	3	4.3	410	-	31,620		14,347	-	
6330	Fire, marine, and casualty insurance	54	43	6.0	3,162	3,141	33,819	38,991	111,018	117,392	11.6
6360	Title insurance	17	11	16.2	62	-	32,452	-	2,302	-	-
6370	Pension, health, and welfare funds	33	27	6.1	112	141	24,893	18,837	3,519	3,245	4.0
6400	Insurance agents, brokers, and service	281	303	6.0	2,082	1,838	36,411	36,226	81,402	76,664	8.1
6500	Real estate	388	394	5.4	2,950	2,513	21,078	19,438	66,853	58,868	5.5
6510	Real estate operators and lessors	131	150	5.2	1,554	1,115	18,386	19,767	30,149	25,662	7.7
6530	Real estate agents and managers	169	191	6.0	946	962	24,520	20,723	24,582	25,079	4.3
6540	Title abstract offices	15	14	5.9	53	54	20,377	18,370	1,294	1,318	2.4
6552	Subdividers and developers, n.e.c.	17	14	4.9	89	36	37,618	29,333	3,580	1,620	4.2
6553	Cemetery subdividers and developers	21	22	3.4	237	344	20,101	13,884	5,168	5,145	9.3
6700	Holding and other investment offices	52	53	5.9	433	294	38,855	54,612	16,895	15,094	3.0
6710	Holding offices	14	17	6.6	151	128	49,748	67,906	7,299	8,371	2.3
6732	Educational, religious, etc. trusts	8	9	4.3	21	-	47,048		1,021		
6733	Trusts, n.e.c.	13	12	5.3	177	86	23,458	41,767	4,676	1,949	6.8
ELK, PA											
60 –	**Finance, insurance, and real estate**	54	55	0.2	277	282	20,361	19,035	5,766	5,860	0.1
6000	Depository institutions	22	22	0.4	157	147	17,503	17,279	2,790	2,731	0.1
6020	Commercial banks	13	13	0.3	105	94	19,429	19,872	2,034	1,949	0.1
6030	Savings institutions	5	5	0.6	39	40	13,949	13,100	595	628	0.2
6060	Credit unions	4	4	0.5	13	13	12,615	11,385	161	154	0.2
6100	Nondepository institutions	3	3	0.2	9	11	24,000	18,545	219	214	0.0
6140	Personal credit institutions	3	3	0.4	9	11	24,000	18,545	219	214	0.1
6400	Insurance agents, brokers, and service	17	17	0.3	56	62	20,000	18,516	1,191	1,371	0.1
6500	Real estate	7	8	0.1	14	22	11,429	15,273	233	446	0.0
6530	Real estate agents and managers	4	4	0.1	-	6	-	6,000	-	41	0.0
ERIE, PA											
60 –	**Finance, insurance, and real estate**	525	506	2.2	5,893	5,213	25,636	24,590	160,782	140,044	1.4
6000	Depository institutions	150	147	2.6	2,023	1,574	19,589	19,375	39,146	31,050	1.2
6020	Commercial banks	86	73	2.0	1,609	1,111	20,574	20,842	32,602	23,336	1.1
6030	Savings institutions	18	18	2.0	212	205	18,019	17,971	3,775	3,923	1.4
6100	Nondepository institutions	43	32	2.5	237	171	24,219	23,836	5,812	4,418	0.8
6140	Personal credit institutions	31	20	3.0	159	124	21,509	22,677	3,433	2,871	1.8
6160	Mortgage bankers and brokers	10	8	1.8	-	36	-	24,556	-	1,254	0.5
6200	Security and commodity brokers	24	23	2.0	144	131	54,194	53,252	7,457	7,307	0.6
6210	Security brokers and dealers	16	11	1.9	103	91	67,379	68,791	6,530	6,501	1.0
6280	Security and commodity services	8	12	2.3	41	40	21,073	17,900	927	806	0.2
6300	Insurance carriers	53	41	1.9	2,131	2,175	26,893	28,785	64,520	68,368	2.3
6310	Life insurance	18	15	2.0	369	314	22,688	24,115	8,443	7,670	0.6
6400	Insurance agents, brokers, and service	120	128	2.5	804	565	34,786	23,540	29,756	15,230	1.6

Source: County Business Patterns, 1992/93, CBP-92/93-1, U.S. Department of Commerce, Washington, D.C., April 1995. SIC categories for which data were suppressed or not available for both 1992 and 1993 are *not* displayed. The employment columns represent mid-March employment in the year. Pay per employee is calculated by dividing 1st Quarter payroll, annualized, by mid-March employment. The columns headed "% State" show the county's percentage of the state total for the SIC in 1993; for example, 0.9% for SIC 6030 means that the county had 0.9 percent of the state's total establishments (or payroll) in SIC 6030 in 1993. A dash (-) is used to indicate that data are not available or cannot be calculated; *nec* means not elsewhere classified.

Continued on next page.

SIC	Industry	No. Establishments			Employment		Pay / Employee		Annual Payroll ($ 000)		
		1992	1993	% State	1992	1993	1992	1993	1992	1993	% State
ERIE, PA - [continued]											
6500	Real estate	117	124	1.7	455	547	13,547	12,088	7,138	8,577	0.8
6510	Real estate operators and lessors	42	52	1.8	209	261	12,727	10,069	2,834	3,193	1.0
6530	Real estate agents and managers	54	52	1.6	161	215	13,441	13,395	2,664	3,760	0.6
6552	Subdividers and developers, n.e.c.	2	4	1.4	-	8		25,000	-	503	1.3
6553	Cemetery subdividers and developers	14	14	2.1	63	61	14,476	14,689	1,058	1,052	1.9
6732	Educational, religious, etc. trusts	3	4	1.9	6	12	30,000	32,667	185	396	1.2
6733	Trusts, n.e.c.	5	3	1.3	17	-	9,882	-	134	-	-
FAYETTE, PA											
60 –	**Finance, insurance, and real estate**	197	195	0.8	1,254	1,340	19,327	19,296	25,405	27,162	0.3
6000	Depository institutions	56	57	1.0	555	589	17,715	17,338	10,219	11,067	0.4
6020	Commercial banks	40	39	1.0	472	492	18,144	17,780	8,810	9,451	0.4
6030	Savings institutions	7	7	0.8	58	61	17,379	17,967	1,137	1,206	0.4
6060	Credit unions	9	11	1.3	25	36	10,400	10,222	272	410	0.4
6100	Nondepository institutions	13	10	0.8	57	64	27,789	21,125	1,575	1,512	0.3
6200	Security and commodity brokers	5	6	0.5	19	30	36,211	28,267	720	901	0.1
6210	Security brokers and dealers	5	5	0.8	19	-	36,211	-	720	-	-
6300	Insurance carriers	22	15	0.7	296	335	22,797	23,475	6,494	7,354	0.2
6310	Life insurance	10	6	0.8	265	316	22,008	22,747	5,505	6,602	0.5
6400	Insurance agents, brokers, and service	45	47	0.9	130	143	15,785	16,336	2,423	2,508	0.3
6500	Real estate	47	50	0.7	178	163	13,056	12,319	2,853	2,778	0.3
6510	Real estate operators and lessors	23	23	0.8	86	59	12,279	13,288	1,402	1,316	0.4
6530	Real estate agents and managers	11	15	0.5	31	47	10,452	10,298	361	593	0.1
6710	Holding offices	3	5	1.9	-	13	-	86,154	-	669	0.2
6733	Trusts, n.e.c.	5	4	1.8	6	-	14,000	-	193	-	-
FOREST, PA											
60 –	**Finance, insurance, and real estate**	8	8	0.0	24	21	10,333	10,667	260	276	0.0
FRANKLIN, PA											
60 –	**Finance, insurance, and real estate**	195	196	0.8	1,386	1,415	20,087	19,935	28,756	29,319	0.3
6000	Depository institutions	64	67	1.2	931	948	19,368	19,608	18,123	18,831	0.7
6020	Commercial banks	52	54	1.4	816	820	19,686	20,015	16,076	16,468	0.8
6030	Savings institutions	3	2	0.2	19	-	20,211	-	303	-	-
6060	Credit unions	9	11	1.3	96	-	16,500	-	1,744	-	-
6100	Nondepository institutions	11	7	0.5	-	28	-	29,000	-	805	0.1
6280	Security and commodity services	2	4	0.8	-	7	-	6,286	-	104	0.0
6300	Insurance carriers	7	6	0.3	37	39	21,946	20,103	859	646	0.0
6400	Insurance agents, brokers, and service	40	39	0.8	155	165	23,535	21,964	3,792	3,758	0.4
6500	Real estate	64	67	0.9	199	204	14,975	14,980	3,511	3,778	0.4
6510	Real estate operators and lessors	21	20	0.7	49	66	12,490	12,606	589	872	0.3
6530	Real estate agents and managers	24	34	1.1	87	94	15,264	14,936	1,592	1,989	0.3
6540	Title abstract offices	2	3	1.3	-	15	-	10,933	-	132	0.2
6552	Subdividers and developers, n.e.c.	3	3	1.0	-	8	-	18,000	-	244	0.6
6553	Cemetery subdividers and developers	7	7	1.1	24	21	22,667	24,381	643	541	1.0
FULTON, PA											
60 –	**Finance, insurance, and real estate**	14	11	0.0	138	54	18,406	15,481	2,656	1,404	0.0
6000	Depository institutions	7	7	0.1	84	39	20,619	16,103	1,653	1,198	0.0
6020	Commercial banks	7	7	0.2	84	39	20,619	16,103	1,653	1,198	0.1
GREENE, PA											
60 –	**Finance, insurance, and real estate**	44	43	0.2	281	301	21,480	17,116	6,303	5,483	0.1
6000	Depository institutions	14	14	0.2	203	210	22,266	17,829	4,710	3,852	0.1

Source: County Business Patterns, 1992/93, CBP-92/93-1, U.S. Department of Commerce, Washington, D.C., April 1995. SIC categories for which data were suppressed or not available for both 1992 and 1993 are *not* displayed. The employment columns represent mid-March employment in the year. Pay per employee is calculated by dividing 1st Quarter payroll, annualized, by mid-March employment. The columns headed "% State" show the county's percentage of the state total for the SIC in 1993; for example, 0.9% for SIC 6030 means that the county had 0.9 percent of the state's total establishments (or payroll) in SIC 6030 in 1993. A dash (-) is used to indicate that data are not available or cannot be calculated; *nec* means not elsewhere classified.

Continued on next page.

SIC	Industry	No. Establishments			Employment		Pay / Employee		Annual Payroll ($ 000)		
		1992	1993	% State	1992	1993	1992	1993	1992	1993	% State
GREENE, PA - [continued]											
6400	Insurance agents, brokers, and service	11	13	0.3	41	51	22,927	16,078	894	923	0.1
6500	Real estate	13	10	0.1	26	28	13,538	11,714	456	390	0.0
6510	Real estate operators and lessors	8	5	0.2	16	14	12,500	14,286	240	226	0.1
HUNTINGDON, PA											
60 –	**Finance, insurance, and real estate**	58	60	0.3	476	590	19,109	17,634	8,213	10,922	0.1
6000	Depository institutions	24	25	0.4	276	269	14,942	17,651	4,446	4,890	0.2
6020	Commercial banks	20	21	0.6	261	254	14,759	17,496	4,178	4,569	0.2
6030	Savings institutions	4	4	0.4	15	15	18,133	20,267	268	321	0.1
6100	Nondepository institutions	3	3	0.2	12	12	23,333	21,000	290	258	0.0
6140	Personal credit institutions	3	3	0.4	12	12	23,333	21,000	290	258	0.2
6300	Insurance carriers	4	2	0.1	16	-	20,000	-	299	-	-
6400	Insurance agents, brokers, and service	11	13	0.3	153	280	27,425	17,629	3,018	5,213	0.5
6510	Real estate operators and lessors	3	5	0.2	2	-	8,000	-	26	-	-
6530	Real estate agents and managers	5	4	0.1	6	5	6,667	9,600	24	56	0.0
INDIANA, PA											
60 –	**Finance, insurance, and real estate**	149	139	0.6	1,371	1,065	24,995	22,411	33,419	24,646	0.2
6000	Depository institutions	42	37	0.7	678	658	19,965	21,058	13,152	13,864	0.5
6100	Nondepository institutions	9	8	0.6	27	-	22,519	-	597	-	-
6140	Personal credit institutions	7	6	0.9	-	19	-	22,737	-	451	0.3
6200	Security and commodity brokers	4	4	0.4	20	-	76,200	-	1,616	-	-
6210	Security brokers and dealers	4	3	0.5	20	-	76,200	-	1,616	-	-
6300	Insurance carriers	14	13	0.6	86	41	27,814	31,122	2,384	1,415	0.0
6310	Life insurance	4	4	0.5	64	-	27,938	-	1,716	-	-
6330	Fire, marine, and casualty insurance	5	6	0.8	-	14	-	32,857	-	555	0.1
6370	Pension, health, and welfare funds	3	2	0.5	1	-	28,000	-	40	-	-
6400	Insurance agents, brokers, and service	35	35	0.7	124	127	21,194	23,307	2,768	3,219	0.3
6500	Real estate	36	37	0.5	145	116	9,766	11,069	1,477	1,448	0.1
6510	Real estate operators and lessors	13	16	0.6	57	57	11,719	10,526	682	662	0.2
6530	Real estate agents and managers	11	15	0.5	28	-	7,143	-	216	-	-
6700	Holding and other investment offices	9	5	0.6	291	86	41,801	30,558	11,425	2,781	0.6
6733	Trusts, n.e.c.	3	2	0.9	11	-	6,182	-	72	-	-
JEFFERSON, PA											
60 –	**Finance, insurance, and real estate**	65	70	0.3	383	398	18,162	18,060	7,061	7,810	0.1
6000	Depository institutions	20	21	0.4	212	194	20,321	19,608	4,224	3,861	0.1
6020	Commercial banks	18	18	0.5	-	182	-	19,758	-	3,645	0.2
6300	Insurance carriers	5	5	0.2	38	73	20,421	20,219	783	1,686	0.1
6400	Insurance agents, brokers, and service	16	17	0.3	61	60	15,213	15,400	947	1,092	0.1
6500	Real estate	20	24	0.3	51	53	11,608	10,943	685	714	0.1
6510	Real estate operators and lessors	6	11	0.4	19	35	6,526	10,400	149	402	0.1
6530	Real estate agents and managers	4	6	0.2	6	6	8,000	10,000	58	119	0.0
6553	Cemetery subdividers and developers	7	7	1.1	-	12	-	13,000	-	193	0.3
JUNIATA, PA											
60 –	**Finance, insurance, and real estate**	35	32	0.1	224	231	17,125	16,329	4,301	4,137	0.0
6000	Depository institutions	12	12	0.2	155	163	16,568	15,117	2,600	2,708	0.1
6300	Insurance carriers	5	6	0.3	14	25	19,143	21,120	666	572	0.0
6400	Insurance agents, brokers, and service	11	9	0.2	42	35	21,333	20,686	930	786	0.1
6500	Real estate	7	5	0.1	13	8	8,000	7,000	105	71	0.0
6510	Real estate operators and lessors	3	1	0.0	4	-	12,000	-	42	-	-
LACKAWANNA, PA											
60 –	**Finance, insurance, and real estate**	381	375	1.6	4,611	5,153	25,468	25,605	121,157	139,070	1.4
6000	Depository institutions	92	96	1.7	2,113	2,451	21,721	22,616	46,221	57,661	2.2
6020	Commercial banks	70	71	1.9	1,946	2,264	22,092	23,155	43,296	54,396	2.6
6030	Savings institutions	10	10	1.1	117	121	18,325	16,959	2,132	2,252	0.8

Source: County Business Patterns, 1992/93, CBP-92/93-1, U.S. Department of Commerce, Washington, D.C., April 1995. SIC categories for which data were suppressed or not available for both 1992 and 1993 are not displayed. The employment columns represent mid-March employment in the year. Pay per employee is calculated by dividing 1st Quarter payroll, annualized, by mid-March employment. The columns headed "% State" show the county's percentage of the state total for the SIC in 1993; for example, 0.9% for SIC 6030 means that the county had 0.9 percent of the state's total establishments (or payroll) in SIC 6030 in 1993. A dash (-) is used to indicate that data are not available or cannot be calculated; nec means not elsewhere classified.

Continued on next page.

SIC	Industry	No. Establishments			Employment		Pay / Employee		Annual Payroll ($ 000)		
		1992	1993	% State	1992	1993	1992	1993	1992	1993	% State
LACKAWANNA, PA - [continued]											
6060	Credit unions	12	15	1.8	50	66	15,200	14,485	793	1,013	1.0
6100	Nondepository institutions	22	15	1.2	91	109	23,121	25,284	1,971	2,754	0.5
6140	Personal credit institutions	17	11	1.6	68	81	22,588	19,259	1,366	1,740	1.1
6200	Security and commodity brokers	14	12	1.1	116	96	67,103	61,583	7,046	7,265	0.6
6210	Security brokers and dealers	9	8	1.3	106	90	71,472	64,978	6,832	7,207	1.1
6280	Security and commodity services	5	4	0.8	10	6	20,800	10,667	214	58	0.0
6300	Insurance carriers	46	46	2.2	1,331	1,476	32,986	33,130	46,312	50,808	1.7
6310	Life insurance	16	18	2.4	1,072	1,216	33,728	33,480	38,130	42,058	3.2
6330	Fire, marine, and casualty insurance	14	12	1.7	212	210	32,774	35,162	7,483	7,792	0.8
6400	Insurance agents, brokers, and service	93	97	1.9	454	438	21,401	23,005	10,784	10,592	1.1
6500	Real estate	99	97	1.3	421	500	14,898	13,160	6,939	7,584	0.7
6510	Real estate operators and lessors	50	47	1.6	301	319	14,645	13,229	4,904	4,668	1.4
6530	Real estate agents and managers	20	29	0.9	39	128	13,026	11,219	567	1,636	0.3
6552	Subdividers and developers, n.e.c.	6	6	2.1	9	10	34,667	28,400	302	353	0.9
6553	Cemetery subdividers and developers	11	13	2.0	42	-	16,667	-	828	-	-
6710	Holding offices	8	3	1.2	75	-	20,427	-	1,624	-	-
6733	Trusts, n.e.c.	3	3	1.3	-	6	-	20,000	-	245	0.9
LANCASTER, PA											
60 –	**Finance, insurance, and real estate**	830	842	3.6	9,277	10,095	24,210	24,865	223,515	267,142	2.7
6000	Depository institutions	202	205	3.6	3,707	3,934	21,453	22,218	76,475	87,903	3.4
6020	Commercial banks	164	161	4.3	3,490	3,659	21,594	22,461	72,137	82,194	3.9
6030	Savings institutions	17	21	2.4	127	163	17,039	15,828	2,313	2,878	1.0
6100	Nondepository institutions	40	42	3.3	428	528	32,234	30,970	15,026	23,536	4.3
6140	Personal credit institutions	21	20	3.0	-	161	-	23,627	-	4,040	2.5
6160	Mortgage bankers and brokers	16	17	3.8	243	275	34,831	34,575	9,887	11,651	4.3
6200	Security and commodity brokers	37	36	3.2	223	240	54,260	50,950	11,746	14,447	1.3
6210	Security brokers and dealers	22	16	2.7	184	178	61,261	61,258	10,672	12,828	1.9
6280	Security and commodity services	15	20	3.8	39	62	21,231	21,355	1,074	1,619	0.3
6300	Insurance carriers	105	93	4.4	1,442	1,661	30,011	30,603	42,321	49,677	1.6
6310	Life insurance	21	17	2.3	405	496	28,958	33,024	12,125	15,623	1.2
6330	Fire, marine, and casualty insurance	35	39	5.4	801	837	32,874	33,907	24,660	27,366	2.7
6370	Pension, health, and welfare funds	39	28	6.3	123	226	17,106	12,602	2,307	3,202	3.9
6400	Insurance agents, brokers, and service	170	181	3.6	1,195	1,030	26,129	26,850	32,197	30,519	3.2
6500	Real estate	235	249	3.4	1,909	2,247	16,920	18,524	34,189	45,344	4.2
6510	Real estate operators and lessors	70	90	3.1	888	864	15,545	13,713	15,198	13,802	4.1
6530	Real estate agents and managers	96	112	3.5	733	1,176	17,735	21,493	13,610	27,409	4.7
6540	Title abstract offices	10	8	3.4	81	64	17,185	20,875	1,610	1,560	2.8
6552	Subdividers and developers, n.e.c.	14	13	4.5	82	68	27,902	32,647	1,787	1,478	3.9
6553	Cemetery subdividers and developers	22	21	3.2	85	71	12,188	11,493	966	873	1.6
6710	Holding offices	7	9	3.5	179	119	39,732	38,185	6,083	5,231	1.4
6732	Educational, religious, etc. trusts	7	6	2.9	48	72	8,917	5,833	580	568	1.7
6733	Trusts, n.e.c.	13	9	4.0	15	-	12,267	-	237	-	-
6794	Patent owners and lessors	6	5	8.6	75	103	16,693	16,621	1,845	2,267	14.4
6799	Investors, n.e.c.	3	5	5.6	4	9	22,000	24,889	92	227	0.8
LAWRENCE, PA											
60 –	**Finance, insurance, and real estate**	155	153	0.7	1,669	1,734	19,641	20,072	34,389	35,407	0.4
6000	Depository institutions	51	54	1.0	654	598	17,719	18,488	10,988	11,105	0.4
6020	Commercial banks	28	29	0.8	427	345	16,131	18,029	6,469	6,376	0.3
6030	Savings institutions	11	11	1.2	201	216	21,831	20,259	4,165	4,255	1.5
6060	Credit unions	12	14	1.6	26	37	12,000	12,432	354	474	0.5
6100	Nondepository institutions	12	10	0.8	42	-	20,571	-	1,087	-	-
6140	Personal credit institutions	9	8	1.2	36	50	20,222	22,560	770	910	0.6
6300	Insurance carriers	16	15	0.7	628	597	18,554	18,372	12,033	11,441	0.4
6310	Life insurance	6	5	0.7	76	69	14,789	15,594	1,214	1,195	0.1
6400	Insurance agents, brokers, and service	36	36	0.7	142	150	23,887	21,653	3,936	3,847	0.4
6500	Real estate	33	33	0.5	90	105	10,622	9,905	1,108	1,295	0.1

Source: County Business Patterns, 1992/93, CBP-92/93-1, U.S. Department of Commerce, Washington, D.C., April 1995. SIC categories for which data were suppressed or not available for both 1992 and 1993 are *not* displayed. The employment columns represent mid-March employment in the year. Pay per employee is calculated by dividing 1st Quarter payroll, annualized, by mid-March employment. The columns headed "% State" show the county's percentage of the state total for the SIC in 1993; for example, 0.9% for SIC 6030 means that the county had 0.9 percent of the state's total establishments (or payroll) in SIC 6030 in 1993. A dash (-) is used to indicate that data are not available or cannot be calculated; *nec* means not elsewhere classified.

Continued on next page.

SIC	Industry	No. Establishments			Employment		Pay / Employee		Annual Payroll ($ 000)		
		1992	1993	% State	1992	1993	1992	1993	1992	1993	% State
LAWRENCE, PA - [continued]											
6510	Real estate operators and lessors	14	14	0.5	37	55	8,108	9,527	324	521	0.2
6530	Real estate agents and managers	11	11	0.3	25	30	13,120	9,600	395	408	0.1
6553	Cemetery subdividers and developers	8	7	1.1	28	20	11,714	11,400	389	283	0.5
LEBANON, PA											
60–	**Finance, insurance, and real estate**	183	179	0.8	1,422	1,636	23,122	22,208	34,642	37,759	0.4
6000	Depository institutions	48	50	0.9	722	808	20,266	21,584	14,713	18,132	0.7
6020	Commercial banks	41	42	1.1	666	750	20,697	22,139	13,833	17,144	0.8
6100	Nondepository institutions	14	16	1.2	-	63	-	26,222	-	1,756	0.3
6140	Personal credit institutions	11	12	1.8	39	41	28,205	28,585	1,057	1,129	0.7
6300	Insurance carriers	14	14	0.7	199	265	28,302	25,781	6,043	6,760	0.2
6310	Life insurance	4	3	0.4	129	195	32,155	27,221	3,894	4,693	0.4
6330	Fire, marine, and casualty insurance	5	4	0.6	-	41	-	27,220	-	1,353	0.1
6370	Pension, health, and welfare funds	5	7	1.6	-	29	-	14,069	-	714	0.9
6400	Insurance agents, brokers, and service	42	40	0.8	187	185	19,594	21,254	4,389	4,215	0.4
6500	Real estate	54	49	0.7	162	250	14,765	12,320	2,726	3,331	0.3
6510	Real estate operators and lessors	20	20	0.7	63	165	16,635	12,339	1,221	2,121	0.6
6530	Real estate agents and managers	16	15	0.5	45	30	13,156	13,600	571	442	0.1
6540	Title abstract offices	3	3	1.3	18	22	15,778	11,818	305	342	0.6
6552	Subdividers and developers, n.e.c.	-	3	1.0	-	9	-	16,444	-	191	0.5
6553	Cemetery subdividers and developers	9	8	1.2	20	24	8,000	9,500	223	235	0.4
6700	Holding and other investment offices	6	4	0.4	70	-	48,800	-	3,372	-	
6710	Holding offices	3	1	0.4	60	-	54,400	-	3,216	-	
LEHIGH, PA											
60–	**Finance, insurance, and real estate**	660	665	2.8	9,590	10,542	26,797	26,599	259,570	286,194	2.9
6000	Depository institutions	142	137	2.4	1,991	1,793	21,901	23,920	44,391	44,455	1.7
6020	Commercial banks	104	105	2.8	1,612	1,459	21,980	24,406	36,288	36,379	1.7
6060	Credit unions	19	19	2.2	194	193	18,206	19,358	3,722	4,251	4.3
6100	Nondepository institutions	55	63	4.9	542	1,101	35,963	29,104	18,914	34,321	6.3
6140	Personal credit institutions	30	32	4.8	354	843	36,011	26,629	11,638	24,350	15.3
6160	Mortgage bankers and brokers	21	23	5.1	-	204	-	35,294	-	8,060	3.0
6200	Security and commodity brokers	39	43	3.8	345	749	67,710	45,757	22,216	29,379	2.6
6210	Security brokers and dealers	19	18	3.0	281	307	75,957	65,029	20,125	21,234	3.2
6280	Security and commodity services	20	24	4.6	64	-	31,500	-	2,091	-	-
6300	Insurance carriers	70	61	2.9	4,683	4,822	25,076	24,406	117,145	120,185	4.0
6310	Life insurance	27	22	3.0	3,002	2,915	23,989	25,154	71,925	72,553	5.5
6321	Accident and health insurance	3	5	10.0	-	136	-	19,000	-	2,738	4.6
6330	Fire, marine, and casualty insurance	27	23	3.2	1,361	1,343	27,603	25,781	37,422	37,845	3.8
6360	Title insurance	4	2	2.9	9	-	30,667	-	300	-	-
6370	Pension, health, and welfare funds	7	8	1.8	-	164	-	2,049	-	397	0.5
6400	Insurance agents, brokers, and service	121	131	2.6	557	605	31,921	29,164	21,468	20,826	2.2
6500	Real estate	211	209	2.9	907	942	16,891	16,964	17,219	17,960	1.7
6510	Real estate operators and lessors	86	85	3.0	434	467	16,645	15,777	7,712	8,197	2.5
6530	Real estate agents and managers	79	88	2.8	277	320	15,495	16,612	5,363	6,231	1.1
6540	Title abstract offices	9	6	2.5	49	33	21,469	26,424	1,138	1,099	2.0
6552	Subdividers and developers, n.e.c.	7	9	3.1	39	52	29,949	33,154	1,214	1,569	4.1
6553	Cemetery subdividers and developers	19	20	3.1	63	70	11,429	10,000	805	804	1.4
6710	Holding offices	9	8	3.1	96	55	32,417	48,000	2,935	3,439	1.0
6733	Trusts, n.e.c.	4	5	2.2	-	57	-	5,193	-	308	1.1
6799	Investors, n.e.c.	4	3	3.3	5	-	8,800	-	47	-	-
LUZERNE, PA											
60–	**Finance, insurance, and real estate**	605	614	2.6	7,077	7,277	24,419	23,346	170,101	169,563	1.7
6000	Depository institutions	167	164	2.9	3,166	2,821	19,903	21,322	63,343	60,474	2.3
6020	Commercial banks	105	105	2.8	2,602	2,237	19,816	20,801	52,193	45,965	2.2
6030	Savings institutions	21	21	2.4	422	444	22,569	26,090	9,074	12,336	4.5
6060	Credit unions	41	38	4.4	142	140	13,577	14,514	2,076	2,173	2.2

Source: County Business Patterns, 1992/93, CBP-92/93-1, U.S. Department of Commerce, Washington, D.C., April 1995. SIC categories for which data were suppressed or not available for both 1992 and 1993 are not displayed. The employment columns represent mid-March employment in the year. Pay per employee is calculated by dividing 1st Quarter payroll, annualized, by mid-March employment. The columns headed "% State" show the county's percentage of the state total for the SIC in 1993; for example, 0.9% for SIC 6030 means that the county had 0.9 percent of the state's total establishments (or payroll) in SIC 6030 in 1993. A dash (-) is used to indicate that data are not available or cannot be calculated; nec means not elsewhere classified.

Continued on next page.

SIC	Industry	No. Establishments			Employment		Pay / Employee		Annual Payroll ($ 000)		
		1992	1993	% State	1992	1993	1992	1993	1992	1993	% State
LUZERNE, PA - [continued]											
6100	Nondepository institutions	38	41	3.2	676	861	21,497	19,377	12,662	18,527	3.4
6140	Personal credit institutions	23	27	4.0	125	193	29,152	19,959	3,648	3,847	2.4
6200	Security and commodity brokers	17	23	2.0	229	265	53,118	65,917	12,243	15,398	1.3
6210	Security brokers and dealers	14	15	2.5	-	143	-	104,559	-	11,912	1.8
6300	Insurance carriers	62	59	2.8	1,258	1,600	23,688	24,668	29,952	36,991	1.2
6310	Life insurance	21	25	3.4	418	539	26,163	28,846	10,988	14,022	1.1
6330	Fire, marine, and casualty insurance	15	14	1.9	192	331	27,354	25,801	5,430	7,184	0.7
6400	Insurance agents, brokers, and service	129	138	2.7	488	558	22,377	21,168	11,428	12,691	1.3
6500	Real estate	169	172	2.4	892	823	16,404	17,468	15,533	16,686	1.6
6510	Real estate operators and lessors	68	70	2.4	453	367	16,865	19,913	7,743	7,859	2.4
6530	Real estate agents and managers	49	58	1.8	269	317	17,755	16,744	5,237	6,506	1.1
6540	Title abstract offices	7	7	2.9	25	35	20,480	17,829	546	844	1.5
6552	Subdividers and developers, n.e.c.	7	7	2.4	39	21	9,026	8,571	401	254	0.7
6553	Cemetery subdividers and developers	26	28	4.3	78	81	12,718	11,605	1,161	1,197	2.2
6700	Holding and other investment offices	20	14	1.6	238	165	96,504	32,533	20,149	3,859	0.8
6710	Holding offices	9	7	2.7	201	126	111,164	38,794	19,554	3,367	0.9
6732	Educational, religious, etc. trusts	4	3	1.4	14	4	8,857	11,000	105	41	0.1
6733	Trusts, n.e.c.	3	2	0.9	14	-	9,143	-	118	-	-
LYCOMING, PA											
60 –	**Finance, insurance, and real estate**	238	223	0.9	3,198	2,546	15,916	20,985	50,624	52,803	0.5
6000	Depository institutions	60	58	1.0	973	1,056	19,922	19,678	18,893	19,253	0.7
6020	Commercial banks	40	38	1.0	877	954	20,178	19,799	17,185	17,231	0.8
6030	Savings institutions	6	6	0.7	45	41	19,467	23,610	866	1,041	0.4
6060	Credit unions	14	14	1.6	51	61	15,922	15,148	842	981	1.0
6140	Personal credit institutions	11	10	1.5	47	55	24,000	21,745	1,087	1,173	0.7
6160	Mortgage bankers and brokers	3	3	0.7	11	9	23,636	26,667	242	378	0.1
6200	Security and commodity brokers	9	7	0.6	74	74	78,865	75,838	5,443	5,663	0.5
6300	Insurance carriers	28	24	1.1	1,686	904	9,514	18,199	15,944	17,075	0.6
6310	Life insurance	9	8	1.1	1,064	251	4,199	17,721	3,595	4,360	0.3
6330	Fire, marine, and casualty insurance	7	6	0.8	407	407	21,179	21,278	9,128	9,282	0.9
6400	Insurance agents, brokers, and service	50	53	1.0	155	176	20,439	19,114	3,627	4,008	0.4
6500	Real estate	70	62	0.8	184	190	13,630	14,379	2,877	3,067	0.3
6510	Real estate operators and lessors	27	23	0.8	72	71	14,500	13,859	1,070	1,142	0.3
6530	Real estate agents and managers	28	29	0.9	60	72	12,067	16,056	919	1,231	0.2
6553	Cemetery subdividers and developers	8	7	1.1	36	-	13,111	-	561	-	-
6732	Educational, religious, etc. trusts	3	3	1.4	-	3	-	17,333	-	67	0.2
MCKEAN, PA											
60 –	**Finance, insurance, and real estate**	86	86	0.4	365	534	19,485	20,225	7,101	11,118	0.1
6000	Depository institutions	32	31	0.5	221	239	18,552	17,238	4,134	4,409	0.2
6020	Commercial banks	18	17	0.5	145	169	21,103	18,414	3,051	3,285	0.2
6100	Nondepository institutions	3	3	0.2	9	-	19,111	-	182	-	-
6140	Personal credit institutions	3	3	0.4	9	-	19,111	-	182	-	-
6400	Insurance agents, brokers, and service	28	29	0.6	64	69	23,500	20,870	1,382	1,431	0.2
6500	Real estate	20	20	0.3	-	42	-	8,667	-	390	0.0
6510	Real estate operators and lessors	6	7	0.2	15	20	11,200	10,400	180	199	0.1
6553	Cemetery subdividers and developers	8	8	1.2	14	14	7,143	7,429	148	148	0.3
MERCER, PA											
60 –	**Finance, insurance, and real estate**	200	197	0.8	1,522	1,609	20,415	21,201	32,641	35,423	0.4
6000	Depository institutions	59	58	1.0	829	856	19,817	19,785	17,130	17,590	0.7
6020	Commercial banks	45	43	1.2	697	752	20,534	20,298	14,931	15,918	0.8
6030	Savings institutions	8	7	0.8	106	68	16,868	17,353	1,861	1,186	0.4
6060	Credit unions	6	8	0.9	26	36	12,615	13,667	338	486	0.5
6100	Nondepository institutions	16	12	0.9	111	55	21,910	23,418	2,477	1,232	0.2
6280	Security and commodity services	3	4	0.8	-	4	-	13,000	-	66	0.0
6300	Insurance carriers	19	15	0.7	194	291	28,021	27,835	5,412	7,819	0.3

Source: County Business Patterns, 1992/93, CBP-92/93-1, U.S. Department of Commerce, Washington, D.C., April 1995. SIC categories for which data were suppressed or not available for both 1992 and 1993 are *not* displayed. The employment columns represent mid-March employment in the year. Pay per employee is calculated by dividing 1st Quarter payroll, annualized, by mid-March employment. The columns headed "% State" show the county's percentage of the state total for the SIC in 1993; for example, 0.9% for SIC 6030 means that the county had 0.9 percent of the state's total establishments (or payroll) in SIC 6030 in 1993. A dash (-) is used to indicate that data are not available or cannot be calculated; *nec* means not elsewhere classified.

Continued on next page.

SIC	Industry	No. Establishments			Employment		Pay / Employee		Annual Payroll ($ 000)		
		1992	1993	% State	1992	1993	1992	1993	1992	1993	% State
MERCER, PA - [continued]											
6310	Life insurance	6	6	0.8	173	272	27,260	27,132	4,633	6,974	0.5
6330	Fire, marine, and casualty insurance	9	6	0.8	-	12		53,667	-	750	0.1
6370	Pension, health, and welfare funds	3	3	0.7	7	7	10,857	10,857	103	95	0.1
6400	Insurance agents, brokers, and service	42	45	0.9	155	156	18,632	19,333	3,527	3,594	0.4
6500	Real estate	54	56	0.8	189	182	10,392	10,681	2,233	2,281	0.2
6510	Real estate operators and lessors	25	27	0.9	117	81	8,855	10,469	1,271	943	0.3
6530	Real estate agents and managers	17	18	0.6	43	50	16,000	13,920	695	870	0.1
6553	Cemetery subdividers and developers	9	11	1.7	-	51		7,843	-	468	0.8
MIFFLIN, PA											
60 –	**Finance, insurance, and real estate**	59	61	0.3	445	472	21,384	19,475	9,970	10,244	0.1
6000	Depository institutions	22	23	0.4	245	250	20,800	18,160	4,935	5,231	0.2
6020	Commercial banks	17	18	0.5	207	212	21,333	18,264	4,189	4,564	0.2
6300	Insurance carriers	6	5	0.2	100	113	25,760	25,204	2,575	2,858	0.1
6310	Life insurance	5	5	0.7	-	113		25,204	-	2,858	0.2
6400	Insurance agents, brokers, and service	16	16	0.3	53	54	18,566	18,593	1,208	1,208	0.1
6500	Real estate	11	13	0.2	-	34		14,471	-	597	0.1
6510	Real estate operators and lessors	4	6	0.2	-	16		17,000	-	315	0.1
6530	Real estate agents and managers	3	3	0.1	3	5	12,000	11,200	46	49	0.0
6553	Cemetery subdividers and developers	4	4	0.6	15	13	13,333	12,615	235	233	0.4
MONROE, PA											
60 –	**Finance, insurance, and real estate**	247	254	1.1	1,764	1,594	17,254	18,806	30,811	34,333	0.3
6000	Depository institutions	55	54	1.0	491	474	16,676	16,819	8,556	8,553	0.3
6020	Commercial banks	39	38	1.0	353	330	16,861	17,115	6,104	5,879	0.3
6030	Savings institutions	10	10	1.1	115	118	16,800	17,051	2,145	2,348	0.9
6060	Credit unions	6	6	0.7	23	26	13,217	12,000	307	326	0.3
6140	Personal credit institutions	7	8	1.2	21	-	28,762	-	559	-	
6160	Mortgage bankers and brokers	11	10	2.2	47	39	18,383	26,462	1,045	1,268	0.5
6300	Insurance carriers	13	12	0.6	51	76	35,922	37,105	1,941	4,395	0.1
6400	Insurance agents, brokers, and service	41	44	0.9	167	162	19,066	21,136	3,112	3,754	0.4
6500	Real estate	114	118	1.6	947	780	14,910	16,318	13,856	14,251	1.3
6510	Real estate operators and lessors	15	18	0.6	73	75	16,548	13,867	1,136	1,291	0.4
6530	Real estate agents and managers	53	70	2.2	656	562	13,293	15,858	8,699	10,090	1.7
6540	Title abstract offices	15	15	6.3	57	58	19,579	23,655	1,274	1,406	2.5
6552	Subdividers and developers, n.e.c.	10	11	3.8	36	73	39,667	17,699	918	1,336	3.5
6553	Cemetery subdividers and developers	3	3	0.5	8	9	12,000	11,111	119	120	0.2
6700	Holding and other investment offices	3	3	0.3	-	1		8,000	-	16	0.0
MONTGOMERY, PA											
60 –	**Finance, insurance, and real estate**	2,421	2,477	10.5	40,202	38,695	31,374	30,235	1,306,521	1,255,101	12.6
6000	Depository institutions	396	384	6.8	6,379	6,423	25,841	25,037	171,569	164,430	6.3
6020	Commercial banks	259	246	6.6	4,042	4,415	25,537	24,033	106,847	110,288	5.2
6030	Savings institutions	96	92	10.3	1,931	1,594	25,154	24,698	50,879	41,004	14.9
6060	Credit unions	34	38	4.4	208	218	19,346	18,550	4,162	4,422	4.5
6100	Nondepository institutions	140	155	12.0	2,549	2,911	41,930	36,471	117,365	131,008	23.9
6140	Personal credit institutions	56	51	7.6	497	599	62,688	43,987	31,012	33,499	21.1
6150	Business credit institutions	20	25	19.4	148	207	32,946	31,768	4,815	6,307	7.3
6160	Mortgage bankers and brokers	62	79	17.6	1,883	2,105	37,268	34,795	80,824	91,202	33.7
6200	Security and commodity brokers	165	170	14.9	1,383	1,490	70,299	69,184	103,617	115,151	10.0
6210	Security brokers and dealers	80	73	12.3	818	878	82,626	80,510	65,378	71,710	10.8
6280	Security and commodity services	82	92	17.5	562	608	52,690	53,230	38,043	42,831	9.2
6300	Insurance carriers	291	248	11.6	19,054	16,428	29,265	29,048	563,233	475,777	15.7
6310	Life insurance	106	114	15.4	12,010	10,854	25,194	26,897	288,169	282,155	21.2
6321	Accident and health insurance	11	9	18.0	-	302		22,887	-	8,104	13.7
6324	Hospital and medical service plans	6	7	10.0	-	695		28,547	-	21,063	4.3
6330	Fire, marine, and casualty insurance	71	69	9.6	4,023	4,093	33,325	35,639	133,833	148,288	14.7
6350	Surety insurance	8	3	11.1	36	10	55,444	72,800	2,232	775	3.2

Source: County Business Patterns, 1992/93, CBP-92/93-1, U.S. Department of Commerce, Washington, D.C., April 1995. SIC categories for which data were suppressed or not available for both 1992 and 1993 are not displayed. The employment columns represent mid-March employment in the year. Pay per employee is calculated by dividing 1st Quarter payroll, annualized, by mid-March employment. The columns headed "% State" show the county's percentage of the state total for the SIC in 1993; for example, 0.9% for SIC 6030 means that the county had 0.9 percent of the state's total establishments (or payroll) in SIC 6030 in 1993. A dash (-) is used to indicate that data are not available or cannot be calculated; nec means not elsewhere classified.

Continued on next page.

SIC	Industry	No. Establishments			Employment		Pay / Employee		Annual Payroll ($ 000)		
		1992	1993	% State	1992	1993	1992	1993	1992	1993	% State
MONTGOMERY, PA - [continued]											
6360	Title insurance	19	13	19.1	75	102	30,453	35,569	3,092	4,824	14.3
6370	Pension, health, and welfare funds	67	32	7.2	377	372	23,533	22,247	12,179	10,563	13.0
6400	Insurance agents, brokers, and service	527	571	11.3	4,400	3,895	34,807	33,053	158,991	148,360	15.6
6500	Real estate	772	814	11.2	4,825	5,672	22,994	22,081	123,085	145,748	13.6
6510	Real estate operators and lessors	277	300	10.5	1,944	1,961	20,235	18,911	41,597	41,516	12.4
6530	Real estate agents and managers	334	420	13.2	2,104	3,183	24,561	23,771	58,521	86,894	14.8
6540	Title abstract offices	27	28	11.8	157	176	26,828	23,409	5,581	6,619	11.9
6552	Subdividers and developers, n.e.c.	29	31	10.8	142	106	33,690	31,660	4,589	4,659	12.2
6553	Cemetery subdividers and developers	26	26	4.0	222	241	23,081	20,498	5,803	5,517	9.9
6700	Holding and other investment offices	125	129	14.4	1,573	1,833	43,830	36,408	66,951	72,198	14.5
6710	Holding offices	47	47	18.3	1,107	1,185	41,875	34,734	42,233	43,024	11.9
6720	Investment offices	8	4	16.7	-	9	-	25,333	-	295	1.6
6732	Educational, religious, etc. trusts	20	18	8.6	93	52	64,430	22,462	5,688	1,579	4.6
6733	Trusts, n.e.c.	20	26	11.6	49	144	15,347	10,417	1,033	2,568	8.9
6794	Patent owners and lessors	7	8	13.8	184	74	31,109	57,784	6,258	3,775	24.1
6798	Real estate investment trusts	3	4	20.0	39	-	68,103	-	1,893	-	-
6799	Investors, n.e.c.	12	20	22.2	26	311	46,769	48,103	1,278	17,516	61.6
MONTOUR, PA											
60 –	**Finance, insurance, and real estate**	29	32	0.1	166	207	17,084	20,155	2,916	4,288	0.0
6000	Depository institutions	10	11	0.2	119	144	16,739	15,806	2,044	2,410	0.1
6020	Commercial banks	7	7	0.2	100	108	16,720	15,741	1,732	1,778	0.1
6400	Insurance agents, brokers, and service	9	9	0.2	23	28	18,261	23,000	470	609	0.1
6500	Real estate	6	7	0.1	9	-	15,556	-	154	-	-
6530	Real estate agents and managers	5	6	0.2	-	9	-	12,889	-	163	0.0
NORTHAMPTON, PA											
60 –	**Finance, insurance, and real estate**	392	385	1.6	3,864	4,165	25,529	25,705	98,197	116,254	1.2
6000	Depository institutions	129	123	2.2	1,999	2,144	24,092	23,873	47,054	52,152	2.0
6020	Commercial banks	100	93	2.5	1,693	1,807	24,645	24,622	40,657	43,814	2.1
6030	Savings institutions	16	16	1.8	242	272	23,124	21,441	5,581	7,434	2.7
6060	Credit unions	11	14	1.6	61	65	12,262	13,231	762	904	0.9
6100	Nondepository institutions	19	16	1.2	80	74	25,050	20,919	2,520	2,093	0.4
6140	Personal credit institutions	11	9	1.3	-	42	-	17,714	-	761	0.5
6160	Mortgage bankers and brokers	7	6	1.3	31	-	29,161	-	1,424	-	-
6200	Security and commodity brokers	10	15	1.3	47	54	61,277	85,556	2,637	9,009	0.8
6210	Security brokers and dealers	5	12	2.0	37	-	73,946	-	2,456	-	-
6280	Security and commodity services	5	3	0.6	10	-	14,400	-	181	-	-
6300	Insurance carriers	32	29	1.4	988	1,039	28,741	29,386	27,699	31,368	1.0
6310	Life insurance	15	12	1.6	466	-	25,236	-	11,535	-	-
6330	Fire, marine, and casualty insurance	12	15	2.1	511	500	32,266	32,880	15,961	16,778	1.7
6400	Insurance agents, brokers, and service	83	80	1.6	352	353	23,750	23,116	8,739	8,692	0.9
6500	Real estate	109	110	1.5	357	405	17,042	17,867	6,609	9,288	0.9
6510	Real estate operators and lessors	38	37	1.3	138	158	17,420	19,949	2,620	3,503	1.0
6530	Real estate agents and managers	37	46	1.4	81	123	12,988	13,626	1,222	2,022	0.3
6540	Title abstract offices	3	3	1.3	8	-	15,500	-	197	-	-
6552	Subdividers and developers, n.e.c.	5	8	2.8	48	49	26,667	27,265	1,356	2,406	6.3
6553	Cemetery subdividers and developers	14	14	2.1	60	67	16,133	12,836	832	1,106	2.0
6700	Holding and other investment offices	10	12	1.3	41	96	67,317	39,375	2,939	3,652	0.7
6710	Holding offices	3	3	1.2	-	59	-	41,492	-	1,976	0.5
6733	Trusts, n.e.c.	3	5	2.2	-	18	-	14,000	-	279	1.0
NORTHUMBERLAND, PA											
60 –	**Finance, insurance, and real estate**	131	129	0.5	1,051	1,157	20,156	20,118	21,755	24,228	0.2
6000	Depository institutions	42	41	0.7	580	634	19,372	18,208	11,161	11,886	0.5
6020	Commercial banks	30	29	0.8	460	479	19,617	18,313	8,536	8,758	0.4
6300	Insurance carriers	14	8	0.4	159	183	24,604	28,546	3,853	5,216	0.2
6310	Life insurance	6	6	0.8	128	-	27,844	-	3,550	-	-

Source: County Business Patterns, 1992/93, CBP-92/93-1, U.S. Department of Commerce, Washington, D.C., April 1995. SIC categories for which data were suppressed or not available for both 1992 and 1993 are *not* displayed. The employment columns represent mid-March employment in the year. Pay per employee is calculated by dividing 1st Quarter payroll, annualized, by mid-March employment. The columns headed "% State" show the county's percentage of the state total for the SIC in 1993; for example, 0.9% for SIC 6030 means that the county had 0.9 percent of the state's total establishments (or payroll) in SIC 6030 in 1993. A dash (-) is used to indicate that data are not available or cannot be calculated; *nec* means not elsewhere classified.

Continued on next page.

SIC	Industry	No. Establishments			Employment		Pay / Employee		Annual Payroll ($ 000)		
		1992	1993	% State	1992	1993	1992	1993	1992	1993	% State
NORTHUMBERLAND, PA - [continued]											
6400	Insurance agents, brokers, and service	29	30	0.6	139	154	22,763	22,494	3,789	3,867	0.4
6500	Real estate	39	40	0.5	133	143	10,797	11,580	1,558	1,790	0.2
6510	Real estate operators and lessors	13	15	0.5	35	-	12,114	-	423	-	-
6530	Real estate agents and managers	14	16	0.5	38	47	12,526	14,553	517	730	0.1
6553	Cemetery subdividers and developers	7	7	1.1	38	-	9,158	-	395	-	-
6700	Holding and other investment offices	1	3	0.3	-	1	-	4,000	-	9	0.0
PERRY, PA											
60 –	**Finance, insurance, and real estate**	55	51	0.2	258	331	16,031	13,837	4,585	4,690	0.0
6000	Depository institutions	19	19	0.3	177	181	16,678	16,331	3,104	3,149	0.1
6300	Insurance carriers	3	2	0.1	4	-	12,000	-	102	-	-
6400	Insurance agents, brokers, and service	13	14	0.3	36	34	22,000	20,706	747	817	0.1
6500	Real estate	17	13	0.2	35	92	7,886	8,391	565	614	0.1
6510	Real estate operators and lessors	6	4	0.1	13	70	12,000	9,143	444	475	0.1
6530	Real estate agents and managers	4	3	0.1	7	7	8,571	10,857	65	76	0.0
PHILADELPHIA, PA											
60 –	**Finance, insurance, and real estate**	2,433	2,343	10.0	61,899	72,258	33,325	30,140	1,954,248	2,250,042	22.5
6000	Depository institutions	628	638	11.3	18,890	20,864	30,539	26,714	523,376	546,811	21.1
6020	Commercial banks	295	317	8.5	13,530	16,301	32,461	27,174	386,979	427,688	20.2
6030	Savings institutions	145	115	12.9	2,381	1,335	23,259	22,427	55,955	32,069	11.6
6090	Functions closely related to banking	109	115	65.0	740	871	22,897	24,358	16,875	21,131	55.2
6100	Nondepository institutions	70	65	5.0	1,681	1,218	31,774	39,461	50,722	54,227	9.9
6140	Personal credit institutions	39	25	3.7	443	355	27,205	47,955	12,254	17,173	10.8
6150	Business credit institutions	9	13	10.1	361	541	31,845	26,810	12,312	19,573	22.7
6160	Mortgage bankers and brokers	22	26	5.8	877	-	34,052	-	26,156	-	-
6200	Security and commodity brokers	200	189	16.5	4,611	4,926	69,807	69,959	318,057	385,636	33.5
6210	Security brokers and dealers	135	123	20.7	3,226	3,196	79,795	81,956	246,345	277,849	41.7
6280	Security and commodity services	55	58	11.0	1,081	1,349	45,636	52,522	57,906	93,449	20.2
6300	Insurance carriers	289	217	10.2	16,659	28,025	39,704	28,802	609,751	818,765	27.0
6310	Life insurance	74	71	9.6	5,334	16,486	44,913	24,078	196,285	392,035	29.5
6321	Accident and health insurance	5	5	10.0	598	588	22,836	16,020	13,571	9,268	15.7
6324	Hospital and medical service plans	7	10	14.3	2,516	3,364	33,506	34,593	82,683	130,964	26.7
6330	Fire, marine, and casualty insurance	64	56	7.8	6,447	6,166	40,227	37,764	246,209	227,304	22.5
6350	Surety insurance	9	5	18.5	320	-	68,238	-	24,161	-	-
6360	Title insurance	16	12	17.6	501	-	33,253	-	18,328	-	-
6370	Pension, health, and welfare funds	112	58	13.1	930	765	27,733	30,588	28,235	24,817	30.5
6400	Insurance agents, brokers, and service	240	255	5.0	2,977	3,513	43,370	37,214	128,769	140,171	14.8
6500	Real estate	848	835	11.4	15,298	12,062	14,292	18,432	223,265	237,027	22.1
6510	Real estate operators and lessors	354	375	13.1	10,132	3,262	8,997	18,402	91,176	63,864	19.1
6530	Real estate agents and managers	361	403	12.6	4,241	8,373	24,789	18,322	108,737	163,069	27.8
6540	Title abstract offices	20	21	8.8	110	161	31,600	21,068	3,532	4,182	7.5
6552	Subdividers and developers, n.e.c.	28	15	5.2	191	52	31,791	16,692	6,228	923	2.4
6553	Cemetery subdividers and developers	25	21	3.2	287	214	21,324	21,607	6,370	4,989	9.0
6700	Holding and other investment offices	152	137	15.3	1,484	1,359	60,838	41,610	88,128	55,937	11.3
6710	Holding offices	30	24	9.3	528	413	60,955	68,087	32,127	23,796	6.6
6720	Investment offices	10	4	16.7	-	40	-	36,900	-	2,039	11.2
6732	Educational, religious, etc. trusts	54	49	23.3	385	346	27,449	31,873	10,407	10,866	31.7
6733	Trusts, n.e.c.	32	33	14.7	96	387	28,917	17,054	3,006	9,693	33.7
6794	Patent owners and lessors	3	7	12.1	-	17	-	26,588	-	826	5.3
6798	Real estate investment trusts	6	5	25.0	116	-	57,759	-	6,013	-	-
6799	Investors, n.e.c.	13	14	15.6	54	96	20,370	52,333	1,166	4,972	17.5
PIKE, PA											
60 –	**Finance, insurance, and real estate**	57	56	0.2	360	553	17,589	14,416	6,398	8,549	0.1
6000	Depository institutions	16	13	0.2	125	94	20,064	20,979	2,396	1,922	0.1
6020	Commercial banks	15	13	0.3	-	94	-	20,979	-	1,922	0.1
6100	Nondepository institutions	4	3	0.2	7	8	18,857	14,000	131	141	0.0

Source: County Business Patterns, 1992/93, CBP-92/93-1, U.S. Department of Commerce, Washington, D.C., April 1995. SIC categories for which data were suppressed or not available for both 1992 and 1993 are not displayed. The employment columns represent mid-March employment in the year. Pay per employee is calculated by dividing 1st Quarter payroll, annualized, by mid-March employment. The columns headed "% State" show the county's percentage of the state total for the SIC in 1993; for example, 0.9% for SIC 6030 means that the county had 0.9 percent of the state's total establishments (or payroll) in SIC 6030 in 1993. A dash (-) is used to indicate that data are not available or cannot be calculated; nec means not elsewhere classified.

Continued on next page.

SIC	Industry	No. Establishments			Employment		Pay / Employee		Annual Payroll ($ 000)		
		1992	1993	% State	1992	1993	1992	1993	1992	1993	% State
PIKE, PA - [continued]											
6400	Insurance agents, brokers, and service	9	8	0.2	34	-	31,294	-	1,043	-	-
6500	Real estate	24	31	0.4	177	420	14,328	11,905	2,745	5,697	0.5
6510	Real estate operators and lessors	5	4	0.1	23	-	22,783	-	570	-	-
6530	Real estate agents and managers	10	19	0.6	75	305	12,747	11,069	1,021	3,916	0.7
6540	Title abstract offices	4	4	1.7	17	15	15,294	16,533	249	268	0.5
POTTER, PA											
60 –	**Finance, insurance, and real estate**	27	25	0.1	116	130	15,724	16,769	1,996	2,220	0.0
6000	Depository institutions	8	8	0.1	73	82	15,616	15,463	1,202	1,183	0.0
6020	Commercial banks	8	8	0.2	73	82	15,616	15,463	1,202	1,183	0.1
6400	Insurance agents, brokers, and service	6	7	0.1	14	15	12,571	10,933	168	182	0.0
6500	Real estate	9	7	0.1	18	24	14,889	22,167	400	649	0.1
6530	Real estate agents and managers	4	3	0.1	12	-	17,333	-	332	-	-
SCHUYLKILL, PA											
60 –	**Finance, insurance, and real estate**	235	229	1.0	1,743	1,938	18,260	20,254	33,070	42,286	0.4
6000	Depository institutions	80	80	1.4	1,006	1,123	18,887	21,122	19,291	25,360	1.0
6020	Commercial banks	62	60	1.6	851	1,000	19,680	21,368	16,754	22,902	1.1
6030	Savings institutions	12	13	1.5	120	97	13,233	20,866	1,724	2,013	0.7
6060	Credit unions	5	7	0.8	-	26	-	12,615	-	445	0.4
6100	Nondepository institutions	12	11	0.9	59	61	25,220	20,131	1,452	1,284	0.2
6300	Insurance carriers	18	15	0.7	205	278	22,244	26,676	4,507	7,469	0.2
6310	Life insurance	7	7	0.9	151	239	23,099	27,732	3,615	6,628	0.5
6400	Insurance agents, brokers, and service	62	63	1.2	290	282	15,545	15,362	5,070	5,189	0.5
6500	Real estate	57	55	0.8	175	185	11,680	12,324	2,400	2,497	0.2
6510	Real estate operators and lessors	22	15	0.5	55	33	9,527	13,212	722	455	0.1
6530	Real estate agents and managers	13	20	0.6	33	70	12,121	12,057	479	1,016	0.2
6540	Title abstract offices	3	3	1.3	5	9	20,800	17,778	99	160	0.3
6552	Subdividers and developers, n.e.c.	3	4	1.4	40	42	12,300	11,714	568	460	1.2
6553	Cemetery subdividers and developers	12	12	1.8	34	31	11,176	11,226	427	391	0.7
SNYDER, PA											
60 –	**Finance, insurance, and real estate**	52	56	0.2	401	417	16,978	15,770	7,554	7,722	0.1
6000	Depository institutions	15	15	0.3	261	250	18,069	16,544	4,555	4,659	0.2
6100	Nondepository institutions	6	4	0.3	21	-	21,524	-	451	-	-
6300	Insurance carriers	5	4	0.2	-	25	-	15,200	-	758	0.0
6400	Insurance agents, brokers, and service	13	14	0.3	37	44	16,216	17,182	676	877	0.1
6500	Real estate	12	18	0.2	69	61	13,797	11,934	1,123	918	0.1
6530	Real estate agents and managers	5	2	0.1	30	-	14,400	-	583	-	-
6553	Cemetery subdividers and developers	3	4	0.6	-	10	-	4,400	-	31	0.1
SOMERSET, PA											
60 –	**Finance, insurance, and real estate**	123	119	0.5	1,144	875	19,147	19,959	22,888	18,297	0.2
6000	Depository institutions	34	36	0.6	435	448	17,959	18,562	8,001	8,665	0.3
6020	Commercial banks	34	36	1.0	435	448	17,959	18,562	8,001	8,665	0.4
6100	Nondepository institutions	4	5	0.4	17	19	26,824	29,474	466	625	0.1
6300	Insurance carriers	10	8	0.4	168	174	25,071	24,253	4,171	4,335	0.1
6400	Insurance agents, brokers, and service	33	33	0.7	101	105	18,059	18,400	1,903	1,898	0.2
6500	Real estate	37	33	0.5	401	105	17,706	16,990	7,655	1,944	0.2
6510	Real estate operators and lessors	20	20	0.7	-	59	-	11,119	-	854	0.3
6553	Cemetery subdividers and developers	6	6	0.9	-	8	-	6,000	-	89	0.2
SULLIVAN, PA											
60 –	**Finance, insurance, and real estate**	12	10	0.0	55	-	11,855	-	762	-	-
6500	Real estate	5	4	0.1	11	6	4,727	6,000	106	77	0.0

Source: County Business Patterns, 1992/93, CBP-92/93-1, U.S. Department of Commerce, Washington, D.C., April 1995. SIC categories for which data were suppressed or not available for both 1992 and 1993 are not displayed. The employment columns represent mid-March employment in the year. Pay per employee is calculated by dividing 1st Quarter payroll, annualized, by mid-March employment. The columns headed "% State" show the county's percentage of the state total for the SIC in 1993; for example, 0.9% for SIC 6030 means that the county had 0.9 percent of the state's total establishments (or payroll) in SIC 6030 in 1993. A dash (-) is used to indicate that data are not available or cannot be calculated; nec means not elsewhere classified.

SIC	Industry	No. Establishments			Employment		Pay / Employee		Annual Payroll ($ 000)		
		1992	1993	% State	1992	1993	1992	1993	1992	1993	% State
SUSQUEHANNA, PA											
60 –	**Finance, insurance, and real estate**	54	53	0.2	395	391	17,671	16,184	7,166	6,298	0.1
6000	Depository institutions	20	20	0.4	253	303	15,763	15,142	3,977	4,152	0.2
6020	Commercial banks	20	20	0.5	253	303	15,763	15,142	3,977	4,152	0.2
6400	Insurance agents, brokers, and service	14	15	0.3	48	47	18,417	22,553	921	1,084	0.1
6500	Real estate	17	16	0.2	46	-	14,696	-	835	-	-
6510	Real estate operators and lessors	5	4	0.1	11	10	7,273	8,800	108	99	0.0
6530	Real estate agents and managers	6	5	0.2	32	15	18,250	9,867	693	366	0.1
6553	Cemetery subdividers and developers	6	7	1.1	3	-	4,000	-	34	-	-
TIOGA, PA											
60 –	**Finance, insurance, and real estate**	55	56	0.2	333	366	21,429	20,109	7,187	7,584	0.1
6000	Depository institutions	16	16	0.3	244	258	22,115	21,566	5,376	5,610	0.2
6020	Commercial banks	13	13	0.3	235	250	22,536	21,904	5,246	5,456	0.3
6060	Credit unions	3	2	0.2	9	-	11,111	-	130	-	-
6100	Nondepository institutions	3	3	0.2	14	15	28,000	25,333	375	349	0.1
6400	Insurance agents, brokers, and service	16	18	0.4	39	46	20,205	15,826	827	856	0.1
6500	Real estate	15	13	0.2	-	17	-	11,059	-	249	0.0
6530	Real estate agents and managers	5	6	0.2	11	-	7,273	-	80	-	-
6553	Cemetery subdividers and developers	4	3	0.5	1	-	8,000	-	40	-	-
UNION, PA											
60 –	**Finance, insurance, and real estate**	64	59	0.3	379	374	18,860	19,176	7,462	7,459	0.1
6000	Depository institutions	16	16	0.3	187	196	17,968	17,776	3,655	3,735	0.1
6020	Commercial banks	13	13	0.3	175	185	18,240	18,011	3,473	3,564	0.2
6200	Security and commodity brokers	4	4	0.4	3	-	12,000	-	55	-	-
6210	Security brokers and dealers	4	3	0.5	3	-	12,000	-	55	-	-
6400	Insurance agents, brokers, and service	14	14	0.3	45	44	16,533	17,273	788	820	0.1
6500	Real estate	22	20	0.3	67	67	6,806	8,299	597	716	0.1
6510	Real estate operators and lessors	7	8	0.3	27	34	3,407	6,588	104	247	0.1
6530	Real estate agents and managers	9	9	0.3	20	28	12,600	11,000	285	426	0.1
6553	Cemetery subdividers and developers	2	3	0.5	-	5	-	4,800	-	43	0.1
VENANGO, PA											
60 –	**Finance, insurance, and real estate**	94	93	0.4	1,113	874	20,870	23,735	22,591	20,576	0.2
6000	Depository institutions	30	28	0.5	802	647	21,282	23,499	16,406	15,017	0.6
6020	Commercial banks	19	18	0.5	652	583	23,681	24,185	15,562	13,763	0.7
6030	Savings institutions	6	5	0.6	130	-	10,800	-	611	-	-
6060	Credit unions	5	5	0.6	20	-	11,200	-	233	-	-
6100	Nondepository institutions	4	4	0.3	-	20	-	22,200	-	423	0.1
6140	Personal credit institutions	4	4	0.6	-	20	-	22,200	-	423	0.3
6200	Security and commodity brokers	6	6	0.5	34	32	45,412	58,875	1,502	1,752	0.2
6210	Security brokers and dealers	6	6	1.0	34	32	45,412	58,875	1,502	1,752	0.3
6300	Insurance carriers	11	7	0.3	105	-	20,952	-	2,242	-	-
6310	Life insurance	5	3	0.4	99	-	20,687	-	2,052	-	-
6400	Insurance agents, brokers, and service	13	20	0.4	50	50	20,800	21,280	1,021	1,083	0.1
6500	Real estate	27	26	0.4	105	77	8,724	11,896	963	961	0.1
6510	Real estate operators and lessors	11	11	0.4	44	27	11,273	9,481	535	257	0.1
6530	Real estate agents and managers	8	8	0.3	46	37	6,522	14,595	290	580	0.1
WARREN, PA											
60 –	**Finance, insurance, and real estate**	85	84	0.4	501	517	20,559	20,015	10,757	11,455	0.1
6000	Depository institutions	23	23	0.4	287	305	19,791	18,374	6,323	6,369	0.2
6100	Nondepository institutions	5	5	0.4	14	19	22,571	21,053	351	539	0.1
6140	Personal credit institutions	5	4	0.6	14	-	22,571	-	351	-	-
6300	Insurance carriers	8	7	0.3	49	62	37,388	22,194	1,314	1,523	0.1
6310	Life insurance	3	3	0.4	-	54	-	22,000	-	1,243	0.1
6400	Insurance agents, brokers, and service	20	20	0.4	52	57	17,385	15,228	866	861	0.1
6500	Real estate	22	22	0.3	79	50	7,595	11,440	656	644	0.1

Source: County Business Patterns, 1992/93, CBP-92/93-1, U.S. Department of Commerce, Washington, D.C., April 1995. SIC categories for which data were suppressed or not available for both 1992 and 1993 are *not* displayed. The employment columns represent mid-March employment in the year. Pay per employee is calculated by dividing 1st Quarter payroll, annualized, by mid-March employment. The columns headed "% State" show the county's percentage of the state total for the SIC in 1993; for example, 0.9% for SIC 6030 means that the county had 0.9 percent of the state's total establishments (or payroll) in SIC 6030 in 1993. A dash (-) is used to indicate that data are not available or cannot be calculated; *nec* means not elsewhere classified.

Continued on next page.

SIC	Industry	No. Establishments			Employment		Pay / Employee		Annual Payroll ($ 000)		
		1992	1993	% State	1992	1993	1992	1993	1992	1993	% State
WARREN, PA - [continued]											
6510	Real estate operators and lessors	8	8	0.3	31	26	14,323	15,231	466	425	0.1
6530	Real estate agents and managers	6	7	0.2	6	10	4,667	4,400	34	67	0.0
6553	Cemetery subdividers and developers	6	6	0.9	40	-	3,000	-	146	-	
WASHINGTON, PA											
60 –	**Finance, insurance, and real estate**	330	323	1.4	2,106	2,038	19,951	22,043	44,801	46,525	0.5
6000	Depository institutions	83	83	1.5	978	765	19,084	17,856	18,823	13,985	0.5
6020	Commercial banks	47	48	1.3	670	445	20,173	19,452	13,077	8,329	0.4
6030	Savings institutions	21	19	2.1	254	260	16,740	15,508	4,760	4,579	1.7
6060	Credit unions	15	16	1.9	54	60	16,593	16,200	986	1,077	1.1
6100	Nondepository institutions	16	18	1.4	69	76	30,319	19,842	2,040	1,617	0.3
6140	Personal credit institutions	12	11	1.6	54	57	23,556	18,947	1,225	1,205	0.8
6200	Security and commodity brokers	15	14	1.2	60	63	39,333	47,810	3,243	3,895	0.3
6210	Security brokers and dealers	8	8	1.3	35	37	41,371	51,351	1,484	1,775	0.3
6280	Security and commodity services	7	6	1.1	25	26	36,480	42,769	1,759	2,120	0.5
6300	Insurance carriers	27	24	1.1	286	294	20,783	23,565	7,026	6,677	0.2
6310	Life insurance	10	8	1.1	162	173	23,556	23,769	3,816	3,330	0.3
6370	Pension, health, and welfare funds	7	7	1.6	113	88	13,168	17,409	2,546	1,813	2.2
6400	Insurance agents, brokers, and service	87	82	1.6	300	289	19,640	19,599	6,374	6,450	0.7
6500	Real estate	94	94	1.3	384	486	14,688	18,708	5,831	9,614	0.9
6510	Real estate operators and lessors	41	42	1.5	168	290	13,000	20,566	2,190	5,721	1.7
6530	Real estate agents and managers	31	32	1.0	114	115	17,649	17,357	2,114	2,298	0.4
6552	Subdividers and developers, n.e.c.	2	6	2.1	-	19	-	22,947	-	663	1.7
6553	Cemetery subdividers and developers	12	14	2.1	-	62	-	11,226	-	932	1.7
6700	Holding and other investment offices	8	8	0.9	29	65	49,103	77,846	1,464	4,287	0.9
6710	Holding offices	2	3	1.2	-	59	-	84,000	-	4,181	1.2
WAYNE, PA											
60 –	**Finance, insurance, and real estate**	97	99	0.4	752	883	16,819	16,852	14,885	17,851	0.2
6000	Depository institutions	27	26	0.5	359	366	17,448	17,585	7,127	7,277	0.3
6100	Nondepository institutions	4	2	0.2	11	-	14,909	-	126	-	-
6400	Insurance agents, brokers, and service	23	23	0.5	93	107	18,753	18,579	1,940	2,305	0.2
6500	Real estate	35	42	0.6	241	374	11,618	12,513	3,926	6,036	0.6
6510	Real estate operators and lessors	6	9	0.3	9	-	5,333	-	53	-	-
6530	Real estate agents and managers	20	28	0.9	211	337	11,280	12,451	3,076	5,402	0.9
WESTMORELAND, PA											
60 –	**Finance, insurance, and real estate**	662	663	2.8	4,449	4,750	20,125	20,515	94,438	103,679	1.0
6000	Depository institutions	178	181	3.2	1,684	1,754	19,057	19,092	32,768	33,941	1.3
6020	Commercial banks	109	113	3.0	1,331	1,417	19,684	20,068	26,887	28,578	1.4
6030	Savings institutions	23	14	1.6	225	161	17,404	16,621	3,849	2,777	1.0
6060	Credit unions	46	54	6.3	128	176	15,438	13,500	2,032	2,586	2.6
6140	Personal credit institutions	34	23	3.4	141	149	27,433	18,577	3,934	3,109	2.0
6160	Mortgage bankers and brokers	3	5	1.1	31	48	29,806	22,750	1,205	1,596	0.6
6200	Security and commodity brokers	22	18	1.6	96	176	56,417	47,045	5,683	9,010	0.8
6210	Security brokers and dealers	13	9	1.5	77	82	59,896	58,732	4,863	5,142	0.8
6280	Security and commodity services	9	8	1.5	19	-	42,316	-	820	-	-
6300	Insurance carriers	64	50	2.3	776	1,081	20,289	21,521	16,368	23,072	0.8
6310	Life insurance	23	18	2.4	608	729	18,533	20,439	10,569	14,677	1.1
6330	Fire, marine, and casualty insurance	27	21	2.9	72	255	36,389	27,200	2,799	7,001	0.7
6370	Pension, health, and welfare funds	9	8	1.8	85	-	16,800	-	2,636	-	-
6400	Insurance agents, brokers, and service	157	176	3.5	759	572	19,863	17,266	15,771	11,935	1.3
6500	Real estate	167	172	2.4	683	661	12,252	14,239	9,449	10,947	1.0
6510	Real estate operators and lessors	73	83	2.9	239	315	13,707	12,597	3,620	4,351	1.3
6530	Real estate agents and managers	58	58	1.8	143	184	14,881	16,457	2,416	3,247	0.6
6540	Title abstract offices	4	6	2.5	25	46	12,800	16,609	464	1,153	2.1
6552	Subdividers and developers, n.e.c.	7	4	1.4	18	14	25,778	18,571	558	247	0.6
6553	Cemetery subdividers and developers	17	19	2.9	98	102	15,878	13,647	1,673	1,783	3.2

Source: County Business Patterns, 1992/93, CBP-92/93-1, U.S. Department of Commerce, Washington, D.C., April 1995. SIC categories for which data were suppressed or not available for both 1992 and 1993 are *not* displayed. The employment columns represent mid-March employment in the year. Pay per employee is calculated by dividing 1st Quarter payroll, annualized, by mid-March employment. The columns headed "% State" show the county's percentage of the state total for the SIC in 1993; for example, 0.9% for SIC 6030 means that the county had 0.9 percent of the state's total establishments (or payroll) in SIC 6030 in 1993. A dash (-) is used to indicate that data are not available or cannot be calculated; *nec* means not elsewhere classified.

Continued on next page.

SIC	Industry	No. Establishments			Employment		Pay / Employee		Annual Payroll ($ 000)		
		1992	1993	% State	1992	1993	1992	1993	1992	1993	% State
WESTMORELAND, PA - [continued]											
6700	Holding and other investment offices	35	33	3.7	252	273	27,381	29,612	8,309	8,627	1.7
6710	Holding offices	4	5	1.9	32	76	100,875	73,895	4,149	5,490	1.5
6732	Educational, religious, etc. trusts	9	10	4.8	64	64	16,188	16,625	1,225	1,337	3.9
6733	Trusts, n.e.c.	17	14	6.2	123	120	20,358	10,700	2,736	1,600	5.6
WYOMING, PA											
60 –	**Finance, insurance, and real estate**	33	33	0.1	211	212	18,882	19,585	4,179	4,274	0.0
6000	Depository institutions	13	14	0.2	137	143	15,737	15,972	2,266	2,412	0.1
6020	Commercial banks	11	11	0.3	-	122	-	16,131	-	2,067	0.1
6400	Insurance agents, brokers, and service	12	11	0.2	51	50	25,412	28,160	1,423	1,450	0.2
YORK, PA											
60 –	**Finance, insurance, and real estate**	588	586	2.5	5,560	5,939	23,548	24,610	136,930	155,075	1.6
6000	Depository institutions	163	165	2.9	2,533	2,849	19,583	20,994	51,340	60,918	2.3
6020	Commercial banks	110	113	3.0	1,972	2,296	20,016	21,916	40,124	49,564	2.3
6030	Savings institutions	26	24	2.7	423	414	19,310	18,126	9,142	9,199	3.3
6060	Credit unions	27	27	3.2	138	-	14,232	-	2,074	-	-
6100	Nondepository institutions	32	27	2.1	169	187	30,249	26,802	5,239	5,549	1.0
6140	Personal credit institutions	22	16	2.4	82	-	28,341	-	2,203	-	-
6160	Mortgage bankers and brokers	9	9	2.0	-	58	-	33,172	-	2,635	1.0
6200	Security and commodity brokers	19	17	1.5	149	151	54,040	65,272	9,621	10,715	0.9
6210	Security brokers and dealers	11	10	1.7	120	-	57,167	-	7,685	-	-
6280	Security and commodity services	8	7	1.3	29	-	41,103	-	1,936	-	-
6300	Insurance carriers	51	43	2.0	1,110	1,135	28,317	30,393	30,413	33,710	1.1
6310	Life insurance	14	14	1.9	232	347	27,672	25,360	6,439	8,411	0.6
6330	Fire, marine, and casualty insurance	18	18	2.5	604	575	34,172	34,762	19,007	20,209	2.0
6400	Insurance agents, brokers, and service	120	122	2.4	761	815	29,209	27,539	24,413	26,569	2.8
6500	Real estate	187	193	2.6	774	730	15,240	16,838	13,180	14,824	1.4
6510	Real estate operators and lessors	53	57	2.0	246	209	12,325	15,215	3,235	3,586	1.1
6530	Real estate agents and managers	88	95	3.0	359	353	18,162	17,632	7,454	8,044	1.4
6540	Title abstract offices	4	8	3.4	26	62	14,923	17,871	491	1,384	2.5
6552	Subdividers and developers, n.e.c.	3	7	2.4	-	11	-	57,091	-	382	1.0
6553	Cemetery subdividers and developers	25	25	3.8	108	95	11,259	12,126	1,274	1,408	2.5
6700	Holding and other investment offices	16	19	2.1	64	72	42,250	31,222	2,724	2,790	0.6
6710	Holding offices	6	5	1.9	-	29	-	54,897	-	1,931	0.5
6732	Educational, religious, etc. trusts	5	5	2.4	6	8	27,333	26,500	154	186	0.5
6733	Trusts, n.e.c.	3	5	2.2	5	11	12,800	9,455	91	179	0.6

Source: County Business Patterns, 1992/93, CBP-92/93-1, U.S. Department of Commerce, Washington, D.C., April 1995. SIC categories for which data were suppressed or not available for both 1992 and 1993 are *not* displayed. The employment columns represent mid-March employment in the year. Pay per employee is calculated by dividing 1st Quarter payroll, annualized, by mid-March employment. The columns headed "% State" show the county's percentage of the state total for the SIC in 1993; for example, 0.9% for SIC 6030 means that the county had 0.9 percent of the state's total establishments (or payroll) in SIC 6030 in 1993. A dash (-) is used to indicate that data are not available or cannot be calculated; *nec* means not elsewhere classified.

RHODE ISLAND

SIC	Industry	No. Establishments			Employment		Pay / Employee		Annual Payroll ($ 000)		
		1992	1993	% State	1992	1993	1992	1993	1992	1993	% State
BRISTOL, RI											
60 –	**Finance, insurance, and real estate**	61	65	3.2	299	296	21,753	21,878	6,576	7,020	0.9
6000	Depository institutions	14	15	4.7	138	137	20,087	19,620	2,425	2,620	1.3
6020	Commercial banks	9	9	5.4	100	92	21,320	21,652	1,761	1,882	1.2
6400	Insurance agents, brokers, and service	10	12	3.0	55	49	30,618	30,939	1,802	1,763	2.5
6500	Real estate	26	25	3.3	66	59	16,364	16,203	1,195	1,195	1.4
6510	Real estate operators and lessors	13	13	4.3	35	-	15,200	-	591	-	
6530	Real estate agents and managers	8	10	2.6	21	17	15,810	15,294	327	368	0.9
KENT, RI											
60 –	**Finance, insurance, and real estate**	380	394	19.6	6,779	5,649	22,034	24,579	157,088	151,389	18.8
6000	Depository institutions	48	50	15.7	1,148	1,091	18,146	20,502	22,218	23,545	11.4
6020	Commercial banks	21	22	13.1	289	298	17,675	19,826	5,036	6,253	4.1
6030	Savings institutions	15	15	20.8	-	563	-	21,258	-	12,751	39.3
6060	Credit unions	12	13	17.8	-	230	-	19,530	-	4,541	24.3
6100	Nondepository institutions	45	49	31.8	349	390	28,573	27,364	10,928	13,108	
6160	Mortgage bankers and brokers	27	34	35.4	182	273	29,846	29,084	6,474	10,253	30.3
6200	Security and commodity brokers	15	17	15.0	-	163	-	35,362	-	5,783	6.6
6210	Security brokers and dealers	3	3	6.8	40	-	17,700	-	469	-	
6300	Insurance carriers	46	44	27.8	3,797	2,751	22,496	25,800	89,084	75,756	28.6
6310	Life insurance	15	13	27.1	2,796	1,436	19,139	24,195	55,643	34,709	55.3
6330	Fire, marine, and casualty insurance	20	22	31.0	951	1,059	31,748	26,470	31,526	31,867	24.2
6400	Insurance agents, brokers, and service	80	89	22.0	387	402	28,217	28,119	10,704	12,584	17.6
6500	Real estate	131	130	17.0	903	722	19,176	20,753	19,222	17,038	20.1
6510	Real estate operators and lessors	37	39	13.0	326	306	12,969	23,046	4,611	7,600	21.3
6530	Real estate agents and managers	59	73	19.2	479	375	22,789	18,091	12,088	7,241	18.5
6552	Subdividers and developers, n.e.c.	8	11	36.7	30	18	17,600	41,333	314	1,623	35.9
6700	Holding and other investment offices	14	14	13.9	127	-	27,307	-	3,753	-	-
NEWPORT, RI											
60 –	**Finance, insurance, and real estate**	165	175	8.7	1,180	1,037	20,603	24,544	25,940	27,577	3.4
6000	Depository institutions	28	30	9.4	430	442	20,056	20,317	9,297	9,582	4.7
6020	Commercial banks	10	11	6.5	110	120	19,818	20,033	2,067	2,170	1.4
6200	Security and commodity brokers	8	11	9.7	21	40	27,238	68,200	556	2,684	3.1
6280	Security and commodity services	5	7	10.4	12	-	25,333	-	354	-	-
6400	Insurance agents, brokers, and service	28	29	7.2	123	119	32,130	36,504	4,178	4,695	6.6
6500	Real estate	74	83	10.9	442	318	15,439	17,849	7,643	6,367	7.5
6510	Real estate operators and lessors	23	25	8.3	111	94	16,252	22,255	2,014	2,444	6.8
6530	Real estate agents and managers	33	49	12.9	278	201	14,820	14,826	4,548	3,450	8.8
6552	Subdividers and developers, n.e.c.	6	4	13.3	11	5	20,727	46,400	304	103	2.3
6700	Holding and other investment offices	14	9	8.9	101	46	19,762	20,783	1,939	1,085	-
PROVIDENCE, RI											
60 –	**Finance, insurance, and real estate**	1,157	1,201	59.6	19,806	18,571	31,129	30,883	611,501	590,020	73.4
6000	Depository institutions	190	194	60.8	6,364	5,653	28,874	27,299	184,266	157,441	76.5
6020	Commercial banks	97	106	63.1	4,776	4,525	29,575	28,153	142,723	130,673	86.2
6030	Savings institutions	51	41	56.9	1,168	633	28,318	23,918	32,456	13,441	41.5
6060	Credit unions	38	41	56.2	-	446	-	20,197	-	10,177	54.4
6090	Functions closely related to banking	3	6	100.0	-	49	-	56,816	-	3,150	100.0
6100	Nondepository institutions	91	93	60.4	1,546	1,414	31,909	32,263	42,522	44,788	-
6140	Personal credit institutions	46	28	63.6	472	-	37,237	-	14,189	-	
6160	Mortgage bankers and brokers	37	55	57.3	589	697	19,083	27,443	12,443	23,044	68.2

Source: *County Business Patterns, 1992/93*, CBP-92/93-1, U.S. Department of Commerce, Washington, D.C., April 1995. SIC categories for which data were suppressed or not available for both 1992 and 1993 are *not* displayed. The employment columns represent mid-March employment in the year. Pay per employee is calculated by dividing 1st Quarter payroll, annualized, by mid-March employment. The columns headed "% State" show the county's percentage of the state total for the SIC in 1993; for example, 0.9% for SIC 6030 means that the county had 0.9 percent of the state's total establishments (or payroll) in SIC 6030 in 1993. A dash (-) is used to indicate that data are not available or cannot be calculated; *nec* means not elsewhere classified.

Continued on next page.

SIC	Industry	No. Establishments			Employment		Pay / Employee		Annual Payroll ($ 000)		
		1992	1993	% State	1992	1993	1992	1993	1992	1993	% State
PROVIDENCE, RI - [continued]											
6200	Security and commodity brokers	53	79	69.9	1,276	1,615	49,577	49,870	61,100	78,354	89.8
6210	Security brokers and dealers	32	36	81.8	1,089	665	43,960	71,405	47,452	45,699	94.5
6300	Insurance carriers	104	92	58.2	5,495	5,638	31,688	31,211	176,008	183,292	69.3
6310	Life insurance	41	31	64.6	883	889	31,361	32,931	29,586	25,422	40.5
6330	Fire, marine, and casualty insurance	35	35	49.3	2,754	2,847	34,797	32,507	94,449	97,051	73.8
6370	Pension, health, and welfare funds	17	15	60.0	75	-	31,360	-	2,430	-	-
6400	Insurance agents, brokers, and service	239	247	61.0	1,545	1,443	29,823	28,532	51,182	46,762	65.3
6500	Real estate	415	430	56.4	2,567	2,470	17,851	20,321	49,061	55,160	65.0
6510	Real estate operators and lessors	164	192	64.0	811	1,004	15,571	22,124	13,427	23,680	66.3
6530	Real estate agents and managers	168	199	52.4	1,076	1,261	20,810	18,994	23,877	25,694	65.6
6540	Title abstract offices	4	5	71.4	-	92	-	10,043	-	1,128	98.6
6552	Subdividers and developers, n.e.c.	12	10	33.3	34	21	14,824	48,762	641	1,995	44.1
6553	Cemetery subdividers and developers	21	21	60.0	104	92	20,038	22,609	2,526	2,530	69.9
6700	Holding and other investment offices	65	66	65.3	1,013	338	53,473	76,071	47,362	24,223	-
6710	Holding offices	15	20	66.7	155	201	74,890	101,871	11,311	17,304	84.8
6732	Educational, religious, etc. trusts	14	14	63.6	-	52	-	25,385	-	1,380	56.5
6733	Trusts, n.e.c.	12	13	56.5	42	44	43,333	44,545	1,885	3,249	-
6799	Investors, n.e.c.	12	16	94.1	94	-	44,085	-	2,564	-	-
WASHINGTON, RI											
60 –	**Finance, insurance, and real estate**	176	180	8.9	1,161	999	22,153	24,092	26,815	27,652	3.4
6000	Depository institutions	33	30	9.4	575	550	21,725	20,924	12,194	12,607	6.1
6020	Commercial banks	20	20	11.9	440	449	21,736	21,416	9,702	10,558	7.0
6030	Savings institutions	5	3	4.2	53	-	22,792	-	978	-	-
6060	Credit unions	8	7	9.6	82	-	20,976	-	1,514	-	-
6100	Nondepository institutions	9	5	3.2	72	-	30,111	-	1,537	-	-
6200	Security and commodity brokers	7	6	5.3	-	13	-	34,154	-	406	0.5
6280	Security and commodity services	4	5	7.5	10	-	60,800	-	619	-	-
6300	Insurance carriers	10	9	5.7	132	52	18,333	51,769	2,362	2,498	0.9
6400	Insurance agents, brokers, and service	25	28	6.9	134	151	31,343	30,543	5,203	5,834	8.1
6500	Real estate	85	95	12.5	225	200	16,018	18,160	4,625	5,097	6.0
6510	Real estate operators and lessors	28	31	10.3	107	-	15,850	-	1,899	-	-
6530	Real estate agents and managers	34	49	12.9	73	104	18,411	15,308	1,849	2,439	6.2
6552	Subdividers and developers, n.e.c.	2	5	16.7	-	7	-	16,571	-	805	17.8
6553	Cemetery subdividers and developers	5	5	14.3	16	16	13,000	12,250	252	249	6.9
6733	Trusts, n.e.c.	5	3	13.0	-	3	-	9,333	-	32	-

Source: County Business Patterns, 1992/93, CBP-92/93-1, U.S. Department of Commerce, Washington, D.C., April 1995. SIC categories for which data were suppressed or not available for both 1992 and 1993 are *not* displayed. The employment columns represent mid-March employment in the year. Pay per employee is calculated by dividing 1st Quarter payroll, annualized, by mid-March employment. The columns headed "% State" show the county's percentage of the state total for the SIC in 1993; for example, 0.9% for SIC 6030 means that the county had 0.9 percent of the state's total establishments (or payroll) in SIC 6030 in 1993. A dash (-) is used to indicate that data are not available or cannot be calculated; *nec* means not elsewhere classified.

SOUTH CAROLINA

SIC	Industry	No. Establishments			Employment		Pay / Employee		Annual Payroll ($ 000)		
		1992	1993	% State	1992	1993	1992	1993	1992	1993	% State
ABBEVILLE, SC											
60 –	**Finance, insurance, and real estate**	32	30	0.4	170	142	15,765	17,127	3,200	2,443	0.2
6000	Depository institutions	13	13	0.9	105	101	16,686	16,713	1,718	1,697	0.4
6020	Commercial banks	7	8	0.8	69	66	16,000	16,242	1,107	1,076	0.3
6100	Nondepository institutions	7	7	0.6	16	20	17,250	15,200	284	325	0.2
6140	Personal credit institutions	7	7	0.8	16	20	17,250	15,200	284	325	0.4
6500	Real estate	4	3	0.1	30	-	9,733	-	285	-	-
AIKEN, SC											
60 –	**Finance, insurance, and real estate**	206	222	3.0	1,214	1,239	20,946	22,883	26,706	29,025	1.8
6000	Depository institutions	48	50	3.4	667	614	19,106	22,599	13,147	13,529	2.8
6020	Commercial banks	27	27	2.9	260	257	19,062	20,311	4,926	4,868	1.5
6100	Nondepository institutions	30	31	2.6	96	127	22,042	18,772	2,332	2,868	1.5
6140	Personal credit institutions	23	21	2.3	74	92	19,946	14,391	1,469	1,483	1.8
6200	Security and commodity brokers	4	5	1.9	15	-	40,267	-	726	-	-
6300	Insurance carriers	19	18	3.3	127	129	34,898	36,930	4,491	5,115	1.3
6310	Life insurance	7	6	2.5	-	117	-	29,504	-	3,565	2.1
6400	Insurance agents, brokers, and service	35	40	2.8	125	134	20,832	24,866	3,141	3,400	1.7
6500	Real estate	67	73	3.1	182	198	15,912	11,677	2,833	2,549	1.0
6510	Real estate operators and lessors	17	23	3.1	37	62	18,162	8,903	735	572	1.1
6530	Real estate agents and managers	33	41	3.1	107	99	15,290	12,687	1,560	1,360	0.9
6552	Subdividers and developers, n.e.c.	9	5	4.0	17	13	15,059	13,231	271	229	0.8
6553	Cemetery subdividers and developers	3	4	4.3	-	24	-	13,833	-	388	3.2
6700	Holding and other investment offices	3	4	2.1	2	-	16,000	-	36	-	-
ALLENDALE, SC											
60 –	**Finance, insurance, and real estate**	12	10	0.1	-	-	-	-	-	-	-
6100	Nondepository institutions	3	3	0.3	-	14	-	23,429	-	305	0.2
ANDERSON, SC											
60 –	**Finance, insurance, and real estate**	248	264	3.6	1,484	1,493	20,884	21,149	31,777	34,245	2.1
6000	Depository institutions	53	53	3.6	645	643	20,081	20,890	13,318	13,864	2.9
6020	Commercial banks	32	32	3.4	429	407	20,065	21,572	8,784	8,731	2.7
6030	Savings institutions	16	16	5.0	194	215	20,351	19,777	4,166	4,697	4.2
6060	Credit unions	4	5	2.8	-	21	-	19,048	-	436	1.2
6100	Nondepository institutions	50	58	4.9	177	194	21,559	19,938	4,096	4,326	2.3
6140	Personal credit institutions	42	48	5.2	152	162	20,500	19,086	3,317	3,421	4.1
6200	Security and commodity brokers	8	10	3.8	27	65	53,481	27,200	1,387	2,484	2.7
6300	Insurance carriers	14	12	2.2	174	180	29,747	33,400	4,861	5,999	1.6
6310	Life insurance	7	6	2.5	161	162	26,186	29,481	4,017	4,832	2.9
6400	Insurance agents, brokers, and service	46	52	3.7	179	169	20,291	21,373	3,843	4,062	2.1
6500	Real estate	70	73	3.1	252	227	11,524	11,013	3,166	3,048	1.2
6510	Real estate operators and lessors	20	22	2.9	44	57	10,000	8,772	607	770	1.4
6530	Real estate agents and managers	30	35	2.7	130	99	11,938	11,838	1,541	1,319	0.9
6540	Title abstract offices	6	5	12.8	15	13	13,600	14,154	220	210	8.8
6552	Subdividers and developers, n.e.c.	4	6	4.8	16	20	11,000	11,800	166	285	1.0
6553	Cemetery subdividers and developers	4	5	5.4	32	38	12,250	10,737	465	464	3.9
6710	Holding offices	4	3	4.6	23	-	41,043	-	946	-	-

Source: County Business Patterns, 1992/93, CBP-92/93-1, U.S. Department of Commerce, Washington, D.C., April 1995. SIC categories for which data were suppressed or not available for both 1992 and 1993 are *not* displayed. The employment columns represent mid-March employment in the year. Pay per employee is calculated by dividing 1st Quarter payroll, annualized, by mid-March employment. The columns headed "% State" show the county's percentage of the state total for the SIC in 1993; for example, 0.9% for SIC 6030 means that the county had 0.9 percent of the state's total establishments (or payroll) in SIC 6030 in 1993. A dash (-) is used to indicate that data are not available or cannot be calculated; *nec* means not elsewhere classified.

Finance, Insurance, and Real Estate U.S.A., 3rd Edition

SIC	Industry	No. Establishments			Employment		Pay / Employee		Annual Payroll ($ 000)		
		1992	1993	% State	1992	1993	1992	1993	1992	1993	% State
BAMBERG, SC											
60 –	**Finance, insurance, and real estate**	26	24	*0.3*	104	109	19,885	17,761	2,176	2,088	*0.1*
6000	Depository institutions	9	9	*0.6*	64	69	21,750	18,377	1,453	1,349	*0.3*
6100	Nondepository institutions	6	5	*0.4*	15	14	22,400	22,000	300	290	*0.2*
6400	Insurance agents, brokers, and service	3	4	*0.3*	14	21	14,286	13,905	280	355	*0.2*
6510	Real estate operators and lessors	3	3	*0.4*	4	-	10,000	-	43	-	-
BARNWELL, SC											
60 –	**Finance, insurance, and real estate**	25	29	*0.4*	128	140	15,438	15,943	2,085	2,227	*0.1*
6000	Depository institutions	9	12	*0.8*	80	88	18,050	19,091	1,444	1,505	*0.3*
6100	Nondepository institutions	6	6	*0.5*	21	21	8,952	8,571	168	200	*0.1*
6140	Personal credit institutions	6	6	*0.7*	21	21	8,952	8,571	168	200	*0.2*
6400	Insurance agents, brokers, and service	2	4	*0.3*	-	17	-	16,706	-	423	*0.2*
6500	Real estate	7	7	*0.3*	13	14	6,769	6,286	94	99	*0.0*
6530	Real estate agents and managers	4	3	*0.2*	10	8	7,600	8,500	76	68	*0.0*
BEAUFORT, SC											
60 –	**Finance, insurance, and real estate**	337	341	*4.6*	2,545	2,858	24,484	26,127	66,530	77,379	*4.8*
6000	Depository institutions	42	46	*3.1*	515	546	24,186	22,579	12,745	12,169	*2.6*
6020	Commercial banks	25	28	*3.0*	354	406	22,836	22,985	8,100	8,939	*2.8*
6030	Savings institutions	13	14	*4.3*	-	101	-	23,208	-	2,437	*2.2*
6100	Nondepository institutions	27	26	*2.2*	99	101	18,586	22,337	2,171	2,993	*1.6*
6140	Personal credit institutions	16	14	*1.5*	72	68	17,500	20,235	1,409	1,526	*1.8*
6160	Mortgage bankers and brokers	8	11	*5.5*	18	-	22,000	-	520	-	-
6200	Security and commodity brokers	16	17	*6.5*	87	81	67,770	85,037	5,316	6,974	*7.7*
6210	Security brokers and dealers	12	13	*7.0*	76	72	66,368	90,389	4,796	6,672	*8.0*
6300	Insurance carriers	8	6	*1.1*	41	95	33,463	17,516	1,360	1,589	*0.4*
6310	Life insurance	4	5	*2.1*	37	-	33,189	-	1,246		
6400	Insurance agents, brokers, and service	33	33	*2.3*	204	177	26,490	26,350	5,688	5,301	*2.7*
6500	Real estate	201	202	*8.6*	1,526	1,782	20,018	20,884	33,112	41,761	*16.8*
6510	Real estate operators and lessors	35	44	*5.8*	194	108	16,495	15,741	2,232	2,200	*4.1*
6530	Real estate agents and managers	118	134	*10.3*	1,090	1,205	20,664	21,228	25,241	27,821	*18.5*
6540	Title abstract offices	4	5	*12.8*	19	18	20,842	22,667	444	478	*20.1*
6552	Subdividers and developers, n.e.c.	14	15	*11.9*	168	449	20,452	21,158	4,002	11,007	*37.4*
6700	Holding and other investment offices	10	11	*5.8*	73	76	65,699	127,053	6,138	6,592	*15.1*
6710	Holding offices	4	4	*6.2*	61	58	72,918	153,379	5,738	5,944	*17.3*
BERKELEY, SC											
60 –	**Finance, insurance, and real estate**	92	101	*1.4*	376	507	17,872	19,006	6,914	10,329	*0.6*
6000	Depository institutions	16	18	*1.2*	143	149	19,385	17,691	2,686	2,709	*0.6*
6020	Commercial banks	7	7	*0.7*	78	84	19,282	18,429	1,491	1,555	*0.5*
6030	Savings institutions	5	5	*1.6*	37	32	17,730	16,250	607	537	*0.5*
6060	Credit unions	4	6	*3.4*	28	33	21,857	17,212	588	617	*1.7*
6100	Nondepository institutions	20	22	*1.9*	66	81	21,879	23,111	1,507	1,931	*1.0*
6140	Personal credit institutions	20	19	*2.1*	66	-	21,879	-	1,507	-	-
6400	Insurance agents, brokers, and service	17	18	*1.3*	73	77	16,658	17,922	1,302	1,434	*0.7*
6500	Real estate	34	36	*1.5*	86	96	11,767	13,000	1,067	1,397	*0.6*
6510	Real estate operators and lessors	16	17	*2.3*	49	50	12,000	13,120	628	740	*1.4*
6530	Real estate agents and managers	11	15	*1.2*	23	-	10,087	-	271	-	-
CALHOUN, SC											
60 –	**Finance, insurance, and real estate**	12	14	*0.2*	-	-	-	-	-	-	-
6000	Depository institutions	3	3	*0.2*	21	-	19,238	-	412	-	-
6100	Nondepository institutions	3	3	*0.3*	8	-	22,000	-	156	-	-
6500	Real estate	3	4	*0.2*	6	5	10,000	13,600	65	69	*0.0*
6510	Real estate operators and lessors	3	4	*0.5*	6	5	10,000	13,600	65	69	*0.1*

Source: County Business Patterns, 1992/93, CBP-92/93-1, U.S. Department of Commerce, Washington, D.C., April 1995. SIC categories for which data were suppressed or not available for both 1992 and 1993 are *not* displayed. The employment columns represent mid-March employment in the year. Pay per employee is calculated by dividing 1st Quarter payroll, annualized, by mid-March employment. The columns headed "% State" show the county's percentage of the state total for the SIC in 1993; for example, 0.9% for SIC 6030 means that the county had 0.9 percent of the state's total establishments (or payroll) in SIC 6030 in 1993. A dash (-) is used to indicate that data are not available or cannot be calculated; *nec* means not elsewhere classified.

SIC	Industry	No. Establishments			Employment		Pay / Employee		Annual Payroll ($ 000)		
		1992	1993	% State	1992	1993	1992	1993	1992	1993	% State
CHARLESTON, SC											
60 –	**Finance, insurance, and real estate**	864	859	*11.6*	7,249	6,948	22,534	23,497	168,386	178,737	*11.0*
6000	Depository institutions	138	152	*10.2*	2,148	2,036	23,562	22,479	50,222	46,026	*9.7*
6020	Commercial banks	64	81	*8.6*	1,087	1,097	22,764	23,938	24,155	24,335	*7.5*
6030	Savings institutions	43	36	*11.2*	676	541	23,905	22,159	16,815	13,081	*11.7*
6060	Credit unions	25	23	*12.8*	368	352	25,783	19,875	8,890	7,983	*21.9*
6090	Functions closely related to banking	6	12	*33.3*	17	46	12,941	11,391	362	627	–
6100	Nondepository institutions	112	106	*8.9*	564	754	26,901	24,562	16,243	21,820	*11.8*
6140	Personal credit institutions	78	73	*8.0*	382	448	24,545	19,759	9,293	9,030	*10.8*
6150	Business credit institutions	2	6	*13.6*	-	22	-	42,364	-	827	–
6160	Mortgage bankers and brokers	30	27	*13.5*	148	284	27,892	30,761	5,642	11,963	*15.3*
6200	Security and commodity brokers	33	32	*12.3*	204	211	59,824	56,019	11,897	16,519	*18.2*
6210	Security brokers and dealers	20	19	*10.2*	179	189	61,453	55,661	10,709	15,011	*18.0*
6280	Security and commodity services	13	13	*18.8*	25	22	48,160	59,091	1,188	1,508	*21.7*
6300	Insurance carriers	62	52	*9.7*	1,318	1,405	25,958	28,575	33,421	40,354	*10.7*
6310	Life insurance	38	29	*12.2*	780	801	23,241	21,618	17,767	16,460	*9.7*
6330	Fire, marine, and casualty insurance	17	17	*8.6*	505	484	30,574	41,289	14,918	20,179	*23.2*
6400	Insurance agents, brokers, and service	143	145	*10.2*	750	810	22,555	22,089	17,774	19,963	*10.2*
6500	Real estate	342	338	*14.4*	2,155	1,628	14,838	16,327	36,242	31,235	*12.6*
6510	Real estate operators and lessors	99	106	*14.1*	540	594	14,296	14,323	8,134	10,224	*19.1*
6530	Real estate agents and managers	175	199	*15.3*	1,309	894	14,442	17,566	22,770	18,111	*12.1*
6540	Title abstract offices	5	5	*12.8*	9	15	18,222	18,667	201	309	*13.0*
6552	Subdividers and developers, n.e.c.	20	18	*14.3*	122	78	14,721	20,308	1,939	1,775	*6.0*
6553	Cemetery subdividers and developers	6	6	*6.5*	51	45	9,412	10,756	535	549	*4.6*
6700	Holding and other investment offices	34	34	*17.8*	110	104	20,509	24,346	2,587	2,820	*6.4*
6710	Holding offices	7	9	*13.8*	38	44	26,632	25,273	1,012	1,131	*3.3*
6720	Investment offices	4	3	*60.0*	7	8	18,286	23,500	147	219	–
6732	Educational, religious, etc. trusts	6	8	*21.6*	28	23	17,429	21,217	502	607	–
6733	Trusts, n.e.c.	5	4	*10.8*	24	17	12,833	25,882	420	515	*25.4*
.6799	Investors, n.e.c.	4	6	*18.8*	6	–	8,000	–	59	–	–
CHEROKEE, SC											
60 –	**Finance, insurance, and real estate**	56	58	*0.8*	310	297	20,877	20,337	6,440	6,305	*0.4*
6000	Depository institutions	9	11	*0.7*	157	147	19,312	20,517	2,940	2,934	*0.6*
6100	Nondepository institutions	14	13	*1.1*	53	65	17,208	14,892	987	1,059	*0.6*
6140	Personal credit institutions	13	13	*1.4*	-	65	-	14,892	-	1,059	*1.3*
6300	Insurance carriers	7	8	*1.5*	-	24	-	33,333	-	835	*0.2*
6400	Insurance agents, brokers, and service	12	12	*0.8*	30	30	24,800	23,200	795	868	*0.4*
6500	Real estate	12	11	*0.5*	28	-	15,286	-	363	-	–
6510	Real estate operators and lessors	5	5	*0.7*	-	13	-	6,462	-	114	*0.2*
6530	Real estate agents and managers	5	5	*0.4*	9	8	13,333	10,500	162	132	*0.1*
CHESTER, SC											
60 –	**Finance, insurance, and real estate**	33	36	*0.5*	164	189	20,390	19,556	3,419	3,661	*0.2*
6000	Depository institutions	11	11	*0.7*	94	95	21,787	21,221	2,009	1,993	*0.4*
6020	Commercial banks	6	6	*0.6*	40	42	21,200	19,524	842	800	*0.2*
6100	Nondepository institutions	6	6	*0.5*	23	24	16,348	15,667	358	382	*0.2*
6140	Personal credit institutions	6	6	*0.7*	23	24	16,348	15,667	358	382	*0.5*
6300	Insurance carriers	3	4	*0.7*	7	-	21,143	-	190	-	–
6330	Fire, marine, and casualty insurance	3	2	*1.0*	7	-	21,143	-	190	-	–
6400	Insurance agents, brokers, and service	9	8	*0.6*	34	27	21,412	23,556	810	613	*0.3*
6500	Real estate	4	6	*0.3*	6	8	7,333	9,500	52	88	*0.0*
CHESTERFIELD, SC											
60 –	**Finance, insurance, and real estate**	48	46	*0.6*	243	232	20,247	18,431	5,122	4,531	*0.3*
6000	Depository institutions	13	13	*0.9*	115	122	19,235	17,869	2,209	2,237	*0.5*
6100	Nondepository institutions	13	11	*0.9*	35	34	19,200	18,000	716	626	*0.3*

Source: County Business Patterns, 1992/93, CBP-92/93-1, U.S. Department of Commerce, Washington, D.C., April 1995. SIC categories for which data were suppressed or not available for both 1992 and 1993 are not displayed. The employment columns represent mid-March employment in the year. Pay per employee is calculated by dividing 1st Quarter payroll, annualized, by mid-March employment. The columns headed "% State" show the county's percentage of the state total for the SIC in 1993; for example, 0.9% for SIC 6030 means that the county had 0.9 percent of the state's total establishments (or payroll) in SIC 6030 in 1993. A dash (-) is used to indicate that data are not available or cannot be calculated; nec means not elsewhere classified.

Continued on next page.

SIC	Industry	No. Establishments			Employment		Pay / Employee		Annual Payroll ($ 000)		
		1992	1993	% State	1992	1993	1992	1993	1992	1993	% State
CHESTERFIELD, SC - [continued]											
6400	Insurance agents, brokers, and service	12	11	0.8	32	-	19,875	-	773	-	-
6500	Real estate	6	7	0.3	-	14	-	10,286	-	154	0.1
6510	Real estate operators and lessors	3	4	0.5	6	7	10,000	13,714	64	96	0.2
CLARENDON, SC											
60 –	**Finance, insurance, and real estate**	36	36	0.5	188	191	18,638	20,712	3,909	4,072	0.3
6000	Depository institutions	5	5	0.3	82	82	16,390	18,829	1,592	1,636	0.3
6100	Nondepository institutions	16	16	1.3	44	44	17,455	17,545	771	795	0.4
6140	Personal credit institutions	16	15	1.6	44	-	17,455	-	771	-	-
6300	Insurance carriers	3	2	0.4	26	-	34,615	-	975	-	-
6400	Insurance agents, brokers, and service	5	6	0.4	20	-	17,200	-	374	-	-
6500	Real estate	7	7	0.3	16	18	9,250	10,667	197	200	0.1
6530	Real estate agents and managers	3	2	0.2	11	-	8,727	-	140	-	-
COLLETON, SC											
60 –	**Finance, insurance, and real estate**	64	75	1.0	410	595	21,512	15,886	8,522	9,934	0.6
6000	Depository institutions	12	13	0.9	126	274	21,238	8,219	2,739	2,371	0.5
6020	Commercial banks	9	10	1.1	96	91	20,292	18,154	1,991	1,693	0.5
6100	Nondepository institutions	16	16	1.3	61	62	21,639	23,161	1,328	1,447	0.8
6140	Personal credit institutions	15	13	1.4	-	47	-	19,404	-	975	1.2
6300	Insurance carriers	4	5	0.9	100	103	29,480	32,233	2,117	3,464	0.9
6310	Life insurance	4	5	2.1	100	103	29,480	32,233	2,117	3,464	2.0
6400	Insurance agents, brokers, and service	13	12	0.8	40	-	17,900	-	779	-	-
6500	Real estate	19	27	1.2	83	120	13,976	14,800	1,559	1,914	0.8
6510	Real estate operators and lessors	4	8	1.1	4	19	8,000	7,579	42	201	0.4
6530	Real estate agents and managers	8	14	1.1	63	90	15,492	16,844	1,341	1,569	1.0
DARLINGTON, SC											
60 –	**Finance, insurance, and real estate**	94	90	1.2	545	449	18,738	19,955	10,331	8,893	0.5
6000	Depository institutions	28	28	1.9	261	250	21,027	22,736	5,558	5,441	1.1
6020	Commercial banks	17	18	1.9	172	169	19,698	20,970	3,568	3,441	1.1
6100	Nondepository institutions	16	13	1.1	50	43	17,600	17,023	878	760	0.4
6300	Insurance carriers	6	6	1.1	65	43	24,185	23,907	1,509	927	0.2
6400	Insurance agents, brokers, and service	19	20	1.4	68	65	13,412	15,015	946	1,023	0.5
6500	Real estate	21	20	0.9	91	40	10,505	7,700	1,029	365	0.1
6510	Real estate operators and lessors	8	10	1.3	21	19	6,286	7,368	142	173	0.3
6530	Real estate agents and managers	7	7	0.5	11	16	17,091	8,250	134	151	0.1
6553	Cemetery subdividers and developers	3	3	3.2	5	5	7,200	7,200	35	41	0.3
DILLON, SC											
60 –	**Finance, insurance, and real estate**	43	45	0.6	286	220	14,364	19,527	4,347	4,542	0.3
6000	Depository institutions	8	7	0.5	74	65	20,649	21,600	1,505	1,383	0.3
6020	Commercial banks	8	7	0.7	74	65	20,649	21,600	1,505	1,383	0.4
6100	Nondepository institutions	10	9	0.8	25	-	17,280	-	421	-	-
6140	Personal credit institutions	10	9	1.0	25	-	17,280	-	421	-	-
6400	Insurance agents, brokers, and service	9	11	0.8	39	-	16,615	-	840	-	-
6510	Real estate operators and lessors	8	10	1.3	19	19	5,895	8,421	151	164	0.3
6530	Real estate agents and managers	4	5	0.4	4	6	8,000	6,667	42	48	0.0
DORCHESTER, SC											
60 –	**Finance, insurance, and real estate**	127	130	1.7	563	629	19,055	17,615	10,946	11,473	0.7
6000	Depository institutions	31	32	2.2	252	257	18,508	17,261	4,604	4,679	1.0
6020	Commercial banks	19	20	2.1	175	179	18,423	17,765	3,150	3,217	1.0
6030	Savings institutions	8	8	2.5	46	48	15,826	14,583	800	867	0.8
6060	Credit unions	4	4	2.2	31	30	22,968	18,533	654	595	1.6
6100	Nondepository institutions	21	21	1.8	72	103	25,778	17,126	1,691	1,997	1.1
6140	Personal credit institutions	17	17	1.9	-	91	-	16,484	-	1,584	1.9
6160	Mortgage bankers and brokers	3	3	1.5	1	-	20,000	-	22	-	-

Source: County Business Patterns, 1992/93, CBP-92/93-1, U.S. Department of Commerce, Washington, D.C., April 1995. SIC categories for which data were suppressed or not available for both 1992 and 1993 are *not* displayed. The employment columns represent mid-March employment in the year. Pay per employee is calculated by dividing 1st Quarter payroll, annualized, by mid-March employment. The columns headed "% State" show the county's percentage of the state total for the SIC in 1993; for example, 0.9% for SIC 6030 means that the county had 0.9 percent of the state's total establishments (or payroll) in SIC 6030 in 1993. A dash (-) is used to indicate that data are not available or cannot be calculated; *nec* means not elsewhere classified.

Continued on next page.

SIC	Industry	No. Establishments			Employment		Pay / Employee		Annual Payroll ($ 000)		
		1992	1993	% State	1992	1993	1992	1993	1992	1993	% State
DORCHESTER, SC - [continued]											
6200	Security and commodity brokers	4	5	1.9	9	8	7,111	9,000	77	103	0.1
6300	Insurance carriers	5	5	0.9	14	-	26,571	-	411	-	-
6400	Insurance agents, brokers, and service	24	27	1.9	88	103	16,000	17,243	1,403	1,751	0.9
6500	Real estate	39	37	1.6	122	139	16,262	16,029	2,428	2,233	0.9
6510	Real estate operators and lessors	14	14	1.9	-	53	-	9,660	-	513	1.0
6530	Real estate agents and managers	18	19	1.5	29	-	14,069	-	509	-	-
6700	Holding and other investment offices	3	3	1.6	6	-	63,333	-	332	-	-
EDGEFIELD, SC											
60 –	**Finance, insurance, and real estate**	28	26	0.3	95	-	17,389	-	1,655	-	-
6000	Depository institutions	8	7	0.5	49	-	20,735	-	1,025	-	-
6100	Nondepository institutions	5	5	0.4	8	9	11,000	11,111	97	109	0.1
6400	Insurance agents, brokers, and service	6	5	0.4	15	13	17,067	16,308	274	263	0.1
6500	Real estate	9	9	0.4	23	25	12,696	9,120	259	257	0.1
6510	Real estate operators and lessors	3	4	0.5	3	10	10,667	7,200	18	94	0.2
6530	Real estate agents and managers	3	5	0.4	7	15	9,714	10,400	69	163	0.1
FAIRFIELD, SC											
60 –	**Finance, insurance, and real estate**	23	24	0.3	96	96	19,500	18,875	1,994	1,889	0.1
6000	Depository institutions	7	7	0.5	61	61	19,410	19,934	1,283	1,226	0.3
6100	Nondepository institutions	5	5	0.4	17	15	24,941	23,200	386	344	0.2
6500	Real estate	3	4	0.2	4	4	18,000	10,000	64	45	0.0
FLORENCE, SC											
60 –	**Finance, insurance, and real estate**	260	269	3.6	3,222	3,742	19,476	18,696	62,289	69,771	4.3
6000	Depository institutions	47	49	3.3	613	626	21,005	20,728	12,981	13,452	2.8
6020	Commercial banks	30	31	3.3	483	485	21,549	21,171	10,378	10,538	3.3
6030	Savings institutions	5	5	1.6	65	74	20,246	19,622	1,484	1,640	1.5
6060	Credit unions	12	13	7.3	65	67	17,723	18,746	1,119	1,274	3.5
6100	Nondepository institutions	52	62	5.2	676	1,171	24,302	19,775	13,333	21,342	11.5
6140	Personal credit institutions	44	49	5.3	259	299	31,320	25,619	6,663	6,205	7.4
6210	Security brokers and dealers	4	6	3.2	-	30	-	88,000	-	2,549	3.1
6300	Insurance carriers	27	21	3.9	1,358	1,352	15,947	16,343	22,967	22,216	5.9
6310	Life insurance	13	13	5.5	228	-	25,614	-	5,875	-	-
6400	Insurance agents, brokers, and service	55	59	4.2	243	256	19,424	20,344	5,127	5,774	3.0
6500	Real estate	69	67	2.9	174	183	16,092	14,863	2,828	3,196	1.3
6510	Real estate operators and lessors	26	26	3.5	46	66	9,913	12,485	546	1,137	2.1
6530	Real estate agents and managers	29	35	2.7	62	79	20,129	17,266	992	1,444	1.0
6553	Cemetery subdividers and developers	4	4	4.3	26	-	6,154	-	406	-	-
GEORGETOWN, SC											
60 –	**Finance, insurance, and real estate**	110	109	1.5	766	695	18,768	19,672	14,911	14,101	0.9
6000	Depository institutions	28	27	1.8	227	245	20,952	21,110	4,879	4,811	1.0
6020	Commercial banks	14	14	1.5	121	135	19,802	19,615	2,543	2,459	0.8
6100	Nondepository institutions	15	17	1.4	-	50	-	16,880	-	869	0.5
6210	Security brokers and dealers	4	4	2.1	17	-	57,176	-	1,010	-	-
6300	Insurance carriers	8	6	1.1	44	-	27,818	-	1,138	-	-
6310	Life insurance	3	3	1.3	33	-	28,727	-	867	-	-
6330	Fire, marine, and casualty insurance	3	2	1.0	6	-	40,000	-	252	-	-
6400	Insurance agents, brokers, and service	11	11	0.8	42	43	21,333	23,535	1,021	1,207	0.6
6500	Real estate	41	41	1.7	325	285	14,412	14,147	4,866	4,331	1.7
6510	Real estate operators and lessors	11	11	1.5	35	40	10,857	9,900	490	587	1.1
6530	Real estate agents and managers	22	24	1.8	180	168	14,822	14,929	3,002	2,714	1.8
GREENVILLE, SC											
60 –	**Finance, insurance, and real estate**	830	886	11.9	11,452	11,449	24,505	24,905	291,376	289,398	17.8
6000	Depository institutions	142	157	10.6	2,765	2,672	24,220	26,403	66,830	69,089	14.5
6020	Commercial banks	89	104	11.0	1,395	1,389	25,459	28,570	35,709	37,452	11.6

Source: County Business Patterns, 1992/93, CBP-92/93-1, U.S. Department of Commerce, Washington, D.C., April 1995. SIC categories for which data were suppressed or not available for both 1992 and 1993 are not displayed. The employment columns represent mid-March employment in the year. Pay per employee is calculated by dividing 1st Quarter payroll, annualized, by mid-March employment. The columns headed "% State" show the county's percentage of the state total for the SIC in 1993; for example, 0.9% for SIC 6030 means that the county had 0.9 percent of the state's total establishments (or payroll) in SIC 6030 in 1993. A dash (-) is used to indicate that data are not available or cannot be calculated; nec means not elsewhere classified.

Continued on next page.

SIC	Industry	No. Establishments			Employment		Pay / Employee		Annual Payroll ($ 000)		
		1992	1993	% State	1992	1993	1992	1993	1992	1993	% State
GREENVILLE, SC - [continued]											
6030	Savings institutions	33	34	10.6	1,252	1,169	23,125	24,270	28,688	29,080	26.1
6060	Credit unions	16	16	8.9	102	100	21,647	22,120	2,110	2,225	6.1
6090	Functions closely related to banking	4	3	8.3	16	14	18,250	20,000	323	332	-
6100	Nondepository institutions	122	128	10.8	652	705	25,313	22,894	16,634	18,803	10.1
6140	Personal credit institutions	92	92	10.0	459	494	23,930	20,283	10,995	11,476	13.7
6150	Business credit institutions	7	8	18.2	42	54	26,095	27,111	1,030	1,659	-
6160	Mortgage bankers and brokers	22	28	14.0	150	157	29,387	29,656	4,593	5,668	7.3
6200	Security and commodity brokers	39	45	17.3	257	340	52,374	55,200	13,639	17,328	19.1
6210	Security brokers and dealers	27	30	16.0	228	276	55,579	62,043	12,563	15,840	19.0
6300	Insurance carriers	92	92	17.1	3,414	3,275	27,704	28,601	95,071	90,513	23.9
6310	Life insurance	40	40	16.8	2,661	2,582	26,868	27,478	70,563	66,483	39.3
6330	Fire, marine, and casualty insurance	38	38	19.2	581	577	31,339	34,267	19,448	21,255	24.4
6350	Surety insurance	3	2	28.6	9	-	19,111	-	188	-	-
6400	Insurance agents, brokers, and service	175	191	13.5	990	1,201	25,636	30,871	28,109	39,118	20.0
6500	Real estate	222	243	10.4	1,020	2,687	19,118	11,402	21,479	31,686	12.7
6510	Real estate operators and lessors	75	86	11.4	415	1,781	15,335	6,509	7,538	10,975	20.5
6530	Real estate agents and managers	92	129	9.9	379	735	20,686	22,732	8,593	18,038	12.0
6552	Subdividers and developers, n.e.c.	14	12	9.5	50	26	28,080	23,231	1,794	704	2.4
6553	Cemetery subdividers and developers	7	8	8.6	73	142	15,068	11,944	1,008	1,771	14.7
6700	Holding and other investment offices	33	25	13.1	2,320	529	17,728	29,671	47,191	19,735	45.1
6710	Holding offices	10	12	18.5	2,257	487	17,714	30,752	45,853	18,938	55.1
6733	Trusts, n.e.c.	10	7	18.9	-	35	-	6,857	-	264	13.0
GREENWOOD, SC											
60 –	**Finance, insurance, and real estate**	142	143	1.9	1,081	873	23,323	23,212	26,565	22,072	1.4
6000	Depository institutions	35	33	2.2	345	347	21,113	22,190	7,524	8,162	1.7
6020	Commercial banks	23	20	2.1	235	227	21,736	22,907	5,133	5,125	1.6
6100	Nondepository institutions	28	27	2.3	108	106	21,704	18,717	2,329	1,985	1.1
6140	Personal credit institutions	25	23	2.5	101	97	21,743	18,639	2,179	1,811	2.2
6200	Security and commodity brokers	7	7	2.7	31	28	73,290	71,000	2,507	2,289	2.5
6300	Insurance carriers	12	12	2.2	130	141	29,415	28,142	3,681	3,880	1.0
6400	Insurance agents, brokers, and service	23	20	1.4	93	74	21,978	25,189	2,691	1,991	1.0
6500	Real estate	33	39	1.7	370	172	19,481	14,558	7,484	3,053	1.2
6510	Real estate operators and lessors	10	13	1.7	-	75	-	10,933	-	993	1.9
6530	Real estate agents and managers	13	21	1.6	58	85	16,690	18,071	1,045	1,857	1.2
6553	Cemetery subdividers and developers	3	4	4.3	-	12	-	12,333	-	172	1.4
6700	Holding and other investment offices	4	5	2.6	4	5	59,000	51,200	349	712	1.6
HAMPTON, SC											
60 –	**Finance, insurance, and real estate**	21	22	0.3	159	166	15,648	16,289	2,703	2,834	0.2
6000	Depository institutions	8	8	0.5	109	124	17,615	17,581	2,101	2,215	0.5
6100	Nondepository institutions	3	4	0.3	8	8	12,000	14,000	89	149	0.1
6140	Personal credit institutions	3	4	0.4	8	8	12,000	14,000	89	149	0.2
6400	Insurance agents, brokers, and service	4	5	0.4	25	22	11,040	12,545	304	320	0.2
6500	Real estate	5	5	0.2	-	12	-	11,333	-	150	0.1
HORRY, SC											
60 –	**Finance, insurance, and real estate**	500	546	7.3	5,067	4,635	16,686	17,980	94,024	94,459	5.8
6000	Depository institutions	72	77	5.2	1,076	1,097	21,320	21,098	23,410	24,303	5.1
6020	Commercial banks	49	54	5.7	733	746	21,512	21,416	15,761	16,480	5.1
6100	Nondepository institutions	30	43	3.6	110	150	23,345	22,053	2,712	3,874	2.1
6140	Personal credit institutions	22	29	3.2	78	107	20,205	16,299	1,649	1,882	2.2
6200	Security and commodity brokers	16	19	7.3	66	73	47,515	45,425	2,896	3,968	4.4
6300	Insurance carriers	22	24	4.5	197	221	28,914	25,810	6,015	4,974	1.3
6310	Life insurance	7	7	2.9	164	137	25,756	28,350	4,414	3,646	2.2
6400	Insurance agents, brokers, and service	66	77	5.4	306	338	22,693	23,822	7,539	9,527	4.9
6500	Real estate	283	295	12.6	3,273	2,709	13,007	14,450	50,718	46,898	18.9
6510	Real estate operators and lessors	51	64	8.5	367	338	14,485	19,195	6,249	8,170	15.3

Source: County Business Patterns, 1992/93, CBP-92/93-1, U.S. Department of Commerce, Washington, D.C., April 1995. SIC categories for which data were suppressed or not available for both 1992 and 1993 are not displayed. The employment columns represent mid-March employment in the year. Pay per employee is calculated by dividing 1st Quarter payroll, annualized, by mid-March employment. The columns headed "% State" show the county's percentage of the state total for the SIC in 1993; for example, 0.9% for SIC 6030 means that the county had 0.9 percent of the state's total establishments (or payroll) in SIC 6030 in 1993. A dash (-) is used to indicate that data are not available or cannot be calculated; nec means not elsewhere classified.

Continued on next page.

SIC	Industry	No. Establishments			Employment		Pay / Employee		Annual Payroll ($ 000)		
		1992	1993	% State	1992	1993	1992	1993	1992	1993	% State
HORRY, SC - [continued]											
6530	Real estate agents and managers	164	210	16.1	1,954	2,219	13,617	13,067	30,547	34,353	22.9
6552	Subdividers and developers, n.e.c.	10	13	10.3	660	139	10,048	23,741	8,809	3,954	13.5
6700	Holding and other investment offices	11	11	5.8	39	47	17,744	14,213	734	915	2.1
6732	Educational, religious, etc. trusts	4	4	10.8	-	15	-	9,067	-	137	-
6733	Trusts, n.e.c.	2	3	8.1	-	1	-	20,000	-	61	3.0
JASPER, SC											
60 –	**Finance, insurance, and real estate**	21	21	0.3	315	325	13,651	15,323	5,097	5,223	0.3
6000	Depository institutions	5	5	0.3	34	33	18,824	18,545	688	527	0.1
6100	Nondepository institutions	4	4	0.3	15	13	11,733	16,000	183	209	0.1
6140	Personal credit institutions	4	4	0.4	15	13	11,733	16,000	183	209	0.2
6400	Insurance agents, brokers, and service	5	5	0.4	15	-	8,267	-	135	-	-
KERSHAW, SC											
60 –	**Finance, insurance, and real estate**	78	80	1.1	471	520	17,834	18,438	9,040	9,989	0.6
6000	Depository institutions	18	22	1.5	163	193	19,902	21,658	3,572	4,154	0.9
6020	Commercial banks	9	11	1.2	68	90	22,824	20,356	1,575	1,679	0.5
6100	Nondepository institutions	16	17	1.4	53	65	19,019	16,985	1,084	1,192	0.6
6140	Personal credit institutions	13	14	1.5	43	-	18,977	-	885	-	-
6500	Real estate	18	19	0.8	-	34	-	10,588	-	499	0.2
6530	Real estate agents and managers	12	11	0.8	26	20	13,538	10,200	425	290	0.2
LANCASTER, SC											
60 –	**Finance, insurance, and real estate**	77	74	1.0	779	890	23,461	24,746	17,419	20,116	1.2
6000	Depository institutions	16	16	1.1	206	215	23,786	24,670	5,134	5,038	1.1
6020	Commercial banks	7	7	0.7	70	74	21,714	18,919	1,680	1,559	0.5
6100	Nondepository institutions	18	17	1.4	80	83	19,950	17,108	1,459	1,484	0.8
6300	Insurance carriers	4	4	0.7	26	-	29,385	-	722	-	-
6400	Insurance agents, brokers, and service	20	15	1.1	361	79	26,981	18,886	8,667	1,865	1.0
6500	Real estate	16	18	0.8	101	97	9,703	11,505	1,050	1,163	0.5
6510	Real estate operators and lessors	6	4	0.5	23	-	13,217	-	298	-	-
6530	Real estate agents and managers	5	11	0.8	67	72	7,343	10,722	558	759	0.5
LAURENS, SC											
60 –	**Finance, insurance, and real estate**	72	65	0.9	450	474	21,111	20,464	10,277	10,392	0.6
6000	Depository institutions	19	18	1.2	269	269	21,665	21,695	6,154	6,197	1.3
6020	Commercial banks	14	13	1.4	233	230	21,803	21,809	5,302	5,299	1.6
6100	Nondepository institutions	19	19	1.6	54	67	17,333	17,493	1,121	1,416	0.8
6140	Personal credit institutions	19	18	2.0	54	-	17,333	-	1,121	-	-
6300	Insurance carriers	3	3	0.6	61	73	23,738	19,945	1,643	1,445	0.4
6400	Insurance agents, brokers, and service	12	12	0.8	-	45	-	14,311	-	720	0.4
6500	Real estate	13	8	0.3	13	12	13,538	12,333	203	173	0.1
6510	Real estate operators and lessors	4	3	0.4	1	4	12,000	13,000	33	52	0.1
6700	Holding and other investment offices	4	3	1.6	8	-	11,500	-	43	-	-
LEE, SC											
60 –	**Finance, insurance, and real estate**	20	25	0.3	74	84	14,541	15,476	1,201	1,382	0.1
6000	Depository institutions	4	4	0.3	33	33	18,303	18,545	596	583	0.1
6020	Commercial banks	4	4	0.4	33	33	18,303	18,545	596	583	0.2
6100	Nondepository institutions	5	7	0.6	12	17	14,000	10,353	189	229	0.1
6140	Personal credit institutions	5	7	0.8	12	17	14,000	10,353	189	229	0.3
6400	Insurance agents, brokers, and service	6	7	0.5	20	25	13,400	18,400	383	501	0.3
6500	Real estate	5	7	0.3	9	9	4,000	5,778	33	69	0.0
LEXINGTON, SC											
60 –	**Finance, insurance, and real estate**	249	273	3.7	1,798	1,914	21,566	23,218	40,647	46,588	2.9
6000	Depository institutions	56	61	4.1	661	653	17,924	20,165	12,410	13,469	2.8
6020	Commercial banks	40	46	4.9	551	556	18,483	20,914	10,604	11,752	3.6

Source: County Business Patterns, 1992/93, CBP-92/93-1, U.S. Department of Commerce, Washington, D.C., April 1995. SIC categories for which data were suppressed or not available for both 1992 and 1993 are not displayed. The employment columns represent mid-March employment in the year. Pay per employee is calculated by dividing 1st Quarter payroll, annualized, by mid-March employment. The columns headed "% State" show the county's percentage of the state total for the SIC in 1993; for example, 0.9% for SIC 6030 means that the county had 0.9 percent of the state's total establishments (or payroll) in SIC 6030 in 1993. A dash (-) is used to indicate that data are not available or cannot be calculated; nec means not elsewhere classified.

Continued on next page.

SIC	Industry	No. Establishments			Employment		Pay / Employee		Annual Payroll ($ 000)		
		1992	1993	% State	1992	1993	1992	1993	1992	1993	% State
LEXINGTON, SC - [continued]											
6030	Savings institutions	11	10	3.1	90	77	13,867	14,390	1,437	1,333	1.2
6060	Credit unions	5	5	2.8	20	20	20,800	21,600	369	384	1.1
6100	Nondepository institutions	41	41	3.5	215	248	25,451	19,855	5,106	5,360	2.9
6140	Personal credit institutions	28	27	2.9	163	160	24,761	19,700	3,665	3,136	3.7
6200	Security and commodity brokers	4	9	3.5	-	28	-	31,857	-	608	0.7
6210	Security brokers and dealers	2	5	2.7	-	9	-	21,333	-	136	0.2
6280	Security and commodity services	2	4	5.8	-	19	-	36,842	-	472	6.8
6300	Insurance carriers	16	17	3.2	401	454	31,162	34,846	13,000	15,646	4.1
6330	Fire, marine, and casualty insurance	11	10	5.1	-	334	-	35,701	-	11,714	13.5
6400	Insurance agents, brokers, and service	61	63	4.4	186	215	18,882	19,665	4,104	5,174	2.6
6500	Real estate	66	78	3.3	284	308	16,324	16,740	5,354	6,068	2.4
6510	Real estate operators and lessors	23	30	4.0	71	128	11,042	19,094	808	2,795	5.2
6530	Real estate agents and managers	26	38	2.9	94	129	20,809	13,364	2,415	1,981	1.3
6540	Title abstract offices	2	3	7.7	-	11	-	22,545	-	309	13.0
6700	Holding and other investment offices	5	4	2.1	-	8	-	31,500	-	263	0.6
6710	Holding offices	3	1	1.5	44	-	9,000	-	441	-	-
MCCORMICK, SC											
60 –	**Finance, insurance, and real estate**	8	11	0.1	116	177	16,621	14,260	1,957	2,937	0.2
6020	Commercial banks	1	3	0.3	-	27	-	22,074	-	733	0.2
MARION, SC											
60 –	**Finance, insurance, and real estate**	49	52	0.7	310	349	19,523	19,862	6,249	6,940	0.4
6000	Depository institutions	13	12	0.8	177	177	19,503	19,254	3,326	3,260	0.7
6100	Nondepository institutions	14	16	1.3	54	64	18,148	17,812	1,047	1,313	0.7
6140	Personal credit institutions	14	16	1.7	54	64	18,148	17,812	1,047	1,313	1.6
6400	Insurance agents, brokers, and service	11	12	0.8	34	39	15,294	16,821	557	732	0.4
6500	Real estate	7	8	0.3	-	21	-	14,667	-	322	0.1
6530	Real estate agents and managers	3	4	0.3	10	11	12,000	14,545	134	166	0.1
MARLBORO, SC											
60 –	**Finance, insurance, and real estate**	35	38	0.5	179	170	18,190	20,282	3,332	3,684	0.2
6000	Depository institutions	7	8	0.5	56	55	18,571	19,927	1,042	1,123	0.2
6100	Nondepository institutions	9	9	0.8	26	29	19,231	17,379	498	502	0.3
6140	Personal credit institutions	9	9	1.0	26	29	19,231	17,379	498	502	0.6
6500	Real estate	8	9	0.4	17	22	8,706	8,545	150	201	0.1
6510	Real estate operators and lessors	4	6	0.8	7	19	9,714	7,158	70	145	0.3
NEWBERRY, SC											
60 –	**Finance, insurance, and real estate**	45	45	0.6	245	240	17,535	17,567	4,648	4,681	0.3
6000	Depository institutions	17	15	1.0	173	159	16,832	17,585	3,094	3,081	0.6
6100	Nondepository institutions	13	13	1.1	38	49	20,421	15,755	860	870	0.5
6400	Insurance agents, brokers, and service	8	8	0.6	18	18	15,333	17,778	321	325	0.2
6500	Real estate	3	4	0.2	5	-	10,400	-	62	-	-
OCONEE, SC											
60 –	**Finance, insurance, and real estate**	93	91	1.2	529	513	19,380	19,454	10,403	10,779	0.7
6000	Depository institutions	22	24	1.6	204	210	21,314	21,867	4,337	4,605	1.0
6020	Commercial banks	14	16	1.7	136	143	23,265	23,608	3,085	3,302	1.0
6100	Nondepository institutions	22	20	1.7	65	75	19,200	16,747	1,260	1,196	0.6
6400	Insurance agents, brokers, and service	17	17	1.2	54	51	17,481	15,922	842	836	0.4
6500	Real estate	25	24	1.0	154	135	16,753	15,822	2,684	2,857	1.1
6530	Real estate agents and managers	9	14	1.1	21	-	29,714	-	409	-	-
6552	Subdividers and developers, n.e.c.	5	4	3.2	6	-	4,667	-	42	-	-

Source: County Business Patterns, 1992/93, CBP-92/93-1, U.S. Department of Commerce, Washington, D.C., April 1995. SIC categories for which data were suppressed or not available for both 1992 and 1993 are *not* displayed. The employment columns represent mid-March employment in the year. Pay per employee is calculated by dividing 1st Quarter payroll, annualized, by mid-March employment. The columns headed "% State" show the county's percentage of the state total for the SIC in 1993; for example, 0.9% for SIC 6030 means that the county had 0.9 percent of the state's total establishments (or payroll) in SIC 6030 in 1993. A dash (-) is used to indicate that data are not available or cannot be calculated; *nec* means not elsewhere classified.

SIC	Industry	No. Establishments			Employment		Pay / Employee		Annual Payroll ($ 000)		
		1992	1993	% State	1992	1993	1992	1993	1992	1993	% State
ORANGEBURG, SC											
60 –	**Finance, insurance, and real estate**	146	148	*2.0*	950	923	19,444	19,567	19,269	19,617	*1.2*
6000	Depository institutions	35	32	*2.2*	499	446	18,429	19,946	9,435	9,418	*2.0*
6020	Commercial banks	27	25	*2.6*	439	398	18,588	19,970	8,362	8,354	*2.6*
6100	Nondepository institutions	34	35	*2.9*	138	149	22,087	18,658	2,866	2,892	*1.6*
6140	Personal credit institutions	30	32	*3.5*	110	124	17,200	14,419	1,878	2,009	*2.4*
6300	Insurance carriers	9	10	*1.9*	106	111	26,604	25,802	3,058	3,122	*0.8*
6400	Insurance agents, brokers, and service	31	28	*2.0*	111	105	20,360	20,952	2,624	2,623	*1.3*
6500	Real estate	32	37	*1.6*	89	104	11,326	10,615	1,133	1,329	*0.5*
6510	Real estate operators and lessors	13	14	*1.9*	20	28	10,400	10,286	250	311	*0.6*
6530	Real estate agents and managers	11	16	*1.2*	17	60	15,529	10,933	356	830	*0.6*
6553	Cemetery subdividers and developers	3	4	*4.3*	12	-	10,000	-	132	-	*-*
PICKENS, SC											
60 –	**Finance, insurance, and real estate**	130	137	*1.8*	798	790	20,872	19,959	17,796	16,841	*1.0*
6000	Depository institutions	30	35	*2.4*	329	345	19,283	19,119	6,832	6,801	*1.4*
6020	Commercial banks	17	22	*2.3*	217	231	20,129	19,481	4,717	4,510	*1.4*
6030	Savings institutions	10	10	*3.1*	102	101	18,196	18,970	1,960	2,104	*1.9*
6060	Credit unions	3	3	*1.7*	10	13	12,000	13,846	155	187	*0.5*
6100	Nondepository institutions	23	23	*1.9*	83	98	22,410	19,143	1,806	1,879	*1.0*
6300	Insurance carriers	7	7	*1.3*	63	45	34,667	34,578	2,200	1,424	*0.4*
6400	Insurance agents, brokers, and service	25	23	*1.6*	90	90	19,600	19,467	1,914	1,950	*1.0*
6500	Real estate	37	41	*1.7*	187	195	16,535	16,021	3,560	3,794	*1.5*
6510	Real estate operators and lessors	7	8	*1.1*	22	23	11,273	10,957	272	274	*0.5*
6530	Real estate agents and managers	18	24	*1.8*	105	135	17,905	16,652	2,213	2,830	*1.9*
RICHLAND, SC											
60 –	**Finance, insurance, and real estate**	974	1,010	*13.6*	15,651	15,802	26,585	27,564	412,242	436,949	*26.8*
6000	Depository institutions	154	176	*11.8*	5,059	5,094	25,591	25,504	127,641	123,354	*26.0*
6020	Commercial banks	76	105	*11.1*	3,957	4,168	26,460	26,323	100,805	100,558	*31.2*
6030	Savings institutions	31	23	*7.1*	613	437	22,852	23,533	15,706	12,515	*11.2*
6060	Credit unions	35	35	*19.6*	360	354	21,800	18,836	8,163	6,992	*19.1*
6100	Nondepository institutions	128	130	*11.0*	1,228	1,900	31,062	30,512	37,774	61,601	*33.2*
6140	Personal credit institutions	65	66	*7.2*	-	648	-	17,364	-	11,944	*14.2*
6160	Mortgage bankers and brokers	54	50	*25.0*	447	827	40,277	39,831	16,742	35,269	*45.2*
6200	Security and commodity brokers	38	40	*15.4*	362	376	62,564	69,053	20,955	23,127	*25.5*
6210	Security brokers and dealers	25	27	*14.4*	340	339	65,600	72,861	20,497	22,037	*26.4*
6280	Security and commodity services	13	13	*18.8*	22	37	15,636	34,162	458	1,090	*15.7*
6300	Insurance carriers	136	127	*23.6*	4,939	4,715	27,288	28,592	128,984	132,494	*35.0*
6310	Life insurance	58	56	*23.5*	1,147	934	26,860	30,874	30,895	28,127	*16.6*
6330	Fire, marine, and casualty insurance	44	39	*19.7*	557	630	44,158	35,759	21,225	20,727	*23.8*
6370	Pension, health, and welfare funds	11	11	*28.9*	111	-	46,342	-	2,566	-	*-*
6400	Insurance agents, brokers, and service	215	232	*16.4*	2,192	2,013	23,626	25,904	54,962	58,040	*29.7*
6500	Real estate	263	270	*11.5*	1,655	1,543	18,847	18,828	32,938	32,560	*13.1*
6510	Real estate operators and lessors	80	92	*12.2*	394	405	12,640	15,980	5,519	6,896	*12.9*
6530	Real estate agents and managers	114	147	*11.3*	938	961	20,179	20,587	20,082	21,929	*14.6*
6540	Title abstract offices	8	7	*17.9*	35	39	18,400	12,103	677	584	*24.5*
6552	Subdividers and developers, n.e.c.	20	13	*10.3*	115	63	26,435	17,905	3,285	1,626	*5.5*
6553	Cemetery subdividers and developers	8	5	*5.4*	52	71	27,462	15,944	1,427	1,335	*11.1*
6710	Holding offices	13	13	*20.0*	112	64	41,393	33,625	4,633	2,157	*6.3*
6732	Educational, religious, etc. trusts	10	10	*27.0*	26	42	34,462	29,810	978	1,380	*-*
6733	Trusts, n.e.c.	7	6	*16.2*	25	7	44,160	28,571	1,894	237	*11.7*
6799	Investors, n.e.c.	5	5	*15.6*	11	-	15,273	-	203	-	*-*
SALUDA, SC											
60 –	**Finance, insurance, and real estate**	18	16	*0.2*	86	91	14,186	14,110	1,278	1,436	*0.1*
6000	Depository institutions	7	6	*0.4*	58	52	15,724	15,615	959	824	*0.2*

Source: County Business Patterns, 1992/93, CBP-92/93-1, U.S. Department of Commerce, Washington, D.C., April 1995. SIC categories for which data were suppressed or not available for both 1992 and 1993 are not displayed. The employment columns represent mid-March employment in the year. Pay per employee is calculated by dividing 1st Quarter payroll, annualized, by mid-March employment. The columns headed "% State" show the county's percentage of the state total for the SIC in 1993; for example, 0.9% for SIC 6030 means that the county had 0.9 percent of the state's total establishments (or payroll) in SIC 6030 in 1993. A dash (-) is used to indicate that data are not available or cannot be calculated; nec means not elsewhere classified.

Continued on next page.

SIC	Industry	No. Establishments			Employment		Pay / Employee		Annual Payroll ($ 000)		
		1992	1993	% State	1992	1993	1992	1993	1992	1993	% State
SALUDA, SC - [continued]											
6100	Nondepository institutions	4	4	0.3	10	22	13,600	14,364	124	420	0.2
6140	Personal credit institutions	4	4	0.4	10	22	13,600	14,364	124	420	0.5
6400	Insurance agents, brokers, and service	4	4	0.3	13	-	8,923	-	153	-	-
SPARTANBURG, SC											
60 –	**Finance, insurance, and real estate**	398	420	5.6	2,763	2,702	23,512	24,816	67,701	70,789	4.3
6000	Depository institutions	82	94	6.3	1,000	922	19,732	21,119	20,904	20,832	4.4
6020	Commercial banks	52	65	6.9	674	626	20,760	22,064	14,591	14,432	4.5
6030	Savings institutions	20	19	5.9	290	262	17,186	18,519	5,569	5,590	5.0
6100	Nondepository institutions	69	74	6.2	246	299	25,626	19,237	6,294	6,204	3.3
6140	Personal credit institutions	61	62	6.8	207	253	22,995	17,565	4,838	4,537	5.4
6200	Security and commodity brokers	16	17	6.5	98	110	56,490	72,618	6,045	6,813	7.5
6300	Insurance carriers	43	37	6.9	452	362	22,619	26,530	10,893	9,837	2.6
6310	Life insurance	16	13	5.5	284	230	22,831	25,009	6,117	5,780	3.4
6330	Fire, marine, and casualty insurance	19	15	7.6	85	-	39,106	-	3,699	-	-
6370	Pension, health, and welfare funds	7	7	18.4	-	57	-	5,895	-	674	22.0
6400	Insurance agents, brokers, and service	77	78	5.5	346	361	26,566	26,548	9,618	10,440	5.3
6500	Real estate	94	102	4.3	445	477	17,861	17,283	8,582	10,576	4.3
6510	Real estate operators and lessors	33	41	5.4	114	97	14,947	10,887	1,849	1,220	2.3
6530	Real estate agents and managers	34	45	3.5	163	217	21,129	19,668	3,682	4,673	3.1
6552	Subdividers and developers, n.e.c.	7	5	4.0	39	72	20,923	20,833	826	729	2.5
6553	Cemetery subdividers and developers	6	7	7.5	70	87	18,343	15,448	1,383	3,778	31.4
6732	Educational, religious, etc. trusts	3	2	5.4	7	-	29,143	-	206	-	-
6733	Trusts, n.e.c.	4	6	16.2	5	-	16,000	-	104	-	-
SUMTER, SC											
60 –	**Finance, insurance, and real estate**	160	160	2.2	1,135	1,130	21,984	21,926	25,776	25,992	1.6
6000	Depository institutions	23	24	1.6	519	508	19,576	20,189	9,816	10,045	2.1
6020	Commercial banks	13	14	1.5	344	332	19,884	20,133	6,583	6,492	2.0
6100	Nondepository institutions	27	28	2.4	109	119	21,688	18,992	2,386	2,480	1.3
6200	Security and commodity brokers	6	6	2.3	-	23	-	56,000	-	1,582	1.7
6210	Security brokers and dealers	3	3	1.6	-	19	-	65,474	-	1,532	1.8
6280	Security and commodity services	3	3	4.3	6	4	9,333	11,000	47	50	0.7
6300	Insurance carriers	14	13	2.4	169	160	26,509	27,800	4,685	4,481	1.2
6400	Insurance agents, brokers, and service	32	34	2.4	111	128	23,532	21,844	2,837	2,961	1.5
6500	Real estate	55	51	2.2	173	158	12,879	12,937	2,687	2,516	1.0
6510	Real estate operators and lessors	22	23	3.1	81	70	12,494	11,429	1,095	1,015	1.9
6530	Real estate agents and managers	22	21	1.6	54	55	13,704	15,200	1,079	1,006	0.7
6700	Holding and other investment offices	3	4	2.1	-	34	-	49,529	-	1,927	4.4
6710	Holding offices	3	4	6.2	-	34	-	49,529	-	1,927	5.6
UNION, SC											
60 –	**Finance, insurance, and real estate**	43	42	0.6	209	217	18,622	18,304	4,016	4,346	0.3
6000	Depository institutions	11	11	0.7	134	131	19,731	19,908	2,726	2,887	0.6
6100	Nondepository institutions	11	11	0.9	29	43	18,483	14,884	496	682	0.4
6140	Personal credit institutions	11	11	1.2	29	43	18,483	14,884	496	682	0.8
6400	Insurance agents, brokers, and service	7	9	0.6	25	29	17,760	17,655	495	544	0.3
6500	Real estate	9	8	0.3	15	-	8,800	-	156	-	-
6510	Real estate operators and lessors	5	4	0.5	7	7	5,714	5,714	52	35	0.1
WILLIAMSBURG, SC											
60 –	**Finance, insurance, and real estate**	37	42	0.6	241	246	19,286	19,106	5,140	5,282	0.3
6000	Depository institutions	9	9	0.6	135	131	18,756	18,473	2,642	2,600	0.5
6100	Nondepository institutions	14	16	1.3	46	51	17,391	15,608	908	962	0.5
6140	Personal credit institutions	13	15	1.6	46	-	17,391	-	881	-	-

Source: County Business Patterns, 1992/93, CBP-92/93-1, U.S. Department of Commerce, Washington, D.C., April 1995. SIC categories for which data were suppressed or not available for both 1992 and 1993 are not displayed. The employment columns represent mid-March employment in the year. Pay per employee is calculated by dividing 1st Quarter payroll, annualized, by mid-March employment. The columns headed "% State" show the county's percentage of the state total for the SIC in 1993; for example, 0.9% for SIC 6030 means that the county had 0.9 percent of the state's total establishments (or payroll) in SIC 6030 in 1993. A dash (-) is used to indicate that data are not available or cannot be calculated; nec means not elsewhere classified.

Continued on next page.

SIC	Industry	No. Establishments			Employment		Pay / Employee		Annual Payroll ($ 000)		
		1992	1993	% State	1992	1993	1992	1993	1992	1993	% State
WILLIAMSBURG, SC - [continued]											
6500	Real estate	5	6	0.3	8	10	9,500	10,000	81	112	0.0
6510	Real estate operators and lessors	2	3	0.4	-	7	-	12,000	-	97	0.2
6553	Cemetery subdividers and developers	3	3	3.2	-	3	-	5,333	-	15	0.1
YORK, SC											
60 –	**Finance, insurance, and real estate**	243	250	3.4	1,500	1,571	21,440	21,232	34,375	36,151	2.2
6000	Depository institutions	58	64	4.3	627	660	20,536	21,176	13,840	14,542	3.1
6020	Commercial banks	35	36	3.8	424	392	19,821	21,265	8,998	8,290	2.6
6030	Savings institutions	19	18	5.6	167	179	21,341	21,073	3,934	4,358	3.9
6060	Credit unions	4	8	4.5	36	-	25,222	-	908	-	-
6100	Nondepository institutions	39	37	3.1	203	184	24,729	19,761	5,119	4,221	2.3
6140	Personal credit institutions	28	26	2.8	140	-	23,314	-	3,352	-	-
6160	Mortgage bankers and brokers	10	10	5.0	-	51	-	29,333	-	2,080	2.7
6300	Insurance carriers	26	24	4.5	231	219	25,004	27,982	6,156	6,456	1.7
6310	Life insurance	8	8	3.4	163	145	25,055	25,434	4,167	3,811	2.3
6370	Pension, health, and welfare funds	2	3	7.9	-	1	-	4,000	-	80	2.6
6400	Insurance agents, brokers, and service	44	46	3.2	192	170	22,875	24,659	4,669	4,768	2.4
6500	Real estate	70	71	3.0	227	316	14,326	14,544	3,747	5,209	2.1
6510	Real estate operators and lessors	23	22	2.9	45	45	13,067	13,689	640	810	1.5
6530	Real estate agents and managers	36	44	3.4	97	251	16,289	14,247	1,885	3,920	2.6

Source: County Business Patterns, 1992/93, CBP-92/93-1, U.S. Department of Commerce, Washington, D.C., April 1995. SIC categories for which data were suppressed or not available for both 1992 and 1993 are *not* displayed. The employment columns represent mid-March employment in the year. Pay per employee is calculated by dividing 1st Quarter payroll, annualized, by mid-March employment. The columns headed "% State" show the county's percentage of the state total for the SIC in 1993; for example, 0.9% for SIC 6030 means that the county had 0.9 percent of the state's total establishments (or payroll) in SIC 6030 in 1993. A dash (-) is used to indicate that data are not available or cannot be calculated; *nec* means not elsewhere classified.

SOUTH DAKOTA

SIC	Industry	No. Establishments			Employment		Pay / Employee		Annual Payroll ($ 000)		
		1992	1993	% State	1992	1993	1992	1993	1992	1993	% State
AURORA, SD											
60 –	**Finance, insurance, and real estate**	8	8	0.4	-	34	-	22,235	-	961	0.3
BEADLE, SD											
60 –	**Finance, insurance, and real estate**	62	62	3.0	357	351	16,840	15,977	5,963	5,742	1.5
6000	Depository institutions	9	12	2.7	144	153	22,806	19,033	3,034	2,895	1.5
6020	Commercial banks	6	6	1.9	129	131	23,783	19,939	2,811	2,565	1.5
6060	Credit unions	3	6	8.0	15	22	14,400	13,636	223	330	-
6140	Personal credit institutions	3	-	-	6	-	15,333	-	91	-	-
6400	Insurance agents, brokers, and service	21	20	3.2	47	41	16,936	17,171	884	766	2.0
6500	Real estate	22	24	3.8	95	98	8,421	8,367	849	881	2.9
6510	Real estate operators and lessors	11	12	4.0	68	54	8,706	7,704	607	440	3.8
6700	Holding and other investment offices	4	3	4.2	56	45	12,286	11,556	752	733	-
6710	Holding offices	3	3	12.0	-	45	-	11,556	-	733	23.7
BENNETT, SD											
60 –	**Finance, insurance, and real estate**	4	4	0.2	21	22	15,048	15,091	366	366	0.1
BON HOMME, SD											
60 –	**Finance, insurance, and real estate**	24	22	1.0	88	83	12,545	13,060	1,271	1,266	0.3
6000	Depository institutions	5	5	1.1	47	47	18,638	18,383	1,042	1,031	0.5
6500	Real estate	4	4	0.6	15	13	3,733	3,077	54	46	0.2
BROOKINGS, SD											
60 –	**Finance, insurance, and real estate**	63	65	3.1	351	394	14,724	15,025	6,383	6,981	1.9
6000	Depository institutions	13	14	3.1	231	266	16,260	16,782	4,779	5,200	2.7
6020	Commercial banks	9	9	2.9	195	229	15,713	16,541	4,035	4,476	2.6
6200	Security and commodity brokers	4	4	3.9	-	6	-	23,333	-	151	0.7
6300	Insurance carriers	6	6	4.3	50	-	12,320	-	507	-	-
6400	Insurance agents, brokers, and service	14	15	2.4	-	33	-	9,939	-	345	0.9
6500	Real estate	22	24	3.8	28	52	10,000	10,154	500	682	2.3
6510	Real estate operators and lessors	6	9	3.0	9	14	5,333	4,857	52	95	0.8
6530	Real estate agents and managers	8	10	4.5	10	31	10,800	11,226	170	383	2.9
6700	Holding and other investment offices	3	2	2.8	8	-	11,000	-	170	-	-
BROWN, SD											
60 –	**Finance, insurance, and real estate**	124	136	6.5	762	1,017	25,617	19,575	18,597	20,903	5.6
6000	Depository institutions	21	22	4.9	261	265	20,690	20,558	5,764	5,463	2.9
6020	Commercial banks	11	11	3.5	200	200	22,100	22,040	4,791	4,400	2.6
6030	Savings institutions	5	5	7.9	37	37	15,568	15,568	576	609	6.1
6060	Credit unions	5	6	8.0	24	28	16,833	16,571	397	454	-
6100	Nondepository institutions	7	6	8.3	162	115	23,457	23,652	3,970	2,489	9.9
6140	Personal credit institutions	4	3	14.3	91	98	20,791	21,061	2,011	2,105	23.8
6200	Security and commodity brokers	10	13	12.6	-	32	-	42,500	-	1,731	8.0
6210	Security brokers and dealers	6	9	14.8	32	29	57,750	45,379	1,777	1,670	9.3
6280	Security and commodity services	3	3	9.7	1	-	16,000	-	32	-	-
6300	Insurance carriers	12	11	8.0	56	135	35,143	28,563	1,925	3,947	6.6
6310	Life insurance	4	3	8.1	-	51	-	38,431	-	1,945	8.4
6370	Pension, health, and welfare funds	3	3	21.4	3	-	9,333	-	27	-	-
6400	Insurance agents, brokers, and service	38	39	6.2	120	110	16,900	16,800	2,163	1,925	4.9
6500	Real estate	31	36	5.7	80	96	10,800	11,083	1,119	1,446	4.8

Source: County Business Patterns, 1992/93, CBP-92/93-1, U.S. Department of Commerce, Washington, D.C., April 1995. SIC categories for which data were suppressed or not available for both 1992 and 1993 are *not* displayed. The employment columns represent mid-March employment in the year. Pay per employee is calculated by dividing 1st Quarter payroll, annualized, by mid-March employment. The columns headed "% State" show the county's percentage of the state total for the SIC in 1993; for example, 0.9% for SIC 6030 means that the county had 0.9 percent of the state's total establishments (or payroll) in SIC 6030 in 1993. A dash (-) is used to indicate that data are not available or cannot be calculated; *nec* means not elsewhere classified.

Continued on next page.

SIC	Industry	No. Establishments			Employment		Pay / Employee		Annual Payroll ($ 000)		
		1992	1993	% State	1992	1993	1992	1993	1992	1993	% State
BROWN, SD - [continued]											
6510	Real estate operators and lessors	17	21	7.0	-	35	-	8,914	-	371	3.2
6530	Real estate agents and managers	10	12	5.5	-	30	-	9,200	-	285	2.2
6700	Holding and other investment offices	5	9	12.5	-	264	-	13,682	-	3,902	-
BRULE, SD											
60 –	**Finance, insurance, and real estate**	19	18	0.9	80	71	18,850	19,718	1,554	1,526	0.4
6000	Depository institutions	5	5	1.1	36	-	25,111	-	840	-	-
6400	Insurance agents, brokers, and service	8	9	1.4	27	28	17,185	17,286	543	523	1.3
BUFFALO, SD											
60 –	**Finance, insurance, and real estate**	3	3	0.1	-	-	-	-	-	-	-
BUTTE, SD											
60 –	**Finance, insurance, and real estate**	24	25	1.2	87	95	21,747	22,021	1,643	1,681	0.4
6000	Depository institutions	5	6	1.3	53	59	25,887	24,475	1,187	1,157	0.6
6020	Commercial banks	3	3	1.0	-	51	-	25,412	-	1,055	0.6
6400	Insurance agents, brokers, and service	6	8	1.3	10	-	11,600	-	129	-	-
6500	Real estate	9	9	1.4	16	-	9,500	-	159	-	-
6510	Real estate operators and lessors	6	6	2.0	8	8	5,500	5,500	44	44	0.4
CAMPBELL, SD											
60 –	**Finance, insurance, and real estate**	3	2	0.1	-	-	-	-	-	-	-
CHARLES MIX, SD											
60 –	**Finance, insurance, and real estate**	17	16	0.8	72	83	19,278	17,494	1,629	1,708	0.5
6000	Depository institutions	6	6	1.3	57	63	22,175	20,889	1,498	1,581	0.8
6400	Insurance agents, brokers, and service	6	6	1.0	10	16	8,800	7,250	91	107	0.3
6500	Real estate	3	2	0.3	2	-	10,000	-	25	-	-
CLARK, SD											
60 –	**Finance, insurance, and real estate**	15	16	0.8	51	53	14,745	13,736	749	734	0.2
6000	Depository institutions	5	5	1.1	36	38	16,667	14,421	588	550	0.3
6020	Commercial banks	5	5	1.6	36	38	16,667	14,421	588	550	0.3
6400	Insurance agents, brokers, and service	3	4	0.6	5	-	16,000	-	85	-	-
6500	Real estate	5	5	0.8	7	7	7,429	8,571	56	63	0.2
CLAY, SD											
60 –	**Finance, insurance, and real estate**	30	30	1.4	126	115	12,698	9,774	1,643	1,509	0.4
6000	Depository institutions	6	6	1.3	60	61	16,400	9,246	1,065	949	0.5
6300	Insurance carriers	3	2	1.4	8	-	8,000	-	68	-	-
6400	Insurance agents, brokers, and service	11	10	1.6	13	14	12,308	12,000	161	170	0.4
6500	Real estate	6	9	1.4	37	28	4,324	5,143	127	126	0.4
6530	Real estate agents and managers	2	3	1.4	-	17	-	4,235	-	62	0.5
CODINGTON, SD											
60 –	**Finance, insurance, and real estate**	81	87	4.1	356	421	24,809	25,330	8,784	9,909	2.6
6000	Depository institutions	13	14	3.1	200	208	22,500	22,346	4,648	4,588	2.4
6100	Nondepository institutions	4	4	5.6	15	-	40,267	-	522	-	-
6200	Security and commodity brokers	6	7	6.8	20	-	35,400	-	825	-	-
6300	Insurance carriers	6	3	2.2	-	4	-	12,000	-	51	0.1
6330	Fire, marine, and casualty insurance	3	1	1.6	6	-	5,333	-	27	-	-
6400	Insurance agents, brokers, and service	29	29	4.6	58	67	17,586	19,224	1,103	1,504	3.8
6500	Real estate	20	28	4.5	28	61	10,714	14,623	396	1,162	3.8
6510	Real estate operators and lessors	5	10	3.3	12	-	9,667	-	181	-	-
6530	Real estate agents and managers	14	17	7.7	14	33	11,143	14,061	186	539	4.1

Source: County Business Patterns, 1992/93, CBP-92/93-1, U.S. Department of Commerce, Washington, D.C., April 1995. SIC categories for which data were suppressed or not available for both 1992 and 1993 are not displayed. The employment columns represent mid-March employment in the year. Pay per employee is calculated by dividing 1st Quarter payroll, annualized, by mid-March employment. The columns headed "% State" show the county's percentage of the state total for the SIC in 1993; for example, 0.9% for SIC 6030 means that the county had 0.9 percent of the state's total establishments (or payroll) in SIC 6030 in 1993. A dash (-) is used to indicate that data are not available or cannot be calculated; nec means not elsewhere classified.

SIC	Industry	No. Establishments			Employment		Pay / Employee		Annual Payroll ($ 000)		
		1992	1993	% State	1992	1993	1992	1993	1992	1993	% State
CORSON, SD											
60 –	**Finance, insurance, and real estate**	5	6	0.3	14	15	15,143	14,133	199	186	0.0
CUSTER, SD											
60 –	**Finance, insurance, and real estate**	18	19	0.9	41	41	17,366	17,659	751	735	0.2
6000	Depository institutions	3	4	0.9	-	24	-	18,333	-	414	0.2
6400	Insurance agents, brokers, and service	5	5	0.8	9	8	12,444	17,000	134	134	0.3
6500	Real estate	8	8	1.3	5	-	5,600	-	38	-	-
6510	Real estate operators and lessors	1	3	1.0	-	1	-	4,000	-	33	0.3
6530	Real estate agents and managers	4	3	1.4	2	3	6,000	5,333	21	19	0.1
DAVISON, SD											
60 –	**Finance, insurance, and real estate**	71	76	3.6	292	318	19,753	20,365	5,854	6,489	1.7
6000	Depository institutions	7	8	1.8	130	149	21,969	23,785	3,005	3,403	1.8
6020	Commercial banks	4	4	1.3	120	137	22,533	24,088	2,840	3,159	1.9
6100	Nondepository institutions	4	4	5.6	-	17	-	35,059	-	498	2.0
6200	Security and commodity brokers	8	6	5.8	18	-	35,111	-	669	-	-
6210	Security brokers and dealers	5	4	6.6	-	15	-	33,600	-	649	3.6
6300	Insurance carriers	6	4	2.9	-	9	-	30,222	-	237	0.4
6330	Fire, marine, and casualty insurance	3	2	3.3	7	-	29,714	-	207	-	-
6400	Insurance agents, brokers, and service	26	30	4.8	75	83	13,707	13,253	1,033	1,162	3.0
6500	Real estate	19	22	3.5	43	38	7,349	7,263	329	338	1.1
6510	Real estate operators and lessors	12	13	4.3	31	-	6,968	-	201	-	-
6530	Real estate agents and managers	3	8	3.6	3	7	8,000	8,000	51	100	0.8
DAY, SD											
60 –	**Finance, insurance, and real estate**	22	21	1.0	94	103	11,064	11,223	1,243	1,730	0.5
6000	Depository institutions	9	8	1.8	71	69	11,662	11,246	911	790	0.4
6500	Real estate	5	4	0.6	10	-	12,400	-	155	-	-
DEUEL, SD											
60 –	**Finance, insurance, and real estate**	11	10	0.5	63	87	17,397	17,609	1,088	1,583	0.4
6000	Depository institutions	4	4	0.9	43	60	22,233	21,400	921	1,354	0.7
6500	Real estate	3	3	0.5	11	-	4,727	-	52	-	-
DEWEY, SD											
60 –	**Finance, insurance, and real estate**	5	5	0.2	70	90	18,857	14,533	1,382	1,515	0.4
DOUGLAS, SD											
60 –	**Finance, insurance, and real estate**	7	8	0.4	32	36	24,125	18,000	753	662	0.2
EDMUNDS, SD											
60 –	**Finance, insurance, and real estate**	13	14	0.7	50	46	13,920	16,261	916	977	0.3
6000	Depository institutions	4	4	0.9	35	32	17,371	20,000	834	860	0.5
6020	Commercial banks	4	4	1.3	35	32	17,371	20,000	834	860	0.5
6400	Insurance agents, brokers, and service	3	4	0.6	3	3	5,333	9,333	14	21	0.1
6500	Real estate	6	6	1.0	12	11	6,000	7,273	68	96	0.3
6510	Real estate operators and lessors	3	3	1.0	7	8	4,000	4,500	29	36	0.3
FALL RIVER, SD											
60 –	**Finance, insurance, and real estate**	14	13	0.6	45	52	21,689	20,000	956	949	0.3
6000	Depository institutions	6	6	1.3	36	43	21,222	19,256	782	738	0.4
6400	Insurance agents, brokers, and service	3	3	0.5	-	5	-	22,400	-	120	0.3
FAULK, SD											
60 –	**Finance, insurance, and real estate**	5	6	0.3	18	-	15,778	-	294	-	-

Source: County Business Patterns, 1992/93, CBP-92/93-1, U.S. Department of Commerce, Washington, D.C., April 1995. SIC categories for which data were suppressed or not available for both 1992 and 1993 are not displayed. The employment columns represent mid-March employment in the year. Pay per employee is calculated by dividing 1st Quarter payroll, annualized, by mid-March employment. The columns headed "% State" show the county's percentage of the state total for the SIC in 1993; for example, 0.9% for SIC 6030 means that the county had 0.9 percent of the state's total establishments (or payroll) in SIC 6030 in 1993. A dash (-) is used to indicate that data are not available or cannot be calculated; nec means not elsewhere classified.

SIC	Industry	No. Establishments			Employment		Pay / Employee		Annual Payroll ($ 000)		
		1992	1993	% State	1992	1993	1992	1993	1992	1993	% State
GRANT, SD											
60 –	**Finance, insurance, and real estate**	21	22	*1.0*	311	283	21,132	20,509	5,950	5,874	*1.6*
6000	Depository institutions	6	6	*1.3*	56	55	23,571	20,655	1,170	1,089	*0.6*
6300	Insurance carriers	4	5	*3.6*	-	205	-	21,463	-	4,462	*7.4*
6330	Fire, marine, and casualty insurance	4	5	*8.2*	-	205	-	21,463	-	4,462	*28.2*
6400	Insurance agents, brokers, and service	6	6	*1.0*	-	13	-	14,769	-	211	*0.5*
6500	Real estate	5	5	*0.8*	13	10	8,000	7,600	102	112	*0.4*
GREGORY, SD											
60 –	**Finance, insurance, and real estate**	16	16	*0.8*	90	91	17,156	17,802	1,733	1,801	*0.5*
6400	Insurance agents, brokers, and service	6	6	*1.0*	14	-	7,714	-	118	-	*-*
6500	Real estate	3	4	*0.6*	17	16	7,294	9,750	127	200	*0.7*
HAAKON, SD											
60 –	**Finance, insurance, and real estate**	7	9	*0.4*	-	56	-	24,643	-	1,469	*0.4*
6400	Insurance agents, brokers, and service	3	4	*0.6*	-	4	-	5,000	-	24	*0.1*
HAMLIN, SD											
60 –	**Finance, insurance, and real estate**	19	17	*0.8*	64	62	18,438	27,097	1,154	1,391	*0.4*
6000	Depository institutions	9	8	*1.8*	52	-	20,308	-	994	-	*-*
6020	Commercial banks	9	8	*2.6*	52	-	20,308	-	994	-	*-*
6400	Insurance agents, brokers, and service	3	3	*0.5*	-	4	-	11,000	-	47	*0.1*
6500	Real estate	5	5	*0.8*	4	8	9,000	8,500	74	48	*0.2*
HAND, SD											
60 –	**Finance, insurance, and real estate**	11	10	*0.5*	64	65	22,000	22,277	1,461	1,466	*0.4*
6400	Insurance agents, brokers, and service	3	4	*0.6*	-	13	-	15,692	-	210	*0.5*
6500	Real estate	4	3	*0.5*	4	-	6,000	-	30	-	*-*
HANSON, SD											
60 –	**Finance, insurance, and real estate**	9	9	*0.4*	36	37	19,222	16,865	675	655	*0.2*
6000	Depository institutions	3	3	*0.7*	28	29	23,714	20,552	645	632	*0.3*
6020	Commercial banks	3	3	*1.0*	28	29	23,714	20,552	645	632	*0.4*
6500	Real estate	3	3	*0.5*	4	4	2,000	2,000	16	9	*0.0*
HARDING, SD											
60 –	**Finance, insurance, and real estate**	5	5	*0.2*	-	14	-	32,000	-	338	*0.1*
HUGHES, SD											
60 –	**Finance, insurance, and real estate**	55	62	*3.0*	375	356	21,984	24,697	7,959	8,454	*2.3*
6000	Depository institutions	9	10	*2.2*	172	172	23,163	24,581	3,957	4,267	*2.3*
6020	Commercial banks	6	6	*1.9*	155	155	23,897	25,342	3,673	3,961	*2.3*
6300	Insurance carriers	7	5	*3.6*	37	31	24,541	27,484	752	713	*1.2*
6400	Insurance agents, brokers, and service	13	19	*3.0*	68	64	20,588	25,062	1,313	1,630	*4.2*
6500	Real estate	15	16	*2.5*	66	53	10,242	10,792	699	570	*1.9*
6510	Real estate operators and lessors	9	9	*3.0*	-	12	-	5,000	-	63	*0.5*
6530	Real estate agents and managers	5	6	*2.7*	51	41	10,980	12,488	589	502	*3.8*
6700	Holding and other investment offices	4	5	*6.9*	7	9	25,143	18,667	172	189	*-*
HUTCHINSON, SD											
60 –	**Finance, insurance, and real estate**	17	20	*1.0*	102	106	19,373	17,962	2,289	2,356	*0.6*
6000	Depository institutions	8	8	*1.8*	74	76	19,784	18,789	1,804	1,853	*1.0*
6400	Insurance agents, brokers, and service	6	6	*1.0*	16	15	22,250	18,933	313	323	*0.8*
6500	Real estate	3	3	*0.5*	12	12	13,000	13,667	172	154	*0.5*
HYDE, SD											
60 –	**Finance, insurance, and real estate**	5	4	*0.2*	9	5	5,333	4,800	27	28	*0.0*

Source: County Business Patterns, 1992/93, CBP-92/93-1, U.S. Department of Commerce, Washington, D.C., April 1995. SIC categories for which data were suppressed or not available for both 1992 and 1993 are *not* displayed. The employment columns represent mid-March employment in the year. Pay per employee is calculated by dividing 1st Quarter payroll, annualized, by mid-March employment. The columns headed "% State" show the county's percentage of the state total for the SIC in 1993; for example, 0.9% for SIC 6030 means that the county had 0.9 percent of the state's total establishments (or payroll) in SIC 6030 in 1993. A dash (-) is used to indicate that data are not available or cannot be calculated; *nec* means not elsewhere classified.

SIC	Industry	No. Establishments			Employment		Pay / Employee		Annual Payroll ($ 000)		
		1992	1993	% State	1992	1993	1992	1993	1992	1993	% State
JACKSON, SD											
60 –	**Finance, insurance, and real estate**	2	2	0.1	-	-	-	-	-	-	-
JERAULD, SD											
60 –	**Finance, insurance, and real estate**	6	6	0.3	19	31	16,632	11,742	381	436	0.1
JONES, SD											
60 –	**Finance, insurance, and real estate**	4	5	0.2	22	25	21,091	20,480	503	529	0.1
KINGSBURY, SD											
60 –	**Finance, insurance, and real estate**	18	20	1.0	101	130	17,901	17,415	2,035	2,475	0.7
6000	Depository institutions	6	6	1.3	58	59	17,034	18,780	1,067	1,166	0.6
6510	Real estate operators and lessors	3	2	0.7	6	-	3,333		28	-	-
LAKE, SD											
60 –	**Finance, insurance, and real estate**	30	30	1.4	117	141	20,855	20,681	2,543	2,946	0.8
6000	Depository institutions	7	8	1.8	50	84	24,720	24,762	1,298	1,967	1.0
6020	Commercial banks	5	5	1.6	-	74	-	26,216	-	1,828	1.1
6400	Insurance agents, brokers, and service	9	9	1.4	29	26	17,103	15,077	549	448	1.1
6500	Real estate	9	9	1.4	26	22	16,769	8,545	457	299	1.0
6510	Real estate operators and lessors	4	4	1.3	10	10	4,400	5,600	47	63	0.5
LAWRENCE, SD											
60 –	**Finance, insurance, and real estate**	55	60	2.9	344	232	15,233	19,741	5,602	4,475	1.2
6000	Depository institutions	12	12	2.7	100	110	24,400	24,036	2,236	2,253	1.2
6020	Commercial banks	8	8	2.6	77	85	26,805	25,647	1,827	1,890	1.1
6400	Insurance agents, brokers, and service	12	14	2.2	50	-	10,080	-	585	-	-
6500	Real estate	25	27	4.3	167	58	10,563	12,690	2,199	866	2.9
6510	Real estate operators and lessors	13	16	5.3	-	35	-	9,143	-	386	3.4
6530	Real estate agents and managers	8	8	3.6	44	17	15,182	21,647	762	447	3.4
LINCOLN, SD											
60 –	**Finance, insurance, and real estate**	32	32	1.5	156	162	16,538	18,074	2,623	2,989	0.8
6000	Depository institutions	12	12	2.7	113	115	17,735	19,965	2,086	2,349	1.2
6400	Insurance agents, brokers, and service	10	9	1.4	16	16	8,750	10,500	156	181	0.5
6500	Real estate	5	6	1.0	15	19	11,733	9,684	187	233	0.8
LYMAN, SD											
60 –	**Finance, insurance, and real estate**	5	5	0.2	27	25	13,778	16,000	379	409	0.1
MCCOOK, SD											
60 –	**Finance, insurance, and real estate**	18	17	0.8	66	64	16,485	14,125	1,119	806	0.2
6000	Depository institutions	6	6	1.3	45	44	21,333	16,545	868	539	0.3
6400	Insurance agents, brokers, and service	7	5	0.8	12	10	6,000	10,400	78	106	0.3
MCPHERSON, SD											
60 –	**Finance, insurance, and real estate**	8	9	0.4	55	55	14,909	20,145	954	1,030	0.3
6500	Real estate	3	4	0.6	1	9	8,000	8,889	13	88	0.3
MARSHALL, SD											
60 –	**Finance, insurance, and real estate**	11	12	0.6	60	55	10,867	10,764	713	657	0.2
6000	Depository institutions	7	7	1.5	39	40	14,974	13,600	657	601	0.3
MEADE, SD											
60 –	**Finance, insurance, and real estate**	29	33	1.6	141	158	18,950	18,304	2,668	3,027	0.8
6000	Depository institutions	8	9	2.0	98	110	20,000	19,927	2,020	2,234	1.2
6020	Commercial banks	4	4	1.3	63	68	21,905	22,118	1,433	1,521	0.9

Source: County Business Patterns, 1992/93, CBP-92/93-1, U.S. Department of Commerce, Washington, D.C., April 1995. SIC categories for which data were suppressed or not available for both 1992 and 1993 are *not* displayed. The employment columns represent mid-March employment in the year. Pay per employee is calculated by dividing 1st Quarter payroll, annualized, by mid-March employment. The columns headed "% State" show the county's percentage of the state total for the SIC in 1993; for example, 0.9% for SIC 6030 means that the county had 0.9 percent of the state's total establishments (or payroll) in SIC 6030 in 1993. A dash (-) is used to indicate that data are not available or cannot be calculated; *nec* means not elsewhere classified.

Continued on next page.

SIC	Industry	No. Establishments			Employment		Pay / Employee		Annual Payroll ($ 000)		
		1992	1993	% State	1992	1993	1992	1993	1992	1993	% State
MEADE, SD - [continued]											
6400	Insurance agents, brokers, and service	9	11	1.7	-	20	-	19,400	-	401	1.0
6500	Real estate	10	13	2.1	21	28	11,619	11,143	257	392	1.3
6530	Real estate agents and managers	6	6	2.7	14	21	10,857	10,095	165	251	1.9
MELLETTE, SD											
60 –	**Finance, insurance, and real estate**	2	2	0.1	-	-	-	-	-	-	-
MINER, SD											
60 –	**Finance, insurance, and real estate**	9	7	0.3	29	33	18,621	22,909	564	847	0.2
6000	Depository institutions	4	4	0.9	18	23	25,556	29,391	468	761	0.4
MINNEHAHA, SD											
60 –	**Finance, insurance, and real estate**	502	512	24.4	9,307	8,832	21,435	22,041	198,291	196,668	52.4
6000	Depository institutions	88	85	18.8	5,276	4,618	20,653	21,355	103,980	96,504	50.9
6020	Commercial banks	60	56	17.9	4,945	4,275	20,558	21,456	96,506	89,340	52.3
6100	Nondepository institutions	23	27	37.5	896	934	17,045	16,869	15,192	16,090	64.2
6140	Personal credit institutions	13	10	47.6	-	312	-	17,833	-	6,056	68.4
6150	Business credit institutions	6	11	57.9	634	562	13,584	14,164	9,155	7,324	90.8
6200	Security and commodity brokers	23	31	30.1	249	335	33,430	36,155	8,087	12,254	56.8
6210	Security brokers and dealers	16	19	31.1	228	220	32,421	41,709	7,162	9,450	52.6
6300	Insurance carriers	60	52	37.7	1,703	1,582	25,602	25,226	46,127	41,324	68.8
6310	Life insurance	25	23	62.2	758	653	26,602	23,975	20,088	16,953	73.5
6321	Accident and health insurance	5	5	62.5	111	72	23,099	24,556	2,399	1,685	-
6330	Fire, marine, and casualty insurance	20	16	26.2	249	243	26,040	26,733	6,980	7,077	44.7
6400	Insurance agents, brokers, and service	147	149	23.6	526	623	26,243	26,273	14,169	17,369	44.3
6500	Real estate	135	145	23.1	583	670	13,592	14,890	8,867	10,959	36.3
6510	Real estate operators and lessors	64	66	21.9	288	186	11,250	12,344	3,531	2,530	22.0
6530	Real estate agents and managers	55	65	29.5	221	432	15,511	15,593	3,975	7,378	56.4
6552	Subdividers and developers, n.e.c.	4	8	33.3	4	12	7,000	14,333	37	247	13.7
6553	Cemetery subdividers and developers	4	4	12.5	22	-	7,636	-	239	-	-
6710	Holding offices	5	7	28.0	10	14	32,800	44,857	338	623	20.1
6733	Trusts, n.e.c.	5	3	23.1	6	-	21,333	-	210	-	-
MOODY, SD											
60 –	**Finance, insurance, and real estate**	10	10	0.5	58	55	19,103	21,818	1,229	1,270	0.3
6000	Depository institutions	3	3	0.7	36	36	24,000	26,556	976	1,049	0.6
6500	Real estate	4	4	0.6	14	11	12,857	16,364	192	158	0.5
PENNINGTON, SD											
60 –	**Finance, insurance, and real estate**	221	239	11.4	1,476	1,488	21,266	22,228	32,091	34,469	9.2
6000	Depository institutions	29	32	7.1	457	519	21,969	21,218	10,298	10,393	5.5
6020	Commercial banks	15	15	4.8	292	327	25,370	22,606	7,355	6,858	4.0
6100	Nondepository institutions	12	13	18.1	51	67	29,961	33,254	1,788	2,447	9.8
6200	Security and commodity brokers	14	15	14.6	72	76	49,278	52,684	3,617	4,135	19.2
6210	Security brokers and dealers	9	11	18.0	66	68	53,030	57,824	3,531	4,061	22.6
6280	Security and commodity services	5	4	12.9	6	8	8,000	9,000	86	74	2.7
6300	Insurance carriers	21	18	13.0	224	229	24,946	25,380	5,561	5,736	9.6
6310	Life insurance	8	7	18.9	139	159	25,496	24,881	3,512	3,845	16.7
6330	Fire, marine, and casualty insurance	10	8	13.1	-	65	-	26,769	-	1,792	11.3
6400	Insurance agents, brokers, and service	54	59	9.4	217	250	21,991	20,928	5,196	6,059	15.4
6500	Real estate	81	95	15.1	276	341	11,957	12,786	4,001	5,339	17.7
6510	Real estate operators and lessors	34	44	14.6	114	138	10,632	12,203	1,341	1,854	16.1
6530	Real estate agents and managers	38	44	20.0	134	159	12,597	12,000	1,884	2,160	16.5
6552	Subdividers and developers, n.e.c.	5	4	16.7	9	25	16,444	19,200	492	908	50.3
6700	Holding and other investment offices	10	7	9.7	179	6	14,592	71,333	1,630	360	-
6799	Investors, n.e.c.	4	4	36.4	-	5	-	84,800	-	342	77.4

Source: County Business Patterns, 1992/93, CBP-92/93-1, U.S. Department of Commerce, Washington, D.C., April 1995. SIC categories for which data were suppressed or not available for both 1992 and 1993 are *not* displayed. The employment columns represent mid-March employment in the year. Pay per employee is calculated by dividing 1st Quarter payroll, annualized, by mid-March employment. The columns headed "% State" show the county's percentage of the state total for the SIC in 1993; for example, 0.9% for SIC 6030 means that the county had 0.9 percent of the state's total establishments (or payroll) in SIC 6030 in 1993. A dash (-) is used to indicate that data are not available or cannot be calculated; *nec* means not elsewhere classified.

SIC	Industry	No. Establishments			Employment		Pay / Employee		Annual Payroll ($ 000)		
		1992	1993	% State	1992	1993	1992	1993	1992	1993	% State
PERKINS, SD											
60–	**Finance, insurance, and real estate**	16	16	0.8	65	71	16,985	13,915	1,132	997	0.3
6000	Depository institutions	4	4	0.9	44	47	20,909	16,511	914	749	0.4
6400	Insurance agents, brokers, and service	5	5	0.8	6	-	14,000	-	85	-	-
6500	Real estate	5	6	1.0	-	13	-	6,769	-	139	0.5
POTTER, SD											
60–	**Finance, insurance, and real estate**	11	13	0.6	57	63	18,105	18,857	1,170	1,305	0.3
6000	Depository institutions	4	4	0.9	-	52	-	19,846	-	1,127	0.6
6400	Insurance agents, brokers, and service	5	6	1.0	9	8	16,000	17,500	143	155	0.4
6500	Real estate	2	3	0.5	-	3	-	5,333	-	23	0.1
ROBERTS, SD											
60–	**Finance, insurance, and real estate**	27	29	1.4	172	175	14,140	14,377	2,580	2,490	0.7
6000	Depository institutions	7	8	1.8	63	70	18,095	16,629	1,249	1,235	0.7
6100	Nondepository institutions	3	3	4.2	9	-	22,222	-	152	-	-
6400	Insurance agents, brokers, and service	7	9	1.4	14	16	9,429	15,250	163	225	0.6
SANBORN, SD											
60–	**Finance, insurance, and real estate**	9	8	0.4	31	30	13,290	16,000	455	480	0.1
6500	Real estate	3	2	0.3	6	-	5,333	-	33	-	-
SHANNON, SD											
60–	**Finance, insurance, and real estate**	1	3	0.1	-	-	-	-	-	-	-
SPINK, SD											
60–	**Finance, insurance, and real estate**	21	22	1.0	88	97	21,182	19,711	1,828	1,813	0.5
6000	Depository institutions	9	9	2.0	65	68	23,938	22,471	1,483	1,448	0.8
6400	Insurance agents, brokers, and service	6	7	1.1	9	-	16,444	-	190	-	-
6500	Real estate	3	4	0.6	6	9	7,333	6,667	47	60	0.2
STANLEY, SD											
60–	**Finance, insurance, and real estate**	3	5	0.2	-	-	-	-	-	-	-
SULLY, SD											
60–	**Finance, insurance, and real estate**	8	8	0.4	33	18	24,000	36,222	593	576	0.2
6400	Insurance agents, brokers, and service	3	3	0.5	6	4	24,667	11,000	62	41	0.1
TODD, SD											
60–	**Finance, insurance, and real estate**	5	4	0.2	40	30	20,100	13,733	886	506	0.1
TRIPP, SD											
60–	**Finance, insurance, and real estate**	21	19	0.9	114	118	18,456	18,644	2,218	2,216	0.6
6000	Depository institutions	5	5	1.1	72	78	20,111	19,590	1,573	1,649	0.9
6400	Insurance agents, brokers, and service	6	6	1.0	21	25	16,190	15,200	388	385	1.0
6500	Real estate	7	5	0.8	-	9	-	10,222	-	67	0.2
6530	Real estate agents and managers	4	3	1.4	10	-	10,000	-	71	-	-
TURNER, SD											
60–	**Finance, insurance, and real estate**	26	27	1.3	92	119	17,609	20,504	1,850	2,334	0.6
6000	Depository institutions	8	8	1.8	63	65	20,127	29,169	1,468	1,833	1.0
6500	Real estate	7	8	1.3	7	31	17,714	10,323	146	263	0.9
6510	Real estate operators and lessors	3	4	1.3	2	-	4,000	-	8	-	-
UNION, SD											
60–	**Finance, insurance, and real estate**	17	18	0.9	111	117	21,802	18,120	2,485	2,220	0.6
6000	Depository institutions	5	5	1.1	68	82	23,706	19,463	1,502	1,535	0.8
6400	Insurance agents, brokers, and service	4	4	0.6	14	16	17,143	19,250	300	403	1.0

Source: County Business Patterns, 1992/93, CBP-92/93-1, U.S. Department of Commerce, Washington, D.C., April 1995. SIC categories for which data were suppressed or not available for both 1992 and 1993 are *not* displayed. The employment columns represent mid-March employment in the year. Pay per employee is calculated by dividing 1st Quarter payroll, annualized, by mid-March employment. The columns headed "% State" show the county's percentage of the state total for the SIC in 1993; for example, 0.9% for SIC 6030 means that the county had 0.9 percent of the state's total establishments (or payroll) in SIC 6030 in 1993. A dash (-) is used to indicate that data are not available or cannot be calculated; *nec* means not elsewhere classified.

SIC	Industry	No. Establishments			Employment		Pay / Employee		Annual Payroll ($ 000)		
		1992	1993	% State	1992	1993	1992	1993	1992	1993	% State
WALWORTH, SD											
60 –	**Finance, insurance, and real estate**	26	23	*1.1*	97	85	16,536	18,306	1,549	1,574	*0.4*
6000	Depository institutions	4	4	*0.9*	-	50	-	20,640	-	1,049	*0.6*
6020	Commercial banks	3	3	*1.0*	45	-	20,000	-	907	-	-
6400	Insurance agents, brokers, and service	11	10	*1.6*	22	24	14,909	12,500	301	304	*0.8*
6500	Real estate	10	7	*1.1*	22	-	5,455	-	132	-	-
6510	Real estate operators and lessors	3	3	*1.0*	7	3	5,143	4,000	17	7	*0.1*
6530	Real estate agents and managers	4	2	*0.9*	5	-	4,800	-	22	-	-
YANKTON, SD											
60 –	**Finance, insurance, and real estate**	56	56	*2.7*	285	441	20,042	18,685	6,062	9,321	*2.5*
6000	Depository institutions	12	12	*2.7*	187	342	19,187	17,965	4,063	7,203	*3.8*
6300	Insurance carriers	5	3	*2.2*	4	-	21,000	-	67	-	-
6400	Insurance agents, brokers, and service	18	21	*3.3*	33	35	15,273	15,543	683	719	*1.8*
6500	Real estate	16	15	*2.4*	35	29	8,114	9,103	305	321	*1.1*
6510	Real estate operators and lessors	8	8	*2.7*	13	18	5,846	8,222	84	199	*1.7*
6530	Real estate agents and managers	4	5	*2.3*	3	-	6,667	-	21	-	-
ZIEBACH, SD											
60 –	**Finance, insurance, and real estate**	1	1	*0.0*	-	-	-	-	-	-	-

Source: County Business Patterns, 1992/93, CBP-92/93-1, U.S. Department of Commerce, Washington, D.C., April 1995. SIC categories for which data were suppressed or not available for both 1992 and 1993 are *not* displayed. The employment columns represent mid-March employment in the year. Pay per employee is calculated by dividing 1st Quarter payroll, annualized, by mid-March employment. The columns headed "% State" show the county's percentage of the state total for the SIC in 1993; for example, 0.9% for SIC 6030 means that the county had 0.9 percent of the state's total establishments (or payroll) in SIC 6030 in 1993. A dash (-) is used to indicate that data are not available or cannot be calculated; *nec* means not elsewhere classified.

TENNESSEE

SIC	Industry	No. Establishments			Employment		Pay / Employee		Annual Payroll ($ 000)		
		1992	1993	% State	1992	1993	1992	1993	1992	1993	% State
ANDERSON, TN											
60 –	**Finance, insurance, and real estate**	132	137	1.3	939	925	18,547	19,157	18,526	19,835	0.7
6000	Depository institutions	39	39	1.8	583	559	18,552	17,996	11,155	11,033	1.2
6020	Commercial banks	20	23	1.5	209	-	20,478	-	4,166	-	-
6030	Savings institutions	7	4	1.9	66	-	17,030		1,107	-	-
6060	Credit unions	12	12	3.1	308	319	17,571	15,774	5,882	5,703	8.7
6100	Nondepository institutions	4	4	0.5	16	14	24,250	29,429	385	435	0.2
6140	Personal credit institutions	4	3	0.6	16	-	24,250	-	385	-	-
6200	Security and commodity brokers	7	7	1.6	12	16	55,000	61,000	750	942	0.3
6210	Security brokers and dealers	3	3	1.1	-	11	-	72,727	-	755	0.3
6280	Security and commodity services	4	4	2.6	-	5	-	35,200	-	187	0.4
6300	Insurance carriers	9	9	1.1	60	47	28,600	32,085	1,909	1,659	0.2
6400	Insurance agents, brokers, and service	26	27	1.2	60	62	19,400	18,581	1,303	1,365	0.4
6500	Real estate	42	48	1.5	194	213	12,680	15,042	2,833	3,953	1.1
6510	Real estate operators and lessors	21	23	1.6	140	160	12,429	15,800	2,011	2,926	2.6
6530	Real estate agents and managers	13	18	1.2	33	36	12,364	12,667	505	692	0.3
6553	Cemetery subdividers and developers	6	4	3.2	17	16	15,765	13,000	277	298	2.7
6700	Holding and other investment offices	5	3	0.7	14	14	15,143	29,143	191	448	0.3
BEDFORD, TN											
60 –	**Finance, insurance, and real estate**	47	48	0.5	317	310	18,019	18,052	5,923	5,520	0.2
6000	Depository institutions	11	11	0.5	194	184	18,227	20,130	3,677	3,543	0.4
6020	Commercial banks	8	8	0.5	177	168	18,486	20,571	3,432	3,302	0.5
6140	Personal credit institutions	4	3	0.6	11	10	20,364	22,000	266	247	0.3
6400	Insurance agents, brokers, and service	13	14	0.6	32	35	18,250	13,486	555	464	0.1
6500	Real estate	14	15	0.5	34	37	8,118	8,432	309	344	0.1
6510	Real estate operators and lessors	3	4	0.3	16	15	6,000	8,533	100	129	0.1
6530	Real estate agents and managers	9	10	0.7	15	-	10,667	-	185	-	-
BENTON, TN											
60 –	**Finance, insurance, and real estate**	17	22	0.2	91	96	21,319	18,167	1,945	2,026	0.1
6000	Depository institutions	8	8	0.4	77	79	23,584	19,646	1,814	1,724	0.2
6400	Insurance agents, brokers, and service	6	8	0.3	10	12	10,000	10,000	110	203	0.1
6500	Real estate	3	6	0.2	4	5	6,000	14,400	21	99	0.0
6530	Real estate agents and managers	3	4	0.3	4	-	6,000	-	21	-	-
BLEDSOE, TN											
60 –	**Finance, insurance, and real estate**	8	8	0.1	33	36	19,273	19,889	671	734	0.0
6400	Insurance agents, brokers, and service	4	4	0.2	5	6	13,600	12,000	76	81	0.0
BLOUNT, TN											
60 –	**Finance, insurance, and real estate**	130	143	1.4	1,114	1,223	18,639	19,853	21,644	25,368	0.8
6000	Depository institutions	37	39	1.8	601	711	18,203	19,561	11,033	12,443	1.4
6020	Commercial banks	28	29	1.8	495	558	17,568	19,104	8,763	9,958	1.4
6030	Savings institutions	5	6	2.9	-	128	-	21,562	-	1,870	2.6
6060	Credit unions	4	4	1.0	-	25	-	19,520	-	615	0.9
6100	Nondepository institutions	13	14	1.6	172	184	18,860	20,761	3,786	5,568	2.4
6140	Personal credit institutions	10	6	1.2	161	164	18,236	20,512	3,544	4,919	5.7
6300	Insurance carriers	8	7	0.8	-	31	-	28,903	-	1,045	0.1
6400	Insurance agents, brokers, and service	22	25	1.1	93	101	24,989	26,297	2,363	2,819	0.9
6500	Real estate	43	50	1.5	194	185	14,062	14,270	2,745	3,086	0.9

Source: County Business Patterns, 1992/93, CBP-92/93-1, U.S. Department of Commerce, Washington, D.C., April 1995. SIC categories for which data were suppressed or not available for both 1992 and 1993 are not displayed. The employment columns represent mid-March employment in the year. Pay per employee is calculated by dividing 1st Quarter payroll, annualized, by mid-March employment. The columns headed "% State" show the county's percentage of the state total for the SIC in 1993; for example, 0.9% for SIC 6030 means that the county had 0.9 percent of the state's total establishments (or payroll) in SIC 6030 in 1993. A dash (-) is used to indicate that data are not available or cannot be calculated; nec means not elsewhere classified.

Continued on next page.

SIC	Industry	No. Establishments			Employment		Pay / Employee		Annual Payroll ($ 000)		
		1992	1993	% State	1992	1993	1992	1993	1992	1993	% State
BLOUNT, TN - [continued]											
6510	Real estate operators and lessors	10	15	1.1	42	54	13,238	16,963	585	987	0.9
6530	Real estate agents and managers	23	27	1.8	74	83	18,378	15,084	1,202	1,497	0.7
6553	Cemetery subdividers and developers	6	5	4.0	46	39	8,435	8,308	369	396	3.6
BRADLEY, TN											
60 –	**Finance, insurance, and real estate**	134	136	1.3	872	895	19,179	20,554	17,694	19,198	0.6
6000	Depository institutions	34	36	1.6	421	418	21,311	23,799	9,211	10,016	1.1
6020	Commercial banks	22	23	1.5	322	341	22,807	25,408	7,623	8,702	1.2
6100	Nondepository institutions	16	16	1.8	176	191	18,750	19,874	3,671	4,148	1.8
6140	Personal credit institutions	11	12	2.4	160	175	18,775	19,886	3,345	3,715	4.3
6300	Insurance carriers	12	8	0.9	60	-	23,533	-	1,475	-	-
6400	Insurance agents, brokers, and service	25	25	1.1	66	88	18,182	18,318	1,399	1,715	0.5
6500	Real estate	42	45	1.4	136	143	10,647	10,126	1,555	1,672	0.5
6510	Real estate operators and lessors	14	19	1.3	43	47	8,837	9,617	423	457	0.4
6530	Real estate agents and managers	15	20	1.3	52	66	12,154	11,152	700	854	0.4
6552	Subdividers and developers, n.e.c.	5	2	1.4	6	-	8,000	-	89	-	-
6700	Holding and other investment offices	3	3	0.7	-	10	-	19,600	-	219	0.2
CAMPBELL, TN											
60 –	**Finance, insurance, and real estate**	36	39	0.4	211	280	19,204	16,214	4,387	5,498	0.2
6000	Depository institutions	11	12	0.5	119	177	23,227	18,757	2,865	3,945	0.4
6400	Insurance agents, brokers, and service	8	8	0.3	36	33	20,889	17,333	730	745	0.2
6500	Real estate	12	14	0.4	46	59	7,739	7,593	558	578	0.2
6510	Real estate operators and lessors	4	4	0.3	4	11	7,000	13,455	44	88	0.1
6530	Real estate agents and managers	3	4	0.3	2	2	4,000	4,000	59	23	0.0
CANNON, TN											
60 –	**Finance, insurance, and real estate**	17	18	0.2	152	215	12,184	14,195	2,024	3,158	0.1
6400	Insurance agents, brokers, and service	6	6	0.3	24	29	14,667	14,207	387	411	0.1
CARROLL, TN											
60 –	**Finance, insurance, and real estate**	39	42	0.4	229	254	16,629	18,283	4,203	4,767	0.2
6000	Depository institutions	17	18	0.8	177	200	18,079	20,100	3,540	4,020	0.4
6400	Insurance agents, brokers, and service	8	9	0.4	26	26	14,615	14,769	394	426	0.1
6500	Real estate	11	13	0.4	22	-	8,727	-	231	-	-
6510	Real estate operators and lessors	2	4	0.3	-	7	-	6,857	-	55	0.0
6530	Real estate agents and managers	6	5	0.3	13	9	10,154	4,889	169	45	0.0
CARTER, TN											
60 –	**Finance, insurance, and real estate**	57	60	0.6	336	359	18,524	20,869	7,577	8,635	0.3
6000	Depository institutions	18	18	0.8	219	230	17,443	21,130	4,476	4,880	0.5
6030	Savings institutions	5	5	2.4	48	49	20,000	27,429	1,069	1,207	1.7
6100	Nondepository institutions	6	7	0.8	28	39	20,000	21,026	553	1,019	0.8
6140	Personal credit institutions	6	7	1.4	28	39	20,000	21,026	553	1,019	1.2
6400	Insurance agents, brokers, and service	15	18	0.8	42	42	12,857	11,048	520	558	0.2
6500	Real estate	9	10	0.3	31	-	12,903	-	428	-	-
6510	Real estate operators and lessors	3	4	0.3	12	-	13,333	-	169	-	-
6530	Real estate agents and managers	4	5	0.3	-	10	-	10,000	-	105	0.1
CHEATHAM, TN											
60 –	**Finance, insurance, and real estate**	22	23	0.2	84	107	20,429	20,411	1,898	1,974	0.1
6000	Depository institutions	8	8	0.4	67	76	20,657	22,842	1,490	1,483	0.2
6400	Insurance agents, brokers, and service	3	5	0.2	9	-	21,778	-	229	-	-
6500	Real estate	8	9	0.3	6	14	16,667	9,143	121	164	0.0
6510	Real estate operators and lessors	3	2	0.1	3	-	22,667	-	73	-	-
6530	Real estate agents and managers	4	6	0.4	2	5	14,000	8,000	41	67	0.0

Source: County Business Patterns, 1992/93, CBP-92/93-1, U.S. Department of Commerce, Washington, D.C., April 1995. SIC categories for which data were suppressed or not available for both 1992 and 1993 are *not* displayed. The employment columns represent mid-March employment in the year. Pay per employee is calculated by dividing 1st Quarter payroll, annualized, by mid-March employment. The columns headed "% State" show the county's percentage of the state total for the SIC in 1993; for example, 0.9% for SIC 6030 means that the county had 0.9 percent of the state's total establishments (or payroll) in SIC 6030 in 1993. A dash (-) is used to indicate that data are not available or cannot be calculated; *nec* means not elsewhere classified.

SIC	Industry	No. Establishments			Employment		Pay / Employee		Annual Payroll ($ 000)		
		1992	1993	% State	1992	1993	1992	1993	1992	1993	% State
CHESTER, TN											
60 –	**Finance, insurance, and real estate**	12	13	0.1	-	75	-	19,467	-	1,679	0.1
6000	Depository institutions	5	5	0.2	64	62	18,938	20,774	1,434	1,488	0.2
6020	Commercial banks	5	5	0.3	64	62	18,938	20,774	1,434	1,488	0.2
6400	Insurance agents, brokers, and service	4	4	0.2	8	8	12,500	13,000	105	117	0.0
CLAIBORNE, TN											
60 –	**Finance, insurance, and real estate**	30	27	0.3	253	313	18,846	13,725	4,839	4,556	0.2
6000	Depository institutions	11	10	0.5	212	169	15,170	16,757	3,564	3,151	0.4
6400	Insurance agents, brokers, and service	6	5	0.2	22	12	27,273	27,667	601	334	0.1
6500	Real estate	11	9	0.3	-	11	-	10,182	-	199	0.1
6510	Real estate operators and lessors	5	2	0.1	7	-	17,143	-	110	-	-
6530	Real estate agents and managers	1	3	0.2	-	4	-	7,000	-	101	0.0
CLAY, TN											
60 –	**Finance, insurance, and real estate**	6	5	0.0	32	21	17,500	21,905	491	396	0.0
6400	Insurance agents, brokers, and service	3	3	0.1	5	-	16,800	-	85	-	-
COCKE, TN											
60 –	**Finance, insurance, and real estate**	38	36	0.3	227	234	16,458	16,462	3,660	3,605	0.1
6000	Depository institutions	13	12	0.5	158	159	17,139	18,214	2,593	2,588	0.3
6100	Nondepository institutions	8	7	0.8	27	29	17,481	15,172	473	451	0.2
6140	Personal credit institutions	8	7	1.4	27	29	17,481	15,172	473	451	0.5
6400	Insurance agents, brokers, and service	5	6	0.3	-	20	-	16,000	-	320	0.1
6500	Real estate	11	11	0.3	21	26	10,095	7,538	252	246	0.1
6510	Real estate operators and lessors	7	6	0.4	9	11	10,667	7,273	102	92	0.1
COFFEE, TN											
60 –	**Finance, insurance, and real estate**	80	87	0.8	556	577	18,842	18,912	11,105	12,366	0.4
6000	Depository institutions	19	22	1.0	303	383	18,350	18,465	5,771	8,017	0.9
6100	Nondepository institutions	11	8	0.9	107	-	20,860	-	2,231	-	-
6140	Personal credit institutions	9	5	1.0	-	30	-	22,133	-	723	0.8
6400	Insurance agents, brokers, and service	19	18	0.8	48	51	21,000	19,373	1,130	1,129	0.4
6500	Real estate	20	29	0.9	52	66	10,538	11,394	588	887	0.2
6510	Real estate operators and lessors	6	11	0.8	18	32	10,444	10,375	197	366	0.3
6530	Real estate agents and managers	11	15	1.0	-	20	-	7,600	-	198	0.1
CROCKETT, TN											
60 –	**Finance, insurance, and real estate**	18	19	0.2	130	134	16,308	16,806	2,353	2,386	0.1
6000	Depository institutions	10	10	0.5	114	113	15,965	16,637	2,048	2,041	0.2
6020	Commercial banks	10	10	0.6	114	113	15,965	16,637	2,048	2,041	0.3
6400	Insurance agents, brokers, and service	5	7	0.3	11	-	18,182	-	200	-	-
CUMBERLAND, TN											
60 –	**Finance, insurance, and real estate**	67	63	0.6	617	710	16,143	17,668	9,439	12,664	0.4
6000	Depository institutions	14	14	0.6	163	174	18,969	19,057	3,147	3,256	0.4
6060	Credit unions	2	3	0.8	-	10	-	12,400	-	146	0.2
6100	Nondepository institutions	6	4	0.5	-	11	-	17,091	-	173	0.1
6140	Personal credit institutions	6	4	0.8	-	11	-	17,091	-	173	0.2
6400	Insurance agents, brokers, and service	13	12	0.5	73	28	26,027	12,857	1,702	411	0.1
6500	Real estate	27	26	0.8	354	445	12,610	15,452	4,036	7,115	2.0
6510	Real estate operators and lessors	5	7	0.5	170	123	14,188	14,699	1,828	1,752	1.5
6530	Real estate agents and managers	14	14	0.9	156	306	10,795	15,908	1,825	5,083	2.4
DAVIDSON, TN											
60 –	**Finance, insurance, and real estate**	1,857	1,838	17.6	28,308	27,961	29,721	28,671	854,960	825,515	27.6
6000	Depository institutions	258	250	11.3	7,688	7,898	26,219	27,624	187,641	204,253	22.8
6020	Commercial banks	176	167	10.6	6,505	5,950	26,275	28,510	165,653	156,571	21.8
6030	Savings institutions	27	14	6.8	511	142	29,894	26,704	6,117	3,739	5.2

Source: County Business Patterns, 1992/93, CBP-92/93-1, U.S. Department of Commerce, Washington, D.C., April 1995. SIC categories for which data were suppressed or not available for both 1992 and 1993 are not displayed. The employment columns represent mid-March employment in the year. Pay per employee is calculated by dividing 1st Quarter payroll, annualized, by mid-March employment. The columns headed "% State" show the county's percentage of the state total for the SIC in 1993; for example, 0.9% for SIC 6030 means that the county had 0.9 percent of the state's total establishments (or payroll) in SIC 6030 in 1993. A dash (-) is used to indicate that data are not available or cannot be calculated; nec means not elsewhere classified.

Continued on next page.

SIC	Industry	No. Establishments			Employment		Pay / Employee		Annual Payroll ($ 000)		
		1992	1993	% State	1992	1993	1992	1993	1992	1993	% State
DAVIDSON, TN - [continued]											
6060	Credit unions	42	52	13.5	347	401	22,582	22,803	8,049	9,887	15.1
6100	Nondepository institutions	171	150	16.9	-	1,439	-	34,263	-	56,398	24.8
6140	Personal credit institutions	92	71	14.4	614	478	29,231	25,473	16,686	11,629	13.5
6150	Business credit institutions	17	18	23.7	354	533	37,831	41,726	13,583	23,825	-
6160	Mortgage bankers and brokers	59	60	22.6	378	428	29,503	34,785	12,649	20,919	22.1
6200	Security and commodity brokers	95	88	19.6	1,022	1,235	57,667	64,531	66,418	84,456	25.5
6210	Security brokers and dealers	51	42	15.2	896	1,088	59,839	63,298	59,532	74,032	27.0
6220	Commodity contracts brokers, dealers	5	2	13.3	6	-	20,667	-	200	-	-
6280	Security and commodity services	39	44	28.2	120	-	43,300		6,686	-	-
6300	Insurance carriers	249	214	25.2	7,369	6,993	29,643	27,754	226,563	200,472	28.6
6310	Life insurance	88	73	24.3	3,625	3,219	29,626	23,505	110,622	79,258	24.2
6330	Fire, marine, and casualty insurance	96	83	22.9	2,660	2,880	32,707	32,326	88,189	95,531	38.9
6350	Surety insurance	3	2	20.0	19	-	45,474	-	962	-	-
6360	Title insurance	12	7	25.0	59	-	24,136	-	1,925	-	-
6370	Pension, health, and welfare funds	33	28	34.6	275	310	12,393	11,871	4,368	3,868	31.8
6400	Insurance agents, brokers, and service	339	377	16.3	3,251	3,075	36,560	33,344	121,006	106,672	33.8
6500	Real estate	639	642	19.4	5,565	5,914	16,653	16,326	97,093	109,895	30.4
6510	Real estate operators and lessors	268	292	20.7	1,705	2,019	13,762	12,884	23,123	29,730	26.0
6530	Real estate agents and managers	272	301	19.6	3,418	3,540	17,623	18,090	64,134	71,718	34.5
6540	Title abstract offices	12	15	21.7	55	103	22,545	21,398	1,824	3,499	27.7
6552	Subdividers and developers, n.e.c.	23	21	14.9	81	84	21,926	11,619	1,627	1,132	8.0
6553	Cemetery subdividers and developers	11	8	6.3	133	165	18,286	19,636	2,589	3,312	30.0
6700	Holding and other investment offices	101	111	27.3	1,613	-	49,369	-	87,004	-	-
6710	Holding offices	28	25	18.7	1,178	385	56,343	44,104	71,684	17,108	20.6
6720	Investment offices	7	3	33.3	23	-	30,261	-	731	-	-
6732	Educational, religious, etc. trusts	13	17	27.9	78	156	16,872	15,923	1,433	2,538	38.1
6733	Trusts, n.e.c.	14	12	17.6	61	33	21,115	14,788	1,547	605	10.8
6794	Patent owners and lessors	25	35	57.4	209	321	30,029	29,583	7,181	12,082	50.5
DECATUR, TN											
60 –	**Finance, insurance, and real estate**	12	13	0.1	86	77	14,558	16,987	1,398	1,511	0.1
6000	Depository institutions	6	6	0.3	74	67	15,297	17,910	1,264	1,388	0.2
6020	Commercial banks	6	6	0.4	74	67	15,297	17,910	1,264	1,388	0.2
DE KALB, TN											
60 –	**Finance, insurance, and real estate**	22	21	0.2	147	110	19,782	18,255	2,725	1,992	0.1
6000	Depository institutions	7	4	0.2	117	78	20,957	20,308	2,265	1,554	0.2
6020	Commercial banks	7	4	0.3	117	78	20,957	20,308	2,265	1,554	0.2
6400	Insurance agents, brokers, and service	6	6	0.3	15	15	22,667	18,400	337	284	0.1
6500	Real estate	9	11	0.3	15	17	7,733	8,706	123	154	0.0
6530	Real estate agents and managers	6	5	0.3	9	9	7,556	6,667	79	58	0.0
DICKSON, TN											
60 –	**Finance, insurance, and real estate**	53	55	0.5	321	345	20,822	19,849	7,784	8,043	0.3
6000	Depository institutions	15	15	0.7	186	194	20,796	19,856	4,058	3,949	0.4
6100	Nondepository institutions	4	4	0.5	27	30	26,519	25,733	719	887	0.4
6400	Insurance agents, brokers, and service	16	15	0.6	79	84	22,582	21,905	2,644	2,774	0.9
6500	Real estate	15	18	0.5	24	33	8,500	9,091	259	342	0.1
6510	Real estate operators and lessors	6	7	0.5	10	14	6,400	8,286	88	106	0.1
6530	Real estate agents and managers	6	10	0.7	8	-	8,500	-	88	-	-
DYER, TN											
60 –	**Finance, insurance, and real estate**	75	75	0.7	542	589	22,332	22,126	12,469	13,499	0.5
6000	Depository institutions	18	18	0.8	310	339	19,574	16,885	6,076	6,377	0.7
6100	Nondepository institutions	9	11	1.2	-	57	-	25,825	-	1,561	0.7
6140	Personal credit institutions	5	6	1.2	-	27	-	23,852	-	604	0.7
6300	Insurance carriers	5	4	0.5	64	57	37,312	47,579	2,195	2,392	0.3
6310	Life insurance	4	4	1.3	-	57	-	47,579	-	2,392	0.7

Source: County Business Patterns, 1992/93, CBP-92/93-1, U.S. Department of Commerce, Washington, D.C., April 1995. SIC categories for which data were suppressed or not available for both 1992 and 1993 are *not* displayed. The employment columns represent mid-March employment in the year. Pay per employee is calculated by dividing 1st Quarter payroll, annualized, by mid-March employment. The columns headed "% State" show the county's percentage of the state total for the SIC in 1993; for example, 0.9% for SIC 6030 means that the county had 0.9 percent of the state's total establishments (or payroll) in SIC 6030 in 1993. A dash (-) is used to indicate that data are not available or cannot be calculated; *nec* means not elsewhere classified.

Continued on next page.

SIC	Industry	No. Establishments			Employment		Pay / Employee		Annual Payroll ($ 000)		
		1992	1993	% State	1992	1993	1992	1993	1992	1993	% State
DYER, TN - [continued]											
6400	Insurance agents, brokers, and service	18	18	0.8	73	74	20,219	20,000	1,837	1,761	0.6
6500	Real estate	23	21	0.6	41	44	15,220	22,273	740	780	0.2
6510	Real estate operators and lessors	17	14	1.0	34	34	16,471	26,353	655	680	0.6
FAYETTE, TN											
60 –	**Finance, insurance, and real estate**	21	21	0.2	127	131	16,409	16,000	2,299	2,426	0.1
6000	Depository institutions	5	5	0.2	98	98	16,816	16,571	1,845	1,888	0.2
6020	Commercial banks	4	5	0.3	-	98	-	16,571	-	1,888	0.3
6400	Insurance agents, brokers, and service	5	6	0.3	10	12	15,200	16,000	174	208	0.1
6500	Real estate	7	8	0.2	9	-	12,000	-	111	-	-
6510	Real estate operators and lessors	5	5	0.4	6	7	13,333	14,857	81	99	0.1
FENTRESS, TN											
60 –	**Finance, insurance, and real estate**	13	14	0.1	111	109	19,207	18,606	2,163	2,254	0.1
6000	Depository institutions	3	3	0.1	72	71	19,222	19,155	1,455	1,501	0.2
6400	Insurance agents, brokers, and service	4	5	0.2	14	17	16,857	16,000	256	291	0.1
6500	Real estate	2	3	0.1	-	10	-	13,200	-	179	0.0
FRANKLIN, TN											
60 –	**Finance, insurance, and real estate**	41	43	0.4	210	231	18,857	17,801	4,022	4,045	0.1
6000	Depository institutions	11	12	0.5	114	162	22,070	18,963	2,572	2,961	0.3
6100	Nondepository institutions	6	5	0.6	40	-	18,900	-	764	-	-
6200	Security and commodity brokers	2	3	0.7	-	3	-	5,333	-	19	0.0
6210	Security brokers and dealers	2	3	1.1	-	3	-	5,333	-	19	0.0
6400	Insurance agents, brokers, and service	9	9	0.4	34	32	14,235	14,875	460	468	0.1
6500	Real estate	11	13	0.4	18	17	8,889	9,176	177	193	0.1
6510	Real estate operators and lessors	2	4	0.3	-	6	-	10,000	-	74	0.1
6530	Real estate agents and managers	8	8	0.5	8	-	6,000	-	64	-	-
GIBSON, TN											
60 –	**Finance, insurance, and real estate**	86	77	0.7	502	440	18,462	19,064	9,643	8,783	0.3
6000	Depository institutions	31	28	1.3	331	313	18,792	19,834	5,967	6,003	0.7
6020	Commercial banks	29	27	1.7	327	-	18,765	-	5,936	-	-
6100	Nondepository institutions	5	5	0.6	15	14	24,000	20,000	288	276	0.1
6400	Insurance agents, brokers, and service	26	22	0.9	78	71	17,026	17,746	1,327	1,428	0.5
6500	Real estate	16	16	0.5	25	29	6,400	8,966	147	248	0.1
6510	Real estate operators and lessors	7	6	0.4	8	-	8,000	-	69	-	-
6530	Real estate agents and managers	8	9	0.6	16	-	5,500	-	75	-	-
GILES, TN											
60 –	**Finance, insurance, and real estate**	28	30	0.3	258	263	19,473	21,019	4,840	5,533	0.2
6000	Depository institutions	9	10	0.5	198	198	21,657	22,808	3,975	4,196	0.5
6020	Commercial banks	7	10	0.6	-	198	-	22,808	-	4,196	0.6
6400	Insurance agents, brokers, and service	7	9	0.4	23	-	15,652	-	363	-	-
6500	Real estate	9	10	0.3	29	39	10,483	14,154	396	858	0.2
6510	Real estate operators and lessors	5	4	0.3	17	-	12,000	-	300	-	-
6530	Real estate agents and managers	3	5	0.3	8	-	7,000	-	53	-	-
GRAINGER, TN											
60 –	**Finance, insurance, and real estate**	7	9	0.1	-	-	-	-	-	-	-
GREENE, TN											
60 –	**Finance, insurance, and real estate**	85	88	0.8	519	524	22,844	21,916	12,731	12,194	0.4
6000	Depository institutions	30	32	1.4	266	284	22,481	18,915	6,116	5,498	0.6
6020	Commercial banks	19	22	1.4	206	231	23,320	19,550	4,875	4,566	0.6
6030	Savings institutions	5	2	1.0	34	-	20,824	-	771	-	-
6060	Credit unions	6	8	2.1	26	-	18,000	-	470	-	-
6100	Nondepository institutions	13	10	1.1	44	36	16,000	20,333	874	976	0.4

Source: County Business Patterns, 1992/93, CBP-92/93-1, U.S. Department of Commerce, Washington, D.C., April 1995. SIC categories for which data were suppressed or not available for both 1992 and 1993 are *not* displayed. The employment columns represent mid-March employment in the year. Pay per employee is calculated by dividing 1st Quarter payroll, annualized, by mid-March employment. The columns headed "% State" show the county's percentage of the state total for the SIC in 1993; for example, 0.9% for SIC 6030 means that the county had 0.9 percent of the state's total establishments (or payroll) in SIC 6030 in 1993. A dash (-) is used to indicate that data are not available or cannot be calculated; *nec* means not elsewhere classified.

Continued on next page.

SIC	Industry	No. Establishments			Employment		Pay / Employee		Annual Payroll ($ 000)		
		1992	1993	% State	1992	1993	1992	1993	1992	1993	% State
GREENE, TN - [continued]											
6300	Insurance carriers	4	3	0.4	-	21	-	32,000	-	649	0.1
6400	Insurance agents, brokers, and service	16	23	1.0	118	126	28,169	27,905	3,719	3,570	1.1
6500	Real estate	19	17	0.5	33	23	9,212	11,130	333	314	0.1
6510	Real estate operators and lessors	7	8	0.6	11	13	8,727	9,231	100	137	0.1
6530	Real estate agents and managers	7	6	0.4	10	6	14,800	17,333	182	127	0.1
GRUNDY, TN											
60 –	**Finance, insurance, and real estate**	12	9	0.1	43	18	12,372	12,889	558	238	0.0
6400	Insurance agents, brokers, and service	3	3	0.1	6	5	8,000	8,800	47	47	0.0
HAMBLEN, TN											
60 –	**Finance, insurance, and real estate**	113	120	1.1	546	527	18,952	19,233	10,746	11,585	0.4
6000	Depository institutions	25	25	1.1	240	235	18,700	20,374	4,432	5,106	0.6
6020	Commercial banks	13	15	1.0	128	135	20,531	23,496	2,416	3,271	0.5
6030	Savings institutions	5	3	1.4	88	-	16,545	-	1,592	-	-
6060	Credit unions	7	7	1.8	24	-	16,833	-	424	-	-
6100	Nondepository institutions	14	15	1.7	63	55	20,063	18,982	1,385	1,190	0.5
6140	Personal credit institutions	12	12	2.4	-	48	-	19,833	-	1,054	1.2
6300	Insurance carriers	8	8	0.9	-	24	-	40,167	-	971	0.1
6400	Insurance agents, brokers, and service	26	29	1.3	111	101	16,721	18,455	2,052	2,195	0.7
6500	Real estate	34	38	1.1	84	91	8,810	9,626	923	1,033	0.3
6510	Real estate operators and lessors	14	13	0.9	35	27	7,086	10,815	282	311	0.3
6530	Real estate agents and managers	15	19	1.2	28	33	11,286	9,333	418	385	0.2
6700	Holding and other investment offices	4	3	0.7	9	-	52,444	-	280	-	-
HAMILTON, TN											
60 –	**Finance, insurance, and real estate**	761	768	7.3	11,444	11,403	26,518	29,155	310,231	334,437	11.2
6000	Depository institutions	145	151	6.8	2,176	2,149	24,096	28,052	51,906	52,663	5.9
6020	Commercial banks	80	85	5.4	1,548	1,470	25,548	29,271	37,172	39,097	5.4
6030	Savings institutions	18	17	8.2	-	301	-	32,664	-	5,484	7.7
6060	Credit unions	44	45	11.7	-	365	-	19,792	-	7,890	12.0
6090	Functions closely related to banking	3	4	8.3	-	13	-	15,385	-	192	0.6
6100	Nondepository institutions	75	75	8.5	431	415	23,852	21,773	10,265	9,536	4.2
6140	Personal credit institutions	46	42	8.5	315	297	22,159	20,741	6,998	5,814	6.8
6150	Business credit institutions	4	4	5.3	9	-	36,889	-	370	-	-
6160	Mortgage bankers and brokers	25	27	10.2	107	104	27,738	23,846	2,897	3,290	3.5
6200	Security and commodity brokers	36	35	7.8	214	244	54,411	43,623	12,304	14,783	4.5
6210	Security brokers and dealers	17	11	4.0	170	169	60,471	53,988	10,703	12,735	4.6
6300	Insurance carriers	101	83	9.8	6,429	6,456	27,697	31,653	182,082	201,949	28.8
6310	Life insurance	39	34	11.3	4,146	4,156	27,983	32,345	118,546	135,826	41.4
6330	Fire, marine, and casualty insurance	30	29	8.0	390	382	37,446	31,602	13,093	12,181	5.0
6370	Pension, health, and welfare funds	11	7	8.6	87	-	44,092	-	3,289	-	-
6400	Insurance agents, brokers, and service	157	160	6.9	738	639	28,054	26,504	21,174	19,746	6.3
6500	Real estate	205	223	6.7	1,275	1,320	19,555	19,342	26,685	28,924	8.0
6510	Real estate operators and lessors	95	114	8.1	674	753	20,938	19,830	13,824	14,026	12.2
6530	Real estate agents and managers	76	85	5.5	404	437	18,277	18,975	8,814	11,666	5.6
6540	Title abstract offices	5	6	8.7	31	48	22,839	21,000	770	1,476	11.7
6552	Subdividers and developers, n.e.c.	9	10	7.1	30	6	25,200	24,000	914	449	3.2
6553	Cemetery subdividers and developers	7	8	6.3	74	76	15,297	15,211	1,347	1,307	11.8
6710	Holding offices	13	12	9.0	66	-	52,242	-	3,622	-	-
6732	Educational, religious, etc. trusts	12	12	19.7	42	41	21,905	25,268	1,007	1,086	16.3
6733	Trusts, n.e.c.	7	6	8.8	53	45	9,887	15,467	634	728	13.0
6799	Investors, n.e.c.	5	5	8.1	5	-	23,200	-	117	-	-
HANCOCK, TN											
60 –	**Finance, insurance, and real estate**	4	4	0.0	-	-	-	-	-	-	-

Source: County Business Patterns, 1992/93, CBP-92/93-1, U.S. Department of Commerce, Washington, D.C., April 1995. SIC categories for which data were suppressed or not available for both 1992 and 1993 are *not* displayed. The employment columns represent mid-March employment in the year. Pay per employee is calculated by dividing 1st Quarter payroll, annualized, by mid-March employment. The columns headed "% State" show the county's percentage of the state total for the SIC in 1993; for example, 0.9% for SIC 6030 means that the county had 0.9 percent of the state's total establishments (or payroll) in SIC 6030 in 1993. A dash (-) is used to indicate that data are not available or cannot be calculated; *nec* means not elsewhere classified.

SIC	Industry	No. Establishments			Employment		Pay / Employee		Annual Payroll ($ 000)		
		1992	1993	% State	1992	1993	1992	1993	1992	1993	% State
HARDEMAN, TN											
60 –	**Finance, insurance, and real estate**	27	28	0.3	219	218	15,087	15,743	3,566	3,815	0.1
6000	Depository institutions	9	9	0.4	158	166	16,937	17,566	2,919	3,209	0.4
6400	Insurance agents, brokers, and service	7	9	0.4	17	22	12,000	10,364	217	243	0.1
6500	Real estate	9	7	0.2	-	25	-	6,400	-	202	0.1
6530	Real estate agents and managers	4	3	0.2	17	-	11,294	-	188	-	-
6553	Cemetery subdividers and developers	2	3	2.4	-	3	-	4,000	-	28	0.3
HARDIN, TN											
60 –	**Finance, insurance, and real estate**	41	37	0.4	147	159	21,932	19,421	3,078	3,500	0.1
6000	Depository institutions	13	14	0.6	89	98	25,438	21,469	2,026	2,170	0.2
6100	Nondepository institutions	4	3	0.3	11	9	23,273	23,111	232	208	0.1
6140	Personal credit institutions	4	3	0.6	11	9	23,273	23,111	232	208	0.2
6400	Insurance agents, brokers, and service	7	7	0.3	19	21	14,316	13,524	270	313	0.1
6500	Real estate	11	9	0.3	19	22	8,632	9,091	182	429	0.1
6530	Real estate agents and managers	7	5	0.3	10	-	8,400	-	94	-	-
HAWKINS, TN											
60 –	**Finance, insurance, and real estate**	41	43	0.4	197	197	16,609	18,640	3,285	3,144	0.1
6000	Depository institutions	13	15	0.7	134	144	17,313	19,333	2,360	2,361	0.3
6020	Commercial banks	11	11	0.7	-	133	-	20,060	-	1,881	0.3
6100	Nondepository institutions	5	4	0.5	-	12	-	35,000	-	262	0.1
6400	Insurance agents, brokers, and service	7	6	0.3	18	-	10,222	-	186	-	-
6500	Real estate	13	16	0.5	25	25	10,880	10,880	308	314	0.1
6510	Real estate operators and lessors	4	5	0.4	11	11	12,000	11,273	136	142	0.1
6530	Real estate agents and managers	3	7	0.5	7	10	12,571	13,200	106	144	0.1
6553	Cemetery subdividers and developers	3	3	2.4	4	-	5,000	-	30	-	-
HAYWOOD, TN											
60 –	**Finance, insurance, and real estate**	28	28	0.3	265	258	15,638	17,380	4,289	4,721	0.2
6000	Depository institutions	6	6	0.3	125	123	18,080	18,472	2,273	2,330	0.3
6020	Commercial banks	6	6	0.4	125	123	18,080	18,472	2,273	2,330	0.3
6400	Insurance agents, brokers, and service	8	9	0.4	24	27	14,000	12,444	355	348	0.1
6500	Real estate	9	6	0.2	29	20	6,759	8,000	222	131	0.0
HENDERSON, TN											
60 –	**Finance, insurance, and real estate**	30	31	0.3	190	183	19,263	19,454	3,598	3,748	0.1
6000	Depository institutions	15	16	0.7	153	148	19,399	19,919	2,806	3,002	0.3
6400	Insurance agents, brokers, and service	6	8	0.3	21	24	18,667	16,667	475	528	0.2
6500	Real estate	4	4	0.1	5	7	13,600	10,286	68	70	0.0
6510	Real estate operators and lessors	4	4	0.3	5	7	13,600	10,286	68	70	0.1
HENRY, TN											
60 –	**Finance, insurance, and real estate**	44	46	0.4	272	294	20,353	18,980	5,789	5,915	0.2
6000	Depository institutions	18	18	0.8	213	238	21,239	18,908	4,601	4,665	0.5
6400	Insurance agents, brokers, and service	9	10	0.4	25	28	15,040	13,000	381	400	0.1
6500	Real estate	11	14	0.4	16	18	6,750	14,222	237	330	0.1
6510	Real estate operators and lessors	3	4	0.3	5	-	6,400	-	32	-	-
6530	Real estate agents and managers	6	8	0.5	10	13	7,200	16,615	195	269	0.1
HICKMAN, TN											
60 –	**Finance, insurance, and real estate**	10	10	0.1	99	100	17,495	18,280	1,810	1,895	0.1
6000	Depository institutions	5	4	0.2	85	-	18,400	-	1,627	-	-
6400	Insurance agents, brokers, and service	1	3	0.1	-	3	-	16,000	-	63	0.0
HOUSTON, TN											
60 –	**Finance, insurance, and real estate**	5	5	0.0	-	21	-	19,810	-	272	0.0

Source: County Business Patterns, 1992/93, CBP-92/93-1, U.S. Department of Commerce, Washington, D.C., April 1995. SIC categories for which data were suppressed or not available for both 1992 and 1993 are not displayed. The employment columns represent mid-March employment in the year. Pay per employee is calculated by dividing 1st Quarter payroll, annualized, by mid-March employment. The columns headed "% State" show the county's percentage of the state total for the SIC in 1993; for example, 0.9% for SIC 6030 means that the county had 0.9 percent of the state's total establishments (or payroll) in SIC 6030 in 1993. A dash (-) is used to indicate that data are not available or cannot be calculated; nec means not elsewhere classified.

SIC	Industry	No. Establishments			Employment		Pay / Employee		Annual Payroll ($ 000)		
		1992	1993	% State	1992	1993	1992	1993	1992	1993	% State
HUMPHREYS, TN											
60 –	Finance, insurance, and real estate	22	22	0.2	103	88	18,330	23,045	2,063	2,432	0.1
6000	Depository institutions	7	8	0.4	64	57	17,938	20,702	1,172	1,195	0.1
6400	Insurance agents, brokers, and service	7	6	0.3	19	18	18,737	20,222	483	455	0.1
6500	Real estate	5	4	0.1	-	9	-	44,444	-	434	0.1
JACKSON, TN											
60 –	Finance, insurance, and real estate	7	5	0.0	45	44	18,400	20,455	921	962	0.0
JEFFERSON, TN											
60 –	Finance, insurance, and real estate	41	42	0.4	177	199	16,316	16,382	2,934	3,274	0.1
6000	Depository institutions	16	16	0.7	121	126	16,893	17,937	2,077	2,220	0.2
6020	Commercial banks	12	12	0.8	113	117	17,310	18,496	1,981	2,112	0.3
6400	Insurance agents, brokers, and service	12	12	0.5	25	21	12,160	13,333	299	253	0.1
6500	Real estate	7	8	0.2	12	33	9,333	7,879	104	291	0.1
6530	Real estate agents and managers	4	3	0.2	4	-	9,000	-	37	-	-
6553	Cemetery subdividers and developers	3	3	2.4	8	10	9,500	4,800	67	59	0.5
JOHNSON, TN											
60 –	Finance, insurance, and real estate	19	20	0.2	92	93	15,870	16,817	1,634	1,838	0.1
6000	Depository institutions	5	5	0.2	63	62	18,159	19,161	1,320	1,440	0.2
6400	Insurance agents, brokers, and service	4	4	0.2	7	6	6,286	7,333	46	54	0.0
6500	Real estate	7	8	0.2	14	17	7,429	8,235	109	158	0.0
6510	Real estate operators and lessors	5	7	0.5	12	-	7,000	-	86	-	-
KNOX, TN											
60 –	Finance, insurance, and real estate	945	951	9.1	7,693	8,013	24,595	25,236	202,469	221,379	7.4
6000	Depository institutions	156	149	6.7	2,486	2,220	21,797	24,191	56,679	53,150	5.9
6020	Commercial banks	92	88	5.6	1,567	1,538	25,090	26,463	39,597	38,767	5.4
6030	Savings institutions	23	19	9.2	392	-	19,031	-	8,560	-	-
6100	Nondepository institutions	96	89	10.0	592	920	28,088	17,396	17,449	19,376	8.5
6140	Personal credit institutions	61	44	8.9	374	681	25,893	13,627	9,512	9,820	11.4
6160	Mortgage bankers and brokers	26	34	12.8	175	188	30,171	26,638	6,192	7,853	8.3
6200	Security and commodity brokers	50	52	11.6	284	355	64,718	55,155	17,396	21,585	6.5
6210	Security brokers and dealers	25	29	10.5	239	277	71,464	59,957	15,916	17,382	6.3
6280	Security and commodity services	25	23	14.7	45	78	28,889	38,103	1,480	4,203	8.8
6300	Insurance carriers	106	96	11.3	1,226	1,276	28,816	29,878	37,623	38,035	5.4
6310	Life insurance	37	35	11.7	839	895	27,933	28,903	24,880	25,155	7.7
6330	Fire, marine, and casualty insurance	47	42	11.6	264	-	31,091	-	8,426	-	-
6400	Insurance agents, brokers, and service	183	211	9.1	926	944	25,996	26,975	25,228	28,833	9.1
6500	Real estate	317	320	9.7	1,776	1,797	16,516	17,790	36,416	41,470	11.5
6510	Real estate operators and lessors	130	134	9.5	697	505	14,743	17,117	10,768	10,612	9.3
6530	Real estate agents and managers	119	148	9.7	690	1,104	17,316	18,286	13,291	25,359	12.2
6540	Title abstract offices	11	14	20.3	50	73	21,200	21,041	1,720	2,322	18.4
6552	Subdividers and developers, n.e.c.	15	13	9.2	152	31	20,868	20,903	6,891	1,908	13.4
6553	Cemetery subdividers and developers	11	7	5.6	108	81	16,370	10,815	1,733	849	7.7
6700	Holding and other investment offices	37	34	8.4	403	501	28,000	34,675	11,678	18,930	14.5
6710	Holding offices	9	10	7.5	222	383	34,775	39,446	8,608	15,881	19.1
6732	Educational, religious, etc. trusts	7	6	9.8	33	39	21,818	14,564	742	827	12.4
6733	Trusts, n.e.c.	8	9	13.2	64	36	14,312	25,333	835	1,168	20.8
LAKE, TN											
60 –	Finance, insurance, and real estate	13	13	0.1	38	39	24,526	22,154	884	883	0.0
6400	Insurance agents, brokers, and service	4	4	0.2	8	6	23,500	18,000	126	120	0.0
LAUDERDALE, TN											
60 –	Finance, insurance, and real estate	29	30	0.3	225	224	20,836	21,821	4,426	4,022	0.1
6000	Depository institutions	12	11	0.5	173	175	21,110	21,920	3,308	2,894	0.3
6020	Commercial banks	11	11	0.7	-	175	-	21,920	-	2,894	0.4

Source: County Business Patterns, 1992/93, CBP-92/93-1, U.S. Department of Commerce, Washington, D.C., April 1995. SIC categories for which data were suppressed or not available for both 1992 and 1993 are *not* displayed. The employment columns represent mid-March employment in the year. Pay per employee is calculated by dividing 1st Quarter payroll, annualized, by mid-March employment. The columns headed "% State" show the county's percentage of the state total for the SIC in 1993; for example, 0.9% for SIC 6030 means that the county had 0.9 percent of the state's total establishments (or payroll) in SIC 6030 in 1993. A dash (-) is used to indicate that data are not available or cannot be calculated; *nec* means not elsewhere classified.

Continued on next page.

SIC	Industry	No. Establishments			Employment		Pay / Employee		Annual Payroll ($ 000)		
		1992	1993	% State	1992	1993	1992	1993	1992	1993	% State
LAUDERDALE, TN - [continued]											
6400	Insurance agents, brokers, and service	7	9	0.4	27	25	13,037	16,320	360	376	0.1
6500	Real estate	7	7	0.2	13	12	16,308	14,000	288	264	0.1
6510	Real estate operators and lessors	5	5	0.4	12	-	17,000	-	279	-	-
LAWRENCE, TN											
60 –	**Finance, insurance, and real estate**	53	59	0.6	272	271	20,412	21,151	5,357	5,724	0.2
6000	Depository institutions	14	15	0.7	169	161	19,621	22,087	3,043	3,203	0.4
6140	Personal credit institutions	6	6	1.2	21	21	20,000	19,429	474	449	0.5
6400	Insurance agents, brokers, and service	17	18	0.8	41	49	24,195	20,980	883	1,061	0.3
6500	Real estate	12	15	0.5	12	15	6,667	8,800	104	220	0.1
6530	Real estate agents and managers	6	10	0.7	6	10	2,667	8,800	32	144	0.1
LEWIS, TN											
60 –	**Finance, insurance, and real estate**	9	9	0.1	73	61	18,247	19,934	1,387	1,150	0.0
6400	Insurance agents, brokers, and service	4	5	0.2	6	-	16,667	-	107	-	-
LINCOLN, TN											
60 –	**Finance, insurance, and real estate**	46	48	0.5	244	262	20,393	20,305	4,932	4,623	0.2
6000	Depository institutions	16	17	0.8	164	178	22,293	22,674	3,576	3,312	0.4
6020	Commercial banks	12	15	1.0	128	-	23,094	-	2,880	-	-
6100	Nondepository institutions	5	4	0.5	17	12	20,235	17,333	330	289	0.1
6400	Insurance agents, brokers, and service	11	10	0.4	31	30	19,613	20,667	574	564	0.2
6500	Real estate	10	13	0.4	14	25	12,571	11,520	227	250	0.1
6510	Real estate operators and lessors	5	6	0.4	7	15	12,000	12,800	137	139	0.1
6530	Real estate agents and managers	5	7	0.5	7	10	13,143	9,600	90	111	0.1
LOUDON, TN											
60 –	**Finance, insurance, and real estate**	60	59	0.6	445	428	17,762	19,607	7,939	9,086	0.3
6000	Depository institutions	20	20	0.9	204	210	18,863	21,333	3,844	4,756	0.5
6020	Commercial banks	13	12	0.8	173	178	18,312	21,483	3,181	4,090	0.6
6100	Nondepository institutions	7	5	0.6	23	18	16,522	20,000	407	420	0.2
6500	Real estate	16	18	0.5	176	169	15,750	18,249	2,801	3,424	0.9
6510	Real estate operators and lessors	4	5	0.4	12	-	26,667	-	234	-	-
6530	Real estate agents and managers	5	8	0.5	-	89	-	13,843	-	1,641	0.8
MCMINN, TN											
60 –	**Finance, insurance, and real estate**	66	70	0.7	436	454	19,936	22,361	9,332	10,284	0.3
6000	Depository institutions	23	25	1.1	277	287	20,072	23,345	5,970	6,504	0.7
6020	Commercial banks	15	15	1.0	193	210	20,622	23,905	4,313	4,674	0.6
6100	Nondepository institutions	7	4	0.5	20	14	18,600	24,286	448	350	0.2
6140	Personal credit institutions	4	2	0.4	11	-	14,909	-	188	-	-
6150	Business credit institutions	3	-	-	9	-	23,111	-	260	-	-
6400	Insurance agents, brokers, and service	10	13	0.6	46	56	24,870	21,500	1,182	1,285	0.4
6500	Real estate	17	18	0.5	43	49	11,907	13,469	585	774	0.2
6510	Real estate operators and lessors	5	8	0.6	14	-	7,143	-	120	-	-
6530	Real estate agents and managers	7	8	0.5	15	9	14,400	21,333	236	244	0.1
MCNAIRY, TN											
60 –	**Finance, insurance, and real estate**	29	27	0.3	157	168	18,089	18,024	3,495	3,675	0.1
6000	Depository institutions	10	10	0.5	114	126	19,439	18,921	2,770	2,960	0.3
6400	Insurance agents, brokers, and service	9	10	0.4	25	27	12,800	12,889	401	405	0.1
6500	Real estate	5	4	0.1	8	8	8,500	7,000	67	63	0.0
6510	Real estate operators and lessors	5	4	0.3	8	8	8,500	7,000	67	63	0.1
MACON, TN											
60 –	**Finance, insurance, and real estate**	20	19	0.2	144	146	18,861	19,342	2,607	2,792	0.1
6000	Depository institutions	8	8	0.4	113	119	19,717	20,807	2,130	2,361	0.3

Source: County Business Patterns, 1992/93, CBP-92/93-1, U.S. Department of Commerce, Washington, D.C., April 1995. SIC categories for which data were suppressed or not available for both 1992 and 1993 are not displayed. The employment columns represent mid-March employment in the year. Pay per employee is calculated by dividing 1st Quarter payroll, annualized, by mid-March employment. The columns headed "% State" show the county's percentage of the state total for the SIC in 1993; for example, 0.9% for SIC 6030 means that the county had 0.9 percent of the state's total establishments (or payroll) in SIC 6030 in 1993. A dash (-) is used to indicate that data are not available or cannot be calculated; nec means not elsewhere classified.

Continued on next page.

SIC	Industry	No. Establishments			Employment		Pay / Employee		Annual Payroll ($ 000)		
		1992	1993	% State	1992	1993	1992	1993	1992	1993	% State
MACON, TN - [continued]											
6400	Insurance agents, brokers, and service	7	6	0.3	14	-	16,286	-	213	-	-
6500	Real estate	3	3	0.1	-	13	-	7,692	-	162	0.0
6530	Real estate agents and managers	3	3	0.2	-	13	-	7,692	-	162	0.1
MADISON, TN											
60 –	**Finance, insurance, and real estate**	213	207	2.0	1,471	1,397	23,459	24,412	35,543	35,421	1.2
6000	Depository institutions	49	49	2.2	567	556	20,099	22,799	11,852	12,961	1.4
6020	Commercial banks	38	36	2.3	525	456	20,465	23,447	11,178	10,735	1.5
6060	Credit unions	10	13	3.4	-	100	-	19,840	-	2,226	3.4
6100	Nondepository institutions	21	20	2.3	117	113	26,359	26,407	3,071	3,636	1.6
6140	Personal credit institutions	14	10	2.0	91	63	22,637	25,270	2,045	1,569	1.8
6160	Mortgage bankers and brokers	7	7	2.6	26	-	39,385	-	1,026	-	-
6200	Security and commodity brokers	7	7	1.6	43	36	65,023	52,889	2,076	1,893	0.6
6210	Security brokers and dealers	7	7	2.5	43	36	65,023	52,889	2,076	1,893	0.7
6300	Insurance carriers	36	28	3.3	407	357	25,985	30,252	11,053	10,716	1.5
6310	Life insurance	18	15	5.0	345	312	25,901	29,077	9,416	9,077	2.8
6400	Insurance agents, brokers, and service	48	46	2.0	148	146	20,622	21,370	3,436	3,103	1.0
6500	Real estate	41	48	1.5	114	133	14,807	14,256	1,847	2,280	0.6
6510	Real estate operators and lessors	13	19	1.3	44	58	10,000	11,448	485	742	0.6
6530	Real estate agents and managers	22	26	1.7	57	68	18,175	16,412	1,139	1,402	0.7
6552	Subdividers and developers, n.e.c.	3	2	1.4	6	-	26,667	-	127	-	-
6700	Holding and other investment offices	11	9	2.2	75	56	25,547	12,929	2,208	832	0.6
6710	Holding offices	4	1	0.7	50	-	27,600	-	1,729	-	-
6794	Patent owners and lessors	2	3	4.9	-	4	-	38,000	-	208	0.9
MARION, TN											
60 –	**Finance, insurance, and real estate**	24	26	0.2	140	171	19,514	21,614	2,614	3,867	0.1
6000	Depository institutions	11	11	0.5	111	130	18,991	23,631	2,074	3,235	0.4
6400	Insurance agents, brokers, and service	5	8	0.3	11	18	25,455	19,111	289	334	0.1
6500	Real estate	5	5	0.2	10	-	12,400	-	76	-	-
MARSHALL, TN											
60 –	**Finance, insurance, and real estate**	31	34	0.3	194	190	20,515	20,253	3,683	3,752	0.1
6000	Depository institutions	12	11	0.5	137	130	23,299	23,077	2,879	2,857	0.3
6100	Nondepository institutions	3	3	0.3	10	-	13,600	-	147	-	-
6400	Insurance agents, brokers, and service	7	8	0.3	-	21	-	19,238	-	428	0.1
6500	Real estate	8	10	0.3	25	25	8,320	9,600	220	243	0.1
6510	Real estate operators and lessors	3	3	0.2	-	12	-	6,000	-	81	0.1
6530	Real estate agents and managers	4	6	0.4	12	-	11,333	-	142	-	-
MAURY, TN											
60 –	**Finance, insurance, and real estate**	115	119	1.1	1,293	1,327	23,623	24,093	31,193	32,280	1.1
6000	Depository institutions	27	30	1.4	419	434	18,625	18,664	8,445	8,467	0.9
6020	Commercial banks	22	23	1.5	390	401	19,323	18,574	8,060	7,777	1.1
6100	Nondepository institutions	14	11	1.2	-	52	-	22,462	-	1,140	0.5
6140	Personal credit institutions	12	9	1.8	61	-	17,311	-	1,016	-	-
6300	Insurance carriers	7	9	1.1	625	-	28,429	-	17,087	-	-
6400	Insurance agents, brokers, and service	23	24	1.0	74	77	22,054	22,442	1,825	2,037	0.6
6500	Real estate	39	40	1.2	91	121	15,868	13,851	1,914	2,494	0.7
6510	Real estate operators and lessors	16	16	1.1	39	54	14,154	10,963	688	684	0.6
6530	Real estate agents and managers	13	18	1.2	27	47	12,148	14,298	538	1,080	0.5
6553	Cemetery subdividers and developers	5	4	3.2	-	6	-	10,000	-	123	1.1
MEIGS, TN											
60 –	**Finance, insurance, and real estate**	5	2	0.0	77	-	21,662	-	1,389	-	-

Source: County Business Patterns, 1992/93, CBP-92/93-1, U.S. Department of Commerce, Washington, D.C., April 1995. SIC categories for which data were suppressed or not available for both 1992 and 1993 are not displayed. The employment columns represent mid-March employment in the year. Pay per employee is calculated by dividing 1st Quarter payroll, annualized, by mid-March employment. The columns headed "% State" show the county's percentage of the state total for the SIC in 1993; for example, 0.9% for SIC 6030 means that the county had 0.9 percent of the state's total establishments (or payroll) in SIC 6030 in 1993. A dash (-) is used to indicate that data are not available or cannot be calculated; nec means not elsewhere classified.

SIC	Industry	No. Establishments			Employment		Pay / Employee		Annual Payroll ($ 000)		
		1992	1993	% State	1992	1993	1992	1993	1992	1993	% State
MONROE, TN											
60 –	**Finance, insurance, and real estate**	49	48	0.5	264	256	23,924	22,109	6,052	5,557	0.2
6000	Depository institutions	21	19	0.9	188	183	20,043	17,596	3,866	3,385	0.4
6400	Insurance agents, brokers, and service	11	11	0.5	30	28	14,267	18,000	422	494	0.2
6500	Real estate	12	14	0.4	16	18	7,250	9,556	149	167	0.0
6510	Real estate operators and lessors	4	5	0.4	5	8	8,000	6,500	26	58	0.1
6530	Real estate agents and managers	6	8	0.5	5	-	4,800	-	39	-	-
MONTGOMERY, TN											
60 –	**Finance, insurance, and real estate**	175	171	1.6	1,116	1,031	17,875	19,507	20,729	22,400	0.7
6000	Depository institutions	41	38	1.7	476	438	18,807	21,132	9,017	9,683	1.1
6020	Commercial banks	25	23	1.5	337	269	19,122	22,424	6,398	6,044	0.8
6030	Savings institutions	6	6	2.9	102	120	19,647	20,033	2,085	2,459	3.4
6060	Credit unions	5	5	1.3	25	26	15,040	14,769	386	407	0.6
6090	Functions closely related to banking	5	4	8.3	12	23	10,667	18,957	148	773	2.5
6100	Nondepository institutions	18	15	1.7	85	76	22,635	25,105	1,944	1,993	0.9
6140	Personal credit institutions	12	8	1.6	60	-	20,400	-	1,149	-	-
6160	Mortgage bankers and brokers	4	5	1.9	20	23	26,600	32,174	623	767	0.8
6300	Insurance carriers	9	9	1.1	79	89	26,278	26,831	2,059	2,467	0.4
6400	Insurance agents, brokers, and service	32	31	1.3	124	115	16,548	19,583	2,479	2,756	0.9
6500	Real estate	60	62	1.9	274	246	11,299	13,350	3,323	3,805	1.1
6510	Real estate operators and lessors	32	32	2.3	120	87	9,833	9,793	1,315	1,159	1.0
6530	Real estate agents and managers	21	27	1.8	117	141	13,709	14,383	1,608	2,248	1.1
MOORE, TN											
60 –	**Finance, insurance, and real estate**	4	3	0.0	-	-	-	-	-	-	-
MORGAN, TN											
60 –	**Finance, insurance, and real estate**	8	8	0.1	46	49	17,304	16,000	813	833	0.0
OBION, TN											
60 –	**Finance, insurance, and real estate**	61	61	0.6	400	397	21,250	21,703	8,039	8,836	0.3
6000	Depository institutions	20	16	0.7	245	189	18,612	20,656	4,315	3,686	0.4
6020	Commercial banks	17	15	1.0	223	-	19,157	-	4,115	-	-
6300	Insurance carriers	3	3	0.4	-	3	-	44,000	-	135	0.0
6400	Insurance agents, brokers, and service	10	12	0.5	40	47	31,500	21,191	892	948	0.3
6500	Real estate	20	19	0.6	51	52	10,039	9,692	604	572	0.2
6510	Real estate operators and lessors	10	10	0.7	26	32	10,000	10,625	306	374	0.3
6530	Real estate agents and managers	8	9	0.6	21	20	9,714	8,200	242	198	0.1
6700	Holding and other investment offices	2	3	0.7	-	27	-	27,556	-	766	0.6
6710	Holding offices	2	3	2.2	-	27	-	27,556	-	766	0.9
OVERTON, TN											
60 –	**Finance, insurance, and real estate**	16	15	0.1	132	120	18,030	23,567	2,504	2,594	0.1
6000	Depository institutions	6	6	0.3	78	90	21,385	22,578	1,793	1,891	0.2
6400	Insurance agents, brokers, and service	5	5	0.2	25	23	19,040	30,957	478	617	0.2
PERRY, TN											
60 –	**Finance, insurance, and real estate**	7	9	0.1	36	37	15,444	15,027	686	784	0.0
PICKETT, TN											
60 –	**Finance, insurance, and real estate**	5	3	0.0	-	-	-	-	-	-	-
POLK, TN											
60 –	**Finance, insurance, and real estate**	13	13	0.1	148	150	20,432	18,613	3,005	2,906	0.1
6000	Depository institutions	7	8	0.4	125	128	20,640	18,594	2,534	2,472	0.3

Source: County Business Patterns, 1992/93, CBP-92/93-1, U.S. Department of Commerce, Washington, D.C., April 1995. SIC categories for which data were suppressed or not available for both 1992 and 1993 are *not* displayed. The employment columns represent mid-March employment in the year. Pay per employee is calculated by dividing 1st Quarter payroll, annualized, by mid-March employment. The columns headed "% State" show the county's percentage of the state total for the SIC in 1993; for example, 0.9% for SIC 6030 means that the county had 0.9 percent of the state's total establishments (or payroll) in SIC 6030 in 1993. A dash (-) is used to indicate that data are not available or cannot be calculated; *nec* means not elsewhere classified.

SIC	Industry	No. Establishments			Employment		Pay / Employee		Annual Payroll ($ 000)		
		1992	1993	% State	1992	1993	1992	1993	1992	1993	% State
PUTNAM, TN											
60 –	**Finance, insurance, and real estate**	100	106	*1.0*	586	635	22,027	21,972	13,413	14,416	*0.5*
6000	Depository institutions	30	27	*1.2*	327	341	22,777	23,672	7,331	7,974	*0.9*
6020	Commercial banks	24	22	*1.4*	306	320	23,046	23,875	6,910	7,531	*1.0*
6100	Nondepository institutions	7	6	*0.7*	-	24	-	26,833	-	627	*0.3*
6200	Security and commodity brokers	5	6	*1.3*	-	15	-	42,667	-	668	*0.2*
6210	Security brokers and dealers	5	6	*2.2*	-	15	-	42,667	-	668	*0.2*
6300	Insurance carriers	5	6	*0.7*	51	66	29,804	25,394	1,542	1,745	*0.2*
6400	Insurance agents, brokers, and service	23	21	*0.9*	87	79	20,092	21,468	1,848	1,713	*0.5*
6500	Real estate	30	37	*1.1*	78	106	12,103	10,868	1,437	1,615	*0.4*
6510	Real estate operators and lessors	11	15	*1.1*	27	-	9,481	-	347	-	*-*
6530	Real estate agents and managers	11	18	*1.2*	18	55	23,111	11,564	597	1,027	*0.5*
6700	Holding and other investment offices	-	3	*0.7*	-	4	-	18,000	-	74	*0.1*
RHEA, TN											
60 –	**Finance, insurance, and real estate**	30	32	*0.3*	157	147	19,159	15,864	3,176	2,499	*0.1*
6000	Depository institutions	8	8	*0.4*	112	104	20,071	15,962	2,422	1,761	*0.2*
6100	Nondepository institutions	5	5	*0.6*	18	16	20,000	21,000	335	357	*0.2*
6400	Insurance agents, brokers, and service	5	6	*0.3*	15	16	13,600	10,750	196	209	*0.1*
6510	Real estate operators and lessors	5	5	*0.4*	5	6	14,400	8,667	80	52	*0.0*
ROANE, TN											
60 –	**Finance, insurance, and real estate**	51	53	*0.5*	286	306	18,951	19,425	5,260	5,767	*0.2*
6000	Depository institutions	20	19	*0.9*	174	176	20,000	21,182	3,145	3,478	*0.4*
6020	Commercial banks	13	13	*0.8*	128	129	21,531	23,473	2,397	2,681	*0.4*
6030	Savings institutions	3	2	*1.0*	30	-	15,467	-	474	-	*-*
6060	Credit unions	4	4	*1.0*	16	-	16,250		274	-	*-*
6500	Real estate	13	15	*0.5*	30	33	12,133	12,485	371	584	*0.2*
6510	Real estate operators and lessors	6	8	*0.6*	9	7	14,222	21,143	125	157	*0.1*
6530	Real estate agents and managers	4	3	*0.2*	8	6	10,500	12,667	90	79	*0.0*
ROBERTSON, TN											
60 –	**Finance, insurance, and real estate**	63	68	*0.7*	247	281	17,700	20,342	4,353	5,518	*0.2*
6000	Depository institutions	17	18	*0.8*	134	136	19,164	21,235	2,476	2,434	*0.3*
6100	Nondepository institutions	5	5	*0.6*	17	16	26,118	27,250	411	513	*0.2*
6400	Insurance agents, brokers, and service	11	12	*0.5*	37	40	15,676	18,500	592	696	*0.2*
6500	Real estate	27	29	*0.9*	53	61	11,245	9,574	691	751	*0.2*
6510	Real estate operators and lessors	10	12	*0.8*	17	28	12,000	9,571	230	299	*0.3*
6530	Real estate agents and managers	14	15	*1.0*	30	-	10,800	-	375	-	*-*
RUTHERFORD, TN											
60 –	**Finance, insurance, and real estate**	206	218	*2.1*	3,151	3,140	27,401	32,060	89,371	95,814	*3.2*
6000	Depository institutions	49	48	*2.2*	553	577	24,043	24,055	12,292	12,705	*1.4*
6020	Commercial banks	38	35	*2.2*	426	416	23,634	23,952	9,089	8,746	*1.2*
6100	Nondepository institutions	24	24	*2.7*	123	112	25,301	24,286	3,244	3,687	*1.6*
6140	Personal credit institutions	16	14	*2.8*	83	62	23,422	21,161	2,004	1,484	*1.7*
6160	Mortgage bankers and brokers	4	6	*2.3*	29	-	30,483	-	923	-	*-*
6300	Insurance carriers	20	19	*2.2*	-	2,020	-	38,349	-	71,297	*10.2*
6310	Life insurance	8	6	*2.0*	234	-	23,573	-	5,895	-	*-*
6400	Insurance agents, brokers, and service	38	40	*1.7*	140	133	15,286	17,594	2,310	2,436	*0.8*
6500	Real estate	65	76	*2.3*	235	247	10,519	11,206	2,948	3,603	*1.0*
6510	Real estate operators and lessors	20	30	*2.1*	62	82	10,194	10,683	743	1,088	*0.9*
6530	Real estate agents and managers	32	41	*2.7*	128	151	10,594	10,517	1,636	1,946	*0.9*
6552	Subdividers and developers, n.e.c.	4	4	*2.8*	7	-	10,857	-	81	-	*-*
SCOTT, TN											
60 –	**Finance, insurance, and real estate**	13	12	*0.1*	131	124	15,878	17,290	2,270	2,383	*0.1*
6000	Depository institutions	5	4	*0.2*	114	-	15,614	-	1,953	-	*-*

Source: County Business Patterns, 1992/93, CBP-92/93-1, U.S. Department of Commerce, Washington, D.C., April 1995. SIC categories for which data were suppressed or not available for both 1992 and 1993 are not displayed. The employment columns represent mid-March employment in the year. Pay per employee is calculated by dividing 1st Quarter payroll, annualized, by mid-March employment. The columns headed "% State" show the county's percentage of the state total for the SIC in 1993; for example, 0.9% for SIC 6030 means that the county had 0.9 percent of the state's total establishments (or payroll) in SIC 6030 in 1993. A dash (-) is used to indicate that data are not available or cannot be calculated; nec means not elsewhere classified.

Continued on next page.

SIC	Industry	No. Establishments			Employment		Pay / Employee		Annual Payroll ($ 000)		
		1992	1993	% State	1992	1993	1992	1993	1992	1993	% State
SCOTT, TN - [continued]											
6020	Commercial banks	5	4	0.3	114	-	15,614	-	1,953	-	-
6400	Insurance agents, brokers, and service	4	4	0.2	-	9	-	14,222	-	144	0.0
6500	Real estate	3	3	0.1	5	-	19,200	-	104	-	-
SEQUATCHIE, TN											
60 –	**Finance, insurance, and real estate**	10	11	0.1	59	84	14,508	13,000	980	1,210	0.0
SEVIER, TN											
60 –	**Finance, insurance, and real estate**	149	169	1.6	1,096	1,418	17,788	16,519	22,258	27,740	0.9
6000	Depository institutions	29	27	1.2	360	381	21,244	20,640	7,243	8,242	0.9
6020	Commercial banks	24	22	1.4	334	356	21,677	20,899	6,798	7,760	1.1
6100	Nondepository institutions	6	5	0.6	-	13	-	18,462	-	203	0.1
6140	Personal credit institutions	4	3	0.6	10	-	20,800	-	191	-	-
6400	Insurance agents, brokers, and service	23	22	0.9	79	84	17,873	18,857	1,591	1,925	0.6
6500	Real estate	81	105	3.2	524	766	15,305	13,561	10,880	13,343	3.7
6510	Real estate operators and lessors	31	35	2.5	222	286	12,306	9,790	3,310	3,519	3.1
6530	Real estate agents and managers	38	58	3.8	274	460	18,234	15,930	7,201	9,533	4.6
6700	Holding and other investment offices	4	5	1.2	77	133	14,234	16,571	1,078	2,935	2.2
SHELBY, TN											
60 –	**Finance, insurance, and real estate**	1,902	1,938	18.5	25,071	23,292	34,176	33,727	842,602	826,389	27.6
6000	Depository institutions	310	331	14.9	6,976	7,850	34,704	30,790	227,518	245,519	27.4
6020	Commercial banks	200	203	12.9	5,535	6,008	36,906	32,788	191,794	199,950	27.8
6030	Savings institutions	27	25	12.1	759	-	30,018	-	18,772	-	-
6060	Credit unions	64	85	22.1	413	777	19,225	25,369	8,088	21,171	32.3
6100	Nondepository institutions	188	173	19.5	-	2,237	-	36,923	-	74,271	32.6
6140	Personal credit institutions	110	84	17.1	1,160	790	28,200	30,643	28,400	23,986	27.9
6160	Mortgage bankers and brokers	60	60	22.6	987	1,302	48,470	40,968	34,834	44,986	47.5
6200	Security and commodity brokers	112	124	27.7	1,534	1,898	96,866	86,095	151,578	191,030	57.8
6210	Security brokers and dealers	60	74	26.8	1,324	1,606	103,018	90,511	122,343	151,705	55.4
6280	Security and commodity services	32	38	24.4	128	-	59,312	-	22,175	-	-
6300	Insurance carriers	226	186	21.9	3,857	3,535	26,071	28,579	101,577	103,370	14.8
6310	Life insurance	84	69	23.0	1,773	1,480	25,128	27,362	43,835	39,596	12.1
6330	Fire, marine, and casualty insurance	89	72	19.8	946	809	32,182	31,876	31,583	27,409	11.1
6370	Pension, health, and welfare funds	29	18	22.2	205	121	22,966	21,620	5,326	3,072	25.3
6400	Insurance agents, brokers, and service	406	431	18.6	2,559	2,269	32,783	31,626	83,903	75,219	23.8
6500	Real estate	562	593	17.9	4,557	4,390	19,974	19,883	96,749	96,045	26.6
6510	Real estate operators and lessors	244	268	19.0	1,521	1,570	16,792	19,944	25,872	32,759	28.6
6530	Real estate agents and managers	215	264	17.2	2,327	2,399	22,615	20,425	54,712	54,160	26.1
6540	Title abstract offices	7	6	8.7	58	61	19,931	20,852	1,135	1,680	13.3
6552	Subdividers and developers, n.e.c.	38	37	26.2	190	230	23,368	18,626	7,314	5,777	40.6
6553	Cemetery subdividers and developers	10	9	7.1	219	128	14,795	10,969	3,247	1,596	14.5
6700	Holding and other investment offices	93	96	23.6	2,967	-	33,708	-	104,854	-	-
6710	Holding offices	26	29	21.6	1,648	751	27,840	34,610	45,794	28,289	34.0
6720	Investment offices	5	4	44.4	42	-	51,714	-	2,101	-	-
6732	Educational, religious, etc. trusts	18	14	23.0	-	80	-	16,500	-	1,506	22.6
6733	Trusts, n.e.c.	13	16	23.5	-	40	-	41,600	-	1,476	26.3
6794	Patent owners and lessors	6	11	18.0	-	127	-	38,835	-	5,175	21.6
SMITH, TN											
60 –	**Finance, insurance, and real estate**	19	18	0.2	118	127	19,322	18,236	2,340	2,418	0.1
6000	Depository institutions	7	7	0.3	78	88	20,308	19,182	1,627	1,695	0.2
6020	Commercial banks	7	7	0.4	78	88	20,308	19,182	1,627	1,695	0.2
6500	Real estate	5	5	0.2	20	-	9,600	-	200	-	-
6510	Real estate operators and lessors	3	3	0.2	-	11	-	11,636	-	146	0.1

Source: County Business Patterns, 1992/93, CBP-92/93-1, U.S. Department of Commerce, Washington, D.C., April 1995. SIC categories for which data were suppressed or not available for both 1992 and 1993 are not displayed. The employment columns represent mid-March employment in the year. Pay per employee is calculated by dividing 1st Quarter payroll, annualized, by mid-March employment. The columns headed "% State" show the county's percentage of the state total for the SIC in 1993; for example, 0.9% for SIC 6030 means that the county had 0.9 percent of the state's total establishments (or payroll) in SIC 6030 in 1993. A dash (-) is used to indicate that data are not available or cannot be calculated; nec means not elsewhere classified.

SIC	Industry	No. Establishments			Employment		Pay / Employee		Annual Payroll ($ 000)		
		1992	1993	% State	1992	1993	1992	1993	1992	1993	% State

STEWART, TN

SIC	Industry	1992	1993	% State	1992	1993	1992	1993	1992	1993	% State
60 –	**Finance, insurance, and real estate**	10	10	0.1	68	64	17,529	18,375	1,161	1,147	0.0
6000	Depository institutions	7	7	0.3	48	43	19,000	20,558	856	836	0.1

SULLIVAN, TN

SIC	Industry	1992	1993	% State	1992	1993	1992	1993	1992	1993	% State
60 –	**Finance, insurance, and real estate**	269	270	2.6	1,878	1,824	20,492	21,728	40,953	42,442	1.4
6000	Depository institutions	66	66	3.0	768	764	18,833	20,105	14,651	17,310	1.9
6020	Commercial banks	41	43	2.7	543	515	16,891	20,598	9,552	10,139	1.4
6030	Savings institutions	15	8	3.9	184	-	25,261	-	4,419	-	-
6060	Credit unions	10	14	3.6	41	-	15,707	-	680	-	-
6100	Nondepository institutions	24	23	2.6	120	111	25,300	23,604	3,318	2,934	1.3
6140	Personal credit institutions	22	17	3.5	-	94	-	24,000	-	2,482	2.9
6200	Security and commodity brokers	7	7	1.6	33	39	45,455	32,410	1,683	1,395	0.4
6300	Insurance carriers	26	24	2.8	428	390	23,121	28,072	10,714	10,326	1.5
6310	Life insurance	9	10	3.3	365	334	20,197	25,090	8,082	7,844	2.4
6400	Insurance agents, brokers, and service	59	62	2.7	251	245	23,936	24,506	6,699	6,553	2.1
6500	Real estate	77	79	2.4	246	246	12,049	11,398	3,312	3,249	0.9
6510	Real estate operators and lessors	30	35	2.5	122	138	9,148	10,522	1,293	1,581	1.4
6530	Real estate agents and managers	36	37	2.4	60	84	13,933	12,190	996	1,261	0.6
6700	Holding and other investment offices	10	9	2.2	32	29	19,250	21,793	576	675	0.5

SUMNER, TN

SIC	Industry	1992	1993	% State	1992	1993	1992	1993	1992	1993	% State
60 –	**Finance, insurance, and real estate**	184	184	1.8	958	906	24,230	23,740	23,428	22,019	0.7
6000	Depository institutions	44	42	1.9	396	356	21,495	22,427	8,362	7,326	0.8
6020	Commercial banks	38	36	2.3	377	331	21,719	22,755	8,010	6,869	1.0
6100	Nondepository institutions	18	17	1.9	72	-	21,556	-	1,561	-	-
6140	Personal credit institutions	13	10	2.0	61	55	18,361	21,018	1,278	1,295	1.5
6160	Mortgage bankers and brokers	3	5	1.9	-	11	-	23,273	-	333	0.4
6200	Security and commodity brokers	6	4	0.9	12	-	15,667	-	200	-	-
6300	Insurance carriers	17	16	1.9	71	72	29,296	28,056	2,008	1,983	0.3
6400	Insurance agents, brokers, and service	47	42	1.8	130	136	22,154	20,647	3,166	3,279	1.0
6500	Real estate	46	56	1.7	147	133	14,150	18,827	2,231	2,587	0.7
6510	Real estate operators and lessors	18	19	1.3	61	57	15,738	18,667	1,090	1,007	0.9
6530	Real estate agents and managers	18	28	1.8	48	54	13,083	18,000	574	1,054	0.5
6540	Title abstract offices	3	2	2.9	12	-	15,667	-	203	-	-
6553	Cemetery subdividers and developers	3	4	3.2	-	14	-	20,857	-	283	2.6
6700	Holding and other investment offices	6	7	1.7	130	131	45,538	33,924	5,900	4,876	3.7

TIPTON, TN

SIC	Industry	1992	1993	% State	1992	1993	1992	1993	1992	1993	% State
60 –	**Finance, insurance, and real estate**	42	44	0.4	310	346	19,806	20,763	6,509	7,517	0.3
6000	Depository institutions	12	13	0.6	219	252	20,457	20,063	4,396	4,996	0.6
6400	Insurance agents, brokers, and service	13	14	0.6	51	49	21,647	29,224	1,511	1,736	0.6
6500	Real estate	13	13	0.4	28	34	7,429	7,882	222	321	0.1
6530	Real estate agents and managers	6	8	0.5	3	8	9,333	8,500	38	89	0.0

TROUSDALE, TN

SIC	Industry	1992	1993	% State	1992	1993	1992	1993	1992	1993	% State
60 –	**Finance, insurance, and real estate**	7	8	0.1	59	72	21,831	21,389	1,288	1,422	0.0

UNICOI, TN

SIC	Industry	1992	1993	% State	1992	1993	1992	1993	1992	1993	% State
60 –	**Finance, insurance, and real estate**	17	17	0.2	89	97	14,517	14,103	1,494	1,437	0.0
6000	Depository institutions	7	6	0.3	62	58	16,129	17,241	1,164	1,047	0.1
6400	Insurance agents, brokers, and service	6	5	0.2	18	27	12,222	10,519	233	291	0.1

UNION, TN

SIC	Industry	1992	1993	% State	1992	1993	1992	1993	1992	1993	% State
60 –	**Finance, insurance, and real estate**	14	14	0.1	77	62	15,013	12,968	1,420	921	0.0

Source: County Business Patterns, 1992/93, CBP-92/93-1, U.S. Department of Commerce, Washington, D.C., April 1995. SIC categories for which data were suppressed or not available for both 1992 and 1993 are *not* displayed. The employment columns represent mid-March employment in the year. Pay per employee is calculated by dividing 1st Quarter payroll, annualized, by mid-March employment. The columns headed "% State" show the county's percentage of the state total for the SIC in 1993; for example, 0.9% for SIC 6030 means that the county had 0.9 percent of the state's total establishments (or payroll) in SIC 6030 in 1993. A dash (-) is used to indicate that data are not available or cannot be calculated; *nec* means not elsewhere classified.

Continued on next page.

SIC	Industry	No. Establishments			Employment		Pay / Employee		Annual Payroll ($ 000)		
		1992	1993	% State	1992	1993	1992	1993	1992	1993	% State
UNION, TN - [continued]											
6000	Depository institutions	6	6	0.3	51	46	15,216	14,522	901	768	0.1
6020	Commercial banks	6	6	0.4	51	46	15,216	14,522	901	768	0.1
6400	Insurance agents, brokers, and service	3	3	0.1	10	10	5,200	5,600	55	68	0.0
VAN BUREN, TN											
60 –	**Finance, insurance, and real estate**	4	4	0.0	-	-	-	-	-	-	-
WARREN, TN											
60 –	**Finance, insurance, and real estate**	54	55	0.5	365	298	17,227	19,973	6,401	6,139	0.2
6000	Depository institutions	17	17	0.8	214	211	22,262	22,028	4,925	4,618	0.5
6020	Commercial banks	11	11	0.7	195	191	23,036	22,660	4,609	4,224	0.6
6100	Nondepository institutions	5	5	0.6	17	-	22,118	-	363	-	-
6400	Insurance agents, brokers, and service	13	13	0.6	29	31	16,276	15,613	506	540	0.2
6500	Real estate	14	16	0.5	97	36	4,536	7,111	352	300	0.1
6510	Real estate operators and lessors	8	9	0.6	-	24	-	7,167	-	220	0.2
6530	Real estate agents and managers	3	4	0.3	-	3	-	6,667	-	27	0.0
WASHINGTON, TN											
60 –	**Finance, insurance, and real estate**	221	230	2.2	2,417	2,136	17,630	19,114	42,693	39,429	1.3
6000	Depository institutions	45	48	2.2	564	540	21,305	23,770	11,616	11,483	1.3
6020	Commercial banks	28	34	2.2	384	461	21,760	25,024	7,859	9,575	1.3
6030	Savings institutions	10	5	2.4	153	-	20,654		3,243		-
6060	Credit unions	6	8	2.1	-	35	18,743			756	1.2
6100	Nondepository institutions	21	19	2.1	990	1,013	13,604	14,105	13,228	12,871	5.7
6200	Security and commodity brokers	22	15	3.3	373	76	20,472	39,000	7,563	3,190	1.0
6210	Security brokers and dealers	19	12	4.3	371	74	20,550	39,784	7,550	3,162	1.2
6280	Security and commodity services	3	3	1.9	2	2	6,000	10,000	13	28	0.1
6300	Insurance carriers	18	19	2.2	164	171	30,024	31,532	5,067	5,740	0.8
6310	Life insurance	8	8	2.7	139	136	30,245	32,118	4,118	4,298	1.3
6500	Real estate	69	76	2.3	203	205	11,015	13,015	2,523	3,152	0.9
6510	Real estate operators and lessors	31	41	2.9	116	123	8,345	10,569	1,010	1,474	1.3
6530	Real estate agents and managers	25	25	1.6	51	52	13,647	15,308	862	967	0.5
6540	Title abstract offices	3	2	2.9	6	-	16,000	-	116	-	-
6552	Subdividers and developers, n.e.c.	2	3	2.1	-	7	-	26,857	-	212	1.5
WAYNE, TN											
60 –	**Finance, insurance, and real estate**	16	14	0.1	99	103	17,010	16,893	1,733	1,865	0.1
6000	Depository institutions	7	7	0.3	91	92	16,571	16,739	1,547	1,642	0.2
6020	Commercial banks	7	7	0.4	91	92	16,571	16,739	1,547	1,642	0.2
6400	Insurance agents, brokers, and service	5	4	0.2	-	4	-	12,000	-	50	0.0
WEAKLEY, TN											
60 –	**Finance, insurance, and real estate**	52	51	0.5	297	278	16,929	16,849	5,318	5,175	0.2
6000	Depository institutions	21	20	0.9	192	201	17,188	15,781	3,480	3,427	0.4
6020	Commercial banks	17	17	1.1	185	197	17,276	15,858	3,418	3,373	0.5
6060	Credit unions	3	3	0.8	-	4	-	12,000	-	54	0.1
6400	Insurance agents, brokers, and service	11	14	0.6	24	28	12,667	12,857	306	411	0.1
6500	Real estate	11	10	0.3	35	22	12,457	8,364	446	199	0.1
6510	Real estate operators and lessors	5	5	0.4	7	8	5,714	5,500	44	49	0.0
6530	Real estate agents and managers	5	5	0.3	26	14	14,308	10,000	378	150	0.1
WHITE, TN											
60 –	**Finance, insurance, and real estate**	23	28	0.3	133	144	17,023	18,000	2,350	3,662	0.1
6000	Depository institutions	7	8	0.4	87	87	18,023	19,356	1,602	1,522	0.2

Source: County Business Patterns, 1992/93, CBP-92/93-1, U.S. Department of Commerce, Washington, D.C., April 1995. SIC categories for which data were suppressed or not available for both 1992 and 1993 are *not* displayed. The employment columns represent mid-March employment in the year. Pay per employee is calculated by dividing 1st Quarter payroll, annualized, by mid-March employment. The columns headed "% State" show the county's percentage of the state total for the SIC in 1993; for example, 0.9% for SIC 6030 means that the county had 0.9 percent of the state's total establishments (or payroll) in SIC 6030 in 1993. A dash (-) is used to indicate that data are not available or cannot be calculated; *nec* means not elsewhere classified.

Continued on next page.

SIC	Industry	No. Establishments			Employment		Pay / Employee		Annual Payroll ($ 000)		
		1992	1993	% State	1992	1993	1992	1993	1992	1993	% State
WHITE, TN - [continued]											
6100	Nondepository institutions	4	5	0.6	9	-	17,778	-	149	-	-
6400	Insurance agents, brokers, and service	7	8	0.3	24	22	14,833	15,636	379	387	0.1
6500	Real estate	2	5	0.2	-	10	-	15,200	-	243	0.1
WILLIAMSON, TN											
60 –	**Finance, insurance, and real estate**	340	361	3.5	2,572	2,324	30,165	28,466	77,267	75,200	2.5
6000	Depository institutions	46	42	1.9	533	517	23,182	23,776	12,196	11,945	1.3
6020	Commercial banks	36	34	2.2	424	435	23,075	23,982	10,052	10,040	1.4
6100	Nondepository institutions	26	36	4.1	174	232	34,368	34,603	6,896	10,707	4.7
6140	Personal credit institutions	11	11	2.2	88	-	27,818	-	2,656	-	-
6160	Mortgage bankers and brokers	12	23	8.6	83	126	41,542	38,889	3,997	7,337	7.7
6200	Security and commodity brokers	15	19	4.2	49	57	33,469	35,579	1,643	2,324	0.7
6210	Security brokers and dealers	10	13	4.7	46	49	34,783	38,122	1,548	2,140	0.8
6280	Security and commodity services	5	5	3.2	3	-	13,333	-	95	-	- -
6300	Insurance carriers	38	39	4.6	531	509	31,774	32,369	16,613	16,987	2.4
6310	Life insurance	6	10	3.3	65	101	30,031	28,950	1,668	3,015	0.9
6321	Accident and health insurance	4	2	6.7	44	-	28,455	-	1,109	-	-
6330	Fire, marine, and casualty insurance	15	17	4.7	331	348	35,275	34,989	11,513	12,421	5.1
6360	Title insurance	3	3	10.7	11	-	22,182	-	378	-	-
6370	Pension, health, and welfare funds	5	5	6.2	13	-	21,846	-	312	-	-
6400	Insurance agents, brokers, and service	77	87	3.8	620	422	24,974	27,678	17,326	15,422	4.9
6500	Real estate	115	116	3.5	482	465	29,037	20,232	13,426	11,983	3.3
6510	Real estate operators and lessors	29	28	2.0	102	66	66,510	19,030	5,061	1,340	1.2
6530	Real estate agents and managers	61	73	4.8	234	341	15,504	19,765	4,127	8,227	4.0
6552	Subdividers and developers, n.e.c.	9	9	6.4	100	29	25,120	28,690	2,526	1,191	8.4
6700	Holding and other investment offices	23	22	5.4	183	122	61,508	51,180	9,167	5,832	4.5
6710	Holding offices	10	7	5.2	141	73	62,610	47,233	6,747	3,117	3.8
WILSON, TN											
60 –	**Finance, insurance, and real estate**	90	102	1.0	491	493	22,134	21,671	11,544	11,553	0.4
6000	Depository institutions	26	30	1.4	288	321	23,236	23,576	6,936	8,120	0.9
6020	Commercial banks	23	26	1.6	-	300	-	22,893	-	7,021	1.0
6100	Nondepository institutions	5	6	0.7	17	20	22,353	23,400	400	459	0.2
6200	Security and commodity brokers	5	6	1.3	-	9	-	40,000	-	425	0.1
6210	Security brokers and dealers	4	6	2.2	-	9	-	40,000	-	425	0.2
6400	Insurance agents, brokers, and service	14	18	0.8	44	50	22,909	20,480	1,005	1,087	0.3
6500	Real estate	33	38	1.1	123	83	18,341	11,614	2,658	1,131	0.3
6510	Real estate operators and lessors	8	14	1.0	18	52	9,556	10,846	224	671	0.6
6530	Real estate agents and managers	20	22	1.4	23	-	17,565	-	422	-	-

Source: County Business Patterns, 1992/93, CBP-92/93-1, U.S. Department of Commerce, Washington, D.C., April 1995. SIC categories for which data were suppressed or not available for both 1992 and 1993 are *not* displayed. The employment columns represent mid-March employment in the year. Pay per employee is calculated by dividing 1st Quarter payroll, annualized, by mid-March employment. The columns headed "% State" show the county's percentage of the state total for the SIC in 1993; for example, 0.9% for SIC 6030 means that the county had 0.9 percent of the state's total establishments (or payroll) in SIC 6030 in 1993. A dash (-) is used to indicate that data are not available or cannot be calculated; *nec* means not elsewhere classified.

TEXAS

SIC	Industry	No. Establishments			Employment		Pay / Employee		Annual Payroll ($ 000)		
		1992	1993	% State	1992	1993	1992	1993	1992	1993	% State
ANDERSON, TX											
60 –	**Finance, insurance, and real estate**	60	58	0.1	359	348	21,259	24,011	8,429	7,692	0.1
6000	Depository institutions	10	11	0.2	210	214	22,990	23,421	4,971	4,642	0.2
6020	Commercial banks	6	6	0.2	188	190	23,660	24,189	4,561	4,207	0.2
6100	Nondepository institutions	6	6	0.2	30	-	19,867	-	680	-	-
6140	Personal credit institutions	3	3	0.2	-	9	-	22,222	-	190	0.1
6300	Insurance carriers	5	5	0.2	16	16	18,250	19,750	285	313	0.0
6400	Insurance agents, brokers, and service	16	14	0.2	48	43	16,750	17,302	804	778	0.1
6500	Real estate	17	16	0.1	35	31	8,229	13,548	273	347	0.0
6530	Real estate agents and managers	5	6	0.1	16	12	7,250	5,667	122	91	0.0
6700	Holding and other investment offices	4	4	0.1	-	12	-	8,000	-	97	0.0
ANDREWS, TX											
60 –	**Finance, insurance, and real estate**	16	15	0.0	106	110	19,170	22,000	2,132	2,427	0.0
6000	Depository institutions	4	4	0.1	65	64	17,908	19,875	1,265	1,324	0.0
6400	Insurance agents, brokers, and service	4	3	0.0	15	15	13,600	26,133	232	325	0.0
6500	Real estate	3	4	0.0	-	14	-	10,000	-	153	0.0
ANGELINA, TX											
60 –	**Finance, insurance, and real estate**	143	148	0.4	1,003	994	19,697	18,901	20,981	21,059	0.2
6000	Depository institutions	19	20	0.4	457	448	20,333	20,402	9,374	10,124	0.3
6020	Commercial banks	6	6	0.2	319	336	21,016	20,786	6,843	7,905	0.4
6030	Savings institutions	5	6	0.9	109	88	18,716	19,273	1,986	1,755	0.6
6060	Credit unions	8	8	0.8	29	24	18,897	19,167	545	464	0.2
6140	Personal credit institutions	9	8	0.6	33	38	16,485	15,579	580	658	0.2
6300	Insurance carriers	13	10	0.3	101	113	22,812	18,478	2,300	2,291	0.1
6310	Life insurance	6	5	0.5	79	-	19,899	-	1,517	-	-
6400	Insurance agents, brokers, and service	45	47	0.5	160	172	17,100	18,628	3,666	3,895	0.3
6500	Real estate	47	52	0.3	176	203	17,045	14,483	3,231	3,329	0.2
6510	Real estate operators and lessors	28	32	0.5	64	88	13,812	13,864	899	1,139	0.2
6530	Real estate agents and managers	14	14	0.2	96	92	20,167	13,217	2,137	1,606	0.1
6700	Holding and other investment offices	6	7	0.3	68	11	14,941	14,909	1,155	171	0.0
6799	Investors, n.e.c.	2	4	0.6	-	8	-	9,500	-	85	0.1
ARANSAS, TX											
60 –	**Finance, insurance, and real estate**	35	36	0.1	188	172	18,660	14,302	4,415	2,211	0.0
6000	Depository institutions	6	4	0.1	103	53	22,291	18,340	2,167	769	0.0
6400	Insurance agents, brokers, and service	8	7	0.1	32	38	16,750	16,316	1,504	437	0.0
6500	Real estate	17	20	0.1	45	70	10,667	9,429	542	729	0.0
6510	Real estate operators and lessors	5	7	0.1	25	10	8,160	13,200	229	119	0.0
6530	Real estate agents and managers	8	8	0.1	17	51	13,176	7,922	256	465	0.0
6552	Subdividers and developers, n.e.c.	1	3	0.4	-	3	-	13,333	-	32	0.0
ARCHER, TX											
60 –	**Finance, insurance, and real estate**	11	11	0.0	58	60	19,724	20,000	1,154	1,215	0.0
6000	Depository institutions	5	5	0.1	36	39	22,778	22,256	806	887	0.0
ARMSTRONG, TX											
60 –	**Finance, insurance, and real estate**	5	5	0.0	-	29	-	18,621	-	540	0.0

Source: County Business Patterns, 1992/93, CBP-92/93-1, U.S. Department of Commerce, Washington, D.C., April 1995. SIC categories for which data were suppressed or not available for both 1992 and 1993 are *not* displayed. The employment columns represent mid-March employment in the year. Pay per employee is calculated by dividing 1st Quarter payroll, annualized, by mid-March employment. The columns headed "% State" show the county's percentage of the state total for the SIC in 1993; for example, 0.9% for SIC 6030 means that the county had 0.9 percent of the state's total establishments (or payroll) in SIC 6030 in 1993. A dash (-) is used to indicate that data are not available or cannot be calculated; *nec* means not elsewhere classified.

SIC	Industry	No. Establishments			Employment		Pay / Employee		Annual Payroll ($ 000)		
		1992	1993	% State	1992	1993	1992	1993	1992	1993	% State
ATASCOSA, TX											
60 –	**Finance, insurance, and real estate**	38	38	*0.1*	316	299	22,139	23,304	6,966	5,536	*0.0*
6000	Depository institutions	7	6	*0.1*	115	109	21,496	22,055	2,409	2,254	*0.1*
6020	Commercial banks	6	6	*0.2*	-	109	-	22,055	-	2,254	*0.1*
6100	Nondepository institutions	7	6	*0.2*	138	105	26,928	33,943	3,642	2,162	*0.2*
6400	Insurance agents, brokers, and service	8	10	*0.1*	23	27	11,652	12,000	266	356	*0.0*
6500	Real estate	10	9	*0.1*	17	-	9,176	-	176	-	-
6510	Real estate operators and lessors	5	6	*0.1*	7	26	6,286	5,077	59	140	*0.0*
6700	Holding and other investment offices	2	3	*0.1*	-	3	-	13,333	-	89	*0.0*
AUSTIN, TX											
60 –	**Finance, insurance, and real estate**	47	50	*0.1*	297	305	16,714	17,823	5,110	5,826	*0.0*
6000	Depository institutions	11	11	*0.2*	172	184	19,163	18,565	3,572	3,828	*0.1*
6020	Commercial banks	7	7	*0.3*	160	171	19,250	18,480	3,331	3,557	*0.2*
6030	Savings institutions	4	4	*0.6*	12	13	18,000	19,692	241	271	*0.1*
6300	Insurance carriers	5	4	*0.1*	50	-	12,000	-	431	-	-
6400	Insurance agents, brokers, and service	9	9	*0.1*	23	33	19,826	19,758	450	695	*0.1*
6500	Real estate	17	19	*0.1*	36	62	9,000	8,581	349	504	*0.0*
6510	Real estate operators and lessors	6	6	*0.1*	16	28	5,750	8,571	95	204	*0.0*
6530	Real estate agents and managers	8	9	*0.1*	16	30	11,000	8,000	197	221	*0.0*
BAILEY, TX											
60 –	**Finance, insurance, and real estate**	14	12	*0.0*	74	61	21,946	27,213	1,627	1,512	*0.0*
6000	Depository institutions	3	2	*0.0*	49	-	24,000	-	1,175	-	-
6020	Commercial banks	3	2	*0.1*	49	-	24,000	-	1,175	-	-
6400	Insurance agents, brokers, and service	6	6	*0.1*	10	12	16,800	16,667	178	201	*0.0*
BANDERA, TX											
60 –	**Finance, insurance, and real estate**	20	21	*0.1*	68	79	21,353	16,506	1,667	1,399	*0.0*
6000	Depository institutions	4	4	*0.1*	-	39	-	22,051	-	794	*0.0*
6400	Insurance agents, brokers, and service	4	5	*0.1*	13	11	35,077	13,091	621	218	*0.0*
6500	Real estate	10	10	*0.1*	17	-	16,941	-	283	-	-
6530	Real estate agents and managers	4	6	*0.1*	5	13	17,600	10,462	64	169	*0.0*
BASTROP, TX											
60 –	**Finance, insurance, and real estate**	42	42	*0.1*	271	267	15,424	15,910	4,413	4,513	*0.0*
6000	Depository institutions	9	8	*0.2*	188	179	15,809	17,296	3,086	3,224	*0.1*
6400	Insurance agents, brokers, and service	11	12	*0.1*	28	32	16,714	14,500	490	532	*0.0*
6500	Real estate	19	18	*0.1*	50	48	13,440	12,500	755	648	*0.0*
6510	Real estate operators and lessors	7	8	*0.1*	9	17	8,444	9,176	86	163	*0.0*
6530	Real estate agents and managers	5	6	*0.1*	23	-	10,087	-	246	-	-
BAYLOR, TX											
60 –	**Finance, insurance, and real estate**	11	10	*0.0*	45	44	16,622	16,818	748	760	*0.0*
6000	Depository institutions	3	3	*0.1*	34	33	18,000	18,788	610	623	*0.0*
6400	Insurance agents, brokers, and service	3	5	*0.1*	6	-	11,333	-	70	-	-
BEE, TX											
60 –	**Finance, insurance, and real estate**	45	46	*0.1*	249	305	17,253	17,967	4,305	5,298	*0.0*
6000	Depository institutions	7	7	*0.1*	142	154	18,704	20,260	2,540	2,943	*0.1*
6020	Commercial banks	4	5	*0.2*	125	-	18,976	-	2,260	-	-
6100	Nondepository institutions	6	5	*0.2*	14	-	15,143	-	179	-	-
6200	Security and commodity brokers	4	4	*0.2*	10	9	13,200	13,778	146	170	*0.0*
6300	Insurance carriers	6	4	*0.1*	28	55	18,000	17,891	560	797	*0.0*
6330	Fire, marine, and casualty insurance	3	1	*0.1*	4	-	18,000	-	68	-	-
6400	Insurance agents, brokers, and service	7	9	*0.1*	27	41	17,630	15,610	570	761	*0.1*

Source: County Business Patterns, 1992/93, CBP-92/93-1, U.S. Department of Commerce, Washington, D.C., April 1995. SIC categories for which data were suppressed or not available for both 1992 and 1993 are not displayed. The employment columns represent mid-March employment in the year. Pay per employee is calculated by dividing 1st Quarter payroll, annualized, by mid-March employment. The columns headed "% State" show the county's percentage of the state total for the SIC in 1993; for example, 0.9% for SIC 6030 means that the county had 0.9 percent of the state's total establishments (or payroll) in SIC 6030 in 1993. A dash (-) is used to indicate that data are not available or cannot be calculated; nec means not elsewhere classified.

Continued on next page.

SIC	Industry	No. Establishments			Employment		Pay / Employee		Annual Payroll ($ 000)		
		1992	1993	% State	1992	1993	1992	1993	1992	1993	% State
BEE, TX - [continued]											
6500	Real estate	11	15	0.1	21	29	10,095	11,310	219	330	0.0
6510	Real estate operators and lessors	8	7	0.1	18	22	10,000	10,364	164	238	0.0
6700	Holding and other investment offices	4	2	0.1	7	-	14,857	-	91	-	-
BELL, TX											
60 –	**Finance, insurance, and real estate**	351	377	0.9	2,890	3,319	15,492	15,238	47,801	56,407	0.4
6000	Depository institutions	49	44	0.9	866	907	19,381	19,568	17,092	19,908	0.7
6020	Commercial banks	25	25	1.0	678	745	20,165	19,893	13,754	16,665	0.7
6030	Savings institutions	7	4	0.6	56	-	16,357	-	985	-	-
6060	Credit unions	8	8	0.8	107	115	17,794	19,061	2,017	2,399	1.1
6090	Functions closely related to banking	9	7	1.4	25	-	11,680	-	336	-	-
6100	Nondepository institutions	33	37	1.2	598	847	15,900	14,564	10,600	13,988	1.2
6140	Personal credit institutions	24	26	1.8	104	183	18,962	11,388	1,864	1,940	0.6
6200	Security and commodity brokers	14	18	0.9	47	79	48,596	26,228	2,173	2,476	0.2
6210	Security brokers and dealers	9	10	0.8	37	66	58,919	29,576	2,056	2,340	0.2
6280	Security and commodity services	5	7	1.0	10	13	10,400	9,231	117	131	0.0
6300	Insurance carriers	30	20	0.6	186	490	18,860	7,682	3,760	3,456	0.1
6310	Life insurance	6	4	0.4	100	-	19,760	-	2,015	-	-
6330	Fire, marine, and casualty insurance	16	14	1.0	25	404	29,280	5,871	873	2,163	0.2
6400	Insurance agents, brokers, and service	70	80	0.9	659	331	9,141	18,175	6,596	6,157	0.5
6500	Real estate	146	173	1.1	508	649	12,276	12,277	6,972	9,549	0.4
6510	Real estate operators and lessors	67	83	1.3	245	323	9,404	9,659	2,357	3,296	0.6
6530	Real estate agents and managers	55	70	1.0	204	238	15,373	14,773	3,505	4,363	0.3
6540	Title abstract offices	1	5	1.3	-	50	-	19,760	-	1,206	1.5
6552	Subdividers and developers, n.e.c.	5	5	0.7	14	10	16,286	10,800	314	419	0.3
6553	Cemetery subdividers and developers	8	8	2.5	22	28	6,909	8,429	165	249	0.5
6700	Holding and other investment offices	9	5	0.2	26	16	16,462	42,000	608	873	0.1
6799	Investors, n.e.c.	3	1	0.1	3	-	21,333	-	181	-	-
BEXAR, TX											
60 –	**Finance, insurance, and real estate**	2,642	2,683	6.8	37,648	35,845	27,874	27,260	1,102,226	1,071,386	8.3
6000	Depository institutions	327	277	5.7	9,689	7,658	22,187	23,772	218,001	190,017	6.5
6020	Commercial banks	155	121	4.6	6,813	4,708	22,816	25,596	151,274	115,548	5.1
6030	Savings institutions	61	30	4.7	1,227	801	21,995	29,029	32,511	32,434	10.7
6060	Credit unions	62	78	7.6	1,338	1,779	19,584	17,619	27,428	34,837	15.6
6100	Nondepository institutions	219	228	7.6	2,190	2,704	29,447	23,075	67,301	73,786	6.3
6140	Personal credit institutions	144	130	9.0	1,010	1,478	22,127	15,981	23,191	27,511	8.1
6150	Business credit institutions	20	30	7.6	162	161	30,346	35,155	6,655	6,134	3.3
6160	Mortgage bankers and brokers	49	68	6.8	1,010	1,065	36,622	31,095	36,960	40,141	6.6
6200	Security and commodity brokers	127	125	6.2	1,329	1,496	48,572	56,939	68,549	83,914	5.5
6210	Security brokers and dealers	93	81	6.4	1,029	701	53,446	80,194	56,962	49,466	4.4
6300	Insurance carriers	277	247	7.9	13,715	13,291	30,061	32,218	440,698	477,091	16.8
6310	Life insurance	98	84	8.6	2,669	2,482	25,819	28,638	72,589	74,968	7.8
6321	Accident and health insurance	10	9	7.2	-	326	-	22,601	-	7,737	6.6
6324	Hospital and medical service plans	11	15	20.0	-	717	-	22,064	-	18,290	10.6
6330	Fire, marine, and casualty insurance	115	114	8.0	9,915	9,450	31,916	34,404	337,876	365,958	26.4
6350	Surety insurance	6	6	16.2	48	-	36,167	-	1,452	-	-
6360	Title insurance	12	8	3.7	174	163	32,851	38,282	6,333	7,398	5.8
6370	Pension, health, and welfare funds	23	10	4.0	150	118	11,973	13,898	3,370	1,735	3.7
6400	Insurance agents, brokers, and service	549	589	6.7	3,063	3,096	25,332	24,487	92,494	83,783	6.4
6500	Real estate	974	1,043	6.9	6,096	6,671	16,940	17,659	114,533	130,377	6.1
6510	Real estate operators and lessors	401	465	7.0	2,213	2,777	13,609	15,294	31,471	45,258	7.9
6530	Real estate agents and managers	425	510	7.3	3,037	3,352	18,344	18,228	63,654	66,413	5.0
6540	Title abstract offices	9	14	3.7	121	209	23,471	25,952	3,390	6,728	8.4
6552	Subdividers and developers, n.e.c.	35	40	6.0	294	256	21,959	28,938	6,391	10,265	8.0
6553	Cemetery subdividers and developers	9	6	1.9	118	76	19,288	18,158	2,341	1,551	3.3
6700	Holding and other investment offices	162	168	6.2	1,435	681	76,201	27,877	97,511	24,658	3.3
6710	Holding offices	18	26	4.6	815	102	117,070	56,275	83,254	10,024	2.7

Source: County Business Patterns, 1992/93, CBP-92/93-1, U.S. Department of Commerce, Washington, D.C., April 1995. SIC categories for which data were suppressed or not available for both 1992 and 1993 are not displayed. The employment columns represent mid-March employment in the year. Pay per employee is calculated by dividing 1st Quarter payroll, annualized, by mid-March employment. The columns headed "% State" show the county's percentage of the state total for the SIC in 1993; for example, 0.9% for SIC 6030 means that the county had 0.9 percent of the state's total establishments (or payroll) in SIC 6030 in 1993. A dash (-) is used to indicate that data are not available or cannot be calculated; nec means not elsewhere classified.

Continued on next page.

SIC	Industry	No. Establishments			Employment		Pay / Employee		Annual Payroll ($ 000)		
		1992	1993	% State	1992	1993	1992	1993	1992	1993	% State
BEXAR, TX - [continued]											
6720	Investment offices	6	5	6.8	-	5	-	22,400	-	114	0.7
6732	Educational, religious, etc. trusts	27	28	8.9	86	111	15,302	15,315	1,445	1,837	3.7
6733	Trusts, n.e.c.	40	39	7.2	144	180	28,972	22,756	3,326	3,917	5.0
6798	Real estate investment trusts	7	2	5.1	125	-	17,504	-	2,532	-	-
6799	Investors, n.e.c.	31	39	5.4	104	127	20,462	23,244	2,176	3,726	3.1
BLANCO, TX											
60 –	**Finance, insurance, and real estate**	18	17	0.0	91	94	16,879	17,787	1,640	1,751	0.0
6000	Depository institutions	5	5	0.1	64	64	18,312	19,500	1,254	1,312	0.0
6400	Insurance agents, brokers, and service	3	4	0.0	5	-	16,000	-	87	-	-
6500	Real estate	10	7	0.0	22	13	12,909	10,462	299	139	0.0
6510	Real estate operators and lessors	5	5	0.1	7	-	8,000	-	67	-	-
BORDEN, TX											
60 –	**Finance, insurance, and real estate**	1	1	0.0	-	-	-	-	-	-	-
BOSQUE, TX											
60 –	**Finance, insurance, and real estate**	33	35	0.1	122	118	18,951	17,458	2,201	2,286	0.0
6000	Depository institutions	9	8	0.2	75	78	20,693	19,436	1,547	1,682	0.1
6020	Commercial banks	9	8	0.3	75	78	20,693	19,436	1,547	1,682	0.1
6300	Insurance carriers	5	2	0.1	4	-	11,000	-	46	-	-
6330	Fire, marine, and casualty insurance	3	1	0.1	3	-	9,333	-	27	-	-
6400	Insurance agents, brokers, and service	6	10	0.1	-	23	-	12,696	-	329	0.0
6500	Real estate	7	8	0.1	7	8	17,714	13,000	126	119	0.0
6510	Real estate operators and lessors	3	4	0.1	-	4	-	17,000	-	67	0.0
6700	Holding and other investment offices	4	4	0.1	10	4	21,200	10,000	137	44	0.0
BOWIE, TX											
60 –	**Finance, insurance, and real estate**	178	172	0.4	1,077	1,103	23,231	22,281	25,624	26,479	0.2
6000	Depository institutions	30	29	0.6	523	540	21,698	19,185	11,658	12,016	0.4
6020	Commercial banks	17	16	0.6	390	385	22,051	20,343	8,739	9,091	0.4
6100	Nondepository institutions	17	19	0.6	63	67	19,175	22,328	1,258	1,423	0.1
6140	Personal credit institutions	16	14	1.0	-	42	-	19,619	-	860	0.3
6200	Security and commodity brokers	5	4	0.2	-	15	-	92,267	-	1,263	0.1
6210	Security brokers and dealers	4	4	0.3	15	15	83,200	92,267	1,093	1,263	0.1
6300	Insurance carriers	23	19	0.6	140	105	27,457	30,705	3,871	3,011	0.1
6310	Life insurance	10	6	0.6	103	68	25,165	32,294	2,646	1,913	0.2
6400	Insurance agents, brokers, and service	50	49	0.6	175	187	32,731	29,305	5,944	6,419	0.5
6500	Real estate	50	48	0.3	150	177	10,133	14,124	1,670	2,209	0.1
6510	Real estate operators and lessors	30	27	0.4	83	120	7,614	11,833	772	1,207	0.2
6530	Real estate agents and managers	12	14	0.2	33	25	14,303	27,040	453	518	0.0
6552	Subdividers and developers, n.e.c.	3	3	0.4	-	9	-	6,667	-	94	0.1
6700	Holding and other investment offices	3	4	0.1	-	12	-	11,000	-	138	0.0
BRAZORIA, TX											
60 –	**Finance, insurance, and real estate**	265	274	0.7	1,573	1,694	19,517	19,341	32,891	34,230	0.3
6000	Depository institutions	44	40	0.8	723	703	20,111	19,789	14,860	14,178	0.5
6020	Commercial banks	30	22	0.8	575	510	20,890	19,529	11,966	10,162	0.5
6100	Nondepository institutions	7	9	0.3	-	28	-	24,857	-	896	0.1
6160	Mortgage bankers and brokers	3	5	0.5	15	-	29,333	-	526	-	-
6200	Security and commodity brokers	5	5	0.2	-	15	-	50,400	-	970	0.1
6300	Insurance carriers	24	23	0.7	113	92	28,708	31,957	3,141	2,928	0.1
6330	Fire, marine, and casualty insurance	14	14	1.0	36	-	39,556	-	1,493	-	-
6400	Insurance agents, brokers, and service	65	67	0.8	237	234	18,380	18,325	4,687	4,308	0.3
6500	Real estate	108	121	0.8	371	551	14,340	15,535	7,069	9,246	0.4
6510	Real estate operators and lessors	46	54	0.8	151	223	10,702	13,399	2,041	3,192	0.6
6530	Real estate agents and managers	40	53	0.8	112	201	15,857	16,100	2,498	3,206	0.2

Source: County Business Patterns, 1992/93, CBP-92/93-1, U.S. Department of Commerce, Washington, D.C., April 1995. SIC categories for which data were suppressed or not available for both 1992 and 1993 are not displayed. The employment columns represent mid-March employment in the year. Pay per employee is calculated by dividing 1st Quarter payroll, annualized, by mid-March employment. The columns headed "% State" show the county's percentage of the state total for the SIC in 1993; for example, 0.9% for SIC 6030 means that the county had 0.9 percent of the state's total establishments (or payroll) in SIC 6030 in 1993. A dash (-) is used to indicate that data are not available or cannot be calculated; nec means not elsewhere classified.

Continued on next page.

SIC	Industry	No. Establishments			Employment		Pay / Employee		Annual Payroll ($ 000)		
		1992	1993	% State	1992	1993	1992	1993	1992	1993	% State
BRAZORIA, TX - [continued]											
6552	Subdividers and developers, n.e.c.	5	7	1.0	6	-	18,667	-	124	-	-
6553	Cemetery subdividers and developers	3	4	1.3	44	56	17,909	21,214	1,261	1,483	3.2
6700	Holding and other investment offices	11	8	0.3	50	-	9,280	-	469	-	-
BRAZOS, TX											
60–	**Finance, insurance, and real estate**	234	249	0.6	1,680	1,834	22,567	22,022	42,049	49,701	0.4
6000	Depository institutions	19	19	0.4	431	473	25,281	23,425	11,080	14,913	0.5
6020	Commercial banks	8	8	0.3	260	238	21,138	17,076	5,761	5,454	0.2
6030	Savings institutions	6	6	0.9	139	200	36,547	33,020	5,082	8,979	3.0
6100	Nondepository institutions	18	20	0.7	97	112	23,216	22,786	2,460	3,168	0.3
6110	Federal and Federally-sponsored credit	3	2	1.4	19	-	22,526	-	524	-	-
6140	Personal credit institutions	11	12	0.8	67	62	23,403	21,935	1,581	1,497	0.4
6160	Mortgage bankers and brokers	4	6	0.6	11	-	23,273	-	355	-	-
6200	Security and commodity brokers	17	20	1.0	65	67	44,800	47,164	3,128	3,462	0.2
6210	Security brokers and dealers	9	11	0.9	51	54	51,608	53,704	2,763	3,132	0.3
6280	Security and commodity services	8	9	1.3	14	13	20,000	20,000	365	330	0.1
6300	Insurance carriers	17	12	0.4	100	77	27,320	32,727	3,010	2,496	0.1
6310	Life insurance	7	4	0.4	67	67	29,015	31,224	2,114	1,994	0.2
6400	Insurance agents, brokers, and service	43	51	0.6	303	366	27,380	30,175	10,900	14,082	1.1
6500	Real estate	106	116	0.8	558	663	12,237	11,759	7,228	9,260	0.4
6510	Real estate operators and lessors	54	61	0.9	342	312	10,386	10,821	3,830	3,924	0.7
6530	Real estate agents and managers	36	44	0.6	168	322	16,048	12,708	2,763	4,807	0.4
6553	Cemetery subdividers and developers	1	3	0.9	-	6	-	10,667	-	96	0.2
6700	Holding and other investment offices	14	11	0.4	126	76	31,714	29,421	4,243	2,320	0.3
BREWSTER, TX											
60–	**Finance, insurance, and real estate**	15	17	0.0	84	85	13,048	14,212	1,186	1,342	0.0
6400	Insurance agents, brokers, and service	2	3	0.0	-	7	-	10,857	-	80	0.0
6500	Real estate	9	10	0.1	13	21	7,077	5,524	95	116	0.0
6510	Real estate operators and lessors	3	4	0.1	3	6	5,333	4,667	20	28	0.0
6530	Real estate agents and managers	3	2	0.0	5	-	4,800	-	30	-	-
BRISCOE, TX											
60–	**Finance, insurance, and real estate**	8	6	0.0	36	31	18,222	19,613	803	750	0.0
6500	Real estate	3	3	0.0	5	-	2,400	-	20	-	-
BROOKS, TX											
60–	**Finance, insurance, and real estate**	12	12	0.0	68	75	14,882	13,920	1,071	1,184	0.0
6000	Depository institutions	3	3	0.1	47	56	16,681	15,357	875	979	0.0
6400	Insurance agents, brokers, and service	4	5	0.1	9	10	10,222	9,600	98	109	0.0
BROWN, TX											
60–	**Finance, insurance, and real estate**	51	55	0.1	243	245	19,737	21,551	4,991	5,074	0.0
6000	Depository institutions	9	9	0.2	140	133	20,171	19,820	2,687	2,633	0.1
6020	Commercial banks	5	4	0.2	116	106	21,655	21,283	2,355	2,243	0.1
6100	Nondepository institutions	4	3	0.1	-	11	-	22,909	-	234	0.0
6140	Personal credit institutions	3	2	0.1	7	-	21,714	-	141	-	-
6300	Insurance carriers	8	6	0.2	22	-	28,364	-	657	-	-
6400	Insurance agents, brokers, and service	17	18	0.2	49	50	14,041	16,480	719	849	0.1
6500	Real estate	11	15	0.1	19	27	11,368	9,333	239	448	0.0
6510	Real estate operators and lessors	2	6	0.1	-	6	-	12,000	-	77	0.0
6530	Real estate agents and managers	6	5	0.1	7	4	10,857	9,000	92	71	0.0
BURLESON, TX											
60–	**Finance, insurance, and real estate**	25	26	0.1	130	145	18,123	18,097	2,615	2,777	0.0
6000	Depository institutions	7	8	0.2	93	108	20,344	20,185	2,183	2,344	0.1
6300	Insurance carriers	7	3	0.1	-	1	-	4,000	-	13	0.0

Source: County Business Patterns, 1992/93, CBP-92/93-1, U.S. Department of Commerce, Washington, D.C., April 1995. SIC categories for which data were suppressed or not available for both 1992 and 1993 are *not* displayed. The employment columns represent mid-March employment in the year. Pay per employee is calculated by dividing 1st Quarter payroll, annualized, by mid-March employment. The columns headed "% State" show the county's percentage of the state total for the SIC in 1993; for example, 0.9% for SIC 6030 means that the county had 0.9 percent of the state's total establishments (or payroll) in SIC 6030 in 1993. A dash (-) is used to indicate that data are not available or cannot be calculated; *nec* means not elsewhere classified.

Continued on next page.

SIC	Industry	No. Establishments			Employment		Pay / Employee		Annual Payroll ($ 000)		
		1992	1993	% State	1992	1993	1992	1993	1992	1993	% State
BURLESON, TX - [continued]											
6330	Fire, marine, and casualty insurance	4	2	0.1	8	-	7,000	-	68	-	-
6400	Insurance agents, brokers, and service	5	8	0.1	12	-	12,000	-	152	-	-
6500	Real estate	4	5	0.0	8	13	6,500	7,385	61	99	0.0
BURNET, TX											
60–	**Finance, insurance, and real estate**	62	62	0.2	235	238	15,932	20,790	4,166	5,402	0.0
6000	Depository institutions	9	9	0.2	126	120	18,095	18,500	2,330	2,379	0.1
6100	Nondepository institutions	3	3	0.1		6		19,333		203	0.0
6400	Insurance agents, brokers, and service	13	13	0.1	30	30	17,600	27,467	775	1,080	0.1
6500	Real estate	33	32	0.2	64	68	8,250	8,000	597	813	0.0
6510	Real estate operators and lessors	19	19	0.3	38	45	5,789	5,956	268	273	0.0
6530	Real estate agents and managers	7	7	0.1	11	-	13,455	-	141	-	-
CALDWELL, TX											
60–	**Finance, insurance, and real estate**	34	36	0.1	194	189	14,619	15,788	2,967	3,199	0.0
6000	Depository institutions	5	5	0.1	102	114	20,000	17,719	2,032	2,060	0.1
6100	Nondepository institutions	4	4	0.1	6	-	26,667	-	145	-	-
6300	Insurance carriers	5	4	0.1	-	6	-	22,000	-	146	0.0
6400	Insurance agents, brokers, and service	6	7	0.1	56	24	4,357	10,833	259	280	0.0
6500	Real estate	12	14	0.1	22	33	9,273	9,333	259	280	0.0
6510	Real estate operators and lessors	4	7	0.1	8	19	5,000	8,421	70	217	0.0
6530	Real estate agents and managers	2	4	0.1	-	6	-	9,333	-	63	0.0
6540	Title abstract offices	3	2	0.5	5	-	18,400	-	113	-	-
CALHOUN, TX											
60–	**Finance, insurance, and real estate**	30	31	0.1	202	199	17,921	18,633	3,680	3,860	0.0
6000	Depository institutions	10	10	0.2	155	156	20,748	20,974	3,216	3,389	0.1
6020	Commercial banks	5	5	0.2	130	129	20,862	21,178	2,693	2,816	0.1
6400	Insurance agents, brokers, and service	8	7	0.1	23	20	9,217	9,400	224	194	0.0
6510	Real estate operators and lessors	4	6	0.1	12	-	4,000	-	75	-	-
6530	Real estate agents and managers	2	4	0.1	-	4	-	5,000	-	28	0.0
CALLAHAN, TX											
60–	**Finance, insurance, and real estate**	14	14	0.0	80	85	18,150	17,459	1,563	1,679	0.0
6000	Depository institutions	5	4	0.1	59	64	20,339	19,250	1,296	1,400	0.0
6020	Commercial banks	4	4	0.2	-	64	-	19,250	-	1,400	0.1
6400	Insurance agents, brokers, and service	4	5	0.1	10	-	10,000	-	102	-	-
6500	Real estate	4	4	0.0	-	7	-	16,000	-	134	0.0
CAMERON, TX											
60–	**Finance, insurance, and real estate**	507	531	1.3	3,616	3,614	18,896	17,630	72,017	68,326	0.5
6000	Depository institutions	56	61	1.3	1,214	1,238	21,977	20,756	28,175	27,425	0.9
6020	Commercial banks	36	37	1.4	1,088	1,098	22,702	21,552	26,071	25,179	1.1
6030	Savings institutions	6	7	1.1	24	28	26,333	21,429	633	598	0.2
6060	Credit unions	8	9	0.9	86	95	14,279	13,600	1,340	1,482	0.7
6090	Functions closely related to banking	6	8	1.5	16	17	7,500	8,235	131	166	-
6100	Nondepository institutions	56	55	1.8	233	347	20,446	16,438	5,217	6,217	0.5
6140	Personal credit institutions	48	48	3.3	214	320	19,813	15,762	4,689	5,469	1.6
6200	Security and commodity brokers	11	13	0.6	-	44	-	68,727	-	3,221	0.2
6210	Security brokers and dealers	8	9	0.7	-	39	-	76,821	-	3,194	0.3
6300	Insurance carriers	31	24	0.8	306	226	24,523	24,619	7,813	5,794	0.2
6310	Life insurance	12	7	0.7	233	171	22,489	20,865	5,282	3,784	0.4
6330	Fire, marine, and casualty insurance	15	12	0.8	46	-	36,957	-	1,753	-	-
6370	Pension, health, and welfare funds	2	3	1.2	-	14	-	16,286	-	101	0.2
6400	Insurance agents, brokers, and service	87	97	1.1	392	406	19,143	20,581	8,026	8,515	0.7
6500	Real estate	254	271	1.8	1,181	1,280	11,265	10,366	13,667	14,997	0.7
6510	Real estate operators and lessors	112	146	2.2	387	472	10,646	10,263	4,363	5,502	1.0
6530	Real estate agents and managers	105	113	1.6	582	767	10,983	10,149	6,555	8,548	0.6

Source: County Business Patterns, 1992/93, CBP-92/93-1, U.S. Department of Commerce, Washington, D.C., April 1995. SIC categories for which data were suppressed or not available for both 1992 and 1993 are *not* displayed. The employment columns represent mid-March employment in the year. Pay per employee is calculated by dividing 1st Quarter payroll, annualized, by mid-March employment. The columns headed "% State" show the county's percentage of the state total for the SIC in 1993; for example, 0.9% for SIC 6030 means that the county had 0.9 percent of the state's total establishments (or payroll) in SIC 6030 in 1993. A dash (-) is used to indicate that data are not available or cannot be calculated; *nec* means not elsewhere classified.

Continued on next page.

SIC	Industry	No. Establishments			Employment		Pay / Employee		Annual Payroll ($ 000)		
		1992	1993	% State	1992	1993	1992	1993	1992	1993	% State
CAMERON, TX - [continued]											
6552	Subdividers and developers, n.e.c.	9	9	1.3	55	-	16,727	-	678	-	-
6700	Holding and other investment offices	12	10	0.4	-	73	-	28,822	-	2,157	0.3
6733	Trusts, n.e.c.	6	4	0.7	-	8	-	8,000	-	71	0.1
CAMP, TX											
60 –	**Finance, insurance, and real estate**	18	16	0.0	105	95	20,876	23,663	1,864	1,951	0.0
6000	Depository institutions	4	4	0.1	76	73	24,368	27,233	1,504	1,600	0.1
6400	Insurance agents, brokers, and service	5	5	0.1	15	13	12,533	12,923	181	180	0.0
6530	Real estate agents and managers	5	3	0.0	6	-	8,667	-	62	-	-
CARSON, TX											
60 –	**Finance, insurance, and real estate**	11	11	0.0	57	88	24,421	22,455	1,297	1,849	0.0
6000	Depository institutions	4	4	0.1	42	44	29,333	27,727	1,120	1,146	0.0
6400	Insurance agents, brokers, and service	4	3	0.0	9	9	10,667	12,444	100	127	0.0
CASS, TX											
60 –	**Finance, insurance, and real estate**	48	43	0.1	246	243	19,447	18,058	4,925	4,868	0.0
6000	Depository institutions	15	14	0.3	153	148	20,810	20,135	3,386	3,432	0.1
6020	Commercial banks	9	9	0.3	115	120	22,157	19,633	2,787	2,836	0.1
6100	Nondepository institutions	5	5	0.2	13	16	13,846	13,500	230	222	0.0
6140	Personal credit institutions	5	5	0.3	13	16	13,846	13,500	230	222	0.1
6400	Insurance agents, brokers, and service	13	13	0.1	44	45	14,091	17,244	594	831	0.1
6500	Real estate	11	8	0.1	21	26	12,571	9,846	301	251	0.0
6530	Real estate agents and managers	8	6	0.1	9	-	10,222	-	111	-	-
CASTRO, TX											
60 –	**Finance, insurance, and real estate**	20	21	0.1	81	84	22,568	21,286	1,754	1,648	0.0
6000	Depository institutions	4	4	0.1	46	45	26,870	26,667	1,104	1,039	0.0
6100	Nondepository institutions	3	3	0.1	12	-	28,000	-	374	-	-
6300	Insurance carriers	4	2	0.1	7	-	13,714	-	123	-	-
6400	Insurance agents, brokers, and service	3	4	0.0	-	13	-	7,385	-	113	0.0
6500	Real estate	5	6	0.0	9	11	4,889	7,636	38	101	0.0
6510	Real estate operators and lessors	2	3	0.0	-	8	-	8,000	-	74	0.0
CHAMBERS, TX											
60 –	**Finance, insurance, and real estate**	26	28	0.1	136	129	15,765	17,085	2,376	2,343	0.0
6000	Depository institutions	4	4	0.1	66	76	20,303	19,737	1,588	1,656	0.1
6020	Commercial banks	4	4	0.2	66	76	20,303	19,737	1,588	1,656	0.1
6400	Insurance agents, brokers, and service	8	9	0.1	19	24	13,474	12,000	296	319	0.0
6500	Real estate	14	12	0.1	51	28	10,745	14,714	492	344	0.0
6510	Real estate operators and lessors	4	2	0.0	19	-	8,842	-	94	-	-
6530	Real estate agents and managers	7	6	0.1	14	11	11,714	13,455	192	88	0.0
CHEROKEE, TX											
60 –	**Finance, insurance, and real estate**	59	58	0.1	344	299	22,535	23,171	7,702	7,280	0.1
6000	Depository institutions	11	12	0.2	188	185	25,936	26,357	4,713	5,224	0.2
6020	Commercial banks	8	8	0.3	-	125	-	27,424	-	3,629	0.2
6140	Personal credit institutions	8	7	0.5	43	28	16,372	16,857	713	553	0.2
6400	Insurance agents, brokers, and service	12	12	0.1	35	32	17,257	11,000	528	350	0.0
6500	Real estate	17	17	0.1	62	39	14,258	13,128	954	525	0.0
6510	Real estate operators and lessors	7	7	0.1	18	14	10,000	9,429	186	157	0.0
6530	Real estate agents and managers	5	7	0.1	12	11	19,000	18,182	249	141	0.0
6700	Holding and other investment offices	5	5	0.2	6	6	42,667	8,667	333	81	0.0
CHILDRESS, TX											
60 –	**Finance, insurance, and real estate**	16	15	0.0	63	64	14,540	17,562	1,044	1,136	0.0

Source: *County Business Patterns, 1992/93*, CBP-92/93-1, U.S. Department of Commerce, Washington, D.C., April 1995. SIC categories for which data were suppressed or not available for both 1992 and 1993 are *not* displayed. The employment columns represent mid-March employment in the year. Pay per employee is calculated by dividing 1st Quarter payroll, annualized, by mid-March employment. The columns headed "% State" show the county's percentage of the state total for the SIC in 1993; for example, 0.9% for SIC 6030 means that the county had 0.9 percent of the state's total establishments (or payroll) in SIC 6030 in 1993. A dash (-) is used to indicate that data are not available or cannot be calculated; *nec* means not elsewhere classified.

Continued on next page.

SIC	Industry	No. Establishments			Employment		Pay / Employee		Annual Payroll ($ 000)		
		1992	1993	% State	1992	1993	1992	1993	1992	1993	% State
HAMILTON, TX											
60–	**Finance, insurance, and real estate**	14	11	0.0	75	62	17,227	17,677	1,342	1,245	0.0
6000	Depository institutions	5	3	0.1	55	46	19,127	19,130	1,051	956	0.0
6020	Commercial banks	5	3	0.1	55	46	19,127	19,130	1,051	956	0.0
6400	Insurance agents, brokers, and service	6	5	0.1	16	13	12,000	13,231	242	234	0.0
6500	Real estate	3	3	0.0	4	3	12,000	14,667	49	55	0.0
HANSFORD, TX											
60–	**Finance, insurance, and real estate**	18	18	0.0	124	132	16,452	16,909	2,220	2,300	0.0
6000	Depository institutions	4	4	0.1	70	71	22,400	24,225	1,658	1,736	0.1
6400	Insurance agents, brokers, and service	6	7	0.1	14	20	14,857	13,800	236	312	0.0
HARDEMAN, TX											
60–	**Finance, insurance, and real estate**	8	8	0.0	55	53	20,655	19,698	1,101	1,130	0.0
6000	Depository institutions	4	3	0.1	45	41	23,467	22,829	1,017	1,008	0.0
6020	Commercial banks	3	3	0.1		41	-	22,829	-	1,008	0.0
HARDIN, TX											
60–	**Finance, insurance, and real estate**	42	47	0.1	247	248	18,591	17,887	4,863	4,667	0.0
6000	Depository institutions	8	9	0.2	140	155	19,257	19,587	3,037	3,177	0.1
6100	Nondepository institutions	4	3	0.1	24	7	16,833	16,000	402	118	0.0
6400	Insurance agents, brokers, and service	15	19	0.2	47	45	17,362	14,133	678	644	0.0
6500	Real estate	10	12	0.1	28	29	12,571	12,828	389	415	0.0
6510	Real estate operators and lessors	4	6	0.1	5	-	10,400	-	53	-	-
6530	Real estate agents and managers	4	4	0.1	-	5	-	4,800	-	19	0.0
HARRIS, TX											
60–	**Finance, insurance, and real estate**	7,469	7,606	19.2	97,790	94,054	33,483	34,233	3,350,043	3,395,632	26.2
6000	Depository institutions	906	870	18.1	23,938	21,231	30,626	30,440	708,257	654,592	22.5
6020	Commercial banks	462	426	16.3	19,101	15,901	30,962	31,289	559,830	495,849	22.1
6030	Savings institutions	148	119	18.5	2,366	2,084	32,556	34,741	80,535	77,532	25.7
6060	Credit unions	139	158	15.4	1,175	1,452	20,984	20,769	25,860	31,642	14.2
6080	Foreign bank and branches and agencies	16	17	81.0	-	371	-	56,733	-	23,753	83.1
6090	Functions closely related to banking	136	149	28.8	696	-	26,443	-	18,501	-	-
6100	Nondepository institutions	441	466	15.5	5,818	6,087	30,789	31,094	200,344	223,449	19.0
6140	Personal credit institutions	147	111	7.6	1,475	1,494	26,967	21,175	39,854	32,880	9.7
6150	Business credit institutions	77	84	21.3	675	766	28,267	32,888	20,587	27,689	15.1
6160	Mortgage bankers and brokers	202	268	26.9	3,588	3,826	32,955	34,614	137,733	162,816	26.9
6200	Security and commodity brokers	418	434	21.4	5,991	6,054	89,403	93,647	583,412	625,360	41.1
6210	Security brokers and dealers	243	242	19.0	3,857	4,100	106,959	100,624	440,480	459,267	40.6
6220	Commodity contracts brokers, dealers	15	15	30.6	56	-	50,714	-	3,472	-	-
6280	Security and commodity services	152	174	24.7	2,018	1,835	56,442	76,660	132,318	147,607	40.0
6300	Insurance carriers	725	558	17.8	16,940	16,251	33,134	33,294	561,898	543,753	19.1
6310	Life insurance	214	193	19.8	8,641	8,601	29,460	29,452	257,185	246,559	25.6
6321	Accident and health insurance	14	15	12.0	158	328	28,911	34,085	5,805	11,908	10.1
6324	Hospital and medical service plans	10	10	13.3	407	414	31,106	32,280	13,135	13,868	8.0
6330	Fire, marine, and casualty insurance	308	267	18.7	5,410	5,246	39,206	38,685	205,756	205,301	14.8
6350	Surety insurance	15	12	32.4	237	-	53,181	-	9,474	-	-
6360	Title insurance	40	26	11.9	1,188	1,053	36,074	37,402	44,947	43,789	34.1
6370	Pension, health, and welfare funds	115	32	13.0	720	351	20,167	28,091	19,423	11,611	24.6
6390	Insurance carriers, n.e.c.	5	2	12.5	169	-	42,201	-	5,927	-	-
6400	Insurance agents, brokers, and service	1,403	1,534	17.3	10,098	9,790	32,294	33,236	335,659	337,577	25.9
6500	Real estate	2,942	3,087	20.5	27,883	26,062	21,220	21,073	606,621	592,319	27.5
6510	Real estate operators and lessors	1,087	1,220	18.4	7,250	6,699	14,945	16,891	115,287	126,505	22.1
6530	Real estate agents and managers	1,359	1,659	23.9	16,333	17,172	21,861	22,005	362,712	405,442	30.8
6540	Title abstract offices	33	40	10.4	209	488	24,000	27,500	5,750	14,877	18.5
6552	Subdividers and developers, n.e.c.	116	116	17.4	2,128	1,143	37,835	29,232	79,870	33,419	26.0
6553	Cemetery subdividers and developers	21	28	8.8	408	506	20,765	20,506	8,841	10,864	23.1
6700	Holding and other investment offices	613	634	23.6	6,263	5,550	44,713	44,044	290,229	262,708	34.7

*Source: County Business Patterns, 1992/93, CBP-92/93-1, U.S. Department of Commerce, Washington, D.C., April 1995. SIC categories for which data were suppressed or not available for both 1992 and 1993 are *not* displayed. The employment columns represent mid-March employment in the year. Pay per employee is calculated by dividing 1st Quarter payroll, annualized, by mid-March employment. The columns headed "% State" show the county's percentage of the state total for the SIC in 1993; for example, 0.9% for SIC 6030 means that the county had 0.9 percent of the state's total establishments (or payroll) in SIC 6030 in 1993. A dash (-) is used to indicate that data are not available or cannot be calculated; *nec* means not elsewhere classified.

Continued on next page.

SIC	Industry	No. Establishments			Employment		Pay / Employee		Annual Payroll ($ 000)		
		1992	1993	% State	1992	1993	1992	1993	1992	1993	% State
HARRIS, TX - [continued]											
6710	Holding offices	153	161	28.7	3,875	2,592	52,000	55,565	198,545	155,582	41.2
6720	Investment offices	26	20	27.4	150	142	27,467	48,085	4,171	6,800	41.2
6732	Educational, religious, etc. trusts	65	60	19.2	469	597	19,846	20,275	10,728	13,884	28.1
6733	Trusts, n.e.c.	91	95	17.6	428	644	28,514	30,068	17,915	22,801	29.2
6792	Oil royalty traders	66	87	25.7	251	286	59,602	51,273	16,967	16,774	36.8
6794	Patent owners and lessors	20	22	25.0	292	350	24,192	26,400	8,075	10,210	26.5
6798	Real estate investment trusts	26	13	33.3	173	168	35,306	21,833	6,968	4,321	40.2
6799	Investors, n.e.c.	131	173	24.0	438	754	41,580	44,939	19,436	31,698	26.6
HARRISON, TX											
60 –	**Finance, insurance, and real estate**	86	88	0.2	597	665	19,236	19,543	13,320	14,818	0.1
6000	Depository institutions	14	14	0.3	238	273	21,765	21,436	5,609	6,051	0.2
6020	Commercial banks	7	7	0.3	215	251	22,102	21,625	5,150	5,593	0.2
6060	Credit unions	5	4	0.4	-	15	-	20,000	-	310	0.1
6100	Nondepository institutions	13	13	0.4	34	30	14,471	19,200	534	588	0.0
6200	Security and commodity brokers	6	6	0.3	15	20	52,800	48,600	795	970	0.1
6210	Security brokers and dealers	4	3	0.2	-	12	-	62,667	-	709	0.1
6280	Security and commodity services	1	3	0.4	-	8	-	27,500	-	261	0.1
6300	Insurance carriers	10	9	0.3	74	80	16,054	15,850	1,187	1,404	0.0
6310	Life insurance	5	5	0.5	60	68	15,667	15,000	932	1,113	0.1
6400	Insurance agents, brokers, and service	16	17	0.2	172	183	14,791	16,175	3,038	3,643	0.3
6500	Real estate	17	18	0.1	52	61	19,231	17,115	1,326	1,678	0.1
6510	Real estate operators and lessors	3	5	0.1	4	9	10,000	8,889	42	82	0.0
6530	Real estate agents and managers	9	8	0.1	28	31	22,571	19,355	902	1,128	0.1
6700	Holding and other investment offices	10	11	0.4	12	18	24,000	18,000	831	484	0.1
HASKELL, TX											
60 –	**Finance, insurance, and real estate**	20	17	0.0	93	87	16,516	18,345	1,723	1,697	0.0
6000	Depository institutions	5	5	0.1	64	67	18,875	19,940	1,310	1,381	0.0
6500	Real estate	5	4	0.0	11	-	8,727	-	68	-	-
HAYS, TX											
60 –	**Finance, insurance, and real estate**	118	124	0.3	595	600	16,632	17,440	10,698	11,056	0.1
6000	Depository institutions	15	16	0.3	265	269	16,438	17,368	4,509	4,564	0.2
6020	Commercial banks	8	8	0.3	200	193	17,260	18,363	3,521	3,402	0.2
6100	Nondepository institutions	11	14	0.5	38	48	20,316	19,333	759	1,196	0.1
6200	Security and commodity brokers	3	4	0.2	5	9	55,200	54,667	295	483	0.0
6300	Insurance carriers	7	4	0.1	49	37	16,000	23,135	990	966	0.0
6400	Insurance agents, brokers, and service	16	21	0.2	48	72	15,667	17,500	756	1,249	0.1
6500	Real estate	60	54	0.4	176	137	14,500	12,642	2,929	1,979	0.1
6510	Real estate operators and lessors	21	25	0.4	50	-	8,000	-	559	-	-
6530	Real estate agents and managers	34	24	0.3	108	79	17,852	13,367	2,075	1,212	0.1
6700	Holding and other investment offices	6	11	0.4	14	28	28,857	18,714	460	619	0.1
HEMPHILL, TX											
60 –	**Finance, insurance, and real estate**	13	13	0.0	71	70	45,915	25,714	2,435	1,855	0.0
6000	Depository institutions	3	3	0.1	43	39	25,860	28,410	999	1,054	0.0
6400	Insurance agents, brokers, and service	3	3	0.0	6	9	10,667	10,222	94	106	0.0
HENDERSON, TX											
60 –	**Finance, insurance, and real estate**	95	91	0.2	608	590	16,664	16,576	10,830	11,866	0.1
6000	Depository institutions	19	16	0.3	267	250	21,034	19,840	5,809	6,479	0.2
6020	Commercial banks	16	13	0.5	255	223	21,176	20,753	5,480	5,845	0.3
6100	Nondepository institutions	3	5	0.2	-	42	-	25,714	-	1,367	0.1
6400	Insurance agents, brokers, and service	23	25	0.3	66	63	11,394	14,667	786	985	0.1
6500	Real estate	39	39	0.3	206	226	10,777	10,602	2,369	2,652	0.1
6510	Real estate operators and lessors	18	16	0.2	55	119	8,073	9,176	443	1,105	0.2

Source: County Business Patterns, 1992/93, CBP-92/93-1, U.S. Department of Commerce, Washington, D.C., April 1995. SIC categories for which data were suppressed or not available for both 1992 and 1993 are *not* displayed. The employment columns represent mid-March employment in the year. Pay per employee is calculated by dividing 1st Quarter payroll, annualized, by mid-March employment. The columns headed "% State" show the county's percentage of the state total for the SIC in 1993; for example, 0.9% for SIC 6030 means that the county had 0.9 percent of the state's total establishments (or payroll) in SIC 6030 in 1993. A dash (-) is used to indicate that data are not available or cannot be calculated; *nec* means not elsewhere classified.

Continued on next page.

SIC	Industry	No. Establishments			Employment		Pay / Employee		Annual Payroll ($ 000)		
		1992	1993	% State	1992	1993	1992	1993	1992	1993	% State
HENDERSON, TX - [continued]											
6530	Real estate agents and managers	12	15	0.2	32	47	13,125	12,085	447	631	0.0
6540	Title abstract offices	3	2	0.5	11	-	20,000	-	231	-	-
6700	Holding and other investment offices	6	2	0.1	24	-	12,667	-	387	-	-
HIDALGO, TX											
60 –	**Finance, insurance, and real estate**	616	661	1.7	4,341	3,857	19,620	18,544	88,598	77,504	0.6
6000	Depository institutions	80	86	1.8	1,899	1,544	20,701	19,964	39,864	32,108	1.1
6020	Commercial banks	48	45	1.7	1,712	1,245	21,343	20,970	37,119	27,125	1.2
6030	Savings institutions	7	8	1.2	41	90	23,610	20,756	878	1,842	0.6
6060	Credit unions	8	13	1.3	121	143	12,496	16,224	1,531	2,378	1.1
6090	Functions closely related to banking	17	20	3.9	25	66	11,680	8,000	336	763	-
6100	Nondepository institutions	81	76	2.5	401	391	18,414	15,519	7,833	6,644	0.6
6140	Personal credit institutions	70	68	4.7	288	325	16,861	13,698	5,159	4,608	1.4
6160	Mortgage bankers and brokers	6	4	0.4	52	58	22,385	24,966	1,394	1,865	0.3
6210	Security brokers and dealers	10	8	0.6	57	52	67,579	85,231	4,006	4,518	0.4
6300	Insurance carriers	37	30	1.0	234	191	24,291	24,963	5,772	5,724	0.2
6310	Life insurance	9	4	0.4	128	87	22,000	19,264	2,634	1,941	0.2
6370	Pension, health, and welfare funds	3	3	1.2	6	-	10,667	-	165	-	-
6400	Insurance agents, brokers, and service	124	130	1.5	568	520	23,479	18,515	13,144	10,100	0.8
6500	Real estate	250	291	1.9	930	921	11,062	12,026	11,457	12,000	0.6
6510	Real estate operators and lessors	117	149	2.2	527	518	10,452	11,197	5,811	6,168	1.1
6530	Real estate agents and managers	86	93	1.3	211	243	11,431	12,790	2,906	3,508	0.3
6552	Subdividers and developers, n.e.c.	17	38	5.7	74	95	11,892	11,705	1,097	1,151	0.9
6553	Cemetery subdividers and developers	7	8	2.5	42	-	15,429	-	689	-	-
6700	Holding and other investment offices	29	32	1.2	229	196	19,633	20,918	5,828	5,543	0.7
6710	Holding offices	6	9	1.6	-	55	-	26,400	-	2,476	0.7
6732	Educational, religious, etc. trusts	7	5	1.6	116	81	10,862	18,914	1,322	1,668	3.4
6733	Trusts, n.e.c.	8	11	2.0	23	25	16,870	16,320	465	459	0.6
HILL, TX											
60 –	**Finance, insurance, and real estate**	53	48	0.1	268	271	19,851	20,959	5,925	6,385	0.0
6000	Depository institutions	11	8	0.2	132	122	23,485	24,787	2,737	2,717	0.1
6020	Commercial banks	10	8	0.3	-	122	-	24,787	-	2,717	0.1
6100	Nondepository institutions	4	3	0.1	11	-	19,636	-	202	-	-
6300	Insurance carriers	8	7	0.2	30	33	16,000	15,273	517	544	0.0
6400	Insurance agents, brokers, and service	8	8	0.1	28	25	14,714	16,960	495	397	0.0
6500	Real estate	18	18	0.1	61	75	15,607	17,227	1,751	2,283	0.1
6510	Real estate operators and lessors	5	8	0.1	13	32	8,923	7,750	230	251	0.0
6530	Real estate agents and managers	5	5	0.1	5	7	10,400	2,857	60	27	0.0
HOCKLEY, TX											
60 –	**Finance, insurance, and real estate**	37	38	0.1	183	203	19,934	20,473	3,881	4,415	0.0
6000	Depository institutions	8	8	0.2	122	115	21,443	21,670	2,686	2,700	0.1
6100	Nondepository institutions	4	4	0.1	-	13	-	26,154	-	377	0.0
6400	Insurance agents, brokers, and service	12	11	0.1	26	36	13,538	17,333	416	513	0.0
6500	Real estate	10	10	0.1	18	20	12,000	14,000	301	367	0.0
6510	Real estate operators and lessors	4	6	0.1	9	14	8,889	8,857	74	183	0.0
6530	Real estate agents and managers	4	2	0.0	4	-	9,000	-	43	-	-
HOOD, TX											
60 –	**Finance, insurance, and real estate**	59	62	0.2	321	409	16,274	18,034	5,695	7,823	0.1
6000	Depository institutions	9	8	0.2	145	159	21,131	20,629	3,345	3,528	0.1
6020	Commercial banks	9	8	0.3	145	159	21,131	20,629	3,345	3,528	0.2
6200	Security and commodity brokers	2	3	0.1	-	6	-	44,000	-	239	0.0
6210	Security brokers and dealers	2	3	0.2	-	6	-	44,000	-	239	0.0
6300	Insurance carriers	5	3	0.1	23	-	12,870	-	348	-	-
6400	Insurance agents, brokers, and service	14	16	0.2	98	48	10,776	21,333	1,010	1,108	0.1

Source: County Business Patterns, 1992/93, CBP-92/93-1, U.S. Department of Commerce, Washington, D.C., April 1995. SIC categories for which data were suppressed or not available for both 1992 and 1993 are not displayed. The employment columns represent mid-March employment in the year. Pay per employee is calculated by dividing 1st Quarter payroll, annualized, by mid-March employment. The columns headed "% State" show the county's percentage of the state total for the SIC in 1993; for example, 0.9% for SIC 6030 means that the county had 0.9 percent of the state's total establishments (or payroll) in SIC 6030 in 1993. A dash (-) is used to indicate that data are not available or cannot be calculated; nec means not elsewhere classified.

Continued on next page.

SIC	Industry	No. Establishments			Employment		Pay / Employee		Annual Payroll ($ 000)		
		1992	1993	% State	1992	1993	1992	1993	1992	1993	% State
HOOD, TX - [continued]											
6500	Real estate	26	28	0.2	47	124	12,681	12,484	794	1,785	0.1
6510	Real estate operators and lessors	11	12	0.2	22	-	13,091	-	375	-	-
6530	Real estate agents and managers	9	15	0.2	13	92	9,231	12,174	222	1,263	0.1
HOPKINS, TX											
60 –	**Finance, insurance, and real estate**	45	49	0.1	354	415	21,819	19,345	7,730	8,610	0.1
6000	Depository institutions	9	9	0.2	236	264	23,169	20,727	5,600	5,947	0.2
6100	Nondepository institutions	8	7	0.2	46	39	25,043	20,718	998	800	0.1
6140	Personal credit institutions	3	4	0.3	9	-	16,444	-	145	-	-
6150	Business credit institutions	3	-	-	23	-	31,304	-	597	-	-
6400	Insurance agents, brokers, and service	11	12	0.1	37	40	15,027	14,300	544	572	0.0
6500	Real estate	14	17	0.1	30	67	10,533	12,119	346	877	0.0
6510	Real estate operators and lessors	5	6	0.1	8	-	5,500	-	41	-	-
6530	Real estate agents and managers	6	7	0.1	9	18	7,111	8,444	74	178	0.0
HOUSTON, TX											
60 –	**Finance, insurance, and real estate**	34	35	0.1	213	182	19,737	21,143	4,307	4,451	0.0
6000	Depository institutions	9	9	0.2	118	113	21,424	22,903	2,588	2,735	0.1
6400	Insurance agents, brokers, and service	9	7	0.1	26	19	14,462	14,947	337	294	0.0
6500	Real estate	9	14	0.1	31	33	10,839	11,394	363	496	0.0
6510	Real estate operators and lessors	3	6	0.1	7	7	9,143	9,714	70	147	0.0
6530	Real estate agents and managers	3	4	0.1	11	13	8,727	10,462	110	161	0.0
HOWARD, TX											
60 –	**Finance, insurance, and real estate**	68	71	0.2	378	393	21,143	20,478	8,117	8,438	0.1
6000	Depository institutions	12	14	0.3	203	209	23,389	21,742	4,766	5,121	0.2
6020	Commercial banks	5	5	0.2	131	128	24,397	22,719	3,264	3,369	0.2
6100	Nondepository institutions	7	7	0.2	19	17	17,053	19,294	324	231	0.0
6140	Personal credit institutions	7	7	0.5	19	17	17,053	19,294	324	231	0.1
6300	Insurance carriers	4	2	0.1	16	-	21,250	-	353	-	-
6400	Insurance agents, brokers, and service	19	23	0.3	63	73	12,889	13,096	867	979	0.1
6500	Real estate	21	22	0.1	50	57	14,320	14,105	718	840	0.0
6510	Real estate operators and lessors	11	13	0.2	22	30	13,091	12,533	313	425	0.1
6530	Real estate agents and managers	6	6	0.1	13	13	12,000	8,923	155	125	0.0
HUDSPETH, TX											
60 –	**Finance, insurance, and real estate**	2	2	0.0	-	-	-	-	-	-	-
HUNT, TX											
60 –	**Finance, insurance, and real estate**	109	109	0.3	617	595	17,588	16,934	11,395	10,506	0.1
6000	Depository institutions	19	14	0.3	294	248	18,871	20,887	5,251	5,000	0.2
6100	Nondepository institutions	7	5	0.2	32	-	25,250	-	835	-	-
6140	Personal credit institutions	7	5	0.3	32	-	25,250	-	835	-	-
6200	Security and commodity brokers	5	5	0.2	-	12	-	27,667	-	424	0.0
6300	Insurance carriers	10	7	0.2	45	32	21,156	18,750	1,089	682	0.0
6310	Life insurance	3	1	0.1	26	-	21,692	-	617	-	-
6400	Insurance agents, brokers, and service	24	31	0.4	66	107	12,182	12,598	980	1,501	0.1
6500	Real estate	41	44	0.3	157	148	12,917	10,730	2,265	1,871	0.1
6510	Real estate operators and lessors	15	18	0.3	77	58	13,299	8,000	1,089	573	0.1
6530	Real estate agents and managers	17	16	0.2	35	38	10,286	9,579	356	381	0.0
6540	Title abstract offices	3	3	0.8	21	29	20,190	18,897	572	670	0.8
HUTCHINSON, TX											
60 –	**Finance, insurance, and real estate**	44	43	0.1	208	193	19,173	19,855	4,255	4,000	0.0
6000	Depository institutions	8	11	0.2	123	130	20,065	20,092	2,529	2,737	0.1
6020	Commercial banks	5	5	0.2	98	94	19,551	18,894	1,908	1,848	0.1
6060	Credit unions	3	6	0.6	25	36	22,080	23,222	621	889	0.4
6100	Nondepository institutions	4	2	0.1	12	-	21,000	-	262	-	-

Source: County Business Patterns, 1992/93, CBP-92/93-1, U.S. Department of Commerce, Washington, D.C., April 1995. SIC categories for which data were suppressed or not available for both 1992 and 1993 are *not* displayed. The employment columns represent mid-March employment in the year. Pay per employee is calculated by dividing 1st Quarter payroll, annualized, by mid-March employment. The columns headed "% State" show the county's percentage of the state total for the SIC in 1993; for example, 0.9% for SIC 6030 means that the county had 0.9 percent of the state's total establishments (or payroll) in SIC 6030 in 1993. A dash (-) is used to indicate that data are not available or cannot be calculated; *nec* means not elsewhere classified.

Continued on next page.

SIC	Industry	No. Establishments			Employment		Pay / Employee		Annual Payroll ($ 000)		
		1992	1993	% State	1992	1993	1992	1993	1992	1993	% State
HUTCHINSON, TX - [continued]											
6140	Personal credit institutions	4	1	0.1	12	-	21,000	-	262	-	-
6300	Insurance carriers	5	2	0.1	12	-	23,333	-	304	-	-
6330	Fire, marine, and casualty insurance	3	1	0.1	5	-	48,800	-	240	-	-
6400	Insurance agents, brokers, and service	10	13	0.1	30	32	13,733	14,375	386	548	0.0
6500	Real estate	14	11	0.1	27	18	14,074	13,333	447	244	0.0
6510	Real estate operators and lessors	4	4	0.1	3	6	21,333	14,000	72	78	0.0
6530	Real estate agents and managers	6	6	0.1	12	-	10,667	-	136	-	-
IRION, TX											
60 –	**Finance, insurance, and real estate**	2	2	0.0	-	-	-	-	-	-	-
JACK, TX											
60 –	**Finance, insurance, and real estate**	12	12	0.0	71	69	20,225	20,696	1,454	1,464	0.0
6000	Depository institutions	4	3	0.1	57	45	22,737	25,689	1,295	1,180	0.0
6400	Insurance agents, brokers, and service	6	6	0.1	-	12	-	9,333	-	105	0.0
JACKSON, TX											
60 –	**Finance, insurance, and real estate**	29	27	0.1	166	101	18,120	16,158	3,073	1,715	0.0
6000	Depository institutions	8	7	0.1	123	60	19,772	17,800	2,478	1,066	0.0
6400	Insurance agents, brokers, and service	6	7	0.1	12	14	9,000	9,714	115	159	0.0
6500	Real estate	10	5	0.0	13	11	7,077	8,000	118	89	0.0
6510	Real estate operators and lessors	6	3	0.0	9	-	6,667	-	73	-	-
JASPER, TX											
60 –	**Finance, insurance, and real estate**	44	46	0.1	363	351	18,303	17,652	7,379	6,923	0.1
6000	Depository institutions	9	10	0.2	252	261	19,746	19,356	5,245	5,699	0.2
6020	Commercial banks	9	9	0.3	252	-	19,746	-	5,245	-	-
6100	Nondepository institutions	6	5	0.2	22	16	28,909	19,750	1,021	365	0.0
6140	Personal credit institutions	4	5	0.3	-	16	-	19,750	-	365	0.1
6400	Insurance agents, brokers, and service	11	14	0.2	35	-	10,057	-	388	-	-
6500	Real estate	13	15	0.1	39	27	12,103	11,259	479	326	0.0
6510	Real estate operators and lessors	5	9	0.1	-	15	-	10,933	-	155	0.0
6530	Real estate agents and managers	6	4	0.1	13	-	10,769	-	154	-	-
JEFF DAVIS, TX											
60 –	**Finance, insurance, and real estate**	4	5	0.0	12	18	22,000	20,222	305	365	0.0
JEFFERSON, TX											
60 –	**Finance, insurance, and real estate**	502	500	1.3	3,729	3,568	22,134	22,554	86,800	86,628	0.7
6000	Depository institutions	69	77	1.6	1,315	1,270	21,192	20,447	26,703	28,882	1.0
6020	Commercial banks	29	29	1.1	960	752	20,921	22,250	19,492	19,296	0.9
6030	Savings institutions	14	12	1.9	93	76	26,581	20,368	1,808	1,532	0.5
6060	Credit unions	23	32	3.1	252	381	20,683	19,874	5,326	7,897	3.5
6090	Functions closely related to banking	3	4	0.8	10	61	10,000	1,902	77	157	
6100	Nondepository institutions	39	29	1.0	-	235	-	17,447	-	5,056	0.4
6140	Personal credit institutions	34	19	1.3	273	194	19,590	14,742	5,343	2,901	0.9
6160	Mortgage bankers and brokers	3	6	0.6	17	-	37,882	-	911	-	-
6200	Security and commodity brokers	17	22	1.1	119	134	61,412	63,313	7,716	9,188	0.6
6210	Security brokers and dealers	14	15	1.2	-	122	-	66,984	-	8,560	0.8
6280	Security and commodity services	3	7	1.0	-	12	-	26,000	-	628	0.2
6300	Insurance carriers	58	53	1.7	541	443	25,671	29,679	13,858	13,100	0.5
6310	Life insurance	23	23	2.4	390	324	23,272	27,049	8,771	8,049	0.8
6330	Fire, marine, and casualty insurance	18	17	1.2	66	59	45,030	49,492	3,199	3,116	0.2
6360	Title insurance	4	1	0.5	50	-	19,920	-	875	-	-
6370	Pension, health, and welfare funds	10	9	3.6	22	23	14,909	15,652	475	894	1.9
6400	Insurance agents, brokers, and service	126	132	1.5	606	620	20,772	20,368	13,418	12,763	1.0
6500	Real estate	157	155	1.0	714	723	15,076	14,949	11,844	11,689	0.5
6510	Real estate operators and lessors	77	84	1.3	309	305	12,350	11,174	4,134	3,580	0.6

Source: County Business Patterns, 1992/93, CBP-92/93-1, U.S. Department of Commerce, Washington, D.C., April 1995. SIC categories for which data were suppressed or not available for both 1992 and 1993 are not displayed. The employment columns represent mid-March employment in the year. Pay per employee is calculated by dividing 1st Quarter payroll, annualized, by mid-March employment. The columns headed "% State" show the county's percentage of the state total for the SIC in 1993; for example, 0.9% for SIC 6030 means that the county had 0.9 percent of the state's total establishments (or payroll) in SIC 6030 in 1993. A dash (-) is used to indicate that data are not available or cannot be calculated; nec means not elsewhere classified.

Continued on next page.

SIC	Industry	No. Establishments			Employment		Pay / Employee		Annual Payroll ($ 000)		
		1992	1993	% State	1992	1993	1992	1993	1992	1993	% State
JEFFERSON, TX - [continued]											
6530	Real estate agents and managers	57	54	0.8	229	245	16,594	17,845	3,886	4,792	0.4
6540	Title abstract offices	3	4	1.0	-	65	-	24,554	-	1,767	2.2
6553	Cemetery subdividers and developers	10	9	2.8	113	-	14,230	-	1,820	-	-
6700	Holding and other investment offices	35	31	1.2	129	-	28,000	-	6,425	-	-
6710	Holding offices	6	5	0.9	76	53	38,632	45,660	5,021	3,045	0.8
6732	Educational, religious, etc. trusts	4	4	1.3	12	-	15,667	-	187	-	-
6733	Trusts, n.e.c.	8	6	1.1	21	13	13,333	18,462	292	259	0.3
6792	Oil royalty traders	7	7	2.1	12	-	10,000	-	184	-	-
6799	Investors, n.e.c.	6	8	1.1	7	11	8,000	7,636	94	117	0.1
JIM HOGG, TX											
60 –	**Finance, insurance, and real estate**	10	9	0.0	85	54	19,765	17,259	1,855	1,018	0.0
6000	Depository institutions	3	2	0.0	68	-	20,941	-	1,582	-	-
6020	Commercial banks	3	2	0.1	68	-	20,941	-	1,582	-	-
JIM WELLS, TX											
60 –	**Finance, insurance, and real estate**	59	56	0.1	442	431	18,271	17,485	8,575	9,082	0.1
6000	Depository institutions	9	9	0.2	192	184	22,812	19,152	4,454	4,699	0.2
6020	Commercial banks	7	6	0.2	-	172	-	19,698	-	4,617	0.2
6100	Nondepository institutions	10	9	0.3	31	35	17,806	18,057	590	696	0.1
6300	Insurance carriers	5	3	0.1	40	-	16,800	-	760	-	-
6400	Insurance agents, brokers, and service	13	17	0.2	63	64	19,937	20,938	1,429	1,451	0.1
6500	Real estate	18	13	0.1	105	95	9,257	8,000	1,004	894	0.0
6510	Real estate operators and lessors	6	5	0.1	25	52	9,120	6,462	223	412	0.1
6530	Real estate agents and managers	6	5	0.1	26	-	12,000	-	280	-	-
JOHNSON, TX											
60 –	**Finance, insurance, and real estate**	124	125	0.3	750	757	18,891	18,964	15,276	15,806	0.1
6000	Depository institutions	26	25	0.5	495	480	20,000	20,983	10,732	10,900	0.4
6020	Commercial banks	21	21	0.8	460	448	20,322	21,438	10,014	10,313	0.5
6100	Nondepository institutions	7	6	0.2	16	16	20,750	23,000	369	397	0.0
6140	Personal credit institutions	5	3	0.2	-	11	-	19,273	-	240	0.1
6200	Security and commodity brokers	4	5	0.2	-	7	-	24,571	-	178	0.0
6210	Security brokers and dealers	3	5	0.4	-	7	-	24,571	-	178	0.0
6300	Insurance carriers	11	9	0.3	67	52	23,403	25,692	1,499	1,515	0.1
6360	Title insurance	4	3	1.4	24	-	28,167	-	641	-	-
6400	Insurance agents, brokers, and service	32	33	0.4	85	86	15,388	14,140	1,323	1,335	0.1
6500	Real estate	38	42	0.3	80	110	9,850	10,364	909	1,425	0.1
6510	Real estate operators and lessors	15	22	0.3	49	79	7,918	9,013	421	805	0.1
6530	Real estate agents and managers	11	12	0.2	14	6	12,286	9,333	153	136	0.0
6552	Subdividers and developers, n.e.c.	4	5	0.7	3	7	28,000	14,286	88	132	0.1
6700	Holding and other investment offices	6	5	0.2	-	6	-	8,667	-	56	0.0
JONES, TX											
60 –	**Finance, insurance, and real estate**	30	28	0.1	131	117	19,908	19,590	2,856	2,435	0.0
6000	Depository institutions	5	4	0.1	67	65	21,731	23,200	1,631	1,678	0.1
6400	Insurance agents, brokers, and service	10	11	0.1	25	25	11,680	12,960	298	295	0.0
6500	Real estate	9	8	0.1	7	11	14,857	9,091	100	94	0.0
6510	Real estate operators and lessors	4	4	0.1	4	4	7,000	7,000	20	13	0.0
KARNES, TX											
60 –	**Finance, insurance, and real estate**	15	16	0.0	116	111	20,759	20,468	2,435	2,366	0.0
6000	Depository institutions	5	5	0.1	79	77	22,835	23,169	1,867	1,850	0.1
6020	Commercial banks	5	5	0.2	79	77	22,835	23,169	1,867	1,850	0.1
6400	Insurance agents, brokers, and service	4	5	0.1	8	10	15,500	10,400	101	118	0.0

Source: County Business Patterns, 1992/93, CBP-92/93-1, U.S. Department of Commerce, Washington, D.C., April 1995. SIC categories for which data were suppressed or not available for both 1992 and 1993 are not displayed. The employment columns represent mid-March employment in the year. Pay per employee is calculated by dividing 1st Quarter payroll, annualized, by mid-March employment. The columns headed "% State" show the county's percentage of the state total for the SIC in 1993; for example, 0.9% for SIC 6030 means that the county had 0.9 percent of the state's total establishments (or payroll) in SIC 6030 in 1993. A dash (-) is used to indicate that data are not available or cannot be calculated; nec means not elsewhere classified.

SIC	Industry	No. Establishments			Employment		Pay / Employee		Annual Payroll ($ 000)		
		1992	1993	% State	1992	1993	1992	1993	1992	1993	% State
KAUFMAN, TX											
60 –	**Finance, insurance, and real estate**	90	85	0.2	487	515	23,228	20,054	11,830	11,334	0.1
6000	Depository institutions	15	16	0.3	262	304	23,969	20,671	6,656	6,751	0.2
6020	Commercial banks	13	13	0.5	-	291	-	20,729	-	6,488	0.3
6100	Nondepository institutions	9	6	0.2	20	10	15,200	16,000	292	145	0.0
6140	Personal credit institutions	7	5	0.3	19	-	15,789	-	283	-	-
6300	Insurance carriers	5	3	0.1	35	-	27,200	-	1,024	-	-
6400	Insurance agents, brokers, and service	19	23	0.3	45	62	15,467	14,258	861	1,126	0.1
6500	Real estate	37	31	0.2	88	88	16,773	16,591	1,661	1,794	0.1
6510	Real estate operators and lessors	13	17	0.3	28	-	19,571	-	783	-	-
6530	Real estate agents and managers	13	7	0.1	24	11	12,500	15,273	299	189	0.0
6540	Title abstract offices	5	5	1.3	18	20	19,111	18,400	351	505	0.6
6552	Subdividers and developers, n.e.c.	4	2	0.3	12	-	17,333	-	154	-	-
KENDALL, TX											
60 –	**Finance, insurance, and real estate**	44	49	0.1	228	177	21,491	20,000	5,207	3,726	0.0
6000	Depository institutions	7	5	0.1	117	59	24,068	25,424	2,877	1,552	0.1
6200	Security and commodity brokers	2	4	0.2	-	6	-	14,000	-	97	0.0
6210	Security brokers and dealers	2	4	0.3	-	6	-	14,000	-	97	0.0
6300	Insurance carriers	5	2	0.1	13	-	11,385	-	177	-	-
6400	Insurance agents, brokers, and service	8	12	0.1	21	25	15,238	20,320	379	606	0.0
6500	Real estate	17	21	0.1	50	55	15,360	15,927	880	963	0.0
6510	Real estate operators and lessors	6	7	0.1	14	18	20,571	18,667	340	332	0.1
6530	Real estate agents and managers	4	9	0.1	13	-	14,462	-	222	-	-
6540	Title abstract offices	3	4	1.0	11	14	13,455	16,857	181	275	0.3
KENT, TX											
60 –	**Finance, insurance, and real estate**	1	1	0.0	-	-	-	-	-	-	-
KERR, TX											
60 –	**Finance, insurance, and real estate**	102	106	0.3	521	485	22,626	23,423	11,813	11,661	0.1
6000	Depository institutions	10	10	0.2	228	199	22,456	20,322	4,992	4,002	0.1
6020	Commercial banks	6	6	0.2	207	185	23,072	20,562	4,600	3,755	0.2
6100	Nondepository institutions	6	3	0.1	12	-	18,000	-	196	-	-
6200	Security and commodity brokers	8	8	0.4	30	30	100,267	111,467	2,955	3,083	0.2
6300	Insurance carriers	6	4	0.1	22	-	20,364	-	456	-	-
6400	Insurance agents, brokers, and service	12	15	0.2	48	47	14,917	13,106	766	677	0.1
6500	Real estate	49	53	0.4	150	147	11,493	14,585	1,809	2,659	0.1
6510	Real estate operators and lessors	19	20	0.3	55	61	14,545	14,164	844	1,085	0.2
6530	Real estate agents and managers	21	25	0.4	72	49	9,056	11,755	675	816	0.1
6540	Title abstract offices	1	3	0.8	-	29	-	19,310	-	597	0.7
6552	Subdividers and developers, n.e.c.	4	5	0.7	4	8	10,000	18,000	38	161	0.1
6700	Holding and other investment offices	11	13	0.5	31	42	17,935	16,476	639	697	0.1
KIMBLE, TX											
60 –	**Finance, insurance, and real estate**	14	12	0.0	71	49	13,296	16,163	1,160	964	0.0
6000	Depository institutions	3	2	0.0	37	-	18,486	-	827	-	-
6500	Real estate	7	6	0.0	32	10	7,625	6,800	291	96	0.0
6530	Real estate agents and managers	2	3	0.0	-	2	-	10,000	-	29	0.0
KINNEY, TX											
60 –	**Finance, insurance, and real estate**	5	4	0.0	16	14	17,250	16,857	233	212	0.0
KLEBERG, TX											
60 –	**Finance, insurance, and real estate**	57	53	0.1	259	273	16,757	16,718	4,589	4,824	0.0
6000	Depository institutions	7	6	0.1	157	163	17,350	16,908	2,839	2,866	0.1
6020	Commercial banks	3	3	0.1	135	146	17,363	16,822	2,465	2,562	0.1
6060	Credit unions	3	3	0.3	-	17	-	17,647	-	304	0.1
6100	Nondepository institutions	5	5	0.2	17	-	23,059	-	393	-	-

Source: County Business Patterns, 1992/93, CBP-92/93-1, U.S. Department of Commerce, Washington, D.C., April 1995. SIC categories for which data were suppressed or not available for both 1992 and 1993 are not displayed. The employment columns represent mid-March employment in the year. Pay per employee is calculated by dividing 1st Quarter payroll, annualized, by mid-March employment. The columns headed "% State" show the county's percentage of the state total for the SIC in 1993; for example, 0.9% for SIC 6030 means that the county had 0.9 percent of the state's total establishments (or payroll) in SIC 6030 in 1993. A dash (-) is used to indicate that data are not available or cannot be calculated; nec means not elsewhere classified.

Continued on next page.

SIC	Industry	No. Establishments			Employment		Pay / Employee		Annual Payroll ($ 000)		
		1992	1993	% State	1992	1993	1992	1993	1992	1993	% State
KLEBERG, TX - [continued]											
6140	Personal credit institutions	5	5	0.3	17	-	23,059	-	393	-	-
6200	Security and commodity brokers	4	3	0.1	6	5	22,000	17,600	115	54	0.0
6300	Insurance carriers	3	1	0.0	6	-	24,000	-	169	-	-
6400	Insurance agents, brokers, and service	14	14	0.2	36	38	14,444	14,737	511	675	0.1
6500	Real estate	18	18	0.1	31	36	9,677	10,889	341	434	0.0
6510	Real estate operators and lessors	11	10	0.2	15	19	7,467	9,263	155	209	0.0
6530	Real estate agents and managers	3	6	0.1	4	-	11,000	-	50	-	-
6700	Holding and other investment offices	6	6	0.2	6	10	21,333	28,800	221	281	0.0
KNOX, TX											
60 –	**Finance, insurance, and real estate**	7	8	0.0	45	48	17,422	17,667	851	1,004	0.0
6400	Insurance agents, brokers, and service	4	4	0.0	-	10	-	5,600	-	65	0.0
LAMAR, TX											
60 –	**Finance, insurance, and real estate**	91	85	0.2	536	568	17,970	18,056	11,006	10,787	0.1
6000	Depository institutions	15	15	0.3	255	256	21,051	20,281	5,856	5,508	0.2
6060	Credit unions	2	3	0.3	-	4	-	10,000	-	40	0.0
6100	Nondepository institutions	8	9	0.3	25	35	19,040	15,086	499	540	0.0
6300	Insurance carriers	9	5	0.2	51	42	21,333	23,048	1,268	1,051	0.0
6400	Insurance agents, brokers, and service	21	19	0.2	68	143	13,118	13,874	1,526	2,066	0.2
6500	Real estate	32	32	0.2	107	75	10,206	11,253	1,082	922	0.0
6510	Real estate operators and lessors	19	21	0.3	67	43	9,373	10,233	634	472	0.1
6530	Real estate agents and managers	8	7	0.1	23	16	9,739	9,500	192	183	0.0
LAMB, TX											
60 –	**Finance, insurance, and real estate**	28	25	0.1	168	149	18,048	18,604	3,196	2,731	0.0
6000	Depository institutions	10	7	0.1	120	85	20,100	23,247	2,459	2,051	0.1
6400	Insurance agents, brokers, and service	5	6	0.1	10	-	11,200	-	120	-	-
6500	Real estate	7	9	0.1	10	23	6,400	10,087	72	157	0.0
6553	Cemetery subdividers and developers	3	3	0.9	6	5	4,667	5,600	34	29	0.1
LAMPASAS, TX											
60 –	**Finance, insurance, and real estate**	22	21	0.1	105	113	16,838	17,699	1,933	2,119	0.0
6000	Depository institutions	5	5	0.1	68	67	19,647	21,134	1,474	1,493	0.1
6400	Insurance agents, brokers, and service	7	6	0.1	16	16	12,250	12,250	198	212	0.0
6510	Real estate operators and lessors	4	4	0.1	10	-	2,400	-	33	-	-
LA SALLE, TX											
60 –	**Finance, insurance, and real estate**	6	7	0.0	32	38	15,375	13,789	516	531	0.0
6500	Real estate	2	3	0.0	-	10	-	4,400	-	39	0.0
LAVACA, TX											
60 –	**Finance, insurance, and real estate**	43	44	0.1	285	301	16,561	19,003	5,617	5,715	0.0
6000	Depository institutions	11	10	0.2	151	167	17,563	16,934	3,482	3,252	0.1
6020	Commercial banks	7	6	0.2	135	151	17,985	17,060	3,231	2,986	0.1
6100	Nondepository institutions	3	3	0.1	6	-	14,000	-	78	-	-
6400	Insurance agents, brokers, and service	9	14	0.2	-	31	-	10,581	-	365	0.0
6500	Real estate	8	8	0.1	15	15	7,200	7,733	123	129	0.0
6510	Real estate operators and lessors	3	3	0.0	5	6	8,800	8,667	50	55	0.0
LEE, TX											
60 –	**Finance, insurance, and real estate**	29	27	0.1	184	202	17,696	18,455	3,743	4,362	0.0
6000	Depository institutions	6	6	0.1	88	95	20,091	18,442	1,868	1,871	0.1
6100	Nondepository institutions	4	4	0.1	12	-	17,333	-	318	-	-

Source: County Business Patterns, 1992/93, CBP-92/93-1, U.S. Department of Commerce, Washington, D.C., April 1995. SIC categories for which data were suppressed or not available for both 1992 and 1993 are *not* displayed. The employment columns represent mid-March employment in the year. Pay per employee is calculated by dividing 1st Quarter payroll, annualized, by mid-March employment. The columns headed "% State" show the county's percentage of the state total for the SIC in 1993; for example, 0.9% for SIC 6030 means that the county had 0.9 percent of the state's total establishments (or payroll) in SIC 6030 in 1993. A dash (-) is used to indicate that data are not available or cannot be calculated; *nec* means not elsewhere classified.

Continued on next page.

SIC	Industry	No. Establishments			Employment		Pay / Employee		Annual Payroll ($ 000)		
		1992	1993	% State	1992	1993	1992	1993	1992	1993	% State
LEE, TX - [continued]											
6400	Insurance agents, brokers, and service	5	6	0.1	-	48	-	22,917	-	1,217	0.1
6500	Real estate	7	6	0.0	9	10	16,889	10,400	159	116	0.0
6510	Real estate operators and lessors	3	3	0.0	4	-	9,000	-	24	-	-
LEON, TX											
60 –	**Finance, insurance, and real estate**	17	16	0.0	86	85	15,256	18,024	1,484	1,699	0.0
6000	Depository institutions	5	5	0.1	55	56	19,345	18,214	1,149	1,164	0.0
6400	Insurance agents, brokers, and service	5	7	0.1	13	12	6,154	30,000	121	332	0.0
LIBERTY, TX											
60 –	**Finance, insurance, and real estate**	79	70	0.2	404	435	17,802	17,306	10,504	7,859	0.1
6000	Depository institutions	12	11	0.2	237	239	19,190	18,979	4,786	4,618	0.2
6300	Insurance carriers	4	4	0.1	3	4	18,667	19,000	559	116	0.0
6400	Insurance agents, brokers, and service	23	24	0.3	77	98	16,364	13,714	1,324	1,353	0.1
6500	Real estate	29	23	0.2	52	63	9,615	15,429	794	1,031	0.0
6510	Real estate operators and lessors	12	12	0.2	15	23	12,267	8,696	147	230	0.0
6530	Real estate agents and managers	4	8	0.1	3	34	25,333	21,882	412	774	0.1
6553	Cemetery subdividers and developers	3	3	0.9	6	6	4,000	4,667	24	27	0.1
6700	Holding and other investment offices	5	2	0.1	14	-	13,143	-	2,377	-	-
LIMESTONE, TX											
60 –	**Finance, insurance, and real estate**	32	29	0.1	177	239	18,011	17,322	3,393	4,376	0.0
6000	Depository institutions	9	9	0.2	106	106	20,264	20,264	2,311	2,312	0.1
6400	Insurance agents, brokers, and service	7	8	0.1	14	15	15,714	14,667	224	229	0.0
6500	Real estate	12	8	0.1	38	-	11,789	-	465	-	-
6530	Real estate agents and managers	5	3	0.0	8	-	4,000	-	21	-	-
LIPSCOMB, TX											
60 –	**Finance, insurance, and real estate**	9	9	0.0	56	57	21,571	19,860	1,324	1,239	0.0
6000	Depository institutions	3	3	0.1	37	38	22,378	20,000	915	859	0.0
6020	Commercial banks	3	3	0.1	37	38	22,378	20,000	915	859	0.0
LIVE OAK, TX											
60 –	**Finance, insurance, and real estate**	16	14	0.0	98	102	18,122	17,059	1,903	1,980	0.0
6000	Depository institutions	3	3	0.1	65	74	21,169	18,703	1,484	1,582	0.1
6020	Commercial banks	3	3	0.1	65	74	21,169	18,703	1,484	1,582	0.1
6400	Insurance agents, brokers, and service	5	4	0.0	19	-	15,158	-	309	-	-
6500	Real estate	7	6	0.0	-	10	-	10,400	-	61	0.0
6530	Real estate agents and managers	3	2	0.0	4	-	3,000	-	9	-	-
LLANO, TX											
60 –	**Finance, insurance, and real estate**	32	34	0.1	157	184	19,669	19,217	3,505	4,685	0.0
6000	Depository institutions	10	10	0.2	88	113	21,591	18,867	1,994	2,783	0.1
6500	Real estate	17	16	0.1	52	47	17,231	21,277	1,167	1,428	0.1
6510	Real estate operators and lessors	4	5	0.1	7	-	6,857	-	54	-	-
6530	Real estate agents and managers	8	9	0.1	15	14	12,000	24,857	202	423	0.0
LUBBOCK, TX											
60 –	**Finance, insurance, and real estate**	589	614	1.5	4,066	4,019	23,642	23,750	96,621	106,138	0.8
6000	Depository institutions	47	50	1.0	1,441	1,330	23,478	26,556	33,396	36,048	1.2
6020	Commercial banks	26	29	1.1	1,258	1,189	24,114	27,670	31,343	33,483	1.5
6060	Credit unions	10	13	1.3	51	76	18,902	18,842	976	1,507	0.7
6100	Nondepository institutions	33	34	1.1	231	-	23,446	-	5,512	-	-
6140	Personal credit institutions	23	21	1.4	195	212	23,036	17,925	4,463	3,817	1.1
6150	Business credit institutions	4	3	0.8	12	-	33,333	-	459	-	-
6160	Mortgage bankers and brokers	6	8	0.8	24	54	21,833	22,741	590	1,863	0.3
6200	Security and commodity brokers	34	41	2.0	164	195	40,049	37,744	7,038	7,967	0.5
6210	Security brokers and dealers	22	26	2.0	131	169	45,374	40,994	6,387	7,429	0.7

Source: County Business Patterns, 1992/93, CBP-92/93-1, U.S. Department of Commerce, Washington, D.C., April 1995. SIC categories for which data were suppressed or not available for both 1992 and 1993 are not displayed. The employment columns represent mid-March employment in the year. Pay per employee is calculated by dividing 1st Quarter payroll, annualized, by mid-March employment. The columns headed "% State" show the county's percentage of the state total for the SIC in 1993; for example, 0.9% for SIC 6030 means that the county had 0.9 percent of the state's total establishments (or payroll) in SIC 6030 in 1993. A dash (-) is used to indicate that data are not available or cannot be calculated; nec means not elsewhere classified.

Continued on next page.

SIC	Industry	No. Establishments			Employment		Pay / Employee		Annual Payroll ($ 000)		
		1992	1993	% State	1992	1993	1992	1993	1992	1993	% State
LUBBOCK, TX - [continued]											
6220	Commodity contracts brokers, dealers	4	4	8.2	9	4	40,000	36,000	416	173	-
6280	Security and commodity services	8	11	1.6	24	22	11,000	13,091	235	365	0.1
6300	Insurance carriers	90	71	2.3	782	637	30,026	27,542	20,781	16,068	0.6
6310	Life insurance	18	17	1.7	371	335	27,590	29,684	8,673	8,400	0.9
6330	Fire, marine, and casualty insurance	37	28	2.0	280	138	37,500	36,870	8,764	4,983	0.4
6370	Pension, health, and welfare funds	27	21	8.5	72	117	13,889	7,521	1,385	855	1.8
6400	Insurance agents, brokers, and service	169	190	2.1	633	701	21,668	22,300	15,589	17,520	1.3
6500	Real estate	167	182	1.2	662	745	13,625	14,513	9,643	12,024	0.6
6510	Real estate operators and lessors	91	104	1.6	292	329	12,370	12,632	3,942	4,701	0.8
6530	Real estate agents and managers	56	63	0.9	285	358	14,919	14,547	4,419	5,771	0.4
6540	Title abstract offices	1	4	1.0	-	37	-	24,216	-	979	1.2
6552	Subdividers and developers, n.e.c.	9	8	1.2	33	-	8,606	-	311	-	-
6700	Holding and other investment offices	48	45	1.7	-	116	-	24,586	-	9,883	1.3
6732	Educational, religious, etc. trusts	6	5	1.6	26	14	10,154	17,714	276	259	0.5
6733	Trusts, n.e.c.	19	17	3.2	48	49	13,083	11,755	687	776	1.0
6792	Oil royalty traders	7	6	1.8	18	-	27,556	-	468	-	-
6798	Real estate investment trusts	2	3	7.7	-	6	-	25,333	-	136	1.3
6799	Investors, n.e.c.	9	9	1.3	23	-	31,130	-	1,009	-	-
LYNN, TX											
60 –	**Finance, insurance, and real estate**	11	12	0.0	69	71	20,812	20,113	1,631	1,795	0.0
6000	Depository institutions	4	4	0.1	52	54	21,923	20,815	1,266	1,402	0.0
6400	Insurance agents, brokers, and service	5	5	0.1	-	13	-	16,000	-	278	0.0
MCCULLOCH, TX											
60 –	**Finance, insurance, and real estate**	15	11	0.0	83	85	20,482	17,882	1,925	1,746	0.0
6000	Depository institutions	4	3	0.1	59	55	22,915	20,800	1,555	1,365	0.0
6400	Insurance agents, brokers, and service	4	3	0.0	13	-	8,923	-	139	-	-
6500	Real estate	5	3	0.0	-	4	-	14,000	-	52	0.0
MCLENNAN, TX											
60 –	**Finance, insurance, and real estate**	429	452	1.1	3,951	4,277	22,229	22,759	98,259	99,004	0.8
6000	Depository institutions	52	57	1.2	1,040	1,147	21,788	20,757	23,572	24,814	0.9
6020	Commercial banks	28	27	1.0	845	884	22,764	21,493	19,639	19,813	0.9
6060	Credit unions	15	20	2.0	98	145	18,571	18,400	2,052	2,908	1.3
6100	Nondepository institutions	45	43	1.4	320	348	22,625	21,862	7,846	6,999	0.6
6140	Personal credit institutions	35	32	2.2	182	170	19,648	21,271	3,716	4,050	1.2
6160	Mortgage bankers and brokers	2	7	0.7	-	145	-	21,848	-	2,068	0.3
6200	Security and commodity brokers	20	19	0.9	116	105	48,897	50,400	5,856	5,261	0.3
6210	Security brokers and dealers	12	12	0.9	98	85	51,265	55,106	5,235	4,515	0.4
6280	Security and commodity services	8	7	1.0	18	20	36,000	30,400	621	746	0.2
6300	Insurance carriers	55	45	1.4	1,226	1,338	24,055	26,009	36,109	34,934	1.2
6310	Life insurance	24	18	1.8	661	665	21,428	21,883	19,433	14,769	1.5
6330	Fire, marine, and casualty insurance	23	19	1.3	522	-	27,801	-	15,521	-	-
6400	Insurance agents, brokers, and service	92	108	1.2	355	436	23,470	27,248	9,598	11,689	0.9
6500	Real estate	131	141	0.9	652	613	14,086	13,325	9,334	8,833	0.4
6510	Real estate operators and lessors	66	72	1.1	269	262	13,918	13,756	3,743	3,748	0.7
6530	Real estate agents and managers	44	53	0.8	268	223	15,209	13,256	4,148	3,293	0.3
6540	Title abstract offices	4	3	0.8	46	-	16,174	-	786	-	-
6553	Cemetery subdividers and developers	4	6	1.9	34	59	10,706	10,441	378	644	1.4
6700	Holding and other investment offices	34	39	1.4	242	290	21,686	19,945	5,944	6,474	0.9
6710	Holding offices	9	11	2.0	44	-	24,909	-	1,304	-	-
6732	Educational, religious, etc. trusts	4	5	1.6	11	13	19,273	20,923	236	314	0.6
6733	Trusts, n.e.c.	9	8	1.5	113	61	12,071	6,033	1,460	465	0.6
6794	Patent owners and lessors	3	6	6.8	-	142	-	21,127	-	3,140	8.2

Source: County Business Patterns, 1992/93, CBP-92/93-1, U.S. Department of Commerce, Washington, D.C., April 1995. SIC categories for which data were suppressed or not available for both 1992 and 1993 are not displayed. The employment columns represent mid-March employment in the year. Pay per employee is calculated by dividing 1st Quarter payroll, annualized, by mid-March employment. The columns headed "% State" show the county's percentage of the state total for the SIC in 1993; for example, 0.9% for SIC 6030 means that the county had 0.9 percent of the state's total establishments (or payroll) in SIC 6030 in 1993. A dash (-) is used to indicate that data are not available or cannot be calculated; nec means not elsewhere classified.

SIC	Industry	No. Establishments			Employment		Pay / Employee		Annual Payroll ($ 000)		
		1992	1993	% State	1992	1993	1992	1993	1992	1993	% State
MCMULLEN, TX											
60 –	**Finance, insurance, and real estate**	2	2	0.0	-	-	-	-		-	-
MADISON, TX											
60 –	**Finance, insurance, and real estate**	16	17	0.0	126	181	18,476	11,823	2,634	2,237	0.0
6000	Depository institutions	5	5	0.1	91	84	19,560	15,381	2,023	1,642	0.1
6500	Real estate	5	7	0.0	19	85	10,737	7,106	229	263	0.0
MARION, TX											
60 –	**Finance, insurance, and real estate**	11	10	0.0	47	53	17,702	16,830	944	901	0.0
6400	Insurance agents, brokers, and service	3	3	0.0	7	11	16,000	12,000	129	150	0.0
6500	Real estate	5	4	0.0	6	7	8,667	5,714	65	45	0.0
6530	Real estate agents and managers	5	4	0.1	6	7	8,667	5,714	65	45	0.0
MARTIN, TX											
60 –	**Finance, insurance, and real estate**	5	5	0.0	40	40	20,200	22,300	972	998	0.0
MASON, TX											
60 –	**Finance, insurance, and real estate**	12	13	0.0	55	46	18,473	15,565	1,076	903	0.0
6000	Depository institutions	3	3	0.1	37	24	19,243	17,667	760	614	0.0
6400	Insurance agents, brokers, and service	5	5	0.1	10	10	8,000	9,600	80	85	0.0
MATAGORDA, TX											
60 –	**Finance, insurance, and real estate**	71	69	0.2	298	350	19,128	17,829	6,184	6,510	0.1
6000	Depository institutions	9	9	0.2	164	164	21,463	22,659	3,702	3,811	0.1
6020	Commercial banks	4	4	0.2	137	131	22,190	23,969	3,197	3,229	0.1
6140	Personal credit institutions	3	3	0.2	-	9	-	16,889	-	156	0.0
6300	Insurance carriers	8	6	0.2	3	10	32,000	10,400	159	114	0.0
6400	Insurance agents, brokers, and service	14	14	0.2	45	51	20,622	24,000	1,021	1,296	0.1
6500	Real estate	32	29	0.2	70	96	11,543	7,708	858	814	0.0
6510	Real estate operators and lessors	11	10	0.2	21	45	11,810	8,267	351	400	0.1
6530	Real estate agents and managers	12	14	0.2	26	38	6,154	4,947	153	226	0.0
6553	Cemetery subdividers and developers	4	4	1.3	9	-	12,444	-	116	-	-
6700	Holding and other investment offices	4	6	0.2	6	15	14,000	7,733	112	107	0.0
6732	Educational, religious, etc. trusts	3	3	1.0	-	6	-	14,667	-	98	0.2
MAVERICK, TX											
60 –	**Finance, insurance, and real estate**	50	45	0.1	337	330	14,184	14,291	5,192	4,979	0.0
6000	Depository institutions	5	4	0.1	147	143	15,891	16,084	2,423	2,416	0.1
6100	Nondepository institutions	11	11	0.4	36	-	13,444	-	674	-	-
6140	Personal credit institutions	10	10	0.7	-	37	-	13,405	-	540	0.2
6300	Insurance carriers	3	2	0.1	55	-	18,836	-	1,147	-	-
6400	Insurance agents, brokers, and service	10	10	0.1	39	43	6,769	7,349	283	341	0.0
6500	Real estate	21	18	0.1	60	48	11,000	11,250	665	673	0.0
6510	Real estate operators and lessors	8	9	0.1	32	-	11,250	-	348	-	-
6530	Real estate agents and managers	6	3	0.0	12	3	9,667	9,333	104	39	0.0
MEDINA, TX											
60 –	**Finance, insurance, and real estate**	44	42	0.1	206	195	16,854	19,508	3,770	3,765	0.0
6000	Depository institutions	14	12	0.2	123	120	21,203	21,667	2,812	2,550	0.1
6100	Nondepository institutions	4	4	0.1	-	11	-	38,545	-	405	0.0
6400	Insurance agents, brokers, and service	10	10	0.1	29	35	10,345	11,200	286	415	0.0
6500	Real estate	8	9	0.1	22	20	4,364	5,400	115	134	0.0
6530	Real estate agents and managers	4	6	0.1	16	16	5,000	5,500	94	112	0.0
6700	Holding and other investment offices	5	4	0.1	9	-	5,778	-	49	-	-

Source: County Business Patterns, 1992/93, CBP-92/93-1, U.S. Department of Commerce, Washington, D.C., April 1995. SIC categories for which data were suppressed or not available for both 1992 and 1993 are *not* displayed. The employment columns represent mid-March employment in the year. Pay per employee is calculated by dividing 1st Quarter payroll, annualized, by mid-March employment. The columns headed "% State" show the county's percentage of the state total for the SIC in 1993; for example, 0.9% for SIC 6030 means that the county had 0.9 percent of the state's total establishments (or payroll) in SIC 6030 in 1993. A dash (-) is used to indicate that data are not available or cannot be calculated; *nec* means not elsewhere classified.

SIC	Industry	No. Establishments			Employment		Pay / Employee		Annual Payroll ($ 000)		
		1992	1993	% State	1992	1993	1992	1993	1992	1993	% State
MENARD, TX											
60 –	**Finance, insurance, and real estate**	6	5	*0.0*	18	26	16,222	12,769	322	365	*0.0*
6500	Real estate	3	2	*0.0*	3	-	5,333	-	13	-	
MIDLAND, TX											
60 –	**Finance, insurance, and real estate**	327	341	*0.9*	2,005	1,977	24,922	25,876	51,310	54,189	*0.4*
6000	Depository institutions	30	35	*0.7*	701	641	24,023	25,691	16,686	18,712	*0.6*
6020	Commercial banks	13	16	*0.6*	594	517	25,199	27,389	14,754	16,225	*0.7*
6100	Nondepository institutions	13	11	*0.4*	51	-	23,843	-	1,270	-	-
6160	Mortgage bankers and brokers	5	4	*0.4*	15	17	24,267	33,412	407	501	*0.1*
6200	Security and commodity brokers	24	25	*1.2*	143	172	50,853	55,116	7,881	9,152	*0.6*
6210	Security brokers and dealers	19	20	*1.6*	131	157	53,618	57,478	7,553	8,708	*0.8*
6280	Security and commodity services	5	5	*0.7*	12	15	20,667	30,400	328	444	*0.1*
6300	Insurance carriers	30	26	*0.8*	233	208	23,622	29,077	6,140	5,915	*0.2*
6310	Life insurance	11	8	*0.8*	134	123	18,836	25,789	2,703	3,164	*0.3*
6330	Fire, marine, and casualty insurance	12	12	*0.8*	77	70	30,649	32,971	2,725	2,262	*0.2*
6400	Insurance agents, brokers, and service	58	62	*0.7*	204	230	23,294	23,670	5,113	6,454	*0.5*
6500	Real estate	119	120	*0.8*	545	536	18,818	16,134	10,317	9,320	*0.4*
6510	Real estate operators and lessors	55	62	*0.9*	195	219	15,528	12,913	3,180	3,192	*0.6*
6530	Real estate agents and managers	46	49	*0.7*	248	244	19,742	18,852	4,673	4,785	*0.4*
6540	Title abstract offices	4	4	*1.0*	58	44	21,172	14,091	1,357	731	*0.9*
6700	Holding and other investment offices	53	61	*2.3*	128	146	32,250	26,000	3,903	3,343	*0.4*
6710	Holding offices	3	4	*0.7*	4	4	17,000	19,000	68	78	*0.0*
6792	Oil royalty traders	22	23	*6.8*	62	65	40,645	23,323	2,298	1,200	*2.6*
MILAM, TX											
60 –	**Finance, insurance, and real estate**	32	31	*0.1*	216	234	21,685	20,325	5,043	5,175	*0.0*
6000	Depository institutions	8	9	*0.2*	137	148	23,620	21,784	3,502	3,577	*0.1*
6400	Insurance agents, brokers, and service	10	11	*0.1*	26	44	20,000	11,909	532	520	*0.0*
6500	Real estate	4	4	*0.0*	10	14	8,800	11,429	80	163	*0.0*
MILLS, TX											
60 –	**Finance, insurance, and real estate**	11	9	*0.0*	132	68	12,727	17,294	1,830	1,288	*0.0*
6400	Insurance agents, brokers, and service	2	3	*0.0*	-	7	-	10,286	-	62	*0.0*
MITCHELL, TX											
60 –	**Finance, insurance, and real estate**	12	14	*0.0*	68	66	18,412	20,303	1,326	1,287	*0.0*
6000	Depository institutions	3	3	*0.1*	52	51	20,308	20,941	1,097	1,003	*0.0*
6020	Commercial banks	3	3	*0.1*	52	51	20,308	20,941	1,097	1,003	*0.0*
6400	Insurance agents, brokers, and service	5	5·	*0.1*	9	-	11,111	-	127	-	-
6500	Real estate	4	5	*0.0*	7	-	13,714	-	102	-	-
6510	Real estate operators and lessors	3	3	*0.0*	-	5	-	15,200	-	82	*0.0*
MONTAGUE, TX											
60 –	**Finance, insurance, and real estate**	27	26	*0.1*	179	176	17,810	18,750	3,331	3,511	*0.0*
6000	Depository institutions	7	6	*0.1*	110	114	19,055	17,649	2,078	2,163	*0.1*
6400	Insurance agents, brokers, and service	8	9	*0.1*	14	27	14,286	11,259	244	341	*0.0*
6500	Real estate	7	5	*0.0*	35	14	8,800	14,286	307	212	*0.0*
MONTGOMERY, TX											
60 –	**Finance, insurance, and real estate**	288	299	*0.8*	1,681	1,651	25,711	26,147	44,662	46,961	*0.4*
6000	Depository institutions	28	26	*0.5*	377	374	23,756	24,289	8,465	8,965	*0.3*
6020	Commercial banks	19	18	*0.7*	324	327	21,296	24,930	7,037	7,854	*0.3*
6100	Nondepository institutions	11	17	*0.6*	103	130	31,456	23,815	3,347	4,012	*0.3*
6140	Personal credit institutions	8	9	*0.6*	36	-	17,000	-	854	-	-
6160	Mortgage bankers and brokers	2	7	*0.7*	-	93	-	26,409	-	3,054	*0.5*
6200	Security and commodity brokers	20	15	*0.7*	89	69	39,371	44,348	4,067	3,594	*0.2*
6210	Security brokers and dealers	10	8	*0.6*	55	43	41,891	44,930	2,590	2,183	*0.2*
6280	Security and commodity services	9	7	*1.0*	- ·	26	-	43,385	-	1,411	*0.4*

Source: County Business Patterns, 1992/93, CBP-92/93-1, U.S. Department of Commerce, Washington, D.C., April 1995. SIC categories for which data were suppressed or not available for both 1992 and 1993 are not displayed. The employment columns represent mid-March employment in the year. Pay per employee is calculated by dividing 1st Quarter payroll, annualized, by mid-March employment. The columns headed "% State" show the county's percentage of the state total for the SIC in 1993; for example, 0.9% for SIC 6030 means that the county had 0.9 percent of the state's total establishments (or payroll) in SIC 6030 in 1993. A dash (-) is used to indicate that data are not available or cannot be calculated; nec means not elsewhere classified.

Continued on next page.

SIC	Industry	No. Establishments			Employment		Pay / Employee		Annual Payroll ($ 000)		
		1992	1993	% State	1992	1993	1992	1993	1992	1993	% State
MONTGOMERY, TX - [continued]											
6300	Insurance carriers	23	20	0.6	137	77	32,613	42,026	4,474	3,303	0.1
6310	Life insurance	3	2	0.2	49	-	16,245	-	826	-	-
6330	Fire, marine, and casualty insurance	16	14	1.0	39	-	61,026	-	2,283	-	-
6400	Insurance agents, brokers, and service	56	67	0.8	160	210	20,300	22,838	3,510	4,681	0.4
6500	Real estate	135	142	0.9	749	724	22,660	23,094	18,067	19,203	0.9
6510	Real estate operators and lessors	37	47	0.7	144	193	12,806	12,062	1,800	3,008	0.5
6530	Real estate agents and managers	63	79	1.1	387	300	28,248	19,893	11,412	7,314	0.6
6540	Title abstract offices	3	4	1.0	46	80	25,478	26,050	1,542	2,284	2.8
6552	Subdividers and developers, n.e.c.	6	8	1.2	32	-	25,250	-	639	-	-
6700	Holding and other investment offices	15	12	0.4	66	67	42,909	47,403	2,732	3,203	0.4
6710	Holding offices	3	4	0.7	5	-	52,800	-	134	-	-
MOORE, TX											
60 –	**Finance, insurance, and real estate**	33	34	0.1	188	159	20,191	20,654	3,420	3,628	0.0
6000	Depository institutions	9	9	0.2	129	105	21,829	22,095	2,235	2,426	0.1
6020	Commercial banks	4	3	0.1	80	-	23,100	-	1,244	-	-
6100	Nondepository institutions	3	3	0.1	7	8	19,429	18,500	147	153	0.0
6400	Insurance agents, brokers, and service	10	11	0.1	29	27	11,586	16,000	371	561	0.0
6500	Real estate	7	8	0.1	15	15	7,733	6,133	86	100	0.0
6510	Real estate operators and lessors	3	6	0.1	6	-	4,667	-	30	-	-
MORRIS, TX											
60 –	**Finance, insurance, and real estate**	14	12	0.0	114	112	19,018	18,786	2,227	2,145	0.0
6000	Depository institutions	8	8	0.2	93	95	20,430	19,832	1,948	1,917	0.1
6020	Commercial banks	4	4	0.2	73	75	19,562	19,893	1,468	1,507	0.1
MOTLEY, TX											
60 –	**Finance, insurance, and real estate**	2	3	0.0	-	12	-	15,000	-	184	0.0
NACOGDOCHES, TX											
60 –	**Finance, insurance, and real estate**	106	107	0.3	592	516	20,000	18,171	11,650	10,244	0.1
6000	Depository institutions	14	14	0.3	309	248	22,434	19,710	6,484	5,263	0.2
6020	Commercial banks	11	11	0.4	-	236	-	19,983	-	5,091	0.2
6060	Credit unions	2	3	0.3	-	12	-	14,333	-	172	0.1
6100	Nondepository institutions	6	8	0.3	31	-	19,097	-	612	-	-
6140	Personal credit institutions	5	4	0.3	-	15	-	21,067	-	334	0.1
6200	Security and commodity brokers	6	6	0.3	14	-	52,286	-	871	-	-
6300	Insurance carriers	7	5	0.2	40	24	16,900	13,167	803	451	0.0
6400	Insurance agents, brokers, and service	25	25	0.3	74	77	20,703	18,597	1,416	1,586	0.1
6500	Real estate	42	43	0.3	115	119	10,713	9,748	1,313	1,294	0.1
6510	Real estate operators and lessors	22	25	0.4	65	71	12,185	9,634	845	822	0.1
6530	Real estate agents and managers	12	14	0.2	34	37	9,294	9,081	315	361	0.0
6552	Subdividers and developers, n.e.c.	3	3	0.4	4	-	10,000	-	35	-	-
6700	Holding and other investment offices	6	6	0.2	9	11	16,000	17,091	151	193	0.0
6732	Educational, religious, etc. trusts	2	3	1.0	-	7	-	18,286	-	133	0.3
NAVARRO, TX											
60 –	**Finance, insurance, and real estate**	81	80	0.2	489	670	18,855	17,934	10,305	12,914	0.1
6000	Depository institutions	17	17	0.4	225	240	20,142	19,200	4,898	4,815	0.2
6020	Commercial banks	13	12	0.5	215	227	20,391	19,489	4,733	4,636	0.2
6100	Nondepository institutions	9	8	0.3	27	25	18,222	29,760	527	508	0.0
6140	Personal credit institutions	6	5	0.3	18	-	13,556	-	256	-	-
6200	Security and commodity brokers	4	4	0.2	9	12	45,333	25,000	493	321	0.0
6210	Security brokers and dealers	4	4	0.3	9	12	45,333	25,000	493	321	0.0
6300	Insurance carriers	5	5	0.2	108	111	20,185	16,793	2,097	2,120	0.1
6400	Insurance agents, brokers, and service	14	16	0.2	36	36	14,444	14,889	533	560	0.0
6500	Real estate	25	22	0.1	71	229	13,239	13,799	1,603	3,662	0.2

Source: County Business Patterns, 1992/93, CBP-92/93-1, U.S. Department of Commerce, Washington, D.C., April 1995. SIC categories for which data were suppressed or not available for both 1992 and 1993 are *not* displayed. The employment columns represent mid-March employment in the year. Pay per employee is calculated by dividing 1st Quarter payroll, annualized, by mid-March employment. The columns headed *"% State"* show the county's percentage of the state total for the SIC in 1993; for example, 0.9% for SIC 6030 means that the county had 0.9 percent of the state's total establishments (or payroll) in SIC 6030 in 1993. A dash (-) is used to indicate that data are not available or cannot be calculated; *nec* means not elsewhere classified.

Continued on next page.

SIC	Industry	No. Establishments			Employment		Pay / Employee		Annual Payroll ($ 000)		
		1992	1993	% State	1992	1993	1992	1993	1992	1993	% State
NAVARRO, TX - [continued]											
6510	Real estate operators and lessors	10	10	0.2	33	197	13,818	13,888	1,138	3,146	0.5
6530	Real estate agents and managers	8	8	0.1	23	18	13,391	15,556	284	355	0.0
6700	Holding and other investment offices	7	8	0.3	13	17	11,385	47,294	154	928	0.1
NEWTON, TX											
60–	**Finance, insurance, and real estate**	8	7	0.0	20	27	20,000	13,185	366	416	0.0
6400	Insurance agents, brokers, and service	3	3	0.0	5	5	8,000	7,200	37	39	0.0
NOLAN, TX											
60–	**Finance, insurance, and real estate**	26	24	0.1	153	163	20,758	23,215	3,520	3,981	0.0
6000	Depository institutions	6	5	0.1	89	91	20,854	22,681	2,012	2,245	0.1
6020	Commercial banks	3	3	0.1	78	-	22,103	-	1,874	-	-
6400	Insurance agents, brokers, and service	10	9	0.1	32	32	15,000	17,875	560	622	0.0
6500	Real estate	7	6	0.0	16	21	14,500	10,286	231	220	0.0
NUECES, TX											
60–	**Finance, insurance, and real estate**	731	749	1.9	5,586	5,855	22,679	20,820	130,142	140,682	1.1
6000	Depository institutions	84	81	1.7	1,860	1,816	25,004	21,278	45,803	43,931	1.5
6020	Commercial banks	41	36	1.4	1,261	1,167	24,400	19,465	30,132	25,019	1.1
6100	Nondepository institutions	64	63	2.1	417	-	23,674	-	10,420	-	-
6140	Personal credit institutions	47	44	3.0	343	324	21,679	16,481	7,703	5,703	1.7
6160	Mortgage bankers and brokers	10	11	1.1	47	59	29,787	27,458	1,670	1,916	0.3
6200	Security and commodity brokers	33	32	1.6	227	219	59,789	60,438	12,874	14,703	1.0
6210	Security brokers and dealers	28	26	2.0	219	190	61,589	68,063	12,780	14,468	1.3
6280	Security and commodity services	4	6	0.9	-	29	-	10,483	-	235	0.1
6300	Insurance carriers	72	54	1.7	588	541	26,027	27,519	15,754	15,345	0.5
6310	Life insurance	24	15	1.5	297	266	23,300	23,744	7,217	6,769	0.7
6330	Fire, marine, and casualty insurance	30	23	1.6	93	70	35,957	42,914	3,495	2,990	0.2
6360	Title insurance	2	3	1.4	-	77	-	21,766	-	1,791	1.4
6370	Pension, health, and welfare funds	6	5	2.0	6	6	12,667	10,667	119	74	0.2
6400	Insurance agents, brokers, and service	144	167	1.9	633	716	21,826	22,240	14,171	17,305	1.3
6500	Real estate	285	301	2.0	1,701	2,008	13,717	13,651	25,537	29,948	1.4
6510	Real estate operators and lessors	121	145	2.2	631	678	12,532	13,540	8,596	9,798	1.7
6530	Real estate agents and managers	116	142	2.0	797	1,207	13,802	13,186	12,069	17,567	1.3
6552	Subdividers and developers, n.e.c.	8	7	1.0	48	13	9,167	17,231	490	239	0.2
6553	Cemetery subdividers and developers	5	5	1.6	106	108	19,245	19,222	2,166	2,302	4.9
6700	Holding and other investment offices	48	49	1.8	-	136	-	27,647	-	10,840	1.4
6710	Holding offices	6	6	1.1	35	26	44,914	42,000	1,806	1,213	0.3
6732	Educational, religious, etc. trusts	8	6	1.9	30	30	21,600	21,333	649	647	1.3
6733	Trusts, n.e.c.	12	9	1.7	56	33	21,786	23,030	2,347	2,625	3.4
6792	Oil royalty traders	6	7	2.1	13	10	14,462	11,600	170	223	0.5
OCHILTREE, TX											
60–	**Finance, insurance, and real estate**	18	18	0.0	138	135	23,855	21,837	3,481	3,290	0.0
6000	Depository institutions	4	4	0.1	101	101	24,317	21,584	2,525	2,336	0.1
6400	Insurance agents, brokers, and service	5	5	0.1	16	11	14,750	16,727	241	228	0.0
6500	Real estate	5	5	0.0	7	9	9,714	7,556	70	82	0.0
OLDHAM, TX											
60–	**Finance, insurance, and real estate**	3	3	0.0	-	-	-	-	-	-	
ORANGE, TX											
60–	**Finance, insurance, and real estate**	108	110	0.3	700	809	20,440	18,443	14,647	14,267	0.1
6000	Depository institutions	18	21	0.4	280	373	19,886	20,622	5,662	6,967	0.2
6020	Commercial banks	7	6	0.2	220	169	18,764	20,071	4,172	3,402	0.2
6030	Savings institutions	4	4	0.6	46	-	25,304	-	1,203	-	-
6060	Credit unions	7	11	1.1	14	-	19,714	-	287	-	-
6100	Nondepository institutions	9	8	0.3	54	28	20,444	10,429	1,056	303	0.0

Source: County Business Patterns, 1992/93, CBP-92/93-1, U.S. Department of Commerce, Washington, D.C., April 1995. SIC categories for which data were suppressed or not available for both 1992 and 1993 are not displayed. The employment columns represent mid-March employment in the year. Pay per employee is calculated by dividing 1st Quarter payroll, annualized, by mid-March employment. The columns headed "% State" show the county's percentage of the state total for the SIC in 1993; for example, 0.9% for SIC 6030 means that the county had 0.9 percent of the state's total establishments (or payroll) in SIC 6030 in 1993. A dash (-) is used to indicate that data are not available or cannot be calculated; nec means not elsewhere classified.

Continued on next page.

SIC	Industry	No. Establishments			Employment		Pay / Employee		Annual Payroll ($ 000)		
		1992	1993	% State	1992	1993	1992	1993	1992	1993	% State
ORANGE, TX - [continued]											
6140	Personal credit institutions	7	5	0.3	-	24	-	9,333	-	221	0.1
6400	Insurance agents, brokers, and service	29	34	0.4	73	108	17,205	13,704	1,323	1,610	0.1
6500	Real estate	32	30	0.2	162	164	14,173	11,390	2,378	2,015	0.1
6510	Real estate operators and lessors	12	13	0.2	44	79	7,455	6,785	375	575	0.1
6530	Real estate agents and managers	10	9	0.1	47	40	16,681	20,200	829	825	0.1
6552	Subdividers and developers, n.e.c.	2	4	0.6	-	34	-	12,235	-	498	0.4
6553	Cemetery subdividers and developers	3	4	1.3	10	11	9,600	9,818	91	117	0.2
6700	Holding and other investment offices	8	9	0.3	103	115	29,942	22,748	3,085	2,379	0.3
6733	Trusts, n.e.c.	5	4	0.7	-	74	-	17,243	-	1,266	1.6
PALO PINTO, TX											
60 –	**Finance, insurance, and real estate**	41	42	0.1	225	209	17,298	18,871	4,082	4,185	0.0
6000	Depository institutions	13	12	0.2	138	127	19,623	20,630	2,732	2,825	0.1
6020	Commercial banks	9	9	0.3	129	118	19,969	21,119	2,612	2,689	0.1
6400	Insurance agents, brokers, and service	6	8	0.1	16	20	10,000	11,800	172	234	0.0
6500	Real estate	16	15	0.1	61	57	12,721	14,526	888	826	0.0
6510	Real estate operators and lessors	6	5	0.1	23	-	9,739	-	239	-	-
6530	Real estate agents and managers	5	6	0.1	5	29	11,200	15,862	83	508	0.0
6540	Title abstract offices	3	3	0.8	10	9	11,600	24,444	119	132	0.2
6700	Holding and other investment offices	2	4	0.1	-	2	-	12,000	-	49	0.0
PANOLA, TX											
60 –	**Finance, insurance, and real estate**	31	30	0.1	185	187	18,724	20,193	3,826	3,903	0.0
6000	Depository institutions	8	8	0.2	114	113	21,333	21,841	2,595	2,754	0.1
6400	Insurance agents, brokers, and service	5	5	0.1	20	18	11,600	13,556	343	333	0.0
6500	Real estate	12	11	0.1	25	28	7,680	6,857	220	225	0.0
6510	Real estate operators and lessors	6	7	0.1	8	13	7,000	8,000	73	108	0.0
6540	Title abstract offices	3	2	0.5	10	-	10,000	-	99	-	-
PARKER, TX											
60 –	**Finance, insurance, and real estate**	78	76	0.2	463	428	17,832	19,738	8,784	9,011	0.1
6000	Depository institutions	13	11	0.2	248	238	21,065	22,739	5,397	5,542	0.2
6020	Commercial banks	10	8	0.3	232	222	21,259	23,027	5,133	5,263	0.2
6200	Security and commodity brokers	3	4	0.2	-	10	-	75,200	-	822	0.1
6400	Insurance agents, brokers, and service	19	17	0.2	54	56	12,296	12,857	726	739	0.1
6500	Real estate	34	34	0.2	122	91	9,607	10,418	1,285	1,123	0.1
6510	Real estate operators and lessors	12	16	0.2	77	54	9,091	9,333	744	551	0.1
6530	Real estate agents and managers	12	12	0.2	18	20	8,889	9,800	181	245	0.0
6552	Subdividers and developers, n.e.c.	3	4	0.6	-	5	-	18,400	-	127	0.1
6700	Holding and other investment offices	6	6	0.2	13	17	8,000	17,647	163	358	0.0
PARMER, TX											
60 –	**Finance, insurance, and real estate**	13	12	0.0	104	99	21,538	21,455	2,608	2,563	0.0
6000	Depository institutions	5	5	0.1	70	72	21,829	22,056	1,888	2,053	0.1
6400	Insurance agents, brokers, and service	3	3	0.0	9	10	12,444	9,600	135	110	0.0
PECOS, TX											
60 –	**Finance, insurance, and real estate**	16	19	0.0	137	148	18,657	16,243	2,533	2,489	0.0
6000	Depository institutions	3	4	0.1	83	86	19,855	20,233	1,611	1,789	0.1
6020	Commercial banks	3	3	0.1	83	-	19,855	-	1,611	-	-
6400	Insurance agents, brokers, and service	5	6	0.1	19	22	16,421	13,455	292	321	0.0
6500	Real estate	3	5	0.0	8	15	7,500	6,933	76	95	0.0
POLK, TX											
60 –	**Finance, insurance, and real estate**	51	55	0.1	266	273	18,602	16,147	5,258	4,807	0.0
6000	Depository institutions	7	7	0.1	151	172	20,371	18,047	3,234	3,258	0.1
6100	Nondepository institutions	3	2	0.1	4	-	18,000	-	71	-	-
6400	Insurance agents, brokers, and service	11	14	0.2	22	29	12,182	11,586	294	321	0.0

Source: County Business Patterns, 1992/93, CBP-92/93-1, U.S. Department of Commerce, Washington, D.C., April 1995. SIC categories for which data were suppressed or not available for both 1992 and 1993 are not displayed. The employment columns represent mid-March employment in the year. Pay per employee is calculated by dividing 1st Quarter payroll, annualized, by mid-March employment. The columns headed "% State" show the county's percentage of the state total for the SIC in 1993; for example, 0.9% for SIC 6030 means that the county had 0.9 percent of the state's total establishments (or payroll) in SIC 6030 in 1993. A dash (-) is used to indicate that data are not available or cannot be calculated; nec means not elsewhere classified.

Continued on next page.

SIC	Industry	No. Establishments			Employment		Pay / Employee		Annual Payroll ($ 000)		
		1992	1993	% State	1992	1993	1992	1993	1992	1993	% State
WEBB, TX - [continued]											
6552	Subdividers and developers, n.e.c.	11	15	2.2	31	-	15,613	-	509	-	-
6700	Holding and other investment offices	13	15	0.6	29	33	17,103	22,788	520	813	0.1
6732	Educational, religious, etc. trusts	3	1	0.3	5	-	19,200	-	85	-	-
6733	Trusts, n.e.c.	7	8	1.5	-	11	-	12,364	-	162	0.2
WHARTON, TX											
60 –	**Finance, insurance, and real estate**	83	81	0.2	573	573	22,750	19,742	13,684	12,164	0.1
6000	Depository institutions	20	21	0.4	263	262	22,068	20,489	6,116	5,682	0.2
6020	Commercial banks	12	12	0.5	236	232	22,797	21,086	5,660	5,074	0.2
6030	Savings institutions	5	5	0.8	18	17	19,111	16,471	373	409	0.1
6060	Credit unions	3	4	0.4	9	13	8,889	15,077	83	199	0.1
6100	Nondepository institutions	6	5	0.2	-	24	-	24,333	-	588	0.0
6300	Insurance carriers	7	6	0.2	55	36	17,527	19,000	1,076	730	0.0
6400	Insurance agents, brokers, and service	19	20	0.2	50	56	15,600	15,000	878	973	0.1
6500	Real estate	25	22	0.1	77	141	14,130	15,206	1,177	2,251	0.1
6510	Real estate operators and lessors	12	9	0.1	34	105	17,412	15,238	617	1,740	0.3
6530	Real estate agents and managers	6	8	0.1	14	-	8,571	-	101	-	-
6700	Holding and other investment offices	5	5	0.2	104	-	35,654	-	3,778	-	-
WHEELER, TX											
60 –	**Finance, insurance, and real estate**	10	12	0.0	62	63	21,097	21,524	1,417	1,482	0.0
6000	Depository institutions	5	5	0.1	50	53	22,240	22,189	1,239	1,289	0.0
6500	Real estate	1	3	0.0	-	2	-	6,000	-	26	0.0
WICHITA, TX											
60 –	**Finance, insurance, and real estate**	309	303	0.8	1,872	1,913	21,203	22,020	40,861	43,378	0.3
6000	Depository institutions	40	42	0.9	745	760	20,993	22,068	16,246	17,441	0.6
6020	Commercial banks	21	18	0.7	562	563	22,797	23,105	12,823	13,462	0.6
6030	Savings institutions	6	6	0.9	33	-	16,242	-	543	-	-
6060	Credit unions	10	14	1.4	142	156	15,549	20,128	2,784	3,185	1.4
6090	Functions closely related to banking	3	4	0.8	8	-	10,500	-	96	-	-
6140	Personal credit institutions	16	11	0.8	52	44	18,462	13,545	951	664	0.2
6160	Mortgage bankers and brokers	3	4	0.4	5	-	14,400	-	71	-	-
6200	Security and commodity brokers	16	15	0.7	90	82	53,422	53,073	5,055	4,653	0.3
6210	Security brokers and dealers	11	10	0.8	55	50	64,436	60,560	3,619	3,119	0.3
6280	Security and commodity services	5	5	0.7	35	32	36,114	41,375	1,436	1,534	0.4
6300	Insurance carriers	35	29	0.9	275	267	21,120	24,914	6,460	6,418	0.2
6310	Life insurance	15	14	1.4	127	135	23,024	31,200	2,999	3,593	0.4
6330	Fire, marine, and casualty insurance	12	9	0.6	99	80	22,869	23,450	2,370	1,982	0.1
6400	Insurance agents, brokers, and service	66	71	0.8	199	225	26,291	26,329	4,312	5,558	0.4
6500	Real estate	100	97	0.6	402	415	11,940	12,742	5,428	5,908	0.3
6510	Real estate operators and lessors	54	54	0.8	247	277	11,012	10,469	3,009	3,248	0.6
6530	Real estate agents and managers	35	37	0.5	79	83	12,253	18,458	1,235	1,671	0.1
6700	Holding and other investment offices	30	30	1.1	95	79	22,400	20,152	2,095	1,695	0.2
6710	Holding offices	4	3	0.5	6	-	27,333	-	182	-	-
6732	Educational, religious, etc. trusts	6	8	2.6	28	22	11,000	12,182	301	279	0.6
6733	Trusts, n.e.c.	7	6	1.1	27	7	28,444	7,429	505	50	0.1
6792	Oil royalty traders	6	6	1.8	-	27	-	29,333	-	863	1.9
6799	Investors, n.e.c.	6	6	0.8	-	15		19,467	-	306	0.3
WILBARGER, TX											
60 –	**Finance, insurance, and real estate**	30	29	0.1	216	196	21,185	21,939	4,292	4,086	0.0
6000	Depository institutions	5	4	0.1	137	140	24,934	24,343	3,027	3,099	0.1
6300	Insurance carriers	4	2	0.1	18	-	7,111	-	170	-	-

Source: County Business Patterns, 1992/93, CBP-92/93-1, U.S. Department of Commerce, Washington, D.C., April 1995. SIC categories for which data were suppressed or not available for both 1992 and 1993 are *not* displayed. The employment columns represent mid-March employment in the year. Pay per employee is calculated by dividing 1st Quarter payroll, annualized, by mid-March employment. The columns headed "% State" show the county's percentage of the state total for the SIC in 1993; for example, 0.9% for SIC 6030 means that the county had 0.9 percent of the state's total establishments (or payroll) in SIC 6030 in 1993. A dash (-) is used to indicate that data are not available or cannot be calculated; *nec* means not elsewhere classified.

Continued on next page.

SIC	Industry	No. Establishments			Employment		Pay / Employee		Annual Payroll ($ 000)		
		1992	1993	% State	1992	1993	1992	1993	1992	1993	% State
WILBARGER, TX - [continued]											
6400	Insurance agents, brokers, and service	9	10	0.1	26	32	13,538	13,000	371	519	0.0
6500	Real estate	6	7	0.0	13	10	20,308	19,200	302	172	0.0
6510	Real estate operators and lessors	3	6	0.1	6	-	22,000	-	144	-	-
WILLACY, TX											
60 -	**Finance, insurance, and real estate**	17	17	0.0	127	121	18,425	19,306	2,403	2,469	0.0
6100	Nondepository institutions	4	4	0.1	9	8	20,444	23,000	202	199	0.0
6400	Insurance agents, brokers, and service	6	6	0.1	21	18	10,857	11,778	238	227	0.0
6500	Real estate	4	3	0.0	8	7	11,000	8,000	76	52	0.0
WILLIAMSON, TX											
60 -	**Finance, insurance, and real estate**	212	232	0.6	959	1,124	20,467	20,772	21,540	27,402	0.2
6000	Depository institutions	31	31	0.6	403	438	20,328	19,333	8,388	9,258	0.3
6020	Commercial banks	21	21	0.8	339	371	21,027	19,655	7,302	8,110	0.4
6060	Credit unions	3	3	0.3	22	25	12,364	12,160	301	314	0.1
6100	Nondepository institutions	9	13	0.4	20	26	22,800	18,615	466	720	0.1
6140	Personal credit institutions	7	9	0.6	-	19	-	17,474	-	376	0.1
6200	Security and commodity brokers	8	10	0.5	16	15	31,000	44,000	517	595	0.0
6300	Insurance carriers	27	23	0.7	126	110	26,413	36,327	3,800	4,679	0.2
6310	Life insurance	4	4	0.4	41	-	31,512	-	1,392	-	-
6360	Title insurance	4	3	1.4	45	-	23,733	-	1,263	-	-
6400	Insurance agents, brokers, and service	56	65	0.7	175	220	18,126	19,236	3,681	5,405	0.4
6500	Real estate	73	82	0.5	198	292	16,263	15,425	3,830	5,450	0.3
6510	Real estate operators and lessors	23	30	0.5	33	79	10,545	10,228	579	1,002	0.2
6530	Real estate agents and managers	38	44	0.6	135	195	18,607	16,862	2,746	3,780	0.3
6552	Subdividers and developers, n.e.c.	3	6	0.9	6	-	6,667	-	41	-	-
6700	Holding and other investment offices	8	8	0.3	21	23	36,381	43,652	858	1,295	0.2
6733	Trusts, n.e.c.	3	1	0.2	9	-	11,111	-	85	-	-
WILSON, TX											
60 -	**Finance, insurance, and real estate**	25	23	0.1	124	131	34,839	21,954	4,801	3,556	0.0
6000	Depository institutions	5	4	0.1	84	88	45,286	26,591	4,238	2,884	0.1
6020	Commercial banks	4	4	0.2	-	88	-	26,591	-	2,884	0.1
6200	Security and commodity brokers	3	3	0.1	4	-	7,000	-	19	-	-
6300	Insurance carriers	3	1	0.0	6	-	8,000	-	56	-	-
6400	Insurance agents, brokers, and service	7	9	0.1	14	20	14,857	13,000	248	382	0.0
6500	Real estate	7	6	0.0	16	19	14,500	13,684	240	267	0.0
WINKLER, TX											
60 -	**Finance, insurance, and real estate**	11	13	0.0	60	59	23,200	22,305	1,122	1,142	0.0
6000	Depository institutions	3	4	0.1	41	-	27,610	-	884	-	-
6020	Commercial banks	3	3	0.1	41	-	27,610	-	884	-	-
6400	Insurance agents, brokers, and service	3	3	0.0	9	9	12,889	15,111	111	120	0.0
6500	Real estate	4	5	0.0	-	5	-	14,400	-	103	0.0
WISE, TX											
60 -	**Finance, insurance, and real estate**	43	44	0.1	278	264	18,129	18,439	5,551	5,644	0.0
6000	Depository institutions	10	10	0.2	156	176	20,923	19,795	3,348	3,907	0.1
6400	Insurance agents, brokers, and service	13	13	0.1	28	38	14,571	16,000	429	720	0.1
6500	Real estate	15	17	0.1	66	30	13,030	12,267	1,062	491	0.0
6510	Real estate operators and lessors	7	10	0.2	10	12	7,600	9,333	90	217	0.0
WOOD, TX											
60 -	**Finance, insurance, and real estate**	57	58	0.1	346	340	16,890	17,929	6,397	6,427	0.0
6000	Depository institutions	14	13	0.3	197	195	19,208	19,815	4,122	3,892	0.1
6100	Nondepository institutions	3	2	0.1	6	-	14,667	-	87	-	-
6140	Personal credit institutions	3	2	0.1	6	-	14,667	-	87	-	-
6400	Insurance agents, brokers, and service	12	16	0.2	32	42	13,000	13,905	429	668	0.1

Source: County Business Patterns, 1992/93, CBP-92/93-1, U.S. Department of Commerce, Washington, D.C., April 1995. SIC categories for which data were suppressed or not available for both 1992 and 1993 are not displayed. The employment columns represent mid-March employment in the year. Pay per employee is calculated by dividing 1st Quarter payroll, annualized, by mid-March employment. The columns headed "% State" show the county's percentage of the state total for the SIC in 1993; for example, 0.9% for SIC 6030 means that the county had 0.9 percent of the state's total establishments (or payroll) in SIC 6030 in 1993. A dash (-) is used to indicate that data are not available or cannot be calculated; nec means not elsewhere classified.

Continued on next page.

SIC	Industry	No. Establishments			Employment		Pay / Employee		Annual Payroll ($ 000)		
		1992	1993	% State	1992	1993	1992	1993	1992	1993	% State
WOOD, TX - [continued]											
6500	Real estate	19	20	0.1	91	83	12,396	14,554	1,259	1,406	0.1
6510	Real estate operators and lessors	2	4	0.1	-	11	-	7,273	-	100	0.0
6530	Real estate agents and managers	11	9	0.1	54	-	14,222	-	861	-	-
6700	Holding and other investment offices	6	5	0.2	10	12	10,400	6,000	122	68	0.0
YOAKUM, TX											
60 –	**Finance, insurance, and real estate**	12	13	0.0	62	65	16,452	16,985	1,117	1,170	0.0
6000	Depository institutions	5	5	0.1	51	51	16,549	18,118	903	970	0.0
6400	Insurance agents, brokers, and service	3	4	0.0	-	7	-	8,571	-	64	0.0
6500	Real estate	4	4	0.0	-	7	-	17,143	-	136	0.0
YOUNG, TX											
60 –	**Finance, insurance, and real estate**	35	34	0.1	379	355	18,596	17,510	6,679	6,398	0.0
6000	Depository institutions	7	7	0.1	298	217	17,705	18,581	4,712	4,225	0.1
6020	Commercial banks	3	4	0.2	71	-	23,324	-	1,601	-	-
6200	Security and commodity brokers	3	1	0.0	10	-	28,000	-	342	-	-
6210	Security brokers and dealers	3	1	0.1	10	-	28,000	-	342	-	-
6400	Insurance agents, brokers, and service	10	10	0.1	36	-	13,778	-	520	-	-
6500	Real estate	9	10	0.1	15	8	8,000	7,500	82	76	0.0
6510	Real estate operators and lessors	6	6	0.1	10	4	6,000	5,000	32	44	0.0
6530	Real estate agents and managers	3	4	0.1	5	4	12,000	10,000	50	32	0.0
6700	Holding and other investment offices	3	4	0.1	-	88	-	15,909	-	1,330	0.2
ZAPATA, TX											
60 –	**Finance, insurance, and real estate**	9	10	0.0	51	55	20,000	16,582	1,024	942	0.0
6400	Insurance agents, brokers, and service	1	3	0.0	-	6	-	10,667	-	65	0.0
6500	Real estate	4	3	0.0	10	7	6,000	6,857	68	42	0.0
ZAVALA, TX											
60 –	**Finance, insurance, and real estate**	10	9	0.0	44	46	16,273	17,478	892	816	0.0
6500	Real estate	4	3	0.0	6	7	10,667	9,714	68	74	0.0

Source: County Business Patterns, 1992/93, CBP-92/93-1, U.S. Department of Commerce, Washington, D.C., April 1995. SIC categories for which data were suppressed or not available for both 1992 and 1993 are *not* displayed. The employment columns represent mid-March employment in the year. Pay per employee is calculated by dividing 1st Quarter payroll, annualized, by mid-March employment. The columns headed "% State" show the county's percentage of the state total for the SIC in 1993; for example, 0.9% for SIC 6030 means that the county had 0.9 percent of the state's total establishments (or payroll) in SIC 6030 in 1993. A dash (-) is used to indicate that data are not available or cannot be calculated; *nec* means not elsewhere classified.

UTAH

SIC	Industry	No. Establishments			Employment		Pay / Employee		Annual Payroll ($ 000)		
		1992	1993	% State	1992	1993	1992	1993	1992	1993	% State
BEAVER, UT											
60 –	**Finance, insurance, and real estate**	15	11	0.3	38	39	14,000	12,821	535	531	0.1
6000	Depository institutions	5	5	0.7	24	25	17,333	14,560	394	375	0.1
6020	Commercial banks	5	4	0.9	24	-	17,333	-	394	-	-
6400	Insurance agents, brokers, and service	5	5	0.6	5	-	10,400	-	56	-	-
BOX ELDER, UT											
60 –	**Finance, insurance, and real estate**	48	51	1.3	256	259	18,047	18,239	4,913	5,045	0.5
6000	Depository institutions	13	14	1.9	133	119	18,165	19,597	2,478	2,479	0.8
6020	Commercial banks	7	7	1.5	94	83	19,404	20,289	1,851	1,768	0.8
6300	Insurance carriers	3	2	0.7	26	-	40,769	-	1,087	-	-
6400	Insurance agents, brokers, and service	16	18	2.1	37	-	11,243	-	548	-	-
6500	Real estate	12	13	0.9	39	46	11,179	9,826	453	516	0.4
6530	Real estate agents and managers	7	8	1.1	21	25	12,000	9,600	268	281	0.3
CACHE, UT											
60 –	**Finance, insurance, and real estate**	111	126	3.1	631	774	19,924	18,770	13,175	16,763	1.7
6000	Depository institutions	24	25	3.4	283	307	20,042	19,270	5,961	6,568	2.2
6020	Commercial banks	18	18	3.9	214	231	20,879	20,035	4,649	5,167	2.2
6100	Nondepository institutions	10	10	3.0	80	115	25,850	25,948	2,678	4,358	2.8
6160	Mortgage bankers and brokers	5	5	2.7	44	94	30,545	27,702	1,994	3,960	4.1
6210	Security brokers and dealers	5	4	4.3	-	8	-	58,000	-	392	0.8
6300	Insurance carriers	12	8	2.9	44	-	25,636	-	1,194	-	-
6400	Insurance agents, brokers, and service	21	26	3.0	42	77	18,762	32,260	766	1,639	1.3
6500	Real estate	35	49	3.4	157	236	9,707	8,458	1,814	2,881	2.0
6510	Real estate operators and lessors	16	20	3.8	52	59	6,231	6,644	414	381	1.1
6530	Real estate agents and managers	14	22	2.9	39	145	7,179	8,138	387	1,898	2.3
CARBON, UT											
60 –	**Finance, insurance, and real estate**	30	33	0.8	133	-	16,602	-	2,266	-	-
6000	Depository institutions	9	10	1.4	72	89	16,611	16,270	1,208	1,565	0.5
6020	Commercial banks	6	6	1.3	58	63	17,517	16,000	1,020	1,112	0.5
6400	Insurance agents, brokers, and service	6	8	0.9	18	32	11,778	12,875	228	468	0.4
6500	Real estate	11	11	0.8	15	37	13,067	6,054	250	306	0.2
6530	Real estate agents and managers	6	6	0.8	7	27	7,429	5,185	57	141	0.2
DAGGETT, UT											
60 –	**Finance, insurance, and real estate**	1	1	0.0	-	-	-	-	-	-	-
DAVIS, UT											
60 –	**Finance, insurance, and real estate**	248	271	6.8	1,668	1,939	19,197	17,582	35,846	38,218	3.9
6000	Depository institutions	50	54	7.4	539	589	17,432	16,156	9,618	10,954	3.6
6020	Commercial banks	36	37	8.1	427	447	18,070	17,638	7,900	8,353	3.6
6100	Nondepository institutions	10	10	3.0	115	104	20,730	20,462	2,344	2,005	1.3
6160	Mortgage bankers and brokers	4	5	2.7	-	25	-	23,840	-	914	0.9
6200	Security and commodity brokers	10	9	4.9	-	229	-	9,362	-	2,854	4.6
6300	Insurance carriers	25	22	7.9	136	62	28,441	34,968	4,373	2,371	1.5
6330	Fire, marine, and casualty insurance	17	16	11.9	91	-	30,813	-	3,216	-	-
6400	Insurance agents, brokers, and service	58	61	7.0	334	499	20,922	16,930	7,610	9,730	7.5
6500	Real estate	88	104	7.2	329	406	16,170	19,655	7,592	8,601	6.0

Source: County Business Patterns, 1992/93, CBP-92/93-1, U.S. Department of Commerce, Washington, D.C., April 1995. SIC categories for which data were suppressed or not available for both 1992 and 1993 are *not* displayed. The employment columns represent mid-March employment in the year. Pay per employee is calculated by dividing 1st Quarter payroll, annualized, by mid-March employment. The columns headed "% State" show the county's percentage of the state total for the SIC in 1993; for example, 0.9% for SIC 6030 means that the county had 0.9 percent of the state's total establishments (or payroll) in SIC 6030 in 1993. A dash (-) is used to indicate that data are not available or cannot be calculated; *nec* means not elsewhere classified.

Continued on next page.

SIC	Industry	No. Establishments			Employment		Pay / Employee		Annual Payroll ($ 000)		
		1992	1993	% State	1992	1993	1992	1993	1992	1993	% State
DAVIS, UT - [continued]											
6510	Real estate operators and lessors	26	37	7.1	133	146	13,594	25,151	2,066	2,954	8.3
6530	Real estate agents and managers	44	52	6.9	122	157	16,656	14,904	2,913	2,705	3.2
6700	Holding and other investment offices	7	11	7.1	-	50	-	34,160	-	1,703	8.1
DUCHESNE, UT											
60 –	**Finance, insurance, and real estate**	15	18	0.4	73	68	12,384	12,588	933	893	0.1
6000	Depository institutions	7	7	1.0	43	36	14,884	16,000	638	580	0.2
6400	Insurance agents, brokers, and service	4	6	0.7	9	-	8,889	-	83	-	-
6500	Real estate	4	4	0.3	21	22	8,762	9,091	212	227	0.2
EMERY, UT											
60 –	**Finance, insurance, and real estate**	8	9	0.2	-	38	-	11,579	-	518	0.1
6000	Depository institutions	6	6	0.8	-	29	-	13,793	-	458	0.2
GARFIELD, UT											
60 –	**Finance, insurance, and real estate**	4	6	0.1	20	-	13,800	-	292	-	-
6000	Depository institutions	3	4	0.5	-	16	-	14,250	-	266	0.1
GRAND, UT											
60 –	**Finance, insurance, and real estate**	16	20	0.5	63	77	14,730	14,597	1,075	1,358	0.1
6500	Real estate	8	11	0.8	19	21	8,000	7,048	213	222	0.2
6510	Real estate operators and lessors	5	5	1.0	11	-	6,545	-	129	-	-
6530	Real estate agents and managers	3	5	0.7	8	10	10,000	8,400	84	86	0.1
IRON, UT											
60 –	**Finance, insurance, and real estate**	42	53	1.3	231	276	14,165	13,377	3,402	4,357	0.4
6000	Depository institutions	7	11	1.5	98	120	19,020	16,767	1,883	2,477	0.8
6020	Commercial banks	6	7	1.5	-	105	-	17,257	-	2,254	1.0
6060	Credit unions	1	4	1.8	-	15	-	13,333	-	223	0.5
6400	Insurance agents, brokers, and service	10	15	1.7	29	67	9,241	12,358	309	1,017	0.8
6500	Real estate	19	22	1.5	83	81	9,735	8,000	818	614	0.4
6510	Real estate operators and lessors	5	6	1.2	13	20	7,692	8,800	105	215	0.6
6530	Real estate agents and managers	11	13	1.7	51	45	7,216	9,422	310	339	0.4
6552	Subdividers and developers, n.e.c.	1	3	3.4	-	16	-	3,000	-	60	0.8
JUAB, UT											
60 –	**Finance, insurance, and real estate**	8	8	0.2	-	33	-	17,091	-	597	0.1
6000	Depository institutions	4	4	0.5	20	20	19,400	21,200	400	445	0.1
KANE, UT											
60 –	**Finance, insurance, and real estate**	12	12	0.3	37	-	14,703	-	641	-	-
6500	Real estate	7	7	0.5	7	13	8,571	8,923	98	134	0.1
6530	Real estate agents and managers	4	3	0.4	5	-	8,800	-	67	-	-
6552	Subdividers and developers, n.e.c.	1	3	3.4	-	1	-	12,000	-	32	0.4
MILLARD, UT											
60 –	**Finance, insurance, and real estate**	15	16	0.4	65	62	16,862	16,903	1,108	1,121	0.1
6000	Depository institutions	6	6	0.8	45	39	17,244	16,821	792	768	0.3
6400	Insurance agents, brokers, and service	4	7	0.8	12	21	18,000	17,524	194	332	0.3
6500	Real estate	2	3	0.2	-	2	-	12,000	-	21	0.0
MORGAN, UT											
60 –	**Finance, insurance, and real estate**	7	7	0.2	-	-	-	-	-	-	-
PIUTE, UT											
60 –	**Finance, insurance, and real estate**	1	1	0.0	-	-	-	-	-	-	-

Source: County Business Patterns, 1992/93, CBP-92/93-1, U.S. Department of Commerce, Washington, D.C., April 1995. SIC categories for which data were suppressed or not available for both 1992 and 1993 are *not* displayed. The employment columns represent mid-March employment in the year. Pay per employee is calculated by dividing 1st Quarter payroll, annualized, by mid-March employment. The columns headed "% State" show the county's percentage of the state total for the SIC in 1993; for example, 0.9% for SIC 6030 means that the county had 0.9 percent of the state's total establishments (or payroll) in SIC 6030 in 1993. A dash (-) is used to indicate that data are not available or cannot be calculated; *nec* means not elsewhere classified.

SIC	Industry	No. Establishments			Employment		Pay / Employee		Annual Payroll ($ 000)		
		1992	1993	% State	1992	1993	1992	1993	1992	1993	% State
RICH, UT											
60 –	**Finance, insurance, and real estate**	1	1	0.0	-	-	-	-	-	-	-
SALT LAKE, UT											
60 –	**Finance, insurance, and real estate**	2,060	2,221	55.4	24,813	27,176	24,779	24,809	630,030	743,434	75.5
6000	Depository institutions	338	351	47.8	7,406	7,680	25,536	25,076	182,636	203,327	67.6
6020	Commercial banks	205	208	45.5	5,908	6,059	26,678	25,967	150,876	163,193	70.6
6030	Savings institutions	22	20	57.1	339	326	29,192	26,454	9,466	9,416	64.4
6060	Credit unions	103	112	49.1	986	1,025	17,602	18,494	17,526	20,439	45.9
6100	Nondepository institutions	192	215	64.4	3,513	4,083	23,658	23,483	94,138	129,176	84.0
6140	Personal credit institutions	78	64	57.7	646	-	23,350	-	15,032	-	-
6150	Business credit institutions	31	32	88.9	1,587	1,635	17,931	17,776	26,619	31,234	98.0
6160	Mortgage bankers and brokers	76	117	63.2	1,216	1,808	30,921	28,097	50,406	77,118	79.4
6200	Security and commodity brokers	121	130	70.3	768	943	50,812	50,011	39,538	49,166	79.7
6210	Security brokers and dealers	58	64	68.1	621	627	57,082	62,960	35,314	39,869	78.0
6280	Security and commodity services	59	64	73.6	138	-	24,928	-	4,094	-	-
6300	Insurance carriers	223	193	68.9	5,285	5,308	25,156	24,843	132,062	138,201	89.4
6310	Life insurance	61	52	75.4	2,054	1,944	24,078	22,074	45,608	41,522	83.8
6321	Accident and health insurance	11	14	100.0	628	447	26,815	24,376	17,412	11,179	100.0
6330	Fire, marine, and casualty insurance	88	81	60.0	1,026	-	30,526	-	31,223	-	-
6360	Title insurance	19	7	63.6	237	-	22,498	-	7,721	-	-
6370	Pension, health, and welfare funds	27	24	80.0	428	428	24,290	24,850	9,671	10,460	99.0
6400	Insurance agents, brokers, and service	412	460	52.9	2,853	3,178	26,343	26,807	76,609	95,250	73.7
6500	Real estate	655	760	52.5	4,070	4,938	16,984	17,265	78,043	92,099	64.4
6510	Real estate operators and lessors	246	280	53.8	1,214	1,458	12,781	12,875	16,810	21,457	60.6
6530	Real estate agents and managers	285	403	53.7	2,064	3,143	18,479	16,795	43,120	59,075	70.1
6540	Title abstract offices	6	9	18.8	79	122	22,430	18,197	2,366	3,717	31.0
6552	Subdividers and developers, n.e.c.	38	42	47.2	428	133	20,785	54,406	9,470	4,922	63.3
6553	Cemetery subdividers and developers	10	10	62.5	65	58	14,400	18,000	1,222	1,420	76.7
6710	Holding offices	26	28	80.0	193	230	36,435	50,678	7,112	11,078	97.2
6732	Educational, religious, etc. trusts	19	18	81.8	62	53	16,258	15,094	1,123	942	-
6733	Trusts, n.e.c.	27	19	55.9	116	101	12,552	12,832	1,701	1,293	61.9
6798	Real estate investment trusts	4	-	-	14	-	8,571	-	57	-	-
6799	Investors, n.e.c.	18	28	70.0	-	101	-	23,168	-	2,846	88.4
SAN JUAN, UT											
60 –	**Finance, insurance, and real estate**	13	11	0.3	56	57	10,500	8,351	666	565	0.1
6000	Depository institutions	6	5	0.7	32	-	15,625	-	508	-	-
6500	Real estate	4	4	0.3	20	26	3,400	3,692	147	110	0.1
SANPETE, UT											
60 –	**Finance, insurance, and real estate**	24	27	0.7	119	127	27,361	13,512	2,252	2,085	0.2
6000	Depository institutions	8	11	1.5	64	74	19,250	16,054	1,309	1,311	0.4
6020	Commercial banks	5	7	1.5	57	65	20,421	17,108	1,238	1,230	0.5
6060	Credit unions	3	4	1.8	7	9	9,714	8,444	71	81	0.2
6400	Insurance agents, brokers, and service	8	8	0.9	17	24	12,941	10,833	274	356	0.3
6500	Real estate	5	5	0.3	-	19	-	10,526	-	232	0.2
SEVIER, UT											
60 –	**Finance, insurance, and real estate**	23	27	0.7	143	142	17,706	15,070	2,518	2,344	0.2
6000	Depository institutions	7	8	1.1	77	60	20,623	16,067	1,609	1,140	0.4
6020	Commercial banks	6	5	1.1	-	52	-	16,308	-	1,011	0.4
6060	Credit unions	1	3	1.3	-	8	-	14,500	-	129	0.3
6400	Insurance agents, brokers, and service	6	9	1.0	22	-	15,455	-	354	-	-
6500	Real estate	6	9	0.6	36	46	14,778	16,261	457	695	0.5
6530	Real estate agents and managers	3	5	0.7	-	8	-	9,000	-	92	0.1

Source: County Business Patterns, 1992/93, CBP-92/93-1, U.S. Department of Commerce, Washington, D.C., April 1995. SIC categories for which data were suppressed or not available for both 1992 and 1993 are *not* displayed. The employment columns represent mid-March employment in the year. Pay per employee is calculated by dividing 1st Quarter payroll, annualized, by mid-March employment. The columns headed "% State" show the county's percentage of the state total for the SIC in 1993; for example, 0.9% for SIC 6030 means that the county had 0.9 percent of the state's total establishments (or payroll) in SIC 6030 in 1993. A dash (-) is used to indicate that data are not available or cannot be calculated; *nec* means not elsewhere classified.

SIC	Industry	No. Establishments			Employment		Pay / Employee		Annual Payroll ($ 000)		
		1992	1993	% State	1992	1993	1992	1993	1992	1993	% State
SUMMIT, UT											
60 –	**Finance, insurance, and real estate**	87	101	2.5	1,050	1,017	18,682	19,351	17,355	20,055	2.0
6000	Depository institutions	8	9	1.2	63	67	19,429	22,627	1,257	1,696	0.6
6020	Commercial banks	8	9	2.0	63	67	19,429	22,627	1,257	1,696	0.7
6100	Nondepository institutions	7	8	2.4	23	-	47,652	-	1,099	-	-
6200	Security and commodity brokers	2	3	1.6	-	1	-	12,000	-	27	0.0
6400	Insurance agents, brokers, and service	9	16	1.8	51	73	25,804	26,247	1,542	2,629	2.0
6500	Real estate	54	61	4.2	874	832	16,810	17,106	12,026	12,950	9.1
6510	Real estate operators and lessors	7	9	1.7	67	147	15,343	21,415	1,005	3,097	8.7
6530	Real estate agents and managers	40	48	6.4	787	663	16,147	15,186	9,745	8,248	9.8
6700	Holding and other investment offices	3	3	1.9	25	-	38,400	-	777	-	-
TOOELE, UT											
60 –	**Finance, insurance, and real estate**	29	31	0.8	144	153	16,444	15,634	2,551	2,638	0.3
6000	Depository institutions	11	12	1.6	103	107	17,165	16,150	1,893	1,922	0.6
6400	Insurance agents, brokers, and service	7	8	0.9	19	27	13,474	15,111	272	443	0.3
6500	Real estate	7	7	0.5	15	11	13,867	9,455	252	144	0.1
6510	Real estate operators and lessors	2	3	0.6	-	3	-	8,000	-	35	0.1
UINTAH, UT											
60 –	**Finance, insurance, and real estate**	32	33	0.8	127	125	22,142	23,104	2,569	2,870	0.3
6000	Depository institutions	6	6	0.8	66	-	20,606	-	1,258	-	-
6400	Insurance agents, brokers, and service	10	15	1.7	20	29	46,600	39,586	671	836	0.6
6500	Real estate	11	10	0.7	26	23	9,846	10,957	308	421	0.3
6510	Real estate operators and lessors	8	6	1.2	15	-	10,400	-	173	-	-
6530	Real estate agents and managers	2	3	0.4	-	4	-	11,000	-	86	0.1
UTAH, UT											
60 –	**Finance, insurance, and real estate**	383	436	10.9	2,700	2,742	19,167	19,205	54,686	61,874	6.3
6000	Depository institutions	75	83	11.3	1,170	1,182	19,299	18,860	23,546	24,902	8.3
6020	Commercial banks	52	56	12.3	900	872	20,400	20,174	19,137	19,499	8.4
6100	Nondepository institutions	34	36	10.8	179	247	29,050	26,283	5,915	9,097	5.9
6160	Mortgage bankers and brokers	16	21	11.4	112	190	35,429	28,800	4,550	7,997	8.2
6200	Security and commodity brokers	20	17	9.2	137	112	40,117	45,893	5,483	5,373	8.7
6210	Security brokers and dealers	11	8	8.5	92	86	48,130	52,977	4,700	4,792	9.4
6280	Security and commodity services	8	9	10.3	-	26	-	22,462	-	581	-
6300	Insurance carriers	42	29	10.4	287	180	24,376	27,133	6,799	5,073	3.3
6310	Life insurance	6	6	8.7	138	134	23,942	25,373	3,317	3,402	6.9
6360	Title insurance	7	-	-	63	-	18,984	-	1,341	-	-
6400	Insurance agents, brokers, and service	73	92	10.6	237	359	16,540	17,136	4,505	7,825	6.1
6500	Real estate	129	164	11.3	664	591	10,898	11,743	8,089	8,807	6.2
6510	Real estate operators and lessors	50	68	13.1	264	329	9,439	9,629	2,866	3,579	10.1
6530	Real estate agents and managers	51	68	9.1	270	153	10,222	11,843	2,641	2,288	2.7
6540	Title abstract offices	6	9	18.8	45	93	21,422	18,839	1,349	2,507	20.9
6552	Subdividers and developers, n.e.c.	6	14	15.7	-	12	-	15,667	-	364	4.7
6700	Holding and other investment offices	10	15	9.6	26	71	12,462	10,704	349	797	3.8
6710	Holding offices	1	3	8.6	-	4	-	19,000	-	74	0.6
WASATCH, UT											
60 –	**Finance, insurance, and real estate**	14	20	0.5	65	71	15,262	15,211	1,071	1,327	0.1
6000	Depository institutions	4	4	0.5	29	-	18,207	-	543	-	-
6020	Commercial banks	3	3	0.7	-	25	-	18,560	-	551	0.2
6400	Insurance agents, brokers, and service	3	4	0.5	13	20	19,385	17,000	298	420	0.3
6500	Real estate	4	9	0.6	-	12	-	3,667	-	131	0.1
6530	Real estate agents and managers	2	6	0.8	-	9	-	2,667	-	59	0.1

Source: County Business Patterns, 1992/93, CBP-92/93-1, U.S. Department of Commerce, Washington, D.C., April 1995. SIC categories for which data were suppressed or not available for both 1992 and 1993 are not displayed. The employment columns represent mid-March employment in the year. Pay per employee is calculated by dividing 1st Quarter payroll, annualized, by mid-March employment. The columns headed "% State" show the county's percentage of the state total for the SIC in 1993; for example, 0.9% for SIC 6030 means that the county had 0.9 percent of the state's total establishments (or payroll) in SIC 6030 in 1993. A dash (-) is used to indicate that data are not available or cannot be calculated; nec means not elsewhere classified.

SIC	Industry	No. Establishments			Employment		Pay / Employee		Annual Payroll ($ 000)		
		1992	1993	% State	1992	1993	1992	1993	1992	1993	% State
WASHINGTON, UT											
60 –	**Finance, insurance, and real estate**	111	138	*3.4*	710	694	17,701	17,262	14,221	15,455	*1.6*
6000	Depository institutions	17	21	*2.9*	247	279	22,818	20,659	5,654	7,185	*2.4*
6020	Commercial banks	15	17	*3.7*	-	221	-	21,104	-	5,080	*2.2*
6100	Nondepository institutions	11	12	*3.6*	76	50	16,842	24,240	2,178	1,497	*1.0*
6140	Personal credit institutions	5	4	*3.6*	43	8	11,814	19,000	643	166	*-*
6160	Mortgage bankers and brokers	6	8	*4.3*	33	42	23,394	25,238	1,535	1,331	*1.4*
6200	Security and commodity brokers	5	3	*1.6*	-	4	-	46,000	-	426	*0.7*
6300	Insurance carriers	8	1	*0.4*	59	-	15,593	-	1,263	-	*-*
6400	Insurance agents, brokers, and service	15	23	*2.6*	60	109	24,467	17,798	1,507	2,976	*2.3*
6500	Real estate	51	76	*5.3*	243	240	10,963	10,267	3,080	2,918	*2.0*
6510	Real estate operators and lessors	13	17	*3.3*	60	68	6,467	7,882	533	551	*1.6*
6530	Real estate agents and managers	25	45	*6.0*	96	121	13,208	10,612	1,286	1,550	*1.8*
6540	Title abstract offices	1	3	*6.3*	-	17	-	14,118	-	273	*2.3*
6552	Subdividers and developers, n.e.c.	6	9	*10.1*	30	-	10,800	-	380	-	*-*
WEBER, UT											
60 –	**Finance, insurance, and real estate**	310	319	*8.0*	2,444	2,634	19,890	19,532	51,574	58,268	*5.9*
6000	Depository institutions	60	65	*8.9*	1,032	1,174	22,430	21,359	23,765	27,680	*9.2*
6020	Commercial banks	25	30	*6.6*	-	483	-	25,739	-	12,918	*5.6*
6030	Savings institutions	13	7	*20.0*	296	-	27,554	-	7,816	-	*-*
6060	Credit unions	21	27	*11.8*	-	595	-	18,245	-	12,631	*28.3*
6100	Nondepository institutions	33	29	*8.7*	270	145	22,400	26,317	6,259	4,524	*2.9*
6140	Personal credit institutions	23	15	*13.5*	214	73	19,458	18,082	4,175	1,366	*-*
6160	Mortgage bankers and brokers	9	14	*7.6*	-	72	-	34,667	-	3,158	*3.3*
6200	Security and commodity brokers	10	12	*6.5*	61	64	52,918	51,375	3,200	3,350	*5.4*
6210	Security brokers and dealers	8	8	*8.5*	-	60	-	52,933	-	3,121	*6.1*
6300	Insurance carriers	34	19	*6.8*	366	290	21,246	23,476	8,006	6,593	*4.3*
6360	Title insurance	6	1	*9.1*	48	-	22,083	-	1,142	-	*-*
6400	Insurance agents, brokers, and service	63	77	*8.9*	170	229	13,176	13,624	2,267	3,580	*2.8*
6500	Real estate	98	108	*7.5*	460	671	10,774	12,775	6,212	10,858	*7.6*
6510	Real estate operators and lessors	38	46	*8.8*	165	186	9,648	9,742	1,713	2,019	*5.7*
6530	Real estate agents and managers	42	52	*6.9*	197	417	8,934	12,403	2,747	7,153	*8.5*
6540	Title abstract offices	3	5	*10.4*	18	45	29,111	25,244	627	1,133	*9.4*

Source: County Business Patterns, 1992/93, CBP-92/93-1, U.S. Department of Commerce, Washington, D.C., April 1995. SIC categories for which data were suppressed or not available for both 1992 and 1993 are *not* displayed. The employment columns represent mid-March employment in the year. Pay per employee is calculated by dividing 1st Quarter payroll, annualized, by mid-March employment. The columns headed "% State" show the county's percentage of the state total for the SIC in 1993; for example, 0.9% for SIC 6030 means that the county had 0.9 percent of the state's total establishments (or payroll) in SIC 6030 in 1993. A dash (-) is used to indicate that data are not available or cannot be calculated; *nec* means not elsewhere classified.

VERMONT

SIC	Industry	No. Establishments			Employment		Pay / Employee		Annual Payroll ($ 000)		
		1992	1993	% State	1992	1993	1992	1993	1992	1993	% State
ADDISON, VT											
60 –	**Finance, insurance, and real estate**	55	52	3.4	311	333	21,711	20,925	6,968	7,601	2.3
6000	Depository institutions	17	17	5.1	132	140	19,000	18,886	2,621	2,765	2.6
6020	Commercial banks	12	11	4.8	111	111	19,532	19,964	2,328	2,350	3.1
6300	Insurance carriers	4	3	2.7	72	-	27,944	-	1,865	-	-
6400	Insurance agents, brokers, and service	15	12	3.8	68	61	21,588	22,623	1,549	1,404	3.4
6500	Real estate	16	15	2.5	-	25	-	15,840	-	480	1.3
6510	Real estate operators and lessors	-	3	1.9	-	5	-	20,800	-	125	1.3
6530	Real estate agents and managers	8	9	2.7	-	18	-	15,778	-	340	1.5
6553	Cemetery subdividers and developers	5	3	5.1	-	2	-	4,000	-	15	-
BENNINGTON, VT											
60 –	**Finance, insurance, and real estate**	93	96	6.3	511	560	22,810	20,279	11,894	12,686	3.8
6000	Depository institutions	21	21	6.3	253	283	20,142	17,583	5,247	5,076	4.7
6020	Commercial banks	16	16	7.0	219	247	19,507	17,296	4,463	4,284	5.7
6100	Nondepository institutions	4	4	9.1	13	-	28,000	-	410	-	-
6160	Mortgage bankers and brokers	4	4	14.3	13	-	28,000	-	410	-	-
6200	Security and commodity brokers	3	4	7.1	-	7	-	66,857	-	609	3.0
6400	Insurance agents, brokers, and service	14	12	3.8	73	67	32,164	30,866	2,368	2,387	5.7
6500	Real estate	46	47	7.9	143	152	19,776	17,053	2,801	3,107	8.5
6510	Real estate operators and lessors	12	13	8.2	37	32	11,784	11,875	399	495	5.1
6530	Real estate agents and managers	24	27	8.2	79	86	24,405	19,721	1,944	1,998	8.5
6553	Cemetery subdividers and developers	4	4	6.8	8	-	10,500	-	143	-	-
6700	Holding and other investment offices	1	5	7.7	-	5	-	38,400	-	391	-
CALEDONIA, VT											
60 –	**Finance, insurance, and real estate**	78	78	5.1	515	507	20,621	22,122	10,825	10,719	3.2
6000	Depository institutions	18	22	6.6	241	222	18,805	20,775	4,618	4,128	3.8
6100	Nondepository institutions	3	2	4.5	12	-	21,000	-	187	-	-
6200	Security and commodity brokers	4	4	7.1	-	11	-	75,636	-	731	3.6
6300	Insurance carriers	6	4	3.6	93	100	26,108	29,360	2,466	2,765	3.2
6400	Insurance agents, brokers, and service	15	17	5.4	70	62	18,686	22,000	1,330	1,390	3.3
6500	Real estate	31	28	4.7	78	94	14,205	11,617	1,279	1,201	3.3
6510	Real estate operators and lessors	8	9	5.7	14	16	11,143	19,000	243	337	3.5
6530	Real estate agents and managers	16	12	3.6	52	72	17,308	10,611	952	824	3.5
6553	Cemetery subdividers and developers	6	7	11.9	10	6	3,600	4,000	77	40	-
CHITTENDEN, VT											
60 –	**Finance, insurance, and real estate**	445	455	30.0	3,929	3,910	29,124	30,073	117,124	125,300	37.6
6000	Depository institutions	71	71	21.2	1,755	1,601	24,807	24,750	43,099	39,912	36.8
6020	Commercial banks	52	40	17.6	1,401	970	23,780	24,120	34,403	23,210	30.8
6100	Nondepository institutions	14	15	34.1	-	167	-	61,437	-	14,188	-
6160	Mortgage bankers and brokers	8	11	39.3	-	101	-	21,149	-	3,227	38.3
6200	Security and commodity brokers	25	23	41.1	220	208	63,509	60,000	16,580	13,216	65.8
6210	Security brokers and dealers	14	10	37.0	180	175	62,867	64,137	11,565	11,761	72.3
6280	Security and commodity services	11	13	46.4	40	33	66,400	38,061	5,015	1,455	-
6300	Insurance carriers	62	54	49.1	420	448	28,486	35,143	11,570	16,096	18.6
6310	Life insurance	19	13	37.1	160	196	29,550	44,102	4,549	8,124	15.1
6330	Fire, marine, and casualty insurance	19	17	43.6	114	110	33,684	36,945	4,034	4,402	23.5
6360	Title insurance	1	3	100.0	-	11	-	33,091	-	316	100.0
6400	Insurance agents, brokers, and service	91	102	32.3	534	556	31,993	31,784	18,130	18,524	44.4
6500	Real estate	160	168	28.4	576	664	21,938	22,898	12,827	14,773	40.3

Source: *County Business Patterns, 1992/93*, CBP-92/93-1, U.S. Department of Commerce, Washington, D.C., April 1995. SIC categories for which data were suppressed or not available for both 1992 and 1993 are *not* displayed. The employment columns represent mid-March employment in the year. Pay per employee is calculated by dividing 1st Quarter payroll, annualized, by mid-March employment. The columns headed "% State" show the county's percentage of the state total for the SIC in 1993; for example, 0.9% for SIC 6030 means that the county had 0.9 percent of the state's total establishments (or payroll) in SIC 6030 in 1993. A dash (-) is used to indicate that data are not available or cannot be calculated; *nec* means not elsewhere classified.

Continued on next page.

SIC	Industry	No. Establishments			Employment		Pay / Employee		Annual Payroll ($ 000)		
		1992	1993	% State	1992	1993	1992	1993	1992	1993	% State
CHITTENDEN, VT - [continued]											
6510	Real estate operators and lessors	54	57	*36.1*	217	206	29,567	28,680	5,256	4,563	*47.0*
6530	Real estate agents and managers	69	87	*26.4*	246	404	17,805	20,317	5,170	8,724	*37.3*
6552	Subdividers and developers, n.e.c.	13	17	*43.6*	31	45	24,774	22,311	1,017	1,361	*49.6*
6553	Cemetery subdividers and developers	4	4	*6.8*	7	7	9,714	10,857	92	98	*-*
6700	Holding and other investment offices	21	22	*33.8*	-	266	-	24,812	-	8,591	*-*
6733	Trusts, n.e.c.	9	5	*33.3*	28	21	31,000	12,952	953	138	*12.1*
ESSEX, VT											
60 –	**Finance, insurance, and real estate**	5	5	*0.3*	14	12	18,857	22,000	254	268	*0.1*
FRANKLIN, VT											
60 –	**Finance, insurance, and real estate**	72	74	*4.9*	335	341	21,767	23,648	6,654	8,325	*2.5*
6000	Depository institutions	18	19	*5.7*	222	197	21,063	19,878	3,985	3,712	*3.4*
6020	Commercial banks	13	12	*5.3*	207	171	21,643	20,772	3,796	3,305	*4.4*
6300	Insurance carriers	7	6	*5.5*	24	-	39,500	-	741	-	*-*
6400	Insurance agents, brokers, and service	10	12	*3.8*	41	41	27,610	26,927	1,234	1,220	*2.9*
6500	Real estate	34	33	*5.6*	-	42	-	10,190	-	635	*1.7*
6510	Real estate operators and lessors	6	9	*5.7*	12	18	6,000	12,000	106	219	*2.3*
6530	Real estate agents and managers	14	13	*3.9*	26	21	10,769	7,238	313	188	*0.8*
6552	Subdividers and developers, n.e.c.	2	3	*7.7*	-	2	-	28,000	-	196	*7.1*
6553	Cemetery subdividers and developers	8	8	*13.6*	1	1	4,000	4,000	37	32	*-*
GRAND ISLE, VT											
60 –	**Finance, insurance, and real estate**	9	7	*0.5*	18	14	19,111	14,000	262	282	*0.1*
6500	Real estate	4	3	*0.5*	3	-	54,667	-	62	-	*-*
LAMOILLE, VT											
60 –	**Finance, insurance, and real estate**	46	48	*3.2*	260	293	18,215	16,724	4,910	5,489	*1.6*
6000	Depository institutions	10	10	*3.0*	143	155	18,853	15,768	2,620	2,763	*2.6*
6020	Commercial banks	10	10	*4.4*	143	155	18,853	15,768	2,620	2,763	*3.7*
6400	Insurance agents, brokers, and service	8	9	*2.8*	-	41	-	26,927	-	1,276	*3.1*
6500	Real estate	24	25	*4.2*	77	92	11,740	14,130	1,077	1,368	*3.7*
6510	Real estate operators and lessors	6	5	*3.2*	17	14	16,471	20,571	411	429	*4.4*
6530	Real estate agents and managers	10	17	*5.2*	16	77	13,000	12,935	246	905	*3.9*
ORANGE, VT											
60 –	**Finance, insurance, and real estate**	44	46	*3.0*	252	227	23,524	21,216	5,524	4,688	*1.4*
6000	Depository institutions	13	17	*5.1*	162	141	24,963	24,142	3,825	3,126	*2.9*
6400	Insurance agents, brokers, and service	10	11	*3.5*	48	55	20,250	18,036	1,061	1,106	*2.6*
6500	Real estate	15	14	*2.4*	20	15	7,400	8,000	186	168	*0.5*
6530	Real estate agents and managers	8	7	*2.1*	18	-	6,667	-	147	-	*-*
6553	Cemetery subdividers and developers	4	5	*8.5*	-	1	-	4,000	17	24	*-*
ORLEANS, VT											
60 –	**Finance, insurance, and real estate**	50	52	*3.4*	235	230	18,774	21,009	4,282	4,830	*1.4*
6000	Depository institutions	15	15	*4.5*	147	127	19,265	22,803	2,648	2,778	*2.6*
6020	Commercial banks	10	10	*4.4*	127	106	20,094	23,887	2,338	2,436	*3.2*
6400	Insurance agents, brokers, and service	11	15	*4.7*	-	35	-	20,000	-	761	*1.8*
6500	Real estate	20	19	*3.2*	-	26	-	9,846	-	306	*0.8*
6510	Real estate operators and lessors	3	5	*3.2*	8	9	6,000	8,889	36	83	*0.9*
6530	Real estate agents and managers	7	7	*2.1*	-	11	-	9,455	-	124	*0.5*
6552	Subdividers and developers, n.e.c.	3	2	*5.1*	4	-	20,000	-	88	-	*-*
6553	Cemetery subdividers and developers	5	5	*8.5*	7	-	3,429	-	33	-	*-*
RUTLAND, VT											
60 –	**Finance, insurance, and real estate**	160	163	*10.7*	1,391	1,319	22,157	22,159	30,027	30,950	*9.3*
6000	Depository institutions	32	33	*9.9*	686	637	20,373	20,364	13,161	13,455	*12.4*
6020	Commercial banks	26	25	*11.0*	499	393	19,760	21,140	8,989	8,385	*11.1*

Source: County Business Patterns, 1992/93, CBP-92/93-1, U.S. Department of Commerce, Washington, D.C., April 1995. SIC categories for which data were suppressed or not available for both 1992 and 1993 are not displayed. The employment columns represent mid-March employment in the year. Pay per employee is calculated by dividing 1st Quarter payroll, annualized, by mid-March employment. The columns headed "% State" show the county's percentage of the state total for the SIC in 1993; for example, 0.9% for SIC 6030 means that the county had 0.9 percent of the state's total establishments (or payroll) in SIC 6030 in 1993. A dash (-) is used to indicate that data are not available or cannot be calculated; nec means not elsewhere classified.

Continued on next page.

SIC	Industry	No. Establishments			Employment		Pay / Employee		Annual Payroll ($ 000)		
		1992	1993	% State	1992	1993	1992	1993	1992	1993	% State
RUTLAND, VT - [continued]											
6100	Nondepository institutions	4	4	9.1	77	-	27,844	-	1,902	-	-
6200	Security and commodity brokers	4	3	5.4	28	-	54,429	-	1,577	-	-
6300	Insurance carriers	13	10	9.1	124	85	19,645	26,400	2,470	2,363	2.7
6310	Life insurance	7	6	17.1	96	81	18,083	23,951	1,712	1,893	3.5
6400	Insurance agents, brokers, and service	40	43	13.6	147	185	23,429	19,178	3,566	3,905	9.4
6500	Real estate	63	66	11.1	237	263	13,063	13,506	3,136	3,611	9.9
6510	Real estate operators and lessors	17	17	10.8	86	70	16,930	14,743	1,353	947	9.7
6530	Real estate agents and managers	24	36	10.9	122	155	10,984	14,839	1,338	2,460	10.5
6552	Subdividers and developers, n.e.c.	5	6	15.4	9	20	10,222	7,400	124	59	2.2
6553	Cemetery subdividers and developers	7	7	11.9	12	18	7,000	4,000	163	145	-
6700	Holding and other investment offices	4	4	6.2	92	-	45,652	-	4,215	-	-
WASHINGTON, VT											
60–	**Finance, insurance, and real estate**	173	171	11.3	2,732	2,521	32,991	32,146	84,527	76,335	22.9
6000	Depository institutions	38	38	11.3	516	389	25,589	20,833	13,908	7,928	7.3
6020	Commercial banks	19	22	9.7	245	174	30,057	19,747	8,130	3,337	4.4
6200	Security and commodity brokers	9	7	12.5	84	53	46,048	58,264	3,707	2,662	13.2
6210	Security brokers and dealers	4	4	14.8	63	-	42,540	-	2,333	-	-
6280	Security and commodity services	5	3	10.7	21	-	56,571	-	1,374	-	-
6300	Insurance carriers	19	21	19.1	1,410	1,687	39,424	36,598	48,611	57,162	66.2
6330	Fire, marine, and casualty insurance	11	11	28.2	-	346	-	26,312	-	9,831	52.4
6400	Insurance agents, brokers, and service	27	27	8.5	421	137	28,684	25,927	12,937	3,837	9.2
6500	Real estate	68	61	10.3	242	189	15,471	14,243	3,825	2,835	7.7
6510	Real estate operators and lessors	13	11	7.0	27	28	8,000	9,571	253	296	3.0
6530	Real estate agents and managers	38	41	12.4	185	156	17,816	15,256	3,295	2,426	10.4
6553	Cemetery subdividers and developers	7	7	11.9	3	-	5,333	-	53	-	-
WINDHAM, VT											
60–	**Finance, insurance, and real estate**	106	113	7.4	1,759	1,330	25,442	22,256	45,492	29,529	8.9
6000	Depository institutions	29	30	9.0	680	791	23,288	24,475	16,350	17,242	15.9
6020	Commercial banks	21	21	9.3	640	730	23,438	25,129	15,523	16,173	21.5
6100	Nondepository institutions	5	6	13.6	-	66	-	25,636	-	2,136	-
6160	Mortgage bankers and brokers	3	4	14.3	54	-	27,185	-	1,647	-	-
6300	Insurance carriers	5	5	4.5	112	110	20,214	22,800	2,480	2,536	2.9
6400	Insurance agents, brokers, and service	16	16	5.1	128	154	17,094	13,273	2,229	2,255	5.4
6500	Real estate	39	41	6.9	138	156	15,043	14,667	2,077	2,610	7.1
6510	Real estate operators and lessors	12	12	7.6	19	-	23,789	-	498	-	-
6530	Real estate agents and managers	19	27	8.2	98	120	12,776	14,267	1,217	2,018	8.6
WINDSOR, VT											
60–	**Finance, insurance, and real estate**	160	159	10.5	794	756	18,887	19,217	15,594	16,347	4.9
6000	Depository institutions	36	39	11.6	288	251	20,306	20,701	5,513	5,120	4.7
6020	Commercial banks	29	29	12.8	256	206	20,312	20,835	4,845	4,129	5.5
6100	Nondepository institutions	5	2	4.5	20	-	29,400	-	645	-	-
6400	Insurance agents, brokers, and service	33	36	11.4	127	137	25,008	23,737	3,240	3,523	8.4
6500	Real estate	72	70	11.8	273	286	14,945	16,168	4,525	5,458	14.9
6510	Real estate operators and lessors	19	15	9.5	145	112	12,690	14,893	1,812	1,650	17.0
6530	Real estate agents and managers	36	43	13.0	76	148	14,947	17,405	1,273	3,172	13.6
6552	Subdividers and developers, n.e.c.	2	5	12.8	-	21	-	17,143	-	514	18.7
6553	Cemetery subdividers and developers	4	6	10.2	2	-	4,000	-	16	-	-
6700	Holding and other investment offices	6	7	10.8	52	51	17,615	18,824	1,412	1,596	-

Source: County Business Patterns, 1992/93, CBP-92/93-1, U.S. Department of Commerce, Washington, D.C., April 1995. SIC categories for which data were suppressed or not available for both 1992 and 1993 are *not* displayed. The employment columns represent mid-March employment in the year. Pay per employee is calculated by dividing 1st Quarter payroll, annualized, by mid-March employment. The columns headed "% State" show the county's percentage of the state total for the SIC in 1993; for example, 0.9% for SIC 6030 means that the county had 0.9 percent of the state's total establishments (or payroll) in SIC 6030 in 1993. A dash (-) is used to indicate that data are not available or cannot be calculated; *nec* means not elsewhere classified.

VIRGINIA

SIC	Industry	No. Establishments			Employment		Pay / Employee		Annual Payroll ($ 000)		
		1992	1993	% State	1992	1993	1992	1993	1992	1993	% State
ACCOMACK, VA											
60 –	**Finance, insurance, and real estate**	53	57	0.4	358	345	20,034	21,426	7,082	7,173	0.1
6000	Depository institutions	18	19	0.6	163	176	23,779	25,864	3,433	3,954	0.3
6400	Insurance agents, brokers, and service	11	10	0.4	51	-	17,333	-	1,001	-	-
6500	Real estate	19	24	0.4	95	84	12,168	11,048	1,270	1,244	0.2
6510	Real estate operators and lessors	4	5	0.3	9	-	13,333	-	147	-	-
6530	Real estate agents and managers	12	16	0.6	65	60	11,569	9,400	748	840	0.2
ALBEMARLE, VA											
60 –	**Finance, insurance, and real estate**	49	80	0.5	176	352	20,841	20,886	5,037	9,503	0.2
6000	Depository institutions	7	9	0.3	31	38	18,581	16,842	587	678	0.1
6020	Commercial banks	5	5	0.2	-	29	-	18,069	-	555	0.1
6060	Credit unions	2	4	1.1	-	9	-	12,889	-	123	0.1
6200	Security and commodity brokers	1	3	0.4	-	5	-	36,800	-	194	0.1
6400	Insurance agents, brokers, and service	9	15	0.5	10	24	21,200	16,333	255	419	0.1
6500	Real estate	23	42	0.8	82	229	16,976	19,057	2,412	6,119	0.8
6510	Real estate operators and lessors	6	13	0.7	8	46	10,000	12,870	83	708	0.4
6530	Real estate agents and managers	11	23	0.8	28	89	11,857	19,281	699	2,259	0.4
6700	Holding and other investment offices	3	5	0.9	-	17	-	26,118	-	595	0.2
ALLEGHANY, VA											
60 –	**Finance, insurance, and real estate**	2	7	0.0	-	-	-	-	-	-	-
6500	Real estate	1	5	0.1	-	11	-	9,455	-	85	0.0
AMELIA, VA											
60 –	**Finance, insurance, and real estate**	6	5	0.0	30	25	19,600	22,720	553	516	0.0
6000	Depository institutions	3	3	0.1	24	-	19,667	-	438	-	-
6020	Commercial banks	3	3	0.1	24	-	19,667	-	438	-	-
AMHERST, VA											
60 –	**Finance, insurance, and real estate**	34	38	0.3	175	197	20,526	20,244	3,772	4,008	0.1
6000	Depository institutions	9	9	0.3	73	87	21,370	21,425	1,786	1,840	0.1
6400	Insurance agents, brokers, and service	7	9	0.3	26	26	15,385	14,308	382	400	0.1
6500	Real estate	11	14	0.3	21	24	9,143	15,167	190	347	0.0
6510	Real estate operators and lessors	3	5	0.3	3	8	12,000	15,500	49	118	0.1
6530	Real estate agents and managers	5	5	0.2	13	12	8,308	12,000	116	174	0.0
APPOMATTOX, VA											
60 –	**Finance, insurance, and real estate**	17	18	0.1	128	137	22,125	20,555	2,740	2,722	0.1
6000	Depository institutions	6	5	0.2	66	72	19,636	19,056	1,165	1,164	0.1
6400	Insurance agents, brokers, and service	5	6	0.2	11	18	12,364	13,333	184	284	0.1
6530	Real estate agents and managers	2	4	0.1	-	6	-	16,000	-	121	0.0
ARLINGTON, VA											
60 –	**Finance, insurance, and real estate**	534	527	3.6	6,669	6,088	26,442	29,999	171,492	190,847	3.8
6000	Depository institutions	114	110	3.7	1,378	1,155	21,660	25,368	29,783	31,653	2.4
6020	Commercial banks	68	71	3.3	824	706	20,034	21,875	15,925	14,545	1.5
6030	Savings institutions	28	16	4.1	405	255	24,978	38,133	10,478	12,707	9.4
6060	Credit unions	16	19	5.1	-	188	-	21,745	-	4,317	3.0
6090	Functions closely related to banking	2	4	5.6	-	6	-	7,333	-	84	-
6100	Nondepository institutions	21	12	1.1	156	114	34,692	49,263	4,727	5,045	0.8
6140	Personal credit institutions	6	-	-	27	-	22,222	-	682	-	-

Source: County Business Patterns, 1992/93, CBP-92/93-1, U.S. Department of Commerce, Washington, D.C., April 1995. SIC categories for which data were suppressed or not available for both 1992 and 1993 are *not* displayed. The employment columns represent mid-March employment in the year. Pay per employee is calculated by dividing 1st Quarter payroll, annualized, by mid-March employment. The columns headed "% State" show the county's percentage of the state total for the SIC in 1993; for example, 0.9% for SIC 6030 means that the county had 0.9 percent of the state's total establishments (or payroll) in SIC 6030 in 1993. A dash (-) is used to indicate that data are not available or cannot be calculated; *nec* means not elsewhere classified.

Continued on next page.

SIC	Industry	No. Establishments			Employment		Pay / Employee		Annual Payroll ($ 000)		
		1992	1993	% State	1992	1993	1992	1993	1992	1993	% State
ARLINGTON, VA - [continued]											
6160	Mortgage bankers and brokers	6	7	1.2	58	-	31,862	-	1,452	-	-
6200	Security and commodity brokers	19	21	3.1	213	122	43,099	57,475	10,282	7,690	2.0
6210	Security brokers and dealers	10	8	2.3	-	18	-	41,778	-	783	0.3
6280	Security and commodity services	8	13	4.0	146	104	38,000	60,192	6,762	6,907	-
6300	Insurance carriers	32	32	2.7	948	917	30,789	32,759	31,453	33,190	3.6
6310	Life insurance	12	11	3.5	846	811	31,215	33,011	28,573	30,126	10.8
6360	Title insurance	4	2	2.3	13	-	28,308	-	366	-	-
6400	Insurance agents, brokers, and service	49	53	1.9	348	226	33,057	33,788	10,897	7,842	2.0
6500	Real estate	278	273	5.1	3,474	3,360	20,116	23,540	68,336	87,821	10.8
6510	Real estate operators and lessors	135	144	7.4	1,313	1,321	16,320	15,976	20,703	22,582	11.8
6530	Real estate agents and managers	91	110	3.8	1,687	1,860	21,048	28,656	35,839	60,055	11.3
6552	Subdividers and developers, n.e.c.	24	14	5.1	373	-	25,244	-	8,677	-	-
6700	Holding and other investment offices	21	26	.4.8	152	194	140,289	123,361	16,014	17,606	5.2
6710	Holding offices	5	7	4.1	47	53	351,404	303,774	10,608	8,332	3.4
AUGUSTA, VA											
60 –	**Finance, insurance, and real estate**	50	87	0.6	160	257	15,025	15,564	2,715	4,327	0.1
6000	Depository institutions	14	16	0.5	84	94	15,143	15,660	1,364	1,483	0.1
6020	Commercial banks	13	13	0.6	-	83	-	16,241	-	1,351	0.1
6060	Credit unions	1	3	0.8	-	11	-	11,273	-	132	0.1
6400	Insurance agents, brokers, and service	6	22	0.8	12	40	12,667	16,500	169	765	0.2
6500	Real estate	20	39	0.7	-	101	-	11,129	-	1,396	0.2
6510	Real estate operators and lessors	8	17	0.9	20	59	10,200	9,763	259	658	0.3
6530	Real estate agents and managers	6	16	0.6	10	37	10,000	12,757	112	538	0.1
6700	Holding and other investment offices	3	3	0.5	11	-	30,909	-	328	-	-
BATH, VA											
60 –	**Finance, insurance, and real estate**	7	7	0.0	27	-	15,556	-	572	-	-
BEDFORD, VA											
60 –	**Finance, insurance, and real estate**	25	38	0.3	82	105	18,195	19,238	1,818	2,391	0.0
6000	Depository institutions	3	5	0.2	11	19	16,364	18,105	193	343	0.0
6400	Insurance agents, brokers, and service	5	5	0.2	12	19	15,333	13,895	177	274	0.1
6500	Real estate	12	21	0.4	49	51	18,041	20,078	1,083	1,217	0.2
6510	Real estate operators and lessors	2	5	0.3	-	5	-	12,000	-	76	0.0
6530	Real estate agents and managers	10	11	0.4	-	24	-	18,167	-	523	0.1
BLAND, VA											
60 –	**Finance, insurance, and real estate**	5	4	0.0	-	-	-	-	-	-	-
BOTETOURT, VA											
60 –	**Finance, insurance, and real estate**	31	35	0.2	134	154	17,015	17,506	2,276	2,630	0.1
6000	Depository institutions	10	10	0.3	91	100	18,945	17,400	1,727	1,736	0.1
6020	Commercial banks	10	10	0.5	91	100	18,945	17,400	1,727	1,736	0.2
6400	Insurance agents, brokers, and service	5	7	0.3	10	11	14,000	7,273	141	86	0.0
6510	Real estate operators and lessors	3	3	0.2	6	7	9,333	14,286	88	92	0.0
6530	Real estate agents and managers	4	6	0.2	7	-	19,429	-	59	-	-
BRUNSWICK, VA											
60 –	**Finance, insurance, and real estate**	18	19	0.1	86	101	17,163	16,317	1,477	1,759	0.0
6400	Insurance agents, brokers, and service	6	6	0.2	24	23	19,167	17,043	443	519	0.1
6500	Real estate	4	5	0.1	14	21	12,286	8,000	164	206	0.0
BUCHANAN, VA											
60 –	**Finance, insurance, and real estate**	32	30	0.2	210	208	17,714	18,538	3,997	4,028	0.1
6000	Depository institutions	14	13	0.4	161	157	18,186	19,185	3,139	3,166	0.2
6020	Commercial banks	14	13	0.6	161	157	18,186	19,185	3,139	3,166	0.3
6400	Insurance agents, brokers, and service	10	8	0.3	25	-	17,280	-	480	-	-

Source: County Business Patterns, 1992/93, CBP-92/93-1, U.S. Department of Commerce, Washington, D.C., April 1995. SIC categories for which data were suppressed or not available for both 1992 and 1993 are *not* displayed. The employment columns represent mid-March employment in the year. Pay per employee is calculated by dividing 1st Quarter payroll, annualized, by mid-March employment. The columns headed "% State" show the county's percentage of the state total for the SIC in 1993; for example, 0.9% for SIC 6030 means that the county had 0.9 percent of the state's total establishments (or payroll) in SIC 6030 in 1993. A dash (-) is used to indicate that data are not available or cannot be calculated; *nec* means not elsewhere classified.

Continued on next page.

SIC	Industry	No. Establishments			Employment		Pay / Employee		Annual Payroll ($ 000)		
		1992	1993	% State	1992	1993	1992	1993	1992	1993	% State
BUCHANAN, VA - [continued]											
6500	Real estate	7	7	0.1	-	25	-	14,080	-	353	0.0
6510	Real estate operators and lessors	3	4	0.2	-	10	-	4,000	-	24	0.0
6530	Real estate agents and managers	3	2	0.1	11	-	22,909	-	273	-	-
BUCKINGHAM, VA											
60 –	**Finance, insurance, and real estate**	12	13	0.1	-	-	-	-	-	-	-
6400	Insurance agents, brokers, and service	5	5	0.2	5	6	10,400	10,667	56	68	0.0
6500	Real estate	3	4	0.1	8	15	7,000	8,000	50	117	0.0
CAMPBELL, VA											
60 –	**Finance, insurance, and real estate**	45	63	0.4	174	216	17,540	18,463	3,323	4,336	0.1
6000	Depository institutions	13	15	0.5	110	124	21,636	21,387	2,531	2,831	0.2
6020	Commercial banks	9	9	0.4	99	100	21,939	21,720	2,342	2,373	0.2
6100	Nondepository institutions	4	5	0.5	9	-	16,444	-	173	-	-
6140	Personal credit institutions	4	4	1.0	9	-	16,444	-	173	-	-
6400	Insurance agents, brokers, and service	13	19	0.7	29	-	10,483	-	338	-	-
6500	Real estate	13	22	0.4	-	42	-	14,571	-	729	0.1
6510	Real estate operators and lessors	3	8	0.4	3	-	5,333	-	20	-	-
6530	Real estate agents and managers	8	12	0.4	12	28	11,000	14,000	183	492	0.1
CAROLINE, VA											
60 –	**Finance, insurance, and real estate**	22	25	0.2	159	151	16,151	19,338	2,906	2,783	0.1
6400	Insurance agents, brokers, and service	4	5	0.2	14	18	20,000	18,667	297	354	0.1
6500	Real estate	8	9	0.2	51	26	11,529	13,077	665	351	0.0
6510	Real estate operators and lessors	1	3	0.2	-	5	-	17,600	-	48	0.0
CARROLL, VA											
60 –	**Finance, insurance, and real estate**	17	22	0.1	-	106	-	17,057	-	1,737	0.0
6000	Depository institutions	4	4	0.1	59	62	15,729	18,452	908	1,050	0.1
6020	Commercial banks	4	4	0.2	59	62	15,729	18,452	908	1,050	0.1
6400	Insurance agents, brokers, and service	8	12	0.4	-	34	-	15,176	-	523	0.1
6500	Real estate	4	5	0.1	4	-	9,000	-	71	-	-
CHARLOTTE, VA											
60 –	**Finance, insurance, and real estate**	13	12	0.1	72	72	17,889	18,167	1,308	1,383	0.0
6000	Depository institutions	6	6	0.2	56	55	19,357	19,927	1,092	1,120	0.1
6020	Commercial banks	6	6	0.3	56	55	19,357	19,927	1,092	1,120	0.1
CHESTERFIELD, VA											
60 –	**Finance, insurance, and real estate**	437	465	3.2	4,609	4,433	26,540	26,055	116,202	121,981	2.5
6000	Depository institutions	87	82	2.7	1,189	1,021	21,346	19,346	22,901	20,673	1.6
6020	Commercial banks	58	57	2.6	518	498	17,544	19,253	9,400	9,213	0.9
6030	Savings institutions	19	10	2.6	558	358	25,068	20,749	11,110	8,604	6.3
6100	Nondepository institutions	32	44	4.1	196	301	30,327	20,930	6,111	8,485	1.4
6160	Mortgage bankers and brokers	13	21	3.7	80	141	38,450	26,979	3,206	6,104	2.0
6200	Security and commodity brokers	13	16	2.3	30	48	78,800	67,917	3,000	3,985	1.0
6210	Security brokers and dealers	6	6	1.7	11	13	38,182	47,385	459	704	0.3
6280	Security and commodity services	7	10	3.0	19	35	102,316	75,543	2,541	3,281	-
6300	Insurance carriers	64	53	4.4	1,972	1,939	32,247	32,485	56,940	61,685	6.7
6330	Fire, marine, and casualty insurance	29	26	4.8	578	579	29,723	25,603	15,589	14,871	3.6
6400	Insurance agents, brokers, and service	96	119	4.3	341	430	28,293	23,600	10,086	11,240	2.9
6500	Real estate	137	144	2.7	834	668	16,134	17,419	15,222	14,307	1.8
6510	Real estate operators and lessors	34	43	2.2	123	228	16,520	15,614	2,285	3,669	1.9
6530	Real estate agents and managers	59	78	2.7	257	300	17,743	18,840	5,662	7,590	1.4
6540	Title abstract offices	6	7	6.4	16	32	25,500	21,000	487	797	4.3

Source: County Business Patterns, 1992/93, CBP-92/93-1, U.S. Department of Commerce, Washington, D.C., April 1995. SIC categories for which data were suppressed or not available for both 1992 and 1993 are *not* displayed. The employment columns represent mid-March employment in the year. Pay per employee is calculated by dividing 1st Quarter payroll, annualized, by mid-March employment. The columns headed "% State" show the county's percentage of the state total for the SIC in 1993; for example, 0.9% for SIC 6030 means that the county had 0.9 percent of the state's total establishments (or payroll) in SIC 6030 in 1993. A dash (-) is used to indicate that data are not available or cannot be calculated; *nec* means not elsewhere classified.

Continued on next page.

SIC	Industry	No. Establishments			Employment		Pay / Employee		Annual Payroll ($ 000)		
		1992	1993	% State	1992	1993	1992	1993	1992	1993	% State
CHESTERFIELD, VA - [continued]											
6552	Subdividers and developers, n.e.c.	11	8	2.9	285	20	13,726	19,000	4,648	736	1.5
6553	Cemetery subdividers and developers	5	5	3.5	78	65	16,513	16,062	1,205	1,112	5.3
6700	Holding and other investment offices	8	7	1.3	47	26	41,277	54,615	1,942	1,606	0.5
CLARKE, VA											
60 –	**Finance, insurance, and real estate**	20	19	0.1	107	100	26,019	26,040	2,883	2,974	0.1
6400	Insurance agents, brokers, and service	3	2	0.1	10	-	27,200	-	256	-	-
6500	Real estate	9	8	0.1	23	15	14,435	13,867	326	230	0.0
6510	Real estate operators and lessors	4	2	0.1	4	-	5,000	-	23	-	-
6530	Real estate agents and managers	3	5	0.2	-	8	-	20,000	-	147	0.0
CRAIG, VA											
60 –	**Finance, insurance, and real estate**	5	4	0.0	-	-	-	-	-	-	-
6500	Real estate	3	2	0.0	1	-	4,000	-	7	-	-
CULPEPER, VA											
60 –	**Finance, insurance, and real estate**	58	57	0.4	499	515	35,423	35,456	17,659	19,401	0.4
6000	Depository institutions	10	10	0.3	264	275	46,136	44,625	12,190	13,471	1.0
6100	Nondepository institutions	7	7	0.6	52	50	26,923	31,200	1,457	1,626	0.3
6160	Mortgage bankers and brokers	3	3	0.5	6	-	42,667	-	265	-	-
6400	Insurance agents, brokers, and service	10	11	0.4	38	45	22,105	24,000	1,015	1,115	0.3
6500	Real estate	23	21	0.4	56	53	13,000	12,226	820	838	0.1
6510	Real estate operators and lessors	8	6	0.3	13	-	9,846	-	148	-	-
6530	Real estate agents and managers	11	14	0.5	28	41	14,143	12,585	454	715	0.1
CUMBERLAND, VA											
60 –	**Finance, insurance, and real estate**	8	7	0.0	-	25	-	17,760	-	595	0.0
DICKENSON, VA											
60 –	**Finance, insurance, and real estate**	13	11	0.1	94	88	15,021	16,864	1,574	1,469	0.0
6000	Depository institutions	5	5	0.2	72	73	15,556	17,863	1,247	1,278	0.1
6020	Commercial banks	5	5	0.2	72	73	15,556	17,863	1,247	1,278	0.1
DINWIDDIE, VA											
60 –	**Finance, insurance, and real estate**	13	17	0.1	82	105	20,732	19,238	1,882	2,137	0.0
6000	Depository institutions	5	5	0.2	59	70	23,593	22,743	1,494	1,672	0.1
6400	Insurance agents, brokers, and service	4	4	0.1	12	15	14,667	13,333	232	232	0.1
6500	Real estate	2	5	0.1	-	10	-	9,200	-	90	0.0
ESSEX, VA											
60 –	**Finance, insurance, and real estate**	22	22	0.1	153	171	19,765	19,018	3,536	3,374	0.1
6000	Depository institutions	7	6	0.2	68	84	16,412	16,952	1,591	1,457	0.1
6020	Commercial banks	7	6	0.3	68	84	16,412	16,952	1,591	1,457	0.1
6400	Insurance agents, brokers, and service	4	4	0.1	-	18	-	31,778	-	585	0.2
6500	Real estate	6	7	0.1	7	11	14,857	13,818	109	157	0.0
FAIRFAX, VA											
60 –	**Finance, insurance, and real estate**	2,271	2,451	16.7	32,100	33,164	35,565	37,301	1,134,587	1,299,277	26.2
6000	Depository institutions	379	357	11.9	7,689	7,493	24,395	27,144	188,818	202,896	15.3
6020	Commercial banks	233	239	11.0	3,930	4,060	25,215	27,090	94,996	106,669	11.0
6030	Savings institutions	108	75	19.4	-	1,277	-	28,066	-	32,290	23.8
6060	Credit unions	29	35	9.4	-	2,112	-	26,515	-	61,987	43.3
6100	Nondepository institutions	240	266	24.6	7,013	7,480	43,490	47,900	301,658	371,487	61.2
6140	Personal credit institutions	49	36	9.4	341	-	29,853	-	10,942	-	-
6150	Business credit institutions	22	21	24.1	753	445	35,501	44,872	29,017	23,608	-
6160	Mortgage bankers and brokers	161	197	34.7	4,858	2,910	49,865	35,162	232,961	146,073	48.8
6200	Security and commodity brokers	118	160	23.4	848	1,072	54,698	53,996	53,042	72,449	18.8
6210	Security brokers and dealers	47	63	18.2	530	595	61,411	62,118	31,645	41,231	14.7

Source: County Business Patterns, 1992/93, CBP-92/93-1, U.S. Department of Commerce, Washington, D.C., April 1995. SIC categories for which data were suppressed or not available for both 1992 and 1993 are not displayed. The employment columns represent mid-March employment in the year. Pay per employee is calculated by dividing 1st Quarter payroll, annualized, by mid-March employment. The columns headed "% State" show the county's percentage of the state total for the SIC in 1993; for example, 0.9% for SIC 6030 means that the county had 0.9 percent of the state's total establishments (or payroll) in SIC 6030 in 1993. A dash (-) is used to indicate that data are not available or cannot be calculated; nec means not elsewhere classified.

Continued on next page.

SIC	Industry	No. Establishments			Employment		Pay / Employee		Annual Payroll ($ 000)		
		1992	1993	% State	1992	1993	1992	1993	1992	1993	% State
FAIRFAX, VA - [continued]											
6220	Commodity contracts brokers, dealers	3	3	*42.9*	3	1	53,333	48,000	141	42	-
6280	Security and commodity services	68	94	*28.7*	315	476	43,416	43,857	21,256	31,176	-
6300	Insurance carriers	202	176	*14.7*	2,587	3,488	36,753	34,026	96,417	129,062	*14.1*
6310	Life insurance	41	32	*10.3*	1,024	942	36,160	38,102	33,253	34,764	*12.5*
6330	Fire, marine, and casualty insurance	83	78	*14.4*	835	1,318	38,189	32,923	34,589	48,480	*11.9*
6350	Surety insurance	3	3	*27.3*	46	-	70,609	-	3,782	-	-
6360	Title insurance	30	17	*19.3*	122	55	33,148	29,309	4,000	2,274	*12.7*
6370	Pension, health, and welfare funds	31	32	*20.5*	133	170	37,594	21,153	5,412	4,405	*33.4*
6400	Insurance agents, brokers, and service	315	372	*13.4*	1,642	1,841	30,677	32,445	52,016	66,316	*17.2*
6500	Real estate	900	982	*18.3*	8,585	8,237	25,232	23,872	216,621	223,980	*27.7*
6510	Real estate operators and lessors	215	220	*11.4*	1,803	1,247	20,424	20,071	37,574	29,778	*15.6*
6530	Real estate agents and managers	500	654	*22.9*	5,617	6,444	24,319	24,304	143,107	174,500	*33.0*
6540	Title abstract offices	18	27	*24.5*	66	83	18,061	29,060	1,541	3,768	*20.5*
6552	Subdividers and developers, n.e.c.	58	58	*21.2*	658	414	43,818	27,768	21,321	14,352	*30.1*
6553	Cemetery subdividers and developers	6	6	*4.2*	105	-	21,943	-	2,121	-	-
6700	Holding and other investment offices	101	121	*22.2*	1,947	2,121	36,006	40,119	68,957	81,442	*24.1*
6710	Holding offices	30	42	*24.4*	1,455	1,592	38,719	44,111	54,747	64,595	*26.0*
6720	Investment offices	6	1	*8.3*	16	-	51,750	-	1,315	-	-
6732	Educational, religious, etc. trusts	30	32	*24.2*	319	297	19,737	20,539	6,554	6,949	*24.2*
6733	Trusts, n.e.c.	12	15	*14.3*	20	-	21,200	-	375	-	-
6794	Patent owners and lessors	3	5	*17.9*	-	68	-	35,824	-	3,010	*33.6*
6798	Real estate investment trusts	3	4	*30.8*	-	4	-	61,000	-	140	*2.5*
6799	Investors, n.e.c.	13	21	*27.3*	89	127	47,640	40,850	3,371	5,387	*13.6*
FAUQUIER, VA											
60 –	**Finance, insurance, and real estate**	100	108	*0.7*	727	774	22,212	21,142	15,218	18,050	*0.4*
6000	Depository institutions	22	21	*0.7*	429	438	23,077	21,763	8,672	10,197	*0.8*
6020	Commercial banks	15	15	*0.7*	287	301	21,477	20,797	4,854	6,615	*0.7*
6300	Insurance carriers	12	9	*0.8*	-	10	-	34,800	-	357	*0.0*
6370	Pension, health, and welfare funds	4	5	*3.2*	7	-	10,286	-	47	-	-
6400	Insurance agents, brokers, and service	19	22	*0.8*	71	79	20,282	23,190	1,573	1,957	*0.5*
6500	Real estate	36	46	*0.9*	83	208	13,783	12,962	1,287	3,392	*0.4*
6510	Real estate operators and lessors	7	11	*0.6*	21	113	10,286	9,876	235	1,357	*0.7*
6530	Real estate agents and managers	15	26	*0.9*	32	78	19,000	16,974	700	1,726	*0.3*
6540	Title abstract offices	2	3	*2.7*	-	5	-	20,800	-	142	*0.8*
6700	Holding and other investment offices	4	3	*0.5*	-	2	-	32,000	-	45	*0.0*
FLOYD, VA											
60 –	**Finance, insurance, and real estate**	10	10	*0.1*	68	67	16,176	18,746	1,161	1,286	*0.0*
FLUVANNA, VA											
60 –	**Finance, insurance, and real estate**	12	11	*0.1*	94	96	17,319	16,000	1,555	1,606	*0.0*
6500	Real estate	7	6	*0.1*	-	72	-	16,278	-	1,256	*0.2*
6530	Real estate agents and managers	6	4	*0.1*	71	-	18,310	-	1,192	-	-
FRANKLIN, VA											
60 –	**Finance, insurance, and real estate**	62	55	*0.4*	334	299	15,174	16,963	5,748	5,536	*0.1*
6000	Depository institutions	17	15	*0.5*	162	164	17,309	17,780	2,870	2,995	*0.2*
6020	Commercial banks	13	13	*0.6*	147	-	17,986	-	2,717	-	-
6140	Personal credit institutions	3	3	*0.8*	6	-	27,333	-	131	-	-
6400	Insurance agents, brokers, and service	12	15	*0.5*	39	44	18,051	18,000	640	787	*0.2*
6500	Real estate	26	19	*0.4*	116	77	10,862	12,779	1,957	1,452	*0.2*
6510	Real estate operators and lessors	6	5	*0.3*	10	6	8,800	9,333	80	113	*0.1*
6530	Real estate agents and managers	9	10	*0.3*	49	44	10,939	12,727	775	852	*0.2*

Source: County Business Patterns, 1992/93, CBP-92/93-1, U.S. Department of Commerce, Washington, D.C., April 1995. SIC categories for which data were suppressed or not available for both 1992 and 1993 are *not* displayed. The employment columns represent mid-March employment in the year. Pay per employee is calculated by dividing 1st Quarter payroll, annualized, by mid-March employment. The columns headed "% State" show the county's percentage of the state total for the SIC in 1993; for example, 0.9% for SIC 6030 means that the county had 0.9 percent of the state's total establishments (or payroll) in SIC 6030 in 1993. A dash (-) is used to indicate that data are not available or cannot be calculated; *nec* means not elsewhere classified.

SIC	Industry	No. Establishments			Employment		Pay / Employee		Annual Payroll ($ 000)		
		1992	1993	% State	1992	1993	1992	1993	1992	1993	% State
FREDERICK, VA											
60 –	**Finance, insurance, and real estate**	36	51	0.3	134	226	18,060	20,124	2,875	5,077	0.1
6000	Depository institutions	10	10	0.3	75	73	19,360	20,712	1,441	1,563	0.1
6020	Commercial banks	10	10	0.5	75	73	19,360	20,712	1,441	1,563	0.2
6370	Pension, health, and welfare funds	6	5	3.2	2	–	4,000	–	91	–	–
6400	Insurance agents, brokers, and service	4	13	0.5	4	46	14,000	20,609	106	1,127	0.3
6500	Real estate	10	20	0.4	46	71	17,826	18,141	1,156	1,670	0.2
6510	Real estate operators and lessors	3	9	0.5	–	50	–	19,440	–	1,298	0.7
6530	Real estate agents and managers	2	6	0.2	–	7	–	8,571	–	55	0.0
6700	Holding and other investment offices	4	2	0.4	6	–	11,333	–	68	–	–
6733	Trusts, n.e.c.	4	2	1.9	6	–	11,333	–	68	–	–
GILES, VA											
60 –	**Finance, insurance, and real estate**	19	19	0.1	98	99	15,184	16,242	1,485	1,510	0.0
6000	Depository institutions	8	8	0.3	71	70	17,634	18,457	1,232	1,203	0.1
6400	Insurance agents, brokers, and service	4	4	0.1	10	–	8,000	–	76	–	–
6500	Real estate	4	5	0.1	8	11	7,500	10,909	66	123	0.0
GLOUCESTER, VA											
60 –	**Finance, insurance, and real estate**	57	52	0.4	184	219	18,130	18,320	3,672	4,174	0.1
6000	Depository institutions	11	12	0.4	94	119	20,128	18,790	1,926	2,290	0.2
6400	Insurance agents, brokers, and service	9	10	0.4	35	34	18,743	21,059	731	787	0.2
6500	Real estate	29	21	0.4	40	52	12,100	12,077	683	749	0.1
6510	Real estate operators and lessors	10	6	0.3	12	13	11,333	11,692	194	174	0.1
6530	Real estate agents and managers	16	13	0.5	22	–	13,636	–	429	–	–
GOOCHLAND, VA											
60 –	**Finance, insurance, and real estate**	18	20	0.1	77	–	51,688	–	3,265	–	–
6400	Insurance agents, brokers, and service	4	4	0.1	7	9	21,714	20,889	209	227	0.1
6500	Real estate	8	11	0.2	27	–	12,593	–	341	–	–
6510	Real estate operators and lessors	3	3	0.2	6	4	14,667	13,000	87	55	0.0
6552	Subdividers and developers, n.e.c.	–	3	1.1	–	5	–	16,000	–	113	0.2
GRAYSON, VA											
60 –	**Finance, insurance, and real estate**	15	12	0.1	74	79	13,730	16,911	1,279	1,427	0.0
6400	Insurance agents, brokers, and service	5	5	0.2	12	–	11,000	–	153	–	–
6500	Real estate	3	1	0.0	4	–	7,000	–	35	–	–
GREENE, VA											
60 –	**Finance, insurance, and real estate**	10	9	0.1	36	40	12,333	13,100	458	480	0.0
6400	Insurance agents, brokers, and service	3	3	0.1	6	6	12,000	14,667	82	89	0.0
HALIFAX, VA											
60 –	**Finance, insurance, and real estate**	10	15	0.1	28	41	23,143	19,512	699	914	0.0
6400	Insurance agents, brokers, and service	2	5	0.2	–	10	–	16,000	–	212	0.1
6500	Real estate	4	5	0.1	3	11	17,333	10,909	72	146	0.0
6530	Real estate agents and managers	3	4	0.1	3	–	17,333	–	55	–	–
HANOVER, VA											
60 –	**Finance, insurance, and real estate**	128	135	0.9	879	964	22,125	22,116	21,263	22,162	0.4
6000	Depository institutions	27	28	0.9	419	426	16,544	18,113	7,159	7,618	0.6
6020	Commercial banks	24	24	1.1	405	408	16,444	18,059	6,943	7,282	0.7
6030	Savings institutions	3	3	0.8	14	–	19,429	–	216	–	–
6100	Nondepository institutions	10	12	1.1	71	135	28,958	26,489	2,461	3,309	0.5
6280	Security and commodity services	3	1	0.3	3	–	118,667	–	179	–	–
6300	Insurance carriers	13	11	0.9	67	74	31,463	26,216	3,357	1,963	0.2
6310	Life insurance	4	2	0.6	55	–	29,382	–	1,675	–	–
6400	Insurance agents, brokers, and service	24	26	0.9	180	169	27,844	27,669	4,988	5,301	1.4

Source: County Business Patterns, 1992/93, CBP-92/93-1, U.S. Department of Commerce, Washington, D.C., April 1995. SIC categories for which data were suppressed or not available for both 1992 and 1993 are *not* displayed. The employment columns represent mid-March employment in the year. Pay per employee is calculated by dividing 1st Quarter payroll, annualized, by mid-March employment. The columns headed "% State" show the county's percentage of the state total for the SIC in 1993; for example, 0.9% for SIC 6030 means that the county had 0.9 percent of the state's total establishments (or payroll) in SIC 6030 in 1993. A dash (-) is used to indicate that data are not available or cannot be calculated; *nec* means not elsewhere classified.

Continued on next page.

SIC	Industry	No. Establishments			Employment		Pay / Employee		Annual Payroll ($ 000)		
		1992	1993	% State	1992	1993	1992	1993	1992	1993	% State
HANOVER, VA - [continued]											
6500	Real estate	45	49	0.9	110	129	14,873	16,186	1,760	2,543	0.3
6510	Real estate operators and lessors	8	13	0.7	15	-	6,133	-	81	-	-
6530	Real estate agents and managers	29	34	1.2	64	94	18,188	18,511	1,248	2,174	0.4
HENRICO, VA											
60 –	**Finance, insurance, and real estate**	515	639	4.3	10,686	12,184	26,931	29,855	296,174	371,031	7.5
6000	Depository institutions	109	112	3.7	3,203	3,510	21,603	22,493	69,950	81,706	6.2
6020	Commercial banks	83	81	3.7	3,077	3,351	21,728	22,693	67,793	78,518	8.1
6030	Savings institutions	14	11	2.8	62	-	16,774	-	810	-	-
6060	Credit unions	12	18	4.8	64	105	20,312	18,095	1,347	2,300	1.6
6100	Nondepository institutions	33	43	4.0	282	409	29,674	34,963	10,515	13,838	2.3
6140	Personal credit institutions	12	13	3.4	69	76	28,696	20,895	2,742	1,872	3.0
6150	Business credit institutions	4	6	6.9	12	18	32,667	46,667	321	735	-
6160	Mortgage bankers and brokers	17	24	4.2	201	315	29,831	37,689	7,452	11,231	3.7
6200	Security and commodity brokers	17	29	4.2	96	268	85,000	86,358	9,086	30,586	7.9
6210	Security brokers and dealers	6	8	2.3	72	92	100,056	26,000	7,570	2,448	0.9
6280	Security and commodity services	11	21	6.4	24	176	39,833	117,909	1,516	28,138	-
6300	Insurance carriers	84	83	6.9	3,896	4,018	30,708	33,929	123,810	133,965	14.6
6310	Life insurance	22	22	7.1	1,004	1,145	30,155	31,043	34,141	34,102	12.3
6330	Fire, marine, and casualty insurance	38	38	7.0	-	1,383	-	34,753	-	49,409	12.1
6400	Insurance agents, brokers, and service	108	160	5.8	1,356	2,371	32,189	30,701	39,770	72,110	18.7
6500	Real estate	148	195	3.6	1,274	1,112	19,589	22,482	29,489	28,055	3.5
6510	Real estate operators and lessors	47	65	3.4	679	348	14,845	17,575	11,582	7,003	3.7
6530	Real estate agents and managers	78	103	3.6	484	594	24,281	23,481	14,475	16,261	3.1
6540	Title abstract offices	6	2	1.8	24	-	33,333	-	796	-	-
6552	Subdividers and developers, n.e.c.	6	17	6.2	-	108	-	33,444	-	3,366	7.1
6553	Cemetery subdividers and developers	3	5	3.5	-	52	-	20,385	-	1,149	5.5
6732	Educational, religious, etc. trusts	2	3	2.3	-	3	-	34,667	-	104	0.4
6733	Trusts, n.e.c.	5	5	4.8	-	9	-	11,111	-	105	1.7
HENRY, VA											
60 –	**Finance, insurance, and real estate**	48	63	0.4	336	389	15,143	14,797	5,328	6,151	0.1
6000	Depository institutions	14	14	0.5	207	192	17,855	16,979	3,764	3,338	0.3
6100	Nondepository institutions	5	4	0.4	17	-	18,588	-	318	-	-
6400	Insurance agents, brokers, and service	15	25	0.9	41	86	16,195	16,977	703	1,545	0.4
6500	Real estate	9	15	0.3	18	32	6,667	12,250	197	483	0.1
6510	Real estate operators and lessors	3	8	0.4	3	-	8,000	-	39	-	-
6530	Real estate agents and managers	3	6	0.2	8	12	7,000	14,333	68	193	0.0
6700	Holding and other investment offices	3	3	0.5	-	44	-	4,909	-	235	0.1
HIGHLAND, VA											
60 –	**Finance, insurance, and real estate**	6	6	0.0	27	-	17,037	-	526	-	-
ISLE OF WIGHT, VA											
60 –	**Finance, insurance, and real estate**	32	33	0.2	141	150	18,610	19,707	2,932	2,948	0.1
6000	Depository institutions	8	9	0.3	85	86	21,788	22,884	1,854	1,853	0.1
6400	Insurance agents, brokers, and service	7	7	0.3	21	22	15,619	19,455	385	424	0.1
6500	Real estate	11	13	0.2	25	27	11,360	12,741	518	453	0.1
6510	Real estate operators and lessors	5	6	0.3	11	11	9,091	13,091	292	191	0.1
JAMES CITY, VA											
60 –	**Finance, insurance, and real estate**	19	51	0.3	600	256	15,993	27,406	11,127	8,150	0.2
6200	Security and commodity brokers	2	3	0.4	-	3	-	32,000	-	116	0.0
6300	Insurance carriers	5	6	0.5	8	13	38,000	32,615	363	446	0.0
6400	Insurance agents, brokers, and service	1	10	0.4	-	14	-	16,000	-	234	0.1

Source: County Business Patterns, 1992/93, CBP-92/93-1, U.S. Department of Commerce, Washington, D.C., April 1995. SIC categories for which data were suppressed or not available for both 1992 and 1993 are not displayed. The employment columns represent mid-March employment in the year. Pay per employee is calculated by dividing 1st Quarter payroll, annualized, by mid-March employment. The columns headed "% State" show the county's percentage of the state total for the SIC in 1993; for example, 0.9% for SIC 6030 means that the county had 0.9 percent of the state's total establishments (or payroll) in SIC 6030 in 1993. A dash (-) is used to indicate that data are not available or cannot be calculated; nec means not elsewhere classified.

Continued on next page.

SIC	Industry	No. Establishments			Employment		Pay / Employee		Annual Payroll ($ 000)		
		1992	1993	% State	1992	1993	1992	1993	1992	1993	% State
FALLS CHURCH, VA - [continued]											
6100	Nondepository institutions	5	3	0.3	28	29	31,571	44,552	1,130	1,518	0.3
6160	Mortgage bankers and brokers	4	3	0.5	-	29	-	44,552	-	1,518	0.5
6200	Security and commodity brokers	9	7	1.0	20	13	27,800	39,077	473	1,098	0.3
6300	Insurance carriers	7	5	0.4	-	10	-	27,600	-	323	0.0
6400	Insurance agents, brokers, and service	9	13	0.5	50	60	25,920	26,133	1,400	1,664	0.4
6500	Real estate	38	28	0.5	234	198	19,897	19,939	4,724	4,611	0.6
6510	Real estate operators and lessors	13	10	0.5	74	68	20,595	19,118	1,562	1,462	0.8
6530	Real estate agents and managers	17	16	0.6	49	-	24,571	-	1,425	-	-
FRANKLIN, VA											
60 –	**Finance, insurance, and real estate**	32	19	0.1	148	128	20,108	22,969	3,048	2,951	0.1
6000	Depository institutions	8	7	0.2	70	78	19,657	19,231	1,348	1,486	0.1
6020	Commercial banks	7	7	0.3	-	78	-	19,231	-	1,486	0.2
6400	Insurance agents, brokers, and service	5	3	0.1	38	-	23,684	-	886	-	-
6500	Real estate	13	6	0.1	25	9	8,480	8,889	265	96	0.0
6510	Real estate operators and lessors	7	5	0.3	11	-	6,909	-	82	-	-
FREDERICKSBURG, VA											
60 –	**Finance, insurance, and real estate**	198	142	1.0	1,208	991	24,050	24,791	30,184	26,089	0.5
6000	Depository institutions	40	30	1.0	448	356	23,768	23,742	10,272	8,729	0.7
6020	Commercial banks	31	26	1.2	367	-	20,676	-	7,795	-	-
6100	Nondepository institutions	16	13	1.2	83	85	28,627	23,435	2,781	2,276	0.4
6140	Personal credit institutions	9	8	2.1	43	59	25,116	14,712	1,282	1,128	1.8
6160	Mortgage bankers and brokers	6	5	0.9	31	26	36,000	43,231	1,308	1,148	0.4
6300	Insurance carriers	26	17	1.4	146	147	26,795	27,510	4,104	3,984	0.4
6310	Life insurance	6	6	1.9	121	123	24,099	26,407	2,939	3,105	1.1
6370	Pension, health, and welfare funds	3	1	0.6	2	-	12,000	-	130	-	-
6400	Insurance agents, brokers, and service	28	26	0.9	129	117	22,326	23,692	2,862	2,969	0.8
6500	Real estate	78	49	0.9	337	208	19,039	18,673	6,909	4,211	0.5
6510	Real estate operators and lessors	21	15	0.8	118	39	18,068	15,179	2,214	675	0.4
6530	Real estate agents and managers	33	23	0.8	96	78	17,750	15,641	1,620	1,382	0.3
GALAX, VA											
60 –	**Finance, insurance, and real estate**	29	24	0.2	120	112	19,267	21,464	2,405	2,501	0.1
6000	Depository institutions	8	8	0.3	73	78	17,699	20,256	1,331	1,465	0.1
6400	Insurance agents, brokers, and service	9	6	0.2	19	14	10,947	12,571	227	222	0.1
6500	Real estate	5	4	0.1	8	3	18,000	4,000	182	190	0.0
HAMPTON, VA											
60 –	**Finance, insurance, and real estate**	206	211	1.4	2,661	2,925	16,663	16,319	48,175	49,823	1.0
6000	Depository institutions	51	52	1.7	715	789	19,474	20,046	14,578	16,448	1.2
6020	Commercial banks	35	33	1.5	413	428	19,874	21,467	8,667	9,389	1.0
6060	Credit unions	8	10	2.7	270	317	19,541	19,192	5,423	6,511	4.5
6100	Nondepository institutions	20	19	1.8	351	376	20,160	20,181	7,383	6,886	1.1
6140	Personal credit institutions	16	12	3.1	-	71	-	16,282	-	1,051	1.7
6200	Security and commodity brokers	6	10	1.5	39	43	55,487	56,837	2,131	2,383	0.6
6210	Security brokers and dealers	6	6	1.7	39	41	55,487	59,415	2,131	2,355	0.8
6280	Security and commodity services	-	4	1.2	-	2	-	4,000	-	28	-
6300	Insurance carriers	16	15	1.3	132	103	29,667	33,126	4,123	2,848	0.3
6310	Life insurance	4	2	0.6	73	-	26,247	-	1,893	-	-
6400	Insurance agents, brokers, and service	28	30	1.1	93	104	19,699	19,077	1,845	2,114	0.5
6500	Real estate	79	78	1.5	1,318	1,471	11,554	10,646	17,728	18,198	2.2
6510	Real estate operators and lessors	36	31	1.6	212	194	13,340	11,464	3,104	2,373	1.2
6530	Real estate agents and managers	33	43	1.5	1,054	1,238	10,824	10,223	13,539	15,016	2.8
6700	Holding and other investment offices	6	7	1.3	13	39	15,385	21,231	387	946	0.3
6710	Holding offices	2	3	1.7	-	29	-	24,138	-	835	0.3

Source: County Business Patterns, 1992/93, CBP-92/93-1, U.S. Department of Commerce, Washington, D.C., April 1995. SIC categories for which data were suppressed or not available for both 1992 and 1993 are *not* displayed. The employment columns represent mid-March employment in the year. Pay per employee is calculated by dividing 1st Quarter payroll, annualized, by mid-March employment. The columns headed "% State" show the county's percentage of the state total for the SIC in 1993; for example, 0.9% for SIC 6030 means that the county had 0.9 percent of the state's total establishments (or payroll) in SIC 6030 in 1993. A dash (-) is used to indicate that data are not available or cannot be calculated; *nec* means not elsewhere classified.

SIC	Industry	No. Establishments			Employment		Pay / Employee		Annual Payroll ($ 000)		
		1992	1993	% State	1992	1993	1992	1993	1992	1993	% State
HARRISONBURG, VA											
60 –	**Finance, insurance, and real estate**	138	96	0.7	1,028	621	19,451	25,456	22,342	16,282	0.3
6000	Depository institutions	35	32	1.1	341	329	21,150	22,991	7,549	7,227	0.5
6020	Commercial banks	30	30	1.4	304	-	21,263	-	6,800	-	-
6100	Nondepository institutions	11	9	0.8	44	32	28,818	36,250	1,530	1,423	0.2
6160	Mortgage bankers and brokers	5	7	1.2	21	-	33,905	-	952	-	-
6200	Security and commodity brokers	9	7	1.0	29	30	58,759	79,333	2,196	2,860	0.7
6280	Security and commodity services	5	2	0.6	8	-	14,000	-	141	-	-
6300	Insurance carriers	9	6	0.5	84	-	21,190	-	2,004	-	-
6400	Insurance agents, brokers, and service	23	16	0.6	129	37	22,295	20,865	3,417	818	0.2
6500	Real estate	43	23	0.4	356	87	12,416	16,138	4,834	1,447	0.2
6510	Real estate operators and lessors	21	8	0.4	280	-	11,886	-	3,458	-	-
6530	Real estate agents and managers	17	12	0.4	64	44	15,812	15,818	1,282	689	0.1
6700	Holding and other investment offices	8	3	0.5	45	-	16,356	-	812	-	-
HOPEWELL, VA											
60 –	**Finance, insurance, and real estate**	41	42	0.3	214	200	20,523	24,980	4,419	4,354	0.1
6000	Depository institutions	8	9	0.3	106	95	18,264	19,495	1,867	1,853	0.1
6020	Commercial banks	4	5	0.2	46	47	19,478	21,106	940	966	0.1
6400	Insurance agents, brokers, and service	9	10	0.4	43	-	28,651	-	1,092	-	-
6500	Real estate	16	17	0.3	50	58	14,480	11,862	911	898	0.1
6510	Real estate operators and lessors	6	11	0.6	23	38	12,522	10,947	301	441	0.2
6530	Real estate agents and managers	8	6	0.2	20	20	16,600	13,600	335	457	0.1
LEXINGTON, VA											
60 –	**Finance, insurance, and real estate**	50	50	0.3	211	190	20,209	19,811	4,311	3,797	0.1
6000	Depository institutions	9	9	0.3	72	78	20,889	21,641	1,528	1,678	0.1
6020	Commercial banks	8	9	0.4	-	78	-	21,641	-	1,678	0.2
6200	Security and commodity brokers	4	4	0.6	12	13	47,667	63,077	497	760	0.2
6210	Security brokers and dealers	4	4	1.2	12	13	47,667	63,077	497	760	0.3
6300	Insurance carriers	4	3	0.3	-	12	-	7,000	-	78	0.0
6400	Insurance agents, brokers, and service	8	10	0.4	27	31	17,926	17,032	510	543	0.1
6500	Real estate	19	20	0.4	39	45	9,231	10,667	459	566	0.1
6510	Real estate operators and lessors	13	13	0.7	32	35	8,250	10,400	312	372	0.2
6530	Real estate agents and managers	3	7	0.2	5	10	15,200	11,600	105	194	0.0
LYNCHBURG, VA											
60 –	**Finance, insurance, and real estate**	254	240	1.6	3,298	2,626	29,235	28,369	97,613	81,334	1.6
6000	Depository institutions	69	63	2.1	1,068	1,036	26,202	29,625	27,690	30,342	2.3
6020	Commercial banks	34	35	1.6	825	813	27,704	31,951	22,752	25,389	2.6
6030	Savings institutions	19	11	2.8	176	154	22,000	23,039	3,645	3,726	2.7
6060	Credit unions	16	17	4.6	67	69	18,746	16,928	1,293	1,227	0.9
6100	Nondepository institutions	16	10	0.9	80	58	22,550	18,000	1,864	1,194	0.2
6140	Personal credit institutions	11	5	1.3	42	-	17,619	-	756	-	-
6160	Mortgage bankers and brokers	4	4	0.7	-	17	-	26,353	-	599	0.2
6200	Security and commodity brokers	11	15	2.2	97	126	59,794	51,778	5,885	8,903	2.3
6210	Security brokers and dealers	6	8	2.3	70	91	55,943	49,890	3,505	5,689	2.0
6280	Security and commodity services	5	7	2.1	27	35	69,778	56,686	2,380	3,214	-
6300	Insurance carriers	34	26	2.2	1,582	947	31,960	27,970	51,279	30,480	3.3
6310	Life insurance	10	9	2.9	917	893	32,345	27,413	28,469	28,393	10.2
6330	Fire, marine, and casualty insurance	17	13	2.4	-	36	-	36,889	-	1,363	0.3
6400	Insurance agents, brokers, and service	44	45	1.6	201	206	23,741	23,262	4,997	5,348	1.4
6500	Real estate	69	73	1.4	186	239	16,344	16,820	3,257	4,431	0.5
6510	Real estate operators and lessors	23	31	1.6	59	92	11,458	11,957	682	1,134	0.6
6530	Real estate agents and managers	32	32	1.1	100	107	18,840	18,617	1,995	2,416	0.5
6552	Subdividers and developers, n.e.c.	3	3	1.1	-	7	-	10,286	-	100	0.2

Source: County Business Patterns, 1992/93, CBP-92/93-1, U.S. Department of Commerce, Washington, D.C., April 1995. SIC categories for which data were suppressed or not available for both 1992 and 1993 are *not* displayed. The employment columns represent mid-March employment in the year. Pay per employee is calculated by dividing 1st Quarter payroll, annualized, by mid-March employment. The columns headed "% State" show the county's percentage of the state total for the SIC in 1993; for example, 0.9% for SIC 6030 means that the county had 0.9 percent of the state's total establishments (or payroll) in SIC 6030 in 1993. A dash (-) is used to indicate that data are not available or cannot be calculated; *nec* means not elsewhere classified.

Continued on next page.

SIC	Industry	No. Establishments			Employment		Pay / Employee		Annual Payroll ($ 000)		
		1992	1993	% State	1992	1993	1992	1993	1992	1993	% State
LYNCHBURG, VA - [continued]											
6553	Cemetery subdividers and developers	3	5	3.5	-	31	-	14,065	-	606	2.9
6700	Holding and other investment offices	11	8	1.5	84	14	29,238	66,857	2,641	636	0.2
6733	Trusts, n.e.c.	5	5	4.8	-	10	-	16,000		112	1.8
MANASSAS, VA											
60 -	**Finance, insurance, and real estate**	143	130	0.9	911	830	27,082	24,622	23,997	21,964	0.4
6000	Depository institutions	30	28	0.9	419	349	24,229	22,980	9,163	8,309	0.6
6020	Commercial banks	16	17	0.8	193	211	22,756	22,483	4,210	4,707	0.5
6030	Savings institutions	9	7	1.8	158	129	27,722	23,938	3,488	2,981	2.2
6100	Nondepository institutions	15	9	0.8	100	62	42,120	30,065	4,731	2,684	0.4
6160	Mortgage bankers and brokers	6	4	0.7	58	34	44,414	25,882	3,063	1,651	0.6
6330	Fire, marine, and casualty insurance	5	6	1.1	-	23	-	40,348	-	1,402	0.3
6400	Insurance agents, brokers, and service	31	34	1.2	117	113	25,812	26,478	3,142	2,968	0.8
6500	Real estate	49	45	0.8	207	209	23,266	21,569	4,537	4,619	0.6
6510	Real estate operators and lessors	12	11	0.6	93	87	17,075	15,954	1,614	1,622	0.9
6530	Real estate agents and managers	28	26	0.9	75	72	32,267	28,000	1,990	1,637	0.3
6540	Title abstract offices	7	8	7.3	28	50	21,286	22,080	692	1,360	7.4
MANASSAS PARK, VA											
60 -	**Finance, insurance, and real estate**	1	2	0.0	-	-	-	-	-	-	-
MARTINSVILLE, VA											
60 -	**Finance, insurance, and real estate**	92	73	0.5	675	643	23,597	23,073	16,263	15,003	0.3
6000	Depository institutions	19	18	0.6	430	450	22,214	22,276	9,475	9,514	0.7
6020	Commercial banks	13	12	0.6	389	401	22,098	22,324	8,467	8,424	0.9
6100	Nondepository institutions	8	8	0.7	51	-	25,176	-	1,417	-	-
6140	Personal credit institutions	4	4	1.0	18	33	27,333	14,424	504	382	0.6
6160	Mortgage bankers and brokers	4	4	0.7	33	-	24,000	-	913	-	-
6200	Security and commodity brokers	3	5	0.7	-	30	-	72,400	-	2,505	0.6
6370	Pension, health, and welfare funds	3	1	0.6	-	-	-	-	7	-	-
6400	Insurance agents, brokers, and service	23	12	0.4	55	19	19,273	19,579	1,265	520	0.1
6500	Real estate	27	20	0.4	86	60	11,442	9,933	1,049	706	0.1
6510	Real estate operators and lessors	12	11	0.6	27	29	13,481	10,621	481	368	0.2
6530	Real estate agents and managers	9	8	0.3	18	-	11,333	-	208	-	-
6700	Holding and other investment offices	7	6	1.1	14	16	24,571	17,250	545	363	0.1
NEWPORT NEWS, VA											
60 -	**Finance, insurance, and real estate**	431	442	3.0	2,720	2,966	22,638	23,338	64,856	75,466	1.5
6000	Depository institutions	74	75	2.5	861	917	21,180	22,233	18,434	20,557	1.6
6020	Commercial banks	43	45	2.1	403	454	22,184	23,639	8,834	10,467	1.1
6030	Savings institutions	13	12	3.1	200	200	21,800	22,040	4,673	4,741	3.5
6060	Credit unions	12	12	3.2	234	239	20,274	20,736	4,695	5,106	3.6
6090	Functions closely related to banking	6	6	8.5	24	24	8,000	12,167	232	243	-
6100	Nondepository institutions	41	39	3.6	260	299	32,046	33,311	10,597	14,500	2.4
6160	Mortgage bankers and brokers	22	21	3.7	176	205	37,341	39,356	8,689	11,499	3.8
6210	Security brokers and dealers	5	6	1.7	53	61	73,736	70,623	3,779	4,345	1.6
6300	Insurance carriers	42	34	2.8	314	307	28,051	28,339	9,466	9,137	1.0
6310	Life insurance	10	9	2.9	162	159	24,370	23,270	4,106	3,917	1.4
6330	Fire, marine, and casualty insurance	19	17	3.1	101	98	37,743	41,388	4,161	4,191	1.0
6400	Insurance agents, brokers, and service	58	78	2.8	191	268	24,063	24,254	4,256	6,411	1.7
6500	Real estate	203	200	3.7	1,022	1,095	17,092	17,450	18,082	20,229	2.5
6510	Real estate operators and lessors	110	105	5.4	515	538	14,128	12,669	7,692	7,238	3.8
6530	Real estate agents and managers	74	88	3.1	440	526	20,209	22,114	9,140	12,324	2.3
6540	Title abstract offices	3	3	2.7	17	-	23,059	-	399	-	-

Source: County Business Patterns, 1992/93, CBP-92/93-1, U.S. Department of Commerce, Washington, D.C., April 1995. SIC categories for which data were suppressed or not available for both 1992 and 1993 are *not* displayed. The employment columns represent mid-March employment in the year. Pay per employee is calculated by dividing 1st Quarter payroll, annualized, by mid-March employment. The columns headed "% State" show the county's percentage of the state total for the SIC in 1993; for example, 0.9% for SIC 6030 means that the county had 0.9 percent of the state's total establishments (or payroll) in SIC 6030 in 1993. A dash (-) is used to indicate that data are not available or cannot be calculated; *nec* means not elsewhere classified.

SIC	Industry	No. Establishments			Employment		Pay / Employee		Annual Payroll ($ 000)		
		1992	1993	% State	1992	1993	1992	1993	1992	1993	% State
NORFOLK, VA											
60 –	**Finance, insurance, and real estate**	618	580	*3.9*	9,695	8,549	24,057	25,871	244,326	239,887	*4.8*
6000	Depository institutions	120	124	*4.1*	4,095	3,945	22,909	24,801	99,105	102,503	*7.7*
6020	Commercial banks	67	73	*3.4*	3,473	3,200	23,277	26,362	86,333	88,195	*9.1*
6030	Savings institutions	20	14	*3.6*	381	456	24,483	20,553	9,104	9,883	*7.3*
6060	Credit unions	23	27	*7.2*	206	258	16,019	14,186	3,262	3,971	*2.8*
6090	Functions closely related to banking	10	10	*14.1*	35	31	9,829	14,452	406	454	*-*
6100	Nondepository institutions	38	31	*2.9*	384	393	24,542	23,562	11,175	11,702	*1.9*
6140	Personal credit institutions	23	17	*4.5*	306	281	24,314	21,922	7,427	6,328	*10.0*
6150	Business credit institutions	5	4	*4.6*	8	23	31,000	14,261	207	311	*-*
6160	Mortgage bankers and brokers	10	10	*1.8*	70	89	24,800	31,146	3,541	5,063	*1.7*
6200	Security and commodity brokers	27	30	*4.4*	339	372	69,735	73,796	26,346	29,309	*7.6*
6210	Security brokers and dealers	15	20	*5.8*	283	315	74,007	74,463	20,775	21,993	*7.9*
6280	Security and commodity services	9	10	*3.0*	46	57	51,217	70,105	5,319	7,316	*-*
6300	Insurance carriers	69	63	*5.3*	2,428	1,493	19,652	20,463	48,792	31,684	*3.5*
6310	Life insurance	30	24	*7.7*	972	759	19,695	20,643	17,845	16,365	*5.9*
6321	Accident and health insurance	4	6	*16.7*	421	-	11,392	-	4,989	-	*-*
6324	Hospital and medical service plans	4	2	*4.3*	64	-	19,000	-	1,181	-	*-*
6330	Fire, marine, and casualty insurance	13	13	*2.4*	783	207	25,492	31,845	22,045	6,329	*1.6*
6350	Surety insurance	3	-	*-*	29	-	7,448	-	194	-	*-*
6360	Title insurance	3	2	*2.3*	45	-	26,578	-	1,184	-	*-*
6370	Pension, health, and welfare funds	12	16	*10.3*	114	-	10,421	-	1,354	-	*-*
6400	Insurance agents, brokers, and service	86	86	*3.1*	469	570	27,412	26,568	13,886	15,714	*4.1*
6500	Real estate	248	219	*4.1*	1,696	1,576	17,830	17,538	31,665	32,665	*4.0*
6510	Real estate operators and lessors	123	110	*5.7*	617	596	12,629	11,725	8,146	7,940	*4.2*
6530	Real estate agents and managers	88	104	*3.6*	908	922	20,740	21,692	20,105	23,991	*4.5*
6710	Holding offices	10	7	*4.1*	166	87	52,964	53,701	8,216	7,319	*2.9*
6732	Educational, religious, etc. trusts	7	6	*4.5*	31	40	22,581	12,600	559	517	*1.8*
6733	Trusts, n.e.c.	8	7	*6.7*	51	12	14,431	10,333	829	509	*8.2*
NORTON, VA											
60 –	**Finance, insurance, and real estate**	25	23	*0.2*	129	-	19,845	-	2,636	-	*-*
6000	Depository institutions	6	6	*0.2*	60	65	19,533	17,969	1,130	1,034	*0.1*
6400	Insurance agents, brokers, and service	7	8	*0.3*	27	25	20,000	24,000	584	610	*0.2*
6510	Real estate operators and lessors	3	3	*0.2*	4	4	7,000	8,000	31	35	*0.0*
PETERSBURG, VA											
60 –	**Finance, insurance, and real estate**	94	75	*0.5*	719	684	23,076	21,105	18,562	17,427	*0.4*
6000	Depository institutions	29	27	*0.9*	366	392	21,311	18,327	9,430	9,462	*0.7*
6020	Commercial banks	16	16	*0.7*	160	167	25,225	20,024	4,222	3,494	*0.4*
6030	Savings institutions	9	8	*2.1*	194	-	18,660	-	5,072	-	*-*
6140	Personal credit institutions	8	5	*1.3*	36	-	22,111	-	851	-	*-*
6300	Insurance carriers	11	8	*0.7*	124	101	26,290	24,832	3,353	2,400	*0.3*
6310	Life insurance	7	4	*1.3*	118	97	26,542	24,948	3,218	2,293	*0.8*
6400	Insurance agents, brokers, and service	15	14	*0.5*	74	79	34,378	28,962	2,637	2,963	*0.8*
6500	Real estate	27	17	*0.3*	107	74	14,355	16,919	1,687	1,307	*0.2*
6510	Real estate operators and lessors	12	10	*0.5*	-	48	-	13,083	-	679	*0.4*
6530	Real estate agents and managers	13	7	*0.2*	32	26	20,125	24,000	678	628	*0.1*
POQUOSON, VA											
60 –	**Finance, insurance, and real estate**	6	10	*0.1*	31	52	20,258	24,231	666	1,216	*0.0*
6400	Insurance agents, brokers, and service	-	3	*0.1*	-	2	-	10,000	-	35	*0.0*
6500	Real estate	1	3	*0.1*	-	23	-	24,522	-	487	*0.1*
PORTSMOUTH, VA											
60 –	**Finance, insurance, and real estate**	149	150	*1.0*	964	1,080	17,589	18,274	18,335	20,127	*0.4*
6000	Depository institutions	49	48	*1.6*	433	463	16,139	18,143	7,172	8,505	*0.6*
6020	Commercial banks	26	25	*1.2*	326	322	16,417	19,975	5,612	6,350	*0.7*
6030	Savings institutions	8	5	*1.3*	45	40	16,533	13,400	604	572	*0.4*

Source: County Business Patterns, 1992/93, CBP-92/93-1, U.S. Department of Commerce, Washington, D.C., April 1995. SIC categories for which data were suppressed or not available for both 1992 and 1993 are *not* displayed. The employment columns represent mid-March employment in the year. Pay per employee is calculated by dividing 1st Quarter payroll, annualized, by mid-March employment. The columns headed "% State" show the county's percentage of the state total for the SIC in 1993; for example, 0.9% for SIC 6030 means that the county had 0.9 percent of the state's total establishments (or payroll) in SIC 6030 in 1993. A dash (-) is used to indicate that data are not available or cannot be calculated; *nec* means not elsewhere classified.

Continued on next page.

SIC	Industry	No. Establishments			Employment		Pay / Employee		Annual Payroll ($ 000)		
		1992	1993	% State	1992	1993	1992	1993	1992	1993	% State
PORTSMOUTH, VA - [continued]											
6060	Credit unions	11	14	3.8	50	88	14,880	14,318	757	1,377	1.0
6090	Functions closely related to banking	4	4	5.6	12	13	12,333	13,231	199	206	-
6100	Nondepository institutions	12	10	0.9	79	57	18,177	22,596	1,509	1,313	0.2
6160	Mortgage bankers and brokers	-	4	0.7	-	36	-	20,889		700	0.2
6300	Insurance carriers	10	10	0.8	98	184	32,041	22,391	3,553	3,975	0.4
6310	Life insurance	4	3	1.0	88	81	28,818	25,284	2,387	1,786	0.6
6400	Insurance agents, brokers, and service	23	22	0.8	86	83	15,209	15,373	1,686	1,381	0.4
6500	Real estate	49	54	1.0	240	267	14,550	14,921	3,785	4,388	0.5
6510	Real estate operators and lessors	24	27	1.4	166	197	13,494	13,523	2,366	2,952	1.5
6530	Real estate agents and managers	21	24	0.8	58	-	17,310	-	1,165	-	-
6732	Educational, religious, etc. trusts	3	3	2.3	5	-	16,000	-	92	-	-
RADFORD, VA											
60 –	**Finance, insurance, and real estate**	43	35	0.2	228	205	20,070	19,415	4,498	4,120	0.1
6000	Depository institutions	13	14	0.5	113	120	18,372	17,733	2,085	2,188	0.2
6020	Commercial banks	10	10	0.5	94	91	18,809	19,165	1,783	1,801	0.2
6100	Nondepository institutions	5	1	0.1	27	-	16,148	-	433	-	-
6400	Insurance agents, brokers, and service	6	4	0.1	32	26	18,500	23,846	615	605	0.2
6500	Real estate	15	12	0.2	40	45	15,700	13,511	731	723	0.1
6510	Real estate operators and lessors	8	7	0.4	-	18	-	13,556	-	309	0.2
6530	Real estate agents and managers	6	5	0.2	23	27	20,522	13,481	500	414	0.1
RICHMOND, VA											
60 –	**Finance, insurance, and real estate**	1,087	973	6.6	22,216	20,480	34,125	37,322	791,200	826,394	16.7
6000	Depository institutions	178	169	5.6	7,894	8,860	34,094	36,840	265,105	328,180	24.8
6020	Commercial banks	116	120	5.5	6,184	7,103	35,310	37,728	210,761	263,850	27.1
6030	Savings institutions	29	16	4.1	340	-	25,047	-	6,524	-	-
6060	Credit unions	23	23	6.2	212	245	22,000	19,837	4,697	5,200	3.6
6140	Personal credit institutions	42	23	6.0	326	155	26,110	25,368	8,652	3,991	6.3
6160	Mortgage bankers and brokers	55	55	9.7	1,409	811	19,089	31,818	31,325	30,461	10.2
6200	Security and commodity brokers	81	85	12.4	1,677	1,775	69,753	65,618	136,342	144,917	37.6
6210	Security brokers and dealers	41	52	15.0	1,360	1,573	69,785	66,083	106,644	133,402	47.6
6280	Security and commodity services	40	33	10.1	317	202	69,615	62,000	29,698	11,515	-
6300	Insurance carriers	137	126	10.5	5,024	3,553	31,822	30,108	157,169	111,752	12.2
6310	Life insurance	50	45	14.4	1,874	1,449	30,549	28,903	52,167	41,633	15.0
6321	Accident and health insurance	6	7	19.4	-	144	-	29,056	-	4,106	28.3
6324	Hospital and medical service plans	1	3	6.4	-	67	-	33,254	-	3,338	1.9
6330	Fire, marine, and casualty insurance	46	45	8.3	2,811	1,699	33,276	31,230	93,712	55,926	13.7
6350	Surety insurance	3	2	18.2	41	-	31,024	-	1,348	-	-
6360	Title insurance	7	8	9.1	86	98	29,209	35,020	2,849	3,470	19.4
6370	Pension, health, and welfare funds	24	16	10.3	79	-	20,152	-	2,468	-	-
6400	Insurance agents, brokers, and service	203	181	6.5	1,514	1,204	33,115	32,618	50,011	40,271	10.4
6500	Real estate	320	268	5.0	3,020	2,505	18,620	19,697	61,421	57,631	7.1
6510	Real estate operators and lessors	121	105	5.4	1,296	642	18,858	18,779	23,636	13,122	6.9
6530	Real estate agents and managers	127	135	4.7	1,368	1,454	18,842	20,765	30,403	35,185	6.6
6540	Title abstract offices	5	5	4.5	9	11	13,333	19,273	181	228	1.2
6552	Subdividers and developers, n.e.c.	24	15	5.5	122	241	18,393	16,946	2,657	4,651	9.7
6553	Cemetery subdividers and developers	8	5	3.5	102	157	14,824	17,809	1,740	4,314	20.6
6700	Holding and other investment offices	64	55	10.1	1,044	1,325	58,460	62,980	71,714	96,501	28.5
6710	Holding offices	27	18	10.5	889	960	64,103	77,633	67,613	88,290	35.6
6720	Investment offices	3	4	33.3	-	6	-	27,333	-	285	30.2
6732	Educational, religious, etc. trusts	15	11	8.3	48	47	17,500	29,021	878	1,412	4.9
6733	Trusts, n.e.c.	13	10	9.5	71	17	15,437	23,059	939	293	4.7
6799	Investors, n.e.c.	4	8	10.4	-	51	-	68,392	-	2,934	7.4

Source: County Business Patterns, 1992/93, CBP-92/93-1, U.S. Department of Commerce, Washington, D.C., April 1995. SIC categories for which data were suppressed or not available for both 1992 and 1993 are *not* displayed. The employment columns represent mid-March employment in the year. Pay per employee is calculated by dividing 1st Quarter payroll, annualized, by mid-March employment. The columns headed "% State" show the county's percentage of the state total for the SIC in 1993; for example, 0.9% for SIC 6030 means that the county had 0.9 percent of the state's total establishments (or payroll) in SIC 6030 in 1993. A dash (-) is used to indicate that data are not available or cannot be calculated; *nec* means not elsewhere classified.

SIC	Industry	No. Establishments			Employment		Pay / Employee		Annual Payroll ($ 000)		
		1992	1993	% State	1992	1993	1992	1993	1992	1993	% State
ROANOKE, VA											
60 –	**Finance, insurance, and real estate**	387	360	2.4	5,502	5,123	27,324	30,172	152,821	148,626	3.0
6000	Depository institutions	77	68	2.3	1,422	1,333	23,519	26,449	33,103	31,703	2.4
6020	Commercial banks	52	50	2.3	1,257	1,197	23,997	27,251	30,143	28,879	3.0
6060	Credit unions	9	9	2.4	78	83	19,231	18,072	1,536	1,648	1.2
6100	Nondepository institutions	26	19	1.8	303	387	26,376	23,080	8,484	7,816	1.3
6160	Mortgage bankers and brokers	8	6	1.1	166	135	20,675	22,756	4,059	3,060	1.0
6200	Security and commodity brokers	21	24	3.5	347	274	33,568	45,066	12,808	14,132	3.7
6210	Security brokers and dealers	10	14	4.0	132	205	54,636	52,644	8,114	12,380	4.4
6280	Security and commodity services	11	10	3.0	215	69	20,633	22,551	4,694	1,752	-
6300	Insurance carriers	74	62	5.2	1,692	1,758	33,593	35,732	55,313	58,900	6.4
6310	Life insurance	30	24	7.7	719	691	39,683	37,436	27,265	25,346	9.1
6330	Fire, marine, and casualty insurance	13	12	2.2	126	99	31,048	34,626	3,716	3,098	0.8
6400	Insurance agents, brokers, and service	67	72	2.6	460	288	26,157	26,986	10,883	8,427	2.2
6500	Real estate	101	98	1.8	549	663	17,144	14,655	9,948	11,072	1.4
6510	Real estate operators and lessors	47	53	2.7	236	370	13,237	10,562	2,967	3,986	2.1
6530	Real estate agents and managers	34	34	1.2	209	174	16,000	16,437	3,708	3,559	0.7
6553	Cemetery subdividers and developers	6	6	4.2	57	-	14,035	-	868	-	-
6700	Holding and other investment offices	21	17	3.1	729	420	26,019	42,219	22,282	16,576	4.9
6732	Educational, religious, etc. trusts	3	3	2.3	11	-	25,455	-	294	-	-
SALEM, VA											
60 –	**Finance, insurance, and real estate**	71	62	0.4	421	812	17,587	19,936	8,405	17,275	0.3
6000	Depository institutions	25	23	0.8	240	251	16,767	16,590	4,224	4,701	0.4
6020	Commercial banks	16	16	0.7	163	177	17,595	17,537	2,972	3,456	0.4
6030	Savings institutions	3	2	0.5	14	-	14,571	-	191	-	-
6060	Credit unions	6	5	1.3	63	-	15,111	-	1,061	-	-
6400	Insurance agents, brokers, and service	17	14	0.5	51	34	23,059	36,941	1,427	1,373	0.4
6500	Real estate	18	17	0.3	98	501	14,327	20,032	1,820	10,402	1.3
6510	Real estate operators and lessors	10	7	0.4	74	-	13,351	-	1,338	-	-
6530	Real estate agents and managers	5	8	0.3	12	-	16,000	-	222	-	-
6700	Holding and other investment offices	3	2	0.4	12	-	10,000	-	141	-	-
SOUTH BOSTON, VA											
60 –	**Finance, insurance, and real estate**	34	27	0.2	165	-	21,939	-	3,656	-	-
6000	Depository institutions	8	8	0.3	74	83	25,459	21,253	1,823	1,614	0.1
6400	Insurance agents, brokers, and service	8	6	0.2	24	20	20,833	16,400	486	394	0.1
6500	Real estate	10	7	0.1	28	16	11,000	9,500	333	162	0.0
6510	Real estate operators and lessors	7	6	0.3	21	-	8,952	-	202	-	-
STAUNTON, VA											
60 –	**Finance, insurance, and real estate**	99	80	0.5	649	563	22,724	25,329	15,090	14,890	0.3
6000	Depository institutions	19	18	0.6	267	252	20,569	24,381	5,830	6,373	0.5
6020	Commercial banks	15	15	0.7	238	-	20,218	-	5,195	-	-
6100	Nondepository institutions	8	8	0.7	35	40	32,343	30,900	1,253	1,351	0.2
6140	Personal credit institutions	5	4	1.0	18	-	24,222	-	437	-	-
6300	Insurance carriers	11	7	0.6	90	87	23,067	24,368	2,241	2,234	0.2
6310	Life insurance	3	2	0.6	59	-	23,051	-	1,468	-	-
6400	Insurance agents, brokers, and service	17	12	0.4	78	59	25,795	26,034	2,026	1,771	0.5
6500	Real estate	38	29	0.5	157	105	14,140	13,524	2,263	1,640	0.2
6510	Real estate operators and lessors	13	7	0.4	75	-	12,800	-	985	-	-
6530	Real estate agents and managers	19	20	0.7	59	54	15,932	12,889	937	849	0.2
SUFFOLK, VA											
60 –	**Finance, insurance, and real estate**	94	92	0.6	470	467	20,672	22,090	10,420	11,236	0.2
6000	Depository institutions	27	26	0.9	176	186	19,864	20,129	3,407	3,675	0.3
6020	Commercial banks	16	17	0.8	129	146	19,535	22,274	2,635	3,165	0.3
6030	Savings institutions	5	3	0.8	23	20	20,870	10,600	439	221	0.2
6060	Credit unions	6	6	1.6	24	20	20,667	14,000	333	289	0.2

Source: County Business Patterns, 1992/93, CBP-92/93-1, U.S. Department of Commerce, Washington, D.C., April 1995. SIC categories for which data were suppressed or not available for both 1992 and 1993 are not displayed. The employment columns represent mid-March employment in the year. Pay per employee is calculated by dividing 1st Quarter payroll, annualized, by mid-March employment. The columns headed "% State" show the county's percentage of the state total for the SIC in 1993; for example, 0.9% for SIC 6030 means that the county had 0.9 percent of the state's total establishments (or payroll) in SIC 6030 in 1993. A dash (-) is used to indicate that data are not available or cannot be calculated; nec means not elsewhere classified.

Continued on next page.

SIC	Industry	No. Establishments			Employment		Pay / Employee		Annual Payroll ($ 000)		
		1992	1993	% State	1992	1993	1992	1993	1992	1993	% State
SUFFOLK, VA - [continued]											
6100	Nondepository institutions	6	8	0.7	27	-	26,519	-	732	-	-
6200	Security and commodity brokers	2	3	0.4	-	11	-	50,909	-	1,063	0.3
6300	Insurance carriers	7	5	0.4	57	52	23,649	27,154	1,507	1,362	0.1
6400	Insurance agents, brokers, and service	14	15	0.5	82	83	28,049	30,361	2,696	2,793	0.7
6500	Real estate	36	33	0.6	117	106	12,855	13,283	1,653	1,602	0.2
6510	Real estate operators and lessors	15	15	0.8	54	58	11,556	11,103	681	743	0.4
6530	Real estate agents and managers	11	12	0.4	24	27	16,500	15,556	450	468	0.1
VIRGINIA BEACH, VA											
60 –	**Finance, insurance, and real estate**	980	988	6.7	7,700	7,935	21,411	22,377	180,220	197,846	4.0
6000	Depository institutions	164	164	5.5	1,772	1,969	19,302	20,837	34,349	41,566	3.1
6020	Commercial banks	101	107	4.9	932	1,073	19,811	22,285	18,737	21,895	2.2
6030	Savings institutions	31	25	6.5	327	357	21,028	24,146	6,803	9,797	7.2
6060	Credit unions	26	26	7.0	471	516	17,367	15,992	8,407	9,668	6.7
6090	Functions closely related to banking	6	6	8.5	42	23	16,286	10,609	402	206	-
6100	Nondepository institutions	86	89	8.2	891	1,003	31,398	29,894	31,161	38,196	6.3
6140	Personal credit institutions	36	33	8.6	279	333	26,151	24,216	7,752	8,481	13.4
6150	Business credit institutions	3	4	4.6	5	20	18,400	22,800	218	562	-
6160	Mortgage bankers and brokers	44	52	9.2	535	650	35,566	33,022	21,572	29,153	9.7
6200	Security and commodity brokers	48	47	6.9	232	293	39,362	36,205	10,403	11,779	3.1
6210	Security brokers and dealers	20	23	6.6	160	190	49,025	43,158	7,538	8,584	3.1
6280	Security and commodity services	25	23	7.0	70	-	18,343	-	2,144	-	-
6300	Insurance carriers	93	83	6.9	987	1,168	28,126	25,914	28,711	30,277	3.3
6310	Life insurance	25	22	7.1	444	443	22,378	22,483	10,093	9,465	3.4
6330	Fire, marine, and casualty insurance	48	41	7.6	291	269	36,165	40,431	11,647	11,265	2.8
6370	Pension, health, and welfare funds	7	5	3.2	53	-	16,453	-	481	-	-
6400	Insurance agents, brokers, and service	171	191	6.9	849	712	24,005	27,770	20,576	20,288	5.3
6500	Real estate	389	384	7.1	2,875	2,725	15,293	16,272	53,188	53,890	6.7
6510	Real estate operators and lessors	133	141	7.3	762	846	13,559	14,946	13,411	15,715	8.2
6530	Real estate agents and managers	176	217	7.6	1,381	1,644	17,665	17,326	29,536	34,390	6.5
6540	Title abstract offices	8	7	6.4	30	31	19,733	20,387	768	916	5.0
6552	Subdividers and developers, n.e.c.	18	13	4.7	451	158	9,836	11,722	4,920	2,059	4.3
6553	Cemetery subdividers and developers	5	4	2.8	53	-	21,660	-	1,146	-	-
6710	Holding offices	7	7	4.1	21	-	22,095	-	620	-	-
6732	Educational, religious, etc. trusts	7	5	3.8	18	10	17,111	26,400	290	309	1.1
6733	Trusts, n.e.c.	7	6	5.7	22	23	7,455	15,478	234	276	4.4
WAYNESBORO, VA											
60 –	**Finance, insurance, and real estate**	59	56	0.4	360	341	20,267	21,853	8,070	8,431	0.2
6000	Depository institutions	16	15	0.5	167	159	17,222	18,591	2,971	2,932	0.2
6020	Commercial banks	9	8	0.4	90	82	18,400	20,244	1,687	1,555	0.2
6100	Nondepository institutions	5	4	0.4	-	13	-	27,692	-	382	0.1
6140	Personal credit institutions	3	3	0.8	9	-	23,556	-	202	-	-
6300	Insurance carriers	6	5	0.4	56	55	25,286	21,164	1,608	1,710	0.2
6400	Insurance agents, brokers, and service	8	7	0.3	42	-	35,619	-	1,845	-	-
6500	Real estate	22	22	0.4	75	61	13,227	15,607	1,107	1,164	0.1
6510	Real estate operators and lessors	12	13	0.7	47	-	10,638	-	555	-	-
6530	Real estate agents and managers	8	8	0.3	25	23	18,720	20,522	527	607	0.1
WILLIAMSBURG, VA											
60 –	**Finance, insurance, and real estate**	111	76	0.5	612	487	26,980	27,713	18,907	14,691	0.3
6000	Depository institutions	26	22	0.7	219	197	20,749	20,853	4,504	4,318	0.3
6020	Commercial banks	19	15	0.7	170	149	21,365	21,101	3,624	3,279	0.3
6030	Savings institutions	5	4	1.0	-	18	-	18,444	-	406	0.3
6060	Credit unions	2	3	0.8	-	30	-	21,067	-	633	0.4
6100	Nondepository institutions	7	4	0.4	23	12	18,261	25,667	437	693	0.1
6140	Personal credit institutions	3	1	0.3	11	-	18,909	-	229	-	-
6200	Security and commodity brokers	5	4	0.6	29	32	69,517	67,250	1,903	2,465	0.6

Source: County Business Patterns, 1992/93, CBP-92/93-1, U.S. Department of Commerce, Washington, D.C., April 1995. SIC categories for which data were suppressed or not available for both 1992 and 1993 are not displayed. The employment columns represent mid-March employment in the year. Pay per employee is calculated by dividing 1st Quarter payroll, annualized, by mid-March employment. The columns headed "% State" show the county's percentage of the state total for the SIC in 1993; for example, 0.9% for SIC 6030 means that the county had 0.9 percent of the state's total establishments (or payroll) in SIC 6030 in 1993. A dash (-) is used to indicate that data are not available or cannot be calculated; nec means not elsewhere classified.

Continued on next page.

SIC	Industry	No. Establishments			Employment		Pay / Employee		Annual Payroll ($ 000)		
		1992	1993	% State	1992	1993	1992	1993	1992	1993	% State
WILLIAMSBURG, VA - [continued]											
6210	Security brokers and dealers	3	3	0.9	28	-	71,286	-	1,878	-	-
6300	Insurance carriers	10	5	0.4	37	9	36,216	80,000	1,334	766	0.1
6400	Insurance agents, brokers, and service	15	10	0.4	43	51	18,512	23,373	749	1,247	0.3
6500	Real estate	45	26	0.5	249	172	27,036	25,000	9,347	4,490	0.6
6510	Real estate operators and lessors	13	5	0.3	38	15	13,579	7,200	613	126	0.1
6530	Real estate agents and managers	22	18	0.6	135	153	23,289	26,980	5,658	4,326	0.8
6552	Subdividers and developers, n.e.c.	4	3	1.1	11	4	36,727	16,000	402	38	0.1
6700	Holding and other investment offices	3	5	0.9	12	14	55,333	51,143	633	712	0.2
WINCHESTER, VA											
60-	**Finance, insurance, and real estate**	160	137	0.9	944	825	22,119	22,996	23,029	20,986	0.4
6000	Depository institutions	39	37	1.2	411	421	20,331	22,100	9,512	9,663	0.7
6020	Commercial banks	34	32	1.5	387	390	20,372	22,636	9,049	9,191	0.9
6100	Nondepository institutions	14	15	1.4	70	70	25,314	21,200	1,844	1,872	0.3
6140	Personal credit institutions	8	8	2.1	30	35	22,000	17,829	672	698	1.1
6160	Mortgage bankers and brokers	5	7	1.2	-	35	-	24,571	-	1,174	0.4
6200	Security and commodity brokers	6	7	1.0	22	25	57,818	54,880	1,314	1,611	0.4
6210	Security brokers and dealers	2	3	0.9	-	18	-	67,556	-	1,442	0.5
6280	Security and commodity services	4	4	1.2	-	7	-	22,286	-	169	-
6300	Insurance carriers	15	12	1.0	83	78	26,120	25,385	2,312	2,294	0.3
6310	Life insurance	4	4	1.3	70	65	23,829	22,585	1,760	1,762	0.6
6370	Pension, health, and welfare funds	3	1	0.6	-	-	-	-	14	-	-
6400	Insurance agents, brokers, and service	31	21	0.8	112	84	23,607	24,667	2,930	2,106	0.5
6500	Real estate	50	42	0.8	225	129	19,556	19,287	4,841	3,144	0.4
6510	Real estate operators and lessors	19	18	0.9	137	48	20,730	24,917	2,937	1,167	0.6
6530	Real estate agents and managers	18	17	0.6	44	48	16,091	16,833	900	1,144	0.2
6700	Holding and other investment offices	5	3	0.5	21	18	12,762	15,111	276	296	0.1

Source: *County Business Patterns, 1992/93*, CBP-92/93-1, U.S. Department of Commerce, Washington, D.C., April 1995. SIC categories for which data were suppressed or not available for both 1992 and 1993 are *not* displayed. The employment columns represent mid-March employment in the year. Pay per employee is calculated by dividing 1st Quarter payroll, annualized, by mid-March employment. The columns headed "% State" show the county's percentage of the state total for the SIC in 1993; for example, 0.9% for SIC 6030 means that the county had 0.9 percent of the state's total establishments (or payroll) in SIC 6030 in 1993. A dash (-) is used to indicate that data are not available or cannot be calculated; *nec* means not elsewhere classified.

WASHINGTON

SIC	Industry	No. Establishments			Employment		Pay / Employee		Annual Payroll ($ 000)		
		1992	1993	% State	1992	1993	1992	1993	1992	1993	% State
ADAMS, WA											
60 –	**Finance, insurance, and real estate**	28	26	0.2	103	103	19,223	16,583	1,935	1,844	0.0
6000	Depository institutions	9	9	0.4	52	48	25,000	21,000	1,237	1,005	0.1
6500	Real estate	11	10	0.2	22	27	5,636	5,926	174	228	0.0
6510	Real estate operators and lessors	7	7	0.3	14	22	5,143	5,455	108	179	0.1
ASOTIN, WA											
60 –	**Finance, insurance, and real estate**	26	27	0.2	108	119	18,667	17,882	2,156	2,184	0.1
6000	Depository institutions	5	5	0.2	53	56	20,981	19,500	1,095	1,050	0.1
6400	Insurance agents, brokers, and service	6	6	0.2	15	18	11,467	14,000	321	330	0.1
6500	Real estate	10	13	0.2	30	39	8,133	10,256	256	421	0.1
6510	Real estate operators and lessors	4	7	0.3	7	18	8,000	9,111	61	160	0.1
BENTON, WA											
60 –	**Finance, insurance, and real estate**	225	249	1.8	1,314	1,631	18,673	19,939	26,970	35,416	0.9
6000	Depository institutions	35	37	1.8	469	591	20,844	19,926	9,974	12,117	1.2
6020	Commercial banks	17	18	1.6	232	331	20,672	18,248	4,685	5,995	1.0
6030	Savings institutions	12	13	2.7	95	111	22,779	24,396	2,306	2,784	1.1
6060	Credit unions	6	6	1.9	142	149	19,831	20,322	2,983	3,338	3.2
6140	Personal credit institutions	7	9	3.8	34	-	20,941	-	764	-	-
6160	Mortgage bankers and brokers	6	9	1.4	-	55	-	49,091	-	2,245	0.8
6200	Security and commodity brokers	11	10	1.4	59	60	54,508	53,733	3,367	3,709	1.0
6210	Security brokers and dealers	8	8	1.9	54	-	58,370	-	3,254	-	-
6280	Security and commodity services	3	2	0.7	5	-	12,800	-	113	-	-
6300	Insurance carriers	21	17	1.9	87	133	28,230	29,053	2,556	4,100	0.5
6330	Fire, marine, and casualty insurance	14	10	2.2	24	18	39,833	48,444	989	895	0.2
6400	Insurance agents, brokers, and service	36	40	1.6	156	180	18,513	19,111	3,373	4,075	0.9
6500	Real estate	108	126	2.0	434	554	11,594	12,065	6,095	8,308	1.4
6510	Real estate operators and lessors	52	71	2.6	170	320	8,329	10,312	1,630	3,585	2.2
6530	Real estate agents and managers	42	42	1.5	184	156	12,043	12,462	2,833	2,563	0.7
6552	Subdividers and developers, n.e.c.	1	5	1.4	-	3	-	12,000	-	339	0.7
CHELAN, WA											
60 –	**Finance, insurance, and real estate**	187	190	1.4	1,086	1,108	20,659	22,119	24,358	25,945	0.7
6000	Depository institutions	30	29	1.4	398	398	25,719	28,121	10,638	10,979	1.1
6020	Commercial banks	17	17	1.5	315	319	27,124	29,818	8,857	9,229	1.6
6030	Savings institutions	8	7	1.4	54	48	22,222	24,417	1,274	1,228	0.5
6060	Credit unions	5	5	1.5	29	31	16,966	16,387	507	522	0.5
6100	Nondepository institutions	8	10	1.0	28	47	27,143	27,149	828	1,574	0.4
6150	Business credit institutions	3	2	1.9	19	-	26,947	-	566	-	-
6160	Mortgage bankers and brokers	2	5	0.8	-	23	-	24,348	-	906	0.3
6200	Security and commodity brokers	9	11	1.6	41	44	56,390	53,909	2,511	2,245	0.6
6210	Security brokers and dealers	7	7	1.7	-	39	-	56,205	-	2,085	0.7
6280	Security and commodity services	2	4	1.5	-	5	-	36,000	-	160	0.2
6300	Insurance carriers	13	10	1.1	47	-	26,043	-	1,299	-	-
6310	Life insurance	5	1	0.5	13	-	21,538	-	270	-	-
6400	Insurance agents, brokers, and service	30	32	1.3	108	141	22,037	21,759	2,503	3,202	0.7
6500	Real estate	91	93	1.5	449	430	11,457	12,195	6,138	6,477	1.1
6510	Real estate operators and lessors	41	41	1.5	116	135	7,069	9,156	1,023	1,481	0.9

Source: County Business Patterns, 1992/93, CBP-92/93-1, U.S. Department of Commerce, Washington, D.C., April 1995. SIC categories for which data were suppressed or not available for both 1992 and 1993 are *not* displayed. The employment columns represent mid-March employment in the year. Pay per employee is calculated by dividing 1st Quarter payroll, annualized, by mid-March employment. The columns headed "% State" show the county's percentage of the state total for the SIC in 1993; for example, 0.9% for SIC 6030 means that the county had 0.9 percent of the state's total establishments (or payroll) in SIC 6030 in 1993. A dash (-) is used to indicate that data are not available or cannot be calculated; *nec* means not elsewhere classified.

Continued on next page.

SIC	Industry	No. Establishments			Employment		Pay / Employee		Annual Payroll ($ 000)		
		1992	1993	% State	1992	1993	1992	1993	1992	1993	% State
CHELAN, WA - [continued]											
6530	Real estate agents and managers	41	43	1.5	278	243	12,619	13,235	3,941	4,120	1.1
6552	Subdividers and developers, n.e.c.	4	7	2.0	3	52	24,000	15,231	224	813	1.8
6700	Holding and other investment offices	6	5	1.0	15	-	25,333	-	441	-	-
CLALLAM, WA											
60 –	**Finance, insurance, and real estate**	147	144	1.0	675	726	19,407	19,267	13,088	14,500	0.4
6000	Depository institutions	27	30	1.4	330	366	19,503	18,831	6,302	6,858	0.7
6020	Commercial banks	14	14	1.2	-	145	-	16,855	-	2,241	0.4
6030	Savings institutions	11	13	2.7	186	204	18,473	19,980	3,560	4,251	1.7
6060	Credit unions	2	3	0.9	-	17	-	21,882	-	366	0.4
6200	Security and commodity brokers	7	8	1.1	-	22	-	54,182	-	1,423	0.4
6210	Security brokers and dealers	6	7	1.7	23	-	30,087	-	802	-	-
6300	Insurance carriers	9	7	0.8	40	47	25,500	19,149	981	1,052	0.1
6400	Insurance agents, brokers, and service	23	24	1.0	86	84	25,302	22,476	1,962	1,818	0.4
6500	Real estate	78	72	1.2	184	204	13,978	15,118	2,850	3,306	0.5
6510	Real estate operators and lessors	27	30	1.1	66	60	7,515	11,333	548	754	0.5
6530	Real estate agents and managers	34	31	1.1	69	76	14,667	12,368	1,086	1,090	0.3
6540	Title abstract offices	5	5	11.1	43	57	23,349	24,772	1,048	1,365	8.5
6552	Subdividers and developers, n.e.c.	2	6	1.7	-	11	-	4,727	-	97	0.2
6700	Holding and other investment offices	2	3	0.6	-	3	-	10,667	-	43	0.0
CLARK, WA											
60 –	**Finance, insurance, and real estate**	580	628	4.6	4,722	4,470	20,545	21,976	106,672	108,196	2.9
6000	Depository institutions	104	109	5.3	1,213	1,237	22,509	21,274	26,449	26,931	2.7
6020	Commercial banks	54	52	4.5	718	688	21,994	20,645	14,948	13,729	2.4
6030	Savings institutions	24	25	5.1	197	-	29,523	-	5,773	-	-
6060	Credit unions	24	30	9.3	-	329	-	21,459	-	7,491	7.2
6100	Nondepository institutions	59	53	5.4	279	299	35,068	35,719	11,280	13,938	3.9
6140	Personal credit institutions	23	13	5.5	136	105	32,441	30,705	4,403	2,783	6.5
6150	Business credit institutions	3	5	4.7	-	5	-	22,400	-	121	-
6160	Mortgage bankers and brokers	32	35	5.6	129	189	39,318	38,857	6,654	11,034	4.1
6200	Security and commodity brokers	31	34	4.8	-	82	-	37,951	-	4,052	1.1
6210	Security brokers and dealers	19	20	4.8	56	57	39,500	50,246	2,172	3,776	1.3
6280	Security and commodity services	12	14	5.2	-	25	-	9,920	-	276	0.4
6300	Insurance carriers	40	33	3.8	1,161	744	20,851	27,968	28,246	20,572	2.4
6330	Fire, marine, and casualty insurance	24	21	4.7	839	503	15,356	29,702	13,008	13,999	3.9
6360	Title insurance	6	3	6.7	177	-	45,605	-	12,227	-	-
6400	Insurance agents, brokers, and service	93	111	4.6	306	402	21,987	20,348	7,435	8,815	2.1
6500	Real estate	242	276	4.5	1,561	1,578	14,398	15,894	25,108	28,085	4.6
6510	Real estate operators and lessors	102	123	4.4	392	525	11,633	12,632	5,032	7,697	4.6
6530	Real estate agents and managers	107	124	4.4	1,032	934	14,337	17,002	15,901	17,218	4.7
6552	Subdividers and developers, n.e.c.	13	23	6.6	36	53	22,556	19,170	1,267	1,118	2.4
6700	Holding and other investment offices	10	12	2.4	107	128	33,757	31,688	5,253	5,803	4.0
6710	Holding offices	4	4	4.2	83	-	32,241	-	3,911	-	-
COLUMBIA, WA											
60 –	**Finance, insurance, and real estate**	9	10	0.1	22	26	19,273	17,231	394	411	0.0
6000	Depository institutions	4	4	0.2	-	16	-	18,750	-	266	0.0
6400	Insurance agents, brokers, and service	2	3	0.1	-	6	-	18,667	-	109	0.0
6500	Real estate	3	3	0.0	3	4	8,000	9,000	30	36	0.0
COWLITZ, WA											
60 –	**Finance, insurance, and real estate**	169	176	1.3	945	1,015	19,297	19,570	19,567	22,093	0.6
6000	Depository institutions	35	33	1.6	460	483	20,991	20,679	9,763	10,676	1.1
6020	Commercial banks	17	16	1.4	171	163	21,637	21,006	3,456	3,657	0.6
6030	Savings institutions	7	5	1.0	36	36	18,667	21,556	871	1,051	0.4
6060	Credit unions	11	12	3.7	253	284	20,885	20,380	5,436	5,968	5.7
6100	Nondepository institutions	6	6	0.6	34	-	20,588	-	784	-	-

Source: County Business Patterns, 1992/93, CBP-92/93-1, U.S. Department of Commerce, Washington, D.C., April 1995. SIC categories for which data were suppressed or not available for both 1992 and 1993 are *not* displayed. The employment columns represent mid-March employment in the year. Pay per employee is calculated by dividing 1st Quarter payroll, annualized, by mid-March employment. The columns headed "% State" show the county's percentage of the state total for the SIC in 1993; for example, 0.9% for SIC 6030 means that the county had 0.9 percent of the state's total establishments (or payroll) in SIC 6030 in 1993. A dash (-) is used to indicate that data are not available or cannot be calculated; *nec* means not elsewhere classified.

Continued on next page.

SIC	Industry	No. Establishments			Employment		Pay / Employee		Annual Payroll ($ 000)		
		1992	1993	% State	1992	1993	1992	1993	1992	1993	% State
COWLITZ, WA - [continued]											
6200	Security and commodity brokers	3	4	0.6	7	7	74,286	81,143	559	679	0.2
6210	Security brokers and dealers	3	4	1.0	7	7	74,286	81,143	559	679	0.2
6300	Insurance carriers	15	10	1.1	77	56	16,727	28,286	1,348	1,676	0.2
6330	Fire, marine, and casualty insurance	8	6	1.3	13	10	34,154	45,600	519	522	0.1
6400	Insurance agents, brokers, and service	32	39	1.6	144	176	21,972	20,364	3,615	3,993	0.9
6500	Real estate	75	81	1.3	218	259	13,064	12,741	3,462	3,993	0.6
6510	Real estate operators and lessors	48	50	1.8	110	137	8,909	8,555	1,190	1,344	0.8
6530	Real estate agents and managers	22	25	0.9	82	75	15,854	16,640	1,568	1,380	0.4
6552	Subdividers and developers, n.e.c.	-	3	0.9	-	19	-	12,211	-	315	0.7
6700	Holding and other investment offices	3	3	0.6	5	-	12,000	-	36	-	-
DOUGLAS, WA											
60 –	**Finance, insurance, and real estate**	45	45	0.3	173	196	17,110	18,673	3,486	3,996	0.1
6000	Depository institutions	10	13	0.6	77	107	20,831	21,271	1,754	2,324	0.2
6020	Commercial banks	6	6	0.5	49	50	21,143	24,880	1,125	1,202	0.2
6400	Insurance agents, brokers, and service	9	8	0.3	-	22	-	12,909	-	298	0.1
6500	Real estate	18	19	0.3	48	61	11,833	14,820	751	1,153	0.2
6510	Real estate operators and lessors	12	13	0.5	35	-	9,943	-	427	-	-
FERRY, WA											
60 –	**Finance, insurance, and real estate**	5	6	0.0	20	20	14,400	12,600	284	289	0.0
FRANKLIN, WA											
60 –	**Finance, insurance, and real estate**	63	58	0.4	342	302	19,883	18,808	6,211	5,025	0.1
6000	Depository institutions	15	14	0.7	184	131	21,848	17,679	3,140	1,808	0.2
6020	Commercial banks	10	9	0.8	157	102	22,803	17,922	2,641	1,244	0.2
6100	Nondepository institutions	3	3	0.3	11	12	31,636	34,333	364	355	0.1
6300	Insurance carriers	4	2	0.2	8	-	12,500	-	107	-	-
6400	Insurance agents, brokers, and service	15	12	0.5	62	57	25,935	25,825	1,524	1,500	0.3
6500	Real estate	26	24	0.4	77	89	9,403	13,618	1,076	1,074	0.2
6510	Real estate operators and lessors	14	13	0.5	45	54	8,711	9,259	516	663	0.4
6530	Real estate agents and managers	7	6	0.2	25	28	11,200	10,429	499	291	0.1
GARFIELD, WA											
60 –	**Finance, insurance, and real estate**	5	6	0.0	18	19	20,444	18,316	346	328	0.0
GRANT, WA											
60 –	**Finance, insurance, and real estate**	109	107	0.8	445	446	18,553	18,215	9,281	9,043	0.2
6000	Depository institutions	23	21	1.0	197	188	20,873	19,787	4,022	3,876	0.4
6020	Commercial banks	17	14	1.2	160	140	21,250	19,486	3,203	2,629	0.5
6100	Nondepository institutions	5	4	0.4	35	34	28,343	33,882	1,000	1,124	0.3
6300	Insurance carriers	5	2	0.2	20	-	17,000	-	354	-	-
6400	Insurance agents, brokers, and service	26	28	1.2	99	112	20,081	18,786	2,279	2,448	0.6
6500	Real estate	45	48	0.8	87	101	6,529	7,089	844	999	0.2
6510	Real estate operators and lessors	27	28	1.0	56	66	5,286	4,788	407	426	0.3
6530	Real estate agents and managers	9	13	0.5	12	26	12,667	12,308	289	457	0.1
6552	Subdividers and developers, n.e.c.	3	4	1.2	-	3	-	8,000	-	48	0.1
6553	Cemetery subdividers and developers	3	3	3.1	-	6	-	9,333	-	68	0.5
GRAYS HARBOR, WA											
60 –	**Finance, insurance, and real estate**	123	132	1.0	745	759	17,793	18,161	14,256	14,299	0.4
6000	Depository institutions	37	37	1.8	324	360	20,284	20,089	6,971	7,290	0.7
6020	Commercial banks	17	16	1.4	147	145	21,061	20,828	3,089	2,861	0.5
6030	Savings institutions	10	10	2.0	132	155	20,121	19,923	2,959	3,288	1.3
6200	Security and commodity brokers	4	5	0.7	17	-	51,529	-	869	-	-
6300	Insurance carriers	7	5	0.6	64	-	21,312	-	1,465	-	-
6400	Insurance agents, brokers, and service	23	29	1.2	79	118	14,785	15,593	1,198	1,776	0.4
6500	Real estate	47	52	0.8	231	221	11,550	12,796	3,151	3,248	0.5

Source: County Business Patterns, 1992/93, CBP-92/93-1, U.S. Department of Commerce, Washington, D.C., April 1995. SIC categories for which data were suppressed or not available for both 1992 and 1993 are *not* displayed. The employment columns represent mid-March employment in the year. Pay per employee is calculated by dividing 1st Quarter payroll, annualized, by mid-March employment. The columns headed "% State" show the county's percentage of the state total for the SIC in 1993; for example, 0.9% for SIC 6030 means that the county had 0.9 percent of the state's total establishments (or payroll) in SIC 6030 in 1993. A dash (-) is used to indicate that data are not available or cannot be calculated; *nec* means not elsewhere classified.

Continued on next page.

SIC	Industry	No. Establishments			Employment		Pay / Employee		Annual Payroll ($ 000)		
		1992	1993	% State	1992	1993	1992	1993	1992	1993	% State
GRAYS HARBOR, WA - [continued]											
6510	Real estate operators and lessors	13	18	0.6	47	71	8,936	12,113	468	1,092	0.7
6530	Real estate agents and managers	27	27	1.0	148	118	11,919	11,525	2,150	1,430	0.4
6552	Subdividers and developers, n.e.c.	3	3	0.9	-	1	-	8,000	-	18	0.0
ISLAND, WA											
60 –	**Finance, insurance, and real estate**	99	108	0.8	759	794	20,142	19,602	16,154	17,055	0.5
6000	Depository institutions	25	26	1.3	492	514	20,959	18,926	10,711	10,512	1.1
6030	Savings institutions	8	8	1.6	208	193	21,346	22,238	4,796	4,913	1.9
6100	Nondepository institutions	4	3	0.3	-	12	-	48,667	-	746	0.2
6160	Mortgage bankers and brokers	3	3	0.5	-	12	-	48,667	-	746	0.3
6300	Insurance carriers	6	3	0.3	26	-	18,923	-	523	-	-
6400	Insurance agents, brokers, and service	16	20	0.8	97	99	20,041	24,283	2,133	2,619	0.6
6500	Real estate	47	54	0.9	122	161	15,016	14,062	1,929	2,614	0.4
6510	Real estate operators and lessors	20	21	0.8	41	50	17,659	10,400	736	545	0.3
6530	Real estate agents and managers	22	27	1.0	68	88	12,059	13,500	940	1,431	0.4
JEFFERSON, WA											
60 –	**Finance, insurance, and real estate**	46	63	0.5	225	249	19,787	19,823	4,691	5,268	0.1
6000	Depository institutions	9	10	0.5	83	88	17,976	19,227	1,479	1,713	0.2
6400	Insurance agents, brokers, and service	6	10	0.4	29	-	23,448	-	712	-	-
6500	Real estate	23	36	0.6	68	101	22,000	19,168	1,768	1,988	0.3
6510	Real estate operators and lessors	7	10	0.4	6	15	6,000	6,400	59	113	0.1
6530	Real estate agents and managers	9	18	0.6	14	43	15,714	15,535	280	763	0.2
6700	Holding and other investment offices	4	4	0.8	39	26	13,128	18,462	525	616	0.4
6732	Educational, religious, etc. trusts	3	3	3.3	-	26	-	18,462	-	501	4.1
KING, WA											
60 –	**Finance, insurance, and real estate**	5,594	5,741	41.8	70,795	69,969	32,293	33,480	2,276,125	2,340,759	62.1
6000	Depository institutions	685	680	32.8	20,464	18,793	29,576	31,731	622,175	534,398	53.9
6020	Commercial banks	398	369	32.1	14,674	10,866	28,814	27,944	419,452	301,775	51.9
6030	Savings institutions	165	175	35.9	3,829	5,585	33,481	39,822	147,095	162,835	63.5
6060	Credit unions	58	69	21.4	1,070	1,315	23,009	22,111	24,939	30,541	29.4
6080	Foreign bank and branches and agencies	6	9	100.0	153	-	44,026	-	7,240	-	-
6090	Functions closely related to banking	54	56	56.0	-	586	-	37,870	-	21,796	69.3
6100	Nondepository institutions	433	495	50.1	3,977	4,780	40,268	37,112	164,973	214,911	59.8
6140	Personal credit institutions	116	91	38.2	766	836	33,295	27,507	25,573	23,425	54.7
6150	Business credit institutions	52	73	68.9	679	704	60,359	59,068	29,674	33,077	-
6160	Mortgage bankers and brokers	259	329	52.5	2,510	3,231	37,146	34,866	109,227	158,278	58.8
6200	Security and commodity brokers	329	362	51.3	3,479	3,633	64,181	73,364	223,984	259,494	73.2
6210	Security brokers and dealers	189	198	47.1	2,561	2,793	72,795	76,546	188,562	205,558	72.2
6220	Commodity contracts brokers, dealers	7	10	71.4	-	15	-	39,733	-	834	75.5
6280	Security and commodity services	129	154	56.8	898	825	40,098	63,205	34,379	53,102	77.6
6300	Insurance carriers	463	386	44.3	18,115	17,952	33,581	36,840	566,560	631,665	74.0
6310	Life insurance	123	108	56.3	4,736	4,570	35,149	39,455	152,122	163,858	77.1
6321	Accident and health insurance	13	11	68.8	293	-	28,082	-	7,736	-	-
6324	Hospital and medical service plans	12	17	33.3	2,289	-	15,554	-	26,585	-	-
6330	Fire, marine, and casualty insurance	226	198	44.5	8,953	8,025	38,221	39,179	319,697	296,095	82.5
6350	Surety insurance	14	9	90.0	166	-	32,795	-	5,952	-	-
6360	Title insurance	16	15	33.3	841	775	33,974	37,806	31,466	32,840	56.7
6400	Insurance agents, brokers, and service	867	932	38.4	6,640	6,559	36,636	34,777	235,711	231,333	53.8
6500	Real estate	2,502	2,586	42.0	14,936	15,365	21,051	20,387	335,404	351,770	57.5
6510	Real estate operators and lessors	1,082	1,170	42.2	4,777	4,790	15,746	16,275	84,928	86,741	52.4
6530	Real estate agents and managers	1,009	1,209	43.3	8,288	9,659	22,918	21,712	196,350	235,954	64.4
6540	Title abstract offices	-	5	11.1	-	8	-	5,000	-	66	0.4
6552	Subdividers and developers, n.e.c.	148	142	41.0	806	704	32,958	29,222	26,943	22,663	49.4
6553	Cemetery subdividers and developers	15	16	16.7	199	189	20,060	24,423	5,608	5,414	35.9
6700	Holding and other investment offices	298	282	56.4	2,816	2,424	42,399	34,398	115,045	99,274	69.0
6710	Holding offices	71	65	67.7	1,577	1,339	52,317	37,204	74,945	60,203	67.1

Source: County Business Patterns, 1992/93, CBP-92/93-1, U.S. Department of Commerce, Washington, D.C., April 1995. SIC categories for which data were suppressed or not available for both 1992 and 1993 are not displayed. The employment columns represent mid-March employment in the year. Pay per employee is calculated by dividing 1st Quarter payroll, annualized, by mid-March employment. The columns headed "% State" show the county's percentage of the state total for the SIC in 1993; for example, 0.9% for SIC 6030 means that the county had 0.9 percent of the state's total establishments (or payroll) in SIC 6030 in 1993. A dash (-) is used to indicate that data are not available or cannot be calculated; nec means not elsewhere classified.

Continued on next page.

SIC	Industry	No. Establishments			Employment		Pay / Employee		Annual Payroll ($ 000)		
		1992	1993	% State	1992	1993	1992	1993	1992	1993	% State
KING, WA - [continued]											
6720	Investment offices	23	13	76.5	141	33	43,887	35,394	5,994	1,323	50.8
6732	Educational, religious, etc. trusts	51	51	55.4	311	329	19,627	21,872	6,151	8,509	69.3
6733	Trusts, n.e.c.	60	60	41.7	334	375	23,174	25,227	8,945	10,139	69.1
6794	Patent owners and lessors	15	17	73.9	156	110	39,231	35,418	6,425	5,415	78.6
6798	Real estate investment trusts	12	6	66.7	25	31	34,240	11,742	1,187	462	81.6
6799	Investors, n.e.c.	48	69	60.5	165	207	45,745	55,459	8,145	13,173	78.1
KITSAP, WA											
60 –	**Finance, insurance, and real estate**	388	413	3.0	2,679	2,764	26,991	22,715	64,306	69,604	1.8
6000	Depository institutions	64	64	3.1	868	836	37,673	20,981	22,182	18,231	1.8
6020	Commercial banks	39	35	3.0	501	533	24,000	21,891	12,176	12,243	2.1
6030	Savings institutions	8	11	2.3	137	-	121,372	-	5,541	-	-
6060	Credit unions	16	17	5.3	-	221	-	19,186	-	4,257	4.1
6100	Nondepository institutions	21	30	3.0	106	219	31,170	32,658	-	9,987	2.8
6140	Personal credit institutions	7	8	3.4	25	31	22,880	20,387	621	682	1.6
6160	Mortgage bankers and brokers	14	22	3.5	81	188	33,728	34,681	3,534	9,305	3.5
6200	Security and commodity brokers	19	23	3.3	-	69	-	49,217	-	3,884	1.1
6210	Security brokers and dealers	12	12	2.9	54	55	48,667	54,618	2,639	3,178	1.1
6280	Security and commodity services	7	11	4.1	-	14	-	28,000	-	706	1.0
6300	Insurance carriers	21	21	2.4	233	216	25,545	29,741	6,387	7,145	0.8
6310	Life insurance	3	2	1.0	26	-	24,154	-	664	-	-
6330	Fire, marine, and casualty insurance	12	13	2.9	-	20	-	67,000	-	1,437	0.4
6360	Title insurance	3	3	6.7	80	-	20,700	-	1,894	-	-
6400	Insurance agents, brokers, and service	68	74	3.1	584	590	25,301	24,312	14,162	15,221	3.5
6500	Real estate	192	193	3.1	814	809	15,111	16,030	14,186	13,958	2.3
6510	Real estate operators and lessors	68	76	2.7	251	274	9,084	9,401	2,336	2,761	1.7
6530	Real estate agents and managers	95	100	3.6	420	412	17,971	17,515	8,673	7,871	2.1
6552	Subdividers and developers, n.e.c.	8	9	2.6	36	45	14,000	19,644	1,197	1,433	3.1
6553	Cemetery subdividers and developers	3	3	3.1	23	26	16,696	16,308	338	371	2.5
6700	Holding and other investment offices	3	8	1.6	-	25	-	38,400	-	1,178	0.8
KITTITAS, WA											
60 –	**Finance, insurance, and real estate**	56	58	0.4	175	229	17,691	18,463	3,536	4,515	0.1
6000	Depository institutions	11	11	0.5	66	99	19,697	18,869	1,371	2,072	0.2
6020	Commercial banks	6	7	0.6	-	81	-	19,309	-	1,730	0.3
6400	Insurance agents, brokers, and service	12	14	0.6	50	55	17,920	18,909	1,030	1,120	0.3
6500	Real estate	27	27	0.4	51	66	13,333	15,455	857	1,031	0.2
6510	Real estate operators and lessors	9	11	0.4	13	20	6,769	10,800	136	162	0.1
KLICKITAT, WA											
60 –	**Finance, insurance, and real estate**	25	27	0.2	113	90	16,673	17,956	1,998	1,900	0.1
6000	Depository institutions	6	6	0.3	46	48	22,609	21,417	1,060	1,113	0.1
6500	Real estate	9	11	0.2	29	15	8,690	8,533	279	220	0.0
6510	Real estate operators and lessors	4	5	0.2	12	10	8,667	9,200	115	100	0.1
LEWIS, WA											
60 –	**Finance, insurance, and real estate**	100	99	0.7	586	595	20,273	22,259	12,041	13,160	0.3
6000	Depository institutions	20	22	1.1	245	271	23,249	24,074	5,529	6,113	0.6
6020	Commercial banks	13	13	1.1	195	204	24,000	25,392	4,365	4,532	0.8
6100	Nondepository institutions	5	4	0.4	-	26	-	31,538	-	766	0.2
6200	Security and commodity brokers	4	4	0.6	7	-	47,429	-	356	-	-
6300	Insurance carriers	6	6	0.7	61	56	8,066	19,857	524	1,196	0.1
6400	Insurance agents, brokers, and service	23	23	0.9	83	81	24,964	27,160	1,889	2,057	0.5
6500	Real estate	41	38	0.6	152	152	15,395	14,842	2,799	2,596	0.4
6510	Real estate operators and lessors	17	16	0.6	54	52	12,889	8,308	832	567	0.3
6530	Real estate agents and managers	19	16	0.6	56	55	15,143	14,764	1,030	950	0.3

Source: County Business Patterns, 1992/93, CBP-92/93-1, U.S. Department of Commerce, Washington, D.C., April 1995. SIC categories for which data were suppressed or not available for both 1992 and 1993 are *not* displayed. The employment columns represent mid-March employment in the year. Pay per employee is calculated by dividing 1st Quarter payroll, annualized, by mid-March employment. The columns headed "% State" show the county's percentage of the state total for the SIC in 1993; for example, 0.9% for SIC 6030 means that the county had 0.9 percent of the state's total establishments (or payroll) in SIC 6030 in 1993. A dash (-) is used to indicate that data are not available or cannot be calculated; *nec* means not elsewhere classified.

SIC	Industry	No. Establishments			Employment		Pay / Employee		Annual Payroll ($ 000)		
		1992	1993	% State	1992	1993	1992	1993	1992	1993	% State
LINCOLN, WA											
60 –	**Finance, insurance, and real estate**	33	31	0.2	107	108	20,112	19,556	1,918	1,965	0.1
6000	Depository institutions	10	11	0.5	60	57	22,933	24,632	1,249	1,254	0.1
6020	Commercial banks	10	9	0.8	60	-	22,933	-	1,249	-	-
6400	Insurance agents, brokers, and service	11	11	0.5	29	32	19,172	17,500	474	516	0.1
6500	Real estate	10	9	0.1	-	19	-	7,789	-	195	0.0
6510	Real estate operators and lessors	4	3	0.1	9	7	3,556	4,000	28	28	0.0
6530	Real estate agents and managers	3	2	0.1	1	-	4,000	-	8	-	-
MASON, WA											
60 –	**Finance, insurance, and real estate**	70	75	0.5	455	454	21,222	17,436	8,664	8,977	0.2
6000	Depository institutions	14	14	0.7	158	183	21,089	18,710	3,337	3,774	0.4
6020	Commercial banks	8	8	0.7	68	73	23,118	19,562	1,586	1,727	0.3
6300	Insurance carriers	4	2	0.2	58	-	53,448	-	1,457	-	-
6500	Real estate	36	43	0.7	172	224	13,605	14,500	2,805	3,746	0.6
6510	Real estate operators and lessors	12	10	0.4	68	68	8,000	8,824	650	608	0.4
6530	Real estate agents and managers	14	23	0.8	-	80	-	12,100	-	1,183	0.3
6540	Title abstract offices	2	3	6.7	-	57	-	22,807	-	1,548	9.6
6552	Subdividers and developers, n.e.c.	3	4	1.2	13	14	20,615	21,714	366	252	0.5
OKANOGAN, WA											
60 –	**Finance, insurance, and real estate**	57	66	0.5	227	269	17,198	16,238	4,261	4,549	0.1
6000	Depository institutions	15	16	0.8	131	140	20,305	18,914	2,713	2,610	0.3
6020	Commercial banks	13	13	1.1	-	123	-	19,122	-	2,254	0.4
6200	Security and commodity brokers	3	3	0.4	4	-	16,000	-	79	-	-
6400	Insurance agents, brokers, and service	10	15	0.6	36	45	13,667	15,289	522	705	0.2
6500	Real estate	26	30	0.5	46	73	11,043	10,466	745	937	0.2
6510	Real estate operators and lessors	13	13	0.5	24	21	4,833	4,762	128	110	0.1
6530	Real estate agents and managers	6	13	0.5	8	-	14,000	-	139	-	-
PACIFIC, WA											
60 –	**Finance, insurance, and real estate**	43	44	0.3	202	206	16,079	17,476	3,328	3,857	0.1
6000	Depository institutions	14	14	0.7	104	114	18,269	18,526	1,992	2,430	0.2
6400	Insurance agents, brokers, and service	9	12	0.5	-	48	-	17,667	-	868	0.2
6500	Real estate	18	18	0.3	40	44	10,900	14,545	511	559	0.1
6510	Real estate operators and lessors	6	5	0.2	5	6	6,400	6,000	42	43	0.0
6530	Real estate agents and managers	9	10	0.4	29	32	11,310	10,625	395	396	0.1
PEND OREILLE, WA											
60 –	**Finance, insurance, and real estate**	19	15	0.1	63	60	16,190	16,600	1,144	1,126	0.0
6000	Depository institutions	5	4	0.2	36	30	19,000	17,200	731	599	0.1
6400	Insurance agents, brokers, and service	5	5	0.2	12	14	15,000	20,571	162	211	0.0
6500	Real estate	9	6	0.1	15	16	10,400	12,000	251	316	0.1
6510	Real estate operators and lessors	3	2	0.1	3	-	2,667	-	10	-	-
6530	Real estate agents and managers	3	2	0.1	2	-	8,000	-	23	-	-
PIERCE, WA											
60 –	**Finance, insurance, and real estate**	1,235	1,288	9.4	11,546	10,722	25,101	25,828	318,119	308,852	8.2
6000	Depository institutions	206	208	10.0	6,022	4,210	26,638	26,294	165,334	119,502	12.1
6020	Commercial banks	137	132	11.5	4,839	2,890	26,781	25,385	136,816	83,474	14.3
6030	Savings institutions	24	25	5.1	698	576	29,330	28,681	18,143	15,805	6.2
6060	Credit unions	29	37	11.5	381	605	22,457	20,952	8,605	13,091	12.6
6090	Functions closely related to banking	16	14	14.0	104	139	17,231	58,532	1,770	7,132	22.7
6100	Nondepository institutions	79	86	8.7	470	530	27,702	27,675	14,724	18,641	5.2
6140	Personal credit institutions	41	31	13.0	297	-	24,848	-	7,271	-	-
6160	Mortgage bankers and brokers	33	51	8.1	167	256	32,743	32,688	7,194	11,766	4.4
6200	Security and commodity brokers	50	51	7.2	-	376	-	44,904	-	21,222	6.0
6210	Security brokers and dealers	28	27	6.4	188	192	53,574	52,083	10,604	11,868	4.2
6280	Security and commodity services	21	23	8.5	86	-	19,349	-	2,052	-	-

Source: County Business Patterns, 1992/93, CBP-92/93-1, U.S. Department of Commerce, Washington, D.C., April 1995. SIC categories for which data were suppressed or not available for both 1992 and 1993 are *not* displayed. The employment columns represent mid-March employment in the year. Pay per employee is calculated by dividing 1st Quarter payroll, annualized, by mid-March employment. The columns headed "% State" show the county's percentage of the state total for the SIC in 1993; for example, 0.9% for SIC 6030 means that the county had 0.9 percent of the state's total establishments (or payroll) in SIC 6030 in 1993. A dash (-) is used to indicate that data are not available or cannot be calculated; *nec* means not elsewhere classified.

Continued on next page.

SIC	Industry	No. Establishments			Employment		Pay / Employee		Annual Payroll ($ 000)		
		1992	1993	% State	1992	1993	1992	1993	1992	1993	% State
PIERCE, WA - [continued]											
6300	Insurance carriers	76	71	8.1	833	916	30,603	30,533	25,948	29,949	3.5
6310	Life insurance	16	14	7.3	164	165	24,902	26,255	4,227	4,105	1.9
6330	Fire, marine, and casualty insurance	36	33	7.4	83	76	49,928	53,105	4,304	4,173	1.2
6360	Title insurance	5	7	15.6	219	280	25,881	28,329	6,060	9,016	15.6
6400	Insurance agents, brokers, and service	203	225	9.3	858	1,578	30,406	37,678	23,951	64,226	14.9
6500	Real estate	566	603	9.8	2,858	2,901	13,966	14,458	43,857	48,429	7.9
6510	Real estate operators and lessors	252	280	10.1	932	1,088	10,781	12,044	12,268	14,864	9.0
6530	Real estate agents and managers	241	272	9.7	1,630	1,625	13,944	14,860	23,865	27,957	7.6
6552	Subdividers and developers, n.e.c.	24	31	9.0	57	35	32,070	20,800	1,916	1,222	2.7
6553	Cemetery subdividers and developers	7	7	7.3	130	131	26,800	26,137	3,483	3,756	24.9
6700	Holding and other investment offices	54	43	8.6	226	-	57,646	-	31,519	-	-
6710	Holding offices	12	5	5.2	29	26	165,241	84,462	22,967	3,339	3.7
6732	Educational, religious, etc. trusts	7	5	5.4	37	12	34,703	55,000	1,340	512	4.2
6733	Trusts, n.e.c.	18	19	13.2	77	39	15,584	17,641	1,387	891	6.1
SAN JUAN, WA											
60 –	**Finance, insurance, and real estate**	52	60	0.4	179	195	24,581	30,256	5,349	6,536	0.2
6000	Depository institutions	8	8	0.4	94	84	26,298	24,286	2,672	2,821	0.3
6400	Insurance agents, brokers, and service	9	8	0.3	31	-	27,484	-	899	-	-
6500	Real estate	27	34	0.6	45	49	13,156	10,041	765	754	0.1
6510	Real estate operators and lessors	12	14	0.5	19	19	5,684	5,895	197	138	0.1
6530	Real estate agents and managers	14	18	0.6	24	-	18,333	-	527	-	-
6700	Holding and other investment offices	5	4	0.8	8	9	59,500	57,333	892	1,005	0.7
SKAGIT, WA											
60 –	**Finance, insurance, and real estate**	212	237	1.7	988	1,120	21,810	19,614	23,058	23,711	0.6
6000	Depository institutions	45	45	2.2	443	457	23,883	19,860	10,413	9,889	1.0
6020	Commercial banks	27	23	2.0	336	315	23,631	19,327	7,838	6,735	1.2
6030	Savings institutions	13	16	3.3	88	102	26,091	23,137	2,198	2,507	1.0
6100	Nondepository institutions	10	14	1.4	52	55	31,615	34,327	1,798	1,871	0.5
6160	Mortgage bankers and brokers	7	10	1.6	26	-	40,154	-	1,146	-	-
6280	Security and commodity services	2	3	1.1	-	5	-	10,400	-	38	0.1
6300	Insurance carriers	6	5	0.6	50	-	28,480	-	1,517	-	-
6400	Insurance agents, brokers, and service	35	40	1.6	119	190	22,286	23,389	3,128	4,666	1.1
6500	Real estate	104	120	2.0	250	350	13,824	11,554	3,950	4,497	0.7
6510	Real estate operators and lessors	37	45	1.6	99	105	12,525	11,162	1,348	1,220	0.7
6530	Real estate agents and managers	53	61	2.2	99	152	14,101	13,842	1,611	2,330	0.6
6552	Subdividers and developers, n.e.c.	6	8	2.3	14	62	11,714	2,774	245	229	0.5
6553	Cemetery subdividers and developers	4	4	4.2	14	-	14,571	-	213	-	-
6700	Holding and other investment offices	3	5	1.0	-	32	-	6,750	-	331	0.2
SKAMANIA, WA											
60 –	**Finance, insurance, and real estate**	9	8	0.1	27	27	10,222	12,296	311	373	0.0
6500	Real estate	4	4	0.1	-	10	-	7,200	-	72	0.0
SNOHOMISH, WA											
60 –	**Finance, insurance, and real estate**	1,093	1,122	8.2	7,975	8,361	26,914	28,138	234,528	243,035	6.4
6000	Depository institutions	181	177	8.5	2,099	2,111	25,433	25,122	52,041	52,074	5.3
6020	Commercial banks	100	94	8.2	1,265	1,278	22,817	22,404	28,495	28,402	4.9
6030	Savings institutions	53	54	11.1	664	614	30,542	30,261	19,764	18,352	7.2
6060	Credit unions	17	18	5.6	132	175	27,576	28,914	3,118	4,535	4.4
6090	Functions closely related to banking	11	11	11.0	38	44	15,789	17,273	664	785	2.5
6100	Nondepository institutions	100	108	10.9	820	878	36,078	41,216	32,754	43,504	12.1
6140	Personal credit institutions	31	25	10.5	188	126	28,085	21,397	5,280	2,686	6.3
6160	Mortgage bankers and brokers	66	78	12.4	626	744	38,613	44,656	27,337	40,583	15.1
6200	Security and commodity brokers	43	37	5.2	174	157	46,391	50,013	7,883	8,664	2.4
6210	Security brokers and dealers	26	24	5.7	148	139	52,243	54,360	7,551	8,337	2.9
6280	Security and commodity services	16	13	4.8	-	18	-	16,444	-	327	0.5

Source: County Business Patterns, 1992/93, CBP-92/93-1, U.S. Department of Commerce, Washington, D.C., April 1995. SIC categories for which data were suppressed or not available for both 1992 and 1993 are *not* displayed. The employment columns represent mid-March employment in the year. Pay per employee is calculated by dividing 1st Quarter payroll, annualized, by mid-March employment. The columns headed "% State" show the county's percentage of the state total for the SIC in 1993; for example, 0.9% for SIC 6030 means that the county had 0.9 percent of the state's total establishments (or payroll) in SIC 6030 in 1993. A dash (-) is used to indicate that data are not available or cannot be calculated; *nec* means not elsewhere classified.

Continued on next page.

SIC	Industry	No. Establishments			Employment		Pay / Employee		Annual Payroll ($ 000)		
		1992	1993	% State	1992	1993	1992	1993	1992	1993	% State
SNOHOMISH, WA - [continued]											
6300	Insurance carriers	81	76	8.7	2,132	2,085	29,563	36,401	73,950	70,578	8.3
6310	Life insurance	15	13	6.8	252	258	31,413	35,721	8,464	9,452	4.5
6330	Fire, marine, and casualty insurance	48	48	10.8	382	390	39,351	41,631	15,170	15,807	4.4
6370	Pension, health, and welfare funds	9	8	7.2	-	15	-	19,200	-	166	0.5
6400	Insurance agents, brokers, and service	186	191	7.9	710	820	23,301	24,244	18,108	20,002	4.7
6500	Real estate	467	501	8.1	1,863	2,163	18,495	18,175	39,913	44,909	7.3
6510	Real estate operators and lessors	191	220	7.9	774	1,049	14,202	12,965	13,139	16,750	10.1
6530	Real estate agents and managers	200	241	8.6	827	990	18,626	21,487	19,417	23,894	6.5
6552	Subdividers and developers, n.e.c.	28	25	7.2	117	84	31,487	37,429	3,602	2,782	6.1
6553	Cemetery subdividers and developers	6	7	7.3	26	29	22,154	22,207	621	618	4.1
6700	Holding and other investment offices	35	32	6.4	177	147	54,056	21,088	9,879	3,304	2.3
6732	Educational, religious, etc. trusts	3	4	4.3	5	-	27,200	-	119	-	-
6798	Real estate investment trusts	4	-	-	35	-	26,971	-	1,350	-	-
SPOKANE, WA											
60 -	**Finance, insurance, and real estate**	1,015	1,081	7.9	9,761	9,433	24,179	25,697	244,478	254,230	6.7
6000	Depository institutions	153	156	7.5	2,443	2,425	23,733	22,656	58,794	55,095	5.6
6020	Commercial banks	83	83	7.2	1,724	1,525	24,413	24,026	42,512	36,894	6.3
6060	Credit unions	43	45	13.9	445	626	19,973	17,789	8,769	11,579	11.1
6100	Nondepository institutions	64	84	8.5	1,013	991	29,639	31,366	32,829	35,125	9.8
6140	Personal credit institutions	30	24	10.1	260	182	25,385	24,879	6,496	4,618	10.8
6160	Mortgage bankers and brokers	28	46	7.3	604	603	30,695	31,688	21,417	22,822	8.5
6200	Security and commodity brokers	66	72	10.2	585	599	48,957	45,703	29,914	28,571	8.1
6210	Security brokers and dealers	42	43	10.2	483	447	53,772	52,635	27,114	24,913	8.7
6220	Commodity contracts brokers, dealers	3	3	21.4	8	-	36,000	-	240	-	-
6280	Security and commodity services	21	26	9.6	94	-	25,319	-	2,560	-	-
6300	Insurance carriers	123	118	13.5	1,953	2,225	24,973	26,413	49,055	57,808	6.8
6310	Life insurance	32	30	15.6	946	1,018	21,869	22,589	20,374	22,325	10.5
6330	Fire, marine, and casualty insurance	40	39	8.8	474	567	32,945	35,675	15,107	19,032	5.3
6360	Title insurance	4	3	6.7	110	102	21,273	19,725	2,533	2,338	4.0
6400	Insurance agents, brokers, and service	203	207	8.5	813	870	27,449	27,577	21,700	24,694	5.7
6500	Real estate	355	403	6.6	2,605	1,992	12,633	13,948	37,418	34,003	5.6
6510	Real estate operators and lessors	142	178	6.4	486	773	10,650	12,279	6,030	10,780	6.5
6530	Real estate agents and managers	162	182	6.5	1,806	1,029	11,973	14,150	25,276	17,979	4.9
6552	Subdividers and developers, n.e.c.	13	23	6.6	39	32	20,615	21,875	678	1,281	2.8
6553	Cemetery subdividers and developers	10	10	10.4	66	66	20,970	20,000	1,548	1,598	10.6
6710	Holding offices	9	7	7.3	116	132	76,759	101,576	7,475	12,752	14.2
6732	Educational, religious, etc. trusts	10	8	8.7	35	31	17,943	18,839	639	568	4.6
6733	Trusts, n.e.c.	19	16	11.1	78	70	16,256	12,457	1,519	868	5.9
6799	Investors, n.e.c.	4	5	4.4	7	4	30,857	10,000	270	86	0.5
STEVENS, WA											
60 -	**Finance, insurance, and real estate**	37	42	0.3	306	190	23,464	18,989	7,431	4,279	0.1
6000	Depository institutions	7	6	0.3	74	70	22,324	19,543	1,595	1,490	0.2
6400	Insurance agents, brokers, and service	8	12	0.5	51	58	25,725	22,069	1,335	1,444	0.3
6500	Real estate	17	20	0.3	43	48	12,093	12,750	646	911	0.1
6510	Real estate operators and lessors	4	6	0.2	7	9	6,857	8,889	37	142	0.1
6530	Real estate agents and managers	9	10	0.4	26	35	15,538	14,514	539	643	0.2
THURSTON, WA											
60 -	**Finance, insurance, and real estate**	391	420	3.1	2,296	2,681	22,916	21,644	55,508	65,005	1.7
6000	Depository institutions	68	72	3.5	815	1,019	24,898	21,441	20,860	24,070	2.4
6020	Commercial banks	31	32	2.8	357	403	24,739	21,310	9,038	9,863	1.7
6030	Savings institutions	25	24	4.9	250	263	26,832	22,662	6,955	6,427	2.5
6060	Credit unions	9	13	4.0	203	344	22,049	20,093	4,646	7,392	7.1
6090	Functions closely related to banking	3	3	3.0	5	9	55,200	43,111	221	388	1.2
6100	Nondepository institutions	24	25	2.5	171	130	23,228	27,846	4,675	4,830	1.3
6140	Personal credit institutions	14	10	4.2	132	-	20,061	-	2,807	-	-

Source: County Business Patterns, 1992/93, CBP-92/93-1, U.S. Department of Commerce, Washington, D.C., April 1995. SIC categories for which data were suppressed or not available for both 1992 and 1993 are not displayed. The employment columns represent mid-March employment in the year. Pay per employee is calculated by dividing 1st Quarter payroll, annualized, by mid-March employment. The columns headed "% State" show the county's percentage of the state total for the SIC in 1993; for example, 0.9% for SIC 6030 means that the county had 0.9 percent of the state's total establishments (or payroll) in SIC 6030 in 1993. A dash (-) is used to indicate that data are not available or cannot be calculated; nec means not elsewhere classified.

Continued on next page.

SIC	Industry	No. Establishments			Employment		Pay / Employee		Annual Payroll ($ 000)		
		1992	1993	% State	1992	1993	1992	1993	1992	1993	% State
THURSTON, WA - [continued]											
6160	Mortgage bankers and brokers	7	12	1.9	-	67	-	37,075	-	3,683	1.4
6200	Security and commodity brokers	12	13	1.8	65	68	55,938	54,588	3,497	4,065	1.1
6300	Insurance carriers	31	31	3.6	336	342	29,286	31,450	10,164	11,400	1.3
6310	Life insurance	5	4	2.1	214	199	31,813	32,281	6,426	6,269	3.0
6330	Fire, marine, and casualty insurance	16	17	3.8	37	44	35,135	36,636	1,452	1,769	0.5
6360	Title insurance	2	3	6.7	-	75	-	28,907	-	2,654	4.6
6370	Pension, health, and welfare funds	6	6	5.4	5	-	20,000	-	407	-	-
6400	Insurance agents, brokers, and service	64	71	2.9	221	230	19,385	18,365	4,592	4,595	1.1
6500	Real estate	180	195	3.2	653	858	14,224	14,569	10,341	14,422	2.4
6510	Real estate operators and lessors	81	90	3.2	244	311	11,311	10,611	2,916	3,658	2.2
6530	Real estate agents and managers	72	88	3.2	251	274	16,510	18,701	4,367	5,568	1.5
6552	Subdividers and developers, n.e.c.	10	10	2.9	54	211	8,815	13,630	757	3,710	8.1
6553	Cemetery subdividers and developers	4	4	4.2	16	16	29,250	11,750	492	207	1.4
6733	Trusts, n.e.c.	4	8	5.6	-	8	-	29,000	-	351	2.4
WAHKIAKUM, WA											
60 –	**Finance, insurance, and real estate**	7	6	0.0	15	18	14,933	12,222	228	272	0.0
6000	Depository institutions	3	2	0.1	8	-	21,500	-	137	-	-
WALLA WALLA, WA											
60 –	**Finance, insurance, and real estate**	83	84	0.6	560	630	26,100	23,981	13,558	15,072	0.4
6000	Depository institutions	21	20	1.0	327	352	27,291	24,284	8,147	8,246	0.8
6020	Commercial banks	9	9	0.8	203	221	25,084	23,077	4,843	5,139	0.9
6100	Nondepository institutions	4	5	0.5	18	-	52,444	-	898	-	-
6200	Security and commodity brokers	5	3	0.4	12	-	41,667	-	406	-	-
6300	Insurance carriers	6	5	0.6	41	25	30,146	32,320	997	874	0.1
6400	Insurance agents, brokers, and service	15	15	0.6	69	75	25,217	27,947	1,703	1,954	0.5
6500	Real estate	32	36	0.6	93	108	13,677	12,407	1,407	1,706	0.3
6510	Real estate operators and lessors	16	16	0.6	35	35	12,800	9,943	582	383	0.2
6530	Real estate agents and managers	10	13	0.5	-	39	-	13,026	-	602	0.2
6552	Subdividers and developers, n.e.c.	2	3	0.9	-	12	-	12,667	-	300	0.7
WHATCOM, WA											
60 –	**Finance, insurance, and real estate**	353	388	2.8	2,680	2,688	22,575	24,921	63,302	71,633	1.9
6000	Depository institutions	60	64	3.1	1,286	992	22,488	22,685	30,164	25,782	2.6
6020	Commercial banks	44	38	3.3	1,045	624	22,320	22,679	24,247	15,761	2.7
6030	Savings institutions	9	15	3.1	131	200	25,924	24,500	3,514	6,239	2.4
6100	Nondepository institutions	18	21	2.1	93	97	25,118	25,649	2,387	2,781	0.8
6140	Personal credit institutions	8	7	2.9	43	-	20,279	-	922	-	-
6160	Mortgage bankers and brokers	8	12	1.9	-	75	-	26,293	-	2,159	0.8
6200	Security and commodity brokers	16	19	2.7	55	59	76,873	76,949	3,919	4,571	1.3
6210	Security brokers and dealers	10	13	3.1	46	47	87,739	88,766	3,718	4,211	1.5
6280	Security and commodity services	6	5	1.8	9	9	21,333	23,111	201	220	0.3
6300	Insurance carriers	30	22	2.5	266	225	26,241	29,831	7,190	6,904	0.8
6310	Life insurance	7	4	2.1	31	-	29,935	-	770	-	-
6330	Fire, marine, and casualty insurance	13	11	2.5	-	21	-	47,619	-	1,119	0.3
6360	Title insurance	5	2	4.4	110	-	19,891	-	2,508	-	-
6370	Pension, health, and welfare funds	3	3	2.7	2	-	14,000	-	16	18	0.1
6400	Insurance agents, brokers, and service	53	62	2.6	205	298	24,137	26,107	5,159	7,667	1.8
6500	Real estate	163	184	3.0	739	912	16,893	16,921	13,848	16,775	2.7
6510	Real estate operators and lessors	69	80	2.9	359	429	12,312	10,508	4,637	4,685	2.8
6530	Real estate agents and managers	67	79	2.8	223	261	16,287	16,307	3,736	4,699	1.3
6552	Subdividers and developers, n.e.c.	12	15	4.3	137	196	30,190	31,551	4,977	6,839	14.9
6700	Holding and other investment offices	13	16	3.2	36	105	16,778	71,733	635	7,153	5.0
6732	Educational, religious, etc. trusts	5	5	5.4	13	-	17,846	-	252	-	-
6733	Trusts, n.e.c.	4	3	2.1	6	-	17,333	-	130	-	-

Source: County Business Patterns, 1992/93, CBP-92/93-1, U.S. Department of Commerce, Washington, D.C., April 1995. SIC categories for which data were suppressed or not available for both 1992 and 1993 are *not* displayed. The employment columns represent mid-March employment in the year. Pay per employee is calculated by dividing 1st Quarter payroll, annualized, by mid-March employment. The columns headed "% State" show the county's percentage of the state total for the SIC in 1993; for example, 0.9% for SIC 6030 means that the county had 0.9 percent of the state's total establishments (or payroll) in SIC 6030 in 1993. A dash (-) is used to indicate that data are not available or cannot be calculated; *nec* means not elsewhere classified.

SIC	Industry	No. Establishments			Employment		Pay / Employee		Annual Payroll ($ 000)		
		1992	1993	% State	1992	1993	1992	1993	1992	1993	% State
WHITMAN, WA											
60 –	**Finance, insurance, and real estate**	91	86	*0.6*	382	365	17,246	17,425	6,918	7,028	*0.2*
6000	Depository institutions	28	28	*1.4*	213	220	19,981	18,891	4,276	4,296	*0.4*
6020	Commercial banks	24	24	*2.1*	177	181	19,977	18,608	3,445	3,364	*0.6*
6400	Insurance agents, brokers, and service	24	22	*0.9*	63	60	14,159	15,533	1,165	1,206	*0.3*
6500	Real estate	32	31	*0.5*	90	74	8,933	11,081	899	968	*0.2*
6510	Real estate operators and lessors	17	16	*0.6*	52	28	6,154	11,143	366	380	*0.2*
6530	Real estate agents and managers	8	8	*0.3*	-	31	-	10,839	-	338	*0.1*
6552	Subdividers and developers, n.e.c.	1	3	*0.9*	-	5	-	1,600	-	22	*0.0*
6553	Cemetery subdividers and developers	3	3	*3.1*	2	-	4,000	-	12	-	-
YAKIMA, WA											
60 –	**Finance, insurance, and real estate**	348	373	*2.7*	2,018	2,148	23,231	24,326	47,003	51,958	*1.4*
6000	Depository institutions	59	60	*2.9*	778	741	24,514	21,555	17,333	17,151	*1.7*
6020	Commercial banks	35	34	*3.0*	539	484	25,106	21,124	11,572	10,441	*1.8*
6030	Savings institutions	13	13	*2.7*	143	147	25,538	23,864	3,847	4,356	*1.7*
6100	Nondepository institutions	15	15	*1.5*	83	84	28,916	27,238	2,530	2,514	*0.7*
6140	Personal credit institutions	9	8	*3.4*	60	-	25,933	-	1,550	-	-
6160	Mortgage bankers and brokers	5	5	*0.8*	-	25	-	37,600	-	1,166	*0.4*
6200	Security and commodity brokers	10	12	*1.7*	64	75	66,000	119,733	4,518	5,221	*1.5*
6300	Insurance carriers	39	31	*3.6*	208	162	24,923	32,049	5,717	4,822	*0.6*
6310	Life insurance	8	7	*3.6*	97	99	28,536	32,485	2,649	3,013	*1.4*
6330	Fire, marine, and casualty insurance	16	13	*2.9*	34	-	35,412	-	1,283	-	-
6360	Title insurance	4	-	-	53	-	18,415	-	1,493	-	-
6370	Pension, health, and welfare funds	7	8	*7.2*	5	19	9,600	18,316	100	142	*0.4*
6400	Insurance agents, brokers, and service	73	92	*3.8*	360	455	25,222	24,747	9,623	12,670	*2.9*
6500	Real estate	138	147	*2.4*	411	487	15,153	12,739	6,363	7,075	*1.2*
6510	Real estate operators and lessors	75	77	*2.8*	170	247	12,329	10,607	2,386	2,898	*1.8*
6530	Real estate agents and managers	48	58	*2.1*	159	177	13,434	12,949	2,252	2,727	*0.7*
6552	Subdividers and developers, n.e.c.	2	3	*0.9*	-	31	-	24,258	-	857	*1.9*
6553	Cemetery subdividers and developers	6	6	*6.3*	-	29	-	16,690	-	523	*3.5*
6700	Holding and other investment offices	14	16	*3.2*	114	144	6,070	16,361	919	2,505	*1.7*
6732	Educational, religious, etc. trusts	5	4	*4.3*	100	81	5,160	9,235	678	727	*5.9*
6733	Trusts, n.e.c.	5	9	*6.3*	7	-	4,571	-	21	-	-

Source: County Business Patterns, 1992/93, CBP-92/93-1, U.S. Department of Commerce, Washington, D.C., April 1995. SIC categories for which data were suppressed or not available for both 1992 and 1993 are *not* displayed. The employment columns represent mid-March employment in the year. Pay per employee is calculated by dividing 1st Quarter payroll, annualized, by mid-March employment. The columns headed "% State" show the county's percentage of the state total for the SIC in 1993; for example, 0.9% for SIC 6030 means that the county had 0.9 percent of the state's total establishments (or payroll) in SIC 6030 in 1993. A dash (-) is used to indicate that data are not available or cannot be calculated; *nec* means not elsewhere classified.

WEST VIRGINIA

SIC	Industry	No. Establishments			Employment		Pay / Employee		Annual Payroll ($ 000)		
		1992	1993	% State	1992	1993	1992	1993	1992	1993	% State
BARBOUR, WV											
60 –	**Finance, insurance, and real estate**	16	16	0.5	102	112	18,510	28,536	1,874	3,223	0.6
6000	Depository institutions	5	5	0.7	85	95	19,765	32,042	1,671	3,048	1.2
6020	Commercial banks	5	5	1.0	85	95	19,765	32,042	1,671	3,048	1.3
6400	Insurance agents, brokers, and service	5	6	0.8	8	11	23,000	12,364	174	146	0.2
6500	Real estate	6	5	0.4	9	6	2,667	2,667	29	29	0.0
BERKELEY, WV											
60 –	**Finance, insurance, and real estate**	110	114	3.6	748	777	19,995	19,753	15,521	16,931	3.0
6000	Depository institutions	26	27	3.9	406	378	19,232	19,280	7,812	7,527	3.0
6020	Commercial banks	17	17	3.4	327	304	18,544	20,053	6,068	6,324	2.7
6100	Nondepository institutions	9	9	8.3	37	-	24,541	-	1,012	-	-
6200	Security and commodity brokers	1	3	3.4	-	9	-	20,889	-	290	0.9
6300	Insurance carriers	13	10	4.0	57	89	25,544	28,180	1,629	2,817	3.1
6330	Fire, marine, and casualty insurance	8	7	8.2	50	-	26,640	-	1,498	-	-
6400	Insurance agents, brokers, and service	11	13	1.7	69	75	23,652	21,920	1,826	1,913	2.1
6500	Real estate	47	50	4.3	166	169	16,627	14,935	2,917	2,752	4.6
6510	Real estate operators and lessors	20	16	2.5	82	82	15,415	11,951	1,464	1,065	3.1
6530	Real estate agents and managers	17	26	7.6	49	59	18,367	16,475	890	1,080	6.6
6553	Cemetery subdividers and developers	3	3	2.7	23	-	16,870	-	381	-	-
BOONE, WV											
60 –	**Finance, insurance, and real estate**	24	27	0.9	175	175	16,297	17,303	3,122	3,234	0.6
6000	Depository institutions	6	6	0.9	111	117	19,351	18,632	2,418	2,313	0.9
6400	Insurance agents, brokers, and service	6	6	0.8	21	21	15,238	14,286	343	332	0.4
6500	Real estate	6	8	0.7	16	14	7,500	16,000	126	239	0.4
6510	Real estate operators and lessors	4	4	0.6	-	8	-	21,000	-	180	0.5
BRAXTON, WV											
60 –	**Finance, insurance, and real estate**	12	14	0.4	-	85	-	15,106	-	1,390	0.2
6400	Insurance agents, brokers, and service	3	3	0.4	-	3	-	17,333	-	47	0.1
6530	Real estate agents and managers	2	3	0.9	-	5	-	6,400	-	30	0.2
BROOKE, WV											
60 –	**Finance, insurance, and real estate**	27	26	0.8	160	137	15,000	14,978	2,719	2,414	0.4
6000	Depository institutions	8	7	1.0	92	75	14,609	14,507	1,444	1,200	0.5
6400	Insurance agents, brokers, and service	7	7	0.9	19	-	14,737	-	311	-	-
6500	Real estate	8	9	0.8	13	16	12,923	10,750	199	190	0.3
6553	Cemetery subdividers and developers	4	4	3.6	7	7	13,714	9,143	115	77	1.1
CABELL, WV											
60 –	**Finance, insurance, and real estate**	273	271	8.5	1,964	1,967	20,684	22,090	43,122	44,914	8.0
6000	Depository institutions	40	42	6.1	879	874	18,799	19,863	17,728	18,268	7.2
6020	Commercial banks	23	22	4.4	707	690	19,474	20,858	14,918	15,144	6.6
6100	Nondepository institutions	17	14	12.8	87	91	23,356	18,549	2,050	1,910	-
6200	Security and commodity brokers	9	12	13.8	68	79	61,588	81,570	4,187	4,704	15.3
6300	Insurance carriers	41	34	13.7	328	267	21,451	21,513	7,086	7,092	7.9
6310	Life insurance	13	10	11.5	202	151	24,000	23,762	4,544	3,713	10.9
6370	Pension, health, and welfare funds	20	18	30.0	93	-	10,667	-	1,182	-	-
6400	Insurance agents, brokers, and service	62	66	8.9	216	236	21,370	20,441	4,896	5,255	5.9
6500	Real estate	92	86	7.4	355	361	14,693	12,909	5,698	4,449	7.4
6510	Real estate operators and lessors	55	51	7.9	196	243	11,612	10,749	2,693	2,261	6.6

Source: County Business Patterns, 1992/93, CBP-92/93-1, U.S. Department of Commerce, Washington, D.C., April 1995. SIC categories for which data were suppressed or not available for both 1992 and 1993 are *not* displayed. The employment columns represent mid-March employment in the year. Pay per employee is calculated by dividing 1st Quarter payroll, annualized, by mid-March employment. The columns headed "% State" show the county's percentage of the state total for the SIC in 1993; for example, 0.9% for SIC 6030 means that the county had 0.9 percent of the state's total establishments (or payroll) in SIC 6030 in 1993. A dash (-) is used to indicate that data are not available or cannot be calculated; *nec* means not elsewhere classified.

Continued on next page.

SIC	Industry	No. Establishments			Employment		Pay / Employee		Annual Payroll ($ 000)		
		1992	1993	% State	1992	1993	1992	1993	1992	1993	% State
CABELL, WV - [continued]											
6530	Real estate agents and managers	21	28	8.2	82	85	24,732	19,765	2,135	1,765	10.9
6700	Holding and other investment offices	12	17	13.0	31	59	32,645	46,305	1,477	3,236	13.8
6710	Holding offices	6	7	18.4	16	-	50,500	-	1,204	-	-
CALHOUN, WV											
60 -	**Finance, insurance, and real estate**	7	6	0.2	-	50	-	14,400	-	779	0.1
CLAY, WV											
60 -	**Finance, insurance, and real estate**	7	5	0.2	-	-	-	-	-	-	-
DODDRIDGE, WV											
60 -	**Finance, insurance, and real estate**	3	3	0.1	-	-	-	-	-	-	-
FAYETTE, WV											
60 -	**Finance, insurance, and real estate**	58	57	1.8	446	344	17,471	18,093	7,734	6,485	1.2
6000	Depository institutions	17	17	2.5	332	234	18,349	19,709	6,044	4,685	1.9
6020	Commercial banks	15	14	2.8	-	218	-	20,018	-	4,435	1.9
6400	Insurance agents, brokers, and service	18	18	2.4	50	-	20,240	-	943	-	-
6500	Real estate	17	18	1.6	52	53	10,154	10,189	529	594	1.0
6510	Real estate operators and lessors	9	11	1.7	17	27	8,000	7,259	123	225	0.7
6530	Real estate agents and managers	4	3	0.9	9	5	7,556	4,800	98	46	0.3
GILMER, WV											
60 -	**Finance, insurance, and real estate**	4	4	0.1	-	-	-	-	-	-	-
GRANT, WV											
60 -	**Finance, insurance, and real estate**	18	19	0.6	112	111	19,250	17,766	2,356	2,278	0.4
6000	Depository institutions	5	5	0.7	76	77	19,947	16,675	1,546	1,456	0.6
6500	Real estate	7	8	0.7	-	9	-	13,333	-	120	0.2
6530	Real estate agents and managers	3	4	1.2	-	8	-	14,500	-	111	0.7
GREENBRIER, WV											
60 -	**Finance, insurance, and real estate**	68	73	2.3	483	396	24,323	18,778	12,215	7,612	1.4
6000	Depository institutions	12	13	1.9	240	259	19,533	20,803	5,112	5,423	2.1
6020	Commercial banks	12	12	2.4	240	-	19,533	-	5,112	-	-
6400	Insurance agents, brokers, and service	20	21	2.8	34	40	17,882	16,900	671	704	0.8
6500	Real estate	28	32	2.8	179	69	32,425	8,870	5,733	720	1.2
6510	Real estate operators and lessors	13	14	2.2	32	21	9,375	8,952	276	225	0.7
6530	Real estate agents and managers	8	9	2.6	-	19	-	9,053	-	173	1.1
6552	Subdividers and developers, n.e.c.	1	4	7.5	-	15	-	12,000	-	224	-
6553	Cemetery subdividers and developers	5	5	4.5	13	14	6,769	5,143	110	98	1.4
HAMPSHIRE, WV											
60 -	**Finance, insurance, and real estate**	23	26	0.8	131	150	19,115	18,427	2,490	2,704	0.5
6000	Depository institutions	6	8	1.2	-	102	-	18,353	-	1,784	0.7
6500	Real estate	9	11	1.0	19	16	4,842	6,250	102	137	0.2
6510	Real estate operators and lessors	2	4	0.6	-	4	-	8,000	-	33	0.1
6530	Real estate agents and managers	1	3	0.9	-	4	-	6,000	-	50	0.3
6552	Subdividers and developers, n.e.c.	3	3	5.7	7	-	4,000	-	38	-	-
HANCOCK, WV											
60 -	**Finance, insurance, and real estate**	53	58	1.8	419	441	17,995	16,018	7,318	7,635	1.4
6000	Depository institutions	19	20	2.9	302	304	18,795	16,566	5,177	5,316	2.1
6020	Commercial banks	7	7	1.4	154	145	17,195	18,234	2,827	2,733	1.2
6400	Insurance agents, brokers, and service	13	15	2.0	62	71	16,323	13,634	1,097	1,044	1.2
6500	Real estate	14	18	1.6	27	-	10,222	-	456	-	-

Source: County Business Patterns, 1992/93, CBP-92/93-1, U.S. Department of Commerce, Washington, D.C., April 1995. SIC categories for which data were suppressed or not available for both 1992 and 1993 are *not* displayed. The employment columns represent mid-March employment in the year. Pay per employee is calculated by dividing 1st Quarter payroll, annualized, by mid-March employment. The columns headed "% State" show the county's percentage of the state total for the SIC in 1993; for example, 0.9% for SIC 6030 means that the county had 0.9 percent of the state's total establishments (or payroll) in SIC 6030 in 1993. A dash (-) is used to indicate that data are not available or cannot be calculated; *nec* means not elsewhere classified.

Continued on next page.

SIC	Industry	No. Establishments			Employment		Pay / Employee		Annual Payroll ($ 000)		
		1992	1993	% State	1992	1993	1992	1993	1992	1993	% State
HANCOCK, WV - [continued]											
6510	Real estate operators and lessors	5	10	*1.6*	11	28	8,727	11,571	142	494	*1.4*
6530	Real estate agents and managers	4	5	*1.5*	8	4	10,500	9,000	154	68	*0.4*
6553	Cemetery subdividers and developers	3	3	*2.7*	6	-	11,333		77	-	
HARDY, WV											
60 –	**Finance, insurance, and real estate**	19	22	*0.7*	129	110	16,341	16,873	2,107	2,009	*0.4*
6000	Depository institutions	5	6	*0.9*	-	83	-	19,084	-	1,667	*0.7*
6020	Commercial banks	5	6	*1.2*	-	83	-	19,084	-	1,667	*0.7*
6400	Insurance agents, brokers, and service	6	6	*0.8*	11	-	9,091	-	102	-	
6500	Real estate	6	8	*0.7*	-	12	-	7,333		179	*0.3*
HARRISON, WV											
60 –	**Finance, insurance, and real estate**	149	154	*4.9*	1,083	1,135	21,440	21,720	23,014	24,671	*4.4*
6000	Depository institutions	34	36	*5.2*	528	523	18,682	21,537	9,741	11,402	*4.5*
6020	Commercial banks	26	26	*5.2*	511	502	18,896	21,841	9,532	11,040	*4.8*
6060	Credit unions	8	9	*6.7*	17	-	12,235	-	209	-	-
6100	Nondepository institutions	15	13	*11.9*	119	77	20,336	15,273	2,507	1,170	-
6140	Personal credit institutions	11	9	*11.4*	102	55	20,157	14,327	2,056	777	*7.8*
6210	Security brokers and dealers	4	3	*4.6*	18	-	41,778	-	820	-	
6300	Insurance carriers	13	14	*5.6*	181	171	31,779	32,187	5,793	5,325	*5.9*
6310	Life insurance	6	6	*6.9*	121	118	30,545	29,525	3,510	3,103	*9.1*
6400	Insurance agents, brokers, and service	41	38	*5.1*	121	185	22,116	19,416	2,334	3,628	*4.1*
6500	Real estate	38	45	*3.9*	104	132	10,885	10,182	1,215	1,490	*2.5*
6510	Real estate operators and lessors	23	28	*4.3*	68	74	10,353	10,216	741	857	*2.5*
6530	Real estate agents and managers	11	14	*4.1*	29	55	12,552	10,473	403	616	*3.8*
6553	Cemetery subdividers and developers	4	3	*2.7*	7	3	9,143	4,000	71	17	*0.3*
JACKSON, WV											
60 –	**Finance, insurance, and real estate**	31	31	*1.0*	194	206	21,196	20,602	4,061	4,159	*0.7*
6000	Depository institutions	10	10	*1.4*	115	123	22,609	23,480	2,596	2,755	*1.1*
6400	Insurance agents, brokers, and service	9	10	*1.3*	53	56	20,075	18,000	1,055	1,024	*1.1*
6500	Real estate	8	9	*0.8*	19	-	12,211	-	257	-	-
6510	Real estate operators and lessors	5	7	*1.1*	15	17	13,067	10,353	211	207	*0.6*
JEFFERSON, WV											
60 –	**Finance, insurance, and real estate**	68	65	*2.1*	386	413	17,440	18,063	7,222	7,954	*1.4*
6000	Depository institutions	17	16	*2.3*	249	254	18,618	18,331	4,907	4,904	*1.9*
6400	Insurance agents, brokers, and service	8	9	*1.2*	29	34	31,172	28,706	987	1,035	*1.2*
6500	Real estate	40	35	*3.0*	103	93	9,709	9,806	1,120	1,018	*1.7*
6510	Real estate operators and lessors	12	13	*2.0*	32	36	7,875	7,222	275	308	*0.9*
6530	Real estate agents and managers	13	13	*3.8*	24	36	13,500	11,667	348	463	*2.8*
6552	Subdividers and developers, n.e.c.	4	4	*7.5*	24	-	9,667	-	263	-	-
6553	Cemetery subdividers and developers	2	3	*2.7*	-	7	-	7,429	-	64	*0.9*
KANAWHA, WV											
60 –	**Finance, insurance, and real estate**	552	575	*18.1*	5,948	6,621	25,775	26,980	152,805	179,443	*32.0*
6000	Depository institutions	76	79	*11.4*	2,073	2,025	23,925	24,488	47,250	49,120	*19.4*
6020	Commercial banks	56	52	*10.3*	1,885	1,801	24,119	24,966	42,636	43,495	*18.9*
6140	Personal credit institutions	20	14	*17.7*	143	130	25,063	20,862	3,545	2,777	*27.8*
6160	Mortgage bankers and brokers	4	4	*25.0*	46	-	20,435	-	1,119	-	-
6200	Security and commodity brokers	21	22	*25.3*	191	216	79,225	88,852	13,638	15,338	*50.0*
6210	Security brokers and dealers	17	16	*24.6*	183	188	82,142	101,277	13,545	15,144	*51.4*
6280	Security and commodity services	4	6	*27.3*	8	28	12,500	5,429	93	194	*15.8*
6300	Insurance carriers	75	70	*28.2*	1,297	1,496	25,412	23,465	32,030	36,974	*41.0*
6310	Life insurance	32	26	*29.9*	568	511	23,394	26,254	13,711	12,444	*36.7*
6330	Fire, marine, and casualty insurance	25	23	*27.1*	222	197	35,495	37,909	8,204	7,417	*32.2*
6400	Insurance agents, brokers, and service	108	121	*16.2*	1,102	1,521	22,886	29,386	27,645	44,643	*49.9*
6500	Real estate	209	227	*19.6*	879	964	19,763	17,900	19,468	20,393	*33.9*

Source: County Business Patterns, 1992/93, CBP-92/93-1, U.S. Department of Commerce, Washington, D.C., April 1995. SIC categories for which data were suppressed or not available for both 1992 and 1993 are *not* displayed. The employment columns represent mid-March employment in the year. Pay per employee is calculated by dividing 1st Quarter payroll, annualized, by mid-March employment. The columns headed "% State" show the county's percentage of the state total for the SIC in 1993; for example, 0.9% for SIC 6030 means that the county had 0.9 percent of the state's total establishments (or payroll) in SIC 6030 in 1993. A dash (-) is used to indicate that data are not available or cannot be calculated; *nec* means not elsewhere classified.

Continued on next page.

SIC	Industry	No. Establishments			Employment		Pay / Employee		Annual Payroll ($ 000)		
		1992	1993	% State	1992	1993	1992	1993	1992	1993	% State
KANAWHA, WV - [continued]											
6510	Real estate operators and lessors	135	155	24.1	499	618	22,469	17,819	12,840	13,210	38.6
6530	Real estate agents and managers	54	55	16.1	292	262	16,425	18,580	5,115	5,649	34.8
6552	Subdividers and developers, n.e.c.	2	4	7.5	-	7	-	15,429	-	141	-
6553	Cemetery subdividers and developers	12	13	11.6	74	77	15,568	16,468	1,225	1,393	20.5
6700	Holding and other investment offices	36	34	26.0	194	214	40,825	41,271	7,574	8,499	36.3
6710	Holding offices	8	6	15.8	138	134	48,812	53,552	6,162	6,835	50.8
6732	Educational, religious, etc. trusts	8	11	44.0	20	31	25,000	22,968	704	771	26.7
6733	Trusts, n.e.c.	11	8	27.6	21	14	9,143	19,143	223	289	-
6792	Oil royalty traders	3	3	23.1	6	24	10,667	15,167	62	316	7.6
6799	Investors, n.e.c.	3	6	30.0	-	11	-	28,364	-	288	-
LEWIS, WV											
60 –	**Finance, insurance, and real estate**	21	23	0.7	123	143	14,276	14,490	1,772	2,190	0.4
6000	Depository institutions	4	4	0.6	90	84	15,022	15,762	1,362	1,336	0.5
6020	Commercial banks	4	4	0.8	90	84	15,022	15,762	1,362	1,336	0.6
6500	Real estate	10	11	1.0	16	16	8,500	8,500	142	152	0.3
6510	Real estate operators and lessors	5	7	1.1	11	10	8,727	6,400	102	70	0.2
LINCOLN, WV											
60 –	**Finance, insurance, and real estate**	14	14	0.4	67	-	14,507	-	1,215	-	-
6500	Real estate	3	3	0.3	-	6	-	8,000	19	31	0.1
LOGAN, WV											
60 –	**Finance, insurance, and real estate**	60	58	1.8	368	421	19,772	19,449	7,803	7,455	1.3
6000	Depository institutions	12	14	2.0	210	244	18,324	19,902	4,449	4,311	1.7
6100	Nondepository institutions	4	3	2.8	18	27	23,778	12,444	445	316	-
6140	Personal credit institutions	4	3	3.8	18	27	23,778	12,444	445	316	3.2
6300	Insurance carriers	5	5	2.0	-	25	-	20,000	-	437	0.5
6310	Life insurance	3	2	2.3	3	-	2,667	-	10	-	-
6400	Insurance agents, brokers, and service	12	12	1.6	35	33	23,314	23,879	856	831	0.9
6500	Real estate	24	20	1.7	90	83	13,689	13,157	1,336	1,152	1.9
6510	Real estate operators and lessors	14	12	1.9	64	58	14,688	12,690	1,005	755	2.2
6530	Real estate agents and managers	6	5	1.5	8	-	9,000	-	77	-	-
MCDOWELL, WV											
60 –	**Finance, insurance, and real estate**	28	28	0.9	202	200	19,287	18,100	4,448	4,202	0.7
6000	Depository institutions	10	10	1.4	142	140	21,296	20,229	3,495	3,358	1.3
6020	Commercial banks	10	10	2.0	142	140	21,296	20,229	3,495	3,358	1.5
6400	Insurance agents, brokers, and service	7	7	0.9	30	31	11,733	10,839	364	335	0.4
6500	Real estate	9	8	0.7	27	24	18,667	18,000	572	488	0.8
6510	Real estate operators and lessors	8	5	0.8	-	19	-	13,053	-	275	0.8
MARION, WV											
60 –	**Finance, insurance, and real estate**	99	103	3.2	865	851	17,114	22,599	15,460	18,468	3.3
6000	Depository institutions	26	26	3.8	556	513	16,475	23,018	8,917	11,905	4.7
6300	Insurance carriers	10	11	4.4	87	101	22,115	22,495	2,173	2,440	2.7
6370	Pension, health, and welfare funds	3	4	6.7	8	27	6,000	9,037	25	149	-
6400	Insurance agents, brokers, and service	19	20	2.7	64	69	17,812	19,246	1,450	1,571	1.8
6500	Real estate	29	33	2.9	94	88	8,511	8,955	834	889	1.5
6510	Real estate operators and lessors	14	18	2.8	63	69	8,381	9,101	537	630	1.8
6530	Real estate agents and managers	7	9	2.6	14	7	7,143	4,571	105	93	0.6
6553	Cemetery subdividers and developers	6	6	5.4	13	12	9,846	10,667	155	166	2.4
6700	Holding and other investment offices	10	9	6.9	50	56	27,360	46,286	1,662	1,209	5.2
MARSHALL, WV											
60 –	**Finance, insurance, and real estate**	34	31	1.0	-	-	-	-	-	-	-

Source: County Business Patterns, 1992/93, CBP-92/93-1, U.S. Department of Commerce, Washington, D.C., April 1995. SIC categories for which data were suppressed or not available for both 1992 and 1993 are not displayed. The employment columns represent mid-March employment in the year. Pay per employee is calculated by dividing 1st Quarter payroll, annualized, by mid-March employment. The columns headed "% State" show the county's percentage of the state total for the SIC in 1993; for example, 0.9% for SIC 6030 means that the county had 0.9 percent of the state's total establishments (or payroll) in SIC 6030 in 1993. A dash (-) is used to indicate that data are not available or cannot be calculated; nec means not elsewhere classified.

Continued on next page.

SIC	Industry	No. Establishments			Employment		Pay / Employee		Annual Payroll ($ 000)		
		1992	1993	% State	1992	1993	1992	1993	1992	1993	% State
MARSHALL, WV - [continued]											
6000	Depository institutions	13	12	*1.7*	184	171	14,348	16,327	2,766	2,868	*1.1*
6020	Commercial banks	8	8	*1.6*	172	160	14,791	16,850	2,672	2,767	*1.2*
6510	Real estate operators and lessors	3	3	*0.5*	6	6	7,333	6,667	44	33	*0.1*
MASON, WV											
60 –	**Finance, insurance, and real estate**	30	34	*1.1*	194	200	17,485	17,360	3,510	3,774	*0.7*
6000	Depository institutions	8	8	*1.2*	142	144	19,521	19,417	2,784	2,996	*1.2*
6500	Real estate	11	15	*1.3*	22	26	10,545	11,692	312	402	*0.7*
6510	Real estate operators and lessors	5	5	*0.8*	11	10	12,727	13,200	146	157	*0.5*
6530	Real estate agents and managers	3	6	*1.8*	4	10	8,000	12,400	97	166	*1.0*
MERCER, WV											
60 –	**Finance, insurance, and real estate**	117	112	*3.5*	824	870	24,995	25,255	20,678	20,816	*3.7*
6000	Depository institutions	21	25	*3.6*	328	408	20,646	19,588	6,975	7,534	*3.0*
6020	Commercial banks	12	16	*3.2*	306	384	21,451	20,188	6,730	7,271	*3.2*
6200	Security and commodity brokers	6	6	*6.9*	-	20	-	47,200	-	1,054	*3.4*
6210	Security brokers and dealers	5	5	*7.7*	18	-	55,778	-	869	-	*-*
6300	Insurance carriers	10	8	*3.2*	75	86	37,653	36,419	2,676	2,957	*3.3*
6310	Life insurance	5	5	*5.7*	65	-	33,662	-	2,032	-	*-*
6400	Insurance agents, brokers, and service	32	30	*4.0*	181	167	28,972	32,431	5,198	4,685	*5.2*
6500	Real estate	37	32	*2.8*	147	100	13,116	14,720	2,069	1,563	*2.6*
6510	Real estate operators and lessors	18	17	*2.6*	94	38	11,532	9,684	1,153	363	*1.1*
6530	Real estate agents and managers	11	7	*2.1*	22	23	13,273	21,217	320	486	*3.0*
6553	Cemetery subdividers and developers	6	6	*5.4*	-	35	-	16,571	-	682	*10.0*
MINERAL, WV											
60 –	**Finance, insurance, and real estate**	33	32	*1.0*	188	180	16,170	15,978	2,999	2,947	*0.5*
6000	Depository institutions	9	11	*1.6*	113	114	17,345	16,386	1,943	1,951	*0.8*
6400	Insurance agents, brokers, and service	11	11	*1.5*	35	-	16,000	-	558	-	*-*
6500	Real estate	10	9	*0.8*	-	21	-	6,286	-	136	*0.2*
6530	Real estate agents and managers	6	8	*2.3*	11	-	4,364	-	53	-	*-*
MINGO, WV											
60 –	**Finance, insurance, and real estate**	31	32	*1.0*	286	297	17,958	18,694	5,592	6,429	*1.1*
6000	Depository institutions	12	12	*1.7*	234	239	18,222	19,849	4,746	5,516	*2.2*
6020	Commercial banks	12	12	*2.4*	234	239	18,222	19,849	4,746	5,516	*2.4*
6400	Insurance agents, brokers, and service	7	8	*1.1*	23	-	15,826	-	419	-	*-*
6500	Real estate	10	11	*1.0*	-	31	-	11,742	-	414	*0.7*
6510	Real estate operators and lessors	5	8	*1.2*	13	-	9,231	-	109	-	*-*
MONONGALIA, WV											
60 –	**Finance, insurance, and real estate**	166	174	*5.5*	1,262	1,324	17,480	17,495	23,015	23,727	*4.2*
6000	Depository institutions	31	31	*4.5*	593	577	17,848	19,882	10,515	11,310	*4.5*
6020	Commercial banks	23	22	*4.4*	551	529	18,185	20,567	9,959	10,623	*4.6*
6100	Nondepository institutions	6	5	*4.6*	22	32	21,636	21,875	511	824	*-*
6200	Security and commodity brokers	3	5	*5.7*	13	13	23,077	22,769	332	226	*0.7*
6300	Insurance carriers	16	11	*4.4*	129	178	25,023	16,337	3,737	2,784	*3.1*
6370	Pension, health, and welfare funds	4	3	*5.0*	20	-	8,000	-	282	-	*-*
6400	Insurance agents, brokers, and service	25	30	*4.0*	97	92	23,670	24,217	2,221	2,123	*2.4*
6500	Real estate	78	82	*7.1*	302	316	12,053	11,962	4,121	4,457	*7.4*
6510	Real estate operators and lessors	47	57	*8.9*	175	229	12,503	11,354	2,473	3,215	*9.4*
6530	Real estate agents and managers	21	20	*5.9*	62	71	14,323	14,028	984	1,006	*6.2*
6700	Holding and other investment offices	7	10	*7.6*	106	116	14,491	15,345	1,578	2,003	*8.6*
6732	Educational, religious, etc. trusts	5	5	*20.0*	103	109	14,680	15,009	1,554	1,838	*63.7*

Source: County Business Patterns, 1992/93, CBP-92/93-1, U.S. Department of Commerce, Washington, D.C., April 1995. SIC categories for which data were suppressed or not available for both 1992 and 1993 are *not* displayed. The employment columns represent mid-March employment in the year. Pay per employee is calculated by dividing 1st Quarter payroll, annualized, by mid-March employment. The columns headed "% State" show the county's percentage of the state total for the SIC in 1993; for example, 0.9% for SIC 6030 means that the county had 0.9 percent of the state's total establishments (or payroll) in SIC 6030 in 1993. A dash (-) is used to indicate that data are not available or cannot be calculated; *nec* means not elsewhere classified.

SIC	Industry	No. Establishments			Employment		Pay / Employee		Annual Payroll ($ 000)		
		1992	1993	% State	1992	1993	1992	1993	1992	1993	% State
MONROE, WV											
60–	**Finance, insurance, and real estate**	12	12	0.4	50	–	16,320	–	856	–	–
6000	Depository institutions	5	5	0.7	42	40	17,429	18,500	778	811	0.3
6020	Commercial banks	5	5	1.0	42	40	17,429	18,500	778	811	0.4
MORGAN, WV											
60–	**Finance, insurance, and real estate**	19	20	0.6	103	103	21,553	16,039	2,348	1,924	0.3
6400	Insurance agents, brokers, and service	4	4	0.5	14	–	21,143	–	336	–	–
6500	Real estate	9	10	0.9	12	10	15,000	18,000	204	254	0.4
6530	Real estate agents and managers	3	4	1.2	6	–	8,000	–	57	–	–
NICHOLAS, WV											
60–	**Finance, insurance, and real estate**	43	46	1.5	239	196	14,879	20,551	4,046	3,939	0.7
6000	Depository institutions	9	10	1.4	151	140	16,583	21,771	2,590	2,743	1.1
6300	Insurance carriers	3	3	1.2	2	4	16,000	26,000	160	137	0.2
6400	Insurance agents, brokers, and service	13	12	1.6	26	25	13,538	15,840	422	514	0.6
6500	Real estate	14	18	1.6	50	21	8,560	12,381	507	358	0.6
6510	Real estate operators and lessors	7	11	1.7	17	–	9,176	–	178	–	–
6530	Real estate agents and managers	4	5	1.5	7	8	10,857	9,500	75	106	0.7
OHIO, WV											
60–	**Finance, insurance, and real estate**	146	150	4.7	1,570	1,698	23,954	20,973	34,671	37,721	6.7
6000	Depository institutions	28	30	4.3	737	789	19,425	19,265	14,748	15,991	6.3
6020	Commercial banks	14	16	3.2	578	651	20,581	19,957	12,109	13,618	5.9
6140	Personal credit institutions	6	4	5.1	24	35	20,000	12,343	489	478	4.8
6200	Security and commodity brokers	7	6	6.9	64	69	142,250	72,348	4,708	4,730	15.4
6210	Security brokers and dealers	7	6	9.2	64	69	142,250	72,348	4,708	4,730	16.1
6300	Insurance carriers	21	21	8.5	410	455	22,429	22,171	9,340	10,538	11.7
6310	Life insurance	6	7	8.0	142	177	22,254	22,147	3,226	3,570	10.5
6330	Fire, marine, and casualty insurance	6	6	7.1	–	23	–	36,696	–	907	3.9
6400	Insurance agents, brokers, and service	25	24	3.2	115	117	19,652	19,453	2,721	2,905	3.2
6500	Real estate	54	60	5.2	170	191	9,718	10,660	1,993	2,476	4.1
6510	Real estate operators and lessors	31	34	5.3	108	130	9,037	10,123	1,102	1,494	4.4
6530	Real estate agents and managers	15	20	5.9	28	28	10,714	11,143	308	399	2.5
PENDLETON, WV											
60–	**Finance, insurance, and real estate**	7	8	0.3	–	–	–	–	–	–	–
PLEASANTS, WV											
60–	**Finance, insurance, and real estate**	10	10	0.3	67	70	16,119	15,657	1,127	1,167	0.2
6000	Depository institutions	5	4	0.6	54	56	16,667	16,571	955	995	0.4
POCAHONTAS, WV											
60–	**Finance, insurance, and real estate**	11	13	0.4	78	114	15,282	14,316	1,289	1,589	0.3
6500	Real estate	4	6	0.5	5	47	8,000	11,660	60	349	0.6
PRESTON, WV											
60–	**Finance, insurance, and real estate**	44	46	1.5	226	230	18,796	22,209	4,530	4,765	0.8
6000	Depository institutions	10	12	1.7	151	164	16,450	15,537	2,636	2,659	1.1
6400	Insurance agents, brokers, and service	10	11	1.5	24	–	17,333	–	470	–	–
6500	Real estate	18	20	1.7	37	–	10,270	–	471	–	–
6510	Real estate operators and lessors	7	10	1.6	–	14	–	9,714	–	134	0.4
6553	Cemetery subdividers and developers	3	5	4.5	5	–	3,200	–	20	–	–
PUTNAM, WV											
60–	**Finance, insurance, and real estate**	54	50	1.6	245	250	19,020	18,800	5,094	5,215	0.9
6000	Depository institutions	9	10	1.4	133	141	23,338	20,738	3,191	3,163	1.2
6020	Commercial banks	6	6	1.2	123	129	24,065	21,147	3,042	2,946	1.3
6100	Nondepository institutions	3	1	0.9	5	–	21,600	–	159	–	–

Source: County Business Patterns, 1992/93, CBP-92/93-1, U.S. Department of Commerce, Washington, D.C., April 1995. SIC categories for which data were suppressed or not available for both 1992 and 1993 are not displayed. The employment columns represent mid-March employment in the year. Pay per employee is calculated by dividing 1st Quarter payroll, annualized, by mid-March employment. The columns headed "% State" show the county's percentage of the state total for the SIC in 1993; for example, 0.9% for SIC 6030 means that the county had 0.9 percent of the state's total establishments (or payroll) in SIC 6030 in 1993. A dash (-) is used to indicate that data are not available or cannot be calculated; nec means not elsewhere classified.

Continued on next page.

SIC	Industry	No. Establishments			Employment		Pay / Employee		Annual Payroll ($ 000)		
		1992	1993	% State	1992	1993	1992	1993	1992	1993	% State
PUTNAM, WV - [continued]											
6400	Insurance agents, brokers, and service	16	16	2.1	40	43	19,000	16,837	732	906	1.0
6500	Real estate	21	20	1.7	57	52	8,000	10,231	562	634	1.1
6510	Real estate operators and lessors	10	9	1.4	29	22	7,172	6,909	246	228	0.7
6530	Real estate agents and managers	3	4	1.2	8	5	10,000	24,000	87	89	0.5
6552	Subdividers and developers, n.e.c.	3	4	7.5	9	-	13,778	-	157	-	-
6553	Cemetery subdividers and developers	3	3	2.7	9	-	3,556	-	45	-	-
RALEIGH, WV											
60 –	**Finance, insurance, and real estate**	138	141	4.4	929	913	22,045	23,049	19,513	21,849	3.9
6000	Depository institutions	21	21	3.0	396	378	18,535	20,815	7,245	8,022	3.2
6020	Commercial banks	16	15	3.0	377	351	18,398	20,991	6,842	7,516	3.3
6100	Nondepository institutions	8	8	7.3	38	60	26,947	15,800	1,049	942	-
6140	Personal credit institutions	8	7	8.9	38	-	26,947	-	1,049	-	-
6200	Security and commodity brokers	4	2	2.3	15	-	50,400	-	765	-	-
6210	Security brokers and dealers	4	2	3.1	15	-	50,400	-	765	-	-
6300	Insurance carriers	17	15	6.0	122	101	18,852	26,139	2,161	2,744	3.0
6310	Life insurance	7	6	6.9	39	40	28,205	24,900	896	967	2.8
6330	Fire, marine, and casualty insurance	5	4	4.7	15	-	60,267	-	922	-	-
6400	Insurance agents, brokers, and service	29	33	4.4	109	127	25,725	22,709	2,663	3,326	3.7
6500	Real estate	50	53	4.6	228	219	23,561	25,461	4,797	5,462	9.1
6510	Real estate operators and lessors	27	34	5.3	90	123	10,222	28,455	1,046	3,398	9.9
6530	Real estate agents and managers	14	12	3.5	58	27	27,655	13,778	836	412	2.5
6700	Holding and other investment offices	9	9	6.9	21	-	42,095	-	833	-	-
6710	Holding offices	5	4	10.5	15	11	56,000	41,091	798	634	4.7
RANDOLPH, WV											
60 –	**Finance, insurance, and real estate**	50	49	1.5	388	345	16,619	16,267	6,612	6,005	1.1
6000	Depository institutions	9	7	1.0	249	212	17,414	16,623	4,372	3,722	1.5
6400	Insurance agents, brokers, and service	15	16	2.1	49	48	19,673	19,917	1,044	1,010	1.1
6500	Real estate	20	20	1.7	64	60	9,062	9,667	602	648	1.1
6510	Real estate operators and lessors	10	9	1.4	49	40	8,408	9,700	426	446	1.3
RITCHIE, WV											
60 –	**Finance, insurance, and real estate**	12	12	0.4	106	104	17,170	18,731	1,700	1,804	0.3
6000	Depository institutions	5	5	0.7	76	75	15,421	16,107	1,157	1,197	0.5
6020	Commercial banks	5	5	1.0	76	75	15,421	16,107	1,157	1,197	0.5
ROANE, WV											
60 –	**Finance, insurance, and real estate**	17	17	0.5	133	133	19,429	17,744	2,566	2,386	0.4
6000	Depository institutions	4	4	0.6	111	109	21,117	19,376	2,308	2,112	0.8
6020	Commercial banks	4	4	0.8	111	109	21,117	19,376	2,308	2,112	0.9
6400	Insurance agents, brokers, and service	6	6	0.8	11	12	13,091	12,667	152	161	0.2
6500	Real estate	7	7	0.6	11	12	8,727	8,000	106	113	0.2
6510	Real estate operators and lessors	4	4	0.6	7	5	8,571	8,000	59	59	0.2
SUMMERS, WV											
60 –	**Finance, insurance, and real estate**	16	15	0.5	112	112	19,536	17,821	2,047	2,032	0.4
6500	Real estate	5	4	0.3	5	-	5,600	-	35	-	-
TAYLOR, WV											
60 –	**Finance, insurance, and real estate**	12	11	0.3	50	-	16,000	-	830	-	-
6000	Depository institutions	4	5	0.7	29	48	19,034	14,167	593	753	0.3
6400	Insurance agents, brokers, and service	3	5	0.7	8	-	10,000	-	83	-	-
TUCKER, WV											
60 –	**Finance, insurance, and real estate**	20	21	0.7	119	163	14,050	12,123	1,945	2,094	0.4
6000	Depository institutions	5	5	0.7	58	62	16,345	15,032	1,182	1,213	0.5
6020	Commercial banks	5	5	1.0	58	62	16,345	15,032	1,182	1,213	0.5

Source: County Business Patterns, 1992/93, CBP-92/93-1, U.S. Department of Commerce, Washington, D.C., April 1995. SIC categories for which data were suppressed or not available for both 1992 and 1993 are not displayed. The employment columns represent mid-March employment in the year. Pay per employee is calculated by dividing 1st Quarter payroll, annualized, by mid-March employment. The columns headed "% State" show the county's percentage of the state total for the SIC in 1993; for example, 0.9% for SIC 6030 means that the county had 0.9 percent of the state's total establishments (or payroll) in SIC 6030 in 1993. A dash (-) is used to indicate that data are not available or cannot be calculated; nec means not elsewhere classified.

Continued on next page.

SIC	Industry	No. Establishments			Employment		Pay / Employee		Annual Payroll ($ 000)		
		1992	1993	% State	1992	1993	1992	1993	1992	1993	% State
TUCKER, WV - [continued]											
6400	Insurance agents, brokers, and service	3	4	0.5	7	10	20,571	14,400	166	169	0.2
6500	Real estate	12	12	1.0	54	91	10,741	9,890	597	712	1.2
6510	Real estate operators and lessors	3	2	0.3	13	-	4,615	-	74	-	-
6530	Real estate agents and managers	7	7	2.1	-	74	-	8,973	-	487	3.0
TYLER, WV											
60 –	**Finance, insurance, and real estate**	11	10	0.3	-	-	-	-	-	-	-
6000	Depository institutions	5	5	0.7	58	57	15,655	15,860	971	999	0.4
UPSHUR, WV											
60 –	**Finance, insurance, and real estate**	26	26	0.8	184	175	17,413	16,800	3,811	3,018	0.5
6000	Depository institutions	5	6	0.9	129	127	17,271	17,795	2,249	2,264	0.9
6020	Commercial banks	5	6	1.2	129	127	17,271	17,795	2,249	2,264	1.0
6400	Insurance agents, brokers, and service	6	7	0.9	21	-	14,857	-	302	-	-
6500	Real estate	9	8	0.7	19	16	9,053	10,250	299	193	0.3
6510	Real estate operators and lessors	4	2	0.3	9	-	14,667	-	132	-	-
6530	Real estate agents and managers	4	6	1.8	9	-	4,000	-	161	-	-
WAYNE, WV											
60 –	**Finance, insurance, and real estate**	40	42	1.3	275	336	18,720	19,548	5,601	6,094	1.1
6000	Depository institutions	11	12	1.7	156	227	20,795	21,093	3,678	4,182	1.7
6020	Commercial banks	7	8	1.6	139	209	21,899	21,895	3,453	3,952	1.7
6400	Insurance agents, brokers, and service	13	12	1.6	76	70	20,000	20,343	1,414	1,362	1.5
6500	Real estate	13	14	1.2	-	38	-	9,263	-	533	0.9
6510	Real estate operators and lessors	9	11	1.7	-	30	-	9,600	-	468	1.4
6530	Real estate agents and managers	4	2	0.6	11	-	8,000	-	87	-	-
WEBSTER, WV											
60 –	**Finance, insurance, and real estate**	5	8	0.3	-	-	-	-	-	-	-
WETZEL, WV											
60 –	**Finance, insurance, and real estate**	35	36	1.1	224	231	15,268	15,740	3,606	3,802	0.7
6000	Depository institutions	14	15	2.2	163	177	15,067	16,339	2,499	2,961	1.2
6020	Commercial banks	10	10	2.0	132	130	15,697	16,523	2,103	2,159	0.9
6500	Real estate	10	10	0.9	15	18	11,467	12,222	215	265	0.4
6510	Real estate operators and lessors	6	7	1.1	9	10	9,778	10,400	92	115	0.3
WIRT, WV											
60 –	**Finance, insurance, and real estate**	4	4	0.1	-	-	-	-	-	-	-
WOOD, WV											
60 –	**Finance, insurance, and real estate**	185	194	6.1	1,516	1,525	20,813	20,808	35,303	34,338	6.1
6000	Depository institutions	39	38	5.5	681	642	19,471	20,019	14,256	12,952	5.1
6020	Commercial banks	26	26	5.2	613	577	19,667	20,506	13,000	11,887	5.2
6100	Nondepository institutions	9	6	5.5	50	25	20,480	20,480	1,128	675	-
6140	Personal credit institutions	6	5	6.3	23	-	24,000	-	617	-	-
6200	Security and commodity brokers	8	13	14.9	32	29	61,750	56,552	1,829	2,044	6.7
6210	Security brokers and dealers	6	10	15.4	-	28	-	58,286	-	2,030	6.9
6280	Security and commodity services	2	3	13.6	-	1	-	8,000	-	14	1.1
6300	Insurance carriers	19	16	6.5	344	411	24,895	24,506	10,491	11,038	12.2
6310	Life insurance	7	7	8.0	130	129	21,508	22,233	2,802	3,153	9.3
6400	Insurance agents, brokers, and service	42	45	6.0	132	131	20,273	17,740	2,649	2,672	3.0
6500	Real estate	60	67	5.8	245	253	13,714	13,992	3,704	3,862	6.4
6510	Real estate operators and lessors	29	41	6.4	113	150	13,451	14,293	1,670	2,278	6.7
6530	Real estate agents and managers	16	17	5.0	47	61	13,787	12,918	769	1,013	6.2
6552	Subdividers and developers, n.e.c.	6	1	1.9	35	-	14,057	-	474	-	-

Source: County Business Patterns, 1992/93, CBP-92/93-1, U.S. Department of Commerce, Washington, D.C., April 1995. SIC categories for which data were suppressed or not available for both 1992 and 1993 are *not* displayed. The employment columns represent mid-March employment in the year. Pay per employee is calculated by dividing 1st Quarter payroll, annualized, by mid-March employment. The columns headed "% State" show the county's percentage of the state total for the SIC in 1993; for example, 0.9% for SIC 6030 means that the county had 0.9 percent of the state's total establishments (or payroll) in SIC 6030 in 1993. A dash (-) is used to indicate that data are not available or cannot be calculated; *nec* means not elsewhere classified.

Continued on next page.

SIC	Industry	No. Establishments			Employment		Pay / Employee		Annual Payroll ($ 000)		
		1992	1993	% State	1992	1993	1992	1993	1992	1993	% State
WOOD, WV - [continued]											
6553	Cemetery subdividers and developers	6	7	6.3	41	39	15,024	14,667	657	521	7.7
6700	Holding and other investment offices	8	9	6.9	32	34	21,625	23,294	1,246	1,095	4.7
6792	Oil royalty traders	1	3	23.1	-	17	-	12,471	-	139	3.4
WYOMING, WV											
60 –	**Finance, insurance, and real estate**	17	22	0.7	151	143	17,219	14,713	2,841	2,388	0.4
6000	Depository institutions	4	7	1.0	113	108	17,274	15,148	2,157	1,854	0.7
6020	Commercial banks	4	7	1.4	113	108	17,274	15,148	2,157	1,854	0.8
6500	Real estate	5	5	0.4	16	16	11,750	12,250	225	219	0.4

Source: *County Business Patterns, 1992/93*, CBP-92/93-1, U.S. Department of Commerce, Washington, D.C., April 1995. SIC categories for which data were suppressed or not available for both 1992 and 1993 are *not* displayed. The employment columns represent mid-March employment in the year. Pay per employee is calculated by dividing 1st Quarter payroll, annualized, by mid-March employment. The columns headed "% State" show the county's percentage of the state total for the SIC in 1993; for example, 0.9% for SIC 6030 means that the county had 0.9 percent of the state's total establishments (or payroll) in SIC 6030 in 1993. A dash (-) is used to indicate that data are not available or cannot be calculated; *nec* means not elsewhere classified.

WISCONSIN

SIC	Industry	No. Establishments			Employment		Pay / Employee		Annual Payroll ($ 000)		
		1992	1993	% State	1992	1993	1992	1993	1992	1993	% State
ADAMS, WI											
60 –	**Finance, insurance, and real estate**	18	17	0.1	90	-	15,378	-	1,406	-	-
6000	Depository institutions	4	4	0.2	56	-	16,714	-	909	-	-
6400	Insurance agents, brokers, and service	5	5	0.2	12	-	13,333	-	156	-	-
6500	Real estate	9	8	0.2	22	22	13,091	14,727	341	415	0.1
ASHLAND, WI											
60 –	**Finance, insurance, and real estate**	42	42	0.4	295	294	17,166	18,980	5,223	5,575	0.1
6000	Depository institutions	9	10	0.4	157	149	19,312	22,067	2,921	3,031	0.3
6060	Credit unions	3	4	0.8	4	9	3,000	6,667	11	64	0.1
6400	Insurance agents, brokers, and service	9	13	0.4	26	29	19,385	16,552	516	621	0.2
6510	Real estate operators and lessors	5	2	0.1	16	-	10,500	-	242	-	-
6530	Real estate agents and managers	4	5	0.3	-	20	-	3,600	-	173	0.1
BARRON, WI											
60 –	**Finance, insurance, and real estate**	84	80	0.7	607	443	18,959	19,847	11,292	9,473	0.2
6000	Depository institutions	22	21	0.9	355	247	19,470	19,870	6,191	5,204	0.6
6020	Commercial banks	13	14	1.1	222	194	20,018	20,000	4,758	4,112	0.6
6030	Savings institutions	6	4	0.8	112	29	18,250	20,552	993	632	0.4
6060	Credit unions	3	3	0.6	21	24	20,190	18,000	440	460	0.6
6400	Insurance agents, brokers, and service	25	30	1.0	74	72	16,324	18,611	1,597	1,722	0.5
6500	Real estate	28	23	0.6	64	69	13,188	14,377	1,014	1,077	0.3
6510	Real estate operators and lessors	10	8	0.5	13	9	8,000	11,111	124	108	0.1
6530	Real estate agents and managers	13	11	0.7	-	27	-	10,667	-	326	0.2
BAYFIELD, WI											
60 –	**Finance, insurance, and real estate**	24	21	0.2	105	98	21,181	19,714	2,286	2,102	0.1
6000	Depository institutions	10	10	0.4	81	81	21,333	21,481	1,829	1,870	0.2
6500	Real estate	11	8	0.2	18	12	23,778	10,667	382	156	0.0
6530	Real estate agents and managers	7	6	0.4	10	-	5,200	-	110	-	-
BROWN, WI											
60 –	**Finance, insurance, and real estate**	463	478	4.1	7,573	7,395	25,468	23,696	188,720	183,862	4.6
6000	Depository institutions	89	89	3.8	1,694	1,802	24,149	21,760	37,297	38,417	4.2
6020	Commercial banks	40	40	3.0	1,177	1,241	26,399	23,017	27,503	27,690	4.2
6030	Savings institutions	26	27	5.6	303	325	21,888	21,625	6,371	6,890	3.9
6060	Credit unions	22	22	4.3	-	236	-	15,339	-	3,837	5.1
6100	Nondepository institutions	23	19	3.8	223	207	26,314	25,237	6,289	6,240	3.3
6160	Mortgage bankers and brokers	8	8	4.5	102	90	28,235	26,178	3,520	3,781	3.4
6200	Security and commodity brokers	26	29	5.1	145	179	48,828	56,670	6,814	8,895	2.6
6210	Security brokers and dealers	16	16	4.5	124	130	55,935	71,631	6,662	7,886	3.4
6300	Insurance carriers	53	39	4.8	3,713	2,744	25,613	24,273	91,228	65,782	3.9
6310	Life insurance	15	10	5.1	153	-	24,471	-	4,399	-	-
6330	Fire, marine, and casualty insurance	19	16	4.3	337	387	31,181	30,243	9,360	8,122	1.6
6400	Insurance agents, brokers, and service	120	138	4.4	1,068	1,685	23,213	22,697	28,365	44,865	12.7
6500	Real estate	138	148	3.9	540	649	13,667	14,681	8,957	11,921	3.7
6510	Real estate operators and lessors	56	63	4.0	274	342	11,139	13,906	3,703	4,817	4.6
6530	Real estate agents and managers	55	65	3.8	175	208	17,714	16,192	3,307	4,551	2.8
6540	Title abstract offices	7	8	5.9	44	83	15,273	14,554	1,178	2,199	8.0
6552	Subdividers and developers, n.e.c.	3	8	6.7	1	7	16,000	8,571	62	120	0.9
6553	Cemetery subdividers and developers	4	4	1.6	11	9	10,909	15,111	196	234	2.2

Source: County Business Patterns, 1992/93, CBP-92/93-1, U.S. Department of Commerce, Washington, D.C., April 1995. SIC categories for which data were suppressed or not available for both 1992 and 1993 are not displayed. The employment columns represent mid-March employment in the year. Pay per employee is calculated by dividing 1st Quarter payroll, annualized, by mid-March employment. The columns headed "% State" show the county's percentage of the state total for the SIC in 1993; for example, 0.9% for SIC 6030 means that the county had 0.9 percent of the state's total establishments (or payroll) in SIC 6030 in 1993. A dash (-) is used to indicate that data are not available or cannot be calculated; nec means not elsewhere classified.

Continued on next page.

SIC	Industry	No. Establishments			Employment		Pay / Employee		Annual Payroll ($ 000)		
		1992	1993	% State	1992	1993	1992	1993	1992	1993	% State
BROWN, WI - [continued]											
6700	Holding and other investment offices	14	16	4.3	190	129	61,811	48,651	9,770	7,742	4.8
6710	Holding offices	7	6	4.2	161	104	69,093	53,192	9,113	7,040	6.5
6732	Educational, religious, etc. trusts	3	3	5.8	5	-	9,600	-	47	-	-
BUFFALO, WI											
60 –	**Finance, insurance, and real estate**	28	28	0.2	126	122	17,111	17,344	2,333	2,402	0.1
6000	Depository institutions	9	9	0.4	86	85	18,233	17,506	1,751	1,685	0.2
6400	Insurance agents, brokers, and service	10	11	0.4	23	22	12,522	13,091	293	328	0.1
6500	Real estate	6	6	0.2	6	-	6,667	-	34	-	-
6530	Real estate agents and managers	4	3	0.2	4	2	7,000	4,000	23	24	0.0
BURNETT, WI											
60 –	**Finance, insurance, and real estate**	19	20	0.2	111	111	17,586	15,856	2,401	1,877	0.0
6000	Depository institutions	5	5	0.2	-	64	-	19,938	-	1,284	0.1
6400	Insurance agents, brokers, and service	2	3	0.1	-	16	-	12,750	-	229	0.1
6500	Real estate	11	12	0.3	-	31	-	9,032	-	364	0.1
6530	Real estate agents and managers	4	6	0.4	5	-	7,200	-	69	-	-
CALUMET, WI											
60 –	**Finance, insurance, and real estate**	65	68	0.6	354	371	20,780	24,507	8,720	9,851	0.2
6000	Depository institutions	17	19	0.8	160	186	18,375	19,935	3,090	3,657	0.4
6020	Commercial banks	11	11	0.8	126	126	18,667	21,302	2,519	2,615	0.4
6100	Nondepository institutions	4	2	0.4	29	-	20,138	-	599	-	-
6300	Insurance carriers	4	2	0.2	12	-	13,667	-	166	-	-
6400	Insurance agents, brokers, and service	21	23	0.7	43	54	23,535	21,037	1,132	1,390	0.4
6500	Real estate	12	13	0.3	68	71	15,294	17,690	1,492	1,542	0.5
6510	Real estate operators and lessors	4	8	0.5	14	-	10,571	-	204	-	-
6530	Real estate agents and managers	7	4	0.2	-	51	-	20,549	-	1,286	0.8
6700	Holding and other investment offices	3	6	1.6	-	34	-	67,294	-	2,508	1.6
CHIPPEWA, WI											
60 –	**Finance, insurance, and real estate**	80	83	0.7	423	464	18,156	18,422	8,590	9,313	0.2
6000	Depository institutions	25	27	1.2	257	291	16,700	16,330	4,605	4,977	0.5
6020	Commercial banks	16	17	1.3	197	203	17,157	17,438	3,652	3,714	0.6
6030	Savings institutions	5	5	1.0	30	-	15,467	-	516	-	-
6060	Credit unions	4	5	1.0	30	-	14,933	-	437	-	-
6300	Insurance carriers	6	6	0.7	64	59	26,000	25,966	1,530	1,685	0.1
6400	Insurance agents, brokers, and service	25	26	0.8	62	68	15,419	16,235	1,626	1,627	0.5
6500	Real estate	19	20	0.5	25	29	10,080	13,103	220	338	0.1
6510	Real estate operators and lessors	8	10	0.6	-	16	-	7,750	-	162	0.2
6530	Real estate agents and managers	8	4	0.2	10	7	16,800	30,857	96	94	0.1
6553	Cemetery subdividers and developers	3	6	2.4	-	6	-	6,667	-	82	0.8
CLARK, WI											
60 –	**Finance, insurance, and real estate**	64	63	0.5	348	330	17,333	16,982	5,862	5,568	0.1
6000	Depository institutions	24	25	1.1	235	249	19,251	18,731	4,337	4,469	0.5
6020	Commercial banks	19	20	1.5	215	228	19,684	19,140	4,043	4,139	0.6
6100	Nondepository institutions	2	3	0.6	-	5	-	16,000	-	95	0.1
6400	Insurance agents, brokers, and service	20	19	0.6	45	-	11,733	-	502	-	-
6500	Real estate	15	14	0.4	56	-	14,857	-	867	-	-
6510	Real estate operators and lessors	3	2	0.1	3	-	2,667	-	17	-	-
6530	Real estate agents and managers	5	6	0.4	-	7	-	6,286	-	74	0.0
6553	Cemetery subdividers and developers	3	3	1.2	4	3	2,000	2,667	7	9	0.1
COLUMBIA, WI											
60 –	**Finance, insurance, and real estate**	98	102	0.9	636	715	17,767	16,179	12,517	13,189	0.3
6000	Depository institutions	26	27	1.2	294	316	20,680	18,190	6,551	6,566	0.7
6020	Commercial banks	21	21	1.6	265	284	21,525	18,831	6,134	6,064	0.9

Source: County Business Patterns, 1992/93, CBP-92/93-1, U.S. Department of Commerce, Washington, D.C., April 1995. SIC categories for which data were suppressed or not available for both 1992 and 1993 are *not* displayed. The employment columns represent mid-March employment in the year. Pay per employee is calculated by dividing 1st Quarter payroll, annualized, by mid-March employment. The columns headed "% State" show the county's percentage of the state total for the SIC in 1993; for example, 0.9% for SIC 6030 means that the county had 0.9 percent of the state's total establishments (or payroll) in SIC 6030 in 1993. A dash (-) is used to indicate that data are not available or cannot be calculated; *nec* means not elsewhere classified.

Continued on next page.

SIC	Industry	No. Establishments			Employment		Pay / Employee		Annual Payroll ($ 000)		
		1992	1993	% State	1992	1993	1992	1993	1992	1993	% State
COLUMBIA, WI - [continued]											
6030	Savings institutions	3	3	0.6	-	28	-	13,286	-	473	0.3
6060	Credit unions	2	3	0.6	-	4	-	7,000	-	29	0.0
6100	Nondepository institutions	3	2	0.4	14	-	23,714	-	320	-	-
6300	Insurance carriers	12	10	1.2	121	113	18,843	20,531	2,510	2,509	0.1
6400	Insurance agents, brokers, and service	24	27	0.9	66	67	12,606	13,075	912	978	0.3
6500	Real estate	28	32	0.8	132	198	11,515	9,172	1,857	2,396	0.8
6510	Real estate operators and lessors	5	9	0.6	11	29	8,727	8,000	131	229	0.2
6530	Real estate agents and managers	14	15	0.9	75	143	11,040	8,531	888	1,663	1.0
CRAWFORD, WI											
60 –	**Finance, insurance, and real estate**	30	31	0.3	187	141	14,631	16,511	2,577	2,509	0.1
6000	Depository institutions	7	7	0.3	143	103	14,993	17,087	1,909	1,874	0.2
6500	Real estate	10	11	0.3	14	11	5,714	6,182	107	103	0.0
6510	Real estate operators and lessors	4	5	0.3	4	-	5,000	-	18	-	-
6530	Real estate agents and managers	3	4	0.2	4	4	12,000	12,000	75	75	0.0
DANE, WI											
60 –	**Finance, insurance, and real estate**	1,059	1,096	9.5	21,153	21,395	25,982	25,446	560,391	599,917	15.0
6000	Depository institutions	153	155	6.6	3,641	3,689	23,355	22,402	84,035	84,057	9.2
6020	Commercial banks	75	77	5.9	2,248	2,282	24,722	24,559	53,680	54,355	8.3
6030	Savings institutions	42	38	7.9	890	859	22,499	19,367	20,439	19,141	10.9
6060	Credit unions	34	40	7.9	-	548	-	18,175	-	10,561	13.9
6100	Nondepository institutions	60	52	10.4	691	1,146	25,279	24,098	17,914	30,881	16.3
6140	Personal credit institutions	29	19	8.7	-	667	-	20,654	-	15,328	34.7
6150	Business credit institutions	10	8	12.3	266	-	26,647	-	6,726	-	-
6160	Mortgage bankers and brokers	19	22	12.4	254	320	25,449	27,550	7,368	10,840	9.7
6200	Security and commodity brokers	45	51	9.0	396	426	60,030	78,864	25,199	33,940	10.0
6210	Security brokers and dealers	28	27	7.6	245	241	81,176	86,622	18,957	17,720	7.7
6300	Insurance carriers	144	123	15.1	12,151	11,937	26,551	25,998	326,821	350,998	20.6
6310	Life insurance	46	34	17.3	3,909	3,791	27,438	29,537	120,624	130,747	14.7
6321	Accident and health insurance	5	5	19.2	-	139	-	30,791	-	4,081	5.2
6324	Hospital and medical service plans	7	13	22.4	-	3,375	-	18,980	-	69,584	46.0
6330	Fire, marine, and casualty insurance	54	46	12.2	4,057	4,300	30,247	28,442	118,129	139,684	27.0
6360	Title insurance	9	2	8.0	390	-	60,800	-	14,801	-	-
6370	Pension, health, and welfare funds	18	18	15.7	105	140	19,733	18,143	2,395	2,615	15.7
6400	Insurance agents, brokers, and service	227	256	8.2	1,156	1,255	29,682	29,122	36,739	38,587	11.0
6500	Real estate	384	417	11.0	2,367	2,719	16,446	17,383	43,648	53,449	16.7
6510	Real estate operators and lessors	156	182	11.6	818	785	12,533	13,885	11,599	12,272	11.8
6530	Real estate agents and managers	183	202	12.0	1,292	1,497	17,433	18,194	24,717	30,777	19.0
6540	Title abstract offices	3	6	4.4	-	199	-	19,658	-	4,777	17.4
6552	Subdividers and developers, n.e.c.	15	15	12.6	84	206	29,952	20,583	3,168	4,140	31.6
6553	Cemetery subdividers and developers	4	6	2.4	-	18	-	15,333	-	356	3.4
6700	Holding and other investment offices	46	42	11.4	751	223	36,559	28,735	26,035	8,005	5.0
6732	Educational, religious, etc. trusts	12	7	13.5	65	45	21,969	29,511	1,644	1,714	20.9
6733	Trusts, n.e.c.	11	15	18.1	50	54	22,320	23,704	1,011	1,364	4.4
6799	Investors, n.e.c.	6	5	9.3	-	58	-	25,724	-	2,042	25.1
DODGE, WI											
60 –	**Finance, insurance, and real estate**	138	140	1.2	862	910	20,719	21,451	18,322	19,092	0.5
6000	Depository institutions	37	40	1.7	395	431	18,927	21,104	7,773	8,370	0.9
6020	Commercial banks	25	25	1.9	338	374	19,669	22,182	6,922	7,512	1.1
6030	Savings institutions	6	6	1.3	38	36	14,316	15,889	563	627	0.4
6060	Credit unions	6	9	1.8	19	21	14,947	10,857	288	231	0.3
6100	Nondepository institutions	7	5	1.0	-	40	-	26,800	-	845	0.4
6140	Personal credit institutions	5	2	0.9	13	-	8,615	-	145	-	-
6200	Security and commodity brokers	5	5	0.9	13	21	31,692	31,048	371	630	0.2
6300	Insurance carriers	14	11	1.3	173	176	28,486	26,295	5,013	5,115	0.3
6330	Fire, marine, and casualty insurance	10	9	2.4	156	-	28,154	-	4,494	-	-

Source: County Business Patterns, 1992/93, CBP-92/93-1, U.S. Department of Commerce, Washington, D.C., April 1995. SIC categories for which data were suppressed or not available for both 1992 and 1993 are not displayed. The employment columns represent mid-March employment in the year. Pay per employee is calculated by dividing 1st Quarter payroll, annualized, by mid-March employment. The columns headed "% State" show the county's percentage of the state total for the SIC in 1993; for example, 0.9% for SIC 6030 means that the county had 0.9 percent of the state's total establishments (or payroll) in SIC 6030 in 1993. A dash (-) is used to indicate that data are not available or cannot be calculated; nec means not elsewhere classified.

Continued on next page.

SIC	Industry	No. Establishments			Employment		Pay / Employee		Annual Payroll ($ 000)		
		1992	1993	% State	1992	1993	1992	1993	1992	1993	% State
DODGE, WI - [continued]											
6400	Insurance agents, brokers, and service	35	41	1.3	131	146	23,206	22,055	2,893	3,081	0.9
6500	Real estate	39	38	1.0	106	96	8,566	8,875	1,117	1,051	0.3
6510	Real estate operators and lessors	15	16	1.0	38	39	7,579	6,769	303	312	0.3
6530	Real estate agents and managers	9	11	0.7	22	-	10,182	-	249	-	
6553	Cemetery subdividers and developers	9	9	3.6	19	21	4,000	4,000	158	171	1.6
DOOR, WI											
60-	**Finance, insurance, and real estate**	79	83	0.7	426	447	16,535	16,886	7,694	7,656	0.2
6000	Depository institutions	17	17	0.7	216	189	18,778	21,206	4,429	3,916	0.4
6200	Security and commodity brokers	4	4	0.7	18	-	42,222	-	705	-	
6400	Insurance agents, brokers, and service	14	16	0.5	50	79	21,040	13,165	1,108	1,113	0.3
6500	Real estate	41	44	1.2	135	160	7,674	9,950	1,310	1,760	0.6
6510	Real estate operators and lessors	7	9	0.6	26	-	8,000	-	205	-	
6530	Real estate agents and managers	28	30	1.8	93	109	8,129	10,092	1,016	1,183	0.7
6553	Cemetery subdividers and developers	3	3	1.2	11	-	2,545	-	31	-	
DOUGLAS, WI											
60-	**Finance, insurance, and real estate**	79	83	0.7	492	468	16,122	17,821	8,411	8,699	0.2
6000	Depository institutions	18	23	1.0	244	275	19,000	19,375	4,723	5,208	0.6
6020	Commercial banks	8	8	0.6	169	176	20,355	21,909	3,461	3,572	0.5
6100	Nondepository institutions	6	1	0.2	29	-	12,552	-	402	-	
6140	Personal credit institutions	6	1	0.5	29	-	12,552	-	402	-	
6300	Insurance carriers	5	5	0.6	-	11	-	28,727	-	348	0.0
6400	Insurance agents, brokers, and service	21	22	0.7	66	81	19,576	18,568	1,387	1,785	0.5
6500	Real estate	27	30	0.8	133	92	9,323	11,304	1,483	1,202	0.4
6510	Real estate operators and lessors	10	12	0.8	56	23	8,714	9,739	597	232	0.2
6530	Real estate agents and managers	8	11	0.7	52	-	7,538	-	461	-	
6553	Cemetery subdividers and developers	5	5	2.0	7	7	10,286	11,429	89	88	0.8
DUNN, WI											
60-	**Finance, insurance, and real estate**	81	82	0.7	371	369	18,081	19,393	7,000	7,421	0.2
6000	Depository institutions	26	23	1.0	230	229	17,478	18,550	4,304	4,540	0.5
6300	Insurance carriers	4	3	0.4	13	9	40,000	73,778	400	450	0.0
6400	Insurance agents, brokers, and service	17	21	0.7	51	55	16,471	18,109	895	1,025	0.3
6500	Real estate	26	29	0.8	49	49	11,184	7,592	610	515	0.2
6510	Real estate operators and lessors	7	7	0.4	14	-	5,429	-	139	-	
6530	Real estate agents and managers	11	16	0.9	18	27	8,222	6,815	158	242	0.1
6553	Cemetery subdividers and developers	4	4	1.6	-	3	-	2,667	-	14	0.1
6700	Holding and other investment offices	3	2	0.5	11	-	12,000	-	103	-	
EAU CLAIRE, WI											
60-	**Finance, insurance, and real estate**	233	245	2.1	1,732	1,896	23,485	21,097	40,343	42,715	1.1
6000	Depository institutions	44	49	2.1	701	772	20,850	17,736	14,487	15,323	1.7
6020	Commercial banks	22	24	1.8	363	413	22,358	20,387	7,560	8,709	1.3
6030	Savings institutions	7	7	1.5	123	132	20,000	16,818	2,804	3,323	1.9
6060	Credit unions	14	18	3.5	-	227	-	13,445	-	3,291	4.3
6100	Nondepository institutions	13	9	1.8	35	36	18,286	15,778	829	764	0.4
6140	Personal credit institutions	9	5	2.3	25	27	16,640	13,926	448	382	0.9
6160	Mortgage bankers and brokers	2	4	2.2	-	9	-	21,333	-	382	0.3
6200	Security and commodity brokers	12	13	2.3	71	79	67,944	59,443	4,550	4,688	1.4
6210	Security brokers and dealers	8	10	2.8	64	73	72,438	63,945	4,378	4,655	2.0
6280	Security and commodity services	3	3	1.5	-	6	-	4,667	-	33	-
6300	Insurance carriers	33	26	3.2	383	376	30,548	30,734	11,161	11,136	0.7
6310	Life insurance	10	7	3.6	119	119	33,815	32,269	3,956	3,684	0.4
6330	Fire, marine, and casualty insurance	12	11	2.9	125	131	32,896	29,740	4,051	4,394	0.9
6400	Insurance agents, brokers, and service	56	68	2.2	250	257	20,752	21,323	5,263	6,045	1.7
6500	Real estate	67	70	1.8	276	343	12,029	10,647	3,785	4,490	1.4
6510	Real estate operators and lessors	25	34	2.2	112	107	12,321	11,738	1,481	1,571	1.5

Source: County Business Patterns, 1992/93, CBP-92/93-1, U.S. Department of Commerce, Washington, D.C., April 1995. SIC categories for which data were suppressed or not available for both 1992 and 1993 are not displayed. The employment columns represent mid-March employment in the year. Pay per employee is calculated by dividing 1st Quarter payroll, annualized, by mid-March employment. The columns headed "% State" show the county's percentage of the state total for the SIC in 1993; for example, 0.9% for SIC 6030 means that the county had 0.9 percent of the state's total establishments (or payroll) in SIC 6030 in 1993. A dash (-) is used to indicate that data are not available or cannot be calculated; nec means not elsewhere classified.

Continued on next page.

SIC	Industry	No. Establishments			Employment		Pay / Employee		Annual Payroll ($ 000)		
		1992	1993	% State	1992	1993	1992	1993	1992	1993	% State
EAU CLAIRE, WI - [continued]											
6530	Real estate agents and managers	21	22	*1.3*	81	193	10,914	9,098	1,113	2,202	*1.4*
6540	Title abstract offices	3	3	*2.2*	11	13	20,364	19,385	280	305	*1.1*
6552	Subdividers and developers, n.e.c.	3	5	*4.2*	8	25	18,500	14,400	178	383	*2.9*
6553	Cemetery subdividers and developers	6	6	*2.4*	9	5	4,000	5,600	31	29	*0.3*
6700	Holding and other investment offices	8	10	*2.7*	16	33	24,250	10,788	268	269	*0.2*
6733	Trusts, n.e.c.	3	2	*2.4*	4	-	34,000	-	87	-	-
FLORENCE, WI											
60 –	**Finance, insurance, and real estate**	5	5	*0.0*	17	16	15,765	17,250	338	359	*0.0*
FOND DU LAC, WI											
60 –	**Finance, insurance, and real estate**	171	186	*1.6*	1,324	1,448	23,091	23,086	31,096	34,082	*0.9*
6000	Depository institutions	32	40	*1.7*	577	621	20,354	22,306	12,935	13,764	*1.5*
6020	Commercial banks	21	25	*1.9*	455	480	21,345	24,333	10,773	11,400	*1.7*
6100	Nondepository institutions	10	6	*1.2*	62	49	24,065	32,082	2,156	2,005	*1.1*
6140	Personal credit institutions	7	3	*1.4*	22	16	16,182	14,250	317	201	*0.5*
6200	Security and commodity brokers	9	10	*1.8*	41	-	52,000	-	2,050	-	-
6210	Security brokers and dealers	8	8	*2.2*	-	38	-	64,632	-	2,439	*1.1*
6300	Insurance carriers	15	12	*1.5*	282	269	36,113	32,877	7,421	7,250	*0.4*
6400	Insurance agents, brokers, and service	54	62	*2.0*	175	237	16,914	16,321	3,384	4,585	*1.3*
6500	Real estate	47	52	*1.4*	183	193	11,126	12,290	3,113	3,468	*1.1*
6510	Real estate operators and lessors	14	13	*0.8*	35	40	9,486	10,700	755	786	*0.8*
6530	Real estate agents and managers	20	24	*1.4*	87	95	10,161	10,863	1,328	1,484	*0.9*
6540	Title abstract offices	3	4	*2.9*	13	16	23,077	21,500	416	513	*1.9*
6700	Holding and other investment offices	4	4	*1.1*	4	-	6,000	-	37	-	-
FOREST, WI											
60 –	**Finance, insurance, and real estate**	13	16	*0.1*	63	76	15,365	14,474	1,077	1,194	*0.0*
6000	Depository institutions	4	4	*0.2*	44	50	17,545	16,800	859	872	*0.1*
6400	Insurance agents, brokers, and service	3	5	*0.2*	10	14	12,000	9,143	123	166	*0.0*
6500	Real estate	6	7	*0.2*	9	12	8,444	11,000	95	156	*0.0*
6510	Real estate operators and lessors	3	3	*0.2*	5	-	6,400	-	27	-	-
GRANT, WI											
60 –	**Finance, insurance, and real estate**	112	117	*1.0*	586	565	18,662	20,821	11,435	11,370	*0.3*
6000	Depository institutions	36	32	*1.4*	346	325	18,844	21,182	7,253	7,114	*0.8*
6020	Commercial banks	29	27	*2.1*	310	301	19,716	21,515	6,706	6,712	*1.0*
6400	Insurance agents, brokers, and service	27	31	*1.0*	89	91	23,236	24,044	1,684	1,795	*0.5*
6500	Real estate	33	42	*1.1*	63	72	8,825	10,611	714	877	*0.3*
6510	Real estate operators and lessors	10	23	*1.5*	16	28	4,500	3,857	76	132	*0.1*
6530	Real estate agents and managers	10	9	*0.5*	21	22	8,571	13,455	207	305	*0.2*
6553	Cemetery subdividers and developers	6	7	*2.8*	4	4	3,000	3,000	39	64	*0.6*
6700	Holding and other investment offices	3	3	*0.8*	47	38	16,511	19,474	797	778	*0.5*
GREEN, WI											
60 –	**Finance, insurance, and real estate**	69	67	*0.6*	422	455	17,450	17,899	8,172	8,626	*0.2*
6000	Depository institutions	15	15	*0.6*	268	314	20,149	19,529	5,876	6,337	*0.7*
6300	Insurance carriers	8	5	*0.6*	55	-	10,764	-	611	-	-
6400	Insurance agents, brokers, and service	25	26	*0.8*	48	63	13,417	13,079	702	920	*0.3*
6500	Real estate	17	17	*0.4*	39	41	10,154	13,268	554	715	*0.2*
6510	Real estate operators and lessors	8	9	*0.6*	10	16	5,600	9,250	60	138	*0.1*
6530	Real estate agents and managers	5	5	*0.3*	14	7	11,429	14,857	176	126	*0.1*
GREEN LAKE, WI											
60 –	**Finance, insurance, and real estate**	39	42	*0.4*	208	218	16,519	15,963	3,854	4,051	*0.1*
6000	Depository institutions	11	12	*0.5*	129	142	19,814	18,423	2,737	2,910	*0.3*
6400	Insurance agents, brokers, and service	14	15	*0.5*	26	29	12,308	12,690	362	393	*0.1*

Source: County Business Patterns, 1992/93, CBP-92/93-1, U.S. Department of Commerce, Washington, D.C., April 1995. SIC categories for which data were suppressed or not available for both 1992 and 1993 are not displayed. The employment columns represent mid-March employment in the year. Pay per employee is calculated by dividing 1st Quarter payroll, annualized, by mid-March employment. The columns headed "% State" show the county's percentage of the state total for the SIC in 1993; for example, 0.9% for SIC 6030 means that the county had 0.9 percent of the state's total establishments (or payroll) in SIC 6030 in 1993. A dash (-) is used to indicate that data are not available or cannot be calculated; nec means not elsewhere classified.

Continued on next page.

SIC	Industry	No. Establishments			Employment		Pay / Employee		Annual Payroll ($ 000)		
		1992	1993	% State	1992	1993	1992	1993	1992	1993	% State
GREEN LAKE, WI - [continued]											
6500	Real estate	10	10	0.3	-	30	-	8,667	-	516	0.2
6510	Real estate operators and lessors	5	3	0.2	19	-	6,737	-	176	-	-
6530	Real estate agents and managers	1	4	0.2	-	5	-	10,400	-	49	0.0
IOWA, WI											
60 –	**Finance, insurance, and real estate**	35	37	0.3	213	182	16,507	17,121	3,822	3,160	0.1
6000	Depository institutions	12	10	0.4	136	112	17,882	17,821	2,597	2,078	0.2
6300	Insurance carriers	3	2	0.2	16	-	10,500	-	133	-	-
6400	Insurance agents, brokers, and service	9	12	0.4	25	26	15,040	13,231	474	592	0.2
6500	Real estate	10	11	0.3	-	18	-	14,222	-	248	0.1
6510	Real estate operators and lessors	6	6	0.4	15	-	7,200	-	106	-	-
6530	Real estate agents and managers	3	4	0.2	3	4	16,000	15,000	133	90	0.1
IRON, WI											
60 –	**Finance, insurance, and real estate**	17	17	0.1	85	72	13,035	13,222	1,032	984	0.0
6000	Depository institutions	5	5	0.2	31	27	14,581	16,593	493	479	0.1
6400	Insurance agents, brokers, and service	4	6	0.2	6	10	23,333	15,600	144	191	0.1
6500	Real estate	8	6	0.2	48	35	10,750	9,943	395	314	0.1
6530	Real estate agents and managers	4	3	0.2	39	-	10,564	-	274	-	-
JACKSON, WI											
60 –	**Finance, insurance, and real estate**	40	42	0.4	166	175	15,518	16,823	3,028	3,156	0.1
6000	Depository institutions	11	11	0.5	100	109	19,000	19,229	2,278	2,233	0.2
6400	Insurance agents, brokers, and service	13	14	0.4	44	39	10,091	15,897	503	640	0.2
6500	Real estate	13	15	0.4	18	-	10,667	-	211	-	-
6530	Real estate agents and managers	3	3	0.2	-	4	-	11,000	-	46	0.0
6553	Cemetery subdividers and developers	5	6	2.4	1	3	4,000	2,667	21	21	0.2
JEFFERSON, WI											
60 –	**Finance, insurance, and real estate**	125	133	1.2	770	813	17,699	17,934	14,532	15,321	0.4
6000	Depository institutions	30	30	1.3	481	467	19,435	20,188	9,562	9,547	1.0
6020	Commercial banks	18	18	1.4	370	354	21,157	22,158	7,974	7,705	1.2
6030	Savings institutions	5	5	1.0	30	28	14,400	15,714	443	510	0.3
6060	Credit unions	7	7	1.4	81	85	13,432	13,459	1,145	1,332	1.8
6100	Nondepository institutions	3	4	0.8	-	22	-	20,182	-	328	0.2
6200	Security and commodity brokers	7	10	1.8	23	-	41,043	-	966	-	-
6210	Security brokers and dealers	4	4	1.1	20	21	43,800	40,571	897	1,086	0.5
6280	Security and commodity services	3	6	3.0	3	-	22,667	-	69	-	-
6300	Insurance carriers	11	8	1.0	52	-	13,154	-	806	-	-
6370	Pension, health, and welfare funds	3	3	2.6	9	-	7,556	-	39	-	-
6400	Insurance agents, brokers, and service	32	36	1.1	67	102	14,866	17,843	1,064	1,775	0.5
6500	Real estate	38	41	1.1	114	136	9,018	8,765	1,312	1,581	0.5
6510	Real estate operators and lessors	12	18	1.1	44	79	8,182	9,367	358	840	0.8
6530	Real estate agents and managers	16	13	0.8	36	24	11,889	11,500	608	421	0.3
6553	Cemetery subdividers and developers	5	7	2.8	17	19	2,588	2,316	96	101	1.0
JUNEAU, WI											
60 –	**Finance, insurance, and real estate**	45	45	0.4	197	212	17,807	16,962	3,633	3,624	0.1
6000	Depository institutions	15	15	0.6	133	144	19,759	18,250	2,678	2,613	0.3
6400	Insurance agents, brokers, and service	11	14	0.4	26	32	16,154	16,250	440	500	0.1
6500	Real estate	16	14	0.4	32	-	10,375	-	436	-	-
6510	Real estate operators and lessors	7	8	0.5	9	23	2,222	11,304	22	306	0.3
6530	Real estate agents and managers	5	3	0.2	15	3	12,267	6,667	248	25	0.0
KENOSHA, WI											
60 –	**Finance, insurance, and real estate**	219	231	2.0	1,461	1,797	19,173	19,136	33,198	38,851	1.0
6000	Depository institutions	51	55	2.4	742	859	17,660	18,906	14,722	16,866	1.8
6020	Commercial banks	25	27	2.1	460	572	18,452	18,161	9,135	10,657	1.6

Source: County Business Patterns, 1992/93, CBP-92/93-1, U.S. Department of Commerce, Washington, D.C., April 1995. SIC categories for which data were suppressed or not available for both 1992 and 1993 are not displayed. The employment columns represent mid-March employment in the year. Pay per employee is calculated by dividing 1st Quarter payroll, annualized, by mid-March employment. The columns headed "% State" show the county's percentage of the state total for the SIC in 1993; for example, 0.9% for SIC 6030 means that the county had 0.9 percent of the state's total establishments (or payroll) in SIC 6030 in 1993. A dash (-) is used to indicate that data are not available or cannot be calculated; nec means not elsewhere classified.

Continued on next page.

SIC	Industry	No. Establishments			Employment		Pay / Employee		Annual Payroll ($ 000)		
		1992	1993	% State	1992	1993	1992	1993	1992	1993	% State
KENOSHA, WI - [continued]											
6100	Nondepository institutions	7	9	1.8	36	48	27,444	28,250	1,533	3,850	2.0
6140	Personal credit institutions	4	4	1.8	-	14	-	21,143	-	1,765	4.0
6200	Security and commodity brokers	9	9	1.6	30	41	67,867	59,902	1,858	2,326	0.7
6210	Security brokers and dealers	9	9	2.5	30	41	67,867	59,902	1,858	2,326	1.0
6300	Insurance carriers	19	14	1.7	64	39	20,125	17,333	2,020	820	0.0
6370	Pension, health, and welfare funds	3	3	2.6	12	-	8,667	-	161	-	-
6400	Insurance agents, brokers, and service	46	58	1.9	167	198	21,916	19,232	4,330	4,725	1.3
6500	Real estate	76	77	2.0	240	279	16,133	16,975	4,360	5,864	1.8
6510	Real estate operators and lessors	30	27	1.7	78	79	12,256	12,861	1,060	1,144	1.1
6530	Real estate agents and managers	27	40	2.4	88	141	15,364	18,298	1,606	2,507	1.5
6552	Subdividers and developers, n.e.c.	4	3	2.5	6	-	9,333	-	80	-	-
6553	Cemetery subdividers and developers	5	5	2.0	23	22	13,217	16,182	372	353	3.3
6700	Holding and other investment offices	11	9	2.4	182	333	16,835	15,363	4,375	4,400	2.8
KEWAUNEE, WI											
60 –	**Finance, insurance, and real estate**	33	33	0.3	198	212	17,091	16,340	3,734	4,139	0.1
6000	Depository institutions	13	13	0.6	148	158	17,892	16,937	2,763	3,093	0.3
6400	Insurance agents, brokers, and service	9	9	0.3	29	30	18,759	19,733	743	803	0.2
6500	Real estate	6	6	0.2	10	13	6,400	6,769	92	115	0.0
LA CROSSE, WI											
60 –	**Finance, insurance, and real estate**	245	253	2.2	1,827	2,045	22,945	22,093	45,946	49,849	1.2
6000	Depository institutions	37	43	1.8	717	793	22,008	20,731	17,044	17,637	1.9
6020	Commercial banks	18	18	1.4	346	352	24,173	24,375	8,482	8,252	1.3
6060	Credit unions	9	15	2.9	74	-	20,378	-	1,537	-	-
6100	Nondepository institutions	13	12	2.4	53	42	14,340	17,048	742	745	0.4
6140	Personal credit institutions	11	7	3.2	-	31	-	13,677	-	446	1.0
6160	Mortgage bankers and brokers	2	5	2.8	-	11	-	26,545	-	299	0.3
6200	Security and commodity brokers	15	18	3.2	63	78	55,302	56,000	3,094	4,024	1.2
6210	Security brokers and dealers	8	9	2.5	50	58	65,120	69,310	2,763	3,583	1.6
6300	Insurance carriers	32	19	2.3	325	132	27,729	28,212	10,074	3,595	0.2
6310	Life insurance	9	4	2.0	115	32	24,452	32,500	3,531	818	0.1
6330	Fire, marine, and casualty insurance	15	10	2.7	176	64	30,773	29,562	5,616	1,826	0.4
6400	Insurance agents, brokers, and service	60	68	2.2	295	319	21,329	20,953	7,359	8,099	2.3
6500	Real estate	81	88	2.3	339	658	16,000	18,304	6,223	14,748	4.6
6510	Real estate operators and lessors	44	53	3.4	242	551	16,793	19,833	4,527	13,270	12.8
6530	Real estate agents and managers	28	30	1.8	68	-	13,706	-	1,177	-	-
6700	Holding and other investment offices	7	5	1.4	35	23	33,371	52,348	1,410	1,001	0.6
LAFAYETTE, WI											
60 –	**Finance, insurance, and real estate**	32	33	0.3	176	139	18,023	24,777	3,616	3,606	0.1
6000	Depository institutions	10	10	0.4	124	99	15,452	20,970	2,056	2,154	0.2
6400	Insurance agents, brokers, and service	10	10	0.3	21	16	10,667	10,750	284	268	0.1
6500	Real estate	6	7	0.2	13	6	9,231	7,333	133	56	0.0
6510	Real estate operators and lessors	3	3	0.2	5	3	4,800	6,667	22	21	0.0
LANGLADE, WI											
60 –	**Finance, insurance, and real estate**	31	32	0.3	201	216	17,174	18,241	3,755	4,262	0.1
6000	Depository institutions	7	8	0.3	128	141	17,906	18,184	2,357	2,584	0.3
6400	Insurance agents, brokers, and service	12	11	0.4	48	42	18,000	21,810	1,020	1,108	0.3
6500	Real estate	7	10	0.3	16	-	8,000	-	194	-	-
6530	Real estate agents and managers	3	6	0.4	3	5	9,333	16,000	47	182	0.1
LINCOLN, WI											
60 –	**Finance, insurance, and real estate**	51	56	0.5	593	611	20,675	23,535	12,957	14,303	0.4
6000	Depository institutions	11	11	0.5	150	142	19,413	21,521	2,898	2,916	0.3
6020	Commercial banks	5	5	0.4	92	83	19,348	23,133	1,769	1,836	0.3

Source: County Business Patterns, 1992/93, CBP-92/93-1, U.S. Department of Commerce, Washington, D.C., April 1995. SIC categories for which data were suppressed or not available for both 1992 and 1993 are not displayed. The employment columns represent mid-March employment in the year. Pay per employee is calculated by dividing 1st Quarter payroll, annualized, by mid-March employment. The columns headed "% State" show the county's percentage of the state total for the SIC in 1993; for example, 0.9% for SIC 6030 means that the county had 0.9 percent of the state's total establishments (or payroll) in SIC 6030 in 1993. A dash (-) is used to indicate that data are not available or cannot be calculated; nec means not elsewhere classified.

Continued on next page.

SIC	Industry	No. Establishments			Employment		Pay / Employee		Annual Payroll ($ 000)		
		1992	1993	% State	1992	1993	1992	1993	1992	1993	% State
LINCOLN, WI - [continued]											
6400	Insurance agents, brokers, and service	18	19	0.6	39	45	12,718	10,133	530	518	0.1
6510	Real estate operators and lessors	4	6	0.4	7	11	2,857	7,636	24	97	0.1
6530	Real estate agents and managers	11	11	0.7	23	19	5,391	6,105	169	246	0.2
MANITOWOC, WI											
60 –	**Finance, insurance, and real estate**	151	156	1.4	855	872	19,888	18,427	16,431	16,240	0.4
6000	Depository institutions	42	46	2.0	531	570	22,252	19,137	11,092	10,969	1.2
6020	Commercial banks	26	27	2.1	453	461	23,232	19,844	9,788	9,061	1.4
6030	Savings institutions	5	5	1.0	32	31	17,875	17,161	570	612	0.3
6060	Credit unions	11	14	2.8	46	78	15,652	15,744	734	1,296	1.7
6100	Nondepository institutions	7	5	1.0	49	20	17,388	27,600	867	490	0.3
6200	Security and commodity brokers	5	4	0.7	16	12	36,000	52,000	520	567	0.2
6300	Insurance carriers	15	11	1.3	46	49	19,913	17,959	901	825	0.0
6330	Fire, marine, and casualty insurance	11	8	2.1	-	29	-	16,966	-	452	0.1
6400	Insurance agents, brokers, and service	36	43	1.4	83	94	14,458	13,149	1,276	1,412	0.4
6500	Real estate	40	42	1.1	118	108	11,322	13,481	1,354	1,564	0.5
6510	Real estate operators and lessors	17	20	1.3	35	42	9,143	8,667	319	386	0.4
6530	Real estate agents and managers	16	17	1.0	66	42	8,242	12,095	612	587	0.4
6700	Holding and other investment offices	6	5	1.4	12	19	25,667	21,684	421	413	0.3
MARATHON, WI											
60 –	**Finance, insurance, and real estate**	249	256	2.2	4,116	4,394	31,046	28,956	119,298	126,522	3.2
6000	Depository institutions	50	62	2.7	694	778	21,141	21,157	14,841	17,245	1.9
6020	Commercial banks	33	36	2.7	526	550	22,251	22,793	11,726	12,810	1.9
6030	Savings institutions	9	9	1.9	93	94	19,269	19,404	1,918	2,211	1.3
6060	Credit unions	8	17	3.3	75	134	15,680	15,672	1,197	2,224	2.9
6100	Nondepository institutions	19	12	2.4	113	87	18,726	20,644	2,337	1,555	0.8
6200	Security and commodity brokers	14	12	2.1	80	85	51,600	40,235	4,041	4,499	1.3
6210	Security brokers and dealers	8	7	2.0	50	56	67,360	48,500	3,220	3,792	1.6
6280	Security and commodity services	6	5	2.5	30	29	25,333	24,276	821	707	-
6300	Insurance carriers	27	23	2.8	2,705	2,887	36,152	33,395	88,460	92,706	5.4
6400	Insurance agents, brokers, and service	70	76	2.4	244	264	20,607	19,212	5,232	5,797	1.6
6500	Real estate	59	62	1.6	259	265	11,351	10,838	3,438	3,625	1.1
6510	Real estate operators and lessors	30	25	1.6	96	73	7,583	8,110	889	773	0.7
6530	Real estate agents and managers	21	28	1.7	128	153	12,719	11,137	1,782	2,038	1.3
6553	Cemetery subdividers and developers	5	7	2.8	16	-	12,500	-	230	-	-
6700	Holding and other investment offices	10	9	2.4	21	28	52,762	42,857	949	1,095	0.7
6710	Holding offices	4	2	1.4	8	-	35,000	-	306	-	-
6733	Trusts, n.e.c.	2	3	3.6	-	13	-	63,692	-	749	2.4
MARINETTE, WI											
60 –	**Finance, insurance, and real estate**	77	82	0.7	463	460	17,322	18,304	7,991	8,335	0.2
6000	Depository institutions	27	28	1.2	341	341	17,830	18,018	5,993	6,116	0.7
6020	Commercial banks	15	15	1.1	264	258	18,439	18,372	4,768	4,792	0.7
6030	Savings institutions	5	6	1.3	-	26	-	16,154	-	442	0.3
6060	Credit unions	7	7	1.4	-	57	-	17,263	-	882	1.2
6400	Insurance agents, brokers, and service	24	27	0.9	57	54	15,228	14,963	859	918	0.3
6500	Real estate	20	20	0.5	38	36	9,474	10,222	430	431	0.1
6510	Real estate operators and lessors	7	9	0.6	8	12	12,500	10,333	110	141	0.1
6530	Real estate agents and managers	6	7	0.4	11	12	8,364	9,667	99	139	0.1
MARQUETTE, WI											
60 –	**Finance, insurance, and real estate**	31	29	0.3	118	102	17,593	16,549	2,141	1,824	0.0
6000	Depository institutions	6	7	0.3	75	68	21,227	19,118	1,599	1,336	0.1
6020	Commercial banks	6	7	0.5	75	68	21,227	19,118	1,599	1,336	0.2
6400	Insurance agents, brokers, and service	9	10	0.3	21	20	16,190	14,600	396	353	0.1

Source: County Business Patterns, 1992/93, CBP-92/93-1, U.S. Department of Commerce, Washington, D.C., April 1995. SIC categories for which data were suppressed or not available for both 1992 and 1993 are *not* displayed. The employment columns represent mid-March employment in the year. Pay per employee is calculated by dividing 1st Quarter payroll, annualized, by mid-March employment. The columns headed "% State" show the county's percentage of the state total for the SIC in 1993; for example, 0.9% for SIC 6030 means that the county had 0.9 percent of the state's total establishments (or payroll) in SIC 6030 in 1993. A dash (-) is used to indicate that data are not available or cannot be calculated; *nec* means not elsewhere classified.

Continued on next page.

SIC	Industry	No. Establishments			Employment		Pay / Employee		Annual Payroll ($ 000)		
		1992	1993	% State	1992	1993	1992	1993	1992	1993	% State
MARQUETTE, WI - [continued]											
6500	Real estate	16	12	0.3	22	14	6,545	6,857	146	135	0.0
6530	Real estate agents and managers	10	7	0.4	-	12	-	7,000	-	115	0.1
6553	Cemetery subdividers and developers	3	3	1.2	1	-	4,000	-	9	-	-
MILWAUKEE, WI											
60 –	**Finance, insurance, and real estate**	2,129	2,127	18.5	43,849	46,775	35,643	34,539	1,515,839	1,623,758	40.6
6000	Depository institutions	321	343	14.7	9,549	10,457	25,981	25,414	245,039	274,703	30.1
6020	Commercial banks	135	145	11.0	6,684	7,407	28,159	27,381	178,577	206,011	31.3
6030	Savings institutions	107	106	22.1	2,087	2,284	20,792	22,095	49,843	55,579	31.7
6060	Credit unions	55	71	13.9	465	606	17,170	16,099	8,149	10,299	13.6
6090	Functions closely related to banking	21	21	72.4	-	160	-	17,025	-	2,814	78.3
6100	Nondepository institutions	150	135	26.9	1,591	2,858	38,165	29,618	73,906	80,922	42.7
6140	Personal credit institutions	82	51	23.3	542	-	22,125	-	12,126	-	-
6150	Business credit institutions	18	24	36.9	-	363	-	32,948	-	11,837	58.7
6160	Mortgage bankers and brokers	48	59	33.1	766	2,156	47,055	30,453	51,114	61,691	55.5
6200	Security and commodity brokers	123	131	23.2	2,553	2,689	72,186	62,865	159,211	176,902	52.2
6210	Security brokers and dealers	75	75	21.1	1,634	1,680	88,624	76,733	118,974	127,695	55.4
6220	Commodity contracts brokers, dealers	2	3	33.3	-	9	-	81,333	-	320	-
6280	Security and commodity services	42	53	26.8	492	1,000	53,463	39,400	29,451	48,887	-
6300	Insurance carriers	215	149	18.3	20,410	19,900	40,345	40,835	791,584	801,541	47.1
6310	Life insurance	69	58	29.6	14,953	14,616	42,550	42,750	616,779	629,653	70.8
6321	Accident and health insurance	10	5	19.2	769	-	33,254	-	21,995	-	-
6324	Hospital and medical service plans	7	15	25.9	1,429	-	33,786	-	40,245	-	-
6330	Fire, marine, and casualty insurance	72	46	12.2	1,918	1,727	33,393	31,863	62,844	55,660	10.8
6370	Pension, health, and welfare funds	42	16	13.9	278	227	24,662	27,542	7,064	6,382	38.2
6400	Insurance agents, brokers, and service	480	519	16.6	2,652	3,070	26,579	27,078	74,402	87,892	25.0
6500	Real estate	722	735	19.4	4,922	5,185	16,570	17,580	87,426	91,813	28.8
6510	Real estate operators and lessors	347	378	24.1	2,741	2,951	12,277	12,863	34,843	37,535	36.1
6530	Real estate agents and managers	295	320	18.9	1,792	2,074	22,690	23,697	44,012	49,864	30.8
6540	Title abstract offices	4	6	4.4	22	27	18,000	19,556	434	610	2.2
6552	Subdividers and developers, n.e.c.	17	9	7.6	69	31	29,391	47,355	2,080	1,346	10.3
6553	Cemetery subdividers and developers	18	18	7.1	98	99	18,000	18,707	2,081	2,391	22.7
6700	Holding and other investment offices	115	110	29.7	-	2,139	-	41,722	-	88,728	55.6
6710	Holding offices	44	42	29.4	1,076	1,154	54,747	50,527	48,461	58,079	53.8
6720	Investment offices	10	-	-	40	-	39,500	-	2,030	-	-
6732	Educational, religious, etc. trusts	22	23	44.2	117	131	24,308	33,924	3,068	3,703	45.1
6733	Trusts, n.e.c.	15	18	21.7	528	702	33,621	30,735	16,020	21,823	69.9
6794	Patent owners and lessors	6	5	26.3	52	-	10,462	-	506	-	-
6798	Real estate investment trusts	4	1	25.0	20	-	13,400	-	295	-	-
6799	Investors, n.e.c.	12	19	35.2	42	131	45,048	34,015	1,742	4,691	57.6
MONROE, WI											
60 –	**Finance, insurance, and real estate**	72	73	0.6	471	444	17,163	18,901	8,294	8,999	0.2
6000	Depository institutions	18	19	0.8	247	276	19,757	18,478	4,915	5,350	0.6
6020	Commercial banks	12	12	0.9	192	195	20,208	19,877	3,914	3,965	0.6
6100	Nondepository institutions	3	4	0.8	23	-	16,696	-	408	-	-
6140	Personal credit institutions	3	3	1.4	23	-	16,696	-	408	-	-
6300	Insurance carriers	6	4	0.5	-	11	-	22,182	-	408	0.0
6330	Fire, marine, and casualty insurance	3	2	0.5	12	-	14,667	-	205	-	-
6400	Insurance agents, brokers, and service	17	18	0.6	75	51	21,973	21,882	1,630	1,050	0.3
6500	Real estate	24	24	0.6	104	57	6,500	8,140	785	612	0.2
6510	Real estate operators and lessors	11	13	0.8	34	29	11,059	8,138	253	282	0.3
6530	Real estate agents and managers	6	6	0.4	14	-	4,857	-	86	-	-
6553	Cemetery subdividers and developers	4	4	1.6	9	8	1,778	2,000	36	39	0.4

Source: County Business Patterns, 1992/93, CBP-92/93-1, U.S. Department of Commerce, Washington, D.C., April 1995. SIC categories for which data were suppressed or not available for both 1992 and 1993 are not *displayed. The employment columns represent mid-March employment in the year. Pay per employee is calculated by dividing 1st Quarter payroll, annualized, by mid-March employment. The columns headed "% State" show the county's percentage of the state total for the SIC in 1993; for example, 0.9% for SIC 6030 means that the county had 0.9 percent of the state's total establishments (or payroll) in SIC 6030 in 1993. A dash (-) is used to indicate that data are not available or cannot be calculated;* nec *means not elsewhere classified.*

SIC	Industry	No. Establishments			Employment		Pay / Employee		Annual Payroll ($ 000)		
		1992	1993	% State	1992	1993	1992	1993	1992	1993	% State
OCONTO, WI											
60 –	**Finance, insurance, and real estate**	60	61	0.5	240	257	15,183	14,739	3,972	4,173	0.1
6000	Depository institutions	16	16	0.7	128	141	18,438	18,496	2,470	2,687	0.3
6400	Insurance agents, brokers, and service	15	16	0.5	46	40	11,913	13,200	623	651	0.2
6500	Real estate	24	25	0.7	49	61	8,571	6,361	553	554	0.2
6510	Real estate operators and lessors	11	12	0.8	12	18	3,000	3,778	50	76	0.1
6530	Real estate agents and managers	4	5	0.3	15	16	13,600	8,000	239	251	0.2
6540	Title abstract offices	4	3	2.2	10	14	14,000	11,143	223	184	0.7
6553	Cemetery subdividers and developers	5	5	2.0	12	13	3,333	2,769	41	43	0.4
ONEIDA, WI											
60 –	**Finance, insurance, and real estate**	91	98	0.9	454	447	21,877	25,235	10,627	10,827	0.3
6000	Depository institutions	17	17	0.7	186	187	21,892	20,064	3,807	3,636	0.4
6020	Commercial banks	9	9	0.7	129	130	23,783	20,954	2,787	2,526	0.4
6200	Security and commodity brokers	4	5	0.9	29	30	65,379	108,267	1,906	1,944	0.6
6210	Security brokers and dealers	4	4	1.1	29	–	65,379	–	1,906	–	–
6300	Insurance carriers	3	3	0.4	10	15	25,600	16,800	223	254	0.0
6400	Insurance agents, brokers, and service	27	30	1.0	73	82	21,260	21,366	1,601	1,687	0.5
6500	Real estate	36	40	1.1	126	99	14,540	17,697	2,482	2,468	0.8
6510	Real estate operators and lessors	6	11	0.7	15	18	5,333	15,556	104	312	0.3
6530	Real estate agents and managers	22	24	1.4	66	49	14,667	14,694	1,557	1,023	0.6
6540	Title abstract offices	4	4	2.9	21	–	21,524	–	491	–	–
OUTAGAMIE, WI											
60 –	**Finance, insurance, and real estate**	361	365	3.2	5,976	6,073	30,025	31,158	166,902	175,824	4.4
6000	Depository institutions	69	71	3.0	1,614	1,595	23,901	25,743	35,291	36,697	4.0
6020	Commercial banks	31	31	2.4	828	774	26,961	26,682	19,771	18,684	2.8
6030	Savings institutions	18	18	3.8	511	515	23,319	29,398	10,813	12,879	7.4
6060	Credit unions	20	22	4.3	275	306	15,767	17,216	4,707	5,134	6.8
6100	Nondepository institutions	22	18	3.6	142	160	35,775	36,425	4,905	5,817	3.1
6160	Mortgage bankers and brokers	9	10	5.6	68	91	49,000	42,637	3,186	4,230	3.8
6200	Security and commodity brokers	25	25	4.4	167	257	48,599	50,070	7,449	11,869	3.5
6210	Security brokers and dealers	14	17	4.8	137	238	55,124	52,521	6,803	11,413	4.9
6280	Security and commodity services	11	8	4.0	30	19	18,800	19,368	646	456	–
6300	Insurance carriers	46	41	5.0	2,997	3,070	31,592	32,777	87,750	91,929	5.4
6330	Fire, marine, and casualty insurance	16	17	4.5	310	307	30,787	31,349	9,081	9,195	1.8
6360	Title insurance	4	2	8.0	59	–	28,136	–	1,724	–	–
6400	Insurance agents, brokers, and service	93	100	3.2	416	402	23,154	24,786	11,083	11,503	3.3
6500	Real estate	91	96	2.5	353	384	18,085	18,094	6,696	7,685	2.4
6510	Real estate operators and lessors	28	31	2.0	81	–	10,765	–	968	–	–
6530	Real estate agents and managers	42	47	2.8	155	215	18,865	21,116	3,503	5,070	3.1
6552	Subdividers and developers, n.e.c.	3	9	7.6	–	22	–	30,364	–	447	3.4
6553	Cemetery subdividers and developers	7	6	2.4	62	57	14,065	12,421	921	960	9.1
6700	Holding and other investment offices	15	14	3.8	287	205	59,108	58,205	13,728	10,324	6.5
6710	Holding offices	10	7	4.9	190	171	66,400	65,029	9,970	9,494	8.8
OZAUKEE, WI											
60 –	**Finance, insurance, and real estate**	200	214	1.9	1,030	1,191	26,388	22,677	28,004	29,899	0.7
6000	Depository institutions	33	35	1.5	441	492	21,007	18,935	9,614	9,955	1.1
6020	Commercial banks	18	19	1.4	324	374	22,420	19,733	7,655	7,997	1.2
6030	Savings institutions	12	12	2.5	109	108	17,688	17,185	1,892	1,878	1.1
6060	Credit unions	3	4	0.8	8	10	9,000	8,000	67	80	0.1
6100	Nondepository institutions	7	4	0.8	32	23	72,375	36,348	1,132	659	0.3
6200	Security and commodity brokers	19	23	4.1	92	102	64,957	58,549	6,145	7,322	2.2
6210	Security brokers and dealers	8	13	3.7	41	61	72,293	58,164	3,007	4,481	1.9
6280	Security and commodity services	11	10	5.1	51	41	59,059	59,122	3,138	2,841	–
6300	Insurance carriers	17	9	1.1	49	36	20,082	23,556	1,001	801	0.0
6310	Life insurance	7	2	1.0	11	–	21,455	–	240	–	–
6330	Fire, marine, and casualty insurance	7	5	1.3	–	18	–	28,000	–	568	0.1

Source: County Business Patterns, 1992/93, CBP-92/93-1, U.S. Department of Commerce, Washington, D.C., April 1995. SIC categories for which data were suppressed or not available for both 1992 and 1993 are not displayed. The employment columns represent mid-March employment in the year. Pay per employee is calculated by dividing 1st Quarter payroll, annualized, by mid-March employment. The columns headed "% State" show the county's percentage of the state total for the SIC in 1993; for example, 0.9% for SIC 6030 means that the county had 0.9 percent of the state's total establishments (or payroll) in SIC 6030 in 1993. A dash (-) is used to indicate that data are not available or cannot be calculated; nec means not elsewhere classified.

Continued on next page.

SIC	Industry	No. Establishments			Employment		Pay / Employee		Annual Payroll ($ 000)		
		1992	1993	% State	1992	1993	1992	1993	1992	1993	% State
OZAUKEE, WI - [continued]											
6400	Insurance agents, brokers, and service	41	56	1.8	158	187	28,304	27,636	4,501	5,231	1.5
6500	Real estate	76	81	2.1	243	336	16,214	14,000	5,272	5,659	1.8
6510	Real estate operators and lessors	31	33	2.1	97	94	18,845	15,404	2,504	1,624	1.6
6530	Real estate agents and managers	23	36	2.1	103	214	14,796	13,121	1,725	3,236	2.0
6552	Subdividers and developers, n.e.c.	5	7	5.9	11	5	14,182	20,000	263	258	2.0
6700	Holding and other investment offices	7	6	1.6	15	15	15,200	10,933	339	272	0.2
6710	Holding offices	4	5	3.5	12	-	13,333	-	219	-	-
PEPIN, WI											
60 –	**Finance, insurance, and real estate**	18	15	0.1	86	83	16,744	18,892	1,681	1,624	0.0
6400	Insurance agents, brokers, and service	8	8	0.3	32	32	9,375	10,250	321	334	0.1
PIERCE, WI											
60 –	**Finance, insurance, and real estate**	66	69	0.6	359	368	20,134	22,435	7,635	8,255	0.2
6000	Depository institutions	15	15	0.6	244	229	20,852	22,725	5,268	5,282	0.6
6400	Insurance agents, brokers, and service	18	19	0.6	42	48	15,810	16,000	706	792	0.2
6500	Real estate	24	26	0.7	31	44	13,419	16,182	587	830	0.3
6510	Real estate operators and lessors	11	12	0.8	7	-	7,429	-	69	-	-
6530	Real estate agents and managers	8	9	0.5	13	15	20,615	22,933	385	460	0.3
6553	Cemetery subdividers and developers	2	3	1.2	-	3	-	4,000	-	30	0.3
6700	Holding and other investment offices	3	2	0.5	8	-	7,000	-	56	-	-
POLK, WI											
60 –	**Finance, insurance, and real estate**	70	71	0.6	360	367	17,333	17,613	6,420	7,098	0.2
6000	Depository institutions	15	16	0.7	246	239	19,821	19,983	4,894	5,350	0.6
6020	Commercial banks	12	13	1.0	211	202	20,227	20,535	4,252	4,673	0.7
6100	Nondepository institutions	3	3	0.6	10	13	26,800	34,769	275	382	0.2
6300	Insurance carriers	6	6	0.7	-	13	-	12,308	-	159	0.0
6330	Fire, marine, and casualty insurance	4	4	1.1	9	-	14,667	-	142	-	-
6400	Insurance agents, brokers, and service	17	17	0.5	-	56	-	13,214	-	794	0.2
6500	Real estate	25	25	0.7	44	44	7,091	7,364	352	386	0.1
6510	Real estate operators and lessors	6	7	0.4	10	15	3,200	3,467	49	60	0.1
6530	Real estate agents and managers	11	12	0.7	22	22	8,000	8,545	192	222	0.1
6553	Cemetery subdividers and developers	4	4	1.6	2	-	6,000	-	11	-	-
PORTAGE, WI											
60 –	**Finance, insurance, and real estate**	140	138	1.2	4,198	3,945	27,365	26,733	103,507	100,544	2.5
6000	Depository institutions	26	30	1.3	909	982	23,657	20,851	21,758	21,437	2.3
6100	Nondepository institutions	7	5	1.0	-	28	-	21,000	-	554	0.3
6400	Insurance agents, brokers, and service	39	39	1.2	245	241	17,714	17,112	5,287	4,724	1.3
6500	Real estate	46	46	1.2	119	121	10,017	12,893	1,540	1,801	0.6
6510	Real estate operators and lessors	26	30	1.9	60	71	9,133	13,577	619	979	0.9
6530	Real estate agents and managers	14	13	0.8	34	30	8,235	9,067	344	342	0.2
6700	Holding and other investment offices	6	3	0.8	247	-	40,113	-	3,219	-	-
PRICE, WI											
60 –	**Finance, insurance, and real estate**	38	41	0.4	275	294	23,375	23,673	7,615	8,057	0.2
6000	Depository institutions	11	11	0.5	114	112	16,526	16,679	1,893	1,843	0.2
6020	Commercial banks	4	4	0.3	69	69	18,493	17,797	1,270	1,162	0.2
6400	Insurance agents, brokers, and service	13	12	0.4	29	34	14,759	14,118	458	508	0.1
6500	Real estate	11	13	0.3	-	139	-	31,597	-	5,545	1.7
RACINE, WI											
60 –	**Finance, insurance, and real estate**	353	362	3.1	2,868	2,642	22,331	22,318	64,518	62,786	1.6
6000	Depository institutions	73	83	3.6	1,157	1,215	20,283	18,305	23,726	21,401	2.3
6020	Commercial banks	43	45	3.4	902	917	21,681	19,075	19,408	16,006	2.4
6030	Savings institutions	16	16	3.3	150	158	16,987	17,747	2,728	3,153	1.8
6100	Nondepository institutions	29	19	3.8	103	72	18,874	20,389	1,866	2,012	1.1

Source: County Business Patterns, 1992/93, CBP-92/93-1, U.S. Department of Commerce, Washington, D.C., April 1995. SIC categories for which data were suppressed or not available for both 1992 and 1993 are *not* displayed. The employment columns represent mid-March employment in the year. Pay per employee is calculated by dividing 1st Quarter payroll, annualized, by mid-March employment. The columns headed "% State" show the county's percentage of the state total for the SIC in 1993; for example, 0.9% for SIC 6030 means that the county had 0.9 percent of the state's total establishments (or payroll) in SIC 6030 in 1993. A dash (-) is used to indicate that data are not available or cannot be calculated; *nec* means not elsewhere classified.

Continued on next page.

SIC	Industry	No. Establishments			Employment		Pay / Employee		Annual Payroll ($ 000)		
		1992	1993	% State	1992	1993	1992	1993	1992	1993	% State
RACINE, WI - [continued]											
6140	Personal credit institutions	21	11	5.0	83	42	15,518	22,095	1,344	1,015	2.3
6160	Mortgage bankers and brokers	8	8	4.5	20	30	32,800	18,000	522	997	0.9
6200	Security and commodity brokers	19	18	3.2	71	61	50,648	62,164	3,211	3,976	1.2
6210	Security brokers and dealers	15	13	3.7	65	54	52,554	66,667	3,025	3,683	1.6
6280	Security and commodity services	4	5	2.5	6	7	30,000	27,429	186	293	-
6300	Insurance carriers	27	20	2.5	315	228	25,041	27,281	6,684	6,128	0.4
6310	Life insurance	8	6	3.1	198	141	22,343	24,284	3,126	2,923	0.3
6330	Fire, marine, and casualty insurance	12	9	2.4	61	-	30,623	-	1,859	-	-
6400	Insurance agents, brokers, and service	77	82	2.6	299	339	22,475	21,062	7,414	8,299	2.4
6500	Real estate	115	127	3.3	570	555	14,182	15,777	9,695	11,511	3.6
6510	Real estate operators and lessors	51	56	3.6	239	216	11,950	14,852	3,422	3,599	3.5
6530	Real estate agents and managers	45	54	3.2	244	256	14,115	14,938	4,351	5,056	3.1
6540	Title abstract offices	4	5	3.7	39	41	25,436	23,805	1,220	1,915	7.0
6552	Subdividers and developers, n.e.c.	3	3	2.5	4	-	10,000	-	24	-	-
6553	Cemetery subdividers and developers	5	7	2.8	-	32	-	17,125	-	665	6.3
6700	Holding and other investment offices	13	13	3.5	353	172	34,969	54,349	11,922	9,459	5.9
6710	Holding offices	6	4	2.8	293	93	35,290	68,774	9,980	6,345	5.9
RICHLAND, WI											
60 –	**Finance, insurance, and real estate**	35	39	0.3	186	151	16,667	17,828	3,267	3,156	0.1
6000	Depository institutions	8	9	0.4	85	59	19,247	18,441	1,637	1,385	0.2
6020	Commercial banks	6	6	0.5	-	38	-	20,211	-	1,028	0.2
6100	Nondepository institutions	3	2	0.4	12	-	19,667	-	243	-	-
6400	Insurance agents, brokers, and service	8	10	0.3	17	27	13,647	16,593	273	467	0.1
6500	Real estate	11	14	0.4	55	43	8,000	10,326	533	563	0.2
6510	Real estate operators and lessors	4	8	0.5	-	10	-	12,000	-	157	0.2
6530	Real estate agents and managers	4	4	0.2	35	-	6,171	-	245	-	-
ROCK, WI											
60 –	**Finance, insurance, and real estate**	264	265	2.3	1,850	1,929	22,134	21,951	40,968	43,220	1.1
6000	Depository institutions	60	68	2.9	873	1,003	20,541	20,387	17,488	20,767	2.3
6020	Commercial banks	29	32	2.4	598	690	22,294	21,832	12,743	14,772	2.2
6030	Savings institutions	15	12	2.5	141	-	19,291	-	2,824	-	-
6060	Credit unions	15	23	4.5	-	216	-	16,815	-	4,103	5.4
6100	Nondepository institutions	17	8	1.6	145	86	22,786	31,116	3,461	2,104	1.1
6200	Security and commodity brokers	13	12	2.1	37	40	55,351	59,900	2,073	2,452	0.7
6300	Insurance carriers	30	21	2.6	373	317	25,705	24,025	8,894	7,055	0.4
6310	Life insurance	9	6	3.1	114	90	40,632	37,778	4,309	2,890	0.3
6330	Fire, marine, and casualty insurance	13	9	2.4	47	-	26,979	-	1,264	-	-
6400	Insurance agents, brokers, and service	71	80	2.6	200	244	20,700	19,459	4,437	5,414	1.5
6500	Real estate	66	67	1.8	208	211	16,365	17,251	4,012	4,470	1.4
6510	Real estate operators and lessors	26	23	1.5	86	69	16,977	16,232	1,625	1,075	1.0
6530	Real estate agents and managers	32	37	2.2	78	90	13,231	16,667	1,183	2,048	1.3
6540	Title abstract offices	4	4	2.9	36	40	21,222	22,200	1,076	1,099	4.0
6553	Cemetery subdividers and developers	1	3	1.2	-	12	-	11,000	-	248	2.4
6700	Holding and other investment offices	7	9	2.4	14	28	38,000	29,286	603	958	0.6
6733	Trusts, n.e.c.	4	6	7.2	-	23	-	25,043	-	681	2.2
RUSK, WI											
60 –	**Finance, insurance, and real estate**	23	22	0.2	128	125	14,375	14,144	1,837	1,784	0.0
6000	Depository institutions	6	6	0.3	89	92	16,629	15,696	1,451	1,396	0.2
6400	Insurance agents, brokers, and service	9	10	0.3	14	16	10,857	10,000	154	172	0.0
6500	Real estate	8	6	0.2	25	17	8,320	9,647	232	216	0.1
6510	Real estate operators and lessors	3	1	0.1	6	-	2,000	-	15	-	-
6530	Real estate agents and managers	3	4	0.2	10	-	5,600	-	59	-	-

Source: County Business Patterns, 1992/93, CBP-92/93-1, U.S. Department of Commerce, Washington, D.C., April 1995. SIC categories for which data were suppressed or not available for both 1992 and 1993 are *not* displayed. The employment columns represent mid-March employment in the year. Pay per employee is calculated by dividing 1st Quarter payroll, annualized, by mid-March employment. The columns headed "% State" show the county's percentage of the state total for the SIC in 1993; for example, 0.9% for SIC 6030 means that the county had 0.9 percent of the state's total establishments (or payroll) in SIC 6030 in 1993. A dash (-) is used to indicate that data are not available or cannot be calculated; *nec* means not elsewhere classified.

SIC	Industry	No. Establishments			Employment		Pay / Employee		Annual Payroll ($ 000)		
		1992	1993	% State	1992	1993	1992	1993	1992	1993	% State
ST. CROIX, WI											
60 –	**Finance, insurance, and real estate**	91	87	0.8	841	561	15,705	22,360	13,950	12,139	0.3
6000	Depository institutions	19	19	0.8	320	346	22,312	26,266	7,175	8,241	0.9
6020	Commercial banks	13	13	1.0	245	268	23,363	28,522	5,597	6,239	0.9
6400	Insurance agents, brokers, and service	25	25	0.8	72	77	17,611	16,675	1,590	1,604	0.5
6500	Real estate	37	32	0.8	427	114	10,126	13,474	4,553	1,582	0.5
6510	Real estate operators and lessors	10	6	0.4	26	-	23,538	-	667	-	-
6530	Real estate agents and managers	19	18	1.1	83	86	12,000	10,093	1,132	799	0.5
6553	Cemetery subdividers and developers	7	7	2.8	2	-	10,000	-	40	-	-
SAUK, WI											
60 –	**Finance, insurance, and real estate**	126	129	1.1	743	872	17,997	19,523	13,995	18,147	0.5
6000	Depository institutions	29	28	1.2	394	428	20,376	20,290	8,095	8,861	1.0
6200	Security and commodity brokers	4	5	0.9	-	11	-	14,909	-	185	0.1
6300	Insurance carriers	8	7	0.9	-	128	-	26,188	-	3,461	0.2
6400	Insurance agents, brokers, and service	36	38	1.2	112	123	18,500	19,350	2,270	2,413	0.7
6500	Real estate	45	48	1.3	165	165	11,297	11,418	2,132	2,571	0.8
6510	Real estate operators and lessors	11	14	0.9	46	53	8,435	8,302	476	546	0.5
6530	Real estate agents and managers	21	21	1.2	86	80	11,953	12,100	1,116	1,401	0.9
6553	Cemetery subdividers and developers	7	7	2.8	-	12	-	5,667	-	90	0.9
SAWYER, WI											
60 –	**Finance, insurance, and real estate**	37	42	0.4	176	194	16,227	16,103	2,985	3,468	0.1
6000	Depository institutions	7	8	0.3	94	96	19,106	17,500	1,709	1,774	0.2
6020	Commercial banks	4	5	0.4	69	71	18,087	18,704	1,280	1,351	0.2
6400	Insurance agents, brokers, and service	12	13	0.4	26	29	13,385	14,483	351	399	0.1
6500	Real estate	15	17	0.4	-	49	-	16,408	-	973	0.3
6510	Real estate operators and lessors	5	7	0.4	19	29	16,000	12,828	386	475	0.5
6530	Real estate agents and managers	7	8	0.5	12	-	9,333	-	176	-	-
SHAWANO, WI											
60 –	**Finance, insurance, and real estate**	78	79	0.7	404	411	26,208	19,105	8,741	8,320	0.2
6000	Depository institutions	20	20	0.9	233	263	20,155	20,259	4,667	5,421	0.6
6020	Commercial banks	17	17	1.3	215	242	20,577	20,628	4,393	5,109	0.8
6100	Nondepository institutions	2	3	0.6	-	8	-	19,000	-	196	0.1
6140	Personal credit institutions	2	3	1.4	-	8	-	19,000	-	196	0.4
6330	Fire, marine, and casualty insurance	3	1	0.3	23	-	77,739	-	755	-	-
6400	Insurance agents, brokers, and service	27	30	1.0	67	72	17,552	15,278	1,049	1,308	0.4
6500	Real estate	18	19	0.5	42	47	11,238	10,979	551	596	0.2
6510	Real estate operators and lessors	4	5	0.3	3	19	4,000	5,474	17	124	0.1
6530	Real estate agents and managers	10	10	0.6	-	25	-	16,160	-	458	0.3
6553	Cemetery subdividers and developers	3	4	1.6	1	3	8,000	2,667	13	14	0.1
SHEBOYGAN, WI											
60 –	**Finance, insurance, and real estate**	215	223	1.9	2,130	2,182	24,759	23,963	52,065	56,847	1.4
6000	Depository institutions	45	48	2.1	735	730	23,559	20,405	16,332	15,719	1.7
6020	Commercial banks	24	22	1.7	540	552	25,630	22,710	12,806	13,163	2.0
6030	Savings institutions	8	8	1.7	79	-	18,532	-	1,489	-	-
6060	Credit unions	13	17	3.3	116	136	17,345	12,353	2,037	1,782	2.4
6100	Nondepository institutions	14	10	2.0	42	-	18,095	-	970	-	-
6140	Personal credit institutions	10	6	2.7	-	27	-	13,778	-	293	0.7
6160	Mortgage bankers and brokers	3	3	1.7	7	-	30,857	-	421	-	-
6200	Security and commodity brokers	10	11	2.0	-	53	-	41,509	-	2,643	0.8
6210	Security brokers and dealers	7	9	2.5	40	-	53,100	-	2,166	-	-
6300	Insurance carriers	19	14	1.7	758	776	25,272	26,562	18,580	21,111	1.2
6400	Insurance agents, brokers, and service	55	67	2.1	189	228	18,709	18,509	3,720	4,741	1.3
6500	Real estate	61	62	1.6	229	161	9,258	11,925	2,660	2,883	0.9
6510	Real estate operators and lessors	24	26	1.7	60	58	8,867	9,862	565	689	0.7
6530	Real estate agents and managers	25	24	1.4	86	89	12,326	11,596	1,407	1,790	1.1

Source: County Business Patterns, 1992/93, CBP-92/93-1, U.S. Department of Commerce, Washington, D.C., April 1995. SIC categories for which data were suppressed or not available for both 1992 and 1993 are *not* displayed. The employment columns represent mid-March employment in the year. Pay per employee is calculated by dividing 1st Quarter payroll, annualized, by mid-March employment. The columns headed "% State" show the county's percentage of the state total for the SIC in 1993; for example, 0.9% for SIC 6030 means that the county had 0.9 percent of the state's total establishments (or payroll) in SIC 6030 in 1993. A dash (-) is used to indicate that data are not available or cannot be calculated; *nec* means not elsewhere classified.

Continued on next page.

SIC	Industry	No. Establishments			Employment		Pay / Employee		Annual Payroll ($ 000)		
		1992	1993	% State	1992	1993	1992	1993	1992	1993	% State
SHEBOYGAN, WI - [continued]											
6553	Cemetery subdividers and developers	7	8	3.2	5	6	9,600	26,667	71	165	1.6
6700	Holding and other investment offices	10	10	2.7	65	63	78,031	60,508	4,941	5,048	3.2
6710	Holding offices	5	6	4.2	41	46	120,098	80,348	4,754	4,933	4.6
TAYLOR, WI											
60 –	**Finance, insurance, and real estate**	36	38	0.3	221	-	20,941	-	4,601	-	-
6000	Depository institutions	13	13	0.6	151	155	21,033	20,826	2,912	3,076	0.3
6020	Commercial banks	8	8	0.6	109	111	22,055	21,586	2,128	2,225	0.3
6400	Insurance agents, brokers, and service	12	13	0.4	43	37	22,233	25,297	1,163	1,318	0.4
6500	Real estate	7	8	0.2	7	35	10,286	5,829	108	228	0.1
6510	Real estate operators and lessors	3	4	0.3	5	28	2,400	3,857	13	112	0.1
TREMPEALEAU, WI											
60 –	**Finance, insurance, and real estate**	65	69	0.6	302	319	17,060	16,238	5,136	5,361	0.1
6000	Depository institutions	18	19	0.8	192	206	19,354	18,563	3,678	3,934	0.4
6020	Commercial banks	12	12	0.9	172	174	19,581	18,828	3,313	3,360	0.5
6100	Nondepository institutions	4	3	0.6	22	-	19,273	-	421	-	-
6300	Insurance carriers	5	3	0.4	12	-	10,000	-	130	-	-
6400	Insurance agents, brokers, and service	16	20	0.6	43	53	14,698	12,302	575	642	0.2
6500	Real estate	22	24	0.6	33	37	7,879	7,243	332	315	0.1
6510	Real estate operators and lessors	9	10	0.6	12	18	2,333	2,667	42	50	0.0
6530	Real estate agents and managers	5	7	0.4	10	9	10,000	11,111	107	112	0.1
6540	Title abstract offices	2	3	2.2	-	8	-	14,500	-	132	0.5
6553	Cemetery subdividers and developers	4	4	1.6	2	2	2,000	2,000	17	21	0.2
VERNON, WI											
60 –	**Finance, insurance, and real estate**	60	61	0.5	257	299	19,222	16,896	5,099	5,411	0.1
6000	Depository institutions	15	16	0.7	144	178	20,000	16,382	2,847	3,171	0.3
6020	Commercial banks	12	12	0.9	-	146	-	16,329	-	2,576	0.4
6300	Insurance carriers	4	3	0.4	14	-	20,286	-	405	-	-
6400	Insurance agents, brokers, and service	17	18	0.6	39	45	18,667	18,133	789	823	0.2
6500	Real estate	22	21	0.6	-	51	-	13,961	-	715	0.2
6510	Real estate operators and lessors	4	4	0.3	10	11	3,200	2,545	33	29	0.0
6530	Real estate agents and managers	6	5	0.3	12	6	8,333	11,333	132	103	0.1
VILAS, WI											
60 –	**Finance, insurance, and real estate**	48	56	0.5	274	363	17,825	17,697	5,147	6,143	0.2
6000	Depository institutions	15	16	0.7	154	174	22,519	25,517	3,357	3,649	0.4
6400	Insurance agents, brokers, and service	7	9	0.3	22	-	12,545	-	310	-	-
6500	Real estate	23	30	0.8	90	139	11,556	10,590	1,365	1,994	0.6
6510	Real estate operators and lessors	3	4	0.3	-	44	-	9,455	-	387	0.4
6530	Real estate agents and managers	16	23	1.4	60	80	9,667	9,500	735	1,109	0.7
WALWORTH, WI											
60 –	**Finance, insurance, and real estate**	165	180	1.6	1,097	1,248	17,429	17,949	21,868	25,091	0.6
6000	Depository institutions	38	39	1.7	507	546	19,637	19,355	10,420	10,818	1.2
6020	Commercial banks	24	25	1.9	427	461	20,440	19,809	9,177	9,318	1.4
6030	Savings institutions	8	8	1.7	60	59	16,533	18,576	998	1,119	0.6
6060	Credit unions	5	6	1.2	-	26	-	13,077	-	381	0.5
6100	Nondepository institutions	7	6	1.2	20	18	29,000	24,444	678	733	0.4
6140	Personal credit institutions	3	2	0.9	10	-	13,600	-	167	-	-
6200	Security and commodity brokers	7	8	1.4	17	32	63,059	54,375	1,202	1,511	0.4
6210	Security brokers and dealers	4	4	1.1	16	19	66,500	72,421	1,132	1,236	0.5
6280	Security and commodity services	3	4	2.0	1	13	8,000	28,000	70	275	-
6300	Insurance carriers	8	8	1.0	-	126	-	23,238	-	2,730	0.2
6370	Pension, health, and welfare funds	3	2	1.7	9	-	7,556	-	83	-	-
6400	Insurance agents, brokers, and service	36	40	1.3	119	133	21,311	20,992	2,675	4,218	1.2
6500	Real estate	67	79	2.1	383	393	10,601	10,005	4,500	5,081	1.6

Source: County Business Patterns, 1992/93, CBP-92/93-1, U.S. Department of Commerce, Washington, D.C., April 1995. SIC categories for which data were suppressed or not available for both 1992 and 1993 are not displayed. The employment columns represent mid-March employment in the year. Pay per employee is calculated by dividing 1st Quarter payroll, annualized, by mid-March employment. The columns headed "% State" show the county's percentage of the state total for the SIC in 1993; for example, 0.9% for SIC 6030 means that the county had 0.9 percent of the state's total establishments (or payroll) in SIC 6030 in 1993. A dash (-) is used to indicate that data are not available or cannot be calculated; nec means not elsewhere classified.

Continued on next page.

SIC	Industry	No. Establishments			Employment		Pay / Employee		Annual Payroll ($ 000)		
		1992	1993	% State	1992	1993	1992	1993	1992	1993	% State
WALWORTH, WI - [continued]											
6510	Real estate operators and lessors	20	26	1.7	212	166	7,377	5,133	1,567	1,164	1.1
6530	Real estate agents and managers	32	41	2.4	138	200	15,884	12,780	2,519	3,264	2.0
6552	Subdividers and developers, n.e.c.	2	6	5.0	-	11	-	37,455	-	513	3.9
6553	Cemetery subdividers and developers	4	6	2.4	16	16	6,750	7,000	114	140	1.3
WASHBURN, WI											
60 –	**Finance, insurance, and real estate**	36	36	0.3	178	182	18,180	16,945	3,197	3,377	0.1
6000	Depository institutions	7	7	0.3	108	112	18,296	16,607	1,997	1,954	0.2
6400	Insurance agents, brokers, and service	9	8	0.3	31	24	21,806	26,667	505	612	0.2
6500	Real estate	20	20	0.5	39	-	14,974	-	695	-	-
6510	Real estate operators and lessors	5	5	0.3	6	8	4,667	4,000	34	37	0.0
6530	Real estate agents and managers	10	11	0.7	26	31	17,385	12,774	500	581	0.4
WASHINGTON, WI											
60 –	**Finance, insurance, and real estate**	187	191	1.7	1,779	1,930	24,297	25,254	44,231	48,505	1.2
6000	Depository institutions	35	36	1.5	535	587	20,740	20,886	11,040	11,422	1.3
6020	Commercial banks	26	27	2.1	422	460	21,498	21,261	8,893	8,999	1.4
6100	Nondepository institutions	11	8	1.6	60	-	19,467	-	1,046	-	-
6140	Personal credit institutions	4	3	1.4	31	19	16,129	20,211	549	312	0.7
6160	Mortgage bankers and brokers	4	2	1.1	10	-	10,800	-	204	-	-
6200	Security and commodity brokers	10	10	1.8	258	280	42,915	46,157	8,723	9,909	2.9
6300	Insurance carriers	18	14	1.7	590	611	22,454	24,242	13,858	15,707	0.9
6310	Life insurance	4	3	1.5	30	-	16,267	-	829	-	-
6400	Insurance agents, brokers, and service	56	60	1.9	129	183	17,209	19,913	2,603	4,613	1.3
6500	Real estate	52	60	1.6	171	201	16,117	18,010	4,549	5,025	1.6
6510	Real estate operators and lessors	19	24	1.5	47	107	6,553	19,402	584	2,981	2.9
6530	Real estate agents and managers	22	24	1.4	63	57	16,635	11,789	1,210	817	0.5
6552	Subdividers and developers, n.e.c.	4	6	5.0	25	3	23,840	34,667	1,225	233	1.8
6700	Holding and other investment offices	5	3	0.8	36	-	46,222	-	2,412	-	-
WAUKESHA, WI											
60 –	**Finance, insurance, and real estate**	1,004	1,067	9.3	9,990	10,113	26,494	28,351	290,243	319,554	8.0
6000	Depository institutions	141	141	6.0	2,254	2,344	21,718	21,727	51,399	50,412	5.5
6020	Commercial banks	85	84	6.4	1,570	1,664	21,455	21,397	34,747	33,783	5.1
6030	Savings institutions	37	37	7.7	483	502	22,311	23,705	12,174	13,113	7.5
6060	Credit unions	17	20	3.9	-	178	-	19,236	-	3,516	4.6
6100	Nondepository institutions	78	81	16.1	737	800	29,596	29,815	23,866	33,060	17.5
6140	Personal credit institutions	31	29	13.2	291	342	23,670	25,953	6,967	8,945	20.2
6150	Business credit institutions	16	18	27.7	-	104	-	36,077	-	3,568	17.7
6160	Mortgage bankers and brokers	29	34	19.1	321	354	32,523	31,706	12,945	20,547	18.5
6200	Security and commodity brokers	65	60	10.6	590	661	49,749	50,796	37,537	45,702	13.5
6210	Security brokers and dealers	32	31	8.7	188	178	55,851	60,225	12,628	10,773	4.7
6280	Security and commodity services	31	29	14.6	401	483	46,973	47,321	24,899	34,929	-
6300	Insurance carriers	117	109	13.4	3,061	3,070	29,964	32,083	95,842	99,000	5.8
6310	Life insurance	33	23	11.7	802	442	29,716	31,348	22,976	14,082	1.6
6330	Fire, marine, and casualty insurance	49	49	13.0	1,952	2,007	30,727	32,331	64,591	64,986	12.6
6360	Title insurance	7	1	4.0	172	-	20,465	-	3,737	-	-
6370	Pension, health, and welfare funds	23	21	18.3	76	-	29,789	-	2,461	-	-
6400	Insurance agents, brokers, and service	286	321	10.2	1,295	1,439	26,944	28,036	39,936	47,376	13.5
6500	Real estate	286	324	8.5	1,509	1,492	15,793	18,954	26,436	31,946	10.0
6510	Real estate operators and lessors	87	109	6.9	479	422	11,716	17,242	6,238	7,767	7.5
6530	Real estate agents and managers	152	184	10.9	671	800	19,905	19,305	14,503	17,455	10.8
6540	Title abstract offices	-	4	2.9	-	143	-	19,608	-	3,182	11.6
6552	Subdividers and developers, n.e.c.	11	12	10.1	91	28	13,626	19,000	1,703	939	7.2
6553	Cemetery subdividers and developers	8	9	3.6	-	85	-	23,624	-	2,316	22.0

Source: County Business Patterns, 1992/93, CBP-92/93-1, U.S. Department of Commerce, Washington, D.C., April 1995. SIC categories for which data were suppressed or not available for both 1992 and 1993 are not displayed. The employment columns represent mid-March employment in the year. Pay per employee is calculated by dividing 1st Quarter payroll, annualized, by mid-March employment. The columns headed "% State" show the county's percentage of the state total for the SIC in 1993; for example, 0.9% for SIC 6030 means that the county had 0.9 percent of the state's total establishments (or payroll) in SIC 6030 in 1993. A dash (-) is used to indicate that data are not available or cannot be calculated; nec means not elsewhere classified.

Continued on next page.

SIC	Industry	No. Establishments			Employment		Pay / Employee		Annual Payroll ($ 000)		
		1992	1993	% State	1992	1993	1992	1993	1992	1993	% State
WAUKESHA, WI - [continued]											
6700	Holding and other investment offices	28	29	7.8	427	-	22,895	-	10,912	-	-
6710	Holding offices	6	7	4.9	351	66	19,373	60,545	7,907	3,775	3.5
6733	Trusts, n.e.c.	8	10	12.0	31	-	29,935		952	-	-
WAUPACA, WI											
60-	**Finance, insurance, and real estate**	110	121	1.0	540	593	18,941	19,460	10,782	11,971	0.3
6000	Depository institutions	27	28	1.2	326	378	20,503	19,810	7,137	7,663	0.8
6020	Commercial banks	20	20	1.5	280	319	21,029	19,636	6,375	6,584	1.0
6030	Savings institutions	5	4	0.8	-	35	-	24,686	-	738	0.4
6060	Credit unions	2	4	0.8	-	24	-	15,000	-	341	0.5
6100	Nondepository institutions	5	2	0.4	26	-	20,769	-	534	-	-
6300	Insurance carriers	5	5	0.6	-	14	-	15,143	-	237	0.0
6400	Insurance agents, brokers, and service	32	36	1.1	86	93	21,628	22,366	1,625	1,911	0.5
6500	Real estate	38	45	1.2	80	83	10,650	11,904	1,166	1,551	0.5
6510	Real estate operators and lessors	12	14	0.9	22	19	9,273	5,053	234	119	0.1
6530	Real estate agents and managers	9	15	0.9	33	39	8,970	12,923	429	905	0.6
6552	Subdividers and developers, n.e.c.	2	4	3.4	-	4	-	5,000	-	64	0.5
6553	Cemetery subdividers and developers	8	9	3.6	-	6	-	3,333	-	39	0.4
6700	Holding and other investment offices	2	3	0.8	-	5	-	2,400	-	15	0.0
WAUSHARA, WI											
60-	**Finance, insurance, and real estate**	38	37	0.3	164	207	17,878	16,676	3,132	3,704	0.1
6000	Depository institutions	9	9	0.4	95	117	17,979	19,043	2,006	2,299	0.3
6020	Commercial banks	9	9	0.7	95	117	17,979	19,043	2,006	2,299	0.3
6400	Insurance agents, brokers, and service	7	8	0.3	22	-	32,727	-	513	-	-
6500	Real estate	17	16	0.4	34	55	10,118	11,855	442	783	0.2
6510	Real estate operators and lessors	6	6	0.4	7	9	3,429	3,556	32	35	0.0
6530	Real estate agents and managers	6	6	0.4	6	7	9,333	10,286	62	96	0.1
WINNEBAGO, WI											
60-	**Finance, insurance, and real estate**	334	344	3.0	3,060	3,231	22,340	21,762	76,021	69,648	1.7
6000	Depository institutions	64	77	3.3	1,068	1,217	21,431	19,283	30,396	23,425	2.6
6020	Commercial banks	29	30	2.3	696	728	23,874	20,934	15,092	14,064	2.1
6030	Savings institutions	14	14	2.9	-	166	-	16,795	-	3,654	2.1
6060	Credit unions	21	33	6.5	-	323	-	16,842	-	5,707	7.5
6100	Nondepository institutions	22	12	2.4	192	105	17,625	19,657	3,743	2,242	1.2
6140	Personal credit institutions	18	8	3.7	166	78	16,000	16,462	2,824	1,223	2.8
6160	Mortgage bankers and brokers	2	4	2.2	-	27	-	28,889	-	1,019	0.9
6200	Security and commodity brokers	20	19	3.4	59	81	47,254	40,148	2,473	3,064	0.9
6210	Security brokers and dealers	9	11	3.1	42	53	60,667	55,396	2,234	2,754	1.2
6280	Security and commodity services	11	8	4.0	17	28	14,118	11,286	239	310	-
6300	Insurance carriers	37	24	2.9	920	836	27,765	29,933	23,737	22,158	1.3
6310	Life insurance	10	7	3.6	315	268	29,956	30,149	8,802	7,523	0.8
6330	Fire, marine, and casualty insurance	16	13	3.5	559	542	27,413	30,731	13,532	14,298	2.8
6400	Insurance agents, brokers, and service	74	86	2.7	219	294	22,247	20,259	5,048	6,729	1.9
6500	Real estate	106	110	2.9	517	606	12,487	12,759	7,792	8,824	2.8
6510	Real estate operators and lessors	47	50	3.2	280	240	11,500	10,450	3,509	2,882	2.8
6530	Real estate agents and managers	44	47	2.8	192	310	14,104	13,394	3,559	5,000	3.1
6540	Title abstract offices	3	2	1.5	8	-	15,000	-	222	-	-
6553	Cemetery subdividers and developers	3	4	1.6	-	27	-	10,370	-	147	1.4
6700	Holding and other investment offices	11	16	4.3	85	92	28,565	30,609	2,832	3,206	2.0
6710	Holding offices	3	5	3.5	-	73	-	33,808	-	2,781	2.6
6733	Trusts, n.e.c.	5	5	6.0	13	-	14,462	-	204	-	-
WOOD, WI											
60-	**Finance, insurance, and real estate**	168	172	1.5	987	1,019	19,818	19,454	19,253	20,947	0.5
6000	Depository institutions	43	49	2.1	592	667	20,703	19,388	11,975	13,656	1.5
6020	Commercial banks	24	24	1.8	419	429	21,298	20,531	8,591	9,292	1.4

Source: County Business Patterns, 1992/93, CBP-92/93-1, U.S. Department of Commerce, Washington, D.C., April 1995. SIC categories for which data were suppressed or not available for both 1992 and 1993 are *not* displayed. The employment columns represent mid-March employment in the year. Pay per employee is calculated by dividing 1st Quarter payroll, annualized, by mid-March employment. The columns headed "% State" show the county's percentage of the state total for the SIC in 1993; for example, 0.9% for SIC 6030 means that the county had 0.9 percent of the state's total establishments (or payroll) in SIC 6030 in 1993. A dash (-) is used to indicate that data are not available or cannot be calculated; *nec* means not elsewhere classified.

Continued on next page.

SIC	Industry	No. Establishments			Employment		Pay / Employee		Annual Payroll ($ 000)		
		1992	1993	% State	1992	1993	1992	1993	1992	1993	% State
WOOD, WI - [continued]											
6030	Savings institutions	8	8	1.7	71	-	21,070	-	1,562	-	-
6060	Credit unions	10	16	3.1	-	150	-	14,427	-	2,316	3.1
6100	Nondepository institutions	10	5	1.0	70	46	19,029	18,348	1,401	590	0.3
6200	Security and commodity brokers	6	6	1.1	19	-	54,526	-	946	-	-
6300	Insurance carriers	11	9	1.1	-	36	-	19,778	-	601	0.0
6330	Fire, marine, and casualty insurance	6	6	1.6	12	15	45,667	32,000	491	502	0.1
6370	Pension, health, and welfare funds	3	2	1.7	11	-	7,636	-	34	-	-
6400	Insurance agents, brokers, and service	41	42	1.3	126	138	19,873	18,580	2,496	2,950	0.8
6500	Real estate	53	58	1.5	146	110	8,110	11,018	1,341	1,585	0.5
6510	Real estate operators and lessors	22	30	1.9	41	45	7,415	8,622	317	573	0.6
6530	Real estate agents and managers	15	18	1.1	36	37	9,333	10,378	382	454	0.3
6540	Title abstract offices	5	5	3.7	16	17	20,250	20,941	385	434	1.6
6553	Cemetery subdividers and developers	4	4	1.6	13	-	5,538	-	113	-	-

Source: County Business Patterns, 1992/93, CBP-92/93-1, U.S. Department of Commerce, Washington, D.C., April 1995. SIC categories for which data were suppressed or not available for both 1992 and 1993 are *not* displayed. The employment columns represent mid-March employment in the year. Pay per employee is calculated by dividing 1st Quarter payroll, annualized, by mid-March employment. The columns headed "% State" show the county's percentage of the state total for the SIC in 1993; for example, 0.9% for SIC 6030 means that the county had 0.9 percent of the state's total establishments (or payroll) in SIC 6030 in 1993. A dash (-) is used to indicate that data are not available or cannot be calculated; *nec* means not elsewhere classified.

WYOMING

SIC	Industry	No. Establishments			Employment		Pay / Employee		Annual Payroll ($ 000)		
		1992	1993	% State	1992	1993	1992	1993	1992	1993	% State
ALBANY, WY											
60 –	**Finance, insurance, and real estate**	69	64	5.1	379	365	19,166	20,318	7,609	8,058	4.6
6000	Depository institutions	8	9	5.0	183	159	18,929	18,792	3,407	3,377	4.3
6020	Commercial banks	4	4	3.7	140	102	19,143	19,020	2,616	2,315	3.7
6400	Insurance agents, brokers, and service	14	13	4.4	28	56	16,286	19,071	458	1,206	6.4
6500	Real estate	31	29	5.5	50	51	9,920	10,431	605	593	3.0
6510	Real estate operators and lessors	16	13	4.7	26	18	9,077	9,556	302	231	3.3
6530	Real estate agents and managers	10	16	7.5	17	33	11,294	10,909	222	362	3.6
6700	Holding and other investment offices	2	3	5.7	-	10		12,400	-	130	-
BIG HORN, WY											
60 –	**Finance, insurance, and real estate**	14	15	1.2	89	94	20,899	20,638	1,741	1,738	1.0
6000	Depository institutions	6	6	3.3	71	73	22,873	22,959	1,494	1,515	1.9
6500	Real estate	4	5	0.9	4	6	6,000	4,667	27	31	0.2
CAMPBELL, WY											
60 –	**Finance, insurance, and real estate**	77	73	5.8	361	425	18,759	18,927	6,924	8,348	4.7
6000	Depository institutions	9	8	4.4	156	160	22,359	23,600	3,436	3,724	4.7
6100	Nondepository institutions	3	3	7.7	7	33	33,714	23,273	199	1,126	-
6200	Security and commodity brokers	6	4	5.6	9	-	33,333	-	245	-	-
6300	Insurance carriers	6	4	5.0	18	41	24,000	20,878	446	492	3.1
6400	Insurance agents, brokers, and service	12	13	4.4	44	49	20,636	18,286	915	971	5.1
6500	Real estate	38	39	7.4	121	130	10,909	11,354	1,590	1,682	8.5
6510	Real estate operators and lessors	16	17	6.2	49	52	11,102	12,154	695	811	11.4
6530	Real estate agents and managers	15	20	9.4	43	-	9,023	-	481	-	-
6700	Holding and other investment offices	3	2	3.8	6	-	14,667	-	93	-	-
CARBON, WY											
60 –	**Finance, insurance, and real estate**	35	36	2.9	165	159	16,630	18,491	2,993	3,219	1.8
6000	Depository institutions	9	7	3.9	107	90	18,131	22,311	2,080	2,213	2.8
6020	Commercial banks	6	6	5.6	102	-	18,627	-	2,040	-	-
6400	Insurance agents, brokers, and service	6	8	2.7	21	28	19,810	15,286	437	453	2.4
6500	Real estate	16	18	3.4	26	31	7,538	8,645	257	288	1.5
6510	Real estate operators and lessors	9	9	3.3	-	17	-	8,706	-	183	2.6
6530	Real estate agents and managers	5	7	3.3	8	-	7,000	-	58	-	-
CONVERSE, WY											
60 –	**Finance, insurance, and real estate**	21	26	2.1	103	112	19,456	18,679	2,229	2,431	1.4
6000	Depository institutions	3	3	1.7	56	57	23,857	24,211	1,548	1,673	2.1
6020	Commercial banks	3	3	2.8	56	57	23,857	24,211	1,548	1,673	2.6
6400	Insurance agents, brokers, and service	7	9	3.1	15	22	12,267	11,818	195	272	1.4
6500	Real estate	5	8	1.5	22	-	14,909	-	331	-	-
CROOK, WY											
60 –	**Finance, insurance, and real estate**	9	8	0.6	41	40	18,634	19,400	847	787	0.4
6400	Insurance agents, brokers, and service	4	4	1.4	8	8	9,000	10,000	84	85	0.4
FREMONT, WY											
60 –	**Finance, insurance, and real estate**	75	71	5.7	278	403	16,043	14,600	5,576	6,581	3.7
6000	Depository institutions	9	11	6.1	102	119	18,745	18,185	2,157	2,439	3.1
6020	Commercial banks	5	5	4.7	-	79	-	19,392	-	1,784	2.8
6100	Nondepository institutions	4	2	5.1	24	-	15,500	-	393	-	-

Source: County Business Patterns, 1992/93, CBP-92/93-1, U.S. Department of Commerce, Washington, D.C., April 1995. SIC categories for which data were suppressed or not available for both 1992 and 1993 are *not* displayed. The employment columns represent mid-March employment in the year. Pay per employee is calculated by dividing 1st Quarter payroll, annualized, by mid-March employment. The columns headed "% State" show the county's percentage of the state total for the SIC in 1993; for example, 0.9% for SIC 6030 means that the county had 0.9 percent of the state's total establishments (or payroll) in SIC 6030 in 1993. A dash (-) is used to indicate that data are not available or cannot be calculated; *nec* means not elsewhere classified.

Continued on next page.

1091

SIC	Industry	No. Establishments			Employment		Pay / Employee		Annual Payroll ($ 000)		
		1992	1993	% State	1992	1993	1992	1993	1992	1993	% State
FREMONT, WY - [continued]											
6300	Insurance carriers	5	4	5.0	11	8	24,000	39,500	290	268	1.7
6400	Insurance agents, brokers, and service	21	22	7.5	56	64	13,500	13,000	844	994	5.2
6500	Real estate	29	27	5.1	72	89	10,056	11,101	866	1,147	5.8
6510	Real estate operators and lessors	14	15	5.5	50	72	10,320	10,722	632	905	12.7
6530	Real estate agents and managers	9	10	4.7	14	-	10,286	-	151	-	-
GOSHEN, WY											
60 –	**Finance, insurance, and real estate**	29	28	2.2	125	145	18,048	16,690	2,458	2,643	1.5
6000	Depository institutions	6	6	3.3	85	94	20,235	18,851	1,888	2,021	2.6
6400	Insurance agents, brokers, and service	10	9	3.1	16	13	12,250	13,538	205	197	1.0
6500	Real estate	9	9	1.7	15	30	6,667	5,467	118	145	0.7
6510	Real estate operators and lessors	5	5	1.8	-	25	-	5,280	-	111	1.6
6530	Real estate agents and managers	3	3	1.4	5	-	5,600	-	31	-	-
HOT SPRINGS, WY											
60 –	**Finance, insurance, and real estate**	11	10	0.8	51	51	16,471	17,176	843	652	0.4
6000	Depository institutions	3	3	1.7	42	41	17,905	18,927	751	554	0.7
6500	Real estate	5	4	0.8	6	7	6,000	6,857	41	45	0.2
JOHNSON, WY											
60 –	**Finance, insurance, and real estate**	20	19	1.5	107	105	21,346	22,438	2,412	2,118	1.2
6000	Depository institutions	4	4	2.2	64	66	21,188	21,152	1,366	1,398	1.8
6500	Real estate	8	8	1.5	13	15	18,154	34,133	168	221	1.1
6510	Real estate operators and lessors	2	3	1.1	-	3	-	8,000	-	42	0.6
6530	Real estate agents and managers	3	4	1.9	2	-	10,000	-	25	-	-
LARAMIE, WY											
60 –	**Finance, insurance, and real estate**	190	204	16.3	1,449	1,786	22,940	23,514	37,432	45,358	25.7
6000	Depository institutions	30	31	17.1	781	834	22,402	22,518	20,716	22,567	28.5
6020	Commercial banks	13	13	12.1	428	451	23,654	23,166	12,808	14,052	22.2
6100	Nondepository institutions	14	14	35.9	155	122	27,639	33,705	4,740	3,845	-
6140	Personal credit institutions	9	10	55.6	-	85	-	25,600	-	2,085	71.1
6160	Mortgage bankers and brokers	4	4	28.6	86	37	29,395	52,324	3,044	1,760	29.0
6200	Security and commodity brokers	13	12	16.9	52	64	55,769	70,000	2,936	3,164	11.7
6300	Insurance carriers	18	17	21.3	166	353	24,723	20,487	4,158	7,890	49.2
6310	Life insurance	6	7	41.2	89	96	27,371	27,917	2,255	2,407	69.1
6330	Fire, marine, and casualty insurance	6	6	25.0	7	-	38,286	-	280	-	-
6400	Insurance agents, brokers, and service	52	61	20.7	127	200	19,276	23,080	2,587	4,766	25.1
6500	Real estate	56	62	11.7	159	-	11,472	-	2,107	-	-
6510	Real estate operators and lessors	27	31	11.3	69	87	9,971	8,920	769	963	13.6
6530	Real estate agents and managers	22	27	12.7	74	103	13,027	16,117	1,114	1,828	18.4
6733	Trusts, n.e.c.	4	2	16.7	3	-	14,667	-	125	-	-
LINCOLN, WY											
60 –	**Finance, insurance, and real estate**	17	16	1.3	112	98	15,464	18,245	1,833	1,952	1.1
6000	Depository institutions	3	3	1.7	62	61	19,419	19,213	1,257	1,327	1.7
6020	Commercial banks	3	3	2.8	62	61	19,419	19,213	1,257	1,327	2.1
6400	Insurance agents, brokers, and service	7	8	2.7	19	-	15,368	-	312	-	-
6500	Real estate	4	3	0.6	21	8	5,714	10,000	127	81	0.4
NATRONA, WY											
60 –	**Finance, insurance, and real estate**	208	203	16.3	1,091	1,202	23,963	24,532	26,006	31,120	17.6
6000	Depository institutions	19	19	10.5	356	425	25,539	22,654	8,985	10,367	13.1
6020	Commercial banks	13	9	8.4	320	374	26,350	23,412	8,334	9,458	15.0
6100	Nondepository institutions	13	8	20.5	69	109	31,594	27,303	2,139	3,334	-
6200	Security and commodity brokers	13	18	25.4	63	86	56,571	49,721	3,801	4,935	18.3
6300	Insurance carriers	32	24	30.0	148	136	22,784	28,294	3,752	3,359	21.0
6330	Fire, marine, and casualty insurance	10	9	37.5	24	11	25,500	28,000	537	376	11.5

Source: County Business Patterns, 1992/93, CBP-92/93-1, U.S. Department of Commerce, Washington, D.C., April 1995. SIC categories for which data were suppressed or not available for both 1992 and 1993 are not displayed. The employment columns represent mid-March employment in the year. Pay per employee is calculated by dividing 1st Quarter payroll, annualized, by mid-March employment. The columns headed "% State" show the county's percentage of the state total for the SIC in 1993; for example, 0.9% for SIC 6030 means that the county had 0.9 percent of the state's total establishments (or payroll) in SIC 6030 in 1993. A dash (-) is used to indicate that data are not available or cannot be calculated; nec means not elsewhere classified.

Continued on next page.

SIC	Industry	No. Establishments			Employment		Pay / Employee		Annual Payroll ($ 000)		
		1992	1993	% State	1992	1993	1992	1993	1992	1993	% State
NATRONA, WY - [continued]											
6370	Pension, health, and welfare funds	4	2	50.0	1	-	4,000	-	46	-	-
6400	Insurance agents, brokers, and service	50	49	16.7	171	172	21,731	21,907	3,709	4,043	21.3
6500	Real estate	69	72	13.6	223	211	13,184	14,540	2,859	3,178	16.1
6510	Real estate operators and lessors	30	33	12.0	95	100	9,474	9,440	982	1,025	14.4
6530	Real estate agents and managers	30	33	15.5	91	87	13,978	15,586	1,192	1,447	14.6
6540	Title abstract offices	3	3	37.5	11	14	43,273	48,857	393	641	56.8
6700	Holding and other investment offices	12	13	24.5	61	63	20,984	30,540	761	1,904	-
6733	Trusts, n.e.c.	4	3	25.0	10	9	12,400	10,222	85	64	3.8
6792	Oil royalty traders	2	3	37.5	-	6	-	16,667	-	96	60.8
NIOBRARA, WY											
60 –	**Finance, insurance, and real estate**	6	6	0.5	27	27	17,037	17,778	508	560	0.3
PARK, WY											
60 –	**Finance, insurance, and real estate**	62	63	5.0	289	309	20,457	18,848	6,676	6,573	3.7
6000	Depository institutions	14	14	7.7	182	208	20,593	18,288	4,074	4,396	5.6
6020	Commercial banks	7	6	5.6	154	167	22,130	19,401	3,681	3,821	6.0
6300	Insurance carriers	3	2	2.5	7	-	16,571	-	135	-	-
6400	Insurance agents, brokers, and service	13	14	4.8	36	49	16,000	13,061	600	735	3.9
6500	Real estate	23	24	4.5	36	31	12,111	11,355	500	458	2.3
6510	Real estate operators and lessors	10	11	4.0	23	-	12,348	-	313	-	-
6530	Real estate agents and managers	8	11	5.2	8	15	11,000	12,000	119	232	2.3
6700	Holding and other investment offices	4	5	9.4	-	4	-	12,000	-	47	-
PLATTE, WY											
60 –	**Finance, insurance, and real estate**	19	17	1.4	63	70	17,778	20,457	1,190	1,451	0.8
6000	Depository institutions	5	5	2.8	44	49	20,818	22,939	971	1,140	1.4
6400	Insurance agents, brokers, and service	6	4	1.4	10	-	13,600	-	145	-	-
6500	Real estate	5	6	1.1	-	7	-	14,286	-	92	0.5
6510	Real estate operators and lessors	3	4	1.5	3	-	5,333	-	23	-	-
SHERIDAN, WY											
60 –	**Finance, insurance, and real estate**	77	134	10.7	462	517	18,961	21,501	8,887	10,924	6.2
6000	Depository institutions	12	12	6.6	195	198	22,749	23,596	4,432	4,619	5.8
6020	Commercial banks	7	6	5.6	156	150	21,949	23,387	3,241	3,314	5.2
6100	Nondepository institutions	3	2	5.1	8	-	21,000	-	128	-	-
6200	Security and commodity brokers	6	6	8.5	26	-	45,077	-	1,197	-	-
6210	Security brokers and dealers	6	6	11.5	26	-	45,077	-	1,197	-	-
6300	Insurance carriers	5	4	5.0	12	7	19,000	21,714	242	156	1.0
6400	Insurance agents, brokers, and service	10	13	4.4	49	55	21,143	20,000	987	1,203	6.3
6500	Real estate	36	91	17.2	160	203	9,500	8,808	1,671	1,901	9.6
6510	Real estate operators and lessors	17	73	26.6	38	143	7,684	6,126	297	797	11.2
6530	Real estate agents and managers	12	14	6.6	89	44	9,483	14,455	922	738	7.4
6700	Holding and other investment offices	5	6	11.3	12	24	16,667	84,167	230	1,595	-
6732	Educational, religious, etc. trusts	3	2	16.7	10	-	18,400	-	212	-	-
SUBLETTE, WY											
60 –	**Finance, insurance, and real estate**	12	12	1.0	60	50	15,133	15,760	964	1,019	0.6
6500	Real estate	5	5	0.9	21	9	12,000	6,667	217	183	0.9
SWEETWATER, WY											
60 –	**Finance, insurance, and real estate**	87	89	7.1	382	438	19,832	18,868	7,963	9,142	5.2
6000	Depository institutions	13	15	8.3	200	229	24,780	23,808	5,119	6,000	7.6
6020	Commercial banks	7	8	7.5	170	186	26,329	24,688	4,601	5,113	8.1
6300	Insurance carriers	6	4	5.0	12	11	26,333	28,364	397	331	2.1
6400	Insurance agents, brokers, and service	22	24	8.2	38	61	16,737	15,475	781	1,070	5.6

Source: County Business Patterns, 1992/93, CBP-92/93-1, U.S. Department of Commerce, Washington, D.C., April 1995. SIC categories for which data were suppressed or not available for both 1992 and 1993 are not displayed. The employment columns represent mid-March employment in the year. Pay per employee is calculated by dividing 1st Quarter payroll, annualized, by mid-March employment. The columns headed "% State" show the county's percentage of the state total for the SIC in 1993; for example, 0.9% for SIC 6030 means that the county had 0.9 percent of the state's total establishments (or payroll) in SIC 6030 in 1993. A dash (-) is used to indicate that data are not available or cannot be calculated; nec means not elsewhere classified.

Continued on next page.

SIC	Industry	No. Establishments			Employment		Pay / Employee		Annual Payroll ($ 000)		
		1992	1993	% State	1992	1993	1992	1993	1992	1993	% State
SWEETWATER, WY - [continued]											
6500	Real estate	37	39	7.4	103	111	10,951	9,369	1,044	1,268	6.4
6510	Real estate operators and lessors	21	24	8.8	62	66	11,871	10,606	683	787	11.1
6530	Real estate agents and managers	11	10	4.7	13	-	9,846	-	130	-	-
TETON, WY											
60 –	**Finance, insurance, and real estate**	89	91	7.3	496	492	28,903	30,439	20,886	25,335	14.3
6000	Depository institutions	4	4	2.2	116	139	26,552	21,353	3,177	3,284	4.1
6020	Commercial banks	4	4	3.7	116	139	26,552	21,353	3,177	3,284	5.2
6160	Mortgage bankers and brokers	3	3	21.4	10	-	26,800	-	373	-	-
6400	Insurance agents, brokers, and service	12	13	4.4	27	42	18,963	21,905	594	977	5.1
6500	Real estate	54	56	10.6	290	231	13,793	15,082	4,401	4,565	23.1
6510	Real estate operators and lessors	13	16	5.8	42	31	9,810	12,000	468	482	6.8
6530	Real estate agents and managers	30	32	15.0	217	186	14,138	15,269	3,373	3,356	33.8
6552	Subdividers and developers, n.e.c.	3	7	33.3	-	14	-	19,429	-	717	-
6700	Holding and other investment offices	7	7	13.2	14	16	37,143	33,500	695	641	-
6799	Investors, n.e.c.	1	3	30.0	-	3	-	5,333	-	28	3.2
UINTA, WY											
60 –	**Finance, insurance, and real estate**	32	28	2.2	142	141	18,873	18,582	3,035	2,865	1.6
6000	Depository institutions	7	7	3.9	90	91	19,422	20,659	2,040	2,080	2.6
6400	Insurance agents, brokers, and service	6	6	2.0	13	-	15,385	-	200	-	-
6500	Real estate	12	13	2.5	28	33	19,571	11,636	546	415	2.1
6510	Real estate operators and lessors	4	5	1.8	4	-	13,000	-	54	-	-
6530	Real estate agents and managers	6	7	3.3	-	18	-	10,444	-	202	2.0
WASHAKIE, WY											
60 –	**Finance, insurance, and real estate**	25	23	1.8	126	128	19,143	19,250	2,389	2,417	1.4
6000	Depository institutions	5	5	2.8	78	80	21,436	20,950	1,610	1,654	2.1
6400	Insurance agents, brokers, and service	7	7	2.4	24	24	19,333	15,167	435	373	2.0
6500	Real estate	9	7	1.3	12	16	10,000	11,750	153	193	1.0
6510	Real estate operators and lessors	3	4	1.5	2	7	14,000	15,429	53	111	1.6
6530	Real estate agents and managers	6	3	1.4	10	9	9,200	8,889	100	82	0.8
WESTON, WY											
60 –	**Finance, insurance, and real estate**	11	12	1.0	80	94	19,400	16,681	1,298	1,358	0.8
6000	Depository institutions	3	3	1.7	65	74	21,538	18,649	1,133	1,150	1.5
6020	Commercial banks	3	3	2.8	65	74	21,538	18,649	1,133	1,150	1.8
6400	Insurance agents, brokers, and service	4	5	1.7	10	14	8,000	8,857	87	123	0.6

Source: County Business Patterns, 1992/93, CBP-92/93-1, U.S. Department of Commerce, Washington, D.C., April 1995. SIC categories for which data were suppressed or not available for both 1992 and 1993 are *not* displayed. The employment columns represent mid-March employment in the year. Pay per employee is calculated by dividing 1st Quarter payroll, annualized, by mid-March employment. The columns headed "% State" show the county's percentage of the state total for the SIC in 1993; for example, 0.9% for SIC 6030 means that the county had 0.9 percent of the state's total establishments (or payroll) in SIC 6030 in 1993. A dash (-) is used to indicate that data are not available or cannot be calculated; *nec* means not elsewhere classified.

SIC INDEX

The SIC Index shows all 4-digit SICs covered in *Finance, Insurance, and Real Estate U.S.A.* in numerical order. A separate section, listing the industries in alphabetical order, follows. Indented names indicate 4-digit SIC categories for which company names are listed separately but for which no other detailed information is provided. In the alphabetical section, each industry name is followed by the SIC number (in parentheses) and then by one or more page numbers. This SIC structure is based on the 1987 definitions published in *Standard Industrial Classification Manual*, 1987, Office of Management and Budget. The abbreviation 'nec' stands for 'not elsewhere classified'.

KEYWORD INDEX

The Keyword Index holds the names of industries, activities, and services that are part of the Finance, Insurance, and Real Estate industries of the U.S. Also included are names of government agencies and institutions. Each keyword is followed by one or more page numbers; these pages refer to the first page of the industry; one or more SIC categories follow in brackets.

Insurance - continued
—information bureaus, p. 275 [SIC 6411]
—inspection and investigation services, p. 275 [SIC 6411]
—liability, p. 231 [SIC 6350]
—life, pp. 173, 275 [SICs 6310, 6411]
—livestock, p. 219 [SIC 6330]
—loss prevention services, p. 275 [SIC 6411]
—marine, p. 219 [SIC 6330]
—medical claims: contract or fee basis, p. 275 [SIC 6411]
—mortgage guaranty, p. 231 [SIC 6350]
—patrol services, p. 275 [SIC 6411]
—plate glass, p. 219 [SIC 6330]
—professional standards services, p. 275 [SIC 6411]
—property damage, p. 219 [SIC 6330]
—rate making organizations, p. 275 [SIC 6411]
—reporting services, p. 275 [SIC 6411]
—research services, p. 275 [SIC 6411]
—savings and loan shares, p. 267 [SIC 6390]
—surety, p. 231 [SIC 6350]
—title, p. 241 [SIC 6360]
—workers' compensation, p. 219 [SIC 6330]
Interbank deposits, foreign banks, p. 69 [SIC 6080]
Interinsurance exchanges, reciprocal
—accident and health, p. 195 [SIC 6321]
—fire, marine, and casualty, p. 219 [SIC 6330]
—surety and fidelity, p. 231 [SIC 6350]
Intermediate investment banks, p. 105 [SIC 6150]
International banking institutions, p. 69 [SIC 6080]
Investigation services, insurance, p. 275 [SIC 6411]
Investment bankers, p. 131 [SIC 6210]
Investment banks, intermediate, p. 105 [SIC 6150]
Investment certificates, sale of, p. 131 [SIC 6210]
Investment clubs, p. 415 [SIC 6799]
Investment companies, small business, p. 105 [SIC 6150]
Investment firms, general brokerage, p. 131 [SIC 6210]
Investment funds, management
—closed-end, p. 363 [SIC 6720]
—open-end, p. 363 [SIC 6720]
Investment holding companies, p. 351 [SIC 6710]
Investment offices, p. 363 [SIC 6720]
Investment trusts
—mortgages, p. 405 [SIC 6798]
—real estate, p. 405 [SIC 6798]
—realty, p. 405 [SIC 6798]
—unit, p. 363 [SIC 6720]
Investment
—advisory services, p. 161 [SIC 6280]
—counseling, p. 161 [SIC 6280]
—investors' syndicates, p. 363 [SIC 6720]
—personal: trust management, p. 379 [SIC 6733]
—research, p. 161 [SIC 6280]
Investors nec, p. 415 [SIC 6799]

Job completion, bonding for guarantee of, p. 231 [SIC 6350]

Land, except cemeteries: subdividers and developers of, p. 331 [SIC 6552]
Landholding offices, p. 287 [SIC 6510]
Leases, oil: buying, selling, or trading on own account, p. 387 [SIC 6792]
Leasing
—autos, p. 105 [SIC 6150]
—machinery and equipment, p. 105 [SIC 6150]
—pari-mutuel totalizer equipment, p. 105 [SIC 6150]
—real estate: time-sharing, p. 305 [SIC 6530]
—trucks, p. 105 [SIC 6150]
Legal reserve life insurance, p. 173 [SIC 6310]
Lessors
—airports: except operators, p. 287 [SIC 6510]
—franchises, patents, and copyrights, p. 395 [SIC 6794]
—piers, docks, and related facilities, p. 287 [SIC 6510]
—property, nec, p. 287 [SIC 6510]
—railroad property, p. 287 [SIC 6510]
—real estate, p. 287 [SIC 6510]
Liability, insurance, p. 231 [SIC 6350]
Licensing
—franchises, patents, and copyrights, p. 395 [SIC 6794]
—music, p. 395 [SIC 6794]
—performance rights, p. 395 [SIC 6794]
Liens, tax: holding, buying, and selling, p. 415 [SIC 6799]
Life insurance, p. 173 [SIC 6310]
—agents, p. 275 [SIC 6411]
—assessment associations, p. 173 [SIC 6310]
—cooperative, p. 173 [SIC 6310]
—fraternal organizations, p. 173 [SIC 6310]
—legal reserve, p. 173 [SIC 6310]
Life insurance funds, savings bank, p. 173 [SIC 6310]
Life reinsurance, p. 173 [SIC 6310]
Listing services, real estate, p. 305 [SIC 6530]
Livestock, insurance, p. 219 [SIC 6330]
Livestock loan companies, p. 105 [SIC 6150]
Loan brokers, p. 119 [SIC 6160]
Loan companies
—livestock, p. 105 [SIC 6150]
—small: licensed, p. 95 [SIC 6140]
Loan correspondents, p. 119 [SIC 6160]
Loan institutions, general and industrial, p. 105 [SIC 6150]
Loan societies, remedial, p. 95 [SIC 6140]
Loans
—agricultural, p. 105 [SIC 6150]
—auto, p. 95 [SIC 6140]
—business, p. 119 [SIC 6160]
—commercial: foreign banks, p. 69 [SIC 6080]
—farm, p. 119 [SIC 6160]
—federally guaranteed, p. 87 [SIC 6110]
—federally insured, p. 87 [SIC 6110]
—industrial, p. 95 [SIC 6140]
—mortgage, p. 119 [SIC 6160]
—real estate construction, p. 119 [SIC 6160]
—to individuals, p. 95 [SIC 6140]

Keyword Index

Securities - continued
—holders' protective committees, p. 161 [SIC 6280]
—services allied with, p. 161 [SIC 6280]
—speculators: on own account, p. 415 [SIC 6799]
—trading, p. 131 [SIC 6210]
—transfer agents, p. 161 [SIC 6280]
Security exchanges, p. 153 [SIC 6230]
Selling agents
—real estate, p. 305 [SIC 6530]
Shopping centers, property operation of, p. 287 [SIC 6510]
Short-term business credit, p. 105 [SIC 6150]
—except agricultural, p. 105 [SIC 6150]
Sick benefit associations, mutual, p. 195 [SIC 6321]
Small business investment companies, p. 105 [SIC 6150]
Speculators, securities: on own account, p. 415 [SIC 6799]
State chartered savings institutions, p. 33 [SIC 6030]
State commercial banks, p. 11 [SIC 6020]
State credit unions, p. 49 [SIC 6060]
Stock exchanges, p. 153 [SIC 6230]
Stock insurance
—fire, marine, and casualty, p. 219 [SIC 6330]
—life, p. 173 [SIC 6310]
Stock options, buying, selling, or trading, p. 153 [SIC 6230]
Stocks
—brokers and dealers, p. 131 [SIC 6210]
—buying, selling, or trading, p. 153 [SIC 6230]
—option dealers, p. 131 [SIC 6210]
—quotation services, p. 161 [SIC 6280]
—transfer agents, p. 161 [SIC 6280]
Student Loan Marketing Administration, p. 87 [SIC 6110]
Subdividers
—cemeteries, p. 343 [SIC 6553]
—real property: except cemeteries, p. 331 [SIC 6552]
Surety bonding, p. 231 [SIC 6350]
Surety insurance, p. 231 [SIC 6350]
—reciprocal interinsurance exchanges, p. 231 [SIC 6350]
Switching, electronic funds transfer, p. 77 [SIC 6090]
Synthetic Fuels Corporation, p. 87 [SIC 6110]

Tax certificates
—dealers, p. 131 [SIC 6210]
—sale and redemption agencies, p. 77 [SIC 6090]
Taxation
—capital gains, p. 405 [SIC 6798]
—corporate, p. 405 [SIC 6798]
Taxes, liens: holding, buying, and selling, p. 415 [SIC 6799]
Theater buildings, owner-operators of, p. 287 [SIC 6510]
Theft, insurance, p. 219 [SIC 6330]
Time-sharing, real estate: sales, leasing, and rentals, p. 305 [SIC 6530]
Title abstract offices, p. 323 [SIC 6540]
Title companies, p. 323 [SIC 6540]
Title reconveyance companies, p. 323 [SIC 6540]
Title search companies, p. 323 [SIC 6540]

Titles
—guaranty of, p. 241 [SIC 6360]
—insurance, p. 241 [SIC 6360]
Trade companies, foreign, p. 69 [SIC 6080]
Traders, commodity contracts, p. 143 [SIC 6220]
Trading companies, commodity contracts, p. 415 [SIC 6799]
Transfer agents
—securities, p. 161 [SIC 6280]
—stock, p. 161 [SIC 6280]
Transfer networks, electronic funds, p. 77 [SIC 6090]
Travelers' checks, issuance, p. 77 [SIC 6090]
Trucks, finance leasing of, p. 105 [SIC 6150]
Trust companies, p. 323 [SIC 6540]
—commercial: national, p. 11 [SIC 6020]
—commercial: state, p. 11 [SIC 6020]
Trust deeds, purchase and sale of, p. 105 [SIC 6150]
Trust facilities
—nondepository, p. 77 [SIC 6090]
—nondepository: federally chartered, p. 77 [SIC 6090]
—nondepository: nationally chartered, p. 77 [SIC 6090]
—nondepository: state chartered, p. 77 [SIC 6090]
Trust funds, union, p. 251 [SIC 6370]
Trustees, except educational, religious, and charitable, p. 379 [SIC 6733]
Trusts
—educational, religious, and charitable: management of, p. 371 [SIC 6732]
—except educational, religious, and charitable: management of, p. 379 [SIC 6733]
—mortgage investments, p. 405 [SIC 6798]
—real estate investment, p. 405 [SIC 6798]
—realty investments, p. 405 [SIC 6798]
—unit investment, p. 363 [SIC 6720]

Underwriting
—fire, marine, and casualty insurance, p. 219 [SIC 6330]
—insurance, p. 267 [SIC 6390]
—life insurance, p. 173 [SIC 6310]
—securities, p. 131 [SIC 6210]
—surety and fidelity insurance, p. 231 [SIC 6350]
—title insurance, p. 241 [SIC 6360]
Unions, trust, benefit, and health funds, p. 251 [SIC 6370]
Unit investment trusts, p. 363 [SIC 6720]
Utilities, holding companies, p. 351 [SIC 6710]

Vacations, funds for employees, p. 379 [SIC 6733]
Vehicles, finance leasing of, p. 105 [SIC 6150]
Venture capital companies, p. 415 [SIC 6799]

Warranties, auto, p. 267 [SIC 6390]
Warranty insurance, home, p. 231 [SIC 6350]
Welfare funds, p. 251 [SIC 6370]
Workers' compensation insurance, p. 219 [SIC 6330]
Working capital, direct financing, p. 105 [SIC 6150]

COMPANY INDEX

This index shows, in alphabetical order, more than 2,900 companies in *Finance, Insurance, and Real Estate U.S.A.* Organizations may be public or private companies, subsidiaries or divisions of companies, joint ventures or affiliates, or corporate groups. Each company entry is followed by one or more page numbers. After the page numbers, the SICs under which the company is listed follow in brackets preceded by "SIC" or "SICs". Some company names are abbreviated.

Company Index

Company Index

Loyola Federal Savings Bank, p. 43 [SIC 6035]
Lumbermens Mutual Casualty Co., p. 228 [SIC 6324]
Lynch Corp., p. 170 [SIC 6231]

M and I Capital Markets Group Inc., p. 423 [SIC 6799]
Mabie and Mintz Inc., p. 298 [SIC 6513]
Mabon Securities Corp., p. 140 [SIC 6163]
MacDill Federal Credit Union, p. 56 [SIC 6061]
Macerich Co., p. 411 [SIC 6798]
Macerich Partnership L.P., p. 314 [SIC 6531]
Madison Dearborn Partners Inc., p. 422 [SIC 6799]
Madison Square Garden Corp., p. 294 [SIC 6512]
Madisonville Realty Co., p. 302 [SIC 6519]
Maestro Latin America Inc., p. 85 [SIC 6099]
Mahoney Group, pp. 240, 314 [SICs 6331, 6531]
Mal Inc., p. 296 [SIC 6512]
Malaco Records Inc., p. 422 [SIC 6799]
Malama Pacific Corp., p. 341 [SIC 6552]
Malan Realty Investors Inc., p. 412 [SIC 6798]
Mall of America Co., p. 314 [SIC 6531]
Managers Funds L.P., p. 369 [SIC 6722]
Manhattan Mortgage Co., p. 129 [SIC 6163]
Manufacturers Alliance Insurance Co., p. 239 [SIC 6331]
Manufacturers and Traders Trust Co., p. 23 [SIC 6022]
Manufacturers Leasing Services Inc., p. 117 [SIC 6159]
Marcus and Millichap Co., p. 314 [SIC 6531]
Margaretten and Company Inc., p. 127 [SIC 6162]
Margaretten Financial Corp., p. 127 [SIC 6162]
Maricopa County Employees Federal Credit Union, p. 59 [SIC 6061]
Marine Petroleum Trust, p. 393 [SIC 6792]
Mariner Group Inc., p. 339 [SIC 6552]
Maritime Capital Corp., p. 117 [SIC 6159]
Markel Corp., pp. 229, 238 [SICs 6324, 6331]
Markel Service Inc., pp. 229, 238 [SICs 6324, 6331]
Market Profile Theorems Inc., p. 172 [SIC 6282]
Marriott Senior Living Services, p. 297 [SIC 6513]
Marsh and McLennan Co. Inc., p. 168 [SIC 6231]
Marsh and McLennan Companies Inc., p. 282 [SIC 6411]
Marsh Associates Inc., p. 302 [SIC 6519]
Marshall and Ilsley Corp., pp. 20, 22, 359 [SICs 6021, 6022, 6712]
Marshall and Ilsley Trust Co., p. 84 [SIC 6091]
Martin Selig Real Estate, p. 296 [SIC 6512]
Maryland National Bank, p. 20 [SIC 6021]
Mason-McDuffie Real Estate Inc., p. 312 [SIC 6531]
Massachusetts Federal Credit Union, p. 58 [SIC 6061]
Massachusetts Minority Enterprise Investment Corp., p. 116 [SIC 6159]
MASSBANK Corp., p. 46 [SIC 6036]
MASSBANK for Savings, p. 46 [SIC 6036]
Mattick and Duke Inc., p. 422 [SIC 6799]
Maxicare Health Plans Inc., p. 217 [SIC 6321]
Maxim Property Management, p. 313 [SIC 6531]
Mayer and Schweitzer Inc., p. 140 [SIC 6163]

Maytag Financial Services Corp., pp. 103, 116 [SICs 6141, 6159]
Mazon Associates Inc., p. 113 [SIC 6153]
Mazzio's Corp., p. 403 [SIC 6794]
MBIA Insurance Corp., p. 238 [SIC 6331]
MBIA Municipal Investors Service Corp., p. 238 [SIC 6331]
MBL Life Assurance Corp., p. 182 [SIC 6289]
MBNA America Bank N.A., p. 20 [SIC 6021]
MBNA Corp., p. 359 [SIC 6712]
MBS Clearing Corp., p. 172 [SIC 6282]
MCC Financial Corp., p. 116 [SIC 6159]
McDonald and Company Investments Inc., p. 140 [SIC 6163]
McDonald and Company Securities Inc., p. 140 [SIC 6163]
McDonald's Corp., p. 401 [SIC 6794]
McDonnell Douglas Corp., p. 338 [SIC 6552]
McDonnell Douglas Finance Corp., p. 114 [SIC 6159]
McDonnell Douglas Financial Services Corp., p. 114 [SIC 6159]
McKeany-Flavell Company Inc., p. 150 [SIC 6211]
McKee and McFarland Inc., p. 423 [SIC 6799]
McLaughlin, Piven, Vogel Inc., p. 171 [SIC 6231]
McNeil Real Estate Management, p. 299 [SIC 6513]
McVean Trading and Investm. Inc., p. 150 [SIC 6211]
M.D. Enterprises of Connecticut Inc., p. 217 [SIC 6321]
Medallion Mortgage Co., p. 127 [SIC 6162]
Medford Savings Bank, p. 45 [SIC 6036]
Media/Professional Insurance, pp. 274, 284 [SICs 6399, 6411]
Medica, p. 217 [SIC 6321]
Medical Professional Liability Agency Ltd., p. 283 [SIC 6411]
MedView Services Inc., p. 283 [SIC 6411]
Mego Financial Corp., pp. 103, 313, 340 [SICs 6141, 6531, 6552]
Mellon Bank Corp., pp. 18, 357 [SICs 6021, 6712]
Memphis Hospital Service and Surgical Association Inc., p. 217 [SIC 6321]
Mercantile Bancorporation Inc., pp. 20, 22, 359 [SICs 6021, 6022, 6712]
Mercantile Bankshares Corp., p. 23 [SIC 6022]
Merchant Factors Corp., p. 113 [SIC 6153]
Mercury Finance Co., p. 102 [SIC 6141]
Mercy Healthcare Arizona, p. 215 [SIC 6321]
Meredith and Grew Inc., p. 129 [SIC 6163]
Meridian Bancorp Inc., pp. 22, 358 [SICs 6022, 6712]
Meridian Bank, p. 22 [SIC 6022]
Meridian Insurance Group Inc., p. 169 [SIC 6231]
Meridian Investments, p. 140 [SIC 6163]
Meridian Mortgage Corp., p. 127 [SIC 6162]
Merrill Lynch and Company Inc., pp. 138, 168, 180, 360 [SICs 6163, 6231, 6289, 6719]
Merrill Lynch Credit Corp., p. 127 [SIC 6162]
Merrill Pickard Anderson and Eyre, p. 423 [SIC 6799]
Merrimack Valley Federal Credit Union, p. 57 [SIC 6061]

Philadelphia Stock Exchange Inc., p. 160 [SIC 6221]

Philip Morris Capital Corp., pp. 114, 338 [SICs 6159, 6552]

Phoenix Equity Planning Corp., p. 369 [SIC 6722]

Phoenixx International Resources Inc., p. 151 [SIC 6211]

Physician Corporation of America, p. 215 [SIC 6321]

Physicians Health Services Inc., p. 216 [SIC 6321]

Physicians Health Services of Connecticut Inc., p. 216 [SIC 6321]

Physicians Mutual Insurance Co., p. 205 [SIC 6311]

P.I.E. Mutual Insurance Co., p. 239 [SIC 6331]

Piedmont Associates Inc., p. 284 [SIC 6411]

Piedmont Management Company Inc., pp. 169, 238 [SICs 6231, 6331]

Pierce, Pace and Associates, p. 299 [SIC 6513]

Pinnacle West Capital Corp., pp. 338, 362, 421 [SICs 6552, 6719, 6799]

Pioneer Financial Services Inc., p. 204 [SIC 6311]

Pioneer Group Inc., pp. 141, 170, 171, 421 [SICs 6163, 6231, 6282, 6799]

Pioneer Life Insurance Company of Illinois, p. 205 [SIC 6311]

Piper Jaffray Companies Inc., pp. 139, 169 [SICs 6163, 6231]

Piper Jaffray Inc., p. 139 [SIC 6163]

Piper Trust Co., p. 84 [SIC 6091]

Pitney Bowes Credit Corp., p. 114 [SIC 6159]

Pizza Hut Inc., p. 401 [SIC 6794]

Playboy Enterprises Inc., p. 403 [SIC 6794]

Plaza Home Mortgage Corp., p. 127 [SIC 6162]

Plus System Inc., p. 85 [SIC 6099]

PM Realty Group, pp. 294, 297, 301 [SICs 6512, 6513, 6514]

PMI Group Inc., p. 238 [SIC 6331]

PNC Bank Corp., pp. 18, 21, 84, 357 [SICs 6021, 6022, 6091, 6712]

Pocatello Railroad Federal Credit Union, p. 58 [SIC 6061]

Podolsky and Associates L.P., p. 295 [SIC 6512]

Poe and Brown Inc., p. 283 [SIC 6411]

Police and Fire Federal Credit Union, p. 56 [SIC 6061]

Portland General Corp., p. 338 [SIC 6552]

Portland Postal Employees Credit Union, p. 61 [SIC 6062]

Portland Teachers Credit Union, p. 60 [SIC 6062]

Poughkeepsie Savings Bank F.S.B., pp. 127, 282 [SICs 6162, 6411]

Premier America Federal Credit Union, p. 56 [SIC 6061]

Premium Financing Specialists Inc., p. 112 [SIC 6153]

Prentiss Properties Limited Inc., p. 314 [SIC 6531]

Presidential Realty Corp., p. 412 [SIC 6798]

Price REIT Inc., p. 411 [SIC 6798]

Primark Corp., p. 127 [SIC 6162]

Prime Rate Premium Finance Corp., p. 112 [SIC 6153]

Prime Residential Inc., p. 411 [SIC 6798]

Prime Retail Inc., p. 411 [SIC 6798]

Primerica Financial Services Inc., p. 169 [SIC 6231]

Principal Financial Group Inc., pp. 126, 180, 202, 226 [SICs 6162, 6289, 6311, 6324]

Principal Mutual Life Insurance Co., pp. 180, 202 [SICs 6289, 6311]

ProCard Inc., p. 104 [SIC 6141]

Proctor Homer Warren Inc., p. 284 [SIC 6411]

Progressive Corp., p. 227 [SIC 6324]

Prokop Industries Inc., p. 300 [SIC 6513]

Promenade Real Estate Co., p. 303 [SIC 6519]

PROMPT Finance Inc., pp. 112, 116 [SICs 6153, 6159]

Property and Casualty Insurance Guaranty Corp., p. 240 [SIC 6331]

Prospect Group Inc., p. 423 [SIC 6799]

Protective Life Corp., pp. 182, 202 [SICs 6289, 6311]

Provident Bancorp Inc., p. 24 [SIC 6022]

Provident Life and Accident Insurance Co., pp. 181, 202 [SICs 6289, 6311]

Provident Life and Accident Insurance Company of America, pp. 180, 202, 360 [SICs 6289, 6311, 6719]

Provident Life Capital Corp., pp. 181, 202, 360 [SICs 6289, 6311, 6719]

Provident Savings Bank, p. 44 [SIC 6036]

Prudential Asset Management Company Inc., p. 171 [SIC 6231]

Prudential Insurance Company of America, pp. 138, 168, 180, 202 [SICs 6163, 6231, 6289, 6311]

Prudential Securities Inc., p. 138 [SIC 6163]

Prudential Summerson-Burrows Realtors, p. 312 [SIC 6531]

PSI Properties Inc., p. 300 [SIC 6513]

Public Employees Credit Union, p. 62 [SIC 6062]

Public Service Enterprise Group Inc., p. 360 [SIC 6719]

Pulte Corp., pp. 126, 139 [SICs 6162, 6163]

Pulte Diversified Companies Inc., p. 421 [SIC 6799]

Pulte Financial Companies Inc., p. 421 [SIC 6799]

Putnam Institutional Management, p. 171 [SIC 6231]

Putnam Investments Inc., p. 169 [SIC 6231]

Pyramid Management Group Inc., p. 294 [SIC 6512]

Quaker State Corp., p. 238 [SIC 6331]

Qual-Med Washington Health Plan Inc. Puget Sound Div., p. 217 [SIC 6321]

Queen City Insurance Agencies Inc., p. 258 [SIC 6371]

Queens County Bancorp Inc., p. 45 [SIC 6036]

Queens County Savings Bank, p. 45 [SIC 6036]

Quick and Reilly Group Inc., p. 140 [SIC 6163]

Quincy Savings Bank, p. 46 [SIC 6036]

R and R Investors Ltd., p. 296 [SIC 6512]

Radnor Corp., p. 340 [SIC 6552]

Radnor Realty Services Inc., p. 295 [SIC 6512]

Railroad Financial Corp., p. 127 [SIC 6162]

Rally's Inc., p. 403 [SIC 6794]

Rancho Carlsbad, p. 302 [SIC 6515]

Rand Financial Services Inc., p. 150 [SIC 6211]

Randall Mortgage Inc., p. 129 [SIC 6163]

Randolph-Brooks Federal Credit Union, p. 56 [SIC 6061]

Rarin Federal Credit Union, p. 59 [SIC 6061]

Rauscher Pierce Refsnes Inc., pp. 140, 171 [SICs 6163, 6282]

OCCUPATION INDEX

This index lists those occupations in the Finance, Insurance, and Real Estate sector that account for 1 percent or more of employment. This limitation excludes many occupations employed in the sector in small numbers. All told, 68 employment groups are shown, translating into 143 specific occupations or their alphabetical rotation. After the name of each occupation, a value in parentheses shows the number of 3-digit manufacturing industry groups in which the occupation occurs. One or more page numbers follow. After the page numbers, the 3-digit SICs are shown inside brackets. *Please note:* page and SIC references are sorted so that they point to industry groups with descending employment (the first page reference is to the largest employing industry group). Only the top ten industry groups are referenced.

Account collectors (4) 99, 91, 109, 123 [SIC 614, 611, 615, 616]

Accountants & auditors (29) 15, 37, 53, 354, 366, 374, 390, 177, 309, 223 [SIC 602, 603, 606, 671, 672, 673, 679, 631, 653, 633]

Accounting clerks (30) 15, 37, 53, 309, 279, 291, 223, 354, 366, 374 [SIC 602, 603, 606, 653, 641, 651, 633, 671, 672, 673]

Adjusters, insurance (8) 223, 279, 199, 177, 235, 245, 255, 271 [SIC 633, 641, 632, 631, 635, 636, 637, 639]

Adjusters & investigators nec (1) 223 [SIC 633]

Adjustment clerks (12) 15, 37, 53, 199, 177, 99, 91, 109, 5, 73 [SIC 602, 603, 606, 632, 631, 614, 611, 615, 601, 608]

Administrators nec (18) 177, 223, 199, 354, 366, 374, 390, 5, 73, 81 [SIC 631, 633, 632, 671, 672, 673, 679, 601, 608, 609]

Analysts, credit (7) 123, 91, 109, 99, 5, 73, 81 [SIC 616, 611, 615, 614, 601, 608, 609]

Analysts, operations research (1) 199 [SIC 632]

Analysts, systems (14) 177, 223, 199, 354, 366, 374, 390, 157, 165, 5 [SIC 631, 633, 632, 671, 672, 673, 679, 623, 628, 601]

Appraisers, real estate (2) 309, 123 [SIC 653, 616]

Assistants, legal (4) 235, 245, 255, 271 [SIC 635, 636, 637, 639]

Auditing clerks (30) 15, 37, 53, 309, 279, 291, 223, 354, 366, 374 [SIC 602, 603, 606, 653, 641, 651, 633, 671, 672, 673]

Auditors (29) 15, 37, 53, 354, 366, 374, 390, 177, 309, 223 [SIC 602, 603, 606, 671, 672, 673, 679, 631, 653, 633]

Bank tellers (7) 15, 37, 53, 5, 73, 81, 99 [SIC 602, 603, 606, 601, 608, 609, 614]

Banking clerks (3) 15, 37, 53 [SIC 602, 603, 606]

Bill & account collectors (4) 99, 91, 109, 123 [SIC 614, 611, 615, 616]

Billing, cost, & rate clerks (1) 223 [SIC 633]

Blue collar worker supervisors (2) 327, 335 [SIC 654, 655]

Bookkeeping, accounting, & auditing clerks (30) 15, 37, 53, 309, 279, 291, 223, 354, 366, 374 [SIC 602, 603, 606, 653, 641, 651, 633, 671, 672, 673]

Brokerage clerks (11) 135, 147, 157, 165, 354, 366, 374, 390, 5, 73 [SIC 621, 622, 623, 628, 671, 672, 673, 679, 601, 608]

Brokers, real estate (1) 309 [SIC 653]

Building service workers (1) 291 [SIC 651]

Carpenters (2) 327, 335 [SIC 654, 655]

Cashiers (4) 99, 5, 73, 81 [SIC 614, 601, 608, 609]

Checkers, credit (2) 91, 109 [SIC 611, 615]

Claims clerks, insurance (8) 177, 223, 199, 279, 235, 245, 255, 271 [SIC 631, 633, 632, 641, 635, 636, 637, 639]

Claims examiners, insurance (8) 223, 279, 199, 177, 235, 245, 255, 271 [SIC 633, 641, 632, 631, 635, 636, 637, 639]

Cleaners (8) 291, 309, 327, 335, 354, 366, 374, 390 [SIC 651, 653, 654, 655, 671, 672, 673, 679]

Cleaning & building service workers nec (1) 291 [SIC 651]

Clerical supervisors & managers (27) 15, 37, 53, 279, 223, 177, 199, 135, 147, 123 [SIC 602, 603, 606, 641, 633, 631, 632, 621, 622, 616]

Clerical support workers nec (25) 15, 37, 53, 223, 177, 199, 279, 135, 147, 123 [SIC 602, 603, 606, 633, 631, 632, 641, 621, 622, 616]

Clerks, accounting & auditing (30) 15, 37, 53, 309, 279, 291, 223, 354, 366, 374 [SIC 602, 603, 606, 653, 641, 651, 633, 671, 672, 673]

Clerks, adjustment (12) 15, 37, 53, 199, 177, 99, 91, 109, 5, 73 [SIC 602, 603, 606, 632, 631, 614, 611, 615, 601, 608]

Clerks, banking (3) 15, 37, 53 [SIC 602, 603, 606]

Clerks, brokerage (11) 135, 147, 157, 165, 354, 366, 374, 390, 5, 73 [SIC 621, 622, 623, 628, 671, 672, 673, 679, 601, 608]

Clerks, correspondence (3) 199, 91, 109 [SIC 632, 611, 615]

Clerks, cost & rate (1) 223 [SIC 633]

Clerks, credit (14) 15, 37, 53, 123, 99, 91, 109, 235, 245, 255 [SIC 602, 603, 606, 616, 614, 611, 615, 635, 636, 637]

Clerks, file (7) 279, 223, 199, 235, 245, 255, 271 [SIC 641, 633, 632, 635, 636, 637, 639]

Clerks, general office (30) 15, 37, 53, 279, 177, 309, 223, 291, 123, 354 [SIC 602, 603, 606, 641, 631, 653, 633, 651, 616, 671]

Clerks, information (21) 309, 279, 291, 123, 135, 147, 354, 366, 374, 390 [SIC 653, 641, 651, 616, 621, 622, 671, 672,

673, 679]

Clerks, insurance (8) 177, 223, 199, 279, 235, 245, 255, 271
   [SIC 631, 633, 632, 641, 635, 636, 637, 639]

Clerks, real estate (1) 309 [SIC 653]

Clerks, statement (3) 15, 37, 53 [SIC 602, 603, 606]

Collectors, account (4) 99, 91, 109, 123 [SIC 614, 611, 615,
   616]

Computer operators, ex peripheral equipment (6) 199, 5, 73,
   81, 157, 165 [SIC 632, 601, 608, 609, 623, 628]

Computer programmers (20) 177, 223, 199, 135, 147, 5, 73,
   81, 157, 165 [SIC 631, 633, 632, 621, 622, 601, 608, 609,
   623, 628]

Correspondence clerks (3) 199, 91, 109 [SIC 632, 611, 615]

Cost clerks (1) 223 [SIC 633]

Counselors, loan (10) 15, 37, 53, 123, 99, 91, 109, 5, 73, 81
   [SIC 602, 603, 606, 616, 614, 611, 615, 601, 608, 609]

Credit analysts (7) 123, 91, 109, 99, 5, 73, 81 [SIC 616, 611,
   615, 614, 601, 608, 609]

Credit checkers (2) 91, 109 [SIC 611, 615]

Credit clerks (14) 15, 37, 53, 123, 99, 91, 109, 235, 245, 255
   [SIC 602, 603, 606, 616, 614, 611, 615, 635, 636, 637]

Data entry keyers, ex composing (13) 199, 223, 157, 165, 5,
   73, 81, 235, 245, 255 [SIC 632, 633, 623, 628, 601, 608, 609,
   635, 636, 637]

Duplicating, mail, & office machine operators (6) 15, 37, 53,
   5, 73, 81 [SIC 602, 603, 606, 601, 608, 609]

Examiners, claims, insurance (8) 223, 279, 199, 177, 235,
   245, 255, 271 [SIC 633, 641, 632, 631, 635, 636, 637, 639]

Examiners, insurance (8) 223, 279, 199, 177, 235, 245, 255,
   271 [SIC 633, 641, 632, 631, 635, 636, 637, 639]

Executives (30) 15, 37, 53, 279, 309, 354, 366, 374, 390, 291
   [SIC 602, 603, 606, 641, 653, 671, 672, 673, 679, 651]

Farming supervisors (2) 327, 335 [SIC 654, 655]

File clerks (7) 279, 223, 199, 235, 245, 255, 271 [SIC 641,
   633, 632, 635, 636, 637, 639]

Financial managers (27) 15, 37, 53, 309, 354, 366, 374, 390,
   99, 279 [SIC 602, 603, 606, 653, 671, 672, 673, 679, 614,
   641]

Financial services workers (18) 135, 147, 15, 37, 53, 157, 165,
   123, 354, 366 [SIC 621, 622, 602, 603, 606, 623, 628, 616,
   671, 672]

Food preparation & service workers nec (3) 291, 327, 335
   [SIC 651, 654, 655]

Forestry supervisors (2) 327, 335 [SIC 654, 655]

Gardeners & groundskeepers, ex farm (4) 291, 327, 335, 309
   [SIC 651, 654, 655, 653]

General managers & top executives (30) 15, 37, 53, 279, 309,
   354, 366, 374, 390, 291 [SIC 602, 603, 606, 641, 653, 671,
   672, 673, 679, 651]

General managers (30) 15, 37, 53, 279, 309, 354, 366, 374,
   390, 291 [SIC 602, 603, 606, 641, 653, 671, 672, 673, 679,

651]

General office clerks (30) 15, 37, 53, 279, 177, 309, 223, 291,
   123, 354 [SIC 602, 603, 606, 641, 631, 653, 633, 651, 616,
   671]

Groundskeepers (4) 291, 327, 335, 309 [SIC 651, 654, 655,
   653]

Guards (7) 291, 309, 327, 335, 5, 73, 81 [SIC 651, 653, 654,
   655, 601, 608, 609]

Health professionals & paraprofessionals nec (1) 199 [SIC
   632]

Information clerks (21) 309, 279, 291, 123, 135, 147, 354,
   366, 374, 390 [SIC 653, 641, 651, 616, 621, 622, 671, 672,
   673, 679]

Insurance adjusters, examiners, & investigators (8) 223, 279,
   199, 177, 235, 245, 255, 271 [SIC 633, 641, 632, 631, 635,
   636, 637, 639]

Insurance claims clerks (8) 177, 223, 199, 279, 235, 245, 255,
   271 [SIC 631, 633, 632, 641, 635, 636, 637, 639]

Insurance claims examiners (8) 223, 279, 199, 177, 235, 245,
   255, 271 [SIC 633, 641, 632, 631, 635, 636, 637, 639]

Insurance policy processing clerks (8) 279, 223, 177, 199,
   235, 245, 255, 271 [SIC 641, 633, 631, 632, 635, 636, 637,
   639]

Insurance sales workers (8) 279, 177, 223, 199, 235, 245, 255,
   271 [SIC 641, 631, 633, 632, 635, 636, 637, 639]

Interviewers, loan (1) 123 [SIC 616]

Investigators, insurance (8) 223, 279, 199, 177, 235, 245, 255,
   271 [SIC 633, 641, 632, 631, 635, 636, 637, 639]

Investigators, nec (1) 223 [SIC 633]

Janitors & cleaners, incl maids (8) 291, 309, 327, 335, 354,
   366, 374, 390 [SIC 651, 653, 654, 655, 671, 672, 673, 679]

Keyers, data entry (13) 199, 223, 157, 165, 5, 73, 81, 235, 245,
   255 [SIC 632, 633, 623, 628, 601, 608, 609, 635, 636, 637]

Labor specialists (4) 354, 366, 374, 390 [SIC 671, 672, 673,
   679]

Law clerks (4) 235, 245, 255, 271 [SIC 635, 636, 637, 639]

Lawyers (5) 223, 354, 366, 374, 390 [SIC 633, 671, 672, 673,
   679]

Legal assistants, law clerks nec (4) 235, 245, 255, 271 [SIC
   635, 636, 637, 639]

Loan & credit clerks (14) 15, 37, 53, 123, 99, 91, 109, 235,
   245, 255 [SIC 602, 603, 606, 616, 614, 611, 615, 635, 636,
   637]

Loan interviewers (1) 123 [SIC 616]

Loan officers & counselors (10) 15, 37, 53, 123, 99, 91, 109,
   5, 73, 81 [SIC 602, 603, 606, 616, 614, 611, 615, 601, 608,
   609]

Maids (8) 291, 309, 327, 335, 354, 366, 374, 390 [SIC 651,
   653, 654, 655, 671, 672, 673, 679]

Occupation Index

655]

Underwriters (9) 223, 279, 177, 123, 235, 245, 255, 271, 199
    [SIC 633, 641, 631, 616, 635, 636, 637, 639, 632]

Word processors (9) 279, 309, 177, 235, 245, 255, 271, 327,
    335 [SIC 641, 653, 631, 635, 636, 637, 639, 654, 655]